TRAVELING WITH YOUR PET
THE AAA PETBOOK®

The AAA guide to more than 13,000
pet-friendly, AAA-RATED® hotels
and campgrounds across the
United States and Canada

10th Edition

AAA PUBLISHING

President & CEO	**Robert Darbelnet**
Executive Vice President, Publishing & Administration	**Rick Rinner**
Managing Director, Travel Information	**Bob Hopkins**
Director, Product Development & Sales	**Bill Wood**
Director, Publishing Marketing & Communications	**Patty Wight**
Director, Manufacturing & Quality Management	**Susan Sears**
Director, Tourism Information Development (TID)	**Michael Petrone**
Director, Publishing Operations/Travel Information	**Jeff Zimmerman**
Director, Publishing/GIS Systems & Development	**Ramin Kalhor**
Director, GIS/Cartography	**Jan Coyne**
Director, Purchasing & Corporate Services	**Becky Barrett**
Director, Business Development	**Gary Sisco**
Product Manager	**Kim Birch**
Manager, Public Relations	**Heather Hunter**
Manager, Retail Marketing	**Renuka Sastri**
Buyer	**Bob Bailes**
TID Regional Managers	**Stacy Brunick, Marquita Dudley, Michel Mousseau, Todd Cronson, Patrick Schardin**
TID Field Operations Manager	**Laurie DiMinico**
Manager, Travel Information Operations	**Dawn Garrison**
Publishing Business & Sales Administration Manager	**Linda Indolfi**
Manager, Advertising Services	**Mike McCrary**
Manager, Prepress, Photo Services & Pagination	**Tim Johnson**
Manager, Travel Information	**Kim Nicastro**
Manager, Application Development	**Scott Chrisien**
Manager, Publishing Systems	**Chris Puccio**
Development Editors	**Maria White, Greg Weekes**
Cover and Photo Insert Design	**Sonya Hester, Kelly Canova**
Supervisor, Graphic Design & Advertising Services	**Barbra Natali**
Photo Research	**Denise Campbell**
Prepress Technician	**Hai Nguyen**
Quality Services	**Terry Lane, Andrea Payne-Lecky**
Paginators	**Cathy Rapp, Janice Simmons**
Technical Specialist	**Roland Levett**
Planning Analyst	**Lorne Corbett**
Programmer	**James Cothrine**
Travel Information Analysts	**Kelly Giewont, Andrea Tlumacki, Jennifer Lopresti, Connie Delle Donne, Amy Watkins-Copeland, Ghazala Syed, William Young**
Proofreader	**Janet D'Amico**

AAA wishes to acknowledge the following for their assistance:
Dogpark.com®
Veterinary Emergency & Critical Care Society

Cover Photos

Cover: Bassett in red car	**StockByte/age fotostock**
Collar portion of front cover image	**© Eg Project / Photonica / Getty Images**
Back Cover: Libby at Peggy's Cove lighthouse, Nova Scotia	**Photo Contest winner Donna Allman**
Spine: Dory ready to kayak on the Colorado River	**Photo Contest winners LaDonna and Dan Ishida**

Published by AAA Publishing
1000 AAA Drive, Heathrow, Florida 32746

Tenth Edition Copyright © 2008 AAA Publishing. All rights reserved.
ISBN 10: 1-59508-267-0 ISBN 13: 978-1-59508-267-1 Stock Number 552208
Printed in the USA by Rose Printing

ABOUT THIS BOOK

Welcome to the 10th edition of **Traveling With Your Pet: The AAA PetBook**®. *Traveling With Your Pet* is a must for the traveler who's also an animal lover. This comprehensive book provides all the information you need to know about taking a four-legged friend on the road. Will Spot be a good car passenger? Is it safe to take Snowball on a plane? What are the important rules of pet etiquette? Is pet insurance a good idea? *Traveling With Your Pet* answers all of these questions and more. Here are just some of the features covered:

- Dog parks where you and your furry friends can play, exercise or just relax.

- An extensive listing of emergency animal clinics compiled by the Veterinary Emergency & Critical Care Society. Names, addresses and phone numbers provide valuable information for unexpected or emergency situations, both en route and at your destination.

- A roundup of pet-friendly attractions.

- National public lands in the United States and Canada that allow pets, along with recreation information.

- Border crossing procedures and tips for travelers — both entering Canada from the United States and vice versa.

- Policies pertaining to service animals.

Traveling With Your Pet lists more than 13,000 AAA-RATED® hotels and campgrounds. And the listings show AAA's trustworthy diamond ratings, the traveler's assurance of quality. Other handy features include:

- Informative highway directions.

- Specific information about lodgings' pet policies: deposits and fees (rounded to the nearest dollar), housekeeping service, designated rooms and other stipulations relating to travelers with pets.

- Additional details about the lodgings themselves, including icons for amenities, recreation, dining and accessibility.

- Icons designating AAA's member discount programs.

- Listings for AAA's highest rated campgrounds, including rate and pet policy information and service/amenity icons.

All of this valuable information is packaged in a contemporary, easy-to-read format, making *Traveling With Your Pet: The AAA PetBook*® as indispensable an on-the-road companion as Spot's water dish or Snowball's litter box. Don't leave home without it, and remember: It always pays to *Travel With Someone You Trust*®.

Have some great pictures from traveling with your pet? The AAA PetBook photo contest gives you a chance at winning some great prizes and seeing your pet's photo on a cover of *Traveling With Your Pet: The AAA PetBook*®. Check out some adorable photos of traveling pets in the middle section of this guide. For details on the annual photo contest, please refer to the entry form on the next page or visit www.AAA.com/petbook.

AAA PetBook® Photo Contest
Entry Form

The next time you go on vacation with your pet, be sure to take along your camera.

The winning entry in the AAA PetBook Photo Contest will appear on a cover of the 11th edition of **Traveling With Your Pet: The AAA PetBook®**. The winner also will receive a $350 AAA VISA Gift Card and five complimentary copies of the book. The second place entry will appear on the book's spine and the winner will receive a $200 AAA VISA Gift Card and two complimentary copies of the book. Contest rules and entries from previous years are online at www.AAA.com/PetBook.

Please print clearly

Name:_____

Address:_____

City: _____ State: _____ Zip code:_____

Daytime phone: _____ Evening phone:_____

Email address:_____

Pet's name/gender: _____ Animal breed:_____

Photo taken:_____

Please answer the following questions:

*1. Why do you travel with your pet?_____
_____

*2. What is your favorite place or city to take your pet, and why?_____
_____

3. Tell us about an adventure you had while traveling with your pet._____
_____

*Required answer

AAA PetBook® Photo Contest Official Rules

1. Email **one** digital photo to Petbookcontest@national.aaa.com. Please send the photo as a .jpeg file attachment no larger than 2 MB, and include the information requested on the entry form in the body of the email. The digital photo must have a minimum resolution of 1200 pixels by 1600 pixels. The entry form information (name, address, phone, pet's name/gender, animal breed and answers to questions) must be included in the email for contest consideration. Minor digital enhancement for cropping, red-eye removal, filters and correction functions are permitted, but images that are determined to be significantly altered will be disqualified. Photographers are not permitted to place borders or frames around their image or to place a watermark, signature, date or copyright notices on the image.

   OR

2. Send printed color 8″ x 10″ unmounted photo that is in focus, along with the completed entry form to:

   AAA PetBook® Photo Contest
   AAA
   1000 AAA Drive, MS 64
   Heathrow, FL 32746

3. Photos must be postmarked by Nov. 26, 2008, and received by Nov. 30, 2008, to be eligible for the contest.

(Official Rules continued)

4. Photo must feature at least one pet and convey a travel theme.

5. Only one photo may be entered per household.

6. The entrant must be the person who took the photo and who has full rights to the photo.

7. The entrant must obtain full consent from all models or persons appearing in the photo for full use of the photo, including use and publishing in this contest and the other uses stated herein.

8. All photos entered in the contest, including the prize-winning photo(s), along with all rights of every kind therein, become the sole and exclusive property of AAA and will not be returned.

9. A panel of judges will choose the winning photo based on the following qualities: impact, lighting, composition and effectively conveying the idea that *Traveling With Your Pet: The AAA PetBook®* is about traveling on vacation with your pet. Posed or studio photographs will be disqualified.

10. The winner will be notified **by mail** early January 2009.

Disclaimer

By participating, entrants agree that: (i) these rules and the decisions of AAA shall be final in all respects, and (ii) AAA may put the winner's photo on the front or back cover or spine of the 11th edition of *Traveling With Your Pet: The AAA PetBook®*. The winner grants AAA the right to use his or her name, likeness, portrait, picture, photo, answers on entry form and/or prize information for advertising, publicity and promotional purposes relating to the book, *Traveling With Your Pet: The AAA PetBook®*, and the contest without compensation or permission (unless prohibited by law). Each entrant agrees to hold harmless and release AAA from any injuries, losses or damages of any kind that may result from taking a photo intended to be submitted. AAA is not responsible for late, lost or misdirected entries or mail; for technical, hardware or software malfunctions, lost or unavailable network connections, or failed, incorrect, inaccurate, incomplete, garbled or delayed electronic communications, whether caused by the sender or by any of the equipment or programming associated with or utilized in this promotion, or by any human error that may occur in the processing of entries; or for loss of or damage to any entries. AAA retains the right to not award the prize should no acceptable photos be received. By participating in the contest, each entrant agrees that AAA becomes the owner of each photo submitted and AAA may use said photo in any manner and medium it chooses and entrant relinquishes all rights in and to said photo(s).

Eligibility

No purchase is necessary to enter the contest or claim the prize. Open to U.S. or Canadian residents 18 years or older. **Employees of AAA, CAA and their clubs are not eligible to enter**.

By submitting an entry I agree that I have read the Contest Rules, assent thereto, and submit the enclosed photo in accordance therewith; I attest that I own all rights to the photo and it has not been published or accepted for publication in any medium; and if the photo portrays any living person or persons, I have secured a model release or releases. I further agree that should my entry be chosen as the winning entry I will execute all necessary paperwork/releases as requested by AAA.

Traveling with Your Pet: The AAA PetBook® contains listings for more than 13,000 pet-friendly, AAA-Rated hotels and campgrounds in the United States and Canada. In addition, the AAA PetBook® lists animal hospitals, dog parks, and pet-accessible federal lands, along with information on preparing your pet for travel, how to pack for your pet, and selecting a carrier or crate. *Traveling With Your Pet: The AAA PetBook®* is available at many AAA offices and at better bookstores.

TABLE OF CONTENTS

AAA PetBook® Photo Contest

Traveling With Pets

Pet-Friendly Places

Pet-Friendly Lodgings

U.S. Lodgings

Canadian Lodgings

Pet-Friendly Campgrounds

Many people view their pets as full-fledged members of the family. Spot and Snowball often have their own beds, premium-quality foods, a basketful of toys and a special place in their humans' heart.

Until it's time to go on vacation, that is. Then the family dog or cat is consigned to "watching the fort" at home while everyone else experiences the joy of traveling. Many animal lovers hesitate to take their pet with them because they don't think they'll be able to find accommodations that accept four-legged guests. Others aren't sure how — or if — their furry friends will adapt.

The truth is, including a pet in the family vacation is fairly easy, so long as you plan ahead. Most pets respond well to travel, a fact that isn't lost on the tourism industry. More than 13,000 AAA-RATED® hotels and campgrounds from coast to coast are pet-friendly, and airline bookings for pet passengers are on the rise. Great companions at home, pets are earning their stripes on the road, too.

So if you've been longing to hit the trail with a canine or feline companion, read the tips on the following pages. You may find that a getaway can be far more enjoyable with than without your pet.

Should Your Pet Travel?

Before you make reservations, determine if your pet is able to travel. Most animals can and do make the most of the experience, but a small percentage simply are not cut out for traveling. Illness, physical condition and temperament are important factors, as is your pet's ability to adjust to such stresses as changes to his environment and routine. When in doubt, check with your veterinarian. If you feel your pet isn't up to the trip, it's better for everyone if he stays home.

❀ **Rule 1: Pets who are very young, very old, pregnant, sick, injured, prone to biting or excessive vocalizing, or who cannot follow basic obedience commands should not travel.**

Even if Spot and Snowball are seasoned travelers, take into account the type of vacation and activities you have planned. No pet is going to be happy (or safe) cooped up in a car or hotel room. Likewise, the family dog may love camping and hiking, but the family cat may not. Putting a little thought toward your animal's needs and safety will pay off in a more enjoyable vacation for everyone.

❀ **Rule 2: If your pet can't actively participate in the trip, she should stay home.**

Most of the information in this book pertains to cats and dogs. If you own a bird, hamster, pig, ferret, lizard or other exotic creature, remember that unusual animals are not always accepted as readily as more conventional pets. Always specify the type of pet you have when making arrangements.

Also check states' animal policies. **Hawaii** imposes 120-day or 5-days-or-less quarantines for all imported dogs, cats and other carnivores to prevent the importation of rabies. Guide dogs and other service animals are exempt from the quarantine provided they have: a standard health certificate; a current rabies vaccination with documentation of the product name, lot number and lot expiration date; and an electronic identification microchip implanted and operational. Upon arrival, guide dogs still must be examined for external parasites and undergo serum antibody testing and a microchip scan. For additional details, obtain the Hawaii Rabies Quarantine Information Brochure from the Hawaii Department of Agriculture, Animal Quarantine Station, 99-951 Halawa Valley St., Aiea, HI 96701-5602; phone (808) 483-7151 or (808) 837-8092, fax (808) 483-7161. The Web site address is http://www.hawaii.gov/hdoa/ai/aqs/info.

North Carolina has stringent restrictions regarding pets in lodgings. Make certain you understand an accommodation's specific policies before making reservations.

❀ **Rule 3: Be specific when making travel plans that include your pet. Nobody wants unpleasant surprises on vacation.**

If Spot and Snowball stay behind, leave them in good hands while you're gone. **Family, friends and neighbors** make good sitters (provided they're willing), especially if they know your pet and can care for him in your home. Provide detailed instructions for feeding, exercise and medication, as well as phone numbers for your destination, your veterinarian and your local animal emergency clinic.

Professional pet sitters offer a range of services, from feeding and walking your pet daily to full-time house sitting while you are gone. Interview several candidates, and always check credentials and references. For additional information, contact the National Association of Professional Pet Sitters or Pet Sitters International. *(See sidebars on p. 8 and p. 9.)*

Kennels board many animals simultaneously and generally are run by professionals who will provide food and exercise according to your instructions. Pets usually are kept in a run (dogs) or cage (cats and small dogs) and may not get the same level of human interaction as at home. **Veterinary clinics** also board pets and may be the best choice if yours is sick, injured or needs special medical care. For further information on how to select a kennel, contact the American Boarding Kennels Association.

Veterinarians, fellow pet owners and professional associations are a good source of referrals for sitters and kennels.

❀ **Rule 4: Never leave your pet with someone you don't trust.**

Travelers Who Have Disabilities

Individuals with disabilities who own service animals to assist them with everyday activities undoubtedly face challenges, but traveling should not be one of them. Service animals (the accepted term for animals trained to help people with disabilities) are not pets and thus are not subject to many of the laws or policies pertaining to pets.

The Americans With Disabilities Act (ADA) defines a service animal as "any guide dog, signal dog or other animal individually trained to provide assistance to an individual with a disability." ADA regulations stipulate that public accommodations are required to modify policies, practices and procedures to permit the use of a service animal by an individual with a disability.

The purpose of these regulations is to provide equal access opportunities for people with disabilities and to ensure that they are not separated from their service animals. A tow truck operator, for example, must allow a service animal to ride in the truck with her owner rather than in the towed vehicle.

Public accommodations may charge a fee or deposit to an individual who has a disability — provided that fee or deposit is required of all customers — but no fees or deposits may be charged for the service animal, even those normally charged for pets.

The handler/owner is responsible for the animal's care and behavior; if the dog creates an altercation or poses a direct threat, the handler may be required to remove it from the premises and pay for any resulting damages.

CHOOSING A PET SITTER

Before hiring a pet sitter, ask:
- Is he or she insured (for commercial liability) and bonded?
- What is included in the fee?
- Does the sitter require that your pet have a current vaccination?
- What kind of animals does the sitter typically care for?
- How will a medical, weather or home emergency be handled?
- Does he or she fully understand your pet's medical or dietary needs?
- How much time will be spent with your pet?

The pet sitter should:
- Have a polished, professional attitude.
- Provide references.
- Have a standard contract outlining terms of service.
- Have experience in caring for animals.
- Insist on current vaccinations.
- Ask about your pet's health, temperament, schedule and needs.
- Visit and interact with your pet before you leave.
- Devote time and attention to your pet.
- Be affiliated with pet care organizations.

Be sure you:
- Explain your pet's personality — favorite toys, good and bad habits, hiding spots, general health, etc.
- Leave care instructions, keys, food and water dishes, extra supplies (food, medication, etc.), and phone numbers for your veterinarian and an emergency contact.
- Bring pets inside before leaving.

CHOOSING A KENNEL

Before reserving a kennel, ask:
- What is included in the fee?
- Are current vaccinations required?
- What kind of animals do they board?
- How will a medical or weather emergency be handled?
- Will your pet be kept in a cage or run?
- Will your pet receive daily exercise?
- Does the kennel fully understand your pet's medical or dietary needs?
- How and how often will staff interact with your pet?

The kennel should:
- Require proof of current vaccinations.
- Be clean, well-ventilated and offer adequate protection from the elements.
- Have separate areas for dogs, cats and other animals, with secure fencing and caging.
- Clean and disinfect facilities daily.
- Give your pet his regular food on his regular schedule.
- Provide soft bedding in runs/cages.
- Understand your pet's medical needs.
- Provide or obtain veterinary care if necessary.
- Offer sufficient supervision.
- Have a friendly, animal-loving staff.

Be sure you:
- Notify staff of behavior quirks (dislike of other animals, children, etc.).
- Provide food and medication.
- Leave a familiar object with your pet.
- Leave phone numbers for your veterinarian and an emergency contact.
- Spend time with your pet before boarding him.

The **Delta Society,** an organization devoted to companion and service animals, has information about laws that affect people and service animals in public accommodations. Phone (425) 679-5500 for a catalog, or visit www.deltasociety.org.

Preparing Your Pet for Travel

Happily, many vacations can be planned to include fun activities for pets. Trips to parks, nature trails, the ocean or lakes offer exposure to the world beyond the window or fence at home, as well as the chance to explore new sights and sounds. Even the streets of an unfamiliar city can provide a smorgasbord of discoveries for your animal friend to enjoy.

Once you decide Spot and Snowball are ready to hit the road, plan accordingly:

❧ **Get a clean bill of health from the veterinarian.** Update your pet's vaccinations, check his general physical condition and obtain a health certificate showing proof of up-to-date inoculations, particularly rabies, distemper and kennel cough. Such documentation will be necessary if you cross state or country lines, and also may come in handy in the unlikely event your pet gets lost and must be retrieved from the local shelter. Don't forget to ask the doctor about potential health risks at your destination (Lyme disease, heartworm infection) and the necessary preventive measures.

If your pet is taking prescribed medicine, pack a sufficient supply plus a few days' extra. Also take the prescription in case you need a refill. Be prepared for emergencies by getting the names and numbers of clinics or doctors at your destination from your veterinarian or the American Animal Hospital Association. **Hint:** Obtain these references before you leave and keep them handy throughout the trip.

Make sure your pet is in good physical shape overall, especially if you are planning an active vacation. If your animal is primarily sedentary or overweight, he may not be up to lengthy hikes through the woods.

Note: Some owners believe a sedated animal will travel more easily than one that is fully aware, but this is rarely the case. In fact, tranquilizing an animal can make travel much more stressful. Always consult a veterinarian about what is best for your pet, and administer sedatives only under the doctor's direction. In addition, never give an animal medication that is specifically prescribed for humans. The dosage may be too high for an animal's much smaller body mass, or may cause dangerous side effects.

❧ **Acclimate your pet to car travel.** Even if you're flying, your pet will have to ride in the car to get to the airport or terminal, and you don't want any unpleasant surprises before departure.

CONTACT INFORMATION

The following organizations offer information, tips, brochures and other travel materials designed to help you and your pet enjoy a happy and safe vacation.

American Animal Hospital Association
12575 W. Bayaud Ave., Lakewood, CO 80228
(303) 986-2800 — www.healthypet.com

American Boarding Kennels Association
1702 E. Pikes Peak Ave.
Colorado Springs, CO 80909
(719) 667-1600 — www.abka.com

American Society for the Prevention of Cruelty to Animals
424 E. 92nd St., New York, NY 10128-6804
(212) 876-7700 — www.aspca.org

American Veterinary Medical Association
1931 N. Meacham Rd., Suite 100
Schaumburg, IL 60173
(847) 925-8070 — www.avma.org

Dogpark.com®
820 Fifth Ave., Suite B, San Rafael, CA 94901
www.dogpark.com

The Humane Society of the United States
2100 L St. N.W., Washington, DC 20037
(202) 452-1100 — www.hsus.org

National Association of Professional Pet Sitters
15000 Commerce Pkwy., Suite C
Mt. Laurel, NJ 08054
(856) 439-0324 — www.petsitters.org

PetGroomer.com
P.O. Box 2489
Yelm, WA 98597
(360) 446-5348 — www.petgroomer.com

Pet Sitters International
201 E. King St., King, NC 27021
(336) 983-9222 — www.petsit.com

USDA-APHIS
USDA-APHIS-Animal Care
4700 River Rd., Unit 84
Riverdale, MD 20737-1234
(301) 734-7833
www.aphis.usda.gov/animal_welfare/index.shtml

3 1833 05631 7529

Some animals are used to riding in the car and even enjoy it. But most associate the inside of the carrier or the car with one thing only: the annual visit to the V-E-T. Considering that these visits usually end with a jab from a sharp needle, it's no wonder that some pets forget their training and act up in the car. If this is your situation, you will have to re-train your animal to view a drive as a reward, not a punishment.

Begin by allowing your pet to become used to the car without actually going anywhere. Then take short trips to places that are fun for animals, such as the park or the drive-through window at a fast-food restaurant. (Keep those indulgent snacks to a minimum!) Be sure to praise her for good behavior with words, petting and healthy treats. It shouldn't take long before you and your furry friend are enjoying leisurely drives without incident. *(See Traveling by Car, p. 12.)*

❧ **Brush up on behavior.** Will Snowball make a good travel companion? Or will he be an absolute terror on the road? Don't wait until the vacation is already under way to find out; review general behavioral guidelines with respect to your animal, keeping in mind that the unfamiliarity of travel situations may test the temperament of even the most well-behaved pet.

It's a good idea to socialize Spot by exposing her to other people and animals (especially if she normally stays inside). You're likely to encounter both on your trip, and it is important that she learns to behave properly in the company of strangers. Make her introduction to the outside world gradual, such as a walk in a new neighborhood or taking her along while you run errands. Exposure to new situations will help reduce fear of the unknown and result in more socially acceptable behavior.

Is your pet housebroken? How is he around children? Does he obey vocal commands? Be honest about your animal's ability to cope in unfamiliar surroundings. Depending on the length and nature of the trip and your pet's level of command response, an obedience refresher course might be a good idea.

❧ **Learn about your destination.** Check into quarantines or other restrictions well in advance, and make follow-up calls as your departure date approaches. Find out what types of documentation will be required — not just en route, but on the way home as well.

Be aware of potential safety or health risks where you're going, and plan accordingly. For example, the southeastern United States — particularly Florida — is home to alligators and heartworm-carrying mosquitoes, and many mountainous and wooded areas may harbor ticks that transmit Lyme disease.

Confirm all travel plans within a few days of your departure, especially with lodgings and airlines; their policies may have changed after you made the reservations. If you plan to visit state parks or attractions that accept pets on the premises, obtain their animal regulations in advance.

WHAT TO TAKE

- ❏ Carrier or crate. *(See Selecting a Carrier or Crate, p. 11, for specifications.)*
- ❏ Nylon or leather collar or harness, license tag, ID tag(s) and leash. All should be sturdy and should fit your pet properly.
- ❏ Food and water dishes.
- ❏ Can opener and spoon (for canned food).
- ❏ An ample supply of food, plus a few days' extra.
- ❏ Bottled water from home. (Many animals are finicky about their drinking water.)
- ❏ Cooler with ice.
- ❏ Healthy treats.
- ❏ Medications, if necessary.
- ❏ Health certificate and other required documents.
- ❏ A blanket or other bedding. (If your pet is used to sleeping on the furniture, bring an old blanket or sheet to place on top of the hotel's bedding.)
- ❏ Litter supplies (for cats or other small animals), a scooper and plastic bags (for dogs).
- ❏ Favorite toys.
- ❏ Carpet deodorizer.
- ❏ Chewing preventative.
- ❏ A recent photograph and a written description including name, breed, gender, height, weight, coloring and distinctive markings.
- ❏ Grooming supplies:
  comb/brush
  nail clippers
  shampoo
  cloth and paper towels
  cotton balls/tissues
- ❏ First-aid kit:
  gauze, bandages and adhesive tape
  hydrogen peroxide
  rubbing alcohol
  ointment
  muzzle
  scissors
  tweezers (for removing ticks, burrs, splinters, etc.)
  local emergency phone numbers
  first-aid guide (such as *Pet First Aid: Cats & Dogs*, published by The Humane Society of the United States and the American Red Cross)

❧ **Determine the best mode of transportation.** Most people traveling with pets drive. Many airlines do accept animals in the passenger cabin or cargo hold, and as more people choose to fly with their pet airlines are becoming more pet-conscious. Restrictions vary as to the type and number of pets an airline will carry, however, so inquire about animal shipping and welfare policies before making reservations. If your pet must travel in the cargo hold, heed the cautionary advice in the Traveling by Air section. *(See p. 13.)*

Flying is really the only major option to car travel. Amtrak, as well as Greyhound and other interstate bus lines, do not accept pets. **Note:** Seeing-eye dogs and other service animals are exempt from the regulations prohibiting pets on Amtrak and interstate bus lines. Local rail and bus companies may allow pets in small carriers, but this is an exception rather than a rule.

The only cruise ship that currently permits pets is the Cunard Line's *Queen Mary 2* (on transatlantic crossings); kennels are provided, but animals are accepted on a very limited basis. Some charter and sightseeing boat companies permit pets onboard, however.

A word of advice: Never try to sneak your pet onto any mode of public transportation where she is not permitted. You may face legal action or fines, and the animal may be confiscated if discovered.

❧ **Pack as carefully for your pet as you do for yourself.** *(See What To Take, p. 10.)* Make sure she has a collar with a license tag and ID tag(s) listing her name and yours, along with your address and phone number. As an added precaution, some owners outfit their dog with a second tag listing the name and number of a contact person at home. Popular backup identification methods are to have your animal tattooed with an ID number (usually a social security number) or to implant a microchip under her skin.

If your pet requires medication, make sure that is specified on his tag. This helps others understand your animal's needs and also may prevent people from keeping a found pet or from stealing one to sell.

Note: Choke chains, collars that tighten when they are pulled, may be useful during training sessions, but they do not make good full-time collars. If the chain catches on something, your pet could choke herself trying to pull free. For regular wear, use a harness or a conventional collar made of nylon or leather.

Selecting a Carrier or Crate

This is one of the most important steps in ensuring your pet's safety when traveling. A good-quality carrier not only contains your pet during transit, it also gives him a safe, reassuring place to stay when confinement is necessary at your destination. Acclimate the animal before the trip so he views the crate as a cozy den, not a place of exile.

If you plan to travel by car, a carrier will confine your pet en route, and also may come in handy if Spot or Snowball must stay in the room unsupervised. A secured crate will prevent your pet from escaping from the room when the cleaning staff arrives, or at night if camping in the open. *(See At Your Destination, p. 16.)*

Some airlines allow small pets to travel in the passenger cabin as carry-on luggage. There are no laws dictating the type of carrier to use, but remember that it must be small enough to fit under a standard airplane seat and should not exceed 45 linear inches (length + width + height), or roughly **22 by 14 by 9 inches.** If your pet will be flying in the cargo hold, you must use a carrier that meets U.S. Department of Agriculture Animal and Plant Health Inspection Service (USDA-APHIS) specifications. *(See Traveling by Air, p. 13.)*

Crates are available at pet supply stores; some airlines also sell carriers. Soft-sided travel bags are handy for flyers with small pets. Before you make the investment, make sure your carrier is airline-approved.

Even if you never take to the skies, these common-sense guidelines provide a good rule of thumb in selecting a crate for other uses. USDA-APHIS rules stipulate the following:

❧ The crate must be enclosed, but with ventilation openings occupying at least 14 percent of total wall space, at least one-third of which must be located on the top half of the kennel. A three-quarter-inch lip or rim must surround the exterior to prevent air holes from being blocked.

❧ The crate must open easily, but must be sufficiently strong to hold up during normal cargo transit procedures (loading, unloading, etc.).

❧ The floor must be solid and leakproof, and must be covered with an absorbent lining or material (such as an old towel or litter).

Ventilation openings

Live animal label

Spacer bar

Name and address label

Food and water dishes

HEATSTROKE
AND
HYPOTHERMIA

The best way to treat heatstroke or hypothermia is to prevent it. Do not leave pets unattended in a car, even if only for a few minutes. Also heed airlines' restrictions on pet travel, and carefully investigate animal welfare policies to make certain the airline has safeguards to protect your pet from both conditions.

Other preventive measures are to avoid strenuous exercise — including such activities as hiking and "fetch" — when the sun is strongest (10 a.m.-2 p.m.), and to provide your pet access to clean, fresh drinking water at all times.

Following are the warning signs and basic first aid for heatstroke and hypothermia. Always be alert to your pet's physical condition and watch for symptoms — immediate attention to the situation may mean the difference between life and death. If your pet is struck with either disorder, take him to an animal hospital or veterinarian as fast as safely possible.

HEATSTROKE

Symptoms
- rapid, shallow breathing
- excessive salivation
- heavy panting
- hot to the touch
- glazed eyes
- unsteadiness, dizziness
- deep red or purple tongue or gums
- vomiting
- body temperature of 104 F or higher

First Aid
- place pet in the shade
- quickly dampen with cool water, especially on the head and neck
- give small amounts of water

HYPOTHERMIA

Symptoms
- shivering
- weakness
- lethargy
- cold to the touch
- body temperature of 95 F or lower

First Aid
- place in a warm area
- wrap in towels or a blanket
- quickly warm by gently massaging the head, chest and extremities

❧ The crate must be just large enough to allow the animal to turn freely while standing, and to have a full range of normal movement while standing or lying down.

❧ The crate must offer exterior grips or handles so that handlers do not have to place their hands or fingers inside.

❧ Food and water dishes must be securely attached and accessible without opening the kennel.

❧ If the carrier has wheels, they must be removed or immobilized prior to loading.

❧ One-inch lettering stating "Live Animal" or "Wild Animal" must be placed visibly on the exterior, and must be accompanied by directional arrows showing the crate's proper orientation. It also is a good idea to label the crate with your name, home address and home phone number, as well as an address and phone number where you can be reached during the trip. **Hint:**Use an adhesive label or an indelible marker and write directly on the crate, as paper may be ripped off accidentally in transit.

❧ Attach a list of care instructions (feeding, watering, etc.) for a 24-hour period to the exterior of the carrier. This will help airport workers care for your pet if he is sent to the wrong destination.

❧ If you are traveling with multiple pets, note that crates may contain only one animal whose weight exceeds 20 pounds. Smaller animals may travel together under the following guidelines: one species to a crate, except compatible dogs and cats of similar size; two puppies or kittens under 6 months of age; 15 guinea pigs or rabbits; 50 hamsters. **Note:** These are federal limits; airlines may impose more stringent regulations.

Traveling by Car

The first step in ensuring your pet's well-being during a vacation is to train her to ride in the car. For safety reasons, pets should be confined to the back seat, either in a carrier or a harness attached to the car's seat belt. This keeps the animal from interfering with or distracting the driver, and also may save her life in the event of an accident. And a restrained animal will not be able to break free and run away the second the car door is opened.

To help prevent car sickness, feed your pet a light meal four to six hours before departing. Do not give an animal food or water in a moving vehicle.

Never allow your pet to ride in the bed of a pickup truck. It's illegal in some states; he also can jump out or be thrown, endangering himself and others on the road. Harnessing or leashing him to the truck bed is not advisable either: If he tries to jump out, he could be dragged along the road or the restraint could become a noose. Avoid placing animals in campers or trailers as well. **If your pet cannot ride in the car with you, leave him at home.**

Don't let your dog stick her head out the window, no matter how enjoyable it seems. Road debris and other flying objects can injure delicate eyes and ears, and the animal is at greater risk for severe injury if the vehicle should stop suddenly or be struck. If it is hot outside, run the air conditioner instead of opening the windows, and be sure that the air flow is reaching your pet.

AAA recommends that drivers stop every two hours to stretch their legs and take a quick break from driving. Your pet will appreciate the same break. Plan to visit a rest stop every four hours or so to let him have a drink and a chance to answer the call of nature. (Cat owners should bring along a litter box; dog owners should clean up afterward.)

Be sure your pet is leashed before opening the car door. This is not merely a courtesy to fellow travelers; it will prevent her from unexpectedly breaking free and running away. Keep in mind that even the most obedient pet may become disoriented during travel or in strange places and set off for home. **Hint:** If your pet is not used to traveling, use a harness instead of a collar; it is more difficult for an animal to wriggle out of a harness.

NEVER leave an animal in a parked car, even if the windows are partially open. Even on pleasant days the temperature inside a car can soar to well over 100 degrees in less than 10 minutes, placing your pet at risk for heatstroke and possibly death. On very cold days, hypothermia is a risk. Also, animals left unattended in parked cars frequently are stolen.

Traveling by Air

(Service animals are normally exempt from most of the regulations and fees specified in this section. Check policies with the airline when making reservations.)

Opinion is divided as to whether air travel is truly safe for pets. Statistically, it is less dangerous than being a passenger in a car, but some experts warn of potentially deadly conditions for animals. The truth lies somewhere in between: Most pets arrive at their destination in fine condition, but death or injury is always a possibility. Before you decide to fly, know the risk factors and the necessary precautions to keep your pet safe.

❧ **Determine whether your pet is fit to fly.** The Animal Welfare Act (AWA), administered by USDA-APHIS, specifies that dogs and cats must be at least 8 weeks old and weaned at least 5 days before air travel. Animals that are very young, very old, pregnant, ill or injured should not fly at all. Cats, snub-nosed dogs (pugs, boxers, etc.) and long-nosed dogs (shelties, collies, etc.) are prone to severe respiratory difficulties in an airplane's poorly ventilated cargo hold and should travel only in the passenger cabin (if size allows) with their owner. Some airlines will not accept snub-nosed breeds if the temperature exceeds 70 degrees anywhere in the routing.

❧ **Decide where your pet will fly.** Most animals fly in the hold as checked baggage when traveling with their owners, or as cargo when they are unaccompanied. The AWA was enacted to ensure animals traveling in this manner are treated humanely and are not subjected to dangerous or life-threatening conditions. For specific requirements pertaining to your animal, check with the airline in advance, as policies vary. Some airlines will not ship dogs as checked baggage, and others will only accept dogs shipped as cargo from "known shippers"; i.e., commercial shippers or licensed pet breeders. Except for service animals, Southwest accepts no pets in the cabin or cargo department.

Items classified as "dangerous goods" (dry ice or toxic chemicals, for example) must be transported in a different part of the hold from where live animals are carried. Some planes are designed to have separate hold areas, but so-called "people mover" airlines that are primarily

AIRLINE CONTACT INFORMATION

Following is a list of the major North American airlines and their toll-free reservation numbers.

Web site addresses include information about flying with animals. **Hint:** Look under links for baggage, cargo or special travel needs, or do a site search for "pets."

Air Canada . . . . (888) 247-2262
www.aircanada.ca (only service animals in cabin)

Alaska Airlines . . . . (800) 252-7522
www.alaskaair.com

American Airlines . . . . (800) 433-7300
www.aa.com

Continental Airlines . . . . (800) 523-3273
www.continental.com

Delta Airlines . . . . (800) 221-1212
www.delta.com

Northwest Airlines . . . . (800) 225-2525
www.nwa.com

Southwest Airlines . . . . (800) 435-9792
www.southwest.com (accepts service animals only)

United Airlines . . . . (800) 864-8331
www.united.com

US Airways . . . . (800) 428-4322
www.usairways.com

interested in getting human passengers from one point to another as quickly as possible may not give priority to this feature. Check your airline's specific baggage policies so you know exactly where in the hold your pet will be traveling.

Small pets may be taken into the passenger cabin with you as carry-on luggage on most airlines. This places the animal's welfare squarely in your hands but is feasible only if he is very well-behaved and fits comfortably in a container that meets standard carry-on regulations. *(See Selecting a Carrier or Crate, p. 11.)* Keep in mind that the carrier — with the animal inside — must be kept under the seat in front of you throughout the flight. Some airlines charge a fee ($50-$95) for carry-on pets. **Note:** AWA regulations do not apply to animals traveling in the cabin.

❧ **Do your homework.** Investigate the airline's animal transport and welfare policies, especially if you are flying with a small or commuter airline. All airlines are subject to basic AWA regulations, but specific standards of care vary greatly from one company to another. Do your research well in advance and confirm the information 24-48 hours before departing.

The more information an airline provides, the better care your pet is likely to receive. Beware of companies that have vague animal welfare guidelines, or none at all. All

major airlines provide information about pet transport on their Web sites. Also talk to fellow travelers and pet owners about their experiences. Finally, keep in mind that airlines are not required to transport live animals and can refuse to carry them for any reason.

❧ **Protect your investment.** Most people think of their pets as part of the family, but the legal system assigns them the same value as a piece of luggage. Inquire about insurance — an airline that won't insure animals in its care may not be the right one for your pet. (Always read the fine print before purchasing any insurance policy.) Also ask if the airline's workers are trained to handle animals. Few are, but it doesn't hurt to check. Remember, it's up to you to choose an airline that values pets and will treat yours with care.

❧ **Understand the potential hazards.** Because a plane's cargo hold is neither cooled nor heated until take-off, the most dangerous time for your pet is that spent on the ground in this unventilated compartment. In summer the space absorbs heat while the plane sits on the tarmac; the reverse is true in winter, when it is no warmer inside the hold than outside. Both instances expose pets to the possibility of serious injury or death from heatstroke or hypothermia. **Note:** The latter also may be a concern during flight if the hold's heater is disabled or turned off, allowing the temperature to drop to near-freezing levels.

To minimize these risks, USDA-APHIS rules prohibit animals from being kept in the hold or on the tarmac for more than 45 minutes when temperatures are above 85 F or below 45 F. Some airlines impose even tighter temperature restrictions and may not permit animals to fly on planes going to cities where the ground temperatures may exceed these limits. Delta, for example, does not carry animals in the cargo hold May 15 through Sept. 15. (Exceptions may be made for animals whose veterinarians certify they are acclimated to colder temperatures, but never warmer.)

❧ **Make stress-free travel arrangements.** Once you decide to fly, reserve space for Spot or Snowball when you arrange your own tickets, preferably well in advance of your travel date. Airlines accept only a limited number of animals per flight — usually two to four in the passenger cabin and one pet per passenger — on a first-come, first-served basis. More animals are generally allowed in the cargo hold.

Prepare to pay an additional fee, about $75-$100 each way; the cost is often greater for large animals traveling on a flight without their owner. (Unfortunately, pets are not eligible for frequent flyer miles.) Always reconfirm your reservations and flight information 24-48 hours before departure.

If your pet will be flying in the hold, travel on the same plane and reserve a nonstop flight. This not only reduces the danger of heatstroke or hypothermia during layovers, it also eliminates the possibility that she will be placed on

PET INSURANCE

Just like their owners, pets can experience major medical problems at some point in their lifetime — even those that live indoors. And if illness strikes while you're on the road, it may be necessary to obtain care quickly. As a result, more and more people who travel with their devoted companion are considering pet health insurance.

Insurance plans run the gamut from basic coverage and routine care for illness and injury to comprehensive health maintenance, vaccinations and exams. Annual premiums range from less than $100 to more than $350, depending on the type of pet and plan. When choosing your plan, consider the following:

- What are the enrollment guidelines (age, breed, specific restrictions, etc.)?
- Which expenses are covered and which are excluded?
- What is the plan's policy concerning existing health problems?
- Does the plan allow you to use your own veterinarian?
- How are veterinary fees paid?
- Is a multiple pet discount offered?

the wrong connecting flight. In summer, fly during the early morning or late evening when temperatures are cooler. Because of large crowds and the chance of heavy air traffic causing delays, avoid holiday travel whenever possible.

Additional precautions may be necessary when traveling outside the United States and Canada. Other countries may impose lengthy quarantines, and airline workers outside North America may not be bound by animal welfare laws. *(See International Travel, p. 18.)*

❀ **Play an active role in your pet's well-being.** Flying safely with your pet requires careful planning and attention to his welfare. See the veterinarian within 10 days of departure for a health certificate (required by most airlines) and a pre-flight check-up.

Address any concerns you have about your pet traveling by air, especially if you are considering tranquilization. Sedation usually is not recommended for cats and dogs, regardless of whether they fly in the cabin or in the hold. Exposure to increased altitude pressure can create respiratory and cardiovascular problems; animals with short, wide heads are particularly susceptible to disorientation and possible injury. Sedation should never be administered without your veterinarian's approval.

Obtain an airline-approved carrier and acclimate your pet to its presence by leaving it open with a familiar object inside. A sturdy, well-ventilated crate adds an additional measure of protection.

Because animals are classified as luggage, they may be loaded on the plane via conveyor belt. If the crate falls off the belt, your pet could be injured or released. Ask that she be hand-carried on and off the plane, and that you be permitted to watch both procedures. Also ask about "counter-to-counter" shipping, in which the animal is loaded immediately before departure and unloaded immediately after arrival. There usually is an additional fee for this service.

Make sure you will have access to your pet if there is a lengthy layover or delay. Think twice about flying on an airline that won't allow you to check on your animal under such circumstances.

❀ **Prepare for the flight.** Keep in mind that traveling with an animal will require additional pre-flight time and preparation on your part. Exercise your pet before the flight, and arrive at least two but not more than four hours before departure. If he is traveling as carry-on luggage, check-in is normally at the passenger terminal; if he is traveling as checked baggage or as cargo in the cargo hold, proceed to the airline's cargo terminal, which is often in a different location. Find this out when making reservations and again when confirming flight information.

Make sure your animal's crate is properly labeled and secured, but do not lock it in case airline personnel have to provide emergency care. Include an ice pack for extra comfort on a hot day or a hot water bottle on a cold day. **Hint:** Wrap in a towel to prevent leaking.

Do not feed your pet less than four hours before departure, but provide water up until boarding. **Hint:** Freeze water in the bowl so that it melts throughout the trip, providing a constant drinking source.

Spot or Snowball should wear a sturdy collar (breakaway collars are recommended for cats) and two identification tags marked with your name, home address and phone number, and travel address and phone number. It's also a good idea to clip your pet's nails before departure so they won't accidentally get caught on any part of the carrier.

Note: You may be required to take your pet out of the carrier as you pass through security on your way to the gate. Make sure the animal is wearing a collar and leash or harness.

Attach food and water dishes inside the carrier so that airline workers can reach them without opening the door. If the trip will take longer than 12 hours, also attach a plastic bag with at least one meal's worth of dry food. Animals under 16 weeks of age must be fed every 12 hours, adult animals every 24 hours. Water must be provided at least every 12 hours, regardless of the animal's age.

Allow your pet to answer the call of nature before boarding, but do not take her out of the carrier while in the terminal. As a courtesy, wait until you are outside and away from fellow travelers. Keep her leash with you — do not leave it inside or attached to the kennel.

If your pet is traveling as carry-on luggage, let the passenger sitting next to you know. Someone with allergies may want to change seats.

Perhaps the most important precaution is to alert the flight crew and the captain that your pet is aboard. The pilot must activate the heater for the cargo hold; make sure this is done once you are in the air. If there are layovers or delays, ask the flight crew to be sure your pet has adequate shelter and/or ventilation; better yet, ask them to allow you to check in person.

If you have arranged to watch your pet being unloaded, ask a flight attendant to call the baggage handlers and let them know you are on the way. Above all, do not hesitate to voice any concerns you have for your pet's welfare — it is your responsibility to do so.

❀ **Be prepared for emergencies.** In the unlikely event your pet gets lost en route, contact the airline, local humane shelters, animal control agencies or USDA-APHIS. Many airlines can trace a pet that was transferred to the wrong flight. If your pet is injured in transit, proceed to the nearest animal hospital; register any complaints with USDA-APHIS. **Hint:** Carry a list of emergency contact numbers and a current photograph of your pet in your wallet or purse, just in case.

At Your Destination

How well you and your companion behave on the road directly affects the way future furry travelers will be treated. Always clean up after your pet and keep him under your control. This is not only a courtesy to fellow human travelers; it's the surest way to enjoy a safe and happy vacation.

Inquire about pet policies before making lodging reservations. Properties may impose restrictions on the type or size of pet allowed, or they may designate only certain rooms, such as smoking rooms, for travelers with animals. If you have a dog, get a room on the first floor with direct access outside, preferably near a walking area; keep her leashed on any excursion.

Lodgings may have supervision policies requiring that pets be crated when unattended or that they may not be left alone at all. Allow your pet only in designated exercise or animal-approved areas; never take him into such off-limits places as the lobby, pool area, patio or restaurant. Prepare to receive limited housekeeping service, or none at all.

Expect to pay some type of additional charge, which may be per room or per pet and may include any of the following: refundable deposit, non-refundable deposit, daily fee, weekly fee.

If staying with friends or relatives, make certain your pet is a welcome guest. Know and respect their "house rules," especially if they have small children or pets of their own.

Once in the room, check for such hazards as chemically treated toilet water, hiding spaces and electrical cords before freeing your pet. Give her time to adjust to her new surroundings under your supervision.

Above all, practice good "petiquette":

❧ Try not to leave your pet alone, but if you must, crate or otherwise confine her.

❧ Crate at night as well.

❧ To keep your pet and the housekeeper from having an unexpected encounter, leave the "Do Not Disturb" sign on the door when you go out without him.

❧ Barking dogs make poor hotel neighbors — keep your pet quiet.

❧ Don't allow your pet on the furniture. If she insists on sleeping on the bed, bring a bedspread or sheet from home and place that on top of the hotel bedding.

❧ Clean up after your pet immediately — inside the room and out — and leave no trace of him behind when checking out.

❧ Dispose of litter and other "accidents" properly — check with housekeeping.

❧ Notify the management immediately if something is damaged, and be ready to pay for repairs.

❧ Add a little extra to the housekeeping tip.

❧ When you take your pet out of the room, keep her leashed, especially in wilderness areas and around small children. No matter how obedient she is at home, new stimuli and distractions may cause her to forget or ignore vocal commands. Know and obey animal policies at parks, beaches and other public areas. Check before arriving to make certain animals still are welcome, even if you've been there before — the rules may have changed.

❧ Look for outdoor cafes when selecting restaurants. For health reasons, pets are not permitted inside eating establishments, but many restaurants allow animals to sit quietly with their owners at outdoor tables. Drive-through restaurants are another alternative.

In Case of Emergency

Be prepared for any turn of events by knowing how to get to the nearest animal hospital. *(See Animal Clinics, p. 50)* Also have the name and number of a local animal shelter and a local veterinarian handy — ask your veterinarian for a recommendation. Take first-aid supplies with you and know how to use them. An animal in pain may become aggressive, so exercise caution at all times.

Emergency evacuation shelters do not accept pets, and domesticated animals do not fare well if left to weather an emergency on their own, especially when far from home. Avert a potential tragedy by planning in advance where you will go with your pet in case of evacuation. Use the listings in this book to find other lodgings willing to take you and your pet. Above all, don't wait for disaster to strike. Leave as soon as the evacuation order is announced, and take your animal with you.

The Great Outdoors

Travelers planning an active or camping vacation should make some additional preparations. Check in advance to be sure your pet is permitted at campgrounds, parks, beaches, trails and anywhere else you will be visiting. If there are restrictions — and there usually are — follow them. Remember that pets other than service animals usually are not allowed in public buildings.

Note: It is not advisable to take animals other than dogs into wilderness areas. For example, bringing a pet is not recommended at some national parks in Alaska. Also keep in mind that rural areas often have few veterinarians and even fewer boarding kennels.

Use common sense. Clean up after your pet, do not allow excessive vocalizing and keep her under your control. If the property requires your pet to be leashed or crated at all times, do so. Few parks or natural areas will allow a pet to be unattended, even when chained — the risk of disagreeable encounters with other travelers or wildlife is too great. The National Park Service may confiscate pets that harm wildlife or other visitors.

If camping, crate your pet at night to protect him from the elements and predators. (Chaining confines the animal but won't keep him from becoming a midnight snack.)

When hiking, stick to the trail and keep your pet on a short leash. It is all too easy for an unleashed pet to wander off and get lost or fall prey to a larger animal. Keep an eye out for such wildlife as alligators, bears, big cats, porcupines and skunks, and avoid other dogs and small children. Be aware of indigenous poisonous plants, such as English ivy and oleander, or those causing physical injury, such as cactus, poison ivy or stinging nettle. Your veterinarian or local poison control center should be able to give you a full list of hazardous flora.

Before setting out on the trail, make sure both of you are in good physical shape. An animal that rarely exercises at home will not suddenly be ready for a 10-mile trek across uneven terrain. Plan a hike well within the limits of your pet's endurance, and don't push — remember, if Spot gets too tired to make it back on her own, you'll have to carry her.

Carry basic first-aid supplies, including a first-aid guide. *(See What to Take, p. 10.)* Also carry fresh drinking water for both of you — "found" water may contain harmful germs or toxins. Drink often, not just when thirst strikes, and have your pet do the same. Watch for signs of dehydration, leg or foot injuries, heat exhaustion or heatstroke. Stop immediately and return home or to camp if any of these occur.

Note: Dogs can carry their own backpacks (check your local pet store for specially designed packs), but should never carry more than one-third of their body weight. Train the dog to accept the pack beforehand, and only use it with a strong, healthy animal in excellent physical condition.

No matter where or how you spend your vacation, visit the veterinarian when you return home to check for injuries, parasites and general health.

Note: Most campgrounds accept pets. The AAA CampBook guides are an excellent source for obtaining detailed information regarding pet policies, restrictions and extra charges for campgrounds in the United States and Canada. AAA members may obtain complimentary copies of the CampBook guides at their local AAA club.

Traveling Between the United States and Canada

Traveling across the international border with your pet — either from the United States into Canada or from Canada into the United States — should prove largely hassle-free, although some basic regulations need to be kept in mind.

Effective Jan. 23, 2007, the Western Hemisphere Travel Initiative requires all persons — including U.S. citizens — traveling by air between the United States and Canada, Mexico, Bermuda and the Caribbean region to present a passport or other accepted secure document. The requirement will be extended to land and sea border crossings by summer 2008, but no exact date has been set. AAA recommends that all travelers carry a passport for visits outside the United States to simplify the travel process. Visit the U.S. State Department's travel Web site at www.travel.state.gov, or phone (877) 487-2778 for more information.

U.S. Customs grants returning U.S. citizens who stay in Canada more than 48 hours an individual $800 duty-free exemption (if not used within the prior 30 days). Any amount over the $800 exemption is subject to duty.

The exemption is based on fair retail value and applies to goods acquired for personal or household use or as gifts but not intended for sale. All items for which the exemption is claimed must accompany you upon return.

A 5 percent Goods and Service Tax (GST) is levied on most items sold and most services rendered in Canada. In New Brunswick, Nova Scotia or Newfoundland and Labrador, a Harmonized Sales Tax (HST) of 13 percent (which includes the GST) is charged on goods and services. Rebates can be claimed on some items. Brochures that explain the GST and contain a rebate form are available at tourist information centers, customs offices and duty free shops at the border and in airports.

U.S. citizens taking pet cats and dogs three months of age and older into Canada must carry a health certificate signed by a licensed veterinarian that describes the animal and provides proof of rabies vaccination within the past 12 or 36 months, depending on the type of vaccine. Collar tags are not sufficient proof of immunization. The certificate also is needed to bring a pet back into the United States; make sure the vaccination doesn't expire while you're in Canada. **Note:** Pit bulls are not permitted into Ontario.

Service animals are exempt from import restrictions. Also exempt are up to two puppies or kittens under three months old; obtain a certificate of health from your veterinarian indicating that the animal is too young to vaccinate. **Note:** For details on pet imports, contact the Canadian Embassy; 501 Pennsylvania Ave. N.W., Washington, DC 20001; phone (202) 682-1740. The Web site address is www.canadianembassy.org.

The Canadian Food Inspection Agency (CFIA) provides additional pet information; phone (613) 225-2342 or visit the Web site at www.inspection.gc.ca. If you need assistance while in Canada, contact the U.S. Embassy, 490 Sussex Dr., P.O. Box 866/Station B, Ottawa, ON, Canada K1N 1G8/K1P 5T1; phone (613) 238-5335.

Canadian Customs allows Canadian citizens to bring back from the United States, duty and tax free, goods valued up to $400 any number of times per year, provided the visit is 48 hours or more. A $50 exemption, excluding alcoholic beverages and tobacco products, may be claimed if the visit is 24 hours or more and no other exemption is being used. If returning from a visit of 7 days or more (not counting the day of departure from Canada), the exemption goes up to $750.

Canadian travelers may take pet cats and dogs into the United States with no restrictions, but U.S. Customs requires that dogs have proof of rabies vaccination no less than 30 days before arrival. For additional information on U.S. regulations, contact the Animal and Veterinary Services department of the USDA-APHIS National Center for Import and Export, (301) 734-3277.

International Travel

If you plan to travel abroad with Spot or Snowball, prepare for a lengthy flight and at least a short quarantine period. Be aware that airline and animal workers in other countries may not be bound by the same animal welfare laws that exist in the United States and Canada. Contact the embassy or consulate at your destination for information about documentation and quarantine requirements, animal control laws and animal welfare regulations.

As with any trip, have your pet checked by your regular veterinarian within 10 days of departure to obtain a health certificate showing proof of rabies and other inoculations. If you are traveling with an animal other than a domesticated dog or cat, check with USDA-APHIS for restrictions or additional documentation required.

The booklet "Pets and Wildlife: Licensing and Health Requirements" has general information about traveling abroad with animals; write U.S. Customs & Border Protection, 1300 Pennsylvania Ave. N.W., Washington, D.C. 20229; phone (202) 354-1000, or visit www.customs.gov.

Note: Island nations such as Australia and the United Kingdom, which are rabies-free, have adopted the Pet Travel Scheme (PETS) to allow entry for dogs and cats from the U.S. and Canada without the usual 6-month quarantine. Pets must be tested and vaccinated for rabies at least 6 months prior to travel, be implanted with microchip identification and receive a certificate of treatment from an official government veterinarian. For information, visit the U.K. Web site for the Department for Environment, Food and Rural Affairs (DEFRA) at www.defra.gov.uk. Hawaii, which has a standard 120-day quarantine for all imported animals except guide dogs, has adopted a similar expedited program of 5 days or less; a pet must have been vaccinated at least *twice* for rabies in its lifetime.

Loss Prevention Tips

Searching the woods or an unfamiliar town for a missing pet is easily prevented by following these helpful tips:

❧ Have your pet wear a sturdy nylon or leather collar with current ID and rabies tags firmly attached. Be sure the ID tag includes the phone number of an emergency contact. Consider having your pet implanted with microchip identification; it's a simple procedure similar to a vaccination.

❧ Keep your pet on a leash or harness. Even trained animals can become agitated or disoriented in unfamiliar surroundings and fail to obey vocal commands.

❧ Attach the leash or harness while your pet is still inside the closed car or crate.

❧ Do not leave your pet unattended at any time, anywhere. A stolen pet is extremely difficult to recover.

❧ Escape-proof your hotel room by crating your pet and asking hotel management to make certain no one enters your room while you are gone. (Inform the property that you're traveling with an animal when making reservations.)

❧ Take along a recent picture and a detailed written description of your pet.

If your pet gets lost these steps will improve your chances of recovery:

❧ If your pet is lost in transit, contact the airline immediately. Ask to trace the animal via the airline's automated baggage tracking system.

❧ Contact local police, animal control, animal shelters, humane organizations and veterinary clinics with a description and a recent photograph. Stay in contact until your pet is found, and provide your home and destination phone numbers.

❧ Post signs and place an ad in the local newspaper so that anyone who comes across your pet knows she is lost and how to reach you.

The Last Word

You are ultimately responsible for your pet's welfare and behavior while traveling. Since animals cannot speak for themselves, it is up to you to focus on your pet's well-being every step of the way. It also is important to make sure he conducts himself properly so that other pets will be welcome visitors in the future. Following the common-sense information in this book will help ensure that both you and your animal companion have a safe and happy trip.

PET-FRIENDLY
PLACES

IN THE UNITED STATES AND CANADA

Dog Parks
Attractions
National Public Lands
Emergency Animal Clinics

DOG PARKS

A dog park is a place where people and their dogs can play together. These places offer dogs an area to play, exercise and socialize with other dogs while their owners enjoy the park-like setting. Dog park size and features vary greatly from location to location, from several hundred square feet in urban areas to several hundred acres in the suburbs and rural locations. Dog owners should remember to always keep their animal leashed until they reach the dog park entrance, to maintain voice control of their animal at all times, to bring their own supply of bags for picking up after their pet (and to be diligent in doing so), and to always have fresh water available for their dog. Please observe all dog park rules.

This list of dog parks in the United States and Canada is provided by Dogpark.com®. Dogpark.com is all about dogs — all breeds, all mixes of breeds, and all shapes, sizes and dispositions. It provides articles and information about dogs and their care, health and play. Online, visit www.dogpark.com.

The dog parks listed here welcome people who travel with their dogs; private parks or parks requiring local residency are not included. **Note:** Fence types and heights vary, and some areas have no fencing at all, requiring that the dog be under firm voice control.

United States

ARIZONA

Chaparral Park - Scottsdale
scottsdaleaz.gov/parks/offleashareas.asp
5401 N. Hayden Rd. (at the southeast corner of McDonald Drive and Hayden Road)
5:30 a.m.-10 p.m., May-Oct.; 6 a.m.-10 p.m., rest of year
Closed for maintenance 8 a.m.-noon Tues. and Fri. and in wet conditions. Phone (480) 312-9963 for status.
Fenced, 4 acres, benches, shade, restroom, water, separate areas for large and small dogs.

Horizon Park - Scottsdale
scottsdaleaz.gov/parks/offLeashareas.asp
15444 N. 100th St. (Thompson Peak Parkway and 100th Street, east of SR 101 off Frank Lloyd Wright Boulevard)
Daily dawn-dusk
Fenced, lighted, benches, little shade, tables, disposal bags, trash cans, parking, phones, restrooms; bring your own water.

Vista del Camino Park - Scottsdale
scottsdaleaz.gov/parks/offleashareas.asp
7700 East Pierce St. (take Pierce Street heading west from Hayden Road)
Daily dawn-dusk
Fenced, lighted, 1/2 acre, grass turf, benches, restrooms nearby, dog and people water fountains, mutt mitt stations.

Creamery Park - Tempe
tempe.gov/parks/pdf/Dog%20Park%20Flyer%202007.pdf
8th Street and Una Avenue (just south of University near Rural)
Daily 6 a.m.-10 p.m.
Fenced, lighted, benches, disposal bags, trash cans, parking, water. For information phone (480) 350-5200.

Jaycee Park - Tempe
tempe.gov/parks/pdf/Dog%20Park%20Flyer%202007.pdf
5th Street and Hardy Drive
Daily 6 a.m.-10 p.m.
Fenced, lighted, trees, benches, disposal bags, trash cans, parking, water. Access for the disabled. For information phone (480) 350-5200.

Mitchell Park - Tempe
tempe.gov/parks/pdf/Dog%20Park%20Flyer%202007.pdf
Mitchell Drive and 9th Street
Daily 6 a.m.-10 p.m.
Fenced, lighted, trees, benches, disposal bags, trash cans, parking, water. Access for the disabled. For information phone (480) 350-5200.

Papago Park - Tempe
tempe.gov/parks/pdf/Dog%20Park%20Flyer%202007.pdf
Curry Road and College Avenue
Daily 6 a.m.-10 p.m.
Fenced, lighted, trees, disposal bags, trash cans, parking, water. For information phone (480) 350-5200.

Tempe Sports Complex - Tempe
tempe.gov/parks/pdf/Dog%20Park%20Flyer%202007.pdf
Warner Road and Hardy Drive
Daily 6 a.m.-midnight
Fenced, lighted, trees, disposal bags, trash cans, parking, water. For information phone (480) 350-5200.

CALIFORNIA

Calabasas Bark Park - Calabasas
cityofcalabasas.com/recreation/barkpark.html
4232 Las Virgenes Rd., south of the Las Virgenes Municipal Water District (approximately 2 miles west of US 101 on the south side)
Daily 5 a.m.-9 p.m.
Fenced, lighted, trees, benches, scoops, trash cans, paved parking, dog water fountain, separate areas for large and small dogs.

Costa Mesa Bark Park - Costa Mesa
cmbarkpark.org
Arlington Drive and Newport Boulevard, across from the Orange County Fairgrounds Equestrian Center
Wed.-Mon. dawn-9 p.m.; phone ahead in rainy conditions, (949) 733-4101
Fenced, 2.1 acres, night lights from dusk until 9 p.m., grass turf, trees, benches, tables, disposal bags, trash cans, parking, restrooms, water. Access for the disabled.

CALIFORNIA (CONT'D)

Ernie Smith Dog Park - El Verano
sonoma-county.org/parks/pk_smith.htm
18776 Gilman Dr.
Daily dawn-dusk. Parking free.
Fenced, double-gated entry, .5 acre, picnic tables, waste bags, garbage can, dog water fountain.

Elizabeth Anne Perrone Dog Park - Glen Ellen
sonoma-county.org/PARKS/foundation/
perrone_dog_park.htm
13630 Sonoma Hwy. in Sonoma Valley Regional Park (SR 12 between Arnold Drive and Madrone Road)
Daily dawn-dusk. Parking fee $5 or annual park pass.
Fenced, 1 acre, double-gated entry, covered gazebo, shade trees, dog water fountain.

Huntington Dog Beach - Huntington Beach
dogbeach.org
Pacific Coast Highway between 21st and Seapoint streets
Daily 5 a.m.-10 p.m.; parking lot closes at 10 p.m.
Unfenced, benches and tables on the bluffs above the beach, disposal bags, trash cans, metered parking, restrooms. Dogs may be off leash anywhere on the beach while under an owner's supervision. Access for the disabled to the sand.

Laguna Niguel Pooch Park - Laguna Niguel
ci.laguna-niguel.ca.us/index.asp?SID=481
31461 Golden Lantern near Chapparosa Park
Tues.-Thurs. and Sat. 7 a.m.-dusk, Sun. 8 a.m.-dusk, Mon. and Fri. noon-dusk
Fenced, 1 acre, Wood chip ground cover, picnic tables, shelters, disposal bag dispenser, parking, restroom, water faucet with hose, separate fenced area for small dogs.

Long Beach Recreation Dog Park - Long Beach
geocities.com/lbdogpark
5201 East 7th St. at Park
Daily dawn-10 p.m.
Fenced, lighted, trees, crushed-granite surface, benches, tables, disposal bags, trash cans, parking, water, separate fenced area for small dogs. Access for the disabled.

Palm Springs Dog Park - Palm Springs
ci.palm-springs.ca.us/dogpark.html
3200 E. Tahquitz Canyon Way, behind City Hall
Daily dawn-10 p.m.
Fenced, lighted, double-gated entry, trees, benches, tables, shelter, disposal bags, trash cans, parking, phones, dual-level drinking fountains, separate areas for large and small dogs, antique fire hydrants. Unusual iron fence created by sculptor Phill Evans. Access for the disabled.

Redondo Beach Dog Park - Redondo Beach
rbdogpark.com
Southeast corner of 190th Street and Flagler Lane
Daily dawn-dusk; closed Wed. dawn-noon for maintenance
Fenced, trees, benches, disposal bags, trash cans, parking, phones, water, separate fenced area for small dogs. Access for the disabled.

Bannon Creek Park - Sacramento
cityofsacramento.org/parksandrecreation/parks/
dogpark1.htm
Bannon Creek Park, 2780 Azevedo Dr. off of Azevedo Dr., near West El Camino
Daily 5 a.m.-10 p.m.
Fenced, double-gated entry, .6 acres, benches, disposal bag dispensers, dog drinking fountain/faucet.

Granite Dog Park - Sacramento
cityofsacramento.org/parksandrecreation/parks/
dogpark1.htm
Ramona Avenue off Power Inn Road in Granite Regional Park
Daily 5 a.m.-10 p.m.
Fenced, double-gated entry, 2 acres, bench, disposal bags, trash cans, water spigot for dogs. Access for the disabled.

Partner Park - Sacramento
cityofsacramento.org/parksandrecreation/parks/
dogpark1.htm
5699 South Land Park Dr. at Fruitridge Road, behind Belle Cooledge Community Center
Daily dawn-10 p.m.
Fenced, lighted, double-gated entry, 2 acres landscaped with turf and mature trees, bench, disposal bags, trash cans, water spigot for dogs. Access for the disabled.

Tanzanite Community Park - Sacramento
cityofsacramento.org/parksandrecreation/parks/
dogpark1.htm
2220 Tanzanite Way in Tanzanite Community Park
Daily 5 a.m.-10 p.m.
Two acres, landscaped with turf and native grass, bench, disposal bags, trash cans, drinking fountain for dogs.

Balboa Park - San Diego
sandiego.gov/park-and-recreation/general-info/dogs.shtml
Two off-leash areas:
(1) Nate's Point at El Prado, on the southwest side of Cabrillo Bridge
(2) Morley Field, northwest of the tennis courts
Daily 24 hours
Unfenced, large field.

Cadman Community Park - San Diego
sandiego.gov/park-and-recreation/general-info/
cadmanleashfree.shtml
4280 Avati Dr.
Phone (858) 581-9929 for specific hours
Unfenced.

Capehart Park (Pacific Beach) - San Diego
sandiego.gov/park-and-recreation/general-info/dogs.shtml
Soledad Mountain Road and Feldspar Street
Daily 24 hours
Fenced, 1 acre, picnic tables, benches, parking, separate grass-turf areas for large and small dogs, areas to provide water for dogs, drinking fountain.

Dog Beach - San Diego
sandiego.gov/park-and-recreation/general-info/dogs.shtml
Voltaire Street in Ocean Beach; enter the parking lot at the west end of Voltaire
Daily 24 hours
Unfenced, disposal bags, trash cans, water, restrooms nearby. Access for the disabled.

CALIFORNIA (CONT'D)

Doyle Community Park - San Diego
sandiego.gov/park-and-recreation/general-info/dogs.shtml
8175 Regents Rd. behind Doyle Recreation Center
Daily 24 hours.
Fenced, no lights, separate grass-turf areas for large and small dogs.

Fiesta Island - San Diego
sandiego.gov/park-and-recreation/general-info/dogs.shtml
Mission Bay Park; this island allows dogs anywhere outside the fenced areas.
Daily 6 a.m.-10 p.m.

Grape Street Park - San Diego
sandiego.gov/park-and-recreation/general-info/dogs.shtml
Grape Street and Granada Avenue
Mon.-Fri. 7:30 a.m.-9 p.m.; Sat.-Sun. and holidays 9-9
Unfenced, 5 acres, lighted, trees, benches, tables, trash cans, parking, restrooms, water.

San Francisco
San Francisco regularly reviews its off-leash ("dog play area") policies. Refer to sfgov.org/site/recpark_page.asp?id=2180 for the most recent information on dog parks.

Alamo Square Park - San Francisco
sfgov.org/site/recpark_page.asp?id=2180
Scott Street between Hayes and Fulton streets in the western half of the park
Daily 6 a.m.-10 p.m.
Unfenced; dogs must be under firm voice control.

Alta Plaza Park - San Francisco
sfgov.org/site/recpark_page.asp?id=2180
Clay Street between Scott and Steiner streets, on the second terrace of the park
Daily 6 a.m.-10 p.m.
Unfenced; dogs must be under firm voice control.

Bernal Heights - San Francisco
sfgov.org/site/recpark_page.asp?id=2180
Bernal Heights Boulevard at the top of the hill
Daily 6 a.m.-10 p.m.
Unfenced; dogs must be under firm voice control.

Brotherhood Mini Park - San Francisco
sfgov.org/site/recpark_page.asp?id=2180
Head Street and Brotherhood Way on Department of Public Works property, improved by Recreation and Parks Dept.
Daily 6 a.m.-10 p.m.
Unfenced; dogs must be under firm voice control.

Buena Vista Park - San Francisco
sfgov.org/site/recpark_page.asp?id=2180
Buena Vista West at Central Avenue
Daily 6 a.m.-10 p.m.
Unfenced; dogs must be under firm voice control.

Corona Heights - San Francisco
sfgov.org/site/recpark_page.asp?id=2180
Roosevelt Way and Museum Way in the field next to Randall Museum
Daily 6 a.m.-10 p.m.
Fenced.

Crocker Amazon Playground - San Francisco
sfgov.org/site/recpark_page.asp?id=2180
Between LaGrande and Dublin streets in the northern portion of park, adjacent to community garden
Daily 6 a.m.-10 p.m.
Unfenced; dogs must be under firm voice control.

Dolores Park - San Francisco
sfgov.org/site/recpark_page.asp?id=2180
Between Church and Dolores streets, south of tennis courts and soccer field to central lawn
Daily 6 a.m.-10 p.m.
Unfenced; dogs must be under firm voice control.

Douglass Park - San Francisco
sfgov.org/site/recpark_page.asp?id=2180
27th and Douglass streets, upper field
Daily 6 a.m.-10 p.m.
Unfenced; dogs must be under firm voice control.

Eureka Valley Recreation Center - San Francisco
sfgov.org/site/recpark_page.asp?id=2180
Collingwood Street, adjacent to the tennis courts, east of baseball diamond
Daily 6 a.m.-10 p.m.
Fenced.

Golden Gate Park - San Francisco
sfgov.org/site/recpark_page.asp?id=2180
Four off-leash areas:
(1) Southeast section bounded by Lincoln Way, King Drive and 2nd and 7th avenues
(2) Northeast section at Fulton and Willard streets
(3) South-central area bounded by Martin Luther King Jr. Drive, Middle Drive and 34th and 38th avenues
(4) Fenced dog-training area near 38th Avenue and Fulton Street

Jefferson Park - San Francisco
sfgov.org/site/recpark_page.asp?id=2180
Eddy and Laguna Streets at the northwest end of the park
Daily 6 a.m.-10 p.m.
Unfenced; dogs must be under firm voice control.

Lafayette Park - San Francisco
sfgov.org/site/recpark_page.asp?id=2180
Near Sacramento Street between Octavia and Gough streets
Daily 6 a.m.-10 p.m.
Unfenced; dogs must be under firm voice control.

Lake Merced - San Francisco
sfgov.org/site/recpark_page.asp?id=2180
Lake Merced Boulevard and Middlefield Drive, northern lake area
Daily 6 a.m.-10 p.m.
Unfenced; dogs must be under firm voice control.

McKinley Square - San Francisco
sfgov.org/site/recpark_page.asp?id=2180
San Bruno Avenue and 20th Street, on the west slope
Daily 6 a.m.-10 p.m.
Unfenced; dogs must be under firm voice control.

CALIFORNIA (CONT'D)

McLaren Park - San Francisco
sfgov.org/site/recpark_page.asp?id=2180
Two off-leash areas:
(1) A 59-acre hilltop bounded by Shelly Drive with trails, open areas, reservoir and fence at roadway. Includes natural area, excludes group picnic facilities, children's play area and custodian housing. Leash restrictions during performances at amphitheater.
(2) South entrance at 1600 block of Geneva adjacent to natural area with open area fenced on roadway
Daily 6 a.m.-10 p.m.

Mountain Lake Park - San Francisco
sfgov.org/site/recpark_page.asp?id=2180
North of Lake Street at 8th Avenue, east end of park
Daily 6 a.m.-10 p.m.
Unfenced; dogs must be under firm voice control.

Pine Lake Park - San Francisco
sfgov.org/site/recpark_page.asp?id=2180
Crestlake and Vale streets, west of and contiguous to Stern Grove and adjacent to the parking lot
Daily 6 a.m.-10 p.m.
Unfenced; dogs must be under firm voice control.

Potrero Hill Mini Park - San Francisco
sfgov.org/site/recpark_page.asp?id=2180
22nd Street between Arkansas and Connecticut streets
Daily 6 a.m.-10 p.m.
Unfenced; dogs must be under firm voice control.

St. Mary's Recreation Center - San Francisco
sfgov.org/site/recpark_page.asp?id=2180
Justin and Benton Streets, lower terrace of the park
Daily 6 a.m.-10 p.m.
Fenced.

Stern Grove - San Francisco
sfgov.org/site/recpark_page.asp?id=2180
Wawona Street between 21st and 23rd avenues, north side
Daily 6 a.m.-10 p.m.
Unfenced; dogs must be under firm voice control.

Upper Noe Recreation Center - San Francisco
sfgov.org/site/recpark_page.asp?id=2180
30th Street between Church and Sanchez streets, behind and along the baseball field
Daily 6 a.m.-10 p.m.
Fenced.

Walter Haas Playground - San Francisco
sfgov.org/site/recpark_page.asp?id=2180
Diamond Heights Boulevard on upper terrace of the park
Daily 6 a.m.-10 p.m.
Unfenced; dogs must be under firm voice control.

Field of Dogs - San Rafael
fieldofdogs.org
3540 Civic Center Dr. near the intersection of US 101 and North San Pedro Road
Daily dawn-dusk
Fenced, double-gated entry, trees, benches, tables, shelter, disposal bags, trash cans, parking, water. Access for the disabled.

DeTurk Roundbarn Park - Santa Rosa
ci.santa-rosa.ca.us/default.aspx?PageId=2074
819 Donahue St. between West 8th and 9th streets
Daily dawn-dusk
Fenced, water (small neighborhood park).

Doyle Park Dog Park - Santa Rosa
ci.santa-rosa.ca.us/default.aspx?PageId=2074
700 Hoen Ave. within Doyle Park (go west on Sonoma Avenue, turn left on Hoen and then turn right into the parking lot; the fenced dog park is behind the stadium)
Daily dawn-dusk
Fenced, 3/4 acre, bench, disposal bags, water, small and large dog areas.

Galvin Dog Park - Santa Rosa
ci.santa-rosa.ca.us/default.aspx?PageId=2074/
3330 Yulupa Ave. in Don Galvin Park, next to Bennet Valley Golf Course
Daily dawn-dusk
Fenced, double-gated entry, 1/2 acre, trees, trash cans, parking, water, picnic tables, restrooms. Access for the disabled.

Northwest Community Dog Park - Santa Rosa
ci.santa-rosa.ca.us/default.aspx?PageId=2074
2620 W. Steele Lane in Northwest Community Park (go west on Gurneville Road, turn right on Marlow and then turn right at the first traffic light into the park's parking lot; walk east along the path to the dog park on the left)
Daily dawn-dusk
Fenced, 1/2 acre, benches, disposal bags, trash cans, restrooms nearby, water, separate area for small dogs.

Rincon Valley Dog Park - Santa Rosa
ci.santa-rosa.ca.us/default.aspx?PageId=2074
5108 Badger Rd. in Rincon Valley Community Park
Daily dawn-dusk
Fenced, 1/2 acre, trees, benches, tables, disposal bags, trash cans, parking, phones, restrooms, water, separate fenced areas for large and small dogs (large-dog area closed during the winter), fenced pond area for dogs (open year-round). Monitors are present during peak hours to enforce rules. Access for the disabled.

Off-leash, unfenced, under voice control areas:

700 Doyle Park Drive - Santa Rosa
ci.santa-rosa.ca.us/default.aspx?PageId=2074
700 Doyle Park Dr. (go west on Sonoma, turn left on Hoen and then turn right into the parking lot; the unfenced, off-leash area is to the right of the fenced dog park)
Daily 6-8 a.m.

Franklin Park - Santa Rosa
ci.santa-rosa.ca.us/default.aspx?PageId=2074
2095 Franklin Ave.
Daily 6-8 a.m.

Southwest Community - Santa Rosa
ci.santa-rosa.ca.us/default.aspx?PageId=2074
1698 Hearn Ave.
Daily 6-8 a.m.

Youth Community - Santa Rosa
ci.santa-rosa.ca.us/default.aspx?PageId=2074
1725 Fulton Rd.
Daily 6-8 a.m.

CALIFORNIA (CONT'D)

Remington Dog Park - Sausalito
www.sausalitodogpark.org/index.htm
Ebbtide at Bridgeway
Mon.-Fri. 7-7, Sat.-Sun. 8-7
Fully fenced, lighted, safety-gated entry, picnic tables, benches, tents for shelter, scoops and scooper cleaning station, trash cans, parking, water, tennis balls and racquets provided.

Animal Care Center Dog Park - Sebastopol
sonoma-county.org/parks/pk_ragle_dog.htm
500 Ragle Rd.
Daily dawn-dusk. Parking fee $5 or annual park pass
Fenced, double-gated entry, .5 acre, waste bags & garbage can, dog water fountain.

Sierra Madre Dog Park - Sierra Madre
cityofsierramadre.com/index.php?mod=police_services
611 East Sierra Madre Blvd. in Sierra Vista Park, south of the tennis courts
Daily 6 a.m.-10 p.m. Permit required; daily permit $5. Daily and annual permits are available at City Hall; the Sierra Madre Police Department, 242 W. Sierra Madre Blvd.; or the Sierra Madre Community Recreation Center, 611 E. Sierra Madre Blvd.
Fenced, lighted, double-gated entry, trees, benches, disposal bags, trash cans, parking, phones, restrooms, water, separate fenced areas for large/active dogs and "special needs" dogs. Access for the disabled.

Baldy View Dog Park - Upland
baldyviewdogpark.com
Located on 11th street in the city of upland between Mountain Ave. and San Antonio Ave.
Daily dawn-dusk.
Fenced, double-gated entry and exit, 1.3 acres, grass turf, shade trees, benches, free parking, small and large dog sections, dog water stations.

COLORADO

Grandview Off-Leash Dog Park - Aurora
auroragov.org For additional information phone (303) 739-7160
17900 E. Quincy Ave., just east of Pitkin Street, adjacent to Quincy Reservoir on the lake's west side
Daily dawn-dusk
Fenced, trash cans, parking, water.

East Boulder Community - Boulder City
bouldercolorado.gov/index.php?option=com
_content&task=view&id=2409&Itemid=1926
5660 Sioux Dr.
Daily dawn-dusk
Fenced, disposal bags, trash cans, parking, water, fenced-off swimming area. Access for the disabled.

Foothills Community Park - Boulder City
bouldercolorado.gov/index.php?option=com
_content&task=view&id=2409&Itemid=1926
Locust Avenue and Lee Hill Road, west of Broadway
Daily dawn-dusk
Fenced, disposal bags, trash cans, parking, water. Access for the disabled.

Howard H. Hueston Park - Boulder City
bouldercolorado.gov/index.php?option=com
_content&task=view&id=2409&Itemid=1926
34th Street near O'Neal Parkway
Daily dawn-dusk
Unfenced, trees, benches, tables, trash cans, parking. Dogs must be under voice and sight control. Access for the disabled.

Valmont Dog Park - Boulder City
bouldercolorado.gov/index.php?option=com
_content&task=view&id=2409&Itemid=1926
Valmont and Airport roads
Daily dawn-dusk
Fenced, disposal bags, trash cans, parking, water. Access for the disabled.

Palmer Park - Colorado Springs
http://www.springsgov.com/Page.asp?NavID=5109
Maizeland Road and Academy Boulevard
Daily 5 a.m.-11 p.m., May-Oct.; 5 a.m.-9 p.m., rest of year
Fenced, benches, tables, disposal bags, trash cans, parking, restrooms, water. Access for the disabled.

Rampart Dog Park - Colorado Springs
http://www.springsgov.com/Page.asp?NavID=5109
8270 Lexington Dr. (from the intersection of Lexington Drive and N. Union Boulevard, go north on Lexington, then turn left into the park entrance)
Daily 5 a.m.-11 p.m., May-Oct.; 5 a.m.-9 p.m., rest of year
Fenced, trees, benches, disposal bags, trash cans, parking, water. Access for the disabled.

Barnum Park - Denver
www.denvergov.org/PRdogsoffleash/ or Dogs-off-leash
hotline: (303) 964-1006
Hooker and West 5th
Daily 5:00 a.m.-11:00 p.m
Natural barriers (turf with split-rail fencing to delineate boundaries), 3 acres, trees, trash bags and cans, parking, restroom, bulletin board.

Berkeley Park - Denver
www.denvergov.org/PRdogsoffleash/ or Dogs-off-leash
hotline: (303) 964-1006
Sheridan and West 46th
Daily 5:00 a.m.-11:00 p.m.
Fenced, 2 acres, turf, double-gate entry, trees, trash bags and cans, parking, bulletin board.

Denver Off-Leash Dog Park - Denver
denvergov.org
678 South Jason St. behind the Denver Municipal Animal Shelter
Daily dawn-dusk
Fenced, grass turf, parking, toys. Access for the disabled.

Fuller Park - Denver
www.denvergov.org/PRdogsoffleash/ or Dogs-off-leash
hotline: (303) 964-1006
Franklin and East 29th
Daily 5:00 a.m.-11:00 p.m.
Fenced, 1 acre, turf, double-gate entry, trash bags and cans, bulletin board, on-street neighborhood parking only.

COLORADO (CONT'D)

Green Valley Ranch East Park - Denver
www.denvergov.org/PRdogsoffleash/ or Dogs-off-leash
hotline: (303) 964-1006
Jebel and East 45th
Daily 5:00 a.m.-11:00 p.m.
Natural barriers (native vegetation and split-rail fencing to
delineate boundaries), 2 acres, trash bags and cans,
parking.

Kennedy Park - Denver
www.denvergov.org/PRdogsoffleash/ or Dogs-off-leash
hotline: (303) 964-1006
Hampden and South Dayton
Daily 5:00 a.m.-11:00 p.m.
Natural barriers (native vegetation and split-rail fencing to
delineate boundaries), 3 acres, trash bags and cans,
bulletin board, very limited parking.

FLORIDA

Happy Tails Canine Park - Bradenton
51st Street West at G.T. Bray Park, about halfway
between Manatee Avenue and Cortez Road
Daily dawn-dusk
Eight-foot fence, 3 acres, trees, benches, tables, disposal
bags, trash cans, parking (including handicapped spaces),
restrooms nearby, water.

Dr. Paul's Memorial Dog Park - Coral Springs
toppetcare.com/petutopiawelcome.htm
Sportsplex Drive in the Sportsplex Regional Park Complex
(park off Sportsplex Drive at the west pedestrian entrance)
Daily dawn-9:30 p.m.
Enclosed, lighted, trees, shaded area, paved running path,
picnic table, gazebo, disposal bag dispensers, trash cans,
indoor restroom, separate areas for large and small dogs,
dog and people water fountains, dog shower, dog statues,
weatherproof dog agility equipment.

Barkley Square Dog Park - DeLand
volusia.org/parks/barkley.htm
1010 N. Ridgewood Ave. (take SR 17/92 north to
Plymouth Avenue, turn left on Plymouth Avenue, then turn
right on N. Ridgewood Avenue; the dog park is on the left)
Daily dawn-dusk
Fenced, 14 acres, trees, parking, dog watering stations,
areas for small and large dogs.

The Dog Park in Lake Ida Park - Delray Beach
pbcgov.com/parks/dogparks/lakeida
2929 Lake Ida Rd. (take the Atlantic Avenue West exit off
I-95, proceed west to Congress Avenue, go north on
Congress for 1 mile, turn right onto Lake Ida Road and
proceed east under I-95; park entrance is on the left)
Daily dawn-dusk; closed Thurs. noon-3 for maintenance
Fenced, 2.5 acres, partial paved pathway, eight shaded
sitting areas, disposal bag dispensers and receptacles,
restrooms and parking nearby, separate fenced areas for
large and small dogs, two canine drinking stations, dog
washing area, information kiosk.

Pooch Pines Dog Park at Okeeheelee Park - Delray Beach
pbcgov.com/parks/dogparks/lakeida
7715 Forest Hill Blvd. (off I-95 exit Forest Hill Boulevard,
west to the main Okeeheelee Park entrance on the north
side of the road; follow the park road to the Pooch Pines
sign, turn right and continue to the top of the hill)
Daily dawn-dusk; closed Wed. noon-3 for maintenance
Fenced, 5 acres, paved pathways, shaded sitting areas,
disposal bag dispensers and receptacles, trash cans,
restrooms and parking nearby, separate areas for large
and small dogs, canine drinking stations, dog washing
area.

Bark Park at Snyder Park - Fort Lauderdale
ci.fort-lauderdale.fl.us/cityparks/snyder/barkpark
3299 S.W. 4th Ave.
Daily 7 a.m.-7:30 p.m., Apr.-Oct.; 7-6:30, rest of year.
Fee Mon.-Fri. $2; $1.50 (senior citizens and ages 6-12).
Fee Sat.-Sun. and holidays $2.50; $2 (senior citizens and
ages 6-12).
Fenced, two open-air pavilions, benches, disposal bags,
trash cans, parking, restrooms, water, separate area for
small dogs, two hose stations, drinking fountains, agility
equipment, small nature area with more than 20 labeled
native trees. Freshwater dog swim Sat.-Sun. and holidays
10-5, first weekend in Mar.-first Sun. in Dec.; fee $1. Dogs
must remain in the car until arrival at Bark Park and are
not permitted in the remainder of Snyder Park. Access for
the disabled.

Dog Wood Off-Leash Park - Gainesville
dogwoodpark.com
5505 S.W. Archer Rd. (1 mile west of I-75)
Tues.-Thurs. 1-4, Fri. 4-6 p.m., Sat.-Sun. 9-5; closed Jan.
1, and Dec. 24-25 and 31.
Fee $9 plus tax for the first dog, $2 plus tax for each
additional dog per family (otherwise $2.50 plus tax for
each additional dog in the group)
Six-foot fence, 15 acres, double-gated entry and exit,
jogging trail, hammocks, gazebo, picnic tables, lounge
chairs, swinging and regular benches, multiple clean-up
stations with disposal bags, indoor restrooms, free bottled
water, soft drinks for sale, two large swimming ponds for
dogs, wading pools, dog shower, agility course, sunny and
shady areas for small dogs, park-provided tennis balls.
Park also offers a do-it-yourself dog wash, a doggie
boutique, dog day care and agility and obedience training.
All male dogs over 7 months must be neutered in order to
enter the park. Children under 4 feet tall are not permitted.
Phone (352) 335-1919 for details.

Paw Park of Historic Sanford - Sanford
pawparksanford.org
427 French Ave. (US 17/92) in Sanford's Historic District,
20 minutes north of downtown Orlando. From I-4, take the
SR 46 exit (exit 101C, Sanford/Mount Dora), proceed east
on SR 46 approximately 4 miles to French Avenue, turn
right (southbound) and get into the left thru-lane; the Paw
Park is on the left just past the Burger King
Daily 7:30 a.m.-8 p.m.
Fenced, double-gated entry, shaded with mature oak trees,
historic lighting, paved walkway, benches, tables, disposal
bag dispensers, parking, self-watering bowls, water misting
station, dog showers, separate area for small dogs,
community bulletin board. Access for the disabled.

FLORIDA (CONT'D)

17th Street Park & Paw Park - Sarasota
scgov.net/CommunityServices/ParksandRecreation/Parks/parks.asp
4570 17th St.
Daily dawn-dusk
Six-foot fence, 6 acres, lighted, double-gated entry, trees, benches, tables, disposal bags, trash cans, parking, restrooms, water, dog shower, separate area for small dogs, community bulletin board.

Lakeview Park - Sarasota
scgov.net/CommunityServices/ParksandRecreation/Parks/parks.asp
7150 Lago St.
Daily dawn-midnight
Six-foot fence, double-gated entry, many trees, benches, tables, disposal bags, trash cans, parking, restrooms, water, dog shower, separate area for small dogs, community bulletin board. Access for the disabled.

Brohard Beach & Paw Park - Venice
venicegov.com/Park_links/paw.htm
1600 Harbor Dr. South
Daily 7 a.m.-dusk
Six-foot fence, trees, benches, tables, shelter, disposal bags, trash cans, parking, water, dog shower, separate area for small dogs, community bulletin board. Dog Beach is accessed by boardwalk from Paw Park. Dogs are permitted in a restricted area along Brohard Beach as indicated by beach signs. Access for the disabled.

Woodmere Park & Woodmere Paw Park - Venice
scgov.net/CommunityServices/ParksandRecreation/RecreationCenters/Woodmere_Park.asp
3951 Woodmere Park Blvd. (two blocks north of U.S. 41 on Jacaranda Boulevard)
Daily dawn-dusk
Fenced, double-gated entry, trees, benches, tables, disposal bags, trash cans, parking, restrooms, water, double-gated section for small dogs near the front gate, dog shower, community bulletin board.

ILLINOIS

Rover's Run Dog Park - Homewood
hfparks.com/parks/roversrun.htm
At 191st St. and Center Ave. in Apollo Park
Daily dawn-dusk.
Membership fee $15 per year for residents, $25 per year for non-residents. A list of current vaccinations is required. Phone (708)957-0300 for details.
Fenced, 3 acres, double-gated entry, separate training area and entrance, benches, covered picnic tables, free parking, walking path, owner/dog drinking fountain.

MICHIGAN

Orion Oaks Bark Park - Lake Orion
oakgov.com/parksrec/activities/dogpark.html
Joslyn Road, south of Clarkston Road (park at the north Joslyn Road entrance and follow the signs)
Daily half-hour before dawn to half-hour after dusk
Resident park pass $7 per day, $30 annual pass. Non-resident park pass $12 per vehicle per day, $46 annual pass. Over 62, park pass $4 per vehicle per day, $28 annual pass. Park pass required; a daily pass is available at the Lake Orion Township office (open Mon.-Fri.) on Joslyn Road south of the park; or at Independence Oaks County Park (open daily) on Sashabaw Road 2.5 miles north of I-75.
Fenced, 7 acres, trees, benches, tables, disposal bags, trash cans, parking, portable toilet, water. A portion of Lake Sixteen is reserved for canine swimmers. Access for the disabled.

Lyon Oaks Bark Park - Lyon Township
oakgov.com/parksrec/activities/dogpark.html
Pontiac Trail between Wixom and Old Plank roads
Daily half-hour before dawn to half-hour after dusk
Resident park pass $7 per day, $30 annual pass. Non-resident park pass $12 per vehicle per day, $46 annual pass. Over 62, park pass $4 per vehicle per day, $28 annual pass. Park pass required; daily and annual passes are available at the park.
Fenced, 13 acres of open fields, benches, tables, disposal bags, trash cans, parking, restrooms, water pump.

MINNESOTA

Note: In the greater Minneapolis area there are multiple off-leash sites within a 15-minute drive of downtown Minneapolis/St. Paul. There are additional sites in rural/suburban areas of the seven-county metropolitan area. Some parks require a permit for use; please read descriptions carefully.

Alimagnet Dog Park - Burnsville (south metro suburb)
alimagnetdogpark.org
1200 Alimagnet Pkwy. (from central St. Paul, go south on I-35E to the CR 42 exit, east to CR 11, then north on CR 11 to Alimagnet Parkway and turn right; the dog park is on the right)
Daily 5 a.m.-10 p.m. Permit required; for information go to burnsville.org/index.asp?NID=287 or phone the Recreation Department at (952) 895-4500.
Fenced, 7 acres, double-gated entry, wooded areas, open fields, mowed prairie-grass trail, benches, tables, disposal bags, trash cans, parking, phones, restrooms, water, pond.

Coates/Dakota County (south metro rural)
www.co.dakota.mn.us/LeisureRecreation/Parks/DogPark/default.htm
Blaine Avenue south of CR 46 (160th Street E.) in the center of Dakota County near Coates
Daily 5 a.m.-10 p.m. Permit required.
Fenced, 16 acres of wooded and open spaces with a walking trail loop, tables, disposal bag dispensers and receptacles, parking, portable toilets, no surface water; bring drinking water for your dog.

MINNESOTA (CONT'D)

Elm Creek Park Reserve - Dayton (northwest metro rural)
threeriversparkdistrict.org/trails/trails_pet.cfm
13080 Territorial Rd.
Daily 5 a.m.-dusk. Permit required; day permits are available at the site. Annual special-use permits may be obtained by phoning Park Guest Services at (763) 559-9000.
Fenced, 30 acres with a mowed trail, trees, tables, trash cans, parking, restrooms.

Battle Creek Off-Leash Site - Maplewood (east central metro)
co.ramsey.mn.us/parks/parks/offleash.asp
Lower Afton and McKnight
Daily dawn-dusk. No permit required.
Partially fenced, 12 acres, tables, trash cans, parking.

Franklin Terrace - Minneapolis
minneapolisparks.org/default.asp?PageID=851
Franklin Terrace and 30th Avenue S.
Daily 6 a.m.-10 p.m. Permit required; phone (612) 348-4250 for information.
Fully fenced, 1.6 acres, double-gated entry at the east and west ends of the site, bench, disposal bag dispensers, on-street parking.

Lake of the Isles Park - Minneapolis
minneapolisparks.org/default.asp?PageID=851
Lake of the Isles Parkway and W. 28th Street
Daily 6 a.m.-10 p.m. Permit required; phone (612) 348-4250 for information.
Fully fenced, 3.6 acres, double-gated entry at the northern end of the site, lighted at the southern end, benches, disposal bag dispensers.

Loring Park - Minneapolis
minneapolisparks.org/default.asp?PageID=851
Maple Street and Harmon Place
Daily 6 a.m.-10 p.m. Permit required.
Fenced, one-quarter acre, disposal bag dispensers, limestone boulders for climbing and sitting, crushed limestone surfce.

Minnehaha Park - Minneapolis
minneapolisparks.org/default.asp?PageID=851
Minnehaha Avenue and E. 54th Street
Daily 6 a.m.-10 p.m. Permit required; phone (612) 348-4250 for information.
Partially fenced, 4.2 acres along the Mississippi River (where dogs can swim), disposal bag dispensers, lighted parking area (parking permit required), portable toilet in parking area.

Saint Anthony Parkway - Minneapolis
minneapolisparks.org/default.asp?PageID=851
St. Anthony Pkwy. off Central Ave.
Daily 6 a.m.-10 p.m. Permit required; phone (612) 348-4250 for information.
Fully fenced, 2 acres, double-gated entry at the east and west ends of the park, bench, disposal bag dispensers, parking.

Egan Park's Off-Leash Area - Plymouth
http://www2.ci.plymouth.mn.us
CR 47 in northwest Plymouth, about two blocks west of Dunkirk Lane on the south side of CR 47
Daily dawn-dusk. No permit required.
Unfenced, 10 acres, trash cans; bring your own drinking water and disposal bags.

Cleary Lake Regional Park - Prior Lake (south metro rural)
threeriversparkdistrict.org/trails/trails_pet.cfm
18106 Texas Ave.
Daily 5 a.m.-dusk. Permit required; day permits are available at the site. Annual special-use permits may be obtained by phoning Park Guest Services at (763) 559-9000.
Fenced, 35 acres, tables, trash cans, parking, restrooms, pond. Trails are mowed in summer, packed in winter.

Lake Sarah Regional Park - Rockford (west metro rural)
threeriversparkdistrict.org/trails/trails_pet.cfm
Lake Sarah Drive, 30 miles west of Minneapolis and east of CR 92 (take US 55 west to CR 92, proceed south to Lake Sarah Drive, turn left and then left again onto the first gravel road; the parking lot for the off-leash area is on the left side)
Daily 5 a.m.-dusk. Permit required; day permits are available at the site. Annual special-use permits may be obtained by phoning Park Guest Services at (763) 559-9000.
Unfenced, 30 acres, trees, mowed parking area, trash cans, restrooms.

Crow-Hassan Park Reserve - Rogers (northwest metro rural)
threeriversparkdistrict.org/trails/trails_pet.fmc
Sylvan Lake Road west of Rogers (from I-94, take the Rogers exit and go south through town to the T intersection, turn right on CR 116 and proceed to CR 203, turn left and follow CR 203 to the park entrance)
Daily 5 a.m.-dusk. Permit required; day permits are available at the site. Annual special-use permits may be obtained by phoning Park Guest Services at (763) 559-9000.
Fenced, 30 acres with a mowed trail, trees, tables, trash cans, parking, restrooms.

Woodview Dog Park - Roseville (central)
co.ramsey.mn.us/parks/parks/offleash.asp
Larpenteur Avenue, just east of Dale Street (access gate to main off-leash area is about 100 yards down the bike trail)
Daily dawn-dusk. No permit required.
Partially fenced (along bike trail only), 3 acres, trees, tables, disposal bags, trash cans, parking, water, separate fenced area for small dogs. Access for the disabled.

Rice Creek Off-Leash Site - Shoreview (northeast metro)
co.ramsey.mn.us/parks/parks/offleash.asp
Lexington Avenue, just south of CR J
Daily dawn-dusk. No permit required.
Unfenced, 12 acres of flat prairie vegetation, tables, trash cans, parking, small pond.

MINNESOTA (CONT'D)

Bass Lake/Belt Line - St. Louis Park (west central)
stlouispark.org/experience/off_leash_dog_park.htm
West 36th Street and Belt Line Boulevard at Bass Lake
Preserve, east of the tennis courts
Daily 7 a.m.-8:30 p.m. Permit required.
Fenced, 1.5 acres; bring drinking water for your dog.

Arlington-Arkwright (ArlArk) Dog Park - St. Paul
stpaul.gov/depts/parks/userguide/dogpark
Arkwright Street at Arlington Avenue (from I-35E, take the
Maryland Avenue exit east to Arkwright Street, then go
north; the park is on the right-hand side)
Daily dawn-9 p.m. No permit required.
Fenced, 4.5 acres with trails and woods, tables, disposal
bags, trash cans, parking. Park users sometimes leave
gates open; keep your dog under voice control to prevent
escapes.

Otter Lake Dog Park - White Bear Township (northeast suburban)
co.ramsey.mn.us/parks/parks/offleash.htm
Otter Lake Road (take I-35E to the CR J exit, then CR J
east to Otter Lake Road, following it south to the dog
park; the entrance is next to the boat launch)
Daily dawn-dusk. No permit required.
Partially fenced, 10 acres of rolling hills with wooded and
open prairie vegetation, separate 1-acre fenced area for
small dogs. The park is fenced adjacent to Otter Lake
Road and along most of the south boundary, bounded on
the east by a large wetland and on the north by Otter
Lake.

NEVADA

All Clark County/Las Vegas dog park areas include
water, seating and waste receptacles.

Desert Breeze Park Dog Park - Clark County/Las Vegas (NW)
accessclarkcounty.com/parks/Dog_Parks.htm
8425 W. Spring Mountain Rd. at Durango
Daily 6 a.m.-11 p.m.

Desert Inn Dog Park - Clark County/Las Vegas (SE)
accessclarkcounty.com/parks/Dog_Parks.htm
3570 Vista del Monte, near Lamb and Boulder Highway
Daily 6 a.m.-11 p.m.

Dog Fancier's Park - Clark County/Las Vegas (SE)
accessclarkcounty.com/parks/Dog_Parks.htm
5800 E. Flamingo Rd., off E. Flamingo and Jimmy
Durante
Daily 6 a.m.-11 p.m.
This 12-acre park is also used for dog shows and training.

Molasky Park Dog Park - Clark County/Las Vegas (SE)
accessclarkcounty.com/parks/Dog_Parks.htm
1065 E. Twain, west of Maryland Parkway; dog run is
south of Twain
Daily 6 a.m.-11 p.m.

Shadow Rock Dog Park - Clark County/Las Vegas (NE)
accessclarkcounty.com/parks/Dog_Parks.htm
2650 Los Feliz (cross streets Lake Mead past Hollywood);
dog run is east of the park area
Daily 6 a.m.-11 p.m.

Sunset Park - Clark County/Las Vegas (SE)
accessclarkcounty.com/parks/Dog_Parks.htm
2601 E. Sunset Rd.; closest parking is off Eastern
between Sunset and Warm Springs roads
Daily 6 a.m.-11 p.m.

NEW HAMPSHIRE

Derry Dog Park - Derry
derry.nh.us
45 Fordway St.
Daily dawn-dusk
Fenced, .5 acres, gazebo, picnic tables, bone-shaped dog
pool in summer only. Tunnel, seesaw, tire jump and other
agility items are provided. Children under 9 are not
permitted. Rules are posted on fence inside and out.
Parking is free but somewhat limited after 25 vehicles.

NEW YORK

New York City (Manhattan and boroughs)
urbanhound.com
nycgovparks.org/sub_things_to_do/facilities/
af_dog_runs.html

Canine Court, Van Cortlandt Park - Bronx
West 252nd Street and Broadway (enter on the path on
252nd and follow it about 100 feet to the left)
Daily dawn-dusk
Fenced with two large runs: a basic dog run and a canine
agility playground with teeter-totter, hurdles, ladder, three
chutes and a hanging tire.

Ewen Park ("John's Run") - Bronx (Riverdale)
Riverdale to Johnson avenues, south of West 232nd
Street and down the steps in the clearing on the right
Daily dawn-dusk
Unfenced, plastic lawn furniture, scenic views.

Seton Park - Bronx (Riverdale)
West 235th Street and Independence Avenue (west of
Independence on 235th Street, near the Spuyten Duyvil
Library)
Daily dawn-dusk

Prospect Park - Brooklyn
fidobrooklyn.org
Grand Army Plaza and Flatbush; off-leash areas may be
accessed from all park entrances
Daily 9 p.m.-9 a.m. At all other times, dogs must be on a
leash, minimum fine for non-compliance $100.
Trees, restrooms (at Long Meadow only; may not be
available early in the morning), water (some fountains
equipped with troughs for dogs). No separate area for
small dogs. Small swimming area in the Long Meadow
near the 9th Street entrance. Note: Use of the park is at
the owner's risk. Dogs may be off-leash with appropriate
supervision in three large meadows at the hours specified
above; please observe all off-leash rules. Rules are posted
online and at park entrances. Dogs must be on a leash at
all other places and times.

Owl's Head Park - Brooklyn (Bay Ridge)
68th Street and Shore Road
Tree, grass surface, disposal bags.

Hillside Park - Brooklyn Heights
Columbia Heights and Middagh Street
Daily 24 hours
Fenced.

NEW YORK (CONT'D)

Palmetto Playground - Brooklyn Heights
Columbia Place and State Street (in the corner by the Brooklyn-Queens Expressway)
Daily 24 hours
Benches, one park light, water.

Tompkins Square Park - Manhattan (East Village)
East 9th Street at Avenue B
Daily 6 a.m.-midnight
Benches, picnic tables, water, a canine memorial.

Madison Square Park - Manhattan (Gramercy/Flatiron/ Union Square)
East 24th Street at Fifth Avenue
Daily 6 a.m.-midnight
Trees, benches, disposal bags, water.

Thomas Jefferson Park - Manhattan (Harlem)
East 112th Street at First Avenue
Daily 24 hours
Benches, wood chips surface.

J. Hood Wright Park - Manhattan (Inwood/Ft. George/ Washington Heights)
West 173rd Street between Fort Washington Avenue and Haven Avenue

Fishbridge Park - Manhattan (Lower East Side)
Dover Street at Pearl Street, just south of the Brooklyn Bridge
Daily dawn-dusk
Benches, water hose, summer wading pool, lockbox for toys, lockbox with newspapers for picking up after your dog.

Peter Detmold Park — Manhattan (Midtown East)
East 49th Street at FDR Drive (behind Beeckman Place)
Daily dawn-9 p.m., June-Sept.; dawn-8 p.m., Mar.-May and Oct.-Nov.; dawn-7 p.m., rest of year
Trees, benches, historical lamps, disposal bags.

Carl Shurz Park - Manhattan (Upper East Side)
East 86th Street at East End Avenue
Daily dawn-1 a.m.
Benches, scoops, pea gravel surface. A second run for small dogs (past the main run, toward the East River) has a scenic view of the river and the 59th Street Bridge.

Riverside Park at 72nd Street - Manhattan (Upper West Side/Morningside Heights)
West 72nd Street
Daily 6 a.m.-1 a.m.
Bench, hanging flowerpots, disposal bags, scoopers.

Riverside Park at 87th Street - Manhattan (Upper West Side/Morningside Heights)
West 87th Street
Daily dawn-dusk
Separate areas for large and small dogs, fountain and hose.

Riverside Park at 105th Street - Manhattan (Upper West Side/Morningside Heights)
riversidedog.org
West 105th Street, Riverside Park Central Promenade
Daily dawn-dusk
Trees, crushed granite surface, benches, disposal bag dispensers, drinking fountain, dog water faucet, separate area for small dogs.

Theodore Roosevelt Park - Manhattan (Upper West Side/Morningside Heights)
West 81st Street at Columbus Avenue
Daily 8 a.m.-10 p.m.
Shade trees, benches, dog water faucet, separate run for small dogs.

Washington Square Park - Manhattan (West Village)
West 4th Street at Thompson Street
Daily 6 a.m.-midnight
Trees, pea gravel surface, benches, scoopers, water hose, water bowls.

Doughboy Plaza - Queens (Woodside)
Woodside Avenue from 54th to 56th streets (also south of Woodside at 56th Street) at Windmuller Park
Daily dawn-dusk
Fenced, trash can.

NORTH CAROLINA

Down East Dog Park - New Bern
newbern-nc.org/RP/parks.php
303 Glenburnie Dr. in Glenburnie Park
Daily dawn-dusk
Annual fee $35 for first dog, $20 each additional dog; weekly passes $5. Proof of current rabies vaccination is required. Contact 252-639-7588 for more information.
Fenced; the main 1-acre area is for large dogs over 25 lbs., but dogs of any size may use it; a separate area is set aside for puppies and small dogs.

OHIO

Mt. Airy Dog Park - Cincinnati
cincinnati-oh.gov/cityparks/pages/-4327-/
Westward Northern Boulevard within Mt. Airy Forest's Highpoint Picnic Area, between Montana Avenue and North Bend Road
Daily dawn-dusk
Fenced, trees, benches, tables, shelter, trash cans, parking, restrooms, water. Access for the disabled.

Big Walnut Dog Park - Columbus
bigwalnutdogpark.com
5000 E. Livingston Ave. in Big Walnut Park, across from Walnut Ridge High School
Daily 7 a.m.-11p.m.
Fenced, 2 double-gate entries, 3 acres, swimming pond, shade trees, picnic tables, paved parking; no restrictions on breeds or spay/neuter.

OREGON

Alton Baker Park - Eugene
www.eugene-or.gov/parks
South of Leo Harris Parkway; park in the lot south of
Autzen Stadium and cross the pedestrian bridge to the
dog park
Daily 6 a.m.-11 p.m.
Fenced, benches, tables, simple shelters for protection
from sun and rain, disposal bag receptacles, water.

Amazon Park - Eugene
www.eugene-or.gov/parks
East of 29th Street and Amazon Parkway
Daily 6 a.m.-11 p.m.
Fenced, benches, tables, simple shelters for protection
from sun and rain, disposal bag receptacles, water,
parking nearby.

Morse Ranch - Eugene
www.eugene-or.gov/parks
Crest Drive and Lincoln Street (park in the main parking
area at 595 Crest Dr. and take the trail east)
Daily 6 a.m.-11 p.m.
Fenced, benches, tables, simple shelters for protection
from sun and rain, disposal bag receptacles, water.

Brentwood Park - Portland
http://www.portlandonline.com/parks/index.cfm?c=39523
SE 60th Avenue and Duke Street
Daily 5 a.m.-midnight
Fenced.

Chimney Park - Portland
http://www.portlandonline.com/parks/index.cfm?c=39523
9360 N. Columbia Blvd.
Daily 5 a.m.-midnight
Unfenced, 6 acres of off-leash meadow and trails. Dogs
should be under excellent voice command.

East Delta Park - Portland
http://www.portlandonline.com/parks/index.cfm?c=39523
N. Denver and Martin Luther King Jr. Boulevard (off I-5
exit 307 across from the East Delta Sports Complex)
Daily 5 a.m.-midnight, May-Oct. (open during dry season
only)
Fenced, 5 acres of off-leash field, trees, benches; bring
drinking water for your dog. Dogs are not allowed on the
sports fields.

Gabriel Park - Portland
http://www.portlandonline.com/parks/index.cfm?c=39523
S.W. 45th Street and Vermont
Daily 5 a.m.-midnight, May-Oct. (open during dry season
only)
Fenced, 1 5 acres of off-leash area, trees, picnic tables,
water. Dogs must remain leashed when not in the
off-leash area.

Normandale Park - Portland
http://www.portlandonline.com/parks/index.cfm?c=39523
NE 57th Avenue and Halsey Street
Daily 5 a.m.-midnight
Fenced.

TEXAS

White Rock Lake Dog Park - Dallas
dallasdogparks.org
Mockingbird Point within White Rock Lake Park
Tues.-Sun. 5 a.m.-midnight (weather permitting)
Fenced, 2.5 acres, trees, benches, disposal bags, trash
cans, parking, restrooms, water fountains, separate fenced
areas for large and small dogs, fenced swimming area for
dogs in White Rock Lake.

Jack Carter Park - Plano
plano.gov/Departments/parksandrecreation
/Parks_Facilities/dog_park.htm
Spring Creek Parkway and Pleasant Valley Drive; park is
half a block north of the intersection on Pleasant Valley
Drive
Daily dawn-dusk, weather permitting; closed for
maintenance first and third Tues. of the month
Fenced, 2 acres, double-gated entry, benches, disposal
bags, trash cans, parking, water fountains for dogs and
people.

VIRGINIA

Note: Disposal bag receptacles are provided at Alexandria
parks; patrons must provide their own bags.

Ben Brenman Park - Alexandria
www3.alexandriava.gov/recreation/parks/dogpark.html
Cameron Station along Backlick Creek
Daily 6 a.m.-10 p.m.
Fenced, disposal bag receptacles, trash cans, parking.

Dog Park - Alexandria
www3.alexandriava.gov/recreation/parks/dogpark.html
5000 block of Duke Street east of the Charles E. Beatley
Jr. Library
Daily 6 a.m.-10 p.m.
Fenced, disposal bag receptacles, trash cans, parking.

Montgomery Park - Alexandria
www3.alexandriava.gov/recreation/parks/dogpark.html
Fairfax and 1st streets
Daily 6 a.m.-10 p.m.
Fenced, disposal bag receptacles, trash cans, parking.

Simpson Stadium Park - Alexandria
www3.alexandriava.gov/recreation/parks/dogpark.html
Monroe Avenue
Daily 6 a.m.-10 p.m.
Fenced, disposal bag receptacles, trash cans, parking, dog
water fountains.

Off-leash, unfenced, under voice control areas:

Braddock Road - Alexandria
www3.alexandriava.gov/recreation/parks/dogpark.html
Southeast corner of Braddock Road and
Commonwealth Avenue
Daily 6 a.m.-10 p.m.
Unfenced.

Chambliss Street - Alexandria
www3.alexandriava.gov/recreation/parks/dogpark.html
Chambliss Street at Grigsby Avenue, south of the
tennis courts
Daily 6 a.m.-10 p.m.
Unfenced; area is marked by traffic barriers.

VIRGINIA (CONT'D)

Chinquapin Park - Alexandria
www3.alexandriava.gov/recreation/parks/dogpark.html
King Street at the east end of the loop road
Daily 6 a.m.-10 p.m.
Unfenced; area is marked by traffic barriers.

Edison Street - Alexandria
www3.alexandriava.gov/recreation/parks/dogpark.html
Edison Street, west of the cul-de-sac between the bike
trail and Berkey Photo Processing
Daily 6 a.m.-10 p.m.
Unfenced; area is marked by traffic barriers.

Ft. Williams - Alexandria
www3.alexandriava.gov/recreation/parks/dogpark.html
Ft. Williams and New Ft. Williams Parkway
Daily 6 a.m.-10 p.m.
Unfenced; area is marked by traffic barriers.

Founders Park - Alexandria
www3.alexandriava.gov/recreation/parks/dogpark.html
Oronoco Street and Union Street, northeast corner
Daily 6 a.m.-10 p.m.
Unfenced; 100-by-100-foot area is marked by traffic
barriers.

Off-leash, unfenced, under voice control areas:

Hooff's Run - Alexandria
www3.alexandriava.gov/recreation/parks/dogpark.html
East of Commonwealth Avenue between Oak and
Chapman streets
Daily 6 a.m.-10 p.m.
Unfenced; area is marked by traffic barriers.

Monticello Park - Alexandria
www3.alexandriava.gov/recreation/parks/dogpark.html
Beverly Drive, east of the entrance
Daily 6 a.m.-10 p.m.
Unfenced; 50-by-200-foot area is marked by traffic
barriers.

North Fort Ward Park - Alexandria
www3.alexandriava.gov/recreation/parks/dogpark.html
Braddock Road, east side of entrance
Daily 6 a.m.-10 p.m.
Unfenced; 100-by-100-foot area is marked by traffic
barriers.

Tarleton Park - Alexandria
www3.alexandriava.gov/recreation/parks/dogpark.html
Old Mill Run west of Gordon Street
Daily 6 a.m.-10 p.m.
Unfenced.

Timberbranch Parkway - Alexandria
www3.alexandriava.gov/recreation/parks/dogpark.html
Median to Timberbranch Parkway between Braddock
Road and Oakley Place
Daily 6 a.m.-10 p.m.
Unfenced; area is marked by traffic barriers.

Windmill Hill Park - Alexandria
www3.alexandriava.gov/recreation/parks/dogpark.html
Gibbon and Union streets
Daily 6 a.m.-10 p.m.
Unfenced.

W&OD Railroad - Alexandria
www3.alexandriava.gov/recreation/parks/dogpark.html
Raymond Avenue (200 feet of the W&OD Railroad
right-of-way south of Raymond)
Daily 6 a.m.-10 p.m.
Unfenced; area is marked by traffic barriers.

Benjamin Banneker Park - Arlington County
arlingtondogs.org
1600 block of North Sycamore Street (take I-66 west to
Sycamore Street/exit 69, turn left on Sycamore and
proceed past the East Falls Church Metro Station, turn
right onto North 16th Street and take the first right, which
dead-ends at the dog exercise area)
Daily dawn to half-hour after dusk
Fully fenced, picnic table and benches, water.

Fort Barnard Park - Arlington County
arlingtondogs.org
South Pollard Street and South Walter Reed Drive (from
Rte. 50, take Glebe Road south, turn right on South
Walter Reed Drive and proceed to Pollard Street; the park
is on the right side)
Daily dawn to half-hour after dusk
Fully fenced, picnic table and benches, water.

Glencarlyn Park - Arlington County
arlingtondogs.org
301 South Harrison St. (from Rte. 50, head west to Carlin
Springs Road, exit right and then turn left at the stop sign,
pass under Rte. 50 and follow Carlin Springs to 4th
Street, turn left on 4th Street and proceed five blocks until
the road ends at the Glencarlyn Park sign, following the
park road until it ends; park and walk over a small bridge
and stream to the exercise area)
Daily dawn to half-hour after dusk
Unfenced area near a creek and woods, picnic table,
benches.

Shirlington Park - Arlington County
arlingtondogs.org
2601 S. Arlington Mill Dr., bordering South Four Mile Run
between Shirlington Road and South Walter Reed Drive
along the bicycle path between a storage facility and the
water, near but not in Jennie Dean Park (from South Four
Mile Run, turn south onto Nelson and park behind the
storage facility; there are no signs indicating the dog park)
Daily dawn to half-hour after dusk
Partially fenced, picnic table, benches, water.

Towers Park - Arlington County
arlingtondogs.org
801 South Scott St. behind the tennis courts
Daily dawn to half-hour after dusk
Fully fenced, separate small dog area, parking.

Red Wing Park - Virginia Beach
vbgov.com
1398 General Booth Blvd.
Daily 7:30 a.m.-dusk; closed Jan. 1, Martin Luther King
Day, Veterans Day, Thanksgiving and Dec. 25
Annual fee for first-time visitors $10; owners must register
at the park office, show proof of pet's rabies shot and
vaccines, and obtain a city dog license.
Fenced, benches, disposal bags, parking, restrooms,
water. Access for the disabled.

VIRGINIA (CONT'D)

Woodstock Community Park - Virginia Beach
vbgov.com
5709 Providence Rd.
Daily 7:30 a.m.-dusk; closed Jan. 1, Martin Luther King Day, Veterans Day, Thanksgiving and Dec. 25
Annual fee for first-time visitors $10; owners must register at the park office, show proof of pet's rabies shot and vaccines, and obtain a city dog license.
Fenced, benches, disposal bags, restrooms, parking. Access for the disabled.

WASHINGTON

I-5 Colonnade Park - Seattle
coladog.org
Lakeview Boulevard and Franklin Avenue East in the Eastlake neighborhood beneath I-5, south of East Howe Street
Daily 6 a.m.-11 p.m.
Fenced, 1.2 acres, double-gated entry, dog water fountain; the I-5 freeway deck provides shelter from the elements.

I-90 "Blue Dog Pond" - Seattle
coladog.org
Martin Luther King Jr. Way and South Massachusetts Street, on the northwest corner
Daily 6 a.m.-11 p.m.
Fenced, 1 acre, parking, dog water fountain, Blue Dog sculpture. No off-leash areas in I-90 Lid Park, just east of Blue Dog Pond.

Dr. Jose Rizal Park - Seattle
coladog.org
1008 12th Ave. S. on North Beacon Hill; off-leash area is in the lower portion of the park
Daily 6 a.m.-11 p.m.
Fenced, 4 acres, double-gated entry, parking, dog water fountain, scenic view of downtown.

Genesee Park - Seattle
coladog.org
46th Avenue South and South Genesee Street
Daily 6 a.m.-11 p.m.
Fenced, 3 acres, double-gated entry, parking, dog water fountain.

Golden Gardens Park - Seattle
coladog.org
8498 Seaview Pl. N.W. in Ballard
Daily 6 a.m.-11 p.m.
Fenced, lighted, 1 acre, parking, dog water fountain. The off-leash area is in the upper (eastern) portion of the park; dogs are not allowed on the lower beach area.

Magnuson Park - Seattle
coladog.org
6500 Sandpoint Way N.E. (enter the park at 74th Street and drive to the end of the road)
Daily 6 a.m.-11 p.m.
Fenced, 9 acres, double-gated entry, shelter, parking, separate area for small/shy dogs, dog water fountain, beach access.

Northacres Park - Seattle
coladog.org
N. 130th Street, west of I-5; off-leash area is in the northeast corner of the park at 12530 Third Ave. N.E., north of the ball field. Parking is available on the west side of the park along 1st Street N.E. and on the south side along North 125th Street
Daily 6 a.m.-11 p.m.
Fenced, double-gated entry, parking, dog water fountain.

Plymouth Pillars Park - Seattle
coladog.org
Boren Avenue and Pike Street on Capitol Hill above I-5
Daily 6 a.m.-11 p.m.
Fenced, 9,800 square feet, double-gated entry, dog water fountain, scenic view of downtown Seattle.

Regrade Park - Seattle
coladog.org
3rd Avenue and Bell Street, downtown
Fenced, 13,000 square feet, double-gated entry, dog water fountain.

Westcrest Park - Seattle
coladog.org
8806 8th Ave. S.W. in West Seattle
Daily 6 a.m.-11 p.m.
Fenced, 5 acres, parking, dog water fountain. The off-leash area is along the east side of the reservoir.

Woodland Park - Seattle
coladog.org
West Green Lake Way North, west of the tennis courts
Daily 6 a.m.-11 p.m.
Fenced, 1 acre, double-gated entry, parking, dog water fountain.

Canada

ALBERTA

91 Street Right of Way - Edmonton
gov.edmonton.ab.ca, (780) 496-1475
Berm east of 91 Street from 10 Avenue north to Whitemud Freeway and east to 76 Street
Unfenced.

Buena Vista Great Meadow - Edmonton
gov.edmonton.ab.ca, (780) 496-1475
North of Laurier Park and Buena Vista Drive and south of Melton Ravine in the vicinity of 88 Avenue
Unfenced; area does not include the pedestrian bridge access trail, Yorath property or the trail north to McKenzie Ravine. This is a hot-air balloon site, so please leash your dog during balloon launches.

ALBERTA (CONT'D)

Hermitage Park North - Edmonton
gov.edmonton.ab.ca, (780) 496-1475
129 Avenue to 137 Avenue; also 22 Street along the riverbank where signs designate an off-leash area. Unfenced. This is a multi-use area in the valley north of the park's fishing pond and picnic area.

Jackie Parker Park - Edmonton
gov.edmonton.ab.ca, (780) 496-1475
Whitemud Freeway and 50th Street
Unfenced. Includes the area south of the 44 Avenue entrance; dogs are not allowed on the golf course.

Keehewin Blackmud - Edmonton
gov.edmonton.ab.ca, (780) 496-1475
Pipeline corridor, 104 Street and 20 Avenue to the south end of 109 Street (excludes Bearspaw Drive West and Blackmud Creek and Ravine)
Unfenced.

Kennedale - Edmonton
gov.edmonton.ab.ca, (780) 496-1475
Ravine west of the 40 Street loop, west to 47 Street and the top of the bank
Unfenced.

Lauderdale - Edmonton
gov.edmonton.ab.ca, (780) 496-1475
South end of Grand Trunk Park, from 127 to 129 Avenue and 113A to 109 Street
Unfenced.

Mill Creek Ravine - Edmonton
gov.edmonton.ab.ca, (780) 496-1475
68 Avenue and 93 Street; access is from the west or north sides of Argyll Park
Unfenced. A granular trail along the bottom of the ravine leads to the Whyte (82) Avenue overpass.

Terwillegar Park - Edmonton
gov.edmonton.ab.ca, (780) 496-1475
Rabbit Hill Road
Unfenced. This is a multi-use area.

MANITOBA

Bourkevale Park - Winnipeg
winnipeg.ca/publicworks/parks/fieldsforfido.asp
100 Ferry Rd., south of the dike along the riverbank
Daily 6 a.m.-10 p.m.
Unfenced, trash cans, parking; bring your own disposal bags.

Juba Park & Pioneer Avenue - Winnipeg
winnipeg.ca/publicworks/parks/fieldsforfido.asp
Pioneer Avenue, all vacant land west of the walkway to Juba Park
Daily 6 a.m.-10 p.m.
Unfenced, trash cans, parking; bring your own disposal bags.

Kil-Cona Park - Winnipeg
winnipeg.ca/publicworks/parks/fieldsforfido.asp
Lagimodiere Boulevard in the area north of the west parking lot
Daily 6 a.m.-10 p.m.
Unfenced, trash cans, parking; bring your own disposal bags.

King's Park - Winnipeg
winnipeg.ca/publicworks/parks/fieldsforfido.asp
King's Drive, south end of park, south of the lake
Daily 6 a.m.-10 p.m.
Unfenced, trash cans, parking; bring your own disposal bags.

Little Mountain Park - Winnipeg
winnipeg.ca/publicworks/parks/fieldsforfido.asp
West side of park adjacent to Klimpike Road entrance
Daily 6 a.m.-10 p.m.
Unfenced, trash cans, parking; bring your own disposal bags.

Maple Grove Park - Winnipeg
winnipeg.ca/publicworks/parks/fieldsforfido.asp
Frobisher Road, north area of park
Daily 6 a.m.-10 p.m.
Unfenced, trash cans, parking; bring your own disposal bags.

Mazenod Park - Winnipeg
winnipeg.ca/publicworks/parks/fieldsforfido.asp
Area surrounding retention pond, bordered by Mazenod Rd., Camiel Sys St. and Beghin St.
Daily 6 a.m.-10 p.m.
Unfenced, trash cans, parking; bring your own disposal bags.

Westview Park - Winnipeg
winnipeg.ca/publicworks/parks/fieldsforfido.asp
Midland Street; entire park is an off-leash area
Daily 6 a.m.-10 p.m.
Unfenced, trash cans, parking; bring your own disposal bags.

Wordsworth Park - Winnipeg
winnipeg.ca/publicworks/parks/fieldsforfido.asp
Northeast of King Edward Avenue and Park Lane
Daily 6 a.m.-10 p.m.
Unfenced, trash cans, parking; bring your own disposal bags.

United States

CALIFORNIA

Disneyland® Resort

(714) 781-4565, 1313 S. Harbor Blvd. via I-5 Disneyland Drive and Disney Way exits, Anaheim
Disneyland® Resort consists of two family-oriented theme parks — Disneyland® and Disney's California Adventure™ — and the shops, restaurants and entertainment of Downtown Disney®. Indoor kennel facilities. Both theme parks are open daily with extended hours during the summer, on some holidays and on weekends. Admission to either park $66; $64 (ages 61+); $56 (ages 3-9). Parking fee. disneyland.disney.go.com

SeaWorld

(619) 226-3901 or (800) 380-3203, 500 SeaWorld Dr., San Diego
SeaWorld offers animal shows, rides and playgrounds, a marina and exhibits featuring marine creatures from around the world. Pet facility provided for a nominal charge on a first-come, first-serve basis. Park open daily at 9, mid-June through Labor Day; at 10, rest of year. Closing times vary. Hours vary and may be extended during summer and holiday periods; phone ahead. Admission $59; $49 (ages 3-9). Parking fee. www.seaworld.com/

Universal Studios Hollywood

(800) 864-8377, off Hollywood Freeway (US 101) at Lankershim Boulevard, Universal City
In addition to thrill rides and attractions, Universal Studios gives visitors a behind-the-scenes look at the workings of a major film and TV studio. Complimentary kennel service. Park open daily 9-9, in summer; 10-6, rest of year. Box office closes nightly at 5, in summer; at 4, rest of year. Closed Thanksgiving and Dec. 25. Admission $64; $54 (under 48 inches tall). Parking fee. www.universalstudioshollywood.com

DISTRICT OF COLUMBIA

Washington Monument

(202) 426-6841, 15th Street and Constitution Avenue N.W., Washington, D.C.
This instantly recognizable 555-foot marble obelisk commemorates our nation's first president and is surrounded by expansive grounds. Pets on leash. Daily 9-4:45; closed Dec. 25. Free. www.nps.gov/wamo

FLORIDA

Busch Gardens Tampa Bay

(866) 353-8622 or (888) 800-5447, 3000 E. Busch Blvd., Tampa
This African-themed family entertainment park and outstanding zoological facility features all kinds of thrill rides and numerous opportunities for animal observation. Indoor kennel facilities. Generally open daily at 9; closing times vary. Phone ahead to confirm hours. Admission $64.95; $54.95 (ages 3-9). Parking fee. www.buschgardens.com

SeaWorld Orlando

(407) 351-3600 or (800) 327-2424, 7007 SeaWorld Dr. at I-4 and SR 528 (Beachline Expressway), Orlando
This marine life adventure park presents crowd-pleasing animal shows starring a family of performing killer whales. SeaWorld also features numerous attractions and rides, including a floorless roller coaster, penguin encounter area and simulated helicopter ride. Air-conditioned kennels. Generally open daily at 9; closing times vary. Phone ahead to confirm hours. Admission $67.95; $57.95 (ages 3-9). Parking fee. www.seaworld.com

Universal Orlando® Resort

(407) 363-8000, off I-4 exit 75A (eastbound) or 74B (westbound) following signs, Orlando
At Universal Orlando you can "ride the movies" at the Universal Studios® theme park, cavort with superheroes and cartoon characters at Universal's Islands of Adventure® theme park, or visit the specialty shops, celebrity-themed restaurants and entertainment venues at Universal CityWalk®. Air-conditioned kennels. Theme parks open daily at 9; closing times vary by season. Phone ahead to confirm hours. CityWalk open daily 11 a.m.-2 a.m. One-day admission to either theme park $71; $60 (ages 3-9). Individual CityWalk venue charges vary. Parking fee. www.universalorlando.com/

Walt Disney World® Resort

(407) 824-4321 or (407) 934-7639, theme parks accessible from US 192, Osceola Parkway and several I-4 exits, Lake Buena Vista
Walt Disney World has — count 'em — four theme parks: Magic Kingdom® Park, Epcot®, Disney's Animal Kingdom® Theme Park and Disney's Hollywood Studios, plus shopping, dining and entertainment at the Downtown Disney® Area. Air-conditioned kennels. Theme parks generally open daily at 9; closing times vary. One-day, one-park admission $71; $60 (ages 3-9). Parking fee. disneyworld.disney.go.com

GEORGIA

Six Flags Over Georgia

(770) 948-9290, 275 Riverside Pkwy. (off I-20), Austell
Six Flags offers more than 100 rides, attractions and shows, a 12,000-seat concert amphitheater, Broadway-style musical shows and a July 4 fireworks display. Kennel facilities (water provided, but not food). Park open daily at 10, late May to mid-Aug.; Sat.-Sun. at 10, mid-Mar. to late May and mid-Aug. to late Oct. Closing times vary. Admission $49.99; $29.99 (under 48 inches tall); free (ages 0-2). Parking fee. www.sixflags.com

ILLINOIS

 Six Flags Great America

(847) 249-4636 or (847) 249-1776, 542 SR 21N, Gurnee
Batman the Ride, Iron Wolf and Raging Bull are among
the thrill rides at this family theme park, which also has a
section of rides and attractions for children under 54
inches tall. Kennel facilities. Park open daily at 10, late
May to mid.-Sept.; Sat.-Sun. at 10, mid-Sept. to late Oct.
Closing times vary; phone ahead to confirm hours.
Admission $54.99; $34.99 (under 48 inches tall); free
(ages 0-2). Parking fee. www.sixflags.com

IOWA

 Pella Historical Village

(641) 628-2409 or (641) 628-4311, 507 Franklin St., Pella
A country store, log cabin, grist mill, windmill, smithy and
other buildings (including Wyatt Earp's boyhood home) are
reminders of this town's Dutch Heritage. Pets on leash
(grounds only). Mon.-Sat. 9-5, Mar.-Dec. Admission $8; $2
(ages 5-18).

MASSACHUSETTS

 Bunker Hill Monument

(617) 242-5641, in Monument Square on Breed's Hill,
Charlestown
Part of Boston National Historical Park, this 221-foot-tall
granite obelisk commemorates the site of the Battle of
Bunker Hill, which occurred on June 17, 1775. Pets on
leash (grounds only); must pick up after pet. Visitor lodge
and exhibits daily 9-5. Free. www.nps.gov/bost/Bunker_Hill/
htm

MISSISSIPPI

 Vicksburg National Military Park

(601) 636-0583, entered via I-20 exit 4B, then .2 miles
west on Clay St. (US 80)
More than 1,260 memorials, monuments, statues, tablets,
bronze portraits and markers honor the Union and
Confederate troops who engaged in the siege of
Vicksburg in 1863. Pets on leash. Grounds open daily
dawn-dusk. Visitor center daily 8-5. Admission $8 per
private vehicle. www.nps.gov/vick

MISSOURI

 The Gateway Arch

(877) 982-1410, Memorial Drive and Market Street, St.
Louis
This curved, stainless steel monument soars 630 feet high
and symbolizes the gateway to the West. A tram ride
takes visitors to an observation deck. Pets on leash
(grounds only). Tram ticket center open daily 8 a.m.-10
p.m., Memorial Day-Labor Day; 9-6, rest of year. Closed
Jan. 1, Thanksgiving and Dec. 25. Tram ride $10; $7
(ages 13-15); $3 (ages 3-12). www.gatewayarch.com

NORTH CAROLINA

 Carowinds Theme Park

(704) 588-2600, (803) 548-5300 or (800) 888-4386, 10
miles south on I-77 to exit 90, Charlotte
Depicting the past and present of the Carolinas, the
themed areas at this park offer roller coasters, water rides,
children's play areas and other family entertainment.
Air-conditioned kennels. Park open daily at 10, early June
to mid-Aug.; Sat.-Sun. at 10, mid-Mar. to early June and
mid-Aug. to early Oct. Closing times vary; phone ahead to
confirm hours. Admission $45.95; $19.95 (ages 3-6, ages
62+ and under 48 inches tall). Parking fee.
www.carowinds.com

OHIO

 Kings Island

(513) 754-5700 or (800) 288-0808, Kings Island Drive (off
I-71 exits 24 and 25), Kings Mills
Kings Island is a family entertainment park featuring 14
hair-raising roller coasters; Boomerang Bay, a water
recreation playground; costumed cartoon characters; and a
variety of live shows. Kennel facilities (fee). Park open
daily at 10, late May-Aug. 31; Sat.-Sun. at 10, late
Mar.-late May and Sept.-Oct. Phone ahead to confirm
hours. Admission $49.99; $26.99 (ages 3-6, ages 62+ and
under 48 inches tall). Parking fee. www.pki.com

PENNSYLVANIA

 Hersheypark

(800) 437-7439, 100 W. Hersheypark Dr. (just off SR 743
and US 422), Hershey
Hersheypark has more than 60 rides and attractions —
including 11 roller coasters — plus live entertainment.
Visitors can enjoy a marine mammal show, song and
dance reviews and concerts highlighting big-name
performers. Zooamerica North American Wildlife Park
covers 11 acres. Kennel facilities. Park open daily at 10,
Memorial Day-Labor Day; Fri.-Sun. at 10, May 1-Sun.
before Memorial Day weekend; Sat.-Sun. at 10, day after
Labor Day-late Sept. Closing times vary; phone ahead to
confirm hours. Admission (Memorial Day weekend-late
Sept.) $47.95; $28.95 (ages 3-8 and 55-69); $19.95 (ages
70+). Admission (early May-late May) $43.95; $24.95
(ages 3-8 and 55-69); $17.95 (ages 70+). Parking fee.
www.hersheypark.com

TEXAS

 ### SeaWorld San Antonio

(800) 700-7786, 10500 SeaWorld Dr. (off SR 151 at the junction of Westover Hills Boulevard and Ellison Drive), San Antonio

A 250-acre marine life adventure park, SeaWorld San Antonio entertains and educates with shark exhibits, a penguin habitat and high-energy whale and dolphin shows. Such thrill rides as Journey to Atlantis, the Steel Eel coaster and Texas Splashdown add to the excitement. Outdoor kennel facilities (owner must provide food and water containers). Park open daily at 10, early Mar.-late Nov.; closing times vary. Phone ahead to confirm hours. Admission $50.99; $42.99 (ages 3-9). Prices may vary. Parking fee. www.seaworld.com

 ### Six Flags Over Texas

(817) 530-6000, 2201 Road to Six Flags (at the junction of I-30 and SR 360 exit 30), Arlington

Themed areas, each featuring thrill rides, food and entertainment, depict Texas under six different flags: Spain, France, Mexico, the Republic of Texas, the Confederate States of America and the United States. Air-conditioned kennels (fee). Park open daily, late May-early Aug.; Sat.-Sun., Mar. 1-late May, early Aug.-last Sun. in Oct. and day after Thanksgiving-Dec. 31. Hours vary; phone ahead. Admission $46.99; $34.99 (under 48 inches tall); free (ages 0-2). Prices may vary. Parking fee. www.sixflags.com

VIRGINIA

 ### Busch Gardens Europe

(800) 343-7946, 3 miles east on US 60 or off I-64 exit 243A, Williamsburg

This European-themed adventure park offers something for the entire family, from thrill rides to dance and music shows to villages representing England, Germany, France and other nations. Kennel facilities (England parking lot); fee $6 per pet per day. Park open daily at 10, Mar.-Oct.; days and closing times vary. Phone ahead to confirm schedule. Admission $56.95; $49.95 (ages 3-6). Parking fee. www.buschgardens.com/va

 ### Kings Dominion

(804) 876-5000, 16000 Theme Park Way (on SR 30 ½ mile east off I-95 exit 98), Doswell

Eight themed areas make up Kings Dominion, a full-scale theme park with thrill rides, children's play areas, costumed characters, live shows and specialty shopping. Kennel facilities (fee); water provided, but not food. Park open daily, Memorial Day-Labor Day; Sat.-Sun., late Mar. to day before Memorial Day and first Sat. after Labor Day-late Oct. Hours vary seasonally; phone ahead. Admission $49.95; $24.95 (ages 62+ and under 48 inches tall); free (ages 0-2). Parking fee. www.kingsdominion.com

WASHINGTON

 ### Hovander Homestead

(360) 384-3444, 1 mile south via Hovander Road, Ferndale

This restored house, dating from 1903 and furnished with antiques, is within a large park encompassing gardens, picnic sites and a children's farm area. Pets on leash (grounds only). Grounds open daily 8 a.m.-dusk. House open Thurs.-Sun. noon-4:30, early June-Labor Day; Sat.-Sun. noon-4:30, in May. House $1; 50 cents (ages 5-12). www.co.whatcom.wa.us/parks/hovander/hovander.jsp

Canada

ONTARIO

 ### Upper Canada Village

(613) 543-4328 or (800) 437-2233, 7 miles (11 kilometers) east on CR 2 off Hwy. 401, Morrisburg

Upper Canada Village re-creates life during the 1860s through a working community of artisans and costumed interpreters who perform chores typical of the era. Pets on leash (grounds only). Daily 9:30-5, late May-early Oct. Village admission $17.95; $16.95 (ages 66+); $11.95 (students with ID); $7.95 (ages 5-12); $2.50 (ages 2-4). www.uppercanadavillage.com

Canada's Wonderland

(905) 832-7000 or (905) 832-8131, off Hwy. 400 (Rutherford Road exit northbound or Major MacKenzie Drive E. exit southbound) at 9580 Jane St., Vaughan

Thrill rides at this theme park include the Great Canadian Minebuster and Drop Zone, a free-fall plunge, while Nickelodeon Central and Hanna-Barbera Land will entertain little ones. Air-conditioned kennels (fee). Park open daily at 10, late May-Labour Day; open some weekends, early to late May and day after Labour Day-late Oct. Closing times vary; phone ahead to confirm hours. Grounds admission $27.26. Passport for grounds admission and most rides $51.40; $26.45 (ages 3-6 and 60+). Parking fee. www.canadaswonderland.com

NATIONAL PUBLIC LANDS

The National Public Lands listed below permit pets on a leash. Keep in mind that animals may be prohibited from entering public buildings and even some areas outdoors, particularly those that are ecologically sensitive. Where swimming is permitted, there are usually no lifeguards on duty; people and pets swim at their own risk. Specific pet policies vary from park to park and are subject to change. Always check in advance regarding any applicable regulations and to confirm that pets are still permitted where you are going.

Be aware of dangers to your pet in natural areas, including snakes, ticks and fast-moving currents in rivers and streams. An unleashed dog may chase after a wild animal and become separated from its owner, increasing the risk of loss or injury. Never leave your pet unattended. Keep him leashed or crated at all times. Follow park guidelines faithfully, and monitor your pet's behavior; the National Park Service may confiscate pets that harm wildlife or other visitors. *For additional information on outdoor vacations, see The Great Outdoors, p. 16.*

United States

ALABAMA

Conecuh National Forest
On the Alabama-Florida border.
(334) 222-2555
🚲 ⛺ 🥾 🧺 🏊

Eufaula National Wildlife Refuge
On the Chattahoochee River.
(334) 687-4065
🚲 🥾 👥

Horseshoe Bend National Military Park
12 mi. north of Dadeville on SR 49.
(256) 234-7111
🚲 🥾 🧺 👥

Talladega National Forest
In central Alabama.
(256) 362-2909
⛺ 🥾 🧺 👥 🍽

Tuskegee National Forest
Northeast of Tuskegee.
(334) 727-2652
⛺ 🥾 🧺 👥

William B. Bankhead National Forest
In northwestern Alabama.
(205) 489-5111
🚲 ⛺ 🥾 🧺 🏊 👥

Wheeler National Wildlife Refuge
Between Decatur and Huntsville.
(256) 350-6639
🚲 🥾 🧺 👥

ALASKA

Chugach National Forest
Along the Gulf of Alaska from Cape Suckling to Seward.
(907) 743-9500
🚲 ⛺ 🥾 🧺 👥

Denali National Park and Preserve
In south-central Alaska.
(907) 683-2294
🚲 ⛺ 🥾 🧺 👥 🍽

Glacier Bay National Park and Preserve
North of Cross Sound to the Canadian border.
(907) 697-2230
🚲 ⛺ 🥾 👥

Kenai Fjords National Park
Southeastern side of the Kenai Peninsula.
(907) 224-7500 or (907) 224-2132
⛺ 🥾 🧺 👥

Lake Clark National Park and Preserve
In southern Alaska.
(907) 781-2218 or (907) 644-3626
⛺ 🥾 👥

Tongass National Forest
In southeastern Alaska.
(907) 586-8800 or (907) 228-6220
🚲 ⛺ 🥾 🧺 🏊 👥

Wrangell-St. Elias National Park and Preserve
In southeastern Alaska, northwest of Tongass National Forest.
(907) 822-5234
🚲 ⛺ 🥾 👥 🍽

ARIZONA

Apache-Sitgreaves National Forests
In east-central Arizona.
(928) 333-4301
🚲 ⛺ 🥾 🧺 👥 🍽

Bill Williams River National Wildlife Refuge
Off SR 95 near Parker.
(928) 667-4144
🥾 🧺 👥

Buenos Aires National Wildlife Refuge
North of Sasabe on SR 286.
(520) 823-4251
🚲 ⛺ 🥾 🧺 👥

🚲 Bicycling Trails ⛺ Camping 🥾 Hiking Trails 🧺 Picnic Facilities
🏊 Swimming 👥 Visitor Center 🍽 Food Service

Coconino National Forest
In north-central Arizona.
(928) 527-3600
🚴 🔺 🥾 🏕 🏊 👫 🍴

Coronado National Forest
In southeastern Arizona and southwestern New Mexico.
(520) 388-8300
🚴 🔺 🥾 🏕 👫

Glen Canyon National Recreation Area
In north-central Arizona.
(928) 608-6200
🔺 🥾 🏕 🏊 👫 🍴

Grand Canyon National Park
In northwestern Arizona.
(928) 638-7888
🔺 🥾 🏕 👫 🍴

Kaibab National Forest
In north-central Arizona.
(928) 635-4061 or (800) 863-0546
🚴 🔺 🥾 🏕 👫 🍴

Lake Mead National Recreation Area
In northwestern Arizona and southeastern Nevada.
(702) 293-8990
🚴 🔺 🥾 🏕 🏊 👫 🍴

Petrified Forest National Park
In east-central Arizona, east of Holbrook.
(928) 524-6228
🥾 🏕 👫 🍴

Prescott National Forest
In central Arizona.
(928) 443-8000
🚴 🔺 🥾 🏕 🍴

Saguaro National Park
Two districts, 15 mi. east and west of Tucson.
(520) 733-5153
🚴 🥾 🏕 👫

Tonto National Forest
In central Arizona.
(602) 225-5200
🚴 🔺 🥾 🏕 🏊 👫 🍴

ARKANSAS

Buffalo National River
In northwestern Arkansas.
(870) 741-5443 or (870) 439-2502
🔺 🥾 🏕 🏊 👫 🍴

Felsenthal National Wildlife Refuge
7 mi. west of Crossett on US 82.
(870) 364-3167
🔺 🥾 👫

Hot Springs National Park
In western Arkansas.
(501) 624-2701, (501) 620-6701 or TDD (501) 624-2308
🔺 🥾 🏕 👫 🍴

Ouachita National Forest
In west-central Arkansas and southeastern Oklahoma.
(501) 321-5202
🚴 🔺 🥾 🏕 🏊 👫 🍴

Ozark-St. Francis National Forests
In northwestern and east-central Arkansas.
(479) 964-7200
🚴 🔺 🥾 🏕 🏊 👫 🍴

Pea Ridge National Military Park
East of Rogers in northwest Arkansas.
(479) 451-8122
🚴 🥾 🏕 👫

CALIFORNIA

Angeles National Forest
In southern California.
(626) 574-5200
🚴 🔺 🥾 🏕 🏊 👫 🍴

Cleveland National Forest
In southwestern California.
(858) 673-6180
🚴 🔺 🥾 🏕 👫 🍴

Death Valley National Park
Along the Nevada border in east-central California.
(760) 786-2331
🚴 🔺 🥾 🏕 👫 🍴

Eldorado National Forest
In central California.
(530) 644-6048
🚴 🔺 🥾 🏕 🏊 👫 🍴

Golden Gate National Recreation Area
North of the Golden Gate Bridge and in northern and western San Francisco.
(415) 561-4730
🚴 🔺 🥾 🏕 🏊 👫 🍴

Inyo National Forest
In east-central California.
(760) 873-2400
🚴 🔺 🥾 🏕 🏊 👫 🍴

Joshua Tree National Park
East of Desert Hot Springs.
(760) 367-5500
🚴 🔺 🥾 🏕 👫

Klamath National Forest
In northern California.
(530) 842-6131
🚴 🔺 🥾 🏕 🏊 🍴

🚴 Bicycling Trails   🔺 Camping   🥾 Hiking Trails   🏕 Picnic Facilities
🏊 Swimming   👫 Visitor Center   🍴 Food Service

Lassen National Forest
In northeastern California.
(530) 257-2151

Lassen Volcanic National Park
In northeastern California.
(530) 595-4444

Los Padres National Forest
In southern California.
(805) 968-6640

Mendocino National Forest
In northwestern California.
(530) 934-2350 or (530) 934-3316, or TDD (530) 934-7724

Modoc National Forest
In northeastern California.
(530) 233-5811

Mojave National Preserve
Between I-15 and I-40 in southeastern California.
(760) 252-6100

Plumas National Forest
In northern California.
(530) 283-2050

Point Reyes National Seashore
Along the California coast just north of San Francisco.
(415) 464-5100

Redwood National and State Parks
On the northern California coast.
(707) 465-7306

San Bernardino National Forest
In southern California.
(909) 382-2600

Santa Monica Mountains National Recreation Area
West from Griffith Park in Los Angeles to the Ventura County line.
(805) 370-2301

Sequoia and Kings Canyon National Parks
In east-central California.
(559) 565-3341

Sequoia National Forest
In south-central California.
(559) 784-1500

Shasta-Trinity National Forests
In northern California.
(530) 226-2500

Sierra National Forest
In central California.
(559) 297-0706

Six Rivers National Forest
In northwestern California.
(707) 442-1721

Smith River National Recreation Area
Within Six Rivers National Forest in northwestern California.
(707) 457-3131

Stanislaus National Forest
In central California.
(209) 532-3671

Tahoe National Forest
In north-central California.
(530) 265-4531

Whiskeytown-Shasta-Trinity National Recreation Area
North and west of Redding.
(530) 242-3400, (530) 275-1589 in Shasta
or (530) 623-2121 in Trinity

Yosemite National Park
In central California.
(209) 372-0200

COLORADO

Arapaho and Roosevelt National Forests and Pawnee National Grassland
In north-central Colorado.
(970) 295-6700

Arapaho National Recreation Area
In north-central Colorado.
(970) 887-4100

Black Canyon of the Gunnison National Park
In western Colorado.
(970) 641-2337

Curecanti National Recreation Area
In south-central Colorado between Gunnison and Montrose, paralleling US 50.
(970) 641-2337

Grand Mesa-Uncompahgre-Gunnison National Forests
In west-central Colorado.
(970) 874-6600
[icons]

Great Sand Dunes National Park and Preserve
Northeast of Alamosa.
(719) 378-6300
[icons]

Mesa Verde National Park
In southwestern Colorado.
(970) 529-4465
[icons]

Pike and San Isabel National Forest
In south-central Colorado.
(719) 553-1400
[icons]

Rio Grande National Forest
In south-central Colorado.
(719) 852-5941
[icons]

Rocky Mountain National Park
In north-central Colorado.
(970) 586-1206 or (970) 586-1333
[icons]

Routt National Forest
In northwestern Colorado.
(970) 879-1870
[icons]

San Juan National Forest
In southwestern Colorado.
(970) 247-4874
[icons]

White River National Forest
In west-central Colorado.
(970) 945-2521
[icons]

DELAWARE

Bombay Hook National Wildlife Refuge
South of Smyrna.
(302) 653-9345
[icons]

Prime Hook National Wildlife Refuge
North of Milton via SR 1.
(302) 684-8419
[icons]

FLORIDA

Apalachicola National Forest
In northwestern Florida.
(850) 926-3561
[icons]

Biscayne National Park
In southeast Florida.
(305) 230-7275
[icons]

J.N. "Ding" Darling National Wildlife Refuge
1 Wildlife Dr. in Sanibel.
(239) 472-1100
[icons]

Ocala National Forest
In north-central Florida.
(352) 236-0288
[icons]

Osceola National Forest
Near the Georgia border.
(386) 752-2577
[icons]

GEORGIA

Chattahoochee and Oconee National Forests
In central and northern Georgia.
(770) 297-3000
[icons]

Chattahoochee River National Recreation Area
North of Atlanta.
(678) 538-1200
[icons]

Chickamauga and Chattanooga National Military Park
On the Georgia-Tennessee border.
(706) 866-9241 or (423) 752-5213, ext 123
[icons]

Kennesaw Mountain National Battlefield Park
Northwest of Marietta.
(770) 427-4686
[icons]

IDAHO

Boise National Forest
In southwestern Idaho.
(208) 373-4007
[icons]

Caribou-Targhee National Forest
In southeastern Idaho.
(208) 524-7500 or (208) 624-3151
[icons]

Clearwater National Forest
In northeastern Idaho.
(208) 476-4541
[icons]

Hells Canyon National Recreation Area
In western Idaho and northeastern Oregon.
(509) 758-0616
[icons]

[🚲] Bicycling Trails   [▲] Camping   [🥾] Hiking Trails   [⛱] Picnic Facilities
[🏊] Swimming   [🏠] Visitor Center   [🍽] Food Service

Idaho Panhandle National Forests
In northern and northwestern Idaho.
(208) 765-7223

Nez Perce National Forest
In northwestern Idaho.
(208) 983-1950

Payette National Forest
In west-central Idaho.
(208) 634-0700

Salmon-Challis National Forest
In east-central Idaho.
(208) 756-5100

Sawtooth National Forest
In south-central Idaho.
(208) 737-3200 or (800) 260-5970

Sawtooth National Recreation Area
In south-central Idaho.
(208) 727-5013 or (800) 260-5970

ILLINOIS
Chautauqua National Wildlife Refuge
Near Havana.
(309) 535-2290

Shawnee National Forest
In southern Illinois.
(618) 253-7114 or (800) 699-6637

INDIANA
George Rogers Clark National Historical Park
Off US 50 and US 41 near Vincennes.
(812) 882-1776, ext. 110

Hoosier National Forest
In southern Indiana.
(812) 275-5987

Indiana Dunes National Lakeshore
On the southern shore of Lake Michigan.
(219) 926-7561, ext. 225

Muscatatuck National Wildlife Refuge
East of jct. I-65 and US 50 near Seymour.
(812)522-4352

KANSAS
Kirwin National Wildlife Refuge
702 E. Xavier Rd.
(785) 543-6673

KENTUCKY
Big South Fork National River and Recreation Area
In southeastern Kentucky and northeastern Tennessee.
(423) 286-7275 or (606) 376-5073

Cumberland Gap National Historical Park
At the borders of Kentucky, Tennessee and Virginia.
(606) 248-2817

Daniel Boone National Forest
Five districts in eastern and southeastern Kentucky.
(859) 745-3100

Land Between the Lakes National Recreation Area
In western Kentucky and Tennessee.
(270) 924-2000 or (800) 525-7077

Mammoth Cave National Park
In south-central Kentucky 10 mi. west of Cave City.
(270) 758-2180

LOUISIANA
Bayou Sauvage National Wildlife Refuge
Within the New Orleans city limits.
(985) 882-2000

Kisatchie National Forest
In central and northern Louisiana.
(318) 473-7160

MAINE
Acadia National Park
Along the Atlantic coast southeast of Bangor.
(207) 288-3338

Moosehorn National Wildlife Refuge
Near Baring and Dennysville.
(207) 454-7161

MARYLAND
Assateague Island National Seashore
In southeastern Maryland south of Ocean City.
(410) 641-1441 or (410) 641-3030

Chesapeake and Ohio Canal National Historical Park
From Georgetown to Cumberland.
(301) 739-4200

MASSACHUSETTS

Cape Cod National Seashore
Occupies 40 miles along the shoreline.
(508)349-3785, ext. 200
🚲 🐾 🌲 ⚓ ♿

MICHIGAN

Hiawatha National Forest
In Michigan's Upper Peninsula.
(906) 786-4062
🚲 ⛺ 🐾 🌲 ⚓ ♿ 🍴

Huron-Manistee National Forests
In the northern part of the Lower Peninsula.
(231) 775-2421 or (800) 821-6263
🚲 ⛺ 🐾 🌲 ⚓ ♿ 🍴

Ottawa National Forest
In Michigan's Upper Peninsula.
(906) 932-1330 or (800) 562-1201
🚲 ⛺ 🐾 🌲 ⚓ ♿ 🍴

Pictured Rocks National Lakeshore
Along Lake Superior in Michigan's Upper Peninsula.
906-387-3700 or (906) 387-2607
⛺ 🐾 🌲 ⚓ ♿

Sleeping Bear Dunes National Lakeshore
Along Lake Michigan in the northwestern part of the Lower Peninsula.
(231) 326-5134
⛺ 🐾 🌲 ⚓ ♿ 🍴

MINNESOTA

Chippewa National Forest
In north-central Minnesota.
(218) 335-8600
🚲 ⛺ 🐾 🌲 ⚓ ♿ 🍴

Minnesota Valley National Wildlife Refuge
3815 E. American Blvd, Bloomington
(952) 854-5900
🚲 🐾 ♿

Superior National Forest
In northeastern Minnesota.
(218) 626-4300
🚲 ⛺ 🐾 🌲 ⚓ ♿ 🍴

MISSISSIPPI

Bienville National Forest
In central Mississippi.
(601) 469-3811
⛺ 🐾 🌲 ⚓ ♿ 🍴

Gulf Islands National Seashore
Along the Gulf of Mexico in southern Mississippi.
(228) 875-9057
🚲 🐾 🌲 ⚓ ♿

MISSOURI

Mark Twain National Forest (Big Bay)
1 mi. southeast of Shell Knob on SR 39, then 3 mi. southeast on CR YY.
(573) 364-4621
🚲 🌲 ⚓

Mark Twain National Forest (Council Bluff)
13 mi. s. of Potosi on CR P, 4 mi. w. on CR C , then 8 mi. s. on CR DD.
(573) 364-4621
🚲 ⛺ 🐾 🌲 ⚓

Mark Twain National Forest (Crane Lake)
12 mi. south of Ironton off SR 49 and CR E.
(573) 364-4621
🚲 🐾 🌲 ⚓

Mark Twain National Forest (Fourche Lake)
18 mi. west of Doniphan on SR 160.
(573) 364-4621
🐾 🌲 ⚓

Mark Twain National Forest (Noblett Lake)
8 mi. west of Willow Springs on SR 76, then 1.5 mi. south on SR 181, 3 mi. southeast on CR AP and 1 mi. southwest on FR 857.
(573) 364-4621
🚲 🐾 🌲

Mark Twain National Forest (Pinewoods Lake)
2 mi. west of Ellsinore on SR 60.
(573) 364-4621
🚲 🐾 🌲 ⚓

Mark Twain National Forest (Red Bluff)
1 mi. east of Davisville on CR V, then 1 mi. north on FR 2011.
(573) 364-4621
⛺ 🐾 🌲 ⚓

Ozark National Scenic Riverways
In southeastern Missouri.
(573) 323-4236
⛺ 🐾 🌲 ⚓ ♿ 🍴

MONTANA

Beaverhead-Deerlodge National Forest
In southwestern Montana.
(406) 683-3900
🚲 ⛺ 🐾 🌲 ⚓ 🍴

Bighorn Canyon National Recreation Area
In southern Montana and northern Wyoming.
(406) 666-2412
⛺ 🐾 🌲 ⚓ ♿ 🍴

Bitterroot National Forest
In western Montana.
(406) 363-7100
⛺ 🐾 🌲 ⚓ ♿

🚲 Bicycling Trails   ⛺ Camping   🐾 Hiking Trails   🌲 Picnic Facilities
⚓ Swimming   ♿ Visitor Center   🍴 Food Service

Custer National Forest
In southeastern Montana.
(406) 657-6200

Flathead National Forest
In northwestern Montana.
(406) 758-5204

Gallatin National Forest
In south-central Montana.
(406) 522-2520

Glacier National Park
In northwestern Montana.
(406) 888-7800

Helena National Forest
In west-central Montana.
(406) 449-5201

Kootenai National Forest
In northwestern Montana.
(406) 293-6211

Lewis and Clark National Forest
In central Montana.
(406) 791-7700

NEBRASKA

Fort Niobrara National Wildlife Refuge
East of Valentine on SR 12.
(402) 376-3789

Nebraska National Forest
In central and northwestern Nebraska.
(308) 432-0300 or TDD (308) 432-0304

Oglala National Grassland
In northwestern Nebraska, 6 mi. north of Crawford via SR 2.
(308) 432-4475 or (308) 665-3900

NEVADA

Great Basin National Park
In central Nevada, 5 mi. west of Baker near the Nevada-Utah border.
(775) 234-7331

Humboldt-Toiyabe National Forest
In central, western, northern and southern Nevada and eastern California.
(775) 331-6444

Lake Mead National Recreation Area
In southeastern Nevada and northwestern Arizona.
(702) 293-8990

NEW HAMPSHIRE

White Mountain National Forest
In northern New Hampshire.
(603) 528-8721 or TDD (603) 528-8722

NEW JERSEY

Edwin B. Forsythe National Wildlife Refuge
US 9 and Great Creek Road near Oceanville
(609) 652-1665

Gateway National Recreation Area (Sandy Hook Unit)
In northeastern New Jersey.
(732) 872-5970

Morristown National Historical Park
Four units in Morristown and southwest.
(973) 539-2016

NEW MEXICO

Carson National Forest
In north-central New Mexico.
(505) 758-6200

Chaco Culture National Historical Park
In northwestern New Mexico.
(505) 786-7014

Cibola National Forest
In central New Mexico.
(505) 346-3900

Gila National Forest
In southwestern New Mexico.
(505) 388-8201

Lincoln National Forest
In south-central New Mexico.
(505) 434-7200

Santa Fe National Forest
In north-central New Mexico between the San Pedro Mountains and the Sangre de Cristo Mountains.
(505) 438-7840

NEW YORK

Finger Lakes National Forest
In south-central New York on a ridge between Seneca and Cayuga lakes, via I-90, I-81 and SR 17.
(607) 546-4470

Fire Island National Seashore
In southeastern New York on Fire Island, off the south shore of Long Island.
(631) 687-4750
[A] [🚶] [🏕] [🏊] [👥] [🍴]

Gateway National Recreation Area (Jamaica Bay Unit)
In Brooklyn and Queens boroughs in New York City.
(718) 338-3799
[🚴] [A] [🚶] [🏕] [🏊] [👥] [🍴]

Gateway National Recreation Area (Staten Island Unit)
On Staten Island borough in New York City.
(718) 354-4500
[🚴] [A] [🚶] [🏕] [🏊] [👥] [🍴]

Saratoga National Historical Park
8 miles south of Schuylerville on US 4.
(518) 664-9821, ext. 224
[🚴] [🚶] [🏕] [👥]

NORTH CAROLINA

Cape Hatteras National Seashore
In eastern North Carolina along the Outer Banks.
(252) 473-2111 or (252) 441-5711
[🚴] [A] [🚶] [🏕] [🏊] [👥] [🍴]

Croatan National Forest
In southeastern North Carolina.
(252) 638-5628
[🚴] [A] [🚶] [🏕] [🏊]

Great Smoky Mountains National Park
In western North Carolina and eastern Tennessee.
(865) 436-1200
[🚴] [A] [🚶] [🏕] [👥]

Nantahala National Forest
At North Carolina's southwestern tip.
(828) 257-4200 or (828) 526-3765
[🚴] [A] [🚶] [🏕] [🏊]

Pisgah National Forest
In western North Carolina.
(828) 257-4200
[🚴] [A] [🚶] [🏕] [🏊] [👥]

Pisgah National Forest (Lake Powhatan)
7 mi. southwest of Asheville on SR 191 and FR 3807.
(828) 257-4200
[🚴] [A] [🚶] [🏕] [🏊]

Pisgah National Forest (Rocky Bluff)
3 mi. south of Hot Springs on SR 209.
(828) 257-4200
[A] [🚶] [🏕]

Uwharrie National Forest
In central North Carolina.
(910) 576-6391
[🚴] [A] [🚶] [🏕] [🏊] [👥]

NORTH DAKOTA

Little Missouri National Grassland
Between the Missouri River and South Dakota.
(701) 227-7800
[🚴] [A] [🚶] [🏕] [👥]

Sheyenne National Grassland
Along the Sheyenne River south of Fargo.
(701) 683-4342
[A] [🚶] [🏕]

Theodore Roosevelt National Park (North Unit)
In western North Dakota.
(701) 842-2333
[🚴] [A] [🚶] [🏕] [👥]

Theodore Roosevelt National Park (South Unit)
In western North Dakota.
(701) 623-4466
[A] [🚶] [🏕] [👥] [🍴]

OHIO

Cuyahoga Valley National Park
In northeastern Ohio.
(216) 524-1497
[🚴] [🚶] [🏕] [👥] [🍴]

Hopewell Culture National Historical Park
About 3 mi. north of Chillicothe on SR 104.
(740) 774-1126
[🚴] [🚶] [🏕] [👥]

Wayne National Forest
In southeast Ohio.
(740) 753-0101
[🚴] [A] [🚶] [🏕] [🏊] [👥]

OKLAHOMA

Chickasaw National Recreation Area
In south-central Oklahoma.
(580) 622-3165 or (580) 622-3161
[🚴] [A] [🚶] [🏕] [🏊] [👥]

Ouachita National Forest
In southeastern Oklahoma and west-central Arkansas.
(501) 321-5202
[🚴] [A] [🚶] [🏕] [🏊] [👥] [🍴]

Salt Plains National Wildlife Refuge
Off SR 38, 2 mi. south of jct. SRs 11 and 38 at Cherokee.
(580) 626-4794
[A] [🚶] [👥]

OREGON

Crater Lake National Park
On the crest of the Cascade Range off SR 62.
(541) 594-3100
[🚴] [A] [🚶] [🏕] [👥] [🍴]

[🚴] Bicycling Trails   [A] Camping   [🚶] Hiking Trails   [🏕] Picnic Facilities
[🏊] Swimming   [👥] Visitor Center   [🍴] Food Service

Deschutes National Forest
In central Oregon 6 mi. south of Bend via US 97.
(541) 383-5300

Fremont-Winema National Forests
In south-central Oregon.
(541) 947-2151

Hells Canyon National Recreation Area
In northeastern Oregon and western Idaho.
(541) 426-5546

Malheur National Forest
In eastern Oregon.
(541) 575-3000

Mount Hood National Forest
In northwestern Oregon.
(888) 622-4822

Ochoco National Forest
In central Oregon off US 26.
(541) 416-6500

Oregon Dunes National Recreation Area
Between North Bend and Florence.
(541) 271-6000

Rogue River-Siskiyou National Forest
In southwestern Oregon off I-5 from Medford.
(541) 858-2200

Siuslaw National Forest
In western Oregon.
(541) 750-7000

Umatilla National Forest
In northeastern Oregon.
(541) 278-3716

Umpqua National Forest
In southwestern Oregon 33 mi. east of Roseburg on SR 138.
(541) 672-6601

Wallowa-Whitman National Forest
In northeastern Oregon.
(541) 523-6391

Willamette National Forest
In western Oregon.
(541) 225-6300

PENNSYLVANIA

Allegheny National Forest
In northwestern Pennsylvania.
(814) 723-5150 or TDD (814) 726-2710

Delaware Water Gap National Recreation Area
In eastern Pennsylvania and northwestern New Jersey.
(570) 426-2457

Gettysburg National Military Park
Surrounding the town of Gettysburg at SR 134.
(717) 334-1124

John Heinz National Wildlife Refuge at Tinicum
I-95S exit 14 near Philadelphia
(215) 365-3118

Valley Forge National Historical Park
Extending east of Valley Forge along SR 23.
(610) 783-1077

SOUTH CAROLINA

Congaree National Park
Southeast of Hopkins.
(803) 776-4396

Francis Marion National Forest
On the Coastal Plain north of Charleston.
(803) 561-4000

Kings Mountain National Military Park
South of Kings Mountain, N.C., off I-85.
(864) 936-7921

Sumter National Forest
In western South Carolina.
(803) 561-4000

SOUTH DAKOTA

Badlands National Park
In southwestern South Dakota.
(605) 433-5361, ext. 100

Black Hills National Forest
In southwestern South Dakota.
(605) 673-9200 or TDD (605) 673-4954

Custer National Forest
In northwestern South Dakota and southeastern Montana.
(605) 797-4432

Wind Cave National Park
In southwestern South Dakota.
(605) 745-4600
[A] [%] [丌] [ℴℴ]

TENNESSEE

Big South Fork National River and Recreation Area
In northeastern Tennessee and southeastern Kentucky.
(423) 286-7275
[ℴ] [A] [%] [丌] [▲] [ℴℴ]

Cherokee National Forest
In eastern Tennessee.
(423) 476-9700
[ℴ] [A] [%] [丌] [▲] [ℴℴ]

Chickamauga and Chattanooga National Military Park
On the Georgia-Tennessee border.
(706) 866-9241
[ℴ] [%] [丌] [ℴℴ]

Great Smoky Mountains National Park
In eastern Tennessee and western North Carolina.
(865) 436-1200
[ℴ] [A] [%] [丌] [ℴℴ]

Land Between the Lakes National Recreation Area
In western Kentucky and Tennessee.
(270) 924-2000 or (800) 525-7077
[ℴ] [A] [%] [丌] [▲] [ℴℴ]

TEXAS

Amistad National Recreation Area
Northwest of Del Rio via US 90.
(830) 775-7491
[A] [%] [丌] [▲] [ℴℴ]

Angelina National Forest
In east Texas.
(936) 897-1068
[A] [%] [丌] [▲]

Big Bend National Park
Southeast of Alpine on SR 118 and US 385.
(432) 477-2251 or (432) 477-1187
[ℴ] [A] [%] [丌] [ℴℴ] [ℴℴ]

Davy Crockett National Forest
In east Texas.
(936) 655-2299
[A] [%] [丌] [▲] [ℴℴ]

Guadalupe Mountains National Park
110 mi. east of El Paso on US 62/180.
(915) 828-3251
[A] [%] [丌] [ℴℴ]

Lake Meredith National Recreation Area
45 mi. northeast of Amarillo and 9 mi. west of Borger via SR 136.
(806) 857-3151
[A] [丌] [▲] [ℴℴ]

Padre Island National Seashore
On Padre Island near Corpus Christi.
(361) 949-8068
[ℴ] [A] [%] [丌] [▲] [ℴℴ] [ℴℴ]

Sabine National Forest
In east Texas.
(409) 787-3870
[A] [%] [丌] [▲]

Sam Houston National Forest
40 mi. north of Houston in east Texas.
(936) 344-6205 or (888) 361-6908
[ℴ] [A] [%] [丌] [▲] [ℴℴ]

UTAH

Ashley National Forest
In northeastern Utah.
(435) 789-1181
[ℴ] [A] [%] [丌] [▲] [ℴℴ]

Canyonlands National Park
In southeastern Utah.
(435) 719-2100 or TTY (435) 259-5279
[A] [%] [丌] [ℴℴ]

Capitol Reef National Park
10 mi. east of Torrey on SR 24.
(435) 425-3791, ext. 111
[ℴ] [A] [%] [丌] [ℴℴ]

Dixie National Forest
In southwestern Utah.
(435) 865-3700
[ℴ] [A] [%] [丌] [▲] [ℴℴ] [ℴℴ]

Fishlake National Forest
In south-central Utah.
(435) 896-9233
[ℴ] [A] [%] [丌] [▲] [ℴℴ] [ℴℴ]

Flaming Gorge National Recreation Area
In northeastern Utah.
(435) 784-3445
[ℴ] [A] [%] [丌] [▲] [ℴℴ] [ℴℴ]

Glen Canyon National Recreation Area
In south-central Utah.
(928) 608-6200
[A] [%] [丌] [▲] [ℴℴ] [ℴℴ]

Manti-La Sal National Forest
In southeastern Utah.
(435) 637-2817
[ℴ] [A] [%] [丌] [▲] [ℴℴ]

Uinta National Forest
In central Utah.
(801) 342-5100
[ℴ] [A] [%] [丌]

[ℴ] Bicycling Trails   [A] Camping   [%] Hiking Trails   [丌] Picnic Facilities
[▲] Swimming   [ℴℴ] Visitor Center   [ℴℴ] Food Service

Wasatch-Cache National Forest
In north-central and northeastern Utah.
(801) 236-3400 or (801) 466-6411

Zion National Park
In southwestern Utah.
(435) 772-3256

VERMONT

Green Mountain National Forest
In south-central Vermont.
(802) 747-6700

Marsh-Billings-Rockefeller National Historical Park
Off SR 12 near Woodstock.
(802) 457-3368, ext. 22

VIRGINIA

George Washington and Jefferson National Forests
In western Virginia and the eastern edge of West Virginia.
(540) 265-5100 or (888) 265-0019

Mount Rogers National Recreation Area
In southwestern Virginia.
(276) 783-5196 or (800) 628-7202

Shenandoah National Park
In northwestern Virginia.
(540) 999-3500

WASHINGTON

Colville National Forest
In northeastern Washington.
(509) 684-7000

Gifford Pinchot National Forest
In southwestern Washington.
(360) 891-5000

Lake Chelan National Recreation Area
In north-central Washington.
(509) 682-2549

Lake Roosevelt National Recreation Area
In northeastern Washington.
(509) 633-9441

Mount Baker-Snoqualmie National Forest
2 mi. east of Glacier on SR 542.
(425) 775-9702, (800) 627-0062, ext. 0, or TTY (425) 744-3577

Okanogan National Forest
In north-central Washington.
(509) 996-4000

Olympic National Forest
In northwestern Washington.
(360) 956-2400

Ross Lake National Recreation Area
Between the north and south sections of North Cascades National Park.
(360) 856-5700, ext. 515, or (360) 206-386-4495, ext. 11

WEST VIRGINIA

Monongahela National Forest
In eastern West Virginia.
(304) 636-1800

New River Gorge National River
Between Fayetteville and Hinton.
(304) 465-0508

Spruce Knob-Seneca Rocks National Recreation Area
In east-central West Virginia.
(304) 257-4488

WISCONSIN

Apostle Islands National Lakeshore
Off northern Wisconsin's Bayfield Peninsula in Lake Superior.
(715) 779-3397

Chequamegon-Nicolet National Forest
In north-central and northeastern Wisconsin.
(715) 762-2461 (Chequamegon) or (715) 362-1300 (Nicolet)

St. Croix National Scenic Riverway
Running 252 mi. from Cable to Prescott.
(715) 483-3284

WYOMING

Bighorn Canyon National Recreation Area
In Montana and northern Wyoming.
(307) 548-2251

Bighorn National Forest
In north-central Wyoming.
(307) 674-2600

Devils Tower National Monument
Between Sundance and Hulett.
(307) 467-5283
🚴 🥾 ⛱ 🏠

Flaming Gorge National Recreation Area
On the Wyoming-Utah border.
(435) 784-3445
🚴 🏕 🥾 ⛱ 🏊 🏠 🍽

Fossil Butte National Monument
14 mi. west of Kemmerer on US 30.
(307) 877-4455
🥾 ⛱ 🏠

Grand Teton National Park
In northwestern Wyoming.
(307) 739-3300
🚴 🏕 🥾 ⛱ 🏊 🏠 🍽

Medicine Bow National Forest
In southeastern Wyoming.
(307) 745-2300
🚴 🏕 🥾 ⛱ 🏠

Shoshone National Forest
In northwestern Wyoming.
(307) 527-6241
🚴 🏕 🥾 ⛱ 🏠 🍽

Yellowstone National Park
In northwestern Wyoming.
(307) 344-7311
🏕 🥾 ⛱ 🏊 🏠 🍽

Canada

ALBERTA

Banff National Park of Canada
In southwestern Alberta, west of Calgary.
(403) 762-1550
🚴 🏕 🥾 ⛱ 🏠 🍽

Elk Island National Park of Canada
In central Alberta, east of Edmonton.
(780) 992-2950
🚴 🏕 🥾 ⛱ 🏠 🍽

Jasper National Park of Canada
In west-central Alberta along the British Columbia border.
(780) 852-6176
🚴 🏕 🥾 ⛱ 🏊 🏠 🍽

Waterton Lakes National Park of Canada
In Alberta's southwestern corner.
(403) 859-5133, or (403) 859-2224 during the winter
🚴 🏕 🥾 ⛱ 🏊 🏠 🍽

BRITISH COLUMBIA

Gulf Islands National Park Reserve of Canada
Off the southeast coast of Vancouver Island.
(250) 654-4000
🏕 🥾 ⛱ 🏊

Glacier National Park of Canada
In southeastern British Columbia.
(250) 837-5100
🏕 🥾 ⛱ 🏠 🍽

Kootenay National Park of Canada
In southeastern British Columbia.
(250) 347-9505 or (888) 773-8888
🚴 🏕 🥾 ⛱ 🏊 🏠 🍽

Mount Revelstoke National Park of Canada
In southeastern British Columbia.
(250) 837-7500
🚴 🏕 🥾 ⛱

Pacific Rim National Park Reserve of Canada
On the southwestern coast of Vancouver Island.
(250) 726-7721 or (250) 726-4212, Jun. 1 to mid-Sept.
🏕 🥾 ⛱ 🏊 🏠 🍽

Yoho National Park of Canada
On the British Columbia-Alberta border.
(250) 343-6783
🚴 🏕 🥾 ⛱ 🏠 🍽

MANITOBA

Riding Mountain National Park of Canada
In southwestern Manitoba.
(204) 848-7275
🚴 🏕 🥾 ⛱ 🏊 🏠 🍽

NEW BRUNSWICK

Fundy National Park of Canada
On Hwy. 114, 130 km. southwest of Moncton.
(506) 887-6000
🚴 🏕 🥾 ⛱ 🏊 🏠 🍽

Kouchibouguac National Park of Canada
On Hwy. 134, north of Moncton.
(506) 876-2443 or TDD (506) 876-4205
🚴 🏕 🥾 ⛱ 🏊 🏠 🍽

NEWFOUNDLAND

Gros Morne National Park of Canada
On Newfoundland's western coast.
(709) 458-2417 or TDD (709) 772-4564
🏕 🥾 ⛱ 🏊 🏠

🚴 Bicycling Trails 🏕 Camping 🥾 Hiking Trails ⛱ Picnic Facilities
🏊 Swimming 🏠 Visitor Center 🍽 Food Service

Terra Nova National Park of Canada
In eastern Newfoundland.
(709) 533-2801

NORTHWEST TERRITORIES

Nahanni National Park Reserve of Canada
145 km. west of Fort Simpson in southwestern Northwest Territories.
(867) 695-3151

Wood Buffalo National Park of Canada
On the Northwest Territories-Alberta border.
(867) 872-7960

NOVA SCOTIA

Cape Breton Highlands National Park of Canada
5 km. northeast of Chéticamp on Cabot Tr.
(902) 224-2306 or (888) 773-8888

Kejimkujik National Park and National Historic Site of Canada
In southwestern Nova Scotia off Hwy. 8 at Maitland Bridge.
(902) 682-2772

ONTARIO

Bruce Peninsula National Park of Canada
In southwestern Ontario.
(519) 596-2233

Georgian Bay Islands National Park
Along the southeastern portion of Georgian Bay.
(705) 526-9804

Point Pelee National Park of Canada
South of Leamington.
(519) 322-2365 or (888) 773-8888

Pukaskwa National Park of Canada
On the north shore of Lake Superior.
(807) 229-0801, ext. 242

St. Lawrence Islands National Park of Canada
In the St. Lawrence River between Kingston and Brockville.
(613) 923-5261

PRINCE EDWARD ISLAND

Port La Joye-Fort Amherst National Historic Site of Canada
West of Charlottetown on Hwy. 1.
(902) 566-7626

Prince Edward Island National Park of Canada
Along the island's northern shore.
(902) 566-7050

QUEBEC

Forillon National Park of Canada
20 km. northeast of Gaspé via Hwy. 132.
(418) 368-5505 or (888) 773-8888

La Mauricie National Park of Canada
North of Trois-Rivières via Hwy. 55.
(819) 538-3232 or (888) 773-8888

SASKATCHEWAN

Grasslands National Park of Canada
Between Val Marie and Killdeer in southern Saskatchewan.
(306) 298-2257

Prince Albert National Park of Canada
In central Saskatchewan.
(306) 663-4522

YUKON TERRITORY

Kluane National Park of Canada
West of Haines Junction.
(867) 634-7250

This list of emergency animal clinics in the United States and Canada is provided by the Veterinary Emergency & Critical Care Society (VECCS) as a service to the community for information purposes only. This is not to be construed as a certification or an endorsement of any clinic listed. For further information, contact the society at (210) 698-5575 or online at www.veccs.org. Note: Hours frequently change, and not all clinics are open 24 hours or in the evening. In addition, not all facilities listed here are emergency clinics. In non-emergency situations, it's best to call first.

If you are traveling to an area not covered in this list, be prepared for an emergency by asking your regular veterinarian to recommend a clinic or veterinarian at your destination. The American Animal Hospital Association also provides a veterinary locator service to clinics that meet the association's high standards for veterinary care. Contact the association at (303) 986-2800 or online at www.healthypet.com.

United States

ALABAMA

Auburn University Small Animal Teaching Hospital
Hoerlein Hall, Wire Rd., Auburn
(334) 844-4690

Emergency & Specialty Animal Medical Center
2864 Acton Rd., Birmingham
(205) 967-7389

Animal Emergency Clinic of North Alabama
2112 Memorial Pkwy. S.W., Huntsville
(256) 533-7600

ALASKA

Pet Emergency Treatment, Inc.
2320 E. Dowling Rd., Anchorage
(907) 274-5636

After Hours Veterinary Emergency Clinic
8 Bonnie Ave., Fairbanks
(907) 479-2700

ARIZONA

First Regional Animal Hospital
1233 W. Warner Rd., Chandler
(480) 732-0018

Emergency Animal Clinic, PLC
86 W. Juniper, Gilbert
(480) 497-0222

1st Emergency Pet Care
1423 S. Higley Rd. #102, Mesa
(480) 924-1123

Emergency Animal Clinic, PLC
9875 W. Peoria Ave., Peoria
(623) 974-1520

Emergency Animal Clinic, PLC
2260 W. Glendale Ave., Phoenix
(602) 995-3757

North Valley Regional Animal Hospital
520 W. Union Hills Dr. #105, Phoenix
(623) 849-0700

Sonora Veterinary Specialists
4015 E. Cactus Rd., Phoenix
(602) 765-3700

Emergency Animal Clinic, PLC
14202 N. Scottsdale Rd., Suite 163, Scottsdale
(480) 949-8001

Ina Road Animal Hospital
7320 N. La Cholla, Suite 114, Tucson
(520) 544-7700

Pima Pet Clinic - Animal Emergency Service
4832 E. Speedway Blvd., Tucson
(520) 327-5624

Southern Arizona Veterinary Specialty and Emergency Center
141 E. Fort Lowell, Tucson
(520) 888-3177, ext. 1

Southern Arizona Veterinary Specialty and Emergency Center
7474 E. Broadway Blvd., Tucson
(520) 888-3177, ext. 2

Veterinary Specialty Center of Tucson
4909 N. La Canada Dr., Tucson
(520) 795-9955

ARKANSAS

Ft. Smith Animal Emergency Clinic
4301 Regions Park Dr., Suite 3, Fort Smith
(479) 649-3100

After Hours Animal Hospital
290 Smokey Ln., North Little Rock
(501) 955-0911

Animal Emergency & Specialty Clinic
8735 Sheltie Dr., Suite G, North Little Rock
(501) 224-3784

Animal Emergency Clinic of Northwest Arkansas
777 Mathias Dr., Suite B, Springdale
(479) 927-0007

CALIFORNIA

East Bay Veterinary Emergency
1312 Sunset Dr., Antioch
(925) 754-5001

Central Coast Pet Emergency Clinic
1558 W. Branch St., Arroyo Grande
(805) 489-6573

Atascadero Pet Hospital and Emergency Center
9575 El Camino Real, Atascadero
(805) 466-3880

Animal Emergency & Urgent Care
4300 Easton Dr., Suite 1, Bakersfield
(661) 322-6019

Pet Emergency Treatment Service
1048 University Ave., Berkeley
(510) 548-6684

United Emergency Animal Clinic
911 Dell Ave., Campbell
(408) 371-6252

Pacific Veterinary Specialists and Emergency Critical Care Center
1980 41st Ave., Capitola
(831) 476-2584

Sacramento Animal Medical Group
4990 Manzanita Ave., Carmichael
(916) 331-7430

Contra Costa Veterinary Emergency Center
1410 Monument Blvd., Suite 108, Concord
(925) 798-2900

Advanced Critical Care
9599 Jefferson Blvd., Culver City
(310) 558-6100

UC Davis Veterinary Medical Teaching Hospital Small Animal Clinic
One Shields Ave., Davis
(530) 752-0186

Vetcare Emergency & Specialty Care Center
7660 Amador Valley Blvd., Dublin
(925) 556-1234

Emergency Pet Clinic of San Gabriel Valley
3254 Santa Anita Ave., El Monte
(626) 579-4550

North Coast Veterinary and Emergency
414 Encinitas Blvd., Encinitas
(760) 632-1072

Animal Urgent Care
2430 A.S. Escondido Blvd., Escondido
(760) 738-9600

Animal Emergency Center
3954 A Jacobs Ave., Eureka
(707) 443-2776

Solano-Napa Pet Emergency Clinic
4437 Central Pl., Fairfield
(707) 864-1444

VCA All-Care Animal Referral Center
18440 Amistad St., Suite E, Fountain Valley
(714) 963-0909

Ohlone Veterinary Emergency Clinic
1618 Washington Blvd., Fremont
(510) 657-6620

Central California Veterinary Specialty Center
6606 N. Blackstone Ave., Fresno
(559) 451-0800

Veterinary Emergency Service, Inc.
1639 N. Fresno St., Fresno
(559) 486-0520

Orange County Emergency Pet Clinic
12750 Garden Grove Blvd., Garden Grove
(714) 537-3032

Animal Emergency Clinic
12022 La Crosse Ave., Grand Terrace
(909) 825-9350

North Orange County Emergency Pet Clinic
1474 S. Harbor Blvd., La Habra
(714) 441-2925

Pet Emergency and Specialty Center
5232 Jackson Dr. #105, La Mesa
(619) 462-4800

Animal Emergency Clinic
1055 W. Avenue M, Suite 101, Lancaster
(661) 723-3959

Animal Specialty Group
4641 Colorado Blvd., Los Angeles
(818) 244-7977

Animal Surgical and Emergency Center (ASEC)
1535 S. Sepulveda Blvd., Los Angeles
(310) 473-5906

Eagle Rock Emergency Pet Clinic
4254 Eagle Rock Blvd., Los Angeles
(323) 254-7382

VCA West Los Angeles Animal Hospital
1818 S. Sepulveda Blvd., Los Angeles
(310) 473-2951

Animal Urgent Care
2805 Hillcrest, Mission Viejo
(949) 364-6228

Modesto Veterinary Emergency Clinic
1800 Prescott Rd., Modesto
(209) 527-8844

Monterey Peninsula-Salinas Vet Emergency Clinic
#2 Harris Ct., Suite A-1, Monterey
(831) 373-7374

Central Orange County Emergency Animal Clinic
3720 Campus Dr., Suite D, Newport Beach
(949) 261-7979

Crossroads Animal Emergency and Referral Clinic
11057 E. Rosecrans Ave., Norwalk
(562) 863-2522

Orange Veterinary Hospital
1100 W. Chapman Ave., Orange
(714) 997-8200

South Peninsula Veterinary Emergency Clinic
3045 Middlefield Rd., Palo Alto
(650) 494-1461

Animal Emergency Clinic of Pasadena
2121 E. Foothill Blvd., Pasadena
(626) 564-0704

Animal Emergency Clinic of San Diego
12775 Poway Rd., Poway
(858) 748-7387

Animal Care Center
6470 Redwood Dr., Rohnert Park
(707) 584-4343

Atlantic St. Veterinary Hospital and Pet Emergency Center
1100 Atlantic St., Roseville
(916) 783-4655

El Camino Veterinary Hospital
4000 El Camino Ave., Sacramento
(916) 488-6878

Mueller Pet Medical Center
6420 Freeport Blvd., Sacramento
(916) 428-9202

Sacramento Veterinary Referral Center
9801 Old Winery Pl., Sacramento
(916) 362-3111

Animal E.R. of San Diego
5610 Kearny Mesa Rd., San Diego
(858) 569-0600

VCA Emergency Animal Hospital and Referral Center
2317 Hotel Cir. S., San Diego
(619) 299-2400

Veterinary Specialty Hospital
10435 Sorrento Valley Rd., San Diego
(858) 875-7500

All Animals Emergency Hospital
1333 Ninth Ave., San Francisco
(415) 566-0531

Pets Unlimited
2343 Fillmore St., San Francisco
(415) 563-6700

San Francisco Veterinary Specialists
600 Alabama St., San Francisco
(415) 401-9200

Emergency Animal Clinic of South San Jose
5440 Thornwood Dr., San Jose
(408) 578-5622

Bay Area Veterinary Emergency Clinic
14790 Washington Ave., San Leandro
(510) 352-6080

California Veterinary Specialists
100 N. Rancho Santa Fe Rd., San Marcos
(760) 734-4433

North Peninsula Veterinary Emergency Clinic, Inc.
227 N. Amphlett Blvd., San Mateo
(650) 348-2576

The Pet Emergency and Specialty Center
901 E. Francisco Blvd., Suite C, San Rafael
(415) 456-7372

California Animal Referral & Emergency Hospital
301 E. Haley St., Santa Barbara
(805) 899-2273

Santa Cruz Veterinary Hospital
2585 Soquel Dr., Santa Cruz
(831) 475-5400

Westside Animal Emergency Hospital
1304 Wilshire Blvd., Santa Monica
(310) 451-8962

Emergency Animal Hospital of Santa Rosa
1946 Santa Rosa Ave., Santa Rosa
(707) 544-1647

PetCare Veterinary Hospital
1370 Fulton Rd., Santa Rosa
(707) 579-5900

TLC Pet Medical Centers-South Pasadena
1412 Huntington Dr., South Pasadena
(626) 441-8555

Associated Veterinary Emergency Services
3008 E. Hammer Ln. #115, Stockton
(209) 952-8387

Animal Emergency Centre
11730 Ventura Blvd., Studio City
(818) 760-3882

Pet Emergency Clinic, Inc.
2967 N. Moorepark Rd., Thousand Oaks
(805) 492-2436

Animal Emergency Referral Center
3511 Pacific Coast Hwy., Torrance
(310) 325-3000

Emergency Pet Clinic of South Bay
2325 Torrance Blvd., Torrance
(310) 320-8300

Monte Vista Small Animal Hospital
901 E. Monte Vista Ave., Turlock
(209) 634-0023

Advanced Critical Care & Internal Medicine
3021 Edinger Ave., Tustin
(949) 654-8950

Inland Valley Emergency Pet Clinic
10 W. 7th St., Upland
(909) 931-7871

Pet Emergency Clinic, Inc.
2301 S. Victoria Ave., Ventura
(805) 642-8562

Veterinary Medical and Surgical Group
2199 Sperry Ave., Ventura
(805) 339-2290

Animal Emergency Clinic
15532 Bear Valley Rd., Victorville
(760) 962-1122

Tulare-Kings Veterinary Emergency Service
4946 W. Mineral King Ave., Visalia
(559) 739-7054

TLC Pet Medical Centers-West Hollywood
8725 Santa Monica Blvd., West Hollywood
(310) 859-4852

COLORADO

Valley Emergency Pet Care
180 Fiou Ln., Suite 101, Basalt
(970) 927-5066

Boulder Emergency Pet Clinic
1658 30th St., Boulder
(303) 440-7722

VCA Douglas County Animal Hospital
531 Jerry St., Castle Rock
(303) 688-2480

Animal Emergency Care Centers, Inc.
3775 Airport Rd., Colorado Springs
(719) 578-9300

Animal Emergency Care, Inc.
5520 N. Nevada Ave., Colorado Springs
(719) 260-7141

VCA Alameda East Veterinary Hospital
9770 E. Alameda Ave., Denver
(303) 366-2639

Central Veterinary Emergency Services
3550 S. Jason St., Englewood
(303) 874-7387

Pet Emergency Treatment Services of N. Colorado
3629 23rd Ave., Evans
(970) 339-8700

Fort Collins Veterinary Emergency Hospital
816 S. Lemay Ave., Fort Collins
(970) 484-8080

James L. Voss Veterinary Teaching Hospital Colorado State University
300 W. Drake Rd., Fort Collins
(970) 221-4535

Grand Valley Veterinary Emergency Center
1660 North Ave., Grand Junction
(970) 255-1911

Animal Hospital Center
5640 County Line Pl., Suite 1, Highland Ranch
(303) 740-9595

Animal Critical Care & Emergency Services, Inc.
1597 Wadsworth Blvd., Lakewood
(303) 239-1200

Animal E.R.
221 W. County Line Rd., Littleton
(720) 283-9348

Columbine Animal Hospital & Emergency Clinic
5546 W. Canyon Tr., Littleton
(303) 979-4040

Animal Emergency Center of Longmont
230 S. Main St., Longmont
(303) 678-8844

Animal Emergency Services of Northern Colorado
201 W. 67th Ct., Loveland
(970) 663-5760

Animal Emergency & Specialty Center
17701 Cottonwood Dr., Parker
(720) 842-5050

Northside Emergency Pet Clinic
945 W. 124th Ave., Westminster
(303) 252-7722

Wheat Ridge Animal Hospital / Wheat Ridge Veterinary Specialists
3695 Kipling St., Wheat Ridge
(303) 424-3325

CONNECTICUT

Farmington Valley Veterinary Emergency Hospital
9 Avonwood Rd., Avon
(860) 674-1886

New Haven Hospital for Veterinary Medicine, Inc.
843 State St., New Haven
(203) 865-0878

Veterinary Referral & Emergency Center
123 W. Cedar St., Norwalk
(203) 854-9960

V-E-T-S (Veterinary Emergency Treatment Services)
8 Enterprise Ln., Oakdale
(860) 444-8870

VCA Shoreline Referral & Emergency Center
895 Bridgeport Ave., Shelton
(203) 929-8600

Connecticut Veterinary Center
470 Oakwood Ave., West Hartford
(860) 233-8564

DELAWARE

VCA Newark Animal Hospital
1360 Marrows Rd., Newark
(302) 737-8100

Veterinary Emergency Center of Delaware
1212 E. Newport Pike, Wilmington
(302) 691-3647

Wincrest Animal Emergency Hospital
3705 Lancaster Pike, Wilmington
(302) 998-2995

DISTRICT OF COLUMBIA

Friendship Hospital for Animals
4105 Brandywire St., Washington
(202) 363-7300

FLORIDA

Animal Emergency Clinic of Brandon
693 W. Lumsden Rd., Brandon
(813) 684-3013

Veterinary Emergency Clinic of Central Florida, Inc.
195 Concord Dr., Casselberry
(407) 740-5500

Animal Emergency and Critical Care Services of S. Florida
9410 Stirling Rd., Cooper City
(954) 432-5611

Coral Springs Animal Hospital
1730 University Dr., Coral Springs
(954) 753-1800

Volusia Animal Emergency Clinic
US 92, Daytona Beach
(386) 252-4300

American Animal Emergency Clinic of Deerfield Beach
103 N. Powerline Rd., Deerfield Beach
(954) 428-9888

Florida Veterinary Referral Center & 24 Hour Emergency & Critical Care
9220 Estero Park Commons Blvd., Suite 7, Estero
(239) 992-8878

Animal Emergency Trauma Center
2200 W. Oakland Park Blvd., Fort Lauderdale
(954) 731-4228

Pet Emergency Center
921 E. Cypress Creek Rd., Fort Lauderdale
(954) 772-0420

Emergency Veterinary Clinic, Inc.
2045 Collier Ave., Fort Myers
(239) 939-5542

Animal Emergency and Referral Center
3984 S. US 1, Fort Pierce
(772) 466-3441

Affiliated Pet Emergency Services
7314 W. University Ave., Gainesville
(352) 373-4444

Hollywood Animal Hospital
2864 Hollywood Blvd., Hollywood
(954) 920-3556

Animal ER
3444 Southside Blvd., Suite 101, Jacksonville
(904) 642-4357

Emergency Pet Care, LLC
14185 Beach Blvd., Suite 7, Jacksonville
(904) 223-8000

Emergency Pet Care of Jupiter
300 Central Blvd., Jupiter
(561) 746-0555

Tampa Bay Veterinary Emergency Service
1501-A Belcher Rd., Suite 1A, Largo
(727) 531-5752

Animal Emergency and Critical Care Center of Brevard
2281 W. Eau Gallie Blvd., Melbourne
(321) 725-5365

AEC-Animal Emergency Clinic South
8429 S.W. 132nd St., Miami
(305) 251-2096

Miami Pet Emergency
11774 S.W. 88th St., Miami
(305) 273-8100

Miami Veterinary Specialists
8601 Sunset Dr., Miami
(305) 665-2820

Snapper Creek Emergency Clinic (Knowles Animal Clinics)
9933 Sunset Dr., Miami
(305) 279-2323

Emergency Pet Hospital of Collier County
6530 Dudley Dr., Naples
(230) 263-8010

Animal ER of SW Florida
15201 N. Cleveland Ave. #1400, North Fort Myers
(239) 995-7755

Clay-Duval Pet Emergency Clinic
275 Corporate Way, Suite 200, Orange Park
(904) 264-8281

Veterinary Emergency Clinic of Central Florida, South Facility
2080 Principal Row, Orlando
(407) 438-4449

Pet Emergency and Critical Care Clinic
3816 Northlake Blvd., Palm Beach Gardens
(561) 691-9999

A.A. Animal ER Center, LLC
36401 US 19N, Palm Harbor
(727) 787-5402

Animal Emergency of Countryside, Inc.
30606 US 19N, Palm Harbor
(727) 786-5755

After Hours Emergency Animal Clinic of Hollywood, Inc.
6602 Pines Blvd., Pembroke Pines
(954) 962-0300

Veterinary Referral Emergency Center
4800 N. Davis Hwy., Pensacola
(850) 477-3914

The Veterinary Emergency Clinic
17829 Murdock Cir., Port Charlotte
(941) 255-5222

Sarasota Emergency Hospital
7517 S. Tamiami Tr., Sarasota
(941) 923-7260

Animal Emergency Clinic of St. Petersburg
3165 22nd Ave. N., St. Petersburg
(727) 323-1311

Noahs Animal Hospital and 24 Hour Emergency
2050 62nd Ave. N., St. Petersburg
(727) 522-6640

Pet Emergency & Critical Care Clinic, Inc.
2239 S. Kanner Hwy., Stuart
(772) 781-3302

Pet Emergency Center
7110 N. University Dr., Tamarac
(954) 726-0998

FVS (Florida Veterinary Specialists)
3000 Busch Lake Blvd., Tampa
(813) 933-8944

Tampa Bay Veterinary Emergency Service
238 E. Bares Ave., Tampa
(813) 265-4043

Animal E.R.
8239 Cooper Creek Blvd., University Park
(941) 355-2884

Palm Beach Veterinary Referral and Critical Care Center
3092 Forest Hill Blvd., West Palm Beach
(561) 434-5700

GEORGIA

All Pets Emergency and Referral Center, P.C.
6460 Hwy. 9N, Alpharetta
(678) 366-2125

University of Georgia - Vet Teaching Hospital
College of Veterinary Medicine, Athens
(706) 542-3221

Animal Emergency Center of Sandy Springs
228 Sandy Springs Pl. N.E., Atlanta
(404) 252-7881

Southern Crescent Animal Emergency
1270 Hwy. 54 E., Fayetteville
(770) 460-8166

An-Emerg Animal Emergency Center
275 #3 Pearl Nix Pkwy., Gainesville
(770) 534-2911

Animal Emergency Center of Gwinnett
1956 Lawrenceville-Suwanee Rd., Lawrenceville
(770) 277 3220

Cobb Emergency Veterinary Clinic
630 Cobb Pkwy. N., Suite C, Marietta
(770) 424-9157

Animal Emergency Center of North Fulton
900 Mansell Rd., Suite 19, Roswell
(770) 594-2266

Georgia Veterinary Specialists and Emergency Care
455 Abernathy Rd. N.E., Sandy Springs
(404) 459-0903

DeKalb-Gwinnet Animal Emergency Clinic
6430 Lawrenceville Hwy., Tucker
(770) 491-0661

Cherokee Emergency Veterinary Clinic
7800 Hwy. 92, Woodstock
(770) 924-3720

IDAHO

WestVet
5019 N. Sawyer Ave., Garden City
(208) 375-1600

North Idaho Pet Emergency
2700 E. Seltice Way #12, Post Falls
(208) 777-2707

ILLINOIS

Animal E.R. of Arlington Heights
1195 E. Palatine Rd., Arlington Heights
(847) 394-6049

VCA Animal Hospital
2600 W. Galena Blvd., Aurora
(630) 896-8541

Animal Emergency Clinic of McLean County
2505 E. Oakland Ave., Bloomington
(309) 665-5020

Veterinary Specialty Center Emergency & Critical Care
1515 Busch Pkwy., Buffalo Grove
(847) 459-7535

Animal Emergency Clinic of Champaign County
1713 S. State St. #4, Champaign
(217) 359-1977

Chicago Veterinary Emergency Service
3123 N. Clybourne Ave., Chicago
(773) 281-7110

Animal Emergency Center
2005 Mall St., Collinsville
(618) 346-1898

Emergency Veterinary Care South Assoc.
13715 S. Cicero Ave., Crestwood
(708) 388-3771

Animal Emergency of McHenry County
1095 Pingree Rd., Suite 120, Crystal Lake
(815) 479-9119

Arboretum View Animal Hospital
2551 Warrenville Rd., Downers Grove
(630) 963-0424

Dundee Animal Hospital
199 Penny Ave., Dundee
(847) 428-6114

VCA Franklin Park Animal Hospital
9846 W. Grand Ave., Franklin Park
(847) 455-4922

Animal Emergency & Treatment Center
1810 E. Belvidere Rd., Grayslake
(847) 548-5300

Emergency Veterinary Services
820 Ogden Ave., Lisle
(630) 960-2900

Animal Emergency of Mokena
19110 S. 88th Ave., Mokena
(708) 326-4800

Animal Emergency and Referral Center
1810 Frontage Rd., Northbrook
(847) 564-5775

Animal Emergency Clinic of Rockford
4236 Maray Dr., Rockford
(815) 229-7791

Animal 911
3735 W. Dempster St., Skokie
(847) 673-9110

Animal Emergency Clinic of Springfield
1333 W. Wabash Ave., Springfield
(217) 698-0870

Emergency Veterinary Services of St. Charles
530 Dunham Rd., St. Charles
(630) 584-7447

University of Illinois College of Veterinary Medicine
1008 W. Hazelwood Dr., Urbana
(217) 333-5300

INDIANA

Northwood Veterinary Hospital
3255 N. SR 9, Anderson
(765) 649-5218

St. Francis Family Pet Health Care
822 W. Plymouth St., Breman
(574) 546-9005

Airport Animal Emergi-Center
5235 W. Washington St., Indianapolis
(317) 248-0832

Indiana Veterinary Specialist & Emergency Center
8250 Bash St., Indianapolis
(317) 849-4925

Indianapolis Veterinary Emergency Center
5425 Victory Dr., Indianapolis
(317) 782-4484

Noahs Animal Hospital, P.C.
5510 Millersville Rd., Indianapolis
(317) 253-1327

Animal Emergency Clinic of Tippecanoe County
1343 Sagamore Pkwy. N., Lafayette
(765) 449-2001

Animal Emergency Clinic
2324 Grape Rd., Mishawaka
(574) 259-8387

Calumet Emergency Veterinary Clinic
216 W. Lincoln Hwy., Schererville
(219) 865-0970

North Central Veterinary Emergency Center
1645 S. US 421, Westville
(219) 785-7300

IOWA

Iowa State University Veterinary Clinical Sciences Teaching Hospital
S. 16th St., Ames
(515) 294-4900

Animal Emergency Center of the Quad Cities
1510 State St., Bettendorf
(563) 344-9599

Eastern Iowa Veterinary Specialty Center
755 Capital Dr. S.W., Cedar Rapids
(319) 841-5161

Animal Emergency & Referral Center of Central Iowa
6110 Creston Ave., Des Moines
(515) 280-3051

KANSAS

Kansas State University Vet. Med. Teaching Hospital
1800 Denison Ave., Manhattan
(785) 532-4100

Mission MedVet
5914 Johnson Dr., Mission
(913) 722-5566

Veterinary Specialty & Emergency Center
11950 W. 110th St., Overland Park
(913) 642-9563

Central Kansas Veterinary Center
515 W. Blanchard Ave., South Hutchinson
(620) 663-8387

Emergency Animal Clinic of Topeka
839 S.W. Fairlawn Rd., Topeka
(785) 272-2926

Veterinary Emergency and Specialty Hospital of Wichita
727 S. Washington, Wichita
(316) 262-5321

KENTUCKY

AA Small Animal Emergency Service
200 Southland Dr., Lexington
(859) 276-2505

Jefferson Animal Hospital and Regional Emergency Center
4504 Outer Loop, Louisville
(502) 966-4104

Louisville Veterinary Specialty and Emergency Services
12905 Shelbyville Rd., Suite 3, Louisville
(502) 244-3036

Greater Cincinnati Veterinary Specialists & Emergency Services
11 Beacon Dr., Wilder
(859) 572-0560

LOUISIANA

Baton Rouge Pet Emergency Hospital
1514 Cottondale Dr., Baton Rouge
(225) 925-5566

Veterinary Emergency and Critical Care
2611 Florida St., Mandeville
(985) 626-4862

Southeast Veterinary Emergency and Critical Care
3409 Division St., Metairie
(504) 219-0444

MAINE

Eastern Maine Emergency Veterinary Clinic
15 Dirigo Dr., Brewer
(207) 989-6267

Animal Emergency Clinic of Mid-Maine
37 Strawberry Ave., Lewiston
(207) 777-1110

Animal Emergency Clinic
739 Warren Ave., Portland
(207) 878-3121

MARYLAND

Anne Arundel Veterinary Emergency Clinic
808 Bestgate Rd., Annapolis
(410) 224-0331

Harford Emergency Veterinary Services
526 Underwood Ln., Bel Air
(410) 420-8000

Emergency Veterinary Clinic, Inc.
32 Mellor Ave., Catonsville
(410) 788-7040

Emergency Animal Hospital of Ellicott City
10270 Baltimore National Pike (SR 40W), Ellicott City
(410) 750-1177

Frederick Emergency Animal Hospital
434 Prospect Blvd., Frederick
(301) 662-6622

Greenbriar Veterinary Referral & Emergency Center
3051 Thurston Rd., Frederick
(301) 874-8880

VCA Veterinary Referral Associates
15021 Dufief Mill Rd., Gaithersburg
(301) 340-3224

Metropolitan Emergency Animal Clinic
12106 Nebel St., Rockville
(301) 770-5226

Pets ER
Gateway Crossing, 329 Tilghman Rd., Suite 100, Salisbury
(410) 543-8400

PET ER
1209 Cromwell Bridge Rd., Towson
(410) 252-8387

Southern Maryland Veterinary Referral Center
3485 Rockefeller Ct., Waldorf
(301) 638-0988

MASSACHUSETTS

Animal Emergency Care
164 Great Rd., Acton
(978) 263-1742

MSPCA Angell Animal Medical Center
350 S. Huntington Ave., Boston
(617) 522-7282

Cape Cod Veterinary Specialists Emergency Service
11 Bourne Bridge Approach, Buzzards Bay
(508) 759-5125

Wignall Animal Hospital
1837 Bridge St., Dracut
(978) 454-8272

Fall River Animal Hospital, Inc.
33 18th St., Fall River
(508) 675-6374

Essex County Veterinary Emergency Hospital
247 Chickering Rd., North Andover
(978) 725-5544

Tufts University Cummings School of Veterinary Medicine
200 Westboro Rd., North Grafton
(508) 839-5395

VCA South Shore Animal Hospital
595 Columbian St., South Weymouth
(781) 337-6622

VCA Boston Road Animal Hospital
1235 Boston Rd., Springfield
(413) 783-1203

TUFTS Veterinary Emergency Treatment and Specialties
525 South St., Walpole
(508) 668-5454

Veterinary Emergency & Specialty Center of New England
180 Bear Hill Rd., Waltham
(781) 684-8387

New England Animal Medical Center
595 W. Center St., West Bridgewater
(508) 580-2515

Massachusetts Veterinary Referral Hospital
20 Cabot Rd., Woburn
(781) 932-5802

Woburn Animal Hospital
373 Russell St., Woburn
(781) 933-0170

MICHIGAN

Animal Emergency Clinic
4126 Packard Rd., Ann Arbor
(734) 971-8774

Ann Arbor Animal Hospital Emergency Service
2150 W. Liberty, Ann Arbor
(734) 662-4474

Michigan Veterinary Specialists
3412 E. Walton Blvd., Auburn Hills
(248) 371-3713

Oakland Veterinary Emergency & Critical Care
1400 Telegraph Rd., Bloomfield Hills
(248) 334-6877

Michigan State University Veterinary Teaching Hospital
Michigan State University, Wilson Rd., East Lansing
(517) 353-5420

Animal Emergency Hospital
1007 S. Ballenger Hwy., Flint
(810) 238 7557

Animal Emergency Hospital
3260 Plainfield Ave. N.E., Grand Rapids
(616) 361-9911

Southwest Michigan Animal Emergency Hospital
3301 S. Burdick, Kalamazoo
(616) 381-5228

Lansing Veterinary Urgent Care
3276 E. Jolly Rd., Lansing
(517) 393-9200

Veterinary Emergency Service-East
28223 John R Rd., Madison Heights
(248) 547-4677

Veterinary Care Specialists
205 Rowe Rd., Milford
(248) 684-0468

Animal Emergency Center
24255 Novi Rd., Novi
(248) 348-1788

Veterinary Emergency Service-West
40850 Ann Arbor Rd., Plymouth
(734) 207-8500

Great Lakes Pet Emergencies
1221 Tittabawassee Rd., Saginaw
(989) 752-1960

Michigan Veterinary Specialists
29080 Inkster Rd., Southfield
(248) 354-6660

Affiliated Veterinary Emergency Clinic
14085 Northline Rd., Southgate
(734) 284-1700

MINNESOTA
South Metro Animal Emergency Care
14690 Pennock Ave., Apple Valley
(952) 953-3737

Midwest Veterinary Specialty Group
11850 Aberdeen St., N.E., Blaine
(763) 754-5000

Affiliated Emergency Veterinary Hospital
1615 Coon Rapids Blvd., Coon Rapids
(763) 754-9434

Affiliated Emergency Veterinary Service
2314 W. Michigan St., Duluth
(218) 302-8000

Affiliated Emergency Veterinary Service
7717 Flying Cloud Dr., Eden Prairie
(952) 942-8272

Affiliated Emergency Veterinary Service
4708 Hwy. 55, Golden Valley
(763) 529-6560

Animal Emergency Clinic
7166 10th St. N., Oakdale
(651) 501-3766

Affiliated Emergency Veterinary Service
121 23rd Ave. S.W., Rochester
(507) 424-3976

Affiliated Emergency Veterinary Service
4180 Thielman Ln., St. Cloud
(320) 258-3481

Animal Emergency Clinic
301 University Ave., St. Paul
(651) 293-1800

University of Minnesota, College of Veterinary Medicine
1365 Gortner Ave., St. Paul
(612) 626-8387

MISSOURI
Animal Emergency Clinic
7095 Metropolitan Blvd., Suite G, Barnhart
(636) 464-2846

Animal Emergency Clinic
12501 Natural Bridge, Bridgeton
(314) 739-1500

University of Missouri-Columbia Veterinary Med. Teaching Hospital
900 E. Campus Dr., Columbia
(573) 882-7821

Animal Emergency Center
8141 N. Oak Trfy., Kansas City
(816) 455-5430

Animal Emergency & Referral Hospital
3495 N.E. Ralph Powell Rd., Lee's Summit
(816) 554-4990

Animal Emergency Clinic
334 Fort Zumwalt Sq., O'Fallon
(636) 240-5496

Emergency Veterinary Clinic of Southwest Missouri
400 S. Glenstone Ave., Springfield
(417) 890-1600

Animal Emergency Clinic
9937 Big Bend Blvd., St. Louis
(314) 822-7600

MONTANA
Western Montana Small Animal Emergency Clinic
1914 S. Reserve St., Missoula
(406) 829-9300

NEBRASKA
Veterinary Emergency Services of Lincoln
3700 S. 9th St., Lincoln
(402) 489-6800

Animal Emergency Clinic
9664 Mockingbird Dr., Omaha
(402) 339-6232

NEVADA
Animal Emergency Center of Las Vegas
3340 E. Patrick Ln., Las Vegas
(702) 457-8050

Las Vegas Animal Emergency Hospital
5231 W. Charleston Blvd., Las Vegas
(702) 822-1045

Animal Emergency Center
6425 S. Virginia St., Reno
(775) 851-3600

NEW HAMPSHIRE
Capital Area Veterinary Emergency Service
22 Bridge St., Concord
(603) 227-1199

Veterinary Emergency Center of Manchester
55 Carl Dr., Manchester
(603) 666-6677

Animal Medical Center of New England
168 Main Dunstable Rd., Nashua
(603) 821-7222

Emergency Veterinary Clinic of the Seacoast Region
300 Gosling Rd., Portsmouth
(603) 431-3600

NEW JERSEY
Veterinary Surgical & Diagnostic Specialists
34 Trenton-Lakewood Rd., Clarksburg
(609) 259-8300

Animal Emergency Referral Associates
1237 Broomfield Ave., Fairfield
(973) 226-3282

Central Jersey Veterinary Emergency Service
643 Rt. 27, Iselin
(732) 283-3535

Jersey Shore Veterinary Emergency Service
1000 Rt. 70, Lakewood
(732) 363-3200

South Jersey Veterinary Emergency Services
535 Maple Ave., Linwood
(609) 926-5300

Animal Emergency Service of South Jersey
220 Moorestown-Mount Laurel Rd., Mount Laurel
(856) 727-1332

Oradell Animal Hospital
580 Winters Ave., Paramus
(201) 262-0010

Alliance Emergency Veterinary Clinic
540 Rt. 10W, Randolph
(973) 328-2844

Animerge
21 Rt. 206N, Raritan
(908) 707-9077

Garden State Veterinary Specialists
1 Pine St., Tinton Falls
(732) 922-0011

Red Bank Veterinary Hospital
197 Hance Ave., Tinton Falls
(732) 747-3636

NEW MEXICO

Veterinary Medical Clinic
1407 Indian Wells Rd., Alamogordo
(505) 437-3063

Albuquerque Animal Emergency Clinic
4000 Montgomery Blvd. N.E., Albuquerque
(505) 884-3433

Urgent Care Veterinary Hospital
9032 Montgomery Blvd. N.E., Albuquerque
(505) 275-2273

Emergency Veterinary Clinic of Santa Fe
1311 Calle Mava, Santa Fe
(505) 984-0625

NEW YORK

Greater Buffalo Veterinary Emergency Services
4949 Main St., Amherst
(716) 839-4043

Veterinary Emergency & Critical Care Center
2115 Downer Street Rd., Baldwinsville
(315) 638-3500

Katonah Bedford Veterinary Center
546 N. Bedford Rd., Bedford Hills
(914) 241-7700

Atlantic Coast Veterinary Specialists
3250 Veterans Hwy., Bohemia
(631) 285-7780

Animal Emergency Service
6230-C Jericho Tpke., Commack
(631) 462-6044

Veterinary Medical Center of Central New York
5841 Bridge St., East Syracuse
(315) 446-7933

New York Veterinary Specialty Center
2233 Broadhollow Rd., Farmingdale
(631) 694-3400

Animal Emergency Clinic
1112 Morton Blvd., Kingston
(845) 336-0713

Capital District Animal Emergency Clinic
222 Troy-Schenectady Rd., Latham
(518) 785-1094

Orange County Animal Emergency Service
517 Rt. 211E, Middletown
(845) 692-0260

The Veterinary Referral Center of Ultravet Diagnostics
220 E. Jericho Tpke., Mineola
(516) 294-6680

Manhattan Veterinary Group
240 E. 80th St., New York
(212) 988-1000

NYC Veterinary Specialists and Cancer Treatment Center
410 W. 55th St., New York
(212) 767-0099

Orchard Park Veterinary Medical Center
3507 Orchard Park Rd., Orchard Park
(716) 662-6660

Long Island Veterinary Specialists & Animal Emergency & Critical Care Center
163 S. Service Rd., Plainview
(516) 501-1700

Animal Emergency Clinic of Hudson Valley
84 Patrick Ln., Poughkeepsie
(845) 471-8242

East End Veterinary Emergency Center
67 Commerce Dr., Riverhead
(631) 369-4513

Animal Hospital of Pittsford (Monroe Emergency Service)
2816 Monroe Ave., Rochester
(585) 271-7700

Veterinary Specialists of Rochester/Animal Emergency Service
825 White Spruce Blvd., Rochester
(585) 424-1277

Animal Emergency Service
280-L Middle Country Rd., Selden
(631) 698-2225

Valley Cottage Animal Hospital
202 Rt. 303, Valley Cottage
(845) 268-9263

Nassau Animal Emergency Hospital
740 Old Country Rd., Westbury
(516) 333-6262

The Center for Specialized Veterinary Care
609-5 Cantiague Rock Rd., Westbury
(516) 420-0000

NORTH CAROLINA

REACH Emergency Animal Hospital
677 Brevard Rd., Asheville
(828) 665-4399

Animal Emergency Clinic of the High Country
1126 Blowing Rock Rd., Suite A, Boone
(828) 268-2833

Animal Emergency Clinic of Cary
220 High House Rd., Cary
(919) 462-8989

Veterinary Specialty Hospital of the Carolinas
6405 Tryon Rd., Cary
(919) 233-4911

Animal Medical Hospital
3832 Monroe Rd., Charlotte
(704) 334-4684

Carolina Veterinary Specialists-Animal Emergency and Trauma Center
2225 Township Rd., Charlotte
(704) 504-9608

Triangle Veterinary Emergency Clinic
3319 Chapel Hill Blvd., Durham
(919) 489-0615

After Hours Veterinary Emergency Clinic
5505 W. Friendly Ave., Greensboro
(336) 851-1990

Carolina Veterinary Specialists-Animal Emergency and Trauma Center
501 Nicholas Rd., Greensboro
(336) 632-0605

After Hours Emergency Veterinary Clinic
126 Hwy. 321 S.W., Hickory
(828) 328-2660

Carolina Veterinary Specialists-Animal Emergency and Trauma Center
12117 Statesville Rd., Huntersville
(704) 949-1100

Cabarrus Emergency Veterinary Clinic
1317 S. Cannon Blvd., Kannapolis
(704) 932-1182

Emergency Veterinary Clinic, PA
2440 Plantation Center Dr., Matthews
(704) 844-6440

After Hours Small Animal Emergency Clinic
409 Vick Ave., Raleigh
(919) 781-5145

Quail Corners Animal Hospital & 24 Hour Emergency Care
1613 E. Millbrook Rd., Raleigh
(919) 876-0739

Eastern Carolina Veterinary Emergency Treatment Service
4909-D Expressway Dr., Wilson
(252) 265-9920

Carolina Veterinary Specialists-Animal Emergency and Trauma Center
1600 Hanes Mall Blvd., Winston-Salem
(336) 896-0902

OHIO

Akron Veterinary Referral & Emergency Center
1321 Centerview Cir., Akron
(330) 665-4996

Metropolitan Veterinary Hospital
1053 S. Cleveland-Massillon Rd., Akron
(330) 666-2976

Veterinary Referral Clinic & Emergency Center
5035 Richmond Rd., Bedford Heights
(216) 831-6789

Animal Emergency Clinic West
5320 W. 140th St., Brook Park
(216) 362-6001

Stark County Veterinary Emergency Clinic, LLC
2705 Fulton Dr. N.W., Canton
(330) 452-5116

Cincinnati Animal Referral and Emergency Center
6995 E. Kemper Rd., Cincinnati
(513) 530-0911

Capital Veterinary Referral & Emergency Clinic
5230 Renner Rd., Columbus
(614) 870-0480

Ohio State University Veterinary Hospital
601 Vernon L. Tharp St., Columbus
(614) 292-3551

Dayton Emergency Veterinary Clinic
2714 Springboro W., Dayton
(937) 293-2714

After Hours Animal Emergency Clinic, Inc.
2680 W. Liberty St., Girard
(330) 530-8387

Animal Emergency Center, Inc.
5152 Grove Ave., Lorain
(440) 240-1400

Aaron Animal Clinic and Emergency Hospital
7640 Broadview Rd., Parma
(216) 901-9980

Animal Emergency & Critical Care Center of Toledo, Inc.
2785 W. Central Ave., Toledo
(419) 473-0328

Green Animal Medical Center
1620 Corporate Woods Cir., Uniontown
(330) 896-4040

MedVet Associates, Ltd.
300 E. Wilson Bridge Rd., Worthington
(614) 846-5800

OKLAHOMA

Animal Emergency Center
931 S.W. 74th, Oklahoma City
(405) 631-7828

Neel Veterinary Hospital
2700 N. MacArthur, Oklahoma City
(405) 947-8387

Veterinary Emergency and Critical Care Hospital
1800 W. Memorial Rd., Oklahoma City
(405) 749-6989

Animal Emergency Center, Inc.
7220 E. 41st St., Tulsa
(918) 665-0508

OREGON

The Animal Emergency Center of Central Oregon
1245 S.E. 3rd St., Suite C3, Bend
(541) 385-9110

Northwest Veterinary Specialists & Emergency Services
16756 S.E. 82nd Dr., Clackamas
(503) 656-3999

Animal Emergency and Critical Care Center
650 S.W. 3rd St., Corvallis
(541) 753-5750

Dove Lewis Emergency Animal Hospital
1945 N.W. Pettygroove, Portland
(503) 228-7281

VCA Southeast Portland Animal Hospital
13830 S.E. Stark St., Portland
(503) 255-8139

Salem Veterinary Emergency Clinic
3215 Market St. N.E., Salem
(503) 588-8082

Springfield-Eugene Emergency Veterinary Hospital
103 W. Q St., Springfield
(541) 746-0112

Emergency Veterinary Clinic of Tualatin
19314 S.W. Mohave Ct., Tualatin
(503) 691-7922

PENNSYLVANIA

Center for Animal Referral and Emergency Services
2010 Cabot Blvd. W., Suite D, Langhorne
(215) 750-2774

Veterinary Specialty & Emergency Center
1900 W. Old Lincoln Hwy., Langhorne
(215) 750-7884

Gwynedd Veterinary Hospital and Emergency Service
1615 W. Point Pike, Lansdale
(215) 699-9294

Allegheny Veterinary Emergency Trauma & Specialty
4224 Northern Pike, Monroeville
(412) 373-4200

Emergency Service, Veterinary Hospital of the University of PA
3900 Delancey St., Philadelphia
(215) 898-4685

VCA Castle Shannon Animal Hospital Service
3610 Library Rd., Pittsburgh
(412) 885-2500

Veterinary Emergency Clinic
882 Butler St., Pittsburgh
(412) 492-9855

Hickory Veterinary Hospital
2303 Hickory Rd., Plymouth Meeting
(610) 828-3054

Metropolitan Emergency Service
2626 Van Buren Ave., Norristown
(610) 666-0914

Bucks County Veterinary Emergency Trauma Service
978 Easton Rd., Warrington
(215) 918-2200

Animal Emergency Center
395 Susquehanna Tr., Watsontown
(570) 742-7400

Valley Central Emergency Veterinary Hospital
210 Fullerton Ave., Whitehall
(610) 435-5588

RHODE ISLAND

Ocean State Veterinary Specialists
1480 S. County Tr., East Greenwich
(401) 886-6787

SOUTH CAROLINA

South Carolina Veterinary Emergency Care
132 Stonemark Ln., Columbia
(803) 798-3837

Palmetto Regional Emergency Hospital for Animals
921 Spears Creek Ct., Elgin
(803) 865-1418

Greater Charleston Emergency Veterinary Clinic
930 Pine Hollow Rd., Mt. Pleasant
(843) 216-7554

Animal Emergency Hospital of the Strand
303 Hwy. 15, Suite 1, Myrtle Beach
(843) 445-9797

Greater Charleston Emergency Veterinary Clinic
3163 W. Montague Ave., North Charleston
(843) 744-3372

Spartanburg Veterinary Emergency Clinic
1291 Asheville Hwy., Spartanburg
(864) 591-1923

SOUTH DAKOTA

Veterinary Emergency Hospital
3508 S. Minnesota Ave., Suite 104, Sioux Falls
(605) 977-6200

TENNESSEE

Midland Pet Emergency Center, Inc.
235 Calderwood St., Alcoa
(865) 982-1007

Airport Pet Emergency Clinic
2436 Hwy. 75, Blountville
(423) 279-0574

Pet Emergency Treatment Service
1668 Mallory Ln., Brentwood
(615) 333-1212, ext. 1

Regional Institute for Veterinary Emergency & Referral
2132 Amnicola Hwy., Chattanooga
(423) 698-4612

Animal Emergency Clinic of Maury County, LLC
1900B Shady Brook St., Columbia
(931) 380-1929

PetMed Emergency Center, LLC
830 N. Germantown Pkwy., Suite 105, Cordova
(901) 624-9002

Knoxville Pet Emergency Clinic
1819 Ailor Ave., Knoxville
(865) 637-0114

University of Tennessee Veterinary Teaching Hospital
2407 River Dr., Knoxville
(865) 974-8387

Animal Emergency Center, PC
3767 Summer Ave., Memphis
(901) 323-4563

TEXAS

I-20 Animal Medical Center
5820 W. I-20, Arlington
(817) 478-9238

Austin Vet Care
4106 N. Lamar, Austin
(512) 459-4336

Emergency Animal Hospital of Northwest Austin
12034 Research Blvd., Suite 8, Austin
(512) 331-6121

Emergency Animal Hospital of Northwest Austin - South Branch
4434 Frontier Tr., Austin
(512) 899-0955

Animal Emergency Clinic of Southeast Texas, Inc.
3420 W. Cardinal Dr., Beaumont
(409) 842-3239

North Texas Emergency Pet Clinic
1712 W. Frankford Rd., Suite 3108, Carrolton
(972) 323-1310

Emergency Animal Clinic
12101 Greenville Ave., Suite 118, Dallas
(972) 994-9110

The E-Clinic, Inc.
3337 Fitzhugh Ave., Dallas
(214) 520-8388

Denton County Animal Emergency Room
4145 S. I-35E, Suite 101, Denton
(940) 271-1200

El Paso Animal Emergency Center
1220 Airway Blvd., El Paso
(915) 545-1148

Airport Frwy. Animal Emergency Clinic
411 N. Main St., Euless
(817) 571-2088

Metro West Emergency Veterinary Center
3201 Hulen St., Fort Worth
(817) 731-3734

Animal Emergency & Urgent Care Center of The Woodlands
27870 I-45N, Houston
(281) 367-5444

Animal Emergency Center of West Houston
4823 Hwy. 6N, Houston
(832) 593-8387

Animal Emergency Clinic
1111 West Loop S. #200, Houston
(713) 693-1100

Animal Emergency Clinic SH 249
19311 SH 249, Houston
(281) 890-8875

VCA Animal Emergency Hospital
10331 Gulf Frwy., Houston
(713) 941-8460

Veterinary Emergency Referral Group, Inc.
8921 Katy Frwy., Houston
(713) 932-9589

VCA Metroplex Animal Hospital & Pet Lodge
700 W. Airport Frwy., Irving
(972) 438-7113

After Hours Veterinary Services
2501 S. W.S. Young, Suite 413, Killeen
(254) 628-5017

VCA Animal Emergency Clinic Southeast-Calder Rd.
1100 Gulf Frwy. S., Suite 104, League City
(281) 332-1678

Lake Ray Hubbard Emergency Pet Care Center
4651 N. Beltline Rd., Mesquite
(972) 226-3377

Lake Ray Hubbard Emergency Pet Care Center
9501 Lakeview Pkwy., Rowlett
(972) 475-5349

Angel of Mercy Animal Critical Care, Inc.
8734 Grissom Rd., San Antonio
(210) 684-2105

Animal Emergency Room
4315 Fredericksburg Rd., Suite 2, San Antonio
(210) 737-7380

Emergency Pet Clinic, Inc.
8503 Broadway #105, San Antonio
(210) 822-2873

Northeast Emergency Animal Clinic
8365 Perrin Beitel, San Antonio
(210) 650-3141

Animal Emergency Hospital of North Texas
2340 W. Southlake Blvd., Southlake
(817) 410-2273

Animal Emergency Clinic 59 Southwest
9920 Hwy. 90A, Suite 100C, Sugar Land
(281) 340-8387

Texas Animal Medical Center
4900 Steinbeck Bend, Waco
(254) 753-0901

UTAH

Central Valley Veterinary Hospital
55 E. Miller Ave., Salt Lake City
(801) 487-1325

Pet E.R. - The Pet Emergency Room
6360 S. Highland Dr., Salt Lake City
(801) 278-3367

Animal Emergency Center
2465 N. Main St., Sunset
(801) 776-8118

VERMONT

Burlington Emergency Veterinary Service
200 Commerce St., Williston
(802) 865-1205

VIRGINIA

Alexandria Veterinary Emergency Service
2660 Duke St., Alexandria
(703) 823-3601

Veterinary Emergency Treatment Services, Inc.
370 Greenbrier Dr., Suite A-2, Charlottesville
(434) 973-3519

Greenbrier Veterinary Emergency Center
1100 Eden Way N., Suite 101B, Chesapeake
(757) 366-9000

SouthPaws Veterinary Specialists & Emergency Center
8500 Arlington Blvd., Fairfax
(703) 752-9100

Animal Emergency Critical Care
165 Fort Evans Rd. N.E., Leesburg
(703) 777-5755

Animal Emergency & Critical Care of Lynchburg
3432 Odd Fellows Rd., Lynchburg
(434) 846-1504

Veterinary Referral & Critical Care (VRCC)
1596 Hockett Rd., Manakin Sabot
(804) 784-8722

Prince William Emergency Veterinary Clinic
8610 Centreville Rd., Manassas
(703) 361-8287

Veterinary Emergency Center South
12501 Hull St., Midlothian
(804) 744-9800

Veterinary Emergency Center, Inc.
3312 W. Cary St., Richmond
(804) 353-9000

Emergency Veterinary Services of Roanoke
4902 Frontage Rd. N.W., Roanoke
(540) 563-8575

Regional Veterinary Referral Center
6651 Backlick Rd., Springfield
(703) 451-8900

The Hope Center for Advanced Veterinary Medicine
140 Park St. S.E., Vienna
(703) 281-5121

Beach Veterinary Emergency Clinic
1124 Lynnhaven Pkwy., Virginia Beach
(757) 468-4900

Tidewater Veterinary Emergency and Critical Care Center
5425 Virginia Beach Blvd., Virginia Beach
(757) 499-5463

Woodbridge Animal Hospital
2703 Caton Hill Rd., Woodbridge
(703) 897-5665

Emergency Veterinary Clinic
1120 George Washington Memorial Hwy., Yorktown
(757) 874-8115

WASHINGTON

After Hours Animal Emergency Clinic
718 Auburn Way N., Auburn
(253) 939-6272

Animal Emergency Care
317 Telegraph Rd., Bellingham
(360) 758-2200

Animal Emergency Clinic of Everett
3625 Rucker Ave., Everett
(425) 258-4466

VCA Alpine Animal Hospital
888 N.W. Sammamish Rd., Issaquah
(425) 392-8888

Animal Emergency Service, East
636 7th Ave., Kirkland
(425) 827-8727

Veterinary Specialty Center of Seattle
20115 44th Ave. W., Lynnwood
(425) 697-6106

Pet Emergency Center
14434 Avon Allen Rd., Mount Vernon
(360) 848-5911

Animal Emergency & Trauma Center
320 Lindvig Way, Poulsbo
(360) 697-7771

Washington State University
Veterinary Teaching Hospital, 100 Grimes Way, Pullman
(509) 335-0711

Animal Critical Care & Emergency Services (ACCES)
11536 Lake City Way, N.E., Seattle
(206) 364-1660

Emerald City Emergency Clinic
4102 Stone Way N., Seattle
(206) 634-9000

Five Corners Veterinary Hospital
15707 1st Ave. S., Seattle
(206) 243-2982

PSCVM Small Animal Emergency and Critical Care Center
11308 92nd St. S.E., Snohomish
(360) 568-9111

Pet Emergency Clinic
21 E. Mission Ave., Spokane
(509) 326-6670

The Animal Emergency Clinic
5608 S. Durango St., Tacoma
(253) 474-0791

Emergency Veterinary Service, Inc.
6818 E. 4th Plain Blvd., Suite C, Vancouver
(360) 694-3007

St. Francis 24 Hr. Animal Hospital
12010 N.E. 65th St., Vancouver
(360) 253-5446

WEST VIRGINIA

Kanawha Valley Animal Emergency Clinic
5304 MacCorkle Ave. S.W., Charleston
(304) 768-2911

Animal Urgent Care, Inc.
4201 Wood St., Wheeling
(304) 233-0002

WISCONSIN

Fox Valley Animal Referral Center
4706 New Horizons Blvd., Appleton
(920) 993-9193

Animal Emergency Center & Specialty Services
2100 W. Silver Spring Dr., Glendale
(414) 540-6710

Green Bay Animal Emergency Center
933 Anderson Dr., Suite F, Green Bay
(920) 494-9400

Crawford Animal Hospital
4607 S. 108th St., Greenfield
(414) 427-1731

Emergency Clinic for Animals
229 W. Beltline Hwy., Madison
(608) 274-7772

Emergency Vets of Central Wisconsin, LLC
1420 Kronenwetter Dr., Mosinee
(715) 693-6934

The Animal ER of Kenosha & Racine
4333 S. Green Bay Rd., Racine
(262) 553-9223

Wisconsin Veterinary Referral Center
360 Bluemound Rd., Waukesha
(262) 542-3241

Canada

ALBERTA

Calgary North Veterinary Hospital and Emergency Service
4204 4th St. N.W., Calgary
(403) 277-0135

Animal Emergency Hospital South, Ltd.
3823 99th St. N.W., Edmonton
(780) 436-5880

Edmonton Veterinarians Emergency Clinic
11104 102nd Ave., Edmonton
(780) 433-9505

BRITISH COLUMBIA

Central Animal Emergency Clinic
812 Roderick Ave., Coquitlam
(604) 931-1911

Animal Emergency Clinic of the Fraser Valley
#306-6325 204th St., Langley
(604) 514-1711

Vancouver Animal Emergency Clinic, Ltd.
1590 W. 4th St., Vancouver
(604) 734-5104

Central Victoria Veterinary Hospital
760 Roderick St., Victoria
(250) 475-2495

MANITOBA

Winnipeg Animal Emergency Hospital
400 Pembina Hwy., Winnipeg
(204) 452-9427

NOVA SCOTIA

Metro Animal Emergency Clinic
201 Brownlow Ave., Unit 9, Dartmouth
(902) 468-0674

ONTARIO

Veterinary Emergency Clinic of York Region
1210 Journey's End Cir., New Market
(905) 953-5351

Huronia Veterinary Emergency Clinic
115 Bell Farm Rd., Barrie
(705) 722-0377

Emergency Veterinary Clinic
#1 Wexford Rd., Brampton
(905) 495-9907

North Town Veterinary Hospital
496 Main St. N., Brampton
(905) 451-2000

Veterinary Emergency Clinic
41 Adelaide St. N., #43, London
(519) 432-7341

Mississauga-Oakville Veterinary Emergency Hospital & Referral Group
2285 Bristol Cir., Oakville
(905) 829-9444

Alta Vista Animal Hospital
2616 Bank St., Ottawa
(613) 731-9911

Niagara Veterinary Emergency Clinic
2F Tremont Dr., Unit 1, St. Catharines
(905) 641-3185

Veterinary Emergency Clinic
920 Yonge St. #117, Toronto
(416) 920-2002

Animal Emergency Clinic
1910 Dundas St. E., Unit B 101, Whitby
(905) 576-3031

QUEBEC

Centre Veterinaire DMV
2300 54th Ave., Montreal
(514) 633-8888

University of Montreal
3200 Sicotte St., St-Hyacinthe
(450) 778-8111

PET-FRIENDLY LODGINGS

How to Use the Listings
U.S. Lodgings
Canadian Lodgings
Campground Listings

HOW TO USE THE LISTINGS

Some 13,000 AAA-RATED® properties across North America accept traveling pets. This guide provides listings for those lodgings in the United States and Canada that roll out the welcome mat for pets as well as the people who love them.

For the purpose of this book, "pets" are domestic cats or dogs. If you are planning to travel with any other kind of animal — particularly such exotic pets as birds or reptiles — check with the property before making definite plans. Expect to keep nontraditional pets crated at all times.

Note: Always inform the management that you are traveling with an animal; you may be fined if you do not declare your pet. Many properties require guests with pets to sign a waiver or release form and to pay for the room with a credit card. Of course, whether you pay in cash or by credit card, you will be held liable for any damages caused by your pet, even if the property does not charge a deposit or pet fee. It is not a good idea to leave your pet unattended in the room, but if you must, crate him and notify the management. When in public areas, keep your pet leashed and do not allow him to disturb other guests.

About the Listings

Geographic listings are used for accuracy and consistency; lodgings are listed under the city or town in which they physically are located — or in some cases under the nearest recognized city or town. For a complete list of all cities within a state or province, see the comprehensive City Index at the beginning of the corresponding section.

U.S. properties are shown first, followed by Canadian properties. Most listings are alphabetically organized by state or province, city and establishment name. Reflecting contemporary travel patterns, properties in some cities or towns may instead be listed within destination cities or areas. Such "vicinity cities" and their listings will be shown alphabetically in the destination city or area, and the vicinity city also will appear in alphabetical order in the City Index, along with the page number on which the listings begin.

Each listing provides the following information *(see sample listing, next page)*:

❶ Symbol denoting Official Appointment (OA) properties. The OA program permits properties to display and advertise the ⚫ or ⚫ logo. OAs have a special interest in serving AAA/CAA members. Ask if they offer special member amenities such as free breakfast, early check-in/ late check-out, free room upgrade, free local phone calls, etc.

❷ Diamond rating

❸ Property name

❹ Lodging classification

❺ Special amenities offered. These properties provide an additional benefit to pets, such as treats, toys or gifts, pet sitting and/or walking, a pet menu, food/water dishes, pet sheets or pillows, pet beds or other extras.

❻ Telephone number

❼ Two-person (2P) rate year-round, and cancellation notice validity period (if more than 48 hours). Rates listed are usually daily, but weekly rates also may be listed. **Note:** Most properties accept any or all of the major credit cards, including American Express, MasterCard and VISA. If a property accepts only cash, the phrase "(no credit cards)" follows the rates.

❽ Physical address and highway location, if available

❾ Exterior or interior corridors

❿ Pet policies. If the phrase "pets accepted" appears, the property does accept pets but specific information was unavailable at press time. Otherwise, pet-specific policies are denoted as follows:

Size. "Very small" denotes pets weighing up to 10 pounds; "small," up to 25 pounds; "medium," up to 50 pounds; and "large," up to 100 pounds. If no size is specified, the property accepts pets of all sizes.

Species. "Other" indicates the property accepts animals other than dogs and cats. Always call ahead and specify the type of pet you plan to bring.

Deposits and fees. Includes the dollar amount, the type of charge (refundable deposit or nonrefundable fee), the frequency of the charge and whether the charge is per pet or per room.

Designated rooms. Guests with pets are placed in certain rooms, often smoking rooms or those on the ground floor.

Housekeeping service. The phrase "service with restrictions" denotes properties that require the pet to be crated, removed or attended by the owner during housekeeping service.

Supervision. The pet is required to be supervised at all times.

Crate. The pet must be crated when the owner is not present.

⓫ **Property discounts and amenities:**

- 🅂🅰🆅🅴 Minimum 10% discount
- 🅰🆂🅺 May offer discount
- 🆂🄳 Senior discount
- ⊠ Non-smoking rooms
- Ⓖ Accessible features (call property for available services and amenities)
- ⊟ Refrigerator
- ▣ Coffee maker

🍽 Restaurant on premises

🏊 Pool

⊠ Recreational activities

🅺 No air conditioning

📺 No TV

☎ No telephones

Please note: Some in-room amenities represented by the icons in the listings may be available only in selected rooms, and may incur an extra fee. Please inquire when making your reservations.

It is important to remember that animal policies do change; always confirm policies, restrictions and fees with the lodging when making reservations and again 1-2 days before departure.

Listing information is subject to change. All listing information was accurate at press time. However, lodging rates and policies change and the publisher cannot be held liable for changes occurring after publication. AAA cannot guarantee the safety of guests or their pets at any facility.

AAA Diamond Ratings

Before a property is listed by AAA, it must satisfy a set of minimum standards regarding basic lodging needs as identified by AAA members. If a property meets those requirements, it is assigned a diamond rating reflecting the overall quality of the establishment.

AAA ratings range from one to five diamonds and indicate the property's physical and service standards as measured against the standards of each diamond level. The rating process takes into account the property's classification; i.e., its physical structure and style of operation.

🔸 These establishments typically appeal to the budget-minded traveler. They provide essential, no-frills accommodations. They meet the basic requirements pertaining to comfort, cleanliness, and hospitality.

🔸🔸 These establishments appeal to the traveler seeking more than the basic accommodations. There are modest enhancements to the overall physical attributes, design elements, and amenities of the facility typically at a modest price.

🔸🔸🔸 These establishments appeal to the traveler with comprehensive needs. Properties are multifaceted with a distinguished style, including marked upgrades in the quality of physical attributes, amenities and level of comfort provided.

🔸🔸🔸🔸 These establishments are upscale in all areas. Accommodations are progressively more refined and stylish. The physical attributes reflect an obvious enhanced level of quality throughout. The fundamental hallmarks at this level include an extensive array of amenities combined with a high degree of hospitality, service, and attention to detail.

🔸🔸🔸🔸🔸 These establishments reflect the characteristics of the ultimate in luxury and sophistication. Accommodations are first-class. The physical attributes are extraordinary in every manner. The fundamental hallmarks at this level are to meticulously serve and exceed all guest expectations while maintaining an impeccable standard of excellence. Many personalized services and amenities enhance an unmatched level of comfort.

Lodging Classifications

🅱 **Bed & Breakfast:** Usually smaller establishments emphasizing a more personal relationship between operators and guests, leading to an "at home" feeling. Guest units tend to be individually decorated. Rooms may not include some modern amenities such as televisions and telephones, and may have a shared bathroom. Usually owner-operated, with a common room or parlor separate from the innkeeper's living quarters, where guests and operators can interact during evening and breakfast hours. Evening office closures are normal. A continental or full, hot breakfast is served and is included in the room rate.

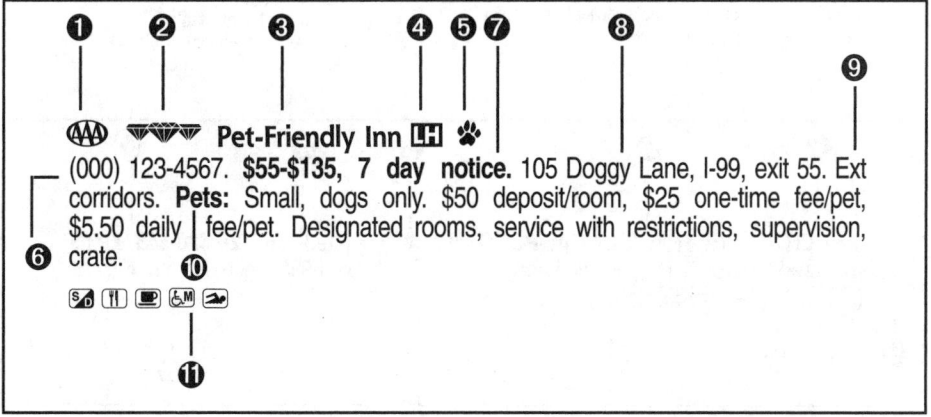

① ② ③ ④ ⑤⑦ ⑧ ⑨

🔺 🔸🔸🔸 **Pet-Friendly Inn** 🅛🅗 🐾

⑥ (000) 123-4567. **$55-$135, 7 day notice.** 105 Doggy Lane, I-99, exit 55. Ext corridors. **Pets:** Small, dogs only. $50 deposit/room, $25 one-time fee/pet, $5.50 daily fee/pet. Designated rooms, service with restrictions, supervision, crate. ⑩

⑪ 🆂 🍽 🖥 ♿ 🏊

CA Cabin/Cottage: Vacation-oriented, small-scale, free-standing houses or cabins. Units vary in design and decor and often contain one or more bedrooms, living room, kitchen, dining area and bathroom. Studio-type models combine the sleeping and living areas into one room. Typically, basic cleaning supplies, kitchen utensils, and complete bed and bath linens are supplied. The guest registration area may be located off-site.

CI Country Inn: Although similar in definition to a bed and breakfast, country inns are usually larger in size, provide more spacious public areas and offer a dining facility that serves at least breakfast and dinner. May be located in a rural setting or downtown area.

CO Condominium: Establishments that primarily offer guest accommodations that are privately owned by individuals and available for rent. These can include apartment-style units or homes. A variety of room styles and decor treatments are offered, and limited housekeeping service is typical. May have off-site registration.

LH Large-scale Hotel: A multistory establishment with interior room entrances. A variety of guest unit styles are offered. Public areas are spacious and include a variety of facilities such as a restaurant, shops, fitness center, spa, business center or meeting rooms.

M Motel: Low-rise or multistory establishment offering limited public and recreational facilities.

RA Ranch: Often offers rustic decor treatments and food and beverage facilities. Entertainment and recreational activities are geared to a Western-style adventure vacation. May provide some meeting facilities.

SH Small-scale Hotel: A multistory establishment typically with interior room entrances. A variety of guest unit styles are offered. Public areas are limited in size and/or the variety of facilities available.

VH Vacation Home: Vacation-oriented or extended-stay, large-scale, freestanding houses that are routinely available for rent through a management company. Houses vary in design and décor and often contain two or more bedrooms, living room, full kitchen, dining room and multiple bathrooms. Typically, basic cleaning supplies, kitchen utensils, and complete bed and bath linens are supplied. The guest registration area may be located off-site.

Campground Listings

Geographic listings are used for accuracy and consistency. Campgrounds are listed under the city or town in which they physically are located — or in some cases under the nearest recognized city or town. Not all listings include physical addresses. U.S. campgrounds are given first, followed by Canadian campgrounds. Listings are alphabetically organized by state or province, city and campground name.

Note: Call first before taking your pet on a camping trip, as campground policies regarding pets may change, including any possible fees that may be assessed.

Each listing provides the following information (see sample listing):

❶ Location

❷ Campground name

❸ Symbol denoting Official Appointment (OA) campgrounds. The OA program permits privately operated campgrounds to display and advertise the AAA or CAA logo. OAs have a special interest in serving AAA/CAA members.

❹ Telephone number

❺ Fee range for a specified number of persons, including the fee for an extra person (XP) staying at the campground.

❻ Most campgrounds accept any or all of the major credit cards, including American Express, MasterCard and Visa. If a campground accepts only cash, the sentence "(no credit cards)." appears.

❼ Physical address (if available), highway location and mailing address (if available).

❽ Campground discounts and amenities:

  SD 10% senior discount for members over 59

  No Tents No Tents

  Pool Pool

  Recreational Recreational activities

  GM Accessible features
  (call property for available
  services and amenities)

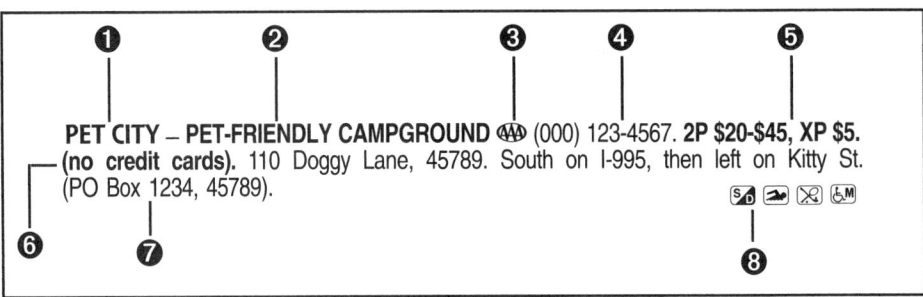

United States Lodgings

ALABAMA

ABBEVILLE

▼▼ Best Western-Abbeville Inn Ⓜ

(334) 585-5060. **$59-$74.** 1237 US Hwy 431. Jct SR 27. Ext corridors. **Pets:** $10 daily fee/pet. Service with restrictions, crate.

Ⓐ$Ⓚ Ⓢ☐ ✕ ☐ ☐ ☜

ALBERTVILLE

▼▼ Jameson Inn Ⓢ🅷

(256) 891-2600. **$70-$90.** 315 Martling Rd. On US 431, just e of SR 75. Ext corridors. **Pets:** Small. $15 daily fee/room. Service with restrictions, crate.

Ⓐ$Ⓚ Ⓢ☐ ✕ ☐ ☐ ☜

ALEXANDER CITY

▼▼ Jameson Inn Ⓢ🅷

(256) 234-7099. **$75-$95.** 4335 US Hwy 280. US 280, just s of jct SR 22; just w of jct SR 63. Ext corridors. **Pets:** Small. $15 daily fee/room. Service with restrictions, crate.

Ⓐ$Ⓚ Ⓢ☐ ✕ ☐ ☐ ☜

ANDALUSIA

▼▼ Days Inn Ⓜ

(334) 427-0050. **$66-$125, 10 day notice.** 1604 Dr. MLK Jr Expwy. On US 84 Bypass. Ext corridors. **Pets:** Accepted.

Ⓐ$Ⓚ Ⓢ☐ ✕ ☐ ☐ ☜

▼ Scottish Inn Ⓜ ❀

(334) 222-7511. **$45-$62, 3 day notice.** 1421 Dr. MLK Jr Expwy. On US 84 Bypass. Ext corridors. **Pets:** Small. $20 daily fee/pet. No service, supervision.

Ⓢ☐ Ⓢ☐ ✕ ☐ ☐ ☜

ANNISTON

▼▼ Long Leaf Lodge at McClellan Ⓜ

(256) 820-9494. **$60.** 74 Exchange Ave. I-20, exit 185, 10 mi n on SR 21, then 1.5 mi e into McClellan-Ballzell Gate. Ext corridors. **Pets:** Accepted.

Ⓐ$Ⓚ Ⓢ☐ ✕ ☐ ☐ ☜

▼▼▼ The Victoria, a Country Inn Ⓒ🅘 ❀

(256) 236-0503. **$89.** 1600 Quintard Ave. I-20, exit 185, 4 mi n on SR 21/US 431. Ext/int corridors. **Pets:** Small. $25 one-time fee/pet. Crate.

✕ ☐ ☐ ⑪ ☜

ARAB

▼▼▼ Jameson Inn Ⓢ🅷

(256) 586-5777. **$70-$90.** 706 N Brindlee Mountain Pkwy. On US 231, 0.5 mi n of jct SR 69. Ext corridors. **Pets:** Small. $15 daily fee/room. Service with restrictions, crate.

Ⓐ$Ⓚ Ⓢ☐ ✕ ☐ ☐ ☜

ATHENS

◉◉◉ ▼▼▼ Best Western Athens Inn Ⓢ🅷

(256) 233-4030. **$59-$99.** 1329 Hwy 72. I-65, exit 351, just w. Ext corridors. **Pets:** Medium. $10 daily fee/pet. Designated rooms, service with supervision.

Ⓢ🄰🄵🄴 Ⓢ☐ ✕ ☐ ☐ ☜

▼▼▼ Comfort Inn Ⓢ🅷

(256) 232-2704. **$70-$95.** 1218 Kelli Dr. I-65, exit 351, just e on US 72, then just s. Ext corridors. **Pets:** Medium. $20 daily fee/pet. Service with restrictions, supervision.

Ⓐ$Ⓚ Ⓢ☐ ✕ ☐ ☐ ☜

▼▼ Sleep Inn Athens Ⓢ🅷

(256) 232-4700. **$74.** 1115 Audubon Ln. I-65, exit 351, just nw. Int corridors. **Pets:** Other species. $10 daily fee/pet. No service, supervision.

Ⓐ$Ⓚ Ⓢ☐ ✕ ☐ ☜

ATTALLA

◉◉◉ ♦ Americas Best Value Inn & Suites Ⓢ🅷

(256) 570-0117. **$35-$80.** 915 E 5th Ave. I-59, exit 183 southbound, just e; exit northbound, through first set of lights, then just e. Ext corridors. **Pets:** Accepted.

Ⓢ🄰🄵🄴 Ⓢ☐ ✕ ☐

▼▼ Days Inn Attalla Ⓢ🅷

(256) 538-7861. **$45-$200.** 801 Cleveland Ave. I-59, exit 183 northbound, just e; exit southbound, through first set of lights, then just e. Ext corridors. **Pets:** Accepted.

Ⓐ$Ⓚ Ⓢ☐ ✕ ☐ ☐ ☜

AUBURN

◉◉◉ ▼▼▼ Best Western University Convention Center Ⓢ🅷

(334) 821-7001. **$89-$225.** 1577 S College St. I-85, exit 51, 1.4 mi n on US 29/SR 147. Ext corridors. **Pets:** Accepted.

Ⓢ🄰🄵🄴 Ⓢ☐ ✕ ☐ ☐ ☜

◉◉◉ ▼▼▼▼ The Hotel at Auburn University & Dixon Conference Center Ⓛ🅗

(334) 821-8200. **$99-$129.** 241 S College St. I-85, exit 51, 3.5 mi n on US 29/SR 147. Int corridors. **Pets:** Accepted.

Ⓢ🄰🄵🄴 ✕ Ⓖ🄼 ☐ ☐ ⑪ ☜ ✕

▼▼ Jameson Inn Ⓜ

(334) 502-5020. **$70-$90.** 1212 Mall Pkwy. I-85, exit 58, 1.5 mi n on US 280 W, then 2.1 mi s on US 29/SR 14. Ext corridors. **Pets:** Small. $15 daily fee/room. Service with restrictions, crate.

Ⓐ$Ⓚ Ⓢ☐ ✕ ☐ ☐ ☜

◉◉◉ ▼▼▼ Microtel Inn & Suites Ⓢ🅷

(334) 826-1444. **$55-$199.** 2174 S College St. I-85, exit 51, just n. Int corridors. **Pets:** Accepted.

Ⓢ🄰🄵🄴 Ⓢ☐ ✕ ☐ ☐

BIRMINGHAM METROPOLITAN AREA

BESSEMER

Best Western Hotel & Suites SH
(205) 481-1950. **$99-$250.** 5041 Academy Ln. I-20/59, exit 108, just sw. Int corridors. **Pets:** Medium, other species. $100 deposit/room, $15 daily fee/pet. Designated rooms, service with restrictions, crate.

Jameson Inn SH
(205) 428-3194. **$75-$95.** 5021 Academy Ln. I-20/59, exit 108, just sw. Ext corridors. **Pets:** Small. $15 daily fee/room. Service with restrictions, crate.

Motel 6 #426 M
(205) 426-9646. **$45-$57.** 1000 Shiloh Ln. I-20/59, exit 108, 1 mi ne on US 11. Ext corridors. **Pets:** Other species. Service with restrictions, supervision.

Sleep Inn SH
(205) 424-0000. **$79-$159.** 1259 Greenmor Dr. I-459, exit 6, just e, then just s. Int corridors. **Pets:** Small. $15 daily fee/pet. Service with restrictions, supervision.

BIRMINGHAM

Best Western Carlton Suites SH
(205) 940-9990. **$109-$169.** 140 State Farm Pkwy. I-65, exit 255, just w to Wildwood Pkwy, then just n. Int corridors. **Pets:** Small, dogs only. $10 daily fee/pet. Designated rooms, no service, supervision.

Best Western Mountain Brook M
(205) 991-9977. **$80-$200.** 4627 Hwy 280 E. I-459, exit 19 (US 280), 1.4 mi e. Ext corridors. **Pets:** Accepted.

Drury Inn & Suites-Birmingham Southeast SH
(205) 967-2450. **$95-$186.** 3510 Grandview Pkwy. I-459, exit 19, just e on US 280; in Grandview. Int corridors. **Pets:** Large, other species. Service with restrictions, supervision.

Embassy Suites Birmingham LH
(205) 879-7400. **$139-$279.** 2300 Woodcrest Pl. Just n of jct US 31 and 280, exit 21st Ave southbound, then 0.3 mi s. Int corridors. **Pets:** Other species. $30 one-time fee/pet. Service with restrictions, crate.

Homestead Studio Suites Hotel-Birmingham Perimeter Park South SH
(205) 967-3800. **$44-$69.** 12 Perimeter Park S. I-459, exit 19 (US 280), 0.5 mi, then just s. Ext corridors. **Pets:** Other species. $75 one-time fee/pet. Service with restrictions.

Homewood Suites by Hilton SH
(205) 995-9823. **Call for rates.** 215 Inverness Center Dr. I-459, exit 19 (US 280), 1.8 mi e, then just s. Int corridors. **Pets:** Large. $75 one-time fee/room. Service with restrictions.

La Quinta Inn & Suites Birmingham SH
(205) 995-9990. **$69-$109.** 513 Cahaba Park Cir. I-459, exit 19 (US 280), 1.2 mi e. Int corridors. **Pets:** Other species. Service with restrictions, supervision.

Residence Inn By Marriott SH
(205) 991-8686. **$159-$269.** 3 Greenhill Pkwy. I-459, exit 19 (US 280), 2 mi e. Ext corridors. **Pets:** Small. $75 one-time fee/room. Service with restrictions, crate.

Sheraton Birmingham Hotel LH
(205) 324-5000. **$129-$159.** 2101 Richard Arrington Jr Blvd N. I-20/59, exit 22nd St. Int corridors. **Pets:** Dogs only. Service with restrictions, supervision.

CALERA

Holiday Inn Express SH
(205) 668-3641. **$99-$119.** 357 Hwy 304. I-65, exit 231, just se. Ext corridors. **Pets:** Other species. $20 daily fee/room. Designated rooms, service with restrictions, supervision.

HOMEWOOD

Drury Inn & Suites-Birmingham Southwest SH
(205) 940-9500. **$86-$166.** 160 State Farm Pkwy. I-65, exit 255, 0.5 mi on northwest frontage road. Int corridors. **Pets:** Large, other species. Service with restrictions, supervision.

La Quinta Inn & Suites Birmingham (Homewood) SH
(205) 290-0150. **$99-$139.** 60 State Farm Pkwy. I-65, exit 255, 0.9 mi on northwest frontage road. Int corridors. **Pets:** Other species. Service with restrictions, supervision.

Motel 6 #2004 M
(205) 942-9414. **$47-$59.** 151 Vulcan Rd. I-65, exit 256 northbound; exit 256A southbound, just nw. Ext corridors. **Pets:** Other species. Service with restrictions, supervision.

Ramada Inn SH
(205) 916-0464. **$65-$199.** 226 Summit Pkwy. I-65, exit 256 northbound; exit 256A southbound, just w. Int corridors. **Pets:** Accepted.

Residence Inn by Marriott SH
(205) 943-0044. **$149-$249.** 50 State Farm Pkwy. I-65, exit 255, 1 mi on northwest frontage road. Int corridors. **Pets:** Accepted.

StudioPLUS M
(205) 290-0102. **$39-$59.** 40 State Farm Pkwy. I-65, exit 255, just e on Lakeshore Pkwy, just n on Wildwood Pkwy, then 0.6 mi w. Int corridors. **Pets:** Other species. $75 one-time fee/pet. Service with restrictions.

Super 8 Motel SH
(205) 945-9888. **$47-$70.** 140 Vulcan Rd. I-65, exit 256 northbound; exit 256A southbound, just nw. Int corridors. **Pets:** Small, other species. $5 daily fee/pet. Service with restrictions, crate.

TownePlace Suites by Marriott SH
(205) 943-0114. **$129-$219.** 500 Wildwood Cir. I-65, exit 255, 0.6 mi w, then just n. Int corridors. **Pets:** Large, other species. $75 one-time fee/room. Service with restrictions, supervision.

HOOVER

△△△▽ ▼▼▼ ▼▼▼ **The Wynfrey Hotel** 🄻🄷
(205) 987-1600. **$160-$1200.** 1000 Riverchase Galleria. I-459, exit 13 (US 31), adjacent to Riverchase Galleria. Int corridors. **Pets:** Accepted.
SAVE 🆂🅳 ⊠ 🛏 🖵 🍴 ➰ ⊠

LEEDS

△△△▽ ▼▼▼ **Days Inn of Leeds** 🅼
(205) 699-9833. **$66-$160, 30 day notice.** 1838 Ashville Rd. I-20, exit 144A eastbound; exit 144B westbound, just s. Ext corridors. **Pets:** Medium, other species. $10 daily fee/pet. Service with restrictions, crate.
SAVE 🆂🅳 ⊠ 🛏 🖵 ➰

ONEONTA

△△△▽ ▼▼▼ **Best Western Colonial Inn** 🅂🄷
(205) 274-2200. **$72-$179, 14 day notice.** 293 Valley Rd. On SR 75, 0.5 mi n of jct US 231. Ext corridors. **Pets:** Accepted.
A$K 🆂🅳 ⊠ 🛏 🖵 ➰

PELHAM

△△△▽ ▼▼▼ **Best Western at Oak Mountain** 🅂🄷
(205) 982-1113. **$99.** 100 Bishop Cir. I-65, exit 246, just sw, then just s on State Park Rd. Int corridors. **Pets:** $125 daily fee/pet. No service.
A$K 🆂🅳 ⊠ 🛏 🖵 ➰

△△△▽ ▼▼▼ **Quality Inn** 🅼
(205) 444-9200. **$79-$89, 14 day notice.** 110 Cahaba Valley Pkwy. I-65, exit 246, just nw. Ext corridors. **Pets:** Small. $25 one-time fee/room. Designated rooms, no service, supervision.
SAVE 🆂🅳 ⊠ 🛏 🖵 ➰

TRUSSVILLE

▼▼▼ **Jameson Inn** 🅂🄷
(205) 661-9323. **$85-$105.** 4730 Norrell Dr. I-59, exit 141, just e on Chalkville Rd, then just n. Ext corridors. **Pets:** Very small. $10 daily fee/pet. Service with restrictions, supervision.
A$K 🆂🅳 ⊠ 🛏 🖵 ➰

END METROPOLITAN AREA

CHILDERSBURG

▼▼▼ **Key West Inn Childersburg** 🅼
(256) 378-0337. **$64.** 32210 US Hwy 280. Just s of jct CR 235. Ext corridors. **Pets:** Very small, dogs only. $25 one-time fee/pet. Designated rooms, service with restrictions, supervision.
A$K 🆂🅳 ⊠ 🛏 🖵 ➰

CLANTON

△△△▽ ▼▼▼ **Best Western Inn** 🅂🄷
(205) 280-1006. **$65-$100, 5 day notice.** 801 Bradberry Ln. I-65, exit 205, 0.5 mi e. Ext corridors. **Pets:** Small. $10 daily fee/pet. Service with restrictions, supervision.
SAVE ⊠ 🛏 🖵 ➰

△△△▽ ▼▼▼ **GuestHouse International Inn** 🅂🄷
(205) 280-0306. **$67-$95.** 946 Lake Mitchell Rd. I-65, exit 208, just w. Ext corridors. **Pets:** Small, other species. $6 one-time fee/pet. Supervision.
SAVE 🆂🅳 ⊠ 🛏 🖵 ➰

CULLMAN

△△△▽ ▼▼▼ **Best Western Fairwinds Inn** 🅂🄷
(256) 737-5009. **$69-$109.** 1917 Commerce Ave NW. I-65, exit 310, just e. Ext corridors. **Pets:** Small. $9 daily fee/room. Service with restrictions.
SAVE 🆂🅳 ⊠ 🛏 🖵 ➰

▼▼▼ **Comfort Inn** 🅂🄷
(256) 734-1240. **Call for rates.** 5917 Alabama Hwy 157 NW. I-65, exit 310, just e. Ext corridors. **Pets:** Accepted.
⊠ 🛏 🖵 ➰

▼▼▼ **Days Inn** 🅼
(256) 739-3800. **$63-$80.** 1841 4th St SW. I-65, exit 308, just e. Ext corridors. **Pets:** Medium, other species. $5 one-time fee/room. Service with restrictions, supervision.
A$K 🆂🅳 ⊠ 🛏 🖵 🍴 ➰

△△△▽ ▼ **Econo Lodge** 🅼 ❀
(256) 734-2691. **$60-$75, 7 day notice.** 1655 CR 437. I-65, exit 304, just e. Ext corridors. **Pets:** Small, dogs only. $10 daily fee/pet. Designated rooms, no service, crate.
SAVE 🆂🅳 ⊠ 🛏 🖵

DECATUR

△△△▽ ▼▼▼ **Best Western River City Hotel** 🅂🄷
(256) 301-1388. **$79.** 1305 Front Ave. I-65, exit 334, 8 mi n. Int corridors. **Pets:** Medium, other species. $50 one-time fee/pet. Service with restrictions, crate.
SAVE 🆂🅳 ⊠ 🔆🄼 🛏 🖵 ➰

△△△▽ ▼▼▼ **Comfort Inn & Suites** 🅂🄷
(256) 355-1999. **$75-$95.** 2212 Danville Rd SW. SR 67, jct Beltline Rd SW. Int corridors. **Pets:** Accepted.
SAVE 🆂🅳 ⊠ 🛏 🖵 ➰

▼▼▼▼ **Holiday Inn Hotel & Suites** 🅂🄷
(256) 355-3150. **$95-$135.** 1101 6th Ave NE. Just w of jct US 31, 72A and SR 20. Ext/int corridors. **Pets:** Small. $15 one-time fee/room. Designated rooms, service with restrictions, supervision.
A$K 🆂🅳 ⊠ 🛏 🖵 🍴 ➰ ⊠

▼▼▼ **Jameson Inn** 🅂🄷
(256) 355-2229. **$65-$85.** 2120 Jameson Pl SW. SR 67, 1.6 mi s of jct US 72A; 3.9 mi n of jct US 31. Ext corridors. **Pets:** Small. $15 daily fee/room. Service with restrictions, crate.
A$K 🆂🅳 ⊠ 🛏 🖵 ➰

▼▼▼ **Microtel Inn & Suites** 🅂🄷 ❀
(256) 301-9995. **$58-$75.** 2226 Beltline Rd SW. On SR 67, 4 mi w of jct US 31. Int corridors. **Pets:** Medium. $25 one-time fee/pet. Service with restrictions, crate.
A$K 🆂🅳 ⊠ 🔆🄼 🛏 🖵 ➰

DOTHAN

△△△▽ ◆ **Americas Best Value Inn & Suites** 🅼
(334) 793-5200. **$45-$99.** 2901 Ross Clark Cir. 0.8 mi s of jct US 84; west end of town. Ext corridors. **Pets:** Very small, dogs only. $10 daily fee/pet. Service with restrictions, supervision.
SAVE 🆂🅳 ⊠ 🛏 🖵 ➰

△△△▽ ◆◆◆ **Comfort Inn** 🅂🄷
(334) 793-9090. **$90-$106.** 3593 Ross Clark Cir. Just w of jct US 231; northwest part of town. Int corridors. **Pets:** Small. $10 daily fee/pet. Service with restrictions, supervision.
SAVE 🆂🅳 ⊠ 🔆🄼 🛏 🖵 ➰

▼▼▼ **Days Inn** 🅼
(334) 793-2550. **Call for rates.** 2841 Ross Clark Cir. 0.9 mi s of jct US 84; west end of town. Ext corridors. **Pets:** Accepted.
⊠ 🛏 🖵 ➰ ⊠

▼▼ Howard Johnson Express Inn **M**
(334) 792-3339. **$62-$70.** 2244 Ross Clark Cir. 1.4 mi s of jct SR 52; west end of town. Ext corridors. **Pets:** Dogs only. $15 daily fee/pet. Designated rooms, service with restrictions, supervision.
[ASK] [S✿] [✕] [🛏] [💻] [🌊]

▼ Motel 6 #1233 **M**
(334) 793-6013. **$39-$51.** 2907 Ross Clark Cir. 0.8 mi s of jct US 84; west end of town. Ext corridors. **Pets:** Other species. Service with restrictions, supervision.
[S✿] [✕] [🛏] [🌊]

▼▼ Quality Inn **M**
(334) 794-6601. **$70.** 3053 Ross Clark Cir. Just s of jct US 84; west end of town. Ext corridors. **Pets:** Accepted.
[ASK] [S✿] [✕] [&M] [🛏] [💻] [🍴] [🌊]

ENTERPRISE

△△△ ▼▼ Comfort Inn **M**
(334) 393-2304. **$70.** 615 Boll Weevil Cir. On US 84 Bypass. Ext corridors. **Pets:** Accepted.
[SAVE] [S✿] [✕] [🛏] [💻] [🌊]

EUFAULA

▼▼▼ Eufaula Comfort Suites **SH**
(334) 616-0114. **$100-$110.** 12 Paul Lee Pkwy. 1.7 mi s on US 431 from jct US 82 E, then just e. Int corridors. **Pets:** $25 one-time fee/room. Service with restrictions, supervision.
[ASK] [S✿] [✕] [&M] [🛏] [💻] [🌊] [✕]

▼▼ Jameson Inn **M**
(334) 687-7747. **$70-$90.** 136 Towne Center Blvd. On US 431, 1 mi s of US 82 E. Ext corridors. **Pets:** Small. $15 daily fee/room. Service with restrictions, crate.
[ASK] [S✿] [✕] [🛏] [💻] [🌊]

EVERGREEN

△△△ ▼▼ Comfort Inn **M**
(251) 578-4701. **$60-$125.** 83 Ted Bates Rd. I-65, exit 96, just w. Ext corridors. **Pets:** Other species. $10 daily fee/pet. Designated rooms, supervision.
[SAVE] [S✿] [✕] [🛏] [💻] [🌊]

▼▼ Days Inn of Evergreen **M** 🐾
(251) 578-2100. **$60-$70.** Rt 2, Box 389. I-65, exit 96, just w. Ext corridors. **Pets:** Service with restrictions, supervision.
[ASK] [S✿] [✕] [🛏] [💻]

FAIRHOPE

▼▼ Key West Inn **M**
(251) 990-7373. **$69-$109.** 231 S Greeno Rd. On US 98, 1.9 mi s of jct SR 104. Ext corridors. **Pets:** Accepted.
[ASK] [S✿] [✕] [🛏] [💻] [🌊]

FLORENCE

▼▼ Jameson Inn **SH**
(256) 764-5326. **$80-$100.** 115 Ana Dr. On US 43/72, just nw of jct SR 133 (Cox Creek Pkwy). Ext corridors. **Pets:** Small. $15 daily fee/room. Service with restrictions, crate.
[ASK] [S✿] [✕] [🛏] [💻] [🌊]

▼ Knights Inn Florence **M**
(256) 766-2620. **$45-$120.** 1915 Florence Blvd (US 72). 2 mi w; jct SR 133 (Cox Creek Pkwy) and US 72. Ext corridors. **Pets:** Small, dogs only. $10 one-time fee/pet. Service with restrictions.
[ASK] [S✿] [✕] [🛏] [💻] [🌊]

▼▼▼ ◇◇◇◇ Marriott Shoals Hotel and Spa **SH**
(256) 246-3600. **$119-$250.** 800 Cox Creek Pkwy S. From jct US 43/72 and SR 133 (Cox Creek Pkwy), 1.5 mi s; at Wilson Dam. Int corridors. **Pets:** Small, other species. $75 one-time fee/pet. Service with restrictions, crate.
[✕] [&M] [🛏] [💻] [🍴] [🌊] [✕]

FOLEY

△△△ ▼▼▼ Holiday Inn Express **SH**
(251) 943-9100. **$90-$190.** 2682 S McKenzie St. On SR 59, 1.9 mi s of jct US 98. Ext corridors. **Pets:** Accepted.
[SAVE] [✕] [&M] [🛏] [💻] [🌊]

▼▼ Key West Inn **M**
(251) 943-1241. **$69-$139.** 2520 S McKenzie St. On SR 59, 1.8 mi s of jct US 98. Ext corridors. **Pets:** Small. $50 deposit/pet, $20 daily fee/pet. Designated rooms, service with restrictions, supervision.
[ASK] [S✿] [✕] [🛏] [💻] [🌊]

GADSDEN

▼▼ Motel 6 #1495 **SH**
(256) 543-1105. **$43-$55.** 1600 Rainbow Dr. I-759, exit 4A, 0.8 mi s on US 411. Ext corridors. **Pets:** Other species. Service with restrictions, supervision.
[S✿] [✕] [🌊]

GENEVA

△△△ ▼▼▼ Briarwood Inn of Geneva **M**
(334) 684-7715. **$69-$102.** 1503 W Magnolia Ave. On SR 52, 0.3 mi w of jct SR 196. Ext corridors. **Pets:** Accepted.
[ASK] [✕] [🛏] [🌊]

GREENVILLE

△△△ ▼▼▼ Days Inn **M**
(334) 382-3118. **$65-$95, 7 day notice.** 946 Fort Dale Rd. I-65, exit 130, just s on SR 185. Ext corridors. **Pets:** Accepted.
[SAVE] [S✿] [✕] [🛏] [💻] [🌊]

▼▼ Jameson Inn **M**
(334) 382-6300. **$70-$90.** 71 Jameson Ln. I-65, exit 130, just n on SR 185, then just w on Cahaba Rd. Ext corridors. **Pets:** Small. $15 daily fee/room. Service with restrictions, crate.
[ASK] [S✿] [✕] [🛏] [💻] [🌊]

GULF SHORES

△△△ ▼▼▼ La Quinta Inn **SH**
(251) 967-3500. **Call for rates.** 213 W Fort Morgan Rd. On SR 180, just w of jct SR 59. Int corridors. **Pets:** Other species. Service with restrictions, supervision.
[SAVE] [✕] [&M] [🛏] [💻] [🌊] [✕]

GUNTERSVILLE

▼ Super 8 Motel-Guntersville **M**
(256) 582-8444. **Call for rates.** 14341 Hwy 431 S. On US 431, 2 mi s of jct SR 69. Ext corridors. **Pets:** Accepted.
[✕] [🛏]

HAMILTON

△△△ ▼▼▼ Days Inn **SH**
(205) 921-1790. **$59-$89.** 1849 Military St S. US 78, exit 14, 1 mi n, then 1 mi w on US 43. Ext corridors. **Pets:** Other species. $10 daily fee/pet. Service with restrictions, supervision.
[SAVE] [S✿] [✕] [🛏] [💻] [🌊]

HUNTSVILLE

 America's Best Inns **M**
(256) 539-9671. **$64-$74.** 1304 N Memorial Pkwy. I-565, exit 19B, 0.5 mi n on US 231/431, Cook Ave exit. Ext corridors. **Pets:** Small. Designated rooms, service with restrictions, supervision.

Extended StayAmerica Huntsville-U.S. Space and Rocket Center M
(256) 830-9110. **$49-$69.** 4751 Govenors House Dr. I-565, exit 17A, just s, then 0.5 mi w. Ext corridors. **Pets:** Other species. $75 one-time fee/pet. Service with restrictions.

Holiday Inn Express Hotel & Suites SH
(256) 721-1000. **$75-$125.** 3808 University Dr. I-565, exit 17A, just e. Int corridors. **Pets:** Accepted.

Holiday Inn Hunstville Downtown LH
(256) 533-1400. **$114-$169.** 401 Williams Ave SW. Just w of Church St; downtown. Int corridors. **Pets:** Accepted.

La Quinta Inn & Suites Huntsville SH
(256) 830-8999. **$69-$109.** 4890 University Dr SE. I-565, exit 14B, 2.6 mi n on Research Park Blvd, then 1 mi e on US 72. Int corridors. **Pets:** Other species. Service with restrictions, supervision.

La Quinta Inn Huntsville (Research Park) SH
(256) 830-2070. **$69-$109.** 4870 University Dr NW. I-565, exit 14B, 2.6 mi n on Research Park Blvd, then 1 mi e on US 72. Ext corridors. **Pets:** Other species. Service with restrictions, supervision.

La Quinta Inn Huntsville (Space Center) SH
(256) 830-0756. **$69-$109.** 3141 University Dr (Hwy 72). I-565, exit 17A, 1.1 mi n on SR 53 (Jordan Ln), then 0.6 mi e on US 72. Ext corridors. **Pets:** Other species. Service with restrictions, supervision.

JACKSON

Econo Lodge M
(251) 246-4111. **$70-$83.** 3680 N College Ave. I-65, exit 19, on US 43. Ext corridors. **Pets:** Other species. Service with restrictions, crate.

JASPER

Jameson Inn SH
(205) 387-7710. **$75-$95.** 1100 Hwy 78/118 E. SR 118, 1.8 mi w of jct SR 69. Ext corridors. **Pets:** Small. $15 daily fee/room. Service with restrictions, crate.

MADISON

Motel 6–1087 M
(256) 772-7479. **$43-$55.** 8995 Madison Blvd. I-565, exit 8, just n on Wall Triana Hwy, then just w. Ext corridors. **Pets:** Other species. Service with restrictions, supervision.

Ramada Inn & Conference Center LH
(256) 772-0701. **Call for rates.** 8716 Madison Blvd. I-565, exit 8, just n on Wall Triana Hwy, then 0.4 mi e. Int corridors. **Pets:** Accepted.

MILLBROOK

Key West Inn M
(334) 309-2004. **$69-$89.** 2275 Cobbs Ford Rd. I-65, exit 179, just w. Ext corridors. **Pets:** Medium. $10 daily fee/pet. Designated rooms, service with restrictions, supervision.

MOBILE

Drury Inn-Mobile SH
(251) 344-7700. **$87-$127.** 824 W I-65 Service Rd S. I-65, exit 3 (Airport Blvd), just w, then just s on service road. Int corridors. **Pets:** Large, other species. Service with restrictions, supervision.

Extended StayAmerica M
(251) 344-2514. **$64-$84.** 508 Spring Hill Plaza Ct. I-65, exit 5A, just w, then just n. Ext corridors. **Pets:** Other species. $75 one-time fee/pet. Service with restrictions.

Holiday Inn-Bellingrath Gardens SH
(251) 666-5600. **Call for rates.** 5465 Hwy 90 W. I-10, exit 15B, just e on US 90, then just s on Coca Cola Rd. Int corridors. **Pets:** Accepted.

La Quinta Inn Mobile M
(251) 343-4051. **$89-$119.** 816 W I-65 Service Rd S. I-65, exit 3 (Airport Blvd), just w, then just s. Ext/int corridors. **Pets:** Other species. Service with restrictions, supervision.

Motel 6 #608 M
(251) 660-1483. **$45-$57.** 5488 Inn Rd. I-10, exit 15B, just e on US 90, then just n. Ext corridors. **Pets:** Accepted.

Olsson Motel M
(251) 661-5331. **$45-$85, 10 day notice.** 4137 Government Blvd. I-65, exit 1, 2 mi w on US 90. Ext corridors. **Pets:** Accepted.

Red Roof Inn North #98 M
(251) 476-2004. **$57-$69.** 33 I-65 Service Rd E. I-65, exit 4, just e on Dauphin St, just s on Springdale Blvd, then just w. Ext corridors. **Pets:** Accepted.

Residence Inn by Marriott Mobile SH
(251) 304-0570. **Call for rates.** 950 W I-65 Service Rd S. I-65, exit 3 (Airport Blvd), just w, then 0.4 mi s. Int corridors. **Pets:** Other species. $75 one-time fee/room.

TownePlace Suites by Marriott SH
(251) 345-9588. **Call for rates.** 1075 Montlimar Dr. I-65, exit 3 (Airport Blvd), 0.5 mi w, then 0.5 mi s. Int corridors. **Pets:** Accepted.

MONROEVILLE

Americas Best Value Inn M
(251) 743-3154. **$50-$200.** 50 Hwy 21 S. On SR 21, just s of jct US 84. Ext corridors. **Pets:** Small. $15 daily fee/pet. Designated rooms, service with restrictions, supervision.

Best Western of Monroeville M
(251) 575-9999. **$66-$90.** 4419 S Alabama Ave. On SR 21, 0.5 mi n of jct US 84. Ext corridors. **Pets:** Accepted.

▼▼▼ Days Inn of Monroeville M
(251) 743-3297. **Call for rates.** 4389 S Alabama Ave. On SR 21, 0.5 mi n of jct US 84. Ext corridors. **Pets:** Accepted.
⊠ 🛏 🖵 🏊

AAA ▼▼▼ Holiday Inn Express SH
(251) 743-3333. **$85-$200.** 120 Hwy 21 S. On SR 21, just s of jct US 84. Int corridors. **Pets:** Accepted.
[SAVE] 🔊 ⊠ 🕭 🛏 🖵 🏊

MONTGOMERY

AAA ▼▼▼ Days Inn Midtown M
(334) 269-9611. **$59-$64.** 2625 Zelda Rd. I-85, exit 3, just s on Ann St. Ext corridors. **Pets:** Other species. $10 daily fee/pet. Service with restrictions, supervision.
[SAVE] 🔊 ⊠ 🛏 🖵 🏊

▼▼▼▼ Drury Inn & Suites-Montgomery SH
(334) 273-1101. **$81-$171.** 1124 Eastern Blvd. I-85, exit 6, just n. Int corridors. **Pets:** Large, other species. Service with restrictions, supervision.
[ASK] ⊠ 🕭 🛏 🖵 🏊

▼▼▼ Econo Lodge M
(334) 284-3400. **$55-$65.** 4135 Troy Hwy. On US 82/231, 0.7 mi e of jct South and East blvds. Ext corridors. **Pets:** Accepted.
[ASK] 🔊 ⊠ 🛏 🖵 🏊

AAA ▼▼▼ Embassy Suites Montgomery Conference Center LH
(334) 269-5055. **$149-$179.** 300 Tallapoosa St. Between Motton and Commerce sts; in historic downtown. Int corridors. **Pets:** Other species. $35 one-time fee/room. Designated rooms, service with restrictions, supervision.
[SAVE] ⊠ 🕭 🛏 🖵 🍴 🏊

▼▼ Extended StayAmerica Montgomery-Eastern Blvd M
(334) 279-1204. **$34-$49.** 2491 Eastern Blvd. I-85, exit 6, 1.3 mi s on US 231. Ext corridors. **Pets:** Other species. $75 one-time fee/pet. Service with restrictions.
[ASK] 🔊 ⊠ 🛏 🖵

AAA ▼▼▼ La Quinta Inn & Suites SH
(334) 277-6000. **$69-$99.** 5225 Carmichael Rd. I-85, exit 6, just s on Eastern Blvd, then just w. Int corridors. **Pets:** Other species. Service with restrictions, supervision.
[SAVE] ⊠ 🕭 🛏 🖵 🏊

AAA ▼▼▼ La Quinta Inn Montgomery M
(334) 271-1620. **$69-$99.** 1280 East Blvd. I-85, exit 6, just s. Ext corridors. **Pets:** Other species. Service with restrictions, supervision.
[SAVE] ⊠ 🛏 🖵 🏊

▼▼▼ The Lexington Hotel by Vantage SH
(334) 272-0370. **$79.** 1185 Eastern Blvd. I-85, exit 6, just n. Ext/int corridors. **Pets:** Large, other species. $25 one-time fee/room. Service with restrictions.
[ASK] 🔊 ⊠ 🕭 🛏 🖵 🍴 🏊 ⊠

AAA ▼▼▼ Quality Inn & Suites SH
(344) 288-2800. **$69.** 2705 E South Blvd. I-85, exit 6, 3.7 mi s on East Blvd. Ext corridors. **Pets:** Accepted.
[SAVE] 🔊 ⊠ 🛏 🖵 🏊

AAA ▼▼▼ Residence Inn by Marriott SH
(334) 270-3300. **$89-$169, 7 day notice.** 1200 Hilmar Ct. I-85, exit 6, just s on Eastern Blvd, then just e. Ext/int corridors. **Pets:** Accepted.
[SAVE] 🔊 ⊠ 🛏 🖵 🏊 ⊠

▼▼▼ StudioPLUS SH
(334) 273-0075. **$34-$54.** 5115 Carmichael Rd. I-85, exit 6, 0.5 mi s on US 231. Int corridors. **Pets:** Other species. $75 one-time fee/pet. Service with restrictions.
[ASK] 🔊 ⊠ 🛏 🖵 🏊

▼▼▼ TownePlace Suites by Marriott SH
(334) 396-5505. **Call for rates.** 5047 Townplace Dr. I-85, exit 6, just s on Eastern Blvd, then just w on Carmichael Rd. Int corridors. **Pets:** Other species. $100 one-time fee/room. Service with restrictions.
⊠ 🕭 🛏 🖵 🏊

OXFORD

▼▼▼ Baymont Inn-Anniston/Oxford SH
(256) 835-1492. **$69.** 1600 Hwy 21 S. I-20, exit 185, just s. Ext corridors. **Pets:** Accepted.
[ASK] 🔊 ⊠ 🛏 🖵 🏊

AAA ▼▼▼ Econo Lodge Oxford M
(256) 831-9480. **$43-$48.** 25 Elm St. I-20, exit 185, just s. Ext corridors. **Pets:** Medium. $10 daily fee/pet. No service, supervision.
[SAVE] 🔊 ⊠ 🛏 🖵 🏊

▼▼ Jameson Inn Oxford M
(256) 835-2170. **$80-$100.** 161 Colonial Dr. I-20, exit 188, just n, then w. Ext corridors. **Pets:** Accepted.
[ASK] 🔊 ⊠ 🛏 🖵 🏊

OZARK

AAA ▼▼▼ All American Ozark Inn M
(334) 774-5166. **$49-$57.** 2064 Hwy 231 S. 1 mi s of jct SR 249. Ext corridors. **Pets:** Accepted.
[SAVE] 🔊 ⊠ 🛏 🖵 🏊

▼▼ Jameson Inn M
(334) 774-0233. **$70-$90.** 1360 S US Hwy 231. 0.3 mi s of jct SR 249. Ext corridors. **Pets:** Small. $15 daily fee/room. Service with restrictions, crate.
[ASK] 🔊 ⊠ 🕭 🛏 🖵 🏊

AAA ▼▼▼ Quality Inn & Suites-Ozark/Ft Rucker SH
(334) 774-7300. **$70.** 858 US 231 S. Just n of jct SR 249. Ext corridors. **Pets:** Accepted.
[SAVE] 🔊 ⊠ 🛏 🖵 🍴 🏊

PRATTVILLE

▼▼ Jameson Inn SH
(334) 361-6463. **$70-$90.** 104 Jameson Ct. I-65, exit 179, 1 mi w. Ext corridors. **Pets:** Small. $15 daily fee/room. Service with restrictions, crate.
[ASK] 🔊 ⊠ 🛏 🖵 🏊

PRICEVILLE

▼▼ Comfort Inn SH
(256) 355-1037. **$60-$300.** 3239 Point Mallard Pkwy. I-65, exit 334, just w. Int corridors. **Pets:** Accepted.
[ASK] 🔊 ⊠ 🛏 🖵 🏊

▼▼ Days Inn SH
(256) 355-3297. **$47-$69.** 63 Marco Dr. I-65, exit 334, just e. Ext corridors. **Pets:** Medium. $10 daily fee/room. Service with restrictions, supervision.
[ASK] 🔊 ⊠ 🛏 🖵 🏊

SCOTTSBORO

▼▼ Jameson Inn SH
(256) 574-6666. **$80-$100.** 208 Micah Way. On US 72, just s of jct SR 35. Ext corridors. **Pets:** Small. $15 daily fee/room. Service with restrictions, crate.
[ASK] 🔊 ⊠ 🛏 🖵 🏊

SELMA

◆◆ Comfort Inn 🆂🅷
(334) 875-5700. **$61-$71.** 1812 Hwy 14 E. Jct SR 14 and US 80 Bypass. Int corridors. **Pets:** Small. $10 daily fee/pet. Designated rooms, service with restrictions, supervision.

A$K 🆂🅾 ⊠ 🅗 💻 ⇌

◆◆ Jameson Inn 🅼
(334) 874-8600. **$70-$90.** 2420 Broad St. On SR 22, just n of jct US 80. Ext corridors. **Pets:** Small. $15 daily fee/room. Service with restrictions, crate.

A$K 🆂🅾 ⊠ 🅗 💻 ⇌

◆◆ Ramada Inn 🆂🅷
(334) 872-0461. **Call for rates.** 1710 W Highland Ave. On US 80. Ext corridors. **Pets:** Accepted.

⊠ 🅗 💻 🍽 ⇌

STEVENSON

◆ Budget Host Inn 🅼
(256) 437-2215. **$45-$65, 3 day notice.** 42973 US Hwy 72. On US 72, just s of CR 85. Ext corridors. **Pets:** Accepted.

A$K 🆂🅾 ⊠ 🅗 💻

SYLACAUGA

◆◆ Jameson Inn 🆂🅷
(256) 245-4141. **$75-$95.** 89 Gene Stewart Blvd. Off US 280, just s. Ext corridors. **Pets:** Small. $15 daily fee/room. Service with restrictions, crate.

A$K 🆂🅾 ⊠ 🅗 💻 ⇌

TROY

◆◆ Holiday Inn Express 🅼
(334) 670-0012. **$80.** Hwy 231 at US 29. On US 231, just n of jct US 29. Ext corridors. **Pets:** Accepted.

A$K 🆂🅾 ⊠ 🅗 💻

◆◆◆ Holiday Inn of Troy 🆂🅷 🐾
(334) 566-1150. **$61-$109.** Hwy 231 at US 29. On US 231, just n of jct US 29. Ext corridors. **Pets:** Medium. $10 one-time fee/pet. Service with restrictions, crate.

A$K 🆂🅾 ⊠ 🅗 💻 🍽 ⇌

TUSCALOOSA

◆◆◆ Americas Best Value Inn 🆂🅷
(205) 556-7950. **$59-$145.** 3501 McFarland Blvd. I-59/20, exit 73, just ne on US 82. Ext corridors. **Pets:** Very small, dogs only. $15 deposit/pet. Designated rooms, service with restrictions, supervision.

SAVE 🆂🅾 ⊠ 🅗 💻 ⇌

◆◆ Jameson Inn 🆂🅷
(205) 345-5018. **$80-$100.** 5021 Oscar Baxter Rd. I-59/20, exit 71A, just s. Ext corridors. **Pets:** Small. $15 daily fee/room. Service with restrictions, crate.

A$K 🆂🅾 ⊠ 🅗 💻 ⇌

◆◆◆ La Quinta Inn Tuscaloosa 🅼
(205) 349-3270. **$79-$109.** 4122 McFarland Blvd E. I-59/20, exit 73, just sw on US 82. Ext corridors. **Pets:** Other species. Service with restrictions, supervision.

SAVE ⊠ 🅗 💻 ⇌

◆◆ Masters Inn 🅼
(205) 556-2010. **$45-$55.** 3600 McFarland Blvd. I-59/20, exit 73, just nw on US 82. Ext corridors. **Pets:** Very small. $10 one-time fee/pet. Designated rooms, no service, supervision.

SAVE 🆂🅾 ⊠ 🅗 ⇌

VANCE

◆◆◆ Baymont Inn & Suites 🆂🅷
(205) 556-3606. **Call for rates.** 11170 Will Walker Rd/Daimler Benz Blvd. I-59/20, exit 89 southbound, just s; exit northbound, 0.8 mi n on Mercedes Dr, 0.3 mi w, then just s. Int corridors. **Pets:** Medium. $25 one-time fee/pet. Designated rooms, service with restrictions, supervision.

SAVE ⊠ ♿ 🅗 💻

ALASKA

CITY INDEX

ANCHORAGE

Best Western Barratt Inn SH
(907) 243-3131. **Call for rates.** 4616 Spenard Rd. International Airport Rd; just ne of jct Jewel Lake and Spenard rds. Ext/int corridors. **Pets:** Accepted.
SAVE ✕ &M 🛏 💻

Comfort Inn Ship Creek SH ☙
(907) 277-6887. **Call for rates.** 111 W Ship Creek Ave. At 3rd and E sts, 0.3 mi n on E St, across the railway, just e on Ship Creek Ave; downtown. Int corridors. **Pets:** Other species. $15 daily fee/room. Designated rooms, service with restrictions, supervision.
✕ &M 🛏 💻 ⛲

Hilton Anchorage LH
(907) 272-7411. **Call for rates.** 500 W 3rd Ave. At E St; downtown. Int corridors. **Pets:** Accepted.
✕ &M 🛏 💻 🍽 ⛲ ✕

Long House Alaskan Hotel SH ☙
(907) 243-2133. **Call for rates.** 4335 Wisconsin St. International Airport Rd, 1.5 mi ne on Spenard Rd, nw on Wisconsin St at 43rd Ave, then just e. Int corridors. **Pets:** Other species. $50 deposit/room, $10 daily fee/pet. Designated rooms, service with restrictions, supervision.
SAVE ✕ &M 🛏 💻

Microtel Inn & Suites SH
(907) 245-5002. **$75-$170.** 5205 Northwood Dr. 1.7 mi e of airport. Int corridors. **Pets:** Accepted.
A$K ✕ &M 🛏 💻

Millennium Alaskan Hotel Anchorage LH
(907) 243-2300. **$170-$310.** 4800 Spenard Rd. International Airport Rd; just ne from jct Jewel Lake and Spenard rds. Int corridors. **Pets:** Other species. $50 deposit/room. Designated rooms, service with restrictions, supervision.
SAVE S🐾 ✕ &M 🛏 💻 🍽 ✕

Motel 6–4216 M
(907) 677-8000. **Call for rates.** 5000 a St. Jct C St and International Airport Rd. Int corridors. **Pets:** Other species. Service with restrictions, supervision.
✕ &M

Ramada Anchorage Downtown SH ☙
(907) 272-7561. **$79-$249.** 115 E 3rd Ave. Jct Barrow St; downtown. Ext/int corridors. **Pets:** Large, dogs only. $10 daily fee/pet. Designated rooms, service with restrictions, crate.
SAVE S🐾 ✕ 🛏 💻

Red Roof Inn M
(907) 274-1650. **Call for rates.** 1104 E 5th Ave. At Karluk St. Ext/int corridors. **Pets:** Accepted.
✕ &M 🛏 💻

Sheraton Anchorage Hotel LH ☙
(907) 276-8700. **$209-$349.** 401 E 6th Ave. 6th Ave and Denali St. Int corridors. **Pets:** Medium, dogs only. Service with restrictions, supervision.
SAVE S🐾 ✕ &M 🛏 💻 🍽 ✕

Westmark Anchorage Hotel LH
(907) 276-7676. **$139-$239.** 720 W 5th Ave. At G St and W 5th Ave; downtown. Int corridors. **Pets:** Accepted.
SAVE ✕ &M 🛏 💻 🍽

CANTWELL

Backwoods Lodge M ☙
(907) 768-2232. **$100-$160, 10 day notice.** Denali Hwy MM 133.8. Parks Hwy, (Milepost 210), just e on Denali Hwy. Ext corridors. **Pets:** Medium. Service with restrictions, supervision.
SAVE S🐾 ✕ 🛏 💻 ✕

DENALI NATIONAL PARK AND PRESERVE

McKinley Chalet Resort LH
(907) 683-8200. **$279, 30 day notice.** Milepost 238 (Parks Hwy). Milepost 238.5 on SR 3 (Parks Hwy). Ext/int corridors. **Pets:** Medium, other species. Service with restrictions, supervision.
SAVE S🐾 ✕ 🛏 💻 🍽 ✕ ✕

EAGLE RIVER

Eagle River Microtel Inn & Suites SH ☙
(907) 622-6000. **$120-$160.** 13049 Old Glenn Hwy. Jct Glenn Hwy (SR 1), exit Eagle River, just e, then just s. Int corridors. **Pets:** Other species. $10 daily fee/pet. Designated rooms, service with restrictions, crate.
SAVE S🐾 ✕ 🛏 💻 ✕

Eagle River Motel M
(907) 694-5000. **$54-$169, 3 day notice.** 11111 Old Eagle River Rd. Glenn Hwy, exit Eagle River, just e; center. Ext corridors. **Pets:** Other species. $10 daily fee/pet. Designated rooms, service with restrictions, crate.
SAVE ✕ 🛏 💻 ✕

FAIRBANKS

Best Western Fairbanks Inn SH
(907) 456-6602. **Call for rates.** 1521 S Cushman St. Just s of Airport Way. Int corridors. **Pets:** Accepted.
✕ &M 🛏 💻 🍽

Comfort Inn-Chena River SH
(907) 479-8080. **Call for rates.** 1908 Chena Landings Loop. Airport Way, just n on Peger Rd, then just e on Phillips Field Rd, follow signs in wooded area south of road. Int corridors. **Pets:** Accepted.
✕ &M 🛏 💻 ⛲

Pike's Waterfront Lodge SH
(907) 456-4500. **$75-$550.** 1850 Hoselton Rd. Jct Airport and Hoselton rds. Ext/int corridors. **Pets:** Accepted.
SAVE ✕ 🛏 💻 🍽 ✕

Super 8 Motel M
(907) 451-8888. **Call for rates.** 1909 Airport Way. Airport Way at Wilbur St. Int corridors. **Pets:** Accepted.
✕ 🛏

GUSTAVUS

Glacier Bay's Bear Track Inn SH
(907) 697-3017. **Call for rates.** 255 Rink Creek Rd. 7 mi e of airport; at end of Rink Creek Rd. Int corridors. **Pets:** Accepted.
✕ 🍽 ✕ 📺 ✉

HAINES

Captain's Choice Inc Motel M
(907) 766-3111. **$86-$182.** 108 2nd Ave N. Jct 2nd Ave and Dalton St. Ext corridors. **Pets:** Other species. $15 one-time fee/room. Service with restrictions, supervision.

HOMER

Best Western Bidarka Inn M
(907) 235-8148. **$89-$189.** 575 Sterling Hwy. 0.3 mi n on (SR 1) Sterling Hwy. Ext/int corridors. **Pets:** Other species. $10 daily fee/pet. Designated rooms, service with restrictions, supervision.

KETCHIKAN

Best Western Landing SH
(907) 225-5166. **$142-$230.** 3434 Tongass Ave. Across from the Alaska Marine Hwy ferry terminal. Ext/int corridors. **Pets:** Other species. $10 daily fee/pet. Designated rooms, service with restrictions, supervision.

Cape Fox Lodge LH
(907) 225-8001. **$110-$200.** 800 Venetia Way. Above Creek St (Tramway from Creek St). Ext/int corridors. **Pets:** Designated rooms, service with restrictions, crate.

KODIAK

Best Western Kodiak Inn SH
(907) 486-5712. **$109-$219.** 236 W Rezanof Dr. 0.3 mi w of ferry terminal; center. Ext/int corridors. **Pets:** Accepted.

Comfort Inn Kodiak SH
(907) 487-2700. **$110-$235.** 1395 Airport Way. Adjacent to airport. Int corridors. **Pets:** Accepted.

PALMER

Peak Inn Motel M
(907) 746-5757. **$55-$105, 7 day notice.** 775 W Evergreen Ave. Just w of Glenn Hwy (SR 1). Ext corridors. **Pets:** Dogs only. $10 daily fee/room. Service with restrictions, supervision.

SITKA

Shee Atika Totem Square Inn SH
(907) 747-3693. **$99-$169.** 201 Katlian St. Center; in Totem Square Complex, near Municipal Office. Int corridors. **Pets:** Small. $50 deposit/pet, $10 daily fee/pet. Service with restrictions, crate.

SKAGWAY

Westmark Inn Skagway SH
(907) 983-6000. **$135-$145.** 3rd & Spring St. Downtown. Ext/int corridors. **Pets:** Accepted.

SOLDOTNA

Alaskan Serenity Bed and Breakfast BB
(907) 262-6648. **$59-$180, 30 day notice.** 41598 Aksala Ln. Sterling Hwy (SR 1), 1.5 mi e, 1.6 mi n on Mackey Lake Rd, then 0.5 mi e on Denise Lake Rd. Ext/int corridors. **Pets:** $30 one-time fee/room. Designated rooms, no service, supervision.

TOK

Cleft of the Rock Bed & Breakfast CA
(907) 883-4219. **$75-$145, 3 day notice.** 122 Sundog Tr. Jct SR 1 and 2 (Alaskan Hwy), 3 mi w on SR 2 (Alaskan Hwy) to Sundog Trail, then 0.5 mi n. Ext/int corridors. **Pets:** Accepted.

Westmark Inn Tok M
(907) 883-5174. **$139.** Jct Alaska Hwy & Glenn Hwy. On SR 1; jct SR 2 (Alaskan Hwy). Ext corridors. **Pets:** Accepted.

TRAPPER CREEK

Gate Creek Cabins CA
(907) 733-1393. **$130, 10 day notice.** Mile 10.5 Petersville Rd. From MM 114 (Parks Hwy), 10.5 mi w at Petersville Rd. Ext corridors. **Pets:** Accepted.

VALDEZ

Best Western Valdez Harbor Inn SH
(907) 835-3434. **$99-$169.** 100 N Harbor Dr. Just s at Meals Dr. Int corridors. **Pets:** Accepted.

WASILLA

Best Western Lake Lucille Inn SH
(907) 373-1776. **Call for rates.** 1300 W Lake Lucille Dr. George Parks Hwy (SR 3), just w on Hallea Ln; center. Int corridors. **Pets:** Accepted.

Grandview Inn & Suites SH
(907) 357-7666. **$80-$160.** 2900 E Parks Hwy. 1 mi n of jct Parks Hwy and Fairview Loop exit. Int corridors. **Pets:** Medium. $50 deposit/room, $10 daily fee/room. Designated rooms, service with restrictions, supervision.

ARIZONA

AJO

▼ La Siesta Motel 🅜
(520) 387-6569. **$46-$60.** 2561 N Ajo-Gila Bend Hwy. On SR 85, 1.8 mi n of town plaza. Ext corridors. **Pets:** Accepted.

BELLEMONT

ⓐⓐⓐ ▼▼▼ Americas Best Value Inn 🆂🅷
(928) 556-9599. **$55-$125.** 12380 W Interstate Hwy 40. I-40, exit 185, just n. Int corridors. **Pets:** Small, dogs only. $75 deposit/pet, $15 daily fee/pet. Designated rooms, service with restrictions, supervision.

BENSON

ⓐⓐⓐ ▼▼▼▼ Best Western-Quail Hollow Inn 🆂🅷 ❀
(520) 586-3646. **$69-$149.** 699 N Ocotillo Rd. I-10, exit 304, just s. Ext corridors. **Pets:** Medium, other species. $10 daily fee/pet. Service with restrictions, supervision.

▼▼ Super 8 Motel 🅜
(520) 586-1530. **Call for rates.** 855 N Ocotillo Rd. I-10, exit 304, just n. Ext corridors. **Pets:** Accepted.

BISBEE

ⓐⓐⓐ ▼▼▼ Audrey's Inn 🅒🅞
(520) 227-6120. **$105.** 20 Brewery Ave. Just ne of Main St; in historic district. Int corridors. **Pets:** Accepted.

ⓐⓐⓐ ▼▼▼ San Jose Lodge 🅜
(520) 432-5761. **$69-$145.** 1002 Naco Hwy. Off of SR 92 W, 1.5 mi s on Naco Hwy. Ext corridors. **Pets:** Medium, dogs only. $10 daily fee/pet. Designated rooms, no service.

BULLHEAD CITY

ⓐⓐⓐ ▼▼▼▼ Best Western Bullhead City Inn 🆂🅷
(928) 754-3000. **$79-$99.** 1126 Hwy 95. 1.8 mi s of Laughlin Bridge. Ext corridors. **Pets:** Large. $20 one-time fee/room. Service with restrictions, supervision.

ⓐⓐⓐ ▼▼ Budget Host Inn 🅜
(928) 763-1002. **$65-$75.** 1616 Hwy 95. Jct SR 68, 3.2 mi s on SR 95. Int corridors. **Pets:** Small, dogs only. $10 daily fee/pet. Designated rooms, service with restrictions, supervision.

ⓐⓐⓐ ▼ Lake Mohave Resort Motel 🅜 ❀
(928) 754-3245. **$90-$125.** 2690 E Katherine Spur Rd. Jct SR 95, 1.5 mi e on SR 68, 1 mi n, then 5.4 mi e; at Katherine Landing; in Lake Mead National Recreation area. Ext corridors. **Pets:** Large, other species. $50 deposit/pet, $10 daily fee/pet. Service with restrictions, supervision.

ⓐⓐⓐ ▼▼▼ Lodge on The River 🅜 ❀
(928) 758-8080. **$45-$65, 7 day notice.** 1717 Hwy 95. 3.8 mi s of Laughlin Bridge. Ext corridors. **Pets:** $10 daily fee/pet. Designated rooms, service with restrictions, supervision.

CAMERON

ⓐⓐⓐ ▼▼▼ Cameron Trading Post Motel, Restaurant & Gift Shop 🆂🅷
(928) 679-2231. **$69-$109.** US 89. 1 mi from the east gate turn off. Ext corridors. **Pets:** Other species. $15 daily fee/pet. No service.

CAMP VERDE

ⓐⓐⓐ ▼▼▼ Comfort Inn-Camp Verde 🆂🅷
(928) 567-9000. **$59-$199.** 340 N Goswick Way. I-17, exit 287, just e, then just s. Int corridors. **Pets:** Medium, other species. $15 daily fee/room. Designated rooms, service with restrictions, supervision.

ⓐⓐⓐ ▼▼▼ Days Inn & Suites of Camp Verde 🆂🅷
(928) 567-3700. **Call for rates.** 1640 W Hwy 260. I-17, exit 287, just e, then just n. Int corridors. **Pets:** Other species. $10 daily fee/pet. Designated rooms, service with restrictions, supervision.

ⓐⓐⓐ ▼▼▼ The Lodge At Cliff Castle Casino 🆂🅷
(928) 567-6611. **$89-$139.** 333 Middle Verde Rd. I-17, exit 289, 0.4 mi se. Ext corridors. **Pets:** Accepted.

ⓐⓐⓐ ▼ Super 8 Motel-Camp Verde 🅜
(928) 567-2622. **Call for rates.** 1550 W Hwy 260. I-17, exit 287, just e. Int corridors. **Pets:** Accepted.

CASA GRANDE

ⓐⓐⓐ ▼▼▼▼ Francisco Grande Hotel & Golf Resort 🅛🅗
(520) 836-6444. **Call for rates.** 26000 W Gila Bend Hwy (SR 84). I-8, exit 172 (Thornton Rd), 3.5 mi n, then 4.2 mi w. Ext corridors. **Pets:** Small. $25 daily fee/pet. Designated rooms, service with restrictions, supervision.

▼▼ Holiday Inn Casa Grande SH
(520) 426-3500. **Call for rates.** 777 N Pinal Ave. I-10, exit 194 (SR 287), 3.9 mi w. Int corridors. **Pets:** Accepted.
⊠ 🖥 🖭 🍴 ➳

▼ Motel 6–1263 M
(520) 836-3323. **$49-$65 (no credit cards).** 4965 N Sunland Gin Rd. I-10, exit 200, just w. Ext corridors. **Pets:** Other species. Service with restrictions, supervision.
🅢 ⊠ 🖥 ➳

AAA ▼▼ Super 8 Motel SH
(520) 836-8800. **Call for rates.** 2066 E Florence Blvd. I-10, exit 194 (SR 287), 0.6 mi w. Int corridors. **Pets:** Accepted.
SAVE ⊠ 🖥 🖭 ➳

CHINLE

▼▼ Thunderbird Lodge M
(928) 674-5841. **$65-$110.** Indian Rt 7. US 191, 3.5 mi e; just e of visitor center. Ext corridors. **Pets:** Accepted.
🅢 ⊠ 🖥 🍴

COTTONWOOD

AAA ▼▼▼ Best Western Cottonwood Inn SH
(928) 634-5575. **$89-$129.** 993 S Main St. On SR 89A, at SR 260. Ext corridors. **Pets:** Accepted.
SAVE 🅢 ⊠ 🖥 🖭 ➳

AAA ▼ Little Daisy Motel M
(928) 634-7865. **$52-$125.** 34 S Main St. On SR 89A, just n. Ext corridors. **Pets:** Dogs only. $10 daily fee/room. Service with restrictions, supervision.
SAVE 🅢 ⊠ 🖥

AAA ▼▼ Pines Motel SH
(928) 634-9975. **$59-$129.** 920 S Camino Real. Jct SR 260, just nw on SR 89A, then just s. Ext corridors. **Pets:** $10 daily fee/pet. Service with restrictions, supervision.
SAVE 🅢 ⊠ 🖥 🖭 ➳

AAA ▼ Quality Inn SH
(928) 634-4207. **$80-$120.** 301 W SR 89A. On SR 89A, 1.8 mi s of jct SR 260. Ext corridors. **Pets:** Small. $10 daily fee/room, $20 one-time fee/room. Designated rooms, service with restrictions, supervision.
SAVE 🅢 ⊠ 🖥 🖭 🍴 ➳

AAA ▼ The View Motel M
(928) 634-7581. **$58-$75.** 818 S Main St. On SR 89A, 0.4 mi nw of jct SR 260. Ext corridors. **Pets:** Accepted.
SAVE ⊠ 🖥 ➳

DOUGLAS

▼ Motel 6 #305 M
(520) 364-2457. **$45-$58 (no credit cards).** 111 16th St (SR 80). 1.2 mi e of jct SR 191. Ext corridors. **Pets:** Other species. Service with restrictions, supervision.
🅢 ⊠ 🖥 ➳

EAGAR

AAA ▼▼ Best Western Sunrise Inn M
(928) 333-2540. **$95-$120.** 128 N Main St. Jct SR 260, just n; jct US 60, 1.5 mi s. Ext corridors. **Pets:** Medium. $10 one-time fee/pet. Service with restrictions, supervision.
SAVE 🅢 ⊠ 🖥 🖭

EHRENBERG

AAA ▼▼ Best Western Flying J Motel SH
(928) 923-9711. **Call for rates.** S Frontage Rd. I-10, exit 1, just s; 0.5 mi e of Colorado River. Int corridors. **Pets:** Accepted.
SAVE ⊠ 🖥 🖭 ➳

FLAGSTAFF

AAA ▼▼ Best Western Kings House M
(928) 774-7186. **$69-$149.** 1560 E Route 66. I-40, exit 198 (Butler Ave), just w, just n on Enterprise, then just w. Ext corridors. **Pets:** Accepted.
SAVE 🅢 ⊠ 🖥 🖭 ➳

AAA ▼▼▼ Best Western Pony Soldier Inn and Suites SH
(928) 526-2388. **Call for rates.** 3030 E Route 66. I-40, exit 201, just n, then 1 mi w. Int corridors. **Pets:** Other species. $15 one-time fee/room. Designated rooms, service with restrictions, supervision.
SAVE ⊠ 🖥 🖭 ➳

AAA ▼▼ Comfort Inn I-17/I-40 SH
(928) 774-2225. **Call for rates.** 2355 S Beulah Blvd. I-40, exit 195, just n to Forest Meadows St, then 1 blk w. Int corridors. **Pets:** Large, other species. $10 daily fee/pet. Service with restrictions, supervision.
SAVE ⊠ 🖥 🖭 ➳

AAA ▼▼ Days Inn East SH
(928) 527-1477. **Call for rates.** 3601 E Lockett Rd. I-40, exit 201, just n, 0.5 mi w on I-40 business loop, then just n. Int corridors. **Pets:** Large. $20 one-time fee/room. No service, supervision.
SAVE ⊠ 🖥 🖭 ➳

AAA ▼▼ Days Inn Route 66 M 🐾
(928) 774-5221. **Call for rates.** 1000 W Route 66. I-40, exit 195, 1.5 mi n on Milton Rd, then just w. Ext corridors. **Pets:** Small, other species. $10 daily fee/pet. Service with restrictions, supervision.
SAVE ⊠ 🖥 🖭 ➳

AAA ▼▼ Econo Lodge-University M
(928) 774-7326. **$49-$109.** 914 S Milton Rd. I-40, exit 195, 1.2 mi n. Ext corridors. **Pets:** Other species. $5 daily fee/pet. Service with restrictions, supervision.
SAVE 🅢 ⊠ 🖥 🖭 ➳

AAA ▼▼ Howard Johnson Inn-Lucky Lane M
(928) 779-5121. **$54-$129.** 2520 E Lucky Ln. I-40, exit 198 (Butler Ave), just n, then just e. Ext corridors. **Pets:** Accepted.
SAVE 🅢 ⊠ 🖥 🖭 ➳

▼▼▼ La Quinta Inn & Suites SH
(928) 556-8666. **$95-$125.** 2015 S Beulah Blvd. I-40, exit 195, just n to Forest Meadow St, then just w. Int corridors. **Pets:** Other species. Service with restrictions, supervision.
ASK 🅢 ⊠ 🖥 🖭 ➳

▼▼ Motel 6-Flagstaff West #1000 M
(928) 779-3757. **$45-$58 (no credit cards).** 2745 S Woodlands Village Blvd. I-40, exit 195, just n to Forest Meadows St, w to Beulah Blvd, just s, then just w. Ext corridors. **Pets:** Other species. Service with restrictions, supervision.
🅢 ⊠ 🅛 🖥 ➳

AAA ▼▼ Quality Inn I-40/I-17 SH 🐾
(928) 774-8771. **$49-$119.** 2000 S Milton Rd. I-40, exit 195, just n to Forest Meadows St, then right. Int corridors. **Pets:** Other species. $10 daily fee/room. Supervision.
SAVE 🅢 ⊠ 🖭 ➳

AAA ▼▼ Quality Inn-Lucky Lane M
(928) 226-7111. **$65-$129.** 2500 E Lucky Ln. I-40, exit 198 (Butler Ave), just n, then just e. Ext corridors. **Pets:** Accepted.
SAVE 🅢 ⊠ 🖥 🖭 ➳

▼▼▼ Residence Inn by Marriott Flagstaff M
(928) 526-5555. **$154-$196.** 3440 N Country Club Dr. I-40, exit 201, 0.5 mi s. Ext/int corridors. **Pets:** Accepted.
ASK 🅢 ⊠ 🖥 🖭 ➳ ⊠

△△△⁷ ▼▼▼ Sleep Inn M
(928) 556-3000. **$55-$125.** 2765 S Woodlands Village Blvd. I-40, exit 195, just n to Forest Meadows St, w to Beulah Rd, just s, then just w. Int corridors. **Pets:** Accepted.
[SAVE] [S🐾] [✕] [👪M] [🛏] [💻] [🏊]

△△△⁷ ▼▼◆ Super 8-Lucky Lane M
(928) 773-4888. **$49-$125.** 2540 E Lucky Ln. I-40, exit 198 (Butler Ave), just n, then just e. Ext corridors. **Pets:** Accepted.
[SAVE] [S🐾] [🛏] [💻] [🏊]

△△△⁷ ▼▼ Super 8 Motel East Flagstaff M
(928) 526-0818. **$49-$59.** 3725 Kasper Ave. I-40, exit 201, just n, 0.5 mi w on I-40 business loop, then just n. Int corridors. **Pets:** Large, other species. $10 daily fee/pet. Designated rooms, no service, supervision.
[SAVE] [✕] [🛏]

△△△⁷ ▼ Travel Inn M
(928) 774-3381. **$39-$119, 3 day notice.** 801 W Route 66. I-40, exit 195, 1.2 mi n on Milton Rd, then just w. Ext corridors. **Pets:** $10 daily fee/room. Service with restrictions, supervision.
[SAVE] [✕] [🛏]

FLORENCE

▼▼ Rancho Sonora Inn M
(520) 868-8000. **Call for rates.** 9198 N Hwy 79. On SR 79, 5 mi s of SR 287. Ext corridors. **Pets:** Accepted.
[✕] [🛏] [💻] [🏊]

FOREST LAKES

△△△⁷ ▼ Forest Lakes Lodge M
(928) 535-4727. **Call for rates.** 876 AZ Hwy 260. On SR 260; between MM 288-289. Ext corridors. **Pets:** Small. $15 one-time fee/pet. Designated rooms, service with restrictions, supervision.
[SAVE] [✕] [🛏] [K̸]

GILA BEND

▼ America's Choice Inn & Suites M
(928) 683-6311. **$65.** 2888 Butterfield Tr. I-8, exit 119, just nw. Int corridors. **Pets:** Accepted.
[ASK] [S🐾] [✕] [🛏] [🏊]

△△△⁷ ▼▼◆ Best Western Space Age Lodge M
(928) 683-2273. **$79-$169.** 401 E Pima St. Business Loop I-8; center. Ext corridors. **Pets:** Other species. Designated rooms, service with restrictions, supervision.
[SAVE] [S🐾] [✕] [🛏] [💻] [🍴] [🏊]

GLOBE

▼▼ Comfort Inn at Round Mountain Park SH
(928) 425-7575. **$69-$289.** 1515 South St. On US 60, 1 mi e of town. Ext corridors. **Pets:** Small, dogs only. $10 daily fee/pet. No service, supervision.
[ASK] [S🐾] [✕] [🛏] [💻] [🏊]

GOLD CANYON

▼▼▼ Gold Canyon Golf Resort LH
(480) 982-9090. **$115-$296, 3 day notice.** 6100 S Kings Ranch Rd. US 60, exit Kings Ranch Rd, 1 mi n. Ext corridors. **Pets:** Accepted.
[ASK] [S🐾] [✕] [💻] [🍴] [🏊] [✗]

GRAND CANYON NATIONAL PARK AREA

GRAND CANYON NATIONAL PARK (SOUTH RIM)

△△△⁷ ▼▼▼ The Grand Hotel SH
(928) 638-3333. **Call for rates.** Hwy 64. On SR 64; 2 mi s of South Rim entrance. Int corridors. **Pets:** Dogs only. $50 deposit/pet, $25 one-time fee/pet. Designated rooms, service with restrictions, supervision.
[SAVE] [✕] [🛏] [💻] [🍴] [🏊]

△△△⁷ ▼▼▼ Red Feather Lodge SH
(928) 638-2414. **$69-$165.** Hwy 64. On SR 64; 2 mi s of South Rim entrance. Ext/int corridors. **Pets:** $50 deposit/pet, $10 daily fee/pet. Designated rooms, supervision.
[SAVE] [S🐾] [✕] [👪M] [🛏] [💻] [🍴] [🏊]

END AREA

HEBER

△△△⁷ ▼▼▼ Best Western Sawmill Inn SH
(928) 535-5053. **$75-$95.** 1877 Hwy 260. 0.5 mi e of center. Ext corridors. **Pets:** Large. $10 daily fee/pet. Designated rooms, service with restrictions, supervision.
[SAVE] [S🐾] [✕] [🛏] [💻]

HOLBROOK

△△△⁷ ▼ American Best Inn M
(928) 524-2654. **$41-$56.** 2211 E Navajo Blvd. I-40, exit 289, 1 mi w. Ext corridors. **Pets:** Other species. $5 one-time fee/pet. No service, crate.
[SAVE] [S🐾] [✕] [🛏] [💻]

△△△⁷ ▼ Best Western Adobe Inn M
(928) 524-3948. **$49-$99.** 615 W Hopi Dr. I-40, exit 285, 1 mi e on US 180 (Hopi Dr). Ext corridors. **Pets:** Medium. $10 one-time fee/pet. Service with restrictions, supervision.
[SAVE] [S🐾] [✕] [🛏] [💻] [🏊]

△△△⁷ ▼▼ Best Western Arizonian Inn SH
(928) 524-2611. **$86-$116.** 2508 Navajo Blvd. I-40, exit 289, 0.5 mi w. Ext corridors. **Pets:** Accepted.
[SAVE] [S🐾] [✕] [🛏] [💻] [🏊]

△△△⁷ ▼▼▼ Comfort Inn SH
(928) 524-6131. **Call for rates.** 2602 E Navajo Blvd. I-40, exit 289, just w. Ext corridors. **Pets:** Accepted.
[SAVE] [✕] [🛏] [💻] [🏊]

△△△⁷ ▼▼ Econo Lodge SH
(928) 524-1448. **$40-$60.** 2596 E Navajo Blvd. I-40, exit 289, just w. Ext corridors. **Pets:** Accepted.
[SAVE] [S🐾] [✕] [🛏] [💻] [🏊]

▼▼ Holbrook Holiday Inn Express M
(928) 524-1466. **Call for rates.** 1308 E Navajo Blvd. I-40, exit 286, just e. Int corridors. **Pets:** Accepted.
[✕] [🛏] [💻] [🏊]

JEROME

▼▼▼▼ Connor Hotel of Jerome 🆂🅷
(928) 634-5006. **$90-$165, 3 day notice.** 164 Main St. Center. Int corridors. **Pets:** Accepted.
A$K Ⓢ🔊 ✕ 🛢 💻 💻

KAYENTA

▼▼▼▼ Hampton Inn of Kayenta 🆂🅷
(928) 697-3170. **Call for rates.** Hwy 160. On US 160, just w. Int corridors. **Pets:** Accepted.
✕ 🔊ᴹ 💻 🍴 ⤳

KINGMAN

🅰🅰🅰⁷ ▼▼▼▼ Best Western a Wayfarer's Inn &
Suites 🆂🅷 ❀
(928) 753-6271. **$87-$115.** 2815 E Andy Devine Ave. I-40, exit 53, 0.5 mi w on Route 66. Ext corridors. **Pets:** Small. $8 one-time fee/room. Service with restrictions, supervision.
SAVE Ⓢ🔊 ✕ 🛢 💻 ⤳

🅰🅰🅰⁷ ▼▼ Brunswick Hotel 🆂🅷
(928) 718-1800. **Call for rates.** 315 E Andy Devine Ave. On Route 66; downtown. Int corridors. **Pets:** Small, dogs only. $10 daily fee/pet. Service with restrictions.
SAVE ✕ 🛢 🍴

▼▼ Comfort Inn 🅼
(928) 718-1717. **Call for rates.** 3129 E Andy Devine Ave. I-40, exit 53, just w on Route 66. Int corridors. **Pets:** Accepted.
✕ 🛢 💻 ⤳

🅰🅰🅰⁷ ▼▼ Days Inn West 🅼
(928) 753-7500. **Call for rates.** 3023 E Andy Devine Ave. I-40, exit 53, just w on Route 66. Ext corridors. **Pets:** Medium. $10 daily fee/pet. Service with restrictions, supervision.
SAVE ✕ 🛢 💻 ⤳

🅰🅰🅰⁷ Hill Top Motel 🅼
(928) 753-2198. **$40-$100, 3 day notice.** 1901 E Andy Devine Ave. I-40, exit 53, 2 mi w on Route 66. Ext corridors. **Pets:** Dogs only. $5 daily fee/pet. Service with restrictions, supervision.
SAVE Ⓢ🔊 ✕ 🛢 ⤳

▼ Motel 6-1114 🅼
(928) 753-9222. **$45-$58 (no credit cards).** 424 W Beale St. I-40, exit 48, just se on Business Loop I-40/US 93. Ext corridors. **Pets:** Other species. Service with restrictions, supervision.
Ⓢ🔊 ✕ ⤳

▼ Motel 6 E-1366 🅼
(928) 757-7151. **$42-$55 (no credit cards).** 3351 E Andy Devine Ave. I-40, exit 53, just e on Route 66. Ext corridors. **Pets:** Other species. Service with restrictions, supervision.
Ⓢ🔊 ✕ ⤳

🅰🅰🅰⁷ ▼▼ Quality Inn 🅼
(928) 753-4747. **$77-$140.** 1400 E Andy Devine Ave. I-40, exit 53, 2.5 mi sw on Route 66. Ext corridors. **Pets:** Accepted.
SAVE ✕ 🛢 💻 ⤳ ✕

🅰🅰🅰⁷ ▼▼▼ Super 8 Motel 🆂🅷
(928) 757-4808. **Call for rates.** 3401 E Andy Devine Ave. I-40, exit 53, just e on Route 66. Int corridors. **Pets:** Accepted.
SAVE ✕ 🛢

🅰🅰🅰⁷ ▼▼▼ Travelodge 🅼
(928) 757-1188. **Call for rates.** 3275 E Andy Devine Ave. I-40, exit 53, just e on Route 66. Ext corridors. **Pets:** Small, dogs only. $10 one-time fee/room. Designated rooms, service with restrictions, supervision.
SAVE ✕ 🛢 💻 ⤳

KOHLS RANCH

▼▼ Kohl's Ranch Lodge 🅲🅾 ❀
(928) 478-4211. **Call for rates (no credit cards).** 202 S Kohl's Ranch Lodge Rd. Jct SR 87 and 260 E, 16.6 mi e, just s. Ext/int corridors. **Pets:** Medium, dogs only. $20 daily fee/pet. Designated rooms, service with restrictions, supervision.
✕ 🛢 💻 🍴 ⤳ ✕

LAKE HAVASU CITY

🅰🅰🅰⁷ ▼ Americas Best Value Inn 🅼
(928) 855-5559. **$49-$99.** 101 London Bridge Rd. Jct SR 95, 0.3 mi nw. Ext corridors. **Pets:** Small, dogs only. $5 daily fee/pet. Service with restrictions, supervision.
SAVE Ⓢ🔊 ✕ 🛢 💻 ⤳

🅰🅰🅰⁷ ▼▼▼ Best Western Lake Place Inn 🆂🅷
(928) 855-2146. **Call for rates.** 31 Wing's Loop. 1 mi e of SR 95 via Swanson Ave; downtown. Ext corridors. **Pets:** $8 daily fee/pet. Service with restrictions.
SAVE ✕ 🛢 💻 ⤳

▼▼ Days Inn Lake Havasu 🅼
(928) 855-7841. **$54-$204.** 1700 N McCulloch Blvd. Just ne of Lake Havasu Ave; center. Ext corridors. **Pets:** Accepted.
A$K ✕ 🛢 💻 ⤳

🅰🅰🅰⁷ ▼▼▼▼ Hampton Inn Lake Havasu 🆂🅷
(928) 855-4071. **$111-$180.** 245 London Bridge Rd. 0.5 mi n of London Bridge. Ext/int corridors. **Pets:** Accepted.
SAVE Ⓢ🔊 ✕ 🛢 💻 ⤳ ✕

🅰🅰🅰⁷ ▼▼ Island Inn Hotel 🆂🅷 ❀
(928) 680-0606. **Call for rates.** 1300 W McCulloch Blvd. 0.7 mi w of London Bridge/SR 95. Int corridors. **Pets:** Other species. $50 deposit/room, $10 daily fee/room. Service with restrictions, supervision.
SAVE ✕ 🛢 🍴 ⤳

🅰🅰🅰⁷ ▼▼ Island Suites 🆂🅷
(928) 855-7333. **Call for rates.** 236 S Lake Havasu Ave. Just s of jct McCulloch Blvd. Int corridors. **Pets:** Accepted.
SAVE ✕ 🛢 ⤳

▼ Lake Havasu City Super 8 🅼
(928) 855-8844. **Call for rates.** 305 London Bridge Rd. Just w of SR 95, exit Palo Verde; 0.5 mi n of London Bridge. Int corridors. **Pets:** Accepted.
✕ 🛢 ⤳

🅰🅰🅰⁷ ▼ Motel 6 Lakeside 🅼
(928) 855-3200. **Call for rates.** 111 London Bridge Rd. 0.3 mi n of London Bridge. Int corridors. **Pets:** Other species. Service with restrictions, supervision.
SAVE ✕

🅰🅰🅰⁷ ▼▼▼ Travelodge-Lake Havasu City 🆂🅷
(928) 680-9202. **Call for rates.** 480 London Bridge Rd. 1 mi n of London Bridge. Int corridors. **Pets:** Accepted.
SAVE ✕ 🛢 💻

MUNDS PARK

🅰🅰🅰⁷ ▼ Motel In The Pines 🅼
(928) 286-9699. **$39-$79.** 80 W Pinewood Rd. I-17, exit 322, just e. Ext corridors. **Pets:** Accepted.
SAVE Ⓢ🔊 ✕ 🛢 💻

NOGALES

▼▼▼ Holiday Inn Express 🆂🅷
(520) 281-0123. **Call for rates.** 850 W Shell Rd. I-19, exit 4, just w to Frank Reed, then just nw. Int corridors. **Pets:** Accepted.
✕ 🛢 💻 ⤳

▼ **Motel 6 Nogales #71**
(520) 281-2951. **$49-$62 (no credit cards).** 141 W Mariposa Rd. I-19, exit 4, 0.9 mi e. Ext corridors. **Pets:** Other species. Service with restrictions, supervision.

PAGE

◈▼ **Americas Best Value Inn**
(928) 645-2858. **$49-$109.** 75 S 7th Ave. 1 mi e of US 89 via SR 89L; just n of Lake Powell Blvd. Ext corridors. **Pets:** $10 daily fee/pet. Designated rooms, service with restrictions, supervision.

◈▼▼ **Best Western Arizona Inn** **SH**
(928) 645-2466. **$49-$129.** 716 Rimview Dr. 0.7 mi e of US 89 via SR 89L. Int corridors. **Pets:** Accepted.

◈▼▼ **Lake Powell Days Inn & Suites** **SH**
(928) 645-2800. **$69-$189.** 961 N Hwy 89. On US 89, just s. Int corridors. **Pets:** Other species. $15 daily fee/pet. Service with restrictions, supervision.

◈▼▼ **Lake Powell Resort and Marina** **LH**
(928) 645-2433. **$123-$203.** 100 Lakeshore Dr. 4 mi n of Glen Canyon Dam via US 89. Int corridors. **Pets:** Accepted.

▼▼ **Linda's Lake Powell Condos** **CO**
(928) 353-4591. **Call for rates.** 1019 Tower Butte. 6 mi n on US 89. Ext corridors. **Pets:** Accepted.

◈▼ **Motel 6-Page/Lake Powell #4013** **SH**
(928) 645-5888. **$39-$79, 3 day notice.** 637 S Lake Powell Blvd. On Business Loop SR 89L, just e of US 89. Int corridors. **Pets:** Small. Designated rooms, no service, supervision.

◈▼▼ **Quality Inn, At Lake Powell** **SH**
(928) 645-8851. **$50-$92.** 287 N Lake Powell Blvd. 0.8 mi e of US 89/SR 89L. Int corridors. **Pets:** $20 daily fee/pet. Designated rooms, service with restrictions, supervision.

◈▼▼ **Super 8 Gateway to Lake Powell** **SH**
(928) 645-5858. **$49-$99, 3 day notice.** 649 S Lake Powell Blvd. On SR 89L, just e of US 89. Int corridors. **Pets:** Small. $10 one-time fee/pet. Service with restrictions, supervision.

PARKER

◈▼▼ **Best Western Parker Inn** **SH**
(928) 669-6060. **$74-$129.** 1012 Geronimo Ave. SR 95, just e. Int corridors. **Pets:** Accepted.

PAYSON

◈▼ **Americas Best Value Inn** **M**
(928) 474-2283. **$49-$120.** 811 S Beeline Hwy. On SR 87, 0.7 mi s of SR 260. Ext/int corridors. **Pets:** Small, dogs only. $15 daily fee/pet. Designated rooms, service with restrictions, supervision.

◈▼▼ **Best Western Payson Inn** **SH**
(928) 474-3241. **$59-$149, 3 day notice.** 801 N Beeline Hwy. On SR 87, 0.6 mi n of SR 260. Ext corridors. **Pets:** $25 daily fee/room. Service with restrictions, supervision.

◈▼▼ **Days Inn & Suites** **SH** ❀
(928) 474-9800. **Call for rates.** 301-A S Beeline Hwy. On SR 87, just s of SR 260. Int corridors. **Pets:** Small. $10 daily fee/pet. Designated rooms, service with restrictions, supervision.

▼▼ **Majestic Mountain Inn** **SH**
(928) 474-0185. **$70-$210, 7 day notice.** 602 E Hwy 260. On SR 260, 0.5 mi e of SR 87. Ext corridors. **Pets:** Accepted.

PHOENIX METROPOLITAN AREA

APACHE JUNCTION

◈▼ **Apache Junction Motel** **M**
(480) 982-7702. **$49-$89.** 1680 W Apache Tr. US 60, exit 195, 2 mi n, then just w. Ext corridors. **Pets:** Accepted.

◈▼▼ **Apache Junction Super 8** **SH** ❀
(480) 288-8888. **Call for rates.** 251 E 29th Ave. US 60, exit 196 (Idaho Rd/SR 88 E), just n. Ext/int corridors. **Pets:** Small, dogs only. $100 deposit/room, $25 daily fee/pet. Designated rooms, service with restrictions, supervision.

BUCKEYE

◈▼▼ **Days Inn-Buckeye** **SH**
(623) 386-5400. **Call for rates.** 25205 W Yuma Rd. I-10, exit 114 (Miller Rd), just sw. Ext corridors. **Pets:** Accepted.

CAREFREE

◈▼▼▼ **The Boulders Resort and Golden Door Spa** **LH**
(480) 488-9009. **Call for rates.** 34631 N Tom Darlington Dr. Scottsdale Rd, 11 mi n of Bell Rd. Ext corridors. **Pets:** Accepted.

◈▼▼▼ **Carefree Resort & Villas** **LH**
(480) 488-5300. **$90-$1200, 3 day notice.** 37220 Mule Train Rd. SR 101, exit 36 (Pima Rd), 12.2 mi n to Cave Creek Rd, 1 mi w, then 0.4 mi n. Ext/int corridors. **Pets:** Large. $50 one-time fee/pet. Designated rooms, service with restrictions, supervision.

CHANDLER

◈▼▼▼ **Chandler Super 8** **SH**
(480) 961-3888. **Call for rates.** 7171 W Chandler Blvd. I-10, exit 160 (Chandler Blvd), just e. Int corridors. **Pets:** Medium, other species. $5 daily fee/pet. No service, supervision.

Comfort Inn SH
(480) 705-8882. **Call for rates.** 255 N Kyrene Rd. I-10, exit 160 (Chandler Blvd), 1.5 mi e, then just n. Int corridors. **Pets:** Accepted.

Crowne Plaza San Marcos Golf Resort SH
(480) 812-0900. **$129-$299.** 1 San Marcos Pl. Jct Chandler Blvd, just s on Arizona Ave, then just w on Buffalo St; in historic downtown. Ext corridors. **Pets:** Small, dogs only. $50 one-time fee/pet. Designated rooms, service with restrictions, supervision.

Hawthorn Suites Chandler SH
(480) 705-8881. **Call for rates.** 5858 W Chandler Blvd. I-10, exit 160 (Chandler Blvd), 1.5 mi e. Int corridors. **Pets:** Accepted.

Homewood Suites by Hilton SH
(480) 753-6200. **Call for rates.** 7373 W Detroit St. I-10, exit 160 (Chandler Blvd), 0.4 mi e, n on 54th St, then just w. Int corridors. **Pets:** Accepted.

Radisson Phoenix-Chandler SH
(480) 961-4444. **$169-$229.** 7475 W Chandler Blvd. I-10, exit 160 (Chandler Blvd), just e, then just s on Southgate Dr. Int corridors. **Pets:** Small. Service with restrictions, supervision.

Red Roof Inn-Chandler SH
(480) 857-4969. **Call for rates.** 7400 W Boston St. I-10, exit 160 (Chandler Blvd), just e, then s on Southgate Dr. Int corridors. **Pets:** Accepted.

Residence Inn-Chandler Fashion Center SH
(480) 782-1551. **$165-$241.** 200 N Federal St. I-10, exit 160 (Chandler Blvd), 4.2 mi e, just n on N Metro Blvd, then just e. Int corridors. **Pets:** Accepted.

Windmill Suites of Chandler SH
(480) 812-9600. **Call for rates.** 3535 W Chandler Blvd. I-10, exit 160 (Chandler Blvd), 4 mi e. Int corridors. **Pets:** Accepted.

FOUNTAIN HILLS

Holiday Inn Hotel & Suites-Fountain Hills/Mayo Clinic SH
(480) 837-6565. **$109-$159, 5 day notice.** 12800 N Saguaro Blvd. Jct Shea Blvd, 2.2 mi n; across from the Fountain; center. Int corridors. **Pets:** Accepted.

GLENDALE

Ramada SH
(623) 412-2000. **Call for rates.** 7885 W Arrowhead Towne Center Dr. Loop 101, exit 14 (Bell Rd), 0.3 mi e, then just n on 79th Ave. Ext corridors. **Pets:** Accepted.

GOODYEAR

Best Western Phoenix Goodyear Inn M
(623) 932-3210. **$89-$189.** 55 N Litchfield Rd. I-10, exit 128, 0.8 mi s. Ext/int corridors. **Pets:** Large, other species. $10 daily fee/room.

Hampton Inn & Suites SH
(623) 536-1313. **Call for rates.** 2000 N Litchfield Rd. I-10, exit 128, 0.5 mi n. Int corridors. **Pets:** Accepted.

Holiday Inn Express SH
(623) 535-1313. **Call for rates.** 1313 N Litchfield Rd. I-10, exit 128, just n. Int corridors. **Pets:** Accepted.

Residence Inn by Marriott SH
(623) 866-1313. **$164-$229.** 2020 N Litchfield Rd. I-10, exit 128, 0.6 mi n. Int corridors. **Pets:** Accepted.

Wingate Inn & Suites SH
(623) 547-1313. **$159-$179.** 1188 N Dysart Rd. I-10, exit 129 (Dysart Rd), just n. Int corridors. **Pets:** Accepted.

LITCHFIELD PARK

The Wigwam Resort LH
(623) 935-3811. **Call for rates.** 300 Wigwam Blvd. I-10, exit 128 (Litchfield Rd), 2.4 mi n, then 0.4 mi e. Ext corridors. **Pets:** Medium, dogs only. Service with restrictions, supervision.

MESA

Arizona Golf Resort & Conference Center LH
(480) 832-3202. **$180-$250.** 425 S Power Rd. 1.3 mi n of US 60 (Superstition Frwy), exit 188 (Power Rd); southeast corner of Broadway and Power rds; entrance on Broadway Rd. Ext corridors. **Pets:** Other species. Service with restrictions.

Best Western Mesa Inn SH
(480) 964-8000. **$79-$350, 14 day notice.** 1625 E Main St. 2 mi n of US 60 (Superstition Frwy), exit Stapley Dr, 0.5 mi e. Ext corridors. **Pets:** Other species. $20 one-time fee/room. Service with restrictions, supervision.

Best Western Mezona Inn SH
(480) 834-9233. **$99-$169.** 250 W Main St. Just e of Country Club Dr; downtown. Ext corridors. **Pets:** Medium. $20 one-time fee/pet. Designated rooms, service with restrictions, supervision.

Best Western Superstition Springs Inn SH
(480) 641-1164. **Call for rates.** 1342 S Power Rd. Just n of US 60 (Superstition Frwy), exit 188 (Power Rd); northwest corner of Power Rd and Hampton Ave. Ext corridors. **Pets:** Accepted.

Days Hotel SH
(480) 844-8900. **$60-$170.** 333 W Juanita. US 60 (Superstition Frwy), exit 179 (Country Club Dr), just s, then just e. Int corridors. **Pets:** Accepted.

Days Inn-East Mesa SH
(480) 981-8111. **$50-$100.** 5531 E Main St. 0.4 mi e of Higley Rd. Ext corridors. **Pets:** Accepted.

Extended StayAmerica-Phoenix/Mesa SH
(480) 632-0201. **$65-$95.** 455 W Baseline Rd. US 60 (Superstition Frwy), exit 179 (Country Club Dr), 0.4 mi s on SR 87, then just w. Int corridors. **Pets:** Other species. $75 one-time fee/pet. Service with restrictions.

Holiday Inn Hotel & Suites LH
(480) 964-7000. **$109-$399, 3 day notice.** 1600 S Country Club Dr. US 60 (Superstition Frwy), exit 179 (Country Club Dr), just s. Ext/int corridors. **Pets:** Accepted.

▼▼▼ **Homestead Studio Suites Hotel Phoenix-Mesa** SH
(480) 752-2266. **$47-$95.** 1920 W Isabella. Just s of US 60 (Superstition Frwy), exit 177 (Dobson Rd). Ext corridors. **Pets:** Other species. $75 one-time fee/pet. Service with restrictions.
A$K Sᴅ ✕ 🛏 🖥

▼▼▼ **La Quinta Inn & Suites Phoenix (Mesa East)** SH
(480) 654-1970. **$149-$179.** 6530 E Superstition Springs Blvd. US 60 (Superstition Frwy), exit 187 (Superstition Springs Blvd) eastbound, just se; exit 188 (Power Rd) westbound, just sw. Int corridors. **Pets:** Other species. Service with restrictions, supervision.
A$K Sᴅ ✕ &ᴹ 🛏 🖥 ⇌

▼▼▼ **La Quinta Inn & Suites Phoenix (Mesa West)** SH
(480) 844-8747. **$112-$142.** 902 W Grove Ave. US 60 (Superstition Frwy), exit 178 (Alma School Rd), just n, then just e. Int corridors. **Pets:** Other species. Service with restrictions, supervision.
A$K Sᴅ ✕ 🛏 🖥 ⇌

▼ **Motel 6-Mesa South #1030** M
(480) 834-0066. **$51-$65 (no credit cards).** 1511 S Country Club Dr. US 60 (Superstition Frwy), exit 179 (Country Club Dr), northeast corner. Ext corridors. **Pets:** Other species. Service with restrictions, supervision.
Sᴅ ✕ 🛏 ⇌

▼ **Quality Inn & Suites Mesa/Phoenix** SH ❀
(480) 964-2897. **$49-$159.** 1410 S Country Club Dr. US 60, exit 179 (Country Club), just n. Ext corridors. **Pets:** Small, other species. $10 daily fee/pet. Service with restrictions, supervision.
A$K Sᴅ ✕ 🛏 🖥 ⇌

▼▼▼ **Residence Inn by Marriott Mesa** SH
(480) 610-0100. **$131-$208.** 941 W Grove Ave. US 60 (Superstition Frwy), exit 178 (Alma School Rd), just n, then just e. Int corridors. **Pets:** Accepted.
A$K Sᴅ ✕ &ᴹ 🛏 🖥 ⇌ ✗

▼ **Sleep Inn of Mesa** SH
(480) 807-7760. **$80-$325, 21 day notice.** 6347 E Southern Ave. US 60 (Superstition Frwy), exit 188 (Power Rd), 0.8 mi n, then 0.4 mi w to mall entrance. Int corridors. **Pets:** Medium, other species. $10 daily fee/room, $25 one-time fee/room. Designated rooms, service with restrictions, supervision.
A$K Sᴅ ✕ 🛏 🖥 ⇌

▲▲▲ ▼ **Super 8 Motel-Mesa/Gilbert Rd** SH
(480) 545-0888. **Call for rates.** 1550 S Gilbert Rd. US 60 (Superstition Frwy), exit 182 (Gilbert Rd), 1 blk n. Int corridors. **Pets:** Other species. $5 daily fee/pet. Designated rooms, service with restrictions, supervision.
SAVE ✕ 🛏 ⇌

▼ **Travelodge Suites Mesa** SH
(480) 832-5961. **Call for rates.** 4244 E Main St. US 60 (Superstition Frwy), exit 185 (Greenfield Rd), 2 mi n, then just w. Ext corridors. **Pets:** Accepted.
✕ 🛏 🖥 ⇌

▲▲▲ ▼▼▼ **Windemere Hotel and Conference Center** SH
(480) 985-3600. **$59-$229.** 5750 E Main St. 0.6 mi e of Higley Rd. Ext corridors. **Pets:** Accepted.
SAVE Sᴅ ✕ 🛏 🖥 🍽 ⇌

PARADISE VALLEY

▼▼▼ **Hermosa Inn** SH
(602) 955-8614. **Call for rates.** 5532 N Palo Cristi Rd. 1 mi s of Lincoln Dr; corner of Stanford Dr. Ext corridors. **Pets:** Accepted.
✕ 🛏 🖥 🍽 ⇌ ✗

▲▲▲ ▼▼▼ ▼▼▼ **Sanctuary on Camelback Mountain** LH ❀
(480) 948-2100. **Call for rates.** 5700 E McDonald Dr. US 101, exit McDonald Dr, 3.9 mi w. Ext corridors. **Pets:** Small, other species. Service with restrictions, supervision.
SAVE ✕ 🖥 🍽 ⇌ ✗

PEORIA

▼▼ **Comfort Suites by Choice Hotels/Sports Complex** SH
(623) 334-3993. **Call for rates.** 8473 W Paradise Ln. Loop 101, exit 14 (Bell Rd), just e to 83rd Ave, just s, then just w. Int corridors. **Pets:** Accepted.
✕ 🛏 🖥 ⇌

▼▼ **Extended StayAmerica Phoenix-Peoria** SH
(623) 487-0020. **$75-$125.** 7345 W Bell Rd. Loop 101, exit 14 (Bell Rd), 1.2 mi e. Int corridors. **Pets:** Other species. $75 one-time fee/pet. Service with restrictions.
A$K Sᴅ ✕ 🛏 🖥

▼▼▼ **Holiday Inn Express Hotel & Suites** SH
(623) 853-1313. **Call for rates.** 16771 N 84th Ave. Loop 101, exit 14 (Bell Rd), just w, then just s. Int corridors. **Pets:** Accepted.
✕ &ᴹ 🛏 🖥 ⇌

▼▼▼ **La Quinta Inn & Suites Phoenix (West/Peoria)** SH
(623) 487-1900. **$139-$169.** 16321 N 83rd Ave. Loop 101, exit 14 (Bell Rd), just e, then just s. Int corridors. **Pets:** Other species. Service with restrictions, supervision.
A$K Sᴅ ✕ 🛏 🖥 ⇌

▼▼▼ **Residence Inn by Marriott** SH
(623) 979-2074. **$175-$274.** 8435 W Paradise Ln. Loop 101, exit 14 (Bell Rd), just e, just s on 83rd Ave, then just w. Int corridors. **Pets:** Accepted.
A$K Sᴅ ✕ 🛏 🖥 ⇌ ✗

PHOENIX

▲▲▲ ▼▼▼ ▼▼▼ **Arizona Biltmore Resort & Spa** LH ❀
(602) 955-6600. **Call for rates.** 2400 E Missouri Ave. Jct Camelback Rd, 0.5 mi n on 24th St, then 0.4 mi e. Ext/int corridors. **Pets:** Medium. $50 deposit/room, $50 one-time fee/room. Designated rooms, service with restrictions, supervision.
SAVE ✕ 🖥 🍽 ⇌ ✗

▲▲▲ ▼▼▼ **Best Western Airport Inn** SH
(602) 273-7251. **$79-$199.** 2425 S 24th St. I-10, exit 150B westbound, just s; exit 151 (University Dr) eastbound, just n to I-10 westbound, 1 mi w to exit 150B (24th St), then just s. Ext/int corridors. **Pets:** Small. $25 one-time fee/room. Designated rooms, service with restrictions, supervision.
SAVE Sᴅ ✕ 🛏 🖥 🍽 ⇌

▲▲▲ ▼▼▼ **Best Western Bell Hotel** SH
(602) 993-8300. **$70-$500.** 17211 N Black Canyon Hwy. I-17, exit 212, just e, then just n. Ext corridors. **Pets:** Accepted.
SAVE Sᴅ ✕ 🛏 🖥 ⇌

▲▲▲ ▼▼▼ **Best Western InnSuites Hotel & Suites Phoenix Northern** SH
(602) 997-6285. **$79-$999.** 1615 E Northern Ave. SR 51, exit 7, 0.6 mi w. Ext corridors. **Pets:** Medium. $25 one-time fee/pet. Designated rooms, service with restrictions, supervision.
SAVE Sᴅ ✕ 🛏 🖥 ⇌

▲▲▲ ▼▼▼ **Best Western Phoenix/I-17 Metrocenter Inn** SH
(602) 864-6233. **$50-$160.** 8101 N Black Canyon Hwy. I-17, exit 206 (Northern Ave), just e, then just n; on east side of freeway. Ext corridors. **Pets:** Small, other species. $25 one-time fee/pet. Service with restrictions, crate.
SAVE Sᴅ ✕ 🛏 🖥 ⇌

▼▼ ▼▼ **Candlewood Suites** 🆂🅷
(602) 861-4900. **Call for rates.** 11411 N Black Canyon Hwy. I-17, exit 208 (Peoria Ave), just e, then 0.4 mi n. Int corridors. **Pets:** Accepted.

🗙 🅗 🖵 🌊

◍◍ ▼▼▼▼ **Clarion Hotel @ Phoenix Tech Center** 🆂🅷
(480) 893-3900. **$69-$189.** 5121 E La Puenta Ave. I-10, exit 157 (Elliot Rd), just w, just n on 51st St, then just e. Ext corridors. **Pets:** Medium, other species. $25 one-time fee/room. Service with restrictions, supervision.

🆂🅰🆅🅴 🆂🅳 🗙 🅗 🖵 🌊

◍◍ ▼▼▼ **Comfort Inn Black Canyon** 🆂🅷
(602) 242-8011. **$59-$469.** 5050 N Black Canyon Hwy. I-17, exit 203 (Camelback Rd), just w, then just n on west side of freeway. Ext corridors. **Pets:** Small, other species. $35 one-time fee/room. Service with restrictions, supervision.

🆂🅰🆅🅴 🆂🅳 🗙 🅗 🖵 🌊

◍◍ ▼▼▼ **Comfort Inn I-10 West/Central** 🆂🅷
(602) 415-1623. **$190-$195.** 1344 N 27th Ave. I-10, exit 27th Ave eastbound, just n; exit 141 (35th Ave) westbound, just n, 1 mi e on McDowell Rd, then s. Int corridors. **Pets:** Accepted.

🆂🅰🆅🅴 🆂🅳 🗙 🅗 🖵 🌊

▼▼ ▼▼ **Comfort Suites by Choice Hotels** 🆂🅷
(602) 861-3900. **Call for rates.** 10210 N 26th Dr. I-17, exit 208 (Peoria Ave), just e, just s on 25th Ave, then 0.3 mi w on W Beryl Ave. Int corridors. **Pets:** Accepted.

🗙 🅛🅼 🅗 🖵 🌊

▼▼ **Crossland Economy Studios-Phoenix West** 🆂🅷
(602) 272-8571. **$55-$75.** 4861 W McDowell Rd. I-10, exit 139, just n, then just e. Ext corridors. **Pets:** Other species. $75 one-time fee/pet. Service with restrictions.

🅰🆂🅺 🆂🅳 🗙 🅗 🖵

◍◍ ▼▼▼▼ **Crowne Plaza Phoenix** 🆂🅷
(602) 943-2341. **$65-$499.** 2532 W Peoria Ave. I-17, exit 208 (Peoria Ave), just e, then just n on 25th Ave. Int corridors. **Pets:** $25 one-time fee/room. Service with restrictions, supervision.

🆂🅰🆅🅴 🆂🅳 🗙 🅛🅼 🅗 🖵 🍴 🌊 🗶

◍◍ ▼▼▼▼ **Crowne Plaza Phoenix Airport** 🆂🅷
(602) 273-7778. **Call for rates.** 4300 E Washington St. Loop 202, exit 2 (44th St), 0.7 mi s. Int corridors. **Pets:** Other species. $50 one-time fee/pet. Service with restrictions, crate.

🆂🅰🆅🅴 🗙 🅗 🖵 🍴 🌊

◍◍ ▼▼ ▼▼ **Days Inn Phoenix I-17 & Thomas** 🆂🅷
(602) 257-0801. **$66-$196.** 2420 W Thomas Rd. I-17, exit 201 (Thomas Rd), just e. Int corridors. **Pets:** Small. $25 one-time fee/pet. Designated rooms, service with restrictions, crate.

🆂🅰🆅🅴 🆂🅳 🗙 🅗 🖵 🌊

◍◍ ▼▼▼▼ **Embassy Suites Phoenix Airport at 24th St** 🆂🅷
(602) 957-1910. **Call for rates.** 2333 E Thomas Rd. SR 51, exit 2, just e. Ext corridors. **Pets:** Large. $15 daily fee/room. Service with supervision.

🆂🅰🆅🅴 🗙 🅗 🖵 🍴 🌊 🗶

▼▼▼▼ **Embassy Suites Phoenix-Biltmore** 🆂🅷
(602) 955-3992. **Call for rates.** 2630 E Camelback Rd. Just n of Camelback Rd, on 26th St. Int corridors. **Pets:** Accepted.

🗙 🅗 🖵 🍴 🌊

◍◍ ▼▼▼▼ **Embassy Suites Phoenix North** 🅻🅷
(602) 375-1777. **Call for rates.** 2577 W Greenway Rd. I-17, exit 211, just e. Ext corridors. **Pets:** Accepted.

🆂🅰🆅🅴 🗙 🅗 🖵 🍴 🌊 🗶

▼▼ ▼▼ **Extended StayAmerica-Chandler** 🆂🅷
(480) 785-0464. **$77-$105.** 14245 S 50th St. I-10, exit 159, just w on Ray Rd, just s, then just e. Int corridors. **Pets:** Other species. $75 one-time fee/pet. Service with restrictions.

🅰🆂🅺 🆂🅳 🗙 🅛🅼 🖵

▼▼ ▼▼ **Extended StayAmerica-Phoenix Airport** 🆂🅷
(602) 438-2900. **$60-$95.** 3421 E Elwood St. I-10, exit 151 (University Dr), just n, then just e. Int corridors. **Pets:** Other species. $75 one-time fee/pet. Service with restrictions.

🅰🆂🅺 🆂🅳 🗙 🅗 🖵

▼▼ ▼▼ **Extended StayAmerica Phoenix/Airport/E Oak St** 🆂🅷
(602) 225-2998. **$65-$105.** 4357 E Oak St. Loop 202, exit 2 (44th St), 1 mi n. Int corridors. **Pets:** Other species. $75 one-time fee/pet. Service with restrictions.

🅰🆂🅺 🆂🅳 🗙 ♿🅼 🅗 🖵 🌊

▼▼ ▼▼ **Extended StayAmerica Phoenix-Chandler-E Chandler Blvd** 🆂🅷
(480) 753-6700. **$75-$110.** 5035 E Chandler Blvd. I-10, exit 160 (Chandler Blvd), just w. Ext corridors. **Pets:** Other species. $75 one-time fee/pet. Service with restrictions.

🅰🆂🅺 🆂🅳 🗙 🅗 🖵 🌊

▼▼ ▼▼ **Extended StayAmerica Phoenix-Deer Valley** 🆂🅷
(623) 879-6609. **$55-$100.** 20827 N 27th Ave. I-10, exit 215 (Rose Garden), just w; exit 215B southbound, just w, then 0.4 mi s. Int corridors. **Pets:** Other species. $75 one-time fee/pet. Service with restrictions.

🅰🆂🅺 🆂🅳 🗙 🅗 🖵

▼▼ ▼▼ **Extended StayAmerica Phoenix-Metro Center** 🆂🅷
(602) 870-2999. **$60-$90.** 11211 N Black Canyon Hwy. I-17, exit 208 (Peoria Ave), just e, then 0.3 mi n; on east side of freeway. Ext corridors. **Pets:** Other species. $75 one-time fee/pet. Service with restrictions.

🅰🆂🅺 🆂🅳 🗙 🅗 🖵 🌊

▼▼▼▼ **Extended Stay Deluxe Phoenix-Biltmore** 🆂🅷
(602) 265-6800. **$85-$135.** 5235 N 16th St. Jct SR 51, just w on Camelback Rd, then just n. Int corridors. **Pets:** Other species. $75 one-time fee/pet. Service with restrictions.

🅰🆂🅺 🆂🅳 🗙 🅗 🖵 🌊

▼▼▼▼ **Extended Stay Deluxe (Phoenix/Midtown)** 🆂🅷
(602) 279-9000. **$90-$130.** 217 W Osborn Rd. Just w of Central Ave; between Indian School and Thomas rds. Int corridors. **Pets:** Other species. $75 one-time fee/pet. Service with restrictions.

🅰🆂🅺 🆂🅳 🗙 🅛🅼 🅗 🖵 🌊

◍◍ ▼▼▼▼ **Fairfield Inn & Suites** 🆂🅷
(602) 716-9900. **$79-$185.** 2520 N Central Ave. I-10, exit 145 (7th St), just n to McDowell Rd, 0.4 mi w, then 0.7 mi n. Int corridors. **Pets:** Other species. $75 one-time fee/room. Service with restrictions, supervision.

🆂🅰🆅🅴 🆂🅳 🗙 🅗 🖵 🌊

▼▼▼▼ **Hilton Suites-Phoenix** 🅻🅷
(602) 222-1111. **Call for rates.** 10 E Thomas Rd. Just e of Central Ave; in Phoenix Plaza. Int corridors. **Pets:** Accepted.

🗙 🅛🅼 🅗 🖵 🍴 🌊 🗶

◍◍ ▼▼▼▼ **Holiday Inn Express Hotel & Suites** 🆂🅷
(480) 785-8500. **$81-$144.** 15221 S 50th St. I-10, exit 160 (Chandler Blvd), just w, then just n. Int corridors. **Pets:** Medium. $25 one-time fee/room. Service with restrictions, crate.

🆂🅰🆅🅴 🆂🅳 🗙 🅗 🖵 🌊

◍◍ ▼▼▼▼ **Holiday Inn West** 🆂🅷
(602) 484-9009. **Call for rates.** 1500 N 51st Ave. I-10, exit 139 (51st Ave), just n. Int corridors. **Pets:** Medium. $75 one-time fee/pet. Service with restrictions, supervision.

🆂🅰🆅🅴 🗙 🅛🅼 🅗 🖵 🍴 🌊

Homestead Studio Suites Hotel-Phoenix North/Metro Center M
(602) 944-7828. **$50-$85.** 2102 W Dunlap Ave. I-17, exit 207, 0.7 mi e. Ext corridors. **Pets:** Other species. $75 one-time fee/pet. Service with restrictions.
A$K S X 8 P

Homewood Suites by Hilton SH
(602) 508-0937. **Call for rates.** 2001 E Highland Ave. Just e of 20th St. Int corridors. **Pets:** Accepted.
X 8 P ➳ X

Homewood Suites Hotel SH ☘
(602) 674-8900. **Call for rates.** 2536 W Beryl Ave. I-17, exit 208 (Peoria Ave), just e, just s on 25th Ave, then just w. Int corridors. **Pets:** Medium. $49 one-time fee/room. Service with restrictions.
SAVE X ᕗM 8 P ➳

La Quinta Inn & Suites Phoenix (Chandler) SH
(480) 961-7700. **$155-$185.** 15241 S 50th St. I-10, exit 160 (Chandler Blvd), just w, then just n. Int corridors. **Pets:** Other species. Service with restrictions, supervision.
A$K S X ᕗM 8 P ➳

La Quinta Inn & Suites Phoenix West SH ☘
(602) 595-7601. **$119-$149.** 4929 W McDowell Rd. I-10, exit 139, just n, then just e. Int corridors. **Pets:** Small. $50 deposit/pet. Service with restrictions, crate.
A$K S X 8 P ➳

La Quinta Inn Phoenix Airport North SH
(602) 956-6500. **$119-$149.** 4727 E Thomas Rd. Just w of 48th St. Ext/int corridors. **Pets:** Other species. Service with restrictions, supervision.
SAVE S X 8 P ➳

La Quinta Inn Phoenix (North) SH
(602) 993-0800. **$124-$154.** 2510 W Greenway Rd. I-17, exit 211, just e. Ext corridors. **Pets:** Other species. Service with restrictions, supervision.
A$K S X 8 P ➳ X

La Quinta Inn Phoenix (Thomas Road) M
(602) 258-6271. **$99-$139.** 2725 N Black Canyon Hwy. I-17, exit 201 (Thomas Rd), just e, then just s on east side of freeway. Ext corridors. **Pets:** Other species. Service with restrictions, supervision.
A$K S X 8 P ➳

MainStay Suites SH
(602) 395-0900. **$79-$159.** 9455 N Black Canyon Hwy. I-17, exit 207, just e, then 0.4 mi n. Int corridors. **Pets:** Accepted.
A$K S X 8 P ➳

Motel 6 Phoenix East #18 M
(602) 267-8555. **$55-$68 (no credit cards).** 5315 E Van Buren St. Loop 202 eastbound, exit 4 (52nd St/Van Buren St) just s, then just e. Ext corridors. **Pets:** Other species. Service with restrictions, supervision.
S X 8 ➳

Motel 6 Phoenix-North #344 M
(602) 993-2353. **$49-$65 (no credit cards).** 2330 W Bell Rd. I-17, exit 212, just e. Ext corridors. **Pets:** Other species. Service with restrictions, supervision.
S ➳

Motel 6 Phoenix West #696 M
(602) 272-0220. **$48-$65 (no credit cards).** 1530 N 52nd Dr. I-10, exit 139, just n to McDowell, just w, then just s. Ext corridors. **Pets:** Other species. Service with restrictions, supervision.
S X ➳

Park Plaza Hotel Phoenix North SH
(602) 978-2222. **Call for rates.** 2641 W Union Hills Dr. I-17, exit 214A (Union Hills Dr), just w. Int corridors. **Pets:** Accepted.
SAVE X 8 P ¶ ➳

Pointe Hilton Squaw Peak Resort LH ☘
(602) 997-2626. **Call for rates.** 7677 N 16th St. Loop 51, exit Glendale Ave, 0.4 mi w, then 0.6 mi n. Ext corridors. **Pets:** $100 deposit/room. Service with restrictions, supervision.
SAVE X 8 P ¶ ➳ X

Pointe Hilton Tapatio Cliffs Resort LH ☘
(602) 866-7500. **Call for rates.** 11111 N 7th St. I-17, exit 207 (Dunlap Ave), 3 mi e, then 2 mi n. Ext corridors. **Pets:** $75 deposit/room. Service with restrictions, supervision.
SAVE X P ¶ ➳ X

Ramada Plaza Hotel and Suites SH
(602) 866-7000. **Call for rates.** 12027 N 28th Dr. I-17, exit 209 (Cactus Rd), just w, then just s. Int corridors. **Pets:** Medium. $35 daily fee/pet. Designated rooms, service with restrictions, supervision.
SAVE X 8 P ¶ ➳

Red Roof Inn SH
(602) 233-8004. **Call for rates.** 5215 W Willetta. I-10, exit 139 (51st Ave), just n, just e on McDowell Rd, then just s. Int corridors. **Pets:** Accepted.
X ᕗM 8 ➳

Red Roof Inn-Camelback SH
(602) 264-9290. **Call for rates.** 502 W Camelback Rd. I-17, exit 203 (Camelback Rd), 1.8 mi e. Int corridors. **Pets:** Accepted.
X 8 ➳

Residence Inn by Marriott SH ☘
(602) 864-1900. **$131-$230.** 8242 N Black Canyon Hwy. I-17, exit 207 (Dunlap Ave), just w, then 0.8 mi s. Ext/int corridors. **Pets:** Medium. $100 one-time fee/room. Service with restrictions, supervision.
SAVE S X ᕗM 8 P ➳ X

Residence Inn by Marriott Phoenix Airport SH
(602) 273-9220. **$153-$296.** 801 N 44th St. Loop 202, exit 2 (44th St), just s. Int corridors. **Pets:** Accepted.
A$K S X ᕗM 8 P ➳ X

The Ritz-Carlton, Phoenix LH
(602) 468-0700. **Call for rates.** 2401 E Camelback Rd. Southeast corner of Camelback Rd and 24th St. Int corridors. **Pets:** Accepted.
X 8 P ¶ ➳ X

Royal Palms Resort and Spa LH
(602) 840-3610. **$169-$599, 7 day notice.** 5200 E Camelback Rd. Just e of 52nd St. Ext/int corridors. **Pets:** Accepted.
SAVE X 8 P ¶ ➳ X

Sheraton Crescent Hotel LH
(602) 943-8200. **$89-$499, 3 day notice.** 2620 W Dunlap Ave. I-17, exit 207 (Dunlap Ave), just e. Int corridors. **Pets:** Service with restrictions, crate.
SAVE S X ᕗM 8 P ¶ ➳ X

Sheraton Wild Horse Pass Resort & Spa LH ☘
(602) 225-0100. **Call for rates.** 5594 W Wild Horse Pass Blvd. I-10, exit 162, 2.4 mi w. Int corridors. **Pets:** Medium, dogs only. Designated rooms, service with restrictions, supervision.
SAVE X 8 P ¶ ➳ X

Sleep Inn Phoenix North SH
(602) 504-1200. **$59-$550.** 18235 N 27th Ave. I-17, exit 214A (Union Hills), just w, then just s. Int corridors. **Pets:** Small. $100 deposit/room, $15 daily fee/pet. Designated rooms, service with restrictions, crate.
SAVE S X ᕗM 8 P ➳

⚐ ▼▼ Sleep Inn Sky Harbor Airport 🆂🅷
(480) 967-7100. **$59-$229.** 2621 S 47th St. I-10, exit 151 (University Dr), 2 mi n, then just w. Int corridors. **Pets:** Small, other species. $25 one-time fee/pet. Service with restrictions, supervision.

[SAVE] 🆂 ☒ 🅗 🖵 🔜

▼▼ Studio 6 Phoenix-Deer Valley #6030 🆂🅷
(602) 843-1151. **$71-$91 (no credit cards).** 18405 N 27th Ave. I-17, exit 214A (Union Hills Dr), just w, then just s. Ext corridors. **Pets:** Other species. Service with restrictions, supervision.

🆂 ☒ 🅗 🖵 🖵

▼▼ Super 8 Motel-Phoenix 🆂🅷
(602) 415-0888. **Call for rates.** 1242 N 53rd Ave. I-10, exit 139 (51st Ave), just s to Latham Rd, then just w. Int corridors. **Pets:** Accepted.

☒ 🅗 🔜

▼▼ TownePlace Suites by Marriott 🆂🅷
(602) 943-9510. **$120-$186.** 9425 N Black Canyon Hwy. I-17, exit 207, just e, then 0.3 mi n. Int corridors. **Pets:** Accepted.

[ASK] 🆂 ☒ 🅗 🖵 🔜

SCOTTSDALE

⚐ ▼▼▼▼ Camelback Inn, a JW Marriott Resort & Spa 🅻🅷
(480) 948-1700. **$208-$593, 7 day notice.** 5402 E Lincoln Dr. 0.5 mi e of Tatum Blvd; on north side of Lincoln Dr. Ext corridors. **Pets:** Small. $250 deposit/pet. Service with restrictions.

[SAVE] 🆂 ☒ 🅜 🅗 🖵 🍴 🔜 🗙

⚐ ▼▼▼▼ The Canyon Suites at the Phoenician 🅻🅷
(480) 423-2880. **Call for rates.** 6000 E Camelback Rd. 0.5 mi w of 64th St; in The Phoenician. Int corridors. **Pets:** Accepted.

[SAVE] ☒ 🅜 🍴 🔜 🗙

⚐ ▼▼▼▼ Chaparral Suites Resort 🆂🅷
(480) 949-1414. **$129-$259.** 5001 N Scottsdale Rd. At Chaparral Rd. Ext corridors. **Pets:** Medium, dogs only. $25 one-time fee/pet. Service with restrictions, supervision.

[SAVE] ☒ 🅜 🅗 🖵 🍴 🔜 🗙

▼▼ Comfort Suites by Choice Hotels-Old Town 🆂🅷
(480) 946-1111. **Call for rates.** 3275 N Drinkwater Blvd. N of Thomas Rd; just e of Scottsdale Rd. Int corridors. **Pets:** Accepted.

☒ 🅜 🅗 🖵 🔜

▼▼▼▼ Country Inn & Suites By Carlson 🆂🅷
(480) 314-1200. **$99-$153, 3 day notice.** 10801 N 89th Pl. Loop 101, exit 41, just e on Shea Blvd, then just n. Int corridors. **Pets:** Accepted.

[ASK] 🆂 ☒ 🅗 🖵 🔜

⚐ ▼▼▼▼ DoubleTree Paradise Valley Resort 🅻🅷
(480) 947-5400. **Call for rates.** 5401 N Scottsdale Rd. Just n of Chaparral Rd; on east side of Scottsdale Rd. Ext corridors. **Pets:** Small. Service with restrictions, supervision.

[SAVE] ☒ 🅗 🖵 🔜 🗙

▼▼ Extended StayAmerica-Phoenix-Scottsdale 🆂🅷
(480) 607-3767. **$70-$95.** 15501 N Scottsdale Rd. Loop 101, exit Frank Lloyd Wright, 2 mi w, 0.5 mi s on Scottsdale Rd, then just e on Tierra Buena Ln. Ext corridors. **Pets:** Other species. $75 one-time fee/pet. Service with restrictions.

[ASK] 🆂 ☒ 🅗 🖵

▼▼ Extended Stay Deluxe Phoenix-Scottsdale 🆂🅷
(480) 483-1333. **$75-$135.** 10660 N 69th St. Jct Scottsdale Rd, just w on Shea Blvd, then just n. Int corridors. **Pets:** Other species. $75 one-time fee/pet. Service with restrictions.

[ASK] 🆂 ☒ 🅗 🖵 🔜 🗙

⚐ ▼▼▼▼ The Fairmont Scottsdale Princess 🅻🅷
(480) 585-4848. **$129-$1179, 7 day notice.** 7575 E Princess Dr. Loop 101, exit 34 (Scottsdale Rd), 0.8 mi s, just e; 0.6 mi n of Bell Rd. Ext/int corridors. **Pets:** Medium. $35 one-time fee/pet. Designated rooms, service with restrictions, supervision.

[SAVE] ☒ 🅜 🅗 🖵 🔜 🗙

⚐ ▼▼▼▼ FireSky Resort & Spa, a Kimpton Hotel 🆂🅷 🐾
(480) 945-7666. **$109-$469, 3 day notice.** 4925 N Scottsdale Rd. Southeast corner of Scottsdale and Chaparral rds. Int corridors. **Pets:** Other species. Service with restrictions.

[SAVE] 🆂 ☒ 🅗 🖵 🍴 🔜 🗙

⚐ ▼▼▼▼ Four Seasons Resort Scottsdale at Troon North 🅻🅷
(480) 515-5700. **$205-$5500, 7 day notice.** 10600 E Crescent Moon Dr. SR 101, exit 36 (Pima Rd), 4.7 mi n, 2 mi e on Happy Valley, then 1.5 mi n on Alma School Rd. Ext corridors. **Pets:** Accepted.

[SAVE] ☒ 🅗 🖵 🍴 🔜 🗙

⚐ ▼▼▼▼ Hilton Scottsdale Resort & Villas 🅻🅷
(480) 948-7750. **Call for rates.** 6333 N Scottsdale Rd. Loop 101, exit 45, 2.1 mi w on McDonald Dr, then 0.3 mi n. Int corridors. **Pets:** Medium. $25 one-time fee/room. Service with restrictions, supervision.

[SAVE] ☒ 🅜 🅗 🖵 🍴 🔜 🗙

⚐ ▼▼▼▼ Holiday Inn Express Hotel & Suites-Scottsdale 🆂🅷
(480) 675-7665. **$79-$229.** 3131 N Scottsdale Rd. Northeast corner of Scottsdale Rd and Earll Dr. Int corridors. **Pets:** Other species. $25 deposit/room. Service with restrictions, supervision.

[SAVE] 🆂 ☒ 🅜 🅗 🖵 🔜

▼▼▼▼ Homestead Studio Suites Hotel-Phoenix-Scottsdale 🆂🅷
(480) 994-0297. **$65-$110.** 3560 N Marshall Way. Just w of Scottsdale Rd on Goldwater, just s. Ext corridors. **Pets:** Other species. $75 one-time fee/pet. Service with restrictions.

[ASK] 🆂 ☒ 🅜 🅗 🖵 🔜

⚐ ▼▼▼▼ Hotel Indigo Scottsdale 🆂🅷 🐾
(480) 941-9400. **$99-$329.** 4415 N Civic Center Plaza. Scottsdale Rd, just e on Camelback Rd, just s on 75th St. Ext/int corridors. **Pets:** Medium, dogs only. $25 deposit/pet. Designated rooms, service with restrictions, crate.

[SAVE] 🆂 ☒ 🅜 🅗 🖵 🍴 🔜

⚐ ▼▼▼▼ Hotel Valley Ho 🆂🅷 🐾
(480) 248-2000. **Call for rates.** 6850 E Main St. 0.4 mi w of Scottsdale Rd, just s of Indian School Rd; on northside of Main St. Ext/int corridors. **Pets:** Designated rooms, service with restrictions, supervision.

[SAVE] ☒ 🖵 🍴 🔜 🗙

▼▼▼▼ Hyatt Summerfield Suites-Scottsdale 🆂🅷
(480) 946-7700. **$99-$799.** 4245 N Drinkwater Blvd. 0.3 mi e of Scottsdale Rd. Ext corridors. **Pets:** Accepted.

[ASK] ☒ 🅗 🖵 🔜 🗙

⚐ ▼▼ The Inn at Pima, a Condominium Suite Hotel 🅲🅾
(480) 948-3800. **$59-$338.** 7330 N Pima Rd. 0.4 mi n of Indian Bend Rd; on west side of Pima Rd. Ext/int corridors. **Pets:** Accepted.

[SAVE] 🆂 ☒ 🅗 🖵 🔜 🗙

▼▼▼▼ La Quinta Inn & Suites Phoenix (Scottsdale) 🆂🅷
(480) 614-5300. **$149-$179.** 8888 E Shea Blvd. Loop 101, exit Shea Blvd, northeast corner. Int corridors. **Pets:** Other species. Service with restrictions, supervision.

[ASK] 🆂 ☒ 🅜 🅗 🖵 🔜 🗙

◇◇ ▼▼◇▼ **Millennium Resort Scottsdale, McCormick Ranch** 🄻🄷
(480) 948-5050. **$89-$319 (no credit cards), 3 day notice.** 7401 N Scottsdale Rd. 0.8 mi n of Indian Bend Rd. Int corridors. **Pets:** Accepted.

🆂🅰 🆂🄳 ⊠ 🛏 💻 🍴 🏊 ⊗

▼ **Motel 6 Scottsdale #29** 🄼
(480) 946-2280. **$55-$91 (no credit cards).** 6848 E Camelback Rd. Just w of Scottsdale Rd. Ext corridors. **Pets:** Other species. Service with restrictions, supervision.

🆂🄳 ⊠ 🍴 🏊

◇◇ ▼◇▼◇▼ **The Phoenician** 🄻🄷
(480) 941-8200. **$229-$815, 7 day notice.** 6000 E Camelback Rd. 0.5 mi w of 64th St. Ext/int corridors. **Pets:** Accepted.

🆂🅰 ⊠ 🛏 💻 🍴 🏊 ⊗

◇◇ ▼◇▼◇▼ **Radisson Fort McDowell Resort & Casino** 🄻🄷
(480) 789-5300. **$119-$309.** 10438 N Fort McDowell Rd. Jct Shea Blvd, 1.6 mi ne on SR 87. Int corridors. **Pets:** Small, dogs only. $10 one-time fee/pet. Designated rooms, service with restrictions, supervision.

🆂🅰 🆂🄳 ⊠ 🄼 🛏 💻 🍴 🏊 ⊗

▼▼ **Ramada Limited Scottsdale** 🄼
(480) 994-9461. **Call for rates.** 6935 5th Ave. Just w of Scottsdale Rd; just n of Indian School Rd; on south side of 5th Ave. Ext corridors. **Pets:** Accepted.

⊠ 🛏 💻 🏊

◇◇ ▼◇▼◇ **Renaissance Scottsdale Resort** 🄻🄷
(480) 991-1414. **$131-$340.** 6160 N Scottsdale Rd. Just n of McDonald Dr. Ext corridors. **Pets:** Accepted.

🆂🅰 🆂🄳 ⊠ 🄼 🛏 💻 🍴 🏊 ⊗

◇◇ ▼◇▼◇ **Residence Inn by Marriott, Scottsdale/ Paradise Valley** 🆂🄷
(480) 948-8666. **$131-$296.** 6040 N Scottsdale Rd. Just n of McDonald Dr. Ext/int corridors. **Pets:** Medium, other species. $100 one-time fee/room. Service with restrictions.

🆂🅰 🆂🄳 ⊠ 🄼 🛏 💻 🏊 ⊗

▼◇▼◇ **Residence Inn Scottsdale North** 🆂🄷
(480) 563-4120. **$142-$307.** 17011 N Scottsdale Rd. SR 101, exit 34 (Scottsdale Rd), 1.1 mi s, then just e on 17050 N. Int corridors. **Pets:** Accepted.

🄰🅂🄺 🆂🄳 ⊠ 🛏 💻 🏊 ⊗

◇◇ ▼◇▼◇▼ **Scottsdale Marriott at McDowell Mountains** 🆂🄷
(480) 502-3836. **$164-$406.** 16770 N Perimeter Dr. Loop 101, exit 36 (Princess Dr), just w to N Perimeter Dr, then 0.6 mi s. Int corridors. **Pets:** Accepted.

🆂🅰 🆂🄳 ⊠ 🄼 🛏 💻 🍴 🏊 ⊗

◇◇ ▼◇▼◇ **Scottsdale Thunderbird Suites** 🆂🄷
(480) 951-4000. **$79-$199.** 7515 E Butherus Dr. 0.8 mi n of Thunderbird Rd; 0.5 mi e of Scottsdale Rd. Ext corridors. **Pets:** Small, other species. $10 daily fee/room. Service with restrictions.

🆂🅰 🆂🄳 ⊠ 🛏 💻 🍴 🏊

◇◇ ▼◇▼ **Sleep Inn** 🆂🄷 🌸
(480) 998-9211. **$69-$189.** 16630 N Scottsdale Rd. Just s of Bell Rd. Int corridors. **Pets:** Medium, other species. $10 daily fee/pet. Service with restrictions, crate.

🆂🅰 🆂🄳 ⊠ 🄼 🛏 💻 🏊

▼◇▼◇ **TownePlace Suites Scottsdale by Marriott** 🆂🄷
(480) 551-1100. **$109-$208.** 10740 N 90th St. Loop 101, exit Shea Blvd, just e to 90th St, then just n. Int corridors. **Pets:** Accepted.

🄰🅂🄺 🆂🄳 ⊠ 🄼 🛏 💻 🏊

◇◇ ▼◇▼◇▼ **The Westin Kierland Resort & Spa** 🄻🄷 🌸
(480) 624-1000. **$179-$699, 7 day notice.** 6902 E Greenway Pkwy. 0.5 mi w of Scottsdale Rd. Int corridors. **Pets:** Medium. Service with restrictions, crate.

🆂🅰 🆂🄳 ⊠ 💻 🍴 🏊 ⊗

SURPRISE

◇◇ ▼◇▼ **Days Inn & Suites** 🆂🄷
(623) 933-4000. **Call for rates.** 12477 W Bell Rd. US 60 (Grand Ave), 1.1 mi e, then just s on Greasewood St. Int corridors. **Pets:** Large. $25 one-time fee/pet. Service with restrictions, supervision.

🆂🅰 ⊠ 🛏 💻 🏊

◇◇ ▼◇▼◇ **Windmill Suites at Sun City West** 🆂🄷
(623) 583-0133. **$79-$179.** 12545 W Bell Rd. US 60 (Grand Ave), 1 mi e. Int corridors. **Pets:** Accepted.

🆂🅰 🆂🄳 ⊠ 🛏 💻 🏊 ⊗

TEMPE

◇◇ ▼◇▼◇ **Best Western Inn of Tempe** 🆂🄷
(480) 784-2233. **Call for rates.** 670 N Scottsdale Rd. SR 202 Loop (Red Mountain Frwy), exit 7, just s. Int corridors. **Pets:** Accepted.

🆂🅰 ⊠ 🛏 💻

◇◇ ▼◇▼◇ **Best Western Tempe by the Mall** 🆂🄷
(480) 820-7500. **$59-$109.** 5300 S Priest Dr. I-10, exit 155 (Baseline Rd), 0.4 mi e, then just s. Int corridors. **Pets:** Small. $25 one-time fee/pet. Designated rooms, service with restrictions, supervision.

🆂🅰 🆂🄳 ⊠ 🛏 💻 🏊

◇◇ ▼◇▼ **Comfort Inn & Suites Tempe/ASU** 🆂🄷
(480) 966-7202. **$69-$149.** 1031 E Apache Blvd. SR 202 Loop (Red Mountain Frwy), exit 7 (Rural Rd S), 1.5 mi s, then just e. Int corridors. **Pets:** Small, other species. $50 deposit/room. Service with restrictions, crate.

🆂🅰 🆂🄳 ⊠ 🛏 💻 🏊 ⊗

▼◇▼◇ **Country Inn & Suites By Carlson** 🆂🄷
(480) 345-8585. **Call for rates.** 1660 W Elliot Rd. I-10, exit 157, just e. Ext corridors. **Pets:** Accepted.

⊠ 🛏 💻 🏊

▼◇▼◇ **Country Inn & Suites By Carlson** 🆂🄷
(480) 858-9898. **$119-$229.** 808 N Scottsdale Rd. SR 202 Loop (Red Mountain Frwy), exit 7, just n. Int corridors. **Pets:** Accepted.

🄰🅂🄺 🆂🄳 ⊠ 🄼 🛏 💻 🏊

◇◇ ▼◇▼◇▼ **Hampton Inn & Suites** 🆂🄷
(480) 675-9799. **$99-$209.** 1429 N Scottsdale Rd. SR 202 Loop (Red Mountain Frwy), exit 7, 0.5 mi n. Ext corridors. **Pets:** Accepted.

🆂🅰 🆂🄳 ⊠ 🛏 💻 🏊 ⊗

◇◇ ▼◇▼◇▼ **Holiday Inn Express Hotel & Suites Tempe** 🆂🄷
(480) 831-9800. **$99-$259.** 1520 W Baseline Rd. I-10, exit 155 (Baseline Rd), 0.4 mi e. Int corridors. **Pets:** Accepted.

🆂🅰 ⊠ 🛏 💻 🏊

▼◇▼ **Holiday Inn Tempe/ASU** 🆂🄷
(480) 968-3451. **Call for rates.** 915 E Apache Blvd. US 60 (Superstition Frwy), exit 174 (Rural Rd), 2 mi n. Int corridors. **Pets:** Accepted.

⊠ 🛏 💻 🍴

▼◇▼ **Homestead Studio Suites Hotel-Phoenix/Airport/Tempe** 🆂🄷
(480) 557-8880. **$80-$100.** 2165 W 15th St. I-10, exit 153 (Broadway Rd), 0.3 mi ne, just nw on S 52nd St, then just w. Int corridors. **Pets:** Other species. $75 one-time fee/pet. Service with restrictions.

🄰🅂🄺 🆂🄳 ⊠ 🛏 💻 🏊

InnSuites Hotels & Suites Tempe/Phoenix Airport SH
(480) 897-7900. **Call for rates.** 1651 W Baseline Rd. I-10, exit 155 (Baseline Rd), just e. Ext corridors. **Pets:** Medium. $25 one-time fee/pet. Designated rooms, service with restrictions, supervision.

La Quinta Inn Phoenix (Sky Harbor South) SH
(480) 967-4465. **$139-$169.** 911 S 48th St. I-10, exit 153 (Broadway Rd) eastbound; exit 153A (University Dr) westbound, 0.8 mi n; on south side of University Dr; east side of SR 143 (Hohokam Expwy). Ext corridors. **Pets:** Other species. Service with restrictions, supervision.

Quality Inn-Phoenix Airport-Tempe SH
(480) 967-3000. **$49-$155.** 1550 S 52nd St. I-10, exit 153B (Broadway Rd) westbound; exit 153A (48th St) eastbound, 0.3 mi ne. Ext corridors. **Pets:** Accepted.

Ramada Limited SH
(480) 413-1188. **Call for rates.** 1701 W Baseline Rd. I-10, exit 155 (Baseline Rd), just e. Ext corridors. **Pets:** Accepted.

Ramada Limited Tempe-University M
(480) 736-1700. **$79-$189.** 1915 E Apache Blvd. US 60 (Superstition Frwy), exit 175, 1.9 mi n on McClintock Dr, then 0.3 mi e. Ext corridors. **Pets:** Small, dogs only. $50 deposit/pet, $15 daily fee/pet. Service with restrictions, supervision.

Red Roof Inn Phoenix Airport SH
(480) 449-3205. **Call for rates.** 2135 W 15th St. I-10, exit 153 (Broadway Rd), just nw on S 52nd St, then just w. Int corridors. **Pets:** Accepted.

Residence Inn by Marriott SH
(480) 756-2122. **$153-$296.** 5075 S Priest Dr. I-10, exit 155 (Baseline Rd), 0.4 mi e, then just n. Ext/int corridors. **Pets:** Accepted.

Sheraton Phoenix Airport Hotel-Tempe LH ❀
(480) 967-6600. **$269-$349.** 1600 S 52nd St. I-10, exit 153B Broadway Rd westbound; exit 153A 48th St eastbound, 0.3 mi ne. Int corridors. **Pets:** Medium, dogs only. $75 one-time fee/room. Supervision.

Studio 6 Extended Stay #6031 SH
(602) 414-4470. **$71-$87 (no credit cards).** 4909 S Wendler Dr. I-10, exit 155 (Baseline Rd), just w, then 0.4 mi n. Ext corridors. **Pets:** Other species. Service with restrictions, supervision.

Tempe Mission Palms Hotel SH
(480) 894-1400. **$296-$315.** 60 E 5th St. Jct University Dr, just n on Mill Ave, then just e; downtown. Int corridors. **Pets:** Small. $25 one-time fee/room. Service with restrictions, supervision.

TOLLESON

Premier Inns SH
(623) 533-4660. **Call for rates.** 8399 W Lynwood St. I-10, exit 135, just n, then just w. Ext corridors. **Pets:** Accepted.

YOUNGTOWN

Best Western Inn & Suites of Sun City SH ❀
(623) 933-8211. **$75-$200.** 11201 Grand Ave. On US 60, just se of 113th Ave. Ext/int corridors. **Pets:** Medium, other species. Designated rooms, service with restrictions, supervision.

END METROPOLITAN AREA

PINETOP-LAKESIDE

Best Western Inn of Pinetop M
(928) 367-6667. **$99-$115.** 404 E White Mountain Blvd. On SR 260. Ext corridors. **Pets:** Medium. $10 daily fee/pet. Service with restrictions, supervision.

Holiday Inn Express SH
(928) 367-6077. **$59-$169, 3 day notice.** 431 E White Mountain Blvd. On SR 260. Int corridors. **Pets:** Very small. $25 daily fee/room. Designated rooms, service with restrictions, supervision.

Lazy Oaks Resort CA
(928) 368-6203. **Call for rates (no credit cards).** 1075 Larson Rd. Jct SR 260, 0.8 mi s on Rainbow Lake Dr, then 0.6 mi w. Ext corridors. **Pets:** Accepted.

Mountain Hacienda Lodge M
(928) 367-4146. **Call for rates.** 1023 E White Mountain Blvd. On SR 260. Ext corridors. **Pets:** Accepted.

Northwoods Resort CA
(928) 367-2966. **Call for rates.** 165 E White Mountain Blvd. On SR 260. Ext corridors. **Pets:** Accepted.

Super 8 Motel SH
(928) 367-3161. **Call for rates.** 1202 E White Mountain Blvd. On SR 260, east end of town. Int corridors. **Pets:** Accepted.

TimberLodge Inn M
(928) 367-4463. **$45-$99.** 1078 E White Mountain Blvd. On SR 260. Ext corridors. **Pets:** Accepted.

Woodland Inn & Suites M
(928) 367-3636. **$74-$169, 3 day notice.** 458 E White Mountain Blvd. On SR 260. Ext corridors. **Pets:** Medium, other species. $10 daily fee/pet. Service with restrictions, supervision.

PRESCOTT

Americas Best Value Inn M ❀
(928) 776-1281. **Call for rates.** 1105 E Sheldon St. 0.4 mi e of jct SR 89. Int corridors. **Pets:** Dogs only. $10 one-time fee/room. Service with restrictions, supervision.

▼▼ Best Western Prescottonian Motel Ⓜ
(928) 445-3096. **$89-$149, 7 day notice.** 1317 E Gurley St. On SR 89, just s of jct SR 69. Ext corridors. **Pets:** Medium. $10 daily fee/pet. Service with restrictions, supervision.

Ⓐ$Ⓚ Ⓢ Ⓧ ⦿ ⬜ ⑪ ⬷

⟨AAA⟩ ▼▼ Comfort Inn of Prescott Ⓜ
(928) 778-5770. **$65-$169.** 1290 White Spar Rd. On SR 89, 1.5 mi s of town center. Ext corridors. **Pets:** Medium, dogs only. $15 one-time fee/room. Service with restrictions, supervision.

Ⓢ$Ⓥ Ⓢ Ⓧ ⦿ ⬜

▼ Motel 6 #0166 Ⓜ
(928) 776-0160. **$43-$55 (no credit cards).** 1111 E Sheldon St. 0.4 mi e of jct SR 89; center. Ext corridors. **Pets:** Other species. Service with restrictions, supervision.

Ⓢ Ⓧ ⦿ ⬷

▼▼ Prescott Cabin Rentals ⒮Ⓗ
(928) 778-9573. **$72-$720, 14 day notice.** 5555 Onyx Dr. Jct SR 89, 5 mi e on SR 69, 0.4 mi s on dirt/gravel road. Ext corridors. **Pets:** Accepted.

Ⓧ ⦿ ⬜ Ⓧ

⟨AAA⟩ ▼▼▼ Quality Inn & Suites and Conference Center ⒮Ⓗ ✤
(928) 777-0770. **$109-$229.** 4499 Hwy 69. On SR 69, 3.6 mi e of jct SR 89. Int corridors. **Pets:** Medium, dogs only. $40 daily fee/pet. Designated rooms, service with restrictions, supervision.

Ⓢ$Ⓥ Ⓧ ⦿ ⬜ ⑪ ⬷ Ⓧ

▼▼▼ SpringHill Suites by Marriott ⒮Ⓗ
(928) 776-0998. **$153-$208.** 200 E Sheldon St. On SR 89, at Marina St. Int corridors. **Pets:** Accepted.

Ⓐ$Ⓚ Ⓢ Ⓧ Ⓜ ⦿ ⬜ ⬷

PRESCOTT VALLEY

⟨AAA⟩ ▼▼ Days Inn/Prescott Valley ⒮Ⓗ
(928) 772-8600. **Call for rates.** 7875 E Hwy 69. On SR 69; corner of Windsong Rd. Ext corridors. **Pets:** Other species. $50 deposit/room. Service with restrictions.

Ⓢ Ⓧ ⦿ ⬜ ⬷

QUARTZSITE

▼ Super 8 Motel-Quartzsite Ⓜ
(928) 927-8080. **Call for rates.** 2050 W Dome Rock Rd. I-10, exit 17, just s to Frontage Rd, then 0.6 mi w. Int corridors. **Pets:** Accepted.

Ⓧ ⦿

RIO RICO

▼▼▼ Esplendor Resort at Rio Rico ⓁⒽ
(520) 281-1901. **$134-$249.** 1069 Camino Caralampi. I-19, exit 17 (Rio Rico Dr), just w to Camino Caralampi, then just s to resort entrance. Ext corridors. **Pets:** Accepted.

Ⓐ$Ⓚ Ⓢ Ⓧ Ⓜ ⦿ ⬜ ⑪ ⬷ Ⓧ

SAFFORD

⟨AAA⟩ ▼▼ Best Western Desert Inn Ⓜ
(928) 428-0521. **Call for rates.** 1391 W Thatcher Blvd. US 191, 1 mi w on US 70. Ext corridors. **Pets:** Accepted.

Ⓢ Ⓧ ⦿ ⬜ ⬷

⟨AAA⟩ ▼▼ Days Inn Ⓜ
(928) 428-5000. **Call for rates.** 520 E Hwy 70. US 191, 0.5 mi e. Ext corridors. **Pets:** Small. $20 daily fee/room. Service with restrictions, crate.

Ⓢ Ⓧ Ⓜ ⦿ ⬜ ⬷

ST. JOHNS

▼ Days Inn Ⓜ
(928) 337-4422. **Call for rates.** 125 E Commercial St. On SR 191/61; center. Ext corridors. **Pets:** Accepted.

Ⓧ ⦿ ⬜

SEDONA

⟨AAA⟩ ▼▼ ▼▼ Amara Resort and Spa ⒮Ⓗ ✤
(928) 282-4828. **$128-$268, 3 day notice.** 310 N Hwy 89A. Jct SR 179, 0.4 mi ne; center. Int corridors. **Pets:** Medium. $75 one-time fee/room. Designated rooms, service with restrictions.

Ⓢ Ⓢ Ⓧ ⦿ ⬜ ⑪ ⬷ Ⓧ

⟨AAA⟩ ▼▼▼ Best Western Inn of Sedona ⒮Ⓗ
(928) 282-3072. **$189-$249.** 1200 W Hwy 89A. Jct SR 179, 1.2 mi w. Ext corridors. **Pets:** Accepted.

Ⓢ Ⓢ Ⓧ ⦿ ⬜ ⬷

⟨AAA⟩ ▼▼▼ Desert Quail Inn Ⓜ
(928) 284-1433. **$69-$189.** 6626 Hwy 179. Jct Bell Rock Blvd, 0.9 mi s. Ext corridors. **Pets:** Small, dogs only. $15 daily fee/pet. Designated rooms, service with restrictions, supervision.

Ⓢ Ⓢ Ⓧ ⦿ ⬜ ⬷

⟨AAA⟩ ▼▼▼ El Portal Sedona Luxury Inn ⒮Ⓗ ✤
(928) 203-9405. **$250-$550, 15 day notice.** 95 Portal Ln. Jct SR 89A, just s on SR 179, then just w. Ext/int corridors. **Pets:** Other species. Designated rooms, supervision.

Ⓢ Ⓧ ⦿

⟨AAA⟩ ▼▼▼ Hilton Sedona Resort & Spa ⓁⒽ
(928) 284-4040. **Call for rates.** 90 Ridge Trail Dr. Jct SR 89A, 7.3 mi s on SR 179. Int corridors. **Pets:** Accepted.

Ⓢ Ⓧ ⦿ ⬜ ⑪ ⬷ Ⓧ

▼▼ King's Ransom Sedona Hotel ⒮Ⓗ ✤
(928) 282-7151. **$125-$225.** 771 Hwy 179. 0.7 mi s of jct SR 89A. Ext/int corridors. **Pets:** Medium. $15 daily fee/room. Designated rooms, service with restrictions, supervision.

Ⓐ$Ⓚ Ⓢ Ⓧ ⦿ ⬜ ⑪ ⬷ Ⓧ

⟨AAA⟩ ▼▼▼ La Quinta Inn Sedona ⒮Ⓗ
(928) 284-0711. **$139-$169.** 6176 Hwy 179. Jct Bell Rock Blvd, just s. Int corridors. **Pets:** Other species. Service with restrictions, supervision.

Ⓢ Ⓢ Ⓧ Ⓜ ⦿ ⬜ ⬷

⟨AAA⟩ ▼▼▼ L'Auberge de Sedona Inn and Spa ⒮Ⓗ ✤
(928) 282-1661. **$229-$359, 7 day notice.** 301 L'Auberge Ln. Jct SR 179, just n on SR 89A, then ne; down the hill. Ext/int corridors. **Pets:** Dogs only. $35 daily fee/pet. Designated rooms, service with restrictions.

Ⓢ Ⓢ Ⓧ ⦿ ⬜ ⑪ Ⓧ

▼▼ ▼▼ The Lodge at Sedona ⒝Ⓑ ✤
(928) 204-1942. **$170-$339, 14 day notice.** 125 Kallof Pl. Jct SR 179, 1.8 mi w on SR 89A, then just s. Ext/int corridors. **Pets:** Medium, dogs only. $35 daily fee/pet. Designated rooms, service with restrictions, supervision.

Ⓧ Ⓧ Ⓩ

▼▼ ▼▼ Los Abrigados Resort & Spa ⒞Ⓞ ✤
(928) 282-1777. **$225-$425, 3 day notice.** 160 Portal Ln. Jct SR 89A, just s on SR 179, just w. Ext corridors. **Pets:** Medium, other species. $250 deposit/room, $20 daily fee/pet. Designated rooms, service with restrictions.

Ⓐ$Ⓚ Ⓧ ⦿ ⬜ ⑪ ⬷ Ⓧ

⟨AAA⟩ ▼▼▼ Matterhorn Inn Ⓜ
(928) 282-7176. **$79-$169.** 230 Apple Ave. Jct SR 179, just ne on SR 89A; uptown. Ext corridors. **Pets:** Large. $10 daily fee/room. Designated rooms, service with restrictions, crate.

Ⓢ Ⓢ Ⓧ ⦿ ⬜ ⬷

△△△ **▽▽** **Quail Ridge Resort** 🆂🅷
(928) 284-9327. **$135-$289, 14 day notice.** 120 Canyon Circle Dr. Jct SR 179, just w on Bell Rock Blvd, just nw. Ext corridors. **Pets:** Accepted.
[SAVE] [✕] [🍽] [💻] [≋]

△△△ **▽▽▽▽** **Sedona Real Inn & Suites** 🆂🅷
(928) 282-1414. **$95-$340.** 95 Arroyo Pinon Dr. Jct SR 179, 3.4 mi w on SR 89A, just sw. Ext corridors. **Pets:** Medium, other species. $20 one-time fee/pet. Designated rooms, service with restrictions, supervision.
[SAVE] [S📍] [✕] [🍽] [💻] [≋]

△△△ **▽▽▽** **▽▽▽** **Sedona Rouge Hotel & Spa** 🆂🅷 ❀
(928) 203-4111. **$249-$279, 3 day notice.** 2250 W Hwy 89A. Jct SR 179, 2 mi w. Ext/int corridors. **Pets:** Medium, dogs only. $100 deposit/pet, $50 one-time fee/pet. Designated rooms, service with restrictions.
[SAVE] [✕] [🍽] [💻] [🍴] [≋] [✕]

▽▽ **Sedona Super 8** 🆂🅷
(928) 282-1533. **Call for rates.** 2545 W Hwy 89A. Jct SR 179, 2.4 mi w. Int corridors. **Pets:** Accepted.
[✕] [🍽] [≋]

▽▽ **Sky Ranch Lodge** 🅼
(928) 282-6400. **Call for rates.** Airport Rd. Jct SR 179, 1 mi w on SR 89A, then 1 mi s. Ext corridors. **Pets:** Accepted.
[✕] [🍽] [💻] [≋]

▽▽ **The Views Inn Sedona** 🅼
(928) 284-2487. **Call for rates.** 65 E Cortez Dr. Jct Bell Rock Blvd, 0.9 mi s on SR 179, just e. Ext corridors. **Pets:** Accepted.
[✕] [🍽] [💻] [≋]

△△△ **▽** **Village Lodge** 🅼
(928) 284-3626. **Call for rates.** 78 Bell Rock Blvd. Jct SR 179, just w. Ext/int corridors. **Pets:** Very small, dogs only. $10 one-time fee/pet. Designated rooms, service with restrictions, supervision.
[SAVE] [✕] [🍽] [💻]

SELIGMAN

△△△ **▽** **Deluxe Inn Motel** 🅼
(928) 422-3244. **$42-$52.** 203 E Chino. I-40, exit 121 eastbound, 1 mi n, then 0.7 mi w on Route 66; exit 123 westbound, just ne on I-40 business loop, then 2.4 mi w. Ext corridors. **Pets:** Other species. $10 one-time fee/room. Designated rooms, service with restrictions, supervision.
[SAVE] [S📍] [✕] [🍽]

SHOW LOW

▽ **Americas Best Value Inn** 🅼
(928) 537-7694. **$49-$120.** 1941 E Deuce of Clubs Ave. Just e of jct SR 260. Ext corridors. **Pets:** Accepted.
[A$K] [S📍] [✕] [🍽]

△△△ **▽▽** **Best Western Paint Pony Lodge** 🅼
(928) 537-5773. **$68-$88.** 581 W Deuce of Clubs Ave. On US 60 and SR 260. Ext corridors. **Pets:** Other species. $10 daily fee/pet. Service with restrictions, supervision.
[SAVE] [S📍] [✕] [🍽] [💻]

△△△ **▽▽** **Days Inn** 🅼
(928) 537-4356. **Call for rates.** 480 W Deuce of Clubs. On US 60 and SR 260. Ext/int corridors. **Pets:** Small. $10 one-time fee/room. Service with restrictions, supervision.
[SAVE] [✕] [🍽] [💻] [🍴] [≋]

△△△ **▽** **Kiva Motel** 🅼
(928) 537-4542. **$58-$68, 3 day notice.** 261 E Deuce of Clubs Ave. On US 60 and SR 260; center. Ext corridors. **Pets:** Small, dogs only. $5 daily fee/pet. Service with restrictions, supervision.
[SAVE] [S📍] [✕] [🍽]

△△△ **▽▽** **Sleep Inn** 🆂🅷
(928) 532-7323. **Call for rates.** 1751 W Deuce of Clubs Ave. Jct SR 260 and US 60, just w. Int corridors. **Pets:** Accepted.
[SAVE] [✕] [🅼] [🍽] [💻] [≋]

SIERRA VISTA

△△△ **▽** **Americas Best Value Inn** 🅼 ❀
(520) 459-5380. **Call for rates.** 100 Fab Ave. Jct Business SR 90 and Fry Blvd, then just e of main gate to Fort Huachuca. Ext corridors. **Pets:** Dogs only. $10 one-time fee/room. Designated rooms, service with restrictions, supervision.
[SAVE] [✕] [🍽] [💻] [≋]

△△△ **▽▽** **Best Western Mission Inn** 🆂🅷
(520) 458-8500. **$75-$99.** 3460 E Fry Blvd. Just w of jct SR 90/92. Ext corridors. **Pets:** Other species. $10 daily fee/pet. Service with restrictions, supervision.
[SAVE] [S📍] [✕] [🅼] [🍽] [💻] [≋]

△△△ **▽▽** **Quality Inn** 🆂🅷
(520) 458-7900. **$84.** 1631 S Hwy 92. On SR 92, 1 mi s of jct SR 90. Int corridors. **Pets:** Large. $10 daily fee/pet. Designated rooms, service with restrictions, crate.
[SAVE] [S📍] [✕] [🍽] [💻] [≋]

▽▽▽ **Windemere Hotel & Conference Center** 🆂🅷
(520) 459-5900. **$139.** 2047 S Hwy 92. 1.5 mi s of jct SR 90. Int corridors. **Pets:** Accepted.
[A$K] [✕] [🍽] [💻] [🍴] [≋]

SNOWFLAKE

▽▽ **Comfort Inn** 🆂🅷
(928) 536-3888. **Call for rates.** 2055 S Main. SR 77, just s of town. Int corridors. **Pets:** Accepted.
[✕] [🍽] [💻] [≋]

TAYLOR

△△△ **▽▽** **Silver Creek Inn-Rodeway Inn** 🅼
(928) 536-2600. **Call for rates.** 825 N Main St. On SR 77. Ext corridors. **Pets:** Accepted.
[SAVE] [✕] [🍽] [💻]

TOMBSTONE

△△△ **▽▽** **Best Western Lookout Lodge** 🆂🅷
(520) 457-2223. **$75-$120.** 801 US Hwy 80 W. On SR 80, 1 mi n. Ext corridors. **Pets:** Accepted.
[SAVE] [S📍] [✕] [💻] [🍴] [≋]

TUBAC

△△△ **▽▽▽▽** **Tubac Golf Resort and Spa** 🆂🅷 ❀
(520) 398-2211. **$159-$289, 7 day notice.** 1 Otero Rd. I-19, exit 40 (Chavez Siding Rd), on east side, then 2 mi s. Ext corridors. **Pets:** Medium. $25 daily fee/room. Designated rooms, service with restrictions, supervision.
[SAVE] [S📍] [✕] [🍽] [💻] [🍴] [≋] [✕]

TUBA CITY

△△△ **▽▽▽** **Quality Inn Navajo Nation** 🆂🅷
(928) 283-4545. **$75-$123.** Main St & Moenave Rd. 1 mi n of US 160. Int corridors. **Pets:** Medium. $10 daily fee/pet. Service with restrictions, supervision.
[SAVE] [S📍] [✕] [🍽] [💻] [🍴]

TUCSON METROPOLITAN AREA

CATALINA

▼▼ Best Western Catalina Inn **M**
(520) 818-9500. **Call for rates.** 15691 N Oracle Rd. 4.6 mi n of Tangerine Rd. Ext/int corridors. **Pets:** Dogs only. $100 deposit/room, $5 daily fee/pet. Service with restrictions, crate.
⊠ 📵 💻 ➰

GREEN VALLEY

AAA ▼▼▼ Baymont Inn & Suites **SH**
(520) 399-3736. **Call for rates.** 90 W Esperanza Blvd. I-19, exit 65, just w. Int corridors. **Pets:** Small. $50 deposit/room, $10 daily fee/room. Designated rooms, service with restrictions, supervision.
SAVE ⊠ 📵 💻 ➰

AAA ▼▼▼ Best Western Green Valley **SH**
(520) 625-2250. **Call for rates.** 111 S La Canada Dr. I-19, exit 65, just w, then just s. Int corridors. **Pets:** Accepted.
SAVE ⊠ 📵 💻 🍴 ➰

AAA ▼▼▼ Holiday Inn Express **SH**
(520) 625-0900. **Call for rates.** 19200 S I-19 Frontage Rd. I-19, exit 69 (Duval Mine Rd), west side of interstate, then just s. Int corridors. **Pets:** Accepted.
SAVE ⊠ 📵 💻 ➰

MARANA

▼▼ La Quinta Inn & Suites **SH**
(520) 572-4235. **$90-$120.** 6020 W Hospitality Rd. I-10, exit 246 (Cortaro Rd), just w, then just n. Int corridors. **Pets:** Other species. Service with restrictions, supervision.
A$K S🔒 ⊠ &M 📵 💻 ➰

▼▼ Red Roof Inn Tucson North **SH**
(520) 744-8199. **Call for rates.** 4940 W Ina Rd. I-10, exit 248 (Ina Rd), just w. Int corridors. **Pets:** Accepted.
⊠ 📵 ➰

▼▼ Super 8 Motel **SH**
(520) 572-0300. **Call for rates.** 8351 N Cracker Barrel Rd. I-10, exit 246 (Cortaro Rd), just w. Int corridors. **Pets:** Accepted.
⊠ 📵 ➰

ORO VALLEY

AAA ▼▼▼ Hilton Tucson El Conquistador Golf & Tennis Resort **LH**
(520) 544-5000. **$109-$658.** 10000 N Oracle Rd. I-10, exit 248 (Ina Rd), jct Ina Rd, 4.4 mi n. Ext/int corridors. **Pets:** Accepted.
SAVE ⊠ &M 📵 💻 🍴 ➰ 🐾

TUCSON

AAA ▼▼ Americas Best Value Inn-Tucson **M**
(520) 884-5800. **Call for rates.** 810 E Benson Hwy. I-10, exit 262, just s. Ext corridors. **Pets:** $25 deposit/room. Service with restrictions, supervision.
SAVE ⊠ 📵 ➰

AAA ▼▼▼ Best Western InnSuites Hotel & Suites Tucson-Catalina Foothills **SH**
(520) 297-8111. **$79-$199.** 6201 N Oracle Rd. I-10, exit 250 (Orange Grove Rd), 4 mi e, then just s. Ext corridors. **Pets:** Medium. $25 one-time fee/pet. Designated rooms, service with restrictions, supervision.
SAVE ⊠ 📵 💻 ➰ 🐾

AAA ▼▼▼ Best Western Las Brisas Hotel Tucson Airport **SH**
(520) 746-0271. **Call for rates.** 7060 S Tucson Blvd. At entrance to Tucson International Airport. Int corridors. **Pets:** Small. $15 daily fee/room, $30 one-time fee/room. Designated rooms, service with restrictions, supervision.
SAVE ⊠ 📵 💻 🍴 ➰

▼▼ Comfort Suites **SH**
(520) 295-4400. **Call for rates.** 6935 S Tucson Blvd. Just n of Tucson International Airport. Int corridors. **Pets:** Medium. $25 one-time fee/room. Service with restrictions, supervision.
⊠ 📵 💻 ➰

AAA ▼▼▼ Comfort Suites at Sabino Canyon **SH**
(520) 298-2300. **$79-$159.** 7007 E Tanque Verde Rd. Jct Grand Rd, 0.4 mi ne. Ext corridors. **Pets:** Accepted.
SAVE S🔒 ⊠ 📵 💻 ➰

AAA ▼▼▼ Comfort Suites at Tucson Mall **SH**
(520) 888-6676. **$89-$189.** 515 W Auto Mall Dr. I-10, exit 254 (Prince Rd), 1.9 mi e, then 1.2 mi n. Int corridors. **Pets:** Other species. $10 one-time fee/pet. Designated rooms, service with restrictions, supervision.
SAVE ⊠ 📵 💻 ➰ 🐾

▼▼▼ Country Inn & Suites By Carlson **SH**
(520) 575-9255. **Call for rates.** 7411 N Oracle Rd. SR 77 (Oracle Rd), just n of Ina Rd. Ext corridors. **Pets:** Accepted.
⊠ &M 📵 💻 ➰ 🐾

▼ Crossland Economy Studios-Tucson-Butterfield Dr **SH**
(520) 745-3612. **$50-$75.** 4800 S Butterfield Dr. I-10, exit 264B eastbound, just n to Irvington, just e to Hotel Dr, just n; exit 264 westbound, just n. Ext corridors. **Pets:** Other species. $75 one-time fee/pet. Service with restrictions.
A$K S🔒 ⊠ 📵 💻

AAA ▼▼▼▼ DoubleTree Hotel at Reid Park **LH**
(520) 881-4200. **Call for rates.** 445 S Alvernon Way. I-10, exit 259 (22nd St), 4 mi e, then just n. Ext/int corridors. **Pets:** Accepted.
SAVE ⊠ 📵 💻 🍴 ➰ 🐾

AAA ▼ Econo Lodge **M**
(520) 622-6714. **$39-$179.** 1136 N Stone Ave. I-10, exit 257 (Speedway Blvd), eastbound, just e, then just n. Ext corridors. **Pets:** Dogs only. $10 deposit/pet, $10 one-time fee/pet. Designated rooms, service with restrictions, crate.
SAVE S🔒 ⊠ 📵 ➰

AAA ▼▼▼ Executive Inn & Suites of Tucson **SH**
(520) 791-7551. **Call for rates.** 333 W Drachman St. I-10, exit 257 (Speedway Blvd), 0.4 mi e to Main St, then 0.3 mi n. Int corridors. **Pets:** Accepted.
SAVE ⊠ 📵 💻 ➰

▼▼ Extended StayAmerica-Tucson-Grant Rd **SH**
(520) 795-9510. **$60-$105.** 5050 E Grand Rd. 0.5 mi e of Swan Rd. Ext corridors. **Pets:** Other species. $75 one-time fee/pet. Service with restrictions.
A$K S🔒 ⊠ 📵 💻

AAA ▼▼▼ Hampton Inn North **SH**
(520) 206-0602. **$79-$159.** 1375 W Grant Rd. I-10, exit 256 (Grant Rd), just w. Int corridors. **Pets:** Accepted.
SAVE S🔒 ⊠ &M 📵 💻 ➰

AAA ▼▼▼ Holiday Inn Express Hotel & Suites Tucson Airport **SH**
(520) 889-6600. **$99-$189.** 2548 E Medina Rd. 0.5 mi n of entrance to Tucson International Airport. Int corridors. **Pets:** Accepted.
SAVE ⊠ &M 📵 💻 ➰

The Hotel Arizona 🏨
(520) 624-8711. **$67-$129 (no credit cards).** 181 W Broadway. I-10, exit 258 (Broadway Blvd/Congress St), just e. Int corridors. **Pets:** Large. $50 one-time fee/room. Service with restrictions.

InnSuites Hotels & Suites Tucson City Center 🆂🅷
(520) 622-3000. **$69-$189.** 475 N Granada Ave. I-10, exit 258 (Broadway Blvd/Congress St), just e, then 0.4 mi n. Ext/int corridors. **Pets:** Medium. $25 one-time fee/pet. Designated rooms, service with restrictions, supervision.

La Posada Lodge & Casitas 🆂🅷
(520) 887-4800. **Call for rates.** 5900 N Oracle Rd. 0.5 mi s of Orange Grove Rd. Ext corridors. **Pets:** Accepted.

La Quinta Inn & Suites Tucson Airport 🆂🅷
(520) 573-3333. **$129-$159.** 7001 S Tucson Blvd. Just n of Tucson International Airport. Int corridors. **Pets:** Other species. Service with restrictions, supervision.

La Quinta Inn Downtown 🆂🅷
(520) 624-4455. **$99-$129.** 750 Starr Pass Blvd. I-10, exit 259 (Starr Pass Blvd), just w. Int corridors. **Pets:** Other species. Service with restrictions, supervision.

La Quinta Inn Tucson (East) 🆂🅷
(520) 747-1414. **$105-$135.** 6404 E Broadway. Just e of Wilmot Rd. Ext corridors. **Pets:** Other species. Service with restrictions, supervision.

The Lodge At Ventana Canyon 🏨
(520) 577-1400. **$99-$799, 21 day notice.** 6200 N Clubhouse Ln. I-10, exit 256 (Grant Rd), 8.6 mi e to Tanque Verde Rd, 0.6 mi e to Sabino Canyon Rd, 2 mi n, then 3.2 mi n on Kolb Rd. Ext/int corridors. **Pets:** Accepted.

Lodge on the Desert 🆂🅷
(520) 325-3366. **Call for rates.** 306 N Alvernon Way. I-10, exit 258 (Broadway Blvd/Congress St), 4 mi e, then just n. Ext corridors. **Pets:** Accepted.

Loews Ventana Canyon Resort 🏨
(520) 299-2020. **Call for rates.** 7000 N Resort Dr. I-10, exit 256 (Grant Rd), 8.6 mi e, 0.6 mi ne on Tanque Verde Rd, 2 mi n on Sabino Canyon Rd, then 3.5 mi n on Kolb Rd. Ext/int corridors. **Pets:** Accepted.

Motel 6 Tucson-Congress Street #50 🅼
(520) 628-1339. **$45-$61 (no credit cards).** 960 S Freeway. I-10, exit 258 (Broadway Blvd/Congress St), 0.7 mi s on west side of interstate. Ext corridors. **Pets:** Other species. Service with restrictions, supervision.

Motel 6 Tucson North #1127 🅼
(520) 744-9300. **$49-$65 (no credit cards).** 4630 W Ina Rd. I-10, exit 248 (Ina Rd), just e to Camino de Oeste, then just n. Int corridors. **Pets:** Other species. Service with restrictions, supervision.

Quality Inn at Tucson Airport 🆂🅷
(520) 294-2500. **$59-$225.** 2803 E Valencia Rd. 1 mi ne of Tucson International Airport; just e of Tucson Blvd. Ext/int corridors. **Pets:** Accepted.

Quality Inn Tucson 🆂🅷
(520) 623-7792. **Call for rates.** 1025 E Benson Hwy. I-10, exit 262, just s. Int corridors. **Pets:** Medium. $15 one-time fee/pet. Designated rooms, service with restrictions, supervision.

Radisson Suites Tucson 🏨
(520) 721-7100. **$109-$269.** 6555 E Speedway Blvd. Just e of Wilmot Rd. Ext corridors. **Pets:** Accepted.

Ramada Inn & Suites Foothills Resort 🆂🅷
(520) 886-9595. **Call for rates.** 6944 E Tanque Verde Rd. Jct Campbell Ave, 5.5 mi e on Grant Rd, then just ne. Ext corridors. **Pets:** Accepted.

Randolph Park Hotel and Suites 🆂🅷
(520) 795-0330. **$70-$165.** 102 N Alvernon Way. Jct Campbell Ave, 2.2 mi e on Broadway, then just n. Ext/int corridors. **Pets:** Medium. $25 one-time fee/pet. Designated rooms, service with restrictions, supervision.

Red Roof Inn-Tucson South 🅼
(520) 571-1400. **Call for rates.** 3704 E Irvington Rd. I-10, exit 264 westbound; exit 264B eastbound. Ext corridors. **Pets:** Accepted.

Residence Inn by Marriott 🆂🅷
(520) 721-0991. **$175-$274.** 6477 E Speedway Blvd. Just e of Wilmot Rd. Ext corridors. **Pets:** Accepted.

Residence Inn by Marriott Williams Centre 🆂🅷
(520) 790-6100. **$153-$219.** 5400 E Williams Cir. Jct Campbell Ave, 3.8 mi e on Broadway Blvd, then just s and just e on Williams Centre. Int corridors. **Pets:** Accepted.

Riverpark Inn 🆂🅷
(520) 239-2300. **$79-$159 (no credit cards).** 350 S Freeway. I-10, exit 158 (Broadway Blvd/Congress St), just w, then 0.4 mi s. Ext/int corridors. **Pets:** Accepted.

Sheraton Tucson Hotel & Suites 🆂🅷
(520) 323-6262. **Call for rates.** 5151 E Grant Rd. Jct Campbell Ave, 3.6 mi e. Ext/int corridors. **Pets:** Accepted.

Studio 6 Extended Stay #6002 🅼
(520) 746-0030. **$57-$73 (no credit cards).** 4950 S Outlet Center Dr. I-10, exit 264A eastbound; exit 264B westbound, just s, then just nw on Julian Dr. Ext corridors. **Pets:** Other species. Service with restrictions, supervision.

TownePlace Suites by Marriott 🆂🅷
(520) 292-9697. **$98-$186.** 405 W Rudasill Rd. Jct Orange Grove Rd, 0.5 mi s on Oracle Rd, then just e. Int corridors. **Pets:** Accepted.

The Westin La Paloma Resort & Spa 🏨
(520) 742-6000. **$129-$549.** 3800 E Sunrise Dr. From SR 77 (Oracle Rd), 4.6 mi e on Ina Rd via Skyline and Sunrise drs, just s on Via Palomita. Ext corridors. **Pets:** Medium, dogs only. Service with restrictions, supervision.

AAA ▼▼ **Westward Look Resort** 🄻🄷 ❀
(520) 297-1151. **$99-$369, 7 day notice.** 245 E Ina Rd. I-10, exit 248
(Ina Rd), 6 mi e, then just n on Westward Look Dr. Ext corridors.
Pets: Small, dogs only. $75 one-time fee/room. Service with restrictions,
crate.
🆂🅰🆅🅴 🆂🄳 ⊠ 🍴 🖥 🍴 ⇄ ⊠

AAA ▼▼▼ **Windmill Suites at St. Philip's**
Plaza 🆂🄷 ❀
(520) 577-0007. **$99-$189.** 4250 N Campbell Ave. I-10, exit 254 (Prince
Rd), 4 mi e, then 1 mi n. Int corridors. **Pets:** Other species. Designated
rooms, service with restrictions, crate.
🆂🅰🆅🅴 🆂🄳 ⊠ 🍴 🖥 ⇄ ⊠

END METROPOLITAN AREA

WELLTON

▼▼ **Microtel Inn & Suites at Coyote Wash** 🆂🄷
(928) 785-3777. **Call for rates.** 28784 Commerce Way. I-8, exit 30, just
s. Int corridors. **Pets:** Accepted.
⊠ 🍴 🖥 ⇄

WICKENBURG

AAA ▼▼ **Best Western Rancho Grande** 🆂🄷 ❀
(928) 684-5445. **Call for rates.** 293 E Wickenburg Way. On US 60;
center. Ext corridors. **Pets:** Other species. $8 daily fee/room. Designated
rooms, service with restrictions, supervision.
🆂🅰🆅🅴 ⊠ 🍴 🖥 ⇄ ⊠

AAA ▼▼ **Super 8 Motel & Suites** 🄼
(928) 684-0808. **Call for rates.** 1021 N Tegner St. 1 mi n of US 60 and
93. Ext/int corridors. **Pets:** Other species. $10 daily fee/pet. Supervision.
🆂🅰🆅🅴 ⊠ 🍴 🖥

AAA ▼▼ **Wickenburg Inn** 🆂🄷
(928) 684-5461. **$69-$95, 5 day notice.** 850 E Wickenburg Way. 1.3 mi
se on US 60. Int corridors. **Pets:** Medium. $10 one-time fee/pet. Service
with restrictions, supervision.
🆂🅰🆅🅴 🆂🄳 ⊠ 🍴 🖥 ⇄

WILLCOX

AAA ▼▼ **Best Western Plaza Inn** 🆂🄷
(520) 384-3556. **$79, 10 day notice.** 1100 W Rex Allen Dr. I-10, exit
340, just s. Ext corridors. **Pets:** $15 daily fee/pet. Service with restrictions,
supervision.
🆂🅰🆅🅴 🆂🄳 ⊠ 🍴 🖥 🍴 ⇄

AAA ▼▼ **Days Inn** 🄼
(520) 384-4222. **Call for rates.** 724 N Bisbee Ave. I-10, exit 340, just s.
Ext corridors. **Pets:** Medium. $7 daily fee/pet. Service with restrictions,
supervision.
🆂🅰🆅🅴 ⊠ 🍴 🖥 ⇄

▼ **Motel 6 Willcox #410** 🄼
(520) 384-2201. **$45-$58 (no credit cards).** 921 N Bisbee Ave. I-10,
exit 340, just s. Ext corridors. **Pets:** Other species. Service with restrictions, supervision.
🆂🄳 ⊠ 🍴 ⇄

WILLIAMS

AAA ▼▼ **Americas Best Value Inn of Williams** 🄼
(928) 635-2202. **$35-$84.** 1001 W Route 66. I-40, exit 161, 0.9 mi e.
Ext/int corridors. **Pets:** Accepted.
🆂🅰🆅🅴 🆂🄳 ⊠ 🍴 ⇄

AAA ▼▼▼ **Best Western Inn of Williams** 🆂🄷
(928) 635-4400. **$159-$209.** 2600 W Route 66. I-40, exit 161, just e. Int
corridors. **Pets:** Accepted.
🆂🅰🆅🅴 🆂🄳 ⊠ 🖥 ⇄

▼ **Canyon Motel & RV Park** 🄼
(928) 635-9371. **$40-$121.** 1900 E Rodeo Rd/Route 66. I-40, exit 165
(Grand Canyon), 1 mi s on Business Loop 40, then just w. Ext corridors. **Pets:** Accepted.
🄰🆂🅺 ⊠ 🍴 🖥 ⇄ 🆉

AAA ▼▼ **Days Inn** 🄼
(928) 635-4051. **Call for rates.** 2488 W Route 66. I-40, exit 161, just e.
Int corridors. **Pets:** Accepted.
🆂🅰🆅🅴 ⊠ 🍴 ⇄

AAA ▼ **El Rancho Motel** 🄼 ❀
(928) 635-2552. **$35-$78.** 617 E Route 66. I-40, exit 163, 0.6 mi s, then
just e. Ext corridors. **Pets:** $5 daily fee/pet. Designated rooms, service
with restrictions, supervision.
🆂🅰🆅🅴 🆂🄳 ⊠ 🍴 ⇄

AAA ▼▼ **Holiday Inn Williams** 🆂🄷
(928) 635-4114. **$95-$170.** 950 N Grand Canyon Blvd. I-40, exit 163,
just s. Int corridors. **Pets:** Other species. Service with restrictions, crate.
🆂🅰🆅🅴 🆂🄳 ⊠ 🅶🄼 🍴 🖥 🍴 ⇄

AAA ▼▼ **Motel 6–4010** 🄼
(928) 635-9000. **Call for rates.** 831 W Route 66. I-40, exit 161, 1 mi e.
Int corridors. **Pets:** Other species. Service with restrictions, supervision.
🆂🅰🆅🅴 ⊠ 🍴 ⇄

AAA ▼▼▼ **Quality Inn Mountain Ranch**
Resort 🆂🄷 ❀
(928) 635-2693. **$79-$149.** 6701 E Mountain Ranch Rd. I-40, exit 171
(Deer Farm Rd), just s. Ext corridors. **Pets:** $45 one-time fee/room.
Designated rooms, service with restrictions, supervision.
🆂🅰🆅🅴 🆂🄳 ⊠ 🍴 🖥 🍴 ⇄ ⊠

AAA ▼▼ **Rodeway Inn** 🄼
(928) 635-2619. **$35-$149.** 334 E Route 66. I-40, exit 163, 0.5 mi s,
then just e. Ext corridors. **Pets:** Accepted.
🆂🅰🆅🅴 🆂🄳 ⊠ 🍴 🖥

AAA ▼ **Travelodge Williams** 🄼
(928) 635-2651. **Call for rates.** 430 E Route 66. I-40, exit 163, 0.5 mi
s, then just e. Ext corridors. **Pets:** Dogs only. $8 daily fee/pet. Designated
rooms, service with restrictions, supervision.
🆂🅰🆅🅴 ⊠ 🍴 🖥 ⇄

WINDOW ROCK

AAA ▼▼ **Quality Inn Navajo Nation Capital** 🆂🄷
(928) 871-4108. **$67-$81.** 48 W Hwy 264. Center. Ext corridors.
Pets: $50 deposit/pet. Service with restrictions, supervision.
🆂🅰🆅🅴 🆂🄳 ⊠ 🍴 🖥 🍴

WINSLOW

AAA ▼▼ **Comfort Inn-Winslow** 🆂🄷
(928) 289-4638. **$70-$100.** 1701 N Park Dr. I-40, exit 253. Int corridors.
Pets: $10 daily fee/pet. Designated rooms, service with restrictions, super-
vision.
🆂🅰🆅🅴 🆂🄳 ⊠ 🍴 🖥 🍴 ⇄

AAA ▼▼ **Econo Lodge** 🆂🄷
(928) 289-4687. **$50-$110.** 1706 N Park Dr. I-40, exit 253, just s. Ext
corridors. **Pets:** Small. $5 one-time fee/room. Service with restrictions,
supervision.
🆂🅰🆅🅴 🆂🄳 ⊠ 🍴 🖥 ⇄

▼▼▼ La Posada Hotel SH
(928) 289-4366. **$99, 3 day notice.** 303 E 2nd St. I-40, exit 253, 1 mi s to Route 66 (2nd St), then just e; in historic downtown. Int corridors. **Pets:** Accepted.
[X] [&M] [🛏] [❒] [☎]

ⒶⒶⒶ ▼▼ Motel 6 Winslow #4012 M
(928) 289-9581. **Call for rates.** 520 W Desmond St. I-40, exit 253, just s on N Park Dr, then just w. Int corridors. **Pets:** Other species. Service with restrictions, supervision.
[SAVE] [X] [🛏]

▼▼ Super 8 Motel M
(928) 289-4606. **Call for rates.** 1916 W Third St. I-40, exit 252, just s, then just e on Route 66. Int corridors. **Pets:** Medium, other species. $10 daily fee/pet. Service with restrictions, supervision.
[X] [🛏] [❒]

YUMA

ⒶⒶⒶ ▼▼ Best Western Coronado Motor Hotel M ❀
(928) 783-4453. **$79-$170.** 233 4th Ave. I-8, exit 4th Ave eastbound, 0.5 mi s; exit 1 (Giss Pkwy) westbound, 1 mi w. Ext corridors. **Pets:** Small. Designated rooms, service with restrictions, supervision.
[SAVE] [S🐾] [X] [🛏] [❒] [❘❘] [🛏]

ⒶⒶⒶ ▼▼▼ Best Western InnSuites Hotel & Suites
Yuma SH
(928) 783-8341. **Call for rates.** 1450 Castle Dome Ave. I-8, exit 2 (16th St/US 95), just e to Yuma Palms Pkwy, just n, then just w. Ext corridors. **Pets:** Medium. $25 one-time fee/pet. Designated rooms, service with restrictions, supervision.
[SAVE] [X] [🛏] [❒] [❘❘] [🛏] [X]

▼▼▼ Clarion Suites SH
(928) 726-4830. **Call for rates.** 2600 S 4th Ave. I-8, exit 2 (16 St/US 95) eastbound, 1 mi w, then 1.3 mi s; exit 3 (SR 280) westbound, 0.5 mi s, then 2 mi w. Ext corridors. **Pets:** Accepted.
[X] [🛏] [❒]

▼▼ Comfort Inn SH
(928) 782-1200. **$109-$209, 7 day notice.** 1691 S Riley Ave. I-8, exit 2 (16th St/US 95), just w. Int corridors. **Pets:** Accepted.
[ASK] [S🐾] [X] [&M] [🛏] [❒] [🛏]

▼▼▼ Holiday Inn SH
(928) 782-9300. **Call for rates (no credit cards).** 1901 E 18th St. I-8, exit 2 (16th St/US 95), 0.4 mi e on 16th St, just s on Pacific Ave, then just w. Int corridors. **Pets:** No service, supervision.
[X] [&M] [🛏] [❒] [❘❘] [🛏]

ⒶⒶⒶ ▼▼ Howard Johnson Inn SH ❀
(928) 344-1420. **Call for rates.** 3181 S 4th Ave. I-8, exit 3E (SR 280 S), 1 mi s to 32nd St, then 2 mi w. Ext corridors. **Pets:** Other species. $10 daily fee/room. Service with restrictions, crate.
[SAVE] [X] [🛏] [❒] [🛏]

▼▼ Microtel Inn & Suites SH
(928) 345-1777. **$57-$140.** 11274 S Fortuna Rd. I-8, exit 12 (Fortuna Rd), just s, then w on frontage road. Int corridors. **Pets:** Accepted.
[ASK] [X] [🛏] [❒] [🛏]

▼▼ Motel 6 Yuma East #1031 M
(928) 782-9521. **$45-$65 (no credit cards).** 1445 E 16th St. I-8, exit 2 (16th St/US 95), just e. Ext corridors. **Pets:** Other species. Service with restrictions, supervision.
[S🐾] [X] [🛏]

▼▼ Oak Tree Inn SH
(928) 539-9000. **$79-$179.** 1731 Sunridge Dr. I-8, exit 2 (16th St/US 95), just e, then just s. Int corridors. **Pets:** Dogs only. $10 one-time fee/pet. Service with restrictions, supervision.
[ASK] [S🐾] [X] [🛏] [❒] [🛏]

ⒶⒶⒶ ▼▼▼ Quality Inn Airport SH
(928) 726-4721. **$79-$159.** 711 E 32nd St. I-8, exit 3E (SR 280), 1.2 mi s, then 1.9 mi w. Ext corridors. **Pets:** $25 one-time fee/room. Service with restrictions, supervision.
[SAVE] [S🐾] [X] [🛏] [❒] [❘❘] [🛏]

ⒶⒶⒶ ▼▼ Shilo Inn Hotel-Yuma SH ❀
(928) 782-9511. **$150-$200.** 1550 S Castle Dome Rd. I-8, exit 2 (16th St/US 95), just e to Yuma Palms Pkwy, just n, then just w. Int corridors. **Pets:** $25 one-time fee/room. Designated rooms, service with restrictions, supervision.
[SAVE] [S🐾] [X] [🛏] [❒] [❘❘] [🛏] [X]

ⒶⒶⒶ ▼▼ Yuma Cabana Motel M
(928) 783-8311. **$46-$120 (no credit cards), 3 day notice.** 2151 S 4th Ave. I-8, exit 2 (16th St/US 95), 1 mi w, then 0.5 mi s. Int corridors. **Pets:** Accepted.
[SAVE] [S🐾] [X] [🛏] [🛏]

▼▼ Yuma Super 8 Motel SH
(928) 782-2000. **$71-$139.** 1688 S Riley Ave. I-8, exit 2 (16th St/US 95), just w. Int corridors. **Pets:** Accepted.
[ASK] [S🐾] [X] [&M] [🛏] [❒] [🛏]

ARKANSAS

CITY INDEX

ALMA

Comfort Inn & Suites SH
(479) 632-4141. **Call for rates.** 439 Hwy 71 N. I-40, exit 13, just n. Ext/int corridors. **Pets:** Accepted.

ARKADELPHIA

 Best Western-Continental Inn SH
(870) 246-5592. **$62-$99.** 136 Valley St. I-30, exit 78, just e. Ext corridors. **Pets:** Large. $9 daily fee/pet. Service with restrictions, crate.

BATESVILLE

Ramada Inn of Batesville SH
(870) 698-1800. **$75-$149.** 1325 N St. Louis St. 1 mi n on US 167. Ext corridors. **Pets:** Accepted.

Super 8 Motel-Batesville M
(870) 793-5888. **$59-$62.** 1287 N St. Louis St. 1 mi n on US 167. Int corridors. **Pets:** Dogs only. $25 one-time fee/pet. Service with restrictions, supervision.

BEEBE

Days Inn SH
(501) 882-2008. **Call for rates.** 100 Tammy Ln. US 67/167, exit 28, just e. Ext corridors. **Pets:** Accepted.

BENTONVILLE

Comfort Suites Bentonville/Rogers SH
(479) 254-9099. **$79-$139.** 2011 SE Walton Blvd. I-540, exit 85, just w. Int corridors. **Pets:** Accepted.

La Quinta Inn & Suites SH
(479) 271-7555. **$158.** 1001 SE Walton Blvd. I-540, exit 85, 0.7 mi w. Int corridors. **Pets:** Other species. Service with restrictions, supervision.

TownePlace Suites by Marriott Bentonville/Rogers SH
(479) 621-0202. **$209-$229.** 3100 SE 14th St. I-540, exit 86, just e. Int corridors. **Pets:** Accepted.

BLYTHEVILLE

Comfort Inn of Blytheville SH
(870) 763-7081. **$63-$70.** 1520 E Main. I-55, exit 67, just w. Ext corridors. **Pets:** Accepted.

Hampton Inn SH
(870) 763-5220. **Call for rates.** 301 N Access Rd. I-55, exit 67, just nw. Ext corridors. **Pets:** Accepted.

Holiday Inn SH
(870) 763-5800. **$99-$139.** 1121 E Main. I-55, exit 67, just w. Ext/int corridors. **Pets:** Accepted.

BRYANT

Americas Best Value Inn & Suites M
(501) 653-7800. **$55-$79.** 407 W Commerce St. I-30, exit 123, just sw. Ext corridors. **Pets:** Accepted.

Super 8 Motel M
(501) 847-7888. **Call for rates.** 201 Dell Dr. I-30, exit 123, just e. Ext corridors. **Pets:** Accepted.

Vista Inn & Suites SH
(501) 847-7120. **$65-$96.** 210 Office Park Dr. I-30, exit 123, just w. Ext corridors. **Pets:** Small. $10 daily fee/pet. Service with restrictions.

CAMDEN

Holiday Inn Express SH
(870) 836-8100. **$95-$105.** 1450 US Hwy 278 W. 1 mi w of jct US 79 and 278. Int corridors. **Pets:** Accepted.

CLARKSVILLE

Best Western Sherwood Inn SH
(479) 754-7900. **$45-$74.** 1203 S Rogers Ave. I-40, exit 58, just n. Ext corridors. **Pets:** Other species. Service with restrictions, supervision.

CONWAY

Best Western Conway SH
(501) 329-9855. **Call for rates.** 816 E Oak St. I-40, exit 127, just n. Ext corridors. **Pets:** Accepted.

Quality Inn SH
(501) 329-0300. **Call for rates.** 150 Hwy 65 N. I-40, exit 125, just n. Ext corridors. **Pets:** Small, other species. $25 one-time fee/pet. Designated rooms, service with restrictions, crate.

EL DORADO

La Quinta Inn El Dorado SH
(870) 863-6677. **$60.** 2303 Junction City Rd. Just e of jct US 167 and 82B. Ext/int corridors. **Pets:** Other species. Service with restrictions, supervision.

EUREKA SPRINGS

1886 Crescent Hotel & Spa SH
(479) 253-9766. **$109-$179, 3 day notice.** 75 Prospect Ave. 1.3 mi n of jct SR 23 on US 62B Historic Loop. Int corridors. **Pets:** Small, other species. $10 daily fee/pet. Service with restrictions, crate.

1905 Basin Park Hotel SH
(479) 253-7837. **Call for rates.** 12 Spring St. 0.7 mi n of jct US 62 via SR 23 N; downtown. Int corridors. **Pets:** Small, other species. $10 daily fee/pet. Designated rooms, service with restrictions, crate.

Arsenic & Old Lace B&B BB
(479) 253-5454. **$119-$269, 15 day notice.** 60 Hillside Ave. 1.2 mi n on SR 23, just sw; downtown. Ext/int corridors. **Pets:** Accepted.

Bavarian Inn SH
(479) 253-8128. **$68-$130, 3 day notice.** 325 W Van Buren St. 1 mi w of jct US 62 and SR 23. Ext corridors. **Pets:** Accepted.

Best Western-Eureka Inn SH
(479) 253-9551. **Call for rates.** 101 E Van Buren St. Just w of jct US 62 and SR 23 N. Ext/int corridors. **Pets:** Small, dogs only. $12 daily fee/pet. Designated rooms, service with restrictions, supervision.

Best Western Inn of the Ozarks SH
(479) 253-9768. **Call for rates.** 207 W Van Buren St. On US 62, 0.5 mi w of jct SR 23. Ext corridors. **Pets:** Large, dogs only. $10 one-time fee/pet. Service with restrictions, supervision.

Brackenridge Lodge M
(479) 253-6803. **$42-$149, 7 day notice.** 352 W Van Buren St. 1 mi w of jct US 62 and SR 23. Ext corridors. **Pets:** Accepted.

Budget Host Inn SH
(479) 253-7300. **$48-$150.** 154 Huntsville Rd. Just s of jct US 62 and SR 23. Ext/int corridors. **Pets:** Small. $4 daily fee/room. Designated rooms, supervision.

Days Inn M
(479) 253-8863. **$49-$179, 3 day notice.** 120 W Van Buren St. On US 62, just w of jct SR 23 N. Ext corridors. **Pets:** Accepted.

Howard Johnson Express SH
(479) 253-6665. **Call for rates.** 4042 E Van Buren St. 1.8 mi e of jct US 62 and SR 23. Ext corridors. **Pets:** Accepted.

Road Runner Inn & Cabins M
(479) 253-8166. **$69-$250, 30 day notice.** 3034 Mundell Rd. On US 62, 4.3 mi w, 3.9 mi s on SR 187, then 3 mi se. Ext corridors. **Pets:** Accepted.

Travelodge SH
(479) 253-8992. **Call for rates.** 110 Huntsville Dr. Jct US 62 and SR 23. Ext corridors. **Pets:** Accepted.

FAYETTEVILLE

Best Western Windsor Suites SH
(479) 587-1400. **$70-$79, 7 day notice.** 1122 S Futrall Dr. I-540, exit 62, just se. Ext corridors. **Pets:** Small, dogs only. $10 one-time fee/pet. Service with restrictions, supervision.

Quality Inn SH
(479) 444-9800. **$65-$120.** 523 S Shiloh Dr. I-540, exit 62, just w. Ext corridors. **Pets:** Accepted.

Sleep Inn by Choice Hotels SH
(479) 587-8700. **$69-$159.** 728 Millsap Rd. I-540, exit 67, 1.6 mi e, then just s on US 71B. Int corridors. **Pets:** Accepted.

FORDYCE

Days Inn SH
(870) 352-2400. **Call for rates.** 2500 W 4th St. On US 79/167; 1 mi w of center. Ext/int corridors. **Pets:** Accepted.

FORREST CITY

Holiday Inn SH
(870) 633-6300. **$81-$90.** 200 Holiday Dr. I-40, exit 241B, just n. Ext corridors. **Pets:** Accepted.

FORT SMITH

Aspen Hotel & Suites SH
(479) 452-9000. **$109-$120 (no credit cards).** 2900 S 68th St. I-540, exit 8B (Rogers Ave), just e. Int corridors. **Pets:** Accepted.

Baymont Inn & Suites Fort Smith SH
(479) 484-5770. **Call for rates.** 2123 Burnham Rd. I-540, exit 8A (Rogers Ave), just w. Int corridors. **Pets:** Other species. Service with restrictions.

Comfort Inn SH
(479) 484-0227. **$99-$169.** 2120 Burnham Rd. I-540, exit 8A (Rogers Ave), just w. Int corridors. **Pets:** Other species. Service with restrictions, crate.

Courtyard by Marriott Downtown Fort Smith SH
(479) 783-2100. **$121-$141.** 900 Rogers Ave. Just s of US 64 (Garrison Ave); downtown. Int corridors. **Pets:** Small, other species. $75 one-time fee/room. Designated rooms, service with restrictions, crate.

Holiday Inn City Center Fort Smith LH
(479) 783-1000. **$109-$149.** 700 Rogers Ave. Just s of US 64 (Garrison Ave); downtown. Int corridors. **Pets:** Accepted.

Holiday Inn Express SH
(479) 452-7500. **$100-$119.** 6813 Phoenix Ave. I-540, exit 8A (Rogers Ave), 0.6 mi e, then 0.5 mi s. Int corridors. **Pets:** Accepted.

Residence Inn by Marriott SH
(479) 478-8300. **$121-$141.** 3005 S 74th. I-540, exit 8A (Rogers Ave), 0.8 mi e. Int corridors. **Pets:** Accepted.

GENTRY

Apple Crest Inn Bed & Breakfast BB
(479) 736-8201. **$110-$180, 14 day notice.** 12758 S Hwy 59. On SR 59, 1 mi s. Int corridors. **Pets:** Accepted.

HARRISON

▼▼ Comfort Inn 🆂🅷
(870) 741-7676. **$65-$95.** 1210 Hwy 62/65 N. 1 mi n on US 62/65/412. Ext/int corridors. **Pets:** Accepted.
🅰🆂🅺 🆂🖥 ❌ 🛎 🖥 ⇆

▼▼▼ Holiday Inn Express Hotel & Suites 🆂🅷
(870) 741-3636. **$80-$125.** 117 Hwy 43 E. Just e from jct US 62/65/412 and SR 43. Int corridors. **Pets:** Accepted.
🅰🆂🅺 🆂🖥 ❌ 🛎 🖥 ⇆ ❌

HOPE

▲▲▲ ▼▼ Best Western of Hope 🆂🅷
(870) 777-9222. **Call for rates.** 1800 Holiday Dr. I-30, exit 30, just nw. Ext corridors. **Pets:** $15 one-time fee/room. Service with restrictions.
🆂🅰🆅🅴 ❌ 🛎 🖥 ⇆

HOT SPRINGS

▲▲▲ ▼▼▼▼ Clarion Resort 🆂🅷
(501) 525-1391. **$89-$229.** 4813 Central Ave. 5.5 mi s of jct US 270 and SR 7. Int corridors. **Pets:** Medium. $10 daily fee/room, $25 one-time fee/room. Designated rooms, service with restrictions, supervision.
🆂🅰🆅🅴 🆂🖥 ❌ 🛎 🖥 🍴 ⇆ ❌

▲▲▲ ▼▼▼▼ Embassy Suites Hot Springs 🅻🅷 🐾
(501) 624-9200. **$199.** 400 Convention Blvd. Just w of jct US 70. Int corridors. **Pets:** Medium. $35 daily fee/pet. Designated rooms, service with restrictions, crate.
🆂🅰🆅🅴 ❌ 🖥ᴹ 🛎 🖥 🍴 ⇆ ❌

▲▲▲ ▼▼ Traveller Inn Ⓜ
(501) 624-4681. **$38-$130.** 1045 E Grand Ave. 1 mi e of jct US 270B and 70. Ext corridors. **Pets:** Small. $15 deposit/pet. Service with restrictions, supervision.
🆂🅰🆅🅴 🆂🖥 ❌ 🛎 ⇆

JONESBORO

▲▲▲ ▼▼▼ Comfort Inn & Suites 🆂🅷
(870) 972-9000. **$75.** 2911 Gilmore Dr. US 63, exit Stadium Blvd/Caraway Rd, just n. Int corridors. **Pets:** Small, other species. $10 daily fee/pet. Service with restrictions, crate.
🆂🅰🆅🅴 🆂🖥 ❌ 🛎 🖥 ⇆

▼▼▼ Holiday Inn Express 🆂🅷
(870) 932-5554. **Call for rates.** 2407 Phillips Dr. US 63, exit Stadium Blvd/Caraway Rd, just n. Int corridors. **Pets:** Accepted.
❌ 🛎 🖥 ⇆

▼▼▼ Holiday Inn of Jonesboro 🆂🅷 🐾
(870) 935-2030. **$60-$85.** 3006 S Caraway Rd. US 63, exit Stadium Blvd/Caraway Rd, just n. Ext/int corridors. **Pets:** Medium. $20 deposit/pet, $20 daily fee/pet. Service with restrictions, supervision.
🅰🆂🅺 🆂🖥 ❌ 🛎 🖥 🍴 ⇆ ❌

LITTLE ROCK

▼▼ Airport Travelodge 🆂🅷
(501) 490-2200. **Call for rates.** 7615 Fluid Dr. I-440, exit 5, just n. Ext corridors. **Pets:** Accepted.
❌ 🛎 🖥

▲▲▲ ▼▼▼▼ Comfort Inn & Suites, Downtown Little Rock @ The Clinton Library 🆂🅷
(501) 687-7700. **$79-$119.** 707 I-30. I-30, exit 140A, just e. Int corridors. **Pets:** Small. $25 one-time fee/room. Service with restrictions, supervision.
🆂🅰🆅🅴 🆂🖥 ❌ 🖥ᴹ 🛎 🖥 ⇆

▲▲▲ ▼▼▼▼ Embassy Suites Hotel Little Rock 🅻🅷
(501) 312-9000. **$119-$229.** 11301 Financial Center Pkwy. Jct I-430 and 630, just w. Int corridors. **Pets:** Accepted.
🆂🅰🆅🅴 ❌ 🖥ᴹ 🛎 🖥 🍴 ⇆ ❌

▼▼▼▼ La Quinta Inn 🆂🅷
(501) 225-7007. **$74-$94.** 1010 Breckenridge Rd. I-430, exit 8, just e to Breckenridge Rd, then just s. Int corridors. **Pets:** Other species. Service with restrictions, supervision.
🅰🆂🅺 🆂🖥 ❌ 🛎 🖥 ⇆

▼▼▼▼ La Quinta Inn Little Rock (West) 🆂🅷
(501) 224-0900. **$82.** 200 S Shackleford Rd. I-430, exit 6; I-630, exit Shackleford Rd N; jct I-430 and 630. Ext corridors. **Pets:** Other species. Service with restrictions, supervision.
🅰🆂🅺 🆂🖥 ❌ ⇆

LONOKE

▲▲▲ ▼▼ Days Inn 🆂🅷
(501) 676-5138. **$60-$75.** 105 Dee Dee Ln. I-40, exit 175, just n. Ext corridors. **Pets:** Medium, other species. $10 daily fee/pet. Designated rooms, service with restrictions, supervision.
🆂🅰🆅🅴 🆂🖥 ❌ 🛎 🖥 ⇆

▲▲▲ ▼▼▼▼ Holiday Inn Express Hotel & Suites 🆂🅷
(501) 676-7800. **$89-$99.** 104 Dee Dee Ln. I-40, exit 175, just n. Int corridors. **Pets:** Small, other species. $25 one-time fee/pet. Designated rooms, service with restrictions, supervision.
🆂🅰🆅🅴 🆂🖥 ❌ 🖥ᴹ 🛎 🖥 ⇆

▲▲▲ ▼▼▼ Super 8 Motel 🆂🅷 🐾
(501) 676-8880. **Call for rates.** 102 Dee Dee Ln. I-40, exit 175, just n. Int corridors. **Pets:** Medium. $10 daily fee/pet. Designated rooms, service with restrictions, supervision.
🆂🅰🆅🅴 ❌ 🛎 🖥 ⇆

MARION

▼▼ Best Western-Regency Motor Inn 🆂🅷
(870) 739-3278. **Call for rates.** 3635 I-55. I-55, exit 10, just nw. Ext corridors. **Pets:** Medium. Service with restrictions, supervision.
❌ 🛎 🖥 ⇆

MAUMELLE

▼▼▼ Quality Inn-Maumelle 🆂🅷
(501) 851-3500. **Call for rates.** 14325 Frontier Dr. I-40, exit 142, just sw. Ext corridors. **Pets:** Accepted.
❌ 🛎 🖥 ⇆

MCGEHEE

▲▲▲ ▼▼▼ Best Western McGehee Ⓜ
(870) 222-3564. **Call for rates.** 1202 Hwy 65 N. Center. Ext corridors. **Pets:** Very small, dogs only. $5 one-time fee/pet. Designated rooms, service with restrictions, supervision.
🆂🅰🆅🅴 ❌ 🛎 🖥 ⇆

MOUNTAIN HOME

▼▼ Days Inn 🆂🅷
(870) 425-1010. **Call for rates.** 1746 E Hwy 62B. On US 62B, 2.3 mi e. Int corridors. **Pets:** Accepted.
❌ 🖥ᴹ 🛎 🖥 ⇆

▼▼▼ Holiday Inn Express 🆂🅷
(870) 425-6200. **$95.** 1005 Coley Dr. 1.4 mi e on US 62B. Int corridors. **Pets:** Accepted.
🅰🆂🅺 🆂🖥 ❌ 🖥ᴹ 🛎 🖥 ⇆

▼▼ Super 8 Motel-Mountain Home Ⓜ
(870) 424-5600. **Call for rates.** 865 Hwy 62 E. 1.3 mi e on US 62B. Int corridors. **Pets:** Accepted.
❌ 🛎

▲▲▲ ▼▼▼ Teal Point Resort 🅲🅰
(870) 492-5145. **$72-$389, 45 day notice.** 715 Teal Point Rd. 7 mi e on US 62, 0.6 mi n on CR 406, follow signs. Ext corridors. **Pets:** $7 daily fee/pet. Service with restrictions, supervision.
🆂🅰🆅🅴 🛎 ⇆ ❌ 🏧

MOUNTAIN VIEW

 Best Western Fiddlers Inn Ⓜ
(870) 269-2828. **Call for rates.** 601 Sylomore. 1 mi n on SR 5, 9 and 14. Ext corridors. **Pets:** Dogs only. $10 one-time fee/pet. Service with restrictions, supervision.

NORTH LITTLE ROCK

 Hampton Inn ⑤Ⓗ
(501) 771-2090. **Call for rates.** 500 W 29th St. I-40, exit 152. Int corridors. **Pets:** Accepted.

Holiday Inn-North ⑤Ⓗ
(501) 758-1851. **$120-$130.** 120 W Pershing Blvd. I-40, exit 152 westbound; exit 153A eastbound. Int corridors. **Pets:** Accepted.

La Quinta Inn ⑤Ⓗ
(501) 758-8888. **$85-$89.** 4100 E McCain Blvd. Jct US 67/167, exit 1A northbound; exit 1 southbound. Ext corridors. **Pets:** Other species. Service with restrictions, supervision.

La Quinta Inn & Suites ⑤Ⓗ
(501) 945-0808. **$99-$104.** 4311 Warden Rd. US 67/167, exit 1B northbound; exit 1 southbound. Int corridors. **Pets:** Other species. Service with restrictions, supervision.

 Red Roof Inn ⑤Ⓗ
(501) 945-0080. **Call for rates.** 5711 Pritchard Dr. I-40, exit 157, just s. Int corridors. **Pets:** Accepted.

Residence Inn by Marriott-North ⑤Ⓗ
(501) 945-7777. **$144-$164.** 4110 Healthcare Dr. I-40, exit 156. Int corridors. **Pets:** Accepted.

PINE BLUFF

 Best Western Presidential Hotel ⑤Ⓗ
(870) 535-6300. **$66-$73, 3 day notice.** 3104 Market St. I-530, exit 46, just n. Int corridors. **Pets:** Accepted.

Comfort Inn ⑤Ⓗ
(870) 535-5300. **$55-$99.** 2809 Pines Mall Dr. I-530, exit 46, just n. Int corridors. **Pets:** Accepted.

Days Inn & Suites ⑤Ⓗ
(870) 534-1800. **Call for rates.** 406 N Blake St. Just n of jct US 65B and 79B. Ext corridors. **Pets:** Accepted.

Holiday Inn Express Hotel & Suites ⑤Ⓗ
(870) 879-3800. **$86.** 3620 Camden Rd. I-530, exit 39, just sw. Int corridors. **Pets:** Accepted.

POCAHONTAS

Days Inn & Suites ⑤Ⓗ
(870) 892-9500. **Call for rates.** 2805 Hwy 67 S. 1.7 mi s. Int corridors. **Pets:** Accepted.

ROGERS

Candlewood Suites ⑤Ⓗ
(479) 636-2783. **$99-$109.** 4601 W Rozell St. I-540, exit 85, 0.5 mi n on 46th St. Int corridors. **Pets:** Accepted.

 Embassy Suites Northwest Arkansas Ⓗ ✿
(479) 254-8400. **$129-$249.** 3303 Pinnacle Hills Pkwy. I-540, exit 83, just w, then 0.6 mi s. Int corridors. **Pets:** Large. $75 one-time fee/room. Designated rooms, service with restrictions, crate.

Residence Inn by Marriott ⑤Ⓗ
(479) 636-5900. **$187-$207.** 4611 W Locust St. I-540, exit 85, 0.4 mi n on 46th St. Int corridors. **Pets:** Accepted.

RUSSELLVILLE

Comfort Inn Ⓜ
(479) 967-7500. **$65-$90.** 3019 E Parkway Dr. I-40, exit 84, just s. Ext corridors. **Pets:** Accepted.

Motel 6 Russellville #265 Ⓜ
(479) 968-3666. **Call for rates.** 215 W Birch St. I-40, exit 81, just n. Ext corridors. **Pets:** Other species. Service with restrictions, supervision.

 Super 8 Motel-Russellville ⑤Ⓗ
(479) 968-8898. **$59-$69.** 2404 N Arkansas Ave. I-40, exit 81, just s. Int corridors. **Pets:** Medium. $10 daily fee/pet, $10 one-time fee/pet. Service with restrictions, supervision.

SEARCY

Hampton Inn ⑤Ⓗ
(501) 268-0654. **Call for rates.** 3204 E Race Ave. US 67, exit 46, just w. Ext/int corridors. **Pets:** Accepted.

SILOAM SPRINGS

Super 8 Motel Ⓜ
(479) 524-8898. **$63-$70.** 1800 Hwy 412 W. Center. Ext corridors. **Pets:** Accepted.

SPRINGDALE

Hampton Inn & Suites ⑤Ⓗ
(479) 756-3500. **Call for rates.** 1700 S 48th St. I-540, exit 72, just e. Int corridors. **Pets:** Accepted.

Holiday Inn Northwest AR Hotel & Convention Center Ⓗ
(479) 751-8300. **$129.** 1500 S 48th St. I-540, exit 72, just e on US 412. Int corridors. **Pets:** Accepted.

Residence Inn by Marriott ⑤Ⓗ
(479) 872-9100. **$132-$152.** 1740 S 48th St. I-540, exit 72, just e to 48th St, then just s. Int corridors. **Pets:** Medium, other species. $75 one-time fee/room. Service with restrictions.

STAR CITY

Super 8 Motel-Star City ⑤Ⓗ
(870) 628-6883. **Call for rates.** 1308 N Lincoln St. Just n on US 425. Int corridors. **Pets:** Accepted.

STUTTGART

 Days Inn & Suites 🅢🅗
(870) 673-3616. **Call for rates.** 708 W Michigan. Just w on US 63/79. Ext corridors. **Pets:** $10 one-time fee/pet. Service with restrictions, supervision.

TEXARKANA

La Quinta Inn & Suites 🅢🅗
(870) 773-1000. **Call for rates.** 5102 N State Line Ave. I-30, exit 223B, just n. Int corridors. **Pets:** Other species. Service with restrictions, supervision.

Remington Hotel 🅢🅗 🐾
(870) 774-3521. **$109-$250.** 5100 N State Line Ave. I-30, exit 223B, just n. Int corridors. **Pets:** Small, other species. $50 one-time fee/pet. Service with restrictions, supervision.

TRUMANN

 Days Inn & Suites 🅢🅗
(870) 483-8383. **$75.** 400 Commerce Dr. US 63, exit 29, just e. Ext/int corridors. **Pets:** Other species. $10 daily fee/pet. Service with restrictions, supervision.

VAN BUREN

Best Western Van Buren Inn 🅢🅗
(479) 474-8100. **$82, 14 day notice.** 1903 N 6th St. I-40, exit 5, just n. Ext corridors. **Pets:** Accepted.

WEST HELENA

Best Western Inn 🅢🅗
(870) 572-2592. **Call for rates.** 1053 Hwy 49 W. US 49, 3 mi w. Ext corridors. **Pets:** Small. $20 deposit/room. Designated rooms, service with restrictions, supervision.

CALIFORNIA

CITY INDEX

ALAMEDA

 Extended StayAmerica Oakland-Alameda 🅂🄷
(510) 864-1333. **$117-$130.** 1350 Marina Village Pkwy. I-880, exit Broadway W, through Webster Tube, s on Atlantic Ave, e on Challenger Dr, then s. Int corridors. **Pets:** Other species. $75 one-time fee/pet. Service with restrictions.

Ⓐ🅂�😾 ☒ 🄼 📶 💻

ALTURAS

 Best Western Trailside Inn 🅼
(530) 233-4111. **$72-$90.** 343 N Main St. On US 395. Ext corridors. **Pets:** Medium, dogs only. $10 daily fee/pet. Designated rooms, service with restrictions, supervision.

🆂🅰🆅🅴 🅂🅾 ☒ 📶 💻 🐾

AAA ▼▼ Rim Rock Motel M
(530) 233-5455. **$58-$75.** Hwy 299. Just e on SR 299 from US 395.
Ext corridors. **Pets:** Small, dogs only. $10 daily fee/room. Designated
rooms, service with restrictions, supervision.
SAVE ✕ 🖥 📺

AAA ▼▼▼ Super 8 Motel M
(530) 233-3545. **$72-$112.** 511 N Main St. On US 395. Ext corridors.
Pets: Dogs only. Service with restrictions, supervision.
SAVE 🕬 ✕ 🖥 📺

ANAHEIM

AAA ▼▼▼ Anabella Hotel SH
(714) 905-1050. **$99-$349, 7 day notice.** 1030 W Katella Ave. I-5, exit
109 (Katella Ave/Disney Way); exit 109A (Katella Ave/
Orangewood Ave) southbound, 1.2 mi w. Ext corridors. **Pets:** Accepted.
SAVE 🕬 ✕ 🖥 📺 🍴 🏊

▼▼▼ Anaheim Candlewood Suites SH
(714) 808-9000. **$149-$199.** 1733 S Anaheim Blvd. I-5, exit 109 (Katella
Ave/Disney Way) northbound; 109A (Katella Ave/Orangewood Ave)
southbound, just w, then just n. Int corridors. **Pets:** Accepted.
ASK 🕬 ✕ 🖥 📺 🏊 ✕

▼▼▼ Anaheim Marriott Hotel LH
(714) 750-8000. **$352-$372.** 700 W Convention Way. I-5, exit 109
(Katella Ave/Disney Way) northbound; exit 109A (Katella Ave/
Orangewood Ave) southbound, 0.8 mi w on Katella Ave, just s on
Harbor Blvd, then just w. Int corridors. **Pets:** Accepted.
ASK 🕬 ✕ 🖥 🖥 📺 🍴 🏊 ✕

AAA ▼▼▼ Anaheim Plaza Hotel & Suites SH
(714) 772-5900. **$89-$218.** 1700 S Harbor Blvd. I-5, exit 110 (Harbor
Blvd/Ball Rd) northbound; exit 110A (Harbor Blvd) southbound, 0.6 mi
s. Ext corridors. **Pets:** Medium. $12 daily fee/pet. Designated rooms,
service with restrictions, supervision.
SAVE 🕬 ✕ 🖥 📺 🍴 🏊

AAA ▼▼▼ Clarion Hotel Anaheim Resort LH
(714) 750-3131. **$69-$199.** 616 Convention Way. I-5, exit 109 (Katella
Ave/Disney Way) northbound; exit 109A (Katella Ave/Orangewood
Ave) southbound, 0.8 mi w to Harbor Blvd, just s, then just w. Int
corridors. **Pets:** Accepted.
SAVE 🕬 ✕ 🖥 📺 🍴 🏊

AAA ▼▼▼ Embassy Suites Hotel Anaheim-North LH
(714) 632-1221. **Call for rates.** 3100 E Frontera St. SR 91, exit 31
(Kraemer Blvd/Glassell St) eastbound; exit 32 westbound just s, then
just e. Int corridors. **Pets:** Accepted.
SAVE ✕ 🖥 📺 🍴 🏊 ✕

**▼▼ Extended StayAmerica-Orange County-Anaheim
Convention Center SH**
(714) 502-9988. **$84-$114.** 1742 S Clementine St. I-5, exit 109 (Katella
Ave/Disney Way) northbound; exit 109A (Katella Ave/Orangewood
Ave) southbound, just w, then just n. Int corridors. **Pets:** Other species.
$75 one-time fee/pet. Service with restrictions.
ASK 🕬 ✕ 🖥 📺

**▼▼ Extended StayAmerica-Orange County-Anaheim
Hills SH**
(714) 630-4006. **$84-$104.** 1031 N Pacificenter Dr. SR 91, exit 33
(Tustin Ave), just n, then just w. Int corridors. **Pets:** Other species. $75
one-time fee/pet. Service with restrictions.
ASK 🕬 ✕ 🖥 📺

▼▼▼ Hotel Menage SH
(714) 758-9000. **$109-$229.** 1221 S Harbor Blvd. I-5, exit 110 (Harbor
Blvd/Ball Rd) northbound; exit 110 a (Harbor Blvd) southbound, just n.
Ext corridors. **Pets:** Accepted.
ASK 🕬 ✕ 🖥 📺 🍴 🏊

▼▼ ▼▼ La Quinta Inn and Suites SH
(714) 635-5000. **$139-$179.** 1752 S Clementine St. I-5, exit 109
(Katella Ave/Disney Way) northbound; exit 109A (Katella Ave/
Orangewood Ave) southbound, just w, then just n. Int corridors.
Pets: Other species. Service with restrictions, supervision.
ASK 🕬 ✕ 🖥 📺 🏊 ✕

AAA ▼▼▼ Lemon Tree Hotel M
(714) 772-0200. **Call for rates.** 1600 E Lincoln Ave. I-5, exit 111 (Lincoln Ave), 2 mi e. Ext/int corridors. **Pets:** Very small, dogs only. $15 daily
fee/pet. Service with restrictions, supervision.
SAVE ✕ 🖥 📺 🏊

▼▼▼ Motel 6 Anaheim-Maingate M
(714) 520-9696. **Call for rates.** 100 Disney Way. I-5, exit 109 (Katella
Ave/Disney Way) northbound; exit 109B (Disney Way/Anaheim Blvd)
southbound, just w. Ext corridors. **Pets:** Other species. Service with
restrictions, supervision.
✕ 🖥 🏊

**AAA ▼▼▼ Residence Inn by Marriott Anaheim
Maingate SH**
(714) 533-3555. **$209-$229.** 1700 S Clementine St. I-5, exit 109
(Katella Ave/Disney Way) northbound; exit 109A (Katella Ave/
Orangewood Ave) southbound, just w on Katella Ave, then just n. Ext
corridors. **Pets:** Accepted.
SAVE 🕬 ✕ 🖥 🖥 📺 🏊 ✕

AAA ▼▼▼ Sheraton Anaheim Hotel LH 🐾
(714) 778-1700. **$145-$285.** 900 S Disneyland Dr. I-5, exit 110 (Harbor
Blvd/Ball Rd) northbound; exit 110A (Harbor Blvd) southbound, just n
on Harbor Blvd, just w on Ball Rd, then just n. Int corridors. **Pets:** Other
species. $25 daily fee/room. Service with restrictions.
SAVE ✕ 🖥 📺 🍴 🏊 ✕

**AAA ▼▼▼ Sheraton Park Hotel at the Anaheim
Resort LH** 🐾
(714) 750-1811. **$129-$275, 3 day notice.** 1855 S Harbor Blvd. I-5, exit
109 (Katella Ave/Disney Way) northbound; exit 109A (Katella Ave/
Orangewood Ave) southbound, 0.8 mi w, then just s. Int corridors.
Pets: Medium. Designated rooms, service with restrictions.
SAVE 🕬 ✕ 🖥 📺 🍴 🏊 ✕

**AAA ▼▼▼ Staybridge Suites by Holiday Inn-Anaheim
Resort SH**
(714) 748-7700. **Call for rates.** 1855 S Manchester Ave. I-5, exit 109
(Katella Ave/Disney Way) northbound; exit 109A (Katella Ave/
Orangewood Ave) southbound, just w on Katella Ave, then 0.3 mi s;
adjacent to west side of freeway. Int corridors. **Pets:** Accepted.
SAVE ✕ 🖥 📺 🏊 ✕

AAA ▼▼▼ TownePlace Suites By Marriott M
(714) 939-9700. **$79-$189.** 1730 S State College Blvd. I-5, exit 109
(Katella Ave/Disney Way) northbound; exit 109A (Katella Ave/
Orangewood Ave) southbound, 0.7 mi e, then just n. Int corridors.
Pets: Other species. $100 one-time fee/room. Service with restrictions,
supervision.
SAVE 🕬 ✕ 🖥 📺 🏊 ✕

ANAHEIM HILLS

▼▼▼ Best Western Anaheim Hills M
(714) 779-0252. **$74-$129.** 5710 E La Palma Ave. SR 91, exit 36
(Imperial Hwy), 0.3 mi n. Ext/int corridors. **Pets:** Accepted.
ASK 🕬 ✕ 🖥 📺 🏊 ✕

ANDERSON

AAA ▼▼▼ AmeriHost Inn-Anderson SH
(530) 365-6100. **$80-$100.** 2040 Factory Outlet Dr. I-5, exit Factory
Outlet Dr, just w. Int corridors. **Pets:** Accepted.
SAVE 🕬 ✕ 🖥 🖥 📺 🏊 ✕

ANGELS CAMP

AAA⧸ ◈◈◈ Angels Inn Motel SH
(209) 736-4242. **$95-$145.** 600 N Main St. SR 49, north end of town. Ext corridors. **Pets:** Dogs only. $10 daily fee/pet. Designated rooms, service with restrictions, supervision.
SAVE ⊠ 🛏 📺 ➰

AAA⧸ ◈◈◈◈ Best Western Cedar Inn & Suites SH
(209) 736-4000. **Call for rates.** 444 S Main St. On SR 49; center. Ext/int corridors. **Pets:** Accepted.
SAVE ⊠ ♿ 🛏 📺 ➰

AAA⧸ ◈◈◈ Gold Country Inn M
(209) 736-4611. **$60-$190.** 720 S Main St. 1 mi s of jct SR 49 and 4. Ext corridors. **Pets:** Medium. $10 daily fee/pet. Service with restrictions, supervision.
SAVE S📶 ⊠ 🛏 📺

AAA⧸ ◈◈ Jumping Frog Motel M
(209) 736-2191. **$60-$150, 3 day notice.** 330 Murphys Grade Rd. SR 49, n of Angels Camp Center, just left. Ext corridors. **Pets:** Small, dogs only. $12 one-time fee/pet. Service with restrictions, supervision.
SAVE S📶 ⊠ 🛏 📺

ANTIOCH

AAA⧸ ◈◈◈◈ Best Western Heritage Inn M
(925) 778-2000. **$94-$104.** 3210 Delta Fair Blvd. SR 4, exit Somersville Rd. Ext corridors. **Pets:** Dogs only. $15 one-time fee/pet. Service with restrictions, supervision.
SAVE S📶 ⊠ 🛏 📺 ➰

APTOS

◈◈ Bayview Hotel CI
(831) 688-8654. **Call for rates.** 8041 Soquel Dr. SR 1, exit State Park Dr E, 0.8 mi s. Int corridors. **Pets:** Accepted.
⊠ 🍴

ARCATA

AAA⧸ ◈◈ Arcata Super 8 SH
(707) 822-8888. **Call for rates.** 4887 Valley West Blvd. US 101, exit Giuntoli Ln/Janes Rd, just e, then just s. Int corridors. **Pets:** Accepted.
SAVE ⊠ 🛏 📺

AAA⧸ ◈◈◈ Best Western Arcata Inn M 🐾
(707) 826-0313. **$69-$175.** 4827 Valley West Blvd. US 101, exit Giuntoli Ln/Janes Rd, just e, then just s. Ext corridors. **Pets:** Dogs only. $20 one-time fee/room. Service with restrictions, supervision.
SAVE S📶 ⊠ 🛏 📺 ➰

AAA⧸ ◈◈◈ Comfort Inn M
(707) 826-2827. **$65-$185.** 4701 Valley West Blvd. US 101, exit Giuntoli Ln/Janes Rd, just e, then 0.3 mi s. Ext corridors. **Pets:** Medium, dogs only. $15 one-time fee/pet. Designated rooms, supervision.
SAVE S📶 ⊠ ♿ 🛏 📺 ➰

AAA⧸ ◈◈◈ Days Inn SH 🐾
(707) 822-4861. **$65-$169.** 4975 Valley West Blvd. US 101, exit Giuntoli Ln/Janes Rd, just e, then s. Int corridors. **Pets:** Medium. $35 one-time fee/room. Designated rooms, service with restrictions, supervision.
SAVE S📶 ⊠ 🛏 📺

AAA⧸ ◈◈◈ Hotel Arcata SH
(707) 826-0217. **Call for rates.** 708 9th St. Corner of G St; downtown; in Plaza. Int corridors. **Pets:** Other species. $50 deposit/pet, $5 daily fee/pet. Service with restrictions, supervision.
SAVE ⊠ 📺 🍴 🏋

AAA⧸ ◈◈◈ Quality Inn Arcata SH
(707) 822-0409. **$79-$220.** 3535 Janes Rd. US 101, exit Giuntoli Ln/Janes Rd, just w. Int corridors. **Pets:** Other species. $10 daily fee/pet. Designated rooms, service with restrictions, crate.
SAVE S📶 ⊠ 🛏 📺 ➰ ⊠

ARROYO GRANDE

AAA⧸ ◈◈◈ Premier Inns M
(805) 481-4774. **$40-$80.** 555 Camino Mercado. US 101, exit 188 (Oak Park Rd), just e, then 0.3 mi s. Ext corridors. **Pets:** Accepted.
SAVE S📶 ⊠ 🛏 ➰

AUBURN

AAA⧸ ◈◈◈◈ Best Western Golden Key SH 🐾
(530) 885-8611. **$90-$135.** 13450 Lincoln Way. I-80, exit Foresthill Rd. Ext corridors. **Pets:** Other species. $15 one-time fee/pet. Designated rooms, service with restrictions, supervision.
SAVE S📶 ⊠ ♿ 🛏 📺

AAA⧸ ◈◈ Foothills Motel M
(530) 885-8444. **$65-$98.** 13431 Bowman Rd. I-80, exit Foresthill Rd. Ext corridors. **Pets:** Dogs only. $50 deposit/room, $10 daily fee/pet. Designated rooms, service with restrictions, supervision.
SAVE S📶 ⊠ 🛏 📺 ➰

AAA⧸ ◈◈◈◈ Holiday Inn-Auburn SH
(530) 887-8787. **$139-$179.** 120 Grass Valley Hwy. I-80, exit SR 49. Int corridors. **Pets:** Small, dogs only. $20 daily fee/pet. Designated rooms, service with restrictions, supervision.
SAVE ⊠ ♿ 🛏 📺 ➰

AAA⧸ ◈◈ Motel 6 #4152 M
(530) 888-7829. **$60-$72.** 1819 Auburn Ravine Rd. I-80, exit Foresthill and Auburn Ravine rds. Int corridors. **Pets:** Designated rooms, service with restrictions, supervision.
SAVE S📶 ⊠ ♿ 🛏 ➰

AAA⧸ ◈◈◈ Travelodge M
(530) 885-7025. **$90-$140.** 13490 Lincoln Way. I-80, exit Foresthill Rd. Ext/int corridors. **Pets:** Very small. $15 daily fee/pet. Designated rooms, service with restrictions, supervision.
SAVE S📶 ⊠ ♿ 🛏 📺 ➰

AVILA BEACH

◈◈◈ Avila Village Inn SH
(805) 627-1810. **$100-$350.** 6655 Bay Laurel Dr. US 101, exit 195 (Avila Beach Dr), 1.2 mi w to San Luis Bay Dr, just n, then just w. Int corridors. **Pets:** Accepted.
ASK S📶 ⊠ ♿ 🛏 📺

BAKERSFIELD

◈◈◈ Bakersfield Red Lion Hotel SH
(661) 327-0681. **$120-$300.** 2400 Camino Del Rio Ct. SR 99, exit 26 (SR 58 W/Rosedale Hwy), just w, then just s. Ext/int corridors. **Pets:** Accepted.
ASK S📶 ⊠ 🛏 📺 🍴 ➰

AAA⧸ ◈◈◈ Best Western Crystal Palace Inn & Suites SH
(661) 327-9651. **$89-$149.** 2620 Buck Owens Blvd. SR 99, exit 26B (Buck Owens Blvd) northbound, just s; exit 26 (SR 58 W/SR 178 E) southbound, just e, then just n. Int corridors. **Pets:** Accepted.
SAVE S📶 ⊠ ♿ 🛏 📺 🍴 ➰

AAA⧸ ◈◈◈ Best Western Heritage Inn M
(661) 764-6268. **$68-$129.** 253 Trask St. I-5, exit 253 (Stockdale Hwy), just e. Ext corridors. **Pets:** Accepted.
SAVE S📶 ⊠ ♿ 🛏 📺 ➰

Best Western Hill House SH ❀
(661) 327-4064. **$79-$139.** 700 Truxton Ave. SR 99, exit 25 (California Ave), 1.2 mi e, 0.4 mi n on Chester Ave, then 0.4 mi e. Int corridors. **Pets:** Medium. $15 one-time fee/pet. Designated rooms, service with restrictions, supervision.
SAVE S⊖ ⊠ 🛡 💻 ❬❭ ⇆

California Best Inn M
(661) 834-3377. **$59-$69.** 1030 Wible Rd. SR 99, exit 23 (Ming Ave), just e, then 0.7 mi n. Ext corridors. **Pets:** Very small. $50 deposit/pet, $10 daily fee/pet. Service with restrictions, supervision.
SAVE S⊖ ⊠ 🛡 💻 ⇆

DoubleTree Hotel Bakersfield LH
(661) 323-7111. **$215-$250.** 3100 Camino Del Rio Ct. SR 99, exit 26 (SR 58 W/Rosedale Hwy), just w, then just s. Int corridors. **Pets:** Accepted.
ASK S⊖ ⊠ 🔥M 🛡 💻 ❬❭ ⇆ ⊠

Econo Lodge Bakersfield M ❀
(661) 392-1511. **$45-$89.** 5200 Olive Tree Ct. SR 99, exit 28 (Olive Dr), just w, then just n on Knudson Dr. Ext corridors. **Pets:** Other species. $6 daily fee/pet. Service with restrictions, supervision.
ASK S⊖ ⊠ 🛡 💻 ⇆

Extended StayAmerica-Bakersfield-California Avenue SH
(661) 322-6888. **$67-$77.** 3318 California Ave. SR 99, exit 25 (California Ave), on east side of freeway, just n. Int corridors. **Pets:** Other species. $75 one-time fee/pet. Service with restrictions.
ASK S⊖ ⊠ 🛡 💻

Extended Stay Deluxe SH
(661) 328-8181. **$90-$100.** 3600 Chester Ln. SR 99, exit 25 (California Ave), just w to Real Rd, just s, then just w. Int corridors. **Pets:** Other species. $75 one-time fee/pet. Service with restrictions.
ASK S⊖ ⊠ 🔥M 🛡 💻

La Quinta Inn & Suites SH
(661) 393-7775. **$120-$140.** 8858 Spectrum Park Way. SR 99, exit 30 (SR 65) northbound, just n to 7th Standard Rd, just w, then just s; exit 31 (7th Standard Rd) southbound, just e, then just s. Int corridors. **Pets:** Other species. Service with restrictions, supervision.
ASK S⊖ ⊠ 🔥M 🛡 💻 ⇆

La Quinta Inn Bakersfield M
(661) 325-7400. **$99-$125.** 3232 Riverside Dr. SR 99, exit 26 (SR 58 W/Rosedale Hwy) southbound, just e, then just n; exit 26B (Buck Owens Blvd) northbound, just s. Ext corridors. **Pets:** Other species. Service with restrictions, supervision.
ASK S⊖ ⊠ 🔥M 🛡 💻 ⇆

Ramada Limited-Central M ❀
(661) 831-1922. **$59-$199.** 830 Wible Rd. SR 99, exit 23 (Ming Ave), just e, then 0.8 mi n. Int corridors. **Pets:** Other species. $10 daily fee/pet. Service with restrictions, crate.
SAVE S⊖ ⊠ 🛡 💻 ⇆

Residence Inn by Marriott SH
(661) 321-9800. **$198-$218.** 4241 Chester Ln. SR 99, exit 25 (California Ave), 0.5 mi w, then just n. Ext corridors. **Pets:** Accepted.
ASK S⊖ ⊠ 🔥M 🛡 💻 ⇆ ⊠

Rodeway Inn M
(661) 764-5221. **$65-$75.** 200 Trask St. I-5, exit 253 (Stockdale Hwy), just e. Ext corridors. **Pets:** Medium. $5 daily fee/pet. Designated rooms, service with restrictions, supervision.
SAVE S⊖ ⊠ 🛡 ⇆

Super 8 M
(661) 833-1000. **$55-$85.** 3620 Wible Rd. SR 99, exit 21 (White Ln), just w, then 0.3 mi n. Ext corridors. **Pets:** Medium. $5 daily fee/pet. Service with restrictions, supervision.
SAVE S⊖ ⊠ 🛡 💻 ⇆

Super 8 Motel Bakersfield M
(661) 322-1012. **Call for rates.** 901 Real Rd. SR 99, exit 25 (California Ave), just w, then just s. Ext corridors. **Pets:** Small. $10 daily fee/pet. Designated rooms, service with restrictions, supervision.
SAVE ⊠ 🛡 ⇆

Travelodge of Bakersfield M
(661) 325-0772. **$64-$72.** 1011 Oak St. SR 99, exit 25 (California Ave), just e, then just s. Ext/int corridors. **Pets:** Accepted.
ASK S⊖ ⊠ 🛡 💻 ⇆

Vagabond Inn South M
(661) 831-9200. **$45-$65.** 6501 Colony St. SR 99, exit 20 (Panama Ln), just e, then just s. Ext corridors. **Pets:** Dogs only. $5 daily fee/pet. Service with restrictions, supervision.
SAVE S⊖ ⊠ 🛡 💻 ⇆

BANNING

Banning Travelodge M
(951) 849-1000. **Call for rates.** 1700 W Ramsey St. I-10, exit 99 (22nd St), just n, then 0.5 mi e. Ext corridors. **Pets:** Medium, dogs only. $10 daily fee/pet. Designated rooms, service with restrictions, supervision.
SAVE ⊠ 🛡 💻 ⇆

Days Inn M
(951) 849-0092. **Call for rates.** 2320 W Ramsey St. I-10, exit 99 (22nd St), just n, then just w. Ext corridors. **Pets:** Accepted.
⊠ 🛡 💻 ⇆

Super 8 Motel M
(951) 849-8888. **Call for rates.** 1690 W Ramsey St. I-10, exit 99 (22nd St), just n, then 0.4 mi e. Int corridors. **Pets:** Medium, dogs only. $10 daily fee/pet. Designated rooms, service with restrictions, supervision.
SAVE ⊠ 🛡 💻 ⇆

BARSTOW

Barstow-Super 8 Motel M
(760) 256-8443. **$72-$77.** 170 Coolwater Ln. I-15, exit 184B (E Main St) northbound; exit 184 (E Main St/I-40 E/Needles) southbound, 0.3 mi w, then just s; I-40 westbound, exit 1 (E Main St), 0.7 mi w, then just s. Ext corridors. **Pets:** $5 daily fee/pet. Service with restrictions, supervision.
SAVE S⊖ ⊠ 🛡 💻 ⇆

Best Western Desert Villa Inn M
(760) 256-1781. **$89-$149.** 1984 E Main St. I-15, exit 184B (E Main St) northbound; exit 184 (E Main St/I-40/Needles) southbound, 0.5 mi e; I-40 westbound, exit 1 (E Main St), just w. Ext corridors. **Pets:** $15 one-time fee/pet. Service with restrictions, supervision.
SAVE S⊖ ⊠ 🔥M 🛡 💻 ⇆

Days Inn M
(760) 256-1737. **Call for rates.** 1590 Coolwater Ln. I-15, exit 184B (E Main St) northbound; exit 184 (E Main St/I-40 E/Needles) southbound, just w, then just s; I-40, exit 1 (E Main St) westbound, 0.7 mi w, then just s. Ext corridors. **Pets:** Small. $10 daily fee/pet. Service with restrictions, supervision.
SAVE ⊠ 🛡 💻 ⇆

Holiday Inn Express, Barstow-Historic Route 66 SH
(760) 256-1300. **$94-$99.** 1861 W Main St. I-15, exit 181 (L St), 0.5 mi n, then just e. Int corridors. **Pets:** Accepted.
ASK ⊠ 🛡 💻 ⇆

Holiday Inn Express Hotel & Suites SH
(760) 253-9200. **$155-$202.** 2700 Lenwood Rd. I-15, exit 178 (Lenwood Rd), just e, then 0.5 mi s. Int corridors. **Pets:** Accepted.
ASK S⊖ ⊠ 🔥M 🛡 💻 ⇆ ⊠

Ⱳ Motel 6 Barstow #1355 **M**

(760) 256-1752. **$45-$55.** 150 N Yucca Ave. I-15, exit 184B (E Main St) northbound; exit 184 (E Main St/I-40 E/Needles) southbound, 0.5 mi w, then just n; I-40, exit 1 (E Main St) westbound, 1 mi w, then just n. Ext corridors. **Pets:** Other species. Service with restrictions, supervision.

⊠ ⤳

Ⱳ Ⱳ Quality Inn **M** ❀

(760) 256-6891. **$80-$180.** 1520 E Main St. I-15, exit 184B (E Main St) northbound; exit 184 (E Main St/I-40 E/Needles) southbound, 0.3 mi w; I-40, exit 1 (E Main St) westbound, 0.8 mi w. Ext corridors. **Pets:** Small, dogs only. $10 one-time fee/room. Designated rooms, service with restrictions.

A$K S✆ ⊠ 🛈 💻 ⍝ ⤳

Ⱳ Ⱳ Ramada Inn **SH**

(760) 256-5673. **$89-$119.** 1511 E Main St. I-15, exit 184B (E Main St) northbound; exit 184 (E Main St/I-40 E/Needles) southbound, 0.3 mi w; I-40, exit 1 (E Main St) westbound, 0.8 mi w. Int corridors. **Pets:** Accepted.

A$K S✆ ⊠ &M 🛈 💻 ⍝ ⤳

ⱭⱭⱭ Ⱳ Ⱳ Red Roof Inn **M**

(760) 253-2121. **Call for rates.** 2551 Commerce Pkwy. I-15, exit 178 (Lenwood Rd), just w; 8 mi s of town. Ext corridors. **Pets:** Accepted.

SAVE ⊠ 🛈 ⤳

ⱭⱭⱭ Ⱳ Ⱳ Ⱳ Rodeway Inn **M**

(760) 256-7581. **$43-$66.** 1261 E Main St. I-15, exit 184B (E Main St) northbound; exit 184 (E Main St/I-40 E/Needles) southbound, 0.8 mi w; I-40, exit 1 (E Main St) westbound, 1.3 mi w. Ext corridors. **Pets:** Accepted.

SAVE S✆ ⊠ 🛈 ⤳

ⱭⱭⱭ Ⱳ Stardust Inn **M**

(760) 256-7116. **Call for rates.** 901 E Main St. I-15, exit 183 (Barstow Rd), 0.8 mi n, then 0.4 mi e. Ext corridors. **Pets:** Small, dogs only. $5 daily fee/pet. Designated rooms, service with restrictions, supervision.

SAVE ⊠ 🛈 ⤳

ⱭⱭⱭ Ⱳ Travelodge **M**

(760) 256-8931. **$55-$85.** 1630 E Main St. I-15, exit 184B (E Main St) northbound; exit 184 (E Main St/I-40 E/Needles) southbound, just e; I-40 westbound, exit 1 (E Main St), just w. Ext corridors. **Pets:** Small, dogs only. $8 one-time fee/pet. Service with restrictions, supervision.

SAVE S✆ ⊠ 🛈 ⤳

BEAUMONT

ⱭⱭⱭ Ⱳ Americas Best Value Inn **M**

(951) 845-2185. **$70-$199.** 625 E 5th St. I-10, exit 94 (SR 79/Beaumont Ave), just n. Ext corridors. **Pets:** Medium. $5 daily fee/pet. Service with restrictions, supervision.

SAVE S✆ ⊠ ⤳

ⱭⱭⱭ Ⱳ Ⱳ Best Western El Rancho Motor Inn **M**

(951) 845-2176. **$95-$200.** 480 E 5th St. I-10, exit 94 (SR 79/Beaumont Ave), just n, then just e. Ext corridors. **Pets:** Very small. $10 daily fee/pet. Designated rooms, service with restrictions, supervision.

SAVE S✆ ⊠ 🛈 💻 ⍝ ⤳

BENICIA

ⱭⱭⱭ Ⱳ Ⱳ Ⱳ Best Western Heritage Inn **SH**

(707) 746-0401. **$101-$159.** 1955 E 2nd St. I-780, exit Central Benicia/E 2nd St, just e. Int corridors. **Pets:** Small. $25 one-time fee/pet. Service with restrictions, supervision.

SAVE S✆ ⊠ 🛈 ⤳

BERKELEY

ⱭⱭⱭ Ⱳ Ⱳ Ⱳ Best Value Golden Bear Inn **M**

(510) 525-6770. **$80-$160.** 1620 San Pablo Ave. I-80, exit Gilman E, 2 mi s. Ext corridors. **Pets:** Other species. $20 daily fee/pet. Designated rooms, service with restrictions, supervision.

SAVE S✆ ⊠ 🛈 💻

ⱭⱭⱭ Ⱳ Ⱳ Ⱳ Ⱳ Claremont Resort and Spa **LH**

(510) 843-3000. **$209-$389.** 41 Tunnel Rd. SR 13 and 24, exit SR 24 (Claremont Ave), 1 mi n; in Berkeley Hills. Int corridors. **Pets:** Small, dogs only. $99 one-time fee/pet. Service with restrictions, supervision.

SAVE S✆ ⊠ 🛈 ⍝ ⤳ ⊠

ⱭⱭⱭ Ⱳ Ⱳ Ⱳ DoubleTree Hotel and Executive Meeting Center Berkeley Marina **SH**

(510) 548-7920. **Call for rates.** 200 Marina Blvd. I-80, exit University Ave, 0.5 mi w; on Berkeley Marina. Int corridors. **Pets:** Accepted.

SAVE ⊠ 🛈 💻 ⍝ ⤳ ⊠

BERRY CREEK

Ⱳ Ⱳ Ⱳ Ⱳ Lake Oroville Bed & Breakfast **BB**

(530) 589-0700. **$145-$165, 5 day notice.** 240 Sunday Dr. SR 162, 15 mi e to Bell Ranch Rd, 0.5 mi w. Int corridors. **Pets:** Accepted.

A$K S✆ ⊠ &M 🛈

BIG BEAR LAKE

Ⱳ Ⱳ Bear Manor Cabins **CA**

(909) 866-6800. **Call for rates.** 40393 Big Bear Blvd. SR 18, 0.8 mi w of village. Ext corridors. **Pets:** Accepted.

⊠ 🛈 🐾

ⱭⱭⱭ Ⱳ Ⱳ Ⱳ Best Western Big Bear Chateau **SH**

(909) 866-6666. **$129-$459.** 42200 Moonridge Rd. SR 18, 1.5 mi e of Pine Knot Ave, then 0.5 mi s. Int corridors. **Pets:** Accepted.

SAVE S✆ ⊠ 🛈 💻 ⍝ ⤳ ⊠

ⱭⱭⱭ Ⱳ Big Bear Lakefront Lodge **M** ❀

(909) 866-8271. **$69-$425.** 40360 Lakeview Dr. SR 18, 0.5 mi w of Pine Knot Ave, 0.5 mi nw. Ext/int corridors. **Pets:** Dogs only. $20 daily fee/pet. Designated rooms, service with restrictions, supervision.

SAVE S✆ ⊠ 🛈 💻 ⊠ 🐾 ⊠

ⱭⱭⱭ Ⱳ Ⱳ Cozy Hollow Lodge **CA**

(909) 866-9694. **Call for rates.** 40409 Big Bear Blvd. SR 18, 0.8 mi w. Ext corridors. **Pets:** Medium, dogs only. $10 daily fee/pet, $25 one-time fee/room. Designated rooms, service with restrictions, supervision.

SAVE ⊠ 🛈 💻 🐾

Ⱳ Ⱳ Eagle's Nest Bed & Breakfast **BB**

(909) 866-6465. **$115-$185, 5 day notice.** 41675 Big Bear Blvd. SR 18, 1 mi e of Pine Knot Ave. Ext/int corridors. **Pets:** Accepted.

A$K S✆ ⊠ 🛈 💻

ⱭⱭⱭ Ⱳ Ⱳ Golden Bear Cottages **CA**

(909) 866-2010. **$99-$799, 90 day notice.** 39367 Big Bear Blvd. SR 18, 2 mi w of village. Ext corridors. **Pets:** Accepted.

SAVE S✆ ⊠ 🛈 💻 ⤳ ⊠ 🐾

ⱭⱭⱭ Ⱳ Ⱳ Grey Squirrel Resort **CA**

(909) 866-4335. **$94, 14 day notice.** 39372 Big Bear Blvd. SR 18, 2.5 mi w of village. Ext corridors. **Pets:** Other species. $10 daily fee/pet. Service with restrictions.

SAVE ⊠ 🛈 💻 ⤳ ⊠ 🐾

Ⱳ Ⱳ Pine Knot Guest Ranch **CA**

(909) 866-6500. **$89-$169.** 908 Pine Knot Ave. Just s of SR 18 and downtown area. Ext corridors. **Pets:** Accepted.

A$K S✆ ⊠ 🛈 💻

⚜ ▼▼▼ Sleepy Forest Cottages CA
(909) 866-7444. **$99-$299, 15 day notice.** 426 Eureka Dr. SR 18, 0.7 mi e of Pine Knot Ave, then just n. Ext corridors. **Pets:** Dogs only. $25 daily fee/pet. Designated rooms, service with restrictions, supervision.
SAVE 🔊 ⊗ 🖥 💻 🐾

⚜ ▼▼▼ Timber Haven Lodge CA ❀
(909) 866-7207. **$89-$320, 14 day notice.** 877 Tulip Ln. SR 18, 1.8 mi w of Pine Knot Ave, 0.4 mi s. Ext corridors. **Pets:** Dogs only. $15 daily fee/pet. Designated rooms, service with restrictions, supervision.
SAVE 🔊 ⊗ 🖥 💻 🐾 🐾

BIG PINE

▼▼ Big Pine Motel M
(760) 938-2282. **Call for rates.** 370 S Main St. On US 395. Ext corridors. **Pets:** Accepted.
⊗ 🖥 💻

⚜ ▼▼▼ Bristlecone Motel M
(760) 938-2067. **$48-$75.** 101 N Main St. On US 395. Ext corridors. **Pets:** Other species. Service with restrictions, supervision.
SAVE 🔊 ⊗ 🖥 💻

BISHOP

⚜ ▼▼▼▼ Best Western Bishop Holiday Spa Lodge M ❀
(760) 873-3543. **$80-$120.** 1025 N Main St. On US 395. Ext corridors. **Pets:** Other species. $10 daily fee/pet. Supervision.
SAVE 🔊 ⊗ 🐾 🖥 💻 🐾

⚜ ▼▼▼▼ Comfort Inn M
(760) 873-4284. **Call for rates.** 805 N Main St. On US 395. Ext corridors. **Pets:** Accepted.
SAVE ⊗ 🐾 🖥 💻 🐾

⚜ ▼▼▼▼ Holiday Inn Express Hotel & Suites SH
(760) 872-2423. **$109-$279.** 636 N Main St. On US 395. Int corridors. **Pets:** Medium, dogs only. $25 daily fee/pet. Designated rooms, service with restrictions, supervision.
SAVE ⊗ 🐾 🖥 💻 🏊 🐾

▼▼ Motel 6–#4094 M
(760) 873-8426. **Call for rates.** 1005 N Main St. On US 395. Ext corridors. **Pets:** Other species. Service with restrictions, supervision.
⊗ 🐾 🖥 🐾

⚜ ▼▼▼▼ Ramada Limited M ❀
(760) 872-1771. **$80-$150.** 155 E Elm St. On US 395, just e. Ext corridors. **Pets:** $15 daily fee/pet. Designated rooms, service with restrictions, supervision.
SAVE 🔊 ⊗ 🐾 🖥 💻 🐾

▼▼ Rodeway Inn M
(760) 873-3564. **Call for rates.** 150 E Elm St. On US 395, just e. Ext/int corridors. **Pets:** Accepted.
⊗ 🖥 💻 🐾

▼▼ Super 8 Motel M
(760) 872-1386. **Call for rates.** 535 S Main St. On US 395. Ext corridors. **Pets:** Accepted.
⊗ 🖥 💻

▼▼ Thunderbird Motel M
(760) 873-4215. **Call for rates.** 190 W Pine St. Just w of US 395. Ext corridors. **Pets:** Accepted.
⊗ 🖥 💻

⚜ ▼▼▼▼ Vagabond Inn M
(760) 873-6351. **Call for rates.** 1030 N Main St. On US 395. Ext corridors. **Pets:** Accepted.
SAVE ⊗ 🐾 💻 🏊 🐾

BLYTHE

⚜ ▼▼▼ Best Western Sahara Motel M ❀
(760) 922-7105. **$89-$159.** 825 W Hobsonway. I-10, exit 239 (Lovekin Blvd), just n, then just w. Ext corridors. **Pets:** Small. Service with restrictions, supervision.
SAVE 🔊 ⊗ 🖥 💻 🐾

⚜ ▼▼▼▼ Comfort Suites M
(760) 922-9209. **$80-$150.** 545 E Hobsonway. I-10, exit 240 (7th St), just n, then just w. Ext corridors. **Pets:** Other species. $15 daily fee/pet. Service with restrictions.
SAVE 🔊 ⊗ 🖥 💻 🐾

⚜ ▼▼▼ Days Inn M
(760) 922-5101. **Call for rates.** 9274 E Hobsonway. I-10, exit 239 (Intake Blvd), just n, then just w. Ext corridors. **Pets:** Medium, other species. $5 one-time fee/pet. Service with restrictions, supervision.
SAVE ⊗ 🖥 💻 🐾

▼▼▼ Regency Inn & Suites M
(760) 922-4146. **$89-$169.** 903 W Hobsonway. I-10, exit 239 (Lovekin Blvd), just n, then just w. Ext corridors. **Pets:** Accepted.
ASK 🔊 ⊗ 🖥 💻 🐾

⚜ ▼▼▼ Super 8 Motel M
(760) 922-8881. **$70-$140.** 550 W Donlon St. I-10, exit 239 (Lovekin Blvd), just e. Int corridors. **Pets:** Accepted.
SAVE 🔊 ⊗ 🖥 💻 🐾

⚜ ▼▼▼ Travelers Inn Express M
(760) 922-3334. **Call for rates.** 1781 E Hobsonway. I-10, exit 241 (Intake Blvd), just n, then just w. Ext corridors. **Pets:** Accepted.
SAVE ⊗ 🖥 💻 🍴 🐾

BORREGO SPRINGS

⚜ ▼▼▼▼ Borrego Springs Resort Hotel SH
(760) 767-5700. **$100-$175.** 1112 Tilting T Dr. SR 22, 1.5 mi s on Borrego Valley Rd, just w. Int corridors. **Pets:** Small, other species. $50 one-time fee/pet. Designated rooms, service with restrictions, supervision.
SAVE 🔊 ⊗ 🖥 💻 🍴 🐾 🐾

⚜ ▼▼▼▼ La Casa del Zorro Desert Resort LH
(760) 767-5323. **$295-$1660, 7 day notice.** 3845 Yaqui Pass Rd. 5.5 mi se on CR S-3; jct Yaqui Pass and Borrego Springs rds. Ext corridors. **Pets:** Other species. $100 deposit/pet, $50 daily fee/pet. Service with restrictions.
SAVE ⊗ 🖥 💻 🍴 🐾 🐾

BREA

▼▼ Homestead Studio Suites Hotel-Orange County-Brea M
(714) 528-2500. **$94-$114.** 3050 E Imperial Hwy. SR 57, exit 9 (SR 90), 1.4 mi e on Imperial Hwy (SR 90). Ext corridors. **Pets:** Other species. $75 one-time fee/pet. Service with restrictions.
ASK 🔊 ⊗ 🖥

⚜ ▼▼▼ Woodfin Suite Hotel M
(714) 579-3200. **$129-$299.** 3100 E Imperial Hwy. SR 57, exit 9 (SR 90), 1.5 mi e on Imperial Hwy (SR 90). Ext corridors. **Pets:** Accepted.
SAVE ⊗ 🖥 💻 🐾

BRIDGEPORT

⚜ ▼▼▼ Redwood Motel M ❀
(760) 932-7060. **$59-$250.** 425 Main St. On US 395; on north side of town. Ext corridors. **Pets:** Large. $10 daily fee/pet. Designated rooms, service with restrictions, supervision.
SAVE 🔊 ⊗ 🖥 💻

△△△⁷ ▽▽▽ Ruby Inn M
(760) 932-7241. **$125-$200.** 333 Main St. On US 395; center. Ext corridors. **Pets:** Accepted.
[SAVE] [S⌀] [✕] [⛶] [💻]

△△△⁷ ▽▽▽ Silver Maple Inn M ❀
(760) 932-7383. **$70-$120.** 310 Main St. On US 395; center. Ext corridors. **Pets:** Other species. Supervision.
[SAVE] [S⌀] [✕] [⛶] [💻] [🐾]

△△△⁷ ▽▽▽ Walker River Lodge M
(760) 932-7021. **$70-$220.** 100 Main St. On US 395; at south end of town. Ext corridors. **Pets:** Large, other species. Service with restrictions, supervision.
[SAVE] [S⌀] [✕] [⛶] [💻] [🐾]

BUELLTON

△△△⁷ ▽▽▽ Quality Inn Solvang/Buellton M
(805) 688-0022. **$69-$179.** 630 Ave of the Flags. US 101, exit 140B (Ave of the Flags) southbound, just s; exit 140A (SR 246) northbound, just w, then just n. Ext/int corridors. **Pets:** Accepted.
[SAVE] [S⌀] [✕] [⛶] [💻]

▽▽▽▽ Santa Ynez Valley Marriott SH
(805) 688-1000. **$197-$219.** 555 McMurray Rd. US 101, exit 140A (SR 246), just e, then just n. Int corridors. **Pets:** Accepted.
[ASK] [S⌀] [✕] [⛶ᴹ] [⛶] [💻] [🍴] [🐾] [✕⛶]

BUENA PARK

△△△⁷ ▽▽ Red Roof Inn M
(714) 670-9000. **Call for rates.** 7121 Beach Blvd. SR 91, exit 23B (Beach Blvd/SR 39), just n. Ext corridors. **Pets:** Accepted.
[SAVE] [✕] [⛶] [🐾] [✕⛶]

BURNEY

△△△⁷ ▽ Charm Motel M ❀
(530) 335-2254. **$59-$99, 3 day notice.** 37363 Main St. 0.8 mi e on SR 299. Ext corridors. **Pets:** Other species. $10 daily fee/pet. Service with restrictions, supervision.
[SAVE] [S⌀] [✕] [⛶] [💻]

△△△⁷ ▽▽▽ Green Gables Motel M ❀
(530) 335-2264. **$69-$129, 3 day notice.** 37385 Main St. 0.8 mi e on SR 299. Ext corridors. **Pets:** Other species. $10 daily fee/pet. Service with restrictions, supervision.
[SAVE] [S⌀] [✕] [⛶] [💻] [🐾]

BUTTONWILLOW

△△△⁷ ▽▽ Super 8 Motel M
(661) 764-5117. **$45-$85.** 20681 Tracy Ave. I-5, exit 257 (SR 58), just e, then just n. Ext corridors. **Pets:** Dogs only. $10 daily fee/pet. Designated rooms, service with restrictions, supervision.
[SAVE] [S⌀] [✕] [⛶ᴹ] [⛶] [🐾]

CALEXICO

△△△⁷ ▽▽▽ Best Western John Jay Inn M
(760) 768-0442. **$89-$124.** 2421 Scaroni Rd. I-8, exit 118A (SR 111 S), 5.5 mi s, just w on W Cole Rd, then just n. Int corridors. **Pets:** Dogs only. $100 deposit/room, $10 daily fee/pet. Designated rooms, service with restrictions, supervision.
[SAVE] [S⌀] [✕] [⛶ᴹ] [⛶] [💻] [🐾]

CALIMESA

△△△⁷ ▽▽ Calimesa Inn Motel M
(909) 795-2536. **$60-$150.** 1205 Calimesa Blvd. I-10, exit 88 (Calimesa Blvd), just ne. Ext corridors. **Pets:** Accepted.
[SAVE] [✕] [⛶] [🐾]

CALIPATRIA

△△△⁷ ▽▽▽ Calipatria Inn & Suites M ❀
(760) 348-7348. **$100-$105.** 700 N Sorenson Ave. On SR 111. Ext corridors. **Pets:** Dogs only. $10 deposit/room, $10 one-time fee/room. Service with restrictions, supervision.
[SAVE] [S⌀] [✕] [⛶] [💻] [🍴] [🐾]

CAMBRIA

▽▽▽▽ Blue Dolphin Inn SH
(805) 927-3300. **$109-$299.** 6470 Moonstone Beach Dr. SR 1, exit Moonstone Beach Dr, 0.7 mi n. Int corridors. **Pets:** Accepted.
[ASK] [✕] [⛶] [💻] [☆]

▽▽▽▽ Cambria Shores Inn M
(805) 927-8644. **$150-$350, 7 day notice.** 6276 Moonstone Beach Dr. SR 1, exit Moonstone Beach Dr, just w, then 0.8 mi s. Ext corridors. **Pets:** Accepted.
[✕] [⛶] [💻]

▽▽▽▽ Fog Catcher Inn M
(805) 927-1400. **Call for rates.** 6400 Moonstone Beach Dr. SR 1, exit Moonstone Beach Dr, just w, then 0.7 mi s. Ext corridors. **Pets:** Accepted.
[✕] [⛶] [💻] [🐾] [☆]

△△△⁷ ▽▽ Mariners Inn by the Sea M
(805) 927-4624. **$89-$239, 3 day notice.** 6180 Moonstone Beach Dr. SR 1, exit Moonstone Beach Dr, just w, then 1 mi s. Ext corridors. **Pets:** Dogs only. $15 daily fee/pet. Designated rooms, service with restrictions, supervision.
[SAVE] [✕] [⛶] [☆]

▽▽▽▽ Sand Pebbles Inn SH
(805) 927-5600. **$109-$299.** 6252 Moonstone Beach Dr. SR 1, exit Moonstone Beach Dr, just w, then 0.9 mi s. Int corridors. **Pets:** Accepted.
[ASK] [✕] [⛶] [💻] [☆]

▽▽▽▽ Sea Otter Inn M
(805) 927-5888. **Call for rates.** 6656 Moonstone Beach Dr. SR 1, exit Moonstone Beach Dr, just w, then 0.5 mi s. Ext corridors. **Pets:** Accepted.
[✕] [⛶] [💻] [🐾] [☆]

CAMERON PARK

▽▽▽▽ Cameron Park Inn & Suites SH
(530) 677-2203. **Call for rates.** 3361 Coach Ln. 12 mi w of Placerville on US 50, exit Cameron Park Dr. Ext corridors. **Pets:** Accepted.
[✕] [⛶ᴹ] [⛶] [💻] [🐾]

CAMINO

△△△⁷ ▽▽▽ Camino Hotel-Seven Mile House BB
(530) 644-7740. **$168-$198, 7 day notice.** 4103 Carson Rd. US 50, exit 54 (Camino), just n. Int corridors. **Pets:** Accepted.
[SAVE] [S⌀] [✕] [⛶ᴹ] [🅿] [☎]

CAMPBELL

△△△⁷ ▽▽▽▽ Larkspur Landing Campbell SH
(408) 364-1514. **$109-$189.** 550 W Hamilton Ave. SR 17, exit Hamilton Ave, 1 mi w. Int corridors. **Pets:** Medium. $75 one-time fee/room. Service with restrictions, crate.
[SAVE] [S⌀] [✕] [⛶ᴹ] [⛶] [💻]

▽▽▽▽ Residence Inn by Marriott-San Jose SH
(408) 559-1551. **$209-$229.** 2761 S Bascom Ave. SR 17, exit Camden Ave E, just n. Ext corridors. **Pets:** Large, other species. $75 one-time fee/pet. Service with restrictions.
[ASK] [S⌀] [✕] [⛶] [💻] [🐾]

▼▼▼▼ TownePlace Suites by Marriott-San
Jose/Campbell **SH**
(408) 370-4510. **$198-$218.** 700 E Campbell Ave. SR 17, exit Hamilton
Ave E, 0.3 mi to Bascom Ave, 0.3 mi s, then 0.3 mi w. Int corridors.
Pets: Accepted.
[ASK] [S🐾] [✕] [🛗] [💻]

CAPITOLA

◈◈◈ ▼▼▼▼ Best Western Capitola By-the-Sea Inn &
Suites **SH**
(831) 477-0607. **Call for rates.** 1435 41st Ave. SR 1, exit 41st Ave, 0.8
mi w. Int corridors. **Pets:** Accepted.
[SAVE] [✕] [&M] [🛗] [💻] [🌊]

CARLSBAD

◈◈◈ ▼▼▼▼▼ Four Seasons Resort Aviara **LH** ❀
(760) 603-6800. **$405-$680, 3 day notice.** 7100 Four Seasons Point.
I-5, exit 45 (Poinsettia Ln/Aviara Pkwy), 1 mi e on Poinsettia Ln, then
1 mi s on Aviara Pkwy. Int corridors. **Pets:** Very small. Service with
restrictions, supervision.
[SAVE] [✕] [💻] [🍴] [🌊] [⊠]

▼▼▼▼ La Quinta Inn Carlsbad **M**
(760) 438-2828. **$119-$139.** 760 Macadamia Dr. I-5, exit 45 (Poinsettia
Ln/Aviara Pkwy), just w to Ave Encinas, just n, then just e. Ext corridors. **Pets:** Other species. Service with restrictions, supervision.
[ASK] [S🐾] [✕] [🛗] [💻] [🌊]

▼▼▼ Quality Inn & Suites **SH**
(760) 931-1185. **$74-$189.** 751 Raintree Dr. I-5, exit 45 (Poinsettia Ln),
just w to Ave Encinas, then just n. Ext corridors. **Pets:** Accepted.
[ASK] [S🐾] [✕] [🛗] [💻] [🍴] [🌊]

◈◈◈ ▼▼▼▼ West Inn & Suites **SH** ❀
(760) 448-4500. **$169-$399, 3 day notice.** 4970 Avenida Encinas. I-5,
exit 48 (Cannon Rd), just w, then just n. Int corridors. **Pets:** $75 daily
fee/room. Designated rooms, service with restrictions, crate.
[SAVE] [S🐾] [✕] [&M] [🛗] [💻] [🍴] [🌊] [⊠]

CARPINTERIA

◈◈◈ ▼▼▼▼ Holiday Inn Express Hotel & Suites **SH**
(805) 566-9499. **Call for rates.** 5606 Carpinteria Ave. US 101, exit 86A
(Casitas Pass Rd), just s, then just e. Int corridors. **Pets:** Accepted.
[SAVE] [✕] [&M] [🛗] [💻] [🌊]

CASSEL

▼▼▼▼ Burney Mountain Guest Ranch **RA**
(530) 335-4087. **Call for rates.** 22800 Hat Creek Powerhouse #2. I-5,
exit 299 E, 2.7 mi; jct SR 89/299 e. Ext corridors. **Pets:** Accepted.
[✕] [🛗] [💻] [🌊] [⊠]

CASTAIC

◈◈◈ ▼▼▼ Days Inn **M** ❀
(661) 295-1070. **Call for rates.** 31410 Castaic Rd. I-5, exit 176A
(Parker Rd) northbound, just e on Ridge Route Rd, then just s; exit
176 (Lake Hughes Rd/Castaic) southbound, just s on The Old Rd, just
e on Sloan Canyon Rd, then 0.6 mi s. Ext corridors. **Pets:** Small, dogs
only. $15 daily fee/pet. Designated rooms, service with restrictions, supervi-
sion.
[SAVE] [✕] [🛗] [💻] [🌊]

◈◈◈ ▼▼▼ Rodeway Inn **M**
(661) 295-1100. **$59-$99.** 31558 Castaic Rd. I-5, exit 175A (Parker Rd)
northbound, just e on Ridge Route Rd, then just n; exit 176 (Lake
Hughes/Castaic) southbound, just s on The Old Rd, just e on Sloan
Canyon Rd, then 0.4 mi s. Ext corridors. **Pets:** Other species. $10
one-time fee/pet. Designated rooms, service with restrictions, supervision.
[SAVE] [S🐾] [✕] [🛗] [💻] [🌊]

CASTRO VALLEY

▼▼▼▼ Holiday Inn Express **SH**
(510) 538-9501. **$109-$139.** 2532 Castro Valley Blvd. I-580, exit Castro
Valley Blvd, 0.3 mi n. Int corridors. **Pets:** Accepted.
[ASK] [S🐾] [✕] [&M] [🛗] [💻] [🌊]

CATHEDRAL CITY

▼▼▼ Comfort Suites **M**
(760) 324-5939. **$69-$279.** 69-151 E Palm Canyon Dr. I-10, exit 126
(Date Palm Dr), 5 mi s, then just e. Ext corridors. **Pets:** Accepted.
[ASK] [S🐾] [✕] [🛗] [💻] [🌊]

▼▼▼▼ Doral Desert Princess Resort, Palm Springs **LH**
(760) 322-7000. **$99-$359, 3 day notice.** 67-967 Vista Chino. I-10, exit
126 (Date Palm Dr), 0.5 mi s, then 1 mi w. Int corridors.
Pets: Accepted.
[ASK] [S🐾] [✕] [🛗] [💻] [🍴] [🌊] [⊠]

CAYUCOS

◈◈◈ ▼▼▼ Beachwalker Inn **M**
(805) 995-2133. **Call for rates.** 501 S Ocean Ave. On SR 1 business
route. Ext corridors. **Pets:** Accepted.
[SAVE] [✕] [🛗] [💻] [🎴]

▼▼▼ Cayucos Beach Inn **M**
(805) 995-2828. **Call for rates.** 333 S Ocean Ave. On SR 1 business
route. Ext corridors. **Pets:** Accepted.
[✕] [&M] [🛗] [💻]

◈◈◈ ▼ Cypress Tree Motel **M** ❀
(805) 995-3917. **$50-$117.** 125 S Ocean Ave. On SR 1 business route.
Ext corridors. **Pets:** Large, other species. $10 one-time fee/room. Service
with restrictions, crate.
[SAVE] [S🐾] [✕] [🛗] [💻] [🎴]

◈◈◈ ▼ Estero Bay Motel **M**
(805) 995-3614. **Call for rates.** 25 S Ocean Ave. On SR 1 business
route. Ext corridors. **Pets:** Medium, dogs only. $10 daily fee/pet. Service
with restrictions, supervision.
[SAVE] [✕] [🛗] [💻] [🎴]

◈◈◈ ▼ Shoreline Inn...On The Beach **M**
(805) 995-3681. **Call for rates.** 1 N Ocean Ave. On SR 1 business
route. Ext corridors. **Pets:** Accepted.
[SAVE] [✕] [&M] [🛗] [💻] [🎴]

CEDARVILLE

◈◈◈ ▼▼ Sunrise Motel **M**
(530) 279-2161. **$65-$75, 7 day notice.** 62271 Hwy 299 W. On SR
299, 0.5 mi w. Ext corridors. **Pets:** Medium. $10 daily fee/pet. Designated
rooms, service with restrictions, supervision.
[SAVE] [S🐾] [✕] [🛗] [💻]

CHESTER

◈◈◈ ▼▼▼▼ Almanor Lakeside Resort **M**
(530) 596-4530. **$125-$175, 30 day notice.** 325 Peninsula Dr. SR 36,
right on CR A-13, left on Peninsula Dr, then 0.5 mi. Ext corridors.
Pets: Accepted.
[SAVE] [S🐾] [✕] [💻] [⊠]

◈◈◈ ▼▼▼▼ Best Western Rose Quartz Inn **SH** ❀
(530) 258-2002. **$119-$180.** 306 Main St. On SR 36; center. Int corridors. **Pets:** $30 daily fee/pet. Designated rooms, service with restrictions,
supervision.
[SAVE] [S🐾] [✕] [🛗] [💻]

CHICO

◭◭◮ ▼▼▼ Best Western Heritage Inn-Chico **SH**
(530) 894-8600. **$95-$120.** 25 Heritage Ln. Just e of SR 99, via Cohasset Rd. Int corridors. **Pets:** Medium. $30 one-time fee/pet. Designated rooms, service with restrictions, supervision.

SAVE **S🐾** ⊗ **&M** 🛗 🖵

◭◭◮ ▼ Budget Inn of Chico **SH**
(530) 342-9472. **$50-$175.** 1717 Park Ave. SR 99, exit 20th St E, then right. Ext corridors. **Pets:** Accepted.

SAVE **S🐾** ⊗ 🛗 ⊠

◭◭◮ ▼▼ Heritage Inn Express **M**
(530) 343-4527. **$89-$109.** 725 Broadway. SR 32, exit SR 99, 1 mi w. Ext corridors. **Pets:** $20 one-time fee/room. Designated rooms, service with restrictions, supervision.

SAVE **S🐾** ⊗ 🛗 🖵 ➿

◭◭◮ ▼▼▼ Holiday Inn of Chico **SH**
(530) 345-2491. **Call for rates.** 685 Manzanita Ct. Just w of SR 99, via Cohasset Rd. Int corridors. **Pets:** Accepted.

SAVE ⊗ **&M** 🛗 🖵 🍴 ➿

▼▼▼▼ Music Express Inn **BB**
(530) 345-8376. **$76-$125.** 1145 El Monte Ave. SR 99, exit SR 32, 1 mi e to El Monte Ave, then just n. Ext/int corridors. **Pets:** Accepted.

⊗ **&M**

▼▼▼▼ Oxford Suites **SH**
(530) 899-9090. **$149-$169.** 2035 Business Ln. SR 99, exit 20th St E. Int corridors. **Pets:** Accepted.

A$K **S🐾** ⊗ **&M** 🛗 🖵 ➿ ⊠

▼▼▼▼ Residence Inn **SH**
(530) 894-5500. **$121-$141.** 2485 Carmichael Dr. SR 99, exit Park Ave, 0.5 mi nw. Int corridors. **Pets:** Accepted.

A$K **S🐾** ⊗ 🛗 🖵 ➿ ⊠

◭◭◮ ▼▼ Super 8 Motel **SH**
(530) 345-2533. **$60-$200.** 655 Manzanita Ct. Just w of SR 99, via Cohasset Rd. Int corridors. **Pets:** $10 daily fee/pet. Service with restrictions, supervision.

SAVE **S🐾** ⊗ 🛗 ➿

CHOWCHILLA

◭◭◮ ▼▼ Days Inn **M** 🐾
(559) 665-4821. **$59-$89.** 220 E Robertson Blvd. SR 99, exit Robertson Blvd W. Ext corridors. **Pets:** Other species. $10 daily fee/pet. Service with restrictions, supervision.

SAVE **S🐾** ⊗ 🛗 🖵 ➿

CLIO

▼▼▼ Molly's Bed & Breakfast **BB**
(530) 836-4436. **Call for rates.** 276 Lower Main St. Just e of SR 89. Int corridors. **Pets:** Accepted.

⊗ 〰 ⊠

COALINGA

◭◭◮ ▼▼▼ Best Western Big Country Inn **M**
(559) 935-0866. **$79-$119.** 25020 W Dorris Ave. I-5, exit SR 198/ Hanford-Lemoore, just w. Ext corridors. **Pets:** Medium. $10 daily fee/pet. Designated rooms, service with restrictions, supervision.

SAVE **S🐾** ⊗ 🛗 🖵 ➿

◭◭◮ ▼▼▼▼ The Inn at Harris Ranch **LH**
(559) 935-0717. **$135-$295.** 24505 W Dorris Ave. I-5, exit SR 198/ Hanford-Lemoore, just e. Ext/int corridors. **Pets:** $20 one-time fee/pet. Designated rooms, service with restrictions, supervision.

SAVE **S🐾** ⊗ **&M** 🛗 🖵 🍴 ➿

COLUMBIA

▼▼ Columbia Gem Motel **M**
(209) 532-4508. **$89-$149.** 22131 Parrotts Ferry Rd. 3 mi n of Sonora; 1 mi from Columbia State Historic Park. Ext corridors. **Pets:** Accepted.

⊗ 🛗 🖵 ⊠

CONCORD

◭◭◮ ▼▼▼ Best Western Heritage Inn **SH**
(925) 686-4466. **$70-$120.** 4600 Clayton Rd. 3 mi e at Wharton Way. Ext corridors. **Pets:** Medium. $100 deposit/room. Service with restrictions, supervision.

SAVE **S🐾** ⊗ 🛗 🖵 ➿

◭◭◮ ▼▼▼ Crowne Plaza Hotel Concord/Walnut Creek **LH**
(925) 825-7700. **$99-$199.** 45 John Glenn Dr. I-680, exit Concord Ave, just e. Int corridors. **Pets:** Accepted.

SAVE **S🐾** ⊗ **&M** 🛗 🖵 🍴 ➿

◭◭◮ ▼▼▼ Holiday Inn Concord **LH**
(925) 687-5500. **$179-$199.** 1050 Burnett Ave. I-680, exit E Concord Ave, just e. Ext/int corridors. **Pets:** Other species. $10 daily fee/pet. Designated rooms, service with restrictions, crate.

SAVE **S🐾** ⊗ 🛗 🖵 🍴 ➿

◭◭◮ ▼▼▼ Premier Inns **M**
(925) 674-0888. **$51-$71.** 1581 Concord Ave. SR 242, exit Clayton Rd northbound; exit Concord Ave southbound, just e. Ext corridors. **Pets:** Accepted.

SAVE **S🐾** ⊗ 🛗 ➿

CORNING

◭◭◮ ▼▼▼ Best Western Inn Corning **M**
(530) 824-2468. **$80-$159.** 2165 Solano St. I-5, exit 631 (Central Corning), just e. Ext corridors. **Pets:** Medium. $10 daily fee/pet. Designated rooms, service with restrictions, supervision.

SAVE **S🐾** ⊗ **&M** 🛗 🖵 ➿

◭◭◮ ▼▼▼ Comfort Inn **SH**
(530) 824-5200. **$64-$149.** 910 Hwy 99 W. I-5, exit 631 (Central Corning), just e. Int corridors. **Pets:** Other species. $10 daily fee/pet. Supervision.

SAVE **S🐾** ⊗ **&M** 🛗 🖵 ➿

◭◭◮ ▼▼▼ Days Inn **SH**
(530) 824-2000. **Call for rates.** 3475 Hwy 99 W. I-5, exit 630 (South Ave), 0.3 mi s. Int corridors. **Pets:** Other species. $50 deposit/room, $5 daily fee/pet. Designated rooms, service with restrictions, supervision.

SAVE ⊗ **&M** 🛗 ➿

◭◭◮ ▼▼▼ Holiday Inn Express Hotel & Suites **SH** 🐾
(530) 824-6400. **Call for rates.** 3350 Sunrise Way. I-5, exit 630 (South Ave), just s. Int corridors. **Pets:** $10 one-time fee/room. Designated rooms, service with restrictions, supervision.

SAVE ⊗ 🛗 🖵 ➿ ⊠

◭◭◮ ▼▼▼▼ Ramada Inn & Suites **SH** 🐾
(530) 824-8300. **Call for rates.** 2645 Barham Ave. I-5, exit 628 (Liberal), just w. Int corridors. **Pets:** Other species. $10 daily fee/room. Designated rooms, service with restrictions, supervision.

SAVE ⊗ 🛗 ➿

CORONA

▼▼ ▼▼ Hotel Paseo "Dynasty Suites" **M**
(951) 371-7185. **$89-$150.** 1805 W 6th St. SR 91, exit 48 (Maple St/W 6th St) eastbound; exit 48 (Maple St) westbound, just s. Ext corridors. **Pets:** Accepted.

A$K ⊗ 🛗 🖵 ➿

▼▼▼▼ **Residence Inn by Marriott Corona** SH
(951) 371-0107. **$177-$197.** 1015 Montecito Dr. I-15, exit 95 (Magnolia Ave), just e, just n on El Camino, just w on Carly Way, then just n. Int corridors. **Pets:** Accepted.

ASK S6 ⊠ 🛈 🖵 �)) 🗵

COSTA MESA

▼▼▼▼ **Costa Mesa Marriott** LH
(714) 957-1100. **$297-$317.** 500 Anton Blvd. I-405, exit 9B (Bristol St), just n, then 3 blks e. Int corridors. **Pets:** Accepted.

ASK S6 ⊠ 🖄 🛈 🖵 ¶¶ �).) 🗵

▼▼▼▼ **Hilton Orange County/Costa Mesa** LH
(714) 540-7000. **Call for rates.** 3050 Bristol St. I-405, exit 9B (Bristol St), just s. Int corridors. **Pets:** Accepted.

⊠ 🛈 🖵 ¶¶ �).) 🗵

AAA ▼▼▼▼ **Holiday Inn-Costa Mesa/Orange County Airport** LH
(714) 557-3000. **$89-$219.** 3131 Bristol St. I-405, exit 9B (Bristol St), just s. Int corridors. **Pets:** Accepted.

SAVE S6 ⊠ 🛈 🖵 ¶¶ �)

▼▼▼▼ **La Quinta Inn Costa Mesa (John Wayne/Orange Co. Airport)** M
(714) 957-5841. **$92-$149.** 1515 S Coast Dr. I-405, exit 11B (Harbor Blvd), just n, then just w. Ext corridors. **Pets:** Other species. Service with restrictions, supervision.

ASK S6 ⊠ 🛈 🖵 �)

AAA ▼▼▼▼ **Ramada Limited & Suites** SH 🐾
(949) 645-2221. **$80-$180.** 1680 Superior Ave. Just w of SR 55 (Newport Blvd) at 17th St. Ext corridors. **Pets:** Small. $100 deposit/room, $5 daily fee/room. Designated rooms, service with restrictions, supervision.

SAVE S6 ⊠ 🖄 🛈 🖵 🚠

▼▼▼▼ **Residence Inn by Marriott** SH
(714) 241-8800. **$264-$284.** 881 W Baker St. SR 73, exit 17B (Bear St); SR 55, exit 5B (Baker St). Ext corridors. **Pets:** Accepted.

ASK S6 ⊠ 🛈 🖵 🚠 🗵

AAA ▼▼ **Travelodge-Orange County Airport** M
(714) 557-8700. **$75-$125.** 1400 SE Bristol St. Adjacent to SR 73, just w of Red Hill Ave. Ext corridors. **Pets:** Accepted.

SAVE S6 ⊠ 🛈 🖵 🚠

AAA ▼▼ **Vagabond Inn** M 🐾
(714) 557-8360. **$79-$119.** 3205 Harbor Blvd. I-405, exit 11 (Harbor Blvd), just s; entrance from Gisler Ave, just w of Harbor. Ext corridors. **Pets:** Small. $15 daily fee/pet. Designated rooms, service with restrictions, supervision.

SAVE S6 ⊠ 🛈 🖵 🚠

▼▼▼▼ **The Westin South Coast Plaza Hotel** LH
(714) 540-2500. **$139-$375.** 686 Anton Blvd. I-405, exit 9B (Bristol St), just n, then just e. Int corridors. **Pets:** Accepted.

ASK S6 ⊠ 🖄 🖵 ¶¶ 🚠 🗵

AAA ▼▼▼▼ **Wyndham Orange County Airport** LH
(714) 751-5100. **$209-$269.** 3350 Ave of the Arts. I-405, exit 9B (Bristol St), n to Anton Blvd, just e, then just n. Int corridors. **Pets:** Accepted.

SAVE S6 ⊠ 🛈 🖵 ¶¶ 🚠

CRESCENT CITY

AAA ▼▼ **Americas Best Value Inn** M
(707) 464-4141. **$50-$125.** 440 Hwy 101 N. Center. Ext corridors. **Pets:** Small, dogs only. $10 daily fee/pet. Designated rooms, service with restrictions, supervision.

SAVE S6 ⊠ 🛈 🖵

AAA ▼▼▼ **Comfort Inn & Suites** SH
(707) 464-3885. **$94-$209.** 100 Walton St. Just w of US 101. Ext corridors. **Pets:** Accepted.

SAVE S6 ⊠ 🛈 🖵

▼ **Hiouchi Motel** M
(707) 458-3041. **$65-$81.** 2097 Hwy 199. On US 199, 5.5 mi e of jct US 101. Ext corridors. **Pets:** Accepted.

ASK S6 ⊠ 🛈 🖄 🗵

AAA ▼ **Super 8** M 🐾
(707) 464-4111. **Call for rates.** 685 Hwy 101 S. On US 101. Ext corridors. **Pets:** Medium, dogs only. $10 daily fee/pet. Designated rooms, service with restrictions, supervision.

SAVE ⊠ 🛈 🖵 🖄

CUPERTINO

AAA ▼▼▼▼ **Cypress Hotel** LH
(408) 253-8900. **$129-$309.** 10050 S De Anza Blvd. I-280, exit De Anza Blvd, just s. Int corridors. **Pets:** Accepted.

SAVE S6 ⊠ 🛈 🖵 🚠

CYPRESS

▼▼ **Homestead Studio Suites Hotel-Orange County-Cypress** SH
(714) 761-2766. **$104-$124.** 5990 Corporate Ave. I-605, exit 1D (Katella Ave) southbound; exit 1B (Katella Ave/Willow St) northbound, 3 mi e, 0.4 mi n on Valley View Ave, then just w. Int corridors. **Pets:** Other species. $75 one-time fee/pet. Service with restrictions.

ASK S6 ⊠ 🛈 🖵

AAA ▼▼▼ **Woodfin Suite Hotel-Cypress** SH
(714) 828-4000. **Call for rates.** 5905 Corporate Ave. I-605, exit 1D (Katella Ave) southbound; exit 1B (Katella Ave/Willow St) northbound, 3 mi e, 0.4 mi n on Valley View Ave, then just w. Int corridors. **Pets:** Accepted.

SAVE ⊠ 🛈 🖵 🚠

DANA POINT

▼▼▼▼ **DoubleTree Guest Suites Doheny Beach** SH
(949) 661-1100. **$139-$369, 3 day notice.** 34402 Pacific Coast Hwy. I-5, exit 79 (Beach Cities Dr) northbound; exit 79 (Pacific Coast Hwy) southbound, 0.6 mi w, U-turn at Doheny Park Plaza Dr, then 0.8 mi s. Int corridors. **Pets:** Accepted.

⊠ 🛈 🖵 ¶¶ 🚠 🗵

AAA ▼▼▼▼ **Holiday Inn Express Hotel & Suites** SH
(949) 248-1000. **$119-$399.** 34280 Pacific Coast Hwy. I-5, exit 79 (Pacific Coast Hwy) southbound; exit 79 (Beach Cities Dr) northbound, 0.6 mi w, then 0.5 mi n. Ext/int corridors. **Pets:** Other species. $75 one-time fee/room. Supervision.

SAVE S6 ⊠ 🖄 🛈 🖵 🚠

AAA ▼▼▼▼ **St. Regis Resort, Monarch Beach** LH 🐾
(949) 234-3200. **$625-$6000, 7 day notice.** One Monarch Beach Resort. I-5, exit 79 (Pacific Coast Hwy) northbound, 3 mi n; exit 86 (Crown Valley Pkwy) southbound, 3 mi w, 1 mi s on Pacific Coast Hwy, then 0.5 mi e on Niguel Rd. Int corridors. **Pets:** Small, dogs only. $150 one-time fee/pet. Designated rooms, no service, supervision.

SAVE ⊠ 🖄 ¶¶ 🚠 🗵

DAVIS

AAA ▼▼ **Best Western University Lodge** SH
(530) 756-7890. **$95-$120.** 123 B St. Just e of University of California Davis campus. Ext corridors. **Pets:** Medium. $100 deposit/pet. Service with restrictions, supervision.

SAVE S6 ⊠ 🖄 🛈 🖵 🗵

WWWW Howard Johnson Hotel SH ❖
(530) 792-0800. **Call for rates.** 4100 Chiles Rd. I-80, exit Mace Blvd, just s, then 0.3 mi w. Int corridors. **Pets:** Medium. $20 daily fee/pet. Designated rooms, service with restrictions, supervision.
[SAVE] [X] [&M] [🏢] [🖥] [🍴] [🏊] [X]

WWWW University Park Inn & Suites SH
(530) 756-0910. **$80-$119.** 1111 Richards Blvd. I-80, exit Richards Blvd, just n. Ext corridors. **Pets:** Medium, other species. $250 deposit/pet, $10 daily fee/pet. Designated rooms, service with restrictions, crate.
[SAVE] [S🐾] [X] [&M] [🏢] [🖥] [🏊]

DEATH VALLEY NATIONAL PARK

W Stovepipe Wells Village M
(303) 297-2757. **Call for rates.** SR 190. On SR 190; 24 mi nw of visitor center. Ext corridors. **Pets:** Accepted.
[X] [&M] [🏢] [🍴] [🏊] [🗲]

DELANO

WWW Rodeway Inn M
(661) 725-1022. **Call for rates.** 2211 Girard St. SR 99, exit 58 (County Line Rd), just e, then just s. Ext corridors. **Pets:** Small. $10 daily fee/pet. Designated rooms, service with restrictions, supervision.
[SAVE] [X] [🏢] [🖥] [🏊]

DINUBA

WWWW Reedley Country Inn BB
(559) 638-2585. **Call for rates.** 43137 Rd 52. SR 99, exit 121 (Manning Ave), 10 mi e, then 1 mi s. Ext/int corridors. **Pets:** Accepted.
[X]

DIXON

WWWWW Best Western Inn Dixon SH
(707) 678-1400. **$95-$185, 3 day notice.** 1345 Commercial Way. I-80, exit Pitt School Rd; 8 mi w of University of California Davis campus. Ext/int corridors. **Pets:** Medium, other species. $15 one-time fee/room. Designated rooms, service with restrictions, supervision.
[SAVE] [S🐾] [X] [&M] [🏢] [🖥] [🏊] [X]

WWWW Microtel Inn & Suites M
(707) 693-0606. **$59-$129.** 1480 Ary Ln. I-80, exit Pitt School Rd, just s. Int corridors. **Pets:** Medium. $10 daily fee/pet. Service with restrictions, supervision.
[SAVE] [S🐾] [X] [&M] [🏢] [🏊]

WW Super 8 SH
(707) 678-3399. **Call for rates.** 2500 Plaza Ct. I-80, exit West a St, just s. Int corridors. **Pets:** Accepted.
[X] [🏢] [🏊]

DORRIS

WWW Golden Eagle Motel SH
(530) 397-3114. **$39-$99.** 100 N Main St. US 97; center. **Pets:** $6 daily fee/pet. Designated rooms, service with restrictions, supervision.
[SAVE] [S🐾] [X] [🏢]

DUBLIN

WWWW Radisson Hotel Dublin/Pleasanton SH
(925) 828-7750. **$79-$249.** 6680 Regional St. At northwest quadrant of I-580 and 680. Int corridors. **Pets:** Accepted.
[ASK] [S🐾] [X] [&M] [🏢] [🖥] [🍴] [🏊] [X]

DUNNIGAN

WWWW Americas Best Value Inn SH ❖
(530) 724-3333. **$66-$79.** 3930 Rd 89. I-5, exit Dunnigan. Int corridors. **Pets:** Large. $10 daily fee/pet. Service with restrictions, supervision.
[SAVE] [S🐾] [X] [&M] [🏢] [🏊]

WWW Best Western Country M ❖
(530) 724-3471. **$89-$125.** 3930 Rd 89. I-5, exit Dunnigan. Ext corridors. **Pets:** Large. $20 daily fee/room. Service with restrictions, supervision.
[SAVE] [S🐾] [X] [&M] [🏢] [🖥] [🏊]

DUNSMUIR

WWWW Caboose Motel-Railroad Park Resort M ❖
(530) 235-4440. **Call for rates.** 100 Railroad Park Rd. I-5, exit 728 (Railroad Park Rd), 1 mi s. **Pets:** Large, dogs only. $14 daily fee/pet. Designated rooms, service with restrictions, supervision.
[SAVE] [X] [🏢] [🖥] [🍴] [🏊]

WW Cedar Lodge Motel M
(530) 235-4331. **$50-$74.** 4201 Dunsmuir Ave. I-5, exit 732, 0.5 mi w. Ext corridors. **Pets:** Accepted.
[SAVE] [S🐾] [X] [🏢] [🖥]

EAST PALO ALTO

WWWWW Four Seasons Hotel Silicon Valley at East Palo Alto LH
(650) 566-1200. **Call for rates.** 2050 University Ave. US 101, exit University Ave. Int corridors. **Pets:** Accepted.
[X] [&M] [🖥] [🍴] [🏊] [X]

EL CENTRO

WWW Barbara Worth Resort SH
(760) 356-2806. **$119-$159.** 2050 Country Club Dr. I-8, exit 120 (Bowker Rd), 2 mi n, then 3 mi e on CR S-80; 9 mi e of SR 86. Ext/int corridors. **Pets:** Accepted.
[ASK] [X] [🏢] [🖥] [🍴] [🏊] [X]

WWW Ramada Inn El Centro M
(760) 352-5152. **$69-$99.** 1455 Ocotillo Dr. I-8, exit 114 (Imperial Ave), just n, then just e. Ext corridors. **Pets:** Accepted.
[SAVE] [S🐾] [X] [🏢] [🖥] [🍴] [🏊]

WWW Rodeway Inn & Suites M
(760) 352-6620. **Call for rates.** 455 W Wake Ave. I-8, exit 115 (4th St/SR 86), just s, then just w. Ext corridors. **Pets:** Small. $5 daily fee/pet. Service with restrictions, supervision.
[SAVE] [X] [🏢] [🏊]

WWW Super Star Inn-El Centro M
(760) 352-0715. **$50-$90.** 611 N Imperial Ave. I-8, exit 114 (Imperial Ave), 1.5 mi n. Ext corridors. **Pets:** Accepted.
[SAVE] [S🐾] [X] [🏢] [🖥]

WW Vacation Inn M
(760) 352-9700. **$65-$95.** 2015 Cottonwood Cir. I-8, exit 114 (Imperial Ave), just n, then just w. Ext corridors. **Pets:** Accepted.
[S🐾] [X] [🏢] [🍴] [🏊]

ELK GROVE

WW Extended StayAmerica-Sacramento-Elk Grove SH
(916) 683-3753. **$99-$110.** 2201 Long Port Ct. I-5, exit Laguna Blvd, 0.5 mi e, just s on Harbour Point Dr, then just w. Int corridors. **Pets:** Other species. $75 one-time fee/pet. Service with restrictions.
[ASK] [S🐾] [X] [🏢]

EL PORTAL

WWWWW Yosemite View Lodge SH
(209) 379-2681. **$95-$729, 14 day notice.** 11136 Hwy 140. Just w of Yosemite National Park West Gate. Ext corridors. **Pets:** Other species. $10 daily fee/pet. Service with restrictions, supervision.
[SAVE] [X] [&M] [🏢] [🖥] [🏊] [X]

EMERYVILLE

WW Extended StayAmerica-Oakland-Emeryville **SH**
(510) 923-1481. **$113-$125.** 3650 Mandela Pkwy. I-80, exit Powell St
W, s on Shellmound St via Horton St to Mandela Pkwy. Int corridors.
Pets: Other species. $75 one-time fee/pet. Service with restrictions.
[ASK] [S$] [X] [■] [■]

**WWW Woodfin Suite Hotel San Francisco Bay
Bridge** **LH**
(510) 601-5880. **$149-$239.** 5800 Shellmound St. I-80, exit Powell St.
Int corridors. **Pets:** Small. $150 deposit/room, $10 daily fee/pet. Designated rooms, service with restrictions, crate.
[SAVE] [S$] [X] [■] [■] [††] [≈]

ENCINITAS

**WWW Best Western Encinitas Inn & Suites at
Moonlight Beach** **M**
(760) 942-7455. **$130-$220, 3 day notice.** 85 Encinitas Blvd. I-5, exit
41B (Encinitas Blvd), just w. Ext corridors. **Pets:** Medium. $75 one-time
fee/room. Designated rooms, service with restrictions, supervision.
[SAVE] [S$] [X] [■] [■] [††] [≈]

WWW Howard Johnson-Encinitas **M**
(760) 944-3800. **Call for rates.** 607 Leucadia Blvd. I-5, exit 43 (Leucadia Blvd), east side. Ext corridors. **Pets:** Medium, other species. $15
daily fee/room. Service with restrictions, supervision.
[X] [■] [■] [≈]

WW Portofino Beach Inn **M**
(760) 944-0301. **$69-$350.** 186 N Coast Hwy. I-5, exit 41B (Encinitas
Blvd), 0.6 mi w, then just n. Ext corridors. **Pets:** Accepted.
[ASK] [S$] [X] [■] [■]

ESCONDIDO

WWW Best Western Escondido **SH**
(760) 740-1700. **$110-$180.** 1700 Seven Oaks Rd. I-15, exit 33 (El
Norte Pkwy), just e. Int corridors. **Pets:** Small, other species. $25 one-time fee/pet. Service with restrictions, supervision.
[SAVE] [S$] [X] [■] [■]

WW Rodeway Inn **M** 🐾
(760) 746-0441. **$54-$129.** 250 W El Norte Pkwy. I-15, exit 33 (El Norte
Pkwy), 1 mi e. Ext corridors. **Pets:** Medium. $30 daily fee/pet. Designated
rooms, service with restrictions, supervision.
[SAVE] [S$] [X] [■] [■]

ETNA

W Motel Etna **M**
(530) 467-5330. **Call for rates.** 317 Collier Way. Just w of SR 3. Ext
corridors. **Pets:** Accepted.
[X] [■]

EUREKA

WW Americas Best Value Inn & Suites **M**
(707) 443-9751. **$55-$150.** 129 4th St. On US 101 southbound; corner
of C St. Ext corridors. **Pets:** Medium, dogs only. $20 deposit/pet, $8 daily
fee/pet. Designated rooms, service with restrictions, supervision.
[SAVE] [S$] [X] [■] [■] [K]

WWW Best Western Bayshore Inn **M**
(707) 268-8005. **$97-$220.** 3500 Broadway. US 101; south end of town.
Ext corridors. **Pets:** Medium, dogs only. $40 one-time fee/room. Service
with restrictions, supervision.
[SAVE] [S$] [X] [■] [■] [††] [≈] [⊠]

WWW Carter House Inns **CI** 🐾
(707) 444-8062. **$190-$612, 3 day notice.** 301 L St. Just w of US 101
S. Int corridors. **Pets:** Large. $50 one-time fee/room. Service with restrictions, supervision.
[SAVE] [S$] [X] [■] [††] [K]

WW Eureka Town House Motel **M**
(707) 443-4536. **$55-$135.** 933 4th St. On US 101 southbound; corner
of K St. Ext corridors. **Pets:** Medium, dogs only. $10 daily fee/pet. Designated rooms, service with restrictions, supervision.
[SAVE] [S$] [X] [■] [■] [K]

W Eureka Travelodge **M**
(707) 443-6345. **Call for rates.** 4 4th St. On US 101; corner of 4th and
B sts. Ext corridors. **Pets:** Accepted.
[X] [■] [■] [≈] [K]

WWW Quality Inn Eureka **M**
(707) 443-1601. **$78-$250.** 1209 4th St. On US 101 southbound;
between M and N sts. Ext corridors. **Pets:** Accepted.
[SAVE] [S$] [X] [■] [■] [≈] [K]

WWWW Red Lion Hotel Eureka **SH** 🐾
(707) 445-0844. **$119-$199.** 1929 4th St. On US 101 southbound;
between T and V sts. Ext corridors. **Pets:** Medium. $20 one-time fee/pet.
Service with restrictions, supervision.
[SAVE] [S$] [X] [■] [■] [††] [≈]

FAIRFIELD

WW Days Inn **M**
(707) 864-1728. **Call for rates.** 4376 Central Pl. I-80, exit Suisun Valley
Rd, just e. Ext corridors. **Pets:** Accepted.
[SAVE] [X] [■] [≈]

WW Extended StayAmerica-Fairfield-Napa Valley **SH**
(707) 438-0932. **$99-$110.** 1019 Oliver Rd. I-80, exit Texas St, just w.
Int corridors. **Pets:** Other species. $75 one-time fee/pet. Service with
restrictions.
[ASK] [S$] [X] [■] [■]

FALLBROOK

WW Fallbrook Country Inn **M**
(760) 728-1114. **Call for rates.** 1425 S Mission Rd. I-15, exit 51 (Mission Rd), 6.4 mi sw. Ext corridors. **Pets:** Accepted.
[X] [■] [■] [≈]

WWW Pala Mesa Resort **LH**
(760) 728-5881. **$149-$225, 3 day notice.** 2001 Old Hwy 395. I-15, exit
46 (SR 76/Pala/Oceanside), just w, then 2 mi n. Ext corridors.
Pets: Accepted.
[SAVE] [S$] [X] [■] [■] [††] [≈] [⊠]

FALL RIVER MILLS

WW Hi-Mont Motel **M** 🐾
(530) 336-5541. **$69-$99, 3 day notice.** 43021 Bridge St. 1 mi w on
SR 299. Ext corridors. **Pets:** Other species. $10 daily fee/pet. Service with
restrictions, supervision.
[SAVE] [S$] [X] [■] [■]

FERNDALE

WWW Collingwood Inn Bed & Breakfast **BB**
(707) 786-9219. **Call for rates.** 831 Main St. Center. Int corridors.
Pets: Accepted.
[X] [K] [Z]

WWW Shaw House Inn Bed & Breakfast **BB**
(707) 786-9958. **Call for rates.** 703 Main St. Center. Ext/int corridors.
Pets: Medium, other species. $30 daily fee/pet. Designated rooms, service
with restrictions, supervision.
[SAVE] [X] [K] [W] [Z]

FILLMORE

WWW Best Western La Posada Motel **M**
(805) 524-0440. **$95-$130.** 827 Ventura Ave. On SR 126. Ext corridors.
Pets: Accepted.
[SAVE] [S$] [X] [■] [■] [≈]

FIREBAUGH

⚜ **▼▼▼** Best Western Apricot Inn **M**
(559) 659-1444. **$72-$110.** 46290 W Panoche Rd. I-5, exit W Panoche Rd, just w. Ext corridors. **Pets:** Small. $10 daily fee/pet. Service with restrictions, supervision.

SAVE [S] ⊠ ⬛ ⬛ ⬅

FISH CAMP

⚜ **▼▼▼▼** Apple Tree Inn **SH** ❀
(559) 683-5111. **Call for rates.** 1110 Hwy 41. 2 mi from South Gate to Yosemite National Park. Ext corridors. **Pets:** Large. $50 one-time fee/pet. Designated rooms, service with restrictions, supervision.

SAVE ⊠ &M ⬛ ⬅ ⊠ ⿻

▼▼ The Narrow Gauge Inn **SH**
(559) 683-7720. **$79-$250, 4 day notice.** 48571 Hwy 41. 4 mi from South Gate to Yosemite National Park. Ext corridors. **Pets:** Accepted.

⊠ ⬛ ⬛ ⿻ ⬅

⚜ **▼▼▼▼** Tenaya Lodge at Yosemite **LH** ❀
(559) 683-6555. **$119-$389, 7 day notice.** 1122 Hwy 41. 2 mi from South Gate to Yosemite National Park. Int corridors. **Pets:** Large, dogs only. $75 one-time fee/room. No service, supervision.

SAVE ⊠ &M ⬛ ⬛ ⿻ ⬅ ⊠

FOLSOM

⚜ **▼▼▼** Lake Natoma Inn **SH** ❀
(916) 351-1500. **$89-$159.** 702 Gold Lake Dr. US 50, exit Folsom Blvd, 3 mi n; behind The Lakes Specialty Shopping Center. Int corridors. **Pets:** Other species. $15 daily fee/pet, $45 one-time fee/room. Service with restrictions, supervision.

SAVE [S] ⊠ &M ⬛ ⬛ ⿻ ⬅ ⊠

⚜ **▼▼▼** Larkspur Landing Folsom **SH** ❀
(916) 355-1616. **$169-$189.** 121 Iron Point Rd. US 50, exit Folsom Blvd, 0.5 mi n to Iron Point Rd, then 0.3 mi e. Int corridors. **Pets:** Medium. $75 one-time fee/pet. Designated rooms, service with restrictions.

SAVE [S] ⊠ &M ⬛ ⬛

▼▼▼ Residence Inn by Marriott **SH**
(916) 983-7289. **$150-$193.** 2555 Iron Point Rd. US 50, exit Bidwell St, just e. Int corridors. **Pets:** Accepted.

A$K [S] ⊠ &M ⬛ ⬛ ⬅ ⊠

FORTUNA

⚜ **▼▼** Best Western Country Inn **M** ❀
(707) 725-6822. **$84-$155.** 2025 Riverwalk Dr. US 101, exit 687 (Kenmar Rd), just w. Ext corridors. **Pets:** Medium, dogs only. $20 one-time fee/pet. Designated rooms, service with restrictions, supervision.

SAVE [S] ⊠ &M ⬛ ⬛ ⬅

⚜ **▼▼** Fortuna Super 8 **M**
(707) 725-2888. **$80-$155.** 1805 Alamar Way. US 101, exit 687 (Kenmar Rd), 0.3 mi w on Riverwalk Dr to Alamar Way. Ext corridors. **Pets:** Small, dogs only. $10 daily fee/pet. Designated rooms, service with restrictions, supervision.

SAVE [S] ⊠ ⬛ ⬛

▼▼▼ Holiday Inn Express **M**
(707) 725-5500. **$90-$120.** 1859 Alamar Way. US 101, exit 687 (Kenmar Rd), 0.3 mi w on Riverwalk Dr to Alamar Way. Ext corridors. **Pets:** Accepted.

A$K [S] ⊠ ⬛ ⬛ ⬅

⚜ **▼▼** Travel Inn **M**
(707) 725-6993. **Call for rates.** 275 12th St. US 101, exit 12th St, 0.5 mi w. Ext corridors. **Pets:** Very small, dogs only. $10 daily fee/pet. Designated rooms, service with restrictions, supervision.

SAVE ⊠ ⬛ ⿻

FOUNTAIN VALLEY

▼▼▼ Residence Inn by Marriott **SH**
(714) 965-8000. **$264-$284.** 9930 Slater Ave. I-405, exit 14 (Brookhurst St), just n, then just w. Ext corridors. **Pets:** Accepted.

A$K [S] ⊠ ⬛ ⬛ ⬅ ⊠

FREMONT

⚜ **▼▼▼** Best Western Garden Court Inn **SH**
(510) 792-4300. **$69-$169.** 5400 Mowry Ave. I-880, exit Mowry Ave, just e. Int corridors. **Pets:** Accepted.

SAVE [S] ⊠ ⬛ ⬛ ⬅

▼ Extended StayAmerica-Fremont **SH**
(510) 979-1222. **$81-$90.** 46312 Mission Blvd. I-680, exit Mission Blvd (SR 262), just w. Int corridors. **Pets:** Other species. $75 one-time fee/pet. Service with restrictions.

A$K [S] ⊠ ⬛

▼ Extended StayAmerica-Fremont-Newark **SH**
(510) 794-8040. **$86-$95.** 5355 Farwell Pl. I-880, exit Mowry Ave, just e. Int corridors. **Pets:** Other species. $75 one-time fee/pet. Service with restrictions.

A$K [S] ⊠ &M ⬛

▼▼ Extended Stay Deluxe-Fremont-Newark **SH**
(510) 794-9693. **$95-$105.** 5375 Farwell Pl. I-880, exit Mowry Ave, just e. Int corridors. **Pets:** Other species. $75 one-time fee/pet. Service with restrictions.

A$K [S] ⊠ ⬛ ⬅

▼▼▼ Fremont Marriott **LH**
(510) 413-3700. **$264-$284.** 46100 Landing Pkwy. I-880, exit Fremont Blvd/Cushing Pkwy, then w. Int corridors. **Pets:** Accepted.

A$K [S] ⊠ ⬛ ⬛ ⿻ ⬅

▼▼ Homestead Studio Suites Hotel-Fremont Blvd. South **SH**
(510) 353-1664. **$86-$95.** 46080 Fremont Blvd. I-880, exit Fremont Blvd/Cushing Pkwy, just w. Int corridors. **Pets:** Other species. $75 one-time fee/pet. Service with restrictions.

A$K [S] ⊠ &M ⬛

▼▼▼ La Quinta Inn & Suites Fremont **SH**
(510) 445-0808. **$115-$155.** 46200 Landing Pkwy. I-880, exit Fremont Blvd/Cushing Pkwy, just w. Int corridors. **Pets:** Other species. Service with restrictions, supervision.

A$K [S] ⊠ &M ⬛ ⬛ ⬅

▼▼▼ Residence Inn by Marriott **SH**
(510) 794-5900. **$187-$207.** 5400 Farwell Pl. I-880, exit Mowry Ave, just e. Ext corridors. **Pets:** Accepted.

A$K [S] ⊠ &M ⬛ ⬅ ⊠

FRESNO

▼ Crossland Economy Studios **SH**
(559) 277-8700. **$77-$85.** 3460 W Shaw Ave. SR 99, exit Shaw Ave, 1.8 mi e. Ext corridors. **Pets:** Other species. $75 one-time fee/pet. Service with restrictions.

A$K [S] ⊠ &M ⬛ ⬛

⚜ **▼▼▼** Days Inn Jensen & 99 **SH**
(559) 237-6644. **Call for rates.** 2640 S Second St. SR 99, exit Jensen Ave, just e. Ext corridors. **Pets:** Accepted.

SAVE ⊠ ⬛ ⬛ ⬅

⚜ **▼▼** Days Inn-Parkway **M**
(559) 268-6211. **$58-$99.** 1101 N Parkway Dr. SR 99, exit Olive Ave, just w. Ext corridors. **Pets:** $10 daily fee/pet. Service with restrictions, supervision.

SAVE [S] ⊠ ⬛ ⬛ ⬅

▼▼ Extended StayAmerica **SH**
(559) 438-7105. **$104-$115.** 7135 N Fresno St. SR 41, exit Herndon Ave, just e, then just n. Ext corridors. **Pets:** Other species. $75 one-time fee/pet. Service with restrictions.
ASK S✆ ✕ ⛾M 🛏 💻 🖵

▼▼▼ La Quinta Inn Fresno/Yosemite **SH**
(559) 442-1110. **$99-$129.** 2926 Tulare St. SR 99, exit Fresno St, 1 mi e to R St, then s, then just e. Ext/int corridors. **Pets:** Other species. Service with restrictions, supervision.
ASK S✆ ✕ ⛾M 🛏 💻 🖦

▼▼ Quality Inn **M**
(559) 275-2727. **$89-$159.** 4278 W Ashlan Ave. SR 99, exit Ashlan Ave, just w. Ext corridors. **Pets:** Accepted.
ASK S✆ ✕ 🛏 💻 🖦

▼ Red Roof Inn **M**
(559) 276-1910. **Call for rates.** 5021 N Barcus Ave. SR 99, exit Shaw Ave, just e. Ext corridors. **Pets:** Accepted.
✕ 🛏 🖦

▼▼ Residence Inn by Marriott **SH**
(559) 222-8900. **$198-$218.** 5322 N Diana St. SR 41, exit Shaw Ave, 0.3 mi w, n on Blackstone Ave, then e on Barstow Ave. Int corridors. **Pets:** Accepted.
ASK S✆ ✕ ⛾M 🛏 💻 🖦 🖵

AAA ▼▼▼ Rodeway Inn **SH**
(559) 431-3557. **Call for rates.** 6730 N Blackstone Ave. SR 41, exit Herndon Ave, then w. Ext corridors. **Pets:** Accepted.
SAVE ✕ 🖦

AAA ▼▼▼ Super 8-Parkway **M**
(559) 268-0741. **$57-$89.** 1087 N Parkway Dr. SR 99, exit Olive Ave, just w. Ext corridors. **Pets:** Medium. $10 daily fee/pet. Service with restrictions, supervision.
SAVE S✆ ✕ 🛏 💻 🖦

AAA ▼▼▼▼ TownePlace Suites by Marriott **SH**
(559) 435-4600. **$126-$146.** 7127 N Fresno St. SR 41, exit Herndon Ave E. Int corridors. **Pets:** Other species. $100 one-time fee/room. Service with restrictions, supervision.
SAVE S✆ ✕ ⛾M 🛏 💻 🖦

AAA ▼▼ University Inn **SH**
(559) 294-0224. **$59-$99.** 2655 E Shaw Ave. SR 168, exit Shaw Ave, just w. Ext corridors. **Pets:** Small, other species. $60 deposit/room, $20 one-time fee/room. Service with restrictions, supervision.
SAVE ✕ 🛏 🖦

AAA ▼ Valley Inn **M**
(559) 233-3913. **$45-$65.** 933 N Parkway Dr. SR 99, exit Olive Ave, then w. Ext corridors. **Pets:** Small, dogs only. $6 daily fee/pet. Designated rooms, service with restrictions, supervision.
SAVE S✆ ✕ 🛏

FULLERTON

▼▼▼▼ Fullerton Marriott Hotel at California State Univ **SH**
(714) 738-7800. **$192-$212.** 2701 E Nutwood Ave. SR 57, exit 7 (Nutwood Ave) northbound; exit 7 (Nutwood Ave/Chapman Ave) southbound, just w. Int corridors. **Pets:** Accepted.
ASK S✆ ✕ ⛾M 🛏 💻 🍽 🖦 🖵

GARBERVILLE

AAA ▼▼▼▼ Best Western Humboldt House Inn **M**
(707) 923-2771. **$92-$142.** 701 Redwood Dr. US 101, exit Garberville, just e. Ext corridors. **Pets:** Small, dogs only. $5 one-time fee/room. Designated rooms, service with restrictions, supervision.
SAVE S✆ ✕ 🛏 💻 🖦

GARDEN GROVE

AAA ▼▼▼▼ Anaheim Marriott Suites **LH** ❀
(714) 750-1000. **$242-$262.** 12015 Harbor Blvd. I-5, exit 107B (Chapman Ave) northbound, 1.5 mi w on Chapman Ave, then just s; exit 107C (State College/The City Dr) southbound, just s on State College Blvd, 1.5 mi w on Chapman Ave, then just s. Int corridors. **Pets:** Other species. $15 daily fee/pet. Designated rooms, service with restrictions, supervision.
SAVE S✆ ✕ 🛏 💻 🍽 🖦 🖵

▼▼ Candlewood Suites Anaheim-South **SH**
(714) 539-4200. **Call for rates.** 12901 Garden Grove Blvd. SR 22, exit 13 (Haster St) westbound; exit 13 (Fairview St) eastbound, just n, then just w. Int corridors. **Pets:** Accepted.
✕ 🛏 💻

AAA ▼▼▼▼ Residence Inn Anaheim Resort Area **SH**
(714) 591-4000. **$186-$208.** 11931 Harbor Blvd. I-5, exit 107B (Chapman Ave) northbound, 1.5 mi w, then just n; exit 107C (State College/The City Dr) southbound, just s on State College Blvd, 1.5 mi w on Chapman Ave, then just n. Int corridors. **Pets:** Small. $75 one-time fee/room. Service with restrictions, supervision.
SAVE S✆ ✕ ⛾M 🛏 💻 🖦 🖵

GILROY

AAA ▼▼▼▼ Best Western Forest Park Inn **SH**
(408) 848-5144. **$79-$259.** 375 Leavesley Rd. US 101, exit Leavesley Rd, just w. Int corridors. **Pets:** Small. $30 daily fee/pet. Designated rooms, service with restrictions, crate.
SAVE S✆ ✕ 🛏 💻 🖦 🖵

AAA ▼▼▼ Quality Inn & Suites **SH**
(408) 847-5500. **$69-$249.** 8430 Murray Ave. US 101, exit Leavesley Rd, just w. Ext corridors. **Pets:** Accepted.
SAVE S✆ ✕ 🛏 💻 🖦

AAA ▼▼ Super 8 Motel **SH**
(408) 848-4108. **$89.** 8435 San Ysidro Ave. US 101, exit Leavesley Rd, just e. Int corridors. **Pets:** Small. $10 daily fee/pet. Designated rooms, service with restrictions, supervision.
SAVE ✕ 🛏 🖦

GLENNVILLE

▼▼ The Bunkhouse Motel **M**
(661) 536-9100. **$65-$75.** 12044 Hwy 155 S. On SR 155 at Granite Rd. Ext corridors. **Pets:** Accepted.
ASK S✆ ✕ 🛏 💻 🍽

GRAEAGLE

▼▼▼ Chalet View Lodge **SH**
(530) 832-5528. **$92-$208, 7 day notice.** 72056 Hwy 70. 5 mi e on SR 70 (Feather River Hwy) from jct SR 89. Ext corridors. **Pets:** Accepted.
ASK ✕ 🛏 💻 🍽 🖦 🖵

GRASS VALLEY

AAA ▼▼▼ Alta Sierra Village Inn **M** ❀
(530) 273-9102. **$69-$195, 7 day notice.** 11858 Tammy Way. 6 mi s, 1.1 mi e on Alta Sierra Dr, 0.8 mi w on Norlene, then 0.5 mi e; follow signs to Alta Sierra Country Club. Ext corridors. **Pets:** Other species. $10 daily fee/room. Designated rooms, service with restrictions, supervision.
SAVE ✕ ⛾M 🛏 💻 🗵

AAA ▼▼▼ Best Western Gold Country Inn **M**
(530) 273-1393. **$89-$149.** 11972 Sutton Way. SR 20 and 49, exit Brunswick Rd, just e; midway between Grass Valley and Nevada City. Ext corridors. **Pets:** Small, other species. $20 one-time fee/pet. Service with restrictions, supervision.
SAVE S✆ ✕ ⛾M 🛏 💻 🖦

Coach N' Four Motel M
(530) 273-8009. **$56-$190, 3 day notice.** 628 S Auburn St. SR 49, exit E Empire St, 0.3 mi e, then just s. Ext corridors. **Pets:** Dogs only. $10 daily fee/pet. Service with restrictions, supervision.

Golden Chain Resort Motel M
(530) 273-7279. **$55-$99.** 13413 State Hwy 49. On SR 49, 2.5 mi s. Ext corridors. **Pets:** Small. $10 one-time fee/pet. Service with restrictions, supervision.

Grass Valley Courtyard Suites SH ☘
(530) 272-7696. **$145-$325, 3 day notice.** 210 N Auburn St. SR 49, exit Central Grass Valley/SR 174. Ext corridors. **Pets:** Large, dogs only. $50 one-time fee/pet. Service with restrictions, supervision.

Stagecoach Motel M
(530) 272-3701. **$60-$109, 3 day notice.** 405 S Auburn St. SR 49, exit Colfax Ave, 0.4 mi s. Ext corridors. **Pets:** Small, dogs only. $10 one-time fee/pet. Designated rooms, service with restrictions, supervision.

GREENVILLE

Yorkshire House B&B BB
(530) 284-1794. **Call for rates.** 421 Main St. N on SR 89, then 1 mi. Int corridors. **Pets:** Small. $25 daily fee/pet. No service, supervision.

GRIDLEY

Pacific Motel M
(530) 846-4580. **Call for rates.** 1308 Hwy 99. On SR 99, 1 mi s. Ext corridors. **Pets:** Accepted.

GROVELAND

Groveland Hotel at Yosemite National Park CI
(209) 962-4000. **$145-$285.** 18767 Main St. Center. Int corridors. **Pets:** Accepted.

HANFORD

Irwin Street Inn BB
(559) 583-8000. **Call for rates.** 522 N Irwin St. Downtown. Ext corridors. **Pets:** Accepted.

Sequoia Inn SH
(559) 582-0338. **Call for rates.** 1655 Mall Dr. SR 198, exit 12th Ave, then n. Int corridors. **Pets:** $100 deposit/room. No service, supervision.

HAYWARD

Comfort Inn SH
(510) 538-4466. **$89-$170.** 24997 Mission Blvd. 1.8 mi e of I-880, exit SR 92 (Jackson St), 0.5 mi s on SR 238 (Mission Blvd). Ext corridors. **Pets:** Small. $100 deposit/room, $15 daily fee/pet. Designated rooms, service with restrictions, supervision.

La Quinta Inn & Suites Hayward/Oakland Airport SH
(510) 732-6300. **$114-$134.** 20777 Hesperian Blvd. I-880, exit a St, 0.5 mi w. Int corridors. **Pets:** Other species. Service with restrictions, supervision.

MainStay Suites SH
(510) 731-3571. **$59-$120.** 835 West a St. I-880, exit a St, just w. Int corridors. **Pets:** Accepted.

HEMET

Best Western Inn of Hemet M
(951) 925-6605. **$109-$139.** 2625 W Florida Ave. 2.4 mi w of SR 79 N (San Jacinto St) on SR 74/79. Ext corridors. **Pets:** Medium, other species. $25 daily fee/room. Designated rooms, service with restrictions, supervision.

Coach Light Motel M
(951) 658-3237. **$60-$80.** 1640 W Florida Ave. 1.7 mi w of SR 74 N (San Jacinto St) on SR 74/79. Ext corridors. **Pets:** Dogs only. $7 daily fee/pet. No service, supervision.

Quality Inn M
(951) 766-1902. **$98-$119.** 1201 W Florida Ave. 1.5 mi w of SR 79 N (San Jacinto St) on SR 74/79. Ext corridors. **Pets:** Small. $20 daily fee/pet. Service with restrictions, supervision.

HESPERIA

Days Inn Suites-Hesperia/Victorville M
(760) 948-0600. **Call for rates.** 14865 Bear Valley Rd. I-15, exit 147 (Bear Valley Rd), 0.5 mi e of Victor Valley Mall. Ext corridors. **Pets:** Accepted.

Holiday Inn Express Hotel & Suites SH
(760) 244-7674. **$99.** 9750 Key Pointe Dr. I-15, exit 143 (Hesperia/Main St), just w on Main St, then just n. Int corridors. **Pets:** Small, other species. $25 daily fee/pet. Service with restrictions, supervision.

La Quinta Inn & Suites Victorville SH
(760) 949-9900. **$110-$140.** 12000 Mariposa Rd. I-15, exit 147 (Bear Valley Rd), just e, then just s. Int corridors. **Pets:** Other species. Service with restrictions, supervision.

Super 8 Motel M
(760) 949-3231. **$83-$125.** 12033 Oakwood Ave. I-15, exit 147 (Bear Valley Rd), just se. Ext corridors. **Pets:** Other species. $10 daily fee/pet. Supervision.

HUNTINGTON BEACH

Extended StayAmerica-Orange County/Huntington Beach SH
(714) 799-4887. **$104-$124.** 5050 Skylab W Cir. I-405, exit 21 (SR 22 Valley View Blvd) northbound, 1.8 mi s; exit 18 (Bolsa Ave) southbound, 2 mi s. Int corridors. **Pets:** Other species. $75 one-time fee/pet. Service with restrictions.

Hilton Waterfront Beach Resort LH
(714) 845-8000. **Call for rates.** 21100 Pacific Coast Hwy. I-405, exit 16 (Beach Blvd), 6 mi s, then just w. Int corridors. **Pets:** Accepted.

IDYLLWILD

Cedar Street Inn CA
(951) 659-4789. **$90-$160, 10 day notice.** 25880 Cedar St. From SR 243 and town center, 0.3 mi ne on N Circle Dr. Ext corridors. **Pets:** Accepted.

▼▼ **Fern Valley Inn and Cabins** 🅒🅐
(951) 659-2205. **$85-$175, 10 day notice.** 25240 Fern Valley Rd. From SR 243 and town center, 0.8 mi ne on N Circle Dr, just s on S Circle Dr, then 0.4 mi ne. Ext corridors. **Pets:** Accepted.
🅰🅢🅚 ☒ 🛈 💻 ⇨ 🅐🅚 🅩

🛸 ▼▼ **Fireside Inn** 🅒🅐 🐾
(951) 659-2966. **$65-$130, 10 day notice.** 54540 N Circle Dr. From SR 243 and town center, 0.3 mi ne. Ext corridors. **Pets:** Medium, other species. $10 daily fee/room. Supervision.
🅢🅐🅥🅔 🅢🅓 ☒ 🛈 💻 🅩

▼▼ **Quiet Creek Inn** 🅜
(951) 659-6110. **$112-$195, 14 day notice.** 26345 Delano Dr. From SR 243, 0.8 mi sw of town center, 0.4 mi w on Toll Gate Rd, then just n. Ext corridors. **Pets:** Accepted.
☒ 🛈 💻 🅩

▼▼ **Woodland Park Manor** 🅜
(951) 659-2657. **$95-$195, 10 day notice.** 55350 S Circle Dr. From SR 243 and town center, 1 mi ne. Ext corridors. **Pets:** Accepted.
🅰🅢🅚 🅢🅓 ☒ 🛈 💻 ⇨ 🅐🅚 🅩

INDEPENDENCE

🛸 ▼ **Independence Courthouse Motel** 🅜
(760) 878-2732. **Call for rates.** 157 N Edwards. On US 395. Ext corridors. **Pets:** Accepted.
🅢🅐🅥🅔 ☒ 🛈 💻

▼▼ **Ray's Den Motel** 🅜
(760) 878-2122. **Call for rates.** 405 N Edwards. On US 395. Ext corridors. **Pets:** Accepted.
☒ 🛈 💻

INDIO

🛸 ▼▼ **Best Western Date Tree Hotel** 🅜
(760) 347-3421. **$79-$199.** 81-909 Indio Blvd. I-10, exit 139 (Jefferson St/Indio Blvd), 2 mi se; eastbound, south across freeway, then 2.8 mi e. Int corridors. **Pets:** Accepted.
🅢🅐🅥🅔 🅢🅓 ☒ 🛈 💻 ⇨

🛸 ▼▼ **Indian Palms Country Club & Resort** 🆂🅷
(760) 775-4444. **$84-$209.** 48-630 Monroe St. I-10, exit 142 (Monroe St), 2 mi s. Ext corridors. **Pets:** Medium, dogs only. $15 daily fee/room. Service with restrictions, crate.
🅢🅐🅥🅔 ☒ 🛈 💻 🍽 ⇨ 🅧

🛸 ▼▼ **Quality Inn** 🅜
(760) 347-4044. **$79-$350.** 43505 Monroe St. I-10, exit 142 (Monroe St), 0.5 mi s. Int corridors. **Pets:** Accepted.
🅢🅐🅥🅔 🅢🅓 ☒ 🛈 💻 ⇨

🛸 ▼▼ **Super 8 Motel** 🅜
(760) 342-0264. **$59-$209.** 81753 Hwy 111. I-10, exit 142 (Monroe St), 1.5 mi s, then 0.5 mi w. Ext corridors. **Pets:** Accepted.
🅢🅐🅥🅔 🅢🅓 ☒ 🛈 💻 ⇨

IRVINE

🛸 ▼▼ **Hilton Irvine/Orange County Airport** 🅻🅷 🐾
(949) 833-9999. **Call for rates.** 18800 MacArthur Blvd. I-405, exit 8 (MacArthur Blvd/John Wayne Airport), 0.5 mi s. Int corridors. **Pets:** Other species. Service with restrictions, supervision.
🅢🅐🅥🅔 ☒ 🛈 💻 🍽 ⇨

▼▼▼ **La Quinta Inn Irvine Spectrum (Old Historic Site)** 🅜
(949) 551-0909. **$114-$134.** 14972 Sand Canyon Ave. I-5, exit 96 (Sand Canyon Ave) northbound; exit 96A (Sand Canyon Ave) southbound, just w. Ext/int corridors. **Pets:** Other species. Service with restrictions, supervision.
🅰🅢🅚 🅢🅓 ☒ 🛈 💻 ⇨

▼▼▼ **Residence Inn by Marriott Irvine John Wayne Airport** 🆂🅷
(949) 261-2020. **$286-$306.** 2855 Main St. I-405, exit 7 (Jamboree Blvd), just n, then just e. Int corridors. **Pets:** Accepted.
🅰🅢🅚 🅢🅓 ☒ 🛈 💻 ⇨ 🅧

▼▼▼ **Residence Inn by Marriott-Irvine Spectrum** 🆂🅷
(949) 380-3000. **$264-$284.** 10 Morgan. I-5, exit 94B (Alton Pkwy) northbound; exit 94 (Alton Pkwy) southbound, 2 mi e. Ext corridors. **Pets:** Accepted.
🅰🅢🅚 🅢🅓 ☒ 🛈 💻 ⇨ 🅧

JACKSON

🛸 ▼ **Amador Motel** 🅜
(209) 223-0970. **Call for rates.** 12408 Kennedy Flat Rd. 1.5 mi n at jct SR 49 and 88 on Frontage Rd. Ext corridors. **Pets:** Dogs only. $10 one-time fee/pet. Service with restrictions, supervision.
🅢🅐🅥🅔 ☒ 🛈 💻 ⇨

🛸 ▼▼ **Best Western Amador Inn** 🆂🅷
(209) 223-0211. **$80-$111.** 200 S Hwy 49. On SR 49. Int corridors. **Pets:** $10 daily fee/pet. Service with restrictions, supervision.
🅢🅐🅥🅔 🅢🅓 ☒ 🛈 💻 ⇨

🛸 ▼▼ **El Campo Casa Resort Motel** 🅜
(209) 223-0100. **Call for rates.** 12548 Kennedy Flat Rd. 1.5 mi w in Martell; jct SR 49 and 88 on Frontage Rd; approach off SR 88. Ext corridors. **Pets:** Accepted.
🅢🅐🅥🅔 ☒ 💻 ⇨ 🅩

🛸 ▼▼ **The Jackson Lodge** 🅜
(209) 223-0486. **Call for rates.** 850 N Hwy 49/88. On SR 88/49, 0.5 mi w. Ext corridors. **Pets:** Medium, dogs only. $100 deposit/pet, $15 daily fee/pet. Designated rooms, service with restrictions, supervision.
🅢🅐🅥🅔 ☒ 🛈 💻 ⇨

JAMESTOWN

🛸 ▼▼▼ **1859 Historic National Hotel, a Country Inn** 🅒🅘
(209) 984-3446. **Call for rates.** 18183 Main St. Downtown. Int corridors. **Pets:** Accepted.
🅢🅐🅥🅔 ☒ 🍽 🅦 🅩

▼▼ **Country Inn Sonora** 🅜
(209) 984-0315. **$48-$189.** 18730 Hwy 108. On SR 108 and 49, 1 mi e of town. Ext corridors. **Pets:** Accepted.
🅰🅢🅚 🅢🅓 ☒ 🛈 💻 ⇨

🛸 ▼▼ **Jamestown Railtown Motel** 🅜
(209) 984-3332. **$40-$80, 3 day notice.** 10301 Willow St. Center. Ext corridors. **Pets:** Medium, dogs only. $10 daily fee/pet. No service.
🅢🅐🅥🅔 🅢🅓 ☒ 🛈 💻 ⇨

🛸 ▼▼ **Royal Carriage Inn / Americas Best Value Inn** 🆂🅷
(209) 984-5271. **Call for rates.** 18239 Main St. SR 108 and 49, exit Central Business District. Ext/int corridors. **Pets:** Other species. $100 deposit/pet. Designated rooms, supervision.
🅢🅐🅥🅔 ☒ 🛈 💻 ⇨

JUNE LAKE

🛸 ▼▼▼ **Double Eagle Resort/Spa** 🅒🅐
(760) 648-7004. **$169-$369, 30 day notice.** 5587 Hwy 158. On SR 158; 3 mi w of village. Ext corridors. **Pets:** $15 daily fee/room. Designated rooms, service with restrictions, supervision.
🅢🅐🅥🅔 ☒ 🅢🅜 🛈 💻 🍽 ⇨ 🅧 🅚

▼▼ **Gull Lake Lodge** 🅜
(760) 648-7516. **Call for rates.** 132 Leonard Ave. Just n of SR 158; via Knoll and Bruce sts; in village. Ext corridors. **Pets:** Accepted.
☒ 🛈 💻 🅚 🅩

▼▼▼ June Lake Villager **M**
(760) 648-7712. **$65-$95.** 85 Boulder Dr. On SR 158; center of village. Ext corridors. **Pets:** Accepted.

(ASK) (S⭐) (✕) (🛏) (🖥) (❄)

KERNVILLE

▼▼ Barewood Motel **M**
(760) 376-1910. **Call for rates.** 7013 Wofford Blvd. In Wofford Heights. Ext corridors. **Pets:** Accepted.

(✕) (🛏) (🖥)

▼▼ River View Lodge **M**
(760) 376-6019. **Call for rates.** 2 Sirretta St. On Kernville Rd; at the bridge. Ext corridors. **Pets:** Accepted.

(✕) (🛏)

KETTLEMAN CITY

◆◆◇ ▼▼▼ Best Western Kettleman Inn and Suites **M**
(559) 386-0804. **Call for rates.** 33410 Powers Dr. E of and adjacent to I-5, exit SR 41 N, 0.3 mi to Bernard, then 0.3 mi n. Ext corridors. **Pets:** Accepted.

(SAVE) (✕) (🛏) (🖥) (≈)

◆◆◇ ▼▼▼ Super 8 **M**
(559) 386-9530. **$59-$99.** 33415 Powers Dr. E of and adjacent to I-5, exit SR 41 N, 0.3 mi to Bernard, then 0.3 mi n. Ext corridors. **Pets:** Accepted.

(SAVE) (S⭐) (✕) (🛏) (≈)

KINGSBURG

◆◆◇ ▼▼▼ Swedish Inn **M**
(559) 897-1022. **Call for rates.** 401 Conejo St. SR 99, exit Conejo St, just w. Ext corridors. **Pets:** Medium. $100 deposit/room. Service with restrictions, crate.

(SAVE) (✕) (🛏) (🖥) (≈)

KLAMATH

◆◆◇ ▼▼ Motel Trees **M**
(707) 482-3152. **$65-$110.** 15495 Hwy 101 N. On US 101, 4.5 mi n. Ext corridors. **Pets:** $10 daily fee/pet. No service, supervision.

(SAVE) (S⭐) (✕) (🛏) (🖥) (🍴) (❄)

KYBURZ

◆◆◇ ▼▼▼ Kyburz Resort Motel **M**
(530) 293-3382. **Call for rates.** 13666 Hwy 50. On US 50; halfway between Placerville and South Lake Tahoe. Ext corridors. **Pets:** Other species. $10 daily fee/room. Service with restrictions, supervision.

(SAVE) (✕) (🔊M) (🛏) (🖥) (❄)

LAGUNA BEACH

◆◆◇ ▼▼▼ Aliso Creek Inn **SH**
(949) 499-2271. **$149-$375.** 31106 S Coast Hwy. SR 133, 3 mi s on SR 1, then 0.3 mi e. Ext corridors. **Pets:** Medium, other species. $50 one-time fee/pet. Service with restrictions.

(SAVE) (S⭐) (✕) (🛏) (🖥) (🍴) (≈) (⊠) (❄)

◆◆◇ ▼▼▼ Best Western Laguna Brisas Spa Hotel **M**
(949) 497-7272. **$119-$499, 3 day notice.** 1600 S Coast Hwy. SR 133, 1 mi s on SR 1. Ext/int corridors. **Pets:** Accepted.

(SAVE) (S⭐) (✕) (🛏) (🖥) (≈)

▼▼▼ The Carriage House-Bed & Breakfast **BB**
(949) 494-8945. **Call for rates.** 1322 Catalina St. SR 133, 1 mi s on S Coast Hwy to Cress St, then just e. Ext corridors. **Pets:** Accepted.

(✕) (🛏) (🖥) (❄) (☎)

▼▼▼ Casa Laguna Inn **BB**
(949) 494-2996. **$200-$650, 5 day notice.** 2510 S Coast Hwy. SR 133, 1.3 mi s on SR 1. Ext corridors. **Pets:** Accepted.

(ASK) (✕) (🛏) (🖥) (≈)

◆◆◇ ▼▼▼ The Tides Inn **M** 🐾
(949) 494-2494. **$99-$285, 3 day notice.** 460 N Coast Hwy. SR 133, 0.5 mi n on SR 1. Ext corridors. **Pets:** $25 daily fee/pet. Designated rooms, supervision.

(SAVE) (S⭐) (✕) (🛏) (🖥)

LAGUNA HILLS

▼▼▼ Holiday Inn Laguna Hills **SH**
(949) 586-5000. **$129-$209.** 25205 La Paz Rd. I-5, exit 89 (La Paz Rd), just w. Int corridors. **Pets:** Small. $100 one-time fee/room. Designated rooms, service with restrictions, crate.

(ASK) (✕) (🔊M) (🛏) (🖥) (🍴) (≈)

LAKE ARROWHEAD

◆◆◇ ▼▼▼ Arrowhead Saddleback Inn **CI**
(909) 336-3571. **$137-$648, 7 day notice.** Hwy 173. On SR 173, jct SR 189; across from entrance to Lake Arrowhead Village. Ext/int corridors. **Pets:** Other species. $8 daily fee/room. Designated rooms, service with restrictions, crate.

(SAVE) (✕) (🛏) (🖥) (🍴)

◆◆◇ ▼▼ Arrowhead Tree Top Lodge **M**
(909) 337-2311. **$169-$217 (no credit cards), 7 day notice.** 27992 Rainbow Dr. 0.3 mi s of Lake Arrowhead Village on SR 173. Ext corridors. **Pets:** Dogs only. $8 daily fee/pet. Service with restrictions, supervision.

(SAVE) (S⭐) (✕) (🛏) (🖥) (≈) (❄) (☎)

▼▼▼ Lake Arrowhead Resort and Spa **LH**
(909) 336-1511. **$159-$429, 3 day notice.** 27984 Hwy 189. Just w of SR 173; in Lake Arrowhead Village. Int corridors. **Pets:** Accepted.

(ASK) (S⭐) (✕) (🔊M) (🖥) (🍴) (≈) (⊠)

▼▼▼ Storybook Inn **BB**
(909) 337-0011. **$99-$299.** 28717 SR 18. SR 18, 1.1 mi e of jct SR 173. Ext/int corridors. **Pets:** Accepted.

(ASK) (S⭐) (✕) (🛏) (🖥) (🍴)

LAKE TAHOE AREA

SOUTH LAKE TAHOE

▼▼▼ Alder Inn Ⓜ
(530) 544-4485. **Call for rates.** 1072 Ski Run Blvd. 2.5 blks s off US 50 on Ski Run Blvd; 0.8 mi below Heavenly Valley Ski Lift Terminal. Ext corridors. **Pets:** Accepted.

⊠ 🛏 💻 ➿ 𝓚

⟨⟨⟨⟩ ▼▼▼ Alpenrose Inn Ⓜ
(530) 544-2985. **Call for rates.** 4074 Pine Blvd. 0.3 mi n of US 50 via Park Ave, 3 blks from casino area. Ext corridors. **Pets:** Medium. $10 daily fee/pet. Designated rooms, service with restrictions, crate.

SAVE ⊠ 🛏 💻 ⊠

⟨⟨⟨⟩ ▼▼ Ambassador Motor Lodge Ⓜ
(530) 544-6461. **$45-$300.** 4130 Manzanita Ave. Just s of US 50 on Stateline Ave. Ext corridors. **Pets:** Accepted.

SAVE S🐾 ⊠ 🛏 💻 ➿ 𝓚

⟨⟨⟨⟩ ▼▼▼▼ Best Western Timber Cove Lodge 🆂🅷
(530) 541-6722. **$86-$240, 14 day notice.** 3411 Lake Tahoe Blvd. 1.5 mi w of casino center; 0.5 mi w of Ski Run Blvd. Ext corridors. **Pets:** Medium. $100 deposit/room, $25 daily fee/pet. Designated rooms, service with restrictions, supervision.

SAVE S🐾 ⊠ ⅏ 💻 🍽 ➿ ⊠

⟨⟨⟨⟩ ▼▼▼ Big Pines Mountain House of Tahoe Ⓜ
(530) 541-5155. **Call for rates.** 4083 Cedar Ave. US 50, exit Friday Ave, toward the lake; near casino area. Ext corridors. **Pets:** Accepted.

SAVE ⊠ ⅏ 🛏 💻 ➿ 𝓚

⟨⟨⟨⟩ ▼▼ Capri Motel Ⓜ
(530) 544-3665. **Call for rates.** 932 Stateline Ave. Just s of US 50; in casino area. Ext corridors. **Pets:** Accepted.

SAVE ⊠ 🛏 💻 ➿ 𝓚

⟨⟨⟨⟩ ▼▼ Days Inn-Casino Area/Lake Resort Ⓜ
(530) 541-4800. **Call for rates.** 968 Park Ave. 3 blks w of casino area; 1 blk n off US 50 toward lake, at Park and Cedar aves. Int corridors. **Pets:** Accepted.

SAVE ⊠ 💻 ➿

⟨⟨⟨⟩ ▼▼ Fireside Lodge B&B 🅱🅱
(530) 544-5515. **$69-$195, 3 day notice.** 515 Emerald Bay Rd. SR 89, 1 mi n of US 50. Ext corridors. **Pets:** Accepted.

SAVE S🐾 ⊠ 🛏 💻 𝓚

⟨⟨⟨⟩ ▼▼▼ High Country Lodge Ⓜ
(530) 541-0508. **Call for rates.** 1227 Emerald Bay Rd. US 50, 0.5 mi n of airport. Ext corridors. **Pets:** Small, dogs only. $10 one-time fee/pet. Service with restrictions, supervision.

SAVE ⊠ 🛏 💻

⟨⟨⟨⟩ ▼▼ Pistantes Coyote Den Ⓜ
(530) 541-2282. **$55-$375, 4 day notice.** 1211 Emerald Bay Rd. US 50, 0.5 mi n of airport. Ext corridors. **Pets:** Dogs only. $50 deposit/room. Designated rooms, service with restrictions, supervision.

SAVE ⊠ 🛏 𝓚

⟨⟨⟨⟩ ▼▼◆▼ Tahoe Keys Resort 🅲🅾 🐾
(530) 544-5397. **$112-$1300.** 599 Tahoe Keys Blvd. US 50, exit Tahoe Keys Blvd, 1 mi w. Ext corridors. **Pets:** Dogs only. $125 deposit/pet, $25 one-time fee/pet. Designated rooms, service with restrictions, supervision.

SAVE S🐾 ⊠ 🛏 💻 ➿ ⊠ 𝓚

⟨⟨⟨⟩ ▼▼◆▼ Tahoe Valley Lodge Ⓜ
(530) 541-0353. **$125-$495, 7 day notice.** 2241 Lake Tahoe Blvd. 0.5 mi e of jct US 50 and SR 89. Ext corridors. **Pets:** Very small, dogs only. $20 daily fee/pet. Designated rooms, service with restrictions, supervision.

SAVE S🐾 ⊠ 🛏 💻 ➿

TAHOE CITY

⟨⟨⟨⟩ ▼▼▼ Mother Nature's Inn Ⓜ 🐾
(530) 581-4278. **$55-$125, 7 day notice.** 551 N Lake Blvd. SR 28, 0.5 mi e of jct SR 89; behind Mother Nature's Store. Int corridors. **Pets:** $15 daily fee/pet. Designated rooms, service with restrictions, supervision.

SAVE ⊠ 🛏 💻

TAHOE VISTA

▼▼ Holiday House Ⓜ
(530) 546-2369. **$125-$225, 14 day notice.** 7276 N Lake Blvd. SR 28, 1 mi w of SR 267. Ext corridors. **Pets:** Accepted.

⊠ ⅏ 🛏 💻 𝓚

TRUCKEE

▼▼◆▼ The Cedar House Sport Hotel 🆂🅷
(530) 582-5655. **$140-$295.** 10918 Brockway Rd. I-80, exit SR 267, 1.5 mi s. Int corridors. **Pets:** Accepted.

A$K S🐾 ⊠ 🛏 💻

END AREA

LANCASTER

⟨⟨⟨⟩ ▼▼▼▼ Best Western Antelope Valley Inn Ⓜ
(661) 948-4651. **$159.** 44055 N Sierra Hwy. SR 14, exit 42 (Ave K), 2.3 mi e. Ext/int corridors. **Pets:** Other species. $35 one-time fee/room. Service with restrictions.

SAVE S🐾 ⊠ 🛏 💻 🍽 ➿

⟨⟨⟨⟩ ▼▼▼▼ Holiday Inn Express 🆂🅷
(661) 951-8848. **$145-$165.** 43719 17th St W. SR 14, exit 42 (Ave K), just e, then just n. Int corridors. **Pets:** Dogs only. $100 deposit/room, $15 daily fee/pet. Designated rooms, service with restrictions, supervision.

SAVE S🐾 ⊠ ⅏ 🛏 💻

▼▼▼▼ Oxford Inn & Suites Ⓜ
(661) 949-3423. **$109-$139.** 1651 W Ave K. SR 14, exit 42 (Ave K), just w. Int corridors. **Pets:** Accepted.

A$K S🐾 ⊠ ⅏ 🛏 💻 ➿

LA PALMA

▼▼▼ La Quinta Inn & Suites Orange County (Buena Park) 🆂🅷
(714) 670-1400. **$129-$169.** 3 Center Pointe Dr. SR 91, exit 21 (Orangethorpe Ave/Valley View St) eastbound; exit 22 (Orangethorpe Ave/Valley View St) westbound, just n. Int corridors. **Pets:** Other species. Service with restrictions, supervision.

A$K S🐾 ⊠ 🛏 💻 ➿

LATHROP

▼▼ Days Inn 🆂🅷
(209) 982-1959. **Call for rates.** 14750 S Harlan Rd. I-5, exit Lathrop Rd, just e. Int corridors. **Pets:** Accepted.

⊠ ⅏ 🛏 ➿

LEBEC

Best Rest Inn M
(661) 248-2700. **$79-$109.** 51541 N Peace Valley Rd. I-5, exit 205 (Frazier Park), just w. Int corridors. **Pets:** Other species. $10 one-time fee/pet. Service with restrictions.

Ramada Limited Grapevine M
(661) 248-1530. **Call for rates.** 9000 Country Side Ct. I-5, exit 215 (Grapevine Rd), just w. Ext corridors. **Pets:** Medium. $10 one-time fee/pet. Designated rooms, service with restrictions, supervision.

LEE VINING

Murphey's Motel M
(760) 647-6316. **$58-$113.** 51493 Hwy 395. US 395; in town. Ext corridors. **Pets:** Medium. $5 one-time fee/pet. Service with restrictions, supervision.

LEMOORE

Days Inn Lemoore M
(559) 924-1261. **Call for rates.** 877 E "D" St. SR 198, exit Houston St, 0.8 ni nw. Ext corridors. **Pets:** Accepted.

LINDSAY

Super 8 Motel M
(559) 562-5188. **Call for rates.** 390 N Hwy 65. SR 65. Ext corridors. **Pets:** Accepted.

LIVERMORE

Hampton Inn SH
(925) 606-6400. **Call for rates.** 2850 Constitution Dr. I-580, exit Airway Blvd/Collier Canyon Rd. Int corridors. **Pets:** Accepted.

La Quinta Inn SH
(925) 373-9600. **$129-$149.** 7700 Southfront Rd. I-580, exit Greenville Rd, just s. Int corridors. **Pets:** Other species. Service with restrictions, supervision.

Residence Inn by Marriott SH
(925) 373-1800. **$176-$196.** 1000 Airway Blvd. I-580, exit Airway Blvd/Collier Canyon Rd, just n. Ext corridors. **Pets:** Accepted.

LODI

El Rancho Motel M ❖
(209) 368-0651. **Call for rates.** 603 N Cherokee Ln. SR 99, exit Turner Rd, just s. Ext corridors. **Pets:** Small. $10 one-time fee/pet. Service with restrictions, supervision.

Microtel Inn & Suites SH ❖
(209) 367-9700. **$69-$99.** 6428 W Banner St. I-5, exit SR 12, just e. Int corridors. **Pets:** $15 daily fee/pet. Designated rooms, service with restrictions, supervision.

Wine & Roses Hotel and Restaurant CI
(209) 334-6988. **Call for rates.** 2505 W Turner Rd. I-5, exit Turner Rd, 5 mi e; SR 99, exit Turner Rd, 2 mi w. Int corridors. **Pets:** Accepted.

LOMA LINDA

Loma Linda Inn M
(909) 583-2500. **$75-$85.** 24532 University Ave. I-10, exit 74 (Anderson St/Tippecanoe Ave) eastbound; exit westbound, 1 mi s, just w on Stewart, just s on Campus, then just w. Ext corridors. **Pets:** Other species. $35 one-time fee/pet. Designated rooms, service with restrictions, supervision.

LOMPOC

Americas Best Value Inn M
(805) 735-3737. **$50-$90 (no credit cards).** 1200 N H St. SR 1, 1.3 mi n of Ocean Ave. Ext corridors. **Pets:** $10 one-time fee/pet. Service with restrictions, crate.

Days Inn M
(805) 735-7744. **Call for rates.** 1122 N H St. SR 1, 1.2 mi n of Ocean Ave. Ext/int corridors. **Pets:** Accepted.

Quality Inn & Executive Suites SH
(805) 735-8555. **$99-$209.** 1621 N H St. SR 1, 1.8 mi n of Ocean Ave. Int corridors. **Pets:** Accepted.

Super 8 Motel M
(805) 735-6444. **Call for rates.** 1020 E Ocean Ave. SR 1, 1.5 mi w of H St. Ext corridors. **Pets:** $15 daily fee/room. Designated rooms, service with restrictions.

White Oaks Hotel M ❖
(805) 733-5000. **Call for rates.** 3955 Apollo Way. SR 1, exit 211 (Constellation Blvd), just e; 3.5 mi n of Ocean Ave. Ext/int corridors. **Pets:** Small, dogs only. $10 daily fee/pet. Designated rooms, service with restrictions, supervision.

LONE PINE

Best Western Frontier Motel M
(760) 876-5571. **$79-$124.** 1008 S Main St. US 395; at south end of town. Ext corridors. **Pets:** Large, other species. Service with restrictions, supervision.

Comfort Inn SH
(760) 876-8700. **$59-$199.** 1920 S Main St. US 395, 1.5 mi s of town. Int corridors. **Pets:** Accepted.

Dow Villa Motel M
(760) 876-5521. **$66-$140.** 310 S Main St. US 395. Ext corridors. **Pets:** Other species. $50 deposit/room. Designated rooms, service with restrictions, supervision.

Lone Pine Budget Inn Motel M
(760) 876-5655. **$45-$99, 3 day notice.** 138 W Willow St. US 395, just w. Ext corridors. **Pets:** Very small, dogs only. $10 daily fee/pet. Designated rooms, service with restrictions, supervision.

National 9 Trails Motel M
(760) 876-5555. **$49-$99, 3 day notice.** 633 S Main St. US 395. Ext corridors. **Pets:** Very small, dogs only. $10 daily fee/pet. Designated rooms, no service, supervision.

Timberline Motel **M**
(760) 876-4555. **Call for rates.** 215 E Post St. US 395, just e. Ext corridors. **Pets:** $10 daily fee/pet. Designated rooms, supervision.
SAVE ⊠ 🛏 💻 🐾

LOS ALAMITOS

Residence Inn by Marriott-Cypress/Orange County **SH**
(714) 484-5700. **$209-$229.** 4931 Katella Ave. I-605, exit 1D (Katella Ave) southbound; exit 1B (Katella Ave/Willow St) northbound, 1.5 mi e. Int corridors. **Pets:** Accepted.
ASK 🐶 ⊠ 🛏 💻 🐾 🗙

LOS ALTOS

Residence Inn-Palo Alto/Los Altos **SH**
(650) 559-7890. **$242-$262.** 4460 El Camino Real. US 101, exit San Antonio Rd, 2 mi w to SR 82, then just n. Int corridors. **Pets:** Accepted.
ASK 🐶 ⊠ 🛏 💻 🐾 🗙

LOS ANGELES METROPOLITAN AREA

ALHAMBRA

 Super 8 Motel **M**
(323) 225-2310. **Call for rates.** 5350 Huntington Dr S. I-10, exit 22 (Fremont Ave), 2.5 mi n, then 0.5 mi w. Ext corridors. **Pets:** $20 daily fee/pet. Designated rooms, service with restrictions.
SAVE ⊠ 🛏 💻

ARCADIA

Extended StayAmerica-Los Angeles-Arcadia **SH**
(626) 446-6422. **$104-$124.** 401 E Santa Clara St. I-210, exit 33 (Huntington Dr), just w to 5th, just n, then just w. Int corridors. **Pets:** Other species. $75 one-time fee/pet. Service with restrictions.
ASK 🐶 ⊠ 🛏 💻

Residence Inn by Marriott **SH**
(626) 446-6500. **$220-$240.** 321 E Huntington Dr. I-210, exit 33 (Huntington Dr), 0.5 mi w, then just n on Gateway Dr. Ext corridors. **Pets:** Accepted.
ASK 🐶 ⊠ 🛏 💻 🐾 🗙

BEVERLY HILLS

Avalon Hotel **SH**
(310) 277-5221. **$319-$399.** 9400 W Olympic Blvd. I-10, exit 6 (Robertson Blvd), 1.7 mi n, then 0.8 mi w. Ext/int corridors. **Pets:** Accepted.
⊠ 💻 🍴 🐾

The Beverly Hills Hotel & Bungalows **LH** ❁
(310) 276-2251. **$485-$6900.** 9641 Sunset Blvd. I-405, exit 57 (Sunset Blvd), 3.7 mi e. Int corridors. **Pets:** Small, dogs only. $250 one-time fee/pet. Designated rooms.
ASK ⊠ 🛏 🍴 🐾 🗙

Beverly Hilton **LH**
(310) 274-7777. **Call for rates.** 9876 Wilshire Blvd. I-405, exit 55 (Wilshire Blvd), 2.2 mi e. Int corridors. **Pets:** Accepted.
⊠ 🛏 🍴 🐾 🗙

Beverly Wilshire Beverly Hills a Four Seasons Hotel **LH**
(310) 275-5200. **$545-$575.** 9500 Wilshire Blvd. I-405, exit 55 (Wilshire Blvd), 4.5 mi e. Int corridors. **Pets:** Accepted.
⊠ 🛏 🍴 🐾 🗙

The Mosaic Hotel **SH**
(310) 278-0303. **$405.** 125 S Spalding Dr. I-405, exit 55 (Wilshire Blvd), 2.2 mi e, then just s. Ext/int corridors. **Pets:** Accepted.
ASK 🐶 ⊠ 💻 🍴 🐾

The Peninsula Beverly Hills **SH**
(310) 551-2888. **$525-$3750.** 9882 S Santa Monica Blvd. I-405, exit 55A (Santa Monica Blvd), 2.2 mi e at Wilshire Blvd. Int corridors. **Pets:** Accepted.
SAVE ⊠ 🛏 💻 🍴 🐾 🗙

Raffles L'Ermitage Beverly Hills **SH** ❁
(310) 278-3344. **Call for rates.** 9291 Burton Way. I-10, exit 6 (Robertson Blvd), 3.1 mi n, then just w. Int corridors. **Pets:** Medium. $150 one-time fee/room. Supervision.
SAVE ⊠ 🛏 💻 🍴 🐾 🗙

BURBANK

Burbank Airport Marriott Hotel & Convention Center **LH**
(818) 843-6000. **$220-$240.** 2500 Hollywood Way. I-5, exit 149 (Hollywood Way), 1 mi s. Int corridors. **Pets:** Accepted.
ASK 🐶 ⊠ 🛏 🛏 💻 🍴 💻 🐾

Extended StayAmerica-Los Angeles-Burbank Airport **SH**
(818) 567-0952. **$129-$149.** 2200 Empire Ave. I-5, exit 146B (Burbank Blvd), just w, then 0.7 mi n on Victory Pl. Int corridors. **Pets:** Other species. $75 one-time fee/pet. Service with restrictions.
ASK 🐶 ⊠ 🛏 💻

The Graciela Burbank **SH**
(818) 842-8887. **$330-$585.** 322 N Pass Ave. SR 134, exit 2 (Hollywood Way) westbound, just w on Alameda Ave, then 0.5 mi n; exit 2 (Pass Ave) eastbound, 0.5 mi n. Ext corridors. **Pets:** Accepted.
ASK 🐶 ⊠ 🛏 💻 🛏 🍴 🐾

Safari Inn, a Coast Hotel **M**
(818) 845-8586. **$129-$299.** 1911 W Olive Ave. I-5, exit 146A (Olive Ave), 1.3 mi sw. Ext corridors. **Pets:** Other species. $200 deposit/room, $25 one-time fee/room. Supervision.
SAVE 🐶 ⊠ 🛏 💻 🍴 🐾

CARSON

Extended StayAmerica-Los Angeles/Carson **SH**
(310) 323-2080. **$99-$119.** 401 E Albertoni St. SR 91, exit 7B (Avalon Blvd) just s, then just w. Int corridors. **Pets:** Other species. $75 one-time fee/pet. Service with restrictions.
ASK 🐶 ⊠ 🛏 💻 🛏 💻

CERRITOS

Sheraton Cerritos Hotel at Towne Center **SH**
(562) 809-1500. **Call for rates.** 12725 Center Court Dr. SR 91, exit 19B (Artesia/Bloomfield Dr), just s to Town Center Dr, just e, then just s. Int corridors. **Pets:** Medium. $50 one-time fee/pet. Service with restrictions, supervision.
⊠ 🛏 💻 🍴 🐾

CHATSWORTH

Ramada Inn **SH**
(818) 998-5289. **$89-$109.** 21340 Devonshire St. SR 118, exit 35 (De Soto Ave), 1.5 mi s, then 0.5 mi w. Int corridors. **Pets:** Accepted.
ASK 🐶 ⊠ 🛏 🛏 💻 🍴 🐾

CHINO

▼▼ **Extended StayAmerica** SH
(909) 597-8675. **$99-$119.** 4325 Corporate Center Ave. SR 71, exit Chino Hills Pkwy, just e to Ramona Ave, just n, then just w. Int corridors. **Pets:** Other species. $75 one-time fee/pet. Service with restrictions.

(ASK) (S&) (X) (&M) (★) (▭)

CLAREMONT

▼▼▼ **DoubleTree Hotel Claremont** LH
(909) 626-2411. **Call for rates.** 555 W Foothill Blvd. I-210, exit Indian Hill Blvd, 0.5 mi s, then just w. Int corridors. **Pets:** Accepted.

(X) (&M) (★) (▭) (¶) (➦) (X)

▼▼ **Hotel Claremont & Tennis Club** M
(909) 621-4831. **$89-$109.** 840 S Indian Hill Blvd. I-10, exit 47 (Indian Hill Blvd), just s; enter on Auto Center Dr. Ext corridors. **Pets:** Accepted.

(ASK) (S&) (X) (★) (▭) (➦) (X)

CULVER CITY

AAA ▼▼▼ **Four Points by Sheraton Culver City** LH
(310) 641-7740. **$115-$220.** 5990 Green Valley Cir. I-405, exit 49 (Howard Hughes Pkwy), just n, then just e. Int corridors. **Pets:** Accepted.

(SAVE) (S&) (X) (★) (▭) (¶) (➦)

▼▼▼ **Radisson Hotel-LA Westside** LH
(310) 649-1776. **$109-$229.** 6161 W Centinela Ave. I-405, exit 50 (Jefferson Blvd), just s, then just nw. Int corridors. **Pets:** Accepted.

(ASK) (S&) (X) (★) (▭) (¶) (➦)

DOWNEY

AAA ▼▼▼ **Embassy Suites Hotel** LH
(562) 861-1900. **$129-$199.** 8425 Firestone Blvd. I-605, exit 10 (Firestone Blvd), 2 mi w. Int corridors. **Pets:** Accepted.

(SAVE) (X) (&M) (★) (▭) (¶) (➦) (X)

EL SEGUNDO

▼▼▼ **Embassy Suites-LAX South** LH
(310) 640-3600. **$139-$281.** 1440 E Imperial Ave. I-405, exit 45B (Imperial Hwy), 1.6 mi w. Int corridors. **Pets:** Accepted.

(X) (★) (▭) (¶) (➦)

▼▼ **Homestead Studio Suites Hotel-Los Angeles-LAX Airport-El Segundo** M
(310) 607-4000. **$134-$154.** 1910 E Mariposa Ave. I-105, exit 1B (Sepulveda Blvd), 1 mi s. Ext corridors. **Pets:** Other species. $75 one-time fee/pet. Service with restrictions.

(ASK) (S&) (X) (&M) (★) (▭)

▼▼▼ **Hyatt Summerfield Suites-El Segundo** M
(310) 725-0100. **Call for rates.** 810 S Douglas St. I-405, exit 43 (Rosecrans Ave), 0.5 mi e, then just n. Ext/int corridors. **Pets:** Medium. $200 one-time fee/room. Service with restrictions.

(X) (&M) (★) (▭) (➦) (X)

AAA ▼▼▼ **Residence Inn by Marriott-LAX/El Segundo** SH 🐾
(310) 333-0888. **$209-$229.** 2135 E El Segundo Blvd. I-405, exit 44 (El Segundo Blvd), 1.4 mi w. Int corridors. **Pets:** $100 one-time fee/pet. Service with restrictions.

(SAVE) (S&) (X) (&M) (★) (▭) (➦) (X)

GLENDALE

▼▼▼ **Homestead Studio Suites Hotel-Los Angeles-Glendale** SH
(818) 956-6665. **$134-$154.** 1377 W Glenoaks Blvd. I-5, exit 145A (Western Ave), 0.4 mi e, then 0.6 mi s. Int corridors. **Pets:** Other species. $75 one-time fee/pet. Service with restrictions.

(ASK) (S&) (X) (&M) (★) (▭)

▼▼ **Los Angeles Days Inn-Glendale** SH
(818) 956-0202. **$94-$149, 7 day notice.** 450 W Pioneer Dr. SR 134, exit 7A (Pacific Ave), just s, then just e. Int corridors. **Pets:** Accepted.

(ASK) (S&) (X) (★) (▭) (¶) (➦)

AAA ▼▼▼ **Vagabond Inn Glendale** M
(818) 240-1700. **$76-$94.** 120 W Colorado St. SR 134, exit 7B (Brand Blvd), 1 mi s, then just w. Ext corridors. **Pets:** Small. $10 daily fee/pet. Designated rooms, service with restrictions, supervision.

(SAVE) (S&) (X) (&M) (★) (▭) (➦)

HAWTHORNE

▼▼ **TownePlace Suites by Marriott** M
(310) 725-9696. **$176-$196.** 14400 Aviation Blvd. I-405, exit 43 (Rosecrans Ave), 0.4 mi w. Int corridors. **Pets:** Accepted.

(ASK) (S&) (X) (★) (▭) (➦)

HOLLYWOOD

AAA ▼▼▼ **Best Western Hollywood Hills Hotel** M
(323) 464-5181. **$109-$225.** 6141 Franklin Ave. US 101, exit Gower St, just n, then just e. Ext/int corridors. **Pets:** $25 daily fee/pet.

(SAVE) (S&) (X) (★) (▭) (¶) (➦)

AAA ▼▼▼ **Hollywood Hotel Near Universal Studios-A Ramada Hotel** SH
(323) 315-1800. **$90-$169.** 1160 N Vermont Ave. US 101, exit 6A (Vermont Ave), 0.5 mi n. Int corridors. **Pets:** Medium. $50 daily fee/pet. Designated rooms, service with restrictions, supervision.

(SAVE) (S&) (X) (&M) (★) (▭) (¶) (➦)

INDUSTRY

▼▼▼ **Pacific Palms Conference Resort** LH
(626) 810-4455. **$229-$259.** One Industry Hills Pkwy. SR 60, exit 18 (Azusa Ave), 1.3 mi n, 0.5 mi w. Int corridors. **Pets:** Accepted.

(ASK) (X) (&M) (▭) (¶) (➦) (X)

LA MIRADA

▼▼▼ **Residence Inn by Marriott** SH
(714) 523-2800. **$170-$190.** 14419 Firestone Blvd. I-5, exit 118 (Valley View), just n, then 0.5 mi e. Ext corridors. **Pets:** Accepted.

(ASK) (S&) (X) (&M) (★) (▭) (➦) (X)

LONG BEACH

AAA ▼▼▼ **The Coast Long Beach Hotel** SH
(562) 435-7676. **Call for rates.** 700 Queensway Dr. I-710, exit 14 (Harbor Scenic Dr/Queen Mary), 1 mi s. Ext corridors. **Pets:** Accepted.

(SAVE) (X) (★) (▭) (¶) (➦) (X)

▼▼ **Extended StayAmerica-Los Angeles-Long Beach** SH
(562) 989-4601. **$109-$129.** 4105 E Willow St. I-405, exit 27 (Lakewood Blvd), 0.3 mi sw. Int corridors. **Pets:** Other species. $75 one-time fee/pet. Service with restrictions.

(ASK) (S&) (X) (&M) (★) (▭)

AAA ▼▼▼ **GuestHouse Hotel Long Beach** M
(562) 597-1341. **$99-$149 (no credit cards).** 5325 E Pacific Coast Hwy. I-405, exit 23 (SR 22/Long Beach) northbound, 2 mi nw; exit 27 (Lakewood Blvd) southbound, 2 mi se on SR 1. Ext corridors. **Pets:** Medium. $10 one-time fee/room. Service with restrictions, crate.

(SAVE) (S&) (X) (★) (▭) (➦)

▼▼▼ **Hilton Long Beach** LH
(562) 983-3400. **$159-$375, 3 day notice.** Two World Trade Center. I-710, exit Downtown/Broadway, just e to Daisy Ave, just s to Ocean Blvd, then just w. Int corridors. **Pets:** Accepted.

(ASK) (X) (&M) (▭) (¶) (X)

Holiday Inn-Long Beach Airport LH ❀
(562) 597-4401. **$199-$219.** 2640 Lakewood Blvd. I-405, exit 27 (Lakewood Blvd), just s. Ext/int corridors. **Pets:** Small. $100 deposit/pet, $25 one-time fee/pet. Designated rooms, service with restrictions, supervision.
SAVE S X 📠 💻 🍴 🌊

Renaissance Long Beach Hotel LH
(562) 437-5900. **$220-$240.** 111 E Ocean Blvd. I-710, exit Downtown/Broadway, 0.8 mi e to Long Beach Blvd, just s, then just w. Int corridors. **Pets:** Accepted.
ASK S X M 💻 🍴 🌊 X

Residence Inn by Marriott Long Beach SH
(562) 595-0909. **$207-$227.** 4111 E Willow St. I-405, exit 27 (Lakewood Blvd), just s, then just w. Ext corridors. **Pets:** Other species. $100 one-time fee/room. Service with restrictions, crate.
ASK S X M 📠 💻 🌊 X

The Westin Long Beach LH ❀
(562) 436-3000. **$199-$389.** 333 E Ocean Blvd. I-710, exit Downtown/Broadway, 0.8 mi e to Long Beach Blvd, then just s. **Pets:** Medium. Service with restrictions, crate.
SAVE S X 💻 🍴 🌊 X

LOS ANGELES

Beverly Laurel Motor Hotel M
(323) 651-2441. **$107-$150.** 8018 Beverly Blvd. I-10, exit 7B (Fairfax Ave), 2.8 mi n, then just w. Ext corridors. **Pets:** Small. $25 daily fee/pet. Service with restrictions, supervision.
SAVE X 📠 🍴 🌊

Extended StayAmerica-Los Angeles/LAX Airport SH
(310) 568-9337. **$124-$144.** 6531 S Sepulveda Blvd. I-405, exit 49 (Howard Hughes Pkwy), 0.9 mi w, then just n. Int corridors. **Pets:** Other species. $75 one-time fee/pet. Service with restrictions.
ASK S X M 📠 💻

Four Points by Sheraton LAX LH
(310) 645-4600. **$255.** 9750 Airport Blvd. I-405, exit 46 (Century Blvd), 1.5 mi w, then just n. Ext/int corridors. **Pets:** Accepted.
SAVE S X 📠 💻 🍴 🌊

Four Seasons Hotel Los Angeles at Beverly Hills LH ❀
(310) 273-2222. **$455-$6500.** 300 S Doheny Dr. I-10, exit 6 (Robertson Blvd), 3 mi n to Burton Way, then just w. Int corridors. **Pets:** Very small. Service with restrictions, supervision.
SAVE X M 💻 🍴 🌊 X

Hotel Bel-Air SH
(310) 472-1211. **$395-$4500.** 701 Stone Canyon Rd. I-405, exit 57 (Sunset Blvd), 2 mi e, then 0.8 mi n. Ext corridors. **Pets:** Accepted.
X 📠 🍴 🌊

Hyatt Regency Century Plaza LH
(310) 228-1234. **$219-$429.** 2025 Avenue of the Stars. I-10, exit 6 (Robertson Blvd), 2.7 mi n to Olympic Blvd, 1.9 mi w, then just n. Int corridors. **Pets:** Accepted.
SAVE X M 💻 🍴 🌊 X

La Quinta Inn & Suites–LAX LH
(310) 645-2200. **$129-$165.** 5249 W Century Blvd. I-405, exit 46 (Century Blvd), just w. Int corridors. **Pets:** Other species. Service with restrictions, supervision.
ASK S X 📠 💻 🍴 🌊

Los Angeles Airport Hilton & Towers LH
(310) 410-4000. **$109-$259.** 5711 W Century Blvd. I-405, exit 46 (Century Blvd), 0.8 mi w. Int corridors. **Pets:** Accepted.
SAVE X 📠 💻 🍴 🌊 X

Los Angeles Airport Marriott Hotel LH
(310) 641-5700. **$253-$273.** 5855 W Century Blvd. I-405, exit 46 (Century Blvd), 1 mi w. Int corridors. **Pets:** Accepted.
ASK S X 📠 💻 🍴 🌊

Luxe Hotel Sunset Boulevard SH
(310) 476-6571. **Call for rates.** 11461 Sunset Blvd. I-405, exit 57 (Sunset Blvd), just w. Int corridors. **Pets:** Accepted.
X M 💻 🍴 🌊 X

Omni Los Angeles Hotel LH
(213) 617-3300. **$309-$575.** 251 S Olive St. SR 110, exit 4th St southbound; exit 6th St northbound, just e, then just n. Int corridors. **Pets:** Small. $50 one-time fee/room. Designated rooms, service with restrictions.
SAVE S X M 📠 💻 🍴 🌊

The Orlando SH
(323) 658-6600. **$279-$329.** 8384 W 3rd St. I-10, exit 7A (La Cienega Blvd), 2.3 mi n, then just e. Int corridors. **Pets:** Accepted.
ASK S X 📠 💻 🍴 🌊 X

Radisson Hotel at Los Angeles Airport LH
(310) 670-9000. **$129-$329.** 6225 W Century Blvd at Sepulveda Blvd. I-405, exit 46 (Century Blvd), 1.6 mi w. Int corridors. **Pets:** Accepted.
ASK S X 📠 💻 🍴 🌊 X

Residence Inn by Marriott-Beverly Hills SH
(310) 277-4427. **$220-$240.** 1177 S Beverly Dr. I-405, exit 6 (Robertson Blvd), 1.6 mi n to Pico Blvd, then 0.6 mi w. Int corridors. **Pets:** Accepted.
ASK S X 📠 💻

Sheraton Gateway Hotel, Los Angeles Airport LH
(310) 642-1111. **Call for rates.** 6101 W Century Blvd. I-405, exit 46 (Century Blvd), 1.3 mi w. Int corridors. **Pets:** Accepted.
X M 💻 🍴 🌊

Sheraton Los Angeles Downtown LH
(213) 488-3500. **$349.** 711 S Hope St. SR 110, exit 6th St southbound, just e, then just s. Int corridors. **Pets:** Accepted.
ASK S X M 📠 💻 🍴

Sofitel Los Angeles LH
(310) 278-5444. **$535-$2000, 3 day notice.** 8555 Beverly Blvd. I-10, exit 7A (La Cienega Blvd), 2.5 mi n. Int corridors. **Pets:** Accepted.
ASK S X 🍴 🌊 X

The Tower–Beverly Hills LH
(310) 277-2800. **Call for rates.** 1224 S Beverwil Dr. I-10, exit 6 (Robertson Blvd), 1.8 mi n, then 0.7 mi e. Int corridors. **Pets:** Accepted.
SAVE X 💻 🍴 🌊

Travelodge Hotel at Lax SH ❀
(310) 649-4000. **$75-$130.** 5547 W Century Blvd. I-405, exit 46 (Century Blvd), 0.5 mi w. Ext/int corridors. **Pets:** $10 daily fee/pet. Designated rooms, service with restrictions, crate.
SAVE X 📠 💻 🍴 🌊

Vagabond Inn Los Angeles-USC M
(213) 746-1531. **$74-$119.** 3101 S Figueroa St. SR 110, exit Adams Blvd, 0.5 mi s. Ext corridors. **Pets:** $10 daily fee/pet. Designated rooms, service with restrictions, supervision.
SAVE S X 📠 💻 🍴 🌊

The Westin Bonaventure Hotel & Suites LH ❀
(213) 624-1000. **$419.** 404 S Figueroa St. SR 110, exit 23A (6th St), just n on Figueroa, e on 4th St, then s on Flower. Int corridors. **Pets:** Medium, dogs only. Service with restrictions, supervision.
ASK S X M 📠 💻 🍴 🌊

The Westin Hotel-Los Angeles Airport LH
(310) 216-5858. **$279-$289.** 5400 W Century Blvd. I-405, exit 46 (Century Blvd), just w. Int corridors. **Pets:** Accepted.
ASK S X M 📠 💻 🍴 🌊 X

MANHATTAN BEACH

▼▼▼ Residence Inn by Marriott SH
(310) 421-3100. **$181-$197.** 1700 N Sepulveda Blvd. I-405, exit 43B (Rosecrans Ave), 1.5 mi w, then 1 mi s on SR 1. Ext corridors. **Pets:** Accepted.

ASK SD ✕ ᏏM 🗄 ▣ ➾ ✕

MARINA DEL REY

▼▼▼▼ The Ritz-Carlton, Marina del Rey LH
(310) 823-1700. **$479.** 4375 Admiralty Way. SR 90 (Marina Frwy), just s on Lincoln Blvd (SR 1), just w on Bali Way. Int corridors. **Pets:** Accepted.

✕ ᏏM ▣ ♦ ➾ ✕

MONROVIA

▼▼▼ Homestead Studio Suites Hotel-Los Angeles-Monrovia SH
(626) 256-6999. **$114-$134.** 930 S Fifth Ave. I-210, exit 33 (Huntington Dr), just w, then just n. Int corridors. **Pets:** Other species. $75 one-time fee/pet. Service with restrictions.

ASK SD ✕ ᏏM 🗄 ▣

NORTHRIDGE

▼▼ Extended StayAmerica-Los Angeles/Northridge SH
(818) 734-1787. **$109-$129.** 19325 Londelius St. SR 118, exit 37 (Tampa Ave), 3 mi s. Int corridors. **Pets:** Other species. $75 one-time fee/pet. Service with restrictions.

ASK SD ✕ ᏏM 🗄 ▣

PASADENA

▼▼◆ Quality Inn Pasadena M
(626) 796-9291. **$85-$199.** 3321 E Colorado Blvd. I-210, exit 29B (Madre St), just s, then 0.3 mi e. Ext corridors. **Pets:** Accepted.

ASK SD ✕ 🗄 ▣ ➾ ✕

▼▼◆▼ The Ritz-Carlton, Huntington Hotel & Spa LH
(626) 568-3900. **Call for rates.** 1401 S Oak Knoll Ave. I-210, exit 26B (Lake Ave), 2 mi s. Ext/int corridors. **Pets:** Accepted.

✕ ᏏM 🗄 ▣ ♦ ➾ ✕

▼▼◆▼ Sheraton Pasadena Hotel LH ❀
(626) 449-4000. **$169-$259.** 303 E Cordova St. I-210, exit 26B (Lake Ave), 0.7 mi s, then just w. Int corridors. **Pets:** Large, dogs only. Service with restrictions, supervision.

ASK ✕ ᏏM 🗄 ▣ ♦ ➾ ✕

AAA ▼▼◆ Super 8 M
(626) 449-3020. **$70-$250.** 2863 E Colorado Blvd. I-210, exit 29A (San Gabriel Blvd), 0.3 mi s, then just e. Ext corridors. **Pets:** Small. $20 daily fee/pet. Designated rooms, no service, supervision.

SAVE SD ✕ 🗄 ➾

AAA ▼▼◆ Vagabond Inn M
(626) 449-3170. **$90-$130.** 1203 E Colorado Blvd. I-210, exit 27A (Hill Ave), just s, then just w. Ext/int corridors. **Pets:** Accepted.

SAVE SD ✕ 🗄 ▣ ➾

AAA ▼▼▼ The Westin-Pasadena LH ❀
(626) 792-2727. **$415.** 191 N Los Robles Ave. I-210, exit Los Robles Ave, just s; in Plaza Las Fuentes. Int corridors. **Pets:** Small, dogs only. Service with restrictions, crate.

SAVE ✕ ᏏM 🗄 ▣ ♦ ➾ ✕

AAA ▼▼▼ Westway Inn M
(626) 304-9678. **$75-$350, 30 day notice.** 1599 E Colorado Blvd. I-210, exit 27B (Allen Ave) westbound; exit 27 (Hill Ave) eastbound, 0.8 mi s. Ext corridors. **Pets:** Accepted.

SAVE ✕ 🗄 ▣ ➾

POMONA

▼▼▼ Sheraton Suites Fairplex LH
(909) 622-2220. **$129-$189.** 601 W McKinley Ave. I-10, exit 45A (White Ave) eastbound, 0.5 mi n, then just w; exit 43 (Fairplex Dr) westbound, 1 mi n, then 0.7 mi e. Int corridors. **Pets:** Accepted.

ASK SD ✕ ᏏM 🗄 ▣ ♦ ➾ ✕

SAN DIMAS

▼▼ Red Roof Inn M
(909) 599-2362. **Call for rates.** 204 N Village Ct. SR 57, exit 45 (Arrow Hwy), just e, then just n. Ext corridors. **Pets:** Accepted.

✕ ᏏM 🗄 ➾

SAN PEDRO

AAA ▼▼▼ DoubleTree Hotel San Pedro LH
(310) 514-3344. **Call for rates.** 2800 Via Cabrillo Marina. I-110, exit Gaffey St, 1.5 mi s, then 0.5 mi e on 22nd St. Int corridors. **Pets:** Accepted.

SAVE ✕ 🗄 ▣ ♦ ➾ ✕

AAA ◆ Vagabond Inn M
(310) 831-8911. **$69-$84.** 215 S Gaffey St. I-110, exit Gaffey St, just s of terminus. Ext corridors. **Pets:** Small. $25 one-time fee/pet. Designated rooms, service with restrictions, supervision.

SAVE SD ✕ 🗄 ▣ ➾

SANTA CLARITA

AAA ▼▼◆ Best Western Valencia Inn M
(661) 255-0555. **$99-$149.** 27413 Wayne Mills Pl. I-5, exit 170 (Magic Mountain Pkwy), just e. Ext corridors. **Pets:** Accepted.

SAVE SD ✕ 🗄 ▣ ➾

▼▼◆ Comfort Suites SH
(661) 254-7700. **Call for rates.** 25380 The Old Road. I-5, exit 167 (Lyons Ave), just w. Int corridors. **Pets:** Medium, other species. $25 one-time fee/pet. Service with restrictions, supervision.

✕ ᏏM 🗄 ▣ ➾

▼▼ Extended StayAmerica SH
(661) 255-1044. **$104-$124.** 24940 W Pico Canyon Rd. I-5, exit 167 (Lyons Ave), just w. Int corridors. **Pets:** Other species. $75 one-time fee/pet. Service with restrictions.

ASK SD ✕ 🗄 ▣

▼▼◆ La Quinta Inn & Suites Stevenson Ranch SH
(661) 286-1111. **$149-$179.** 25201 The Old Rd. I-5, exit 167 (Lyons Ave), just w to Chiquella Ln, just n, then just w. Int corridors. **Pets:** Other species. Service with restrictions, supervision.

ASK SD ✕ 🗄 ➾

▼▼◆ Residence Inn by Marriott SH
(661) 290-2800. **$181-$197.** 25320 The Old Rd. I-5, exit 167 (Lyons Ave), just w. Int corridors. **Pets:** Accepted.

ASK SD ✕ ᏏM 🗄 ▣ ➾ ✕

SANTA MONICA

AAA ▼▼◆ ▼▼◆ The Fairmont Miramar Hotel Santa Monica LH
(310) 576-7777. **$309-$429.** 101 Wilshire Blvd. I-10, exit 1B (Lincoln Blvd), 0.6 mi n, then 0.6 mi w. Ext/int corridors. **Pets:** Medium. $25 one-time fee/pet. Designated rooms, service with restrictions, supervision.

SAVE ✕ ᏏM ▣ ♦ ➾ ✕

▼▼▼ The Georgian SH
(310) 395-9945. **$272-$320.** 1415 Ocean Ave. I-10, exit 1B (Lincoln Blvd), just n, then 0.5 mi w on Broadway. Int corridors. **Pets:** Accepted.

ASK SD ✕ ▣

Le Merigot–A JW Marriott Beach Hotel & Spa LH
(310) 395-9700. **Call for rates.** 1740 Ocean Ave. I-10, exit 1B (Lincoln Blvd), 0.3 mi s, 0.6 mi w on Pico Blvd, then just n. Int corridors. **Pets:** Accepted.

Loews Santa Monica Beach Hotel LH
(310) 458-6700. **$299-$2600.** 1700 Ocean Ave. I-10, exit 1B (Lincoln Blvd), 0.3 mi s, 0.6 mi w on Pico Blvd, then just n. Int corridors. **Pets:** Small. $25 one-time fee/room. Service with restrictions, supervision.

Sheraton Delfina Santa Monica LH
(310) 399-9344. **$469.** 530 Pico Blvd. I-10, exit 1B (Lincoln Blvd), just s. Int corridors. **Pets:** Accepted.

Travelodge-Santa Monica/Pico Blvd M
(310) 450-5766. **$99-$199.** 3102 W Pico Blvd. I-10, exit 2 (Centinela Ave), just n, then just w. Ext corridors. **Pets:** Small. $100 deposit/pet. Designated rooms, service with restrictions, supervision.

SEAL BEACH

The Pacific Inn SH
(562) 493-7501. **$109-$169.** 600 Marina Dr. SR 1 (Pacific Coast Hwy), just s. Ext/int corridors. **Pets:** Medium, other species. $75 one-time fee/room. Designated rooms, service with restrictions, crate.

SHERMAN OAKS

Best Western Carriage Inn M
(818) 787-2300. **$99-$199.** 5525 Sepulveda Blvd. I-405, exit 64 (Burbank Blvd), just e, then just s. Ext/int corridors. **Pets:** Accepted.

SOUTH EL MONTE

Rodeway Inn South El Monte M
(626) 579-4490. **Call for rates.** 1228 N Durfee Rd. SR 60, exit 11 (Peck Rd), just s, then just e. Ext corridors. **Pets:** Accepted.

TARZANA

St. George Inn & Suites M
(818) 345-6911. **$74-$98.** 19454 Ventura Blvd. US 101, exit 24 (Tampa Ave), just s, then just w. Ext corridors. **Pets:** Accepted.

TORRANCE

Extended StayAmerica-Los Angeles-Torrance SH
(310) 540-5442. **$109-$129.** 3525 Torrance Blvd. I-405, exit 42A (Hawthorne Blvd), 3.5 mi, then 0.4 mi e. Int corridors. **Pets:** Other species. $75 one-time fee/pet. Service with restrictions.

Extended StayAmerica-Los Angeles/Torrance Harbor Gateway SH
(310) 328-6000. **$104-$124.** 19200 Harborgate Way. I-405, exit 38A (Normandie Ave), just s, then just w via 190th St. Int corridors. **Pets:** Other species. $75 one-time fee/pet. Service with restrictions.

Holiday Inn Torrance LH
(310) 781-9100. **$119-$209.** 19800 S Vermont Ave. I-110, exit 9 (190th St), just e, then 0.4 mi n. Int corridors. **Pets:** Accepted.

Homestead Studio Suites Hotel-Los Angeles-Torrance SH
(310) 543-0048. **$114-$134.** 3995 Carson St. I-405, exit 42A (Hawthorne Blvd), 3.6 mi s; I-110, exit 7B (Carson St), 4.5 mi w. Int corridors. **Pets:** Other species. $75 one-time fee/pet. Service with restrictions.

Ramada Inn M
(310) 325-0660. **$99-$109.** 2880 Pacific Coast Hwy. I-405, exit 39 (Crenshaw Blvd), 5 mi s, then just w. Ext corridors. **Pets:** Medium. $10 daily fee/pet, $50 one-time fee/room. Designated rooms, service with restrictions, supervision.

Residence Inn by Marriott SH
(310) 543-4566. **$220-$440.** 3701 Torrance Blvd. I-405, exit 42A (Hawthorne Blvd), 3.2 mi s, then just e. Ext corridors. **Pets:** Accepted.

Staybridge Suites M
(310) 371-8525. **Call for rates.** 19901 Prairie Ave. I-405, exit 39 (Crenshaw Blvd), just s to 190th St, 1 mi w, then just s. Ext/int corridors. **Pets:** Accepted.

UNIVERSAL CITY

Sheraton Universal Hotel, at Universal Studios LH
(818) 980-1212. **$409-$449.** 333 Universal Hollywood Dr. US 101, exit 12A (Lankershim Blvd), just n, then just e. Int corridors. **Pets:** Medium, other species. Designated rooms, service with restrictions, supervision.

WEST HOLLYWOOD

The Grafton on Sunset SH
(323) 654-4600. **$185-$335.** 8462 Sunset Blvd. I-10, exit 7A (La Cienega Blvd), 4.4 mi n, then just e. Int corridors. **Pets:** Small, other species. $100 one-time fee/room. Designated rooms, service with restrictions.

Le Montrose Suite Hotel SH
(310) 855-1115. **$440-$635.** 900 Hammond St at Cynthia St. I-10, exit 7A (La Cienega Blvd), 2.6 mi n to San Vicente Blvd, 1.3 mi nw, then just w on Cynthia St. Int corridors. **Pets:** Accepted.

Le Parc Suite Hotel LH
(310) 855-8888. **$219-$440.** 733 N West Knoll Dr. I-10, exit 7A (La Cienega Blvd), 3.5 mi n, just w on Melrose Ave, then just n. Int corridors. **Pets:** Accepted.

WHITTIER

Radisson Hotel Whittier LH
(562) 945-8511. **Call for rates.** 7320 Greenleaf Ave. I-605, exit 15 (Whittier Blvd), 2.5 mi e, then 0.6 mi n. Int corridors. **Pets:** $50 one-time fee/pet. Designated rooms, service with restrictions, supervision.

Vagabond Inn M
(562) 698-9701. **Call for rates.** 14125 E Whittier Blvd. I-605, exit 15 (Whittier Blvd), 3.5 mi e. Ext corridors. **Pets:** Accepted.

WOODLAND HILLS

▼▼ ◆◆ Extended StayAmerica-Los Angeles-Woodland Hills **SH**
(818) 710-1170. **$99-$119.** 20205 Ventura Blvd. US 101, exit 25 (Winnetka Ave), just s, then just w. Int corridors. **Pets:** Other species. $75 one-time fee/pet. Service with restrictions.

ASK 🖀 ✕ 🖀 🖳

▧▧▱ ▼▼▼ Warner Center Marriott Hotel **LH** ❀
(818) 887-4800. **$286-$306.** 21850 Oxnard St. US 101, exit 27A (Topanga Canyon Blvd N), 0.6 mi n, then just e. Int corridors. **Pets:** Other species. $75 one-time fee/room. Service with restrictions, crate.

SAVE 🖀 ✕ 🖳 🖀 🖳 ⑪ ⇌ ✕

END METROPOLITAN AREA

LOS BANOS

▧▧▱ ▼▼▼ Best Western Executive Inn **SH**
(209) 827-0954. **$70-$99.** 301 W Pacheco Blvd. On SR 152. Int corridors. **Pets:** Medium, dogs only. $20 daily fee/pet. Service with restrictions, supervision.

SAVE 🖀 ✕ 🖳 🖀 🖳 ⇌ ✕

LOS GATOS

▧▧▱ ▼▼▼▼ Los Gatos Lodge **SH** ❀
(408) 354-3300. **$139-$179.** 50 Los Gatos/Saratoga Rd. SR 17, exit E Los Gatos, just e. Ext/int corridors. **Pets:** Medium, other species. $50 one-time fee/room. Service with restrictions, supervision.

SAVE 🖀 ✕ 🖳 🖀 🖳 ⑪ ⇌

▧▧▱ ▼▼▼▼ Toll House, a Larkspur Collection Hotel **SH** ❀
(408) 395-7070. **$188-$405.** 140 S Santa Cruz Ave. I-880/SR 17, exit SR 9, 0.3 mi w. Int corridors. **Pets:** $250 deposit/room, $25 daily fee/pet. Service with restrictions, crate.

SAVE 🖀 ✕ 🖀 🖳 ⑪ ✕

MADERA

▧▧▱ ▼▼▼ Madera Valley Inn **SH**
(559) 664-0100. **Call for rates.** 317 North G St. SR 99, exit Central Madera, just e. Int corridors. **Pets:** $15 one-time fee/room. Designated rooms, service with restrictions, supervision.

SAVE ✕ 🖀 🖳 ⑪ ⇌

▼ Super 8 **M**
(559) 661-1131. **$65-$79.** 1855 W Cleveland Ave. SR 99, exit Cleveland Ave, just w. Ext corridors. **Pets:** Accepted.

ASK 🖀 ✕ 🖀 🖳 ⇌

MAMMOTH LAKES

▧▧▱ ▼▼▼ Econo Lodge Wildwood Inn **M**
(760) 934-6855. **$89-$199.** 3626 Main St. On SR 203, 0.7 mi w of Old Mammoth Rd. Ext corridors. **Pets:** $10 daily fee/pet. Designated rooms, service with restrictions, supervision.

SAVE 🖀 ✕ 🖀 🖳 ⇌ 🖳

▼▼▼ Mammoth Mountain Inn **LH**
(760) 934-2581. **Call for rates.** 1 Minaret Rd. 5 mi w of town on SR 203. Int corridors. **Pets:** Accepted.

✕ 🖳 🖀 🖳 ⑪ ⇌ ✕ 🖳

▼▼▼ Mammoth Ski & Racquet Club **CO**
(760) 934-7368. **$110-$485, 30 day notice.** 248 Mammoth Slopes Dr. From Old Mammoth Rd, 1 mi w on SR 203, just n; Canyon Blvd, 0.8 mi w, then just s. Int corridors. **Pets:** Accepted.

ASK 🖀 ✕ 🖀 🖳 ⇌ ✕ 🖳

▼▼▼ Shilo Inn **SH** ❀
(760) 934-4500. **$180-$225.** 2963 Main St. On SR 203, just e of Old Mammoth Rd. Int corridors. **Pets:** $25 one-time fee/room. Designated rooms, service with restrictions, supervision.

ASK 🖀 ✕ 🖳 🖀 🖳 ⇌ ✕

▧▧▱ ▼▼▼ Sierra Lodge **SH** ❀
(760) 934-8881. **$59-$199.** 3540 Main St. On SR 203, 0.6 mi w of Old Mammoth Rd. Int corridors. **Pets:** $10 daily fee/pet. Designated rooms, service with restrictions.

SAVE 🖀 ✕ 🖀 🖳

▼▼▼ Sierra Nevada Rodeway Inn **SH**
(760) 934-2515. **Call for rates.** 164 Old Mammoth Rd. Just s of SR 203. Ext/int corridors. **Pets:** Accepted.

✕ 🖀 🖳 ⇌

MANTECA

▧▧▱ ▼▼▼▼ Best Western Executive Inn & Suites **SH**
(209) 825-1415. **$85-$99.** 1415 E Yosemite Ave. Jct SR 99 and 120, exit E Yosemite Ave. Ext corridors. **Pets:** Medium. $25 one-time fee/pet. Designated rooms, service with restrictions, supervision.

SAVE 🖀 ✕ 🖳 🖀 🖳 ⇌

MARIPOSA

▧▧▱ ▼▼▼ Americas Best Value Inn–Mariposa Lodge **SH**
(209) 966-3607. **$149.** 5052 Hwy 140. Center. Ext corridors. **Pets:** Medium, other species. $10 daily fee/pet. Supervision.

SAVE 🖀 ✕ 🖀 🖳 ⇌

▧▧▱ ▼▼▼ Best Western Yosemite Way Station Motel **SH**
(209) 966-7545. **Call for rates.** 4999 Hwy 140. SR 140 at SR 49 S. Ext corridors. **Pets:** Small. $7 daily fee/pet. Designated rooms, service with restrictions, supervision.

SAVE ✕ 🖳 🖳 ⇌

▧▧▱ ▼▼▼ Comfort Inn Yosemite Valley Gateway **SH**
(209) 966-4344. **$79-$109.** 4994 Bullion St. Jct SR 140 and 49 S, just e. Ext corridors. **Pets:** Accepted.

SAVE 🖀 ✕ 🖳 ⇌

▧▧▱ ▼▼▼ Miners Inn **SH**
(209) 742-7777. **$63-$174.** 5181 Hwy 49 N. On SR 49, n at SR 140. Ext/int corridors. **Pets:** Other species. $10 daily fee/pet. Designated rooms, service with restrictions, supervision.

SAVE 🖀 ✕ 🖀 🖳 ⑪ ⇌

MERCED

▧▧▱ ▼▼▼ Merced-Yosemite Travelodge **M**
(209) 722-6224. **Call for rates.** 1260 Yosemite Pkwy. SR 99, exit SR 140, just e. Ext corridors. **Pets:** $10 daily fee/pet. No service, crate.

SAVE 🖀 🖳 🖀 🖳 ⇌

MILPITAS

▧▧▱ ▼▼ Americas Best Value Inn & Suites **M**
(408) 946-8383. **$72-$130.** 485 S Main St. I-880, exit Calaveras Blvd (SR 237), 0.5 mi e, then just s. Ext corridors. **Pets:** Small, dogs only. $10 daily fee/pet. Service with restrictions, supervision.

SAVE 🖀 ✕ 🖀 🖳

AAA ◆◆◆ Best Western Brookside Inn SH
(408) 263-5566. **$89-$149.** 400 Valley Way. I-880, exit Calaveras Blvd (SR 237), just e. Ext/int corridors. **Pets:** Accepted.
[SAVE] [S◇] [✕] [🛏] [💻] [🏊] [✕]

AAA ◆◆◆ Beverly Heritage Hotel LH
(408) 943-9080. **$65-$189.** 1820 Barber Ln. Northwest quadrant of I-880 and Montague Expwy. Int corridors. **Pets:** Accepted.
[SAVE] [S◇] [✕] [🛏] [💻] [🍴] [🏊] [✕]

◆◆◆◆ Embassy Suites Milpitas/Silicon Valley LH
(408) 942-0400. **Call for rates.** 901 E Calaveras Blvd. I-680, exit Calaveras Blvd (SR 237), just w. Int corridors. **Pets:** Accepted.
[✕] [🛏] [💻] [🍴] [🏊] [✕]

◆◆◆ Extended StayAmerica-San Jose/Milpitas SH
(408) 941-9977. **$131-$149.** 1000 Hillview Ct. I-680, exit Calaveras Blvd W (SR 237), just n. Int corridors. **Pets:** Other species. $75 one-time fee/pet. Service with restrictions.
[ASK] [S◇] [✕] [💻]

◆◆◆ Homestead Studio Suites Hotel-San Jose-Milpitas SH
(408) 433-9700. **$131-$145.** 330 Cypress Dr. SR 237, exit McCarthy S. Ext/int corridors. **Pets:** Other species. $75 one-time fee/pet. Service with restrictions.
[ASK] [S◇] [✕] [💻]

◆◆◆ Residence Inn by Marriott SH
(408) 941-9222. **$231-$251.** 1501 California Cir. I-880, exit Dixon Landing Rd E, just s. Int corridors. **Pets:** Accepted.
[ASK] [S◇] [✕] [💻] [🏊] [✕]

AAA ◆◆◆◆ Sheraton San Jose at Silicon Valley LH
(408) 943-0600. **Call for rates.** 1801 Barber Ln. 4 mi n of San Jose International Airport; 0.3 mi nw of I-880 and Montague Expwy. Ext/int corridors. **Pets:** Accepted.
[SAVE] [✕] [🛏] [💻] [🍴] [🏊] [✕]

◆◆◆ TownePlace Suites by Marriott SH
(408) 719-1959. **$187-$207.** 1428 Falcon Dr. I-680, exit Montague Expwy, just w, then just n. Int corridors. **Pets:** Accepted.
[ASK] [S◇] [✕] [🛏] [💻] [🏊]

MIRANDA

AAA ◆◆◆ Miranda Gardens Resort CA
(707) 943-3011. **$95-$265, 7 day notice.** 6766 Ave of the Giants. US 101, exit 650 (Miranda), just e on French Rd, 0.3 mi s on Maple Hills Rd, then 1.5 mi e. Ext corridors. **Pets:** Medium. $150 deposit/room, $15 daily fee/pet. Designated rooms, service with restrictions, supervision.
[SAVE] [S◇] [✕] [🛏] [💻] [🏊] [X] [Z]

MI-WUK VILLAGE

AAA ◆◆ Christmas Tree Inn SH
(209) 586-1005. **$89-$129, 3 day notice.** 24685 Hwy 108. On SR 108, 15 mi e of Sonora. Ext corridors. **Pets:** Small, dogs only. $15 daily fee/pet. Designated rooms, service with restrictions, supervision.
[SAVE] [S◇] [✕] [🛏] [💻] [🏊]

AAA ◆◆◆ Mi Wuk Village Inn & Conference Center SH ❖
(209) 586-3031. **$99-$255.** 24680 SR 108. On SR 108, 15 mi e of Sonora. Ext corridors. **Pets:** Dogs only. $150 deposit/room, $20 daily fee/pet. Designated rooms, service with restrictions, supervision.
[SAVE] [S◇] [✕] [🛏] [💻] [🏊]

MODESTO

AAA ◆◆◆ Best Western Town House Lodge SH
(209) 524-7261. **$91-$120.** 909 16th St. SR 99, exit Central Modesto, 1 mi e, at I St. Ext corridors. **Pets:** Accepted.
[SAVE] [S◇] [✕] [♿] [🛏] [💻] [🏊]

AAA ◆◆◆ Days Inn SH
(209) 527-1010. **Call for rates.** 1312 McHenry Ave. SR 99, exit Briggsmore Ave, 2.3 mi e, then 0.5 mi s. Ext/int corridors. **Pets:** Accepted.
[SAVE] [✕] [♿] [🛏] [💻] [🏊]

AAA ◆◆◆ Microtel Inn & Suites SH
(209) 538-6466. **$66-$110.** 1760 Herndon Rd. SR 99, exit Hatch Rd E, just s. Int corridors. **Pets:** Very small, other species. $75 deposit/pet. Designated rooms, service with restrictions, supervision.
[SAVE] [S◇] [✕] [♿] [🛏] [💻] [🏊]

MOJAVE

AAA ◆◆◆ Americas Best Value Inn M
(661) 824-9317. **$59-$65.** 16352 Sierra Hwy. On SR 14 and 58. Ext corridors. **Pets:** Accepted.
[SAVE] [S◇] [✕] [🛏] [💻] [🏊]

AAA ◆◆◆ Best Western Desert Winds M
(661) 824-3601. **$79-$89.** 16200 Sierra Hwy. On SR 14 and 58. Ext corridors. **Pets:** Very small. $10 daily fee/pet. Service with restrictions, supervision.
[SAVE] [S◇] [✕] [🛏] [💻] [🏊]

AAA ◆◆◆ Days Inn-Mojave M ❖
(661) 824-2621. **Call for rates.** 16100 Sierra Way. On SR 14. Ext corridors. **Pets:** Small. $10 daily fee/pet. Designated rooms, service with restrictions, supervision.
[SAVE] [✕] [🛏] [💻] [🏊]

AAA ◆◆◆ Desert Inn M
(661) 824-2518. **$45-$65.** 1954 Hwy 58. Just e of SR 14. Ext corridors. **Pets:** Medium. Service with restrictions, crate.
[SAVE] [✕] [🛏] [💻]

◆◆ Econo Lodge M
(661) 824-2463. **$49-$62.** 2145 Hwy 58. Just e of SR 14. Ext corridors. **Pets:** Accepted.
[ASK] [S◇] [✕] [🛏] [💻] [🏊]

AAA ◆◆◆ Mariah Country Inn & Suites SH
(661) 824-4980. **$100-$125.** 1385 Hwy 58. 1.5 mi e of SR 14. Int corridors. **Pets:** Medium, other species. $10 daily fee/room. Service with restrictions, supervision.
[SAVE] [S◇] [✕] [♿] [🛏] [💻] [🍴] [🏊]

MONTEREY PENINSULA AREA

CARMEL-BY-THE-SEA

Best Western Carmel Mission Inn SH
(831) 624-1841. **$129-$529.** 3665 Rio Rd. 1 mi s on SR 1. Ext/int corridors. **Pets:** Medium. $35 one-time fee/room. Designated rooms, service with restrictions, supervision.

Briarwood Inn BB
(831) 626-9056. **$105-$285, 7 day notice.** San Carlos St. 3 blks n of Ocean Ave; at jct 4th Ave. Ext corridors. **Pets:** Medium, dogs only. $25 daily fee/pet. Designated rooms, service with restrictions, supervision.

Carmel Country Inn BB
(831) 625-3263. **$165-$395, 7 day notice.** Dolores & 3rd Ave. 4 blks n of Ocean Ave. Ext corridors. **Pets:** Accepted.

Carmel Fireplace Inn Bed & Breakfast BB
(831) 624-4862. **$105-$295, 7 day notice.** San Carlos at 4th. 3 blks n of Ocean Ave. Ext corridors. **Pets:** Medium, dogs only. $25 daily fee/pet. Designated rooms, service with restrictions, supervision.

Carmel Garden Court BB 🐾
(831) 624-6926. **Call for rates.** 4th & Torres. 3 blks n of Ocean Ave. Ext corridors. **Pets:** Medium. $50 one-time fee/pet. Designated rooms, service with restrictions, supervision.

Carmel River Inn M
(831) 624-1575. **$99-$179, 3 day notice.** Hwy One. 1 mi s on SR 1; n of Carmel River Bridge at Oliver Rd. Ext corridors. **Pets:** Accepted.

Coachman's Inn SH
(831) 624-6421. **$145-$435, 3 day notice.** San Carlos St at 7th Ave. Just s of Ocean Ave on San Carlos St; between 7th and 8th aves. Ext corridors. **Pets:** Dogs only. $25 daily fee/pet. Designated rooms, service with restrictions, supervision.

Cypress Inn SH
(831) 624-3871. **Call for rates.** Lincoln & 7th St. Just s off Ocean Ave. Ext/int corridors. **Pets:** Accepted.

Hofsas House SH 🐾
(831) 624-2745. **$100-$350, 3 day notice.** San Carlos St. 3 blks n off Ocean Ave; between 3rd and 4th aves. Ext corridors. **Pets:** Dogs only. $20 daily fee/pet. Designated rooms, supervision.

Horizon Inn & Ocean View Lodge SH
(831) 624-5327. **$126-$350, 3 day notice.** 3rd Ave & Junipero SWC. 4 blks n off Ocean Ave. Ext corridors. **Pets:** Medium, dogs only. $20 daily fee/pet. Designated rooms, service with restrictions, supervision.

Quail Lodge SH
(831) 624-2888. **$380-$575, 3 day notice.** 8205 Valley Greens Dr. 3.5 mi e of SR 1, via Carmel Valley Rd. Ext corridors. **Pets:** Accepted.

Svendsgaard's SH 🐾
(831) 624-1511. **$149-$269, 7 day notice.** 4th & San Carlos. 3 blks n off Ocean Ave. Ext corridors. **Pets:** Other species. Designated rooms, service with restrictions, supervision.

Tradewinds Carmel SH
(831) 624-2776. **$225-$550, 3 day notice.** Mission St and 3rd Ave. 4 blks n off Ocean Ave. Ext corridors. **Pets:** Accepted.

CARMEL VALLEY

Acacia Lodge-Country Garden Inns M
(831) 659-5361. **$129-$195, 3 day notice.** 20 Via Contenta. 12.8 mi e of SR 1. Ext corridors. **Pets:** Accepted.

Hidden Valley Inn-Country Garden Inns M
(831) 659-5361. **Call for rates.** 102 W Carmel Valley Rd. 11 mi e of SR 1. Ext corridors. **Pets:** Accepted.

Los Laureles Lodge SH
(831) 659-2233. **$79-$650, 3 day notice.** 313 W Carmel Valley Rd. 10.5 mi e of SR 1. Ext corridors. **Pets:** Accepted.

MONTEREY

Bay Park Hotel SH 🐾
(831) 649-1020. **$89-$350.** 1425 Munras Ave. SR 1, exit Soledad Dr/Munras Ave, just w. Int corridors. **Pets:** Medium, other species. $20 daily fee/pet. Designated rooms, service with restrictions, supervision.

Best Western Beach Resort Monterey SH 🐾
(831) 394-3321. **$99-$469.** 2600 Sand Dunes Dr. SR 1, exit Del Rey Oaks, just w. Ext corridors. **Pets:** Other species. $50 daily fee/room. Service with restrictions, crate.

Best Western Victorian Inn SH 🐾
(831) 373-8000. **Call for rates.** 487 Foam St. SR 1, exit Monterey, 3.4 mi w. Ext/int corridors. **Pets:** Other species. $30 daily fee/room. Designated rooms, service with restrictions, crate.

Casa Munras, a Larkspur Collection Hotel SH
(831) 375-2411. **$129-$269, 3 day notice.** 700 Munras Ave. SR 1, exit Soledad Dr/Munras Ave, 0.8 mi w. Ext/int corridors. **Pets:** Accepted.

El Adobe Inn M 🐾
(831) 372-5409. **$49-$199, 3 day notice.** 936 Munras Ave. SR 1, exit Soledad Dr/Munras Ave, 0.6 mi w. Ext corridors. **Pets:** Medium, dogs only. $15 daily fee/pet. Designated rooms, service with restrictions, supervision.

Hyatt Regency-Monterey Resort & Conference Center LH 🐾
(831) 372-1234. **$195-$385.** 1 Old Golf Course Rd. SR 1, exit Aguajito Rd northbound; exit Monterey southbound, just e. Int corridors. **Pets:** Other species. $65 one-time fee/pet. Designated rooms, service with restrictions, supervision.

Mariposa Inn SH
(831) 649-1414. **Call for rates.** 1386 Munras Ave. SR 1, exit Soledad Dr/Munras Ave, just w. Ext/int corridors. **Pets:** Medium, dogs only. $40 daily fee/pet. Service with restrictions, supervision.

Monterey Bay Lodge SH
(831) 372-8057. **Call for rates.** 55 Camino Aguajito. SR 1, exit Aguajito Rd, just w. Ext corridors. **Pets:** Accepted.
SAVE ✕ 🛏 💻 🍽 🏊

Monterey Bay Travelodge SH
(831) 373-3381. **$169.** 2030 N Fremont St. Jct SR 1 and Fremont St, at SR 68. Ext corridors. **Pets:** Other species. $20 daily fee/pet. Designated rooms, service with restrictions, supervision.
SAVE ✕ 🛏 💻 🍽 🏊 🐾

Monterey Fireside Lodge M
(831) 373-4172. **$69-$599, 3 day notice.** 1131 10th St. SR 1, exit Aguajito Rd or Monterey, just w. Ext corridors. **Pets:** Other species. $20 daily fee/pet. Designated rooms, service with restrictions, supervision.
SAVE ✕ 🛏 🐾

PACIFIC GROVE

Bide-A-Wee Inn & Cottages M ❀
(831) 372-2330. **$59-$289, 3 day notice.** 221 Asilomar Ave. 1 mi n of SR 68. Ext corridors. **Pets:** Medium. $14 daily fee/pet. Designated rooms, service with restrictions, supervision.
SAVE S🐾 ✕ 🛏 💻 🐾

Deer Haven Inn & Suites SH
(831) 373-7784. **$79-$209, 3 day notice.** 740 Crocker Ave. Just e of SR 68 via Sinex Ave. Ext corridors. **Pets:** Accepted.
ASK S🐾 ✕ 🛏 💻 🐾

Olympia Lodge SH
(831) 373-2777. **Call for rates.** 1140 Lighthouse Ave. 1 mi w. Ext corridors. **Pets:** Accepted.
✕ 🛏 💻 🏊 🐾

Sea Breeze Inn and Cottages SH
(831) 372-7771. **$79-$399.** 1100 Lighthouse Ave. Just w of Seventeen Mile Dr; jct Lighthouse Ave and Grove Acre. Ext/int corridors. **Pets:** Accepted.
✕ 🛏 💻 🍽 🐾

Sea Breeze Lodge M
(831) 372-3431. **$79-$399.** 1100 Lighthouse Ave. Just w of Seventeen Mile Dr. Ext corridors. **Pets:** Accepted.
✕ 🛏 💻 🏊 🐾

PEBBLE BEACH

The Lodge at Pebble Beach LH ❀
(831) 624-3811. **Call for rates.** 1700 Seventeen Mile Dr. Off SR 1. Ext/int corridors. **Pets:** Medium, dogs only.
✕ �&M 💻 🍽 🏊 ✕ 🐾

SEASIDE

Econo Lodge Bay Breeze M
(831) 899-7111. **$45-$120.** 2049 Fremont Blvd. SR 1, exit Sand City/Seaside, just e. Ext/int corridors. **Pets:** Accepted.
SAVE S🐾 ✕ 🛏 💻 🐾

Thunderbird Motel M
(831) 394-6797. **Call for rates.** 1933 Fremont Blvd. SR 1 business route, 0.3 mi n. Ext corridors. **Pets:** Small. $50 deposit/pet. Designated rooms, service with restrictions, supervision.
SAVE ✕ 🛏 🏊 🐾

END AREA

MORENO VALLEY

Comfort Inn M
(951) 242-0699. **$70-$139.** 23330 Sunnymead Blvd. SR 60, exit 62 (Perris Blvd) westbound, just s, then 1.3 mi w; eastbound, 1 mi w. Ext/int corridors. **Pets:** Medium, other species. $50 deposit/pet, $10 daily fee/pet. Service with restrictions, crate.
SAVE S🐾 ✕ 🛏 💻 🏊

MORGAN HILL

Extended StayAmerica-Morgan Hill SH
(408) 779-9660. **$86-$95.** 605 Jarvis Dr. US 101, exit Cochrane W, s on Sutter Blvd, then just e. Int corridors. **Pets:** Other species. $75 one-time fee/pet. Service with restrictions.
ASK S🐾 ✕ 🛏 💻

Quality Inn SH
(408) 779-0447. **$69-$150.** 16525 Condit Rd. US 101, exit Tennant or E Dunne aves, just e. Int corridors. **Pets:** Small. $15 daily fee/pet. No service, supervision.
SAVE S🐾 ✕ 🛏 💻 🏊

Residence Inn by Marriott SH
(408) 782-8311. **$160-$176.** 18620 Madrone Pkwy. US 101, exit Cochrane W, just n. Int corridors. **Pets:** Accepted.
ASK S🐾 ✕ 🛏 💻 🏊

MORRO BAY

Best Western El Rancho M
(805) 772-2212. **$85-$205, 3 day notice.** 2460 Main St. SR 1, exit SR 41, 0.5 mi n. Ext corridors. **Pets:** Accepted.
SAVE S🐾 ✕ ⅃M 🛏 💻 🏊 🐾

Days Inn M
(805) 772-2711. **$59-$169, 3 day notice.** 1095 Main St. SR 1, exit Morro Bay Blvd, 0.7 mi w, then just n. Ext corridors. **Pets:** Accepted.
ASK S🐾 ✕ 🛏 💻 🐾

Econo Lodge South M
(805) 772-7503. **$50-$200, 3 day notice.** 540 Main St. SR 1, exit Morro Bay Blvd, 0.7 mi w, then 0.4 mi s. Ext corridors. **Pets:** Medium. $15 daily fee/room. Designated rooms, service with restrictions, supervision.
SAVE S🐾 ✕ ⅃M 🛏 💻 🐾

Sundown Inn M
(805) 772-7381. **$39-$159.** 640 Main St. SR 1, exit Morro Bay Blvd, 0.7 mi w, then just s. Ext corridors. **Pets:** Accepted.
SAVE S🐾 ✕ ⅃M 🛏 💻 🐾

MOUNTAIN VIEW

Homestead Studio Suites Hotel-San Jose, Mountain View SH
(650) 962-1500. **$126-$140.** 190 E El Camino Real. On SR 82, just w of SR 85. Ext corridors. **Pets:** Other species. $75 one-time fee/pet. Service with restrictions.
ASK S🐾 ✕ ⅃M 🛏 💻

Tropicana Lodge M
(650) 961-0220. **$75-$95.** 1720 El Camino Real W. US 101, exit Shoreline Blvd, 2 mi to SR 82, then just n. Ext/int corridors. **Pets:** Other species. Designated rooms, service with restrictions, crate.

MOUNT SHASTA

A-1 Choice Inn M
(530) 926-4811. **Call for rates.** 1340 S Mount Shasta Blvd. I-5, exit McCloud/SR 89, just n at 1st left, then 1 mi. Ext corridors. **Pets:** Very small, dogs only. $10 daily fee/pet. Designated rooms, service with restrictions, supervision.

Best Western Tree House Motor Inn SH
(530) 926-3101. **$119-$209.** 111 Morgan Way. I-5, exit 738 (Central Mount Shasta), just e. Ext/int corridors. **Pets:** Large, other species. $10 daily fee/pet. Service with restrictions, supervision.

Cold Creek Inn M ❀
(530) 926-9851. **$69-$129, 3 day notice.** 724 N Mt Shasta Blvd. I-5, exit 738. Ext corridors. **Pets:** Other species. $10 daily fee/pet. Service with restrictions, supervision.

Mt Shasta Ranch Bed & Breakfast BB
(530) 926-3870. **Call for rates.** 1008 W a Barr Rd. I-5, exit 738 (Central Mount Shasta), 1.5 mi w. Ext/int corridors. **Pets:** Accepted.

Swiss Holiday Lodge M ❀
(530) 926-3446. **$65-$180.** 2400 S Mount Shasta Blvd. I-5, exit McCloud/SR 89, just n at 1st left. Ext corridors. **Pets:** Small. $10 daily fee/pet. Designated rooms, service with restrictions, supervision.

MYERS FLAT

Myers Inn BB
(707) 943-3259. **$165-$225, 14 day notice.** 12913 Ave of the Giants. US 101, exit Myers Flat, just w. Int corridors. **Pets:** Accepted.

NEEDLES

Americas Best Value Inn M
(760) 326-4501. **$36-$77, 3 day notice.** 1102 E Broadway. I-40, exit 144 (US 95/E Broadway), just sw. Ext corridors. **Pets:** Accepted.

Best Western Colorado River Inn M
(760) 326-4552. **$74-$96.** 2371 W Broadway. I-40, exit 141 (W Broadway/River Rd), 0.3 mi e; on Business Loop I-40. Ext corridors. **Pets:** Medium, other species. $25 deposit/pet. Designated rooms, service with restrictions, supervision.

Best Western Royal Inn M
(760) 326-5660. **$74-$96.** 1111 Pashard St. I-40, exit 141 (W Broadway/River Rd). Ext corridors. **Pets:** Medium, other species. $25 deposit/pet. Designated rooms, service with restrictions, supervision.

Days Inn & Suites M
(760) 326-5836. **Call for rates.** 1215 Hospitality Ln. I-40, exit 142 (J St), just se. Ext corridors. **Pets:** Medium. $10 daily fee/pet. Designated rooms, service with restrictions, supervision.

Travelers Inn M
(760) 326-4900. **$59-$139.** 1195 3rd St Hill. I-40, exit 142 (J St), just e, then just s. Ext corridors. **Pets:** Small, other species. $10 one-time fee/room. Designated rooms, service with restrictions, supervision.

NEVADA CITY

Nevada City Inn M
(530) 265-2253. **$55-$120.** 760 Zion St. SR 20 and 49, exit Gold Flat/Ridge Rd, 0.3 mi w, then 0.3 mi n. Ext corridors. **Pets:** Medium, other species. $10 daily fee/pet. Service with restrictions, supervision.

NEWARK

Homewood Suites by Hilton SH
(510) 791-7700. **$149-$229.** 39270 Cedar Blvd. I-880, exit Mowry Ave, w to Cedar Blvd, then 0.3 mi s. Int corridors. **Pets:** Accepted.

Residence Inn by Marriott Newark/Silicon Valley SH
(510) 739-6000. **$220-$240.** 34566 Dumbarton Ct. SR 84, exit Newark Blvd, just s. Int corridors. **Pets:** Accepted.

Woodfin Suites SH
(510) 795-1200. **Call for rates.** 39150 Cedar Blvd. I-880, exit Mowry Ave, just w, then 0.3 mi s. Int corridors. **Pets:** Accepted.

NEWPORT BEACH

Best Western Newport Beach Inn M
(949) 642-8252. **$159-$299, 3 day notice.** 6208 W Coast Hwy. SR 55, 1 mi nw on SR 1. Int corridors. **Pets:** Accepted.

Extended StayAmerica-Orange County/John Wayne Airport SH
(949) 851-2711. **$114-$134.** 4881 Birch St. I-405, exit 8 (MacArthur Blvd), 0.8 mi s, then just e. Int corridors. **Pets:** Other species. $75 one-time fee/pet. Service with restrictions.

Fairmont Newport Beach LH
(949) 476-2001. **$129-$399.** 4500 MacArthur Blvd. I-405, exit 8 (MacArthur Blvd), 1 mi s. Int corridors. **Pets:** Medium. $35 one-time fee/pet. Designated rooms, service with restrictions, supervision.

The Island Hotel Newport Beach LH ❀
(949) 759-0808. **$420-$735.** 690 Newport Center Dr. SR 73, exit 14 (MacArthur Blvd) northbound, 3 mi s to San Joaquin Hills Rd, then 0.5 mi w; exit 15 (Jamboree Rd) southbound, 2.5 mi s to San Joaquin Hills Rd, then 0.5 mi e. Int corridors. **Pets:** Small, other species. $100 one-time fee/pet. Service with restrictions, supervision.

NIPOMO

Kaleidoscope Inn & Gardens B&B BB
(805) 929-5444. **Call for rates.** 130 E Dana St. US 101, exit 179 (Tefft St), 0.7 mi e, just s on Thompson Rd, then just e. Ext/int corridors. **Pets:** Accepted.

NOVATO

AAA ▼▼▼▼ **Inn Marin** SH ❀
(415) 883-5952. **$109-$169.** 250 Entrada Dr. US 101, exit Ignacio Blvd, just w, then just n on Enfrente Rd. Ext corridors. **Pets:** Other species. $20 daily fee/pet. Service with restrictions, supervision.
[SAVE] [S🐾] [✕] [⎙M] [🛏] [💻] [🍴] [🏊]

AAA ▼▼▼ **Novato Days Inn** SH
(415) 897-7111. **$71-$96.** 8141 Redwood Blvd. US 101, exit San Marin Dr, 1 mi n. Ext corridors. **Pets:** Small, dogs only. $10 daily fee/pet. Designated rooms, service with restrictions, supervision.
[SAVE] [S🐾] [✕] [⎙M] [🛏] [💻] [🍴] [🏊]

OAKDALE

AAA ▼▼ **Holiday Motel** M ❀
(209) 847-7023. **$65-$85.** 950 East F St. 1 mi e on SR 108 and 120. Ext corridors. **Pets:** Other species. $10 daily fee/pet, $30 one-time fee/room. Designated rooms, service with restrictions, supervision.
[SAVE] [S🐾] [✕] [🛏] [🏊]

AAA ▼▼ **Quality Inn** SH
(209) 847-8181. **$89-$109.** 825 East F St. 0.8 mi e on SR 108 and 120. Ext corridors. **Pets:** Accepted.
[SAVE] [S🐾] [✕] [⎙M] [🛏] [🏊]

OAKHURST

AAA ▼▼▼ **Americas Best Value Inn** SH
(559) 658-5500. **$59-$259.** 48800 Royal Oaks Dr. SR 41, just s of SR 49. Int corridors. **Pets:** Small. $10 daily fee/pet. Service with restrictions, supervision.
[SAVE] [S🐾] [✕] [⎙M] [🛏] [💻] [🏊]

AAA ▼▼▼ **Best Western Yosemite Gateway Inn** SH
(559) 683-2378. **$59-$119.** 40530 Hwy 41. SR 49, 0.8 mi n. Ext corridors. **Pets:** Accepted.
[SAVE] [S🐾] [✕] [⎙M] [🛏] [💻] [🍴] [🏊] [✕]

AAA ▼▼▼▼ **Chateau du Sureau** CI
(559) 683-6860. **$375-$575, 14 day notice.** 48688 Victoria Ln. Just w of jct SR 41 and 49. Int corridors. **Pets:** Accepted.
[SAVE] [✕] [🍴] [🏊]

AAA ▼▼▼ **Comfort Inn Yosemite Area** SH
(559) 683-8282. **$59-$159.** 40489 Hwy 41. SR 49, 0.5 mi n. Ext corridors. **Pets:** Other species. $10 daily fee/room. Designated rooms, service with restrictions, supervision.
[SAVE] [S🐾] [✕] [🛏] [💻] [🏊]

AAA ▼▼▼ **Days Inn** M
(559) 642-2525. **$60-$160.** 40662 Hwy 41. SR 49, 0.8 mi n. Ext corridors. **Pets:** Small. $50 deposit/pet, $10 daily fee/pet. Designated rooms, service with restrictions, supervision.
[SAVE] [S🐾] [✕] [🛏] [💻] [🏊]

OAKLAND

▼▼▼ **Hilton Oakland Airport** LH
(510) 635-5000. **Call for rates.** 1 Hegenberger Rd. I-880, exit Hegenberger Rd, 1 mi w; 1.3 mi e of Metropolitan Oakland International Airport. Int corridors. **Pets:** Accepted.
[✕] [⎙M] [🛏] [💻] [🍴] [🏊]

AAA ▼▼▼ **Homewood Suites** SH
(510) 663-2700. **Call for rates.** 1103 Embarcadero. I-880, exit 16th Ave/Embarcadero southbound; exit 5th Ave/Embarcadero northbound, just w. Int corridors. **Pets:** Accepted.
[SAVE] [✕] [🛏] [💻] [🏊]

AAA ▼▼▼ **The Inn at Jack London Square** SH
(510) 452-4565. **Call for rates.** 233 Broadway. I-880, exit Broadway, 0.3 mi w. Int corridors. **Pets:** Accepted.
[SAVE] [✕] [🛏] [💻] [🏊]

AAA ▼▼▼ **Quality Inn** SH
(510) 562-4888. **$69-$129.** 8471 Enterprise Way. I-880, exit Hegenberger Rd, just e. Ext corridors. **Pets:** Small. $100 deposit/room, $10 daily fee/pet. Service with restrictions, crate.
[SAVE] [S🐾] [✕] [🛏] [💻] [🏊]

OCEANO

AAA ▼▼▼ **Oceano Inn** M
(805) 473-0032. **$69-$219.** 1252 Pacific Blvd. On SR 1. Ext corridors. **Pets:** Accepted.
[SAVE] [S🐾] [✕] [⎙M] [🛏] [💻]

OCEANSIDE

AAA ▼▼▼ **Best Western Marty's Valley Inn** M
(760) 757-7700. **$95-$155.** 3240 E Mission Ave. I-5, exit 53 (Mission Ave), 2 mi e. Ext/int corridors. **Pets:** Small. $10 daily fee/pet. Designated rooms, service with restrictions, crate.
[SAVE] [S🐾] [✕] [🛏] [💻] [🏊]

▼▼▼▼ **Best Western Oceanside Inn Hotel & Suites** M
(760) 722-1821. **Call for rates.** 1680 Oceanside Blvd. I-5, exit 52 (Oceanside Blvd), just w. Ext/int corridors. **Pets:** Accepted.
[✕] [🛏] [💻] [🏊]

▼▼ **Extended StayAmerica-San Diego/Oceanside** SH
(760) 439-1499. **$94-$164.** 3190 Vista Way. I-5, exit 51B (SR 78 E) 1.5 mi e to El Camino Real, just n, then just e. Int corridors. **Pets:** Other species. $75 one-time fee/pet. Service with restrictions.
[ASK] [S🐾] [✕] [⎙M] [🛏] [💻]

▼▼ **La Quinta Inn** SH
(760) 450-0730. **$119-$139.** 937 N Coast Hwy. I-5, exit 54 (Coast Hwy), just w. Int corridors. **Pets:** Other species. Service with restrictions, supervision.
[ASK] [S🐾] [✕] [⎙M] [🛏] [💻]

AAA ▼▼▼ **Motel 6 #4208** M
(760) 721-1543. **$50-$100, 7 day notice.** 909 N Coast Hwy. I-5, exit 54B (Coast Hwy), just w. Int corridors. **Pets:** Other species. Service with restrictions, supervision.
[SAVE] [S🐾] [✕] [⎙M] [🛏] [🏊]

OJAI

AAA ▼▼▼▼ **Best Western Casa Ojai** M
(805) 646-8175. **$81-$180.** 1302 E Ojai Ave. 0.8 mi e on SR 150. Ext corridors. **Pets:** Dogs only. $25 daily fee/pet. Designated rooms, service with restrictions, supervision.
[SAVE] [S🐾] [✕] [🛏] [💻] [🏊]

▼▼▼▼ **Blue Iguana Inn** M
(805) 646-5277. **$109-$269, 7 day notice.** 11794 N Ventura Ave. 2.5 mi w of town on SR 33. Ext corridors. **Pets:** Accepted.
[ASK] [S🐾] [🛏] [💻] [🏊] [✕]

AAA ▼▼ **Oakridge Inn** M
(805) 649-4018. **Call for rates.** 780 N Ventura Ave. 4 mi s on SR 33; 2 mi e of Lake Casitas; in Oak View. Ext corridors. **Pets:** Medium. $100 deposit/pet, $15 one-time fee/pet. Designated rooms, service with restrictions, supervision.
[SAVE] [✕] [🛏] [💻]

AAA ▼▼▼▼ **Ojai Valley Inn & Spa** LH ❀
(805) 646-1111. **$400-$3000, 3 day notice.** 905 Country Club Rd. 1 mi w on SR 150, 0.3 mi s. Ext/int corridors. **Pets:** Dogs only. $50 daily fee/pet. Service with restrictions.
[SAVE] [S🐾] [✕] [⎙M] [🛏] [💻] [🍴] [🏊] [✕]

ONTARIO

Best Western InnSuites Ontario SH
(909) 466-9600. **$90-$130.** 3400 Shelby St. I-10, exit 56 (Haven Ave), just n to Inland Empire Blvd, just w, then just se. Ext corridors. **Pets:** Medium. $25 one-time fee/pet. Designated rooms, service with restrictions, supervision.

Country Inn & Suites by Carlson M
(909) 937-6000. **$110-$214.** 231 N Vineyard Ave. I-10, exit 54 (Vineyard Ave), just s. Ext corridors. **Pets:** $50 one-time fee/room. Service with restrictions.

DoubleTree Hotel Ontario LH
(909) 937-0900. **$99-$290.** 222 N Vineyard Ave. I-10, exit 54 (Vineyard Ave), 0.4 mi s. Int corridors. **Pets:** Accepted.

Extended StayAmerica-Los Angeles-Ontario Airport SH
(909) 944-8900. **$94-$114.** 3990 E Inland Empire Blvd. I-10, exit 56 (Haven Ave), just n, then 0.5 mi e. Int corridors. **Pets:** Other species. $75 one-time fee/pet. Service with restrictions.

Hilton Ontario Airport LH
(909) 980-0400. **Call for rates.** 700 N Haven Ave. I-10, exit 56 (Haven Ave), just n. Int corridors. **Pets:** Accepted.

La Quinta Inn & Suites Ontario (Airport) SH
(909) 476-1112. **$145-$179.** 3555 Inland Empire Blvd. I-10, exit 56 (Haven Ave), just n, then just e. Int corridors. **Pets:** Other species. Service with restrictions, supervision.

Residence Inn by Marriott SH
(909) 937-6788. **$176-$196.** 2025 Convention Center Way. I-10, exit 54 (Vineyard Ave), just s, then 1 blk e. Ext corridors. **Pets:** Accepted.

Sheraton Ontario Airport Hotel LH ❖
(909) 937-8000. **$99-$269.** 429 N Vineyard Ave. I-10, exit 54 (Vineyard Ave), just s. Int corridors. **Pets:** Small. Service with restrictions, supervision.

ORANGE

Howard Johnson Express Inn M
(714) 639-1121. **$69-$109.** 1930 E Katella Ave. SR 55, exit 15 (Katella Ave), just w. Ext corridors. **Pets:** Medium. $50 deposit/pet. Designated rooms, service with restrictions, supervision.

ORLAND

Amber Light Inn Motel M ❖
(530) 865-7655. **$52-$65.** 828 Newville Rd. I-5, exit Chico (SR 32), 0.3 mi e. Ext corridors. **Pets:** Small. $5 daily fee/pet. Designated rooms, service with restrictions, supervision.

Orland Inn M
(530) 865-7632. **$59-$69.** 1052 South St. I-5, exit South St northbound; exit CR 16 southbound, just e; in Stony Creek Shopping Center. Ext corridors. **Pets:** Medium, other species. $5 daily fee/pet. Service with restrictions, supervision.

OROVILLE

Americas Best Value Inn M ❖
(530) 533-7070. **$60-$125.** 580 Oro Dam Blvd. SR 70, exit Oroville Dam Blvd, 0.3 mi e. Ext corridors. **Pets:** Other species. $20 deposit/ room, $10 daily fee/pet. Designated rooms, service with restrictions, crate.

Comfort Inn SH
(530) 533-9673. **$80-$165.** 1470 Feather River Blvd. SR 70, exit E Montgomery St. Int corridors. **Pets:** Dogs only. $100 deposit/room, $10 daily fee/pet. Designated rooms, service with restrictions, supervision.

Days Inn-Oroville M
(530) 533-3297. **$60-$99.** 1745 Feather River Blvd. SR 70, exit E Montgomery St, just e to Feather River Blvd, then 0.5 mi s. Ext corridors. **Pets:** Medium. $10 daily fee/pet. Designated rooms, service with restrictions, supervision.

Sunset Inn M
(530) 533-8201. **$55-$150.** 1835 Feather River Blvd. SR 70, exit E Montgomery St, 0.5 mi s. Ext corridors. **Pets:** Accepted.

OXNARD

Residence Inn At River Ridge SH
(805) 278-2200. **$159-$179.** 2101 W Vineyard Ave. US 101, exit 62A (Vineyard Ave), 1.8 mi w. Ext corridors. **Pets:** Accepted.

Vagabond Inn Oxnard M ❖
(805) 983-0251. **$66-$80.** 1245 N Oxnard Blvd. US 101, exit 62A (Vineyard Ave) northbound; exit 62B (Oxnard Blvd) southbound, 1.5 mi s. Ext corridors. **Pets:** Other species. $5 daily fee/room. Service with restrictions, supervision.

PALMDALE

Residence Inn by Marriott SH
(661) 947-4204. **$199-$219.** 514 W Ave P. SR 14, exit Ave P, just w. Int corridors. **Pets:** Accepted.

Super 8 Motel M
(661) 273-8000. **Call for rates.** 200 W Palmdale Blvd. SR 14, exit 35 (Palmdale Blvd), just e. Int corridors. **Pets:** Accepted.

PALM DESERT

Best Western Palm Desert Resort M
(760) 340-4441. **$79-$209.** 74-695 Hwy 111. I-10, exit 134 (Cook St), 4.4 mi s, then 0.3 mi w. Ext corridors. **Pets:** Other species. $10 daily fee/room. Service with restrictions, supervision.

Comfort Suites M
(760) 360-3337. **$89-$349.** 39-585 Washington St. I-10, exit 137 (Washington St), just n. Int corridors. **Pets:** Medium, other species. $20 one-time fee/room. Service with restrictions, supervision.

Embassy Suites Hotel LH
(760) 340-6600. **Call for rates.** 74-700 Hwy 111. I-10, exit 134 (Cook St), 4.4 mi s, then 0.3 mi w. Ext corridors. **Pets:** Accepted.

Fairfield Inn **M**
(760) 341-9100. **$98-$186.** 72-322 Hwy 111. I-10, exit 131 (Monterey Ave), 5.7 mi s, then 0.6 mi w. Int corridors. **Pets:** Other species. $75 one-time fee/room. Service with restrictions, supervision.

The Inn at Deep Canyon **M**
(760) 346-8061. **$47-$127, 3 day notice.** 74-470 Abronia Tr. I-10, exit 134 (Cook St), 4.4 mi s to SR 111, 0.5 mi w, then just s on Deep Canyon Rd. Ext corridors. **Pets:** Accepted.

International Lodge **CO**
(760) 346-6161. **$116-$178, 3 day notice.** 74-380 El Camino. I-10, exit 134 (Cook St), 4.4 mi s to SR 111, 0.6 mi w to Panorama Dr, just s, then just e. Ext corridors. **Pets:** Small, other species. $10 daily fee/pet. Designated rooms, no service, crate.

Residence Inn by Marriott **SH**
(760) 776-0050. **$131-$219.** 38-305 Cook St. I-10, exit 134 (Cook St), 0.8 mi s. Ext corridors. **Pets:** Accepted.

PALM SPRINGS

A Place In The Sun **M**
(760) 325-0254. **$79-$299, 7 day notice.** 754 San Lorenzo Rd. Just e of Palm Canyon Dr via Mesquite Ave and Random Rd. Ext corridors. **Pets:** Accepted.

Best Western Las Brisas Hotel **M**
(760) 325-4372. **$69-$259.** 222 S Indian Canyon Dr. 0.3 mi s of Tahquitz Canyon Way. Ext corridors. **Pets:** Dogs only. $35 daily fee/pet. Service with restrictions, supervision.

Casa Cody Country Inn **M**
(760) 320-9346. **Call for rates.** 175 S Cahuilla Rd. SR 111, just w on Tahquitz Canyon Way, then just s. Ext corridors. **Pets:** Accepted.

Hilton Palm Springs Resort **LH**
(760) 320-6868. **$80-$355, 3 day notice.** 400 E Tahquitz Canyon Way. Just e of Indian Canyon Dr. Int corridors. **Pets:** Accepted.

Hotel California **M**
(760) 322-8855. **$89-$250, 3 day notice.** 424 E Palm Canyon Dr. 1.5 mi s of Tahquitz Canyon Way. Ext corridors. **Pets:** Accepted.

Hotel Zoso **LH**
(760) 325-9676. **$109-$349, 3 day notice.** 150 S Indian Canyon Dr. Just s of Tahquitz Canyon Way. Int corridors. **Pets:** Accepted.

Quality Inn Resort **M**
(760) 323-2775. **$59-$189.** 1269 E Palm Canyon Dr. 2.3 mi se of Tahquitz Canyon Way. Ext corridors. **Pets:** Accepted.

Ramada Palm Springs **M**
(760) 320-0555. **Call for rates.** 2000 N Palm Canyon Dr. 1.5 mi n of Tahquitz Canyon Way. Ext/int corridors. **Pets:** Very small, dogs only. $100 deposit/room, $15 daily fee/pet. Designated rooms, service with restrictions, supervision.

Shilo Inn Suites **M** 🐾
(760) 320-7676. **$185-$225.** 1875 N Palm Canyon Dr. 1.5 mi n of Tahquitz Canyon Way. Ext corridors. **Pets:** $25 one-time fee/room. Designated rooms, service with restrictions, supervision.

Vagabond Inn Palm Springs **M**
(760) 325-7211. **$49-$249.** 1699 S Palm Canyon Dr. 1.5 mi s of Tahquitz Canyon Way. Ext corridors. **Pets:** $10 daily fee/pet. Designated rooms, service with restrictions, supervision.

Wyndham Palm Springs **LH**
(760) 322-6000. **Call for rates.** 888 Tahquitz Canyon Way. 0.4 mi e of Indian Canyon Dr. Int corridors. **Pets:** Accepted.

PALO ALTO

Crowne Plaza Cabana Hotel **SH**
(650) 857-0787. **$204-$279.** 4290 El Camino Real. US 101, exit San Antonio Rd, 0.4 mi n. Ext/int corridors. **Pets:** Accepted.

Sheraton Palo Alto Hotel **LH**
(650) 328-2800. **Call for rates.** 625 El Camino Real. US 101, exit Embarcadero, 1.8 mi w, then just n on SR 82. Int corridors. **Pets:** Accepted.

The Westin Palo Alto **LH**
(650) 321-4422. **Call for rates.** 675 El Camino Real. US 101, exit Embarcadero, 1.8 mi w, then just n on SR 82. Int corridors. **Pets:** Accepted.

PARADISE

Comfort Inn **SH**
(530) 876-0191. **$79-$159.** 5475 Clark Rd. SR 191, 0.5 mi s of Pearson Rd. Int corridors. **Pets:** Dogs only. $100 deposit/room, $10 daily fee/pet. Designated rooms, service with restrictions, supervision.

Lantern Inn **M**
(530) 877-5553. **$65.** 5799 Wildwood Ln. 1 blk w off Skyway. Ext corridors. **Pets:** Medium. $10 daily fee/pet. Service with restrictions, supervision.

Paradise Inn **M**
(530) 877-2127. **Call for rates.** 5423 Skyway. 1.5 mi w. Ext corridors. **Pets:** $10 daily fee/pet.

Ponderosa Gardens Motel **M** 🐾
(530) 872-9094. **$79-$119.** 7010 Skyway. 2 blks e; center. Ext corridors. **Pets:** Other species. $10 daily fee/pet. Designated rooms, service with restrictions, supervision.

PASO ROBLES

Hampton Inn & Suites **SH**
(805) 226-9988. **$129-$219.** 212 Alexa Ct. US 101, exit 231B (SR 46/Fresno/Bakersfield), just sw. Int corridors. **Pets:** Accepted.

La Quinta Inn & Suites **SH**
(805) 239-3004. **$129-$169.** 2615 Buena Vista Dr. US 101, exit 234 northbound; exit 231B (SR 46 E) southbound, 0.3 mi e, then just n. Int corridors. **Pets:** Other species. Service with restrictions, supervision.

PATTERSON

Best Western Villa Del Lago Inn **SH**
(209) 892-5300. **$79-$139.** 2959 Speno Dr. I-5, exit Sperry Rd, just e. Int corridors. **Pets:** Medium. Service with restrictions, crate.

PHELAN

♨♨ ▼▼▼ Best Western Cajon Pass M
(760) 249-6777. **Call for rates.** 8317 Hwy 138. I-15, exit 131 (SR 138/Palmdale), just w. Ext corridors. **Pets:** Medium. $25 one-time fee/room. Service with restrictions, supervision.

SAVE ✕ 🛏 💻 🏊

PISMO BEACH

▼▼▼▼ Cliffs Resort SH
(805) 773-5000. **Call for rates.** 2757 Shell Beach Rd. US 101, exit 193 (Spyglass Dr) northbound; exit 193 (Shell Beach Rd) southbound, just w, then just n. Int corridors. **Pets:** Accepted.

✕ ♿M 🛏 💻 🍴 🏊 ✕

▼▼▼▼ Cottage Inn by the Sea M
(805) 773-4617. **Call for rates.** 2351 Price St. US 101, exit 191B (Shell Beach Rd) northbound, just w, 0.5 mi s; exit 191B (Price St) southbound, just w, then just s. Ext corridors. **Pets:** Accepted.

✕ ♿M 🛏 💻 🏊 ⚓

♨♨ ▼▼▼ Oxford Suites SH 🐾
(805) 773-3773. **$109-$259.** 651 Five Cities Dr. US 101, exit 189 (4th St), just w, then just n. Ext corridors. **Pets:** Medium. $10 daily fee/pet. Designated rooms, service with restrictions, supervision.

SAVE 🛏 ✕ ♿M 🛏 💻 🏊 ✕

▼▼▼▼ Sandcastle Inn M
(805) 773-2422. **Call for rates.** 100 Stimson Ave. US 101, exit 190 (Price St) northbound, 0.3 mi s, then just w; exit 190B (Hinds Ave) southbound, just w, then just s. Ext/int corridors. **Pets:** Accepted.

✕ ♿M 🛏 💻

▼▼ Sea Gypsy Motel CO
(805) 773-1801. **$55-$220.** 1020 Cypress St. US 101, exit 191A (Wadsworth Ave) northbound, 0.3 mi w to Cypress St, then just s; exit 191A (SR 1) southbound, just w on Wadsworth Ave, then just s. Ext/int corridors. **Pets:** Accepted.

✕ 🛏 💻 🏊 ⚓

♨♨ ▼▼▼ Shell Beach Inn M
(805) 773-4373. **Call for rates.** 653 Shell Beach Rd. US 101, exit 191B (Shell Beach Rd) northbound, just w, then 1.2 mi s; exit 191B (Price St) southbound, just w, then 1 mi n. Ext corridors. **Pets:** Accepted.

SAVE ✕ 🛏 💻 🏊 ⚓

▼▼▼▼ Spyglass Inn SH
(805) 773-4855. **Call for rates.** 2705 Spyglass Dr. US 101, exit 193 (Spyglass Dr) northbound; exit 193 (Shell Beach Rd) southbound, just w, then just n. Ext corridors. **Pets:** Accepted.

✕ ♿M 🛏 💻 🍴 🏊 ⚓

PLACENTIA

♨♨ ▼▼▼▼ Residence Inn by Marriott SH
(714) 996-0555. **$220-$240.** 700 W Orangethorpe Ave. SR 57, exit 6 (Orangethorpe Ave) southbound; exit 6A (Orangethorpe Ave) northbound, just w, just n on Placentia Ave, then just e. Ext corridors. **Pets:** Medium, other species. $75 one-time fee/pet. Service with restrictions, supervision.

SAVE 🛏 ✕ 🛏 🛏 💻 🏊 ✕

PLACERVILLE

♨♨ ▼▼▼▼ Best Western Placerville Inn SH
(530) 622-9100. **$109-$349.** 6850 Green Leaf Dr. US 50, exit Missouri Flat Rd S, just e. Int corridors. **Pets:** $25 daily fee/pet. Service with restrictions.

SAVE 🛏 ✕ ♿M 🛏 💻 🏊 ✕

♨♨ ▼ Mother Lode Motel M
(530) 622-0895. **Call for rates.** 1940 Broadway. US 50, exit Point View Dr, just e. Ext corridors. **Pets:** Medium, dogs only. $20 daily fee/pet. Designated rooms, service with restrictions, supervision.

SAVE ✕ ♿M 🛏 💻 🏊

PLEASANT HILL

▼▼▼ Extended StayAmerica-Pleasant Hill SH
(925) 945-6788. **$113-$125.** 3220 Buskirk Ave. I-680, exit Treat Blvd/Geary Rd E, just n. Int corridors. **Pets:** Other species. $75 one-time fee/pet. Service with restrictions.

ASK 🛏 ✕ 🛏 💻

▼▼▼▼ Hyatt Summerfield Suites SH 🐾
(925) 934-3343. **$114-$500.** 2611 Contra Costa Blvd. I-680, exit Contra Costa Blvd, then w. Int corridors. **Pets:** Medium. $200 one-time fee/room. Designated rooms, service with restrictions, crate.

ASK ✕ ♿M 💻 🏊 ✕

▼▼▼▼ Residence Inn by Marriott-Pleasant Hill SH 🐾
(925) 689-1010. **$264-$284.** 700 Ellinwood Way. I-680, exit Willow Pass Rd W to S Contra Costa Blvd, e on Ellinwood Dr, then n. Ext/int corridors. **Pets:** Other species. $100 one-time fee/room. Service with restrictions.

ASK 🛏 ✕ 💻 🏊 ✕

PLEASANTON

▼▼ ▼▼ Best Western Pleasanton Inn M
(925) 463-1300. **Call for rates.** 5375 Owens Ct. I-580, exit Hopyard Rd, just s. Ext corridors. **Pets:** Accepted.

✕ 🛏 💻 🏊 ✕

♨♨ ▼▼▼▼ Crowne Plaza Hotel Pleasanton LH
(925) 847-6000. **Call for rates.** 11950 Dublin Canyon Rd. I-580, exit Foothill Rd, 0.3 mi s. Int corridors. **Pets:** Accepted.

SAVE ✕ ♿M 💻 🍴 🏊

▼▼ Extended Stay Deluxe SH
(925) 730-0000. **$113-$125.** 4555 Chabot Dr. I-580, exit Hopyard Rd, 1 mi s, e on Stoneridge Dr, then s. Int corridors. **Pets:** Other species. $75 one-time fee/pet. Service with restrictions.

ASK 🛏 ✕ 💻 🏊

▼▼▼▼ Hyatt Summerfield Suites SH
(925) 730-0070. **$99-$450.** 4545 Chabot Dr. I-580, exit Hopyard Rd, 1 mi s, e on Stoneridge Dr, then s. Ext corridors. **Pets:** Accepted.

ASK ✕ ♿M 💻 🏊 ✕

♨♨ ▼▼▼▼ Larkspur Landing Pleasanton SH
(925) 463-1212. **$189-$209.** 5535 Johnson Dr. I-580, exit Hopyard Rd S, w on Owen. Int corridors. **Pets:** Large, other species. $75 one-time fee/pet. Service with restrictions, crate.

SAVE 🛏 ✕

♨♨ ▼▼▼▼ Residence Inn by Marriott SH
(925) 227-0500. **$187-$207.** 11920 Dublin Canyon Rd. I-580, exit Foothill Blvd S, then w. Int corridors. **Pets:** Medium. $100 one-time fee/pet. Service with restrictions.

ASK 🛏 ✕ ♿M 💻 🏊 ✕

♨♨ ▼▼▼▼ Sheraton Pleasanton Hotel SH
(925) 463-3330. **$239.** 5990 Stoneridge Mall Rd. Jct I-580 and 680, 0.5 mi sw; I-580, exit Foothill Rd, 0.3 mi s, then 0.3 mi e on Canyon Way. Int corridors. **Pets:** Accepted.

SAVE 🛏 ✕ 🛏 💻 🍴 🏊 ✕

PLYMOUTH

♨♨ ▼▼ ▼ Shenandoah Inn M
(209) 245-4491. **$92-$150.** 17674 Village Dr. 1 mi s on SR 49. Ext corridors. **Pets:** Small, dogs only. $25 one-time fee/pet. Designated rooms, service with restrictions, supervision.

SAVE 🛏 ✕ 🛏 💻 🏊

POLLOCK PINES

Best Western Stagecoach Inn Ⓜ
(530) 644-2029. **$123-$143.** 5940 Pony Express Tr. US 50, exit Pollock Pines eastbound, 1 mi e; exit Sly Park westbound. Ext corridors. **Pets:** Accepted.

Westhaven Inn Ⓜ
(530) 644-7800. **Call for rates.** 5658 Pony Express Tr. US 50, exit Pollock Pines, just n. Ext corridors. **Pets:** Accepted.

PORTERVILLE

Best Western Porterville Inn ⑤Ⓗ
(559) 781-7411. **$105-$129.** 350 W Montgomery Ave. SR 65, 0.8 mi e on SR 190, just s on Jaye St, then just e. Int corridors. **Pets:** Accepted.

PORTOLA

Sleepy Pines Motel Ⓜ
(530) 832-4291. **$72-$180.** 74631 Hwy 70. On SR 70. Ext corridors. **Pets:** Accepted.

QUINCY

Pine Hill Motel Ⓜ
(530) 283-1670. **Call for rates.** 42075 Hwy 70. 1 mi n. Ext corridors. **Pets:** Medium. $5 daily fee/pet. Service with restrictions, supervision.

RAMONA

Ramona Valley Inn Ⓜ
(760) 789-6433. **$62-$68.** 416 Main St. On SR 78, 0.5 mi e of jct SR 67. Ext corridors. **Pets:** Very small, dogs only. $100 one-time fee/pet. Designated rooms, service with restrictions, supervision.

RANCHO CORDOVA

Crossland Studios-Sacramento-Point East Dr ⑤Ⓗ
(916) 859-0280. **$68-$75.** 11299 Point East Dr. US 50, exit Sunrise Blvd, just s, e on Folsom Blvd, then just n. Ext corridors. **Pets:** Other species. $75 one-time fee/pet. Service with restrictions.

Days Inn ⑤Ⓗ
(916) 351-1213. **$70-$90, 4 day notice.** 12249 Folsom Blvd. US 50, exit Hazel Ave, just s. Ext corridors. **Pets:** Large, other species. $20 daily fee/room. Designated rooms, service with restrictions, crate.

Extended StayAmerica-Sacramento-White Rock Rd ⑤Ⓗ
(916) 635-2363. **$86-$95.** 10721 White Rock Rd. US 50, exit Zinfandel Dr, just s. Ext corridors. **Pets:** Other species. $75 one-time fee/pet. Service with restrictions.

Fairfield Inn & Suites ⑤Ⓗ
(916) 858-8680. **$61-$169.** 10745 Gold Center Dr. US 50, exit Zinfandel Dr, just s. Int corridors. **Pets:** Other species. $75 one-time fee/room. Service with restrictions, supervision.

Hawthorn Suites ⑤Ⓗ
(916) 351-9192. **$119.** 12180 Tributary Point Dr. US 50, exit Hazel Ave, just n. Int corridors. **Pets:** Medium. $50 one-time fee/room. Service with restrictions, supervision.

Holiday Inn Rancho Cordova ⑤Ⓗ
(916) 635-4040. **Call for rates.** 11269 Point East Dr. US 50, exit Sunrise Blvd S, e on Folsom Blvd, then just n. Int corridors. **Pets:** Small. $10 daily fee/room, $25 one-time fee/room. Designated rooms, service with restrictions, crate.

La Quinta Inn & Suites ⑤Ⓗ
(916) 638-1111. **$129-$159.** 11131 Folsom Blvd. US 50, exit Sunrise Blvd S. Int corridors. **Pets:** Other species. Service with restrictions, supervision.

Red Roof Inn-Rancho Cordova-Sacramento East Ⓜ
(916) 638-2500. **Call for rates.** 10800 Olson Dr. I-5, exit 17, just e. Ext corridors. **Pets:** Accepted.

Residence Inn by Marriott ⑤Ⓗ
(916) 851-1550. **$166-$186.** 2779 Prospect Park Dr. US 50, exit Zinfandel Dr, just s, then e. Int corridors. **Pets:** Accepted.

Vagabond Inn Executive-Rancho Cordova ⑤Ⓗ
(916) 631-7500. **Call for rates.** 10713 White Rock Rd. US 50, exit Zinfandel Dr, just s; 11 mi e of Sacramento. Ext/int corridors. **Pets:** Large. Designated rooms, service with restrictions, crate.

RANCHO CUCAMONGA

Homewood Suites ⑤Ⓗ
(909) 481-6480. **Call for rates (no credit cards).** 11433 Mission Vista Dr. I-15, exit 110 (4th St), just w to Richmond Pl, just n, then just w. Int corridors. **Pets:** Accepted.

TownePlace Suites by Marriott ⑤Ⓗ
(909) 466-1100. **$132-$152.** 9625 Milliken Ave. I-10, exit 57 (Milliken Ave), 0.6 mi n. Int corridors. **Pets:** Other species. $100 one-time fee/room. Service with restrictions, supervision.

RANCHO MIRAGE

The Westin Mission Hills Resort & Spa Ⓛ Ⓗ
(760) 328-5955. **$99-$500, 7 day notice.** 71-333 Dinah Shore Dr. I-10, exit 130 (Ramon Rd), 0.3 mi w on Ramon Rd, 1 mi s on Bob Hope Dr, then 0.6 mi w. Ext corridors. **Pets:** Accepted.

RED BLUFF

Best Western Antelope Inn ⑤Ⓗ
(530) 527-8882. **$80-$160.** 203 Antelope Blvd. I-5, exit SR 36 W (Central District). Int corridors. **Pets:** Other species. $10 daily fee/pet. Designated rooms, service with restrictions, supervision.

Comfort Inn ⑤Ⓗ ❁
(530) 529-7060. **Call for rates.** 90 Sale Ln. I-5, exit Susanville/Lassen Park, 0.3 mi e. Int corridors. **Pets:** Other species. $15 daily fee/pet. Designated rooms, service with restrictions.

Sportsman Lodge Ⓜ
(530) 527-2888. **Call for rates.** 768 Antelope Blvd. I-5, exit SR 36 W (Central District), 1.5 mi e. Ext corridors. **Pets:** $7 one-time fee/pet. No service, supervision.

Super 8 Motel Red Bluff M
(530) 529-2028. **$55-$150.** 30 Gilmore Rd. I-5, exit 649 (Central Red Bluff), just sw on SR 36. Ext corridors. **Pets:** Medium. $10 daily fee/pet. Designated rooms, service with restrictions, supervision.

Travelodge Red Bluff M
(530) 527-6020. **$55-$150.** 38 Antelope Blvd. I-5, exit 649 (Central Red Bluff), just w. Ext corridors. **Pets:** Medium. $10 daily fee/pet. Designated rooms, service with restrictions, supervision.

REDCREST

Redcrest Resort CA
(707) 722-4208. **$60-$205, 14 day notice.** 26459 Ave of the Giants. US 101, exit Redcrest southbound; exit Redcrest/Holmes northbound, just e, then just n. Ext corridors. **Pets:** Accepted.

REDDING

AmeriHost Inn & Suites-Redding SH
(530) 722-9100. **$79-$130.** 2600 Larkspur Ln. I-5, exit Cypress Ave, just e, then right at Larkspur Ln. Int corridors. **Pets:** Accepted.

Grand Manor Inn & Suites SH
(530) 221-4472. **Call for rates.** 850 Mistletoe Ln. I-5, exit Cypress Ave E, 0.8 mi n on Hilltop Dr. Int corridors. **Pets:** Medium. $10 daily fee/pet. Designated rooms, service with restrictions, supervision.

Holiday Inn SH
(530) 221-7500. **$124-$159.** 1900 Hilltop Dr. I-5, exit Hilltop Dr, just s. Int corridors. **Pets:** Dogs only. $100 deposit/room, $10 daily fee/pet. Designated rooms, service with restrictions, supervision.

Holiday Inn Express SH
(530) 241-5500. **$99-$299.** 1080 Twin View Blvd. I-5, exit Twin View Blvd, just w. Int corridors. **Pets:** Accepted.

La Quinta Inn Redding SH
(530) 221-8200. **$109-$139.** 2180 Hilltop Dr. I-5, exit Cypress Ave E, 0.5 mi n. Int corridors. **Pets:** Other species. Service with restrictions, supervision.

Oxford Suites SH
(530) 221-0100. **$105-$159.** 1967 Hilltop Dr. I-5, exit Cypress Ave E, 0.5 mi n. Ext/int corridors. **Pets:** Accepted.

Quality Inn M
(530) 221-6530. **$85-$140.** 2059 Hilltop Dr. I-5, exit Cypress Ave E, 0.3 mi n. Ext corridors. **Pets:** Small. $15 daily fee/room. Service with restrictions, supervision.

Ramada Limited SH
(530) 246-2222. **$75-$160.** 1286 Twin View Blvd. I-5, exit Twin View Blvd E, just n. Int corridors. **Pets:** Accepted.

Redding Travelodge SH
(530) 243-5291. **Call for rates.** 540 N Market St. I-5, exit Lake Blvd northbound, just w, 0.5 mi to Market St, then 0.5 mi s; exit Market St southbound, 2 mi s. Ext corridors. **Pets:** Large, other species. $8 daily fee/pet. Designated rooms, service with restrictions, supervision.

Red Lion Hotel Redding SH
(530) 221-8700. **$99-$179.** 1830 Hilltop Dr. I-5, exit SR 44/ Hilltop Dr. Int corridors. **Pets:** Accepted.

Rodeway Inn SH
(530) 241-6464. **Call for rates.** 532 N Market St. I-5, exit Lake Blvd northbound, just w, 0.5 mi to Market St, then 0.5 mi s; exit Market St southbound, 2 mi s. Ext corridors. **Pets:** Medium, dogs only. $20 daily fee/room. Designated rooms, service with restrictions, supervision.

REDLANDS

Best Western Sandman Motel M
(909) 793-2001. **Call for rates.** 1120 W Colton Ave. I-10, exit 77C (Tennessee St) eastbound; exit 77B (Tennessee St) westbound, just s, then just e. Ext corridors. **Pets:** Accepted.

Dynasty Suites-Redlands M
(909) 793-6648. **$89-$159 (no credit cards), 3 day notice.** 1235 W Colton Ave. I-10, exit 77C (Tennessee St) eastbound; exit 77B (Tennessee St) westbound, just s, then just w. Ext corridors. **Pets:** Small. $15 daily fee/pet. Service with restrictions, supervision.

REDWAY

Dean Creek Resort M
(707) 923-2555. **$80-$140.** 4112 Redwood Dr. US 101, exit Redwood Dr northbound; exit Redway/Shelter Cove southbound, just w. Ext corridors. **Pets:** Dogs only. $10 daily fee/pet. Service with restrictions, supervision.

REDWOOD CITY

Sofitel San Francisco Bay LH
(650) 598-9000. **$369-$599.** 223 Twin Dolphin Dr. US 101, exit Marine Pkwy E, 0.5 mi s. Int corridors. **Pets:** Accepted.

TownePlace Suites by Marriott SH
(650) 593-4100. **$198-$218.** 1000 Twin Dolphin Dr. US 101, exit Redwood Shores Pkwy, 0.3 mi e, then just s. Int corridors. **Pets:** Accepted.

REEDLEY

Edgewater Inn M
(559) 637-7777. **$75-$79.** 1977 W Manning Ave. 12 mi e of SR 99 via Manning Ave. Ext corridors. **Pets:** Supervision.

RIALTO

Best Western Empire Inn M
(909) 877-0690. **$79-$200, 3 day notice.** 475 W Valley Blvd. I-10, exit 68 (Riverside Ave), just n, then 0.5 mi w. Ext corridors. **Pets:** Accepted.

RIDGECREST

Best Western China Lake Inn M
(760) 371-2300. **$95-$105.** 400 S China Lake Blvd. On US 395 business route. Ext corridors. **Pets:** Small. $10 one-time fee/pet. Service with restrictions, supervision.

Carriage Inn M
(760) 446-7910. **$143.** 901 N China Lake Blvd. On SR 178 and US 395 business route. Ext corridors. **Pets:** Small, dogs only. $25 one-time fee/pet. Service with restrictions, supervision.

▼▼▼▼ **Comfort Inn** Ⓜ
(760) 375-9731. **$90-$100.** 507 S China Lake Blvd. On US 395 business route. Ext corridors. **Pets:** Accepted.
Ⓐ$K S♦ ☒ ᠘M 🖥 💻 ⌲

⟨AAA⟩ ▼▼▼▼ **Econo Lodge Inn & Suites** Ⓜ
(760) 446-2551. **$70-$97.** 201 Inyokern Rd. On SR 178 and US 395 business route, just w of China Lake Blvd. Ext corridors. **Pets:** Small. Service with restrictions, supervision.
ⓈAVE S♦ ☒ 🖥 💻 ⌲

⟨AAA⟩ ▼▼▼ **Heritage Inn & Suites** 🆂🅷
(760) 446-7951. **$75.** 1050 N Norma. On US 395 business route, just w. Int corridors. **Pets:** Other species. $100 deposit/room. Service with restrictions, crate.
ⓈAVE S♦ ☒ ᠘M 🖥 💻 ⌈🍴 ⌲

▼▼ ▼▼ **Rodeway Inn** Ⓜ
(760) 384-3575. **$49-$99.** 131 W Upjohn Ave. On US 395 business route, just w. Ext corridors. **Pets:** Accepted.
Ⓐ$K S♦ ☒ 🖥 💻

⟨AAA⟩ ▼▼ ▼▼ **Vagabond Inn** Ⓜ
(760) 375-2220. **$65-$89.** 426 China Lake Blvd. On US 395 business route. Ext corridors. **Pets:** $10 one-time fee/pet. Service with restrictions, supervision.
ⓈAVE S♦ ☒ ᠘M 🖥 💻

RIO DELL

⟨AAA⟩ ▼▼ **Humboldt Gables Motel** Ⓜ
(707) 764-5609. **$40-$80.** 40 W Davis St. US 101, exit Wildwood Ave, 0.5 mi w. Ext corridors. **Pets:** Accepted.
ⓈAVE S♦ ☒ ᠘M 🖥 💻 🎿

RIPON

⟨AAA⟩ ▼▼▼▼ **La Quinta Inn & Suites** 🆂🅷
(209) 599-8999. **$97-$117.** 1524 Colony Rd. SR 99, exit Jack Tone Rd, just e. Int corridors. **Pets:** Other species. Service with restrictions, supervision.
ⓈAVE S♦ ☒ 🖥 💻 ⌲

RIVERSIDE

⟨AAA⟩ ▼▼ ▼▼ **Eco Inn** Ⓜ
(951) 359-0770. **Call for rates.** 10518 Magnolia Ave. SR 91, exit 56 (Tyler St), 0.5 mi nw, then 0.3 mi sw. Ext corridors. **Pets:** Other species. $20 daily fee/pet. Designated rooms, service with restrictions, supervision.
ⓈAVE ☒ 🖥 💻 ⌲

ROCKLIN

⟨AAA⟩ ▼▼ ▼▼ **Heritage Inn Express, Rocklin** 🆂🅷
(916) 632-3366. **$69-$99.** 4480 Rocklin Rd. I-80, exit Rocklin Rd, just w, then just s. Int corridors. **Pets:** Medium, other species. $25 one-time fee/room. Designated rooms, service with restrictions, supervision.
ⓈAVE S♦ ☒ 🖥 💻 ⌲

⟨AAA⟩ ▼▼ ▼▼ **Howard Johnson Hotel** 🆂🅷 ❈
(916) 624-4500. **$81-$100.** 4420 Rocklin Rd. I-80, exit Rocklin Rd, just w, then just s. Ext corridors. **Pets:** Small. $100 deposit/pet, $25 one-time fee/pet. Designated rooms, service with restrictions, supervision.
ⓈAVE S♦ ☒ ᠘M 🖥 💻 ⌲

ROSEVILLE

⟨AAA⟩ ▼▼ ▼▼ **Best Western Roseville Inn** 🆂🅷
(916) 782-4434. **Call for rates.** 220 Harding Blvd. I-80, exit Douglas Blvd, just w, then just n. Ext corridors. **Pets:** Accepted.
ⓈAVE ☒ ᠘M 🖥 💻 ⌲

▼▼ ▼▼ **Extended StayAmerica-Sacramento-Roseville** 🆂🅷
(916) 781-9001. **$99-$110.** 1000 Lead Hill Blvd. I-80, exit Douglas Blvd W, just n to Harding Blvd. Int corridors. **Pets:** Other species. $75 one-time fee/pet. Service with restrictions.
Ⓐ$K S♦ ☒ 🖥 💻

▼▼ ▼▼ **Heritage Inn Express** 🆂🅷
(916) 782-4466. **Call for rates.** 204 Harding Blvd. I-80, exit Douglas Blvd, just w, then just n. Ext corridors. **Pets:** Medium. $30 daily fee/pet. Service with restrictions, supervision.
ⓈAVE ☒ ᠘M 🖥 💻 ⌈🍴 ⌲

▼▼▼▼ **Homewood Suites by Hilton** 🆂🅷
(916) 783-7455. **Call for rates.** 401 Creekside Ridge Ct. I-80, exit SR 65, 1 mi w to Galleria Blvd, 0.5 mi s to Antelope Creek Rd, then just e to Creekside Ridge Ct. Int corridors. **Pets:** Accepted.
☒ ᠘M 🖥 💻 ⌲

▼▼▼▼ **Larkspur Landing Roseville** 🆂🅷
(916) 773-1717. **$109-$179.** 1931 Taylor Rd. I-80, exit Eureka-Taylor Rd, 0.3 mi ne. Int corridors. **Pets:** Medium. $75 one-time fee/pet. Designated rooms, service with restrictions, supervision.
ⓈAVE S♦ ☒ ᠘M 🖥 💻

⟨AAA⟩ ▼▼▼▼ **Orchid Suites Roseville** 🆂🅷
(916) 784-2222. **$119-$209.** 130 N Sunrise Ave. I-80, exit Douglas Blvd, just e, then 0.3 mi n. Ext/int corridors. **Pets:** Medium. $20 daily fee/pet. Designated rooms, service with restrictions, supervision.
ⓈAVE S♦ ☒ ᠘M 🖥 💻 ⌲

▼▼▼▼ **Residence Inn by Marriott** 🆂🅷
(916) 772-5500. **$177-$197.** 1930 Taylor Rd. I-80, exit Eureka-Taylor Rd, just s. Int corridors. **Pets:** Accepted.
Ⓐ$K S♦ ☒ ᠘M 💻 ⌲ ☒

SACRAMENTO

⟨AAA⟩ ▼▼ ▼▼ **Best Western Expo Inn** 🆂🅷
(916) 922-9833. **$95-$250.** 1413 Howe Ave. Jct SR 16 and US 50, exit Howe Ave, 2.5 mi n. Int corridors. **Pets:** Accepted.
ⓈAVE S♦ ☒ 🖥 💻 ⌲

⟨AAA⟩ ▼▼▼▼ **Best Western Harbor Inn & Suites** 🆂🅷
(916) 371-2100. **$89-$119.** 1250 Halyard Dr. 4 mi w; exit Business Rt I-80 via Harbor Blvd. Ext/int corridors. **Pets:** Accepted.
ⓈAVE S♦ ☒ ᠘M 🖥 💻 ⌈🍴 ⌲

⟨AAA⟩ ▼▼ ▼▼ **Clarion Hotel Mansion Inn** 🆂🅷
(916) 444-8000. **$89-$169, 21 day notice.** 700 16th St. On SR 160, 1.3 mi n of Business Rt I-80, exit 16th St. Int corridors. **Pets:** $50 one-time fee/pet. Service with restrictions, crate.
ⓈAVE S♦ ☒ ᠘M 🖥 💻 ⌈🍴 ⌲

⟨AAA⟩ ▼▼ ▼▼ **Clarion Hotel Near Calexpo** 🆂🅷
(916) 487-7600. **$79-$149.** 2600 Auburn Blvd. Business Rt I-80, exit Fulton Ave. Int corridors. **Pets:** Accepted.
ⓈAVE S♦ ☒ ᠘M 🖥 💻 ⌈🍴 ⌲

▼▼▼▼ **DoubleTree Hotel** 🅻🅷
(916) 929-8855. **Call for rates.** 2001 Point West Way. 1 blk off Business Rt I-80, exit via Arden Way. Int corridors. **Pets:** Accepted.
☒ ᠘M 🖥 💻 ⌈🍴 ⌲

⟨AAA⟩ ▼▼ **Econo Lodge** Ⓜ
(916) 443-6631. **$59-$129.** 711 16th St. Business Rt I-80, exit 15th St eastbound; exit 16th St westbound; I-5, exit J St (Old Sacramento). Ext corridors. **Pets:** $6 daily fee/pet. Designated rooms, service with restrictions.
ⓈAVE S♦ ☒ ᠘M 🖥

▼▼ ▼▼ **Extended StayAmerica-Sacramento-Arden Way** 🆂🅷
(916) 921-9942. **$86-$95.** 2100 Harvard St. I-80 business route, exit Arden Way, just w. Ext corridors. **Pets:** Other species. $75 one-time fee/pet. Service with restrictions.
Ⓐ$K S♦ 🖥 💻

Holiday Inn Express Sacramento SH
(916) 444-4436. **Call for rates.** 728 16th St. On SR 160. Int corridors.
Pets: $50 one-time fee/pet. Service with restrictions, crate.

Homestead Studio Suites Hotel-Sacramento-S. Natomas M
(916) 564-7500. **$95-$105.** 2810 Gateway Oaks Dr. I-5, exit W El
Camino Ave, just w, then 0.4 mi n. Ext corridors. **Pets:** Other species.
$75 one-time fee/pet. Service with restrictions.

Host Airport Hotel SH
(916) 922-8071. **$109-$169.** 6945 Airport Blvd. 11 mi nw of state capitol; 6 mi nw of I-80; off I-5. Ext corridors. **Pets:** Accepted.

La Quinta Inn Sacramento (Downtown) SH
(916) 448-8100. **$109-$142.** 200 Jibboom St. I-5, exit Richards Blvd W,
2.3 mi nw of Business Loop I-80. Ext corridors. **Pets:** Other species.
Service with restrictions, supervision.

La Quinta Inn Sacramento (North) SH
(916) 348-0900. **$112-$139.** 4604 Madison Ave. I-80, exit Madison Ave,
0.3 mi e. Ext corridors. **Pets:** Other species. Service with restrictions,
supervision.

Larkspur Landing Sacramento SH
(916) 646-1212. **$99-$179 (no credit cards).** 555 Howe Ave. US 50,
exit Howe Ave, 1.5 mi n. Int corridors. **Pets:** Small. $75 one-time fee/pet.
Service with restrictions, supervision.

Quality Inn Natomas SH
(916) 927-7117. **$72.** 3796 Northgate Blvd. I-80, exit Northgate Blvd,
just s. Ext corridors. **Pets:** Medium. $25 daily fee/room. Service with
restrictions, supervision.

Radisson Hotel SH
(916) 922-2020. **Call for rates.** 500 Leisure Ln. Business Rt I-80, exit
Exposition Blvd, 0.4 mi w. Ext corridors. **Pets:** Accepted.

Ramada Limited-Discovery Park SH
(916) 442-6971. **$69-$150.** 350 Bercut Dr. I-5, exit E Richards Blvd, 2.3
mi nw of Business Loop I-80. Ext corridors. **Pets:** Accepted.

Red Lion Hotel Sacramento SH
(916) 922-8041. **$150-$249.** 1401 Arden Way. I-80, exit Arden Way; in
Arden Fair Shopping Plaza. Ext/int corridors. **Pets:** Accepted.

Residence Inn By Marriott-Capitol Sacramento SH
(916) 443-0500. **Call for rates (no credit cards).** 150 L St. Downtown;
just e of state capitol; entrance 15th and L sts. Int corridors.
Pets: Accepted.

Residence Inn By Marriott-Sacramento Airport Natomas SH
(916) 649-1300. **$187-$207.** 2410 W El Camino Ave. I-5, exit W El
Camino Ave. Ext corridors. **Pets:** Accepted.

Residence Inn By Marriott-Sacramento Cal Expo SH
(916) 920-9111. **$176-$196.** 1530 Howe Ave. 2.5 mi n of jct SR 16 and
US 50, exit Howe Ave. Ext corridors. **Pets:** Accepted.

TownePlace Suites by Marriott Sacramento Cal Expo SH
(916) 920-5400. **$129-$249.** 1784 Tribute Rd. I-5, exit Business Rt I-80
N, exit Exposition Blvd, just w. Int corridors. **Pets:** $100 one-time fee/
room. Service with restrictions.

Vagabond Executive Inn Old Town SH
(916) 446-1481. **$99-$169.** 909 3rd St. I-5, exit J St (Old Sacramento);
8 blks w of state capitol. Ext corridors. **Pets:** Medium. $10 daily fee/pet.
Designated rooms, service with restrictions, supervision.

SALIDA

La Quinta Inn & Suites SH
(209) 579-8723. **$124-$146.** 4909 Sisk Rd. SR 99, exit SR 219, just e.
Int corridors. **Pets:** $100 deposit/pet. Service with restrictions, supervision.

SALINAS

Residence Inn by Marriott-Salinas SH
(831) 775-0410. **$170-$191.** 17215 El Rancho Way. US 101, exit Laurel
Dr, just w. Int corridors. **Pets:** Accepted.

Vagabond Inn M
(831) 758-4693. **Call for rates.** 131 Kern St. US 101, exit Market St,
just e. Ext corridors. **Pets:** Accepted.

SAN ANDREAS

The Robins Nest BB
(209) 754-1076. **$150-$175, 7 day notice.** 247 W St. Charles St. SR
49; north end of town. Int corridors. **Pets:** Accepted.

SAN BERNARDINO

Best Western Hospitality Lane M
(909) 381-1681. **$105-$159.** 294 E Hospitality Ln. I-10, exit 73 (Waterman Ave) westbound; exit 73B (Waterman Ave) eastbound, just nw.
Ext corridors. **Pets:** Small, other species. $10 daily fee/pet. Service with
restrictions, supervision.

Econo Lodge M
(909) 383-1188. **Call for rates.** 606 N "H" St. I-215, exit 44 (SR 66
W/5th St) southbound; exit 44A (SR 66 W/5th St) northbound, just e,
then just n. Ext corridors. **Pets:** Accepted.

Hilton-San Bernardino LH
(909) 889-0133. **Call for rates.** 285 E Hospitality Ln. I-10, exit 73
(Waterman Ave) westbound; exit 73B (Waterman Ave) eastbound, just
n, then just w. Int corridors. **Pets:** Accepted.

La Quinta Inn San Bernardino M
(909) 888-7571. **$122-$142.** 205 E Hospitality Ln. I-10, exit 73 (Waterman Ave) westbound; 73B (Waterman Ave N) eastbound, just n, then
0.3 mi w. Ext corridors. **Pets:** Other species. Service with restrictions,
supervision.

Quality Inn Hospitality Lane Area M ❀
(909) 888-4827. **$94-$169.** 1750 S Waterman Ave. I-10, exit 73 (Waterman Ave), 0.5 mi n. Ext corridors. **Pets:** Medium, dogs only. $25 one-
time fee/pet. Service with restrictions, supervision.

▼▼▼▼ **Residence Inn San Bernardino** SH
(909) 382-4564. **$177-$197.** 1040 E Harriman Pl. I-10, exit 74 (Tippecanoe Ave) eastbound; exit 74 (Anderson St/Tippecanoe Ave) westbound, just n, then just w. Int corridors. **Pets:** Accepted.

ASK S⚡ ✕ 🛏 💻 ➰ ⊠

SAN CLEMENTE

◈◈◈ ▼▼▼▼ **Best Western Casablanca Inn** SH
(949) 361-1644. **$89-$199.** 1601 N El Camino Real. I-5, exit 76
(Avenida Pico), 0.8 mi sw, then just s. Ext corridors. **Pets:** Medium. $25
daily fee/room. Designated rooms, supervision.

SAVE S⚡ ✕ 🛏 💻 ➰

◈◈◈ ▼▼▼▼ **Country Plaza Inn** SH
(949) 498-8800. **$80-$249.** 35 Via Pico Plaza. I-5, exit 76 (Avenida
Pico), just w, then just s. Int corridors. **Pets:** $15 daily fee/room. Desig-
nated rooms, service with restrictions, supervision.

SAVE S⚡ ✕ ⚡M 🛏 💻 ➰

▼▼▼▼ **Holiday Inn-San Clemente Resort** SH
(949) 361-3000. **$139-$189.** 111 S Avenida de la Estrella. I-5, exit 75
(Avenida Palizada) southbound; exit 75 (Avenida Presidio) northbound, just s, then just w. Int corridors. **Pets:** Accepted.

ASK S⚡ ✕ ⚡M 🛏 💻 🍴 ➰

SAN DIEGO METROPOLITAN AREA

CHULA VISTA

▼▼▼▼ **La Quinta Inn San Diego (Chula Vista)** M
(619) 691-1211. **$129-$159.** 150 Bonita Rd. I-805, exit 7C (E St/Bonita
Rd), just w. Ext corridors. **Pets:** Other species. Service with restrictions,
supervision.

ASK S⚡ ✕ 🛏 💻 ➰

CORONADO

▼▼▼▼ **Coronado Island Marriott Resort** LH
(619) 435-3000. **$230-$314.** 2000 2nd St. I-5, exit 14A (Coronado
Bridge), 1.5 mi w to Glorietta Blvd, then just ne. Ext corridors.
Pets: Accepted.

ASK S⚡ ✕ ⚡M 🛏 💻 🍴 ➰ ⊠

▼▼ **Crown City Inn** M
(619) 435-3116. **$100-$299.** 520 Orange Ave. I-5, exit 14A (Coronado
Bridge), 1.5 mi w, then just s. Ext corridors. **Pets:** Accepted.

✕ ⚡M 🛏 💻 🍴 ➰

◈◈◈ ▼▼▼▼ **Loews Coronado Bay Resort** LH 🐾
(619) 424-4000. **$199-$399.** 4000 Coronado Bay Rd. I-5, exit 14A
(Coronado Bridge), 1.7 mi w to Orange Ave, 1 mi sw to Silver Strand
Blvd, then 4.5 mi s to Coronado Cays. Ext/int corridors. **Pets:** Large,
other species. $25 one-time fee/room. Service with restrictions, supervision.

SAVE S⚡ ✕ 🛏 💻 🍴 ➰ ⊠

DEL MAR

▼▼▼▼ **DoubleTree Hotel Del Mar** LH
(858) 481-5900. **Call for rates.** 11915 El Camino Real. I-5, exit 33
(Carmel Valley Rd), 0.3 mi e. Int corridors. **Pets:** Accepted.

✕ 🛏 💻 🍴 ➰

▼▼▼▼ **Hilton San Diego Del Mar** LH
(858) 792-5200. **Call for rates.** 15575 Jimmy Durante Blvd. I-5, exit 36
(Via de la Valle), just w. Int corridors. **Pets:** Accepted.

✕ 🛏 💻 🍴 ➰

EL CAJON

◈◈◈ ▼▼▼ **Best Western Courtesy Inn** M
(619) 440-7378. **Call for rates.** 1355 E Main St. I-8, exit 19 (2nd St),
0.5 mi s, then just e. Ext corridors. **Pets:** Accepted.

SAVE ✕ 🛏 💻 ➰

◈◈◈ ▼▼▼ **Quality Inn & Suites Grossmont** SH 🐾
(619) 588-8808. **$75-$225.** 1250 El Cajon Blvd. I-8, exit 14C (Severin
Dr) westbound, 1 mi w on Murray Rd; exit 15 (El Cajon Blvd) eastbound, 0.5 mi w. Ext corridors. **Pets:** Medium. $10 daily fee/room. Des-
ignated rooms, service with restrictions, supervision.

SAVE S⚡ ✕ 🛏 💻 ➰

LA JOLLA

◈◈◈ ▼▼▼ **La Jolla Cove Suites** SH 🐾
(858) 459-2621. **$199-$615.** 1155 Coast Blvd. I-5, exit 28 (La Jolla
Village Dr), 1 mi w to Torrey Pines Rd, 2.5 mi to Prospect St, 0.5 mi s
to Girard Ave, then just w. Ext corridors. **Pets:** Medium. $25 daily
fee/pet. Designated rooms, service with restrictions, supervision.

SAVE S⚡ ✕ 🛏 💻 ➰ ⊠

▼▼▼ ▼▼▼ **La Valencia Hotel** LH 🐾
(858) 454-0771. **$248-$275.** 1132 Prospect St. I-5, exit 26A (La Jolla
Pkwy) northbound, 1.5 mi w to Torrey Pines Rd, 1 mi w, then 0.6 mi
sw; exit 28 (La Jolla Village Dr) southbound, 1 mi w to Torrey Pines
Rd, 2.7 mi sw, then 0.6 mi sw. Ext/int corridors. **Pets:** Medium. $75
one-time fee/pet. Service with restrictions.

ASK S⚡ ✕ 🛏 💻 🍴 ➰ ⊠

▼▼▼▼ **Residence Inn by Marriott La Jolla** SH
(858) 587-1770. **$241-$296.** 8901 Gilman Dr. I-5, exit 27 (Gilman Dr),
1.5 mi nw. Ext corridors. **Pets:** Accepted.

ASK S⚡ ✕ 🛏 💻 ➰ ⊠

▼▼▼▼ **San Diego Marriott La Jolla** LH
(858) 587-1414. **$296-$307.** 4240 La Jolla Village Dr. I-5, exit 28 (La
Jolla Village Dr), 0.5 mi e. Int corridors. **Pets:** Accepted.

ASK S⚡ ✕ ⚡M 🛏 💻 🍴 ➰ ⊠

POWAY

▼▼▼ **Best Western Country Inn** M
(858) 748-6320. **$109-$169.** 13845 Poway Rd. I-15, exit 18 (Poway
Rd), 4 mi e. Ext corridors. **Pets:** Accepted.

ASK S⚡ ✕ ⚡M 🛏 💻 ➰

◈◈◈ ▼▼▼ **Ramada Hotel** SH 🐾
(858) 748-7311. **Call for rates.** 12448 Poway Rd. I-15, exit 18 (Poway
Rd), 3 mi e. Ext corridors. **Pets:** Other species. $15 daily fee/pet. No
service.

SAVE ✕ 🛏 💻 ➰

RANCHO BERNARDO

▼▼▼▼ **La Quinta Inn San Diego (Rancho
Penasquitos)** SH
(858) 484-8800. **$115-$155.** 10185 Paseo Montril. I-15, exit 18 (Rancho
Penasquitos Blvd), just w. Ext corridors. **Pets:** Other species. Service
with restrictions, supervision.

ASK S⚡ ✕ ⚡M 🛏 💻 ➰

◈◈◈ ▼▼▼▼ **Radisson Suite Hotel** LH
(858) 451-6600. **$189-$219.** 11520 W Bernardo Ct. I-15, exit 24 (Rancho Bernardo Rd), just w, then 0.5 mi s. Ext corridors. **Pets:** Accepted.

SAVE S⚡ ✕ ⚡M 🛏 💻 🍴 ➰

▼▼▼▼ **Staybridge Suites Carmel Mountain** SH
(858) 487-0900. **Call for rates.** 11855 Ave of Industry. I-15, exit 21 (Carmel Mountain Rd), 1 mi ne to second Rancho Carmel Dr, just w to Innovation Dr, just n, then just e. Int corridors. **Pets:** Accepted.

⊠ ⓜ 🛏 🖥 ⊠

RANCHO SANTA FE

▼▼▼▼ **The Inn at Rancho Santa Fe** SH
(858) 756-1131. **$249-$1250, 3 day notice.** 5951 Linea del Cielo. I-5, exit 37 (Lomas Sante Fe Dr), 4 mi e on CR S-8. Ext/int corridors. **Pets:** Accepted.

ASK Sõ ⊠ 🛏 🖥 🍴 ⊷ ⊠

▼▼▼▼ **Morgan Run Resort & Club** SH
(858) 756-2471. **$139-$329.** 5690 Cancha de Golf. I-5, exit 36 (Via De La Valle), 3 mi e. Ext/int corridors. **Pets:** Accepted.

ASK Sõ ⊠ 🛏 🖥 🍴 ⊷ ⊠

SAN DIEGO

ⓐⓐⓐ ▼▼▼ **Best Western Lamplighter Inn & Suites** M
(619) 582-3088. **$90-$185.** 6474 El Cajon Blvd. I-8, exit 11 (70th St), 0.5 mi s, then 1 mi w. Ext corridors. **Pets:** Medium, other species. $10 daily fee/pet. Service with restrictions, crate.

SAVE Sõ ⊠ 🛏 🖥 ⊷

▼▼▼▼ **Best Western Mission Bay Inn** M
(619) 275-5700. **$99-$189.** 2575 Clairemont Dr. I-5, exit 22 (Clairemont Dr/Mission Bay Dr), just e. Ext corridors. **Pets:** Small, dogs only. $20 daily fee/pet. Designated rooms, service with restrictions, supervision.

ASK Sõ ⊠ 🛏 🖥 ⊷

ⓐⓐⓐ ▼▼▼▼ **DoubleTree Club Hotel San Diego Zoo/ SeaWorld Area** LH
(619) 881-6900. **$129-$249.** 1515 Hotel Cir S. I-8, exit 4A (Hotel Cir), south side. Int corridors. **Pets:** Accepted.

SAVE Sõ ⊠ ⓜ 🛏 🖥 🍴 ⊷ ⊠

▼▼▼▼ **DoubleTree Hotel San Diego-Mission Valley** LH
(619) 297-5466. **$159-$359, 3 day notice.** 7450 Hazard Center Dr. SR 163, exit 4 (Friars Rd), 0.3 mi e to Frazee Rd, then just s. Int corridors. **Pets:** Accepted.

ASK Sõ ⊠ 🛏 🖥 🍴 ⊷ ⊠

▼▼ ▼▼ **Extended StayAmerica-San Diego/Hotel Circle** SH
(619) 296-5570. **$114-$169.** 2087 Hotel Cir S. I-8, exit 4A (Hotel Cir), south side. Int corridors. **Pets:** Other species. $75 one-time fee/pet. Service with restrictions.

ASK Sõ ⊠ ⓜ 🛏 🖥

▼▼ ▼▼ **Extended StayAmerica–San Diego/Mission Valley Stadium** SH
(858) 292-8927. **$99-$149.** 3860 Murphy Canyon Dr. I-15, exit 8 (Aero Dr), just w, then 1 mi n. Int corridors. **Pets:** Other species. $75 one-time fee/pet. Service with restrictions.

ASK Sõ ⊠ ⓜ 🛏 🖥

▼▼▼▼ **Hampton Inn-San Diego/Kearny Mesa** SH
(858) 292-1482. **Call for rates.** 5434 Kearny Mesa Rd. SR 163, exit 8 (Clairemont Mesa Blvd), just w. Int corridors. **Pets:** Accepted.

⊠ 🛏 🖥 ⊷

▼▼▼▼ **Hawthorn Suites** M
(619) 299-3501. **$129-$199.** 1335 Hotel Cir S. I-8, exit 4A (Hotel Cir), south side. Ext/int corridors. **Pets:** Accepted.

ASK Sõ ⊠ 🛏 🖥

▼▼▼▼ **The Hillcrest Bed and Breakfast @ Kasa Korbett** BB
(619) 291-3962. **Call for rates.** 4050 Front St. SR 163, exit 2B (Washington St), 0.4 mi w to 1st Ave, just n to Montecito St, just w, then just s. Int corridors. **Pets:** Small, dogs only. $25 deposit/pet. Service with restrictions, supervision.

⊠ 🐾 🕸

ⓐⓐⓐ ▼▼▼▼ **Holiday Inn on the Bay** LH
(619) 232-3861. **$149-$209.** 1355 N Harbor Dr at Ash St. I-5, exit 17 (Hawthorn St) northbound, 0.4 mi w, then 0.4 mi s; exit 17 (Front St) southbound, 0.5 mi s to Ash St, then just w. Int corridors. **Pets:** Accepted.

SAVE ⊠ 🛏 🖥 🍴 ⊷

▼▼▼▼ **Homestead Studio Suites Hotel-San Diego/Mission Valley** M
(619) 299-2292. **$104-$159.** 7444 Mission Valley Rd. SR 163, exit 4 (Friars Rd), 1 mi ne via Mission Center Dr. Ext corridors. **Pets:** Other species. $75 one-time fee/pet. Service with restrictions.

ASK Sõ ⊠ ⓜ 🛏 🖥

▼▼▼▼ **Homestead Studio Suites Hotel-San Diego/Sorrento Mesa** M
(858) 623-0100. **$114-$174.** 9880 Pacific Heights Blvd. I-805, exit 27 (Mira Mesa Blvd), 1 mi e. Int corridors. **Pets:** Other species. $75 one-time fee/pet. Service with restrictions.

ASK Sõ ⊠ ⓜ 🛏 🖥

ⓐⓐⓐ ▼▼▼▼ **Kona Kai Resort** SH
(619) 221-8000. **$189-$289.** 1551 Shelter Island Dr. I-5, exit 20 (Rosecrans St) southbound, 3 mi sw; exit 17 (Hawthorn St) northbound, 3 mi nw on Harbor Dr to Scott Rd, then 0.5 mi w. Ext/int corridors. **Pets:** Small. $75 one-time fee/room. Designated rooms, service with restrictions, supervision.

SAVE Sõ ⊠ 🛏 🖥 🍴 ⊷ ⊠

▼▼ ▼▼ **Mission Valley Resort** SH
(619) 298-8281. **$99-$179.** 875 Hotel Cir S. I-8, exit 4A (Hotel Cir), south side. Ext corridors. **Pets:** Accepted.

ASK Sõ ⊠ 🛏 🖥 🍴 ⊠

ⓐⓐⓐ ▼▼▼▼ **Ocean Villa Inn** M 🐾
(619) 224-3481. **$99-$399.** 5142 W Point Loma Blvd. I-8, exit Sunset Cliff Blvd, 1.5 mi sw. Ext corridors. **Pets:** Dogs only. $25 one-time fee/pet. Designated rooms, service with restrictions.

SAVE Sõ ⊠ 🛏 🖥 ⊷

ⓐⓐⓐ ▼▼ ▼▼ **Old Town Inn** M
(619) 260-8024. **$69-$154.** 4444 Pacific Hwy. I-5, exit 21 (SeaWorld Dr), just w, then 1 mi s. Ext corridors. **Pets:** Medium, other species. $10 daily fee/pet. Service with restrictions, crate.

SAVE ⊠ ⓜ 🛏 🖥 ⊷

▼▼▼▼ **Omni San Diego Hotel** LH 🐾
(619) 231-6664. **Call for rates.** 675 L St. I-5, exit 17 (Front St/Civic Center), 0.3 mi s, 0.3 mi e on a St, 0.6 mi s on Sixth Ave, then just e; connected via skybridge to Petco Park. Int corridors. **Pets:** Medium. $50 one-time fee/room. Designated rooms, service with restrictions, supervision.

⊠ ⓜ 🖥 🍴 ⊷ ⊠

ⓐⓐⓐ ▼▼ **Premier Inn-Sports Arena/Mission Bay** M
(619) 223-9500. **$50-$109.** 3333 Channel Way. I-5/8, exit 20 (Rosecrans St), 0.5 mi s, 1 mi nw on Sports Arena Blvd, then just e. Ext corridors. **Pets:** Medium, other species. Designated rooms, service with restrictions, supervision.

SAVE Sõ ⊠ ⓜ 🛏 🖥 ⊷

ⓐⓐⓐ ▼▼▼▼ **Premier Inns Sports Arena/Mission Bay** M
(619) 291-8252. **$50-$109.** 2484 Hotel Circle Pl. I-8, exit 3 (Taylor St), just n. Ext corridors. **Pets:** Accepted.

SAVE Sõ ⊠ 🛏 🖥 ⊷

▼▼▼▼ **Residence Inn by Marriott-San Diego Central** SH
(858) 278-2100. **$219-$241.** 5400 Kearny Mesa Rd. SR 163, exit 8 (Clairemont Mesa Blvd). Ext corridors. **Pets:** Accepted.

ASK Sõ ⊠ 🛏 🖥 ⊷ ⊠

Residence Inn by Marriott San Diego Downtown SH
(619) 338-8200. **$253-$273.** 1747 Pacific Hwy. I-5, exit 17 (Front St) southbound, just s to Grape St, 0.3 mi w, then just n; exit 17 (Hawthorn St) northbound, 0.4 mi w, then just s. Int corridors. **Pets:** Accepted.

ASK SAVE X ⌂ 🐾 ≈

Residence Inn San Diego/Mission Valley/ SeaWorld Area SH
(619) 881-3600. **$252-$296.** 1865 Hotel Cir S. I-8, exit 4A (Hotel Cir), south side. Int corridors. **Pets:** Accepted.

SAVE SAVE X ⌂M ⌂ 🐾 ≈ X

Residence Inn San Diego Ranch Bernardo/Scripps Poway SH
(858) 635-5724. **$215-$235.** 12011 Scripps Highland Dr. I-805, exit 17 (Mercy Rd/Scripps Poway Pkwy), just e, then just n. Int corridors. **Pets:** Accepted.

ASK SAVE X ⌂M ⌂ 🐾 ≈ X

Residence Inn San Diego-Sorrento Mesa SH
(858) 552-9100. **$231-$307.** 5995 Pacific Mesa Ct. I-805, exit 27 (Mira Mesa Blvd), 1.5 mi e. Int corridors. **Pets:** Accepted.

ASK SAVE X ⌂ 🐾 ≈ X

San Diego Marriott Hotel & Marina LH
(619) 234-1500. **$337-$357.** 333 W Harbor Dr. I-5, exit 17 (Front St), 1.3 mi s, then just w. Int corridors. **Pets:** Accepted.

ASK SAVE X ⌂ 🐾 ⍨ ≈ X

Sheraton San Diego Hotel, Mission Valley LH ❀
(619) 260-0111. **$139-$269.** 1433 Camino del Rio S. I-8, exit 5 (Mission Center Rd), south side. Int corridors. **Pets:** Medium, dogs only. $75 one-time fee/room. Service with restrictions, crate.

SAVE SAVE X ⌂M 🐾 ⍨ ≈

Sheraton Suites San Diego LH ❀
(619) 696-9800. **$189-$339.** 701 a St/7th Ave. I-5, exit 17 (Front St), 0.5 mi s. Int corridors. **Pets:** Medium, other species. Designated rooms, service with restrictions, supervision.

SAVE SAVE X ⌂M 🐾 ⍨ ≈ X

Sommerset Suites Hotel SH
(619) 692-5200. **Call for rates.** 606 Washington St. SR 163, exit 2B (Washington St), just w. Ext/int corridors. **Pets:** Accepted.

X ⌂M ⌂ 🐾 ≈

Staybridge Suites by Holiday Inn-Sorrento Mesa SH
(858) 453-5343. **Call for rates.** 6639 Mira Mesa Blvd. I-805, exit 27 (Mira Mesa Blvd), 2.3 mi e. Int corridors. **Pets:** Accepted.

X ⌂M ⌂ 🐾 ≈

The US Grant LH
(619) 232-3121. **$589-$3500.** 326 Broadway. I-5, exit 17 (Front St) southbound, 0.9 mi s to Broadway, just e; exit 16B (6th Ave) northbound, 0.6 mi s, just w. Int corridors. **Pets:** Large. $150 one-time fee/room. Service with restrictions, supervision.

ASK X ⌂M 🐾 ⍨ X

Vagabond Inn-Point Loma M ❀
(619) 224-3371. **$79-$305.** 1325 Scott St. I-8, exit Nimintz Blvd, 2 mi s to Rosecrans St, just w to Jarvis St, then just s; in Point Loma area. Ext corridors. **Pets:** Medium. $10 daily fee/pet. Designated rooms, service with restrictions, supervision.

SAVE SAVE X ⌂ 🐾 ≈

The Westin Horton Plaza LH
(619) 239-2200. **Call for rates.** 910 Broadway Cir. I-5, exit 17 (Front St) southbound, 0.9 mi s to Broadway, just e, then just s; exit 16B (6th Ave) northbound, 0.6 mi s, just w, then just s. Int corridors. **Pets:** Accepted.

X ⌂M ⌂ 🐾 ⍨ ≈ X

The Westin San Diego LH ❀
(619) 239-4500. **$215-$449.** 400 W Broadway. Between Columbia and State sts. Int corridors. **Pets:** Medium, dogs only. Designated rooms, service with restrictions, supervision.

ASK SAVE X ⌂M 🐾 ⍨ ≈ X

Woodfin Suite Hotel SH ❀
(858) 597-0500. **$399 (no credit cards).** 10044 Pacific Mesa Blvd. I-805, exit 27 (Mira Mesa Blvd), 1.1 mi e, then just n. Int corridors. **Pets:** Other species. $200 deposit/room, $10 daily fee/pet. Designated rooms, service with restrictions, crate.

SAVE SAVE X ⌂M ⌂ 🐾 ⍨ ≈

END METROPOLITAN AREA

SAN FRANCISCO METROPOLITAN AREA

BELMONT

▼▼▼▼ Hyatt Summerfield Suites-Belmont/Redwood Shores SH
(650) 591-8600. **$129-$450.** 400 Concourse Dr. US 101, exit Marine World Pkwy, just e, then just n on Oracle Pkwy. Ext corridors. **Pets:** Accepted.

(ASK) (X) (&M) (□) (➜)

BRISBANE

▼▼▼▼ Homewood Suites By Hilton SH
(650) 589-1600. **Call for rates.** 2000 Shoreline Ct. US 101, exit Sierra Point Pkwy, just e. Int corridors. **Pets:** Accepted.

(X) (&M) (➊) (□) (➜)

BURLINGAME

▼▼▼ Crowne Plaza LH
(650) 342-9200. **$89-$189.** 1177 Airport Blvd. US 101, exit Broadway-Burlingame or Old Bayshore Hwy, just e. Int corridors. **Pets:** Accepted.

(ASK) (Sₐ) (X) (&M) (➊) (□) (¶¶) (➜)

⟨AAA⟩ ▼▼▼▼ DoubleTree Hotel-San Francisco Airport LH
(650) 344-5500. **$99-$269.** 835 Airport Blvd. US 101, exit Broadway-Burlingame or Anza Blvd, just e. Int corridors. **Pets:** Medium. $25 daily fee/pet. Service with restrictions, supervision.

(SAVE) (X) (&M) (➊) (□) (¶¶)

▼▼▼▼ Embassy Suites-San Francisco Airport-Burlingame LH
(650) 342-4600. **Call for rates.** 150 Anza Blvd. US 101, exit Broadway-Burlingame, just e. Int corridors. **Pets:** Accepted.

(X) (&M) (➊) (□) (¶¶) (➜) (X)

▼▼ Red Roof Inn M
(650) 342-7772. **Call for rates.** 777 Airport Blvd. US 101, exit Broadway-Burlingame or E Anza Blvd; just s of airport. Ext corridors. **Pets:** Accepted.

(X) (&M) (➊) (➜)

▼▼▼ ▼▼▼ San Francisco Airport Marriott LH
(650) 692-9100. **$242-$262.** 1800 Old Bayshore Hwy. US 101, exit Millbrae Ave, just e. Int corridors. **Pets:** Medium. $75 one-time fee/room. Service with restrictions, supervision.

(ASK) (Sₐ) (X) (&M) (➊) (□) (¶¶) (➜) (X)

⟨AAA⟩ ▼▼▼▼ Sheraton Gateway Hotel-San Francisco International Airport LH ❀
(650) 340-8500. **Call for rates.** 600 Airport Blvd. US 101, exit Broadway-Burlingame or Anza Blvd, 0.3 mi e. Int corridors. **Pets:** Designated rooms, service with restrictions.

(SAVE) (X) (&M) (➊) (□) (¶¶) (➜)

⟨AAA⟩ ▼▼▼ Vagabond Inn-SFO SH
(650) 692-4040. **$69-$199.** 1640 Bayshore Hwy. US 101, exit Millbrae Ave, just e. Ext corridors. **Pets:** Small. $10 daily fee/pet. Designated rooms, service with restrictions, supervision.

(SAVE) (Sₐ) (X) (&M) (➊) (□)

CORTE MADERA

⟨AAA⟩ ▼▼▼ Marin Suites Hotel SH
(415) 924-3608. **$159-$209.** 45 Tamal Vista Blvd. US 101, exit Tamalpais Rd/Paradise Dr. Ext corridors. **Pets:** Accepted.

(SAVE) (Sₐ) (X) (&M) (□) (➜) (X) (K)

HALF MOON BAY

⟨AAA⟩ ▼▼▼▼ Best Western Half Moon Bay Lodge SH
(650) 726-9000. **$159-$249.** 2400 S Cabrillo Hwy. 2.5 mi s of jct SR 92 and 1, just w. Ext corridors. **Pets:** Accepted.

(SAVE) (Sₐ) (X) (&M) (➊) (□) (➜) (X) (K)

⟨AAA⟩ ▼▼▼▼ Comfort Inn Half Moon Bay SH ❀
(650) 712-1999. **$89-$249.** 2930 N Cabrillo Hwy. On SR 1. Ext corridors. **Pets:** Medium. $10 daily fee/pet. Designated rooms, service with restrictions, supervision.

(SAVE) (Sₐ) (X) (&M) (➊) (□)

⟨AAA⟩ ▼▼ Days Inn M
(650) 726-9700. **$70-$300.** 3020 N Cabrillo Hwy. 2 mi n of jct SR 92 and 1; w of SR 1. Ext corridors. **Pets:** Dogs only. $15 daily fee/pet. Service with restrictions, supervision.

(SAVE) (Sₐ) (X) (&M) (➊) (□)

⟨AAA⟩ ▼▼ Harbor View Inn M
(650) 726-2329. **$86-$170.** 51 Ave Alhambra. 4 mi n of jct SR 92 and 1; e of SR 1. Ext corridors. **Pets:** Accepted.

(SAVE) (Sₐ) (X) (&M) (➊) (K)

⟨AAA⟩ ▼▼▼▼ Holiday Inn Express M
(650) 726-3400. **$105-$169.** 230 S Cabrillo Hwy. On SR 1, just s of SR 92. Ext corridors. **Pets:** $10 daily fee/pet. Designated rooms, service with restrictions, supervision.

(SAVE) (Sₐ) (X) (&M) (➊) (□)

▼▼▼▼ Landis Shores Oceanfront Inn BB
(650) 726-6642. **Call for rates.** 211 Mirada Rd. 3 mi n of jct SR 92 and 1, exit SR 1 W at Medio Ave, just n. Int corridors. **Pets:** Accepted.

(X) (&M) (➊) (K)

▼▼▼▼ The Ritz-Carlton, Half Moon Bay LH ❀
(650) 712-7000. **Call for rates.** 1 Miramontes Point Rd. 3 mi s of jct SR 92 and 1; w of SR 1 at Miramontes Point Rd. Ext/int corridors. **Pets:** Small, other species. $125 one-time fee/room. Designated rooms, service with restrictions.

(X) (□) (¶¶) (➜) (X)

MILLBRAE

▼▼▼▼ Clarion Hotel-San Francisco Airport LH
(650) 692-6363. **Call for rates.** 401 E Millbrae Ave. US 101, exit Millbrae Ave, just e. Int corridors. **Pets:** Accepted.

(X) (&M) (➊) (□) (¶¶) (➜)

▼▼▼▼ The Westin Hotel-San Francisco Airport LH
(650) 692-3500. **$379.** 1 Old Bayshore Hwy. Just e of US 101, exit Millbrae Ave. Int corridors. **Pets:** Accepted.

(ASK) (Sₐ) (X) (&M) (□) (¶¶) (➜) (X)

SAN BRUNO

⟨AAA⟩ ▼▼▼ Regency Inn M
(650) 589-7535. **$89-$99.** 411 E San Bruno Ave. US 101, exit San Bruno Ave, 0.4 mi w. Ext corridors. **Pets:** Medium, other species. $15 daily fee/pet. Service with restrictions, supervision.

(SAVE) (X) (&M) (➊) (□)

⟨AAA⟩ ▼▼▼ Staybridge Suites SH
(650) 588-0770. **$199-$279.** 1350 Huntington Ave. I-380, exit El Camino Real N, e on Sneath Ln. Ext corridors. **Pets:** Other species.

(SAVE) (Sₐ) (X) (&M) (➊) (□) (➜) (X)

SAN CARLOS

◆◆ **Homestead Studio Suites Hotel-San Francisco San Carlos** SH
(650) 368-2600. **$99-$110.** 3 Circle Star Way. US 101, exit Whipple Ave, w to Industrial, then just n. Int corridors. **Pets:** Other species. $75 one-time fee/pet. Service with restrictions.
A$K S✿ ⊠ ⓖ☰ 🔒 ▣

SAN FRANCISCO

◆◇ ◆◆ ◆◆ **Argonaut Hotel** LH ❧
(415) 563-0800. **$209-$429.** 495 Jefferson St. Fisherman's Wharf; adjacent to The Cannery. Int corridors. **Pets:** Small, other species. Service with restrictions, supervision.
SAVE S✿ ⊠ ⓖ☰ ▣ ⑪

◆◇ ◆◆◆ **Beresford Arms** SH ❧
(415) 673-2600. **$108-$158.** 701 Post St. 3 blks w of Union Square. Int corridors. **Pets:** Other species. $25 one-time fee/room. Designated rooms, service with restrictions, supervision.
SAVE S✿ ⊠ ⓖ☰ 🔒 ▣ ⒦

◆◇ ◆◆◆ **Best Western Tuscan Inn at Fisherman's Wharf** SH ❧
(415) 561-1100. **Call for rates.** 425 Northpoint St. Just s of Fisherman's Wharf at Mason St. Int corridors. **Pets:** Other species. Designated rooms, service with restrictions.
SAVE ⊠ ▣ ⑪

◆◆◆ ◆◆◆ **Campton Place Hotel** SH ❧
(415) 781-5555. **Call for rates.** 340 Stockton St. Just n of Union Square. Int corridors. **Pets:** Other species. $100 one-time fee/room. Service with restrictions, supervision.
⊠ ⓖ☰ ⑪

◆◇ ◆◆ ◆◆ **The Cartwright, a Larkspur Hotel** SH
(415) 421-2865. **$145-$229.** 524 Sutter St. Union Square at Powell St. Int corridors. **Pets:** Accepted.
SAVE S✿ ⊠ ⓖ☰ ▣

◆◇ ◆◆◆ **Crowne Plaza Union Square** LH
(415) 398-8900. **$239-$299.** 480 Sutter St. Just n off Union Square; corner of Powell St. Int corridors. **Pets:** Accepted.
SAVE S✿ ⊠ ⓖ☰ 🔒 ▣ ⑪

◆◆ ◆◆◆ **The Fairmont San Francisco** LH
(415) 772-5000. **$189-$750.** 950 Mason St. Atop Nob Hill at California St. Int corridors. **Pets:** Medium. $35 one-time fee/pet. Designated rooms, service with restrictions, supervision.
A$K S✿ ⊠ ⓖ☰ ⑪

◆◆◆ ◆◆◆ **Four Seasons San Francisco** LH ❧
(415) 633-3000. **$480-$7000.** 757 Market St. Between 3rd and 4th sts. Int corridors. **Pets:** Other species. Service with restrictions, crate.
⊠ ⓖ☰ 🔒 ▣ ⑪ 🐾 ⊠

◆◇ ◆◆◆ **Galleria Park Hotel** SH ❧
(415) 781-3060. **$299-$549.** 191 Sutter St. 2 blks ne of Union Square. Int corridors. **Pets:** Medium.
SAVE S✿ ⊠ ⓖ☰ ▣ ⑪

◆◇ ◆◆◆ **Harbor Court Hotel** SH
(415) 882-1300. **Call for rates.** 165 Steuart St. On Embarcadero; between Howard and Mission sts. Int corridors. **Pets:** Accepted.
SAVE ⊠ ⓖ☰ ⑪

◆◆◆ ◆◆◆ **Hilton San Francisco Financial District** LH
(415) 433-6600. **Call for rates.** 750 Kearny St. Between Clay and Washington sts. Int corridors. **Pets:** Accepted.
⊠ ⓖ☰ 🔒 ▣ ⑪

◆◆ ◆◆◆ **Holiday Inn Civic Center** LH
(415) 626-6103. **$89-$249.** 50 8th St. 2 blks from Civic Auditorium; just s of Market St and BART Station. Int corridors. **Pets:** Accepted.
SAVE ⊠ ⓖ☰ 🔒 ⑪ 🐾

◆◆ ◆◆◆ **Holiday Inn Fisherman's Wharf** LH
(415) 771-9000. **$124-$299.** 1300 Columbus Ave. Jct North Point St. Int corridors. **Pets:** Accepted.
SAVE ⊠ ⓖ☰ 🔒 ▣ ⑪ 🐾

◆◇ ◆◆◆ **Hotel Beresford** SH ❧
(415) 673-9900. **$98-$138.** 635 Sutter St. 1 blk nw of Union Square at Mason St. Int corridors. **Pets:** Other species. $25 one-time fee/room. Designated rooms, service with restrictions, supervision.
SAVE S✿ ⊠ ⓖ☰ ⑪ ⒦

◆◇ ◆◆◆ **Hotel Carlton** LH
(415) 673-0242. **$189.** 1075 Sutter St. 0.5 mi w of Union Square; between Hyde and Larkin sts. Int corridors. **Pets:** Accepted.
SAVE S✿ ⊠ ⓖ☰ ▣ ⑪ ⒦

◆◇ ◆◆◆ **Hotel Diva** SH
(415) 885-0200. **$119-$329.** 440 Geary St. Just w of Union Square. Int corridors. **Pets:** Medium, dogs only. $250 deposit/room, $75 one-time fee/room. Service with restrictions, supervision.
SAVE S✿ ⊠ ⑪

◆◇ ◆◆◆ **Hotel Metropolis** SH
(415) 775-4600. **Call for rates.** 25 Mason St. Jct Market St. Int corridors. **Pets:** Medium, dogs only. $250 deposit/room, $75 one-time fee/room. Service with restrictions, supervision.
SAVE ⊠ ⓖ☰ 🔒 ⒦

◆◇ ◆◆◆ ◆◆◆ **Hotel Monaco** LH ❧
(415) 292-0100. **$179-$429.** 501 Geary St. Just w of Union Square at Taylor St. Int corridors. **Pets:** Other species. Service with restrictions.
SAVE S✿ ⊠ ⓖ☰ ▣ ⑪ ⊠

◆◆ ◆◆◆ ◆◆◆ **Hotel Nikko San Francisco** LH
(415) 394-1111. **Call for rates.** 222 Mason St. Just w of Union Square. Int corridors. **Pets:** Accepted.
SAVE ⊠ ⓖ☰ ▣ ⑪ 🐾 ⊠

◆◇ ◆◆◆ **Hotel Palomar** SH
(415) 348-1111. **$179-$429.** 12 Fourth St. At Market St. Int corridors. **Pets:** Accepted.
SAVE S✿ ⊠ ⓖ☰ 🔒 ⑪

◆◇ ◆◆◆ **Hotel Triton** SH
(415) 394-0500. **$139-$349.** 342 Grant Ave. Near Union Square at Bush St. Int corridors. **Pets:** Accepted.
SAVE S✿ ⊠ ⓖ☰ ▣

◆◇ ◆◆◆ **Hotel Union Square** SH
(415) 397-3000. **Call for rates.** 114 Powell St. US 101 (Van Ness Ave), exit Market St E to Powell St; just n of cable car turnaround. Int corridors. **Pets:** Accepted.
SAVE ⊠ ⒦

◆◆◆ ◆◆◆ **Hotel Vitale** SH
(415) 278-3700. **$369-$799.** 8 Mission St. At Embarcadero. Int corridors. **Pets:** Accepted.
A$K ⊠ ⓖ☰ ⑪ ⊠

◆◇ ◆◆◆ ◆◆◆ **JW Marriott Hotel San Francisco** LH ❧
(415) 771-8600. **$319-$339.** 500 Post St. Just w of Union Square at Mason St. Int corridors. **Pets:** Small. $75 one-time fee/room.
SAVE S✿ ⊠ ⓖ☰ ▣ ⑪

Kensington Park Hotel SH
(415) 788-6400. **Call for rates.** 450 Post St. Just w of Union Square. Int corridors. **Pets:** Accepted.
SAVE ✕ 🛏 ▥ 🍽 🐾

The Laurel Inn SH ❖
(415) 567-8467. **Call for rates.** 444 Presidio Ave. 1 mi w of US 101 (Van Ness Ave); 1 mi e of Park Presidio Blvd (SR 1) at California St. Int corridors. **Pets:** Service with restrictions, supervision.
SAVE ✕ ♿ 🛏 ▥ 🐾

Le Meridien San Francisco LH
(415) 296-2900. **$189-$549, 10 day notice.** 333 Battery St. At Clay St; in financial district. Int corridors. **Pets:** Accepted.
SAVE S✕ ✕ ♿ 🛏 🍽

Mandarin Oriental, San Francisco LH ❖
(415) 276-9888. **Call for rates.** 222 Sansome St. US 101, 1.2 mi e on Bush St, then just n. Int corridors. **Pets:** Small, dogs only. $25 daily fee/pet. Service with restrictions, supervision.
✕ ▥ 🍽 🐾

Motel 6 SH
(415) 441-8220. **Call for rates.** 895 Geary St. Just e of US 101 (Van Ness Ave), exit Larkin St. Int corridors. **Pets:** Service with restrictions, supervision.
SAVE ✕ ♿ 🛏

Omni San Francisco Hotel LH ❖
(415) 677-9494. **$499-$799.** 500 California St. At Montgomery St; downtown; in financial district. Int corridors. **Pets:** Medium. $50 one-time fee/room. Service with restrictions.
ASK ✕ ♿ ▥ 🍽

The Opal San Francisco SH
(415) 673-4711. **Call for rates.** 1050 Van Ness Ave. On US 101 (Van Ness Ave). Int corridors. **Pets:** Accepted.
SAVE ✕ ♿ ▥

Palace Hotel LH ❖
(415) 512-1111. **Call for rates.** 2 New Montgomery St. Just e of Union Square at Market St. Int corridors. **Pets:** Medium. $100 one-time fee/room.
✕ ♿ 🍽 🐾

The Powell Hotel SH
(415) 398-3200. **$119-$134.** 28 Cyril Magnin St. At Powell St cable car turnaround. Int corridors. **Pets:** Accepted.
ASK S✕ ✕ ♿ ▥ 🍽 🐾

The Prescott Hotel SH ❖
(415) 563-0303. **$189-$369.** 545 Post St. Just w of Union Square. Int corridors. **Pets:** Other species. $250 deposit/room. Service with restrictions, supervision.
SAVE S✕ ✕ 🍽

The Ritz-Carlton, San Francisco LH ❖
(415) 296-7465. **Call for rates.** 600 Stockton St. Just n of Union Square at California St. Int corridors. **Pets:** Very small, dogs only. $125 one-time fee/pet. Service with restrictions, supervision.
SAVE ✕ ♿ ▥ 🍽 🐾

St. Regis Hotel San Francisco LH
(415) 284-4000. **Call for rates.** 125 3rd St. At Mission St. Int corridors. **Pets:** Accepted.
✕ ♿ 🍽 🐾

San Francisco Marriott Fisherman's Wharf LH ❖
(415) 775-7555. **$208-$263.** 1250 Columbus Ave. Just s of Fisherman's Wharf at Bay St. Int corridors. **Pets:** $100 one-time fee/room. Service with restrictions, supervision.
SAVE S✕ ✕ ♿ 🛏 ▥ 🍽

Serrano Hotel SH
(415) 885-2500. **$139-$329.** 405 Taylor St. Just w of Union Square at O'Farrell St. Int corridors. **Pets:** Accepted.
SAVE S✕ ✕ ♿ 🍽 🐾

Sheraton Fisherman's Wharf LH
(415) 362-5500. **$399.** 2500 Mason St. Just se of Fisherman's Wharf at Beach St. Int corridors. **Pets:** Accepted.
ASK S✕ ✕ ♿ 🛏 ▥ 🍽 🏊

Sir Francis Drake Hotel LH
(415) 392-7755. **$189-$439.** 450 Powell St. Just n of Union Square at Sutter St. Int corridors. **Pets:** Accepted.
SAVE S✕ ✕ ♿ 🍽

The Stanford Court, a Renaissance Hotel LH
(415) 989-3500. **$251-$295.** 905 California St. Atop Nob Hill; corner of California and Powell sts. Int corridors. **Pets:** Accepted.
SAVE S✕ ✕ ♿ 🛏 🍽

Travelodge By The Bay M ❖
(415) 673-0691. **$59-$250.** 1450 Lombard St. On US 101 (Lombard St). Ext/int corridors. **Pets:** Dogs only. $22 daily fee/pet. Designated rooms, service with restrictions.
SAVE ✕ ♿ 🛏 ▥

The Vertigo SH
(415) 885-6800. **$119-$299.** 940 Sutter St. Just w of Union Square. Int corridors. **Pets:** Small, dogs only. $75 one-time fee/room. Service with restrictions, supervision.
SAVE S✕ ✕ ♿ ▥ 🐾

Villa Florence, a Larkspur Collection Hotel SH
(415) 397-7700. **$159-$289.** 225 Powell St. Just s of Union Square; between O'Farrell and Geary sts. Int corridors. **Pets:** Accepted.
SAVE S✕ ✕ ♿ ▥ 🍽

The Westin St. Francis LH ❖
(415) 397-7000. **$149-$599.** 335 Powell St. On Union Square. **Pets:** Small, dogs only. Service with restrictions, supervision.
SAVE S✕ ✕ ♿ ▥ 🍽 🐾

Westin San Francisco Market Street LH ❖
(415) 974-6400. **$299-$1800.** 50 3rd St. 1 1/2 blks n of Moscone Convention Center. Int corridors. **Pets:** Medium, dogs only. Service with restrictions, supervision.
SAVE S✕ ✕ ♿ ▥ 🍽

W San Francisco LH ❖
(415) 777-5300. **$219-$649.** 181 3rd St. At Howard St. Int corridors. **Pets:** Medium, other species. $100 one-time fee/room.
ASK ✕ 🛏 ▥ 🍽 🏊 🐾

SAN MATEO

Homestead Studio Suites Hotel-San Francisco-SFO SH
(650) 574-1744. **$108-$120.** 1830 Gateway Dr. SR 92, exit Edgewater Blvd; se of jct US 101 and SR 92. Ext corridors. **Pets:** Other species. $75 one-time fee/pet. Service with restrictions.
ASK ✕ ♿ 🛏 ▥

▼▼▼ **Residence Inn by Marriott** 🆂🅷
(650) 574-4700. **$242-$262.** 2000 Winward Way. 0.8 mi se from jct US 101 and SR 92; exit SR 92 via Edgewater Blvd. Ext corridors. **Pets:** Accepted.
A$K 🆂 ✕ ⓜ 🖥 🖵 ➳ ✕

SAN RAFAEL

▼ ▼ **Villa Inn** Ⓜ
(415) 456-4975. **$75-$160.** 1600 Lincoln Ave. Off US 101 at Lincoln Ave off-ramp; exit Central San Rafael northbound, 0.3 mi w on 4th St, then 0.5 mi n. Ext corridors. **Pets:** Accepted.
✕ ⓜ 🖥 🖵

SOUTH SAN FRANCISCO

▼▼▼ **Embassy Suites San Francisco Airport-South San Francisco** 🅻🅷
(650) 589-3400. **Call for rates.** 250 Gateway Blvd. US 101, exit Grand Ave, just e. Int corridors. **Pets:** Accepted.
✕ ⓜ 🖥 🖵 🍴 ➳ ✕

▼▼▼ **La Quinta Inn San Francisco (Airport)** 🆂🅷
(650) 583-2223. **$112-$142.** 20 S Airport Blvd. US 101, exit S Airport Blvd, just w. Int corridors. **Pets:** Other species. Service with restrictions, supervision.
A$K 🆂 ✕ ⓜ 🖥 🖵 ➳

END METROPOLITAN AREA

SAN JOSE

🆇🆇 ▼▼▼ **Crowne Plaza San Jose–Downtown** 🅻🅷
(408) 998-0400. **$149-$299.** 282 Almaden Blvd. I-280, exit Almaden-Vine, 6 blks n. Int corridors. **Pets:** Accepted.
SAVE ✕ ⓜ 🖥 🖵 🍴

🆇🆇 ▼▼▼▼ **DoubleTree Hotel San Jose** 🅻🅷
(408) 453-4000. **Call for rates.** 2050 Gateway Pl. 0.3 mi e of San Jose International Airport via Airport Blvd; w of US 101, exit N 1st St; US 101 northbound, exit Brokaw Rd. Int corridors. **Pets:** $50 deposit/room. Service with restrictions, supervision.
SAVE ✕ 🖥 🖵 🍴 ➳

▼▼▼ **Extended Stay Deluxe San Jose** 🆂🅷
(408) 229-9188. **Call for rates.** 6189 San Ignacio Ave. US 101, exit Bernal Rd E, just n. Int corridors. **Pets:** Other species. $75 one-time fee/pet. Service with restrictions.
✕ 🖥 🖵 ➳

▼▼▼ **Extended Stay Deluxe-San Jose-Downtown** 🆂🅷
(408) 453-3000. **$135-$150.** 55 E Brokaw Rd. US 101, exit 1st St/Brokaw Rd, just e. Int corridors. **Pets:** Other species. $75 one-time fee/pet. Service with restrictions.
A$K 🆂 ✕ 🖵 ➳

▼▼▼ **Fairfield Inn and Suites** 🆂🅷
(408) 453-3133. **$121-$141.** 1755 N 1st St. US 101, exit N 1st St, just w. Int corridors. **Pets:** Accepted.
A$K 🆂 ✕ 🖥 🖵 ➳

▼▼▼▼ **The Fairmont San Jose** 🅻🅷
(408) 998-1900. **$129-$350.** 170 S Market St. At Fairmont Plaza. Int corridors. **Pets:** Medium. $35 one-time fee/pet. Designated rooms, service with restrictions, supervision.
A$K 🆂 ✕ 🖵 🍴 ➳ ✕

🆇🆇 ▼▼▼ **Hilton San Jose** 🅻🅷
(408) 287-2100. **Call for rates.** 300 Almaden Blvd.. Int corridors. **Pets:** Medium. Service with restrictions, supervision.
SAVE ✕ ⓜ 🖥 🖵 🍴 ➳

🆇🆇 ▼▼▼ **Holiday Inn** 🅻🅷
(408) 793-3300. **Call for rates.** 1740 N 1st St. W of US 101, exit N 1st St; 0.5 mi e of San Jose International Airport via Airport Pkwy. Int corridors. **Pets:** Accepted.
SAVE ✕ 🖥 🖵 🍴 ➳ ✕

▼▼ **Homestead Studio Suites Hotel-San Jose-Downtown** 🆂🅷
(408) 573-0648. **$117-$130.** 1560 N 1st St. 1 mi e of San Jose International Airport; US 101, exit N 1st St, then s. Int corridors. **Pets:** Other species. $75 one-time fee/pet. Service with restrictions.
A$K 🆂 ✕ 🖵

▼▼▼ **Homewood Suites by Hilton** 🆂🅷
(408) 428-9900. **Call for rates.** 10 W Trimble Rd. 2 mi ne of San Jose International Airport; US 101, exit Trimble Rd, 1.3 mi e. Ext/int corridors. **Pets:** Accepted.
✕ ⓜ 🖥 🖵 ➳ ✕

🆇🆇 ▼▼▼▼ **Hotel De Anza** 🅻🅷
(408) 286-1000. **Call for rates.** 233 W Santa Clara St. SR 87, exit Santa Clara St, just e. Int corridors. **Pets:** Small. $50 one-time fee/room. Service with restrictions.
SAVE ✕ 🖥 🍴

🆇🆇 ▼▼ **Howard Johnson Inn** Ⓜ
(408) 280-5300. **Call for rates.** 1215 S 1st St. Jct I-280 and SR 82, 0.8 mi s. Ext corridors. **Pets:** Small. Service with restrictions, supervision.
SAVE ✕ 🖥 🖵

🆇🆇 ▼▼▼▼ **La Quinta Inn San Jose Airport** 🆂🅷
(408) 435-8800. **$109-$119, 7 day notice.** 2585 Seaboard Ave. US 101, exit Trimble Rd E; 1 mi ne of San Jose International Airport. Int corridors. **Pets:** Other species. Service with restrictions, supervision.
SAVE 🆂 ✕ 🖥 🖵 ➳

▼▼▼ **Residence Inn by Marriott** 🆂🅷
(408) 226-7676. **$209-$229.** 6111 San Ignacio Ave. US 101, exit Bernal Rd, then e. Int corridors. **Pets:** Accepted.
A$K 🆂 ✕ ⓜ 🖥 🖵 ➳ ✕

▼▼▼ **Staybridge Suites San Jose** 🆂🅷
(408) 436-1600. **Call for rates.** 1602 Crane Ct. US 101, exit 1st St/Brokaw Rd, 0.4 mi e to Bering S, then 0.5 mi. Ext corridors. **Pets:** Accepted.
✕ 🖥 🖵 ➳

▼▼ **TownePlace Suites by Marriott San Jose/Cupertino** 🆂🅷
(408) 984-5903. **$198-$218.** 440 Saratoga Ave. I-280, exit Saratoga Ave, just n. Int corridors. **Pets:** Accepted.
A$K 🆂 ✕ 🖥 🖵 ➳

SAN JUAN BAUTISTA

🆇🆇 ▼▼ **San Juan Inn** Ⓜ
(831) 623-4380. **$69-$99.** 410 The Alameda. Jct SR 156. Ext corridors. **Pets:** Medium. $15 daily fee/pet. Designated rooms.
SAVE 🆂 ✕ 🖥 🖵 ➳

SAN JUAN CAPISTRANO

🆇🆇 ▼▼▼ **Best Western Capistrano Inn** Ⓜ
(949) 493-5661. **$90-$160.** 27174 Ortega Hwy. I-5, exit 82 (SR 74/Ortega Hwy), just e. Ext corridors. **Pets:** Accepted.
SAVE 🆂 ✕ 🖥 🖵 ➳

SAN LUIS OBISPO

⚋⚋⚋ ▼▼▼ Best Western Royal Oak Hotel 🅜 ❀
(805) 544-4410. **Call for rates.** 214 Madonna Rd. US 101, exit 201 (Madonna Rd), just s. Ext/int corridors. **Pets:** Large. $15 one-time fee/pet. Service with restrictions, supervision.

(SAVE) ⊠ &M 🖥 🖵 ⇌

⚋⚋⚋ ▼▼▼ Days Inn 🅜
(805) 549-9911. **$69-$219.** 2050 Garfield St. US 101, exit 204 (Monterey St), just sw. Ext corridors. **Pets:** Small, dogs only. $75 deposit/pet, $10 daily fee/pet. Designated rooms, service with restrictions, supervision.

(SAVE) (S₆) ⊠ &M 🖥 🖵 ⇌

▼▼ Heritage Inn Bed & Breakfast 🄱🄱
(805) 544-7440. **Call for rates.** 978 Olive St. US 101, exit 203B (SR 1/Morro Bay) northbound, just w on Santa Rosa St, then just s; exit 203A (Santa Rosa St) southbound, just ne. Int corridors. **Pets:** Accepted.

⊠ ⿻ ⿻ ⿻

▼▼▼ Holiday Inn Express 🆂🄷
(805) 544-8600. **Call for rates.** 1800 Monterey St. US 101, exit 204 (Monterey St), just w. Int corridors. **Pets:** Accepted.

⊠ &M 🖥 🖵 ⇌

⚋⚋⚋ ▼▼▼ Ramada Inn Olive Tree 🅜
(805) 544-2800. **$79-$399.** 1000 Olive St. US 101, exit 203B (Morro Bay) northbound, just w on Santa Rosa St, then just s; exit 203A (Santa Rosa St) southbound, just ne. Ext corridors. **Pets:** Accepted.

(SAVE) (S₆) ⊠ &M 🖥 🖵 ⇌

⚋⚋⚋ ▼▼▼ Sands Suites & Motel 🅜
(805) 544-0500. **$79-$229.** 1930 Monterey St. US 101, exit 204 (Monterey St), just sw. Ext corridors. **Pets:** Other species. $25 one-time fee/pet. Designated rooms, service with restrictions, supervision.

(SAVE) (S₆) ⊠ &M 🖥 🖵 ⊠

⚋⚋⚋ ▼▼▼ Super 8 Motel 🅜
(805) 544-6888. **$49-$199.** 1951 Monterey St. US 101, exit 204 (Monterey St), just e. Ext corridors. **Pets:** Medium, other species. $10 daily fee/pet. Service with restrictions, supervision.

(SAVE) (S₆) ⊠ &M 🖥 🖵 ⇌

SAN MARCOS

⚋⚋⚋ ▼▼▼▼ Lake San Marcos Resort 🆂🄷
(760) 744-0120. **$249-$469.** 1025 La Bonita Dr. SR 78, exit Rancho Santa Fe Rd, 2 mi s, then 0.5 mi e via Lake San Marcos Dr and San Marino Dr; at Lake San Marcos. Ext/int corridors. **Pets:** Accepted.

(SAVE) (S₆) ⊠ 🖥 🖵 🍽 ⇌ ⊠

SAN RAMON

▼▼ Extended StayAmerica-San Ramon-Bishop Ranch 🆂🄷
(925) 242-0991. **$95-$105.** 2100 Camino Ramon. I-680, exit Crow Canyon E, then just n. Int corridors. **Pets:** Other species. $75 one-time fee/pet. Service with restrictions.

(ASK) (S₆) ⊠ 🖵 ⇌

▼▼ Homestead Studio Suites Hotel-San Ramon-Bishop Ranch 🆂🄷
(925) 277-0833. **$90-$100.** 18000 San Ramon Valley Blvd. I-680, exit Bollinger Canyon Rd E, just n. Ext corridors. **Pets:** Other species. $75 one-time fee/pet. Service with restrictions.

(ASK) (S₆) ⊠ 🖥 ⇌

▼▼▼ Residence Inn by Marriott 🆂🄷
(925) 277-9292. **$253-$273.** 1071 Market Pl. I-680, exit Bollinger Canyon Rd E, 0.5 mi e. Ext corridors. **Pets:** Accepted.

(ASK) (S₆) ⊠ 🖵 ⇌ ⊠

▼▼▼ San Ramon Marriott at Bishop Ranch 🄻🄷
(925) 867-9200. **$275-$295.** 2600 Bishop Dr. I-680, exit Bollinger Canyon Rd E, n on Sunset, then just w. Int corridors. **Pets:** Accepted.

(ASK) (S₆) ⊠ 🖥 🖵 🍽 ⇌ ⊠

SAN SIMEON

⚋⚋⚋ ▼▼▼ Courtesy Inn 🅜
(805) 927-4691. **$89-$119.** 9450 Castillo Dr. East side of SR 1. Ext corridors. **Pets:** Medium, dogs only. $10 one-time fee/pet. Designated rooms, no service, supervision.

(SAVE) (S₆) ⊠ 🖥 🖵 ⇌

▼▼ Motel 6 Premiere–1212 🆂🄷
(805) 927-8691. **$45-$55.** 9070 Castillo Dr. Just e of SR 1. Int corridors. **Pets:** Other species. Service with restrictions, supervision.

(S₆) ⊠ &M 🖥 🍽 ⇌

⚋⚋⚋ ▼▼▼ San Simeon Lodge 🆂🄷
(805) 927-4601. **Call for rates.** 9520 Castillo Dr. On SR 1. Ext corridors. **Pets:** Small, dogs only. $10 daily fee/pet. Service with restrictions, supervision.

(SAVE) ⊠ 🖥 🖵 🍽 ⇌ ⿻

⚋⚋⚋ ▼▼▼ Silver Surf Motel 🅜
(805) 927-4661. **$59-$189.** 9390 Castillo Dr. Just e of SR 1. Ext corridors. **Pets:** Medium. $10 daily fee/pet. Designated rooms, service with restrictions, supervision.

(SAVE) (S₆) ⊠ 🖥 🖵 ⇌ ⿻

SANTA ANA

▼▼▼ La Quinta Inn & Suites Santa Ana 🅜
(714) 540-1111. **$129-$169.** 2721 Hotel Terrace Rd. SR 55, exit 8 (Dyer Rd) northbound; exit 8B (Dyer Rd W) southbound, just w, then just s. Ext corridors. **Pets:** Other species. Service with restrictions, supervision.

(ASK) (S₆) ⊠ 🖥 🖵 ⇌

▼▼ Motel 6 #738 🅜
(714) 558-0500. **$47-$55.** 1623 E 1st St. I-5, exit 103C (1st St/4th St) northbound; exit 104A (1st St/4th St) southbound, just w. Ext corridors. **Pets:** Other species. Service with restrictions, supervision.

(S₆) ⊠

▼▼ Red Roof Inn 🅜
(714) 542-0311. **Call for rates.** 2600 N Main St. I-5, exit 105B (Main St), 0.3 mi n. Ext/int corridors. **Pets:** Accepted.

⊠ 🖥 ⇌

SANTA BARBARA

⚋⚋⚋ ▼▼ Best Western Beachside Inn 🅜
(805) 965-6556. **Call for rates.** 336 W Cabrillo Blvd. US 101, exit 97 (Bath St) northbound, just w on Haley St to Castillo St, then 0.4 mi s; exit 97 (Castillo St) southbound, 0.3 mi s. Ext corridors. **Pets:** Accepted.

(SAVE) ⊠ 🖵 ⇌

⚋⚋⚋ ▼▼ Blue Sands Motel 🅜
(805) 965-1624. **$85-$275, 3 day notice.** 421 S Milpas St. US 101, exit 96A (Milpas St), 0.3 mi s. Ext corridors. **Pets:** Dogs only. $10 daily fee/pet. Service with restrictions.

(SAVE) ⊠ 🖥 🖵 ⇌ ⿻

▼▼ Extended StayAmerica 🆂🄷
(805) 692-1882. **$144-$174.** 4870 Calle Real. US 101, exit Turnpike Rd, just e, then just n. Int corridors. **Pets:** Other species. $75 one-time fee/pet. Service with restrictions.

(ASK) (S₆) ⊠ &M 🖥 🖵

⚋⚋⚋ ▼▼ ▼▼ Fess Parker's DoubleTree Resort 🄻🄷
(805) 564-4333. **Call for rates.** 633 E Cabrillo Blvd. US 101, exit 96A (Milpas St), just s, then just w. Ext/int corridors. **Pets:** Accepted.

(SAVE) ⊠ &M 🖥 🖵 🍽 ⇌ ⊠

▼▼✕▼▼ Four Seasons Biltmore Santa Barbara LH
(805) 969-2261. **$650 (no credit cards), 3 day notice.** 1260 Channel Dr. US 101, exit 94A (Olive Mill Rd), 0.3 mi s. Ext/int corridors. **Pets:** Accepted.
✕ 🔊 🛡 📷 🍴 ➰ ✕

▲▲▲⁷ ▼▼▼▼ Harbor House Inn M
(805) 962-9745. **$129-$349.** 104 Bath St. US 101, exit 94B (Cabrillo Blvd) (left hand exit), 3 mi n, then just e; exit 97 (Castillo St) southbound, 0.4 mi w, just s on Cabrillo Blvd, then just e. Ext corridors. **Pets:** Dogs only. $15 daily fee/pet. Designated rooms, service with restrictions, supervision.
SAVE 🔊 ✕ 🛡 📷 🍴

▲▲▲⁷ ▼▼▼▼ Hotel MarMonte LH 🐾
(805) 963-0744. **Call for rates.** 1111 E Cabrillo Blvd. US 101, exit 96A (Milpas St), 0.3 mi s, then just e. Int corridors. **Pets:** Dogs only. $50 one-time fee/room. Designated rooms, service with restrictions, crate.
SAVE ✕ 🔊 🛡 📷 🍴 ➰ ✕

▼▼▼ Marina Beach Motel M
(805) 963-9311. **$99-$324.** 21 Bath St. US 101, exit 96B (Garden St), 0.3 mi w to Cabrillo Blvd, 0.4 mi n to Bath St, then just e. Ext corridors. **Pets:** Accepted.
ASK 🔊 ✕ 🛡 📷

▼▼▼ Pacifica Suites SH
(805) 683-6722. **Call for rates.** 5490 Hollister Ave. US 101, exit 104A (Patterson Ave), 0.5 mi w, then 0.5 mi n. Ext/int corridors. **Pets:** Accepted.
✕ 🔊 🛡 📷 ➰

▼▼▼▼ The Parkside Inn M
(805) 963-0744. **Call for rates.** 424 Por La Mar. US 101, exit 96A (Milpas St), 0.3 mi s, just e on Cabrillo Blvd, then just n. Int corridors. **Pets:** Accepted.
✕ 🛡 📷 ➰ ✕

SANTA CATALINA ISLAND

▲▲▲⁷ ▼▼▼▼ Catalina Canyon Resort & Spa M
(310) 510-0325. **Call for rates.** 888 Country Club Dr. 0.5 mi from harbor via Sumner Ave. Ext corridors. **Pets:** Accepted.
SAVE ✕ 🛡 📷 🍴 ➰ ✕

SANTA CLARA

▲▲▲⁷ ▼▼▼ Quality Inn & Suites M
(408) 241-3010. **$85-$139.** 2930 El Camino Real. SR 82, 0.5 mi w of San Tomas Expwy; US 101, exit S Bowers Ave. Ext corridors. **Pets:** Small. $20 daily fee/pet. Designated rooms, service with restrictions, supervision.
SAVE 🔊 ✕ 🔊 🛡 📷 ➰

▼▼▼ Ramada Limited SH
(408) 244-8313. **$79-$109.** 1655 El Camino Real. I-880, exit The Alameda, 2 mi w. Ext corridors. **Pets:** Accepted.
ASK 🔊 ✕ 🛡 ➰

▼▼▼▼ Santa Clara Marriott Hotel LH
(408) 988-1500. **$308-$328.** 2700 Mission College Blvd. 0.5 mi e off US 101, exit Great America Pkwy; 0.8 mi s of Great America Theme Park. Int corridors. **Pets:** Accepted.
ASK 🔊 ✕ 🔊 🛡 📷 🍴 ➰ ✕

▲▲▲⁷ ▼▼▼ The Vagabond Inn M
(408) 241-0771. **$69-$199.** 3580 El Camino Real. On SR 82, southeast corner of Lawrence Expwy Cloverleaf. Ext corridors. **Pets:** Accepted.
SAVE 🔊 ✕ 🛡 📷 ➰

SANTA CRUZ

▲▲▲⁷ ▼▼▼▼ GuestHouse International Pacific Inn SH 🐾
(831) 425-3722. **$70-$220.** 330 Ocean St. 1 mi from jct SR 1 and 17. Int corridors. **Pets:** Dogs only. $15 daily fee/pet. Service with restrictions, supervision.
SAVE 🔊 ✕ 🛡 📷 ➰

▲▲▲⁷ ▼▼▼▼ Hilton Santa Cruz/Scotts Valley SH 🐾
(831) 440-1000. **Call for rates.** 6001 La Madrona Dr. SR 17, exit Mt. Hermon Rd. Int corridors. **Pets:** Dogs only. $25 daily fee/pet. Designated rooms, service with restrictions, supervision.
SAVE ✕ 🔊 🛡 📷 🍴 ➰

▲▲▲⁷ ▼▼▼▼ The Inn at Pasatiempo SH
(831) 423-5000. **$145-$220.** 555 Hwy 17. 0.8 mi n of jct SR 1 and 17; exit SR 17, exit Pasatiempo Dr. Ext corridors. **Pets:** Medium, dogs only. $25 daily fee/pet. Designated rooms, service with restrictions, supervision.
SAVE 🔊 ✕ 🛡 📷 🍴 ➰ ✕

▲▲▲⁷ ▼▼▼ Santa Cruz Beach Inn SH
(831) 458-9660. **Call for rates.** 600 Riverside Ave. 4 blks from beach. Ext corridors. **Pets:** $15 daily fee/pet. Designated rooms, service with restrictions, supervision.
SAVE ✕ 🛡 📷 ➰ ✕

SANTA MARIA

▲▲▲⁷ ▼▼▼ Best Western Big America M
(805) 922-5200. **$109-$169.** 1725 N Broadway. US 101, exit 173 (SR 135/S Broadway), 0.5 mi s. Ext corridors. **Pets:** Accepted.
SAVE 🔊 ✕ 🛡 📷 ➰

▲▲▲⁷ ▼▼▼ Comfort Inn M
(805) 922-5891. **Call for rates.** 210 S Nicholson Ave. US 101, exit 171 (Main St), just e, then just s. Int corridors. **Pets:** $25 one-time fee/pet. Service with restrictions, supervision.
SAVE ✕ 🔊 🛡 📷 ➰

▼▼▼ Historic Santa Maria Inn LH
(805) 928-7777. **$124-$154.** 801 S Broadway. US 101, exit 171 (Main St), 1 mi w, then 0.5 mi s. Int corridors. **Pets:** Accepted.
ASK 🔊 ✕ 🔊 🛡 📷 🍴 ➰ ✕

▲▲▲⁷ ▼▼▼ Holiday Inn Hotel & Suites LH
(805) 928-6000. **$129-$229.** 2100 N Broadway. US 101, exit 173 (SR 135/S Broadway), just s. Int corridors. **Pets:** Medium. $25 daily fee/room. Designated rooms, service with restrictions, supervision.
SAVE 🔊 ✕ 🔊 🛡 📷 🍴 ➰

SANTA NELLA

▲▲▲⁷ ▼▼▼▼ Holiday Inn Express SH
(209) 826-8282. **$80-$99.** 28976 Plaza Dr. I-5, exit 407 (SR 33), just e. Ext corridors. **Pets:** $8 daily fee/room. Designated rooms, no service, supervision.
SAVE 🔊 ✕ 🛡 📷 ➰

▲▲▲⁷ ▼▼▼ Ramada Mission de Oro M
(209) 826-4444. **$65-$106.** 13070 State Hwy 33. I-5, exit 407 (SR 33), just w. Ext/int corridors. **Pets:** Other species. $10 daily fee/pet. Service with restrictions.
SAVE 🔊 ✕ 🛡 📷 🍴 ➰

▲▲▲⁷ ▼▼▼ Super 8 Motel SH
(209) 827-8700. **$69-$99.** 28821 W Gonzaga Rd. 2.5 mi w of I-5; SR 152, exit Gonzaga Rd, just s. Ext corridors. **Pets:** Accepted.
SAVE 🔊 ✕ 🛡 📷 ➰

SCOTTS VALLEY

∰ **▼▼▼** Best Western Inn Scotts Valley **SH**
(831) 438-6666. **Call for rates.** 6020 Scotts Valley Dr. SR 17, exit Granite Creek, just w. Ext corridors. **Pets:** Large, dogs only. $200 deposit/pet, $15 daily fee/pet. Designated rooms, service with restrictions, supervision.
SAVE ✕ &M █ ▆ ⇌

SELMA

∰ **▼** Super 8 Motel **SH**
(559) 896-2800. **$90-$145.** 3142 S Highland Ave. SR 99, exit Floral Ave. Int corridors. **Pets:** Accepted.
SAVE S◯ ✕ █ ⇌

SHASTA LAKE

∰ **▼▼** Bridge Bay Resort **SH** ❀
(530) 275-3021. **Call for rates.** 10300 Bridge Bay Rd. I-5, exit 690; e of I-5, exit Bridge Bay Rd; 12 mi n of Redding. Ext corridors. **Pets:** $50 deposit/pet, $10 daily fee/pet. Designated rooms, service with restrictions, supervision.
SAVE ✕ █ ▆ ¶¶ ⇌ ✕

∰ **▼▼** Fawndale Lodge & RV Resort **M**
(530) 275-8000. **$63-$115.** 15215 Fawndale Rd. I-5, exit 689, 1 mi s of Shasta Lake; e of I-5, exit Fawndale Rd; 10 mi n of Redding. Ext corridors. **Pets:** Accepted.
SAVE S◯ ✕ █ ▆ ⇌ ✕

SHAVER LAKE

▼▼ Dinkey Creek Inn & Chalets **CA**
(559) 841-3435. **Call for rates.** 53861 Dinkey Creek Rd. SR 168, 13.5 mi e. Ext corridors. **Pets:** Accepted.
✕ █ ▆ ¶¶ ✕ K̲ Z̲

SHELTER COVE

∰ **▼▼▼** Inn of the Lost Coast **M**
(707) 986-7521. **$150-$260.** 205 Wave Dr. US 101, exit Shelter Cove, 1.7 mi s on Redwood Dr, 21.1 mi w on Briceland Rd/Shelter Cove Rd, 0.4 mi n on Upper Pacific Rd, then just w on Lower Pacific Rd. Ext corridors. **Pets:** $10 daily fee/pet. Designated rooms, service with restrictions, supervision.
SAVE S◯ ✕ █ ▆ ¶¶ K̲ Z̲

SIERRA CITY

∰ **▼▼** Herrington's Sierra Pines **M**
(530) 862-1151. **Call for rates.** 104 Main St. 0.5 mi w on SR 49; 12 mi n of Downieville Center. Ext corridors. **Pets:** Other species. Supervision.
SAVE ✕ █ ▆ ¶¶ ✕ K̲ Z̲

SIMI VALLEY

▼▼ Extended StayAmerica-Los Angeles-Simi Valley **SH**
(805) 584-8880. **$94-$114.** 2498 Stearns St. SR 118, exit Stearns St, just s. Int corridors. **Pets:** Other species. $75 one-time fee/pet. Service with restrictions.
ASK S◯ ✕ █ ▆

SMITH RIVER

▼ Ship Ashore Motel **M**
(707) 487-3141. **Call for rates.** 12370 Hwy 101. On US 101, 3.7 mi s of Oregon border. Ext corridors. **Pets:** Accepted.
✕ █ ▆ ¶¶ K̲

SOLEDAD

∰ **▼▼** Best Western Valley Harvest Inn **SH**
(831) 678-3833. **$89-$189.** 1155 Front St. US 101, exit Soledad, just e. Ext/int corridors. **Pets:** Accepted.
SAVE ✕ █ ▆ ¶¶ ⇌

SOLVANG

▼▼ Meadowlark Inn **M**
(805) 688-4631. **Call for rates.** 2644 Mission Dr. On SR 246, 1.6 mi e. Ext corridors. **Pets:** Accepted.
✕ █ ▆ ⇌

∰ **▼▼** Royal Copenhagen Inn **M**
(805) 688-5561. **$85-$225, 3 day notice.** 1579 Mission Dr. On SR 246. Ext/int corridors. **Pets:** Accepted.
SAVE ✕ █ ▆ ⇌

∰ **▼▼▼** Wine Valley Inn & Cottages **SH**
(805) 688-2111. **Call for rates.** 1564 Copenhagen Dr. SR 246, just s on 5th St. Ext/int corridors. **Pets:** $25 daily fee/pet. Designated rooms, no service, supervision.
SAVE ✕ █ ▆ ✕

SONORA

∰ **▼▼** Aladdin Motor Inn **SH** ❀
(209) 533-4971. **Call for rates.** 14260 Mono Way (Hwy 108). On SR 108, 3.5 mi e. Ext/int corridors. **Pets:** Medium, other species. $15 one-time fee/pet. Designated rooms, service with restrictions, supervision.
SAVE ✕ █ ▆ ⇌

∰ **▼▼▼** Best Western Sonora Oaks **SH** ❀
(209) 533-4400. **$110-$132.** 19551 Hess Ave. 3.5 mi e on SR 108. Ext/int corridors. **Pets:** Medium. $25 daily fee/room. Designated rooms, service with restrictions, supervision.
SAVE S◯ ✕ █ ▆ ⇌

∰ **▼** Miners Motel **M**
(209) 532-7850. **$40-$80, 3 day notice.** 18740 SR 108. On SR 108 and 49, 1 mi e of Jamestown. Ext corridors. **Pets:** Small, dogs only. $10 daily fee/pet. Service with restrictions.
SAVE S◯ ✕ █ ▆ ⇌

∰ **▼▼** Sonora Days Inn **SH**
(209) 532-2400. **$74-$164.** 160 S Washington St. Downtown. Ext/int corridors. **Pets:** Accepted.
SAVE S◯ ✕ █ ▆ ⇌

∰ **▼** Sonora Gold Lodge **M**
(209) 532-3952. **$39-$99.** 480 Stockton St. 0.5 mi sw on SR 108/49 business route. Ext corridors. **Pets:** Accepted.
SAVE S◯ ✕ █ ▆ ⇌

▼▼▼ Union Hill Inn **BB**
(209) 533-1494. **$150-$195, 3 day notice.** 21645 Parrotts Ferry Rd. Jct SR 49 and Parrotts Ferry Rd; 3 mi n of downtown. Ext corridors. **Pets:** Accepted.
ASK S◯ ✕ █ ▆ ⇌ Z̲

STANTON

∰ **▼▼▼** Best Western Cypress Inn & Suites **M**
(714) 527-6680. **$99-$139.** 7161 W Katella Ave. SR 22, exit 7 (Knott Ave/Golden West St.), 2 mi n, then just w. Ext/int corridors. **Pets:** Accepted.
SAVE S◯ ✕ █ ▆ ⇌

STOCKTON

∰ **▼▼** Comfort Inn **SH**
(209) 478-4300. **$49-$120.** 2654 W March Ln. I-5, exit March Ln, just e. Ext corridors. **Pets:** Accepted.
SAVE S◯ ✕ &M █ ▆ ⟋

∰ **▼** Econo Lodge of Stockton **SH**
(209) 466-5741. **$49-$69.** 2210 S Manthey Rd. I-5, exit 8th St W, 0.3 mi s of jct SR 4. Int corridors. **Pets:** Small, dogs only. $10 daily fee/pet. Designated rooms, service with restrictions, supervision.
SAVE S◯ ✕ &M █ ⇌

Extended StayAmerica-Stockton **SH**
(209) 472-7588. **Call for rates.** 2844 W March Ln. I-5, exit March Ln, just w. Int corridors. **Pets:** Other species. $75 one-time fee/pet. Service with restrictions.

AAA ▼▼▼ Holiday Inn **SH**
(209) 474-3301. **Call for rates.** 111 E March Ln. I-5, exit March Ln, 2.5 mi e; corner of El Dorado St. Int corridors. **Pets:** Medium, other species. $30 daily fee/pet. Designated rooms, service with restrictions, supervision.

▼▼ Howard Johnson Express Inn-Marina **SH**
(209) 948-6151. **$65-$99.** 33 N Center St. 1 blk n; w off El Dorado St via Weber; SR 99, exit Wilson Way southbound; exit northbound, w via Mariposa Rd to Charter Way; I-5, exit downtown. Ext corridors. **Pets:** Accepted.

▼▼▼ La Quinta Inn Stockton **SH**
(209) 952-7800. **$105-$125.** 2710 W March Ln. I-5, exit March Ln, just w. Ext corridors. **Pets:** Other species. Service with restrictions, supervision.

▼▼ Red Roof Inn Stockton **M**
(209) 466-7777. **$63-$75.** 1707 W Fremont St. I-5, exit Fremont St southbound; exit Pershing Ave northbound, just w. Ext corridors. **Pets:** Accepted.

▼▼▼ Residence Inn by Marriott **SH**
(209) 472-9800. **$165-$185.** 3240 W March Ln. I-5, exit March Ln, 0.5 mi w. Int corridors. **Pets:** Medium. $100 one-time fee/room. Service with restrictions, supervision.

SUNNYVALE

▼▼ Homestead Studio Suites Hotel-San Jose-Sunnyvale **SH**
(408) 734-3431. **$113-$125.** 1255 Orleans Dr. N of SR 237, exit Mathilda Ave, e on Moffett Park Dr. Ext corridors. **Pets:** Other species. $75 one-time fee/pet. Service with restrictions.

AAA ▼▼▼ Maple Tree Inn **SH** ❀
(408) 720-9700. **$109-$169.** 711 E El Camino Real. On SR 82; between Fair Oaks and Wolfe Rd; 2.5 mi w of US 101. Int corridors. **Pets:** Medium. $20 daily fee/pet. Designated rooms, service with restrictions, supervision.

▼▼▼ Quality Inn-Sunnyvale **SH**
(408) 744-1100. **Call for rates.** 1280 Persian Dr. US 101, exit Lawrence Expwy N, 1 mi n to Persian Dr, then 0.3 mi w. Int corridors. **Pets:** Accepted.

AAA ▼▼▼ Ramada Inn-Silicon Valley **SH**
(408) 245-5330. **$99-$159.** 1217 Wildwood Ave. US 101, exit Lawrence Expwy N, just n. Ext corridors. **Pets:** Small. $200 deposit/room, $10 daily fee/pet. Service with restrictions, supervision.

▼▼▼ Residence Inn by Marriott **SH**
(408) 720-8893. **$275-$295.** 1080 Stewart Dr. US 101, exit Lawrence Expwy S, w on Duane Ave W. Ext corridors. **Pets:** Accepted.

▼▼▼ Residence Inn by Marriott **SH**
(408) 720-1000. **$275-$295.** 750 Lakeway Dr. US 101, exit Lawrence Expwy S, e on Oakmead. Ext corridors. **Pets:** Accepted.

AAA ▼▼▼ Staybridge Suites **SH**
(408) 745-1515. **Call for rates.** 900 Hamlin Ct. SR 237, exit Mathilda Ave S, w on Ross Dr. Ext corridors. **Pets:** Accepted.

▼▼▼ TownePlace Suites by Marriott Sunnyvale/Mountain View **SH**
(408) 733-4200. **$209-$229.** 606 S Bernardo Ave. SR 85, exit SR 82, 0.5 mi s. Int corridors. **Pets:** Accepted.

AAA ▼▼ Vagabond Inn **M**
(408) 734-4607. **$59-$259.** 816 Ahwanee Ave. US 101, exit Mathilda Ave S, then s. Ext corridors. **Pets:** Accepted.

SUSANVILLE

▼ America's Best Inns **M**
(530) 257-4522. **Call for rates.** 2705 Main St. 1.5 mi e on SR 36. Ext corridors. **Pets:** Accepted.

AAA ▼▼ River Inn **M**
(530) 257-6051. **$75.** 1710 Main St. 0.8 mi e on SR 36. Ext corridors. **Pets:** Accepted.

▼▼▼ The Roseberry House Bed & Breakfast **BB**
(530) 257-5675. **$110-$135, 5 day notice.** 609 North St. Just n on N Lassen St from jct SR 36. Int corridors. **Pets:** Accepted.

AAA ▼▼ Super 8 Motel **M**
(530) 257-2782. **$80-$90.** 2975 Johnstonville Rd. SR 36, 1.8 mi e. Ext corridors. **Pets:** Large. $10 daily fee/pet. Designated rooms, service with restrictions, supervision.

SUTTER CREEK

AAA ▼▼ Sutter Creek Days Inn **SH**
(209) 267-9177. **$79-$129.** 271 Hanford St, Hwy 49. SR 49, 0.5 mi n of historic district. Int corridors. **Pets:** Other species. $10 daily fee/pet. Designated rooms, service with restrictions, supervision.

TEHACHAPI

AAA ▼▼ Best Western Mountain Inn **M**
(661) 822-5591. **$89-$99.** 418 W Tehachapi Blvd. SR 58, exit 148 (SR 202), 1 mi e. Ext corridors. **Pets:** Other species. $500 deposit/room. No service, supervision.

AAA ▼▼ Tehachapi Summit Travelodge **M**
(661) 823-8000. **Call for rates.** 500 Steuber Rd. SR 58, exit 151 (Monolith/Tehachapi Blvd), just s. Int corridors. **Pets:** Other species. Service with restrictions, supervision.

TEMECULA

▼▼ Extended StayAmerica-Temecula-Wine Country **M**
(951) 587-8881. **$94-$154.** 27622 Jefferson Ave. I-15, exit 61 (SR 79 N), just w on Winchester Rd, then 0.4 mi s. Int corridors. **Pets:** Other species. $75 one-time fee/pet. Service with restrictions.

▼▼ Quality Inn Temecula Wine Country **M**
(951) 296-3788. **$77-$189.** 27338 Jefferson Ave. I-15, exit 61 (Winchester Rd/79 N), just w on Winchester Rd, then just n. Ext corridors. **Pets:** Accepted.

THOUSAND OAKS

▼▼▼▼ Best Western Thousand Oaks Inn SH ❀
(805) 497-3701. **$117-$165.** 75 W Thousand Oaks Blvd. US 101, exit 44 (Moorpark Rd), just n, then just w. Ext corridors. **Pets:** Small, other species. $45 one-time fee/pet. Designated rooms, service with restrictions, supervision.

ASK SD ✕ ⊛M 🛗 ▤ 🍴 ⟿

AAA⬦ ▼▼▼▼ La Quinta Inn & Suites M
(805) 499-5910. **$149-$189.** 1320 Newbury Rd. US 101, exit 46 (Ventu Park Rd), just se. Ext corridors. **Pets:** Other species. Service with restrictions, supervision.

SAVE SD ✕ ⊛M 🛗 ▤ 🏊

▼ Motel 6 #1360 Thousand Oaks M
(805) 499-0711. **$49-$58.** 1516 Newbury Rd. US 101, exit 46 (Ventu Park Rd), just w, then just n. Ext corridors. **Pets:** Other species. Service with restrictions, supervision.

SD ✕ ⟿

AAA⬦ ▼▼▼ Premier Inns M
(805) 499-0755. **$50-$70.** 2434 W Hillcrest Dr. US 101, exit 47A (Borchard Rd), just e, then just n. Ext corridors. **Pets:** Medium. Designated rooms, service with restrictions, supervision.

SAVE SD ✕ ⊛M 🛗 ⟿

▼▼▼▼ TownePlace Suites by Marriott SH
(805) 499-3111. **$170-$191.** 1712 Newbury Rd. US 101, exit 46 (Ventu Park Rd), just s, then just w. Int corridors. **Pets:** Accepted.

ASK SD ✕ 🛗 ▤ ⟿

THOUSAND PALMS

AAA⬦ ▼▼▼ Red Roof Inn M
(760) 343-1381. **$51-$189.** 72-215 Varner Rd. I-10, exit 130 (Ramon Rd), just n, then just w. Ext corridors. **Pets:** Other species. $25 deposit/room. Service with restrictions, supervision.

SAVE SD ✕ ▤ ⟿

THREE RIVERS

AAA⬦ ▼▼▼ Americas Best Value Inn–Lazy J Ranch M
(559) 561-4449. **$100-$110, 3 day notice.** 39625 Sierra Dr. SR 198, 3 mi sw of town center. Ext corridors. **Pets:** $5 one-time fee/pet. Service with restrictions, supervision.

SAVE SD ✕ 🛗 ▤ ⟿ ✕

AAA⬦ ▼▼▼ Buckeye Tree Lodge M
(559) 561-5900. **$69-$132, 7 day notice.** 46000 Sierra Dr. SR 198, 6 mi ne of town center; 0.5 mi sw of entrance to Sequoia National Park. Ext corridors. **Pets:** $10 daily fee/pet. Service with restrictions, crate.

SAVE SD ✕ 🛗 ▤ 🏊

AAA⬦ ▼▼▼ Gateway Lodge M
(559) 561-4133. **$79-$179, 3 day notice.** 45978 Sierra Dr. SR 198, 6 mi ne of town center; 0.5 mi sw of entrance to Sequoia National Park. Ext corridors. **Pets:** Other species. $10 daily fee/pet.

SAVE SD ✕ 🛗 ▤ 🍴 🐾

▼▼▼ Sequoia River Dance Bed & Breakfast BB ❀
(559) 561-4411. **$95-$135, 10 day notice.** 40534 Cherokee Oaks Dr. SR 198, 2 mi sw of town center, then 0.3 mi e. Int corridors. **Pets:** $15 daily fee/pet. Supervision.

ASK ✕ 🐾 🐾

AAA⬦ ▼▼▼ Sequoia Village Inn CA
(559) 561-3652. **$69-$269, 7 day notice.** 45971 Sierra Dr. SR 198, 6 mi ne of town center; 0.5 mi sw of entrance to Sequoia National Park. Ext corridors. **Pets:** Accepted.

SAVE SD ✕ 🛗 ▤ ⟿ 🐾

AAA⬦ ▼▼▼ Western Holiday Lodge Three Rivers M
(559) 561-4119. **$59-$109.** 40105 Sierra Dr. SR 198, 2 mi sw of town center. Ext corridors. **Pets:** Dogs only. $15 daily fee/pet. Designated rooms, supervision.

SAVE SD ✕ 🛗 ▤ ⟿ ✕

TRINIDAD

AAA⬦ ▼ Bishop Pine Lodge CA
(707) 677-3314. **$100-$140, 7 day notice.** 1481 Patrick's Point Dr. US 101, exit Seawood Dr, just w, then 0.8 mi s. Ext corridors. **Pets:** Accepted.

SAVE SD ✕ 🛗 ▤ 🐾

▼▼▼ Lost Whale Bed & Breakfast Inn BB
(707) 677-3425. **Call for rates.** 3452 Patrick's Point Dr. US 101, exit Patrick's Point Dr, 1.1 mi w. Int corridors. **Pets:** Accepted.

✕ 🐾

AAA⬦ ▼▼▼ Trinidad Inn SH
(707) 677-3349. **$110-$180.** 1170 Patrick's Point Dr. US 101, exit Trinidad, just w on Main St, then 1.3 mi n. Ext corridors. **Pets:** Accepted.

SAVE ✕ 🛗 ▤ 🐾

TULARE

AAA⬦ ▼▼▼▼ Best Western Town & Country Lodge M
(559) 688-7537. **$89-$199.** 1051 N Blackstone St. SR 99, exit 88 (Prosperity Ave/Blackstone St), just w. Int corridors. **Pets:** Accepted.

SAVE SD ✕ 🛗 ▤ ⟿

▼▼▼ Charter Inn SH
(559) 685-9500. **$89-$139.** 1016 E Prosperity Ave. SR 99, exit 88 (Prosperity Ave/Blackstone St), just e. Int corridors. **Pets:** Accepted.

ASK SD ✕ ⊛M 🛗 ▤ ⟿

▼▼▼ Microtel Inn & Suites SH
(559) 685-8900. **Call for rates (no credit cards).** 1500 Cherry Ct. SR 99, exit 88 (Prosperity Ave/Blackstone St), just w. Int corridors. **Pets:** Small. $20 one-time fee/pet. Designated rooms, service with restrictions, supervision.

✕ 🛗 ▤ ⟿

AAA⬦ ▼▼▼ Quality Inn M
(559) 686-3432. **$79-$150.** 1010 E Prosperity Ave. SR 99, exit 88 (Prosperity Ave/Blackstone St), just e. Int corridors. **Pets:** Small, dogs only. $10 daily fee/pet. Service with restrictions, supervision.

SAVE SD ✕ 🛗 ▤ ⟿ ✕

TURLOCK

AAA⬦ ▼▼▼ Best Western Orchard Inn SH
(209) 667-2827. **$89-$109, 14 day notice.** 5025 N Golden State Blvd. SR 99, exit Taylor Rd, just e. Ext corridors. **Pets:** $25 one-time fee/pet. Service with restrictions, crate.

SAVE SD ✕ ⊛M 🛗 ▤ ⟿

AAA⬦ ▼▼▼ Travelodge SH
(209) 668-3400. **$69-$99.** 201 W Glenwood Ave. SR 99, exit Lander W. Ext corridors. **Pets:** Small. $10 daily fee/pet. Service with restrictions, supervision.

SAVE SD ✕ ⊛M 🛗 ▤ ⟿

TWAIN HARTE

AAA⬦ ▼▼▼ ▼▼▼ McCaffrey House B & B Inn BB
(209) 586-0757. **$145-$165, 7 day notice.** 23251 Hwy 108. 0.5 mi on SR 108; just beyond 4000' elevation marker. Int corridors. **Pets:** Other species. $25 daily fee/pet. Designated rooms, service with restrictions, supervision.

SAVE ✕

TWENTYNINE PALMS

♦♦ ♦♦♦♦ Roughley Manor BB
(760) 367-3238. **Call for rates.** 74744 Joe Davis Rd. SR 62, 0.5 mi n on Utah Tr, 0.5 mi e on Joe Davis Rd, then just n. Ext/int corridors. **Pets:** Dogs only. Designated rooms, supervision.
SAVE ✕ ▤ ▣ ⇒ ✍

♦♦♦ Sunnyvale Garden Suites Hotel CO
(760) 361-3939. **$103.** 73843 Sunnyvale Dr. SR 62, 0.7 mi n on Adobe Rd, just e on S Slope, just n on Ocotillo, then just e. Ext corridors. **Pets:** Accepted.
ASK S⅋ ✕ ▤ ▣ ✕

UNION CITY

♦♦♦ Extended StayAmerica-Union City SH
(510) 441-9616. **$95-$105.** 31950 Dyer St. I-880, exit Alvarado-Niles Rd, just w, then just n; in Union Landing Shopping Center. Int corridors. **Pets:** Other species. $75 one-time fee/pet. Service with restrictions.
ASK S⅋ ✕ ▤ ▣ ⇒

VACAVILLE

♦♦♦ ♦♦♦ Best Western Heritage Inn M
(707) 448-8453. **$85-$115.** 1420 E Monte Vista Ave. I-80, exit Monte Vista Ave, just n. Ext corridors. **Pets:** Medium. Designated rooms, service with restrictions, supervision.
SAVE S⅋ ✕ ৬M ▤ ▣ ⇒

♦♦♦♦ Extended StayAmerica-Sacramento-Vacaville SH
(707) 469-1371. **$90-$100.** 799 Orange Dr. I-80, exit Leisure Town Rd. Int corridors. **Pets:** Other species. $75 one-time fee/pet. Service with restrictions.
ASK S⅋ ✕ ▤ ▣

♦♦♦♦ Residence Inn by Marriott SH
(707) 469-0300. **$154-$176.** 360 Orange Dr. I-80, exit Orange Dr eastbound, 0.5 mi; exit Monte Vista westbound, freeway overpass to E Nut Tree Pkwy. Int corridors. **Pets:** Accepted.
ASK S⅋ ✕ ৬M ▤ ▣ ⇒ ✕

VALLEJO

♦♦♦ ♦♦♦♦ Best Western Inn & Suites at Discovery Kingdom SH
(707) 554-9655. **$60-$160.** 1596 Fairgrounds Dr. I-80, exit SR 37 (Marine World Pkwy) N, 0.3 mi w. Int corridors. **Pets:** $35 one-time fee/pet. Designated rooms, service with restrictions, supervision.
SAVE S⅋ ✕ ৬M ▤ ▣ ⇒

♦♦♦♦ Courtyard by Marriott SH
(707) 644-1200. **$165-$187.** 1000 Fairgrounds Dr. I-80, exit SR 37 (Marine World Pkwy), 0.3 mi n. Int corridors. **Pets:** Accepted.
ASK S⅋ ✕ ৬M ▤ ▣ ▯▯ ⇒

♦♦♦ Ramada Inn SH
(707) 643-2700. **$72-$89.** 1000 Admiral Callaghan Ln. I-80, exit Columbus Pkwy, 0.5 mi w. Ext corridors. **Pets:** Accepted.
ASK S⅋ ✕ ৬M ▤ ▣ ⇒

VENTURA

♦♦♦ ♦♦♦♦ Crowne Plaza Ventura Beach Resort LH
(805) 648-7731. **Call for rates.** 450 E Harbor Blvd. US 101, exit 70A (California St) northbound, just s; exit 71 (Main St) southbound, 0.5 mi e to California St, then just s. Int corridors. **Pets:** Accepted.
SAVE ✕ ৬M ▤ ▣ ▯▯ ⇒

♦♦♦♦ Four Points by Sheraton Ventura Harbortown SH
(805) 658-1212. **$134-$175.** 1050 Schooner Dr. US 101, exit 68 (Seaward Ave), just w, then 1.5 mi s; at Ventura Harbor. Ext corridors. **Pets:** Large, other species. $75 one-time fee/room. Designated rooms, service with restrictions, supervision.
✕ ৬M ▤ ▣ ▯▯ ⇒ ✕

♦♦♦♦ Holiday Inn Express Ventura Harbor SH
(805) 856-9533. **$129-$200.** 1080 Navigator Dr. US 101, exit 68 (Seaward Ave), just w, then 1.5 mi s; at Ventura Harbor. Ext/int corridors. **Pets:** Accepted.
ASK ✕ ৬M ▤ ▣

♦♦♦♦ La Quinta Inn Ventura M
(805) 658-6200. **$105-$145.** 5818 Valentine Rd. US 101, exit 64 (Victoria Ave), just s, then just n. Ext/int corridors. **Pets:** Other species. Service with restrictions, supervision.
ASK S⅋ ✕ ৬M ▤ ▣ ⇒

♦♦♦ Marriott Ventura Beach Hotel LH
(805) 643-6000. **$208-$230.** 2055 Harbor Blvd. US 101, exit 68 (Seaward Ave), just w, then 0.5 mi n. Int corridors. **Pets:** Accepted.
ASK S⅋ ✕ ৬M ▤ ▣ ▯▯ ⇒

♦♦ ♦♦♦ Vagabond Inn Ventura M
(805) 648-5371. **$79-$249.** 756 E Thompson Blvd. US 101, exit 70A (California St) northbound, just n, then just e; exit 70A (Ventura Ave) southbound, 0.6 mi e. Ext corridors. **Pets:** Other species. $10 daily fee/pet. Service with restrictions.
SAVE S⅋ ✕ ▤ ▣ ▯▯ ⇒

VICTORVILLE

♦♦♦ ♦♦♦♦ Comfort Suites Hotel SH
(760) 245-6777. **$99-$139.** 12281 Mariposa Rd. I-15, exit 147 (Bear Valley Rd), just e, then just n. Int corridors. **Pets:** $25 daily fee/room. Service with restrictions, supervision.
SAVE S⅋ ✕ ৬M ▤ ▣ ⇒

♦♦♦ ♦♦♦♦ Hawthorn Suites by Hyatt SH
(760) 949-4700. **Call for rates.** 11750 Dunia Rd. I-15, exit 147 (Bear Valley Rd), just w, just s on Amargosa Rd, then just w. Int corridors. **Pets:** Accepted.
SAVE ✕ ৬M ▤ ▣ ⇒ ✕

♦♦♦ Red Roof Inn M
(760) 241-1577. **Call for rates.** 13409 Mariposa Rd. I-15, exit 147 (Bear Valley Rd) northbound, just e, then 1.5 mi n; exit 150 (SR 18 W/Palmdale Rd) southbound, just e, then 1.5 mi s. Ext corridors. **Pets:** Accepted.
✕ ▤ ▣ ⇒

♦♦♦ ♦♦♦ Travelodge Victorville M
(760) 241-7200. **$59-$89.** 12175 Mariposa Rd. I-15, exit 147 (Bear Valley Rd), just e, then just n. Ext corridors. **Pets:** Very small, dogs only. $8 one-time fee/pet. Service with restrictions, supervision.
SAVE S⅋ ✕ ▤ ▣

VISALIA

♦♦♦ ♦♦♦ Best Western Visalia Inn M
(559) 732-4561. **$69-$140.** 623 W Main St. SR 198, exit 105B (SR 63 S/Mooney Blvd), just n, then 0.9 mi e. Ext corridors. **Pets:** Accepted.
SAVE S⅋ ✕ ▤ ▣ ⇒

♦♦♦ ♦♦♦ Holiday Inn Hotel & Conference Center LH
(559) 651-5000. **$149.** 9000 W Airport Dr. SR 198, exit 102 (Plaza Dr), then just s. Int corridors. **Pets:** Large. $25 daily fee/pet. Designated rooms, service with restrictions, supervision.
SAVE S⅋ ✕ ৬M ▤ ▣ ▯▯ ⇒ ✕

♦♦♦ ♦♦♦ Lamp Liter Inn M
(559) 732-4511. **$79-$129.** 3300 W Mineral King Ave. SR 198, exit 105B (SR 63 S/Mooney Blvd) westbound, 0.5 mi w; exit eastbound, just n, then 0.5 mi w. Ext corridors. **Pets:** Accepted.
SAVE S⅋ ✕ ▤ ▣ ▯▯ ⇒

♦♦♦♦ La Quinta Inn & Suites SH
(559) 739-9800. **$93-$118.** 5438 W Cypress Ave. SR 198, exit 104 (Akers St), just s, then just w. Int corridors. **Pets:** Other species. Service with restrictions, supervision.
ASK ✕ ▤ ▣ ⇒

VISTA

▼▼▼▼ La Quinta Inn San Diego (Vista)
(760) 727-8180. **$112-$149.** 630 Sycamore Ave. SR 78, exit Sycamore Ave, just sw. Ext/int corridors. **Pets:** Other species. Service with restrictions, supervision.

(ASK) (S⌀) (✕) (🛏) (🖥) (🐾)

WALNUT CREEK

(AAA) ▼▼▼▼ Holiday Inn Walnut Creek [SH]
(925) 932-3332. **Call for rates.** 2730 N Main St. I-680, exit N Main St, just n. Int corridors. **Pets:** Accepted.

(SAVE) (✕) (🛏) (🖥) (🍴) (🐾)

WATSONVILLE

(AAA) ▼▼▼▼ Best Western Rose Garden Inn [SH]
(831) 724-3367. **$69-$199.** 740 Freedom Blvd. On SR 152. Ext corridors. **Pets:** Accepted.

(SAVE) (S⌀) (✕) (🛏) (🖥)

(AAA) ▼▼▼▼ Comfort Inn Watsonville [SH]
(831) 728-2300. **$79-$450.** 112 Airport Blvd. SR 1, exit Airport Blvd, 1 mi e. Int corridors. **Pets:** Small. $35 one-time fee/pet. Designated rooms, service with restrictions, supervision.

(SAVE) (S⌀) (✕) (🛏) (🖥)

(AAA) ▼▼▼ Red Roof Inn [SH]
(831) 740-4520. **Call for rates.** 1620 W Beach St. SR 1, exit Riverside Dr (SR 129), just w. Int corridors. **Pets:** Accepted.

(SAVE) (✕) (&M) (🛏) (🖥) (🐾)

WEAVERVILLE

(AAA) ▼▼▼ 49er Gold Country Inn
(530) 623-4937. **Call for rates.** 880 Main St (Hwy 299). On SR 299. Ext corridors. **Pets:** Service with restrictions, supervision.

(SAVE) (✕) (🛏) (🖥) (🐾) (✕)

(AAA) ▼ Motel Trinity
(530) 623-2129. **$70-$95, 3 day notice.** 1270 Main St. Just s on SR 3. Ext corridors. **Pets:** Dogs only. $5 daily fee/pet. Service with restrictions, supervision.

(SAVE) (S⌀) (✕) (🛏) (🖥) (🐾)

▼ Red Hill Motel
(530) 623-4331. **Call for rates.** Red Hill Rd. SR 299, just w of SR 3. Ext corridors. **Pets:** Accepted.

(🛏) (🖥)

(AAA) ▼▼▼▼ Weaverville Victorian Inn [SH]
(530) 623-4432. **$79-$159.** 1709 Main St. On SR 299. Ext corridors. **Pets:** Small, dogs only. $25 one-time fee/room. Designated rooms, service with restrictions, supervision.

(SAVE) (S⌀) (✕) (🛏) (🖥) (🍴) (🐾)

WEED

(AAA) ▼▼▼ Quality Inn and Suites [SH]
(530) 938-1308. **$79-$89.** 1830 Black Butte Dr. I-5, exit S Weed, just e. Int corridors. **Pets:** Accepted.

(SAVE) (S⌀) (✕) (🛏) (🖥)

(AAA) ▼ Sis-Q-Inn Motel ❖
(530) 938-4194. **$65-$150.** 1825 Shastina Dr. I-5, exit S Weed. Int corridors. **Pets:** Small. $10 daily fee/pet. Designated rooms, service with restrictions, supervision.

(SAVE) (S⌀) (✕) (🛏)

WESTLAKE VILLAGE

▼▼▼▼▼ Four Seasons Hotel Westlake Village [LH]
(818) 575-3000. **Call for rates.** Two Dole Dr. US 101, exit Lindero Canyon Rd, just e, then just n on Via Colinas. Int corridors. **Pets:** Accepted.

(✕) (&M) (🛏) (🖥) (🍴) (🐾)

WESTLEY

(AAA) ▼▼ Econo Lodge
(209) 894-3900. **$55-$95, 3 day notice.** 7100 McCracken Rd. I-5, exit Westley, just e. Ext corridors. **Pets:** Medium. $10 daily fee/pet. No service, supervision.

(SAVE) (S⌀) (✕) (🛏) (🖥) (🐾)

(AAA) ▼▼▼▼ Holiday Inn Express [SH] ❖
(209) 894-8940. **$74-$109.** 4525 Howard Rd. I-5, exit Westley, just e. Int corridors. **Pets:** Small, other species. $25 one-time fee/pet. Service with restrictions, supervision.

(SAVE) (S⌀) (✕) (🛏) (🖥) (🐾)

WESTMORLAND

(AAA) ▼▼ Super 8 Motel
(760) 351-7100. **Call for rates.** 351 W Main St. On SR 86. Int corridors. **Pets:** Accepted.

(SAVE) (✕) (🛏) (🖥) (🐾)

WEST SACRAMENTO

▼▼ Extended StayAmerica-Sacramento-West Sacramento [SH]
(916) 371-1270. **$99-$110.** 795 Stillwater Ave. I-80, exit Reed Ave, just w. Int corridors. **Pets:** Other species. $75 one-time fee/pet. Service with restrictions.

(ASK) (S⌀) (✕) (🛏) (🖥)

WILLIAMS

(AAA) ▼▼ Comfort Inn
(530) 473-2381. **$79-$149.** 400 C St. I-5, exit Williams, just w on E St, then just n on 4th St. Ext corridors. **Pets:** Accepted.

(SAVE) (S⌀) (✕) (&M) (🛏) (🖥) (🐾)

(AAA) ▼▼▼▼ Granzella's Inn
(530) 473-3310. **$85-$110.** 391 6th St. I-5, exit Williams, 0.5 mi w. Int corridors. **Pets:** Other species. $10 one-time fee/room. Service with restrictions, supervision.

(SAVE) (S⌀) (✕) (&M) (🛏) (🖥) (🍴) (🐾)

(AAA) ▼▼▼ Holiday Inn Express Hotel & Suites ❖
(530) 473-5120. **Call for rates.** 374 Ruggieri Way. I-5, exit Williams, just e. Int corridors. **Pets:** Small. $25 one-time fee/room. Designated rooms, service with restrictions, supervision.

(SAVE) (✕) (&M) (🛏) (🖥)

(AAA) ▼ Stage Stop Inn
(530) 473-2281. **$45-$55.** 330 7th St. I-5, exit SR 20 business route, 3 blks w. Ext corridors. **Pets:** Accepted.

(SAVE) (✕) (🛏) (🖥) (🐾)

WILLOW CREEK

(AAA) ▼ Bigfoot Motel
(530) 629-2142. **$125.** 39039 Hwy 299. On SR 299; just e of SR 96; center. Ext corridors. **Pets:** Medium. $50 deposit/pet. Service with restrictions, supervision.

(SAVE) (✕) (🛏) (🐾)

WILLOWS

AAA ◇◇◇ Baymont Inns & Suites Willows SH
(530) 934-9700. **$69-$99.** 199 N Humboldt Ave. I-5, exit 162 (Willows-Elk Creek-Glenn Rd), then right. Int corridors. **Pets:** Accepted.
[SAVE] [S⊘] [✕] [🛏] [🖵] [⇌]

AAA ◇◇ Days Inn M
(530) 934-4444. **Call for rates.** 475 N Humboldt Ave. I-5, exit 162 (Willows-Elk Creek-Glenn Rd), just e. Ext corridors. **Pets:** $10 daily fee/pet. Service with restrictions, supervision.
[SAVE] [✕] [ㄴM] [🛏] [🖵] [⇌]

AAA ◇◇ Economy Inn M
(530) 934-4224. **$50-$75.** 435 N Tehama St. I-5, exit SR 162 (Willows-Elk Creek-Glenn Rd), 1 mi e. Ext corridors. **Pets:** Small. $7 one-time fee/pet. Designated rooms, service with restrictions, supervision.
[SAVE] [S⊘] [✕] [🛏]

AAA ◇ Motel 6 #4273 M
(530) 934-7026. **$55-$59.** 452 N Humboldt Ave. I-5, exit 162 (Willows-Elk Creek-Glenn Rd), just e. Ext corridors. **Pets:** Medium. $7 daily fee/pet. Designated rooms, service with restrictions, supervision.
[SAVE] [S⊘] [✕] [🛏] [⇌]

AAA ◇◇ Super 8 Motel of Willows SH
(530) 934-2871. **$49-$64.** 457 Humboldt Ave. I-5, exit 162 (Willows-Elk Creek-Glenn Rd). Int corridors. **Pets:** Medium. $10 daily fee/pet. Designated rooms, service with restrictions, supervision.
[SAVE] [S⊘] [✕] [🛏] [⇌]

WINE COUNTRY AREA

ALBION

◇◇ Fensalden Inn BB
(707) 937-4042. **$139-$253, 7 day notice.** 33810 Navarro Ridge Rd. 0.5 mi e of jct SR 1. Ext/int corridors. **Pets:** Accepted.
[✕] [🛏] [🖵] [ⓚ] [ⓦ] [☎]

CALISTOGA

AAA ◇◇◇ Brannan Cottage Inn BB
(707) 942-4200. **$155-$230.** 109 Wapoo Ave. At Lincoln Ave. Ext corridors. **Pets:** Other species. $100 deposit/room, $25 daily fee/pet. Designated rooms, service with restrictions, crate.
[SAVE] [✕] [🛏] [☎]

◇◇◇◇ Garnett Creek Inn BB
(707) 942-9797. **$108-$325.** 1139 Lincoln Ave. On SR 29. Int corridors. **Pets:** Accepted.
[ASK] [S⊘] [✕] [ㄴM] [🖵]

CLOVERDALE

AAA ◇ Cloverdale Oaks Inn M
(707) 894-2404. **$59-$139.** 123 S Cloverdale Blvd. US 101, exit Citrus Fair Dr, 0.4 mi w to S Cloverdale Blvd, then just n. Ext corridors. **Pets:** Accepted.
[SAVE] [S⊘] [✕] [ㄴM] [🛏] [🖵]

FORT BRAGG

AAA ◇◇◇◇ Beach House Inn M
(707) 961-1700. **Call for rates.** 100 Pudding Creek Rd. 0.7 mi n on SR 1. Int corridors. **Pets:** Accepted.
[SAVE] [✕] [🛏] [🖵] [ⓚ]

◇◇◇◇ Emerald Dolphin Inn & Mini Golf SH
(707) 964-6699. **$59-$200, 7 day notice.** 1211 S Main St. On SR 1. Ext corridors. **Pets:** Accepted.
[ASK] [S⊘] [✕] [ㄴM] [🛏] [🖵] [✕] [ⓚ]

AAA ◇◇◇ Quality Inn & Suites/Tradewinds SH
(707) 964-4761. **$69-$259.** 400 S Main St. 6 blks s on SR 1. Ext corridors. **Pets:** Other species. $10 daily fee/room. Designated rooms, service with restrictions, supervision.
[SAVE] [S⊘] [✕] [ㄴM] [🛏] [🖵] [🍴] [⇌] [ⓚ]

AAA ◇◇ Seabird Lodge M
(707) 964-4731. **$85-$145.** 191 South St. 0.8 mi n of Noyo River Bridge; 1 blk e off SR 1. Ext corridors. **Pets:** Medium. $10 daily fee/pet. Designated rooms, service with restrictions, supervision.
[SAVE] [S⊘] [✕] [🛏] [🖵] [⇌] [ⓚ]

◇◇ Super 8 M
(707) 964-4003. **$56-$140.** 888 S Main St. 0.5 mi s on SR 1; north end of Noyo River Bridge. Ext corridors. **Pets:** Accepted.
[ASK] [S⊘] [✕] [ㄴM] [🛏] [🖵]

AAA ◇◇◇ Surf Motel and Gardens M 🐾
(707) 964-5361. **$59-$139, 3 day notice.** 1220 S Main St. 1 mi s on SR 1; s of Noyo River Bridge; 0.3 mi n of jct SR 20. Ext corridors. **Pets:** Other species. $10 daily fee/pet. Service with restrictions, supervision.
[SAVE] [S⊘] [✕] [🛏] [🖵] [ⓚ]

GUALALA

◇◇ Gualala Country Inn M
(707) 884-4343. **$95-$175.** 47955 Center St. East side of SR 1. Ext/int corridors. **Pets:** Accepted.
[✕] [🛏] [🖵] [ⓚ]

AAA ◇◇◇ North Coast Country Inn BB 🐾
(707) 884-4537. **$164-$225, 5 day notice.** 34591 S Hwy 1. On SR 1, 4.5 mi n. Ext corridors. **Pets:** Dogs only. $25 one-time fee/pet. Designated rooms, service with restrictions, supervision.
[SAVE] [✕] [🛏] [🖵] [ⓚ] [ⓦ] [☎]

◇◇ Surf Motel M
(707) 884-3571. **$105-$190.** 39170 S Hwy 1. Center. Ext/int corridors. **Pets:** Accepted.
[✕] [🛏] [🖵] [ⓚ]

GUERNEVILLE

AAA ◇◇◇ Ferngrove Cottages CA 🐾
(707) 869-8105. **$89-$269, 3 day notice.** 16650 Hwy 116. On SR 116, just sw. Ext corridors. **Pets:** Other species. $15 daily fee/pet. Designated rooms, service with restrictions, supervision.
[SAVE] [S⊘] [✕] [ㄴM] [🛏] [🖵] [⇌] [✕] [ⓚ] [☎]

HEALDSBURG

AAA ◇◇◇ Americas Best Value Inn & Suites M
(707) 433-5548. **$89-$249.** 74 Healdsburg Ave. US 101, exit Central Healdsburg, just e. Ext corridors. **Pets:** Small, dogs only. $10 daily fee/pet. Service with restrictions, supervision.
[SAVE] [S⊘] [✕] [ㄴM] [🛏] [🖵]

AAA ◇◇◇ Best Western Dry Creek Inn SH 🐾
(707) 433-0300. **$105-$299.** 198 Dry Creek Rd. US 101, exit Dry Creek Rd, just e. Ext corridors. **Pets:** $25 daily fee/room. Designated rooms, service with restrictions, supervision.
[SAVE] [S⊘] [✕] [ㄴM] [🛏] [🖵] [⇌]

▼▼▼▼ Hotel Healdsburg **SH**
(707) 431-2800. **Call for rates.** 25 Matheson St. On the Plaza. Int corridors. **Pets:** Accepted.

[X] [&M] [■] [■] [¶] [≈] [X]

JENNER

◇◇◇ ▼▼▼▼ Jenner Inn & Cottages **CI**
(707) 865-2377. **$118-$378, 21 day notice.** 10400 Hwy 1. On SR 1 at SR 116. Ext corridors. **Pets:** Accepted.

[SAVE] [S○] [X] [&M] [■] [■] [¶] [X] [W]

LAKEPORT

▼▼ Konocti Vista Casino Resort & Marina **M**
(707) 262-1900. **Call for rates.** 2755 Mission Rancheria Rd. 3 mi se on Soda Bay Rd. Ext corridors. **Pets:** Accepted.

[X] [■] [≈]

LEGGETT

◇◇◇ ▼▼ Redwoods River Resort **CA**
(707) 925-6249. **$69-$150, 7 day notice.** 75000 Hwy 101. 6.5 mi n of jct SR 1. Ext corridors. **Pets:** Accepted.

[SAVE] [X] [■] [■] [≈] [X] [X] [Z]

LITTLE RIVER

◇◇◇ ▼▼▼▼ Auberge Mendocino-Rachel's Inn **BB** ❀
(707) 937-0088. **$355, 21 day notice.** 8200 N Hwy 1. On SR 1, 2 mi s of Mendocino. Ext/int corridors. **Pets:** Medium, dogs only. $100 deposit/room, $35 one-time fee/pet. Designated rooms, service with restrictions, supervision.

[SAVE] [S○] [X] [■] [■] [X] [Z]

▼▼▼▼ The Inn at Schoolhouse Creek **BB**
(707) 937-5525. **$145-$250, 7 day notice.** 7051 N Hwy 1. On SR 1, 0.8 mi s of Van Damme State Park entrance. Ext corridors. **Pets:** Accepted.

[A$K] [S○] [X] [■] [■] [X]

▼▼▼▼ Little River Inn **CI**
(707) 937-5942. **$95-$325, 5 day notice.** 7901 N Hwy 1. On N SR 1. Ext/int corridors. **Pets:** Accepted.

[A$K] [X] [■] [■] [¶] [X] [X]

◇◇◇ ▼▼▼▼ Stevenswood Spa Resort **CI** ❀
(707) 937-2810. **$159-$965.** 8211 SR 1. 2 mi s of Mendocino. Int corridors. **Pets:** Other species. $50 one-time fee/room.

[SAVE] [S○] [X] [■] [■] [¶] [X] [X]

MENDOCINO

▼▼▼▼ Abigail's Bed & Breakfast **BB**
(707) 937-0934. **Call for rates.** 951 Ukiah St. Just e of Lansing St; center. Ext/int corridors. **Pets:** Accepted.

[X] [■] [■] [X] [Z]

▼▼▼▼ Agate Cove Inn **CA**
(707) 937-0551. **$149-$339, 14 day notice.** 11201 N Lansing St. Just w on Little Lake Rd from jct SR 1, 0.6 mi n. Ext corridors. **Pets:** Accepted.

[A$K] [X] [■] [X] [Z]

◇◇◇ ▼▼▼ Blackberry Inn **M** ❀
(707) 937-5281. **Call for rates.** 44951 Larkin Rd. Just e of jct SR 1. Ext corridors. **Pets:** $10 daily fee/pet. Designated rooms, supervision.

[SAVE] [X] [■] [■] [X]

▼▼▼▼ Hill House Inn **CI**
(707) 937-0554. **Call for rates.** 10701 Pallette Dr. Just w on Little Lake St from jct SR 1, just n on Lansing St. Ext corridors. **Pets:** Accepted.

[X] [■] [■] [¶] [X]

▼▼▼▼ MacCallum House Inn **CI**
(707) 937-0289. **$95-$395, 7 day notice.** 45020 Albion St. Just w of Lansing St; center. Ext/int corridors. **Pets:** Accepted.

[A$K] [S○] [X] [■] [■] [¶] [X] [X]

◇◇◇ ▼▼▼ ▼▼▼ Stanford Inn by the Sea & Spa **CI** ❀
(707) 937-5615. **$215-$470, 7 day notice.** 44850 Comptche-Ukiah Rd. SR 1, exit Comptche-Ukiah Rd, just e. Ext corridors. **Pets:** Other species. $30 one-time fee/pet. Supervision.

[SAVE] [S○] [X] [&M] [■] [■] [¶] [≈] [X] [X]

NAPA

◇◇◇ ▼▼▼ The Chablis Inn **M** ❀
(707) 257-1944. **$89-$199, 3 day notice.** 3360 Solano Ave. Just w off SR 29 via Redwood Rd, then just s. Ext corridors. **Pets:** Dogs only. $10 daily fee/pet. Designated rooms, service with restrictions, supervision.

[SAVE] [S○] [X] [&M] [■] [■] [≈]

◇◇◇ ▼ Discovery Inn **M**
(707) 253-0892. **$75-$190, 3 day notice.** 500 Silverado Tr. 1.5 mi s of Lincoln Ave. Ext corridors. **Pets:** Small. $15 one-time fee/pet. Supervision.

[SAVE] [S○] [X] [■]

◇◇◇ ▼▼▼▼ Embassy Suites Napa Valley **SH** ❀
(707) 253-9540. **$129-$379.** 1075 California Blvd. SR 29, exit 1st St E. Ext/int corridors. **Pets:** Medium, other species. $75 one-time fee/room. Designated rooms, service with restrictions.

[SAVE] [X] [&M] [■] [■] [¶] [≈] [X]

◇◇◇ ▼▼▼▼ The Napa Inn **BB**
(707) 257-1444. **$120-$295, 10 day notice.** 1137 Warren St. SR 29, exit 1st St, 0.5 mi e, then 0.3 mi n. Int corridors. **Pets:** $20 daily fee/pet. Designated rooms, service with restrictions, supervision.

[SAVE] [S○] [X] [&M] [■] [■]

▼▼▼▼ Napa River Inn **SH**
(707) 251-8500. **$199-$599.** 500 Main St. Downtown. Int corridors. **Pets:** Accepted.

[A$K] [S○] [X] [&M] [■] [■]

◇◇◇ ▼ Napa Valley Redwood Inn **M** ❀
(707) 257-6111. **$67-$150, 3 day notice.** 3380 Solano Ave. Just w off SR 29 via Redwood Rd, just s. Ext corridors. **Pets:** $10 daily fee/pet. Service with restrictions, supervision.

[SAVE] [S○] [X] [&M] [■] [≈]

OCCIDENTAL

◇◇◇ ▼▼▼ Occidental Lodge **M**
(707) 874-3623. **$94-$145.** 3610 Bohemian Hwy. In the village. Ext corridors. **Pets:** Medium. $8 daily fee/pet. Service with restrictions, supervision.

[SAVE] [X] [&M] [■] [■] [≈]

PETALUMA

◇◇◇ ▼▼▼▼ Best Western Petaluma Inn **SH**
(707) 763-0994. **$89-$179.** 200 S McDowell Blvd. US 101, exit Washington St, 1 blk e. Ext corridors. **Pets:** $10 one-time fee/pet. Service with restrictions, supervision.

[SAVE] [S○] [X] [&M] [■] [■] [≈]

◇◇◇ ▼▼▼▼ Quality Inn-Petaluma **SH**
(707) 664-1155. **$99-$219.** 5100 Montero Way. US 101, exit Old Redwood Hwy-Penngrove northbound; exit Petaluma Blvd N-Penngrove southbound (east side). Ext/int corridors. **Pets:** $15 daily fee/room. Service with restrictions, supervision.

[SAVE] [S○] [X] [&M] [■] [■] [≈] [X]

Sheraton Sonoma County-Petaluma 🆂🅷 🐾
(707) 283-2888. **Call for rates.** 745 Baywood Dr. US 101, exit SR 116 (Lakeville Hwy), just se. Int corridors. **Pets:** Medium. Designated rooms, service with restrictions, supervision.
SAVE ⬛ ⬛ ⬛ ⬛ ⬛ ⬛ ⬛ ⬛

ROHNERT PARK

Best Western Inn 🆂🅷
(707) 584-7435. **$89-$130.** 6500 Redwood Dr. US 101, exit Rohnert Park Expwy, just w. Ext corridors. **Pets:** Accepted.
SAVE ⬛ ⬛ ⬛ ⬛ ⬛

ST. HELENA

El Bonita Motel 🆂🅷
(707) 963-3216. **Call for rates.** 195 Main St. 0.8 mi s on SR 29. Ext corridors. **Pets:** Medium, other species. $15 daily fee/pet. Service with restrictions.
SAVE ⬛ ⬛ ⬛ ⬛ ⬛

Harvest Inn 🆂🅷
(707) 963-9463. **$469-$749, 7 day notice.** One Main St. 1.5 mi s on SR 29. Ext corridors. **Pets:** Accepted.
SAVE ⬛ ⬛ ⬛ ⬛ ⬛ ⬛

SANTA ROSA

Americas Best Value Inn Ⓜ
(707) 523-3480. **$70-$149.** 1800 Santa Rosa Ave. US 101, exit Baker Ave northbound; exit Corby Ave southbound. Ext corridors. **Pets:** Accepted.
SAVE ⬛ ⬛ ⬛ ⬛

Best Western Garden Inn 🆂🅷 🐾
(707) 546-4031. **$89-$149.** 1500 Santa Rosa Ave. US 101, exit Baker Ave northbound; exit Corby Ave southbound. Ext corridors. **Pets:** Medium, dogs only. $15 daily fee/pet. Designated rooms, service with restrictions, supervision.
SAVE ⬛ ⬛ ⬛ ⬛ ⬛ ⬛ ⬛

Days Inn 🆂🅷
(707) 568-1011. **$59-$139.** 3345 Santa Rosa Ave. US 101, exit Todd Rd, 0.5 mi n. Ext corridors. **Pets:** $10 daily fee/pet. Designated rooms, service with restrictions, supervision.
SAVE ⬛ ⬛ ⬛ ⬛

Flamingo Resort and Spa 🆂🅷
(707) 545-8530. **Call for rates.** 2777 4th St. Off SR 12; at Farmers Ln. Int corridors. **Pets:** Accepted.
SAVE ⬛ ⬛ ⬛ ⬛ ⬛ ⬛ ⬛

Hillside Inn Motel Ⓜ
(707) 546-9353. **$84-$99, 3 day notice.** 2901 4th St. US 101, 2.5 mi e on SR 12; at Farmers Ln and 4th St. Ext corridors. **Pets:** Accepted.
SAVE ⬛ ⬛ ⬛ ⬛ ⬛

Hilton Sonoma Wine Country 🆂🅷
(707) 523-7555. **Call for rates.** 3555 Round Barn Blvd. 2.5 mi n on US 101, exit Mendocino Ave/Old Redwood Hwy; just ne at top of hill. Int corridors. **Pets:** Accepted.
⬛ ⬛ ⬛ ⬛ ⬛ ⬛

Holiday Inn Express 🆂🅷
(707) 545-9000. **$119-$269.** 870 Hopper Ave. US 101, exit Mendocino Ave/Old Redwood Hwy northbound, just w; exit Hopper Ave southbound. Ext corridors. **Pets:** Medium, dogs only. $25 one-time fee/room. Designated rooms, service with restrictions, supervision.
SAVE ⬛ ⬛ ⬛ ⬛ ⬛

Sandman Inn 🆂🅷 🐾
(707) 544-8570. **$89-$125, 3 day notice.** 3421 Cleveland Ave. US 101, exit W Mendocino Ave/Old Redwood Hwy. Ext corridors. **Pets:** Dogs only. $25 one-time fee/room. Service with restrictions, supervision.
SAVE ⬛ ⬛ ⬛ ⬛ ⬛

Santa Rosa Downtown Travelodge Ⓜ
(707) 544-4141. **Call for rates.** 635 Healdsburg Ave. 3 blks off US 101 via College Ave; at Mendocino Ave. Ext corridors. **Pets:** Accepted.
SAVE ⬛ ⬛ ⬛ ⬛ ⬛

Travelodge Ⓜ
(707) 542-3472. **$65-$150.** 1815 Santa Rosa Ave. 1.5 mi s on US 101 business route; US 101, exit Baker Ave northbound; exit Corby Ave southbound. Ext corridors. **Pets:** $15 daily fee/pet. Service with restrictions, supervision.
SAVE ⬛ ⬛ ⬛ ⬛ ⬛

SONOMA

Best Western Sonoma Valley Inn 🆂🅷 🐾
(707) 938-9200. **$169-$349, 3 day notice.** 550 2nd St W. 1 blk w of town plaza. Ext corridors. **Pets:** Other species. $30 one-time fee/room. Service with restrictions, crate.
SAVE ⬛ ⬛ ⬛ ⬛ ⬛

THE SEA RANCH

Sea Ranch Lodge 🆂🅷 🐾
(707) 785-2371. **$230-$495, 7 day notice.** 60 Sea Walk Dr. Just w of SR 1. Ext corridors. **Pets:** Medium, dogs only. $50 one-time fee/pet. Designated rooms, service with restrictions, supervision.
SAVE ⬛ ⬛ ⬛ ⬛ ⬛ ⬛ ⬛

UKIAH

Americas Best Value Inn Ⓜ
(707) 462-6657. **$49-$109.** 1070 S State St. US 101, exit Talmage Rd, 1 mi w. Ext corridors. **Pets:** Other species. $10 daily fee/pet. Service with restrictions, crate.
SAVE ⬛ ⬛ ⬛ ⬛

Days Inn Ⓜ
(707) 462-7584. **$69-$199, 7 day notice.** 950 N State St. US 101, exit N State St, 0.5 mi s. Ext corridors. **Pets:** Medium, other species. $10 daily fee/pet. Designated rooms, service with restrictions, supervision.
SAVE ⬛ ⬛ ⬛ ⬛

Discovery Inn 🆂🅷 🐾
(707) 462-8873. **$79-$110.** 1340 N State St. 1.5 mi n on US 101 business route; US 101, exit N State St. Ext corridors. **Pets:** $25 one-time fee/room. Designated rooms, service with restrictions, supervision.
SAVE ⬛ ⬛ ⬛ ⬛ ⬛

Rodeway Inn Ⓜ
(707) 462-2906. **$59-$89.** 1050 S State St. US 101, exit Talmage Rd, 0.5 mi w. Ext corridors. **Pets:** Accepted.
SAVE ⬛ ⬛ ⬛ ⬛ ⬛

Super 8 Ⓜ 🐾
(707) 468-8181. **$49-$119.** 693 S Orchard Ave. US 101, exit Gobbi St W. Ext corridors. **Pets:** Other species. $10 daily fee/pet. Designated rooms, supervision.
SAVE ⬛ ⬛ ⬛ ⬛ ⬛

UPPER LAKE

Super 8 Motel Ⓜ
(707) 275-0888. **$59-$169, 3 day notice.** 450 E Hwy 20. SR 29, 0.5 mi e. Ext corridors. **Pets:** Dogs only. $10 daily fee/pet. Service with restrictions, supervision.
SAVE ⬛ ⬛ ⬛ ⬛ ⬛ ⬛

WILLITS

 Baechtel Creek Inn & Spa 🅜 ❀
(707) 459-9063. **$90-$200.** 101 Gregory Ln. US 101, just w. Ext corridors. **Pets:** Small, dogs only. $25 one-time fee/pet. Designated rooms, service with restrictions, supervision.

[SAVE] [S◐] [✕] [🛏] [💻] [🏊]

YOUNTVILLE

 Vintage Inn 🆂🅷
(707) 944-1112. **$280-$695, 7 day notice.** 6541 Washington St. SR 29, exit Yountville; center. Ext corridors. **Pets:** Accepted.

[SAVE] [S◐] [✕] [⅄M] [🛏] [💻] [🏊] [✕]

END AREA

WOODLAND

📐 ▼▼ Days Inn 🆂🅷
(530) 666-3800. **$75-$109.** 1524 E Main St. I-5, exit Main St (Woodland) northbound; exit SR 113 (Davis) southbound. Int corridors. **Pets:** Dogs only. $10 daily fee/pet. Designated rooms, service with restrictions, supervision.

[SAVE] [S◐] [✕] [⅄M] [🛏] [💻] [🏊]

YERMO

📐 ▼▼▼ Oak Tree Inn 🆂🅷
(760) 254-1148. **$65-$75.** 35450 Yermo Rd. I-15, exit 191 (Ghost Town Rd), just e, then just s. Int corridors. **Pets:** Accepted.

[SAVE] [S◐] [✕] [🛏] [💻] [🍴] [🏊]

YOSEMITE NATIONAL PARK

▼▼ The Redwoods In Yosemite 🆅🅷
(209) 375-6666. **$172-$282, 30 day notice.** 8038 Chilnualna Falls Rd. 6 mi inside the southern entrance via SR 41 and Chilnualna Falls Rd. Ext corridors. **Pets:** Accepted.

[A$K] [S◐] [✕] [🛏] [💻]

YREKA

📐 ▼▼▼ Baymont Inn & Suites 🆂🅷
(530) 841-1300. **Call for rates.** 148 Moonlit Oaks Ave. I-5, exit SR 3 (Fort Jones Rd). Int corridors. **Pets:** Small. $10 one-time fee/pet. Designated rooms, service with restrictions, supervision.

[SAVE] [✕] [🛏] [💻] [🏊] [✕]

📐 ▼▼▼ Best Western Miner's Inn 🆂🅷 🐾
(530) 842-4355. **$90-$138.** 122 E Miner St. I-5, exit Central Yreka, just w. Ext corridors. **Pets:** $10 daily fee/pet. Service with restrictions, supervision.

[SAVE] [S◐] [✕] [🛏] [💻] [🏊] [✕]

📐 ▼▼ Comfort Inn 🆂🅷
(530) 842-1612. **Call for rates.** 1804-B Fort Jones Rd. I-5, exit SR 3 (Fort Jones Rd). Int corridors. **Pets:** Medium, other species. $50 deposit/pet, $10 one-time fee/pet. Designated rooms, service with restrictions, supervision.

[SAVE] [✕] [⅄M] [🛏] [💻] [🏊]

📐 ▼ Econo Lodge Inn & Suites 🅜
(530) 842-4404. **Call for rates.** 526 S Main St. I-5, exit Central Yreka, 0.3 mi s. Ext corridors. **Pets:** Medium. $20 deposit/pet, $10 daily fee/pet. Designated rooms, service with restrictions, supervision.

[SAVE] [✕] [⅄M] [🛏] [💻] [🏊]

📐 ▼ Mountain View Inn/Motel 🅜
(530) 842-1940. **$55-$58.** 801 N Main St. I-5, exit Montague Rd, 0.5 mi w. Ext corridors. **Pets:** Very small. $5 daily fee/pet. Service with restrictions, supervision.

[SAVE] [S◐] [✕] [🛏] [💻]

📐 ▼ Rodeway Inn 🅜 🐾
(530) 842-4412. **$47-$67.** 1235 S Main St. I-5, exit 775 southbound, 0.5 mi s on SR 3; exit 773 northbound, 0.9 mi n on SR 3. Ext corridors. **Pets:** Other species. $25 deposit/room, $5 daily fee/pet. Service with restrictions, supervision.

[SAVE] [S◐] [✕] [🛏] [🏊]

📐 ▼▼▼ Super 8-Yreka 🅜
(530) 842-5781. **$59-$75.** 136 Montague Rd. I-5, exit Montague Rd, just w. Ext corridors. **Pets:** $10 daily fee/pet. Service with restrictions, supervision.

[SAVE] [S◐] [✕] [🛏] [💻] [🏊]

YUBA CITY

▼▼ Quality Inn & Suites 🆂🅷
(530) 674-0201. **Call for rates.** 4228 S Hwy 99. On SR 99, 4.5 mi s of SR 20. Ext corridors. **Pets:** Accepted.

[✕] [⅄M] [🛏] [💻] [🍴] [🏊]

YUCCA VALLEY

📐 ▼▼ Americas Best Value Inn & Suites-Oasis of Eden 🅜
(760) 365-6321. **$56-$136.** 56377 Twentynine Palms Hwy. 1 mi w of jct SR 62 and 247. Ext corridors. **Pets:** Accepted.

[SAVE] [S◐] [✕] [🛏] [💻] [🏊]

📐 ▼ Super 8 Motel 🅜
(760) 228-1773. **$69-$129.** 57096 Twentynine Palms Hwy. On SR 62, 0.3 mi w of jct SR 247. Int corridors. **Pets:** Accepted.

[SAVE] [✕] [🛏] [💻] [🏊]

COLORADO

ALAMOSA

◆◇◇ ▽▽▽ Best Western Alamosa Inn 🅂🄷 ❀
(719) 589-2567. **$70-$105.** 2005 W Main St. 1 mi w on US 160 and
285. Ext corridors. **Pets:** Medium. $15 one-time fee/pet. Service with
restrictions, supervision.
🆂🅰🆅🅴 🆂🔟 ⊠ 🖥 💻 ➰

▽▽▽ Holiday Inn Express Hotel & Suites 🅂🄷
(719) 589-4026. **$75-$150.** 3418 Mariposa St. 1.8 mi w on US 160. Int
corridors. **Pets:** Accepted.
🄰🅂🄺 ⊠ 🖥 💻 ➰ ⊗

◆◆◇ ▽▽▽ Inn of the Rio Grande 🅂🄷
(719) 589-5833. **$70-$89.** 333 Santa Fe Ave. Just e of jct SR 17 on US
160. Int corridors. **Pets:** Other species. $15 deposit/pet. Supervision.
🆂🅰🆅🅴 🆂🔟 ⊠ 🔟🄼 🖥 💻 🍴 ➰ ⊗

ASPEN

**▽▽▽▽ Aspen Meadows Resort, a Dolce Conference
Destination** 🄻🄷
(970) 925-4240. **$175-$600, 30 day notice.** 845 Meadows Rd. 3 blks n
of SR 82 via 7th Ave, just w. Ext/int corridors. **Pets:** Accepted.
🄰🅂🄺 🆂🔟 ⊠ 🖥 💻 🍴 ⊗ 🅺

▽▽▽▽ Aspen Mountain Lodge 🅂🄷
(970) 925-7650. **$116-$435, 7 day notice.** 311 W Main St. Just w on
SR 82; between 2nd and 3rd sts. Int corridors. **Pets:** Accepted.
🄰🅂🄺 ⊠ 🖥 💻 ➰

◆◆◇ ▽▽▽ ▽▽ Hotel Jerome 🅂🄷
(970) 920-1000. **Call for rates.** 330 E Main St. On SR 82; downtown.
Int corridors. **Pets:** Accepted.
🆂🅰🆅🅴 ⊠ 🍴 ➰ ⊗

▽▽▽▽ Hotel Lenado 🅂🄷 ❀
(970) 925-6246. **Call for rates.** 200 S Aspen St. Just s of SR 82 via
Aspen St at jct Hopkins St. Ext/int corridors. **Pets:** Designated rooms.
⊠ 🖥 💻

◆◆◇ ▽▽▽▽▽ The Little Nell 🄻🄷 ❀
(970) 920-4600. **$510-$5775, 30 day notice.** 675 E Durant Ave. Beside
the gondola at base of Aspen Mountain. Int corridors. **Pets:** Dogs only.
$50 daily fee/room. Service with restrictions, supervision.
🆂🅰🆅🅴 🆂🔟 🖥 💻 🍴 ➰ ⊗

▽▽▽▽ ▽▽ St. Regis Resort, Aspen 🄻🄷 ❀
(970) 920-3300. **$465-$1740, 30 day notice.** 315 E Dean St. SR 82, s
on Monarch St, then just e. Int corridors. **Pets:** $100 one-time fee/room.
Designated rooms, service with restrictions, supervision.
⊠ 🍴 ➰ ⊗

◆◆◇ ▽▽▽▽ Sky Hotel 🄻🄷
(970) 925-6760. **$199-$709, 30 day notice.** 709 E Durant Ave. At base
of Aspen Mountain. Ext/int corridors. **Pets:** Accepted.
🆂🅰🆅🅴 ⊠ 💻 🍴 ➰ ⊗

AVON

▽▽▽▽ Comfort Inn-Vail/Beaver Creek 🅂🄷
(970) 949-5511. **$79-$219.** 161 W Beaver Creek Blvd. I-70, exit 167,
just s on Avon Rd, then just w. Int corridors. **Pets:** Accepted.
🄰🅂🄺 🆂🔟 ⊠ 🖥 💻 ➰

BEAVER CREEK

**◆◆◇ ▽▽▽▽▽▽ The Ritz-Carlton, Bachelor
Gulch** 🄻🄷 ❀
(970) 748-6200. **$273-$394, 9 day notice.** 130 Daybreak Ridge. I-70,
exit 167, s on Avon and Village rds (beyond gatehouse), w on Prater
Rd, follow signs to Bachelor Gulch Village. Int corridors. **Pets:** Large,
dogs only. $125 one-time fee/room. Service with restrictions, supervision.
🆂🅰🆅🅴 🆂🔟 ⊠ 🔟🄼 💻 🍴 ➰ ⊗

BOULDER

◆◆◇ ▽▽▽▽ Best Western Boulder Inn 🅂🄷
(303) 449-3800. **$89-$149.** 770 28th St. US 36 (28th St) at Baseline Rd
(SR 93). Int corridors. **Pets:** Medium. $100 deposit/room. Designated
rooms, supervision.
🆂🅰🆅🅴 🆂🔟 ⊠ 🖥 💻 🍴 ➰ ⊗

▽▽▽▽ Boulder Broker Inn 🅂🄷
(303) 444-3330. **$79-$299.** 555 30th St. US 36 (28th St), exit Baseline
Rd (SR 93), 0.3 mi e to 30th St, then just s. Int corridors.
Pets: Accepted.
🄰🅂🄺 🆂🔟 ⊠ 🖥 💻 🍴 ➰ ⊗

◆◆◇ ▽▽▽▽ Boulder Outlook Hotel & Suites 🅂🄷 ❀
(303) 443-3322. **$69-$199.** 800 28th St. US 36 (28th St), exit Baseline
Rd (SR 93) via Frontage Rd. Ext/int corridors. **Pets:** $10 daily fee/room.
Designated rooms, service with restrictions, crate.
🆂🅰🆅🅴 🆂🔟 ⊠ 🖥 💻 🍴 ➰ ⊗

◆◆◇ ▽▽▽ Boulder University Inn 🄼 ❀
(303) 417-1700. **$60-$119.** 1632 Broadway. US 36 (28th St), exit Baseline (SR 93) Rd, 0.3 mi s, then 3 mi nw. Ext corridors. **Pets:** Medium,
other species. $100 deposit/pet, $15 daily fee/pet. Designated rooms,
service with restrictions, supervision.
🆂🅰🆅🅴 🆂🔟 ⊠ 🖥 💻 ➰

◇◇ ▼▼◇ Foot of The Mountain Motel Ⓜ
(303) 442-5688. **$70-$90.** 200 Arapahoe Ave. 1.8 mi w of US 36 (28th St). Ext corridors. **Pets:** Large. $50 deposit/room, $5 daily fee/pet. Designated rooms, service with restrictions, supervision.
[SAVE] [✕] [🛢] [💻] [🐾]

▼▼◇ Holiday Inn Express 🆂🅷
(303) 442-6600. **$103-$189.** 4777 N Broadway. 3 mi n of Pearl Street Pedestrian Mall; jct US 36 (28th St), 0.3 mi s. Int corridors. **Pets:** Accepted.
[ASK] [S🌀] [✕] [🛢] [💻] [🌊]

▼▼◇◇ Homewood Suites by Hilton 🆂🅷
(303) 499-9922. **$189.** 4950 Baseline Rd. 1.2 mi e of US 36 (28th St); Jct SR 157 (Foothills Pkwy), just w; entry off Baseline Rd. Ext/int corridors. **Pets:** Accepted.
[ASK] [S🌀] [✕] [🛢] [💻] [🌊] [✕]

◇◇ ▼▼◇◇ Millennium Harvest House Boulder 🅻🅷
(303) 443-3850. **$109-$265.** 1345 28th St. Just s of jct Arapahoe Ave and US 36 (28th St). Int corridors. **Pets:** Accepted.
[SAVE] [S🌀] [✕] [💻] [🍽] [🌊] [✕]

◇◇ ▼▼◇◇ Quality Inn & Suites Boulder
　　　　　Creek 🆂🅷 🐾
(303) 449-7550. **$79-$149.** 2020 Arapahoe Ave. US 36 (28th St), 0.5 mi w. Ext/int corridors. **Pets:** Medium, other species. $100 deposit/room, $15 daily fee/pet. Designated rooms, service with restrictions, supervision.
[SAVE] [S🌀] [✕] [🛢] [💻] [🌊] [✕]

▼▼◇▼ Residence Inn by Marriott 🆂🅷
(303) 449-5545. **$208-$230.** 3030 Center Green Dr. 0.5 mi e of US 36 (28th St), e on Valmont Rd; from Foothills Pkwy, just w on Valmont Rd. Ext corridors. **Pets:** Accepted.
[ASK] [S🌀] [✕] [🛢] [💻] [🌊] [✕]

BRECKENRIDGE

▼◇▼◇ Great Divide Lodge 🅻🅷
(970) 547-5550. **$118-$450, 21 day notice.** 550 Village Rd. Jct Main St, just w on S Park Ave, then just sw. Int corridors. **Pets:** Accepted.
[ASK] [S🌀] [✕] [🅼] [🛢] [💻] [🍽] [🌊] [✕] [🐾]

▼◇▼◇ The Village at Breckenridge Hotel 🆂🅷
(970) 453-2000. **Call for rates.** 535 S Park Ave. 0.3 mi w of Main St. Int corridors. **Pets:** Accepted.
[✕] [🅼] [🛢] [💻] [✕]

BROOMFIELD

▼◇ ▼◇ Hilltop Inn Guesthouse & Suites 🅶🅸
(303) 469-3900. **$109-$129 (no credit cards).** 9009 Jeffco Airport Ave. US 36 (Boulder Tpke), exit US 287/CR 121, 0.4 mi s, then just w. Ext corridors. **Pets:** Accepted.
[ASK] [S🌀] [✕] [🛢] [🍽]

◇◇ ▼◇▼◇▼◇ Omni Interlocken Resort 🅻🅷
(303) 438-6600. **$117-$315.** 500 Interlocken Blvd. US 36 (Boulder Tpke), exit Interlocken Loop, 0.4 mi s, they 0.4 mi e. Int corridors. **Pets:** Accepted.
[SAVE] [S🌀] [✕] [🅼] [🛢] [💻] [🍽] [🌊] [✕]

▼◇ ▼◇ TownePlace Suites by Marriott
　　　　Boulder/Broomfield 🆂🅷
(303) 466-2200. **$164-$175.** 480 Flatiron Blvd. US 36 (Boulder Tpke), exit Interlocken Loop, 0.4 mi s, just w on Interlocken Blvd, then just s. Int corridors. **Pets:** Accepted.
[ASK] [S🌀] [✕] [🅼] [🛢] [💻] [🌊]

BRUSH

▼◇ ▼◇ Econo Lodge Brush 🆂🅷
(970) 842-5146. **$56-$80.** 1208 N Colorado Ave. I-76, exit 90B, just n. Ext/int corridors. **Pets:** Accepted.
[ASK] [S🌀] [✕] [🛢] [💻] [🌊]

▼◇ ▼◇ Microtel Inn 🆂🅷
(970) 842-4241. **$62-$82, 7 day notice.** 975 N Colorado Ave. I-76, exit 90A, just s. Int corridors. **Pets:** Accepted.
[ASK] [S🌀] [✕] [🛢] [💻] [🌊]

BUENA VISTA

◇◇ ▼◇ ◇ Alpine Lodge Ⓜ
(719) 395-2415. **Call for rates.** 12845 Hwy 24 & 285. 2 mi s on US 24, 0.5 mi e on US 24 and 285. Ext corridors. **Pets:** Accepted.
[SAVE] [✕]

◇◇ ▼◇ ▼◇ Super 8 Motel Buena Vista 🆂🅷
(719) 395-8888. **Call for rates.** 530 N US 24. On US 24, 0.3 mi n. Ext/int corridors. **Pets:** Accepted.
[SAVE] [✕] [🛢] [💻] [🌊]

BURLINGTON

▼◇ ▼◇ Burlington Comfort Inn 🆂🅷
(719) 346-7676. **$75-$120.** 282 S Lincoln St. I-70, exit 437, just n on US 385. Int corridors. **Pets:** Accepted.
[ASK] [S🌀] [✕] [🛢] [💻] [🌊]

◇◇ ◇ Chaparral Motor Inn Ⓜ
(719) 346-5361. **$45-$59.** 405 S Lincoln St. I-70, exit 437, just n on jct US 385. Ext corridors. **Pets:** $10 daily fee/pet. Designated rooms, service with restrictions, crate.
[SAVE] [✕] [🛢] [💻] [🌊]

CANON CITY

◇◇ ▼◇ ▼◇ Budget Host Royal Gorge Inn Ⓜ
(719) 269-1100. **$55-$129.** 217 N Raynolds Ave. 1 mi e on US 50, just n. Int corridors. **Pets:** Accepted.
[SAVE] [S🌀] [✕] [🛢] [💻] [🌊]

▼◇ ▼◇ Comfort Inn 🆂🅷
(719) 276-6900. **Call for rates.** 311 Royal Gorge Blvd. On US 50; just w of downtown. Int corridors. **Pets:** Accepted.
[✕] [🅼] [🛢] [💻] [🌊]

▼◇ ▼◇ Holiday Inn Express 🆂🅷
(719) 275-2400. **$100-$115, 7 day notice.** 110 Latigo Ln. 2.5 mi e of SR 115 on US 50. Int corridors. **Pets:** Accepted.
[ASK] [S🌀] [✕] [🅼] [🛢] [💻] [🌊]

▼◇ ▼◇ Quality Inn & Suites 🆂🅷
(719) 275-8676. **$59-$129.** 3075 E Hwy 50. 12 mi w of jct SR 115; center. Int corridors. **Pets:** Accepted.
[ASK] [S🌀] [✕] [🛢] [💻] [🍽] [🌊]

CARBONDALE

◇◇ ▼◇▼◇ Comfort Inn & Suites 🆂🅷 🐾
(970) 963-8880. **$119-$240.** 920 Cowen Dr. Jct of SR 82 and 133, just s via signs. Int corridors. **Pets:** Medium. $25 daily fee/pet. Designated rooms, service with restrictions, supervision.
[SAVE] [S🌀] [✕] [🛢] [💻] [🌊] [✕]

◇◇ ▼◇ ▼◇ Days Inn-Carbondale 🆂🅷
(970) 963-9111. **$109-$209, 3 day notice.** 950 Cowen Dr. Jct SR 82 and 133. Int corridors. **Pets:** $10 daily fee/pet. Service with restrictions, supervision.
[SAVE] [S🌀] [✕] [🛢] [🌊] [✕]

CASTLE ROCK

◇◇ ▼◇▼◇ Best Western Inn & Suites of Castle
　　　　　Rock 🆂🅷 🐾
(303) 814-8000. **$69-$149.** 595 Genoa Way. I-25, exit 184 (Meadows Pkwy), just w to Castleton Way, just s, then e. Int corridors. **Pets:** Medium. $15 daily fee/pet. Designated rooms, service with restrictions, supervision.
[SAVE] [S🌀] [🛢] [💻] [🌊]

△△△▽ ▽▼▽ Castle Rock Days Inn and Suites 🆂🅷
(303) 814-5825. **$54-$99, 30 day notice.** 4961 Castleton Way. I-25, exit 184 (Meadows Pkwy), 0.5 mi e, just s on Castleton Way, then just se. Int corridors. **Pets:** Medium. $10 daily fee/room. Service with restrictions, supervision.
🆂🅰🅴🅭🅭 🆂🆉 ☒ 🖥 💻 🏊

▽▼▽▼▽ Comfort Suites 🆂🅷
(303) 814-9999. **$64-$119.** 4755 Castleton Way. I-25, exit 184 (Meadows Pkwy), w to Castleton Way; entry on east side. Int corridors. **Pets:** Accepted.
🄰🅂🄺 🆂🅰 ☒ 🅶🅼 🖥 💻 🏊 ☒

▽▼▽▼▽ Hampton Inn 🆂🅷
(303) 660-9800. **Call for rates.** 4830 Castleton Way. I-25, exit 184 (Meadows Pkwy), sw to N Castleton Rd, just s, then e. Int corridors. **Pets:** Accepted.
☒ 🅶🅼 🖥 💻 🏊

▽▼▽▼▽ Holiday Inn Express 🆂🅷
(303) 660-9733. **$79-$139.** 884 Park St. I-25, exit 182, just w. Int corridors. **Pets:** Accepted.
🄰🅂🄺 🆂🅰 ☒ 🖥 💻 🏊

CEDAREDGE

△△△▽ ▽▼▽ Howard Johnson Express Inn 🆂🅷
(970) 856-7824. **Call for rates.** 530 S Grand Mesa Dr. Just s on SR 65. Int corridors. **Pets:** $10 daily fee/pet. Designated rooms, service with restrictions, supervision.
🆂🅰🅴🅭 ☒ 🖥 💻 🏊

CIMARRON

△△△▽ ▽▼▽ The Inn at Arrowhead 🅱🅱 🐾
(970) 862-8206. **$125-$175, 14 day notice.** 21401 Alpine Plateau Rd. 11 mi e; from US 50, 5.3 mi s on Dirt Rd; look for signs. Int corridors. **Pets:** Dogs only. $25 daily fee/pet. No service, supervision.
🆂🅰🅴 🆂🅰 ☒ 🍴 ☒ 🅺 🆆 🚗

COLORADO SPRINGS METROPOLITAN AREA

CHIPITA PARK

▽▼▽▼▽ Chipita Lodge B&B 🅱🅱
(719) 684-8454. **$100-$175, 7 day notice.** 9090 Chipita Park Rd. Jct US 24, just s on Fountain Blvd (Pine Peak Hwy), then 1.5 mi w; go right at fork. Ext/int corridors. **Pets:** Accepted.
🄰🅂🄺 🆂🅰 ☒ 🖥 💻 🅺

COLORADO SPRINGS

△△△▽ ▽▼▽ Airport Value Inn & Suites 🆂🅷
(719) 596-5588. **$60-$90.** 6875 Space Village Ave. I-25, exit 141, 1 mi e on Cimarron Ave, 0.7 mi n on Wahsatch Ave, 6.3 mi e on Platte Ave, then exit Space Village Ave. Ext/int corridors. **Pets:** Medium. $35 one-time fee/room. Service with restrictions, supervision.
🆂🅰🅴 🆂🅰 ☒ 🅶🅼 🖥 💻

△△△▽ ▽▼▽ Apollo Park Executive Suites 🅲🅾
(719) 634-0286. **$49-$105.** 805 S Circle Dr, 2-B. I-25, exit 138, 2.5 mi e. Int corridors. **Pets:** Small. $7 daily fee/pet. Designated rooms, service with restrictions, supervision.
🆂🅰🅴 🆂🅰 ☒ 🖥 💻 🏊

△△△▽ ▽▼▽ Best Western Airport Inn 🆂🅷
(719) 574-7707. **$79-$94.** 1780 Aeroplaza Dr. I-25, exit 139, 4.5 mi e on US 24 Bypass. Int corridors. **Pets:** Very small. $10 daily fee/pet. Designated rooms, service with restrictions, supervision.
🆂🅰🅴 🆂🅰 ☒ 🅶🅼 🖥 💻 🏊

△△△▽ ▽▼▽ Best Western Executive Inn & Suites 🆂🅷
(719) 576-2371. **Call for rates.** 1440 Harrison Rd. I-25, exit 138, just w; on northwest corner of interchange; entry through restaurant. Int corridors. **Pets:** Small, dogs only. $10 daily fee/pet. Designated rooms, service with restrictions, supervision.
🆂🅰🅴 ☒ 🅶🅼 🖥 💻 🏊

△△△▽ ▽▼▽▼▽ Best Western The Academy Hotel 🅻🅷
(719) 598-5770. **Call for rates.** 8110 N Academy Blvd. I-25, exit 150, just s. Int corridors. **Pets:** Accepted.
🆂🅰🅴 ☒ 🅶🅼 🖥 💻 🍴 🏊 ☒

△△△▽ ▽▼▽▼▽▼▽ The Broadmoor 🅻🅷 🐾
(719) 634-7711. **$290-$2500, 7 day notice.** 1 Lake Ave. I-25, exit 138, 3 mi w on Circle Dr (which becomes Lake Ave). Int corridors. **Pets:** Other species. $35 daily fee/pet. Service with restrictions, supervision.
🆂🅰🅴 ☒ 🅶🅼 🖥 💻 🍴 🏊 ☒

△△△▽ ▽▼▽▼▽ Cheyenne Mountain Resort 🅻🅷 🐾
(719) 538-4000. **$109-$279.** 3225 Broadmoor Valley Rd. I-25, exit 138, 1.4 mi w to SR 115, 0.5 mi s, just w on Clubhouse Dr, then just s. Ext/int corridors. **Pets:** Medium, dogs only. $35 deposit/room. Service with restrictions, crate.
🆂🅰🅴 ☒ 🖥 💻 🍴 🏊 ☒

△△△▽ ▽▼▽▼▽ Clarion Hotel Downtown 🆂🅷 🐾
(719) 471-8680. **$69-$199.** 314 W Bijou St. I-25, exit 142, just w. Int corridors. **Pets:** Medium, other species. $10 daily fee/pet. Designated rooms, service with restrictions.
🆂🅰🅴 🆂🅰 ☒ 🖥 💻 🍴 🏊

△△△▽ ▽▼▽▼▽ Comfort Inn North 🆂🅷
(719) 262-9000. **$69-$119.** 6450 Corporate Dr. I-25, exit 149 (Woodmen Rd), just w, then 0.3 mi s. Int corridors. **Pets:** Small, other species. $10 daily fee/pet. Designated rooms, service with restrictions, supervision.
🆂🅰🅴 🆂🅰 ☒ 🅶🅼 🖥 💻 🏊

△△△▽ ▽▼▽▼▽ Comfort Inn South 🆂🅷
(719) 579-6900. **$69-$149.** 1410 Harrison Rd. I-25, exit 138, just w to Rand Rd, then ne. Int corridors. **Pets:** Large, other species. $25 deposit/pet. Designated rooms, service with restrictions, supervision.
🆂🅰🅴 🆂🅰 ☒ 🖥 💻 🏊

△△△▽ ▽▼▽▼▽ Crowne Plaza Colorado Springs 🅻🅷
(719) 576-5900. **$89-$199.** 2886 S Circle Dr. I-25, exit 138, just e. Int corridors. **Pets:** Dogs only. $25 deposit/room, $25 one-time fee/room. Service with restrictions, supervision.
🆂🅰🅴 🆂🅰 ☒ 🖥 💻 🍴 🏊 ☒

▽▼▽ Days Inn-Air Force Academy 🆂🅷
(719) 266-1317. **Call for rates.** 8350 Razorback Rd. I-25, exit 150, just s, then e. Int corridors. **Pets:** Accepted.
☒ 🅶🅼 🖥 💻 🏊

▽▼▽▼▽ DoubleTree Hotel Colorado Springs, World Arena 🆂🅷
(719) 576-8900. **Call for rates.** 1775 E Cheyenne Mountain Blvd. I-25, exit 138, just w. Int corridors. **Pets:** Accepted.
☒ 🅶🅼 🖥 💻 🍴 🏊 ☒

▽▼▽▼▽ Drury Inn-Pikes Peak 🆂🅷
(719) 598-2500. **$63-$133.** 8155 N Academy Blvd. I-25, exit 150, just s, then e. Int corridors. **Pets:** Large, other species. Service with restrictions, supervision.
🄰🅂🄺 ☒ 🖥 💻 🏊

▼▼▼▼ Fairfield Inn by Marriott-South SH
(719) 576-1717. **$69-$139.** 2725 Geyser Dr. I-25, exit 138, just w to E Cheyenne Mountain Blvd, then just s. Int corridors. **Pets:** Accepted.
(ASK) (S∕D) (✕) (♿M) (🛏) (💻) (🏊)

◈◈◈ **▼▼▼▼ Hampton Inn & Suites Colorado Springs Air Force Academy** SH
(719) 598-6911. **$79-$169.** 1307 Republic Dr. I-25, exit 153, 0.5 mi e, then just s. Int corridors. **Pets:** Accepted.
(SAVE) (S∕D) (✕) (🛏) (💻) (🏊)

◈◈◈ **▼▼▼▼ Holiday Inn Express Air Force Academy** SH
(719) 592-9800. **$89-$199.** 7110 Commerce Center Dr. I-25, exit 149, just w on Woodmen Rd, then just n. Int corridors. **Pets:** Medium, dogs only. $25 daily fee/pet. Designated rooms, service with restrictions, supervision.
(SAVE) (S∕D) (✕) (♿M) (🛏) (💻) (🏊) (🐾)

◈◈◈ **▼▼▼▼ Homewood Suites by Hilton** SH
(719) 265-6600. **$99-$179.** 9130 Explorer Dr. I-25, exit 151, 0.8 mi e; across from Focus on the Family. Int corridors. **Pets:** Small, other species. $20 one-time fee/pet. Service with restrictions, crate.
(SAVE) (S∕D) (✕) (♿M) (🛏) (💻) (🏊)

▼▼▼▼ Homewood Suites by Hilton Colorado Springs Airport SH
(719) 574-2701. **$112-$134.** 2875 Zeppelin Rd. I-25, exit 139, 4 mi e on US 24 Bypass, 1.1 mi s on Powers Blvd, then just e. Int corridors. **Pets:** Small. $50 one-time fee/pet. Service with restrictions, crate.
(ASK) (S∕D) (✕) (🛏) (💻) (🏊) (🐾)

▼▼▼▼ Hyatt Summerfield Suites SH
(719) 268-9990. **Call for rates.** 5805 Delmonico Dr. I-25, exit 147, just nw, then e on Delmonico Dr; entry around the bank. Int corridors. **Pets:** Accepted.
(✕) (🛏) (💻) (🏊) (🐾)

▼▼▼▼ La Quinta Inn & Suites Colorado Springs (South/Airport) SH
(719) 527-4788. **$125.** 2750 Geyser Dr. I-25, exit 138 (Circle Dr), just w to Cheyenne Mountain Blvd, then just s. Int corridors. **Pets:** Other species. Service with restrictions, supervision.
(ASK) (S∕D) (✕) (♿M) (🛏) (💻) (🏊)

▼▼▼ La Quinta Inn Colorado Springs (Garden of the Gods) SH
(719) 528-5060. **$69-$109.** 4385 Sinton Rd. I-25, exit 146, just e. Ext/int corridors. **Pets:** Other species. Service with restrictions, supervision.
(ASK) (✕) (🛏) (💻) (🏊)

◈◈◈ **▼▼▼ Microtel Inn & Suites** SH 🐾
(719) 598-7500. **$59-$120.** 7265 Commerce Center Dr. I-25, exit 149, just w, then n. Int corridors. **Pets:** Other species. $20 one-time fee/room. Designated rooms, service with restrictions.
(SAVE) (S∕D) (✕) (♿M) (🛏) (💻) (🏊)

◈◈◈ **▼▼▼▼ Radisson Hotel Colorado Springs Airport** LH
(719) 597-7000. **$119-$185.** 1645 N Newport Rd. I-25, exit 139, 4.5 mi e on US 24 Bypass. Int corridors. **Pets:** Medium. $100 deposit/room, $25 one-time fee/pet. Designated rooms, service with restrictions, crate.
(SAVE) (S∕D) (✕) (♿M) (🛏) (💻) (🍴) (🏊) (🐾)

◈◈◈ **▼▼▼ Rainbow Lodge and Inn** M
(719) 632-4551. **Call for rates.** 3709 W Colorado Ave. I-25, exit 141, 2.5 mi w on US 24, just n on 31st St, then 0.7 mi w. Ext corridors. **Pets:** Accepted.
(SAVE) (✕) (🛏) (🏊)

▼▼▼ Ramada Limited East-Airport SH
(719) 596-7660. **Call for rates.** 520 N Murray Blvd. I-25, exit 141, 1 mi e on Cimarron Ave, 0.7 mi n on Wahsatch Ave, 3.7 mi e on Platte Ave, then just n. Ext/int corridors. **Pets:** Accepted.
(✕) (🛏) (💻) (🏊)

▼▼▼ Residence Inn by Marriott-Central SH
(719) 574-0370. **$164-$241.** 3880 N Academy Blvd. I-25, exit 146, 4.5 mi e on Garden of the Gods/Austin Bluffs Pkwy, then 0.3 mi s. Ext corridors. **Pets:** Large. $75 one-time fee/room.
(ASK) (S∕D) (✕) (🛏) (💻) (🏊) (🐾)

▼▼▼ Residence Inn by Marriott Colorado Springs North at Interquest Pkwy SH
(719) 388-9300. **$131-$164.** 9805 Federal Dr. I-25, exit 153, just e, then s. Int corridors. **Pets:** Accepted.
(ASK) (S∕D) (✕) (♿M) (🛏) (💻) (🏊) (🐾)

▼▼▼ Residence Inn by Marriott-Colorado Springs South SH
(719) 576-0101. **$89-$299.** 2765 Geyser Dr. I-25, exit 138, just w to E Cheyenne Mountain Blvd, then just s. Int corridors. **Pets:** Accepted.
(ASK) (S∕D) (✕) (♿M) (🛏) (💻) (🏊) (🐾)

◈◈◈ **▼▼▼ Rodeway Inn & Suites** SH 🐾
(719) 632-6651. **$40-$120.** 1623 S Nevada Ave. I-25, exit 140, just s. Ext corridors. **Pets:** Other species. $10 deposit/pet, $10 one-time fee/pet. Service with restrictions, supervision.
(SAVE) (S∕D) (✕) (🛏) (💻) (🏊)

◈◈◈ **▼▼▼ Sleep Inn** SH
(719) 260-6969. **$49-$149.** 1075 Kelly Johnson Blvd. I-25, exit 150, just s on Academy Blvd to Kelly Johnson Blvd, then w. Int corridors. **Pets:** Accepted.
(SAVE) (S∕D) (✕) (♿M) (💻)

◈◈◈ **▼▼ Stagecoach Motel** M 🐾
(719) 633-3894. **$39-$69, 4 day notice.** 1647 S Nevada Ave. I-25, exit 140, just s. Ext corridors. **Pets:** Small. $5 daily fee/pet. Service with restrictions, supervision.
(SAVE) (S∕D) (✕) (🛏) (💻)

◈◈◈ **▼▼▼▼ Staybridge Suites-Air Force Academy** SH
(719) 590-7829. **$119-$179.** 7130 Commerce Center Dr. I-25, exit 149, just w, then n. Int corridors. **Pets:** Accepted.
(SAVE) (S∕D) (✕) (♿M) (🛏) (💻) (🏊) (🐾)

▼▼▼▼ TownePlace Suites by Marriott-Colorado Springs SH 🐾
(719) 594-4447. **$175-$208.** 4760 Centennial Blvd. I-25, exit 146, 1 mi w on Garden of the Gods Rd, just n on Centennial Blvd, then first left. Int corridors. **Pets:** Other species. $100 one-time fee/room. Service with restrictions.
(ASK) (S∕D) (✕) (♿M) (🛏) (💻) (🏊)

▼▼▼▼ TownePlace Suites Colorado Springs South SH
(719) 638-0800. **Call for rates.** 1530 N Newport Rd. I-25, exit 139, 5 mi e on US 24 Bypass, then just n. Int corridors. **Pets:** Accepted.
(✕) (🛏) (💻) (🏊)

◈◈◈ **▼ Travel Inn** M
(719) 636-3986. **$40-$99.** 512 S Nevada Ave. I-25, exit 141, 0.7 mi e to Nevada Ave, then just s. Ext/int corridors. **Pets:** Other species. $20 deposit/pet, $5 daily fee/pet. Service with restrictions, supervision.
(SAVE) (S∕D) (✕) (🛏)

◈◈◈ **▼▼ Travelodge** SH
(719) 632-4600. **$50-$95.** 2625 Ore Mill Rd. I-25, exit 141, 2.3 mi nw on US 24; entry via 26th St. Int corridors. **Pets:** Large. $20 one-time fee/room. Service with restrictions, supervision.
(SAVE) (✕) (🛏) (💻) (🏊)

MANITOU SPRINGS

ⒶⒶⒶ ◈◈◈◈ Best Western Skyway Inn & Suites 🆂🅷
(719) 685-5991. **Call for rates.** 311 Manitou Ave. I-25, exit 141, 4 mi w on US 24, then just sw on US 24 business route. Ext corridors. **Pets:** Accepted.
🆂🅰🆅🅴 ⊠ 🔋 💻 ⊅

ⒶⒶⒶ ◈◈◈ El Colorado Lodge 🅒🅐
(719) 685-5485. **$56-$136.** 23 Manitou Ave. I-25, exit 141, 4 mi w on US 24, then just ne on US 24 business route. Ext corridors. **Pets:** Large. $75 deposit/room. Designated rooms, service with restrictions, crate.
🆂🅰🆅🅴 ⊠ 🔋 💻 ⊅ ⊠

ⒶⒶⒶ ◈◈◈ Park Row Lodge 🅼 ❀
(719) 685-5216. **$49-$79.** 54 Manitou Ave. I-25, exit 141, 4 mi w on US 24, then just ne on US 24 business route. Ext corridors. **Pets:** Small. $25 deposit/pet. Service with restrictions, supervision.
🆂🅰🆅🅴 🆂🅳 ⊠ 🔋

ⒶⒶⒶ ◈◈◈ Red Wing Motel 🅼
(719) 685-5656. **$39-$119.** 56 El Paso Blvd. I-25, exit 141, 4 mi w on US 24, just ne on US 24 business route/Manitou Ave, then just w on Beckers Ln. Ext corridors. **Pets:** Accepted.
🆂🅰🆅🅴 🆂🅳 ⊠ 🔋 💻 ⊅

ⒶⒶⒶ ◈◈◈ Silver Saddle Motel 🅼
(719) 685-5611. **$60-$90.** 215 Manitou Ave. I-25, exit 141, 4 mi w on US 24, then just sw on US 24 business route. Ext corridors. **Pets:** Other species. Service with restrictions, supervision.
🆂🅰🆅🅴 🆂🅳 ⊠ 🔋 💻 ⊅

END METROPOLITAN AREA

CORTEZ

ⒶⒶⒶ ◈◈◈◈ Best Western Turquoise Inn & Suites 🆂🅷 ❀
(970) 565-3778. **$80-$162.** 535 E Main St. On US 160. Ext corridors. **Pets:** $15 one-time fee/room. Designated rooms, service with restrictions.
🆂🅰🆅🅴 🆂🅳 ⊠ 🔋 💻 ⊅

ⒶⒶⒶ ◈◈ Budget Host Inn 🅼
(970) 565-3738. **$42-$98.** 2040 E Main St. 1.3 mi e on US 160, w of jct SR 145. Ext corridors. **Pets:** Other species. $10 daily fee/pet. Designated rooms, service with restrictions, supervision.
🆂🅰🆅🅴 ⊠ 🔋 💻 ⊅

ⒶⒶⒶ ◈◈◈ Comfort Inn 🆂🅷 ❀
(970) 565-3400. **Call for rates.** 2321 E Main St. 1.3 mi e on US 160. Ext/int corridors. **Pets:** Large, other species. $10 one-time fee/room. Designated rooms, service with restrictions, supervision.
🆂🅰🆅🅴 ⊠ 🔋 💻 ⊅

◈◈ Econo Lodge 🅼
(970) 565-3474. **$39-$139.** 2020 E Main St. 1.3 mi e on US 160. Ext corridors. **Pets:** Accepted.
🅰🆂🅺 🆂🅳 ⊠ 🔋 💻 ⊅

ⒶⒶⒶ ◈◈◈◈ Holiday Inn Express 🆂🅷
(970) 565-6000. **$99-$159.** 2121 E Main St. 1.3 mi e on US 160. Int corridors. **Pets:** Small. Designated rooms, service with restrictions, supervision.
🆂🅰🆅🅴 ⊠ 🔋 💻 ⊪ ⊅ ⊠

ⒶⒶⒶ ◈◈◈ Rodeway Inn 🅼
(970) 565-3761. **$59-$109.** 1120 E Main St. 0.3 mi e on US 160. Ext/int corridors. **Pets:** Other species. $10 daily fee/pet. Designated rooms, service with restrictions, supervision.
🆂🅰🆅🅴 🆂🅳 ⊠ 🔋 💻 ⊅

ⒶⒶⒶ ◈◈◈ Tomahawk Lodge 🅼
(970) 565-8521. **$49-$99.** 728 S Broadway. 1 mi sw on US 160 and 491. Ext corridors. **Pets:** Dogs only. $25 deposit/pet. Designated rooms, service with restrictions, supervision.
🆂🅰🆅🅴 🆂🅳 ⊠ 💻 ⊅

CRAIG

ⒶⒶⒶ ◈◈◈◈ Best Western Deer Park Inn and Suites 🆂🅷
(970) 824-9282. **$89-$199.** 262 Commerce St (Hwy 13). Jct US 40, just 0.3 mi s on SR 13. Int corridors. **Pets:** Accepted.
🆂🅰🆅🅴 🆂🅳 ⊠ 🄼 🔋 💻 ⊅

ⒶⒶⒶ ◈◈◈ Black Nugget Motel 🅼
(970) 824-8161. **$69-$89, 7 day notice.** 2855 W Victory Way. 1.5 mi w on US 40, 0.3 mi w of jct SR 13. Ext corridors. **Pets:** Accepted.
🆂🅰🆅🅴 🆂🅳 ⊠ 🔋 💻

◈◈◈ Craig Holiday Inn 🆂🅷
(970) 824-4000. **$109-$209.** 300 S Hwy 13. Jct US 40, 0.3 mi s on SR 13. Int corridors. **Pets:** Accepted.
🅰🆂🅺 🆂🅳 ⊠ 🔋 💻 ⊪ ⊅ ⊠

CRESTED BUTTE

◈◈◈ Grand Lodge Crested Butte 🅛🅗
(970) 349-8000. **$89-$235, 3 day notice.** 6 Emmons Loop. 2.5 mi n on SR 135. Int corridors. **Pets:** Accepted.
🅰🆂🅺 🆂🅳 ⊠ 🔋 💻 ⊪ ⊅ ⊠ 🅰🅒

◈◈◈ Old Town Inn 🆂🅷
(970) 349-6184. **$79-$149, 14 day notice.** 708 6th St. Se on SR 135. Int corridors. **Pets:** Accepted.
🅰🆂🅺 🆂🅳 ⊠ 🔋

DELTA

ⒶⒶⒶ ◈◈◈ Best Western Sundance 🆂🅷
(970) 874-9781. **$90-$116, 7 day notice.** 903 Main St. 0.5 mi s on US 50. Ext corridors. **Pets:** Other species. $10 daily fee/pet. Service with restrictions, crate.
🆂🅰🆅🅴 🆂🅳 ⊠ 🔋 💻 ⊪ ⊅

◈◈◈ Comfort Inn 🆂🅷
(970) 874-1000. **Call for rates.** 180 Gunnison River Dr. Just n, w of jct US 50 and 92. Int corridors. **Pets:** Accepted.
⊠ 🔋 💻

ⒶⒶⒶ ◈◈ Riverwood Inn 🅼
(970) 874-5787. **$46-$90.** 677 US 50. 0.5 mi n. Int corridors. **Pets:** Accepted.
🆂🅰🆅🅴 🆂🅳 ⊠ 🔋 💻

ⒶⒶⒶ ◈◈◈ Southgate Inns 🅼
(970) 874-9726. **$56-$90.** 2124 S Main St. 1.5 mi s on US 50. Ext corridors. **Pets:** Small. $10 daily fee/pet. Service with restrictions, supervision.
🆂🅰🆅🅴 🆂🅳 ⊠ 🔋 💻 ⊅

DENVER METROPOLITAN AREA

AURORA

Best Western Gateway Inn & Suites SH
(720) 748-4800. **$69-$149.** 800 S Abilene St. I-225, exit 7 (Mississippi Ave), just e, then 3 blks n. Int corridors. **Pets:** Accepted.

SAVE SD X GM FI IP A X

Comfort Inn Denver Southeast SH
(303) 755-8000. **$69-$179.** 14071 E Iliff Ave. I-225, exit 5, just e. Int corridors. **Pets:** Accepted.

ASK SD X GM FI IP

Comfort Inn DIA Airport SH
(303) 367-5000. **Call for rates.** 16921 E 32nd Ave. I-70, exit 285, just s on Airport Blvd; on southeast corner. Int corridors. **Pets:** Large, other species. $10 daily fee/pet. Designated rooms, service with restrictions, supervision.

SAVE X GM FI IP A

Crestwood Suites Extended Stay Hotels SH
(303) 481-0379. **Call for rates.** 14090 E Evans Ave. I-225, exit 5 (E Iliff Ave), e to Blackhawk St, then 0.4 mi nw. Int corridors. **Pets:** Accepted.

X FI IP

Crystal Inn DIA SH
(303) 340-3800. **$149-$169.** 3300 N Ouray St. I-70, exit 285, just s on Airport Blvd, then w on 32nd Ave. Int corridors. **Pets:** Small. $25 one-time fee/room.

SAVE SD X GM FI IP A

Extended Stay Deluxe SH
(303) 337-7000. **Call for rates.** 14095 E Evans Ave. I-225, exit 5 (E Iliff Ave), just e to Blackhawk St, then 0.4 mi nw. Int corridors. **Pets:** Other species. $75 one-time fee/pet. Service with restrictions.

X GM FI IP A

Homestead Studio Suites Hotel-Denver/Aurora M
(303) 750-9116. **Call for rates.** 13941 E Harvard Ave. I-225, exit 5 (Iliff Ave), just e to Blackhawk St, then just s. Ext corridors. **Pets:** Other species. $75 one-time fee/pet. Service with restrictions.

X GM FI IP

La Quinta Inn Denver (Aurora) M
(303) 337-0206. **$72-$99.** 1011 S Abilene St. I-225, exit 7, just e, then n. Ext corridors. **Pets:** Other species. Service with restrictions, supervision.

ASK X GM FI IP A

Sleep Inn Denver International Airport SH
(303) 373-1616. **$70-$175.** 15900 E 40th Ave. I-70, exit 283; from airport, Pena Blvd S to 40th Ave W. Int corridors. **Pets:** Other species. $10 daily fee/room. Supervision.

SAVE SD X GM FI IP A

CENTENNIAL

Bradford HomeSuites Denver Tech Center SH
(303) 858-9990. **Call for rates.** 7150 S Clinton St. I-25, exit 197, just e to S Clinton St, then just s. Int corridors. **Pets:** Accepted.

X GM FI IP A

Days Inn Denver Tech Center SH
(303) 768-9400. **Call for rates.** 9719 E Geddes Ave. I-25, exit 196 (Dry Creek Rd), just e to S Clinton St, just n, then just e. Int corridors. **Pets:** Medium. $25 one-time fee/room. Service with restrictions.

X GM FI IP

Embassy Suites Denver Tech Center SH
(303) 792-0433. **$109-$500.** 10250 E Costilla Ave. I-25, exit 197, 1 mi e on Arapahoe Rd, 0.3 mi s on Havana St, then w. Int corridors. **Pets:** Accepted.

SAVE SD X GM FI IP TI A

DENVER

Brown Palace Hotel and Spa LH
(303) 297-3111. **$189-$569.** 321 17th St. I-25, exit 210 (E Colfax Ave) to Lincoln St, just n on Lincoln St, just w on 18th St, then s. Int corridors. **Pets:** Accepted.

SAVE SD X FI IP TI

Comfort Inn Central SH ✿
(303) 297-1717. **$89-$114.** 401 E 58th Ave. I-25, exit 215, just e, then n on Logan St; connected to Denver Merchandise Mart. Int corridors. **Pets:** Large, other species. $10 daily fee/pet. Designated rooms, service with restrictions, crate.

SAVE SD X GM FI IP TI A

Comfort Inn Downtown Denver SH
(303) 296-0400. **$99-$259.** 401 17th St. I-25, exit 210 (E Colfax Ave) to Lincoln St, then just w; opposite Brown Palace Hotel & Spa. Int corridors. **Pets:** Accepted.

ASK SD X IP TI

Crowne Plaza DIA LH
(303) 371-9494. **$159-$189, 14 day notice.** 15500 E 40th Ave. I-70, exit 283 (Chambers Rd), just n, then just e. Int corridors. **Pets:** Other species. $25 one-time fee/pet. Service with restrictions, crate.

SAVE X FI IP TI A X

DoubleTree Hotel Denver LH
(303) 321-3333. **Call for rates.** 3203 Quebec St. I-70, exit 278, 0.5 mi s; I-270, exit 4. Int corridors. **Pets:** Accepted.

X FI IP TI A X

Drury Inn-Denver East SH
(303) 373-1983. **$76-$113.** 4380 E Peoria St. I-70, exit 281, just n. Int corridors. **Pets:** Large, other species. Service with restrictions, supervision.

ASK X FI IP

Embassy Suites Denver-Aurora LH
(303) 375-0400. **$199.** 4444 N Havana St. I-70, exit 280, just n. Int corridors. **Pets:** Accepted.

SAVE SD X GM FI IP TI A X

The Four Points by Sheraton Denver Southeast LH
(303) 758-7000. **Call for rates.** 6363 E Hampden Ave. I-25, exit 201, just e. Ext/int corridors. **Pets:** Accepted.

X GM FI IP A X

Hampton Inn & Suites Denver Tech Center SH
(303) 804-9900. **$89-$189.** 5001 S Ulster St. I-25, exit 199, e to Ulster St, then just n. Int corridors. **Pets:** Accepted.

ASK SD X GM FI IP A

Hampton Inn DIA SH
(303) 371-0200. **$140-$175.** 6290 Tower Rd. I-70, exit 286 (Tower Rd), 3.5 mi n. Int corridors. **Pets:** Small. Designated rooms, service with restrictions, supervision.

SAVE SD X GM IP A

Holiday Chalet a Victorian Bed & Breakfast BB
(303) 437-8245. **Call for rates.** 1820 E Colfax Ave. I-25, exit 210 (Colfax Ave), 2.3 mi e on US 40. Int corridors. **Pets:** Accepted.

SAVE X FI IP

Holiday Inn-Denver Central LH
(303) 292-9500. **Call for rates.** 4849 Bannock St. I-25, exit 215 north-bound; exit 214B southbound, just w to Broadway, then 1.2 mi s. Ext/int corridors. **Pets:** Accepted.

X GM FI IP TI A

Hotel Monaco Denver SH ❀
(303) 296-1717. **$349-$369.** 1717 Champa St. I-25, exit 210A (W Colfax Ave), 1 mi e to Kalamath St, 0.7 mi ne, just nw on 18th St, then just sw. Int corridors. **Pets:** Other species. Designated rooms, service with restrictions, supervision.

Hotel Teatro SH ❀
(303) 228-1100. **$189-$319.** 1100 14th St. I-25, exit 212 (Speer Blvd), just ne on Lawrence St, then e to 14th St; exit Auraria Pkwy northbound. Int corridors. **Pets:** Dogs only. $50 one-time fee/room.

The Inn at Cherry Creek SH ❀
(303) 350-4440. **$189-$345.** 233 Clayton St. Entrance on Clayton St; between 2nd and 3rd aves; in Cherry Creek Village. Int corridors. **Pets:** Medium, dogs only. $15 daily fee/pet. Designated rooms, service with restrictions, supervision.

JW Marriott Denver At Cherry Creek SH ❀
(303) 316-2700. **$299-$399.** 150 Clayton Ln. I-25, exit 205 (University Blvd), 2.4 mi n to 1st Ave, just e, then just n. Int corridors. **Pets:** Dogs only. Service with restrictions, supervision.

La Quinta Inn & Suites Denver (Airport/DIA) SH
(303) 371-0888. **$135.** 6801 Tower Rd. I-70, exit 286, 4.2 mi n; 0.8 mi s of Pena Blvd. Int corridors. **Pets:** Other species. Service with restrictions, supervision.

La Quinta Inn Denver (Central) SH
(303) 458-1222. **$99.** 3500 Park Ave W. I-25, exit 213, just s on Park Ave W, then just e on Globeville Rd. Ext/int corridors. **Pets:** Other species. Service with restrictions, supervision.

La Quinta Inn Denver (Cherry Creek) SH
(303) 758-8886. **$100.** 1975 S Colorado Blvd. I-25, exit 204, just s. Ext corridors. **Pets:** Other species. Service with restrictions, supervision.

Magnolia Hotel-Downtown SH
(303) 607-9000. **Call for rates.** 818 17th St. I-25, exit 212A (Speer Blvd S) to Market St, e to 17th St, then s to jct 17th and Stout sts. Int corridors. **Pets:** Accepted.

Microtel Inn D.I.A SH
(303) 371-8300. **$66-$81.** 18600 E 63rd Ave. I-70, exit 286 (Tower Rd), 3.6 mi n. Int corridors. **Pets:** Medium. $10 one-time fee/pet. Supervision.

The Oxford Hotel SH
(303) 628-5400. **Call for rates.** 1600 17th St. Corner of 17th and Wazee sts. Int corridors. **Pets:** Accepted.

Quality Inn & Suites SH
(303) 371-5300. **$59-$129.** 6890 Tower Rd. I-70, exit 286, 4.2 mi n; 0.8 mi s of Pena Blvd. Int corridors. **Pets:** Other species. $25 deposit/room. Service with restrictions, supervision.

Quality Inn Central SH
(303) 296-4000. **$59-$139.** 200 W 48th Ave. I-25, exit 215 northbound; exit 214B southbound, just w to Broadway, then 1.2 mi s. Int corridors. **Pets:** Accepted.

Quality Inn Denver East SH
(303) 371-5640. **$79.** 3975 Peoria Way. I-70, exit 281 eastbound; exit 282 westbound, just s. Ext corridors. **Pets:** Designated rooms, supervision.

Radisson Hotel Denver Stapleton Plaza LH
(303) 321-3500. **$129-$299.** 3333 Quebec St. I-70, exit 278, 0.3 mi s; I-270, exit 4. Int corridors. **Pets:** Medium. $50 daily fee/pet. Service with restrictions, supervision.

Ramada Inn Denver Downtown LH
(303) 831-7700. **Call for rates.** 1150 E Colfax Ave. I-25, exit 210 (E Colfax Ave), 1 mi e on US 40; 0.5 mi e of State Capitol. Int corridors. **Pets:** Other species. $100 deposit/room. Service with restrictions.

Red Lion Denver Central SH
(303) 321-6666. **$189.** 4040 Quebec St. I-70, exit 278, s on Quebec St, exit Smith Rd, then e to Frontage Rd; I-270, exit 4. Int corridors. **Pets:** Accepted.

Red Lion Hotel Denver Downtown at Invesco Field SH
(303) 433-8331. **$149.** 1975 Bryant St. I-25, exit 210B, just w. Int corridors. **Pets:** Medium. $10 daily fee/room. Service with restrictions, supervision.

Residence Inn by Marriott Denver City Center SH
(303) 296-3444. **$259-$899.** 1725 Champa St. I-25, exit 212 a (Speer Blvd S), 1.3 mi s to Stout St, 0.6 mi e, just n on 18th St, then just s. Int corridors. **Pets:** Accepted.

Residence Inn by Marriott Denver Downtown SH
(303) 458-5318. **$198-$218.** 2777 Zuni St. I-25, exit 212B, just w, then just n. Ext corridors. **Pets:** Accepted.

TownePlace Suites by Marriott Downtown Denver SH
(303) 722-2322. **$208-$230.** 685 Speer Blvd. I-25, exit Speer Blvd S, 2.2 mi s, stay in right lane, just past second Bannock St, exit towards Broadway, then right on Acoma St. Int corridors. **Pets:** Accepted.

Warwick Denver Hotel SH ❀
(303) 861-2000. **$189-$400.** 1776 Grant St. I-25, exit 210 a (E Colfax Ave), 1.7 mi to Logan St, just n to 18th St, then just w. Int corridors. **Pets:** Small, dogs only. $50 one-time fee/room. Designated rooms, service with restrictions, supervision.

The Westin Tabor Center Denver LH ❀
(303) 572-9100. **Call for rates.** 1672 Lawrence St. I-25, exit 212A (Speer Blvd S), 1 mi s to Lawrence St, then e. Int corridors. **Pets:** Medium, dogs only. Service with restrictions, supervision.

ENGLEWOOD

Clarion Hotel Denver South SH
(303) 790-7770. **$79-$399.** 7770 S Peoria St. I-25, exit 197 (Arapahoe Rd), 2 mi e, then 1.3 mi s; follow signs. Int corridors. **Pets:** Accepted.

Comfort Suites SH
(303) 858-0700. **$69-$299.** 7374 S Clinton St. I-25, exit 196 (Dry Creek Rd), just e, then n. Int corridors. **Pets:** Accepted.

▼▼▼▼ Drury Inn & Suites-Denver Near the Tech Center SH
(303) 694-3400. **$156.** 9445 E Dry Creek Rd. I-25, exit 196 (Dry Creek Rd), just w, on northwest corner. Int corridors. **Pets:** Large, other species. Service with restrictions, supervision.

[ASK] [X] [🛏] [💻] [🏊]

▼▼ Extended Stay Deluxe-Denver Tech Center South SH
(303) 858-0292. **Call for rates (no credit cards).** 9604 E Easter Ave. I-25, exit 197. Int corridors. **Pets:** Other species. $75 one-time fee/pet. Service with restrictions.

[X] [🛏] [💻] [🏊]

▼▼▼▼ Holiday Inn Express Hotel & Suites SH
(303) 662-0777. **$124-$135.** 7380 S Clinton St. I-25, exit 196 (Dry Creek Rd), e to S Clinton St, then just n. Int corridors. **Pets:** Medium. $50 one-time fee/pet. Designated rooms, service with restrictions, crate.

[ASK] [S🐾] [X] [🛏] [💻] [🏊]

▼▼▼▼ Residence Inn by Marriott-Denver Tech Center SH
(303) 740-7177. **$209-$229.** 6565 S Yosemite St. I-25, exit 197, just w on Arapahoe Rd, then n. Ext corridors. **Pets:** Accepted.

[ASK] [S🐾] [X] [🛏] [💻] [🏊] [X]

▼▼▼▼ Residence Inn Park Meadows SH
(720) 895-0200. **$208-$230.** 8322 S Valley Hwy. I-25, exit 195 (County Line Rd), just e to S Valley Hwy, then just s. Int corridors. **Pets:** Accepted.

[ASK] [S🐾] [X] [&M] [🛏] [💻] [🏊] [X]

▼▼▼ TownePlace Suites Denver Tech Center SH
(720) 875-1113. **$164-$184.** 7877 S Chester St. I-25, exit 196 (Dry Creek Rd), just w to Chester St, then 0.3 mi s. Int corridors. **Pets:** Accepted.

[ASK] [S🐾] [X] [&M] [🛏] [💻] [🏊]

GLENDALE

◆ Crossland Studios-Denver/Cherry Creek M
(303) 333-2545. **Call for rates.** 4850 Leetsdale Dr. I-25, exit 204, 1.2 mi n, just e on Alameda, then 0.3 mi se. Ext corridors. **Pets:** Other species. $75 one-time fee/pet. Service with restrictions.

[X] [🛏] [💻]

AAA ▼▼▼▼ Loews Denver Hotel LH
(303) 782-9300. **$239-$309.** 4150 E Mississippi Ave. I-25, exit 204, 1 mi n on Colorado Blvd, then just e. Int corridors. **Pets:** Accepted.

[SAVE] [S🐾] [X] [&M] [🛏] [💻] [🍴]

▼▼▼ Staybridge Suites Denver/Cherry Creek SH
(303) 321-5757. **$125-$199.** 4220 E Virginia Ave. I-25, exit 204, 1.5 mi n on Colorado Blvd to Virginia Ave, then just e. Int corridors. **Pets:** Accepted.

[ASK] [S🐾] [X] [&M] [🛏] [💻] [X]

GOLDEN

AAA ▼▼▼ Clarion Collection The Golden Hotel SH
(303) 279-0100. **$149-$289.** 800 11th St. At 11th St and Washington Ave; downtown. Int corridors. **Pets:** Accepted.

[ASK] [X] [🛏] [💻] [🍴]

▼▼ Days Inn Denver West SH
(303) 277-0200. **$69-$139.** 15059 W Colfax Ave. I-70, exit 262 (Colfax Ave), just e. Int corridors. **Pets:** Accepted.

[ASK] [S🐾] [X] [🛏] [💻] [🍴] [🏊] [X]

▼▼▼ Denver Marriott West LH
(303) 279-9100. **$186-$206.** 1717 Denver W Blvd. I-70, exit 263, just n, then w. Int corridors. **Pets:** Accepted.

[ASK] [S🐾] [X] [&M] [🛏] [💻] [🍴] [🏊] [X]

▼▼▼▼ La Quinta Inn Denver (Golden) SH
(303) 279-5565. **$72-$102.** 3301 Youngfield Service Rd. I-70, exit 264 (32nd Ave) westbound, just w, then n; exit eastbound, just e, n on 32nd, then just e. Ext corridors. **Pets:** Other species. Service with restrictions, supervision.

[ASK] [X] [🛏] [💻] [🏊]

▼▼▼▼ Residence Inn by Marriott Denver West/Golden SH
(303) 271-0909. **$153-$173.** 14600 W 6th Ave Frontage Rd. US 6, exit Indiana Ave to frontage road, just e. Int corridors. **Pets:** Accepted.

[ASK] [S🐾] [X] [&M] [🛏] [💻] [🏊] [X]

AAA ▼▼▼▼ Table Mountain Inn SH
(303) 277-9898. **$121-$209.** 1310 Washington Ave. US 6, exit 19th St, 0.5 mi n to Washington Ave, 0.5 mi w; downtown, just s of arch. Int corridors. **Pets:** Accepted.

[SAVE] [S🐾] [X] [&M] [🛏] [💻] [🍴]

GREENWOOD VILLAGE

▼▼▼▼ Hampton Inn Denver Southeast SH
(303) 792-9999. **Call for rates.** 9231 E Arapahoe Rd. I-25, exit 197, just e. Int corridors. **Pets:** Accepted.

[X] [&M] [🛏] [💻] [🏊]

▼▼ Homestead Studio Suites Hotel-Denver/Tech Center South-Greenwood Village SH
(303) 858-1669. **Call for rates.** 9253 E Costilla Ave. I-25, exit 197, just e on Arapahoe Rd, se on Clinton St to Costilla St, then w. Int corridors. **Pets:** Other species. $75 one-time fee/pet. Service with restrictions.

[X] [&M] [🛏] [💻]

AAA ▼▼▼▼ Hyatt Summerfield Suites Hotel SH
(303) 706-1945. **$99-$399.** 9280 E Costilla Ave. I-25, exit 197, e to Clinton St, then just s. Int corridors. **Pets:** Large, other species. $150 one-time fee/room. Service with restrictions, crate.

[SAVE] [X] [&M] [🛏] [💻] [🏊]

▼▼▼▼ La Quinta Inn & Suites Denver Tech Center SH
(303) 649-9969. **$129.** 7077 S Clinton St. I-25, exit 197, e to Clinton St, then s. Int corridors. **Pets:** Other species. Service with restrictions, supervision.

[ASK] [S🐾] [X] [&M] [🛏] [💻] [🏊]

▼▼▼▼ La Quinta Inn & Suites Englewood SH
(303) 799-4555. **$122-$132.** 9009 E Arapahoe Rd. I-25, exit 197, just e to Boston, n to Southtech, then just w. Int corridors. **Pets:** Other species. Service with restrictions, supervision.

[ASK] [S🐾] [X] [&M] [🛏] [💻] [🏊] [X]

▼▼▼▼ Sheraton Denver Tech Center Hotel SH
(303) 799-6200. **$79-$299.** 7007 S Clinton St. I-25, exit 197, e on Arapahoe Rd, then s. Int corridors. **Pets:** Accepted.

[ASK] [S🐾] [X] [&M] [🛏] [🍴] [🏊]

HIGHLANDS RANCH

▼▼▼▼ Residence Inn Denver South Highlands Ranch SH
(303) 683-5500. **$187-$207.** 93 Centennial Blvd. SR 470, exit Broadway, just s, then w. Int corridors. **Pets:** Accepted.

[ASK] [S🐾] [X] [&M] [🛏] [💻] [🏊] [X]

LAKEWOOD

AAA ▼▼▼▼ Best Western-Denver Southwest SH
(303) 989-5500. **$70-$95.** 3440 S Vance St. Just ne of jct US 285 (Hampden Ave) and S Wadsworth Blvd, e on Girton Dr, then just s. Int corridors. **Pets:** Designated rooms, service with restrictions, supervision.

[SAVE] [S🐾] [X] [🛏] [💻] [🏊]

▼▼ ▼▼ Comfort Suites Lakewood SH
(303) 988-8600. **$79-$149.** 7260 W Jefferson Ave. Just se of US 285 (W Hampden Ave) and Wadsworth Blvd, then e. Int corridors. **Pets:** Medium. $10 daily fee/pet. Designated rooms, service with restrictions, crate.

(ASK) (S&) (X) 🔒 💻 🛥

◆◆◆ ▼▼▼▼ Comfort Suites–Lakewood/Golden SH
(303) 231-9929. **$99-$149.** 11909 W 6th Ave. US 6, exit Simms/Union, westbound travelers must turn right at stop light, but do not use right turn lane, follow signs to frontage road. Int corridors. **Pets:** Accepted.

(SAVE) (S&) (X) (&M) 🔒 💻 🛥 (X)

▼▼▼▼ La Quinta Inn & Suites Denver
(Southwest/Lakewood) M
(303) 969-9700. **$107.** 7190 W Hampden Ave. Just se of jct US 285 (W Hampden Ave) and Wadsworth Blvd, e on Jefferson Ave, just n, then e on frontage road. Int corridors. **Pets:** Other species. Service with restrictions, supervision.

(ASK) (S&) (X) (&M) 🔒 💻 🛥

▼▼▼▼ Residence Inn by Marriott Denver
SW/Lakewood SH
(303) 985-7676. **$142-$162.** 7050 W Hampden Ave. Just se of jct US 285 (W Hampden Ave) and Wadsworth Blvd, e on Jefferson Ave, then n on frontage road. Int corridors. **Pets:** Accepted.

(ASK) (S&) (X) (&M) 🔒 💻 🛥 (X)

▼▼▼▼ Sheraton-Denver West Hotel LH
(303) 987-2000. **$219.** 360 Union Blvd. US 6, exit Simms/Union, s on Union Blvd; 3 mi e of jct I-70, exit 261. Int corridors. **Pets:** Accepted.

(ASK) (S&) (X) 🔒 💻 (TI) 🛥 (X)

▼▼ ▼▼ TownePlace Suites by Marriott-Denver West/Federal
Center SH
(303) 232-7790. **$131-$153.** 800 Tabor St. US 6, exit Simms/Union, just n to 8th, then w. Int corridors. **Pets:** Accepted.

(ASK) (S&) (X) (&M) 🔒 💻 🛥

LITTLETON

◆◆◆ ▼▼▼▼ Holiday Inn Express SH
(720) 981-1000. **$99-$129.** 12683 W Indore Pl. I-70 to SR 470 and Ken Caryl Ave; I-25 to SR 470 and Ken Caryl Ave, to Shaffer Ave, just n, then w. Int corridors. **Pets:** Accepted.

(SAVE) (S&) (X) (&M) 🔒 💻 🛥

LONE TREE

▼▼▼▼ Staybridge Suites Denver South-Lone Tree SH
(303) 649-1010. **$185.** 7820 Park Meadows Dr. I-25, exit 195 (County Line Rd), w on County Line Rd to Acres Green, s to E Park Meadows Dr, then just w; SR 470, exit Quebec St, just s on Quebec St, then just e. Int corridors. **Pets:** Medium, other species. $100 one-time fee/room. Service with restrictions, crate.

(ASK) (S&) (X) (&M) 🔒 💻 🛥 (X)

THORNTON

▼▼ Crossland Studios-Denver-Thornton SH
(303) 430-4474. **Call for rates (no credit cards).** 8750 Grant St. I-25, exit 219, e to Grant St, then 0.5 mi n. Ext corridors. **Pets:** Other species. $75 one-time fee/pet. Service with restrictions.

(X) 🔒 💻

◆◆◆ ▼▼▼ Sleep Inn North Denver SH 🐾
(303) 280-9818. **$64-$159.** 12101 Grant St. I-25, exit 223, e to Grant St, then n. Int corridors. **Pets:** Large, other species. $10 daily fee/room. Service with restrictions.

(SAVE) (S&) (X) (&M) 🔒 💻 🛥

WESTMINSTER

◆◆◆ ▼▼▼ Comfort Inn Northwest SH
(303) 428-3333. **$69-$210.** 8500 Turnpike Dr. US 36 (Boulder Tpke), exit Sheridan Ave, just s, left on Turnpike Dr at 87th Ave, then 0.4 mi. Int corridors. **Pets:** $10 daily fee/pet. Designated rooms, service with restrictions, supervision.

(SAVE) (S&) (X) (&M) 🔒 💻 🛥

▼▼ ▼▼ Comfort Suites Denver North SH
(303) 429-5500. **$70-$130.** 12085 Delaware St. I-25, exit 223, just w. Int corridors. **Pets:** Accepted.

(ASK) (S&) (X) 🔒 💻 🛥

▼▼ ▼▼ Denver North-Westminster-Super 8 SH
(303) 451-7200. **Call for rates.** 12055 Melody Dr. I-25, exit 223, just w. Int corridors. **Pets:** Accepted.

(X) 🔒 💻 (X)

◆◆◆ ▼▼▼▼ DoubleTree Hotel Denver North SH 🐾
(303) 427-4000. **$99-$189.** 8773 Yates Dr. US 36 (Boulder Tpke), exit Sheridan Ave, n to 92nd Ave, e to Yates Dr, then 0.5 mi s. Int corridors. **Pets:** $25 one-time fee/pet. Service with restrictions, supervision.

(SAVE) (S&) (X) 💻 (TI) 🛥 (X)

◆◆◆ ▼▼▼▼ La Quinta Inn & Suites Westminster
(Promenade) SH
(303) 438-5800. **$80.** 10179 Church Ranch Way. US 36 (Boulder Tpke), exit Church Ranch Blvd, just s to 103rd Pl, then e. Int corridors. **Pets:** Other species. Service with restrictions, supervision.

(SAVE) (S&) (X) (&M) 🔒 💻 🛥

▼▼ ▼▼ La Quinta Inn Denver (Northglenn) SH
(303) 252-9800. **$65-$92.** 345 W 120th Ave. I-25, exit 223, just w. Ext/int corridors. **Pets:** Other species. Service with restrictions, supervision.

(ASK) (X) 🔒 💻 🛥

▼▼ ▼▼ La Quinta Inn Denver (Westminster Mall) SH
(303) 425-9099. **$80-$100.** 8701 Turnpike Dr. US 36 (Boulder Tpke), exit Sheridan Ave, just s, then left on Turnpike Dr at 87th Ave. Ext/int corridors. **Pets:** Other species. Service with restrictions, supervision.

(ASK) (X) (&M) 🔒 💻 🛥

▼▼▼ ▼▼▼ Residence Inn by Marriott SH
(303) 427-9500. **$198-$219.** 5010 W 88th Pl. US 36 (Boulder Tpke), exit Sheridan Ave, n to 92nd Ave, e to Yates Dr, then s. Int corridors. **Pets:** Accepted.

(ASK) (S&) (X) (&M) 🔒 💻 🛥 (X)

▼▼▼ ▼▼▼ The Westin Westminster LH
(303) 410-5000. **$119-$329.** 10600 Westminster Blvd. US 36 (Boulder Tpke), exit 104th Ave, just n. Int corridors. **Pets:** Accepted.

(ASK) (S&) (X) (&M) 🔒 💻 (TI) 🛥 (X)

WHEAT RIDGE

▼▼▼ Holiday Inn Express Hotel & Suites SH
(303) 424-8300. **$100-$185.** 10101 W 48th Ave. I-70, exit 267, just sw.
Int corridors. **Pets:** Accepted.

ASK ⊠ 🛎 💻 🐾

END METROPOLITAN AREA

DILLON

🔷 ▼▼ Best Western Ptarmigan Lodge SH
(970) 468-2341. **$75-$180, 3 day notice.** 652 Lake Dillon Dr. I-70, exit
205, 1.3 mi se on US 6, then 0.3 mi s. Ext/int corridors.
Pets: Accepted.

SAVE S🐕 ⊠ 🛎 💻 ⊠ 🎾

🔷 ▼ Dillon Super 8 Motel SH
(970) 468-8888. **$59-$159.** 808 Little Beaver Tr. I-70, exit 205, just s,
then e. Int corridors. **Pets:** Medium. $15 one-time fee/pet. Designated
rooms, service with restrictions, supervision.

SAVE S🐕 ⊠ 🛎 💻

DURANGO

🔷 ▼ Caboose Motel M
(970) 247-1191. **$58-$150.** 3363 Main Ave. On US 550, 2.5 mi n. Ext
corridors. **Pets:** Small, dogs only. $10 daily fee/pet. Designated rooms,
service with restrictions, supervision.

SAVE S🐕 ⊠ 🛎 💻

🔷 ▼▼ Comfort Inn SH 🐾
(970) 259-5373. **$69-$149.** 2930 N Main Ave. On US 550, 2.1 mi n. Ext
corridors. **Pets:** Medium, other species. $10 daily fee/pet. Designated
rooms, service with restrictions, supervision.

SAVE S🐕 ⊠ 💻 🐾

▼▼▼ DoubleTree Hotel Durango SH
(970) 259-6580. **Call for rates.** 501 Camino Del Rio. Jct US 160 and
550. Int corridors. **Pets:** Accepted.

⊠ 🅜 🛎 💻 🍴 🐾 ⊠

🔷 ▼▼▼ Holiday Inn SH
(970) 247-5393. **$99-$159.** 800 Camino Del Rio. On US 550, just n of
jct US 160. Ext corridors. **Pets:** Accepted.

SAVE S🐕 ⊠ 💻 🍴 🐾 ⊠

🔷 ▼▼▼ Residence Inn by Marriott SH
(970) 259-6200. **$258-$278, 3 day notice.** 21691 Hwy 160 W. On US
160, just w. Int corridors. **Pets:** Accepted.

SAVE S🐕 ⊠ 🛎 💻 🐾 ⊠

▼▼▼ The Rochester Hotel BB
(970) 385-1920. **$119-$349, 14 day notice.** 726 E 2nd Ave. Just e of
Main Ave via 7th St, then just n. Int corridors. **Pets:** Accepted.

ASK S🐕 ⊠ 🛎 💻

🔷 ▼ Siesta Motel M
(970) 247-0741. **$58-$145.** 3475 N Main Ave. 2.6 mi n of jct US 160 W
and 550, on US 550. Ext corridors. **Pets:** Medium, dogs only. $10 daily
fee/pet. Designated rooms, service with restrictions, supervision.

SAVE ⊠ 🛎 💻

EAGLE

🔷 ▼▼▼ Best Western Eagle Lodge & Suites SH
(970) 328-6316. **Call for rates.** 200 Loren Ln. I-70, exit 147, just s. Int
corridors. **Pets:** $50 deposit/pet, $10 daily fee/pet. Service with restrictions,
supervision.

SAVE 🛎 💻 🐾 ⊠

EDWARDS

🔷 ▼▼▼ Inn and Suites at Riverwalk SH
(970) 926-0606. **$100-$800, 14 day notice.** 27 Main St. I-70, exit 163,
0.3 mi s. Int corridors. **Pets:** Large. $5 daily fee/pet, $25 one-time fee/pet.
Designated rooms, service with restrictions, crate.

SAVE S🐕 ⊠ 🛎 💻 🍴 🐾

ESTES PARK

🔷 ▼▼ Budget Host Four Winds Motor Lodge M
(970) 586-3313. **$55-$115, 5 day notice.** 1120 Big Thompson Ave. 1
mi n on US 34. Ext corridors. **Pets:** $15 daily fee/pet. Designated rooms,
service with restrictions, supervision.

SAVE S🐕 ⊠ 🛎 💻 🐾 ⊠

🔷 ▼▼ Castle Mountain Lodge CA
(970) 586-3664. **$95-$425, 30 day notice.** 1520 Fall River Rd. 1 mi w
on US 34. Ext corridors. **Pets:** Dogs only. $15 daily fee/pet. Designated
rooms, supervision.

SAVE S🐕 ⊠ 🛎 💻 ⊠ 🎾 ⊠

🔷 ▼▼▼ Holiday Inn Rocky Mountain Park SH
(970) 586-2332. **Call for rates.** 101 S St Vrain Ave. 0.5 mi se; on SR 7
at US 36. Int corridors. **Pets:** Accepted.

SAVE ⊠ 🅜 🛎 💻 🍴 🐾

🔷 ▼▼ Lake Estes Inn & Suites M
(970) 586-3386. **$59-$259, 7 day notice.** 1650 Big Thompson Ave. 1.7
mi e on US 34. Ext corridors. **Pets:** Accepted.

SAVE S🐕 ⊠ 🛎 💻 🐾 ⊠ 🎾

🔷 ▼▼ McGregor Mountain Lodge CA
(970) 586-3457. **$79-$385, 30 day notice.** 2815 Fall River Rd. 3.5 mi w
on US 34. Ext corridors. **Pets:** Dogs only. $20 daily fee/pet. Designated
rooms, supervision.

SAVE ⊠ 🛎 💻 ⊠ 🎾 ⊠

🔷 ▼▼ Silver Moon Inn M
(970) 586-6006. **$80-$159.** 175 Spruce Dr. Just w on US 34, then just
ne. Ext corridors. **Pets:** Dogs only. Designated rooms, service with restrictions,
supervision.

SAVE ⊠ 🛎 💻 🐾 ⊠

EVANS

🔷 ▼ Americas Best Value Inn SH
(970) 339-2492. **$39-$79.** 800 31st St. Jct US 85 and 31st St. Ext
corridors. **Pets:** Other species. $10 daily fee/pet. Designated rooms, service
with restrictions, supervision.

SAVE S🐕 ⊠ 🛎 🐾

🔷 ▼▼ Sleep Inn Greeley/Evans SH 🐾
(970) 356-2180. **$59-$149.** 3025 8th Ave. Just sw of jct US 34 and 85
Bypass. Int corridors. **Pets:** Other species. $15 one-time fee/pet. Service
with restrictions, crate.

SAVE S🐕 ⊠ 🅜 🛎 💻 🐾

EVERGREEN

☾ ▼▼▼▼ Quality Suites at Evergreen Parkway 🏠 ❀
(303) 526-2000. **$109-$189.** 29300 US Hwy 40. I-70, exit 252 (Evergreen Pkwy), on west side of El Rancho Restaurant; exit 251 eastbound. Int corridors. **Pets:** Large, other species. $50 deposit/pet, $10 daily fee/room. Designated rooms, service with restrictions, supervision.

SAVE ⬛ ✕ ⬛ ⬛ ⬛ ⬛ ✕

FORT COLLINS

☾ ▼▼▼ AmericInn Lodge & Suites 🏠
(970) 226-1232. **$89-$169.** 7645 Westgate Dr. I-25, exit 262, just se off SR 392. Int corridors. **Pets:** Medium. $10 daily fee/room. Designated rooms, service with restrictions, supervision.

SAVE ⬛ ✕ ⬛ ⬛ ⬛ ⬛ ✕

☾ ▼▼▼ Best Western Kiva Inn 🏠 ❀
(970) 484-2444. **$69-$119.** 1638 E Mulberry St (Hwy 14). I-25, exit 269B, 1.5 mi w on SR 14. Ext/int corridors. **Pets:** Medium, dogs only. $10 daily fee/pet. Designated rooms, service with restrictions, supervision.

SAVE ⬛ ✕ ⬛ ⬛ ⬛ ✕

☾ ▼▼ Best Western University Inn 🅼
(970) 484-1984. **$69-$149.** 914 S College Ave. I-25, exit 268, 4 mi w to College Ave, then just n on US 287. Ext/int corridors. **Pets:** $10 daily fee/pet. Designated rooms, supervision.

SAVE ⬛ ✕ ⬛ ⬛ ⬛

▼▼▼ Comfort Suites by Choice Hotels 🏠
(970) 206-4597. **$99-$159, 14 day notice.** 1415 Oakridge Dr. I-25, exit 265, 3.3 mi w to McMurray Ave, just s, then w. Int corridors. **Pets:** Accepted.

ASK ⬛ ✕ ⬛ ⬛ ⬛

▼▼▼ Fort Collins Marriott 🅛🅗
(970) 226-5200. **$169-$191.** 350 E Horsetooth Rd. I-25, exit 265, 4 mi w to John F Kennedy, then n; just beyond Horsetooth Rd. Int corridors. **Pets:** Accepted.

ASK ⬛ ✕ ⬛ ⬛ ⬛ ⬛ ⬛

▼▼▼ Hampton Inn 🏠
(970) 229-5927. **Call for rates.** 1620 Oakridge Dr. I-25, exit 265, 3.3 mi w, s on McMurray Ave to Oakridge Dr, then just e. Int corridors. **Pets:** Accepted.

✕ ⬛ ⬛ ⬛ ⬛

☾ ▼▼▼▼ Hilton Ft Collins 🏠
(970) 482-2626. **Call for rates.** 425 W Prospect Rd. I-25, exit 268, 4.3 mi w. Int corridors. **Pets:** Accepted.

SAVE ✕ ⬛ ⬛ ⬛ ⬛ ✕

▼▼▼ Quality Inn & Suites 🏠
(970) 282-9047. **$109-$209.** 4001 S Mason St. I-25, exit 265, 4.6 mi w to Mason St, then 0.5 mi n. Int corridors. **Pets:** Accepted.

ASK ⬛ ✕ ⬛ ⬛ ⬛ ⬛

▼▼▼ Residence Inn Fort Collins 🏠
(970) 223-5700. **$191-$219.** 1127 Oakridge Dr. I-25, exit 265, 3.3 mi w on Harmony Rd to Lemay Ave, then s to Oakridge Dr. Int corridors. **Pets:** Accepted.

ASK ⬛ ✕ ⬛ ⬛ ⬛ ✕

▼▼ Sleep Inn 🏠
(970) 484-5515. **$89-$129.** 3808 E Mulberry St. I-25, exit 269B, just nw. Int corridors. **Pets:** Accepted.

ASK ⬛ ✕ ⬛ ⬛

▼▼ Super 8 Motel 🏠
(970) 493-7701. **$60-$125.** 409 Centro Way. I-25, exit 269B, just w. Int corridors. **Pets:** Accepted.

✕ ⬛ ✕

FORT MORGAN

☾ ▼▼ Best Western Park Terrace Inn 🏠
(970) 867-8256. **$73-$91.** 725 Main St. I-76, exit 80, 0.5 mi s. Ext corridors. **Pets:** Medium. $10 one-time fee/pet. Designated rooms, service with restrictions, supervision.

SAVE ⬛ ✕ ⬛ ⬛ ⬛ ⬛

☾ ▼▼ Central Motel 🅼 ❀
(970) 867-2401. **$47-$65.** 201 W Platte Ave. I-76, exit 80, 0.6 mi s, then w on US 34. Ext corridors. **Pets:** $10 one-time fee/room. Supervision.

SAVE ⬛ ✕ ⬛ ⬛

▼▼ Rodeway Inn 🅼
(970) 867-9481. **$79-$129.** 1409 Barlow Rd. I-76, exit 82, just n. Ext/int corridors. **Pets:** Accepted.

✕ ⬛ ⬛ ⬛

FRISCO

☾ ▼▼▼▼ Best Western Lake Dillon Lodge 🏠
(970) 668-5094. **$79-$279.** 1202 Summit Blvd. I-70, exit 203, just s. Int corridors. **Pets:** Accepted.

SAVE ⬛ ✕ ⬛ ⬛ ⬛ ⬛ ✕

☾ ▼▼▼▼ Holiday Inn-Frisco 🏠
(970) 668-5000. **$69-$179, 3 day notice.** 1129 N Summit Blvd. I-70, exit 203, just s. Ext/int corridors. **Pets:** Accepted.

SAVE ⬛ ✕ ⬛ ⬛ ⬛ ⬛ ⬛ ✕

▼▼ Hotel Frisco 🏠
(970) 668-5009. **$59-$319, 14 day notice.** 308 Main. I-70, exit 201, 0.7 mi s; center. Ext/int corridors. **Pets:** Accepted.

ASK ⬛ ✕ ⬛ ⬛ ⬛

☾ ▼▼ New Summit Inn 🏠
(970) 668-3220. **$49-$159, 15 day notice.** 1205 N Summit Blvd. I-70, exit 203, just s, then just e. Int corridors. **Pets:** Accepted.

SAVE ✕ ⬛ ⬛

☾ ▼▼ Ramada Limited Frisco 🏠 ❀
(970) 668-8783. **Call for rates.** 990 Lakepoint Dr. I-70, exit 203, just s. Int corridors. **Pets:** Other species. $10 daily fee/room. Designated rooms, no service, supervision.

SAVE ✕ ⬛ ⬛ ⬛

☾ ▼▼ Snowshoe Motel 🅼
(970) 668-3444. **$49-$140.** 521 Main St. I-70, exit 203 westbound, 1 mi s to Main St, then just w; exit 201 eastbound. Ext corridors. **Pets:** $10 one-time fee/pet. Designated rooms, supervision.

SAVE ✕ ⬛ ⬛ ⬛

FRUITA

☾ ▼▼ Balanced Rock Motel 🅼
(970) 858-7333. **$55-$65.** 126 S Coulson. I-70, exit 19, just n to Aspen Ave, then just w. Ext corridors. **Pets:** $5 daily fee/pet. Designated rooms, service with restrictions, supervision.

SAVE ✕ ⬛

☾ ▼▼ Comfort Inn 🏠
(970) 858-1333. **$55-$135.** 400 Jurassic Ave. I-70, exit 19, 0.3 mi s; just e of Dinosaur Journey Museum. Int corridors. **Pets:** Large, other species. Designated rooms, supervision.

SAVE ⬛ ✕ ⬛ ⬛ ⬛ ⬛

▼▼▼ La Quinta Inn & Suites 🏠
(970) 858-8850. **$94.** 570 Raptor Rd. I-70, exit 19, 0.3 mi s; next to Dinosaur Journey Museum. Int corridors. **Pets:** Other species. Service with restrictions, supervision.

ASK ⬛ ✕ ⬛ ⬛ ⬛

AAA ◆◆◆ Super 8 SH ❖
(970) 858-0808. **Call for rates.** 399 Jurassic Ave. I-70, exit 19, 0.3 mi s; just e of Dinosaur Journey Museum. Int corridors. **Pets:** Medium. $5 daily fee/pet. Designated rooms, service with restrictions, supervision.
SAVE ✕ ᴸᴹ 🔌 ➿

GEORGETOWN

AAA ◆◆ Georgetown Mountain Inn M
(303) 569-3201. **$54-$110.** 1100 Rose St. I-70, exit 228, just s, then 0.3 mi w. Ext corridors. **Pets:** Other species. $10 one-time fee/room. Designated rooms, service with restrictions, supervision.
SAVE Sᴅ ✕ 🔌 ➿ ⚿

GLENWOOD SPRINGS

◆◆◆◆ Americinn Lodge & Suites At The Cavern SH
(970) 928-8188. **Call for rates.** 52000 Two Rivers Plaza Rd. I-70, exit 116, just w on US 6 and 24. Int corridors. **Pets:** Accepted.
✕ 🔌 ➿ ✕

AAA ◆◆◆ Hotel Colorado M
(970) 945-6511. **$164-$725.** 526 Pine St. I-70, exit 116, just ne. Int corridors. **Pets:** Medium. $50 one-time fee/room. No service, supervision.
SAVE Sᴅ ✕ 🔌 ✕ ⚿

◆◆◆◆ Quality Inn & Suites SH
(970) 945-5995. **$99-$169.** 2650 Gilstrap. I-70, exit 114, just s, then w. Int corridors. **Pets:** Accepted.
A$K Sᴅ ✕ 🔌 ➿

◆◆◆ Ramada Inn & Suites SH
(970) 945-2500. **$107-$170.** 124 W 6th St. I-70, exit 116, just w. Ext/int corridors. **Pets:** Accepted.
A$K Sᴅ ✕ 🔌 ❚❚ ➿

AAA ◆◆ Silver Spruce Motel M
(970) 945-5458. **$45-$129.** 162 W 6th St. I-70, exit 116, just w on frontage road. Ext corridors. **Pets:** Accepted.
SAVE Sᴅ ✕ 🔌

GRANBY

AAA ◆◆◆ The Inn at Silver Creek LH
(970) 887-2131. **$89-$219, 15 day notice.** 62927 Hwy 40. 2 mi se on US 40. Int corridors. **Pets:** Accepted.
SAVE Sᴅ ✕ 🔌 ❚❚ ➿ ✕ ⚿

GRAND JUNCTION

AAA ◆◆◆ Americas Best Value Inn SH
(970) 245-1410. **$52-$109.** 754 Horizon Dr. I-70, exit 31, 0.3 mi n. Ext corridors. **Pets:** Other species. Designated rooms, service with restrictions, supervision.
SAVE Sᴅ ✕ 🔌 ➿

AAA ◆◆ Best Western Sandman Motel SH ❖
(970) 243-4150. **$65-$130.** 708 Horizon Dr. I-70, exit 31, 0.3 mi s. Ext/int corridors. **Pets:** Medium, dogs only. $25 one-time fee/pet. Service with restrictions, supervision.
SAVE ✕ 🔌 ➿

AAA ◆◆ Grand Junction Super 8 SH
(970) 248-8080. **Call for rates.** 728 Horizon Dr. I-70, exit 31, just s. Int corridors. **Pets:** Large. $5 daily fee/pet. Designated rooms, service with restrictions, supervision.
SAVE ✕ 🔌 ➿

AAA ◆◆◆ Grand Vista Hotel SH
(970) 241-8411. **$79-$109.** 2790 Crossroads Blvd. I-70, exit 31, 0.3 mi n. Int corridors. **Pets:** Other species. $10 daily fee/room. Designated rooms, service with restrictions, supervision.
SAVE Sᴅ ✕ 🔌 ❚❚ ➿ ✕

◆◆◆ Hawthorn Suites SH
(970) 242-2525. **Call for rates.** 225 Main St. At 2nd and Main sts; downtown. Int corridors. **Pets:** Accepted.
✕ 🔌 ➿ ✕

AAA ◆◆◆ Holiday Inn SH ❖
(970) 243-6790. **$89-$109.** 755 Horizon Dr. I-70, exit 31; northwest corner. Ext/int corridors. **Pets:** Other species. Service with restrictions, supervision.
SAVE Sᴅ ✕ 🔌 ❚❚ ➿ ✕

◆◆◆ La Quinta Inn & Suites Grand Junction SH
(970) 241-2929. **$137.** 2761 Crossroads Blvd. I-70, exit 31, n to Crossroads Blvd, then just w. Int corridors. **Pets:** Other species. Service with restrictions, supervision.
A$K Sᴅ ✕ 🔌 ➿

AAA ◆ Mesa Inn M
(970) 245-3080. **Call for rates.** 704 Horizon Dr. I-70, exit 31, 0.5 mi s. Ext corridors. **Pets:** Accepted.
SAVE ✕ 🔌 ➿

AAA ◆◆◆ Quality Inn of Grand Junction SH
(970) 245-7200. **$79-$199.** 733 Horizon Dr. I-70, exit 31, just s. Int corridors. **Pets:** $10 one-time fee/room. Designated rooms, service with restrictions, supervision.
SAVE Sᴅ ✕ 🔌 ❚❚ ➿

AAA ◆◆◆ Ramada Inn SH
(970) 243-5150. **$89-$179.** 752 Horizon Dr. I-70, exit 31, just n. Int corridors. **Pets:** Accepted.
SAVE Sᴅ ✕ 🔌 ➿

GRAND LAKE

AAA ◆◆◆ Spirit Lake Lodge M
(970) 627-3344. **$55-$200, 7 day notice.** 829 Grand Ave. Just e of US 34; downtown. Ext corridors. **Pets:** Medium. $15 daily fee/pet. No service, supervision.
SAVE Sᴅ ✕ 🔌 ⚿

GREAT SAND DUNES NATIONAL PARK AND PRESERVE

◆◆ Great Sand Dunes Lodge M
(719) 378-2900. **$89-$100.** 7900 Hwy 150 N. From Alamosa, 16 mi e on US 160, then 16 mi n on SR 150. Ext corridors. **Pets:** Accepted.
✕ ➿

GREELEY

AAA ◆◆◆ Comfort Inn-Greeley SH
(970) 330-6380. **$79-$139.** 2467 W 29th St. US 34 Bypass, exit 23rd Ave, just sw. Int corridors. **Pets:** Other species. $50 deposit/pet, $15 daily fee/pet. Service with restrictions.
SAVE Sᴅ ✕ 🔌 ➿

◆◆◆ Country Inn & Suites By Carlson SH
(970) 330-3404. **$83-$102.** 2501 W 29th St. US 34 Bypass, exit 23rd Ave, just s, then w. Int corridors. **Pets:** Small, other species. $15 daily fee/pet. Designated rooms, service with restrictions, supervision.
A$K Sᴅ ✕ ᴸᴹ 🔌 ➿

AAA ◆◆◆ Days Inn SH
(970) 392-1530. **Call for rates.** 5630 W 10th St. 5 mi w on US 34 business route; entry via 54th Ave off 10th St. Int corridors. **Pets:** Large. $15 daily fee/pet. Service with restrictions, supervision.
SAVE ✕ ᴸᴹ 🔌

AAA ◆◆◆ Regency Hotel SH
(970) 353-8444. **$80-$100, 15 day notice.** 701 8th St. On US 85 business route; downtown. Int corridors. **Pets:** Accepted.
SAVE Sᴅ ✕ ᴸᴹ ❚❚ ➿

GUNNISON

AAA ▽ ABC Motel M
(970) 641-2400. **$49-$89.** 212 E Tomichi Ave. On US 50; near Western State College. Ext corridors. **Pets:** Accepted.
[SAVE] [S&] [✕] [🛏] [💻]

▽ Alpine Inn SH
(970) 641-2804. **$39-$139.** 1011 W Rio Grande. Jct US 50 and SR 135, 1.1 mi w. Int corridors. **Pets:** Accepted.
[ASK] [S&] [✕] [🛏] [💻] [🏊]

AAA ▽ Gunnison Inn M
(970) 641-0700. **$55-$85.** 412 E Tomichi Ave. On US 50; near Western State College. Ext corridors. **Pets:** Dogs only. $5 daily fee/pet. Service with restrictions, supervision.
[SAVE] [S&] [✕]

▽ Rodeway Inn SH
(970) 641-0500. **$55-$109.** 37760 W Hwy 50. US 50, 2.3 mi w. Ext corridors. **Pets:** Small. $5 daily fee/pet. Designated rooms, no service, supervision.
[ASK] [S&] [✕] [🛏] [💻]

AAA ▽▽ Water Wheel Inn SH 🐾
(970) 641-1650. **$64-$104.** 37478 W Hwy 50. Jct SR 135, 2.5 mi w. Ext/int corridors. **Pets:** Other species. $5 daily fee/pet. Designated rooms, service with restrictions, supervision.
[SAVE] [S&] [✕] [🛏] [💻]

HOT SULPHUR SPRINGS

AAA ▽ Canyon Motel M 🐾
(970) 725-3395. **$49-$99.** 221 Byers Ave. On US 40. Ext corridors. **Pets:** Other species. $10 daily fee/room. Service with restrictions, crate.
[SAVE] [S&] [✕] [🛏] [💻] [🎬]

JULESBURG

AAA ▽ Budget Host Platte Valley Inn SH
(970) 474-3336. **$53-$65.** 15225 Hwy 385 & I-76. I-76, exit 180, just n. Ext corridors. **Pets:** Dogs only. $7 daily fee/pet. Designated rooms, service with restrictions, supervision.
[SAVE] [S&] [✕] [🛏] [💻] [🍴] [🏊]

KEYSTONE

AAA ▽▽▽ The Inn at Keystone SH 🐾
(970) 496-4825. **$109-$319, 21 day notice.** 23044 Hwy 6. I-70, exit 205, 6.5 mi e on US 6; at Keystone Ski area. Int corridors. **Pets:** Other species. $25 daily fee/room. Service with restrictions.
[SAVE] [✕] [🛏] [💻] [🍴]

LA JUNTA

▽▽▽ Holiday Inn Express M
(719) 384-2900. **$109-$124.** 27994 US Hwy 50 Frontage Rd. On US 50, 0.8 mi w. Int corridors. **Pets:** Accepted.
[ASK] [S&] [✕] [🛏] [💻] [🏊]

LAKE CITY

AAA ▽ Matterhorn Mountain Motel M
(970) 944-2210. **$85-$125, 14 day notice.** 409 Bluff St. Just w of SR 149 via 4th St. Ext corridors. **Pets:** Small, dogs only. $20 one-time fee/pet. Designated rooms, no service, supervision.
[SAVE] [✕] [🛏] [💻] [🎬] [📷]

LAKE GEORGE

AAA ▽▽▽ Mule Creek Outfitters/M Lazy C Ranch RA
(719) 748-3398. **$75-$110, 30 day notice.** 801 CR 453. 5 mi w on US 24, 0.8 mi n on dirt road. Ext corridors. **Pets:** Accepted.
[SAVE] [✕] [🛏] [💻] [📷] [🎬] [📺] [📷]

LAMAR

AAA ▽▽▽ Best Western Cow Palace Inn M
(719) 336-7753. **$84-$104.** 1301 N Main St. 0.8 mi n on US 50 and 287. Ext/int corridors. **Pets:** Accepted.
[SAVE] [S&] [✕] [🛏] [💻] [🍴] [🏊]

AAA ▽ Blue Spruce Motel M
(719) 336-7454. **$45-$75.** 1801 S Main St. 1.3 mi s on US 287 and 385. Ext corridors. **Pets:** Medium, other species. $5 daily fee/pet. Designated rooms, service with restrictions, supervision.
[SAVE] [S&] [✕] [🛏] [💻] [🏊]

AAA ▽ Chek Inn M
(719) 336-4331. **$45-$75.** 1210 S Main St. 1 mi s on US 287 and 385. Ext corridors. **Pets:** Medium, other species. $5 daily fee/pet. Designated rooms, service with restrictions, supervision.
[SAVE] [S&] [✕] [🛏] [💻] [🏊]

LAS ANIMAS

AAA ▽▽▽ Best Western Bent's Fort Inn M
(719) 456-0011. **$64-$84.** 10950 E US 50. On US 50, 1.5 mi e on frontage road. Int corridors. **Pets:** Other species. $10 daily fee/pet. Service with restrictions, crate.
[SAVE] [S&] [✕] [💻] [🍴] [🏊]

LEADVILLE

AAA ▽▽▽ Alps Motel M
(719) 486-1223. **$60-$85, 5 day notice.** 207 Elm St. Just s on US 24. Int corridors. **Pets:** Other species. $18 daily fee/pet. Service with restrictions, supervision.
[SAVE] [S&] [✕] [🛏] [💻] [🎬]

AAA ▽▽▽ Silver King Inn SH
(719) 486-2610. **$119-$150.** 2020 N Poplar. US 24, just s of jct SR 91. Ext/int corridors. **Pets:** Medium, other species. $35 daily fee/pet. Designated rooms, service with restrictions, supervision.
[SAVE] [S&] [✕] [🛏] [💻] [🎬]

LIMON

AAA ▽▽ Best Western Limon Inn SH
(719) 775-0277. **$80-$100.** 925 T Ave. I-70, exit 359, just s. Int corridors. **Pets:** Accepted.
[SAVE] [S&] [✕] [🛏] [💻] [🏊]

AAA ▽ Safari Motel M
(719) 775-2363. **$48-$96.** 637 Main St. I-70, exit 361, 0.8 mi w. Ext corridors. **Pets:** Other species. $5 daily fee/pet. Designated rooms, service with restrictions, supervision.
[SAVE] [S&] [✕] [💻] [🏊]

AAA ▽▽ Tyme Square Inn SH
(719) 775-0700. **Call for rates.** 2505 6th St. I-70, exit 359, then s. Int corridors. **Pets:** Accepted.
[SAVE] [✕] [&M] [🛏] [💻] [🏊]

LONGMONT

AAA ▽▽▽ Hawthorn Suites SH
(303) 774-7100. **$89-$189.** 2000 Sunset Way. Jct US 287, 1.3 mi w on SR 119, just n on Sunset St, then just w on Korte Pkwy. Int corridors. **Pets:** Large, other species. $50 one-time fee/room. Service with restrictions, crate.
[SAVE] [✕] [&M] [🛏] [💻] [🏊] [📷]

AAA ▽▽▽ Radisson Hotel & Conference Center Longmont-Boulder SH
(303) 776-2000. **$139-$189.** 1900 Ken Pratt Blvd. Jct US 287, 1.3 mi sw on SR 119. Int corridors. **Pets:** Other species. $75 deposit/room. Designated rooms, service with restrictions, crate.
[SAVE] [S&] [✕] [🛏] [💻] [🍴] [🏊] [📷]

▼▼▼ **Residence Inn by Marriott Boulder/Longmont** 🆂🅷
(303) 702-9933. **$164-$186.** 1450 Dry Creek Dr. I-25, exit 235, jct Hover Rd and SR 119. Int corridors. **Pets:** Accepted.
🄰🄵🄺 🆂 🆇 🄶🄼 🄱 🄻 🛥 🆇

▼▼ **Super 8 Motel** 🄼
(303) 772-0888. **Call for rates.** 10805 Turner Blvd. I-25, exit 240, jct SR 119; 7 mi e of town. Int corridors. **Pets:** Accepted.
🆇

▼ **Twin Peaks Super 8** 🆂🅷
(303) 772-8106. **$65-$198.** 2446 N Main St. 2.5 mi n on US 287 at SR 66. Int corridors. **Pets:** Accepted.
🄰🄵🄺 🆂 🆇 🄱 🄻

LOUISVILLE

🄰🄰🄰 ▼▼▼ **Comfort Inn in Boulder County** 🆂🅷
(303) 604-0181. **$60-$200.** 1196 Dillon Rd. US 36 (Boulder Tpke), exit Superior (SR 170), just n on McCaslin Blvd, then just w. Int corridors. **Pets:** Medium, other species. $10 daily fee/pet. Designated rooms, service with restrictions, supervision.
🅂🄰🅅🄴 🆂 🆇 🄶🄼 🄱 🄻

▼▼▼ **La Quinta Inn & Suites Denver**
(Louisville/Boulder) 🆂🅷
(303) 664-0100. **$132.** 902 Dillon Rd. US 36 (Boulder Tpke), exit Superior (SR 170), just n on McCaslin Blvd, then e. Int corridors. **Pets:** Other species. Service with restrictions, supervision.
🄰🄵🄺 🆂 🆇 🄶🄼 🄱 🄻 🛥

▼▼ **Quality Inn & Suites** 🆂🅷
(303) 327-1215. **$59-$129.** 960 W Dillon Rd. US 36 (Boulder Tpke), exit Superior (SR 170), n on McCaslin Blvd to Dillon Rd, then e. Int corridors. **Pets:** Accepted.
🄰🄵🄺 🆂 🆇 🄱 🄻 🛥

▼▼▼▼ **Residence Inn by Marriott-Boulder/Louisville** 🆂🅷
(303) 665-2661. **$153-$173.** 845 Coal Creek Cir. US 36 (Boulder Tpke), exit Superior (SR 170), n on McCaslin Blvd to Dillon Rd, then 0.6 mi e. Int corridors. **Pets:** Accepted.
🄰🄵🄺 🆂 🆇 🄶🄼 🄱 🄻 🛥 🆇

LOVELAND

🄰🄰🄰 ▼▼▼ **Best Western Crossroads Inn & Conference**
Center 🆂🅷 🐾
(970) 667-7810. **$80-$150.** 5542 E US Hwy 34. I-25, exit 257B, just w. Ext/int corridors. **Pets:** Other species. $15 daily fee/pet. Service with restrictions, supervision.
🅂🄰🅅🄴 🆂 🆇 🄱 🄻 🍴 🛥

🄰🄰🄰 ▼ **Budget Host Exit 254 Inn** 🄼
(970) 667-5202. **$55-$99.** 2716 SE Frontage Rd. I-25, exit 254, just e, then just n. Ext corridors. **Pets:** Dogs only. $6 daily fee/pet. Crate.
🅂🄰🅅🄴 🆇 🄱 🛥

▼▼▼ **Residence Inn By Marriott Loveland** 🆂🅷
(970) 622-7000. **$153-$186.** 5450 McWhinney Blvd. I-25, exit 257B, 0.5 mi w to Outlet Mall entry, just n, then just e. Int corridors. **Pets:** Accepted.
🄰🄵🄺 🆂 🆇 🄱 🄻 🛥 🆇

MESA VERDE NATIONAL PARK

🄰🄰🄰 ▼▼▼ **Far View Lodge in Mesa Verde** 🄼
(970) 529-4421. **$90-$148.** 1 Navajo Hill, MM 15. 15 mi from park gate; near park visitors center. Ext corridors. **Pets:** Accepted.
🅂🄰🅅🄴 🆂 🆇 🄱 🄻 🍴 🄼

MONTE VISTA

🄰🄰🄰 ▼▼▼ **Best Western Movie Manor Motel** 🆂🅷
(719) 852-5921. **$55-$120, 7 day notice.** 2830 W Hwy 160. On US 160, 2 mi w. Ext corridors. **Pets:** Accepted.
🅂🄰🅅🄴 🆂 🆇 🄻 🍴

🄰🄰🄰 ▼▼▼ **Pecosa Inn** 🆂🅷
(719) 852-0612. **$80-$110.** 1519 Grande Ave. On US 160, 0.3 mi e. Int corridors. **Pets:** Other species. Service with restrictions, supervision.
🅂🄰🅅🄴 🆂 🆇 🛥

MONTROSE

🄰🄰🄰 ▼▼▼▼ **Best Western Red Arrow** 🆂🅷
(970) 249-9641. **Call for rates.** 1702 E Main St. 1 mi e on US 50. Ext/int corridors. **Pets:** $10 daily fee/pet. Designated rooms, service with restrictions, supervision.
🅂🄰🅅🄴 🆇 🄱 🄻 🛥 🆇

🄰🄰🄰 ▼▼▼ **Black Canyon Motel** 🆂🅷 🐾
(970) 249-3495. **$45-$95.** 1605 E Main St. 1 mi e on US 50. Ext corridors. **Pets:** Other species. $5 daily fee/pet. Service with restrictions.
🅂🄰🅅🄴 🆂 🆇 🄱 🄻

🄰🄰🄰 ▼ **Canyon Trails Inn** 🄼
(970) 249-3426. **$50-$80.** 1225 E Main St. 0.8 mi e on US 50. Ext corridors. **Pets:** Accepted.
🅂🄰🅅🄴 🆂 🆇 🄱 🄻

▼▼▼▼ **Hampton Inn Montrose** 🆂🅷
(970) 252-3300. **$123-$153.** 1980 N Townsend Ave. On US 550, just n of jct US 50. Int corridors. **Pets:** Accepted.
🄰🄵🄺 🆂 🆇 🄻 🛥 🆇

🄰🄰🄰 ▼▼▼▼ **Holiday Inn Express Hotel & Suites** 🆂🅷
(970) 240-1800. **$129-$139.** 1391 S Townsend Ave. 1 mi s on US 550, e on Niagara Ave. Int corridors. **Pets:** Designated rooms, supervision.
🅂🄰🅅🄴 🆇 🄶🄼 🄱 🄻

▼▼▼ **Quality Inn & Suites-Montrose** 🆂🅷
(970) 249-1011. **$79-$139.** 2751 Commercial Way. 2 mi s on US 550, w on O'Delle. Int corridors. **Pets:** Accepted.
🄰🄵🄺 🆂 🆇 🄱 🄻 🛥

▼▼ **Uncompahgre Bed & Breakfast** 🅱🅱
(970) 240-4000. **$90-$150.** 21049 Uncompahgre Rd. 8 mi s on US 550. Int corridors. **Pets:** Accepted.
🄰🄵🄺 🆂 🆇 🄱 🄩

▼ **Western Motel** 🄼
(970) 249-3481. **$50-$150.** 1200 E Main St. 0.8 mi e on US 50. Ext corridors. **Pets:** Accepted.
🄰🄵🄺 🆂 🆇 🄱 🄻 🛥

NEDERLAND

🄰🄰🄰 ▼▼▼▼ **Best Western Lodge at Nederland** 🆂🅷
(303) 258-9463. **$110-$160, 7 day notice.** 55 Lakeview Dr. SR 119; across street from Visitor's Center. Int corridors. **Pets:** Accepted.
🅂🄰🅅🄴 🆂 🆇 🄱 🄻 🆇

NEW CASTLE

▼▼ **New Castle Rodeway Inn** 🆂🅷
(970) 984-2363. **$90-$179.** 781 Burning Mountain Ave. I-70, exit 105, just n, then w. Int corridors. **Pets:** Accepted.
🄰🄵🄺 🆂 🆇 🄱 🄻 🛥

OURAY

(AAA) ▼▼▼▼ Best Western Twin Peaks Hot Springs 🆂🅷
(970) 325-4427. **$69-$300.** 125 3rd Ave. Just w of US 550. Ext corridors. **Pets:** Medium, dogs only. Designated rooms, service with restrictions, supervision.
🆂🅰🆅🅴 ⑤₀ ⊠ 🔒 💻 🔁

(AAA) ▼▼▼ Comfort Inn 🅼
(970) 325-7203. **$69-$159.** 191 5th Ave. Just w of US 550. Ext corridors. **Pets:** Dogs only. $15 daily fee/pet. Designated rooms, service with restrictions, supervision.
🆂🅰🆅🅴 ⑤₀ ⊠ 🅰🅼 🔒 💻

(AAA) ▼▼▼ Ouray Riverside Inn & Cabins 🆂🅷
(970) 325-4061. **$55-$195.** 1805 N Main St. Just n on US 550. Ext corridors. **Pets:** Accepted.
🆂🅰🆅🅴 ⊠ 🔒 💻

(AAA) ▼◆ Ouray Victorian Inn 🆂🅷
(970) 325-7222. **$65-$275.** 50 3rd Ave. Just w of US 550. Ext corridors. **Pets:** Accepted.
🆂🅰🆅🅴 ⑤₀ ⊠ 🔒 💻 🅺

(AAA) ▼▼▼ Rivers Edge Motel 🅼
(970) 325-4621. **$59-$249.** 110 7th Ave. Just w of US 550. Ext corridors. **Pets:** Medium, dogs only. $10 daily fee/pet. Service with restrictions, supervision.
🆂🅰🆅🅴 ⑤₀ ⊠ 🔒 💻 🅺

PAGOSA SPRINGS

(AAA) ▼▼ Americas Best Value High Country Lodge 🆂🅷
(970) 264-4181. **Call for rates.** 3821 E Hwy 160. On US 160, 3 mi e. Ext corridors. **Pets:** Accepted.
🆂🅰🆅🅴 ⊠ 🔒 💻 🆇

(AAA) ▼▼▼ Best Western Oak Ridge Lodge 🆂🅷
(970) 264-4173. **$68-$150, 3 day notice.** 158 Hot Springs Blvd. Just s of US 160. Int corridors. **Pets:** Other species. $100 deposit/pet, $15 one-time fee/pet. Service with restrictions, supervision.
🆂🅰🆅🅴 ⑤₀ ⊠ 🔒 💻 🍴 🔁 🆇

▼▼ Fireside Inn Cabins 🅲🅰
(970) 264-9204. **$105-$180.** 1600 E Hwy 160. On US 160, 1.3 mi e. Ext corridors. **Pets:** Accepted.
🅰🆂🅺 ⊠ 🔒 💻 🆇 🅺

(AAA) ▼▼▼ Pagosa Lodge 🆂🅷
(970) 731-4141. **$95-$125.** 3505 W Hwy 160. On US 160, 3.5 mi w. Int corridors. **Pets:** Medium, dogs only. $75 one-time fee/pet. Service with restrictions, supervision.
🆂🅰🆅🅴 ⊠ 🔒 💻 🔁 🆇

▼◆ The Pagosa Springs Inn & Suites 🆂🅷
(970) 731-3400. **$60-$169.** 519 Village Dr. 3.8 mi w on US 160. Int corridors. **Pets:** Accepted.
🅰🆂🅺 ⑤₀ ⊠ 🔒 💻 🔁

(AAA) ▼ Super 8 Motel 🅼
(970) 731-4005. **Call for rates.** 8 Solomon Dr. 2.5 mi w on US 160. Ext/int corridors. **Pets:** Other species. Service with restrictions, supervision.
🆂🅰🆅🅴 ⊠ 🔒 💻

PARKER

▼▼ Super 8 Motel-Parker 🆂🅷
(720) 851-2644. **$79-$89.** 6230 E Pine Ln. E-470 toll road, exit 5 (Parker Rd/SR 83), 0.4 mi se, then just e. Int corridors. **Pets:** Accepted.
🅰🆂🅺 ⑤₀ ⊠ 🔒 💻

PLACERVILLE

(AAA) ▼◆▼ The Blue Jay Lodge & Cafe 🆂🅷
(970) 728-0830. **$105-$200.** 22332 Hwy 145. Just n on SR 145, 13.5 mi s of Telluride. Int corridors. **Pets:** Dogs only. $25 one-time fee/pet. Designated rooms, no service.
🆂🅰🆅🅴 ⊠ 🔒 💻 🍴 🆇

PUEBLO

▼▼▼ Best Western Eagle Ridge Inn & Suites 🆂🅷
(719) 543-4644. **$85-$150.** 4727 N Elizabeth St. I-25, exit 102, just w, then just n. Int corridors. **Pets:** Large, other species. $15 daily fee/room. Designated rooms, service with restrictions, supervision.
🅰🆂🅺 ⑤₀ ⊠ 🔒 💻 🔁 🆇

▼▼▼ La Quinta Inn & Suites Pueblo 🆂🅷
(719) 542-3500. **$98.** 4801 N Elizabeth St. I-25, exit 102, just nw. Int corridors. **Pets:** Other species. Service with restrictions, supervision.
🅰🆂🅺 ⑤₀ ⊠ 🔒 💻 🔁

▼▼ Microtel Inn & Suites 🆂🅷
(719) 242-2020. **$65-$99.** 3343 Gateway Dr. I-25, exit 94. Int corridors. **Pets:** Accepted.
🅰🆂🅺 ⊠ 🅰🅼 🔒 💻

▼ Motel 6–1186 🅼
(719) 543-8900. **$43-$55.** 960 Hwy 50 W. I-25, exit 101, 0.3 mi w. Ext corridors. **Pets:** Other species. Service with restrictions, supervision.
⑤₀ ⊠ 🔒

▼▼ Ramada of Pueblo 🆂🅷
(719) 544-4700. **$69-$119.** 4703 N Freeway. I-25, exit 102, just w. Ext corridors. **Pets:** Accepted.
⑤₀ ⊠ 🔒 💻 🔁

▼▼ Sleep Inn 🆂🅷
(719) 583-4000. **$59-$139.** 3626 N Freeway. I-25, exit 101, just ne on frontage road. Int corridors. **Pets:** Accepted.
🅰🆂🅺 ⑤₀ ⊠ 🅰🅼 🔒 💻 🔁

RIDGWAY

(AAA) ▼▼▼ Chipeta Sun Lodge and Spa 🆂🅷 🐾
(970) 626-3737. **$125-$250.** 304 S Lena St. Jct US 550, just w on SR 62, then just s. Ext/int corridors. **Pets:** $35 one-time fee/pet. Designated rooms, service with restrictions, supervision.
🆂🅰🆅🅴 ⑤₀ ⊠ 🔒 💻 🍴 🆇

▼▼ Ridgway-Ouray Lodge & Suites 🆂🅷
(970) 626-5444. **$70-$93.** 373 Palomino Tr. From US 550, just ne on SR 62, then just e. Int corridors. **Pets:** Accepted.
🅰🆂🅺 ⑤₀ ⊠ 🔒 💻 🔁 🆇

RIFLE

▼▼▼ La Quinta Inns & Suites Rifle CO 🆂🅷
(970) 625-2676. **$109-$119.** 600 Wapiti Ct. I-70, exit 90, just s, then just e. Int corridors. **Pets:** Other species. Service with restrictions, supervision.
🅰🆂🅺 ⑤₀ ⊠ 🔒 💻

(AAA) ▼▼ Rusty Cannon Motel 🅼
(970) 625-4004. **$78-$86.** 701 Taughenbaugh Blvd. I-70, exit 90, just s. Ext corridors. **Pets:** Dogs only. $25 one-time fee/pet. Designated rooms, service with restrictions.
🆂🅰🆅🅴 ⑤₀ ⊠ 🔒 💻 🔁

SALIDA

(AAA) ▼ Aspen Leaf Lodge 🅼 🐾
(719) 539-6733. **$59-$99.** 7350 W Hwy 50. Just w of Hot Springs Pool. Ext corridors. **Pets:** Medium, other species. $5 daily fee/pet. Service with restrictions, supervision.
🆂🅰🆅🅴 ⊠ 🔒

AAA ▼ Circle R Motel **M**
(719) 539-6296. **$59-$105.** 304 E US Hwy 50. On US 50. Ext corridors. **Pets:** Dogs only. $5 daily fee/pet. No service, supervision.
[SAVE] [✕] [📋] [🖥]

AAA ▼▼ Gateway Inn & Suites **SH**
(719) 539-2895. **$39-$179.** 1310 E Hwy 50. Just e on US 50; between Blake and Palmer sts. Ext corridors. **Pets:** Accepted.
[SAVE] [S🔧] [✕] [📋] [🖥]

AAA ▼▼ Great Western Colorado Lodge **M**
(719) 539-2514. **$39-$120.** 352 W Rainbow Blvd. On US 50. Ext corridors. **Pets:** $10 daily fee/pet. Designated rooms, service with restrictions, supervision.
[SAVE] [S🔧] [✕] [📋] [🖥] [🏊]

AAA ▼▼▼ Silver Ridge Lodge **M** 🐾
(719) 539-2553. **$49-$119, 3 day notice.** 545 W Rainbow Blvd. On US 50, just w of Chamber of Commerce. Ext corridors. **Pets:** Small. $10 daily fee/pet. Designated rooms, service with restrictions, supervision.
[SAVE] [S🔧] [✕] [📋] [🖥] [🏊]

▼▼ Super 8 Motel **M**
(719) 539-6689. **$69-$149.** 525 W Rainbow Blvd. On US 50. Ext corridors. **Pets:** Accepted.
[ASK] [S🔧] [✕] [📋] [🖥] [🏊]

AAA ▼▼▼ Travelodge **M**
(719) 539-2528. **$59-$109.** 7310 Hwy 50. On US 50 W, just w of Hot Springs Pool. Ext corridors. **Pets:** Accepted.
[SAVE] [S🔧] [✕] [📋] [🖥] [🏊]

▼▼▼ The Tudor Rose Bed & Breakfast **BB**
(719) 539-2002. **$77-$180, 7 day notice.** 6720 CR 104. Just e on US 50, s on CR 104, 0.5 mi up the hill, follow signs. Int corridors. **Pets:** Accepted.
[✕] [📋] [✕] [🌡]

AAA ▼▼▼ Woodland Motel **M** 🐾
(719) 539-4980. **$50-$145.** 903 W 1st St. From center of historic downtown, 0.5 mi w on 1st St (SR 291). Ext corridors. **Pets:** Other species.
[SAVE] [S🔧] [✕] [📋] [🖥]

SILVERTHORNE

AAA ▼▼ Days Inn Summit County **SH**
(970) 468-8661. **$51-$193, 3 day notice.** 580 Silverthorne Ln. I-70, exit 205, just n on SR 9, just e on Rainbow Dr, then just e on Tanglewood Ln. Int corridors. **Pets:** Other species. $10 daily fee/pet. Supervision.
[SAVE] [✕] [&M] [📋] [🖥]

▼▼ Quality Inn & Suites **SH**
(970) 513-1222. **Call for rates.** 530 Silverthorne Ln. I-70, exit 205, just n on SR 9, just e on Rainbow Dr, then just e on Tanglewood Ln. Int corridors. **Pets:** Medium. $50 deposit/pet, $10 daily fee/pet. Designated rooms, service with restrictions, supervision.
[✕] [&M] [📋] [🖥] [🏊]

SILVERTON

AAA ▼▼▼▼ Silverton's Inn of the Rockies at the Historic Alma House **BB**
(970) 387-5336. **$89-$139, 7 day notice.** 220 E 10th St. On 10th St, just se of Greene St (Main St). Int corridors. **Pets:** Accepted.
[SAVE] [S🔧] [✕] [🌡] [☎]

▼▼ Villa Dallavalle B & B **BB**
(970) 387-5555. **$75-$125.** 1257 Blair St. Corner of 13th and Blair sts. Int corridors. **Pets:** Accepted.
[ASK] [S🔧] [✕] [🖥] [🌡]

AAA ▼▼▼▼ The Wyman Hotel & Inn **BB**
(970) 387-5372. **Call for rates.** 1371 Greene St. Corner of Greene (Main St) and 14th sts. Int corridors. **Pets:** Accepted.
[SAVE] [✕] [📋] [🍴] [🌡]

SNOWMASS VILLAGE

▼▼ Snowmass Mountain Chalet **SH**
(970) 923-3900. **$99-$340, 45 day notice.** 115 Daly Ln. 4 mi sw of SR 82 via Brush Creek and Lower Village rds, Lot 5. Ext/int corridors. **Pets:** Accepted.
[ASK] [S🔧] [✕] [📋] [🖥] [🏊] [✕] [🌡]

SOUTH FORK

AAA ▼▼▼ Americas Best Value Inn Wolf Creek Lodge **SH**
(719) 873-5547. **Call for rates.** 31042 Hwy 160 W. On US 160. Ext corridors. **Pets:** Accepted.
[SAVE] [✕] [📋] [🖥] [✕]

▼ Ute Bluff Lodge and RV Park **M**
(719) 873-5595. **$44-$198, 14 day notice.** 27680 W Hwy 160. 2.5 mi e of jct US 160 and SR 149. Ext corridors. **Pets:** Accepted.
[ASK] [S🔧] [✕] [📋] [🖥] [🌡]

STEAMBOAT SPRINGS

AAA ▼▼ The Alpiner Lodge **M**
(970) 879-1430. **$69-$119, 5 day notice.** 424 Lincoln Ave. US 40, just w of Hot Springs Pool. Ext/int corridors. **Pets:** $15 one-time fee/room. Designated rooms, service with restrictions, supervision.
[SAVE] [S🔧] [✕] [📋] [🖥]

▼▼ Comfort Inn **SH**
(970) 879-6669. **$79-$499, 3 day notice.** 1055 Walton Creek Rd. 2.8 mi e on US 40. Int corridors. **Pets:** Accepted.
[ASK] [S🔧] [✕] [&M] [📋] [🖥] [🏊]

AAA ▼▼▼▼ Fairfield Inn & Suites by Marriott **SH** 🐾
(970) 870-9000. **$142-$252.** 3200 S Lincoln Ave. 3 mi e on US 40. Int corridors. **Pets:** $25 one-time fee/room. Designated rooms, service with restrictions, supervision.
[SAVE] [S🔧] [✕] [&M] [📋] [🖥] [🏊]

AAA ▼▼▼▼ Holiday Inn Steamboat **SH**
(970) 879-2250. **$119-$219, 3 day notice.** 3190 S Lincoln Ave. 3 mi e on US 40. Int corridors. **Pets:** Accepted.
[SAVE] [S🔧] [✕] [&M] [📋] [🖥] [🍴] [🏊] [✕]

AAA ▼▼ Nordic Lodge **M**
(970) 879-0531. **$69-$299, 14 day notice.** 1036 Lincoln Ave. Between 10th and 11th sts; downtown. Ext corridors. **Pets:** $10 daily fee/pet. Service with restrictions, supervision.
[SAVE] [✕] [📋] [🏊]

AAA ▼▼ Rabbit Ears Motel **M**
(970) 879-1150. **$79-$169, 3 day notice.** 201 Lincoln Ave. Just e on US 40. Ext corridors. **Pets:** $15 one-time fee/room. Service with restrictions, supervision.
[SAVE] [S🔧] [✕] [📋] [🖥]

▼▼▼ Sheraton Steamboat Resort **LH**
(970) 879-2220. **$219-$499, 30 day notice.** 2200 Village Inn Ct. 2.3 mi e on US 40, 1 mi n on Mt Werner Rd; at ski area. Int corridors. **Pets:** Accepted.
[ASK] [S🔧] [✕] [📋] [🖥] [🍴] [🏊] [✕]

AAA ▼▼ Super 8 Motel **SH**
(970) 879-5230. **$59-$98.** 3195 S Lincoln Ave. 3 mi e on US 40. Int corridors. **Pets:** Accepted.
[ASK] [S🔧] [✕] [📋] [🖥] [🏊]

STERLING

Best Western Sundowner Ⓜ
(970) 522-6265. **$80-$121.** 125 Overland Trail St. I-76, exit 125, just w. Ext/int corridors. **Pets:** $10 daily fee/room. Designated rooms, service with restrictions, supervision.
SAVE S❄ ⊠ 🛢 💻 ➥

Colonial Motel Ⓜ
(970) 522-3382. **$50-$68.** 915 S Division. I-76, exit 125, 1.8 mi w on US 6 to 3rd traffic light (4th St), then 0.7 mi s. Ext corridors. **Pets:** Dogs only. $5 daily fee/pet. Service with restrictions, supervision.
SAVE S❄ ⊠ 🛢

Ramada Inn SH
(970) 522-2625. **$76-$120.** 22140 E Hwy 6. I-76, exit 125, 0.5 mi e on US 6. Ext/int corridors. **Pets:** Accepted.
ASK S❄ ⊠ 🛢 💻 ¶¶ ➥ ⊠

STRATTON

Best Western Golden Prairie Inn SH
(719) 348-5311. **$79-$99.** 700 Colorado Ave. I-70, exit 419, just n. Ext corridors. **Pets:** $10 one-time fee/pet. Designated rooms, service with restrictions, crate.
SAVE S❄ ⊠ 🛢 💻 ¶¶ ➥

TELLURIDE

Fairmont Heritage Place Franz Klammer Lodge
(970) 728-3318. **Call for rates (no credit cards).** 567 Mountain Village Blvd. SR 145 S, take left on Mountain Village Blvd, then 2.3 mi to entrance; SR 145 N, take right on Mountain Village Blvd, then 2.3 mi to entrance. Int corridors. **Pets:** Medium. $35 one-time fee/pet. Designated rooms, service with restrictions, supervision.
⊠ 🛢 💻 ➥ ⊠ 🅐

Hotel Columbia SH ❀
(970) 728-0660. **$150-$340, 30 day notice.** 300 W San Juan Ave. Just s of SR 145 (Colorado Ave); corner of Aspen St and San Juan Ave; opposite gondola. Int corridors. **Pets:** Dogs only. $20 daily fee/room. Designated rooms, service with restrictions.
SAVE S❄ ⊠ 🛢 💻 ¶¶ ⊠

The Hotel Telluride SH ❀
(970) 369-1188. **$169-$499.** 199 N Cornet St. Just n of jct SR 145 (Colorado Ave). Int corridors. **Pets:** $100 one-time fee/room. Service with restrictions, supervision.
SAVE ⊠ ♿M 🛢 💻 ¶¶ ⊠

TRINIDAD

Best Western Trinidad Inn Ⓜ
(719) 846-2215. **Call for rates.** 900 W Adams St. I-25, exit 13A northbound; exit Cross Bridge southbound, just ne. Ext corridors. **Pets:** Accepted.
SAVE ⊠ 🛢 💻 ➥

Budget Host Derrick Motel Ⓜ
(719) 846-3307. **$79-$99.** 10301 Santa Fe Trail Dr. I-25, exit 11, 0.5 mi ne. Ext corridors. **Pets:** Medium, dogs only. Service with restrictions, supervision.
SAVE S❄ ⊠ 🛢 💻

Quality Inn Trinidad SH
(719) 846-4491. **$89-$119.** 3125 Toupal Dr. I-25, exit 11, just w. Int corridors. **Pets:** Medium. $15 daily fee/pet. Designated rooms, service with restrictions, supervision.
SAVE S❄ ⊠ 🛢 💻 ¶¶ ➥ ⊠

Super 8 Motel Ⓜ
(719) 846-8280. **Call for rates.** 1924 Freedom Rd. I-25, exit 15, just ne. Int corridors. **Pets:** Accepted.
⊠ 🛢 💻

VAIL

Antlers at Vail CO
(970) 476-2471. **$190-$725, 60 day notice.** 680 W Lionshead Pl. I-70, exit 176, 0.5 mi w, then just s on Lionshead Cir. Ext corridors. **Pets:** Other species. $15 daily fee/pet. Designated rooms, service with restrictions, crate.
SAVE ⊠ 🛢 💻 ➥ ⊠ 🅐

Evergreen Lodge at Vail SH
(970) 476-7810. **$120-$450, 30 day notice.** 250 S Frontage Rd W. I-70, exit 176, just w. Int corridors. **Pets:** Accepted.
ASK S❄ ⊠ 🛢 💻 ¶¶ ➥ ⊠ 🅐

Holiday Inn Apex Vail SH
(970) 476-2739. **$99-$599.** 2211 N Frontage Rd. I-70, exit 173, just e. Int corridors. **Pets:** Accepted.
ASK S❄ ⊠ ♿M 🛢 💻 ¶¶ ➥ ⊠

The Lodge at Vail, a RockResort SH ❀
(970) 476-5011. **$149-$686, 45 day notice.** 174 E Gore Creek Dr. I-70, exit 176, s on Vail Rd to center of village. Ext/int corridors. **Pets:** Dogs only. $25 daily fee/pet. Designated rooms, service with restrictions.
SAVE ⊠ 🛢 💻 ➥ ⊠

WALSENBURG

Best Western Rambler SH ❀
(719) 738-1121. **$90-$175.** 457 US Hwy 85-87. I-25, exit 52, just w. Ext corridors. **Pets:** Medium. $10 daily fee/pet. Designated rooms, service with restrictions, crate.
SAVE S❄ ⊠ 🛢 💻 ¶¶ ➥

WELLINGTON

Comfort Inn Wellington SH
(970) 568-0444. **Call for rates.** 7860 6th St. I-25, exit 278, just w, then just s. Int corridors. **Pets:** Accepted.
⊠ 🛢 💻 ➥

WINDSOR

Super 8 Motel SH
(970) 686-5996. **$60-$125.** 1265 Main St. I-25, exit 262, 3.8 mi e; in shopping/restaurant complex. Int corridors. **Pets:** Accepted.
ASK S❄ ⊠ ♿M 🛢 💻

WINTER PARK

Best Western Alpenglo Lodge SH
(970) 726-8088. **$72-$179, 30 day notice.** 78665 US Hwy 40. On US 40; center. Int corridors. **Pets:** Accepted.
SAVE S❄ ⊠ ♿M 🛢 💻

Winter Park Mountain Lodge SH
(970) 726-4211. **$67-$379, 21 day notice.** 81699 US Hwy 40. 2.3 mi se on US 40; near Winter Park ski area. Int corridors. **Pets:** Accepted.
SAVE S❄ ⊠ ♿M 🛢 💻 ¶¶ ➥ ⊠

YAMPA

Oak Tree Inn SH
(970) 638-1000. **$85-$95.** 98 Moffat Ave. Just off SR 131. Int corridors. **Pets:** Accepted.
ASK S❄ ⊠ 🛢 💻 ¶¶

CONNECTICUT

BETHEL

▼▼▼ Microtel Inn & Suites 🆂🅷 ❀
(203) 748-8318. $79-$89. 80 Benedict Rd. I-84, exit 8, 1 mi e on US 6.
Int corridors. **Pets:** Other species. $100 deposit/room, $10 daily fee/pet.
Service with restrictions, crate.

Ⓐ🆂🅺 🆂🔟 ⊠ 🛏 💻

BRIDGEPORT

▼▼▼▼ Bridgeport Holiday Inn & Convention Center 🆂🅷
(203) 334-1234. $159. 1070 Main St. SR 8, exit 2 northbound, 0.7 mi
se; exit southbound, just s, then just e. Int corridors. **Pets:** $10 daily
fee/room. Service with restrictions, supervision.

Ⓐ🆂🅺 🆂🔟 ⊠ 🅰🅼 🛏 💻 🍴 🏊

BROOKFIELD

▼▼ Newbury Inn 🅼
(203) 775-0220. $99-$109. 1030 Federal Rd (Rt 7 & 202). Jct SR 25,
0.9 mi nw on US 7 and 202. Ext/int corridors. **Pets:** Small. $10 daily
fee/pet. Service with restrictions, crate.

Ⓐ🆂🅺 🆂🔟 ⊠ 🛏

DANBURY

▼▼▼ Ethan Allen Hotel 🆂🅷
(203) 744-1776. $95-$135. 21 Lake Ave Extension. I-84, exit 4, 0.3 mi
w on US 6 and 202. Int corridors. **Pets:** Dogs only. $15 daily fee/room.
Designated rooms, no service, supervision.

Ⓐ🆂🅺 🆂🔟 ⊠ 🛏 💻 🍴 🏊

🔷 ▼▼▼▼ Holiday Inn 🆂🅷
(203) 792-4000. $109-$154. 80 Newtown Rd. I-84, exit 8 (Newtown
Rd), 0.5 mi s on US 6 W. Int corridors. **Pets:** Large. $15 daily fee/pet.
Designated rooms, service with restrictions, supervision.

🆂🅰🆅🅴 🆂🔟 ⊠ 🛏 💻 🍴 🏊

🔷 ▼▼▼▼ Maron Hotel & Suites 🆂🅷
(203) 791-2200. $99-$189. 42 Lake Ave Extension. I-84, exit 4, 0.5 mi
w on US 6 and 202. Int corridors. **Pets:** Accepted.

🆂🅰🆅🅴 🆂🔟 ⊠ 🅰🅼 🛏 💻 🍴

🔷 ▼▼▼▼ Residence Inn by Marriott 🆂🅷 ❀
(203) 797-1256. $181-$207. 22 Segar St. I-84, exit 4 eastbound, just n;
exit westbound, just e on Lake Ave Extension, then just s. Int corridors. **Pets:** Other species. Service with restrictions.

🆂🅰🆅🅴 🆂🔟 ⊠ 🛏 💻 🏊

▼▼▼ Sheraton Danbury 🅻🅷
(203) 794-0600. $139. 18 Old Ridgebury Rd. I-84, exit 2 eastbound;
exit 2A westbound. Int corridors. **Pets:** Accepted.

Ⓐ🆂🅺 🆂🔟 ⊠ 🛏 💻 🍴 🏊 ⊠

DAYVILLE

▼▼▼ Holiday Inn Express 🆂🅷
(860) 779-3200. $120-$140. 16 Tracy Rd. I-395, exit 94, just w. Int
corridors. **Pets:** Medium. $10 daily fee/pet. Service with restrictions, crate.

Ⓐ🆂🅺 🆂🔟 ⊠ 🅰🅼 🛏 💻 🏊

FAIRFIELD

🔷 ▼▼▼▼ Best Western Black Rock Inn 🆂🅷
(203) 659-2200. $119-$229. 100 Kings Hwy Cutoff. I-95, exit 24, just
sw. Int corridors. **Pets:** Small, dogs only. $20 one-time fee/pet. Designated
rooms, service with restrictions, supervision.

🆂🅰🆅🅴 🆂🔟 ⊠ 🅰🅼 🛏 💻

GREENWICH

🔷 ▼▼▼▼ The Stanton House Inn 🅱🅱
(203) 869-2110. $169-$249, 7 day notice. 76 Maple Ave. Just n of US
1; center. Ext/int corridors. **Pets:** Accepted.

🆂🅰🆅🅴 ⊠ 🛏 🏊

GRISWOLD

▼▼▼ AmericInn Lodge & Suites 🆂🅷
(860) 376-3200. $69-$179. 375 Voluntown Rd. I-395, exit 85, w on SR
138. Int corridors. **Pets:** Accepted.

Ⓐ🆂🅺 🆂🔟 ⊠ 🅰🅼 🛏 💻 🏊

HAMDEN

▼▼▼ Clarion Hotel & Suites Hamden-New Haven 🅼
(203) 288-3831. $129-$179, 7 day notice. 2260 Whitney Ave. Just n
off SR 15, exit 61. Int corridors. **Pets:** Small, dogs only. $50 deposit/
room. Service with restrictions, supervision.

Ⓐ🆂🅺 🆂🔟 ⊠ 🛏 💻 🏊

HARTFORD METROPOLITAN AREA

AVON

▼▼▼▼ Avon Old Farms Hotel SH ❀
(860) 677-1651. **$159-$209.** 279 Avon Mountain Rd. Jct US 44 and SR
10. Ext/int corridors. **Pets:** Large. $50 deposit/room. Designated rooms,
service with restrictions, crate.

(A$K) (S🐾) (✕) (🛏) (🖥) (🍴) (🏊) (🐾)

▼▼▼ Residence Inn by Marriott Hartford-Avon SH
(860) 678-1666. **$187-$207.** 55 Simsbury Rd (SR 202). Jct US 44, just
n. Int corridors. **Pets:** Other species. $100 one-time fee/room. Service with
restrictions, supervision.

(A$K) (S🐾) (✕) (�&M) (🛏) (🖥) (🏊) (🐾)

BERLIN

🔷🔷 ▼▼▼ Hawthorne Inn SH
(860) 828-4181. **$89-$99.** 2387 Berlin Tpke. I-91, exit 17 northbound,
4.7 mi n on SR 15 (Berlin Tpke); exit 22N southbound, 2.5 mi n on SR
9 to exit 22, follow signs onto US 5 and SR 15 (Berlin Tpke), then 3
mi s. Int corridors. **Pets:** Accepted.

(SAVE) (S🐾) (✕) (🛏) (🍴) (🏊)

CROMWELL

▼▼ ▼▼ Comfort Inn SH
(860) 635-4100. **Call for rates.** 111 Berlin Rd. I-91, exit 21, just e on
SR 372. Int corridors. **Pets:** Accepted.

(✕) (🛏) (🖥)

EAST HARTFORD

🔷🔷 ▼▼▼▼ Sheraton Hartford Hotel SH
(860) 528-9703. **$89-$169.** 100 E River Dr. I-84, exit 53 eastbound, just
s; exit 54 westbound to exit 3 (Darlin St), just n. Int corridors.
Pets: Accepted.

(SAVE) (S🐾) (✕) (�&M) (🛏) (🖥) (🍴) (🏊)

EAST WINDSOR

**🔷🔷 ▼▼▼▼ Holiday Inn Express Hartford Airport
Area** M
(860) 627-6585. **$95-$109.** 260 Main St (US 5). I-91, exit 44, just s. Int
corridors. **Pets:** Accepted.

(SAVE) (S🐾) (✕) (�&M) (🛏) (🖥)

ENFIELD

▼▼ ▼▼ Red Roof Inn # 7105 M
(860) 741-2571. **Call for rates.** 5 Hazard Ave. I-91, exit 47E. Ext
corridors. **Pets:** Accepted.

(✕) (�&M) (🛏)

FARMINGTON

🔷🔷 ▼▼▼▼ Centennial Inn Suites CO
(860) 677-4647. **$121-$181.** 5 Spring Ln. US 6, 0.3 mi e of jct SR 177.
Ext/int corridors. **Pets:** Accepted.

(SAVE) (S🐾) (✕) (�&M) (🛏) (🖥) (🏊)

**▼▼ ▼▼ Extended StayAmerica Deluxe
Hartford-Farmington** SH
(860) 676-2790. **$125-$175.** 1 Batterson Park Rd. I-84, exit 37, just ne.
Int corridors. **Pets:** Other species. $75 one-time fee/pet. Service with
restrictions.

(A$K) (S🐾) (✕) (🛏) (🖥)

▼▼▼▼ Homewood Suites by Hilton SH
(860) 321-0000. **Call for rates.** 2 Farm Glen Blvd. I-84, exit 39, 0.6 mi
e on SR 4. Int corridors. **Pets:** Accepted.

(✕) (�&M) (🛏) (🖥) (🏊)

GLASTONBURY

**🔷🔷🔷 ▼▼▼▼ Homewood Suites by Hilton Hartford
South-Glastonbury** SH
(860) 652-8111. **$109-$299.** 65 Glastonbury Blvd. SR 3, exit Main St,
just se. Int corridors. **Pets:** Other species. $100 one-time fee/room. Serv-
ice with restrictions.

(SAVE) (S🐾) (✕) (�&M) (🛏) (🖥) (🏊) (🐾)

HARTFORD

▼▼▼▼ Crowne Plaza Hartford Downtown LH
(860) 549-2400. **$129-$209.** 50 Morgan St. I-91, exit 32B; I-84, exit 50
eastbound; exit 52 westbound. Int corridors. **Pets:** Small. $50 one-time
fee/room. Service with restrictions, crate.

(A$K) (S🐾) (✕) (�&M) (🛏) (🖥) (🍴) (🏊)

▼▼▼▼ Goodwin Hotel SH ❀
(860) 246-7500. **$139-$1200.** 1 Haynes St. Downtown; entrance on
Asylum St. Int corridors. **Pets:** Large, other species. $25 one-time fee/
room. Service with restrictions.

(A$K) (✕) (�&M) (🛏) (🖥) (🍴)

▼▼▼▼ Holiday Inn Express Downtown SH
(860) 246-9900. **$109-$189.** 440 Asylum St. I-84, exit 48, just se via
Spring St. Int corridors. **Pets:** Accepted.

(A$K) (✕) (🛏) (🖥)

**▼▼▼▼ Residence Inn by Marriott Downtown
Hartford** SH ❀
(860) 524-5550. **$285-$318.** 942 Main St. I-91, exit 29A northbound;
exit 31 southbound. Int corridors. **Pets:** $100 one-time fee/pet. Desig-
nated rooms.

(A$K) (S🐾) (✕) (🛏) (🖥)

MANCHESTER

▼▼ ▼▼ Extended StayAmerica SH
(860) 643-5140. **$108-$158.** 340 Tolland Tpke. I-84, exit 63, 0.3 mi se
on SR 30, then just sw. Int corridors. **Pets:** Other species. $75 one-time
fee/pet. Service with restrictions.

(A$K) (S🐾) (✕) (�&M) (🛏) (🖥)

🔷🔷🔷 ▼▼▼▼ Residence Inn Manchester SH
(860) 432-4242. **$197-$285.** 201 Hale Rd. I-84, exit 63, 0.5 mi nw, then
0.6 mi sw. Int corridors. **Pets:** Accepted.

(SAVE) (S🐾) (✕) (�&M) (🛏) (🖥) (🏊) (🐾)

ROCKY HILL

▼▼▼▼ Residence Inn by Marriott Hartford-Rocky Hill SH
(860) 257-7500. **$186-$207.** 680 Cromwell Ave. I-91, exit 23, 0.4 mi w
on West St, then just n. Int corridors. **Pets:** $100 one-time fee/room.
Service with restrictions.

(A$K) (S🐾) (✕) (�&M) (🛏) (🖥) (🏊) (🐾)

SIMSBURY

▼▼▼▼ Simsbury 1820 House CI
(860) 658-7658. **$169-$229.** 731 Hopmeadow St. US 202/SR 10, 2 mi
n of jct SR 185; center. Ext/int corridors. **Pets:** Accepted.

(A$K) (✕) (🛏) (🖥) (🍴)

SOUTHINGTON

🔷🔷🔷 ▼▼▼▼ Residence Inn by Marriott SH
(860) 621-4440. **$153-$186.** 778 West St. I-84, exit 31, just s. Int
corridors. **Pets:** Medium. $100 one-time fee/room. Designated rooms, serv-
ice with restrictions, crate.

(SAVE) (S🐾) (✕) (�&M) (🛏) (🖥) (🏊) (🐾)

VERNON

🐾 ◈◈◈ Quality Inn & Conference Center SH
(860) 646-5700. **$70-$120.** 51 Hartford Tpke (SR 83). I-84, exit 64, se on SR 30, then 0.8 mi s. Int corridors. **Pets:** Accepted.

SAVE Sℱ ⊠ ⅀M 🛏 🖵 ⇀ ⊠

WETHERSFIELD

🐾 ◈◈◈ Best Western Camelot Inn SH
(860) 563-2311. **$109-$159.** 1330 Silas Deane Hwy. I-91, exit 24, 0.4 mi n. Int corridors. **Pets:** Small. $50 one-time fee/pet. Designated rooms, service with restrictions, supervision.

SAVE Sℱ ⊠ ⅀M 🛏 🖵 ⇀ ⊠

WINDSOR

◈◈◈ The Residence Inn by Marriott
    Hartford-Windsor SH
(860) 688-7474. **$264-$284.** 100 Dunfey Ln. I-91, exit 37, just w on SR 305 to Dunfey Ln, then 0.3 mi n. Ext corridors. **Pets:** Accepted.

ASK Sℱ ⊠ ⅀M 🛏 🖵 ⇀ ⊠

WINDSOR LOCKS

◈◈◈ Candlewood Suites SH
(860) 623-2000. **$119-$129.** 149 Ella T Grasso Tpke. I-91, exit 40, 2.5 mi w on SR 20, then 0.6 mi n on SR 75. Int corridors. **Pets:** Large, other species. $75 one-time fee/room. Designated rooms, service with restrictions, crate.

ASK Sℱ ⊠ ⅀M 🛏 🖵 ⇀

END METROPOLITAN AREA

IVORYTON

🐾 ◈◈◈ The Copper Beech Inn CI
(860) 767-0330. **$225-$400, 14 day notice.** 46 Main St. SR 9, exit 3, 1.7 mi w. Int corridors. **Pets:** Accepted.

SAVE ⊠ 🍽

LAKEVILLE

🐾 ◈◈ Inn at Iron Masters M
(860) 435-9844. **$100-$205, 3 day notice.** 229 Main St (Rt 44 & 41). 0.5 mi ne. Ext corridors. **Pets:** Accepted.

SAVE ⊠ 🖵 ⇀

🐾 ◈◈◈ Interlaken Inn Resort and Conference
    Center SH ❖
(860) 435-9878. **$149-$259, 7 day notice.** 74 Interlaken Rd. On SR 112, 0.5 mi w of jct SR 41. Ext/int corridors. **Pets:** Dogs only. $15 daily fee/room. Designated rooms, service with restrictions, supervision.

SAVE ⊠ 🛏 🖵 🍽 ⇀ ⊠

LEDYARD

◈◈ Almost In Mystic/Mares Inn BB ❖
(860) 572-7556. **$125-$225, 14 day notice.** 333 Colonel Ledyard Hwy. I-95, exit 89, 1 mi ne to Gold Star Hwy, 0.6 mi w, then 0.7 mi n. Int corridors. **Pets:** Other species. Designated rooms.

ASK ⊠ 🛏 🖵 🗹

LITCHFIELD

🐾 ◈◈ Litchfield Inn CI ❖
(860) 567-4503. **$170-$312, 3 day notice.** 432 Bantam Rd. 1.5 mi w on US 202. Int corridors. **Pets:** Medium. $25 daily fee/pet. Designated rooms, service with restrictions, supervision.

SAVE Sℱ ⊠ 🛏 🖵 🍽

🐾 ◈◈◈ Homewood Suites by Hilton SH
(860) 627-8463. **Call for rates.** 65 Ella T Grasso Tpke. I-91, exit 40, 2.5 mi w on SR 20, then just n on SR 75. Ext/int corridors. **Pets:** Accepted.

⊠ ⅀M 🛏 🖵 ⇀ ⊠

◈◈◈ La Quinta Inn Hartford-Airport SH
(860) 623-3336. **$89-$95.** 64 Ella T Grasso Tpke. I-91, exit 40, 2.5 mi w on SR 20, then just n on SR 75. Int corridors. **Pets:** Other species. Service with restrictions, supervision.

ASK Sℱ ⊠ ⅀M 🛏 🖵

◈◈ Ramada Inn Bradley International Airport SH ❖
(860) 623-9494. **Call for rates.** 5 Ella T Grasso Tpke. I-91, exit 40, 2.5 mi w on SR 20, then just n on SR 75. Int corridors. **Pets:** Medium. $49 one-time fee/room. Service with restrictions, supervision.

⊠ 🛏 🖵 🍽 ⇀

🐾 ◈◈◈ Sheraton Hotel At Bradley International
    Airport LH
(860) 627-5311. **$299-$359, 3 day notice.** 1 Bradley International Airport. At Bradley International Airport terminal. Int corridors. **Pets:** Accepted.

SAVE Sℱ ⊠ ⅀M 🛏 🖵 🍽 ⇀

MERIDEN

◈◈ Extended StayAmerica Hartford-Meriden SH
(203) 630-1927. **$110-$160.** 366 Bee St. I-91, exit 17 northbound, just e on E Main St, then 0.7 mi n; exit 19 southbound, 0.5 mi w on Baldwin Ave, then 0.6 mi s. Int corridors. **Pets:** Other species. $75 one-time fee/pet. Service with restrictions.

ASK Sℱ ⊠ 🛏 🖵

◈◈ Residence Inn by Marriott SH
(203) 634-7770. **$187-$212.** 390 Bee St. I-91, exit 16 northbound, just e on E Main St, then 0.7 mi n; exit 19 southbound, 0.5 mi w on Baldwin Ave, then 0.5 mi s. Ext/int corridors. **Pets:** Accepted.

ASK Sℱ ⊠ ⅀M 🛏 🖵 ⇀ ⊠

MILFORD

◈◈ Residence Inn by Marriott SH
(203) 283-2100. **$159-$180.** 62 Rowe Ave. I-95, exit 35, just nw. Int corridors. **Pets:** Large. $100 one-time fee/room. Service with restrictions, supervision.

ASK Sℱ ⊠ 🛏 🖵 ⇀

MYSTIC

🐾 ◈◈◈ Comfort Inn of Mystic SH ❖
(860) 572-8531. **$99-$199.** 48 Whitehall Ave. I-95, exit 90, just n on SR 27. Int corridors. **Pets:** Medium. $100 deposit/room, $25 one-time fee/pet. Designated rooms, service with restrictions, crate.

SAVE Sℱ ⊠ ⅀M 🛏 🖵

🐾 ◈◈◈ Inn at Mystic M
(860) 536-9604. **$95-$295.** 3 Williams Ave. On US 1 at SR 27. Ext/int corridors. **Pets:** Accepted.

SAVE ⊠ 🛏 🖵 🍽 ⇀ ⊠

🐾 ◈◈◈ Residence Inn by Marriott SH
(860) 536-5150. **$164-$274.** 40 Whitehall Ave. I-95, exit 90, just n on SR 27. Int corridors. **Pets:** Accepted.

SAVE Sℱ ⊠ 🛏 🖵 ⇀ ⊠

NEW HAVEN

◇◇◇ Omni New Haven Hotel at Yale LH
(203) 772-6664. **$219-$459.** 155 Temple St. Center of downtown. Int corridors. **Pets:** Accepted.

SAVE S X M 🔒 💻 ⑪

NEW LONDON

◇◇ Red Roof Inn #7145 M
(860) 444-0001. **Call for rates.** 707 Colman St. I-95, exit 82A northbound, 0.4 mi e, then just n; exit 83 southbound, 0.6 mi s. Ext corridors. **Pets:** Accepted.

X 🔒

NEW MILFORD

◇◇ The Homestead Inn BB
(860) 354-4080. **$105-$220.** 5 Elm St. Just e of village green off Main St; center. Ext/int corridors. **Pets:** Other species. $10 daily fee/room. Designated rooms, service with restrictions, supervision.

ASK S X 🔒

NIANTIC

◇ Motel 6-1063 M
(860) 739-6991. **Call for rates.** 269 Flanders Rd. I-95, exit 74, just s. Ext corridors. **Pets:** Other species. Service with restrictions, supervision.

X 🔒 ⮑

NORTH STONINGTON

◇◇◇ Antiques and Accommodations BB
(860) 535-1736. **$149-$269 (no credit cards).** 32 Main St. I-95, exit 92, 2.5 mi nw on SR 2, then 0.3 mi n. Int corridors. **Pets:** Accepted.

ASK S X ⊘

◇◇◇ The Inn at Lower Farm B & B BB
(860) 535-9075. **$100-$175, 7 day notice.** 119 Mystic Rd. I-95, exit 90, 1.5 mi n on SR 27, 1.4 mi e on SR 184, then 3.4 mi n on SR 201. Int corridors. **Pets:** Medium. $10 daily fee/room. Designated rooms, service with restrictions, supervision.

ASK S X 🅿 ⊘

NORWALK

◇◇◇ Four Points by Sheraton Norwalk SH
(203) 849-9828. **$100-$190.** 426 Main Ave. I-95, exit 15, 3.5 mi n via US 7, just e, then 0.7 mi s. Int corridors. **Pets:** Accepted.

SAVE X M 🔒 💻 ⑪

◇◇ Homestead Studio Suites Hotel-Norwalk SH
(203) 847-6888. **$148-$200.** 400 Main Ave. I-95, exit 15, 3.5 mi n via US 7, just e, then 1 mi s. Int corridors. **Pets:** Other species. $75 one-time fee/pet. Service with restrictions.

ASK S X M 🔒 💻

◇◇◇ The Silvermine Tavern CI
(203) 847-4558. **$140-$190, 3 day notice.** 194 Perry Ave. Merritt Pkwy, exit 40A, 0.5 mi s on Main Ave, then 1.7 mi ne. Int corridors. **Pets:** Accepted.

SAVE X 🔒 💻 ⑪ 🅿

OLD SAYBROOK

◇◇◇ Days Inn M
(860) 388-3453. **Call for rates.** 1430 Boston Post Rd. I-95, exit 66, 0.3 mi s on SR 166, then 0.5 mi e on US 1 N. Ext corridors. **Pets:** Small, dogs only. $15 daily fee/room. Designated rooms, service with restrictions, supervision.

SAVE X 🔒 💻

◇◇◇ Liberty Inn M
(860) 388-1777. **$58-$130.** 55 Spring Brook Rd. I-95, exit 68 southbound; exit 67 northbound, 0.9 mi n on US 1, then w. Ext corridors. **Pets:** Accepted.

SAVE S X 🔒 💻

◇◇◇ Saybrook Point Inn & Spa SH ❀
(860) 395-2000. **$229-$899, 3 day notice.** 2 Bridge St. On SR 154, 2.2 mi s of jct US 1; at Saybrook Point. Int corridors. **Pets:** Medium, dogs only. $50 daily fee/room. Designated rooms, service with restrictions, supervision.

SAVE X M 🔒 💻 ⑪ ⮑ 🔀

RIVERTON

◇◇ Old Riverton Inn CI
(860) 379-8678. **$95-$220, 10 day notice.** 436 E River Rd (SR 20). Center. Int corridors. **Pets:** Accepted.

X 🔒 ⑪

SHELTON

◇◇ Homestead Studio Suites Hotel-Shelton-Fairfield County SH
(203) 926-6868. **$150-$200.** 945 Bridgeport Ave. SR 8, exit 11, 0.5 mi w. Int corridors. **Pets:** Other species. $75 one-time fee/pet. Service with restrictions.

ASK S X M 🔒 💻

◇◇ Residence Inn by Marriott SH
(203) 926-9000. **$242-$262.** 1001 Bridgeport Ave. SR 8, exit 11, 0.3 mi w. Ext corridors. **Pets:** Accepted.

ASK S X M 🔒 💻 ⮑ 🔀

SOUTHBURY

◇◇◇ Cornucopia at Oldfield Bed and Breakfast BB
(203) 267-6772. **$100-$250, 14 day notice.** 782 Main St N. I-84, exit 15, 1.5 mi n. Int corridors. **Pets:** Medium, dogs only. Designated rooms, supervision.

ASK S X ⮑ ⊘

◇◇◇ Crowne Plaza Southbury SH
(203) 598-7600. **$99-$169.** 1284 Strongtown Rd. I-84, exit 16, just n on SR 188. Int corridors. **Pets:** Medium. $25 one-time fee/room. Designated rooms, service with restrictions, supervision.

SAVE S X M 🔒 💻 ⑪ ⮑ 🔀

◇◇◇ Heritage Hotel LH
(203) 264-8200. **$190.** 522 Heritage Rd. I-84, exit 15, 0.4 mi n on SR 67, then 1 mi w. Int corridors. **Pets:** Accepted.

SAVE S X M 🔒 💻 ⑪ ⮑ 🔀

STAMFORD

◇◇◇ Amsterdam Hotel–Greenwich/Stamford SH
(203) 327-4300. **$90-$170.** 19 Clark Ave. I-95, exit 8 northbound, just n on Atlantic St, 0.6 mi ne on Tresser Blvd, then just s; exit southbound, just nw on Elm St, ne on Main St, then just s. Int corridors. **Pets:** Accepted.

SAVE X 🔒 💻

◇◇◇ Hilton Stamford LH
(203) 967-2222. **$109-$349.** 1 First Stamford Pl. I-95, exit 7 northbound, just s on Greenwich Ave, then just w; exit 6 southbound, just s on West Ave, 0.3 mi w on Baxter Ave, just n on Fairfield Ave, then just e. Int corridors. **Pets:** Medium, dogs only. $75 deposit/pet. Service with restrictions, supervision.

ASK S X 🔒 💻 ⑪ ⮑ 🔀

◇◇◇ Holiday Inn Select LH
(203) 358-8400. **$239-$264.** 700 Main St. I-95, exit 8 southbound, just n on Elm; exit northbound, n on Atlantic St, 0.3 mi e on Tresser Blvd, then just n on Elm; downtown. Int corridors. **Pets:** Accepted.

ASK S X 🔒 💻 ⑪ ⮑

◇◇ La Quinta Inn & Suites Stamford SH
(203) 357-7100. **$145.** 135 Harvard Ave. I-95, exit 6 northbound, just s; exit southbound, just w on Grenhart Rd, then just s. Int corridors. **Pets:** Other species. Service with restrictions, supervision.

ASK S X M 🔒 💻 ⑪ ⮑

▼▼▼ **Marriott Stamford Hotel & Spa** LH
(203) 357-9555. **$292-$318.** Two Stamford Forum. I-95, exit 8, just n under viaduct, then n on Tresser Blvd. Int corridors. **Pets:** Accepted.

ASK S∅ ⊠ &M 🔲 🖭 ¶¶ ⊷ ⊠

▼▼▼ **Sheraton Stamford Hotel** LH
(203) 359-1300. **$159-$319.** 2701 Summer St. I-95, exit 8 northbound, 1.7 mi w on Atlantic and Bedford sts; exit 7 southbound, n on Atlantic and Bedford sts. Int corridors. **Pets:** Medium, dogs only. Service with restrictions, crate.

ASK S∅ ⊠ 🔲 🖭 ¶¶ ⊷ ⊠

STONINGTON

◈◈◈ ▼▼▼ **Another Second Penny Inn** BB
(860) 535-1710. **$80-$195, 7 day notice.** 870 Pequot Tr. I-95, exit 91, 0.8 mi s on SR 234. Int corridors. **Pets:** Accepted.

SAVE S∅ ⊠ 🔲

STRATFORD

▼▼▼ **Homewood Suites by Hilton** SH
(203) 377-3322. **$179-$219.** 6905 Main St. SR 15, exit 53, just n. Int corridors. **Pets:** Accepted.

ASK S∅ ⊠ &M 🔲 🖭 ⊷

WATERBURY

▼▼▼ **House on the Hill Bed & Breakfast** BB
(203) 757-9901. **$175-$250, 14 day notice.** 92 Woodlawn Terr. I-84, exit 21, 0.6 mi n on Meadow St, then 0.4 mi ne on Pine St. Int corridors. **Pets:** Service with restrictions, supervision.

ASK S∅ ⊠ 🔲 🖭

WATERFORD

◈◈◈ ▼ **Oakdell Motel** M
(860) 442-9446. **$65-$160.** 983 Hartford Tpke. I-95, exit 82, 2 mi n on SR 85. Ext/int corridors. **Pets:** Accepted.

SAVE ⊠ 🔲 ⊷

▼ **Rodeway Inn at Crossroad** M
(860) 442-7227. **$60-$150.** 211 Parkway N. I-95, exit 81 northbound, just nw; exit southbound, 0.6 mi w. Ext corridors. **Pets:** Other species. $15 daily fee/pet. Designated rooms.

ASK S∅ ⊠ 🔲 ⊷

WESTPORT

▼▼▼ **The Westport Inn** M ❀
(203) 259-5236. **$169-$399.** 1595 Post Rd E. I-95, exit 18 northbound, n to US 1, then 1.5 mi e; exit 19 southbound, 1 mi w. Ext/int corridors. **Pets:** Large. $49 one-time fee/room. Designated rooms, service with restrictions.

ASK S∅ ⊠ 🔲 🖭 ⊷

DELAWARE

CLAYMONT

▼▼▼ Holiday Inn Select Wilmington 🔛
(302) 792-2700. **$109-$145.** 630 Naamans Rd. I-95, exit 11, just w on SR 92; I-495, exit 6 (Naamans Rd). Int corridors. **Pets:** Medium, other species. $50 deposit/pet. No service, supervision.
(ASK) 🔲 ⊠ 🔲 🔲 🔲 🔲 🔲

DEWEY BEACH

⨮⨮⨮ ▼▼▼ Atlantic Oceanside Motel 🅼 ☙
(302) 227-8811. **$45-$269, 7 day notice.** 1700 Hwy 1. Jct SR 1 and McKinley St. Ext corridors. **Pets:** Dogs only. $5 daily fee/pet. Service with restrictions, crate.
(SAVE) ⊠ 🔲 🔲

▼▼ Bellbuoy Motel 🅼 ☙
(302) 227-6000. **$55-$375, 3 day notice.** 21 Van Dyke St. SR 1, on oceanside block of Van Dyke St. Ext corridors. **Pets:** Dogs only. $10 daily fee/pet. Designated rooms, service with restrictions.
⊠ 🔲 🔲

⨮⨮⨮ ▼▼ Best Western Gold Leaf 🔛
(302) 226-1100. **Call for rates.** 1400 Hwy 1. On SR 1; center. Int corridors. **Pets:** Accepted.
(SAVE) ⊠ 🔲 🔲 🔲

⨮⨮⨮ ▼ Sea-Esta Motel I 🅼
(302) 227-7666. **$49-$199.** 2306 Hwy 1. SR 1 at Houston St. Ext corridors. **Pets:** Accepted.
(SAVE) ⊠ 🔲

⨮⨮⨮ ▼▼ Sea-Esta Motel III 🅼
(302) 227-4343. **$55-$229.** 1409 Hwy 1. Jct SR 1 and Rodney St. Ext corridors. **Pets:** Accepted.
(SAVE) ⊠ 🔲 🔲

DOVER

⨮⨮⨮ ▼▼▼ Comfort Inn-Dover 🅼
(302) 674-3300. **$89-$129.** 222 S DuPont Hwy. SR 1, exit 95, 2 mi n on US 113, then 0.3 mi n on US 13. Ext corridors. **Pets:** Medium, other species. $35 one-time fee/room. Designated rooms, service with restrictions, crate.
(SAVE) 🔲 ⊠ 🔲 🔲 🔲

⨮⨮⨮ ▼▼▼▼ Sheraton Dover Hotel 🔛
(302) 678-8500. **Call for rates.** 1570 N DuPont Hwy. SR 1, exit 104, 1 mi s on US 13. Int corridors. **Pets:** Accepted.
(SAVE) ⊠ 🔲 🔲 🔲

GEORGETOWN

⨮⨮⨮ ▼▼▼▼ Comfort Inn & Suites-Georgetown 🔛
(302) 854-9400. **$90-$280, 3 day notice.** 20530 DuPont Blvd. On US 113, 0.5 mi n of jct SR 404. Int corridors. **Pets:** $15 daily fee/room. Designated rooms, service with restrictions, supervision.
(SAVE) ⊠ 🔲 🔲 🔲

HARRINGTON

▼▼▼▼ AmericInn Lodge & Suites of Harrington 🔛 ☙
(302) 398-3900. **$99-$139.** 1259 Corn Crib Rd. On US 13, 0.6 mi s of jct SR 14. Int corridors. **Pets:** Dogs only. $20 daily fee/room. Designated rooms, service with restrictions, crate.
(ASK) 🔲 ⊠ 🔲 🔲 🔲 🔲

LEWES

⨮⨮⨮ ▼▼▼ The Inn at Canal Square 🔛
(302) 644-3377. **$105-$300, 7 day notice.** 122 Market St. On the canal. Int corridors. **Pets:** Medium. Designated rooms, service with restrictions, supervision.
(SAVE) 🔲 ⊠ 🔲 🔲 🔲

⨮⨮⨮ ▼▼▼ Sleep Inn & Suites 🔛
(302) 645-6464. **$59-$259.** 18451 Coastal Hwy. On SR 1, 1.5 mi s. Int corridors. **Pets:** Accepted.
(SAVE) 🔲 ⊠ 🔲 🔲 🔲

LONG NECK

⨮⨮⨮ ▼▼▼ Sea Esta II 🅼
(302) 945-5900. **$49-$169.** A19 Long Neck Rd. On SR 23, 1.1 mi s of jct SR 24, 5 and 23. Ext corridors. **Pets:** Accepted.
(SAVE) ⊠ 🔲 🔲 🔲

MILLSBORO

▼▼ Atlantic Inn-Millsboro 🅼
(302) 934-6711. **$65-$189.** 210 E DuPont Hwy. US 113, just s of SR 24. Ext corridors. **Pets:** Accepted.
(ASK) ⊠ 🔲 🔲

NEWARK

⨮⨮⨮ ▼▼▼ Days Inn Wilmington/Newark 🅼
(302) 368-2400. **Call for rates.** 900 Churchmans Rd. I-95, exit 4B, 0.3 mi n on SR 7, exit 166, then 0.3 mi w on SR 58 (Churchmans Rd). Ext corridors. **Pets:** Small. $10 daily fee/pet. Service with restrictions, supervision.
(SAVE) ⊠ 🔲 🔲 🔲

▼▼▼ Hilton Wilmington/Christiana 🔛 ☙
(302) 454-1500. **Call for rates.** 100 Continental Dr. I-95, exit 4B, 0.3 mi n on SR 7, exit 166, then 0.4 mi w on SR 58 (Churchmans Rd). Int corridors. **Pets:** Medium. $49 one-time fee/room. Service with restrictions, supervision.
⊠ 🔲 🔲 🔲 🔲 🔲

▼▼ Homestead Studio Suites Hotel-Newark/Christiana 🔛
(302) 283-0800. **$114-$124.** 333 Continental Dr. I-95, exit 4B, 0.3 mi n on SR 7, exit 166, then 0.4 mi w on SR 58 (Churchmans Rd). Int corridors. **Pets:** Other species. $75 one-time fee/pet. Service with restrictions.
(ASK) 🔲 ⊠ 🔲 🔲 🔲

▼▼▼ Homewood Suites by Hilton Newark/Wilmington South 🔛
(302) 453-9700. **Call for rates.** 640 S College Ave. I-95, exit 1B southbound; exit 1 northbound, 0.8 mi n on SR 896. Int corridors. **Pets:** Small. $150 one-time fee/pet. Designated rooms, service with restrictions.
⊠ 🔲 🔲 🔲 🔲

⨮⨮⨮ ▼▼ Howard Johnson Inn & Suites–Wilmington/Newark 🔛
(302) 368-8521. **Call for rates.** 1119 S College Ave. I-95, exit 1B southbound; exit 1 northbound, 0.3 mi n on SR 896. Int corridors. **Pets:** Accepted.
(SAVE) ⊠ 🔲 🔲 🔲

▼▼ ▼▼ **Quality Inn University** Ⓜ
(302) 368-8715. **$59-$349.** 1120 S College Ave. I-95, exit 1B south-bound; exit 1 northbound, 0.3 mi n on SR 896. Ext corridors. **Pets:** Medium, other species. $10 daily fee/pet. Designated rooms, service with restrictions, supervision.

[A$K] [S🐾] [✕] [🕭M] [📦] [🖭] [⇌]

▼▼ ▼▼ **Red Roof Inn-Wilmington** Ⓜ
(302) 292-2870. **Call for rates.** 415 Stanton Christiana Rd. I-95, exit 4B, 0.5 mi n on SR 7. Ext corridors. **Pets:** Accepted.

[✕] [🕭M] [📦]

▼▼ ▼▼▼ **Residence Inn by Marriott** 🆂🅷
(302) 453-9200. **$219-$230.** 240 Chapman Rd. I-95, exit 3 southbound; exit 3A northbound, 0.3 mi e on SR 273 E, then 0.5 mi s. Ext corridors. **Pets:** Accepted.

[A$K] [S🐾] [✕] [📦] [🖭] [⇌] [✕]

▼▼ ▼▼▼ **Staybridge Suites-Newark/Wilmington** 🆂🅷
(302) 366-8097. **$190-$200.** 270 Chapman Rd. I-95, exit 3 southbound; exit 3A northbound, 0.3 mi e on SR 273 E, then just n. Int corridors. **Pets:** Accepted.

[A$K] [S🐾] [✕] [🕭M] [📦] [🖭] [⇌]

🅐🅐🅐⁄ ▼▼▼▼ **TownePlace Suites by Marriott-Wilmington/Newark** 🆂🅷
(302) 369-6212. **$158-$193.** 410 Eagle Run Rd. I-95, exit 3 south-bound; exit 3A northbound, just e. Int corridors. **Pets:** Small. $100 one-time fee/room. Designated rooms, service with restrictions, supervision.

[SAVE] [S🐾] [✕] [📦] [⇌]

NEW CASTLE

🅐🅐🅐⁄ ▼▼ ▼▼ **Quality Inn Skyways** Ⓜ
(302) 328-6666. **$109-$184.** 147 N DuPont Hwy. I-95, exit 5A, 0.8 mi s on SR 141, exit 1B, 0.5 mi s on US 13, 40 and 301; I-295, exit New Castle Airport/US 13 S, 1.8 mi s on US 13, 40 and 301. Ext/int corridors. **Pets:** Other species. $10 daily fee/room. Designated rooms, service with restrictions, supervision.

[SAVE] [S🐾] [✕] [🕭M] [📦] [🖭] [⇌]

▼▼ ▼▼ **Super 8 Motel** Ⓜ
(302) 322-9480. **Call for rates.** 215 S DuPont Hwy. I-95, exit 3A, 4.3 mi e on SR 273, then 0.8 mi s on US 13. Int corridors. **Pets:** Small, dogs only. $11 daily fee/pet. Service with restrictions, supervision.

[✕] [📦]

REHOBOTH BEACH

▼▼ ▼▼ **AmericInn Lodge & Suites of Rehoboth Beach** 🆂🅷 🐾
(302) 226-0700. **$69-$249.** 329Z Airport Rd. Just w of SR 1; just w on Miller Rd, then just s. Int corridors. **Pets:** Dogs only. $20 daily fee/pet. Designated rooms, service with restrictions.

[A$K] [S🐾] [✕] [🕭M] [📦] [🖭] [⇌]

▼▼ ▼▼ **The Atlantis Inn** Ⓜ
(302) 227-9446. **$85-$275, 7 day notice.** 154 Rehoboth Ave. At Rehoboth Ave and 2nd St; downtown. Ext corridors. **Pets:** Accepted.

[A$K] [S🐾] [✕] [📦] [🖭] [⇌]

▼▼▼▼ **The Breakers Hotel & Suites** Ⓜ 🐾
(302) 227-6688. **Call for rates.** 105 2nd St. Just n of Rehoboth Ave. Ext corridors. **Pets:** Dogs only. $50 daily fee/pet. Designated rooms, service with restrictions.

[✕] [📦] [🖭] [⇌]

🅐🅐🅐⁄ ▼▼▼▼ **Sea-Esta IV** Ⓜ
(302) 227-5882. **$47-$189.** 3101 Hwy 1. 1 mi s. Ext corridors. **Pets:** Other species. $8 daily fee/pet. Service with restrictions, crate.

[SAVE] [✕] [📦] [🖭] [⇌]

🅐🅐🅐⁄ ▼▼▼▼ **Sea Witch, Bewitched & Bedazzled** 🅱🅱 🐾
(302) 226-9482. **Call for rates.** 771 Lake Ave. Jct Rehoboth Ave, just ne. Int corridors. **Pets:** Medium, dogs only. $15 daily fee/pet. Designated rooms, service with restrictions.

[SAVE] [✕] [📦]

WILMINGTON

🅐🅐🅐⁄ ▼▼▼▼ **Best Western Brandywine Valley Inn** 🆂🅷
(302) 656-9436. **$99-$117.** 1807 Concord Pike. I-95, exit 8, 1 mi n on US 202. Ext corridors. **Pets:** Medium, other species. $25 one-time fee/pet. Designated rooms, service with restrictions, supervision.

[SAVE] [S🐾] [✕] [📦] [🖭] [⇌]

🅐🅐🅐⁄ ▼▼ ▼▼ **Days Inn Wilmington** Ⓜ
(302) 478-0300. **Call for rates.** 5209 Concord Pike. I-95, exit 8, 4 mi n on US 202; jct SR 92 (Naamans Rd). Ext corridors. **Pets:** Accepted.

[SAVE] [✕] [📦] [🖭]

🅐🅐🅐⁄ ▼▼▼▼ **Hotel du Pont** 🅻🅷
(302) 594-3100. **$457-$565.** 1007 Market St. I-95, exit 7, 0.5 mi se; downtown at 11th St. Int corridors. **Pets:** Small, dogs only. $100 one-time fee/pet. Service with restrictions, crate.

[SAVE] [✕] [🖭] [🍴] [✕]

🅐🅐🅐⁄ ▼▼▼▼ **Sheraton Suites Wilmington** 🅻🅷 🐾
(302) 654-8300. **$209-$330.** 422 Delaware Ave. I-95, exit 7, 0.3 mi e; downtown. Int corridors. **Pets:** Medium, dogs only. Service with restrictions, supervision.

[SAVE] [S🐾] [✕] [🕭M] [📦] [🖭] [🍴] [⇌]

DISTRICT OF COLUMBIA

DISTRICT OF COLUMBIA METROPOLITAN AREA

WASHINGTON

▼▼▼▼▼ DoubleTree Guest Suites, Washington DC 🆂🅷
(202) 785-2000. **Call for rates.** 801 New Hampshire Ave NW. Just sw at Washington Circle. Int corridors. **Pets:** Large, other species. $20 daily fee/room. Service with restrictions.
[icons]

🆐 ▼▼▼▼ The Fairfax at Embassy Row Washington, DC a Starwood Luxury Collection Hotel 🆂🅷
(202) 293-2100. **$219-$759.** 2100 Massachusetts Ave NW. Just w of Dupont Circle; at 21st St. Int corridors. **Pets:** Accepted.
[icons]

▼▼▼▼ The Fairmont Washington, D.C. 🅻🅷
(202) 429-2400. **$189-$699.** 2401 M St NW. 24th and M sts NW. Int corridors. **Pets:** Medium. $35 one-time fee/pet. Designated rooms, service with restrictions, supervision.
[icons]

🆐 ▼▼▼▼ Four Seasons Hotel Washington D.C. 🅻🅷
(202) 342-0444. **$695-$725.** 2800 Pennsylvania Ave NW. In Georgetown. Int corridors. **Pets:** Small. Designated rooms, service with restrictions, supervision.
[icons]

▼▼▼▼ Hamilton Crowne Plaza Hotel Washington DC 🅻🅷
(202) 682-0111. **$99-$650.** 1001 14th St NW. 14th and K sts NW. Int corridors. **Pets:** Medium. $150 deposit/pet. Service with restrictions, supervision.
[icons]

▼▼▼▼ The Hay-Adams 🆂🅷
(202) 638-6600. **$700-$6600.** 800 16th St NW. 16th and H sts NW; just n of the White House. Int corridors. **Pets:** Accepted.
[icons]

🆐 ▼▼▼▼ The Hotel George 🆂🅷
(202) 347-4200. **$169-$529.** 15 E St NW. On Capitol Hill, just n of Capitol grounds. Int corridors. **Pets:** Other species. Service with restrictions, crate.
[icons]

🆐 ▼▼▼▼ Hotel Helix 🆂🅷
(202) 462-9001. **$139-$389 (no credit cards).** 1430 Rhode Island Ave NW. Just e of Scott Circle. Int corridors. **Pets:** Other species. Service with restrictions, crate.
[icons]

🆐 ▼▼▼▼ Hotel Madera 🆂🅷
(202) 296-7600. **$149-$429.** 1310 New Hampshire Ave NW. Between 20th and N sts NW. Int corridors. **Pets:** Accepted.
[icons]

🆐 ▼▼▼▼ Hotel Monaco Washington DC 🆂🅷
(202) 628-7177. **$169-$1200.** 700 F St NW. Between 7th and 8th sts NW. Int corridors. **Pets:** Other species. Service with restrictions, crate.
[icons]

🆐 ▼▼▼▼ Hotel Palomar-A Kimpton Hotel 🆂🅷
(202) 448-1800. **$319-$549.** 2121 P St NW. Between 21st and 22nd sts NW; just w of Dupont Circle. Int corridors. **Pets:** Accepted.
[icons]

🆐 ▼▼▼▼ Hotel Rouge 🆂🅷
(202) 232-8000. **$139-$389.** 1315 16th St NW. Just n of Scott Circle. Int corridors. **Pets:** Other species. Service with restrictions, crate.
[icons]

▼▼▼▼ L'Enfant Plaza Hotel 🅻🅷
(202) 484-1000. **$109-$409.** 480 L'Enfant Plaza SW. I-395, exit L'Enfant Plaza/12th St. Int corridors. **Pets:** Large, other species. $250 deposit/room, $25 daily fee/pet. Supervision.
[icons]

🆐 ▼▼▼▼ The Madison, a Loews Hotel 🅻🅷
(202) 862-1600. **$189-$459.** 1177 15th St NW. 15th and M sts NW. Int corridors. **Pets:** Accepted.
[icons]

▼▼▼▼ Mandarin Oriental, Washington D.C. 🅻🅷
(202) 554-8588. **$495-$8000.** 1330 Maryland Ave SW. Jct Independence Ave SW, just s on 12th St SW. Int corridors. **Pets:** Small. $50 daily fee/room, $50 one-time fee/room. Designated rooms, service with restrictions, crate.
[icons]

▼▼▼▼ Marriott Wardman Park Hotel 🅻🅷
(202) 328-2000. **Call for rates.** 2660 Woodley Rd NW. Just w of Connecticut Ave; at Woodley Park/Zoo Metro Station. Int corridors. **Pets:** Accepted.
[icons]

🆐 ▼▼▼▼ The Mayflower, a Renaissance Hotel 🅻🅷
(202) 347-3000. **$406-$483.** 1127 Connecticut Ave NW. Just n of K St NW; in business district. Int corridors. **Pets:** Accepted.
[icons]

🆐 ▼▼▼▼ The Melrose Hotel, Washington DC 🆂🅷
(202) 955-6400. **$189-$449.** 2430 Pennsylvania Ave NW. Between 24th and 25th sts NW. Int corridors. **Pets:** Medium, other species. $100 one-time fee/pet. Service with restrictions.
[icons]

🆐 ▼▼▼▼ Omni Shoreham Hotel 🅻🅷
(202) 234-0700. **$199-$529.** 2500 Calvert St NW. Just w of Connecticut Ave. Int corridors. **Pets:** Other species. $50 one-time fee/room. Service with restrictions, supervision.
[icons]

🆐 ▼▼▼▼ Park Hyatt Washington, D.C. 🅻🅷
(202) 789-1234. **$249-$599.** 1201 24th St NW. 24th and M sts NW. Int corridors. **Pets:** Medium. $150 one-time fee/pet. Service with restrictions.
[icons]

▼▼ The Quincy 🆂🅷
(202) 223-4320. **$109-$289.** 1823 L St NW. Between 18th and 19th sts NW. Int corridors. **Pets:** Small. $100 one-time fee/pet. Service with restrictions.
[icons]

▼▼▼ Red Roof Inn Downtown Washington, D.C. 🆂🅷
(202) 289-5959. **Call for rates.** 500 H St NW. At 5th and H sts NW; in Chinatown. Int corridors. **Pets:** Accepted.
[icons]

▼▼▼ Residence Inn by Marriott Capitol 🆂🅷
(202) 484-8280. **$285-$362.** 333 E St SW. Between 3rd and 4th sts SW. Int corridors. **Pets:** Medium. $10 daily fee/pet, $200 one-time fee/room. Service with restrictions, crate.
[icons]

▼▼▼ Residence Inn by Marriott-Dupont Circle 🖼️
(202) 466-6800. **$285-$373.** 2120 P St NW. Between 21st and 22nd sts NW; just w of Dupont Circle. Int corridors. **Pets:** Accepted.
(ASK) (S🔒) (X) (&M) (🔲) (💻)

▼▼▼ Residence Inn by Marriott-Washington DC-Vermont Ave 🖼️
(202) 898-1100. **$296-$373.** 1199 Vermont Ave NW. Jct 14th St and Vermont Ave NW, at Thomas Circle. Int corridors. **Pets:** Accepted.
(ASK) (S🔒) (X) (&M) (🔲) (💻)

▼▼▼▼ The Ritz-Carlton, Georgetown 🖼️
(202) 912-4100. **Call for rates.** 3100 South St NW. Just s of jct M St and Wisconsin Ave; off Wisconsin Ave, just e; in Georgetown. Int corridors. **Pets:** Accepted.
(X) (🔲) (🍴) (🏊)

▼▼▼ The Ritz-Carlton, Washington, DC 🏛️
(202) 835-0500. **Call for rates.** 1150 22nd St NW. At 22nd and M sts NW. Int corridors. **Pets:** Accepted.
(X) (💻) (🍴) (🏊) (🏊)

▼▼▼ The River Inn 🖼️
(202) 337-7600. **Call for rates.** 924 25th St NW. Between K and I sts NW. Int corridors. **Pets:** Medium. $150 one-time fee/room. Service with restrictions.
(X) (🔲) (💻) (🍴)

🏅 ▼▼▼ Sofitel Lafayette Square Washington DC 🖼️ 🐾
(202) 730-8800. **Call for rates.** 806 15th St NW. Jct 15th and H sts NW. Int corridors. **Pets:** Large. Service with restrictions, crate.
(SAVE) (X) (&M) (🍴)

🏅 ▼▼▼ Topaz Hotel 🖼️
(202) 393-3000. **$139-$409.** 1733 N St NW. Just e of Connecticut Ave. Int corridors. **Pets:** Accepted.
(SAVE) (S🔒) (X) (🍴)

🏅 ▼▼▼ Washington Suites Georgetown 🖼️
(202) 333-8060. **$169-$394.** 2500 Pennsylvania Ave NW. Jct 25th St NW and Pennsylvania Ave; 2 blks from Foggy Bottom metro station. Int corridors. **Pets:** Small. $20 daily fee/pet. Designated rooms, crate.
(SAVE) (S🔒) (X) (&M) (🔲) (💻)

▼▼▼ The Westin Grand 🏛️
(202) 429-0100. **$179-$569, 3 day notice.** 2350 M St NW. 24th and M sts NW. Int corridors. **Pets:** Accepted.
(ASK) (S🔒) (X) (💻) (🍴) (🏊)

🏅 ▼▼▼ The Westin Washington DC City Center Hotel 🏛️
(202) 429-1700. **$119-$439.** 1400 M St NW. Just w of Thomas Circle. Int corridors. **Pets:** Accepted.
(SAVE) (X) (💻) (🍴)

▼▼▼ The Willard InterContinental 🏛️
(202) 628-9100. **$299-$879.** 1401 Pennsylvania Ave NW. Just e of the White House. Int corridors. **Pets:** Small, dogs only. $100 one-time fee/room. Service with restrictions, supervision.
(S🔒) (X) (&M) (💻) (🍴) (🏊)

END METROPOLITAN AREA

FLORIDA

CITY INDEX

ALACHUA

▼▼▼ **Alachua Inn** SH
(386) 462-2414. **$75-$85, 7 day notice.** 15920 NW Hwy 441. I-75, exit 399, just e. Ext corridors. **Pets:** Dogs only. $10 daily fee/pet. Designated rooms, service with restrictions, supervision.

A$K S☐ ✕ ☐ ☐ ☞

▲▲▲ ▼▼▼ **Quality Inn Alachua** SH
(386) 462-2244. **$100-$110, 3 day notice.** 15960 NW Hwy 441. I-75, exit 399, just e. Ext corridors. **Pets:** Accepted.

SAVE S☐ ✕ ☐ ☐ ☞

APALACHICOLA

▲▲▲ ▼▼▼ **Coombs House Inn** BB ❖
(850) 653-9199. **$79-$229, 7 day notice.** 80 6th St. Corner of US 98 and 6th St; center. Int corridors. **Pets:** Medium. $25 daily fee/pet. Designated rooms, service with restrictions.

SAVE S☐ ✕ ☐ ☐

▲▲▲ ▼▼▼ **Gibson Inn** CI
(850) 653-2191. **$105-$250, 14 day notice.** Market St & Ave C. On US 98 at west end of bridge. Int corridors. **Pets:** $25 daily fee/pet. Designated rooms, service with restrictions, supervision.

SAVE ✕ ☐

ARCADIA

▲▲▲ ▼▼▼ **Best Western Arcadia Inn** M
(863) 494-4884. **$79-$129.** 504 S Brevard Ave. 0.6 mi s of SR 70; on US 17. Ext corridors. **Pets:** Accepted.

SAVE S☐ ✕ ☐ ☐ ☞

AVON PARK

▲▲▲ ▼▼▼ **Econo Lodge** M
(863) 453-2000. **$69-$110.** 2511 US Hwy 27 S. On US 27; 2.5 mi s of jct SR 17 and 64. Ext corridors. **Pets:** Other species. $10 daily fee/room. Service with restrictions.

SAVE S☐ ✕ ☞

BOCA RATON

▲▲▲ ▼▼▼▼ **Boca Raton Bridge Hotel** LH
(561) 368-9500. **$99-$409, 3 day notice.** 999 E Camino Real. Just w of SR A1A, 1 mi s of jct SR 798 (Palmetto Park Rd). Int corridors. **Pets:** Accepted.

SAVE S☐ ✕ ☐ ☐ ☐ ☞ ✕

▲▲▲ ▼▼▼ **Fairfield Inn & Suites by Marriott** SH
(561) 417-8585. **$131-$241.** 3400 Airport Rd. I-95, exit 45 (SR 808/ Glades Rd), just e, then 1.1 mi n. Int corridors. **Pets:** Accepted.

SAVE S☐ ✕ ☐ ☐ ☞

▼▼ **Homestead Studio Suites Hotel-Boca Raton/Commerce** M
(561) 994-2599. **$72-$131.** 501 NW 77th St. I-95, exit 50, just s on Congress Ave to NW 6th Ave. Ext corridors. **Pets:** Other species. $75 one-time fee/pet. Service with restrictions.

A$K S☐ ✕ ☐ ☐

▲▲▲ ▼▼▼ **Residence Inn-By Marriott-Boca Raton** SH
(561) 994-3222. **$175-$296.** 525 NW 77th St. I-95, exit 50, W on Congress Ave to NW 6th Ave, then to NW 77th St. Ext corridors. **Pets:** $100 one-time fee/room. Service with restrictions.

SAVE S☐ ✕ ☐ ☐ ☞ ✕

▼▼▼ **TownePlace Suites by Marriott** SH ❖
(561) 994-7232. **$164-$285.** 5110 NW 8th Ave. I-95, exit 48B (Yamato Rd), just w; in Arvida Corporate Park. Int corridors. **Pets:** $100 one-time fee/room. Service with restrictions, crate.

A$K S☐ ✕ ☐M ☐ ☐ ☞

BONITA SPRINGS

▼▼▼ **AmericInn Hotel & Suites** SH ❖
(239) 495-9255. **Call for rates.** 28600 Trails Edge Blvd. I-75, exit 116, 3.5 mi w on CR 865 (Bonita Beach Rd SE), 0.7 mi s on US 41 (Tamiami Tr), then just w; in Woods Edge. Int corridors. **Pets:** Small. $10 daily fee/pet. Designated rooms, service with restrictions, supervision.

✕ ☐M ☐ ☐ ☞

▼▼ Comfort Inn Hotel 🆂🅷
(239) 992-5001. **$130-$180.** 9800 Bonita Beach Rd SE. I-75, exit 116, 2.3 mi w on CR 865 (Bonita Beach Rd SE). Int corridors. **Pets:** Accepted.

Ⓐ$ⓀＳⓓ ☒ 🏢 💻 🍴 ⤳

▲ ▼▼▼ Hyatt Regency Coconut Point Resort & Spa 🅻🅷
(239) 444-1234. **$179-$555, 3 day notice.** 5001 Coconut Rd. I-75, exit 123, 1.9 mi w on CR 850 (Corkscrew Rd), 2.3 mi s on US 41, then 1.5 mi w. Int corridors. **Pets:** Accepted.

ＳⒶⓋⒺ ☒ 🏢 💻 🍴 ⤳ ☒

▲ ▼▼▼ Inn at the Springs 🅲🅾
(239) 949-5913. **Call for rates.** 8901 Highland Woods Blvd. I-75, exit 116, 3.5 mi w on CR 865 (Bonita Beach Rd SE), 1.4 mi n on US 41 (Tamiami Tr), then e. Int corridors. **Pets:** Large. $100 one-time fee/room. Designated rooms, service with restrictions.

ＳⒶⓋⒺ ☒ Ⓜ 🏢 💻 ⤳

BRADENTON

▼▼ Days Inn Bradenton 🅼
(941) 746-1141. **$59-$139.** 3506 1st St W. On US 41, just e of jct US 301. Ext corridors. **Pets:** Accepted.

Ⓐ$ⓀＳⓓ ☒ 🏢 💻 🍴 ⤳

▲ ▼▼ Howard Johnson Express Inn 🅼
(941) 756-8399. **$45-$144.** 6511 14th St W. On US 41, 1.5 mi s of jct SR 70. Ext corridors. **Pets:** Small, dogs only. $10 daily fee/pet. Service with restrictions, supervision.

ＳⒶⓋⒺ Ｓⓓ ☒ 🏢 💻 ⤳

▲ ▼▼ Quality Inn 🅼
(941) 758-7199. **$59-$189.** 6727 14th St W. On US 41, 2 mi s of jct SR 70. Ext corridors. **Pets:** Small, dogs only. $10 daily fee/pet. Service with restrictions, supervision.

ＳⒶⓋⒺ Ｓⓓ ☒ 🏢 💻 ⤳

BRADENTON BEACH

▲ ▼▼▼ Tortuga Inn Beach Resort 🅲🅾
(941) 778-6611. **Call for rates.** 1325 Gulf Dr N. On SR 789, 0.3 mi n of jct SR 684. Ext corridors. **Pets:** Accepted.

ＳⒶⓋⒺ ☒ 🏢 💻 ⤳

▲ ▼▼▼ Tradewinds Resort 🅲🅰
(941) 779-0010. **$120-$300, 14 day notice.** 1603 Gulf Dr N. On SR 789, 0.5 mi n of jct SR 684. Ext corridors. **Pets:** Accepted.

ＳⒶⓋⒺ ☒ 🏢 💻 ⤳

BROOKSVILLE

▲ ▼▼ Best Western Brooksville I-75 🅼
(352) 796-9481. **$79-$129.** 30307 Cortez Blvd. I-75, exit 301, just w on US 98/SR 50. Ext corridors. **Pets:** Large, other species. $25 one-time fee/room. Designated rooms, service with restrictions, supervision.

ＳⒶⓋⒺ Ｓⓓ ☒ Ⓜ 💻 🍴 ≋

▲ ▼▼ Days Inn Heritage Inn 🅼
(352) 796-9486. **$79-$99.** 6320 Windmere Rd. I-75, exit 301, just e on US 98/SR 50. Ext corridors. **Pets:** Other species. $25 one-time fee/room. Service with restrictions, crate.

ＳⒶⓋⒺ Ｓⓓ ☒ Ⓜ 🏢 💻 ⤳

CAPE CANAVERAL

▲ ▼▼▼ Residence Inn by Marriott Cape Canaveral/ Cocoa Beach 🆂🅷
(321) 323-1100. **$153-$197.** 8959 Astronaut Blvd. On SR A1A, 0.3 mi s of jct SR 528. Int corridors. **Pets:** $75 one-time fee/room.

ＳⒶⓋⒺ Ｓⓓ ☒ Ⓜ 🏢 💻 ⤳ ☒

CAPE CORAL

▲ ▼▼ Dockside Inn 🅼 ❀
(239) 542-0061. **$75-$145, 7 day notice.** 3817 Del Prado Blvd. 1.2 mi n of jct Cape Coral Pkwy. Ext corridors. **Pets:** Other species. $25 one-time fee/room.

ＳⒶⓋⒺ Ｓⓓ ☒ 🏢 ⤳ ☒

▼▼▼ Quality Hotel 🆂🅷
(239) 542-2121. **$75-$175.** 1538 Cape Coral Pkwy. Jct Del Prado Blvd. Int corridors. **Pets:** Small, other species. $15 daily fee/room. Designated rooms, service with restrictions, supervision.

Ⓐ$ⓀＳⓓ ☒ 🏢 💻 ⤳

CEDAR KEY

▲ ▼▼ Park Place Motel & Condominiums 🅼
(352) 543-5737. **$65-$110.** 211 2nd St. At a St. Ext corridors. **Pets:** Small, other species. $7 daily fee/pet. Designated rooms, service with restrictions, supervision.

ＳⒶⓋⒺ ☒ 🏢 💻

▲ ▼▼ Seahorse Landing Condominiums 🅲🅾
(352) 543-5860. **$160-$185, 3 day notice.** 4050 G St. Just w on 6th St. Ext corridors. **Pets:** Medium, dogs only. $15 daily fee/room. Designated rooms, service with restrictions, crate.

ＳⒶⓋⒺ ☒ 🏢 💻 ⤳ ☒

CHARLOTTE HARBOR

▼ Banana Bay On Charlotte Harbor 🅼
(941) 743-4441. **Call for rates.** 23285 Bayshore Rd. Jct US 41. Ext corridors. **Pets:** Accepted.

☒ 🏢 💻

CHIEFLAND

▼▼ Holiday Inn Express 🆂🅷
(352) 493-9400. **Call for rates.** 809 NW 21st Ave. US 19/98, 1.5 mi n of jct US 129. Ext corridors. **Pets:** Accepted.

☒ Ⓜ 🏢 ⤳

CHIPLEY

▼▼ Super 8 Motel 🅼
(850) 638-8530. **$60-$70.** 1150 Motel Dr. I-10, exit 120, just n. Ext corridors. **Pets:** Accepted.

Ⓐ$ⓀＳⓓ ☒ 🏢

COCOA

▼▼ Best Western Cocoa Inn 🆂🅷
(321) 632-1065. **$69-$129.** 4225 W King St. I-95, exit 201 (SR 520), 0.3 mi e. Ext corridors. **Pets:** Medium, other species. $10 daily fee/room. Service with restrictions, crate.

Ⓐ$ⓀＳⓓ ☒ 🏢 💻 ⤳

▲ ▼▼▼ Econo Lodge-Space Center 🆂🅷
(321) 632-4561. **$59-$159.** 3220 N Cocoa Blvd. US 1, just n of jct SR 528. Ext corridors. **Pets:** Small. $50 deposit/pet, $15 one-time fee/pet. Designated rooms, service with restrictions, supervision.

ＳⒶⓋⒺ Ｓⓓ ☒ 🏢 💻 🍴 ⤳

COCOA BEACH

▼▼▼ Four Points by Sheraton Cocoa Beach 🆂🅷
(321) 783-8717. **$120-$160.** 4001 N Atlantic Ave. SR A1A, just s of jct SR 520. Int corridors. **Pets:** Accepted.

Ⓐ$ⓀＳⓓ ☒ Ⓜ 🏢 💻 🍴 ⤳

▲ ▼▼ Holiday Inn Cocoa Beach Oceanfront Resort 🆂🅷
(321) 783-2271. **$99-$189.** 1300 N Atlantic Ave. SR A1A, 1.8 mi s of jct SR 520. Ext corridors. **Pets:** Accepted.

ＳⒶⓋⒺ Ｓⓓ ☒ Ⓜ 🏢 💻 🍴 ⤳ ☒

△△△⌀ ▼▼▼ La Quinta Inn Cocoa Beach 🆂🅷
(321) 783-2252. **$144-$154.** 1275 N Atlantic Ave. On SR A1A, 1.7 mi s. Ext corridors. **Pets:** Other species. Service with restrictions, supervision.
🆂🅰🆅🅴 🆂🅾 ☒ 🔒 💻 🍽 ⊇

▼▼▼▼ Quality Suites Cocoa Beach 🆂🅷
(321) 783-6868. **$89-$189.** 3655 N Atlantic Ave. SR A1A, 0.3 mi s of jct SR 520. Int corridors. **Pets:** Medium, other species. $100 deposit/room. Designated rooms, service with restrictions, supervision.
🅰🆂🅺 🆂🅾 ☒ 🛂 🔒 💻

▼▼ Surf Studio Beach Resort Ⓜ
(321) 783-7100. **Call for rates.** 1801 S Atlantic Ave. SR A1A northbound, 5 mi s of jct SR 520 at Francis St; 1.3 mi n of Partrick AFB. Ext corridors. **Pets:** Medium. $20 daily fee/pet. Designated rooms, no service, supervision.
🔒 💻 ⊇

CRESCENT BEACH

△△△⌀ ▼▼▼ Beacher's Lodge 🆂🅷
(904) 471-8849. **$89-$225, 3 day notice.** 6970 A1A S. Just s of jct SR 206. Ext corridors. **Pets:** Small. $50 one-time fee/pet. Designated rooms, service with restrictions, crate.
🆂🅰🆅🅴 🆂🅾 ☒ 🔒 💻 ⊇

CRESCENT CITY

▼ Lake View Motel Ⓜ
(386) 698-1090. **Call for rates.** 1004 N Summit St. 1 mi n on US 17. Ext corridors. **Pets:** Small. $10 daily fee/pet. Designated rooms, service with restrictions, supervision.
☒ 🔒 💻 ⊇

CRESTVIEW

▼▼▼ Jameson Inn 🆂🅷
(850) 683-1778. **Call for rates.** 151 Cracker Barrel Dr. I-10, exit 56, just s. Int corridors. **Pets:** Small. $15 daily fee/room. Service with restrictions, crate.
☒ 🔒 💻 ⊇

△△△⌀ ▼ ◆ Super 8 Motel Ⓜ
(850) 682-9649. **$53-$78.** 3925 S Ferdon Blvd. I-10, exit 56, 0.3 mi s. Ext corridors. **Pets:** Accepted.
🆂🅰🆅🅴 🆂🅾 ☒ 🔒

CRYSTAL RIVER

△△△⌀ ▼▼◆ Best Western Crystal River Resort 🆂🅷
(352) 795-3171. **$110-$160.** 614 NW Hwy 19. On US 19/98, 0.8 mi n of jct SR 44. Ext corridors. **Pets:** Medium, other species. $5 daily fee/pet. Service with restrictions, supervision.
🆂🅰🆅🅴 🆂🅾 ☒ 🔒 💻 ☒

△△△⌀ ▼▼◆ Days Inn 🆂🅷
(352) 795-2111. **$55-$140.** 2380 NW Hwy 19. US 19, 2.2 mi n of jct SR 44. Ext corridors. **Pets:** Other species. $10 daily fee/pet. Service with restrictions, supervision.
🆂🅰🆅🅴 🆂🅾 ☒ 🔒 🍽

DAYTONA BEACH

△△△⌀ ▼ Days Inn Speedway Ⓜ
(386) 255-0541. **Call for rates.** 2900 W International Speedway Blvd. I-95, exit 261B southbound; exit 261 northbound, just w on US 92. Ext corridors. **Pets:** Medium. $15 daily fee/pet. Designated rooms, service with restrictions, supervision.
🆂🅰🆅🅴 ☒ 🔒 🍽 ⊇

▼▼ Extended Stay Deluxe Daytona Beach-International Speedway 🆂🅷
(386) 257-4311. **$77-$84.** 255 Bill France Blvd. I-95, exit 261, 2.5 mi e, then just n. Int corridors. **Pets:** Other species. $75 one-time fee/pet. Service with restrictions.
🅰🆂🅺 🆂🅾 ☒ 🔒 💻 ⊇

▼▼▼ Homewood Suites by Hilton Daytona Speedway/Airport 🆂🅷
(386) 258-2828. **$139-$699.** 165 Bill France Blvd. I-95, exit 261, 2.5 mi e, then just n. Int corridors. **Pets:** Accepted.
🅰🆂🅺 🆂🅾 ☒ 🛂 🔒 💻 ⊇ ☒

△△△⌀ ▼▼◆ LaPlaya Resort & Suites 🆂🅷
(386) 672-0990. **$89-$459, 7 day notice.** 2500 N Atlantic Ave. On SR A1A, 3.3 mi n of jct US 92. Ext corridors. **Pets:** Accepted.
🆂🅰🆅🅴 🆂🅾 ☒ 🔒 💻 🍽 ⊇ ☒

△△△⌀ ▼▼▼ La Quinta Inn & Suites 🆂🅷
(386) 944-0060. **$109-$119.** 816 N Atlantic Ave. On SR A1A, 1.4 mi n of US 92. Ext corridors. **Pets:** Other species. Service with restrictions, supervision.
🆂🅰🆅🅴 🆂🅾 ☒ 🔒 💻 ⊇

△△△⌀ ▼▼◆ Plaza Ocean Club 🆂🅷 🐾
(386) 239-9800. **$89-$499, 7 day notice.** 640 N Atlantic Ave. On SR A1A, 1 mi n of jct SR 90. Int corridors. **Pets:** Small, dogs only. $50 deposit/pet, $20 daily fee/pet. Designated rooms, service with restrictions.
🆂🅰🆅🅴 🆂🅾 ☒ 🛂 🔒 💻 🍽 ⊇

▼▼ Ramada Inn Speedway 🆂🅷
(386) 255-2422. **Call for rates.** 1798 W International Speedway Blvd. I-95, exit 261A southbound; exit 261 northbound, 2 mi e on US 92. Ext corridors. **Pets:** Accepted.
☒ 🔒 💻 🍽 ⊇

△△△⌀ ▼▼◆ Residence Inn by Marriott 🆂🅷
(386) 252-3949. **$153-$208.** 1725 Richard Petty Blvd. I-95, exit 261, 2.6 mi e, then just s. Int corridors. **Pets:** Other species. $75 one-time fee/room. Service with restrictions, supervision.
🆂🅰🆅🅴 🆂🅾 ☒ 🛂 🔒 💻 ⊇ ☒

▼ Scottish Inns Ⓜ
(386) 258-5742. **$39-$250, 15 day notice.** 1515 S Ridgewood Ave. I-95, exit 260A, 2.5 mi e on SR 400, then just n on US 1. Ext corridors. **Pets:** Accepted.
🅰🆂🅺 🆂🅾 ☒ 🔒 ⊇

DAYTONA BEACH SHORES

△△△⌀ ▼▼ Atlantic Ocean Palm Inn Ⓜ
(386) 761-8450. **$59-$139, 30 day notice.** 3247 S Atlantic Ave. On SR A1A, 5 mi s of jct US 92. Ext corridors. **Pets:** Small. $15 daily fee/pet. Designated rooms, service with restrictions, supervision.
🆂🅰🆅🅴 🆂🅾 ☒ 🔒 ⊇

△△△⌀ ▼▼▼◆ The Shores Resort & Spa 🅻🅷 🐾
(386) 767-7350. **$129-$369, 3 day notice.** 2637 S Atlantic Ave. On SR A1A, 3.2 mi s of jct US 92. Int corridors. **Pets:** Medium. $250 deposit/room, $25 daily fee/room. Designated rooms, service with restrictions, supervision.
🆂🅰🆅🅴 🆂🅾 ☒ 🛂 💻 🍽 ⊇ ☒

DE FUNIAK SPRINGS

△△△⌀ ▼▼ Best Western Crossroads Inn 🆂🅷
(850) 892-5111. **$69-$99.** 2343 Freeport Rd. I-10, exit 85, just s. Ext/int corridors. **Pets:** Small. $20 one-time fee/room. Designated rooms, service with restrictions, supervision.
🅰🆂🅺 🆂🅾 ☒ 🔒 💻 🍽 ⊇

DELAND

△△△⌀ ▼▼▼ University Inn Ⓜ
(386) 734-5711. **$79-$199.** 644 N Woodland Blvd. US 17, 0.9 mi n of jct SR 44. Ext corridors. **Pets:** Very small, dogs only. $10 daily fee/pet. Designated rooms, service with restrictions, supervision.
🆂🅰🆅🅴 🆂🅾 ☒ 🔒 ⊇

DELRAY BEACH

(AAA) ◆◆◆◆ **Colony Hotel & Cabana Club** SH ❀
(561) 276-4123. **$125-$349, 3 day notice.** 525 E Atlantic Ave. On SR 806 (Atlantic Ave) at US 1 northbound; center. Int corridors. **Pets:** Other species. $25 daily fee/pet. Designated rooms.
SAVE S🐾 ✕

(AAA) ◆◆◆◆ **Residence Inn Delray Beach** SH
(561) 276-7441. **$197-$340.** 1111 E Atlantic Ave. I-95, exit 52 (SR 806/Atlantic Ave), 1.7 mi e. Int corridors. **Pets:** Accepted.
A$K S🐾 ✕ ♿M 🍴 ➘ ➿

DELTONA

(AAA) ◆◆◆ **Best Western Deltona Inn** SH
(386) 860-3000. **$79-$269.** 481 Deltona Blvd. I-4, exit 108, just ne. Ext corridors. **Pets:** Accepted.
SAVE S🐾 ✕ 🍴 ➘ 🍽

DESTIN

◆◆◆ **Beachside Inn** SH ❀
(850) 650-9099. **Call for rates.** 2931 Scenic Hwy 98. 1 mi s of US 98. Ext corridors. **Pets:** Other species. $25 one-time fee/room. Designated rooms.
✕ 🍴 ➘ 🍽 ➿

(AAA) ◆◆◆ **Inn on Destin Harbor** SH
(850) 837-7326. **$59-$299.** 402 Harbor Blvd. US 98, 2.5 mi w. Int corridors. **Pets:** Medium, other species. $75 one-time fee/room. Designated rooms, service with restrictions, supervision.
SAVE S🐾 ✕ 🍴 ➘ 🍽 ➿

◆◆◆◆ **Residence Inn Sandestin at Grand Boulevard** LH
(850) 650-7811. **$142-$230.** 300 Grand Blvd. 6 mi w on US 98 from jct US 331. Int corridors. **Pets:** Accepted.
A$K S🐾 ✕ ♿M 🍴 ➘ ➿ ✕

DUNDEE

(AAA) ◆◆◆ **Quality Inn-Dundee** SH
(863) 438-9800. **$64-$89.** 28610 US Hwy 27. On US 27; center. Ext corridors. **Pets:** Accepted.
SAVE S🐾 ✕ 🍴 ➘ 🍽 ➿

ELKTON

(AAA) ◆◆◆ **Comfort Inn St. Augustine** SH
(904) 829-3435. **$79-$109.** 2625 SR 207. I-95, exit 311, just w. Ext corridors. **Pets:** Accepted.
SAVE S🐾 ✕ 🍴 ➘ ➿

ELLENTON

◆◆◆ **GuestHouse International Inn** M
(941) 729-0600. **$70-$120.** 4915 17th St E. I-75, exit 224, 0.3 mi s on US 301, just w on 51st Ave E, then just n. Ext corridors. **Pets:** Small. $10 daily fee/pet. Designated rooms, no service, crate.
A$K S🐾 ✕ ♿M 🍴 ➘ ➿

(AAA) ◆◆◆ **Sleep Inn & Suites Riverfront** M ❀
(941) 721-4933. **$79-$179.** 5605 18th St E. I-75, exit 224, just n on US 301, just e on 19th St E, then 0.3 mi sw. Int corridors. **Pets:** Large, other species. $20 daily fee/room. Service with restrictions, crate.
SAVE S🐾 ✕ ♿M 🍴 ➘ ➿

FLAGLER BEACH

◆◆◆ **Beach Front Motel** M
(386) 439-0089. **$54-$89, 3 day notice.** 1544 S A1A. On SR A1A, 1 mi s of SR 100. Ext corridors. **Pets:** Medium. $15 one-time fee/room. Service with restrictions, crate.
A$K S🐾 ✕ 🍴 ➘

(AAA) ◆◆◆ **Topaz Motel** SH
(386) 439-3301. **$70-$185, 14 day notice.** 1224 S Oceanshore Blvd. On SR A1A, 0.5 mi s of SR 100. Ext/int corridors. **Pets:** Accepted.
SAVE ✕ 🍴 ➘ 🍽 ➿

FLORAL CITY

◆◆◆ **Moonrise Resort** CA
(352) 726-2553. **$75-$1800 (no credit cards).** 8801 E Moonrise Ln, Lot 18. Just e on CR 48, then 1.5 mi n on Old Floral City Rd. Ext corridors. **Pets:** Dogs only. $20 daily fee/pet. No service.
🍴 ➘ ✕ ☎

THE FLORIDA KEYS AREA

KEY LARGO

(AAA) ◆◆◆◆ **Key Largo Grande Resort & Beach Club** LH
(305) 852-5553. **$99-$378.** 97000 S Overseas Hwy. US 1 at MM 97. Ext corridors. **Pets:** Accepted.
SAVE ✕ 🍴 ➘ 🍴 ➿ ✕

(AAA) ◆◆◆◆ **Marina Del Mar Resort & Marina** SH
(305) 451-4107. **$99-$299, 3 day notice.** 527 Caribbean Dr. US 1 at MM 100. Ext corridors. **Pets:** Accepted.
SAVE S🐾 ✕ 🍴 ➘ 🍴 ➿ ✕

KEY WEST

◆◆◆◆ **Ambrosia Too At Fleming St** BB
(305) 296-9838. **$209-$609, 30 day notice.** 622 Fleming St. Just n of Simonton St; in Old Town. Ext corridors. **Pets:** Other species. $25 one-time fee/pet. Service with restrictions, supervision.
A$K S🐾 ✕ 🍴 ➘ ➿

◆◆◆ **Center Court Historic Inn & Cottages** BB
(305) 296-9292. **$118-$608, 30 day notice.** 1075 Duval, C-19 St. Just e of Truman Ave; in Duval Square. Ext/int corridors. **Pets:** Other species. $15 daily fee/pet. Designated rooms, no service, supervision.
✕ 🍴 ➿

(AAA) ◆◆◆◆ **Chelsea House Pool & Gardens** BB
(305) 296-2211. **$119-$369, 7 day notice.** 709 Truman Ave. Corner of Elizabeth St and Truman Ave. Ext/int corridors. **Pets:** Accepted.
SAVE ✕ 🍴 ➘ ➿

◆◆◆◆ **Courtney's Place Historic Cottages & Inn** CA ❀
(305) 294-3480. **Call for rates.** 720 Whitmarsh Ln. Just e of jct Petronia and Simonton sts; in Old Town. Ext corridors. **Pets:** Other species. $25 daily fee/pet. Designated rooms, service with restrictions.
✕ 🍴 ➘ ➿

◆◆◆◆ **The Cuban Club Suites** M
(305) 294-5269. **Call for rates.** 1108 Duval St. Corner of Duval and Amelia sts; in Old Town. Int corridors. **Pets:** Accepted.
✕ 🍴 ➿

(AAA) ◆◆◆◆ **Curry Mansion Inn** BB
(305) 294-5349. **$215-$365, 14 day notice.** 511 Caroline St. Just n of jct Duval St; in Old Town. Ext/int corridors. **Pets:** Very small, dogs only. Service with restrictions, supervision.
SAVE ✕ 🍴 ➿

AAA ▼▼▼▼ **Frances Street Bottle Inn** BB
(305) 294-8530. **$125-$1000.** 535 Frances St. US 1/Roosevelt Blvd, w on White St, then just s on Southard St; corner of Frances and Southard sts; in Old Town. Int corridors. **Pets:** Accepted.
[SAVE] [S🖊] [✕] [🖥] [☎]

AAA ▼▼▼▼ **Hyatt Key West Resort & Marina** LH
(305) 809-1234. **$252-$590, 7 day notice.** 601 Front St. Simonton and Front sts; just n of Mallory Square; in Old Town. Ext corridors. **Pets:** $250 deposit/room, $100 one-time fee/room. Service with restrictions, crate.
[SAVE] [✕] [🖥] [🖦] [🍴] [🛌] [✕]

AAA ▼▼▼ **The Palms Hotel** BB 🐾
(305) 294-3146. **$120-$420, 7 day notice.** 820 White St. Just w of Truman Ave. Ext corridors. **Pets:** Small, other species. Service with restrictions, crate.
[SAVE] [S🖊] [🛌]

AAA ▼▼▼▼ **Sheraton Suites-Key West** LH
(305) 292-9800. **$189-$399, 3 day notice.** 2001 S Roosevelt Blvd. Jct US 1 and SR A1A, 3 mi s. Ext/int corridors. **Pets:** Accepted.
[SAVE] [✕] [🖦M] [🖥] [🖦] [🍴] [🛌] [✕]

AAA ▼▼▼▼ **The Westin Key West Resort & Marina** LH
(305) 294-4000. **$229-$2225, 3 day notice.** 245 Front St. Adjacent to Mallory Square; in Old Town. Ext/int corridors. **Pets:** Accepted.
[SAVE] [✕] [🖥] [🖦] [🍴] [🛌] [✕]

END AREA

FORT LAUDERDALE METROPOLITAN AREA

CORAL SPRINGS

(AAA) ▼▼▼▼ La Quinta Inn Coral Springs North SH
(954) 753-9000. **$129-$189.** 3701 University Dr. SR 817, just n of jct SR 834 (Sample Rd). Int corridors. **Pets:** Other species. Service with restrictions, supervision.

(SAVE) (S⌀) (✕) (&M) 🚪 💻 ⇌

(AAA) ▼▼▼ La Quinta Inn South SH
(954) 344-2200. **$139-$189.** 3100 N University Dr. SR 817, just s of jct SR 834 (Sample Rd). Int corridors. **Pets:** Other species. Service with restrictions, supervision.

(SAVE) (S⌀) (✕) 🚪 💻 ⇌

▼▼ Studio 6 #6027 M
(954) 796-0011. **$89-$103.** 5645 University Dr. SR 869 (Sawgrass Expwy), exit 12 (University Dr), just s. Ext corridors. **Pets:** Other species. Service with restrictions, supervision.

(S⌀) (✕) 🚪 💻

DANIA BEACH

▼ Motel 6 E. Dania Beach Blvd #376 M
(954) 921-5505. **$65-$95.** 825 E Dania Beach Blvd. I-95, exit 22, 1.1 mi e on Stirling Rd, just n on US 1 (Federal Hwy), then 0.8 mi e. Ext corridors. **Pets:** Other species. Service with restrictions, supervision.

(S⌀) (✕) ⇌

▼▼▼▼ Sheraton Fort Lauderdale Airport Hotel LH
(954) 920-3500. **$89-$319.** 1825 Griffin Rd. I-95, exit 23. Int corridors. **Pets:** Accepted.

(SAVE) (S⌀) (✕) (&M) 🚪 💻 ¶ ⇌ (✕)

DAVIE

▼▼ Homestead Studio Suites Hotel-Fort Lauderdale-Plantation M
(954) 476-1211. **$91-$131.** 7550 SR 84 E. I-595, exit 5, 0.3 mi. Ext corridors. **Pets:** Other species. $75 one-time fee/pet. Service with restrictions.

(ASK) (S⌀) (✕) (&M) 🚪 💻

DEERFIELD BEACH

(AAA) ▼▼▼▼ Comfort Inn-Oceanside M ❀
(954) 428-0650. **$130-$240.** 50 S Ocean Dr. SR A1A, jct SR 810 (Hillsboro Blvd). Int corridors. **Pets:** Medium, other species. $25 daily fee/room. Designated rooms, service with restrictions, supervision.

(ASK) (S⌀) (✕) 🚪 💻 ⇌

(AAA) ▼▼▼▼ Comfort Suites SH
(954) 570-8887. **$89-$199.** 1040 E Newport Center Dr. I-95, exit 41, jct SW 10th St to SW 12th Ave, then s; in Newport Center Complex. Ext corridors. **Pets:** Accepted.

(SAVE) (S⌀) (✕) 🚪 💻 ⇌

(AAA) ▼▼▼▼ Embassy Suites-Deerfield Beach Resort LH
(954) 426-0478. **$139-$799.** 950 Ocean Dr (SR A1A). SR A1A, 0.5 mi s of SR 810 (Hillsboro Blvd). Int corridors. **Pets:** Accepted.

(SAVE) (✕) 🚪 💻 ¶ ⇌ (✕)

▼▼ Extended StayAmerica-Deerfield Beach SH
(954) 428-5997. **$77-$131.** 1200 FAU Research Park Blvd. I-95, exit 41, just e to FAU Research Park Rd, then just s. Int corridors. **Pets:** Other species. $75 one-time fee/pet. Service with restrictions.

(ASK) (S⌀) (✕) (&M) 🚪 💻

(AAA) ▼▼▼▼ La Quinta Inn & Suites SH
(954) 428-0661. **$169-$209.** 100 SW 12th Ave. I-95, exit 42B, just w on SR 810 (Hillsboro Blvd), then just s. Int corridors. **Pets:** Other species. Service with restrictions, supervision.

(SAVE) (S⌀) (✕) (&M) 🚪 💻 ⇌

(AAA) ▼▼▼▼ La Quinta Inn Ft. Lauderdale (Deerfield Beach) M
(954) 421-1004. **$129-$189.** 351 W Hillsboro Blvd. I-95, exit 42A, 0.3 mi e on SR 810 (Hillsboro Blvd). Ext corridors. **Pets:** Other species. Service with restrictions, supervision.

(SAVE) (S⌀) (✕) (&M) 🚪 💻 ⇌

FORT LAUDERDALE

▼▼ Angela's Beach Resort M
(954) 563-7926. **$59-$230, 21 day notice.** 3016 Windamar St. On SR A1A, 6 blks s of SR 838 (Sunrise Blvd); west corner of Breakers Ave and Windamar St. Ext corridors. **Pets:** Small, other species. $100 deposit/room, $20 daily fee/pet, $25 one-time fee/room. Designated rooms, service with restrictions, crate.

(ASK) (✕) 🚪 💻 ⇌

▼▼ Crossland Studios-Fort Lauderdale/Commercial Blvd M
(954) 484-5115. **Call for rates.** 3031 W Commercial Blvd. I-95, exit 32 SR 870 (Commercial Blvd), 2 mi w; Florida Tpke, exit 62, 1.5 mi e. Ext corridors. **Pets:** Other species. $75 one-time fee/pet. Service with restrictions.

(✕) 🚪

▼▼▼▼ Embassy Suites-Fort Lauderdale LH
(954) 527-2700. **Call for rates.** 1100 SE 17th St Cswy. On SR A1A, just e of jct US 1 (Federal Hwy). Int corridors. **Pets:** Accepted.

(✕) 🚪 💻 ¶ ⇌ (✕)

▼▼ Extended StayAmerica-Cypress Creek/Andrews Ave M
(954) 776-9447. **$67-$105.** 5851 N Andrews Ave. I-95, exit 33 (Cypress Creek), just w, 0.3 mi s on N Andrews Ave, then left. Ext corridors. **Pets:** Other species. $75 one-time fee/pet. Service with restrictions.

(ASK) (S⌀) (✕) 🚪 💻

▼▼ Extended StayAmerica-Marina/Convention Center SH
(954) 761-9055. **$100-$152.** 1450 SE 17th St Cswy. 1 mi e of US 1 (Federal Hwy) on SR A1A. Int corridors. **Pets:** Other species. $75 one-time fee/pet. Service with restrictions.

(ASK) (S⌀) (✕) 🚪 💻

▼▼▼▼ Hampton Inn Fort Lauderdale Airport North SH
(954) 524-9900. **$99-$269.** 2301 SW 12th Ave. I-95, exit 25 (SR 84), 0.7 mi e to SW 12th Ave, then just n. Int corridors. **Pets:** Accepted.

(ASK) (S⌀) (✕) (&M) 🚪 💻 ⇌

(AAA) ▼▼▼▼ La Quinta Inn Fort Lauderdale (Cypress Creek/I-95) SH
(954) 491-7666. **$119-$169.** 999 W Cypress Creek Rd. I-95, exit 33 southbound, 0.8 mi; exit 33B northbound, at Powerline Rd. Int corridors. **Pets:** Other species. Service with restrictions, supervision.

(SAVE) (S⌀) (✕) 🚪 💻 ⇌

(AAA) ▼▼▼▼ La Quinta Inn-Ft Lauderdale NE SH
(954) 491-2500. **$129-$169.** 5727 N Federal Hwy. 0.5 mi n on US 1 (Federal Hwy) from SR 870 (Commercial Blvd). Ext corridors. **Pets:** Other species. Service with restrictions, supervision.

(SAVE) (S⌀) (✕) (&M) 💻 ⇌ (✕)

▼▼ Motel 6–Ft Lauderdale #55 SH
(954) 760-7999. **$76-$96.** 1801 SR 84. I-95, exit 25 (SR 84 E), just e, then u-turn at light. Int corridors. **Pets:** Other species. Service with restrictions, supervision.

(✕) ⇌

▼▼ Red Roof Inn SH
(954) 776-6333. **Call for rates.** 4800 Powerline Rd. I-95, exit 32, just w of jct Commercial Blvd, then n. Int corridors. **Pets:** Accepted.

(✕) 🚪 ⇌

◆◆◆ ▼▼▼ **Royal Saxon Apartments** Ⓜ
(954) 566-7424. **$65-$175, 30 day notice.** 551 Breakers Ave. Just w of SR A1A, 0.5 mi s of SR 838 (Sunrise Blvd); corner of Breakers Ave and Terramar St. Ext corridors. **Pets:** Accepted.
🆂🅰🆅🅴 🆂🅳 ⊠ 🕻 ➿

◆◆◆ ▼▼▼▼ **Sheraton Suites Cypress Creek** ⅬⒽ
(954) 772-5400. **$269-$329.** 555 NW 62nd St. I-95, exit 33B northbound, then w; exit 33 southbound, then w SR 811 (Cypress Creek Rd). Int corridors. **Pets:** Accepted.
🆂🅰🆅🅴 🆂🅳 ⊠ 🕻 💭 🍽 ➿

◆◆◆ ▼▼▼▼ **Sheraton Yankee Clipper Hotel** ⅬⒽ
(954) 524-5551. **$199-$330.** 1140 Seabreeze Blvd (A1A). SR A1A, just s of Bahia Mar Marina. Ext/int corridors. **Pets:** Medium, dogs only. Service with restrictions, supervision.
🆂🅰🆅🅴 🆂🅳 ⊠ 🔗ᴹ 🕻 💭 🍽 ➿ ⊠

◆◆◆ ▼▼▼▼ **Sheraton Yankee Trader Hotel** ⅬⒽ
(954) 467-1111. **$199-$330.** 321 N Fort Lauderdale Beach Blvd, A1A. On SR A1A, 0.8 mi s of SR 838 (Sunrise Blvd). Int corridors. **Pets:** Medium, dogs only. Service with restrictions, supervision.
🆂🅰🆅🅴 🆂🅳 ⊠ 🔗ᴹ 🕻 💭 🍽 ➿

▼▼▼▼ **TownePlace Suites by Marriott** 🆂🅷
(954) 484-2214. **$175-$285.** 3100 Prospect Rd. I-95, exit 33, 2.7 mi w, then 0.5 mi s on NW 31st St. Int corridors. **Pets:** Accepted.
🅰🆂🅺 🆂🅳 ⊠ 🕻 💭 ➿

▼▼▼▼ **Westin, Fort Lauderdale** ⅬⒽ
(954) 772-1331. **$229-$359.** 400 Corporate Dr. I-95, exit 33 southbound, then e; exit 33A northbound; in Radice Corporate Park. Int corridors. **Pets:** Accepted.
🅰🆂🅺 🆂🅳 ⊠ 🕻 💭 🍽 ➿ ⊠

HOLLYWOOD

▼▼▼▼ **Days Inn Fort Lauderdale/Hollywood Airport South** 🆂🅷
(954) 923-7300. **$98-$299.** 2601 N 29th Ave. I-95, exit 21, just nw on SR 822 (Sheridan St). Int corridors. **Pets:** Large, other species. $10 one-time fee/pet. Designated rooms, service with restrictions, supervision.
🅰🆂🅺 🆂🅳 ⊠ 🕻 💭 ➿

◆◆◆ ▼▼▼▼ **La Quinta Inn & Suites Ft. Lauderdale (Airport)** 🆂🅷
(954) 922-2295. **$145-$199.** 2620 N 26th Ave. I-95, exit 21, just e to Oakwood, then just left. Int corridors. **Pets:** Other species. Service with restrictions, supervision.
🆂🅰🆅🅴 🆂🅳 ⊠ 🔗ᴹ 🕻 💭 ➿ ⊠

◆◆◆ ▼▼▼ **Quality Inn & Suites Hollywood Blvd** Ⓜ 🐾
(954) 981-1800. **$70-$290.** 4900 Hollywood Blvd. I-95, exit 20, 1.6 mi w; Florida Tpke, exit 49, 1.3 mi e. Ext corridors. **Pets:** Other species. $50 deposit/room. Service with restrictions, supervision.
🆂🅰🆅🅴 🆂🅳 ⊠ 🕻 💭 ➿

▼ **Sandy Shores Motel & Family Lodging** Ⓜ
(954) 923-3750. **Call for rates.** 342 Van Buren St. From SR 820 (Hollywood Blvd), just s on SR A1A (S Ocean Dr), then e. Ext corridors. **Pets:** Accepted.
⊠ 🕻

◆◆◆ ▼▼▼ ▼▼▼ **Seminole Hard Rock Hotel & Casino Hollywood** ⅬⒽ
(954) 327-7625. **$299-$399.** 1 Seminole Way. I-95, exit 22, 2.9 mi w, then just n on SR 7/US 441; Florida Tpke, exit 53, 0.5 mi e, then 0.8 mi s. Int corridors. **Pets:** Accepted.
🆂🅰🆅🅴 ⊠ 🔗ᴹ 🕻 💭 🍽 ➿ ⊠

MIRAMAR

▼▼▼▼ **Residence Inn by Marriott Fort Lauderdale SW/Miramar** 🆂🅷 🐾
(954) 450-2717. **$197-$263.** 14700 Hotel Rd. I-75, exit 7A (Miramar Pkwy), just e to SW 145th Ave, then n. Int corridors. **Pets:** Large, other species. $100 one-time fee/room. Designated rooms, service with restrictions, crate.
🅰🆂🅺 🆂🅳 ⊠ 🔗ᴹ 🕻 💭 ➿ ⊠

PLANTATION

◆◆◆ ▼▼▼▼ **Best Western Plantation-Sawgrass** 🆂🅷
(954) 556-8200. **$65-$149.** 1711 N University Dr. On SR 817 (University Dr), just s of Sunrise Blvd (SR 838). Ext/int corridors. **Pets:** Accepted.
🅰🆂🅺 🆂🅳 ⊠ 🕻 💭 🍽 ➿

▼▼▼ **Extended StayAmerica-Fort Lauderdale/Plantation** 🆂🅷
(954) 382-8888. **$85.** 7755 SW 6th St. Just w of SR 817 (University Dr); next to Broward Mall. Int corridors. **Pets:** Other species. $75 one-time fee/pet. Service with restrictions.
🅰🆂🅺 ⊠ 🕻 💭 ➿

▼▼▼▼ **Holiday Inn Express Plantation Hotel & Suites** 🆂🅷
(954) 472-5600. **$149-$259.** 1701 N University Dr. SR 817 (University Dr), just s of jct SR 838 (Sunrise Blvd). Int corridors. **Pets:** Accepted.
🅰🆂🅺 ⊠ 🕻 💭 ➿

◆◆◆ ▼▼▼▼ **La Quinta Inn** 🆂🅷
(954) 473-8257. **$139-$189.** 7901 SW 6th St. 0.3 mi w of SR 817 (University Dr); 0.5 mi sw of jct SR 842 (Broward Blvd). Int corridors. **Pets:** Other species. Service with restrictions, supervision.
🆂🅰🆅🅴 🆂🅳 ⊠ 🕻 💭 ➿

◆◆◆ ▼▼▼▼ **La Quinta Inn & Suites Ft. Lauderdale (Plantation)** 🆂🅷
(954) 476-6047. **$149-$199.** 8101 Peters Rd. I-595, exit 5 (SR 817 N/University Dr), just n, then just w; in Crossroad Office Park. Int corridors. **Pets:** Other species. Service with restrictions, supervision.
🆂🅰🆅🅴 🆂🅳 ⊠ 🔗ᴹ 🕻 💭 ➿

◆◆◆ ▼▼▼▼ **Sheraton Suites-Plantation** ⅬⒽ
(954) 424-3300. **$359-$419.** 311 N University Dr. I-595, exit 5 (SR 817/University Dr), 0.7 mi n; 0.3 mi n of jct Broward Blvd (SR 842); at Fashion Mall. Int corridors. **Pets:** Accepted.
🆂🅰🆅🅴 🆂🅳 ⊠ 🕻 💭 🍽 ➿ ➿

▼▼▼▼ **Staybridge Suites Ft Lauderdale-Plantation** 🆂🅷
(954) 577-9696. **$230-$450.** 410 N Pine Island Rd. I-595, exit 4 (Pine Island Rd), 1.7 mi n. Int corridors. **Pets:** Accepted.
🅰🆂🅺 🆂🅳 ⊠ 🔗ᴹ 🕻 💭 ➿

POMPANO BEACH

▼▼▼▼ **Extended Stay Deluxe–Cypress Creek Park North** 🆂🅷
(954) 783-1050. **$81-$143.** 1401 SW 15th St. I-95, exit 33B (Cypress Creek Rd) to Andrews Ave, just s, then left on McNab St. Int corridors. **Pets:** Other species. $75 one-time fee/pet. Service with restrictions.
🅰🆂🅺 🆂🅳 ⊠ 🕻 💭 ➿

SUNRISE

◆◆◆ ▼▼ ▼ **La Quinta Inn & Suites Sunrise** 🆂🅷
(954) 845-9929. **$165-$209.** 13600 NW 2nd St. SW 136th Ave, 0.3 mi n of jct I-595, exit 1A and SR 84; 0.5 mi e of jct I-75 and SR 869 (Sawgrass Expwy). Int corridors. **Pets:** Other species. Service with restrictions, supervision.
🆂🅰🆅🅴 🆂🅳 ⊠ 🕻 💭 ➿

La Quinta Inn-Sawgrass Mills Outlet Mall 🆂🅷

(954) 846-1200. **$145-$189.** 13651 NW 2nd St. SW 136th Ave, 0.3 mi n of jct I-595, exit 1A and SR 84; 0.5 mi e of jct I-75 and SR 869 (Sawgrass Expwy). Int corridors. **Pets:** Other species. Service with restrictions, supervision.

🆂🅰🆅🅴 ✖ ▤ 💻 🌊

TAMARAC

 Homestead Studio Suites Hotel-Ft Lauderdale-Tamarac Ⓜ

(954) 733-6644. **$62-$100.** 3873 W Commercial Blvd. SR 870 (Commercial Blvd), 0.7 mi e of Florida Tpke, exit 62; just e of jct US 441 and SR 7. Ext corridors. **Pets:** Other species. $75 one-time fee/pet. Service with restrictions.

🅰🆂🅺 🆂🅰 ✖ ▤ 💻

 La Quinta Inn 🆂🅷

(954) 485-7900. **$104-$149.** 3800 W Commercial Blvd. On SR 870 (Commercial Blvd), 0.8 mi e of Florida Tpke, exit 62; just e of jct SR 7 and US 441. Int corridors. **Pets:** Other species. Service with restrictions, supervision.

🆂🅰🆅🅴 🆂🅰 ✖ ▤ 💻 🌊

La Quinta Inn & Suites 🆂🅷

(954) 484-6909. **$119-$179.** 5070 N SR 7. SR 7 and US 441, just n of jct SR 870 (Commercial Blvd); 0.5 mi e of Florida Tpke, exit 62, then n. Int corridors. **Pets:** Other species. Service with restrictions, supervision.

🆂🅰🆅🅴 🆂🅰 ✖ ▤ 💻 🌊

WESTON

Hawthorn Suites 🆂🅷

(954) 659-1555. **$100-$300, 3 day notice.** 2201 N Commerce Pkwy. I-75, exit 15, 0.5 mi w on Arvida Pkwy to Weston Rd, n to N Commerce Pkwy, then just e. Int corridors. **Pets:** Accepted.

🆂🅰🆅🅴 ✖ 🅰🅼 ▤ 💻 🌊

Hyatt Regency Bonaventure Conference Center and Spa 🅻🅷 🐾

(954) 616-1234. **$119-$599, 3 day notice.** 250 Racquet Club Rd. I-75, exit 21 (Indian Trace) southbound, 1.6 mi e on SR 84 to E Mall Dr, then just s; exit northbound, U-turn to SR 84, 1.6 mi to E Mall Dr, then just s. Ext corridors. **Pets:** Very small. $50 one-time fee/pet. Service with restrictions, supervision.

🆂🅰🆅🅴 ✖ ▤ 💻 🍽 🌊 ✖

Residence Inn by Marriott Weston 🆂🅷

(954) 659-8585. **$175-$219.** 2605 Weston Rd. I-75, exit 15 to Weston Rd, just s. Int corridors. **Pets:** Other species. $100 one-time fee/room. Service with restrictions, crate.

🅰🆂🅺 🆂🅰 ✖ 🅰🅼 ▤ 💻 🌊 ✖

TownePlace Suites by Marriott Weston 🆂🅷

(954) 659-2234. **$241-$296.** 1545 Three Village Rd. I-75, exit 15, 1 mi e on Arvida Pkwy to Bonaventure Blvd, n to Three Village Rd, then w. Int corridors. **Pets:** Accepted.

🅰🆂🅺 🆂🅰 ✖ 🅰🅼 ▤ 💻 🌊

END METROPOLITAN AREA

FORT MYERS

Best Western Airport Inn 🆂🅷

(239) 561-7000. **$100-$230.** 8955 Daniels Pkwy. I-75, exit 131, 0.6 mi w, on CR 879 (Daniels Pkwy). Int corridors. **Pets:** Small. $15 daily fee/pet. Designated rooms, service with restrictions, supervision.

🆂🅰🆅🅴 🆂🅰 ✖ ▤ 💻 🌊 ✖

Best Western Springs Resort Ⓜ 🐾

(239) 267-7900. **$99-$159, 30 day notice.** 18051 S Tamiami Trail. On US 41 at Constitution Blvd. Ext corridors. **Pets:** Other species. $15 daily fee/pet. Service with restrictions, crate.

🆂🅰🆅🅴 🆂🅰 ✖ ▤ 💻 🍽 🌊

Comfort Suites Airport/University Ⓜ

(239) 768-0005. **$80-$160.** 13651 Indian Paint Ln. I-75, exit 131, just w on CR 879 (Daniels Pkwy). Int corridors. **Pets:** Accepted.

🅰🆂🅺 🆂🅰 ✖ ▤ 💻 🌊

Country Inn & Suites By Carlson Sanibel-Gateway 🆂🅷

(239) 454-9292. **$109-$249.** 13901 Shell Point Plaza. Just w of jct McGregor Blvd. Int corridors. **Pets:** Accepted.

🆂🅰🆅🅴 🆂🅰 ✖ 🅰🅼 ▤ 💻 🌊

Crowne Plaza 🆂🅷 🐾

(239) 482-2900. **$169-$339, 7 day notice.** 13051 Bell Tower Dr. Jct Daniels Pkwy; just e of jct US 41; in Bell Tower Shops. **Pets:** Medium. $50 one-time fee/room. Designated rooms, service with restrictions, supervision.

🆂🅰🆅🅴 🆂🅰 ✖ 🅰🅼 ▤ 💻 🍽 🌊 ✖

Holiday Inn Downtown Historic District 🆂🅷

(239) 332-3232. **Call for rates.** 2431 Cleveland Ave. On US 41, just s of jct Edison Ave. Int corridors. **Pets:** Medium. $75 one-time fee/pet. Designated rooms, service with restrictions, crate.

✖ 🅰🅼 ▤ 💻 🍽 🌊

Homewood Suites by Hilton-Ft. Myers 🆂🅷

(239) 275-6000. **$109-$339.** 5255 Big Pine Way. Just e of jct US 41; just n of jct Daniels Pkwy; in Bell Tower Shops. Int corridors. **Pets:** Medium. $75 one-time fee/room. Service with restrictions, supervision.

🅰🆂🅺 🆂🅰 ✖ 🅰🅼 ▤ 💻 🌊

La Quinta Inn & Suites 🆂🅷

(239) 466-1200. **$129-$199.** 20091 Summerlin Rd SW. Jct John Morris Rd. Ext corridors. **Pets:** Other species. Service with restrictions, supervision.

🆂🅰🆅🅴 🆂🅰 ✖ ▤ 💻 🌊

La Quinta Inn Fort Myers Ⓜ

(239) 275-3300. **$99-$189.** 4850 S Cleveland Ave. On US 41, just s of jct N Airport Rd. Ext corridors. **Pets:** Other species. Service with restrictions, supervision.

🆂🅰🆅🅴 ✖ 🅰🅼 ▤ 💻 🌊

Residence Inn by Marriott 🆂🅷 🐾

(239) 936-0110. **$154-$274.** 2960 Colonial Blvd. I-75, exit 136, 3.5 mi w on SR 884 (Colonial Blvd). Int corridors. **Pets:** Other species. $100 one-time fee/room. Service with restrictions.

🅰🆂🅺 🆂🅰 ✖ 🅰🅼 ▤ 💻 🌊 ✖

Suburban Extended Stay Hotel 🆂🅷

(239) 938-0100. **$74-$144.** 10150 Metro Pkwy. I-75, exit 136, 3.4 mi w on SR 884 (Colonial Blvd); just s on SR 739. Int corridors. **Pets:** Medium. $15 daily fee/pet. Designated rooms, service with restrictions, supervision.

🅰🆂🅺 🆂🅰 ✖ 🅰🅼 ▤ 💻 🌊

Wynstar Inn & Suites 🆂🅷 🐾

(239) 791-5000. **$69-$259.** 10150 Daniels Pkwy. I-75, exit 131, just e on CR 879 (Daniels Pkwy). Int corridors. **Pets:** Small, dogs only. $15 daily fee/pet. Designated rooms, service with restrictions, supervision.

🅰🆂🅺 🆂🅰 ✖ 🅰🅼 ▤ 💻 🌊

FORT MYERS BEACH

⚑ ▼▼▼ Best Western Beach Resort SH
(239) 463-6000. **$119-$409, 7 day notice.** 684 Estero Blvd. 0.4 mi n of Matanzas Pass Bridge (SR 865). Ext corridors. **Pets:** Small, other species. $10 daily fee/pet. Designated rooms, service with restrictions, supervision.
SAVE Sᴅ ✕ 🛗 💻 ⟲ ⊠

▼▼▼▼ Casa Playa All Suite Resort CO ❀
(239) 765-0510. **$99-$299, 14 day notice.** 510 Estero Blvd. 0.5 mi n of Matanzas Pass Bridge (SR 865) via 5th St. Ext corridors. **Pets:** Medium. $25 deposit/pet, $25 daily fee/pet. Designated rooms, service with restrictions, supervision.
A$K Sᴅ ✕ 🛗 💻

⚑ ▼▼▼ Lighthouse Resort Inn & Suites SH
(239) 463-9392. **$72-$325, 3 day notice.** 1051 5th St. Jct Matanzas Pass Bridge (SR 865). Ext corridors. **Pets:** Small, other species. $25 daily fee/room. Service with restrictions, supervision.
SAVE ✕ 🛗 💻 ⑪ ⟲

FORT PIERCE

⚑ ▼▼ Dockside Inn & Resort SH
(772) 468-3555. **$75-$155.** 1160 Seaway Dr. SR A1A southbound, 2 mi e of jct US 1. Ext corridors. **Pets:** Small, other species. $50 one-time fee/pet. Designated rooms, service with restrictions.
SAVE Sᴅ ✕ 🛗 💻 ⟲ ⊠

⚑ ▼ Fountain Resort M
(772) 466-7041. **$79-$109.** 4889 N US 1. I-95, exit 138 (Indrio Rd), 5.5 mi e, then just n. Ext corridors. **Pets:** Accepted.
A$K ✕ 🛗 💻 ⟲ ⊠

▼ Holiday Inn Express SH
(772) 464-5000. **Call for rates.** 7151 Okeechobee Rd. I-95, exit 129, 0.7 mi w on SR 70; Florida Tpke, exit 152. Ext corridors. **Pets:** Small. $25 one-time fee/room. Service with restrictions, supervision.
✕ ᴸᴹ 🛗 💻 ⟲

▼ Motel 6-Fort Pierce #1207 M
(772) 461-9937. **$51-$71.** 2500 Peters Rd. I-95, exit 129, just w, then n. Ext corridors. **Pets:** Other species. Service with restrictions, supervision.
Sᴅ ✕ 🛗 ⟲

⚑ ▼ Royal Inn M ❀
(772) 464-0405. **$79-$129.** 222 Hernando St. 2.5 mi e on SR A1A southbound to Hernando St, then just s. Ext corridors. **Pets:** Small, other species. Designated rooms, service with restrictions.
SAVE Sᴅ ✕ 🛗

⚑ ▼▼ The Sandhurst Hotel & Suites SH
(772) 595-0711. **$139-$199.** 1230 Seaway Dr. Jct US 1 and SR A1A southbound, 2 mi e. Int corridors. **Pets:** Large, other species. $50 one-time fee/room. Service with restrictions, supervision.
SAVE Sᴅ ✕ 🛗 💻 ⟲ ⊠

GAINESVILLE

⚑ ▼▼▼ A Newberry Inn & Conference Center SH
(352) 332-8001. **$109.** 7413 W Newberry Rd. I-75, exit 387, just w. Ext corridors. **Pets:** Accepted.
SAVE Sᴅ ✕ 🛗 💻 ⑪ ⟲

⚑ ▼▼▼▼ Best Western Gateway Grand SH ❀
(352) 331-3336. **$119-$169.** 4200 NW 97th Blvd. I-75, exit 390, just n of SR 222, then just w. Int corridors. **Pets:** $20 daily fee/room. Designated rooms, supervision.
SAVE Sᴅ ✕ ᴸᴹ 🛗 💻 ⑪ ⟲ ⊠

⚑ ▼▼▼▼ Clarion Inn & Conference Center SH
(352) 332-7500. **$99-$219.** 7417 Newberry Rd. I-75, exit 387, just w. Ext corridors. **Pets:** Accepted.
SAVE Sᴅ ✕ 🛗 💻 ⑪ ⟲

⚑ ▼▼▼ Comfort Inn SH
(352) 373-6500. **$68-$81.** 2435 SW 13th St. I-75, exit 382, 2 mi ne on SR 331, then 1 mi n on US 441. Ext corridors. **Pets:** Small. $10 daily fee/pet. Service with restrictions, crate.
SAVE Sᴅ ✕ 🛗 💻 ⟲

▼▼▼ Comfort Inn West SH ❀
(352) 264-1771. **$99-$229.** 3440 SW 40th Blvd. I-75, exit 384, just e, then just n. Int corridors. **Pets:** $10 daily fee/pet. Designated rooms, service with restrictions, supervision.
A$K Sᴅ ✕ ᴸᴹ 🛗 💻 ⟲

▼▼▼ Extended StayAmerica SH
(352) 375-0073. **$75-$79.** 3600 SW 42nd St. I-75, exit 384, just e. Ext corridors. **Pets:** Other species. $75 one-time fee/pet. Service with restrictions.
A$K Sᴅ ✕ 🛗 💻

⚑ ▼▼▼ Holiday Inn Express SH
(352) 376-0004. **$100.** 3905 SW 43rd St. I-75, exit 384, just w; behind Cracker Barrel Restaurant. Int corridors. **Pets:** Medium. $10 daily fee/pet. Designated rooms, service with restrictions, supervision.
SAVE Sᴅ ✕ ᴸᴹ 🛗 💻 ⟲

▼▼▼ Homewood Suites SH
(352) 335-3133. **$139-$289.** 3333 SW 42nd St. I-75, exit 384, just e. Int corridors. **Pets:** Other species. $100 one-time fee/room. Service with restrictions.
A$K ✕ ᴸᴹ 🛗 💻 ⟲ ⊠

▼▼ Red Roof Inn-Gainesville SH
(352) 336-3311. **Call for rates.** 3500 SW 42nd St. I-75, exit 384, just e. Int corridors. **Pets:** Accepted.
✕ ᴸᴹ 🛗 ⟲

⚑ ▼▼▼ Sweetwater Branch Inn Bed & Breakfast BB
(352) 373-6760. **$95-$245.** 625 E University Ave. 1.3 mi e of the University on SR 26; 7.3 mi e of I-75, exit 387. Int corridors. **Pets:** Accepted.
SAVE ✕ 🛗 💻

HAINES CITY

⚑ ▼▼▼ Best Western Lake Hamilton M
(863) 421-6929. **$65-$120.** 605 B Moore Rd. On US 27, just s of jct SR 544; 2 mi s of jct US 17-92. Ext corridors. **Pets:** Small. $20 daily fee/pet. Designated rooms, service with restrictions, supervision.
SAVE Sᴅ ✕ ᴸᴹ 🛗 💻 ⟲ ⊠

HERNANDO

▼▼ Best Western Citrus Hills Lodge SH
(352) 527-0015. **$105-$115.** 350 E Norvell Bryant Hwy. CR 486 at Citrus Hills Blvd, 3.3 mi w of US 41. Ext corridors. **Pets:** Accepted.
A$K Sᴅ ✕ ᴸᴹ 🛗 💻 ⑪ ⟲

HOLMES BEACH

⚑ ▼▼▼ Haley's Motel M
(941) 778-5405. **$89-$259, 30 day notice.** 8102 Gulf Dr N. On CR 789, 1.2 mi n of jct SR 64, jct Palm Dr; on Anna Maria Island. Ext corridors. **Pets:** Other species. $30 one-time fee/room.
SAVE ✕ 🛗 ⟲

HORSESHOE BEACH

▼▼ Horseshoe Beach-Vacation Rentals VH
(352) 498-2400. **Call for rates (no credit cards).** 96 Main St. 20 mi s of US 19; north side of town. Ext corridors. **Pets:** Large.
✕ 🛗 💻

INDIALANTIC

♦♦♦♦ DoubleTree Guest Suites Melbourne Beach Oceanfront SH
(321) 723-4222. **$149-$279.** 1665 N SR A1A. On SR A1A, 1.5 mi n of jct US 192. Ext corridors. **Pets:** Medium. $75 one-time fee/room. Designated rooms, service with restrictions, supervision.

⊠ 🖪 💷 🍴 🕿

♦♦♦♦ Oceanfront Cottages CA
(321) 725-8474. **Call for rates.** 612 Wavecrest Ave. Just s of east end of US 192. Ext corridors. **Pets:** Small. $30 one-time fee/room. Service with restrictions, supervision.

⊠ 🖪 🕿

INDIAN HARBOUR BEACH

♦♦♦ Lexington Hotel on the Island SH
(321) 773-0325. **$79-$95.** 1894 S Patrick Dr. I-95, exit 183 (SR 518), 8 mi e on Eau Gallie Blvd, then 1 mi n on SR 513. Ext/int corridors. **Pets:** Medium, other species. $50 one-time fee/pet. Service with restrictions, crate.

SAVE 🖪 ⊠ 🖪 💷 🕿

INGLIS

♦♦♦ Pine Lodge Bed & Breakfast BB
(352) 447-7463. **$149-$179, 7 day notice.** 649 Hwy 40 W. 1.5 mi w of US 19. Ext/int corridors. **Pets:** Small. $25 one-time fee/pet. Designated rooms, service with restrictions, supervision.

SAVE 🖪 ⊠ 🖪 💷 🕿 🖉

JACKSONVILLE METROPOLITAN AREA

BALDWIN

♦♦♦ Best Western Baldwin Inn M
(904) 266-9759. **$75.** 1088 US 301 S. I-10, exit 343, just s. Ext corridors. **Pets:** Accepted.

SAVE 🖪 ⊠ 💷 🕿

FERNANDINA BEACH

♦♦♦♦ Amelia Island Plantation-Inn & Beach Club LH
(904) 261-6161. **$289-$419, 14 day notice.** 6800 First Coast Hwy. SR A1A, 6.5 mi s of the bridge. Ext corridors. **Pets:** Accepted.

SAVE ⊠ 💷 🍴 🕿 🐾

♦♦ Hampton Inn Amelia Island SH 🐾
(904) 321-1111. **Call for rates.** 2549 Sadler Rd. Just w of jct SR A1A and Sadler Rd. Int corridors. **Pets:** Medium, other species. $35 one-time fee/pet. Designated rooms, service with restrictions, crate.

⊠ 🖪 🖪 💷 🕿

♦♦♦ Hoyt House BB 🐾
(904) 277-4300. **Call for rates.** 804 Atlantic Ave. On Atlantic Ave/SR 200 at Centre and S 8th sts; in historic district. Int corridors. **Pets:** Small. $35 one-time fee/pet. Designated rooms.

⊠ 🕿

JACKSONVILLE

♦♦♦ Best Western Hotel JTB/Southpoint LH 🐾
(904) 281-0900. **$79-$169.** 4660 Salisbury Rd. I-95, exit 344 (SR 202), just ne, then just s. Int corridors. **Pets:** Small. $10 daily fee/pet. Designated rooms, service with restrictions, supervision.

SAVE 🖪 ⊠ 🖪 💷 🕿 🖾

♦♦♦ Best Western Jacksonville Airport SH
(904) 741-4980. **$79-$149.** 1170 Airport Entrance Rd. I-95, exit 363B, just w, then just s on Duval Rd. Ext corridors. **Pets:** Medium. $15 daily fee/pet. Service with restrictions, crate.

SAVE 🖪 ⊠ 🖪 🖪 💷 🕿

♦♦ Candlewood Suites SH
(904) 296-7785. **$90.** 4990 Belfort Rd. I-95, exit 344 (SR 202), ne to Belfort Rd, then just s. Int corridors. **Pets:** Accepted.

ASK 🖪 ⊠ 🖪 🖪 💷

♦♦ Extended StayAmerica-Jacksonville-Butler Blvd SH
(904) 296-0181. **$67-$74.** 6961 Lenoir Ave. I-95, exit 344 (SR 202), just sw, then 0.3 mi n. Int corridors. **Pets:** Other species. $75 one-time fee/pet. Service with restrictions.

ASK 🖪 ⊠ 🖪 💷

♦♦ Extended Stay Deluxe-Butler Blvd SH
(904) 332-6512. **$77-$84.** 4699 Lenoir Ave S. I-95, exit 344 (SR 202), just sw, then just n. Int corridors. **Pets:** Other species. $75 one-time fee/pet. Service with restrictions.

ASK 🖪 ⊠ 🖪 💷 🕿

♦♦♦ Extended Stay Deluxe (Jacksonville/Deerwood Park) SH
(904) 620-9008. **$77-$84.** 8801 Perimeter Park Blvd. I-95, exit 344 (SR 202), 2.5 mi e on J Turner Butler Blvd to Southside Blvd, then just n on west side of road. Int corridors. **Pets:** Other species. $75 one-time fee/pet. Service with restrictions.

ASK 🖪 ⊠ 🖪 🖪 💷 🏊

♦♦♦ Hampton Inn Central SH
(904) 396-7770. **$109-$209.** 1331 Prudential Dr. South side of Main St Bridge. Int corridors. **Pets:** Accepted.

ASK 🖪 ⊠ 🖪 🖪 💷

♦♦♦ Holiday Inn Express & Suites Jacksonville SH 🐾
(904) 696-3333. **$109-$259.** 10148 New Berlin Rd. I-95, exit 362A southbound, 4.9 mi s on SR 9A to Heckscher Dr, then just w; exit 358A northbound, 5.8 mi ne on Hecksher Dr; 0.6 mi from Jaxport Cruise Terminal. Int corridors. **Pets:** $30 one-time fee/room. Service with restrictions, supervision.

ASK 🖪 ⊠ 🖪 💷 🕿 🖾

♦♦ Homestead Jacksonville-Salisbury Rd-Southpoint SH
(904) 296-0661. **$72-$79.** 4693 Salisbury Rd S. I-95, exit 344 (SR 202), e on J Turner Butler Blvd, then just s. Int corridors. **Pets:** Other species. $75 one-time fee/pet. Service with restrictions.

ASK 🖪 ⊠ 🖪 🖪 💷 🕿

♦♦ Homestead Jacksonville-Southside-St Johns Towne Center M
(904) 642-9911. **$58-$65.** 10020 Skinner Lake Rd. I-95, exit 344 (SR 202), 3.5 mi e on J Turner Butler Blvd to Gate Pkwy, just n, then just w. Ext corridors. **Pets:** Other species. $75 one-time fee/pet. Service with restrictions.

ASK 🖪 ⊠ 🖪 🖪 💷

▼▼ Homestead Studio Suites Hotel-Jacksonville/Baymeadows SH
(904) 739-1881. **$72-$79.** 8300 Western Way. I-95, exit 341, just e to Western Way, then just s. Int corridors. **Pets:** Other species. $75 one-time fee/pet. Service with restrictions.

▼▼▼ Homewood Suites by Hilton Jacksonville South/Town Center SH
(904) 641-7988. **Call for rates (no credit cards).** 10434 Midtown Pkwy. I-95, exit 344 (SR 202), 3.5 mi e on J Turner Butler Blvd to Gate Blvd, 0.3 mi n to Town Center Pkwy, 0.5 mi e to Midtown Pkwy, then 0.3 mi s. Int corridors. **Pets:** Accepted.

▼▼ Howard Johnson Inn & Suites M
(904) 281-0198. **$60-$120.** 4300 Salisbury Rd N. I-95, exit 344 (SR 202), just nw to Salisbury Rd, then just n. Ext corridors. **Pets:** Small. $10 daily fee/pet. Service with restrictions.

▼▼ Jameson Inn SH
(904) 296-0968. **Call for rates.** 7030 Bonneval Rd. I-95, exit 344 (SR 202), just w. Int corridors. **Pets:** Small. $15 daily fee/room. Service with restrictions, crate.

⟨AAA⟩ ▼▼ La Quinta Inn SH
(904) 268-9999. **$89-$99.** 3199 Hartley Rd. I-295, exit 5A northbound; exit 5 southbound at SR 13. Int corridors. **Pets:** Other species. Service with restrictions, supervision.

⟨AAA⟩ ▼▼▼▼ La Quinta Inn & Suites Jacksonville (Butler Blvd) SH
(904) 296-0703. **$129-$139.** 4686 Lenoir Ave S. I-95, exit 344 (SR 202), just sw, then just nw. Int corridors. **Pets:** Other species. Service with restrictions, supervision.

⟨AAA⟩ ▼▼▼ La Quinta Inn Jacksonville (Airport/North) SH
(904) 751-6960. **$92-$109.** 812 Dunn Ave. I-95, exit 360, southwest corner. Ext corridors. **Pets:** Other species. Service with restrictions, supervision.

⟨AAA⟩ ▼▼▼ La Quinta Inn Jacksonville (Orange Park) SH
(904) 778-9539. **$104-$114.** 8555 Blanding Blvd. I-295, exit 12, just s on SR 21. Ext corridors. **Pets:** Other species. Service with restrictions, supervision.

▼▼ Microtel Inn & Suites Butler Blvd/Southpoint SH
(904) 281-2244. **$49-$79.** 4940 Mustang Rd. I-95, exit 344 (SR 202), just sw, then just nw. Int corridors. **Pets:** Medium, other species. $15 daily fee/pet. Designated rooms, service with restrictions, supervision.

⟨AAA⟩ ▼▼▼ ▼▼▼ Omni Jacksonville Hotel LH ❖
(904) 355-6664. **$299-$349.** 245 Water St. Corner of Pearl and Water sts; on northside of St. Johns River; downtown; adjacent to The Landing. Int corridors. **Pets:** Small. $50 one-time fee/pet. Service with restrictions, supervision.

▼▼ Ramada Conference Center Mandarin SH
(904) 268-8080. **$99-$109.** 3130 Hartley Rd. I-295, exit 5A northbound; exit 5 southbound, just n on SR 13. Ext corridors. **Pets:** $20 one-time fee/room. No service, supervision.

▼▼ Residence Inn by Marriott SH
(904) 996-8900. **$144-$184.** 10551 Deerwood Park Blvd. I-95, exit 344 (SR 202), 3.5 mi e on J Turner Butler Blvd to Gate Blvd, just s, then just w. Int corridors. **Pets:** Accepted.

⟨AAA⟩ ▼▼▼ ▼ Residence Inn by Marriott SH 🐾
(904) 733-8088. **$166-$206.** 8365 Dix Ellis Tr. I-95, exit 341 (SR 152), just w to Freedom Commerce Pkwy, then just s. Ext corridors. **Pets:** Large, other species. $75 one-time fee/room. Service with restrictions.

JACKSONVILLE BEACH

⟨AAA⟩ ▼▼▼ ▼ Quality Suites Oceanfront SH ❖
(904) 435-3535. **$179-$349.** 11 1st St N. Just n of Beach Blvd (US 90). Int corridors. **Pets:** Medium. $35 daily fee/pet. Designated rooms, service with restrictions, supervision.

ORANGE PARK

▼▼ Comfort Inn SH
(904) 644-4444. **$65-$95.** 341 Park Ave. I-295, exit 10 (US 17), just s. Ext corridors. **Pets:** $30 one-time fee/pet. Service with restrictions, supervision.

PONTE VEDRA BEACH

⟨AAA⟩ ▼▼▼ ▼ Sawgrass Marriott Resort & Spa LH
(904) 285-7777. **$197-$307.** 1000 PGA Tour Blvd. 2.5 mi s of J Turner Butler Blvd. Ext/int corridors. **Pets:** Accepted.

YULEE

▼▼ Comfort Inn SH
(904) 225-2600. **Call for rates.** 76043 Sidney Pl. I-95, exit 373, just e on SR 200/A1A. Int corridors. **Pets:** Accepted.

END METROPOLITAN AREA

JUPITER

▼▼▼ Fairfield Inn & Suites by Marriott SH
(561) 748-5252. **$120-$252.** 6748 W Indiantown Rd. I-95, exit 87A, 0.8 mi e on SR 706 (Indiantown Rd). Int corridors. **Pets:** Small. $50 one-time fee/pet. Service with restrictions, crate.

LAKE CITY

⟨AAA⟩ ▼▼▼ Best Western Lake City Inn SH
(386) 752-3801. **$69-$110.** 3598 W Hwy 90. I-75, exit 427, just w. Ext corridors. **Pets:** Medium, other species. $10 daily fee/pet. Designated rooms, service with restrictions, supervision.

Days Inn I-10 SH
(386) 758-4224. **$59-$120.** 3430 N Hwy 441. I-10, exit 303, just s. Ext corridors. **Pets:** Medium. $10 daily fee/pet. Designated rooms, service with restrictions, supervision.

Driftwood Inn M
(386) 755-3545. **$42-$70.** 2764 W Hwy 90. I-75, exit 427, 0.7 mi e. Ext corridors. **Pets:** Small, dogs only. $10 daily fee/pet. Designated rooms, service with restrictions, supervision.

Rodeway Inn M
(386) 755-5203. **$46-$55.** 205 SW Commerce Dr. I-75, exit 427, just e. Ext corridors. **Pets:** Dogs only. $5 one-time fee/pet. Designated rooms, service with restrictions, crate.

LAKELAND

Holiday Inn Lakeland Hotel & Conference Center SH
(863) 688-8080. **$100-$125.** 3260 US Hwy 98 N. I-4, exit 32, just e. Int corridors. **Pets:** Accepted.

Jameson Inn SH
(863) 858-9070. **Call for rates.** 4375 Lakeland Park Dr. I-4, exit 33, just nw. Int corridors. **Pets:** Small. $15 daily fee/room. Service with restrictions, crate.

Lakeland Residence Inn by Marriott SH
(863) 680-2323. **$153-$216.** 3701 Harden Blvd. I-4, exit 27 (Polk Pkwy), se on SR 570 (toll road) to exit 5, then just n. Int corridors. **Pets:** Accepted.

La Quinta Inn & Suites Lakeland SH
(863) 859-2866. **$115-$139.** 1024 Crevasse St. I-4, exit 32, just n on US 98. Int corridors. **Pets:** Other species. Service with restrictions, supervision.

La Quinta Inn East SH
(863) 815-0606. **$109-$139.** 4315 Lakeland Park Dr. I-4, exit 33; jct SR 33, just nw. Int corridors. **Pets:** Other species. Service with restrictions, supervision.

Quality Inn & Sutes SH
(863) 858-1411. **$79-$179, 3 day notice.** 4645 Socrum Loop Rd. I-4, exit 33, just nw. Ext corridors. **Pets:** Very small. $10 daily fee/pet. Designated rooms, service with restrictions, supervision.

LAKE WORTH

Lago Motor Inn M
(561) 585-5246. **$63-$195, 14 day notice.** 714 S Dixie Hwy. I-95, exit 63, 0.7 mi e, then just s on US 1, just s of jct 6th Ave S. Ext corridors. **Pets:** $10 daily fee/pet. Designated rooms, service with restrictions, supervision.

LANTANA

Motel 6 Lantana #688 M
(561) 585-5833. **$66-$82.** 1310 W Lantana Rd. I-95, exit 61 (SR 812), just e, then s. Ext corridors. **Pets:** Other species. Service with restrictions, supervision.

LIVE OAK

Econo Lodge SH
(386) 362-7459. **$62-$85.** 6811 N US 129 & I-10. I-10, exit 283, just s. Ext corridors. **Pets:** Large, other species. $10 one-time fee/pet. Service with restrictions, supervision.

Suwannee River Best Western Inn SH
(386) 362-6000. **$49-$150, 7 day notice.** 6819 US 129 N. I-10, exit 283, 0.3 mi s. Ext corridors. **Pets:** Small, other species. Service with restrictions, supervision.

LONGBOAT KEY

Cedars Tennis Resort CO
(941) 383-4621. **$850-$2375, 90 day notice.** 645 Cedars Ct, Suite A. Just e of jct SR 789 (Gulf of Mexico Dr), on Campanion Way. Ext corridors. **Pets:** Small. $200 one-time fee/pet. Supervision.

Riviera Beach Resort M
(941) 383-2552. **Call for rates.** 5451 Gulf of Mexico Dr. On SR 789, 5 mi se of jct SR 684 (Cortez Rd). Ext corridors. **Pets:** Small, other species. $100 deposit/pet, $15 daily fee/pet. No service, supervision.

LYNN HAVEN

Wingate Inn SH ❖
(850) 248-8080. **$95-$150.** 2610 Lynn Haven Pkwy. Jct 23rd St, 2.3 mi n on SR 77. Int corridors. **Pets:** Small, dogs only. $50 one-time fee/pet. Designated rooms, service with restrictions, crate.

MACCLENNY

Econo Lodge M
(904) 259-3000. **$58-$80.** 151 Woodlawn Rd. I-10, exit 335, just s of jct SR 121. Ext corridors. **Pets:** Large, other species. $10 one-time fee/pet. Service with restrictions, supervision.

MANALAPAN

The Ritz-Carlton, Palm Beach LH ❖
(561) 533-6000. **$175-$439, 15 day notice.** 100 S Ocean Blvd. On SR A1A; 9 mi s of Palm Beach. Int corridors. **Pets:** Small. $35 daily fee/pet. Service with restrictions.

MARIANNA

Americas Best Value Inn SH
(850) 526-5666. **$65-$95.** 2086 Hwy 71 S. I-10, exit 142, 0.3 mi s. Ext corridors. **Pets:** $10 daily fee/pet. Service with restrictions.

Quality Inn SH
(850) 526-5600. **$55-$89.** 2175 Hwy 71 S. I-10, exit 142, just n. Ext corridors. **Pets:** Accepted.

MELBOURNE

Crane Creek Inn Waterfront Bed & Breakfast BB ❖
(321) 768-6416. **Call for rates.** 907 E Melbourne Ave. Jct US 192, just s on Babcock, then 0.9 mi e. Ext/int corridors. **Pets:** Dogs only. $10 daily fee/pet. Designated rooms, supervision.

▼▼▼▼ Hilton Melbourne Rialto Place SH
(321) 768-0200. **Call for rates.** 200 Rialto Pl. 1 mi w of US 1, 0.8 mi n of US 192 via Airport Blvd. Int corridors. **Pets:** $50 deposit/pet. Service with restrictions, supervision.
⊠ 🏃 🛏 💻 🍴 🏊 🏋

ⒶⒶ▼ ▼▼▼ La Quinta Inn & Suites Melbourne SH
(321) 242-9400. **$135-$169.** 7200 George T Edwards Dr. I-95, exit 191 (CR 509), just w. Int corridors. **Pets:** Other species. Service with restrictions, supervision.
SAVE 🏃 ⊠ 🛏 💻 🏊

MIAMI-MIAMI BEACH METROPOLITAN AREA

AVENTURA

ⒶⒶ▼ ▼▼▼ ▼▼ The Fairmont Turnberry Isle Resort & Club LH
(305) 932-6200. **$199-$5639, 3 day notice.** 19999 W Country Club Dr. 0.5 mi w of SR A1A via SR 856; from US 1 at NE 199th St and Biscayne Blvd. Ext/int corridors. **Pets:** Medium. $35 one-time fee/pet. Designated rooms, service with restrictions, supervision.
SAVE 🏃 ⊠ 🛏 💻 🍴 🏊 🏋

ⒶⒶ▼ ▼▼▼ Residence Inn by Marriott-Aventura Mall SH 🐾
(786) 528-1001. **$144-$296.** 19900 W Country Club Dr. 0.5 mi w of SR A1A via SR 856; from US 1 at NE 199th St and Biscayne Blvd. Int corridors. **Pets:** Medium. $100 one-time fee/room. Service with restrictions.
SAVE 🏃 ⊠ 🏃 🛏 💻 🏊

COCONUT GROVE

ⒶⒶ▼ ▼▼▼ ▼▼ Grand Bay-Miami SH
(305) 858-9600. **Call for rates.** 2669 S Bayshore Dr. On Water Front Dr. Int corridors. **Pets:** Accepted.
SAVE ⊠ 🏃 🛏 💻 🍴 🏊 🏋

ⒶⒶ▼ ▼▼▼ ▼▼ Mayfair Hotel & Spa SH
(305) 441-0000. **$159-$259.** 3000 Florida Ave. At Florida Ave and Virginia St; center. Ext/int corridors. **Pets:** Accepted.
SAVE 🏃 ⊠ 💻 🍴 🏊 🏋

▼▼▼ Residence Inn by Marriott SH
(305) 285-9303. **$142-$228.** 2835 Tigertail Ave. S Bayshore Dr, w on SW 27th Ave/Cornelia Dr, then s. Ext corridors. **Pets:** Other species. $100 one-time fee/pet. Service with restrictions.
ASK 🏃 ⊠ 🛏 💻 🏊

ⒶⒶ▼ ▼▼▼▼ The Ritz-Carlton Coconut Grove, Miami LH
(305) 644-4680. **$219-$439.** 3300 SW 27th Ave. 7 mi s of jct US 1. Int corridors. **Pets:** Accepted.
SAVE 🏃 ⊠ 🏃 🛏 💻 🍴 🏊 🏋

CORAL GABLES

▼▼▼ ▼▼▼ The Biltmore Hotel Coral Gables LH
(305) 445-1926. **Call for rates.** 1200 Anastasia Ave. 1 mi w of Le Jeune Rd. Int corridors. **Pets:** Accepted.
⊠ 🛏 🍴 🏊 🏋

▼▼ ▼▼ Extended StayAmerica-Miami-Coral Gables SH
(305) 443-7444. **$91-$143.** 3640 Coral Way/SW 22nd St. Just e of Douglas Rd. Int corridors. **Pets:** Other species. $75 one-time fee/pet. Service with restrictions.
ASK 🏃 ⊠ 🏃 🛏 💻

CUTLER RIDGE

ⒶⒶ▼ ▼▼▼ Best Western Floridian Hotel SH
(305) 253-9960. **$79-$259.** 10775 Caribbean Blvd. Florida Tpke, exit 12 (US 1), then w. Ext corridors. **Pets:** Accepted.
SAVE 🏃 ⊠ 🛏 💻 🏊

ⒶⒶ▼ ▼▼▼ La Quinta Inn & Suites SH
(305) 278-0001. **$109-$149.** 10821 Caribbean Blvd. Florida Tpke, exit 12 (US 1), northwest corner. Int corridors. **Pets:** Other species. Service with restrictions, supervision.
SAVE 🏃 ⊠ 🏃 🛏 💻 🏊

FLORIDA CITY

ⒶⒶ▼ ▼▼▼ Coral Roc Motel M
(305) 246-2888. **$39-$149.** 1100 N Krome Ave. On SR 997; just w of US 1; 0.5 mi s of Homestead. Ext corridors. **Pets:** Small, dogs only. $50 deposit/pet. Service with restrictions, supervision.
SAVE 🏃 ⊠ 🛏 🏊

▼▼▼ Ramada M
(305) 247-8833. **Call for rates.** 124 E Palm Dr. On US 1, 0.3 mi s of Florida Tpke terminus. Ext corridors. **Pets:** Accepted.
⊠ 🛏 🏊

ⒶⒶ▼ ▼▼ Travelodge M
(305) 248-9777. **$65-$225.** 409 SE 1st Ave. On US 1, just s of Florida Tpke terminus. Ext corridors. **Pets:** $10 daily fee/pet. Designated rooms, service with restrictions, supervision.
SAVE 🏃 ⊠ 🏃 🛏 💻

HIALEAH GARDENS

ⒶⒶ▼ ▼▼▼ Howard Johnson Plaza Hotel & Conference Center-Miami Airport LH
(305) 825-1000. **$84-$139.** 7707 NW 103rd St. SR 826 (Palmetto Expwy), exit NW 103rd St, just w. Int corridors. **Pets:** Accepted.
SAVE 🏃 ⊠ 🛏 💻 🍴 🏊 🏋

HOMESTEAD

ⒶⒶ▼ ▼▼ Everglades Motel M
. **Call for rates.** 605 S Krome Ave. Just w of US 1; between Lucy and 6th sts; on SR 997, 0.5 mi s of center of town. Ext corridors. **Pets:** Other species. $7 daily fee/pet. Supervision.
SAVE ⊠ 🛏 🏊

KENDALL

ⒶⒶ▼ ▼▼▼ Hyatt Place Miami/Kendall SH
(305) 279-8688. **$129-$239, 3 day notice.** 11520 SW 88th St. Florida Tpke, exit 20 (SW 88th/Kendall Dr), just e on SR 94, then 0.3 mi s. Int corridors. **Pets:** Accepted.
SAVE ⊠ 🏃 🛏 💻 🏊

KEY BISCAYNE

◆◆◆◆◆ The Ritz-Carlton, Key Biscayne [LH]
(305) 365-4500. **$263-$681, 7 day notice.** 455 Grand Bay Dr. Crandon Blvd, just e. Int corridors. **Pets:** Accepted.

[SAVE] [S🐾] [✕] [👤M] [🛏] [🖥] [🍴] [🏊] [✕]

MIAMI

◆◆ America's Best Inn-Miami Airport [M]
(305) 592-5440. **$63-$99.** 7330 NW 36th St. Just e of jct SR 826 (Palmetto Expwy). Int corridors. **Pets:** Accepted.

[ASK] [S🐾] [✕] [🖥] [🏊]

◆◆◆◆ Candlewood Suites Miami Airport West [SH]
(305) 591-9099. **$169-$200.** 8855 NW 27th St. SR 826 (Palmetto Expwy), 0.8 mi w on nw 36th St, 0.4 mi s. Int corridors. **Pets:** Other species. $75 one-time fee/pet. Service with restrictions.

[ASK] [✕] [👤M] [🛏] [🖥] [🏊]

◆◆◆ Extended StayAmerica-Airport at Doral [SH]
(786) 331-7717. **$86-$126.** 8655 NW 21 Terrace. SR 836 (Dolphin Expwy), exit 87th Ave NW, then just n. Int corridors. **Pets:** Other species. $75 one-time fee/pet. Service with restrictions.

[ASK] [S🐾] [✕] [🖥] [🏊]

◆◆ Extended StayAmerica-Miami-Brickell-Port of Miami [SH]
(305) 856-3700. **$100-$143.** 298 SW 15th Rd/Broadway Rd. I-95, exit 1B (SW 7th St) to SW 8th St, then e, s on SW 2nd Ave, then w. Int corridors. **Pets:** Other species. $75 one-time fee/pet. Service with restrictions.

[ASK] [S🐾] [✕] [👤M] [🛏] [🖥]

◆◆ Extended Stay Deluxe-Miami Airport [SH]
(305) 716-9005. **$96-$163.** 7750 NW 25th St. From SR 836 (Dolphin Expwy), exit NW 25th St, then w; turn into The Shoppes at MICC Center. Int corridors. **Pets:** Other species. $75 one-time fee/pet. Service with restrictions.

[ASK] [S🐾] [✕] [👤M] [🛏] [🖥] [🏊]

◆◆◆ Four Seasons Hotel Miami [LH] 🐾
(305) 358-3535. **$350-$450.** 1435 Brickell Ave. On US 1; jct 14th St. Int corridors. **Pets:** Small. Service with restrictions, supervision.

[SAVE] [✕] [👤M] [🛏] [🖥] [🍴] [🏊] [✕]

◆◆ Homestead Studio Suites Hotel-Miami/Airport at Doral [M]
(305) 436-1811. **$81-$121.** 8720 NW 33rd St. SR 826 (Palmetto Expwy), 0.8 mi w on NW 36th St, just s. Ext corridors. **Pets:** Other species. $75 one-time fee/pet. Service with restrictions.

[ASK] [S🐾] [✕] [🛏] [🖥] [🏊]

◆◆ Homestead Studio Suites Hotel–Miami Airport–Blue Lagoon [M]
(305) 260-0085. **$77-$110.** 6605 NW 7th St. SR 836 (Dolphin Expwy), exit Milam Dairy Rd S, 0.3 mi e; in Blue Lagoon Office Park. Ext corridors. **Pets:** Other species. $75 one-time fee/pet. Service with restrictions.

[ASK] [S🐾] [✕] [👤M] [🛏] [🖥]

◆◆◆ Hyatt Summerfield Suites-Miami Airport [SH]
(305) 269-1922. **$139-$259, 3 day notice.** 5710 Blue Lagoon Dr. Se of jct SR 836 (Dolphin Expwy), exit Red Rd, just w. Int corridors. **Pets:** $250 one-time fee/room. Service with restrictions, supervision.

[SAVE] [✕] [👤M] [🖥] [🏊]

◆◆◆ La Quinta Inn & Suites Miami (Airport West) [SH]
(305) 436-0830. **$149-$179.** 8730 NW 27th St. SR 836 (Dolphin Expwy), just n on 87th NW Ave. Int corridors. **Pets:** Other species. Service with restrictions, supervision.

[SAVE] [S🐾] [✕] [🛏] [🖥] [🏊]

◆◆◆◆ La Quinta Inn Miami (Airport North) [M]
(305) 599-9902. **$109-$145.** 7401 NW 36th St. Just e of jct SR 826 (Palmetto Expwy). Ext corridors. **Pets:** Other species. Service with restrictions, supervision.

[SAVE] [S🐾] [✕] [🛏] [🖥] [🏊]

◆◆◆◆ Mandarin Oriental, Miami [LH] 🐾
(305) 913-8288. **$465-$6500.** 500 Brickell Key Dr. US 1 (Brickell Ave), just e on SE 8th St (Brickell Key Dr). Int corridors. **Pets:** Small. $100 deposit/room, $100 one-time fee/room. Supervision.

[SAVE] [✕] [👤M] [🛏] [🍴] [🏊] [✕]

◆◆ Miami River Inn [BB]
(305) 325-0045. **$89-$299, 7 day notice.** 118 SW South River Dr. I-95, exit 1B (SW 7th St), just w to SW 5th Ave, just n to SW 2nd St, then e. Ext/int corridors. **Pets:** Medium, other species. $25 one-time fee/pet.

[ASK] [S🐾] [✕] [🏊]

◆◆◆ Quality Inn-South at The Falls [M]
(305) 251-2000. **$82-$172.** 14501 S Dixie Hwy (US 1). US 1 at SW 145th St. Ext corridors. **Pets:** Small. $10 daily fee/room. Service with restrictions.

[SAVE] [S🐾] [✕] [🛏] [🖥] [🍴] [🏊]

◆◆◆◆ Residence Inn by Marriott [SH]
(305) 591-2211. **$131-$175.** 1212 NW 82nd Ave. SR 836 (Dolphin Expwy), exit 87th Ave NW, just n to NW 82nd Ave, then e. Ext corridors. **Pets:** Accepted.

[ASK] [S🐾] [✕] [🛏] [🖥] [🏊] [✕]

◆◆◆◆ Sheraton Miami Mart Hotel [LH]
(305) 261-3800. **$179-$259.** 711 NW 72nd Ave. At Milam Dairy Rd off SR 836 (Dolphin Expwy). Int corridors. **Pets:** Accepted.

[SAVE] [S🐾] [✕] [🛏] [🖥] [🍴] [🏊]

◆◆◆◆ Sofitel Miami [LH]
(305) 264-4888. **$430-$540.** 5800 Blue Lagoon Dr. Just sw of jct SR 836 (Dolphin Expwy), exit Red Rd. Int corridors. **Pets:** Accepted.

[SAVE] [S🐾] [✕] [🛏] [🍴] [🏊] [✕]

◆◆◆◆ Staybridge Suites Miami/Doral Area [SH] 🐾
(305) 500-9100. **Call for rates.** 3265 NW 87th Ave. 0.4 mi s of jct NW 36th St. Int corridors. **Pets:** Medium. $125 one-time fee/room. Service with restrictions, crate.

[✕] [🛏] [🖥] [🏊]

◆◆◆◆ TownePlace Suites by Marriott [SH] 🐾
(305) 718-4144. **$164-$219.** 10505 NW 36th St. Florida Tpke, exit 29, 1.2 mi e to 107th Ave, then just s. Int corridors. **Pets:** $100 one-time fee/room. Service with restrictions, supervision.

[SAVE] [S🐾] [✕] [🛏] [🖥] [🏊]

MIAMI BEACH

◆◆◆◆ Casa Grande Suite Hotel [SH]
(305) 672-7003. **Call for rates.** 834 Ocean Dr. E of SR A1A (Collins Ave) and 8th St. Int corridors. **Pets:** Accepted.

[🛏] [🖥]

◆◆◆◆ Fontainebleau Resort [LH]
(305) 538-2000. **Call for rates.** 4441 Collins Ave. On SR A1A. Int corridors. **Pets:** Accepted.

[✕] [🛏] [🖥] [🍴] [🏊] [✕]

◆◆◆◆ Greenview Hotel [SH]
(305) 531-6588. **Call for rates (no credit cards).** 1671 Washington Ave. From SR A1A (Collins Ave), just e on Lincoln Rd, then just n. Int corridors. **Pets:** Accepted.

[SAVE]

◆◆◆◆ Hotel Ocean [SH]
(305) 672-2579. **$375-$495, 7 day notice.** 1230 Ocean Dr. E of jct SR A1A (Collins Ave) and 12th St. Int corridors. **Pets:** Accepted.

[SAVE] [S🐾] [✕] [🛏] [🍴]

◆◆◆◆ The Kent Hotel **SH**
(305) 604-5068. **Call for rates.** 1131 Collins Ave. On SR A1A, jct Collins Ave and 11th St. Int corridors. **Pets:** Medium. Service with restrictions, supervision.

⊠

🪐 ◆◆◆ ◆◆ Loews Miami Beach Hotel **LH**
(305) 604-1601. **Call for rates.** 1601 Collins Ave. On SR A1A, jct Collins and 16th aves. Int corridors. **Pets:** Accepted.

SAVE ⊠ &M 📵 🖃 ¶ ⇌ ⊠

◆◆◆◆ The Marlin **SH**
(305) 604-3595. **Call for rates.** 1200 Collins Ave. On SR A1A, at Collins Ave and 12th St. Int corridors. **Pets:** Accepted.

📵 🖃

🪐 ◆◆◆ Marriott South Beach **LH**
(305) 536-7700. **$285-$406, 3 day notice.** 161 Ocean Dr. Just e of SR A1A (Collins Ave); just s of 2nd St. Int corridors. **Pets:** Large. $150 one-time fee/room. Service with restrictions.

SAVE S⊘ ⊠ 📵 🖃 ¶ ⇌ ⊠

◆◆◆ ◆◆ The Ritz-Carlton, South Beach **LH**
(786) 276-4000. **$274-$824, 3 day notice.** 1 Lincoln Rd. Jct SR A1A. Int corridors. **Pets:** Accepted.

ASK S⊘ ⊠ &M 📵 🖃 ¶ ⇌ ⊠

◆◆◆◆ The Setai **LH**
(305) 520-6100. **Call for rates (no credit cards).** 2001 Collins Ave. On SR A1A (Collins Ave); at 20th St. Int corridors. **Pets:** Accepted.

⊠ &M 📵 🖃 ¶ ⇌ ⊠

🪐 ◆◆◆ ◆◆ The Tides Hotel **SH**
(305) 604-5070. **Call for rates.** 1220 Ocean Dr. E of jct SR A1A (Collins Ave) and 12th St. Int corridors. **Pets:** Accepted.

SAVE ⊠ &M 📵 ¶ ⇌

MIAMI LAKES

🪐 ◆◆◆ La Quinta Inn & Suites **SH**
(305) 821-8274. **$139-$189.** 7925 NW 154th St. Jct SR 826 (Palmetto Expwy), just w. Int corridors. **Pets:** Other species. Service with restrictions, supervision.

SAVE S⊘ ⊠ 📵 🖃 ⇌

🪐 ◆◆◆ TownePlace Suites by Marriott **SH**
(305) 512-9191. **$175-$208.** 8079 NW 154th St. SR 826 (Palmetto Expwy), exit 154th St, 0.4 mi w. Int corridors. **Pets:** Accepted.

SAVE S⊘ ⊠ 📵 🖃 ⇌

MIAMI SPRINGS

◆◆◆◆ Homestead Studio Suites Hotel-Miami/Airport/Miami Springs **SH**
(305) 870-0448. **$110-$152.** 101 Fairway Dr. I-95 to SR 112 W, exit NW 36th St, then w, right on Palmetto Dr, then w; between Le Jeune Rd and SR 826 (Palmetto Expwy); behind Clarion Hotel. Int corridors. **Pets:** Other species. $75 one-time fee/pet. Service with restrictions.

ASK S⊘ ⊠ 📵 🖃 ⇌

🪐 ◆◆◆ La Quinta Inn **SH**
(305) 871-1777. **$129-$179.** 3501 NW Le Jeune Rd. SR 953 (Le Jeune Rd) at jct SR 112. Int corridors. **Pets:** Other species. Service with restrictions, supervision.

SAVE S⊘ ⊠ 📵 🖃 ⇌

◆◆◆◆ Red Roof Inn Miami Airport **SH**
(305) 871-4221. **Call for rates.** 3401 NW Le Jeune Rd. On SR 953 at SR 112; 0.5 mi n of airport entrance. Int corridors. **Pets:** Accepted.

⊠ ⇌

SUNNY ISLES BEACH

◆◆◆ ◆◆ Acqualina, a Rosewood Resort **LH**
(305) 918-8000. **Call for rates.** 17875 Collins Ave. On SR A1A (Collins Ave); corner of 178th St, just s of The William Lehman Cswy. Int corridors. **Pets:** Accepted.

⊠ &M 📵 ¶ ⇌ ⊠

🪐 ◆◆◆ ◆◆ Le Meridien Sunny Isles Beach Miami **CO**
(305) 503-6000. **$409-$479, 3 day notice.** 18683 Collins Ave. From north, just s from William Lehman Cswy, U-turn at 186th St, then just n; from south, SR 826, 1.3 mi n. Int corridors. **Pets:** Accepted.

SAVE S⊘ ⊠ 📵 🖃 ¶ ⇌ ⊠

🪐 ◆◆◆ Newport Beachside Hotel & Resort **LH**
(305) 949-1300. **$99-$299, 3 day notice.** 16701 Collins Ave. SR A1A, jct SR 826 and Sunny Isles Blvd. Int corridors. **Pets:** Small. $75 one-time fee/pet. Service with restrictions, supervision.

SAVE S⊘ 📵 🖃 ¶ ⇌ ⊠

🪐 ◆◆◆ ◆◆ Trump International Sonesta Beach Resort **LH**
(305) 692-5600. **$159-$409, 3 day notice.** 18001 Collins Ave. On SR A1A, just s of The William Lehman Cswy. Int corridors. **Pets:** Accepted.

SAVE S⊘ ⊠ 📵 🖃 ¶ ⇌ ⊠

END METROPOLITAN AREA

MILTON

◆◆◆ Comfort Inn **SH**
(850) 623-1511. **Call for rates.** 8936 S Hwy 87. I-10, exit 31, just s. Int corridors. **Pets:** Medium, other species. $15 daily fee/pet. Designated rooms, service with restrictions, supervision.

⊠ &M 📵 🖃 ⇌

◆◆◆ Red Roof Inn & Suites **SH**
(850) 995-6100. **Call for rates.** 2672 Avalon Blvd. I-10, exit 22, just s. Int corridors. **Pets:** Accepted.

⊠ &M 📵 🖃 ⇌

MOSSY HEAD

◆◆◆ Rodeway Inn **M**
(850) 951-9780. **$54-$90.** 326 Green Acres Dr. I-10, exit 70, just s. Ext corridors. **Pets:** $25 daily fee/pet. Service with restrictions, supervision.

ASK S⊘ ⊠ 🖃 ¶

NAPLES

🪐 ◆◆◆ The Fairways Resort **M**
(239) 597-8181. **$75-$275.** 103 Palm River Blvd. I-75, exit 111, 2.2 mi w on CR 846 (Immokalee Rd). Ext corridors. **Pets:** Small. $50 one-time fee/pet. Designated rooms, no service, supervision.

SAVE S⊘ ⊠ 📵 🖃 ⇌

🪐 ◆◆◆ Hawthorn Suites of Naples **SH**
(239) 593-1300. **$134-$329.** 3557 Pine Ridge Rd. I-75, exit 107, 0.5 mi w on CR 896. Int corridors. **Pets:** Large. $125 one-time fee/room. Designated rooms, service with restrictions, supervision.

SAVE S⊘ ⊠ &M 📵 🖃 ⇌ ⊠

🪐 ◆◆◆ Holiday Inn of Naples **M**
(239) 263-3434. **$89-$219.** 1100 Tamiami Tr N. I-75, exit 107, 3.8 mi w on CR 896 (Pine Ridge Rd); 3.8 mi s on US 41. Ext corridors. **Pets:** Medium. $25 daily fee/room. Designated rooms, service with restrictions, supervision.

SAVE S⊘ ⊠ 📵 🖃 ¶ ⇌

▼▼▼ ▼▼▼ LaPlaya Beach & Golf Resort 🆑
(239) 597-3123. **$319-$549.** 9891 Gulf Shore Dr. US 41 (Tamiami Tr), 1.3 mi w on CR 862 (Vanderbilt Beach Rd), 0.5 mi n. Ext/int corridors. **Pets:** Accepted.

(A$K) ✕ 🔲 ⍾⍾ ⇌ ✕

♠♠♠ ▼▼▼ La Quinta Inn & Suites 🆂🅷
(239) 352-8400. **$149-$189.** 185 Bedzel Cir. I-75, exit 101, just w on SR 84 (Davis Blvd). Int corridors. **Pets:** Other species. Service with restrictions, supervision.

(SAVE) (S⌀) ✕ (⌖M) 🔲 🔲 ⇌

♠♠♠ ▼▼▼ La Quinta Inns & Suites 🆂🅷
(239) 793-4646. **$119-$199.** 1555 5th Ave S. I-75, exit 101, 6.8 mi w on SR 84. Int corridors. **Pets:** Other species. Service with restrictions, supervision.

(SAVE) (S⌀) ✕ 🔲 🔲 ⇌

▼▼ Red Roof Inn 🆂🅷
(239) 774-3117. **Call for rates.** 1925 Davis Blvd. I-75, exit 101, 6.4 mi w on SR 84; just e of jct US 41 (Tamiami Tr). Ext corridors. **Pets:** Accepted.

✕ 🔲 🔲 ⇌

▼▼▼ Residence Inn by Marriott, Naples 🆂🅷 🐾
(239) 659-1300. **$221-$261.** 4075 Tamiami Tr N. I-75, exit 107, 3.8 mi w on CR 896 (Pine Ridge Rd), then 1 mi s on US 41. Int corridors. **Pets:** Other species. $75 one-time fee/room. Service with restrictions.

(A$K) (S⌀) ✕ (⌖M) 🔲 🔲 ⇌ ✕

♠♠♠ ▼▼▼▼ The Ritz-Carlton Golf Resort 🆑 🐾
(239) 593-2000. **$307-$604, 7 day notice.** 2600 Tiburon Dr. I-75, exit 111, 1.6 mi w on CR 846 (Immokalee Rd), 1.3 mi s on CR 31 (Airport-Pulling Rd), then just e. Int corridors. **Pets:** Small. $150 one-time fee/room. Designated rooms, service with restrictions, supervision.

(SAVE) (S⌀) ✕ (⌖M) 🔲 🔲 ⍾⍾ ⇌ ✕

♠♠♠ ▼▼▼ Staybridge Suites by Holiday Inn 🆂🅷
(239) 643-8002. **$59-$350.** 4805 Tamiami Tr N. I-75, exit 107, 3.8 mi w on CR 896 (Pine Ridge Rd), then 0.9 mi s on US 41. Int corridors. **Pets:** Accepted.

(SAVE) (S⌀) ✕ (⌖M) 🔲 🔲 ⇌

NEW SMYRNA BEACH

♠♠♠ ▼▼▼ Longboard Inn 🅱🅱
(386) 428-3499. **$115-$160, 14 day notice.** 312 Washington St. 0.25 mi w of jct N Riverside Dr. Ext corridors. **Pets:** $10 daily fee/room. Designated rooms, crate.

(SAVE) (S⌀) ✕ 🔲

▼▼▼ Night Swan Intracoastal Bed & Breakfast 🅱🅱 🐾
(386) 423-4940. **$110-$200, 3 day notice.** 512 S Riverside Dr. Just s of SR 44 Intracoastal Waterway bridge; west side of Intracoastal Waterway. Ext/int corridors. **Pets:** Medium, other species. Designated rooms.

(A$K) (S⌀) ✕ 🔲 🔲 ✕

NORTH FORT MYERS

♠♠♠ ▼▼▼ Best Western Fort Myers Waterfront 🆂🅷
(239) 997-5511. **$90-$180.** 13021 N Cleveland Ave. On US 41, 0.6 mi s of SR 78A (Pondella Rd), jct N Bay Dr and Caloosahatchee Bridge. Ext corridors. **Pets:** Accepted.

(SAVE) (S⌀) ✕ 🔲 🔲 ⍾⍾ ✕

♠♠♠ ▼▼▼ Econo Lodge Ⓜ
(239) 995-0571. **$49-$149.** 13301 N Cleveland Ave. On US 41, 1.1 mi n of Caloosahatchee Bridge. Ext corridors. **Pets:** Accepted.

(SAVE) (S⌀) ✕ 🔲 🔲 ⇌

OCALA

♠♠♠ ▼▼▼ Budget Host Inn Ⓜ
(352) 732-6940. **Call for rates.** 4013 NW Bonnie Heath Blvd. I-75, exit 354, 0.3 mi n on US 27. Ext corridors. **Pets:** Accepted.

(SAVE) ✕ 🔲

♠♠♠ ▼▼ Days Inn 🆂🅷
(352) 629-7041. **$60-$110.** 3811 NW Bonnie Heath Blvd. I-75, exit 354, just n on US 27. Ext/int corridors. **Pets:** Other species. $5 daily fee/pet. Service with restrictions, supervision.

(SAVE) (S⌀) ✕ 🔲 🔲 ⇌

▼▼▼ Hilton Ocala 🆑
(352) 854-1400. **$99-$209, 3 day notice.** 3600 SW 36th Ave. I-75, exit 350, 0.3 mi e on SR 200. Int corridors. **Pets:** Accepted.

(A$K) (S⌀) ✕ 🔲 🔲 ⍾⍾ ⇌ ✕

♠♠♠ ▼▼▼▼ Howard Johnson Inn & Restaurant Ⓜ
(352) 629-7021. **$60-$200.** 3951 NW Bonnie Heath Blvd. I-75, exit 354, just w. Ext corridors. **Pets:** Other species. $20 daily fee/pet. Designated rooms, service with restrictions, supervision.

(SAVE) (S⌀) ✕ 🔲 🔲 ⍾⍾ ✕

♠♠♠ ▼▼▼▼ La Quinta Inn & Suites Ocala 🆂🅷
(352) 861-1137. **$119-$169.** 3530 SW 36th Ave. I-75, exit 350, just e on SR 200. Int corridors. **Pets:** Other species. Service with restrictions, supervision.

(SAVE) (S⌀) ✕ (⌖M) 🔲 🔲 ⍾⍾ ⇌

▼▼▼ Quality Inn Ocala Hotel and Conference Center 🆂🅷
(352) 629-0381. **$59-$150.** 3621 W Silver Springs Blvd. I-75, exit 352, just e on SR 40. Ext corridors. **Pets:** Small. $10 daily fee/pet. Designated rooms, service with restrictions, crate.

(A$K) (S⌀) ✕ 🔲 🔲 ⍾⍾ ⇌

♠♠♠ ▼▼ Ramada Inn & Conference Center 🆂🅷
(352) 732-3131. **Call for rates.** 3810 NW Bonnie Heath Blvd. I-75, exit 354, just w. Ext corridors. **Pets:** Accepted.

(SAVE) ✕ 🔲 🔲 ⍾⍾ ⇌ ✕

♠♠♠ ▼▼▼ Red Roof Inn & Suites 🆂🅷
(352) 732-4590. **Call for rates.** 120 NW 40th Ave. I-75, exit 352, just w. Int corridors. **Pets:** Accepted.

(SAVE) ✕ 🔲 🔲 ⇌

▼▼▼ Residence Inn by Marriott Ocala 🆂🅷 🐾
(352) 547-1600. **$164-$186.** 3610 SW 38th Ave. I-75, exit 350, just w on SR 200, then n. Int corridors. **Pets:** Medium. $75 one-time fee/room. Service with restrictions, supervision.

(A$K) (S⌀) ✕ 🔲 🔲 ⇌ ✕

▼▼▼ Seven Sisters Inn 🅱🅱
(352) 867-1170. **Call for rates.** 820 SE Fort King St. Just s of jct SR 40 on SE Winona Ave; in downtown historic district. Int corridors. **Pets:** Accepted.

✕

♠♠♠ ▼▼▼ Travelodge 🆂🅷
(352) 629-8850. **$69-$129.** 4040 W Silver Springs Blvd. I-75, exit 352, just w on SR 40. Ext corridors. **Pets:** Small. $20 daily fee/pet. Service with restrictions.

(SAVE) (S⌀) ✕ 🔲 🔲 ⇌

OKEECHOBEE

♠♠♠ ▼ Budget Inn Ⓜ
(863) 763-3185. **$69-$185.** 201 S Parrott Ave (US 441). US 98 and 441, just s of jct SR 70. Ext corridors. **Pets:** Very small, dogs only. $10 daily fee/pet. Designated rooms, service with restrictions, supervision.

(SAVE) (S⌀) ✕ 🔲 ⇌

OLD TOWN

Suwanee Gables Motel **M** ❀
(352) 542-7752. **$98-$210.** 27659 SE Hwy 19, Alt 27. US 19, 98 and 27A; 2 mi s of jct SR 349. Ext corridors. **Pets:** Small, other species. $10 daily fee/pet. Service with restrictions, supervision.

ORANGE CITY

Comfort Inn **M**
(386) 775-7444. **$79-$249.** 445 S Volusia Ave. I-4, exit 114, 2.8 mi w on SR 472, then 2 mi s on US 17-92. Ext corridors. **Pets:** Medium. $25 deposit/room, $15 daily fee/pet. Service with restrictions, crate.

Days Inn **M**
(386) 775-4522. **$65-$250.** 2501 N Volusia Ave. I-4, exit 114, 2.8 mi w on SR 472, then 0.3 mi s on US 17-92. Ext corridors. **Pets:** Accepted.

ORLANDO METROPOLITAN AREA

ALTAMONTE SPRINGS

Candlewood Suites **SH**
(407) 767-5757. **Call for rates.** 644 Raymond Ave. I-4, exit 92, just w to Douglas Ave, 0.8 mi n to Central Pkwy, then just e. Int corridors. **Pets:** Accepted.

Days Inn Altamonte Springs **SH**
(407) 788-1411. **$99-$130.** 150 S Westmonte Dr. I-4, exit 92, 0.3 mi w on SR 436, then just s. Ext corridors. **Pets:** $10 daily fee/pet. Designated rooms, service with restrictions, supervision.

Embassy Suites Orlando North **SH** ❀
(407) 834-2400. **$115-$229.** 225 Shorecrest Dr. I-4, exit 92, 0.3 mi e on SR 436, then just n on North Lake Blvd. Int corridors. **Pets:** Medium. $20 daily fee/pet. Designated rooms, service with restrictions, supervision.

Holiday Inn Orlando North/Altamonte Springs **SH** ❀
(407) 862-4455. **$99-$169.** 230 W SR 436. I-4, exit 92, just sw. Ext/int corridors. **Pets:** Medium. $40 one-time fee/room. Designated rooms, service with restrictions, crate.

Homestead Studio Suites Hotel-Orlando/Altamonte Springs **SH**
(407) 332-9300. **$62-$68.** 302 S North Lake Blvd. I-4, exit 92, just e, then 0.3 mi s. Int corridors. **Pets:** Other species. $75 one-time fee/pet. Service with restrictions.

Residence Inn by Marriott **SH**
(407) 788-7991. **$199-$239.** 270 Douglas Ave. I-4, exit 92, just w on SR 436, then just n. Ext corridors. **Pets:** Medium, other species. $75 one-time fee/pet. Service with restrictions, crate.

DAVENPORT

Best Western Main Gate South **SH**
(863) 424-2596. **$77-$94.** 2425 Frontage Rd. I-4, exit 55, just s on US 27. Ext corridors. **Pets:** Accepted.

Calabay Parc-The Florida Store **VH**
(352) 243-2853. **$129-$189, 30 day notice.** 325 Calabay Parc Blvd. Jct US 192 and 27, 4 mi s. Ext corridors. **Pets:** Accepted.

Hampton Inn Orlando-South of Walt Disney World Resorts **SH**
(863) 420-9898. **Call for rates.** 44117 Hwy 27. I-4, exit 55, just nw. Int corridors. **Pets:** Accepted.

Omni Orlando Resort at ChampionsGate **LH**
(407) 390-6664. **$249-$329, 3 day notice.** 1500 Masters Blvd. I-4, exit 58, 0.3 mi w. Int corridors. **Pets:** Accepted.

Regal Palms Resort & Spa **CO**
(863) 424-6141. **$119-$239, 3 day notice.** 2700 Sand Mine Rd. 0.5 mi s of jct US 27 and 192. Ext corridors. **Pets:** Accepted.

Southern Dunes-The Florida Store **VH**
(352) 243-2853. **$129-$189.** 2684 Hemingway Dr. I-4, exit 68, 3.5 mi s on SR 535, then 3.8 mi e on US 192. Ext corridors. **Pets:** Accepted.

Super 8 Motel Maingate South **SH**
(863) 420-8888. **$60-$80.** 44199 Hwy 27. I-4, exit 55, 0.5 mi n. Ext corridors. **Pets:** Accepted.

KISSIMMEE

Baymont Inn Kissimmee **SH**
(407) 994-1900. **$79-$99.** 4156 W Vine St. I-4, exit 64A, 6 mi e. Ext corridors. **Pets:** Very small, dogs only. $10 daily fee/pet. Designated rooms, service with restrictions, supervision.

Best Western Maingate East Hotel & Suites **SH**
(407) 870-2000. **$59-$129.** 4018 W Vine St. I-4, exit 64A, 7 mi e on US 192. Ext corridors. **Pets:** Accepted.

Calypso Cay Hotel & Suites **SH**
(407) 997-1300. **$100-$300, 3 day notice.** 4991 Calypso Cay Way. I-4, exit 68, 3 mi s on SR 535. Int corridors. **Pets:** Accepted.

Clarion Resort & Water Park-Conference Center **LH**
(407) 846-2221. **$140-$350.** 2261 E Irlo Bronson Memorial Pkwy. Florida Tpke exit 244, then just w. Ext corridors. **Pets:** Accepted.

Country Inn & Suites Orlando-Maingate at Calypso Cay SH
(407) 997-1400. **$89-$179.** 5001 Calypso Cay Way. I-4, exit 68, 3 mi s on SR 535; just s of Osceola Pkwy; just n of US 192. Int corridors. **Pets:** Accepted.

Days Inn-Kissimmee SH
(407) 846-7136. **Call for rates.** 2095 E Irlo Bronson Memorial Hwy. Florida Tpke, exit 244, 0.3 mi w on US 192. Ext corridors. **Pets:** Accepted.

Hampton Lakes-The Florida Store VH
(352) 243-2853. **$129-$189, 30 day notice.** 1740 Bloomingdale Dr. I-4, exit 68, 3.5 mi s on SR 535, then 3.8 mi e on US 192. Ext corridors. **Pets:** Accepted.

Howard Johnson Inn & Suites–Kissimmee Heritage Park SH
(407) 705-5070. **$100-$180.** 201 Simpson Rd. Florida Tpke, exit 244, 0.5 mi w to Simpson Rd, then just n. Ext corridors. **Pets:** Accepted.

Howard Johnson Maingate Resort West LH 🐾
(407) 396-4500. **$49-$119.** 8660 W Irlo Bronson Memorial Hwy. I-4, exit 64B, 5.6 mi w on US 192. Ext corridors. **Pets:** Medium. $35 one-time fee/room. Designated rooms, service with restrictions, crate.

Indian Creek-The Florida Store VH
(407) 846-1722. **$129-$189, 30 day notice.** 8009 Bow Creek Rd. I-4, exit 64B, 3.2 mi on US 192 to Formosa Gardens Blvd, then 1.2 mi s. Ext corridors. **Pets:** Accepted.

La Quinta Inn & Suites Kissimmee (Orlando Maingate) SH
(407) 997-1700. **$114-$169.** 3484 Polynesian Isle Blvd. I-4, exit 68, s on SR 535, then just e. Int corridors. **Pets:** Other species. Service with restrictions, supervision.

Masters Inn-Kissimmee SH
(407) 396-4020. **$40-$90.** 5367 W Irlo Bronson Memorial Hwy. I-4, exit 25, 2.5 mi e on US 192. Ext corridors. **Pets:** Small. $20 one-time fee/pet. Designated rooms, service with restrictions, supervision.

Masters Inn-Main Gate SH
(407) 396-7743. **$45-$150.** 2945 Entry Point Blvd. I-4, exit 25, 2.5 mi w on US 192; 1 mi w of Disney World main gate. Ext corridors. **Pets:** Small. $20 one-time fee/pet. Service with restrictions, crate.

Motel 6–#0436 SH
(407) 396-6422. **$42-$50.** 7455 W Irlo Bronson Memorial Hwy. I-4, exit 64B, 1.3 mi w on US 192. Ext corridors. **Pets:** Other species. Service with restrictions, supervision.

Motel 6–#0464 M
(407) 396-6333. **$39-$52.** 5731 W Hwy 192. I-4, exit 64A, 2 mi e. Ext corridors. **Pets:** Other species. Service with restrictions, supervision.

The Palms Hotel and Villas CO
(407) 396-2229. **$99-$139.** 3100 Parkway Blvd. I-4, exit 64A, 0.3 mi e on US 192, then 0.5 mi n. Ext/int corridors. **Pets:** Medium. $100 one-time fee/pet. Service with restrictions, crate.

Radisson Resort WorldGate LH
(407) 396-1400. **$89-$169, 3 day notice.** 3011 Maingate Ln. US 192, 2.8 mi w of I-4, 1 mi w of Disney World main gate access road. Int corridors. **Pets:** Medium. $75 one-time fee/room. Service with restrictions.

Red Roof Inn SH
(407) 396-0065. **Call for rates.** 4970 Kyngs Heath Rd. I-4, exit 64A, 3.6 mi e on US 192; jct SR 535. Ext corridors. **Pets:** Accepted.

Rodeway Inn Eastgate M
(407) 396-1212. **$35-$89.** 4559 W Hwy 192. I-4, exit 68, 4 mi s on SR 535, then 3 mi e. Ext corridors. **Pets:** Small. $50 deposit/pet, $5 daily fee/pet. Designated rooms, service with restrictions.

Rodeway Inn Maingate SH
(407) 396-4300. **$39-$99.** 5995 W Irlo Bronson Memorial Hwy. I-4, exit 64A, 1 mi e. Ext corridors. **Pets:** Medium. $50 deposit/pet. Designated rooms, no service, supervision.

Seralago Hotel & Suites Main Gate East SH
(407) 396-4488. **$50-$109.** 5678 W Irlo Bronson Memorial Hwy. I-4, exit 64A; between MM 9 and 10. Ext corridors. **Pets:** Medium. $40 one-time fee/room. Designated rooms, service with restrictions, crate.

Ventian Bay–Ventura Resort Rentals CO
(407) 273-8770. **$124-$320.** 4008 San Gallo Dr. SR 417, exit 11, 3 mi s on Orange Blossom Tr, then 2 mi w on West Carroll. Ext corridors. **Pets:** Accepted.

Wonderland Inn M
(407) 847-2477. **Call for rates.** 3601 S Orange Blossom Tr. US 192, 3 mi s on US 17-92 (John Young Pkwy/Bermuda Ave). Ext corridors. **Pets:** Accepted.

LADY LAKE

Comfort Suites in the Villages SH
(352) 259-6578. **$99-$119.** 1202 Avenida Central N. Just n on US 441. Int corridors. **Pets:** Medium, other species. $35 one-time fee/pet. Service with restrictions, supervision.

Holiday Inn Express Hotel & Suites SH
(352) 750-3888. **$99-$155.** 1205 Avenida Central N. Just n on US 441. Int corridors. **Pets:** Medium, other species. $35 one-time fee/pet. Designated rooms, service with restrictions, supervision.

Microtel Inn & Suites SH 🐾
(352) 259-0184. **Call for rates.** 850 US 27/441. 1 mi s. Int corridors. **Pets:** Small. $25 one-time fee/pet. Service with restrictions, supervision.

LAKE BUENA VISTA

Buena Vista Suites SH
(407) 239-8588. **$109-$159.** 8203 World Center Dr. I-4, exit 67, 1.3 mi e; jct SR 535 and 536. Int corridors. **Pets:** Small, other species. $50 deposit/pet, $10 daily fee/pet. Designated rooms, service with restrictions, supervision.

Comfort Inn Lake Buena Vista LH 🐾
(407) 996-7300. **$59-$89.** 8442 Palm Pkwy. I-4, exit 68, 0.6 mi n on SR 535, then 0.5 mi e. Ext corridors. **Pets:** Medium. $50 deposit/room, $10 daily fee/pet. Designated rooms, service with restrictions, supervision.

Disney's Animal Kingdom Lodge [LH]
(407) 938-3000. **$215-$490, 6 day notice.** 2901 Osceola Pkwy. I-4, exit 64 or 65; n of US 192 on World Dr, follow signs. Int corridors. **Pets:** Accepted.

Disney's Wilderness Lodge [LH]
(407) 824-3200. **$215-$550, 6 day notice.** 901 W Timberline Dr. I-4, exit 67, follow signs to Disney's Magic Kingdom; in Walt Disney World. Int corridors. **Pets:** Accepted.

Extended Stay Deluxe Orlando Lake Buena Vista [SH]
(407) 239-4300. **$81-$89.** 8100 Palm Pkwy. I-4, exit 68, 0.6 mi n on SR 535, then 0.7 mi e. Int corridors. **Pets:** Other species. $75 one-time fee/pet. Service with restrictions.

Holiday Inn Express Lake Buena Vista [SH]
(407) 239-8400. **$99-$189.** 8686 Palm Pkwy. I-4, exit 68, 0.5 mi n on CR 535, then 0.3 mi e. Int corridors. **Pets:** Medium, other species. $50 one-time fee/room. Designated rooms, service with restrictions, supervision.

Holiday Inn-SunSpree Resort-Lake Buena Vista [LH]
(407) 239-4500. **Call for rates.** 13351 SR 535. I-4, exit 68, 0.3 mi se. Ext corridors. **Pets:** Small. $40 one-time fee/pet. Service with restrictions, crate.

Residence Inn Orlando Lake Buena Vista [SH]
(407) 465-0075. **$122-$162, 3 day notice.** 11450 Marbella Palms Ct. I-4, exit 68, 0.4 mi n on SR 535, then 0.5 mi e on Palm Pkwy. Int corridors. **Pets:** Small. $100 one-time fee/room. Service with restrictions, supervision.

Sheraton Safari Hotel & Suites [SH] ❖
(407) 239-0444. **$119-$299.** 12205 Apopka-Vineland Rd. I-4, exit 68, 0.5 mi n on SR 535. Ext/int corridors. **Pets:** Medium, dogs only. Designated rooms, service with restrictions, supervision.

LAKE MARY

Candlewood Suites Lake Mary-Heathrow [SH]
(407) 585-3000. **Call for rates.** 1130 Greenwood Blvd. I-4, exit 98, just e to Lake Emma Rd, 0.5 mi s to Greenwood Blvd, then 0.6 mi w. Int corridors. **Pets:** Accepted.

Extended StayAmerica-Lake Mary [SH]
(407) 833-0011. **$72-$79.** 1036 Greenwood Blvd. I-4, exit 98, just e to Lake Emma Rd, then 0.5 mi. Int corridors. **Pets:** Other species. $75 one-time fee/pet. Service with restrictions.

Homestead Studio Suites-Orlando/Lake Mary [SH]
(407) 829-2332. **$77-$89.** 1040 Greenwood Blvd. I-4, exit 98, 0.5 mi s on Lake Emma Rd; in Commerce Park. Int corridors. **Pets:** Other species. $75 one-time fee/pet. Service with restrictions.

Homewood Suites by Hilton [SH] ❖
(407) 805-9111. **$109-$189.** 755 Currency Cir. I-4, exit 98, just ne via Lake Mary Blvd and Primera. Int corridors. **Pets:** Medium, other species. $49 one-time fee/room. Service with restrictions, crate.

LEESBURG

Super 8 Motel [SH]
(352) 787-6363. **$50-$175.** 1392 North Blvd W. Jct US 27 and 441. Int corridors. **Pets:** Accepted.

MAITLAND

Extended StayAmerica-Orlando-Maitland Pembrook Dr [SH]
(407) 667-0474. **$62-$68.** 1760 Pembrook Dr. I-4, exit 90B, 0.5 mi w. Int corridors. **Pets:** Other species. $75 one-time fee/pet. Service with restrictions.

Extended Stay Deluxe-Maitland [SH]
(407) 475-1675. **$72-$84.** 1776 Pembrook Dr. I-4, exit 90B, 0.5 mi w. Int corridors. **Pets:** Other species. $75 one-time fee/pet. Service with restrictions.

Homewood Suites by Hilton Orlando North [SH]
(407) 875-8777. **Call for rates.** 290 Southhall Ln. I-4, exit 90, just w, then just s on Lake Destiny. Int corridors. **Pets:** Medium. $75 one-time fee/room. Service with restrictions, supervision.

Sheraton Orlando North [LH]
(407) 660-9000. **$269-$289.** 600 N Lake Destiny Dr. I-4, exit 90B, just w. Int corridors. **Pets:** Accepted.

MOUNT DORA

Heron Cay Lakeview Bed & Breakfast [BB] ❖
(352) 383-4050. **$175-$295, 15 day notice.** 495 Old Hwy 441. On CR 441 (Old US 441), 0.3 mi w. Int corridors. **Pets:** Large, other species. $25 daily fee/room. Service with restrictions, supervision.

OCOEE

Best Western Turnpike West-Orlando [SH]
(407) 656-5050. **Call for rates.** 10945 W Colonial Dr. I-4, exit 84, 10 mi w on SR 50; 0.5 mi e of Florida Tpke, exit 267B. Ext corridors. **Pets:** Accepted.

Red Roof Inn Orlando West [SH]
(407) 347-0140. **Call for rates.** 11241 W Colonial Dr. I-4, exit 84, 10 mi w on SR 50; 0.6 mi e of Florida Tpke, exit 267. Int corridors. **Pets:** Accepted.

ORLANDO

Best Western Orlando West [SH] ❖
(407) 841-8600. **Call for rates.** 2014 W Colonial Dr. I-4, exit 84, 1.5 mi w on SR 50; 0.4 mi e of SR 423. Int corridors. **Pets:** Small. $5 daily fee/pet. Designated rooms, service with restrictions, supervision.

Clarion Hotel Universal [LH] ❖
(407) 351-5009. **$89-$149.** 7299 Universal Blvd. I-4, exit 75A, just e of International Dr. Int corridors. **Pets:** Large. $10 daily fee/pet, $25 one-time fee/room. Service with restrictions, crate.

Comfort Inn Universal Studios [SH]
(407) 363-7886. **$55-$79.** 6101 Sand Lake Rd. I-4, exit 74A, 0.3 mi e on SR 482 (Sand Lake Rd), at Universal Blvd. Ext corridors. **Pets:** Medium. $10 daily fee/pet. No service, supervision.

Comfort Suites Orlando SH 🐾
(407) 351-5050. **$99-$149.** 9350 Turkey Lake Rd. I-4, exit 74A, just w on SR 482 (Sand Lake Rd), then 1.5 mi s. Ext corridors. **Pets:** Medium, dogs only. $49 one-time fee/room. Designated rooms, service with restrictions, supervision.

SAVE S⃝ ✕ ⌖ⁿ ☐ ⊑ ⇝

Country Inn & Suites by Carlson-Orlando International Airport SH
(407) 856-8896. **$135-$150.** 5440 Forbes Pl. SR 528 (Beachline Expwy), exit 11, 0.6 mi n on SR 436, then just w. Int corridors. **Pets:** Accepted.

A$K S⃝ ✕ ☐ ⊑ ⇝

Courtyard by Marriott Orlando International Airport SH
(407) 240-7200. **$186-$230.** 7155 N Frontage Rd. SR 436, 0.3 mi n of SR 528 (Beachline Expwy). Int corridors. **Pets:** $25 one-time fee/pet. Service with restrictions, supervision.

SAVE S⃝ ✕ ⌖ⁿ ☐ ⊑ ⍾ ⇝

Crossland Economy Studios-University of Central Florida SH
(407) 282-7112. **Call for rates (no credit cards).** 12350 E Colonial Dr. SR 417, exit 34, 4 mi e. Ext corridors. **Pets:** Other species. $75 one-time fee/pet. Service with restrictions.

✕ ☐ ⊑

Days Inn North of Universal SH
(407) 841-3731. **$59-$99.** 2500 W 33rd St. I-4, exit 79, just e. Ext corridors. **Pets:** Medium. $15 one-time fee/room. Service with restrictions, supervision.

A$K S⃝ ✕ ☐ ⍾ ⇝

Extended StayAmerica Orlando Convention Center Westwood Blvd SH
(407) 352-3454. **$62-$74.** 6451 Westwood Blvd. I-4, exit 72, just e on SR 528 (Beachline Expwy) to exit 1 (International Dr), just s, then just w. Int corridors. **Pets:** Other species. $75 one-time fee/pet. Service with restrictions.

A$K S⃝ ✕ ☐ ⊑

Extended Stay Deluxe Orlando Convention Center/ Pointe Orlando SH
(407) 903-1500. **$100-$110.** 8750 Universal Blvd. I-4, exit 74A, 0.5 mi e on SR 482 (Sand Lake Rd), then 0.7 mi s. Int corridors. **Pets:** Other species. $75 one-time fee/pet. Service with restrictions.

A$K S⃝ ✕ ⌖ⁿ ☐ ⊑ ⇝ ✕

Extended Stay Deluxe/Orlando Convention Center/ Westwood Blvd. SH
(407) 351-1982. **$72-$84.** 6443 Westwood Blvd. I-4, exit 72, just e on SR 528 (Beachline Expwy) to exit 1 (International Dr), just s, then just w. Int corridors. **Pets:** Other species. $75 one-time fee/pet. Service with restrictions.

A$K S⃝ ✕ ☐ ⊑ ⇝

Extended Stay Deluxe Orlando-John Young Parkway SH
(407) 248-8010. **$77-$84.** 8687 Commodity Cir. Just sw of jct SR 423 (John Young Pkwy) and 482 (Sand Lake Rd). Int corridors. **Pets:** Other species. $75 one-time fee/pet. Service with restrictions.

A$K S⃝ ✕ ☐ ⊑ ⇝

Extended Stay Deluxe Orlando-Universal Studios SH
(407) 370-4428. **$67-$84.** 5610 Vineland Ave. I-4, exit 75B, just n, then e. Int corridors. **Pets:** Other species. $75 one-time fee/pet. Service with restrictions.

A$K S⃝ ✕ ⌖ⁿ ☐ ⊑ ⇝

The Grand Bohemian Hotel LH
(407) 313-9000. **$199-$599.** 325 S Orange Ave. Corner of Jackson St. Int corridors. **Pets:** Accepted.

SAVE ✕ ⌖ⁿ ⊑ ⍾ ⇝ ✕

Hawthorn Suites Orlando Airport SH
(407) 438-2121. **$109-$299.** 7450 Augusta National Dr. SR 528 (Beachline Expwy), exit 11, 0.5 mi n on SR 436, just e, then just s. Int corridors. **Pets:** Accepted.

SAVE S⃝ ✕ ⌖ⁿ ☐ ⊑ ⇝ ✕

Holiday Inn & Suites At Universal Orlando SH
(407) 351-3333. **$89-$169, 3 day notice.** 5905 S Kirkman Rd. I-4, exit 75B, 0.5 mi n on SR 435 (Kirkman Rd). Int corridors. **Pets:** Accepted.

SAVE S⃝ ✕ ⌖ⁿ ☐ ⊑ ⍾ ⇝

Holiday Inn Express Florida Mall SH
(407) 851-8200. **$90-$159.** 8820 S Orange Blossom Tr. Florida Tpke, exit 254, just n. Int corridors. **Pets:** Accepted.

SAVE ✕ ⌖ⁿ ☐ ⊑ ⇝

Holiday Inn Express Orlando International Airport SH
(407) 581-7900. **$109-$139, 14 day notice.** 7900 Conway Rd. SR 528 (Beachline Expwy), exit 9, just n. Int corridors. **Pets:** Accepted.

A$K S⃝ ✕ ⌖ⁿ ☐ ⊑ ⇝

Holiday Inn-International Drive Resort SH
(407) 351-3500. **$79-$169.** 6515 International Dr. I-4, exit 74A, just e on SR 482 (Sand Lake Rd), then 0.5 mi n. Ext/int corridors. **Pets:** Large. $200 deposit/room, $15 daily fee/room. Service with restrictions, crate.

SAVE ✕ ⌖ⁿ ☐ ⊑ ⍾ ⇝ ✕

Homestead Studio Suites Hotel-Orlando/John Young Parkway SH
(407) 352-5577. **$67-$74.** 4101 Equity Row. Just sw of jct SR 423 (John Young Pkwy) and 482 (Sand Lake Rd). Int corridors. **Pets:** Other species. $75 one-time fee/pet. Service with restrictions.

A$K S⃝ ✕ ⌖ⁿ ☐ ⊑ ⇝

Howard Johnson Inn SH
(407) 851-1050. **$60-$100.** 9393 S Orange Blossom Tr. Florida Tpke, exit 254, just s. Ext corridors. **Pets:** Accepted.

A$K S⃝ ✕ ☐ ⊑

International Plaza Resort & Spa LH
(407) 352-1100. **Call for rates.** 10100 International Dr. I-4, exit 72, just s on International Dr; SR 528 (Beachline Expwy), exit 1, just e. Ext/int corridors. **Pets:** Accepted.

✕ ⌖ⁿ ☐ ⊑ ⍾ ⇝ ✕

La Quinta Inn & Suites Orlando (Airport North) SH
(407) 240-5000. **$139-$149.** 7160 N Frontage Rd. SR 528 (Beachline Expwy), exit 11, 0.5 mi n on SR 436, then just w. Int corridors. **Pets:** Other species. Service with restrictions, supervision.

SAVE S⃝ ✕ ⌖ⁿ ☐ ⊑ ⇝

La Quinta Inn & Suites Orlando (Convention Center) SH
(407) 345-1365. **$129-$149.** 8504 Universal Blvd. I-4, exit 74A, 0.5 mi e on SR 482 (Sand Lake Rd), then 0.5 mi s. Int corridors. **Pets:** Other species. Service with restrictions, supervision.

SAVE S⃝ ✕ ⌖ⁿ ☐ ⊑ ⇝

La Quinta Inn & Suites Orlando (U.C.F.) SH
(407) 737-6075. **$139-$149.** 11805 Research Pkwy. Just se of jct University Blvd and SR 434 (Alafaya Trail). Int corridors. **Pets:** Other species. Service with restrictions, supervision.

SAVE S⃝ ✕ ⌖ⁿ ☐ ⊑ ⇝

La Quinta Inn International Dr North SH
(407) 351-4100. **$99-$109.** 5825 International Dr. I-4, exit 75A, just w. Int corridors. **Pets:** Other species. Service with restrictions, supervision.

SAVE S⃝ ✕ ☐ ⊑ ⇝

La Quinta Inn Orlando (Airport West) 🆂🅷
(407) 857-9215. **$115-$130.** 7931 Daetwyler Dr. SR 528 (Beachline Expwy), exit 9 (Tradeport), via McCoy Rd. Ext corridors. **Pets:** Other species. Service with restrictions, supervision.
(SAVE) 🆂 💻 🏊

La Quinta Inn Orlando (International Drive) 🆂🅷
(407) 351-1660. **$104-$129.** 8300 Jamaican Ct. I-4, exit 74A, just e on SR 482 (Sand Lake Rd), then just s on International Dr. Ext corridors. **Pets:** Other species. Service with restrictions, supervision.
(SAVE) 🆂 ✖ 🅜 🍴 💻 🏊 ✖

Microtel Inn & Suites 🆂🅷
(407) 226-9887. **Call for rates.** 7531 Canada Ave. I-4, exit 74A, just e on SR 482 (Sand Lake Rd), then n. Int corridors. **Pets:** Accepted.
✖ 🍴 💻 🏊

Motel 6 Orlando-International Drive #1079 🆂🅷
(407) 351-6500. **$51-$65.** 5909 American Way. I-4, exit 75A, just w of SR 435, then just n. Int corridors. **Pets:** Other species. Service with restrictions, supervision.
🆂 ✖ 🏊

Quality Inn & Suites 🆂🅷
(407) 996-4600. **$90-$200.** 8700 S Orange Blossom Tr. On US 17-92 and 441, 0.5 mi n of SR 528 and Florida Tpke, exit 254. Ext corridors. **Pets:** Small. $10 daily fee/pet. Service with restrictions, supervision.
(SAVE) 🆂 ✖ 🍴 💻 🏊

Quality Inn International 🅻🅷 🐾
(407) 996-1600. **$59-$109.** 7600 International Dr. I-4, exit 74A, just e on SR 482 (Sand Lake Rd), then just n. Ext corridors. **Pets:** Medium. $10 daily fee/room. Service with restrictions, supervision.
(ASK) 🆂 ✖ 🅜 🍴 💻 🍴 🏊

Quality Inn Plaza 🅻🅷 🐾
(407) 996-8585. **$49-$129.** 9000 International Dr. I-4, exit 74A, just e on SR 482 (Sand Lake Rd), then 1 mi s. Ext corridors. **Pets:** Medium, other species. $10 daily fee/pet. Service with restrictions, supervision.
(ASK) 🆂 ✖ 🅜 🍴 💻 🍴 🏊 ✖

Red Roof Inn Convention Center 🆂🅷
(407) 352-1507. **Call for rates.** 9922 Hawaiian Ct. I-4, exit 72, 0.9 mi e on SR 528 (Beachline Expwy) to exit 1, then just n. Ext corridors. **Pets:** Accepted.
✖ 🅜 🍴 🏊

Residence Inn by Marriott Orlando Convention Center 🆂🅷
(407) 226-0288. **$139-$159.** 8800 Universal Blvd. I-4, exit 74A, 0.5 mi e on SR 482 (Sand Lake Rd), then 0.8 mi s. Int corridors. **Pets:** Accepted.
(SAVE) 🆂 ✖ 🅜 🍴 💻 🏊 ✖

Residence Inn by Marriott-Orlando International Dr 🆂🅷
(407) 345-0117. **$175-$219.** 7975 Canada Ave. I-4, exit 74A, just e on SR 482 (Sand Lake Rd). Ext corridors. **Pets:** Medium, other species. $75 one-time fee/room. Service with restrictions.
(SAVE) 🆂 ✖ 🍴 💻 🏊 ✖

Residence Inn by Marriott SeaWorld International Center 🆂🅷
(407) 313-3600. **$190-$229.** 11000 Westwood Blvd. I-4, exit 72. Int corridors. **Pets:** Accepted.
(SAVE) 🆂 ✖ 🅜 🍴 💻 🍴 🏊 ✖

Rodeway Inn International 🆂🅷
(407) 996-4444. **$50-$90.** 6327 International Dr. I-4, exit 74A, just e on SR 482 (Sand Lake Rd), then 0.7 mi n. Ext/int corridors. **Pets:** Medium. $10 daily fee/pet. Designated rooms, service with restrictions, supervision.
(ASK) 🅜 🍴 💻 🍴 🏊

Sheraton Downtown 🆂🅷
(407) 425-4455. **$129-$299.** 60 Ivanhoe Blvd. I-4, exit Ivanhoe Blvd. Int corridors. **Pets:** Small, dogs only. Service with restrictions, supervision.
(SAVE) 🆂 ✖ 🍴 💻 🍴 🏊 ✖

Sheraton Suites Orlando Airport 🆂🅷
(407) 240-5555. **$109-$289.** 7550 Augusta National Dr. 2 mi n of airport terminal via SR 436 and TG Lee Blvd. Int corridors. **Pets:** Accepted.
(SAVE) 🆂 ✖ 🅜 🍴 💻 🍴 🏊

Universal's Hard Rock Hotel 🅻🅷 🐾
(407) 503-2000. **Call for rates.** 5800 Universal Blvd. I-4, exit 75A, 1 mi n, follow signs. Int corridors. **Pets:** Other species. $25 one-time fee/pet. Designated rooms, no service.
(SAVE) ✖ 🅜 🍴 💻 🍴 🏊 ✖

Universal's Portofino Bay Hotel, a Loews Hotel 🅻🅷 🐾
(407) 503-1000. **Call for rates.** 5601 Universal Blvd. I-4, exit 74B westbound; exit 75A eastbound, 1 mi n, follow signs. Int corridors. **Pets:** Other species. $25 one-time fee/room. Designated rooms, service with restrictions.
(SAVE) ✖ 🍴 💻 🍴 🏊 ✖

Universal's Royal Pacific Resort, a Loews Hotel 🅻🅷
(407) 503-3000. **Call for rates.** 6300 Hollywood Way. I-4, exit 74B, just n. Int corridors. **Pets:** Accepted.
(SAVE) ✖ 🍴 💻 🍴 🏊 ✖

Ventura Country Club-Ventura Resort Rentals 🆅🅷
(407) 273-8770. **$101-$180.** 5946 Curry Ford Rd. 0.6 mi e of SR 436. Ext corridors. **Pets:** Accepted.
(ASK) 🆂 🍴 💻 🏊 ✖

Wyndham Orlando Resort 🅻🅷
(407) 351-2420. **$83-$194, 3 day notice.** 8001 International Dr. I-4, exit 74A, just e at SR 482 (Sand Lake Rd). Ext/int corridors. **Pets:** Accepted.
(SAVE) 🆂 ✖ 🅜 🍴 💻 🍴 🏊 ✖

ST. CLOUD

Budget Inn of St Cloud 🅼
(407) 892-2858. **$35-$90, 3 day notice.** 602 13th St. On US 192, 0.5 mi e of The Water Tower, 2 mi w of jct CR 15. Ext corridors. **Pets:** Very small, dogs only. $10 daily fee/pet. No service, crate.
(SAVE) 🆂 ✖ 🍴

TAVARES

AAA ▼▼▼▼ **Best Western Lake County Inn & Suites** SH
(352) 253-2378. **$69-$249.** 1380 E Burleigh Blvd. On US 441 N. Int corridors. **Pets:** Medium, dogs only. $25 daily fee/pet. Designated rooms, service with restrictions, supervision.
SAVE S⊘ ☒ 🖪 🖵 ⊅

▼▼▼ **Budget Inn** M
(352) 343-4666. **Call for rates.** 101 W Burleigh Blvd. On US 441, 0.3 mi e of jct SR 19 S. Ext corridors. **Pets:** Accepted.
☒ 🖪 ⊅

END METROPOLITAN AREA

ORMOND BEACH

AAA ▼▼▼ **Econo Lodge Interstate** SH
(386) 672-8621. **$45-$300, 10 day notice.** 1567 N US 1. I-95, exit 273, just e. Ext corridors. **Pets:** Accepted.
SAVE ☒ 🖪 🖵 ⊅

▼▼▼ **Jameson Inn** SH
(386) 672-3675. **Call for rates.** 175 Interchange Blvd. I-95, exit 268, just w, then just s. Int corridors. **Pets:** Small. $15 daily fee/room. Service with restrictions, crate.
☒ Ġ 🖪 🖵 ⊅

OSPREY

AAA ▼▼▼ **Osprey Inn** M
(941) 966-2121. **$79-$179.** 1660 S Tamiami Tr. On US 41, 1.8 mi n of jct SR 681. Ext/int corridors. **Pets:** Small, dogs only. $50 one-time fee/room. Designated rooms, service with restrictions, supervision.
SAVE ☒ 🖪 🖵 Ⓣ ⊅

PALM BAY

▼▼▼ **Jameson Inn** SH
(321) 725-2952. **Call for rates.** 890 Palm Bay Rd. I-95, exit 176. Int corridors. **Pets:** Small. $15 daily fee/room. Service with restrictions, crate.
☒ Ġ 🖪 🖵 ⊅

PALM BEACH

AAA ▼▼▼▼ **Brazilian Court Hotel** SH
(561) 655-7740. **$400-$2300, 7 day notice.** 301 Australian Ave. From Royal Palm Way (SR 704), s on Cocoanut Row, 2 blks to Australian Ave, then just e; corner of Hibiscus and Australian aves. Int corridors. **Pets:** Accepted.
SAVE S⊘ ☒ Ⓣ ⊠

▼▼▼▼ **The Chesterfield Hotel** SH
(561) 659-5800. **Call for rates.** 363 Cocoanut Row. Just w of SR A1A; at Australian Ave and Cocoanut Row. Int corridors. **Pets:** Accepted.
☒ 🖪 Ⓣ ⊅ ⊠

AAA ▼▼▼▼ **The Four Seasons Resort, Palm Beach** LH ❖
(561) 582-2800. **Call for rates.** 2800 S Ocean Blvd. SR A1A, 0.3 mi n of jct SR 802. Int corridors. **Pets:** Small. Service with restrictions, crate.
SAVE ☒ Ġ 🖪 🖵 Ⓣ ⊅ ⊠

AAA ▼▼▼▼ **The OC Beach Resort** SH
(561) 586-6542. **Call for rates.** 2842 S Ocean Blvd. On SR A1A; just n of jct SR 802. Int corridors. **Pets:** Accepted.
SAVE ☒ 🖵 Ⓣ ⊅ ⊠

▼▼▼▼ **The Palm House** SH
(561) 655-5600. **$250-$2995, 4 day notice.** 160 Royal Palm Way. Just e of SR A1A; center. Int corridors. **Pets:** Accepted.
ASK S⊘ ☒ 🖪 🖵 Ⓣ ⊅

PALM BEACH SHORES

AAA ▼▼▼ **Best Western Seaspray Inn** SH
(561) 844-0233. **$120-$250, 14 day notice.** 123 S Ocean Ave. On Singer Island; 0.5 mi s of SR A1A. Int corridors. **Pets:** Medium. $15 daily fee/pet. Service with restrictions, supervision.
SAVE S⊘ ☒ 🖪 🖵 Ⓣ ⊅

PALM COAST

▼▼▼ **European Village Resort** CO
(386) 597-5200. **Call for rates.** 101 Palm Harbor Pkwy. I-95, exit 289, 3 mi e, then 0.3 mi e; Palm Harbor Pkwy is before the toll bridge. Int corridors. **Pets:** Accepted.
☒ 🖪 🖵 ⊅ ⊠

▼▼▼ **Microtel Inn & Suites** SH
(386) 445-8976. **Call for rates.** 16 Kingswood Dr. I-95, exit 289, 0.5 mi se via Old Kings Rd. Int corridors. **Pets:** Accepted.
☒ Ġ 🖪 🖵 ⊅

AAA ▼▼▼ **Palm Coast Villas** M ❖
(386) 445-3525. **$69-$79, 7 day notice.** 5454 N Oceanshore Blvd. I-95, exit 289, 2.8 mi e to SR A1A, then 1.8 mi n. Ext corridors. **Pets:** Other species. $5 daily fee/pet. Designated rooms, service with restrictions, supervision.
SAVE S⊘ ☒ 🖪 🖵 ⊅

PANAMA CITY

AAA ▼▼▼ **La Quinta Inn & Suites Panama City** SH
(850) 914-0022. **$119-$144.** 1030 E 23rd St. Jct US 231 and CR 390A. Int corridors. **Pets:** Other species. Service with restrictions, supervision.
SAVE S⊘ ☒ Ġ 🖪 🖵 ⊅

▼▼▼ **Super 8 Motel** M
(850) 784-1988. **$58-$100.** 207 Hwy 231 N. Just n of jct US 98. Ext/int corridors. **Pets:** Small, dogs only. $15 daily fee/pet. Designated rooms, service with restrictions, crate.
ASK S⊘ ☒ 🖪 ⊅

PANAMA CITY BEACH

AAA ▼▼▼ **La Quinta Inn & Suites** SH
(850) 234-3133. **$99-$149.** 1000 Thomas Dr. 2 mi s of US 98. Int corridors. **Pets:** Other species. Service with restrictions, supervision.
SAVE S⊘ ☒ 🖪 🖵 ⊅

PENSACOLA

AAA ▼▼▼ **Americas Best Value Inn & Suites** SH
(850) 479-1099. **$59-$89.** 8240 N Davis Hwy. I-10, exit 13, 0.8 mi n. Ext/int corridors. **Pets:** Medium. $10 one-time fee/pet. Service with restrictions, crate.
SAVE S⊘ ☒ 🖪 🖵 ⊅

▼▼▼ **Ashton Inn & Suites** SH
(850) 454-0280. **Call for rates.** 4 New Warrington Rd. Just n of jct US 98 and SR 295. Int corridors. **Pets:** Accepted.
☒ 🖪 🖵 ⊅

▼▼▼ **Extended StayAmerica-Pensacola-University Mall** SH
(850) 473-9323. **$67-$74.** 809 Bloodworth Ln. I-10, exit 13, just s on Davis Hwy, then e. Int corridors. **Pets:** Other species. $75 one-time fee/pet. Service with restrictions.
ASK S⊘ ✕ 🗄 💻 📺

Q⚶D ▼▼▼ **La Quinta Inn Pensacola** SH
(850) 474-0411. **$119-$139.** 7750 N Davis Hwy. I-10, exit 13, just n. Ext corridors. **Pets:** Other species. Service with restrictions, supervision.
SAVE S⊘ ✕ 🗄 💻 ➣

▼ **Motel 6 #1105** M
(850) 474-1060. **$45-$61.** 7226 Plantation Rd. I-10, exit 13, sw on Mall Rd. Ext corridors. **Pets:** Other species. Service with restrictions, supervision.
S⊘ ✕ ➣

▼ **Motel 6 Pensacola North** M
(850) 476-5386. **$46-$61.** 7827 N Davis Hwy. I-10, exit 13, 0.3 mi n. Ext corridors. **Pets:** Other species. Service with restrictions, supervision.
S⊘ ✕ ➣

Q⚶D ▼▼▼ **Quality Inn Pensacola West** SH
(850) 944-0333. **$65-$75, 3 day notice.** 8060 Lavalle Way. I-10, exit 7, just s. Ext corridors. **Pets:** Accepted.
SAVE S⊘ ✕ 🗄 💻 ➣

▼▼ **Red Roof Inn** M
(850) 476-7960. **Call for rates.** 7340 Plantation Rd. I-10, exit 13, just s. Ext corridors. **Pets:** Accepted.
✕ 🗄

Q⚶D ▼▼▼ **Residence Inn By Marriott** SH
(850) 479-1000. **$160-$200.** 7230 Plantation Rd. I-10, exit 13, just s. Ext corridors. **Pets:** Small. $100 one-time fee/room. Service with restrictions.
SAVE S⊘ ✕ ⬜M 🗄 💻 ➣ ✕

PERRY

Q⚶D ▼ **Best Budget Inn** M
(850) 584-6231. **$56-$62.** 2220 US 19 S. US 19 and 98, 0.4 mi s of jct US 221. Ext corridors. **Pets:** Other species. $10 daily fee/pet. Service with restrictions, supervision.
SAVE S⊘ ✕ 🗄 ➣

PORT CHARLOTTE

Q⚶D ▼▼ **Days Inn of Port Charlotte** SH
(941) 627-8900. **$69-$139.** 1941 Tamiami Tr. On US 41, 2.3 mi s of jct Toledo Blade Blvd (CR 779). Ext corridors. **Pets:** Accepted.
SAVE S⊘ ✕ 🗄 💻 ⫯⫯ ➣

PORT ST. LUCIE

▼▼▼ **Holiday Inn-Port St Lucie** SH
(772) 337-2200. **$129-$249.** 10120 S Federal Hwy, Rt 1. US 1, 0.5 mi n of jct SR 716, Port St Lucie Blvd. Int corridors. **Pets:** Medium. $50 one-time fee/room. Designated rooms, service with restrictions, crate.
ASK S⊘ ✕ 🗄 💻 ⫯⫯ ➣

QUINCY

▼▼▼ **Allison House Inn** BB ❖
(850) 875-2511. **$90-$150, 21 day notice.** 215 N Madison St. Just e of town center; in historic district. Int corridors. **Pets:** Small, dogs only. Designated rooms, service with restrictions, supervision.
ASK S⊘ ✕

ST. AUGUSTINE

Q⚶D ▼▼▼ **Avenida Inn Saint Augustine** SH
(904) 829-6581. **$69-$115.** 2800 N Ponce de Leon Blvd. US 1 at SR 16; in historic district. Ext corridors. **Pets:** Medium, dogs only. $10 daily fee/pet. Designated rooms, service with restrictions.
SAVE S⊘ ✕ 🗄 💻 ⫯⫯ ➣

▼▼▼ **Bayfront Westcott House** BB
(904) 824-4301. **Call for rates.** 146 Avenida Menendez. 1 blk s of Bridge of Lions. Ext/int corridors. **Pets:** Accepted.
✕

Q⚶D ▼▼▼ **Casablanca Inn on the Bay** BB
(904) 829-0928. **$99-$379, 7 day notice.** 24 Avenida Menendez. US 1 business route and SR A1A, then just n. Int corridors. **Pets:** Accepted.
SAVE ✕ 🗄 💻

Q⚶D ▼▼▼ **The Cozy Inn** M
(904) 824-2449. **$49-$209, 30 day notice.** 202 San Marco Ave. 0.3 mi s of jct SR 16. Ext corridors. **Pets:** Accepted.
SAVE S⊘ ✕ 🗄 💻

Q⚶D ▼▼▼ **Days Inn-West** SH
(904) 824-4341. **$59-$199.** 2560 SR 16. I-95, exit 318, just w. Ext corridors. **Pets:** Accepted.
SAVE S⊘ ✕ 🗄 💻 ⫯⫯ ➣

▼▼ **The Inn At Camachee Harbor** SH ❖
(904) 825-0003. **$109-$179.** 201 Yacht Club Dr. On Intracoastal Waterway at west side of Usine Bridge; 1 mi e of jct N SR A1A and San Marco Blvd. Ext/int corridors. **Pets:** Other species. $15 daily fee/room. Designated rooms, service with restrictions.
✕ 🗄 💻 ✕

Q⚶D ▼▼▼ **St. Francis Inn** BB ❖
(904) 824-6068. **$99-$319.** 279 St George St. Just s; in historic district. Ext/int corridors. **Pets:** Medium, other species. $15 daily fee/pet. Designated rooms, supervision.
SAVE S⊘ ✕ 🗄 💻 ➣

ST. AUGUSTINE BEACH

Q⚶D ▼▼▼ **Comfort Inn at St. Augustine Beach** SH
(904) 471-1474. **$79-$169.** 901 A1A Beach Blvd. On Business Rt SR A1A, 1.6 mi s of jct SR 312 and A1A. Ext corridors. **Pets:** Other species. $15 daily fee/pet. Service with restrictions, supervision.
SAVE S⊘ ✕ 🗄 💻 ➣

Q⚶D ▼▼▼ **Holiday Inn-St Augustine Beach** SH
(904) 471-2555. **$114-$209.** 860 A1A Beach Blvd. On Business Rt SR A1A, 1.8 mi s of jct SR 312 and A1A. Int corridors. **Pets:** Accepted.
SAVE S⊘ ✕ 🗄 💻 ⫯⫯ ➣

SARASOTA

Q⚶D ▼▼▼ **Coquina on the Beach Resort** M
(941) 388-2141. **$119-$279.** 1008 Benjamin Franklin Dr. On St. Armands Key of Lido Beach; 0.9 mi s of St. Armands Circle. Ext corridors. **Pets:** Accepted.
SAVE S⊘ ✕ 🗄 💻 ➣

Q⚶D ▼▼▼ **Hibiscus Suites Inn** M
(941) 921-5797. **$89-$249, 3 day notice.** 1735 Stickney Point Rd. On SR 72, 0.3 mi sw of jct US 41. Ext corridors. **Pets:** $25 daily fee/room. Service with restrictions, crate.
ASK S⊘ ✕ ⬜M 🗄 💻 ➣

Q⚶D ▼▼▼ **Holiday Inn Express Sarasota Siesta Key** SH
(941) 924-4900. **$89-$199.** 6600 S Tamiami Tr. On US 41, just s of jct SR 72 (Clark Rd/Stickney Point Rd). Ext corridors. **Pets:** Medium, dogs only. $50 one-time fee/room. Service with restrictions, crate.
ASK S⊘ ✕ ⬜M 🗄 💻 ➣

Q⚶D ▼▼▼ **Homewood Suites by Hilton** SH ❖
(941) 365-7300. **$99-$229.** 3470 Fruitville Rd. I-75, exit 210, 3.2 mi w on SR 780 (Fruitville Rd). Int corridors. **Pets:** Medium. $100 one-time fee/pet. Designated rooms, service with restrictions.
SAVE S⊘ ✕ ⬜M 🗄 💻 ➣ ✕

▼▼▼ **Hotel Indigo** SH ❀
(941) 487-3800. **$169-$289.** 1223 Boulevard of the Arts. Jct US 41 (N Tamiami Tr). Int corridors. **Pets:** Medium. $75 one-time fee/room. Designated rooms, service with restrictions, supervision.

(ASK) (S✿) ⊠ (&M) 🛆 🖵 ᵀ📶

ⓐⓐⓐ ▼▼▼ **Hyatt Sarasota** LH
(941) 953-1234. **$159-$435, 3 day notice.** 1000 Boulevard of the Arts. Just w of jct US 41 (Tamiami Tr). Int corridors. **Pets:** Medium. $150 one-time fee/pet. Designated rooms.

(SAVE) ⊠ (&M) 🛆 🖵 ᵀ📶 ⧂⊠

ⓐⓐⓐ ▼▼▼ **La Quinta Inn & Suites Sarasota Airport** SH
(941) 366-5128. **$119-$189.** 1803 N Tamiami Tr. On US 41, 1 mi n of jct SR 780 (Fruitville Rd). Int corridors. **Pets:** Other species. Service with restrictions, supervision.

(SAVE) (S✿) ⊠ (&M) 🛆 🖵 📶

▼▼▼▼ **The Ritz-Carlton, Sarasota** LH
(941) 309-2000. **$362-$549.** 1111 Ritz-Carlton Dr. On US 41, jct John Ringling Blvd. Int corridors. **Pets:** Accepted.

(ASK) (S✿) ⊠ 🛆 🖵 ᵀ📶 ⧂⊠

▼▼▼▼ **Sarasota Cay Club Resort & Marina** CO
(941) 355-2781. **Call for rates.** 7150 N Tamiami Tr. On US 41, 2.4 mi n of jct University Pkwy. Ext/int corridors. **Pets:** Accepted.

⊠ (&M) 🛆 🖵 ᵀ📶 ⧂⊠

SEBRING

▼▼▼ **Four Points by Sheraton Sebring Chateau Elan** SH
(863) 655-6252. **Call for rates.** 150 Midway Dr. From US 27, 2.2 mi e on US 98; at entrance to Sebring International Raceway. Int corridors. **Pets:** Accepted.

⊠ 🛆 🖵 ᵀ📶 ⧂⊠

ⓐⓐⓐ ▼▼▼ **Inn On The Lakes** SH ❀
(863) 471-9400. **$94-$109, 3 day notice.** 3100 Golfview Rd. On US 27, 1.5 mi n of jct SR 17. Ext/int corridors. **Pets:** Other species. $40 one-time fee/room. Designated rooms, service with restrictions, supervision.

(SAVE) (S✿) ⊠ 🛆 🖵 ᵀ📶

ⓐⓐⓐ ▼ **Kenilworth Lodge** SH
(863) 385-0111. **$75-$200, 3 day notice.** 1610 Lakeview Dr. US 27, 1 mi e on SR 17. Ext/int corridors. **Pets:** Large, other species. $15 daily fee/room. Designated rooms, service with restrictions, crate.

(SAVE) (S✿) ⊠ 🛆 🖵 📶 ⧂⊠

SIESTA KEY

ⓐⓐⓐ ▼▼▼ **Tropical Breeze Resort of Siesta Key** CO
(941) 349-1125. **$129-$365.** 153 Avenida Messina. I-75, exit 205, jct Ocean Blvd; in Siesta Village. Ext corridors. **Pets:** $75 one-time fee/pet. No service, crate.

(SAVE) (S✿) ⊠ 🛆 🖵 📶 ⧂⊠

▼▼▼ **Tropical Breeze Vacations** M
(941) 349-1125. **$119-$495.** 153 Avenida Messina. I-75, exit 205, jct Ocean Blvd; in Siesta Village. Ext corridors. **Pets:** $75 one-time fee/pet. No service, crate.

(ASK) (S✿) ⊠ 🛆 🖵 📶 ⧂⊠

SPRING HILL

ⓐⓐⓐ ▼▼▼ **Weeki Wachee Resort** M
(352) 596-2007. **$89-$149.** 6172 Commercial Way. On US 19, jct SR 50 (Cortez Blvd). Ext corridors. **Pets:** Accepted.

(SAVE) (S✿) ⊠ 🛆 🖵 ᵀ📶

STARKE

ⓐⓐⓐ ▼▼▼ **Best Western Motor Inn** SH
(904) 964-6744. **$81-$130, 14 day notice.** 1290 N Temple Ave. 1 mi n on US 301 from jct SR 100. Ext corridors. **Pets:** Medium. $10 daily fee/pet. Service with restrictions, supervision.

(SAVE) (S✿) ⊠ 🛆 🖵 📶

STEINHATCHEE

▼▼▼ **Steinhatchee Landing Resort** CO
(352) 498-3513. **$136-$594, 14 day notice.** SR 51. SR 51, 8 mi w of jct US 19/98. Ext corridors. **Pets:** Small, dogs only. $100 deposit/room. Service with restrictions, supervision.

(ASK) ⊠ 🛆 🖵 📶 ⧂⊠

▼▼ **Steinhatchee River Inn** M
(352) 498-4049. **$69-$139, 14 day notice.** 1111 Riverside Dr. Center. Ext corridors. **Pets:** Small, dogs only. $10 daily fee/pet. Designated rooms, service with restrictions, supervision.

(ASK) (S✿) ⊠ 🛆 🖵 📶

STUART

ⓐⓐⓐ ▼▼◇ **Pirates Cove Resort & Marina** SH
(772) 287-2500. **$130-$225.** 4307 SE Bayview St. 0.3 mi e of SR A1A. Ext corridors. **Pets:** Other species. $20 one-time fee/pet. Designated rooms, service with restrictions, supervision.

(SAVE) (S✿) 🛆 🖵 ᵀ📶 ⧂⊠

TALLAHASSEE

ⓐⓐⓐ ▼▼▼ **Best Western Pride Inn & Suites** SH
(850) 656-6312. **$64-$169, 3 day notice.** 2016 Apalachee Pkwy. 1 mi se of US 27. Ext corridors. **Pets:** Medium, other species. $10 daily fee/pet. Service with restrictions, crate.

(SAVE) (S✿) ⊠ 🛆 🖵 📶

ⓐⓐⓐ ▼◇◇ **Best Western Seminole Inn** M
(850) 656-2938. **$59-$150, 7 day notice.** 6737 Mahan Dr. I-10, exit 209A, just w on US 90. Ext corridors. **Pets:** Accepted.

(SAVE) ⊠ 🛆 🖵 📶

ⓐⓐⓐ ▼▼▼ **Days Inn** SH
(850) 222-3219. **Call for rates.** 1350 W Tennessee St. 1.6 mi w of US 27. Int corridors. **Pets:** $10 daily fee/pet. Service with restrictions, supervision.

(SAVE) ⊠ 🛆 🖵 📶

ⓐⓐⓐ ◇ **Econo Lodge** M
(850) 385-6155. **$55-$95.** 2681 N Monroe St. I-10, exit 199, 0.5 mi s. Ext corridors. **Pets:** Large, other species. $10 one-time fee/pet. Service with restrictions, supervision.

(SAVE) (S✿) ⊠ 🛆 🖵 📶

▼▼▼ **Holiday Inn Capital East** SH
(850) 877-3171. **$109-$174.** 1355 Apalachee Pkwy. 1.3 mi se on US 27. Int corridors. **Pets:** Medium, other species. $50 one-time fee/room. Service with restrictions.

(ASK) (S✿) ⊠ 🛆 🖵 ᵀ📶

▼▼▼ **Homewood Suites by Hilton** SH
(850) 402-9400. **Call for rates.** 2987 Apalachee Pkwy. US 27, 3.5 mi s. Int corridors. **Pets:** Accepted.

⊠ 🛆 🖵 📶 ⧂⊠

ⓐⓐⓐ ▼▼◇ **La Quinta Inn Tallahassee (North)** SH
(850) 385-7172. **$102-$115.** 2905 N Monroe St. I-10, exit 199, just s on US 27. Ext corridors. **Pets:** Other species. Service with restrictions, supervision.

(SAVE) (S✿) ⊠ 🛆 🖵 📶

ⓐⓐⓐ ▼▼◇ **La Quinta Inn Tallahassee (South)** SH
(850) 878-5099. **$99-$115.** 2850 Apalachee Pkwy. 3 mi se on US 27. Ext corridors. **Pets:** Other species. Service with restrictions, supervision.

(SAVE) (S✿) ⊠ (&M) 🛆 🖵 📶

▼▼ Motel 6 #1073 🅂🄷
(850) 877-6171. **$47-$85.** 1027 Apalachee Pkwy. 1 mi se on US 27. Ext corridors. **Pets:** Other species. Service with restrictions, supervision.
🅂👁 ✖ 🍴 🖵 🏊

▼▼ Motel 6 #1191 🅂🄷
(850) 386-7878. **$43-$75.** 2738 N Monroe St. I-10, exit 199, just s on US 27. Ext corridors. **Pets:** Other species. Service with restrictions, supervision.
🅂👁 ✖ 🍴 🖵 🏊

▼▼ Motel 6 #420 🄼
(850) 668-2600. **$45-$75.** 1481 Timberlane Rd. I-10, exit 203, just n, then w. Ext corridors. **Pets:** Other species. Service with restrictions, supervision.
🅂👁 ✖ 🏊

▼▼ Ramada Conference Center 🄻🄷
(850) 386-1027. **Call for rates.** 2900 N Monroe St. I-10, exit 199, just s. Ext/int corridors. **Pets:** $15 daily fee/pet. Designated rooms, service with restrictions.
✖ 🍴 🖵 🍴 🏊

▼▼ StudioPLUS-Tallahassee-Killearn 🅂🄷
(850) 383-1700. **$77-$84.** 1950 Raymond Diehl Rd. I-10, exit 203, 2.4 mi s, then just n. Int corridors. **Pets:** Other species. $75 one-time fee/pet. Service with restrictions.
🄰🅂🄺 🅂👁 ✖ 🅂🄼 🍴 🖵 🏊

TAMPA BAY METROPOLITAN AREA

BRANDON

▼▼ Homestead Studio Suites Hotel-Tampa/Brandon 🄼
(813) 643-5900. **$77-$110.** 330 Grand Regency Blvd. I-75, exit 257, just e on SR 60, then 0.4 mi n; in Regency Office Park. Ext corridors. **Pets:** Other species. $75 one-time fee/pet. Service with restrictions.
🄰🅂🄺 🅂👁 ✖ 🅂🄼 🍴 🖵

◈◈◈ ▼▼▼▼ La Quinta Inn & Suites Tampa Bay (Brandon) 🅂🄷
(813) 643-0574. **$129-$165.** 310 Grand Regency Blvd. I-75, exit 257, just e on SR 60, then 0.5 mi n; in Regency Office Park. Int corridors. **Pets:** Other species. Service with restrictions, supervision.
🅂🄰🅅🄴 🅂👁 ✖ 🅂🄼 🍴 🖵 🏊

CLEARWATER

◈◈◈ ▼▼▼▼ Belleview Biltmore Resort & Spa 🅂🄷 ✻
(727) 373-3000. **$99-$239.** 25 Belleview Blvd. 2 mi s on US Alternate 19 (Ft Harrison Ave); from jct SR 60, 0.5 mi w. Int corridors. **Pets:** Medium. $75 one-time fee/room. Designated rooms, service with restrictions, crate.
🅂🄰🅅🄴 🅂👁 ✖ 🍴 🍴 🏊 🏊

◈◈◈ ▼▼▼ Days Inn Clearwater/St. Petersburg Airport 🅂🄷
(727) 573-3334. **$59-$104.** 3910 Ulmerton Rd. I-275, exit 31 southbound; exit 30 northbound, 2 mi w on SR 688. Int corridors. **Pets:** Small, other species. $25 one-time fee/pet. Designated rooms, service with restrictions, crate.
🅂🄰🅅🄴 🅂👁 ✖ 🅂🄼 🍴 🖵 🏊

▼▼ Extended StayAmerica-St. Petersburg-Clearwater 🅂🄷
(727) 561-9032. **$67-$89.** 3089 Executive Dr. I-275, exit 31 southbound; exit 30 northbound, 1.8 mi w on SR 699, just n on 34th St N, then 0.3 mi ne. Int corridors. **Pets:** Other species. $75 one-time fee/pet. Service with restrictions.
🄰🅂🄺 🅂👁 ✖ 🅂🄼 🍴 🖵

◈◈◈ ▼▼▼ Holiday Inn Express 🅂🄷 ✻
(727) 536-7275. **$89-$179.** 13625 Icot Blvd. 0.5 mi e of jct US 19; just n of Ulmerton Rd (SR 688); in Icot Center Business Park. Int corridors. **Pets:** Medium. $49 one-time fee/room. Service with restrictions.
🅂🄰🅅🄴 🅂👁 ✖ 🍴 🖵 🏊

▼▼ Homestead Studio Suites Hotel-St Petersburg-Clearwater 🄼
(727) 572-4800. **$67-$95.** 2311 Ulmerton Rd. I-275, exit 31 southbound; exit 30 northbound, 1.3 mi w on SR 688. Ext corridors. **Pets:** Other species. $75 one-time fee/pet. Service with restrictions.
🄰🅂🄺 🅂👁 ✖ 🅂🄼 🍴 🖵 🏊

▼▼▼ Homewood Suites by Hilton 🅂🄷
(727) 573-1500. **Call for rates.** 2233 Ulmerton Rd. I-275, exit 31 southbound; exit 30 northbound, 1.3 mi w on SR 688 (Ulmerton Rd). Int corridors. **Pets:** Accepted.
✖ 🅂🄼 🍴 🖵 🏊

▼▼ Howard Johnson Inn & Suites 🄼
(727) 796-0135. **$80-$130.** 27988 US Hwy 19 N. On US 19, 0.6 mi n of jct SR 580. Ext corridors. **Pets:** Small. $50 deposit/room, $10 daily fee/pet. Designated rooms, service with restrictions, supervision.
🄰🅂🄺 🅂👁 ✖ 🍴 🖵 🏊

◈◈◈ ▼▼▼▼ La Quinta Inn Tampa Bay (Clearwater-Airport) 🅂🄷
(727) 572-7222. **$114-$139.** 3301 Ulmerton Rd. I-275, exit 31 southbound; exit 30 northbound, 1.7 mi w on SR 688; in The Centres Office Park. Int corridors. **Pets:** Other species. Service with restrictions, supervision.
🅂🄰🅅🄴 🅂👁 ✖ 🍴 🖵 🏊 🏊

▼▼▼▼ Radisson Hotel Clearwater Central 🅂🄷
(727) 799-1181. **Call for rates.** 20967 US 19 N. On US 19, just n of jct SR 60. Ext/int corridors. **Pets:** Accepted.
✖ 🅂🄼 🍴 🖵 🍴 🏊 🏊

◈◈◈ ▼▼▼ Residence Inn by Marriott 🅂🄷 ✻
(727) 573-4444. **$186-$241.** 5050 Ulmerton Rd. On SR 688, 1 mi e of jct US 19. Ext corridors. **Pets:** Large. $75 one-time fee/room. Service with restrictions.
🅂🄰🅅🄴 🅂👁 ✖ 🍴 🖵 🏊 🏊

◈◈◈ ▼▼▼ Super 8 Clearwater/St. Petersburg Airport 🅂🄷
(727) 572-8881. **$50-$100.** 13260 34th St N. I-275, exit 31 southbound; exit 30 northbound, 1.8 mi w on SR 688 (Ulmerton Rd), then just s. Int corridors. **Pets:** Small, other species. $10 daily fee/pet. Designated rooms, service with restrictions, supervision.
🅂🄰🅅🄴 🅂👁 ✖ 🍴 🖵 🏊

▼▼▼ TownePlace Suites by Marriott St. Petersburg/Clearwater 🅂🄷
(727) 299-9229. **$142-$197.** 13200 49th St N. I-275, exit 31 southbound; exit 30 northbound, 3 mi w on SR 688, then just s; in Turtle Creek. Int corridors. **Pets:** Accepted.
🄰🅂🄺 🅂👁 ✖ 🅂🄼 🍴 🖵 🏊

CLEARWATER BEACH

◈◈◈ ▼▼▼▼ Sheraton Sand Key Resort 🄻🄷
(727) 595-1611. **$299-$335.** 1160 Gulf Blvd. 2 mi s on SR 699; at south end of Clearwater Pass Bridge. Int corridors. **Pets:** Accepted.
🅂🄰🅅🄴 🅂👁 ✖ 🅂🄼 🍴 🖵 🍴 🏊 🏊

INDIAN ROCKS BEACH

▼▼▼▼ Sea Star Motel & Apartments **M** ❀
(727) 596-2525. **$70-$1960.** 1805 Gulf Blvd. On SR 699, 1.2 mi n of jct SR 688 (Walsingham Rd). Ext corridors. **Pets:** Other species. $10 daily fee/pet. No service, crate.

⊠ 🛏 💻 ⊠ 🗹

INDIAN SHORES

𝄞 ▼▼▼▼ Sea Club Resort Condominiums **CO** ❀
(727) 596-2046. **$135-$170, 45 day notice.** 19725 Gulf Blvd. On SR 699, 1.1 mi n of jct CR 694. Ext corridors. **Pets:** Small. $50 one-time fee/pet. Designated rooms, no service, supervision.

SAVE ⊠ 🛏 ⇌ ⊠

LARGO

𝄞 ▼▼▼▼ Hampton Inn & Suites **SH**
(727) 585-3333. **$109-$229.** 100 E Bay Dr. On SR 686, 3.4 mi w of jct US 19; at jct US Alt 19. Int corridors. **Pets:** Other species. Service with restrictions, supervision.

SAVE S🐾 ⊠ 🐾M 🛏 💻 ⇌

MADEIRA BEACH

𝄞 ▼▼▼ Snug Harbor Inn Waterfront Bed & Breakfast **M** ❀
(727) 395-9256. **$74-$374, 21 day notice.** 13655 Gulf Blvd. On SR 699, 0.9 mi s of jct Tom Stuart Cswy. Ext corridors. **Pets:** Other species. Service with restrictions, supervision.

SAVE ⊠ 🛏 💻 ⇌ ⊠

NEW PORT RICHEY

𝄞 ▼▼▼ Riverside Inn **M**
(727) 845-4990. **$50-$100.** 7631 US 19. On US 19, 0.8 mi n of jct Main St. Ext corridors. **Pets:** Small. $6 daily fee/room. Designated rooms, no service, supervision.

SAVE S🐾 ⊠ 🛏 💻 ⇌

OLDSMAR

𝄞 ▼▼▼▼ Residence Inn Tampa/Oldsmar **SH**
(813) 818-9400. **$153-$219.** 4012 Tampa Rd. On SR 580; jct St. Pete Dr. Int corridors. **Pets:** Accepted.

SAVE S🐾 ⊠ 🐾M 🛏 💻 ⇌ ⊠

PALM HARBOR

𝄞 ▼▼▼▼ Best Western Lake Tarpon Hotel **CO**
(727) 942-0358. **$69-$115.** 37611 US 19 N. On US 19, 3 mi s of jct SR 582. Ext corridors. **Pets:** Medium, other species. $10 daily fee/pet. Service with restrictions, crate.

SAVE S🐾 ⊠ 🛏 💻 🍴 ⇌ ⊠

𝄞 ▼▼▼▼ Innisbrook Resort & Golf Club **CO**
(727) 942-2000. **$109-$509, 3 day notice.** 36750 US Hwy 19 N. On US 19, 2.8 mi s of jct SR 582; at jct Olde Post Rd, follow signs. Int corridors. **Pets:** Accepted.

ASK S🐾 ⊠ 🛏 💻 🍴 ⇌ ⊠

▼▼ Knights Inn-Clearwater/Palm Harbor **M**
(727) 789-2002. **$45-$56.** 34106 US 19 N. On US 19, 1.8 mi n of CR 752 (Tampa Rd). Ext corridors. **Pets:** Medium. $10 daily fee/room. Designated rooms, service with restrictions, supervision.

ASK S🐾 ⊠ 🐾M 🛏 💻 ⊠

𝄞 ▼▼▼ Red Roof Inn **M**
(727) 786-2529. **Call for rates.** 32000 US 19 N. On US 19, 0.4 mi s of jct CR 752 (Tampa Rd). Ext corridors. **Pets:** Accepted.

SAVE ⊠ 🛏 💻 ⇌

PINELLAS PARK

𝄞 ▼▼▼▼ La Quinta Inn Tampa (Pinellas Park/Clearwater) **SH**
(727) 545-5611. **$99-$115.** 7500 US Hwy 19 N. I-275, exit 28, 1.4 mi s on Gandy Blvd (SR 694), then just n. Ext/int corridors. **Pets:** Other species. Service with restrictions, supervision.

SAVE S🐾 ⊠ 🐾M 🛏 💻 ⇌

PLANT CITY

𝄞 ▼▼▼▼ Comfort Inn of Plant City **SH** ❀
(813) 707-6000. **$79-$339.** 2003 S Frontage Rd. I-4, exit 22, just e. Int corridors. **Pets:** Other species. $10 daily fee/pet. Service with restrictions, crate.

SAVE S🐾 ⊠ 🐾M 🛏 💻 ⇌

▼▼▼▼ Ramada Plantation House **M**
(813) 752-3141. **Call for rates.** 2011 N Wheeler St. I-4, exit 21, 0.4 mi ne; at jct SR 39. Ext corridors. **Pets:** Accepted.

⊠ 🐾M 🛏 💻 🍴 ⇌

PORT RICHEY

▼▼ Comfort Inn **M**
(727) 863-3336. **Call for rates.** 11810 US 19. On US 19, just s of jct SR 52. Ext corridors. **Pets:** Accepted.

⊠ 🛏 💻 ⇌

RUSKIN

▼▼▼ Southern Comfort Bed & Breakfast **BB**
(813) 645-6361. **Call for rates.** 2409 Ravine Dr W. Jct US 41, 1.1 mi sw on 1st St, just w on 24th Ave SW, then just s. Ext/int corridors. **Pets:** Accepted.

⊠ 🛏 💻 ⇌ ⊠ 🗹

ST. PETE BEACH

𝄞 ▼▼▼ Bayview Plaza Waterfront Resort **M**
(727) 367-1387. **$49-$199, 14 day notice.** 4321 Gulf Blvd. On SR 699; 0.8 mi n of Pinellas Bayway. Ext/int corridors. **Pets:** Small, other species. $10 daily fee/room.

SAVE S🐾 ⊠

𝄞 ▼▼▼▼ Beach House Suites By The Don Cesar **SH**
(727) 363-0001. **$194-$524.** 3860 Gulf Blvd. On SR 699, 0.4 mi n of jct Pinellas Bayway. Ext corridors. **Pets:** Accepted.

SAVE S🐾 ⊠ 🛏 💻 ⇌ ⊠

𝄞 ▼▼▼▼▼ Don CeSar Beach Resort, a Loews Hotel **LH** ❀
(727) 360-1881. **Call for rates.** 3400 Gulf Blvd. On SR 699, jct Pinellas Bayway. Int corridors. **Pets:** Small. $25 one-time fee/room. Designated rooms, service with restrictions.

SAVE ⊠ 🐾M 🛏 💻 🍴 ⇌ ⊠

ST. PETERSBURG

𝄞 ▼▼▼▼ La Quinta Inn Tampa Bay Area (St. Petersburg) **M**
(727) 527-8421. **$102-$112.** 4999 34th St N. I-275, exit 26 southbound; exit 26B northbound, just w on 54th Ave N, then just s on US 19. Ext corridors. **Pets:** Other species. Service with restrictions, supervision.

SAVE S🐾 ⊠ 🐾M 🛏 💻 ⇌

▼▼▼▼ Mansion House B & B **BB**
(727) 821-9391. **$159-$260.** 105 5th Ave NE. 0.5 mi n at 1st St N; downtown. Ext/int corridors. **Pets:** Accepted.

ASK ⊠ 🛏 ⇌

(AAA) ▼▼▼ Ramada Inn Mirage Ⓜ
(727) 525-1181. **$75-$95.** 5005 34th St N. I-275, exit 26 southbound; exit 26B northbound, 0.8 mi w on 54th Ave N, then 0.3 mi s on US 19. Ext corridors. **Pets:** Accepted.
SAVE 🅂🄳 ✕ 🔋 💻 🍴 ⇨

SEFFNER

(AAA) ▼▼▼ Hampton Inn & Suites Tampa-East SH
(813) 630-4321. **$129-$169.** 11740 Tampa Gateway Blvd. I-4, exit 10, just n of CR 579. Int corridors. **Pets:** Small. Designated rooms, service with restrictions, supervision.
SAVE 🅂🄳 ✕ 🄼 🔋 💻 ⇨

TAMPA

(AAA) ▼▼▼ Best Western Brandon Hotel & Conference Center Ⓜ 🐾
(813) 621-5555. **$68-$85.** 9331 Adamo Dr. I-75, exit 257, 1.2 mi w on SR 60. Ext corridors. **Pets:** Large, other species. $35 one-time fee/pet. Service with restrictions, supervision.
SAVE 🅂🄳 ✕ 🔋 💻 🍴 ⇨

(AAA) ▼▼▼▼ Chase Suite Hotel by Woodfin Ⓜ
(813) 281-5677. **$149-$239.** 3075 N Rocky Point Dr. I-275, exit 39 southbound; exit 39B northbound, 3 mi w on SR 60, then just n; in Rocky Point Harbor. Ext corridors. **Pets:** Accepted.
ASK 🅂🄳 ✕ 🄼 🔋 💻 ⇨ ✕

(AAA) ▼▼▼▼ Clarion Hotel & Conference Center Tampa SH 🐾
(813) 971-4710. **$99-$199, 3 day notice.** 2701 E Fowler Ave. I-275, exit 51, 1.5 mi e on SR 582. Ext/int corridors. **Pets:** Small. $75 one-time fee/room. Designated rooms, service with restrictions, crate.
SAVE 🅂🄳 ✕ 🄼 🔋 💻 🍴 ⇨

▼▼▼ Comfort Inn Hotel & Suites Tampa Stadium/Airport Ⓜ 🐾
(813) 877-6061. **$80-$159.** 4732 N Dale Mabry Hwy. I-275, exit 41B, 2 mi n. Ext corridors. **Pets:** Small. $25 one-time fee/room. Service with restrictions, crate.
ASK 🅂🄳 ✕ 🄼 🔋 💻 ⇨ ✕

▼▼▼ Extended StayAmerica-Tampa Airport-West Shore SH
(813) 873-2850. **$81-$116.** 4312 W Spruce St. I-275, exit 40B, 0.6 mi n on Lois Ave, then just w. Int corridors. **Pets:** Other species. $75 one-time fee/pet. Service with restrictions.
ASK 🅂🄳 ✕ 🄼 🔋 💻

▼▼▼ Extended Stay Deluxe Tampa–Airport SH
(813) 886-5253. **$77-$116.** 4811 Memorial Hwy. Veteran's Expwy, exit 3, just sw on CR 576. Int corridors. **Pets:** Other species. $75 one-time fee/pet. Service with restrictions.
ASK 🅂🄳 ✕ 🄼 🔋 💻 ⇨

▼▼▼ Extended Stay Deluxe-Tampa-Airport-N West Shore Blvd SH
(813) 637-8990. **$91-$126.** 1805 N Westshore Blvd. I-275, exit 40A southbound, 0.5 mi n; exit 39A northbound, 1 mi e on Kennedy Blvd, then 1.3 mi n. Int corridors. **Pets:** Other species. $75 one-time fee/pet. Service with restrictions.
ASK 🅂🄳 ✕ 🄼 🔋 💻 ⇨

(AAA) ▼▼▼ ▼▼ Grand Hyatt Tampa Bay LH
(813) 874-1234. **$149-$425, 3 day notice.** 2900 Bayport Plaza. SR 60, east end of Courtney Campbell Cswy. Ext/int corridors. **Pets:** Small. $75 one-time fee/room. Designated rooms, service with restrictions, supervision.
SAVE ✕ 🄼 🔋 💻 🍴 ⇨ ✕

▼▼▼ Hampton Inn Veterans Expressway SH
(813) 901-5900. **$99-$189.** 5628 W Waters Ave. SR 589 (Veteran's Expwy), exit 6A, just e on CR 584. Int corridors. **Pets:** Medium, other species. $10 daily fee/room. Service with restrictions, supervision.
ASK 🅂🄳 ✕ 🔋 💻 ⇨

(AAA) ▼▼▼▼ Holiday Inn Express & Suites SH 🐾
(813) 910-7171. **$129-$179.** 8310 Galbraith Rd. I-75, exit 270, 0.3 mi n on CR 581 (Bruce B Downs Blvd), just w on Highwoods Preserve Pkwy, then just n; in Highwoods Preserve. Int corridors. **Pets:** Medium, other species. $50 one-time fee/room. Designated rooms, service with restrictions.
SAVE 🅂🄳 ✕ 🄼 🔋 💻 ⇨ ✕

▼▼ Homestead Studio Suites Hotel-Tampa/North Airport Ⓜ
(813) 243-1913. **$67-$100.** 5401 Beaumont Ctr Blvd. SR 589 (Veterans Expwy), exit 4, just w on SR 580. Ext/int corridors. **Pets:** Other species. $75 one-time fee/pet. Service with restrictions.
ASK 🅂🄳 ✕ 🄼 🔋 💻

▼▼▼ Homewood Suites Brandon/Tampa SH
(813) 685-7099. **$149-$199.** 10230 Palm River Rd. I-75, exit 257, 0.4 mi w on SR 60, just s on S Falkenburg Rd, then 0.3 mi e. Int corridors. **Pets:** Accepted.
ASK 🅂🄳 ✕ 🄼 🔋 💻 ⇨ ✕

(AAA) ▼▼▼ La Quinta Inn & Suites Tampa Bay (U.S.F./ Near Busch Gardens) SH
(813) 910-7500. **$139-$149.** 3701 E Fowler Ave. I-275, exit 51, 2.2 mi e on SR 582. Int corridors. **Pets:** Other species. Service with restrictions, supervision.
SAVE 🅂🄳 ✕ 🄼 🔋 💻 ⇨

(AAA) ▼▼▼ La Quinta Inn & Suites Tampa/near Busch Gardens SH
(813) 930-6900. **$99-$109.** 9202 N 30th St. I-275, exit 50, 2 mi e on SR 580, then just n. Ext corridors. **Pets:** Other species. Service with restrictions, supervision.
SAVE 🅂🄳 ✕ 🔋 💻 ⇨

(AAA) ▼▼▼ La Quinta Inn Tampa Bay (Airport) Ⓜ
(813) 287-0440. **$109-$149.** 4730 Spruce St. I-275, exit 40A, 0.7 mi w on Westshore Blvd; exit 39A, 1 mi e on Kennedy Blvd, 1.2 mi n on Westshore Blvd, then just w. Ext corridors. **Pets:** Other species. Service with restrictions, supervision.
SAVE 🅂🄳 ✕ 🔋 💻 ⇨

(AAA) ▼▼▼ La Quinta Inn Tampa East Fairgrounds SH
(813) 626-0885. **$89-$109.** 4811 US 301 N. I-4, exit 6 westbound; exit 6A eastbound, just se. Int corridors. **Pets:** Other species. Service with restrictions, supervision.
SAVE 🅂🄳 ✕ 🔋 💻 ⇨

(AAA) ▼▼▼ La Quinta Inn Tampa South SH
(813) 835-6262. **$120-$130.** 4620 W Gandy Blvd. Just e of jct S West Shore Blvd. Int corridors. **Pets:** Other species. Service with restrictions, supervision.
SAVE 🅂🄳 ✕ 🄼 🔋 💻 ⇨

(AAA) ▼▼▼ La Quinta Inn West Tampa-Brandon SH
(813) 684-4007. **$109-$139.** 602 S Falkenburg Rd. I-75, exit 257, just w on SR 60, then just n. Int corridors. **Pets:** Other species. Service with restrictions, supervision.
SAVE 🅂🄳 ✕ 🔋 💻 ⇨

▼▼▼ Mainsail Suites Hotel & Conference Center SH
(813) 243-2600. **Call for rates.** 5108 Eisenhower Blvd. SR 589 (Veteran's Expwy), exit 4, just w on SR 580; main entrance on Hillsborough Ave. Ext corridors. **Pets:** Accepted.
✕ 🄼 🔋 💻 🍴 ⇨ ✕

◆◆ Motel 6 #1192 [M]
(813) 628-0888. $49-$65. 6510 US 301 N. I-4, exit 7 westbound; exit 7B eastbound, 0.7 mi n. Ext corridors. Pets: Other species. Service with restrictions.
[SD] [X] [≈]

◆◆ Red Roof Inn-Fairgrounds [M]
(813) 623-5245. Call for rates. 5001 N US 301. I-4, exit 7 westbound; exit 7A eastbound, just se. Ext corridors. Pets: Accepted.
[X] [🖬]

◆◆◆ Residence Inn by Marriott Sabal Park [SH]
(813) 627-8855. $132-$186. 9719 Princess Palm Ave. I-75, exit 260 southbound; exit 260B northbound, just w on SR 574 (Dr. Martin Luther King Jr Blvd), just s on Falkenburg Rd, then 0.4 mi w; in Sabal Corporate Center. Int corridors. Pets: Accepted.
[ASK] [SD] [X] [&M] [🖬] [≈] [X]

◆◆◆ Seminole Hard Rock Hotel and Casino Tampa [LH]
(813) 627-7625. $299-$399. 5223 N Orient Rd. I-4, exit 6, just w. Int corridors. Pets: Accepted.
[SAVE] [SD] [X] [&M] [≈] [II] [≈] [X]

◆◆◆ Sheraton Suites Tampa Airport [LH]
(813) 873-8675. $305. 4400 W Cypress St. I-275, exit 40A southbound, just nw on CR 587; exit 39A northbound, just nw on Westshore Blvd (CR 587), then just e. Int corridors. Pets: Accepted.
[SAVE] [SD] [X] [🖬] [≈] [II] [≈]

◆◆ Tahitian Inn [SH]
(813) 877-6721. Call for rates. 601 S Dale Mabry Hwy. I-275, exit 41A, 1.1 mi s. Ext/int corridors. Pets: Accepted.
[SAVE] [X] [🖬] [≈] [II] [≈]

◆◆◆ The Westin Tampa Harbour Island [LH]
(813) 229-5000. Call for rates. 725 S Harbour Island Blvd. I-275, exit 44, just e, then 2 mi s on Tampa St, follow signs to Convention Center and Harbour Island. Int corridors. Pets: Accepted.
[SAVE] [X] [&M] [🖬] [≈] [II] [≈] [X]

TEMPLE TERRACE

◆◆ Extended StayAmerica–Temple Terrace [SH]
(813) 989-2264. $72-$100. 12242 Morris Bridge Rd. I-75, exit 266, just w on Fletcher Ave (CR 582A). Int corridors. Pets: Other species. $75 one-time fee/pet. Service with restrictions.
[ASK] [SD] [X] [&M] [🖬] [≈]

END METROPOLITAN AREA

TITUSVILLE

◆◆ Best Western Space Shuttle Inn Kennedy Space Center [SH]
(321) 269-9100. $69-$149. 3455 Cheney Hwy. I-95, exit 215 (SR 50), just e. Ext corridors. Pets: Accepted.
[ASK] [SD] [X] [🖬] [≈] [II] [≈] [X]

◆◆ Comfort Inn Titusville [SH]
(321) 269-7110. $69-$250. 3655 Cheney Hwy. I-95, exit 215 (SR 50), just w. Ext corridors. Pets: Small. $10 daily fee/pet. Service with restrictions, supervision.
[SAVE] [SD] [🖬] [≈] [≈]

◆◆ Ramada Inn & Suites-Kennedy Space Center [SH]
(321) 269-5510. $79-$89. 3500 Cheney Hwy. I-95, exit 215 (SR 50), just e. Int corridors. Pets: Large. $10 daily fee/pet. Service with restrictions.
[SAVE] [SD] [X] [🖬] [≈] [II] [≈] [X]

VENICE

◆◆◆ Holiday Inn Venice [M] ✿
(941) 485-5411. $69-$179. 455 US 41 Bypass N. 0.5 mi s of jct US 41. Ext/int corridors. Pets: Small, other species. $30 one-time fee/pet. Crate.
[SAVE] [SD] [X] [&M] [🖬] [≈] [II] [≈] [X]

◆◆ Horse and Chaise Inn a Bed & Breakfast [BB]
(941) 488-2702. Call for rates. 317 Ponce de Leon. Just s of jct Venice Ave on Nassau St, just sw; downtown. Ext/int corridors. Pets: Medium. $10 one-time fee/room. Designated rooms, supervision.
[SAVE] [X] [🖬] [Z]

◆ Motel 6–364 [M]
(941) 485-8255. $55-$71. 281 US 41 Bypass N. Just n of jct Venice Ave. Ext corridors. Pets: Accepted.
[SD] [X] [≈]

WEST MELBOURNE

◆◆ Extended Stay Deluxe [SH]
(321) 733-6050. $100-$110. 1701 Evans Rd. I-95, exit 180 (US 192), 3 mi e, then 0.3 mi n. Int corridors. Pets: Other species. $75 one-time fee/pet. Service with restrictions.
[ASK] [SD] [X] [🖬] [🖬] [≈]

◆◆ Howard Johnson [SH] ✿
(321) 768-8439. $64-$100. 4431 W New Haven Ave. I-95, exit 180, just e on US 192. Ext corridors. Pets: Other species. $35 one-time fee/pet. Designated rooms, service with restrictions, supervision.
[ASK] [SD] [X] [🖬] [🖬] [≈]

WEST PALM BEACH

◆◆◆ Comfort Inn & Conference Center [M]
(561) 689-6100. $109-$199. 1901 Palm Beach Lakes Blvd. I-95, exit 71, just w. Int corridors. Pets: Accepted.
[SAVE] [SD] [X] [🖬] [🖬] [≈]

◆◆ Extended Stay Deluxe-Northpoint Corporate Park [SH]
(561) 683-5332. $100-$143. 700 Northpoint Pkwy. I-95, exit 74 (45th St), just w, then n. Int corridors. Pets: Other species. $75 one-time fee/pet. Service with restrictions.
[ASK] [SD] [X] [🖬] [🖬] [≈]

◆◆◆ Hibiscus House Bed & Breakfast [BB]
(561) 863-5633. Call for rates. 501 30th St. 1.2 mi n on Flagler Dr from jct Palm Beach Lakes Blvd, 0.3 mi w. Int corridors. Pets: Other species.
[X] [🖬] [≈]

◆◆ Red Roof Inn-West Palm Beach [M]
(561) 697-7710. Call for rates. 2421 Metrocenter Blvd E. I-95, exit 74 (45th St), just w on CR 702; in Metrocenter Corporate Park. Ext/int corridors. Pets: Accepted.
[X] [&M] [🖬] [≈]

Residence Inn by Marriott West Palm
Beach 🆂🅷
(561) 687-4747. **$175-$329.** 2461 Metrocenter Blvd. I-95, exit 74, just w
on 45th St; in Metrocenter Corporate Park. Int corridors.
Pets: Accepted.

🆂🅰🆅🅴 🆂🅾 ☒ ᕕᴹ 🅱 🔲 🏊 ☒

WINTER HAVEN

  Best Western Admiral's Inn and Conference
Center 🆂🅷
(863) 324-5950. **$98-$350.** 5665 Cypress Gardens Blvd. SR 540, 3 mi
e of jct US 17; 3.9 mi w of jct US 27. Ext/int corridors. **Pets:** Accepted.

🆂🅰🆅🅴 🆂🅾 ☒ 🅱 🔲 🍽 🏊 ☒

GEORGIA

ADAIRSVILLE

Comfort Inn 🆂🅷
(770) 773-2886. **$50-$90.** 107 Princeton Blvd. I-75, exit 306, just w. Ext corridors. **Pets:** Small. $10 daily fee/pet. Service with restrictions, supervision.

Ramada Limited 🆂🅷 ☙
(770) 769-9726. **$65-$130.** 500 Georgia North Cir. I-75, exit 306, 0.3 mi w. Ext corridors. **Pets:** Large. $10 daily fee/pet. Designated rooms, service with restrictions, supervision.

ADEL

Hampton Inn 🆂🅷
(229) 896-3099. **$86-$90.** 1500 W 4th St. I-75, exit 39, just w. Int corridors. **Pets:** Medium. $10 daily fee/pet. Designated rooms, service with restrictions, supervision.

Super 8 Motel I-75 🅼
(229) 896-2244. **Call for rates.** 1103 W 4th St. I-75, exit 39, just e. Ext corridors. **Pets:** Small. $10 daily fee/pet. Service with restrictions.

ALBANY

Jameson Inn 🆂🅷
(229) 435-3737. **$63-$95.** 2720 Dawson Rd. 0.5 mi s of jct US 82 and SR 520. Ext corridors. **Pets:** Small. $15 daily fee/room. Service with restrictions, crate.

Quality Inn-Merry Acres 🅼
(229) 435-7721. **$65-$85.** 1500 Dawson Rd. 3.3 mi w. Ext corridors. **Pets:** Small, dogs only. $10 daily fee/room. Service with restrictions, crate.

Wingate Inn 🆂🅷
(229) 883-9800. **Call for rates.** 2735 Dawson Rd. Jct US 82 and SR 520, 0.4 mi s. Int corridors. **Pets:** Accepted.

AMERICUS

1906 Pathway Inn Bed & Breakfast 🅱🅱
(229) 928-2078. **Call for rates.** 501 S Lee St. 0.5 mi s of US 280 on SR 377. Int corridors. **Pets:** Small. $50 deposit/room, $20 daily fee/pet. Designated rooms, supervision.

Holiday Inn Express 🆂🅷
(229) 928-5400. **Call for rates.** 1611 E Lomar St. On US 280, just w of jct US 27. Ext corridors. **Pets:** Small, other species. $15 one-time fee/pet. Service with restrictions, supervision.

Quality Inn 🆂🅷
(229) 924-4431. **$74.** 1205 Martin Luther King Jr Blvd. On US 19 S, 1 mi w of downtown. Ext corridors. **Pets:** Small. $10 daily fee/pet. Designated rooms, service with restrictions, crate.

ASHBURN

Best Western Ashburn Inn 🆂🅷
(229) 567-0080. **$59-$89.** 820 Shoney's Dr. I-75, exit 82, just w. Ext corridors. **Pets:** Small, dogs only. $10 daily fee/pet. Designated rooms, service with restrictions, supervision.

Days Inn 🆂🅷
(229) 567-3346. **Call for rates.** 823 E Washington Ave. I-75, exit 82, just w on SR 112. Ext corridors. **Pets:** Small, dogs only. $10 daily fee/pet. Designated rooms, service with restrictions, supervision.

Howard Johnson Inn 🆂🅷
(229) 567-3295. **$49-$60.** 156 Whittle Cir. I-75, exit 82, just w. Ext corridors. **Pets:** Accepted.

Super 8 Motel 🆂🅷
(229) 567-4688. **$56-$70.** 749 E Washington Ave. I-75, exit 82, just w. Ext corridors. **Pets:** Very small. $5 daily fee/pet. Service with restrictions, supervision.

ATHENS

♥♥ Best Western-Colonial Inn M
(706) 546-7311. **$59-$159.** 170 N Milledge Ave. Jct US 78 business route (Broad St), 0.5 mi w on SR 15. Ext corridors. **Pets:** Accepted.
(ASK) (S♂) ✕ 🛇 📖 🍃

♥♥♥ Comfort Inn SH
(706) 227-9700. **Call for rates.** 3980 Atlanta Hwy. SR 10 Loop, exit 3, 0.7 mi w. Int corridors. **Pets:** Accepted.
✕ 📶 🛇 📖 🍃

♥♥♥ Comfort Suites Athens SH
(706) 995-4000. **$89-$109.** 255 North Ave. SR 10 Loop, exit 11B (Dougherty St/North Ave); 1 mi n of downtown. Int corridors. **Pets:** Medium. $25 daily fee/pet. Service with restrictions, supervision.
(SAVE) (S♂) ✕ 🛇 📖 🍃

♥♥♥♥ Holiday Inn LH
(706) 549-4433. **Call for rates.** 197 E Broad St. On US 78 business route (Broad St); jct N Hull St; center. Ext/int corridors. **Pets:** Accepted.
✕ 🛇 📖 🍴 🍃

♥♥♥ Microtel Inn SH
(706) 548-5676. **$54-$130.** 1050 Ultimate Dr. Jct US 78 business route (Broad St) and SR 10 Loop, 1.4 mi e. Int corridors. **Pets:** Medium, dogs only. $25 one-time fee/room. Designated rooms, service with restrictions.
(SAVE) (S♂) ✕ 📶 🛇 📖

ATLANTA METROPOLITAN AREA

ACWORTH

♥♥♥ America's Best Inn M
(770) 974-5400. **$45-$50, 7 day notice.** 5320 Cherokee St. I-75, exit 278, just w. Ext corridors. **Pets:** Small. $5 one-time fee/pet. Service with restrictions, supervision.
(SAVE) (S♂) ✕ 🛇 🍃

♥♥♥ Best Western Acworth Inn M
(770) 974-0116. **$54-$74.** 5155 Cowan Rd. I-75, exit 277, just w. Ext corridors. **Pets:** Medium, other species. $10 daily fee/pet. Service with restrictions, supervision.
(SAVE) (S♂) ✕ 🛇 📖 🍃

♥♥ Days Inn M
(770) 974-1700. **Call for rates.** 5035 Cowan Rd. I-75, exit 277, just w. Ext corridors. **Pets:** Accepted.
(SAVE) ✕ 🛇 📖 🍃

♥♥ Deerfield Lodge M
(770) 974-0000. **Call for rates.** 6055 Lake Acworth Dr. I-75, exit 277, just w. Ext corridors. **Pets:** Accepted.
✕ 🛇

♥♥♥ Econo Lodge M
(770) 974-1922. **$55-$65.** 4980 Cowan Rd. I-75, exit 277, just w. Ext corridors. **Pets:** Accepted.
(SAVE) ✕ 🛇 📖 🍃

♥♥♥ Super 8 Motel M
(770) 966-9700. **$54-$75.** 4970 Cowan Rd. I-75, exit 277, just w. Ext corridors. **Pets:** $10 daily fee/pet. Service with restrictions, supervision.
(SAVE) ✕ 🛇 🍃

ALPHARETTA

♥♥♥ Extended StayAmerica SH
(770) 475-2676. **$58-$63.** 1950 Rock Mill Rd. SR 400, exit 9, just e. Int corridors. **Pets:** Other species. $75 one-time fee/pet. Service with restrictions.
(ASK) (S♂) (&M) 🛇 📖

♥♥♥♥ Extended Stay Deluxe
Atlanta-Alpharetta-Northpoint SH
(770) 569-1730. **$72-$79.** 3329 Old Milton Pkwy. SR 400, exit 10, just e. Int corridors. **Pets:** Other species. $75 one-time fee/pet. Service with restrictions.
(ASK) (S♂) ✕ (&M) 🛇 📖 🍃

♥♥♥♥ Homewood Suites SH
(770) 998-1622. **Call for rates.** 10775 Davis Dr. SR 400, exit 8, northwest corner. Int corridors. **Pets:** Accepted.
✕ (&M) 🛇 📖 🍃

♥♥♥ La Quinta Inn & Suites Atlanta
(Alpharetta) SH
(770) 754-7800. **$112.** 1350 North Point Dr. SR 400, exit 9, 0.5 mi e. Int corridors. **Pets:** Other species. Service with restrictions, supervision.
(SAVE) (S♂) ✕ 🛇 📖

♥♥♥ Residence Inn by Marriott SH
(770) 664-0664. **$169-$189.** 5465 Windward Pkwy W. SR 400, exit 11, 0.4 mi w. Ext/int corridors. **Pets:** Accepted.
(SAVE) (S♂) ✕ (&M) 🛇 📖 🍃 ✕

♥♥♥ Staybridge Suites SH
(770) 569-7200. **$135-$171.** 3980 North Point Pkwy. SR 400, exit 10, 0.5 mi e. Int corridors. **Pets:** Medium. $150 one-time fee/room. Service with restrictions, crate.
(ASK) (S♂) ✕ (&M) 🛇 📖 🍃

♥♥ StudioPLUS SH
(770) 475-7871. **$62-$68.** 3331 Old Milton Pkwy. SR 400, exit 10, just e. Int corridors. **Pets:** Other species. $75 one-time fee/pet. Service with restrictions.
(ASK) (S♂) ✕ (&M) 🛇 📖 🍃

♥♥♥ TownePlace Suites by Marriott SH
(770) 664-1300. **$129-$149.** 7925 S Westside Pkwy. SR 400, exit 9, 0.3 mi w. Int corridors. **Pets:** Other species. $75 one-time fee/room. Service with restrictions.
(ASK) (S♂) ✕ (&M) 🛇 📖 🍃

♥♥♥ Wingate Inn SH
(770) 649-0955. **Call for rates.** 1005 Kingswood Pl. SR 400, exit 8, 0.7 mi w. Int corridors. **Pets:** Accepted.
✕ (&M) 🛇 📖

ATLANTA

♥♥♥ Best Western Granada Suite Hotel SH
(404) 876-6100. **Call for rates.** 1302 W Peachtree St. I-75/85, exit 250 (14th St), just e, then just n on W Peachtree St to 16th St. Int corridors. **Pets:** Accepted.
✕ 🛇 📖

♥♥♥ Best Western Inn at the Peachtrees SH
(404) 577-6970. **$99-$119, 7 day notice.** 330 W Peachtree St. I-75/85, exit 248C northbound, 0.4 mi w to Peachtree St, then 0.3 mi n; exit 249C southbound, just s to Peachtree Pl, then just e. Ext/int corridors. **Pets:** Medium. $75 one-time fee/pet. Service with restrictions.
(SAVE) (S♂) ✕ 🛇 📖

♥♥ Beverly Hills Inn BB
(404) 233-8520. **$129-$249, 3 day notice.** 65 Sheridan Dr NE. Jct Piedmont and Peachtree rds, 1.1 mi s on Peachtree Rd to Sheridan Dr, then just e. Int corridors. **Pets:** Accepted.
(ASK) 🛇 📖

▼▼▼▼ **Crowne Plaza Atlanta Perimeter NW** 🔲
(770) 955-1700. **$85-$209.** 6345 Powers Ferry Rd NW. I-285, exit 22, southeast corner. Int corridors. **Pets:** Small, other species. $75 one-time fee/room. Designated rooms, service with restrictions, supervision.

🅰🆂🅺 🆂 ⊠ 🖩 🎔 🖵 🍴 ⇌

▼▼▼ **Embassy Suites Centennial Olympic Park** 🔲
(404) 223-2300. **$169-$469, 7 day notice.** 267 Marietta St. Just w of International Blvd and Marietta St. Int corridors. **Pets:** Accepted.

🅰🆂🅺 🖩 🎔 🖵 🍴 ⇌ ⊠

▼▼ **Extended StayAmerica** 🆂🅷
(770) 396-5600. **$58-$63.** 905 S Crestline Pkwy. I-285, exit 28 westbound, 0.7 mi n; exit 26 eastbound, 0.5 mi n to Hammond Dr, 0.5 mi e, then 0.3 mi n. Int corridors. **Pets:** Other species. $75 one-time fee/pet. Service with restrictions.

🅰🆂🅺 🆂 ⊠ 🖩 🎔 🖵

▼▼ **Extended StayAmerica** 🆂🅷
(404) 679-4333. **$62-$68.** 3115 Clairmont Rd. I-85, exit 91, 0.6 mi w. Int corridors. **Pets:** Other species. $75 one-time fee/pet. Service with restrictions.

🅰🆂🅺 🆂 ⊠ 🖩 🎔 🖵

▼▼▼ **Extended Stay Deluxe Atlanta-Lenox** 🆂🅷
(404) 237-9100. **$72-$79.** 3967 Peachtree Rd. I-85, exit 89, 2.8 mi w. Int corridors. **Pets:** Other species. $75 one-time fee/pet. Service with restrictions.

🅰🆂🅺 🆂 ⊠ 🎔 🖩 🖵 ⇌

▼▼▼ **Extended Stay Deluxe (Atlanta/Marietta/Powers Ferry Rd)** 🆂🅷
(770) 933-8010. **$77-$84.** 2010 Powers Ferry Rd. I-75, exit 260 (Windy Hill Rd), 0.5 mi e, then just s. Int corridors. **Pets:** Other species. $75 one-time fee/pet. Service with restrictions.

🅰🆂🅺 🆂 ⊠ 🎔 🖩 🖵 ⇌

▼▼▼ **Extended Stay Deluxe (Atlanta/Marietta/Windy Hill/Int N Pkwy)** 🆂🅷
(770) 226-0242. **$77-$84.** 2225 Interstate North Pkwy. I-75, exit 260 (Windy Hill Rd), just e to Interstate North Pkwy, then just s. Int corridors. **Pets:** Other species. $75 one-time fee/pet. Service with restrictions.

🅰🆂🅺 🆂 ⊠ 🎔 🖩 🖵 ⇌

▼▼▼ **Extended Stay Deluxe Atlanta-Perimeter** 🆂🅷
(770) 379-0111. **$72-$79.** 6330 Peachtree-Dunwoody Rd NE. I-285, exit 28 westbound, 0.7 mi n; exit 26 eastbound, 0.5 mi n to Hammond Dr, 0.5 mi e, then 0.3 mi n. Int corridors. **Pets:** Other species. $75 one-time fee/pet. Service with restrictions.

🅰🆂🅺 🆂 ⊠ 🎔 🖩 🖵 ⇌

🔺🔺🔺 ▼▼▼▼ **Four Seasons Hotel Atlanta** 🔲
(404) 881-9898. **Call for rates.** 75 14th St. I-75/85, exit 250 (14th St), 0.3 mi e. Int corridors. **Pets:** Accepted.

⊠ 🎔 🍴 ⇌ ⊠

▼▼▼▼ **The Glenn Hotel** 🆂🅷
(404) 521-2250. **$229-$439.** 110 Marietta St NW. I-75/85, exit 248C northbound, 0.8 mi w, then just n; exit 249A southbound, just s to Baker St, just w, then just n. Int corridors. **Pets:** Accepted.

🅰🆂🅺 🆂 ⊠ 🎔 🖵 🍴

🔺🔺🔺 ▼▼▼▼ **Grand Hyatt Atlanta** 🔲
(404) 365-8100. **$189-$459, 3 day notice.** 3300 Peachtree Rd. Corner of Peachtree and Piedmont rds. Int corridors. **Pets:** $100 one-time fee/room. Service with restrictions, supervision.

🆂🅰🆅🅴 ⊠ 🎔 🖩 🖵 🍴 ⇌ ⊠

🔺🔺🔺 ▼▼▼▼ **Hampton Inn-Perimeter Center** 🆂🅷
(404) 303-0014. **Call for rates.** 769 Hammond Dr. I-285, exit 26 eastbound, 0.5 mi n to Hammond Dr, then 0.5 mi e; exit 28 westbound, 0.5 mi n to Hammond Dr then 0.5 mi w. Int corridors. **Pets:** Accepted.

🆂🅰🆅🅴 ⊠ 🎔 🖩 🖵

🔺🔺🔺 ▼▼▼ **Hawthorn Suites-Atlanta NW** 🆂🅷 🐾
(770) 952-9595. **$129-$149.** 1500 Parkwood Cir. I-75, exit 260 (Windy Hill Rd), 0.5 mi e, then 0.3 mi s on Powers Ferry Rd. Ext corridors. **Pets:** Medium. $125 one-time fee/room. Service with restrictions, supervision.

🆂🅰🆅🅴 🆂 ⊠ 🖩 🖵 ⇌ ⊠

▼▼▼ **Holiday Inn Atlanta Central** 🆂🅷
(404) 321-4174. **Call for rates.** 2061 N Druid Hills Rd. I-85, exit 89, just w. Int corridors. **Pets:** Accepted.

⊠ 🎔 🖩 🖵 🍴 ⇌

▼▼▼ **Holiday Inn Select Atlanta Perimeter** 🆂🅷
(770) 457-6363. **$69-$139.** 4386 Chamblee-Dunwoody Rd. I-285, exit 30 eastbound, southwest corner; exit westbound, follow access road 1.3 mi to Chamblee-Dunwoody Rd, then just s. Int corridors. **Pets:** Medium. $75 one-time fee/room. Service with restrictions.

🅰🆂🅺 🆂 ⊠ 🎔 🖩 🖵 🍴 ⇌

▼▼ **Homestead Studio Suites Hotel-Atlanta/North Druid Hills** 🆂🅷
(404) 325-1223. **$62-$68.** 1339 Executive Park Dr NE. I-85, exit 89, just e to Executive Park Dr, then just s. Ext corridors. **Pets:** Other species. $75 one-time fee/pet. Service with restrictions.

🅰🆂🅺 🆂 ⊠ 🎔 🖩 🖵

▼▼▼ **Homestead Studio Suites Hotel-Atlanta/Perimeter** 🆂🅷
(770) 522-0025. **$53-$58.** 1050 Hammond Dr. I-285, exit 26 eastbound, 0.5 mi n to Hammond Dr, then 0.5 mi e; exit 28 westbound, just n to Hammond Dr, then just w. Ext corridors. **Pets:** Other species. $75 one-time fee/pet. Service with restrictions.

🅰🆂🅺 🆂 ⊠ 🎔 🖩 🖵

▼▼▼ **Homewood Suites-Cumberland** 🆂🅷
(770) 988-9449. **$129-$240.** 3200 Cobb Pkwy SW. I-285, exit 19 eastbound; exit 20 westbound, 0.7 mi se on US 41 (Cobb Pkwy). Ext/int corridors. **Pets:** Accepted.

🅰🆂🅺 🆂 ⊠ 🎔 🖩 🖵 ⇌ ⊠

▼▼▼ **Hotel Indigo** 🆂🅷
(404) 874-9200. **Call for rates.** 683 Peachtree St NE. I-75/85, exit 249D, 0.5 mi e to Peachtree St, then just n. Int corridors. **Pets:** Accepted.

⊠ 🖵 🍴

🔺🔺🔺 ▼▼▼▼ **InterContinental Buckhead Atlanta** 🔲
(404) 946-9000. **$219-$499.** 3315 Peachtree Rd NE. Jct Piedmont and Peachtree rds NE, just e. Int corridors. **Pets:** Accepted.

🆂🅰🆅🅴 🆂 ⊠ 🎔 🖵 🍴 ⇌ ⊠

🔺🔺🔺 ▼▼▼▼ **La Quinta Inn & Suites Atlanta (Paces Ferry/Vinings)** 🆂🅷
(770) 801-9002. **$125.** 2415 Paces Ferry Rd SE. I-285, exit 18, just w. Int corridors. **Pets:** Other species. Service with restrictions, supervision.

🆂🅰🆅🅴 🆂 ⊠ 🎔 🖩 🖵 ⇌

🔺🔺🔺 ▼▼▼▼ **La Quinta Inn & Suites Atlanta (Perimeter/Medical Center)** 🆂🅷
(770) 350-6177. **$125-$130.** 6260 Peachtree-Dunwoody. I-285, exit 28 westbound, 0.7 mi n; exit 26 eastbound, 0.5 mi n to Hammond Dr, 0.7 mi e, then 0.5 mi n. Int corridors. **Pets:** Other species. Service with restrictions, supervision.

🆂🅰🆅🅴 🆂 ⊠ 🎔 🖩 🖵 ⇌

🔺🔺🔺 ▼▼▼ **La Quinta Inn-Buckhead** 🆂🅷
(404) 321-0999. **$99-$104.** 2535 Chantilly Dr NE. I-85, exit 88 southbound; exit 86 northbound, 2 mi on Buford Hwy to Lenox Rd, then just e under highway. Int corridors. **Pets:** Other species. Service with restrictions, supervision.

🆂🅰🆅🅴 🆂 ⊠ 🎔 🖵

Omni Hotel at CNN Center LH
(404) 659-0000. **$159-$199.** 100 CNN Center. I-75/85, exit 248C northbound, 0.8 mi w; exit 249C southbound to International Blvd, then 0.5 mi w. Int corridors. **Pets:** Accepted.

Red Roof Inn-Druid Hills M
(404) 321-1653. **Call for rates.** 1960 N Druid Hills Rd. I-85, exit 89, just w. Ext corridors. **Pets:** Accepted.

Residence Inn Atlanta Midtown at 17th Street SH
(404) 745-1000. **$199-$219.** 1365 Peachtree St. I-75/85, exit 250 (14th St), 0.5 mi e to Peachtree St, then 0.3 mi n. Int corridors. **Pets:** Accepted.

Residence Inn-Buckhead/Lenox SH
(404) 467-1660. **$239-$259.** 2220 Lake Blvd. I-85, exit 89, 1.6 mi w on N Druid Hills (becomes E Roxboro), then just n on Lenox Park Blvd. Int corridors. **Pets:** Other species. Supervision.

Residence Inn by Marriott-Atlanta/Buckhead SH
(404) 239-0677. **$202-$222.** 2960 Piedmont Rd NE. Jct Piedmont and Pharr rds, just s. Ext corridors. **Pets:** Other species. $100 one-time fee/room. Service with restrictions, supervision.

Residence Inn by Marriott-Atlanta Downtown SH
(404) 522-0950. **$189-$209.** 134 Peachtree St NW. I-75/85, exit 248C northbound, 0.4 mi w, then just s; exit 249A southbound to International Blvd, just w, then just s. Int corridors. **Pets:** Small. $75 one-time fee/room. Service with restrictions, supervision.

Residence Inn by Marriott Atlanta Dunwoody SH ❖
(770) 455-4446. **$199-$219.** 1901 Savoy Dr. I-285, exit 30, just e. Ext corridors. **Pets:** Other species. $100 one-time fee/room. Service with restrictions, crate.

Residence Inn by Marriott Midtown SH
(404) 872-8885. **$204-$224.** 1041 W Peachtree St. I-75/85, exit 250 (10th St), just e to W Peachtree St, then just n; corner of 11th St. Int corridors. **Pets:** Medium, other species. $100 one-time fee/pet. Service with restrictions, supervision.

Residence Inn by Marriott-Perimeter Center SH
(404) 252-5066. **$229-$249.** 6096 Barfield Rd. I-285, exit 26 eastbound, 0.5 mi n on Glenridge to Hammond Dr, then 0.3 mi e to Barfield Rd; exit 28 westbound (Peachtree-Dunwoody Rd), 0.5 mi n to Hammond Dr, then just w. Ext corridors. **Pets:** Accepted.

The Ritz-Carlton, Buckhead LH
(404) 237-2700. **$459-$479.** 3434 Peachtree Rd NE. I-85, exit 86, 1.8 mi n on Cheshire Bridge-Lenox Rd. Int corridors. **Pets:** Small. $250 one-time fee/room. Supervision.

Sheraton Atlanta Hotel LH ❖
(404) 659-6500. **Call for rates.** 165 Courtland St. I-75/85, exit 249A southbound; exit 248C northbound, just w. Int corridors. **Pets:** Other species. Service with restrictions, supervision.

Sheraton Buckhead Hotel Atlanta LH
(404) 261-9250. **$279-$319.** 3405 Lenox Rd NE. I-85, exit 88 southbound; exit 86 northbound, 1.8 mi n. Int corridors. **Pets:** Accepted.

Sheraton Midtown Atlanta Hotel at Colony Square LH
(404) 892-6000. **Call for rates.** 188 14th St NE. I-75/85, exit 250 (14th St), 0.5 mi e. Int corridors. **Pets:** Accepted.

Sheraton Suites Galleria LH
(770) 955-3900. **$309, 3 day notice.** 2844 Cobb Pkwy SE. I-285, exit 20 westbound; exit 19 eastbound, just s on US 41 (Cobb Pkwy). Int corridors. **Pets:** Accepted.

Staybridge Suites SH
(404) 842-0800. **$169-$269.** 540 Pharr Rd. Jct Pharr and Piedmont rds, just w. Int corridors. **Pets:** $150 one-time fee/room. Service with restrictions, supervision.

Staybridge Suites-Atlanta-Mt. Vernon SH
(404) 250-0110. **$90-$229.** 760 Mt Vernon Hwy NE. I-285, exit 25, 0.8 mi n on Roswell Rd, then 1 mi e. Ext/int corridors. **Pets:** Accepted.

Staybridge Suites Atlanta Perimeter SH
(678) 320-0111. **Call for rates.** 4601 Ridgeview Rd. I-285, exit 29 (Ashford-Dunwoody Rd), 0.5 mi n, 0.5 mi w on Perimeter Center W to Crowne Pointe Dr, then just n. Int corridors. **Pets:** Accepted.

StudioPLUS-Atlanta-Vinings SH
(770) 436-1511. **$72-$79.** 2474 Cumberland Pkwy SE. I-285, exit 18, just e. Int corridors. **Pets:** Other species. $75 one-time fee/pet. Service with restrictions.

Super 8 Motel M
(404) 873-5731. **$79-$109.** 1641 Peachtree St NE. I-75/85, exit 250 (10th St), 0.3 mi e to W Peachtree St, then 1 mi n. Ext/int corridors. **Pets:** Accepted.

TownePlace Suites Atlanta Buckhead SH
(404) 949-4820. **$169-$189.** 820 Sidney Marcus Blvd. I-85, exit 86 northbound, 1.9 mi n to Sidney Marcus Blvd, then just w; exit 88 southbound, just w to Sidney Marcus Blvd, then just w. Int corridors. **Pets:** Small. $75 one-time fee/pet. Service with restrictions.

University Inn at Emory SH ❖
(404) 634-7327. **$89-$200.** 1767 N Decatur Rd. I-85, exit 91, 3.8 mi s on Clairmont Rd to N Decatur Rd, then 0.8 mi w. Ext corridors. **Pets:** Large, other species. $25 daily fee/pet. Service with restrictions.

The Westin Atlanta North LH
(770) 395-3900. **Call for rates.** 7 Concourse Pkwy. I-285, exit 28 westbound; exit 26 eastbound, 0.5 mi n to Hammond Dr, then 0.4 mi e. Int corridors. **Pets:** Accepted.

The Westin Buckhead Atlanta LH
(404) 365-0065. **$459.** 3391 Peachtree Rd NE. Adjacent to Lenox Mall. Int corridors. **Pets:** Accepted.

The Westin Peachtree Plaza LH ❖
(404) 659-1400. **$395.** 210 Peachtree St. I-75/85, exit 248C northbound, 0.4 mi w; exit 249C southbound, 0.5 mi s. Int corridors. **Pets:** Medium. Service with restrictions, supervision.

AUSTELL

▼▼▼▼ Baymont Inn-Six Flags 🆂🅗
(770) 944-2110. **Call for rates.** 7377 Six Flags Dr. I-20, exit 46 eastbound; exit 46B westbound, just n. Ext/int corridors. **Pets:** Accepted.
⊠ 🔧 🖵 🐾

COLLEGE PARK

▼▼ Econo Lodge 🅜
(404) 768-1241. **$50-$55.** 4874 Old National Hwy. I-285, exit 62, just n. Ext corridors. **Pets:** Accepted.
🅰🆂🅺 🆂🗓 ⊠ 🐾

◈◈◈ ▼▼◈◈ Holiday Inn Express-Atlanta Airport 🆂🅗
(404) 761-6500. **$79-$159.** 4601 Best Rd. I-85, exit 71, northwest corner. Int corridors. **Pets:** Medium. $50 one-time fee/pet. Service with restrictions, supervision.
🆂🅰🆅🅴 ⊠ 🐾ᴹ 🔧 🖵 🐾

◈◈◈ ▼◈◈ Quality Inn & Suites 🆂🅗
(404) 761-8371. **$74-$79.** 2451 Old National Pkwy. I-85, exit 69; I-285, exit 62, just s. Ext/int corridors. **Pets:** Accepted.
🆂🅰🆅🅴 🆂🗓 ⊠ 🐾ᴹ 🔧 🖵 🐾

▼▼ Ramada Hotel Atlanta Airport South 🆂🅗
(770) 996-4321. **$109, 7 day notice.** 1551 Phoenix Blvd. I-285, exit 60 (Riverdale Rd N), just sw. Ext/int corridors. **Pets:** Accepted.
🅰🆂🅺 🆂🗓 ⊠ 🔧 🖵 🍽 🐾

◈◈◈ ▼◈◈◈ Sheraton Gateway Hotel, Atlanta Airport 🅻🅗
(770) 997-1100. **$339.** 1900 Sullivan Rd. I-85, exit 71, just e to Sullivan Rd, then just s. Int corridors. **Pets:** Accepted.
🆂🅰🆅🅴 🆂🗓 ⊠ 🔧 🖵 🍽 🐾

◈◈◈ ▼◈◈◈ The Westin Hotel-Atlanta Airport 🅻🅗 ✿
(404) 762-7676. **$99-$279.** 4736 Best Rd. I-85, exit 71, just w, se on access road to Best Rd, then just s. Int corridors. **Pets:** Service with restrictions, crate.
🆂🅰🆅🅴 ⊠ 🐾ᴹ 🔧 🖵 🍽 🐾 ⊠

DECATUR

▼▼ America's Best Inn & Suites 🅜
(404) 286-2500. **$65.** 4095 Covington Hwy. I-285, exit 43, just w. Ext corridors. **Pets:** $10 daily fee/pet. Service with restrictions, supervision.
🅰🆂🅺 🆂🗓 ⊠ 🐾ᴹ 🔧 🐾

▼▼▼▼ Holiday Inn Select 🆂🅗
(404) 371-0204. **Call for rates.** 130 Clairmont Ave. Downtown. Int corridors. **Pets:** Accepted.
⊠ 🔧 🖵 🍽 🐾

DORAVILLE

◈◈◈ ▼▼◈◈ Holiday Inn Northwest/Doraville 🆂🅗
(770) 455-3700. **$99-$169.** 2001 Clearview Ave. I-285, exit 32, southeast corner. Int corridors. **Pets:** Accepted.
🆂🅰🆅🅴 🆂🗓 ⊠ 🔧 🖵 🍽 🐾

DOUGLASVILLE

▼▼ Days Inn 🅜
(770) 949-1499. **Call for rates.** 5489 Westmoreland Plaza. I-20, exit 37, just n. Ext corridors. **Pets:** Large. $20 daily fee/pet. Service with restrictions, supervision.
⊠ 🔧 🐾

DULUTH

▼▼▼▼ Candlewood Suites-Atlanta 🆂🅗
(678) 380-0414. **Call for rates.** 3665 Shackleford Rd. I-85, exit 104, just e, then just s. Int corridors. **Pets:** Large, other species. $150 one-time fee/room. Service with restrictions, crate.
⊠ 🐾ᴹ 🔧 🖵

▼▼ Days Inn Gwinnett Place 🆂🅗
(770) 476-8700. **Call for rates.** 1920 Pleasant Hill Rd. I-85, exit 104; northwest corner. Int corridors. **Pets:** Accepted.
⊠

▼▼▼▼ Extended Stay Deluxe 🆂🅗
(770) 623-6800. **$77-$84.** 3390 Venture Pkwy NW. I-85, exit 104, just w to Venture Pkwy, then just n. Int corridors. **Pets:** Other species. $75 one-time fee/pet. Service with restrictions.
🅰🆂🅺 🆂🗓 ⊠ 🐾ᴹ 🔧 🖵 🐾

◈◈◈ ▼▼◈◈ Hampton Inn & Suites-Gwinnett 🆂🅗 ✿
(770) 931-9800. **$89-$179.** 1725 Pineland Rd. I-85, exit 104, 0.3 mi e to Crestwood, then just s. Int corridors. **Pets:** Medium, other species. Designated rooms, service with restrictions, crate.
🆂🅰🆅🅴 🆂🗓 ⊠ 🐾ᴹ 🔧 🖵 🐾

▼▼▼▼ Holiday Inn-Gwinnett Center 🆂🅗
(770) 476-2022. **$84-$169.** 6310 Sugarloaf Pkwy. I-85, exit 108, just w. Int corridors. **Pets:** Accepted.
🅰🆂🅺 🆂🗓 ⊠ 🐾ᴹ 🔧 🖵 🍽 🐾

◈◈◈ ▼▼◈◈ La Quinta Inn Duluth 🆂🅗
(678) 957-0500. **$104-$114.** 2370 Stephen Center Dr. I-85, exit 107, just w. Int corridors. **Pets:** Other species. Service with restrictions, supervision.
🆂🅰🆅🅴 🆂🗓 ⊠ 🐾ᴹ 🔧 🖵 🐾

▼▼ Quality Inn–Gwinnett Mall 🆂🅗
(770) 623-9300. **$60-$129.** 3500 Venture Pkwy. I-85, exit 104, just w to Venture Pkwy, then just n. Ext/int corridors. **Pets:** Other species. $10 daily fee/pet. Service with restrictions, supervision.
🅰🆂🅺 🆂🗓 ⊠ 🐾ᴹ 🔧 🖵 🐾

▼▼▼▼ Residence Inn-Atlanta Gwinnett 🆂🅗
(770) 921-2202. **$179-$249.** 1760 Pineland Rd. I-85, exit 104, just e to Shackleford Rd, just s to Pineland Rd, then just e. Int corridors. **Pets:** Accepted.
🅰🆂🅺 🆂🗓 ⊠ 🐾ᴹ 🔧 🖵 🐾 ⊠

▼▼▼▼ Studio 6 #6023 🆂🅗
(770) 931-3113. **$57-$63.** 3525 Breckinridge Blvd. I-85, exit 104, just e to Breckinridge Blvd, then just n. Ext corridors. **Pets:** Other species. Service with restrictions, supervision.
🆂🗓 ⊠ 🐾ᴹ 🔧 🖵

EAST POINT

▼▼▼▼ Comfort Inn & Suites Atlanta Airport Camp Creek 🆂🅗
(404) 762-5566. **$79-$119.** 3601 N Desert Dr. I-285, exit 2, just e. Int corridors. **Pets:** Accepted.
🅰🆂🅺 🆂🗓 ⊠ 🐾ᴹ 🔧 🖵 🐾

▼▼▼▼ Crowne Plaza Hotel and Resort Atlanta Airport 🅻🅗
(404) 768-6660. **Call for rates.** 1325 Virginia Ave. I-85, exit 73 southbound; exit 73B northbound, just w. Int corridors. **Pets:** Accepted.
⊠ 🐾ᴹ 🔧 🖵 🍽 🐾

▼▼▼▼ Drury Inn & Suites-Atlanta Airport 🆂🅗
(404) 761-4900. **$93-$160.** 1270 Virginia Ave. I-85, exit 73 southbound; exit 73A northbound, just e. Int corridors. **Pets:** Large, other species. Service with restrictions, supervision.
🅰🆂🅺 ⊠ 🐾ᴹ 🔧 🖵 🐾

◈◈◈ ▼▼◈◈ Holiday Inn Atlanta Airport North 🅻🅗
(404) 762-8411. **Call for rates.** 1380 Virginia Ave. I-85, exit 73 southbound; exit 73B northbound, just w. Ext/int corridors. **Pets:** Accepted.
🆂🅰🆅🅴 ⊠ 🐾ᴹ 🔧 🖵 🍽 🐾

▼▼ Red Roof Inn-Atlanta Airport North 🆂🅗
(404) 209-1800. **Call for rates.** 1200 Virginia Ave. I-85, exit 73 southbound; exit 73A northbound, just e. Int corridors. **Pets:** Accepted.
⊠ 🐾ᴹ 🔧 🐾

◆◆◆◆ Wellesley Inn (Atlanta/Hartsfield Int'l Airport) SH
(404) 762-5111. **$99-$110.** 1377 Virginia Ave. I-85, exit 73 southbound; exit 73B northbound, just w. Int corridors. **Pets:** Small. $10 daily fee/pet. Service with restrictions, supervision.
SAVE ✕ 🛏 🖵 🍴 ⊃

FOREST PARK

◆◆ Days Inn-Airport East M
(404) 768-6400. **$53-$95.** 5116 Hwy 85. I-75, exit 237A southbound; exit 237 northbound, 0.5 mi w. **Pets:** Other species. $25 deposit/room, $25 daily fee/pet. No service, supervision.
✕ 🛏 🖵 ⊃

◆◆ Super 8 Motel M
(404) 363-8811. **Call for rates.** 410 Old Dixie Way. I-75, exit 235, just e. Ext corridors. **Pets:** Small. $10 daily fee/pet. Service with restrictions, supervision.
✕ 🛏 ⊃

HAPEVILLE

◆◆◆◆ Hilton Atlanta Airport LH
(404) 767-9000. **Call for rates.** 1031 Virginia Ave. I-85, exit 73 southbound; exit 73A northbound, just e. Int corridors. **Pets:** Accepted.
SAVE ✕ 🛏 🖵 🍴 ⊃ ✕

◆◆◆◆ Residence Inn Atlanta Airport SH
(404) 761-0511. **$249-$269.** 3401 International Blvd. I-85, exit 73 southbound; exit 73A northbound, 0.5 mi e to International Blvd, then just n. Ext/int corridors. **Pets:** Other species. $75 one-time fee/room.
SAVE ✕ 🛏 🖵 ⊃ ✕

JONESBORO

◆◆◆◆ Holiday Inn Atlanta South Jonesboro LH
(770) 968-4300. **$75-$175.** 6288 Old Dixie Hwy. I-75, exit 235, just w. Int corridors. **Pets:** $15 daily fee/room. Service with restrictions, supervision.
SAVE ✕ 🛏 🖵 🍴 ⊃

KENNESAW

◆◆◆ Best Western Kennesaw Inn SH
(770) 424-7666. **$79-$99.** 3375 Busbee Dr. I-75, exit 271, just e. Ext corridors. **Pets:** Large, other species. $10 daily fee/pet. Designated rooms, no service, supervision.
SAVE ✕ 🛏 🖵 ⊃

◆◆ Extended StayAmerica SH
(770) 422-1403. **$53-$58.** 3000 George Busbee Pkwy. I-75, exit 269, just e to George Busbee Pkwy, then 0.8 mi n. Int corridors. **Pets:** Other species. $75 one-time fee/pet. Service with restrictions.
ASK ✕ 🛏 🖵

◆◆◆ Green Roof Inn & Suites M
(770) 529-3370. **$45-$120.** 3027 Cobb Pkwy NW. I-75, exit 271, 2.5 mi w, then 2.2 mi n on US 41. Ext corridors. **Pets:** Other species. $10 daily fee/pet. Service with restrictions, supervision.
SAVE ✕ 🛏 🖵

◆◆◆◆ La Quinta Inn SH
(770) 426-0045. **$100.** 2625 George Busbee Pkwy. I-75, exit 269, just e to George Busbee Pkwy, then just n. Int corridors. **Pets:** Other species. Service with restrictions, supervision.
SAVE ✕ 🛏 🖵 ⊃

◆◆ Red Roof Inn-Town Center Mall M
(770) 429-0323. **Call for rates.** 520 Roberts Ct NW. I-75, exit 269, just e. Ext corridors. **Pets:** Accepted.
✕ 🖵

◆◆◆◆ Residence Inn by Marriott Town Center SH
(770) 218-1018. **$199-$219.** 3443 Busbee Dr. I-75, exit 271, just e. Int corridors. **Pets:** Accepted.
SAVE ✕ 🛏 🖵 ⊃ ✕

◆◆ StudioPLUS SH
(770) 425-6101. **$53-$58.** 3316 Busbee Dr. I-75, exit 271, just e to Busbee Dr, then just s. Int corridors. **Pets:** Other species. $75 one-time fee/pet. Service with restrictions.
ASK ✕ 🛏 🖵 ⊃

◆◆◆◆ TownePlace Suites by Marriott SH
(770) 794-8282. **$139-$159.** 1074 Cobb Place Blvd NW. I-75, exit 269, 1.1 mi w to Second Cobb Place Blvd entrance. Int corridors. **Pets:** Accepted.
SAVE ✕ 🛏 🖵 ⊃

◆◆ Travelodge M
(770) 590-0519. **$49-$79.** 1460 George Busbee Pkwy. I-75, exit 273, just e. Ext corridors. **Pets:** Accepted.
ASK ✕ 🛏 🖵 ⊃

LAWRENCEVILLE

◆◆◆ Days Inn M
(770) 995-7782. **$70-$121.** 731 Duluth Hwy. Jct SR 316, just e on SR 120. Ext corridors. **Pets:** $20 one-time fee/pet. Service with restrictions, crate.
SAVE ✕ 🛏

◆◆ Extended StayAmerica Atlanta-Lawrenceville SH
(770) 962-5660. **$53-$58.** 474 W Pike St. SR 316, exit SR 120, 0.8 mi s. Ext corridors. **Pets:** Other species. $75 one-time fee/pet. Service with restrictions.
ASK ✕ 🛏 🖵

◆◆◆ Hampton Inn SH
(770) 338-9600. **Call for rates.** 1135 Lakes Pkwy. I-85, exit 106 northbound, 4 mi e to Riverside Pkwy, then just n; exit 115 southbound, 4.4 mi s on SR 20 to SR 316, then 1.1 mi w. Int corridors. **Pets:** Other species. $50 one-time fee/room. No service, supervision.
✕ 🛏 🖵 ⊃

LITHONIA

◆◆ Red Roof Inn SH
(800) 843-7663. **Call for rates (no credit cards).** 5400 Fairington Rd. I-20, exit 71, just s to Fairington Rd, then just ne. Int corridors. **Pets:** Accepted.
✕

MARIETTA

◆◆◆ Comfort Inn-Marietta SH
(770) 952-3000. **$69-$99.** 2100 Northwest Pkwy. I-75, exit 261, 0.3 mi w to Franklin Rd, then just s. Ext corridors. **Pets:** Medium. $25 one-time fee/pet. Service with restrictions, crate.
ASK ✕ 🛏 🖵 ⊃

◆◆◆ Drury Inn & Suites-Atlanta Northwest SH
(770) 612-0900. **$86-$126.** 1170 Powers Ferry Pl. I-75, exit 261, just e. Int corridors. **Pets:** Large, other species. Service with restrictions, supervision.
ASK ✕ 🛏 🖵 ⊃

◆◆◆ Econo Lodge Northwest SH
(770) 952-0052. **$50-$100.** 1940 Leland Dr. I-75, exit 260, just e, then 0.3 mi n. Ext/int corridors. **Pets:** Small. $5 daily fee/pet. No service, crate.
SAVE ✕ 🛏 🖵

◆◆ **Extended StayAmerica Atlanta-Marietta Windy Hill** SH
(770) 690-9477. **$58-$63.** 1967 Leland Dr. I-75, exit 260, just e to Leland Dr, then just n. Int corridors. **Pets:** Other species. $75 one-time fee/pet. Service with restrictions.
A$K S🐾 ✕ 🔥M 🛏 🖥

◆◆◆ **Homestead Studio Suites Hotel-Atlanta-Marrietta-Powers Ferry Rd** SH
(770) 303-0043. **$67-$74.** 2239 Powers Ferry Rd. I-285, exit 22, just n. Int corridors. **Pets:** Other species. $75 one-time fee/pet. Service with restrictions.
A$K S🐾 ✕ 🔥M 🛏 🖥

◉ ◆◆◆◆ **Hyatt Regency Suites Perimeter Northwest** LH
(770) 956-1234. **$108-$283, 3 day notice.** 2999 Windy Hill Rd. I-75, exit 260, 0.5 mi e at Powers Ferry Rd. Int corridors. **Pets:** Small, other species. $50 one-time fee/room. Service with restrictions, crate.
SAVE ✕ 🛏 🖥 🍴 ≈

◉ ◆◆◆ **La Quinta Inn** SH
(770) 951-0026. **$85-$94.** 2170 Delk Rd. I-75, exit 261, 0.3 mi w. Ext/int corridors. **Pets:** Other species. Service with restrictions, supervision.
SAVE S🐾 ✕ 🛏 🖥 ≈

◉ ◆ **Masters Inn Marietta** M
(770) 951-2005. **$45-$52, 5 day notice.** 2682 Windy Hill Rd. I-75, exit 260, just w to Circle 75 Pkwy, then just s. Ext corridors. **Pets:** Small. $20 one-time fee/pet. Service with restrictions, crate.
SAVE S🐾 ✕ 🛏

MORROW

◉ ◆◆ **Best Western Southlake Inn** SH
(770) 961-6300. **$54-$139.** 6437 Jonesboro Rd. I-75, exit 233, just e. Ext corridors. **Pets:** Small. $10 daily fee/pet. Designated rooms, service with restrictions, crate.
A$K S🐾 ✕ 🛏 🖥 ≈

◆◆◆◆ **Drury Inn & Suites-Atlanta South** SH
(770) 960-0500. **$81-$141, 3 day notice.** 6520 S Lee St. I-75, exit 233, just e. Int corridors. **Pets:** Large, other species. Service with restrictions, supervision.
A$K ✕ 🔥M 🛏 🖥 ≈

◆◆ **Extended StayAmerica-Atlanta-Morrow** SH
(770) 472-0727. **$72-$79.** 2265 Mt. Zion Pkwy. I-75, exit 231, just w, then 1.3 mi s. Int corridors. **Pets:** Other species. $75 one-time fee/pet. Service with restrictions.
A$K S🐾 ✕ 🛏 🖥

◆◆◆ **Hampton Inn Southlake** SH
(770) 968-8990. **Call for rates.** 1533 Southlake Pkwy. I-75, exit 233, just w, then just s. Int corridors. **Pets:** Accepted.
✕ 🛏 🖥 ≈

◆◆ **Red Roof Inn-South** M
(770) 968-1483. **Call for rates.** 1348 Southlake Plaza Dr. I-75, exit 233, just e to Southlake Plaza Dr, then just n. Ext corridors. **Pets:** Accepted.
✕ 🛏

◉ ◆◆◆ **Sleep Inn** SH
(770) 472-9800. **$60-$70.** 2185 Mt Zion Pkwy. I-75, exit 231, just w to Mt Zion Pkwy, then just s. Int corridors. **Pets:** $10 daily fee/pet. Designated rooms, service with restrictions, supervision.
SAVE S🐾 ✕ 🔥M 🛏 🖥 ≈

NORCROSS

◉ ◆◆◆ **Best Western Diplomat Inn** SH
(770) 448-8686. **$55-$99, 7 day notice.** 6187 Dawson Blvd. I-85, exit 99, just e to McDonough Dr, then just s. Ext corridors. **Pets:** Accepted.
SAVE S🐾 ✕ 🛏 🖥 ≈

◆◆ **Comfort Inn & Suites** SH 🐾
(770) 662-8175. **$80-$90.** 5985 Oakbrook Pkwy. I-85, exit 99, 0.5 mi e to Live Oak Pkwy, 0.8 mi n, then w. Int corridors. **Pets:** Medium, other species. $20 one-time fee/room. Service with restrictions, supervision.
A$K S🐾 ✕ 🛏 ≈

◉ ◆◆ **Comfort Inn & Suites** SH
(770) 263-8883. **$79-$99.** 5200 Peachtree Industrial Blvd. I-285, exit 31B, 5.5 mi n; I-85, exit 99, 4 mi w to Peachtree Industrial Blvd, then 1.5 mi n. Int corridors. **Pets:** $20 daily fee/pet. Service with restrictions, supervision.
SAVE S🐾 ✕ 🔥M 🛏 🖥 ≈

◆◆ **Days Inn & Suites** SH
(770) 416-9021. **Call for rates.** 5385 Peachtree Industrial Blvd. I-285, exit 31B, 5.5 mi n; I-85, exit 99, 4 mi w to Peachtree Industrial Blvd, then 1.5 mi n. Int corridors. **Pets:** Small. $20 daily fee/pet. Service with restrictions, supervision.
✕ 🔥M 🛏 🖥 ≈

◉ ◆◆ **Days Inn Atlanta NE** M
(770) 368-0218. **$54-$60.** 5990 Western Hills Dr. I-85, exit 99, 0.8 mi w to Norcross Tucker Rd to Western Hills Dr, then just n. Ext corridors. **Pets:** Accepted.
SAVE S🐾 ✕ 🛏 🖥 ≈

◆◆◆ **Drury Inn & Suites-Atlanta Northeast** SH
(770) 729-0060. **$66-$133.** 5655 Jimmy Carter Blvd. I-85, exit 99, just w. Int corridors. **Pets:** Large, other species. Service with restrictions, supervision.
A$K ✕ 🔥M 🛏 🖥 ≈

◆◆ **Extended StayAmerica Atlanta-Jimmy Carter Blvd.** SH
(770) 446-9245. **$48-$53.** 6295 Jimmy Carter Blvd. I-85, exit 99, 2.5 mi w. Ext corridors. **Pets:** Other species. $75 one-time fee/pet. Service with restrictions.
A$K S🐾 ✕ 🔥M 🛏 🖥

◆◆ **Extended StayAmerica Atlanta-Norcross** SH
(770) 729-8100. **$53-$58.** 200 Lawrenceville St. Downtown; behind post office. Ext corridors. **Pets:** Other species. $75 one-time fee/pet. Service with restrictions.
A$K S🐾 ✕ 🔥M 🛏 🖥

◉ ◆◆◆ **GuestHouse Inn** SH
(770) 564-0492. **$49-$89.** 2050 Willowtrail Pkwy. I-85, exit 101, just e. Ext corridors. **Pets:** Small. $10 daily fee/pet. Designated rooms, service with restrictions, supervision.
SAVE S🐾 ✕ 🛏 🖥 ≈

◆◆◆◆ **Hilton Atlanta Northeast** LH
(770) 447-4747. **Call for rates.** 5993 Peachtree Industrial Blvd. I-285, exit 31B, 4.5 mi ne. Int corridors. **Pets:** Small. $50 one-time fee/pet. Service with restrictions, supervision.
✕ 🔥M 🛏 🖥 🍴 ≈ ✕

◆◆ **Homestead Studio Suites Hotel-Atlanta/Peachtree Corners** SH
(770) 449-9966. **$53-$58.** 7049 Jimmy Carter Blvd. I-85, exit 99, 4 mi n; I-285, exit 31B, 4 mi n. Ext corridors. **Pets:** Other species. $75 one-time fee/pet. Service with restrictions.
A$K S🐾 ✕ 🔥M 🛏

◆◆◆◆ **Homewood Suites by Hilton** SH
(770) 448-4663. **Call for rates.** 450 Technology Pkwy. I-85, exit 99, 4 mi w to Peachtree Industrial Blvd, 0.4 mi n, w on Holcomb Bridge Rd, then 2 blks n on Peachtree Pkwy; I-285, exit 31B, 5 mi n on SR 141. Ext/int corridors. **Pets:** Other species. $100 one-time fee/room. Service with restrictions, supervision.
✕ 🔥M 🛏 🖥 ≈ ✕

◇◇◇ ▼▼▼▼ La Quinta Inn 🆂🅷
(770) 368-9400. **$79-$89.** 5945 Oakbrook Pkwy. I-85, exit 99, 0.5 mi e to Live Oak Pkwy, then 0.8 mi w. Int corridors. **Pets:** Other species. Service with restrictions, supervision.
🆂🅰🆅🅴 Ⓢ💰 ⊠ 🔌 ▣ 🏊

▼▼ Ramada Limited 🆂🅷
(770) 449-7322. **$59-$79.** 6045 Oakbrook Pkwy. I-85, exit 99, just e to Live Oak Pkwy, 1 mi n, then w. Ext/int corridors. **Pets:** Small, other species. $9 one-time fee/pet. Service with restrictions, supervision.
🅰Ⓢ🅺 Ⓢ💰 ⊠ 🔌 ▣ 🏊

▼▼ Red Roof Inn & Suites 🆂🅷
(770) 446-2882. **Call for rates.** 5395 Peachtree Industrial Blvd. I-285, exit 31B, 5.5 mi n; I-85, exit 99, 4 mi w to Peachtree Industrial Blvd, then 1.5 mi n. Int corridors. **Pets:** Accepted.
⊠ 🔌 ▣ 🏊

▼▼ Red Roof Inn-Indian Trail 🅼
(770) 448-8944. **Call for rates.** 5171 Brook Hollow Pkwy. I-85, exit 101, just w to Brook Hollow Pkwy, then just s. Ext corridors. **Pets:** Accepted.
⊠

▼▼ StudioPlus 🆂🅷
(770) 582-9984. **$62-$68.** 7065 Jimmy Carter Blvd. I-85, exit 99, 4 mi n; I-285, exit 31B, 4 mi n. Int corridors. **Pets:** Other species. $75 one-time fee/pet. Service with restrictions.
🅰Ⓢ🅺 Ⓢ💰 ⊠ 🅶🅼 🔌 ▣ 🏊

ROSWELL

▼▼ Days Inn- Perimeter 🆂🅷
(770) 587-5161. **Call for rates.** 9995 Old Dogwood Rd. SR 400, exit 7B, just w to Old Dogwood Rd, then just n. Ext corridors. **Pets:** Accepted.
⊠ 🔌 ▣ 🏊

◇◇◇ ▼▼▼▼ La Quinta Inn 🆂🅷
(770) 552-0200. **$85-$94.** 575 Old Holcomb Bridge Rd. SR 400, exit 7B, just w. Int corridors. **Pets:** Other species. Service with restrictions, supervision.
🆂🅰🆅🅴 Ⓢ💰 ⊠ 🅶🅼 🔌 ▣ 🏊

▼▼ Studio 6 #6025 🆂🅷
(770) 992-9449. **$55-$62.** 9955 Old Dogwood Rd. SR 400, exit 7B, just w. Ext corridors. **Pets:** Other species. Service with restrictions, supervision.
Ⓢ💰 🅶🅼 🔌 ▣

SMYRNA

◇◇◇ ▼▼▼▼ Holiday Inn Express Cobb Galleria 🆂🅷
(770) 435-4990. **$80.** 2855 Springhill Pkwy. I-285, exit 20 westbound; exit 19 eastbound, just n on US 41 (Cobb Pkwy), then just w on Spring Rd. Int corridors. **Pets:** $25 one-time fee/room. Service with restrictions.
🆂🅰🆅🅴 Ⓢ💰 ⊠ 🅶🅼 🔌 ▣ 🏊

▼▼ Homestead Studio Suites Hotel-Atlanta/Cumberland Mall 🆂🅷
(770) 432-4000. **$67-$74.** 3103 Sports Ave. I-285, exit 20 westbound; exit 19 eastbound, just n to Spring Rd, then 0.3 mi w. Ext corridors. **Pets:** Other species. $75 one-time fee/pet. Service with restrictions.
🅰Ⓢ🅺 Ⓢ💰 ⊠ 🅶🅼 🔌 ▣

▼▼ Red Roof Inn-North 🅼
(770) 952-6966. **Call for rates.** 2200 Corporate Plaza. I-75, exit 260, just w to Corporate Plaza, then just s. Ext corridors. **Pets:** Accepted.
⊠ 🅶🅼 🔌

◇◇◇ ▼▼▼▼ Residence Inn-Atlanta Cumberland 🆂🅷
(770) 433-8877. **$179-$199.** 2771 Cumberland Blvd. I-285, exit 20 westbound; exit 19 eastbound, just n to Spring Rd, 0.3 mi w to Cumberland Blvd, then just n. Ext corridors. **Pets:** Accepted.
🆂🅰🆅🅴 Ⓢ💰 ⊠ 🅶🅼 🔌 ▣ 🏊 ⊠

STONE MOUNTAIN

◇◇◇ ▼▼▼ Best Western Stone Mountain 🆂🅷
(770) 465-1022. **$83-$129.** 1595 E Park Place Blvd. US 78, exit E Park Place Blvd, just n. Ext corridors. **Pets:** Medium. $25 daily fee/pet. Designated rooms, service with restrictions, supervision.
🆂🅰🆅🅴 Ⓢ💰 ⊠ 🔌 ▣ 🏊

SUWANEE

▼▼ Comfort Inn 🆂🅷
(770) 945-1608. **$75-$129.** 2945 Hwy 317. I-85, exit 111, just e. Ext corridors. **Pets:** Accepted.
🅰Ⓢ🅺 Ⓢ💰 ⊠ 🔌 ▣ 🏊

TUCKER

◇◇◇ ▼▼▼▼ Atlanta Northlake TownePlace Suites 🆂🅷
(770) 938-0408. **$144-$164.** 3300 Northlake Pkwy. I-285, exit 36 southbound; exit 37 northbound, just w to Parklake Dr, 0.5 mi n, then just w. Int corridors. **Pets:** Large, other species. $75 one-time fee/room.
🆂🅰🆅🅴 Ⓢ💰 ⊠ 🅶🅼 🔌 ▣ 🏊

◇◇◇ ▼▼▼ Econo Lodge 🅼
(770) 939-8440. **Call for rates.** 1820 Mountain Industrial Blvd. US 78, exit 4, just n. Int corridors. **Pets:** Accepted.
🆂🅰🆅🅴 ⊠ 🔌 ▣

◇◇◇ ▼▼▼▼ Holiday Inn Atlanta Northlake 🆂🅷
(770) 934-6000. **$129.** 2158 Ranchwood Dr. I-285, exit 37, 0.4 mi w to Ranchwood Dr, then just n. Int corridors. **Pets:** Accepted.
🆂🅰🆅🅴 Ⓢ💰 ⊠ 🅶🅼 🔌 ▣ 🍽 🏊

◇◇◇ ▼▼▼ Masters Inn Tucker 🅼
(770) 938-3552. **$42-$75.** 1435 Montreal Rd. I-285, exit 38, just w. Ext corridors. **Pets:** Small. $10 daily fee/pet. Designated rooms, service with restrictions, supervision.
🆂🅰🆅🅴 ⊠ 🔌 🏊

▼▼ Motel 6 🅼
(770) 496-1311. **$45-$55.** 2810 Lawrenceville Hwy. I-285, exit 38, just w. Ext corridors. **Pets:** Other species. Service with restrictions, supervision.
Ⓢ💰 ⊠

◇◇◇ ▼▼▼ Quality Inn Atlanta/Northlake 🆂🅷
(770) 491-7444. **$69-$99.** 2155 Ranchwood Dr. I-285, exit 37, 0.4 mi w, then just n. Ext/int corridors. **Pets:** Small, other species. $10 daily fee/pet. Designated rooms, service with restrictions.
🆂🅰🆅🅴 Ⓢ💰 ⊠ 🅶🅼 🔌 ▣ 🏊

UNION CITY

▼▼▼ Baymont Inn & Suites 🆂🅷
(770) 969-4567. **Call for rates.** 6743 Shannon Pkwy. I-85, exit 64, 0.3 mi w, then just n. Int corridors. **Pets:** Accepted.
❌ 👪 🔋 💻 🏊

⚫⚫⚫ ▼▼▼ Microtel Inn & Suites 🆂🅷
(770) 306-3800. **Call for rates.** 6690 Shannon Pkwy. I-85, exit 64, 0.3 mi w to Shannon Pkwy, then just n. Int corridors. **Pets:** Small. $5 daily fee/pet. Service with restrictions, supervision.
❌ 👪 🔋 💻

END METROPOLITAN AREA

AUGUSTA

⚫⚫⚫ ▼▼▼ Comfort Inn Medical Center 🆂🅷
(706) 722-2224. **$75.** 1455 Walton Way. I-20, exit 199 (Washington Rd), 4.5 mi e on SR 28, then just sw on 15th St. Ext corridors. **Pets:** Large, other species. $25 one-time fee/room. Designated rooms, service with restrictions, supervision.
🆂🅰🆅🅴 🆂🅳 ❌ 🔋 💻 🏊

▼▼▼▼ DoubleTree Hotel Augusta 🆂🅷
(706) 855-8100. **Call for rates.** 2651 Perimeter Pkwy. I-520, exit 1C (Wheeler Rd), just w to Perimeter Pkwy, then just n. Int corridors. **Pets:** Other species. $25 one-time fee/room. No service, supervision.
❌ 👪 🔋 💻 🏊 ❌

▼▼▼ Holiday Inn Gordon Highway at Bobby Jones 🆂🅷
(706) 737-2300. **$110.** 2155 Gordon Hwy. I-520, exit 3A (US 78), just w. Ext corridors. **Pets:** Accepted.
🅰🆂🅺 🆂🅳 ❌ 🔋 💻 🍴 🏊

▼▼ Jameson Suites 🆂🅷
(706) 733-4656. **Call for rates.** 1062 Claussen Rd. I-20, exit 200 west-bound, 0.4 mi sw on service road; exit 199 eastbound, 0.3 mi w, then 0.6 mi nw on service road. Int corridors. **Pets:** Accepted.
❌ 👪 🔋 💻 🏊

⚫⚫⚫ ▼▼▼▼ La Quinta Inn Augusta 🆂🅷
(706) 733-2660. **$89-$95.** 3020 Washington Rd. I-20, exit 199 (Washington Rd), just w. Ext/int corridors. **Pets:** Other species. Service with restrictions, supervision.
🆂🅰🆅🅴 🆂🅳 ❌ 👪 🔋 💻 🏊

⚫⚫⚫ ▼▼▼▼ Marriott Augusta Hotel & Suites 🅻🅷
(706) 722-8900. **$159-$179.** 2 10th St. I-20, exit 200 (River Watch Pkwy), 5.4 mi se, then just n; downtown. Int corridors. **Pets:** Medium. $25 one-time fee/room. Service with restrictions, crate.
🆂🅰🆅🅴 🆂🅳 ❌ 👪 🔋 💻 🍴 🏊 ❌

⚫⚫⚫ ▼▼▼▼ The Partridge Inn 🆂🅷 🐾
(706) 737-8888. **$119-$199.** 2110 Walton Way. 1.3 mi w off 15th St. Int corridors. **Pets:** Medium, dogs only. $250 deposit/room, $50 one-time fee/room. Service with restrictions, supervision.
🆂🅰🆅🅴 ❌ 🔋 💻 🍴 🏊

BAINBRIDGE

▼▼ ▼▼ Jameson Inn 🆂🅷
(229) 243-7000. **$75-$100.** 1403 Tallahassee Hwy. Just s of US 84 Bypass on US 27. Ext corridors. **Pets:** Small. $15 daily fee/room. Service with restrictions, crate.
🅰🆂🅺 🆂🅳 ❌ 🔋 💻 🏊

BARNESVILLE

⚫⚫⚫ ▼▼ Country Hearth Inn 🆂🅷
(770) 358-0967. **$55-$95.** 648 Hwy 341 S. Jct US 341 and 41, 2.3 mi s. Int corridors. **Pets:** Accepted.
🆂🅰🆅🅴 🆂🅳 ❌ 🔋 💻

BLUE RIDGE

⚫⚫⚫ ▼▼▼ Douglas Inn & Suites 🅼
(706) 258-3600. **$45-$69.** 1192 Windy Ridge Rd. Just off SR 515 and US 76. Ext corridors. **Pets:** Accepted.
🆂🅰🆅🅴 🆂🅳 ❌ 🔋 💻 🏊

BRASELTON

⚫⚫⚫ ▼▼▼ Chateau Elan Lodge by Holiday Inn Express 🆂🅷 ❄
(770) 867-8100. **$90-$130.** 2069 Hwy 211 NW. I-85, exit 126, just w. Int corridors. **Pets:** $20 one-time fee/room. Service with restrictions, supervision.
🅰🆂🅺 🆂🅳 💻 🏊

BREMEN

⚫⚫⚫ ▼▼▼ Days Inn 🆂🅷 ❄
(770) 537-4646. **Call for rates.** 35 Price Creek Rd. I-75, exit 11, just n. Ext corridors. **Pets:** Medium, dogs only. $10 daily fee/pet. Service with restrictions, supervision.
🆂🅰🆅🅴 ❌ 🔋 💻 🏊

⚫⚫⚫ ▼▼▼▼ Holiday Inn Express Hotel & Suites 🆂🅷
(770) 537-3770. **$94-$99.** 125 US Hwy 27 Bypass. I-20, exit 11, just n. Int corridors. **Pets:** Accepted.
🆂🅰🆅🅴 🆂🅳 ❌ 👪 🔋 💻 🏊

BRUNSWICK

⚫⚫⚫ ▼▼▼ Best Western Brunswick Inn 🆂🅷 🐾
(912) 264-0144. **$70-$138.** 5323 New Jesup Hwy. I-95, exit 36B (New Jesup Hwy/US 25), just nw. Ext corridors. **Pets:** Small, other species. Service with restrictions, supervision.
🆂🅰🆅🅴 🆂🅳 ❌ 🔋 💻 🍴 🏊

⚫⚫⚫ ▼▼▼▼ Clarion Inn Brunswick 🆂🅷
(912) 264-4033. **Call for rates.** 5252 New Jesup Hwy. I-95, exit 36B (New Jesup Hwy/US 25), just nw. Ext corridors. **Pets:** Accepted.
🆂🅰🆅🅴 ❌ 🔋 💻 🏊

⚫⚫⚫ ▼▼▼ Hampton Inn 🆂🅷
(912) 261-0002. **$99-$119.** 230 Warren Mason Blvd. I-95, exit 36A (New Jesup Hwy/US 25), just se, then just sw on Tourist Dr. Ext/int corridors. **Pets:** Small. $25 one-time fee/pet. Designated rooms, service with restrictions, supervision.
🆂🅰🆅🅴 🆂🅳 ❌ 🔋 💻 🏊

▼▼▼ Jameson Inn Brunswick 🆂🅷
(912) 267-0800. **Call for rates.** 661 Scranton Rd. I-95, exit 38 (Golden Isles Pkwy), 1.6 mi se, then just sw. Ext corridors. **Pets:** Small. $15 daily fee/room. Service with restrictions, crate.
❌ 🔋 💻 🏊

⚫⚫⚫ ▼▼▼ La Quinta Inn & Suites Brunswick 🆂🅷
(912) 265-7725. **$85.** 165 Warren Mason Blvd. I-95, exit 36A (New Jesup Hwy/US 25), just se, then sw on Tourist Dr. Int corridors. **Pets:** Other species. Service with restrictions, supervision.
🆂🅰🆅🅴 🆂🅳 ❌ 🔋 💻 🏊

⚫⚫⚫ ▼▼ Super 8 Motel 🆂🅷
(912) 264-8800. **$45-$125.** 5280 New Jesup Hwy. I-95, exit 36B (New Jesup Hwy/US 25), just nw. Int corridors. **Pets:** Medium. $10 daily fee/pet. Service with restrictions, supervision.
🆂🅰🆅🅴 🆂🅳 ❌ 🔋

BYRON

Best Western Inn and Suites 🆂🅷 🐾
(478) 956-3056. **$59-$69.** 101 Dunbar Rd. I-75, exit 149 (SR 49), just ne. Ext corridors. **Pets:** Medium. $10 daily fee/pet. Designated rooms, service with restrictions, crate.

Comfort Inn 🆂🅷
(478) 956-1600. **$70-$115.** 115 Chapman Rd. I-75, exit 149 (SR 49), just sw, then n. Ext corridors. **Pets:** Accepted.

CALHOUN

Americas Best Inn Ⓜ
(706) 625-1511. **$45-$60.** 1438 US Hwy 41 N. I-75, exit 318, just w. Ext corridors. **Pets:** Accepted.

Comfort Inn 🆂🅷
(706) 629-8271. **$60-$70.** 742 Hwy 53 SE. I-75, exit 312, just w. Ext corridors. **Pets:** Large, other species. $10 daily fee/pet, $20 one-time fee/pet. Service with restrictions, supervision.

Country Inn & Suites 🆂🅷 🐾
(706) 625-6500. **$76-$149.** 1033 Fairmount Hwy. I-75, exit 312, just e. Int corridors. **Pets:** Small. Service with restrictions, supervision.

Jameson Inn 🆂🅷
(706) 629-8133. **$68-$100.** 189 Jameson St. I-75, exit 312, just w. Ext corridors. **Pets:** Small. $15 daily fee/room. Service with restrictions, crate.

Quality Inn Calhoun 🆂🅷 🐾
(706) 629-9501. **$55-$75.** 915 Hwy 53 E SE. I-75, exit 312, just e. Ext corridors. **Pets:** Small. $6 daily fee/pet. Service with restrictions, crate.

Ramada Limited Ⓜ
(706) 629-9207. **$55-$100.** 1204 Red Bud Rd NE. I-75, exit 315, just w. Ext corridors. **Pets:** Small. $7 daily fee/pet. Service with restrictions, supervision.

Smith Motel Ⓜ 🐾
(706) 629-8427. **$30-$33.** 1437 US Hwy 41 N. I-75, exit 318, just w. Ext corridors. **Pets:** Small. $5 daily fee/pet. Designated rooms.

CARROLLTON

Jameson Inn 🆂🅷
(770) 834-2600. **$63-$95.** 700 S Park St. On US 27, just s of downtown. Ext corridors. **Pets:** Small. $15 daily fee/room. Service with restrictions, crate.

CARTERSVILLE

Best Western Garden Inn & Suites 🆂🅷
(770) 386-1569. **$59-$89.** 5663 Hwy 20 NE. I-75, exit 290, 0.3 mi e. Ext corridors. **Pets:** Small. $10 daily fee/pet. Service with restrictions, supervision.

Budget Host Inn Ⓜ
(770) 386-0350. **$44.** 851 Cass-White Rd. I-75, exit 296, just w. Ext corridors. **Pets:** Accepted.

Comfort Inn Ⓜ
(770) 387-1800. **$55-$60.** 28 SR 20 Spur. I-75, exit 290, 0.3 mi se. Ext corridors. **Pets:** $5 daily fee/pet. Service with restrictions, supervision.

Country Inn & Suites by Carlson 🆂🅷
(770) 386-5888. **$76-$149.** 43 SR 20 Spur. I-75, exit 290, 0.3 mi se. Int corridors. **Pets:** Small. Service with restrictions, supervision.

Days Inn 🆂🅷
(770) 382-1824. **$60.** 5618 Hwy 20 SE. I-75, exit 290, just w. Ext corridors. **Pets:** Other species. $10 one-time fee/pet.

Holiday Inn 🆂🅷
(770) 386-0830. **Call for rates.** 2336 Hwy 411. I-75, exit 293, southwest corner. Int corridors. **Pets:** Other species. $10 daily fee/pet. Service with restrictions, supervision.

Howard Johnson Express Ⓜ
(770) 386-0700. **Call for rates.** 25 Carson Loop NW. I-75, exit 296, just w. Ext corridors. **Pets:** Accepted.

Knights Inn Ⓜ
(770) 386-7263. **$55-$75.** 420 E Church St. I-75, exit 288, 1.5 mi w. Ext corridors. **Pets:** Medium. $10 daily fee/pet. Service with restrictions, crate.

Motel 6-4046 Ⓜ
(770) 386-1449. **Call for rates.** 5657 Hwy 20 NE. I-75, exit 290, 0.3 mi e. Ext corridors. **Pets:** Other species. Service with restrictions, supervision.

Quality Inn 🆂🅷
(770) 386-0510. **$65-$70.** 235 Dixie Ave. I-75, exit 288, 2.5 mi w. Ext corridors. **Pets:** Accepted.

Sleep Inn 🆂🅷
(770) 386-9259. **$80.** 11 Kent Dr. I-75, exit 296, just e. Ext corridors. **Pets:** Medium, other species. $10 daily fee/pet. Designated rooms, service with restrictions, supervision.

Super 8 Motel Ⓜ
(770) 382-8881. **$48-$65.** 41 SR 20 Spur SE. I-75, exit 290, 0.3 mi e. Int corridors. **Pets:** $5 daily fee/pet. Service with restrictions, supervision.

CEDARTOWN

Country Hearth Inn 🆂🅷
(770) 749-9951. **Call for rates.** 925 N Main St. 1.5 mi n on US 27. Int corridors. **Pets:** Other species. $10 daily fee/pet. Service with restrictions, supervision.

CHATSWORTH

Key West Inn Ⓜ
(706) 517-1155. **Call for rates.** 501 GI Maddox Pkwy. Jct SR 76 and US 411. Ext corridors. **Pets:** Accepted.

CLAYTON

Americas Best Value Inn 🆂🅷
(706) 782-4702. **$45-$95.** 698 Hwy 441 S. 0.8 mi s. Int corridors. **Pets:** Very small. $10 daily fee/pet. Designated rooms, service with restrictions, supervision.

Regal Inn Ⓜ
(706) 782-4269. **$37-$95.** 707 Hwy 441 S. 0.8 mi s. Ext corridors. **Pets:** Small, dogs only. $5 daily fee/pet. Designated rooms, service with restrictions, crate.

COLUMBUS

▼▼ Extended StayAmerica-Columbus-Airport 🆂🅷
(706) 653-0131. **$62-$68.** 5020 Armour Rd. I-185, exit 8, 1.5 mi e, then just 0.5 mi n. Ext corridors. **Pets:** Other species. $75 one-time fee/pet. Service with restrictions.
🅰🆂🅺 🆂🔌 ✖ 🖥 🖵

▼▼ Extended StayAmerica-Columbus-Bradley Park 🆂🅷
(706) 653-9938. **$72-$79.** 1721 Rollins Way. US 80 and SR 22, exit 3A, just s to Whittlesey Rd, 0.3 mi e to Rollins Way, then just n. Int corridors. **Pets:** Other species. $75 one-time fee/pet. Service with restrictions.
🅰🆂🅺 🆂🔌 ✖ 🖥 🖵

▼▼ Howard Johnson Express Inn & Suites 🆂🅷
(706) 322-6641. **$65-$99.** 1011 Veterans Pkwy. I-185, exit 7 southbound; exit 7A northbound, 1.2 mi w to Veterans Pkwy, then 3.2 mi s. Ext corridors. **Pets:** $15 one-time fee/room. Service with restrictions, crate.
🅰🆂🅺 🆂🔌 ✖ 🖥 🍴 ⤫

▲▲▲ ▼▼ La Quinta Inn Columbus Midtown 🆂🅷
(706) 568-1740. **$92-$129.** 3201 Macon Rd. I-185, exit 6, just w. Ext/int corridors. **Pets:** Other species. Service with restrictions, supervision.
🆂🅰🆅🅴 🆂🔌 ✖ 🖥 🖵 ⤫

▲▲▲ ▼▼ La Quinta Inn Columbus State University 🆂🅷
(706) 323-4344. **$99-$105.** 2919 Warm Springs Rd. I-185, exit 7 southbound; exit 7A northbound, just e. Int corridors. **Pets:** Other species. Service with restrictions, supervision.
🆂🅰🆅🅴 🆂🔌 ✖ 🖥 🖵 ⤫

▼ Motel 6 #58 🅼
(706) 687-7214. **$49-$59.** 3050 Victory Dr. I-185, exit 1B, 3 mi w. Ext corridors. **Pets:** Other species. Service with restrictions, supervision.
🆂🔌 ✖ ⤫

◆◆◆ ◆◆◆ Rothschild-Pound House Inn 🅱🅱
(706) 322-4075. **$185-$350.** 201 7th St. Jct US 27 (Veterans Pkwy/7th St), just w; downtown. Ext/int corridors. **Pets:** Accepted.
🅰🆂🅺 ✖ 🖥 🍴 ⤫ ✆

COMMERCE

▲▲▲ ▼▼ Comfort Inn 🅼
(706) 335-9001. **$70-$150.** 165 Eisenhower Dr. I-85, exit 149, just ne. Ext corridors. **Pets:** Small. $10 daily fee/pet. Service with restrictions, supervision.
🆂🅰🆅🅴 🆂🔌 ✖ 🖥 🖵 ⤫

▼▼ Howard Johnson Inn & Suites 🅼
(706) 335-5581. **$53-$140.** 148 Eisenhower Dr. I-85, exit 149, just ne. Ext corridors. **Pets:** Medium. $10 one-time fee/pet. Service with restrictions, supervision.
🅰🆂🅺 🆂🔌 ✖ 🖥 🖵 ⤫

▼▼ Super 8 Motel 🅼
(706) 336-8008. **$49-$140.** 152 Eisenhower Dr. I-85, exit 149, just ne. Ext corridors. **Pets:** Medium. $10 one-time fee/pet. Service with restrictions, supervision.
✖

CONYERS

▲▲▲ ▼▼▼ Comfort Inn 🆂🅷
(770) 760-0300. **$79-$129.** 1363 Klondike Rd. I-20, exit 80, just s. Int corridors. **Pets:** Accepted.
🆂🅰🆅🅴 🆂🔌 ✖ 🅶🅼 🖥 🖵 ⤫

▼▼▼ Hampton Inn 🆂🅷
(770) 483-8838. **$119-$129.** 1340 Dogwood Dr. I-20, exit 82, just n, then just e. Int corridors. **Pets:** Small. $25 one-time fee/room. Designated rooms, service with restrictions, supervision.
🅰🆂🅺 🆂🔌 ✖ 🅶🅼 🖥 🖵 ⤫

▼▼ Jameson Inn 🆂🅷
(770) 760-1230. **$78-$105.** 1164 Dogwood Dr. I-20, exit 82, just n, then just w. Ext corridors. **Pets:** Small. $15 daily fee/room. Service with restrictions, crate.
🅰🆂🅺 🆂🔌 ✖ 🖥 🖵 ⤫

▲▲▲ ▼▼▼ La Quinta Inn & Suites Atlanta (Conyers) 🆂🅷
(770) 918-0092. **$112-$125.** 1184 Dogwood Dr. I-20, exit 82, just n, then just w. Int corridors. **Pets:** Other species. Service with restrictions, supervision.
🆂🅰🆅🅴 🆂🔌 ✖ 🅶🅼 🖥 🖵 ⤫

CORDELE

▲▲▲ ▼▼ Best Western Colonial Inn 🆂🅷
(229) 273-5420. **$69-$72.** 1706 E 16th Ave (US 280). I-75, exit 101 (US 280), just w. Ext/int corridors. **Pets:** Accepted.
🆂🅰🆅🅴 🆂🔌 ✖ 🖥 ⤫

▲▲▲ ▼▼▼ Lake Blackshear Resort & Golf Club 🆂🅷
(229) 276-1004. **$99-$199, 7 day notice.** 2459-H US 280 W. I-75, exit 101 (US 280), 10 mi w. Ext/int corridors. **Pets:** Other species. $50 one-time fee/room. Designated rooms, supervision.
🆂🅰🆅🅴 🆂🔌 ✖ 🅶🅼 🖥 🖵 🍴 ⤫ ✖

▲▲▲ ▼▼▼ Ramada Inn 🆂🅷 🐾
(229) 273-5000. **$69-$79.** 2016 E 16th Ave (US 280). I-75, exit 101 (US 280), just e. Ext corridors. **Pets:** Medium. $10 daily fee/pet. Service with restrictions, supervision.
🆂🅰🆅🅴 🆂🔌 ✖ 🖥 ⤫

▲▲▲ ▼ Travelodge 🅼 🐾
(229) 273-2456. **$40-$55.** 1618 16th Ave E (US 280). I-75, exit 101 (US 280), just w. Ext corridors. **Pets:** Small. Designated rooms, no service, crate.
🆂🅰🆅🅴 🆂🔌 ✖ 🖥

CORNELIA

▼▼ Comfort Inn 🆂🅷
(706) 778-9573. **$79-$109.** 2965 J Warren Rd. Jct SR 365 and US 441 business route, just w. Int corridors. **Pets:** Medium. $50 one-time fee/pet. Service with restrictions, crate.
🅰🆂🅺 🆂🔌 ✖ 🅶🅼 🖥 🖵 ⤫

COVINGTON

▲▲▲ ▼▼ Best Western Executive Inn 🅼
(770) 787-4900. **$70-$150.** 10111 Alcovy Rd. I-20, exit 92, just n. Ext corridors. **Pets:** Accepted.
🅰🆂🅺 🆂🔌 ✖ 🅶🅼 🖥 🖵 ⤫

▼▼ Super 8 Motel-Covington 🅼
(770) 786-5800. **Call for rates.** 10130 Alcovy Rd. I-20, exit 92, just n. Ext corridors. **Pets:** Accepted.
✖ 🖥 🖵

DAHLONEGA

▼▼ Super 8 Motel 🅼
(706) 864-4343. **Call for rates.** 20 Mountain Dr. 0.5 mi s on US 19 and SR 60. Ext corridors. **Pets:** Accepted.
✖ 🖥 ⤫

DALLAS

▲▲▲ ▼▼ Days Inn 🅼
(770) 505-4567. **$53-$70.** 1007 Old Harris Rd. Jct Business Rt SR 6 (Atlanta Hwy). Ext corridors. **Pets:** Medium. $15 daily fee/pet. Service with restrictions, supervision.
🆂🅰🆅🅴 🆂🔌 ✖ 🅶🅼 🖥

DALTON

America's Best Inn M ❀
(706) 226-1100. **$44-$69.** 1529 W Walnut Ave. I-75, exit 333, just e. Ext corridors. **Pets:** Medium, other species. $10 daily fee/pet. Service with restrictions, crate.
SAVE SⒹ ✕ 📞 💻 🏊

Best Western Inn of Dalton SH
(706) 226-5022. **$53.** 2106 Chattanooga Rd. I-75, exit 336, just w. Ext corridors. **Pets:** Very small, dogs only. $5 one-time fee/pet. No service, supervision.
SAVE SⒹ ✕ ⓂⒸ 📞 💻 🍴 🏊

Comfort Inn & Suites SH
(706) 259-2583. **$89-$219.** 905 Westbridge Rd. I-75, exit 333, just w to Westbridge Rd, then just s. Int corridors. **Pets:** Accepted.
SAVE SⒹ ✕ ⓂⒸ 📞 💻 🏊

Econo Lodge M
(706) 278-4300. **$43-$100.** 2007 Tampico Way. I-75, exit 336, just e. Int corridors. **Pets:** Accepted.
SAVE SⒹ ✕ 📞 💻 🏊

Jameson Inn SH
(706) 281-1880. **$60-$90.** 790 College Dr. I-75, exit 333, just w, then 0.3 mi n. Ext corridors. **Pets:** Small. $15 daily fee/room. Service with restrictions, crate.
ASK SⒹ ✕ 📞 💻 🏊

Wingate Inn SH
(706) 272-9099. **Call for rates.** 715 College Dr. I-75, exit 333, just w to Holiday Dr, then 0.5 mi n. Int corridors. **Pets:** Accepted.
✕ ⓂⒸ 📞 💻 🏊

DARIEN

Comfort Inn SH
(912) 437-4200. **$85-$250.** 703 Frontage Rd. I-95, exit 49 (SR 251), just nw. Int corridors. **Pets:** Medium. $10 daily fee/pet. Service with restrictions, supervision.
SAVE SⒹ ✕ 📞 💻 🏊

Quality Inn SH
(912) 437-5373. **Call for rates.** GA Hwy 251 & I-95 exit 49. I-95, exit 49 (SR 251), just w. Int corridors. **Pets:** Accepted.
✕ 📞 💻 🏊

DAWSONVILLE

Best Western (Dawson Village Inn) SH
(706) 216-4410. **$69-$159, 7 day notice.** 76 N Georgia Ave. Jct SR 400/53, 0.5 mi s. Int corridors. **Pets:** Small, dogs only. $10 daily fee/pet. Designated rooms, service with restrictions, supervision.
SAVE SⒹ ✕ ⓂⒸ 📞 💻 🏊

Comfort Inn SH
(706) 216-1900. **$71-$134, 15 day notice.** 127 Beartooth Pkwy. Jct SR 400/53, 0.5 mi s. Int corridors. **Pets:** Accepted.
ASK SⒹ ✕ ⓂⒸ 📞 💻 🏊

Super 8 Motel SH
(706) 216-6801. **$49-$99.** 205 N 400 Center Ln. Jct SR 400/53, just n. Int corridors. **Pets:** Accepted.
ASK ✕ ⓂⒸ 📞 💻 🏊

DILLARD

Dillard House SH
(706) 746-5348. **$59-$149, 3 day notice.** 768 Franklin St. US 441, just e via Old Dillard Rd. Ext corridors. **Pets:** Medium, dogs only. $5 one-time fee/pet. Designated rooms, service with restrictions, crate.
SAVE ✕ 📞 💻 🍴 🏊 ✕

Mountain Valley Inn M
(706) 746-5373. **$40-$98.** 13 Royalty Ln. Just n of town center. Ext corridors. **Pets:** Medium. $10 daily fee/pet. Designated rooms, service with restrictions, supervision.
SAVE SⒹ ✕ 📞 💻 🏊

Ramada Limited M
(706) 746-5321. **Call for rates.** 3 Best Inn Way. Center. Ext corridors. **Pets:** Very small, dogs only. $10 daily fee/pet. Service with restrictions, supervision.
✕ 📞 💻 🏊

DOUGLAS

Jameson Inn M
(912) 384-9432. **Call for rates.** 1628 S Peterson Ave. Jct US 221/441/SR 31 and SR 206/353, just s. Ext corridors. **Pets:** Accepted.
✕ 📞 💻 🏊

DUBLIN

Best Western Executive Inn & Suites SH
(478) 275-2650. **Call for rates.** 2121 Hwy 441 S. I-16, exit 51 (US 441), 0.5 mi n. Ext corridors. **Pets:** Accepted.
✕ 📞 💻 🏊

Comfort Inn SH
(478) 274-8000. **Call for rates.** 2110 Hwy 441 S. I-16, exit 51 (US 441), 0.6 mi n. Ext corridors. **Pets:** Accepted.
✕ ⓂⒸ 📞 💻 🏊

Econo Lodge M
(478) 296-1223. **$50-$65.** 2184 Hwy 441 S. I-16, exit 51 (US 441), just n. Ext corridors. **Pets:** Accepted.
ASK SⒹ ✕ 📞

Jameson Inn M
(478) 275-3008. **$63-$95.** 100 PM Watson Dr. I-16, exit 51 (US 441), just n. Ext corridors. **Pets:** Small. $15 daily fee/room. Service with restrictions, crate.
ASK SⒹ ✕ 📞 💻 🏊

EAST ELLIJAY

Stratford Motor Inn SH
(706) 276-1080. **$60-$100.** 79 Maddox Cir. Jct Maddox Cir and SR 515; behind KFC. Ext corridors. **Pets:** Medium. $10 daily fee/pet. Designated rooms, service with restrictions, supervision.
SAVE SⒹ ✕ 📞 🏊

FITZGERALD

Country Hearth Inn SH
(229) 409-9911. **$45-$70.** 125 Stuart Way. Just n of US 319/107, just e. Int corridors. **Pets:** Medium, other species. Service with restrictions, crate.
ASK SⒹ ✕ 📞 💻

Western Motel SH
(229) 424-9500. **Call for rates.** 111 Bull Run Rd. Just n of US 319/107, on US 129. Ext corridors. **Pets:** Accepted.
✕ 📞 💻 🏊

FORSYTH

Best Western Hilltop Inn SH
(478) 994-9260. **$50-$99.** 951 Hwy 42 N. I-75, exit 188 (SR 42), just ne via Frontage Rd. Ext corridors. **Pets:** Accepted.
SAVE SⒹ ✕ 💻 🏊

Econo Lodge SH ❀
(478) 994-5603. **$44-$80.** 320 Cabiness Rd. I-75, exit 187 (SR 83), just ne. Int corridors. **Pets:** Medium. $6 daily fee/pet. No service, supervision.
SAVE SⒹ 💻 🏊

▼▼▼ Holiday Inn Express SH
(478) 994-9697. **$89-$159.** 520 Holiday Cir. I-75, exit 186 (Juliette Rd), just w, then just s on Aaron St. Int corridors. **Pets:** Accepted.

ASK SÐ ✕ ⬥M 🛆 💻

▼▼▼ Holiday Inn Forsyth SH
(478) 994-5691. **$96.** 480 Holiday Cir. I-75, exit 186 (Juliette Rd), just w, then just s on Aaron St. Ext corridors. **Pets:** Accepted.

ASK SÐ ✕ 🛆 💻 ⬥ ⬟

AAA ▼▼▼ Super 8 Motel SH
(478) 994-5101. **$58-$100.** 436 Tift College Dr. I-75, exit 186 (Juliette Rd), just w. Ext/int corridors. **Pets:** Small, dogs only. $15 daily fee/pet. Designated rooms, no service, supervision.

SAVE SÐ ✕ 🛆 ⬟

FORT OGLETHORPE

AAA ▼▼▼ Best Western Battlefield Inn SH
(706) 866-0222. **$49-$99.** 2120 Lafayette Rd. Jct US 27 and SR 2, just n. Ext corridors. **Pets:** Medium. $10 daily fee/pet. Designated rooms, service with restrictions, supervision.

SAVE SÐ ✕ 🛆 💻 ⬟

GAINESVILLE

AAA ▼▼▼ Days Inn SH
(770) 535-8100. **Call for rates.** 520 Queen City Pkwy SW. I-985, exit 20, 1.8 mi nw on SR 60/Queen City Pkwy. Ext corridors. **Pets:** Accepted.

SAVE ✕ 🛆 💻 ⬟

GOLDEN ISLES AREA

JEKYLL ISLAND

AAA ▼▼▼ Quality Inn & Suites SH
(912) 635-2202. **$90-$140.** 700 N Beachview Dr. Jct Ben Fortson Pkwy (SR 520)/Beachview Dr, 1.5 mi n. Ext corridors. **Pets:** $10 daily fee/pet. Service with restrictions, crate.

SAVE SÐ ✕ 🛆 💻 ⬟

END AREA

GREENSBORO

**▼▼▼▼ The Ritz-Carlton Lodge, Reynolds
Plantation** LH
(706) 467-0600. **$219-$319.** One Lk Oconee Tr. I-20, exit 130, 7.2 mi sw on SR 44 (Old Eatonton Rd), 1.5 mi e on Linger Longer Rd, then 2 mi ne. Ext/int corridors. **Pets:** Accepted.

ASK SÐ ✕ ⬥M 🛆 💻 ⬟ ⬟ ✕

HAHIRA

▼▼ Knights Inn M
(229) 794-8000. **Call for rates.** 1300 Georgia Hwy 122 W. I-75, exit 29, just w. Ext corridors. **Pets:** Accepted.

✕ 🛆

HARTWELL

**AAA ▼▼▼ Best Western Lake Hartwell Inn &
Suites** SH
(706) 376-4700. **$79-$189.** 1357 E Franklin St. I-85, exit 177, 2 mi on US 29 E. Int corridors. **Pets:** $20 one-time fee/pet. Service with restrictions, crate.

SAVE SÐ ✕ 🛆 💻 ⬟

▼▼ Ramada Limited M
(770) 287-3205. **Call for rates.** 766 Jesse Jewell Pkwy. I-985, exit 20, 1.9 mi w to Jesse Jewell Pkwy, then just s. Ext corridors. **Pets:** Accepted.

✕ 🛆 💻

GARDEN CITY

AAA ▼▼▼ Baymont Inn & Suites SH
(912) 964-8669. **Call for rates.** 357 Main St. I-95, exit 109 (SR 21), 6.5 mi se to Spur SR 21 (Brampton Rd), 0.3 mi n to Coastal Hwy/Main St, then just se. Int corridors. **Pets:** Small. $25 one-time fee/pet. Designated rooms, no service, supervision.

SAVE ✕ 🛆 💻 ⬟

GLENNVILLE

AAA ▼▼ Cheeri-O Inn M
(912) 654-2176. **Call for rates.** 820 Musgrove St. 0.8 mi s on US 25 and 301. Ext corridors. **Pets:** Medium. $7 daily fee/pet. Service with restrictions, supervision.

SAVE ✕ 🛆 💻

HELEN

▼▼▼ The Helendorf River Inn & Conference Center SH
(706) 878-2271. **Call for rates.** 33 Munichstrasse. SR 17 and 75; center. Ext corridors. **Pets:** Other species. $10 daily fee/pet. Designated rooms, service with restrictions, supervision.

✕ 🛆 💻 ⬟

▼▼ Kountry Peddler Tanglewood Resort Cabins CA
(706) 878-3286. **$89-$169, 14 day notice.** 3387 Hwy 356. 1 mi n on SR 75, then 3 mi ne. Ext corridors. **Pets:** Accepted.

ASK ✕ 🛆 💻 ✕

AAA ▼▼▼▼ Premier Vacation Rentals VH
(706) 348-8323. **$99-$495, 14 day notice.** 5156 Helen Hwy. 3.5 mi s on SR 75. Ext corridors. **Pets:** Dogs only. $15 daily fee/pet. Designated rooms, service with restrictions, supervision.

SAVE 🛆 💻

HIAWASSEE

▼▼ Enota B & B, Cabins & Conference Lodge CA ✤
(706) 896-9966. **$80-$165.** 1000 Hwy 180. E on US 76 to SR 75/17, 6 mi s to SR 180, then 3 mi w. Ext corridors. **Pets:** Other species. $15 daily fee/pet. No service, supervision.

✕ 🛆 💻 ✕ ⬚

HINESVILLE

Best Western Ft. Stewart Inn & Suites SH
(912) 408-4444. **$69-$179.** 773 Frank Cochran Dr. Jct SR 119/196, 1 mi sw on SR 196, then just nw. Int corridors. **Pets:** Small. $20 one-time fee/pet. Designated rooms, service with restrictions, supervision.

HIRAM

Country Inn & Suites by Carlson SH
(770) 222-0456. **Call for rates.** 70 Enterprise Path. Jct SR 92/6 and US 278, 0.3 mi w. Int corridors. **Pets:** Accepted.

HOGANSVILLE

Econo Lodge SH
(706) 637-9395. **$60-$120.** 1888 E Main St. I-85, exit 28, just w. Ext corridors. **Pets:** Small, dogs only. $10 daily fee/pet. Designated rooms, service with restrictions, supervision.

JASPER

Super 8 Motel M
(706) 253-3297. **Call for rates.** 100 Whitfield Dr. Jct SR 515/53; in Lawsons Crossing. Ext corridors. **Pets:** Accepted.

JESUP

Jameson Inn of Jesup M
(912) 427-6800. **Call for rates.** 205 N Hwy 301. Jct US 341, just n. Ext corridors. **Pets:** Small. $15 daily fee/room. Service with restrictions, crate.

KINGSLAND

Best Western/Kings Bay Inn SH
(912) 729-7666. **$58-$80.** 1353 Hwy 40 E. I-95, exit 3 (SR 40), just se. Ext corridors. **Pets:** Small, other species. $10 one-time fee/pet. Designated rooms, service with restrictions, crate.

Econo Lodge M
(912) 673-7336. **$60.** 1135 E King Ave. I-95, exit 3 (SR 40), just nw. Ext corridors. **Pets:** Small. $5 one-time fee/pet. Service with restrictions, supervision.

Jameson Inn M
(912) 729-9600. **$68-$95.** 105 May Creek Dr. I-95, exit 3 (SR 40), just w, then s at Boone Ave. Ext corridors. **Pets:** Small. $15 daily fee/room. Service with restrictions, crate.

Magnolia Inn M
(912) 576-4777. **$60-$100.** 1325 Hospitality Ave. I-95, exit 3 (SR 40), 0.5 mi e, then just n on JSJ Ave. Ext corridors. **Pets:** Small. $15 daily fee/pet. Designated rooms, service with restrictions, supervision.

Microtel Inn & Suites SH
(912) 729-1555. **$49-$79.** 1325 E King Ave. I-95, exit 3, just ne. Int corridors. **Pets:** Other species. $10 daily fee/pet. Designated rooms, service with restrictions, supervision.

Super 8 Motel M
(912) 729-6888. **$50-$100.** 120 Robert L Edenfield Dr. I-95, exit 3 (SR 40), just se. Int corridors. **Pets:** Other species. $10 daily fee/pet. Service with restrictions.

LA FAYETTE

Days Inn M
(706) 639-9362. **$50-$65.** 2209 N Main St. 2.5 mi n on US 27. Ext corridors. **Pets:** Accepted.

Key West Inn M
(706) 638-8200. **$47-$60.** 2221 N Main St. 2.5 mi n on US 27. Ext corridors. **Pets:** Large, other species. $10 daily fee/pet. Service with restrictions, supervision.

LAGRANGE

Days Inn-LaGrange/Callaway Gardens SH
(706) 882-8881. **$60.** 2606 Whitesville Rd. I-85, exit 13, just e. Ext corridors. **Pets:** Medium, other species. $10 one-time fee/pet. Service with restrictions, supervision.

Jameson Inn SH
(706) 882-8700. **$63-$95.** 110 Jameson Dr. I-85, exit 18 (Lafayette Pkwy), 0.3 mi w. Ext corridors. **Pets:** Accepted.

LAKE PARK

Quality Inn SH
(229) 559-5181. **$59-$115.** 1198 Lakes Blvd. I-75, exit 5, just e. Ext corridors. **Pets:** Large, other species. $12 daily fee/pet. Service with restrictions, supervision.

Super 8 Motel SH
(229) 559-8111. **$55-$70.** 4907 Timber Dr. I-75, exit 5, just w, then n. Ext corridors. **Pets:** Accepted.

LAVONIA

Super 8 Motel-Lavonia SH
(706) 356-8848. **$45-$90.** 14227 Jones St. I-85, exit 173, just nw. Ext corridors. **Pets:** Accepted.

LOCUST GROVE

Econo Lodge M
(770) 957-2601. **$45-$130, 3 day notice.** 4829 Bill Gardner Pkwy. I-75, exit 212, just e. Ext corridors. **Pets:** Small. $7 daily fee/pet. Designated rooms, service with restrictions, supervision.

Red Roof Inn & Suites SH
(678) 583-0004. **Call for rates.** 4832 Bill Gardner Pkwy. I-75, exit 212, just e. Int corridors. **Pets:** Accepted.

MACON

The Baymont Inn and Suites of Macon M
(478) 474-8004. **Call for rates.** 150 Plantation Inn Dr. I-475, exit 9 (Zebulon Rd), just e to Peake Rd, then just s. Ext corridors. **Pets:** Accepted.

Best Western Inn & Suites of Macon M
(478) 781-5300. **$59-$79.** 4681 Chambers Rd. I-475, exit 3 (Eisenhower Pkwy/US 80), just ne, then just se. Ext corridors. **Pets:** Medium. $10 daily fee/pet. Service with restrictions, crate.

Best Western Riverside Inn 🅢🅗
(478) 743-6311. **$64.** 2400 Riverside Dr. I-75, exit 167 (Riverside Dr), just w, then 0.4 mi se. Int corridors. **Pets:** Medium. $15 daily fee/pet. Designated rooms, supervision.
[SAVE] 🆂 ☒ 🖥 💻 🍴 🏊

La Quinta Inn & Suites Macon 🅢🅗
(478) 475-0206. **$119-$124.** 3944 River Place Dr. I-75, exit 169 (Arkwright Rd), just n, then e. Int corridors. **Pets:** Other species. Service with restrictions, supervision.
[SAVE] 🆂 ☒ 🅼 🖥 💻 🏊

Rodeway Inn 🏅 🐾
(478) 781-4343. **$49-$59.** 4999 Eisenhower Pkwy. I-475, exit 3 (Eisenhower Pkwy/US 80), just ne. Ext corridors. **Pets:** Medium. $10 daily fee/pet. Designated rooms, service with restrictions.
[SAVE] 🆂 ☒ 🖥 💻 🏊

Sleep Inn I-475 🅢🅗
(478) 476-8111. **$69-$85.** 140 Plantation Inn Dr. I-475, exit 9 (Zebulon Rd), just e to Peake Rd, then just s. Int corridors. **Pets:** Accepted.
[ASK] 🆂 ☒ 🅼 🖥 💻 🏊

MCDONOUGH

Comfort Inn 🅢🅗
(770) 954-9110. **$85-$175.** 80 Hwy 81 W. I-75, exit 218, just nw. Ext corridors. **Pets:** Medium. $10 daily fee/pet. Designated rooms, service with restrictions, supervision.
[SAVE] 🆂 ☒ 🖥 💻 🏊

Days Inn 🅢🅗
(770) 957-5261. **Call for rates.** 744 Hwy 155 S. I-75, exit 216, just e. Ext corridors. **Pets:** Large. $7 daily fee/room. Service with restrictions, crate.
[SAVE] ☒ 🖥 💻 🏊

Econo Lodge 🏅
(770) 957-2651. **$42-$150.** 1279 Hwy 20 W. I-75, exit 218, just w. Ext corridors. **Pets:** Accepted.
[SAVE] 🆂 ☒ 🖥 💻

Quality Inn & Suites Conference Center 🏅
(770) 957-5291. **$85-$199.** 930 Hwy 155 S. I-75, exit 216, just w. Ext corridors. **Pets:** Medium. $10 daily fee/room. Service with restrictions.
[SAVE] 🆂 ☒ 🅼 🖥 💻 🍴 🏊

MILLEDGEVILLE

Holiday Inn Express Hotel & Suites 🅢🅗
(478) 454-9000. **Call for rates.** 1839 N Columbia St. US 441, 2 mi n of downtown. Int corridors. **Pets:** Accepted.
☒ 🅼 🖥 💻 🏊

NEWNAN

Best Western-Shenandoah Inn 🏅
(770) 304-9700. **$69-$74, 7 day notice.** 620 Hwy 34 E. I-85, exit 47, just w. Ext corridors. **Pets:** Medium. $10 daily fee/pet. Designated rooms, service with restrictions, supervision.
[SAVE] 🆂 ☒ 🅼 🖥 💻 🏊

Howard Johnson Inn 🏅
(770) 683-1499. **$50-$55.** 1310 Hwy 29 S. I-85, exit 41, just w. Ext corridors. **Pets:** Accepted.
[ASK] 🆂 ☒ 🖥 💻 🏊

OAKWOOD

Country Inn & Suites by Carlson 🅢🅗
(770) 535-8080. **Call for rates.** 4535 Oakwood Rd. I-985, exit 16, just sw. Int corridors. **Pets:** Accepted.
☒ 🖥 💻 🏊

PEACHTREE CITY

Sleep Inn 🅢🅗
(770) 486-0044. **$95.** 109 City Cir. Jct SR 74 and 54; in The Avenue Shopping Center. Int corridors. **Pets:** Small. $45 one-time fee/pet. Service with restrictions, supervision.
[ASK] 🆂 ☒ 🅼 🖥 💻

PERRY

Henderson Village 🅒🅘
(478) 988-8696. **$159-$297.** 125 S Langston Cir. I-75, exit 127 (SR 26), 1.3 mi w. Ext/int corridors. **Pets:** Accepted.
[SAVE] 🆂 ☒ 🖥 💻 🍴 🏊 ☒

New Perry Hotel 🅢🅗
(478) 987-1000. **Call for rates.** 800 Main St. I-75, exit 136 (Sam Nunn Blvd) southbound, 1.2 mi se on US 341, then just w; exit 135 (US 41) northbound, 1.5 mi ne, then just s. Ext/int corridors. **Pets:** $15 daily fee/pet. Service with restrictions, crate.
☒ 🖥 💻 🍴 🏊

Quality Inn 🏅
(478) 987-1345. **$65-$95, 30 day notice.** 1504 Sam Nunn Blvd. I-75, exit 136 (Sam Nunn Blvd), just w. Ext corridors. **Pets:** Medium. $15 daily fee/room. Designated rooms, service with restrictions, supervision.
[SAVE] 🆂 ☒ 🖥 💻 🍴 🏊

Super 8 Motel 🅢🅗
(478) 987-0999. **Call for rates.** 102 Plaza Dr. I-75, exit 136 (Sam Nunn Blvd), just e. Ext corridors. **Pets:** Accepted.
[SAVE] ☒ 🖥 🏊

PINE MOUNTAIN

The Inn at Callaway Gardens 🅛🅗
(706) 663-2281. **$99-$159, 7 day notice.** Hwy 27. US 27 and SR 354, 2.8 mi s; in Callaway Gardens. Ext corridors. **Pets:** Accepted.
[SAVE] 🆂 ☒ 🅼 🖥 💻 🍴 🏊

White Columns Motel 🏅 🐾
(706) 663-2312. **$80, 3 day notice.** 524 S Main Ave. 1 mi s on US 27. Ext corridors. **Pets:** Large. $10 daily fee/pet. Designated rooms, service with restrictions, supervision.
[ASK] 🆂 ☒ 🖥

POOLER

Best Western Bradbury Suites 🅢🅗 🐾
(912) 330-0330. **$119-$159.** 155 Bourne Ave. I-95, exit 102 (US 80), just e. Int corridors. **Pets:** Small. Service with restrictions.
[SAVE] 🆂 ☒ 🅼 🖥 💻 🏊 ☒

Holiday Inn Savannah West 🅢🅗
(912) 330-5100. **$125-$135.** 103 San Dr. I-95, exit 102 (US 80), just w. Int corridors. **Pets:** Accepted.
[SAVE] 🆂 ☒ 🖥 💻 🍴 🏊

Jameson Inn 🅢🅗
(912) 748-0017. **$83-$115.** 125 Bourne Ave. I-95, exit 102 (US 80), just e. Int corridors. **Pets:** Small. $15 daily fee/room. Service with restrictions, crate.
[ASK] 🆂 ☒ 🖥 💻 🏊

Red Roof Inn & Suites 🅢🅗
(912) 748-4050. **Call for rates.** 20 Mill Creek Cir. I-95, exit 104 (Pooler Pkwy), just w. Int corridors. **Pets:** Accepted.
☒ 🖥 💻 🏊

Travelodge Suites 🅢🅗
(912) 748-6363. **$59-$149.** 130 Continental Blvd. I-95, exit 102 (US 80), just e. Int corridors. **Pets:** Other species. $10 daily fee/pet. Service with restrictions, supervision.
[SAVE] 🆂 ☒ 🖥 💻 🏊

PORT WENTWORTH

▼▼▼▼ Wingate Inn 🆂🅷
(912) 964-0840. **$79-$129.** 115 O' Leary Rd. I-95, exit 109 (SR 21), just e, then just n. Int corridors. **Pets:** Other species. $25 daily fee/pet. Service with restrictions, crate.

🅰🆂🅺 🆂🅳 ✕ 🕹 🖥 🖵

RICHMOND HILL

🛆🛆🛆⟋ ▼▼▼▼ Best Western Richmond Hill Inn 🆂🅷
(912) 756-7070. **$80-$160.** 4564 Hwy. I-95, exit 87 (Ocean Hwy/US 17), just w. Int corridors. **Pets:** Accepted.

🆂🅰🆅🅴 🆂🅳 ✕ 🖥 🖵 ⤳

🛆🛆🛆⟋ ▼▼▼▼ Comfort Suites 🆂🅷
(912) 756-6668. **$89-$109.** 4601 Hwy 17. I-95, exit 87 (Ocean Hwy/US 17), 0.4 mi sw. Int corridors. **Pets:** Medium. $20 daily fee/pet. Designated rooms, service with restrictions, supervision.

🆂🅰🆅🅴 🆂🅳 ✕ 🖥 🖵 ⤳ ✕

RINGGOLD

🛆🛆🛆⟋ ▼▼▼▼ Comfort Inn 🆂🅷
(706) 935-4000. **$70-$109.** 177 Industrial Blvd. I-75, exit 348, just w. Int corridors. **Pets:** Accepted.

🆂🅰🆅🅴 🆂🅳 ✕ 🖥 🖵 ⤳

🛆🛆🛆⟋ ▼▼ Hometown Inn 🆂🅷
(706) 937-7070. **$60-$75.** 22 Gateway Business Park Dr. I-75, exit 350, just e. Int corridors. **Pets:** $10 daily fee/pet. Designated rooms, service with restrictions, supervision.

🆂🅰🆅🅴 🆂🅳 ✕ 🅻🅼 🖥 🖵 ⤳

▼▼ Super 8 Motel 🅼
(706) 965-7080. **$60-$90.** 5400 Alabama Hwy. I-75, exit 348, just e. Ext corridors. **Pets:** Large, other species. $10 daily fee/pet. Designated rooms, service with restrictions, supervision.

🅰🆂🅺 🆂🅳 ✕ 🅻🅼 🖥 🖵 ⤳

ROCKMART

▼▼ Days Inn 🅼
(770) 684-9955. **Call for rates.** 105 GTM Pkwy. Jct US 278 and SR 101, just n. Ext corridors. **Pets:** Accepted.

✕ 🅻🅼 🖥

ROME

▼▼▼▼ Holiday Inn-Sky Top Center 🆂🅷
(706) 295-1100. **$94.** 20 US 411 E. 2 mi e. Ext corridors. **Pets:** Accepted.

🅰🆂🅺 🆂🅳 ✕ 🅻🅼 🖥 🖵 🍴 ⤳

▼▼▼▼ Jameson Inn 🆂🅷
(706) 291-7797. **$78-$110.** 40 Grace Dr. On US 411, 2.2 mi e. Int corridors. **Pets:** Small. $15 daily fee/room. Service with restrictions, crate.

🅰🆂🅺 🆂🅳 ✕ 🅻🅼 🖥 🖵 ⤳

SANDERSVILLE

🛆🛆🛆⟋ ▼▼ Days Inn Sandersville 🅼
(478) 553-0393. **Call for rates (no credit cards).** 128 Commerce St. On SR 15 at jct SR 77, just s. Ext corridors. **Pets:** $25 one-time fee/room. Designated rooms, service with restrictions, crate.

🆂🅰🆅🅴 ✕ 🅻🅼 🖥 🖵 ⤳

SAVANNAH

▼▼▼▼ Catherine Ward House Inn 🅱🅱
(912) 234-8564. **$369, 3 day notice.** 118 E Waldburg St. Between Drayton and Abercorn sts. Ext/int corridors. **Pets:** Accepted.

✕ 🖥

🛆🛆🛆⟋ ▼▼▼▼ Clarion Inn & Suites 🆂🅷
(912) 920-3200. **$79-$169.** 16 Gateway Blvd E. I-95, exit 94 (SR 204), just e. Int corridors. **Pets:** Other species. $35 daily fee/pet. Designated rooms, service with restrictions, supervision.

🆂🅰🆅🅴 🆂🅳 ✕ 🅻🅼 🖥 🖵 ⤳

🛆🛆🛆⟋ ▼▼▼▼ East Bay Inn 🅲🅸
(912) 238-1225. **$189-$250, 7 day notice.** 225 E Bay St. I-16, exit 167 (Montgomery St), 0.8 mi ne, then 0.4 mi se; in historic district. Int corridors. **Pets:** Small, dogs only. $45 one-time fee/pet. Designated rooms, no service, supervision.

🆂🅰🆅🅴 🆂🅳 ✕ 🖥 🍴

▼▼▼▼ Extended StayAmerica-Midtown 🆂🅷
(912) 692-0076. **$77-$84.** 5511 Abercorn St. Jct SR 21 and 204, just s. Int corridors. **Pets:** Other species. $75 one-time fee/pet. Service with restrictions.

🅰🆂🅺 🆂🅳 ✕ 🖥 🖵

▼▼▼▼ The Forsyth Park Inn 🅱🅱 ❀
(912) 233-6800. **$175-$275, 7 day notice.** 102 W Hall St. Between Whitaker and Howard sts; on Forsyth Park. Int corridors. **Pets:** Small. $40 daily fee/room. Designated rooms, service with restrictions.

🅰🆂🅺 ✕ 🖥

▼▼▼▼ Four Points by Sheraton 🆂🅷 ❀
(912) 629-1500. **$240.** 15 Jay R Turner Dr. I-95, exit 104, 0.4 mi e. Int corridors. **Pets:** Large, other species. $50 one-time fee/room. Service with restrictions, supervision.

✕ 🖥 🖵 🍴 ⤳

🛆🛆🛆⟋ ▼▼▼▼ Hamilton-Turner Inn 🅱🅱
(912) 233-1833. **$179-$359, 7 day notice.** 330 Abercorn St. Between E Charlton and E Harris sts; overlooking Lafayette Square; in historic district. Ext/int corridors. **Pets:** Small, other species. $50 one-time fee/room. Designated rooms, service with restrictions, crate.

🆂🅰🆅🅴 ✕

▼▼▼▼ Homewood Suites by Hilton 🆂🅷
(912) 353-8500. **$139-$229.** 5820 White Bluff Rd. Jct SR 21/204, 0.5 mi s. Ext/int corridors. **Pets:** Medium, other species. $45 one-time fee/room. Service with restrictions, crate.

🅰🆂🅺 ✕ 🖥 🖵 ⤳ ✕

▼▼ Joan's on Jones B & B 🅱🅱 ❀
(912) 234-3863. **$160-$185 (no credit cards), 7 day notice.** 17 W Jones St. Between Whitaker and Bull sts. Ext corridors. **Pets:** Dogs only. $50 one-time fee/room.

✕ 🖥 🖵

🛆🛆🛆⟋ ▼▼▼ La Quinta Inn Savannah (I-95) 🆂🅷
(912) 925-9505. **$95-$102.** 6 Gateway Blvd S. I-95, exit 94 (SR 204), just e, then s. Ext corridors. **Pets:** Other species. Service with restrictions, supervision.

🆂🅰🆅🅴 🆂🅳 ✕ 🅻🅼 🖥 ⤳

🛆🛆🛆⟋ ▼▼▼ La Quinta Inn Savannah (Midtown) 🆂🅷
(912) 355-3004. **$89-$114.** 6805 Abercorn St. 1 mi s of jct SR 21/204 (Abercorn St). Ext/int corridors. **Pets:** Other species. Service with restrictions, supervision.

🆂🅰🆅🅴 🆂🅳 ✕ 🖥 🖵 ⤳

🛆🛆🛆⟋ ▼▼▼▼ The Mansion on Forsyth Park 🅻🅷 ❀
(912) 238-5158. **$229-$509, 3 day notice.** 700 Drayton St. Between E Hall and E Gwinnett sts; on Forsyth Park. Int corridors. **Pets:** Small, dogs only. $100 one-time fee/room. Designated rooms, service with restrictions, crate.

🆂🅰🆅🅴 ✕ 🖥 🖵 🍴 ⤳

🛆🛆🛆⟋ ▼▼▼▼ Olde Harbour Inn 🅱🅱
(912) 234-4100. **$199-$279, 7 day notice.** 508 E Factors Walk. Lincoln St ramp off E Bay St; in historic riverfront district. Ext corridors. **Pets:** Medium, other species. $40 one-time fee/room. Designated rooms, service with restrictions, supervision.

🆂🅰🆅🅴 🆂🅳 ✕ 🖥 🖵

ΑΑΑ ▼▼▼ Quality Inn Savannah South **SH** ❀
(912) 925-2770. **$69-$79.** 3 Gateway Blvd S. I-95, exit 94 (SR 204), just e, then just s. Ext corridors. **Pets:** Medium. $10 daily fee/pet. Designated rooms, service with restrictions, crate.
SAVE S✺ ✕ 🛏 💻 🍴 🌊

ΑΑΑ ▼▼▼ Red Roof Inn **SH**
(912) 920-3535. **Call for rates.** 405 Al Henderson Blvd. I-95, exit 94 (SR 204), just e. Int corridors. **Pets:** Accepted.
SAVE ✕ 🛖M 🛏 💻 🌊

▼▼▼ Savannah Residence Inn by Marriott **SH**
(912) 356-3266. **$149-$159.** 5710 White Bluff Rd. Jct SR 21, 0.5 mi s. Int corridors. **Pets:** Small. $100 one-time fee/room. Service with restrictions, supervision.
ASK S✺ ✕ 🛏 💻 🌊 ⊠

▼▼▼ Suites on Lafayette **CO**
(912) 233-7815. **$139-$299, 14 day notice.** 201-205 E Charlton St. Off Abercorn St at Lafayette Square. Int corridors. **Pets:** Accepted.
✕ 🛏

ΑΑΑ ▼▼▼ Travelodge **M**
(912) 925-2640. **$40-$299.** 1 Fort Argyle Rd. I-95, exit 94 (SR 204), just w. Ext corridors. **Pets:** Small. $10 daily fee/pet. Designated rooms, service with restrictions, supervision.
SAVE S✺ ✕ 🛏 💻 🌊

ΑΑΑ ▼▼▼▼ Westin Savannah Harbor Golf Resort and Spa **LH**
(912) 201-2000. **$459, 3 day notice.** 1 Resort Dr. On Hutchinson Island; 1 mi se of first exit after Eugene Talmadge Memorial Bridge and US 17. Int corridors. **Pets:** Accepted.
SAVE S✺ ✕ 🛖M 🛏 💻 🍴 🌊 ⊠

STATESBORO

▼▼▼ Best Western University Inn **M**
(912) 681-7900. **$65-$72.** 1 Jameson Ave. Jct US 25/301 and SR 67, 0.9 mi s on US 25/301. Ext corridors. **Pets:** Accepted.
ASK S✺ ✕ 🛏 💻 🌊

▼▼▼ Hometown Inn **M**
(912) 681-4663. **Call for rates.** 126 Rushing Ln. Jct US 301 Bypass and SR 67, just n, then w. Ext corridors. **Pets:** Accepted.
✕ 🛏

ΑΑΑ ▼▼▼▼ La Quinta Inn Statesboro **SH**
(912) 871-2525. **$90.** 225 Lanier Dr. Jct US 301 Bypass and SR 67, 1.2 mi w on US 301, just n of Georgia Southern University. Int corridors. **Pets:** Other species. Service with restrictions, supervision.
SAVE S✺ ✕ 🛖M 🛏 💻 🌊

▼▼▼▼ Statesboro Inn & Restaurant **CI**
(912) 489-8628. **$95-$135.** 106 S Main St (US 301/25). US 301/25, just s of town center; downtown. Int corridors. **Pets:** $25 daily fee/pet. Designated rooms, service with restrictions, crate.
ASK S✺ ✕ 🛏 💻 🍴

▼▼ Trellis Garden Inn **SH**
(912) 489-8781. **$65-$95.** 107 S Main St (US 301/25). On US 301/25, just s of center; downtown. Ext corridors. **Pets:** Dogs only. Designated rooms, service with restrictions, supervision.
ASK S✺ ✕ 🛏 🌊

STOCKBRIDGE

ΑΑΑ ▼▼▼ Baymont Inn & Suites **SH**
(770) 507-6500. **$59-$99.** 100 N Park Ct. I-75, exit 224, just e, then just n on Rock Quarry Rd. Int corridors. **Pets:** Accepted.
SAVE S✺ ✕ 🛏 💻 🌊

ΑΑΑ ▼▼▼▼ La Quinta Inn & Suites **SH**
(770) 506-9991. **$114.** 3581 Cameron Pkwy. I-75, exit 228, 0.7 mi e; I-675, exit 1, just w. Int corridors. **Pets:** Other species. Service with restrictions, supervision.
SAVE S✺ ✕ 🛖M 🛏 💻 🌊 ⊠

ΑΑΑ ▼▼▼ Super 8 Motel Atlanta South **SH**
(770) 474-5758. **$54-$60.** 1451 Hudson Bridge Rd. I-75, exit 224, just w. Ext corridors. **Pets:** Accepted.
SAVE S✺ ✕ 🛏 💻 🌊

SWAINSBORO

ΑΑΑ ▼▼▼ Best Western Bradford Inn **M** ❀
(478) 237-2400. **$59-$89.** 688 S Main St. I-16, exit 90 (US 1), 12.4 mi n. Ext corridors. **Pets:** Small. $10 daily fee/pet. Service with restrictions, supervision.
SAVE S✺ ✕ 🛏 💻 🌊

THOMASTON

▼▼ Jameson Inn **SH**
(706) 648-2232. **$58-$90.** 1010 Hwy 19 N. Jct SR 74, 2.3 mi n. Ext corridors. **Pets:** Small. $15 daily fee/room. Service with restrictions, crate.
ASK S✺ ✕ 🛏 💻 🌊

THOMASVILLE

▼▼ Comfort Inn **M**
(229) 228-5555. **$75-$83.** 14866 US 19 S. Jct SR 300/US 19 and 84/SR 122. Ext corridors. **Pets:** Accepted.
ASK S✺ ✕ 🛏 💻 🌊

▼▼ Jameson Inn **M**
(229) 227-9500. **$63-$95.** 1470 Remington Ave. US 19, just w on CR 122. Ext corridors. **Pets:** Small. $15 daily fee/room. Service with restrictions, crate.
ASK S✺ ✕ 🛖M 🛏 💻 🌊

ΑΑΑ ▼▼▼▼ Quality Inn & Suites Conference Center **M**
(229) 225-2134. **$60-$120.** 15138 Hwy 19 S. 0.3 mi s of US 319. Ext corridors. **Pets:** Medium. $10 daily fee/pet. Designated rooms, no service, supervision.
SAVE S✺ ✕ 🛖M 🛏 💻 🍴 🌊

THOMSON

ΑΑΑ ▼▼▼▼ Best Western White Columns Inn **SH**
(706) 595-8000. **$68-$140.** 1890 Washington Rd. I-20, exit 172 (US 78), just s. Ext corridors. **Pets:** Other species. $10 daily fee/pet. Designated rooms, service with restrictions, crate.
SAVE S✺ ✕ 🛏 💻 🍴 🌊 ⊠

TIFTON

▼▼ Days Inn & Suites **SH**
(229) 382-8505. **Call for rates.** 1199 Hwy 82 W. I-75, exit 62, just w. Int corridors. **Pets:** Accepted.
✕ 🛏 💻 🌊

▼▼▼ Hampton Inn **SH**
(229) 382-8800. **$98-$106.** 720 Hwy 319 S. I-75, exit 62, just e. Ext corridors. **Pets:** Medium, other species. No service, supervision.
ASK S✺ ✕ 🛏 💻 🌊

ΑΑΑ ▼▼ Holiday Inn **SH**
(229) 382-6687. **$80-$109.** 1208 Hwy 82 W. I-75, exit 62, at jct US 82 and 319. Ext corridors. **Pets:** Other species. Service with restrictions, supervision.
SAVE S✺ ✕ 🛏 💻 🍴 🌊

▼▼ Microtel Inns & Suites **SH**
(229) 387-0112. **$45-$199.** 196 S Virginia Ave. I-75, exit 62, just n. Int corridors. **Pets:** Accepted.
ASK S✺ ✕ 🛖M 🛏 💻 🌊

◆ Motel 6 #4074 **SH**
(229) 388-8777. **Call for rates.** 579 Old Omega Rd. I-75, exit 61, just w. Int corridors. **Pets:** Other species. Service with restrictions, supervision.
⊠ ➷

◆◆ **Ramada Limited and Conference Center SH**
(229) 382-8500. **$59-$109.** 1211 Hwy 82 W. I-75, exit 62, just w. Ext corridors. **Pets:** Accepted.
A$K S✗ ⊠ ⊟ ▣ ➷

TOWNSEND

◆ Days Inn **M**
(912) 832-4411. **$50-$65.** Hwy 57. I-95, exit 58 (SR 57), just nw. Ext corridors. **Pets:** Accepted.
A$K S✗ ⊠ ⊟ ➷

TRENTON

◆◆ Days Inn **SH**
(706) 657-2550. **$51-$60.** 95 Killian Ave. I-59, exit 11, just e. Ext corridors. **Pets:** Accepted.
A$K ⊠ ⊑M ⊟ ▣ ➷

VALDOSTA

◆◆◆ ◆◆◆ **Best Western King of the Road SH** ❀
(229) 244-7600. **$69-$89.** 1403 N St Augustine Rd. I-75, exit 18, just w off of SR 94. Ext corridors. **Pets:** Small. $10 daily fee/pet. Designated rooms, no service, supervision.
A$K S✗ ⊠ ⊟ ▣ ¶¶ ➷

◆◆◆ ◆◆◆ **Comfort Inn Conference Center SH**
(229) 242-1212. **$95-$100.** 2101 W Hill Ave. I-75, exit 16, just w. Ext/int corridors. **Pets:** Large. Designated rooms, service with restrictions, supervision.
SAVE S✗ ⊠ ⊟ ▣ ¶¶ ➷ ⊠

◆◆ **Days Inn I-75 North SH**
(229) 244-4460. **$49-$69.** 4598 N Valdosta Rd. I-75, exit 22, just w. Ext corridors. **Pets:** Accepted.
A$K S✗ ⊠ ⊟ ▣ ➷

◆◆◆ ◆◆◆ **Econo Lodge SH**
(229) 671-1511. **$60-$110.** 3022 James Rd. I-75, exit 18, just w. Int corridors. **Pets:** Accepted.
SAVE S✗ ⊠ ⊟ ▣ ➷

◆◆◆◆ **Holiday Inn Hotel and Conference Center SH**
(229) 244-1111. **$99-$169.** 1805 W Hill Ave. I-75, exit 16, 0.4 mi e. Int corridors. **Pets:** Accepted.
A$K S✗ ⊠ ⊑M ⊟ ▣ ¶¶ ➷

◆◆◆ ◆◆◆◆ **La Quinta Inn & Suites Valdosta SH**
(229) 247-7755. **$89-$149.** 1800 Clubhouse Dr. I-75, exit 18, 0.3 mi e, then just s off SR 94. Int corridors. **Pets:** Other species. Service with restrictions, supervision.
SAVE S✗ ⊠ ⊟ ▣ ➷

◆◆◆ ◆◆◆ **Quality Inn North SH**
(229) 244-8510. **Call for rates.** 1209 St Augustine Rd. I-75, exit 18, 0.3 mi e on SR 94. Ext corridors. **Pets:** Accepted.
SAVE ⊠ ⊟ ▣ ➷

◆◆ **Quality Inn South SH**
(229) 244-4520. **$50-$90.** 1902 W Hill Ave. I-75, exit 16, just e on US 84. Ext corridors. **Pets:** Medium, other species. $8 daily fee/pet. Service with restrictions, crate.
A$K S✗ ⊠ ⊟ ▣ ➷

◆◆ **Ramada Limited M**
(229) 242-1225. **Call for rates.** 2008 W Hill Ave. I-75, exit 16, just e on US 84. Ext corridors. **Pets:** Accepted.
⊠ ⊟ ▣ ➷

VIDALIA

◆◆◆ ◆◆◆ Days Inn **SH**
(912) 537-9251. **$79.** 1503 Lyons E. 1 mi e on US 280. Ext corridors. **Pets:** Medium. $5 daily fee/pet. Service with restrictions, supervision.
SAVE S✗ ⊠ ⊟ ▣ ➷

◆◆◆ **Holiday Inn Express SH**
(912) 537-9000. **$79-$102.** 2619 E First St. 2.5 mi e on US 280. Ext corridors. **Pets:** Medium, other species. Service with restrictions, crate.
A$K S✗ ⊠ ⊟ ▣ ➷

VILLA RICA

◆◆ Days Inn **SH**
(770) 459-8888. **$55-$115.** 195 Hwy 61 Connector. I-20, exit 24, just n. Int corridors. **Pets:** Medium, dogs only. $10 daily fee/pet. Designated rooms, service with restrictions, supervision.
A$K S✗ ⊠ ⊑M ⊟ ➷

◆◆◆ ◆◆◆ Super 8 Motel **SH**
(770) 459-8000. **$54-$154.** 128 Hwy 61 Connector. I-20, exit 24, just n. Ext corridors. **Pets:** Accepted.
SAVE S✗ ⊠ ⊟ ▣ ➷

WARNER ROBINS

◆◆◆ ◆◆◆ **Best Western Peach Inn SH**
(478) 953-3800. **$47-$65.** 2739 Watson Blvd. I-75, exit 146 (SR 247C), 4.1 mi e. Ext corridors. **Pets:** Small, other species. $15 daily fee/pet. Designated rooms, no service, crate.
SAVE S✗ ⊠ ⊟ ▣ ➷

◆◆◆ ◆◆◆ **Comfort Inn & Suites SH**
(478) 922-7555. **Call for rates.** 95 S Hwy 247. Jct SR 247C and US 129/SR 247, 1.6 mi s on US 129/SR 247. Ext/int corridors. **Pets:** Accepted.
SAVE ⊠ ⊟ ▣ ➷

◆◆◆ **Jameson Inn-Warner Robins SH**
(478) 953-5522. **Call for rates.** 2731 Watson Blvd. I-75, exit 146 (SR 247C), 4.1 mi e. Ext corridors. **Pets:** Small. $15 daily fee/room. Service with restrictions, crate.
⊠ ⊟ ▣ ➷

WASHINGTON

◆◆◆ ◆◆◆◆ Lafayette Manor Inn **CI**
(706) 678-5922. **$135-$195, 14 day notice.** 219 E Robert Toombs Ave (SR 17). Downtown; just e of town square. Int corridors. **Pets:** Dogs only. Designated rooms, service with restrictions.
SAVE ⊠ ⊟ ▣ ¶¶ 🗷 🐾

WAYCROSS

◆◆ **Holiday Inn Waycross SH**
(912) 283-4490. **$79.** 1725 Memorial Dr. Jct US 1 and 82. Ext corridors. **Pets:** Accepted.
A$K S✗ ⊠ ⊟ ▣ ¶¶ ➷ ⊠

◆◆ **Jameson Inn M**
(912) 283-3800. **$60-$95.** 950 City Blvd. Between US 1 and 82, east of city. Ext corridors. **Pets:** Small. $15 daily fee/room. Service with restrictions, crate.
A$K S✗ ⊠ ⊑M ⊟ ▣ ➷

WAYNESBORO

◆◆ **Jameson Inn M**
(706) 437-0500. **$63-$95.** 1436 N Liberty St. 0.9 mi n of downtown center on US 25. Ext corridors. **Pets:** Small. $10 daily fee/pet. Service with restrictions, supervision.
A$K S✗ ⊠ ⊟ ▣ ➷

WINDER

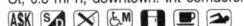 Comfort Inn **SH**
(770) 868-5303. **$67-$121, 15 day notice.** 177 W Athens St. Jct Broad St, 0.8 mi n; downtown. Int corridors. **Pets:** Accepted.

 Jameson Inn **M**
(770) 867-1880. **$73-$100.** 9 Stafford St. Jct SR 81, 11, 53 and 8; center. Ext corridors. **Pets:** Small. $15 daily fee/room. Service with restrictions, crate.

YOUNG HARRIS

 Brasstown Valley Resort **LH**
(706) 379-9900. **Call for rates.** 6321 US Hwy 76. US 76 and US 76/SR 515. Int corridors. **Pets:** Accepted.

HAWAII

HONOLULU

 The Kahala Hotel & Resort 🎖 ❀
(808) 739-8888. **$395-$4700, 3 day notice.** 5000 Kahala Ave. E of Diamond Head at end of Kahala Ave. Int corridors. **Pets:** Small. Service with restrictions, supervision.
[SAVE] [S👁] [✕] [👤M] [🍴] [🏊] [✕]

KAUPULEHU

Four Seasons Resort Hualalai at Historic Ka'upulehu 🎖
(808) 325-8000. **Call for rates.** 100 Ka'upulehu Dr. Off SR 19, 6 mi n of Kona International Airport. Ext corridors. **Pets:** Accepted.
[✕] [👤M] [🔒] [🖥] [🍴] [🏊] [✕]

WAILEA

Four Seasons Resort, Maui at Wailea 🎖
(808) 874-8000. **$440-$12880, 21 day notice.** 3900 Wailea Alanui Dr. From end of SR 31, 0.5 mi s. Int corridors. **Pets:** Accepted.
[SAVE] [✕] [👤M] [🖥] [🍴] [🏊] [✕]

IDAHO

CITY INDEX

AHSAHKA

⬥⬥ ▼▼▼ The High Country Inn 🅱🅱 🐾

(208) 476-7570. **$95-$125, 7 day notice.** 4231 Old Ahsahka Grade. 0.5 mi w to Dworshak Visitors Center Rd, 2 mi n, just w. Ext/int corridors. **Pets:** Other species. $25 one-time fee/room. Supervision.

BLACKFOOT

⬥⬥ ▼▼ Best Western Blackfoot Inn 🆂🅷

(208) 785-4144. **$79-$119.** 750 Jensen Grove Dr. I-15, exit 93, just e on Bergener, then 0.4 mi n on Parkway. Int corridors. **Pets:** Other species. Service with restrictions, supervision.

▼▼ Super 8 🆂🅷

(208) 785-9333. **$66-$85.** 1279 Parkway Dr. I-15, exit 93, just e; shared driveway with McDonald's. Int corridors. **Pets:** Accepted.

BLISS

⬥⬥ ▼ Amber Inn Motel 🆂🅷

(208) 352-4441. **Call for rates.** 17286 US Hwy 30. I-84, exit 141, just s. Int corridors. **Pets:** Accepted.

BOISE

⬥⬥ ▼▼ Comfort Inn Airport 🆂🅷

(208) 336-0077. **$68-$85.** 2526 Airport Way. I-84, exit 53 (Vista Ave), just s. Ext/int corridors. **Pets:** Medium. $15 one-time fee/pet. Service with restrictions, supervision.

▼▼▼ DoubleTree Club Hotel 🆂🅷

(208) 345-2002. **Call for rates.** 475 W Parkcenter Blvd. I-84, exit 54 (Broadway Ave), 2 mi n, then 0.3 mi e on Beacon and Parkcenter Blvd. Int corridors. **Pets:** Accepted.

⬥⬥ ▼▼▼ DoubleTree Hotel Boise Riverside 🆂🅷

(208) 343-1871. **$69-$159.** 2900 Chinden Blvd. I-184, exit 3 (Fairview Ave), just n, then just w on Garden. Int corridors. **Pets:** Medium. $25 one-time fee/room. Designated rooms, service with restrictions, crate.

▼▼ Fairfield Inn by Marriott 🆂🅷

(208) 331-5656. **$110-$130.** 3300 S Shoshone St. I-84, exit 53 (Vista Ave), just n to Elder St, then just w. Int corridors. **Pets:** Accepted.

▼▼▼ Holiday Inn Boise Airport 🆂🅷

(208) 343-4900. **$89-$109.** 3300 Vista Ave. I-84, exit 53 (Vista Ave), just n. Int corridors. **Pets:** Accepted.

▼▼ Holiday Inn Express 🆂🅷

(208) 388-0800. **$119-$129.** 2613 S Vista Ave. I-84, exit 53 (Vista Ave), 0.5 mi n. Int corridors. **Pets:** Accepted.

▼▼▼▼ Oxford Suites 🆂🅷

(208) 322-8000. **$109-$169.** 1426 S Entertainment Ave. I-84, exit 50A westbound; exit 50B eastbound, just s to Spectrum St, just w, then n. Int corridors. **Pets:** Accepted.

▼▼▼ Red Lion Hotel Boise Downtowner 🅻🅷

(208) 344-7691. **$89-$159.** 1800 Fairview Ave. I-184, exit 3 (Fairview Ave), 1 mi n. Int corridors. **Pets:** Accepted.

▼▼▼ Residence Inn by Marriott-Boise Central 🆂🅷

(208) 344-1200. **$176-$197.** 1401 Lusk Ave. I-84, exit 53 (Vista Ave), 2.4 mi n, just w on Ann Morrison, then just s on Lois. Ext corridors. **Pets:** Accepted.

▼▼▼ Residence Inn by Marriott-Boise West 🆂🅷

(208) 385-9000. **$165-$185.** 7303 W Denton. I-84, exit 50A westbound; exit 50B eastbound, 2 mi n on Cole Rd, then just w. Int corridors. **Pets:** Accepted.

⬥⬥ ▼▼▼ Safari Inn Downtown 🆂🅷 🐾

(208) 344-6556. **$79-$89.** 1070 Grove St. At 11th and Grove sts; center. Int corridors. **Pets:** $10 one-time fee/room. Designated rooms, service with restrictions, supervision.

⬥⬥ ▼▼▼ Shilo Inn Suites-Boise Airport 🆂🅷 🐾

(208) 343-7662. **$115.** 4111 Broadway Ave. I-84, exit 54 (Broadway Ave), just sw. Int corridors. **Pets:** $25 one-time fee/room. Designated rooms, service with restrictions, supervision.

▼▼▼ SpringHill Suites by Marriott-Boise ParkCenter 🆂🅷

(208) 342-1044. **$143-$163.** 424 E Parkcenter Blvd. I-84, exit 54 (Broadway Ave), 2.3 mi n, then just e on Beacon and Parkcenter Blvd. Int corridors. **Pets:** Large, other species. $50 one-time fee/room. Service with restrictions, supervision.

BONNERS FERRY

⬥⬥ ▼▼▼ Best Western Kootenai River Inn Casino & Spa 🆂🅷

(208) 267-8511. **Call for rates.** 7169 Plaza St. On US 95; city center. Int corridors. **Pets:** Small. $15 daily fee/pet. Service with restrictions, supervision.

BURLEY

⬥⬥ ▼▼▼ Best Western Burley Inn & Convention Center 🆂🅷

(208) 678-3501. **$69-$79.** 800 N Overland Ave. I-84, exit 208, just s. Ext/int corridors. **Pets:** Accepted.

AAA **WWW** Budget Motel **M**
(208) 678-2200. **$56-$73.** 900 N Overland Ave. I-84, exit 208, just s. Ext corridors. **Pets:** Accepted.
[SAVE] [S] [X] [&M] [B] [≈]

CALDWELL

AAA **WWWW** Best Western Caldwell Inn & Suites **M** ❖
(208) 454-7225. **$79-$169.** 908 Specht Ave. I-84, exit 29, just s. Int corridors. **Pets:** Medium. $10 daily fee/pet. Designated rooms, service with restrictions, supervision.
[SAVE] [S] [X] [B] [▢] [≈]

AAA **WWW** La Quinta Inn Caldwell **SH**
(208) 454-2222. **$94.** 901 Specht Ave. I-84, exit 29, just s. Int corridors. **Pets:** Other species. Service with restrictions, supervision.
[SAVE] [S] [X] [B] [▢] [≈]

COEUR D'ALENE

AAA **WWWW** Best Western Coeur d'Alene Inn & Conference Center **SH** ❖
(208) 765-3200. **$89-$189.** W 506 Appleway Ave. I-90, exit 12, just nw. Int corridors. **Pets:** Large, other species. $25 daily fee/room. Service with restrictions, supervision.
[SAVE] [S] [X] [&M] [B] [▢] [¶] [≈]

WWW The Coeur d'Alene Resort **LH**
(208) 765-4000. **$119-$460.** 115 S 2nd St. I-90, exit 11, 2 mi s. Ext/int corridors. **Pets:** Large, dogs only. $75 one-time fee/pet. Service with restrictions, supervision.
[ASK] [S] [X] [▢] [¶] [≈] [X]

AAA **WWW** Days Inn-Coeur d'Alene **SH** ❖
(208) 667-8668. **$65-$170.** 2200 Northwest Blvd. I-90, exit 11, just se. Int corridors. **Pets:** Medium, other species. $10 daily fee/pet. Service with restrictions, supervision.
[SAVE] [S] [X] [&M] [B] [▢] [X]

WWW Guest House Inn & Suites **SH**
(208) 765-3011. **Call for rates.** 330 W Appleway Ave. I-90, exit 12, just n, then just e. Int corridors. **Pets:** Accepted.
[X] [B] [▢]

WWW Holiday Inn Express Hotel & Suites Coeur d'Alene **SH**
(208) 667-3100. **Call for rates (no credit cards).** 2300 W Seltice Way. I-90, exit 11, just s. Int corridors. **Pets:** Accepted.
[X] [B] [▢] [≈]

AAA **WWW** La Quinta Inn & Suites Coeur D'Alene (East) **SH**
(208) 667-6777. **$74.** 2209 E Sherman Ave. I-90, exit 15 (Sherman Ave), just s. Int corridors. **Pets:** Other species. Service with restrictions, supervision.
[SAVE] [S] [X] [&M] [B] [▢] [≈]

WWWW La Quinta Inn Coeur D'Alene (Appleway) **SH**
(208) 765-5500. **$77.** 280 W Appleway Ave. I-90, exit 12, just ne. Int corridors. **Pets:** Other species. Service with restrictions, supervision.
[ASK] [S] [X] [&M] [B] [▢] [≈] [X]

AAA **WWWW** The Roosevelt Inn, Inc **BB**
(208) 765-5200. **$89-$319, 14 day notice.** 105 Wallace Ave. I-90, exit 13, 2 mi s, then just w; downtown. Int corridors. **Pets:** Accepted.
[SAVE] [S] [X] [X] [W] [Z]

AAA **WWWW** Shilo Inn Suites Coeur d'Alene **SH** ❖
(208) 664-2300. **$89-$230.** 702 W Appleway Ave. I-90, exit 12, just n, then just w. Int corridors. **Pets:** $25 one-time fee/room. Designated rooms, service with restrictions, supervision.
[SAVE] [S] [X] [&M] [B] [▢] [≈] [X]

HAGERMAN

AAA **WWW** Hagerman Valley Inn **M**
(208) 837-6196. **$58-$108.** 661 Frog's Landing. South end of town on US 30. Ext/int corridors. **Pets:** $6 daily fee/pet. Service with restrictions, supervision.
[SAVE] [S] [X] [B]

HAILEY

WWW Airport Inn **M**
(208) 788-2477. **Call for rates.** 820 4th Ave S. Just n of SR 75 at 4th Ave; near airport. Ext corridors. **Pets:** Accepted.
[X] [B] [▢]

WWWW AmericInn Lodge & Suites of Hailey **SH** ❖
(208) 788-7950. **$99-$150.** 51 Cobblestone Ln. Just n on SR 75, then just e. Int corridors. **Pets:** Dogs only. $15 one-time fee/pet. Designated rooms, service with restrictions, supervision.
[ASK] [S] [X] [&M] [B] [▢] [≈] [X]

WWWW Wood River Inn **SH**
(208) 578-0600. **$105-$138.** 603 N Main. Just n of downtown on SR 75. Int corridors. **Pets:** $25 one-time fee/room. Service with restrictions, crate.
[ASK] [X] [&M] [B] [▢] [≈] [X]

HAYDEN

WWWW Holiday Inn Express Hotel & Suites **SH**
(208) 772-7900. **$90-$150.** 151 W Orchard Ave. I-90, exit 12, 3.5 mi n. Int corridors. **Pets:** Accepted.
[ASK] [X] [&M] [B] [▢] [≈] [X]

HEYBURN

WWW Super 8–Burley **SH**
(208) 678-7000. **$65-$80.** 336 S 600 W. I-84, exit 208, just n. Int corridors. **Pets:** Accepted.
[ASK] [S] [X] [&M] [B] [≈]

IDAHO FALLS

AAA **WWWW** Best Western Driftwood Inn **SH** ❖
(208) 523-2242. **$69-$129.** 575 River Pkwy. I-15, exit 118 (Broadway), 0.5 mi e, then 0.3 mi n. Ext corridors. **Pets:** Medium, cats only. $10 one-time fee/room. Service with restrictions, supervision.
[SAVE] [S] [X] [B] [▢] [≈] [X]

WWW Comfort Inn **SH**
(208) 528-2804. **$85-$105.** 195 S Colorado Ave. I-15, exit 118 (Broadway), just w to Colorado Ave, then just s. Int corridors. **Pets:** Accepted.
[ASK] [S] [X] [B] [▢] [≈]

WWW GuestHouse Inn & Suites **SH**
(208) 523-6260. **$59-$150.** 850 Lindsay Blvd. I-15, exit 119, just e. Ext/int corridors. **Pets:** Accepted.
[ASK] [S] [X] [B] [▢] [¶] [≈]

AAA **WWWW** Le Ritz Hotel & Suites **SH**
(208) 528-0880. **$105-$129.** 720 Lindsay Blvd. I-15, exit 118 (Broadway), 0.5 mi e, then just n. Int corridors. **Pets:** Accepted.
[SAVE] [S] [X] [B] [▢] [≈]

WWW Red Lion Hotel on the Falls **SH**
(208) 523-8000. **$80-$150.** 475 River Pkwy. I-15, exit 118 (Broadway), 0.5 mi e, then just n. Ext/int corridors. **Pets:** Accepted.
[ASK] [S] [X] [B] [▢] [¶] [≈] [X]

AAA **WWW** Shilo Inn Suites Conference Hotel **SH** ❖
(208) 523-0088. **$170.** 780 Lindsay Blvd. I-15, exit 119, just se. Int corridors. **Pets:** $25 one-time fee/room. Designated rooms, service with restrictions, supervision.
[SAVE] [S] [X] [B] [▢] [¶] [≈] [X]

JACKSON HOLE AREA (NEARBY WYOMING)

DRIGGS

Teton Valley Cabins CA
(208) 354-8153. **$79-$119, 7 day notice.** 34 Ski Hill Rd. 0.8 mi e on Little Ave from SR 33 E. Ext corridors. **Pets:** Accepted.
⊠ 🔒 💻 ⊠ 🐾

END AREA

JEROME

Best Western Sawtooth Inn and Suites SH
(208) 324-9200. **$85-$140.** 2653 S Lincoln. I-84, exit 168, just n on SR 79. Int corridors. **Pets:** Accepted.
SAVE 🔊 ⊠ 🔒 💻 ➿

KELLOGG

Baymont Inn & Suites SH 🐾
(208) 783-1234. **$59-$79.** 601 Bunker Ave. I-90, exit 49, 0.5 mi s. Int corridors. **Pets:** Large. Service with restrictions, supervision.
SAVE 🔊 ⊠ 🔊 🔒 💻 ➿

Morning Star Lodge SH
(208) 783-0202. **Call for rates.** 602 Bunker Ave. I-90, exit 49, 0.5 mi se. Int corridors. **Pets:** Accepted.
⊠ 🔒 💻 🍴 ⊠

Silverhorn Motor Inn SH
(208) 783-1151. **$63-$87.** 699 W Cameron Ave. I-90, exit 49, just ne. Int corridors. **Pets:** Accepted.
ASK ⊠ 🔒 🍴

KETCHUM

Best Western Tyrolean Lodge SH
(208) 726-5336. **Call for rates.** 260 Cottonwood. South end of town; just w of SR 75 (Main St) on Rivers St, just s on 3rd Ave. Int corridors. **Pets:** Accepted.
SAVE ⊠ 🔒 💻 ➿ ⊠

Tamarack Lodge M
(208) 726-3344. **$89-$164, 3 day notice.** 291 Walnut Ave N. Just ne on Sun Valley Rd from jct SR 75 (Main St); downtown. Ext/int corridors. **Pets:** Accepted.
ASK 🔊 ⊠ 🔒 💻 ➿

KOOSKIA

River Dance Lodge CA
(208) 765-0841. **$129-$159, 45 day notice.** 7743 Hwy 12. 16 mi e on US 12. Ext corridors. **Pets:** Accepted.
ASK ⊠ 🔒 💻 🍴 🐾 🐾 Z

LEWISTON

Comfort Inn SH
(208) 798-8090. **Call for rates.** 2128 8th Ave. 1.2 mi s on US 12 from jct US 95, just s on 21st St. Int corridors. **Pets:** Medium. $10 daily fee/room. Designated rooms, service with restrictions, supervision.
⊠ 🔊 🔒 💻 ➿

GuestHouse Inn & Suites SH
(208) 746-3311. **$55-$89.** 1325 Main St. Downtown. Int corridors. **Pets:** Accepted.
ASK 🔊 ⊠ 🔒 💻 ➿

JEROME

Holiday Inn Express SH 🐾
(208) 750-1600. **$79-$189.** 2425 Nez Perce Dr. 1.2 mi s on US 12 from jct US 95, 1.2 mi s on 21st St, then just e. Int corridors. **Pets:** Large, other species. $10 daily fee/room. Service with restrictions, supervision.
SAVE 🔊 ⊠ 🔊 🔒 💻 ➿ ⊠

Super 8 Motel SH
(208) 743-8808. **$52-$67.** 3120 North & South Hwy. Just e on US 12 from jct US 95. Int corridors. **Pets:** Accepted.
ASK 🔊 ⊠ 🔒

LOWER STANLEY

Salmon River Cabins & Motel CA
(208) 774-3566. **$70-$135, 7 day notice.** 55 Lower Stanley (Hwy US 75). 1 mi n on US 75 from jct SR 21. Ext corridors. **Pets:** $10 daily fee/pet. Service with restrictions, supervision.
SAVE ⊠ 🔒 💻 🍴

MCCALL

AmericInn Lodge & Suites SH 🐾
(208) 634-2230. **$130.** 211 S 3rd St. On SR 55; south end of town. Int corridors. **Pets:** Dogs only. $30 deposit/pet, $10 daily fee/pet. Designated rooms, service with restrictions, supervision.
ASK 🔊 ⊠ 🔊 🔒 💻 ➿ ⊠

Super 8 Motel–McCall M 🐾
(208) 634-4637. **$89-$109.** 303 S 3rd St. South end of town on SR 55. Int corridors. **Pets:** Other species. $10 daily fee/pet. Designated rooms, service with restrictions, supervision.
SAVE 🔊 ⊠ 🔊 🔒 💻

Western Mountain Lodge SH
(208) 634-6300. **$94-$160.** 415 N 3rd St. SR 55, just s of jct Lake St. Ext/int corridors. **Pets:** Large, dogs only. $10 one-time fee/pet. No service, supervision.
SAVE 🔊 ⊠ 🔊 🔒 💻 ➿

MONTPELIER

Clover Creek Inn SH
(208) 847-1782. **$53-$83.** 243 N 4th St. Just n on US 30 from jct US 89 S. Ext corridors. **Pets:** Dogs only. $8 daily fee/pet. Designated rooms, supervision.
SAVE 🔊 ⊠ 🔒 💻

MOSCOW

Best Western University Inn SH
(208) 882-0550. **$99-$119.** 1516 Pullman Rd. Jct US 95, 1 mi w on SR 8. Int corridors. **Pets:** Small, other species. $25 daily fee/room. Designated rooms, service with restrictions, crate.
SAVE 🔊 ⊠ 🔊 🔒 💻 🍴 ➿ ⊠

La Quinta Inn SH
(208) 882-5365. **$89.** 185 Warbonnet Dr. 1.6 mi w on SR 8 from jct US 93, just n. Int corridors. **Pets:** Other species. Service with restrictions, supervision.
ASK 🔊 ⊠ 🔒 💻 ➿

▼▼▼ Super 8 Motel SH
(208) 883-1503. **Call for rates.** 175 Peterson Dr. Jct US 95, 0.8 mi w on SR 8, just n. Int corridors. **Pets:** Accepted.
⊗ ▯

MOUNTAIN HOME

AAA ▼▼▼ Best Western Foothills Motor Inn SH
(208) 587-8477. **$79-$99.** 1080 Hwy 20. I-84, exit 95, just n. Ext corridors. **Pets:** Accepted.
SAVE S⊘ ⊗ ⅏ ▯ ▱ ⇌

▼▼ Sleep Inn SH
(208) 587-9743. **$66-$78.** 1180 Hwy 20. I-84, exit 95, just n. Int corridors. **Pets:** Accepted.
ASK S⊘ ⊗ ▯ ▱

NAMPA

AAA ▼▼▼ Shilo Inn Nampa Suites SH ❧
(208) 465-3250. **$115.** 1401 Shilo Dr. I-84, exit 36, just nw. Int corridors. **Pets:** $25 one-time fee/room. Designated rooms, service with restrictions, supervision.
SAVE S⊘ ⊗ ▯ ▱ ▥ ⇌ ⊠

OROFINO

▼▼▼ Best Western Lodge at River's Edge SH
(208) 476-9999. **$77-$220.** 615 Main St. Downtown. Int corridors. **Pets:** Accepted.
ASK S⊘ ⊗ ▯ ▱ ▥ ⇌ ⊠

AAA ▼▼ Konkolville Motel M
(208) 476-5584. **$55-$85.** 2000 Konkolville Rd. 2.7 mi e on Michigan Ave. Ext corridors. **Pets:** Other species. $15 daily fee/pet. Designated rooms, service with restrictions, supervision.
SAVE S⊘ ⊗ ▯ ⇌

POCATELLO

AAA ▼▼▼ Best Western CottonTree Inn SH ❧
(208) 237-7650. **Call for rates.** 1415 Bench Rd. I-15, exit 71, just e. Int corridors. **Pets:** Other species. $25 deposit/room. Service with restrictions, crate.
SAVE ⊗ ▯ ▱ ⇌

AAA ▼▼ Comfort Inn SH ❧
(208) 237-8155. **$70-$100.** 1333 Bench Rd. I-15, exit 71, just e. Int corridors. **Pets:** Small, dogs only. $10 daily fee/pet. Designated rooms, service with restrictions, supervision.
SAVE S⊘ ⊗ ▯ ▱ ⇌

▼▼▼▼ Holiday Inn-Pocatello SH
(208) 237-1400. **$79-$99.** 1399 Bench Rd. I-15, exit 71, just e. Ext/int corridors. **Pets:** Accepted.
ASK S⊘ ⊗ ▯ ▱ ▥ ⇌ ⊠

AAA ▼▼ Pocatello Super 8 Motel SH
(208) 234-0888. **$65-$115.** 1330 Bench Rd. I-15, exit 71, just e. Int corridors. **Pets:** Other species. $10 one-time fee/room. Designated rooms, service with restrictions, supervision.
SAVE S⊘ ⊗ ▯

AAA ▼▼ Ramada Inn & Convention Center SH
(208) 237-0020. **$60-$100.** 133 W Burnside. I-86, exit 61, just n. Int corridors. **Pets:** Large, dogs only. $10 daily fee/pet. Designated rooms, service with restrictions, supervision.
SAVE S⊘ ⊗ ▯ ▱ ▥ ⇌ ⊠

AAA ▼▼ Red Lion Hotel Pocatello SH ❧
(208) 233-2200. **$110.** 1555 Pocatello Creek Rd. I-15, exit 71, just e. Int corridors. **Pets:** Other species. $10 daily fee/room. Designated rooms, service with restrictions, supervision.
SAVE S⊘ ⊗ ▯ ▱ ▥ ⇌ ⊠

▼ Thunderbird Motel M
(208) 232-6330. **$40-$69.** 1415 S 5th Ave. I-15, exit 67, 1.3 mi n; just s of Idaho State University. Ext corridors. **Pets:** Accepted.
ASK S⊘ ⊗ ▯ ⇌

PONDERAY

AAA ▼▼▼ GuestHouse Inn & Suites–Sandpoint SH
(208) 263-5383. **$49-$89.** 477255 Hwy 95 N. 1.2 mi n on US 95 from jct SR 200. Int corridors. **Pets:** Accepted.
SAVE S⊘ ⊗ ⅏ ▯

▼▼ Super 8 Motel SH
(208) 263-2210. **Call for rates.** 476841 Hwy 95 N. 0.7 mi n on US 95 from jct SR 200. Int corridors. **Pets:** Accepted.
⊗ ⅏ ▯

POST FALLS

AAA ▼▼▼ Howard Johnson Express SH
(208) 773-4541. **Call for rates.** 3647 W 5th Ave. I-90, exit 2, just ne. Int corridors. **Pets:** Accepted.
SAVE ⊗ ⅏ ▯ ▱ ⇌

AAA ▼▼▼ Post Falls Comfort Inn SH ❧
(208) 773-8900. **$69-$119.** 3175 E Seltice Way. I-90, exit 7, just sw. Int corridors. **Pets:** $20 one-time fee/room. Supervision.
SAVE S⊘ ⊗ ⅏ ▯ ▱

AAA ▼▼▼ Red Lion Templin's Hotel on the River–Post Falls SH
(208) 773-1611. **$190.** 414 E First Ave. I-90, exit 5 eastbound, just s to First Ave; exit 6 westbound, 0.7 mi w on Seltice Way to Spokane St, 0.5 mi s, then just e. Int corridors. **Pets:** Dogs only. $20 daily fee/pet. Service with restrictions, supervision.
SAVE S⊘ ⊗ ⅏ ▯ ▱ ▥ ⇌ ⊠

AAA ▼▼▼ Sleep Inn SH ❧
(208) 777-9394. **$59-$139.** 157 S Pleasant View Rd. I-90, exit 2, just s. Int corridors. **Pets:** Medium. $20 one-time fee/room. Designated rooms, service with restrictions, supervision.
SAVE S⊘ ⊗ ▱ ⇌

PRIEST RIVER

▼▼ Eagle's Nest Motel M
(208) 448-2000. **$50-$99.** 1007 Albeni Hwy (US 2). US 2, 0.5 mi w. Ext corridors. **Pets:** Accepted.
ASK ⊗ ⅏ ▯ ▱

REXBURG

▼▼▼ AmericInn Lodge & Suites SH
(208) 356-5333. **$80-$210.** 1098 Golden Beauty Dr. US 20, exit 332 (S Rexburg). Int corridors. **Pets:** Other species. $20 one-time fee/room. Designated rooms, service with restrictions, supervision.
ASK ⊗ ▯ ⇌ ⊠

AAA ▼▼ Best Western CottonTree Inn SH
(208) 356-4646. **Call for rates.** 450 W 4th St S. US 20, exit 332 (S Rexburg), 1 mi e. Int corridors. **Pets:** Small. $15 one-time fee/room. Service with restrictions, supervision.
SAVE ⊗ ▯ ▱ ▥ ⇌

AAA ▼▼▼ Comfort Inn SH
(208) 359-1311. **$69-$109.** 885 W Main St. US 20, exit 333 (Salmon), just e. Int corridors. **Pets:** Other species. Service with restrictions, supervision.
SAVE S⊘ ⊗ ▯ ▱ ⇌

RIGGINS

Best Western Salmon Rapids Lodge SH
(208) 628-2743. **Call for rates.** 1010 S Main St. Just e of US 95; downtown. Int corridors. **Pets:** Accepted.

Pinehurst Resort Cabins CA
(208) 628-3323. **$55-$95.** 5604 Hwy 95. On US 95, 13 mi s. Ext corridors. **Pets:** Accepted.

SAGLE

Bottle Bay Resort & Marina CA
(208) 263-5916. **Call for rates.** 115 Resort Rd. 8.3 mi e on Bottle Bay Rd from US 95. Ext corridors. **Pets:** Accepted.

SALMON

Motel DeLuxe M
(208) 756-2231. **$46-$56.** 112 S Church St. Just s of Main St; downtown. Ext corridors. **Pets:** Accepted.

Stagecoach Inn M
(208) 756-2919. **$61-$85, 7 day notice.** 201 Hwy 93 N. Just n on US 93 from jct SR 28. Int corridors. **Pets:** Accepted.

SANDPOINT

Best Western Edgewater Resort SH
(208) 263-3194. **$139-$299.** 56 Bridge St. Just e of US 95 N; downtown. Int corridors. **Pets:** Dogs only. $10 daily fee/pet. Service with restrictions, supervision.

The K2 Inn M
(208) 263-3441. **Call for rates.** 501 N Fourth Ave. US 95, just e. Ext corridors. **Pets:** Accepted.

La Quinta Inn Sandpoint SH
(208) 263-9581. **$109.** 415 Cedar St. Jct US 2 and 95; downtown. Ext/int corridors. **Pets:** Other species. Service with restrictions, supervision.

Quality Inn Sandpoint SH
(208) 263-2111. **$79-$179.** 807 N 5th. US 2 and 95, just s of jct SR 200. Int corridors. **Pets:** Accepted.

TWIN FALLS

Comfort Inn SH
(208) 734-7494. **$79-$200.** 1893 Canyon Springs Rd. I-84, exit 173, 3.5 mi s on US 93. Int corridors. **Pets:** Accepted.

Days Inn SH
(208) 324-6400. **$69-$85.** 1200 Centennial Spur. I-84, exit 173, just n on US 93. Int corridors. **Pets:** Accepted.

Red Lion Hotel Canyon Springs SH ☙
(208) 734-5000. **$169.** 1357 Blue Lakes Blvd N. I-84, exit 173, 4 mi s on US 93. Int corridors. **Pets:** Medium, other species. $20 daily fee/pet. Service with restrictions, supervision.

Shilo Inn Suites Twin Falls SH ☙
(208) 733-7545. **$170.** 1586 Blue Lakes Blvd N. I-84, exit 173, 3.7 mi s on US 93. Int corridors. **Pets:** $25 one-time fee/room. Designated rooms, service with restrictions, supervision.

Twin Falls Super 8 Motel M
(208) 734-5801. **Call for rates.** 1260 Blue Lakes Blvd N. I-84, exit 173, 4.1 mi s on US 93. Int corridors. **Pets:** Accepted.

WALLACE

Stardust Motel M
(208) 752-1213. **$52-$90.** 410 Pine St. I-90, exit 61 (Business Rt 90), 0.7 mi e; downtown. Ext corridors. **Pets:** Other species. $15 daily fee/pet. Service with restrictions, supervision.

The Wallace Inn SH
(208) 752-1252. **$78-$108.** 100 Front St. I-90, exit 61 (Business Rt 90), just se. Int corridors. **Pets:** Other species. $15 daily fee/pet. Service with restrictions, supervision.

WHITE BIRD

Hells Canyon Jet Boat Trips & Lodging M
(208) 839-2255. **Call for rates (no credit cards).** 3252 Waterfront Dr. 1 mi s of White Bird on Old Hwy 95. Ext corridors. **Pets:** $15 daily fee/pet. Service with restrictions, supervision.

WORLEY

Coeur d'Alene Casino Resort Hotel SH
(208) 686-0248. **Call for rates.** 27068 S Hwy 95. On US 95, 3 mi n. Int corridors. **Pets:** Accepted.

ILLINOIS

ALTON

▼▼ Comfort Inn SH
(618) 465-9999. **$85-$99.** 11 Crossroads Ct. Off SR 3, jct SR 140. Int corridors. **Pets:** Other species. Service with restrictions, supervision.
(ASK) (S/o) (X) (&M) 🛗 💻 ≈

▼ Super 8 Motel SH
(618) 465-8885. **$54-$80.** 1800 Homer Adams Pkwy. On SR 111, 1.8 mi e or jct US 67. Int corridors. **Pets:** $50 deposit/room. Service with restrictions, supervision.
(ASK) (S/o) (X) (&M) 🛗 💻

ARCOLA

▼▼ Comfort Inn SH
(217) 268-4000. **$45-$120.** 610 E Springfield Rd. I-57, exit 203 (SR 133), just w. Int corridors. **Pets:** Accepted.
(ASK) (S/o) (X) 🛗 💻 ≈

BELLEVILLE

◆◆◆◆ ▼ The Shrine Hotel SH
(618) 397-1162. **$73.** 451 S Demazenod Dr. I-255, exit 17A, 1 mi e on SR 15; in Shrine of Our Lady of the Snows Complex. Int corridors. **Pets:** Medium, other species. Service with restrictions, crate.
(SAVE) (S/o) (X) 🛗 💻 🍽 (X)

BLOOMINGTON

▼▼ Baymont Inn & Suites SH
(309) 662-2800. **$62-$92.** 604 1/2 IAA Dr. I-55, exit 167 southbound, follow I-55 business route (Veterans Pkwy), 2.8 mi s to jct SR 9, just e, then just n via service road; exit 157B (Veterans Pkwy) northbound, 4 mi n to SR 9. Int corridors. **Pets:** Accepted.
(ASK) (S/o) (X) 🛗 💻 ≈

▼▼▼▼ Country Inn & Suites By Carlson Bloomington/Normal-Airport SH
(309) 662-3100. **$102-$125.** 2403 E Empire St. Jct I-55 business route (Veterans Pkwy) and SR 9, 0.8 mi e. Int corridors. **Pets:** Accepted.
(ASK) (S/o) (X) 🛗 💻 ≈ (X)

▼▼▼▼ DoubleTree Hotel Bloomington LH
(309) 664-6446. **Call for rates.** 10 Brickyard Dr. I-55 business route (Veterans Pkwy), just n of US 150. Int corridors. **Pets:** Large. $50 one-time fee/pet. No service.
(X) 🛗 💻 🍽 ≈ (X)

▼▼▼ Eastland Suites Hotel & Conference Center SH
(309) 662-0000. **$99-$169.** 1801 Eastland Dr. Jct I-55 business route (Veterans Pkwy) and SR 9, just s to Eastland Dr, then just e. Ext/int corridors. **Pets:** Accepted.
(ASK) (S/o) (X) 🛗 💻 ≈ (X)

▼▼ Econo Lodge by Choice Hotels M
(309) 829-3100. **$45-$105.** 403 Brock Dr. I-55/74, exit 160 (SR 9), just e. Ext corridors. **Pets:** Accepted.
(ASK) (X) 🛗 💻

▼▼▼ Holiday Inn Express SH
(309) 820-9990. **$129.** 1031 Wylie Dr. I-55/74, exit 160 (SR 9), just w, then just n. Int corridors. **Pets:** Accepted.
(ASK) (S/o) (X) 🛗 💻 ≈

▼▼▼ Ramada Limited & Suites Bloomington/Normal-West SH
(309) 828-0900. **$69-$129.** 919 Maple Hill Rd. I-55/74, exit 160 (SR 9), 0.3 mi w to Wylie Rd, just n, then just e. Int corridors. **Pets:** Accepted.
(ASK) (S/o) (X) 🛗 💻 ≈

BOURBONNAIS

▼▼ Hampton Inn Bradley/Kankakee SH
(815) 932-8369. **Call for rates.** 60 Ken Hayes Dr. I-57, exit 315 (SR 50). Int corridors. **Pets:** Accepted.
(X) 🛗 💻 ≈

CARBONDALE

▼▼▼ Hampton Inn SH
(618) 549-6900. **$89-$169.** 2175 Reed Station Pkwy. I-57, exit 54B, 11.7 mi w on SR 13. Int corridors. **Pets:** Accepted.
(ASK) (S/o) (X) (&M) 🛗 💻 ≈

▼▼▼ Holiday Inn Hotel and Conference Center SH
(618) 549-2600. **$119-$149.** 2300 Reed Station Pkwy. I-57, exit 54B, 12 mi w. Int corridors. **Pets:** Accepted.
(ASK) (S/o) (X) (&M) 🛗 💻 🍽 ≈

▼ Super 8 Motel SH
(618) 457-8822. **$56-$95.** 1180 E Main St. I-57, exit 54B, 13.9 mi w on SR 13. Int corridors. **Pets:** Service with restrictions, supervision.
(ASK) (S/o) (X) 🛗 💻

CARLINVILLE

Best Western Carlinville Inn 🆂🅷
(217) 324-2100. **$77.** 19067 W Frontage Rd. I-55, exit 60 (SR 108), just w. Int corridors. **Pets:** Accepted.
🆂🅰🆅🅴 🆂📬 🗙 🔳 🔳 🍴 🏊

CASEY

Comfort Inn 🆂🅷
(217) 932-2212. **$81-$84.** 933 SR 49 N. I-70, exit 129, 0.3 mi se. Int corridors. **Pets:** Other species. $10 daily fee/pet. Service with restrictions, supervision.
🆂🅰🆅🅴 🆂📬 🗙 🔳 🔳 🏊

CHAMPAIGN

Baymont Inn & Suites 🆂🅷
(217) 356-8900. **$79-$150.** 302 W Anthony Dr. I-74, exit 182 (Neil St), just nw. Int corridors. **Pets:** Medium. $50 deposit/pet, $10 daily fee/pet. Designated rooms, service with restrictions, supervision.
🆂🅰🆅🅴 🆂📬 🗙 🔳 🔳

Country Inn & Suites by Carlson 🆂🅷
(217) 355-6666. **$100.** 602 W Marketview Dr. I-74, exit 181 (Prospect Rd), just n, then just e. Int corridors. **Pets:** Small. $15 daily fee/room. Designated rooms, service with restrictions, supervision.
🆂🅰🆅🅴 🆂📬 🗙 🅼 🔳 🔳 🏊

Drury Inn & Suites-Champaign 🆂🅷
(217) 398-0030. **$91-$162.** 905 W Anthony Dr. I-74, exit 181 (Prospect Blvd), just n. Int corridors. **Pets:** Large, other species. Service with restrictions, supervision.
🅰🆂🅺 🗙 🅼 🔳 🔳 🏊

Extended StayAmerica-Champaign-Urbana 🆂🅷
(217) 351-8899. **$73-$135.** 610 W Marketview Dr. I-74, exit 181 (Prospect Rd), just n, then just e. Int corridors. **Pets:** Other species. $75 one-time fee/pet. Service with restrictions.
🅰🆂🅺 🆂📬 🗙 🔳 🔳

La Quinta Inn Champaign 🆂🅷
(217) 356-4000. **$72-$86.** 1900 Center Dr. I-74, exit 182B (Neil St), just n. Int corridors. **Pets:** Other species. Service with restrictions, supervision.
🅰🆂🅺 🆂📬 🗙 🅼 🔳 🔳 🏊

CHESTER

Best Western Reids' Inn 🆂🅷
(618) 826-3034. **$75-$105.** 2150 State St. SR 150, 1 mi e of SR 3. Int corridors. **Pets:** Very small, dogs only. $25 deposit/pet. Designated rooms, service with restrictions, supervision.
🆂🅰🆅🅴 🆂📬 🗙 🔳 🔳 🏊

CHICAGO METROPOLITAN AREA

ALGONQUIN

Holiday Inn Express Hotel & Suites 🆂🅷
(847) 458-6000. **$85-$110, 7 day notice.** 2595 Bunker Hill Rd. I-90, exit Randall Rd N, 6.1 mi n to Bunker Hill Rd, then just w. Int corridors. **Pets:** Very small. $50 one-time fee/room. Designated rooms, service with restrictions, supervision.
🆂🅰🆅🅴 🆂📬 🗙 🅼 🔳 🔳 🏊 🗙

ALSIP

Baymont Inn-Midway South 🆂🅷
(708) 597-3900. **Call for rates.** 12801 S Cicero Ave. I-294, exit SR 50 (Cicero Ave S). Int corridors. **Pets:** Accepted.
🗙 🔳 🔳

ANTIOCH

Regency Inn 🆂🅷
(847) 395-3606. **$96.** 350 Rt 173. SR 173, 0.5 mi w of jct SR 83. Int corridors. **Pets:** Medium. $50 deposit/pet, $15 daily fee/pet. Service with restrictions, crate.
🆂🅰🆅🅴 🆂📬 🗙 🔳 🔳 🏊

ARLINGTON HEIGHTS

DoubleTree Hotel Chicago-Arlington Heights 🅻🅷
(847) 364-7600. **$89-$299.** 75 W Algonquin Rd. I-90, exit Arlington Heights Rd, just n to Algonquin Rd, then just w. Int corridors. **Pets:** Accepted.
🅰🆂🅺 🆂📬 🗙 🅼 🔳 🔳 🍴 🏊 🗙

Jameson Suites 🆂🅷
(847) 956-1400. **Call for rates.** 2111 S Arlington Heights Rd. I-90, exit Arlington Heights Rd, 0.6 mi n. Int corridors. **Pets:** Accepted.
🗙 🔳 🔳 🗙

La Quinta Inn Chicago (Arlington Heights) 🆂🅷
(847) 253-8777. **$90-$104.** 1415 W Dundee Rd. SR 53, exit Dundee Rd, just e. Int corridors. **Pets:** Other species. Service with restrictions, supervision.
🅰🆂🅺 🆂📬 🗙 🔳 🔳 🏊

Motel 6–1048 🆂🅷
(847) 806-1230. **$55-$65.** 441 W Algonquin Rd. I-90, exit Arlington Heights Rd, 0.5 mi n, then 0.5 mi w. Int corridors. **Pets:** Other species. Service with restrictions, supervision.
🆂📬 🗙 🅼 🔳

Red Roof Inn #7102 🅼
(847) 228-6650. **Call for rates.** 22 W Algonquin Rd. I-90, exit Arlington Heights Rd, 0.5 mi n, then just w. Ext corridors. **Pets:** Accepted.
🗙

Sheraton Chicago Northwest and CoCo Key Water Resort 🅻🅷
(847) 394-2000. **$139-$319.** 3400 W Euclid Ave. SR 53, exit Euclid Ave, just e. Int corridors. **Pets:** Accepted.
🆂🅰🆅🅴 🗙 🔳 🔳 🍴 🏊 🗙

AURORA

Staybridge Suites by Holiday Inn Aurora/Naperville 🆂🅷
(630) 978-2222. **$169-$199.** 4320 Meridian Pkwy. I-88, exit SR 59, 2 mi s to Meridian Pkwy, then just w. Int corridors. **Pets:** Other species. $75 one-time fee/pet. Service with restrictions, crate.
🅰🆂🅺 🆂📬 🗙 🅼 🔳 🔳 🏊 🗙

BANNOCKBURN

La Quinta Inn & Suites Deerfield 🆂🅷
(847) 317-7300. **$119-$155.** 2000 S Lakeside Dr. I-94, exit Half Day Rd (SR 22), just e to Lakeside Dr, then just s. Int corridors. **Pets:** Other species. Service with restrictions, supervision.
🅰🆂🅺 🆂📬 🗙 🅼 🔳 🔳 🏊 🗙

BEDFORD PARK

Extended StayAmerica Chicago-Midway 🆂🅷
(708) 496-8211. **$100-$110.** 7524 State Rd. Jct SR 50, just w. Int corridors. **Pets:** Other species. $75 one-time fee/pet. Service with restrictions.
🅰🆂🅺 🆂📬 🗙 🅼 🔳 🔳

BLOOMINGDALE

▼▼▼ Residence Inn by Marriott SH
(630) 893-9200. **$121-$143.** 295 Knollwood Dr. I-355, exit Army Trail Rd, 4 mi w, then just n. Int corridors. **Pets:** Accepted.
(ASK) (Sᴅ) (✕) (&M) (🛏) (▐) (🏊) (🌀)

BOLINGBROOK

▼▼▼ AmericInn Lodge & Suites SH ❖
(630) 378-5300. **$89-$119.** 175 W Remington Blvd. I-55, exit 267, just n on SR 53. Int corridors. **Pets:** Dogs only. $10 daily fee/pet. Service with restrictions.
(SAVE) (Sᴅ) (✕) (&M) (🛏) (▐) (🏊)

▼▼ La Quinta Inn Chicago-Bolingbrook SH
(630) 226-0000. **$114-$139.** 225 W South Frontage Rd. I-55, exit 267, 0.5 mi sw. Int corridors. **Pets:** Other species. Service with restrictions, supervision.
(ASK) (Sᴅ) (✕) (🛏) (▐) (🏊)

BRIDGEVIEW

▼▼ Exel Inn of Bridgeview SH
(708) 430-1818. **$69-$89.** 9625 S 76th Ave. I-294, exit 95th St, just s. Int corridors. **Pets:** Accepted.
(SAVE) (Sᴅ) (✕) (🛏) (▐)

BUFFALO GROVE

▼▼ Extended StayAmerica-Chicago-Buffalo Grove-Deerfield SH
(847) 215-0641. **$90-$100.** 1525 Busch Pkwy. I-94, exit Lake Cook Rd, 2 mi w to Milwaukee Ave (US 45/SR 21), then 1.3 mi n. Int corridors. **Pets:** Other species. $75 one-time fee/pet. Service with restrictions.
(ASK) (Sᴅ) (✕) (🛏) (▐)

BURR RIDGE

▼▼ Extended StayAmerica Chicago-Burr Ridge SH
(630) 323-6630. **$76-$84.** 15 W 122nd S Frontage Rd. I-55, exit 276A (County Line Rd), just sw. Int corridors. **Pets:** Other species. $75 one-time fee/pet. Service with restrictions.
(ASK) (Sᴅ) (✕) (🛏) (▐)

▼▼ The Oaks Hotel & Conference Center SH
(630) 325-2900. **$109-$179.** 300 S Frontage Rd. I-55, exit 276A (County Line Rd), just sw. Int corridors. **Pets:** Accepted.
(SAVE) (Sᴅ) (✕) (🛏) (▐) (🍽) (🏊) (🌀)

CHICAGO

▼▼▼ Affinia Chicago SH ❖
(312) 787-6000. **$329-$599.** 166 E Superior St. Just e of Michigan Ave. Int corridors. **Pets:** Other species. Service with restrictions, crate.
(SAVE) (Sᴅ) (✕) (🛏) (▐)

▼▼▼ Allegro Chicago, a Kimpton Hotel SH
(312) 236-0123. **$199-$559.** 171 W Randolph St. Jct La Salle St; in theater district. Int corridors. **Pets:** Accepted.
(SAVE) (Sᴅ) (✕) (🛏) (▐) (🍽)

▼▼▼ Allerton Hotel LH
(312) 440-1500. **$99-$999.** 701 N Michigan Ave. Jct Huron St. Int corridors. **Pets:** Accepted.
(SAVE) (✕) (▐) (🍽) (🌀)

▼▼▼ Amalfi Hotel Chicago SH ❖
(312) 395-9000. **$149-$549.** 20 W Kinzie St. Between State and Dearborn sts. Int corridors. **Pets:** Dogs only. Service with restrictions, supervision.
(SAVE) (Sᴅ) (✕) (&M) (🛏) (▐) (🌀)

▼▼▼ Avenue Hotel Chicago LH ❖
(312) 787-2900. **$239-$439.** 160 E Huron St. Just e of N Michigan Ave. Int corridors. **Pets:** Small. $75 one-time fee/room. Service with restrictions, supervision.
(SAVE) (Sᴅ) (✕) (🛏) (▐) (🍽) (🏊)

▼▼▼ Best Western Hawthorne Terrace SH
(773) 244-3434. **$149-$279.** 3434 N Broadway St. Between Belmont Ave and Addison St. Int corridors. **Pets:** Accepted.
(SAVE) (Sᴅ) (✕) (🛏) (▐) (🌀)

▼▼▼ Carlton Inn Midway M ❖
(773) 582-0900. **$109-$159.** 4944 S Archer Ave. I-55, exit 287 (Pulaski), 1.8 mi s to Archer Ave, then just e. Ext corridors. **Pets:** Medium. $50 deposit/pet. Designated rooms, service with restrictions, supervision.
(SAVE) (✕) (🛏) (▐)

▼▼▼▼ Conrad Chicago LH ❖
(312) 645-1500. **$215-$555.** 521 N Rush St at Michigan Ave. Jct Grand Ave. Int corridors. **Pets:** Small, dogs only. Service with restrictions, supervision.
(SAVE) (Sᴅ) (✕) (&M) (🛏) (▐) (🍽) (🌀)

▼▼▼ Crowne Plaza Chicago Metro SH
(312) 829-5000. **$139-$459.** 733 W Madison St. I-90/94, exit 51D (Madison St), at Monroe St. Int corridors. **Pets:** Small. $30 one-time fee/pet. Service with restrictions, crate.
(SAVE) (✕) (▐) (🍽)

▼▼▼▼ The Fairmont Chicago LH
(312) 565-8000. **$169-$509.** 200 N Columbus Dr. Jct Michigan Ave and Wacker Dr, just e. Int corridors. **Pets:** Medium. $35 one-time fee/pet. Designated rooms, service with restrictions, supervision.
(SAVE) (✕) (▐) (🍽)

▼▼▼▼ Four Seasons Hotel Chicago LH
(312) 280-8800. **$495-$715.** 120 E Delaware Pl. Jct Michigan Ave; just nw of John Hancock building. Int corridors. **Pets:** Accepted.
(SAVE) (✕) (&M) (🛏) (▐) (🍽) (🏊) (🌀)

▼▼▼ Hard Rock Hotel Chicago-A Preferred Hotel LH ❖
(312) 345-1000. **$209-$509.** 230 N Michigan Ave. Between Lake St and Wacker Dr. Int corridors. **Pets:** Medium. $50 one-time fee/pet. Service with restrictions.
(SAVE) (Sᴅ) (✕) (&M) (▐) (🍽) (🌀)

▼▼▼ Hilton Chicago LH
(312) 922-4400. **Call for rates.** 720 S Michigan Ave. I-290 (Congress Pkwy), just s. Int corridors. **Pets:** Accepted.
(SAVE) (✕) (▐) (🍽) (🏊) (🌀)

▼▼▼ Hilton Chicago O'Hare Airport LH
(773) 686-8000. **$149-$409.** O'Hare Intl Airport. Opposite and connected to terminal buildings at O'Hare International Airport, accessed via I-190. Int corridors. **Pets:** Accepted.
(SAVE) (✕) (▐) (🍽) (🏊) (🌀)

▼▼▼ Holiday Inn Chicago Mart Plaza LH
(312) 836-5000. **$129-$379, 3 day notice.** W Mart Center Dr. Jct N Orleans St; atop the Mart Center along the Chicago River. Int corridors. **Pets:** Accepted.
(SAVE) (Sᴅ) (✕) (🛏) (▐) (🍽) (🏊) (🌀)

▼▼▼ Hotel Burnham Chicago SH
(312) 782-1111. **$209-$519.** One W Washington St. Jct State St. Int corridors. **Pets:** Accepted.
(SAVE) (Sᴅ) (✕) (▐) (🍽)

◆◆◆ ▼▼▼▼ **Hotel Indigo Chicago-Downtown Gold Coast** SH
(312) 787-4980. **$179-$369.** 1244 N Dearborn St. Just s of Goethe St. Int corridors. **Pets:** Accepted.

SAVE ✕ 🖃 ¶¶

◆◆◆ ▼▼▼▼ **Hotel Monaco Chicago** SH ❖
(312) 960-8500. **$169-$599.** 225 N Wabash Ave. Jct Wacker Dr. Int corridors. **Pets:** Other species. Designated rooms.

SAVE S🖍 ✕ 🖃 ¶¶ ✕

◆◆◆ ▼▼▼▼ **Hotel Sax Chicago** LH ❖
(312) 245-0333. **$169-$849.** 333 N Dearborn St. Between Dearborn and State sts. Int corridors. **Pets:** Medium, other species. $50 one-time fee/room. Service with restrictions, supervision.

SAVE S🖍 ✕ 🛢 ¶¶ ✕

◆◆◆ ▼▼▼▼ **InterContinental Chicago** LH ❖
(312) 944-4100. **$159-$2700.** 505 N Michigan Ave. Just n of Chicago River. Int corridors. **Pets:** $50 deposit/room, $50 one-time fee/room. Service with restrictions, crate.

SAVE ✕ 🖃 ¶¶ ⤳ ✕

▼▼▼▼ **The James** LH
(312) 337-1000. **$539.** 55 E Ontario. At Ontario St, just w of N Michigan Ave. Int corridors. **Pets:** Accepted.

ASK ✕ 🖍M 🖃 ¶¶

◆◆◆ ▼▼▼▼ **Omni Chicago Hotel** LH
(312) 944-6664. **$359-$539 (no credit cards).** 676 N Michigan Ave. Jct Huron St. Int corridors. **Pets:** Small, dogs only. $50 one-time fee/room. Service with restrictions, crate.

SAVE S🖍 ✕ 🖍M 🖃 ⤳ ✕

◆◆◆ ▼▼▼▼ **The Palmer House Hilton** LH ❖
(312) 726-7500. **Call for rates.** 17 E Monroe St. Between State St and Wabash Ave. Int corridors. **Pets:** Medium, other species. Service with restrictions, supervision.

SAVE ✕ 🖃 ¶¶ ⤳ ✕

▼▼▼▼ **Park Hyatt Chicago** LH ❖
(312) 335-1234. **$310-$565, 3 day notice.** 800 N Michigan Ave. Jct Chicago and Michigan aves at Water Tower Square. Int corridors. **Pets:** Small, dogs only. $200 one-time fee/room.

ASK ✕ ¶¶ ✕

◆◆◆ ▼▼▼▼ **The Peninsula Chicago** LH
(312) 337-2888. **$525-$695.** 108 E Superior St. Jct Michigan Ave. Int corridors. **Pets:** Accepted.

SAVE ✕ 🛢 ¶¶ ⤳ ✕

◆◆◆ ▼▼▼▼ **Ramada Plaza Hotel Chicago O'Hare** SH
(773) 693-5800. **$117-$207, 3 day notice.** 5615 N Cumberland Ave. I-90, exit 79B (N Cumberland Ave S), just s. Int corridors. **Pets:** Accepted.

SAVE S🖍 ✕ 🖍M 🛢 🖃 ¶¶ ⤳

◆◆◆ ▼▼▼▼ **Renaissance Chicago Hotel** LH
(312) 372-7200. **$285-$428.** One W Wacker Dr. Jct State St. Int corridors. **Pets:** Accepted.

SAVE S🖍 ✕ 🖍M 🖃 ⤳ ✕

▼▼▼▼ **Residence Inn by Marriott Chicago Downtown/ Magnificent Mile** SH
(312) 943-9800. **$153-$307.** 201 E Walton Pl. Just e of Michigan Ave at Mies van der Rohe. Int corridors. **Pets:** Accepted.

ASK S🖍 ✕ 🖍M 🛢 🖃

◆◆◆ ▼▼▼▼ **The Ritz-Carlton, Chicago (A Four Seasons Hotel)** LH
(312) 266-1000. **$510-$4300.** 160 E Pearson St. Jct N Michigan Ave. Int corridors. **Pets:** Accepted.

SAVE S🖍 ✕ 🖃 ¶¶ ✕

◆◆◆ ▼▼▼▼ **Sheraton Chicago Hotel & Towers** LH ❖
(312) 464-1000. **$149-$549.** 301 E North Water St. Columbus Dr at Chicago River; just e of Michigan Ave. Int corridors. **Pets:** Dogs only. Service with restrictions, supervision.

SAVE S🖍 ✕ 🖃 ¶¶ ⤳ ✕

◆◆◆ ▼▼▼▼ **Sofitel Chicago Water Tower** LH ❖
(312) 324-4000. **$530.** 20 E Chestnut St. Jct Wabash Ave and Chestnut St, 1/2 blk w of Rush St. Int corridors. **Pets:** Medium, dogs only. $100 deposit/room. Service with restrictions, supervision.

SAVE S🖍 ✕ 🖍M ¶¶ ✕

◆◆◆ ▼▼▼▼ **The Sutton Place Hotel** LH
(312) 266-2100. **$270-$590.** 21 E Bellevue Pl. Jct Rush St. Int corridors. **Pets:** Accepted.

SAVE S🖍 ✕ 🛢 ¶¶

▼▼▼▼ **W Chicago-City Center** LH ❖
(312) 332-1200. **$699.** 172 W Adams St. Between La Salle and Wells sts. Int corridors. **Pets:** Medium. $100 one-time fee/room. Service with restrictions.

ASK S🖍 ✕ 🛢 ¶¶

▼▼▼▼ **W Chicago Lakeshore** LH
(312) 943-9200. **$699.** 644 N Lakeshore Dr. Jct Ontario St. Int corridors. **Pets:** Accepted.

ASK S🖍 ✕ ¶¶ ⤳

◆◆◆ ▼▼▼▼ **The Westin Chicago River North** LH ❖
(312) 744-1900. **$149-$599.** 320 N Dearborn St. Just n of Chicago River; between Dearborn and Clark sts; in River North area. Int corridors. **Pets:** Medium. Service with restrictions, crate.

SAVE S🖍 ✕ 🛢 🖃 ¶¶ ✕

◆◆◆ ▼▼▼▼ **The Westin Michigan Avenue Chicago** LH
(312) 943-7200. **$559-$569.** 909 N Michigan Ave. Across from John Hancock Center. Int corridors. **Pets:** Accepted.

SAVE S🖍 ✕ 🖍M 🖃 ¶¶

▼▼▼▼ **Wyndham Garden O'Hare** SH
(773) 693-2323. **Call for rates.** 8201 W Higgins Rd. I-90, exit 79B (Cumberland Ave N), just n to Higgins Rd (SR 72), then just e. Int corridors. **Pets:** Medium. $10 one-time fee/pet. Service with restrictions, supervision.

✕ 🛢 🖃 ¶¶ ⤳

CRESTWOOD

▼▼ **Hampton Inn-Chicago/Crestwood** SH
(708) 597-3330. **Call for rates (no credit cards).** 13330 S Cicero Ave. On SR 50 and 83, 0.8 mi s of jct I-294. Int corridors. **Pets:** Medium. Service with restrictions.

✕ 🛢 🖃 ⤳

CRYSTAL LAKE

◆◆◆ ▼▼▼ **Comfort Inn by Choice Hotels** SH
(815) 444-0040. **$79-$100.** 595 E Tracy Tr. Jct US 14 and SR 31, 0.4 mi w, then just s on Pingree St. Int corridors. **Pets:** Accepted.

SAVE S🖍 ✕ 🛢 🖃 ⤳

DARIEN

▼▼ **Extended StayAmerica Chicago-Darien** SH
(630) 985-4708. **$72-$79.** 2345 Sokol Ct. I-55, exit 271A, 0.5 mi s to Westgate Rd, then 0.5 mi ne via frontage road. Int corridors. **Pets:** Other species. $75 one-time fee/pet. Service with restrictions.

ASK S🖍 ✕ 🛢 🖃

DEERFIELD

▼ Red Roof Inn #7188 M
(847) 205-1755. **Call for rates.** 340 S Waukegan Rd. I-94, exit SR 43 (Waukegan Rd). Ext corridors. **Pets:** Accepted.
⊠ 🛢

DES PLAINES

AAA ▼▼▼ Comfort Inn O'Hare SH
(847) 635-1300. **$90-$300.** 2175 E Touhy Ave. I-294, exit Touhy Ave westbound, just w; exit Golf Rd (SR 58) eastbound, 0.3 mi w to River Rd, then 5.5 mi s. Int corridors. **Pets:** Medium. $20 daily fee/pet. Service with restrictions, supervision.
SAVE S⊙ ⊠ 🛢 💻

▼▼ Extended StayAmerica-Chicago-O'Hare SH
(847) 294-9693. **$95-$105.** 1201 E Touhy Ave. At SR 72 (Higgins Rd), 0.6 mi, w of US 12/45 (Mannheim Rd). Int corridors. **Pets:** Other species. $75 one-time fee/pet. Service with restrictions.
ASK S⊙ ⊠ ⑤M 🛢 💻

▼▼ Extended Stay Deluxe Chicago-O'Hare SH
(847) 768-0395. **$104-$115.** 1207 E Touhy Ave. At SR 72 (Higgins Rd), 0.6 mi w of US 12/45 (Mannheim Rd). Int corridors. **Pets:** Other species. $75 one-time fee/pet. Service with restrictions.
ASK S⊙ ⊠ ⑤M 🛢 💻

AAA ▼▼▼ Hilton Garden Inn Chicago-O'Hare Airport SH
(847) 296-8900. **$109-$249, 3 day notice.** 2930 S River Rd. I-294, exit Touhy Ave westbound, just s on River Rd, then 0.3 mi s; exit SR 58 (Golf Rd) eastbound, 0.3 mi w to River Rd, then 6 mi s. Int corridors. **Pets:** Large. $50 deposit/room. Designated rooms, service with restrictions, supervision.
SAVE S⊙ ⊠ ⑤M 🛢 💻 ⑪ ⌇

DOWNERS GROVE

▼ Red Roof Inn #7087 M
(630) 963-4205. **Call for rates.** 1113 Butterfield Rd. I-355, exit Butterfield Rd (SR 56), on frontage road; I-88, exit Highland Ave N, just w. Ext corridors. **Pets:** Accepted.
⊠ 🛢

ELGIN

AAA ▼▼▼ Quality Inn-Elgin SH
(847) 608-7300. **$75-$100.** 500 Tollgate Rd. I-90, exit SR 31 N, just n. Int corridors. **Pets:** Accepted.
SAVE S⊙ ⊠ ⑤M 🛢 💻

ELK GROVE VILLAGE

AAA ▼ Exel Inn of Elk Grove Village SH
(847) 895-2085. **$66-$86.** 1000 W Devon Ave. I-290, exit Thorndale Ave, 0.5 mi w to Rohlwing Rd, 0.3 mi n to Devon Ave, then 0.3 mi e. Int corridors. **Pets:** Accepted.
SAVE S⊙ ⊠ 🛢 💻

AAA ▼ Exel Inn of O'Hare SH
(847) 803-9400. **$69-$89.** 2881 Touhy Ave. Jct SR 72 (Higgins Rd) and 83 (Busse Rd), 1.5 mi e on SR 72 (Higgins Rd). Int corridors. **Pets:** Accepted.
SAVE S⊙ ⊠ 🛢 💻

▼▼▼ La Quinta Inn SH
(847) 439-6767. **$109-$139.** 1900 E Oakton St. Jct SR 72 (Higgins Rd) and 83 (Busse Rd). Int corridors. **Pets:** Other species. Service with restrictions, supervision.
ASK S⊙ ⊠ 🛢 💻 ⌇

AAA ▼▼▼ Quality Inn & Suites O'Hare/Elk Grove SH
(847) 593-8600. **$79-$300.** 100 Busse Rd. Just n of jct SR 72 (Higgins Rd). Int corridors. **Pets:** Small, other species. $30 one-time fee/pet. Designated rooms, service with restrictions, crate.
SAVE S⊙ ⊠ ⑤M 🛢 💻

AAA ▼▼▼ Super 8 Motel O'Hare SH
(847) 827-3133. **$70-$89.** 2951 Touhy Ave. Jct SR 72 (Higgins Rd) and 83 (Busse Rd), 1.5 mi e on SR 72 (Higgins Rd). Int corridors. **Pets:** Accepted.
SAVE S⊙ ⊠ ⑤M 🛢 💻 ⌇

ELMHURST

▼▼▼ Extended StayAmerica Chicago-Elmhurst SH
(630) 530-4353. **$85-$95.** 550 W Grand Ave. Jct US 20 (Lake St), 0.4 mi ne; adjacent to I-290 overpass. Int corridors. **Pets:** Other species. $75 one-time fee/pet. Service with restrictions.
ASK S⊙ ⊠ ⑤M 🛢 💻

EVANSTON

AAA ▼▼▼▼ Hotel Orrington LH 🐾
(847) 866-8700. **$119-$339.** 1710 Orrington Ave. Jct Church St. Int corridors. **Pets:** Medium. $50 one-time fee/pet. Service with restrictions, supervision.
SAVE S⊙ ⊠ ⑤M 🛢 💻 ⑪

GLENVIEW

▼▼ Baymont Inn & Suites Chicago-Glenview SH
(847) 635-8300. **Call for rates.** 1625 Milwaukee Ave. I-294, exit Willow Rd, 0.4 mi e to Landwehr Rd, 1.3 mi s to Lake Ave, then 0.5 mi w. Int corridors. **Pets:** Accepted.
⊠ 🛢 💻

▼▼▼ Staybridge Suites SH
(847) 657-0002. **Call for rates.** 2600 Lehigh Ave. I-294, exit Willow Rd, 2.4 mi e. Int corridors. **Pets:** Accepted.
⊠ ⑤M 🛢 💻 ⌇

GURNEE

▼▼ Comfort Suites by Choice Hotels SH
(847) 782-0890. **$79-$199.** 5430 Grand Ave. I-94, exit Grand Ave (SR 132 E), 0.5 mi e. Int corridors. **Pets:** Accepted.
ASK S⊙ ⊠ ⑤M 🛢 💻 ⌇

▼▼▼ Country Inn & Suites By Carlson SH
(847) 625-9700. **$79-$179.** 5420 Grand Ave. I-94, exit Grand Ave (SR 132), 0.5 mi e. Int corridors. **Pets:** Accepted.
⊠ ⑤M 🛢 💻 ⌇

▼▼ Extended StayAmerica-Chicago-Gurnee SH
(847) 662-3060. **$76-$84.** 5724 Northridge Dr. I-94, exit Grand Ave (SR 132 E), just e via service road. Int corridors. **Pets:** Other species. $75 one-time fee/pet. Service with restrictions.
ASK S⊙ ⊠ ⑤M 🛢 💻

▼▼ La Quinta Inn Chicago-Gurnee SH
(847) 662-7600. **$75-$104.** 5688 Northridge Dr. I-94, exit Grand Ave (SR 132), just e via service road. Int corridors. **Pets:** Other species. Service with restrictions, supervision.
ASK S⊙ ⊠ ⑤M 🛢 💻 ⌇

HANOVER PARK

▼▼ Extended StayAmerica-Chicago-Hanover Park SH
(630) 893-4823. **$86-$95.** 1075 Lake St. On US 20; between Gary Ave and Elgin-O'Hare Expwy. Int corridors. **Pets:** Other species. $75 one-time fee/pet. Service with restrictions.
ASK S⊙ ⊠ 🛢 💻

HARVEY

▼▼ **Sleep Inn by Choice Hotels-Chicago Southland** 🆂🅷
(708) 331-3400. **$60-$75.** 16940 Halsted St. I-80/294, exit Halsted St, just n. Int corridors. **Pets:** Accepted.

HOFFMAN ESTATES

▼▼ **La Quinta Inn Chicago (Hoffman Estates)** 🆂🅷
(847) 882-3312. **$92-$104.** 2280 Barrington Rd. I-90, exit Barrington Rd westbound, 0.3 mi s; exit SR 59 eastbound, 0.5 mi n to SR 72 (Higgins Rd), 2 mi e to Barrington Rd, then just n. Int corridors. **Pets:** Other species. Service with restrictions, supervision.

▼ **Red Roof Inn #7199** Ⓜ
(847) 885-7877. **Call for rates.** 2500 Hassell Rd. I-90, exit Barrington Rd westbound, 0.3 mi s; exit SR 59 eastbound, 0.5 mi n to SR 72 (Higgins Rd), 2 mi e to Barrington Rd, then just n. Ext corridors. **Pets:** Accepted.

ITASCA

▼▼ **Extended StayAmerica-Chicago-Itasca** 🆂🅷
(630) 250-1111. **$76-$84.** 1181 Rohlwing Rd. I-290, exit Thorndale Ave, 0.5 mi w. Int corridors. **Pets:** Other species. $75 one-time fee/pet. Service with restrictions.

Ⓐ ▼▼ ▼▼ **The Westin Chicago Northwest** 🅻🅷
(630) 773-4000. **$349.** 400 Park Blvd. I-290, exit Thorndale Ave, just e. Int corridors. **Pets:** Accepted.

JOLIET

▼▼ **Comfort Inn by Choice Hotels North** 🆂🅷
(815) 436-5141. **Call for rates.** 3235 Norman Ave. I-55, exit 257, just e. Int corridors. **Pets:** Accepted.

▼▼ **Comfort Inn by Choice Hotels-South** 🆂🅷
(815) 744-1770. **Call for rates.** 135 S Larkin Ave. I-80, exit 130B, 0.5 mi n. Int corridors. **Pets:** Accepted.

▼▼▼ **Holiday Inn Convention Center-Joliet** 🆂🅷
(815) 729-2000. **$94-$159.** 411 S Larkin Ave. I-80, exit 130B, just nw. Int corridors. **Pets:** Accepted.

▼ **Red Roof Inn #7071** Ⓜ
(815) 741-2304. **Call for rates.** 1750 McDonough St. I-80, exit 130B, just off Larkin Ave. Ext corridors. **Pets:** Accepted.

LANSING

▼▼ **Extended StayAmerica-Chicago-Lansing** 🆂🅷
(708) 895-6402. **$76-$84.** 2520 173rd St. I-80, exit 161 (Torrence Ave), just n. Int corridors. **Pets:** Other species. $75 one-time fee/pet. Service with restrictions.

▼ **Red Roof Inn #7078** Ⓜ
(708) 895-9570. **Call for rates.** 2450 E 173rd St. I-80/94, exit 161 (Torrence Ave), just n. Ext corridors. **Pets:** Accepted.

LIBERTYVILLE

▼▼▼ **Holiday Inn Express Hotel & Suites** 🆂🅷
(847) 549-7878. **$135-$205.** 77 Buckley Rd. I-94, exit SR 137 (Buckley Rd), 2.3 mi w. Int corridors. **Pets:** Accepted.

LINCOLNSHIRE

▼▼▼ **Homewood Suites by Hilton Chicago-Lincolnshire** 🆂🅷
(847) 945-9300. **Call for rates.** 10 Westminister Way. I-94, exit Half Day Rd, just w. Int corridors. **Pets:** Accepted.

LISLE

▼▼ **Extended StayAmerica-Chicago-Lisle** 🆂🅷
(630) 434-7710. **$76-$84.** 445 Warrenville Rd. I-355, exit Ogden Ave E. Int corridors. **Pets:** Other species. $75 one-time fee/pet. Service with restrictions.

LOMBARD

▼▼ **Extended Stay Deluxe-Chicago-Lombard-Oak Brook** 🆂🅷
(630) 424-1000. **$85-$94.** 260 E 22nd St. I-88, exit Highland Ave, 0.8 mi n to 22nd St, then just e. Int corridors. **Pets:** Other species. $75 one-time fee/pet. Service with restrictions.

▼▼ **Homestead Studio Suites Hotel-Chicago/Lombard-Oak Brook** 🆂🅷
(630) 928-0202. **$76-$84.** 2701 Technology Dr. I-88, exit Highland Ave, just n, 0.6 mi e on Butterfield Rd (SR 56), then just s. Int corridors. **Pets:** Other species. $75 one-time fee/pet. Service with restrictions.

▼▼▼ **Residence Inn by Marriott Chicago Lombard** 🆂🅷
(630) 629-7800. **Call for rates.** 2001 S Highland Ave. I-88, exit Highland Ave, 0.8 mi n. Ext corridors. **Pets:** Accepted.

▼▼ **Towne Place Suites by Marriott Chicago Lombard** 🆂🅷
(630) 932-4400. **Call for rates.** 455 E 22nd St. I-88, exit Highland, 0.8 mi, then 0.3 mi. Int corridors. **Pets:** Accepted.

MATTESON

▼▼▼ **Country Inn & Suites by Carlson** 🆂🅷
(708) 748-4740. **Call for rates.** 950 Lake Superior Dr. I-57, exit 340A, 0.3 mi e, then 0.3 mi n. Int corridors. **Pets:** Accepted.

▼▼ **La Quinta Inn Chicago-Matteson** 🆂🅷
(708) 503-0999. **$69-$79.** 5210 W Southwick Dr. I-57, exit 340A, 0.3 mi e on US 30, then 0.3 mi s on Cicero Ave (SR 50). Int corridors. **Pets:** Other species. Service with restrictions, supervision.

MUNDELEIN

▼▼▼ **Crowne Plaza Chicago North Shore** 🆂🅷
(847) 949-5100. **$100-$300.** 510 SR 83 E. Jct US 45 and SR 83. Int corridors. **Pets:** Accepted.

NAPERVILLE

Best Western Naperville Inn SH
(630) 505-0200. **$70-$120.** 1617 Naperville Rd. I-88, exit Naperville Rd, 0.5 mi s. Ext/int corridors. **Pets:** Dogs only. $10 daily fee/pet. Designated rooms, service with restrictions, crate.

Exel Inn of Naperville SH
(630) 357-0022. **$59-$79.** 1585 Naperville/Wheaton Rd. I-88, exit Naperville Rd, 0.5 mi s. Int corridors. **Pets:** Accepted.

Extended StayAmerica-Chicago-Naperville SH
(630) 983-0000. **$76-$84.** 1575 Bond St. I-88, exit SR 59, just s. Int corridors. **Pets:** Other species. $75 one-time fee/pet. Service with restrictions.

Homestead Studio Suites Hotel-Chicago-Naperville SH
(630) 577-0200. **$76-$84.** 1827 Centre Point Cir. I-88, exit Naperville Rd, just s to Diehl Rd, 0.8 mi w, then just n. Int corridors. **Pets:** Other species. $75 one-time fee/pet. Service with restrictions.

Red Roof Inn #7195 M
(630) 369-2500. **Call for rates.** 1698 W Diehl Rd. I-88, exit SR 59, just s. Ext corridors. **Pets:** Accepted.

TownePlace Suites by Marriott Naperville SH
(630) 548-0881. **$144-$164.** 1843 W Diehl Rd. I-88, exit SR 59, just s to Diehl Rd, then just w. Int corridors. **Pets:** Accepted.

NORTHBROOK

Radisson Hotel Northbrook LH
(847) 298-2525. **$169-$219.** 2875 N Milwaukee Ave. I-294, exit Willow Rd, 1 mi w to SR 21 and US 45, then 0.6 mi s. Int corridors. **Pets:** Small. $25 one-time fee/room. Designated rooms, supervision.

OAK BROOK

Residence Inn by Marriott Chicago/Oak Brook SH
(630) 571-0200. **$208-$241.** 790 Jorie Blvd. I-88, exit Midwest Rd eastbound, just n to 22nd St (Cermak Rd), 1.7 mi e to Jorie Blvd, then just sw; exit 22nd St (Cermak Rd) westbound, 0.4 mi e to Jorie Blvd. Int corridors. **Pets:** Accepted.

OAKBROOK TERRACE

La Quinta Inn Chicago (Oak Brook) SH
(630) 495-4600. **$94-$115.** 1 S 666 Midwest Rd. I-88, exit Midwest Rd eastbound, 0.4 mi n, then just n of 22nd St (Cermak Rd); exit 22nd St (Cermak Rd) westbound, 1.1 mi w to Midwest Rd, then just n. Int corridors. **Pets:** Other species. Service with restrictions, supervision.

Staybridge Suites Chicago-Oakbrook Terrace SH
(630) 953-9393. **Call for rates.** 200 Royce Blvd. I-88, exit Midwest Rd eastbound to 22nd St (Cermak Rd), 0.4 mi w to SR 56, just n, then just n on Renaissance Blvd; exit 22nd St (Cermak) westbound, 2.5 mi w on 22nd St to SR 56, just n, then just n on Renaissance Blvd. Int corridors. **Pets:** Accepted.

PALATINE

Holiday Inn Express Palatine/Arlington Heights SH
(847) 934-4900. **$94-$169.** 1550 E Dundee Rd. SR 53, exit Dundee Rd (SR 68), just w. Int corridors. **Pets:** Accepted.

Hotel Indigo Chicago-Schaumburg North SH
(847) 359-6900. **$119-$179.** 920 E Northwest Hwy (US 14). SR 53, exit Northwest Hwy (US 14), just w. Int corridors. **Pets:** Medium. $25 daily fee/pet. Service with restrictions, supervision.

PROSPECT HEIGHTS

Exel Inn of Prospect Heights SH
(847) 459-0545. **$64-$84.** 540 Milwaukee Ave. Jct SR 21 and US 45. Int corridors. **Pets:** Accepted.

RICHMOND

Save Inn Richmond/Geneva Lakes SH
(815) 678-4711. **$89-$115.** 11200 N Rt 12. 0.5 mi n of jct SR 173. Int corridors. **Pets:** Accepted.

ROLLING MEADOWS

Extended StayAmerica #530 Chicago-Rolling Meadows-Schaumburg-Convention Center SH
(847) 357-1000. **$76-$84.** 2400 Golf Rd. I-90, exit Arlington Heights Rd, just n to Algonquin Rd, 0.7 mi nw to Golf Rd, then 0.8 mi w. Int corridors. **Pets:** Other species. $75 one-time fee/pet. Service with restrictions.

Holiday Inn Rolling Meadows LH
(847) 259-5000. **$102-$295.** 3405 Algonquin Rd. On SR 62, just e of SR 53, 0.3 mi ne of I-90. Ext/int corridors. **Pets:** Other species. $50 one-time fee/room. Designated rooms, service with restrictions, supervision.

ROMEOVILLE

Comfort Inn by Choice Hotels Bolingbrook/Romeoville SH
(630) 226-1900. **Call for rates.** 1235 Lake View Dr. I-55, exit 263, just n. Int corridors. **Pets:** Accepted.

Extended StayAmerica Chicago-Romeoville SH
(630) 226-8966. **$85-$95.** 1225 Lakeview Dr. I-55, exit 263, just n. Int corridors. **Pets:** Other species. $75 one-time fee/pet. Service with restrictions.

ROSEMONT

Crowne Plaza Chicago O'Hare LH
(847) 671-6350. **$99-$339.** 5440 N River Rd. I-190, exit 1B (River Rd), just s. Int corridors. **Pets:** Large. $50 one-time fee/pet. Service with restrictions, supervision.

DoubleTree Hotel Chicago O'Hare Airport-Rosemont LH
(847) 292-9100. **$199-$209.** 5460 N River Rd. I-190, exit 1B (River Rd), just s. Int corridors. **Pets:** Accepted.

Embassy Suites Hotel O'Hare Rosemont LH
(847) 678-4000. **$109-$400.** 5500 N River Rd. I-190, exit 1B, just s. Int corridors. **Pets:** Small. $100 deposit/pet, $25 one-time fee/pet. Designated rooms, service with restrictions, crate.

▼▼▼▼ Residence Inn by Marriott Chicago-O'Hare **SH**
(847) 375-9000. **$253-$273.** 7101 Chestnut St. Jct US 12 and 45 and Touhy Ave. Int corridors. **Pets:** Accepted.

ASK 🛇 ✗ 🖬 📮 🎵 🏊

▼▼▼▼ Sheraton Gateway Suites O'Hare **LH**
(847) 699-6300. **$99-$349.** 6501 N Mannheim Rd. On US 12 and 45, at SR 72 (Higgins Rd). Int corridors. **Pets:** Accepted.

ASK ✗ 🖬 📮 🍽 🏊 🗶

🚗 ▼▼▼▼ The Westin O'Hare **LH**
(847) 698-6000. **$349.** 6100 N River Rd. I-190, exit 1B, just n. Int corridors. **Pets:** Accepted.

SAVE ✗ 🛗 📮 🍽 🏊 🗶

🚗 ▼▼▼▼ Wyndham O'Hare **LH**
(847) 297-1234. **Call for rates.** 6810 N Mannheim Rd. On US 12 and 45, 0.3 mi n of SR 72 (Higgins Rd). Int corridors. **Pets:** Accepted.

SAVE ✗ 🖬 📮 🍽 🏊 🗶

ST. CHARLES

🚗 ▼▼▼ Best Western Inn of St. Charles **SH**
(630) 584-4550. **$79-$149.** 1635 E Main St. On SR 64, 0.5 mi e of SR 25. Ext/int corridors. **Pets:** Dogs only. $10 daily fee/pet. Designated rooms, service with restrictions, supervision.

SAVE 🛇 ✗ 🖬 📮 🏊

🚗 ▼▼▼▼ Courtyard by Marriott Chicago-St Charles **SH** 🐾
(630) 377-6370. **$99-$149.** 700 Courtyard Dr. Jct SR 59 and 64, 3.4 mi w on SR 64, just n on Kirk Rd, then just w on Foxfield. Int corridors. **Pets:** Medium, other species. $75 one-time fee/room. Service with restrictions, crate.

SAVE 🛇 ✗ 🛗 🖬 📮 🍽 🏊 🗶

▼▼ Days Inn St. Charles **SH**
(630) 513-6500. **$70-$170.** 100 S Tyler Rd. Jct SR 25, 0.5 mi e on SR 64, then just s. Int corridors. **Pets:** Medium, other species. $10 daily fee/pet. No service, supervision.

ASK 🛇 ✗ 📮 🏊

🚗 ▼▼ Holiday Inn Express **SH**
(630) 584-5300. **$89-$129.** 1600 E Main St. On SR 64, 0.5 mi e of SR 25. Int corridors. **Pets:** Accepted.

SAVE 🛇 ✗ 🖬 📮

🚗 ▼▼▽ Pheasant Run Resort & Spa **LH**
(630) 584-6300. **$109-$199.** 4051 E Main St. On SR 64, 2.4 mi w of SR 59. Ext/int corridors. **Pets:** Accepted.

SAVE 🛇 ✗ 🖬 📮 🍽 🏊 🗶

🚗 ▼ Super 8 Motel-St. Charles **SH**
(630) 377-8388. **$70-$80.** 1520 E Main St. On SR 64, 1 mi e. Int corridors. **Pets:** Very small. $50 deposit/pet. Designated rooms, service with restrictions, supervision.

SAVE 🛇 ✗ 🖬

SCHAUMBURG

▼▼ Extended StayAmerica #4190 Chicago-Schaumburg-Convention Center **SH**
(847) 882-7011. **$81-$89.** 2000 N Roselle Rd. I-90, exit Roselle Rd, just sw. Int corridors. **Pets:** Other species. $75 one-time fee/pet. Service with restrictions.

ASK 🛇 ✗ 🖬 📮

▼▼ Homestead Studio Suites #9653 HSD-Chicago-Schaumburg-Convention Center **SH**
(847) 882-6900. **$90-$100.** 51 E State Pkwy. I-90, exit Roselle Rd, 0.8 mi s, then just e. Int corridors. **Pets:** Other species. $75 one-time fee/pet. Service with restrictions.

ASK 🛇 ✗ 🛗 🖬 📮

▼▼▼▼ Homewood Suites by Hilton-Schaumburg **SH**
(847) 605-0400. **Call for rates.** 815 E American Ln. I-290, exit SR 72 (Higgins Rd), 1.5 mi w, then 0.4 mi n on Plum Grove Rd. Ext/int corridors. **Pets:** Accepted.

✗ 🛗 🖬 📮 🏊 🗶

🚗 ▼▼▼▼ Hyatt Summerfield Suites **SH**
(847) 706-9007. **$188-$231.** 1251 E American Ln. I-290, exit SR 72 (Higgins Rd), 0.5 mi w to Meacham Rd, 0.5 mi n to American Ln, then just w. Int corridors. **Pets:** Accepted.

SAVE 🛇 ✗ 🛗 🖬 📮 🏊 🗶

▼▼▼▼ La Quinta Inn (Schaumburg) **SH**
(847) 517-8484. **$92-$114.** 1730 E Higgins Rd. I-290, exit SR 72 (Higgins Rd), just w. Int corridors. **Pets:** Other species. Service with restrictions, supervision.

ASK 🛇 ✗ 🖬 📮 🏊

🚗 ▼▼▼ Quality Inn **SH**
(847) 517-7737. **$99.** 600 N Martingale Rd. I-290, exit SR 72 (Higgins Rd), just w, then just n. Int corridors. **Pets:** Accepted.

SAVE 🛇 ✗ 🖬 📮 🏊

▼▼▼ Residence Inn by Marriott-Chicago/Schaumburg **SH**
(847) 517-9200. **$197-$219.** 1610 McConnor Pkwy. I-290, exit 1A (Woodfield/Golf rds) northbound, follow signs just n to Golf Rd, just w to McConnor Pkwy, then 0.8 mi n; exit 1B (Woodfield/Golf rds) southbound. Int corridors. **Pets:** Accepted.

ASK 🛇 ✗ 🛗 🖬 📮 🏊 🗶

▼▼▼▼ Staybridge Suites Chicago/Schaumburg **SH**
(847) 619-6677. **Call for rates.** 901 E Woodfield Office Ct. I-290, exit SR 72 (Higgins Rd), 1.5 mi w, then 0.3 mi n on Plum Grove Rd. Ext/int corridors. **Pets:** Accepted.

✗ 🖬 📮 🏊 🗶

SCHILLER PARK

▼▼▼▼ Comfort Suites by Choice Hotels at O'Hare **SH**
(847) 233-9000. **$99-$249.** 4200 N River Rd. Jct SR 19 (Irving Park Rd) and Des Plaines St/River Rd, just n. Int corridors. **Pets:** Medium. $50 one-time fee/room. Service with restrictions, supervision.

ASK 🛇 ✗ 🛗 🖬 📮 🍽

🚗 ▼▼▼▼ Four Points by Sheraton Chicago O'Hare Airport **LH**
(847) 671-6000. **$250.** 10249 W Irving Park Rd. Jct US 12 and 45 and SR 19 (Irving Park Rd). Int corridors. **Pets:** Accepted.

SAVE 🛇 ✗ 🛗 🖬 📮 🍽 🏊 🗶

SKOKIE

▼▼▼ Extended StayAmerica-Chicago-Skokie **SH**
(847) 663-9031. **$114-$126.** 5211 Old Orchard Rd. I-94, exit 35 (Old Orchard Rd). Int corridors. **Pets:** Other species. $75 one-time fee/pet. Service with restrictions.

ASK 🛇 ✗ 🖬 📮

▼▼▼▼ Holiday Inn Chicago North Shore **SH**
(847) 679-8900. **Call for rates.** 5300 W Touhy Ave. I-94, exit 39A, 0.5 mi w. Ext/int corridors. **Pets:** Accepted.

✗ 🖬 📮 🍽 🏊 🗶

TINLEY PARK

▼▼▼▼ La Quinta Inn & Suites Chicago-Tinley Park **SH**
(708) 633-1200. **$75-$89.** 7255 W 183rd St. I-80, exit 148B, 0.5 mi n to 183rd St, then just w to North Creek Business Center. Int corridors. **Pets:** Other species. Service with restrictions, supervision.

ASK 🛇 ✗ 🛗 🖬 📮 🏊

VERNON HILLS

▼▼ Homestead Studio Suites Hotel-Chicago/Vernon Hills-Lincolnshire 🆂🅷
(847) 955-1111. **$90-$100.** 675 Woodlands Pkwy. I-94, exit SR 60 (Townline Rd), 2.1 mi w to SR 21 (Milwaukee Ave), 1.9 mi s to Woodlands Pkwy, then just w. Int corridors. **Pets:** Other species. $75 one-time fee/pet. Service with restrictions.

🅰🆂🅺 🆂�‍ ⊠ 🛏 🖵

WARRENVILLE

▼▼▼ Residence Inn by Marriott Chicago Naperville/Warrenville 🆂🅷 🐾
(630) 393-3444. **$219-$230.** 28500 Bella Vista Pkwy. I-88, exit Winfield Rd, just n to Ferry Rd, then just e. Int corridors. **Pets:** Large. $100 one-time fee/room. Service with restrictions, crate.

🅰🆂🅺 🆂🙍 ⊠ 🆖 🛏 🖵 ⇥ ⊠

WAUKEGAN

▼▼ Candlewood Suites Chicago/Waukegan 🆂🅷
(847) 578-5250. **Call for rates.** 1151 S Waukegan Rd. I-94, exit SR 137 (Buckley Rd), 0.5 mi e to SR 43 (Waukegan Rd), then 1.9 mi n. Int corridors. **Pets:** Medium. Service with restrictions, supervision.

⊠ 🛏 🖵

▼ Crossland Studios-Chicago-Waukegan Ⓜ
(847) 688-0402. **$62-$68.** 1177 S Northpoint Blvd. At US 41; between US 41 and SR 43. Ext corridors. **Pets:** Other species. $75 one-time fee/pet. Service with restrictions.

🅰🆂🅺 🆂🙍 ⊠ 🛏 🖵

▼▼ Quality Inn Waukegan-Great Lakes 🆂🅷
(847) 662-3200. **$59-$109.** 619 S Green Bay Rd. I-94, exit SR 120 (Belvidere Rd) eastbound, 2.3 mi e. Int corridors. **Pets:** Accepted.

🅰🆂🅺 🆂🙍 ⊠ 🛏 🖵

▼▼▼ Residence Inn by Marriott-Waukegan/Gurnee 🆂🅷
(847) 689-9240. **$169-$224.** 1440 S White Oak Dr. I-94, exit SR 137 (Buckley Rd), 0.5 mi e to SR 43 (Waukegan Rd), 1.5 mi n to Lakeside Dr, then just e. Int corridors. **Pets:** Accepted.

🅰🆂🅺 🆂🙍 ⊠ 🆖 🛏 🖵 ⇥ ⊠

WEST DUNDEE

▼▼ TownePlace Suites by Marriott-Chicago/Elgin 🆂🅷
(847) 608-6320. **$89-$139.** 2185 Marriott Dr. I-90, exit SR 31, 0.4 mi n to Marriott Dr, then just e. Int corridors. **Pets:** Accepted.

🅰🆂🅺 🆂🙍 ⊠ 🛏 🖵 ⇥

WESTMONT

🅰🅰🅰 ▼▼▼ ClubHouse Inn & Suites 🆂🅷
(630) 920-2200. **$89-$129.** 630 Pasquinelli Dr. Just off US 34 (Ogden Ave), 0.3 mi nw of jct SR 83. Int corridors. **Pets:** Accepted.

🆂🅰🆅🅴 🆂🙍 ⊠ 🛏 🖵 ⇥ ⊠

▼▼ Homestead Studio Suites Hotel-Chicago/Westmont-Oak Brook 🆂🅷
(630) 323-9292. **$76-$84.** 855 Pasquinelli Dr. SR 83, exit US 34 (Ogden Ave), just w to Pasquinelli Dr, then 0.5 mi n. Int corridors. **Pets:** Other species. $75 one-time fee/pet. Service with restrictions.

🅰🆂🅺 🆂🙍 ⊠ 🆖 🛏 🖵

WILLOWBROOK

▼ Red Roof Inn #7167 Ⓜ
(630) 323-8811. **Call for rates.** 7535 Kingery Hwy. I-55, exit 274, 0.5 mi n on SR 83. Ext corridors. **Pets:** Accepted.

⊠ 🛏

▼▼ Super 8 Motel-Willowbrook 🆂🅷
(630) 789-6300. **$64-$99.** 820 W 79th St. I-55, exit 274, 0.3 mi n to Midway Dr, then e on frontage road. Ext/int corridors. **Pets:** Accepted.

🅰🆂🅺 🆂🙍 ⊠ 🛏 🖵 ⇥

WOODSTOCK

▼ Super 8 Motel 🆂🅷
(815) 337-8808. **Call for rates.** 1220 Davis Rd. On SR 47, s of jct US 14. Int corridors. **Pets:** Accepted.

⊠ 🛏

END METROPOLITAN AREA

CHILLICOTHE

▼ Super 8 Motel 🆂🅷
(309) 274-2568. **Call for rates.** 615 S Fourth St. 1.1 mi s on SR 29. Int corridors. **Pets:** Accepted.

⊠ 🛏 🖵

COLLINSVILLE

▼▼ Drury Inn-St. Louis/Collinsville 🆂🅷
(618) 345-7700. **$80-$126.** 602 N Bluff Rd. I-55/70, exit 11 (SR 157), just n. Int corridors. **Pets:** Large, other species. Service with restrictions, supervision.

🅰🆂🅺 ⊠ 🆖 🛏 🖵 ⇥

DANVILLE

🅰🅰🅰 ▼▼▼ Best Western Regency Inn 🆂🅷
(217) 446-2111. **$55-$165.** 360 Eastgate Dr. I-74, exit 220 (Lynch Dr), just n. Ext/int corridors. **Pets:** Very small, dogs only. $10 daily fee/pet. Designated rooms, service with restrictions, supervision.

🆂🅰🆅🅴 🆂🙍 ⊠ 🛏 🖵 ⇥

▼▼ Comfort Inn by Choice Hotels 🆂🅷
(217) 443-8004. **Call for rates.** 383 Lynch Dr. I-74, exit 220 (Lynch Dr), just n. Int corridors. **Pets:** Accepted.

⊠ 🛏 🖵 ⇥

▼▼ Sleep Inn & Suites 🆂🅷
(217) 442-6600. **$69-$109.** 361 Lynch Dr. I-74, exit 220 (Lynch Dr), just n. Int corridors. **Pets:** Accepted.

🅰🆂🅺 🆂🙍 ⊠ 🛏 🖵 ⇥

▼▼ Super 8 🆂🅷
(217) 443-4499. **Call for rates.** 377 Lynch Dr. I-74, exit 220 (Lynch Dr), just n. Int corridors. **Pets:** Accepted.

⊠ 🛏 🖵

DECATUR

▼▼▼ Decatur Conference Center & Hotel 🅻🅷
(217) 422-8800. **$99.** 4191 W Hwy 36. I-72, exit 133A (US 36), 1 mi e. Int corridors. **Pets:** Accepted.

🅰🆂🅺 🆂🙍 ⊠ 🆖 🛏 🖵 🍽 ⇥ ⊠

▼▼ Sleep Inn of Decatur 🆂🅷
(217) 872-7700. **Call for rates.** 3920 E Hospitality Ln. I-72, exit 144 (SR 48), just s to Brush College Rd, then just e. Int corridors. **Pets:** Accepted.

⊠ 🛏 🖵 ⇥

DEKALB

▼▼ Baymont Inn & Suites Dekalb/Sycamore SH
(815) 748-4800. **Call for rates.** 1314 W Lincoln Hwy. I-88, exit Annie Glidden Rd, 2 mi n to W Lincoln Hwy (SR 38), then 0.4 mi w. Int corridors. **Pets:** Accepted.
⊠ 🖂 🛢 🖃 🏊

AAA ▼▼ Best Western DeKalb Inn & Suites SH
(815) 758-8661. **$89, 14 day notice.** 1212 W Lincoln Hwy. I-88, exit Annie Glidden Rd, 2 mi n to W Lincoln Hwy (SR 38), then just w. Ext/int corridors. **Pets:** Medium. $50 deposit/room, $10 daily fee/room. Designated rooms, no service, supervision.
SAVE 🖂 ⊠ 🛢 🖃 🏊

DIXON

AAA ▼▼ Comfort Inn by Choice Hotels SH
(815) 284-0500. **$65-$159.** 136 Plaza Dr. I-88, exit SR 26, just n, then just e. Int corridors. **Pets:** Medium, other species. $15 daily fee/pet. Service with restrictions, supervision.
SAVE 🖂 ⊠ 🛢 🖃 🏊

AAA ▼▼▼ Quality Inn & Suites by Choice Hotels SH
(815) 288-2001. **$69-$169.** 154 Plaza Dr. I-88, exit SR 26, just n, then just e. Int corridors. **Pets:** Medium, other species. $15 daily fee/pet. Service with restrictions, supervision.
SAVE 🖂 ⊠ 🛢 🖃 🏊 ⊠

EAST MOLINE

▼▼▼ Ramada-East Moline SH
(309) 792-4660. **Call for rates.** 2209 John Deere Rd. I-74, exit 4B (John Deere Rd), 5 mi e; I-80, exit 4A, 6 mi w. Int corridors. **Pets:** Accepted.
⊠ 🖂 🛢 🖃 🏊

▼ Super 8 Motel-East Moline SH
(309) 796-1999. **$54-$60, 4 day notice.** 2201 John Deere Rd. I-74, exit 4B (John Deere Rd), 5.5 mi e on SR 5. Int corridors. **Pets:** Accepted.
ASK 🖂 ⊠ 🛢 🖃

EAST PEORIA

▼▼ Super 8 Motel SH
(309) 698-8889. **$57-$97.** 725 Taylor St. I-74, exit 96, just e. Int corridors. **Pets:** Medium. $50 deposit/room. Service with restrictions, supervision.
ASK 🖂 ⊠ 🛢 🖃

EFFINGHAM

AAA ▼▼▼ Best Western Raintree Inn SH
(217) 342-4121. **$54-$70.** 1811 W Fayette Ave. I-57/70, exit 159, just n. Ext/int corridors. **Pets:** Medium, other species. Designated rooms, service with restrictions, supervision.
SAVE 🖂 ⊠ 🛢 🖃 🏊

▼▼ Comfort Inn SH
(217) 347-5050. **$59-$75 (no credit cards).** 1304 W Evergreen Dr. I-57/70, exit 160 (SR 32/33), just e, then just n. Int corridors. **Pets:** Accepted.
⊠ 🖂 🛢 🖃 🏊 ⊠

▼▼▼▼ Comfort Suites SH
(217) 342-3151. **$59-$90.** 1310 W Fayette Ave. I-57/70, exit 159, 0.4 mi e. Int corridors. **Pets:** Accepted.
ASK 🖂 ⊠ 🖂 🛢 🖃 🏊

▼▼▼▼ Fairfield Inn & Suites SH
(217) 540-5454. **Call for rates.** 1111 Henritta St. I-70/57, exit 160, just se. Int corridors. **Pets:** Accepted.
⊠ 🖂 🛢 🖃 🏊

HOLIDAY INN EXPRESS

AAA ▼▼▼ Holiday Inn Express SH
(217) 540-1111. **$89-$159.** 1103 Ave of Mid-America. I-57/70, exit 160 (SR 32/33), just n. Int corridors. **Pets:** Accepted.
SAVE 🖂 ⊠ 🖂 🛢 🖃 🏊

AAA ▼▼▼ Rodeway Inn M
(217) 342-9271. **$39-$79.** 1412 W Fayette Ave. I-57/70, exit 159, just e. Ext corridors. **Pets:** Accepted.
SAVE 🖂 ⊠ 🛢 🖃 🏊

▼▼ Super 8 Motel-Effingham M
(217) 342-6888. **$59-$88.** 1400 Thelma Keller Ave. I-57/70, exit 160 (SR 32/33), 0.5 mi n. Int corridors. **Pets:** Service with restrictions, supervision.
ASK 🖂 ⊠ 🛢 🖃

FAIRVIEW HEIGHTS

▼▼▼▼ Comfort Suites SH
(618) 394-0202. **$100-$130.** 137 Ludwig Dr. I-64, exit 12 (SR 159), just n to Ludwig Dr, then 0.4 mi w. Int corridors. **Pets:** Medium. $50 deposit/pet. Service with restrictions, crate.
ASK 🖂 ⊠ 🖂 🛢 🖃 🏊

▼▼▼▼ Drury Inn & Suites-Fairview Heights SH
(618) 398-8530. **$96-$144.** 12 Ludwig Dr. I-64, exit 12 (SR 159). Int corridors. **Pets:** Large, other species. Service with restrictions, supervision.
ASK ⊠ 🛢 🖃 🏊

FLORA

AAA ▼▼ Best Western Lorson Inn SH
(618) 662-3054. **$65-$85.** 201 Hagen Dr. Jct US 45 and 50. Int corridors. **Pets:** Large. $5 daily fee/room. Designated rooms, service with restrictions, supervision.
SAVE 🖂 ⊠ 🖂 🛢 ⊠

FORSYTH

▼▼ Comfort Inn by Choice Hotels SH
(217) 875-1166. **Call for rates.** 134 Barnett Ave. I-72, exit 141B (US 51), 0.5 mi n. Int corridors. **Pets:** Accepted.
⊠ 🛢 🖃 🏊

FREEPORT

AAA ▼▼ Baymont Inn & Suites-Freeport SH
(815) 599-8510. **$70-$150.** 1060 Riverside Dr. Jct US 20 Bypass and SR 26, just s. Int corridors. **Pets:** $25 one-time fee/room. Service with restrictions, crate.
SAVE 🖂 ⊠ 🛢 🖃 🏊

▼▼ Hampton Inn SH
(815) 232-7100. **$99-$125.** 109 S Galena Ave. Jct Main St; downtown. Int corridors. **Pets:** Accepted.
ASK ⊠ 🖂 🛢 🖃

GALENA

AAA ▼▼▼▼ Eagle Ridge Resort & Spa LH 🐾
(815) 777-5000. **$159-$2509, 7 day notice.** 444 Eagle Ridge Dr. 6 mi e on US 20, 4.5 mi n. Ext/int corridors. **Pets:** Medium, dogs only. $75 one-time fee/pet. Designated rooms, service with restrictions, crate.
SAVE ⊠ 🛢 🖃 🍴 🏊 ⊠

GALESBURG

AAA ▼▼▼▼ Best Western Prairie Inn SH
(309) 343-7151. **$110-$200, 7 day notice.** 300 S Soangetaha Rd. I-74, exit 48 (Main St), just e, then just s. Int corridors. **Pets:** Other species. Designated rooms, service with restrictions, crate.
SAVE 🖂 ⊠ 🛢 🖃 🍴 🏊 ⊠

▼▼ **Comfort Inn by Choice Hotels** SH
(309) 344-5445. **$59-$109.** 907 W Carl Sandburg Dr. US 34, exit US 150 E. Int corridors. **Pets:** Accepted.
ASK S⊘ ✕ &M 🛢 💷 ☞

▼▼ **Holiday Inn Express** SH
(309) 343-7100. **$77-$100.** 2285 Washington St. I-74, exit 48A (US 150), just w to Michigan Ave, just s to Washington St, then just e. Int corridors. **Pets:** Accepted.
ASK ✕ &M 🛢 💷 ☞

GILMAN

AAA ▼▼ **Super 8 Motel** SH
(815) 265-7000. **$63-$85.** 1301 S Crescent St. I-57, exit 283, 0.3 mi e. Int corridors. **Pets:** Small, other species. $25 deposit/pet, $6 daily fee/pet. Service with restrictions, supervision.
SAVE S⊘ ✕ 🛢

▼ **Travel Inn** M
(815) 265-7283. **$60-$70.** 834 US 24 W. I-57, exit 283, just e. Ext/int corridors. **Pets:** Accepted.
S⊘ ✕ ☞

GRAYVILLE

▼▼ **Best Western Windsor Oaks Inn** SH
(618) 375-7930. **Call for rates.** 2200 S Court St. I-64, exit 130 (SR 1), just n. Int corridors. **Pets:** Other species. $5 daily fee/room. Service with restrictions, crate.
✕ 🛢 💷 ▮↾ ☞

▼▼ **Super 8 Motel** SH
(618) 375-7288. **$68-$91.** 2060 CR 2450 N. I-64, exit 130 (SR 1), just n. Int corridors. **Pets:** Accepted.
ASK S⊘ ✕ &M 🛢 💷

GREENVILLE

▼ **Super 8 Motel-Greenville** SH
(618) 664-0800. **$55-$66.** 1700 Rt 127 S. I-70, exit 45, just n. Int corridors. **Pets:** Accepted.
ASK S⊘ ✕ 🛢 💷

HIGHLAND

AAA ▼▼ **Michael's Swiss Inn & Coffee Shop** SH
(618) 654-8646. **$65-$75, 3 day notice.** 425 Broadway. On SR 160, 1.8 mi s of jct US 40/SR 143. Ext corridors. **Pets:** Other species. Service with restrictions, crate.
SAVE S⊘ ✕ 🛢 💷 ▮↾ ☞

JACKSONVILLE

▼▼ **Country Hearth Inn** SH
(217) 245-4500. **$71.** 1709 W Morton Ave. I-72, exit 64, 2.3 mi n on SR 267 (Main St) to SR 104 (Morton Ave), then 1.5 mi w. Int corridors. **Pets:** Accepted.
ASK S⊘ ✕ 🛢 💷 ☞ ✕

AAA ▼ **Starlite Motel** M 🐾
(217) 245-7184. **$40-$65.** 1910 W Morton Ave. I-72, exit 64, 2.3 mi n on SR 267 (Main St) to SR 104 (Morton Ave), then 1.8 mi w. Ext corridors. **Pets:** Very small. $7 daily fee/pet. Service with restrictions, crate.
SAVE S⊘ ✕ 🛢

▼ **Super 8 Motel** SH
(217) 479-0303. **$45-$90.** 1003 W Morton Ave. I-72, exit 64, 2.3 mi n on SR 267 (Main St) to SR 104 (Morton Ave), then 0.8 mi w. Int corridors. **Pets:** Accepted.
ASK S⊘ ✕ 🛢 💷

LINCOLN

▼▼ **Holiday Inn Express** SH
(217) 735-5800. **Call for rates.** 130 Olson Dr. I-55, exit 126 (US 121), just e to Heitman Dr, just w to Olson Dr, then just n. Int corridors. **Pets:** Accepted.
✕ 🛢 💷 ☞

LITCHFIELD

AAA ▼▼▼ **Hampton Inn** SH
(217) 324-4441. **$79-$134.** 11 Thunderbird Cir. I-55, exit 52 (SR 16), on Corvette Dr, then just e. Int corridors. **Pets:** Medium. $100 deposit/room. Service with restrictions, supervision.
SAVE S⊘ ✕ &M 🛢 💷 ☞

▼▼ **Holiday Inn Express** SH
(217) 324-4556. **$81-$94.** 1405 W Hudson Dr. I-55, exit 52 (SR 16), just e to Ohren Ln, just s to W Hudson Dr, then just w. Int corridors. **Pets:** Accepted.
ASK S⊘ ✕ 🛢 💷 ☞

LOVES PARK

▼▼ **Days Inn & Suites Rockford/Loves Park** SH
(815) 282-9300. **Call for rates.** 4313 Bell School Rd. I-39/90, exit E Riverside Blvd, just nw. Int corridors. **Pets:** Small, other species. $10 daily fee/pet. No service, supervision.
✕ &M 🛢 💷 ☞

MACOMB

▼▼ **Rodeway Inn-Macomb** SH
(309) 837-2220. **$69-$139.** 1646 N Lafayette St. Jct US 67 and 136, 1.9 mi n on US 67. Int corridors. **Pets:** Accepted.
ASK S⊘ ✕ 🛢 💷 ☞ ✕

▼ **Super 8 Motel** SH
(309) 836-8888. **$59-$125.** 313 University Dr. 1.1 mi n on US 67 to University Dr, 0.5 mi w. Int corridors. **Pets:** Accepted.
ASK S⊘ ✕ 🛢 💷

MANTENO

AAA ▼▼▼ **Country Inn & Suites by Carlson** SH
(815) 468-2600. **$79-$199.** 380 S Cypress St. I-57, exit 322, just se via frontage road. Int corridors. **Pets:** Accepted.
SAVE S⊘ ✕ &M 🛢 💷 ☞

MARION

▼▼ **Comfort Inn** SH
(618) 993-6221. **$76-$99.** 2600 W Main St. I-57, exit 53 (Main St), just w. Int corridors. **Pets:** Accepted.
ASK S⊘ ✕ 🛢 💷 ☞

▼▼ **Drury Inn-Marion** SH
(618) 997-9600. **$86-$136.** 2706 W DeYoung St. I-57, exit 54B (SR 13), 0.5 mi w. Int corridors. **Pets:** Large, other species. Service with restrictions, supervision.
ASK ✕ &M 🛢 💷 ☞ ✕

▼ **Super 8 Motel** SH 🐾
(618) 993-5577. **$60-$90.** 2601 W DeYoung St. I-57, exit 54B (SR 13), just w. Int corridors. **Pets:** Service with restrictions, supervision.
ASK S⊘ ✕ 🛢 💷

MATTOON

▼▼ **Super 8 Motel** M
(217) 235-8888. **$59-$79.** 205 McFall Rd. I-57, exit 190B, just w. Int corridors. **Pets:** Accepted.
ASK S⊘ ✕ 🛢 💷

METROPOLIS

▼▼ ▼▼ Isle of View Bed & Breakfast BB
(618) 524-5838. **Call for rates.** 205 Metropolis St. I-24, exit 37 (US 45), 3.4 mi w, then just s. Int corridors. **Pets:** Accepted.

MONTICELLO

▼▼▼▼ Best Western Monticello Gateway Inn SH
(217) 762-9436. **$50-$99, 7 day notice.** 805 Iron Horse Pl. I-72, exit 166, just s. Ext/int corridors. **Pets:** Other species. $10 daily fee/pet. Designated rooms, service with restrictions, supervision.

A$K S⌀ ✕ 🛏 🖵 ⌷

MORRIS

▼▼ ▼▼ Comfort Inn by Choice Hotels SH
(815) 942-1433. **Call for rates.** 70 Gore Rd W. I-80, exit 112, 0.3 mi nw. Int corridors. **Pets:** Accepted.

✕ 🛏 🖵 ⌷

▼▼ ▼▼ Holiday Inn SH
(815) 942-6600. **Call for rates.** 200 Gore Rd. I-80, exit 112, 0.3 mi nw. Int corridors. **Pets:** Accepted.

✕ 🛏 🖵 ❟❟ ⌷ ⊠

MORTON

AAA ▼▼▼▼▼ Best Western Ashland House Inn &
Conference Center SH
(309) 263-5116. **$79-$109.** 201 E Ashland St. I-74, exit 102, 0.3 mi ne. Int corridors. **Pets:** Accepted.

SAVE S⌀ ✕ 🛏 🖵 ❟❟ ⌷

AAA ▼▼ ▼▼ Comfort Inn by Choice Hotels SH
(309) 266-8888. **$70-$120.** 210 E Ashland St. I-74, exit 102, 0.4 mi ne. Int corridors. **Pets:** Small. $10 daily fee/pet. Designated rooms, service with restrictions, supervision.

SAVE ✕ 🛏 🖵 ⌷

MOUNT VERNON

AAA ▼▼▼▼▼ Holiday Inn LH
(618) 244-7100. **$94-$125.** 222 Potomac Blvd. I-57/64, exit 95 (SR 15), just w to Potomac Blvd, then just n. Int corridors. **Pets:** Accepted.

SAVE S⌀ ✕ 🔊M 🛏 🖵 ❟❟ ⌷ ⊠

NASHVILLE

AAA ▼▼ Best Western U.S. Inn SH
(618) 478-5341. **$65-$85.** 11640 SR 127. I-64, exit 50 (SR 127), 0.3 mi s. Int corridors. **Pets:** Small. $10 daily fee/pet. Designated rooms, service with restrictions, supervision.

SAVE S⌀ ✕ 🔊M 🛏 🖵 ⌷

NORMAL

AAA ▼▼ ▼▼ Best Western University Inn SH
(309) 454-4070. **$59-$159.** 6 Traders Cir. I-55, exit 165A (US 51), just s, then return on frontage road. Int corridors. **Pets:** Other species. $10 daily fee/room. Service with restrictions, crate.

SAVE S⌀ ✕ 🛏 🖵 ⌷

▼▼ ▼▼ Comfort Suites by Choice Hotels
Bloomington/Normal SH
(309) 452-8588. **$89-$130.** 310 B Greenbriar Dr. I-55, exit 167, follow I-55 business route (Veterans Pkwy), 1.3 mi s; jct Fort Jesse Rd. Int corridors. **Pets:** Accepted.

A$K S⌀ ✕ 🔊M 🛏 🖵 ⌷

▼▼ ▼▼ Days Inn & Suites SH
(309) 454-6600. **$65-$80.** 202 Landmark Dr. I-55, exit 167, follow I-55 business route (Veterans Pkwy), 1.3 mi s. Ext/int corridors. **Pets:** Accepted.

A$K S⌀ ✕ 🛏 🖵 ⌷

▼▼▼▼ Holiday Inn Express Hotel & Suites
Bloomington/Normal SH
(309) 862-1600. **$79-$129.** 1715 Parkway Plaza Dr. I-55, exit 167, follow I-55 business route (Veterans Pkwy), 1.7 mi s to Parkway Plaza Dr, then just e. Int corridors. **Pets:** Accepted.

A$K S⌀ ✕ 🛏 🖵 ⌷

O'FALLON

▼▼ ▼▼ Drury Inn & Suites-O'Fallon SH
(618) 624-2211. **$81-$151.** 1118 Central Park Dr. I-64, exit 16, just s. Int corridors. **Pets:** Large, other species. Service with restrictions, supervision.

A$K ✕ 🔊M 🛏 🖵 ⌷ ⊠

▼▼ ▼▼ Extended StayAmerica-O'Fallon Illinois SH
(618) 624-1757. **$82-$105.** 154 Regency Park Dr. I-64, exit 14, just w to Regency Park Dr, then 0.4 mi s. Int corridors. **Pets:** Other species. $75 one-time fee/pet. Service with restrictions.

A$K S⌀ ✕ 🔊M 🛏 🖵

AAA ▼▼ ▼▼ Settle Inn & Suites SH
(618) 624-6060. **$69-$149.** 1100 Eastgate Dr. I-64, exit 19B (SR 158), 0.5 mi n, then just sw. Int corridors. **Pets:** Other species. $50 deposit/pet. Service with restrictions, crate.

SAVE S⌀ ✕ 🛏 🖵 ⌷

OGLESBY

AAA ▼▼ ▼▼ Holiday Inn Express SH
(815) 883-3535. **Call for rates.** 900 Holiday St. I-39, exit 54, just e. Int corridors. **Pets:** Accepted.

SAVE ✕ 🛏 🖵 ⌷

OTTAWA

▼▼▼▼ Hampton Inn-Starved Rock Area SH
(815) 434-6040. **Call for rates.** 4115 Holiday Ln. I-80, exit 90 (SR 23), just n. Int corridors. **Pets:** Accepted.

✕ 🔊M 🛏 🖵 ⌷

▼▼▼▼ Holiday Inn Express SH
(815) 433-0029. **$109-$159.** 120 W Stevenson Rd. I-80, exit 90 (SR 23), just n. Int corridors. **Pets:** Accepted.

A$K ✕ 🛏 🖵 ⌷

PEORIA

▼▼ ▼▼ AmericInn Lodge & Suites SH
(309) 692-9200. **Call for rates.** 9106 N Lindbergh Dr. SR 6, exit 6, 0.5 mi s. Int corridors. **Pets:** Accepted.

✕ 🛏 🖵 ⌷ ⊠

▼▼ ▼▼ Baymont Inn & Suites SH
(309) 686-7600. **Call for rates.** 2002 W War Memorial Dr. I-74, exit 89 (US 150/War Memorial Dr), just n; entrance through Northwoods Mall. Ext/int corridors. **Pets:** Service with restrictions.

✕ 🛏 🖵 ⌷

▼▼▼▼ Comfort Suites by Choice Hotels SH
(309) 688-3800. **Call for rates.** 1812 W War Memorial Dr. I-74, exit 89 (US 150/War Memorial Dr), just e, then just s. Int corridors. **Pets:** Accepted.

✕ 🛏 🖵 ⌷

▼▼ ▼▼ Extended StayAmerica-Peoria-North SH
(309) 688-3110. **$77-$125.** 4306 N Brandywine Dr. I-74, exit 89 (US 150/War Memorial Dr), just w to Brandywine Dr, then just ne. Int corridors. **Pets:** Other species. $75 one-time fee/pet. Service with restrictions.

A$K S⌀ ✕ 🛏 🖵

▼▼ Red Roof Inn #7057 M
(309) 685-3911. **Call for rates.** 1822 W War Memorial Dr. I-74, exit 89 (US 150/War Memorial Dr), just e. Ext corridors. **Pets:** Accepted.

✕ 🛏

WWW Residence Inn by Marriott SH
(309) 681-9000. **$198-$219.** 2000 W War Memorial Dr. I-74, exit 89
(US 150/War Memorial Dr), just w; entrance through Northwoods Mall.
Int corridors. **Pets:** Accepted.
ASK SO X 🛏 💻 🌊 ⊠

W Super 8 Motel SH
(309) 688-8074. **$61-$90.** 1816 W War Memorial Dr. I-74, exit 89 (US
150/War Memorial Dr), just e. Int corridors. **Pets:** Medium, other species.
$50 deposit/room. Designated rooms, service with restrictions, crate.
ASK SO X 🛏 💻

PERU

WW La Quinta Inn Peru SH
(815) 224-9000. **$94.** 4389 Venture Dr. I-80, exit 75 (SR 251), 0.4 mi s
to 38th St, just w to Venture Dr, then 0.4 mi nw. Int corridors.
Pets: Other species. Service with restrictions, supervision.
ASK X 🛏 💻 🌊 ⊠

QUAD CITIES AREA

MOLINE

WW Comfort Inn by Choice Hotels SH
(309) 762-7000. **Call for rates.** 2600 52nd Ave. I-280/74, exit 18A
eastbound; exit 5B westbound, just s on US 6 and 150, then 0.5 mi
nw on 27th St. Int corridors. **Pets:** Accepted.
X 🛏 💻 🌊

AAA WW Exel Inn of Moline SH
(309) 797-5580. **$52-$72.** 2501 52nd Ave. I-280/74, exit 18A eastbound; exit 5B westbound, just s on US 6 and 150, then 1 mi nw on
27th St. Int corridors. **Pets:** Accepted.
SAVE SO X 🛏 💻

WW Fairfield Inn by Marriott SH
(309) 762-9083. **$78-$99.** 2705 48th Ave. I-280/74, exit 5B westbound;
exit 18A eastbound, just s on US 6 to traffic light, then 1 mi nw on
27th St. Int corridors. **Pets:** Accepted.
ASK SO X ♨M 🛏 💻 🌊

WW Holiday Inn Express-Moline Airport SH
(309) 762-8300. **Call for rates.** 6910 27th St. I-280/74, exit 18A eastbound; exit 5B westbound, just s on US 6 and 150, then just nw. Int
corridors. **Pets:** Accepted.
X 🛏 💻

WWW La Quinta Inn Moline SH
(309) 762-9008. **$69-$85.** 5450 27th St. I-280/74, exit 18A eastbound;
exit 5B westbound, just s on US 6 and 150 to traffic light, then just nw.
Int corridors. **Pets:** Other species. Service with restrictions, supervision.
ASK SO X 🛏 💻 🌊

ROCK ISLAND

**AAA WWW Holiday Inn Rock Island Hotel & Conference
Center** LH
(309) 794-1212. **$109-$139.** 226 17th St. Just e of Centennial Bridge;
at 3rd Ave and 17th St; downtown. Int corridors. **Pets:** Small. $30
one-time fee/room. Service with restrictions, crate.
SAVE SO X 🛏 💻 🍴 🌊 ⊠

END AREA

QUINCY

WW Comfort Inn by Choice Hotels SH
(217) 228-2700. **$89-$104.** 4122 Broadway. I-172, exit 14 (SR 104), 1.3
mi w. Int corridors. **Pets:** Accepted.
ASK SO X 🛏 💻 🌊

WWW Country Inn & Suites By Carlson SH
(217) 222-8949. **$95-$500.** 110 N 54th St. I-172, exit 14 (SR 104), just
w. Int corridors. **Pets:** Accepted.
ASK SO X 🛏 💻 🌊 ⊠

AAA W Super 8 Motel SH
(217) 228-8808. **Call for rates.** 224 N 36th St. I-172, exit 14 (SR 104),
1.8 mi w, then just s. Int corridors. **Pets:** Accepted.
SAVE X ♨M 🛏 💻

RANTOUL

AAA WW Best Western Heritage Inn SH
(217) 892-9292. **$57-$62.** 420 S Murray Rd. I-57, exit 250 (US 136),
0.5 mi e, then just s. Ext corridors. **Pets:** Very small. $7 daily fee/pet.
Service with restrictions, supervision.
SAVE SO X 🛏 💻

WW Super 8 Motel SH
(217) 893-8888. **Call for rates.** 207 S Murray Rd. I-57, exit 250 (US
136), just e. Int corridors. **Pets:** Accepted.
X 🛏 💻

ROBINSON

WW Best Western Robinson Inn SH
(618) 544-8448. **$75-$90.** 1500 W Main St. 1.2 mi w on SR 33. Int
corridors. **Pets:** Medium, other species. $5 daily fee/pet. Service with
restrictions, crate.
ASK SO X 🛏 💻

ROCHELLE

AAA WW Comfort Inn & Suites by Choice Hotels SH
(815) 562-5551. **$79-$189.** 1131 N 7th St. I-39, exit 99 (SR 38), 2.5 mi
w; jct SR 38 and 251; downtown. Int corridors. **Pets:** Small, other
species. $25 one-time fee/pet. Service with restrictions, supervision.
SAVE SO X 🛏 💻 🍴 🌊 ⊠

AAA WW Lincoln Highway Hotel SH
(815) 562-9530. **$79-$100.** 567 E Hwy 38. I-39, exit 99 (SR 38), 1 mi
w. Int corridors. **Pets:** Accepted.
SAVE SO X 🛏 💻 🌊

WWW Rochelle U S Express SH
(815) 562-9994. **Call for rates.** 1240 Dement Rd. I-39, exit 99 (SR 38),
just nw. Int corridors. **Pets:** Accepted.
X ♨M 🛏 💻 🌊

ROCKFORD

(AAA) ▽▽▽ **Baymont Inn & Suites Rockford** SH
(815) 229-8200. **Call for rates.** 662 N Lyford Rd. I-90, exit US 20 business route, just e, then just n. Int corridors. **Pets:** Accepted.
SAVE ✕ 🛄 🖵 ⇌ ✕

▽▽ **Candlewood Suites** SH
(815) 229-9300. **$119-$149.** 7555 Walton St. I-90, exit US 20 business route, 0.3 mi e to Bell School Rd, just s to Walton St, then just e. Int corridors. **Pets:** Accepted.
A$K ✕ 🛄 🖵

▽▽ **Comfort Inn by Choice Hotels** SH
(815) 398-7061. **Call for rates.** 7392 Argus Dr. I-90, exit US 20 business route, just w to Bell School Rd, then just n. Int corridors. **Pets:** Accepted.
✕ 🛄 🖵 ⇌

(AAA) ▽ **Exel Inn of Rockford** SH
(815) 332-4915. **$53-$89.** 220 S Lyford Rd. I-90, exit US 20 business route, just e, then just s. Int corridors. **Pets:** Accepted.
SAVE S🐾 ✕ 🛄 🖵

▽▽ **Extended StayAmerica-Rockford East** SH
(815) 226-8969. **$81-$89.** 653 Clark Dr. I-90, exit US 20 business route, just w. Int corridors. **Pets:** Other species. $75 one-time fee/pet. Service with restrictions.
A$K S🐾 ✕ 🛄 🖵

(AAA) ▽▽ **Quality Suites** SH
(815) 227-1300. **Call for rates.** 7401 Walton St. I-90, exit US 20 business route, just w to Bell School Rd, then just s. Int corridors. **Pets:** Accepted.
SAVE ✕ 🛄 🖵 ⇌ ✕

▽ **Red Roof Inn #7035** M
(815) 398-9750. **Call for rates.** 7434 E State St. I-90, exit US 20 business route, just w. Ext corridors. **Pets:** Accepted.
✕ 🛄

▽▽▽ **Residence Inn by Marriott** SH
(815) 227-0013. **$187-$231.** 7542 Colosseum Dr. I-90, exit US 20 business route, just w. Int corridors. **Pets:** Accepted.
A$K S🐾 ✕ 🛄 🖵 ⇌ ✕

(AAA) ▽▽ **Sleep Inn-Rockford** SH
(815) 398-8900. **$79-$179.** 725 Clark Dr. I-90, exit US 20 business route, just w to Bell School Rd, just n to Clark Dr, then 0.4 mi ne. Int corridors. **Pets:** Large, other species. $15 daily fee/room. Designated rooms, service with restrictions, supervision.
SAVE S🐾 ✕ 🛄 🖵

▽▽ **StudioPLUS Deluxe Studios** SH
(815) 397-8316. **$76-$84.** 747 N Bell School Rd. I-90, exit US 20 Business, just w to Bell School Rd, then 0.3 mi n. Int corridors. **Pets:** Other species. $75 one-time fee/pet. Service with restrictions.
A$K S🐾 ✕ 🛄 🖵

SALEM

▽ **Super 8 Motel of Salem** SH
(618) 548-5882. **$60-$87.** 118 Woods Ln. I-57, exit 116 (US 50), just w. Ext/int corridors. **Pets:** Large. Designated rooms, service with restrictions, supervision.
A$K S🐾 ✕ ♿M 🛄 🖵

SAVOY

(AAA) ▽▽▽ **Best Western Paradise Inn** SH
(217) 356-1824. **$75-$90, 3 day notice.** 709 N Dunlap Ave. I-57, exit 229, 1 mi e to US 45, then 2.5 mi n. Ext corridors. **Pets:** Small. $25 deposit/pet, $5 daily fee/pet. Designated rooms, service with restrictions, crate.
SAVE S🐾 ✕ 🛄 🖵 ⇌

SOUTH JACKSONVILLE

(AAA) ▽▽▽ **Comfort Inn-South Jacksonville** SH
(217) 245-8372. **$89-$109.** 200 Comfort Dr. I-72, exit 64, just n. Int corridors. **Pets:** Accepted.
SAVE S🐾 ✕ 🛄 🖵 ⇌

(AAA) ▽▽▽ **Econo Lodge Inn & Suites by Choice Hotels** SH
(217) 245-9575. **$65-$70.** 1914 Southbrooke Rd. I-72, exit 64, just n. Int corridors. **Pets:** Other species. $20 one-time fee/room. Service with restrictions, supervision.
SAVE S🐾 ✕ ♿M 🛄 🖵

SPRINGFIELD

▽▽▽ **Baymont Inn & Suites Springfield** SH
(217) 529-6655. **$85-$95.** 5871 S 6th St. I-55, exit 90 (Toronto Rd), just e to 6th St, then just n. Int corridors. **Pets:** Accepted.
A$K S🐾 ✕ ♿M 🛄 🖵 ⇌

(AAA) ▽▽▽ **Best Western Clearlake Plaza** SH
(217) 525-7420. **$75-$149.** 3440 E Clearlake Ave. I-55, exit 98B, just w. Int corridors. **Pets:** $25 one-time fee/pet. Service with restrictions, supervision.
SAVE S🐾 ✕ ♿M 🛄 🖵 ⇌

▽▽▽▽ **Drury Inn & Suites-Springfield** SH
(217) 529-3900. **$83-$131.** 3180 S Dirksen Pkwy. I-55, exit 94 (Stevenson Dr), just w to Dirksen Pkwy, then just n. Int corridors. **Pets:** Large, other species. Service with restrictions, supervision.
A$K ✕ ♿M 🛄 🖵 ⇌

(AAA) ▽▽▽ **Holiday Inn Express Hotel & Suites** SH
(217) 529-7771. **$89-$106.** 3050 S Dirksen Pkwy. I-55, exit 94 (Stevenson Dr), just w to S Dirksen Pkwy, then 0.4 mi n. Int corridors. **Pets:** Accepted.
SAVE ✕ ♿M 🛄

(AAA) ▽▽▽ **Mansion View Inn & Suites** SH
(217) 544-7411. **$89.** 529 S 4th St. I-55, exit 92 (6th St), 3.9 mi n to Edwards St, then just w, follow signs. Ext/int corridors. **Pets:** Other species. $25 one-time fee/room. Service with restrictions, supervision.
SAVE S🐾 ✕ 🛄 🖵 🍴

▽▽ **Microtel Inn & Suites** SH
(217) 753-2636. **$69-$99.** 2636 Sunrise Dr. I-55, exit 94 (Stevenson Dr), just w to Dirksen Pkwy, then 0.4 mi n. Int corridors. **Pets:** Accepted.
A$K ✕ ♿M 🛄 🖵 ⇌

▽▽ **Pear Tree Inn by Drury-Springfield** SH
(217) 529-9100. **$58-$83.** 3190 S Dirksen Pkwy. I-55, exit 94 (Stevenson Dr), just w. Int corridors. **Pets:** Large, other species. Service with restrictions, supervision.
A$K ✕ 🖵

▽▽ **Red Roof Inn #7040** M
(217) 753-4302. **Call for rates.** 3200 Singer Ave. I-55, exit 96B, just w. Ext corridors. **Pets:** Accepted.
✕

▽▽ **Sleep Inn by Choice Hotels** SH
(217) 787-6200. **Call for rates.** 3470 Freedom Dr. I-72, exit 93 (Veterans Pkwy), 0.7 mi n to Lindbergh Blvd, just w to Freedom Dr, then just s. Int corridors. **Pets:** Accepted.
✕ 🛄 🖵

(AAA) ▽▽▽▽ **The State House Inn-A Clarion Collection Hotel** SH
(217) 528-5100. **$109.** 101 E Adams St. Jct 1st and Adams sts; just n of State House. Int corridors. **Pets:** Small. $25 one-time fee/pet. Designated rooms, service with restrictions, crate.
SAVE S🐾 ✕ ♿M 🛄 🖵

▼▼▼▼ **Staybridge Suites Springfield South** SH
(217) 793-6700. **$119-$169.** 4231 Schooner Dr. I-72, exit 93, 0.4 mi se.
Int corridors. **Pets:** Accepted.
ASK SD ✕ ⚙M 🖥 💻 ➘ ⊗

STAUNTON

▼▼ **Staunton Super 8** SH
(618) 635-5353. **$54.** 1527 Herman Rd. I-55, exit 41, 0.5 mi w. Int
corridors. **Pets:** Accepted.
ASK SD ✕ 🖥 💻

STOCKTON

▼▼▼ **Country Inn & Suites By Carlson** SH
(815) 947-6060. **$88-$105.** 200 Dillon Ave. On US 20, just e of SR 78.
Int corridors. **Pets:** Accepted.
ASK SD ✕ ⚙M 🖥 💻 ➘

SYCAMORE

▼▼ **Americas Best Value Inn & Suites** SH
(815) 899-6500. **$69-$109.** 1860 Dekalb Ave. On SR 23, 0.9 mi s of
Peace Rd. Int corridors. **Pets:** Accepted.
ASK SD ✕ ⚙M 🖥 💻

▲▲▲ ▼▼▼ **Comfort Inn by Choice Hotels** SH
(815) 895-4979. **$80-$105.** 1475 S Peace Rd. I-88, exit Peace Rd, 5.5
mi n to jct SR 23. Int corridors. **Pets:** Accepted.
SAVE SD ✕ ⚙M 🖥 💻 ➘

TUSCOLA

▼▼ **Baymont Inn & Suites** SH
(217) 253-3500. **Call for rates.** 1006 Southline Rd. I-57, exit 212 (US
36), 0.3 mi w. Int corridors. **Pets:** Accepted.
✕ ⚙M 🖥 💻 ➘

▼▼ **Holiday Inn Express** SH
(217) 253-6363. **$85.** 1201 Tuscola Blvd. I-57, exit 212 (US 36), 0.3 mi
w to Progress Blvd, just s to Tuscola Blvd, then 0.4 mi se. Int corridors. **Pets:** Accepted.
ASK SD ✕ ⚙M 🖥 💻 ➘

▼▼ **Super 8 Motel-Tuscola** SH
(217) 253-5488. **Call for rates.** 1007 E Southline Dr. I-57, exit 212 (US
36), 0.4 mi w. Int corridors. **Pets:** Other species. $10 one-time fee/pet. No
service, supervision.
✕ 🖥 💻

URBANA

▲▲▲ ▼▼▼ **Ramada Limited-Urbana/Champaign** SH ❀
(217) 328-4400. **$80-$105.** 902 W Killarney St. I-74, exit 183 (Lincoln
Ave), just s to Killarney St, then just w. Int corridors. **Pets:** $50 deposit/
room. Service with restrictions, crate.
SAVE SD ✕ 🖥 💻 ➘

▲▲▲ ▼▼ **Sleep Inn** SH ❀
(217) 367-6000. **$68-$129.** 1908 N Lincoln Ave. I-74, exit 183 (Lincoln
Ave), 0.5 mi s. Int corridors. **Pets:** Other species. $7 one-time fee/room.
Service with restrictions, supervision.
SAVE SD ✕ 🖥 💻 ➘

VANDALIA

▲▲▲ ▼▼▼ **Days Inn** M
(618) 283-4400. **$69-$81.** 1920 Kennedy Blvd. I-70, exit 63 (US 51),
0.6 mi n. Ext corridors. **Pets:** Other species. $10 deposit/room. Service
with restrictions.
SAVE SD ✕ 🖥 💻 ➘

▲▲▲ ▼▼▼ **Jay's Inn** M
(618) 283-1200. **$54-$65.** 720 Gochenour St. I-70, exit 63 (US 51), just
s. Ext corridors. **Pets:** Other species. Service with restrictions.
SAVE SD ✕ 🖥 💻

▲▲▲ ▼▼▼ **Ramada Vandalia** SH
(618) 283-1400. **$64-$115.** 2707 Veterans Ave. I-70, exit 61, just s. Int
corridors. **Pets:** Other species. $10 one-time fee/pet. Designated rooms,
no service, crate.
SAVE ✕ 🖥 💻 ➘

WASHINGTON

▼▼ **Super 8 Motel** SH
(309) 444-8881. **Call for rates.** 1884 Washington Rd. On Business Rt
SR 24, 1.5 mi w. Int corridors. **Pets:** Accepted.
✕ 🖥

WATSEKA

▲▲▲ ▼▼▼ **Super 8 Motel** SH
(815) 432-6000. **$63-$85.** 710 W Walnut. On US 24; center of downtown. Int corridors. **Pets:** Small. $25 deposit/pet, $6 daily fee/pet. Service
with restrictions, supervision.
SAVE SD ✕ 🖥

WENONA

▼▼ **Super 8 Motel** SH
(815) 853-4371. **Call for rates.** 5 Cavalry Dr. I-39, exit 35. Int corridors.
Pets: Accepted.
✕ 🖥 💻

INDIANA

ANGOLA

Ramada Inn SH
(260) 665-9471. **$75-$155.** 3855 N SR 127. I-69, exit 154, just e, then 0.4 mi s. Int corridors. **Pets:** $25 daily fee/room. Service with restrictions, supervision.

AUBURN

Best Western Auburn Inn SH
(260) 925-6363. **$90-$120.** 225 Touring Dr. I-69, exit 129 (SR 8), just e, then just s. Int corridors. **Pets:** Accepted.

Holiday Inn Express SH ✿
(260) 925-1900. **$79-$109.** 404 Touring Dr. I-69, exit 129 (SR 8), just e, then just s. Int corridors. **Pets:** Other species. Service with restrictions, supervision.

La Quinta Inn Auburn SH
(260) 920-1900. **$80.** 306 Touring Dr. I-69, exit 129, 0.5 mi e on SR 8. Int corridors. **Pets:** Other species. Service with restrictions, supervision.

Super 8 Motel-Auburn SH
(260) 927-8800. **Call for rates.** 503 Ley Dr. I-69, exit 129 (SR 8), just e, then just s. Int corridors. **Pets:** Accepted.

BEDFORD

Bedford Super 8 SH
(812) 275-8881. **$65-$125.** 501 Bell Back Rd. Jct SR 37 and 58, just e on SR 58. Int corridors. **Pets:** $10 daily fee/pet. No service, supervision.

BERNE

Black Bear Inn & Suites SH
(260) 589-8955. **Call for rates.** 1335 US 27 N. On US 27, 1 mi n. Int corridors. **Pets:** Accepted.

BLOOMINGTON

Fairfield Inn by Marriott SH
(812) 331-1122. **$109-$142.** 120 Fairfield Dr. Just e from SR 37 at 3rd St. Int corridors. **Pets:** Accepted.

Hampton Inn SH
(812) 334-2100. **$119-$299.** 2100 N Walnut St. 1 mi e of jct SR 37 on SR 45/46 Bypass, then just s on College Ave/Walnut St. Int corridors. **Pets:** Accepted.

TownePlace Suites By Marriott SH
(812) 334-1234. **$109-$142.** 105 S Franklin Rd. Just e from SR 37 at 3rd St, then 0.3 mi n. Int corridors. **Pets:** Accepted.

CHESTERTON

Gray Goose Inn BB ✿
(219) 926-5781. **$100-$190, 10 day notice.** 350 Indian Boundary Rd. I-94, exit 26A, 0.6 mi s, then just w. Int corridors. **Pets:** $25 deposit/room. Service with restrictions, crate.

CINCINNATI METROPOLITAN AREA (NEARBY OHIO)

LAWRENCEBURG

Comfort Inn & Suites SH
(812) 539-3600. **$80-$130.** 1610 Flossie Dr. I-275, exit 16, 0.3 mi e. Int corridors. **Pets:** Accepted.

Quality Inn & Suites SH
(812) 539-4770. **Call for rates.** 1000 E Eads Pkwy. I-275, exit 16, 0.5 mi w on US 50. Int corridors. **Pets:** Other species. $25 one-time fee/pet. Service with restrictions.

END METROPOLITAN AREA

CLARKSVILLE

Best Western Green Tree Inn M
(812) 288-9281. **$75-$250.** 1425 Broadway St. I-65, exit 4, just w. Ext corridors. **Pets:** Medium, dogs only. Service with restrictions, crate.

CLOVERDALE

▼▼ Super 8 Motel Cloverdale/Greencastle SH
(765) 795-7373. **$60-$145.** 1020 N Main St. I-70, exit 41, just s on US 231. Int corridors. **Pets:** Dogs only. Service with restrictions, supervision.

(ASK) (S&) (X) (&M) (🛏) (💻) (🛍)

COLUMBIA CITY

AAA ▼▼ AmeriHost Inn & Suites SH
(260) 248-4551. **Call for rates.** 701 W Connexion Way. 1 mi w of SR 9, just off US 30. Int corridors. **Pets:** Accepted.

(SAVE) (X) (&M) (🛏) (💻) (🛍)

COLUMBUS

▼▼▼ Columbus Holiday Inn and Conference Center LH
(812) 372-1541. **$101-$143.** 2480 Jonathan Moore Pike. I-65, exit 68, just e on SR 46. Ext/int corridors. **Pets:** Accepted.

(X) (&M) (🛏) (💻) (🍴) (🛍) (X)

▼▼▼ Comfort Inn & Suites SH
(812) 376-8000. **$119-$149.** 2485 Jonathan Moore Pike. I-65, exit 68, just e on SR 46. Int corridors. **Pets:** $10 daily fee/pet. Service with restrictions, crate.

(ASK) (S&) (X) (🛏) (💻) (🛍)

AAA ▼▼ Days Inn Columbus SH
(812) 376-9951. **Call for rates.** 3445 Jonathan Moore Pike. I-65, exit 68, just w. Int corridors. **Pets:** Accepted.

(SAVE) (X) (🛏) (💻) (🛍)

CRAWFORDSVILLE

AAA ▼▼▼ Comfort Inn SH
(765) 361-0665. **$89-$175.** 2991 N Gandhi Dr. I-74, exit 34, just s on US 231. Int corridors. **Pets:** $15 daily fee/pet. Designated rooms, service with restrictions, supervision.

(SAVE) (S&) (X) (🛏) (💻) (🛍)

▼▼ Holiday Inn-Crawfordsville SH
(765) 362-8700. **$80-$145.** 2500 N Lafayette Rd. I-74, exit 34, 0.3 mi s on US 231. Ext corridors. **Pets:** Accepted.

(ASK) (S&) (X) (&M) (🛏) (💻) (🍴) (🛍)

DALE

▼▼ Baymont Inn & Suites Dale SH
(812) 937-7000. **Call for rates.** 1339 N Washington St. I-64, exit 57 (US 231), just s. Int corridors. **Pets:** $25 deposit/room. Designated rooms, service with restrictions, supervision.

(X) (&M) (🛏) (💻) (🛍)

DALEVILLE

▼ Americas Best Value Inn SH
(765) 378-0888. **Call for rates.** 15701 W Commerce Rd. I-69, exit 34, just w. Ext/int corridors. **Pets:** $25 deposit/room, $10 one-time fee/room. Service with restrictions, supervision.

(X) (🛏)

DECATUR

▼▼ Americas Best Value Inn SH
(260) 728-2196. **$55-$69.** 1033 N 13th St. On US 27 and 33, 0.5 mi n of jct US 224. Ext/int corridors. **Pets:** Medium, dogs only. $5 daily fee/pet. Service with restrictions, crate.

(ASK) (S&) (X) (🛏) (💻) (🛍)

▼▼ Baymont Inn & Suites SH
(260) 728-4600. **$84.** 1201 S 13th St. On US 27 and 33, 1 mi s of jct US 224. Int corridors. **Pets:** Accepted.

(ASK) (S&) (X) (&M) (🛏) (💻) (🛍)

▼▼ Comfort Inn of Decatur SH
(260) 724-8888. **$75-$95, 7 day notice.** 1302 S 13th St. 1 mi s on US 27 and 33. Int corridors. **Pets:** Accepted.

(ASK) (S&) (X) (&M) (🛏) (💻) (🛍)

ELKHART

▼▼▼ Candlewood Suites SH
(574) 262-8600. **Call for rates (no credit cards).** 300 Northpointe Blvd. I-80/90, exit 92, just n on SR 19, then w. Int corridors. **Pets:** Accepted.

(X) (&M) (🛏) (💻)

▼▼ Jameson Inn Elkhart SH
(574) 264-7222. **Call for rates.** 3010 Brittany Ct. I-80/90, exit 92, 0.3 mi s on SR 19. Int corridors. **Pets:** Small. $15 daily fee/room. Service with restrictions, crate.

(X) (&M) (🛏) (💻) (🛍)

EVANSVILLE

AAA ▼▼▼ Baymont Inn & Suites Evansville East SH ❀
(812) 477-2677. **$79.** 8005 E Division St. I-164, exit 7B (SR 66/Lloyd Expwy), 0.5 mi w to Cross Pointe Blvd, just n to Division St, then 0.5 mi e. Int corridors. **Pets:** Small, other species. $10 daily fee/room. Service with restrictions, crate.

(SAVE) (S&) (X) (&M) (🛏) (💻) (🛍)

AAA ▼▼▼ Best Western Gateway Inn & Suites SH ❀
(812) 868-8000. **$55-$126.** 324 Rusher Creek Rd. I-64, exit 25A (US 41), 0.5 mi s, then just w. Int corridors. **Pets:** Other species. $15 one-time fee/pet. Service with restrictions, supervision.

(SAVE) (S&) (X) (&M) (🛏) (💻) (🛍)

AAA ▼▼▼ Casino Aztar Hotel LH
(812) 433-4000. **$109-$159.** 421 NW Riverside Dr. SR 62 (Lloyd Expwy), just s on Fulton. Int corridors. **Pets:** Accepted.

(SAVE) (X) (&M) (🛏) (💻) (🍴)

▼▼▼ Comfort Inn East SH
(812) 476-3600. **$79-$249.** 8331 E Walnut St. I-164, exit 7B (SR 66/Lloyd Expwy), 0.5 mi w to Eagle Crest Blvd, 0.3 mi se to Fuquay St, just s to Walnut St, then 0.4 mi e. Int corridors. **Pets:** Medium. $10 one-time fee/room. Designated rooms, service with restrictions, supervision.

(ASK) (S&) (X) (&M) (🛏) (💻) (🛍)

AAA ▼▼▼ Comfort Inn North SH
(812) 867-1600. **$60-$100.** 19622 Elpers Rd. I-64, exit 25A (US 41), 0.5 mi s, then just w. Int corridors. **Pets:** Accepted.

(SAVE) (S&) (X) (🛏) (💻) (🛍)

▼▼▼ Drury Inn & Suites-Evansville East SH
(812) 471-3400. **$76-$138.** 100 Cross Pointe Blvd. I-164, exit 7B (SR 66/Lloyd Expwy), 0.5 mi w. Int corridors. **Pets:** Large, other species. Service with restrictions, supervision.

(ASK) (X) (&M) (🛏) (💻) (🛍) (X)

▼▼▼ Drury Inn & Suites-Evansville North SH
(812) 423-5818. **$86-$126.** 3901 US 41 N. On US 41, 2.5 mi n of jct SR 62 and 66 (Lloyd Expwy), 3.3 mi sw of Regional Airport entrance. Int corridors. **Pets:** Large, other species. Service with restrictions, supervision.

(ASK) (X) (🛏) (💻) (🛍) (X)

▼▼▼ Holiday Inn Express–Evansville West SH ❀
(812) 421-9773. **$109-$209.** 5737 Pearl Dr. Jct US 41 and SR 62, 5.7 mi w on SR 62, then just s on Boehne Camp Rd. Int corridors. **Pets:** Large, other species. $15 one-time fee/room. Service with restrictions, supervision.

(ASK) (S&) (X) (&M) (🛏) (💻) (🛍)

HomeLife Studios & Suites
(812) 475-1700. **Call for rates.** 100 S Green River Rd. I-164, exit 7B (SR 66/Lloyd Expwy), 2 mi w to Green River Rd, then just s. Ext corridors. **Pets:** Accepted.

Jameson Inn Evansville SH
(812) 476-9626. **$90.** 1101 N Green River Rd. I-164, exit 9 (SR 62 E/Morgan Ave), 1.5 mi w on SR 62, then just s. Int corridors. **Pets:** Small. $15 daily fee/room. Service with restrictions, crate.

Residence Inn Hotel SH
(812) 471-7191. **$115-$135.** 8283 E Walnut St. I-164, exit 7B (SR 66/Lloyd Expwy), 0.5 mi w to Eagle Crest Blvd, 0.3 mi se to Fuquay St, then 0.3 mi e. Int corridors. **Pets:** Accepted.

Studio Plus Evansville East SH
(812) 479-0103. **$75-$105.** 301 Eagle Crest Dr. I-164, exit 7B (SR 66/Lloyd Expwy), 0.5 mi w to Eagle Crest Blvd, 0.5 mi s, then just e. Int corridors. **Pets:** Other species. $75 one-time fee/pet. Service with restrictions.

FERDINAND

Comfort Inn SH
(812) 367-1122. **Call for rates.** 440 S Main St. I-64, exit 63. Int corridors. **Pets:** Medium. $10 daily fee/room. Designated rooms, supervision.

FORT WAYNE

Baymont Inn Fort Wayne SH
(260) 489-2220. **Call for rates.** 1005 W Washington Center Rd. I-69, exit 111B, just n on SR 3, then 0.4 mi e. Int corridors. **Pets:** Medium. $50 deposit/pet. Designated rooms, service with restrictions, crate.

Best Western Luxbury Inn Fort Wayne SH
(260) 436-0242. **$88-$94.** 5501 Coventry Ln. I-69, exit 102. Int corridors. **Pets:** $15 daily fee/pet. Designated rooms, service with restrictions, supervision.

Candlewood Suites SH
(260) 484-1400. **Call for rates (no credit cards).** 5250 Distribution Dr. I-69, exit 111A, just e. Int corridors. **Pets:** Accepted.

Don Hall's Guesthouse SH
(260) 489-2524. **$79-$89.** 1313 W Washington Center Rd. I-69, exit 111B, just n on SR 3, then 0.3 mi e. Ext/int corridors. **Pets:** Accepted.

Extended StayAmerica-Fort Wayne-South SH
(260) 432-1916. **$85-$125.** 8309 W Jefferson Blvd. I-69, exit 102, 0.4 mi e on US 24, then 0.6 mi s. Int corridors. **Pets:** Other species. $75 one-time fee/pet. Service with restrictions.

Hilton Fort Wayne at Grand Wayne Convention Center SH
(260) 420-1100. **$99-$199.** 1020 S Calhoun St. Jct Jefferson Blvd; center. Int corridors. **Pets:** Medium. Service with restrictions, crate.

Residence Inn by Marriott Fort Wayne SH
(260) 484-4700. **$139-$159.** 4919 Lima Rd. I-69, exit 111A, 0.4 mi s on US 27. Ext corridors. **Pets:** $100 one-time fee/room. Service with restrictions, crate.

Residence Inn Southwest SH 🐾
(260) 432-8000. **$165-$185.** 7811 W Jefferson Blvd. I-69, exit 102, 0.5 mi e. Int corridors. **Pets:** Other species. $100 one-time fee/room. Service with restrictions, crate.

FRENCH LICK

French Lick Resort & Casino LH 🐾
(812) 936-9300. **$129-$299.** 8670 W SR 56. On SR 56 at SR 145. Int corridors. **Pets:** $50 one-time fee/room. Designated rooms, service with restrictions.

GOSHEN

Best Western Inn
(574) 533-0408. **$88.** 900 Lincolnway E. 1 mi se on US 33. Ext corridors. **Pets:** Accepted.

GREENCASTLE

College Inn
(765) 653-4167. **Call for rates.** 315 Bloomington St. I-70, exit 41, 8 mi n on US 231. Ext corridors. **Pets:** Accepted.

GREENSBURG

Holiday Inn Express SH
(812) 663-5500. **$99-$169.** 915 Ann Blvd. I-74, exit 134A, 1.4 mi s on SR 3. Int corridors. **Pets:** Other species. $20 deposit/room. Designated rooms, service with restrictions, supervision.

HAMMOND

Best Western Northwest Indiana Inn SH
(219) 844-2140. **$70-$110.** 3830 179th St. I-80/94, exit 5, 0.6 mi s on Cline Ave (SR 912), then 0.6 mi n on frontage road (179th St). Int corridors. **Pets:** Medium, other species. $30 deposit/room, $5 daily fee/pet. Designated rooms, service with restrictions, supervision.

Residence Inn by Marriott Chicago Southeast SH
(219) 844-8440. **$149-$299.** 7740 Corinne Dr. I-80/94, exit 3 (Kennedy Ave S), just s. Int corridors. **Pets:** Other species. $100 one-time fee/room. Service with restrictions, crate.

HUNTINGTON

AmeriHost Inn & Suites Huntington SH
(260) 359-9000. **Call for rates.** 2820 Hotel Ave. 0.6 mi nw of jct US 24/224 and SR 5. Int corridors. **Pets:** Accepted.

Super 8 Motel SH
(260) 358-8888. **Call for rates.** 2801 Guilford St. From US 24, just n. Int corridors. **Pets:** Accepted.

INDIANAPOLIS METROPOLITAN AREA

CARMEL

Jameson Inn Carmel SH
(317) 816-1616. **Call for rates.** 10201 N Meridian St. I-465, exit 31, 0.3 mi n on US 31. Int corridors. **Pets:** Small. $15 daily fee/room. Service with restrictions, crate.

Residence Inn by Marriott Indianapolis/Carmel SH
(317) 846-2000. **$164-$186.** 11895 N Meridian St. I-465, exit 31, 2 mi n on US 31, just e on 116th St, then just n on Pennsylvania Rd. Int corridors. **Pets:** Accepted.

SpringHill Suites by Marriott Indianapolis/Carmel SH
(317) 846-1800. **$164-$186.** 11855 N Meridian St. I-465, exit 31, 2 mi n on US 31, just e on 116th St, then just n on Pennsylvania Rd. Int corridors. **Pets:** Accepted.

EDINBURGH

Best Western Horizon Inn SH
(812) 526-9883. **$89-$169.** 11780 N US 31. I-65, exit 76B, just n. Int corridors. **Pets:** Medium. $20 one-time fee/room. Supervision.

FISHERS

Comfort Suites SH
(317) 578-1200. **$70-$180.** 9760 Crosspoint Blvd. I-69, exit 3, just w on 96th St, then just n. Int corridors. **Pets:** Large, other species. $10 daily fee/pet. Service with restrictions, crate.

Residence Inn by Marriott Indianapolis/Fishers SH
(317) 842-1111. **$143-$163.** 9765 Crosspoint Blvd. I-69, exit 3, just nw. Int corridors. **Pets:** Accepted.

Staybridge Suites Indianapolis-Fishers SH
(317) 577-9500. **Call for rates.** 9780 Crosspoint Blvd. I-69, exit 3, just nw. Int corridors. **Pets:** Accepted.

GREENWOOD

Red Roof Inn M
(317) 887-1515. **Call for rates.** 110 Sheek Rd. I-65, exit 99, just w. Ext corridors. **Pets:** Accepted.

INDIANAPOLIS

Baymont Inn & Suites SH
(317) 322-2000. **$89-$159.** 1540 Brookville Crossing Way. I-465, exit 47, 0.3 mi e. Int corridors. **Pets:** Other species. Service with restrictions, supervision.

Best Western Airport Suites SH
(317) 246-1505. **Call for rates.** 55 S High School Rd. I-465, exit 13B, just w. Int corridors. **Pets:** Accepted.

Candlewood Suites SH
(317) 595-9292. **$89-$189.** 8111 Bash St. I-69, exit 1, just w. Int corridors. **Pets:** Other species. $25 one-time fee/room.

Conrad Indianapolis LH ❀
(317) 713-5000. **Call for rates.** 50 W Washington St. Jct Illinois St. Int corridors. **Pets:** Small, dogs only. $100 deposit/room, $150 one-time fee/room. Service with restrictions, crate.

Drury Inn-Indianapolis SH
(317) 876-9777. **$76-$111.** 9320 N Michigan Rd. I-465, exit 27, just s. Int corridors. **Pets:** Large, other species. Service with restrictions, supervision.

Extended StayAmerica Castleton SH
(317) 596-1288. **$75-$105.** 7940 N Shadeland Ave. I-69, exit 1, 0.5 mi s. Int corridors. **Pets:** Other species. $75 one-time fee/pet. Service with restrictions.

Extended StayAmerica-Indianapolis North SH
(317) 843-1181. **$90-$120.** 9750 Lakeshore Dr. I-465, exit 33, 0.4 mi n on Keystone Dr, 0.6 mi e on 96th St, then just n on Bauer Dr. Int corridors. **Pets:** Other species. $75 one-time fee/pet. Service with restrictions.

Extended StayAmerica-Indianapolis-Northwest-College Park SH
(317) 872-3090. **$65-$95.** 9030 Wesleyan Rd. I-465, exit 27, just s to Depauw Blvd, just e, then just s. Int corridors. **Pets:** Other species. $75 one-time fee/pet. Service with restrictions.

Hilton Indianapolis LH
(317) 972-0600. **Call for rates.** 120 W Market St. Jct Illinois St. Int corridors. **Pets:** Small. $20 one-time fee/pet. Service with restrictions, supervision.

Holiday Inn East LH
(317) 359-5341. **$69-$159.** 6990 E 21st St. I-70, exit 89, 0.5 mi w of jct I-465. Int corridors. **Pets:** Medium. $35 one-time fee/room. Service with restrictions, supervision.

Holiday Inn Express Hotel & Suites City Centre SH
(317) 822-6400. **$139-$299.** 410 S Missouri St. Jct Missouri and South sts. Int corridors. **Pets:** Other species. $25 one-time fee/pet. Service with restrictions, supervision.

Homestead Studio Suites Hotel-Indianapolis/Northwest SH
(317) 334-7829. **$75-$105.** 8520 Northwest Blvd. I-465, exit 23, just e. Int corridors. **Pets:** Other species. $75 one-time fee/pet. Service with restrictions.

Indianapolis Marriott East LH
(317) 352-1231. **$109-$199.** 7202 E 21st St. I-70, exit 89, 0.3 mi se; 0.5 mi w of jct I-465. Int corridors. **Pets:** Other species. $75 one-time fee/room. Service with restrictions, crate.

Jameson Inn Indianapolis Castleton SH
(317) 849-8555. **Call for rates.** 8380 Kelly Ln. I-465, exit 35 (Allisonville Rd), just s. Int corridors. **Pets:** Small. $15 daily fee/room. Service with restrictions, crate.

♦♦ Jameson Inn of Indianapolis South SH
(317) 784-7006. **Call for rates.** 4402 E Creekview Dr. I-65, exit 103, just w. Int corridors. **Pets:** Small. $15 daily fee/room. Service with restrictions, crate.

⊠ 🖥 💻 ➿

♦♦ La Quinta Inn & Suites Indianapolis-Airport SH
(317) 244-8100. **$82-$97.** 2650 Executive Dr. I-465, exit 11A southbound; exit 11B northbound, 0.3 mi e. Int corridors. **Pets:** Other species. Service with restrictions, supervision.

ASK ⊠ ⚹M 🖥 💻

♦♦ La Quinta Inn Indianapolis Airport SH
(317) 247-4281. **$99-$102.** 5316 W Southern Ave. I-465, exit 11A, 0.5 mi e on Airport Expwy to Lynhurst Dr. Int corridors. **Pets:** Other species. Service with restrictions, supervision.

ASK S⊘ ⊠ 🖥 💻 ➿

♦♦ La Quinta Inn Indianapolis (East) SH
(317) 359-1021. **$79.** 7304 E 21st St. I-70, exit 89, just s, then just e; 0.5 mi w of jct I-465. Int corridors. **Pets:** Other species. Service with restrictions, supervision.

ASK S⊘ ⊠ ⚹M 🖥 💻 ➿

♦♦ Microtel Inn & Suites SH
(317) 870-7765. **$45-$160.** 9140 N Michigan Rd. I-465, exit 27, just s. Int corridors. **Pets:** Accepted.

⊠ 🖥 💻

♦♦♦ Omni Severin Hotel LH
(317) 634-6664. **$129-$299.** 40 W Jackson Pl. Opposite Union Station. Int corridors. **Pets:** Small, dogs only. $50 one-time fee/room. Service with restrictions, crate.

SAVE S⊘ ⊠ 🖥 💻 🍴 ➿

♦♦ Quality Inn & Suites Airport SH
(317) 381-1000. **Call for rates.** 2631 S Lynhurst Dr. I-465, exit 11A, 0.5 mi e on Airport Expwy to Lynhurst Dr. Int corridors. **Pets:** Accepted.

⊠ 🖥 💻 ➿

♦♦ Ramada Limited SH
(317) 297-1848. **$79-$199, 30 day notice.** 3851 Shore Dr. I-465, exit 17, just w on 38th St, then just n. Ext corridors. **Pets:** Other species. $15 daily fee/pet. No service, supervision.

ASK S⊘ ⊠ 🖥 💻 ➿

♦♦♦ Residence Inn by Marriott Indianapolis Airport SH
(317) 244-1500. **$165-$185.** 5224 W Southern Ave. I-465, exit 11A, 0.5 mi e on Airport Expwy to Lynhurst Dr. Int corridors. **Pets:** Accepted.

ASK S⊘ ⊠ ⚹M 🖥 💻 ➿ ⊠

♦♦♦ Residence Inn by Marriott Indianapolis Downtown on the Canal SH
(317) 822-0840. **$187-$207.** 350 W New York St. At New York St and Senate Ave. Int corridors. **Pets:** Medium, other species. $100 one-time fee/room. Service with restrictions, crate.

ASK S⊘ ⊠ ⚹M 🖥 💻 ➿

♦♦♦ Residence Inn by Marriott Northwest-Indianapolis SH
(317) 275-6000. **$129-$189.** 6220 Digital Way. I-465, exit 21, just w. Int corridors. **Pets:** Accepted.

ASK S⊘ ⊠ ⚹M 🖥 💻 ➿ ⊠

♦♦♦ Sheraton Indianapolis City Centre LH ❀
(317) 635-2000. **$189-$349, 4 day notice.** 31 W Ohio St. Meridian and Ohio sts; just n of Monument Cir. Int corridors. **Pets:** Medium. Service with restrictions, supervision.

ASK S⊘ ⊠ ⚹M 🖥 💻 🍴 ➿

♦♦♦ Sheraton Indianapolis Hotel & Suites LH
(317) 846-2700. **$169-$219.** 8787 Keystone Crossing. I-465, exit 33, 0.5 mi s on SR 431, just e on 86th St, then just n. Int corridors. **Pets:** Accepted.

ASK S⊘ ⊠ ⚹M 🖥 💻 🍴 ➿

♦♦ TownePlace Suites by Marriott Keystone SH
(317) 255-3700. **$143-$163.** 8468 Union Chapel Rd. I-465, exit 33, 0.5 mi s on SR 431, just e on 86th st, then just s. Int corridors. **Pets:** Accepted.

ASK S⊘ ⊠ 🖥 💻 ➿

♦♦ TownePlace Suites by Marriott Park 100 SH
(317) 290-8900. **$165-$185.** 5802 W 71st St. I-465, exit 21, 0.3 mi e. Int corridors. **Pets:** Accepted.

ASK S⊘ ⊠ 🖥 💻 ➿

♦♦♦ ♦♦♦♦ The Westin Indianapolis LH ❀
(317) 262-8100. **$414.** 50 S Capitol Ave. At Washington and Maryland sts and Capitol Ave. Int corridors. **Pets:** Small. Service with restrictions, crate.

SAVE S⊘ ⊠ ⚹M 💻 🍴 ➿ ⊠

♦♦ Wingate Inn-Airport SH
(317) 243-8310. **$89-$99.** 5797 Rockville Rd. I-465, exit 13A, just e. Int corridors. **Pets:** Other species. $25 one-time fee/room.

ASK S⊘ ⊠ ⚹M 🖥 💻 ➿

LEBANON

♦♦♦ ♦♦ Comfort Inn SH
(765) 482-4800. **$75-$169.** 210 N Sam Ralston Rd. I-65, exit 140. Int corridors. **Pets:** Medium. $15 daily fee/pet. Designated rooms, service with restrictions, supervision.

SAVE S⊘ ⊠ 🖥 💻 ➿

♦♦ Holiday Inn Express SH
(765) 483-4100. **$90-$180.** 335 N Mt. Zion Rd. I-65, exit 140, just w. Int corridors. **Pets:** Accepted.

ASK S⊘ ⊠ ⚹M 🖥 💻 ➿

♦♦ Super 8 Motel SH
(765) 482-9999. **$53-$57.** 405 N Mount Zion Rd. I-65, exit 140, just w. Int corridors. **Pets:** Accepted.

ASK S⊘ ⊠ 🖥 ➿

MARTINSVILLE

♦♦ Best Western Martinsville Inn M
(765) 342-1842. **$89-$149.** 50 Bill's Blvd. SR 37 to Ohio St, just w. Int corridors. **Pets:** Small. $10 daily fee/pet. Service with restrictions, supervision.

ASK S⊘ ⊠ ⚹M 🖥 💻

NOBLESVILLE

♦♦ Quality Inn & Suites SH ❀
(317) 770-6772. **$69-$149.** 16025 Prosperity Dr. I-69, exit 5, 4 mi n on SR 37. Int corridors. **Pets:** Other species. $25 one-time fee/room.

ASK S⊘ ⊠ 🖥 💻 ➿

PLAINFIELD

♦♦♦ Staybridge Suites Indianapolis Airport SH
(317) 839-2700. **$139-$249.** 6295 Cambridge Way. I-70, exit 66, 0.4 mi n on SR 267, just e on Hadley Rd, then just s. Int corridors. **Pets:** $75 one-time fee/room. Designated rooms, service with restrictions.

ASK S⊘ ⊠ ⚹M 🖥 💻 ➿

SHELBYVILLE

Americas Best Value Inn SH
(317) 398-0472. **$59-$99.** 68 E Rampart St. I-74, exit 113, just w. Int corridors. **Pets:** Accepted.
SAVE S⊘ ✕ 🗚 🔒 🖵 ⚓

END METROPOLITAN AREA

JASPER

Days Inn Jasper SH
(812) 482-6000. **$67-$95.** 272 Brucke Strasse. Jct SR 164, just w. Ext/int corridors. **Pets:** Accepted.
SAVE S⊘ ✕ 🔒 🖵 🍽 ⚓ ✕

JEFFERSONVILLE

Comfort Suites Louisville North SH
(812) 282-2100. **$90-$325.** 360 Eastern Blvd. I-65, exit 2 (Eastern Blvd), just e. Int corridors. **Pets:** Accepted.
ASK S⊘ ✕ 🗚 🔒 🖵

TownePlace Suites by Marriott SH
(812) 280-8200. **$89-$189.** 703 N Shore Dr. I-65, exit 0, just w. Int corridors. **Pets:** Accepted.
ASK S⊘ ✕ 🔒 🖵 ⚓

KENDALLVILLE

Best Western Kendallville Inn SH
(260) 347-5263. **$79-$129, 3 day notice.** 621 Professional Way. 1 mi e on US 6. Int corridors. **Pets:** Medium, dogs only. $25 one-time fee/pet. Service with restrictions, supervision.
SAVE ✕ 🔒 🖵 ⚓ ✕

KOKOMO

Comfort Inn by Choice Hotels SH
(765) 452-5050. **Call for rates.** 522 Essex Dr. Jct US 35, 0.3 mi n on US 31. Int corridors. **Pets:** Accepted.
✕ 🔒 🖵 ⚓

Days Inn & Suites M
(765) 453-7100. **$56-$80.** 264 S 00 EW. US 31, 2.8 mi s of jct US 35. Ext corridors. **Pets:** $10 one-time fee/room. Service with restrictions, supervision.
ASK S⊘ ✕ 🔒 🖵 🍽 ⚓

Hampton Inn & Suites SH
(765) 455-2900. **$99-$129.** 2920 S Reed Rd (US Hwy 31). US 31, 2 mi s of jct US 35. Int corridors. **Pets:** Other species. Designated rooms, service with restrictions, crate.
ASK S⊘ ✕ 🗚 🔒 🖵 ⚓ ✕

LAFAYETTE

Best Western Lafayette Executive Plaza & Conference Center SH
(765) 447-0575. **$89-$251, 30 day notice.** 4343 SR 26 E. I-65, exit 172, just w. Int corridors. **Pets:** Small. $25 daily fee/room. Designated rooms, service with restrictions, supervision.
SAVE S⊘ ✕ 🗚 🔒 🖵 🍽 ⚓ ✕

Days Inn & Suites SH
(765) 446-8558. **$80-$90.** 151 Frontage Rd. I-65, exit 172, just e. Int corridors. **Pets:** $75 deposit/room. Designated rooms, no service, crate.
ASK S⊘ ✕ 🔒 🖵

Holiday Inn Express SH
(765) 449-4808. **$95-$170.** 201 Frontage Rd. I-65, exit 172, just e on SR 26, then just n. Int corridors. **Pets:** Accepted.
SAVE S⊘ ✕ 🔒 🖵

Homewood Suites by Hilton SH ❀
(765) 448-9700. **$109-$114.** 3939 SR 26 E. I-65, exit 172, 0.8 mi w. Ext/int corridors. **Pets:** Other species. $50 one-time fee/pet. Service with restrictions, crate.
ASK S⊘ ✕ 🔒 🖵 ⚓ ✕

Loeb House Inn BB
(765) 420-7737. **$105-$185, 5 day notice.** 708 Cincinnati St. SR 38, 0.4 mi n on 9th St, then just w. Int corridors. **Pets:** Small, other species. Service with restrictions, crate.
ASK ✕

Motel 6 M
(765) 447-7566. **Call for rates.** 139 Frontage Rd. I-65, exit 172. Ext corridors. **Pets:** Other species. Service with restrictions, supervision.
SAVE ✕ 🔒

Red Roof Inn-Lafayette #7062 M
(765) 448-4671. **Call for rates.** 4201 SR 26 E. I-65, exit 172, 0.3 mi w. Ext corridors. **Pets:** Accepted.
✕ 🔒

TownePlace Suites by Marriott SH
(765) 446-8668. **$165-$185.** 163 Frontage Rd. I-65, exit 172, just e. Int corridors. **Pets:** $75 one-time fee/room. No service, crate.
ASK S⊘ ✕ 🔒 🖵 ⚓

LOGANSPORT

Ramada SH
(574) 753-6351. **$85-$95.** 3550 E Market St. 2.5 mi e on Business Rt US 24. Int corridors. **Pets:** Accepted.
ASK S⊘ ✕ 🗚 🔒 🖵 🍽 ⚓

MADISON

Country Hearth Inn SH ❀
(812) 273-0757. **$59-$99.** 308 Demaree Dr. Jct SR 7 and 62, 2 mi e on SR 62. Int corridors. **Pets:** Other species. $10 daily fee/pet. Service with restrictions, crate.
SAVE S⊘ ✕ 🔒 🖵

MARION

Comfort Suites-Marion SH
(765) 651-1006. **$79-$125.** 1345 N Baldwin Ave. 1.5 mi n of jct SR 9 and 18. Int corridors. **Pets:** Other species. $10 one-time fee/pet. Designated rooms, service with restrictions, supervision.
SAVE S⊘ ✕ 🔒 🖵 ⚓ ✕

MERRILLVILLE

Best Western Inn & Suites of Merrillville SH
(219) 756-2378. **$70-$190.** 8293 Louisiana St. I-65, exit 253, 0.3 mi e on US 30, just s on Mississippi St, then 0.4 mi w on 83rd Ave. Int corridors. **Pets:** Accepted.
SAVE ✕ 🔒 🖵 ⚓

Country Inn & Suites by Carlson SH
(219) 736-1300. **$99-$129.** 8311 Ohio St. I-65, exit 253 (US 30), 0.3 mi e, just s on Mississippi St, 0.4 mi w on 83rd Ave, then just s. Int corridors. **Pets:** Accepted.
ASK S⊘ ✕ 🔒 🖵 ⚓

▼▼ ▼▼ **Extended StayAmerica-Merrillville-US Rte 30** 🆂🅷
(219) 769-4740. **$76-$84.** 1355 E 83rd Ave. I-65, exit 253, 0.3 mi e on US 30, just s on Mississippi St, then 0.4 mi w. Int corridors. **Pets:** Other species. $75 one-time fee/pet. Service with restrictions.
(ASK) (S🔂) (✕) (🖥) (💻)

▼▼▼▼ **Residence Inn by Marriott Merrillville** 🆂🅷 🐾
(219) 791-9000. **$175-$194.** 8018 Delaware Pl. I-65, exit 253 (US 30), 0.3 mi nw. Int corridors. **Pets:** Medium. $100 one-time fee/room. Service with restrictions.
(ASK) (S🔂) (✕) (&M) (🖥) (💻) (🏊) (✕)

⬥⬥⬥ ▼ **Super 8 Motel** 🆂🅷
(219) 736-8383. **$55-$90.** 8300 Louisiana St. I-65, exit 253 (US 30), 0.3 mi e, just s on Mississippi St, then just w on 83rd Ave. Int corridors. **Pets:** Medium, other species. $50 deposit/room. Designated rooms, service with restrictions, supervision.
(SAVE) (✕) (&M) (🖥) (💻)

MONTGOMERY

▼▼ **Gasthof Amish Village Inn** 🆂🅷
(812) 486-2600. **Call for rates.** 6747 E Garth of Village Rd E. US 50, 0.8 mi n on First St. Int corridors. **Pets:** Accepted.
(✕) (🖥) (💻) (🍴) (🏊) (✕)

MOUNT VERNON

▼▼ **Four Seasons Motel** Ⓜ
(812) 838-4821. **$54-$94.** 70 Hwy 62 W. 1.8 mi w. Ext corridors. **Pets:** Accepted.
(ASK) (✕) (🖥) (💻) (🏊)

MUNCIE

▼▼ **Days Inn Muncie** 🆂🅷
(765) 288-2311. **Call for rates.** 3509 N Everbrook Ln. I-69, exit 41, 6.3 mi e on SR 332, then just n. Int corridors. **Pets:** Dogs only. $10 one-time fee/pet. Service with restrictions, supervision.
(✕) (🖥) (💻)

▼▼▼▼ **Signature Inn-Muncie** 🆂🅷
(765) 284-4200. **Call for rates.** 3400 N Chadam Ln. I-69, exit 41, 6.3 mi e on SR 332. Int corridors. **Pets:** Small. $15 daily fee/room. Service with restrictions, crate.
(✕) (🖥) (💻) (🏊)

▼▼ **Super 8 Motel** 🆂🅷
(765) 286-4333. **$45-$85.** 3601 W Fox Ridge Ln. I-69, exit 41, 6.3 mi e on SR 332. Int corridors. **Pets:** Medium, dogs only. $10 daily fee/pet. Service with restrictions, supervision.
(ASK) (S🔂) (✕) (🖥) (💻)

NEW ALBANY

⬥⬥⬥ ▼▼▼▼ **Holiday Inn Express** 🆂🅷
(812) 945-2771. **$100-$400.** 411 W Spring St. I-64, exit 123. Int corridors. **Pets:** Accepted.
(SAVE) (S🔂) (✕) (🖥) (💻) (🏊)

NEW CASTLE

⬥⬥⬥ ▼▼▼▼ **Best Western Raintree Inn** 🆂🅷
(765) 521-0100. **Call for rates.** 2836 S SR 3. I-70, exit 123, 2.8 mi n. Ext/int corridors. **Pets:** Accepted.
(SAVE) (✕) (🖥) (💻) (🏊)

NORTH VERNON

▼▼ **Comfort Inn** 🆂🅷
(812) 352-9999. **$79-$109.** 150 FDR Dr. Jct US 50, 0.6 mi n on SR 7. Int corridors. **Pets:** Small, dogs only. $25 deposit/room. Service with restrictions, crate.
(ASK) (S🔂) (✕) (🖥) (💻) (🏊)

PERU

▼▼▼▼ **Best Western Circus City Inn** 🆂🅷
(765) 473-8800. **Call for rates.** 2642 Business 31 S. Just e of jct US 31. Int corridors. **Pets:** Accepted.
(✕) (🖥) (💻) (🏊)

PLYMOUTH

▼▼ **Super 8 Motel** 🆂🅷
(574) 936-8856. **Call for rates.** 2160 N Oak Rd. US 30, just s. Int corridors. **Pets:** Accepted.
(✕) (🖥) (💻) (🏊)

▼▼▼▼ **Swan Lake Resort** 🆂🅷
(574) 935-5680. **Call for rates.** 5203 Plymouth-LaPorte Tr. 2.5 mi w on US 30, 4 mi nw on Queen Rd/Plymouth-LaPorte Tr. Int corridors. **Pets:** Accepted.
(✕) (🖥) (💻) (🍴) (🏊) (✕)

PORTAGE

▼▼ **Comfort Inn** 🆂🅷
(219) 763-7177. **$69-$179.** 2300 Willow Creek Rd. I-80/90, exit 23; I-94, exit 19, 1.5 mi s on CR 249. Int corridors. **Pets:** Small, dogs only. $20 one-time fee/pet. Designated rooms, service with restrictions, supervision.
(ASK) (S🔂) (✕) (🖥) (💻)

▼▼ **Super 8 Motel Portage** 🆂🅷
(219) 762-8857. **Call for rates.** 6118 Melton Rd. I-94, exit 19, just s on CR 249, then just w on US 20; I-80, exit 23, 1.2 mi n on CR 249, then just w on US 20. Int corridors. **Pets:** Other species. $5 daily fee/pet. Service with restrictions, supervision.
(✕) (🖥) (💻)

PORTLAND

▼▼ **Hoosier Inn** Ⓜ
(260) 726-7113. **$38-$90.** 1620 Meridian St. 1.4 mi n on US 27. Ext corridors. **Pets:** Small, dogs only. $5 daily fee/pet. Service with restrictions, supervision.
(ASK) (S🔂) (✕) (🖥) (💻)

PRINCETON

▼▼ **Fairfield Inn by Marriott** 🆂🅷
(812) 385-4300. **$78-$98.** 2828 Dixon St. Jct US 41 and SR 64, 0.3 mi w. Int corridors. **Pets:** Other species. $25 one-time fee/room. Service with restrictions, supervision.
(ASK) (S🔂) (✕) (&M) (🖥) (💻) (🏊)

RICHMOND

▼▼ **Days Inn** Ⓜ
(765) 966-4900. **$45-$70.** 5775 National Rd E. I-70, exit 156A, just s. Ext corridors. **Pets:** $10 daily fee/pet. Service with restrictions, supervision.
(ASK) (S🔂) (✕) (🖥) (💻)

▼▼▼▼ **Holiday Inn-Richmond** 🆂🅷 🐾
(765) 966-7511. **$89-$325.** 5501 National Rd E. I-70, exit 156A, 0.3 mi w. Int corridors. **Pets:** Large, other species. $20 daily fee/room. Service with restrictions, supervision.
(ASK) (S🔂) (✕) (&M) (🖥) (💻) (🍴) (🏊) (✕)

⬥⬥⬥ ▼▼ **Knights Inn** 🆂🅷
(765) 966-1505. **$55-$89.** 3020 E Main St. I-70, exit 156A, 2 mi w. Ext corridors. **Pets:** Small. $8 daily fee/pet. Service with restrictions, supervision.
(SAVE) (S🔂) (✕) (🖥) (💻) (🏊)

⬥⬥⬥ ▼▼▼▼ **Lees Inn & Suites** 🆂🅷
(765) 966-6559. **$89-$99.** 6030 National Rd E. I-70, exit 156A, jct US 40. Int corridors. **Pets:** Other species. Designated rooms, service with restrictions, crate.
(SAVE) (S🔂) (✕) (&M) (🖥) (💻) (🏊)

▼▼ Motel 6 Richmond #4170 **M**
(765) 966-6682. **Call for rates.** 419 Commerce Dr. I-70, exit 156A, just s on US 40. Ext corridors. **Pets:** Other species. Service with restrictions, supervision.
⊠ ➤

ROCKVILLE

▼ Parke Bridge Motel **M**
(765) 569-3525. **Call for rates.** 304 E Ohio St. US 36, just e of center, 0.5 mi e of jct US 41. Ext corridors. **Pets:** Accepted.
SAVE ⊠ ▣

ROSELAND

▼▼ Quality Inn-University Area **M**
(574) 272-6600. **Call for rates.** 515 N Dixie Way. I-80/90, exit 77, 0.8 mi n on SR 933. Ext/int corridors. **Pets:** Accepted.
⊠ 🛇 ▣ ⑪ ➤

SCOTTSBURG

▼▼▼ Mariann Travel Inn **M**
(812) 752-3396. **$53-$62.** I-65 and SR 56. I-65, exit 29A, just e. Ext corridors. **Pets:** Accepted.
SAVE 🛇 ⊠ 🛇 ⑪ ➤ ⊠

SELLERSBURG

▼▼ Home Lodge **SH**
(812) 246-6332. **$59.** 363 Triangle Dr. I-65, exit 9, just e. Int corridors. **Pets:** Accepted.
A$K ⊠ 🛇 ▣

▼▼▼ Ramada Limited & Suites **SH**
(812) 246-3131. **$79.** 360 Triangle Dr. I-65, exit 9, just e. Int corridors. **Pets:** Accepted.
A$K 🛇 ⊠ 🛇 ▣ ➤

SEYMOUR

▼ Motel 6 Seymour #4153 **SH**
(812) 524-7443. **Call for rates.** 365 Tanger Blvd. I-65, exit 50A. Int corridors. **Pets:** Other species. Service with restrictions, supervision.
⊠ 🛇 🛇 ▣ ➤

▼▼▼ Seymour Quality Inn **SH**
(812) 522-6767. **$79-$99.** 2025 E Tipton St. I-65, exit 50B, 0.5 mi w on US 50. Ext corridors. **Pets:** Medium. Supervision.
A$K 🛇 ⊠ 🛇 ▣ ➤

SOUTH BEND

▼▼▼ Comfort Suites South Bend **SH**
(574) 272-1500. **$100-$165.** 52939 SR 933 N. I-80/90, exit 77, just e to Business Rt US 31/SR 933, then 1 mi n. Int corridors. **Pets:** Very small. $10 daily fee/pet. Designated rooms, no service, crate.
SAVE 🛇 ⊠ 🛇 ▣ ➤ ⊠

▼▼ ▼▼ Cushing Manor Inn **BB**
(574) 288-1990. **$95-$165, 7 day notice.** 508 W Washington St. 0.4 mi w of jct SR 933 and US 31 business. Int corridors. **Pets:** Accepted.
SAVE 🛇 ⊠

▼▼▼ The English Rose Bed & Breakfast Guest House **BB**
(574) 288-1990. **Call for rates.** 116 S Taylor St. Business Rt US 31, 0.3 mi w on Washington St to Taylor St, then just s. Int corridors. **Pets:** Accepted.
⊠ ✍

▼▼▼ Oliver Inn Bed & Breakfast **BB**
(574) 232-4545. **$90-$339, 14 day notice.** 630 W Washington St. 0.3 mi w of SR 933 and US 31 business route. Int corridors. **Pets:** $10 one-time fee/pet. Designated rooms, service with restrictions, supervision.
A$K 🛇 ⊠ 🛇 ▣

▼▼ Quality Inn & Suites **SH**
(574) 288-3800. **$69-$299.** 4124 Lincolnway W. I-80/90, exit 72, 1.5 mi s on US 31 to South Bend Airport exit, then 2 mi e. Int corridors. **Pets:** Accepted.
SAVE 🛇 ⊠ 🛇 🛇 ▣ ➤

▼▼ ▼ Super 8 Motel–South Bend **SH**
(574) 243-0200. **$79-$249.** 4124 Ameritech Dr. I-80/90, exit 72, 0.7 mi n on US 31, just e on Cleveland Rd, then just s. Int corridors. **Pets:** Medium. $10 daily fee/pet. Designated rooms, service with restrictions, supervision.
SAVE 🛇 ⊠ 🛇 ▣ ➤

TAYLORSVILLE

▼▼ Red Roof Inn **M**
(812) 526-9747. **Call for rates.** 10330 US 31. I-65, exit 76A, just s. Ext corridors. **Pets:** Accepted.
⊠ 🛇 ▣ ➤

TELL CITY

▼▼ Ramada Limited **SH**
(812) 547-3234. **$62-$89.** 235 Orchard Hill Dr. Just off SR 66, 1.7 mi se of jct SR 37. Int corridors. **Pets:** Medium, other species. $50 deposit/room, $15 one-time fee/pet. Service with restrictions, supervision.
A$K 🛇 ⊠ 🛇 ▣ ➤

TERRE HAUTE

▼▼ Drury Inn-Terre Haute **SH**
(812) 238-1206. **$91-$126.** 3040 Hwy 41 S. I-70, exit 7 (US 41/150), just n. Int corridors. **Pets:** Large, other species. Service with restrictions, supervision.
A$K ⊠ 🛇 🛇 ▣ ➤ ⊠

▼ Econo Lodge **M**
(812) 234-9931. **$59-$125.** 401 E Margaret Ave. I-70, exit 7 (US 41/150), just n, then e. Ext corridors. **Pets:** Large. $10 one-time fee/room. Service with restrictions.
A$K 🛇 ⊠ 🛇 ▣ ➤

▼▼ Holiday Inn **LH**
(812) 232-6081. **$115-$180.** 3300 US 41 S. I-70, exit 7 (US 41/150), just s. Int corridors. **Pets:** Accepted.
A$K 🛇 ⊠ 🛇 ▣ ⑪ ➤ ⊠

▼▼ Pear Tree Inn by Drury-Terre Haute **SH**
(812) 234-4268. **$78-$93.** 3050 US 41 S. I-70, exit 7 (US 41/150), just n. Int corridors. **Pets:** Large, other species. Service with restrictions, supervision.
A$K ⊠ ▣

▼ Super 8 Motel-Terre Haute **SH**
(812) 232-4890. **$44-$69.** 3089 S 1st St. I-70, exit 7 (US 41/150), just nw. Int corridors. **Pets:** $10 one-time fee/pet. Designated rooms, no service, crate.
A$K 🛇 ⊠ 🛇

VALPARAISO

▼▼▼ Courtyard by Marriott Valparaiso **SH**
(219) 465-1700. **$99-$119.** 2301 E Morthland Dr. On US 30, just w of jct SR 49. Int corridors. **Pets:** Medium, other species. $75 one-time fee/room. Service with restrictions, supervision.
A$K 🛇 ⊠ 🛇 ▣ ➤

WARREN

▼▼ Comfort Inn Warren **SH**
(260) 375-4800. **$55-$199, 7 day notice.** 7275 S 75 E. I-69, exit 78, just n on SR 5. Int corridors. **Pets:** Accepted.
A$K ⊠ 🛇 🛇 ▣ ➤

WARSAW

 Comfort Inn & Suites-Warsaw SH
(574) 269-6655. **$69-$199.** 3328 E Center St. 3.2 mi e of SR 15 on US 30. Int corridors. **Pets:** Small. $10 daily fee/pet. Designated rooms, no service, crate.

(SAVE) ⊠ 🔋 💻 🏊 🔀

 Ramada Plaza of Warsaw SH 🐾
(574) 269-2323. **$99-$110.** 2519 E Center St. 2.8 mi e of SR 15 on US 30, just s. Int corridors. **Pets:** Medium. Service with restrictions, crate.

(ASK) (S🔒) ⊠ 🔋 💻 🍴 🏊 🔀

WASHINGTON

 Baymont Inn & Suites Washington SH
(812) 254-7000. **Call for rates.** 7 Cumberland Dr. Just ne of jct US 50 and SR 257. Int corridors. **Pets:** Medium. $50 deposit/room. Service with restrictions, supervision.

⊠ 🔋 💻 🏊 🔀

WEST BADEN SPRINGS

 West Baden Springs Hotel LH 🐾
(812) 936-1902. **$180-$325, 3 day notice.** 8538 W Baden Ave. On SR 56. Int corridors. **Pets:** Medium, dogs only. Supervision.

(SAVE) (S🔒) ⊠ (🚹M) 🔋 💻 🍴 🏊 🔀

IOWA

ADAIR

Adair Budget Inn M
(641) 742-5553. **$33-$54.** 100 S 5th St. I-80, exit 76. Ext corridors.
Pets: $20 deposit/room. Designated rooms, service with restrictions, supervision.

SAVE SØ ✕ ■

Adair Super 8 SH
(641) 742-5251. **Call for rates.** 111 S 5th St. I-80, exit 76. Int corridors.
Pets: Accepted.
✕ ■ ▣

ALBIA

Indian Hills Inn SH
(641) 932-7181. **Call for rates.** 100 Hwy 34 E. Just e of jct US 34 and SR 5. Ext/int corridors. **Pets:** Accepted.
SAVE ✕ ■ ▣ ¶ ⇌

ALGONA

AmericInn Motel SH
(515) 295-3333. **$82-$135.** 600 Hwy 18 W. Just w of jct US 169/18. Int corridors. **Pets:** Accepted.
ASK SØ ✕ ⑥M ■ ▣ ⇌ ✕

ALTOONA

Motel 6 Des Moines East #1420 SH
(515) 967-5252. **$45-$65.** 3225 Adventureland Dr. I-80, exit 142A. Int corridors. **Pets:** Other species. Service with restrictions, supervision.
SØ ✕ ■ ⇌

Settle Inn & Suites-Altoona SH
(515) 967-7888. **$79-$99.** 2101 Adventureland Dr. I-80, exit 142A, just se. Int corridors. **Pets:** Accepted.
ASK SØ ✕ ■ ▣ ⇌

AMES

AmericInn & Suites SH
(515) 233-1005. **$79-$125.** 2507 SE 16th St. I-35, exit 111B, just w on US 30, then exit 150. Int corridors. **Pets:** $50 deposit/room. Service with restrictions, supervision.
SAVE SØ ✕ ⑥M ■ ▣ ⇌ ✕

Best Western University Park Inn & Suites SH
(515) 296-2500. **$100-$125.** 2500 University Blvd. I-35, exit 111B, 3.5 mi w on US 30, exit 146 (Elwood Dr), then just s. Int corridors. **Pets:** Accepted.
ASK SØ ✕ ■ ▣ ⇌

Comfort Inn-Ames SH 🐾
(515) 232-0689. **$69-$125.** 1605 S Dayton Ave. I-35, exit 111B, just w on US 30, then exit 150. Int corridors. **Pets:** Medium. $10 daily fee/pet. Service with restrictions, supervision.
SAVE ✕ ■ ▣ ⇌

Gateway Hotel & Conference Center LH
(515) 292-8600. **$139-$189.** 2100 Green Hills Dr. I-35, exit 111B, 3.5 mi w on US 30, exit 146 (Elwood Dr). Int corridors. **Pets:** Accepted.
ASK SØ ✕ ⑥M ■ ▣ ¶ ⇌ ✕

GrandStay Residential Suites SH
(515) 232-8363. **Call for rates.** 1606 S Kellogg Ave. I-35, exit 111, 1 mi w, then just nw on Duff Ave to Kellogg Ave. Int corridors.
Pets: Accepted.
✕ ⑥M ■ ▣ ⇌ ✕

Holiday Inn SH
(515) 268-8808. **$99-$170.** 2609 Elwood Dr. I-35, exit 111B, 3.5 mi w on US 30, exit 146 (Elwood Dr), then just s. Int corridors.
Pets: Accepted.
ASK ✕ ⑥M ■ ▣ ¶ ⇌

Microtel Inn & Suites SH
(515) 233-4444. **$49-$149.** 2216 SE 16th St. I-35, exit 111B, just w on US 30, then exit 150. Int corridors. **Pets:** Accepted.
ASK SØ ✕ ⑥M ■ ▣

Quality Inn & Suites Starlite Village Conference Center SH
(515) 232-9260. **Call for rates.** 2601 E 13th St. I-35, exit 113 (13th St), 0.5 mi w. Int corridors. **Pets:** Other species. $10 one-time fee/room. Service with restrictions, crate.
SAVE ✕ ■ ▣ ¶ ⇌ ✕

ANAMOSA

Super 8 Motel-Anamosa SH
(319) 462-3888. **$55-$68.** 100 Grant Wood Dr. Just e on US 64 from US 151 (exit 54). Int corridors. **Pets:** Medium. $10 one-time fee/pet. Service with restrictions, supervision.
ASK SØ ✕ ■ ▣

ANKENY

Best Western Metro North SH
(515) 964-1717. **$90.** 133 SE Delaware Ave. I-35, exit 92, just w. Int corridors. **Pets:** Accepted.
SAVE SØ ✕ ■ ▣ ¶ ⇌ ✕

◀◀▶ ▼▼▼▼ **Comfort Inn** SH
(515) 963-1100. **$69-$189.** 2602 SE Creekview Dr. I-35, exit 90, just ne. Int corridors. **Pets:** Very small. $10 daily fee/pet. Designated rooms, no service, supervision.
SAVE S🔴 ✕ 🔌 🖥 🏊

ARNOLDS PARK

▼▼▼▼ **Bridges Bay Resort** CO
(712) 332-2202. **$99-$699.** 630 Linden Dr. Just e of US 71. Int corridors. **Pets:** Other species. Service with restrictions, crate.
ASK S🔴 ✕ 🔌 🖥 🏊 ✕

▼▼ **Fillenwarth Beach** SH
(712) 332-5646. **$70-$912 (no credit cards), 30 day notice.** 87 Lake Shore Dr. Just w of US 71; on West Lake Okoboji. Ext corridors. **Pets:** Accepted.
✕ 🔌 🖥 🏊 ✕

ATLANTIC

▼▼▼ **Days Inn** SH
(712) 243-4067. **Call for rates.** 64968 Boston Rd. I-80, exit 60 (US 71), 0.5 mi s. Int corridors. **Pets:** Accepted.
✕ 🔌 🖥 🏊

▼▼▼ **Super 8 Motel** SH
(712) 243-4723. **Call for rates.** 1902 E 7th St. I-80, exit 60 (US 71), 6 mi s, then 2 mi w; east side of town. Int corridors. **Pets:** Accepted.
✕ 🔌 🖥 🏊

BURLINGTON

◀◀▶ ▼▼▼▼ **Comfort Suites Hotel & Conference Center** SH
(319) 753-1300. **$99-$112.** 1780 Stonegate Center Dr. On US 61, 2 mi s of US 34. Int corridors. **Pets:** Accepted.
SAVE S🔴 ✕ 🚹M 🔌 🖥 🍽 🏊 ✕

◀◀▶ ▼▼ **Quality Inn** SH
(319) 753-0000. **$60-$90.** 3051 Kirkwood Ave. Jct US 61 and 34, just n. Int corridors. **Pets:** $10 daily fee/pet. Service with restrictions, supervision.
SAVE S🔴 ✕ 🔌 🖥 🏊

▼▼ **Super 8 Motel-Burlington** SH
(319) 752-9806. **$45-$79.** 3001 Kirkwood St. Jct US 61 and 34, just n. Int corridors. **Pets:** Small. $25 daily fee/pet. Service with restrictions, supervision.
ASK S🔴 ✕ 🔌 🖥

CARROLL

▼▼ **Super 8 Motel** SH
(712) 792-4753. **Call for rates.** 1757 US 71 N. Just n of jct US 30 and 71. Int corridors. **Pets:** Accepted.
✕ 🖥

CARTER LAKE

◀◀▶ ▼▼▼▼ **Holiday Inn Express Hotel & Suites** SH
(402) 505-4900. **$89-$259.** 2510 Abbott Plaza. I-480 W, exit 4 to 10th St, 2 mi n, follow Eppley Airfield signs. Int corridors. **Pets:** Medium, other species. $10 daily fee/room. Designated rooms, service with restrictions, crate.
SAVE ✕ 🚹M 🔌 🖥 🏊

▼▼▼▼ **La Quinta Inn & Suites** SH
(712) 347-6595. **$93.** 1201 Ave H. I-480 W, exit 4 to 10th St, 2 mi n, follow Eppley Airfield signs. Int corridors. **Pets:** Other species. Service with restrictions, supervision.
ASK S🔴 ✕ 🚹M 🔌 🖥 🏊

◀◀▶ ▼▼▼ **Super 8 Motel** SH
(712) 347-5588. **$77-$154.** 3000 Airport Dr. I-480 W, exit 4 to 10th St, 2.3 mi n, follow Eppley Airfield signs. Int corridors. **Pets:** $10 one-time fee/room. Service with restrictions, crate.
SAVE S🔴 ✕ 🚹M 🔌 🖥

CEDAR FALLS

▼▼▼▼ **Comfort Suites** SH
(319) 273-9999. **$89-$134.** 7402 Nordic Dr. US 20, exit 225, just nw. Int corridors. **Pets:** Accepted.
ASK S🔴 ✕ 🚹M 🔌 🖥 🏊

◀◀▶ ▼▼▼ **Days Inn** SH
(319) 266-1222. **Call for rates.** 5826 University Ave, Suite 2. 0.7 mi e of jct SR 58. Int corridors. **Pets:** Accepted.
SAVE ✕ 🔌 🖥

◀◀▶ ▼▼ **University Inn** SH
(319) 277-1412. **Call for rates.** 4711 University Ave. 1.6 mi e of jct SR 58. Ext/int corridors. **Pets:** $30 deposit/pet. Designated rooms, service with restrictions, supervision.
SAVE ✕ 🔌 🖥

CEDAR RAPIDS

▼▼▼ **Best Western Cooper's Mill Hotel & Restaurant** SH
(319) 366-5323. **$70-$90.** 100 F Ave NW. I-380, exit 19C northbound, take right at end of exit, make immediate U-turn and go under I-380; exit 20A southbound, cross river, right on 1st St NW. Int corridors. **Pets:** Accepted.
ASK S🔴 ✕ 🔌 🖥 🍽 🏊 ✕

◀◀▶ ▼▼▼▼ **Best Western Longbranch Hotel & Convention Center** SH
(319) 377-6386. **$90-$110.** 90 Twixt Town Rd NE. I-380, exit 24A (SR 100/Collins Rd), 2.5 mi e, then just n. Int corridors. **Pets:** Medium, other species. $5 daily fee/pet. Designated rooms, service with restrictions, supervision.
SAVE S🔴 ✕ 🔌 🖥 🍽 🏊 ✕

◀◀▶ ▼▼ **Clarion Hotel & Convention Center** LH 🐾
(319) 366-8671. **$93-$99.** 525 33rd Ave SW. I-380, exit 17 (33rd Ave SW), just w. Int corridors. **Pets:** Medium. $100 deposit/room, $15 daily fee/room. Designated rooms, service with restrictions, crate.
SAVE S🔴 ✕ 🔌 🖥 🍽 🏊 ✕

▼▼ **Comfort Inn by Choice Hotels North** SH
(319) 393-8247. **Call for rates.** 5055 Rockwell Dr NE. I-380, exit 24A (SR 100/Collins Rd), 1 mi e. Int corridors. **Pets:** Accepted.
✕ 🔌 🖥

▼▼ **Comfort Inn by Choice Hotels South** SH
(319) 363-7934. **Call for rates.** 390 33rd Ave SW. I-380, exit 17 (33rd Ave SW), just w. Int corridors. **Pets:** Accepted.
✕ 🔌 🖥

◀◀▶ ▼▼▼ **Country Inn & Suites Cedar Rapids Airport** SH 🐾
(319) 363-3789. **$109-$149.** 9100 Atlantic Dr SW. I-380, exit 13, just w. Int corridors. **Pets:** Medium, other species. $10 daily fee/pet. Service with restrictions, crate.
SAVE S🔴 ✕ 🚹M 🔌 🖥 🏊

◀◀▶ ▼▼▼ **Exel Inn of Cedar Rapids** M
(319) 366-2475. **$45-$65.** 616 33rd Ave SW. I-380, exit 17 (33rd Ave SW), 0.3 mi w. Int corridors. **Pets:** Accepted.
SAVE S🔴 ✕ 🔌 🖥

▼▼▼ **Hawthorn Suites** SH
(319) 294-8700. **$98-$117.** 4444 Czech Ln NE. I-380, exit 24A (SR 100/Collins Rd), just s. Int corridors. **Pets:** Other species. Service with restrictions, crate.
ASK S🔴 ✕ 🚹M 🔌 🖥 🏊

AAA ▽▽▽ Mainstay Suites SH
(319) 363-7829. **$89-$149.** 5145 Rockwell Dr NE. I-380, exit 24A (SR 100/Collins Rd), 1 mi e, then just n. Int corridors. **Pets:** Medium. $15 one-time fee/pet. Service with restrictions.
⟦SAVE⟧ ⟦S⟧ ⟦✕⟧ ⟦&M⟧ ⟦🛏⟧ ⟦▯⟧ ⟦≈⟧ ⟦✕⟧

AAA ▽▽▽ Marriott Cedar Rapids LH
(319) 393-6600. **$192-$213.** 1200 Collins Rd NE. I-380, exit 24A (SR 100/Collins Rd), 1 mi e. Int corridors. **Pets:** Accepted.
⟦SAVE⟧ ⟦S⟧ ⟦✕⟧ ⟦&M⟧ ⟦🛏⟧ ⟦▯⟧ ⟦¶⟧ ⟦≈⟧

▽▽ Motel 6 #1485 M
(319) 366-7523. **$39-$49.** 3325 Southgate Ct SW. I-380, exit 17 (33rd Ave SW), just sw. Ext corridors. **Pets:** Other species. Service with restrictions, supervision.
⟦S⟧ ⟦✕⟧ ⟦&M⟧ ⟦🛏⟧

▽▽ Quality Inn & Suites SH
(319) 378-8888. **$68-$110.** 2025 Werner Ave NE. I-380, exit 24A (SR 100/Collins Rd), just se. Int corridors. **Pets:** Accepted.
⟦ASK⟧ ⟦S⟧ ⟦✕⟧ ⟦🛏⟧ ⟦▯⟧ ⟦≈⟧

AAA ▽▽ Quality Inn of Cedar Rapids SH
(319) 393-8800. **$60-$100, 3 day notice.** 4747 1st Ave SE. I-380, exit 24A (SR 100/Collins Rd), 2.5 mi e, then 1st Ave SE. Int corridors. **Pets:** Accepted.
⟦SAVE⟧ ⟦S⟧ ⟦✕⟧ ⟦&M⟧ ⟦🛏⟧ ⟦▯⟧ ⟦≈⟧

▽▽ Ramada Limited SH
(319) 396-5000. **$68-$115.** 4011 16th Ave SW. I-380, exit 16 (US 30), 2.4 mi w, 1.4 mi n (exit 250) on Edgewood Rd to 16th Ave, then just w. Int corridors. **Pets:** Accepted.
⟦ASK⟧ ⟦S⟧ ⟦✕⟧ ⟦&M⟧ ⟦🛏⟧ ⟦▯⟧ ⟦≈⟧

▽▽▽▽ Residence Inn by Marriott SH
(319) 395-0111. **$149-$170.** 1900 Dodge Rd NE. I-380, exit 24A (SR 100/Collins Rd), just e. Int corridors. **Pets:** Accepted.
⟦ASK⟧ ⟦S⟧ ⟦✕⟧ ⟦&M⟧ ⟦🛏⟧ ⟦▯⟧ ⟦≈⟧ ⟦✕⟧

▽▽ Super 8 Motel SH
(319) 363-1755. **Call for rates.** 400 33rd Ave SW. I-380, exit 17 (33rd Ave SW), just w. Int corridors. **Pets:** Accepted.
⟦✕⟧ ⟦&M⟧

▽▽ Super 8 Motel SH
(319) 362-6002. **Call for rates.** 720 33rd Ave SW. I-380, exit 17 (33rd Ave SW), 0.4 mi w. Int corridors. **Pets:** Accepted.
⟦✕⟧ ⟦&M⟧ ⟦🛏⟧

CHARLES CITY

AAA ▽ Hartwood Inn M 🐾
(641) 228-4352. **$40-$60, 4 day notice.** 1312 Gilbert St. Jct US 18 and CR B35, exit 212, 2.2 mi e. Ext corridors. **Pets:** Medium. $10 daily fee/pet. Designated rooms, service with restrictions, supervision.
⟦SAVE⟧ ⟦S⟧ ⟦✕⟧ ⟦🛏⟧ ⟦▯⟧

▽▽▽ Sleep Inn & Suites SH
(641) 257-6700. **Call for rates.** 1416 S Grand Ave. Jct US 18 and 218 (exit 218), 0.7 mi n on US 218 business route; south side of town. Int corridors. **Pets:** Accepted.
⟦✕⟧ ⟦🛏⟧ ⟦▯⟧ ⟦≈⟧

▽▽ Super 8 Motel-Charles City SH 🐾
(641) 228-2888. **$55-$74.** 1411 S Grand Ave. Jct US 18 and 218 (exit 118), 0.8 mi n on US 218 business route; south side of town. Int corridors. **Pets:** Medium. $10 one-time fee/pet. Service with restrictions, crate.
⟦ASK⟧ ⟦S⟧ ⟦✕⟧ ⟦&M⟧ ⟦🛏⟧ ⟦▯⟧

CHEROKEE

▽▽▽ Best Western La Grande Hacienda SH
(712) 225-5701. **$70-$90.** 1401 N 2nd St. Jct US 59 and SR 3, 0.4 mi s. Int corridors. **Pets:** Medium, other species. $25 one-time fee/room. Service with restrictions, supervision.
⟦SAVE⟧ ⟦S⟧ ⟦✕⟧ ⟦&M⟧ ⟦▯⟧ ⟦¶⟧ ⟦≈⟧

CLARINDA

▽▽ Clarinda Super 8 Motel SH
(712) 542-6333. **$55-$88.** 1203 S 12th St. Jct US 71 and SR 2, just e. Int corridors. **Pets:** No service, crate.
⟦ASK⟧ ⟦S⟧ ⟦✕⟧ ⟦&M⟧ ⟦🛏⟧ ⟦▯⟧ ⟦≈⟧

CLEAR LAKE

▽▽ AmericInn Lodge & Suites of Clear Lake SH
(641) 357-8954. **$84-$109.** 1406 N 25th St. I-35, exit 194 (SR 122). Int corridors. **Pets:** Accepted.
⟦ASK⟧ ⟦✕⟧ ⟦🛏⟧ ⟦▯⟧ ⟦≈⟧

AAA ▽▽ Best Western Holiday Lodge SH
(641) 357-5253. **$74-$129.** 2023 7th Ave N. I-35, exit 194 (SR 122), 0.3 mi w. Ext/int corridors. **Pets:** Accepted.
⟦SAVE⟧ ⟦S⟧ ⟦✕⟧ ⟦&M⟧ ⟦🛏⟧ ⟦▯⟧ ⟦¶⟧ ⟦≈⟧ ⟦✕⟧

AAA ▽▽ Budget Inn M
(641) 357-8700. **$40-$70.** 1306 N 25th St. I-35, exit 194 (US 18), just nw. Int corridors. **Pets:** Medium. $3 one-time fee/room. Service with restrictions, supervision.
⟦SAVE⟧ ⟦S⟧ ⟦✕⟧ ⟦🛏⟧ ⟦≈⟧

▽ Lake Country Inn M
(641) 357-2184. **Call for rates.** 518 Hwy 18. I-35, exit 194 (US 18), 2 mi w. Ext corridors. **Pets:** Accepted.
⟦✕⟧ ⟦🛏⟧

▽▽ Microtel Inn SH
(641) 357-0966. **$58-$95.** 1305 N 25th St. I-35, exit 194 (SR 122), just nw. Int corridors. **Pets:** Accepted.
⟦ASK⟧ ⟦S⟧ ⟦✕⟧ ⟦&M⟧ ⟦🛏⟧ ⟦▯⟧

▽▽ Super 8 Motel SH
(641) 357-7521. **$45-$80.** 2809 4th Ave S. I-35, exit 193, just e. Int corridors. **Pets:** Accepted.
⟦ASK⟧ ⟦S⟧ ⟦✕⟧ ⟦&M⟧

CLINTON

AAA ▽▽▽ Best Western-Frontier Motor Inn SH
(563) 242-7112. **$89-$119.** 2300 Lincoln Way. On US 30, just e of jct US 30 and 67. Int corridors. **Pets:** Medium, other species. $10 daily fee/pet. Service with restrictions, crate.
⟦SAVE⟧ ⟦S⟧ ⟦✕⟧ ⟦🛏⟧ ⟦▯⟧ ⟦¶⟧ ⟦≈⟧ ⟦✕⟧

AAA ▽▽▽▽ Country Inn & Suites By Carlson SH
(563) 244-9922. **$89-$119.** 2224 Lincoln Way. On US 30, just e of jct US 30 and 67. Int corridors. **Pets:** Accepted.
⟦SAVE⟧ ⟦S⟧ ⟦✕⟧ ⟦&M⟧ ⟦🛏⟧ ⟦▯⟧ ⟦≈⟧

AAA ▽▽▽ Oak Tree Inn SH
(563) 243-1000. **Call for rates (no credit cards).** 2300 Valley West Ct. Just n of jct US 30 and 67, west side of town. Int corridors. **Pets:** Accepted.
⟦SAVE⟧ ⟦✕⟧ ⟦&M⟧ ⟦🛏⟧ ⟦▯⟧

▽▽ Super 8 Motel-Clinton SH 🐾
(563) 242-8870. **$50-$70.** 1711 Lincoln Way. On US 30, 0.7 mi e of jct US 67. Int corridors. **Pets:** Other species. $10 one-time fee/pet. Service with restrictions, crate.
⟦ASK⟧ ⟦S⟧ ⟦✕⟧ ⟦&M⟧ ⟦🛏⟧

CLIVE

◆◆◇ ▼▼▼▼ Best Western Des Moines West SH
(515) 221-2345. **$59-$89, 14 day notice.** 1450 NW 118th St. I-80/35, exit 124 (University Ave), just nw. Int corridors. **Pets:** Accepted.
SAVE SÒ ✕ ⎙M 🛇 ▣ ⇌ ⊠

◆◆◇ ▼▼▼▼ Chase Suite Hotel by Woodfin SH
(515) 223-7700. **Call for rates.** 11428 Forest Ave. I-80/35, exit 124 (University Ave), just ne. Ext corridors. **Pets:** Other species. $150 deposit/pet, $10 daily fee/pet. Service with restrictions, crate.
SAVE ✕ ⎙M 🛇 ⇌

▼▼▼▼ La Quinta Inn & Suites West Des Moines-Clive SH
(515) 221-9200. **$72-$89.** 1390 NW 118th St. I-80/35, exit 124 (University Ave). Int corridors. **Pets:** Other species. Service with restrictions, supervision.
ASK SÒ ✕ ⎙M 🛇 ▣ ⇌ ⊠

COLFAX

◆◆◇ ▼▼▼ Comfort Inn SH
(515) 674-4455. **$70-$149.** 1402 N Walnut. I-80, exit 155, just ne. Int corridors. **Pets:** Accepted.
SAVE SÒ ✕ ⎙M 🛇 ▣ ⇌

▼▼▼ Microtel Inn & Suites SH
(515) 674-0600. **$69-$79.** 11000 Federal Ave. I-80, exit 155 (SR 117). Int corridors. **Pets:** Accepted.
ASK SÒ ✕ 🛇 ▣

CORALVILLE

◆◆◇ ▼▼▼ Best Western-Cantebury Inn & Suites SH
(319) 351-0400. **$79-$99.** 704 1st Ave. I-80, exit 242, just s. Int corridors. **Pets:** Small. $10 daily fee/pet. Designated rooms, service with restrictions.
SAVE SÒ ✕ 🛇 ▣ ¶ ⇌ ⊠

▼▼▼ Comfort Inn by Choice Hotels SH
(319) 351-8144. **Call for rates.** 209 W 9th St. I-80, exit 242, just s. Int corridors. **Pets:** Accepted.
✕ ⎙M 🛇 ▣ ⇌

▼▼▼ Days Inn M
(319) 354-4400. **Call for rates.** 205 2nd St. I-80, exit 242, 1 mi s to 2nd St, then just w. Ext corridors. **Pets:** Accepted.
✕ 🛇 ▣

◆◆◇ ▼▼▼▼ Holiday Inn SH
(319) 351-5049. **$89-$269.** 1220 1st Ave. I-80, exit 242, just n. Int corridors. **Pets:** Accepted.
SAVE SÒ ✕ ⎙M 🛇 ▣ ¶ ⇌

◆◆◇ ▼▼▼ Super 8 Motel-Iowa City SH ✿
(319) 337-8388. **$60-$130.** 611 1st Ave. I-80, exit 242, 0.4 mi s. Int corridors. **Pets:** $10 daily fee/pet. Designated rooms, service with restrictions, supervision.
SAVE SÒ ✕ ⎙M 🛇

COUNCIL BLUFFS

◆◆◇ ▼▼▼ Best Western Crossroads of the Bluffs SH
(712) 322-3150. **$89-$129.** 2216 27th Ave. I-29/80, exit 1B (24th St), just ne. Int corridors. **Pets:** Medium. $10 daily fee/pet. Designated rooms, service with restrictions, supervision.
SAVE SÒ ✕ 🛇 ▣ ⇌

◆◆◇ ▼▼▼ Days Inn SH
(712) 323-2200. **$50-$80.** 3619 9th Ave. I-29, exit 53A (9th Ave). Int corridors. **Pets:** Accepted.
SAVE ✕ 🛇 ▣

▼▼▼ Days Inn SH
(712) 366-9699. **Call for rates.** 3208 S 7th St. I-29/80, exit 3 (US 92), just sw. Int corridors. **Pets:** Accepted.
✕ 🛇 ▣

▼▼▼ Motel 6 Council Bluffs, IA #1153 SH
(712) 366-2405. **$45-$61.** 3032 S Expressway St. I-29/80, exit 3 (US 92). Int corridors. **Pets:** Other species. Service with restrictions, supervision.
SÒ ✕ 🛇 ▣ ⇌

◆◆◇ ▼▼▼ Quality Inn & Suites SH
(712) 328-3171. **$59-$68.** 3537 W Broadway. I-29, exit 53A (9th Ave), just e, 0.5 mi n on S 35th St, then just w. Ext/int corridors. **Pets:** Other species. $10 daily fee/pet. Service with restrictions, supervision.
SAVE SÒ ✕ 🛇 ▣ ⇌

▼▼▼ Super 8 Motel SH
(712) 322-2888. **$65-$80.** 2712 S 24th St. I-29/80, exit 1B (24th St), just nw. Int corridors. **Pets:** Accepted.
ASK SÒ ✕ ⎙M 🛇 ▣

◆◆◇ ▼▼▼ Western Inn SH
(712) 322-4499. **$59-$109.** 1842 Madison Ave. I-80, exit 5 (Madison Ave), just s. Int corridors. **Pets:** Small. $10 one-time fee/room. Service with restrictions, supervision.
SAVE SÒ ✕ 🛇 ▣ ⇌

CRESCO

◆◆◇ ▼ Cresco Motel M ✿
(563) 547-2240. **$53-$81.** 620 2nd Ave SE. On SR 9; on east side of town. Ext corridors. **Pets:** Other species. Supervision.
SAVE SÒ ✕ ⎙M 🛇

CRESTON

▼▼▼ Super 8 Motel-Creston SH
(641) 782-6541. **$55-$75.** 804 W Taylor. Jct US 34 and SR 25, on US 34. Int corridors. **Pets:** Small. $10 daily fee/pet. Designated rooms, no service, crate.
ASK SÒ ✕ ⎙M 🛇 ▣

DENISON

▼▼▼ Denison Super 8 SH
(712) 263-5081. **$75-$85.** 502 Boyer Valley Rd. Jct US 30/59 and SR 141, 0.3 mi sw. Int corridors. **Pets:** Accepted.
ASK SÒ ✕ 🛇

DES MOINES

◆◆◇ ▼▼▼▼ Best Western Des Moines Airport SH
(515) 287-6464. **Call for rates.** 1810 Army Post Rd. Across from airport. Int corridors. **Pets:** Accepted.
SAVE ✕ ⎙M 🛇 ▣ ¶ ⇌

▼▼▼ Comfort Inn by Choice Hotels SH
(515) 287-3434. **Call for rates.** 5231 Fleur Dr. Opposite the airport. Int corridors. **Pets:** Accepted.
✕ ⎙M 🛇 ▣ ⇌

▼▼▼ Econo Lodge SH
(515) 278-8858. **Call for rates.** 4755 Merle Hay Rd. I-80/35, exit 131 (Merle Hay Rd), just s. Int corridors. **Pets:** Accepted.
✕ 🛇

▼▼▼ Motel 6–30 M
(515) 287-6364. **$45-$55.** 4817 Fleur Dr. Opposite the airport. Ext corridors. **Pets:** Other species. Service with restrictions, supervision.
SÒ ✕ 🛇

▼▼▼▼ Quality Inn & Suites SH
(515) 278-2381. **$59-$129.** 4995 Merle Hay Rd. I-35/80, exit 131 (Merle Hay Rd), just s. Int corridors. **Pets:** Accepted.
ASK SÒ ✕ ⎙M 🛇 ▣ ⇌

Quality Inn & Suites Event Center LH
(515) 282-5251. **$70-$275.** 929 3rd St. I-235, exit 3rd St; downtown. Int corridors. **Pets:** Medium. $10 daily fee/pet. Service with restrictions, supervision.
SAVE Sꝏ ✕ 🖥 💻 ⍾ ⇀

Red Roof Inn & Suites SH
(515) 266-6800. **Call for rates.** 4950 NE 14th St. I-80, exit 136 (US 69). Int corridors. **Pets:** Accepted.
SAVE ✕ ♿ 🖥 💻 ⇀

DE SOTO

Edgetowner Motel M
(515) 834-2641. **$48.** 804 Guthrie. I-80, exit 110, just s. Ext corridors. **Pets:** Accepted.
ASK Sꝏ ✕ 🖥

DUBUQUE

Best Western Midway Hotel SH
(563) 557-8000. **$100-$110, 30 day notice.** 3100 Dodge St. US 20, 2.3 mi w of jct US 52/61/151 and Mississippi Bridge. Int corridors. **Pets:** $10 daily fee/pet. Designated rooms.
SAVE Sꝏ ✕ 🖥 💻 ⍾ ⇀ ⊠

Comfort Inn by Choice Hotels SH
(563) 556-3006. **Call for rates.** 4055 McDonald Dr. US 20, 3.8 mi w of jct US 52/61/151 and Mississippi Bridge. Int corridors. **Pets:** Accepted.
✕ 🖥 💻 ⇀

Holiday Inn Dubuque/Galena LH
(563) 556-2000. **$119-$159.** 450 Main St. At Main and 4th sts; downtown. Int corridors. **Pets:** Small. $25 one-time fee/room. Service with restrictions, supervision.
SAVE ✕ ♿ 🖥 💻 ⍾ ⇀ ⊠

MainStay Suites SH
(563) 557-7829. **$79-$170.** 1275 Associates Dr. Just n of jct US 20 and NW Arterial Rd; west side of town. Int corridors. **Pets:** Accepted.
ASK Sꝏ ✕ ♿ 🖥 💻

DYERSVILLE

Comfort Inn-Dyersville SH
(563) 875-7700. **$81-$160.** 527 16th Ave SE. US 20, exit 294 (SR 136), just nw. Int corridors. **Pets:** Accepted.
ASK Sꝏ ✕ ♿ 🖥 💻 ⇀ ⊠

Super 8 Motel-Dyersville SH
(563) 875-8885. **$39-$99.** 925 15th Ave SE. US 20, exit 294 (SR 136), just n. Int corridors. **Pets:** Accepted.
ASK Sꝏ ✕ ♿ 🖥 💻

ELDRIDGE

Quality Inn & Suites SH ❀
(563) 285-4600. **$59-$159.** 1000 E Iowa St. I-80, exit 295B (US 61), 4 mi n to exit 127 (CR F45). Int corridors. **Pets:** Other species. $13 daily fee/pet. Service with restrictions, crate.
SAVE Sꝏ ✕ 🖥 💻 ⇀

ELK HORN

AmericInn Motel & Suites SH
(712) 764-4000. **$85-$130.** 4037 Main St. I-80, exit 54 (SR 173), 6.4 mi n. Int corridors. **Pets:** $10 daily fee/room. Designated rooms, service with restrictions, supervision.
SAVE ✕ ♿ 🖥 💻 ⇀

ESTHERVILLE

Sleep Inn & Suites SH
(712) 362-5522. **$79-$109.** 2008 Central Ave. Jct SR 4 and 9, 1 mi e. Int corridors. **Pets:** $20 one-time fee/room. Service with restrictions, supervision.
SAVE Sꝏ ✕ 🖥 💻 ⇀

Super 8 Motel SH
(712) 362-2400. **$50-$60.** 1919 Central Ave. Jct SR 4 and 9, 1 mi e. Int corridors. **Pets:** Accepted.
ASK Sꝏ ✕ ♿ 🖥 💻

EVANSDALE

Days Inn SH
(319) 235-1111. **Call for rates.** 450 Evansdale Dr. I-380/20, exit 68, just n. Int corridors. **Pets:** Accepted.
✕ ♿ 🖥 💻 ⇀

FAIRFIELD

Best Western Fairfield Inn SH
(641) 472-2200. **$94-$150.** 2200 W Burlington Ave. On US 34, 1 mi w of jct SR 1. Int corridors. **Pets:** $25 one-time fee/room. Supervision.
SAVE Sꝏ ✕ 🖥 💻 ⍾ ⇀

Super 8 Motel SH
(641) 469-2000. **Call for rates.** 3001 W Burlington Ave. On US 34, 1.5 mi w of jct SR 1. Int corridors. **Pets:** Medium. $50 deposit/room, $5 daily fee/pet. Service with restrictions, supervision.
SAVE ✕ ♿ 🖥 💻 ⇀

FORT DODGE

AmericInn Lodge & Suites SH
(515) 576-2100. **Call for rates.** 100 Kenyon Rd W. 3 mi n of jct US 20 and US 169. Int corridors. **Pets:** Medium, other species. $10 daily fee/room. Designated rooms, service with restrictions, supervision.
✕ ♿ 🖥 💻 ⇀

Comfort Inn SH
(515) 573-5000. **$90-$150.** 2938 5th Ave S. US 20, exit 124 (Coalville), 3.5 mi n on CR P59, then 1.3 mi w on 5th Ave and Business Rt US 20. Int corridors. **Pets:** Accepted.
SAVE Sꝏ ✕ ♿ 🖥 💻 ⇀

Days Inn SH
(515) 576-8000. **Call for rates.** 3040 5th Ave S. US 20, exit 124 (Coalville), 3.5 mi n on CR P59, then 1.2 mi w on Business Rt US 20. Int corridors. **Pets:** Accepted.
✕ 💻

FORT MADISON

Comfort Inn & Suites SH
(319) 372-6800. **$85-$141.** 6169 Reve Ct. Just e of jct US 61 and SR 2, on US 61. Int corridors. **Pets:** Accepted.
SAVE Sꝏ ✕ 🖥 💻 ⇀ ⊠

Knights Inn M
(319) 372-7740. **Call for rates.** 3440 Ave L. 2.1 mi e of jct US 61 and SR 2. Ext corridors. **Pets:** Accepted.
✕ 🖥 💻

Super 8 Motel-Ft Madison SH
(319) 372-8500. **$50-$69.** US 61 W, 5107 Ave O. 1 mi e of jct US 61 and SR 2. Ext/int corridors. **Pets:** $10 daily fee/pet. Service with restrictions, supervision.
ASK Sꝏ ✕ 🖥 💻

GRIMES

 AmericInn Lodge & Suites SH
(515) 986-9900. **Call for rates.** 251 Gateway Cir. Just sw of jct US 44 and SR 141. Int corridors. **Pets:** Medium, dogs only. $50 deposit/room, $10 one-time fee/room. Designated rooms, service with restrictions, supervision.

GRINNELL

Comfort Inn & Suites SH
(641) 236-5236. **$99-$189.** 1630 West St S. I-80, exit 182 (SR 146), 0.7 mi n. Int corridors. **Pets:** Accepted.

HAMPTON

 AmericInn Lodge & Suites SH ❀
(641) 456-5559. **$80-$160.** 702 Central Ave W. On SR 3 (Central Ave W), 0.7 mi w of jct US 65 and SR 3. Int corridors. **Pets:** Medium. $50 deposit/room, $10 daily fee/pet. Designated rooms, service with restrictions, supervision.

Country Heritage Bed & Breakfast BB
(641) 456-4036. **$50-$100, 5 day notice.** 1034 Hwy 3. I-35, exit 165, 4 mi e. Int corridors. **Pets:** Accepted.

IDA GROVE

Delux Motel M
(712) 364-3317. **$45-$60.** 5981 US Hwy 175. Jct US 59 S and 175. Ext corridors. **Pets:** Accepted.

INDEPENDENCE

Super 8 Motel SH
(319) 334-7041. **$66-$125.** 2000 1st St W. US 20, exit 252, 1.4 mi n. Int corridors. **Pets:** Accepted.

IOWA CITY

Alexis Park Inn & Suites SH
(319) 337-8665. **$70-$200, 3 day notice.** 1165 S Riverside Dr. I-80, exit 239 (US 218), 5 mi s, 2 mi e on US 6, then just s. Ext corridors. **Pets:** $10 daily fee/pet. Designated rooms, service with restrictions, crate.

hotelVetro conference center SH
(319) 337-4961. **$159-$329.** 201 S Linn St. I-80, exit 244, s on Dubuque St, e on Washington St, then s. Int corridors. **Pets:** Accepted.

Quality Inn & Suites LH
(319) 354-2000. **$79-$169.** 2525 N Dodge. I-80, exit 246, just ne. Int corridors. **Pets:** Accepted.

Sheraton Iowa City Hotel LH ❀
(319) 337-4058. **$119-$239.** 210 S Dubuque St. Dubuque and Burlington sts (SR 1); downtown. Int corridors. **Pets:** Medium, dogs only. Service with restrictions, supervision.

IOWA FALLS

Iowa Falls Super 8 Motel SH
(641) 648-4618. **Call for rates.** 839 S Oak. 1 mi s of jct US 65/20 and Washington Ave; south side of town. Int corridors. **Pets:** Accepted.

JOHNSTON

America's Best Inn SH
(515) 270-1111. **$55-$99.** 5050 Merle Hay Rd. I-80/35, exit 131 (Merle Hay Rd), just n. Int corridors. **Pets:** Other species. $10 daily fee/pet. Service with restrictions, supervision.

Best Western-Des Moines North SH
(515) 276-5411. **Call for rates.** 5055 Merle Hay Rd. I-80/35, exit 131 (Merle Hay Rd), just n. Int corridors. **Pets:** Accepted.

KEOKUK

Hampton Inn SH
(319) 524-6700. **Call for rates.** 3201 Main St. 1.8 mi n of jct US 136. Int corridors. **Pets:** Accepted.

Holiday Inn Express SH
(319) 524-8000. **$80-$89.** 327 Main St. 4th and Main sts; downtown. Int corridors. **Pets:** Accepted.

Super 8 Motel-Keokuk SH
(319) 524-3888. **$50-$79.** 3511 Main St. On Business US 61/US 218, 2 mi n of jct US 136. Int corridors. **Pets:** $10 daily fee/pet. Service with restrictions, supervision.

LE CLAIRE

Comfort Inn & Suites-Riverview SH ❀
(563) 289-4747. **$75-$170.** 902 Mississippi View Ct. I-80, exit 306 (US 67), 0.5 mi n to Eagle Ridge Rd, then just sw. Int corridors. **Pets:** Medium. $25 deposit/room. Service with restrictions, crate.

Holiday Inn Express SH
(563) 289-9978. **$80-$180.** 1201 Canal Shore Dr SW. I-80, exit 306 (US 67), just n. Int corridors. **Pets:** Small. $12 daily fee/pet. Designated rooms, service with restrictions, supervision.

Super 8 of LeClaire SH ❀
(563) 289-5888. **$66-$113.** 1552 Welcome Center Dr. I-80, exit 306 (US 67), 0.5 mi n to Eagle Ridge Rd, then just sw to Mississippi View Ct. Int corridors. **Pets:** Medium. $25 deposit/room. Service with restrictions, crate.

LE MARS

Super 8 Motel SH
(712) 546-8800. **$59-$70.** 1201 Hawkeye Ave SW. 1.2 mi s of jct US 75/SR 3, on US 75; south end of town. Int corridors. **Pets:** Accepted.

MANCHESTER

Super 8 of Manchester SH
(563) 927-2533. **Call for rates.** 1020 W Main. Jct US 20 and SR 13, exit 275, 1.3 mi n, then 0.3 mi e. Int corridors. **Pets:** Accepted.

MARION

Microtel Inn & Suites SH
(319) 373-7400. **$55-$85.** 5500 Dyer Ave. Jct US 151 and SR 13. Int corridors. **Pets:** Accepted.

MARQUETTE

The Frontier Motel M
(563) 873-3497. **$55-$120.** 101 S 1st St. Just s of jct US 18 and SR 76; between Mississippi River Bridge and casino. Ext corridors. **Pets:** Accepted.

MARSHALLTOWN

Best Western Regency Inn SH
(641) 752-6321. **$72-$92.** 3303 S Center St. Jct US 30 and SR 14. Int corridors. **Pets:** Accepted.

Comfort Inn SH
(641) 752-6000. **Call for rates.** 2613 S Center St. 0.5 mi n of jct US 30 and SR 14. Int corridors. **Pets:** Accepted.

Days Inn SH
(641) 753-8181. **Call for rates.** 18 E Berle Rd. Just n of jct US 30 and SR 14. Int corridors. **Pets:** Accepted.

Super 8 Motel SH
(641) 753-3333. **Call for rates.** 3315 S Center St. Just n of jct US 30 and SR 14. Int corridors. **Pets:** Accepted.

MASON CITY

Days Inn Mason City SH
(641) 424-0210. **Call for rates.** 2301 4th St SW. I-35, exit 194 (SR 122), 6 mi e. Int corridors. **Pets:** Accepted.

Holiday Inn SH
(641) 423-1640. **$89-$169.** 2101 4th St SW (Hwy 122). I-35, exit 194 (SR 122), 6 mi e. Ext/int corridors. **Pets:** $15 one-time fee/room. Service with restrictions, crate.

Mason City Super 8 Motel & Suites SH
(641) 423-8855. **$65-$80.** 3010 4th St SW. I-35, exit 194 (SR 122), 5 mi e. Int corridors. **Pets:** Accepted.

MISSOURI VALLEY

Oak Tree Inn SH
(712) 642-3000. **$63-$84.** 128 S Willow Rd. I-29, exit 75, just ne. Int corridors. **Pets:** Small. $5 daily fee/pet. Service with restrictions, supervision.

MONTICELLO

The Blue Inn SH
(319) 465-6116. **Call for rates.** 250 N Main St. North end of town on Business Rt US 151. Int corridors. **Pets:** Accepted.

MOUNT PLEASANT

Brazelton Hotel & Suites SH
(319) 385-0571. **$74-$89.** 1200 E Baker. US 218/27, exit 45, 0.6 mi s on Grand Ave. Int corridors. **Pets:** Accepted.

Super 8 Motel Mt Pleasant SH
(319) 385-8888. **$55-$65.** 1000 N Grand Ave. US 218/27, exit 45, 0.6 mi s. Int corridors. **Pets:** Small. $10 daily fee/pet. Service with restrictions, supervision.

MOUNT VERNON

Sleep Inn & Suites SH
(319) 895-0055. **$79-$149.** 310 Virgil Ave. Jct US 30 and SR 1, just se. Int corridors. **Pets:** Large. $13 daily fee/room. Service with restrictions, supervision.

MUSCATINE

Super 8 Motel-Muscatine SH
(563) 263-9100. **$53-$64.** 2900 N Hwy 61. Jct US 61 and SR 38. Int corridors. **Pets:** Small. $10 daily fee/pet. Designated rooms, no service, crate.

NEWTON

Days Inn of Newton SH
(641) 792-2330. **Call for rates.** 1605 W 19th St S. I-80, exit 164 (SR 14), just n. Int corridors. **Pets:** Accepted.

Econo Lodge Inn & Suites SH
(641) 792-8100. **$30-$140.** 1405 W 19th St S. I-80, exit 164 (SR 14), just n. Int corridors. **Pets:** Accepted.

Holiday Inn Express SH
(641) 792-3333. **$90.** 208 W 4th St N. Downtown. Int corridors. **Pets:** Accepted.

Quality Inn of Newton Iowa SH
(641) 792-7722. **$69-$99, 30 day notice.** 1700 W 19th St S. I-80, exit 164 (SR 14), just nw. Int corridors. **Pets:** Accepted.

NORTH LIBERTY

Sleep Inn & Suites SH
(319) 665-2700. **$70-$110.** 485 Madison Ave N. I-380, exit 4. Int corridors. **Pets:** Medium. $12 daily fee/pet. Service with restrictions, supervision.

NORTHWOOD

Country Inn & Suites By Carlson SH
(641) 323-7000. **$90-$95.** 711 Diamond Jo Ln. I-35, exit 214, just nw. Int corridors. **Pets:** Accepted.

OELWEIN

Super 8 Motel-Oelwein M
(319) 283-2888. **$65-$95.** 210 10th St SE. Jct SR 3 and 150, 1 mi s. Int corridors. **Pets:** Accepted.

OKOBOJI

AmericInn Lodge & Suites SH
(712) 332-9000. **$79-$269, 7 day notice.** 1005 Brooks Park Dr. Jct US 71 and SR 9, 2.5 mi s on US 71. Int corridors. **Pets:** Medium, dogs only. $10 one-time fee/room. Service with restrictions, supervision.

Arrowwood Resort & Conference Center SH
(712) 332-2161. **$81-$171.** 1405 US 71 S. Jct US 71 and SR 9, 3 mi s. Ext/int corridors. **Pets:** Other species. Service with restrictions, crate.

OSCEOLA

▼▼ AmericInn Lodge & Suites 🆂🅷
(641) 342-9400. **$80-$150.** 111 Ariel Cir. I-35, exit 33. Int corridors. **Pets:** Accepted.
⊠ &ᴹ 🛏 🖵 ⋙

▼▼ Days Inn 🆂🅷
(641) 342-6666. **Call for rates.** 710 Warren Ave. I-35, exit 33, just e. Int corridors. **Pets:** Accepted.
⊠ &ᴹ 🖵 ⋙

OSKALOOSA

🆔 ▼▼ Americas Best Value Inn 🅼
(641) 673-8351. **Call for rates.** 1315 a Ave E. On SR 92, just w of jct SR 23. Ext/int corridors. **Pets:** Medium, dogs only. $10 daily fee/pet. Designated rooms, service with restrictions, crate.
🆂🅰🆅🅴 ⊠ 🛏 🖵

▼▼ Comfort Inn 🆂🅷
(641) 676-6000. **Call for rates.** 2401 a Ave W. SR 163, exit 57 (SR 92), just e. Int corridors. **Pets:** Accepted.
⊠ 🛏 🖵 ⋙

▼▼ Super 8 Motel-Oskaloosa 🆂🅷
(641) 673-8481. **Call for rates.** 306 S 17th St. Just s of SR 92 and 23. Int corridors. **Pets:** Accepted.
⊠ &ᴹ 🛏 🖵

OTTUMWA

▼▼ Days Inn 🆂🅷
(641) 683-3000. **Call for rates.** 2824 N Court St. 2 mi n on US 63; from jct US 34. Int corridors. **Pets:** Accepted.
⊠ 🛏 🖵 ⋙

▼▼ Super 8 Motel 🆂🅷
(641) 684-5055. **Call for rates.** 2823 N Court Rd. 2 mi n on US 63; from jct US 34. Int corridors. **Pets:** Accepted.
⊠ 🛏 🖵 ⋙

PELLA

🆔 ▼▼ Baymont Inn & Suites 🆂🅷
(641) 628-0085. **Call for rates.** 2104 Washington St. SR 163, exit 40, just n. Int corridors. **Pets:** Accepted.
🆂🅰🆅🅴 ⊠ &ᴹ 🛏 🖵 ⋙

▼ Super 8 Motel-Pella 🆂🅷
(641) 628-8181. **$45-$65.** 105 E Oskaloosa St. SR 163, exit 42, 1 mi n, then 0.5 mi e. Int corridors. **Pets:** Small. $10 daily fee/pet. Designated rooms, no service, crate.
🅰🆂🅺 🆂🅰🆅🅴 ⊠ &ᴹ 🛏 🖵

PERCIVAL

🆔 ▼▼ Americas Best Value Inn & Suites 🆂🅷
(712) 382-2100. **$73-$110.** 2113 Sapp Brothers Dr. I-29, exit 10 (SR 2), just w. Int corridors. **Pets:** Small, dogs only. $20 daily fee/pet. Designated rooms, service with restrictions, supervision.
🆂🅰🆅🅴 🆂🅰🆅🅴 ⊠ 🛏 🖵 ⋙

🆔 ▼▼ Nebraska City Super 8 Motel 🆂🅷
(712) 382-2828. **$69.** 2103 249th St. I-29, exit 10, just w. Int corridors. **Pets:** $10 one-time fee/room. Service with restrictions.
🆂🅰🆅🅴 🆂🅰🆅🅴 ⊠ &ᴹ 🛏 🖵

PLEASANT HILL

🆔 ▼▼▼ Sleep Inn & Suites 🆂🅷
(515) 299-9922. **$89-$169.** 5850 Morning Star Ct. US 65, exit 79 (SR 163/E University Ave), just e. Int corridors. **Pets:** Medium. $13 daily fee/pet. Service with restrictions, supervision.
🆂🅰🆅🅴 🆂🅰🆅🅴 ⊠ &ᴹ 🛏 🖵 ⋙

QUAD CITIES AREA

BETTENDORF

▼▼▼ The Lodge-Hotel & Conference Center 🅻🅷
(563) 359-7141. **$90.** 900 Spruce Hills Dr. I-74, exit 2, just e. Int corridors. **Pets:** Accepted.
🅰🆂🅺 🆂🅰🆅🅴 ⊠ 🛏 🖵 🍴 ⋙ ✂

🆔 ▼▼▼ Ramada Inn 🆂🅷
(563) 355-7575. **Call for rates.** 3020 Utica Ridge Rd. I-74, exit 2, just e. Int corridors. **Pets:** Small. $10 daily fee/pet. Designated rooms, service with restrictions, supervision.
🆂🅰🆅🅴 ⊠ &ᴹ 🛏 🖵 ⋙ ✂

DAVENPORT

▼▼ Baymont Inn & Suites Davenport 🆂🅷
(563) 386-1600. **Call for rates.** 400 Jason Way Ct. I-80, exit 295A (US 61), just s to 65th St, then 0.5 mi ne on frontage road. Int corridors. **Pets:** Accepted.
⊠ 🛏 🖵 ⋙

🆔 ▼▼▼ Best Western SteepleGate Inn 🆂🅷
(563) 386-6900. **$100-$190.** 100 W 76th St. I-80, exit 295A (US 61), 0.5 mi s to 65th St and West frontage road entrance, then just nw. Int corridors. **Pets:** Medium. $10 daily fee/pet. Designated rooms, service with restrictions, supervision.
🆂🅰🆅🅴 🆂🅰🆅🅴 ⊠ 🛏 🖵 🍴 ⋙ ✂

🆔 ▼▼▼ Clarion Hotel & Conference Center 🆂🅷
(563) 391-1230. **$79-$159.** 5202 Brady St. I-80, exit 295A (US 61), 1.6 mi s. Int corridors. **Pets:** Accepted.
🆂🅰🆅🅴 🆂🅰🆅🅴 ⊠ &ᴹ 🛏 🖵 🍴 ⋙ ✂

🆔 ▼▼▼ Comfort Inn & Suites-Davenport 🆂🅷 🐾
(563) 324-8300. **$99-$149.** 8300 Northwest Blvd. I-80, exit 292, just n. Int corridors. **Pets:** Small, dogs only. $50 one-time fee/room. Designated rooms, service with restrictions, supervision.
🆂🅰🆅🅴 🆂🅰🆅🅴 ⊠ &ᴹ 🛏 🖵

▼▼ Country Inn & Suites by Carlson 🆂🅷
(563) 388-6444. **Call for rates.** 140 E 55th St. I-80, exit 295A (US 61), 1.4 mi s. Int corridors. **Pets:** Accepted.
⊠ &ᴹ 🛏 🖵 ⋙

🆔 ▼▼▼ Davenport Super 8 Motel 🆂🅷
(563) 388-9810. **Call for rates.** 410 E 65th St. I-80, exit 295A (US 61), 0.5 mi s, then just e. Int corridors. **Pets:** Accepted.
🆂🅰🆅🅴 ⊠ &ᴹ 🛏 🖵

▼▼ Econo Lodge Inn & Suites 🆂🅷
(563) 391-8222. **$60-$80.** 7222 Northwest Blvd. I-80, exit 292 (Northwest Blvd), 0.3 mi s. Ext corridors. **Pets:** Accepted.
🅰🆂🅺 🆂🅰🆅🅴 ⊠ 🛏 🖵

🆔 ▼▼ Exel Inn of Davenport 🆂🅷
(563) 386-6350. **$46-$66.** 6310 N Brady Ave. I-80, exit 295A (US 61), 0.5 mi s; use frontage road on west side. Int corridors. **Pets:** Accepted.
🆂🅰🆅🅴 🆂🅰🆅🅴 ⊠ 🛏 🖵

Fairfield Inn by Marriott SH
(563) 355-2264. **$83-$103.** 3206 E Kimberly Rd. I-74, exit 2, just w. Int corridors. **Pets:** Accepted.
ASK S X 🖥 💻 🏊

Howard Johnson Plaza Hotel LH
(563) 326-1786. **Call for rates.** 227 LeClare St. Downtown. Int corridors. **Pets:** Accepted.
X 🖥 💻 🏊

La Quinta Inn SH
(563) 359-3921. **$88.** 3330 E Kimberly Rd. I-74, exit 2, just w, then just s. Int corridors. **Pets:** Other species. Service with restrictions, supervision.
ASK S X 🖥 💻 🏊

Residence Inn by Marriott SH
(563) 391-8877. **$121-$143.** 120 E 55th St. I-80, exit 295 (US 61), 1.4 mi s. Int corridors. **Pets:** Accepted.
ASK S X 🗼 🖥 💻 🏊 ⊠

END AREA

RED OAK

Super 8-Red Oak SH
(712) 623-6919. **Call for rates.** 800 Senate Ave. Just e of jct US 34 and SR 48 on US 34. Int corridors. **Pets:** $5 daily fee/pet. Supervision.
SAVE X 🖥 💻 🏊

SIBLEY

Super 8 Motel SH
(712) 754-3603. **Call for rates.** 1108 2nd Ave. On SR 60. Int corridors. **Pets:** Accepted.
X 🗼 🖥

SIOUX CITY

AmericInn Lodge & Suites SH
(712) 255-1800. **$79-$151.** 4230 S Lewis Blvd. I-29, exit 143, just e. Int corridors. **Pets:** Accepted.
ASK S X 🗼 🖥 💻 🏊 ⊠

Clarion Hotel and Conference Center LH
(712) 277-4101. **Call for rates.** 707 4th St. Downtown. Int corridors. **Pets:** Accepted.
SAVE X 🖥 💻 🍴 🏊 ⊠

Comfort Inn by Choice Hotels SH
(712) 274-1300. **Call for rates.** 4202 S Lakeport St. I-29, exit 144A, 1 mi e on US 20, then just s; do not use Business Rt US 20. Int corridors. **Pets:** Accepted.
X 🖥 💻 🏊

Quality Inn Hotel & Conference Center M
(712) 277-3211. **$59-$89.** 1401 Zenith Dr. I-29, exit 149 (Hamilton Blvd). Int corridors. **Pets:** Accepted.
ASK S X 🖥 💻 🍴 🏊 ⊠

Super 8 Motel SH
(712) 274-1520. **$54-$78.** 4307 Stone Ave. I-29, exit 144A northbound, US 75 to exit 4B, 1 mi n on Gordon Dr; exit 147B southbound to Gordon Dr, 3 mi s. Int corridors. **Pets:** Accepted.
ASK S X 🗼 🖥 💻

SLOAN

Winna Vegas Inn SH
(712) 428-4280. **Call for rates.** 1862 Hwy 141. I-29, exit 127, just e. Int corridors. **Pets:** Accepted.
X 🗼 🖥 💻

SPIRIT LAKE

Ramada Limited SH
(712) 336-3984. **$79-$179, 3 day notice.** 2704 17th St. Jct US 71 and SR 9, just w. Int corridors. **Pets:** Dogs only. $10 one-time fee/room. Service with restrictions, supervision.
X 🖥 💻 🏊

Shamrock Inn SH
(712) 336-2668. **Call for rates.** 1905 18th St. 0.6 mi e on SR 9 from jct US 71. Ext/int corridors. **Pets:** Accepted.
X 🖥 💻 🏊

Spirit Lake Super 8 SH
(712) 336-4901. **$59-$119, 3 day notice.** 2203 Circle Dr W. Jct US 71 and SR 9. Int corridors. **Pets:** $10 one-time fee/room. Service with restrictions, supervision.
ASK S X 🗼 🖥 💻

SPRINGDALE

Econo Lodge M
(319) 627-2171. **$55-$60.** 1943 Garfield Ave. I-80, exit 259, just sw. Ext corridors. **Pets:** Accepted.
SAVE S X

STORY CITY

Comfort Inn SH
(515) 733-6363. **Call for rates.** 425 Timberland Dr. I-35, exit 124, just sw. Int corridors. **Pets:** Large, other species. $13 daily fee/room. Service with restrictions, supervision.
SAVE X 🗼 🖥 💻 🏊 ⊠

Super 8 Motel SH
(515) 733-5281. **Call for rates.** 515 Factory Outlet Dr. I-35, exit 124, just sw. Int corridors. **Pets:** Accepted.
X 🗼 🖥

Viking Hotel M
(515) 733-4306. **Call for rates.** 1520 Broad St. I-35, exit 124, just w. Int corridors. **Pets:** Accepted.
X 🖥

STUART

AmericInn Motel & Suites SH
(515) 523-9000. **$70-$99.** 420 SW 8th St. I-80, exit 93, just w. Int corridors. **Pets:** Accepted.
ASK X 🗼 🖥 💻 🏊 ⊠

Super 8 Motel SH
(515) 523-2888. **Call for rates.** 203 SE 7th St. I-80, exit 93. Int corridors. **Pets:** Accepted.
X 🗼 🖥 💻 🏊

TOLEDO

Designer Inn & Suites SH
(641) 484-5678. **$63-$69.** 403 US 30 W. On US 30, just w of jct US 63 and 30. Int corridors. **Pets:** Accepted.
SAVE S X 🖥 🏊

Super 8 Motel-Toledo SH
(641) 484-5888. **Call for rates.** 207 Hwy 30 W. On US 30, just w of jct US 63 and 30. Ext/int corridors. **Pets:** Accepted.
SAVE X 🗼 🖥 💻

URBANA

Super 8 Urbana Iowa SH
(319) 443-8888. **Call for rates.** 5369 Hutton Dr. I-380, exit 43, just s on east access road. Int corridors. **Pets:** Accepted.
X 🖥 💻 🏊 ⊠

URBANDALE

▼▼ Extended StayAmerica 🆂🅷
(515) 276-1929. **$81-$90.** 3940 114th St. I-35/80, exit 126 (Douglas Ave), just e to 114th St, then 0.4 mi nw. Int corridors. **Pets:** Other species. $75 one-time fee/pet. Service with restrictions.

🄰🅂🄺 🆂🗗 ⊠ 🐾ᴹ 🛗 🖵

⚛ ▼▼▼ Holiday Inn Hotel & Suites Northwest 🅻🅷
(515) 278-4755. **$119.** 4800 Merle Hay Rd. I-35/80, exit 131 (Merle Hay Rd), just s. Int corridors. **Pets:** Accepted.

🆂🅰🆅🅴 ⊠ 🐾ᴹ 🛗 🖵 🍴 🏊 ⊠

▼▼ Microtel Inn and Suites 🆂🅷
(515) 727-5424. **$55-$105.** 8711 Plum Dr. I-35/80, exit 129. Int corridors. **Pets:** Accepted.

🄰🅂🄺 🆂🗗 ⊠ 🐾ᴹ 🛗 🖵

▼▼▼ Ramada Inn Northwest 🆂🅷
(515) 278-0271. **Call for rates.** 5000 Merle Hay Rd. I-35/80, exit 131 (Merle Hay Rd), just s. Ext/int corridors. **Pets:** Accepted.

⊠ 🐾ᴹ 🛗 🖵 🍴 🏊 ⊠

▼▼ Sleep Inn 🆂🅷
(515) 270-2424. **$79-$119.** 11211 Hickman Rd. I-35/80, exit 125 (Hickman Rd), just ne. Int corridors. **Pets:** Accepted.

🄰🅂🄺 🆂🗗 ⊠ 🐾ᴹ 🛗 🖵 🏊 ⊠

⚛ ▼▼ Super 8-Merle Hay 🆂🅷
(515) 270-1037. **$60-$90.** 5900 Sutton Dr. I-80, exit 131 (Merle Hay Rd), just s, then w. Int corridors. **Pets:** Other species. $5 daily fee/pet. Service with restrictions, supervision.

🆂🅰🆅🅴 🆂🗗 ⊠ 🛗 🖵 🏊

WALNUT

▼▼ Super 8 Motel 🆂🅷
(712) 784-2221. **$50-$90.** 2109 Antique City Dr. I-80, exit 46, just n. Int corridors. **Pets:** Accepted.

🄰🅂🄺 🆂🗗 ⊠ 🐾ᴹ 🛗 🖵 🏊

WATERLOO

▼▼ Comfort Inn by Choice Hotels 🆂🅷
(319) 234-7411. **Call for rates.** 1945 La Porte Rd. I-380, exit 72 (E San Marnan). Int corridors. **Pets:** Accepted.

⊠ 🛗 🖵 🏊

▼▼ Holiday Inn Express 🆂🅷
(319) 233-9191. **Call for rates.** 2141 La Porte Rd. I-380, exit 72 (E San Marnan). Int corridors. **Pets:** Accepted.

⊠ 🐾ᴹ 🛗 🖵 🏊

▼▼ Ramada Hotel & Convention Center 🅻🅷
(319) 233-7560. **Call for rates.** 205 W 4th St. 4th and Commercial sts; downtown. Int corridors. **Pets:** Accepted.

⊠ 🐾ᴹ 🛗 🖵 🍴 🏊 ⊠

▼▼ Super 8 Motel 🆂🅷
(319) 233-1800. **Call for rates.** 1825 La Porte Rd. I-380, exit 72 (E San Marnan), just nw. Int corridors. **Pets:** Accepted.

⊠ 🛗

WAVERLY

▼▼ Americas Best Value Inn & Suites 🆂🅷
(319) 352-5330. **$65-$135.** 1900 Heritage Way. On SR 3, 2 mi e of jct US 218 and SR 3 (exit 203). Ext/int corridors. **Pets:** Other species. $8 daily fee/pet. Service with restrictions, supervision.

🄰🅂🄺 ⊠ 🛗 🖵 🍴 🏊

▼▼ Comfort Inn 🆂🅷
(319) 352-0399. **$80-$169.** 404 29th Ave SW. Business Rt US 218, exit 198, 0.5 mi n. Int corridors. **Pets:** Accepted.

🄰🅂🄺 🆂🗗 ⊠ 🐾ᴹ 🛗 🖵 🏊 ⊠

▼▼ Super 8 Waverly 🆂🅷
(319) 352-0888. **$65-$129.** 301 13th Ave SW. Business Rt US 218 S, exit 198, 1.2 mi n. Int corridors. **Pets:** Accepted.

🄰🅂🄺 🆂🗗 ⊠ 🐾ᴹ 🛗 🖵

WEBSTER CITY

▼▼ AmericInn Motel & Suites of Webster City 🆂🅷
(515) 832-3999. **$75.** 411 Closz Dr. Just s of jct US 20 and SR 17. Int corridors. **Pets:** Accepted.

🄰🅂🄺 ⊠ 🐾ᴹ 🛗 🖵 🏊

▼▼ Super 8 Motel 🆂🅷
(515) 832-2000. **$50-$75.** 305 Closz Dr. Just s of jct US 20 and SR 17. Int corridors. **Pets:** Accepted.

🄰🅂🄺 🆂🗗 ⊠ 🛗 🏊

WEST BEND

⚛ ▼▼ Park View Inn & Suites and Conference Center 🆂🅷
(515) 887-3611. **$65-$120.** 13 4th St NE. Jct CR B63, 1 mi n on SR 15, then just w. Int corridors. **Pets:** Small. $10 one-time fee/room. Designated rooms, service with restrictions, supervision.

🆂🅰🆅🅴 ⊠ 🛗 🏊

WEST BURLINGTON

▼▼ AmericInn 🆂🅷
(319) 758-9000. **$70-$90.** 628 S Gear Ave. US 34, exit 260 (Gear Ave), just ne. Int corridors. **Pets:** Accepted.

🄰🅂🄺 🆂🗗 ⊠ 🐾ᴹ 🛗 🖵 🏊 ⊠

WEST DES MOINES

▼▼▼ Candlewood Suites-West Des Moines 🆂🅷
(515) 221-0001. **$89-$159.** 7625 Office Plaza Dr N. I-80, exit 121 (Jordan Creek Pkwy), just sw. Int corridors. **Pets:** Accepted.

🄰🅂🄺 🆂🗗 ⊠ 🐾ᴹ 🛗 🖵

▼▼ Motel 6–1408 🆂🅷
(515) 267-8885. **$45-$59.** 7655 Office Plaza Dr N. I-80, exit 121 (Jordan Creek Pkwy), just sw. Int corridors. **Pets:** Other species. Service with restrictions, supervision.

🆂🗗 ⊠ 🐾ᴹ 🏊

▼▼▼ Residence Inn-Des Moines West 🆂🅷
(515) 267-0338. **$171-$192.** 160 S Jordan Creek Pkwy. I-35, exit 70 (Mills Civic Pkwy), 1.2 mi w to 68th, then just nw. Int corridors. **Pets:** Accepted.

🄰🅂🄺 🆂🗗 ⊠ 🛗 🖵 🏊 ⊠

⚛ ▼▼▼ Sheraton West Des Moines 🅻🅷
(515) 223-1800. **$99-$199.** 1800 50th St. I-80/35, exit 124 (University Ave), just e. Int corridors. **Pets:** Accepted.

🆂🅰🆅🅴 ⊠ 🐾ᴹ 🛗 🖵 🍴 🏊 ⊠

▼▼▼ Staybridge Suites 🆂🅷
(515) 223-0000. **$119.** 6905 Lake Dr. I-80, exit 121 (Jordan Creek Pkwy), just ne. Int corridors. **Pets:** Service with restrictions, crate.

🄰🅂🄺 🆂🗗 ⊠ 🐾ᴹ 🛗 🖵 🏊 ⊠

▼▼ StudioPLUS 🆂🅷
(515) 327-9100. **$86-$95.** 2701 Westown Pkwy. I-235, exit 2 (22nd St), just n to Westown Pkwy, then just w. Int corridors. **Pets:** Other species. $75 one-time fee/pet. Service with restrictions.

🄰🅂🄺 🆂🗗 ⊠ 🐾ᴹ 🛗 🖵 🏊

▼▼▼ Valley West Inn 🆂🅷
(515) 225-2524. **$79.** 3535 Westown Pkwy. I-235, exit 1 (Valley West Dr), just nw. Int corridors. **Pets:** Accepted.

🄰🅂🄺 🆂🗗 ⊠ 🛗 🖵 🍴 🏊 ⊠

WWWW **West Des Moines Marriott** LH
(515) 267-1500. **$209-$229.** 1250 Jordan Creek Pkwy. I-80, exit 121 (Jordan Creek Pkwy), just sw. Int corridors. **Pets:** Accepted.
ASK SD X &M 🅗 🖵 🍴 ᴈ ✗

WWWW **West Des Moines SpringHill Suites by Marriott** SH
(515) 223-9005. **$143-$163.** 1236 Jordan Creek Pkwy. I-80, exit 121 (Jordon Creek Pkwy), just s. Int corridors. **Pets:** Accepted.
ASK SD X &M 🅗 🖵 ᴈ ✗

WILLIAMS

WW **Best Western Norseman Inn** M
(515) 854-2281. **$66-$77.** 3086 220th St. I-35, exit 144, just e. Int corridors. **Pets:** Accepted.
ASK SD X 🅗 🖵

WILLIAMSBURG

WWW **Amana Holiday Inn** SH
(319) 668-1175. **$99-$249.** 2211 U Ave. I-80, exit 225 (US 151). Int corridors. **Pets:** Accepted.
ASK SD X &M 🅗 🖵 🍴 ᴈ ✗

AAA WWW **Best Western Quiet House Suites** SH
(319) 668-9777. **$99-$159.** 1708 N Highland St. I-80, exit 220, 0.8 mi n. Int corridors. **Pets:** Accepted.
SAVE SD X 🅗 🖵 ᴈ

AAA WWW **Crest Country Inn** M
(319) 668-1522. **$60-$85.** 340 W Evans St. I-80, exit 220, just nw. Ext corridors. **Pets:** Accepted.
SAVE SD X

WW **Heritage Inn Hotel & Suites Amana Colonies** SH
(319) 668-2700. **$69-$160.** 2185 U Ave. I-80, exit 225 (US 151), just n. Int corridors. **Pets:** Accepted.
ASK SD X &M 🅗 🖵 ᴈ

AAA WWW **Super 8 Motel** SH
(319) 668-9718. **Call for rates.** 1708 N Highland St. I-80, exit 220, 0.8 mi n. Ext/int corridors. **Pets:** Accepted.
SAVE X 🅗

KANSAS

ABILENE

Americas Best Value Inn /President's Inn SH
(785) 263-2050. **Call for rates.** 2210 N Buckeye. I-70, exit 275, just s. Ext corridors. **Pets:** Small. $10 daily fee/room. Service with restrictions, supervision.

Holiday Inn Express Hotel & Suites SH
(785) 263-4049. **$87.** 110 E Lafayette Ave. I-70, exit 275, just n. Int corridors. **Pets:** Accepted.

Super 8 Motel SH
(785) 263-4545. **Call for rates.** 2207 N Buckeye. I-70, exit 275, just s. Int corridors. **Pets:** Accepted.

ANDOVER

Andover Express Inn M
(316) 733-8881. **$57-$63.** 222 W US Hwy 54. 2.2 mi e of jct SR 96. Ext corridors. **Pets:** Medium, dogs only. $5 daily fee/pet. Service with restrictions, supervision.

ATCHISON

AmericInn Lodge & Suites SH
(913) 367-4000. **$74-$85.** 500 US 73. Just s at US 59 and 73. Int corridors. **Pets:** Small. $50 deposit/room. Designated rooms, service with restrictions, supervision.

BAXTER SPRINGS

Baxter Inn-4-Less SH
(620) 856-2106. **$39-$60.** 2451 Military Ave. On US 69 alternate route, 1 mi s of jct US 166. Int corridors. **Pets:** Accepted.

BELLEVILLE

Americas Best Value Inn M
(785) 527-2231. **$63.** 215 Hwy 36. Jct US 81 and 36; northwest corner; just up hill. Ext corridors. **Pets:** Accepted.

Super 8 Motel SH
(785) 527-2112. **$62-$101.** 1410 28th St. On US 36, 0.5 mi e of jct US 81. Int corridors. **Pets:** Medium, other species. $10 daily fee/pet. Service with restrictions, supervision.

BELOIT

Super 8 Motel-Beloit SH
(785) 738-4300. **Call for rates.** 3018 US 24 Hwy. Just e of jct SR 14. Ext/int corridors. **Pets:** Accepted.

BURLINGTON

Country Haven Inn SH
(620) 364-8260. **$60-$70.** 207 Cross St. Just e of US 75; 1 mi n of center. Int corridors. **Pets:** Accepted.

CHANUTE

Chanute Safari Inn M
(620) 431-9460. **$40-$50.** 3428 S Santa Fe. US 169, exit 35th St, 1.5 mi e. Ext corridors. **Pets:** Accepted.

Guest House Motor Inn M
(620) 431-0600. **$40-$50.** 1814 S Santa Fe. US 169, exit 35th St, 2.5 mi ne. Ext corridors. **Pets:** Accepted.

CLAY CENTER

Cedar Court Motel SH
(785) 632-2148. **$49-$75.** 905 Crawford. On US 24, just e of jct SR 15. Ext corridors. **Pets:** Accepted.

COFFEYVILLE

Super 8 Motel M
(620) 251-2250. **Call for rates.** 104 W 11th St. On US 169 and 166; center. Ext corridors. **Pets:** Accepted.

COLBY

Comfort Inn SH
(785) 462-3833. **$84-$130.** 2225 S Range. I-70, exit 53 (SR 25), just s. Int corridors. **Pets:** Other species. $10 daily fee/pet. Designated rooms, service with restrictions, supervision.

Days Inn SH
(785) 462-8691. **$66-$93.** 1925 S Range. I-70, exit 53 (SR 25), 0.3 mi n. Int corridors. **Pets:** Small, other species. $5 daily fee/pet. Designated rooms, service with restrictions, supervision.

Holiday Inn Express Hotel & Suites SH
(785) 462-8787. **$89-$149, 14 day notice.** 645 W Willow. I-70, exit 53 (SR 25), just ne. Int corridors. **Pets:** Accepted.

Motel 6 #4245 SH
(785) 462-8201. **$40-$51.** 1985 S Range. I-70, exit 53 (SR 25), just n. Ext/int corridors. **Pets:** Other species. Service with restrictions, supervision.
SAVE SD X

Quality Inn SH
(785) 462-3933. **$55-$70, 7 day notice.** 1950 S Range. I-70, exit 53 (SR 25), just n. Ext/int corridors. **Pets:** Medium. $5 daily fee/pet. Designated rooms, service with restrictions, supervision.
SAVE SD X 🛏 💻 🏊

Super 8 Motel SH
(785) 462-8248. **$45-$89.** 1040 Zelfer Ave. I-70, exit 53 (SR 25), 0.3 mi n, then just w. Int corridors. **Pets:** Other species. $10 one-time fee/room. Designated rooms, supervision.
ASK SD X 🛏 💻

CONCORDIA

Super 8 Motel-Concordia SH
(785) 243-4200. **Call for rates.** 1320 Lincoln. On US 81, 1 mi s of center. Ext/int corridors. **Pets:** Large, other species. $10 one-time fee/room. Service with restrictions, supervision.
SAVE X 🛏 💻

COTTONWOOD FALLS

Grand Central Hotel CI
(620) 273-6763. **$160-$190.** 215 Broadway. Just w of US 177; center of downtown. Int corridors. **Pets:** Service with restrictions, supervision.
SAVE SD X 💻 🍴

COUNCIL GROVE

The Cottage House Hotel & Motel SH
(620) 767-6828. **$50-$175, 7 day notice.** 25 N Neosho. Just n of Main St; downtown. Ext/int corridors. **Pets:** $15 daily fee/pet. Designated rooms, service with restrictions, supervision.
SAVE X 🛏 💻

DODGE CITY

Holiday Inn Express SH
(620) 227-5000. **$109-$129.** 2320 W Wyatt Earp Blvd. 1.4 mi w on US 50 business route. Int corridors. **Pets:** Other species. Service with restrictions, crate.
ASK SD X 🛏 💻 🏊

Super 8 Motel SH
(620) 225-3924. **$96-$137.** 1708 W Wyatt Earp Blvd. 1.2 mi w on US 50 business route. Int corridors. **Pets:** Other species. Service with restrictions, crate.
ASK SD X 🛏 💻 🏊

EL DORADO

Best Western Red Coach Inn SH
(316) 321-6900. **Call for rates.** 2525 W Central Ave. I-35, exit 71, 0.5 mi e. Ext corridors. **Pets:** Small. $15 one-time fee/room. Designated rooms, service with restrictions, supervision.
SAVE X 🛏 💻 🍴 🏊

Super 8 Motel-El Dorado M
(316) 321-4888. **$45-$95.** 2530 W Central Ave. I-35, exit 71, 0.5 mi e. Int corridors. **Pets:** Small. $15 daily fee/pet. Designated rooms, no service, crate.
ASK SD X 🛏 💻

ELLSWORTH

Best Western Garden Prairie Inn SH
(785) 472-3116. **Call for rates.** 1414 Foster Rd. Jct SR 140 and 156. Ext/int corridors. **Pets:** Accepted.
SAVE X 🛏 💻 🏊

EMPORIA

Americas Best Value Inn M
(620) 342-7567. **$51-$71.** 2913 W Hwy 50. I-35, exit 127, 0.8 mi e. Int corridors. **Pets:** Dogs only. $10 one-time fee/room. Designated rooms, service with restrictions, supervision.
SAVE SD X 💻

Best Western Hospitality House SH
(620) 342-7587. **$66-$86.** 3021 W Hwy 50. I-35, exit 127, just e. Ext/int corridors. **Pets:** Accepted.
ASK SD X 🛏 💻 🍴 🏊

Candlewood Suites SH
(620) 343-7756. **Call for rates.** 2602 Candlewood Dr. I-35, exit 128 (Industrial St), just n, then e. Int corridors. **Pets:** Accepted.
X 🛏 💻

Comfort Inn SH
(620) 342-9700. **Call for rates (no credit cards).** 2836 W 18th Ave. I-35, exit 128 (Industrial St), just nw. Int corridors. **Pets:** Accepted.
X 🛏 💻 🏊

FORT SCOTT

Fort Scott Inn SH
(620) 223-0100. **$48-$71.** 101 State St. On US 69 Bypass, exit US 54 southbound; exit 3rd St northbound. Ext/int corridors. **Pets:** Medium. $10 daily fee/pet. Service with restrictions, supervision.
SAVE SD X 🛏 💻 🍴 🏊 🐾

GARDEN CITY

AmericInn Lodge & Suites SH
(620) 272-9860. **$89-$165.** 3020 E Kansas Ave. Jct US 50, 83 and SR 156. Int corridors. **Pets:** Accepted.
ASK SD X 🛏 💻 🏊 🐾

Best Western Red Baron Hotel SH
(620) 275-4164. **Call for rates.** 2205 E Hwy 50. 2.3 mi e on US 50 business route, at US 83 Bypass. Ext corridors. **Pets:** Other species. Service with restrictions, crate.
SAVE X 🛏 💻 🍴 🏊

Best Western Wheat Lands Hotel & Conference Center SH
(620) 276-2387. **Call for rates.** 1311 E Fulton. 1 mi e on US 50 business route. Ext corridors. **Pets:** Other species. Service with restrictions, crate.
SAVE X 🛏 💻 🍴 🏊

Comfort Inn SH
(620) 275-5800. **$70-$149.** 2608 E Kansas Ave. Jct US 50, 83 and SR 156. Int corridors. **Pets:** Medium, other species. $10 daily fee/room. Service with restrictions, supervision.
SAVE SD X 🛏 💻 🏊 🐾

Holiday Inn Express Hotel & Suites SH
(620) 275-5900. **$98-$112.** 2502 E Kansas Ave. Jct US 50, 83 and SR 156. Int corridors. **Pets:** Other species. Service with restrictions, crate.
ASK SD X 🛏 💻 🏊

GARNETT

Garnett Inn & Suites & RV Park SH
(785) 448-6800. **$55-$80.** 109 Prairie Plaza Pkwy. On US 169, 1.6 mi n of jct US 59. Int corridors. **Pets:** Accepted.
ASK SD X 🐾 🛏 💻

GODDARD

Express Inn M
(316) 794-3366. **Call for rates.** 19941 W Kellogg Dr. Just se of jct US 54/400 and 199th St. Ext corridors. **Pets:** Small. $10 one-time fee/pet. Service with restrictions, supervision.
SAVE X 🛏

GOODLAND

◈◈◈ **▼▼** Americas Best Value Inn 🅂🄷
(785) 899-3621. **$76-$86, 7 day notice.** 830 W Hwy 24. I-70, exit 17 or 19, n to jct US 24 and SR 27. Ext corridors. **Pets:** Accepted.
[SAVE] [S🐾] [✕] [🛗] [💻] [🍴] [🏊]

◈◈◈ **▼▼** Comfort Inn 🅂🄷
(785) 899-7181. **$79-$120.** 2519 Enterprise Rd. I-70, exit 17 (SR 27), just n. Int corridors. **Pets:** Small. $15 one-time fee/pet. Designated rooms, service with restrictions, supervision.
[SAVE] [S🐾] [✕] [&M] [🛗] [💻] [🏊] [✕]

▼▼ Super 8 Motel-Goodland 🅂🄷
(785) 890-7566. **Call for rates.** 2520 Commerce Rd. I-70, exit 17 (SR 27), just n. Ext corridors. **Pets:** Accepted.
[✕] [🛗] [💻]

GREAT BEND

◈◈◈ **▼▼** Best Western Angus Inn 🅂🄷
(620) 792-3541. **Call for rates.** 2920 10th St. 0.8 mi w on US 56 and SR 96/156. Ext/int corridors. **Pets:** Large, other species. $5 daily fee/room. Designated rooms, service with restrictions, crate.
[SAVE] [✕] [🛗] [💻] [🍴] [🏊] [✕]

◈◈◈ **▼▼** Highland Hotel & Convention Center 🅂🄷
(620) 792-2431. **$64-$85.** 3017 W 10th St. 1 mi w on US 56 and SR 96/156. Ext/int corridors. **Pets:** $10 daily fee/room. Designated rooms, service with restrictions, supervision.
[SAVE] [S🐾] [✕] [🛗] [💻] [🍴] [🏊] [✕]

HAYS

▼▼ Baymont Inn & Suites 🅂🄷
(785) 625-8103. **Call for rates.** 3801 Vine St. I-70, exit 159 (US 183), just sw. Ext/int corridors. **Pets:** Other species. No service, supervision.
[✕] [💻]

▼▼ Best Western Vagabond Motel 🄼
(785) 625-2511. **$65-$80.** 2524 Vine St. I-70, exit 159 (US 183), 1 mi s. Ext corridors. **Pets:** Medium, other species. Designated rooms, service with restrictions, supervision.
[ASK] [S🐾] [✕] [🛗] [💻] [🍴] [🏊]

HESSTON

▼▼ AmericInn Lodge & Suites-Hesston 🅂🄷
(620) 327-2053. **$70-$130.** 2 Leonard Ct. I-135, exit 40, just e. Int corridors. **Pets:** Accepted.
[ASK] [S🐾] [✕] [🛗] [💻] [🏊]

HILLSBORO

▼▼ Country Haven Inn 🅂🄷
(620) 947-2929. **$62-$73.** 804 Western Heights. On US 56; center. Int corridors. **Pets:** Accepted.
[ASK] [S🐾] [✕] [🛗]

HUTCHINSON

◈◈◈ **▼** Americas Best Value Inn 🅂🄷 ✿
(620) 662-6394. **$70-$90.** 1315 E 11th Ave. Just se of jct SR 61. Int corridors. **Pets:** Dogs only. $10 one-time fee/room. Designated rooms, service with restrictions, supervision.
[SAVE] [S🐾] [✕] [💻]

▼▼ Comfort Inn 🅂🄷
(620) 663-7822. **$55-$159.** 1621 Super Plaza. Just w of jct SR 61 and N 17th Ave. Int corridors. **Pets:** Accepted.
[ASK] [S🐾] [✕] [🛗] [💻] [🏊]

▼▼ Holiday Inn Express Hotel & Suites 🅂🄷
(620) 669-5200. **$96-$153.** 1601 Super Plaza. Just w of jct SR 61 and N 17th Ave. Int corridors. **Pets:** Other species. Service with restrictions, crate.
[ASK] [S🐾] [✕] [&M] [🛗] [💻] [🏊]

▼ Microtel Inn & Suites 🅂🄷
(620) 665-3700. **$65-$85.** 1420 N Lorraine. Just nw of jct SR 61 and N 11th Ave. Int corridors. **Pets:** Accepted.
[ASK] [S🐾] [✕] [🛗] [💻]

INDEPENDENCE

▼▼ Appletree Inn 🅂🄷
(620) 331-5500. **$80-$130.** 201 N 8th St. At 8th and Laurel sts. Ext/int corridors. **Pets:** Accepted.
[✕] [🛗] [💻] [🏊]

IOLA

◈◈◈ **▼▼** Best Western Inn 🄼
(620) 365-5161. **Call for rates.** 1315 N State St. Jct US 54 and 169, 1.5 mi w on US 54, then 0.8 mi n. Ext corridors. **Pets:** Very small, dogs only. $500 daily fee/pet. Designated rooms, service with restrictions, supervision.
[SAVE] [✕] [&M] [🛗] [💻] [🍴] [🏊]

▼▼ Super 8 Iola 🅂🄷
(620) 365-3030. **Call for rates.** 200 Bills Way. Jct US 54 and 169. Int corridors. **Pets:** Accepted.
[✕] [&M] [🛗] [💻] [🏊]

JUNCTION CITY

▼▼▼▼ Candlewood Suites by Flint Hotels, LLC 🅂🄷 ✿
(785) 238-1454. **$109-$149.** 100 S Hammons. I-70, exit 298, just w. Int corridors. **Pets:** Other species. $75 one-time fee/pet. Service with restrictions, crate.
[ASK] [✕] [&M] [🛗] [💻]

◈◈◈ **▼▼▼** Courtyard by Marriott Junction City 🅂🄷
(785) 210-1500. **$99-$119.** 310 Hammons Dr. I-70, exit 298, just w. Int corridors. **Pets:** Medium. $75 one-time fee/room. Service with restrictions, supervision.
[SAVE] [S🐾] [✕] [&M] [🛗] [💻] [🏊]

▼▼▼▼ Holiday Inn Express 🅂🄷
(785) 762-4200. **$95.** 120 N East St. I-70, exit 298, just nw. Int corridors. **Pets:** Accepted.
[ASK] [S🐾] [✕] [&M] [🛗] [💻] [🏊] [✕]

KANSAS CITY METROPOLITAN AREA

GARDNER

▼▼ Super 8 Motel SH
(913) 856-8887. **$65-$150.** 2001 E Santa Fe. I-35, exit 210. Int corridors. **Pets:** Accepted.

ASK S♂ ✕ ♿M 📶

KANSAS CITY

AAA ▼▼▼ Best Western Inn and Conference Center SH
(913) 677-3060. **$89-$99.** 501 Southwest Blvd. I-35, exit 234 (7th St), just s. Int corridors. **Pets:** Accepted.

SAVE S♂ ✕ 📶 🖥 ➤

▼▼ Microtel Inn & Suites at the Speedway SH
(913) 334-3028. **$60-$95.** 7721 Elizabeth Ave. I-70, exit 414 (78th St N), just ne. Int corridors. **Pets:** Other species. $50 deposit/room, $10 daily fee/room. Service with restrictions, crate.

ASK S♂ ✕ ♿M 📶 🖥 ➤

LENEXA

▼▼▼ Extended StayAmerica -Kansas City-Lenexa-87th St SH
(913) 894-5550. **$55-$75.** 8015 Lenexa Dr. I-35, exit 227 (75th St), 1 mi s on east frontage road. Ext corridors. **Pets:** Other species. $75 one-time fee/pet. Service with restrictions.

ASK S♂ ✕ ♿M 📶 🖥 ➤

▼▼▼▼ La Quinta Inn Kansas City (Lenexa) SH
(913) 492-5500. **$65-$85.** 9461 Lenexa Dr. I-35, exit 224 (95th St), just ne; entrance left on Monrovia Rd, off 95th St. Int corridors. **Pets:** Other species. Service with restrictions, supervision.

ASK S♂ ✕ 📶 🖥 ➤

▼▼ Super 8 Motel-Lenexa SH
(913) 888-8899. **$60-$70.** 9601 Westgate Dr. I-35, exit 224 (95th St), just se. Int corridors. **Pets:** Small. $10 daily fee/pet. Designated rooms, no service, crate.

ASK S♂ ✕ ♿M 📶 🖥

MERRIAM

AAA ▼▼ Comfort Inn-Merriam SH
(913) 262-2622. **$44-$99.** 6401 E Frontage Rd. I-35, exit 228B (Shawnee Mission Pkwy), just se. Int corridors. **Pets:** Small, other species. $10 daily fee/pet. Designated rooms, service with restrictions, supervision.

SAVE S♂ ✕ 📶 🖥 ➤

▼▼▼▼ Drury Inn-Merriam/Shawnee Mission Parkway SH
(913) 236-9200. **$76-$99.** 9009 W Shawnee Mission Pkwy. I-35, exit 228B (Shawnee Mission Pkwy). Int corridors. **Pets:** Large, other species. Service with restrictions, supervision.

ASK ✕ ♿M 📶 🖥 ➤

▼▼▼▼ Hampton Inn & Suites SH
(913) 722-0800. **$106-$139.** 7400 W Frontage Rd. I-35, exit 227, just nw. Int corridors. **Pets:** Small, other species. Service with restrictions, crate.

ASK S♂ ✕ ♿M 📶 🖥 ➤

▼▼ Homestead Studio Suites Hotel-Kansas City-Shawnee Mission M
(913) 236-6006. **$50-$70.** 6451 E Frontage Rd. I-35, exit 228B (Shawnee Mission Pkwy), just se. Ext corridors. **Pets:** Other species. $75 one-time fee/pet. Service with restrictions.

ASK S♂ ✕ ♿M 📶 🖥

AAA ▼▼▼ Quality Inn SH
(913) 262-4448. **$39-$179.** 6601 E Frontage Rd. I-35, exit 228A, just ne. Ext/int corridors. **Pets:** Small. $10 daily fee/pet. Designated rooms, service with restrictions, supervision.

SAVE S♂ ✕ ♿M 📶 🖥 ➤

OLATHE

▼▼▼▼ Holiday Inn SH
(913) 829-4000. **$98-$130.** 101 W 151st St. I-35, exit 215 (151st St). Int corridors. **Pets:** Other species. Service with restrictions, crate.

ASK S♂ ✕ 📶 🖥 ♨ ➤ ✗

▼▼ Microtel Inn Olathe SH
(913) 397-9455. **$75-$95.** 1501 S Hamilton Cir. I-35, exit 215 (151st St), jct 151st St and CR 7 N, just nw of jct I-35. Int corridors. **Pets:** Small. $10 daily fee/pet. Designated rooms, service with restrictions, supervision.

ASK ✕ ♿M ➤

AAA ▼▼▼ Sleep Inn SH
(913) 390-9500. **$80-$85.** 20662 W 151st St. I-35, exit 215 (151st St), 0.4 mi sw, follow signs. Int corridors. **Pets:** Small, other species. $10 daily fee/pet. Service with restrictions, crate.

SAVE S♂ ✕ ♿M 📶 🖥 ➤

OVERLAND PARK

▼▼▼ Candlewood Suites SH
(913) 469-5557. **$95-$115.** 11001 Oakmont. I-435, exit 82 (Quivira Rd), 0.5 mi s, 0.3 mi w on College Ave, then just n. Int corridors. **Pets:** Accepted.

ASK S♂ ✕ ♿M 📶 🖥

AAA ▼▼▼▼ Chase Suites by Woodfin SH
(913) 491-3333. **$182-$242.** 6300 W 110th. I-435, exit 79 (Metcalf Ave/US 169), 0.3 mi s on US 169, 0.5 mi e on College Blvd to Lamar Ave, then just n. Ext corridors. **Pets:** Other species. $10 daily fee/pet. Designated rooms, service with restrictions, crate.

SAVE S♂ ✕ ♿M 📶 🖥 ➤ ✗

▼▼▼ Comfort Inn & Suites SH
(913) 648-7858. **$100-$200.** 7200 W 107th St. I-435, exit 79 (Metcalf Ave/US 169), just nw. Int corridors. **Pets:** Accepted.

ASK S♂ ✕ ♿M 📶 🖥 ➤

▼▼▼ Drury Inn & Suites-Overland Park SH
(913) 345-1500. **$86-$156.** 10963 Metcalf Ave. I-435, exit 79 (Metcalf Ave/US 169), just se. Int corridors. **Pets:** Large, other species. Service with restrictions, supervision.

ASK ✕ ♿M 📶 🖥 ➤ ✗

▼▼ Extended StayAmerica-Kansas City-Overland Park SH
(913) 661-9299. **$65-$80.** 10750 Quivira Rd. I-435, exit 82 (Quivira Rd), just sw. Int corridors. **Pets:** Other species. $75 one-time fee/pet. Service with restrictions.

ASK S♂ ✕ ♿M 📶 🖥

▼▼▼ Extended Stay Deluxe Kansas City-Overland Park-Metcalf SH
(913) 642-2299. **$75-$90.** 7201 W 106th St. I-435, exit 79 (Metcalf Ave/US 169), just nw. Int corridors. **Pets:** Other species. $75 one-time fee/pet. Service with restrictions.

ASK S♂ ✕ ♿M 📶 🖥

▼▼▼ Holiday Inn of Mission-Overland Park LH
(913) 262-3010. **$99-$119.** 7240 Shawnee Mission Pkwy. I-35, exit 228B (Shawnee Mission Pkwy), 1 mi e. Ext/int corridors. **Pets:** Accepted.

ASK ✕ ♿M 📶 🖥 ♨ ➤ ✗

◆◆◆ ▼▼▼ Holtze Executive Village SH
(913) 344-8100. **$189-$219.** 11400 College Blvd. I-435, exit 82 (Quivira Rd), 0.5 mi s, then just e. Ext/int corridors. **Pets:** Other species. $250 deposit/room, $8 daily fee/pet. Service with restrictions, crate.
(SAVE) (S📶) (✕) (🖩M) 🛏 💻 🐾 (✕)

▼▼▼ Homestead Studio Suites Hotel-Kansas City-Overland Park SH
(913) 661-7111. **$65-$85.** 5401 W 110th St. I-435, exit 77B (Nall Ave), just s. Int corridors. **Pets:** Other species. $75 one-time fee/pet. Service with restrictions.
(A$K) (S📶) (✕) (🖩M) 🛏 💻

▼▼▼ La Quinta Inn & Suites SH
(913) 648-5555. **$98.** 10610 Marty Ave. I-435, exit 79 (Metcalf Ave/US 169), just nw. Int corridors. **Pets:** Other species. Service with restrictions, supervision.
(A$K) (S📶) (✕) 🛏 💻 🐾 (✕)

▼▼▼ Pear Tree Inn by Drury-Overland Park SH
(913) 451-0200. **$63-$103.** 10951 Metcalf Ave. I-435, exit 79 (Metcalf Ave/US 169), just se. Int corridors. **Pets:** Large, other species. Service with restrictions, supervision.
(A$K) (✕) (🖩M) 🛏 💻 🐾

▼▼ Red Roof Inn-Overland Park M
(913) 341-0100. **Call for rates.** 6800 W 108th St. I-435, exit 79 (Metcalf Ave/US 169), just ne. Ext corridors. **Pets:** Accepted.
(✕) (🖩M)

▼▼▼▼ Residence Inn by Marriott SH
(913) 491-4444. **$219-$241.** 12010 Blue Valley Pkwy. I-435, exit 79 (Metcalf Ave/US 169), 1.3 mi s. Int corridors. **Pets:** Accepted.
(A$K) (S📶) (✕) (🖩M) 🛏 💻 🐾 (✕)

◆◆◆ ▼▼▼ Settle Inn SH
(913) 381-5700. **$74-$85.** 4401 W 107th St. I-435, exit 77A (Roe Ave), just ne. Ext/int corridors. **Pets:** Small, dogs only. $15 daily fee/pet. Designated rooms, service with restrictions, supervision.
(SAVE) (S📶) (✕) (🖩M) 🛏 💻 🐾

▼▼▼▼ Sheraton Overland Park Hotel at the Convention Center LH
(913) 234-2100. **$269.** 6100 College Blvd. I-435, exit 79 (Metcalf Ave/US 169), just s to College Blvd, then 0.6 mi e. Int corridors. **Pets:** Accepted.
(A$K) (S📶) (✕) (🖩M) 🛏 💻 🍴 🐾

◆◆◆ ▼▼▼ Super 8 Motel SH
(913) 341-4440. **$49-$60.** 10750 Barkley St. I-435, exit 79 (Metcalf Ave/US 169), just n to 107th St, then just e. Int corridors. **Pets:** Medium. $10 one-time fee/pet. Service with restrictions, supervision.
(SAVE) (S📶) (✕) (🖩M) 🛏 🐾

END METROPOLITAN AREA

LANSING

◆◆◆ ▼▼▼ Econo Lodge SH
(913) 727-2777. **Call for rates.** 504 N Main. I-70, exit 224 (Leavenworth), 10 mi n on US 73 and SR 7. Int corridors. **Pets:** Accepted.
(SAVE) (✕) 🛏 💻

LARNED

◆◆◆ ▼▼▼ Best Western Townsman Inn SH
(620) 285-3114. **$58-$68.** 123 E 14th St. Jct US 56 and SR 156. Ext corridors. **Pets:** Small, dogs only. $10 daily fee/pet. Service with restrictions, supervision.
(SAVE) (S📶) (✕) 🛏 💻 🐾

LAWRENCE

◆◆◆ ▼▼▼ Americas Best Value Inn SH 🐾
(785) 842-5721. **$72-$92.** 515 McDonald Dr. I-70, exit 202, 0.8 mi s, then just w. Int corridors. **Pets:** Dogs only. $10 one-time fee/room. Designated rooms, service with restrictions, supervision.
(SAVE) (S📶) (✕) 🛏 💻

◆◆◆ ▼▼▼ Best Western Lawrence SH
(785) 843-9100. **$69-$129.** 2309 Iowa St. On US 59; jct SR 10. Ext/int corridors. **Pets:** Dogs only. $8 daily fee/room. Designated rooms, supervision.
(SAVE) (S📶) (✕) 🛏 💻 🐾

◆◆◆ ▼▼▼ Econo Lodge SH
(785) 842-7030. **$55-$110.** 2222 W 6th St. I-70, exit 202, 1 mi s. Int corridors. **Pets:** Other species. $10 one-time fee/room. Service with restrictions, crate.
(SAVE) (S📶) (✕) 🛏 💻 🍴 🐾

◆◆◆ ▼▼▼▼ Holiday Inn SH
(785) 841-7077. **$79-$159.** 200 McDonald Dr. I-70, exit 202, 0.5 mi s on US 59. Int corridors. **Pets:** Accepted.
(SAVE) (S📶) (✕) 🛏 💻 🍴 🐾 (✕)

◆◆◆ ▼▼▼ Quality Inn SH
(785) 842-5100. **$69-$149.** 801 Iowa St. I-70, exit 202, 1 mi s on US 59. Ext/int corridors. **Pets:** Dogs only. $10 daily fee/room. Service with restrictions, supervision.
(SAVE) (S📶) (✕) 🛏 💻 🐾

LIBERAL

◆◆◆ ▼▼ Americas Best Value Inn M
(620) 624-6203. **$54-$64.** 564 E Pancake Blvd. 0.8 w of jct US 54 and 83. Ext corridors. **Pets:** $5 one-time fee/pet. Designated rooms, service with restrictions, supervision.
(SAVE) (S📶) (✕) 🛏 💻

◆◆◆ ▼▼ Liberal Inn SH
(620) 624-7254. **$62-$77.** 603 E Pancake Blvd. 0.5 mi w of jct US 54 and 83. Int corridors. **Pets:** Medium. Designated rooms, service with restrictions, crate.
(SAVE) (S📶) (✕) 🛏 💻 🍴 🐾

LINDSBORG

▼▼ Viking Motel M
(785) 227-3336. **Call for rates.** 446 Harrison. I-135, exit 78, 4 mi sw. Ext corridors. **Pets:** Accepted.
(✕) 🐾

MANHATTAN

◆◆◆ ▼▼▼▼ Best Western Manhattan Inn SH
(785) 537-8300. **Call for rates (no credit cards).** 601 E Poyntz Ave. SR 177, 0.4 mi e on US 24 (Frontage Rd). Int corridors. **Pets:** Accepted.
(SAVE) (✕) (🖩M) 💻 🐾

◆◆◆ ▼▼▼▼ Clarion Hotel LH
(785) 539-5311. **$70-$250, 14 day notice.** 530 Richards Dr. On SR 18 (Ft. Riley Blvd), 0.3 mi e of jct SR 113. Ext/int corridors. **Pets:** Other species. $10 one-time fee/room. Service with restrictions, crate.
(SAVE) (S📶) (✕) 🛏 💻 🍴 🐾 (✕)

▼▼▼ **Holiday Inn at the Campus** SH
(785) 539-7531. **Call for rates.** 1641 Anderson. 1 mi n of SR 18 (Ft. Riley Blvd). Int corridors. **Pets:** Accepted.
✕ ⌂ ▣ ⑪ ⊇

▼ **Motel 6–152** M
(785) 537-1022. **Call for rates.** 510 Tuttle Creek Blvd. 0.3 mi ne on US 24 (Frontage Rd) and SR 177. Ext corridors. **Pets:** Other species. Service with restrictions, supervision.
✕ ⑅ ⊇

▼▼ **Super 8 Motel-Manhattan** SH
(785) 537-8468. **$65-$125.** 200 Tuttle Creek Blvd. Jct US 24 (Frontage Rd) and SR 177. Int corridors. **Pets:** Small. $25 one-time fee/pet. Designated rooms, no service, crate.
ASK S⌀ ✕ ⌂ ▣

MARYSVILLE

▼▼ **Best Western Surf Motel** SH
(785) 562-2354. **Call for rates.** 2105 Center St. 1 mi e on US 36 (Pony Express Hwy). Ext/int corridors. **Pets:** Medium. $10 daily fee/pet. Designated rooms, no service, supervision.
✕ ⌂ ▣ ⊗

▼▼ **Super 8 Motel** SH
(785) 562-5588. **$55-$70.** 1155 Pony Express Hwy. 2 mi e on US 36 (Pony Express Hwy). Int corridors. **Pets:** Accepted.
ASK S⌀ ✕ ⑅ ⌂ ▣

MCPHERSON

◈◈◈ ▼▼ **Americas Best Value Inn** M ❀
(620) 241-8881. **$46-$66.** 2110 E Kansas Ave. I-135, exit 60, just w. Int corridors. **Pets:** Dogs only. $10 one-time fee/room. Designated rooms, service with restrictions, supervision.
SAVE S⌀ ✕ ⑅ ▣

◈◈◈ ▼▼ **Best Western Holiday Manor Motel** SH
(620) 241-5343. **Call for rates.** 2211 E Kansas Ave. I-135, exit 60, just w. Ext/int corridors. **Pets:** $10 daily fee/pet. Service with restrictions, supervision.
SAVE ✕ ⌂ ▣ ⑪ ⊇

NEWTON

▼▼ **Days Inn Newton** SH
(316) 283-3330. **Call for rates.** 105 Manchester St. I-135, exit 31, just e. Int corridors. **Pets:** Accepted.
✕ ⌂ ▣ ⊇

OTTAWA

▼▼ **Best Western Ottawa Inn** SH
(785) 242-2224. **Call for rates.** 606 E 23rd St. I-35, exit 183 (US 59). Ext/int corridors. **Pets:** Accepted.
✕ ⑅ ⌂ ▣ ⊇

▼▼ **Days Inn** M
(785) 242-4842. **Call for rates.** 1641 S Main. I-35, exit 183 (US 59), 1 mi n. Ext corridors. **Pets:** Accepted.
✕ ⑅ ⌂ ▣ ⊇

◈◈◈ ▼▼◈ **Econo Lodge** SH
(785) 242-3400. **$60-$90.** 2331 S Cedar Rd. I-35, exit 183 (US 59). Int corridors. **Pets:** Accepted.
SAVE S⌀ ✕ ⌂ ▣ ⊇

PARK CITY

◈◈◈ ▼▼◈ **Best Western Hotel & Suites** SH
(316) 832-9387. **$81-$90.** 915 E 53rd St N. I-135, exit 13, just w. Ext/int corridors. **Pets:** Other species. $20 one-time fee/pet. Service with restrictions, crate.
SAVE S⌀ ✕ ⌂ ▣ ⑪ ⊇ ⊗

▼ **Days Inn Wichita North** SH
(316) 832-1131. **Call for rates.** 901 E 53rd St N. I-135, exit 13, just w. Int corridors. **Pets:** Very small. $10 daily fee/pet. Designated rooms, service with restrictions, supervision.
✕ ⌂ ▣

▼ **Super 8 Motel-Wichita North/Park City** SH
(316) 744-2071. **$45-$84.** 6075 Air Cap Dr. I-135, exit 14, just sw. Int corridors. **Pets:** $10 daily fee/pet. Service with restrictions, supervision.
ASK S⌀ ✕ ⌂

PHILLIPSBURG

◈◈◈ ▼▼◈ **Cottonwood Inn** M
(785) 543-2125. **$65-$99, 7 day notice.** 1200 State St. 1 mi e on US 36/183. Ext corridors. **Pets:** Accepted.
SAVE S⌀ ✕ ⊇

PITTSBURG

◈◈◈ ▼▼ **Econo Lodge** SH
(620) 231-8300. **$55-$90.** 2408 S Broadway. Jct US 69 and Broadway; south side of town. Ext corridors. **Pets:** Small. $10 daily fee/pet. Designated rooms, service with restrictions, supervision.
SAVE S⌀ ✕ ⌂ ⊇

▼▼ **Super 8 Motel-Pittsburg** SH
(620) 232-1881. **$53-$69.** 3108 N Broadway St. 2.1 mi n on US 69 from jct SR 126. Int corridors. **Pets:** Small. $10 daily fee/pet. Designated rooms, no service, crate.
ASK S⌀ ✕ ⌂ ▣

PRATT

▼ **Evergreen Inn** M
(620) 672-6431. **$63-$73.** 20001 W US Hwy 54. On US 54, 3 mi w. Ext corridors. **Pets:** Accepted.
✕ ⌂ ⊇

▼ **Leisure Hotel** SH
(620) 672-9433. **$83-$105.** 1401 W Hwy 54. On US 54, 2 mi w. Int corridors. **Pets:** Other species. Service with restrictions, supervision.
ASK S⌀ ✕ ⌂ ▣ ⊇

RUSSELL

◈◈◈ ▼▼▼ **AmericInn Lodge & Suites** SH
(785) 483-4200. **$80-$95.** 1430 S Fossil St. I-70, exit 184 (US 281), just n. Int corridors. **Pets:** $10 one-time fee/room. Designated rooms, service with restrictions, supervision.
SAVE ✕ ⑅ ⌂ ▣ ⊇ ⊗

▼ **Days Inn** M
(785) 483-6660. **Call for rates.** 1225 S Fossil St. I-70, exit 184 (US 281), just n. Ext corridors. **Pets:** Accepted.
✕ ⌂ ▣ ⊇

SABETHA

▼▼ **Sabetha Country Inn** SH
(785) 284-2300. **Call for rates.** 1423 S 75 Hwy (Old Hwy 75). South side of town. Int corridors. **Pets:** Accepted.
✕ ⌂

SALINA

▼▼ **America's Best Inn** SH
(785) 825-2500. **$56-$79.** 429 W Diamond Dr. I-70, exit 252, just n. Int corridors. **Pets:** Accepted.
ASK S⌀ ✕ ⑅ ⌂

◈◈◈ ▼▼▼ **Best Western Mid-America Inn** SH
(785) 827-0356. **$78-$95.** 1846 N 9th St. I-70, exit 252, just s. Ext corridors. **Pets:** $50 deposit/pet. Designated rooms, service with restrictions, crate.
SAVE S⌀ ✕ ⑅ ▣ ⑪ ⊇

▼▼▼▼ Candlewood Suites SH
(785) 823-6939. **$59-$129.** 2650 Planet Ave. I-135, exit 89 (Schilling Rd), just e to S 9th St, 0.5 mi n to Belmont, then just w. Int corridors. **Pets:** Accepted.

(A$K) (X) (&M) (🛏) (🖥)

▼▼ Comfort Inn SH
(785) 826-1711. **$60-$120.** 1820 W Crawford St. I-135, exit 92, just e. Int corridors. **Pets:** Accepted.

(A$K) (S🐾) (X) (&M) (🛏) (🖥) (🏊)

◬◬ ▼▼▼ Econo Lodge SH
(785) 825-8211. **$45-$89.** 1949 N 9th St. I-70, exit 252, just s. Ext corridors. **Pets:** $10 daily fee/pet. Designated rooms, service with restrictions, crate.

(SAVE) (S🐾) (X) (🛏) (🖥) (🏊)

▼▼▼▼ Holiday Inn Express Hotel & Suites-Salina SH
(785) 827-9000. **$89-$149.** 201 E Diamond Dr. I-70, exit 252, just ne. Int corridors. **Pets:** Other species. $10 one-time fee/pet. Service with restrictions, crate.

(A$K) (S🐾) (X) (&M) (🛏) (🖥) (🏊)

▼▼▼ Holiday Inn of Salina SH
(785) 823-1739. **$95.** 1616 W Crawford St. I-135, exit 92, 0.5 mi e. Int corridors. **Pets:** Dogs only. $25 one-time fee/room. Designated rooms, no service, supervision.

(A$K) (S🐾) (X) (&M) (🛏) (🖥) (🍴) (🏊) (X)

◬◬◬ ▼▼▼ Quality Inn & Suites SH 🐾
(785) 825-2111. **$69-$99.** 2110 W Crawford St. I-135, exit 92, just w. Int corridors. **Pets:** $15 daily fee/pet. Designated rooms, service with restrictions, supervision.

(SAVE) (S🐾) (X) (&M) (🛏) (🖥) (🍴) (🏊) (X)

◬◬◬ ▼▼▼ Super 8 I-70 SH
(785) 823-8808. **Call for rates.** 120 E Diamond Dr. I-70, exit 252, just ne. Int corridors. **Pets:** Accepted.

(SAVE) (X) (&M) (🛏) (🖥) (🏊)

SHARON SPRINGS

▼▼ Oak Tree Inn SH
(785) 852-4664. **$73-$79.** 801 N Hwy 27. Jct US 40 and SR 27. Ext/int corridors. **Pets:** Accepted.

(A$K) (S🐾) (X) (🛏) (🖥) (🍴)

SMITH CENTER

◬◬◬ ▼ U.S. Center Motel M
(785) 282-6611. **$44-$53.** 116 E Hwy 36. Jct US 36 and 281. Ext corridors. **Pets:** Accepted.

(SAVE) (S🐾) (X) (🛏) (🏊)

TOPEKA

▼▼▼ Candlelight Inn Hotel M
(785) 272-9550. **$60-$110.** 2831 SW Fairlawn Rd. I-470, exit 3. Ext corridors. **Pets:** Accepted.

(A$K) (S🐾) (X) (🛏) (🖥) (🏊) (X)

◬◬◬ ▼▼▼▼ Capitol Plaza Hotel LH
(785) 431-7200. **$119.** 1717 SW Topeka Blvd. I-70, exit SE 8th Ave, 1.6 mi s; I-470, exit Topeka Blvd, 2.9 mi n. Int corridors. **Pets:** Large, other species. Service with restrictions, crate.

(SAVE) (S🐾) (X) (&M) (🛏) (🖥) (🍴) (🏊) (X)

◬◬◬ ▼▼▼▼ ClubHouse Inn & Suites SH
(785) 273-8888. **$89-$119.** 924 SW Henderson. I-70, exit 356 (Wanamaker Rd). Int corridors. **Pets:** Medium. $10 daily fee/pet. Service with restrictions, supervision.

(SAVE) (S🐾) (X) (🛏) (🖥) (🏊)

▼▼ Comfort Inn by Choice Hotels SH
(785) 273-5365. **$70-$130.** 1518 SW Wanamaker Rd. I-470, exit 1 (Wanamaker Rd). Int corridors. **Pets:** Accepted.

(A$K) (S🐾) (X) (🛏) (🖥) (🏊)

▼▼▼ Country Inn & Suites By Carlson-Topeka-West SH
(785) 478-9800. **Call for rates.** 6020 SW 10th St. I-70, exit 356 (Wanamaker Rd). Int corridors. **Pets:** Accepted.

(X) (&M) (🛏) (🖥) (🏊)

◬◬◬ ▼▼▼ Quality Inn SH
(785) 273-6969. **Call for rates.** 1240 SW Wanamaker Rd. I-470, exit 1 (Wanamaker Rd), just ne; I-70, exit 356A (Wanamaker Rd), 1 mi s. Int corridors. **Pets:** Accepted.

(SAVE) (X) (🛏) (🖥) (🏊)

▼▼ Ramada Hotel & Convention Center LH
(785) 234-5400. **Call for rates.** 420 SE Sixth St. I-70, exit 362B, just e. Int corridors. **Pets:** Accepted.

(X) (&M) (🛏) (🖥) (🍴) (🏊) (X)

▼▼▼▼ Residence Inn by Marriott SH
(785) 271-8903. **$198-$253.** 1620 SW Westport Dr. I-470, exit 1 (Wanamaker Rd), just se. Int corridors. **Pets:** Accepted.

(A$K) (S🐾) (X) (&M) (🛏) (🖥) (🏊) (X)

▼▼▼▼ The Senate Luxury Suites SH
(785) 233-5050. **$80-$120.** 900 SW Tyler. Just w of state capitol; downtown. Int corridors. **Pets:** Accepted.

(A$K) (S🐾) (X) (🛏) (🖥)

◬◬◬ ▼▼▼ Sleep Inn & Suites SH
(785) 228-2500. **$69-$99.** 1024 SW Wanamaker Rd. I-70, exit 356 (Wanamaker Rd), just s. Int corridors. **Pets:** Medium, other species. $10 daily fee/pet. Designated rooms, service with restrictions, supervision.

(SAVE) (S🐾) (X) (&M) (🛏) (🖥) (🏊)

◬◬◬ ▼▼▼ Super 8 at Forbes Landing SH
(785) 862-2222. **$70-$140.** 5922 S Topeka Blvd. I-470, exit 6, 2.2 mi s. Int corridors. **Pets:** Dogs only. $20 one-time fee/room. Service with restrictions.

(SAVE) (S🐾) (X) (&M) (🛏) (🖥) (🏊)

ULYSSES

▼▼ Single Tree Inn SH
(620) 356-1500. **$75-$118.** 2033 W Oklahoma St. 1.5 mi w on US 160. Int corridors. **Pets:** Other species. $25 deposit/room. Service with restrictions, crate.

(A$K) (S🐾) (X) (🛏) (🖥)

UNIONTOWN

▼ Wyatt Earp Inn & B&B SH
(620) 756-4990. **$65-$100.** 100 5th St. On SR 3; on west side of town. Int corridors. **Pets:** Accepted.

(A$K) (X)

WAKEENEY

▼▼▼▼ Best Western Wakeeney Inn & Suites SH
(785) 743-2700. **Call for rates.** 525 S 1st. I-70, exit 127, just n. Int corridors. **Pets:** Accepted.

(X) (&M) (🛏) (🖥) (🏊)

▼▼▼ Super 8 Motel SH
(785) 743-6442. **Call for rates.** 709 S 13th St. I-70, exit 128, just n. Int corridors. **Pets:** Accepted.

(X) (🛏) (🖥)

WAMEGO

◬◬◬ ▼▼ Simmer Motel M
(785) 456-2304. **$43-$80.** 1215 Hwy 24 W. Jct SR 99, 0.5 mi w. Ext corridors. **Pets:** Accepted.

(SAVE) (X) (🛏) (🖥) (🏊)

WICHITA

Best Western Airport Inn & Conference Center SH
(316) 942-5600. **$90.** 6815 W Kellogg. I-235, exit 7, 0.6 mi w on US 54 (S Frontage Rd). Int corridors. **Pets:** Accepted.

Candlewood Suites SH
(316) 942-0400. **$79-$139.** 570 S Julia. I-235, exit 7, 0.4 mi nw on Dugan Rd. Int corridors. **Pets:** Accepted.

Candlewood Suites-Wichita Northeast SH
(316) 634-6070. **Call for rates.** 3141 N Webb Rd. SR 96, exit Webb Rd, just nw. Int corridors. **Pets:** Accepted.

Clarion Inn & Suites SH
(316) 942-7911. **$82.** 5805 W Kellogg. I-235, exit 7A, just w. Int corridors. **Pets:** Small. $35 one-time fee/pet. Service with restrictions, supervision.

Comfort Inn SH 🐾
(316) 522-1800. **$59-$109, 3 day notice.** 4849 S Laura. I-135, exit 1A/B (47th St S), just e. Int corridors. **Pets:** Other species. $10 one-time fee/room. Service with restrictions, supervision.

Comfort Inn by Choice Hotels SH
(316) 686-2844. **Call for rates.** 9525 E Corporate Hills Dr. I-35, exit 50, just ne. Int corridors. **Pets:** Accepted.

Cresthill Suites Hotel SH
(316) 689-8000. **$99.** 12111 E Central Ave. 1.7 mi e of jct Webb Rd. Int corridors. **Pets:** Accepted.

Hampton Inn by Hilton SH
(316) 686-3576. **Call for rates.** 9449 E Corporate Hills Dr. I-35, exit 50, just ne. Int corridors. **Pets:** Accepted.

Holiday Inn Express SH
(316) 529-4848. **$94.** 4848 S Laura. I-135, exit 1 A/B (47th St S), just ne. Int corridors. **Pets:** Other species. $25 one-time fee/room. Service with restrictions, supervision.

Holiday Inn Hotel & Suites Convention Center SH
(316) 269-2090. **$89-$119.** 221 E Kellogg. Just sw of jct US 54/400 and Broadway. Int corridors. **Pets:** Accepted.

Holiday Inn Select SH
(316) 686-7131. **$89-$119.** 549 S Rock Rd. I-35, exit 50, 0.5 mi w. Ext/int corridors. **Pets:** Very small. $25 one-time fee/room. Designated rooms, service with restrictions, supervision.

Homewood Suites by Hilton@The Waterfront SH
(316) 260-8844. **Call for rates.** 1550 Waterfront Pkwy. Just e of Jct 13th and Webb rds. Int corridors. **Pets:** Accepted.

Hyatt Regency Wichita LH
(316) 293-1234. **$105-$212.** 400 W Waterman. Just w of jct Main St and Waterman; downtown. Int corridors. **Pets:** Accepted.

Quality Suites Airport SH
(316) 945-2600. **$90-$159, 3 day notice.** 658 Westdale. Jct I-235 and US 54. Int corridors. **Pets:** Very small. $10 daily fee/pet. Designated rooms, service with restrictions, supervision.

Residence Inn by Marriott SH
(316) 686-7331. **Call for rates.** 411 S Webb Rd. I-35, exit 50, just ne. Ext corridors. **Pets:** Accepted.

Residence Inn by Marriott at Plazzio SH
(316) 682-7300. **$209-$229.** 1212 N Greenwich. SR 96, exit 13th St, 0.5 mi sw. Int corridors. **Pets:** Accepted.

Super 8 Motel-Wichita/East SH
(316) 686-3888. **$51-$73.** 527 S Webb Rd. I-35, exit 50, just e. Int corridors. **Pets:** Small. $10 daily fee/pet. Designated rooms, no service, crate.

TownePlace Suites by Marriott SH
(316) 631-3773. **$143-$163.** 9444 E 29th St N. SR 96, exit Webb Rd, just sw. Int corridors. **Pets:** Accepted.

Wesley Inn SH
(316) 858-3343. **$87.** 3343 E Central Ave. Just e of jct Hillside. Int corridors. **Pets:** Accepted.

WINFIELD

Comfort Inn SH
(620) 221-7529. **Call for rates.** Hwy 77 at Quail Ridge Dr. On US 77, 1 mi s. Ext/int corridors. **Pets:** Accepted.

Econo Lodge M
(620) 221-9050. **$65-$85.** 1710 Main St. 0.5 mi s of jct US 77 and 160. Ext corridors. **Pets:** Accepted.

KENTUCKY

ASHLAND

▼▼▼▼ Holiday Inn Express Hotel & Suites SH
(606) 929-1720. $100-$150. 13131 Slone Ct. I-64, exit 185, just n. Int corridors. Pets: Other species. $25 daily fee/pet. Service with restrictions, supervision.
[A$K] [S⭕] [✕] [⭡M] [🖥] [▆] [⇌]

BARDSTOWN

ⒶⒶⒶ ▼▼▼ Bardstown-Parkview Motel M
(502) 348-5983. $50-$90. 418 E Stephen Foster Ave. 0.5 mi e on US 150; e of jct US 62. Ext corridors. Pets: Accepted.
[SAVE] [S⭕] [✕] [🖥] [¶|] [⇌]

ⒶⒶⒶ ▼▼▼ Best Western General Nelson Motel SH
(502) 348-3977. $59-$79, 7 day notice. 411 W Stephen Foster Ave. 0.5 mi w on US 62. Ext corridors. Pets: Small. $10 one-time fee/room. Service with restrictions, crate.
[A$K] [S⭕] [✕] [🖥] [▆] [⇌]

ⒶⒶⒶ ▼▼▼▼ Hampton Inn SH
(502) 349-0100. $89-$119. 985 Chambers Blvd. Just s of US 245. Int corridors. Pets: Small. $50 one-time fee/room. Service with restrictions, supervision.
[SAVE] [S⭕] [✕] [⭡M] [🖥] [▆] [⇌]

BEAVER DAM

▼▼ Days Inn Beaver Dam SH
(270) 274-0851. Call for rates. 1750 US Hwy 231. Kentucky Pkwy, exit 75, just n. Int corridors. Pets: Accepted.
[✕] [🖥] [▆] [⇌]

BENTON

▼▼▼▼ Holiday Inn Express Hotel & Suites SH
(270) 527-5300. $79-$129. 173 Carroll Rd. Purchase Pkwy, exit 47. Int corridors. Pets: Large. $10 one-time fee/pet. Designated rooms, service with restrictions, supervision.
[A$K] [S⭕] [✕] [⭡M] [🖥] [▆] [⇌]

BEREA

ⒶⒶⒶ ▼▼▼▼ Boone Tavern Hotel-Berea College SH ❖
(859) 985-3700. $102-$142. 100 Main St. I-75, exit 76, 1.5 mi ne on SR 21. Int corridors. Pets: Medium. $50 one-time fee/room. Designated rooms, service with restrictions, crate.
[SAVE] [S⭕] [✕] [▆] [¶|]

▼▼▼▼ Comfort Inn & Suites SH
(859) 985-5500. $59-$99. 1003 Paint Lick Rd. I-75, exit 76, just w. Int corridors. Pets: Small. $10 daily fee/pet. Service with restrictions, supervision.
[A$K] [S⭕] [✕] [⭡M] [🖥] [▆] [⇌]

BOWLING GREEN

ⒶⒶⒶ ▼▼▼ Country Hearth Inn SH
(270) 783-4443. $45-$90. 395 Corvette Dr. I-65, exit 28, just w. Int corridors. Pets: Small. $5 one-time fee/pet. Service with restrictions, supervision.
[SAVE] [S⭕] [✕] [⭡M] [🖥] [▆]

▼▼▼▼ Drury Inn-Bowling Green SH
(270) 842-7100. $138. 3250 Scottsville Rd. I-65, exit 22 (Scottsville Rd), just w. Int corridors. Pets: Large, other species. Service with restrictions, supervision.
[A$K] [✕] [⭡M] [🖥] [▆] [⇌]

ⒶⒶⒶ ▼▼▼▼ Holiday Inn University Plaza LH
(270) 745-0088. $129. 1021 Wilkinson Trace. I-65, exit 22 (Scottsville Rd), 2.5 mi w, then just n. Int corridors. Pets: Accepted.
[SAVE] [S⭕] [✕] [🖥] [▆] [¶|] [⊠]

ⒶⒶⒶ ▼▼▼ News Inn of Bowling Green M
(270) 781-3460. $49-$89. 3160 Scottsville Rd. I-65, exit 22 (Scottsville Rd). Ext corridors. Pets: Large. $5 daily fee/pet. Service with restrictions, crate.
[SAVE] [✕] [🖥] [⇌]

ⒶⒶⒶ ▼▼ Red Roof Inn SH
(270) 781-6550. Call for rates. 3140 Scottsville Rd. I-65, exit 22 (Scottsville Rd), 0.3 mi w. Ext corridors. Pets: Medium. Service with restrictions, crate.
[SAVE] [✕] [🖥]

CADIZ

▼▼▼▼ Holiday Inn Express SH
(270) 522-3700. $72-$80. 153 Broad Bent Blvd. I-24, exit 65, just s. Int corridors. Pets: Small, other species. $20 one-time fee/room. Designated rooms, service with restrictions, supervision.
[A$K] [S⭕] [✕] [🖥] [▆] [⇌]

CAMPBELLSVILLE

▼▼▼ Holiday Inn Express SH
(270) 465-2727. $80. 102 Plantation Dr. Jct US 68 and SR 55, 0.5 mi n. Int corridors. Pets: Other species. $10 daily fee/pet. Service with restrictions, crate.
[A$K] [S⭕] [✕] [⭡M] [🖥] [▆] [⇌]

CARROLLTON

ⒶⒶⒶ ▼▼▼▼ Best Western Executive Inn SH
(502) 732-8444. $65-$119. 10 Slumber Ln. I-71, exit 44, just nw. Int corridors. Pets: Other species. $10 daily fee/pet. Service with restrictions.
[SAVE] [S⭕] [✕] [⭡M] [🖥] [▆] [⇌]

▼▼ Days Inn Carrollton SH
(502) 732-9301. Call for rates. 61 Inn Rd. I-71, exit 44, just nw. Int corridors. Pets: Accepted.
[✕] [🖥] [▆] [⇌]

▼▼ ▼▼ **Super 8 Carrollton** SH
(502) 732-0252. **Call for rates.** 130 Slumber Ln. I-71, exit 44, just nw. Int corridors. **Pets:** Accepted.

☒ 🏠

CATLETTSBURG

▼▼▼ **Ramada Limited Hotel** SH ❀
(606) 739-5700. **Call for rates.** 6000 Crider Dr. I-64, exit 191, 0.5 mi n on US 23. Int corridors. **Pets:** Other species. $10 daily fee/pet. Designated rooms, supervision.

☒ 🏠 💻 🏊

CAVE CITY

🐾 ▼▼ **Best Western Kentucky Inn** SH
(270) 773-3161. **$35-$125.** 1009 Doyle Ave. I-65, exit 53, just e. Ext corridors. **Pets:** Accepted.

SAVE 🐾 ☒ 🏠 💻 🏊

🐾 ▼▼ **Comfort Inn** SH
(270) 773-2030. **$30-$140, 3 day notice.** 801 Mammoth Cave St. I-65, exit 53, just ne. Ext corridors. **Pets:** Very small. $10 daily fee/pet. Service with restrictions, supervision.

SAVE 🐾 ☒ 🏠 💻 🏊

🐾 ▼▼ **Super 8 Motel** SH
(270) 773-2500. **Call for rates.** 799 Mammoth Cave St. I-65, exit 53, just ne. Ext corridors. **Pets:** Accepted.

SAVE ☒ 🏠 🏠 💻

CENTRAL CITY

▼▼ ▼▼ **Days Inn** SH
(270) 754-1222. **Call for rates.** 640 S 2nd St. Western Kentucky Pkwy, exit 58, just n. Int corridors. **Pets:** Accepted.

☒ 🏠 💻

CORBIN

🐾 ▼▼ **Best Western-Corbin Inn** SH
(606) 528-2100. **$65-$99.** 2630 Cumberland Falls Hwy. I-75, exit 25. Ext corridors. **Pets:** Medium. $10 daily fee/pet. Designated rooms, service with restrictions, supervision.

SAVE 🐾 ☒ 🏠 💻 🏊

COVINGTON

▼▼▼ **Embassy Suites Cincinnati RiverCenter** LH
(859) 261-8400. **Call for rates.** 10 E RiverCenter Blvd. I-71/75, exit 192, 0.8 mi e on 5th St, then 0.3 mi n on Madison Ave. Int corridors. **Pets:** Small, other species. $25 one-time fee/room. Service with restrictions.

☒ 🐾 🏠 💻 🍽 🏊

▼▼ **Extended StayAmerica** SH
(859) 581-3000. **$95-$145.** 650 W 3rd St. I-71/75, exit 192, 0.5 mi ne on SR 8. Int corridors. **Pets:** Other species. $75 one-time fee/pet. Service with restrictions.

ASK 🐾 ☒ 🐾 🏠 💻

DANVILLE

▼▼▼ **Holiday Inn Express-Danville** SH
(859) 236-8600. **$69-$109.** 96 Daniel Dr. Just e of US 127 on US 150 Bypass. Int corridors. **Pets:** Other species. $20 one-time fee/room. Service with restrictions, supervision.

ASK 🐾 ☒ 🐾 🏠 💻 🏊

DRY RIDGE

▼▼ **Holiday Inn Express** SH
(859) 824-7121. **$69-$89.** 1050 Fashion Ridge Rd. I-75, exit 159, just nw. Int corridors. **Pets:** Medium. $10 one-time fee/pet. Designated rooms, service with restrictions, supervision.

ASK 🐾 ☒ 🏠 💻

EDDYVILLE

▼▼ ▼▼ **Eddy Creek Resort & Marina** CA
(270) 388-2271. **$74-$170, 45 day notice.** 7612 SR 93 S. I-24, exit 45, 4 mi s. Ext corridors. **Pets:** Large. $15 daily fee/pet. Service with restrictions, crate.

☒ 🏠 💻 🍽 🏊 ☒ 🏋

ELIZABETHTOWN

🐾 ▼▼▼ **Best Western Atrium Gardens** SH
(270) 769-3030. **Call for rates.** 1043 Executive Dr. I-65, exit 94, just nw. Int corridors. **Pets:** Other species. $25 one-time fee/room. Designated rooms, service with restrictions, crate.

SAVE ☒ 🏠 💻 🏊

▼▼ ▼▼ **Comfort Inn** SH
(270) 765-4166. **Call for rates.** 2009 N Mulberry St. I-65, exit 94, just sw. Int corridors. **Pets:** Medium. $10 one-time fee/pet. Designated rooms, service with restrictions, supervision.

☒ 🐾 🏠 💻 🏊

▼▼ ▼▼ **Country Hearth Inn & Suites** SH
(270) 769-2344. **$69-$119.** 1058 N Mulberry St. I-65, exit 94, just nw. Ext corridors. **Pets:** Service with restrictions, supervision.

ASK 🐾 ☒ 🏠 💻 🍽 🏊

▼▼ ▼▼ **Holiday Inn Express** SH
(270) 769-1334. **$89-$109.** 107 Buffalo Creek Dr. I-65, exit 94, just w. Int corridors. **Pets:** Small. $25 one-time fee/pet. Designated rooms, service with restrictions, crate.

ASK 🐾 ☒ 🐾 🏠 💻 🏊

🐾 ▼▼▼ **La Quinta Inn Elizabethtown** SH
(270) 765-4747. **$100-$130.** 210 Commerce Dr. I-65, exit 94, just nw. Int corridors. **Pets:** Other species. Service with restrictions, supervision.

SAVE 🐾 ☒ 🐾 🏠 💻 🏊

ERLANGER

🐾 ▼▼ **Days Inn** SH
(859) 342-7111. **Call for rates.** 599 Donaldson Ave. I-75, exit 184. Ext corridors. **Pets:** Small, dogs only. $15 daily fee/pet. Designated rooms, service with restrictions, supervision.

SAVE ☒ 🏠 💻 🍽 🏊

▼▼▼ **Residence Inn by Marriott, Cincinnati Airport** SH
(859) 282-7400. **$139-$159.** 2811 Circleport Dr. I-275, exit 2. Int corridors. **Pets:** Other species. $100 one-time fee/room. Service with restrictions, crate.

ASK 🐾 ☒ 🐾 🏠 💻 🏊 ☒

FLORENCE

▼▼▼ **Ashley Quarters** SH ❀
(859) 525-9997. **Call for rates.** 4880 Houston Rd. I-71/75, exit 182, 0.6 mi w on Turfway and Houston rds. Int corridors. **Pets:** Other species. $75 one-time fee/room.

☒ 🏠 💻 🏊

🐾 ▼▼▼ **Best Western Inn Florence** SH
(859) 525-0090. **$60-$125, 7 day notice.** 7821 Commerce Dr. I-71/75, exit 181, just ne. Int corridors. **Pets:** Medium, dogs only. $15 daily fee/pet. Service with restrictions, supervision.

SAVE 🐾 ☒ 🐾 🏠 💻 🏊

▼▼ ▼▼ **Extended StayAmerica** SH
(859) 282-7829. **$63-$115.** 7350 Turfway Rd. I-71/75, exit 182, just w. Int corridors. **Pets:** Other species. $75 one-time fee/pet. Service with restrictions.

ASK 🐾 ☒ 🐾 🏠 💻

Florence Super 8 🅂🄷 ❧
(859) 283-1221. **$59-$89.** 7928 Dream St. I-71/75, exit 180, just e on US 42, then just n. Int corridors. **Pets:** Other species. $5 daily fee/pet. Designated rooms, service with restrictions.

La Quinta Inn & Suites 🅂🄷
(859) 282-8212. **$109-$149.** 350 Meijer Dr. I-71/75, exit 182, 0.4 mi sw. Int corridors. **Pets:** Other species. Service with restrictions, supervision.

Red Roof Inn Ⓜ
(859) 647-2700. **Call for rates.** 7454 Turfway Rd. I-71/75, exit 182, 0.8 mi sw. Int corridors. **Pets:** Medium. Service with restrictions, supervision.

FRANKFORT

Americas Best Value Inn 🅂🄷 ❧
(502) 875-3220. **$60-$80.** 1225 US Hwy 127 S. I-64, exit 53B, 1.2 mi n. Int corridors. **Pets:** Dogs only. $10 one-time fee/room. Designated rooms, service with restrictions, supervision.

Capital Plaza Hotel 🄻🄷
(502) 227-5100. **$89.** 405 Wilkinson Blvd. Adjacent to Frankfort Convention Center. Int corridors. **Pets:** $25 one-time fee/pet. Supervision.

FRANKLIN

Comfort Inn 🅂🄷
(270) 586-6100. **$50-$100.** 3794 Nashville Rd. I-65, exit 2. Ext corridors. **Pets:** Small. $20 daily fee/pet. Designated rooms, service with restrictions, supervision.

Super 8 Motel 🅂🄷
(270) 586-5090. **Call for rates.** 3811 Nashville Rd. I-65, exit 2, just w. Ext corridors. **Pets:** Accepted.

GLASGOW

Comfort Inn 🅂🄷
(270) 651-9099. **$60-$129.** 210 Calvary Dr. Cumberland Pkwy, exit 11, just n. Ext corridors. **Pets:** Accepted.

Days Inn-Glasgow Ⓜ ❧
(270) 651-1757. **Call for rates.** 105 Days Inn Blvd. Cumberland Pkwy, exit 11, just n. Int corridors. **Pets:** Medium, other species. $10 daily fee/pet. Service with restrictions, supervision.

GRAND RIVERS

Best Western Kentucky-Barkley Lakes Inn 🅂🄷
(270) 928-2700. **$65, 30 day notice.** 720 Complex Dr. I-24, exit 31 (SR 453), just s. Ext/int corridors. **Pets:** Accepted.

Microtel Inn & Suites 🅂🄷
(270) 928-2740. **$54-$74, 7 day notice.** 1017 Dover Rd. I-24, exit 31 (SR 453), just n. Int corridors. **Pets:** Accepted.

GRAYSON

Super 8 Motel 🅂🄷
(606) 474-8811. **Call for rates.** 125 Super 8 Ln. I-64, exit 172, just s. Int corridors. **Pets:** Small. $10 daily fee/pet. Designated rooms, service with restrictions, supervision.

HARLAN

Holiday Inn Express Harlan 🅂🄷
(606) 573-3385. **$69-$99.** 2608 S Hwy 421. On US 421, 2.8 mi s. Int corridors. **Pets:** Small. $7 daily fee/room. Designated rooms, service with restrictions, supervision.

HARRODSBURG

Country Hearth Inn 🅂🄷
(859) 734-2400. **$58-$94.** 105 Commercial Dr. 0.6 mi n on College St. Int corridors. **Pets:** Small. $20 one-time fee/pet. Service with restrictions, supervision.

HOPKINSVILLE

Holiday Inn 🅂🄷
(270) 886-4413. **Call for rates.** 2910 Ft Campbell Blvd. Pennyrile Pkwy, exit 7A, 0.6 mi n on US 41A. Int corridors. **Pets:** Accepted.

Hopkinsville Best Western 🅂🄷
(270) 886-9000. **Call for rates.** 4101 Ft Campbell Blvd. Pennyrile Pkwy, exit 7A, just s on US 41A. Int corridors. **Pets:** Accepted.

KUTTAWA

Days Inn 🅂🄷
(270) 388-4060. **Call for rates.** 139 Days Inn Dr. I-24, exit 40 (US 62), just s. Ext corridors. **Pets:** Accepted.

LEBANON

Hampton Inn Lebanon 🅂🄷
(270) 699-4000. **Call for rates.** 1125 Loretto Rd. Jct SR 49 and 84. Int corridors. **Pets:** Medium, other species. $25 one-time fee/room. Service with restrictions, supervision.

LEITCHFIELD

Hatfield Inn 🅂🄷
(270) 259-0464. **Call for rates.** 769 White St. Western Kentucky Pkwy, exit 107, just nw. Int corridors. **Pets:** Other species. $10 daily fee/room. Service with restrictions, supervision.

LEWISPORT

Best Western Hancock Inn Ⓜ
(270) 295-3234. **Call for rates.** 9040 US Hwy 60 W. On US 60. Int corridors. **Pets:** Medium. $15 daily fee/pet. Designated rooms, service with restrictions, supervision.

LEXINGTON

Days Inn-South 🅂🄷
(859) 263-3100. **Call for rates.** 5575 Athens-Boonesboro Rd. I-75, exit 104, just e. Ext corridors. **Pets:** Small. $10 daily fee/pet. Designated rooms, no service, supervision.

Doubletree Guest Suites Lexington 🄻🄷
(859) 268-0060. **Call for rates.** 2601 Richmond Rd. I-75, exit 104, 5.5 mi w. Int corridors. **Pets:** Accepted.

Extended StayAmerica-Nicholasville Rd 🅂🄷
(859) 278-9600. **$59-$65.** 2650 Wilhite Dr. Jct US 27 and SR 4. Ext corridors. **Pets:** Other species. $75 one-time fee/pet. Service with restrictions.

▼▼ **Extended StayAmerica-Tates Creek** SH
(859) 271-6160. **$63-$70.** 3575 Tates Creek Rd. New Circle Rd (SR 4), exit 18, 0.4 mi s. Int corridors. **Pets:** Other species. $75 one-time fee/pet. Service with restrictions.

ASK SD ⊠ 🛏 🖵

▼▼▼▼ **Four Points Sheraton Hotel** LH
(859) 259-1311. **Call for rates.** 1938 Stanton Way. I-75/64, exit 115, just se on SR 922. Int corridors. **Pets:** Accepted.

⊠ ♿ 🛏 🖵 ❙❙ ⇆

▼▼ ▼▼▼ **Griffin Gate Marriott Resort** LH
(859) 231-5100. **$189-$239.** 1800 Newtown Pike. I-75/64, exit 115, 0.5 mi sw. Int corridors. **Pets:** Accepted.

ASK SD ⊠ ♿ 🛏 🖵 ❙❙ ⇆ ⊠

▼▼▼▼ **Hampton Inn I-75** SH
(859) 299-2613. **Call for rates.** 2251 Elkhorn Rd. I-75, exit 110, 0.4 mi nw. Int corridors. **Pets:** Large, other species. Service with restrictions, supervision.

⊠ ♿ 🛏 🖵 ⇆

▼▼▼▼ **Holiday Inn Express Hotel & Suites-Lexington** SH
(859) 389-6800. **$89-$189.** 1000 Export St. I-75, exit 113, 4.5 mi s, then just e. Int corridors. **Pets:** Accepted.

ASK SD ⊠ ♿ 🛏 🖵 ⇆

🐾 ▼▼▼▼ **Holiday Inn-Lexington North** LH
(859) 233-0512. **$109-$184.** 1950 Newtown Pike. I-75/64, exit 115, just s. Ext/int corridors. **Pets:** Accepted.

SAVE SD ⊠ ♿ 🛏 🖵 ❙❙ ⇆ ⊠

🐾 ▼▼▼▼ **Radisson Plaza Hotel Lexington** LH
(859) 231-9000. **$99-$209.** 369 W Vine St. Corner of Vine St and Broadway. Int corridors. **Pets:** Accepted.

SAVE SD ⊠ ♿ 🛏 🖵 ❙❙ ⇆ ⊠

▼▼ ▼▼ **Red Roof Inn-North** SH
(859) 293-2626. **Call for rates.** 1980 Haggard Ct. I-75/64, exit 113, 0.3 mi nw. Ext corridors. **Pets:** Accepted.

⊠

▼▼ ▼▼ **Red Roof Inn South** SH
(859) 277-9400. **Call for rates.** 2651 Wilhite Dr. Jct US 27 and SR 4. Ext corridors. **Pets:** Accepted.

⊠ ♿ 🛏

▼▼ ▼▼ **Red Roof Inn Southeast** SH
(859) 543-1877. **Call for rates.** 100 Canebrake Dr. I-75, exit 104, just e. Int corridors. **Pets:** Accepted.

⊠ 🛏 🖵 ⇆

▼▼▼▼ **Residence Inn by Marriott** SH
(859) 231-6191. **$209-$229.** 1080 Newtown Pike. I-75/64, exit 115, 1 mi s on SR 922. Ext corridors. **Pets:** Accepted.

ASK SD ⊠ 🛏 🖵 ⇆ ⊠

▼▼▼▼ **Residence Inn South @ Hamburg** SH 🐾
(859) 263-9979. **$129-$144.** 2688 Pink Pigeon Pkwy. I-75, exit 108, just se. Int corridors. **Pets:** Large, other species.

ASK SD ⊠ ♿ 🛏 🖵 ❙❙ ⇆ ⊠

▼▼▼ **Sleep Inn Lexington** SH
(859) 543-8400. **Call for rates.** 1920 Plaudit Pl. I-75, exit 108, just sw. Int corridors. **Pets:** Accepted.

⊠ 🛏 🖵 ⇆

LONDON

▼▼ **Budget Host Westgate Inn** SH 🐾
(606) 878-7330. **$40-$62, 3 day notice.** 254 Russell Dyche Memorial Hwy. I-75, exit 41, just w on SR 80. Ext/int corridors. **Pets:** Small. Designated rooms, service with restrictions, supervision.

SD ⊠ ♿ 🛏 ⇆

▼▼▼▼ **Holiday Inn Express** SH
(606) 862-0077. **Call for rates.** 506 Minton Dr. I-75, exit 38, just e. Int corridors. **Pets:** Accepted.

⊠ ♿ 🛏 🖵 ⇆

▼▼ ▼▼ **Red Roof Inn** SH
(606) 862-8444. **Call for rates.** 110 Melcon Ln. I-75, exit 41, southwest corner. Int corridors. **Pets:** Accepted.

⊠ ♿ 🛏 🖵 ⇆

LOUISA

▼▼ ▼▼ **Super 8 Motel-Louisa** SH
(606) 638-7888. **Call for rates.** 191 Falls Creek Dr. Jct US 23 and SR 3. Int corridors. **Pets:** Accepted.

⊠ ♿ 🛏

LOUISVILLE METROPOLITAN AREA

BROOKS

▼▼ ▼▼ **Comfort Inn** SH
(502) 957-6900. **$59-$265.** 149 Willabrook Dr. I-65, exit 121, just nw. Int corridors. **Pets:** Other species. $10 daily fee/pet. Service with restrictions, crate.

ASK SD ⊠ 🛏 🖵 ⇆ ⊠

HURSTBOURNE

▼▼▼▼ **Drury Inn & Suites-Louisville** SH
(502) 326-4170. **$141.** 9501 Blairwood Rd. I-64, exit 15. Int corridors. **Pets:** Large, other species. Service with restrictions, supervision.

ASK ⊠ ♿ 🛏 🖵 ⇆

▼▼ ▼▼ **Red Roof Inn Louisville–East #034** SH
(502) 426-7621. **Call for rates.** 9330 Blairwood Rd. I-64, exit 15, 0.3 mi nw of Hurstbourne Pkwy. Ext corridors. **Pets:** Accepted.

⊠ ♿ 🛏

JEFFERSONTOWN

▼▼ ▼▼ **Extended StayAmerica** SH
(502) 499-6215. **$54-$195.** 9801 Bunsen Way. I-64, exit 15A, 0.5 mi e on Hurstbourne Pkwy. Int corridors. **Pets:** Other species. $75 one-time fee/pet. Service with restrictions.

ASK SD ⊠ 🛏 🖵 ⇆

▼▼ ▼▼ **Homestead Studio Suites Louisville–Alliant Drive** SH
(502) 267-4454. **$68-$205.** 1650 Alliant Ave. I-64, exit 17, just s. Int corridors. **Pets:** Other species. $75 one-time fee/pet. Service with restrictions.

ASK SD ⊠ ♿ 🛏 🖵 ⇆

▼▼▼▼ **Jameson Inn Louisville East** SH
(502) 267-8100. **Call for rates.** 1301 Kentucky Mills Dr. I-64, exit 17. Ext/int corridors. **Pets:** Small. $15 daily fee/room. Service with restrictions, crate.

⊠ ♿ 🛏 🖵 ⇆ ⊠

♨ ▼▼▼ Microtel Inn Louisville East SH
(502) 266-6590. **$60-$65.** 1221 Kentucky Mills Dr. I-64, exit 17. Int corridors. **Pets:** Small. $20 one-time fee/pet. Service with restrictions, supervision.
SAVE S☐ ✕ ☐M

▼▼ Super 8 Motel & Suites SH
(502) 267-8889. **Call for rates.** 1501 Alliant Ave. I-64, exit 17, just e. Int corridors. **Pets:** Small, cats only. $20 daily fee/pet. Designated rooms, no service, supervision.
✕ ☐M ☐ ☐ ⇆

LA GRANGE

▼▼▼ Comfort Suites SH ❁
(502) 225-4125. **$59-$149.** 1500 Crystal Dr E. I-71, exit 22, just e. Int corridors. **Pets:** Large, other species. $50 deposit/pet, $10 daily fee/pet. Service with restrictions, supervision.
ASK S☐ ✕ ☐M ☐ ☐ ⇆ ✕

♨ ▼▼▼ Holiday Inn Express SH
(502) 222-5678. **$90.** 1001 Paige Pl. I-71, exit 22, just se. Int corridors. **Pets:** Medium. $20 one-time fee/pet. Designated rooms, service with restrictions, supervision.
SAVE S☐ ✕ ☐ ☐ ⇆

LOUISVILLE

▼▼▼ Aleksander House Bed and Breakfast BB ❁
(502) 637-4985. **$109-$185.** 1213 S 1st St. I-65, exit 135 (St Catherine St), just s. Int corridors. **Pets:** Other species. $20 one-time fee/pet. Supervision.
✕ ☐ ☐

▼▼▼ Executive West LH
(502) 367-2251. **$159.** 830 Phillips Ln. I-264, exit 11 (Fairgrounds/Expo Center Main Gate). Int corridors. **Pets:** $100 daily fee/room. Designated rooms, service with restrictions, supervision.
ASK S☐ ✕ ☐ ☐ ☐ ⇆ ✕

▼▼▼ Holiday Inn South-Airport LH
(502) 964-3311. **$110-$145.** 2715 Fern Valley Rd. I-65, exit 128 (Fern Valley Rd), northeast corner. Int corridors. **Pets:** $35 one-time fee/room. Service with restrictions, crate.
ASK S☐ ✕ ☐M ☐ ☐ ☐ ⇆

▼▼▼ Homewood Suites SH
(502) 429-9070. **Call for rates.** 9401 Hurstbourne Tr. I-64, exit 15, 2.5 mi n. Int corridors. **Pets:** Accepted.
✕ ☐M ☐ ☐ ⇆ ✕

▼▼▼ Jameson Inn Airport South SH
(502) 968-4100. **Call for rates.** 6515 Signature Dr. I-65, exit 128 (Fern Valley Rd), southeast corner. Int corridors. **Pets:** Small. $15 daily fee/room. Service with restrictions, crate.
✕ ☐ ⇆

♨ ▼▼▼ La Quinta Inn & Suites Airport & Expo-Louisville SH
(502) 368-0007. **$99-$129.** 4125 Preston Hwy. I-65, exit 130, 1 mi w. Int corridors. **Pets:** Other species. Service with restrictions, supervision.
SAVE S☐ ✕ ☐M ☐ ☐ ⇆

▼▼ Red Roof Inn-Airport-Fairgrounds SH
(502) 968-0151. **Call for rates.** 4704 Preston Hwy. I-65, exit 130, northeast corner. Ext corridors. **Pets:** Accepted.
✕

▼▼ Red Roof Inn-Southeast-Fairgrounds SH
(502) 456-2993. **Call for rates.** 3322 Red Roof Inn Pl. I-264, 15B westbound, 0.3 mi s; exit 15 eastbound. Ext corridors. **Pets:** Accepted.
✕ ☐

▼▼▼ Residence Inn by Marriott-Louisville Airport SH
(502) 363-8800. **$129-$189.** 700 Phillips Ln. I-264, exit 11 (Fairgrounds/Expo Center Main Gate), 0.4 mi w. Int corridors. **Pets:** Accepted.
ASK S☐ ✕ ☐M ☐ ☐ ⇆

▼▼▼ Residence Inn by Marriott Louisville Downtown SH
(502) 589-8998. **$155-$199.** 333 E Market St. Corner of Preston and E Market. Int corridors. **Pets:** Accepted.
ASK S☐ ✕ ☐M ☐ ☐ ⇆

▼▼▼ Residence Inn by Marriott-Louisville NE SH
(502) 412-1311. **$199-$219.** 3500 Springhurst Commons Dr. I-265, exit 32, 0.5 mi w on Westport Rd, then just n. Int corridors. **Pets:** Accepted.
ASK S☐ ✕ ☐M ☐ ☐ ⇆ ✕

▼▼▼ Residence Inn Louisville East SH
(502) 425-1821. **$129-$169.** 120 N Hurstbourne Pkwy. I-64, exit 15, 1.8 mi n. Ext corridors. **Pets:** Accepted.
ASK S☐ ✕ ☐ ☐ ⇆ ✕

♨ ▼▼▼ The Seelbach Hilton Louisville LH
(502) 585-3200. **Call for rates.** 500 4th St. I-65, exit 136C (Muhammad Ali), 0.3 mi w, then just s. Int corridors. **Pets:** Medium. $50 deposit/pet. Service with restrictions, crate.
SAVE ✕ ☐M ☐ ☐ ☐ ✕

▼▼ Sleep Inn Fairgrounds SH ❁
(502) 368-9597. **$69-$325.** 3330 Preston Hwy. I-264, exit 11 (Fairgrounds/Expo Center Main Gate), 0.5 mi e on Phillips Ln, then just n. Int corridors. **Pets:** Large, other species. $10 daily fee/pet. Service with restrictions, crate.
ASK S☐ ✕ ☐ ☐ ⇆

▼▼▼ Staybridge Suites by Holiday Inn SH
(502) 244-9511. **$110-$119.** 11711 Gateworth Way. I-64, exit 17, just n. Int corridors. **Pets:** Accepted.
ASK S☐ ✕ ☐M ☐ ☐ ⇆

ST. MATTHEWS

▼▼ Extended StayAmerica SH
(502) 897-2559. **$54-$195.** 1401 Browns Ln. I-264, exit 18B, just e, 1 mi e on Dutchmans Ln, then just s. Int corridors. **Pets:** Other species. $75 one-time fee/pet. Service with restrictions.
ASK S☐ ✕ ☐ ☐ ⇆

SHEPHERDSVILLE

♨ ▼▼ Best Western South SH
(502) 543-7097. **$73-$89, 30 day notice.** 211 S Lakeview Dr. I-65, exit 117 (SR 44 W), just se. Int corridors. **Pets:** Medium. Service with restrictions, crate.
SAVE S☐ ✕ ☐ ☐ ⇆

▼▼ Super 8 SH
(502) 543-8870. **Call for rates.** 275 Keystone Crossroads. I-65, exit 117, just w. Int corridors. **Pets:** Medium, dogs only. $10 daily fee/pet. Service with restrictions.
✕ ☐ ⇆

SHIVELY

▼▼▼▼ Holiday Inn-Southwest 🇱🇭
(502) 448-2020. **Call for rates.** 4110 Dixie Hwy. I-264, exit 8B, just n on US 31 W and 60. Int corridors. **Pets:** Accepted.
✕ 🛏 💻 🍴 ≈

END METROPOLITAN AREA

MAYSVILLE

🅰️ ▼▼▼ Best Western Maysville Inn 🅂🄷
(606) 759-5696. **Call for rates.** 1428 a US 68. Jct US 68 and SR 9 (AA Hwy). Ext corridors. **Pets:** Accepted.
🆂🅰🆅🅴 ✕ ♿ 🛏 💻 ≈

▼▼▼ Super 8 Motel, Maysville KY 🅂🄷
(606) 759-8888. **Call for rates.** 550 Tucker Dr. Just e of US 68. Int corridors. **Pets:** Accepted.
✕ 🛏

MOREHEAD

🅰️ ▼▼▼▼ Comfort Inn & Suites 🅂🄷
(606) 780-7378. **$62-$99.** 2650 Kentucky 801 N. I-64, exit 133, just s. Int corridors. **Pets:** Accepted.
🆂🅰🆅🅴 ✕ ♿ 🛏 💻 ≈

🅰️ ▼▼▼▼ Holiday Inn Express of Morehead 🅂🄷
(606) 784-5796. **$79-$99.** 110 Toms Dr. I-64, exit 137 (SR 32), just sw. Int corridors. **Pets:** Accepted.
🆂🅰🆅🅴 🆂🅾 ✕ ♿ 🛏 💻 ≈

MORTONS GAP

🅰️ ▼▼▼ Best Western Pennyrile Inn 🅂🄷 ✿
(270) 258-5201. **$60-$72, 3 day notice.** White City Rd. Pennyrile Pkwy, exit 37 (US 41). Ext corridors. **Pets:** Medium. $10 daily fee/pet. Designated rooms, service with restrictions, supervision.
🆂🅰🆅🅴 🆂🅾 ✕ 🛏 💻 ≈

MOUNT VERNON

▼▼ Kastle Inn Motel 🅼
(606) 256-5156. **$56-$62.** Hwy 25 S. I-75, exit 59. Ext corridors. **Pets:** Accepted.
🅰🆂🅺 🆂🅾 ✕ ≈

MUNFORDVILLE

▼▼ Super 8 🅂🄷 ✿
(270) 524-4888. **Call for rates.** 88 Bull Run Rd. I-65, exit 65, 0.5 mi s. Int corridors. **Pets:** Other species. $10 one-time fee/room. Service with restrictions, supervision.
✕ 🛏

MURRAY

▼▼▼ Days Inn-Murray, KY 🅂🄷
(270) 753-6706. **Call for rates.** 517 S 12th St. 1 mi s on US 641. Ext corridors. **Pets:** $10 daily fee/pet. Service with restrictions, supervision.
✕ 🛏 💻 ≈

OAK GROVE

▼▼▼ Comfort Inn-Oak Grove 🅂🄷
(270) 439-3311. **$69-$89.** 201 Auburn St. I-24, exit 86, just s. Ext corridors. **Pets:** $20 daily fee/pet. Designated rooms, service with restrictions, supervision.
🅰🆂🅺 🆂🅾 ✕ ♿ 🛏 💻 ≈

▼▼▼▼ Holiday Inn Express 🅂🄷
(270) 439-0022. **$91, 7 day notice.** 12759 Ft Campbell Blvd. I-24, exit 86. Int corridors. **Pets:** Small. $10 one-time fee/pet. Designated rooms, service with restrictions, supervision.
🅰🆂🅺 ✕ ♿ 🛏 💻 ≈

OLIVE HILL

▼ Spanish Manor Inn 🅼
(606) 286-4141. **Call for rates.** 10095 US Rt 60. I-64, exit 161, 0.4 mi n. Ext corridors. **Pets:** No service, supervision.
✕ 🛏 💻

OWENSBORO

▼ Motel 6 #205 🅂🄷
(270) 686-8606. **$43-$45.** 4585 Frederica St. US 60 Bypass, exit 4 at US 431, just n. Ext corridors. **Pets:** Other species. Service with restrictions, supervision.
🆂🅾 ✕ ♿ 🛏 ≈

▼▼▼ Super 8 Motel-Owensboro 🅂🄷
(270) 685-3388. **Call for rates.** 1027 Goetz Dr. US 60 Bypass, exit 4 at US 431. Int corridors. **Pets:** Accepted.
✕ ♿ 🛏 💻

OWINGSVILLE

▼▼ Super 8 Owingsville 🅂🄷
(606) 674-2200. **Call for rates.** 201 Williams Ave. I-64, exit 121, just n. Int corridors. **Pets:** Accepted.
✕ ♿ 🛏

PADUCAH

🅰️ ▼▼▼ Americas Best Value Inn 🅂🄷
(270) 575-9605. **$60-$70.** 5125 Old Cairo Rd. I-24, exit 3 (SR 305), just e. Ext corridors. **Pets:** Accepted.
🆂🅰🆅🅴 🆂🅾 ✕ 🛏

▼▼ Days Inn 🅂🄷
(270) 442-7500. **Call for rates.** 3901 Hinkleville Rd. I-24, exit 4 (US 60), just e. Ext corridors. **Pets:** Accepted.
✕ 🛏 💻 ≈

▼▼▼▼ Drury Inn-Paducah 🅂🄷
(270) 443-3313. **$129.** 3975 Hinkleville Rd. I-24, exit 4 (US 60), just e. Int corridors. **Pets:** Large, other species. Service with restrictions, supervision.
🅰🆂🅺 ✕ 🛏 💻 ≈

▼▼▼▼ Drury Suites-Paducah 🅂🄷
(270) 441-0024. **$135.** 2930 James-Sanders Blvd. I-24, exit 4 (US 60), just w. Int corridors. **Pets:** Large, other species. Service with restrictions, supervision.
🅰🆂🅺 ✕ ♿ 🛏 💻 ≈

▼▼▼ Holiday Inn Express 🅂🄷
(270) 442-8874. **Call for rates.** 3994 Hinkleville Rd. I-24, exit 4 (US 60), just e. Int corridors. **Pets:** Accepted.
✕ 🛏 💻 ≈

▼▼▼ Pear Tree Inn-Paducah SH
(270) 442-4500. **$91.** 5006 Hinkleville Rd. I-24, exit 4 (US 60), just w. Int corridors. **Pets:** Accepted.
ASK ✕ 🛌M 💻 ⇌

▼▼▼ Thrifty Inn SH
(270) 444-7200. **$81.** 5002 Hinkleville Rd. I-24, exit 4 (US 60), just w. Ext corridors. **Pets:** Large, other species. Service with restrictions, supervision.
ASK ✕ 🛏 💻 ⇌

PRESTONSBURG

▼▼▼▼ Best Western-Prestonburg SH
(606) 886-0001. **Call for rates.** 1887 N US 23. 2 mi s. Ext corridors. **Pets:** Accepted.
✕ 🛌M 🛏 💻 ⇌ ⊠

RICHMOND

▼▼▼ Holiday Inn Express Hotel & Suites SH
(859) 624-4055. **$89-$159.** 1990 Colby Taylor Dr. I-75, exit 87, just w. Int corridors. **Pets:** $25 daily fee/pet. Service with restrictions, crate.
ASK S⊘ ✕ 🛌M 🛏 💻 ⇌

▼▼▼ Jameson Inn SH
(859) 623-0063. **Call for rates.** 1007 Colby Taylor Dr. I-75, exit 87, just w. Int corridors. **Pets:** Small. $15 daily fee/room. Service with restrictions, crate.
✕ 🛌M 🛏 💻 ⇌

(AAA)◇ ▼▼▼ Super 8 Motel SH
(859) 624-1550. **Call for rates.** 107 N Keeneland Dr. I-75, exit 90. Int corridors. **Pets:** Very small. $6 daily fee/pet. Designated rooms, service with restrictions, supervision.
SAVE ✕ 🛌M 🛏 💻

SCOTTSVILLE

(AAA)◇ ▼▼▼ Executive Inn SH
(270) 622-7770. **$55.** 57 Burnley Rd. US 31 E, jct SR 231. Ext corridors. **Pets:** $6 daily fee/pet. Service with restrictions, crate.
SAVE ✕ 🛏 ⇌

SHELBYVILLE

▼▼▼▼ Best Western Shelbyville Lodge SH
(502) 633-4400. **$72-$175, 14 day notice.** 115 Isaac Shelby Dr. I-64, exit 32, 0.5 mi n on SR 55. Int corridors. **Pets:** Large. $10 daily fee/room. Designated rooms, service with restrictions, supervision.
ASK ✕ 🛏 💻 ⇌

(AAA)◇ ▼▼▼ Holiday Inn Express SH
(502) 647-0109. **$84-$95.** 110 Club House Dr. I-64, exit 35, just s. Int corridors. **Pets:** $20 one-time fee/room. Designated rooms, service with restrictions, supervision.
SAVE ✕ 🛌M 🛏 💻 ⇌

▼▼▼ Ramada SH
(502) 633-9933. **Call for rates (no credit cards).** 251 Breighton Cir. I-64, exit 32, just s. Int corridors. **Pets:** Medium. $25 one-time fee/room. Service with restrictions.
✕ 🛌M 🛏 💻 ⇌

SMITHS GROVE

(AAA)◇ ▼▼▼ Bryce Inn SH
(270) 563-5141. **$49-$65.** 592 S Main St. I-65, exit 38, 0.3 mi w. Ext corridors. **Pets:** Small, dogs only. $7 one-time fee/pet. Service with restrictions, supervision.
SAVE ✕ 🛏 💻 ⇌

SPARTA

▼▼▼ Ramada at the Kentucky Speedway SH
(859) 567-7223. **Call for rates.** 525 Dale Dr. I-71, exit 57, just w. Int corridors. **Pets:** Medium. $25 one-time fee/room. Service with restrictions.
✕ 🛌M 🛏 💻 ⇌

VERSAILLES

▼▼▼▼ 1823 Historic Rose Hill Inn BB
(859) 873-5957. **$109-$179.** 233 Rose Hill. Just s on SR 33 (S Main St), then just w. Ext/int corridors. **Pets:** Accepted.
✕ 🛏 💻 ⇌

WEST LIBERTY

▼▼▼ Days Inn SH
(606) 743-4206. **Call for rates.** 1613 W Main St. Jct SR 519 and 460, just w. Int corridors. **Pets:** Accepted.
✕ 🛌M 💻

WILLIAMSBURG

▼▼▼ Cumberland Inn SH
(606) 539-4100. **$89-$94.** 649 S 10th St. I-75, exit 11. Int corridors. **Pets:** Small. $20 one-time fee/room. Designated rooms, service with restrictions, supervision.
ASK S⊘ ✕ 🛌M 🛏 💻 🍴 ⇌

LOUISIANA

CITY INDEX

ALEXANDRIA

Best Western Inn & Suites & Conference Center of Alexandria SH
(318) 445-5530. **$89-$120, 3 day notice.** 2720 W MacArthur Dr. I-49, exit 86 (MacArthur Dr), 1.3 mi sw. Ext/int corridors. **Pets:** Small. $10 daily fee/pet. Designated rooms, service with restrictions, supervision.

La Quinta Inn & Suites Alexandria SH
(318) 442-3700. **$141-$151.** 6116 W Calhoun Dr. I-49, exit 90 (Air Base Rd), just w. Int corridors. **Pets:** Other species. Service with restrictions, supervision.

Ramada Limited SH
(318) 448-1611. **$75-$93.** 742 MacArthur Dr. 0.4 mi s of jct SR 28 and US 71/165 (MacArthur Dr). Ext corridors. **Pets:** Medium. $10 daily fee/ room. Designated rooms, service with restrictions, supervision.

BATON ROUGE

Best Western Richmond Suites Hotel–Baton Rouge SH
(225) 924-6500. **$109-$219.** 5668 Hilton Ave. I-10, exit 158, just ne. Int corridors. **Pets:** Accepted.

Chase Suites by Woodfin SH
(225) 927-5630. **$149-$209.** 5522 Corporate Blvd. I-10, exit 158, just n on College Dr, then just e. Ext corridors. **Pets:** Large, other species. $250 deposit/pet, $10 daily fee/pet. Designated rooms, service with restrictions.

Crestwood Suites Hotel SH
(225) 291-5200. **Call for rates.** 5222 S Sherwood Forest Blvd. I-12, exit 4, 1.7 mi s. Int corridors. **Pets:** Accepted.

Holiday Inn Select Executive Center Baton Rouge LH 🐾
(225) 925-2244. **$139-$199.** 4728 Constitution Ave. I-10, exit 158, just se on frontage road. Int corridors. **Pets:** Medium. $25 one-time fee/room. Service with restrictions, supervision.

La Quinta Inn Baton Rouge SH
(225) 291-6600. **$103-$113.** 10555 Rieger Rd. I-10, exit 163 (Siegen Ln), just n, then just e. Int corridors. **Pets:** Other species. Service with restrictions, supervision.

La Quinta Inn Baton Rouge SH
(225) 924-9600. **$97-$107.** 2333 S Acadian Thruway. I-10, exit 157B. Ext corridors. **Pets:** Other species. Service with restrictions, supervision.

Ramada I-12/Airline Highway SH
(225) 706-5500. **Call for rates.** 10045 Gwenadele Ave. I-12, exit 2B, just n on US 61. Ext corridors. **Pets:** Accepted.

Residence Inn by Marriott-Baton Rouge SH
(225) 293-8700. **Call for rates.** 10333 N Mall Dr. I-10, exit 163 west-bound, just s on Siegen Ln, then just e; exit eastbound, 0.5 mi to S Mall Dr, just e to Andrea (at Lowe's), then just n. Int corridors. **Pets:** Accepted.

Sheraton Baton Rouge Convention Center Hotel LH
(225) 242-2600. **$225.** 102 France St. I-110, exit 1A (Government St), 0.8 mi w to St. James, then just s. Int corridors. **Pets:** Accepted.

TownePlace Suites by Marriott SH
(225) 819-2112. **Call for rates.** 8735 Summa Ave. I-10, exit 162 (Blue-bonnet Blvd), just s to Picardy, just w to Summa Ave, then 0.5 mi nw. Int corridors. **Pets:** Accepted.

BOSSIER CITY

Best Western-Airline Motor Inn SH
(318) 742-6000. **$95-$125.** 1984 Airline Dr. I-20, exit 22 (Airline Dr), just n. Ext corridors. **Pets:** Small, other species. $10 daily fee/pet. Service with restrictions, crate.

Crossland Studios Shreveport-Bossier City SH
(318) 747-5800. **Call for rates (no credit cards).** 3070 E Texas St. I-20, exit 22, just s. Ext corridors. **Pets:** Other species. $75 one-time fee/pet. Service with restrictions.

Hampton Inn SH
(318) 752-1112. **Call for rates.** 1005 Gould Dr. I-20, exit 21, 0.5 mi ne on service road. Int corridors. **Pets:** Small. Service with restrictions, crate.

La Quinta Inn Bossier City SH
(318) 747-4400. **$90-$103.** 309 Preston Blvd. I-20, exit 21, just n. Ext corridors. **Pets:** Other species. Service with restrictions, supervision.

Microtel Inn & Suites SH
(318) 742-7882. **$65-$119.** 2713 Village Ln. I-20, exit 22 (Airline Dr), just s, then just w. Int corridors. **Pets:** Accepted.

Quality Inn & Suites SH
(318) 742-7890. **$94-$195.** 2717 Village Ln. I-20, exit 22 (Airline Dr), just s, then just w. Int corridors. **Pets:** Accepted.

▼▼▼ Residence Inn by Marriott-Shreveport/Bossier City **SH**

(318) 747-6220. **Call for rates.** 1001 Gould Dr. I-20, exit 21, just ne. Ext corridors. **Pets:** Other species. $100 one-time fee/room. Service with restrictions.

☒ 🕯 ▣ ⚲ ⊠

BREAUX BRIDGE

◈ ▼▼▼ Holiday Inn Express of Breaux Bridge **SH**

(337) 667-8913. **$85.** 2942 H Grand Point Hwy. I-10, exit 115, just n. Int corridors. **Pets:** Accepted.

A$K S🔥 ☒ ⬆M 🕯 ▣ ⚲

CONVENT

▼▼▼▼ Poche Plantation Bed & Breakfast and RV Resort **BB**

(225) 562-7728. **$119-$198, 15 day notice.** 6554 Louisiana Hwy 44. Jct SR 44 and 641; 10.1 mi s of Sunshine Bridge (SR 70), then 10.2 mi n. Ext/int corridors. **Pets:** Accepted.

☒ 🕯 ▣ ⚲

CROWLEY

◈◈ **▼▼▼** Days Inn **SH**

(337) 783-2378. **$59-$99.** 9571 Egan Hwy. I-10, exit 80. Ext corridors. **Pets:** Accepted.

SAVE S🔥 ☒ 🕯 ▣ ⚲

DERIDDER

◈◈ **▼▼▼** Stagecoach Inn **SH**

(337) 462-0022. **$69.** 505 E 1st St. 2 mi on east side; between US 171. Ext corridors. **Pets:** Small. $25 daily fee/pet. Service with restrictions.

SAVE S🔥 ☒ ⬆M 🕯 ▣ ⚲

HAMMOND

◈◈ **▼▼▼** Best Western Hammond Inn & Suites **SH**

(985) 419-2001. **$70-$105.** 107 Duo Dr. I-12, exit 40 (US 51), just ne. Ext corridors. **Pets:** Small. $10 daily fee/pet. Service with restrictions, crate.

SAVE S🔥 ☒ 🕯 ▣ ⚲

◈◈ **▼▼▼** Michabelle Inn **CI**

(985) 419-0550. **$75-$125, 4 day notice.** 1106 S Holly St. I-12, exit 40 (US 51), 0.8 mi n, just e on Old Covington Hwy, then n, follow signs. Ext/int corridors. **Pets:** Accepted.

SAVE S🔥 ☒ 🕯 ▣ ⊤⊤ ✍

HOUMA

◈◈ **▼▼▼▼** La Quinta Inn & Suites Houma **SH**

(985) 879-1646. **Call for rates.** 189 Synergy Center Blvd. US 90, exit 202, 3.4 mi s on Main St to Martin Luther King Jr Blvd, then just w. Int corridors. **Pets:** Other species. Service with restrictions, supervision.

SAVE ☒ ⬆M 🕯 ▣ ⚲

KINDER

◈◈ **▼▼▼▼** Best Western Inn At Coushatta **SH**

(337) 738-4800. **$79-$169.** 12102 US Hwy 165 N. 5 mi n of jct US 190/165. Int corridors. **Pets:** Very small, other species. $25 deposit/room. Service with restrictions, supervision.

SAVE S🔥 ☒ 🕯 ▣ ⚲

▼▼▼ Holiday Inn Express Hotel & Suites **SH**

(337) 738-3381. **Call for rates.** 11750 US Hwy 165. 5.2 mi n of jct US 190/165, 5.1 mi on US 165. Ext/int corridors. **Pets:** Accepted.

☒ ⬆M 🕯 ▣ ⚲

LAFAYETTE

▼▼▼ America's Best Suites of Lafayette **SH**

(337) 235-1367. **$99-$109.** 125 E Kaliste Saloom Rd. I-10, exit 103A, 1 mi w of jct E Kaliste Saloom Rd and US 90 (SW Evangeline Thruway). Int corridors. **Pets:** Accepted.

A$K S🔥 ☒ 🕯 ▣ ⚲

◈◈◈ **▼▼◈** Best Western-Lafayette **SH**

(337) 289-9907. **$76-$111.** 126 Alcide Dominique. I-10, exit 101, just s. Int corridors. **Pets:** Accepted.

A$K ☒ ▣ ⚲

▼▼▼▼ Drury Inn & Suites-Lafayette **SH**

(337) 262-0202. **$81-$151.** 120 Alcide Dominique. I-10, exit 101 (SR 182), just s on University Ave, then just w. Int corridors. **Pets:** Large, other species. Service with restrictions, supervision.

A$K ☒ ⬆M 🕯 ▣ ⚲

◈◈◈ **▼▼▼▼** Holiday Inn Lafayette **SH**

(337) 233-6815. **$79-$179.** 2032 NE Evangeline Thruway. I-10, exit 103A, just s. Ext/int corridors. **Pets:** Accepted.

SAVE ☒ 🕯 ▣ ⊤⊤ ⚲ ⊠

▼▼◈ Jameson Inn of Lafayette **SH**

(337) 291-2916. **$85-$105.** 2200 NE Evangeline Thruway. I-10, exit 103A, just s. Int corridors. **Pets:** Small. $15 daily fee/room. Service with restrictions, crate.

A$K S🔥 ☒ 🕯 ▣ ⚲

◈◈◈ **▼▼▼▼** La Quinta Inn & Suites Lafayette Oil Center **SH**

(337) 291-1088. **$109-$149.** 1015 W Pinhook Rd. I-10, exit 101 (University Ave), 3.5 mi to SR 182 (Pinhook Rd), then 0.5 mi w. Int corridors. **Pets:** Other species. Service with restrictions, supervision.

SAVE S🔥 ☒ 🕯 ▣ ⚲

▼▼◈ Ramada Inn **SH**

(337) 235-0858. **$75-$82.** 120 E Kaliste Saloom Rd. I-10, exit 103A, 4.4 mi e on US 90 (Evangeline Thruway), then 1 mi s. Ext corridors. **Pets:** Accepted.

A$K S🔥 ☒ 🕯 ▣ ⚲

LAKE CHARLES

▼▼◈ America's Best Suites **SH**

(337) 439-2444. **Call for rates.** 401 Lakeshore Dr. I-10, exit 29 (business district/tourist bureau) eastbound; exit 30B (Ryan St business district) westbound, just s to Pine, then just w. Int corridors. **Pets:** Accepted.

☒ 🕯 ▣ ⚲

▼▼◈ Baymont Inn & Suites **SH**

(337) 310-7666. **Call for rates (no credit cards).** 1004 MLK Hwy (171 N). I-10, exit 33, just n. Ext corridors. **Pets:** Accepted.

☒ 🕯 ▣

◈◈◈ **▼▼▼▼** Best Western Richmond Suites Hotel **SH**

(337) 433-5213. **$89-$139.** 2600 Moeling St. I-10, exit 33, just n. Ext/int corridors. **Pets:** Small, other species. $75 daily fee/room. Service with restrictions, crate.

SAVE ☒ 🕯 ▣ ⚲ ⊠

◈◈◈ **▼▼▼▼** La Quinta Inn Lake Charles **SH**

(337) 436-5998. **$70-$160.** 1320 MLK Hwy 171 N. I-10, exit 33, 0.8 mi n. Int corridors. **Pets:** Other species. Service with restrictions, supervision.

SAVE S🔥 ☒ 🕯 ▣ ⚲

LIVONIA

▼▼◈ Oak Tree Inn **SH**

(225) 637-2590. **Call for rates.** 7875 Airline Hwy. Jct SR 77 and US 190, 0.3 mi w. Ext corridors. **Pets:** Accepted.

☒ 🕯 ▣

MANY

AAA **▼▼▼** Cypress Bend Golf Resort & Conference Center **LH**
(318) 590-1500. **$129-$159, 7 day notice.** 2000 Cypress Bend Pkwy. 13 mi w on SR 6, 3 mi s on SR 191, 3 mi w on Cypress Bend Dr, then 1.5 mi w. Int corridors. **Pets:** Accepted.

SAVE S$ ✕ &M ❚ 🖵 ❘❙ ⋙ ✕

MINDEN

AAA **▼▼▼** Best Western Minden Inn **SH**
(318) 377-1001. **$70-$85.** 1411 Sibley Rd. I-20, exit 47, just n. Ext corridors. **Pets:** Medium. $10 daily fee/pet. Service with restrictions, supervision.

SAVE S$ ✕ ❚ 🖵 ⋙

MONROE

▼▼ Holiday Inn Hotel & Suites Conference Center **SH**
(318) 387-5100. **$69-$149.** 1051 Hwy 165 Bypass. I-20, exit 118B, just ne on US 165 service road. Ext/int corridors. **Pets:** Accepted.

S$ ✕ ❚ 🖵 ❘❙ ⋙ ✕

AAA **▼▼▼** La Quinta Inn Monroe **SH**
(318) 322-3900. **$86-$107.** 1035 Hwy 165 Bypass. I-20, exit 118B, just ne on US 165 service road. Ext corridors. **Pets:** Other species. Service with restrictions, supervision.

SAVE ✕ 🖵 ⋙

▼▼▼ Residence Inn by Marriott **SH**
(318) 387-0210. **Call for rates.** 4960 Millhaven Rd. I-20, exit 120, just n of Pecanland Mall. Int corridors. **Pets:** Accepted.

✕ &M ❚ 🖵 ⋙ ✕

MORGAN CITY

▼▼▼ Holiday Inn-Morgan City **SH**
(985) 385-2200. **$92-$119.** 520 Roderick St. 1.5 mi s of jct US 90 and SR 70. Ext corridors. **Pets:** Accepted.

ASK S$ ✕ &M ❚ 🖵 ❘❙ ⋙

NEW IBERIA

▼▼▼ Holiday Inn New Iberia-Avery Island **SH**
(337) 367-1201. **$81-$99.** 2915 Hwy 14. SR 14, just e of jct US 90. Ext corridors. **Pets:** Accepted.

ASK ✕ ❚ 🖵 ❘❙ ⋙

NEW ORLEANS METROPOLITAN AREA

GRETNA

AAA **▼▼▼** La Quinta Inn New Orleans (West Bank) **SH**
(504) 368-5600. **$114-$124.** 50 Terry Pkwy. S US 90 business route, exit 9A (Terry Pkwy); N US 90 (Westbank Expwy), exit 9 (Terry Pkwy/General DeGaulle). Ext corridors. **Pets:** Other species. Service with restrictions, supervision.

SAVE ✕ ❚ 🖵 ⋙

KENNER

AAA **▼▼▼** La Quinta Inn New Orleans (Airport) **SH**
(504) 466-1401. **$130-$140.** 2610 Williams Blvd. I-10, exit 223A (Williams Blvd), 0.3 mi s. Int corridors. **Pets:** Other species. Service with restrictions, supervision.

SAVE ✕ ❚ 🖵 ⋙

LA PLACE

AAA **▼▼** Best Western La Place Inn **SH**
(985) 651-4000. **$119.** 4289 Main St. I-10, exit 209, just s. Ext corridors. **Pets:** Other species. $25 daily fee/pet. Service with restrictions, crate.

SAVE S$ ✕ ❚ 🖵 ⋙

▼▼▼ Quality Inn-La Place **SH**
(985) 652-5544. **$85-$130.** 3900 Hwy 51. I-10, exit 209, 0.5 mi s. Ext corridors. **Pets:** Accepted.

ASK S$ ✕ ❚ 🖵 ❘❙ ⋙

METAIRIE

AAA **▼▼▼** La Quinta Inn New Orleans (Causeway) **SH**
(504) 835-8511. **$108-$118.** 3100 I-10 Service Rd. I-10, exit 228 (Causeway Blvd), just s. Ext corridors. **Pets:** Other species. Service with restrictions, supervision.

SAVE ✕ ❚ 🖵 ⋙

AAA **▼▼▼** La Quinta Inn New Orleans (Veterans) **SH**
(504) 456-0003. **$119-$129.** 5900 Veterans Memorial Blvd. I-10, exit 225, just n. Ext corridors. **Pets:** Other species. Service with restrictions, supervision.

SAVE ✕ 🖵 ⋙

AAA **▼▼▼▼** Residence Inn by Marriott-Metairie **SH**
(504) 832-0888. **$179.** 3 Galleria Blvd. I-10, exit 228 (Causeway Blvd), just se to 36th St, then just e. Int corridors. **Pets:** Medium. $100 one-time fee/pet. Service with restrictions, supervision.

SAVE S$ ✕ ❚ 🖵 ⋙ ✕

AAA **▼▼▼▼** Sheraton Metairie New Orleans **SH**
(504) 837-6707. **Call for rates.** 4 Galleria Blvd. I-10, exit 228 (Causeway Blvd), just s to 36th St, just e, then just n. Int corridors. **Pets:** Accepted.

SAVE ✕ 🖵 ❘❙

NEW ORLEANS

AAA **▼▼▼** Best Western St. Christopher Hotel **SH**
(504) 648-0444. **$99-$129.** 114 Magazine St. Between Canal and Common sts. Int corridors. **Pets:** Accepted.

SAVE S$ ✕ 🖵

▼▼▼ Chateau Sonesta Hotel **LH**
(504) 586-0800. **$119-$309, 3 day notice.** 800 Iberville St. Between Dauphine and Bourbon sts. Int corridors. **Pets:** Accepted.

ASK S$ ✕ 🖵 ❘❙ ⋙

▼▼▼ Drury Inn & Suites-New Orleans **SH**
(504) 529-7800. **$96-$226.** 820 Poydras St. Between Baronne and Carondelet sts. Int corridors. **Pets:** Large, other species. Service with restrictions, supervision.

ASK ✕ &M ❚ 🖵 ⋙

AAA **▼▼** **▼▼** Elysian Fields Inn **BB**
(504) 948-9420. **$99-$215, 15 day notice.** 930 Elysian Fields Ave. I-610, exit 3 (Elysian Fields Ave), 1.2 mi s. Int corridors. **Pets:** $10 daily fee/pet. Service with restrictions, crate.

SAVE ✕

▼▼ French Quarter Suites Hotel **SH**
(504) 524-7725. **$79-$229, 7 day notice.** 1119 N Rampart St. Between Ursuline and Governor Nicholls. Ext corridors. **Pets:** Accepted.

✕ ❚ 🖵 ⋙

▼▼▼▼ Holiday Inn Express-New Orleans French Quarter
Downtown ⬛
(504) 962-0800. **Call for rates.** 221 Carondelet St. Between Common and Gravier sts. Int corridors. **Pets:** Accepted.

⊠ 🖥 💻 ➿

◢◢◢ ▼▼▼▼ Holiday Inn French Quarter ⬛
(504) 529-7211. **$89-$309.** 124 Royal St. Between Iberville and Canal sts. Int corridors. **Pets:** Medium, other species. $150 deposit/pet, $75 one-time fee/pet. Designated rooms, service with restrictions, crate.

⟦SAVE⟧ ⟦S🐾⟧ ⊠ ⟦&M⟧ 🖥 💻 ⟦†⟧ ➿

◢◢◢ ▼▼▼▼ Hotel Monteleone ⬛
(504) 523-3341. **$160-$399, 3 day notice.** 214 Royal St. Between Iberville and Bienville sts. Int corridors. **Pets:** $100 one-time fee/room. Service with restrictions, supervision.

⟦SAVE⟧ ⟦S🐾⟧ ⊠ 🖥 💻 ⟦†⟧ ➿

◢◢◢ ▼▼▼ ▼▼▼ The Iberville Suites ⬛
(504) 523-2400. **$89-$449, 3 day notice.** 910 Iberville St. Between Burgundy and Dauphine sts. Int corridors. **Pets:** Accepted.

⟦SAVE⟧ ⟦S🐾⟧ ⊠ 🖥 💻

◢◢◢ ▼▼▼▼ La Quinta Inn & Suites New Orleans–
Downtown Flagship ⬛
(504) 598-9977. **$125-$151.** 301 W Camp St. Corner of Gravier and Camp sts. Int corridors. **Pets:** Other species. Service with restrictions, supervision.

⟦SAVE⟧ ⊠ ⟦&M⟧ 🖥 💻 ➿

◢◢◢ ▼▼▼ ▼▼▼ Loews New Orleans Hotel ⬛ ❀
(504) 595-3300. **$149-$499, 3 day notice.** 300 Poydras St. Corner of S Peters St. Int corridors. **Pets:** Large, other species. Service with restrictions, supervision.

⟦SAVE⟧ ⊠ 💻 ⟦†⟧ ⊠

▼▼▼▼ Maison St. Charles Quality Inn & Suites ⬛
(504) 522-0187. **$79-$268.** 1319 St. Charles Ave. I-90 business, exit St. Charles Ave, just w; between Thalia and Erato sts. Ext corridors. **Pets:** Accepted.

⟦ASK⟧ ⟦S🐾⟧ ⊠ 🖥 💻 ➿

▼▼▼▼ Omni Royal Crescent Hotel ⬛
(504) 527-0006. **$109-$299, 3 day notice.** 535 Gravier St. 0.3 mi w of Canal St. Int corridors. **Pets:** Small. $50 one-time fee/pet. Service with restrictions, supervision.

⟦ASK⟧ ⟦S🐾⟧ ⊠ 🖥 💻 ⟦†⟧ ⊠

◢◢◢ ▼▼▼ ▼▼▼ Omni Royal Orleans Hotel ⬛
(504) 529-5333. **$109-$329, 3 day notice.** 621 St. Louis St. At Royal and St. Louis sts. Int corridors. **Pets:** Small. $50 one-time fee/room. Service with restrictions, crate.

⟦SAVE⟧ ⟦S🐾⟧ ⊠ 🖥 💻 ⟦†⟧ ➿

◢◢◢ ▼▼▼ Residence Inn by Marriott ⬛
(504) 522-1300. **Call for rates.** 345 St. Joseph's St. Jct Tchoupitoulas St. Int corridors. **Pets:** Accepted.

⟦SAVE⟧ ⊠ ⟦&M⟧ 🖥 💻 ➿ ⊠

◢◢◢ ▼▼▼ ▼▼▼ The Ritz-Carlton New Orleans ⬛ ❀
(504) 524-1331. **$459, 3 day notice.** 921 Canal St. Between Dauphine and Burgundy sts. Int corridors. **Pets:** Other species. $150 daily fee/pet. Service with restrictions, supervision.

⟦SAVE⟧ ⊠ ⟦&M⟧ 💻 ⟦†⟧ ➿ ⊠

◢◢◢ ▼▼▼ ▼▼▼ Royal Sonesta Hotel New Orleans ⬛
(504) 586-0300. **$129-$329, 3 day notice.** 300 Bourbon St. Garage entrance on Conti or Bienville sts. Ext/int corridors. **Pets:** Small, other species. $50 one-time fee/room. No service, supervision.

⟦SAVE⟧ ⟦S🐾⟧ ⊠ ⟦&M⟧ 🖥 💻 ⟦†⟧ ➿

▼▼▼▼ St. James Hotel ⬛
(504) 304-4000. **Call for rates.** 330 Magazine St. Jct Magazine and Natchez sts. Int corridors. **Pets:** Accepted.

⊠ 💻 ⟦†⟧

◢◢◢ ▼▼▼ ▼▼▼ The Sheraton New Orleans Hotel ⬛
(504) 525-2500. **$389, 3 day notice.** 500 Canal St. Between Camp and Magazine sts. Int corridors. **Pets:** Accepted.

⟦SAVE⟧ ⟦S🐾⟧ ⊠ ⟦&M⟧ 💻 ⟦†⟧ ➿ ⊠

◢◢◢ ▼▼▼ ▼▼▼ W French Quarter ⬛
(504) 581-1200. **$469, 3 day notice.** 316 Chartres St. Between Conti and Bienville sts. Int corridors. **Pets:** Accepted.

⟦SAVE⟧ ⟦S🐾⟧ ⊠ ⟦†⟧ ➿

◢◢◢ ▼▼▼ ▼▼▼ Windsor Court Hotel ⬛
(504) 523-6000. **$199-$600.** 300 Gravier St. Between Magazine and Tchoupitoulas sts. Int corridors. **Pets:** Small. $250 one-time fee/pet. Designated rooms, service with restrictions, supervision.

⟦SAVE⟧ ⊠ 🖥 💻 ⟦†⟧ ➿ ⊠

◢◢◢ ▼▼▼ ▼▼▼ W New Orleans ⬛
(504) 525-9444. **$469, 3 day notice.** 333 Poydras St. Close to Riverfront area/convention center; jct Poydras and S Peters sts. Int corridors. **Pets:** Accepted.

⟦SAVE⟧ ⟦S🐾⟧ ⊠ ⟦&M⟧ ⟦†⟧ ➿

SLIDELL

◢◢◢ ▼▼▼▼ La Quinta Inn New Orleans/Slidell ⬛
(985) 643-9770. **$115-$125.** 794 E I-10 Service Rd. I-10, exit 266 (Gause Blvd), just se. Ext corridors. **Pets:** Other species. Service with restrictions, supervision.

⟦SAVE⟧ ⊠ 🖥 💻 ➿

END METROPOLITAN AREA

PONCHATOULA

▼▼ Microtel Inn & Suites ⬛
(985) 370-7378. **$79-$109.** 727 W Pine St. I-55, exit 26, just e on SR 22. Int corridors. **Pets:** Accepted.

⟦ASK⟧ ⊠ ⟦&M⟧ 🖥 💻 ➿

PORT ALLEN

◢◢◢ ▼▼▼ Best Western Magnolia Manor ⬛
(225) 344-3638. **$75-$85.** 234 Lobdell Hwy. I-10, exit 151, just n. Int corridors. **Pets:** Accepted.

⟦SAVE⟧ ⊠ 🖥 💻 ➿

RUSTON

▼▼ Howard Johnson ⬛ ❀
(318) 255-5901. **$79.** 401 N Service Rd. I-20, exit 85, just ne. Ext corridors. **Pets:** Other species. $10 one-time fee/room. Service with restrictions, crate.

⊠ 🖥 💻 ⟦†⟧ ➿

ST. FRANCISVILLE

◢◢◢ ▼▼▼ Best Western St. Francis Hotel on the
Lake ⬛
(225) 635-3821. **$79-$109.** US Hwy 61 at Louisiana Hwy 10. Just s of jct US 61 and SR 10. Ext corridors. **Pets:** Accepted.

⟦SAVE⟧ ⟦S🐾⟧ ⊠ 🖥 💻 ➿

Lake Rosemound Inn Bed & Breakfast **BB**
(225) 635-3176. **$80-$135, 3 day notice.** 10473 Lindsey Ln. 13 mi n on SR 61, then 3 mi w using Rosemound Loop, Sligo Rd, Lake Rosemound Rd and Lindsey Ln, follow signs. Ext/int corridors. **Pets:** Accepted.
⊠ ⊠

SCOTT

▼▼ **Howard Johnson** **SH**
(337) 593-0849. **$70-$80.** 103 Harold Gauthe Dr. I-10, exit 97. Int corridors. **Pets:** Medium. $15 deposit/room. Designated rooms, service with restrictions, supervision.
ASK S⊘ ⊠ 🛏 ▯ ⊅

SHREVEPORT

⊕⌁ ▼▼▼ **Best Western Richmond Suites Hotel** **SH**
(318) 635-6431. **$129, 21 day notice.** 5101 Monkhouse Dr. I-20, exit 13 (Monkhouse Rd), just s. Int corridors. **Pets:** Accepted.
SAVE S⊘ ⊠ 🛏 ▯ ⊅ ⊠

⊕⌁ ▼▼▼ **Clarion Hotel Shreveport** **LH**
(318) 797-9900. **$99-$149.** 1419 E 70th St. I-20, exit 19A (SR 1 S), 6 mi s to E 70th St, then 0.4 mi w. Int corridors. **Pets:** Accepted.
ASK S⊘ ⊠ 🛏 ▯ ▯▯ ⊅

▼▼▼ **Holiday Inn Downtown** **LH**
(318) 222-7717. **$99-$124.** 102 Lake St. I-20, exit 19A (Spring St), just n. Int corridors. **Pets:** Accepted.
ASK S⊘ ⊠ ⊾M 🛏 ▯ ▯▯ ⊅

▼▼▼ **Holiday Inn Financial Plaza** **LH**
(318) 688-3000. **$99-$159.** 5555 Financial Plaza. I-20, exit 10 (Pines Rd), 1 mi e on frontage road. Int corridors. **Pets:** Accepted.
ASK S⊘ ⊠ 🛏 ▯ ▯▯ ⊅ ⊠

⊕⌁ ▼▼▼ **La Quinta Inn & Suites Shreveport** **SH**
(318) 671-1100. **$114-$136.** 6700 Financial Cir. I-20, exit 10 (Pines Rd), 0.5 mi e on frontage road. Int corridors. **Pets:** Other species. Service with restrictions, supervision.
SAVE ⊠ ⊾M 🛏 ▯ ⊅

▼▼▼ **Residence Inn by Marriott** **SH**
(318) 635-8000. **Call for rates.** 4910 W Monkhouse. I-20, exit 13, just nw. Int corridors. **Pets:** Accepted.
⊠ ⊾M 🛏 ▯ ⊅ ⊠

SPRINGFIELD

▼▼▼▼ **The Villas at Carter Plantation** **SH**
(225) 294-7555. **Call for rates.** 23475 Carter Trace. I-12, exit 32, 2.7 mi s on SR 43, 1.1 mi e on SR 42, then 1.5 mi s on Carter Cemetery Rd. Ext corridors. **Pets:** Accepted.
⊠ 🛏 ▯ ▯▯ ⊅

SULPHUR

▼▼▼ **Wingate Inn** **SH**
(337) 527-5151. **$109.** 300 Arena Rd. I-10, exit 20 (SR 27), just s, then just w. Int corridors. **Pets:** Accepted.
ASK S⊘ ⊠ 🛏 ▯ ⊅

VILLE PLATTE

⊕⌁ ▼▼ **Best Western Ville Platte** **SH**
(337) 360-9961. **$84-$108.** 1919 E Main St (Hwy 167). Jct SR 1168. Int corridors. **Pets:** Accepted.
ASK ⊠ 🛏 ▯ ⊅

WEST MONROE

▼▼ **Jameson Inn** **SH**
(318) 361-0750. **$85-$105.** 213 Constitution Dr. I-20, exit 114 (Thomas Rd), just s to Constitution Dr, then just w. Int corridors. **Pets:** Small. $15 daily fee/room. Service with restrictions, crate.
ASK S⊘ ⊠ 🛏 ▯ ⊅

▼▼ **Quality Inn & Suites-West Monroe** **SH**
(318) 387-2711. **$70-$115.** 503 Constitution Dr. I-20, exit 114 (Thomas Rd), just s to Constitution Dr, then 0.6 mi w. Int corridors. **Pets:** Accepted.
ASK S⊘ ⊠ ⊾M 🛏 ▯ ▯▯ ⊅

ZACHARY

⊕⌁ ▼▼▼ **Best Western Zachary Inn** **SH**
(225) 658-2550. **$77-$130.** 4030 Hwy 19. Just s of jct SR 64. Int corridors. **Pets:** Other species. $50 one-time fee/room. Service with restrictions, supervision.
SAVE S⊘ ⊠ 🛏 ▯ ⊅

MAINE

AUBURN

▼▼ A Fireside Inn & Suites SH
(207) 777-1777. **$70-$180.** 1777 Washington St. I-95 (Maine Tpke), exit 75, 0.5 mi s on US 202, SR 4 and 100. Ext/int corridors. **Pets:** Medium, dogs only. $10 daily fee/pet. Designated rooms, service with restrictions, supervision.

▼ Sleepy Time Motel M
(207) 783-1435. **$72-$95.** 46 Danville Corner Rd. I-95 (Maine Tpke), exit 75, 0.5 mi ne on US 202, just e. Ext corridors. **Pets:** Accepted.

AUGUSTA

◆▼▼ Best Western Senator Inn & Spa SH
(207) 622-5804. **$89-$279.** 284 Western Ave. I-95, exit 109 (Augusta-Winthrop) northbound; exit 109A southbound, on US 202, SR 11 and 100. Ext/int corridors. **Pets:** Small. $50 deposit/room, $9 one-time fee/room. Designated rooms, service with restrictions, supervision.

▼▼▼ Comfort Inn SH
(207) 623-1000. **$99-$199, 3 day notice.** 281 Civic Center Dr. I-95, exit 112B northbound; exit 112 southbound. Int corridors. **Pets:** Accepted.

▼▼▼ Holiday Inn SH
(207) 622-4751. **$95-$199, 3 day notice.** 110 Community Dr. I-95, exit 112A northbound; exit 112 southbound, just s on SR 8, 11 and 27. Int corridors. **Pets:** Accepted.

BANGOR

▼▼▼ Best Western White House SH ❖
(207) 862-3737. **$100-$150.** 155 Littlefield Ave. I-95, exit 180 (Coldbrook Rd), 5.5 mi s of downtown. Ext/int corridors. **Pets:** Large. $100 deposit/room. Designated rooms, service with restrictions, supervision.

▼▼ Econo Lodge M ❖
(207) 945-0111. **$79-$129.** 327 Odlin Rd. I-95, exit 182B, just e on US 2 and SR 100. Int corridors. **Pets:** Other species. $10 one-time fee/pet. Service with restrictions, supervision.

▼▼ Fireside Inn and Suites SH
(207) 942-1234. **$79-$159.** 570 Main St. I-395, exit 3B. Int corridors. **Pets:** Other species. Service with restrictions, supervision.

▼▼▼ Four Points by Sheraton Bangor SH
(207) 947-6721. **$140-$190.** 308 Godfrey Blvd. At Bangor International Airport. Int corridors. **Pets:** Medium. $20 one-time fee/room. Service with restrictions, supervision.

▼▼ Holiday Inn-Bangor SH
(207) 947-0101. **$129-$179.** 404 Odlin Rd. I-95, exit 182B, jct Odlin Rd and I-395. Int corridors. **Pets:** Accepted.

◆▼ ▼▼ Howard Johnson Inn SH
(207) 942-5251. **Call for rates.** 336 Odlin Rd. I-95, exit 182B, jct Odlin Rd and I-395. Int corridors. **Pets:** Accepted.

▼▼ Ramada SH
(207) 947-6961. **Call for rates.** 357 Odlin Rd. I-95, exit 182B, jct Odlin Rd and I-395. Int corridors. **Pets:** Accepted.

▼▼ Riverside Inn SH
(207) 973-4100. **Call for rates.** 495 State St. Adjacent to Eastern Maine Medical Center. Int corridors. **Pets:** Accepted.

BAR HARBOR

◆▼ ▼ Anchorage Motel M
(207) 288-3959. **$59-$129, 4 day notice.** 51 Mt Desert St. In town on SR 3. Ext corridors. **Pets:** Accepted.

◆▼ ▼▼▼ Atlantic Oakes By-The-Sea SH ❖
(207) 288-5801. **$78-$207, 14 day notice.** 119 Eden St. 1.8 mi w on SR 3. Ext/int corridors. **Pets:** Large, other species. $35 one-time fee/room. Service with restrictions, supervision.

▼▼ A Wonder View Inn & Suites SH
(207) 288-3358. **$49-$220, 3 day notice.** 50 Eden St. 0.5 mi w on SR 3. Ext corridors. **Pets:** Medium. $10 daily fee/pet. Service with restrictions, supervision.

◆▼ ▼▼▼ Balance Rock Inn 1903 BB
(207) 288-2610. **$155-$625, 14 day notice.** 21 Albert Meadow. S on Main St, just e; center. Ext/int corridors. **Pets:** Accepted.

◆▼ ▼▼ Best Western Inn SH
(207) 288-5823. **$85-$155.** 452 State Hwy 3. 4.8 mi w. Ext corridors. **Pets:** Medium, dogs only. $10 daily fee/room. Designated rooms, service with restrictions, supervision.

◆▼ ▼▼ Days Inn M
(207) 288-3321. **Call for rates.** 120 Eden St. 1 mi w on SR 3. Ext corridors. **Pets:** Accepted.

▼ Hutchins Mountain View Cottages CA
(207) 288-4833. **$62-$98, 14 day notice.** 286 State Rt 3. 4 mi w. Ext corridors. **Pets:** Other species. Service with restrictions.

BATH

The Galen C Moses House BB
(207) 442-8771. **$109-$189, 7 day notice.** 1009 Washington St. US 1, exit historic district. 0.5 mi n; downtown. Ext/int corridors. **Pets:** Dogs only. $15 daily fee/pet. Designated rooms, service with restrictions, supervision.

SAVE ⊠ 🖾 🖉

Holiday Inn Bath/Brunswick SH
(207) 443-9741. **Call for rates.** 139 Richardson St. 0.3 mi s on US 1. Int corridors. **Pets:** Accepted.

SAVE ⊠ 🖾 🖽 🖵 🍽 🐾 ⊠

BELFAST

Belfast Harbor Inn SH ❀
(207) 338-2740. **$59-$149.** 91 Searsport Ave (Rt 1). On US 1, 1.2 mi n from jct SR 3. Ext/int corridors. **Pets:** Dogs only. $10 daily fee/pet. Designated rooms, service with restrictions, supervision.

ASK 🖾 ⊠ 🐾

Comfort Inn Ocean's Edge SH ❀
(207) 338-2090. **$79-$389.** 159 Searsport Ave. On US 1, 2 mi n from jct SR 3. Int corridors. **Pets:** $10 daily fee/pet. Designated rooms, service with restrictions, supervision.

ASK 🖾 ⊠ 🖾 🖽 🖵 🍽 🐾 ⊠

Gull Motel M
(207) 338-4030. **$59-$99, 3 day notice.** 196 Searsport Ave. On US 1, 3 mi n from jct SR 3. Ext corridors. **Pets:** Small. Designated rooms, service with restrictions, supervision.

ASK 🖾 ⊠ 🖽

BETHEL

Briar Lea Inn & The Jolly Drayman English Pub CI
(207) 824-4717. **$89-$159, 14 day notice.** 150 Mayville Rd (US 2). 1 mi n of jct US 2, SR 5 and 26. Int corridors. **Pets:** Dogs only. $10 daily fee/pet. Service with restrictions, supervision.

ASK ⊠ 🍽

The Inn At the Rostay M
(207) 824-3111. **$65-$130, 14 day notice.** 186 Mayville Rd (US 2). On US 2, 2 mi e. Ext corridors. **Pets:** Other species. $10 one-time fee/pet. Designated rooms, service with restrictions, supervision.

ASK 🖾 ⊠ 🖽 🍽 🐾

L'Auberge Country Inn & Bistro CI
(207) 824-2774. **Call for rates.** 15 L Ln. Center. Int corridors. **Pets:** Accepted.

SAVE ⊠ 🍽 🖾 🖉

BOOTHBAY

The 1828 Vintage House and Cottages M ❀
(207) 633-3411. **$79-$219, 30 day notice.** 301 Adams Pond Rd. US 1, 9 mi s on SR 27, then just w. Ext/int corridors. **Pets:** Other species. $10 daily fee/pet. Designated rooms, service with restrictions, crate.

⊠ 🖽 🖵 🐾 🖉

White Anchor Inn M
(207) 633-3788. **$59-$89.** 609 Wiscasset Rd. US 1 to SR 27, 7.5 mi s. Ext/int corridors. **Pets:** Other species. $14 one-time fee/room. Designated rooms, service with restrictions, supervision.

SAVE ⊠ 🖽

BOOTHBAY HARBOR

Welch House Inn BB
(207) 633-3431. **$95-$225, 14 day notice.** 56 McKown St. Center. Ext/int corridors. **Pets:** Accepted.

SAVE ⊠

BRIDGTON

Pleasant Mountain Inn M ❀
(207) 647-4505. **$70-$200, 7 day notice.** 656 N High St. On US 302, 3 mi w of center. Ext corridors. **Pets:** Dogs only. $10 daily fee. Service with restrictions, crate.

ASK 🖾 ⊠ 🖽 🖵 🍽

BRUNSWICK

Viking Motor Inn M
(207) 729-6661. **Call for rates.** 287 Bath Rd. US 1, exit Cooks Corner, left on Bath Rd, then 1 mi w. Ext/int corridors. **Pets:** Accepted.

SAVE ⊠ 🖽 🖵

BRYANT POND

Mollyockett Motel & Swim Spa M
(207) 674-2345. **$70-$95.** 1132 S Main St. 1.3 mi n on SR 26 from jct SR 219. Ext/int corridors. **Pets:** Dogs only. Service with restrictions, supervision.

ASK 🖾 ⊠ 🖽 🖵 🐾 ⊠

BUCKSPORT

Bucksport Motor Inn M
(207) 469-3111. **$59-$109.** 70 Main St. On US 1; center. Ext corridors. **Pets:** $15 one-time fee/room. Designated rooms, service with restrictions, supervision.

ASK 🖾 ⊠ 🖽 🖵

CAMDEN

Blackberry Inn at Blackberry Common BB
(207) 236-6060. **$99-$275, 14 day notice.** 82 Elm St. Center. Ext/int corridors. **Pets:** Small, dogs only. $30 one-time fee/pet. Designated rooms, service with restrictions, supervision.

⊠ 🖽 🖵 🖉

The Camden Riverhouse Hotel & Inns SH ❀
(207) 236-0500. **$99-$250.** 11 Tannery Ln. Center. Int corridors. **Pets:** Dogs only. $10 daily fee/pet. Designated rooms, service with restrictions, supervision.

ASK 🖾 ⊠ 🖽 🖵 🐾

Elms Bed & Breakfast at Blackberry Common BB
(207) 236-6060. **$149-$229, 14 day notice.** 84 Elm St. Center. Ext/int corridors. **Pets:** Accepted.

⊠

Lord Camden Inn BB ❀
(207) 236-4325. **$99-$289, 4 day notice.** 24 Main St. Center. Int corridors. **Pets:** Dogs only. $20 daily fee/pet. Supervision.

SAVE 🖾 ⊠ 🖵

CARIBOU

Caribou Inn & Convention Center SH
(207) 498-3733. **$98-$146.** 19 Main St. 3 mi s on US 1. Int corridors. **Pets:** Other species.

SAVE ⊠ 🖽 🖵 🍽 🐾 ⊠

CASTINE

Pentagoet Inn CI
(207) 326-8616. **$95-$245, 14 day notice.** 26 Main St. Center. Int corridors. **Pets:** Accepted.

ASK 🖾 ⊠ 🍽 🎔 🖾 🖉

DEDHAM

The Lucerne Inn CI
(207) 843-5123. **$59-$199.** 2517 Main Rd. On US 1A. Int corridors. **Pets:** Accepted.

SAVE 🖾 ⊠ 🖽 🖵 🍽 🐾

EAGLE LAKE

▼▼▼ **Overlook Motel & Lakeside Cabins** [M]
(207) 444-4535. **$67.** 3232 Aroostook Rd. On SR 11; center. Ext/int corridors. **Pets:** $5 daily fee/pet. Service with restrictions, supervision.

⊠ 🛢 💻 🔀

EAST BOOTHBAY

▼▼▼ **Smuggler's Cove Inn** [SH]
(207) 633-2800. **$70-$220, 14 day notice.** 727 Ocean Point Rd. Jct SR 27, 4.5 mi e on SR 96. Ext corridors. **Pets:** $25 one-time fee/room. Designated rooms, service with restrictions, supervision.

[ASK] ⊠ 🛢 💻 🔀

EDGECOMB

▼▼▼ **Sheepscot Harbour Village & Resort** [SH]
(207) 882-6343. **$79-$349, 7 day notice.** 306 Eddy Rd. 1 mi w on US 1; on east side of Davies Bridge, 1 mi e of Wiscasset. Ext/int corridors. **Pets:** Accepted.

[ASK] [S🕹] ⊠ 🛢 💻 🔀

ELLSWORTH

▼ **The Colonial Inn** [SH]
(207) 667-5548. **$78-$159.** 321 High St. 1.3 mi e on SR 3. Ext/int corridors. **Pets:** Accepted.

⊠ 🛢 💻 🔀

▼▼▼ **Holiday Inn** [SH]
(207) 667-9341. **Call for rates.** 215 High St. Jct US 1, 1A and SR 3. Int corridors. **Pets:** Accepted.

⊠ [&M] 🛢 💻 🔀 🔀 🔀

◆◆◆◇ ▼▼▼ **Twilite Motel** [M] 🐾
(207) 667-8165. **$59-$112.** 147 Bucksport Rd. Jct US 1A, 1.5 mi w on US 1/SR 3. Ext corridors. **Pets:** Medium, dogs only. $10 daily fee/room. Designated rooms, service with restrictions, supervision.

[SAVE] [S🕹] ⊠ 🛢 💻

FREEPORT

◆◆◆◇ ▼▼▼ **Best Western Freeport Inn** [SH] 🐾
(207) 865-3106. **$89-$179.** 31 US 1 S. I-295, exit 17, 1 mi n. Ext/int corridors. **Pets:** Other species. Designated rooms, service with restrictions.

[SAVE] [S🕹] ⊠ 🛢 💻 🔀 🔀

▼▼▼ **Captain Briggs House B & B** [BB]
(207) 865-1868. **$95-$225.** 8 Maple Ave. Just n of downtown, then just w. Int corridors. **Pets:** Dogs only.

[ASK] [S🕹] ⊠ 🔀

▼▼ **Econo Lodge** [M]
(207) 865-3777. **$59-$169.** 537 US Rt 1. I-295, exit 20, 0.3 mi s. Ext corridors. **Pets:** Medium, other species. $10 daily fee/pet. Designated rooms.

[ASK] [S🕹] ⊠

▼▼▼ **White Cedar Inn** [BB] 🐾
(207) 865-9099. **$120-$230, 7 day notice.** 178 Main St. I-295, exit 22, 0.5 mi e, just n on US 1. Ext/int corridors. **Pets:** Dogs only. $25 one-time fee/room. Designated rooms, service with restrictions, supervision.

[ASK] ⊠ 🔀

GREENVILLE

▼▼▼ **Chalet Moosehead Lakefront Motel** [M]
(207) 695-2950. **$71-$140, 7 day notice.** 12 N Birch St. 1.5 mi w on SR 15. Ext corridors. **Pets:** Accepted.

⊠ 🛢 💻 🔀

◆◆◆◇ ▼▼▼ **Kineo View Motor Lodge** [M]
(207) 695-4470. **$69-$199.** 50 Overlook Dr. 2.5 mi s on SR 15; gravel access road from highway. Ext corridors. **Pets:** Other species. $10 daily fee/room. Designated rooms, service with restrictions, supervision.

[SAVE] ⊠ 🛢 💻

HANCOCK

▼▼▼▼ **Le Domaine Inn** [CI]
(207) 422-3395. **Call for rates.** US Rt 1, #1513. On US 1, 9 mi e of Ellsworth; center. Ext corridors. **Pets:** Accepted.

⊠ 🍽 🅆

HOULTON

◆◆◆◇ ▼▼▼ **Shiretown Inn & Suites** [SH]
(207) 532-9421. **$79-$130.** 282 North St. I-95, exit 302, 0.3 mi n on US 1. Ext/int corridors. **Pets:** Accepted.

[SAVE] [S🕹] ⊠ 🛢 💻 🍽 🔀

KENNEBUNK

◆◆◆◇ ▼▼▼ **Turnpike Motel** [M]
(207) 985-4404. **$49-$125, 3 day notice.** 77 Old Alewive Rd. I-95 (Maine Tpke), exit 25, just e on SR 35, then just n. Ext/int corridors. **Pets:** Accepted.

[SAVE] [S🕹] ⊠ 🛢 💻

KENNEBUNKPORT

◆◆◆◇ ▼▼▼ **The Captain Jefferds Inn** [BB]
(207) 967-2311. **$125-$360, 14 day notice.** 5 Pearl St. From Dock Square, 0.3 mi s on Ocean Ave, just ne; corner of Pearl and Pleasant sts. Ext/int corridors. **Pets:** Accepted.

[SAVE] ⊠ 🛢

◆◆◆◇ ▼▼▼ **The Colony Hotel** [SH] 🐾
(207) 967-3331. **$199-$500, 7 day notice.** 140 Ocean Ave. From Dock Square, 1 mi s. Int corridors. **Pets:** Other species. $25 daily fee/pet. Supervision.

[SAVE] [S🕹] ⊠ 🛢 🍽 🔀

◆◆◆◇ ▼▼▼▼ **Lodge At Turbat's Creek** [M]
(207) 967-8700. **$79-$199, 14 day notice.** 7 Turbat Rd. From Dock Square, 0.5 mi se on Maine St, 0.6 mi ne on Wildes, then just se. Ext corridors. **Pets:** Accepted.

[SAVE] [S🕹] ⊠ [&M] 🛢 🔀

◆◆◆◇ ▼▼▼▼ **The Yachtsman Lodge & Marina** [M]
(207) 967-2511. **$125-$400, 30 day notice.** 57 Ocean Ave. From Dock Square, just s. Ext corridors. **Pets:** Accepted.

[SAVE] ⊠ 🛢 💻 🔀

LINCOLNVILLE

▼▼▼ **Abbingtons Seaview Motel & Cottages** [M] 🐾
(207) 236-3471. **$59-$139, 5 day notice.** 4 Seaview Dr. On US 1, 1.2 mi s of jct SR 173. Ext corridors. **Pets:** Other species. $15 daily fee/pet. Designated rooms, service with restrictions, supervision.

[ASK] [S🕹] ⊠ 🛢 💻 🔀

▼▼▼ **Pine Grove Cottages** [CA]
(207) 236-2929. **$80-$185, 7 day notice.** 2076 Atlantic Hwy. On US 1, 2 mi s of jct SR 173. Ext corridors. **Pets:** Medium, other species. Service with restrictions, crate.

⊠ 🛢 💻

LUBEC

▼ **The Eastland Motel** [M]
(207) 733-5501. **$56-$76.** 395 County Rd. Jct US 1 and SR 189, 8.4 mi e on SR 189. Ext/int corridors. **Pets:** Medium, dogs only. $10 daily fee/pet. Designated rooms, service with restrictions, supervision.

⊠ 🛢

MACHIAS

◆◆◆◇ ▼▼ **The Bluebird Motel** [M]
(207) 255-3332. **$65-$80.** Dublin St. On US 1, 1 mi s. Ext corridors. **Pets:** Accepted.

[SAVE] [S🕹] ⊠ [&M] 🛢

◆◆◆ ▼▼▼ **Machias Motor Inn** Ⓜ
(207) 255-4861. **$69-$99.** 26 E Main St. 0.5 mi e on US 1. Ext corridors. **Pets:** Dogs only. $5 daily fee/pet. Designated rooms, supervision.
[SAVE] ⊠ 🛢 💻

MEDWAY

▼▼ **Katahdin Shadows Motel** Ⓜ
(207) 746-5162. **$54, 5 day notice.** 2166 Medway Rd. I-95, exit 244, 1.5 mi w on SR 157. Ext corridors. **Pets:** Large, dogs only. $5 daily fee/pet. Designated rooms, service with restrictions, supervision.
[ASK] ⊠ 🛢 ≈ ⊠

MILFORD

▼▼ **Milford Motel On The River** Ⓜ
(207) 827-3200. **$59-$115, 3 day notice.** 174 Main Rd. 0.5 mi n on US 2. Ext/int corridors. **Pets:** Medium, dogs only. Service with restrictions, supervision.
[ASK] ⊠ 🛢 💻

MILLINOCKET

▼▼ **America's Best Value Heritage Inn** SH
(207) 723-9777. **$79-$109.** 935 Central St. 0.8 mi e on SR 11 and 157. Int corridors. **Pets:** $100 deposit/room, $10 daily fee/pet. Service with restrictions, supervision.
[ASK] S🔊 ⊠ 🛢 💻 ≈

NAPLES

◆◆◆ ▼▼▼ **Augustus Bove House** BB
(207) 693-6365. **$99-$250, 30 day notice.** 11 Sebago Rd. Corner of US 302 and SR 114. Int corridors. **Pets:** Accepted.
[SAVE] S🔊 ⊠ 🛢 💻

OGUNQUIT

▼▼ **Studio East Motor Inn** Ⓜ
(207) 646-7297. **Call for rates.** 267 Main St. On US 1; center. Ext corridors. **Pets:** Accepted.
⊠ 🛢

OLD ORCHARD BEACH

◆◆◆ ▼▼▼ **Alouette Beach Resort** Ⓜ
(207) 934-4151. **$50-$186, 14 day notice.** 91 E Grand Ave. 0.9 mi e on SR 9 (E Grand Ave). Ext/int corridors. **Pets:** Accepted.
[SAVE] ⊠ 🛢 💻 ⏹ ≈

◆◆◆ ▼▼▼ **Beach Walk Ocean Front Inn** SH
(207) 934-2381. **$50-$186, 14 day notice.** 109 E Grand Ave. 1 mi e on SR 9 (E Grand Ave), just e on Morrison St. Ext/int corridors. **Pets:** Accepted.
[SAVE] ⊠ 🛢 💻 ≈

◆◆◆ ▼▼▼ **Grand Beach Inn** SH
(207) 934-4621. **$59-$239, 3 day notice.** 198 E Grand Ave (SR 9). 1.4 mi ne of center. Ext corridors. **Pets:** Accepted.
[SAVE] S🔊 ⊠ 🛢 💻 ⏹ ≈

◆◆◆ ▼▼▼ **Old Colonial Motel** Ⓜ
(207) 934-9862. **$80-$250, 14 day notice.** 61 W Grand Ave. On SR 9 (W Grand Ave), 0.5 mi w. Ext corridors. **Pets:** Accepted.
[SAVE] ⊠ 🛢 💻 ≈ ⊠

◆◆◆ ▼▼▼ **Sea View Motel** SH
(207) 934-4180. **$55-$300, 14 day notice.** 65 W Grand Ave. 0.5 mi w on SR 9 (W Grand Ave). Ext corridors. **Pets:** Accepted.
[SAVE] S🔊 ⊠ 🛢 💻 ≈

ORONO

▼▼▼ **Best Western Black Bear Inn & Conference Center** SH
(207) 866-7120. **$79-$159.** 4 Godfrey Dr. I-95, exit 193 (Stillwater Ave). Int corridors. **Pets:** $5 daily fee/room. Designated rooms, service with restrictions, supervision.
[ASK] S🔊 ⊠ ⚓ 🛢 💻

▼▼ ▼▼ **University Inn Academic Suites** SH
(207) 866-4921. **$62-$99.** 5 College Ave. I-95, exit 191, 1.6 mi n on US 2; 8 mi n of Bangor. Int corridors. **Pets:** Accepted.
⊠ 🛢 💻 ≈

PORTLAND

▼▼▼▼ **Clarion Hotel** LH
(207) 774-5611. **Call for rates.** 1230 Congress St. I-295, exit 5, w on SR 22. Int corridors. **Pets:** Medium. $50 one-time fee/pet. Service with restrictions, supervision.
⊠ ⚓ 🛢 💻 ⏹ ≈

◆◆◆ ▼▼▼▼ **Eastland Park Hotel** LH 🐾
(207) 775-5411. **$79-$229.** 157 High St. At Congress Square; center. Int corridors. **Pets:** Medium. $25 daily fee/room. Service with restrictions, crate.
[SAVE] S🔊 ⊠ 🛢 💻 ⏹ ⊠

◆◆◆ ▼▼▼▼ **Embassy Suites Hotel** LH
(207) 775-2200. **Call for rates.** 1050 Westbrook St. At Portland International Jetport. Int corridors. **Pets:** Medium, dogs only. Designated rooms, service with restrictions, supervision.
[SAVE] ⊠ ⚓ 🛢 💻 ⏹ ≈ ⊠

▼▼▼ **Hilton Garden Inn Portland Downtown Waterfront** SH
(207) 780-0780. **Call for rates.** 65 Commercial St. In the Old Port; across from Casco Bay ferry terminal. Int corridors. **Pets:** Medium. $50 one-time fee/pet. Designated rooms, service with restrictions, supervision.
⊠ ⚓ 🛢 💻 ⏹

◆◆◆ ▼▼▼ **Holiday Inn-West** SH
(207) 774-5601. **$120-$220.** 81 Riverside St. I-95 (Maine Tpke), exit 48. Int corridors. **Pets:** Accepted.
[SAVE] S🔊 ⊠ ⚓ 🛢 💻 ⏹ ≈ ⊠

◆◆◆ ▼▼▼ **Howard Johnson Plaza Hotel** SH
(207) 774-5861. **$80-$225.** 155 Riverside St. I-95 (Maine Tpke), exit 48, jct SR 25. Int corridors. **Pets:** $50 deposit/room. Service with restrictions, supervision.
[SAVE] ⊠ 🛢 💻 ⏹ ≈

▼▼▼ ▼▼▼ **La Quinta Inn & Suites Portland** SH
(207) 871-0611. **$95-$125.** 340 Park Ave. I-295, exit 5A southbound; exit 5 northbound, e on SR 22. Int corridors. **Pets:** Other species. Service with restrictions, supervision.
[ASK] S🔊 ⊠ ⚓ 🛢 💻 ≈

◆◆◆ ▼▼▼ ▼▼▼ **Portland Harbor Hotel** SH
(207) 775-9090. **$179-$379.** 468 Fore St. In the Old Port. Int corridors. **Pets:** Medium. $35 one-time fee/room. Designated rooms, service with restrictions, supervision.
[SAVE] S🔊 ⊠ ⚓ 🛢 ⏹

PRESQUE ISLE

▼▼ **Northern Lights Motel** Ⓜ
(207) 764-4441. **$69-$89, 3 day notice.** 72 Houlton Rd. 2 mi s on US 1. Ext corridors. **Pets:** $10 daily fee/pet. Designated rooms, crate.
⊠ 🛢

◆◆◆ ▼▼▼ **Presque Isle Inn & Convention Center** SH
(207) 764-3321. **$88-$150.** 116 Main St. 1 mi s on US 1. Int corridors. **Pets:** Large, other species. Supervision.
[SAVE] ⊠ 🛢 💻 ⏹ ≈

ROCKLAND

♨️ ▼▼▼ Trade Winds Motor Inn SH
(207) 596-6661. **$59-$199.** 2 Park Dr. On US 1; center. Ext/int corridors. **Pets:** Accepted.

SAVE 🐾 ✕ 🛏 🍽 ➰ 🏊

ROCKPORT

♨️ ▼▼▼ The Country Inn At Camden/Rockport SH
(207) 236-2725. **$94-$209.** 8 Country Inn Way. Jct SR 90, 0.9 mi n on US 1. Ext/int corridors. **Pets:** Accepted.

SAVE 🐾 ✕ 🛏 🍽 ➰ 🏊

♨️ ▼▼ Glen Cove Inn & Suites M
(207) 594-4062. **$79-$209.** 866 Commercial St. Jct SR 90, 3 mi s on US 1. Ext corridors. **Pets:** Accepted.

SAVE 🐾 ✕ 🛏 ➰

RUMFORD

♨️ ▼▼▼ Linnell Motel & RestInn Conference Center SH
(207) 364-4511. **Call for rates.** 986 Prospect Ave. 2 mi w, just off US 2. Ext/int corridors. **Pets:** Accepted.

SAVE ✕ 🛏 🍽

SACO

♨️ ▼▼▼▼ Hampton Inn SH
(207) 282-7222. **$89-$229.** 48 Industrial Park Rd. I-95 (Maine Tpke), exit 36 (I-195), exit 1 (Industrial Park Rd), just ne. Int corridors. **Pets:** Other species. Designated rooms, service with restrictions, supervision.

SAVE 🐾 ✕ 🅼 🛏 🍽 ➰

♨️ ▼▼▼ Holiday Inn Express Hotel & Suites SH 🐾
(207) 286-9600. **$80-$269.** 352 North St (SR 112). I-95 (Maine Tpke), exit 36 (I-195), exit 1 (Industrial Park Rd), 0.6 mi sw to SR 112, then 0.4 mi nw. Int corridors. **Pets:** Designated rooms, service with restrictions, crate.

SAVE ✕ 🅼 🛏 🍽 ➰

♨️ ▼ Saco Motel M
(207) 284-6952. **$50-$90, 3 day notice.** 473 Main St. I-95 (Maine Tpke), exit 36 (I-195), exit 2A (US 1), just sw. Ext corridors. **Pets:** Accepted.

SAVE 🐾 ✕ 🛏 ➰

▼▼ Wagon Wheel Motel M
(207) 284-6387. **$48-$150, 3 day notice.** 726 Portland Rd (US 1). I-95 (Maine Tpke), exit 36 (I-195), 1.5 mi se to US 1, then 0.7 mi ne. Ext corridors. **Pets:** Accepted.

ASK ✕ 🛏 🍽 ➰

SANFORD

▼▼ Super 8 Motel SH
(207) 324-8823. **Call for rates.** 1892 Main St (Rt 109). I-95 (Maine Tpke), exit 19, 7 mi nw. Int corridors. **Pets:** Accepted.

✕ 🛏

SCARBOROUGH

▼▼ Extended StayAmerica Portland-Scarborough SH
(207) 883-0554. **$73-$140.** 2 Ashley Dr. I-95, exit 42, just n. Int corridors. **Pets:** Other species. $75 one-time fee/pet. Service with restrictions.

ASK 🐾 ✕ 🛏 🍽

▼ Pride Motel & Cottages CA
(207) 883-4816. **$55-$190, 7 day notice.** 677 US Rt 1. I-95 (Maine Tpke), exit 36, 0.5 mi e to US 1, then 4.5 mi n. Ext corridors. **Pets:** Other species. $15 daily fee/room. Service with restrictions, supervision.

✕ 🛏 ➰ 🏊

▼▼▼▼ Residence Inn by Marriott SH 🐾
(207) 883-0400. **$186-$230.** 800 Roundwood Dr. I-95 (Maine Tpke), exit 42, 1.5 mi n on Payne Rd. Int corridors. **Pets:** Other species. $75 one-time fee/room. Service with restrictions, crate.

ASK 🐾 ✕ 🅼 🛏 🍽 ➰ 🏊

▼▼▼▼ TownePlace Suites by Marriott SH 🐾
(207) 883-6800. **$164-$219.** 700 Roundwood Dr. I-95 (Maine Tpke), exit 42, 1.5 mi n on Payne Rd. Int corridors. **Pets:** Other species. $75 one-time fee/room. Service with restrictions, crate.

ASK 🐾 ✕ 🅼 🛏 🍽 ➰

SKOWHEGAN

♨️ ▼ Breezy Acres Motel M
(207) 474-2703. **Call for rates.** 315 Waterville Rd. 1.5 mi s on US 201. Ext corridors. **Pets:** Accepted.

SAVE ✕ 🛏 🍽 ➰ 🏊

SOUTHPORT

▼▼ The Lawnmere Inn CI 🐾
(207) 633-2544. **Call for rates.** 65 Hendricks Hill Rd. 2 mi s of Boothbay Harbor on SR 27, just s of bridge to Southport Island. Ext/int corridors. **Pets:** Large. $20 daily fee/pet. Designated rooms, service with restrictions, crate.

✕ 🛏 🍽

♨️ ▼▼ Ocean Gate Resort SH
(207) 633-3321. **$89-$399, 7 day notice.** 70 Ocean Gate Rd. SR 27, 2.5 mi s of Boothbay Harbor, 0.5 mi s of bridge to Southport Island. Ext corridors. **Pets:** Medium. $25 one-time fee/pet. Designated rooms, supervision.

SAVE 🐾 ✕ 🛏 🍽 ➰ 🏊

SOUTH PORTLAND

▼▼▼ Best Western Merry Manor Inn SH
(207) 774-6151. **$100-$170.** 700 Main St. I-95 (Maine Tpke), exit 45, 1.3 mi e to US 1. Ext/int corridors. **Pets:** Dogs only. Designated rooms, service with restrictions, supervision.

ASK 🐾 ✕ 🅼 🛏 🍽 🍴 ➰ 🏊

♨️ ▼▼ Comfort Inn SH
(207) 775-0409. **$79-$199.** 90 Maine Mall Rd. I-95 (Maine Tpke), exit 45, 1 mi n. Int corridors. **Pets:** Other species. $25 one-time fee/room. Service with restrictions, supervision.

SAVE 🐾 ✕ 🅼 🛏 🍽

▼▼▼ Hampton Inn Hotel SH
(207) 773-4400. **Call for rates.** 171 Philbrook Ave. I-95 (Maine Tpke), exit 45, just ne. Int corridors. **Pets:** Accepted.

✕ 🅼 🛏 🍽 ➰ 🏊

♨️ ▼▼▼▼ Holiday Inn Express & Suites SH
(207) 775-3900. **Call for rates.** 303 Sable Oaks Dr. I-95 (Maine Tpke), exit 45, just n on Maine Mall Rd, then just w on Running Hill Rd. Int corridors. **Pets:** Accepted.

SAVE ✕ 🛏 🍽 ➰

▼▼▼ Howard Johnson Hotel SH
(207) 775-5343. **$79-$179.** 675 Main St. I-95 (Maine Tpke), exit 45, 1.3 mi e to US 1. Int corridors. **Pets:** Medium, other species. Designated rooms, service with restrictions, supervision.

ASK ✕ 🛏 🍽 ➰

▼▼▼ Portland Marriott Hotel & Golf Resort LH
(207) 871-8000. **$186-$219.** 200 Sable Oaks Dr. I-95 (Maine Tpke), exit 45, just n on Maine Mall Rd, then just w on Running Hill Rd. Int corridors. **Pets:** Accepted.

ASK 🐾 ✕ 🅼 🛏 🍽 🍴 ➰ 🏊

SPRUCE HEAD

(AAA) ▼▼▼ Craignair Inn CI ❀
(207) 594-7644. **$80-$159, 14 day notice.** 5 Third St. 2.5 mi w on SR 73, 1.5 mi s on Clark Island Rd; 10 mi s of Rockland. Ext/int corridors. **Pets:** $10 daily fee/room. Designated rooms, service with restrictions, supervision.
SAVE ✕ ❍

WATERVILLE

▼▼▼ Holiday Inn SH
(207) 873-0111. **$99-$219.** 375 Main St. I-95, exit 130 (Main St) on SR 104. Int corridors. **Pets:** Other species. Service with restrictions, supervision.
ASK ✕ ❒ ▣ ❍ ⇌ ✕

WELLS

(AAA) ▼▼▼ Ne'r Beach Motel M
(207) 646-2636. **$49-$219, 14 day notice.** 395 Post Rd (Rt 1). I-95 (Maine Tpke), exit 19, jct SR 109/US 1, 2.7 mi s. Ext corridors. **Pets:** Accepted.
SAVE S❍ ✕ ❒ ▣ ⇌ ✕

WEST FORKS

(AAA) ▼▼ Inn by the River CI
(207) 663-2181. **$85-$250, 30 day notice.** 2777 US Rt 201. Center. Int corridors. **Pets:** Accepted.
SAVE ✕ ▣ ❍ ✕ 🅦 ⧖

WESTPORT

▼▼▼ The Squire Tarbox Inn CI
(207) 882-7693. **$110-$198, 14 day notice.** 1181 Main Rd. Jct US 1 and SR 144; in Wiscasset; 8.5 mi s on SR 144, follow signs. Ext/int corridors. **Pets:** Accepted.
✕ ❍ ✕ 🅦 ⧖

YARMOUTH

(AAA) ▼▼ Down-East Village Motel M
(207) 846-5161. **$75-$125.** 705 US Rt 1. I-295, exit 15 northbound; exit 17 southbound. Ext corridors. **Pets:** Accepted.
SAVE S❍ ✕ ❒ ▣ ❍ ⇌

MARYLAND

BALTIMORE METROPOLITAN AREA

ABERDEEN

Clarion Aberdeen SH
(410) 273-6300. **$89-$119.** 980 Hospitality Way. I-95, exit 85, just e on SR 22. Int corridors. **Pets:** Other species. Service with restrictions, supervision.

La Quinta Inn Aberdeen SH
(410) 272-6000. **$100-$130.** 793 W Bel Air Ave. I-95, exit 85, just e. Int corridors. **Pets:** Other species. Service with restrictions, supervision.

Red Roof Inn M
(410) 273-7800. **Call for rates.** 988 Hospitality Way. I-95, exit 85, just e on SR 22. Ext corridors. **Pets:** Accepted.

Super 8 Motel Aberdeen SH
(410) 272-5420. **Call for rates.** 1008 Beards Hill Rd. I-95, exit 85, just e on SR 22. Int corridors. **Pets:** Accepted.

ANNAPOLIS

DoubleTree Hotel Annapolis SH
(410) 224-3150. **Call for rates.** 210 Holiday Ct. 2.3 mi sw on US 50 and 301, exit 22 to Riva Rd, 0.3 mi n. Int corridors. **Pets:** Accepted.

Extended StayAmerica-Annapolis/Naval Academy SH
(410) 571-9988. **$95-$144.** 1 Womack Dr. 2.3 mi sw on US 50 and 301, exit 22, just s on Admiral Cochrane Dr, then just n on Spruill Rd. Int corridors. **Pets:** Other species. $75 one-time fee/pet. Service with restrictions.

Historic Inns of Annapolis SH
(410) 263-2641. **$139-$259.** 58 State Circle. Facing the State Capitol; in historic district. Int corridors. **Pets:** Accepted.

Homestead Studio Suites Hotel-Annapolis SH
(410) 571-6600. **$100-$154.** 120 Admiral Cochrane Dr. 2.3 mi sw on US 50 and 301, exit 22, just s, then just e. Int corridors. **Pets:** Other species. $75 one-time fee/pet. Service with restrictions.

Loews Annapolis Hotel LH ❀
(410) 263-7777. **$143-$323.** 126 West St. US 50 and 301, exit 24 eastbound; exit 24A westbound, 1.4 mi s on SR 70, just sw on Calvert St, then just w. Int corridors. **Pets:** Other species. Service with restrictions.

Residence Inn by Marriott-Annapolis SH
(410) 573-0300. **$176-$207.** 170 Admiral Cochrane Dr. 2.3 mi sw on US 50 and 301, exit 22 to Riva Rd, just s on Riva Rd, then just e. Ext corridors. **Pets:** Accepted.

Sheraton Annapolis Hotel LH ❀
(410) 266-3131. **$369.** 173 Jennifer Rd. North side of US 50 and 301, exit 23B westbound; exit 23 eastbound. Int corridors. **Pets:** Medium, dogs only. Designated rooms, service with restrictions, crate.

ANNAPOLIS JUNCTION

TownePlace Suites by Marriott-Baltimore/Ft. Meade SH
(301) 498-7477. **$158-$193.** 120 National Business Pkwy. I-95, exit 38A, 2.5 mi e on SR 32 to exit 11 (Dorsey Run Rd), then 1.3 mi e. Int corridors. **Pets:** Accepted.

BALTIMORE

Admiral Fell Inn SH
(410) 522-7377. **$149-$269.** 888 S Broadway St. Corner of Broadway and Thames sts; facing the waterfront. Int corridors. **Pets:** Accepted.

Baltimore's Tremont Park Hotel SH
(410) 576-1200. **Call for rates.** 8 E Pleasant St. Just s of US 40 E, off Charles St. Int corridors. **Pets:** Accepted.

Brookshire Suites SH ❀
(410) 625-1300. **$129-$249.** 120 E Lombard St. Corner of Calvert and Lombard sts. Int corridors. **Pets:** Other species. $49 one-time fee/room. Service with restrictions, supervision.

Hampton Inn & Suites Baltimore Inner Harbor SH 🐾
(410) 539-7888. **Call for rates.** 131 E Redwood St. Between Lombard and Baltimore sts; corner of Calvert and E Redwood sts. Int corridors. **Pets:** Medium. Service with restrictions, supervision.

Pier 5 Hotel SH
(410) 539-2000. **$179-$299.** 711 Eastern Ave. On the Inner Harbor, at Pier 5. Int corridors. **Pets:** Accepted.

▼▼▼ **Residence Inn by Marriott-Baltimore Downtown/Inner Harbor** SH ❀
(410) 962-1220. **$198-$273.** 17 Light St. Between Mercer and E Redwood sts. Int corridors. **Pets:** Medium. $100 one-time fee/room. Service with restrictions.
(ASK) (S🐾) ⊠ (&M) 🖥 🖥 🖥

▼▼▼▼ **Sheraton Baltimore City Center Hotel** LH
(410) 752-1100. **$380.** 101 W Fayette St. Between Charles and Liberty sts. Int corridors. **Pets:** Accepted.
(ASK) (S🐾) ⊠ 🖥 🖥 🖥 ¶ ⇄

BELCAMP

▼▼ **Extended StayAmerica-Bel Air** SH
(410) 273-0194. **$114-$124.** 1361 James Way. I-95, exit 80 (SR 543), just ne. Int corridors. **Pets:** Other species. $75 one-time fee/pet. Service with restrictions.
(ASK) (S🐾) ⊠ (&M) 🖥 🖥 🖥

COLUMBIA

▼▼ **Extended StayAmerica-Columbia 100 Parkway** SH
(410) 772-8800. **$119-$129.** 8870 Columbia 100 Pkwy. I-95, exit 43B, 4 mi w on SR 100, exit 1B, then just e. Int corridors. **Pets:** Other species. $75 one-time fee/pet. Service with restrictions.
(ASK) (S🐾) ⊠ (&M) 🖥 🖥 🖥

▼▼ **Extended Stay Deluxe Columbia Corporate Park** SH
(410) 872-2994. **$129-$139.** 8890 Stanford Blvd. I-95, exit 41B, 1.3 mi w on SR 175 (Little Patuxent Pkwy), 0.5 mi s on Snowden River Pkwy, just w on McGaw Rd, then 0.3 mi nw. Int corridors. **Pets:** Other species. $75 one-time fee/pet. Service with restrictions.
(ASK) (S🐾) ⊠ 🖥 🖥 🖥

▼▼ **Homewood Suites by Hilton Columbia** SH
(410) 872-9200. **Call for rates.** 8320 Benson Dr. I-95, exit 41B, 0.5 mi w on SR 175 (Little Patuxent Pkwy), just nw on SR 108, then just w on Lark Brown Rd. Int corridors. **Pets:** Other species. $75 one-time fee/room. Service with restrictions.
⊠ (&M) 🖥 🖥 🖥 ⇄ 🔀

▼▼ **Sheraton Columbia Hotel** LH ❀
(410) 730-3900. **$279-$314.** 10207 Wincopin Cir. 1.2 mi w on SR 175 (Little Patuxent Pkwy) from jct US 29, then just s; center. Int corridors. **Pets:** Medium, dogs only. Designated rooms, service with restrictions, supervision.
(ASK) ⊠ 🖥 🖥 🖥 ¶ ⇄

▼▼▼ **Staybridge Suites Baltimore-Columbia** SH
(410) 964-9494. **$205-$226.** 8844 Columbia 100 Pkwy. I-95, exit 43B, 4 mi w on SR 100, exit 1B, then just e. Int corridors. **Pets:** Medium. $75 one-time fee/room. Service with restrictions, supervision.
(ASK) ⊠ (&M) 🖥 🖥 🖥 ⇄

▼▼ **StudioPLUS Columbia Gateway Drive** SH
(410) 312-1557. **$124-$134.** 6620 Eli Whitney Dr. I-95, exit 41, 1 mi w on SR 175, then just se on Columbia Gateway Dr. Int corridors. **Pets:** Other species. $75 one-time fee/pet. Service with restrictions.
(ASK) (S🐾) ⊠ 🖥 🖥

EDGEWOOD

AAA ▼▼ **Best Western Invitation Inn** M
(410) 679-9700. **$69-$119.** 1709 Edgewood Rd. I-95, exit 77A, just e on SR 24. Ext corridors. **Pets:** Other species. $15 daily fee/room. Service with restrictions, crate.
(SAVE) (S🐾) ⊠ 🖥 🖥 🖥 ⇄

ELLICOTT CITY

▼▼▼ **Residence Inn by Marriott Columbia** SH
(410) 997-7200. **$231-$252.** 4950 Beaver Run Way. I-95, exit 43B, 4 mi w on SR 100, exit 1B (Executive Park Dr). Int corridors. **Pets:** Accepted.
(ASK) (S🐾) ⊠ (&M) 🖥 🖥 🖥 ⇄ 🔀

ESSEX

▼ **Super 8 Motel Baltimore/Essex** SH
(410) 780-0030. **Call for rates.** 98 Stemmers Run Rd. I-695, exit 36 (SR 702 S) to SR 150 E (Chase exit). Int corridors. **Pets:** Small. $11 daily fee/pet. Service with restrictions, supervision.
⊠ 🖥

GLEN BURNIE

AAA ▼▼▼ **Days Inn-Glen Burnie** SH
(410) 761-8300. **Call for rates.** 6600 Ritchie Hwy. I-695, exit 3B eastbound; exit 2 westbound, 0.5 mi s on SR 2. Ext corridors. **Pets:** Small. $25 daily fee/pet. Designated rooms, service with restrictions, supervision.
(SAVE) ⊠ 🖥 🖥 🖥 ⇄

▼▼ **Extended StayAmerica Baltimore-Glen Burnie** SH
(410) 761-2708. **$129-$139.** 104 Chesapeake Centre Ct. I-695, exit 3B, 0.9 mi s on SR 2, just e on E Ordance Rd, then just s. Int corridors. **Pets:** Other species. $75 one-time fee/pet. Service with restrictions.
(ASK) (S🐾) ⊠ (&M) 🖥 🖥 🖥

HANOVER

▼▼ **Red Roof Inn-BWI Parkway** M
(410) 712-4070. **Call for rates.** 7306 Parkway Dr S. I-95, exit 43A, 2 mi e on SR 100, exit 8 (Coca-Cola Dr), then 0.5 mi se. Ext corridors. **Pets:** Accepted.
⊠ (&M) 🖥

▼▼▼ **Residence Inn by Marriott-Arundel Mills/BWI** SH ❀
(410) 799-7332. **$207-$253.** 7035 Arundel Mills Cir. I-95, exit 43A, 3.6 mi e on SR 100, exit 10A (Arundel Mills Blvd). Int corridors. **Pets:** Other species. $75 one-time fee/room. Service with restrictions.
(ASK) (S🐾) ⊠ 🖥 🖥 🖥 ⇄ 🔀

JESSUP

▼▼ **Extended StayAmerica-Jessup** SH
(301) 725-3877. **$124-$134.** 8550 Washington Blvd. I-95, exit 38A, 1.4 mi e on SR 32, 0.5 mi n on US 1. Int corridors. **Pets:** Other species. $75 one-time fee/pet. Service with restrictions.
(ASK) (S🐾) ⊠ 🖥 🖥

▼▼ **Red Roof Inn-Columbia/Jessup** M
(410) 796-0380. **Call for rates.** 8000 Washington Blvd. I-95, exit 41A; 0.3 mi s of jct US 1 and SR 175. Ext corridors. **Pets:** Accepted.
⊠ (&M) 🖥

LINTHICUM

▼▼▼ **Sheraton Baltimore Washington Airport Hotel** SH
(443) 577-2100. **$219-$289.** 1100 Old Elkridge Landing Rd. I-695, exit 7A, 1 mi s on SR 295, 1.3 mi e on W Nursery Rd, then 0.4 mi w on Winterson Rd. Int corridors. **Pets:** Accepted.
(ASK) (S🐾) ⊠ 🖥 🖥 🖥 ¶ ⇄

LINTHICUM HEIGHTS

▼▼▼ **Candlewood Suites-BWI** SH ❀
(410) 850-9214. **$135.** 1247 Winterson Rd. I-695, exit 7A, 1 mi s on SR 295, 1.3 mi e on W Nursery Rd, then 0.3 mi w. Int corridors. **Pets:** Medium, other species. $75 one-time fee/pet. Service with restrictions, supervision.
(ASK) ⊠ 🖥 🖥 🖥

AAA ▼▼▼ **Comfort Inn Airport** SH
(410) 789-9100. **$129-$189.** 6921 Baltimore Annapolis Blvd. I-695, exit 6A eastbound; exit 5 westbound, at SR 170 and 648. Int corridors. **Pets:** Accepted.
(SAVE) (S🐾) ⊠ (&M) 🖥 🖥 🖥 ¶ 🔀

Comfort Suites-BWI Airport SH ❀
(410) 691-1000. **Call for rates.** 815 Elkridge Landing Rd. I-695, exit 7A, 1 mi s on SR 295, then 1.3 mi e on W Nursery Rd. Int corridors. **Pets:** Medium. $25 one-time fee/room. Service with restrictions, crate.
SAVE ✕ 🅼 🛏 🖵

Four Points by Sheraton BWI Airport SH
(410) 859-3300. **$98-$240.** 7032 Elm Rd. I-195, exit 1A, 0.5 mi n on SR 170, then just e. Int corridors. **Pets:** Small, other species. $25 daily fee/pet. Service with restrictions, supervision.
SAVE 🆂 ✕ 🛏 🖵 🍴 ⊰

Hampton Inn BWI Airport SH
(410) 850-0600. **Call for rates.** 829 Elkridge Landing Rd. I-695, exit 7A, 1 mi s on SR 295, 1.3 mi e on W Nursery Rd, then just w. Int corridors. **Pets:** Accepted.
✕ 🅼 🛏 🖵

Holiday Inn-BWI Airport Conference Center LH
(410) 859-8400. **$109-$229.** 890 Elkridge Landing Rd. I-695, exit 7A, 1 mi s on SR 295, 1.3 mi e on W Nursery Rd, then 0.5 mi w. Int corridors. **Pets:** Large. $50 one-time fee/pet. Service with restrictions, crate.
SAVE 🆂 ✕ 🅼 🛏 🖵 🍴 ⊰

Homestead Studio Suites Hotel-Baltimore-BWI Airport M
(410) 691-2500. **$109-$119.** 939 International Dr. I-695, exit 7A, 1 mi s on SR 295, then 0.6 mi e on W Nursery Rd. Ext corridors. **Pets:** Other species. $75 one-time fee/pet. Service with restrictions.
A$K 🆂 ✕ 🅼 🛏 🖵

Homewood Suites by Hilton-BWI Airport SH
(410) 684-6100. **Call for rates.** 1181 Winterson Rd. I-695, exit 7A, 1 mi s on SR 295, 0.7 mi e on W Nursery Rd, then just n. Int corridors. **Pets:** Accepted.
✕ 🅼 🛏 🖵 ⊰ ✕

Motel 6 Baltimore-Linthicum Heights #1201 M
(410) 636-9070. **$65-$78 (no credit cards).** 5179 Raynor Ave. I-695, exit 8, just e on SR 168. Ext corridors. **Pets:** Other species. Service with restrictions, supervision.
🆂 ✕ ⊰

Red Roof Inn-BWI Airport M
(410) 850-7600. **Call for rates.** 827 Elkridge Landing Rd. I-695, exit 7A, 1 mi s on SR 295, 1.3 mi e on W Nursery Rd, then just w. Ext corridors. **Pets:** Accepted.
✕ 🛏

Residence Inn by Marriott-BWI Airport SH
(410) 691-0255. **$227-$277.** 1160 Winterson Rd. I-695, exit 7A, 1 mi s on SR 295, 0.7 mi e on W Nursery Rd, then just n. Int corridors. **Pets:** Accepted.
A$K 🆂 ✕ 🅼 🛏 🖵 ⊰ ✕

Sleep Inn & Suites Airport SH
(410) 789-7223. **$99-$189.** 6055 Belle Grove Rd. I-695, exit 6A east-bound; exit 5 westbound, 0.3 mi n to jct SR 170/648. Int corridors. **Pets:** Accepted.
SAVE 🆂 ✕ 🅼 🛏 🖵

Staybridge Suites BWI SH ❀
(410) 850-5666. **$169-$699.** 1301 Winterson Rd. I-695, exit 7A, 1 mi s on SR 295, 1.3 mi e on Nursery Rd, then 0.4 mi w. Int corridors. **Pets:** Medium. $100 one-time fee/pet. Service with restrictions, crate.
A$K 🆂 ✕ 🅼 🛏 🖵 ⊰

TownePlace Suites Baltimore/BWI Airport SH ❀
(410) 694-0060. **$109-$299.** 1171 Winterson Rd. I-695, exit 7A, 1 mi s on SR 295, 0.7 mi e on W Nursery Rd, then just n. Int corridors. **Pets:** Other species. $100 one-time fee/room. Service with restrictions, supervision.
A$K 🆂 ✕ 🅼 🛏 🖵 ⊰

ROSEDALE

La Quinta Inn & Suites Baltimore North SH
(410) 574-8100. **$139-$169.** 4 Philadelphia Ct. I-695, exit 34, just n. Int corridors. **Pets:** Other species. Service with restrictions, supervision.
A$K 🆂 ✕ 🛏 🖵 ⊰

SYKESVILLE

Inn at Norwood BB ❀
(410) 549-7868. **$130-$220, 7 day notice.** 7514 Norwood Ave. I-70, exit 80 (SR 32), 8 mi n, just w on Main St, then just w on Church St. Int corridors. **Pets:** Dogs only. $20 daily fee/pet. Designated rooms, no service, crate.
A$K ✕ 🛏 🖵 🆉

TIMONIUM

Extended StayAmerica-Timonium SH
(410) 628-1088. **$114-$124.** 9704 Beaver Dam Rd. I-83, exit 17, just e, follow signs to Beaver Dam Rd. Int corridors. **Pets:** Other species. $75 one-time fee/pet. Service with restrictions.
A$K 🆂 ✕ 🅼 🛏 🖵

Red Roof Inn-Timonium M
(410) 666-0380. **Call for rates.** 111 W Timonium Rd. I-83, exit 16A northbound; exit 16 southbound, just e. Ext corridors. **Pets:** Accepted.
✕ 🛏

TOWSON

Holiday Inn Baltimore-Towson SH ❀
(410) 823-4410. **$109-$179.** 1100 Cromwell Bridge Rd. I-695, exit 29A, just s. Int corridors. **Pets:** Medium. $40 one-time fee/pet. Designated rooms, service with restrictions, crate.
SAVE 🆂 ✕ 🛏 🖵 🍴 ⊰

Sheraton Baltimore North Hotel LH
(410) 321-7400. **$233-$259.** 903 Dulaney Valley Rd. I-695, exit 27A, 0.3 mi s. Int corridors. **Pets:** Accepted.
SAVE 🆂 ✕ 🛏 🖵 🍴 ⊰ ✕

WESTMINSTER

The Boston Inn M
(410) 848-9095. **$59-$75.** 533 Baltimore Blvd. 0.9 mi se on SR 97/140 from jct SR 27. Ext corridors. **Pets:** Dogs only. $50 deposit/pet. Service with restrictions, supervision.
A$K 🆂 ✕ 🛏 ⊰

WHITE MARSH

Residence Inn by Marriott Baltimore/White Marsh SH
(410) 933-9554. **$165-$196.** 4980 Mercantile Rd. I-95, exit 67B, 0.5 mi w on SR 43 (White Marsh Blvd), just s to Mercantile Rd, then just e. Int corridors. **Pets:** Accepted.
A$K 🆂 ✕ 🅼 🛏 🖵 ⊰ ✕

END METROPOLITAN AREA

CAMBRIDGE

(AAA) ▽▽ ▽▽ Hyatt Regency Chesapeake Bay Golf Resort, Spa and Marina 🈁 ❀
(410) 901-1234. **$169-$419, 3 day notice.** 100 Heron Blvd. US 50 E, 1.2 mi e of Frederick C Malkus Jr Bridge. Int corridors. **Pets:** Medium. $50 daily fee/pet. Designated rooms, service with restrictions.
🆂🅰🆅🅴 ⊠ 🔖 🔋 🖵 🍴 🌬 ⊠

CUMBERLAND

▽▽ ▽ Holiday Inn 🈁
(301) 724-8800. **$109-$159, 3 day notice.** 100 S George St. I-68, exit 43C, just n; downtown. Int corridors. **Pets:** Accepted.
🄰🅂🄺 ⊠ 🔋 🖵 🍴 🌬

DISTRICT OF COLUMBIA METROPOLITAN AREA

BELTSVILLE

(AAA) ▽▽▽▽ Sheraton College Park Hotel 🈁 ❀
(301) 937-4422. **$99-$249.** 4095 Powder Mill Rd. I-95, exit 29B, just w on SR 212; 2 mi n of I-495 (Capital Beltway). Int corridors. **Pets:** Medium, dogs only. Designated rooms, service with restrictions, crate.
🆂🅰🆅🅴 🆂🔟 ⊠ 🔟🅼 🔋 🖵 🍴 🌬

BETHESDA

▽▽▽ Residence Inn by Marriott-Bethesda Downtown 🈁 ❀
(301) 718-0200. **Call for rates.** 7335 Wisconsin Ave. I-495, exit 34, 2.5 mi s on SR 355; entrance on Waverly St. Int corridors. **Pets:** Medium. $10 daily fee/room, $200 one-time fee/room. Designated rooms, service with restrictions, supervision.
⊠ 🔋 🖵 🌬

BOWIE

▽▽▽ Comfort Inn Hotel & Conference Center-Bowie 🈁
(301) 464-0089. **$130-$163.** 4500 NW Crain Hwy. US 50, exit 13A, jct US 50/301 and SR 3. Int corridors. **Pets:** Medium, other species. $15 daily fee/pet. Designated rooms, service with restrictions, supervision.
🄰🅂🄺 🆂🔟 ⊠ 🔟🅼 🔋 🖵 🍴 🌬

(AAA) ▽▽▽▽ Hampton Inn-Bowie 🈁
(301) 809-1800. **Call for rates.** 15202 Major Lansdale Blvd. US 50, exit 11, 0.4 mi s on SR 197. Int corridors. **Pets:** Accepted.
🆂🅰🆅🅴 ⊠ 🔟🅼 🔋 🖵 🌬

COLLEGE PARK

▽ Super 8 Motel-College Park 🈁
(301) 474-0894. **Call for rates.** 9150 Baltimore Ave. I-95/495, exit 25 northbound; exit 25B southbound, 0.9 mi s on US 1. Int corridors. **Pets:** Accepted.
⊠ 🔋

GAITHERSBURG

(AAA) ▽▽▽▽ Comfort Inn Shady Grove 🈁 ❀
(301) 330-0023. **$69-$149.** 16216 Frederick Rd. I-270, exit 8, 1 mi e on Shady Grove Rd at SR 355. Int corridors. **Pets:** Large, other species. $15 daily fee/pet. Service with restrictions, crate.
🆂🅰🆅🅴 🆂🔟 ⊠ 🔋 🖵 🌬

▽▽ ▽ Extended Stay Deluxe-Washington, DC-Gaithersburg 🈁
(301) 963-3539. **$119-$129.** 201 Professional Dr. I-270, exit 11, 0.4 mi e, then 0.9 mi n on SR 355. Int corridors. **Pets:** Other species. $75 one-time fee/pet. Service with restrictions.
🄰🅂🄺 🆂🔟 ⊠ 🔋 🖵

▽▽▽ Hilton Washington DC North/Gaithersburg 🈁
(301) 977-8900. **Call for rates.** 620 Perry Pkwy. I-270, exit 11, then e. Int corridors. **Pets:** Accepted.
⊠ 🔋 🖵 🍴 🌬

(AAA) ▽▽▽▽ Holiday Inn-Gaithersburg 🈁
(301) 948-8900. **$129-$219.** 2 Montgomery Village Ave. I-270, exit 11, 0.3 mi e. Int corridors. **Pets:** Small, other species. Service with restrictions.
🆂🅰🆅🅴 🆂🔟 ⊠ 🔟🅼 🔋 🖵 🍴 🌬 ⊠

▽▽ ▽ Homestead Studio Suites Hotel-Gaithersburg/Rockville 🈁
(301) 987-9100. **$119-$129.** 2621 Research Blvd. I-270, exit 8, just w, then just n. Int corridors. **Pets:** Other species. $75 one-time fee/pet. Service with restrictions.
🄰🅂🄺 🆂🔟 ⊠ 🔟🅼 🔋 🖵

▽▽▽▽ Hyatt Summerfield Suites-Gaithersburg 🈁
(301) 527-6000. **$119-$399.** 200 Skidmore Blvd. I-370, exit SR 355, just n to Westland Rd. Ext corridors. **Pets:** Medium. $150 one-time fee/room. Designated rooms, crate.
🄰🅂🄺 ⊠ 🔟🅼 🔋 🖵 🌬 ⊠

▽▽▽▽ Residence Inn by Marriott-Gaithersburg 🈁
(301) 590-3003. **$227-$277.** 9721 Washingtonian Blvd. I-270, exit 9B (I-370/Sam Eig Hwy), just w to Fields Rd, 0.8 mi se, then just ne. Int corridors. **Pets:** Accepted.
🄰🅂🄺 🆂🔟 ⊠ 🔟🅼 🔋 🖵 🌬 ⊠

(AAA) ▽▽▽▽ TownePlace Suites by Marriott-Gaithersburg 🈁
(301) 590-2300. **$89-$239.** 212 Perry Pkwy. I-270, exit 10 northbound, just e; exit 11 southbound, just e on SR 355, 0.3 mi s, then 0.5 mi sw. Int corridors. **Pets:** Accepted.
🆂🅰🆅🅴 🆂🔟 ⊠ 🔟🅼 🔋 🖵 🌬

GERMANTOWN

▽▽ ▽ Extended StayAmerica-Washington, DC-Germantown 🈁
(301) 540-9369. **$94-$104.** 12450 Milestone Center Dr. I-270, exit 16, 0.6 mi e on SR 27 (Father Hurley Blvd), 0.7 mi n on Observation Dr, then just w. Int corridors. **Pets:** Other species. $75 one-time fee/pet. Service with restrictions.
🄰🅂🄺 🆂🔟 ⊠ 🔟🅼 🔋 🖵

▽▽ ▽ Homestead Studio Suites Hotel-Germantown Ⓜ
(301) 515-4500. **$94-$104.** 20141 Century Blvd. I-270, exit 15B (SR 118 S/Germantown Rd), just w to Aircraft Dr, then just n. Ext corridors. **Pets:** Other species. $75 one-time fee/pet. Service with restrictions.
🄰🅂🄺 🆂🔟 ⊠ 🔟🅼 🔋 🖵

GREENBELT

▽▽▽▽ Residence Inn by Marriott-Greenbelt 🈁
(301) 982-1600. **Call for rates.** 6320 Golden Triangle Dr. I-95/495, exit 23, 0.5 mi sw of jct SR 201; off SR 193, just n on Walker Dr. Int corridors. **Pets:** Accepted.
⊠ 🔟🅼 🔋 🖵 🌬 ⊠

LAUREL

(AAA) ▽▽▽ Comfort Suites Laurel Lakes 🈁
(301) 206-2600. **$79-$179.** 14402 Laurel Pl. On US 1, 0.9 mi s of jct SR 198. Int corridors. **Pets:** Accepted.
🆂🅰🆅🅴 🆂🔟 ⊠ 🔋 🖵 🌬

AAA ▼▼▼ Quality Inn & Suites Laurel **SH**
(301) 725-8800. **$79-$199.** One Second St. On US 1, 0.5 mi n of jct SR 198. Ext/int corridors. **Pets:** Small. $15 daily fee/pet. Designated rooms, service with restrictions, supervision.
SAVE S✪ ✕ 🛏 💻 ➹

ROCKVILLE

AAA ▼▼▼▼ Best Western Washington Gateway Hotel & Suites **SH**
(301) 424-4940. **$90-$170.** 1251 W Montgomery Ave. I-270, exit 6B, just w on SR 28. Int corridors. **Pets:** Accepted.
SAVE S✪ ✕ 🛏 💻 🍴 ➹

▼▼ Red Roof Inn-Rockville **SH**
(301) 987-0965. **Call for rates.** 16001 Shady Grove Rd. I-270, exit 8 (Shady Grove Rd), 0.5 mi e. Ext corridors. **Pets:** Accepted.
✕ ♿ 🛏

▼▼▼▼ Sheraton Rockville **SH**
(240) 912-8200. **Call for rates.** 920 King Farm Blvd. I-270, exit 8 northbound (Redland Rd), left on Piccard, then left on King Farm Blvd. Int corridors. **Pets:** Accepted.
✕ ♿ 🛏 💻 🍴 ➹

AAA ▼▼▼▼ Woodfin Suites Hotel **SH**
(301) 590-9880. **$159, 3 day notice.** 1380 Piccard Dr. I-270, exit 8 (Shady Grove Rd), 0.3 mi s; 1 mi w of SR 355 via Redland Rd. Ext corridors. **Pets:** $10 daily fee/pet. Supervision.
SAVE S✪ ✕ 🛏 💻 ➹ ✕

SILVER SPRING

▼▼▼▼ Residence Inn by Marriott Silver Spring **SH**
(301) 572-2322. **Call for rates (no credit cards).** 12000 Plum Orchard Dr. I-95, exit 29B, 1.2 mi w on SR 212, then 1 mi n on Cherry Hill Rd. Int corridors. **Pets:** Accepted.
✕ ♿ 🛏 💻 ➹ ✕

END METROPOLITAN AREA

ELKTON

AAA ▼▼▼▼ Hawthorn Suites **SH**
(410) 620-9494. **Call for rates.** 304 Belle Hill Rd. I-95, exit 109A, just e. Int corridors. **Pets:** Accepted.
SAVE ✕ ♿ 🛏 💻 ➹

EMMITSBURG

AAA ▼▼▼ Sleep Inn & Suites in Emmitsburg **SH**
(301) 447-0044. **$75-$199.** 501 Silo Hill Pkwy. US 15, exit SR 140, just w, then just n on Silo Hill Pkwy. Int corridors. **Pets:** $25 daily fee/room. Designated rooms, no service, crate.
SAVE S✪ ✕ 🛏 💻 ➹

FREDERICK

▼▼▼▼ Comfort Inn **SH**
(301) 668-7272. **$99-$129.** 7300 Executive Way. I-270, exit 31B, 0.9 mi sw on SR 85. Int corridors. **Pets:** Other species. $10 daily fee/room. Service with restrictions, crate.
ASK S✪ ✕ ♿ 🛏 💻

▼▼ Extended StayAmerica-Frederick-Westview Dr **M**
(301) 668-0808. **$119-$129.** 5240 Westview Dr. I-270, exit 31B, 0.5 mi sw on SR 85, then 0.4 mi n. Int corridors. **Pets:** Other species. $75 one-time fee/pet. Service with restrictions.
ASK S✪ ✕ 🛏 💻

▼▼▼▼ Frederick Residence Inn by Marriott **SH**
(301) 360-0010. **$188-$219.** 5230 Westview Dr. I-270, exit 31B, 0.5 mi sw on SR 85, then 0.3 mi n on Crestwood Blvd. Int corridors. **Pets:** Other species. $100 one-time fee/room. Service with restrictions, crate.
ASK S✪ ✕ 🛏 💻 ➹ ✕

AAA ▼▼▼ Hampton Inn **SH** ❀
(301) 698-2500. **$89-$139.** 5311 Buckeystown Pike (SR 85). I-270, exit 31B, 0.6 mi w. Int corridors. **Pets:** Medium. Designated rooms, service with restrictions, supervision.
SAVE S✪ ✕ 🛏 💻 🍴 ➹

AAA ▼▼▼▼ Holiday Inn & Conference Center **SH**
(301) 694-7500. **$139-$199.** 5400 Holiday Dr. I-270, exit 31A, just se of SR 85. Int corridors. **Pets:** Accepted.
SAVE ✕ 🛏 💻 🍴 ➹ ✕

AAA ▼▼▼ Holiday Inn Express-FSK Mall **SH**
(301) 695-2881. **Call for rates.** 5579 Spectrum Dr. I-270, exit 31A, just e on SR 85. Int corridors. **Pets:** Other species. $10 daily fee/room. Service with restrictions, crate.
SAVE ✕ 🛏 💻

AAA ▼▼▼▼ MainStay Suites **SH**
(301) 668-4600. **$100-$149.** 7310 Executive Way. I-270, exit 31B, 0.7 mi sw on SR 85. Int corridors. **Pets:** Small. $10 daily fee/pet, $100 one-time fee/room. Designated rooms, service with restrictions, supervision.
SAVE S✪ ✕ 🛏 💻 ➹

FROSTBURG

AAA ▼▼▼ Days Inn & Suites **SH**
(301) 689-2050. **Call for rates.** 11100 New Georges Creek Rd. I-68, exit 34, 1 mi n on SR 36. Int corridors. **Pets:** Medium. $15 daily fee/pet, $15 one-time fee/pet. Service with restrictions, supervision.
SAVE ✕ 🛏 💻

GRANTSVILLE

▼▼▼▼ The Stonebow Inn **BB**
(301) 895-4250. **$155-$195, 14 day notice.** 146 Casselman Rd. I-68, exit 22 westbound, 0.5 mi n on US 219, then 2.1 mi w on US 40; exit 19 eastbound, just n, then 0.9 mi w on US 40; behind Penn Alps Restaurant. Ext/int corridors. **Pets:** Accepted.
ASK ✕ 🛏 💻 ✕

GRASONVILLE

AAA ▼▼▼ Best Western Kent Narrows Inn **M** ❀
(410) 827-6767. **$79-$219.** 3101 Main St. US 50 and 301, exit 42; at Kent Narrows Bridge. Ext corridors. **Pets:** Medium, other species. $10 daily fee/pet. Service with restrictions, crate.
SAVE S✪ ✕ 🛏 💻 ➹ ✕

HAGERSTOWN

▼▼ Halfway Hagerstown Super 8 **SH**
(301) 582-1992. **$63-$71.** 16805 Blake Rd. I-81, exit 5B, just w. Int corridors. **Pets:** Dogs only. $20 one-time fee/pet. Service with restrictions, supervision.
ASK S✪ ✕ 🛏 💻

AAA ▼▼▼ **Sleep Inn & Suites** SH
(301) 766-9449. **$95-$169.** 18216 Col Henry K Douglas Dr. I-70, exit 29, just s. Int corridors. **Pets:** Other species. $10 daily fee/pet. Designated rooms, service with restrictions, supervision.
SAVE S⃞ X⃞ 🛏 💻 🏊

HANCOCK

AAA ▼ **Super 8 Motel** SH
(301) 678-6101. **Call for rates.** 118 Limestone Rd. I-70, exit 1B, just s. Ext/int corridors. **Pets:** $10 one-time fee/pet. Service with restrictions, supervision.
SAVE X⃞ 🛏 💻

INDIAN HEAD

AAA ▼ **Super 8 Motel** SH
(301) 753-8100. **Call for rates.** 4694 Indian Head Hwy. SR 210, 0.6 mi s of jct SR 225. Int corridors. **Pets:** Small, dogs only. $10 daily fee/pet. Service with restrictions, supervision.
SAVE X⃞ 🔧 🛏

LA VALE

AAA ▼▼ **Red Roof Inn** SH
(301) 729-6700. **Call for rates.** 12310 Winchester Rd SW. I-68, exit 40, 0.6 mi s. Ext/int corridors. **Pets:** Accepted.
SAVE X⃞ 🛏

▼ **Super 8 Motel** M
(301) 729-6265. **Call for rates.** 1301 National Hwy. I-68, exit 40, 0.4 mi n. Int corridors. **Pets:** Small. $10 daily fee/pet. Service with restrictions, supervision.
X⃞ 🛏

LEXINGTON PARK

▼▼ **Extended StayAmerica Lexington Park-Pax River** SH
(240) 725-0100. **$114-$124.** 46565 Expedition Park Dr. SR 235, just s to Lexington Park. Int corridors. **Pets:** Other species. $75 one-time fee/pet. Service with restrictions.
ASK S⃞ X⃞ 🔧 🛏 💻

▼ **Super 8 Motel** SH
(301) 862-9822. **Call for rates.** 22801 Three Notch Rd. On SR 235, 3.3 mi n of jct SR 246. Int corridors. **Pets:** Medium, other species. $11 daily fee/pet. Service with restrictions, supervision.
X⃞ 🛏

MCHENRY

▼▼▼ **Wisp Mountain Resort/Hotel & Conference Center** SH
(301) 387-5581. **$89-$369, 14 day notice.** 290 Marsh Hill Rd. 1 mi s on US 219 from jct SR 42, just w on Sang Run Rd, then 0.3 mi s. Int corridors. **Pets:** Medium, dogs only. $50 one-time fee/pet. Designated rooms, service with restrictions, crate.
ASK X⃞ 🛏 💻 🍴 🏊 🐾

NORTH EAST

▼▼ **Comfort Inn & Suites North East** SH 🐾
(410) 287-7100. **$89-$189.** 1 Center Dr. I-95, exit 100 southbound; exit 100A northbound, just e on SR 272. Int corridors. **Pets:** Small, dogs only. $25 one-time fee/pet. Designated rooms, service with restrictions, supervision.
ASK S⃞ X⃞ 🛏 💻 🏊

OCEAN CITY

AAA ▼▼▼ **Clarion Resort Fontainebleau Hotel** LH 🐾
(410) 524-3535. **$89-$399, 3 day notice.** 10100 Coastal Hwy. 101st St and the ocean. Int corridors. **Pets:** Large. $35 daily fee/pet. Designated rooms, service with restrictions, supervision.
SAVE S⃞ X⃞ 🛏 💻 🍴 🏊 🐾

AAA ▼▼ **Fenwick Inn** SH
(410) 250-1100. **$49-$259, 3 day notice.** 13801 Coastal Hwy. 138th St and Coastal Hwy. Int corridors. **Pets:** Small, other species. $10 daily fee/pet. Designated rooms, service with restrictions.
SAVE S⃞ X⃞ 🛏 🍴 🏊

PERRYVILLE

AAA ▼▼▼ **Ramada Perryville** M 🐾
(410) 642-2866. **$75-$87.** 61 Heather Ln. I-95, exit 93, just e. Ext corridors. **Pets:** Medium. $20 daily fee/room. Designated rooms, service with restrictions, supervision.
SAVE S⃞ X⃞ 🛏 💻

ROCK HALL

▼▼▼ **Inn at Huntingfield Creek** BB
(410) 639-7779. **$149-$269, 14 day notice.** 4928 Eastern Neck Rd. 1.8 mi s on SR 445 from jct SR 20. Ext/int corridors. **Pets:** Designated rooms, no service, crate.
ASK S⃞ X⃞ 🛏 💻 🏊 🐾 🗲

▼ **Mariners Motel** M 🐾
(410) 639-2291. **$70-$85.** 5681 S Hawthorne Ave. 0.3 mi e of SR 20. Ext corridors. **Pets:** Other species. Service with restrictions, supervision.
X⃞ 🛏 💻 🏊

ST. MICHAELS

AAA ▼▼ **The Parsonage Inn** BB
(410) 745-5519. **Call for rates.** 210 N Talbot St. 0.3 mi w on SR 33. Ext/int corridors. **Pets:** Medium, dogs only. $25 one-time fee/pet. Designated rooms, service with restrictions, supervision.
SAVE X⃞ 🗲

SALISBURY

AAA ▼▼▼ **Best Western Salisbury Plaza** M
(410) 546-1300. **$55-$135.** 1735 N Salisbury Blvd. US 13 business route, 0.5 mi s of US 50 Bypass. Ext corridors. **Pets:** Other species. $10 daily fee/pet. Service with restrictions, crate.
SAVE S⃞ X⃞ 🛏 💻 🏊

AAA ▼▼▼ **Comfort Inn Salisbury** SH 🐾
(410) 543-4666. **$49-$159.** 2701 N Salisbury Blvd. US 13, 0.5 mi n of jct US 13 business route and Bypass. Int corridors. **Pets:** Other species. Service with restrictions, supervision.
SAVE S⃞ X⃞ 🛏 💻

▼▼ **Ramada Inn and Conference Center** LH
(410) 546-4400. **Call for rates.** 300 S Salisbury Blvd. US 13 business route, 0.4 mi s of jct Business US 50; downtown. Int corridors. **Pets:** Accepted.
X⃞ 🛏 💻 🍴 🏊

▼▼▼ **Residence Inn by Marriott Salisbury** SH 🐾
(410) 543-0033. **$111-$141.** 140 Centre Rd. Just off US 13 business route at US 50. Int corridors. **Pets:** Other species. $100 one-time fee/room. Service with restrictions, supervision.
ASK S⃞ X⃞ 🔧 🛏 💻 🏊 🐾

SNOW HILL

AAA ▼▼▼▼ **River House Inn** BB 🐾
(410) 632-2722. **$125-$300, 7 day notice.** 201 E Market St. 1 mi w on SR 394 from jct SR 113. Ext/int corridors. **Pets:** Dogs only. $15 daily fee/pet. Designated rooms, service with restrictions.
SAVE S⃞ X⃞ 🛏 💻 🏊 🗲

WILLIAMSPORT

AAA ▼▼▼ **Red Roof Inn** SH
(301) 582-3500. **$50-$80.** 310 E Potomac St. I-81, exit 2, 0.3 mi sw on US 11. Ext corridors. **Pets:** Medium. Designated rooms, service with restrictions, supervision.
SAVE S⃞ X⃞ 🛏

MASSACHUSETTS

AMHERST

The Lord Jeffery Inn SH
(413) 253-2576. $79-$239. 30 Boltwood Ave. I-91, exit 19, 6 mi e on SR 9 to Commons. Int corridors. **Pets:** Accepted.

University Lodge M
(413) 256-8111. $59-$159. 345 N Pleasant St. 0.6 mi n. Ext corridors. **Pets:** Accepted.

AUBURN

Comfort Inn SH
(508) 832-8300. $80-$139. 426 Southbridge St. I-90, exit 10, 1 mi n on SR 12; I-290, exit 9 to SR 12. Int corridors. **Pets:** $20 one-time fee/pet. Designated rooms, service with restrictions, supervision.

La Quinta Inn & Suites SH
(508) 832-7000. $72-$104. 446 Southbridge St. I-90, exit 10, 1.2 mi n on SR 12. Int corridors. **Pets:** Medium, other species. Service with restrictions, crate.

BARRE

Jenkins Inn CI
(978) 355-6444. $170-$195, 7 day notice. 7 West St. On SR 122 and 32. Int corridors. **Pets:** Dogs only. Service with restrictions, supervision.

BOSTON METROPOLITAN AREA

ANDOVER

Comfort Suites SH
(978) 475-6000. $99-$139. 4 Riverside Dr. I-93, exit 45, 0.5 mi e. Int corridors. **Pets:** Small, other species. $75 one-time fee/pet. Designated rooms, service with restrictions, crate.

La Quinta Inn & Suites SH
(978) 685-6200. $115-$125. 131 River Rd. I-93, exit 45, just w; I-495, exit 40B, 2 mi n. Int corridors. **Pets:** Other species. Service with restrictions, supervision.

Residence Inn by Marriott
Boston-Andover SH 🐾
(978) 683-0382. $202-$219. 500 Minuteman Rd. I-93, exit 45, 0.3 mi w, then 0.5 mi n. Int corridors. **Pets:** $100 one-time fee/room. Service with restrictions, crate.

Staybridge Suites Boston/Andover SH
(978) 686-2000. $155-$195. 4 Tech Dr. I-93, exit 45, just sw via Shattuck Rd. Int corridors. **Pets:** Accepted.

Wyndham Boston/Andover Hotel LH
(978) 975-3600. Call for rates. 123 Old River Rd. I-93, exit 45, just e on River Rd. Int corridors. **Pets:** Accepted.

ARLINGTON

Hawthorn Suites Ltd SH
(781) 643-7258. Call for rates. 1 Massachusetts Ave. On SR 2A, just n of SR 16. Int corridors. **Pets:** Accepted.

BILLERICA

Homewood Suites by Hilton SH
(978) 670-7111. Call for rates. 35 Middlesex Tpke. I-95, exit 32B, 2.5 mi n. Int corridors. **Pets:** Accepted.

BOSTON

Best Western Roundhouse Suites SH
(617) 989-1000. $109-$299. 891 Massachusetts Ave. I-93, exit 18, just sw; just n of Newmarket Square. Int corridors. **Pets:** Medium. $100 deposit/room, $20 daily fee/pet. Designated rooms, service with restrictions, supervision.

Boston Harbor Hotel LH
(617) 439-7000. $290-$650. 70 Rowes Wharf. At Rowes Wharf. Int corridors. **Pets:** Accepted.

Boston Omni Parker House Hotel LH
(617) 227-8600. **$159-$599.** 60 School St. Corner of Tremont and School sts; northeast corner of Boston Common. Int corridors. **Pets:** Accepted.

[SAVE] [S6] [X] [💻] [🍴]

Bulfinch Hotel SH
(617) 624-0202. **$189-$399.** 107 Merrimac St. At Lancaster St. Int corridors. **Pets:** Accepted.

[SAVE] [X] [💻] [🍴]

The Colonnade Boston LH
(617) 424-7000. **$219-$599.** 120 Huntington Ave. Just s of Copley Square. Int corridors. **Pets:** Accepted.

[ASK] [S6] [X] [💻] [🍴] [🏊]

Comfort Inn Boston SH
(617) 287-9200. **$109-$199.** 900 William T Morrissey Blvd. I-93, exit 13 northbound, 0.5 mi sw; exit 12 southbound, follow signs. Int corridors. **Pets:** Service with restrictions, supervision.

[SAVE] [S6] [X] [🛁] [💻]

Courtyard by Marriott Boston, Copley Square SH
(617) 437-9300. **$274-$472.** 88 Exeter St. I-90, exit 22, just n; between Huntington Ave and Boylston St. Int corridors. **Pets:** Small. $50 daily fee/pet. Service with restrictions, supervision.

[ASK] [S6] [X] [S,M] [🛁] [💻]

DoubleTree Guest Suites-Boston/Cambridge SH
(617) 783-0090. **Call for rates.** 400 Soldiers Field Rd. I-90, exit 20 westbound; exit 18 eastbound. Int corridors. **Pets:** Service with restrictions, crate.

[X] [🛁] [💻] [🍴] [🏊] [X]

The Eliot Hotel SH
(617) 267-1607. **$355-$645.** 370 Commonwealth Ave. Corner of Commonwealth and Massachusetts aves. Int corridors. **Pets:** Accepted.

[SAVE] [X] [🍴]

The Fairmont Copley Plaza Boston LH
(617) 267-5300. **$209-$579.** 138 St. James Ave. At Copley Square. Int corridors. **Pets:** $25 daily fee/room. Service with restrictions, supervision.

[SAVE] [S6] [X] [S,M] [🛁] [💻] [🍴]

Fifteen Beacon SH
(617) 670-1500. **$395-$1400.** 15 Beacon St. Just e of State House; just ne of Boston Common; center. Int corridors. **Pets:** Accepted.

[SAVE] [X] [🍴] [X]

Four Seasons Hotel Boston LH
(617) 338-4400. **$495-$695.** 200 Boylston St. Between Arlington and Charles sts. Int corridors. **Pets:** Accepted.

[SAVE] [X] [S,M] [🍴] [🏊] [X]

Hilton Boston Logan Airport LH
(617) 568-6700. **$149-$999.** One Hotel Dr. At General Edward Lawrence Logan International Airport. Int corridors. **Pets:** Accepted.

[SAVE] [X] [S,M] [🛁] [💻] [🍴] [🏊] [X]

Hotel Commonwealth LH
(617) 933-5000. **$209-$498.** 500 Commonwealth Ave. On SR 2 at Beacon St and Brookline Ave. Int corridors. **Pets:** Accepted.

[SAVE] [S6] [X] [S,M] [🛁] [🍴]

Howard Johnson Hotel Fenway SH
(617) 267-8300. **Call for rates.** 1271 Boylston St. I-90, exit Brookline Ave S, backing onto Fenway Park. Int corridors. **Pets:** Accepted.

[X] [🛁] [💻] [🍴] [🏊]

Hyatt Regency Boston LH
(617) 912-1234. **$189-$519.** One Ave de Lafayette. Just e of Boston Common at Lafayette Pl. Int corridors. **Pets:** Accepted.

[SAVE] [X] [S,M] [💻] [🍴] [🏊] [X]

InterContinental Boston LH
(617) 747-1000. **$250-$800.** 510 Atlantic Ave. I-93, exit 23 southbound; exit 20 northbound. Int corridors. **Pets:** Accepted.

[SAVE] [S6] [X] [S,M] [🍴] [🏊] [X]

The Langham, Boston LH
(617) 451-1900. **$185-$505.** 250 Franklin St. Center; on Post Office Square. Int corridors. **Pets:** Accepted.

[SAVE] [S6] [X] [💻] [🍴] [🏊] [X]

The Lenox Hotel SH
(617) 536-5300. **$215-$455.** 61 Exeter St. I-90, exit 22, just n at Boylston. Int corridors. **Pets:** Accepted.

[SAVE] [S6] [X] [🛁] [🍴]

Nine Zero Hotel SH 🐾
(617) 772-5800. **$329-$599.** 90 Tremont St. Just ne of Boston Common; motor entrance on Bosworth, just s of property; center. Int corridors. **Pets:** Other species. Designated rooms, crate.

[SAVE] [S6] [X] [S,M] [💻] [🍴]

Onyx Hotel SH
(617) 557-9955. **Call for rates.** 155 Portland St. Just n of corner of Merrimac and Traverse sts; 3 blks s of Fleet Center. Int corridors. **Pets:** Accepted.

[SAVE] [X] [🍴]

Ramada Boston SH
(617) 287-9100. **$109-$189.** 800 William T Morrissey Blvd. I-93, exit 13 northbound, 0.5 mi sw; exit 12 southbound, follow signs. Int corridors. **Pets:** Service with restrictions, supervision.

[SAVE] [S6] [X] [🛁] [💻] [🏊]

Residence Inn by Marriott Boston Harbor on Tudor Wharf SH
(617) 242-9000. **$285-$406.** 34-44 Charles River Ave. Just se of SR 99 at Charlestown Bridge. Int corridors. **Pets:** Accepted.

[SAVE] [S6] [X] [S,M] [🛁] [💻] [🍴] [🏊]

The Ritz-Carlton, Boston Common SH 🐾
(617) 574-7100. **$479-$899.** 10 Avery St. At Washington and Avery sts; 1 blk e of Boston Common. Int corridors. **Pets:** $125 one-time fee/pet. Service with restrictions, supervision.

[X] [S,M] [🍴] [🏊] [X]

Seaport Hotel LH
(617) 385-4000. **$179-$499.** 1 Seaport Ln. At Seaport World Trade Center; MBTA-Silverline, World Trade Center Shop. Int corridors. **Pets:** Medium, other species. Designated rooms, supervision.

[SAVE] [S6] [X] [S,M] [🛁] [💻] [🍴] [X]

Sheraton Boston LH 🐾
(617) 236-2000. **$369-$1500.** 39 Dalton St. I-90, exit 22. Int corridors. **Pets:** Medium, dogs only. Service with restrictions, supervision.

[SAVE] [S6] [X] [S,M] [🛁] [💻] [🍴] [🏊] [X]

Taj Boston LH
(617) 536-5700. **$695-$725.** 15 Arlington St. At Arlington and Newbury sts; overlooks the Public Gardens. Int corridors. **Pets:** Accepted.

[SAVE] [S6] [X] [🍴] [X]

Westin Boston Waterfront LH
(617) 532-4600. **$459-$599.** 425 Summer St. I-93, exit 23, se via Purchase St to Summer St. Int corridors. **Pets:** Accepted.

[ASK] [S6] [X] [💻] [🍴] [🏊]

The Westin Copley Place Boston LH
(617) 262-9600. **$529-$569.** 10 Huntington Ave. I-90, exit 22, at Copley Square. Int corridors. **Pets:** Accepted.

SAVE ✕ ▣ 🍴 ⇆ ✕

BOXBOROUGH

Holiday Inn Boxborough Woods SH
(978) 263-8701. **$99-$169.** 242 Adams Pl. I-495, exit 28, just e on SR 111. Int corridors. **Pets:** Small. $25 one-time fee/room. Service with restrictions, supervision.

ASK ✕ ▤ ▣ 🍴 ⇆

BRAINTREE

Candlewood Suites Boston–Braintree SH
(781) 849-7450. **$79-$169.** 235 Wood Rd. I-93, exit 6, just n on SR 37, then 0.5 mi w. Int corridors. **Pets:** Accepted.

✕ ▤ ▣

Extended StayAmerica Boston-Braintree SH
(781) 356-8333. **$109-$150.** 20 Rockdale St. I-93, exit 6, just se. Int corridors. **Pets:** Other species. $75 one-time fee/pet. Service with restrictions.

ASK S✪ ✕ ♿ ▤ ▣

Hampton Inn Braintree SH
(781) 380-3300. **$119-$289.** 215 Wood Rd. I-93, exit 6, just n on SR 37, then 0.5 mi w. Int corridors. **Pets:** Accepted.

SAVE S✪ ✕ ♿ ▤ ▣ ⇆

Holiday Inn Express-Braintree SH
(781) 848-1260. **$109-$299.** 190 Wood Rd. I-93, exit 6, just n on SR 37, then 0.4 mi w. Int corridors. **Pets:** Accepted.

SAVE S✪ ✕ ▤ ▣

Sheraton Braintree Hotel LH
(781) 848-0600. **$99-$349.** 37 Forbes Rd. I-93, exit 6, just s on SR 37, then just w. Int corridors. **Pets:** Accepted.

ASK ✕ ▤ ▣ 🍴 ⇆ ✕

BROOKLINE

Holiday Inn Brookline SH
(617) 277-1200. **$139-$329.** 1200 Beacon St. 1 mi sw of Kenmore Square; at Beacon and St. Paul sts. Int corridors. **Pets:** Accepted.

SAVE S✪ ✕ ♿ ▤ ▣ 🍴 ⇆

BURLINGTON

Candlewood Suites Boston-Burlington SH 🐾
(781) 229-4300. **Call for rates.** 130 Middlesex Tpke. I-95, exit 32B, just n. Int corridors. **Pets:** Medium. $75 one-time fee/pet. Service with restrictions, supervision.

✕ ♿ ▤ ▣

Hilton Garden Inn Boston/Burlington SH
(781) 272-8800. **$109-$199.** 5 Wheeler Rd. I-95, exit 32B, just s on Middlesex Tpke. Int corridors. **Pets:** Accepted.

SAVE S✪ ✕ ♿ ▤ ▣ 🍴 ⇆

Hyatt Summerfield Suites SH
(781) 270-0800. **$99-$299.** 2 Van de Graaff Dr. I-95, exit 33A, just s on US 3, then 0.5 mi w on Wayside Rd. Int corridors. **Pets:** Accepted.

ASK ✕ ♿ ▤ ▣ ⇆ ✕

Staybridge Suites Boston-Burlington SH
(781) 221-2233. **$149-$199.** 11 Old Concord Rd. I-95, exit 32B, just s on Middlesex Tpke. Int corridors. **Pets:** Medium, other species. $75 one-time fee/room. Service with restrictions.

ASK S✪ ✕ ♿ ▤ ▣ ⇆

CAMBRIDGE

Best Western Hotel Tria SH
(617) 491-8000. **$189-$279.** 220 Alewife Brook Pkwy. Jct SR 2, 16 and US 3; in N Cambridge; I-90 (Massachusetts Tpke), exit Cambridge/Allston to SR 2 W (Fresh Pond Pkwy). Int corridors. **Pets:** Accepted.

ASK S✪ ✕ ▤ ▣ 🍴 ⇆

The Charles Hotel, Harvard Square LH
(617) 864-1200. **$199-$700.** One Bennett St. Just s of Harvard Square, at Eliot St. Int corridors. **Pets:** Accepted.

SAVE S✪ ✕ ♿ ▤ 🍴 ⇆ ✕

Hotel Marlowe SH 🐾
(617) 868-8000. **$169-$639.** 25 Edwin H Land Blvd. Just sw of jct SR 28. Int corridors. **Pets:** Other species. Designated rooms.

SAVE S✪ ✕ ♿ 🍴 ✕

Hyatt Regency Cambridge LH
(617) 492-1234. **$179-$399.** 575 Memorial Dr. On US 3 and SR 2. Int corridors. **Pets:** Medium. $50 one-time fee/room. Service with restrictions, supervision.

SAVE ✕ ♿ ▤ ▣ 🍴 ⇆ ✕

Le Meridien Cambridge SH
(617) 577-0200. **Call for rates.** 20 Sidney St. On SR 2A, 1 mi n of the river. Int corridors. **Pets:** Accepted.

SAVE ✕ ▤ ▣ 🍴

Residence Inn by Marriott Cambridge LH 🐾
(617) 349-0700. **$296-$461.** 6 Cambridge Center. Corner of Ames St and Broadway. Int corridors. **Pets:** $150 one-time fee/room. Service with restrictions, supervision.

ASK S✪ ✕ ♿ ▤ ▣ ⇆

Sheraton Commander Hotel SH 🐾
(617) 547-4800. **$129-$449.** 16 Garden St. Just n of Harvard Square. Int corridors. **Pets:** Medium, dogs only. Designated rooms, service with restrictions, supervision.

ASK S✪ ✕ ▤ ▣ 🍴

CONCORD

Best Western at Historic Concord SH
(978) 369-6100. **Call for rates.** 740 Elm Rd. 1.8 mi w, just off SR 2 and 2A. Int corridors. **Pets:** Other species. Designated rooms, supervision.

SAVE ✕ ▤ ▣ ⇆

DANVERS

Comfort Inn North Shore SH
(978) 777-1700. **$79-$179.** 50 Dayton St. Just w of US 1; 0.8 mi n of jct SR 114, exit Center St northbound, w under US 1; exit Dayton St southbound. Int corridors. **Pets:** Small. $10 daily fee/pet, $25 one-time fee/room. Designated rooms, service with restrictions, crate.

SAVE S✪ ✕ ♿ ▤ ▣ ⇆

Extended StayAmerica Boston-Danvers SH
(978) 762-7414. **$72-$115.** 102 Newbury St. On US 1 southbound. Int corridors. **Pets:** Other species. $75 one-time fee/pet. Service with restrictions.

ASK S✪ ✕ ♿ ▤ ▣

Residence Inn by Marriott SH
(978) 777-7171. **$175-$202.** 51 Newbury St (Rt 1). US 1 N, just s of jct SR 114. Ext corridors. **Pets:** Accepted.

ASK S✪ ✕ ▤ ▣ ⇆ ✕

TownePlace Suites by Marriott SH
(978) 777-6222. **$164-$197.** 238 Andover St. Southwest corner of jct US 1 and SR 114; SR 114 eastbound, enter just w of US 1 (no westbound entrance); US 1 southbound, enter through shopping center. Int corridors. **Pets:** Accepted.

ASK S✪ ✕ ♿ ▤ ▣ ⇆

DEDHAM

WWWW Hilton Boston Dedham 🅛🅗
(781) 329-7900. **Call for rates.** 25 Allied Dr. I-95, exit 14, just e. Int corridors. **Pets:** Medium. $50 one-time fee/room. Designated rooms, service with restrictions, supervision.
SAVE ✕ 🛈 🖃 🍽 ⤳ ✕

WWWW Residence Inn by Marriott 🅢🅗 ❄
(781) 407-0999. **$230-$252.** 259 Elm St. I-95, exit 15A, just n, then 0.4 mi e. Int corridors. **Pets:** $75 one-time fee/pet. Service with restrictions, supervision.
SAVE 🔒 ✕ 🛈 🖃 ⤳ ✕

FOXBORO

WWWW Foxborough Residence Inn by Marriott 🅢🅗
(508) 698-2800. **$175-$197.** 250 Foxborough Blvd. I-95, exit 7A, 0.6 mi s on SR 140, 0.7 mi e, then just n. Int corridors. **Pets:** Accepted.
ASK 🔒 ✕ 🛈 🖃 ⤳ ✕

FRAMINGHAM

WW Best Western Framingham 🅢🅗
(508) 872-8811. **$79-$129.** 130 Worcester Rd. I-90, exit 13, 0.5 mi s to SR 9; 1 mi w of Speen St; just w of Shopper's World Mall. Int corridors. **Pets:** Designated rooms, service with restrictions, supervision.
ASK 🔒 ✕ 🛈 🖃 🍽 ⤳

WW Red Roof Inn #7068 🅜
(508) 872-4499. **Call for rates.** 650 Cochituate Rd. I-90, exit 13, follow SR 30 E. Ext corridors. **Pets:** Accepted.
✕ 🛈 🖃

WWW Residence Inn by Marriott 🅢🅗 ❄
(508) 370-0001. **$242-$262.** 400 Staples Dr. SR 9 W to Crossing Blvd, then s. Int corridors. **Pets:** Other species. $75 one-time fee/room. Service with restrictions.
SAVE 🔒 ✕ 🛈 🖃 ⤳

WWWW Sheraton Hotel Framingham 🅛🅗
(508) 879-7200. **$89-$289.** 1657 Worcester Rd. I-90, exit 12, follow signs to SR 9 W. Int corridors. **Pets:** Medium, dogs only. Designated rooms, service with restrictions, supervision.
ASK 🔒 ✕ 🛈 🖃 🍽 ⤳ ✕

FRANKLIN

WWWW Franklin Residence Inn by Marriott 🅢🅗
(508) 541-8188. **$164-$186.** 4 Forge Pkwy. I-495, exit 17, 0.7 mi nw off SR 140 N. Int corridors. **Pets:** Medium. $100 one-time fee/room. Service with restrictions, crate.
ASK 🔒 ✕ 🛈 🖃 ⤳ ✕

WWWW Hawthorn Suites Ltd 🅢🅗 ❄
(508) 553-3500. **$129-$149.** 835 UpperUnion St. I-495, exit 16, just s, then 0.3 mi e. Int corridors. **Pets:** Small. $100 one-time fee/room. Designated rooms, service with restrictions, crate.
SAVE 🔒 ✕ 🛈 🖃 ⤳ ✕

GLOUCESTER

WW Cape Ann Motor Inn 🅜 ❄
(978) 281-2900. **$75-$160.** 33 Rockport Rd. 2 mi n of terminus of SR 128 via SR 127A. Ext corridors. **Pets:** Other species. Designated rooms, service with restrictions, supervision.
✕ 🛈 🎿

HAVERHILL

WWWW Best Western Merrimack Valley 🅢🅗 ❄
(978) 373-1511. **$109-$159.** 401 Lowell Ave. I-495, exit 49 (SR 110). Int corridors. **Pets:** Medium, other species. $20 daily fee/pet. Designated rooms, service with restrictions, supervision.
SAVE 🔒 ✕ 🛈 🖃 ⤳

LEXINGTON

WWW Quality Inn & Suites 🅢🅗
(781) 861-0850. **$99-$129.** 440 Bedford St. I-95, exit 31B, just n on SR 4 and 225, continue n and use jug handle to reverse direction. Ext corridors. **Pets:** Accepted.
SAVE 🔒 ✕ 🛦 🛈 🖃 ⤳

MARLBOROUGH

WWW Courtyard by Marriott Marlborough 🅛🅗
(508) 480-0015. **$176-$196.** 75 Felton St. I-495, exit 24B, just w; just off US 20. Int corridors. **Pets:** Accepted.
ASK 🔒 ✕ 🛦 🛈 🖃 🍽 ⤳ ✕

WWW Embassy Suites Hotel-Boston Marlborough 🅛🅗
(508) 485-5900. **Call for rates.** 123 Boston Post Rd W. I-495, exit 24B, 0.5 mi w; just off US 20. Int corridors. **Pets:** Accepted.
✕ 🛦 🛈 🖃 🍽 ⤳ ✕

WWW Residence Inn By Marriott Boston Marlborough 🅢🅗
(508) 481-1500. **$263-$285.** 112 Donald Lynch Blvd. I-290, exit 25B, 3 mi ne. Int corridors. **Pets:** Accepted.
ASK 🔒 ✕ 🛦 🛈 🖃 ⤳ ✕

METHUEN

WW GuestHouse Inn 🅢🅗
(978) 686-2971. **$75-$145.** 159A Pelham St. I-93, exit 47, just w. Int corridors. **Pets:** Medium. $25 one-time fee/room. Designated rooms, service with restrictions, supervision.
ASK 🔒 ✕ 🛈 🖃 🍽 ⤳

NATICK

WWW Crowne Plaza Boston-Natick 🅛🅗 ❄
(508) 653-8800. **$149-$289.** 1360 Worcester St. I-90, exit 12, 5 mi e; SR 9, 4 mi e of Framingham Center. Int corridors. **Pets:** Medium. Designated rooms, service with restrictions, supervision.
✕ 🛦 🛈 🖃 🍽

NEEDHAM

WWW Sheraton Needham Hotel 🅛🅗
(781) 444-1110. **Call for rates.** 100 Cabot St. I-95, exit 19A, just e. Int corridors. **Pets:** Accepted.
✕ 🛈 🖃 🍽 ⤳ ✕

NEWTON

WWW Sheraton Newton Hotel 🅛🅗
(617) 969-3010. **$299-$329.** 320 Washington St. I-90 (Massachusetts Tpke), exit 17 (SR 16). Int corridors. **Pets:** Accepted.
SAVE 🔒 ✕ 🛈 🖃 🍽 ⤳

NORTH CHELMSFORD

WWW Hawthorn Suites 🅢🅗 ❄
(978) 256-5151. **Call for rates.** 25 Research Pl. US 3, exit 32, 0.3 mi ne on SR 4. Int corridors. **Pets:** Medium. $10 daily fee/room, $50 one-time fee/room. Service with restrictions.
✕ 🛦 🛈 🖃 ⤳

NORWOOD

WWW Hampton Inn 🅢🅗
(781) 769-7000. **$99-$169.** 434 Boston Providence Hwy. I-95, exit 15B, 2.3 mi s. Int corridors. **Pets:** Small. $25 one-time fee/pet. Service with restrictions, supervision.
ASK 🔒 ✕ 🛦 🛈 🖃 ⤳

▼▼▼ Residence Inn Boston-Norwood 🅂🄷 ❧
(781) 278-9595. **$209-$229.** 275 Norwood Park S. I-95, exit 9, on US 1 southbound. Int corridors. **Pets:** Medium. $75 one-time fee/pet. Service with restrictions, crate.

A$K S🄳 ⊠ ⓜ 🔒 💻 ⤳ ⊠

PEABODY

🅐🅐🅐 ▼▼▼ Holiday Inn Hotel & Suites 🅂🄷
(978) 535-4600. **$99-$175.** 1 Newbury St. I-95, exit 44 a northbound, U-turn before lights to US 1 N; exit 44 southbound, just s on US 1, then U-turn to US 1 N. Int corridors. **Pets:** Accepted.

SAVE S🄳 ⊠ 🔒 💻 ¶¶ ⤳

▼▼▼ Homewood Suites by Hilton 🅂🄷
(978) 536-5050. **Call for rates.** 57 Newbury St. On US 1 northbound. Int corridors. **Pets:** Accepted.

⊠ ⓜ 🔒 💻 ⤳

REVERE

▼▼▼ Comfort Inn & Suites Boston Airport 🅂🄷
(781) 485-3600. **$99-$239.** 85 American Legion Hwy. Jct SR 1A and 60, 3 mi n of General Edward Lawrence Logan International Airport. Int corridors. **Pets:** Medium, other species. $10 daily fee/room. Service with restrictions.

A$K S🄳 ⊠ 🔒 💻 ¶¶ ⤳

▼▼▼ Hampton Inn Boston Logan Airport 🅂🄷
(781) 286-5665. **$109-$299.** 230 Lee Burbank Hwy. On SR 1A, 1.9 mi n of General Edward Lawrence Logan International Airport; 0.6 mi s of terminus SR 60. Int corridors. **Pets:** Accepted.

A$K ⊠ ⓜ 🔒 💻 ¶¶ ⤳

SALEM

▼▼▼ Hawthorne Hotel 🅂🄷 ❧
(978) 744-4080. **$104-$212, 3 day notice.** 18 Washington Square W. On SR 1A. Int corridors. **Pets:** Other species. $100 deposit/room, $10 daily fee/pet. Designated rooms, service with restrictions, supervision.

A$K ⊠ 🔒 ¶¶

▼▼▼ The Salem Inn 🄱🄱
(978) 741-0680. **$119-$199, 7 day notice.** 7 Summer St. On SR 114 at Essex St; SR 128, exit 25A, 3 mi e. Int corridors. **Pets:** Other species. $15 daily fee/pet. Designated rooms, service with restrictions.

⊠ 🔒 💻

SAUGUS

▼▼ Red Roof Inn #7305 🅂🄷
(781) 941-1400. **Call for rates.** 920 Broadway. I-95, exit 44 northbound, 3.2 mi s on US 1; exit Main St/Saugus southbound to U-turn. Int corridors. **Pets:** Accepted.

⊠ ⓜ 🔒

SOMERVILLE

▼▼▼ La Quinta Inn & Suites Boston/ Somerville 🅂🄷
(617) 625-5300. **$115-$185.** 23 Cummings St. I-93, exit 29 northbound, just ne on SR 28, then just s on Middlesex Ave; exit 31 southbound, 1 mi e on SR 16, then 0.5 mi s on SR 28 to Middlesex Ave. Int corridors. **Pets:** Other species. Service with restrictions, supervision.

A$K S🄳 ⊠ ⓜ 🔒 💻

SUDBURY

🅐🅐🅐 ▼▼▼ Clarion Carriage House Inn 🅂🄷 ❧
(978) 443-2223. **$139-$279.** 738 Boston Post Rd. I-495, exit 24A, 7.5 mi e on US 20; 4.7 mi w of jct SR 27 on US 20. Int corridors. **Pets:** Other species. $10 one-time fee/pet. Service with restrictions, supervision.

SAVE S🄳 ⊠ 🔒 💻

TEWKSBURY

▼▼ Extended StayAmerica Boston-Tewksbury 🅂🄷
(978) 863-9888. **$86-$110.** 1910 Andover St. I-93, exit 43B, just w; I-495, exit 39, just e. Int corridors. **Pets:** Other species. $75 one-time fee/pet. Service with restrictions.

A$K S🄳 ⊠ 🔒 💻

▼ Motel 6 Boston-Tewksbury #1403 🅼
(978) 851-8677. **Call for rates.** 95 Main St. I-495, exit 38, just s on SR 38. Ext corridors. **Pets:** Other species. Service with restrictions, supervision.

⊠ ⤳

▼▼▼ Residence Inn by Marriott Boston-Tewksbury 🅂🄷
(978) 640-1003. **$191-$208.** 1775 Andover St. I-495, exit 39, 0.3 mi w on SR 133. Ext corridors. **Pets:** Other species. $75 one-time fee/room. Service with restrictions.

A$K S🄳 ⊠ ⓜ 🔒 💻 ⤳ ⊠

▼▼▼ TownePlace Suites by Marriott 🅂🄷
(978) 863-9800. **$164-$186.** 20 International Pl. I-495, exit 39, 0.3 mi nw. Int corridors. **Pets:** Accepted.

A$K S🄳 ⊠ ⓜ 🔒 💻 ⤳

WAKEFIELD

🅐🅐🅐 ▼▼▼ Sheraton Colonial Hotel & Golf Club Boston North 🅻🄷
(781) 245-9300. **$89-$239.** 1 Audubon Rd. I-95, exit 42, just n. Int corridors. **Pets:** Accepted.

SAVE S🄳 ⊠ 🔒 💻 ¶¶ ⤳ ⊠

WALTHAM

▼▼▼ Courtyard by Marriott Boston-Waltham 🅂🄷
(781) 419-0900. **$186-$215.** 387 Winter St. I-95, exit 27A, on northeast corner. Int corridors. **Pets:** Other species. $50 one-time fee/room. Service with restrictions, supervision.

A$K S🄳 ⊠ ⓜ 🔒 💻 ¶¶ ⤳

▼▼▼ Extended Stay Deluxe Boston-Waltham 🅂🄷
(781) 622-1900. **$109-$150.** 32 Fourth Ave. I-95, exit 27A, just se. Int corridors. **Pets:** Other species. $75 one-time fee/pet. Service with restrictions.

A$K S🄳 ⊠ ⓜ 🔒 💻 ⤳

▼▼▼ Holiday Inn Express Boston/Waltham 🅂🄷
(781) 890-2800. **$119-$169.** 385 Winter St. I-95, exit 27A, just ne. Ext/int corridors. **Pets:** Other species. $50 one-time fee/room. Service with restrictions, supervision.

A$K S🄳 ⊠ ⓜ 🔒 💻

▼▼▼ Home Suites Inn of Boston-Waltham 🅂🄷
(781) 890-3000. **$109-$169.** 455 Totten Pond Rd. I-95, exit 27A, just s. Int corridors. **Pets:** Other species. $50 one-time fee/room. Service with restrictions, supervision.

A$K S🄳 ⊠ 🔒 💻 ¶¶ ⤳

▼▼▼ The Westin Waltham-Boston 🅻🄷
(781) 290-5600. **$349.** 70 Third Ave. I-95, exit 27A, just se. Int corridors. **Pets:** Accepted.

A$K S🄳 ⊠ ⓜ 💻 ¶¶ ⤳ ⊠

WESTFORD

▼▼▼ Residence Inn by Marriott 🅂🄷
(978) 392-1407. **$209-$229.** 7 Lan Dr. I-495, exit 32, just s, then 0.5 w on SR 110. Int corridors. **Pets:** Accepted.

A$K S🄳 ⊠ ⓜ 🔒 💻 ⤳ ⊠

WOBURN

(AAA) ▼▼◆▼ **Best Western New Englander** SH
(781) 935-8160. **Call for rates.** 1 Rainin Rd. I-93, exit 36, just e. Int corridors. **Pets:** Accepted.
SAVE ⊠ &M 🛏 🖵 ⫯⫯ ⊜

▼▼▼▼ **Hilton Boston/Woburn** LH
(781) 932-0999. **Call for rates.** 2 Forbes Rd. I-95, exit 36, 0.5 mi s via Washington St, then just e at Lukoil; jct Cedar St. Int corridors. **Pets:** Accepted.
⊠ 🛏 🖵 ⫯⫯ ⊜

▼▼▼ **Holiday Inn Select** SH
(781) 935-8760. **$79-$159.** 15 Middlesex Canal Park Rd. I-95, exit 35, s via SR 38. Int corridors. **Pets:** Accepted.
ASK SD ⊠ &M 🛏 🖵 ⫯⫯ ⊜

▼▼◆▼ **Red Roof Inn Woburn #7238** SH
(781) 935-7110. **Call for rates.** 19 Commerce Way. I-95, exit 36, just n, then just w on Mishawum Rd. Int corridors. **Pets:** Accepted.
⊠ &M 🛏 ⊜

(AAA) ▼▼◆▼ **Residence Inn by**
           Marriott-Boston/Woburn SH
(781) 376-4000. **$197-$219.** 300 Presidential Way. I-93, exit 37C, just nw. Int corridors. **Pets:** Accepted.
SAVE SD ⊠ &M 🛏 🖵 ⊜ ⊠

END METROPOLITAN AREA

BROCKTON

▼▼▼▼ **Residence Inn by Marriott** SH 🐾
(508) 583-3600. **$219-$241.** 124 Liberty St. SR 24, exit 17B, just w, just s on Pearl St, then 0.3 mi se via Mill St connector. Int corridors. **Pets:** Large. $100 one-time fee/room. Service with restrictions, supervision.
ASK SD ⊠ &M 🛏 🖵 ⫯⫯ ⊜ ⊠

CAPE COD AREA

BUZZARDS BAY

(AAA) ▼▼ **Bay Motor Inn** CA
(508) 759-3989. **$62-$139, 7 day notice.** 223 Main St. SR 25, 0.5 mi w of Bourne rotary, exit 3. Ext corridors. **Pets:** $15 daily fee/pet. Service with restrictions, supervision.
SAVE SD ⊠ 🛏 ⊜

EAST FALMOUTH

▼▼ **Capewind Waterfront Resort** M 🐾
(508) 548-3400. **$68-$237, 30 day notice.** 34 Maravista Extension. 2.2 mi e via SR 28, then just s, follow signs. Ext corridors. **Pets:** Medium, dogs only. $10 daily fee/pet. Designated rooms, no service.
ASK ⊠ 🛏 🖵 ⊜ ⊠

FALMOUTH

(AAA) ▼▼▼ **Mariner Motel** M
(508) 548-1331. **$59-$189, 14 day notice.** 555 Main St. 0.5 mi e on SR 28. Ext corridors. **Pets:** Accepted.
SAVE ⊠ 🛏 ⊜

HYANNIS

▼▼ **Cape Cod Harbor House Inn** M
(508) 771-1880. **Call for rates.** 119 Ocean St. Opposite ferry docks. Ext corridors. **Pets:** Dogs only. $25 daily fee/pet. Designated rooms, service with restrictions.
⊠ 🛏 🖵

▼▼▼ **Comfort Inn** SH
(508) 771-4804. **$89-$210.** 1470 Iyanough Rd. US 6, exit 6, 1.3 mi se on SR 132. Ext/int corridors. **Pets:** Accepted.
ASK SD ⊠ 🛏 🖵 ⊜ ⊠

ORLEANS

▼▼ **Orleans Inn** CI
(508) 255-2222. **$175-$300.** 21 Rt 6A. On SR 28 and 6A, exit rotary, just w. Int corridors. **Pets:** Other species.
⊠ 🛏 ⫯⫯

(AAA) ▼▼ **Skaket Beach Motel** M 🐾
(508) 255-1020. **$60-$165, 10 day notice.** 203 Cranberry Hwy (Rt 6A). US 6, exit 12, just e. Ext corridors. **Pets:** $12 daily fee/pet. Designated rooms, service with restrictions, supervision.
SAVE ⊠ 🛏 🖵 ⊜

PROVINCETOWN

▼▼▼▼ **Anchor Inn Beach House** SH
(508) 487-0432. **$150-$400.** 175 Commercial St. 2 blks se of SR 6A, just sw of the post office; center. Ext/int corridors. **Pets:** Accepted.
⊠ 🛏

▼▼▼▼ **Bayshore & Chandler** CO
(508) 487-9133. **Call for rates.** 493 Commercial St. 0.8 mi e of Town Hall. Ext corridors. **Pets:** $15 daily fee/room. Service with restrictions.
⊠ 🛏

(AAA) ▼▼ **Cape Inn** SH
(508) 487-1711. **$69-$209, 7 day notice.** 698 Commercial St. 1.5 mi se on SR 6A. Ext corridors. **Pets:** Accepted.
SAVE ⊠ 🛏 🖵 ⫯⫯ ⊜

(AAA) ▼▼▼ **Surfside Hotel & Suites** SH 🐾
(508) 487-1726. **$109-$299.** 542-543 Commercial St. 1 mi e of Town Hall. Ext/int corridors. **Pets:** Dogs only. $40 daily fee/room. Service with restrictions.
SAVE SD ⊠ 🛏 🖵 ⊜

▼▼▼▼ **White Wind Inn** BB
(508) 487-1526. **$85-$295, 14 day notice.** 174 Commercial St. Just w of Town Hall. Int corridors. **Pets:** Accepted.
⊠ 🛏 🖵

SANDWICH

(AAA) ▼ **Shady Nook Inn & Motel** M
(508) 888-0409. **Call for rates.** 14 Old Kings Hwy (SR 6A). On SR 6A, 1.5 mi w. Ext corridors. **Pets:** Accepted.
SAVE ⊠ 🛏 ⊜

SOUTH YARMOUTH

AAA **WWWW** Best Western Blue Rock Resort 🅼 🐾
(508) 398-6962. **Call for rates.** 39 Todd Rd. SR 28, 1 mi ne via N Main St and High Bank Rd, then 0.5 mi nw on Country Club Dr, follow signs. Ext corridors. **Pets:** Dogs only. $25 daily fee/pet. Designated rooms, service with restrictions, crate.

SAVE ⊠ 📱 💻 🍴 ➿

AAA **WWWW** Best Western Blue Water on The
Ocean 🆂🅷
(508) 398-2288. **$100-$440, 10 day notice.** 291 S Shore Dr. 1 mi s off SR 28. Ext/int corridors. **Pets:** $25 daily fee/pet. Designated rooms, service with restrictions.

SAVE 🆂 ⊠ 📱 💻 🍴 ➿ ⊠

WEST YARMOUTH

AAA **WWW** Tidewater Inn 🅼
(508) 775-6322. **$59-$159.** 135 Main St. On SR 28, 0.8 mi e of jct SR 132. Ext/int corridors. **Pets:** Accepted.

SAVE 🆂 ⊠ 📱 💻 🍴 ➿ ⊠

END AREA

CHICOPEE

AAA **WW** Quality Inn-Chicopee 🆂🅷
(413) 592-6171. **$69-$99.** 463 Memorial Dr. I-90 (Massachusetts Tpke), exit 5, just ne; upon exiting, use jug handle overpass to SR 33 N. Int corridors. **Pets:** Accepted.

SAVE 🆂 ⊠ 📱 💻 ➿

DARTMOUTH

WW Comfort Inn 🆂🅷
(508) 996-0800. **$89-$169.** 171 Faunce Corner Rd. I-195, exit 12A westbound; exit 12 eastbound, then s. Int corridors. **Pets:** Medium, other species. $50 one-time fee/room. Crate.

ASK 🆂 ⊠ 📱 💻 ➿

WWW Residence Inn by Marriott 🆂🅷
(508) 984-5858. **$90-$110.** 181 Faunce Corner Rd. I-195, exit 12A westbound; exit 12 eastbound, just s. Int corridors. **Pets:** Accepted.

ASK 🆂 ⊠ 🆂🅼 📱 💻 ➿ ⊠

EAST WAREHAM

AAA **WW** Atlantic Motel 🅼
(508) 295-0210. **$69-$199, 10 day notice.** 7 Depot St. Between eastbound and westbound lanes of US 6/SR 28; jct SR 25, exit 1. Ext corridors. **Pets:** Accepted.

SAVE 🆂 ⊠ 📱 ➿

FAIRHAVEN

AAA **WWWW** Holiday Inn Express Harborfront 🆂🅷
(508) 997-1281. **$89-$159.** 110 Middle St. I-195, exit 15, 1 mi s, then just off US 6. Int corridors. **Pets:** Other species. $10 one-time fee/room. Service with restrictions, crate.

SAVE 🆂 ⊠ 📱 💻

FITCHBURG

AAA **WWWW** Best Western Royal Plaza Hotel & Trade
Center 🅻🅷
(978) 342-7100. **$109-$129.** 150 Royal Plaza Dr. SR 2, exit 28, just s on SR 31. Int corridors. **Pets:** Accepted.

SAVE 🆂 ⊠ 📱 💻 🍴 ➿ ⊠

GARDNER

WWW Colonial Hotel 🆂🅷
(978) 630-2500. **$99-$139.** 625 Betty Spring Rd. SR 2, exit 24 eastbound; exit 24B, 0.9 mi n on SR 140, then 0.5 mi w. Int corridors. **Pets:** Accepted.

ASK 🆂 ⊠ 📱 💻 🍴 ➿ ⊠

WW Super 8 Motel 🅼
(978) 630-2888. **Call for rates.** 22 Pearson Blvd. SR 2, exit 23, just n. Int corridors. **Pets:** Medium. $15 daily fee/pet. Service with restrictions, supervision.

⊠ 📱 💻

GREAT BARRINGTON

AAA **WW** Monument Mountain Motel 🅼
(413) 528-3272. **$59-$199, 14 day notice.** 247 Stockbridge Rd (Rt 7). On US 7, 1.2 mi s of jct SR 183. Ext corridors. **Pets:** Accepted.

SAVE 🆂 ⊠ 📱 ➿

AAA **WW** Travelodge 🅼
(413) 528-2340. **Call for rates.** 400 Stockbridge Rd. On US 7, 1.2 mi s of jct SR 183. Ext corridors. **Pets:** $10 daily fee/pet. Designated rooms, service with restrictions.

SAVE ⊠ 📱 💻 ➿

GREENFIELD

AAA **WWW** The Brandt House B&B 🅱🅱
(413) 774-3329. **$95-$295, 30 day notice.** 29 Highland Ave. I-91, exit 26, 1.8 mi e on SR 2A, then se via Crescent St. Int corridors. **Pets:** Accepted.

SAVE 🆂 ⊠ 📱

HADLEY

AAA **WWW** Howard Johnson Inn 🆂🅷
(413) 586-0114. **$79-$179.** 401 Russell St. I-91, exit 19 northbound, 4.3 mi e on SR 9; exit 24 southbound, 10 mi s on SR 116, then just w on SR 9. Int corridors. **Pets:** Accepted.

SAVE 🆂 ⊠ 🆂🅼 📱 💻 ➿

AAA **WW** Quality Inn 🆂🅷
(413) 584-9816. **$69-$155.** 237 Russell St (SR 9). I-91, exit 19 northbound; exit 20 southbound, 3 mi e on SR 9. Int corridors. **Pets:** Accepted.

SAVE ⊠ 📱 💻 ➿

HOLLAND

WWW The Inn at Restful Paws 🅱🅱 🐾
(413) 245-7792. **$174, 14 day notice.** 70 Allen Hill Rd. SR 20, 2.1 mi s on E Brimfield Rd, 0.4 mi on Alexander Rd, then 0.7 mi n. Int corridors. **Pets:** Service with restrictions, supervision.

ASK ⊠ 💻 🐾 🐾

HOLYOKE

Homewood Suites by Hilton Holyoke-Springfield SH
(413) 532-3100. **$119-$299.** 375 Whitney Ave. I-91, exit 15, just w on Lower Westfield Rd, then 0.4 mi s. Int corridors. **Pets:** Other species. $100 one-time fee/room. Service with restrictions, crate.

KINGSTON

Plymouth Bay Inn & Suites M
(781) 585-3831. **$89-$169.** 149 Main St. SR 3, exit 9, just w. Int corridors. **Pets:** Accepted.

LANESBOROUGH

The Weathervane Motel M
(413) 443-3230. **$35-$110, 15 day notice.** 475 S Main St. 1.3 mi s on US 7. Ext corridors. **Pets:** Accepted.

LENOX

Blantyre CI
(413) 637-3556. **$575-$1850, 30 day notice.** 16 Blantyre Rd. On US 20, 1 mi s from jct SR 183. Int corridors. **Pets:** Accepted.

LEOMINSTER

Super 8 Motel M
(978) 537-2800. **Call for rates.** 482 N Main St. SR 2, exit 31B, just n on SR 12. Int corridors. **Pets:** Accepted.

MANSFIELD

Holiday Inn Mansfield SH
(508) 339-2200. **$110-$190.** 31 Hampshire St. I-95, exit 7A, 0.5 mi s on SR 140, then 1 mi w on Forbes Rd; I-495, exit 12, 2 mi n on SR 140, then w on Forbes Rd. Int corridors. **Pets:** Medium. $10 daily fee/pet. Service with restrictions, supervision.

MARTHA'S VINEYARD AREA

EDGARTOWN

Colonial Inn of Martha's Vineyard CI
(508) 627-4711. **$95-$425, 14 day notice.** 38 N Water St. Just n from Main St. Int corridors. **Pets:** Accepted.

VINEYARD HAVEN

The Doctor's House BB
(508) 696-0859. **$150-$325.** 60 Mt. Aldworth Rd. 0.4 mi sw to road to Edgartown, 1 blk e. Int corridors. **Pets:** Accepted.

END AREA

MIDDLEBORO

Days Inn-Plymouth/Middleboro SH
(508) 946-4400. **$69-$99.** 30 E Clark St. I-495, exit 4, at SR 105. Int corridors. **Pets:** Large, other species. $10 daily fee/pet. Designated rooms, service with restrictions, crate.

MILFORD

Holiday Inn Express SH
(508) 634-1054. **$99-$129.** 50 Fortune Blvd. I-495, exit 20, just sw on SR 85, then just se. Int corridors. **Pets:** Medium. $25 one-time fee/pet. Designated rooms, service with restrictions, supervision.

La Quinta Inn & Suites SH
(508) 478-8243. **$95-$115.** 24 Beaver St. I-495, exit 19, just w on SR 109. Int corridors. **Pets:** Other species. Service with restrictions, supervision.

NANTUCKET ISLAND

Seven Sea Street Inn BB
(508) 228-3577. **$99-$299, 15 day notice.** 7 Sea St. Center. Int corridors. **Pets:** Accepted.

NEW BEDFORD

Days Inn SH
(508) 997-1231. **$69-$149, 3 day notice.** 500 Hathaway Rd. SR 140, exit 3, just w. Ext/int corridors. **Pets:** Small. $15 daily fee/pet. Service with restrictions, supervision.

NORTH ADAMS

Jae's Inn BB
(413) 664-0100. **$95-$160, 3 day notice.** 1111 S State St. 2 mi s on SR 8; center. Int corridors. **Pets:** Accepted.

NORTHAMPTON

Clarion Hotel & Conference Center SH
(413) 586-1211. **$89-$175.** One Atwood Dr. I-91, exit 18, just s on US 5. Int corridors. **Pets:** Other species. $20 daily fee/room. Designated rooms, service with restrictions, crate.

NORTON

Extended StayAmerica-Boston-Norton SH
(508) 285-7800. **$91-$115.** 271 S Washington St. I-495, exit 9, 0.3 mi se on Bay St, then 0.5 mi nw via Industrial Park Rd. Int corridors. **Pets:** Other species. $75 one-time fee/pet. Service with restrictions.

ORANGE

Executive Inn M
(978) 544-8864. **$45-$80, 7 day notice.** 110 Daniel Shay Hwy. US 202, exit 16, just n of jct SR 2. Ext/int corridors. **Pets:** Accepted.

PITTSFIELD

Berkshire Inn M
(413) 443-3000. **$79-$199.** 150 W Housatonic St. On US 20, 0.4 mi w of jct US 7. Ext corridors. **Pets:** Accepted.

WWWW Crowne Plaza Hotel and Resort Pittsfield Berkshires LH
(413) 499-2000. **$119-$450, 14 day notice.** 1 West St, Berkshire Common. Center. Int corridors. **Pets:** Small, dogs only. $50 one-time fee/room. Designated rooms, service with restrictions, supervision.

PLYMOUTH

WW WWW Best Western Cold Spring M
(508) 746-2222. **$99-$199, 3 day notice.** 188 Court St. Jct US 44, 0.5 mi n on SR 3A. Ext corridors. **Pets:** Medium. $10 daily fee/pet. Designated rooms, service with restrictions, supervision.

RAYNHAM

WW WW Days Inn Taunton M
(508) 824-8647. **Call for rates.** 164 New State Hwy. SR 24, exit 13B, 0.8 mi w on US 44. Ext/int corridors. **Pets:** $10 daily fee/pet. Designated rooms, service with restrictions, supervision.

REHOBOTH

WWWW Five Bridge Inn Bed & Breakfast BB
(508) 252-3190. **$98-$145, 3 day notice.** 154 Pine St. 1.6 mi n of US 44; 3.3 mi w of jct SR 118; US 44, n on Blanding, e on Broad, n on Salisbury, then w. Int corridors. **Pets:** Accepted.

RICHMOND

WWWW The Inn at Richmond BB
(413) 698-2566. **Call for rates.** 802 State Rd (SR 41). 2.5 mi s of jct US 20. Ext/int corridors. **Pets:** Accepted.

ROCKLAND

WW WWWW Best Western Rockland SH ❖
(781) 871-5660. **$109-$169.** 909 Hingham St. SR 3, exit 14, 0.3 mi sw on SR 228. Int corridors. **Pets:** $20 daily fee/pet. Service with restrictions, supervision.

SCITUATE

WW The Inn at Scituate Harbor M
(781) 545-5550. **$115-$235, 3 day notice.** 7 Beaver Dam Rd. Jct Front St; at Scituate Harbor. Int corridors. **Pets:** Accepted.

SEEKONK

WW Motel 6–1289 M
(508) 336-7800. **Call for rates.** 821 Fall River Ave. I-195, exit 1, just n on SR 114A. Int corridors. **Pets:** Other species. Service with restrictions, supervision.

WW WWW Ramada Inn-Providence SH
(508) 336-7300. **$89-$150.** 940 Fall River Ave. I-195, exit 1, just s. Int corridors. **Pets:** Large. $10 daily fee/pet. Designated rooms, service with restrictions, supervision.

SOMERSET

WW WWWW Quality Inn-Fall River/Somerset SH ❖
(508) 678-4545. **$69-$209.** 1878 Wilbur Ave. Jct SR 103 and I-195, exit 4 eastbound; exit 4A westbound. Int corridors. **Pets:** Other species. Designated rooms, supervision.

SOUTHBOROUGH

WWWW Red Roof Inn # 7075 M
(508) 481-3904. **Call for rates.** 367 Turnpike Rd. I-495, exit 23A, just e on SR 9. Ext corridors. **Pets:** Accepted.

SPRINGFIELD

WW WWWW Holiday Inn LH
(413) 781-0900. **$99-$179.** 711 Dwight St. I-291, exit 2A, just e. Int corridors. **Pets:** Other species. $35 one-time fee/room. Service with restrictions, supervision.

WWWW Sheraton Springfield Monarch Place LH
(413) 781-1010. **$229-$239.** 1 Monarch Pl. I-91, exit 6 northbound; exit 7 southbound, just n; downtown. Int corridors. **Pets:** Accepted.

STURBRIDGE

WW WWW American Motor Lodge M
(508) 347-9121. **$89-$109.** 350 Main St. Jct US 20 and SR 131. Int corridors. **Pets:** Accepted.

WW WWWW Comfort Inn & Suites Colonial SH
(508) 347-3306. **$89-$269.** 215 Charlton Rd. I-90 (Massachusetts Tpke), exit 9, 0.5 mi e; I-84, exit 3A. Ext/int corridors. **Pets:** Other species. $15 daily fee/pet. Designated rooms, service with restrictions.

WW WW Days Inn M
(508) 347-3391. **$59-$159.** 66-68 Haynes St (SR 15). I-84, exit 2, 0.5 mi n, follow signs to SR 131, on I-84 service road. Ext/int corridors. **Pets:** Accepted.

WW WWWW Motel 6 M
(508) 347-7327. **$59-$149.** 408 Main St. I-90 (Massachusetts Tpke), exit 9, 0.8 mi w on US 20; I-84, exit 3B. Ext corridors. **Pets:** $10 daily fee/pet. Designated rooms, no service, supervision.

WW WW Publick House Historic Inn & Country Lodge SH ❖
(508) 347-3313. **$79-$209.** 295 Main St. I-90 (Massachusetts Tpke), exit 9; I-84, exit 3B, 0.5 mi s of jct US 20. Ext/int corridors. **Pets:** Other species. $15 daily fee/room. Designated rooms, service with restrictions.

WW WW Quality Inn SH
(508) 347-1978. **Call for rates.** 400 Haynes Rd (SR 15). I-84, exit 1, 0.5 mi w. Int corridors. **Pets:** Accepted.

WW WW Scottish Inns M
(508) 347-9514. **$50-$79.** 142 Main St. On SR 131, 1.5 mi s of jct US 20. Ext corridors. **Pets:** Small, dogs only. $10 daily fee/pet. Service with restrictions, supervision.

WW WWWW Sturbridge Host Hotel and Conference Center on Cedar Lake LH
(508) 347-7393. **$115-$199.** 366 Main St. I-90 (Massachusetts Tpke), exit 9, just w on US 20; I-84, exit 3B. Int corridors. **Pets:** $25 daily fee/pet. Designated rooms, service with restrictions, supervision.

WW WW Super 8 M
(508) 347-9000. **Call for rates.** 358 Main St. I-90 (Massachusetts Tpke), exit 9; I-84, exit 3B on US 20. Ext corridors. **Pets:** Medium. $20 daily fee/pet. Service with restrictions, supervision.

WESTBOROUGH

AAA ▼▼▼▼ **Doubletree Hotel Boston/Westborough** LH
(508) 366-5511. **Call for rates.** 5400 Computer Dr. I-495, exit 23B, just w on SR 9, exit Computer/Research Dr. Int corridors. **Pets:** Accepted.
SAVE ⊠ ⓜ ⯐ ▣ ⑪ ⇌ ⊠

▼▼ **Extended Stay Deluxe-Boston-Westborough** SH
(508) 616-9213. **$91-$140.** 180 E Main St. I-495, exit 23B, 1.4 mi w, then just sw on SR 30. Int corridors. **Pets:** Other species. $75 one-time fee/pet. Service with restrictions.
ASK ⓢ ⊠ ⓜ ⯐ ▣

▼▼ **Extended Stay Deluxe Boston-Westborough-Computer Dr** SH
(508) 366-6100. **$104-$130.** 1800 Computer Dr. I-495, exit 23B, just w; north side of SR 9. Int corridors. **Pets:** Other species. $75 one-time fee/pet. Service with restrictions.
ASK ⓢ ⊠ ⓜ ⯐ ▣ ⇌

▼▼▼▼ **Residence Inn by Marriott Boston/Westborough** SH
(508) 366-7700. **$236-$257.** 25 Connector Rd. I-495, exit 23B, just w on SR 9, exit Computer/Research Dr, then 0.3 mi s. Ext/int corridors. **Pets:** Accepted.
ASK ⓢ ⊠ ⓜ ⯐ ▣ ⇌ ⊠

WESTFIELD

AAA ▼▼▼ **Econo Lodge & Suites** SH
(413) 568-2821. **$64-$129.** 2 Southampton Rd. I-90, exit 3, at US 202 and SR 10. Ext/int corridors. **Pets:** Medium. $25 one-time fee/pet. Service with restrictions, supervision.
SAVE ⓢ ⊠ ⯐ ▣ ⇌

WESTMINSTER

AAA ▼▼▼▼ **Wachusett Village Inn & Conference Center** SH
(978) 874-2000. **$99-$169.** 9 Village Inn Rd. 0.7 mi w on Village Inn Rd; SR 2, exit 27 westbound, 0.3 mi e; exit 26 eastbound. Ext/int corridors. **Pets:** Accepted.
SAVE ⓢ ⊠ ⯐ ▣ ⑪ ⇌ ⊠

WEST SPRINGFIELD

▼▼▼ **Hampton Inn** SH
(413) 732-1300. **Call for rates.** 1011 Riverdale St (US 5). I-91, exit 13B, 0.3 mi s. Int corridors. **Pets:** Accepted.
⊠ ⓜ ⯐ ▣ ⇌

AAA ▼▼▼ **Quality Inn** SH
(413) 739-7261. **$59-$169.** 1150 Riverdale St. I-91, exit 13B, jct US 5. Int corridors. **Pets:** Medium, other species. $15 daily fee/pet. Service with restrictions, crate.
SAVE ⓢ ⊠ ⯐ ▣ ⑪ ⇌

AAA ▼ **Red Carpet Inn** M
(413) 733-6678. **$58-$99.** 560 Riverdale St. I-91, exit 13B, 1.3 mi s. Ext corridors. **Pets:** Small, dogs only. $10 daily fee/pet. Designated rooms, no service, supervision.
SAVE ⓢ ⊠ ⓜ ⯐ ⇌

▼▼ **Red Roof Inn #7193** M
(413) 731-1010. **Call for rates.** 1254 Riverdale St. I-91, exit 13A. Ext corridors. **Pets:** Accepted.
⊠ ⓜ ⯐

▼▼▼ **Residence Inn by Marriott** SH
(413) 732-9543. **$154-$198.** 64 Border Way. I-91, exit 13A, on US 5. Int corridors. **Pets:** Accepted.
ASK ⓢ ⊠ ⓜ ⯐ ▣ ⇌ ⊠

WEST STOCKBRIDGE

AAA ▼ **Pleasant Valley Motel** M
(413) 232-8511. **$45-$165, 15 day notice.** 42 Stockbridge Rd. I-90 (Massachusetts Tpke), exit B3 eastbound, 0.5 mi s on SR 22, then 3.5 mi e on SR 102; exit 1 westbound, 0.4 mi e. Ext corridors. **Pets:** Accepted.
SAVE ⓢ ⊠ ⯐ ⇌

WILLIAMSTOWN

▼ **Cozy Corner Motel** M
(413) 458-8006. **$45-$135, 10 day notice.** 284 Sand Springs Rd (US 7). On US 7, 1.5 mi n of jct SR 2. Ext corridors. **Pets:** Other species. $10 daily fee/pet. Service with restrictions, supervision.
⊠ ⯐

AAA ▼ **The Villager Motel** M
(413) 458-4046. **$55-$125, 14 day notice.** 953 Simonds Rd. On US 7, 1.7 n of jct SR 2. Ext corridors. **Pets:** Accepted.
SAVE ⓢ ⊠ ⯐

WORCESTER

AAA ▼▼▼▼ **Beechwood Hotel** SH
(508) 754-5789. **$245-$325.** 363 Plantation St. I-290, exit 22 westbound, 0.5 mi w on Lincoln St, then 1.5 mi s; exit 21 eastbound, 1.3 mi s. Int corridors. **Pets:** Accepted.
SAVE ⊠ ⓜ ⯐ ▣ ⑪ ⊠

AAA ▼▼▼▼ **Crowne Plaza Hotel** LH
(508) 791-1600. **$119-$199.** 10 Lincoln Square. I-290, exit 17 eastbound; exit 18 westbound, 0.3 mi s. Int corridors. **Pets:** Accepted.
SAVE ⓢ ⊠ ⓜ ⯐ ▣ ⑪ ⇌ ⊠

▼▼▼ **Residence Inn by Marriott Worcester** SH
(508) 753-6300. **$164-$186.** 503 Plantation St. I-290, exit 21, 0.5 mi sw. Int corridors. **Pets:** Accepted.
ASK ⓢ ⊠ ⓜ ⯐ ▣ ⇌

MICHIGAN

ALGONAC

▼▼ Linda's Lighthouse Inn BB ❖
(810) 794-2992. **$95-$135, 14 day notice.** 5965 Pointe Tremble Rd (SR 29). I-94, exit 243 (23 Mile Rd), 14.3 mi e. Int corridors. **Pets:** Other species. $15 daily fee/pet. Crate.
⊠ ⊠ ⚠ ☎

ALLEGAN

▼▼▼ Castle In The Country B & B Inn BB
(269) 673-8054. **$100-$225, 7 day notice.** 340 SR 40 S. SR 40 S, 6 mi s. Int corridors. **Pets:** Accepted.
⊠ ⊠ ☎

ALLENDALE

▼▼ Sleep Inn & Suites SH
(616) 892-8000. **$69-$179.** 4869 Becker Dr. I-96, exit 16, 6 mi s, then 2.5 mi e on SR 45. Int corridors. **Pets:** Accepted.
ASK S⊘ ⊠ &M ☎ ⚟ ⚟

ALPENA

▼▼ Days Inn SH
(989) 356-6118. **$80-$120.** 1496 Hwy 32 W. 2.5 mi w of jct US 23. Int corridors. **Pets:** Accepted.
ASK S⊘ ⊠ ☎ ⚟ ⚟ ⊠

▼▼ Holiday Inn SH
(989) 356-2151. **Call for rates.** 1000 Hwy 23 N. On US 23, 1 mi n. Int corridors. **Pets:** Accepted.
⊠ ☎ ⚟ ⅊ ⚟ ⊠

ANN ARBOR

▼▼ Candlewood Suites SH
(734) 663-2818. **Call for rates.** 701 Waymarket Way. I-94, exit 175 (Ann Arbor/Saline Rd), just e on Eisenhower Rd. Int corridors. **Pets:** Accepted.
⊠ &M ☎ ⚟

AAA ▼▼▼ Courtyard by Marriott SH ❖
(734) 995-5900. **$142-$164.** 3205 Boardwalk St. I-94, exit 177 (State St), just n, then just e on Victors Way. Int corridors. **Pets:** Medium. $75 one-time fee/room. Designated rooms, service with restrictions, supervision.
SAVE S⊘ ⊠ ☎ ⚟ ⚟

▼▼ Extended StayAmerica SH
(734) 332-1980. **$85-$120.** 1501 Briarwood Circle Dr. I-94, exit 177 (State St), just ne. Int corridors. **Pets:** Other species. $75 one-time fee/pet. Service with restrictions.
ASK S⊘ ⊠ &M ☎ ⚟

▼▼ Extended Stay Deluxe Detroit-Ann Arbor SH
(734) 997-7623. **$90-$120.** 3265 Boardwalk Dr. I-94, exit 177 (State St), just n, then e on Victors Way. Int corridors. **Pets:** Other species. $75 one-time fee/pet. Service with restrictions.
ASK S⊘ ⊠ ☎ ⚟

AAA ▼▼◆ Fairfield Inn by Marriott SH ❖
(734) 995-5200. **$126-$147.** 3285 Boardwalk St. I-94, exit 177 (State St), just n, then e on Victors Way. Int corridors. **Pets:** Medium. $75 one-time fee/room. Designated rooms, service with restrictions, supervision.
SAVE S⊘ ⊠ ☎ ⚟ ⚟

▼▼▼ Hampton Inn-North SH
(734) 996-4444. **Call for rates.** 2300 Green Rd. US 23, exit 41 (Plymouth Rd), just nw. Int corridors. **Pets:** Accepted.
⊠ &M ☎ ⚟ ⅊ ⚟

▼▼▼ Hawthorn Suites SH
(734) 327-0011. **$125-$250.** 3535 Green Ct. US 23, exit 41 (Plymouth Rd), just sw. Int corridors. **Pets:** Accepted.
ASK S⊘ ⊠ &M ☎ ⚟ ⚟ ⊠

▼▼ Red Roof Inn #7045 M
(734) 996-5800. **Call for rates.** 3621 Plymouth Rd. US 23, exit 41 (Plymouth Rd), just nw. Ext corridors. **Pets:** Accepted.
⊠ ☎

▼▼ Residence Inn by Marriott SH
(734) 996-5666. **$181-$202.** 800 Victors Way. I-94, exit 177 (State St), just ne. Ext/int corridors. **Pets:** Accepted.
ASK S⊘ ⊠ ☎ ⚟ ⚟ ⊠

AU GRES

▼▼ Econo Lodge Inn SH
(989) 876-4060. **Call for rates.** 510 W US 23. On US 23, just w. Int corridors. **Pets:** Accepted.
⊠ ☎ ⚟ ⚟

BAD AXE

Econo Lodge Inns & Suites SH
(989) 269-3200. **Call for rates.** 898 N Van Dyke Rd. Just s of jct SR 142 and 53 (Van Dyke Rd). Int corridors. **Pets:** Accepted.
SAVE ⊠ ⵏ 🐾

BATTLE CREEK

Baymont Inn & Suites-Battle Creek SH
(269) 979-5400. **Call for rates.** 4725 Beckley Rd. I-94, exit 97 (Capital Ave), just sw. Int corridors. **Pets:** Accepted.
SAVE ⊠ 🛆 🖵 🐾

BAY VIEW

Comfort Inn SH 🐾
(231) 347-3220. **$50-$250.** 1314 US 31 N. Jct US 31 and SR 119. Int corridors. **Pets:** Other species. Service with restrictions, supervision.
SAVE S🛆 ⊠ 🛆 🖵

BEAR LAKE

Bella Vista Inn M
(231) 864-3000. **$60-$109.** 12273 US 31. On US 31; center. Ext corridors. **Pets:** Large, dogs only. $10 daily fee/pet. Designated rooms, service with restrictions, supervision.
SAVE S🛆 ⊠ 🛆 🐾

BEULAH

Best Western Scenic Hill Resort SH
(231) 882-7754. **$76-$186.** 1400 US 31 Hwy. 0.8 mi e on US 31. Int corridors. **Pets:** Medium, dogs only. $50 deposit/room, $20 daily fee/room. Designated rooms, supervision.
SAVE S🛆 ⊠ 🛆 🖵 🐾 🚫

BIG RAPIDS

Holiday Inn Hotel & Conference Center SH
(231) 796-4400. **$99-$150.** 1005 Perry St. US 131, exit 139, 1.3 mi e on SR 20. Int corridors. **Pets:** Accepted.
ASK S🛆 ⊠ 🛆M 🛆 🖵 ⵏ 🐾 🚫

Quality Inn & Suites M
(231) 592-5150. **$59-$129.** 1705 S State St. US 131, exit 139, 2.1 mi e on SR 20, then 1 mi s. Ext/int corridors. **Pets:** $10 daily fee/pet. Designated rooms, service with restrictions, supervision.
SAVE S🛆 ⊠ 🛆 🖵 🐾

BIRCH RUN

Super 8 Motel SH
(989) 624-4440. **$50-$120.** 9235 E Birch Run Rd. I-75, exit 136 (Birch Run Rd), just e. Int corridors. **Pets:** Small. No service, supervision.
SAVE S🛆 ⊠ 🛆 🖵 🚫

BRIDGEPORT

Baymont Inn & Suites-Frankenmuth/Bridgeport SH
(989) 777-3000. **Call for rates.** 6460 Dixie Hwy. I-75, exit 144A. Int corridors. **Pets:** Accepted.
SAVE ⊠ 🛆 🖵 🐾

BROOKLYN

Super 8 Motel SH
(517) 592-0888. **$65-$130.** 155 Wamplers Rd. Jct Main St (SR 50) and SR 124; downtown. Int corridors. **Pets:** Accepted.
ASK S🛆 ⊠ 🛆M 🛆

CADILLAC

Econo Lodge SH
(231) 775-6700. **$55-$95.** 2501 Sunnyside Dr. Jct SR 55 and 115. Ext/int corridors. **Pets:** Accepted.
SAVE S🛆 ⊠ 🛆 🖵

McGuires Resort SH 🐾
(231) 775-9947. **$79-$99, 7 day notice.** 7880 Mackinaw Tr. US 131, exit 177, 0.7 mi n, then 0.5 mi w. Int corridors. **Pets:** Large. $20 daily fee/room. Designated rooms, service with restrictions, crate.
SAVE ⊠ 🛆 🖵 ⵏ 🐾 🚫

CALUMET

AmericInn of Calumet SH
(906) 337-6463. **Call for rates.** 56925 S 6th St. On US 41, just w of Visitors Center. Int corridors. **Pets:** Accepted.
⊠ 🛆 🖵 🐾 🚫

CASCADE

AmeriSuites Grand Rapids/Airport SH
(616) 940-8100. **Call for rates.** 5401 28th St Ct SE. I-96, exit 43B, just e on SR 11. Int corridors. **Pets:** Accepted.
⊠ 🛆 🖵 🐾 🚫

Baymont Inn-Grand Rapids Airport SH
(616) 956-3300. **Call for rates.** 2873 Kraft Ave SE. I-96, exit 43B, just e. Int corridors. **Pets:** Accepted.
⊠ 🛆 🖵

Country Inn & Suites by Carlson of Grand Rapids SH
(616) 977-0909. **Call for rates.** 5399 28th St. I-96, exit 43B, just e on SR 11. Int corridors. **Pets:** Accepted.
⊠ 🛆M 🛆 🖵 🐾

Crowne Plaza Grand Rapids LH
(616) 957-1770. **$189.** 5700 28th St SE. I-96, exit 43B, 0.3 mi e on SR 11. Int corridors. **Pets:** Accepted.
ASK S🛆 ⊠ 🛆 🖵 ⵏ 🐾 🚫

Days Inn SH
(616) 956-9304. **$69-$79.** 4981 28th St SE. I-96, exit 43A, 0.5 mi w on SR 11. Int corridors. **Pets:** Accepted.
ASK S🛆 ⊠ 🛆 🖵 🐾

Exel Inn of Grand Rapids SH
(616) 957-3000. **$46-$66.** 4855 28th St SE. I-96, exit 43A, 0.5 mi w on SR 11. Int corridors. **Pets:** Accepted.
SAVE S🛆 ⊠ 🛆 🖵

CHARLEVOIX

AmericInn Lodge & Suites SH
(231) 237-0988. **Call for rates.** 11800 US 31 N. On US 31, 2.4 mi n. Int corridors. **Pets:** Other species. $50 deposit/room, $10 daily fee/pet. Service with restrictions, supervision.
⊠ 🛆M 🛆 🖵 🐾

CHARLOTTE

Super 8 Motel SH
(517) 543-8288. **Call for rates.** 828 E Shepherd St. I-69, exit 60 (SR 50), just w. Int corridors. **Pets:** Accepted.
⊠ 🛆

CHEBOYGAN

Best Western River Terrace Motel M
(231) 627-5688. **$49-$199.** 847 S Main St. 1 mi s on SR 27. Ext/int corridors. **Pets:** Medium, dogs only. $10 daily fee/pet. Designated rooms, service with restrictions, supervision.
SAVE S🛆 ⊠ 🛆 🖵 🐾 🚫

◈◈◈ ◈ Birch Haus Motel Ⓜ
(231) 627-5862. **$40-$80.** 1301 Mackinaw Ave. On US 23, 0.8 mi nw. Ext corridors. **Pets:** Small. $5 daily fee/pet. Service with restrictions, supervision.
[SAVE] [S🐾] [✕] [🔌]

◈ Continental Inn Ⓜ
(231) 627-7164. **$39-$99.** 613 N Main St. Jct US 23 and SR 27. Ext corridors. **Pets:** Accepted.
[ASK] [S🐾] [✕] [🔌] [⊷]

◈◈◈ ◈ Pine River Motel Ⓜ
(231) 627-5119. **$35-$80, 3 day notice.** 102 Lafayette. On US 23, 0.5 mi e. Ext corridors. **Pets:** $10 one-time fee/pet. Service with restrictions, supervision.
[SAVE] [✕] [🔌]

CHELSEA

◈◈◈◈ Chelsea Comfort Inn & Village Conference Center [SH]
(734) 433-8000. **$99-$289.** 1645 Commerce Park Dr. I-94, exit 159 (SR 52/Main St), just n. Int corridors. **Pets:** Accepted.
[ASK] [S🐾] [✕] [&M] [🔌] [🔌] [⊷]

CHESANING

◈◈◈ ◈ Colonial Motel Ⓜ
(989) 845-3292. **$60-$130.** 9475 E M-57. On SR 57, 0.5 mi e. Ext corridors. **Pets:** Medium. $10 daily fee/pet. Designated rooms, service with restrictions, supervision.
[SAVE] [S🐾] [✕] [🔌]

CLARE

◈ ◈ Days Inn [SH]
(989) 802-0144. **Call for rates.** 10100 S Clare Ave. On Business Rt US 10 and 127, just w of jct US 127 and Old US 27. Int corridors. **Pets:** Accepted.
[✕] [&M] [🔌] [🔌] [✕]

COLDWATER

◈◈◈ ◈ ◈ Red Roof Inn [SH]
(517) 279-1199. **Call for rates.** 348 S Willowbrook Rd. I-69, exit 13 (US 12), just e. Int corridors. **Pets:** Accepted.
[SAVE] [✕] [&M] [🔌] [🔌]

◈◈◈ ◈ ◈ Super 8 Motel [SH]
(517) 278-8833. **Call for rates.** 600 Orleans Blvd. I-69, exit 13 (US 12), 0.3 mi w on E Chicago St, just n on N Michigan Ave, then just e. Int corridors. **Pets:** Accepted.
[SAVE] [✕] [&M] [🔌]

COPPER HARBOR

◈ Lake Fanny Hooe Resort Ⓜ
(906) 289-4451. **$75-$105, 7 day notice.** 505 2nd St. Just s on Manganese Rd. Ext corridors. **Pets:** Accepted.
[✕] [🔌] [🔌] [✕] [🎿] [✉]

DETROIT METROPOLITAN AREA

ALLEN PARK

◈◈◈ ◈ ◈ ◈ Best Western Greenfield Inn [SH]
(313) 271-1600. **$105-$110.** 3000 Enterprise Dr. I-94, exit 206 (Oakwood Blvd), just s, then just w. Int corridors. **Pets:** Medium, dogs only. $50 deposit/room. Designated rooms, service with restrictions, supervision.
[SAVE] [S🐾] [✕] [🔌] [🔌] [🍽] [⊷] [✕]

AUBURN HILLS

◈ ◈ Candlewood Suites [SH]
(248) 373-3342. **Call for rates.** 1650 N Opdyke Rd. I-75, exit 79 (University Dr), just w, then 0.4 mi n. Int corridors. **Pets:** Accepted.
[✕] [🔌] [🔌]

◈ ◈ Homestead Studio Suites Hotel-Detroit/Auburn Hills [SH]
(248) 340-8888. **$69-$77.** 3315 University Dr. I-75, exit 79 (University Dr), 0.9 mi e. Int corridors. **Pets:** Other species. $75 one-time fee/pet. Service with restrictions.
[ASK] [S🐾] [✕] [🔌] [🔌]

◈ ◈ ◈ Staybridge Suites [SH]
(248) 322-4600. **$130-$450.** 2050 Featherstone Rd. I-75, exit 79 (University Dr), just w, 0.5 mi s on Opdyke Rd, then just e. Int corridors. **Pets:** Accepted.
[ASK] [S🐾] [✕] [🔌] [🔌] [⊷]

BELLEVILLE

◈ ◈ Red Roof Inn Metro Airport #7183 Ⓜ
(734) 697-2244. **Call for rates.** 45501 N I-94 Service Dr. I-94, exit 190 (Belleville Rd), just n. Ext corridors. **Pets:** Accepted.
[✕] [🔌]

BIRMINGHAM

◈ ◈ ◈ Barclay Inn Birmingham [SH]
(248) 646-7300. **$84-$129.** 34952 Woodward Ave. On SR 1, jct Woodward Ave and Maple Rd; center. Ext/int corridors. **Pets:** $25 one-time fee/room. Designated rooms, service with restrictions, crate.
[ASK] [S🐾] [✕] [&M] [🔌] [🔌]

◈◈◈ ◈ ◈ ◈ Holiday Inn Express–Birmingham [SH]
(248) 642-6200. **$139-$169.** 35270 Woodward Ave. Jct Woodward Ave and Maple Rd; center. Int corridors. **Pets:** Small, other species. $50 one-time fee/pet. Service with restrictions, supervision.
[SAVE] [S🐾] [✕] [🔌] [🔌]

◈◈◈ ◈ ◈ ◈ The Townsend Hotel [SH]
(248) 642-7900. **$299-$369.** 100 Townsend St. Center. Int corridors. **Pets:** Accepted.
[SAVE] [✕] [&M] [🔌] [🔌] [🍽] [✕]

CANTON

◈ ◈ La Quinta Inn [SH]
(734) 981-1808. **$79-$95.** 41211 Ford Rd. I-275, exit 25 (Ford Rd), just w to jct Haggerty Rd. Int corridors. **Pets:** Other species. Service with restrictions, supervision.
[ASK] [S🐾] [✕] [🔌] [🔌]

DEARBORN

◈ ◈ Extended StayAmerica [SH]
(313) 336-0021. **$95-$125.** 260 Towne Center Dr. SR 39 (Southfield Frwy); between Ford Rd and Michigan Ave exits; just w of jct Service and Hubbard drs. Int corridors. **Pets:** Other species. $75 one-time fee/pet. Service with restrictions.
[ASK] [S🐾] [✕] [&M] [🔌] [🔌]

▼▼ ▼▼ Red Roof Inn-Dearborn #7182 **M**
(313) 278-9732. **Call for rates.** 24130 Michigan Ave. Jct US 24 (Telegraph Rd) and 12 (Michigan Ave). Ext corridors. **Pets:** Accepted.
⊠ 🖶 🖬

♨♨ ▼▼▼ ▼▼▼ The Ritz-Carlton, Dearborn **LH**
(313) 441-2000. **$291-$312.** 300 Town Center Dr. SR 39 (Southfield Frwy); between Ford Rd and Michigan Ave exits, on Service Dr. Int corridors. **Pets:** Medium. $150 one-time fee/pet. Service with restrictions.
[SAVE] 🖬 ⊠ 🖬 🖬 🍴 🏊 ⊠

▼▼ ▼▼ TownePlace Suites **SH**
(313) 271-0200. **$165-$198.** 6141 Mercury Dr. SR 39 (Southfield Frwy), exit 7 (Ford Rd), just e, then 0.8 mi n. Int corridors. **Pets:** Accepted.
[ASK] 🖬 ⊠ 🖬 🖬 🖬 🏊

DETROIT

♨♨ ▼▼▼ ▼▼▼ Hilton Garden Inn Detroit/Downtown **LH**
(313) 967-0900. **Call for rates.** 351 Gratiot Ave. Jct Randolph St and Gratiot Ave, just e; in Harmonie Park. Int corridors. **Pets:** Accepted.
[SAVE] ⊠ 🖬 🖬 🖬 🍴 🏊

♨♨ ▼▼▼ ▼▼▼ Holiday Inn Express **LH**
(313) 887-7000. **$129-$199.** 1020 Washington Blvd. Corner of Washington Blvd and Michigan Ave. Int corridors. **Pets:** Accepted.
[SAVE] ⊠ 🖬 🖬 🍴 🏊

▼▼▼ ▼▼▼ Omni Detroit River Place **LH**
(313) 259-9500. **$179-$199.** 1000 River Place Dr. 1.5 mi on E Jefferson Ave, 4 blks s on McDougall. Int corridors. **Pets:** Accepted.
[ASK] 🖬 ⊠ 🖬 🖬 🏊 ⊠

▼▼▼ ▼▼▼ Residence Inn By Marriott-Dearborn **SH**
(313) 441-1700. **$197-$230.** 5777 Southfield Service Dr. SR 39 (Southfield Frwy), exit Ford Rd, just w. Ext corridors. **Pets:** Accepted.
[ASK] 🖬 ⊠ 🖬 🖬 🏊 ⊠

▼▼▼ ▼▼▼ Sheraton Detroit Riverside **LH**
(313) 965-0200. **$119-$600.** 2 Washington Blvd. Opposite Cobo Hall. Int corridors. **Pets:** Accepted.
[ASK] 🖬 ⊠ 🖬 🖬 🍴 🏊 ⊠

▼▼ ▼▼ Woodbridge Star Bed & Breakfast **BB**
(313) 831-9668. **$125-$175, 10 day notice.** 3985 Trumbull St. Jct Alexandrine St. Int corridors. **Pets:** Accepted.
[ASK] 🖬 ⊠ ☎

FARMINGTON HILLS

▼▼ ▼▼ Candlewood Suites **SH**
(248) 324-0540. **$110-$259.** 37555 Hills Tech Dr. I-696, exit I-96 E/I-275 S/SR 5, just s to SR 5 N, 2 mi n to 12 Mile Rd, 1.3 mi e, then 0.3 mi s on Halsted Rd. Int corridors. **Pets:** Accepted.
[ASK] 🖬 ⊠ 🖬 🖬 🖬

▼▼ ▼▼ Extended StayAmerica-Detroit-Farmington Hills **SH**
(248) 473-4000. **$95-$125.** 27775 Stansbury Blvd. I-696, exit 5 (Orchard Lake Rd), just n, just e on 12 Mile Rd, then just s. Int corridors. **Pets:** Other species. $75 one-time fee/pet. Service with restrictions.
[ASK] 🖬 ⊠ 🖬 🖬 🖬

▼▼ ▼▼ Red Roof Inn-Farmington Hills #7038 **M**
(248) 478-8640. **Call for rates.** 24300 Sinacola Ct. I-96/275 and SR 5, exit 165 (Grand River Ave), just w. Ext corridors. **Pets:** Accepted.
⊠ 🖬 🖬

LAKE ORION

♨♨♨ ▼▼ ▼▼ Best Western Palace Inn **SH**
(248) 391-2755. **Call for rates.** 2755 N Lapeer Rd. I-75, exit 81 (Lapeer Rd), 3.3 mi n. Ext/int corridors. **Pets:** Accepted.
[SAVE] ⊠ 🖬 🖬 🖬 🏊

LIVONIA

▼▼▼ ▼▼▼ Livonia Marriott **SH**
(734) 462-3100. **$208-$230.** 17100 Laurel Park Dr N. I-275, exit 170 (6 Mile Rd), just w. Int corridors. **Pets:** Accepted.
[ASK] 🖬 ⊠ 🖬 🖬 🍴 🏊 ⊠

♨♨ ▼▼▼ ▼▼▼ Residence Inn Detroit-Livonia **SH**
(734) 462-4201. **$230-$252.** 17250 Fox Dr. I-275, exit 170 (6 Mile Rd), just w. Int corridors. **Pets:** Other species. $75 one-time fee/room. Service with restrictions.
[SAVE] 🖬 ⊠ 🖬 🖬 🖬 🏊 ⊠

▼▼ ▼▼ TownePlace Suites by Marriott **SH**
(734) 542-7400. **$182-$203.** 17450 Fox Dr. I-275, exit 170 (6 Mile Rd), just nw. Int corridors. **Pets:** Other species. $75 one-time fee/room. Service with restrictions.
[ASK] 🖬 ⊠ 🖬 🖬 🖬 🏊

MADISON HEIGHTS

▼▼ Motel 6 Madison Heights #1109 **M**
(248) 583-0500. **$55-$65.** 32700 Barrington Rd. I-75, exit 65A (14 Mile Rd), just e. Ext corridors. **Pets:** Other species. Service with restrictions, supervision.
🖬 ⊠ 🖬

▼▼▼ ▼▼ Red Roof Inn #7084 **M**
(248) 583-4700. **Call for rates.** 32511 Concord Dr. I-75, exit 65A (14 Mile Rd), just e, then just s. Ext corridors. **Pets:** Accepted.
⊠ 🖬

▼▼▼ ▼▼▼ Residence Inn by Marriott-Detroit Troy/Madison
Heights **SH**
(248) 583-4322. **$177-$197.** 32650 Stephenson Hwy. I-75, exit 65B (14 Mile Rd), just w, then just s. Ext corridors. **Pets:** Accepted.
[ASK] 🖬 ⊠ 🖬 🖬 🏊 ⊠

NOVI

▼▼ ▼▼ Extended StayAmerica-Detroit-Novi **SH**
(248) 305-9955. **$81-$90.** 21555 Haggerty Rd. I-275, exit 167 (8 Mile Rd), just w, then 0.5 mi n. Int corridors. **Pets:** Other species. $75 one-time fee/pet. Service with restrictions.
[ASK] 🖬 ⊠ 🖬 🖬 🖬

▼▼▼ ▼▼▼ Residence Inn by Marriott-Detroit/Novi **SH**
(248) 735-7400. **$186-$208.** 27477 Caberet Dr. I-96, exit 162 (Novi Rd), just n to 12 Mile Rd, then just w. Int corridors. **Pets:** Accepted.
[ASK] 🖬 ⊠ 🖬 🖬 🏊

▼▼▼ ▼▼▼ Sheraton-Detroit-Novi **LH**
(248) 349-4000. **Call for rates.** 21111 Haggerty Rd. I-275, exit 167 (8 Mile Rd), just w to Haggerty Rd, then just n. Int corridors. **Pets:** Accepted.
⊠ 🖬 🖬 🖬 🍴 🏊

▼▼ ▼▼ TownePlace Suites **SH**
(248) 305-5533. **$164-$186.** 42600 11 Mile Rd. I-96, exit 162 (Novi Rd), just s, 0.5 mi e on Crescent Dr, then just s on Town Center Dr. Int corridors. **Pets:** Accepted.
[ASK] 🖬 ⊠ 🖬 🖬 🏊

PLYMOUTH

▼▼▼ ▼▼ Red Roof Inn-Plymouth #7016 **M**
(734) 459-3300. **Call for rates.** 39700 Ann Arbor Rd. I-275, exit 28 (Ann Arbor Rd), just e. Ext corridors. **Pets:** Accepted.
⊠ 🖬

PONTIAC

◆◆◆ Residence Inn by Marriott Detroit Pontiac/Auburn Hills SH
(248) 858-8664. **$208-$230.** 3333 Centerpoint Pkwy. I-75, exit 75 (Square Lake Rd), w via Opdyke Rd. Int corridors. **Pets:** Accepted.

ASK SD X ⊟ ⬛ ⩗ X

ROCHESTER HILLS

◆◆ Red Roof Inn #7191 M
(248) 853-6400. **Call for rates.** 2580 Crooks Rd. Jct Hall (SR 59) and Crooks rds. Ext corridors. **Pets:** Accepted.

X ⊟

ROMULUS

◆◆ Americas Best Value Inn & Suites SH
(734) 595-7400. **$60-$70.** 9095 Wickham Rd. I-94, exit 198 (Merriman Rd), just n, then just w. Int corridors. **Pets:** Accepted.

ASK SD X ⊟ ⬛

◆◆ Baymont Inn & Suites Detroit-Airport SH
(734) 722-6000. **Call for rates.** 9000 Wickham Rd. I-94, exit 198 (Merriman Rd), just n, then just w. Int corridors. **Pets:** Accepted.

X ⊟ ⬛

◆◆◆ Clarion Hotel Detroit Metro Airport SH
(734) 728-7900. **$89-$149.** 8600 Merriman Rd. I-94, exit 198 (Merriman Rd), just n. Int corridors. **Pets:** Accepted.

SAVE SD X ⊟ ⬛ ⓘ ⩗

◆◆◆ Detroit Metro Airport Marriott SH
(734) 729-7555. **$209-$229.** 30559 Flynn Dr. I-94, exit 198 (Merriman Rd), just n, then 0.3 mi e. Int corridors. **Pets:** Accepted.

ASK SD X ⓜ ⊟ ⬛ ⓘ ⩗

◆◆ Extended StayAmerica SH
(734) 722-7780. **$75-$105.** 30325 Flynn Dr. I-94, exit 198 (Merriman Rd), just n, then 0.4 mi e. Int corridors. **Pets:** Other species. $75 one-time fee/pet. Service with restrictions.

ASK SD X ⬛

◆◆ Four Points by Sheraton Detroit Metro Airport SH
(734) 729-9000. **$150-$175.** 8800 Wickham Rd. I-94, exit 198 (Merriman Rd), just n, then just e. Int corridors. **Pets:** Accepted.

ASK SD X ⊟ ⬛ ⓘ ⩗

◆◆ La Quinta Inn Detroit-Metro Airport SH
(734) 641-9006. **$89.** 7680 Merriman Rd. I-94, exit 198 (Merriman Rd), 0.4 mi n. Int corridors. **Pets:** Other species. Service with restrictions, supervision.

ASK SD X ⊟

◆◆◆ Romulus Quality Inn & Suites SH
(734) 946-1400. **$69-$134.** 9555 Middlebelt Rd. I-94, exit 199 (Middlebelt Rd), 0.4 mi s. Int corridors. **Pets:** Accepted.

SAVE SD X ⊟ ⬛

◆◆◆◆ The Westin Detroit Metropolitan Airport LH ♣
(734) 942-6500. **Call for rates.** 2501 Worldgateway Pl. I-94, exit 198 (Merriman Rd); at McNamara Terminal. Int corridors. **Pets:** Medium, dogs only. Designated rooms, service with restrictions, supervision.

SAVE X ⓜ ⊟ ⬛ ⓘ ⩗

ROSEVILLE

◆◆◆ Baymont Inn & Suites Detroit-Roseville SH
(586) 296-6910. **Call for rates.** 20675 13 Mile Rd. I-94, exit 232 (Little Mack Ave), just s. Int corridors. **Pets:** Accepted.

SAVE X ⊟ ⬛

◆◆ ◆◆ Best Western Georgian Inn M
(586) 294-0400. **$89-$199.** 31327 Gratiot Ave. I-94, exit 232 (Little Mack Ave), just s, 0.5 mi n on 13 Mile Rd, then just n. Ext corridors. **Pets:** Medium, dogs only. $8 daily fee/pet. Service with restrictions, supervision.

SAVE SD X ⊟ ⬛ ⓘ ⩗

◆◆ Microtel Inn & Suites SH
(586) 415-1000. **$55-$65.** 20313 13 Mile Rd. I-94, exit 232 (Little Mack Ave), just s, then 0.4 mi w. Int corridors. **Pets:** Other species. $35 deposit/room.

ASK SD X ⓜ ⊟ ⬛ ⩗

◆◆ Red Roof Inn #7012 M
(586) 296-0310. **Call for rates.** 31800 Little Mack Ave. I-94, exit 232 (Little Mack Ave), just n. Ext corridors. **Pets:** Accepted.

X ⊟

SOUTHFIELD

◆◆ Candlewood Suites SH
(248) 945-0010. **Call for rates.** 1 Corporate Dr. SR 10 (Northwestern Hwy), exit Lasher Rd, just e. Int corridors. **Pets:** Accepted.

X ⓜ ⊟ ⬛

◆◆ ◆◆◆ Holiday Inn Express Hotel & Suites SH
(248) 350-2400. **$119-$169.** 25100 Northwestern Hwy. SR 10 (Northwestern Hwy), exit 10 Mile Rd. Int corridors. **Pets:** Very small, dogs only. $150 one-time fee/pet. No service, supervision.

SAVE SD X ⓜ ⊟ ⬛ ⩗

◆◆ Holiday Resort Hotel LH
(248) 353-7700. **Call for rates.** 26555 Telegraph Rd. I-696, exit 9 (Telegraph Rd), just s on US 24 (Telegraph Rd). Int corridors. **Pets:** Accepted.

X ⓜ ⊟ ⬛ ⓘ ⩗ X

◆◆ ◆◆ Marvin's Garden Inn M
(248) 353-6777. **Call for rates.** 27650 Northwestern Hwy. I-696, exit 9 (Telegraph Rd), just nw. Ext/int corridors. **Pets:** Accepted.

SAVE X ⊟ ⬛

◆◆ Red Roof Inn-Southfield #7133 M
(248) 353-7200. **Call for rates.** 27660 Northwestern Hwy. I-696, exit 9 (Telegraph Rd), just nw. Ext corridors. **Pets:** Accepted.

X ⓜ

◆◆ Residence Inn by Marriott SH
(248) 352-8900. **$209-$229.** 26700 Central Park Blvd. I-696, exit 11 (Evergreen Rd), just sw of jct 11 Mile and Evergreen rds. Ext corridors. **Pets:** Accepted.

ASK SD X ⓜ ⊟ ⬛ ⩗

◆◆ ◆◆◆ ◆◆◆ Westin Hotel Southfield-Detroit LH
(248) 827-4000. **$99-$309.** 1500 Town Center. SR 10 (Northwestern Hwy), exit 10 (Mile/Evergreen rds), 0.3 mi n. Int corridors. **Pets:** Accepted.

SAVE SD X ⓜ ⊟ ⬛ ⓘ ⩗

SOUTHGATE

◆◆◆ La Quinta Inn & Suites Detroit-Southgate SH
(734) 374-3000. **$74-$87.** 12888 Reeck Rd. I-75, exit 37 (Northline Rd), just w. Int corridors. **Pets:** Other species. Service with restrictions, supervision.

ASK SD X ⊟ ⬛

◆◆ ◆◆ Motel 6 Detroit-Southgate M
(734) 287-8340. **$45-$169.** 18777 Northline Rd. I-75, exit 37 (Northline Rd), just w. Ext corridors. **Pets:** Other species. Service with restrictions, supervision.

SAVE SD X ⊟ ⬛ ⩗

STERLING HEIGHTS

▼▼ **TownePlace Suites** 🆂🅷
(586) 566-0900. **$165-$187.** 14800 Lakeside Cir. 1 mi e of jct SR 53 (Van Dyke Ave) and 59 (Hall Rd). Int corridors. **Pets:** Other species. $75 one-time fee/room. Crate.
(A$K) (S🐾) (✕) (&M) 🅗 💻 🐾

TAYLOR

▼▼ **Red Roof Inn-Taylor #7189** Ⓜ
(734) 374-1150. **Call for rates.** 21230 Eureka Rd. I-75, exit 36 (Eureka Rd), just w. Ext corridors. **Pets:** Accepted.
(✕) 🅗

TROY

▼▼ **Drury Inn & Suites-Troy** 🆂🅷
(248) 528-3330. **$81-$216.** 575 W Big Beaver Rd. I-75, exit 69 (Big Beaver Rd), just e. Int corridors. **Pets:** Large, other species. Service with restrictions, supervision.
(A$K) (✕) 🅗 💻 (🍴) 🐾

🐕‍ ▼▼▼ **Hilton/Detroit/Troy** 🆂🅷
(248) 879-2100. **Call for rates.** 5500 Crooks Rd. I-75, exit 72 (Crooks Rd), just n. Int corridors. **Pets:** Accepted.
(SAVE) (✕) (&M) 🅗 💻 (🍴) 🐾

▼▼ **Holiday Inn-Troy** 🆂🅷
(248) 689-7500. **$72-$134.** 2537 Rochester Ct. I-75, exit 67 (Rochester Rd), 0.3 mi sw, then just w. Int corridors. **Pets:** $30 one-time fee/room. Service with restrictions, crate.
(A$K) (S🐾) (✕) 🅗 💻 (🍴) 🐾

▼▼ **Red Roof Inn-Troy #7021** Ⓜ
(248) 689-4391. **Call for rates.** 2350 Rochester Ct. I-75, exit 67 (Rochester Rd), 0.3 mi sw. Ext corridors. **Pets:** Accepted.
(✕) (&M) 🅗

▼▼▼ **Residence Inn by Marriott** 🆂🅷
(248) 689-6856. **$209-$229.** 2600 Livernois Rd. I-75, exit 69 (Big Beaver Rd), 0.5 mi e to Livernois Rd, then 0.5 mi s. Ext corridors. **Pets:** Accepted.
(A$K) (S🐾) (✕) 🅗 💻 🐾 (✕)

UTICA

▼▼ **Comfort Inn** 🆂🅷
(586) 739-7111. **$89-$119.** 11401 Hall Rd. Jct Van Dyke Ave (SR 53) and Hall Rd (SR 59). Int corridors. **Pets:** Accepted.
(A$K) (S🐾) (✕) 🅗 💻

▼▼ **La Quinta Inn & Suites** 🆂🅷
(586) 731-4700. **$95-$100.** 45311 Park Ave. Jct Van Dyke Ave (SR 53) and Hall Rd (SR 59), just n. Int corridors. **Pets:** Other species. Service with restrictions, supervision.
(A$K) (S🐾) (✕) 🅗 💻 🐾

▼▼▼ **Staybridge Suites-Utica** 🆂🅷
(586) 323-0101. **$150-$190.** 46155 Utica Park Blvd. Jct Van Dyke Ave (SR 53) and Hall Rd (SR 59), just n. Int corridors. **Pets:** Accepted.
(A$K) (✕) (&M) 🅗 💻 🐾

WARREN

▼▼ **Candlewood Suites-Detroit Warren** 🆂🅷
(586) 978-1261. **$85-$105.** 7010 Convention Blvd. I-696, exit 23 (Van Dyke Ave), 2.8 mi n. Int corridors. **Pets:** Accepted.
(A$K) (S🐾) (✕) (&M) 🅗 💻

▼▼ **Extended Stay Deluxe** 🆂🅷
(586) 558-5554. **$90-$120.** 30125 N Civic Center Blvd. I-696, exit 23 (Van Dyke Ave), 1.5 mi n, then just e. Int corridors. **Pets:** Other species. $75 one-time fee/pet. Service with restrictions.
(A$K) (S🐾) (✕) (&M) 🅗 💻

▼▼ **Homewood Suites by Hilton** 🆂🅷
(586) 558-7870. **Call for rates.** 30180 N Civic Center Blvd. I-696, exit 23 (Van Dyke Ave), 2 mi n. Ext/int corridors. **Pets:** Accepted.
(✕) (&M) 🅗 💻 🐾

▼▼ **La Quinta Inn** 🆂🅷
(586) 574-0550. **$65-$74.** 30900 Van Dyke Ave. I-696, exit 23 (Van Dyke Ave), 2 mi n on SR 53. Int corridors. **Pets:** Other species. Service with restrictions, supervision.
(A$K) (S🐾) (✕) 🅗 💻

▼▼ **Red Roof Inn-Warren #7070** Ⓜ
(586) 573-4300. **Call for rates.** 26300 Dequindre Rd. I-696, exit 20 (Dequindre Rd), just ne. Ext corridors. **Pets:** Accepted.
(✕) 🅗

▼▼▼ **TownePlace Suites by Marriott** 🆂🅷
(586) 264-8800. **$99-$129.** 7601 Chicago Rd. I-696, exit 23 (Van Dyke Ave), 1.8 mi n. Int corridors. **Pets:** Accepted.
(A$K) (S🐾) (✕) (&M) 🅗 💻 🐾

END METROPOLITAN AREA

DEWITT

🐕‍ ▼▼ **Sleep Inn** 🆂🅷
(517) 669-8823. **$59-$109.** 1101 Commerce Park Dr. I-69, exit 87 (Business Rt US 127), 0.8 mi n. Int corridors. **Pets:** Small, dogs only. $10 daily fee/pet. Service with restrictions, supervision.
(SAVE) (S🐾) (✕) 🅗 💻 🐾

DOUGLAS

▼▼ **AmericInn of Saugatuck/Douglas** 🆂🅷 🐾
(269) 857-8581. **$90-$260, 7 day notice.** 2905 Blue Star Hwy. I-196, exit 36, 0.3 mi n. Int corridors. **Pets:** Medium, dogs only. $20 daily fee/pet. Designated rooms, service with restrictions, supervision.
(A$K) (✕) (&M) 🅗 💻 🐾

DOWAGIAC

🐕‍ ▼▼▼ **Baymont Inn & Suites of Dowagiac** 🆂🅷
(269) 782-4270. **$89-$169.** 29291 Amerihost Dr. 0.4 mi s of jct SR 51 and 62. Int corridors. **Pets:** $25 deposit/room. Designated rooms, service with restrictions, crate.
(SAVE) (S🐾) (✕) (&M) 🅗 💻 🐾

EAST LANSING

🐕‍ ▼▼▼ **Candlewood Suites** 🆂🅷 🐾
(517) 351-8181. **$79-$149.** 3545 Forest Rd. I-496, exit 11 (Jolly Rd), just e to Collins Rd, 0.3 mi n, then just e. Int corridors. **Pets:** Medium. $75 one-time fee/room. Service with restrictions, supervision.
(SAVE) (S🐾) (✕) (&M) 🅗 💻 (🍴)

▼▼▼ **Residence Inn by Marriott** 🆂🅷
(517) 332-7711. **$181-$201.** 1600 E Grand River Ave. US 127, exit Grand River Ave, 2.6 mi se on SR 43. Ext corridors. **Pets:** Accepted.
(A$K) (S🐾) (✕) 🅗 💻 🐾 (✕)

ESCANABA

Hiawatha Motel M
(906) 786-1341. **$50-$125.** 2400 Ludington St. 0.5 mi w on US 2/41. Ext corridors. **Pets:** $5 daily fee/pet. No service, supervision.

FENTON

Holiday Inn Express Hotel & Suites SH
(810) 714-7171. **$89-$159.** 17800 Silver Pkwy. US 23, exit 78 (Owen Rd), just w, then 0.4 mi n. Int corridors. **Pets:** Accepted.

FLINT

Baymont Inn & Suites-Flint SH
(810) 732-2300. **Call for rates.** 4160 Pier North Blvd. I-75, exit 122 (Pierson Rd), just w. Int corridors. **Pets:** Other species. $10 daily fee/room.

Holiday Inn Express SH
(810) 238-7744. **$89-$149.** 1150 Robert T Longway Blvd. I-475, exit 8A (Robert T Longway Blvd), just w. Int corridors. **Pets:** Medium, other species. $25 daily fee/pet. Service with restrictions, supervision.

Residence Inn by Marriott SH
(810) 424-7000. **$177-$197.** 2202 W Hill Rd. US 23, exit 90 (Hill Rd), just e. Int corridors. **Pets:** Accepted.

FRANKENMUTH

Drury Inn & Suites-Frankenmuth SH
(989) 652-2800. **$75-$173.** 260 S Main St. On SR 83; downtown. Int corridors. **Pets:** Large, other species. Service with restrictions, supervision.

GAYLORD

Best Western Alpine Lodge SH ❖
(989) 732-2431. **$69-$109.** 833 W Main St. I-75, exit 282, 0.3 mi e on SR 32. Ext/int corridors. **Pets:** Medium, dogs only. Service with restrictions, supervision.

Downtown Motel M
(989) 732-5010. **$46-$80.** 208 S Otsego Ave. I-75, exit 282, 0.5 mi e, then 0.3 mi s on I-75 business loop. Ext corridors. **Pets:** Dogs only. $5 daily fee/pet. Service with restrictions, supervision.

Quality Inn SH ❖
(989) 732-7541. **$70-$100.** 137 West St. I-75, exit 282, 0.3 mi e on SR 32. Int corridors. **Pets:** Other species. $10 daily fee/room. Designated rooms, service with restrictions, supervision.

Royal Crest Motel SH ❖
(989) 732-6451. **$59-$99.** 803 S Otsego Ave. I-75, exit 279, 2.3 mi ne on I-75 business loop. Int corridors. **Pets:** Medium, dogs only. Service with restrictions, supervision.

Timberly Motel M
(989) 732-5166. **Call for rates.** 881 S Otsego Ave. I-75, exit 279, 2.5 mi n on I-75 business loop (Old US 27). Ext corridors. **Pets:** Accepted.

GRAND MARAIS

Voyageur's Motel M
(906) 494-2389. **$65-$85.** 21914 E Wilson St. 0.5 mi e of SR 77. Ext corridors. **Pets:** Accepted.

GRAND RAPIDS

Best Western Hospitality Hotel & Suites SH
(616) 949-8400. **$69-$129.** 5500 28th St SE. I-96, exit 43B, just e on SR 11. Int corridors. **Pets:** Accepted.

Homewood Suites by Hilton SH
(616) 285-7100. **Call for rates.** 3920 Stahl Dr SE. I-96, exit 43A (28th St SW), 1.5 mi w to E Paris Ave, then just n. Int corridors. **Pets:** Accepted.

Radisson Hotel Grand Rapids Riverfront LH
(616) 363-9001. **$92-$129.** 270 Ann St NW. US 131, exit 88, 1.8 mi n. Int corridors. **Pets:** Accepted.

GRANDVILLE

Residence Inn by Marriott Grand Rapids West SH
(616) 538-1100. **$186-$202.** 3451 Rivertown Point Ct SW. I-196, exit 67, 1.7 mi e. Int corridors. **Pets:** Accepted.

GRAYLING

North Country Lodge M
(989) 348-8471. **$57-$180.** 617 N I-75 Business Loop. 1 mi n. Ext corridors. **Pets:** Accepted.

Ramada Inn of Grayling SH
(989) 348-7611. **Call for rates.** 2650 S Business Loop. I-75 business loop, 0.8 mi s. Ext/int corridors. **Pets:** Accepted.

Super 8 Motel SH
(989) 348-8888. **Call for rates.** 5828 Nelson a Miles Pkwy. I-75, exit 251, just w. Int corridors. **Pets:** Accepted.

GREENVILLE

AmericInn Lodge and Suites SH
(616) 754-4500. **$90-$100.** 2525 W Washington. US 131, exit 101 (SR 57), 13 mi e. Int corridors. **Pets:** Small, dogs only. $15 daily fee/pet. Designated rooms, service with restrictions, supervision.

HANCOCK

Best Western Copper Crown Motel SH
(906) 482-6111. **Call for rates.** 235 Hancock Ave. On US 41 S; downtown. Ext/int corridors. **Pets:** Accepted.

HARRISON

Lakeside Motel & Cottages M ❖
(989) 539-3796. **$58.** 515 E Park St, Business US 127, M-61. US 127, exit US 127 business route/SR 61, 2.2 mi w. Ext corridors. **Pets:** Other species. Crate.

HART

◆◆ **Budget Host Motel** 🆂🅷
(231) 873-1855. **$49-$124, 14 day notice.** 4143 Polk Rd. US 31, exit Mears/Hart, just e on US 31 business route. Int corridors. **Pets:** Accepted.
⊠ 🛏 💻

HOLLAND

◆◆ **Microtel Inn & Suites** Ⓜ
(616) 392-3235. **$54-$89.** 643 Hastings Ave. Just w of US 31 and 32nd St. Int corridors. **Pets:** Accepted.
🄰🅂🄺 🅂🄳 ⊠ 🛗 🛏 💻

◆◆◆ **Residence Inn by Marriott** 🆂🅷
(616) 393-6900. **$142-$164.** 631 Southpoint Ridge Rd. I-196, exit 49, 0.7 mi n on SR 40. Int corridors. **Pets:** Accepted.
🄰🅂🄺 🅂🄳 ⊠ 🛗 🛏 💻 ♒ ⊠

HOUGHTON

◆◆◆ **Best Western-Franklin Square Inn** 🆂🅷
(906) 487-1700. **$90-$110.** 820 Shelden Ave. On US 41; downtown. Int corridors. **Pets:** Accepted.
🅂🄰🅅🄴 🅂🄳 ⊠ 🛏 💻 🍴 ♒ ⊠

◆◆◆ **Country Inn & Suites** 🆂🅷 ☙
(906) 487-6700. **$99-$209.** 919 Razorback Dr. 1.3 mi w on SR 26. Int corridors. **Pets:** Medium, dogs only. $25 daily fee/room. Designated rooms, service with restrictions, supervision.
🅂🄰🅅🄴 🅂🄳 ⊠ 🛗 🛏 💻 ♒ ⊠

HOUGHTON LAKE

◆◆ **Super 8 Motel** 🆂🅷
(989) 422-3119. **Call for rates.** 9580 W Lake City Rd. Jct US 127 and SR 55. Int corridors. **Pets:** Accepted.
⊠ 🛏 ♒ ⊠

HOWELL

◆◆◆ **Best Western Howell** Ⓜ
(517) 548-2900. **Call for rates.** 1500 Pinckney Rd. I-96, exit 137 (Pinckney Rd), just s on CR D19. Ext corridors. **Pets:** Accepted.
🅂🄰🅅🄴 ⊠ 🛏 💻 ♒

HUDSONVILLE

◆◆ **Quality Inn-Hudsonville** 🆂🅷
(616) 662-4000. **$79-$169, 30 day notice.** 3301 Highland Dr. I-196, exit 62 (32nd Ave), just nw. Int corridors. **Pets:** Accepted.
🄰🅂🄺 🅂🄳 ⊠ 🛏 💻 ♒

◆ **Super 8 Motel** 🆂🅷
(616) 896-6710. **$74-$130.** 3005 Corporate Grove Dr. I-196, exit 62 (32nd Ave), just se. Int corridors. **Pets:** Accepted.
🄰🅂🄺 🅂🄳 ⊠ 🛏 💻 ♒

IMLAY CITY

◆◆◆ **Days Inn** 🆂🅷
(810) 724-8005. **$69-$139.** 6692 Newark Rd. I-69, exit 168 (SR 53/Van Dyke Rd), just n, then just w. Int corridors. **Pets:** Small. $12 one-time fee/pet. Service with restrictions, supervision.
🅂🄰🅅🄴 🅂🄳 ⊠ 🛏 💻 ♒

◆◆ **Super 8 Motel-Imlay City** 🆂🅷
(810) 724-8700. **Call for rates.** 6951 Newark Rd. I-69, exit 168 (SR 53/Van Dyke Rd), just n, then just e. Int corridors. **Pets:** Accepted.
⊠ 🛏 💻

IONIA

◆◆ **Super 8 Motel** 🆂🅷
(616) 527-2828. **Call for rates.** 7245 S State Rd. I-96, exit 67 (SR 66). Int corridors. **Pets:** Accepted.
⊠ 🛗 🛏 💻

IRON MOUNTAIN

◆◆◆ ◆◆ **Budget Host Inn** Ⓜ ☙
(906) 774-6797. **$52-$60.** 1663 N Stephenson Ave. 1.5 mi nw on US 2 and 141. Ext corridors. **Pets:** Medium. $5 one-time fee/pet. Designated rooms, service with restrictions, supervision.
🅂🄰🅅🄴 🅂🄳 ⊠ 🛏

IRON RIVER

◆◆◆ **AmericInn of Iron River** 🆂🅷
(906) 265-9100. **$84-$136.** 40 E Adams St. On US 2; downtown. Int corridors. **Pets:** Accepted.
🄰🅂🄺 ⊠ 🛏 💻 ♒ ⊠

IRONWOOD

◆◆◆ ◆◆ **AmericInn of Ironwood** 🆂🅷
(906) 932-7200. **$85-$102.** 1117 E Cloverland Dr. 0.8 mi e on US 2. Int corridors. **Pets:** Accepted.
🅂🄰🅅🄴 🅂🄳 ⊠ 🛗 🛏 💻 ♒ ⊠

◆◆◆ **Crestview Motel** Ⓜ
(906) 932-4845. **Call for rates.** 424 W Cloverland Dr. 0.4 mi w on US 2. Ext corridors. **Pets:** Accepted.
🅂🄰🅅🄴 ⊠ 🛏

◆◆ **Super 8 Motel** 🆂🅷
(906) 932-3395. **Call for rates.** 160 E Cloverland Dr. Jct US 2 and 2 business route. Int corridors. **Pets:** Accepted.
⊠ 🛏 💻 ⊠

ISHPEMING

◆◆◆ ◆◆ **Best Western Country Inn** 🆂🅷
(906) 485-6345. **$90-$108.** 850 US 41 W. On US 41, just n of town. Int corridors. **Pets:** Accepted.
🅂🄰🅅🄴 🅂🄳 ⊠ 💻 🍴 ♒ ⊠

JACKSON

◆◆◆ ◆◆ **Baymont Inn-Jackson** 🆂🅷
(517) 789-6000. **Call for rates.** 2035 Holiday Inn Dr. I-94, exit 138 (US 127), just nw. Int corridors. **Pets:** Large, other species. $10 daily fee/pet. Service with restrictions, crate.
🅂🄰🅅🄴 ⊠ 🛏 💻

◆◆ **Motel 6–1088** Ⓜ
(517) 789-7186. **Call for rates.** 830 Royal Dr. I-94, exit 138 (US 127), just se. Ext corridors. **Pets:** Other species. Service with restrictions, supervision.
⊠ ♒

KALAMAZOO

◆◆◆ ◆◆ **Baymont Inn & Suites-Kalamazoo** 🆂🅷
(269) 372-7999. **$69-$99.** 2203 S 11th St. US 131, exit 36B (Stadium Dr), just w. Int corridors. **Pets:** Very small. $10 daily fee/room. Designated rooms, service with restrictions, supervision.
🅂🄰🅅🄴 🅂🄳 ⊠ 🛏 💻

◆◆◆ ◆◆ **Comfort Inn** 🆂🅷
(269) 381-7000. **Call for rates.** 3820 Sprinkle Rd. I-94, exit 80 (Sprinkle Rd), 0.3 mi s. Int corridors. **Pets:** Accepted.
🅂🄰🅅🄴 ⊠ 🛏 💻 ♒

(AAA) ▼▼▼▼ **Holiday Inn-West** SH
(269) 375-6000. **$129-$159.** 2747 S 11th St. US 131, exit 36B (Stadium Dr), just w. Int corridors. **Pets:** Accepted.
SAVE ⟨S⟩ ✕ ⟨M⟩ 🖥 💻 ¶¶ ⤳ ✕

▼▼▼ **Red Roof Inn-West #7025** SH
(269) 375-7400. **Call for rates.** 5425 W Michigan Ave. US 131, exit 36B (Stadium Dr), just nw. Ext corridors. **Pets:** Accepted.
✕

▼▼▼ **Residence Inn by Marriott** SH
(269) 349-0855. **$186-$208.** 1500 E Kilgore Rd. I-94, exit 78 (Portage Rd), just n, then just w. Int corridors. **Pets:** Accepted.
ASK ⟨S⟩ ✕ ⟨M⟩ 🖥 💻 ⤳ ✕

▼▼▼ **Staybridge Suites-Kalamazoo** SH
(269) 372-8000. **$129-$199.** 2001 Seneca Ln. US 131, exit 36A (Stadium Dr), 0.3 mi e. Int corridors. **Pets:** Accepted.
ASK ⟨S⟩ ✕ ⟨M⟩ 🖥 💻 ⤳

KENTWOOD

▼▼ **Comfort Inn** SH
(616) 957-2080. **$66-$140.** 4155 28th St SE. I-96, exit 43A, 1.5 mi w on SR 11. Int corridors. **Pets:** Accepted.
ASK ⟨S⟩ ✕ 🖥 💻

▼▼ **Residence Inn by Marriott East** SH
(616) 957-8111. **$176-$196.** 2701 E Beltline Ave. Jct SR 11 and E Beltline Ave (SR 37). Ext corridors. **Pets:** Accepted.
ASK ⟨S⟩ ✕ 🖥 💻 ⤳ ✕

▼▼ **Staybridge Suites by Holiday Inn** SH
(616) 464-3200. **$149-$189.** 3000 Lake Eastbrook Blvd SE. I-96, exit 43A, 2 mi w on SR 11, then just s. Int corridors. **Pets:** Accepted.
ASK ⟨S⟩ ✕ ⟨M⟩ 🖥 💻 ⤳

LAKE CITY

(AAA) ▼ **Northcrest Motel** M
(231) 839-2075. **$59-$79, 15 day notice.** 1341 S Lakeshore. 1 mi s on SR 55 and 66. Ext corridors. **Pets:** Accepted.
SAVE ⟨S⟩ 🖥 💻

LAKESIDE

▼▼▼ **White Rabbit Inn** BB
(269) 469-4620. **$95-$200, 7 day notice.** 14634 Red Arrow Hwy. I-94, exit 6 (Union Pier Rd), 1 mi w, then 2 mi n. Ext corridors. **Pets:** Accepted.
✕ 🖥 💻 ☒

LANSING

(AAA) ▼▼▼ **Best Western Midway Hotel** SH
(517) 627-8471. **$65-$85.** 7711 W Saginaw Hwy. I-96, exit 93B (SR 43/Saginaw Hwy), just e. Int corridors. **Pets:** Accepted.
SAVE ⟨S⟩ ✕ 🖥 💻 ¶¶ ⤳ ✕

(AAA) ▼▼▼▼ **Hampton Inn of Lansing** SH
(517) 627-8381. **$99-$129.** 525 N Canal Rd. I-96, exit 93B (SR 43/Saginaw Hwy), just e. Int corridors. **Pets:** Large, other species. $100 deposit/room. Designated rooms, service with restrictions, crate.
SAVE ⟨S⟩ ✕ 🖥 💻

▼ **Motel 6 Lansing West #1089** M
(517) 321-1444. **$45-$55.** 7326 W Saginaw Hwy. I-96, exit 93B (SR 43/Saginaw Hwy), just e. Ext corridors. **Pets:** Other species. Service with restrictions, supervision.
⟨S⟩ ✕ ⤳

(AAA) ▼▼▼ **Quality Suites Hotel** SH
(517) 886-0600. **$99-$119.** 901 Delta Commerce Dr. I-96, exit 93B (SR 43/Saginaw Hwy), 0.3 mi e to Bennigan's Restaurant, then just n. Int corridors. **Pets:** Other species. $25 one-time fee/room. Service with restrictions.
SAVE ⟨S⟩ ✕ 🖥 💻 ✕

▼▼ **Red Roof Inn-West #7020** SH
(517) 321-7246. **Call for rates.** 7412 W Saginaw Hwy. I-96, exit 93B (SR 43/Saginaw Hwy), just e. Ext corridors. **Pets:** Accepted.
✕

▼▼▼ **Residence Inn by Marriott West** SH
(517) 886-5030. **$188-$208.** 922 Delta Commerce Dr. I-96, exit 93B (SR 43/Saginaw Hwy), 0.4 mi e; behind Bennigans. Int corridors. **Pets:** Accepted.
ASK ⟨S⟩ ✕ ⟨M⟩ 🖥 💻 ⤳ ✕

▼▼▼ **Sheraton Lansing Hotel** SH
(517) 323-7100. **$190-$300.** 925 S Creyts Rd. I-496, exit 1 (Creyts Rd), just n. Int corridors. **Pets:** Accepted.
ASK ⟨S⟩ ✕ 🖥 💻 ¶¶ ⤳ ✕

LAPEER

▼▼ **Fairfield Inn Flint-Lapeer** SH ❀
(810) 245-7700. **$100-$120.** 927 Demille Rd. I-69, exit 155 (SR 24), 1.2 mi n, then just e. Int corridors. **Pets:** Other species. $15 daily fee/room, $25 one-time fee/room. Service with restrictions, supervision.
ASK ⟨S⟩ ✕ ⟨M⟩ 🖥 💻 ⤳

LUDINGTON

(AAA) ▼▼▼ **Best Western Splash Park Inn** SH
(231) 843-2140. **$62-$319.** 5005 W US 10. Jct US 31, 1 mi w. Int corridors. **Pets:** Large, other species. Service with restrictions, crate.
SAVE ⟨S⟩ ✕ 🖥 💻 ⤳ ✕

▼▼ **Holiday Inn Express** SH
(231) 845-7004. **$89-$199.** 5323 W US 10. Jct US 31, 1.3 mi w on US 10. Int corridors. **Pets:** Accepted.
ASK ⟨S⟩ ✕ 🖥 💻 ⤳ ✕

MACKINAW CITY

▼▼ **Baymont Inn & Suites-Mackinaw City** SH
(231) 436-7737. **Call for rates.** 109 S Nicolet St. I-75, exit 338 southbound, just n. Int corridors. **Pets:** Medium. $50 deposit/room, $10 daily fee/pet. Designated rooms, service with restrictions, supervision.
✕ 🖥 💻 ⤳

(AAA) ▼ **Beachcomber Motel on the Water** M ❀
(231) 436-8451. **$39-$125, 3 day notice.** 1011 S Huron Ave. 1 mi s on US 23. Ext corridors. **Pets:** Small, dogs only. $5 one-time fee/pet. Designated rooms, service with restrictions, supervision.
SAVE ⟨S⟩ ✕ 🖥

(AAA) ▼ **The Beach House** CA
(231) 436-5353. **$44-$170, 14 day notice.** 11490 W US 23. 1.3 mi s. Ext corridors. **Pets:** Medium, dogs only. $15 one-time fee/pet. Designated rooms, service with restrictions.
SAVE 🖥 ⤳ ✕ ☒

(AAA) ▼ **Budget Inns-Starlite** M
(231) 436-5959. **$35-$199, 3 day notice.** 116 Old US 31. I-75, exit 338 southbound, 0.3 mi e; exit 337 northbound, just ne. Ext corridors. **Pets:** Accepted.
SAVE ⟨S⟩ ✕ 🖥 💻 ⤳ ✕

(AAA) ▼ **Capri Motel** M
(231) 436-5498. **$39-$99, 3 day notice.** 801 S Nicolet St. I-75, exit 338 southbound, just s. Ext corridors. **Pets:** Accepted.
SAVE ⟨S⟩ ✕ 🖥 💻 ⤳ ✕

Days Inn & Suites "Bridgeview Lodge" M
(231) 436-8961. **$44-$250.** 206 N Nicolet St. I-75, exit 339; at bridge. Ext/int corridors. **Pets:** Dogs only. Designated rooms, service with restrictions, supervision.
SAVE SO X B C D

Days Inn Lakeview M
(231) 436-5557. **$49-$219.** 825 S Huron Ave. I-75, exit 337 northbound, 0.5 mi n to US 23, then 0.3 mi e; exit 338 southbound, 0.8 mi se on US 23. Ext corridors. **Pets:** Small. $50 deposit/pet. Service with restrictions, supervision.
SAVE SO X B D TI C

Econo Lodge at the Bridge M
(231) 436-5026. **$49-$189.** 412 N Nicolet St. I-75, exit 339. Ext corridors. **Pets:** Accepted.
SAVE SO X B D

Holiday Inn Express at the Bridge SH
(231) 436-7100. **$65-$270.** 364 Louvigny. I-75, exit 339. Int corridors. **Pets:** Medium, dogs only. $50 deposit/room. Designated rooms, service with restrictions, supervision.
SAVE SO X LM B D C X

Super 8 Motel Bridgeview SH
(231) 436-5252. **$38-$198, 3 day notice.** 601 N Huron Ave. I-75, exit 339 northbound, just n, then just e. Ext/int corridors. **Pets:** Medium. $100 deposit/room. Designated rooms, supervision.
SAVE SO X B D C X

MANISTIQUE

Beachcomber Motel M
(906) 341-2567. **$35-$85.** 751 E Lakeshore Dr. 1 mi e on US 2. Ext corridors. **Pets:** Accepted.
SAVE SO X B

Comfort Inn SH
(906) 341-6981. **$79-$189.** 617 E Lakeshore Dr. 0.5 mi e on US 2. Int corridors. **Pets:** Accepted.
ASK SO X B D X

Econo Lodge Lakeshore M
(906) 341-6014. **$59-$119.** 1101 E Lakeshore Dr. 1.5 mi e on US 2. Ext/int corridors. **Pets:** Accepted.
ASK SO X B D X

MARQUETTE

Birchmont Motel M
(906) 228-7538. **$46-$76.** 2090 US 41 S. On US 41 and SR 28, 4.3 mi s. Ext corridors. **Pets:** Other species. $8 daily fee/room. Designated rooms, service with restrictions, supervision.
SAVE X B C

Holiday Inn SH
(906) 225-1351. **$114-$119.** 1951 US 41 W. On US 41 and SR 28, 1.8 mi w. Int corridors. **Pets:** Accepted.
ASK SO X LM B D TI C X

Travelodge SH
(906) 249-1712. **$62-$138.** 1010 M-28 E. Jct US 41 S and SR 28 E. Int corridors. **Pets:** $10 one-time fee/room. Designated rooms, service with restrictions, supervision.
SAVE SO X B D C

MARSHALL

Arbor Inn of Historic Marshall M
(269) 781-7772. **$45-$69.** 15435 W Michigan Ave. I-69, exit 36 (Michigan Ave), just w. Ext corridors. **Pets:** Accepted.
SAVE SO X B C

MENOMINEE

Econo Lodge On The Bay SH ❀
(906) 863-4431. **$50-$150.** 2516 10th St. 1 mi n on US 41. Int corridors. **Pets:** Medium, other species. $25 daily fee/pet. Designated rooms, service with restrictions, supervision.
SAVE X B C

MIDLAND

Best Western Valley Plaza Resort SH
(989) 496-2700. **$89-$199.** 5221 Bay City Rd. US 10, exit Midland/Bay City Rd. Int corridors. **Pets:** Small. Service with restrictions, supervision.
SAVE SO X B D TI C X

Fairview Inn & Suites SH
(989) 631-0070. **$85-$109.** 2200 W Wackerly St. Jct US 10 and Eastman Rd. Int corridors. **Pets:** Accepted.
ASK SO X B D C

Holiday Inn SH
(989) 631-4220. **Call for rates.** 1500 W Wackerly St. Jct US 10 and Eastman Rd. Ext/int corridors. **Pets:** Accepted.
X B D TI C X

MIO

Mio Motel M
(989) 826-3248. **$60-$75, 3 day notice.** 415 N Morenci St. Just n on SR 33 and 72. Ext corridors. **Pets:** Accepted.
X B

MONROE

Americas Best Value Inn & Suites M
(734) 289-1080. **$60-$100.** 1885 Welcome Way. I-75, exit 15 (SR 50), just e. Ext corridors. **Pets:** Other species. $10 daily fee/pet. Service with restrictions, supervision.
SAVE SO X B D

Baymont Inn & Suites SH
(734) 384-1600. **Call for rates.** 14774 Laplaisance Rd. I-75, exit 11 (Laplaisance Rd), just w. Int corridors. **Pets:** Accepted.
X B D C

Best Western Prestige Inn M
(734) 289-2330. **$63-$110.** 1900 Welcome Way. I-75, exit 15 (SR 50), just e. Ext corridors. **Pets:** Other species. $10 daily fee/room. Service with restrictions, supervision.
SAVE SO X B D C

MOUNT PLEASANT

Comfort Inn & Suites Hotel and Conference Center SH
(989) 772-4000. **Call for rates.** 2424 S Mission St. 2 mi s on US 127 business route. Int corridors. **Pets:** Accepted.
SAVE X B D C

Fairfield Inn and Suites SH
(989) 775-5000. **$82-$102.** 2525 S University Park Dr. 2 mi s on US 127 business route. Int corridors. **Pets:** Accepted.
ASK SO X B D C X

Soaring Eagle Inn & Conference Center SH
(989) 772-2905. **$99-$229.** 5665 E Pickard Ave. Jct US 127 and SR 20 E. Ext/int corridors. **Pets:** Accepted.
ASK SO X LM B D TI C X

Super 8 Motel SH
(989) 773-8888. **$69-$149.** 2323 S Mission St. 1.8 mi s on US 127 business route. Int corridors. **Pets:** Accepted.
X LM B D

MUNISING

(AAA) ▼ Alger Falls Motel M
(906) 387-3536. **$45-$68.** E9427 E Hwy M-28. 2 mi e on SR 28 and 94. Ext corridors. **Pets:** Small, dogs only. $5 one-time fee/pet. Designated rooms, service with restrictions, supervision.
[SAVE] [S🐾] [✕] [🛏]

(AAA) ▼▼ AmericInn of Munising SH
(906) 387-2000. **Call for rates.** E9926 E Hwy M-28. On SR 28, 2.7 mi e. Int corridors. **Pets:** Accepted.
[SAVE] [✕] [&M] [🛏] [💻] [🛬] [✕]

(AAA) ▼ Sunset Motel on the Bay M 🐾
(906) 387-4574. **$53-$88.** 1315 Bay St. 1 mi e on E Munising Ave (CR H58). Ext corridors. **Pets:** Medium, dogs only. $10 one-time fee/pet. Designated rooms, service with restrictions, supervision.
[SAVE] [✕] [🛏] [💻] [✕]

(AAA) ▼ Terrace Motel M
(906) 387-2735. **$40-$55.** 420 Prospect. 0.5 mi e, just off SR 28. Ext corridors. **Pets:** Accepted.
[SAVE] [S🐾] [✕] [✕] [🚗] [☎]

MUSKEGON

▼▼ Holiday Inn-Muskegon Harbor SH
(231) 722-0100. **Call for rates.** 939 3rd St. Center. Int corridors. **Pets:** Accepted.
[✕] [🛏] [💻] [🍽] [🛬] [✕]

NEW BUFFALO

▼▼▼ Holiday Inn Express Hotel & Suites SH
(269) 469-1400. **$99-$299.** 11500 Holiday Dr. I-94, exit 1 (La Porte Rd), just w. Int corridors. **Pets:** Accepted.
[ASK] [S🐾] [✕] [&M] [🛏] [💻] [🛬] [✕]

NORWAY

▼▼ AmericInn of Norway SH
(906) 563-7500. **$79-$86.** W 6002 US Hwy 2. 0.7 mi w. Int corridors. **Pets:** Accepted.
[ASK] [✕] [🛏] [💻] [🛬] [✕]

OKEMOS

▼▼▼ Holiday Inn Express-E Lansing/Okemos SH
(517) 349-8700. **$100-$190.** 2209 University Park Dr. I-96, exit 110 (Okemos Rd), just n, then just e. Int corridors. **Pets:** Accepted.
[ASK] [S🐾] [✕] [&M] [🛏] [💻] [🛬] [✕]

PAW PAW

▼▼ Comfort Inn & Suites SH
(269) 655-0303. **$59-$119.** 153 Ampey Rd. I-94, exit 60 (SR 40), just nw. Int corridors. **Pets:** Accepted.
[ASK] [S🐾] [✕] [&M] [🛏] [💻] [🛬]

(AAA) ▼▼ Econo Lodge M 🐾
(269) 657-2578. **$50-$100.** 139 Ampey Rd. I-94, exit 60 (SR 40), just nw. Ext corridors. **Pets:** Other species. $25 one-time fee/room. No service, supervision.
[SAVE] [S🐾] [✕] [🛏] [💻]

(AAA) ▼▼ Super 8 Motel SH
(269) 657-1111. **$55-$169.** 111 Ampey Rd. I-94, exit 60 (SR 40). Int corridors. **Pets:** Medium. $15 one-time fee/room. Service with restrictions, supervision.
[SAVE] [S🐾] [✕] [&M] [🛏] [💻] [🛬]

PELLSTON

(AAA) ▼▼ Holiday Inn Express Pellston SH
(231) 539-7000. **$59-$199.** 1600 US 31 N. 1.2 mi n. Int corridors. **Pets:** Accepted.
[SAVE] [✕] [🛏] [💻] [🛬] [✕]

PETOSKEY

(AAA) ▼ Days Inn Petoskey M
(231) 348-3900. **$49-$149.** 1420 US 131 S. 1.3 mi s. Ext corridors. **Pets:** Large, other species. $9 daily fee/pet. Designated rooms, service with restrictions, supervision.
[SAVE] [✕] [🛏] [💻] [🍽]

(AAA) ▼ Econo Lodge M
(231) 348-3324. **$49-$135.** 1859 US 131 S. 2 mi s of US 31. Ext corridors. **Pets:** Medium, other species. $10 daily fee/pet. Designated rooms, service with restrictions, supervision.
[SAVE] [S🐾] [✕] [🛏] [💻] [🛬]

(AAA) ▼▼▼ Holiday Inn Express Hotel & Suites SH
(231) 487-0991. **$69-$299.** 1751 S US 131. I-75, exit 282, w on M-32 to US 131N. Int corridors. **Pets:** Accepted.
[SAVE] [S🐾] [✕] [🛏] [💻] [🛬] [✕]

PLAINWELL

(AAA) ▼▼▼ Comfort Inn SH
(269) 685-9891. **$90-$200.** 622 Allegan St. US 131, exit 49A, just e. Int corridors. **Pets:** Medium. $25 daily fee/pet. Service with restrictions, supervision.
[SAVE] [S🐾] [✕] [🛏] [💻] [🛬]

PORT HURON

(AAA) ▼▼ Baymont Inn & Suites SH
(810) 364-8000. **$59-$89.** 1611 Range Rd. I-94, exit 269 (Range Rd), just w. Int corridors. **Pets:** Small. $8 daily fee/pet. Crate.
[SAVE] [S🐾] [✕] [🛏] [💻] [🛬] [✕]

▼▼▼ Hampton Inn SH
(810) 966-9000. **$99-$169.** 1655 Yeager St. I-94, exit 274 (Water St), just s, then just w. Int corridors. **Pets:** Small, other species. $25 one-time fee/room. Designated rooms, service with restrictions, supervision.
[ASK] [S🐾] [✕] [🛏] [💻] [🛬]

PORTLAND

(AAA) ▼▼▼ Best Western American Heritage Inn SH
(517) 647-2200. **$69-$149.** 1681 Grand River Ave. I-96, exit 77, just n. Int corridors. **Pets:** Small, dogs only. $10 daily fee/pet. Service with restrictions, supervision.
[SAVE] [S🐾] [✕] [&M] [🛏] [💻] [🛬]

SAGINAW

▼▼ Best Western–Saginaw SH
(989) 755-0461. **$69-$139.** 1408 S Outer Dr. I-75, exit 149B (SR 46). Int corridors. **Pets:** Large, other species. $25 one-time fee/room. Service with restrictions, supervision.
[ASK] [S🐾] [✕] [🛏] [💻] [🍽] [🛬] [✕]

▼ Motel 6 Saginaw #4354 M
(989) 754-8414. **Call for rates.** 966 S Outer Dr. I-75, exit 149B (SR 46). Ext corridors. **Pets:** Other species. Service with restrictions, supervision.
[✕] [🛏]

(AAA) ▼▼ Ramada Inn & Suites SH
(989) 793-7900. **$69-$149.** 3325 Davenport Ave. I-675, exit 3, 2 mi w on SR 58. Int corridors. **Pets:** $20 daily fee/pet. Service with restrictions, supervision.
[SAVE] [S🐾] [✕] [🛏] [💻] [🍽]

Residence Inn by Marriott SH ❖
(989) 799-9000. **$144-$149.** 5230 Fashion Square Blvd. I-675, exit 6, 0.8 mi w, then just n. Int corridors. **Pets:** Large. $100 one-time fee/room.
ASK ⊠ 🛢 💻 ⇌ ⊠

ST. IGNACE

Budget Host Inn SH
(906) 643-9666. **$62-$150.** 700 N State St. 1.8 mi n of bridge tollgate on I-75 business route. Ext/int corridors. **Pets:** Other species. $40 deposit/room. Service with restrictions, supervision.
SAVE S🔊 ⊠ 🛢 ⇌ ⊠

SAULT STE. MARIE

Best Western Sault Ste. Marie SH
(906) 632-2170. **$69-$169.** 4335 I-75 Business Spur. I-75, exit 392, 0.3 mi ne. Int corridors. **Pets:** Accepted.
SAVE S🔊 ⊠ 🛢 💻 ⇌ ⊠

Budget Host Crestview Inn M
(906) 635-5213. **$59-$79.** 1200 Ashmun St. I-75, exit 392, 2.8 mi ne on I-75 business loop. Ext corridors. **Pets:** Other species. $10 one-time fee/room. Designated rooms, service with restrictions, supervision.
SAVE S🔊 ⊠ 🛢

Comfort Inn SH
(906) 635-1118. **$70-$200, 30 day notice.** 4404 I-75 Business Spur. I-75, exit 392, at business loop. Int corridors. **Pets:** Service with restrictions, supervision.
SAVE ⊠ 🛢 💻 ⇌ ⊠

Days Inn SH
(906) 635-5200. **$69-$199.** 3651 I-75 Business Spur. I-75, exit 392, 0.8 mi ne on I-75 business loop. Int corridors. **Pets:** $5 daily fee/room. Service with restrictions, supervision.
SAVE S🔊 ⊠ 🛢 💻 ⇌ ⊠

La France Terrace Motel M
(906) 632-7823. **$42-$75, 7 day notice.** 1608 Ashmun St. I-75, exit 392, 2.3 mi ne on I-75 business loop. Ext corridors. **Pets:** Accepted.
SAVE S🔊 ⊠ 🛢 ⇌

Mid-City Motel M
(906) 632-6832. **Call for rates.** 304 E Portage Ave. Just e of town, on I-75 business loop. Ext corridors. **Pets:** Accepted.
SAVE ⊠ 🛢

Park Inn SH ❖
(906) 632-6000. **$65-$115.** 3525 I-75 Business Spur. I-75, exit 392, 0.7 mi ne. Int corridors. **Pets:** Other species. $10 daily fee/room. Designated rooms, service with restrictions, supervision.
ASK S🔊 ⊠ 🛢 🛢 💻 ⇌ ⊠

Quality Inn & Suites SH
(906) 635-6918. **$59-$159.** 3290 I-75 Business Loop. I-75, exit 392, 1 mi ne. Int corridors. **Pets:** Medium, other species. $15 daily fee/pet. Designated rooms, service with restrictions.
SAVE S🔊 ⊠ 🛢 💻 🍴 ⇌ ⊠

Royal Motel M
(906) 632-6323. **$43-$99, 5 day notice.** 1707 Ashmun St. I-75, exit 392, 2 mi ne on I-75 business loop. Ext corridors. **Pets:** Accepted.
ASK S🔊 ⊠ 🛢 💻

Super 8 Motel SH ❖
(906) 632-8882. **Call for rates.** 3826 I-75 Business Loop. I-75, exit 392, 0.5 mi ne. Int corridors. **Pets:** Other species. $15 deposit/pet. Service with restrictions, supervision.
SAVE ⊠ 🛢 💻

TraveLodge Sault Ste Marie M ❖
(906) 632-4366. **$55-$155.** 4281 I-75 Business Loop. I-75, exit 392, 0.3 mi ne. Ext corridors. **Pets:** $20 one-time fee/room. Service with restrictions, supervision.
SAVE S🔊 ⊠ 🛢 💻

SILVER CITY

AmericInn Lodge & Suites SH
(906) 885-5311. **$105-$145.** 120 Lincoln Ave. On SR 107, 0.3 mi w of SR 64. Int corridors. **Pets:** Accepted.
ASK S🔊 ⊠ 🛢 💻 🍴 ⇌ ⊠

Mountain View Lodges CA
(906) 885-5256. **$134-$165, 30 day notice.** 34042 M-107. Jct SR 107 and 64, 0.8 mi w. Ext corridors. **Pets:** Accepted.
⊠ 🛢 💻 🅰️

SOUTH HAVEN

Comfort Suites SH
(269) 639-2014. **$79-$209.** 1755 Phoenix St. I-196, exit 20, 0.5 mi e. Int corridors. **Pets:** Medium, other species. $25 daily fee/pet. Crate.
SAVE S🔊 ⊠ 🛢M 🛢 💻 ⇌

SPRING LAKE

Grand Haven Waterfront Holiday Inn SH
(616) 846-1000. **Call for rates.** 940 W Savidge St. On SR 104, just e of US 31. Int corridors. **Pets:** Accepted.
⊠ 🛢 💻 🍴 ⇌ ⊠

STEVENSVILLE

Hampton Inn of St. Joseph I-94 SH
(269) 429-2700. **Call for rates.** 5050 Red Arrow Hwy. I-94, exit 23 (Red Arrow Hwy), just se. Int corridors. **Pets:** Accepted.
⊠ 🛢M 🛢 💻

SUTTONS BAY

Red Lion Motor Lodge M
(231) 271-6694. **$59-$195.** 4290 S West Bay Shore Rd. 5 mi s on SR 22. Ext corridors. **Pets:** Accepted.
⊠ 🛢 💻 🗐

TAWAS CITY

Tawas Motel-Resort M
(989) 362-3822. **$35-$139.** 1124 US 23 S. On US 23, 1.8 mi s. Ext corridors. **Pets:** Accepted.
SAVE S🔊 ⊠ 🛢 💻 ⇌ ⊠

TECUMSEH

Tecumseh Inn Motel M
(517) 423-7401. **$60-$125.** 1445 W Chicago Blvd. On SR 50, 1.5 mi w of city center. Ext corridors. **Pets:** Accepted.
⊠ 🛢 💻

THREE RIVERS

Super 8 Motel SH
(269) 279-8888. **$77-$82.** 711 US 131. Jct US 131 and SR 60 (W Broadway St). Int corridors. **Pets:** Accepted.
ASK S🔊 ⊠ 🛢M 🛢 💻 ⇌

TRAVERSE CITY

Best Western Four Seasons M
(231) 946-8424. **$49-$249.** 305 Munson Ave. 2 mi e on US 31. Ext/int corridors. **Pets:** $10 daily fee/room. Service with restrictions, supervision.
SAVE S🔊 ⊠ 🛢 💻 ⇌

▼▼ **Days Inn & Suites** SH
(231) 941-0208. **$55-$210.** 420 Munson Ave. 2 mi e on US 31. Int corridors. **Pets:** Accepted.

ASK S◐ ✕ 🛢 💻 ➻ ⊠

▼▼ **Holiday Inn** SH
(231) 947-3700. **$90-$250, 3 day notice.** 615 E Front St. 0.5 mi on US 31. Int corridors. **Pets:** Accepted.

ASK S◐ ✕ &M 🛢 💻 ❨❩ ➻ ⊠

▼▼ **Park Place Hotel** SH ✿
(231) 946-5000. **$99-$329.** 300 E State St. Corner of E State and Park sts; downtown. Int corridors. **Pets:** Medium. $20 daily fee/pet. Designated rooms, service with restrictions, supervision.

ASK S◐ ✕ 🛢 💻 ❨❩ ➻ ⊠

Ⓐ ▼▼ **Quality Inn** SH ✿
(231) 929-4423. **$50-$190.** 1492 US 31 N. On US 31, 3.3 mi e. Ext/int corridors. **Pets:** Other species. $10 daily fee/room. Designated rooms, service with restrictions, supervision.

SAVE S◐ ✕ 🛢 💻 ➻

▼▼ **Traverse Victorian Inn** SH
(231) 947-5525. **$69-$149.** 461 Munson Ave. 2.4 mi e on US 31. Int corridors. **Pets:** Accepted.

ASK ✕ 🛢 💻 ➻

WALKER

▼▼ **Baymont Inn & Suites-Grand Rapids North** SH
(616) 735-9595. **Call for rates.** 2151 Holton Ct NW. I-96, exit 28 (Walker Ave), just s. Int corridors. **Pets:** Large, other species. $25 deposit/room. Designated rooms, service with restrictions, crate.

✕ 🛢 💻 ➻

Ⓐ ▼▼ **Quality Inn Grand Rapids North** SH ✿
(616) 791-8500. **$65-$149.** 2171 Holton Ct. I-96, exit 28 (Walker Ave), just s. Int corridors. **Pets:** Medium. $10 daily fee/pet. Service with restrictions, supervision.

SAVE S◐ ✕ 🛢 💻 ➻

WATERSMEET

▼▼ **Dancing Eagles Resort Lac Vieux Desert Casino** SH
(906) 358-4949. **$50-$90.** N5384 US Hwy 45. 1.8 mi n of US 2. Int corridors. **Pets:** Accepted.

ASK S◐ ✕ 🛢 💻 ➻ ⊠

WHITMORE LAKE

Ⓐ ▼▼ **Best Western Whitmore Lake** M
(734) 449-2058. **$89-$109.** 9897 Main St. US 23, exit 53, just e. Ext corridors. **Pets:** Other species. $25 daily fee/pet. Service with restrictions, crate.

SAVE S◐ ✕ 🛢 💻 ➻

WYOMING

Ⓐ ▼▼ **Howard Johnson Plaza Hotel** SH
(616) 241-6444. **$65.** 255 28th St SW. On SR 11, 0.3 mi e of jct US 131, exit 28th St. Int corridors. **Pets:** Other species. $25 one-time fee/room. Service with restrictions, supervision.

SAVE S◐ ✕ 🛢 💻 ❨❩ ➻ ⊠

▼ **Super 8 Motel** SH
(616) 530-8588. **$60-$100.** 727 44th St SW. US 131, exit 79. Int corridors. **Pets:** Accepted.

ASK S◐ ✕ 🛢

MINNESOTA

AITKIN

Ripple River Motel & RV Park
(218) 927-3734. **$55-$90.** 701 Minnesota Ave S. US 169, 0.8 mi s of jct SR 210. Ext corridors. **Pets:** Accepted.

ALBERT LEA

Albert Lea Countryside Inn Motel
(507) 373-2446. **$39-$79, 3 day notice.** 2102 E Main St. I-35, exit 11, 1.3 mi w on CR 46. Ext/int corridors. **Pets:** Accepted.

Albert Lea Inn
(507) 373-8291. **$65-$85.** 2301 E Main St. I-35, exit 11, 1 mi w on CR 46. Int corridors. **Pets:** Medium, other species. $10 daily fee/pet. Service with restrictions, crate.

Comfort Inn
(507) 377-1100. **$80-$90.** 810 Happy Trails Ln. I-35, exit 11, just se. Int corridors. **Pets:** $10 one-time fee/pet. Designated rooms, service with restrictions, supervision.

Country Inn & Suites By Carlson
(507) 373-5513. **$94-$129.** 2214 E Main St. I-35, exit 12 southbound; exit 11 northbound, 1 mi w. Int corridors. **Pets:** Small. $20 one-time fee/pet. Designated rooms, service with restrictions, supervision.

ALEXANDRIA

Country Inn & Suites By Carlson
(320) 763-9900. **$78-$141.** 5304 Hwy 29 S. I-94, exit 103, just sw. Int corridors. **Pets:** $10 one-time fee/room. Designated rooms, supervision.

Holiday Inn Alexandria
(320) 763-6577. **$90-$155.** 5637 State Hwy 29 S. I-94, exit 103, just s. Int corridors. **Pets:** Accepted.

Super 8 Motel
(320) 763-6552. **Call for rates.** 4620 Hwy 29 S. I-94, exit 103, 0.3 mi nw. Int corridors. **Pets:** Accepted.

AUSTIN

Country Side Inn
(507) 437-7774. **$39-$90.** 3303 Oakland Ave W. I-90, exit 175 (Oakland Ave), just nw. Int corridors. **Pets:** Accepted.

Days Inn
(507) 433-8600. **Call for rates.** 700 16th Ave NW. I-90, exit 178A (4th St NW), just nw. Int corridors. **Pets:** Accepted.

Holiday Inn & Austin Conference Center
(507) 433-1000. **$92-$149.** 1701 4th St NW. I-90, exit 178A (4th St NW), just nw. Int corridors. **Pets:** Other species. $25 one-time fee/room. Service with restrictions.

BABBITT

Timber Bay Lodge & Houseboats
(218) 827-3682. **$615-$2060, 60 day notice.** 8347 Timber Bay Rd. 2.8 mi e of jct CR 21 via CR 70 and 623. Ext corridors. **Pets:** $15 daily fee/pet. Supervision.

BAUDETTE

AmericInn Lodge & Suites Lake of the Woods
(218) 634-3200. **$72-$145.** 1179 Main St W. 0.5 mi w on SR 11. Int corridors. **Pets:** Accepted.

BAXTER

Country Inn & Suites by Carlson
(218) 828-2161. **$89-$139.** 15058 Dellwood Dr N. Jct SR 371 and 210, 1 mi n on SR 371. Int corridors. **Pets:** Accepted.

Hawthorn Inn & Suites
(218) 822-1133. **$80-$350.** 7208 Fairview Rd. Just nw of jct SR 371 on SR 210. Int corridors. **Pets:** Accepted.

(AAA) ▼▼▼ Holiday Inn Express, Three Bear Lodge Water & Theme Park SH ☙

(218) 824-3232. **$79-$219.** 15739 Audubon Way. Just se of jct SR 371 and CR 77. Int corridors. **Pets:** Small, dogs only. $150 deposit/room, $25 daily fee/pet. Designated rooms, service with restrictions, supervision.

SAVE S○ ☒ ⌖M ⊟ ◰

BEMIDJI

(AAA) ▼▼▼ Americinn Lodge & Suites SH

(218) 751-3000. **$75-$90.** 1200 Paul Bunyan Dr NW. 0.5 mi e of northwest jct US 2, 71 and SR 197. Int corridors. **Pets:** Medium. $30 one-time fee/room. Designated rooms, service with restrictions, supervision.

SAVE S○ ☒ ⊟ ◰ ↝ ☒

(AAA) ▼▼▼ Best Western Bemidji SH

(218) 751-0390. **$59-$120.** 2420 Paul Bunyan Dr. Jct US 71 N and SR 197. Int corridors. **Pets:** Accepted.

SAVE S○ ☒ ⊟ ◰ ↝ ☒

(AAA) ▼▼▼▼ Ruttger's Birchmont Lodge CA

(218) 444-3463. **$44-$375, 30 day notice.** 7598 Bemidji Rd NE. Jct SR 197, 3.6 mi n on CR 21 (Bemidji Ave N). Ext/int corridors. **Pets:** Other species. $10 daily fee/pet. Designated rooms, service with restrictions.

SAVE S○ ☒ ⊟ ◰ ⑪ ≋ ☒

BLUE EARTH

▼▼ Super 8 Motel SH

(507) 526-7376. **Call for rates.** 1420 Giant Dr. I-90, exit 119 (US 169), just s. Int corridors. **Pets:** Accepted.

☒ ⊟ ◰

BRAINERD

(AAA) ▼▼▼ Ramada Inn Brainerd SH

(218) 829-1441. **Call for rates.** 2115 S 6th St. On SR 371 business route, 1.8 mi s of jct SR 210. Ext/int corridors. **Pets:** Accepted.

SAVE ☒ ⌖M ⊟ ◰ ⑪ ≋ ☒

BRECKENRIDGE

(AAA) ▼▼▼ Select Inn of Breckenridge/Wahpeton SH

(218) 643-9201. **$50-$120.** 821 Hwy 75 N. Just sw of jct US 75 N and 210. Int corridors. **Pets:** Medium. $10 daily fee/pet. Designated rooms, service with restrictions, supervision.

ASK S○ ☒ ⊟ ◰ ≋

CALEDONIA

▼▼▼▼ Americinn Lodge & Suites SH

(507) 725-8000. **Call for rates.** 508 N Kruckow Ave. Just n of Main St on SR 44, just w on Esch Dr. Int corridors. **Pets:** Accepted.

☒ ⊟ ◰ ≋ ☒

▼▼ Crest Red Carpet Inn M

(507) 724-3311. **$65.** 15944 State 76. Jct SR 44 and 76; on north end of town, 1.9 mi s. Ext/int corridors. **Pets:** Accepted.

ASK ☒ ⊟

CANNON FALLS

(AAA) ▼▼▼ Best Western Saratoga Inn SH

(507) 263-7272. **Call for rates.** 31591 64th Ave. From jct SR 19, 1 mi sw on US 52. Int corridors. **Pets:** Very small. $15 daily fee/pet. Designated rooms, service with restrictions, supervision.

SAVE ☒ ⊟ ◰ ≋

CLOQUET

▼▼ Super 8 Motel SH

(218) 879-1250. **$66-$94.** 121 Big Lake Rd. I-35, exit 237 (SR 33), 2 mi nw. Int corridors. **Pets:** Accepted.

ASK S○ ☒ ⌖M ⊟ ◰

CROOKSTON

▼▼ Northland Inn of Crookston SH

(218) 281-5210. **Call for rates.** 2200 University Ave. On US 2 W and 75 N, 1.5 mi n. Int corridors. **Pets:** Accepted.

☒ ⊟ ⑪ ≋

CROSSLAKE

▼▼▼ Pine Peaks Lodge and Suites SH

(218) 692-4100. **Call for rates.** 14047 Swann Dr. Jct CR 66 and Swann Dr. Int corridors. **Pets:** Accepted.

☒ ⊟ ◰ ⑪ ≋ ☒

DEER RIVER

(AAA) ▼▼▼ White Oak Inn & Suites SH

(218) 246-9400. **$57-$160.** 201 4th Ave NW. On US 2. Int corridors. **Pets:** $100 deposit/room. Service with restrictions, supervision.

SAVE S○ ☒ ⊟ ◰ ≋ ☒

DEERWOOD

▼▼▼ Country Inn By Carlson SH

(218) 534-3101. **$79-$109.** 23884 Front St. On SR 6 and 210, e of jct CR 12. Int corridors. **Pets:** Accepted.

ASK S○ ☒ ⌖M ⊟ ◰ ≋

DETROIT LAKES

(AAA) ▼▼▼ Americinn Lodge & Suites SH

(218) 847-8795. **$69-$180.** 777 Hwy 10 E. 1.4 mi se. Int corridors. **Pets:** Other species. $10 daily fee/room. Service with restrictions, supervision.

SAVE S○ ☒ ⌖M ⊟ ◰ ≋ ☒

(AAA) ▼▼▼▼ Best Western Holland House & Suites SH ☙

(218) 847-4483. **$89-$229, 3 day notice.** 615 Hwy 10 E. 1.3 mi se. Ext/int corridors. **Pets:** Medium. $15 daily fee/pet. Designated rooms, service with restrictions, supervision.

SAVE ☒ ⊟ ◰ ≋

(AAA) ▼▼ Budget Host Inn M

(218) 847-4454. **$52-$120.** 895 Hwy 10 E. 1.5 mi se. Ext corridors. **Pets:** $10 daily fee/room. Designated rooms, service with restrictions, crate.

SAVE S○ ☒ ⊟ ◰

(AAA) ▼▼▼ Country Inn & Suites By Carlson SH ☙

(218) 847-2000. **$75-$165.** 1330 Hwy 10 E. Just e of jct US 10 and CR 54 E. Int corridors. **Pets:** $20 one-time fee/pet. Service with restrictions, supervision.

SAVE S○ ☒ ⌖M ⊟ ◰ ≋

DULUTH

(AAA) ▼▼▼▼ Americinn Hotel & Suites of Duluth/Proctor SH

(218) 624-1026. **$85-$210.** 185 US 2. Jct I-35 and US 2, 0.8 mi n. Int corridors. **Pets:** Accepted.

SAVE S○ ☒ ⊟ ◰ ⑪ ≋

(AAA) ▼▼▼ Best Western Downtown Motel M

(218) 727-6851. **$49-$132.** 131 W 2nd St. 2nd St at 2nd Ave W; center. Ext/int corridors. **Pets:** Other species. Service with restrictions, supervision.

SAVE ☒ ⊟ ◰

▼▼▼▼ Country Inn & Suites By Carlson SH

(218) 628-0668. **$79-$170.** 9330 W Skyline Pkwy. I-35, exit 249 (Boundary Ave), just se. Int corridors. **Pets:** Accepted.

ASK S○ ☒ ⊟ ◰ ≋ ☒

Country Inn & Suites-Duluth North SH ❖
(218) 740-4500. **$99-$209.** 4257 Haines Rd. Just n of US 53 at jct Haines Rd. **Pets:** Medium, other species. $10 daily fee/pet. Designated rooms, service with restrictions, supervision.

Days Inn-Duluth SH
(218) 727-3110. **$69-$199.** 909 Cottonwood Ave. SR 194, just n of jct US 53. Int corridors. **Pets:** Large, other species. Service with restrictions, supervision.

Duluth Spirit Mountain Red Roof Inn SH ❖
(218) 628-3691. **$49-$229, 3 day notice.** 9315 Westgate Blvd. I-35, exit 249 (Boundary Ave), just sw. Int corridors. **Pets:** Medium. Designated rooms, service with restrictions, supervision.

Econo Lodge Airport SH
(218) 722-5522. **$75-$155.** 4197 Haines Rd. West side on US 53 and SR 194. Int corridors. **Pets:** $50 deposit/room, $10 one-time fee/room. Designated rooms, supervision.

Edgewater Resort & Waterpark SH
(218) 728-3601. **$99-$359.** 2400 London Rd. I-35, exit 258 (21st Ave E), just nw. Ext/int corridors. **Pets:** Accepted.

The Inn on Lake Superior SH ❖
(218) 726-1111. **$125-$399.** 350 Canal Park Dr. In Canal Park area. Int corridors. **Pets:** Other species. $25 daily fee/room. Service with restrictions, supervision.

Radisson Hotel Duluth-Harborview LH
(218) 727-8981. **$109-$199.** 505 W Superior St. At 5th Ave W; center. Int corridors. **Pets:** Accepted.

Sheraton Duluth Hotel SH
(218) 733-5660. **$229-$349.** 301 E Superior St. I-35, exit 256B (Lake Ave), just nw. Int corridors. **Pets:** Accepted.

The Suites Hotel in Canal Park SH
(218) 727-4663. **$89-$379.** 325 Lake Ave S. In Canal Park area. Int corridors. **Pets:** $15 daily fee/room. Service with restrictions, supervision.

Voyageur Lakewalk Inn M
(218) 722-3911. **$45-$74.** 333 E Superior St. I-35, exit 256 (Superior St), just n at jct 4th Ave E and Superior St. Ext corridors. **Pets:** Accepted.

ELY

Grand Ely Lodge Resort and Conference Center SH
(218) 365-6565. **$109-$300, 14 day notice.** 400 N Pioneer Rd. SR 169 to Central Ave, just n to Pioneer Rd, then 1 mi n. Ext/int corridors. **Pets:** $15 daily fee/pet. Designated rooms, service with restrictions, supervision.

Motel Ely-Budget Host M
(218) 365-3237. **$50-$120, 3 day notice.** 1047 E Sheridan St. SR 1 and 169. Ext corridors. **Pets:** Dogs only. $10 one-time fee/room. Designated rooms, service with restrictions, supervision.

EVELETH

Super 8 Motel SH
(218) 744-1661. **$70-$139.** 1080 Industrial Park Dr. On US 53, 0.5 mi n of jct SR 37. Int corridors. **Pets:** Accepted.

FAIRMONT

Comfort Inn SH
(507) 238-5444. **$90-$95.** 2225 N State St. I-90, exit 102 (SR 15), just sw. Int corridors. **Pets:** Accepted.

Holiday Inn SH
(507) 238-4771. **$95-$175.** 1201 Torgerson Dr. I-90, exit 102 (SR 15), just se. Int corridors. **Pets:** Accepted.

Super 8 Motel SH
(507) 238-9444. **$63-$73.** 1200 Torgerson Dr. I-90, exit 102 (SR 15), just se. Int corridors. **Pets:** Accepted.

FARIBAULT

AmericInn Motel SH
(507) 334-9464. **$90-$180.** 1801 Lavender Dr. I-35, exit 59 (SR 21), 0.3 mi e. Int corridors. **Pets:** $25 one-time fee/pet. Designated rooms, service with restrictions, supervision.

Days Inn & Suites SH
(507) 334-6835. **$65-$95.** 1920 Cardinal Ln. I-35, exit 59 (SR 21), just ne. Int corridors. **Pets:** Medium. $10 daily fee/room. Service with restrictions, crate.

Select Inn M
(507) 334-2051. **$46-$77.** 4040 SR 60 W. I-35, exit 56, just w. Int corridors. **Pets:** Accepted.

FERGUS FALLS

AmericInn Lodge & Suites SH ❖
(218) 739-3900. **$77-$140.** 526 Western Ave N. I-94, exit 54 (SR 210), just se. Int corridors. **Pets:** Other species. $50 deposit/room, $10 one-time fee/room. Designated rooms, service with restrictions, crate.

Comfort Inn SH
(218) 736-5787. **Call for rates.** 425 Western Ave. I-94, exit 54 (SR 210), just se. Int corridors. **Pets:** Accepted.

Motel 7 M
(218) 736-2554. **Call for rates.** 616 Frontier Dr. I-94, exit 54 (SR 210), just ne. Int corridors. **Pets:** Accepted.

FINLAYSON

Americas Best Value Inn SH
(320) 245-5284. **Call for rates.** 60671 State Hwy 23. I-35, exit 195 (SR 23), just ne. Int corridors. **Pets:** Accepted.

FOSSTON

Super 8 Motel SH
(218) 435-1088. **Call for rates.** 108 S Amber. US 2, 0.5 mi e. Int corridors. **Pets:** Accepted.

GARRISON

▼▼▼▼ Garrison Inn & Suites by Ruttger's **SH**
(320) 692-4050. **$75-$149.** 9243 Hwy 169. SR 169, just s of jct SR 18. Int corridors. **Pets:** Accepted.

⊠ 🖬 💻 🏊

GAYLORD

▼▼ Gold Leaf Inn & Suites **M**
(507) 237-5860. **$58-$111.** 330 Main Ave E. 1.5 mi e. Int corridors. **Pets:** Accepted.

⊠ 🖬

GRAND MARAIS

◬ ▼▼▼▼ Best Western Superior Inn & Suites **SH** ❀
(218) 387-2240. **$89-$329, 3 day notice.** 104 1st Ave E. SR 61, just ne of center. Int corridors. **Pets:** Medium. $10 daily fee/room. Designated rooms, service with restrictions, supervision.

SAVE S🗗 ⊠ 🖬 💻

◬ ▼▼▼▼ Gunflint Lodge **VH**
(218) 388-2294. **$109-$599, 31 day notice.** 143 S Gunflint Lake. 43 mi n of town; 0.8 mi e of jct CR 12 (Gunflint Trail) and 50. Ext corridors. **Pets:** Accepted.

SAVE 🗲M 🖬 💻 🍴 ⊠ 🐾 🌊

▼▼ Nor'Wester Lodge and Outfitter **CA**
(218) 388-2252. **Call for rates.** 7778 Gunflint Trail. 30 mi nw on CR 12 (Gunflint Trail) from jct SR 61. Ext corridors. **Pets:** Accepted.

🖬 💻 ⊠ 🐾 🌊 🌊

▼▼ Outpost Motel **M**
(218) 387-1833. **$49-$99, 7 day notice.** 2935 SR 61 E. 9 mi ne. Ext corridors. **Pets:** Accepted.

⊠ 🖬 💻 ⊠ 🐾

◬ ▼▼ Wedgewood Motel **M**
(218) 387-2944. **$49-$69.** 1663 E Hwy 61. On SR 61, 2.5 mi ne. Ext corridors. **Pets:** Dogs only. $5 daily fee/pet. Designated rooms, service with restrictions, supervision.

SAVE S🗗 ⊠ 🖬 🐾 🌊

GRAND RAPIDS

◬ ▼▼▼▼ Budget Host Inn **M** ❀
(218) 326-3457. **$60-$86.** 311 E Hwy 2. Jct US 2 E and 169 N. Ext/int corridors. **Pets:** $10 one-time fee/room. Designated rooms, service with restrictions, crate.

SAVE S🗗 ⊠ 🖬

▼▼▼▼ Country Inn By Carlson **SH**
(218) 327-4960. **$95-$136.** 2601 S Hwy 169. US 2, 2 mi s. Int corridors. **Pets:** Accepted.

ASK S🗗 ⊠ 🗲M 🖬 💻 🌊

◬ ▼▼▼▼ Sawmill Inn **SH** ❀
(218) 326-8501. **$69-$109.** 2301 S Hwy 169. US 2, 2 mi s on US 169. Ext/int corridors. **Pets:** Other species. Service with restrictions, supervision.

SAVE S🗗 ⊠ 🖬 💻 🍴 🌊 ⊠

GRANITE FALLS

▼▼▼▼ Granite Falls Super Motel **SH**
(320) 564-4075. **Call for rates.** 845 W SR 212. 0.5 mi w of Jct SR 23. Int corridors. **Pets:** Accepted.

⊠ 🗲M 🖬 🌊

HIBBING

▼▼▼▼ Super 8 Motel **SH**
(218) 263-8982. **Call for rates.** 1411 E 40th St. Just e of US 169 and SR 37. Int corridors. **Pets:** Accepted.

⊠ 🖬 💻

HINCKLEY

▼▼ Days Inn **SH**
(320) 384-7751. **Call for rates.** 104 Grindstone Ct. I-35, exit 183 (SR 48), just e. Int corridors. **Pets:** Accepted.

⊠ 🖬 💻 🌊

HUTCHINSON

◬ ▼▼▼▼ AmericInn Lodge & Suites **SH**
(320) 587-5515. **$82-$130.** 1115 Hwy 7 E. 1.0 mi e of jct SR 15. Int corridors. **Pets:** Accepted.

SAVE ⊠ 🗲M 🖬 💻 🌊 ⊠

◬ ▼▼▼▼ Best Western Victorian Inn **SH**
(320) 587-6030. **$73-$114.** 1000 Hwy 7 W. SR 15, 1 mi w. Int corridors. **Pets:** $10 daily fee/room. Service with restrictions, supervision.

SAVE S🗗 ⊠ 🖬 💻 🌊

INTERNATIONAL FALLS

◬ ▼▼▼▼ Hilltop Motel **M**
(218) 283-2505. **$49-$84.** 2002 2nd Ave W. US 53, 1 mi s of jct US 53 and SR 11. Ext corridors. **Pets:** Small, dogs only. $10 daily fee/room. Designated rooms, service with restrictions, supervision.

SAVE S🗗 ⊠

▼▼▼▼ Holiday Inn **SH**
(218) 283-9000. **$99-$119.** 1500 US 71 W. 1.5 mi w on US 71 and SR 11 W. Int corridors. **Pets:** Accepted.

ASK S🗗 ⊠ 🖬 💻 🍴 🌊 ⊠

JACKSON

◬ ▼▼▼▼ AmericInn Lodge & Suites **SH**
(507) 847-2444. **$75-$159.** 110 Belmont Ln. I-90, exit 73 (US 71), just sw. Int corridors. **Pets:** Dogs only. $50 deposit/room. Designated rooms, service with restrictions, supervision.

SAVE S🗗 ⊠ 🗲M 🖬 💻 🌊

▼▼ Econo Lodge **SH**
(507) 847-3110. **$60-$95.** 2007 Hwy 71 N. I-90, exit 73 (US 71), just n. Ext/int corridors. **Pets:** Accepted.

ASK S🗗 ⊠ 🖬 💻 🍴 🌊

LAMBERTON

▼▼ Lamberton Motel **M**
(507) 752-7242. **Call for rates.** 601 1st Ave W. Just s of jct US 14 and Ilex St. Ext corridors. **Pets:** Accepted.

⊠ 🖬 💻

LITCHFIELD

▼▼▼ ScotWood Motel **M**
(320) 693-2496. **Call for rates.** 1017 E Frontage Rd. On US 12. Int corridors. **Pets:** Accepted.

⊠ 🖬 🌊

LONG PRAIRIE

◬ ▼▼▼ Budget Host Inn **M**
(320) 732-6118. **$60-$79, 3 day notice.** 417 Lake St. On US 71 and SR 27, just s of jct SR 287. Ext corridors. **Pets:** $5 daily fee/room. Service with restrictions, supervision.

SAVE S🗗 ⊠ 🖬 💻

LUTSEN

AAA ▼▼▼ **Cascade Lodge** 🄲
(218) 387-1112. **$45-$275, 14 day notice.** 3719 W SR 61. On SR 61, 7 mi ne of jct CR 4 (Caribou Trail). Ext/int corridors. **Pets:** Dogs only. $10 daily fee/pet. Designated rooms, service with restrictions.
SAVE 🆂🄳 ⊗ 🔒 ▣ 🍽 ⊠

AAA ▼▼▼ **Solbakken Resort** Ⓜ
(218) 663-7566. **$55-$95, 14 day notice.** 4874 W SR 61. On SR 61, 1.3 mi n of jct CR 4 (Caribou Trail). Ext corridors. **Pets:** $10 daily fee/pet. Designated rooms, no service, supervision.
SAVE 🆂🄳 ⊗ 🔒 ▣ ⊠ 🄚

MANKATO

▼▼ **AmericInn of Mankato at MSU** 🆂🄷
(507) 345-8011. **$100-$190.** 240 Stadium Rd. From jct US 14, 2 mi s on SR 22, 0.4 mi w on SR 83, just s on Victory Dr, then 1.5 mi w. Int corridors. **Pets:** Accepted.
A$K 🆂🄳 ⊗ 🄻🄼 🔒 ▣ ⊇ ⊠

AAA ▼▼▼ **Best Western Hotel & Restaurant** 🆂🄷
(507) 625-9333. **$79-$195.** 1111 Range St. 0.6 mi s of jct US 169 and 14. Int corridors. **Pets:** Designated rooms, service with restrictions, supervision.
SAVE 🆂🄳 ⊗ 🔒 ▣ 🍽 ⊇ ⊠

▼▼ **Comfort Inn by Choice Hotels** 🆂🄷
(507) 388-5107. **Call for rates.** 131 Apache Pl. Just s of jct US 14 and SR 22 S. Int corridors. **Pets:** Accepted.
⊗ 🔒 ▣ ⊇

AAA ▼▼ **Days Inn** 🆂🄷 ❀
(507) 387-3332. **Call for rates.** 1285 Range St. 0.3 mi s of jct US 169 and 14. Int corridors. **Pets:** Other species. $10 daily fee/pet. Designated rooms, service with restrictions, supervision.
SAVE ⊗ 🔒 ▣ ⊇

▼▼▼ **GrandStay Residential Suites** 🆂🄷
(507) 388-8688. **$109-$129.** 1000 Raintree Rd. 0.4 mi se of jct US 14 and CR 3. Int corridors. **Pets:** Accepted.
A$K ⊗ 🔒 ▣ ⊇ ⊠

▼▼▼ **Holiday Inn** 🆂🄷
(507) 345-1234. **$90-$120.** 101 E Main St. Main St at Riverfront Dr; downtown. Int corridors. **Pets:** Accepted.
A$K 🆂🄳 ⊗ 🄻🄼 🔒 ▣ 🍽 ⊇ ⊠

▼▼ **Microtel Inn & Suites** 🆂🄷
(507) 388-2818. **$59-$81.** 200 St. Andrews Dr. US 14, exit CR 3, 0.4 mi n. Int corridors. **Pets:** Accepted.
A$K 🆂🄳 ⊗ 🔒 ▣

▼▼ **Super 8 Motel** 🆂🄷
(507) 387-4041. **$68-$98.** 51578 US Hwy 169 N. Jct US 169 and 14, just n. Int corridors. **Pets:** Accepted.
A$K 🆂🄳 ⊗ 🔒 ▣

MARSHALL

AAA ▼▼▼ **Best Western Marshall Inn** 🆂🄷
(507) 532-3221. **Call for rates.** 1500 E College Dr. SR 19, just w of jct SR 23. Int corridors. **Pets:** Accepted.
SAVE ⊗ 🔒 ▣ 🍽 ⊇ ⊠

▼▼▼ **Comfort Inn** 🆂🄷
(507) 532-3070. **$80-$120.** 1511 E College Dr. SR 19, w of jct SR 23. Int corridors. **Pets:** Accepted.
A$K 🆂🄳 ⊗ 🄻🄼 🔒 ▣ ⊇

▼▼ **Super 8 Motel** 🆂🄷
(507) 537-1461. **Call for rates.** 1106 E Main St. 0.3 mi se on US 59 from jct SR 23. Int corridors. **Pets:** Accepted.
⊗ 🔒 ▣

MCGREGOR

▼▼ **Country Meadows Inn** 🆂🄷
(218) 768-7378. **Call for rates.** 403 Meadows Dr. Jct SR 65 and 210. Int corridors. **Pets:** Accepted.
⊗ 🔒 ▣ ⊇

MILACA

▼▼ **Super 8 Motel** 🆂🄷
(320) 983-2660. **Call for rates.** 215 10th Ave SE. Jct SR 23 and 169. Int corridors. **Pets:** Accepted.
⊗ 🄻🄼 🔒 ▣

MINNEAPOLIS-ST. PAUL METROPOLITAN AREA

ANNANDALE

▼▼ **AmericInn Lodge & Suites** 🆂🄷
(320) 274-3006. **$70-$120.** 620 Elm St E. On SR 55. Int corridors. **Pets:** Accepted.
A$K 🆂🄳 ⊗ 🄻🄼 🔒 ▣ ⊇

BECKER

AAA ▼▼▼ **Sleep Inn & Suites** 🆂🄷
(763) 262-7700. **$80-$100.** 14435 Bank St. Just e on US 10. Int corridors. **Pets:** Medium, dogs only. $150 deposit/pet, $10 daily fee/pet. Service with restrictions, supervision.
SAVE 🆂🄳 ⊗ 🔒 ▣ ⊇ ⊠

BLAINE

▼▼▼ **Comfort Suites** 🆂🄷
(763) 792-0750. **$89-$199.** 10580 Baltimore St NE. 1.5 mi n of jct SR 65 and US 10 to 107th Ave NE, just e to Baltimore St NE, then just s. Int corridors. **Pets:** Small, dogs only. $25 one-time fee/room. Designated rooms, service with restrictions, supervision.
A$K 🆂🄳 ⊗ 🄻🄼 🔒 ▣ ⊇

▼▼ **Super 8 Motel** 🆂🄷
(763) 786-8888. **Call for rates.** 9410 Baltimore St NE. Just n of jct US 10 and SR 65 to 93 ln (Post Office), just e to Baltimore St ne, then just n. Int corridors. **Pets:** Accepted.
⊗ 🄻🄼 🔒 ▣ ⊇

BLOOMINGTON

▼▼ **Extended StayAmerica Minneapolis-Bloomington** 🆂🄷
(952) 884-1400. **$82-$100.** 7956 Lyndale Ave. I-494, exit 4B (Lyndale Ave), just sw. Int corridors. **Pets:** Other species. $75 one-time fee/pet. Service with restrictions.
A$K 🆂🄳 ⊗ 🔒 ▣

AAA ▼▼▼ **Homewood Suites by Hilton** 🆂🄷
(952) 854-0900. **$159-$279.** 2261 Killebrew Dr. I-494, exit 2A (24th Ave), 1 mi s, then just w. Int corridors. **Pets:** Medium, other species. $100 one-time fee/room. Service with restrictions.
SAVE 🆂🄳 ⊗ 🔒 ▣ ⊇

▼▼ ▼▼ La Quinta Inn Minneapolis-Airport (Bloomington) SH
(952) 881-7311. **$69-$84.** 7815 Nicollet Ave S. I-494, exit 4A (Nicollet Ave), just s. Int corridors. **Pets:** Other species. Service with restrictions, supervision.
ASK 🍲 ✕ 🖥 ▣

▲▲▲ ▼▼▼▼ Le Bourget Aero Suites SH
(952) 893-9999. **$99-$204.** 7770 Johnson Ave. I-494, exit 6B (France Ave), 0.5 mi nw on frontage road (78th St). Int corridors. **Pets:** Other species. $10 daily fee/room. Service with restrictions, crate.
SAVE ✕ 🔥M 🖥 ▣ ¶¶ 🏊 ❎

▲▲▲ ▼▼ ▼▼ Ramada Inn Mall of America SH
(952) 854-3411. **Call for rates.** 2300 E American Blvd. I-494, exit 2A (24th Ave), just s. Int corridors. **Pets:** Accepted.
SAVE ✕ 🔥M 🖥 ▣ ¶¶ 🏊

▼▼▼▼ Residence Inn by Marriott SH
(952) 876-0900. **$219-$252.** 7850 Bloomington Ave S. I-494, exit 3 on south frontage road. Int corridors. **Pets:** Accepted.
ASK 🍲 ✕ 🖥 ▣ 🏊

▼▼▼▼ Sheraton Bloomington Hotel Minneapolis South LH ❖
(952) 835-7800. **Call for rates.** 7800 Normandale Blvd. I-494, exit 7A (SR 100). Int corridors. **Pets:** Large, other species. Service with restrictions, supervision.
✕ 🖥 ▣ ¶¶ 🏊 ❎

▲▲▲ ▼▼▼ ▼▼▼ Sofitel Minneapolis LH
(952) 835-1900. **$109-$299.** 5601 W 78th St. Just nw of jct I-494 and SR 100, access via SR 100 and Industrial Blvd. Int corridors. **Pets:** Service with restrictions.
SAVE 🍲 ✕ 🔥M 🖥 ¶¶ ❎

▼▼▼▼ Staybridge Suites SH
(952) 831-7900. **$179-$299.** 5150 American Blvd. I-494, exit 6B (France Ave), just se of SR 100, then 1 mi w on frontage road. Int corridors. **Pets:** Accepted.
✕ 🔥M 🖥 ▣ 🏊 ❎

▲▲▲ ▼▼▼ Super 8 Hotel SH
(952) 888-8800. **$59-$85.** 7800 S 2nd Ave. I-494, exit 4A (Nicollet Ave), just se. Int corridors. **Pets:** $10 daily fee/pet. Service with restrictions, supervision.
SAVE 🍲 ✕ 🖥 ▣ ❎

BROOKLYN CENTER

▼▼ ▼▼ Comfort Inn by Choice Hotels SH
(763) 560-7464. **Call for rates.** 1600 James Cir N. I-694, exit 34 (Shingle Creek Pkwy), just ne. Int corridors. **Pets:** Accepted.
✕ 🔥M 🖥 ▣

▲▲▲ ▼▼▼▼ Crowne Plaza Minneapolis North SH
(763) 566-8000. **$129-$154.** 2200 Freeway Blvd. I-94/694, exit 34 (Shingle Creek Pkwy). Int corridors. **Pets:** Accepted.
SAVE 🍲 ✕ 🖥 ▣ ¶¶ 🏊 ❎

BROOKLYN PARK

▼▼ ▼▼ La Quinta Inn & Suites SH
(763) 971-8000. **$67.** 7011 Northland Cir. I-94/694, exit 30 (Boone Ave), just ne. Int corridors. **Pets:** Other species. Service with restrictions, supervision.
ASK 🍲 ✕ 🔥M 🖥 ▣ 🏊

BURNSVILLE

▲▲▲ ▼▼▼ Americas Best Value Inn M ❖
(952) 894-3400. **$63-$83.** 1101 Burnsville Pkwy. I-35W, exit 2 (Burnsville Pkwy), just sw. Int corridors. **Pets:** Dogs only. $10 one-time fee/room. Designated rooms, service with restrictions, supervision.
SAVE 🍲 ✕ 🖥

CHANHASSEN

▲▲▲ ▼▼▼▼ AmericInn Hotel & Suites SH
(952) 934-3888. **$99-$169.** 570 Pond Promenade. Just se of jct SR 5 and 101 S. Int corridors. **Pets:** Medium, dogs only. $100 deposit/room, $30 one-time fee/room. Designated rooms, service with restrictions, crate.
SAVE ✕ 🔥M 🖥 ▣ 🏊 ❎

CHASKA

▲▲▲ ▼▼▼▼ Best Western Chaska River Inn & Suites SH ❖
(952) 448-7877. **$75-$165.** One Riverbend. Jct US 212, 0.3 mi s on SR 41. Int corridors. **Pets:** Other species. Service with restrictions, supervision.
SAVE 🍲 ✕ 🔥M 🖥 ▣ ¶¶ 🏊 ❎

COON RAPIDS

▼▼ ▼▼ Comfort Inn-Northtown SH
(763) 785-4746. **$59-$199.** 9052 University Ave NE. US 10, exit Foley Blvd, 0.6 mi. Int corridors. **Pets:** Accepted.
✕ 🖥 ▣ 🏊

▲▲▲ ▼▼▼▼ Country Suites By Carlson SH
(763) 780-3797. **$120-$199.** 155 Coon Rapids Blvd. SR 10, exit Foley Blvd, 0.8 mi s to Coon Rapids Blvd, 0.5 mi e to Springbrook Dr, then just n. Int corridors. **Pets:** Medium. $20 daily fee/pet. Designated rooms, service with restrictions, supervision.
SAVE 🍲 ✕ 🖥 ▣ 🏊

EAGAN

▼▼ ▼▼ Days Inn SH
(651) 681-1770. **$69-$149.** 4510 Erin Dr. Just ne of jct SR 77 and Cliff Rd. Int corridors. **Pets:** Accepted.
ASK 🍲 ✕ 🔥M 🖥 ▣ 🏊 ❎

▼▼ ▼▼ Extended StayAmerica SH
(651) 681-9991. **$90-$100.** 3384 Norwest Ct. I-35E, exit 97, just nw. Int corridors. **Pets:** Other species. $75 one-time fee/pet. Service with restrictions.
ASK 🍲 ✕ 🖥 ▣

▼▼ ▼▼ Homestead Studio Suites Hotel-Minneapolis-Airport-Eagan SH
(651) 905-1778. **$95-$105.** 3015 Denmark Ave. I-35E, exit 98 (Lone Oak Rd), just se. Int corridors. **Pets:** Other species. $75 one-time fee/pet. Service with restrictions.
ASK 🍲 ✕ 🖥 ▣

▼▼ ▼▼ Microtel Inn & Suites SH
(651) 405-0988. **$64-$109.** 3000 Denmark Ave. I-35E, exit 98 (Lone Oak Rd), just se. Int corridors. **Pets:** Accepted.
ASK 🍲 ✕ 🖥 ▣

▼▼▼▼ Residence Inn by Marriott-Mpls/St. Paul Airport SH
(651) 688-0363. **$214-$235.** 3040 Eagandale Pl. I-35E, exit 98 (Lone Oak Rd), just sw. Ext corridors. **Pets:** Accepted.
ASK 🍲 ✕ 🖥 ▣ 🏊 ❎

▼▼ ▼▼ Staybridge Suites SH
(651) 994-7810. **$129-$229.** 4675 Rahncliff Rd. I-35E, exit 93 (Cliff Rd), just w, then just s. Int corridors. **Pets:** Accepted.
ASK 🍲 ✕ 🖥 ▣ 🏊

▼▼▼▼ TownePlace Suites SH ❖
(651) 994-4600. **$143-$176.** 3615 Crestridge Dr. I-35E, exit 71 (Pilot Knob Rd), just se. Int corridors. **Pets:** Large. $75 one-time fee/room. Service with restrictions, crate.
ASK 🍲 ✕ 🔥M 🖥 ▣ 🏊

EDEN PRAIRIE

AAA ♦♦♦ **Best Western Eden Prairie Inn** SH
(952) 829-0888. **$72-$99, 3 day notice.** 11500 W 78th St. I-494, exit 11A, just sw. Int corridors. **Pets:** Accepted.
SAVE S⌀ ✕ 🛏 💻 🌊

♦♦♦ **Extended StayAmerica** SH
(952) 941-1113. **$95-$105.** 7550 Office Ridge Cir. I-494, exit 12, just se. Int corridors. **Pets:** Other species. $75 one-time fee/pet. Service with restrictions.
ASK S⌀ ✕ 🛏 💻

♦♦♦ **Homestead Studio Suites Hotel-Minneapolis-Eden Prairie** SH
(952) 942-6818. **$104-$115.** 11905 Technology Dr. Just sw of jct I-494 and US 212 (Flying Cloud Dr). Int corridors. **Pets:** Other species. $75 one-time fee/pet. Service with restrictions.
ASK S⌀ ✕ 🛦M 🛏 💻

♦♦♦♦ **The Residence Inn by Marriott-Minneapolis SW** SH
(952) 829-0033. **Call for rates.** 7780 Flying Cloud Dr. I-494, exit 11A, on US 169 S and 212 (Flying Cloud Dr). Int corridors. **Pets:** $100 one-time fee/room. Service with restrictions, supervision.
✕ 🛏 💻 🌊

EDINA

♦♦♦♦ **Residence Inn Minneapolis-Edina** SH
(952) 893-9300. **$197-$219.** 3400 Edinborough Way. I-494, exit 6B (France Ave), 0.3 mi n to Minnesota Dr, then just e. Int corridors. **Pets:** Accepted.
ASK S⌀ ✕ 🛏 💻

ELK RIVER

♦♦ **AmericInn Lodge & Suites of Elk River** M ❀
(763) 441-8554. **Call for rates.** 17432 Hwy 10. 1.5 mi se on US 10/169. Int corridors. **Pets:** Large. $10 daily fee/pet. Designated rooms, service with restrictions, supervision.
✕ 🛏 💻

FOREST LAKE

♦♦ **AmericInn Motel** SH
(651) 464-1930. **$79-$119.** 1291 W Broadway. I-35, exit 131 (CR 2), just ne. Int corridors. **Pets:** Accepted.
ASK S⌀ ✕ 🛏 💻 🌊

HASTINGS

♦♦ **AmericInn Lodge & Suites** SH
(651) 437-8877. **$89-$140.** 2400 Vermillion St. 1.5 mi s on US 61. Int corridors. **Pets:** Accepted.
ASK S⌀ ✕ 🛏 💻 🌊

♦♦♦ **Country Inn & Suites By Carlson** SH
(651) 437-8870. **$97.** 300 33rd St. 1.7 mi s on US 61, just e. Int corridors. **Pets:** Accepted.
ASK S⌀ ✕ 🛏 💻

MAPLE GROVE

♦♦ **Extended StayAmerica** SH
(763) 694-9747. **$90-$100.** 12970 63rd Ave N. I-494, exit 26, just ne. Int corridors. **Pets:** Other species. $75 one-time fee/pet. Service with restrictions.
ASK S⌀ ✕ 🛦M 🛏 💻

♦♦ **Select Inn** SH
(763) 493-2277. **$69-$119.** 7285 Forest View Ln N. I-94, exit 28 (CR 61/Hemlock Ln), just se. Int corridors. **Pets:** Accepted.
ASK S⌀ ✕ 🛏 💻

♦♦♦♦ **Staybridge Suites Minneapolis-Maple Grove** SH
(763) 494-8856. **$179-$399.** 7821 Elm Creek Blvd. Just ne of jct I-94/494/694. Int corridors. **Pets:** Accepted.
ASK S⌀ ✕ 🛦M 🛏 💻 🌊 🗙

MINNEAPOLIS

AAA ♦♦♦ **Days Inn-University** SH
(612) 623-3999. **Call for rates.** 2407 University Ave SE. I-35W, exit University Ave, 1 mi se. Int corridors. **Pets:** $20 one-time fee/room. Service with restrictions, supervision.
SAVE ✕ 🛏 💻

AAA ♦♦♦♦ **Graves 601 Hotel** LH
(612) 677-1100. **Call for rates.** 601 1st Ave N. Between 6th and 7th sts. Int corridors. **Pets:** Accepted.
SAVE ✕ 🛏 🍴 🗙

AAA ♦♦♦♦ **Hilton Minneapolis** LH
(612) 376-1000. **$109-$369.** 1001 Marquette Ave. Between S 10th and S 11th sts. Int corridors. **Pets:** Small. $100 deposit/pet. Service with restrictions, supervision.
SAVE ✕ 🛏 💻 🍴 🌊 🗙

♦♦♦♦ **Holiday Inn Minneapolis Metrodome** LH
(612) 333-4646. **$149-$289.** 1500 Washington Ave S. Jct Washington and S 15th aves. Int corridors. **Pets:** Accepted.
ASK S⌀ ✕ 🛏 💻 🍴 🌊 🗙

AAA ♦♦♦♦ **The Marquette Hotel** LH
(612) 333-4545. **$149.** 710 Marquette Ave. Jct Marquette Ave and S 7th St. Int corridors. **Pets:** Accepted.
SAVE S⌀ ✕ 🛏 💻 🍴

AAA ♦♦♦♦ **Millennium Hotel Minneapolis** LH
(612) 332-6000. **$135-$260.** 1313 Nicollet Mall. Jct Nicollet Ave and Grant St. Int corridors. **Pets:** Accepted.
SAVE S⌀ ✕ 🛦M 🛏 💻 🍴 🌊 🗙

♦♦♦♦ **Minneapolis Marriott City Center** LH
(612) 349-4000. **$230-$285.** 30 S 7th St. Between Hennepin and Nicollet aves; in City Center Shopping Complex. Int corridors. **Pets:** Accepted.
ASK S⌀ ✕ 🛦M 🛏 💻 🍴 🗙

AAA ♦♦♦♦ **Radisson Plaza Hotel Minneapolis** LH
(612) 339-4900. **$89-$399.** 35 S 7th St. Between Nicollet and Hennepin aves. Int corridors. **Pets:** Medium. $50 one-time fee/room. Designated rooms, service with restrictions, supervision.
SAVE S⌀ ✕ 🛦M 🛏 💻 🍴 🗙

AAA ♦♦♦♦ **Residence Inn by Marriott Minneapolis Downtown City Center** SH
(612) 677-1000. **$348-$368.** 45 S 8th St. At 8th St and LaSalle Ave. Int corridors. **Pets:** Medium. $100 one-time fee/pet. Service with restrictions, crate.
SAVE S⌀ ✕ 🛏 💻

♦♦♦ **Residence Inn Milwaukee Road Depot** SH
(612) 340-1300. **$291-$312.** 425 S 2nd St. Jct S 2nd St and 5th Ave S. Int corridors. **Pets:** Accepted.
ASK S⌀ ✕ 🛏 💻

AAA ♦♦♦♦ **Sheraton Minneapolis Midtown Hotel** SH
(612) 821-7600. **$149-$299, 3 day notice.** 2901 Chicago Ave S. At Lake St. Int corridors. **Pets:** Accepted.
SAVE S⌀ ✕ 🛦M 🛏 💻 🍴 🌊

AAA ♦♦♦♦ **The Westin Minneapolis** LH ❀
(612) 333-4006. **$679.** 88 S 6th St. At Marquette Ave. Int corridors. **Pets:** Medium, dogs only. Service with restrictions, supervision.
SAVE S⌀ ✕ 💻 🍴 🌊 🗙

MINNETONKA

(AAA) ▼▼▼▼ **Minneapolis Marriott-Southwest** 🏩 ❖
(952) 935-5500. **$186-$208.** 5801 Opus Pkwy. Just nw of jct US 169 and Cross Town SR 62, exit Bren Rd off US 169. Int corridors. **Pets:** Medium. $250 deposit/pet. Service with restrictions, crate.
SAVE 🐾 ☒ 🛏 💻 🍽 🏊 ⊠

(AAA) ▼▼▼▼ **Sheraton Minneapolis West Hotel** 🆂🅷
(952) 593-0000. **$99-$179.** 12201 Ridgedale Dr. I-394, exit 1C (Plymouth Rd), 0.3 mi s. Int corridors. **Pets:** Accepted.
SAVE 🐾 ☒ 🛏 💻 🍽 🏊 ⊠

MONTICELLO

(AAA) ▼▼▼ **Best Western Chelsea Inn & Suites** 🆂🅷
(763) 271-8880. **Call for rates.** 89 Chelsea Rd. I-94, exit 193, 0.3 mi se. Int corridors. **Pets:** Accepted.
SAVE ☒ 🛏 💻 🏊 ⊠

(AAA) ▼▼▼ **Days Inn** 🆂🅷
(763) 295-1111. **$59-$79.** 200 E Oakwood Dr. I-94, exit 193, 0.3 mi se. Int corridors. **Pets:** Accepted.
SAVE 🐾 ☒ 🛏 💻

▼▼ **Select Inn of Monticello** 🆂🅷
(763) 295-4000. **$50-$80.** 1114 Cedar St. I-94, exit 193, 0.3 mi se. Int corridors. **Pets:** Accepted.
ASK 🐾 ☒ 🛏 💻 🏊

NORTH BRANCH

(AAA) ▼▼▼ **AmericInn Lodge & Suites** 🆂🅷 ❖
(651) 674-8627. **$79-$180.** 38675 14th Ave. I-35, exit 147 (SR 95), just e, then s on Oakview, then w on Oak St. Int corridors. **Pets:** $30 one-time fee/room. Service with restrictions, supervision.
SAVE ☒ 🛏 💻 🏊 ⊠

(AAA) ▼▼▼ **Budget Host Inn & Suites** 🆂🅷
(651) 277-8000. **$65-$135.** 6010 Main St. I-35, exit 147 (SR 95), just e. Int corridors. **Pets:** Accepted.
SAVE ☒ 🛏 💻 🏊 ⊠

OAKDALE

▼▼▼ **Wingate Inn** 🆂🅷
(651) 578-8466. **Call for rates.** 970 Helena Ave N. I-694, exit 57, just e, then just s. Int corridors. **Pets:** Accepted.
☒ ⑹ᴹ 🛏 💻

OAK PARK HEIGHTS

▼▼ **AmericInn Lodge & Suites** 🆂🅷 ❖
(651) 275-0980. **Call for rates.** 13025 60th St N. SR 36 at Stillwater Blvd, just se. Int corridors. **Pets:** Large, other species. $15 one-time fee/room. Service with restrictions, supervision.
☒ 🛏 💻 🏊 ⊠

PLYMOUTH

(AAA) ▼▼▼ **Best Western Kelly Inn** 🆂🅷
(763) 553-1600. **$89-$139.** 2705 N Annapolis Ln. I-494, exit 22 (SR 55), just e. Int corridors. **Pets:** Medium, other species. Service with restrictions, crate.
SAVE 🐾 ☒ 🛏 💻 🍽 🏊 ⊠

(AAA) ▼▼▼▼ **Radisson Hotel & Conference Center Minneapolis** 🏩 ❖
(763) 559-6600. **$99-$199.** 3131 Campus Dr. I-494, exit 22 (SR 55), just e to CR 61 (Northwest Blvd), then 0.8 mi nw. **Pets:** Service with restrictions, supervision.
SAVE 🐾 ☒ 💻 🍽 🏊 ⊠

▼▼ **Red Roof Inn** 🅼
(763) 553-1751. **Call for rates.** 2600 Annapolis Ln N. I-494, exit 22 (SR 55), just se. Ext corridors. **Pets:** Accepted.
☒

RICHFIELD

▼▼▼ **Candlewood Suites** 🆂🅷
(612) 869-7704. **$110-$135.** 351 W 77th St. I-494, exit 4B (Lyndale Ave), just ne. Int corridors. **Pets:** Large. $75 one-time fee/pet. Service with restrictions, crate.
ASK 🐾 ☒ ⑹ᴹ 🛏 💻

ROGERS

▼▼ **AmericInn Lodge & Suites** 🆂🅷 ❖
(763) 428-4346. **$87-$148.** 21800 Industrial Blvd. I-94, exit 207 (SR 101), just sw. Int corridors. **Pets:** Other species. $100 deposit/room, $10 daily fee/pet. Designated rooms, supervision.
ASK ☒ 🛏 💻 🏊

ROSEVILLE

▼▼▼ **Residence Inn** 🆂🅷
(651) 636-0680. **$192-$213.** 2985 Centre Pointe Dr. I-35W, exit 25A (CR D), just se. Int corridors. **Pets:** Accepted.
ASK 🐾 ☒ ⑹ᴹ 🛏 💻 🏊 ⊠

ST. LOUIS PARK

▼▼▼ **DoubleTree Hotel Minneapolis Park Place** 🏩
(952) 542-8600. **$79-$219.** 1500 Park Place Blvd. I-394, exit 5 (Park Place Blvd), just sw. Int corridors. **Pets:** Accepted.
☒ 🛏 💻 🍽 🏊

(AAA) ▼▼ **Lakeland Inn** 🆂🅷
(952) 926-6575. **Call for rates.** 4025 Hwy 7. SR 7, 0.5 mi e of SR 100. Int corridors. **Pets:** Accepted.
SAVE ☒ 🛏

▼▼▼ **TownePlace Suites-Minneapolis West** 🆂🅷
(952) 847-6900. **$171-$192.** 1400 Zarthan Ave S. I-394, exit 5 (Park Place Blvd), 0.3 mi w on 16th, then just n. Int corridors. **Pets:** Accepted.
ASK 🐾 ☒ 🛏 💻 🏊

ST. PAUL

(AAA) ▼▼▼▼ **Best Western Bandana Square** 🆂🅷
(651) 647-1637. **$89-$159, 30 day notice.** 1010 Bandana Blvd W. I-94, exit 239B (Lexington Pkwy), 1.3 mi n, then 0.3 mi w on Energy Park Dr. Int corridors. **Pets:** Accepted.
SAVE 🐾 ☒ ⑹ᴹ 🛏 💻 🏊 ⊠

(AAA) ▼▼▼ **Best Western Kelly Inn** 🆂🅷
(651) 227-8711. **$119.** 161 St. Anthony Ave. Jct I-35E and 94. Int corridors. **Pets:** Medium, other species. Service with restrictions, crate.
SAVE 🐾 ☒ 🛏 💻 🍽 🏊

(AAA) ▼▼ **Exel Inn of St. Paul** 🆂🅷
(651) 771-5566. **$61-$89.** 1739 Old Hudson Rd. I-94, exit 245 (White Bear Ave), just nw. Int corridors. **Pets:** Accepted.
SAVE 🐾 ☒ 🛏 💻

SHAKOPEE

(AAA) ▼▼▼ **AmericInn Lodge & Suites** 🆂🅷
(952) 445-6775. **$89-$179.** 4100 12th Ave E. Just ne of US 169. Int corridors. **Pets:** Other species. $30 deposit/pet. Supervision.
SAVE ☒ 🛏 💻 🏊 ⊠

(AAA) ▼▼▼▼ **Country Inn & Suites By Carlson** 🆂🅷
(952) 445-0200. **$85-$115.** 1204 Ramsey St. Just ne of US 169. Int corridors. **Pets:** Small. $100 deposit/pet, $30 one-time fee/pet. Service with restrictions, crate.
SAVE 🐾 ☒ ⑹ᴹ 🛏 💻 🏊

A family vacation should include the whole family.

At over 1,100 Best Westerns pets are more than allowed, they're welcomed.

Best Western® invites you to bring your pet on your next family trip. Your best friend will love being part of the fun, while the rest of you enjoy the 17 standard services and amenities that have made Best Western your choice for vacation travel. Visit our website and click on "Trip Planner" to find one of our pet-friendly hotels. And plan your getaway today.

bestwestern.com/aaa | bestwestern.com/caa
1.866.430.9022

THE WORLD'S LARGEST HOTEL CHAIN.®

Discounts.
Free Nights.
Reward Points.
One card does it all.

More points. Low rates.

Get the card that does it all! Join our exclusive frequent guest program for AAA/CAA members, AAA/CAA Preferred Gold Crown Club® International and start earning the most award points ever toward free rooms, dining, shopping, and more. Best of all, you always get the lowest rate available and earn 10% bonus points with each qualified stay*. Membership is FREE, so join today!

bestwestern.com/aaa | bestwestern.com/caa
Over 1,100 AAA/CAA Offices | 1.866.430.9022

THE WORLD'S LARGEST HOTEL CHAIN®

AAA PetBook Photo Contest Entries

Each year, the winning entry in AAA's *PetBook®* Photo Contest appears on a cover of *Traveling With Your Pet: The AAA PetBook®* and also receives other great prizes. You have already met Libby on the back cover and Dory on the spine of this book. Here are more great entries that we just had to make room for!

Check out AAA.com/PetBook for pictures, contest rules and an entry form for next year's contest.

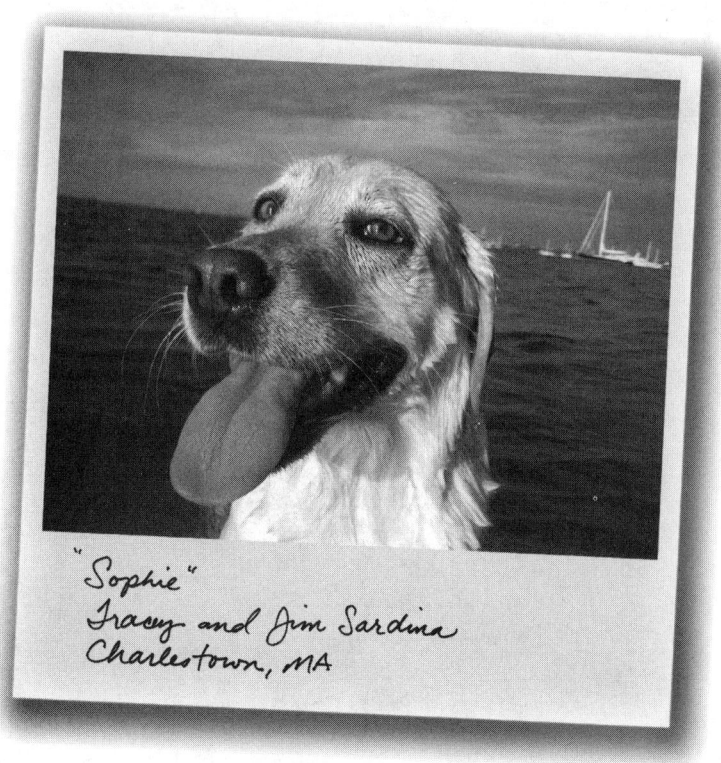

"Sophie"
Tracy and Jim Sardina
Charlestown, MA

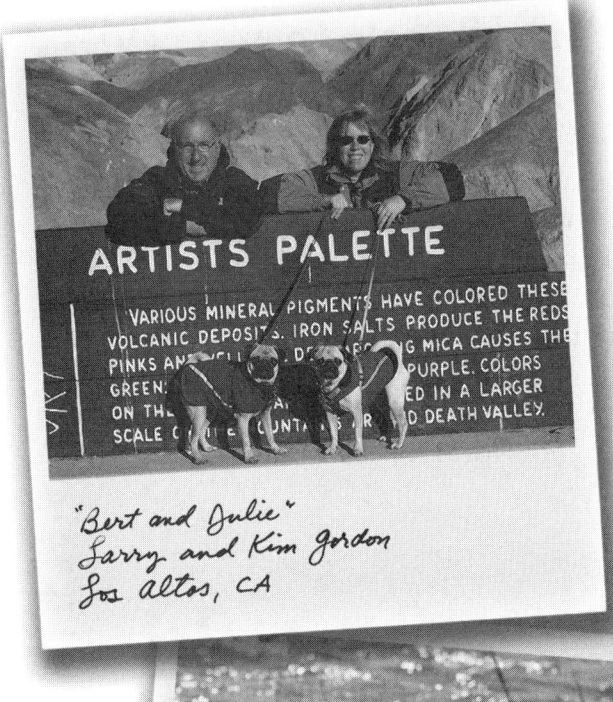

"Bert and Julie"
Larry and Kim Gordon
Los Altos, CA

"Ashley"
Dave Gauntlett
Barrington, RI

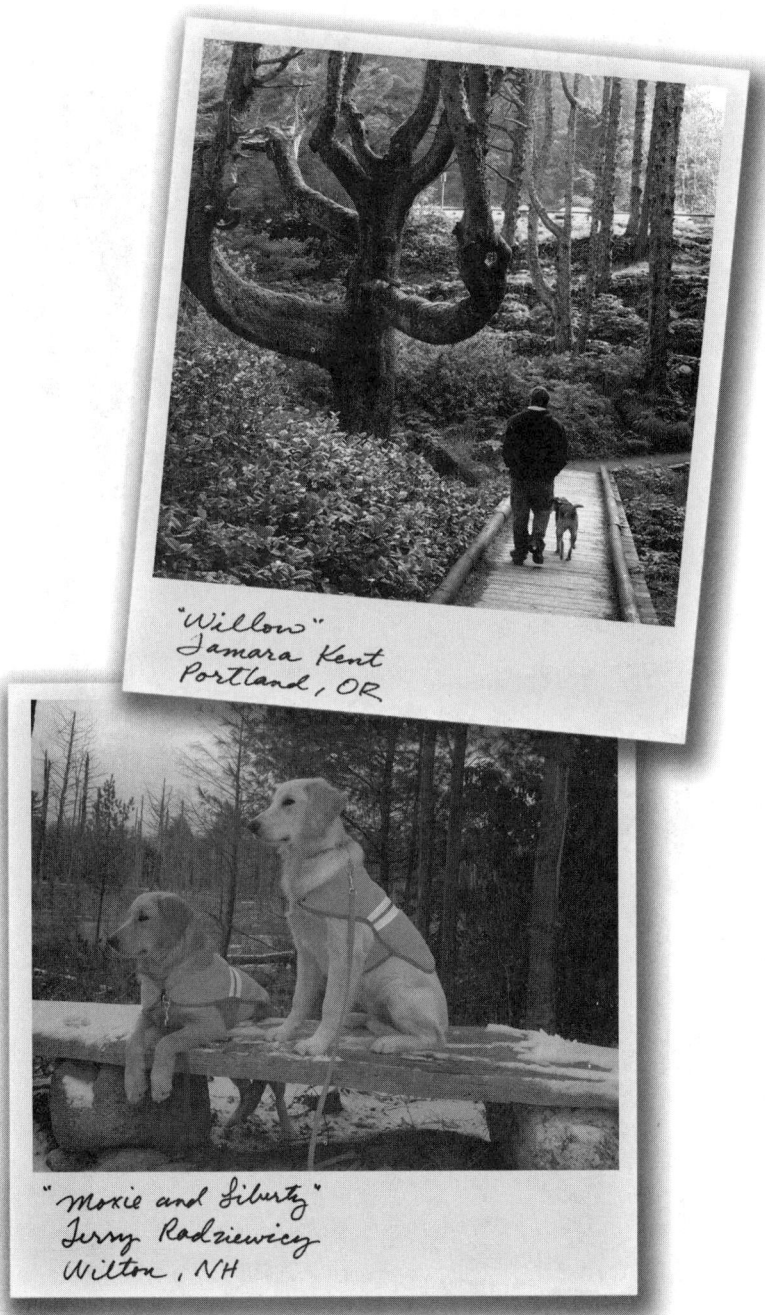

"Willow"
Tamara Kent
Portland, OR

"Moxie and Liberty"
Terry Radziewicz
Wilton, NH

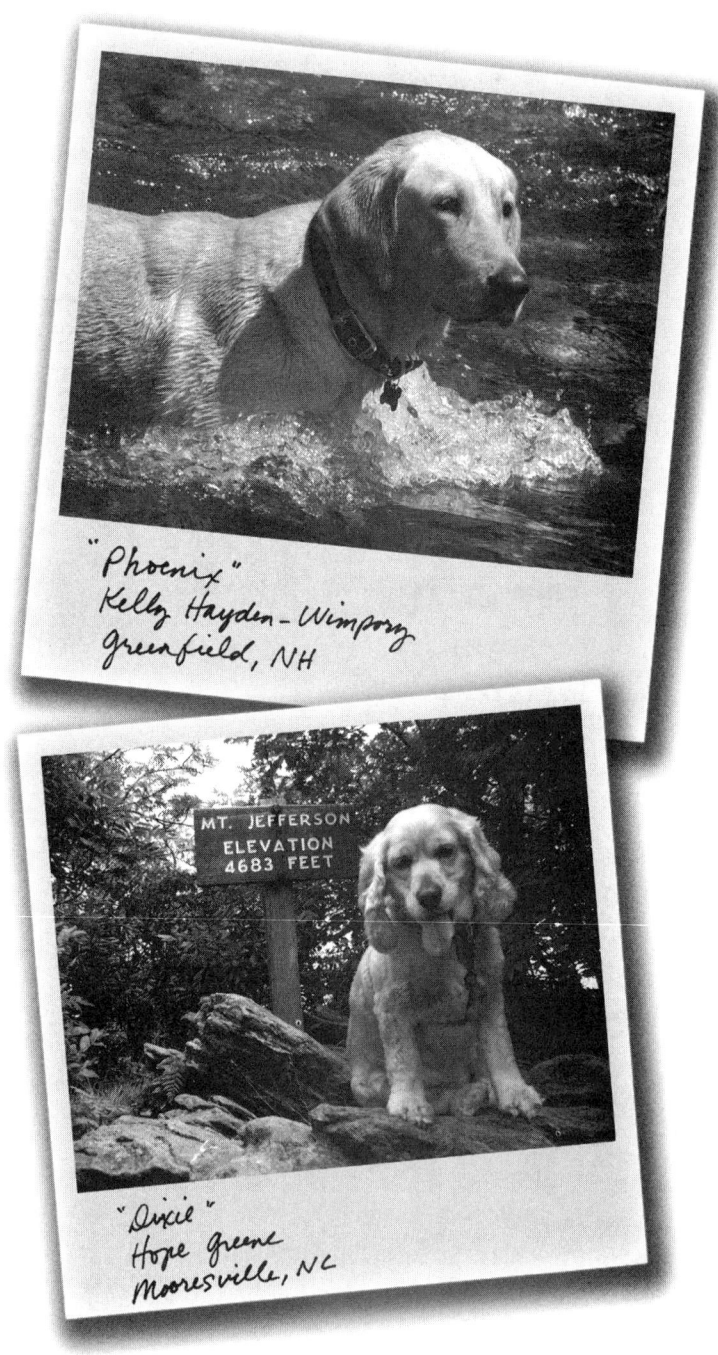

"Phoenix"
Kelly Hayden - Wimpory
Greenfield, NH

"Dixie"
Hope Greene
Mooresville, NC

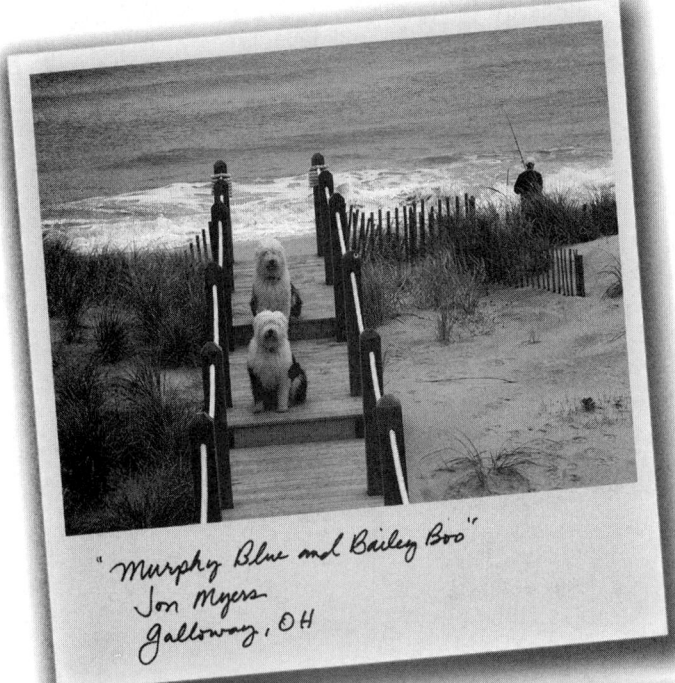

"Murphy Blue and Bailey Boo"
Jon Myers
Galloway, OH

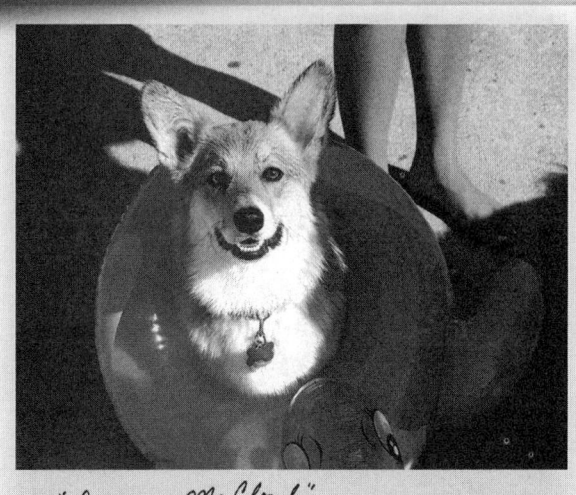

"Duncan McCloud"
Christine Ponczek
Citrus Heights, CA

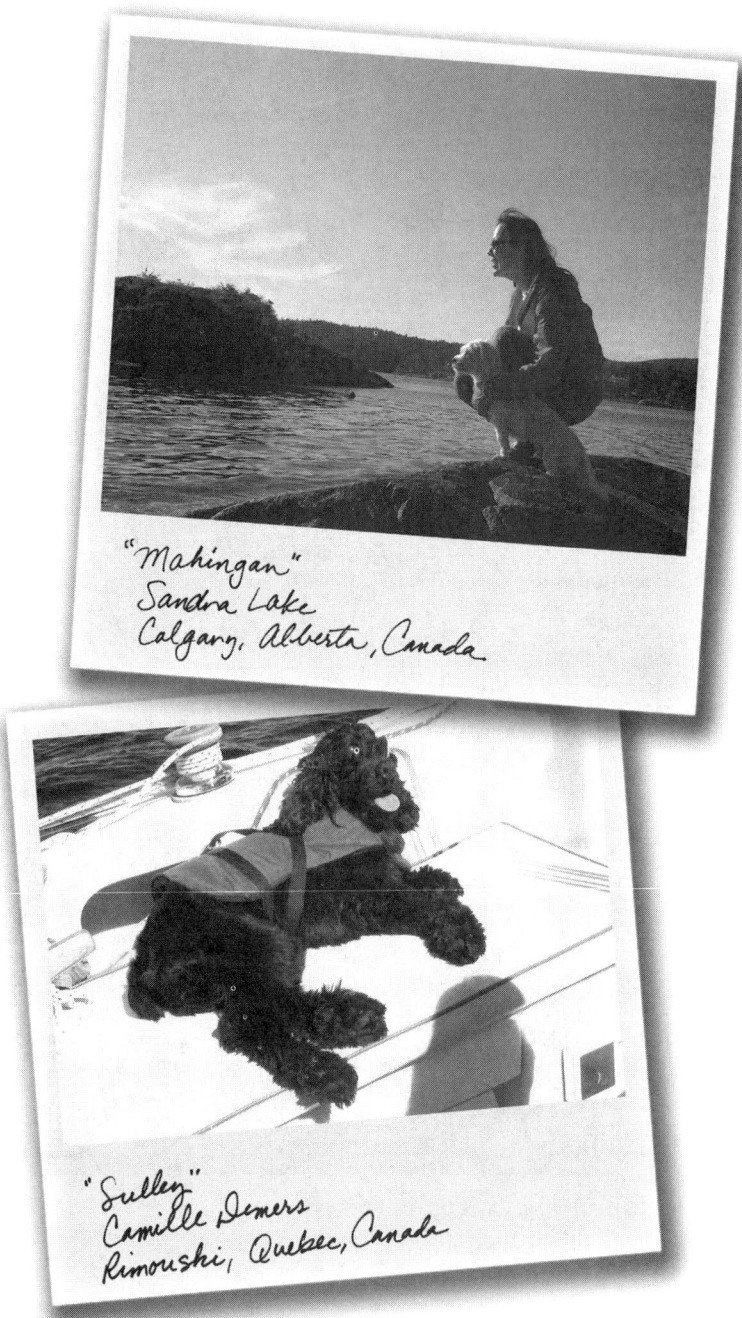

"Mahingan"
Sandra Lake
Calgary, Alberta, Canada

"Sulley"
Camille Demers
Rimouski, Quebec, Canada

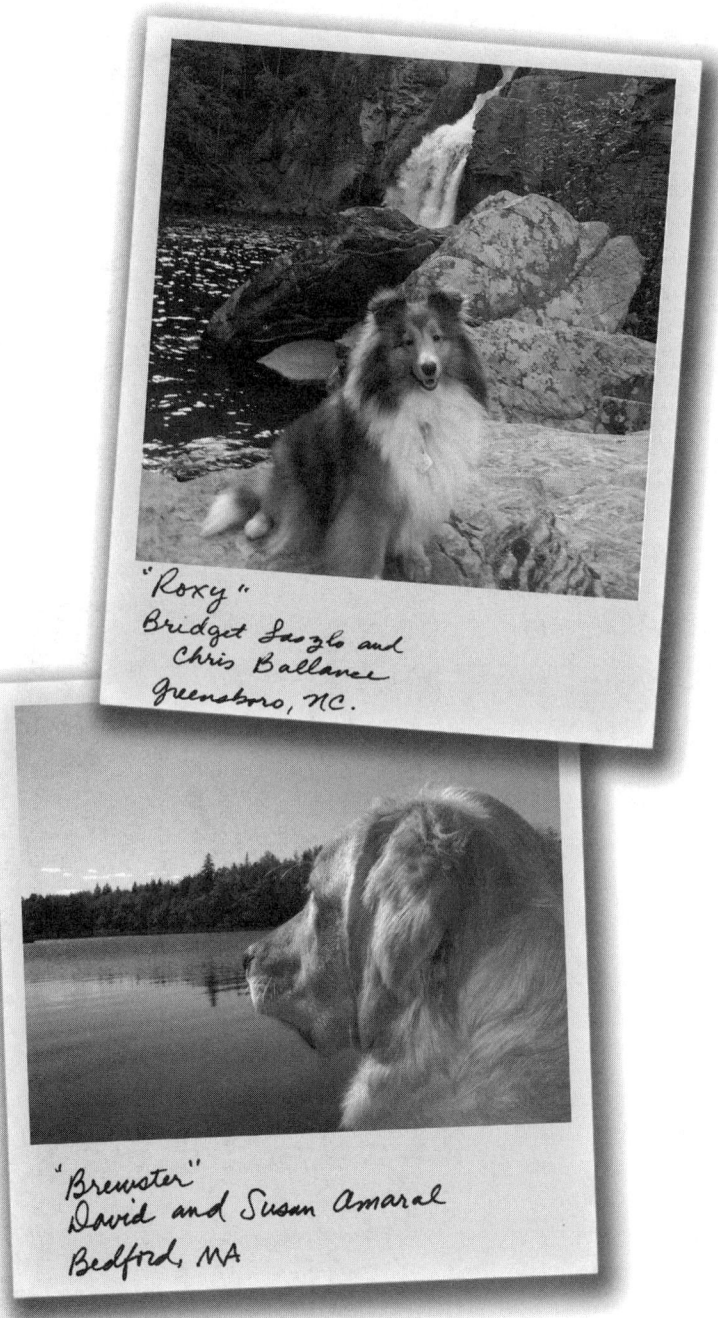

"Roxy"
Bridget Laszlo and
Chris Ballance
Greensboro, NC.

"Brewster"
David and Susan Amaral
Bedford, MA

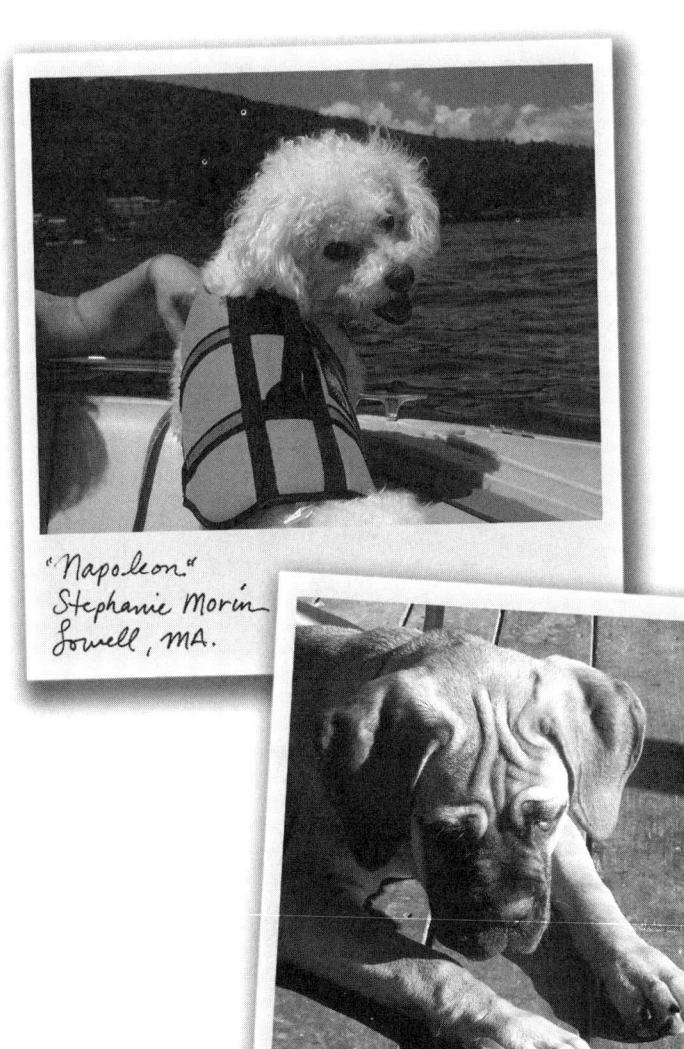

"Napoleon"
Stephanie Morin
Lowell, MA.

"Zane Taylor"
Jacque Hudson
Glendale, AZ

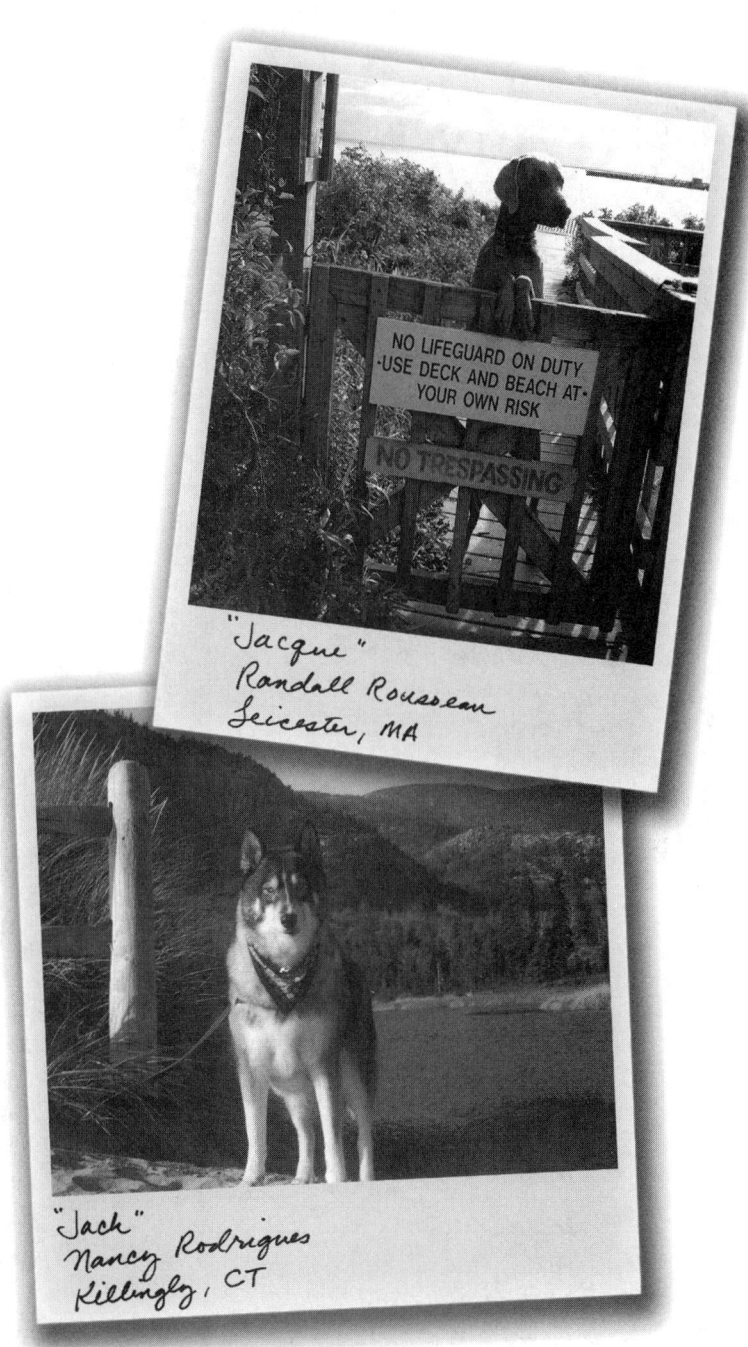

"Jacque"
Randall Rousseau
Leicester, MA

"Jack"
Nancy Rodrigues
Killingly, CT

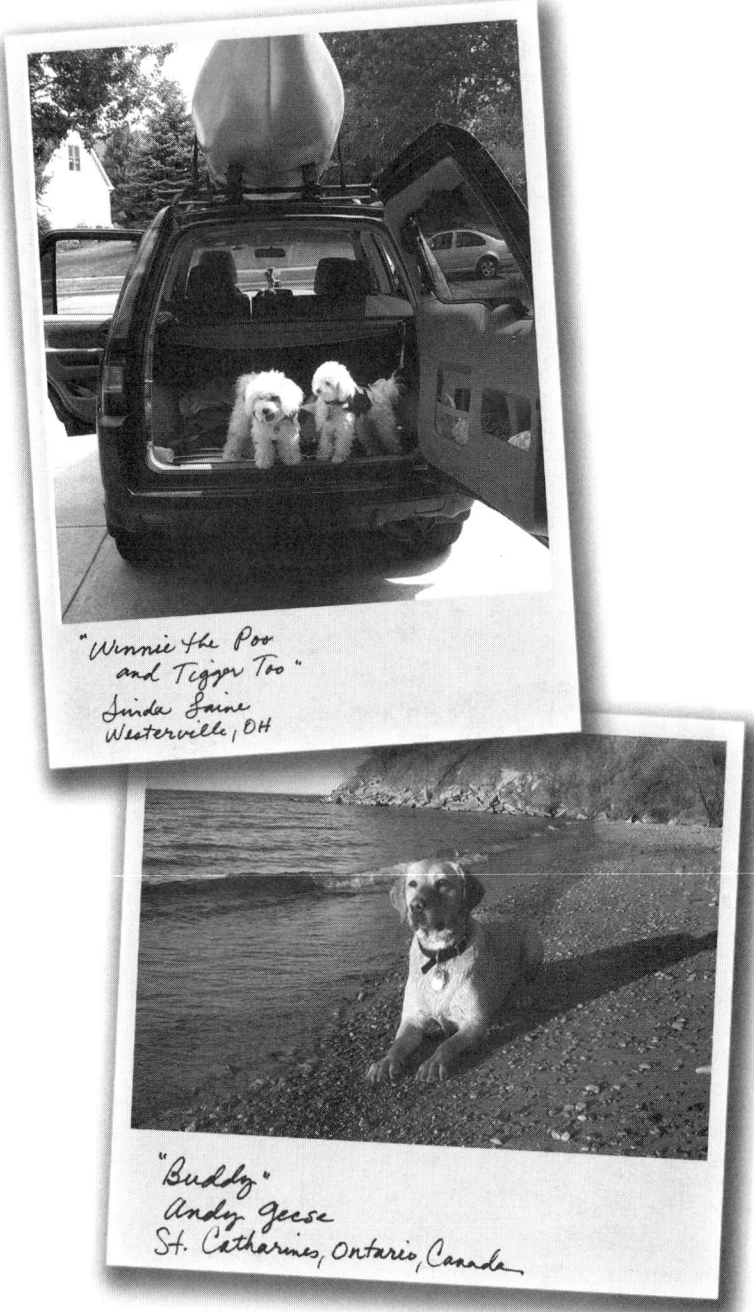

"Winnie the Poo
and Tigger Too"
Linda Laine
Westerville, OH

"Buddy"
Andy Geese
St. Catharines, Ontario, Canada

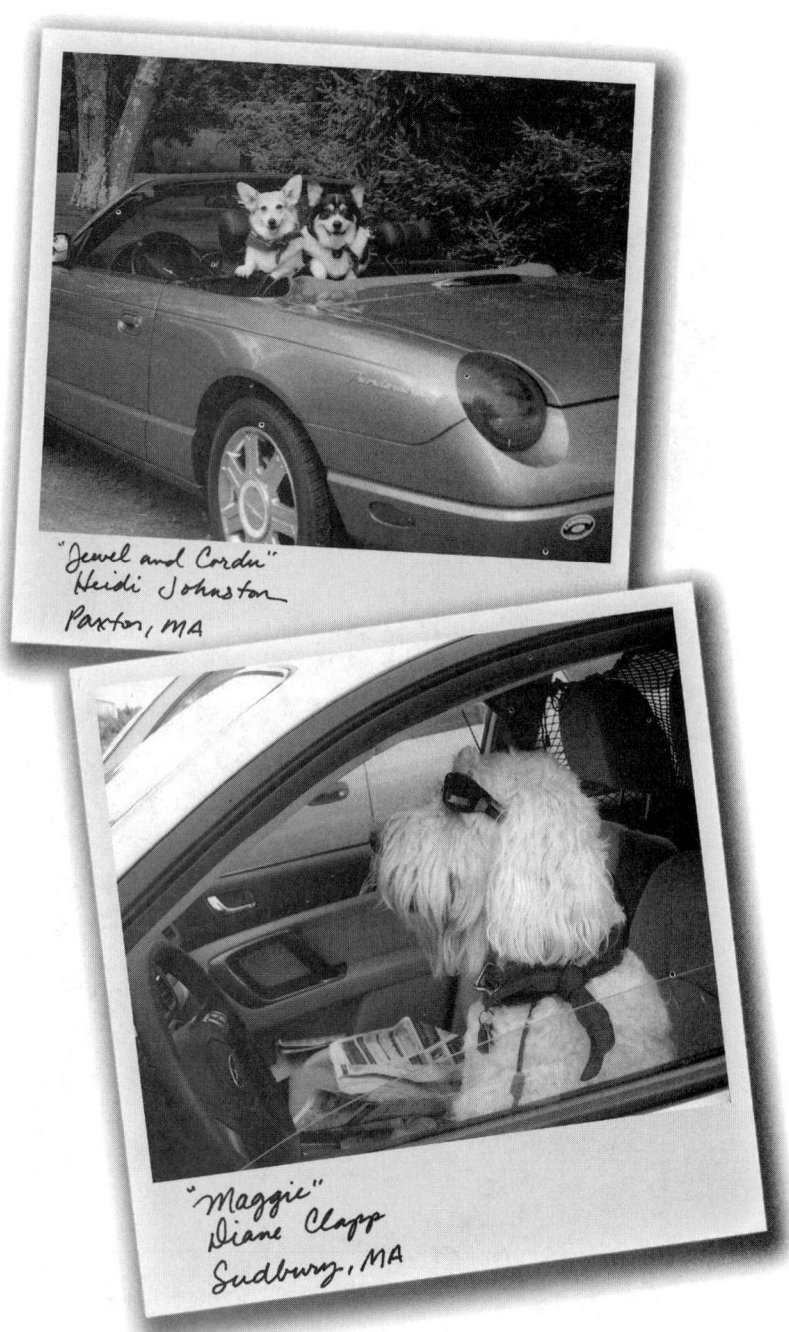

"Jewel and Corda"
Heidi Johnston
Paxton, MA

"Maggie"
Diane Clapp
Sudbury, MA

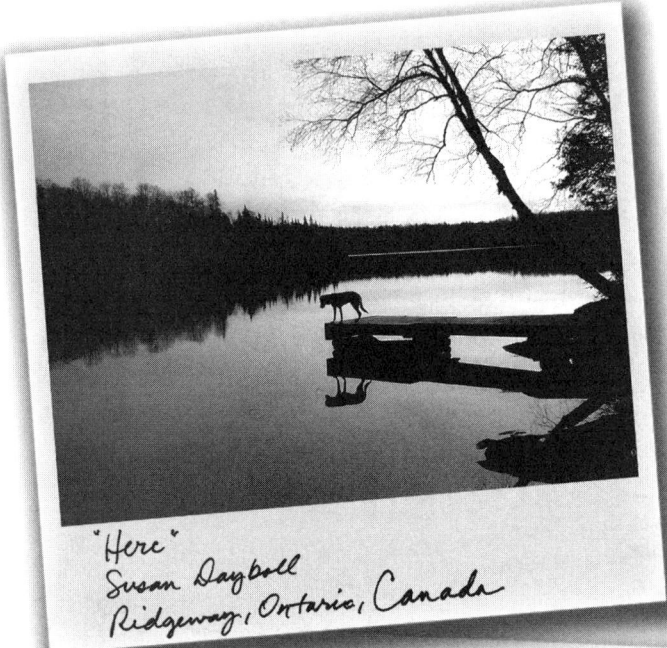

"Here"
Susan Dayboll
Ridgeway, Ontario, Canada

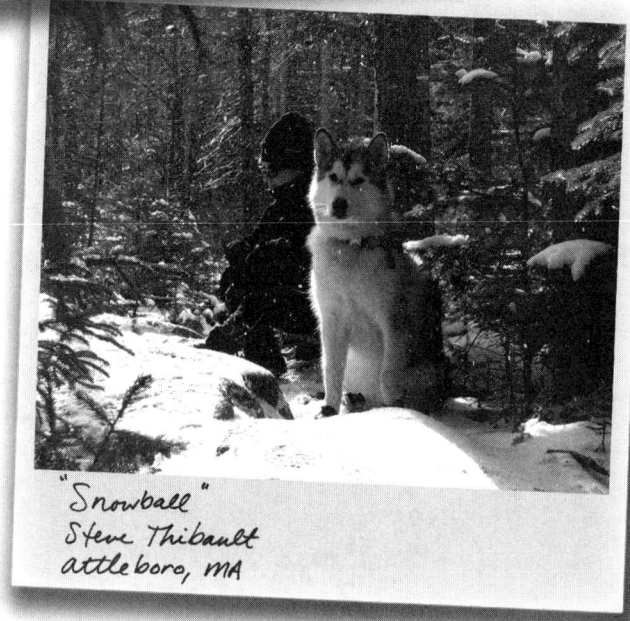

"Snowball"
Steve Thibault
attleboro, MA

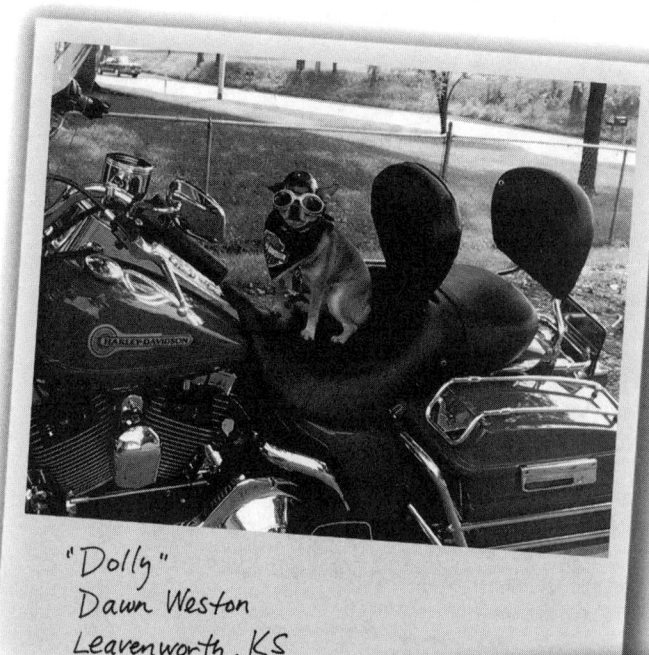

"Dolly"
Dawn Weston
Leavenworth, KS

"Nadia"
Timothy Parker
Portland, OR

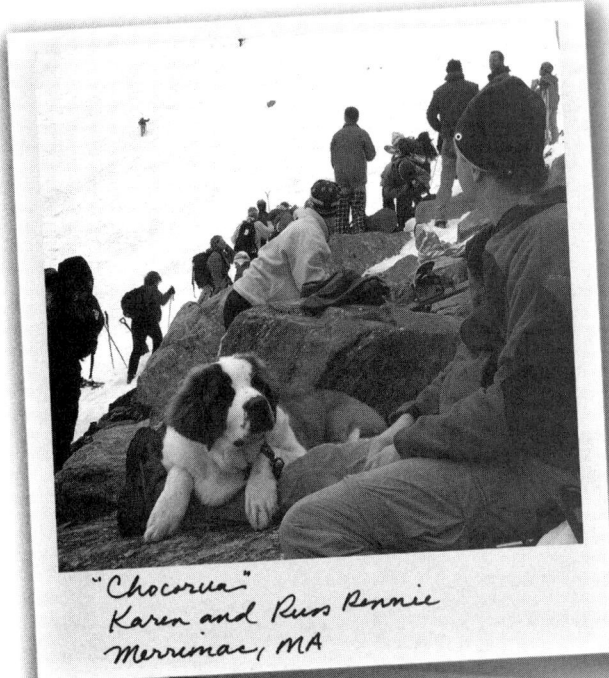

"Chocorua"
Karen and Russ Rennie
Merrimac, MA

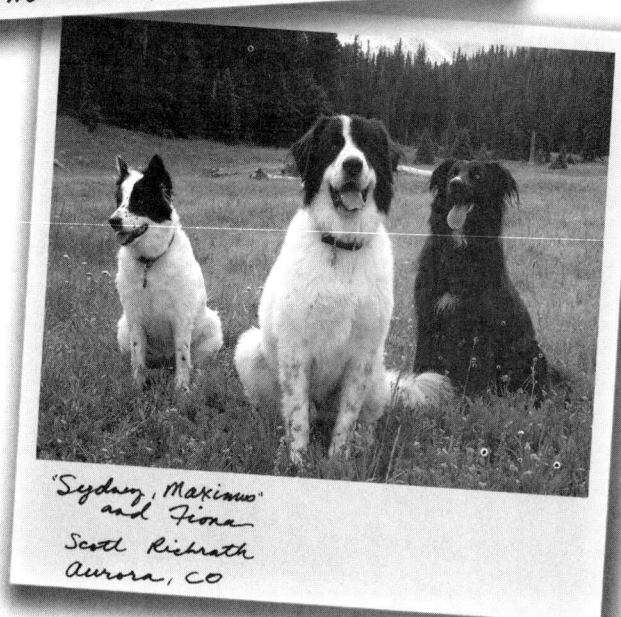

"Sydney, Maximus"
and Fiona
Scott Richrath
Aurora, CO

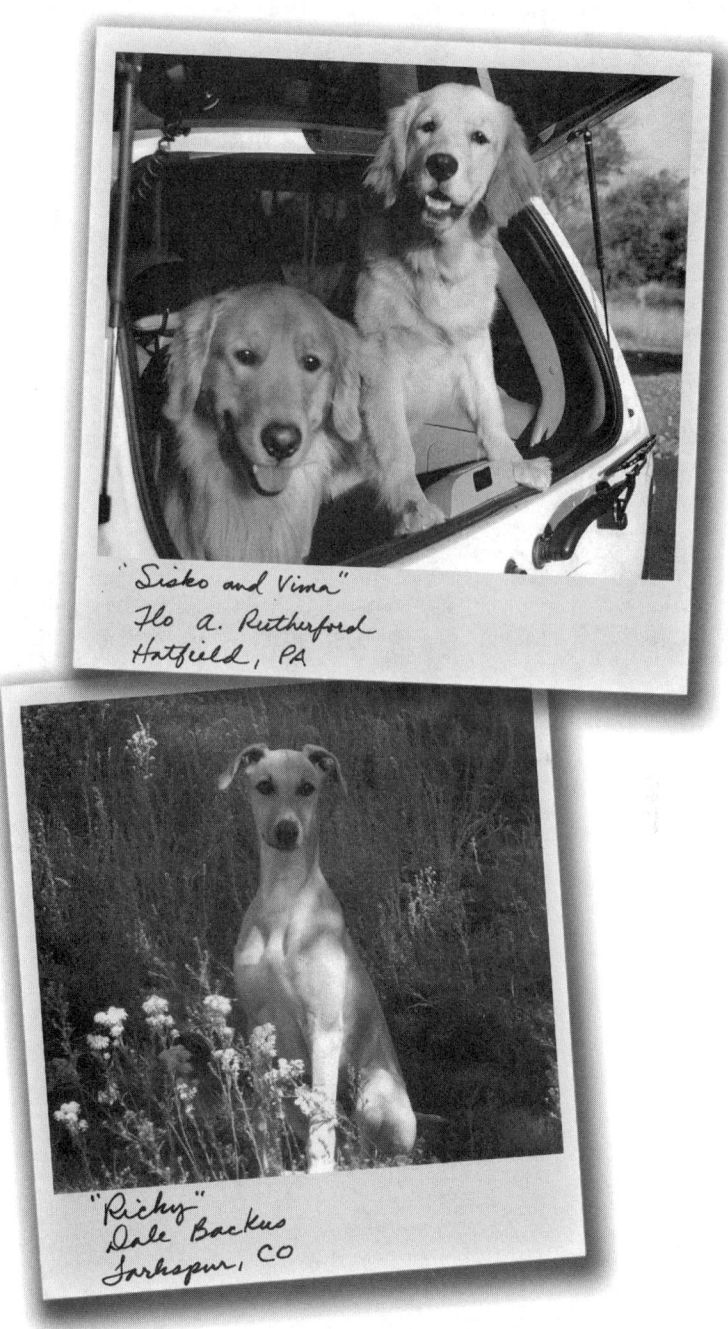

"Sisko and Vima"
Flo A. Rutherford
Hatfield, PA

"Ricky"
Dale Backus
Larkspur, CO

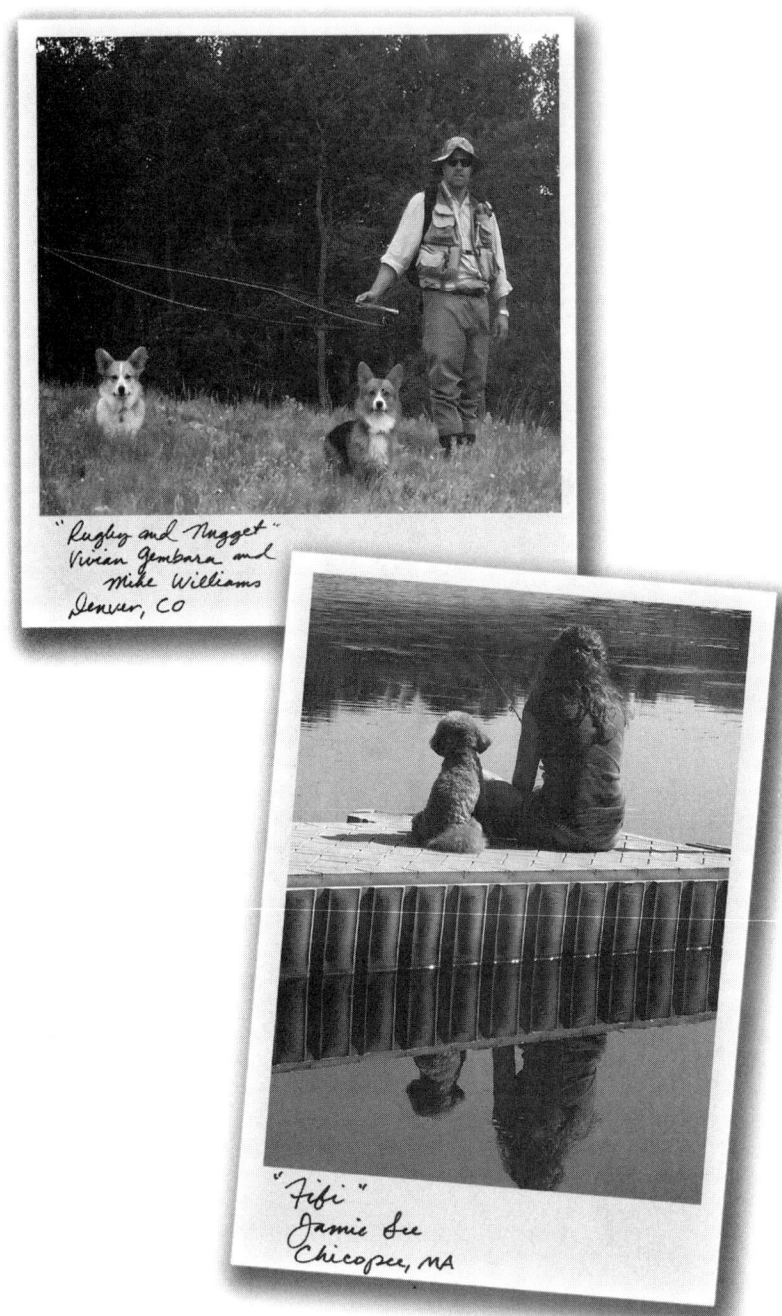

"Rugby and Nugget"
Vivian Gembara and
Mike Williams
Denver, CO

"Fifi"
Jamie Lee
Chicopee, MA

(AAA) ▼▼ **Sandalwood Studios & Suites** SH
(952) 277-0100. **$39-$109.** 3910 12th Ave E. Just nw of US 169. Int corridors. **Pets:** $10 daily fee/room. Designated rooms, service with restrictions, supervision.
SAVE S X H

STILLWATER

▼▼ **Days Inn-Stillwater** SH
(651) 430-1300. **Call for rates.** 1750 W Frontage Rd. SR 36 at Washington Ave, just ne. Int corridors. **Pets:** Accepted.
X M H

▼▼ **Super 8 Motel** SH
(651) 430-3990. **$56-$99.** 2190 W Frontage Rd. SR 36 at Washington Ave. Int corridors. **Pets:** Accepted.
ASK S X H

WACONIA

▼▼ **Super 8 Motel** M
(952) 442-5147. **Call for rates.** 301 E Frontage Rd. On SR 5 at jct CR 10. Int corridors. **Pets:** Accepted.
X H

WHITE BEAR LAKE

(AAA) ▼▼▼ **Best Western White Bear Country Inn** SH
(651) 429-5393. **$89-$109.** 4940 N Hwy 61. Jct SR 96, 1 mi n. Int corridors. **Pets:** Accepted.
SAVE S X H

WOODBURY

(AAA) ▼▼▼▼ **Holiday Inn Express Hotels & Suites** SH
(651) 702-0200. **$119.** 9840 Norma Ln. I-94, exit 251, just sw. Int corridors. **Pets:** Accepted.
SAVE S X H

▼▼ **Red Roof Inn #7063** M
(651) 738-7160. **Call for rates.** 1806 Wooddale Dr. I-494, exit 59 (Valley Creek Rd), just se. Ext corridors. **Pets:** Accepted.
X

END METROPOLITAN AREA

MONTEVIDEO

▼▼▼▼ **Country Inn & Suites By Carlson** SH
(320) 269-8000. **$83-$149, 30 day notice.** 1805 E Hwy 7. On SR 7. Int corridors. **Pets:** Accepted.
ASK S X H

MOORHEAD

(AAA) ▼▼ **Grand Inn Of Moorhead** SH
(218) 233-7501. **$38-$53.** 810 Belsly Blvd. I-94, exit 1A (US 75), 0.5 mi s. Int corridors. **Pets:** Other species. $25 deposit/room. Designated rooms, no service, supervision.
SAVE X

▼▼ **Super 8 Motel** SH
(218) 233-8880. **Call for rates.** 3621 S 8th St. I-94, exit 1A (US 75), 0.5 mi s. Int corridors. **Pets:** Accepted.
X H

(AAA) ▼▼▼ **Travelodge & Suites** SH
(218) 233-5333. **Call for rates.** 3027 S Frontage Rd. Just s of US 10 E; east of downtown. Int corridors. **Pets:** Designated rooms, service with restrictions, supervision.
SAVE X M H

MOOSE LAKE

▼▼▼ **AmericInn Lodge & Suites** SH
(218) 485-8885. **$75-$175.** 400 Park Place Dr. I-35, exit 214 (SR 73), just sw. Int corridors. **Pets:** Other species. $50 deposit/room, $10 one-time fee/room. Designated rooms, service with restrictions, crate.
ASK S X H

MORRIS

▼▼ **Best Northland Prairie Inn** SH
(320) 589-3030. **Call for rates.** 200 SR 28 E. 1.1 mi sw of jct US 59. Int corridors. **Pets:** Accepted.
X H

NEW ULM

▼▼▼ **Holiday Inn** SH
(507) 359-2941. **$84-$199.** 2101 S Broadway. SR 15/68, 1.8 mi se. Int corridors. **Pets:** Accepted.
ASK X H

(AAA) ▼▼ **Microtel Inn & Suites** SH
(507) 354-9800. **Call for rates.** 424 20th St S. Just e of jct SR 15/68 and CR 37. Int corridors. **Pets:** Accepted.
SAVE X M H

NISSWA

(AAA) ▼▼ **Nisswa Motel** M
(218) 963-7611. **$59-$85, 5 day notice.** 5370 Merrill Ave. Just sw of Main St; center. Ext corridors. **Pets:** Dogs only. $5 daily fee/pet. Designated rooms, service with restrictions, crate.
SAVE X H

NORTHFIELD

▼▼ **Super 8 Motel** SH
(507) 663-0371. **Call for rates.** 1420 Riverview Dr. 1.3 mi w of jct SR 19 and 3. Int corridors. **Pets:** Accepted.
X H

ONAMIA

▼▼ **Econo Lodge** SH
(320) 532-3838. **Call for rates.** 40847 US 169. On US 169; 6 mi n. Int corridors. **Pets:** Accepted.
X H

ORR

▼▼▼ **AmericInn Lodge & Suites** SH
(218) 757-3613. **$80-$200.** 4675 Hwy 53. Just n. Int corridors. **Pets:** Accepted.
ASK S X H

▼▼ **North Country Inn** SH
(218) 757-3778. **$68-$94.** 4483 Hwy 53. 0.3 mi s. Int corridors. **Pets:** Accepted.
X M H

OWATONNA

▼▼▼▼ **Comfort Inn** SH ❀
(507) 444-0818. **$90-$140.** 2345 43rd St NW. I-35, exit 45 (Clinton Falls), just sw. Int corridors. **Pets:** $5 daily fee/room. Supervision.
ASK S X M H

◇◇◇ Microtel Inn & Suites SH
(507) 446-0228. **$55-$80.** 150 St. John Dr NW. I-35, exit 41 (Bridge St), just nw. Int corridors. **Pets:** Accepted.

SAVE S🐾 ✕ 🕭M 🍴

PEQUOT LAKES

◇◇◇ AmericInn Lodge & Suites SH
(218) 568-8400. **Call for rates.** 32912 Paul Bunyan Trail Dr (SR 371/CR 16). SR 371; 2 mi n of downtown. Int corridors. **Pets:** Accepted.

✕ 🕭 🍴 ⊃ ✕

PERHAM

◇◇ Super 8 Motel SH
(218) 346-7888. **Call for rates.** 106 Jake St SE. SR 78, just nw of jct US 10. Int corridors. **Pets:** Accepted.

✕ 🕭

PINE RIVER

◇◇ Trail Side Inn M
(218) 587-4499. **Call for rates.** 2684 State 371 SW. 1 mi s. Ext corridors. **Pets:** Accepted.

✕ 🕭 🍴 ✕

RED WING

◇◇◇ Best Western Quiet House & Suites SH
(651) 388-1577. **$99-$180.** 752 Withers Harbor Dr. 1.5 mi n on US 61, at Withers Harbor Dr; opposite side of US 61 from Pottery Mall. Ext/int corridors. **Pets:** $15 daily fee/pet. Designated rooms, service with restrictions, supervision.

SAVE S🐾 ✕ 🕭M 🕭 🍴 ⊃

◇◇ Days Inn M
(651) 388-3568. **Call for rates.** 955 E 7th St. US 61/63, 1.7 mi se. Ext corridors. **Pets:** Accepted.

✕ 🕭 🍴 ⊃

ROCHESTER

◇◇◇ Econo Lodge-South SH
(507) 282-9905. **$62-$102.** 1850 S Broadway. 0.8 mi s of jct US 14 and 63 (Broadway). Int corridors. **Pets:** Dogs only. $10 daily fee/pet. Designated rooms, service with restrictions, crate.

SAVE S🐾 ✕ 🕭

◇◇◇ Holiday Inn South SH
(507) 288-1844. **Call for rates.** 1630 S Broadway. 0.5 mi s of jct US 14 and 63 (Broadway). Ext/int corridors. **Pets:** Accepted.

✕ 🕭 🍴 🍴 ⊃ ✕

◇◇◇ International Hotel SH 🐾
(507) 328-8000. **$425-$2800.** 20 SW Second Ave. Opposite Mayo Clinic and Methodist Hospital; 12th Floor of Kahler Grand Hotel. Int corridors. **Pets:** Large. $150 one-time fee/room. Service with restrictions, crate.

SAVE ✕ 🕭 ⊃ ✕

◇◇◇ The Kahler Grand Hotel LH
(507) 282-2581. **$115-$125.** 20 2nd Ave SW. Opposite Mayo Clinic and Methodist Hospital. Int corridors. **Pets:** Other species. Service with restrictions, crate.

SAVE S🐾 ✕ 🕭 🍴 🍴 ⊃ ✕

◇◇◇ Kahler Inn & Suites SH
(507) 289-8646. **$89-$119.** 9 NW 3rd Ave. Just n of Mayo Clinic. Int corridors. **Pets:** Accepted.

SAVE S🐾 ✕ 🕭 🍴 🍴 ⊃ ✕

◇◇◇ Marriott Hotel LH
(507) 280-6000. **$242-$262.** 101 1st Ave SW. Just e of Mayo Clinic. Int corridors. **Pets:** Accepted.

A$K S🐾 ✕ 🕭 🍴 ⊃ ✕

◇◇ Microtel Inn & Suites SH
(507) 286-8780. **$80-$90.** 4210 Hwy 52 N. US 52, exit 58 (41st St NW), just w. Int corridors. **Pets:** Accepted.

A$K ✕ 🕭

◇◇◇ Quality Inn & Suites SH
(507) 282-8091. **Call for rates.** 1620 1st Ave SE. On US 63 (Broadway) from jct US 14, 0.5 mi s, just e on 16th St, then just s. Ext/int corridors. **Pets:** Other species. $5 daily fee/pet.

SAVE ✕ 🕭 🍴

◇◇◇◇ Radisson Plaza Hotel LH
(507) 281-8000. **$155-$175.** 150 S Broadway. On US 63 (Broadway); downtown. Int corridors. **Pets:** Accepted.

SAVE S🐾 ✕ 🕭 🍴 🍴 ⊃ ✕

◇◇◇ Staybridge Suites SH
(507) 289-6600. **$149-$234.** 1211 2nd St SW. US 52/14, exit 55B (2nd St SW), just e. Int corridors. **Pets:** Accepted.

✕ 🕭M 🕭 🍴 ⊃

ROSEAU

◇◇◇ AmericInn Lodge & Suites SH
(218) 463-1045. **$65-$80.** 1110 3rd St NW. 1 mi w on SR 11. Int corridors. **Pets:** Accepted.

A$K ✕ 🕭M 🕭 🍴 ⊃ ✕

◇◇ North Country Inn SH
(218) 463-9444. **$60-$100.** 902 3rd St NW. 0.8 mi w on SR 11. Int corridors. **Pets:** $5 daily fee/pet. Service with restrictions, supervision.

A$K S🐾 ✕

ST. CLOUD

◇◇◇ AmericInn Lodge & Suites SH
(320) 253-6337. **Call for rates.** 4385 Clearwater Rd. I-94, exit 171 (CR 75), just ne. Int corridors. **Pets:** Accepted.

SAVE ✕ 🕭M 🕭 🍴 ⊃ ✕

◇◇◇ Best Western Americanna Inn & Conference Center SH
(320) 252-8700. **$70-$128.** 520 S US Hwy 10. Jct SR 23, 0.3 mi s. Ext/int corridors. **Pets:** Other species. $10 one-time fee/room. Service with restrictions, supervision.

SAVE S🐾 ✕ 🕭 🍴 🍴 ⊃ ✕

◇◇◇ Best Western Kelly Inn SH
(320) 253-0606. **$79-$139.** 100 4th Ave S. SR 23 at 4th Ave S; center. Int corridors. **Pets:** Medium, other species. Service with restrictions, crate.

SAVE S🐾 ✕ 🕭M 🕭 🍴 🍴 ⊃ ✕

◇◇ Comfort Inn SH
(320) 251-1500. **$65-$139.** 4040 2nd St S. Jct SR 15 and 23 W, just w. Int corridors. **Pets:** Accepted.

A$K S🐾 ✕ 🕭M 🕭 🍴 🍴 ⊃ ✕

◇◇◇ Country Inn & Suites By Carlson SH
(320) 259-8999. **Call for rates.** 235 S Park Ave. Jct SR 15 and 23 W, just w. Int corridors. **Pets:** Small, other species. $15 daily fee/pet. Designated rooms, service with restrictions, supervision.

✕ 🕭M 🕭 🍴 ⊃

◇◇◇ Days Inn Hotel and Waterslide SH
(320) 253-4444. **Call for rates.** 70 37th Ave S. Jct SR 15 and 23, just e. Int corridors. **Pets:** $10 daily fee/pet. Supervision.

SAVE ✕ 🕭M 🕭 🍴 ⊃

◇◇◇ GrandStay Residential Suites SH
(320) 251-5400. **Call for rates.** 213 6th Ave S. SR 23 at 6th Ave S; center. Int corridors. **Pets:** Accepted.

✕ 🕭 🍴 ⊃ ✕

▽▽▽▽ **Holiday Inn Express** SH
(320) 240-8000. **$95.** 4322 Clearwater Rd. I-94, exit 171 (CR 75), just ne. Int corridors. **Pets:** Accepted.
(ASK) (S✿) (✕) (�&M) (🖥) (🖵) (🏊)

▽▽▽ **Holiday Inn Hotel & Suites** SH
(320) 253-9000. **$90-$115.** 75 S 37th Ave. Jct SR 15 and 23. Int corridors. **Pets:** Accepted.
(ASK) (S✿) (✕) (🖥) (🖵) (🍴) (🏊) (✕)

▽ **Thrifty Motel** M
(320) 253-6320. **Call for rates.** 130 14th Ave NE. Jct US 10 and SR 23, 0.3 mi e. Int corridors. **Pets:** Accepted.
(✕) (🖥)

SAUK CENTRE

▲▲▲ ▽▽▽ **AmericInn Lodge & Suites** SH ✿
(320) 352-2800. **$72-$139.** 1230 Timberlane Dr. I-94, exit 127, just ne. Int corridors. **Pets:** Medium, dogs only. $10 one-time fee/pet. Designated rooms, service with restrictions, supervision.
(SAVE) (✕) (🖥) (🖵) (🏊) (✕)

SILVER BAY

▽▽▽ **AmericInn Lodge & Suites** SH
(218) 226-4300. **Call for rates.** 150 Mensing Dr. On SR 61, 0.5 mi ne of jct SR 61 and Outer Dr. Int corridors. **Pets:** Accepted.
(✕) (�&M) (🖥) (🖵) (🏊) (✕)

▲▲▲ ▽▽ **Mariner Motel** M ✿
(218) 226-4488. **$55-$75, 3 day notice.** 46 Outer Dr. Just w off SR 61; at traffic signal. Ext corridors. **Pets:** Dogs only. $5 daily fee/pet. Service with restrictions, supervision.
(SAVE) (✕) (🖥) (🖵) (🗲)

SLEEPY EYE

▲▲▲ ▽▽▽ **Inn of Seven Gables** SH
(507) 794-5390. **Call for rates.** 1100 E Main St. US 14, 0.8 mi e of jct CR 4 and US 14. Int corridors. **Pets:** Accepted.
(SAVE) (✕) (🖥) (🖵) (🏊)

SPICER

▽▽ ▽▽ **Northern Inn Hotel & Suites** SH
(320) 796-2091. **$60-$100.** 154 Lake Ave S. Just e of jct SR 23 and CR 10. Int corridors. **Pets:** Accepted.
(ASK) (✕) (🖥) (🖵) (🏊)

SPRING VALLEY

▲▲▲ ▽▽▽ **Spring Valley Inn & Suites** SH
(507) 346-7788. **$70-$104.** 745 N Broadway. Just w on US 63. Int corridors. **Pets:** Medium, other species. $10 one-time fee/pet. Service with restrictions, supervision.
(SAVE) (S✿) (✕) (Ꮖ) (🖥) (🖵)

STEWARTVILLE

▲▲▲ ▽▽▽ **AmericInn Motel** M
(507) 533-4747. **$65-$85.** 1700 NW 2nd Ave. I-90, exit 209A, 1 mi s on US 63. Int corridors. **Pets:** Small, dogs only. $10 daily fee/pet. Designated rooms, service with restrictions, supervision.
(SAVE) (S✿) (✕) (Ꮖ) (🖥) (🖵)

TOFTE

▲▲▲ ▽▽▽ **AmericInn Lodge & Suites** SH ✿
(218) 663-7899. **$80-$130.** 7231 W SR 61. On SR 61. Int corridors. **Pets:** $10 daily fee/pet. Designated rooms, service with restrictions, supervision.
(SAVE) (✕) (🖥) (🖵) (🏊) (✕)

▲▲▲ ▽▽▽ **Bluefin Bay on Lake Superior** CO
(218) 663-7296. **$59-$299, 7 day notice.** 7198 W SR 61. On SR 61. Ext corridors. **Pets:** Accepted.
(SAVE) (✕) (🖥) (🖵) (🍴) (🏊) (✕) (🗲)

TWO HARBORS

▽▽▽ **AmericInn Lodge & Suites** SH
(218) 834-3000. **$70-$220.** 1088 SR 61 N. On SR 61, 0.7 mi s. Int corridors. **Pets:** Dogs only. $20 daily fee/pet. Designated rooms, service with restrictions, supervision.
(ASK) (✕) (Ꮖ) (🖥) (🖵) (🏊) (✕)

▲▲▲ ▽▽▽ **Superior Shores Resort** CO
(218) 834-5671. **$49-$479.** 1521 Superior Shores Dr. On SR 61, 1.5 mi n of center. Ext/int corridors. **Pets:** Accepted.
(SAVE) (✕) (🖥) (🖵) (🍴) (🏊) (✕)

VERGAS

▽▽▽ **The Log House & Homestead on Spirit Lake** BB
(218) 342-2318. **$110-$215, 8 day notice.** 44854 Fredholm Rd. 5 mi sw on CR 4. Ext/int corridors. **Pets:** Accepted.
(✕) (🖥) (🖵) (✕) (🗲) (☎)

VIRGINIA

▽▽▽ **AmericInn Lodge & Suites** SH
(218) 741-7839. **$104-$179.** 5480 Mountain Iron Dr. US 53, just s of jct US 169. Int corridors. **Pets:** Accepted.
(✕) (Ꮖ) (🖥) (🖵) (🏊) (✕)

▽ **Lakeshor Motor Inn** M
(218) 741-3360. **Call for rates.** 404 6th Ave N. Just n of Chestnut St; center. Ext corridors. **Pets:** Accepted.
(✕) (🖥) (🖵)

▲▲▲ ▽ **Pine View Inn** M
(218) 741-8918. **$55-$85.** 903 N 17th St. Jct US 53 and 169, 0.5 mi n on US 53, 0.7 mi e on 9th St N, then 0.5 mi n on 9th Ave W. Ext/int corridors. **Pets:** Accepted.
(SAVE) (S✿) (✕) (🖵)

WABASHA

▽▽▽ **AmericInn Lodge & Suites** SH
(651) 565-5366. **Call for rates.** 150 Commerce Dr. Just ne of jct US 61 and SR 60. Int corridors. **Pets:** Accepted.
(✕) (Ꮖ) (🖥) (🖵) (🏊) (✕)

WALKER

▽▽▽ **Country Inn & Suites By Carlson** SH
(218) 547-1400. **Call for rates.** 442 Walker Bay Blvd. 1 mi s on SR 371. Int corridors. **Pets:** Accepted.
(✕) (Ꮖ) (🖥) (🖵) (🏊)

WARROAD

▽▽ **Can-Am Motel** SH
(218) 386-3807. **$55-$71.** 406 Main Ave NE. 0.5 mi w on SR 11. Int corridors. **Pets:** Accepted.
(ASK) (S✿) (✕) (Ꮖ) (🖥)

▽▽ **The Patch Motel** SH
(218) 386-2723. **Call for rates.** 801 State Ave N. 0.6 mi w on SR 11. Int corridors. **Pets:** Accepted.
(✕) (Ꮖ) (🖥) (🍴)

WILLMAR

▽▽▽ **Comfort Inn** SH
(320) 231-2601. **Call for rates.** 2200 E US 12. 1.8 mi e. Int corridors. **Pets:** Accepted.
(✕) (🖥) (🖵) (🏊)

Days Inn-Willmar SH
(320) 231-1275. **Call for rates.** 225 28th St SE. 2.3 mi e on US 12. Int corridors. **Pets:** Accepted.

 Holiday Inn & Willmar Conference Center SH
(320) 235-6060. **Call for rates.** 2100 US 12 E. 1.8 mi e. Int corridors. **Pets:** Accepted.

WINONA

 Express Suites Riverport Inn SH
(507) 452-0606. **$69-$129.** 900 Bruski Dr. Jct US 14/61 and SR 43. Int corridors. **Pets:** Other species. $25 daily fee/room. Designated rooms, service with restrictions, supervision.

Holiday Inn Hotel and Suites SH
(507) 453-0303. **$125-$199.** 1025 Hwy 61 E. Jct SR 43, just sw. Int corridors. **Pets:** Accepted.

Quality Inn SH
(507) 454-4390. **$59-$99.** 956 Mankato Ave. Jct US 14/61 and SR 43. Ext/int corridors. **Pets:** Large, other species. $10 one-time fee/room. Designated rooms, service with restrictions, crate.

WORTHINGTON

AmericInn Motel SH
(507) 376-4500. **$75-$90.** 1475 Darling Dr. I-90, exit 43 (US 59), just se. Int corridors. **Pets:** Other species. $10 one-time fee/pet. Supervision.

MISSISSIPPI

ABERDEEN

Best Western Aberdeen Inn M
(662) 369-4343. **$67-$80.** 801 E Commerce St. On US 45, just n of jct SR 25 and Tenn-Tom Bridge. Ext corridors. **Pets:** Accepted.

BATESVILLE

Comfort Inn SH
(662) 563-1188. **$65-$95.** 290 Power Dr. I-55, exit 243B, just ne on frontage road. Ext corridors. **Pets:** Accepted.

BOONEVILLE

Super 8 Motel SH
(662) 720-1688. **$55-$65.** 110 Hospitality Ave. Jct US 45 and SR 4/30, 1.7 mi e to SR 145, then 0.5 mi s. Int corridors. **Pets:** Accepted.

CANTON

Best Western-Canton Inn SH
(601) 859-8600. **7 day notice.** 137 Soldier Colony Rd. I-55, exit 119, just se. Int corridors. **Pets:** Accepted.

Comfort Inn SH
(601) 859-7575. **$80-$100.** 145 Soldier Colony Rd. I-55, exit 119, just se. Int corridors. **Pets:** Accepted.

Econo Lodge SH
(601) 859-2643. **$55-$65.** 119 Soldier Colony Rd. I-55, exit 119, just se. Ext corridors. **Pets:** Accepted.

CLEVELAND

Econo Lodge of Cleveland M
(662) 843-4060. **Call for rates.** 721 N Davis Ave. On US 61, 1 mi n of jct US 61 and SR 8. Ext corridors. **Pets:** Medium. $50 deposit/pet. Service with restrictions, supervision.

COLUMBIA

Comfort Inn SH
(601) 731-9955. **$84-$119.** 820 Hwy 98 Bypass. Just e of jct US 98 Bypass and SR 13. Int corridors. **Pets:** Accepted.

COLUMBUS

Master Hosts Inns & Suites SH
(662) 328-5202. **$54-$64.** 506 Hwy 45 N. US 82, exit US 45 N, just s. Ext corridors. **Pets:** Accepted.

FOREST

Americas Best Value Inn SH
(601) 469-2640. **$54-$69.** 1846 Hwy 35 S. I-20, exit 88, just n. Ext corridors. **Pets:** Small. $10 one-time fee/pet. Service with restrictions, supervision.

Comfort Inn SH
(601) 469-2100. **$65-$75.** 1250 Hwy 35 S. I-20, exit 88, just n. Ext corridors. **Pets:** Accepted.

GREENVILLE

Econo Lodge of Greenville SH
(662) 378-4976. **$70-$85.** 3080 US 82 E. 3 mi e of center. Ext corridors. **Pets:** Accepted.

GREENWOOD

Econo Lodge Inn & Suites SH
(662) 453-5974. **Call for rates.** 401 Hwy 82 W. 0.4 mi w of Main St. Ext corridors. **Pets:** Accepted.

GRENADA

Country Inn & Suites by Carlson SH
(662) 227-8444. **$71-$169.** 255 SW Frontage Rd. I-55, exit 206, just sw. Int corridors. **Pets:** Large. $25 one-time fee/room. Designated rooms, service with restrictions, supervision.

GULFPORT

Americas Best Value Inn SH
(228) 868-8500. **Call for rates.** 9375 Hwy 49. I-10, exit 34A, just sw. Ext corridors. **Pets:** Accepted.

Best Western Seaway Inn SH
(228) 864-0050. **$79-$139.** 9475 Hwy 49. I-10, exit 34A, just sw. Ext corridors. **Pets:** Large, other species. $12 daily fee/pet. Service with restrictions, supervision.

Holiday Inn Airport SH
(228) 868-8200. **Call for rates.** 9415 Hwy 49. I-10, exit 34A, 0.6 mi s. Ext corridors. **Pets:** Medium, other species. $35 one-time fee/room. Service with restrictions, supervision.

Motel 6 #416 M
(228) 863-1890. **$65-$77.** 9355 US Hwy 49. I-10, exit 34A, just s. Ext corridors. **Pets:** Other species. Service with restrictions, supervision.

▼▼ Quality Inn Gulfport SH
(228) 864-7222. **$79-$129.** 9435 Hwy 49. I-10, exit 34A, 0.6 mi s. Ext corridors. **Pets:** Small. $15 daily fee/pet. Service with restrictions, supervision.

ASK Sᴅ ✕ 🛏 🖥

HATTIESBURG

▼▼ Comfort Inn University-The Lodge SH
(601) 264-1881. **$89-$139.** 6541 US Hwy 49. I-59, exit 67A, just s. Ext/int corridors. **Pets:** Accepted.

ASK Sᴅ ✕ 🛏 🖥 ≈

AAA ▼▼▼ Inn on the Hill at Convention Center SH
(601) 599-2001. **$79-$120.** 6595 Hwy 49 N. I-59, exit 67A, just se. Ext corridors. **Pets:** Accepted.

SAVE Sᴅ ✕ 🛏 🖥 🍴 ≈

AAA ▼▼▼▼ La Quinta Inn SH
(601) 268-2850. **$79-$109.** 6563 Hwy 49 N. I-59, exit 67A, just se. Int corridors. **Pets:** Small. Service with restrictions, crate.

SAVE Sᴅ ✕ 🛏 🖥 ≈

HOLLY SPRINGS

▼▼▼▼ Le' Brooks Inn SH
(662) 252-5444. **Call for rates.** 100 Brooks Rd. US 78, exit 30, just sw. Int corridors. **Pets:** Other species. $10 daily fee/room. Supervision.

✕ 🛏 🖥 ≈

HORN LAKE

▼▼▼▼ Drury Inn & Suites-Memphis South SH
(662) 349-6622. **$91-$166.** 735 Goodman Rd W. I-55, exit 289, just sw. Int corridors. **Pets:** Large, other species. Service with restrictions, supervision.

ASK ✕ &M 🛏 🖥 ≈

JACKSON

▼▼▼▼ Clarion Hotel LH
(601) 366-9411. **$60-$110.** 5075 I-55 N. I-55, exit 102A, s on west frontage road. Ext/int corridors. **Pets:** Accepted.

ASK Sᴅ ✕ 🛏 🖥 🍴 ≈

▼▼▼▼ The Edison Walthall Hotel LH
(601) 948-6161. **$99.** 225 E Capitol St. I-55, exit 96A (Pearl St), 0.8 mi w; between West and Lamar sts; downtown. Ext/int corridors. **Pets:** Accepted.

ASK Sᴅ ✕ 🛏 🖥 🍴 ≈

▼▼ Extended StayAmerica Jackson-North M
(601) 956-4312. **$34-$54.** 5354 I-55 N. I-55, exit 100, just n. Ext corridors. **Pets:** Other species. $75 one-time fee/pet. Service with restrictions.

ASK Sᴅ ✕ 🛏 🖥 ≈

AAA ▼▼▼ Jameson Inn SH
(601) 206-8923. **$80-$100.** 585 Beasley Rd. I-55, exit 102, just w. Int corridors. **Pets:** Small. $15 daily fee/room. Service with restrictions, crate.

SAVE Sᴅ ✕ 🛏 🖥 ≈

AAA ▼▼▼ La Quinta Inn Jackson (North) SH
(601) 957-1741. **$49-$89.** 616 Briarwood Dr. I-55, exit 102A northbound, just ne on Frontage Rd. Ext corridors. **Pets:** Other species. Service with restrictions, supervision.

SAVE ✕ &M 🛏 🖥 ≈

AAA ▼▼▼ Quality Inn & Suites SH
(601) 969-2230. **$90-$100.** 400 Greymont Ave. I-55, exit 96B (High St), just w, then just s. Ext corridors. **Pets:** Accepted.

SAVE Sᴅ ✕ 🛏 🖥

▼▼ Red Roof Inn Fairgrounds #131 M
(601) 969-5006. **$44-$57.** 700 Larson St. I-55, exit 96B (High St), e to Greymont, then just ne. Ext corridors. **Pets:** Accepted.

Sᴅ ✕ 🛏

▼▼▼▼ Regency Hotel & Conference Center SH
(601) 969-2141. **$89-$109.** 400 Greymont Ave. I-55, exit 96B, just w, then just s. Ext/int corridors. **Pets:** Small, dogs only. $25 daily fee/pet. Service with restrictions, supervision.

ASK Sᴅ ✕ &M 🛏 🖥 🍴 ≈

AAA ▼▼▼ Residence Inn by Marriott SH
(601) 355-3599. **$134-$157.** 881 E River Pl. I-55, exit 96C, just e. Ext corridors. **Pets:** Medium. $75 one-time fee/room. Service with restrictions, supervision.

SAVE ✕ 🛏 🖥 ≈ ✕

KOSCIUSKO

AAA ▼▼▼ Americas Best Value Inn M
(662) 289-6252. **$55-$62.** 1052 Veterans Memorial Dr/Hwy 35 Bypass. Just sw of jct SR 35 and Natchez Trace Pkwy. Ext corridors. **Pets:** Small, other species. $5 daily fee/pet. Service with restrictions, supervision.

SAVE Sᴅ ✕ 🛏 🖥 ≈

▼▼ Super 8 Motel Kosciusko M
(662) 289-7880. **Call for rates.** 718 Veterans Memorial Dr. Just sw of jct SR 35 and Natchez Trace Pkwy. Ext corridors. **Pets:** Accepted.

✕ 🛏 ≈

MCCOMB

AAA ▼▼▼▼ Hawthorn Inn & Suites SH
(601) 684-8655. **$90.** 2001 Veteran's Blvd. I-55, exit 18, just off interstate. Int corridors. **Pets:** Medium, other species. $125 one-time fee/room. Service with restrictions, crate.

SAVE Sᴅ ✕ &M 🛏 🖥 🍴 ≈

MERIDIAN

AAA ▼▼▼▼ Best Western of Meridian SH
(601) 693-3210. **$67-$69.** 2219 S Frontage Rd. I-20/59, exit 153, just sw. Ext/int corridors. **Pets:** Small, dogs only. $10 daily fee/pet. Service with restrictions, crate.

SAVE Sᴅ ✕ 🛏 🖥 ≈

▼▼▼ Econo Lodge M
(601) 693-9393. **Call for rates.** 2405 S Frontage Rd. I-20/59, exit 153, 0.5 mi sw. Ext corridors. **Pets:** Accepted.

✕ 🛏 🖥

▼▼▼▼ Holiday Inn Meridian SH
(601) 485-5101. **$89-$105.** 111 US 11 & 80. I-20/59, exit 154 westbound, just n to frontage road, then just e; exit 154B eastbound. Ext corridors. **Pets:** Medium, other species. $25 one-time fee/room. Service with restrictions.

ASK Sᴅ ✕ &M 🛏 🖥 🍴 ≈

▼▼ Jameson Inn SH
(601) 483-3315. **$75-$95.** 524 Bonita Lakes Dr. I-20/59, exit 154 southbound; exit 154A northbound, just s. Ext corridors. **Pets:** Small. $15 daily fee/room. Service with restrictions, crate.

ASK Sᴅ ✕ &M 🛏 🖥 ≈

▼▼ Motel 6 #0424 M
(601) 482-1182. **$45-$57.** 2309 S Frontage Rd. I-20/59, exit 153, 0.5 mi sw. Ext corridors. **Pets:** Other species. Service with restrictions, supervision.

Sᴅ ✕ ≈

MOSS POINT

AAA ▼▼▼ Quality Inn SH
(228) 475-2477. **$59-$89.** 6800 Hwy 63 N. I-10, exit 69, just s. Ext corridors. **Pets:** Accepted.

SAVE Sᴅ ✕ 🛏 🖥 ≈

NATCHEZ

Days Inn of Natchez SH
(601) 445-8291. **$74-$87.** 109 US Hwy 61 S. Just se of jct US 61, 84 and 98. Ext corridors. **Pets:** Small, other species. $7 daily fee/pet. Service with restrictions, supervision.

NEWTON

Days Inn M
(601) 683-3361. **$75.** 261 Eastside Dr. I-20, exit 109, just s on SR 15. Ext corridors. **Pets:** Accepted.

OCEAN SPRINGS

Quality Inn Ocean Springs SH
(228) 875-7555. **$70-$150.** 7304 Washington Ave. I-10, exit 50, 0.4 mi s on SR 609. Ext corridors. **Pets:** Medium, other species. $20 daily fee/ room. Service with restrictions, crate.

Ramada Limited SH
(228) 872-2323. **$69-$169.** 8011 Tucker Rd. I-10, exit 50, just n. Ext corridors. **Pets:** Medium, other species. $15 daily fee/pet. Designated rooms, no service, supervision.

OLIVE BRANCH

Comfort Inn SH
(662) 895-0456. **$84-$94.** 7049 Enterprise. US 78, exit 2 (SR 302) just w. Int corridors. **Pets:** Accepted.

Whispering Woods Hotel and Conference Center LH
(662) 895-2941. **$89-$129.** 11200 E Goodman Rd. US 78, exit 2 (SR 302), 3.6 mi e. Int corridors. **Pets:** Accepted.

PASCAGOULA

LaFont Inn SH ❀
(228) 762-7111. **Call for rates.** 2703 Denny Ave. I-10, exit 69, 3.5 mi s on SR 63, then 2 mi w on US 90. Ext corridors. **Pets:** Small, other species. $30 one-time fee/room. Service with restrictions.

Super 8 Motel M
(228) 762-9414. **$99-$150.** 4919 Denny Ave. I-10, exit 69, 3.5 mi s on SR 63, then just w on US 90. Int corridors. **Pets:** Accepted.

PEARL

Jameson Inn of Pearl SH
(601) 932-6030. **$90-$110.** 434 Riverwind Dr. I-20, exit 48, just nw. Int corridors. **Pets:** Accepted.

La Quinta Inn & Suites Jackson Airport (Pearl) SH
(601) 664-0065. **$75-$119.** 501 S Pearson Rd. I-20, exit 48, just s. Int corridors. **Pets:** Other species. Service with restrictions, supervision.

PHILADELPHIA

Deluxe Inn & Suites SH
(601) 656-0052. **$50-$150.** 1004 Central Dr. Jct SR 15 and 16. Ext corridors. **Pets:** Small, dogs only. $10 daily fee/pet. Service with restrictions, crate.

PICAYUNE

Days Inn SH
(601) 799-1339. **Call for rates.** 450 S Lofton Ave. I-59, exit 4, just nw. Ext corridors. **Pets:** Medium. $20 daily fee/pet. Service with restrictions, supervision.

RICHLAND

Executive Inn & Suites SH
(601) 664-3456. **$45-$59.** 390 Hwy 49 S. I-20, exit 47, just s. Ext corridors. **Pets:** Accepted.

RIDGELAND

Drury Inn & Suites-Jackson, MS SH
(601) 956-6100. **$91-$158.** 610 E County Line Rd. I-55, exit 103 (County Line Rd), just w. Int corridors. **Pets:** Large, other species. Service with restrictions, supervision.

Econo Lodge M
(601) 956-7740. **Call for rates.** 839 Ridgewood Rd. I-55, exit 103 (County Line Rd), just e, then just n. Ext corridors. **Pets:** Accepted.

Homewood Suites by Hilton SH
(601) 899-8611. **$139.** 853 Centre St. I-55, exit 103 (County Line Rd), just e to Ridgewood Rd, 0.4 mi ne, then just e. Int corridors. **Pets:** Small, dogs only. $100 one-time fee/room. Designated rooms, service with restrictions, supervision.

Quality Inn North SH
(601) 956-6203. **Call for rates.** 839 Ridgewood Rd. I-55, exit 103 (County Line Rd), just ne. Ext corridors. **Pets:** Accepted.

Red Roof Inn Ridgeland #128 M
(601) 956-7707. **$49-$59.** 810 Adcock St. I-55, exit 103 (County Line Rd), just ne on Frontage Rd. Ext corridors. **Pets:** Accepted.

RIPLEY

Best Western Ripley M
(662) 837-0002. **$70-$73.** 922 City Ave S. Jct US 4 and 15, 0.5 mi s. Ext corridors. **Pets:** Small, dogs only. $5 daily fee/room. Designated rooms, service with restrictions, supervision.

SOUTHAVEN

Residence Inn Memphis Southaven SH ❀
(662) 996-1500. **$139-$169.** 7165 Sleepy Hollow Dr. I-55, exit 289, just ne. Int corridors. **Pets:** Medium, other species. $100 one-time fee/pet. Service with restrictions, crate.

STARKVILLE

Comfort Suites Starkville SH
(662) 324-9595. **Call for rates.** 801 Russell St. 0.5 mi w of jct US 82 and SR 12. Int corridors. **Pets:** Accepted.

Days Inn & Suites SH
(662) 324-5555. **$105-$125.** 119 Hwy 12 W. SR 12, 1.5 mi w of jct US 82. Ext corridors. **Pets:** Accepted.

TUNICA

▼ Key West Inn Tunica M
(662) 363-0021. **$50-$100.** 11635 Hwy 61 N. US 61, 0.3 mi n of SR 304. Ext corridors. **Pets:** Small, dogs only. $10 daily fee/pet. Designated rooms, service with restrictions, supervision.

ASK S6 ✕ 🛗 💻

TUPELO

▼▼ Baymont Inn & Suites SH
(662) 844-7660. **$64-$74.** 625 Spicer Dr. On SR 145, 0.4 mi n of McCullough Blvd. Int corridors. **Pets:** Accepted.

SAVE S6 ✕ 6M 🛗 💻 ≈ ✕

▼▼ Comfort Inn SH
(662) 842-5100. **$77.** 1190 N Gloster St. Jct McCullough Blvd and SR 145, 1.3 mi s to McCullough Blvd, w to N Gloster St, then 0.3 mi n. Ext corridors. **Pets:** Small. $25 deposit/pet. Service with restrictions, crate.

ASK S6 ✕ 🛗 💻

▼▼ Jameson Inn SH
(662) 840-2380. **$75-$95.** 879 Mississippi Dr. US 45, exit Barnes Crossing, 1 mi sw. Ext corridors. **Pets:** Small. $15 daily fee/room. Service with restrictions, crate.

ASK S6 ✕ 🛗 💻 ≈

▼▼ Super 8 Motel M
(662) 842-0448. **$52-$99.** 3898 McCullough Blvd. US 78, exit 81, just sw. Ext corridors. **Pets:** Medium, dogs only. $10 one-time fee/pet. Service with restrictions, supervision.

SAVE S6 ✕ 🛗 ≈

VICKSBURG

▼▼▼ Annabelle Bed & Breakfast BB
(601) 638-2000. **$125-$195, 7 day notice.** 501 Speed St. I-20, exit 1A, 2.3 mi n on Washington St, just w. Ext/int corridors. **Pets:** Accepted.

✕ 🛗 💻 ≈

▼▼ Battlefield Inn SH
(601) 638-5811. **$79.** 4137 I-20 N Frontage Rd. I-20, exit 4B, 1 mi ne. Ext/int corridors. **Pets:** Other species. $10 daily fee/pet. Service with restrictions.

SAVE S6 ✕ 🛗 💻 ¶¶ ≈ ✕

▼▼▼▼ Cedar Grove Mansion CI
(601) 636-1000. **$100-$215, 3 day notice.** 2200 Oak St. I-20, exit 1A, 2.3 mi n on Washington St, then w on Klein St; to gated entrance. Ext/int corridors. **Pets:** Accepted.

SAVE S6 ✕ 🛗 💻 ¶¶ ≈ ✕

▼▼▼ Corners Mansion Bed & Breakfast Inn BB ❀
(601) 636-7421. **$110-$190, 3 day notice.** 601 Klein St. I-20, exit 1A, 2.3 mi n on Washington St, just w. Ext/int corridors. **Pets:** $25 one-time fee/room. Designated rooms, service with restrictions, crate.

ASK S6 ✕ 🛗 💻

▼▼ Jameson Inn SH
(601) 619-7799. **$85-$105.** 3975 S Frontage Rd. I-20, exit 4A, on southeast frontage road. Ext corridors. **Pets:** Small. $15 daily fee/room. Service with restrictions, crate.

ASK S6 ✕ 6M 🛗 💻 ≈

▼ Motel 6 #4189 SH
(601) 638-5077. **Call for rates.** 4127 N Frontage Rd. I-20, exit 4B (Clay St), just ne. Int corridors. **Pets:** Other species. Service with restrictions, supervision.

✕ ≈

▼▼▼ Quality Inn and Suites M
(601) 636-0804. **$80-$155.** 3332 Clay St. I-20, exit 4B (Clay St), just n. Ext corridors. **Pets:** Accepted.

ASK S6 ✕ 🛗 💻 ≈

MISSOURI

CITY INDEX

AVA

▼▼▼ Ava Super 8 🅂🄷
(417) 683-1343. **$60-$80.** 1711 S Jefferson St. Jct SR 5 S and 76; 1.5 mi s of SR 14. Int corridors. **Pets:** Accepted.
🄰🅂🄺 🅂🄳 ⊗ &M 🔋 🖵

BETHANY

🆀🆀🅍 ▼▼🅍 Best Western Bethany Inn 🅂🄷
(660) 425-8006. **Call for rates.** 496 S 39th St. I-35, exit 92, just nw. Int corridors. **Pets:** Medium. $10 daily fee/pet. Designated rooms, service with restrictions, supervision.
🆂🄰🆅🄴 ⊗ 🔋 🖵 ⤳

🆀🆀🅍 ▼▼ Family Budget Inn Ⓜ
(660) 425-7915. **$45-$54.** 4014 Miller St. I-35, exit 92. Int corridors. **Pets:** $20 deposit/pet, $5 daily fee/pet. Designated rooms, service with restrictions, supervision.
🆂🄰🆅🄴 ⊗ 🔋 ⤳

BOONVILLE

🆀🆀🅍 ▼▼ Boonville Comfort Inn 🅂🄷 🐾
(660) 882-5317. **$49-$139.** 2427 Mid America Industrial Dr. I-70, exit 101, just sw. Int corridors. **Pets:** Small, dogs only. $10 daily fee/pet. Designated rooms, service with restrictions, supervision.
🆂🄰🆅🄴 🅂🄳 ⊗ 🔋 🖵 ⤳

BRANSON METROPOLITAN AREA

BRANSON

🆀🆀🅍 ▼▼▼ ▼▼▼ Chateau on the Lake Resort Spa & Convention Center 🄻🄷
(417) 334-1161. **$129-$364, 3 day notice.** 415 N State Hwy 265. Just n of jct SR 165 and 265. Int corridors. **Pets:** Small, dogs only. $30 one-time fee/room. Designated rooms, service with restrictions, supervision.
🆂🄰🆅🄴 ⊗ &M 🔋 🖵 🍴 ⤳ ⊗

🆀🆀🅍 ▼ Eagle's Lodge 🅂🄷
(417) 336-2666. **$45-$85.** 3221 Shepherd of the Hills Expy. 0.3 mi e of jct SR 76. Ext corridors. **Pets:** Accepted.
🆂🄰🆅🄴 🅂🄳 ⊗ 🔋 🖵 ⤳

🆀🆀🅍 ▼▼ Fall Creek Inn & Suites 🅂🄷 🐾
(417) 348-1683. **$39-$69.** 995 Hwy 165. Jct SR 76 (Country Music Blvd), 1.5 mi s on SR 165. Ext corridors. **Pets:** Medium, other species. $50 deposit/pet, $8 daily fee/pet. Designated rooms.
🆂🄰🆅🄴 🅂🄳 ⊗ 🔋 🖵 ⤳

▼▼▼ Howard Johnson 🅂🄷
(417) 336-5151. **Call for rates.** 3027-A W Hwy 76. On SR 76 (Country Music Blvd), 3.5 mi w of jct US 65. Ext corridors. **Pets:** Accepted.
⊗ 🔋 🖵 ⤳

▼▼▼▼ La Quinta Inn Branson (Music City Centre) 🅂🄷
(417) 336-1600. **$64-$84.** 1835 W Hwy 76. 1.6 mi w of jct US 65. Ext/int corridors. **Pets:** Other species. Service with restrictions, supervision.
🄰🅂🄺 🅂🄳 ⊗ 🔋 🖵 ⤳ ⊗

🆀🆀🅍 ▼ Ozark Valley Inn Ⓜ
(417) 336-4666. **Call for rates.** 2693 Shepherd of the Hills Expwy. Jct SR 76 (Country Music Blvd), 0.9 mi e. Ext corridors. **Pets:** Accepted.
🆂🄰🆅🄴 ⊗ 🔋 🖵 ⤳

▼▼▼ Ramada Inn & Conference Center 🅂🄷
(417) 334-1000. **Call for rates.** 1700 Hwy 76 W. Jct SR 76 (Country Music Blvd) and US 65, 1.5 mi w. Ext corridors. **Pets:** Accepted.
⊗ 🔋 🖵 🍴 ⤳ ⊗

▼▼ Residence Inn by Marriott 🅂🄷
(417) 336-4077. **$153-$230.** 280 Wildwood Dr S. 2 mi w on SR 76 (Country Music Blvd), just s. Int corridors. **Pets:** Accepted.
🄰🅂🄺 🅂🄳 ⊗ &M 🔋 🖵 ⤳ ⊗

▼ Rock View Resort Ⓜ
(417) 334-4678. **$56-$92, 21 day notice.** 1049 Park View Dr. Jct US 65, 4.4 mi w on SR 165, 0.3 mi s via Dale Dr, then 0.7 mi w. Ext corridors. **Pets:** Medium, dogs only. $7 daily fee/pet. No service, crate.
⊗ 🔋 🖵 ⤳ ⊗ 🐾

🆀🆀🅍 ▼▼ Scenic Hills Inn 🅂🄷 🐾
(417) 336-8855. **$46-$80.** 2422 Shepherd of the Hills Expwy. Jct SR 76 (Country Music Blvd), 1.1 mi e. Int corridors. **Pets:** Small. $10 daily fee/room. Designated rooms, service with restrictions, crate.
🆂🄰🆅🄴 🅂🄳 ⊗ 🔋 🖵 ⤳

🆀🆀🅍 ▼▼▼ Stone Castle Hotel and Conference Center 🅂🄷
(417) 335-4700. **$69-$119.** 3050 Green Mountain Dr. Jct SR 76 (Country Music Blvd) and US 65, 3 mi w on SR 76, 0.8 mi s. Int corridors. **Pets:** Large, other species. $12 daily fee/pet. Designated rooms, service with restrictions, supervision.
🆂🄰🆅🄴 🅂🄳 ⊗ 🔋 🖵 🍴 ⤳ ⊗

🆀🆀🅍 ▼▼▼ The Village At Indian Point 🄲🄾
(417) 338-8800. **$100-$235, 30 day notice.** 24 Village Tr. 2.5 mi s of jct SR 76 on Indian Point Rd. Ext corridors. **Pets:** Medium, dogs only. $10 daily fee/room. Designated rooms, no service, supervision.
🆂🄰🆅🄴 ⊗ 🔋 ⤳ ⊗

BRANSON WEST

Best Western Branson Inn & Conference Center SH
(417) 338-2141. **$62-$79.** 8514 State Hwy 76. Jct SR 265, 1.1 mi w on SR 76. Int corridors. **Pets:** Accepted.

Shady Acre Motel M
(417) 338-2316. **Call for rates.** 8722 Hwy 76. Jct SR 265, 1.3 mi w. Ext corridors. **Pets:** Accepted.

END METROPOLITAN AREA

BUTLER

Super 8 Motel–Butler M
(660) 679-6183. **Call for rates.** 1114 W Fort Scott St. Just e of jct US 71 and SR 52. Ext corridors. **Pets:** Accepted.

CAMERON

Best Western Acorn Inn M ✤
(816) 632-2187. **Call for rates.** 2210 E US 36. I-35, exit 54, 0.3 mi e. Ext corridors. **Pets:** Other species. Service with restrictions, supervision.

Comfort Inn SH
(816) 632-5655. **$84-$129.** 1803 Comfort Ln. I-35, exit 54, just e. Int corridors. **Pets:** Accepted.

Econo Lodge M
(816) 632-6571. **$49-$79.** 220 E Grand. I-35, exit 54, 0.5 mi w on US 36, then just s on US 69. Ext corridors. **Pets:** Medium. $5 daily fee/pet. Service with restrictions, supervision.

Super 8 Motel SH
(816) 632-8888. **$62-$78 (no credit cards).** 1710 N Walnut St. I-35, exit 54, 0.5 mi w on US 36. Int corridors. **Pets:** Accepted.

CANTON

Comfort Inn Canton SH
(573) 288-8800. **$69-$89.** 1701 Oak St. US 61, exit US 61 business route/CR P, just e. Int corridors. **Pets:** Accepted.

CAPE GIRARDEAU

Drury Lodge-Cape Girardeau SH
(573) 334-7151. **$79-$109.** 104 S Vantage Dr. I-55, exit 96 (William St), just e. Ext/int corridors. **Pets:** Large, other species. Service with restrictions, supervision.

Drury Suites-Cape Girardeau SH
(573) 339-9500. **$110-$132.** 3303 Campster Dr. I-55, exit 96 (William St), just w. Int corridors. **Pets:** Large, other species. Service with restrictions, supervision.

Hampton Inn-Cape Girardeau SH
(573) 651-3000. **$99-$129.** 103 Cape W Pkwy. I-55, exit 96 (William St), 0.3 mi sw. Int corridors. **Pets:** Other species. Service with restrictions, crate.

Pear Tree Inn by Drury-Cape Girardeau SH
(573) 334-3000. **$70-$86.** 3248 William St. I-55, exit 96 (William St), just e. Int corridors. **Pets:** Large, other species. Service with restrictions, supervision.

Victorian Inn & Suites SH
(573) 651-4486. **$60-$109.** 3265 William St. I-55, exit 96 (William St), just e. Ext/int corridors. **Pets:** Accepted.

CARTHAGE

Best Western Precious Moments Hotel SH ✤
(417) 359-5900. **Call for rates.** 2701 Hazel St. Just e of jct US 71 and SR HH. Int corridors. **Pets:** Medium, dogs only. $10 daily fee/room. Designated rooms, service with restrictions, crate.

Econo Lodge SH
(417) 358-3900. **$56-$149.** 1441 W Central. On SR 96; jct US 71. Ext/int corridors. **Pets:** Medium, other species. $10 daily fee/pet. Designated rooms, service with restrictions, supervision.

Super 8 Motel SH
(417) 359-9000. **Call for rates.** 416 W Fir Rd. Just e of jct US 71 and SR HH. Int corridors. **Pets:** Accepted.

CHILLICOTHE

Best Western Inn SH
(660) 646-0572. **Call for rates.** 1020 S Washington St. Jct US 36 and 65 (Washington St). Ext/int corridors. **Pets:** $10 one-time fee/pet. Designated rooms, service with restrictions, supervision.

Chillicothe Super 8 Motel SH
(660) 646-7888. **Call for rates.** 580 Old Hwy 36 E. Jct US 36 and 65 (Washington St), 0.8 mi e. Int corridors. **Pets:** Accepted.

CLINTON

Best Western Colonial Motel M
(660) 885-2206. **$59-$69.** 106 S Baird St. Jct SR 7 and 13. Ext corridors. **Pets:** Medium, dogs only. $10 daily fee/pet. Designated rooms, service with restrictions.

Motel USA Inn M
(660) 885-2267. **$35-$55.** 1508 N 2nd St. Jct SR 7 and 13. Ext corridors. **Pets:** Small, dogs only. $10 daily fee/pet. Designated rooms, service with restrictions, supervision.

COLUMBIA

Best Western Columbia Inn SH
(573) 474-6161. **$69-$101.** 3100 I-70 Dr SE. I-70, exit 128A, just s, then just e. Int corridors. **Pets:** $10 one-time fee/room. Designated rooms, service with restrictions, supervision.

▼▼ **Candlewood Suites** SH
(573) 817-0525. **Call for rates.** 3100 Wingate Ct. I-70, exit 128A, just s on US 63, just e on I-70 Dr SE, then just s on Keene St. Int corridors. **Pets:** Other species. $150 one-time fee/room. Service with restrictions.
⊠ Ⓜ 🛏 ▣

▼▼▼ **Drury Inn-Columbia** SH
(573) 445-1800. **$93-$153.** 1000 Knipp St. I-70, exit 124 (Stadium Blvd), just s. Int corridors. **Pets:** Large, other species. Service with restrictions, supervision.
A$K ⊠ 🛏 ▣ ⇌

▼▼▼ **Extended StayAmerica-Columbia-Stadium Blvd** SH
(573) 445-6800. **$68-$115.** 2000 W Business Loop 70. I-70, exit 124 (Stadium Blvd), just ne. Int corridors. **Pets:** Other species. $75 one-time fee/pet. Service with restrictions.
A$K ⑤ ⊠ 🛏 ▣

▼▼▼ **Holiday Inn Select Executive Center** LH
(573) 445-8531. **$105-$300.** 2200 I-70 Dr SW. I-70, exit 124 (Stadium Blvd), just w. Int corridors. **Pets:** Other species. $35 one-time fee/room. Designated rooms, service with restrictions, supervision.
A$K ⑤ ⊠ Ⓜ ▣ 🍴 ⇌ ⊗

▼ **Red Roof Inn-Columbia** M
(573) 442-0145. **Call for rates.** 201 E Texas Ave. I-70, exit 126 (Providence Rd), just n. Ext corridors. **Pets:** Accepted.
⊠ 🛏

▼ **Super 8 Motel-Clark Lane in Columbia** M
(573) 474-8488. **Call for rates.** 3216 Clark Ln. I-70, exit 128A, northeast corner. Int corridors. **Pets:** Accepted.
⊠ 🛏 ▣

CUBA

▼ **Super 8 Motel** M
(573) 885-2087. **Call for rates.** 28 Hwy P. I-44, exit 208 (SR 19), just nw. Ext/int corridors. **Pets:** Accepted.
⊠ 🛏 ▣

FESTUS

▼▼ **Comfort Inn Festus** SH
(636) 937-2888. **Call for rates.** 1303 Veterans Blvd. I-55, exit 175, just w. Int corridors. **Pets:** Accepted.
⊠ 🛏 ▣

▼▼ **Drury Inn-Festus** SH
(636) 933-2400. **$85-$122.** 1001 Veterans Blvd. I-55, exit 175, just e. Int corridors. **Pets:** Large, other species. Service with restrictions, supervision.
A$K ⊠ 🛏 ▣ ⇌

FULTON

▼▼▼ **Loganberry Inn Bed & Breakfast** BB
(573) 642-9229. **$99-$189, 14 day notice.** 310 W 7th St. Jct US 54, exit CR F, 1 mi e, just n to Westminster, then just e. Int corridors. **Pets:** Accepted.
A$K ⑤ ⊠ 🛏 ▣

HANNIBAL

✈ ▼▼▼ **Quality Inn & Suites** SH
(573) 221-4001. **$79-$129.** 120 Lindsey Dr. 2 mi w on US 36, exit Shinn Ln to south service road, then 0.6 mi e. Int corridors. **Pets:** Medium. $10 daily fee/pet. Designated rooms, service with restrictions.
SAVE ⑤ ⊠ 🛏 ▣ ⇌ ⊗

▼ **Super 8 Motel** M
(573) 221-5863. **$55-$90.** 120 Huckleberry Heights. Jct US 36, 1.5 mi s on US 61. Int corridors. **Pets:** Accepted.
A$K ⑤ ⊠ 🛏 ⇌

HARRISONVILLE

✈ ▼▼▼ **Harrisonville Inn & Suites** M
(816) 884-3200. **$55-$98.** 2201 Rockhaven Rd. Just n of jct US 71 and SR 291. Ext corridors. **Pets:** Small, dogs only. $10 daily fee/pet. Designated rooms, service with restrictions, supervision.
SAVE ⑤ ⊠ 🛏 ▣ ⇌

HAYTI

▼▼ **Drury Inn & Suites-Hayti Caruthersville** SH
(573) 359-2702. **$82-$121.** 1317 Hwy 84. I-55, exit 19 (US 412/SR 84), just w. Int corridors. **Pets:** Large, other species. Service with restrictions, supervision.
A$K ⊠ 🛏 ▣ ⇌

HIGGINSVILLE

▼▼ **Super 8 Motel-Higginsville** SH
(660) 584-7781. **Call for rates.** 6471 Oakview Ln. I-70, exit 49 (SR 13), just se. Int corridors. **Pets:** Accepted.
⊠ ▣

JACKSON

▼▼▼ **Drury Inn & Suites-Jackson,MO** SH
(573) 243-9200. **$76-$126.** 225 Drury Ln. I-55, exit 105 (SR 61), 0.3 mi w. Int corridors. **Pets:** Large, other species. Service with restrictions, supervision.
A$K ⊠ Ⓜ 🛏 ▣ ⇌

JANE

▼▼ **Booneslick Lodge** SH
(417) 226-1888. **$64-$79.** 21140 US Hwy 71. just s on US 71. Int corridors. **Pets:** $10 one-time fee/pet. Designated rooms, service with restrictions, supervision.
A$K ⑤ ⊠ 🛏 ⇌

JEFFERSON CITY

▼▼ **Super 8 Motel-Jefferson City** SH
(573) 636-5456. **$50-$89.** 1710 Jefferson St. US 54, exit Ellis Blvd, 0.3 mi nw on frontage road. Int corridors. **Pets:** $10 daily fee/pet. Designated rooms, no service, supervision.
A$K ⑤ ⊠ 🛏 ▣

✈ ▼▼▼ **Truman Hotel & Conference Center** SH
(573) 635-7171. **$80-$92.** 1510 Jefferson St. US 54, exit Ellis Blvd, 0.5 mi nw. Ext/int corridors. **Pets:** Other species. $10 daily fee/pet. Service with restrictions, crate.
SAVE ⊠ 🛏 ▣ 🍴 ⇌

JOPLIN

✈ ▼▼ **Baymont Inn & Suites** SH
(417) 623-0000. **$66-$96.** 3510 S Range Line Rd. I-44, exit 8B, just n. Ext/int corridors. **Pets:** Accepted.
SAVE ⑤ ⊠ 🛏 ▣ ⇌

✈ ▼▼▼ **Best Western Oasis Inn & Suites** SH
(417) 781-6776. **$59-$99.** 3508 S Range Line Rd. I-44, exit 8B, just nw. Ext corridors. **Pets:** Small. $10 daily fee/pet. Service with restrictions, supervision.
SAVE ⑤ ⊠ 🛏 ▣ ⇌

▼▼▼ **Drury Inn & Suites-Joplin** SH
(417) 781-8000. **$83-$138.** 3601 Range Line Rd. I-44, exit 8B, just ne. Int corridors. **Pets:** Large, other species. Service with restrictions, supervision.
A$K ⊠ Ⓜ 🛏 ▣ ⇌ ⊗

✈ ▼▼▼ **Holiday Inn** SH
(417) 782-1000. **$75-$149.** 3615 Range Line Rd. I-44, exit 8B, just ne. Int corridors. **Pets:** Accepted.
SAVE ⑤ ⊠ 🛏 ▣ 🍴 ⇌ ⊗

▼ Microtel Inn & Suites Joplin 🆂🅷
(417) 626-8282. **Call for rates.** 4101 Richard Joseph Blvd. I-44, exit 8A, just s. Int corridors. **Pets:** Accepted.

⊗ 🖥 💻 ➾

▼▼▼▼ Residence Inn by Marriott-Joplin 🆂🅷
(417) 782-0908. **$154-$174.** 3128 E Hammons Blvd. I-44, exit 8B, just ne. Int corridors. **Pets:** Accepted.

A$K 🆂 ⊗ ⌁ᴹ 🖥 💻 ➾ ⊠

⟨ΑΑΑ⟩ ▼▼▼ Sleep Inn 🆂🅷
(417) 782-1212. **$69-$95.** I-44 & State Hwy 43 S. I-44, exit 4, just s. Int corridors. **Pets:** Accepted.

SAVE 🆂 ⊗ 💻

KANSAS CITY METROPOLITAN AREA

BLUE SPRINGS

▼▼▼ Hampton Inn Blue Springs 🆂🅷
(816) 220-3844. **Call for rates.** 900 NW South Outer Rd. I-70, exit 20, just s on SR 7, then just w. Int corridors. **Pets:** Accepted.

⊗ 🖥 💻 ➾

INDEPENDENCE

⟨ΑΑΑ⟩ ▼▼▼ Best Western Truman Inn 🅼 🐾
(816) 254-0100. **$50-$95.** 4048 S Lynn Court Dr. I-70, exit 12, just n on Noland Rd, then just w. Ext corridors. **Pets:** Medium, other species. $50 deposit/room, $8 daily fee/pet. Service with restrictions, supervision.

SAVE 🆂 ⊗ 🖥 💻 ➾

⟨ΑΑΑ⟩ ▼▼▼ Super 8 Motel 🆂🅷 🐾
(816) 833-1888. **$60-$90.** 4032 S Lynn Court Dr. I-70, exit 12, just n on Noland Rd, then just w. Int corridors. **Pets:** Medium, other species. $50 deposit/room, $8 daily fee/pet. Service with restrictions, supervision.

SAVE 🆂 ⊗ 🖥 ➾

KANSAS CITY

⟨ΑΑΑ⟩ ▼▼▼ Baymont Inn & Suites Kansas City South 🆂🅷
(816) 822-7000. **Call for rates.** 8601 Hillcrest Rd. I-435, exit 69 (87th St), just e, then just n. Int corridors. **Pets:** Accepted.

SAVE ⊗ ⌁ᴹ 🖥 💻

⟨ΑΑΑ⟩ ▼▼▼ Best Western Country Inn-North 🅼
(816) 459-7222. **$49-$199.** 2633 NE 43rd St. I-35, exit 8C (Antioch Rd), just s on SR 1, then just e. Ext corridors. **Pets:** Small, other species. $10 daily fee/pet. Designated rooms, service with restrictions, supervision.

SAVE 🆂 ⊗ 🖥 💻 ➾

⟨ΑΑΑ⟩ ▼▼▼▼ Best Western Seville Plaza Hotel 🆂🅷
(816) 561-9600. **Call for rates.** 4309 Main St. Jct 43rd St, just s. Int corridors. **Pets:** Accepted.

SAVE ⊗ ⌁ᴹ 🖥 💻

⟨ΑΑΑ⟩ ▼▼▼▼ Chase Suites by Woodfin 🆂🅷
(816) 891-9009. **Call for rates.** 9900 NW Prairie View Rd. I-29, exit 10, just w, then just n. Ext corridors. **Pets:** Accepted.

SAVE ⊗ 🖥 💻 ➾ ⊠

▼▼▼▼ Comfort Inn Kansas City/Worlds of Fun 🆂🅷
(816) 454-3500. **$54-$139.** 7300 NE Parvin Rd. I-435, exit 54, just w. Int corridors. **Pets:** Accepted.

A$K 🆂 ⊗ ⌁ᴹ 🖥 💻 ➾

⟨ΑΑΑ⟩ ▼▼▼▼ Courtyard by Marriott-Country Club Plaza 🆂🅷 🐾
(816) 285-9755. **$186-$219.** 4600 J C Nichols Pkwy. Jct 47th St, just n. Int corridors. **Pets:** Medium. $75 one-time fee/room. Service with restrictions.

SAVE 🆂 ⊗ 🖥 💻 🍴 ➾

▼ Crossland Economy Studios Kansas City-Worlds of Fun 🅼
(816) 413-0060. **$50-$70.** 4301 N Corrington Ave. I-435, exit 54 northbound, just w; exit southbound, 1 mi s on service road, just w on Parvin Dr, then just n. Ext corridors. **Pets:** Other species. $75 one-time fee/pet. Service with restrictions.

A$K 🆂 ⊗ 🖥 💻

⟨ΑΑΑ⟩ ▼▼▼▼ Crowne Plaza Kansas City Downtown 🆂🅷
(816) 474-6664. **Call for rates.** 1301 Wyandotte St. Just s of I-70, US 24 and 40. Int corridors. **Pets:** Accepted.

SAVE ⊗ 🖥 💻 🍴 ➾

▼▼▼▼ Drury Inn & Suites-Kansas City Airport 🆂🅷
(816) 880-9700. **$77-$163.** 7900 NW Tiffany Springs Pkwy. I-29, exit 10, just w. Int corridors. **Pets:** Large, other species. Service with restrictions, supervision.

A$K ⊗ ⌁ᴹ 🖥 💻 ➾ ⊠

▼▼▼▼ Drury Inn & Suites-Kansas City Stadium 🆂🅷
(816) 923-3000. **$73-$129.** 3830 Blue Ridge Cutoff. I-70, exit 9 (Blue Ridge Cutoff), just nw. Int corridors. **Pets:** Large, other species. Service with restrictions, supervision.

A$K ⊗ ⌁ᴹ 🖥 💻 ➾

⟨ΑΑΑ⟩ ▼▼▼▼ Embassy Suites Hotel KCI Airport 🆂🅷
(816) 891-7788. **Call for rates.** 7640 NW Tiffany Springs Pkwy. I-29, exit 10, just e. Int corridors. **Pets:** Small. $10 daily fee/room. Service with restrictions, crate.

SAVE ⊗ ⌁ᴹ 🖥 💻 🍴 ➾ ⊠

▼ Extended StayAmerica-Kansas City Airport 🆂🅷
(816) 270-7829. **$50-$70.** 11712 NW Plaza Cir. I-29, exit 13, just e on CR D, just s on Ambassador Dr, then just w. Int corridors. **Pets:** Other species. $75 one-time fee/pet. Service with restrictions.

A$K 🆂 ⊗ 🖥 💻

▼ Extended StayAmerica-Kansas City South 🆂🅷
(816) 943-1315. **$55-$75.** 550 E 105th St. I-435, exit 74, just s on Holmes Rd, then just w. Int corridors. **Pets:** Other species. $75 one-time fee/pet. Service with restrictions.

A$K 🆂 ⊗ 🖥 💻

▼▼▼ Hilton Kansas City Airport 🅻🅷
(816) 891-8900. **Call for rates.** 8801 NW 112th St. I-29, exit 12, just se. Int corridors. **Pets:** Accepted.

⊗ ⌁ᴹ 🖥 💻 🍴 ➾ ⊠

⟨ΑΑΑ⟩ ▼▼▼▼ Holiday Inn At The Plaza, Kansas City 🆂🅷
(816) 753-7400. **$129-$169.** One E 45th St. Jct Main St; in Country Club Plaza. Int corridors. **Pets:** Accepted.

SAVE 🆂 ⊗ ⌁ᴹ 💻 🍴 ➾

▼▼▼ Holiday Inn Express Westport 🆂🅷
(816) 931-1000. **Call for rates.** 801 Westport Rd. Jct Main St, 0.5 mi w; in Westport Plaza area. Int corridors. **Pets:** Accepted.

⊗ ⌁ᴹ 🖥 💻

Holiday Inn-Kansas City Northeast SH
(816) 455-1060. **$99-$139.** 7333 NE Parvin Rd. I-435, exit 54, just w.
Int corridors. **Pets:** Accepted.
⟦SAVE⟧ ⟦Sᴅ⟧ ⟦✕⟧ ⟦ᴄᴹ⟧ ⟦🖷⟧ ⟦🖳⟧ ⟦¶⟧ ⟦≈⟧ ⟦✕⟧

Holiday Inn KCI & Expo Center SH
(816) 801-8400. **$89-$149.** 11728 N Ambassador Dr. I-29, exit 13, just
e on CR D, then just s. Int corridors. **Pets:** Accepted.
⟦SAVE⟧ ⟦Sᴅ⟧ ⟦✕⟧ ⟦🖷⟧ ⟦🖳⟧ ⟦¶⟧ ⟦≈⟧

Holiday Inn-Sports Complex SH
(816) 353-5300. **$129.** 4011 Blue Ridge Cutoff. I-70, exit 9 (Blue Ridge
Cutoff), just se. Int corridors. **Pets:** Accepted.
⟦SAVE⟧ ⟦Sᴅ⟧ ⟦✕⟧ ⟦ᴄᴹ⟧ ⟦🖷⟧ ⟦🖳⟧ ⟦¶⟧ ⟦≈⟧ ⟦✕⟧

**Homestead Studio Suites Hotel-Kansas City/Country
Club Plaza** SH
(816) 531-2212. **$85-$105.** 4535 Main St. Jct 45th St, just s; just ne of
Country Club Plaza. Int corridors. **Pets:** Other species. $75 one-time
fee/pet. Service with restrictions.
⟦ASK⟧ ⟦Sᴅ⟧ ⟦✕⟧ ⟦ᴄᴹ⟧ ⟦🖷⟧ ⟦🖳⟧

Homewood Suites by Hilton SH
(816) 880-9880. **Call for rates.** 7312 NW Polo Dr. I-29, exit 10, just e.
Int corridors. **Pets:** Accepted.
⟦SAVE⟧ ⟦✕⟧ ⟦🖷⟧ ⟦🖳⟧ ⟦≈⟧ ⟦✕⟧

**The InterContinental Kansas City at the
Plaza** LH
(816) 756-1500. **$149-$369.** 401 Ward Pkwy. Jct Wornall Rd; in Country Club Plaza. Int corridors. **Pets:** Small. $25 daily fee/room. Service with
restrictions, supervision.
⟦SAVE⟧ ⟦Sᴅ⟧ ⟦✕⟧ ⟦🖷⟧ ⟦🖳⟧ ⟦¶⟧ ⟦≈⟧ ⟦✕⟧

La Quinta Inn SH
(816) 483-7900. **$85.** 1051 N Cambridge Ave. I-435, exit 57, just w,
then just s. Int corridors. **Pets:** Other species. Service with restrictions,
supervision.
⟦SAVE⟧ ⟦Sᴅ⟧ ⟦✕⟧ ⟦🖷⟧ ⟦🖳⟧ ⟦≈⟧ ⟦✕⟧

Quality Inn & Suites Airport SH
(816) 587-6262. **$79-$99, 7 day notice.** 6901 NW 83rd St. I-29, exit 8,
just w, just s on NW Prairie View Dr, then just w. Int corridors.
Pets: Accepted.
⟦ASK⟧ ⟦Sᴅ⟧ ⟦✕⟧ ⟦🖷⟧ ⟦🖳⟧ ⟦≈⟧

Radisson Hotel Kansas City Airport SH
(816) 464-2423. **Call for rates.** 11828 NW Plaza Cir. I-29, exit 13, just
e on CR D, just s on Ambassador Dr, then just w. Int corridors.
Pets: Accepted.
⟦✕⟧ ⟦ᴄᴹ⟧ ⟦🖷⟧ ⟦🖳⟧ ⟦¶⟧ ⟦≈⟧

Red Roof Inn-North M
(816) 452-8585. **Call for rates.** 3636 NE Randolph Rd. I-435, exit 55B
northbound; exit 55 southbound, just e on SR 210, then just n. Ext
corridors. **Pets:** Accepted.
⟦✕⟧ ⟦ᴄᴹ⟧

**Residence Inn by Marriott Downtown/Union
Hill** SH
(816) 561-3000. **$220-$240.** 2975 Main St. Jct 31st St, just n. Ext
corridors. **Pets:** Accepted.
⟦ASK⟧ ⟦Sᴅ⟧ ⟦✕⟧ ⟦🖷⟧ ⟦🖳⟧ ⟦≈⟧

**Residence Inn Kansas City Country Club
Plaza** SH
(816) 753-0033. **$169-$189.** 4601 Broadway Blvd. Jct JC Nichols Pkwy,
just w on 46th Terr; in Country Club Plaza. Int corridors.
Pets: Accepted.
⟦SAVE⟧ ⟦Sᴅ⟧ ⟦✕⟧ ⟦🖷⟧ ⟦🖳⟧ ⟦≈⟧ ⟦✕⟧

**Sheraton Suites Country Club
Plaza** LH ❀
(816) 931-4400. **$129-$249.** 770 W 47th St. Jct Summit St; in Country
Club Plaza. Int corridors. **Pets:** Service with restrictions, supervision.
⟦SAVE⟧ ⟦Sᴅ⟧ ⟦✕⟧ ⟦ᴄᴹ⟧ ⟦🖷⟧ ⟦🖳⟧ ⟦¶⟧ ⟦≈⟧

The Westin Crown Center LH
(816) 474-4400. **Call for rates.** 1 E Pershing Rd. 0.5 mi s. Int corridors.
Pets: Accepted.
⟦SAVE⟧ ⟦✕⟧ ⟦ᴄᴹ⟧ ⟦🖳⟧ ⟦¶⟧ ⟦≈⟧ ⟦✕⟧

KEARNEY

Best Western Kearney Inn SH
(816) 628-5000. **$70-$150.** 601 Centerville Ave. I-35, exit 26, just w. Int
corridors. **Pets:** Other species. $10 one-time fee/pet. Designated rooms,
service with restrictions, supervision.
⟦SAVE⟧ ⟦Sᴅ⟧ ⟦✕⟧ ⟦🖷⟧ ⟦🖳⟧ ⟦≈⟧

Kearney Super 8 Motel SH
(816) 628-6800. **Call for rates.** 210 Platte Clay Way. I-35, exit 26, just
e on SR 92, then just n. Int corridors. **Pets:** Accepted.
⟦✕⟧ ⟦🖷⟧

LEE'S SUMMIT

Comfort Inn by Choice Hotels SH
(816) 524-8181. **Call for rates.** 607 SE Oldham Pkwy. Jct US 50 and
SR 291 N. Int corridors. **Pets:** Accepted.
⟦✕⟧ ⟦ᴄᴹ⟧ ⟦🖷⟧ ⟦🖳⟧ ⟦≈⟧

Fairfield Inn by Marriott SH
(816) 524-7572. **$74-$94.** 1301 NE Windsor Dr. I-470, exit 10B, 0.5 mi
s on SR 291. Int corridors. **Pets:** Accepted.
⟦ASK⟧ ⟦Sᴅ⟧ ⟦✕⟧ ⟦ᴄᴹ⟧ ⟦🖷⟧ ⟦🖳⟧ ⟦≈⟧

Lee's Summit Holiday Inn Express SH
(816) 795-6400. **$90-$130.** 4825 NE Lakewood Way. I-470, exit 14, just
e on Bowlin Rd, then 0.4 mi s. Int corridors. **Pets:** Accepted.
⟦SAVE⟧ ⟦Sᴅ⟧ ⟦✕⟧ ⟦ᴄᴹ⟧ ⟦🖷⟧ ⟦🖳⟧ ⟦≈⟧

NORTH KANSAS CITY

La Quinta Inn Kansas City North SH
(816) 221-1200. **$82-$102.** 2214 Taney Rd. I-29/35, exit 6A, just e on
SR 210, then just n. Int corridors. **Pets:** Other species. Service with
restrictions, supervision.
⟦ASK⟧ ⟦Sᴅ⟧ ⟦✕⟧ ⟦🖷⟧ ⟦🖳⟧

OAK GROVE (JACKSON COUNTY)

Econo Lodge M
(816) 690-3681. **$59-$89.** 410 SE 1st St. I-70, exit 28, just s on Broadway St, just e on SE 4th St, then just n. Ext corridors. **Pets:** Small,
dogs only. $10 daily fee/pet. Service with restrictions, supervision.
⟦SAVE⟧ ⟦✕⟧ ⟦🖷⟧

END METROPOLITAN AREA

KIRKSVILLE

Super 8 Motel-Kirksville M
(660) 665-8826. **$56-$73.** 1101 Country Club Dr. On US 63 and SR 6.
Int corridors. **Pets:** Other species. $10 daily fee/pet. Designated rooms,
service with restrictions, supervision.
⟦ASK⟧ ⟦Sᴅ⟧ ⟦✕⟧ ⟦🖷⟧

LAMAR

◆◆ **Super 8 Motel-Lamar** 🄢🄷
(417) 682-6888. **$67-$74.** 45 SE 1st Ln. Jct US 71 and 160. Int corridors. **Pets:** Accepted.
[A$K] [S🐕] [✕] [🛏] [💻] [🏊]

LEBANON

🅰🅰🅰 ◆◆ **Best Western Wyota Inn Lebanon** 🄢🄷
(417) 532-6171. **$73-$140.** 1225 Mill Creek Rd. I-44, exit 130, just nw. Ext corridors. **Pets:** Medium. $15 daily fee/pet. Designated rooms, service with restrictions, crate.
[SAVE] [S🐕] [✕] [🛏] [💻] [🍴] [🏊]

◆◆ **Holiday Inn Express** 🄢🄷
(417) 532-1111. **$103.** 1955 W Elm St. I-44, exit 127, just n. Int corridors. **Pets:** Accepted.
[S🐕] [✕] [🛏] [💻] [🏊]

LICKING

◆ **Scenic Rivers Inn** 🄼
(573) 674-4809. **$54-$60 (no credit cards).** 209 S Hwy 63. On US 63. Ext corridors. **Pets:** Accepted.
[A$K] [S🐕] [✕] [🛏] [💻] [🏊] [✕]

LOUISIANA

🅰🅰🅰 ◆ **River's Edge Motel** 🄼
(573) 754-4522. **$50-$65.** 201 Mansion St. On US 54; at Champ Clark Bridge. Ext corridors. **Pets:** Dogs only. $8 one-time fee/pet. Service with restrictions, crate.
[SAVE] [S🐕] [✕] [🛏] [💻]

MACON

◆ **Super 8 Motel** 🄢🄷
(660) 385-5788. **$64.** 203 E Briggs Dr. Jct US 36 and 63. Int corridors. **Pets:** Accepted.
[A$K] [✕] [🛏] [💻]

MARSHFIELD

◆◆ **Holiday Inn Express** 🄢🄷
(417) 859-6000. **$89-$99, 7 day notice.** 1301 Banning St. I-44, exit 100 (SR 38), on southeast corner. Int corridors. **Pets:** Accepted.
[A$K] [S🐕] [✕] [&M] [🛏] [💻] [🏊]

MARYVILLE

◆◆ **Super 8 Motel-Maryville** 🄢🄷
(660) 582-8088. **Call for rates.** 222 Summit Dr. On Business Rt US 71; just n of US 71 Bypass. Int corridors. **Pets:** Accepted.
[✕] [🛏] [💻]

MINER

◆◆ **Drury Inn-Sikeston** 🄢🄷
(573) 471-4100. **$86-$126.** 2602 E Malone. I-55, exit 67, just sw. Int corridors. **Pets:** Large, other species. Service with restrictions, supervision.
[A$K] [✕] [&M] [💻] [🏊]

◆◆ **Pear Tree Inn by Drury-Sikeston** 🄢🄷
(573) 471-8660. **$48-$84.** 2602 E Malone. I-55, exit 67, just sw. Ext corridors. **Pets:** Large, other species. Service with restrictions, supervision.
[A$K] [✕] [&M] [💻] [🏊]

MOBERLY

🅰🅰🅰 ◆◆◆ **Best Western Moberly Inn** 🄢🄷
(660) 263-6540. **Call for rates.** 1200 Hwy 24 E. Jct US 24 and 63 business route. Ext/int corridors. **Pets:** Small, dogs only. $30 one-time fee/room. Designated rooms, service with restrictions, supervision.
[SAVE] [✕] [&M] [🛏] [💻] [🍴] [🏊]

MOUNTAIN GROVE

🅰🅰🅰 ◆ **Days Inn of Mountain Grove** 🄢🄷
(417) 926-5555. **Call for rates.** 300 E 19th St. Jct US 60 and 95, just se. Ext corridors. **Pets:** Accepted.
[SAVE] [✕] [💻] [🏊]

◆ **TraveLodge** 🄼
(417) 926-3152. **Call for rates.** 111 E 17th St. Jct US 60 and 95, just s. Ext corridors. **Pets:** Accepted.
[✕] [💻] [🏊]

NEOSHO

◆◆ **Super 8 Motel-Neosho** 🄢🄷
(417) 455-1888. **$60-$65.** 3085 Gardner/Edgewood Dr. Just s of jct US 60B and 71B. Int corridors. **Pets:** Small. $10 daily fee/pet. Designated rooms, no service, crate.
[A$K] [S🐕] [✕] [🛏]

NEW FLORENCE

◆◆ **Days Inn Booneslick Lodge** 🄢🄷
(573) 835-7777. **Call for rates.** 403 Booneslick Rd. I-70, exit 175, just w. Int corridors. **Pets:** Accepted.
[✕] [🛏] [💻] [🏊]

NIXA

◆ **Super 8 Motel** 🄢🄷
(417) 725-0880. **Call for rates.** 418 Massey Blvd. 0.5 mi n of jct SR 14 and 160; US 65, 4.7 mi w on SR 14, then 0.4 mi n on SR 160. Int corridors. **Pets:** Accepted.
[✕] [🛏] [💻] [🏊]

OSAGE BEACH

🅰🅰🅰 ◆◆ **Best Western Dogwood Hills Resort Inn** 🄢🄷
(573) 348-1735. **$52-$114.** 1252 State Hwy KK. 0.5 mi n, off US 54. Ext corridors. **Pets:** Other species. $25 one-time fee/pet. No service, supervision.
[SAVE] [S🐕] [✕] [🛏] [💻] [🍴] [🏊]

PACIFIC

🅰🅰🅰 ◆ **Quality Inn Near Six Flags** 🄢🄷
(636) 257-8400. **$69-$109.** 1400 W Osage St. I-44, exit 257, just se. Ext/int corridors. **Pets:** Medium. $15 daily fee/room. Service with restrictions, supervision.
[SAVE] [S🐕] [✕] [🛏] [💻] [🏊]

POPLAR BLUFF

◆◆ **Comfort Inn by Choice Hotels** 🄢🄷
(573) 686-5200. **$81-$120.** 2582 N Westwood Blvd. 1.3 mi s from jct US 60 E. Int corridors. **Pets:** Accepted.
[A$K] [S🐕] [✕] [&M] [🛏] [💻] [🏊]

◆◆ **Drury Inn-Poplar Bluff** 🄢🄷
(573) 686-2451. **$79-$99.** 2220 N Westwood Blvd. On US 67, 1.4 mi s from jct US 60 E. Int corridors. **Pets:** Large, other species. Service with restrictions, supervision.
[A$K] [✕] [🛏] [💻] [🏊]

◆ **Pear Tree Inn by Drury-Poplar Bluff** 🄼
(573) 785-7100. **$53-$73.** 2218 N Westwood Blvd. On US 67, 1.4 mi s from jct US 60 E. Ext corridors. **Pets:** Large, other species. Service with restrictions, supervision.
[A$K] [✕] [🛏] [💻] [🏊]

◆ **Super 8** 🄢🄷
(573) 785-0176. **$60-$66.** 2831 N Westwood Blvd. On US 67, 0.8 mi s from jct US 60 E. Int corridors. **Pets:** Accepted.
[A$K] [S🐕] [✕] [🛏] [💻]

POTOSI

▼ **Potosi Super 8** 🆂🅷
(573) 438-8888. **Call for rates.** 820 E High St. Jct SR 8 and 21. Ext/int corridors. **Pets:** Accepted.
⊠ 🔋 💻

REPUBLIC

▼▼ **AmericInn Lodge & Suites of Republic** 🆂🅷
(417) 732-5335. **$80.** 950 Austin Ln. I-44, exit 67, 4.4 mi s to SR 174 (flashing red light/4-way stop), then 0.7 mi e to Highland Park Town Center; just nw of jct US 60, SR 413 and 174. Int corridors. **Pets:** Accepted.
🅰🆂🅺 ⊠ 🔋 💻 🐾

ROLLA

◈ ▼▼ **Best Western Coachlight** 🅼
(573) 341-2511. **Call for rates.** 1403 Martin Springs Dr. Jct I-44 and Business Rt 44 S, exit 184. Ext corridors. **Pets:** Other species. $20 daily fee/pet. Designated rooms, service with restrictions, crate.
🆂🅰🆅🅴 ⊠ 🔋 💻 🐾

▼ **Days Inn** 🅼
(573) 341-3700. **Call for rates.** 1207 Kingshighway. I-44, exit 184, just s. Ext corridors. **Pets:** Accepted.
⊠ 🔋 💻 🐾

▼▼ **Drury Inn-Rolla** 🆂🅷
(573) 364-4000. **$78-$108.** 2006 N Bishop Ave. I-44, exit 186 (US 63), just ne. Int corridors. **Pets:** Large, other species. Service with restrictions, supervision.
🅰🆂🅺 ⊠ 🔋 💻 🐾

ST. CLAIR

◈◈ ▼▼ **Budget Lodging** 🅼
(636) 629-1000. **$64-$69.** 866 S Outer Rd W. I-44, exit 240, just w. Ext/int corridors. **Pets:** Other species. $10 daily fee/pet. Designated rooms, service with restrictions, supervision.
🆂🅰🆅🅴 🆂🅰 ⊠ 🔋 💻 🐾

ST. JOSEPH

▼▼▼ **Drury Inn & Suites-St. Joseph** 🆂🅷
(816) 364-4700. **$66-$116.** 4213 Frederick Blvd. I-29, exit 47. Int corridors. **Pets:** Large, other species. Service with restrictions, supervision.
🅰🆂🅺 ⊠ 🅶🅼 🔋 💻 🐾 ⊠

◈ ▼▼ **Ramada Inn** 🅻🅷
(816) 233-6192. **$81-$85.** 4016 Frederick Blvd. I-29, exit 47, just w. Int corridors. **Pets:** Accepted.
🅰🆂🅺 ⊠ 🔋 💻 🍴 🐾 ⊠

◈◈ ▼▼▼ **St. Joseph Holiday Inn-Riverfront** 🅻🅷
(816) 279-8000. **$85-$99.** 102 S Third St. I-229, exit Edmond St northbound; exit Felix St southbound; downtown. Int corridors. **Pets:** Medium. $15 daily fee/room. Service with restrictions, supervision.
🆂🅰🆅🅴 🆂🅰 ⊠ 🅶🅼 🔋 💻 🍴 🐾 ⊠

ST. LOUIS METROPOLITAN AREA

CHESTERFIELD

▼▼▼ **Drury Plaza Hotel-Chesterfield** 🆂🅷
(636) 532-3300. **$96-$266.** 355 Chesterfield Center E. I-64/US 40, exit 19B (Clarkson Rd/Olive Blvd); jct I-64/US 40 and Clarkson Rd; southwest corner. Int corridors. **Pets:** Large, other species. Service with restrictions, supervision.
🅰🆂🅺 ⊠ 🅶🅼 🔋 💻 🍴 🐾

▼▼▼ **Homewood Suites by Hilton** 🆂🅷
(636) 530-0305. **Call for rates.** 840 Chesterfield Pkwy W. I-64, exit 20, 1 mi n. Int corridors. **Pets:** Accepted.
⊠ 🔋 💻 🐾

CLAYTON

◈◈ ▼▼▼ **Crowne Plaza St. Louis-Clayton** 🆂🅷
(314) 726-5400. **$119-$269.** 7750 Carondelet Ave. I-64/US 40, exit 31 (Brentwood Blvd), 1.3 mi n, then 0.7 mi e. Int corridors. **Pets:** Designated rooms, service with restrictions, crate.
🆂🅰🆅🅴 🆂🅰 ⊠ 💻 🍴 🐾 ⊠

◈◈ ▼▼ ▼▼ **The Ritz-Carlton, St. Louis** 🅻🅷
(314) 863-6300. **$425-$525.** 100 Carondelet Plaza. I-64, exit 32B, 1.2 mi n on Hanley Rd, then just e. Int corridors. **Pets:** Accepted.
🆂🅰🆅🅴 ⊠ 🍴 🐾 ⊠

▼▼ **Seven Gables Inn-Clayton** 🆂🅷
(314) 863-8400. **$299.** 26 N Meramec Ave. I-64/US 40, exit 31 (Brentwood Blvd), 1.3 mi n to Bonhomme Ave, just e to N Meramec, then 0.3 mi n. Int corridors. **Pets:** Accepted.
🅰🆂🅺 🆂🅰 ⊠ 🍴

◈◈ ▼▼▼ **Sheraton Clayton Plaza Hotel** 🆂🅷
(314) 863-0400. **$89-$249.** 7730 Bonhomme Ave. I-64/US 40, exit 31 (Brentwood Blvd), 1.3 mi n, then 0.7 mi e. Int corridors. **Pets:** Accepted.
🆂🅰🆅🅴 🆂🅰 ⊠ 🔋 💻 🍴 🐾 ⊠

CREVE COEUR

▼▼▼ **Drury Inn & Suites-Creve Coeur** 🆂🅷
(314) 989-1100. **$101-$166.** 11980 Olive Blvd. I-270, exit 14 (Olive Blvd). Int corridors. **Pets:** Large, other species. Service with restrictions, supervision.
🅰🆂🅺 ⊠ 🅶🅼 🔋 💻 🐾 ⊠

EARTH CITY

◈◈ ▼▼▼ **Residence Inn St. Louis Airport/Earth City** 🆂🅷
(314) 209-0995. **$170-$197.** 3290 Rider Tr S. I-70, exit 231B (Earth City Expwy N), just e. Int corridors. **Pets:** Accepted.
🆂🅰🆅🅴 🆂🅰 ⊠ 🅶🅼 🔋 💻 🐾 ⊠

EDMUNDSON

▼▼ **Drury Inn-St. Louis Airport** 🆂🅷
(314) 423-7700. **$99-$153.** 10490 Natural Bridge Rd. I-70, exit 236 (Lambert Airport), just se. Int corridors. **Pets:** Large, other species. Service with restrictions, supervision.
🅰🆂🅺 ⊠ 🅶🅼 🔋 💻 🐾

EUREKA

◈◈ ▼▼▼ **Holiday Inn at Six Flags** 🆂🅷
(636) 938-6661. **$109-$269, 3 day notice.** 4901 Six Flags Rd. I-44, exit 261 (Allenton Rd). Ext/int corridors. **Pets:** Large, other species. $25 daily fee/room. Service with restrictions, crate.
🆂🅰🆅🅴 🆂🅰 ⊠ 💻 🍴 🐾 ⊠

FENTON

▼▼▼ Drury Inn & Suites-Fenton 🆂🅷
(636) 343-7822. **$76-$153.** 1088 S Highway Dr. I-44, exit 274 (Bowles Ave), just se. Int corridors. **Pets:** Large, other species. Service with restrictions, supervision.

🄰🅂🄺 ⊠ 🔋 💻 ⇌ ⊠

▼▼ Pear Tree Inn by Drury-Fenton 🆂🅷
(636) 343-8820. **$63-$103.** 1100 S Highway Dr. I-44, exit 274 (Bowles Ave), just s. Int corridors. **Pets:** Large, other species. Service with restrictions, supervision.

🄰🅂🄺 ⊠ 🔋 💻 ⇌

▼▼ TownePlace Suites by Marriott 🆂🅷
(636) 305-7000. **$154-$174.** 1662 Fenton Business Park Ct. I-44, exit 275 westbound; exit 274 eastbound to S Highway Dr, just s. Int corridors. **Pets:** Other species. $100 one-time fee/room. Designated rooms, service with restrictions, crate.

🄰🅂🄺 🅂🄳 ⊠ 🄶🄼 🔋 💻 ⇌

FORISTELL

🄰🄰🄰 ▼▼▼ Best Western West 70 Inn 🆂🅷 ❈
(636) 673-2900. **$65-$95.** 12 Hwy W. I-70, exit 203 (CR W), just n. Int corridors. **Pets:** $15 one-time fee/pet. Service with restrictions, crate.

🅂🄰🅅🄴 🅂🄳 ⊠ 🔋 💻 ⇌

HAZELWOOD

▼▼ La Quinta Inn St. Louis (Airport) 🆂🅷
(314) 731-3881. **$92.** 5781 Campus Ct. I-270, exit 23 (McDonnell Blvd), just s. Int corridors. **Pets:** Other species. Service with restrictions, supervision.

🄰🅂🄺 🅂🄳 ⊠ 🔋 💻 ⇌

KIRKWOOD

▼▼ Best Western Kirkwood Inn 🆂🅷 ❈
(314) 821-3950. **$80-$120, 7 day notice.** 1200 S Kirkwood Rd. I-44, exit 277B (Lindbergh Blvd), just n. Int corridors. **Pets:** Medium. $10 daily fee/pet. Designated rooms, service with restrictions, supervision.

🄰🅂🄺 🅂🄳 ⊠ 🔋 💻 🍴 ⇌

MARYLAND HEIGHTS

▼▼▼ DoubleTree Hotel St. Louis at Westport 🆂🅷
(314) 434-0100. **Call for rates.** 1973 Craigshire Rd. I-270, exit 16A (Page Ave), just e to Lackland Rd, then 0.4 mi sw on Lackland and Craigshire rds. Int corridors. **Pets:** Accepted.

⊠ 🄶🄼 🔋 💻 🍴 ⇌ ⊠

▼▼ Drury Inn & Suites-St. Louis-Westport 🆂🅷
(314) 576-9966. **$75-$142.** 12220 Dorsett Rd. I-270, exit 17 (Dorsett Rd), just se. Int corridors. **Pets:** Large, other species. Service with restrictions, supervision.

🄰🅂🄺 ⊠ 🔋 💻 ⇌

🄰🄰🄰 ▼▼▼ Sheraton Westport Hotel-Lakeside Chalet 🄻🄷
(314) 878-1500. **$89-$249.** 191 Westport Plaza Dr. I-270, exit 16A (Page Ave), 0.8 mi e to Lackland Rd exit, just w to Craig Rd, then 0.4 mi n. Int corridors. **Pets:** Accepted.

🅂🄰🅅🄴 🅂🄳 ⊠ 🄶🄼 🔋 💻 🍴 ⇌

🄰🄰🄰 ▼▼▼ The Sheraton Westport Plaza Tower 🄻🄷
(314) 878-1500. **$99-$269.** 900 Westport Plaza Dr. I-270, exit 16A (Page Ave), 0.8 mi e; exit Lackland Rd, just w to Craig Rd, then 0.4 mi n. Int corridors. **Pets:** Accepted.

🅂🄰🅅🄴 🅂🄳 ⊠ 🄶🄼 🔋 💻 🍴 ⇌ ⊠

▼▼▼ Staybridge Suites 🆂🅷
(314) 878-1555. **$136-$180.** 1855 Craigshire Rd. I-270, exit 16A (Page Ave), 0.8 mi e, exit Lackland Rd, 1 mi w, then s via Lackland and Craigshire rds. Ext/int corridors. **Pets:** Large. $100 one-time fee/room. Service with restrictions.

🄰🅂🄺 🅂🄳 ⊠ 🔋 💻 ⇌ ⊠

MEHLVILLE

▼▼▼▼ Holiday Inn St. Louis-South I-55 🆂🅷
(314) 894-0700. **$89-$129.** 4234 Butler Hill Rd. I-55, exit 195 (Butler Hill Rd), just se. Ext/int corridors. **Pets:** Accepted.

🄰🅂🄺 🅂🄳 ⊠ 🔋 💻 🍴 ⇌ ⊠

O'FALLON

🄰🄰🄰 ▼▼▼ Country Inn & Suites 🆂🅷
(636) 300-4844. **$100.** 1175 Technology Dr. US 40/61, exit 9 (CR K), just nw. Int corridors. **Pets:** Small. $15 one-time fee/pet. Designated rooms, crate.

🅂🄰🅅🄴 🅂🄳 ⊠ 🄶🄼 🔋 💻 ⇌

🄰🄰🄰 ▼▼▼ Hilton Garden Inn St. Louis/O'Fallon 🆂🅷
(636) 625-2700. **Call for rates.** 2310 Technology Dr. US 40/61, exit 6 (Wing Haven Blvd/CR DD), just ne; I-70, exit 216 (Bryan Rd), 4.2 mi s. Int corridors. **Pets:** Accepted.

🅂🄰🅅🄴 ⊠ 🄶🄼 🔋 💻 🍴 ⇌

▼▼▼ Staybridge Suites O'Fallon 🆂🅷
(636) 300-0999. **$109-$179.** 1155 Technology Dr. US 40/64, exit 9 (CR K), just nw. Int corridors. **Pets:** Accepted.

🄰🅂🄺 ⊠ 🄶🄼 🔋 💻 ⇌

RICHMOND HEIGHTS

🄰🄰🄰 ▼▼▼ Residence Inn By Marriott-St. Louis Galleria 🆂🅷 ❈
(314) 862-1900. **$220-$240.** 1100 McMorrow Ave. I-170, exit 1C (Brentwood Ave) northbound; exit southbound, 0.5 mi e of Galleria via Galleria Pkwy. Ext corridors. **Pets:** Other species. $100 one-time fee/room. Service with restrictions, crate.

🅂🄰🅅🄴 🅂🄳 ⊠ 🄶🄼 🔋 💻 ⇌ ⊠

ST. ANN

▼▼▼ Hampton Inn-St. Louis Airport 🆂🅷
(314) 429-2000. **$82-$152.** 10820 Pear Tree Ln. I-70, exit 236 (Airport Dr), just sw. Int corridors. **Pets:** Service with restrictions, supervision.

⊠ 🔋 💻 ⇌

▼▼ Pear Tree Inn by Drury-St. Louis Airport 🆂🅷
(314) 427-3400. **$82-$116.** 10810 Pear Tree Ln. I-70, exit 236 (Airport Dr), just sw. Int corridors. **Pets:** Large, other species. Service with restrictions, supervision.

⊠ 🔋 💻 ⇌

ST. CHARLES

▼▼▼ Comfort Suites-St. Charles 🆂🅷 ❈
(636) 949-0694. **$100-$130.** 1400 S 5th St. I-70, exit 229 (5th St), just ne. Int corridors. **Pets:** Large, other species. Designated rooms, service with restrictions, supervision.

🄰🅂🄺 🅂🄳 ⊠ 🔋 💻 ⇌

🄰🄰🄰 ▼▼▼ Country Inn & Suites St. Charles 🆂🅷
(636) 724-5555. **$120-$152.** 1190 S Main St. I-70, exit 229A (5th St S), to S Main St, then 0.7 mi ne. Int corridors. **Pets:** Small. $25 daily fee/pet. Designated rooms, no service, crate.

🅂🄰🅅🄴 🅂🄳 ⊠ 🔋 💻 ⇌ ⊠

▼▼ TownePlace Suites by Marriott 🆂🅷
(636) 949-6800. **$140-$158.** 1800 Zumbehl Rd. I-70, exit 227 (Zumbehl Rd), 0.6 mi s, adjacent to Zumbehl Crossing Shopping Center, just se. Int corridors. **Pets:** Accepted.

🄰🅂🄺 🅂🄳 ⊠ 🔋 💻 ⇌

ST. LOUIS

▼▼▼▼ Drury Inn & Suites-St. Louis-Convention Center [LH]
(314) 231-8100. **$106-$166.** 711 N Broadway. I-70, exit 250B (Stadium/Memorial Dr), at convention center. Int corridors. **Pets:** Large, other species. Service with restrictions, supervision.
[ASK] [✕] [🛏] [💻] [🍽] [≈] [✕]

▼▼▼▼ Drury Inn-St. Louis/Union Station [SH]
(314) 231-3900. **$96-$166.** 201 S 20th St. Just e of Jefferson Ave; between Market St and Clark Ave. Int corridors. **Pets:** Large, other species. Service with restrictions, supervision.
[ASK] [✕] [🛏] [💻] [🍽] [≈]

(AAA) ▼▼▼▼ Drury Plaza Hotel-St. Louis At the Arch [SH]
(314) 231-3003. **$96-$266.** 4th & Market Sts. I-70, 250B (Stadium/Memorial Dr), just w on Pine St to Broadway, just s to Walnut St, just e to 4th St, then just n. Int corridors. **Pets:** Large, other species. Service with restrictions, supervision.
[SAVE] [✕] [&M] [🛏] [💻] [🍽] [≈]

▼▼▼▼ Hampton Inn-St. Louis/Union Station [SH]
(314) 241-3200. **$92-$150.** 2211 Market St. I-64/US 40, exit 39, just n on Jefferson Ave, then just e. Int corridors. **Pets:** Large. Service with restrictions, supervision.
[ASK] [✕] [🛏] [💻] [🍽] [≈]

(AAA) ▼▼▼▼ Sheraton St. Louis City Center Hotel & Suites [LH]
(314) 231-5007. **$419.** 400 S 14th St. I-40, exit 39B (14th St), just ne. Int corridors. **Pets:** Accepted.
[SAVE] [✕] [&M] [🛏] [💻] [🍽] [≈] [✕]

(AAA) ▼▼▼▼▼ The Westin St. Louis [LH] ❀
(314) 621-2000. **$379.** 811 Spruce St. Just w of Busch Stadium. Int corridors. **Pets:** Medium, dogs only. Service with restrictions, supervision.
[SAVE] [S🐾] [✕] [&M] [💻] [🍽]

ST. PETERS

▼▼▼▼ Drury Inn-St. Charles/St. Peters [SH]
(636) 397-9700. **$96-$146.** 170 Westfield Dr. I-70, exit 222 (Mid Rivers Mall Dr), just se. Int corridors. **Pets:** Large, other species. Service with restrictions, supervision.
[✕] [&M] [🛏] [💻] [≈]

SUNSET HILLS

(AAA) ▼▼▼▼ Holiday Inn-Southwest & Viking Conference Center [SH]
(314) 821-6600. **$104-$139.** 10709 Watson Rd. I-44, exit 277B, just s. Int corridors. **Pets:** Medium. $25 one-time fee/room. Service with restrictions, supervision.
[SAVE] [S🐾] [✕] [🛏] [💻] [🍽] [≈] [✕]

TOWN AND COUNTRY

(AAA) ▼▼▼▼ St. Louis Marriott West [LH]
(314) 878-2747. **$188-$208.** 660 Maryville Centre Dr. I-64/US 40, exit 23 (Maryville Centre Dr), just n. Int corridors. **Pets:** Accepted.
[SAVE] [S🐾] [✕] [&M] [🛏] [💻] [🍽] [≈] [✕]

VALLEY PARK

▼▼▼▼ Drury Inn & Suites-St. Louis Southwest [SH]
(636) 861-8300. **$89-$156.** 5 Lambert Drury Pl. I-44, exit 272 (SR 141), just sw. Int corridors. **Pets:** Large, other species. Service with restrictions, supervision.
[ASK] [✕] [🛏] [💻] [≈]

▼▼▼▼ Hampton Inn-St. Louis Southwest [SH]
(636) 529-9020. **$86-$119.** 9 Lambert Drury Pl. I-44, exit 272 (SR 141), just sw. Int corridors. **Pets:** Medium. Service with restrictions, supervision.
[ASK] [✕] [🛏] [💻] [≈]

END METROPOLITAN AREA

ST. ROBERT

▼▼▼ MainStay Suites [SH]
(573) 451-2700. **$80-$100.** 227 St. Robert Blvd. I-44, exit 159, 0.8 mi nw. Ext/int corridors. **Pets:** Accepted.
[ASK] [S🐾] [✕] [🛏] [💻] [≈]

▼▼▼ Microtel Inn & Suites [SH]
(573) 336-7705. **$60-$80.** 562 Old Route 66. I-44, exit 161 westbound to Business Loop 44/Old Route 66, 0.9 mi w; exit 159 eastbound, 0.4 mi se. Int corridors. **Pets:** Accepted.
[✕] [&M] [🛏] [💻]

(AAA) ▼ Motel 6 #4211 [SH] ❀
(573) 336-3610. **$50-$65.** 545 Hwy Z. I-44, exit 161, just s, then 0.3 mi e on frontage road. Int corridors. **Pets:** Other species. Service with restrictions, crate.
[SAVE] [S🐾] [✕] [&M] [🛏] [💻]

SEDALIA

(AAA) ▼▼▼▼ Hotel Bothwell, a Clarion Collection [SH]
(660) 826-5588. **$60-$190.** 103 E 4th St. Corner of 4th and S Ohio sts; downtown. Int corridors. **Pets:** Accepted.
[SAVE] [S🐾] [✕] [💻] [🍽] [✕]

SPRINGFIELD

(AAA) ▼▼▼ Baymont Inn & Suites [SH]
(417) 889-8188. **$76-$106.** 3776 S Glenstone Ave. On US 60. Int corridors. **Pets:** Accepted.
[SAVE] [S🐾] [✕] [&M] [🛏] [💻] [≈]

▼▼ Best Western Coach House Inn [SH]
(417) 862-0701. **$59-$99.** 2535 N Glenstone Ave. I-44, exit 80A, just s. Ext corridors. **Pets:** Small, other species. $10 daily fee/room. Service with restrictions, supervision.
[ASK] [S🐾] [✕] [🛏] [💻] [≈]

(AAA) ▼▼ Best Western Route 66 Rail Haven [M]
(417) 866-1963. **$64-$104.** 203 S Glenstone Ave. I-44, exit 80A, 3 mi s. Ext corridors. **Pets:** Accepted.
[SAVE] [S🐾] [✕] [&M] [🛏] [💻] [≈]

(AAA) ▼▼▼▼ Courtyard by Marriott Airport [SH]
(417) 869-6700. **$132-$152.** 3527 W Kearney. I-44, exit 75 (US 160 W Bypass), just se to SR 744, then just w. Int corridors. **Pets:** Accepted.
[SAVE] [S🐾] [✕] [&M] [🛏] [💻] [🍽] [≈]

▼▼▼▼ Drury Inn & Suites-Springfield [SH]
(417) 863-8400. **$93-$163.** 2715 N Glenstone Ave. I-44, exit 80A (Glenstone Ave), just s. Int corridors. **Pets:** Large, other species. Service with restrictions, supervision.
[ASK] [✕] [&M] [🛏] [💻] [≈]

(AAA) ▼▼▼▼ Holiday Inn Express Hotel & Suites SH
(417) 862-0070. **$119-$169.** 1117 E St. Louis St. Just w of National Ave. Int corridors. **Pets:** Accepted.
[SAVE] [X] [🛏] [💻] [⇆]

(AAA) ▼▼▼ Krystal Aire-A Non-Smoking Hotel SH
(417) 869-0001. **$65-$95.** 2745 N Glenstone Ave. I-44, exit 80A, just sw. Ext/int corridors. **Pets:** Designated rooms, service with restrictions, supervision.
[SAVE] [S🐾] [X] [🛏] [💻] [⇆]

▼▼ La Quinta Inn Springfield SH
(417) 520-8800. **$88.** 1610 E Evergreen. I-44, exit 80A. Int corridors. **Pets:** Other species. Service with restrictions, supervision.
[ASK] [S🐾] [X] [&M] [🛏] [💻] [⇆]

(AAA) ▼▼▼ Quality Inn & Suites SH
(417) 888-0898. **$79-$129.** 3930 S Overland Ave. US 60 (James River Expwy), exit Kansas Expwy, just n to Chesterfield Blvd, then just w. Int corridors. **Pets:** Small. $10 daily fee/pet. Designated rooms, service with restrictions, supervision.
[SAVE] [S🐾] [X] [&M] [🛏] [💻] [⇆]

(AAA) ▼▼▼ Sleep Inn of Springfield SH
(417) 886-2464. **$69-$84.** 233 El Camino Alto. US 60 (James River Expwy), exit Campbell Ave, just se. Int corridors. **Pets:** Medium, other species. $20 one-time fee/room. Designated rooms, service with restrictions, supervision.
[SAVE] [S🐾] [X] [🛏] [💻] [⇆]

(AAA) ▼▼▼▼ University Plaza Hotel and Convention Center LH
(417) 864-7333. **$159-$209.** 333 John Q Hammons Pkwy. 0.5 mi e on St. Louis St. Int corridors. **Pets:** Small. $25 one-time fee/room. Service with restrictions, supervision.
[SAVE] [X] [&M] [🛏] [💻] [🍽] [⇆]

SULLIVAN

▼▼▼ Baymont Inn SH 🐾
(573) 860-3333. **Call for rates.** 275 N Service Rd W. I-44, exit 225. Int corridors. **Pets:** Designated rooms, service with restrictions, supervision.
[X] [🛏] [💻] [⇆]

SWEET SPRINGS

(AAA) ▼ People's Choice Motel M
(660) 335-6315. **$33-$41.** 1001 N Locust St. I-70, exit 66, just se. Ext corridors. **Pets:** Other species. $20 deposit/room, $5 one-time fee/room. Service with restrictions, supervision.
[SAVE] [S🐾] [X]

TRENTON

▼ Trenton Knights Inn SH
(660) 359-2988. **$66-$79.** 1845A E 28th St. US 65, 1 mi n of jct SR 6 and US 65. Int corridors. **Pets:** Accepted.
[ASK] [S🐾] [X] [🛏]

UNION

▼▼ Super 8 Motel SH
(636) 583-8808. **$76-$125.** 1015 E Main St. I-44, exit 247 (US 50), 4.7 mi w; just w of jct SR 47. Int corridors. **Pets:** Accepted.
[ASK] [X] [&M] [⇆]

WARSAW

▼ Super 8 Motel-Warsaw SH
(660) 438-2882. **Call for rates.** 1603 Commercial St. US 65 and SR 7, exit Clinton. Ext corridors. **Pets:** Accepted.
[X] [🛏] [💻] [⇆]

WASHINGTON

▼ Super 8 Washington SH
(636) 390-0088. **$76-$125.** 2081 Eckelkamp Ct. I-44, exit 251, 10 mi, w on SR 100; just s of SR 100 and 47. Int corridors. **Pets:** Accepted.
[ASK] [X] [🛏] [💻]

WEST PLAINS

▼ Super 8 Motel-West Plains SH
(417) 256-8088. **$55-$60.** 1210 Porter Wagoner Blvd. On US 63B, 0.8 mi s of jct US 63. Int corridors. **Pets:** Small. $25 one-time fee/pet. Service with restrictions, supervision.
[ASK] [S🐾] [X] [💻]

MONTANA

ALBERTON

(AAA) ▼▼ **The Ghost Rails Inn B & B** BB
(406) 722-4990. **$49-$99, 3 day notice.** 702 Railroad Ave. Downtown.
Int corridors. **Pets:** Accepted.
SAVE S✗ ✗ ✗ ✗

BELGRADE

▼▼▼ **Gallatin River Lodge** CI
(406) 388-0148. **$170-$450, 7 day notice.** 9105 Thorpe Rd. I-90, exit
298, 2.7 mi s on SR 85, 1 mi w on Valley Center Rd (gravel), then 0.5
mi s, follow sign. Int corridors. **Pets:** Accepted.
✗ ✗ ✗ ✗

(AAA) ▼▼ **Holiday Inn Express** SH ✿
(406) 388-0800. **$69-$169.** 6261 Jackrabbit Ln. I-90, exit 298, just s on
SR 85. Int corridors. **Pets:** Medium, other species. $50 deposit/room.
Service with restrictions, supervision.
SAVE S✗ ✗ ✗ ✗ ✗ ✗

(AAA) ▼▼▼ **La Quinta Inn & Suites Belgrade**
     (Bozeman/Belgrade) SH
(406) 388-2222. **$104.** 6445 Jackrabbit Ln. I-90, exit 298, just s on SR
85. Int corridors. **Pets:** Other species. Service with restrictions, supervision.
SAVE S✗ ✗ ✗ ✗ ✗ ✗

(AAA) ▼▼▼ **Super 8 Motel-Belgrade/Bozeman Airport** SH
(406) 388-1493. **Call for rates.** 6450 Jackrabbit Ln. I-90, exit 298, just
s. Int corridors. **Pets:** $5 one-time fee/pet. Designated rooms, service with
restrictions.
SAVE ✗ ✗ ✗

BIGFORK

(AAA) ▼▼▼ **Mountain Lake Lodge** SH ✿
(406) 837-3800. **$89-$285, 7 day notice.** 14735 Sylvan Dr. On US 35,
5 mi s. Ext corridors. **Pets:** Other species. $15 daily fee/pet. Designated
rooms, service with restrictions, supervision.
SAVE ✗ ✗ ✗ ✗ ✗ ✗ ✗

(AAA) ▼▼▼ **Timbers Motel** M
(406) 837-6200. **$58-$124, 7 day notice.** 8540 Hwy 35. Just n on US
35 from jct SR 209. Ext corridors. **Pets:** $10 daily fee/pet. Service with
restrictions, supervision.
SAVE ✗ ✗

BIG SKY

(AAA) ▼▼▼ **Buck's T-4 Lodge** SH
(406) 995-4111. **$99-$199.** 46625 Gallatin Rd. US 191, 1 mi s of Big
Sky entrance. Ext/int corridors. **Pets:** $10 daily fee/pet. Service with
restrictions, supervision.
SAVE S✗ ✗ ✗ ✗ ✗ ✗

(AAA) ▼▼▼ **Rainbow Ranch Lodge** RA ✿
(406) 995-4132. **$185-$385.** 42950 Gallatin Rd. 5 mi s on US 191. Ext
corridors. **Pets:** $40 daily fee/room. Service with restrictions, supervision.
SAVE S✗ ✗ ✗ ✗ ✗ ✗ ✗

BIG TIMBER

▼▼ **Big Timber Super 8 Motel** SH
(406) 932-8888. **Call for rates.** 20A Big Timber Loop Rd. I-90, exit 367.
Int corridors. **Pets:** Accepted.
✗ ✗ ✗

▼▼ **River Valley Inn** M
(406) 932-4943. **$68-$90.** 600 W 2nd St. I-90, exit 367, just n, then 0.6
mi e. Int corridors. **Pets:** Accepted.
✗ ✗

BILLINGS

(AAA) ▼▼▼ **Best Western Clocktower Inn** SH
(406) 259-5511. **$89-$149.** 2511 1st Ave N. On I-90 business loop;
downtown. Ext/int corridors. **Pets:** Accepted.
SAVE S✗ ✗ ✗ ✗ ✗

▼▼▼ **Best Western Kelly Inn & Suites** SH
(406) 256-9400. **$119-$159.** 4915 Southgate Dr. I-90, exit 447, just w.
Ext/int corridors. **Pets:** Other species. Service with restrictions, supervision.
ASK S✗ ✗ ✗ ✗

▼▼▼ **Billings Hotel and Convention Center** SH
(406) 248-7151. **Call for rates.** 1223 Mullowney Ln. I-90, exit 446, just
s. Int corridors. **Pets:** Accepted.
✗ ✗ ✗ ✗ ✗ ✗

▼▼ **Billings Super 8 Motel** SH
(406) 248-8842. **$35-$81.** 5400 Southgate Dr. I-90, exit 447, just n on S
Billings Blvd, 0.8 mi w on King Ave, then just s on Parkway Ln. Int
corridors. **Pets:** Medium. $10 one-time fee/pet. No service, crate.
ASK S✗ ✗ ✗ ✗

(AAA) ▼▼▼ **Cherry Tree Inn** SH
(406) 252-5603. **$61.** 823 N Broadway. I-90, exit 450, 2 mi n on 27th
St, then just w on 9th Ave. Int corridors. **Pets:** Other species. Service
with restrictions, supervision.
SAVE S✗ ✗ ✗ ✗

▼▼ **Clubhouse Inn & Suites** SH
(406) 248-9800. **$93-$119.** 5610 S Frontage Rd. I-90, exit 446, just s.
Ext/int corridors. **Pets:** Accepted.
ASK S✗ ✗ ✗ ✗ ✗

▼▼ **Comfort Inn by Choice Hotels** SH
(406) 652-5200. **Call for rates.** 2030 Overland Ave. I-90, exit 446, 0.5
mi n, then just s. Int corridors. **Pets:** Accepted.
✗ ✗ ✗ ✗ ✗

Days Inn SH
(406) 252-4007. **Call for rates.** 843 Parkway Ln. I-90, exit 447, just n on S Billings Blvd, 0.8 mi w on King Ave, then just s. Int corridors. **Pets:** Accepted.

Dude Rancher Lodge M
(406) 259-5561. **Call for rates.** 415 N 29th St. Just w of the 400 block of N 27th st; downtown. Ext/int corridors. **Pets:** Accepted.

Extended StayAmerica-Billings-West End SH
(406) 245-3980. **Call for rates.** 4950 Southgate Dr. I-90, exit 447, just w. Int corridors. **Pets:** Other species. $75 one-time fee/pet. Service with restrictions.

Hilltop Inn SH
(406) 245-5000. **$65-$75.** 1116 N 28th St. I-90, exit 450, 2 mi n on 27th St, just w on 11th Ave, then just n. Int corridors. **Pets:** Other species. $7 daily fee/pet. Designated rooms, service with restrictions, supervision.

Holiday Inn Grand Montana Billings LH
(406) 248-7701. **$109-$149.** 5500 Midland Rd. I-90, exit 446. Int corridors. **Pets:** Accepted.

Kelly Inn SH
(406) 252-2700. **$69-$129.** 5425 Midland Rd. I-90, exit 446, just se. Ext/int corridors. **Pets:** Other species. Service with restrictions, crate.

Motel 6 #178 M
(406) 252-0093. **Call for rates.** 5400 Midland Rd. I-90, exit 446, just se. Ext corridors. **Pets:** Other species. Service with restrictions, supervision.

Quality Inn Homestead SH
(406) 652-1320. **$79-$199.** 2036 Overland Ave. I-90, exit 446, n on King Ave W, then just s, first stoplight. Int corridors. **Pets:** Accepted.

Red Roof Inn #269 SH
(406) 248-7551. **Call for rates.** 5353 Midland Rd. I-90, exit 446, just se. Int corridors. **Pets:** Accepted.

Rimview Inn M
(406) 248-2622. **Call for rates.** 1025 N 27th St. I-90, exit 450, 2 mi n. Ext/int corridors. **Pets:** Large, dogs only. $10 one-time fee/pet. Service with restrictions, supervision.

Riverstone Billings Inn SH
(406) 252-6800. **$65-$75.** 880 N 29th St. I-90, exit 450, 2 mi n on 27th St, then just w on 9th Ave. Int corridors. **Pets:** Other species. $7 daily fee/pet. Designated rooms, service with restrictions, supervision.

Western Executive Inn SH
(406) 294-8888. **$60-$107.** 3121 King Ave W. I-90, exit 446, 2.5 mi w. Int corridors. **Pets:** Small. $10 daily fee/pet. Service with restrictions, supervision.

BOZEMAN

Americas Best Value Inn SH
(406) 585-7888. **$68-$115.** 817 Wheat Dr. I-90, exit 306, just n. Int corridors. **Pets:** Accepted.

AmericInn Lodge & Suites SH
(406) 522-8686. **$99-$189.** 1121 Reeves Rd W. I-90, exit 305, just n. Int corridors. **Pets:** Accepted.

Best Western GranTree Inn SH
(406) 587-5261. **$99-$179.** 1325 N 7th Ave. I-90, exit 306, just s. Int corridors. **Pets:** Service with restrictions, supervision.

Bozeman Days Inn & Suites SH
(406) 587-5251. **$69-$199.** 1321 N 7th Ave. I-90, exit 306, just s. Int corridors. **Pets:** Accepted.

Bozeman Inn SH
(406) 587-3176. **$52-$92.** 1235 N 7th Ave. I-90, exit 306, just s. Ext corridors. **Pets:** $5 one-time fee/pet. Service with restrictions, supervision.

Bozeman's Western Heritage Inn SH
(406) 587-3344. **$78-$118.** 1200 E Main St. I-90 business loop, exit 309, 0.5 mi w. Int corridors. **Pets:** Dogs only. $5 daily fee/pet. Service with restrictions, supervision.

Holiday Inn Bozeman SH
(406) 587-4561. **$89-$139.** 5 E Baxter Ln. I-90, exit 306, just s of jct I-90. Int corridors. **Pets:** Other species. Service with restrictions.

Microtel Inn & Suites SH
(406) 586-3797. **$64-$105.** 612 Nikles Dr. I-90, exit 306, just ne. Int corridors. **Pets:** Accepted.

Rainbow Motel M
(406) 587-4201. **$50-$75.** 510 N 7th Ave. I-90, exit 306, 0.8 mi s. Ext corridors. **Pets:** Medium, dogs only. $10 daily fee/pet. Designated rooms, supervision.

Ramada Limited M
(406) 585-2626. **$65-$125.** 2020 Wheat Dr. I-90, exit 306, just n, then just w. Ext/int corridors. **Pets:** $10 daily fee/room. Service with restrictions, crate.

Royal "7" Budget Inn M
(406) 587-3103. **Call for rates.** 310 N 7th Ave. I-90, exit 306, 0.8 mi s. Ext corridors. **Pets:** Other species. $2 daily fee/pet. Designated rooms, service with restrictions, supervision.

Super 8 SH
(406) 586-1521. **$64-$99.** 800 Wheat Dr. I-90, exit 306, just n, then just w. Int corridors. **Pets:** Other species. $10 one-time fee/room. Service with restrictions, crate.

BROWNING

Western Motel LLC M
(406) 338-7572. **$65-$110, 4 day notice.** 121 Central Ave E. On US 2; center. Ext corridors. **Pets:** Other species. $10 daily fee/pet. Service with restrictions, supervision.

BUTTE

Best Western Butte Plaza Inn 🆂🅷
(406) 494-3500. **$95-$160.** 2900 Harrison Ave. I-90/15, exit 127 (Harrison Ave). Int corridors. **Pets:** Medium. $50 deposit/room. Designated rooms, service with restrictions, supervision.
SAVE ⓢ ⊗ 🛑 🖳 🍽 ⤳ ⊗

Butte War Bonnet Hotel 🆂🅷 🐾
(406) 494-7800. **$89-$109.** 2100 Cornell Ave. I-90/15, exit 127B (Harrison Ave), just n, then just e. Int corridors. **Pets:** Small. $25 deposit/room. Designated rooms, service with restrictions, supervision.
SAVE ⓢ ⊗ 🛑 🖳 🍽 ⤳ ⊗

Comfort Inn of Butte 🆂🅷 🐾
(406) 494-8850. **$99-$120.** 2777 Harrison Ave. I-90/15, exit 127 (Harrison Ave), just s. Int corridors. **Pets:** Other species. $5 daily fee/room. Designated rooms, service with restrictions, supervision.
SAVE ⓢ ⊗ 🛑 🖳 ⤳ ⊗

Copper King Hotel & Convention Center 🆂🅷
(406) 494-6666. **$85-$95.** 4655 Harrison Ave S. I-90/15, exit 127A (Harrison Ave), 2 mi s on SR 2. Int corridors. **Pets:** $20 one-time fee/room. Service with restrictions, supervision.
SAVE ⊗ ⅙ᴹ 🛑 🖳 🍽 ⤳ ⊗

Days Inn 🆂🅷
(406) 494-7000. **Call for rates.** 2700 Harrison Ave. I-90/15, exit 127 (Harrison Ave), just n. Int corridors. **Pets:** Accepted.
⊗ ⅙ᴹ 🛑 🖳 ⤳

Rocker Inn Ⓜ
(406) 723-5464. **$46-$57.** 122001 W Brown's Gulch Rd. I-90/15, exit 122 (Rocker). Int corridors. **Pets:** Medium. $5 daily fee/room. Designated rooms, service with restrictions, supervision.
SAVE ⊗ 🛑

Super 8 Motel of Butte 🆂🅷
(406) 494-6000. **$70-$87.** 2929 Harrison Ave. I-90/15, exit 127 (Harrison Ave), just s. Int corridors. **Pets:** Medium. $50 deposit/pet, $5 daily fee/pet. Designated rooms, service with restrictions, supervision.
SAVE ⊗

CHINOOK

Chinook Motor Inn 🆂🅷
(406) 357-2248. **$69-$79.** 100 Indiana St. On US 2. Int corridors. **Pets:** $10 daily fee/pet. Service with restrictions, supervision.
SAVE ⓢ ⊗ 🖳 🍽

CHOTEAU

Big Sky Motel Ⓜ
(406) 466-5318. **$59.** 209 S Main Ave. Just s of town center on US 89. Ext corridors. **Pets:** Large. $5 daily fee/pet. Service with restrictions.
SAVE ⓢ ⊗ 🛑 🖳

COLUMBUS

Super 8 of Columbus 🆂🅷
(406) 322-4101. **$77-$85.** 602 8th Ave N. I-90, exit 408, just s on SR 78. Int corridors. **Pets:** Accepted.
ASK ⓢ ⊗ ⅙ᴹ 🛑 🖳

CONRAD

Super 8 Motel 🆂🅷
(406) 278-7676. **$70-$77.** 215 N Main. I-15, exit 339, just w. Int corridors. **Pets:** Accepted.
ASK ⓢ ⊗ 🛑 🖳

COOKE CITY

Elk Horn Lodge Ⓜ
(406) 838-2332. **$64-$94, 7 day notice.** 103 Main St. Center. Ext corridors. **Pets:** Accepted.
⊗ 🛑 🖳 🎿 🝢

CUT BANK

Cut Bank Super 8 Ⓜ
(406) 873-5662. **$68-$88.** 609 W Main St. On US 2, 0.3 mi w. Int corridors. **Pets:** Very small, dogs only. $50 deposit/room, $10 daily fee/room. Designated rooms, service with restrictions, supervision.
SAVE ⓢ ⊗ 🛑 🖳 ⤳

Glacier Gateway Inn 🆂🅷
(406) 873-5544. **$59-$85.** 1121 E Railroad St. US 2, just e from town center. Int corridors. **Pets:** Other species. $6 daily fee/pet. Service with restrictions, supervision.
SAVE ⓢ ⊗ 🛑 🖳

DEER LODGE

Super 8 Motel Ⓜ
(406) 846-2370. **Call for rates.** 1150 N Main St. I-90, exit 184, 0.3 mi s. Int corridors. **Pets:** Accepted.
SAVE ⊗ 🛑 🖳

Western Big Sky Inn Ⓜ
(406) 846-2590. **$50-$66.** 210 N Main St. I-90, exit 184, 1 mi w. Ext corridors. **Pets:** Accepted.
ASK ⓢ ⊗ 🛑 🖳

DILLON

Best Western Paradise Inn 🆂🅷 🐾
(406) 683-4214. **$79-$120.** 650 N Montana St. I-15, exit 63, 0.3 mi s on SR 41. Ext corridors. **Pets:** Other species. $10 daily fee/room. Service with restrictions, supervision.
SAVE ⓢ ⊗ 🛑 🖳 🍽 ⤳

Comfort Inn of Dillon 🆂🅷
(406) 683-6831. **$99-$109.** 450 N Interchange. I-15, exit 63. Int corridors. **Pets:** Accepted.
ASK ⓢ ⊗ 🛑 🖳 ⤳

GuestHouse International Inns & Suites 🆂🅷
(406) 683-3636. **Call for rates.** 580 Sinclair St. I-15, exit 63. Int corridors. **Pets:** Accepted.
⊗ ⅙ᴹ 🛑 🖳 ⤳

Sundowner Motel Ⓜ
(406) 683-2375. **$41-$44.** 500 N Montana St. I-15, exit 63, just s. Ext corridors. **Pets:** Accepted.
SAVE ⊗ 🛑

Super 8 Motel 🆂🅷
(406) 683-4288. **$62-$78.** 550 N Montana St. I-15, exit 63, just n on US 91. Int corridors. **Pets:** Dogs only. $10 daily fee/pet. Designated rooms, service with restrictions, supervision.
SAVE ⓢ ⊗ 🛑

EAST GLACIER PARK

Dancing Bears Inn LLC Ⓜ
(406) 226-4402. **$49-$110, 4 day notice.** 40 Montana Ave. Just off US 2, follow signs; center. Ext/int corridors. **Pets:** Accepted.
SAVE ⓢ ⊗ 🛑

ENNIS

Fan Mountain Inn Ⓜ
(406) 682-5200. **$60-$85, 7 day notice.** 204 N Main. US 287, just nw of city center. Ext corridors. **Pets:** Medium, dogs only. $10 daily fee/pet. Designated rooms, service with restrictions, supervision.
SAVE ⊗ ⅙ᴹ 🛑

QAD Riverside Motel & Outfitters **M**
(406) 682-4240. **$50-$145, 14 day notice.** 346 Main St. US 287, east of town. Ext corridors. **Pets:** Accepted.

SAVE X 🛏 🖵 ⚿

FORSYTH

QAD WWW Best Western Sundowner Inn **M** ❀
(406) 346-2115. **Call for rates.** 1018 Front St. I-94, exit 95, 0.5 mi nw on north frontage road. Ext corridors. **Pets:** Dogs only. $10 daily fee/pet. Service with restrictions, supervision.

SAVE X 🛏 🖵

QAD WW Rails Inn Motel **SH**
(406) 346-2042. **$66-$77.** 3rd & Front sts. I-94, exit 93, just n, then 0.5 mi e on frontage road. Int corridors. **Pets:** Large, other species. $6 daily fee/pet. Service with restrictions, supervision.

SAVE Sₒ X 🛏 🍽

QAD WW Restwel Motel **M**
(406) 346-2771. **$53-$67.** 810 Front St. I-94, exit 95, 0.8 mi nw on north frontage road. Ext corridors. **Pets:** Accepted.

SAVE Sₒ X 🛏

QAD WW Westwind Motor Inn **M**
(406) 346-2038. **$61-$72.** 225 Westwind Ln. I-94, exit 93, 0.3 mi n. Int corridors. **Pets:** Large, other species. $6 daily fee/pet. Service with restrictions, supervision.

SAVE Sₒ X 🛏

GARDINER

QAD WWWW Best Western by Mammoth Hot Springs **SH**
(406) 848-7311. **Call for rates.** S Hwy 89. 0.5 mi n. Ext/int corridors. **Pets:** Other species. $10 daily fee/room. Designated rooms, service with restrictions, supervision.

SAVE X 🛏 🖵 🍽 ≈ ⚿

WW Travelodge Yellowstone Park North **M**
(406) 848-7520. **Call for rates.** 109 Hellroaring St. North entrance, just s on US 89; 0.5 mi n of Yellowstone north gate. Ext corridors. **Pets:** Accepted.

X 🖵

QAD WW Yellowstone River Motel **M**
(406) 848-7303. **$50-$95.** 14 E Park St. Just e of US 89. Ext corridors. **Pets:** Other species. $5 one-time fee/room. Service with restrictions, crate.

SAVE Sₒ X ⚙ᴹ 🛏 🖵

WWW Yellowstone Super 8-Gardiner **SH**
(406) 848-7401. **$49-$129.** Hwy 89 S. On US 89. Int corridors. **Pets:** Accepted.

ASK Sₒ X 🛏 🖵 ≈

GLASGOW

WW Cottonwood Inn **SH**
(406) 228-8213. **$68-$80.** 45 1st Ave NE. 0.5 mi e on US 2. Int corridors. **Pets:** Accepted.

ASK Sₒ X 🛏 🖵 🍽 ≈

GLENDIVE

QAD WWW Best Western Glendive Inn **SH**
(406) 377-5555. **Call for rates.** 222 N Kendrick Ave. I-94, exit 215, on I-94 business loop; downtown. Ext/int corridors. **Pets:** Medium. $10 daily fee/room. Designated rooms, service with restrictions, supervision.

SAVE X 🛏 🖵 ≈

WW Super 8 Glendive **M**
(406) 365-5671. **$55-$80.** 1904 Merrill Ave. I-94, exit 215, just n. Int corridors. **Pets:** Accepted.

ASK Sₒ X

GREAT FALLS

QAD WWW Best Western Heritage Inn **SH**
(406) 761-1900. **$99-$159.** 1700 Fox Farm Rd. I-15, exit 278, 0.8 mi e on 10th Ave S and US 87/89 and SR 3/200. Int corridors. **Pets:** Small. $15 one-time fee/room. Designated rooms, no service, supervision.

SAVE Sₒ X 🛏 🖵 🍽 ≈ ⚿

WWW Comfort Inn by Choice Hotels **SH**
(406) 454-2727. **Call for rates.** 1120 9th St S. I-15, exit 278, 3 mi e on 10th Ave S and US 87/89 and SR 3/200, then just s. Int corridors. **Pets:** Accepted.

X ⚙ᴹ 🛏 🖵 ≈

QAD WWWW Crystal Inn **SH**
(406) 727-7788. **$119-$139.** 3701 31st St SW. I-15, exit 277, just e. Int corridors. **Pets:** Large. $10 one-time fee/room. Designated rooms, service with restrictions, supervision.

SAVE Sₒ X 🛏 🖵 ≈

WWW Days Inn of Great Falls **M**
(406) 727-6565. **$60-$95.** 101 14th Ave NW. I-15, exit 280 (Central Ave), 1.3 mi e on Central Ave/Business Rt I-15, 0.8 mi n on 3rd St NW, then just w. Int corridors. **Pets:** Accepted.

ASK Sₒ X 🛏 🖵

WWW Extended StayAmerica-Great Falls **SH**
(406) 761-7524. **Call for rates.** 800 River Dr S. I-15, exit 278, 1.7 mi e on 10th Ave S, then 0.7 mi n. Int corridors. **Pets:** Other species. $75 one-time fee/pet. Service with restrictions.

X ⚙ᴹ 🛏 🖵

QAD WWW The Great Falls Inn **SH** ❀
(406) 453-6000. **$74-$84.** 1400 28th St S. I-15, exit 278, 5.3 mi e on 10th Ave S, 0.3 mi s on 26th St S, then just e on 15th Ave S. Int corridors. **Pets:** $7 daily fee/pet. Designated rooms, supervision.

SAVE Sₒ X ⚙ᴹ 🛏 🖵

WWWW Hampton Inn **SH**
(406) 453-2675. **$89-$139.** 2301 14th St SW. I-15, exit 278, just sw. Int corridors. **Pets:** Accepted.

ASK X ⚙ᴹ 🛏 🖵 ≈

QAD WWWW La Quinta Inn & Suites Great Falls **SH**
(406) 761-2600. **$89.** 600 River Dr S. I-15, exit 278, 1.7 mi e on 10th Ave S, then 0.8 mi n. Int corridors. **Pets:** Other species. Service with restrictions, supervision.

SAVE Sₒ X ⚙ᴹ 🛏 🖵 ≈ ⚿

QAD WW Motel 6 #4238 **M**
(406) 453-1602. **$59-$81.** 2 Treasure State Dr. I-15, exit 278, 0.8 mi e on 10th Ave S and US 87/89 and SR 3/200; next to Best Western. Int corridors. **Pets:** Other species. Supervision.

SAVE Sₒ X

QAD WW Quality Inn **SH**
(406) 761-3410. **$69-$89.** 220 Central Ave. Downtown. Ext/int corridors. **Pets:** Small. Service with restrictions, supervision.

SAVE Sₒ X 🛏 🖵 ≈

WW TownHouse Inn of Great Falls **SH**
(406) 761-4600. **Call for rates.** 1411 10th Ave S. I-15, exit 278, 2.6 mi e on 10th Ave S and US 87/89 and SR 3/200. Int corridors. **Pets:** Accepted.

X 🛏 🖵 ≈ ⚿

HAMILTON

QAD WWW Town House Inns **SH** ❀
(406) 363-6600. **$60-$90.** 1113 N 1st St. On US 93, north of city center. Int corridors. **Pets:** Other species. $10 daily fee/pet. Designated rooms, service with restrictions, supervision.

SAVE Sₒ X ⚙ᴹ 🛏 🖵

HARDIN

American Inn of Hardin SH
(406) 665-1870. **$50-$95.** 1324 N Crawford Ave. I-90, exit 495, just s on SR 47. Ext corridors. **Pets:** Accepted.

Western Motel M
(406) 665-2296. **Call for rates.** 830 W 3rd St. I-90, exit 495 eastbound, 1.3 mi s on SR 47 and CR 313, then just e; exit 497 westbound, 0.3 mi w on I-90 business loop, continue straight on 3rd St for 0.7 mi. Ext corridors. **Pets:** Accepted.

HARLOWTON

Countryside Inn M
(406) 632-4119. **$52-$60.** 309 3rd St NE. US 12 E. Ext corridors. **Pets:** Accepted.

HAVRE

AmericInn of Havre SH
(406) 395-5000. **Call for rates (no credit cards).** 2520 Hwy 2 W. On US 2, west side of town. Int corridors. **Pets:** Dogs only. $20 one-time fee/room. Designated rooms, service with restrictions, supervision.

HELENA

Barrister Bed & Breakfast BB
(406) 443-7330. **$114-$129, 4 day notice.** 416 N Ewing St. I-15, exit 192 (Prospect Ave), 1.5 mi sw via Prospect and Montana aves to 9th Ave, 0.8 mi w, then just s. Int corridors. **Pets:** Accepted.

Best Western Helena Great Northern Hotel SH
(406) 457-5500. **$123-$169.** 835 Great Northern Blvd. I-15, exit 193 (Cedar St), 2 mi w, just w on Lyndale Ave, then just s on Getchell; downtown. Int corridors. **Pets:** Small. $15 daily fee/pet. Designated rooms, service with restrictions, supervision.

Days Inn Helena SH
(406) 442-3280. **$69-$129.** 2001 Prospect Ave. I-15, exit 192 (Prospect Ave), just w. Int corridors. **Pets:** Accepted.

Elkhorn Mountain Inn SH
(406) 442-6625. **Call for rates.** 1 Jackson Creek Rd. I-15, exit 187 (Montana City), just w. Int corridors. **Pets:** $5 daily fee/pet. Supervision.

GuestHouse Inn & Suites SH
(406) 443-2300. **Call for rates.** 2101 E 11th Ave. I-15, exit 192B (capitol area), just sw. Ext/int corridors. **Pets:** Accepted.

Red Lion Colonial Hotel SH
(406) 443-2100. **$155.** 2301 Colonial Dr. I-15, exit 192 southbound; exit 192B northbound. Int corridors. **Pets:** Medium. $20 one-time fee/pet. Service with restrictions, crate.

Super 8 Motel SH
(406) 443-2450. **Call for rates.** 2200 11th Ave. I-15, exit 192B (capitol area) northbound; exit west business district southbound on US 12. Int corridors. **Pets:** $10 one-time fee/pet. Designated rooms, service with restrictions, supervision.

Wingate by Wyndham SH
(406) 449-3000. **$119-$139.** 2007 Oakes. I-15, exit 193 (Cedar St), just sw. Int corridors. **Pets:** Accepted.

HUNGRY HORSE

Mini Golden Inns Motel M
(406) 387-4313. **$86-$160, 30 day notice.** 8955 US 2 E. East end of town. Ext corridors. **Pets:** Accepted.

KALISPELL

Aero Inn SH
(406) 755-3798. **$49-$99.** 1830 US 93 S. 1.3 mi s on US 93 from jct US 2. Int corridors. **Pets:** $20 deposit/pet. Designated rooms, service with restrictions, supervision.

Days Inn Kalispell SH
(406) 756-3222. **Call for rates.** 1550 Hwy 93 N. 1.3 mi n on US 93 from jct US 2. Int corridors. **Pets:** Accepted.

Holiday Inn Express & Suites SH
(406) 755-7405. **Call for rates.** 275 Treeline Rd. 3 mi n on US 93 from jct US 2, just w. Int corridors. **Pets:** Accepted.

Kalispell/Glacier Int'l Airport area Super 8 Motel SH
(406) 755-1888. **Call for rates.** 1341 1st Ave E. 1.2 mi s on US 93 from jct US 2. Int corridors. **Pets:** Accepted.

Kalispell Grand Hotel SH
(406) 755-8100. **$68-$140.** 100 Main St. On US 93; downtown. Int corridors. **Pets:** Accepted.

La Quinta Inn & Suites Kalispell SH
(406) 257-5255. **$174.** 255 Montclair Dr. Jct US 93 and 2, 1 mi e. Int corridors. **Pets:** Other species. Service with restrictions, supervision.

The Outlaw Inn SH
(406) 755-6100. **$60-$189, 3 day notice.** 1701 Hwy 93 S. 1.4 mi s on US 93 from jct US 2. Int corridors. **Pets:** Accepted.

Red Lion Hotel Kalispell SH
(406) 751-5050. **$199.** 20 N Main St. Just s on US 93 from jct of US 2; connected to Kalispell Center Mall. Int corridors. **Pets:** Large. $20 one-time fee/pet. Designated rooms, service with restrictions, supervision.

Rodeway Inn SH
(406) 755-6700. **Call for rates.** 1330 Hwy 2 W. 1 mi w on US 2 from jct US 93. Int corridors. **Pets:** Accepted.

Travelodge SH
(406) 755-6123. **$59-$119.** 350 N Main St. US 93, just n of jct US 2. Ext/int corridors. **Pets:** Accepted.

LAKESIDE

Bayshore Resort Motel Inc M
(406) 844-3131. **$55-$115.** 616 Lakeside Blvd. On US 93; center. Ext corridors. **Pets:** Accepted.

LAUREL

Best Western Yellowstone Crossing SH
(406) 628-6888. **$72-$108.** 205 SE 4th St. I-90, exit 434, just n, then just e. Int corridors. **Pets:** Medium. $10 daily fee/pet. Designated rooms, service with restrictions, supervision.

[SAVE] [S🐾] [X] [&M] [🍴] [💻] [🏊]

LEWISTOWN

B & B Motel M
(406) 535-5496. **$50-$80.** 520 E Main St. Downtown. Ext corridors.
Pets: Accepted.

[SAVE] [X] [🍴]

LIBBY

Caboose Motel and Sportsman Information Center M
(406) 293-6201. **$55-$75.** 714 W 9th St. Just w on US 2 from jct SR 37. Ext corridors. **Pets:** Accepted.

[A$K] [X] [🍴] [💻]

Sandman Motel M
(406) 293-8831. **$55-$80.** 688 US Hwy 2 W. Just w on US 2 from jct SR 37. Ext corridors. **Pets:** Accepted.

[A$K] [S🐾] [X] [🍴]

Super 8 Motel SH
(406) 293-2771. **Call for rates.** 448 US 2 W. Just w on US 2 from jct SR 37. Int corridors. **Pets:** Accepted.

[SAVE] [X] [🍴] [🏊]

LINCOLN

Leeper's Ponderosa Motel M ❀
(406) 362-4333. **$61-$78 (no credit cards).** Hwy 200 & 1st Ave. On SR 200, just w. Ext corridors. **Pets:** Other species. $5 daily fee/room. Service with restrictions, supervision.

[SAVE] [S🐾] [X] [🍴] [💻] [AC]

LIVINGSTON

Best Western Yellowstone Inn & Conference Center SH ❀
(406) 222-6110. **$79-$135.** 1515 W Park St. I-90, exit 333, just n. Int corridors. **Pets:** Medium, other species. $10 daily fee/pet. Service with restrictions, supervision.

[SAVE] [S🐾] [X] [🍴] [💻] [🏊]

Livingston Rodeway Inn M
(406) 222-6320. **$70-$125.** 102 Rogers Ln. I-90, exit 333, just n on US 89, then just w. Ext/int corridors. **Pets:** Accepted.

[A$K] [S🐾] [X] [🍴] [💻] [🍴] [🏊]

Quality Inn SH
(406) 222-0555. **$69-$160.** 111 Rogers Ln. I-90, exit 333, just n on US 89, then just w. Int corridors. **Pets:** Accepted.

[A$K] [S🐾] [X] [&M] [🍴] [💻] [🏊]

MALTA

Maltana Motel M
(406) 654-2610. **$69-$109.** 138 S 1st Ave W. Just s of US 2 via US 191, just w; downtown. Ext corridors. **Pets:** Dogs only. $10 one-time fee/room. Service with restrictions, supervision.

[SAVE] [X] [🍴] [💻]

MILES CITY

Best Western War Bonnet Inn SH ❀
(406) 234-4560. **$70-$150, 5 day notice.** 1015 S Haynes Ave. I-94, exit 138 (Broadus), 0.3 mi n. Ext corridors. **Pets:** Other species. $5 daily fee/pet. Service with restrictions, supervision.

[SAVE] [S🐾] [X] [🍴] [💻] [🏊] [X]

GuestHouse International Inn & Suites SH
(406) 232-3661. **Call for rates.** 3111 Steel St. I-94, exit 138 (Broadus), just s. Int corridors. **Pets:** Accepted.

[X] [&M] [🍴] [💻] [🏊]

MISSOULA

Best Western Grant Creek Inn SH ❀
(406) 543-0700. **$119-$219.** 5280 Grant Creek Rd. I-90, exit 101 (Reserve St), just n. Int corridors. **Pets:** Small. $10 daily fee/room. Service with restrictions, supervision.

[SAVE] [S🐾] [X] [&M] [🍴] [💻] [🏊] [X]

Broadway Inn Conference Center SH
(406) 532-3300. **$99-$119.** 1609 W Broadway. I-90, exit 104 (Orange St), 0.5 mi s, then 1 mi w. Int corridors. **Pets:** Accepted.

[SAVE] [S🐾] [X] [🍴] [💻] [🍴] [🏊]

Campus Inn M
(406) 549-5134. **$50-$100.** 744 E Broadway. I-90, exit 105 (Van Buren St), just s to Broadway, then just w. Ext/int corridors. **Pets:** Accepted.

[A$K] [X] [🍴] [🏊]

Comfort Inn SH
(406) 542-0888. **$79-$169.** 4545 N Reserve St. I-90, exit 101 (Reserve St), 0.5 mi s. Int corridors. **Pets:** Accepted.

[A$K] [S🐾] [X] [&M] [🍴] [💻] [🏊]

Days Inn/Missoula Airport SH
(406) 721-9776. **Call for rates.** 8600 Truck Stop Rd. I-90, exit 96, just n. Int corridors. **Pets:** Accepted.

[SAVE] [X] [💻]

Days Inn University SH
(406) 543-7221. **Call for rates.** 201 E Main St. I-90, exit 104 (Orange St), 0.5 mi s to Broadway, 0.5 mi e to Washington, just s to Main St, then just w. Int corridors. **Pets:** Very small, dogs only. $20 daily fee/pet. Service with restrictions, supervision.

[SAVE] [X] [🍴] [💻] [🏊]

Doubletree Hotel Missoula/Edgewater SH
(406) 728-3100. **Call for rates.** 100 Madison. I-90, exit 105 (Van Buren St), just s, then w on Front St. Int corridors. **Pets:** Accepted.

[SAVE] [X] [&M] [💻] [🍴] [🏊]

Econo Lodge SH
(406) 542-7550. **$75-$120.** 4953 N Reserve St. I-90 W, exit 101 (Reserve St), just s. Int corridors. **Pets:** Medium, other species. $10 daily fee/pet. Designated rooms, service with restrictions.

[SAVE] [S🐾] [X] [🍴] [💻]

Family Inn M ❀
(406) 543-7371. **$70-$86.** 1031 E Broadway. I-90, exit 105 (Van Buren St), just s, then just e. Ext corridors. **Pets:** $10 daily fee/room. Supervision.

[SAVE] [S🐾] [X] [🍴] [💻] [🏊]

Hampton Inn SH ❀
(406) 549-1800. **Call for rates.** 4805 N Reserve St. I-90, exit 101 (Reserve St), just s. Int corridors. **Pets:** Other species. $15 one-time fee/room. Designated rooms, supervision.

[X] [&M] [🍴] [💻] [🏊]

Holiday Inn Missoula-Downtown at the Park SH ❀
(406) 721-8550. **$129-$189.** 200 S Pattee St. I-90, exit 104 (Orange St), 0.5 mi s to Broadway, just e to Pattee St, then just s. Int corridors. **Pets:** Other species. $20 one-time fee/pet. Designated rooms, service with restrictions, supervision.

[SAVE] [S🐾] [X] [🍴] [💻] [🍴] [🏊] [X]

▼▼▼ **Microtel Inn & Suites** SH
(406) 543-0959. **Call for rates.** 5059 N Reserve St. I-90, exit 101 (Reserve St), just s. Int corridors. **Pets:** Accepted.
⊠ Ⓛᴹ 🖥 💻

ⓐⓐⓐ⁄ ▼ **Ponderosa Lodge** M
(406) 543-3102. **$50-$80.** 800 E Broadway. I-90, exit 105 (Van Buren St), just s to Broadway, then w. Ext/int corridors. **Pets:** Accepted.
SAVE Ⓢ▵ ⊠ 🖥

ⓐⓐⓐ⁄ ▼▼ **Quality Inn & Conference Center** SH
(406) 251-2665. **$85-$130.** 3803 Brooks St. I-90, exit 101 (Reserve St), 5 mi s to Brooks St, then just w. Int corridors. **Pets:** Medium, other species. $10 daily fee/pet. Designated rooms, service with restrictions.
SAVE Ⓢ▵ ⊠ Ⓛᴹ 🖥 💻

ⓐⓐⓐ⁄ ▼▼▼ **Red Lion Inn** SH
(406) 728-3300. **$149.** 700 W Broadway. I-90, exit 104 (Orange St), just s, then just w. Ext corridors. **Pets:** Accepted.
SAVE Ⓢ▵ ⊠ 🖥 💻 🏊

ⓐⓐⓐ⁄ ▼▼ **Redwood Lodge** M
(406) 721-2110. **$60-$120.** 8060 Hwy 93 N. I-90, exit 96, just s. Ext corridors. **Pets:** Other species. $5 daily fee/pet. Service with restrictions, supervision.
SAVE Ⓢ▵ ⊠ 🖥

ⓐⓐⓐ⁄ ▼▼▼ **Ruby's Inn & Convention Center** SH
(406) 721-0990. **$60-$120.** 4825 N Reserve St. I-90, exit 101 (Reserve St), just s. Ext/int corridors. **Pets:** Large, other species. $10 one-time fee/pet. Service with restrictions, supervision.
SAVE Ⓢ▵ ⊠ Ⓛᴹ 🖥 💻 🏊 ✕

▼▼ **Sleep Inn by Choice Hotels** SH
(406) 543-5883. **Call for rates.** 3425 Dore Ln. I-90, exit 101 (Reserve St), 5 mi s, then just e on Brooks St. Int corridors. **Pets:** Accepted.
⊠ Ⓛᴹ 🖥 💻 🏊

ⓐⓐⓐ⁄ ▼▼ **Southgate Inn** SH
(406) 251-2250. **$60-$125.** 3530 Brooks St. I-90, exit 101 (Reserve St), 5 mi s to Brooks St, then just e. Ext corridors. **Pets:** Other species. $10 daily fee/pet. Designated rooms, supervision.
SAVE Ⓢ▵ ⊠ 🖥 🏊 ✕

▼▼▼ **Super 8-Brooks St** SH
(406) 251-2255. **Call for rates.** 3901 Brooks St. I-90, exit 101 (Reserve St), 5 mi s to Brooks St, then just w. Int corridors. **Pets:** Accepted.
⊠ 🖥

ⓐⓐⓐ⁄ ▼ **Travelers Inn Motel Inc** M
(406) 728-8330. **$56-$78.** 4850 N Reserve St. I-90, exit 101 (Reserve St), just s. Ext corridors. **Pets:** Small, dogs only. $5 daily fee/pet. Designated rooms, service with restrictions, supervision.
SAVE Ⓢ▵ ⊠ 🖥

OVANDO

▼▼▼ **Lake Upsata Guest Ranch** RA
(406) 793-5890. **Call for rates.** 201 Lower Lakeside Ln. 7.5 mi w on SR 200 to MM 38, 3.4 mi n on Woodworth Rd, then 1 mi e. Ext corridors. **Pets:** Accepted.
⊠ 🖥 💻 ✕ Ⓚ 🄿 🄯

POLSON

ⓐⓐⓐ⁄ ▼▼▼ **Best Western KwaTaqNuk Resort** SH 🐾
(406) 883-3636. **$79-$145, 3 day notice.** 49708 US Hwy 93 E. Just s of downtown. Int corridors. **Pets:** Medium, dogs only. $25 daily fee/pet. Designated rooms, service with restrictions, crate.
SAVE Ⓢ▵ ⊠ Ⓛᴹ 🖥 💻 🏊 ✕

RED LODGE

ⓐⓐⓐ⁄ ▼▼▼ **Beartooth Hideaway Inn & Cabins** M
(406) 446-2288. **Call for rates.** 1223 S Broadway Ave. Just s on US 212. Ext/int corridors. **Pets:** Other species. $5 daily fee/pet. Designated rooms, service with restrictions, supervision.
SAVE ⊠ 🖥 💻 🏊

▼▼ **Best Western Lu Pine Inn** SH
(406) 446-1321. **Call for rates.** 702 S Hauser. 0.4 mi s, just w of US 212. Int corridors. **Pets:** Accepted.
⊠ 🖥 💻 🏊 ✕

▼▼ **Comfort Inn of Red Lodge** SH
(406) 446-4469. **$60-$160.** 612 N Broadway. Jct US 212 and SR 78, north entrance. Int corridors. **Pets:** Accepted.
ASK Ⓢ▵ ⊠ Ⓛᴹ 🖥 💻 🏊

▼▼ **Yodeler Motel** M
(406) 446-1435. **$55-$139.** 601 S Broadway. Just s on US 212. Ext corridors. **Pets:** Accepted.
ASK Ⓢ▵ ⊠ 🖥 💻

RONAN

▼▼ **Starlite Motel** M
(406) 676-7000. **$50-$74.** 18 Main St SW. Just w of jct US 93 and Main St. Ext corridors. **Pets:** Accepted.
ASK ⊠ 🖥 💻

ST. IGNATIUS

▼▼ **Sunset Motel** M
(406) 745-3900. **$60-$80.** 333 Mountain View. Just s of downtown, exit on US 93. Ext corridors. **Pets:** Dogs only. $5 daily fee/pet. Service with restrictions, supervision.
ASK Ⓢ▵ ⊠ 🖥

ST. REGIS

ⓐⓐⓐ⁄ ▼▼ **Little River Motel** M
(406) 649-2713. **$45-$80.** 50 Old US Hwy 10 W. I-90, exit 33, just n to flashing light, just w, then just sw. Ext corridors. **Pets:** Small. $5 daily fee/pet. Designated rooms, service with restrictions, supervision.
SAVE Ⓢ▵ ⊠ 🖥 Ⓚ 🄯

ⓐⓐⓐ⁄ ▼▼ **Super 8 Motel-St. Regis** SH
(406) 649-2422. **$67-$88.** 9 Old Hwy 10 E. I-90, exit 33, just n. Ext/int corridors. **Pets:** Accepted.
SAVE ⊠ 🖥 💻

SHELBY

▼▼ **Comfort Inn of Shelby** SH
(406) 434-2212. **$99-$109.** 455 McKinley Ave. I-15, exit 363, just e, then just s. Int corridors. **Pets:** Accepted.
ASK Ⓢ▵ ⊠ 🖥 💻 ✕

ⓐⓐⓐ⁄ ▼ **O'Haire Manor Motel** M
(406) 434-5555. **$52-$80.** 204 2nd St S. Just s of Main St via Maple St. Ext/int corridors. **Pets:** $5 daily fee/pet. Designated rooms, service with restrictions, supervision.
SAVE Ⓢ▵ ⊠ 🖥 💻

SHERIDAN

▼▼ **Moriah Motel** M
(406) 842-5491. **$62-$78.** 220 S Main St. On SR 287; center. Ext corridors. **Pets:** Accepted.
ASK ⊠ 🖥

SIDNEY

ⓐⓐⓐ⁄ ▼▼▼ **Richland Motor Inn** M
(406) 433-6400. **$86.** 1200 S Central Ave. 1.5 mi n of jct SR 200 and 16. Int corridors. **Pets:** Accepted.
SAVE ⊠ 🖥 💻

SUPERIOR

Budget Host Big Sky Motel M
(406) 822-4831. **$50-$75.** 103 4th Ave E. I-90, exit 47, just n. Ext corridors. **Pets:** Accepted.

THOMPSON FALLS

The Riverfront M
(406) 827-3460. **$45-$125.** 4907 Hwy 200 W. 1 mi w of city center. Ext corridors. **Pets:** Medium. $7 daily fee/pet. Service with restrictions, supervision.

THREE FORKS

Broken Spur Motel M
(406) 285-3237. **$56-$79.** 124 W Elm (Hwy 2). I-90, exit 278 westbound, 1.3 mi sw; exit 274 eastbound, 1 mi s on SR 287 to jct SR 2, then 3 mi se. Ext corridors. **Pets:** Accepted.

Fort Three Forks Motel & RV Park M
(406) 285-3233. **$56-$120.** 10776 Hwy 287. I-90, exit 274. Ext corridors. **Pets:** Other species. $5 one-time fee/pet. Designated rooms, service with restrictions, supervision.

VICTOR

Wildlife Adventures Guest Ranch RA
(406) 642-3262. **$125-$185, 7 day notice.** 1765 Pleasant View Dr. Jct US 93 and Fifth St, 0.9 mi w, 3.2 mi s. Int corridors. **Pets:** Accepted.

WEST YELLOWSTONE

Best Western Cross Winds Motor Inn SH ❀
(406) 646-9557. **$79-$165, 3 day notice.** 201 Firehole Ave. Just w of US 191 and 287, on US 20 at Dunraven St and Firehole Ave. Ext corridors. **Pets:** Designated rooms, service with restrictions, supervision.

Best Western Desert Inn SH ❀
(406) 646-7376. **$79-$200, 3 day notice.** 133 Canyon Ave. US 191 at US 20; corner of Canyon and Firehole aves. Int corridors. **Pets:** Designated rooms, service with restrictions, supervision.

Brandin' Iron Inn SH
(406) 646-9411. **$79-$129.** 201 Canyon Ave. Just w and n of park entrance. Ext corridors. **Pets:** Other species. $15 one-time fee/room. Designated rooms, no service, crate.

City Center Motel M
(406) 646-7337. **$59-$89, 3 day notice.** 214 Madison Ave. W off US 191 at Madison Ave and Dunraven St; just nw of park entrance. Ext corridors. **Pets:** Other species. $15 one-time fee/room. Service with restrictions, supervision.

ClubHouse Inn SH
(406) 646-4892. **$89-$199.** 105 S Electric St. Just sw of jct US 191, 187 and 20; just w of park entrance. Int corridors. **Pets:** Other species. Service with restrictions, crate.

Gray Wolf Inn & Suites SH
(406) 646-0000. **$79-$179.** 250 S Canyon Ave. Just w of Yellowstone National Park entrance. Int corridors. **Pets:** Other species. $50 deposit/room. Designated rooms, service with restrictions, supervision.

Holiday Inn SunSpree Resort West Yellowstone Conference Hotel SH
(406) 646-7365. **$99-$179.** 315 Yellowstone Ave. Just w of park entrance. Int corridors. **Pets:** Accepted.

Kelly Inn SH
(406) 646-4544. **$89-$199.** 104 S Canyon Ave. S of jct US 191, 287 and 20; just w of park entrance. Ext/int corridors. **Pets:** Other species. Service with restrictions, crate.

Stage Coach Inn SH
(406) 646-7381. **$59-$169.** 209 Madison Ave. Corner of Dunraven St and Madison Ave, just w of park entrance. Ext/int corridors. **Pets:** Other species. $50 deposit/room. Designated rooms, service with restrictions.

The Three Bear Lodge M
(406) 646-7353. **$74-$115.** 217 Yellowstone Ave. Just w of park entrance. Ext/int corridors. **Pets:** $15 daily fee/pet. Service with restrictions, supervision.

Yellowstone Lodge SH
(406) 646-0020. **$69-$169.** 251 S Electric St. Just w of park entrance. Int corridors. **Pets:** $50 deposit/pet. Designated rooms, service with restrictions, crate.

WHITEFISH

Best Western Rocky Mountain Lodge SH ❀
(406) 862-2569. **Call for rates.** 6510 Hwy 93 S. 1.3 mi s on US 93 from jct SR 487. Ext/int corridors. **Pets:** $20 one-time fee/room. Designated rooms, service with restrictions, supervision.

Kristianna Mountain Homes CO ❀
(406) 862-2860. **$125-$1100, 30 day notice.** 3842 Winter Ln. Jct US 93 and SR 487, 2.4 mi n on SR 487, at flashing light go 5.2 mi on Big Mountain Rd, just n on Gelande, then just w on Kristanna Close. Ext/int corridors. **Pets:** Medium, dogs only. $20 daily fee/pet. Designated rooms, service with restrictions.

North Forty Resort CA
(406) 862-7740. **Call for rates.** 3765 Hwy 40 W. 2.5 mi e on SR 40 from jct US 93. Ext corridors. **Pets:** Accepted.

Pine Lodge SH
(406) 862-7600. **$79-$170.** 920 Spokane Ave. 1 mi s on US 93. Int corridors. **Pets:** Service with restrictions, supervision.

Super 8 Motel SH
(406) 862-8255. **Call for rates.** 800 Spokane Ave. 1 mi s on US 93 from jct SR 487. Int corridors. **Pets:** Accepted.

WHITE SULPHUR SPRINGS

AAA ◆◆ All Seasons Inn & Suites **M** ❀
(406) 547-8888. **$65-$140.** 808 3rd Ave SW. On US 89, south end of town. Int corridors. **Pets:** $10 one-time fee/pet. Service with restrictions, supervision.
[SAVE] [S/D] [X] [&M] [▪]

WIBAUX

AAA ◆ Beaver Creek Inn & Suites **M**
(406) 796-2666. **$78-$125.** 400 W 2nd Ave N. I-94, exit 241 westbound; exit 242 eastbound. Int corridors. **Pets:** Other species. $8 daily fee/pet. Designated rooms, service with restrictions, supervision.
[SAVE] [S/D] [X] [▪] [▭]

AINSWORTH

 Comfort Inn ▩
(402) 387-1050. **Call for rates.** 1124 E 4th St. 0.5 mi e on US 20. Int corridors. **Pets:** Accepted.

▼ Super 8 Motel ▩
(402) 387-0700. **Call for rates.** 1025 E 4th St. 0.5 mi e on US 20. Int corridors. **Pets:** Other species. $50 deposit/room, $10 one-time fee/room. Service with restrictions, crate.

BEATRICE

▼▼ Beatrice Super 8 Motel ▩
(402) 228-8808. **Call for rates.** 3721 N 6th St. 1 mi n on US 77. Int corridors. **Pets:** Accepted.

▼▼▼ Holiday Inn Express Hotel & Suites ▩
(402) 228-7000. **$95.** 4005 N 6th St. 1 mi n on US 77. Int corridors. **Pets:** Accepted.

BELLEVUE

▼▼ Settle Inn and Suites ▩
(402) 292-1155. **$69-$175.** 2105 Pratt Ave. US 75, exit Cornhusker, just w. Int corridors. **Pets:** Accepted.

BROKEN BOW

▼▼ Americas Best Value Inn & Suites ▩
(308) 872-6428. **$66-$83.** 215 E South E St. On SR 2/92, just e of town. Ext/int corridors. **Pets:** Accepted.

▼▼▼ The Arrow Hotel ▩
(308) 872-6662. **$95-$150.** 509 S 9th Ave. On SR 2/92; downtown. Int corridors. **Pets:** Other species. $10 daily fee/room. Designated rooms, service with restrictions.

CENTRAL CITY

▼▼ Super 8 Motel ▩
(308) 946-5055. **Call for rates.** 1701 31st St. SR 14, 1 mi s of jct US 30. Ext/int corridors. **Pets:** Accepted.

CHADRON

▼▼▼ Best Western West Hills Inn ▩
(308) 432-3305. **$51-$150.** 1100 W 10th St. Just s of jct US 385 and 20. Ext/int corridors. **Pets:** $15 one-time fee/room. Service with restrictions, crate.

▼ Grand Westerner Motel ▥
(308) 432-5595. **$55-$64.** 1050 W Hwy 20. 0.8 mi w on US 20; just e of jct US 385. Ext corridors. **Pets:** Accepted.

▼▼▼ Motel 6 of Chadron #4259 ▩
(308) 432-3000. **$45-$75.** 755 Microtel Dr. Just s of jct US 385 and 20. Int corridors. **Pets:** Other species. Service with restrictions, supervision.

▼▼ Westerner Motel ▥
(308) 432-5577. **$55-$64.** 300 Oak St. On US 20, 0.5 mi e of jct US 385 and SR 87. Ext corridors. **Pets:** Other species. $5 one-time fee/pet. Designated rooms, service with restrictions, supervision.

COLUMBUS

▼▼ Sleep Inn & Suites Hotel ▩
(402) 562-5200. **$77-$130.** 303 23rd St. On US 30, 2 mi e of jct US 30 and 81; east side of town. Int corridors. **Pets:** Accepted.

▼▼ Super 8 Motel-Columbus ▩
(402) 563-3456. **$50-$56.** 3324 20th St. On US 30 and 81, just s. Int corridors. **Pets:** Small. $10 daily fee/pet. Designated rooms, no service, crate.

COZAD

▼▼ Rodeway Inn ▩
(308) 784-4900. **$50-$85.** 809 S Meridian. I-80, exit 222, just n. Int corridors. **Pets:** Medium, other species. Service with restrictions, supervision.

CRETE

▼▼ Super 8 Motel ▩
(402) 826-3600. **$55-$65.** 1880 W 12th St. 1.3 mi sw at jct SR 33/103; west end of town. Int corridors. **Pets:** Accepted.

FULLERTON

▼▼▼ Fullerton Inn ▥
(308) 536-2699. **$56-$60.** 1007 Johnson St. Just s of center, on SR 14. Int corridors. **Pets:** Accepted.

GERING

▼▼ Microtel Inn & Suites ▩
(308) 436-1950. **Call for rates.** 1130 M St. On SR 92, 1 mi e of SR 71. Int corridors. **Pets:** Accepted.

GOTHENBURG

AAA ▼▼▼ **Gothenburg Super 8** 🆂🅷
(308) 537-2684. **$52-$72.** 401 Platte River Dr. I-80, exit 211 (SR 47), just n. Int corridors. **Pets:** Accepted.
SAVE ⊠ 🛏 💷 🏊

GRAND ISLAND

▼▼▼ **Holiday Inn-Interstate 80** 🆂🅷
(308) 384-7770. **$59-$129.** 7838 S US Hwy 281. I-80, exit 312 (US 281), just s. Int corridors. **Pets:** Accepted.
ASK ⊠ 🖢 🛏 💷 🍴 🏊 ⊠

▼ **Rodeway Inn** 🅼
(308) 384-1333. **Call for rates.** 3205 S Locust St. I-80, exit 314, 4 mi s. Int corridors. **Pets:** Accepted.
⊠ 🛏 💷

▼▼ **Super 8 Motel** 🆂🅷
(308) 384-4380. **Call for rates.** 2603 S Locust St. I-80, exit 314, 4.7 mi n. Int corridors. **Pets:** Accepted.
⊠ 🛏 💷 🏊

▼▼ **Travelodge** 🆂🅷
(308) 382-5003. **Call for rates.** 1311 S Locust St. I-80, exit 314 (US 281), 5.2 mi n. Int corridors. **Pets:** Accepted.
⊠ 🛏 💷

HASTINGS

AAA ▼▼▼ **Holiday Inn-Hastings** 🆂🅷
(402) 463-6721. **Call for rates.** 2205 Osborne Dr E. Jct US 34 and 281, 2 mi n. Ext/int corridors. **Pets:** Accepted.
SAVE ⊠ 🖢 🛏 💷 🍴 🏊 ⊠

▼ **Midlands Lodge** 🅼
(402) 463-2428. **Call for rates.** 910 W J St. Jct US 6, 34 and 281. Ext corridors. **Pets:** Accepted.
⊠ 🛏 🏊

▼▼ **Super 8** 🆂🅷
(402) 463-8888. **$54-$84.** 2200 N Kansas Ave. Jct US 34 and 281, 2 mi n. Int corridors. **Pets:** Accepted.
ASK 🆂🅾 ⊠ 🛏 💷

HOLDREGE

▼▼ **Super 8** 🆂🅷
(308) 995-2793. **Call for rates.** 420 Broadway. US 183, 0.5 mi w on US 6/34. Int corridors. **Pets:** Accepted.
⊠ 🛏 💷 🏊

KEARNEY

AAA ▼▼▼ **AmericInn Lodge & Suites of Kearney** 🆂🅷
(308) 234-7800. **$80-$105.** 215 W Talmadge Rd. I-80, exit 272 (SR 44), just n. Int corridors. **Pets:** Medium, dogs only. $10 daily fee/pet. Designated rooms, service with restrictions, supervision.
SAVE 🆂🅾 ⊠ 🖢 🛏 💷 🏊

AAA ▼▼▼ **Best Western Inn of Kearney** 🆂🅷 ❀
(308) 237-5185. **$69-$109.** 1010 3rd Ave. I-80, exit 272 (SR 44), 1 mi n, then just w. Ext/int corridors. **Pets:** Large, other species. $15 one-time fee/room. Supervision.
SAVE 🆂🅾 ⊠ 🛏 💷 🍴 🏊 ⊠

▼▼ **Fairfield Inn-Kearney** 🆂🅷 ❀
(308) 237-0838. **$84-$104.** 121 3rd Ave. I-80, exit 272 (SR 44), 0.3 mi n. Int corridors. **Pets:** Medium, other species. $25 one-time fee/room. Designated rooms, service with restrictions, supervision.
ASK 🆂🅾 ⊠ 🛏 💷 🏊

▼▼ **Super 8 Motel** 🅼 ❀
(308) 234-5513. **$54-$84.** 15 W 8th St. I-80, exit 272 (SR44), 1 mi n, then just e. Int corridors. **Pets:** Dogs only. $10 one-time fee/room. Designated rooms, service with restrictions, supervision.
SAVE 🆂🅾 ⊠ 🛏 💷

KIMBALL

▼▼ **Days Inn-Kimball** 🅼
(308) 235-4671. **Call for rates.** 611 E 3rd St. I-80, exit 20, 1.5 ne on SR 71, then 0.5 mi e on US 30. Ext corridors. **Pets:** Accepted.
⊠ 🛏 💷

LEXINGTON

▼▼ **Days Inn** 🆂🅷
(308) 324-6440. **Call for rates.** 2506 Plum Creek Pkwy. I-80, exit 237 (US 283), 0.6 mi n. Int corridors. **Pets:** Accepted.
⊠ 🛏

AAA ▼▼▼ **Holiday Inn Express Hotel & Suites** 🆂🅷
(308) 324-9900. **Call for rates.** 2605 Plum Creek Pkwy. I-80, exit 237 (US 283), 0.5 mi n. Int corridors. **Pets:** Other species. $11 daily fee/room. Designated rooms, service with restrictions, supervision.
SAVE ⊠ 🖢 🛏 💷 🏊

LINCOLN

AAA ▼▼▼ **Best Western Crown Inn** 🆂🅷
(402) 438-4700. **$79-$145.** 6501 N 28th St. I-80, exit 403 (27th St), 0.3 mi s via Wildcat Dr. Int corridors. **Pets:** Medium, dogs only. $15 daily fee/room. Service with restrictions, supervision.
SAVE 🆂🅾 ⊠ 🛏 💷 🏊

▼▼▼ **Candlewood Suites** 🆂🅷
(402) 420-0330. **$86-$130.** 4100 Pioneer Woods Dr. 4.6 mi e on SR 2, 2.2 mi n via 70th St, e on Pioneers Blvd, then just n. Int corridors. **Pets:** Accepted.
ASK 🆂🅾 ⊠ 🖢 🛏 💷

AAA ▼▼▼▼ **Chase Suites Hotel** 🆂🅷 ❀
(402) 483-4900. **Call for rates.** 200 S 68th St Pl. On US 34, 4.3 mi e, just s of jct 68th St. Ext corridors. **Pets:** Other species. $200 deposit/room, $5 daily fee/pet. Designated rooms, service with restrictions.
SAVE ⊠ 🖢 🛏 💷 🏊 ⊠

AAA ▼ **Cobbler Inn** 🆂🅷
(402) 475-4800. **$49-$75.** 4808 West O St. I-80, exit 395. Int corridors. **Pets:** Medium, other species. $7 daily fee/pet. Designated rooms, service with restrictions, supervision.
SAVE ⊠ 💷

▼▼ **Comfort Suites** 🆂🅷
(402) 476-8080. **Call for rates.** 4231 Industrial Ave. I-80, exit 403 (27th St), 2.3 mi s. Int corridors. **Pets:** Accepted.
⊠ 🛏 💷 🏊

AAA ▼▼▼▼ **Country Inns & Suites By Carlson** 🆂🅷
(402) 476-5353. **$99-$139.** 5353 N 27th St. I-80, exit 403 (27th St), 1.5 mi s. Int corridors. **Pets:** $75 deposit/room, $10 daily fee/pet. Service with restrictions, supervision.
SAVE 🆂🅾 ⊠ 🖢 🛏 💷 🍴 🏊 ⊠

AAA ▼▼▼ **Countryside Suites** 🆂🅷
(402) 742-7575. **$70-$85.** 6750 Wildcat Dr. I-80, exit 403 (27th St), just s, then e. Int corridors. **Pets:** Very small, dogs only. $20 deposit/pet, $10 daily fee/pet. Service with restrictions, crate.
SAVE 🆂🅾 ⊠ 🖢 🛏 💷 🏊

AAA ▼▼▼ **Days Inn South** 🆂🅷
(402) 423-7111. **Call for rates.** 1140 Calvert St. 2.5 mi s on SR 2. Ext/int corridors. **Pets:** Medium, dogs only. $5 daily fee/pet. Designated rooms, service with restrictions, supervision.
SAVE ⊠ 🛏 💷

⚛ ▽▽ Econo Lodge M
(402) 475-4511. **$49-$79.** 1140 W Cornhusker Hwy. I-80, exit 399 (Airport), just w. Ext/int corridors. **Pets:** Medium, dogs only. $10 daily fee/pet. Service with restrictions, supervision.
[SAVE] [✕] [⊟] [▭]

⚛ ▽▽▽ Holiday Inn Express SH ❀
(402) 435-0200. **$85-$90.** 1133 Belmont Ave. I-80, exit 401; exit 401A; 2 mi s on I-180, exit 2 (Cornhusker Hwy e), then just n on 11th St. Int corridors. **Pets:** Service with restrictions, supervision.
[SAVE] [S✿] [✕] [⚷M] [⊟] [▭] [➣] [✕]

▽▽ New Victorian Suites SH
(402) 464-4400. **$69-$129.** 216 N 48th St. 2.5 mi e on US 6 and 34; just ne of jct O St; entrance off 48th St. Int corridors. **Pets:** Accepted.
[ASK] [S✿] [✕] [⊟] [▭]

▽▽ Ramada Limited-South SH
(402) 423-3131. **$75-$95.** 1511 Center Park Rd. I-80, exit 397 (US 77), 5.7 mi s, then 1.7 mi ne on SR L55W. Int corridors. **Pets:** Accepted.
[ASK] [S✿] [✕] [⊟] [▭] [➣]

▽▽ Settle Inn & Suites SH
(402) 435-8100. **$69-$109.** 7333 Husker Cir. I-80, exit 403 (27th St), just s to Wildcat Dr, just e, then just n. Int corridors. **Pets:** Accepted.
[✕] [⚷M] [⊟] [▭]

▽▽▽ Staybridge Suites Lincoln-I-80 SH
(402) 438-7829. **$120-$295.** 2701 Fletcher Ave. I-80, exit 403 (27th St), 0.4 mi s. Int corridors. **Pets:** Accepted.
[ASK] [✕] [⚷M] [⊟] [▭] [➣] [✕]

▽▽ Super 8 Motel-Lincoln/Cornhusker SH ❀
(402) 467-4488. **$49-$80.** 2545 Cornhusker Hwy. I-80, exit 403 (27th St), 2.5 mi s. Int corridors. **Pets:** Medium, dogs only. $10 one-time fee/room. Service with restrictions, supervision.
[ASK] [S✿] [✕] [⚷M] [⊟] [▭]

⚛ ▽ Super 8 Motel-Lincoln/West "O" Street SH
(402) 476-8887. **$55-$67.** 2635 West O St. I-80, exit 396 eastbound, 0.5 mi e; exit 397 westbound, 0.5 mi w. Int corridors. **Pets:** Small. $10 daily fee/pet. Designated rooms, no service, crate.
[SAVE] [S✿] [✕] [⚷M] [⊟] [▭]

MCCOOK

▽▽ Days Inn-McCook SH
(308) 345-7115. **Call for rates.** 901 N Hwy 83. Jct US 6 and 34, 0.3 mi n. Int corridors. **Pets:** Accepted.
[✕] [⊟] [▭] [➣]

▽▽ Holiday Inn Express SH
(308) 345-4505. **Call for rates.** 1 Holiday Bison Dr. On US 83, just n of jct US 6 and 34. Int corridors. **Pets:** Accepted.
[✕] [⚷M] [⊟] [▭]

MORRILL

▽▽ Oak Tree Inn SH
(308) 247-2111. **Call for rates.** 707 E Webster. 0.5 mi e on US 26. Ext/int corridors. **Pets:** Accepted.
[✕] [⚷M] [⊟] [▭] [†|]

NEBRASKA CITY

⚛ ▽▽ Apple Inn SH
(402) 873-5959. **$60-$67.** 502 S 11th St. Jct 11th St and 4th Corso; center. Ext/int corridors. **Pets:** Small, dogs only. $10 daily fee/room. Designated rooms, service with restrictions, crate.
[SAVE] [S✿] [✕] [⊟] [▭] [➣]

NORFOLK

⚛ ▽▽▽ Norfolk Lodge & Suites- a Clarion Collection Hotel SH
(402) 379-3833. **$90-$160 (no credit cards).** 4200 W Norfolk Ave. On US 275 Bypass, 3 mi w of jct US 81. Ext/int corridors. **Pets:** Small, dogs only. $20 one-time fee/pet. Designated rooms, service with restrictions, crate.
[SAVE] [S✿] [✕] [⚷M] [⊟] [▭] [†|] [➣] [✕]

◇ Super 8 Motel-Norfolk SH
(402) 379-2220. **$45-$67.** 1223 Omaha Ave. Jct US 275 Bypass and 81. Int corridors. **Pets:** Other species. $10 one-time fee/pet. Service with restrictions, crate.
[ASK] [S✿] [✕] [⊟] [▭]

NORTH PLATTE

⚛ ▽ Americas Best Value Travelers Inn M
(308) 534-4020. **$40-$60.** 602 E 4th St. I-80, exit 177 (US 83), 1.5 mi n, then 0.3 mi e. Ext corridors. **Pets:** Medium, other species. Service with restrictions, supervision.
[SAVE] [S✿] [✕] [⊟] [➣]

▽▽ Comfort Inn SH
(308) 532-6144. **$70-$120.** 2901 S Jeffers St. I-80, exit 177 (US 83), just s. Int corridors. **Pets:** Accepted.
[ASK] [S✿] [✕] [⊟] [▭] [➣]

⚛ ▽▽▽ Holiday Inn Express Hotel & Suites SH
(308) 532-9500. **$95-$115.** 300 Holiday Frontage Rd. I-80, exit 177 (US 83), just s. Int corridors. **Pets:** Accepted.
[SAVE] [✕] [⚷M] [⊟] [▭] [➣] [✕]

▽▽▽ La Quinta Inn & Suites SH
(308) 534-0700. **$79-$109.** 2600 Eagles Wings Pl. I-80, exit 179, just n, then just w. Int corridors. **Pets:** Other species. Service with restrictions, supervision.
[ASK] [S✿] [✕] [⚷M] [⊟] [▭] [➣]

⚛ ▽▽▽ Quality Inn & Suites SH
(308) 532-9090. **Call for rates.** 2102 S Jeffers St. I-80, exit 177 (US 83), just n. Ext/int corridors. **Pets:** Accepted.
[SAVE] [✕] [⚷M] [⊟] [▭] [†|] [➣] [✕]

⚛ ▽▽ Ramada Inn SH
(308) 534-3120. **Call for rates.** 3201 S Jeffers St. I-80, exit 177 (US 83), 0.3 mi s. Int corridors. **Pets:** Accepted.
[SAVE] [✕] [⊟] [▭] [†|] [➣]

⚛ ▽▽ Rodeway Inn M
(308) 532-2313. **$69-$89.** 920 N Jeffers St. I-80, exit 177 (US 83), 2 mi n on US 30 and 83. Ext corridors. **Pets:** Other species. $7 daily fee/pet. Service with restrictions, supervision.
[SAVE] [S✿] [✕] [⊟] [▭] [➣]

OGALLALA

⚛ ▽▽ Best Western Stagecoach Inn SH ❀
(308) 284-3656. **Call for rates.** 201 Stagecoach Tr. I-80, exit 126 (US 26/SR 61), just n, then e on Frontage Rd. Ext corridors. **Pets:** Other species. $7 daily fee/pet. Designated rooms, service with restrictions, crate.
[SAVE] [✕] [⊟] [▭] [†|] [➣] [✕]

⚛ ▽▽ Days Inn M ❀
(308) 284-6365. **Call for rates.** 601 Stagecoach Trail. I-80, exit 126 (US 26/SR 61), just n, then e on Frontage Rd. Int corridors. **Pets:** Dogs only. $6 daily fee/room. Designated rooms, service with restrictions, supervision.
[SAVE] [✕] [⊟] [▭]

▼▼ **Holiday Inn Express** SH
(308) 284-2266. **$89-$94, 10 day notice.** 501 Stagecoach Trail. I-80, exit 126 (US 26/SR 61), just n, then e on Frontage Rd. Ext/int corridors. **Pets:** Accepted.
A$K S⭕ ✕ 📧 📺

▼▼ **Ogallala Comfort Inn** SH
(308) 284-4028. **$74-$129.** 110 Pony Express Rd. I-80, exit 126 (US 26/SR 61), just s. Ext/int corridors. **Pets:** Accepted.
A$K S⭕ ✕ 📧 📺 ➿

OMAHA

▲▲▲ ▼▼▼ **Baymont Inn & Suites** SH
(402) 391-8129. **Call for rates.** 3301 S 72nd St. I-80, exit 449 (72nd St), just n. Ext/int corridors. **Pets:** Accepted.
SAVE ✕ &M 📧 📺

▲▲▲ ▼▼▼ **Best Western Kelly Inn Omaha** SH ❀
(402) 339-7400. **$109-$139.** 4706 S 108th St. I-80, exit 445 (L St E), 0.3 mi e, then just s. Int corridors. **Pets:** Service with restrictions, supervision.
SAVE S⭕ ✕ 📧 📺 ⑪ ➿ ⊠

▲▲▲ ▼▼▼ **Best Western Seville Plaza** SH
(402) 345-2222. **Call for rates.** 3001 Chicago. I-480, exit 2B westbound; exit 2A northbound, just w on Dodge St, then just n on 30th St. Int corridors. **Pets:** Small. $40 one-time fee/pet. Designated rooms, service with restrictions, crate.
SAVE ✕ &M 📧 📺

▼▼ **Candlewood Suites** SH
(402) 758-2848. **Call for rates.** 360 S 108th Ave. I-680, exit 3 (Dodge St W), 0.7 mi to 108th St, then 0.8 mi s. Int corridors. **Pets:** Accepted.
✕ &M 📧 📺

▲▲▲ ▼▼▼ **Comfort Inn & Suites** SH
(402) 343-1000. **$85-$159.** 8736 W Dodge Rd. I-680, exit 3 (Dodge St E), 1.5 mi e. Int corridors. **Pets:** Medium. $30 one-time fee/pet. Designated rooms, service with restrictions, supervision.
SAVE S⭕ ✕ &M 📧 📺 ➿

▲▲▲ ▼▼▼ **Comfort Inn-Southwest** SH
(402) 593-2380. **$59-$150, 14 day notice.** 10728 L St. I-80, exit 445 (L St E), just n on 108th St, then e. Int corridors. **Pets:** Medium, other species. $10 daily fee/pet. Designated rooms, no service, supervision.
SAVE S⭕ ✕ 📧 📺 ➿

▲▲▲ ▼▼ **Countryside Suites** M
(402) 884-2644. **$70-$85.** 9477 S 142nd St. I-80, exit 440, just ne. Ext corridors. **Pets:** Very small, dogs only. $20 deposit/pet, $10 daily fee/pet. Service with restrictions, supervision.
SAVE ✕ &M 📧 📺

▼▼▼ **Crowne Plaza Hotel** LH
(402) 496-0850. **$79-$189.** 655 N 108th Ave. I-680, exit 3 (Dodge St W), 0.7 mi to 108th St to 108th Ave and N Old Mill Rd exits, then just n. Int corridors. **Pets:** Accepted.
A$K ✕ 📧 📺 ⑪ ➿ ⊠

▼▼▼ **DoubleTree Guest Suites Omaha** LH
(402) 397-5141. **$119-$349.** 7270 Cedar St. I-80, exit 449 (72nd St), 1.3 mi n. Int corridors. **Pets:** Medium, other species. $50 one-time fee/ room. Service with restrictions, crate.
A$K ✕ 📧 📺 ⑪ ➿

▲▲▲ ▼▼▼ **Hawthorn Suites** SH
(402) 331-0101. **$119-$149.** 11025 M St. I-80, exit 445 (L St E), 0.3 mi e, just s on 108th St, then just w. Ext corridors. **Pets:** Medium. $6 daily fee/pet. Service with restrictions.
SAVE S⭕ ✕ 📧 📺 ➿ ⊠

▲▲▲ ▼▼▼ **Hilton Omaha** LH ❀
(402) 998-3400. **$129-$334.** 1001 Cass St. Cass and 10th sts; downtown. Int corridors. **Pets:** Small, other species. $100 one-time fee/room. Service with restrictions, crate.
SAVE ✕ &M 📧 📺 📺 ⑪ ➿ ⊠

▼▼▼ **Holiday Inn Express Hotel & Suites-West** SH
(402) 333-5566. **Call for rates (no credit cards).** 17677 Wright St. I-80, exit 445 (L St W), 5.5 mi w, then just s. Int corridors. **Pets:** Accepted.
✕ &M 📧 📺 ➿

▲▲▲ ▼▼▼ **Homewood Suites** SH
(402) 397-7500. **Call for rates.** 7010 Hascall St. I-80, exit 449 (72nd St), just n, then just e. Ext/int corridors. **Pets:** Small. $50 one-time fee/room. Service with restrictions, crate.
SAVE ✕ 📧 📺 ➿

▼▼▼ **La Quinta Inn Omaha** SH
(402) 493-1900. **$69-$76.** 3330 N 104th Ave. I-680, exit 4 (Maple St), just w to 108th St, just n to Bedford, then just e. Int corridors. **Pets:** Other species. Service with restrictions, supervision.
A$K S⭕ ✕ 📧 📺 ➿

▼▼▼ **La Quinta Inn Omaha Southwest** SH
(402) 592-5200. **$62.** 10760 M St. I-80, exit 445 (L St E), 0.3 mi e, s on 108th St, then just e. Int corridors. **Pets:** Other species. Service with restrictions, supervision.
A$K S⭕ ✕ 📧 📺

▲▲▲ ▼▼ **Relax Inn Motel & Suites** M ❀
(402) 731-7300. **$55-$70.** 4578 S 60th St. I-80, exit 450 (60th St), 0.8 mi s. Ext corridors. **Pets:** Very small, dogs only. $20 deposit/pet, $10 daily fee/pet. Service with restrictions, supervision.
SAVE ✕ 📧 📺

▲▲▲ ▼▼▼ **Residence Inn by Marriott** SH
(402) 553-8898. **$225-$246.** 6990 Dodge St. I-680, exit 3 (Dodge St E), 3 mi e. Ext corridors. **Pets:** Accepted.
SAVE S⭕ ✕ 📧 📺 ➿

▲▲▲ ▼▼ **Satellite Motel** M
(402) 733-7373. **$45-$60.** 6006 L St. I-80, exit 450 (60th St), 0.8 mi s; just n of US 275 and SR 92. Ext/int corridors. **Pets:** Accepted.
SAVE ✕ 📧 📺

▼▼ **StudioPLUS-Omaha-West** SH
(402) 343-9000. **$90-$100.** 9006 Burt St. I-680, exit 3 (Dodge St E), 1.1 mi e, then just n. Int corridors. **Pets:** Other species. $75 one-time fee/pet. Service with restrictions.
A$K S⭕ ✕ 📧 📺

▼▼ **Super 8 Motel-Omaha/Aksarben** SH
(402) 390-0700. **$49-$85.** 7111 Spring St. I-80, exit 449 (72nd St), 0.3 mi n. Int corridors. **Pets:** Small. $10 daily fee/pet. Designated rooms, no service, crate.
A$K S⭕ ✕ 📧 📺

O'NEILL

▲▲▲ ▼ **Elms Motel** M
(402) 336-3800. **Call for rates.** 414 E Hwy 20. 1 mi se on US 20/275. Ext corridors. **Pets:** Accepted.
SAVE ✕ 📧 📺

▼▼▼ **Holiday Inn Express Hotel & Suites** SH
(402) 336-4500. **$85.** 1020 E Douglas St. 0.4 mi e on US 20/275. Int corridors. **Pets:** Accepted.
A$K ✕ &M 📧 📺 ➿

▼▼ **Super 8 Motel-O'Neill** SH
(402) 336-3100. **$50-$56.** 106 E Hwy 20. 0.5 mi e on US 20/275. Int corridors. **Pets:** Small. $10 daily fee/pet. Designated rooms, no service, crate.
A$K S⭕ ✕ &M 📧 📺

PAXTON

AAA ▼▼▼ **Paxton Days Inn** M
(308) 239-4510. **Call for rates.** 851 Paxton Rd. I-80, exit 145, just n. Ext corridors. **Pets:** $10 one-time fee/room. Service with restrictions, supervision.

[SAVE] ⊠ 🛏 🖵 ⑪

ST. PAUL

AAA ▼ **Bel-Air Motel & RV Park** M
(308) 754-4466. **Call for rates.** 1158 Highway 281. On US 281, 1 mi s. Ext corridors. **Pets:** $5 one-time fee/pet. Service with restrictions, crate.

[SAVE] ⊠ 🛏 🖵

SCOTTSBLUFF

▼▼ **Comfort Inn** SH
(308) 632-7510. **$69-$109.** 1902 21st Ave. 1.8 mi e on US 26, just n. Ext/int corridors. **Pets:** Accepted.

[ASK] [Sₒ] ⊠ 🛏 🖵 ⇌

▼ **Lamplighter American Inn** SH
(308) 632-7108. **Call for rates.** 606 E 27th St. US 26 business route, 0.5 mi e of jct SR 71, just s. Int corridors. **Pets:** Accepted.

⊠ 🛏 🖵 ⑪ ⇌

▼▼ **Scottsbluff Super 8 Motel** SH
(308) 635-1600. **Call for rates.** 2202 Delta Dr. 1.8 mi e on US 26. Int corridors. **Pets:** Accepted.

⊠ 🛏 🖵 ⇌

SIDNEY

AAA ▼ **Americas Best Value Inn & Suites** M
(308) 254-2081. **$56-$90.** 2115 W Illinois. On US 30, west side of town. Int corridors. **Pets:** Medium. $10 daily fee/pet. Designated rooms, service with restrictions, supervision.

[SAVE] ⊠ 🛏

AAA ▼▼▼ **AmericInn Lodge & Suites of Sidney** SH
(308) 254-0100. **Call for rates.** 645 Cabela Dr. I-80, exit 59, just nw. Int corridors. **Pets:** Accepted.

[SAVE] ⊠ 🛁 🛏 🖵 ⇌

▼▼▼ **Holiday Inn & Conference Center** SH
(308) 254-2000. **$91-$125.** 664 Chase Blvd. I-80, exit 59, just s. Int corridors. **Pets:** Accepted.

[ASK] ⊠ 🛁 🛏 🖵 ⑪ ⇌

SOUTH SIOUX CITY

▼▼▼ **Americas Best Value Inn** SH 🐾
(402) 494-4114. **$45-$80.** 4402 Dakota Ave. US 20, exit 2, just s. Int corridors. **Pets:** Medium, dogs only. $50 deposit/room. Service with restrictions, supervision.

[ASK] [Sₒ] ⊠ 🛏 🖵

▼▼▼ **Marina Inn Conference Center** SH
(402) 494-4000. **$119-$129.** 4th & B sts. I-29, exit 149 southbound, exit 148 northbound, on banks of Missouri River; e at stop light by Nebraska side of bridge. Int corridors. **Pets:** $10 daily fee/room. Service with restrictions, supervision.

[ASK] [Sₒ] ⊠ 🛁 🛏 🖵 ⑪ ⇌

SYRACUSE

AAA ▼▼▼ **Sleep Inn & Suites** SH
(402) 269-2700. **Call for rates.** 130 N 30th Rd. Jct SR 2, 1 mi n on SR 50. Int corridors. **Pets:** Accepted.

[SAVE] ⊠ 🛁 🛏 🖵 ⇌

THEDFORD

AAA ▼▼▼ **Roadside Inn** SH
(308) 645-2284. **$66-$85.** 39357 E Hwy 2. 1 mi e on SR 2, just w of US 83. Int corridors. **Pets:** Other species. $5 daily fee/room. Service with restrictions, supervision.

[SAVE] [Sₒ] ⊠ 🛁 🛏 🖵

VALENTINE

▼▼ **Dunes Lodge & Suites** M
(402) 376-3131. **$44-$139.** 340 E Hwys 20 & 83. Jct US 20/83, 0.3 mi e. Ext corridors. **Pets:** Accepted.

[ASK] [Sₒ] ⊠ 🛏 🖵

AAA ▼▼▼ **Trade Winds Motel** M
(402) 376-1600. **$45-$84.** E Hwys 20 & 83. Jct US 20/83, 1 mi se. Ext corridors. **Pets:** $5 daily fee/pet. Service with restrictions, supervision.

[SAVE] [Sₒ] ⊠ 🛏 🖵 ⇌

WAHOO

▼▼◆ **Wahoo Heritage Inn** SH
(402) 443-1288. **$52-$70.** 950 N Chestnut. On US 77 and SR 92, just nw of downtown. Ext/int corridors. **Pets:** Accepted.

[ASK] [Sₒ] ⊠ 🛁 🛏 🖵

YORK

AAA ▼▼◆ **Best Western Palmer Inn** M
(402) 362-5585. **$70-$95.** 2426 S Lincoln Ave. I-80, exit 353 (US 81), 1 mi n. Ext corridors. **Pets:** Medium, other species. $10 daily fee/room. Designated rooms, service with restrictions, supervision.

[SAVE] [Sₒ] ⊠ 🛏 🖵 ⇌

AAA ▼▼▼ **Holiday Inn** SH
(402) 362-6661. **Call for rates.** 4619 S Lincoln Ave. I-80, exit 353 (US 81), just s. Int corridors. **Pets:** Small. $25 one-time fee/room. Service with restrictions, supervision.

[SAVE] ⊠ 🛁 🛏 🖵 ⑪ ⇌

AAA ▼▼▼ **Yorkshire Inn Motel** M 🐾
(402) 362-6633. **$42-$79.** 3402 S Lincoln Ave. I-80, exit 353 (US 81), 0.5 mi n. Ext/int corridors. **Pets:** Other species. $5 daily fee/pet. Service with restrictions, supervision.

[SAVE] [Sₒ] ⊠ 🛏

NEVADA

BATTLE MOUNTAIN

▼▼▼ Comfort Inn SH
(775) 635-5880. **$65-$85.** 521 E Front St. I-80, exit 229 or 233, just n. Int corridors. **Pets:** Large. $10 daily fee/pet. Service with restrictions, supervision.

BEATTY

▼▼▼ Exchange Club Motel M
(775) 553-2333. **$53-$73.** 119 Main St. US 95 at SR 374; downtown. Ext corridors. **Pets:** Other species. $25 deposit/room, $5 daily fee/room. Service with restrictions, supervision.

▼▼▼ Stagecoach Hotel Casino M 🐾
(775) 553-2419. **$52-$67.** 900 E Hwy 95 N. North end of town; west side of US 95. Ext/int corridors. **Pets:** Medium. $10 deposit/pet, $5 one-time fee/pet. Designated rooms, service with restrictions, supervision.

CARLIN

▼▼▼ Comfort Inn SH
(775) 754-6110. **$69.** 1018 Fir St. I-80, exit 280, just s. Int corridors. **Pets:** Medium. $100 deposit/pet, $10 daily fee/pet. Service with restrictions, supervision.

CARSON CITY

◆ Carson City Super 8 SH
(775) 883-7800. **$44-$124.** 2829 S Carson St. South end of town. Int corridors. **Pets:** Accepted.

▼▼▼ Days Inn M
(775) 883-3343. **$50-$150.** 3103 N Carson St. US 395 N, north end of town. Ext corridors. **Pets:** Large. $15 daily fee/pet. Service with restrictions, supervision.

▼▼▼ Holiday Inn Express & Suites SH
(775) 283-4055. **Call for rates.** 4055 N Carson St. US 395; north end of town. Int corridors. **Pets:** Accepted.

▼▼▼ The Plaza Hotel & Conference Center SH
(775) 883-9500. **$49-$79.** 801 S Carson St. South end of town. Ext/int corridors. **Pets:** Dogs only. $25 daily fee/pet. Designated rooms, service with restrictions, supervision.

▼▼▼ Quality Inn M
(775) 883-7300. **$79-$300.** 1300 N Carson St. 0.5 mi n on US 395. Ext corridors. **Pets:** Medium, other species. $50 deposit/room, $10 daily fee/pet. Service with restrictions, supervision.

ELKO

▼▼▼▼ Best Western Gold Country Motor Inn SH
(775) 738-8421. **$99-$159.** 2050 Idaho St. I-80, exit 303, just s. Ext corridors. **Pets:** Other species. $15 one-time fee/room. Designated rooms, service with restrictions, crate.

▼ Econo Lodge Inn & Suites SH
(775) 777-8000. **$55-$119.** 3320 E Idaho St. I-80, exit 303, just s. Int corridors. **Pets:** Medium, other species. $15 daily fee/pet. Service with restrictions, supervision.

▼▼ High Desert Inn SH
(775) 738-8425. **Call for rates.** 3015 Idaho St. I-80, exit 303, just n. Ext/int corridors. **Pets:** Accepted.

▼▼▼ Oak Tree Inn SH
(775) 777-2222. **Call for rates.** 95 Spruce Rd. I-80, exit 301, just n. Int corridors. **Pets:** $10 one-time fee/pet. Service with restrictions, supervision.

▼▼▼▼ Red Lion Inn & Casino Elko SH
(775) 738-2111. **$99-$129.** 2065 Idaho St. I-80, exit 303, just s. Int corridors. **Pets:** Accepted.

▼ Rodeway Inn M
(775) 738-7152. **$39-$99.** 736 Idaho St. I-80, exit 301 or 303, 1 mi s. Ext corridors. **Pets:** Medium. $20 daily fee/pet. Designated rooms, service with restrictions, supervision.

▼▼▼ Shilo Inn SH 🐾
(775) 738-5522. **$130.** 2401 Mountain City Hwy. I-80, exit 301, just n. Int corridors. **Pets:** $25 one-time fee/room. Designated rooms, service with restrictions, supervision.

▼▼▼ Thunderbird Motel M
(775) 738-7115. **Call for rates.** 345 Idaho St. I-80, exit 301 or 303, 1 mi s. Ext corridors. **Pets:** Accepted.

ELY

◆ 4 Sevens Motel M
(775) 289-4747. **$44.** 500 High St. Just n of 5th St; downtown. Ext corridors. **Pets:** Other species. Designated rooms, service with restrictions.

▼ Fireside Inn M
(775) 289-3765. **$41.** McGill Hwy. 2 mi n on US 93. Ext corridors. **Pets:** Accepted.

▼▼▼ Historic Hotel Nevada & Gambling Hall SH
(775) 289-6665. **$39-$49.** 501 Aultman St. Downtown. Int corridors. **Pets:** Other species. Designated rooms, service with restrictions.

△△△▽ ▽▽▽▽ Prospector Hotel and Casino SH
(775) 289-8900. **$79-$99.** 1501 E Aultman St. 1.5 mi n on US 93. Int corridors. **Pets:** Designated rooms, service with restrictions.

[SAVE] [S6] [✕] [&M] [⊟] [⊑] [¶] [⇌]

△△△▽ ▽▽▽▽ Ramada Inn-Copper Queen Casino SH
(775) 289-4884. **$94-$199.** 805 Great Basin Blvd. 0.3 mi s of jct US 6, 50 and 93. Ext/int corridors. **Pets:** Large, other species. Designated rooms, service with restrictions, supervision.

[SAVE] [S6] [✕] [&M] [⊟] [⊑] [¶] [⇌]

EUREKA

△△△▽ ▽▽▽▽ Best Western Eureka Inn SH
(775) 237-5247. **$99.** 251 N Main St. On east side of Main St; center. Int corridors. **Pets:** Medium. $15 daily fee/pet. Designated rooms, service with restrictions, supervision.

[SAVE] [S6] [✕] [&M] [⊟] [⊑]

FALLON

△△△▽ ▽▽▽ Comfort Inn SH
(775) 423-5554. **$63-$150.** 1830 W Williams Ave. US 50, 1 mi w of US 95. Int corridors. **Pets:** Small. $15 daily fee/pet. Designated rooms, service with restrictions, supervision.

[SAVE] [S6] [✕] [&M] [⊟] [⊑] [⇌]

△△△▽ ▽▽ Motel 6 #4140 M
(775) 423-2277. **$43-$89.** 1705 S Taylor St. 0.5 mi s of US 50. Ext corridors. **Pets:** Medium. $50 deposit/room. Service with restrictions, supervision.

[SAVE] [S6] [✕] [⊟] [⇌]

△△△▽ ▽▽▽ Super 8 Motel SH
(775) 423-6031. **Call for rates.** 855 W Williams Ave. US 50, 0.5 mi w of US 95. Ext/int corridors. **Pets:** Accepted.

[SAVE] [✕] [¶]

FERNLEY

△△△▽ ▽▽▽ Best Western Fernley Inn M
(775) 575-6776. **$80-$108.** 1405 E Newlands Dr. I-80, exit 48, just s. Ext corridors. **Pets:** Other species. $10 daily fee/room. Designated rooms, service with restrictions, crate.

[SAVE] [S6] [✕] [&M] [⊟] [⊑] [⇌]

GARDNERVILLE

△△△▽ ▽▽▽ Best Western Topaz Lake Inn M
(775) 266-4661. **$80-$150.** 3410 Sandy Bowers Ave. US 395 at Topaz Lake, 20 mi s. Ext/int corridors. **Pets:** Accepted.

[SAVE] [S6] [✕] [&M] [⊟] [⊑]

△△△▽ ▽▽▽ Topaz Lodge SH
(775) 266-3338. **Call for rates.** 1979 US 395 S. US 395 S at Topaz Lake, 22 mi s. Ext corridors. **Pets:** Accepted.

[SAVE] [✕] [¶] [⇌]

△△△▽ ▽▽ Westerner Motel M
(775) 782-3602. **$58-$99, 7 day notice.** 1353 US 395. On US 395, south end of town. Ext corridors. **Pets:** Accepted.

[SAVE] [S6] [✕] [⊟] [⊑] [⇌]

HAWTHORNE

△△△▽ ▽▽▽ El Capitan Resort Casino M
(775) 945-3321. **$45-$75.** 540 F St. Just n of US 95. Ext corridors. **Pets:** Other species. $10 daily fee/room. Designated rooms, service with restrictions.

[SAVE] [S6] [✕] [⊟] [⊑] [¶] [⇌]

JACKPOT

△△△▽ ▽▽▽▽ Horseshu Hotel & Casino SH
(775) 755-7777. **$37-$160.** 1385 Hwy 93. On US 93. Int corridors. **Pets:** Accepted.

[SAVE] [✕] [⊑] [¶] [⇌] [✕]

▽▽▽ West Star Resort M
(775) 755-2600. **Call for rates.** Hwy 93 & Poker St. Just w of US 93. Int corridors. **Pets:** Accepted.

[✕] [&M] [⊑]

LAKE TAHOE AREA

STATELINE

△△△▽ ▽▽▽▽ Lake Village Resort CO
(775) 589-6065. **$99-$495, 30 day notice.** 301 Hwy 50. 1 mi e of casino center. Ext corridors. **Pets:** Dogs only. $20 daily fee/pet. No service, supervision.

[SAVE] [✕] [⊟] [⊑] [⇌] [✕] [🐾]

ZEPHYR COVE

△△△▽ ▽▽▽ Zephyr Cove Resort CA
(775) 589-4907. **Call for rates.** 760 Hwy 50. US 50. Ext corridors. **Pets:** Accepted.

[SAVE] [✕] [⊟] [⊑] [¶] [✕]

END AREA

LAS VEGAS METROPOLITAN AREA

BOULDER CITY

▼▼ Boulder Inn & Suites M
(702) 369-1000. $79-$229. 704 Nevada Way. On US 93. Ext corridors. Pets: Accepted.

ASK SAVE X ⊟ 🖵 ⛆

◈ ▼▼ El Rancho Boulder Motel M
(702) 293-1085. $70-$110, 3 day notice. 725 Nevada Way. On US 93. Ext corridors. Pets: Accepted.

SAVE X ⊟ ⛆

◈ ▼ Sands Motel M ❖
(702) 293-2589. $64-$99. 809 Nevada Way. On US 93. Ext corridors. Pets: Small, dogs only. $10 one-time fee/room. Designated rooms, service with restrictions, supervision.

SAVE SAVE X ⊟

ECHO BAY

◈ ▼▼ Echo Bay Resort M
(702) 394-4000. $70-$125, 3 day notice. North Shore Rd. 4 mi e of SR 167; on Lake Mead. Int corridors. Pets: Medium, other species. $50 deposit/room, $10 daily fee/pet. Service with restrictions, supervision.

SAVE SAVE X ᵫ ⊟ 🍴 ⊠

HENDERSON

◈ ▼▼ ▼▼ Green Valley Ranch LH
(702) 617-7777. $400-$475. 2300 S Paseo Verde Dr. I-215, exit Green Valley Pkwy, just s. Pets: Accepted.

SAVE X ᵫ 🖵 🍴 ⛆ ⊠

◈ ▼▼▼ Hawthorn Inn & Suites M
(702) 568-7800. Call for rates. 910 S Boulder Hwy. S of Lake Mead Pkwy. Int corridors. Pets: Accepted.

SAVE X ⊟ 🖵 ⛆

◈ ▼▼▼ Loews Lake Las Vegas Resort LH ❖
(702) 567-6000. $179-$299. 101 Montelago Blvd. I-215, e to end, then n on Lake Las Vegas Pkwy. Int corridors. Pets: Large, other species. $25 one-time fee/room. Designated rooms, service with restrictions, supervision.

SAVE SAVE X ᵫ ⊟ 🖵 🍴 ⛆ ⊠

◈ ▼▼▼ Residence Inn-Green Valley M
(702) 434-2700. $197-$219. 2190 Olympic Ave. I-215, exit Green Valley Pkwy N, 3 mi n at Sunset Rd. Int corridors. Pets: Accepted.

SAVE SAVE X ᵫ ⊟ 🖵 ⛆ ⊠

◈ ▼▼ ▼▼ The Ritz-Carlton, Lake Las Vegas LH
(702) 567-4700. Call for rates. 1610 Lake Las Vegas Pkwy. I-215, e to end, n on Lake Las Vegas Pkwy, then 0.5 mi. Int corridors. Pets: Accepted.

SAVE X ᵫ 🖵 🍴 ⛆ ⊠

INDIAN SPRINGS

◈ ▼ Indian Springs Motor Hotel M
(702) 879-3700. $49-$54. 300 Tonopah Hwy. On US 95. Int corridors. Pets: Medium. $50 deposit/room, $5 daily fee/pet. Designated rooms, service with restrictions, supervision.

SAVE SAVE X ⊟ 🍴

LAS VEGAS

◈ ▼▼ ▼ Best Western Main Street Inn M
(702) 382-3455. $49-$179. 1000 N Main St. I-15, exit 43E northbound; exit 44E southbound. Ext corridors. Pets: Medium, other species. $15 daily fee/pet. Service with restrictions, supervision.

SAVE SAVE X ⊟ 🖵 🍴 ⛆

◈ ▼▼ Best Western Nellis Motor Inn M
(702) 643-6111. $69-$99. 5330 E Craig Rd. I-15, exit 48, 2.8 mi e; 0.3 mi from Nellis AFB. Ext corridors. Pets: Small. $20 daily fee/pet. Service with restrictions, supervision.

SAVE SAVE X ⊟ 🖵 ⛆

◈ ▼▼ Best Western Parkview Inn M
(702) 385-1213. $56-$200, 7 day notice. 921 Las Vegas Blvd N. I-15, exit US 93/95, 0.3 mi n at Washington. Ext corridors. Pets: Large, other species. $8 daily fee/pet. Service with restrictions, supervision.

SAVE SAVE X ⊟ 🖵 ⛆

▼▼▼ Candlewood Suites SH
(702) 836-3660. $89-$149. 4034 S Paradise Rd. I-15, exit E Flamingo Rd to Paradise Rd, just ne. Int corridors. Pets: Accepted.

ASK SAVE X ᵫ ⊟ 🖵 ⛆

◈ ▼▼▼ Comfort Inn M
(702) 399-1500. Call for rates. 910 E Cheyenne Ave. I-15, exit Cheyenne Ave W, just w. Int corridors. Pets: Accepted.

SAVE X ᵫ ⊟ 🖵 ⛆

▼▼ Extended StayAmerica-Valley View SH
(702) 221-7600. $95-$105. 4270 S Valley View Blvd. I-15, exit W Flamingo Rd, just sw. Ext corridors. Pets: Other species. $75 one-time fee/pet. Service with restrictions.

ASK SAVE X ⊟ 🖵 ⛆

▼▼▼ Extended Stay Deluxe-Las Vegas-East Flamingo M
(702) 731-3111. $95-$105. 1550 E Flamingo Rd. I-15, exit E Flamingo Rd, 2 mi. Int corridors. Pets: Other species. $75 one-time fee/pet. Service with restrictions.

ASK SAVE X ᵫ ⊟ 🖵 ⛆

◈ ▼▼▼▼ Four Seasons Hotel Las Vegas LH
(702) 632-5000. $295-$5000. 3960 Las Vegas Blvd S. I-15, exit E Tropicana Ave, just s on the Strip. Int corridors. Pets: Accepted.

SAVE X ᵫ 🖵 🍴 ⛆ ⊠

◈ ▼ Highland Inn Motel M
(702) 896-4333. $50-$130. 8025 Dean Martin Dr. I-15, exit W Blue Diamond Rd, just nw. Ext corridors. Pets: Very small. $100 deposit/room, $10 daily fee/pet. Service with restrictions.

SAVE SAVE X ⊟ 🖵

▼▼ Homestead Studio Suites Hotel-Las Vegas/Midtown M
(702) 369-1414. Call for rates. 3045 S Maryland Pkwy. I-15, exit Sahara Ave E, just s. Int corridors. Pets: Other species. $75 one-time fee/pet. Service with restrictions.

X ᵫ ⊟ 🖵

◈ ▼▼▼ Howard Johnson Las Vegas Strip M
(702) 388-0301. $50-$100. 1401 Las Vegas Blvd S. I-15, exit Las Vegas Blvd, just n. Ext/int corridors. Pets: Accepted.

SAVE X ⊟ 🖵 🍴 ⛆

◈ ▼▼▼ La Quinta Inn & Suites Las Vegas (Lakes/West) M
(702) 243-0356. $145-$167. 9570 W Sahara Ave. Just w of Fort Apache Rd. Int corridors. Pets: Other species. Service with restrictions, supervision.

SAVE SAVE X ᵫ ⊟ 🖵 ⛆

▼▼▼ La Quinta Inn & Suites Las Vegas (Summerlin Tech Center) M
(702) 360-1200. $129-$159. 7101 Cascade Valley Ct. US 95, exit W Cheyenne Ave. Int corridors. Pets: Other species. Service with restrictions, supervision.

ASK SAVE X ᵫ ⊟ 🖵 ⛆

▼▼▼▼ La Quinta Inn Las Vegas (Convention Center) M
(702) 796-9000. **$115-$165.** 3970 Paradise Rd. I-15, exit E Flamingo Rd, 0.8 mi s of convention center; 0.5 mi e of the Strip. Int corridors. **Pets:** Other species. Service with restrictions, supervision.

🄰🅂🄺 🆂🄳 ✕ 🄼 🍽 💻 🍴 🐾

♠♠♠ ▼▼▼▼ La Quinta Inn Las Vegas (Nellis) M
(702) 632-0229. **$109-$129.** 4288 N Nellis Blvd. I-15, exit Craig Rd, e to N Las Vegas Blvd. Int corridors. **Pets:** Other species. Service with restrictions, supervision.

🅂🄰🆅🄴 🆂🄳 ✕ 🄼 🍽 💻 🐾

▼▼▼▼ La Quinta Inn Las Vegas (Tropicana) M
(702) 798-7736. **$149-$161.** 4975 S Valley View Blvd. I-15, exit Tropicana Ave W, just w. Int corridors. **Pets:** Other species. Service with restrictions, supervision.

🄰🅂🄺 🆂🄳 ✕ 🄼 🍽 💻 🐾

▼ Motel 6 Boulder Highway #1337 M
(702) 457-8051. **$79-$85.** 4125 Boulder Hwy. Just s of Sahara Ave. Ext corridors. **Pets:** Other species. Service with restrictions, supervision.

🆂🄳 ✕ 🐾

▼▼▼ ▼▼▼ Red Rock Casino Resort & Spa LH
(702) 797-7777. **$149-$699.** 11011 W Charleston Blvd. I-215, exit Charleston Blvd, just e. Int corridors. **Pets:** Accepted.

✕ 🄼 🍴 🐾 ✕

▼▼▼▼ Residence Inn by Marriott Las Vegas South SH
(702) 795-7378. **$153-$175.** 5875 Dean Martin Rd. I-15, exit Russell Rd, just sw. Int corridors. **Pets:** Accepted.

🄰🅂🄺 🆂🄳 ✕ 🄼 🍽 💻 🐾 ✕

▼▼▼▼ Residence Inn-Hughes Center SH
(702) 650-0040. **$242-$262.** 370 Hughes Center Dr. I-15, exit Paradise Rd. Int corridors. **Pets:** Accepted.

🄰🅂🄺 🆂🄳 ✕ 🄼 🍽 💻 🐾 ✕

▼▼▼▼ Residence Inn Las Vegas Convention Center M
(702) 796-9300. **$219-$241.** 3225 Paradise Rd. Opposite the convention center. Ext corridors. **Pets:** Accepted.

🄰🅂🄺 🆂🄳 ✕ 🄼 🍽 💻 🐾 ✕

♠♠♠ ▼▼▼ Sahara Westwood Hotel M
(702) 733-0001. **$69-$99.** 2601 Westwood Dr. I-15, exit Sahara Ave E, just se. Int corridors. **Pets:** Accepted.

🆂🄰🆅🄴 🆂🄳 ✕ 🍽 💻 🐾

▼▼▼ Super 8 Motel Las Vegas Strip M
(702) 794-0888. **$50-$175.** 4250 Koval Ln. I-15, exit S Koval Ln. Int corridors. **Pets:** Accepted.

🄰🅂🄺 🆂🄳 ✕ 🍽 💻 🐾

END METROPOLITAN AREA

LOVELOCK

▼▼▼▼ Sturgeon's Inn & Casino SH
(775) 273-2971. **$39-$75.** 1420 Cornell Ave. I-80, exit 105 or 107, just n. Ext corridors. **Pets:** Accepted.

🄰🅂🄺 🆂🄳 ✕ 🄼 🍽 💻 🍴 🐾

MINDEN

♠♠♠ ▼▼▼ Best Western Minden Inn M
(775) 782-7766. **$70-$114.** 1795 Ironwood Dr. US 395, exit Ironwood Dr W, 0.5 mi n of jct US 395 and SR 88. Ext corridors. **Pets:** Dogs only. $12 daily fee/pet. Designated rooms, service with restrictions, supervision.

🆂🄰🆅🄴 🆂🄳 ✕ 🄼 🍽 💻 🐾

♠♠♠ ▼▼▼▼ The Westin Casuarina Las Vegas Hotel, Casino and Spa LH ✿
(702) 836-5900. **$134-$524.** 160 E Flamingo Rd. I-15, exit Flamingo Rd E, 1.1 mi. Int corridors. **Pets:** Large. $139 deposit/room, $35 one-time fee/room. Designated rooms, service with restrictions.

🆂🄰🆅🄴 🆂🄳 ✕ 🄼 🍽 💻 🍴 🐾 ✕

MESQUITE

♠♠♠ ▼▼▼ Best Western Mesquite Inn M
(702) 346-7444. **$69-$150.** 390 N Sandhill Blvd. I-15, exit 122. Ext corridors. **Pets:** Medium. $15 daily fee/pet. Designated rooms, service with restrictions, supervision.

🆂🄰🆅🄴 🆂🄳 ✕ 🍽 💻 🐾

▼▼▼▼ Falcon Ridge Hotel SH
(702) 346-2200. **Call for rates.** 1030 W Pioneer Blvd. I-15, exit 120, just w. Int corridors. **Pets:** Accepted.

✕ 🄼 🍽 💻 🐾 ✕

▼▼ Virgin River Hotel Casino Bingo M
(702) 346-7777. **Call for rates.** 100 Pioneer Blvd. I-15, exit 122, just w. Ext corridors. **Pets:** Accepted.

✕ 🄼 🍴 🐾

OVERTON

▼▼▼▼ Best Western North Shore Inn at Lake Mead M
(702) 397-6000. **$70-$90.** 520 N Moapa Valley Blvd. I-15, exit 93, 10 mi ne on SR 169. Int corridors. **Pets:** Accepted.

🄰🅂🄺 🆂🄳 ✕ 🍽 💻 🐾

PAHRUMP

♠♠♠ ▼▼▼ Best Western Pahrump Station M
(775) 727-5100. **$70-$136.** 1101 S Hwy 160. Downtown. Ext/int corridors. **Pets:** Accepted.

🆂🄰🆅🄴 🆂🄳 ✕ 🄼 🍽 💻 🍴 🐾

♠♠♠ ▼▼▼ Saddle West Hotel & Casino M
(775) 727-1111. **Call for rates.** 1220 S Hwy 160. Downtown. Ext corridors. **Pets:** Accepted.

🆂🄰🆅🄴 ✕ 🄼 🍽 💻 🍴 🐾

▼ Holiday Lodge M
(775) 782-2288. **$45-$70.** 1591 US 395 N. Center. Ext corridors. **Pets:** Accepted.

✕ 🍽 🐾

RENO

♠♠♠ ▼▼▼▼ Atlantis Casino Resort Spa Reno LH
(775) 825-4700. **$69-$279.** 3800 S Virginia St. 3 mi s on US 395. Ext/int corridors. **Pets:** Accepted.

🆂🄰🆅🄴 🆂🄳 ✕ 🄼 🍽 💻 🍴 🐾 ✕

♠♠♠ ▼▼▼▼ Best Western Airport Plaza Hotel SH ✿
(775) 348-6370. **Call for rates.** 1981 Terminal Way. US 395, exit E Plumb Villanova. Int corridors. **Pets:** Other species. $50 deposit/room, $10 daily fee/room. Designated rooms, service with restrictions, supervision.

🆂🄰🆅🄴 ✕ 🄼 🍽 💻 🍴 🐾 ✕

AAA **WWW** **Days Inn** **M** ❀
(775) 786-4070. **$40-$189.** 701 E 7th St. I-80, exit Wells Ave, just s. Ext corridors. **Pets:** Large. $10 daily fee/pet. Designated rooms, service with restrictions, crate.
SAVE S X 🖥 ➥

AAA **WWW** **Desert Rose Inn** **M**
(775) 329-3451. **Call for rates.** 655 W 4th St. I-80, exit Keystone, just e. Ext corridors. **Pets:** Accepted.
SAVE X 🖥 💻 ➥

WWW **Extended StayAmerica-Reno-South Meadows** **SH**
(775) 852-5611. **$113-$125.** 9795 Gateway Dr. US 395, S Meadows Pkwy, then e. Int corridors. **Pets:** Other species. $75 one-time fee/pet. Service with restrictions.
ASK S X 🖥 💻

AAA **WWW** **GateKeeper Inn** **M**
(775) 786-3500. **$45-$109.** 221 W 5th St. Corner of West and 5th sts. Ext corridors. **Pets:** Other species. $15 daily fee/pet. Service with restrictions, supervision.
SAVE S X

AAA **WWWWW** **Holiday Inn-Downtown** **SH**
(775) 786-5151. **$69-$99.** 1000 E 6th St. I-80, exit Wells Ave, 2 blks e. Int corridors. **Pets:** Accepted.
SAVE X 🅶M 🖥 💻 🍴 ➥

WWWW **La Quinta Inn Reno (Airport)** **M**
(775) 348-6100. **$92-$115.** 4001 Market St. US 395, exit airport northbound; exit Villanova Dr southbound. Ext corridors. **Pets:** Other species. Service with restrictions, supervision.
ASK S X 🅶M 🖥 💻 ➥

AAA **WWWW** **Quality Inn South** **SH**
(775) 329-1001. **$66-$139.** 1885 S Virginia St. US 395, exit Plumb Ln Villanova, 1 mi w. Ext/int corridors. **Pets:** Accepted.
SAVE S X 🅶M 🖥 💻 🍴 ➥

AAA **WWWW** **Residence Inn by Marriott** **SH** ❀
(775) 853-8800. **$153-$191.** 9845 Gateway Dr. US 395, exit S Meadows Pkwy, then e. Int corridors. **Pets:** Large, other species. $100 one-time fee/room. Service with restrictions.
SAVE S X 🅶M 🖥 💻 ➥ X

SPARKS

AAA **WWW** **Quality Inn** **SH** ❀
(775) 358-6900. **$69-$189.** 55 E Nugget Ave. I-80, exit E McCarran Blvd, just s. Int corridors. **Pets:** $15 daily fee/pet. Designated rooms, service with restrictions, supervision.
SAVE S X 🖥 💻 🍴 ➥

AAA **WWW** **Sparks Super 8** **SH**
(775) 358-8884. **Call for rates.** 1900 E Greg St. I-80, exit 20, 0.6 mi ne. Int corridors. **Pets:** $10 daily fee/pet. Service with restrictions, supervision.
SAVE X 🖥 💻 ➥

TONOPAH

AAA **WWWW** **Best Western Hi-Desert Inn** **M**
(775) 482-3511. **$79-$139.** 320 Main St. On US 6 and 95. Int corridors. **Pets:** Dogs only. Designated rooms, service with restrictions, supervision.
SAVE S X 🅶M 🖥 💻 ➥

AAA **WWWW** **Ramada Inn-Tonopah Station** **M**
(775) 482-9777. **Call for rates.** 1100 Main St. On US 6 and 95. Int corridors. **Pets:** Other species. Service with restrictions, supervision.
SAVE X 🅶M 💻 🍴

UNIONVILLE

AAA **WWW** **Old Pioneer Garden** **BB** ❀
(775) 538-7585. **Call for rates (no credit cards).** 2805 Unionville Rd. I-80, exit 149, 16 mi s, then 2.5 mi w. Int corridors. **Pets:** Service with restrictions, supervision.
SAVE X 🅟🅦 🌫

WELLS

AAA **WWW** **Super 8 Motel** **M**
(775) 752-3384. **Call for rates.** 930 6th St. I-80, exit 351 eastbound, 1 mi n, then 0.8 mi e; exit 352A westbound, 0.3 mi n, then 0.5 mi w. Ext corridors. **Pets:** Accepted.
SAVE X 🖥 ➥

WEST WENDOVER

WWW **Wendover Super 8** **M**
(775) 664-2888. **Call for rates.** 1325 Wendover Blvd. I-80, exit 410, 0.5 mi w. Int corridors. **Pets:** Accepted.
X 🖥

WINNEMUCCA

AAA **WWWW** **Best Western Gold Country Inn** **SH**
(775) 623-6999. **Call for rates.** 921 W Winnemucca Blvd. I-80, exit 176 or 178, just s. Int corridors. **Pets:** Other species. $10 one-time fee/room. Supervision.
SAVE X 🖥 💻 ➥

AAA **WWWW** **Best Western Holiday Motel** **M**
(775) 623-3684. **$69-$129.** 670 W Winnemucca Blvd. I-80, exit 176 or 178, just s. Ext corridors. **Pets:** Other species. $20 deposit/room. Service with restrictions, supervision.
SAVE S X 🖥 💻 ➥

AAA **WWWW** **Days Inn** **M**
(775) 623-3661. **Call for rates.** 511 W Winnemucca Blvd. I-80, exit 176, just s. Ext corridors. **Pets:** Accepted.
SAVE X 🖥 💻 ➥

WWWW **Holiday Inn Express** **SH**
(775) 625-3100. **$89-$199.** 1987 W Winnemucca Blvd. I-80, exit 178, just s. Int corridors. **Pets:** Accepted.
S X 🅶M 🖥 💻 ➥

AAA **WWWW** **Red Lion Hotel & Casino** **SH**
(775) 623-2565. **$89-$139.** 741 W Winnemucca Blvd. I-80, exit 176 or 178, just s. Int corridors. **Pets:** Other species. Service with restrictions, supervision.
SAVE S X 🖥 💻 🍴 ➥

AAA **WWW** **Scott Shady Court Motel** **M**
(775) 623-3646. **$42-$60.** 400 1st St. I-80, exit 176 or 178, 0.3 mi n on Pavilion. Ext corridors. **Pets:** Accepted.
SAVE X 💻 ➥

WWW **Super 8 Motel** **SH**
(775) 625-1818. **Call for rates.** 1157 W Winnemucca Blvd. I-80, exit 176, 0.5 mi e. Int corridors. **Pets:** Accepted.
X 🖥 💻

AAA **WWWW** **Town House Motel** **M**
(775) 623-3620. **$68-$75.** 375 Monroe St. I-80, exit 176 or 178, just s. Ext corridors. **Pets:** Small, dogs only. Service with restrictions, supervision.
SAVE S X 🖥 💻 ➥

NEW HAMPSHIRE

ANDOVER

▼▼▼ Highland Lake Inn Bed & Breakfast BB
(603) 735-6426. **$145-$200.** 32 Maple St. I-93, exit 17, 15.5 mi nw on US 4, 3.5 mi e on SR 11, then just w. Int corridors. **Pets:** Accepted.

SAVE ✕ 🗗

ASHLAND

▼▼▼ Glynn House Inn BB
(603) 968-3775. **Call for rates.** 59 Highland St. I-93, exit 24 (SR 25 and US 3), 0.8 mi e to flag pole in center of town (Highland), then 0.3 mi nw. Ext/int corridors. **Pets:** Accepted.

✕ 🗗

BARTLETT

▼▼▼ The Bartlett Inn BB
(603) 374-2353. **$109-$248, 14 day notice.** 1477 US Rt 302. On US 302, 7 mi w of jct SR 16. Ext/int corridors. **Pets:** Accepted.

SAVE S🔊 ✕ 🖥 🖥 ✕ 🗗

▼▼▼ The Villager Motel M
(603) 374-2742. **$49-$249, 10 day notice.** 1126 US Rt 302. 1 mi e on US 302; 1.3 mi w of Attitash Mountain. Ext corridors. **Pets:** Accepted.

SAVE S🔊 ✕ 🖥 🖥 ✕

BRETTON WOODS

▼▼▼ Bretton Arms Inn CI 🐾
(603) 278-1000. **$199-$799, 15 day notice.** US 302. Center. Int corridors. **Pets:** Dogs only. $30 daily fee/pet. Designated rooms, service with restrictions.

✕ 🖥 🖥 🍴 ✕

▼▼▼ The Townhomes VH
(603) 278-2000. **$199-$999, 21 day notice.** US 302. Center. Ext corridors. **Pets:** Accepted.

✕ 🖥 🖥 ✕

CAMPTON

▼▼▼ Days Inn Campton/Plymouth SH
(603) 536-3520. **$45-$149.** 1513 Rt 3. I-93, exit 27, just e, then just n. Int corridors. **Pets:** Other species. $20 daily fee/pet. Designated rooms, service with restrictions, supervision.

SAVE S🔊 ✕ 🖥 🖥 ✕

CHESTERFIELD

▼▼▼ Chesterfield Inn CI
(603) 256-3211. **$150-$320, 5 day notice.** 20 Cross Rd. I-91, exit 3, 2 mi e on SR 9. Ext/int corridors. **Pets:** Large, other species. Service with restrictions, supervision.

ASK S🔊 ✕ 🖥 🖥 🍴

CLAREMONT

▼▼▼ Best Budget Inn M
(603) 542-9567. **Call for rates.** 24 Sullivan St. Just n of jct SR 11/12/103/120; center. Ext corridors. **Pets:** Accepted.

SAVE ✕ 🖥

COLEBROOK

▼▼▼ Northern Comfort Motel M
(603) 237-4440. **$69-$89, 3 day notice.** 1 Trooper Scott Phillips Hwy. 1.5 mi s on US 3. Ext corridors. **Pets:** Accepted.

SAVE ✕ 🖥 🖥 ✕

CONCORD

▼▼▼ Concord Comfort Inn SH
(603) 226-4100. **$70-$240.** 71 Hall St. I-93, exit 13, just n on Main St, then 0.3 mi w. Int corridors. **Pets:** Dogs only. $15 daily fee/pet. Designated rooms, supervision.

ASK S🔊 ✕ 🔊M 🖥 🖥 🖥 ✕

▼▼▼ Days Inn M
(603) 224-2511. **Call for rates.** 406 S Main St. I-93, exit 12S on SR 3A. Ext corridors. **Pets:** Medium. $20 daily fee/room. Designated rooms, service with restrictions, supervision.

SAVE ✕ 🖥 🖥 ✕

CONWAY

▼▼▼ White Deer Motel M
(603) 447-5366. **$49-$179, 7 day notice.** 379 White Mountain Hwy. 2.1 mi s of jct US 302; 0.5 mi n of village center on SR 16. Ext/int corridors. **Pets:** Accepted.

ASK S🔊 ✕ 🖥 🖥

DIXVILLE NOTCH

▼▼▼▼ The Balsams Grand Resort Hotel LH
(603) 255-3400. **$278-$578, 7 day notice.** 105 Cold Spring Rd.. Int corridors. **Pets:** Accepted.

ASK ✕ 🖥 🍴 ✕ ✕

DOVER

▼▼▼ Days Inn M
(603) 742-0400. **$89-$179.** 481 Central Ave. Spaulding Tpke, exit 7, 2 mi n on SR 108; downtown. Ext/int corridors. **Pets:** Other species. $50 deposit/room, $10 daily fee/pet. Service with restrictions, supervision.

ASK S🔊 ✕ 🖥 🖥 ✕

DURHAM

▼▼▼ Hickory Pond Inn CI 🐾
(603) 659-2227. **$99-$189, 3 day notice.** 1 Stagecoach Rd. 2.8 mi s on SR 108. Int corridors. **Pets:** Dogs only. $25 one-time fee/pet. Designated rooms, crate.

ASK S🔊 ✕ ✕

FRANCONIA

◇◇ ▽▽▽ Best Western White Mountain Resort SH
(603) 823-7422. **$89-$169.** 87 Wallace Hill Rd. I-93, exit 38, just e. Int corridors. **Pets:** Accepted.
SAVE S⊘ ✕ ⊟ ⊑ ⇌ ✕

◇◇ ▽ Gale River Motel M ✿
(603) 823-5655. **Call for rates.** 1 Main St. I-93, exit 38, 0.8 mi n on SR 18. Ext corridors. **Pets:** Other species. $10 daily fee/pet. Designated rooms, service with restrictions, supervision.
SAVE ✕ ⊟ ⊑ ⇌ ✕

▽▽▽ Lovetts Inn by Lafayette Brook CI
(603) 823-7761. **Call for rates.** 1474 Profile Rd. I-93, exit 38, just w on Wallace Hill Rd, then 2.1 mi s on SR 18. Ext/int corridors. **Pets:** Accepted.
✕ ⊟ ⊑ ⌟⌞ ⇌ ✕ ⊿

GILFORD

▽▽ Fireside Resort Inn & Suites SH
(603) 293-7526. **$100-$260.** 17 Harris Shore Rd. Jct SR 11 and 11B, 2.5 mi e of jct US 3 N. Int corridors. **Pets:** Other species. $10 daily fee/pet. Designated rooms, service with restrictions, supervision.
ASK ✕ ⌂M ⊟ ⊑ ⇌ ✕

GORHAM

▽ Moose Brook Motel M
(603) 466-5400. **$49-$89, 7 day notice.** 65 Lancaster Rd. Jct SR 16, 0.5 mi w on US 2. Ext corridors. **Pets:** $5 one-time fee/pet. Designated rooms, service with restrictions, crate.
✕ ⊟ ⊑ ⇌

▽▽ Royalty Inn SH
(603) 466-3312. **$56-$153.** 130 Main St. On US 2 and SR 16; center. Ext/int corridors. **Pets:** Other species. $5 daily fee/pet. Designated rooms, service with restrictions.
✕ ⌂M ⊟ ⊑ ⌟⌞ ⇌ ✕

◇◇ ▽▽ Top Notch Inn M
(603) 466-5496. **$49-$149.** 265 Main St. On US 2 and SR 16; center. Ext/int corridors. **Pets:** Accepted.
SAVE S⊘ ✕ ⊟ ⊑ ⇌

▽▽ Town & Country Motor Inn SH
(603) 466-3315. **$78-$118.** 20 SR 2. 0.5 mi e of jct SR 16. Ext/int corridors. **Pets:** Accepted.
✕ ⊟ ⊑ ⌟⌞ ⇌ ✕

HAMPTON

◇◇ ▽▽▽ Best Western The Inn at Hampton SH
(603) 926-6771. **$100-$215.** 815 Lafayette Rd. 0.5 mi n on US 1. Int corridors. **Pets:** Medium. Designated rooms, service with restrictions, supervision.
SAVE S⊘ ✕ ⌂M ⊟ ⊑ ⌟⌞ ⇌ ✕

◇◇ ▽▽▽ Lamie's Inn and The Old Salt CI
(603) 926-0330. **$105-$160, 3 day notice.** 490 Lafayette Rd. Jct SR 27 on US 1. Int corridors. **Pets:** Accepted.
SAVE S⊘ ✕ ⊟ ⌟⌞

HAMPTON FALLS

◇◇ ▽▽▽ Hampton Falls Inn M
(603) 926-9545. **$79-$119.** 11 Lafayette Rd. I-95, exit 1, 0.5 mi e on SR 107, then 1 mi n on US 1. Int corridors. **Pets:** Accepted.
SAVE ✕ ⊟ ⌟⌞ ⇌ ✕

HANCOCK

▽▽▽ The Hancock Inn CI
(603) 525-3318. **$125-$290, 15 day notice.** 33 Main St. Jct of SR 123 and 137; center. Int corridors. **Pets:** Accepted.
✕ ⌟⌞

HARTS LOCATION

▽▽▽ Notchland Inn CI
(603) 374-6131. **$195-$385, 14 day notice.** US 302. On US 302, 6.4 mi w of town. Ext/int corridors. **Pets:** Other species. $15 daily fee/pet. Designated rooms, service with restrictions, supervision.
✕ ⊟ ⊑ ⌟⌞ ✕

HENNIKER

◇◇ ▽▽ Henniker Motel M
(603) 428-3536. **$90-$149.** 61 Craney Pond Rd. I-89, exit 5, 6.5 mi w on US 202 and SR 9 to jct SR 114, 3 mi s on SR 114 to Flanders Rd, then 0.5 mi w, follow signs; adjacent to Pat's Peak. Ext/int corridors. **Pets:** Accepted.
SAVE S⊘ ✕ ⊟ ⊑ ⇌

JEFFERSON

◇◇ ▽▽▽ Jefferson Inn BB ✿
(603) 586-7998. **$95-$155, 14 day notice.** 6 Renaissance Ln. US 2, 0.5 mi e of SR 116. Int corridors. **Pets:** Other species. $10 one-time fee/pet. Designated rooms, service with restrictions, crate.
SAVE S⊘ ✕ ⊟ ✕ ⌐K ⊿

KEENE

▽▽ Best Western Sovereign Hotel SH
(603) 357-3038. **$105-$189.** 401 Winchester St. SR 10, just s of jct SR 12 and 101. Int corridors. **Pets:** Accepted.
ASK S⊘ ✕ ⊟ ⊑ ⌟⌞ ⇌

▽▽▽ Holiday Inn Express SH ✿
(603) 352-7616. **$129-$299.** 175 Key Rd. SR 101, just n, via Winchester St, 0.3 mi w. Int corridors. **Pets:** Large, dogs only. $25 daily fee/pet. Designated rooms, service with restrictions, supervision.
ASK S⊘ ✕ ⌂M ⊟ ⊑ ⇌

◇◇ ▽▽ Super 8 Keene SH ✿
(603) 352-9780. **$72-$200.** 3 Ashbrook Rd. Jct SR 9 and 12, just w. Int corridors. **Pets:** $20 one-time fee/room. Service with restrictions, supervision.
SAVE S⊘ ✕ ⌂M ⊟ ⊑

LANCASTER

◇◇ ▽▽ Coos Motor Inn SH
(603) 788-3079. **$45-$100.** 209 Main St. On US 2 and 3; center. Int corridors. **Pets:** Medium. $10 daily fee/pet. Service with restrictions, supervision.
SAVE ✕ ⊟ ⊑

LEBANON

◇◇ ▽▽ Days Inn M
(603) 448-5070. **Call for rates.** 135 SR 120. I-89, exit 18, 0.8 mi n. Ext/int corridors. **Pets:** Accepted.
SAVE ✕ ⊟

▽▽▽ Residence Inn by Marriott-Lebanon SH
(603) 643-4511. **$186-$208.** 32 Centerra Pkwy. I-89, exit 18, 2.5 mi n on SR 120. Int corridors. **Pets:** Accepted.
ASK S⊘ ✕ ⌂M ⊟ ⊑ ⇌ ✕

LINCOLN

AAA ▼▼▼ Comfort Inn & Suites **SH** ❀
(603) 745-6700. **$99-$299, 3 day notice.** 21 Railroad St. I-93, exit 32, just e. on SR 112; at Hobo Railroad. Int corridors. **Pets:** $15 daily fee/pet. Designated rooms, service with restrictions, supervision.
[SAVE] [✕] [&M] [🖥] [💻] [✕]

AAA ▼▼ Econo Lodge Inn & Suites **M**
(603) 745-3661. **$59-$250.** 381 US Rt 3. I-93, exit 33 (US 3), 0.3 mi ne. Ext/int corridors. **Pets:** Medium, dogs only. $15 daily fee/pet. Designated rooms, service with restrictions, crate.
[SAVE] [S🐾] [✕] [🖥] [🏊] [✕]

AAA ▼ Parker's Motel **M**
(603) 745-8341. **$49-$99.** 750 US Rt 3. I-93, exit 33 (US 3), 2 mi ne. Ext corridors. **Pets:** Accepted.
[SAVE] [S🐾] [✕] [🖥] [💻] [🏊] [✕]

AAA ▼▼ Woodward's Resort **M**
(603) 745-8141. **$70-$139, 7 day notice.** 527 US 3. I-93, exit 33 (US 3), 1.4 mi ne. Ext/int corridors. **Pets:** Accepted.
[SAVE] [✕] [🖥] [💻] [🍴] [🏊] [✕]

LITTLETON

▼▼▼ Beal House Inn and Restaurant **CI**
(603) 444-2661. **Call for rates.** 2 W Main St. I-93, exit 42, 0.8 mi e on US 302 and SR 10. Int corridors. **Pets:** Accepted.
[✕] [🖥] [💻] [🍴]

AAA ▼▼▼ Eastgate Motor Inn **M**
(603) 444-3971. **$69-$119.** 335 Cottage St. I-93, exit 41, just e. Ext/int corridors. **Pets:** Accepted.
[SAVE] [✕] [💻] [🍴] [🏊] [✕]

AAA ▼▼ Thayers Inn **SH**
(603) 444-6469. **$69-$169, 15 day notice.** 111 Main St. I-93, exit 42, 1.3 mi e on US 302 and SR 10; center. Int corridors. **Pets:** Accepted.
[SAVE] [S🐾] [✕] [🖥] [💻] [🍴]

LOUDON

AAA ▼▼▼ Red Roof Inn **SH**
(603) 225-8399. **Call for rates.** 2 Staniels Rd. I-393, exit 3, 1.5 mi n. Int corridors. **Pets:** Accepted.
[SAVE] [✕] [&M] [🖥] [🏊]

MANCHESTER

▼▼ Comfort inn **SH**
(603) 668-2600. **$99-$299.** 298 Queen City Ave. I-293, exit 4, just w. Int corridors. **Pets:** Medium. $25 daily fee/room. Designated rooms, service with restrictions, supervision.
[ASK] [S🐾] [✕] [&M] [🖥] [🏊]

AAA ▼▼▼ Holiday Inn Express Hotel & Suites–Manchester Airport **SH**
(603) 669-6800. **$99-$199.** 1298 S Porter St. I-293, exit 1. Int corridors. **Pets:** Accepted.
[SAVE] [S🐾] [✕] [&M] [🖥] [💻] [🏊]

▼▼▼ Homewood Suites by Hilton **SH** ❀
(603) 668-2200. **$109-$179.** 1000 N Perimeter Rd. I-293, exit 2, follow signs to Manchester Airport. Int corridors. **Pets:** Other species. $25 daily fee/pet. Service with restrictions.
[ASK] [S🐾] [✕] [&M] [🖥] [💻] [🏊] [✕]

▼▼▼ Radisson Hotel Manchester **LH**
(603) 625-1000. **$149-$199.** 700 Elm St. Jct Granite St; downtown. Int corridors. **Pets:** Accepted.
[ASK] [S🐾] [✕] [&M] [🖥] [💻] [🍴] [🏊] [✕]

TownePlace Suites by Marriott Manchester

▼▼ ▼▼ TownePlace Suites by Marriott Manchester Airport **SH** ❀
(603) 641-2288. **$170-$191.** 686 Huse Rd. I-293, exit 1, 0.5 mi se on SR 28. Int corridors. **Pets:** Other species. $100 one-time fee/room. Service with restrictions, crate.
[ASK] [S🐾] [✕] [&M] [🖥] [💻] [🏊]

MERRIMACK

▼▼▼ Residence Inn by Marriott **SH** ❀
(603) 424-8100. **$164-$186.** 246 Daniel Webster Hwy. Everett Tpke, exit 11, just e, then 0.6 mi s on US 3. Ext/int corridors. **Pets:** Other species. $75 one-time fee/room. Designated rooms.
[ASK] [S🐾] [✕] [&M] [🖥] [💻] [🏊] [✕]

NASHUA

AAA ▼▼ Best Western's Granite Inn **SH** ❀
(603) 883-7700. **$80-$120.** 10 St. Laurent St. US 3 (Everett Tpke), exit 7E, just e. Int corridors. **Pets:** Medium. $50 one-time fee/pet. Designated rooms, service with restrictions, supervision.
[SAVE] [S🐾] [✕] [🖥] [💻] [🏊]

▼▼ Extended StayAmerica-Nashua **SH**
(603) 577-9900. **$72-$110.** 2000 Southwood Dr. US 3 (Everett Tpke), exit 8, just w. Int corridors. **Pets:** Other species. $75 one-time fee/pet. Service with restrictions.
[ASK] [S🐾] [✕] [&M] [🖥] [💻]

▼▼ Holiday Inn Nashua **SH**
(603) 888-1551. **Call for rates.** 9 Northeastern Blvd. US 3 (Everett Tpke), exit 4, just w, then 0.3 mi n. Int corridors. **Pets:** Accepted.
[✕] [&M] [🖥] [💻] [🍴] [🏊]

▼▼ Red Roof Inn #7122 **M**
(603) 888-1893. **Call for rates.** 77 Spitbrook Rd. US 3 (Everett Tpke), exit 1, just e. Ext corridors. **Pets:** Accepted.
[✕] [&M]

NEWBURY

AAA ▼▼ Best Western Sunapee Lake Lodge **SH**
(603) 763-2010. **$109-$349, 14 day notice.** 1403 SR 103. Jct SR 103B, just e. Int corridors. **Pets:** $10 deposit/pet. Designated rooms, service with restrictions, supervision.
[SAVE] [S🐾] [✕] [&M] [🖥] [💻] [🍴] [🏊] [✕]

NEW CASTLE

AAA ▼▼ ▼▼ Wentworth By The Sea Marriott Hotel & Spa **LH**
(603) 422-7322. **$197-$329, 3 day notice.** 588 Wentworth Rd. On SR 1B, 2 mi e of SR 1A. Ext/int corridors. **Pets:** Small, dogs only. $100 deposit/room. Designated rooms, service with restrictions, supervision.
[SAVE] [S🐾] [✕] [🖥] [💻] [🍴] [🏊] [✕]

NORTH CONWAY

AAA ▼▼▼ Best Western Red Jacket Mountain View and Conference Center **SH** ❀
(603) 356-5411. **$109-$439, 10 day notice.** 2251 White Mountain Hwy. 1 mi s on US 302/SR 16. Ext/int corridors. **Pets:** $25 daily fee/pet. Designated rooms, service with restrictions, supervision.
[SAVE] [✕] [&M] [🖥] [💻] [🍴] [🏊] [✕]

AAA ▼▼ Mt Washington Valley Inn **SH**
(603) 356-5486. **$49-$199.** 1567 White Mountain Hwy. 2.5 mi s on US 302/SR 16; village center. Int corridors. **Pets:** Accepted.
[SAVE] [S🐾] [✕] [🖥] [💻] [🏊]

▼▼▼ North Conway Hampton Inn & Suites **SH**
(603) 356-7736. **$139-$259.** 1788 White Mountain Hwy. Jct US 302/SR 16, 1 mi n. Int corridors. **Pets:** Accepted.
[ASK] [S🐾] [✕] [🖥] [💻] [✕]

ⒶⒶⒶ ▼▼▼ North Conway Mountain Inn **Ⓜ**
(603) 356-2803. **$79-$125, 3 day notice.** 2114 White Mountain Hwy. 1 mi s on US 302/SR 16. Ext corridors. **Pets:** Accepted.
[SAVE] [✕]

PITTSBURG

▼ The Glen **ⒸⒶ**
(603) 538-6500. **$204-$266 (no credit cards), 7 day notice.** 118 Glen Rd. 9 mi n on US 3, from jct SR 145 to Varney Rd, then 0.3 mi s to Glen Rd, follow signs. Ext/int corridors. **Pets:** Other species. Designated rooms, service with restrictions, supervision.
[✕] [🛏] [💻] [🍴] [✕] [Ⓚ] [🐾] [☎]

PORTSMOUTH

▼▼▼▼ Hampton Inn-Portsmouth **ⓈⒽ**
(603) 431-6111. **$89-$249.** 99 Durgin Ln. I-95, exit 7, 1 mi w via Market St and Woodbury Ave to Durgin Ln, then 0.3 mi s. Int corridors. **Pets:** Accepted.
[ASK] [S🐾] [✕] [&M] [🛏] [💻] [🏊] [✕]

▼▼▼▼ Hilton Garden Inn Portsmouth Downtown **ⓈⒽ**
(603) 431-1499. **Call for rates.** 100 High St. Downtown. Int corridors. **Pets:** Accepted.
[✕] [&M] [🛏] [💻] [🍴] [🏊]

▼ Motel 6 Portsmouth #1424 **Ⓜ**
(603) 334-6606. **Call for rates.** 3 Gosling Rd. I-95, exit 4 to Spaulding Tpke (US 4 and SR 16), exit 1, just e. Int corridors. **Pets:** Other species. Service with restrictions, supervision.
[✕] [&M] [🛏] [🏊]

▼▼▼▼ Residence Inn by Marriott **ⓈⒽ**
(603) 436-8880. **$175-$241.** 1 International Dr. SR 4/16, exit 1, just s. Int corridors. **Pets:** Accepted.
[ASK] [S🐾] [✕] [&M] [🛏] [💻] [🏊] [✕]

▼▼▼▼ Sheraton Harborside Portsmouth Hotel & Conference Center **ⓁⒽ** 🐾
(603) 431-2300. **Call for rates.** 250 Market St. Downtown. Int corridors. **Pets:** Medium, dogs only. Designated rooms, service with restrictions, supervision.
[✕] [&M] [🛏] [💻] [🍴] [🏊] [✕]

ROCHESTER

ⒶⒶⒶ ▼ Anchorage Inn **Ⓜ** 🐾
(603) 332-3350. **$69-$129.** 13 Wadleigh Rd. Jct Spaulding Tpke and SR 125, exit 12. Ext corridors. **Pets:** Medium. $50 deposit/room, $15 daily fee/pet. Designated rooms, service with restrictions, supervision.
[SAVE] [S🐾] [✕] [🛏] [🏊]

▼▼▼ The Governor's Inn **ⒸⒾ**
(603) 332-0107. **Call for rates.** 78 Wakefield St. On SR 125 and 108, just n of monument; center. Int corridors. **Pets:** Accepted.
[✕] [🛏] [💻] [🍴]

SALEM

▼▼▼ Holiday Inn-Salem New Hampshire **ⓈⒽ**
(603) 893-5511. **$99-$199.** 1 Keewaydin Dr. I-93, exit 2, just sw. Int corridors. **Pets:** Medium. $25 one-time fee/room. Service with restrictions, supervision.
[ASK] [S🐾] [✕] [&M] [🛏] [💻] [🍴] [🏊] [✕]

▼▼ La Quinta Inn & Suites **ⓈⒽ**
(603) 893-4722. **$99-$115.** 8 Keewaydin Dr. I-93, exit 2, just sw. Int corridors. **Pets:** Other species. Service with restrictions, supervision.
[ASK] [S🐾] [✕] [&M] [🛏] [💻] [🍴] [🏊] [✕]

▼▼ Red Roof Inn #7151 **Ⓜ**
(603) 898-6422. **Call for rates.** 15 Red Roof Ln. I-93, exit 2, just se. Ext corridors. **Pets:** Accepted.
[✕] [&M] [🛏]

SNOWVILLE

▼▼▼▼ Snowvillage Inn **ⒸⒾ**
(603) 447-2818. **Call for rates.** 136 Stewart Rd. Jct SR 16, 5 mi s on SR 153, turn at Crystal Lake, then 1.5 mi s, follow signs. Ext/int corridors. **Pets:** Dogs only. $25 one-time fee/pet. Designated rooms, service with restrictions, crate.
[✕] [🍴] [✕] [🐾] [☎]

SUGAR HILL

▼▼▼▼ The Hilltop Inn **ⒷⒷ** 🐾
(603) 823-5695. **$100-$195, 8 day notice.** 9 Norton Ln. I-93, exit 38, 0.5 mi n on SR 18, then 2.8 mi w on SR 117. Int corridors. **Pets:** Dogs only. $10 daily fee/room. Supervision.
[✕] [🛏] [Ⓚ] [🐾]

▼▼▼▼ Sugar Hill Inn **ⒸⒾ** 🐾
(603) 823-5621. **$115-$360, 14 day notice.** 116 SR 117. I-93, exit 38, 0.5 mi n on SR 18, then 0.4 mi w. Ext/int corridors. **Pets:** Dogs only. $25 daily fee/pet. Designated rooms, service with restrictions, supervision.
[✕] [💻] [🍴] [🏊] [☎]

SUNAPEE

▼▼ Dexter's Inn **ⒸⒾ**
(603) 763-5571. **$110-$200, 14 day notice.** 258 Stagecoach Rd. Jct SR 103B and 11, 0.4 mi w on SR 11, 1.8 mi s (Winn Hill Rd). Ext/int corridors. **Pets:** Other species. $10 daily fee/pet. Designated rooms.
[ASK] [✕] [🛏] [💻] [🍴] [🏊] [✕]

THORNTON

▼ Shamrock Motel **Ⓜ**
(603) 726-3534. **$58-$85, 7 day notice.** 2913 US 3. I-93, exit 29, 2.3 mi n. Ext corridors. **Pets:** Accepted.
[ASK] [S🐾] [✕] [🛏] [💻] [🏊] [Ⓚ] [☎]

TILTON

ⒶⒶⒶ ▼▼▼▼ Black Swan Inn **ⒷⒷ**
(603) 286-4524. **$99-$150, 10 day notice.** 354 W Main St. I-93, exit 20 southbound, 1.5 mi w on SR 3 and 11. Int corridors. **Pets:** Accepted.
[SAVE] [S🐾] [✕] [🛏] [💻]

TROY

ⒶⒶⒶ ▼▼▼ The Inn at East Hill Farm **ⒸⒾ**
(603) 242-6495. **$79-$120, 21 day notice.** 460 Monadnock St. Jct SR 12 and Monadock St, 2 mi e. Ext/int corridors. **Pets:** Accepted.
[SAVE] [✕] [🛏] [🍴] [🏊] [✕] [☎]

WATERVILLE VALLEY

ⒶⒶⒶ ▼▼▼ Best Western Silver Fox Inn **ⓈⒽ**
(603) 236-3699. **$99-$159, 15 day notice.** 14 Snowsbrook Rd. I-93, exit 28, 11 mi e on SR 49, then just n. Int corridors. **Pets:** Small. Designated rooms, service with restrictions, supervision.
[SAVE] [S🐾] [✕] [💻]

WEST LEBANON

ⒶⒶⒶ ▼▼▼ Baymont Inn **Ⓜ**
(603) 298-8888. **Call for rates.** 45 Airport Rd. I-89, exit 20 (SR 12A), just s, then just e. Int corridors. **Pets:** Large. $10 one-time fee/room. Service with restrictions, supervision.
[SAVE] [✕] [&M] [🛏] [💻] [🏊]

▼▼▼▼ Fireside Inn and Suites **ⓈⒽ**
(603) 298-5900. **$120-$200.** 25 Airport Rd. I-89, exit 20 (SR 12A), just s. Int corridors. **Pets:** Accepted.
[ASK] [S🐾] [✕] [🛏] [💻] [🍴] [🏊] [✕]

WOLFEBORO

▼ The Lake Motel [M]
(603) 569-1100. **Call for rates.** 280 S Main St. 0.5 mi se on SR 28. Ext/int corridors. **Pets:** Accepted.

⊠ 🔒 💻 ⊠

WOODSVILLE

⚛ ▼ All Seasons Motel [M]
(603) 747-2157. **$60-$105.** 36 Smith St. I-91, exit 17, 4.1 mi e on US 302, then just s. Ext corridors. **Pets:** Accepted.

[SAVE] [S📶] ⊠ 🔒 💻 🏊

⚛ ▼▼ Nootka Lodge [M]
(603) 747-2418. **$70-$190.** 4982 Dartmouth College Hwy. I-91, exit 17, 4.5 mi e on US 302. Ext corridors. **Pets:** Accepted.

[SAVE] [S📶] ⊠ 🔒 🏊 ⊠

NEW JERSEY

ALLAMUCHY

The Inn at Panther Valley-A Clarion Collection Hotel SH
(908) 852-6000. **$124-$139.** 1627 SR 517. I-80, exit 19, 0.8 mi s. Ext/int corridors. **Pets:** Medium. $20 daily fee/pet. Designated rooms, service with restrictions, crate.

SAVE SØ ✕ 🗄 🖵 ¶

ATLANTIC CITY METROPOLITAN AREA

ABSECON

Knights Inn-Atlantic City/ Absecon M
(609) 407-1919. **Call for rates.** 531 Absecon Blvd. Garden State Pkwy, exit 40, 6 mi e on US 30 (White Horse Pike). Ext corridors. **Pets:** Dogs only. $75 daily fee/pet. Designated rooms, service with restrictions, supervision.

✕ 🗄

ATLANTIC CITY

Sheraton Atlantic City Convention Center Hotel LH
(609) 344-3535. **Call for rates.** 2 Miss America Way. Garden State Expwy, exit 38 to Atlantic City Expwy to Artic Ave, just e to Michigan Ave, then just n. Int corridors. **Pets:** Accepted.

SAVE ✕ 🗄 🖵 ¶ ⊃

BUENA

Econo Lodge M ❧
(856) 697-9000. **Call for rates.** 102 Tuckahoe Rd. Corner of SR 40 and 54. Int corridors. **Pets:** Other species. $15 daily fee/pet. Service with restrictions, supervision.

SAVE ✕ 🗄

SOMERS POINT

Residence Inn by Marriott SH
(609) 927-6400. **$230-$285.** 900 Mays Landing Rd. Garden State Pkwy, exit 30 southbound; exit 29 northbound, 1 mi e. Ext corridors. **Pets:** Accepted.

ASK SØ ✕ 🗄 🖵 ⊃ ✕

WEST ATLANTIC CITY

Quality Hotel Bayside Resort SH
(609) 641-3546. **$59-$299, 30 day notice.** 8029 Black Horse Pike. In West Atlantic City; Garden State Pkwy, exit 38 (Atlantic City Expwy), 2 mi e to exit 5, 0.5 mi s on US 9 to US 40/322, then 1.8 mi e. Int corridors. **Pets:** Accepted.

SAVE SØ ✕ 🗄 🖵 ¶ ⊃ ✕

Ramada-West Atlantic City SH
(609) 646-5220. **$59-$249.** 8037 Black Horse Pike. In West Atlantic City; Garden State Pkwy, exit 38 (Atlantic City Expwy), 2 mi e to exit 5, 0.5 mi s on US 9 to US 40/322, then 1.8 mi e. Ext/int corridors. **Pets:** Medium. $15 daily fee/pet. Service with restrictions, crate.

SAVE SØ ✕ 🗄 🖵 ⊃

END METROPOLITAN AREA

BASKING RIDGE

The Inn at Somerset Hills SH
(908) 580-1300. **$99-$259.** 80 Allen Rd. I-78, exit 33, 0.3 mi n on CR 525, then 0.3 mi w. Int corridors. **Pets:** Accepted.

ASK SØ ✕ 🗄 🖵 ¶

BEACH HAVEN

Engleside Inn SH
(609) 492-1251. **$97-$446, 30 day notice.** 30 Engleside Ave. 6.9 mi s of SR 72 Cswy to Engleside Ave, then just e. Ext corridors. **Pets:** Accepted.

SAVE ✕ 🗄 🖵 ¶ ⊃

BRIDGEWATER

Days Inn SH
(908) 526-9500. **Call for rates.** 1260 Rt 22 E. I-287, exit 17 to US 202/206 S, just s, exit US 22, then 2 mi e; exit 14B northbound, 1 mi w on US 22, U-turn at Adamsville Rd, then 1 mi e. Int corridors. **Pets:** Accepted.

SAVE ✕ 🗄 🖵 ⊃

Hyatt Summerfield Suites SH
(908) 725-0800. **$89-$229.** 530 Rt 22 E. I-287, exit 14B northbound; exit 17 southbound to US 22 W, then 0.8 mi. Ext corridors. **Pets:** Accepted.

ASK ✕ ⊠M 🗄 🖵 ⊃ ✕

BUDD LAKE

◆◆ ◆◆ Extended StayAmerica Mt. Olive-Budd Lake SH
(973) 347-5522. **$96-$150.** 71 International Dr S. I-80, exit 25, just n, follow signs for International Trade Center; just e of jct US 46. Int corridors. **Pets:** Other species. $75 one-time fee/pet. Service with restrictions.

ASK SÒ ✕ ⊟ ▭

CAPE MAY

◆◆ ◆◆◆ Marquis de Lafayette Hotel SH
(609) 884-3500. **$109-$489.** 501 Beach Ave. Between Decatur and Ocean sts. Ext/int corridors. **Pets:** Accepted.

SAVE SÒ ✕ ⊟ ▭ ⓵ ⌔

◆◆ ◆◆◆ Palace Hotel of Cape May SH
(609) 898-8100. **$149-$289, 14 day notice.** 1101 Beach Ave. Jct Beach and Philadelphia aves. Int corridors. **Pets:** Accepted.

SAVE ✕ ⊟ ▭

◆◆◆ White Dove Cottage BB
(609) 884-0613. **Call for rates (no credit cards).** 619 Hughes St. Between Franklin and Ocean sts. Ext/int corridors. **Pets:** Accepted.

✕ ⊟ ▭ ⓩ

CAPE MAY COURT HOUSE

◆◆ ◆◆◆ The Doctors Inn BB
(609) 463-9330. **$100-$350, 14 day notice.** 2 N Main St. At Main (US 9) and Mechanic sts; just s of Garden State Pkwy. Int corridors. **Pets:** Accepted.

SAVE ✕ ⊟ ⓵

CLINTON

◆◆◆ Hampton Inn SH
(908) 713-4800. **Call for rates.** 16 Frontage Dr. I-78, exit 15, 0.3 mi s on CR 513, then left at next light. Int corridors. **Pets:** Accepted.

✕ Ⓜ ⊟ ▭ ⌔

◆◆◆ Holiday Inn Select-Clinton SH
(908) 735-5111. **$139-$179.** 111 Rt 173. I-78, exit 15, just nw. Int corridors. **Pets:** Accepted.

ASK ✕ ⊟ ▭ ⓵ ⌔

CRANBURY

◆◆◆ Residence Inn by Marriott/Cranbury-South Brunswick SH ☙
(609) 395-9447. **$198-$218.** 2662 US 130. New Jersey Tpke, exit 8A to SR 32 W toward town, 2 mi w on S River Rd. Int corridors. **Pets:** Small. $100 one-time fee/room. Service with restrictions, supervision.

ASK SÒ ✕ Ⓜ ⊟ ▭ ⌔ ⌧

◆◆◆ Staybridge Suites/Cranbury SH
(609) 409-7181. **$109-$249.** 1272 S River Rd. New Jersey Tpke, exit 8A to SR 32 toward Cranbury, 2 mi w. Int corridors. **Pets:** $75 one-time fee/pet. Service with restrictions, supervision.

ASK SÒ ✕ ⊟ ▭ ⌔

EAST BRUNSWICK

◆ Motel 6, East Brunswick #1083 SH
(732) 390-4545. **$63-$73.** 244 SR 18 N. New Jersey Tpke, exit 9 (SR 18) to SR 18 S, 1 mi, exit Edgeboro Rd, w at U-turn, then just e. Ext/int corridors. **Pets:** Other species. Service with restrictions, supervision.

SÒ ✕ Ⓜ

◆ Studio 6 East Brunswick #6020 SH
(732) 238-3330. **$81-$91 (no credit cards).** 246 Rt 18 at Edgeboro Rd. New Jersey Tpke, exit 9 (SR 18) to SR 18 S, 1 mi, exit Edgeboro Rd, w at U-turn, then just e. Int corridors. **Pets:** Other species. Service with restrictions, supervision.

SÒ ✕ Ⓜ ⊟ ▭

EAST RUTHERFORD

◆◆ ◆◆ Homestead Studio Suites Hotel-Meadowlands/East Rutherford SH
(201) 939-8866. **$118-$168.** 300 SR 3 E. New Jersey Tpke, exit 16W (from western spur), sports complex right after toll. Int corridors. **Pets:** Other species. $75 one-time fee/pet. Service with restrictions.

ASK SÒ ✕ Ⓜ ⊟ ▭

◆◆◆ Residence Inn by Marriott Meadowlands–East Rutherford SH
(201) 939-0020. **$269-$290.** 10 Murray Hill Pkwy. New Jersey Tpke, exit 16W to SR 3 W to SR 17 N, 1.5 mi n to Paterson Plank Rd (SR 120), then just e. **Pets:** Accepted.

ASK SÒ ✕ Ⓜ ⊟ ▭ ⌔ ⌧

◆◆ ◆◆◆ Sheraton Meadowlands Hotel & Conference Center LH
(201) 896-0500. **$119-$399.** 2 Meadowlands Plaza. New Jersey Tpke, exit 16W (from western spur), sports complex right after toll to Sheraton Plaza Dr. Int corridors. **Pets:** Accepted.

SAVE ✕ ⓂM ⊟ ▭ ⓵ ⌔ ⌧

EATONTOWN

◆◆◆ Staybridge Suites Hotel Eatontown-Tinton Falls SH
(732) 380-9300. **$179-$269.** 4 Industrial Way E. Garden State Pkwy, exit 105, 0.7 mi e on SR 36, then 0.7 mi s on SR 35. Int corridors. **Pets:** Medium. $100 one-time fee/pet. Service with restrictions, crate.

ASK SÒ ✕ ⊟ ▭ ⌔

EDISON

◆◆◆ Clarion Hotel & Towers LH ☙
(732) 287-3500. **$159-$179.** 2055 Lincoln Hwy (SR 27). I-287, exit 2B (SR 27 S) northbound, 1 mi s; exit 3 (New Durham/Metuchen) southbound, 0.5 mi w, then 1 mi s on Talmadge Rd. Int corridors. **Pets:** Small, dogs only. $20 daily fee/room. Designated rooms, service with restrictions, crate.

ASK SÒ ✕ ⓂM ⊟ ▭ ⓵

◆◆◆ Courtyard by Marriott Edison/Woodbridge SH
(732) 738-1991. **$170-$191.** 3105 Woodbridge Ave. New Jersey Tpke, exit 10, 0.5 mi se on CR 514, then just e. Int corridors. **Pets:** Accepted.

ASK SÒ ✕ ⓂM ⊟ ▭ ⌔

◆◆ ◆◆ Extended StayAmerica-Edison-Raritan Center SH
(732) 346-9366. **$92-$125.** 1 Fieldcrest Ave. I-287, exit SR 514 to King Georges Post Rd, then just w. Int corridors. **Pets:** Other species. $75 one-time fee/pet. Service with restrictions.

ASK SÒ ✕ ⓂM ⊟ ▭

◆ Red Roof Inn #7194 M
(732) 248-9300. **Call for rates.** 860 New Durham Rd. I-287, exit 2A northbound, 0.3 mi w via Bridge St, then left; exit 3 southbound, just w. Ext corridors. **Pets:** Accepted.

✕ ⓂM ⊟

◆◆◆ Sheraton Edison LH
(732) 225-8300. **$279.** 125 Raritan Center Pkwy. New Jersey Tpke, exit 10, 0.5 mi se on CR 514, keep right after tolls. Int corridors. **Pets:** Accepted.

ASK ✕ ⓂM ⊟ ▭ ⓵ ⌔ ⌧

ELIZABETH

◆◆ ◆◆ Extended StayAmerica SH
(908) 355-4300. **$105-$147.** 45 Glimcher Realty Way. New Jersey Tpke, exit 13A, after toll follow signs to Jersey Garden Blvd; 1 mi, left on Kapkowski Rd, then just e. Int corridors. **Pets:** Other species. $75 one-time fee/pet. Service with restrictions.

ASK SÒ ✕ ⓂM ⊟ ▭

▼▼▼▼ **Residence Inn by Marriott** SH ❖
(908) 352-4300. **$198-$218.** 83 Glimcher Realty Way. New Jersey Tpke, exit 13A, after toll follow signs to Jersey Garden Blvd, 1 mi, left on Kapkowski Rd, then just e. Int corridors. **Pets:** $100 one-time fee/room. Designated rooms, service with restrictions, crate.
ASK S☐ ✕ ☝M ⊟ ▦ ➣

FAIRFIELD

▼▼▼▼ **La Quinta Inn & Suites Fairfield** SH
(973) 575-1742. **$109-$139.** 38 Two Bridges Rd. I-80, exit 52 westbound; exit 47B (Caldwells) eastbound, 7 mi e on US 46, exit Passaic Ave. Int corridors. **Pets:** Other species. Service with restrictions, supervision.
ASK S☐ ✕ ☝M ⊟ ▦ ⬚ ➣ ⬚

FLEMINGTON

△△△ ▼▼▼ **Ramada** M
(908) 782-7472. **Call for rates.** 250 US 202 & SR 31. 0.5 mi s of the circle. Ext corridors. **Pets:** Medium. $10 daily fee/pet. Designated rooms, service with restrictions, supervision.
SAVE ✕ ⊟ ▦ ⬚ ➣

HAZLET

△△△ ▼▼▼▼ **Holiday Inn/Hazlet** SH
(732) 888-2000. **$69-$249.** 2870 SR 35. Garden State Pkwy, exit 117 to SR 35 S, 2.5 mi s. Int corridors. **Pets:** Accepted.
SAVE ✕ ⊟ ▦ ⬚ ➣

HILLSBOROUGH

▼▼ **Days Inn Hillsborough Executive Inn** SH
(908) 685-9000. **Call for rates.** 118 Rt 206 S. 2.6 mi s of jct SR 28, US 202 and 206, at circle. Int corridors. **Pets:** Accepted.
✕ ⊟ ▦ ⬚ ➣

ISELIN

△△△ ▼▼▼▼ **Woodbridge Hotel & Conference Center** LH
(732) 634-3600. **$105-$189.** 515 Rt 1 S. Garden State Pkwy, exit 131A northbound, 0.7 mi e, s on Middlesex Essex Tpke, 0.4 mi to Gill Ln, then 1.5 mi w; exit 130 southbound, 0.7 mi on US 1 N to Gill Ln, then U-turn; diagonal to Woodbridge Center. Int corridors. **Pets:** Accepted.
SAVE S☐ ✕ ⊟ ▦ ⬚ ➣

LAWRENCEVILLE

▼ **Red Roof Inn-Princeton #7111** M
(609) 896-3388. **Call for rates.** 3203 Brunswick Pike (US 1). I-295, exit 67A, just n. Ext corridors. **Pets:** Accepted.
✕ ⊟

LEDGEWOOD

▼▼ **Days Inn** SH
(973) 347-5100. **Call for rates.** 1691 US 46 W. I-80, exit 27, 2 mi e via US 206 N and 183 N. Int corridors. **Pets:** Accepted.
✕ ⊟ ▦ ➣

LONG BRANCH

▼▼▼ **Ocean Place Resort & Spa** LH
(732) 571-4000. **$125-$629, 7 day notice.** 1 Ocean Blvd. 2.5 mi e from jct SR 71, 0.5 mi s. Int corridors. **Pets:** $250 one-time fee/room. Designated rooms, service with restrictions, supervision.
ASK S☐ ✕ ⊟ ▦ ▦ ➣ ⬚

MAHWAH

▼▼▼ **Homewood Suites by Hilton** SH
(201) 760-9994. **$119-$249.** 375 Corporate Dr. I-287, exit 66, 1.7 mi on SR 17 S to MacArthur Blvd, then 0.4 mi w. Int corridors. **Pets:** Other species. $150 one-time fee/room.
ASK ✕ ⊟ ▦ ➣

△△△ ▼▼▼▼ **Sheraton Mahwah Hotel** LH ❖
(201) 529-1660. **$269-$289.** 1 International Blvd (Rt 17). I-287, exit 66, at SR 17 N. Int corridors. **Pets:** Dogs only. Designated rooms, service with restrictions, supervision.
SAVE ✕ ⊟ ▦ ▦ ➣ ⬚

MIDDLETOWN

△△△ ▼▼▼▼ **Comfort Inn Middletown** M ❖
(732) 671-3400. **$125-$189.** 750 Hwy 35 S. Garden State Pkwy, exit 114, 2 mi on Red Hill Rd, 1 mi s on King's Hwy to SR 35, then 0.3 mi s. Int corridors. **Pets:** Other species. $25 daily fee/room. Service with restrictions, supervision.
SAVE S☐ ✕ ⊟ ▦ ➣

MONMOUTH JUNCTION

▼▼ **Extended StayAmerica Princeton/South Brunswick** SH
(732) 438-5010. **$88-$140.** 4230 US 1 S. 0.5 mi s of jct US 1 and Raymond Rd. Int corridors. **Pets:** Other species. $75 one-time fee/pet. Service with restrictions.
ASK S☐ ✕ ☝M ⊟ ▦

▼ **Red Roof Inn/North Princeton #7198** M
(732) 821-8800. **Call for rates.** 208 New Rd. On US 1 S. Ext corridors. **Pets:** Accepted.
✕ ⊟

▼▼▼ **Residence Inn by Marriott** SH
(732) 329-9600. **$253-$273.** 4225 Rt 1 S. 0.5 mi s of Raymond Rd. Int corridors. **Pets:** Accepted.
ASK S☐ ✕ ☝M ⊟ ▦ ➣ ⬚

MORRIS PLAINS

▼▼▼ **Candlewood Suites Parsippany-Morris Plains** SH
(973) 984-9960. **Call for rates.** 100 Candlewood Dr. I-287, exit 39 northbound; exit 39B southbound, 2 mi w on SR 10. Int corridors. **Pets:** Accepted.
✕ ☝M ⊟ ▦

MORRISTOWN

△△△ ▼▼▼▼ **Hyatt Summerfield Suites Morristown** SH
(973) 971-0008. **$89-$309.** 194 Park Ave. SR 24, exit 2A (Morristown), stay in far left lane. Int corridors. **Pets:** Accepted.
SAVE S☐ ✕ ☝M ⊟ ▦ ➣ ⬚

△△△ ▼▼▼▼ **The Westin Governor Morris** LH ❖
(973) 539-7300. **$129-$349.** 2 Whippany Rd. I-287, exit 36 southbound, left lane to light, left to stop, then left 1 mi; exit 36A northbound thru Morris Ave, 0.8 mi, follow signs. Int corridors. **Pets:** Medium. $50 one-time fee/room. No service.
SAVE S☐ ✕ ⊟ ▦ ▦ ➣

MOUNT OLIVE

▼▼▼ **Residence Inn Mt Olive at the International Trade Center** SH
(973) 691-1720. **$197-$219.** 271 Continental Dr. I-80, exit 25, just n, follow signs for International Trade Center. Int corridors. **Pets:** Other species. $100 one-time fee/room. Service with restrictions, supervision.
ASK S☐ ✕ ⊟ ▦ ➣ ⬚

NEWARK

▼▼▼ **Sheraton Newark Airport Hotel** LH
(973) 690-5500. **Call for rates.** 128 Frontage Rd. New Jersey Tpke, exit 14 via Frontage Rd, 2nd right after toll booth. Int corridors. **Pets:** Accepted.
✕ ☝M ⊟ ▦ ▦ ➣ ⬚

◆◆◆◇ ▼▼▼▼ **SpringHill Suites by Marriott** SH
(973) 624-5300. **$164-$185.** 652 Rt 1 & 9 S. I-95, exit 14, 1 mi sw via US 1 and 9 S. Int corridors. **Pets:** Accepted.

[SAVE] [S✿] [✕] [&M] [📶] [💻] [🐾]

NORTH BERGEN

▼▼ **Days Inn** SH
(201) 348-3600. **$119-$159.** 2750 Tonnelle Ave (US 1 & 9). Jct SR 3, 0.4 mi s. Int corridors. **Pets:** Medium. $100 deposit/pet. Designated rooms, service with restrictions, supervision.

[ASK] [S✿] [✕] [📶] [💻] [♕]

PARAMUS

▼▼ **La Quinta Inn** SH
(201) 265-4200. **$119.** 393 Rt 17 S. Garden State Pkwy, exit 163 northbound to SR 17 N, 0.6 mi to Midland Ave, then U-turn to SR 17 S; exit 165 southbound to Richwood Ave, 1 mi. Int corridors. **Pets:** Other species. Service with restrictions, supervision.

[ASK] [S✿] [✕] [📶] [💻]

PARSIPPANY

▼▼▼▼ **Embassy Suites** LH
(973) 334-1440. **Call for rates.** 909 Parsippany Blvd. I-80, exit 42 to US 202 N; just ne of jct US 202 and 46 W. Int corridors. **Pets:** Accepted.

[✕] [📶] [💻] [♕] [🐾] [✕]

▼▼ **Red Roof Inn #7072** M
(973) 334-3737. **Call for rates.** 855 US 46 E. I-80, exit 47 westbound; exit 45 eastbound, 0.5 mi e. Ext corridors. **Pets:** Accepted.

[✕] [📶]

▼▼▼▼ **Residence Inn by Marriott Parsippany** SH 🐾
(973) 984-3313. **$280-$300.** 3 Gatehall Dr. I-287, exit 39 northbound; exit 39B southbound, 2 mi w on SR 10. Int corridors. **Pets:** Other species. $100 one-time fee/room. Service with restrictions.

[ASK] [S✿] [✕] [&M] [📶] [💻] [🐾] [✕]

◆◆◆◇ ▼▼▼▼ **Sheraton Parsippany Hotel** LH 🐾
(973) 515-2000. **$385-$405.** 199 Smith Rd. I-287, exit 41A northbound; exit 42 to US 46 E, 0.4 mi s. Int corridors. **Pets:** Medium. Designated rooms, service with restrictions, supervision.

[SAVE] [S✿] [✕] [📶] [💻] [♕] [🐾] [✕]

▼▼▼▼ **Staybridge Suites Parsippany** SH
(973) 334-2907. **$194-$269, 3 day notice.** 61 Interpace Pkwy. I-80, exit 42, 0.3 mi s on Cherry Hill Rd, then just w. Int corridors. **Pets:** Accepted.

[ASK] [S✿] [✕] [&M] [📶] [💻] [🐾]

PHILADELPHIA METROPOLITAN AREA (NEARBY PENNSYLVANIA)

BORDENTOWN

◆◆◆◇ ▼ **Imperial Inn** M
(609) 298-3355. **$55-$100.** 3312 US 206 S. New Jersey Tpke, exit 7, 0.8 mi s. Ext corridors. **Pets:** Accepted.

[SAVE] [S✿] [✕] [📶]

CARNEYS POINT

◆◆◆◇ ▼▼▼▼ **Comfort Inn & Suites** SH 🐾
(856) 299-8282. **$69-$99.** 634 Sodders Rd. I-295, exit 2B, just e on Pennsville-Auburn Rd, then 0.3 mi s. Int corridors. **Pets:** Medium. $15 daily fee/pet. Service with restrictions, supervision.

[SAVE] [S✿] [✕] [&M] [📶] [💻]

◆◆◆◇ ▼▼▼▼ **Holiday Inn Express Hotel & Suites** SH
(856) 351-9222. **$125.** 506 Pennsville-Auburn Rd. I-295, exit 2B, just e. Int corridors. **Pets:** Other species. Service with restrictions, supervision.

[SAVE] [✕] [📶] [💻]

CHERRY HILL

▼▼▼▼ **Clarion Hotel & Conference Center** LH
(856) 428-2300. **$119-$159.** 1450 SR 70 E. I-295, exit 34B, just w. Int corridors. **Pets:** Other species. $50 one-time fee/pet. Service with restrictions.

[ASK] [S✿] [✕] [&M] [📶] [💻] [♕] [✕]

▼▼ **Extended StayAmerica-Philadelphia-Cherry Hill** SH
(856) 616-1200. **$87-$110.** 1653 SR 70 (Marlton Pike). I-295, exit 34A, just e. Int corridors. **Pets:** Other species. $75 one-time fee/pet. Service with restrictions.

[ASK] [S✿] [✕] [📶] [💻]

◆◆◆◇ ▼▼▼▼ **Holiday Inn Philadelphia-Cherry Hill** SH
(856) 663-5300. **$115-$149.** 2175 Marlton Pike. I-295, exit 34B, 2.5 mi w. Int corridors. **Pets:** Other species. $50 deposit/room. Service with restrictions.

[SAVE] [✕] [📶] [💻] [♕] [🐾]

DEPTFORD

▼▼▼▼ **Residence Inn by Marriott** SH
(856) 686-9188. **$166-$186.** 1154 Hurffville Rd. In Deptford; SR 42, exit Deptford, Woodbury, Runnemede to CR 544, just e to CR 415. Int corridors. **Pets:** Accepted.

[ASK] [S✿] [✕] [📶] [💻] [🐾] [✕]

HADDONFIELD

▼▼▼ **Haddonfield Inn** BB 🐾
(856) 428-2195. **$199-$299, 7 day notice.** 44 W End Ave. I-295, exit 28, 0.7 mi n on SR 168, 2.6 mi e on Kings Hwy, then just n. Int corridors. **Pets:** Dogs only. $30 daily fee/pet. Designated rooms, service with restrictions, supervision.

[ASK] [✕] [📶]

MOUNT HOLLY

◆◆◆◇ ▼▼▼ **Best Western Burlington Inn** SH
(609) 261-3800. **$104-$129.** 2020 Rt 541, Rd 1. New Jersey Tpke, exit 5, just n. Int corridors. **Pets:** Accepted.

[SAVE] [S✿] [✕] [📶] [💻] [🐾]

MOUNT LAUREL

◆◆◆◇ ▼▼▼ **Candlewood Suites** SH
(856) 642-7567. **Call for rates.** 4000 Crawford Pl. New Jersey Tpke, exit 4, 1 mi s on SR 73 S. Int corridors. **Pets:** Accepted.

[SAVE] [✕] [📶] [💻]

▼▼ **Extended StayAmerica Philadelphia-Mt. Laurel** SH
(856) 778-4100. **$92-$115.** 101 Diemer Dr. New Jersey Tpke, exit 4, 1 mi se on SR 73, just n on Crawford Pl, then just e. Int corridors. **Pets:** Other species. $75 one-time fee/pet. Service with restrictions.

[ASK] [S✿] [✕] [📶] [💻]

▼▼ **Extended Stay Deluxe-Mt. Laurel** SH
(856) 608-9820. **$107-$130.** 500 Diemer Dr. New Jeresy Tpke, exit 4, 1 mi se on SR 73, just n on Crawford Pl, then just e. Int corridors. **Pets:** Other species. $75 one-time fee/pet. Service with restrictions.

[ASK] [S✿] [✕] [📶] [💻]

▼▼◆▼ **Hyatt Summerfield Suites-Mount Laurel** 〔SH〕
(856) 222-1313. **$89-$149.** 3000 Crawford Pl. New Jersey Tpke, exit 4, 1 mi s on SR 73; I-295, exit 36A, 1.5 mi s on SR 73. Ext corridors. **Pets:** Medium. $200 one-time fee/room. Service with restrictions, crate.

ⓐⓢⓚ ⊠ ⓢⓜ 🛏 💻 🍴 ⊃ 🐾

▼ **Red Roof Inn #7066** 〔M〕
(856) 234-5589. **Call for rates.** 603 Fellowship Rd. New Jersey Tpke, exit 4, just nw on SR 73 to Fellowship Rd, then just s; I-295, exit 36A, just se on SR 73 to Fellowship Rd, then just s. Ext corridors. **Pets:** Accepted.

⊠ 🛏

▲▲◆ ▼▼◆▼ **Staybridge Suites** 〔SH〕
(856) 722-1900. **$60-$124.** 4115 Church Rd. New Jersey Tpke, exit 4, 0.5 mi s on SR 73, then 0.5 mi w. Int corridors. **Pets:** $75 one-time fee/pet. No service, supervision.

ⓢⓐⓥⓔ ⓢⓜ ⊠ 🛏 💻 ⊃ 🐾

▲▲◆ ▼▼◆▼ **Wyndham Mount Laurel** 〔LH〕
(856) 234-7000. **Call for rates.** 1111 Rt 73. New Jersey Tpke, exit 4; I-295, exit 36A, 0.5 mi se. Int corridors. **Pets:** Accepted.

ⓢⓐⓥⓔ ⊠ 🛏 💻 🍴 ⊃ 🐾

END METROPOLITAN AREA

PISCATAWAY

▼▼◆▼ **Embassy Suites Hotel** 〔LH〕 ❀
(732) 980-0500. **$129-$229.** 121 Centennial Ave. I-287, exit 9 (Highland Park), just s to Centennial Ave. Int corridors. **Pets:** Medium, other species. $20 daily fee/room. Designated rooms, service with restrictions, supervision.

ⓐⓢⓚ ⊠ 🛏 💻 🍴 ⊃ 🐾

▼ **Motel 6 Piscataway #1084** 〔SH〕
(732) 981-9200. **$65-$75.** 1012 Stelton Rd. I-287, exit 5, just e. Ext/int corridors. **Pets:** Other species. Service with restrictions, supervision.

ⓢⓜ

▼▼◆▼ **Radisson Hotel Piscataway** 〔LH〕
(732) 980-0400. **Call for rates.** 21 Kingsbridge Rd. I-287, exit 9 (Highland Park) to Centennial Ave via River Rd S, then 0.4 mi s. Int corridors. **Pets:** Accepted.

⊠ 🛏 💻 🍴 ⊃

PLAINSBORO

▼▼◆▼ **Courtyard by Marriott Princeton** 〔SH〕
(609) 716-9100. **$205-$225.** 3815 US 1 S. 0.4 mi s of Scudders Mill Rd at Mapleton Rd. Int corridors. **Pets:** Accepted.

ⓐⓢⓚ ⓢⓜ ⊠ ⓢⓜ 🛏 💻 ⊃

PRINCETON

▲▲◆ ▼▼◆▼ **Clarion Hotel-The Palmer Inn** 〔SH〕
(609) 452-2500. **$119-$300, 3 day notice.** 3499 US 1 S. 2 mi s of jct CR 526 and 571. Ext/int corridors. **Pets:** Other species. $20 daily fee/room. Service with restrictions, crate.

ⓢⓐⓥⓔ ⓢⓜ ⊠ 🛏 💻 🍴 ⊃

▼▼ **Extended StayAmerica Princeton-West Windsor** 〔SH〕
(609) 919-9000. **$108-$160.** 3450 Brunswick Pike N. 0.5 mi s of Meadow Rd. Int corridors. **Pets:** Other species. $75 one-time fee/pet. Service with restrictions.

ⓐⓢⓚ ⓢⓜ ⊠ ⓢⓜ 🛏 💻

▲▲◆ ▼▼◆▼ **Holiday Inn Princeton** 〔SH〕
(609) 520-1200. **$194.** 100 Independence Way. I-295, exit 67A (SR 1) northbound; exit 67 (SR 1) southbound, 7 mi n. Int corridors. **Pets:** Medium. $75 one-time fee/room. Designated rooms, service with restrictions, crate.

ⓢⓐⓥⓔ ⓢⓜ ⊠ 🛏 💻 🍴 ⊃ 🐾

▲▲◆ ▼▼◆▼ **Homewood Suites** 〔SH〕 ❀
(609) 720-0550. **$169-$219.** 3819 US 1 S. 0.4 mi s of Scudders Mill Rd at Mapleton Rd. Int corridors. **Pets:** Medium. $49 one-time fee/room. Service with restrictions, supervision.

ⓢⓐⓥⓔ ⓢⓜ ⊠ 🛏 💻 ⊃ 🐾

▲▲◆ ▼▼◆▼ **Nassau Inn** 〔SH〕
(609) 921-7500. **$199-$245.** 10 Palmer Square. Center. Int corridors. **Pets:** Accepted.

ⓢⓐⓥⓔ ⓢⓜ ⊠ 🛏 💻 🍴

▼▼◆▼ **Residence Inn by Marriott-Princeton at Carnegie Center** 〔SH〕
(609) 799-0550. **$231-$251.** 3563 US 1 S. 1.5 mi s of jct CR 527 and 571. Int corridors. **Pets:** Accepted.

ⓐⓢⓚ ⓢⓜ ⊠ ⓢⓜ 🛏 💻 ⊃ 🐾

▼▼◆▼ **Staybridge Suites** 〔SH〕
(609) 951-0009. **$109-$370.** 4375 US 1 S. Just past Ridge Rd. Ext corridors. **Pets:** Medium, other species. $10 daily fee/pet. Service with restrictions, crate.

ⓐⓢⓚ ⊠ 🛏 💻 ⊃ 🐾

▲▲◆ ▼▼◆▼ **Westin Princeton at Forrestal Village** 〔LH〕 ❀
(609) 452-7900. **$349-$399.** 201 Village Blvd. On US 1 southbound, 1.5 mi n of CR 571. Int corridors. **Pets:** Small, dogs only. $60 one-time fee/room. Service with restrictions, crate.

ⓢⓐⓥⓔ ⓢⓜ ⊠ ⓢⓜ 🛏 💻 🍴 ⊃ 🐾

RAMSEY

▲▲◆ ▼▼◆▼ **Best Western-The Inn at Ramsey** 〔SH〕
(201) 327-6700. **$79-$119, 14 day notice.** 1315 Rt 17 S. Jct I-287 and SR 17 S, 3 mi s. Int corridors. **Pets:** Medium, dogs only. $25 deposit/pet, $10 daily fee/pet. Designated rooms, service with restrictions, supervision.

ⓢⓐⓥⓔ ⓢⓜ ⊠ 🛏 💻 🍴

▼▼ **Extended StayAmerica Ramsey** 〔SH〕
(201) 236-9996. **$117-$175.** 112 SR 17 N. Just s of Lake St exit. Int corridors. **Pets:** Other species. $75 one-time fee/pet. Service with restrictions.

ⓐⓢⓚ ⓢⓜ ⊠ ⓢⓜ 🛏 💻

RED BANK

▼▼ **Extended StayAmerica Red Bank-Middletown** 〔SH〕
(732) 450-8688. **$110-$255.** 329 Newman Springs Rd. Garden State Pkwy, exit 109, just e. Int corridors. **Pets:** Other species. $75 one-time fee/pet. Service with restrictions.

ⓐⓢⓚ ⓢⓜ ⊠ ⓢⓜ 🛏 💻

ROCKAWAY

▲▲◆ ▼▼◆ **Best Western at Rockaway** 〔SH〕 ❀
(973) 625-1200. **$85-$219.** 14 Green Pond Rd. I-80, exit 37, just n. Int corridors. **Pets:** $25 daily fee/room. Crate.

ⓢⓐⓥⓔ ⓢⓜ ⊠ 🛏 💻

RUTHERFORD

▼▼ **Extended StayAmerica-Meadowlands** 〔SH〕
(201) 635-0266. **$113-$154.** 750 Edwin L Ward Sr Memorial Hwy. I-95, exit 16W, 1.5 mi w on SR 3 to SR 17 N service road exit, then 0.5 mi e. Int corridors. **Pets:** Other species. $75 one-time fee/pet. Service with restrictions.

ⓐⓢⓚ ⓢⓜ ⊠ 🛏 💻

SECAUCUS

▼▼ Extended StayAmerica-Secaucus-Meadowlands 🆂🅷
(201) 617-1711. **$133-$183.** 1 Meadowlands Pkwy. Between eastern and western spurs of New Jersey Tpke; exits 16E, 17, or 16W to SR 3, exit Meadowlands Pkwy, just n. Int corridors. **Pets:** Other species. $75 one-time fee/pet. Service with restrictions.

🄰🅂🄺 🆂🛋 ⊠ 🛏🄼 🛏 ▣

AAA ▼▼▼▼ The Holiday Inn Harmon Meadow 🅻🅷 🐾
(201) 348-2000. **$240-$280.** 300 Plaza Dr. New Jersey Tpke, exits 16E, 17, or 16W via SR 3 to Harmon Meadow Blvd. Int corridors. **Pets:** Large, dogs only. $49 one-time fee/room. Service with restrictions, crate.

🆂🄰🆅🄴 🆂🛋 ⊠ 🛏 ▣ ⊺⊺

▼▼ Homestead Studio Suites Hotel-Secaucus/Meadowlands 🆂🅷
(201) 553-9700. **$177-$295.** 1 Plaza Dr. New Jersey Tpke, exit 16E northbound; exit 17E southbound, 0.3 mi e. Int corridors. **Pets:** Other species. $75 one-time fee/pet. Service with restrictions.

🄰🅂🄺 🆂🛋 ⊠ 🛏🄼 🛏 ▣

▼▼▼▼ La Quinta Suites Secaucus 🅻🅷
(201) 863-8700. **$145-$175.** 300 Rt 3 W at Mill Creek Dr. Between eastern and western spurs of New Jersey Tpke, exits 16E, 17 or 16W via SR 3 W and Harmon Meadow Blvd; in Mill Creek Mall. Int corridors. **Pets:** Other species. Service with restrictions, supervision.

🄰🅂🄺 🆂🛋 ⊠ 🛏 ▣ ⊺⊺ ⊅

▼▼ Red Roof Inn-Meadowlands #7150 🅼
(201) 319-1000. **Call for rates.** 15 Meadowlands Pkwy. Between eastern and western spurs of New Jersey Tpke, exits 16E, 17 or 16W to SR 3, exit Meadowlands Pkwy. Ext corridors. **Pets:** Accepted.

⊠ 🛏 ⊠

SOMERSET

▼▼ Candlewood Suites 🆂🅷
(732) 748-1400. **Call for rates (no credit cards).** 41 Worlds Fair Dr. I-287, exit 10 (CR 527), left on Ramp (CR 527 S/Easton Ave), 0.3 mi, then 0.5 mi w. Int corridors. **Pets:** Accepted.

⊠ 🛏 ▣

▼▼ Extended StayAmerica-Franklin 🆂🅷
(732) 469-8080. **$98-$158.** 30 World Fair Dr. I-287, exit 10 (CR 527), left on ramp (CR 527 S/Easton Ave), 0.3 mi, then 0.5 mi w. Int corridors. **Pets:** Other species. $75 one-time fee/pet. Service with restrictions.

🄰🅂🄺 🆂🛋 ⊠ 🛏 ▣

▼▼▼▼ Holiday Inn-Somerset 🆂🅷 🐾
(732) 356-1700. **$120-$140.** 195 Davidson Ave. I-287, exit 10 (CR 527), just n (direction Bound Brook), then 0.5 mi sw. Int corridors. **Pets:** Small, other species. $15 daily fee/pet. Designated rooms, service with restrictions, supervision.

🄰🅂🄺 🆂🛋 ⊠ 🛏🄼 🛏 ▣ ⊺⊺ ⊅

▼▼▼▼ Homewood Suites by Hilton-Somerset 🆂🅷
(732) 868-9155. **Call for rates.** 101 Pierce St. I-287, exit 10 (CR 527), left on ramp (CR 527 S/Easton Ave), 0.3 mi, 0.7 mi w on World Fair Dr, then just s. Int corridors. **Pets:** Accepted.

⊠ 🛏🄼 🛏 ▣ ⊅ ⊠

▼▼▼▼ Residence Inn by Marriott-Somerset 🆂🅷
(732) 627-0881. **$203-$224.** 37 World Fair Dr. I-287, exit 10 (CR 527), left on ramp (CR 527 S/Easton Ave) 0.3 mi, then 0.5 mi w. Int corridors. **Pets:** Accepted.

🄰🅂🄺 🆂🛋 ⊠ 🛏🄼 🛏 ▣ ⊅ ⊠

▼▼▼▼ Somerset Marriott Hotel 🅻🅷
(732) 560-0500. **Call for rates.** 110 Davidson Ave. I-287, exit 10 (CR 527), just n (direction Bound Brook) to Davidson Ave, then just sw. Int corridors. **Pets:** Accepted.

⊠ 🛏 ▣ ⊺⊺ ⊅ ⊠

▼▼▼▼ Staybridge Suites Somerset 🆂🅷
(732) 356-8000. **Call for rates.** 260 Davidson Ave. I-287, exit 10 (CR 527), just n (direction Bound Brook) to Davidson Ave, then 0.8 mi sw. Ext corridors. **Pets:** Accepted.

⊠ 🛏 ▣ ⊅ ⊠

TINTON FALLS

▼▼ Red Roof Inn #7211 🅼
(732) 389-4646. **Call for rates.** 11 Centre Plaza. Garden State Pkwy, exit 105, just right at 1st light after toll. Ext corridors. **Pets:** Accepted.

⊠ 🛏🄼 🛏

▼▼▼▼ Residence Inn by Marriott 🆂🅷
(732) 389-8100. **$176-$196.** 90 Park Rd. Garden State Pkwy, exit 105, 1st jughandle after toll, immediate left before Courtyard by Marriott, just n, then e. Ext corridors. **Pets:** Accepted.

🄰🅂🄺 🆂🛋 ⊠ 🛏 ▣ ⊅ ⊠

TOMS RIVER

AAA ▼▼▼ Howard Johnson Hotel-Toms River 🆂🅷 🐾
(732) 244-1000. **$99-$199.** 955 Hooper Ave. Garden State Pkwy, exit 82, 1 mi e on SR 37. Int corridors. **Pets:** Medium. $100 daily fee/pet. Designated rooms, service with restrictions.

🆂🄰🆅🄴 🆂🛋 🛏 🛏 ▣ ⊺⊺ ⊅

VINELAND

▼▼ Ramada Inn Vineland 🆂🅷
(856) 696-3800. **Call for rates.** 2216 W Landis Ave. SR 55, exit 32A, just e. Int corridors. **Pets:** Accepted.

⊠ 🛏 ▣ ⊺⊺ ⊅

WANTAGE

▼ High Point Country Inn 🅼 🐾
(973) 702-1860. **$89.** 1328 SR 23 N. 1 mi n of Colesville Village Center. Ext corridors. **Pets:** Dogs only. $10 daily fee/pet. Designated rooms, service with restrictions.

🄰🅂🄺 🆂🛋 ⊠ 🛏 ⊅ ⊘

WARREN

▼▼▼ Somerset Hills Hotel 🆂🅷
(908) 647-6700. **$99-$259.** 200 Liberty Corner Rd. I-78, exit 33, just n on CR 525. Int corridors. **Pets:** Accepted.

🄰🅂🄺 🆂🛋 ⊠ 🛏 ▣ ⊺⊺ ⊅

WAYNE

▼▼▼ Residence Inn by Marriott Wayne 🆂🅷
(973) 872-7100. **$219-$241.** 30 Nevins Rd. From jct CR 640 (Riverview Dr) and 681 (Valley Rd), 3.5 mi n, just w on Barbour Pond Dr, then just n. Int corridors. **Pets:** Accepted.

🄰🅂🄺 🆂🛋 ⊠ 🛏 ▣ ⊅ ⊠

WEEHAWKEN

AAA ▼▼▼▼ Sheraton Suites On The Hudson 🅻🅷
(201) 617-5600. **$169-$579.** 500 Harbor Blvd. I-495 E toward Lincoln Tunnel, exit Weekawken/Hoboken, bear right at bottom of hill, then 0.4 mi e to Lincoln Harbor Complex; on 19th St. Int corridors. **Pets:** Accepted.

🆂🄰🆅🄴 ⊠ 🛏 ▣ ⊺⊺ ⊅

WEST ORANGE

▼▼▼ Residence Inn by Marriott-West Orange 🆂🅷
(973) 669-4700. **$247-$268.** 107 Prospect Ave. I-280, exit 8B, 1 mi n on CR 527 (Prospect Ave). Int corridors. **Pets:** Accepted.

🄰🅂🄺 🆂🛋 ⊠ 🛏 ▣ ⊅

WHIPPANY

◆◆ **Homestead Studio Suites Hotel-Hanover/Parsippany** SH
(973) 463-1999. **$128-$178.** 125 Rt 10 E. I-287, exit 39, 3.6 mi e. Int corridors. **Pets:** Other species. $75 one-time fee/pet. Service with restrictions.

[ASK] [S🐾] [✕] [&M] [🛏] [🖵]

⊛ ◆◆◆ **Hyatt Summerfield Suites Parsippany/Whippany** SH 🐾
(973) 605-1001. **$89-$309.** 1 Ridgedale Ave N. I-287, exit 39, just nw. Int corridors. **Pets:** Other species. $100 one-time fee/room. Service with restrictions, crate.

[SAVE] [✕] [&M] [🛏] [🖵] [🏊]

WOODBRIDGE

◆◆ **Homestead Studio Suites Hotel-Woodbridge-Newark** SH
(732) 442-8333. **$92-$145.** 1 Hoover Way. New Jersey Tpke, exit 11, 1.4 mi to US 9 N, then just w on King Georges Post Rd. Int corridors. **Pets:** Other species. $75 one-time fee/pet. Service with restrictions.

[ASK] [S🐾] [✕] [&M] [🛏] [🖵]

ALAMOGORDO

▼▼ Quality Inn SH
(505) 437-7100. **Call for rates.** 1401 S White Sands Blvd. 1.6 mi s of jct US 54/70 and 82. Int corridors. **Pets:** Accepted.

▼▼ Super 8 Motel-Alamogordo SH
(505) 434-4205. **Call for rates.** 3204 N White Sands Blvd. Just s of jct US 54/70 and 82. Int corridors. **Pets:** Accepted.

ALBUQUERQUE

▼▼ American Motor Inn SH
(505) 298-7426. **Call for rates.** 12999 Central Ave NE. I-40, exit 167 westbound, 0.3 mi w on Central Ave; exit 166 eastbound, right on Juan Tabo, left on Central Ave, then 0.5 mi e. Ext corridors. **Pets:** Accepted.

▼▼ Best Western InnSuites Hotel & Suites-Airport Albuquerque SH
(505) 242-7022. **$69-$129, 7 day notice.** 2400 Yale Blvd SE. I-25, exit 222 northbound; exit 222A southbound, 1 mi e, then just s. Int corridors. **Pets:** Medium. $25 one-time fee/pet. Designated rooms, service with restrictions, supervision.

▼▼▼ Best Western Rio Grande Inn SH
(505) 843-9500. **$98-$128.** 1015 Rio Grande Blvd NW. I-40, exit 157A, just s. Int corridors. **Pets:** Accepted.

▼▼▼ Brittania & W E Mauger Estate Bed & Breakfast BB ❖
(505) 242-8755. **$143-$179, 10 day notice.** 701 Roma Ave NW. I-25, exit 225, 1 mi w, then just s on 7th Ave. Int corridors. **Pets:** Dogs only. $30 one-time fee/room. Designated rooms, service with restrictions, crate.

▼▼▼ Candlewood Suites SH
(505) 888-3424. **Call for rates.** 3025 Menaul Blvd NE. I-40, exit 160, just n to Menaul Blvd, then 0.5 mi w. Int corridors. **Pets:** Accepted.

▼▼▼ ClubHouse Inn & Suites SH
(505) 345-0010. **Call for rates.** 1315 Menaul Blvd NE. I-25, exit 227A, just e to University Blvd, 0.5 mi s to Menaul Blvd, then 0.5 mi w. Int corridors. **Pets:** Medium, other species. $10 daily fee/pet. Service with restrictions, supervision.

▼▼ Comfort Inn-Airport SH
(505) 243-2244. **Call for rates.** 2300 Yale Blvd SE. I-25, exit 222A southbound; exit 222 northbound, 1 mi n, then just s. Ext/int corridors. **Pets:** Accepted.

▼▼ Comfort Inn & Suites by Choice Hotels SH
(505) 822-1090. **Call for rates.** 5811 Signal Ave NE. I-25, exit 233, just e via Alameda. Int corridors. **Pets:** Accepted.

▼▼ Comfort Inn East M
(505) 294-1800. **Call for rates.** 13031 Central Ave NE. I-40, exit 167, just w. Ext corridors. **Pets:** Accepted.

▼▼ Comfort Inn-Midtown SH
(505) 881-3210. **Call for rates.** 2015 Menaul Blvd NE. I-25, exit 225 northbound, 1.6 mi n of Frontage Rd to Menaul Blvd, then just e; exit 227 (Commanche Rd) southbound, s on Frontage Rd, 0.8 mi n to Menaul Blvd, then just e. Ext corridors. **Pets:** Accepted.

▼▼ Country Inn & Suites SH
(505) 246-9600. **$69-$129.** 2601 Mulberry SE. I-25, exit 222 (Gibson Blvd), just e. Int corridors. **Pets:** Accepted.

▼▼ Days Inn-Hotel Circle SH
(505) 275-3297. **Call for rates.** 10321 Hotel Ave NE. I-40, exit 165 (Eubank Blvd), just n. Ext corridors. **Pets:** Other species. $20 daily fee/pet. Service with restrictions, supervision.

▼▼ Days Inn West M
(505) 836-3297. **$59-$65, 3 day notice.** 6031 Iliff Rd NW. I-40, exit 155, just s on Coors Rd, then just w. Ext corridors. **Pets:** Other species. $10 daily fee/pet. Designated rooms, service with restrictions.

▼▼ Drury Inn & Suites-Albuquerque SH
(505) 341-3600. **Call for rates.** 4310 The 25 Way NE. I-25, exit Jefferson St NE, northwest quadrant of exchange. Int corridors. **Pets:** Large, other species. Service with restrictions, supervision.

▼▼ Econo Lodge Downtown/University M ❖
(505) 243-1321. **$49-$99.** 817 Central Ave NE. I-25, exit 224A northbound; exit 224B southbound, just e. Ext corridors. **Pets:** Medium. $25 deposit/room, $5 daily fee/pet. Designated rooms, service with restrictions, supervision.

▼▼ Econo Lodge East M
(505) 292-7600. **$45-$99.** 13211 Central Ave NE. I-40, exit 167 (Central Ave), just w. Ext corridors. **Pets:** Medium, other species. $5 daily fee/pet. Service with restrictions, supervision.

▼▼ Econo Lodge Midtown SH
(505) 880-0080. **Call for rates.** 2412 Carlisle Blvd NE. I-40, exit 160, just n. Ext corridors. **Pets:** Other species. $10 one-time fee/pet. Service with restrictions, supervision.

(AAA) ♦♦♦ Econo Lodge Old Town SH
(505) 243-8475. **$45-$125.** 2321 Central Ave NW. I-40, exit 157A, 0.6 mi s on Rio Grande Blvd, then 0.4 mi w. Ext corridors. **Pets:** Medium, dogs only. $10 daily fee/pet. Designated rooms, service with restrictions, crate.
SAVE ✕ 🛏 🖵 🐾

(AAA) ♦♦♦♦ Fairfield Inn Airport SH
(505) 247-1621. **$64-$149.** 2300 Centre Ave SE. I-25, exit 222 northbound; exit 222A southbound, 1 mi e to Yale Blvd; northeast jct of Gibson and Yale blvds. Int corridors. **Pets:** Other species. $75 one-time fee/room. Service with restrictions, supervision.
SAVE S🐾 ✕ 🖑M 🛏 🖵 🐾

(AAA) ♦ GuestHouse Inn & Suites SH ❀
(505) 271-8500. **$40-$99.** 10331 Hotel Ave NE. I-40, exit 165, 2 blks n. Int corridors. **Pets:** Very small. $10 daily fee/pet. Service with restrictions, supervision.
SAVE S🐾 ✕ 🛏 🖵

(AAA) ♦♦♦♦ Hacienda Antigua Inn BB
(505) 345-5399. **$139-$209, 10 day notice.** 6708 Tierra Dr NW. I-25, exit 230 (Osuna Dr), 2 mi w, then just n. Ext/int corridors. **Pets:** Other species. $30 one-time fee/pet. Designated rooms, service with restrictions, supervision.
SAVE S🐾 ✕ 🛏 🖵 🐾

(AAA) ♦♦♦ Hampton Inn-North SH
(505) 344-1555. **Call for rates.** 5101 Ellison NE. I-25, exit 231, just w. Ext corridors. **Pets:** Medium. Service with restrictions, supervision.
SAVE ✕ 🖑M 🛏 🖵 🐾

(AAA) ♦♦♦ Hawthorn Inn & Suites SH
(505) 242-1555. **Call for rates.** 1511 Gibson Blvd SE. I-25, exit 222 northbound; exit 222A southbound, just e. Int corridors. **Pets:** Medium. $25 daily fee/pet. Designated rooms, service with restrictions, supervision.
SAVE ✕ 🖑M 🛏 🖵 🐾

(AAA) ♦♦♦ Holiday Inn Express SH
(505) 275-8900. **Call for rates.** 10330 Hotel Ave NE. I-40, exit 165 (Eubank Blvd), 2 blks n. Ext corridors. **Pets:** Medium. $25 one-time fee/pet. Service with restrictions.
SAVE ✕ 🛏 🖵 🐾 ✕

(AAA) ♦♦♦ Holiday Inn Express-West SH
(505) 836-8600. **$95.** 6100 Iliff Rd NW. I-40, exit 155, just sw. Ext/int corridors. **Pets:** Accepted.
SAVE S🐾 ✕ 🖑M 🛏 🖵 🐾 ✕

♦♦♦ Howard Johnson Express Inn SH
(505) 828-1600. **Call for rates.** 7630 Pan American Frwy NE. I-25, exit 231, 0.8 mi n on frontage road. Int corridors. **Pets:** Other species. $15 daily fee/pet. Designated rooms, service with restrictions, supervision.
✕ 🛏 🖵 🐾

♦♦♦♦ La Quinta Inn Albuquerque (Airport) SH
(505) 243-5500. **$99-$129.** 2116 Yale Blvd SE. I-25, exit 222 northbound; exit 222A southbound, 1 mi e. Ext/int corridors. **Pets:** Other species. Service with restrictions, supervision.
ASK S🐾 ✕ 🖑M 🛏 🖵 🐾

♦♦♦ La Quinta Inn Albuquerque (I-40 East) SH
(505) 884-3591. **$82-$112.** 2424 San Mateo Blvd NE. I-40, exit 161 westbound; exit 161B eastbound, just n. Ext corridors. **Pets:** Other species. Service with restrictions, supervision.
ASK S🐾 ✕ 🛏 🖵 🐾

♦♦♦ La Quinta Inn Albuquerque (North) M
(505) 821-9000. **$99-$139.** 5241 San Antonio Dr NE. I-25, exit 231, just e. Ext corridors. **Pets:** Other species. Service with restrictions, supervision.
ASK S🐾 ✕ 🖑M 🛏 🖵 🐾

♦♦♦ La Quinta Inn & Suites Albuquerque (West) SH
(505) 839-1744. **$122-$152.** 6101 Iliff Rd NW. I-40, exit 155, just sw. Int corridors. **Pets:** Other species. Service with restrictions, supervision.
ASK S🐾 ✕ 🖑M 🛏 🖵 🐾

♦♦♦ La Quinta Inn & Suites Northwest SH
(505) 345-7500. **$94-$124.** 7439 Pan American Frwy NE. I-25, exit 231, just w. Int corridors. **Pets:** Other species. Service with restrictions, supervision.
ASK S🐾 ✕ 🛏 🖵 🐾

♦♦♦ La Quinta Suites Midtown/University SH
(505) 761-5600. **$105-$135.** 2011 Menaul Blvd. Jct University Blvd NE and Menaul Blvd, just e. Int corridors. **Pets:** Other species. Service with restrictions, supervision.
ASK S🐾 ✕ 🖑M 🛏 🖵 🐾

♦ Motel 6 Albuquerque North #1290 SH
(505) 821-1472. **$45-$58 (no credit cards).** 8510 Pan American Frwy NE. I-25, exit 232 (Paseo del Norte), just n on Frontage Rd. Int corridors. **Pets:** Other species. Service with restrictions, supervision.
S🐾 ✕ 🖑M 🐾

(AAA) ♦ Motel 76 M
(505) 836-3881. **$38-$65.** 1521 Coors Blvd NW. I-40, exit 155 (Coors Blvd), just s. Ext corridors. **Pets:** Small. $25 deposit/room. Designated rooms, service with restrictions, supervision.
SAVE ✕

♦♦♦ Nativo Lodge SH
(505) 798-4300. **$89-$209.** 6000 Pan American Frwy NE. I-25, exit 230, just e. Int corridors. **Pets:** Accepted.
ASK S🐾 ✕ 🛏 🖵 🍴 🐾 ✕

(AAA) ♦♦ Plaza Inn Albuquerque SH
(505) 243-5693. **Call for rates.** 900 Medical Arts NE. I-25, exit 225, just e. Int corridors. **Pets:** Medium. $25 daily fee/room. Service with restrictions, supervision.
SAVE ✕ 🖑M 🛏 🖵 🍴 🐾

(AAA) ♦♦ Quality Inn & Suites Albuquerque Downtown SH
(505) 242-5228. **$59-$150.** 411 McKnight Ave NW. I-40, exit 159A, just s via 4th St N. Int corridors. **Pets:** Accepted.
SAVE S🐾 ✕ 🖵 🐾

(AAA) ♦♦♦ Quality Suites SH
(505) 797-0850. **Call for rates.** 5251 San Antonio Dr NE. I-25, exit 231, just e. Int corridors. **Pets:** Medium. $50 deposit/room, $10 daily fee/pet. Service with restrictions, supervision.
SAVE ✕ 🛏 🖵 🐾

♦♦ Ramada Limited SH
(505) 858-3297. **Call for rates.** 5601 Alameda Blvd NE. I-25, exit 233, just w. Int corridors. **Pets:** Accepted.
✕ 🖑M 🛏 🖵 🐾

♦♦♦ Residence Inn North by Marriott SH
(505) 761-0200. **$122-$162.** 4331 The Lane at 25 NE. I-25, exit 229 (Jefferson St), just w, just n to The Lane at 25 NE, then just e. Int corridors. **Pets:** Medium, other species. $100 one-time fee/room. Service with restrictions.
ASK S🐾 ✕ 🖑M 🛏 🖵 🐾 ✕

♦♦ Sandia Peak Inn SH
(505) 831-5036. **Call for rates.** 4614 Central Ave SW. I-40, exit 159A (Rio Grande Blvd), just s, then 2 mi w. Ext corridors. **Pets:** Accepted.
✕ 🛏 🐾

(AAA) ♦♦♦♦ Sheraton Albuquerque Uptown LH ❀
(505) 881-0000. **$99-$249.** 2600 Louisiana Blvd NE. I-40, exit 162, 0.8 mi n. Int corridors. **Pets:** Medium. Designated rooms, service with restrictions, supervision.
SAVE S🐾 ✕ 🖑M 🛏 🖵 🍴 🐾 ✕

Stardust Inn **M**
(505) 243-2891. **$45-$75.** 801 Central Ave NE. I-25, 224A northbound; exit 224B southbound, just e. Ext corridors. **Pets:** Medium, dogs only. $25 deposit/pet, $10 daily fee/pet. Service with restrictions, supervision.

Suburban Extended Stay Hotels by Choice Hotels **M**
(505) 883-8888. **$79.** 2401 Wellsley Dr NE. I-40, exit 160, just n to Menaul Blvd, just w, then just s. Ext corridors. **Pets:** Accepted.

Super 8 Motel East **SH**
(505) 271-4807. **Call for rates.** 450 Paisano NE. I-40, exit 166 (Juan Tabo Blvd), just n to Copper, then just s. Int corridors. **Pets:** Accepted.

Super 8 Motel of Albuquerque **SH**
(505) 888-4884. **Call for rates.** 2500 University Blvd NE. I-25, exit 225 northbound, 1.9 mi n on frontage road to Menaul Blvd, then just e; exit 227 (Comanche Rd) southbound, 0.9 mi s to Menaul Blvd, then just e. Int corridors. **Pets:** Accepted.

Super 8 Motel West (Albuquerque) **SH**
(505) 836-5560. **Call for rates.** 6030 Iliff Rd NW. I-40, exit 155, 0.5 mi s. Int corridors. **Pets:** Accepted.

TownePlace Suites by Marriott **SH**
(505) 232-5800. **$79-$149.** 2400 Centre Ave SE. I-25, exit 222 northbound; exit 222A southbound, 1 mi e to Yale Blvd, at northeast jct of Gibson and Yale blvds, then just e. Int corridors. **Pets:** Other species. $100 one-time fee/room. Service with restrictions, supervision.

Vagabond Inn Executive **SH**
(505) 247-0512. **$59-$149, 7 day notice.** 1901 University Blvd SE. I-25, exit 222A southbound; exit 222 northbound, just e. Int corridors. **Pets:** Accepted.

Wyndham Albuquerque at International Sunport **LH**
(505) 843-7000. **Call for rates.** 2910 Yale Blvd SE. I-25, exit 225 northbound; exit 222A southbound, 1 mi e on Gibson Blvd, then 0.5 mi s. Int corridors. **Pets:** Accepted.

ALGODONES

Hacienda Vargas Bed and Breakfast Inn **BB** ❖
(505) 867-9115. **$89-$169, 10 day notice.** 1431 SR 313 (El Camino Real). I-25, exit 248, 0.5 mi w. Int corridors. **Pets:** Other species. $15 one-time fee/room. Crate.

ARROYO SECO

Adobe and Stars B & B **BB**
(505) 776-2776. **Call for rates.** 584 State Hwy 150. 1.1 mi ne on SR 150 at Valdez Rd. Ext/int corridors. **Pets:** Accepted.

Cottonwood Inn Bed & Breakfast **BB**
(505) 776-5826. **Call for rates.** 02 SR 230. On SR 150 at SR 230. Ext/int corridors. **Pets:** Accepted.

ARTESIA

Artesia Inn **M**
(505) 746-9801. **$50-$70.** 1820 S 1st St. 1.5 mi s on US 285. Ext corridors. **Pets:** Other species. $12 one-time fee/room.

Best Western Pecos Inn **SH**
(505) 748-3324. **$89-$109.** 2209 W Main. 1.5 mi w on US 82. Int corridors. **Pets:** Accepted.

BERNALILLO

Days Inn-Bernalillo **SH**
(505) 771-7000. **Call for rates.** 107 N Camino del Pueblo. I-25, exit 242, just w. Int corridors. **Pets:** Medium. $30 deposit/pet. Service with restrictions, supervision.

Hyatt Regency Tamaya Resort and Spa **LH** ✿
(505) 867-1234. **$165-$425, 3 day notice.** 1300 Tuyuna Tr. I-25, exit 242, 1 mi w on SR 44 to Tamaya Rd, then 1 mi n, follow signs. Int corridors. **Pets:** Medium. $50 one-time fee/room. Service with restrictions.

La Hacienda Grande **BB**
(505) 867-1887. **$89-$129, 10 day notice.** 21 Barros Rd. I-25, exit 242, 0.3 mi w to Camino del Pueblo, then 0.5 mi n. Ext/int corridors. **Pets:** Accepted.

Quality Inn & Suites **SH**
(505) 771-9500. **$55-$155.** 210 N Hill Rd. I-25, exit 242, just w. Int corridors. **Pets:** Very small. $10 daily fee/pet. Designated rooms, service with restrictions, supervision.

BLOOMFIELD

Super 8 Motel **M**
(505) 632-8886. **Call for rates.** 525 W Broadway Blvd. Jct of US 64 and 550. Int corridors. **Pets:** Accepted.

CARLSBAD

Best Western Stevens Inn **SH**
(505) 887-2851. **Call for rates.** 1829 S Canal St. 1 mi s on US 62, 180 and 285. Ext corridors. **Pets:** Small. $20 daily fee/pet. Designated rooms, service with restrictions.

Carlsbad Inn **M**
(505) 887-1171. **$49-$69.** 2019 S Canal St. 1.5 mi s on US 62, 180 and 285. Ext corridors. **Pets:** Medium. $10 daily fee/pet. Service with restrictions, crate.

Continental Inn & Suites **M**
(505) 887-0341. **$49-$69.** 3820 National Parks Hwy. 3.5 mi sw on US 62 and 180. Ext corridors. **Pets:** $10 one-time fee/room. Designated rooms, service with restrictions.

Days Inn of Carlsbad **SH**
(505) 887-7800. **$80-$90.** 3910 National Parks Hwy. 3.5 mi sw on US 62 and 180. Ext corridors. **Pets:** Very small, dogs only. $10 daily fee/pet. Designated rooms, service with restrictions, supervision.

CHAMA

AAA ▼▼◆ Vista del Rio Lodge M
(505) 756-2138. **$60-$105, 3 day notice.** 2595 US Hwy 84/64. 0.5 mi s of SR 17. Ext corridors. **Pets:** Small, dogs only. Service with restrictions, supervision.
(SAVE) (S⊘) (✕) (🔡) (🖵) (✕) (AC)

CHIMAYO

▼▼ Casa Escondida Bed & Breakfast BB
(505) 351-4805. **$95-$155, 14 day notice.** 64 CR 0100. Jct SR 76 and 98, just w on SR 76, then 0.5 mi ne on CR 100, follow signs. Ext/int corridors. **Pets:** Accepted.
(ASK) (✕) (🔡) (🖵) (W) (Z)

CIMARRON

AAA ▼ Cimarron Inn & RV Park M
(505) 376-2268. **Call for rates.** 212 10th St. On US 64. Ext corridors. **Pets:** Other species. Designated rooms, supervision.
(SAVE) (✕) (🔡) (🖵)

CLAYTON

AAA ▼▼▼ Best Western Kokopelli Lodge SH ❀
(505) 374-2589. **$105, 10 day notice.** 702 S 1st St. US 87, 0.5 mi se of jct US 56 and 64. Ext corridors. **Pets:** $5 daily fee/pet. Service with restrictions, supervision.
(SAVE) (S⊘) (✕) (🔡) (🖵) (≈)

AAA ▼▼ Days Inn & Suites SH
(505) 374-0133. **Call for rates.** 1120 S 1st St. US 87, 1 mi s of jct US 56 and 64. Int corridors. **Pets:** Medium. $8 daily fee/pet. Service with restrictions, supervision.
(SAVE) (✕) (🔡) (🖵) (≈)

▼▼ Super 8 Motel M
(505) 374-8127. **Call for rates.** 1425 S 1st St. US 87, 1 mi se of jct US 56 and 64. Int corridors. **Pets:** Accepted.
(✕) (🔡) (🖵)

CLOUDCROFT

AAA ▼▼▼ The Lodge Resort SH
(505) 682-2566. **$130-$365, 14 day notice.** 1 Corona Pl. US 82, 0.3 mi s. Int corridors. **Pets:** Medium. $25 one-time fee/room. Designated rooms, service with restrictions, supervision.
(SAVE) (S⊘) (✕) (&M) (🔡) (🖵) (🍴) (≈) (✕)

CLOVIS

▼▼ Econo Lodge M
(505) 763-3439. **$59-$109.** 1400 E Mabry Dr. 0.5 mi e on US 60, 70 and 84. Ext corridors. **Pets:** Small. $10 one-time fee/pet. Service with restrictions, supervision.
(ASK) (S⊘) (✕) (🔡) (🖵) (≈)

▼▼▼ Holiday Inn Clovis SH
(505) 762-4491. **$70.** 2700 E Mabry Dr. 1.5 mi e on US 60, 70 and 84. Ext corridors. **Pets:** Accepted.
(ASK) (S⊘) (✕) (&M) (🔡) (🖵) (🍴) (≈) (✕)

AAA ▼▼▼ La Quinta Inn & Suites Clovis SH
(505) 763-8777. **$99-$139.** 4521 N Prince St. Jct US 60/84 and Prince St, 3 mi n. Int corridors. **Pets:** Other species. Service with restrictions, supervision.
(SAVE) (S⊘) (✕) (🔡) (🖵) (≈)

DEMING

AAA ▼▼ Best Western Mimbres Valley Inn SH
(505) 546-4544. **$59-$119, 7 day notice.** 1500 W Pine. I-10, exit 81, just e. Ext corridors. **Pets:** $15 daily fee/pet. Designated rooms, service with restrictions, supervision.
(SAVE) (S⊘) (✕) (🔡) (🖵) (≈)

AAA ▼▼◆ Days Inn M
(505) 546-8813. **Call for rates.** 1601 E Pine St. I-10, exit 85 westbound, 2 mi w on business loop; exit 81 eastbound, 1 mi e on business loop. Ext corridors. **Pets:** Accepted.
(SAVE) (✕) (🔡) (🖵) (🍴) (≈)

AAA ▼▼◆ Grand Motor Inn SH ❀
(505) 546-2632. **$49-$54.** 1721 E Pine St. I-10, exit 85 westbound, 2 mi w on business loop; exit 82 eastbound, 1 mi e on business loop. Ext corridors. **Pets:** Small, other species. $5 daily fee/room. Service with restrictions, supervision.
(SAVE) (S⊘) (✕) (🔡) (🍴) (≈)

AAA ▼▼▼▼ Holiday Inn SH
(505) 546-2661. **Call for rates.** 4600 E Pine St. I-10, exit 85, just w. Ext corridors. **Pets:** Other species. Designated rooms.
(SAVE) (✕) (&M) (🔡) (🖵) (🍴) (≈)

AAA ▼▼▼▼ La Quinta Inn & Suites SH
(505) 546-0600. **$79-$109.** 4300 E Pine St. I-10, exit 85, just w. Int corridors. **Pets:** Other species. Service with restrictions, supervision.
(SAVE) (S⊘) (✕) (&M) (🔡) (🖵) (≈)

EDGEWOOD

▼▼▼▼ Alta Mae's Heritage Inn BB
(505) 281-5000. **$109, 7 day notice.** 1950-C Old Route 66. I-40, exit 187, just s to stop sign, then just e. Ext corridors. **Pets:** Accepted.
(ASK) (✕) (✕) (Z)

ELEPHANT BUTTE

AAA ▼▼▼ Elephant Butte Inn & Spa SH ❀
(505) 744-5431. **$79-$129.** 401 Hwy 195. I-25, exit 83, 4 mi e. Ext corridors. **Pets:** Medium, dogs only. $25 one-time fee/pet. Designated rooms, service with restrictions, supervision.
(SAVE) (S⊘) (✕) (&M) (🔡) (🖵) (🍴) (≈)

▼▼ Marina Suites Motel M
(505) 744-5269. **Call for rates.** 200 Country Club Dr. I-25, exit 83, 4.7 mi e. Ext corridors. **Pets:** Accepted.
(🔡) (🖵) (Z)

ESPANOLA

AAA ▼▼▼ Comfort Inn SH
(505) 753-2419. **Call for rates.** 604-B S Riverside Dr. US 84 and 285, just s of jct SR 68. Int corridors. **Pets:** Small, other species. $10 daily fee/pet. Service with restrictions, supervision.
(SAVE) (✕) (🔡) (🖵) (≈)

AAA ▼▼ Motel 6 SH
(505) 753-5374. **Call for rates.** 811 S Riverside Dr. US 84 and 285, 0.5 mi s of jct SR 68. Int corridors. **Pets:** Other species. Service with restrictions, supervision.
(SAVE) (✕) (🔡)

FARMINGTON

AAA ▼▼▼ Americas Best Value Inn SH
(505) 325-2288. **Call for rates.** 600 E Broadway. 1 mi e; at Broadway and Scott Ave. Int corridors. **Pets:** Accepted.
(SAVE) (✕) (🔡) (🖵) (≈) (✕)

AAA ▼▼◆ Best Western Inn & Suites SH
(505) 327-5221. **Call for rates.** 700 Scott Ave. 1 mi e on SR 516 (Main St), just s. Int corridors. **Pets:** Other species. $25 one-time fee/pet. Designated rooms, service with restrictions, supervision.
(SAVE) (✕) (🔡) (🖵) (🍴) (≈) (✕)

AAA ▼▼◆ Comfort Inn SH
(505) 325-2626. **$70-$130.** 555 Scott Ave. 1 mi e on SR 516 (Main St), just s. Int corridors. **Pets:** Accepted.
(SAVE) (S⊘) (✕) (🔡) (🖵) (≈)

▼▼▼▼ **Holiday Inn Express** SH
(505) 325-2545. **$99-$139.** 2110 Bloomfield Blvd. 1.6 mi e on US 64 (Bloomfield Blvd), just past jct Broadway, on Frontage Rd. Int corridors. **Pets:** Small. $25 one-time fee/room. Service with restrictions, supervision.

ASK SD ⊠ &M 🛏 🖵 ⇌

▼▼▼▼ **La Quinta Inn Farmington** SH
(505) 327-4706. **$94-$124.** 675 Scott Ave. 1 mi e on SR 516 (Main St), just s. Ext/int corridors. **Pets:** Other species. Service with restrictions, supervision.

ASK SD ⊠ 🛏 🖵 ⇌

GALLUP

▼▼ **Americas Best Value Inn & Suites** SH
(505) 722-0757. **$49-$72, 3 day notice.** 2003 Hwy 66 W. I-40, exit 20, 1 mi w. Ext/int corridors. **Pets:** Accepted.

SAVE SD ⊠ &M 🛏 🖵 ⍾

▼▼▼ **Best Western Inn & Suites** SH ❀
(505) 722-2221. **$70-$90.** 3009 US 66 W. I-40, exit 16, 1 mi e. Int corridors. **Pets:** Large, other species. $10 one-time fee/room. Designated rooms, service with restrictions, supervision.

SAVE SD ⊠ 🛏 🖵 ⍾ ⇌

▼▼▼ **Best Western Red Rock Inn** SH
(505) 722-7600. **Call for rates.** 3010 US 66 E. I-40, exit 26, 1 mi w. Int corridors. **Pets:** Accepted.

SAVE ⊠ 🛏 🖵 ⇌

▼▼▼ **Best Western Royal Holiday Motel** M
(505) 722-4900. **Call for rates.** 1903 W Hwy 66. I-40, exit 20, 0.5 mi s to US 66, then 0.8 mi w. Int corridors. **Pets:** $7 daily fee/pet. Service with restrictions, supervision.

SAVE ⊠ 🛏 🖵 ⇌

▼▼ **Comfort Inn** M
(505) 722-0982. **$55-$106.** 3208 US 66 W. I-40, exit 16, 0.3 mi e. Int corridors. **Pets:** Accepted.

SAVE ⊠ 🛏 🖵 ⇌

▼ **Days Inn-West** SH
(505) 863-6889. **Call for rates.** 3201 W Hwy 66. I-40, exit 16, 0.3 mi e. Ext corridors. **Pets:** Medium. $10 daily fee/pet. Designated rooms, service with restrictions, supervision.

SAVE ⊠ 🛏 🖵 ⇌

▼ **Economy Inn** M
(505) 863-9301. **$35-$49.** 1709 US 66 W. I-40, exit 20, s to US 66, then 0.5 mi w. Ext corridors. **Pets:** Very small, other species. $5 daily fee/pet. Designated rooms, service with restrictions, supervision.

SAVE ⊠ 🛏

▼▼▼▼ **La Quinta Inn & Suites** SH
(505) 722-2233. **$109-$149.** 3880 Hwy 66 E. I-40, exit 26, just e. Int corridors. **Pets:** Other species. Service with restrictions, supervision.

ASK SD ⊠ &M 🛏 🖵 ⇌ ⊠

▼▼▼ **Quality Inn & Suites** SH
(505) 726-1000. **Call for rates.** 1500 W Maloney Ave. I-40, exit 20, just n on Munoz Dr, then just w. Ext/int corridors. **Pets:** Accepted.

SAVE ⊠ &M 🛏 🖵 ⇌

▼▼ **Ramada Limited** SH
(505) 726-2700. **Call for rates.** 1440 W Maloney Ave. I-40, exit 20, 1 mi w. Int corridors. **Pets:** Accepted.

⊠ &M 🛏 🖵 ⇌

▼▼▼ **Red Roof Inn** M
(505) 722-7765. **$33-$60.** 3304 W Hwy 66. I-40, exit 16, just se. Ext corridors. **Pets:** Accepted.

SAVE SD ⊠ 🛏 🖵 ⇌

▼▼▼ **Super 8 Motel** M
(505) 722-5300. **$40-$90 (no credit cards).** 1715 W US Hwy 66. I-40, exit 20, s to US 66, then 0.5 mi w. Int corridors. **Pets:** Medium. $10 daily fee/pet. Designated rooms, service with restrictions, supervision.

SAVE ⊠ 🛏 🖵 ⇌

GRANTS

▼▼▼ **Comfort Inn** SH
(505) 287-8700. **$59-$109.** 1551 E Santa Fe Ave. I-40, exit 85, 0.3 mi n. Int corridors. **Pets:** Accepted.

ASK SD ⊠ &M 🛏 🖵 ⇌

▼▼▼ **Days Inn** SH
(505) 287-8883. **Call for rates.** 1504 E Santa Fe Ave. I-40, exit 85, 0.3 mi n. Ext corridors. **Pets:** Small. $15 daily fee/pet. Service with restrictions, supervision.

SAVE ⊠ 🛏 🖵

▼▼▼ **Holiday Inn Express** SH
(505) 285-4676. **$100-$129, 7 day notice.** 1496 E Sante Fe Ave. I-40, exit 85, 0.3 mi n. Int corridors. **Pets:** Small. $20 daily fee/pet. Service with restrictions, supervision.

SAVE SD ⊠ 🛏 🖵 ⇌

▼ **Sands Motel** M
(505) 287-2996. **$31-$45.** 112 McArthur St. I-40, exit 85, 1.5 mi w on Business Loop 40. Ext corridors. **Pets:** Other species. $6 one-time fee/pet. No service, crate.

SAVE ⊠ 🛏

▼▼ **Super 8 Grants** SH
(505) 287-8811. **$49-$89.** 1604 E Santa Fe Ave. I-40, exit 85, just n. Int corridors. **Pets:** Medium. $10 daily fee/pet. Service with restrictions, supervision.

ASK SD ⊠ 🛏 🖵 ⇌

HOBBS

▼▼ **Americas Best Value Inn** M
(505) 393-4101. **$65-$79.** 200 N Marland Blvd. On US 62 and 180, 2 mi e. Ext corridors. **Pets:** Accepted.

SAVE SD ⊠ 🛏 🖵 ⇌

▼▼ **Best Western Executive Inn** SH
(505) 397-7171. **Call for rates.** 309 N Marland Blvd. US 62 and 180 and Snyder St. Ext corridors. **Pets:** Accepted.

⊠ 🛏 🖵 ⇌

▼▼ **Days Inn** M
(505) 397-6541. **Call for rates.** 211 N Marland Blvd. 2 mi e on US 62 and 180. Ext corridors. **Pets:** Small. $10 daily fee/pet. Service with restrictions, supervision.

SAVE ⊠ 🛏 🖵 ⇌

▼▼ **Econo Lodge** SH
(505) 397-3591. **Call for rates.** 619 N Marland Blvd. 2.5 mi e on US 62 and 180. Ext corridors. **Pets:** Accepted.

SAVE ⊠ 🖵 ⇌

▼▼ **Hobbs Family Inn** SH
(505) 397-3251. **$60-$75.** 501 N Marland Blvd. 2.5 mi e on US 62 and 180. Ext/int corridors. **Pets:** Small, dogs only. $25 deposit/pet. No service, crate.

SAVE ⊠ 🛏 🖵 ⍾ ⇌

LAS CRUCES

▼▼▼ **Best Western Mesilla Valley Inn** SH
(505) 524-8603. **Call for rates.** 901 Avenida de Mesilla. I-10, exit 140, just n. Ext/int corridors. **Pets:** Accepted.

SAVE ⊠ 🛏 🖵 ⍾ ⇌

◈ ◈◈◈ **Best Western Mission Inn** SH
(505) 524-8591. **$81.** 1765 S Main St. I-10, exit 142, 1 mi n. Ext corridors. **Pets:** Large, other species. $10 daily fee/pet. Service with restrictions, supervision.
SAVE S🐾 ✕ 📶 📺 🍴 🏊

◈ ◈◈◈◈ **Comfort Inn & Suites de Mesilla** SH
(505) 527-1050. **Call for rates.** 1300 Avenida de Mesilla. I-10, exit 140, just s. Int corridors. **Pets:** Small, other species. $10 daily fee/pet. Designated rooms, service with restrictions, supervision.
SAVE ✕ 🚷 📶 📺 🏊

◈ ◈◈◈ **Comfort Inn of Las Cruces** SH
(505) 527-2000. **$80-$130.** 2585 S Valley Dr. I-10, exit 142, just n. Int corridors. **Pets:** Small, dogs only. $10 daily fee/pet. Designated rooms, service with restrictions, supervision.
SAVE S🐾 ✕ 📶 🏊

◈◈◈◈ **Comfort Suites by Choice Hotels** SH
(505) 522-1300. **Call for rates.** 2101 S Triviz. I-25, exit 1, just w on University Ave, then just n. Int corridors. **Pets:** Accepted.
✕ 🚷 📶 📺

◈◈◈◈ **DreamCatcher Inn Bed & Breakfast de Las Cruces** BB
(505) 522-3035. **$125-$150, 5 day notice.** 10201 Starfly Rd. US 70 E to Nasa/Baylor Canyon Rd, 0.5 mi s, then 0.5 mi w. Ext corridors. **Pets:** Accepted.
✕ 🚷

◈ ◈◈◈ **Hampton Inn** SH
(505) 526-8311. **Call for rates.** 755 Avenida de Mesilla. I-10, exit 140. Ext corridors. **Pets:** Accepted.
SAVE ✕ 📶 📺 🏊

◈◈◈ **Hilltop Hacienda B & B** BB
(505) 382-3556. **$95-$135, 14 day notice.** 2600 Westmoreland Ave. I-25, exit 6 (US 70), just e to Del Rey Blvd, 3 mi n, then 1 mi e. Int corridors. **Pets:** Accepted.
ASK S🐾 ✕ 📺

◈ ◈◈◈ **Hotel Encanto de Las Cruces** LH
(505) 522-4300. **$98-$159.** 705 S Telshor Blvd. I-25, exit 3 (Lohman Ave), just e on Lohman, then just s. Int corridors. **Pets:** Medium. $15 daily fee/room. Designated rooms, service with restrictions, supervision.
SAVE ✕ 🚷 📶 📺 🍴 🏊

◈◈◈◈ **La Quinta Inn & Suites Las Cruces** SH
(505) 523-0100. **$94-$124.** 1500 Hickory Dr. I-10, exit 140, just se of jct I-25 and Avenida de Mesilla. Int corridors. **Pets:** Other species. Service with restrictions, supervision.
ASK S🐾 ✕ 🚷 📶 📺 🏊

◈◈◈◈ **La Quinta Inn Las Cruces** SH
(505) 524-0331. **$102-$132.** 790 Avenida de Mesilla. I-10, exit 140. Int corridors. **Pets:** Other species. Service with restrictions, supervision.
ASK S🐾 ✕ 🚷 📶 📺 🏊

◈◈◈ **Lundeen's Inn of the Arts** BB
(505) 526-3326. **$79-$89.** 618 S Alameda Blvd. Jct Lohman, just s; center. Int corridors. **Pets:** Accepted.
ASK ✕ 📶 📺

◈◈ **Quality Inn & Suites** SH
(505) 524-4663. **$59-$189.** 2200 S Valley Dr. I-10, exit 142, 2 blks w. Ext corridors. **Pets:** Accepted.
ASK S🐾 ✕ 🚷 📶 📺 🏊

◈ ◈◈◈ **Ramada Palms de Las Cruces** SH 🐾
(505) 526-4411. **Call for rates.** 201 E University Ave. I-10, exit 142, just n. Int corridors. **Pets:** Medium, dogs only. $25 one-time fee/pet. Designated rooms, service with restrictions, supervision.
SAVE ✕ 🚷 📺 🍴 🏊

◈◈ **Royal Host Motel** M
(505) 524-8536. **$47-$54.** 2146 W Picacho St. I-10, exit 139, 1 mi n on Motel Dr, then 0.5 mi e. Ext corridors. **Pets:** Accepted.
✕ 📶 🍴

◈◈◈ **Sleep Inn by Choice Hotels** SH
(505) 522-1700. **Call for rates.** 2121 S Triviz. I-25, exit 1, just w on University Ave, then just n. Int corridors. **Pets:** Accepted.
✕ 🚷 📶 📺 🏊

◈◈◈ **Staybridge Suites** SH
(505) 521-7999. **$129-$199.** 2651 Northrise Dr. I-25, exit 6, just e. Int corridors. **Pets:** Other species. $50 deposit/room, $50 one-time fee/room. Service with restrictions.
ASK S🐾 ✕ 🚷 📶 📺 🏊 ✕🐾

◈ ◈◈◈ **Super 8 Motel** M
(505) 523-8695. **Call for rates.** 245 La Posada Ln. I-10, exit 142, just n on Valley Dr, then just e. Int corridors. **Pets:** Accepted.
SAVE ✕ 📶

LAS VEGAS

◈ ◈◈◈ **Comfort Inn** SH 🐾
(505) 425-1100. **$75-$125.** 2500 N Grand Ave. I-25, exit 347, just sw, US 85 and I-25 business route. Int corridors. **Pets:** Medium. $25 one-time fee/room. Designated rooms, service with restrictions, supervision.
SAVE S🐾 ✕ 📶 📺 🏊

◈ ◈◈ **El Camino Motel** M
(505) 425-5994. **Call for rates.** 1152 N Grand Ave. I-25, exit 345, 0.3 mi w, US 85 and I-25 business route. Ext corridors. **Pets:** Accepted.
SAVE ✕ 📶

◈◈ **Inn on the Santa Fe Trail** M
(505) 425-6791. **Call for rates.** 1133 N Grand Ave. I-25, exit 345, 0.5 mi n; I-25 business route and US 84, 0.3 mi w. Ext corridors. **Pets:** Accepted.
✕ 📶 📺 🍴 🏊

◈ ◈◈◈ **Plaza Hotel** SH 🐾
(505) 425-3591. **$79-$153.** 230 Plaza St. I-25, exit 343 W, just w, follow signs to Old Town Plaza. Int corridors. **Pets:** Other species. $10 daily fee/room. Service with restrictions.
SAVE S🐾 ✕ 📶 📺 🍴

◈ ◈◈◈ **Super 8 Motel-Las Vegas** M
(505) 425-5288. **Call for rates.** 2029 N Grand Ave. I-25, exit 347, 0.8 mi sw, US 85 and I-25 business route. Int corridors. **Pets:** Other species. $10 one-time fee/pet. Designated rooms, service with restrictions, supervision.
SAVE ✕ 📶 📺

LORDSBURG

◈ ◈◈◈ **Best Western-Western Skies Inn** SH 🐾
(505) 542-8807. **$79-$99.** 1303 S Main St. I-10, exit 22, just s. Ext corridors. **Pets:** Small. $10 one-time fee/pet. Designated rooms, service with restrictions, supervision.
SAVE S🐾 ✕ 📶 📺 🍴 🏊

◈◈◈ **Holiday Inn Express** SH
(505) 542-3666. **Call for rates.** 1408 S Main St. I-10, exit 22, just s. Ext corridors. **Pets:** Other species. $15 daily fee/pet. Service with restrictions.
✕ 🚷 📶 📺 🏊

◈ ◈◈ **Super 8 Motel** SH
(505) 542-8882. **Call for rates.** 110 E Maple. I-10, exit 22, just s. Int corridors. **Pets:** Other species. $25 deposit/pet, $10 daily fee/pet. No service, supervision.
SAVE ✕ 📶

LOS ALAMOS

▼▼ Ashley Hotel and Suites 🆂🅷
(505) 662-7211. **$69-$79.** 2175 Trinity Dr. Center. Int corridors.
Pets: Accepted.
[A$K] [S🐾] [✕] [🛏] [💻]

LOS LUNAS

▼▼ Western Skies Inn & Suites 🆂🅷
(505) 865-0001. **$65-$95.** 2258 Sun Ranch Village Loop. I-25, exit 203,
just n. Int corridors. **Pets:** Accepted.
[A$K] [S🐾] [✕] [⛰M] [🛏] [🏊]

LOVINGTON

◈◈◈ ▼▼◈ Lovington Inn 🆂🅷
(505) 396-5346. **$59-$65.** 1600 W Ave D. Jct US 82 and SR 18, 1 mi
w. Ext corridors. **Pets:** $10 deposit/room. Service with restrictions, crate.
[SAVE] [S🐾] [✕] [🛏] [💻] [🍴]

MORIARTY

◈◈◈ ▼▼◈ Comfort Inn 🆂🅷
(505) 832-6666. **$69-$109.** 119 Route 66 E. I-40, exit 196, just s, then
just e. Int corridors. **Pets:** Accepted.
[SAVE] [S🐾] [✕] [⛰M] [🛏] [💻] [🏊]

◈◈◈ ▼◈ Days Inn 🆂🅷
(505) 832-4451. **Call for rates.** 1809 Route 66 W. I-40, exit 194. Int
corridors. **Pets:** Small. $10 daily fee/pet. Designated rooms, service with
restrictions, supervision.
[SAVE] [✕] [🛏]

◈◈◈ ▼▼◈ Econo Lodge 🆂🅷
(505) 832-4457. **$52-$95.** 1316 Route 66 W. I-40, exit 194, 0.5 mi se
on US 66 and I-40 business loop. Int corridors. **Pets:** Large, other
species. $7 daily fee/pet. Service with restrictions, supervision.
[SAVE] [S🐾] [✕] [🛏] [💻]

◈◈◈ ▼◈ Holiday Inn Express 🆂🅷
(505) 832-5000. **$88-$96.** 1507 Route 66. I-40, exit 194, 0.4 mi e. Int
corridors. **Pets:** Other species. $10 one-time fee/room. Service with restric-
tions, supervision.
[SAVE] [S🐾] [✕] [⛰M] [🛏] [💻] [🏊]

◈◈◈ ▼▼◈ Super 8 Motel 🆂🅷
(505) 832-6730. **$55-$89.** 1611 W Old Route 66. I-40, exit 194, 0.5 mi
e on Central Ave. Int corridors. **Pets:** Large, other species. $5 daily
fee/pet. Service with restrictions, supervision.
[SAVE] [S🐾] [✕] [🛏]

PINOS ALTOS

▼▼ Bear Creek Motel & Cabins 🅲🅰 🐾
(505) 388-4501. **Call for rates.** 88 Main St. 1 mi n of Pinos Altos on SR
15. Ext corridors. **Pets:** Other species. $10 daily fee/pet.
[✕] [🛏] [💻] [🦮]

POJOAQUE PUEBLO

◈◈◈ ▼▼◈ Cities of Gold Hotel 🆂🅷
(505) 455-0515. **$79-$99, 3 day notice.** 10A Cities of Gold Rd. On US
84/265, just n. Int corridors. **Pets:** Accepted.
[SAVE] [✕] [⛰M] [🛏] [💻] [🍴]

RANCHOS DE TAOS

◈◈◈ ▼◈ Budget Host Inn 🅼
(505) 758-2524. **Call for rates.** 1798 Paseo Del Pueblo Sur (SR 68).
On SR 68; center. Ext corridors. **Pets:** Accepted.
[SAVE] [✕] [🛏] [💻]

RATON

◈◈◈ ▼▼◈ Best Western Sands 🅼
(505) 445-2737. **Call for rates.** 300 Clayton Rd. I-25, exit 451, just w.
Ext/int corridors. **Pets:** Accepted.
[SAVE] [✕] [🛏] [💻] [🍴] [🏊]

◈◈◈ ▼◈ Budget Host Raton 🅼
(505) 445-3655. **$47-$67.** 136 Canyon Dr. I-25, exit 454, 0.8 mi s on
I-25 business loop. Ext corridors. **Pets:** Medium. $5 daily fee/pet. Service
with restrictions, supervision.
[SAVE] [S🐾] [✕] [⛰M] [🛏]

◈◈◈ ▼◈ Raton Pass Inn 🅼
(505) 445-3641. **$48-$54.** 308 Canyon Dr. I-25, exit 454, 0.8 mi s. Ext
corridors. **Pets:** Dogs only. $2 daily fee/pet. Service with restrictions, super-
vision.
[SAVE] [S🐾] [✕] [🛏]

RIO RANCHO

◈◈◈ ▼▼◈ Best Western Rio Rancho Inn & Conference
Center 🆂🅷
(505) 892-1700. **Call for rates.** 1465 Rio Rancho Blvd. I-25, exit 233
(Alameda Blvd), 6.5 mi w; I-40, exit 155, 10 mi n on Coors Rd/Coors
Bypass to SR 528, then 1 mi n. Ext corridors. **Pets:** $15 daily fee/room.
Service with restrictions, supervision.
[SAVE] [✕] [🛏] [💻] [🏊]

◈◈◈ ▼▼◈ Days Inn-Rio Rancho 🆂🅷
(505) 892-8800. **Call for rates.** 4200 Crestview Dr. I-25, exit 233
(Alameda Blvd), 8 mi w on SR 528; I-40, exit 155, 8 mi n on Coors Rd
(SR 448). Ext corridors. **Pets:** Small. $15 one-time fee/pet. Service with
restrictions, supervision.
[SAVE] [✕] [🛏] [🏊]

▼▼ Extended StayAmerica 🆂🅷
(505) 792-1338. **$58-$68.** 2608 The American Rd NW. Corner of SR
528 and Cottonwood, just n, then just w. Int corridors. **Pets:** Other
species. $75 one-time fee/pet. Service with restrictions.
[A$K] [S🐾] [✕] [🛏] [💻]

▼▼◈ Extended Stay Deluxe 🆂🅷
(505) 892-7900. **$75-$85.** 2221 Rio Rancho Blvd. I-25, exit 233
(Alameda Blvd), 6 mi w (becomes SR 528/Rio Rancho Blvd). Int
corridors. **Pets:** Other species. $75 one-time fee/pet. Service with restric-
tions.
[A$K] [S🐾] [✕] [🛏] [💻] [🏊]

▼▼ Rio Rancho Super 8 Motel 🆂🅷
(505) 896-8888. **Call for rates.** 4100 Barbara Loop SE. I-25, exit 233
(Alameda Blvd), 0.5 mi w, 3.8 mi nw on SR 528, then just e. Int
corridors. **Pets:** Accepted.
[✕]

ROSWELL

◈◈◈ ▼▼◈ Best Western El Rancho Palacio 🆂🅷
(505) 622-2721. **$70-$110.** 2205 N Main St. 1.8 mi n on US 70 and
285. Ext corridors. **Pets:** Service with restrictions, supervision.
[SAVE] [S🐾] [✕] [🛏] [💻] [🏊]

◈◈◈ ▼▼◈▼ Best Western Sally Port Inn & Suites 🆂🅷
(505) 622-6430. **Call for rates.** 2000 N Main St. 1.5 mi n on US 70 and
285. Int corridors. **Pets:** Medium, other species. $10 daily fee/room. Des-
ignated rooms, service with restrictions, supervision.
[SAVE] [✕] [🛏] [💻] [🍴] [🏊] [🦮]

◈◈◈ ▼▼◈ Budget Inn-North 🅼 🐾
(505) 623-6050. **$45-$50.** 2101 N Main St. 1.8 mi n on US 70 and 285.
Ext corridors. **Pets:** $5 daily fee/pet. Service with restrictions, supervision.
[SAVE] [S🐾] [✕] [🛏] [🏊]

Comfort Inn SH
(505) 623-4567. **$99-$159.** 3595 N Main St. On US 70 and 285, 3 mi n. Int corridors. **Pets:** Small. $10 one-time fee/pet. Designated rooms, service with restrictions, supervision.

Days Inn SH
(505) 623-4021. **Call for rates.** 1310 N Main St. 0.8 mi n on US 70 and 285. Ext corridors. **Pets:** Other species. Service with restrictions, supervision.

Holiday Inn Express SH
(505) 627-9900. **$115-$160.** 2300 N Main St. US 70. Int corridors. **Pets:** Accepted.

La Quinta Inn and Suites SH
(505) 622-8000. **$119-$149.** 200 E 19th St. Jct N Main and 19th St, 2 blks e. Int corridors. **Pets:** Other species. Service with restrictions, supervision.

Leisure Inn SH
(505) 622-2575. **$48-$55.** 2700 W 2nd St. 2.5 mi w on US 70 and 380. Ext corridors. **Pets:** Small, dogs only. $5 daily fee/pet. Designated rooms, service with restrictions, supervision.

Ramada Limited SH 🐾
(505) 623-9440. **$74-$85.** 2803 W 2nd St. 2.5 mi w on US 70 and 380. Ext/int corridors. **Pets:** Other species. $10 daily fee/room. Supervision.

Western Inn M
(505) 623-9425. **Call for rates.** 2331 N Main St. Jct US 70/285/380, 2.2 mi n. Ext corridors. **Pets:** Accepted.

RUIDOSO

Dan Dee Cabins CA
(505) 257-2165. **$84-$199, 14 day notice.** 310 Main Rd. 0.8 mi w on Upper Canyon Rd. Ext corridors. **Pets:** $10 one-time fee/pet. No service, crate.

The Lodge at Sierra Blanca SH
(505) 258-5500. **Call for rates.** 107 Sierra Blanca Dr. 2.5 mi n on SR 48. Int corridors. **Pets:** Designated rooms, service with restrictions, supervision.

Quality Inn SH
(505) 378-4051. **$79-$200.** 307 Hwy 70 W. Jct US 70 and SR 48. Int corridors. **Pets:** Small, dogs only. $10 one-time fee/pet. Designated rooms, service with restrictions, supervision.

Travelodge SH
(505) 378-4471. **Call for rates.** 159 W Hwy 70. Jct of US 70 and SR 48. Ext corridors. **Pets:** Accepted.

The Village Lodge CO
(505) 258-5442. **$89-$159, 7 day notice.** 1000 Mechem Dr. 2 mi n on SR 48. Ext corridors. **Pets:** Medium. $10 one-time fee/room. Crate.

Whispering Pine Cabins CA
(505) 257-4311. **$89-$265, 14 day notice.** 422 Main Rd. 0.9 mi w of jct SR 48 and Suddenth Dr. Ext corridors. **Pets:** Other species. $10 one-time fee/pet. No service.

RUIDOSO DOWNS

Best Western Pine Springs Inn SH
(505) 378-8100. **Call for rates.** 1420 W Hwy 70. Just n; center. Ext corridors. **Pets:** Accepted.

SANTA FE

Alexander's Inn BB
(505) 986-1431. **$170-$240, 14 day notice.** 529 E Palace Ave. Just e of jct Paseo de Peralta; 6 blks e of historic plaza. Ext/int corridors. **Pets:** Accepted.

Best Western Inn of Santa Fe SH
(505) 438-3822. **Call for rates.** 3650 Cerrillos Rd. I-25, exit 278, 2.8 mi n. Int corridors. **Pets:** Accepted.

Bishop's Lodge Ranch Resort & Spa SH 🐾
(505) 983-6377. **$299-$599, 3 day notice.** 1297 N Bishop's Lodge Rd. 3.5 mi n of jct Paseo de Peralta. Ext/int corridors. **Pets:** $75 deposit/room. Supervision.

Camel Rock Suites M
(505) 989-3600. **Call for rates.** 3007 S St. Frances Dr. 0.8 mi n on S St. Francis Dr, just e on Zia via access drive. Ext corridors. **Pets:** Other species. $10 daily fee/room. Service with restrictions, supervision.

Casapueblo Inn BB
(505) 988-4455. **Call for rates.** 138 Park Ave. Jct Guadalupe St. Ext corridors. **Pets:** Accepted.

Comfort Inn Santa Fe SH
(505) 474-7330. **$69-$219.** 4312 Cerrillos Rd. I-25, exit 278, 1.6 mi n. Int corridors. **Pets:** Other species. $5 daily fee/pet. Service with restrictions, supervision.

Econo Lodge SH
(505) 474-7570. **Call for rates.** 3470 Cerrillos Rd. I-25, exit 278, 3 mi n. Int corridors. **Pets:** Accepted.

Eldorado Hotel & Spa LH
(505) 988-4455. **Call for rates.** 309 W San Francisco. Just w of The Plaza at Sandoval St. Int corridors. **Pets:** Accepted.

El Paradero Bed & Breakfast BB
(505) 988-1177. **$95-$180, 14 day notice.** 220 W Manhattan Ave. 0.3 mi s on Cerrillos Rd, 1/2 blk e. Ext/int corridors. **Pets:** Dogs only. $20 daily fee/pet. Designated rooms, service with restrictions, supervision.

Hacienda Nicholas BB 🐾
(505) 986-1431. **$120-$240, 14 day notice.** 320 E Marcy St. Just e of jct Paseo de Peralta; 4 blks e of historic plaza. Ext/int corridors. **Pets:** Other species. $20 one-time fee/pet. Service with restrictions, crate.

Hampton Inn Santa Fe SH
(505) 474-3900. **$79-$219.** 3625 Cerrillos Rd. I-25, exit 278, 2.5 mi n. Int corridors. **Pets:** Accepted.

▼▼▼▼ Hilton of Santa Fe SH
(505) 988-2811. **Call for rates.** 100 Sandoval St. Just sw of The Plaza; between San Francisco and W Alameda sts. Ext/int corridors. **Pets:** Accepted.

⊠ 🖪 💻 🍴 ➿

AAA ▼▼▼▼ Holiday Inn SH
(505) 473-4646. **$79-$139.** 4048 Cerrillos Rd. I-25, exit 278, 2.3 mi n just n of Rodeo Dr. Int corridors. **Pets:** Medium. $50 one-time fee/pet. Service with restrictions, crate.

SAVE S🐾 ⊠ ♿M 🖪 💻 🍴 ➿ ⊠

▼▼▼▼ Hotel Plaza Real SH
(505) 988-4900. **$109-$269, 3 day notice.** 125 Washington Ave. Just ne of The Plaza; center. Ext/int corridors. **Pets:** Accepted.

ASK S🐾 ⊠ 🖪 💻 🍴

AAA ▼▼▼▼ Hotel Santa Fe SH 🐾
(505) 982-1200. **$129-$379.** 1501 Paseo de Peralta. At Cerrillos Rd, 0.6 mi s of The Plaza. Int corridors. **Pets:** Dogs only. $20 daily fee/pet. Service with restrictions, supervision.

SAVE S🐾 ⊠ 🖪 💻 🍴 ➿ ⊠

AAA ▼▼ Inn at Santa Fe SH 🐾
(505) 474-9500. **Call for rates.** 8376 Cerrillos Rd. I-25, exit 278, 0.3 mi n. Int corridors. **Pets:** Other species. $20 one-time fee/room. Service with restrictions, supervision.

⊠ ♿M 🖪 💻 ➿

AAA ▼▼▼▼ Inn of the Anasazi, a Rosewood Hotel SH 🐾
(505) 988-3030. **Call for rates.** 113 Washington Ave. Just ne of The Plaza. Int corridors. **Pets:** $40 daily fee/pet. Service with restrictions, supervision.

SAVE ⊠ 💻 🍴

AAA ▼▼▼▼ Inn On The Alameda SH 🐾
(505) 984-2121. **$120-$375, 3 day notice.** 303 E Alameda. Just e of The Plaza; at jct Paseo de Peralta. Ext/int corridors. **Pets:** Small, other species. $20 daily fee/room. Designated rooms, service with restrictions, supervision.

SAVE S🐾 ⊠ 🖪 💻 ⊠

▼▼ La Quinta Inn Santa Fe SH
(505) 471-1142. **$92-$122.** 4298 Cerrillos Rd. I-25, exit 278, 1.8 mi n. Ext/int corridors. **Pets:** Other species. Service with restrictions, supervision.

ASK S🐾 ⊠ 🖪 💻 ➿

AAA ▼▼▼▼ Las Palomas SH 🐾
(505) 982-5560. **$119-$379.** 460 W San Francisco St. Just w of jct Guadalupe St. Ext corridors. **Pets:** Dogs only. $20 daily fee/pet. Service with restrictions, supervision.

SAVE S🐾 ⊠ 🖪 💻 ⊠

▼▼ Motel 6-150 M
(505) 473-1380. **$45-$58 (no credit cards).** 3007 Cerrillos Rd. I-25, exit 278, 3.8 mi n. Ext corridors. **Pets:** Other species. Service with restrictions, supervision.

S🐾 ⊠ 🖪 ➿

▼▼▼▼ The Old Santa Fe Inn M
(505) 995-0800. **$89-$300, 3 day notice.** 320 Galisteo St. Just sw of Historic Santa Fee Plaza; center. Ext/int corridors. **Pets:** Medium. $25 daily fee/pet. Designated rooms, service with restrictions, supervision.

ASK S🐾 ⊠ 🖪 💻

▼▼▼ Park Inn SH 🐾
(505) 471-3000. **Call for rates.** 2907 Cerrillos Rd. I-25, exit 278, 7 mi n. Ext corridors. **Pets:** Medium, other species. $10 daily fee/room. Designated rooms, service with restrictions, supervision.

⊠ 🖪 💻 🍴 ➿

AAA ▼▼▼ Quality Inn SH
(505) 471-1211. **$60-$200.** 3011 Cerrillos Rd. I-25, exit 278B, 3.8 mi n. Int corridors. **Pets:** Small, other species. $10 daily fee/pet. Service with restrictions, supervision.

SAVE S🐾 ⊠ 🖪 💻 🍴 ➿

▼▼▼▼ Residence Inn by Marriott SH
(505) 988-7300. **$131-$208.** 1698 Galisteo St. I-25, exit 282, 1.7 mi n on St Francis Dr to St Michaels Dr, just e, then just n. Ext corridors. **Pets:** Accepted.

ASK S🐾 ⊠ 🖪 💻 ➿ ⊠

AAA ▼▼▼ Sage Inn M
(505) 982-5952. **Call for rates.** 725 Cerrillos Rd. 0.4 mi ne of St. Francis Dr (US 84). Ext corridors. **Pets:** Large. $25 one-time fee/pet. Designated rooms, service with restrictions, supervision.

SAVE ⊠ 🖪 💻 ➿

AAA ▼▼▼ Santa Fe Plaza Travelodge SH
(505) 982-3551. **Call for rates.** 646 Cerrillos Rd. 0.8 mi sw of The Plaza. Ext/int corridors. **Pets:** Very small. $10 one-time fee/pet. Service with restrictions, supervision.

SAVE ⊠ 🖪 💻 ➿

SANTA ROSA

▼▼ Baymont Inn & Suites SH
(505) 472-5412. **Call for rates.** 3300 Historic Route 66. I-40, exit 277, 0.3 mi w. Int corridors. **Pets:** Accepted.

⊠ 🖪 💻 ➿

AAA ▼▼▼ Best Western Adobe Inn SH
(505) 472-3446. **$62-$75.** 1501 Historic Route 66. I-40, exit 275. Ext corridors. **Pets:** Small. Service with restrictions, supervision.

SAVE S🐾 ⊠ 🖪 💻 ➿

AAA ▼▼▼ Best Western Santa Rosa Inn M
(505) 472-5877. **$59-$99.** 3022 Historic Route 66. I-40, exit 277, 0.5 mi w. Ext corridors. **Pets:** Medium. $10 daily fee/room. Designated rooms, service with restrictions, supervision.

SAVE S🐾 ⊠ 🖪 💻 ➿

AAA ▼▼▼ Comfort Inn SH
(505) 472-5570. **Call for rates.** 3343 E Historic Route 66. I-40, exit 277, 0.3 mi w. Ext corridors. **Pets:** Medium. $15 one-time fee/pet. Service with restrictions, supervision.

SAVE ⊠ 🖪 💻 ➿

AAA ▼▼▼ Days Inn of Santa Rosa SH
(505) 472-5985. **$65-$125, 7 day notice.** 1830 Historic Route 66. I-40, exit 275. Ext corridors. **Pets:** Accepted.

SAVE S🐾 ⊠ 🖪 ➿

AAA ▼▼▼ Holiday Inn Express SH
(505) 472-5411. **$75-$199.** 3202 Historic Route 66. I-40, exit 277, 0.4 mi w. Int corridors. **Pets:** $25 one-time fee/pet. Designated rooms, service with restrictions, supervision.

SAVE ⊠ ♿M 🖪 💻 ➿ ⊠

AAA ▼▼▼▼ La Quinta Inn-Santa Rosa SH
(505) 472-4800. **$75-$105.** 1701 Historic Route 66. I-40, exit 275, just e. Int corridors. **Pets:** Other species. Service with restrictions, supervision.

SAVE S🐾 ⊠ 🖪 💻 ➿

▼▼▼ Motel 6-273 M
(505) 472-3045. **$43-$56 (no credit cards).** 3400 Historic Route 66. I-40, exit 277, 0.3 mi w. Ext corridors. **Pets:** Other species. Service with restrictions, supervision.

S🐾 ⊠ 🖪 ➿

▼▼▼ Super 8 Motel-Santa Rosa M
(505) 472-5388. **Call for rates.** 1201 Historic Route 66. I-40, exit 275, just w. Int corridors. **Pets:** Accepted.

⊠ ♿M 🖪

Travelodge SH

(505) 472-3494. **Call for rates.** 1819 Historic Route 66. I-40, exit 275, just n. Ext corridors. **Pets:** Small. $5 one-time fee/pet. Designated rooms, service with restrictions, supervision.

SAVE X 🖥 💻

SILVER CITY

Econo Lodge Silver City SH

(505) 534-1111. **$55-$129.** 1120 Hwy 180 E. 1.5 mi ne on US 180 and SR 90. Int corridors. **Pets:** Large, other species. $7 one-time fee/pet. Designated rooms, service with restrictions, supervision.

SAVE S X LM 🖥 💻 ➤

Holiday Inn Express SH

(505) 538-2525. **$109.** 1103 Superior St. 3 mi ne on US 180 and SR 90. Int corridors. **Pets:** Other species. Designated rooms, service with restrictions, supervision.

SAVE X 💻

SOCORRO

Best Western Socorro Hotel & Suites SH

(505) 838-0556. **Call for rates.** 1100 California Ave NE. Center. Ext/int corridors. **Pets:** Small. $10 daily fee/pet. Designated rooms, service with restrictions.

X LM 🖥 💻 ➤

Comfort Inn & Suites SH

(505) 838-4400. **$70-$100.** 1259 Frontage Rd NW. I-25, exit 150. Int corridors. **Pets:** Accepted.

ASK S X 🖥 💻 ➤

Motel 6 #392 SH

(505) 835-4300. **$39-$51 (no credit cards).** 807 S US 85. I-25, exit 147. Ext corridors. **Pets:** Other species. Service with restrictions, supervision.

S X LM 🖥 ➤

TAOS

American Artists Gallery House Bed & Breakfast BB

(505) 758-4446. **$95-$225, 14 day notice.** 132 Frontier Ln. 1 mi s of jct US 64 and Taos Plaza, 0.3 mi e. Ext/int corridors. **Pets:** Dogs only. $25 one-time fee/pet. Designated rooms, service with restrictions, supervision.

SAVE S X 🖥 💻 X AC

Burch Street Casitas CA

(505) 737-9038. **$120-$150, 21 day notice.** 310 Burch St. US 64, just e of jct SR 68, then just s. Ext corridors. **Pets:** Medium, dogs only. Service with restrictions, supervision.

SAVE X 🖥 💻 AC

El Monte Sagrado Living Resort and Spa SH ❖

(505) 758-3502. **Call for rates.** 317 Kit Carson Rd. 0.5 mi e of jct US 64 and 68. Ext corridors. **Pets:** Medium, dogs only. $150 one-time fee/pet. Supervision.

X 💻 ⑪ ➤

Inn on La Loma Plaza BB

(505) 758-1717. **$150-$425, 15 day notice.** 315 Ranchitos Rd. 0.3 mi sw on Ranchitos Rd, just w of Taos Plaza; in La Loma Plaza Historic District. Ext/int corridors. **Pets:** Accepted.

SAVE S X 🖥 💻 X

Inn On The Rio BB

(505) 758-7199. **$99-$130, 14 day notice.** 910 Kit Carson Rd. US 64, 1.5 mi e of jct SR 68 and Taos Plaza. Ext corridors. **Pets:** Accepted.

SAVE S X 💻 ➤ AC

Orinda Bed & Breakfast BB

(505) 758-8581. **$99-$165, 14 day notice.** 461 Valverde St. Just w from jct Don Fernando and Camino de la Placita, then just s; look for Orinda sign. Ext/int corridors. **Pets:** Accepted.

SAVE X 🖥 💻

Quality Inn SH

(505) 758-2200. **$75-$104.** 1043 Paseo del Pueblo Sur. SR 68, 2 mi sw of jct US 64 and Taos Plaza. Ext/int corridors. **Pets:** Accepted.

ASK S X 🖥 💻 ⑪ ➤

Sagebrush Inn SH

(505) 758-2254. **$79-$219.** 1508 Paseo del Pueblo Sur. SR 68, 3 mi sw of jct US 64 and Taos Plaza. Ext corridors. **Pets:** Accepted.

ASK S X 🖥 💻 ⑪ ➤

San Geronimo Lodge BB

(505) 751-3776. **$95-$160, 10 day notice.** 1101 Witt Rd. 1.3 mi e of jct SR 68 and Taos Plaza on US 64 (Kit Carson Rd), 0.6 mi s. Ext/int corridors. **Pets:** Medium, dogs only. $25 one-time fee/room. Designated rooms, service with restrictions, supervision.

SAVE S X ➤ AC

THOREAU

Zuni Mountain Lodge BB

(505) 862-7616. **$95 (no credit cards), 7 day notice.** 40 W Perch Dr. I-40, exit 53, 13 mi s on SR 612, then w. Ext/int corridors. **Pets:** Accepted.

ASK X AC W Z

TRUTH OR CONSEQUENCES

Best Western Hot Springs Motor Inn M ❖

(505) 894-6665. **Call for rates.** 2270 N Date St. I-25, exit 79. Ext corridors. **Pets:** Large, other species. Service with restrictions, supervision.

X 🖥 💻 ➤

Comfort Inn & Suites SH

(505) 894-1660. **$70-$200.** 2250 N Date St. I-25, exit 79, just e. Int corridors. **Pets:** Accepted.

ASK S LM 🖥 💻 ➤

Super 8 Motel M

(505) 894-7888. **Call for rates.** 2151 N Date St. I-25, exit 79, just s. Int corridors. **Pets:** Accepted.

SAVE X 🖥 💻

TUCUMCARI

Americana Motel M

(505) 461-0431. **$27-$33.** 406 E Tucumcari Blvd. I-40, exit 332, 1.5 mi n on SR 18, then 0.5 mi e on US Route 66. Ext corridors. **Pets:** Very small. $10 one-time fee/pet. Designated rooms, service with restrictions, supervision.

SAVE S X 🖥 💻

Best Western Discovery Inn SH

(505) 461-4884. **Call for rates.** 200 E Estrella. I-40, exit 332. Ext corridors. **Pets:** Accepted.

SAVE X 🖥 💻 ➤

Budget Inn M ❖

(505) 461-4139. **Call for rates.** 824 W Tucumcari Blvd. I-40, exit 332, 1 mi n to Tucumcari Blvd, then 1 mi w. Ext corridors. **Pets:** Medium. $5 one-time fee/pet. Service with restrictions, supervision.

SAVE X 🖥

Comfort Inn SH

(505) 461-4094. **$69-$99.** 2800 E Tucumcari Blvd. I-40, exit 335, 0.5 mi w. Ext corridors. **Pets:** Accepted.

ASK S X 🖥 💻 ➤

(AAA) ▼▼▼ Days Inn SH
(505) 461-3158. **Call for rates.** 2623 S 1st St. I-40, exit 332, just n. Ext/int corridors. **Pets:** Other species. $7 daily fee/pet. Service with restrictions, supervision.

[SAVE] [✕] [🛏] [💻]

(AAA) ▼▼▼ Econo Lodge SH
(505) 461-4194. **$50-$75.** 3400 Route 66 Blvd. I-40, exit 335, just n, then just w. Int corridors. **Pets:** Medium. $5 daily fee/pet. Designated rooms, service with restrictions, supervision.

[SAVE] [S⭕] [✕] [🛏]

(AAA) ▼▼▼ Microtel Inn-Tucumcari SH
(505) 461-0600. **Call for rates.** 2420 S 1st St. I-40, exit 332, just n. Int corridors. **Pets:** Accepted.

[SAVE] [✕] [🛏] [💻] [🐾]

(AAA) ▼▼▼ Quality Inn SH 🐾
(505) 461-3780. **$70-$100.** 3716 E Tucumcari Blvd. I-40, exit 335, 0.3 mi w on Route 66. Ext corridors. **Pets:** Medium, other species. $10 one-time fee/room. Designated rooms, service with restrictions, supervision.

[SAVE] [S⭕] [✕] [&M] [🛏] [💻] [🍴] [🐾] [✕]

(AAA) ▼▼▼ Super 8 Motel M
(505) 461-4444. **Call for rates.** 4001 E Tucumcari Blvd. I-40, exit 335, just w. Int corridors. **Pets:** Small. $5 one-time fee/pet. Service with restrictions, supervision.

[SAVE] [✕] [🛏] [🐾]

(AAA) ▼▼▼ Tucumcari Inn SH
(505) 461-0088. **Call for rates.** 1700 E Route 66 Blvd. I-40, exit 333, 0.5 mi n to Tucumcari Blvd, then just w. Ext corridors. **Pets:** $8 daily fee/pet. Designated rooms, service with restrictions, supervision.

[SAVE] [✕] [🛏] [🐾]

VAUGHN

(AAA) ▼▼▼ Oak Tree Inn SH
(505) 584-8733. **$65-$75.** Jct State Hwy 54/60 & 285. 1.5 mi e on US 54, 60 and 285. Ext/int corridors. **Pets:** Accepted.

[SAVE] [S⭕] [✕] [&M] [🛏] [💻] [🍴]

NEW YORK

ALBANY

▼▼▼▼ CrestHill Suites SH

(518) 454-0007. **$129.** 1415 Washington Ave. I-90, exit 2 westbound, just s on Fuller Rd, then just e; exit eastbound, just e. Int corridors. **Pets:** Large, other species. $15 daily fee/pet. Designated rooms, service with restrictions, crate.

A$K S☐ ✕ ᴸᴹ 🛏 💻 ⇌

▼▼ Days Inn-Albany/Guilderland M

(518) 489-4423. **$84-$104.** 1230 Western Ave. I-90, exit 2, 0.7 mi s, follow signs to US 20 (Western Ave). Int corridors. **Pets:** Medium. $10 daily fee/pet. Service with restrictions, supervision.

A$K S☐ ✕ ᴸᴹ 💻

▼▼ Extended StayAmerica SH

(518) 446-0680. **$90-$110.** 1395 Washington Ave. I-90, exit 2 westbound, just s on Fuller Rd, then 0.5 mi e; exit eastbound, just e. Int corridors. **Pets:** Other species. $75 one-time fee/pet. Service with restrictions.

A$K S☐ ✕ 🛏 💻

▼▼▼▼ TownePlace Suites by Marriott SH

(518) 435-1900. **$198-$231.** 1379 Washington Ave. I-90, exit 2 westbound, just s on Fuller Rd, then 0.6 mi e; exit eastbound, just e. Int corridors. **Pets:** Accepted.

A$K S☐ ✕ ᴸᴹ 🛏 💻 ⇌

ALLEGANY

▼▼ Microtel Inn & Suites-Olean/Allegany SH

(716) 373-5333. **$55-$109.** 3234 NYS Rt 417. I-86, exit 24, 2.1 mi e on SR 417 (State St). Int corridors. **Pets:** Accepted.

A$K S☐ ✕ ᴸᴹ 🛏 💻

ANGELICA

▼▼ Angelica Inn B&B BB

(585) 466-3063. **Call for rates.** 64 W Main St. I-86, exit 31, 0.5 mi w. Ext/int corridors. **Pets:** Accepted.

✕ 🛏 💻 ⚄ ⊠

APALACHIN

AAA ▼▼▼▼ Quality Inn SH

(607) 625-4441. **$84-$209.** 7666 SR 434. SR 17, exit 66, just e. Int corridors. **Pets:** Accepted.

SAVE S☐ ✕ 🛏 💻

AUBURN

AAA ▼▼▼▼ Holiday Inn-Auburn/Finger Lakes SH

(315) 253-4531. **$89-$159.** 75 North St. SR 34, just n of US 20/SR 5. Int corridors. **Pets:** Accepted.

SAVE S☐ ✕ ᴸᴹ 🛏 💻 ¶¶ ⇌

▼▼ Inn at the Finger Lakes SH

(315) 253-5000. **$99-$159.** 12 Seminary Ave. Jct SR 34/38, just e on US 20/SR 5; center. Int corridors. **Pets:** $20 one-time fee/pet. Designated rooms, service with restrictions, supervision.

A$K S☐ ✕ ᴸᴹ 🛏 💻

AVERILL PARK

▼▼▼ La Perla at the Gregory House Country Inn & Restaurant CI

(518) 674-3774. **$110-$175, 7 day notice.** 3016 SR 43. Center. Int corridors. **Pets:** Very small, dogs only. Service with restrictions, supervision.

✕ ¶¶ ⇌

BALDWINSVILLE

AAA ▼▼ Microtel Inn & Suites SH

(315) 635-9556. **$60-$150.** 131 Downer St. SR 690, exit SR 31 W, 0.4 mi e. Int corridors. **Pets:** Large, other species. $10 daily fee/pet. Service with restrictions, supervision.

SAVE S☐ ✕ ᴸᴹ 🛏 💻

BATAVIA

♦♦♦⁷ ◈ Budget Inn Ⓜ
(585) 343-7921. **$49-$129.** 301 Oak St. I-90, exit 48, just n. Int corridors. **Pets:** Medium. $6 daily fee/pet. Designated rooms, service with restrictions, supervision.
[SAVE] [S🐾] [✕] [♿]

♦♦♦⁷ ◈◈◈ Comfort Inn Ⓢ🅷
(585) 344-9999. **$59-$139.** 4371 Federal Dr. I-90, exit 48, just n on SR 98. Int corridors. **Pets:** $10 one-time fee/pet. Service with restrictions, supervision.
[SAVE] [S🐾] [✕] [♿ᴹ] [💻] [🏊]

◈◈ Days Inn Ⓢ🅷
(585) 343-6000. **Call for rates.** 200 Oak St. I-90, exit 48, just s. Ext/int corridors. **Pets:** Accepted.
[✕] [♿] [💻] [🍴] [🏊]

♦♦♦⁷ ◈◈◈ Holiday Inn-Darien Lake Ⓢ🅷
(585) 344-2100. **$69-$159.** 8250 Park Rd. I-90, exit 48, just w. Int corridors. **Pets:** $20 one-time fee/room. Service with restrictions, supervision.
[SAVE] [✕] [♿] [💻] [🍴] [🏊] [✕]

♦♦♦⁷ ◈◈◈ Quality Inn & Suites Ⓢ🅷
(585) 344-7000. **$80-$135.** 8200 Park Rd. I-90, exit 48, just w. Int corridors. **Pets:** Accepted.
[SAVE] [S🐾] [✕] [♿ᴹ] [♿] [💻] [🏊]

♦♦♦⁷ ◈◈ Ramada Limited Ⓢ🅷
(585) 343-1000. **$45-$99.** 8204 Park Rd. I-90, exit 48, just w. Int corridors. **Pets:** Accepted.
[SAVE] [S🐾] [✕] [💻] [🍴]

BATH

◈◈ Bath Super 8 Ⓢ🅷
(607) 776-2187. **$56-$99, 3 day notice.** 333 W Morris St. I-86, exit 38, just n. Int corridors. **Pets:** $10 one-time fee/room. Service with restrictions, supervision.
[ASK] [S🐾] [✕] [♿]

◈◈ Days Inn Ⓢ🅷
(607) 776-7644. **$69-$199.** 330 W Morris St. I-86, exit 38, just n. Int corridors. **Pets:** Other species. Service with restrictions, supervision.
[ASK] [S🐾] [✕] [♿] [💻] [🍴] [🏊]

BINGHAMTON

♦♦♦⁷ ◈◈◈ Comfort Inn of Binghamton Ⓢ🅷
(607) 724-3297. **$89-$169.** 1000 Front St. I-81, exit 5, 1 mi n on US 11 (Front St). Int corridors. **Pets:** Accepted.
[SAVE] [S🐾] [✕] [♿ᴹ] [♿] [💻] [🏊]

◈◈◈ Grand Royale Hotel-A Clarion Collection Hotel Ⓛ🅷
(607) 722-0000. **$73-$250.** 80 State St. Just n of jct Hawley St; downtown. Int corridors. **Pets:** Medium. $10 daily fee/pet. Service with restrictions, supervision.
[✕] [♿] [💻]

◈◈ Motel 6-1222 Ⓢ🅷
(607) 771-0400. **Call for rates.** 1012 Front St. I-81, exit 6 southbound, 2 mi s on US 11 (Front St); exit 5 northbound, 1 mi n on US 11 (Front St). Int corridors. **Pets:** Other species. Service with restrictions, supervision.
[✕] [♿ᴹ]

BOHEMIA

◈◈◈ La Quinta Inn & Suites-Islip Ⓢ🅷
(631) 881-7700. **$129-$159.** 10 Aero Rd. I-495, exit 57, 5.1 mi se on SR 454, just s on Johnson Ave, then just e. Int corridors. **Pets:** Other species. Service with restrictions, supervision.
[ASK] [S🐾] [✕] [♿ᴹ] [♿] [💻]

BOONVILLE

♦♦♦⁷ ◈ Headwaters Motor Lodge Ⓜ
(315) 942-4493. **$63-$89.** 13524 Rt 12. Jct SR 12 and 120, 0.7 mi n. Int corridors. **Pets:** Medium. Service with restrictions, supervision.
[SAVE] [S🐾] [✕] [♿]

BROCKPORT

◈◈◈ Holiday Inn Express Ⓢ🅷
(585) 395-1000. **$85-$155.** 4908 Lake Rd S. Just s of jct SR 31, on SR 195. Int corridors. **Pets:** Accepted.
[ASK] [✕] [♿ᴹ] [♿] [💻]

BUFFALO METROPOLITAN AREA

AMHERST

♦♦♦⁷ ◈◈◈ Comfort Inn University Ⓢ🅷 🐾
(716) 688-0811. **$69-$149.** 1 Flint Rd. I-290, exit 5B, just n on SR 263 (Millersport Hwy), then just w. Int corridors. **Pets:** Medium, other species. $20 daily fee/pet. Designated rooms, service with restrictions.
[SAVE] [S🐾] [✕] [♿] [💻] [🏊]

◈◈◈ Homewood Suites Buffalo/Amherst Ⓢ🅷
(716) 833-2277. **$149-$199.** 1138 Millersport Hwy. I-290, exit 5A, just w. Int corridors. **Pets:** Small. $75 one-time fee/room. Service with restrictions, crate.
[ASK] [✕] [♿ᴹ] [♿] [💻] [🏊]

◈◈◈ Hotel Indigo Buffalo-Amherst Ⓢ🅷
(716) 689-4414. **$139-$199.** 10 Flint Rd. I-290, exit 5B, just n on SR 263 (Millersport Hwy). Int corridors. **Pets:** Other species. $75 one-time fee/room. Designated rooms, service with restrictions, crate.
[ASK] [✕] [♿ᴹ] [♿] [💻] [🏊]

♦♦♦⁷ ◈◈ Lord Amherst Hotel Ⓜ
(716) 839-2200. **$69-$135.** 5000 Main St. I-290, exit 7A, just w on SR 5. Ext/int corridors. **Pets:** Service with restrictions, supervision.
[SAVE] [S🐾] [✕] [♿ᴹ] [♿] [💻] [🏊]

◈ Motel 6 Buffalo-Amherst #1298 Ⓜ
(716) 834-2231. **Call for rates.** 4400 Maple Rd. I-290, exit 5B, just n to Maple Rd, then 0.7 mi w. Int corridors. **Pets:** Other species. Service with restrictions, supervision.
[✕]

◈◈ Red Roof Inn #7104 Ⓜ
(716) 689-7474. **Call for rates.** 42 Flint Rd. I-290, exit 5B, just n on SR 263 (Millersport Hwy). Ext corridors. **Pets:** Accepted.
[✕] [♿ᴹ]

BLASDELL

♦♦♦⁷ ◈◈ Clarion Hotel Ⓢ🅷
(716) 648-5700. **$69-$169.** 3950 McKinley Pkwy. I-90, exit 56, 0.4 mi e on SR 179, then 0.8 mi s. Int corridors. **Pets:** Accepted.
[SAVE] [S🐾] [♿] [💻]

♦♦♦⁷ ◈◈ Econo Lodge South Ⓜ
(716) 825-7530. **$49-$110.** 4344 Milestrip Rd. I-90, exit 56, just e on SR 179. Ext corridors. **Pets:** $10 daily fee/room. Designated rooms, service with restrictions, supervision.
[SAVE] [S🐾] [✕] [♿] [💻]

BOWMANSVILLE

▼▼ Red Roof Inn-Buffalo Airport #7137 M
(716) 633-1100. **Call for rates.** 146 Maple Dr. Just e of SR 78; just n of entrance to I-90 (New York State Thruway), exit 49. Ext corridors. **Pets:** Accepted.
⊠ 🛄

BUFFALO

⚴ ▼▼▼ Best Western Inn-On The Avenue SH
(716) 886-8333. **$129-$179.** 510 Delaware Ave. Between Virginia and Allen sts; downtown. Int corridors. **Pets:** Medium, dogs only. Designated rooms, service with restrictions.
SAVE S⊡ ⊠ 🛄 🖵

▼▼▼▼ Holiday Inn-Downtown SH
(716) 886-2121. **$149-$229.** 620 Delaware Ave. Between Allen and North sts; downtown. Int corridors. **Pets:** Accepted.
ASK ⊠ 🛄 🖵 ⊤ ⇝

CHEEKTOWAGA

⚴ ▼▼▼▼ Comfort Suites-Buffalo Airport SH
(716) 633-6000. **$99-$159.** 901 Dick Rd. SR 33, exit Dick Rd, just sw. Int corridors. **Pets:** Medium, dogs only. Service with restrictions, supervision.
SAVE S⊡ ⊠ ⑤M 🛄 🖵 ⇝

▼▼▼▼ Holiday Inn Express Hotel & Suites-Buffalo Airport SH
(716) 631-8700. **$140-$200.** 131 Buell Ave. I-90, exit 51 (SR 33), just e on Genesee St (SR 33), then just s. Int corridors. **Pets:** Small, other species. $30 one-time fee/room. Service with restrictions, supervision.
ASK ⊠ ⑤M 🛄 🖵 ⇝ ⊠

▼▼▼▼ Homewood Suites by Hilton SH
(716) 685-0700. **Call for rates.** 760 Dick Rd. SR 33, exit Dick Rd, 0.3 mi sw. Int corridors. **Pets:** Accepted.
⊠ 🛄 🖵 ⇝

⚴ ▼▼▼ Oak Tree Inn SH
(716) 681-2600. **$69-$95.** 3475 Union Rd. I-90, exit 52, 0.3 mi e on Walden Ave, just n on SR 277 (Union Rd). Int corridors. **Pets:** Accepted.
SAVE S⊡ ⊠ ⑤M 🛄 🖵

▼▼▼▼ Residence Inn by Marriott SH
(716) 892-5410. **$176-$220.** 107 Anderson Rd. I-90, exit 52 westbound, stay to left off exit ramp. Int corridors. **Pets:** Other species. $100 one-time fee/room. Service with restrictions, supervision.
ASK S⊡ ⊠ ⑤M 🛄 🖵 ⇝ ⊠

CLARENCE

⚴ ▼▼▼▼ Asa Ransom House CI ❀
(716) 759-2315. **$108-$185, 7 day notice.** 10529 Main St. Jct SR 78 (Transit Rd), 5.3 mi e on SR 5 (Main St). Int corridors. **Pets:** Large, dogs only. $75 deposit/room. Designated rooms, service with restrictions, crate.
SAVE S⊡ ⊠ ⑤M 🛄 ⊤

GRAND ISLAND

⚴ ▼▼▼▼ Holiday Inn Grand Island Resort LH
(716) 773-1111. **$99-$159.** 100 Whitehaven Rd. I-190, exit 19, 4 mi e. Int corridors. **Pets:** $75 deposit/pet, $25 one-time fee/room. Service with restrictions, crate.
SAVE S⊡ ⊠ 🛄 🖵 ⊤ ⇝ ⊠

HAMBURG

⚴ ▼▼▼ Comfort Inn & Suites SH
(716) 648-2922. **$79-$179.** 3615 Commerce Pl. I-90, exit 57, just w. Int corridors. **Pets:** Other species. $10 daily fee/room. Service with restrictions, crate.
SAVE S⊡ ⊠ ⑤M 🛄 🖵 ⇝

⚴ ▼▼▼ Holiday Inn Buffalo-Hamburg SH
(716) 649-0500. **$110-$159.** 5440 Camp Rd. I-90, exit 57, 0.3 mi se on SR 75 (Camp Rd). Int corridors. **Pets:** Other species. $15 daily fee/room. Service with restrictions, crate.
SAVE S⊡ ⊠ 🛄 🖵 ⊤ ⇝

▼▼ Red Roof Inn #7055 M
(716) 648-7222. **Call for rates.** 5370 Camp Rd. I-90, exit 57, just se on SR 75. Ext corridors. **Pets:** Accepted.
⊠ 🛄

KENMORE

▼▼ Super 8-Buffalo/Niagara Falls SH
(716) 876-4020. **Call for rates.** 1288 Sheridan Dr. I-190, exit 15, 1.5 mi e on SR 324 (Sheridan Dr). Int corridors. **Pets:** Medium, dogs only. Service with restrictions, supervision.
⊠ 🛄

SPRINGVILLE

▼▼ Microtel Inn & Suites SH
(716) 592-3141. **Call for rates.** 270 S Cascade Dr. On US 219 S. Int corridors. **Pets:** Other species. $10 one-time fee/room. Service with restrictions, crate.
⊠ 🛄 🖵

TONAWANDA

⚴ ▼▼▼ Econo Lodge M
(716) 694-6696. **Call for rates.** 2000 Niagara Falls Blvd. I-290, exit 3 (Niagara Falls Blvd), 0.5 mi n on US 62. Ext corridors. **Pets:** $10 daily fee/pet. Designated rooms, service with restrictions, supervision.
SAVE ⊠ 🛄 🖵

▼▼ Microtel-Tonawanda SH
(716) 693-8100. **$50-$100.** 1 Hospitality Centre Way. I-290, exit 1B westbound; exit 1 eastbound, 0.5 mi e on Crestmount Ave, then just n on SR 384 (Delaware St). Int corridors. **Pets:** Accepted.
ASK ⊠ ⑤M 🛄

WILLIAMSVILLE

▼▼▼ Residence Inn by Marriott Buffalo/Amherst SH
(716) 632-6622. **$165-$197.** 100 Maple Rd. I-290, exit 5B, just n (on Millersport Hwy) to Maple Rd exit, then just e. Ext corridors. **Pets:** Accepted.
ASK S⊡ ⊠ ⑤M 🛄 🖵 ⇝ ⊠

END METROPOLITAN AREA

CALCIUM

▼▼▼ Microtel Inn Watertown 🆂🅷
(315) 629-5000. **$79.** 8000 Virginia Smith Dr. 4 mi e on SR 342; jct US 11. Int corridors. **Pets:** Medium. $100 deposit/room. Service with restrictions, supervision.

ⒶⓈⓀ 🆂🔟 ✖ 🔋

CANANDAIGUA

▲▲▲ ▼▼▼▼ The Inn On The Lake 🆂🅷
(585) 394-7800. **$109-$359.** 770 S Main St. I-90, exit 44 (Canandaigua/SR 332), just s across US 20 and SR 5. Int corridors. **Pets:** Medium. $25 daily fee/room. Service with restrictions, supervision.

🆂🅰🆅🅴 🆂🔟 ✖ 🔊 🔋 🖥 🍽 🐾 🐾

▼▼ Super 8 🆂🅷
(585) 396-7224. **Call for rates.** 4450 Eastern Blvd. Jct SR 332, 5 and US 20, 0.5 mi e. Int corridors. **Pets:** $10 daily fee/pet. Service with restrictions, supervision.

✖ 🔋 🖥

CANASTOTA

▼▼ Days Inn 🆂🅷
(315) 697-3309. **Call for rates.** 377 N Peterboro St. I-90, exit 34 on SR 13. Int corridors. **Pets:** Large, other species. $15 one-time fee/room. Service with restrictions, supervision.

✖ 🔋 🖥

CATSKILL

▲▲▲ ▼▼▼ Catskill Quality Inn & Conference Center 🆂🅷 🐾
(518) 943-5800. **$60-$350.** 704 Rt 23B. I-87 (New York State Thruway), exit 21, just w. Ext/int corridors. **Pets:** Large. $20 daily fee/pet. Designated rooms, service with restrictions, supervision.

🆂🅰🆅🅴 🆂🔟 ✖ 🔋 🖥 🍽 🐾

CHESTER

▲▲▲ ▼▼▼▼ Holiday Inn Express Hotel & Suites 🆂🅷
(845) 469-3000. **$109-$189.** 2 Bryle Pl. SR 17, exit 126, just n on SR 94, then just w on SR 17M (Brookside Ave). Int corridors. **Pets:** Other species. $30 one-time fee/room. Designated rooms, service with restrictions, supervision.

🆂🅰🆅🅴 🆂🔟 ✖ 🔊 🔋 🖥 🐾 🐾

CICERO

▲▲▲ ▼ Budget Inn 🅼
(315) 458-3510. **$49-$120, 7 day notice.** 901 S Bay Rd. I-481, exit 10, just n. Ext corridors. **Pets:** Small, dogs only. $10 daily fee/pet. Service with restrictions, supervision.

🆂🅰🆅🅴 🆂🔟 ✖ 🔋 🖥

CLAYTON

▲▲▲ ▼▼▼ Fair Wind Lodge 🅼
(315) 686-5251. **$50-$80, 3 day notice.** 38201 NYS Rt 12E. 2.3 mi sw. Ext corridors. **Pets:** Accepted.

🆂🅰🆅🅴 ✖ 🖥 🐾 🐾

CLINTON

▼▼▼ Amidst the Hedges 🅱🅱 🐾
(315) 853-3031. **$95-$200, 7 day notice.** 180 Sanford Ave. College St, 0.3 mi n on Elm St. Int corridors. **Pets:** Medium, dogs only. No service, supervision.

✖ 🔋 🖥 🐾

COBLESKILL

▲▲▲ ▼▼▼▼ Best Western Inn of Cobleskill 🆂🅷
(518) 234-4321. **$79-$169.** 121 Burgin Dr. I-88, exit 21 eastbound on SR 7, 0.8 mi e of jct SR 10; exit 22 westbound, 2.9 mi w on SR 27. Int corridors. **Pets:** Accepted.

🆂🅰🆅🅴 🆂🔟 ✖ 🔊 🔋 🖥 🍽 🐾

▼▼ Super 8 🆂🅷
(518) 234-4888. **Call for rates.** 955 E Main St. I-88, exit 22 westbound, 2.4 mi w on SR 7; exit 21 eastbound, 3.1 mi e on SR 7. Int corridors. **Pets:** Other species. $10 one-time fee/room. Service with restrictions.

✖ 🔊

COLONIE

▲▲▲ ▼▼▼ Cocca's Inn & Suites, Wolf Rd 🅼
(518) 459-2240. **$69-$149.** 2 Wolf Rd. I-87, exit 2E, just e. Ext/int corridors. **Pets:** $10 daily fee/pet. Service with restrictions, supervision.

🆂🅰🆅🅴 🆂🔟 ✖ 🔋 🖥

▼▼▼ Holiday Inn Albany on Wolf Road 🆂🅷
(518) 458-7250. **$179-$230.** 205 Wolf Rd. I-87, exit 4, 0.3 mi se. Int corridors. **Pets:** Accepted.

ⒶⓈⓀ 🆂🔟 ✖ 🔊 🔋 🖥 🍽 🐾 🐾

▼▼ Red Roof Inn #7112 🅼
(518) 459-1971. **Call for rates.** 188 Wolf Rd. I-87, exit 4, just se to Wolf Rd, then just sw. Ext corridors. **Pets:** Accepted.

✖ 🔊 🔋

CORNING

▼▼▼▼ Radisson Hotel Corning 🆂🅷
(607) 962-5000. **$99-$169.** 125 Denison Pkwy E. Downtown. Int corridors. **Pets:** Accepted.

ⒶⓈⓀ 🆂🔟 ✖ 🔋 🖥 🍽 🐾

▼▼▼▼ Staybridge Suites by Holiday Inn 🆂🅷
(607) 936-7800. **$145-$240.** 201 Townley Ave. I-86/SR 17, exit 46, just s. Int corridors. **Pets:** Accepted.

ⒶⓈⓀ 🆂🔟 ✖ 🔊 🔋 🖥 🐾 🐾

CORTLAND

▼▼▼ Comfort Inn 🆂🅷
(607) 753-7721. **$89-$199.** 2 1/2 Locust Ave. I-81, exit 11, just e off SR 13. Int corridors. **Pets:** Medium. $10 one-time fee/pet. Service with restrictions, supervision.

ⒶⓈⓀ 🆂🔟 ✖ 🔋 🖥 🍽

▲▲▲ ▼ Econo Lodge 🅼
(607) 756-2856. **$49-$209.** 10 Church St. I-81, exit 11, 0.8 mi s on SR 13/41 and US 11. Ext corridors. **Pets:** Accepted.

🆂🅰🆅🅴 🆂🔟 ✖ 🔋 🖥

▲▲▲ ▼▼ Quality Inn Cortland 🆂🅷
(607) 756-5622. **$79-$189.** 188 Clinton Ave. I-81, exit 11, just n. Int corridors. **Pets:** Other species. $20 daily fee/room. Designated rooms, service with restrictions, supervision.

🆂🅰🆅🅴 🆂🔟 ✖ 🔋 🖥

▼▼▼ Ramada Cortland 🆂🅷
(607) 756-4431. **$69-$189.** 2 River St. I-81, exit 11, just s on SR 13. Int corridors. **Pets:** Other species. $15 daily fee/pet. Service with restrictions, supervision.

ⒶⓈⓀ 🆂🔟 ✖ 🔋 🖥 🍽 🐾

CUBA

▲▲▲ ▼▼ Cuba Econo Lodge 🅼
(585) 968-1992. **$49-$149.** 1 North Branch Rd. I-86, exit 28, just n to N Branch Rd, then e. Int corridors. **Pets:** Medium. $10 daily fee/pet. Service with restrictions, supervision.

🆂🅰🆅🅴 🆂🔟 ✖ 🔋

DELHI

 Buena Vista Motel **M**
(607) 746-2135. **$69-$110.** 18718 State Hwy 28. Jct SR 10, 0.8 mi s.
Ext corridors. **Pets:** Small, dogs only. $15 daily fee/pet. Designated rooms,
service with restrictions, supervision.
SAVE ⊠ 🖬

DEWITT

Econo Lodge **M**
(315) 446-3300. **$69-$160, 3 day notice.** 3400 Erie Blvd E. I-481, exit
3, 1.2 mi w on SR 5; I-690, exit 17 S (Bridge St), just e on Erie Blvd
(SR 5). Ext corridors. **Pets:** Accepted.
SAVE S❺ ⊠ 🖬 💻

DUNKIRK

Best Western Dunkirk/Fredonia **SH**
(716) 366-7100. **Call for rates.** 3912 Vineyard Dr. I-90, exit 59, just w.
Int corridors. **Pets:** Medium, other species. $10 daily fee/pet. Designated
rooms, service with restrictions, supervision.
SAVE ⊠ 🖬 💻 ⊶

Comfort Inn **SH**
(716) 672-4450. **$79-$159.** 3925 Vineyard Dr. I-90, exit 59, just se on
SR 75 (Camp Rd), then just w. Int corridors. **Pets:** Other species. $10
daily fee/pet. Service with restrictions, supervision.
SAVE S❺ ⊠ 🖬 💻

EAST GREENBUSH

Residence Inn by Marriott **SH** 🐾
(518) 720-3600. **$219-$263.** 3 Tech Valley Dr. I-90, exit 9, just e. Int
corridors. **Pets:** Other species. $75 one-time fee/room.
A$K S❺ ⊠ 🖬 ❖M 🖬 💻 ⊶ ⊠

EAST SYRACUSE

Candlewood Suites Syracuse **SH**
(315) 432-1684. **$109-$199, 14 day notice.** 6550 Baptist Way. I-90, exit
35 (Carrier Cir) to SR 298 E to Old Collamer Rd, just n. Int corridors.
Pets: Accepted.
A$K S❺ ⊠ ❖M 🖬 💻

CrestHill Suites **SH**
(315) 432-5595. **$119-$225.** 6410 New Venture Gear Dr. I-90, exit 35
(Carrier Cir) to SR 298 E, just s. Int corridors. **Pets:** Accepted.
A$K ⊠ 🖬 💻 ⊶

Extended StayAmerica Hotels-Syracuse-Dewitt **SH**
(315) 463-1958. **$73-$95.** 6630 Old Collamer Rd S. I-90, exit 35 (Carrier Cir) to SR 298 E, just n. Int corridors. **Pets:** Other species. $75
one-time fee/pet. Service with restrictions.
A$K S❺ ⊠ 🖬 💻

Holiday Inn East-Carrier Circle **SH**
(315) 437-2761. **$109-$179.** 6555 Old Collamer Rd. I-90, exit 35 (Carrier Cir) to SR 298 E, just n. Ext/int corridors. **Pets:** Accepted.
SAVE ⊠ 🖬 💻 🍴 ⊶ ⊠

Red Roof Inn #7157 **M**
(315) 437-3309. **Call for rates.** 6614 N Thompson Rd. I-90, exit 35
(Carrier Cir), just n. Ext corridors. **Pets:** Accepted.
⊠ 🖬

Residence Inn by Marriott **SH** 🐾
(315) 432-4488. **$242-$262.** 6420 Yorktown Cir. I-90, exit 35 (Carrier
Cir) to SR 298, just e to Old Collamer Rd, then 0.5 mi n. Ext corridors.
Pets: Other species. $100 one-time fee/room. Service with restrictions.
A$K S❺ ⊠ ❖M 🖬 💻 ⊶ ⊠

ELLICOTTVILLE

The Jefferson Inn of Ellicottville **BB**
(716) 699-5869. **$79-$229, 30 day notice.** 3 Jefferson St. Western jct
US 219 and SR 242, just n; eastern jct US 219 and 242, 0.8 mi w;
downtown. Ext/int corridors. **Pets:** Other species. $15 daily fee/pet. Des-
ignated rooms, no service.
SAVE ⊠ 🖬

Sugar Pine Lodge **BB**
(716) 699-4855. **Call for rates.** 6158 Jefferson St, Rt 219 S. Jct US
219 and SR 242, 0.5 mi s on US 219. Ext/int corridors. **Pets:** Accepted.
SAVE ⊠ 🖬 💻 ⊶

ELMIRA

Coachman Motor Lodge **M**
(607) 733-5526. **$80-$120.** 908 Pennsylvania Ave. SR 17, exit 56
(Church St), 0.5 mi w on SR 352, 0.5 mi s on Madison Ave, then 1.4
mi s. Ext corridors. **Pets:** Medium. Service with restrictions, supervision.
SAVE S❺ 🖬 💻

Holiday Inn-Elmira Riverview **SH**
(607) 734-4211. **$100-$250.** 760 E Water St. SR 17, exit 56 (Water St),
0.5 mi s. Ext/int corridors. **Pets:** Accepted.
A$K S❺ ⊠ 🖬 💻 🍴 ⊶ ⊠

FALCONER

Red Roof Inn Jamestown/Falconer #7273 **SH**
(716) 665-3670. **Call for rates.** 1980 E Main St. I-86, exit 13, just w. Int
corridors. **Pets:** Accepted.
⊠ 🖬

FARMINGTON

Budget Inn **M**
(585) 924-5020. **$49-$99, 3 day notice.** 6001 Rt 96. I-90, exit 44, 1 mi
s on SR 332, then just e. Ext corridors. **Pets:** Small, dogs only. $10 daily
fee/pet. Service with restrictions, supervision.
SAVE S❺ ⊠ 🖬 🖬

FAYETTEVILLE

Craftsman Inn **SH**
(315) 637-8000. **$109-$199.** 7300 E Genesee St (SR 5). Across from
Fayetteville Towne Center. Int corridors. **Pets:** Accepted.
A$K ⊠ ❖M 🖬 💻 🍴

FISHKILL

Extended StayAmerica-Fishkill-Poughkeepsie **SH**
(845) 896-0592. **$135-$155.** 55 W Merritt Blvd. I-84, exit 13, just n. Int
corridors. **Pets:** Other species. $75 one-time fee/pet. Service with restric-
tions.
A$K S❺ ⊠ ❖M 🖬 💻

Homestead Studio Suites
Hotel-Fishkill-Poughkeepsie **SH**
(845) 897-2800. **$135-$185.** 25 Merritt Blvd. I-84, exit 13, just n. Int
corridors. **Pets:** Other species. $75 one-time fee/pet. Service with restric-
tions.
A$K S❺ ⊠ 🖬 💻

Ramada Fishkill Poughkeepsie **SH**
(845) 896-4995. **Call for rates.** 20 Schuyler Blvd. I-84, exit 13, just n.
Int corridors. **Pets:** Small. $25 daily fee/pet. Designated rooms, service
with restrictions, supervision.
SAVE ⊠ ❖M 🖬 💻

Residence Inn by Marriott **SH**
(845) 896-5210. **$187-$207.** 14 Schuyler Blvd. I-84, exit 13, just n. Ext
corridors. **Pets:** $100 one-time fee/room. Service with restrictions, supervi-
sion.
A$K S❺ ⊠ ❖M 🖬 💻 ⊶ ⊠

FREDONIA

Days Inn Dunkirk-Fredonia SH
(716) 673-1351. **Call for rates.** 10455 Bennett Rd. I-90, exit 59, just s on SR 60. Int corridors. **Pets:** Accepted.

SAVE X 🏨 💻 ❍ 🏊

The White Inn CI
(716) 672-2103. **$79-$199.** 52 E Main St. I-90, exit 59, 0.5 mi s on SR 60, then 1.3 mi sw on US 20 (Main St); center. Int corridors. **Pets:** Other species. $20 one-time fee/room. Designated rooms.

SAVE S X 🏨 ❍

FULTON

Riverside Inn SH
(315) 593-2444. **$59-$159, 7 day notice.** 930 S 1st St. On SR 481. Int corridors. **Pets:** Other species. Service with restrictions, supervision.

ASK S X 🏨 💻 ❍ 🏊

GARDEN CITY

La Quinta Garden City SH
(516) 705-9000. **$195-$199.** 821 Stewart Ave. Meadowbrook Pkwy, exit 3, 0.5 mi w. Int corridors. **Pets:** Other species. Service with restrictions, supervision.

ASK S X ㎝ 🏨 💻

GATES

Comfort Inn Central SH
(585) 436-4400. **$89-$139.** 395 Buell Rd. I-390, exit 18B (SR 204), 0.3 mi w; opposite entrance to Greater Rochester International Airport. Int corridors. **Pets:** Small, dogs only. $15 daily fee/pet. Service with restrictions, supervision.

SAVE S X 🏨 💻

Holiday Inn-Rochester Airport SH
(585) 328-6000. **$139-$209, 14 day notice.** 911 Brooks Ave. I-390, exit 18A (SR 204), just e. Int corridors. **Pets:** Large. $50 deposit/room. Designated rooms, service with restrictions, crate.

ASK S X 🏨 💻 ❍ 🏊 ⊗

GENESEO

Quality Inn Geneseo SH
(585) 243-0500. **$89-$159.** 4242 Lakeville Rd. I-390, exit 8, 3.4 mi w on SR 20A. Int corridors. **Pets:** Large. $15 daily fee/pet. Designated rooms, service with restrictions, crate.

ASK S X 🏨 💻 🏊

GENEVA

Cobtree Vacation Rental Homes VH 🐾
(315) 789-1144. **$139-$428, 90 day notice.** 440-446 Armstrong Rd. 3 mi n on SR 14. **Pets:** $35 one-time fee/pet. Designated rooms, service with restrictions, supervision.

SAVE S X 🏨 💻

Hampton Inn Geneva SH
(315) 781-2035. **$112-$182.** 43 Lake St. Corner of US 20/SR 5 and 14. Int corridors. **Pets:** Accepted.

ASK X ㎝ 🏨 💻 🏊

Ramada Geneva Lakefront SH
(315) 789-0400. **$82-$180.** 41 Lakefront Dr. Just e of SR 14, 5 and 20; downtown. Int corridors. **Pets:** Accepted.

SAVE S X 🏨 💻 ❍ 🏊

GREAT NECK

The Andrew Hotel SH 🐾
(516) 482-2900. **$299-$309.** 75 N Station Plaza. Jct SR 25A, 0.8 mi n on Middle Neck Rd, just e. Int corridors. **Pets:** Small. $150 one-time fee/room. Service with restrictions.

ASK S X 🏨 💻

Inn at Great Neck SH
(516) 773-2000. **$225-$275.** 30 Cutter Mill Rd. Jct SR 25A, 0.8 mi n on Middle Neck Rd, just w. Int corridors. **Pets:** Small, dogs only. $250 deposit/pet. Service with restrictions, supervision.

ASK S X 🏨 💻 ❍

GREECE

Extended StayAmerica-Rochester-Greece SH
(585) 663-5558. **$95-$110.** 600 Center Place Dr. I-390, exit 24A, just e on SR 104 (Ridge Rd), then just n on Buckman Rd. Int corridors. **Pets:** Other species. $75 one-time fee/pet. Service with restrictions.

ASK S X ㎝ 🏨 💻

Hampton Inn-Rochester North SH
(585) 663-6070. **Call for rates.** 500 Center Place Dr. I-390, exit 24A, just e on SR 104 (Ridge Rd), then just n on Buckman Rd. Int corridors. **Pets:** Accepted.

X ㎝ 🏨 💻

Residence Inn by Marriott-West SH 🐾
(585) 865-2090. **$192-$212.** 500 Paddy Creek Cir. I-390, exit 24A, just e on SR 104 (Ridge Rd), just s on Hoover Dr, then just w. Int corridors. **Pets:** $100 one-time fee/room. Service with restrictions, crate.

ASK S X 🏨 💻 🏊 ⊗

GUILDERLAND

Best Western Sovereign Hotel Albany SH
(518) 489-2981. **Call for rates.** 1228 Western Ave. I-87/90, exit 24, follow signs to US 20 (Western Ave), then 1 mi e. Int corridors. **Pets:** Small. $15 daily fee/pet. Designated rooms, service with restrictions, supervision.

SAVE X 🏨 💻 ❍ 🏊 ⊗

HANCOCK

Smith's Colonial Motel M
(607) 637-2989. **$80-$130.** 23085 State Hwy 97. SR 17, exit 87, 2.7 mi s. Ext corridors. **Pets:** $10 daily fee/room. Supervision.

X

HAUPPAUGE

Residence Inn by Marriott SH
(631) 724-4188. **$204-$226.** 850 Veterans Memorial Hwy. I-495, exit 57, 1.2 mi nw. Int corridors. **Pets:** Accepted.

SAVE S X ㎝ 🏨 💻 🏊 ⊗

Sheraton Long Island Hotel LH 🐾
(631) 231-1100. **$109-$269.** 110 Vanderbilt Motor Pkwy. I-495, exit 53 (Wicks Rd), just n, then 0.3 mi e. Int corridors. **Pets:** Medium, dogs only. $200 deposit/room. Designated rooms, service with restrictions, supervision.

SAVE S X ㎝ 🏨 💻 ❍ 🏊 ⊗

HENRIETTA

Comfort Suites by Choice Hotels of Rochester SH
(585) 334-6620. **Call for rates.** 2085 Hylan Dr. I-390, exit 13, just e. Int corridors. **Pets:** Accepted.

X ㎝ 🏨 💻 🏊

Homewood Suites by Hilton-Rochester SH
(585) 334-9150. **Call for rates.** 2095 Hylan Dr. I-390, exit 13, just e. Int corridors. **Pets:** Accepted.

X ㎝ 🏨 💻 🏊

Microtel-Rochester SH
(585) 334-3400. **$65-$109.** 905 Lehigh Station Rd. I-390, exit 12 northbound; exit 12A southbound, just w on SR 253. Int corridors. **Pets:** $75 deposit/pet, $10 daily fee/pet. Service with restrictions, supervision.

ASK S X 🏨

▼▼▼▼ **Radisson Rochester Airport** SH
(585) 475-1910. **$129-$189, 3 day notice.** 175 Jefferson Rd. I-390, exit 14A southbound; exit 14 northbound, 3 mi w on SR 252 (Jefferson Rd). Int corridors. **Pets:** Accepted.
ASK S✿ ⊠ &M 🛏 💻 ¶¶ ⊇

▼▼ **Red Roof Inn-Henrietta #7042** M
(585) 359-1100. **Call for rates.** 4820 W Henrietta Rd. I-390, exit 12 northbound; exit 12A southbound, 0.5 mi w on SR 253, then just s on SR 15 (Henrietta Rd). Ext corridors. **Pets:** Accepted.
⊠ 🛏

▼▼▼▼ **Residence Inn by Marriott** SH
(585) 272-8850. **$176-$196.** 1300 Jefferson Rd. I-390, exit 14A southbound, 0.5 mi e on SR 252 (Jefferson Rd); exit 14 northbound, just n on SR 15A, then 0.5 mi e on SR 252 (Jefferson Rd). Ext/int corridors. **Pets:** $100 one-time fee/room. Service with restrictions, crate.
ASK S✿ ⊠ 🛏 💻 ⊇ ⊠

▼▼▼▼ **R I T Inn & Conference Center** SH
(585) 359-1800. **$89-$149.** 5257 W Henrietta Rd. I-390, exit 12 northbound; exit 12A southbound, 0.5 mi w on SR 253, then 0.7 mi s. Int corridors. **Pets:** Medium. $50 one-time fee/room. Service with restrictions, supervision.
ASK S✿ ⊠ 🛏 💻 ⊇ ⊠

HERKIMER

▲ ▼▼▼ **Herkimer Motel** M
(315) 866-0490. **$68-$98.** 100 Marginal Rd. I-90, exit 30, just n on SR 28. Ext/int corridors. **Pets:** Medium. Service with restrictions, supervision.
SAVE S✿ ⊠ 🛏 💻 ⊇

HIGHLAND

▼▼ **Super 8 Motel** M
(845) 691-6888. **Call for rates.** 3423 Rt 9W. Just s of jct SR 299 and US 9W. Int corridors. **Pets:** Accepted.
⊠ &M 🛏

HORNELL

▲ ▼▼ **Econo Lodge** M
(607) 324-0800. **$65-$85.** 7462 Seneca Rd. Jct I-86 and SR 36, exit 34, just s to SR 21, just e to Seneca Rd, then just s. Ext/int corridors.
Pets: $7 daily fee/pet. Service with restrictions, crate.
SAVE S✿ ⊠ 🛏 💻 ¶¶

HUNTER

▼▼▼ **Hunter Inn** SH
(518) 263-3777. **$90-$310, 14 day notice.** Rt 23A. Jct SR 296, 1.9 mi e. Int corridors. **Pets:** Accepted.
ASK ⊠ 🛏 ⊠

HUNTINGTON STATION

▲ ▼▼▼ **Whitman Motor Lodge** M
(631) 271-2800. **$90-$150.** 295 E Jericho Tpke. On SR 25 (Jericho Tpke), 0.6 mi e of SR 110. Ext/int corridors. **Pets:** Very small. $20 daily fee/pet. Service with restrictions, crate.
SAVE S✿ ⊠ 🛏 💻

INLET

▲ ▼ **Marina Motel** M
(315) 357-3883. **$89-$160, 14 day notice.** 6 S Shore Rd. Center. Ext corridors. **Pets:** $50 deposit/room, $15 daily fee/pet. Crate.
SAVE ⊠ 🛏

IRONDEQUOIT

▼▼▼▼ **Holiday Inn Express** SH
(585) 342-0430. **Call for rates.** 2200 Goodman St N. SR 104, exit Goodman St, just n. Int corridors. **Pets:** Accepted.
⊠ 🛏 💻 ⊇

ITHACA

▲ ▼▼▼▼ **Best Western University Inn** M
(607) 272-6100. **Call for rates.** 1020 Ellis Hollow Rd. From SR 79 E, 1 mi ne on Pine Tree Rd, just n; in East Hill Plaza. Int corridors.
Pets: Medium, dogs only. $10 daily fee/pet. Designated rooms, service with restrictions, supervision.
SAVE ⊠ 🛏 💻 ⊇

▲ ▼▼▼ **Comfort Inn** SH ✿
(607) 272-0100. **$79-$249.** 356 Elmira Rd. Jct SR 96, 89 and 79, 1.5 mi sw on SR 13. Int corridors. **Pets:** $25 one-time fee/pet. Designated rooms, service with restrictions, supervision.
SAVE S✿ ⊠ &M 🛏 💻

▲ ▼▼▼▼ **Hampton Inn** SH
(607) 277-5500. **$109-$225.** 337 Elmira Rd. On SR 13. Int corridors.
Pets: Accepted.
SAVE S✿ ⊠ &M 🛏 💻 ⊇

▼▼▼▼ **Holiday Inn Ithaca Downtown** SH
(607) 272-1000. **$169-$209.** 222 S Cayuga St. Just n of SR 96B. Int corridors. **Pets:** Accepted.
ASK ⊠ 🛏 💻 ¶¶ ⊇

▼▼▼ **La Tourelle Resort and Spa** CI
(607) 273-2734. **$125-$375, 3 day notice.** 1150 Danby Rd. 2.7 mi s on SR 96B. Int corridors. **Pets:** Other species. $100 deposit/pet. Designated rooms, service with restrictions, supervision.
ASK S✿ ⊠ 🛏 💻 ¶¶ ⊠

▲ ▼▼▼ **Meadow Court Inn** M
(607) 273-3885. **$65-$175.** 529 S Meadow St. 1.5 mi s on SR 13 and 96. Ext/int corridors. **Pets:** $10 one-time fee/pet. Designated rooms, service with restrictions, crate.
SAVE ⊠ &M 🛏 💻 ¶¶

▲ ▼▼▼ **Rodeway Inn & Suites** M
(607) 272-5252. **$60-$100.** 654 Elmira Rd. On SR 13 S (Elmira Rd).
Ext/int corridors. **Pets:** Accepted.
SAVE S✿ ⊠ 🛏 💻

JAMESTOWN

▲ ▼▼▼ **Best Western Downtown Jamestown** SH ✿
(716) 484-8400. **$79-$140.** 200 W 3rd St. I-86, exit 12, 2 mi s on SR 60 (Washington St). Int corridors. **Pets:** Medium, other species. $25 one-time fee/room. Service with restrictions.
SAVE S✿ ⊠ &M 🛏 💻 ⊇

▲ ▼▼▼ **Comfort Inn** SH ✿
(716) 664-5920. **$80-$150.** 2800 N Main St. I-86, exit 12, just s on SR 60. Int corridors. **Pets:** Other species. $15 one-time fee/pet. Service with restrictions, supervision.
SAVE S✿ ⊠ 🛏 💻

JOHNSON CITY

▲ ▼▼▼ **Best Western of Johnson City** SH
(607) 729-9194. **Call for rates.** 569 Harry L Dr. SR 17, exit 70N, 0.3 mi n. Int corridors. **Pets:** Accepted.
SAVE ⊠ 🛏 💻

▼▼▼ **La Quinta Inn** SH
(607) 770-9333. **$109.** 581 Harry L Dr. SR 17, exit 70, 0.3 mi n. Int corridors. **Pets:** Other species. Service with restrictions, supervision.
ASK S✿ ⊠ 🛏 💻

▼▼ **Red Roof Inn-Binghamton #7203** M
(607) 729-8940. **Call for rates.** 590 Fairview St. SR 17, exit 70, 0.3 mi n, then just n on Reynolds Rd. Ext corridors. **Pets:** Accepted.
⊠ 🛏

JOHNSTOWN

◈◈◈ Holiday Inn SH
(518) 762-4686. **$96-$160.** 308 N Comrie Ave. Jct SR 30A and 29 E, 1.3 mi n. Ext/int corridors. **Pets:** Accepted.

(ASK) (✕) (&M) (🛏) (💲) (🍴) (🏊)

KINGSTON

◈◈◈ Holiday Inn SH
(845) 338-0400. **$139-$179, 3 day notice.** 503 Washington Ave. I-87, exit 19, just e of traffic circle. Int corridors. **Pets:** Accepted.

(SAVE) (SD) (✕) (🛏) (💲) (🍴) (🏊) (✕)

LAKE GEORGE

◈◈ Balmoral Hotel/Lake George Inn M
(518) 668-4408. **$49-$129, 10 day notice.** 444 Canada St. I-87, exit 22, 0.3 mi s on US 9. Ext corridors. **Pets:** Other species. $15 daily fee/pet. Designated rooms, crate.

(ASK) (SD) (✕) (🛏) (💲) (🏊)

◈ Green Haven M
(518) 668-2489. **$59-$134, 10 day notice.** 3136 Lake Shore Dr. I-87, exit 22, 0.8 mi n on SR 9N. Ext corridors. **Pets:** Dogs only. $10 one-time fee/pet. Service with restrictions, supervision.

(ASK) (✕) (🛏) (💲) (🏊) (✕)

◈◈ Lake Haven Motel M
(518) 668-2260. **$49-$127, 10 day notice.** 442 Canada St. I-87, exit 22, 0.4 mi s on US 9. Ext corridors. **Pets:** Dogs only. $10 daily fee/pet. Designated rooms, service with restrictions, crate.

(SD) (✕) (🛏) (💲)

◈◈◈ Travelodge of Lake George M
(518) 668-5421. **Call for rates.** 2011 SR 9. I-87, exit 21, just s. Ext corridors. **Pets:** Medium, dogs only. $20 daily fee/pet. Service with restrictions, supervision.

(SAVE) (✕) (🛏) (💲) (🍴) (🏊)

LAKE LUZERNE

◈◈◈ Luzerne Court M 🐾
(518) 696-2734. **$75-$180, 14 day notice.** 508 Lake Ave. I-87, exit 21, 8.7 mi s on SR 9N. Ext corridors. **Pets:** Dogs only. $25 one-time fee/room. Service with restrictions, supervision.

(SAVE) (✕) (🛏) (🍴) (🏊) (Z)

LAKE PLACID

◈◈◈ Art Devlin's Olympic Motor Inn, Inc. M
(518) 523-3700. **$68-$208, 14 day notice.** 2764 Main St. 0.5 mi e on SR 86. Ext corridors. **Pets:** Dogs only. $4 daily fee/pet. Supervision.

(SAVE) (✕) (🛏) (🏊)

◈◈◈ Comfort Inn on Lake Placid SH
(518) 523-9555. **$85-$210.** 2125 Saranac Ave. 0.5 mi w on SR 86. Ext/int corridors. **Pets:** Other species. Service with restrictions, supervision.

(SAVE) (SD) (✕) (🛏) (💲) (🍴) (🏊) (✕)

◈◈◈ Crowne Plaza Resort & Golf Club Lake Placid SH
(518) 523-2556. **$119-$299, 30 day notice.** 1 Olympic Dr. Downtown. Ext/int corridors. **Pets:** Other species. $10 daily fee/pet. Service with restrictions, supervision.

(SAVE) (✕) (🛏) (💲) (🍴) (🏊) (✕)

◈◈◈ Golden Arrow Lakeside Resort SH 🐾
(518) 523-3353. **$99-$259, 7 day notice.** On SR 86; center. Int corridors. **Pets:** Other species. $150 deposit/pet, $50 one-time fee/pet. Designated rooms, service with restrictions, supervision.

(SAVE) (SD) (✕) (🛏) (💲) (🍴) (🏊) (✕)

◈◈◈ Hilton Lake Placid Resort SH
(518) 523-4411. **Call for rates.** 1 Mirror Lake Dr. 0.3 mi w on SR 86. Int corridors. **Pets:** Accepted.

(✕) (&M) (🛏) (💲) (🍴) (🏊) (✕)

◈◈◈ Swiss Acres Inn SH
(518) 523-3040. **$49-$149, 7 day notice.** 1970 Saranac Ave. 1 mi w on SR 86. Ext/int corridors. **Pets:** Accepted.

(SAVE) (SD) (✕) (🛏) (💲) (🍴) (🏊)

LANSING

◈◈ Econo Lodge SH
(607) 257-1400. **$65-$209.** 2303 N Triphammer Rd. SR 13, exit Triphammer Rd. Int corridors. **Pets:** Other species. $15 daily fee/pet. Designated rooms, service with restrictions, crate.

(ASK) (SD) (✕) (🛏) (💲)

◈◈◈ Homewood Suites by Hilton SH 🐾
(607) 266-0000. **Call for rates.** 36 Cinema Dr. SR 13, exit Triphammer Rd, just e, then just n on Sheraton Dr (becomes Cinema Dr). Int corridors. **Pets:** Other species. $100 one-time fee/pet. Service with restrictions, supervision.

(✕) (&M) (🛏) (💲) (🏊) (✕)

◈◈◈ Ramada Inn Executive Training & Conference Ctr SH
(607) 257-3100. **$99-$259.** 2310 N Triphammer Rd. Jct SR 13 and 34, 3.5 mi n on SR 13, exit Triphammer Rd, just w. Int corridors. **Pets:** Accepted.

(SAVE) (SD) (✕) (🛏) (💲) (🍴) (🏊) (✕)

LATHAM

◈◈◈ The Century House, a Clarion Hotel SH
(518) 785-0931. **Call for rates.** 997 New Loudon Rd. I-87, exit 7 (SR 7), just e, then 0.5 mi n on US 9 (New Loudon Rd). Int corridors. **Pets:** Accepted.

(SAVE) (✕) (🛏) (💲) (🍴) (🏊)

◈◈ Cocca's Inn & Suites SH
(518) 785-6626. **$89-$129.** 831 SR 9. I-87, exit 6, just n of jct SR 2 and 9. Ext corridors. **Pets:** $10 daily fee/pet. Service with restrictions, supervision.

(ASK) (SD) (✕) (🛏) (💲) (🏊)

◈◈◈ Comfort Inn Albany Airport & Conference Center SH
(518) 783-1900. **$109-$149.** 20 Airport Park Blvd. I-87, exit 4, 2.2 mi nw on Albany Shaker Rd. Int corridors. **Pets:** Medium. $15 daily fee/pet. Designated rooms, service with restrictions.

(SAVE) (SD) (✕) (🛏) (💲)

◈◈◈ Hampton Inn-Latham SH
(518) 785-0000. **Call for rates.** 981 New Loudon Rd. I-87, exit 7 (SR 7), just e, then just n on US 9 (New Loudon Rd). Int corridors. **Pets:** Accepted.

(✕) (&M) (🛏) (💲) (🏊)

◈◈◈ Holiday Inn Express-Airport SH
(518) 783-6161. **Call for rates.** 946 New Loudon Rd. I-87, exit 7 (SR 7), just e, then just n on US 9 (New Loudon Rd). Ext corridors. **Pets:** Accepted.

(SAVE) (✕) (🛏) (💲) (🏊)

◈◈◈ La Quinta Inn & Suites–Albany Airport SH
(518) 640-2200. **$119-$129.** 833 New Loudon Rd. I-87, exit 7, just s on US 9 to Latham Circle, then n on US 9. Int corridors. **Pets:** Other species. Service with restrictions, supervision.

(SAVE) (SD) (✕) (🛏) (💲)

Microtel Inn, Albany Airport SH
(518) 782-9161. **$50-$169.** 7 Rensselaer Ave. I-87, exit 6, just w. Int corridors. **Pets:** Small, dogs only. $10 daily fee/pet. Service with restrictions, supervision.
SAVE S0 X &M 🖶 💻

Quality Inn & Suites SH
(518) 785-5891. **$110-$210.** 611 Troy-Schenectady Rd. I-87, exit 6, just w on SR 7. Ext/int corridors. **Pets:** Medium. $35 one-time fee/room. Designated rooms, service with restrictions, crate.
SAVE S0 X 🖶 💻 🏊

Residence Inn by Marriott Albany Airport SH
(518) 783-0600. **$219-$263.** 1 Residence Inn Dr. I-87, exit 6, 2 mi w on SR 7. Ext corridors. **Pets:** Other species. $75 one-time fee/room. No service.
ASK S0 X 🖶 💻 🏊 🐾

LITTLE FALLS

Best Western Little Falls Motor Inn SH
(315) 823-4954. **$75-$120, 3 day notice.** 20 Albany St. On SR 5 and 167. Int corridors. **Pets:** Other species. $10 deposit/pet. Service with restrictions, crate.
SAVE S0 X 💻 🍴

LIVERPOOL

Best Western Liverpool Grace Inn & Suites SH
(315) 701-4400. **$79-$189.** 136 Transistor Pkwy. I-90, exit 37 (Electronics Pkwy), just n; I-81, exit 25 (7th North St), 1.3 mi w, just n on Electronics Pkwy, then just w. Int corridors. **Pets:** Accepted.
SAVE S0 X 🖶 💻 🏊

Homewood Suites SH
(315) 451-3800. **Call for rates.** 275 Elwood Davis Rd. I-81, exit 25 (7th North St), 1 mi w; I-90, exit 36. Int corridors. **Pets:** Accepted.
X &M 🖶 💻 🏊 🐾

Knights Inn M
(315) 453-6330. **Call for rates.** 430 Electronics Pkwy. I-90, exit 37 (Electronics Pkwy), just w; I-81, exit 25 (7th North St), 1.3 mi nw, then just w. Ext corridors. **Pets:** Accepted.
SAVE X 🖶

Super 8 Motel Route 57 SH
(315) 451-8550. **$59-$119.** 7360 Oswego Rd. I-90, exit 38, 1 mi n on CR 57. Int corridors. **Pets:** Medium, dogs only. $10 daily fee/pet. Service with restrictions, supervision.
SAVE S0 X 💻

LONG LAKE

Journey's End Cottages CA
(518) 624-5381. **$125-$150, 60 day notice.** 941 Deerland Rd (Rt 30). On SR 30/28 N, 1 mi s. Ext corridors. **Pets:** Medium. $25 one-time fee/room. Service with restrictions, supervision.
SAVE 🖶 💻 🐾 🌐 🐾

Long View Lodge CI
(518) 624-2862. **$60-$180, 7 day notice.** 681 Deerland Rd. On SR 30/28 N, 2.2 mi s. Ext/int corridors. **Pets:** $10 daily fee/room. Designated rooms, service with restrictions.
X 🖶 🍴 🐾 🌐

MALONE

Econo Lodge of Malone M
(518) 483-0500. **$55-$115.** 227 W Main St. Just w of jct US 11 and SR 30. Ext/int corridors. **Pets:** Accepted.
ASK S0 X 🖶

Four Seasons Motel M
(518) 483-3490. **$59-$99.** 206 W Main St. 1 mi w on US 11. Ext corridors. **Pets:** Medium. $10 daily fee/pet. Service with restrictions, supervision.
SAVE S0 X 🖶 💻 🐾

Super 8 Motel at Jons SH
(518) 483-8123. **Call for rates.** 42 Finney Blvd. On SR 30, just s of jct US 11. Int corridors. **Pets:** Accepted.
SAVE X &M 🖶

MALTA

Fairfield Inn & Suites by Marriott SH
(518) 899-6900. **$120-$274.** 101 Saratoga Village Blvd. I-87, exit 12, just e. Int corridors. **Pets:** Accepted.
ASK S0 X &M 🖶 💻 🏊

MASSENA

Econo Lodge-Meadow View Motel SH
(315) 764-0246. **$72-$99.** 15054 SR 37. On SR 37, 2.7 mi sw. Ext/int corridors. **Pets:** Accepted.
SAVE S0 X 🖶 💻 🍴

MCGRAW

Cortland Days Inn SH
(607) 753-7594. **$54-$149.** 3775 US Rt 11. I-81, exit 10 (McGraw/Cortland), just n. Int corridors. **Pets:** Small. $15 daily fee/pet. Service with restrictions, supervision.
SAVE S0 X 🖶 💻

MELVILLE

Extended StayAmerica-Melville-New York SH
(631) 777-3999. **Call for rates.** 100 Spangnoli Rd. I-495, exit 49 S eastbound, 0.5 mi e on south service road, then 1.1 mi s on SR 110; exit westbound, 1.5 mi s on SR 110. Int corridors. **Pets:** Other species. $75 one-time fee/pet. Service with restrictions.
X &M 🖶 💻

MONTOUR FALLS

Relax Inn M
(607) 535-7183. **$45-$159, 4 day notice.** 100 Clawson Blvd. Jct SR 14 and 224. Ext corridors. **Pets:** Small, dogs only. $10 daily fee/pet. Designated rooms, service with restrictions, supervision.
SAVE S0 X 🖶

NEWARK

Quality Inn Fingerlakes Region SH 🐾
(315) 331-9500. **$79-$169, 3 day notice.** 125 N Main St. Jct SR 31, just n on SR 88. Int corridors. **Pets:** Other species. $25 deposit/room. Service with restrictions, crate.
ASK S0 X 🖶 💻 🍴 🐾

NEWBURGH

Super 8 M
(845) 564-5700. **Call for rates.** 1287 Rt 300. I-87, exit 17, just w; I-84, exit 6, 2 mi e. Int corridors. **Pets:** Small, other species. $25 daily fee/pet. Designated rooms, service with restrictions, supervision.
X &M

NEW HAMPTON

Days Inn M
(845) 374-2411. **Call for rates.** 4939 Rt 17M. I-84, exit 3, 0.8 mi e on US 6 and SR 17M; SR 17, exit 123, 4 mi w. Ext/int corridors. **Pets:** Medium. $10 daily fee/pet. Designated rooms, service with restrictions, supervision.
SAVE X 🖶 💻 🐾

NEW HARTFORD

▼▼▼ Holiday Inn Utica 🅂🄷
(315) 797-2131. **$89-$189.** 1777 Burrstone Rd. I-90 (New York State Thruway), exit 31, 4.5 mi w on SR 5 W and 12 S, exit Burrstone Rd, then 1 mi nw. Int corridors. **Pets:** Accepted.
🄰🅂🄺 🆂🅾 🅇 🕭 🄼 🛏 🖵 🍴 🛋 🖾

▼▼ Ramada 🅂🄷
(315) 735-3392. **$89-$149.** 141 New Hartford St. SR 8, 12 and 5, exit French Rd, just w, then just n. Int corridors. **Pets:** Small. $20 daily fee/pet. Designated rooms, service with restrictions, crate.
🄰🅂🄺 🆂🅾 🅇 🕭 🖵 🍴 🛋

NEW YORK METROPOLITAN AREA

ARMONK

▼▼▼▼ La Quinta Inn & Suites 🅂🄷 ❧
(914) 273-9090. **$149-$159.** 94 Business Park Dr. I-684, exit 3S northbound; exit 3 southbound, 0.3 mi s on SR 22 to Business Park Dr. Int corridors. **Pets:** Medium. Supervision.
🄰🅂🄺 🅇 🄼 🕭 🖵 🍴 🛋 🖾

BROOKLYN

▼▼▼ Comfort Inn Brooklyn Bridge 🅂🄷
(718) 855-9600. **Call for rates.** 279 Butler St. Between 3rd and Nevins; in Park Slope. Int corridors. **Pets:** Small. $50 one-time fee/room. Designated rooms, service with restrictions, supervision.
🅇 🕭 🖵

▼▼▼ Holiday Inn Express Brooklyn 🅂🄷
(718) 797-1133. **$159-$399.** 625 Union St. Between 3rd and 4th aves. Int corridors. **Pets:** Medium. $50 one-time fee/room. Service with restrictions, supervision.
🄰🅂🄺 🅇 🕭 🖵

EAST ELMHURST

▼▼▼▼ Courtyard by Marriott New York/La Guardia Airport 🄻🄷
(718) 446-4800. **$329-$406.** 90-10 Grand Central Pkwy.Grand Central Pkwy, exit 6 (94th St) eastbound; exit 7 westbound, 0.5 mi s on 94th St to 23rd Ave, then just w to 90th St. Int corridors. **Pets:** Accepted.
🄰🅂🄺 🆂🅾 🅇 🄼 🕭 🖵 🍴 🛋

ELMSFORD

▼▼ Extended StayAmerica-White Plains-Elmsford 🅂🄷
(914) 347-8073. **$150-$255.** 118 Tarrytown Rd. I-87, exit 8, just w. Int corridors. **Pets:** Other species. $75 one-time fee/pet. Service with restrictions.
🄰🅂🄺 🆂🅾 🅇 🄼 🕭 🖵

🐾 ▼▼▼▼ Hampton Inn White Plains/Tarrytown 🅂🄷 ❧
(914) 592-5680. **Call for rates.** 200 Tarrytown Rd. I-287, exit 1; I-87, exit 8, just w. Int corridors. **Pets:** Medium. Service with restrictions, supervision.
🆂🄰🆅🄴 🅇 🄼 🕭 🖵 🛋

FLUSHING

▼▼▼ Extended StayAmerica-Whitestone 🅂🄷
(718) 357-3661. **$180-$255.** 18-30 Whitestone Expwy. I-678, exit 15, just w; in Whitestone. Int corridors. **Pets:** Other species. $25 daily fee/pet. Service with restrictions, supervision.
🄰🅂🄺 🆂🅾 🅇 🕭 🖵

🐾 ▼▼▼▼ Sheraton La Guardia East Hotel 🄻🄷 ❧
(718) 460-6666. **$199-$219.** 135-20 39th Ave. Grand Central Pkwy to Northern Blvd, 1 mi e to Main St, 0.3 mi s to 39th Ave, then just w. Int corridors. **Pets:** Medium. Service with restrictions, supervision.
🆂🄰🆅🄴 🆂🅾 🅇 🕭 🖵 🍴

NEW PALTZ

▼▼ Rodeway Inn & Suites 🄼
(845) 883-7373. **$89-$219, 3 day notice.** 601 Main St (SR 299). I-87, exit 18, 0.5 mi e on SR 299. Ext/int corridors. **Pets:** Accepted.
🄰🅂🄺 🆂🅾 🅇 🕭

JAMAICA

▼▼▼▼ Crowne Plaza Hotel-JFK Airport 🅂🄷
(718) 489-1000. **$189-$369.** 151-20 Baisley Blvd. Belt Pkwy E to Farmer's Blvd exit, just n to N Conduit Ave, then just w to Baisley Blvd; Van Wyck Expwy S, exit 2 (Rockaway Blvd), e to Baisley Blvd. Int corridors. **Pets:** Accepted.
🄰🅂🄺 🅇 🕭 🖵 🍴

▼▼ Ramada Plaza Hotel at JFK 🄻🄷
(718) 995-9000. **Call for rates.** Bldg 144/JFK International Airport. Van Wyck Expwy at Belt Pkwy; southwest corner. Int corridors. **Pets:** Accepted.
🅇 🕭 🖵 🍴

MOUNT KISCO

▼▼▼ Holiday Inn 🅂🄷
(914) 241-2600. **Call for rates.** 1 Holiday Inn Dr. Saw Mill River Pkwy, exit 37, just e. Int corridors. **Pets:** Accepted.
🅇 🄼 🕭 🖵 🍴 🛋

NANUET

▼▼▼ Candlewood Suites 🅂🄷
(845) 371-4445. **$129-$159.** 20 Overlook Blvd. I-287/87 (New York State Thruway), exit 14 (SR 59 W) to New Clarkstown Rd. Int corridors. **Pets:** Accepted.
🄰🅂🄺 🆂🅾 🅇 🕭 🖵

NEW YORK

🐾 ▼▼▼ 70 Park Avenue Hotel 🅂🄷
(212) 973-2400. **$299-$795.** 70 Park Ave. At 38th St. Int corridors. **Pets:** Accepted.
🆂🄰🆅🄴 🆂🅾 🅇 🄼 🍴

🐾 ▼▼▼▼ Affinia 50 🅂🄷 ❧
(212) 751-5710. **$189-$769.** 155 E 50th St. Between 3rd and Lexington aves. Int corridors. **Pets:** Other species. Designated rooms.
🆂🄰🆅🄴 🅇 🕭 🖵

🐾 ▼▼▼▼ Affinia Dumont 🅂🄷 ❧
(212) 481-7600. **$249-$689.** 150 E 34th St. Between Lexington and 3rd aves. Int corridors. **Pets:** Other species. Service with restrictions, crate.
🆂🄰🆅🄴 🅇 🕭 🖵 🍴

🐾 ▼▼▼ Affinia Gardens 🅂🄷
(212) 355-1230. **$279-$769.** 215 E 64th St. Between 2nd and 3rd aves. Int corridors. **Pets:** Accepted.
🆂🄰🆅🄴 🅇 🕭 🖵 🖾

🐾 ▼▼▼ Affinia Manhattan 🄻🄷 ❧
(212) 563-1800. **$189-$519.** 371 7th Ave. At 31st St. Int corridors. **Pets:** $250 deposit/room. Service with restrictions, crate.
🆂🄰🆅🄴 🅇 🕭 🖵 🍴

The Alex SH ☘
(212) 867-5100. **$950-$2090.** 205 E 45th St. At 3rd Ave. Int corridors. **Pets:** Dogs only. $1000.00 deposit/room, $250 one-time fee/room.

Algonquin Hotel LH
(212) 840-6800. **$299-$950.** 59 W 44th St. Between 5th and 6th (Ave of the Americas) aves. Int corridors. **Pets:** Accepted.

Beekman Tower Hotel SH
(212) 355-7300. **$770-$1220.** 3 Mitchell Pl. 49th St and 1st Ave. Int corridors. **Pets:** Accepted.

The Benjamin Hotel SH ☘
(212) 715-2500. **$239-$869.** 125 E 50th St. Between Lexington and 3rd aves. Int corridors. **Pets:** Other species. Service with restrictions, crate.

The Bryant Park Hotel SH
(212) 869-0100. **$395-$2500.** 40 W 40th St. Between 5th and 6th (Ave of the Americas) aves. Int corridors. **Pets:** Accepted.

The Carlyle, a Rosewood Hotel SH
(212) 744-1600. **$755-$1135.** 35 E 76th St. At Madison Ave. Int corridors. **Pets:** Accepted.

Eastgate Tower Hotel SH
(212) 687-8000. **$179-$559.** 222 E 39th St. Between 2nd and 3rd aves. Int corridors. **Pets:** Accepted.

Embassy Suites Hotel New York City LH
(212) 945-0100. **$209-$899.** 102 N End Ave. Between Murray and Vesey sts. Int corridors. **Pets:** Accepted.

Four Seasons Hotel New York LH
(212) 758-5700. **Call for rates.** 57 E 57th St. Between Park and Madison aves. Int corridors. **Pets:** Accepted.

The Franklin Hotel SH
(212) 369-1000. **Call for rates.** 164 E 87th St. Between 3rd and Lexington aves. Int corridors. **Pets:** Accepted.

Hampton Inn-Madison Square Garden Area SH
(212) 947-9700. **Call for rates.** 116 W 31st St. Between 6th (Ave of the Americas) and 7th aves. Int corridors. **Pets:** Small. $50 one-time fee/pet. Service with restrictions, supervision.

Hampton Inn-Manhattan/Chelsea SH
(212) 414-1000. **$169-$519.** 108 W 24th St. Between 6th (Ave of the Americas) and 7th aves. Int corridors. **Pets:** Accepted.

Hampton Inn-Manhattan/Seaport/Financial District SH ☘
(212) 571-4400. **$149-$809, 30 day notice.** 320 Pearl St. Between deck slip and Dover St. Int corridors. **Pets:** Other species. $40 one-time fee/pet. Service with restrictions.

Hilton New York LH
(212) 586-7000. **Call for rates.** 1335 Ave of the Americas. Between 53rd and 54th sts. Int corridors. **Pets:** Accepted.

Hilton Times Square LH
(212) 642-2500. **$279-$999.** 234 W 42nd St. Between 7th and 8th aves. Int corridors. **Pets:** Accepted.

Holiday Inn Express Fifth Ave SH ☘
(212) 302-9088. **$249-$459.** 15 W 45th St. At 5th Ave. **Pets:** Medium, other species. $50 one-time fee/room. Service with restrictions.

Holiday Inn Express Manhattan/Madison Square Garden SH
(212) 695-7200. **Call for rates.** 232 W 29th St. Between 7th and 8th aves. Int corridors. **Pets:** Accepted.

Hotel Gansevoort SH ☘
(212) 660-6700. **$395-$895, 3 day notice.** 18 9th Ave. At 13th St. Int corridors. **Pets:** $100 one-time fee/room. Service with restrictions.

Hotel Plaza Athenee SH ☘
(212) 734-9100. **$695-$1250.** 37 E 64th St. Between Madison and Park aves. Int corridors. **Pets:** Small. $60 one-time fee/pet.

Hotel Wales SH
(212) 876-6000. **$459-$959.** 1295 Madison Ave. Between 92nd and 93rd sts E. Int corridors. **Pets:** Accepted.

Jolly Hotel Madison Towers LH
(212) 802-0600. **Call for rates.** 22 E 38th St. Between Park and Madison aves. Int corridors. **Pets:** Small. Service with restrictions, supervision.

Jumeirah-Essex House LH
(212) 247-0300. **$709-$1169.** 160 Central Park S. Between 6th (Ave of the Americas) and 7th aves. Int corridors. **Pets:** Accepted.

Le Parker Meridien New York LH ☘
(212) 245-5000. **$799-$3020.** 118 W 57th St. Between 6th (Ave of the Americas) and 7th aves; vehicle entrance on 56th St. Int corridors. **Pets:** Other species. Service with restrictions, supervision.

Loews Regency Hotel LH
(212) 759-4100. **$489-$4500.** 540 Park Ave. At 61st St. Int corridors. **Pets:** Accepted.

The London NYC LH
(212) 307-5000. **Call for rates.** 151 W 54th St. Between 6th (Ave of the Americas) and 7th aves. Int corridors. **Pets:** Accepted.

The Lowell Hotel SH ☘
(212) 838-1400. **$575-$750.** 28 E 63rd St. Between Park and Madison aves. Int corridors. **Pets:** Medium. Service with restrictions, supervision.

Mandarin Oriental, New York LH
(212) 805-8800. **$895-$1400.** 80 Columbus Circle at 60th St. At 60th St. Int corridors. **Pets:** Accepted.

Millennium Broadway LH
(212) 768-4400. **$499-$999.** 145 W 44th St. Between 6th (Ave of the Americas) and 7th aves; in Times Square. Int corridors. **Pets:** Accepted.

◉ ◈◈◈ **The Muse Hotel** 🔲
(212) 485-2400. **$299-$1800.** 130 W 46th St. Between 6th (Ave of the Americas) and 7th aves. Int corridors. **Pets:** Accepted.
[SAVE] [S🔲] [✕] [❢]

◉ ◈◈◈◈ **The New York Helmsley Hotel** 🔲
(212) 490-8900. **$335-$415.** 212 E 42nd St. Between 2nd and 3rd aves. Int corridors. **Pets:** Medium. Service with restrictions, crate.
[SAVE] [✕] [❚] [❢]

◈◈◈◈ **New York Marriott Marquis** 🔲
(212) 398-1900. **$461-$747.** 1535 Broadway. Between 45th and 46th sts; motor entrance on 46th St. Int corridors. **Pets:** Accepted.
[A$K] [S🔲] [✕] [❚] [❑] [❢]

◉ ◈◈◈◈ **The New York Palace** 🔲
(212) 888-7000. **$625-$815.** 455 Madison Ave. Between 50th and 51st sts. Int corridors. **Pets:** Accepted.
[SAVE] [✕] [🅶M] [❚] [❑] [❢] [🐾]

◉ ◈◈◈ **Novotel New York** 🔲
(212) 315-0100. **Call for rates.** 226 W 52nd St. At Broadway. Int corridors. **Pets:** Accepted.
[SAVE] [✕] [❚] [❢]

◈◈◈◈ **Omni Berkshire Place** 🔲
(212) 753-5800. **$499-$659.** 21 E 52nd St. Between Madison and 5th aves. Int corridors. **Pets:** Accepted.
[A$K] [S🔲] [✕] [🅶M] [❚] [❢] [🐾]

◈◈◈◈ **On The Ave Hotel** 🔲
(212) 362-1100. **$209-$799.** 2178 Broadway. At 77th St. Int corridors. **Pets:** Accepted.
[S🔲] [✕] [❚] [❑]

◉ ◈◈◈◈ **The Peninsula New York** 🔲 🐾
(212) 956-2888. **$875-$925.** 700 5th Ave. At 55th St. Int corridors. **Pets:** Large. Service with restrictions, supervision.
[SAVE] [✕] [❚] [❢] [🏊] [🐾]

◉ ◈◈◈◈ **The Pierre New York-A Taj Hotel** 🔲
(212) 838-8000. **$815-$7500.** 2 E 61st St. At 5th Ave. Int corridors. **Pets:** Accepted.
[SAVE] [✕] [🅶M] [❚] [❢] [🐾]

◉ ◈◈◈ **Radisson Martinique on Broadway** 🔲
(212) 736-3800. **$259-$569.** 49 W 32nd St. Between Broadway and Fifth Ave. Int corridors. **Pets:** Accepted.
[SAVE] [S🔲] [✕] [🅶M] [❚] [❑] [❢]

◉ ◈◈◈◈ **Renaissance New York Hotel Times Square** 🔲
(212) 765-7676. **$439-$725.** 2 Times Square, 7th Ave at W 48th St. Broadway and 7th Ave; auto access from 7th Ave, s of W 48th St. Int corridors. **Pets:** Accepted.
[SAVE] [S🔲] [✕] [❑] [❢]

◉ ◈◈◈◈ **The Ritz Carlton-New York, Battery Park** 🔲
(212) 344-0800. **Call for rates.** Two West St. Jct Battery Park. Int corridors. **Pets:** Accepted.
[SAVE] [✕] [🅶M] [❚] [❢]

◉ ◈◈◈◈ **The Ritz Carlton-New York, Central Park** 🔲
(212) 308-9100. **Call for rates.** 50 Central Park S. Between 5th and 6th (Ave of the Americas) aves. Int corridors. **Pets:** Accepted.
[SAVE] [✕] [🅶M] [❚] [❢] [🐾]

◉ ◈◈◈◈ **The St. Regis Hotel, New York** 🔲
(212) 753-4500. **$995-$1295.** 2 E 55th St. Between Madison and 5th aves. Int corridors. **Pets:** Accepted.
[SAVE] [✕] [🅶M] [❚] [❑] [❢] [🐾]

◈◈◈◈ **Shelburne Murray Hill Hotel** 🔲 🐾
(212) 689-5200. **$179-$669.** 303 Lexington Ave. Between 37th and 38th sts. Int corridors. **Pets:** Other species. Service with restrictions, crate.
[A$K] [✕] [❚] [❑] [❢]

◈◈◈◈ **Sheraton Manhattan at Times Square** 🔲
(212) 581-3300. **Call for rates.** 790 7th Ave. Between 51st and 52nd sts. Int corridors. **Pets:** Accepted.
[✕] [🅶M] [❚] [❑] [❢] [🏊] [🐾]

◈◈◈◈ **Sheraton New York Hotel & Towers** 🔲
(212) 581-1000. **Call for rates.** 811 7th Ave. At 52nd St. Int corridors. **Pets:** Service with restrictions.
[✕] [🅶M] [❚] [❑] [❢] [🐾]

◉ ◈◈◈◈ **Sofitel New York** 🔲
(212) 354-8844. **$369-$1299.** 45 W 44th St. Between 5th and 6th (Ave of the Americas) aves. Int corridors. **Pets:** Accepted.
[SAVE] [✕] [❚] [❢] [🐾]

◈◈◈◈ **The SoHo Grand Hotel** 🔲
(212) 965-3000. **Call for rates.** 310 W Broadway. In SoHo; jct Grand St. Int corridors. **Pets:** Accepted.
[✕] [❢]

◉ ◈◈◈◈ **Surrey Hotel** 🔲 🐾
(212) 288-3700. **$359-$649.** 20 E 76th St. E 76th St and Madison Ave. Int corridors. **Pets:** Very small, other species. Service with restrictions, crate.
[SAVE] [✕] [❚] [❑] [❢]

◈◈◈◈ **The Time** 🔲
(212) 246-5252. **$229-$929.** 224 W 49th St. Between 8th Ave and Broadway. Int corridors. **Pets:** Accepted.
[✕] [❢] [🐾]

◈◈◈◈ **Tribeca Grand Hotel** 🔲
(212) 519-6600. **Call for rates.** 2 Ave of the Americas. At 6th Ave (Ave of the Americas) and White St. Int corridors. **Pets:** Accepted.
[✕] [❢]

◉ ◈◈◈◈ **Trump International Hotel & Tower** 🔲
(212) 299-1000. **Call for rates.** 1 Central Park W. Jct Central Park S; at Columbus Circle. Int corridors. **Pets:** Accepted.
[SAVE] [✕] [❚] [❑] [❢] [🐾]

◈◈◈ **The Wall Street District Hotel** 🔲
(212) 232-7700. **Call for rates.** 15 Gold St. Corner of Gold and Platt sts. Int corridors. **Pets:** Accepted.
[✕] [🅶M] [❚] [❑] [❢]

◉ ◈◈◈◈ **The Westin New York at Times Square** 🔲
(212) 201-2700. **$299-$899.** 270 W 43rd St. Corner of 8th Ave. Int corridors. **Pets:** Accepted.
[SAVE] [✕] [🅶M] [❚] [❑] [❢] [🐾]

◈◈◈ **W New York** 🔲
(212) 755-1200. **Call for rates.** 541 Lexington Ave. At 49th St. Int corridors. **Pets:** Accepted.
[✕] [🅶M] [❚] [❢]

◈◈◈◈ **W New York Times Square** 🔲
(212) 930-7400. **Call for rates.** 1567 Broadway at 47th St. Corner of 47th St. Int corridors. **Pets:** Accepted.
[✕] [🅶M] [❚] [❑] [❢]

◈◈◈◈ **W New York-Union Square** 🔲 🐾
(212) 253-9119. **Call for rates.** 201 Park Ave S. At 17th St. Int corridors. **Pets:** Small. $25 daily fee/pet, $150 one-time fee/room. No service, supervision.
[✕] [🅶M] [❚] [❢] [🐾]

ORANGEBURG

▼▼▼▼ Orangeburg Holiday Inn & Registry Hotel SH
(845) 359-7000. $109-$169. 329 Rt 303. I-87/287, exit 12, 4 mi s on SR 303; 1 mi n of Palisades Interstate Pkwy, exit 5 northbound; 1 mi e of exit 6. Int corridors. **Pets:** Accepted.

(ASK) (SG) (✕) (♿) (💻) (⑪) (🌊)

RYE BROOK

AAA ▼▼▼▼ Hilton Rye Town LH
(914) 939-6300. $139-$359. 699 Westchester Ave. I-287 (Cross Westchester Expwy), exit 10 eastbound, 0.6 mi ne on SR 120A; exit westbound, 0.3 mi n on Webb Ave, then 0.4 mi ne on SR 120A. Int corridors. **Pets:** Small, dogs only. $50 one-time fee/room. Designated rooms, service with restrictions, supervision.

(SAVE) (✕) (♿) (💻) (⑪) (🌊) (✕)

STATEN ISLAND

AAA ▼▼▼▼ Hilton Garden Inn Staten Island SH
(718) 477-2400. **Call for rates.** 1100 South Ave. I-278, exit 6 (South Ave) westbound, just s; exit 5 eastbound to SR 440 S, exit South Ave, just s to South Ave, 1 mi n to Lois Ln, then just w. Int corridors. **Pets:** Accepted.

(SAVE) (✕) (♿) (💻) (⑪) (🌊) (✕)

AAA ▼▼▼▼ The Staten Island Hotel LH
(718) 698-5000. $159-$208. 1415 Richmond Ave. I-278, exit Richmond Ave, 0.5 mi se. Int corridors. **Pets:** Medium. Service with restrictions.

(SAVE) (SG) (✕) (♿) (💻) (⑪)

SUFFERN

AAA ▼▼▼▼ Holiday Inn-Suffern SH ❖
(845) 357-4800. $113. 3 Executive Blvd. I-87 (New York State Thruway), exit 14B, just n. Int corridors. **Pets:** Other species. $50 one-time fee/room. No service, crate.

(SAVE) (SG) (✕) (♿) (💻) (⑪) (🌊) (✕)

TARRYTOWN

▼▼▼▼ Sheraton Tarrytown Hotel SH
(914) 332-7900. **Call for rates.** 600 White Plains Rd. I-87, exit 9 northbound, 0.8 mi e on SR 119; exit southbound, just n on US 9, then 1 mi e on SR 119. Int corridors. **Pets:** Accepted.

(✕) (♿M) (💻) (⑪) (🌊)

▼▼▼▼ Westchester Marriott Hotel LH ❖
(914) 631-2200. $286-$306. 670 White Plains Rd. I-87 (New York State Thruway), exit 9 northbound, 0.8 mi e on SR 119; exit southbound, just n on US 9, then 1 mi e on SR 119. Int corridors. **Pets:** Large. $75 one-time fee/pet. Designated rooms, service with restrictions, crate.

(ASK) (SG) (✕) (♿) (💻) (⑪) (🌊) (✕)

WHITE PLAINS

▼▼▼▼ Hyatt Summerfield Suites SH
(914) 251-9700. $99-$519. 101 Corporate Park Dr. I-287 (Cross Westchester Expwy), exit 9A eastbound, 0.6 mi e on Westchester Ave, then 0.3 mi n; exit 9N-S westbound, 0.9 mi w on Westchester Ave. Int corridors. **Pets:** Medium, other species. $200 one-time fee/room.

(ASK) (✕) (♿) (💻) (🌊) (✕)

END METROPOLITAN AREA

NIAGARA FALLS METROPOLITAN AREA

LOCKPORT

⨺⨺⨺ Comfort Inn SH
(716) 434-4411. **$69-$139.** 551 S Transit Rd. 1 mi s on SR 78. Int corridors. **Pets:** Medium. $10 daily fee/pet. Service with restrictions, supervision.

SAVE S⨺ ✕ ⨺M ⬛ 🖥

⨺⨺⨺ Holiday Inn Lockport SH
(716) 434-6151. **$89-$189.** 515 S Transit Rd. 1 mi s on SR 78. Int corridors. **Pets:** Large. $10 daily fee/room. Service with restrictions, supervision.

SAVE ✕ ⨺M ⬛ 🖥 🍴 🐾

NEWFANE

⨺ Lake Ontario Motel M
(716) 778-5004. **$57-$75.** 3330 Lockport-Olcott Rd. 2.5 mi n of jct SR 104 on SR 78. Int corridors. **Pets:** Other species. $5 daily fee/room. Service with restrictions, supervision.

ASK S⨺ ✕ ⬛

NIAGARA FALLS

⨺⨺⨺ Best Western Summit Inn SH
(716) 297-5050. **$70-$200.** 9500 Niagara Falls Blvd. I-190, exit 22, 2.1 mi e on US 62 S. Int corridors. **Pets:** $10 daily fee/room. Designated rooms, service with restrictions, crate.

SAVE S⨺ ✕ ⬛ 🖥 🐾

⨺⨺⨺ Fallside Hotel & Conference Center SH
(716) 285-2541. **Call for rates.** 401 Buffalo Ave. I-190, exit 21 (Robert Moses Pkwy), exit City Traffic, just n. Int corridors. **Pets:** Accepted.

SAVE ✕ ⬛ 🖥 🍴 🐾

⨺⨺⨺ Howard Johnson Inn Closest to the Falls SH
(716) 285-5261. **$59-$275.** 454 Main St. I-190, exit 21 (Robert Moses Pkwy), exit City Traffic, just n to Rainbow Blvd, then just w. Int corridors. **Pets:** Accepted.

SAVE S⨺ ✕ ⨺M ⬛ 🖥 🐾

⨺⨺⨺ Quality Hotel and Suites "At the Falls" SH
(716) 282-1212. **$59-$399.** 240 Rainbow Blvd. I-190, exit 21 (Robert Moses Pkwy), eastbound use City Traffic exit, just w; downtown. Int corridors. **Pets:** Large. $20 daily fee/pet. Service with restrictions, crate.

✕ ⬛ 🖥 🍴 🐾

END METROPOLITAN AREA

NORTH SYRACUSE

⨺⨺⨺⨺ Candlewood Suites Syracuse Airport SH 🐾
(315) 454-8999. **$128-$148.** 5414 South Bay Rd. I-90, exit 36; I-81, exit 26 (Mattydale Rd), follow South Bay Rd signs, just n. Int corridors. **Pets:** Medium, other species. $5 daily fee/pet. Service with restrictions, crate.

ASK S⨺ ✕ ⬛ 🖥

⨺⨺⨺⨺ Comfort Inn & Suites/Syracuse Airport SH
(315) 457-4000. **$79-$219.** 6701 Buckley Rd. I-81, exit 25 (7th North St), just w. Int corridors. **Pets:** Large, other species. $10 daily fee/room. Service with restrictions, supervision.

SAVE S⨺ ✕ ⬛ 🖥 🐾 🐾

NORWICH

⨺⨺ Super 8 Motel of Norwich SH
(607) 336-8880. **Call for rates.** 6067 State Hwy 12. On SR 12, 0.9 mi n. Int corridors. **Pets:** $10 daily fee/room. Service with restrictions, supervision.

✕ ⬛ 🖥

OGDENSBURG

⨺⨺⨺⨺ Quality Inn Gran-View M
(315) 393-4550. **$82-$192.** 6765 State Hwy 37. On SR 37, 3 mi sw. Ext/int corridors. **Pets:** Other species. $10 daily fee/room. Designated rooms, service with restrictions, crate.

SAVE S⨺ ✕ ⬛ 🖥 🍴 🐾 🐾

⨺⨺⨺⨺ The Stonefence Resort & Motel M
(315) 393-1545. **$69-$199.** 7191 SR 37. Jct SR 68, 0.5 mi w. Ext/int corridors. **Pets:** Medium. $25 one-time fee/room. Designated rooms, service with restrictions, supervision.

SAVE S⨺ ✕ ⬛ 🖥 🍴 🐾 🐾

⨺⨺ Windjammer Lodge M
(315) 393-6300. **$80-$100.** 5843 SR 37. On SR 37, 5 mi sw. **Pets:** Other species. $10 daily fee/room. Service with restrictions, crate.

ASK S⨺ ✕ ⬛ 🖥 🐾

OLD FORGE

⨺⨺ Best Western Sunset Inn M
(315) 369-6836. **$69-$209, 7 day notice.** 2752 SR 28. 0.3 mi s. Ext/int corridors. **Pets:** Dogs only. Designated rooms, service with restrictions, supervision.

ASK S⨺ ✕ ⬛ 🖥 🐾 ✕

ONEONTA

⨺⨺⨺⨺ Holiday Inn Oneonta/Cooperstown Area SH
(607) 433-2250. **$89-$189.** 5206 State Hwy 23. I-88, exit 15 (SR 23 and 28), 1.5 mi e. Int corridors. **Pets:** Accepted.

SAVE S⨺ ✕ ⬛ 🖥 🍴 🐾 ✕

⨺⨺ Super 8 Motel SH
(607) 432-9505. **$95-$140.** 4973 SR 23. I-88, exit 15 (SR 23 and 28), 0.3 mi e. Int corridors. **Pets:** Other species. $5 daily fee/room. Service with restrictions, supervision.

ASK S⨺ ✕ ⨺M ⬛ 🖥

OWEGO

⨺⨺ Sunrise Motel M
(607) 687-5667. **$55-$65.** 3778 Waverly Rd. SR 17, exit 64 (SR 96 N), across river, w to SR 17C, 2 mi w. Ext corridors. **Pets:** Very small. $5 daily fee/pet. Service with restrictions, crate.

SAVE S⨺ ✕

PAINTED POST

Americas Best Value Inn Lodge on the Green M ✿
(607) 962-2456. **$50-$94.** 196 S Hamilton Rd. SR 17, exit 44; US 15, exit 3, 1 mi n. Ext corridors. **Pets:** Medium. $50 deposit/room. Service with restrictions, crate.
SAVE S⊘ ✕ 🛏 🖵 ⌘

Corning Inn SH
(607) 937-5383. **Call for rates.** 255 S Hamilton St. SR 17, exit 44; US 15, exit 3, 0.5 mi n. Int corridors. **Pets:** Accepted.
✕ ⑤M 🛏

Econo Lodge SH
(607) 962-4444. **$69-$99.** 200 Robert Dann Dr. I-86, exit 44, US 15 S, exit 3, just n on S Hamilton St (SR 417), then just w. Int corridors. **Pets:** $10 daily fee/pet. Service with restrictions, supervision.
ASK S⊘ ✕ ⑤M 🛏 🖵

Erwin Motel M ✿
(607) 962-7411. **$29-$79.** 806 Addison Rd. US 15, exit Erwin Addison, just e on SR 417. Ext corridors. **Pets:** Dogs only. $10 daily fee/pet. Designated rooms, service with restrictions, supervision.
SAVE S⊘ ✕ 🛏 🖵

PEMBROKE

Darien Lakes Econo Lodge SH
(585) 599-4681. **$59-$159.** 8493 SR 77. I-90, exit 48A, in Pembroke; just s. Int corridors. **Pets:** Accepted.
ASK S⊘ ✕ 🛏 🖵

PENN YAN

Best Western Vineyard Inn & Suites SH
(315) 536-8473. **$110-$190.** 142 Lake St. I-90, exit 43, SR 14 S to SR 54 N; corner of SR 54 and 14A. Int corridors. **Pets:** Small, other species. $10 daily fee/pet. Designated rooms, service with restrictions, supervision.
SAVE S⊘ ✕ 🛏 🖵 ⌘

PINE VALLEY

Best Western Marshall Manor M
(607) 739-3891. **Call for rates.** 3527 Watkins Rd. SR 17, exit 52, 5 mi n on SR 14. Ext corridors. **Pets:** Other species. $15 daily fee/room. Designated rooms, service with restrictions.
SAVE ✕ 🛏 🖵 ⌘

PLAINVIEW

Homewood Suites Long Island Melville SH
(516) 293-4663. **$229-$359.** 1585 Round Swamp Rd. I-495, exit 48, just s. Int corridors. **Pets:** Other species. $150 one-time fee/room.
ASK S⊘ ✕ ⑤M 🛏 🖵 ⌘ ✕

Residence Inn by Marriott SH ✿
(516) 433-6200. **$208-$241.** 9 Gerhard Rd. I-495, exit 44, 1.6 mi s on SR 135, exit 10, then just e on Old Country Rd. Int corridors. **Pets:** Large, other species. $100 one-time fee/room. Service with restrictions, supervision.
ASK S⊘ ✕ ⑤M 🛏 🖵 ⌘ ✕

PLATTSBURGH

Best Western The Inn at Smithfield SH ✿
(518) 561-7750. **$80-$130.** 446 Rt 3. I-87, exit 37, just w. Int corridors. **Pets:** Other species. $10 one-time fee/room. Service with restrictions, supervision.
SAVE S⊘ ✕ 🛏 🖵 ⌘ ✕

La Quinta Inn & Suites Plattsburgh SH
(518) 562-4000. **$85-$100.** 16 Plaza Blvd. I-87, exit 37, just w. Int corridors. **Pets:** Medium. Service with restrictions, supervision.
ASK ✕ ⑤M 🛏 🖵 ⌘

Microtel Inn and Suites SH
(518) 324-3800. **$64-$114.** 554 SR 3. I-87, exit 37, just w. Int corridors. **Pets:** Medium. $10 daily fee/pet. Service with restrictions, supervision.
SAVE S⊘ ✕ ⑤M 🛏 🖵

Super 8 Motel M
(518) 562-8888. **Call for rates.** 7129 Rt 9 N. I-87, exit 39, just e, then just n. Int corridors. **Pets:** Accepted.
✕ ⑤M 🛏 🖵 ⌘

PORT JERVIS

Comfort Inn SH
(845) 856-6611. **$69-$149.** 2247 Greenville Tpke. I-84, exit 1, just se. Int corridors. **Pets:** Medium, dogs only. $20 one-time fee/room. Service with restrictions, supervision.
SAVE S⊘ ✕ 🛏 🖵 ⌘

POUGHKEEPSIE

Best Western Inn & Conference Center SH
(845) 462-4600. **$99-$179.** 2170 South Rd (Rt 9). I-84, exit 13N, 4.7 mi s of Mid Hudson Bridge. Int corridors. **Pets:** $50 deposit/pet. Service with restrictions, supervision.
SAVE S⊘ ✕ 🛏 🖵 ¶ ⌘

Econo Lodge SH
(845) 452-6600. **$70-$150.** 2625 US 9. I-84, exit 13N, 1.6 mi s of Mid-Hudson Bridge. Ext corridors. **Pets:** Accepted.
ASK S⊘ ✕ ⑤M 🛏

QUEENSBURY

Alpenhaus Motel M
(518) 792-6941. **$49-$149.** 851 US 9. I-87, exit 19, 0.4 mi e, then just n. Ext corridors. **Pets:** Accepted.
ASK S⊘ ✕ 🛏 🖵

Budget Inn M
(518) 792-9576. **$59-$165, 7 day notice.** 932 US 9 (Lake George Rd). I-87, exit 19, 0.8 mi ne. Ext corridors. **Pets:** Medium, dogs only. $10 daily fee/pet. Service with restrictions, supervision.
S⊘ ✕ 🛏 🖵 ⌘

RHINEBECK

Beekman Arms & Delamater Inn and Conference Center CI
(845) 876-7077. **$120-$300.** 6387 Mill St (Rt 9). Jct US 9 and SR 308; center of village. Ext/int corridors. **Pets:** $15 daily fee/pet. Designated rooms, service with restrictions, supervision.
✕ 🛏 🖵 ¶

RIVERHEAD

Best Western East End SH
(631) 369-2200. **Call for rates.** 1830 SR 25. I-495, exit 72 (SR 25 E). Int corridors. **Pets:** Accepted.
SAVE ✕ 🛏 🖵 ¶ ⌘

Holiday Inn Express East End SH
(631) 548-1000. **$179-$299, 3 day notice.** 1707 Old Country Rd (SR 58). I-495, exit 73, 0.5 mi e. Int corridors. **Pets:** Medium, dogs only. $50 one-time fee/pet. Service with restrictions, crate.
ASK S⊘ ✕ ⑤M 🛏 🖵

ROCHESTER

Clarion Riverside Hotel LH
(585) 546-6400. **$109-$169.** 120 E Main St. Downtown. Int corridors. **Pets:** $50 one-time fee/room. Designated rooms, service with restrictions, supervision.
ASK S⊘ ✕ ⑤M 🛏 🖵 ¶ ⌘ ✕

▼▼▼▼ Strathallan Hotel **SH**
(585) 461-5010. **$184-$194.** 550 East Ave. I-490, exit 17, 0.8 mi n on Goodman St, then just w. Int corridors. **Pets:** Medium. $75 one-time fee/room. Service with restrictions.
ASK ✕ ❚ 🖵 ⅋

ROCK HILL

▲▲▲ ▼▼▼▼ The Lodge at Rock Hill **SH**
(845) 796-3100. **$109-$259.** 283 Rock Hill Dr. SR 17, exit 109, just e. Int corridors. **Pets:** Medium. $25 one-time fee/pet. Designated rooms, no service, supervision.
SAVE S🔯 ✕ ❚ 🖵 ⤳

ROCKVILLE CENTRE

▲▲▲ ▼▼▼ Best Western Mill River Manor **SH**
(516) 678-1300. **$136-$144.** 173 Sunrise Hwy. On SR 27; between N Village and N Centre aves. Ext corridors. **Pets:** Accepted.
SAVE S🔯 ✕ ⅃M ❚ 🖵 ⅋ ⤳

ROME

▼ Econo Lodge **M**
(315) 337-9400. **$60-$109.** 145 E Whitesboro St. Just s of jct SR 26 and 46. Ext corridors. **Pets:** Small. $25 one-time fee/pet. Service with restrictions, supervision.
ASK S🔯 ✕ ❚ 🖵

▲▲▲ ▼▼▼▼ Inn at the Beeches **M**
(315) 336-1776. **$82-$295, 14 day notice.** 7900 Turin Rd. Jct SR 46, 2 mi n on SR 26 (Turin Rd). Ext corridors. **Pets:** $10 daily fee/room. Designated rooms, service with restrictions, supervision.
SAVE S🔯 ✕ ❚ ⅋ ⤳

▲▲▲ ▼▼▼ Quality Inn of Rome **SH**
(315) 336-4300. **$70-$109.** 200 S James St. On SR 49; downtown. Ext/int corridors. **Pets:** Medium. $25 daily fee/pet. Designated rooms, service with restrictions, supervision.
SAVE S🔯 ✕ ❚ 🖵 ⅋ ⤳

ROSCOE

▲▲▲ ▼ Roscoe Motel **M**
(607) 498-5220. **$60-$100, 7 day notice.** 2054 Old Rt 17. SR 17, exit 94, 0.5 mi n on SR 206, then just w. Ext corridors. **Pets:** $10 daily fee/pet. Service with restrictions, supervision.
SAVE S🔯 ❚ 🖵

ROTTERDAM

▼▼ Super 8 Schenectady **SH**
(518) 355-2190. **Call for rates.** 3083 Carman Rd. I-890, exit 9 (Curry Rd), 0.4 mi w; I-90, exit 25. Int corridors. **Pets:** Other species. $10 daily fee/pet. Service with restrictions, supervision.
✕

SACKETS HARBOR

▼▼▼ Ontario Place Hotel **SH** ❀
(315) 646-8000. **$89-$350.** 103 General Smith Dr. Center. Int corridors. **Pets:** $10 one-time fee/room. Designated rooms, service with restrictions, crate.
ASK ✕ ❚ 🖵

SALAMANCA

▼▼▼▼ Holiday Inn Express Hotel & Suites **SH**
(716) 945-7600. **$134-$160.** 779 Broad St. I-86, exit 20, just n. Int corridors. **Pets:** $25 one-time fee/room. Designated rooms, service with restrictions, supervision.
ASK S🔯 ✕ ⅃M ❚ 🖵 ⤳

SARANAC LAKE

▲▲▲ ▼ Adirondack Motel **M**
(518) 891-2116. **$69-$215.** 248 Lake Flower Ave. 0.7 mi e on SR 86. Ext corridors. **Pets:** Dogs only. $10 daily fee/pet. Service with restrictions, supervision.
SAVE ✕ ❚ 🖵 ✕

▲▲▲ ▼▼▼ Best Western Mountain Lake Inn **SH**
(518) 891-1970. **$70-$210.** 487 Lake Flower Ave. 0.8 mi e on SR 86. Int corridors. **Pets:** Other species. $20 one-time fee/room. Designated rooms, service with restrictions, supervision.
SAVE S🔯 ✕ ⅃M 🖵 ⅋ ⤳

▲▲▲ ▼▼▼ The Hotel Saranac **SH**
(518) 891-2200. **$65-$275, 3 day notice.** 100 Main St. Center. Int corridors. **Pets:** Accepted.
SAVE S🔯 ✕ ❚ 🖵 ⅋

▼ Lake Flower Inn **M**
(518) 891-2310. **$58-$128, 14 day notice.** 234 Lake Flower Ave. 0.6 mi e on SR 86. Ext corridors. **Pets:** Dogs only. Designated rooms, supervision.
✕ ❚ ⤳ ✕

▼ Lake Side Motel **M**
(518) 891-4333. **$59-$139, 7 day notice.** 256 Lake Flower Ave. 0.6 mi e on SR 86. Ext corridors. **Pets:** Dogs only. Designated rooms, supervision.
✕ ❚ ⤳ ✕

SARATOGA SPRINGS

▲▲▲ ▼▼▼▼ Best Western Park Inn **SH** ❀
(518) 584-2350. **$100-$320, 7 day notice.** 3291 S Broadway. I-87, exit 13N, 1.1 mi n on US 9. Int corridors. **Pets:** Medium, dogs only. $15 daily fee/pet. Designated rooms, service with restrictions, supervision.
SAVE S🔯 ✕ ❚ 🖵 ✕

▲▲▲ ▼▼▼ Holiday Inn **SH** ❀
(518) 584-4550. **$140-$580, 3 day notice.** 232 Broadway. On US 9, jct SR 50. Int corridors. **Pets:** Other species. Service with restrictions.
SAVE S🔯 ✕ ❚ 🖵 ⅋ ⤳

▼▼▼ Residence Inn by Marriott-Saratoga Springs **LH**
(518) 584-9600. **$208-$472.** 295 Excelsior Ave. I-87, exit 15, just n, just s, then just e. Int corridors. **Pets:** Accepted.
ASK S🔯 ✕ ⅃M ❚ 🖵 ⤳ ✕

▲▲▲ ▼▼▼ The Saratoga Hotel & Conference Center **SH**
(518) 584-4000. **Call for rates.** 534 Broadway. I-87, exit 15, on SR 50. Int corridors. **Pets:** Accepted.
SAVE ✕ ❚ 🖵 ⅋ ⤳

▼ Saratoga Motel **M**
(518) 584-0920. **$79-$209, 14 day notice.** 440 Church St. On SR 9N, 2.3 mi w of jct US 9/SR 50. Ext corridors. **Pets:** Accepted.
ASK S🔯 ✕ ❚ 🖵

▲▲▲ ▼▼▼▼ Union Gables Bed & Breakfast **BB**
(518) 584-1558. **$140-$375, 15 day notice.** 55 Union Ave. I-87, exit 14, 1.5 mi w. Int corridors. **Pets:** Accepted.
SAVE ✕ ❚

SAUGERTIES

▲▲▲ ▼▼▼ Comfort Inn **SH** ❀
(845) 246-1565. **$89-$160.** 2790 SR 32. I-87, exit 20, just n. Int corridors. **Pets:** Other species. $25 one-time fee/room. Designated rooms, service with restrictions, supervision.
SAVE S🔯 ✕ ❚ 🖵

SCHENECTADY

▼▼ Days Inn SH
(518) 370-3297. **Call for rates.** 167 Nott Terrace. Jct State St (SR 5) and Nott Terrace, 2 blks e; downtown. Int corridors. **Pets:** Accepted.
⊗ 🔋 🖵

SCHOHARIE

▼▼◆◆ Holiday Inn Express Hotel & Suites Schoharie SH
(518) 295-6088. **$139-$169.** 160 Holiday Way. I-88, exit 23, just e to Park Pl, then just s. Int corridors. **Pets:** Dogs only. $17 daily fee/pet. Designated rooms, service with restrictions, supervision.
A$K 🔊 ⊗ 🔋 🖵

SCHROON LAKE

◆◆◆ ▼ Blue Ridge Motel M
(518) 532-7521. **$80-$110, 14 day notice.** 2455 US Rt 9. I-87, exit 28, 4 mi n. Ext/int corridors. **Pets:** Medium. $25 one-time fee/room. Service with restrictions, supervision.
SAVE 🔊 ⊗ 🔋 🖵 ⇨ 🚲

SKANEATELES

◆◆◆ ▼▼▼ Skaneateles Suites M
(315) 685-7568. **$99-$175.** 4114 E Genesee Rd. On US 20, 2 mi w. Ext corridors. **Pets:** Other species. $35 one-time fee/pet. Designated rooms, service with restrictions, crate.
SAVE ⊗ 🔋 🖵

SOLVAY

▼▼◆ Holiday Inn/Farrell Road SH
(315) 457-8700. **$109-$119.** 100 Farrell Rd. I-690, exit 4 (John Glenn Blvd). Int corridors. **Pets:** Other species. $25 one-time fee/room. Service with restrictions, crate.
A$K 🔊 ⊗ 🔋 🖵 🍴 ⇨

SOUTHAMPTON

◆◆◆ ▼▼▼ Southampton Inn SH 🐾
(631) 283-6500. **$149-$489.** 91 Hill St. 0.3 mi n from corner of Main St and Jobs Ln. Ext corridors. **Pets:** Other species. $39 one-time fee/pet. Designated rooms, service with restrictions, supervision.
SAVE 🔊 ⊗ 🔋 🍴 ⇨ ⊗

SYLVAN BEACH

▼ Cinderella's Cafe & Suites M
(315) 762-4280. **Call for rates.** 1208 N Main St. On SR 13; center. Ext corridors. **Pets:** Accepted.
⊗ 🔋 🖵 🍴

SYRACUSE

◆◆◆ ▼▼▼▼ Renaissance Syracuse Hotel LH
(315) 479-7000. **$186-$230.** 701 E Genesee St. Jct Almond St; downtown. Int corridors. **Pets:** Accepted.
SAVE 🔊 ⊗ ⳗ 🔋 🖵 🍴

◆◆◆ ▼▼▼◆ Sheraton Syracuse University Hotel & Conference Center LH
(315) 475-3000. **$119-$359.** 801 University Ave. I-81, exit 18. Int corridors. **Pets:** Accepted.
SAVE 🔊 ⊗ 🔋 🖵 🍴 ⇨ ⊗

TICONDEROGA

◆◆◆ ▼ Circle Court Motel M
(518) 585-7660. **$60-$99.** 6 Montcalm St. SR 9N; at Liberty Monument traffic circle. Ext corridors. **Pets:** $10 daily fee/pet. Designated rooms, service with restrictions, supervision.
SAVE 🔊 ⊗ 🔋 🖵

TROY

◆◆◆ ▼▼◆ Rensselaer Inn SH
(518) 274-3210. **$89-$99.** 1800 6th Ave. I-787, exit 9, 0.5 mi e, exit downtown, then 0.5 mi s. Int corridors. **Pets:** Accepted.
SAVE 🔊 ⊗ 🔋 🖵 🍴 ⇨

TUPPER LAKE

◆◆◆ ▼ Red Top Inn M
(518) 359-9209. **$50-$90, 7 day notice.** 1562 SR 30. 3 mi s. Ext/int corridors. **Pets:** Accepted.
SAVE ⊗ 🔋 🖵

UTICA

▼▼◆ Best Western Gateway Adirondack Inn SH
(315) 732-4121. **$89-$189.** 175 N Genesee St. I-90 (New York State Thruway), exit 31, 0.5 mi s. Int corridors. **Pets:** Large. $25 one-time fee/pet. Service with restrictions, crate.
A$K 🔊 ⊗ 🔋 🖵

▼▼◆ Red Roof Inn #7180 M
(315) 724-7128. **Call for rates.** 20 Weaver St. I-90 (New York State Thruway), exit 31. Ext corridors. **Pets:** Accepted.
⊗ 🔋

VALATIE

◆◆◆ ▼▼ Blue Spruce Inn & Suites M
(518) 758-9711. **$75-$105, 3 day notice.** 3093 Rt 9. I-90 (New York State Thruway), exit 12, 4 mi s on US 9 via New York State Thruway Extension, exit B1. Ext corridors. **Pets:** Service with restrictions, supervision.
SAVE 🔊 ⊗ 🔋 🖵 🍴 ⇨

VESTAL

▼▼◆▼ Holiday Inn at the University SH
(607) 729-6371. **$115-$250.** 4105 Vestal Pkwy E. SR 17, exit 70, 2.5 mi s on US 201 to SR 434 W, then right on Bunn Hill Rd. Int corridors. **Pets:** Accepted.
A$K 🔊 ⊗ ⳗ 🔋 🖵 🍴 ⇨

VICTOR

◆◆◆ ▼▼▼ Hampton Inn and Suites-Rochester/Victor SH
(585) 924-4400. **$139-$259.** 7637 SR 96. I-90 (New York State Thruway), exit 45, just n. Int corridors. **Pets:** Small. Service with restrictions, supervision.
SAVE 🔊 ⊗ 🔋 🖵 ⇨

▼▼◆▼ Holiday Inn Express Hotel & Suites SH
(585) 672-2100. **$119-$155.** 7502 County Rd 42. I-90, exit 45, just s on SR 96, then just w. Int corridors. **Pets:** Accepted.
A$K 🔊 ⊗ ⳗ 🔋 🖵 ⇨ ⊗

WARRENSBURG

▼▼ Super 8 Warrensburg/Lake George M
(518) 623-2811. **Call for rates.** 3619 SR 9. I-87, exit 23, just w. Int corridors. **Pets:** Accepted.
⊗

WATERLOO

◆◆◆ ▼▼▼▼ Holiday Inn Waterloo-Seneca Falls SH
(315) 539-5011. **$89-$179.** 2468 SR 414. I-90 (New York State Thruway), exit 41, 4 mi s; just n of jct SR 414/5 and US 20. Int corridors. **Pets:** Accepted.
SAVE ⊗ 🔋 🖵 🍴 ⇨ ⊗

△△△ ▽▽▽ Microtel Inn & Suites SH
(315) 539-8438. **$56-$120.** 1966 Rt 5 & 20. I-90 (New York State Thruway), exit 41, 4 mi s on SR 414, then just e. Int corridors. **Pets:** Other species. $15 daily fee/room. Supervision.

SAVE 🐾 ✕ ⊑M 🔒 💻

WATERTOWN

△△△ ▽▽▽ Best Western Carriage House Inn & Conference Center SH
(315) 782-8000. **$90-$105.** 300 Washington St. Center. Int corridors. **Pets:** Medium, other species. $15 daily fee/room. Designated rooms, service with restrictions, supervision.

SAVE 🐾 ✕ 🔒 💻 🍴 ⇌

△△△ ▽▽ Davidson's Motel M
(315) 782-3861. **$75-$110.** 26177 NYS Rt 3. From Town Square, 3.5 mi e. Ext corridors. **Pets:** Accepted.

SAVE 🐾 ✕ 🔒 ⇌

△△△ ▽▽▽ Ramada SH
(315) 788-0700. **$97, 7 day notice.** 21000 NYS Rt 3. I-81, exit 45, just w. Int corridors. **Pets:** Accepted.

SAVE 🐾 ✕ 🔒 💻 🍴 ⇌ ✕

WATKINS GLEN

△△△ ▽▽▽ Anchor Inn and Marina M
(607) 535-4159. **$69-$169, 10 day notice.** 3425 Salt Point Rd. Just n on SR 14, 0.8 mi n. Ext corridors. **Pets:** Medium. $25 deposit/pet. Service with restrictions, supervision.

SAVE 🐾 ✕ 🔒 ✕

△△△ ▽▽▽ Chieftain Motel M
(607) 535-4159. **$69-$169, 10 day notice.** 3815 SR 14. Jct SR 14A; 3 mi n of town. Ext corridors. **Pets:** Accepted.

SAVE 🐾 ✕ 🔒 💻

WELLSVILLE

△△△ ▽ Long Vue Inn & Suites M
(585) 593-2450. **$54-$98.** 5081 Rt 417 W. Jct SR 19, 3 mi w. Ext corridors. **Pets:** Large. $10 daily fee/pet. Service with restrictions, supervision.

SAVE 🐾 ✕ 🔒 💻

▽▽ Microtel Inn & Suites SH
(585) 593-3449. **Call for rates.** 30 W Dyke St. Just n off SR 19 and 417. Int corridors. **Pets:** Other species. $10 daily fee/pet. Service with restrictions.

✕ ⊑M 🔒 💻

WEST COXSACKIE

△△△ ▽▽▽ Best Western New Baltimore Inn SH
(518) 731-8100. **Call for rates.** 12600 Rt 9W. I-87 (New York State Thruway), exit 21B, 0.5 mi s. Int corridors. **Pets:** Medium. $10 daily fee/pet. Service with restrictions, crate.

SAVE ✕ 🔒 💻 ⇌ ✕

WESTMORELAND

△△△ ▽ Carriage Motor Inn M
(315) 853-3561. **$35-$85, 5 day notice.** 5370 SR 233. I-90 (New York State Thruway), exit 32, just n. Ext corridors. **Pets:** Small. $15 daily fee/pet. Service with restrictions, supervision.

SAVE 🐾 ✕ 🔒

WILMINGTON

△△△ ▽▽ Grand View Motel M
(518) 946-2209. **$65-$99.** 5941 NYS Rt 86. On SR 86, 1 mi e. Ext corridors. **Pets:** Accepted.

SAVE 🐾 ✕ 🔒 💻 ⇌ ✕

▽▽ Green Mountain Lodge M
(518) 946-8232. **$59-$139, 7 day notice.** 5675 SR 86. Jct SR 86 and 431 (Whiteface Mt Hwy). Ext corridors. **Pets:** Other species. $10 daily fee/pet. Service with restrictions, supervision.

A$K 🐾 ✕ 🔒 💻 ✕

△△△ ▽▽▽ Hungry Trout Resort M
(518) 946-2217. **$69-$129, 7 day notice.** 5239 Rt 86. On SR 86, 2 mi w. Ext corridors. **Pets:** Accepted.

SAVE 🐾 ✕ 🔒 💻 🍴 ⇌ ✕

▽▽▽▽ Ledge Rock at Whiteface Mountain M 🐾
(518) 946-2379. **$79-$129, 10 day notice.** 5078 NYS Rt 86. On SR 86, 3 mi w. Ext corridors. **Pets:** $5 daily fee/pet, $25 one-time fee/pet.

SAVE ✕ 🔒 💻 ⇌ ✕

▽▽ Mountain Brook Lodge M
(518) 946-2262. **$74-$84, 10 day notice.** 5712 Rt 86. Center. Ext corridors. **Pets:** Accepted.

🐾 ✕ 🔒 💻 ⇌

△△△ ▽▽▽ North Pole Inn M
(518) 946-7733. **$65-$199, 7 day notice.** 5636 NYS Rt 86. On SR 86, just w of jct CR 431. Ext corridors. **Pets:** Dogs only. $10 daily fee/pet. Service with restrictions, supervision.

SAVE 🐾 ✕ 🔒 💻 ⇌ ✕

△△△ ▽▽▽ Willkommen Hof Bed & Breakfast BB
(518) 946-7669. **Call for rates.** 5367 Rt 86. On SR 86, 1.5 mi of jct CR 431. Int corridors. **Pets:** Accepted.

SAVE ✕ 🔒 💻 ✕ ✉

WOODBURY

△△△ ▽▽▽ Best Western Woodbury Inn M 🐾
(516) 921-6900. **$119-$159.** 7940 Jericho Tpke (SR 25). Jct SR 25 and 135, 0.9 mi e. Ext/int corridors. **Pets:** $50 one-time fee/room. Service with restrictions, supervision.

SAVE 🐾 ✕ 🔒 💻 🍴 ⇌

△△△ ▽▽▽ Executive Inn at Woodbury M 🐾
(516) 921-8500. **$99-$209.** 8030 Jericho Tpke (SR 25). Jct SR 25 and 135, 1 mi e. Ext corridors. **Pets:** $50 one-time fee/room. Service with restrictions, supervision.

SAVE 🐾 ✕ 🔒 💻 ⇌

NORTH CAROLINA

ABERDEEN

ⒶⒶⒶ ▼▼▼ Best Western Pinehurst Motor Inn Ⓜ
(910) 944-2367. **$79-$129.** 1500 Sandhills Blvd. Jct US 15/501 N, just s on US 1. Ext corridors. **Pets:** Accepted.
SAVE Ⓢ ✕ 🖬 💻 ≋

▼▼ Country Hearth Inn & Suites Ⓜ
(910) 944-2324. **$69-$89, 3 day notice.** 1405 N Sandhills Blvd. Jct US 15/501 N, just s on US 1. Ext/int corridors. **Pets:** Small. $10 daily fee/pet. Service with restrictions, supervision.
ASK Ⓢ ✕ 🖬 ≋

▼ Motel 6-1234 Ⓜ
(910) 944-5633. **$45-$57.** 1408 Sandhills Blvd. Jct US 15/501 N, just s on US 1. Ext corridors. **Pets:** Other species. Service with restrictions, supervision.
Ⓢ ✕ 🖬 💻 ≋

ALBEMARLE

▼▼ Best Western Executive Inn ⓈⒽ
(704) 983-6990. **$62-$89.** 735 Hwy 24/27 Bypass. Jct US 52 S, 1.4 mi e. Ext corridors. **Pets:** Accepted.
ASK Ⓢ ✕ 🖬 💻 ≋

ANDREWS

▼▼▼ Hawkesdene House Mountain Retreat ⒷⒷ
(828) 321-6027. **Call for rates.** 381 Phillips Creek Rd. US 19 business route, 3.2 mi s on Cherry St, then 0.5 mi s. Ext/int corridors. **Pets:** Accepted.
✕ 🖬 💻

ARCHDALE

ⒶⒶⒶ ▼▼▼ Best Western-High Point ⓈⒽ
(336) 861-3000. **$69-$199.** 1202 Liberty Rd. I-85, exit 113, just s on SR 62. Int corridors. **Pets:** Accepted.
✕ 🖬 💻 ≋

ⒶⒶⒶ ▼▼▼ Comfort Inn Archdale ⓈⒽ
(336) 434-4797. **$80.** 10123 N Main St. I-85, exit 111, just n on US 311, then just sw on Balfour Dr. Int corridors. **Pets:** Small. $25 one-time fee/pet. Service with restrictions, supervision.
SAVE Ⓢ ✕ ⒻⓂ 🖬 💻 ≋

▼▼▼▼ Hampton Inn-High Point ⓈⒽ
(336) 434-5200. **$79-$109, 3 day notice.** 10066 N Main St. I-85, exit 111, just n on US 311. Int corridors. **Pets:** Small, other species. $10 one-time fee/room. Service with restrictions.
ASK Ⓢ ✕ 🖬 💻 ≋

▼▼▼ Holiday Inn Express Hotel & Suites ⓈⒽ
(336) 861-3310. **$79-$109, 3 day notice.** 10050 N Main St. I-85, exit 111, just n on US 311. Int corridors. **Pets:** Small, other species. $10 one-time fee/room. Service with restrictions.
ASK Ⓢ ✕ 🖬 💻 ≋

▼▼ Innkeeper High Point Ⓜ
(336) 434-5151. **$39-$69, 3 day notice.** 10002 S Main St. I-85, exit 111, just s on US 311. Ext/int corridors. **Pets:** Small, other species. $10 one-time fee/room. Service with restrictions.
ASK Ⓢ ✕ 🖬 ≋

ARDEN

▼▼▼ Quality Inn & Suites Biltmore South ⓈⒽ
(828) 684-6688. **$70-$179.** 1 Skyline Inn Dr. I-26, exit 37. Int corridors. **Pets:** Accepted.
✕ 🖬 💻 ≋ ✕

ASHEBORO

ⒶⒶⒶ ▼▼▼ Comfort Inn ⓈⒽ
(336) 626-3680. **$73-$120.** 242 Lakecrest Rd. US 64, just nw on SR 42. Ext corridors. **Pets:** Medium, other species. $15 daily fee/pet. Service with restrictions, crate.
SAVE Ⓢ ✕ 🖬 💻 ≋

ASHEVILLE

▼▼▼ 1889 WhiteGate Inn & Cottage ⒷⒷ
(828) 253-2553. **$150-$360.** 173 E Chestnut St. I-240, exit 5B (Charlotte St), just n, then just w; in historic district. Ext/int corridors. **Pets:** Medium, dogs only. $50 one-time fee/room. Designated rooms, service with restrictions, supervision.
✕ 🖬 💻

ⒶⒶⒶ ▼▼▼ 1891 Cedar Crest Inn ⒷⒷ
(828) 252-1389. **$150-$300, 14 day notice.** 674 Biltmore Ave. I-40, exit 50, 1.1 mi n. Ext/int corridors. **Pets:** Accepted.
SAVE ✕ 🖬 💻

▼▼▼ 1900 Inn on Montford ⒷⒷ ✿
(828) 254-9569. **$145-$625, 14 day notice.** 296 Montford Ave. I-240, exit 4C (Montford Ave/Haywood St), 0.7 mi n; in historic district. Ext/int corridors. **Pets:** Designated rooms.
✕ 🖬 💻

Abbington Green Bed & Breakfast Inn BB
(828) 251-2454. **$150-$450, 30 day notice.** 46 Cumberland Cir. I-240, exit 4C (Montford Ave/Haywood St), n to W Chestnut St, just e to Cumberland Ave, then 0.3 mi n; in historic district. Ext/int corridors. **Pets:** Dogs only. $10 daily fee/pet. Designated rooms, service with restrictions, crate.

⟨SAVE⟩ ⟨✕⟩ ⟨🛏⟩ ⟨▥⟩ ⟨✆⟩

Applewood Manor Inn Bed & Breakfast BB
(828) 254-2244. **$162-$225, 7 day notice.** 62 Cumberland Cir. I-240, exit 4C (Montford Ave/Haywood St), n on Montford Ave, e on W Chestnut, n on Cumberland, then ne; in historic district. Ext/int corridors. **Pets:** Large, dogs only. $30 daily fee/pet. Designated rooms.

⟨SAVE⟩ ⟨S🐾⟩ ⟨✕⟩ ⟨✆⟩

Best Western Asheville Biltmore SH
(828) 253-1851. **Call for rates.** 22 Woodfin St. I-240, exit 5A (Merrimon Ave). Int corridors. **Pets:** Accepted.

⟨✕⟩ ⟨🛏⟩ ⟨▥⟩ ⟨≈⟩

Best Western of Asheville Biltmore East M
(828) 298-5562. **$45-$199.** 501 Tunnel Rd. I-240, exit 7, 0.5 mi e on US 70 (Tunnel Rd). Ext corridors. **Pets:** Small, dogs only. No service, supervision.

⟨SAVE⟩ ⟨S🐾⟩ ⟨✕⟩ ⟨🛏⟩ ⟨▥⟩ ⟨≈⟩

Biltmore Village Inn BB
(828) 274-8707. **$220-$325, 14 day notice.** 119 Dodge St. I-40, exit 50/50B (US 25 N), 0.5 mi n, just e on Lula St, just n on Reed St, just e on Warren Ave, then just s. Ext/int corridors. **Pets:** Accepted.

⟨SAVE⟩ ⟨S🐾⟩ ⟨✕⟩ ⟨🛏⟩ ⟨▥⟩

Black Walnut B&B Inn BB 🐾
(828) 254-3878. **Call for rates.** 288 Montford Ave. I-40, exit 4C (Montford Ave/Haywood St), 0.5 mi n; in historic district. Ext/int corridors. **Pets:** Other species. Designated rooms, crate.

⟨SAVE⟩ ⟨✕⟩ ⟨🛏⟩ ⟨▥⟩ ⟨✆⟩

Carolina Bed & Breakfast BB
(828) 254-3608. **$120-$225.** 177 Cumberland Ave. I-240, exit 4C (Montford Ave/Haywood St), 0.5 mi n on Montford Ave, just e on Chestnut St, then just n. Ext/int corridors. **Pets:** Other species. $10 daily fee/room. Designated rooms, service with restrictions.

⟨✕⟩ ⟨🛏⟩ ⟨▥⟩ ⟨✆⟩

Comfort Suites-Biltmore Square Mall SH
(828) 665-4000. **Call for rates.** 890 Brevard Rd. I-26, exit 33, 0.3 mi w. Int corridors. **Pets:** Other species. $20 daily fee/room. Designated rooms.

⟨SAVE⟩ ⟨✕⟩ ⟨&M⟩ ⟨🛏⟩ ⟨▥⟩ ⟨≈⟩

Crowne Plaza Resort SH
(828) 254-3211. **Call for rates.** 1 Holiday Inn Dr. I-240, exit 3B (Holiday Inn Dr), just w. Int corridors. **Pets:** $20 daily fee/pet. Service with restrictions, supervision.

⟨SAVE⟩ ⟨✕⟩ ⟨🛏⟩ ⟨▥⟩ ⟨🍴⟩ ⟨≈⟩ ⟨✕⟩

Days Inn-Biltmore East SH
(828) 298-4000. **$42-$199.** 1435 Tunnel Rd. I-40, exit 55, just n. Int corridors. **Pets:** Small, dogs only. $10 daily fee/pet. Service with restrictions, supervision.

⟨SAVE⟩ ⟨S🐾⟩ ⟨✕⟩ ⟨🛏⟩ ⟨▥⟩ ⟨≈⟩

Extended StayAmerica SH
(828) 253-3483. **$68-$119.** 6 Kenilworth Knoll. I-240, exit 6, 0.7 mi e on US 70 (Tunnel Rd), then just n. Int corridors. **Pets:** Other species. $75 one-time fee/pet. Service with restrictions.

⟨ASK⟩ ⟨S🐾⟩ ⟨✕⟩ ⟨&M⟩ ⟨▥⟩

Holiday Inn-Biltmore East at the Blue Ridge Parkway SH
(828) 298-5611. **$69-$169.** 1450 Tunnel Rd. I-40, exit 55, just n. Int corridors. **Pets:** Accepted.

⟨ASK⟩ ⟨S🐾⟩ ⟨✕⟩ ⟨🛏⟩ ⟨▥⟩ ⟨🍴⟩ ⟨≈⟩

The Log Cabin Motor Court CA
(828) 645-6546. **Call for rates.** 330 Weaverville Hwy. US 19/23, exit 21 (New Stock Rd), 1 mi s on Weaverville Hwy. Ext corridors. **Pets:** Accepted.

⟨SAVE⟩ ⟨✕⟩ ⟨🛏⟩ ⟨▥⟩ ⟨🍴⟩ ⟨✆⟩

Motel 6–1134 M
(828) 299-3040. **$45-$58.** 1415 Tunnel Rd. I-40, exit 55. Ext corridors. **Pets:** Other species. Service with restrictions, supervision.

⟨S🐾⟩ ⟨✕⟩ ⟨≈⟩

Quality Inn & Suites M
(828) 298-5519. **$55-$199.** 1430 Tunnel Rd. I-40, exit 55, just n. Ext corridors. **Pets:** Other species. $20 daily fee/room. Designated rooms, service with restrictions, supervision.

⟨SAVE⟩ ⟨S🐾⟩ ⟨✕⟩ ⟨🛏⟩ ⟨▥⟩ ⟨≈⟩

Ramada SH 🐾
(828) 298-9141. **$74-$129.** 800 Fairview Rd. I-240, exit 8; jct I-40 and US 74. Ext/int corridors. **Pets:** $15 daily fee/pet, $10 one-time fee/pet. Designated rooms, service with restrictions, supervision.

⟨SAVE⟩ ⟨S🐾⟩ ⟨✕⟩ ⟨🛏⟩ ⟨▥⟩ ⟨≈⟩ ⟨✕⟩

Red Roof Inn-West M
(828) 667-9803. **Call for rates.** 16 Crowell Rd. I-40, exit 44, just n on US 19 and 23, just w on Old Haywood Rd, then just s. Ext corridors. **Pets:** Accepted.

⟨✕⟩ ⟨🛏⟩

Sleep Inn Biltmore SH 🐾
(828) 277-1800. **$69-$159.** 117 Hendersonville Rd. I-40, exit 50 eastbound; exit 50B westbound, just n on US 25. Int corridors. **Pets:** Small, dogs only. $25 daily fee/pet. Designated rooms, service with restrictions, crate.

⟨ASK⟩ ⟨S🐾⟩ ⟨✕⟩ ⟨&M⟩ ⟨▥⟩

Super 8 Biltmore East M
(828) 298-7952. **$49-$139.** 1329 Tunnel Rd. I-40, exit 55, 0.3 mi w. Ext corridors. **Pets:** Accepted.

⟨ASK⟩ ⟨S🐾⟩ ⟨✕⟩ ⟨&M⟩ ⟨🛏⟩ ⟨▥⟩ ⟨≈⟩

Super 8 Motel at Biltmore Square SH
(828) 670-8800. **$135-$150.** 9 Wedgefield Dr. I-26, exit 33, just nw. Int corridors. **Pets:** Accepted.

⟨ASK⟩ ⟨S🐾⟩ ⟨✕⟩ ⟨&M⟩ ⟨🛏⟩ ⟨▥⟩

Super 8 Motel Central M
(828) 667-8706. **Call for rates.** 8 Crowell Rd. I-40, exit 44, just n on US 19 and 23. Int corridors. **Pets:** Medium. $15 one-time fee/pet. Service with restrictions, supervision.

⟨✕⟩ ⟨&M⟩ ⟨🛏⟩ ⟨▥⟩

BANNER ELK

Banner Elk Inn B&B and Cottages BB
(828) 898-6223. **$90-$250, 30 day notice.** 407 Main St E. Jct SR 184 and 194, 0.3 mi n on SR 194. Int corridors. **Pets:** Large. Designated rooms, no service, supervision.

⟨✕⟩ ⟨🛏⟩ ⟨▥⟩

Best Western Mountain Lodge at Banner Elk SH 🐾
(828) 898-4571. **$79-$189, 3 day notice.** 1615 Tynecastle Hwy. 1 mi se on SR 184. Ext corridors. **Pets:** Other species. Service with restrictions.

⟨SAVE⟩ ⟨S🐾⟩ ⟨✕⟩ ⟨&M⟩ ⟨🛏⟩ ⟨▥⟩ ⟨🍴⟩ ⟨≈⟩

BLOWING ROCK

Hillwinds Inn M
(828) 295-7660. **$89-$359, 3 day notice.** 315 Sunset Dr. Just e of Main St. Ext/int corridors. **Pets:** Medium. $25 daily fee/room. Designated rooms, service with restrictions, crate.

⟨ASK⟩ ⟨S🐾⟩ ⟨✕⟩ ⟨🛏⟩ ⟨▥⟩

▼▼▼ The Village Inn **M**
(828) 295-3380. **Call for rates.** 7876 Valley Blvd. On US 321 Bypass, just e of city park. Ext corridors. **Pets:** Medium. $25 daily fee/room. Designated rooms, service with restrictions, crate.
⊠ 🖥 📖

BREVARD

▼▼▼ Holiday Inn Express **SH**
(828) 862-8900. **Call for rates.** 1570 Asheville Hwy. 3 mi e on US 64. Int corridors. **Pets:** Medium. $50 one-time fee/pet. Designated rooms, service with restrictions, supervision.
⊠ ⅏M 🖥 📖 🏊

BURLINGTON

AAA ▼▼ Econo Lodge **SH**
(336) 227-1270. **$54-$59.** 2133 W Hanford Rd. I-40/85, exit 145, just s on SR 49, then just w. Int corridors. **Pets:** Accepted.
SAVE S🐾 ⊠ 🖥 🏊

▼ Motel 6–1257 **M**
(336) 226-1325. **$41-$53.** 2155 Hanford Rd. I-40/85, exit 145, just s on SR 49, then just w. Ext corridors. **Pets:** Other species. Service with restrictions, supervision.
S🐾 ⊠ 🏊

CANDLER

AAA ▼▼▼ Owl's Nest Inn and Engadine Cabins **BB** 🐾
(828) 665-8325. **Call for rates.** 2630 Smoky Park Hwy. I-40, exit 37, 0.5 mi w on SR 19/23. Ext/int corridors. **Pets:** Other species. $50 one-time fee/pet. Designated rooms, no service.
SAVE ⊠ 🖥 📖

CARY

AAA ▼▼▼ Best Western Cary Inn & Extended Stay Suites **SH**
(919) 481-1200. **$80.** 1722 Walnut St. I-40, exit 293A, just s on US 1, exit 101A, then just e. Ext/int corridors. **Pets:** Accepted.
SAVE S🐾 ⊠ 🖥 📖 🏊 ⊠

▼▼▼ Candlewood Suites-Raleigh/Cary **SH**
(919) 468-4222. **$93-$100.** 1020 Buck Jones Rd. I-40, exit 293A, just s on US 1, exit 101B, 0.5 mi nw; in Buck Jones Village. Int corridors. **Pets:** Other species. $12 daily fee/pet. Service with restrictions, crate.
ASK S🐾 ⊠ 🖥 📖

▼▼▼ Comfort Suites Hotel **SH**
(919) 852-4318. **$79-$129.** 350 Ashville Ave. US 1, exit 98A, 0.8 mi e on Tryon Rd, then just n. Int corridors. **Pets:** Accepted.
ASK S🐾 ⊠ ⅏M 🖥 📖 🏊 ⊠

▼▼ Extended StayAmerica-Raleigh/Cary **SH**
(919) 468-5828. **$72-$80.** 1500 Regency Pkwy. US 1, exit 98A, 0.5 mi e on Tryon Rd, then just s. Int corridors. **Pets:** Other species. $75 one-time fee/pet. Service with restrictions.
ASK S🐾 ⊠ 🖥 📖

▼▼ Extended Stay Deluxe Raleigh-Cary-Regency Parkway **SH**
(919) 460-1161. **$86-$95.** 3100 Regency Pkwy. US 1, exit 98A, 0.5 mi e on Tryon Rd, then just s. Int corridors. **Pets:** Other species. $75 one-time fee/pet. Service with restrictions.
ASK S🐾 ⊠ 🖥 📖 🏊

AAA ▼▼▼ Hampton Inn **SH** 🐾
(919) 859-5559. **Call for rates.** 201 Ashville Ave. US 1, exit 98A, 0.8 mi e on Tryon Rd, then just n. Int corridors. **Pets:** Medium. Designated rooms, service with restrictions, crate.
SAVE ⊠ ⅏M 🖥 📖 🏊

AAA ▼▼▼ Homewood Suites **SH** 🐾
(919) 467-4444. **$89-$169.** 100 MacAlyson Ct. US 1, exit 98B, just w on US 64, then just s on Edinburgh Dr; in MacGregor Park. Int corridors. **Pets:** Medium. $49 one-time fee/room. Service with restrictions, crate.
SAVE S🐾 ⊠ ⅏M 🖥 📖 🏊 ⊠

AAA ▼▼▼ La Quinta Inn & Suites Raleigh (Cary) **SH**
(919) 851-2850. **$109-$149.** 191 Crescent Commons Dr. US 1, exit 98A, 0.5 mi e on Tryon Rd, then just n. Int corridors. **Pets:** Other species. Service with restrictions, supervision.
SAVE S🐾 ⊠ ⅏M 🖥 📖 🏊 ⊠

▼▼▼ Residence Inn **SH**
(919) 467-4080. **$144-$154.** 2900 Regency Pkwy. US 1, exit 98A, 0.5 mi e on Tryon Rd, then just s. Int corridors. **Pets:** $75 one-time fee/room. Service with restrictions.
ASK S🐾 ⊠ ⅏M 🖥 📖 🏊 ⊠

▼▼ StudioPLUS-Harrison Ave **SH**
(919) 677-9910. **$90-$100.** 600 Weston Pkwy. I-40, exit 287, 0.5 mi s on Harrison Ave, then just w. Int corridors. **Pets:** Other species. $75 one-time fee/pet. Service with restrictions.
ASK S🐾 ⊠ 🖥 📖 🏊

AAA ▼▼▼ TownePlace Suites **SH**
(919) 678-0005. **$149-$169.** 120 Sage Commons Way. I-40, exit 287, 0.5 mi s on Harrison Ave, 2.3 w on Weston Pkwy, then just n. Int corridors. **Pets:** Medium, other species. $100 one-time fee/room. Designated rooms, service with restrictions, crate.
ASK S🐾 ⊠ ⅏M 🖥 📖 🏊

AAA ▼▼▼▼ The Umstead Hotel & Spa **SH**
(919) 447-4000. **$199-$425.** 100 Woodland Pond Dr. I-40, exit 287, just s on Harrison Ave, just e on SAS Campus Dr, then just n. Int corridors. **Pets:** Accepted.
SAVE S🐾 ⊠ 🍴 🏊 ⊠

CASHIERS

AAA ▼▼▼▼ High Hampton Inn & Country Club **SH** 🐾
(828) 743-2411. **Call for rates.** 1525 Hwy 107 S. Jct US 64, 1.5 mi s. Ext/int corridors. **Pets:** Dogs only. $50 one-time fee/pet. Designated rooms, service with restrictions, crate.
SAVE ⊠ 🖥 📖 🍴 ⊠ 🎾 ♟ 🏌

▼▼▼ Laurelwood Mountain Inn **M**
(828) 743-9939. **$69-$99, 3 day notice.** 58 Hwy 107. Jct US 64, just n. Ext corridors. **Pets:** Medium, other species. $25 one-time fee/room. Designated rooms, service with restrictions, supervision.
ASK S🐾 ⊠ 🖥 📖

CHAPEL HILL

AAA ▼▼▼ Courtyard by Marriott-Chapel Hill **SH**
(919) 883-0700. **$149-$179.** 100 Marriott Way. I-40, exit 273 & 273A, 1.8 mi w on SR 54, just s on Friday Center Dr, then just e. Int corridors. **Pets:** Accepted.
SAVE S🐾 ⊠ ⅏M 🖥 📖 🍴 🏊

▼▼▼ Holiday Inn **SH**
(919) 929-2171. **$89-$109.** 1301 N Fordham Blvd. I-40, exit 270, 2 mi s on US 15/501. Ext corridors. **Pets:** Accepted.
ASK S🐾 ⊠ 🖥 📖 🍴 🏊

AAA ▼▼▼ Residence Inn by Marriott **SH**
(919) 933-4848. **$137-$169.** 101 Erwin Rd. I-40, exit 270, 1.2 mi s on US 15/501, then just w. Int corridors. **Pets:** Accepted.
ASK S🐾 ⊠ ⅏M 🖥 📖 🏊 ⊠

AAA ▼▼▼ The Siena Hotel **SH** 🐾
(919) 929-4000. **$166-$209.** 1505 E Franklin St. I-40, exit 270, 2 mi s on US 15/501, then 0.5 mi w. Int corridors. **Pets:** Dogs only. $75 one-time fee/room. Service with restrictions.
SAVE S🐾 ⊠ ⅏M 🖥 🍴

CHARLOTTE METROPOLITAN AREA

CHARLOTTE

▼▼▼▼ Candlewood Suites-Coliseum SH ❀
(704) 529-7500. **Call for rates.** 5840 Westpark Dr. I-77, exit 5 (Tyvola Rd), just e, then 0.5 mi s. Int corridors. **Pets:** Medium. $75 one-time fee/pet. Service with restrictions, supervision.

[X] [&M] [🛏] [💻]

△△△ ▼▼▼▼ Comfort Inn-Executive Park SH
(704) 525-2626. **$54-$64.** 5822 Westpark Dr. I-77, exit 5 (Tyvola Rd), just e, then 0.5 mi s. Int corridors. **Pets:** Medium. $25 one-time fee/pet. Service with restrictions, supervision.

[SAVE] [$ð] [X] [🛏] [💻] [🏊]

△△△ ▼▼▼ Comfort Inn-UNCC SH
(704) 598-0007. **Call for rates.** 5111 Equipment Dr. I-85, exit 41, just w, then just s. Int corridors. **Pets:** Small. $50 deposit/pet, $10 one-time fee/pet. Service with restrictions, supervision.

[SAVE] [X] [&M] [🛏] [💻] [🏊]

▼▼▼▼ Comfort Suites-University SH
(704) 547-0049. **$100-$200.** 7735 University City Blvd. I-85, exit 45A, 1 mi e on SR 24, then 0.5 mi s on SR 49. Int corridors. **Pets:** Accepted.

[ASK] [$ð] [X] [&M] [🛏] [💻] [🏊]

▼▼▼▼ Country Inn & Suites-Charlotte University SH ❀
(704) 549-8770. **$89-$249.** 131 E McCullough Dr. I-85, exit 45A, 0.5 mi e on SR 24, 0.4 mi s on US 29 (N Tryon St), then just e. Int corridors. **Pets:** Small. $50 one-time fee/pet. Designated rooms, service with restrictions.

[ASK] [$ð] [X] [&M] [🛏] [💻] [🏊] [X]

△△△ ▼▼▼▼ Crowne Plaza–Charlotte SH
(704) 372-7550. **$119-$289.** 201 S McDowell St. I-277, exit 2A, just w on 4th St, then just s. Int corridors. **Pets:** Accepted.

[SAVE] [$ð] [X] [🛏] [💻] [¶] [🏊]

△△△ ▼▼▼▼ DoubleTree Guest Suites-South Park SH
(704) 364-2400. **$99-$289.** 6300 Morrison Blvd. I-77, exit 5 (Tyvola Rd), 3.3 mi e on Tyvola/Fairview rds, just n on Barclay Downs, then just e. Int corridors. **Pets:** Other species. Service with restrictions, supervision.

[SAVE] [X] [🛏] [💻] [¶] [🏊]

△△△ ▼▼▼▼ DoubleTree Hotel Charlotte-Gateway Village SH
(704) 347-0070. **Call for rates.** 895 W Trade St. I-77, exit 10 or 10B, just e. Int corridors. **Pets:** Accepted.

[X] [&M] [🛏] [💻] [¶] [🏊]

▼▼▼▼ Drury Inn & Suites-Charlotte North SH
(704) 593-0700. **$83-$130.** 415 W WT Harris Blvd. I-85, exit 45A, just e on SR 24. Int corridors. **Pets:** Large, other species. Service with restrictions, supervision.

[ASK] [X] [&M] [🛏] [💻] [🏊]

▼▼ Extended StayAmerica-Charlotte-Pineville SH
(704) 341-0929. **$81-$90.** 10930 Park Rd. I-485, exit 64A, just n on SR 51, then just e; behind Terraces at Park Place Shopping Center. Int corridors. **Pets:** Other species. $75 one-time fee/pet. Service with restrictions.

[ASK] [$ð] [X] [&M] [🛏] [💻]

▼▼ Extended StayAmerica-Charlotte-University Place SH
(704) 510-1636. **$86-$95.** 8211 University Executive Park Dr. I-85, exit 45A, 0.5 mi e on SR 24, then 0.5 mi s on US 29 (N Tryon St). Int corridors. **Pets:** Other species. $75 one-time fee/pet. Service with restrictions.

[ASK] [$ð] [X] [🛏] [💻]

▼▼▼▼ Extended Stay Deluxe-Charlotte/Pineville SH
(704) 542-9521. **$99-$110.** 8405 Pineville-Matthews Rd. I-485, exit 64A, 0.7 mi n on SR 51. Int corridors. **Pets:** Other species. $75 one-time fee/pet. Service with restrictions.

[ASK] [$ð] [X] [🛏] [💻] [🏊]

▼▼▼▼ Four Points by Sheraton-Charlotte SH
(704) 522-0852. **$130-$195.** 315 E Woodlawn Rd. I-77, exit 6A, 0.5 mi e. Int corridors. **Pets:** Accepted.

[ASK] [$ð] [X] [🛏] [💻] [🏊]

△△△ ▼▼▼▼ Hampton Inn University Place SH ❀
(704) 548-0905. **$99-$169.** 8419 N Tryon St. I-85, exit 45A, 0.5 mi e on SR 24, then just s on US 29 (N Tryon St). Int corridors. **Pets:** Medium. Service with restrictions, crate.

[SAVE] [$ð] [X] [&M] [🛏] [💻] [🏊]

▼▼▼▼ Holiday Inn Airport SH
(704) 394-4301. **$119-$199.** 2707 Little Rock Rd. I-85, exit 32, just e. Int corridors. **Pets:** Accepted.

[ASK] [$ð] [X] [🛏] [💻] [¶] [🏊]

▼▼▼▼ Holiday Inn at University Executive Park SH
(704) 547-0999. **$119.** 8520 University Executive Park Dr. I-85, exit 45A, just e on SR 24, then just s. Int corridors. **Pets:** Accepted.

[ASK] [$ð] [X] [&M] [🛏] [💻] [¶] [🏊]

▼▼▼▼ Homestead Studio Suites Hotel-Charlotte/Airport SH
(704) 676-0083. **$90-$100.** 710 Yorkmont Rd. I-77, exit 6B northbound, just w, just s on S Tryon St, then just w; exit southbound, just s on S Tryon St, then just w. Ext corridors. **Pets:** Other species. $75 one-time fee/pet. Service with restrictions.

[ASK] [$ð] [X] [🛏] [💻]

▼▼▼▼ Homewood Suites by Hilton Airport/Coliseum SH
(704) 357-0500. **$169.** 2770 Yorkmont Rd. I-77, exit 6B, 2 mi nw on Billy Graham Pkwy, exit Coliseum/Tyvola Rd, just se on Tyvola Rd, then just w. Int corridors. **Pets:** Very small, dogs only. $200 one-time fee/room. Designated rooms, service with restrictions, crate.

[ASK] [$ð] [X] [&M] [🛏] [💻]

△△△ ▼▼▼▼ Hyatt Summerfield Suites SH
(704) 525-2600. **$79-$299.** 4920 S Tryon St. I-77, exit 6B northbound, just w, then just s; exit southbound, just s. Int corridors. **Pets:** Accepted.

[SAVE] [X] [&M] [🛏] [💻] [🏊] [X]

△△△ ▼▼▼▼ La Quinta Inn- Airport North SH
(704) 392-1600. **$89-$139.** 3127 Sloan Dr. I-85, exit 33, just w, then just s. Int corridors. **Pets:** Other species. Service with restrictions, supervision.

[SAVE] [$ð] [X] [🛏] [💻]

△△△ ▼▼▼▼ La Quinta Inn & Suites Charlotte Airport South SH
(704) 523-5599. **$99-$144.** 4900 S Tryon St. I-77, exit 6B northbound, just w, then just s; exit southbound, just s. Int corridors. **Pets:** Other species. Service with restrictions, supervision.

[SAVE] [$ð] [X] [&M] [🛏] [💻] [🏊]

▼▼ MainStay Suites SH
(704) 521-3232. **Call for rates.** 7926 Forest Pine Dr. I-77, exit 3 southbound; exit 2 northbound, just e, then just s. Int corridors. **Pets:** Medium. $35 daily fee/room. Service with restrictions, supervision.

[X] [&M] [🛏] [💻] [🏊]

△△△ ▼▼▼▼ Marriott-Charlotte Southpark SH
(704) 364-8220. **$169-$189.** 2200 Rexford Rd. I-77, exit 5 (Tyvola Rd), 3.6 mi e on Tyvola/Fairview rds, just n on Sharon Rd, just w on Morrison Blvd, just n on Roxborough Rd, then just w. Int corridors. **Pets:** Medium, other species. $75 one-time fee/pet. Service with restrictions, supervision.

[SAVE] [$ð] [X] [&M] [🛏] [💻] [¶] [🏊] [X]

△△△ ▼▼▼▼ **Omni Charlotte Hotel** LH
(704) 377-0400. **$237-$267.** 132 E Trade St. I-77, exit 10 or 10B, 0.8
mi e; jct Tryon St. Int corridors. **Pets:** Accepted.
SAVE S6 X ⊟ 🖭 ¶1 🏊 ⊠

▼▼▼ **Quality Inn & Suites Airport** SH
(704) 393-5306. **Call for rates.** 3100 Queen City Dr. I-85, exit 33, just
w, then just n. Ext/int corridors. **Pets:** Medium. $20 one-time fee/room.
Service with restrictions, supervision.
X 🕭 ⊟ 🖭 🏊

▼▼▼ **Quality Inn-Executive Park** SH
(704) 525-0747. **Call for rates.** 440 Griffith Rd. I-77, exit 5 (Tyvola Rd),
just e, just s on Westpark Dr, then just e. Int corridors. **Pets:** Accepted.
X 🖭 🏊

▼▼▼ **Ramada Conference Center "Airport South"** SH
(704) 525-8350. **Call for rates.** 212 W Woodlawn Rd. I-77, exit 6A, just
e. Int corridors. **Pets:** Accepted.
X ⊟ 🖭 ¶1 🏊

△△△ ▼▼▼ **Ramada Northeast** SH
(704) 596-2999. **$49-$54.** 5415 Equipment Dr. I-85, exit 41, just w, then
0.4 mi n. Ext/int corridors. **Pets:** Medium. $25 one-time fee/pet. Desig-
nated rooms, service with restrictions, crate.
SAVE S6 X 🕭 🖭 🏊

▼▼▼ **Red Roof Inn-Airport** M
(704) 392-2316. **Call for rates.** 3300 Queen City Dr. I-85, exit 33, just
w, then just s. Ext corridors. **Pets:** Accepted.
X 🕭 ⊟

▼▼▼▼ **Residence Inn by Marriott-Charlotte South** SH
(704) 527-8110. **$149-$169.** 5816 Westpark Dr. I-77, exit 5 (Tyvola Rd),
just e, then 0.4 mi s. Ext/int corridors. **Pets:** Accepted.
A$K S6 X 🕭 ⊟ 🖭 🏊 ⊠

△△△ ▼▼▼▼ **Residence Inn by Marriott-Charlotte**
Uptown SH ❁
(704) 340-4000. **$219-$229.** 404 S Mint St. I-77, exit 10 or 10B, 0.6 mi
e on Trade St, then just s. Int corridors. **Pets:** Large, other species. $75
one-time fee/room. Service with restrictions, crate.
A$K S6 X 🕭 ⊟ 🖭 ¶1

▼▼▼▼ **Residence Inn by Marriott-Piper Glen** SH ❁
(704) 319-3900. **$154-$199.** 5115 Piper Station Dr. I-485, exit 59, just s
on Rea Rd, then just e. Int corridors. **Pets:** Other species. $75 one-time
fee/room. Service with restrictions, supervision.
A$K S6 X 🕭 ⊟ 🖭 🏊 ⊠

▼▼▼▼ **Residence Inn by Marriott-University Research**
Park SH
(704) 547-1122. **$149-$169.** 8503 N Tryon St. I-85, exit 45A, 0.5 mi e
on SR 24, then just s on US 29 (N Tryon St). Ext corridors.
Pets: Accepted.
A$K S6 X 🕭 ⊟ 🖭 🏊 ⊠

△△△ ▼▼▼▼ **Sheraton Charlotte Airport Hotel** LH
(704) 392-1200. **$129-$249.** 3315 Scott Futrell Dr. I-85, exit 33, just e,
then just s. Int corridors. **Pets:** Medium, dogs only. Service with restrictions, crate.
SAVE S6 X ⊟ 🖭 ¶1 🏊

△△△ ▼▼▼ **Sleep Inn** SH
(704) 549-4544. **$59-$179.** 8525 N Tryon St. I-85, exit 45A, 0.5 mi e on
SR 24, just s on US 29 (N Tryon St). Int corridors. **Pets:** Other species.
$25 one-time fee/room. Service with restrictions, crate.
SAVE S6 X 🕭 ⊟ 🖭 🏊

▼▼▼ **Sleep Inn-Yorkmont** SH
(704) 525-5005. **$70-$80.** 701 Yorkmont Rd. I-77, exit 6B northbound,
just w, just s on S Tryon St, then just w; exit southbound, just s on
Tryon St, then just w. Int corridors. **Pets:** Small. $20 daily fee/pet. Des-
ignated rooms, service with restrictions, crate.
S6 X 🕭 ⊟ 🖭 🏊

▼▼▼▼ **Staybridge Suites-Arrowood** SH
(704) 527-6767. **Call for rates.** 7924 Forest Pine Dr. I-77, exit 3 southbound; exit 2 northbound, just e, then just s. Int corridors. **Pets:** Large.
$100 one-time fee/pet. Service with restrictions.
X 🕭 ⊟ 🖭 🏊

▼▼▼▼ **Staybridge Suites Charlotte-Ballantyne** SH
(704) 248-5000. **$129-$349.** 15735 John J Delaney Dr. I-485, exit 61 or
61B, just s. Int corridors. **Pets:** $200 one-time fee/room. Service with
restrictions, supervision.
A$K S6 X 🕭 ⊟ 🖭 🏊 ⊠

▼▼▼ **Studio 6 Airport-#6006** SH
(704) 394-4993. **$53-$63.** 3420 Queen City Dr. I-85, exit 33, just w,
then just s. Int corridors. **Pets:** Other species. Service with restrictions,
supervision.
S6 X 🕭 ⊟ 🖭

▼▼▼ **StudioPLUS-Tyvola** SH
(704) 527-1960. **$86-$95.** 5830 Westpark Dr. I-77, exit 5 (Tyvola Rd),
just e, then 0.4 mi s. Int corridors. **Pets:** Other species. $75 one-time
fee/pet. Service with restrictions.
A$K S6 X 🕭 ⊟ 🖭 🏊

△△△ ▼▼▼▼ **TownePlace Suites by Marriott** SH
(704) 548-0388. **$149-$164.** 8710 Research Dr. I-85, exit 45B, just w
on SR 24, then just n. Int corridors. **Pets:** Other species. $75 one-time
fee/room. Service with restrictions, supervision.
A$K S6 X 🕭 ⊟ 🖭 🏊

△△△ ▼▼▼ **TownePlace Suites by Marriott-Arrowood** SH
(704) 227-2000. **$99-$119.** 7805 Forest Point Blvd. I-77, exit 3 southbound; exit 2 northbound, just e. Int corridors. **Pets:** Accepted.
A$K S6 X 🕭 ⊟ 🖭 🏊

△△△ ▼▼▼▼ **The Westin Charlotte** LH ❁
(704) 375-2600. **Call for rates.** 601 S College St. I-277, exit College St,
just n; jct E Stonewall St. Int corridors. **Pets:** Medium, dogs only. Service
with restrictions.
SAVE X 🕭 ⊟ 🖭 ¶1 🏊 ⊠

CONCORD

△△△ ▼▼▼ **Americas Best Value Inn** M
(704) 788-8550. **$135.** 2451 Kannapolis Hwy. I-85, exit 58, just s on US
29, then just w. Ext corridors. **Pets:** Small. $25 one-time fee/room. Des-
ignated rooms, service with restrictions, supervision.
A$K S6 X ⊟ 🖭

▼▼ **Sleep Inn** SH
(704) 788-2150. **Call for rates.** 1120 Copperfield Blvd. I-85, exit 60, just
e. Int corridors. **Pets:** Large. $25 one-time fee/pet. Service with restric-
tions, crate.
X 🕭 ⊟ 🖭 🏊

CORNELIUS

▼▼ **Clarion Inn** SH
(704) 896-0660. **$79-$109.** 19608 Liverpool Pkwy. I-77, exit 28, just w,
then s. Int corridors. **Pets:** Medium. $25 one-time fee/room. Service with
restrictions, supervision.
A$K S6 X ⊟ 🖭 🏊

△△△ ▼▼▼ **Days Inn-Lake Norman** SH
(704) 892-9120. **$65-$139.** 19901 Holiday Ln. I-77, exit 28, just e, then
just n. Ext corridors. **Pets:** $25 one-time fee/room. Service with restric-
tions, crate.
SAVE S6 X 🕭 ⊟ 🖭 ¶1 🏊

▼▼ Econo Lodge Lake Norman M ❀
(704) 892-3500. **$69-$180.** 20740 Torrence Chapel Rd. I-77, exit 28, just w, then just n. Ext corridors. **Pets:** Medium. $15 daily fee/pet. Designated rooms, service with restrictions, supervision.

Ⓐ$Ⓚ Ⓢ▸ Ⓧ ⬛ ⬛ ⤳

HUNTERSVILLE

▼▼▼ Candlewood Suites 🆂🅷
(704) 895-3434. **$110-$170.** 16530 Northcross Dr. I-77, exit 25, just w on SR 73, then just s. Int corridors. **Pets:** Large, other species. $75 one-time fee/pet. Service with restrictions, crate.

Ⓐ$Ⓚ Ⓢ▸ Ⓧ ⬛ ⬛

▼▼ Quality Inn 🆂🅷
(704) 892-6597. **$60-$169, 14 day notice.** 16825 Caldwell Creek Dr. I-77, exit 25, just e on SR 73, just n on US 21, then just w. Ext/int corridors. **Pets:** $25 one-time fee/room. Designated rooms, service with restrictions, crate.

Ⓐ$Ⓚ Ⓢ▸ Ⓧ ⬛ ⬛

▼▼▼ Residence Inn by Marriott-Lake Norman 🆂🅷
(704) 584-0000. **$179-$199.** 16830 Kenton Dr. I-77, exit 25, 1 mi w on SR 73, then just n. Int corridors. **Pets:** Accepted.

Ⓐ$Ⓚ Ⓢ▸ Ⓧ Ⓜ ⬛ ⬛ ⤳ ⊠

▼▼▼ Sleep Inn 🆂🅷
(704) 766-2500. **$99-$109.** 16508 Northcross Dr. I-77, exit 25, just w on SR 73, then just s. Int corridors. **Pets:** Accepted.

Ⓐ$Ⓚ Ⓢ▸ Ⓧ ⬛ ⬛

MATTHEWS

ⒶⒶⒶ ▼▼▼ Country Inn & Suites-Matthews 🆂🅷 ❀
(704) 846-8000. **$99-$109.** 2001 Mount Harmony Church Rd. I-485, exit 51B, 0.5 mi e on US 74, just n on Independence Commerce Dr, then just w. Int corridors. **Pets:** Large. $20 daily fee/pet. Designated rooms, service with restrictions, crate.

Ⓢ🅰🆅🅴 Ⓢ▸ Ⓧ Ⓜ ⬛ ⬛ ⤳

END METROPOLITAN AREA

CHEROKEE

** ⒶⒶⒶ ▼▼▼ Best Western Great Smokies Inn M**
(828) 497-2020. **$39-$149.** 1636 Acquoni Rd. US 441 N, 2.5 mi n; downtown. Ext corridors. **Pets:** Small, other species. $15 daily fee/pet. Designated rooms, service with restrictions, supervision.

Ⓢ🅰🆅🅴 Ⓢ▸ Ⓧ ⬛ ⬛ ⓣⓣ ⤳

ⒶⒶⒶ ▼▼▼ Microtel Inn & Suites 🆂🅷 ❀
(828) 497-7800. **$35-$139.** 674 Casino Tr. Jct US 441 and Business Rt US 441 S. Int corridors. **Pets:** Other species. $25 daily fee/room. Designated rooms, service with restrictions.

Ⓢ🅰🆅🅴 Ⓢ▸ Ⓧ Ⓜ ⬛ ⬛ ⤳

ⒶⒶⒶ ▼ Pioneer Motel M
(828) 497-2435. **Call for rates.** 122 Tsalagi Rd. 0.8 mi w on US 19 S. Ext corridors. **Pets:** Accepted.

Ⓢ🅰🆅🅴 Ⓧ ⬛ ⬛ ⤳ ⊠

▼ Two Rivers Lodge M
(828) 488-2284. **$35-$120.** 5280 Ela Rd. 5 mi e on US 19 S. Ext corridors. **Pets:** Medium, dogs only. $20 one-time fee/room. Designated rooms, no service, crate.

Ⓐ$Ⓚ Ⓢ▸ Ⓧ ⬛ ⬛ ⤳ ⊠

CHIMNEY ROCK

ⒶⒶⒶ ▼▼ Mountain Village Chalets 🅲🅰
(828) 625-9783. **$67-$336, 14 day notice.** 950 Main St. 1 mi w on US 74A. Ext corridors. **Pets:** Other species. $50 one-time fee/pet. Supervision.

Ⓢ🅰🆅🅴 Ⓢ▸ ⬛ ⬛ ⊠

CLAREMONT

ⒶⒶⒶ ▼▼▼ Super 8 Motel M
(828) 459-7777. **$66-$85.** 3054 N Oxford St. I-40, exit 135, just s. Ext/int corridors. **Pets:** Small, dogs only. $100 deposit/room, $15 daily fee/pet. Service with restrictions, supervision.

Ⓢ🅰🆅🅴 Ⓢ▸ Ⓧ ⬛ ⬛ ⤳

CLAYTON

▼▼ Sleep Inn 🆂🅷
(919) 772-7771. **Call for rates.** 105 Commerce Pkwy. I-40, exit 312, just w on SR 42, then just s. Int corridors. **Pets:** Accepted.

Ⓧ Ⓜ ⬛ ⬛ ⤳

▼▼ Super 8 Motel 🆂🅷
(919) 661-1991. **$60-$70.** 101 Leone Ct. I-40, exit 312, just e on SR 42, then just s. Ext corridors. **Pets:** $5 daily fee/pet. Service with restrictions, supervision.

Ⓐ$Ⓚ Ⓢ▸ Ⓧ ⬛ ⬛ ⤳

CLEMMONS

▼▼ The Village Inn Golf & Conference Center 🆂🅷
(336) 766-9121. **$66-$79.** 6205 Ramada Dr. I-40, exit 184, just s, then just e. Int corridors. **Pets:** Accepted.

Ⓐ$Ⓚ Ⓢ▸ Ⓧ ⬛ ⬛ ⓣⓣ ⤳

COLUMBUS

ⒶⒶⒶ ▼▼ Days Inn M
(828) 894-3303. **$49-$100.** 626 W Mills St. I-26, exit 67, just w on SR 108. Ext corridors. **Pets:** Medium. $20 one-time fee/room. Service with restrictions, supervision.

Ⓢ🅰🆅🅴 Ⓢ▸ Ⓧ ⬛ ⬛ ⤳

CONOVER

▼▼ Days Inn 🆂🅷
(828) 465-2378. **Call for rates.** 1710 Fairgrove Church Rd SE. I-40, exit 128, just s. Ext corridors. **Pets:** Other species. $10 one-time fee/pet. Service with restrictions, crate.

Ⓧ Ⓜ ⬛ ⬛ ⤳

DUNN

▼▼ Jameson Inn M
(910) 891-5758. **$73-$100.** 901 Jackson Rd. I-95, exit 73, just w, then just s. Ext corridors. **Pets:** Small. $15 daily fee/room. Service with restrictions, crate.

Ⓐ$Ⓚ Ⓢ▸ Ⓧ Ⓜ ⬛ ⬛ ⤳

DURHAM

ⒶⒶⒶ ▼▼▼ Americas Best Value Carolina Duke Inn M ❀
(919) 286-0771. **$53-$58.** 2517 Guess Rd. I-85, exit 175, just e. Ext corridors. **Pets:** Other species. $5 daily fee/room. Service with restrictions, crate.

Ⓢ🅰🆅🅴 Ⓢ▸ Ⓧ ⬛ ⬛ ⤳

ⒶⒶⒶ ▼▼▼ Best Western Skyland Inn M ❀
(919) 383-2508. **$80-$100, 7 day notice.** 5400 US 70 W. I-85, exit 170, 0.3 mi e on US 70, then just n. Ext corridors. **Pets:** Other species. $10 daily fee/pet. Service with restrictions.

Ⓢ🅰🆅🅴 Ⓢ▸ Ⓧ ⬛ ⬛ ⤳

Candlewood Suites SH
(919) 484-9922. **Call for rates.** 1818 E NC Hwy 54. I-40, exit 278, just s, then just w. Int corridors. **Pets:** Accepted.
⊠ ⑤ᴹ 🛏 💻

Comfort Inn University SH ❀
(919) 490-4949. **$89-$119.** 3508 Mt Moriah Rd. I-40, exit 270, just n on US 15/501, then just e. Int corridors. **Pets:** Medium. $49 one-time fee/room. Designated rooms, service with restrictions, crate.
SAVE ⑤ᴅ ⊠ 🛏 💻 ⇌

Extended Stay Deluxe-Durham-RTP-Miami Blvd North SH
(919) 941-2878. **$90-$100.** 4610 S Miami Blvd. I-40, exit 281, just n. Int corridors. **Pets:** Other species. $75 one-time fee/pet. Service with restrictions.
ASK ⑤ᴅ ⊠ 🛏 💻 ⇌

Extended Stay Deluxe-RTP-Miami Blvd-South SH
(919) 998-0400. **$99-$110.** 4919 S Miami Blvd. I-40, exit 281, just s. Int corridors. **Pets:** Other species. $75 one-time fee/pet. Service with restrictions.
ASK ⑤ᴅ ⊠ ⑤ᴹ 🛏 💻 ⇌

Four Points by Sheraton SH
(919) 806-8200. **Call for rates.** 7807 Leonardo Dr. I-40, exit 274, just s on SR 751. Int corridors. **Pets:** Large, other species. $50 one-time fee/room. Designated rooms.
⊠ ⑤ᴹ 🛏 💻 🍽 ⇌

Hampton Inn SH ❀
(919) 471-6100. **$99-$139.** 1816 Hillandale Rd. I-85, exit 174A, just w. Int corridors. **Pets:** Large, other species. Designated rooms, service with restrictions, crate.
SAVE ⑤ᴅ ⊠ 🛏 💻 ⇌

Holiday Inn Express SH
(919) 313-3244. **$89-$139, 3 day notice.** 2516 Guess Rd. I-85, exit 175, just e. Int corridors. **Pets:** Small, other species. $10 one-time fee/room. Service with restrictions.
ASK ⑤ᴅ ⊠ 🛏 💻 ⇌

Holiday Inn Express Hotel & Suites-RTP SH
(919) 474-9800. **$89-$149, 3 day notice.** 4912 S Miami Blvd. I-40, exit 281, just s. Int corridors. **Pets:** Small, other species. $10 one-time fee/room. Service with restrictions.
ASK ⑤ᴅ ⊠ ⑤ᴹ 🛏 💻

Homestead Studio Suites Hotel-Durham/University SH
(919) 402-1700. **$72-$80.** 1920 Ivy Creek Blvd. I-40, exit 270, 2 mi n on US 15/501, exit 105B, then just e on Martin Luther King Jr Pkwy; in University Place. Ext corridors. **Pets:** Other species. $75 one-time fee/pet. Service with restrictions.
ASK ⑤ᴅ ⊠ 🛏 💻

Homewood Suites Durham/Chapel Hill SH ❀
(919) 401-0610. **$114-$164.** 3600 Mt Moriah Rd. I-40, exit 270, just n on US 15/501, then just e. Int corridors. **Pets:** Medium. $49 one-time fee/room. Service with restrictions, supervision.
SAVE ⑤ᴅ ⊠ ⑤ᴹ 🛏 💻 ⇌

La Quinta Inn & Suites Raleigh (Durham-Chapel Hill) SH
(919) 401-9660. **$112-$155.** 4414 Durham Chapel Hill Blvd. I-40, exit 270, 1.7 mi n on US 15/501. Int corridors. **Pets:** Other species. Service with restrictions, supervision.
SAVE ⑤ᴅ ⊠ ⑤ᴹ 🛏 💻 ⇌

La Quinta Inn & Suites Raleigh (Research Triangle Park) SH
(919) 484-1422. **$112-$152.** 1910 W Park Dr. I-40, exit 278, just n on SR 55, then just e. Int corridors. **Pets:** Other species. Service with restrictions, supervision.
SAVE ⑤ᴅ ⊠ ⑤ᴹ 🛏 💻 ⇌

Quality Inn & Suites SH
(919) 382-3388. **$72-$77.** 3710 Hillsborough Rd. I-85, exit 173, just e on Cole Mill Rd, then just w on US 70 business route. Ext/int corridors. **Pets:** Small. $25 daily fee/room. Designated rooms, service with restrictions, crate.
SAVE ⑤ᴅ ⊠ 🛏 💻 ⇌

Residence Inn by Marriott SH
(919) 361-1266. **$174-$194.** 201 Residence Inn Blvd. I-40, exit 278, just s, then just w. Ext/int corridors. **Pets:** Accepted.
ASK ⑤ᴅ ⊠ ⑤ᴹ 🛏 💻 ⇌ ⊠

Sleep Inn-RTP SH
(919) 993-3393. **$79-$149.** 5208 Page Rd. I-40, exit 282, just s. Int corridors. **Pets:** Designated rooms, service with restrictions, supervision.
ASK ⑤ᴅ ⊠ ⑤ᴹ 🛏 💻 ⇌

StudioPLUS-Research Triangle Park SH
(919) 361-1853. **$77-$85.** 2504 NC Hwy 54. I-40, exit 278, just s on SR 55, then just e. Int corridors. **Pets:** Other species. $75 one-time fee/pet. Service with restrictions.
ASK ⑤ᴅ ⊠ 🛏 💻 ⇌

Wyndham Hotel-Research Triangle Park SH
(919) 941-6066. **Call for rates.** 4620 S Miami Blvd. I-40, exit 281, just n. Int corridors. **Pets:** Accepted.
⊠ 🛏 💻 🍽 ⇌

EDEN

Jameson Inn SH
(336) 627-0472. **$60-$85.** 716 Linden Dr. Jct SR 700/770, 1.4 mi s on SR 87/14, then just e. Ext corridors. **Pets:** Small. $15 daily fee/room. Service with restrictions, crate.
ASK ⑤ᴅ ⊠ ⑤ᴹ 🛏 💻 ⇌

FAYETTEVILLE

Comfort Inn Cross Creek SH ❀
(910) 867-1777. **$99-$109.** 1922 Skibo Rd. All American Frwy, exit US 401 Bypass, 0.8 mi s. Int corridors. **Pets:** Medium. $49 one-time fee/room. Service with restrictions.
SAVE ⑤ᴅ ⊠ 🛏 💻 ⇌

Comfort Inn-Fayetteville M
(910) 323-8333. **$72-$99.** 1957 Cedar Creek Rd. I-95, exit 49, just w. Ext corridors. **Pets:** $10 one-time fee/pet. Designated rooms, no service, crate.
ASK ⑤ᴅ ⊠ 🛏 💻 ⇌

Econo Lodge I-95 M
(910) 433-2100. **$60-$90.** 1952 Cedar Creek Rd. I-95, exit 49, just w. Ext corridors. **Pets:** Accepted.
SAVE ⑤ᴅ ⊠ 🛏 ⇌

Extended StayAmerica M
(910) 485-2747. **$90-$100.** 408 Owen Dr. Jct All American Frwy. Ext corridors. **Pets:** Other species. $75 one-time fee/pet. Service with restrictions.
ASK ⑤ᴅ ⊠ 🛏 💻

Extended Stay Deluxe Fayetteville-Cross Creek Mall SH
(910) 868-5662. **$108-$120.** 4105 Sycamore Dairy Rd. All American Frwy, exit Morganton Rd, just e, then just n. Int corridors. **Pets:** Other species. $75 one-time fee/pet. Service with restrictions.
ASK ⑤ᴅ ⊠ 🛏 💻 ⇌

Holiday Inn Bordeaux 🆂🅷
(910) 323-0111. **Call for rates.** 1707 Owen Dr. Jct I-95 business route/US 301 S, 2.3 mi w. Ext/int corridors. **Pets:** Small, other species. $50 one-time fee/pet. Designated rooms, service with restrictions, crate.

ⓧ 🅗 🖵 🍽 🏊

🆎 💎💎💎 **Holiday Inn I-95** 🆂🅷 🐾
(910) 323-1600. **$103-$111.** 1944 Cedar Creek Rd. I-95, exit 49, just w. Ext/int corridors. **Pets:** Medium. $25 one-time fee/room. Service with restrictions, crate.

🆂🅰🆅🅴 🆂🅾 ⓧ 🅗 🖵 🍽 🏊

💎💎 **Innkeeper-Cross Creek** 🅼
(910) 867-7659. **$59-$89, 3 day notice.** 1720 Skibo Rd. All American Frwy, exit US 401 Bypass, just s; enter thru Cross Creek Plaza entrance. Ext/int corridors. **Pets:** Small, other species. $10 one-time fee/room. Service with restrictions.

🅰🆂🅺 🆂🅾 ⓧ 🅗 🏊

🆎 💎💎💎 **Red Roof Inn** 🆂🅷
(910) 321-1460. **$49-$70.** 1569 Jim Johnson Rd. I-95, exit 49, just w on SR 53, then just n. Int corridors. **Pets:** Medium, dogs only. Designated rooms, service with restrictions, supervision.

🆂🅰🆅🅴 🆂🅾 ⓧ 🅗 🅼 🏊

💎💎💎 **Residence Inn by Marriott-Fayetteville-Cross Creek-Ft. Bragg** 🆂🅷
(910) 868-9005. **$129-$179.** 1468 Skibo Rd. Jct SR 24/87, just s on US 401 Bypass. Int corridors. **Pets:** Other species. $100 one-time fee/room. Service with restrictions, crate.

🅰🆂🅺 🆂🅾 ⓧ 🅼 🅗 🖵 🏊 ⓧ

FLAT ROCK

💎💎💎 **Highland Lake Inn-A Country Retreat** 🆂🅷
(828) 693-6812. **$79-$259, 7 day notice.** 180 Highland Lake Rd. I-26, exit 53, 2.1 mi w. Ext/int corridors. **Pets:** Medium, dogs only. $25 daily fee/pet. Designated rooms, no service.

🅰🆂🅺 🆂🅾 ⓧ 🅗 🖵 🍽 🏊 ⓧ

FLETCHER

🆎 💎💎💎 **Holiday Inn Asheville-Airport** 🆂🅷
(828) 684-1213. **$79-$169.** 550 Airport Rd. I-26, exit 40, just e. Int corridors. **Pets:** Accepted.

🆂🅰🆅🅴 🆂🅾 ⓧ 🅗 🖵 🍽 🏊

FOREST CITY

💎💎 **Jameson Inn** 🅼
(828) 287-8788. **$63-$95.** 164 Jameson Dr. US 74 Bypass, exit 181, 1.8 mi nw on US 74A. Ext corridors. **Pets:** Small. $15 daily fee/room. Service with restrictions, crate.

🅰🆂🅺 🆂🅾 ⓧ 🅼 🅗 🖵 🏊

FRANKLIN

💎 **The Franklin Motel** 🅼
(828) 524-4431. **Call for rates.** 17 W Palmer St. Jct US 441 Bypass, 1 mi n on US 441 business route; downtown. Ext corridors. **Pets:** Other species. $10 one-time fee/room. Service with restrictions.

ⓧ 🅗 🏊

💎💎 **Microtel Inn & Suites** 🆂🅷
(828) 349-9000. **$50-$100.** 81 Allman Dr. Jct US 441 Bypass, 0.4 mi s on US 441 and 23. Int corridors. **Pets:** Accepted.

🅰🆂🅺 🆂🅾 ⓧ 🅗 🖵

💎 **Sapphire Inn** 🅼
(828) 524-4406. **Call for rates.** 761 E Main St. 0.5 mi w of US 441 and 64 on SR 28. Ext corridors. **Pets:** Accepted.

ⓧ 🅗 🏊

GARNER

💎💎 **Holiday Inn Express** 🆂🅷
(919) 662-4890. **Call for rates.** 1595 Mechanical Blvd. I-40, exit 298A, 1.9 mi e on US 70, then just n. Int corridors. **Pets:** Accepted.

ⓧ 🅗 🖵

GASTONIA

💎💎 **Ramada Limited** 🅼
(704) 864-8744. **Call for rates.** 1400 E Franklin Blvd. I-85, exit 20, 0.5 mi s on SR 279, then just w on US 29/74. Ext corridors. **Pets:** Small. $20 daily fee/room. Service with restrictions, supervision.

ⓧ 🅗 🖵

GOLDSBORO

🆎 💎 💎💎 **Best Western Goldsboro Inn** 🅼
(919) 735-7911. **$60-$100.** 801 US 70 E Bypass. US 70 E Bypass, exit Wayne Memorial Dr eastbound, just n, just w on Eleventh St, then 0.4 mi sw on service road; exit westbound, straight on Eleventh St, then 0.4 mi sw on service road. Ext corridors. **Pets:** Small, dogs only. $10 daily fee/pet. Designated rooms, service with restrictions, supervision.

🆂🅰🆅🅴 🆂🅾 ⓧ 🅗 🖵 🍽 🏊

💎💎💎 **Comfort Suites** 🆂🅷
(919) 759-0098. **$81.** 2613 N Park Dr. US 70 E Bypass, exit Spence Ave, just n, then just e. Int corridors. **Pets:** Other species. $50 one-time fee/pet. Service with restrictions, crate.

🅰🆂🅺 🆂🅾 ⓧ 🅼 🅗 🖵 🏊

🆎 💎💎💎 **Holiday Inn Express Goldsboro** 🆂🅷 🐾
(919) 751-1999. **$105-$195.** 909 N Spence Ave. US 70 E Bypass, exit Spence Ave, just s. Int corridors. **Pets:** Other species. $20 one-time fee/room. Service with restrictions, supervision.

🆂🅰🆅🅴 ⓧ 🅗 🖵 🏊

💎💎 **Jameson Inn** 🆂🅷
(919) 778-9759. **$68-$100.** 1408 Harding Dr. US 70 E Bypass, exit Spence Ave, just n, then just e on North Park Dr. Int corridors. **Pets:** Small. $15 daily fee/room. Service with restrictions, crate.

🅰🆂🅺 🆂🅾 ⓧ 🅼 🅗 🖵 🏊

GREENSBORO

🆎 💎💎💎 **Best Western Deep River** 🆂🅷
(336) 454-0333. **Call for rates.** 7800 National Service Rd. I-40, exit 210 (SR 68), just s, just w on Thorndike Rd, then just n. Int corridors. **Pets:** Accepted.

ⓧ 🅗 🖵 🏊

🆎 💎💎💎 **Best Western Wendover Plaza** 🆂🅷
(336) 297-1055. **$79-$209.** 1103 Lanada Rd. I-40, exit 214 or 214A, just sw on Wendover Ave, then just e on Stanley Rd. Int corridors. **Pets:** Accepted.

🅰🆂🅺 🆂🅾 ⓧ 🅗 🖵 🏊

🆎 💎💎💎 **Best Western Windsor Suites** 🆂🅷
(336) 294-9100. **$99-$185.** 2006 Veasley St. I-40, exit 217, just s on High Point Rd, then just w. Int corridors. **Pets:** Accepted.

🅰🆂🅺 🆂🅾 ⓧ 🅗 🖵 🏊

💎💎💎 **Candlewood Suites** 🆂🅷
(336) 454-0078. **$90-$120, 24 day notice.** 7623 Thorndike Rd. I-40, exit 210 (SR 68), just s, then just w. Int corridors. **Pets:** Accepted.

🅰🆂🅺 🆂🅾 ⓧ 🅼 🅗 🖵

🆎 💎💎💎 **Clarion Hotel-Airport** 🆂🅷
(336) 299-7650. **Call for rates.** 415 Swing Rd. I-40, exit 213, just n, then just w. Int corridors. **Pets:** Accepted.

🆂🅰🆅🅴 ⓧ 🅗 🖵 🍽 🏊

🆎 💎💎 **Comfort Inn** 🆂🅷
(336) 294-6220. **$68-$84.** 2001 Veasley St. I-40, exit 217, just s on High Point Rd, then just w. Int corridors. **Pets:** Accepted.

🆂🅰🆅🅴 🆂🅾 ⓧ 🅗 🖵 🏊

▼▼▼▼ **Comfort Suites Airport** 🆂🅷
(336) 882-6666. **$99-$229.** 7619 Thorndike Rd. I-40, exit 210 (SR 68), just s, then just w. Int corridors. **Pets:** Small. $20 daily fee/room. Designated rooms, service with restrictions, supervision.
⊠ ♿ 🛡 💻 ➴

▼▼ **Crestwood Suites** 🆂🅷
(336) 886-1250. **Call for rates (no credit cards).** 501 Americhase Dr. I-40, exit 210 (SR 68), 0.5 mi s. Int corridors. **Pets:** Accepted.
⊠ 🛡 💻

▼▼▼ **Drury Inn & Suites-Greensboro** 🆂🅷
(336) 856-9696. **$76-$140.** 3220 High Point Rd. I-40, exit 217, just s. Int corridors. **Pets:** Large, other species. Service with restrictions, supervision.
🅰🆂🅺 ⊠ 🛡 💻 ➴

▼▼ **Extended StayAmerica-Greensboro-Wendover Ave** Ⓜ
(336) 299-0200. **$68-$75.** 4317 Big Tree Way. I-40, exit 214 or 214B, just ne on Wendover Ave, then just w. Ext corridors. **Pets:** Other species. $75 one-time fee/pet. Service with restrictions.
🅰🆂🅺 🆂 ⊠ 🛡 💻

▼▼ **Extended Stay Deluxe** 🆂🅷
(336) 454-0080. **$90-$100.** 7617 Thorndike Rd. I-40, exit 210 (SR 68), just s, then just w. Int corridors. **Pets:** Other species. $75 one-time fee/pet. Service with restrictions.
🅰🆂🅺 🆂 ⊠ 🛡 💻 ➴

▼▼▼ **Holiday Inn Express** 🆂🅷
(336) 854-0090. **$84-$119, 3 day notice.** 4305 Big Tree Way. I-40, exit 214 or 214B, just ne on Wendover Ave, then just w. Int corridors. **Pets:** Small, other species. $10 one-time fee/room. Service with restrictions.
🅰🆂🅺 🆂 ⊠ ♿ 🛡 💻 ➴

🆀🆀🆀 ▼▼▼▼ **La Quinta Inn & Suites Greensboro** 🆂🅷
(336) 316-0100. **$125-$164.** 1201 Lanada Rd. I-40, exit 214 or 214A, just sw on Wendover Ave, then just e on Stanley Rd. Int corridors. **Pets:** Other species. Service with restrictions, supervision.
🆂🅰🆅🅴 🆂 ⊠ ♿ 🛡 💻 ➴

▼▼ **Ramada Inn-Conference Center** 🆂🅷
(336) 294-9922. **$55-$199.** 2003 Athena Ct. I-40, exit 217, just s on High Point Rd, just w on Veasley St, then just n on Isler Ct. Ext/int corridors. **Pets:** Accepted.
🅰🆂🅺 🆂 ⊠ ♿ 🛡 💻 ➴

▼▼ **Red Roof Inn Airport** Ⓜ
(336) 271-2636. **Call for rates.** 615 Regional Rd S. I-40, exit 210 (SR 68), just s, then just e. Ext corridors. **Pets:** Accepted.
⊠ ♿ 🛡

▼▼▼ **Residence Inn by Marriott** 🆂🅷
(336) 294-8600. **$104-$124.** 2000 Veasley St. I-40, exit 217, just s on High Point Rd, then 0.4 mi w. Ext corridors. **Pets:** Accepted.
🅰🆂🅺 🆂 ⊠ 🛡 💻 ➴ ⊠

GREENVILLE

▼▼ **Home-Towne Suites** 🆂🅷
(252) 752-3411. **$59-$89.** 2111 W Arlington Blvd. Jct US 13/SR 11, 0.4 mi w on Stantonsburg Rd, then just s. Int corridors. **Pets:** Accepted.
🅰🆂🅺 🆂 ⊠ 🛡 💻

▼▼ **Jameson Inn** Ⓜ
(252) 752-7382. **$55-$85.** 920 Crosswinds St. Jct US 264 business route, just s on US 13/SR 11, then just w. Ext corridors. **Pets:** Small. $15 daily fee/room. Service with restrictions, crate.
🅰🆂🅺 🆂 ⊠ ♿ 🛡 💻 ➴

HAYESVILLE

▼▼ **Chatuge Mountain Inn** Ⓜ
(828) 389-9340. **Call for rates.** 4238 Hwy 64 E. Jct SR 69, 4.2 mi e. Ext corridors. **Pets:** Accepted.
⊠ 🛡 💻

▼▼▼ **Deerfield Inn** Ⓜ
(828) 389-8272. **$70-$100.** 40 Chatuge Ln. 3 mi e on US 64. Ext corridors. **Pets:** Accepted.
⊠ 🛡 💻

HENDERSON

▼▼ **Jameson Inn** 🆂🅷
(252) 430-0247. **$63-$95.** 400 N Cooper Dr. I-85, exit 212, just w on Ruin Creek Rd, then just n. Int corridors. **Pets:** Small. $15 daily fee/room. Service with restrictions, crate.
🅰🆂🅺 🆂 ⊠ ♿ 🛡 💻 ➴

▼▼ **Lamplight Inn B&B** 🅱🅱 ❀
(252) 438-6311. **Call for rates.** 1680 Flemingtown Rd. I-85, exit 220, 1.5 mi nw. Int corridors. **Pets:** Small. Service with restrictions, supervision.
⊠ 🆉

🆀🆀🆀 ▼▼ **Sleep Inn** 🆂🅷
(252) 433-9449. **$59-$85.** 18 Market Pl. I-85, exit 212, just w on Ruin Creek Rd, then just se on Zeb Robinson Rd. Int corridors. **Pets:** Small. $15 daily fee/pet. Designated rooms, service with restrictions, supervision.
🆂🅰🆅🅴 ⊠ 🛡 💻

HENDERSONVILLE

🆀🆀🆀 ▼▼▼ **Best Western Hendersonville Inn** Ⓜ
(828) 692-0521. **Call for rates.** 105 Sugarloaf Rd. I-26, exit 49A, just e. Ext corridors. **Pets:** Accepted.
🆂🅰🆅🅴 ⊠ 🛡 💻 🍴 ➴

🆀🆀🆀 ▼▼▼ **Comfort Inn** 🆂🅷
(828) 693-8800. **$55-$149.** 206 Mitchell Dr. I-26, exit 49B, just w. Ext corridors. **Pets:** Large, other species. $15 daily fee/pet. Service with restrictions, supervision.
🆂🅰🆅🅴 ⊠ 🛡 💻 ➴

HICKORY

▼▼ **Jameson Inn** Ⓜ
(828) 304-0410. **$63-$95.** 1120 13th Ave Dr SE. I-40, exit 125, just s, then 0.4 mi w. Ext corridors. **Pets:** Small. $15 daily fee/room. Service with restrictions, crate.
🅰🆂🅺 🆂 ⊠ ♿ 🛡 💻 ➴

▼▼ **Red Roof Inn Hickory** Ⓜ
(828) 323-1500. **Call for rates.** 1184 Lenoir Rhyne Blvd. I-40, exit 125, just n. Ext corridors. **Pets:** Accepted.
⊠ 🛡

HIGHLANDS

🆀🆀🆀 ▼▼▼ **Mountain High Lodge** Ⓜ ❀
(828) 526-2790. **$49-$189, 7 day notice.** 200 Main St. Just w on US 64; downtown. Ext corridors. **Pets:** Other species. Designated rooms, service with restrictions, supervision.
🆂🅰🆅🅴 🆂 ⊠ 🛡 💻

HILLSBOROUGH

🆀🆀🆀 ▼▼▼ **Holiday Inn Express** 🆂🅷
(919) 644-7997. **$90-$200.** 202 Cardinal Dr. I-85, exit 164, just e, then just s. Int corridors. **Pets:** Accepted.
🆂🅰🆅🅴 🆂 ⊠ ♿ 🛡 💻 ➴

JACKSONVILLE

Americas Best Value Inn 🅂🄷 ❀
(910) 455-6888. **$70-$90.** 2149 N Marine Blvd. Jct Western Blvd, just n on US 17. Int corridors. **Pets:** Dogs only. $10 one-time fee/room. Designated rooms, service with restrictions, supervision.

Extended StayAmerica 🅂🄷
(910) 347-7684. **$90-$100.** 20 McDaniel Dr. Jct Western Blvd, just n on US 17, then just w. Int corridors. **Pets:** Other species. $75 one-time fee/pet. Service with restrictions.

Hampton Inn 🅂🄷 ❀
(910) 347-6500. **$79-$129.** 474 Western Blvd. Jct US 17. Ext corridors. **Pets:** Medium, other species. Service with restrictions, crate.

Innkeeper 🅂🄷
(910) 938-0800. **$69-$109, 3 day notice.** 2139 N Marine Blvd. Jct Western Blvd, just n on US 17. Int corridors. **Pets:** Small, other species. $10 one-time fee/room. Service with restrictions.

JONESVILLE

Comfort Inn 🅂🄷
(336) 835-9400. **$79-$150.** 1633 Winston Rd. I-77, exit 82, just w. Ext corridors. **Pets:** Medium. $10 daily fee/pet. Designated rooms, service with restrictions, supervision.

Days Inn Jonesville-Elkin 🄼
(336) 526-6777. **$69-$109.** 1540 SR 67. I-77, exit 82, 0.3 mi w. Ext corridors. **Pets:** Medium. $10 daily fee/pet. Service with restrictions, supervision.

Holiday Inn Express 🅂🄷
(336) 835-6000. **$79-$99.** 1713 NC 67 Hwy. I-77, exit 82, just e. Int corridors. **Pets:** Small. $10 daily fee/pet. Designated rooms, no service, supervision.

KENLY

Super 8 🄼
(919) 284-3800. **Call for rates.** 843 Johnston Pkwy. I-95, exit 106, just w, then just s. Ext corridors. **Pets:** Accepted.

KINGS MOUNTAIN

Quality Inn 🄼
(704) 739-7070. **$59-$169.** 722-A York Rd. I-85, exit 8, just n on SR 161. Ext corridors. **Pets:** Accepted.

LAURINBURG

Jameson Inn 🄼
(910) 277-0080. **$60-$90.** 14 Jameson Inn Ct. Jct US 74 Bypass, just n on US 15/401 Bypass, just e. Ext corridors. **Pets:** Small. $15 daily fee/room. Service with restrictions, crate.

LENOIR

Days Inn 🅂🄷
(828) 754-0731. **Call for rates.** 206 Blowing Rock Blvd. Jct US 321, just n of SR 18. Ext corridors. **Pets:** Accepted.

LEXINGTON

Comfort Suites of Lexington 🅂🄷 ❀
(336) 357-2333. **Call for rates.** 1620 Cotton Grove Rd. I-85, exit 91, just s on SR 8, then just ne. Ext/int corridors. **Pets:** Small, dogs only. $25 daily fee/pet. Designated rooms, service with restrictions, supervision.

Econo Lodge 🄼 ❀
(336) 249-0111. **$75-$125.** 418 Piedmont Dr. I-85, exit 96, 3.9 mi w on US 64. Ext corridors. **Pets:** Medium, other species. $25 one-time fee/room. Service with restrictions, supervision.

LINCOLNTON

Days Inn 🄼
(704) 735-8271. **Call for rates.** 614 Clark Dr. US 321, exit 24, 1 mi w on SR 150, then just s on US 321 business route. Ext corridors. **Pets:** $10 daily fee/room. Designated rooms, no service, supervision.

LITTLE SWITZERLAND

Switzerland Inn 🄲🄸
(828) 765-2153. **$110-$220, 7 day notice.** 86 High Ridge Rd. Jct SR 226A and Blue Ridge Pkwy, MM 334. Ext/int corridors. **Pets:** Large, other species. $20 daily fee/room. Designated rooms.

LUMBERTON

Best Western Inn 🄼
(910) 618-9799. **$89-$169.** 201 Jackson Ct. I-95, exit 22, just e, then just s. Ext corridors. **Pets:** Other species. $10 daily fee/pet. Service with restrictions, supervision.

Quality Inn and Suites 🅂🄷
(910) 738-8261. **$60-$99.** 3608 Kahn Dr. I-95, exit 20, just e, then just n. Ext/int corridors. **Pets:** Accepted.

MAGGIE VALLEY

Best Western Mountainbrook Inn 🄼
(828) 926-3962. **$49-$149.** 3811 Soco Rd. US 19, 4 mi w of US 276. Ext corridors. **Pets:** Accepted.

Castlewood Inn 🄼
(828) 926-1480. **$50-$100, 7 day notice.** 3695 Soco Rd. US 19, 3.6 mi w of US 276. Ext corridors. **Pets:** Small, dogs only. $15 daily fee/pet. Designated rooms, service with restrictions, crate.

MARION

Hampton Inn 🅂🄷
(828) 652-5100. **Call for rates.** 3560 US 221 S. I-40, exit 85, just n. Int corridors. **Pets:** $35 one-time fee/room. Designated rooms, service with restrictions, supervision.

MOCKSVILLE

Comfort Inn & Suites 🅂🄷
(336) 751-5966. **Call for rates.** 629 Madison Rd. I-40, exit 170, just s on US 601, then just w. Int corridors. **Pets:** Medium. $20 one-time fee/pet. Service with restrictions, supervision.

▼▼ Quality Inn SH ❖
(336) 751-7310. **$64-$80.** 1500 Yadkinville Rd. I-40, exit 170, just s on US 601. Ext corridors. **Pets:** Other species. $25 one-time fee/room. Service with restrictions, supervision.
ASK SÒ ✕ ⊟ ⊒ ⇔

MOORESVILLE

▼▼▼▼ Holiday Inn Express Hotel & Suites SH
(704) 662-6900. **Call for rates.** 130 Norman Station Blvd. I-77, exit 36, just e on SR 150, then just s. Int corridors. **Pets:** Accepted.
✕ ⒧M ⊟ ⊒ ⇔

MOREHEAD CITY

▼▼▼ Holiday Inn Express Hotel & Suites SH
(252) 247-5001. **$73-$124.** 5063 Executive Dr. Jct US 70 and SR 24. Int corridors. **Pets:** Accepted.
✕ ⊟ ⊒ ⇔

MORGANTON

ⒶⒶⒶ ▼▼▼ Comfort Inn & Suites SH
(828) 430-4000. **$79-$169.** 1273 Burkemont Ave. I-40, exit 103, just s. Int corridors. **Pets:** Medium. $25 one-time fee/pet. Designated rooms, service with restrictions, crate.
SAVE SÒ ✕ ⒧M ⊟ ⊒ ⇔

▼▼▼ Holiday Inn-Morganton SH
(828) 437-0171. **$75-$89.** 2400 S Sterling St. I-40, exit 105 (SR 18), just s. Ext corridors. **Pets:** Other species. $25 one-time fee/room. Service with restrictions, crate.
ASK SÒ ✕ ⒧M ⊟ ⊒ ⍾ ⇔

▼▼ Sleep Inn SH
(828) 433-9000. **Call for rates.** 2400A S Sterling St. I-40, exit 105 (SR 18), just s. Int corridors. **Pets:** Accepted.
✕ ⊟ ⊒ ⇔

MORRISVILLE

▼▼ Extended StayAmerica-RDU Airport Ⓜ
(919) 380-1499. **$81-$90.** 2700 Slater Rd. I-40, exit 284 or 284A, 0.4 mi s on Airport Blvd, then just w. Ext corridors. **Pets:** Other species. $75 one-time fee/pet. Service with restrictions.
ASK SÒ ✕ ⊟ ⊒

▼▼▼ Holiday Inn Express SH
(919) 653-2260. **$89-$149, 3 day notice.** 1014 Airport Blvd. I-40, exit 284 or 284A, just s. Int corridors. **Pets:** Small, other species. $10 one-time fee/room. Service with restrictions.
ASK SÒ ✕ ⒧M ⊟ ⊒ ⇔

ⒶⒶⒶ ▼▼▼▼ La Quinta Inn SH
(919) 481-3600. **$112-$154.** 1001 Aerial Center Pkwy. I-40, exit 284 or 284A, just s, then just e. Int corridors. **Pets:** Other species. Service with restrictions, supervision.
SAVE SÒ ✕ ⒧M ⊟ ⊒ ⇔

ⒶⒶⒶ ▼▼▼▼ La Quinta Inn & Suites (Raleigh-Durham Int'l Airport) SH
(919) 461-1771. **$149-$189.** 1001 Hospitality Ct. I-40, exit 284 or 284A, just s, just e on Aerial Center Pkwy, then just ne; in Aerial Center Park. Int corridors. **Pets:** Other species. Service with restrictions, supervision.
SAVE SÒ ✕ ⒧M ⊟ ⊒ ⇔

▼▼▼▼ Staybridge Suites Raleigh Durham Airport SH
(919) 468-0180. **$99-$169, 3 day notice.** 1012 Airport Blvd. I-40, exit 284 or 284A, just s; enter between Hampton Inn and Holiday Inn Express. Int corridors. **Pets:** Small, other species. $10 one-time fee/room. Service with restrictions.
ASK SÒ ✕ ⒧M ⊟ ⊒ ✕

MOUNT AIRY

▼▼ Quality Inn Ⓜ
(336) 789-2000. **$60-$125.** 2136 Rockford St. Jct US 52, 0.6 mi s on US 601. Ext corridors. **Pets:** Medium. $25 one-time fee/room. Designated rooms, service with restrictions, supervision.
ASK SÒ ✕ ⊟ ⊒ ⇔

MURPHY

ⒶⒶⒶ ▼▼ Best Western of Murphy Ⓜ ❖
(828) 837-3060. **$63-$119.** 1522 Andrews Rd. US 74, 19 and SR 129, exit Andrews Rd. Ext corridors. **Pets:** Medium, other species. $20 daily fee/pet. Designated rooms, service with restrictions.
SAVE SÒ ✕ ⊟ ⊒ ⇔

ⒶⒶⒶ ▼▼ Days Inn Ⓜ
(828) 837-8030. **Call for rates.** 754 Hwy 64 W. US 64 W/19 S/74 W and 129 S. Ext corridors. **Pets:** Accepted.
SAVE ✕ ⊟ ⊒ ⇔

NEW BERN

▼▼ Days Hotel SH ❖
(252) 672-0222. **$129-$147.** 925 Broad St. US 70 Bypass, exit Trent Woods/Pembroke Rd, 0.7 mi w on SR 55, then 0.4 mi e. Int corridors. **Pets:** Large, other species. $20 daily fee/pet. Designated rooms, service with restrictions, supervision.
ASK SÒ ✕ ⒧M ⊟ ⊒ ⍾ ⇔

OUTER BANKS AREA

KILL DEVIL HILLS

▼▼▼ Clarion Oceanfront Hotel-Nags Head Beach SH
(252) 441-6333. **$59-$249.** 1601 S Virginia Dare Tr. SR 12, at MM 9.5. Int corridors. **Pets:** Accepted.
ASK SÒ ✕ ⊟ ⊒ ⍾ ⇔ ✕

▼▼ Quality Inn-John Yancey Ⓜ
(252) 441-7141. **$49-$270.** 2009 S Virginia Dare Tr. SR 12, at MM 10.3. Ext/int corridors. **Pets:** Accepted.
ASK SÒ ✕ ⊟ ⊒ ⇔

ⒶⒶⒶ ▼▼▼ Ramada Plaza Outer Banks Resort & Conference Center SH ❖
(252) 441-2151. **$79-$259.** 1701 S Virginia Dare Tr. SR 12, at MM 9.5. Int corridors. **Pets:** $20 daily fee/pet. Designated rooms.
SAVE SÒ ✕ ⊟ ⊒ ⍾ ⇔ ✕

ⒶⒶⒶ ▼▼▼ Travelodge-Nags Head Beach SH
(252) 441-0411. **Call for rates.** 804 N Virginia Dare Tr. SR 12, at MM 8.1. Ext/int corridors. **Pets:** Accepted.
SAVE ✕ ⊟ ⊒ ⇔

NAGS HEAD

▼▼▼ Comfort Inn Oceanfront South SH
(252) 441-6315. **Call for rates.** 8031 Old Oregon Inlet Rd. SR 12, at MM 17. Int corridors. **Pets:** Accepted.
✕ ⊟ ⊒ ⇔ ✕

OCRACOKE

◬◬ **▼▼▼** The Anchorage Inn ⨳
(252) 928-1101. **Call for rates.** 205 Irvin Garrish Hwy (SR 12). From Cedar Island Ferry, just n. Ext corridors. **Pets:** Other species. $20 daily fee/room. Designated rooms, service with restrictions, crate.
⌧✕🗑📺🏊⤬

END AREA

PINEHURST

◬◬ **▼▼▼▼** Homewood Suites by Hilton ⨳ 🐾
(910) 255-0300. **$119-$179.** 250 Central Park Ave. Jct SR 5 and 211; in Olmsted Village. Int corridors. **Pets:** $50 one-time fee/room. Designated rooms.
⌧✕🅼🗑📺🏊

RALEIGH

◬◬ **▼▼▼▼** Best Western Raleigh North ⨳
(919) 872-5000. **$92-$100, 14 day notice.** 2715 Capital Blvd. I-440, exit 11 or 11B, just n on US 1. Int corridors. **Pets:** Accepted.
⌧🅢✕🗑📺🏊

▼▼▼▼ Candlewood Suites-Crabtree ⨳
(919) 789-4840. **$109.** 4433 Lead Mine Rd. I-440, exit 7 or 7B, just w, then just n. Int corridors. **Pets:** Accepted.
Ⓐ⑊✕🅼🗑📺

◬◬ **▼▼▼▼** Comfort Suites ⨳
(919) 876-2211. **$94-$150.** 4400 Capital Blvd. I-440, exit 11 and 11B, 2.5 mi n on US 1. Int corridors. **Pets:** Accepted.
⌧🅢✕🗑📺

◬◬ **▼▼▼** Days Inn Ⓜ
(919) 878-9310. **$61, 7 day notice.** 3201 Wake Forest Rd. I-440, exit 10 (Wake Forest Rd), just n, then just w. Ext corridors. **Pets:** $10 daily fee/pet. Designated rooms, service with restrictions.
⌧🅢✕🗑📺🏊

▼▼ **▼▼** Extended StayAmerica-North Raleigh ⨳
(919) 829-7271. **$68-$75.** 911 Wake Towne Dr. I-440, exit 10 (Wake Forest Rd), just s, then w. Int corridors. **Pets:** Other species. $75 one-time fee/pet. Service with restrictions.
Ⓐ🅢✕🗑📺

◬◬ **▼▼▼▼** Fairfield Inn & Suites–Crabtree ⨳
(919) 881-9800. **$149-$159.** 2201 Summit Park Ln. I-440, exit 7 or 7B, just w on US 70, just s on Blue Ridge Rd, then just e. Int corridors. **Pets:** Large, other species. $100 one-time fee/room. Designated rooms, service with restrictions, supervision.
Ⓐ🅢✕🅼🗑📺🏊

◬◬ **▼▼▼▼** Hampton Inn Crabtree ⨳ 🐾
(919) 782-1112. **$89-$149.** 6209 Glenwood Ave. I-440, exit 7 or 7B, 2.5 mi w on US 70. Int corridors. **Pets:** Large. Service with restrictions, crate.
⌧🅢✕🅼🗑📺🏊⤬

▼▼▼▼ Holiday Inn Crabtree Valley Ⓛ 🐾
(919) 782-8600. **$89-$169.** 4100 Glenwood Ave. I-440, exit 7, just w on US 70. Int corridors. **Pets:** Medium, other species. $50 one-time fee/room. Service with restrictions, supervision.
Ⓐ🅢✕🅼🗑📺🍽🏊⤬

◬◬ **▼▼▼▼** Holiday Inn Raleigh-North Ⓛ
(919) 872-3500. **$120-$139.** 2805 Highwoods Blvd. I-440, exit 11 or 11B, just n on US 1, then just w. Int corridors. **Pets:** Accepted.
⌧✕🅼🗑📺🍽🏊⤬

▼▼ **▼▼** Homestead Studio Suites Hotel-Raleigh/Crabtree Valley ⨳
(919) 510-8551. **$68-$75.** 4810 Bluestone Dr. I-440, exit 7 or 7B, 1.6 mi w on US 70, then just s. Ext corridors. **Pets:** Other species. $75 one-time fee/pet. Service with restrictions.
Ⓐ🅢✕🗑📺

▼▼▼▼ Homestead Studio Suites Hotel-Raleigh/Northeast ⨳
(919) 807-9970. **$72-$80.** 2601 Appliance Ct. I-440, exit 11 or 11B, just n on US 1, then just e. Int corridors. **Pets:** Other species. $75 one-time fee/pet. Service with restrictions.
Ⓐ🅢✕🗑📺🏊

▼▼ **▼▼** Homestead Studio Suites Hotel-Raleigh/North Raleigh ⨳
(919) 981-7353. **$68-$75.** 3531 Wake Forest Rd. I-440, exit 10 (Wake Forest Rd), 0.5 mi n. Ext corridors. **Pets:** Other species. $75 one-time fee/pet. Service with restrictions.
Ⓐ🅢✕🅼🗑📺

◬◬ **▼▼▼▼** Homewood Suites by Hilton ⨳ 🐾
(919) 785-1131. **$89-$179.** 5400 Homewood Banks Dr. I-440, exit 7 or 7B, just w on US 70, just s on Blue Ridge Rd, just w on Crabtree Valley, then just s. Int corridors. **Pets:** Medium, dogs only. $49 one-time fee/room. Service with restrictions, crate.
⌧🅢✕🅼🗑📺

◬◬ **▼▼▼▼** La Quinta Inn & Suites Raleigh (Crabtree) ⨳
(919) 785-0071. **$112-$174.** 2211 Summit Park Ln. I-440, exit 7 or 7B, just w on US 70, just s on Blue Ridge Rd, then just e. Int corridors. **Pets:** Other species. Service with restrictions, supervision.
⌧🅢✕🅼🗑📺🏊

▼▼▼▼ Red Roof Inn-South ⨳
(919) 833-6005. **Call for rates.** 1813 S Saunders St. I-40, exit 298B, just n. Int corridors. **Pets:** Accepted.
✕🅼🗑

◬◬ **▼▼▼▼** Residence Inn by Marriott Crabtree ⨳
(919) 279-3000. **$174-$194.** 2200 Summit Park Ln. I-440, exit 7 or 7B, just w on US 70, just s on Blue Ridge Rd, then just e. Int corridors. **Pets:** Accepted.
Ⓐ🅢✕🅼🗑📺🏊⤬

◬◬ **▼▼▼▼** Residence Inn by Marriott-North Raleigh ⨳
(919) 878-6100. **$139-$159.** 1000 Navaho Dr. I-440, exit 10 (Wake Forest Rd), just n, then w. Ext corridors. **Pets:** Accepted.
Ⓐ🅢✕🅼🗑📺🏊⤬

◬◬ **▼▼▼▼** Sheraton Raleigh Ⓛ
(919) 834-9900. **$130.** 421 S Salisbury St. Just s; downtown. Int corridors. **Pets:** Accepted.
⌧🅢✕🗑📺🍽🏊

▼▼ **▼▼** StudioPLUS-North Raleigh ⨳
(919) 546-0879. **$72-$80.** 921 Wake Towne Dr. I-440, exit 10 (Wake Forest Rd), just s, then just w. Int corridors. **Pets:** Other species. $75 one-time fee/pet. Service with restrictions.
Ⓐ🅢✕🗑📺🏊

REIDSVILLE

Colonial Inn & Suites M
(336) 342-0341. **$45-$149.** 2100 Barnes St. US 29, exit 150 (Barnes St), just e. Ext corridors. **Pets:** Small. $10 daily fee/pet. Designated rooms, service with restrictions.
SAVE SD X ♿ 🛢 🖳 🐾

Comfort Inn M
(336) 634-1275. **$69-$179.** 2203 Barnes St. US 29, exit 150 (Barnes St), just e. Ext corridors. **Pets:** Very small. $15 daily fee/pet. Designated rooms, service with restrictions, supervision.
SAVE SD X ♿ 🛢 🖳 🐾

RESEARCH TRIANGLE PARK

Radisson Hotel in Research Triangle Park SH
(919) 549-8631. **$199-$239.** 150 Park Dr. I-40, exit 280, just s, then just w. Int corridors. **Pets:** Accepted.
ASK SD X 🛢 🖳 ▥ 🐾 ⊠

ROANOKE RAPIDS

Jameson Inn M
(252) 533-0022. **$68-$100.** 101 S Old Farm Rd. I-95, exit 173, 0.5 mi w on US 158, then just s. Ext corridors. **Pets:** Small. $15 daily fee/room. Service with restrictions, crate.
ASK SD X 🛢 🖳 🐾

ROBBINSVILLE

Microtel Inn & Suites SH
(828) 479-6772. **$70-$100.** 111 Rodney Orr Bypass (US 129). Center of downtown. Int corridors. **Pets:** Accepted.
ASK SD X ♿ 🛢 🖳

ROCKY MOUNT

Best Western Inn I-95 Gold Rock M
(252) 985-1450. **$65-$95.** 7095 NC 4. I-95, exit 145, just e. Ext corridors. **Pets:** Medium, other species. $20 daily fee/pet. Designated rooms, service with restrictions, supervision.
SAVE SD X 🛢 🖳 🐾

Comfort Inn SH
(252) 937-7765. **$70-$105.** 200 Gateway Blvd. I-95, exit 138, 1 mi e on US 64, exit Winstead Ave, then just s. Int corridors. **Pets:** Other species. $25 one-time fee/room. Service with restrictions.
SAVE SD X 🛢 🖳 🐾

Motel 6 SH
(252) 984-0907. **$37-$45.** 1370 N Weslyan Blvd. Jct US 64 Bypass, 1.5 mi n on US 301. Int corridors. **Pets:** Other species. Service with restrictions, supervision.
SD X 🛢 🐾

Quality Inn Rocky Mount SH
(252) 972-9400. **$59-$79.** 1200 Benvenue Rd. Jct US 301 Bypass, just n on SR 43/48. Ext/int corridors. **Pets:** Accepted.
ASK SD X ♿ 🛢 🐾

Residence Inn by Marriott SH ❀
(252) 451-5600. **$144-$164.** 230 Gateway Blvd. I-95, exit 138, 1 mi e on US 64, exit Winstead Ave, just s, then just e. Int corridors. **Pets:** Other species. $75 one-time fee/room. Service with restrictions, crate.
ASK SD X ♿ 🛢 🖳 🐾 ⊠

Super 8 Motel M
(252) 442-8075. **Call for rates (no credit cards).** 7522 Hwy 48. I-95, exit 145, just e, then just s. Ext corridors. **Pets:** Accepted.
X 🛢 🐾

ROXBORO

Hampton Inn SH
(336) 599-8800. **$79-$119, 3 day notice.** 920 Durham Rd. Jct US 158, n on US 501. Int corridors. **Pets:** Small, other species. $10 one-time fee/room. Service with restrictions.
ASK SD X 🛢 🖳 🐾

Innkeeper Roxboro M
(336) 599-3800. **$49-$79, 3 day notice.** 906 Durham Rd. Jct US 158, just n on US 501. Ext/int corridors. **Pets:** Small, other species. $10 one-time fee/room. Service with restrictions.
ASK SD X 🛢 🐾

SALISBURY

Hampton Inn SH
(704) 637-8000. **$109-$159, 3 day notice.** 1001 Klumac Rd. I-85, exit 75, just n on US 601, then just sw. Int corridors. **Pets:** Designated rooms, service with restrictions, supervision.
X 🛢 🖳 🐾

Holiday Inn SH
(704) 637-3100. **$90-$200.** 530 Jake Alexander Blvd S. I-85, exit 75, 0.5 mi n on US 601. Ext/int corridors. **Pets:** Small. $15 one-time fee/room. Service with restrictions, supervision.
ASK SD X ♿ 🛢 🖳 ▥ 🐾 ⊠

SALUDA

The Oaks Bed & Breakfast BB
(828) 749-9613. **Call for rates.** 339 Greenville St. I-26, exit 59, 1.1 mi sw, 0.3 mi w on US 176, then cross railway tracks. Ext/int corridors. **Pets:** Accepted.
X 🛢 🖳 ☑

SANFORD

Hampton Inn SH
(919) 775-2000. **$84-$109, 3 day notice.** 1904 S Horner Blvd. Jct US 1, 3.2 mi s on US 421 and SR 87. Int corridors. **Pets:** Small, other species. $10 one-time fee/room. Service with restrictions.
ASK SD X ♿ 🛢 🖳 🐾

Jameson Inn M
(919) 708-7400. **$68-$100.** 2614 S Horner Blvd. Jct US 1, 4.1 mi s on US 421 and SR 87. Ext corridors. **Pets:** Small. $15 daily fee/room. Service with restrictions, crate.
ASK SD X ♿ 🛢 🖳 🐾

SHELBY

Super 8 M
(704) 484-2101. **$50-$80.** 1716 E Dixon Blvd. Jct SR 180, 0.4 mi w on US 74 Bypass. Ext corridors. **Pets:** Small. $10 daily fee/pet. Service with restrictions, crate.
SAVE SD X 🛢 🖳

SMITHFIELD

Jameson Inn M
(919) 989-5901. **$68-$95.** 125 S Equity Dr. I-95, exit 95, just w, just n on Industrial Park Blvd, then just w. Ext corridors. **Pets:** Small. $15 daily fee/room. Service with restrictions, crate.
ASK SD X ♿ 🛢 🖳 🐾

Log Cabin Motel M
(919) 934-1534. **$45-$47.** 2491 US 70 E (Business Route). I-95, exit 95, 0.5 mi e. Ext corridors. **Pets:** Other species. $5 daily fee/pet. Designated rooms, service with restrictions.
SAVE X 🛢 🐾

Super 8 Motel SH
(919) 989-8988. **$62-$120.** 735 Industrial Park Dr. I-95, exit 95, just w, then just n. Int corridors. **Pets:** Small. $10 daily fee/room. Designated rooms, service with restrictions, supervision.
SAVE SD X ♿ 🛢 🖳 🐾

SOUTHERN PINES

▼▼ Econo Lodge Inn & Suites 🆂🅷
(910) 692-2063. **$60-$75.** 408 W Morganton Rd. US 1, exit Morganton Rd, just w. Int corridors. **Pets:** Other species. $20 daily fee/pet. Service with restrictions, crate.

🄰🅂🄺 🆂🍴 ✕ 🛏 💻

▼▼▼ Residence Inn by Marriott 🆂🅷
(910) 693-3400. **$189-$209.** 105 Brucewood Rd. Jct US 1, 1.2 mi n on US 15/501, then just e. Int corridors. **Pets:** Accepted.

🄰🅂🄺 🆂🍴 ✕ 🛏 💻 🏊 ✕

SOUTHPORT

◆◆◆◆ Comfort Suites 🆂🅷
(910) 454-7444. **$89-$149.** 4963 Southport Supply Rd (SR 211). Jct SR 87, 1.8 mi n. Int corridors. **Pets:** Medium, other species. $20 daily fee/pet. Service with restrictions, supervision.

🆂🄰🆅🄴 🆂🍴 ✕ 🛏 💻 🏊

SPRING LAKE

◆◆◆◆ Holiday Inn Express Hotel & Suites 🆂🅷
(910) 436-1900. **$94.** 103 Brook Ln. Jct SR 210, 0.9 mi nw on SR 24/87. Int corridors. **Pets:** Other species. $65 one-time fee/pet. Service with restrictions.

🆂🄰🆅🄴 🆂🍴 ✕ 🛏 💻 🏊 ✕

▼▼ Super 8 Motel 🆂🅷
(910) 436-8588. **Call for rates.** 256 S Main St. Jct SR 210, just se on SR 24/87, just s. Int corridors. **Pets:** Accepted.

✕ 🛏

SPRUCE PINE

◆◆◆◆ Richmond Inn 🅱🅱
(828) 765-6993. **Call for rates.** 51 Pine Ave. Exit off US 19 E and 226 to Oak Ave, just n on Walnut Ave, follow signs; center. Int corridors. **Pets:** $15 deposit/pet.

🆂🄰🆅🄴 ✕ 🛏 💻 🅩

STATESVILLE

◆◆◆ Best Western Statesville Inn 🆂🅷
(704) 881-0111. **$70-$140.** 1121 Morland Dr. I-77, exit 49A, just e on US 70 E. Ext corridors. **Pets:** Small. $15 daily fee/room. Designated rooms, service with restrictions, supervision.

🆂🄰🆅🄴 🆂🍴 ✕ 🛏 💻 🏊

◆◆ Econo Lodge Inn & Suites 🅼
(704) 872-4101. **$54-$100.** 740 Sullivan Rd. I-40, exit 151, just s. Ext corridors. **Pets:** Accepted.

🄰🅂🄺 ✕ ♿ 🛏 💻 🏊

▼▼ Quality Inn 🆂🅷
(704) 878-2721. **Call for rates.** 715 Sullivan Rd. I-40, exit 151, just s. Ext corridors. **Pets:** Accepted.

✕ 🛏 💻 🏊

◆▼ Super 8 Motel 🅼
(704) 878-9888. **$46-$99.** 1125 Greenland Dr. I-77, exit 49A, just e. Ext/int corridors. **Pets:** Small, dogs only. $10 daily fee/pet. Designated rooms, service with restrictions, supervision.

🄰🅂🄺 🆂🍴 ✕

SUNSET BEACH

◆◆◆ ◆◆◆◆ Sea Trail Golf Resort & Convention Center 🄲🅾
(910) 287-1100. **$75-$199, 3 day notice.** 211 Clubhouse Rd. US 17, 2.2 mi e on SR 904, then 1.5 mi s on SR 179. Ext corridors. **Pets:** $75 one-time fee/room. Designated rooms, service with restrictions, supervision.

🆂🄰🆅🄴 🆂🍴 ✕ 🛏 💻 🍴 🏊 ✕

THOMASVILLE

◆◆◆ ▼▼ Days Inn 🆂🅷
(336) 472-6600. **Call for rates.** 895 Lake Rd. I-85, exit 102, just w, then just s. Int corridors. **Pets:** Medium. $25 daily fee/pet. Designated rooms, service with restrictions, supervision.

🆂🄰🆅🄴 ✕ 🛏 🍴 🏊

▼▼ Microtel Inn & Suites 🆂🅷
(336) 474-4515. **$60-$130.** 959 Lake Rd. I-85, exit 102, just w, then just s. Int corridors. **Pets:** Small, dogs only. $25 one-time fee/pet. Designated rooms, service with restrictions, supervision.

🄰🅂🄺 🆂🍴 ✕ ♿ 🛏 💻

TRYON

◆◆◆ ◆◆◆◆ 1906 Pine Crest Inn & Restaurant 🄲🄸
(828) 859-9135. **Call for rates.** 85 Pine Crest Ln. I-26, exit 67, 4 mi e on SR 108, just s on New Market Rd, then just e. Ext/int corridors. **Pets:** Accepted.

🆂🄰🆅🄴 ✕ 🛏 💻 🍴

WAYNESVILLE

▼▼ Days Inn-Waynesville 🅼
(828) 452-9009. **Call for rates.** 232 Phillips Rd. US 23/74, exit 102, just sw. Ext corridors. **Pets:** Accepted.

✕ 🛏 💻 🏊

▼▼ The Lodge of Waynesville 🅼
(828) 452-0353. **$49-$125.** 909 Russ Ave. US 23/74, exit 102, just se. Ext corridors. **Pets:** Accepted.

✕ 🛏 💻 🏊

WELDON

◆◆◆ ▼▼ Days Inn 🅼
(252) 536-4867. **Call for rates.** 1611 Julian R Allsbrook Hwy. I-95, exit 173, just e on US 158. Ext corridors. **Pets:** Accepted.

🆂🄰🆅🄴 ✕ 🛏 🏊

WEST JEFFERSON

◆◆◆ ▼▼▼ Nation's Inn 🅼
(336) 246-2080. **$67-$73.** 107 Beaver Creek School Rd. Jct US 221, just n on SR 194, then just w. Ext corridors. **Pets:** Accepted.

🆂🄰🆅🄴 ✕ ♿ 🛏

WHITEVILLE

◆◆◆ ▼▼ Best Western Premiere Inn 🅼
(910) 642-2378. **Call for rates.** 503 N J K Powell Blvd. Jct US 74/76, 1 mi s on US 701 Bypass. Ext corridors. **Pets:** Accepted.

✕ 💻 🏊

WILLIAMSTON

▼▼▼ Hampton Inn 🆂🅷
(252) 809-1100. **Call for rates.** 1099 Hampton Ct. US 64, exit 514, just s on US 17, then just w. Int corridors. **Pets:** Accepted.

✕ 🛏 💻 🏊

▼▼▼ Holiday Inn 🆂🅷
(252) 792-3184. **$89.** 101 East Blvd. US 64, exit 514, 1.5 mi n on US 17 business route. Ext/int corridors. **Pets:** Other species. No service, supervision.

🄰🅂🄺 🆂🍴 ✕ 🛏 💻 🍴 🏊

WILMINGTON

▼▼ Baymont Inn 🅼
(910) 392-6767. **$71-$109.** 306 S College Rd. Jct US 17 business route, just s on SR 132. Ext/int corridors. **Pets:** Accepted.

🄰🅂🄺 🆂🍴 ✕ 🛏 💻 🏊

Comfort Inn Wilmington SH
(910) 791-4841. **Call for rates.** 151 S College Rd. Jct US 17 business route, just s on SR 132. Int corridors. **Pets:** Accepted.
SAVE ✕ 🛏 🖵 🐾

Courtyard by Marriott SH ❀
(910) 395-8224. **$99-$159.** 151 Van Campen Blvd. Jct US 17 business route, 0.3 mi s on SR 132, just se on Imperial Dr, then just w. Int corridors. **Pets:** Medium. $75 one-time fee/pet. Service with restrictions, crate.
SAVE S📵 ✕ 🐾M 🛏 🖵 🐾 ✕

Days Inn M
(910) 799-6300. **Call for rates.** 5040 Market St. Jct SR 132, 0.6 mi s on US 17 business route. Ext corridors. **Pets:** $15 daily fee/room. Service with restrictions, crate.
✕ 🛏 🖵 🍽 🐾

Extended StayAmerica-Wilmington-New Centre Drive
(910) 793-4508. **$76-$95.** 4929 New Centre Dr. Jct SR 132, 0.4 mi s on US 17 business route, just e. Int corridors. **Pets:** Other species. $75 one-time fee/pet. Service with restrictions.
ASK S📵 ✕ 🐾M 🛏 🖵

Innkeeper SH
(910) 799-4292. **$69-$119, 3 day notice.** 5345 W Market St. Jct SR 132, just s on US 17 business route. Int corridors. **Pets:** Small, other species. $10 one-time fee/room. Service with restrictions.
ASK S📵 ✕ 🛏 🐾

Jameson Inn SH
(910) 452-5660. **$71-$105.** 5102 Dunlea Ct. Jct SR 132, 0.5 mi s on US 17 business route, just w on New Centre Dr. Int corridors. **Pets:** Small. $15 daily fee/room. Service with restrictions, crate.
ASK S📵 ✕ 🛏 🖵 🐾

MainStay Suites SH
(910) 392-1741. **$89-$350, 7 day notice.** 5229 Market St. Jct SR 132, just s on US 17 business route. Int corridors. **Pets:** Small. $100 one-time fee/room. Designated rooms, service with restrictions, crate.
ASK S📵 ✕ 🐾M 🛏 🖵

Quality Inn M
(910) 791-8850. **Call for rates.** 4926 Market St. Jct SR 132, 0.9 mi s on US 17 business route. Ext corridors. **Pets:** Small. $25 daily fee/pet. Designated rooms, service with restrictions, supervision.
✕ 🛏 🖵 🐾

Residence Inn-Landfall SH
(910) 256-0098. **$149-$174.** 1200 Culbreth Dr. Jct US 17 business route, 2.4 mi e on US 74, 0.4 mi n on Military Cutoff Rd, then just e. Int corridors. **Pets:** Medium. $75 one-time fee/room. Designated rooms, service with restrictions.
ASK S📵 ✕ 🐾M 🛏 🖵 🐾 ✕

WILSON

Best Western-Wilson M
(252) 237-8700. **$54-$120.** 817-A Ward Blvd. US 264, exit 42, 2.6 mi n on Downing St, then just w. Ext corridors. **Pets:** Small. $10 daily fee/pet. Designated rooms, service with restrictions.
SAVE S📵 ✕ 🛏 🖵 🐾

Days Inn SH
(252) 291-2323. **$64-$89.** 1801 S Tarboro St. US 264, exit 40, 3.3 mi e on SR 42. Ext corridors. **Pets:** Accepted.
SAVE S📵 ✕ 🛏 🖵 🐾

Jameson Inn M
(252) 234-7172. **Call for rates.** 5016 Hayes Pl. I-95, exit 121, just w, then just n. Ext corridors. **Pets:** Small. $10 daily fee/pet. Service with restrictions, crate.
✕ 🛏 🖵 🐾

WINSTON-SALEM

Augustus T Zevely Inn BB
(336) 748-9299. **$95-$240, 14 day notice.** 803 S Main St. I-40 business route, exit 5D eastbound, 0.5 mi s on Liberty St to Old Salem Rd, just e on Academy St, then just s; exit 5C westbound, just n on Cherry St, just e on 2nd St, 1 mi s on Liberty St to Old Salem Rd, just e on Academy St, then just s. Ext/int corridors. **Pets:** Small. $20 daily fee/pet. Designated rooms, service with restrictions, supervision.
SAVE S📵 ✕ 🛏

Best Western Salem Inn & Suites SH
(336) 725-8561. **$75-$82.** 127 S Cherry St. I-40 business route, exit 5C (Cherry St) eastbound, just e on High St, then just s; exit westbound, just w on 1st St, just s on Marshall St, just e on High St, then just s. Ext corridors. **Pets:** Medium. $25 one-time fee/pet. Designated rooms, service with restrictions, supervision.
ASK S📵 ✕ 🛏 🖵 🐾

Crossland Economy Studios M
(336) 759-7780. **$63-$70.** 7910 North Point Blvd. US 52, exit 115B, 2 mi s on University Pkwy, then just e. Ext corridors. **Pets:** Other species. $75 one-time fee/pet. Service with restrictions.
ASK S📵 ✕

Extended StayAmerica Winston-Salem-Hanes Mall Blvd M
(336) 768-0075. **$72-$80.** 1995 Hampton Inn Ct. I-40, exit 189 (Stratford Rd), just s, just e on Hanes Mall Blvd, then just n. Ext corridors. **Pets:** Other species. $75 one-time fee/pet. Service with restrictions.
ASK S📵 ✕ 🛏 🖵

The Hawthorne Inn & Conference Center SH
(336) 777-3000. **$79-$129.** 420 High St. I-40 business route, exit 5C (Cherry St) eastbound, just e; exit westbound, just w on 1st St, then just s on Marshall St. Int corridors. **Pets:** Medium, other species. $15 daily fee/pet. Designated rooms, service with restrictions, crate.
SAVE S📵 ✕ 🐾M 🛏 🖵 🍽 🐾

Innkeeper M
(336) 721-0062. **$39-$69, 3 day notice.** 2115 Peters Creek Pkwy. I-40, exit 192 (Peters Creek Pkwy), just e on SR 150. Ext/int corridors. **Pets:** Small, other species. $10 one-time fee/room. Service with restrictions.
ASK S📵 ✕ 🛏 🐾

La Quinta Inns & Suites Winston-Salem SH
(336) 765-8777. **$112-$149.** 2020 Griffith Rd. I-40, exit 189 (Stratford Rd), just s, just e on Hanes Mall Blvd, then just s. Int corridors. **Pets:** Other species. Service with restrictions, supervision.
SAVE S📵 ✕ 🐾M 🛏 🖵 🐾

Quality Inn & Suites-Hanes Mall SH
(336) 765-6670. **$69-$150.** 2008 S Hawthorne Rd. I-40 business route, exit 2A, 0.5 mi s on Silas Creek Pkwy, then just e. Ext corridors. **Pets:** Accepted.
SAVE S📵 ✕ 🐾M 🛏 🖵 🍽 🐾

Quality Inn-Coliseum SH
(336) 767-8240. **$65-$110.** 531 Akron Dr. US 52, exit 112, just e. Int corridors. **Pets:** Small. $15 daily fee/pet. Service with restrictions, supervision.
SAVE S📵 ✕ 🛏 🖵 🍽 🐾

Quality Inn University SH
(336) 767-9009. **Call for rates.** 5719 University Pkwy. US 52, exit 115B, 0.4 mi w. Ext corridors. **Pets:** Other species. $25 one-time fee/room. Designated rooms, service with restrictions, supervision.
SAVE ✕ 🖵 🐾

Residence Inn by Marriott SH
(336) 759-0777. **$155-$175.** 7835 N Point Blvd. US 52 N, exit 115B, 2 mi s on University Pkwy, then just e. Ext corridors. **Pets:** Accepted.
ASK S📵 ✕ 🛏 🖵 🐾 ✕

Sundance Plaza Hotel and Spa 🆂🅷
(336) 723-2911. **$150.** 3050 University Pkwy. I-40 business route, exit 5C (Cherry St), 3 mi n. Int corridors. **Pets:** Small. $25 one-time fee/room. Service with restrictions, supervision.
[SAVE] [S🄳] [✕] [🖥] [🖵] [🍴] [⇌]

YADKINVILLE

◈◈ Days Inn 🆂🅷
(336) 679-5000. **Call for rates.** 220 Sharon Dr. US 421, exit 257, just s on US 601, then just e. Int corridors. **Pets:** Accepted.
[✕] [🄼] [🖥] [🖵] [⇌]

YANCEYVILLE

 Days Inn 🅼
(336) 694-9494. **$65-$170.** 1858 NC Hwy 86 N. Jct SR 62, 1.6 mi nw on US 158/SR 86. Ext corridors. **Pets:** Medium. $10 daily fee/pet. Designated rooms, service with restrictions, supervision.
[A$K] [S🄳] [✕] [🖥] [⇌]

NORTH DAKOTA

CITY INDEX

BEULAH

▼▼▼ AmericInn Lodge & Suites SH
(701) 873-2220. $62-$79. 2100 2nd Ave NW. Jct SR 49/200, 1.2 mi s. Int corridors. **Pets:** Accepted.
ASK SÒ ⊠ ⫶M 🖥 💻 ⤼

BISMARCK

⨀ ▼▼▼ Best Western Doublewood Inn SH
(701) 258-7000. $60-$110. 1400 E Interchange Ave. I-94, exit 159 (US 83), just s. Int corridors. **Pets:** Other species. $10 daily fee/room. Designated rooms, service with restrictions, crate.
SAVE SÒ ⊠ ⫶M 🖥 💻 🍴 ⤼ ⊠

⨀ ▼▼▼▼ Best Western Ramkota Hotel SH
(701) 258-7700. $109-$125. 800 S 3rd St. Just s of jct I-94 business loop (Bismarck Expy) and S 3rd St. Int corridors. **Pets:** Accepted.
SAVE SÒ ⊠ ⫶M 🖥 💻 🍴 ⤼ ⊠

▼▼ Comfort Inn SH
(701) 223-1911. $70-$80. 1030 Interstate Ave. I-94, exit 159 (US 83), 0.3 mi nw. Int corridors. **Pets:** Accepted.
ASK SÒ ⊠ 🖥 💻 ⤼ ⊠

⨀ ▼▼▼ Days Inn-Bismarck SH
(701) 223-9151. $69-$139. 1300 E Capitol Ave. I-94, exit 159 (US 83), just s. Int corridors. **Pets:** Accepted.
SAVE SÒ ⊠ 🖥 💻 ⤼ ⊠

▼▼ Expressway Inn SH
(701) 222-2900. $70-$95. 200 Bismarck Expwy. Jct I-94 business loop (Bismarck Expwy) and S 3rd St. Int corridors. **Pets:** Accepted.
ASK SÒ ⊠ ⫶M 🖥 💻 ⤼ ⊠

▼▼ Kelly Inn SH
(701) 223-8001. $65-$125. 1800 N 12th St. I-94, exit 159 (US 83), 0.3 mi s. Int corridors. **Pets:** Accepted.
ASK SÒ ⊠ ⫶M 🖥 💻 🍴 ⤼ ⊠

⨀ ▼▼▼▼ Radisson Hotel Bismarck LH
(701) 255-6000. $97. 605 E Broadway Ave. Jct 6th St; center. Int corridors. **Pets:** Other species. $20 one-time fee/room. Service with restrictions, supervision.
SAVE SÒ ⊠ ⫶M 🖥 💻 🍴 ⤼ ⊠

⨀ ▼▼▼ Ramada Limited SH
(701) 221-3030. $84-$105. 3808 E Divide Ave. I-94, exit 161 (Bismarck Expwy), just s. Int corridors. **Pets:** Other species. $10 daily fee/room. Service with restrictions, crate.
SAVE SÒ ⊠ ⫶M 🖥 💻 ⤼ ⊠

⨀ ▼▼ Select Inn SH
(701) 223-8060. $50-$71. 1505 Interchange Ave. I-94, exit 159 (US 83), just se. Int corridors. **Pets:** Medium. $25 deposit/room. Designated rooms, service with restrictions, supervision.
SAVE SÒ ⊠ 🖥 💻

CARRINGTON

▼▼ Carrington Inn & Suites SH
(701) 652-3982. $58-$86. 101 4th Ave S. Jct US 52 and 281, 0.5 mi e on US 52; just s of jct SR 200. Int corridors. **Pets:** Accepted.
ASK SÒ ⊠ 🖥

▼▼ Chieftain Conference Center SH
(701) 652-3131. $60-$100. 60 4th Ave S. Jct US 52 and 281, 0.5 mi e on US 52; just s of jct SR 200. Ext/int corridors. **Pets:** Accepted.
ASK SÒ ⊠ 🖥 🍴

CASSELTON

⨀ ▼▼▼ Governors' Inn SH
(701) 347-4524. $28-$48. 2050 Governors Dr. I-94, exit 331 (SR 18), just n. Int corridors. **Pets:** Other species. $9 daily fee/pet. Designated rooms, service with restrictions, crate.
SAVE ⊠ ⫶M 🖥 💻 🍴 ⤼ ⊠

DEVILS LAKE

⨀ ▼▼▼ Fireside Inn & Suites SH 🐾
(701) 662-6760. $69-$89. 215 Hwy 2 E. Jct US 2 and SR 20. Int corridors. **Pets:** $10 one-time fee/pet. Service with restrictions, supervision.
SAVE SÒ ⊠ 🖥 💻 ⤼ ⊠

⨀ ▼ Trails West Motel M
(701) 662-5011. $50-$55. 111 1st St W. 0.8 mi sw on US 2. Int corridors. **Pets:** $5 daily fee/pet. Service with restrictions, supervision.
SAVE SÒ ⊠ 🖥

DICKINSON

▼▼ AmericInn Motel & Suites of Dickinson SH
(701) 225-1400. **Call for rates.** 229 15th St W. I-94, exit 61 (SR 22), just n, then e. Int corridors. **Pets:** Accepted.
⊠ ⫶M 🖥 💻 ⤼

▼▼ Comfort Inn SH
(701) 264-7300. $69-$170. 493 Elks Dr. I-94, exit 61 (SR 22), just n, then w. Int corridors. **Pets:** Accepted.
ASK SÒ ⊠ ⫶M 🖥 💻 ⤼ ⊠

⨀ ▼▼▼▼ Hartfiel Inn BB 🐾
(701) 225-6710. $89-$109. 509 3rd Ave W. I-94, exit 61 (SR 22), 0.8 mi s. Int corridors. **Pets:** Medium, dogs only. Designated rooms, service with restrictions, supervision.
SAVE ⊠ 🖥 💻

EDGELEY

▼▼ Prairie Rose Inn SH
(701) 493-2075. $55-$80. 111 Frontage Rd. Jct US 281 and SR 13. Ext/int corridors. **Pets:** Accepted.
ASK SÒ ⊠ 🖥

FARGO

⨀ ▼▼▼ AmericInn Lodge & Suites SH
(701) 234-9946. $78-$142. 1423 35th St SW. I-29, exit 64 (13th Ave S), just se. Int corridors. **Pets:** $10 daily fee/pet. Designated rooms, service with restrictions, supervision.
SAVE ⊠ 🖥 💻 ⤼ ⊠

⨀ ▼▼▼ Best Western Fargo Doublewood Inn SH
(701) 235-3333. $77-$81. 3333 13th Ave S. I-29, exit 64 (13th Ave S), 0.3 mi e. Int corridors. **Pets:** Medium, dogs only. $25 deposit/room. Service with restrictions, supervision.
SAVE SÒ ⊠ ⫶M 🖥 💻 🍴 ⤼ ⊠

WYWY Candlewood Suites 🅢🅗 🐾
(701) 235-8200. **$99-$139.** 1831 NDSU Research Park Dr. I-29, exit 67 (19th Ave), 1.6 mi e. Int corridors. **Pets:** Other species. $75 one-time fee/room. Service with restrictions, crate.
🆂🅰🆅🅴 🆂🖭 ✖ 🔥🅼 🔋 💻 ➳

WY Comfort Inn by Choice Hotels East 🅢🅗
(701) 280-9666. **Call for rates.** 1407 35th St S. I-29, exit 64 (13th Ave S), just se. Int corridors. **Pets:** Accepted.
✖ 🔋 💻 ➳

WY Comfort Inn by Choice Hotels West 🅢🅗
(701) 282-9596. **Call for rates.** 3825 9th Ave SW. I-29, exit 64 (13th Ave S), just nw. Int corridors. **Pets:** Accepted.
✖ 🔋 💻 ➳

WY Comfort Suites by Choice Hotels 🅢🅗
(701) 237-5911. **Call for rates.** 1415 35th St SW. I-29, exit 64 (13th Ave S), just se. Int corridors. **Pets:** Accepted.
✖ 🔥🅼 🔋 💻 ➳

WYWY Country Inn & Suites By Carlson 🅢🅗
(701) 234-0565. **Call for rates.** 3316 13th Ave S. I-29, exit 64 (13th Ave S), 0.3 mi e. Int corridors. **Pets:** Accepted.
✖ 🔋 💻 ➳ ✖

WY Econo Lodge by Choice Hotels 🅢🅗
(701) 232-3412. **Call for rates.** 1401 35th St S. I-29, exit 64 (13th Ave S), just se. Int corridors. **Pets:** Accepted.
✖ 🔋 💻

WY Expressway Inn 🅢🅗
(701) 235-3141. **$82.** 1340 21st Ave S. I-94, exit 351 (University Dr), just sw. Ext/int corridors. **Pets:** Accepted.
🅰🆂🅺 ✖ 🔥🅼 🔋 💻 🍴 ➳ ✖

WY Holiday Inn 🅛🅗
(701) 282-2700. **$99-$169.** 3803 13th Ave S. I-29, exit 64 (13 Ave S), just nw. Int corridors. **Pets:** Other species. $10 one-time fee/room. Service with restrictions, supervision.
🆂🅰🆅🅴 ✖ 🔥🅼 🔋 💻 🍴 ➳ ✖

WYWY Holiday Inn Express Fargo 🅢🅗
(701) 282-2000. **$110.** 1040 40th St S. I-29, exit 64 (13th Ave S), just nw. Int corridors. **Pets:** Accepted.
✖ 🔥🅼 🔋 💻 ➳ ✖

WY Kelly Inn 13th Avenue 🅢🅗
(701) 277-8821. **$79-$120.** 4207 13th Ave SW. I-29, exit 64 (13th Ave S), 0.5 mi w. Ext/int corridors. **Pets:** Medium, other species. Service with restrictions, crate.
🅰🆂🅺 🆂🖭 ✖ 🔥🅼 🔋 💻 ➳

WY Kelly Inn on Main Avenue 🅢🅗
(701) 282-9700. **$70-$115.** 3800 Main Ave. I-29, exit 65 (Main Ave), just w. Ext/int corridors. **Pets:** Medium, other species. Service with restrictions, crate.
🅰🆂🅺 🆂🖭 ✖ 🔋 💻 🍴 ➳ ✖

WYWY MainStay Suites 🅢🅗
(701) 277-4627. **$85-$149.** 1901 44th St SW. I-94, exit 348 (45th St), just n, then just e. Int corridors. **Pets:** Accepted.
🅰🆂🅺 🆂🖭 ✖ 🔥🅼 🔋 💻 ➳ ✖

WY Select Inn 🅢🅗 🐾
(701) 282-6300. **Call for rates.** 1025 38th St SW. I-29, exit 64 (13th Ave S), just w, then n. Int corridors. **Pets:** Large. $25 deposit/room. Service with restrictions, supervision.
🆂🅰🆅🅴 ✖ 💻

WY Sleep Inn 🅢🅗
(701) 281-8240. **$60-$89.** 1921 44 St SW. I-94, exit 348 (45th St), just n, then just e. Int corridors. **Pets:** Accepted.
✖ 🔥🅼 🔋 💻 ➳ ✖

WY Staybridge Suites 🅢🅗
(701) 281-4900. **$109-$299.** 4300 20th Ave S. I-94, exit 348 (45th St), just n, then e. Int corridors. **Pets:** Accepted.
🆂🅰🆅🅴 🆂🖭 ✖ 🔥🅼 🔋 💻 ➳ ✖

WY Super 8 Motel 🅢🅗
(701) 232-9202. **$51-$130.** 3518 Interstate Blvd. I-29, exit 64 (13th Ave S), just n on east frontage road. Int corridors. **Pets:** Accepted.
🅰🆂🅺 🆂🖭 ✖ 🔋 💻 ➳

GRAFTON

WY AmericInn Motel & Suites 🅢🅗
(701) 352-2788. **$79-$199.** 1015 12th St W. SR 17, 1.2 mi w. Int corridors. **Pets:** Accepted.
🅰🆂🅺 🆂🖭 ✖ 🔥🅼 🔋 💻 ➳ ✖

GRAND FORKS

WY Americas Best Value Inn of Grand Forks 🅜
(701) 775-0555. **$42-$80.** 1000 N 42nd St. I-29, exit 141 (Gateway Dr), jct US 2, then just se. Int corridors. **Pets:** Medium. $25 deposit/pet, $10 daily fee/pet. Designated rooms, service with restrictions, supervision.
🆂🅰🆅🅴 🆂🖭 ✖ 🔋

WY Best Western Town House 🅢🅗
(701) 746-5411. **$60-$100, 15 day notice.** 710 1st Ave N. I-29, exit 140 (DeMers Ave), 3 mi e; downtown. Int corridors. **Pets:** Medium. $15 daily fee/room. Designated rooms, service with restrictions, supervision.
🅰🆂🅺 ✖ 🔋 💻 🍴 ➳ ✖

WY Days Inn 🅢🅗
(701) 775-0060. **Call for rates.** 3101 34th St S. I-29, exit 138 (32nd Ave), 0.5 mi e. Int corridors. **Pets:** $5 daily fee/pet. Designated rooms, service with restrictions, supervision.
🆂🅰🆅🅴 ✖ 🔋 💻 ➳

WY Ramada Inn 🅢🅗
(701) 775-3951. **Call for rates.** 1205 N 43rd St. I-29, exit 141 (Gateway Dr), just se of US 2. Int corridors. **Pets:** Medium. Designated rooms, service with restrictions, supervision.
🆂🅰🆅🅴 ✖ 🔋 💻 🍴 ➳ ✖

WY Travelodge 🅢🅗
(701) 772-8151. **Call for rates.** 2100 S Washington St. I-29, exit 140 (Demers Ave), 2.5 mi e, then 1.5 mi s. Int corridors. **Pets:** Accepted.
✖ 🔋 💻 ➳ ✖

JAMESTOWN

WY Comfort Inn by Choice Hotels 🅢🅗
(701) 252-7125. **Call for rates.** 811 20th St SW. I-94, exit 258 (US 281), just n, then just w. Int corridors. **Pets:** Accepted.
✖ 🔋 💻 ➳

WY Quality Inn & Suites 🅢🅗 🐾
(701) 252-3611. **$60-$100.** 507 25th St SW. I-94, exit 258 (US 281), just s. Int corridors. **Pets:** Medium. $10 one-time fee/room. Designated rooms, service with restrictions, supervision.
🆂🅰🆅🅴 🆂🖭 ✖ 🔋 💻 ➳

KENMARE

WY Quilt Inn 🅢🅗
(701) 385-4100. **$55-$65.** 1232 Central Ave N. Just n on US 52. Int corridors. **Pets:** Accepted.
🅰🆂🅺 🆂🖭 ✖ 🔋 ➳

MANDAN

WY Best Western Seven Seas Hotel & Waterpark 🅢🅗
(701) 663-7401. **$95-$104.** 2611 Old Red Tr. I-94, exit 152 (Sunset Dr), just nw. Int corridors. **Pets:** Accepted.
🆂🅰🆅🅴 🆂🖭 ✖ 🔥🅼 🔋 💻 🍴 ➳ ✖

MEDORA

AmericInn Motel & Suites SH
(701) 623-4800. **Call for rates.** 75 E River Rd S. I-94, exit 24, just se of downtown. Int corridors. **Pets:** Accepted.
(SAVE) (X) (&M) (🛏) (💻) (🌊) (X)

MINOT

Best Western Kelly Inn SH
(701) 852-4300. **$79-$199.** 1510 26th Ave SW. US 2 and 52 Bypass, at 16th St SW. Ext/int corridors. **Pets:** Other species. Service with restrictions, crate.
(ASK) (S0) (X) (🛏) (💻) (🌊) (X)

Comfort Inn SH
(701) 852-2201. **$90-$200.** 1515 22nd Ave SW. US 2 and 52 Bypass, at 16th St SW. Int corridors. **Pets:** Small. $10 daily fee/room. Service with restrictions, supervision.
(SAVE) (S0) (X) (🛏) (💻) (🌊) (X)

Days Inn SH
(701) 852-3646. **Call for rates.** 2100 4th St SW. Jct US 2 and 52 Bypass, just n. Int corridors. **Pets:** Accepted.
(X) (🛏) (💻) (🌊)

Fairfield Inn by Marriott SH
(701) 838-2424. **$78-$98.** 900 24th Ave SW. 0.5 mi e of jct US 2, 52 Bypass and 16th St SW. Int corridors. **Pets:** Accepted.
(ASK) (S0) (X) (&M) (🛏) (💻) (🌊)

Sleep Inn & Suites LH
(701) 837-3100. **$109-$199.** 2400 10th St SW. US 2 and 52 Bypass at 16th St SW; southeast corner of Dakota Square Mall. Int corridors. **Pets:** Accepted.
(ASK) (S0) (X) (&M) (🛏) (💻) (🌊) (X)

VALLEY CITY

AmericInn Lodge & Suites SH
(701) 845-5551. **Call for rates.** 280 Winter Show Rd SE. I-94, exit 292, just ne. Int corridors. **Pets:** Accepted.
(SAVE) (X) (&M) (🛏) (💻) (🌊) (X)

Super 8 Motel-Valley City M
(701) 845-1140. **$55-$75.** 860 11th St SW. I-94, exit 292, just nw. Int corridors. **Pets:** Accepted.
(ASK) (S0) (X) (🛏) (💻)

WAHPETON

AmericInn Lodge & Suites SH
(701) 642-8365. **Call for rates.** 2029 Two-Ten Dr. 1 mi n on SR 210 Bypass. Int corridors. **Pets:** Accepted.
(X) (🛏) (💻) (🌊)

Rodeway Inn SH
(701) 642-1115. **$50-$80, 15 day notice.** 209 13th St S. SR 13, 0.3 mi e of jct SR 210 Bypass. Int corridors. **Pets:** Accepted.
(X) (🛏) (💻) (🌊)

Wahpeton Super 8 SH
(701) 642-8731. **Call for rates.** 995 21st Ave N. 1.5 mi n on SR 210 Bypass. Int corridors. **Pets:** Accepted.
(X) (🛏) (💻) (🌊)

WATFORD CITY

McKenzie Inn M
(701) 444-3980. **$56-$110.** 132 SW 3rd St. US 85, just w. Ext corridors. **Pets:** Medium. $5 daily fee/room. Designated rooms, service with restrictions, supervision.
(SAVE) (S0) (X) (🛏)

Roosevelt Inn & Suites SH
(701) 842-3686. **$58-$66.** 600 2nd Ave SW. US 85, 0.3 mi w. Int corridors. **Pets:** Medium. $5 daily fee/pet. Service with restrictions, supervision.
(SAVE) (S0) (X) (🛏) (💻) (🌊)

WILLISTON

El Rancho Motor Hotel SH
(701) 572-6321. **$49-$80.** 1623 2nd Ave W. 1 mi n on US 2 and 85 N Bypass. Ext/int corridors. **Pets:** Accepted.
(SAVE) (S0) (X) (🛏) (💻) (🍴)

Marquis Plaza & Suites SH
(701) 774-3250. **$76-$82.** 1525 9th Ave NW. US 2 and 85, 4 mi e of jct US 85. Int corridors. **Pets:** Small, dogs only. $10 daily fee/pet. Designated rooms, service with restrictions, supervision.
(SAVE) (S0) (X) (🛏) (💻) (🌊)

AKRON

▼▼▼ Red Roof Inn-Akron South #0207 M
(330) 644-7748. **Call for rates.** 2939 S Arlington Rd. I-77, exit 120, just n. **Pets:** Accepted.

ALLIANCE

▼▼ Comfort Inn SH ❀
(330) 821-5555. **$75-$95.** 2500 W State St. 2.5 mi w on US 62. Int corridors. **Pets:** $10 daily fee/pet. Designated rooms, service with restrictions, supervision.

▼▼▼▼ Holiday Inn Express Hotel & Suites SH
(330) 821-6700. **$99-$199.** 2341 W State St. 2 mi w on US 62. Int corridors. **Pets:** Small. $10 one-time fee/pet. Designated rooms, service with restrictions, crate.

▼▼▼ Super 8 Motel M
(330) 821-5688. **$56-$92.** 2330 W State St. 2 mi w on US 62. Ext corridors. **Pets:** $5 daily fee/pet. Service with restrictions.

AMHERST

▼▼ Days Inn M
(440) 985-1428. **Call for rates.** 934 N Leavitt Rd. SR 58, 0.3 mi n of SR 2. Ext/int corridors. **Pets:** Accepted.

ASHLAND

▼▼▼ Days Inn M
(419) 289-0101. **$43-$89.** 1423 CR 1575. I-71, exit 186, just w. Ext corridors. **Pets:** Other species. Service with restrictions, supervision.

▼▼ The Surrey Inn SH ❀
(419) 289-7700. **$69-$79.** 1065 Claremont Ave. 1 mi s. Int corridors. **Pets:** Medium, dogs only. $15 one-time fee/room. Designated rooms, supervision.

ASHTABULA

▼▼ Cedars Motel M ❀
(440) 992-5406. **$80.** 2015 W Prospect Rd. Jct SR 11, 3 mi w on US 20. Ext corridors. **Pets:** Other species. $5 one-time fee/pet. Service with restrictions, supervision.

▼▼ Ho Hum Motel M
(440) 969-1136. **$55-$80.** 3801 N Ridge Rd W. I-90, exit 223, 3 mi n on SR 45, then 1 mi e on SR 20. Ext corridors. **Pets:** Other species. $5 one-time fee/pet. Service with restrictions, supervision.

ATHENS

▼▼ Budget Host-Coach Inn M
(740) 594-2294. **$55-$115, 3 day notice.** 100 Albany Rd (Hwy 50 W). US 50, exit westbound, just past Richland Ave exit; exit eastbound, on Township Rd 60. Ext corridors. **Pets:** Small, dogs only. $10 daily fee/pet. Designated rooms, service with restrictions, supervision.

▼▼▼▼ The Ohio University Inn & Conference Center SH
(740) 593-6661. **$99-$189, 6 day notice.** 331 Richland Ave. 1 mi w on US 33 and 50. Int corridors. **Pets:** Accepted.

AUSTINBURG

▼▼ Comfort Inn-Ashtabula SH
(440) 275-2711. **Call for rates.** 1860 Austinburg Rd. I-90, exit 223, just n. Int corridors. **Pets:** Accepted.

AUSTINTOWN

▼▼ Austintown Super 8 Motel M
(330) 793-7788. **$42-$85.** 5280 76 Dr. I-80, exit 223, just s on SR 46. Int corridors. **Pets:** $10 daily fee/pet. Service with restrictions, supervision.
ASK SO X B B

▼▼ Best Western Meander Inn SH
(330) 544-2378. **$69-$86, 7 day notice.** 870 N Canfield-Niles Rd. I-80, exit 223, 0.3 mi s on SR 46. Int corridors. **Pets:** Other species. $10 daily fee/pet. Service with restrictions, supervision.
SAVE SO X B B TI

▼▼▼ Comfort Inn & Suites M
(330) 792-9740. **Call for rates.** 5425 Clarkins Dr. I-80, exit 223B, just n. Ext corridors. **Pets:** Accepted.
X B B

BEAVERCREEK

▼▼▼ Residence Inn by Marriott Beavercreek SH
(937) 427-3914. **$171-$209.** 2779 Fairfield Commons. I-675, exit 17, just e, just s on New Germany-Trebein, then just e. Int corridors. **Pets:** Accepted.
ASK SO X SM B B

BELLEFONTAINE

▼▼ Comfort Inn Bellefontaine SH
(937) 599-5555. **$78-$87.** 260 Northview Dr. Jct US 33 and SR 68, just ne. Int corridors. **Pets:** Accepted.
ASK SO X B B

BLUFFTON

▼▼▼ Comfort Inn SH
(419) 358-6000. **$80-$105.** 117 Commerce Ln. I-75, exit 142, just w on SR 103. Int corridors. **Pets:** Medium, other species. $25 one-time fee/pet. Service with restrictions, supervision.
SAVE SO X B B

BOARDMAN

▼▼▼ Americas Best Value Inn & Suites SH
(330) 549-0157. **$49-$121.** 9988 Market St. 0.5 mi n on SR 7. Int corridors. **Pets:** Accepted.
SAVE SO X SM B B

▼▼ Days Inn M
(330) 758-2371. **Call for rates.** 8392 Market St. I-76, exit 232, 1.8 mi n on SR 7. Ext corridors. **Pets:** Accepted.
X B B

▼▼ Microtel Inn Youngstown SH
(330) 758-1816. **Call for rates.** 7393 South Ave. Jct I-680 and US 224, 0.3 mi w. Int corridors. **Pets:** Accepted.
X B

BOSTON HEIGHTS

▼▼▼ Comfort Inn SH
(330) 650-2040. **$55-$99.** 6731 Industrial Pkwy. I-80/90, exit 180, 0.3 mi n on SR 8. Int corridors. **Pets:** Other species. $10 daily fee/pet. Service with restrictions.
SAVE SO X SM B B

BOTKINS

▼▼ Budget Host Western Ohio Inn M
(937) 693-6911. **$45-$60.** 505 E State St. I-75, exit 104 (SR 219), just w. Ext corridors. **Pets:** $40 deposit/pet. Designated rooms, service with restrictions, supervision.
SAVE SO X B TI

BOWLING GREEN

▼▼ Days Inn of Bowling Green M
(419) 352-5211. **$39-$180.** 1550 E Wooster St. I-75, exit 181, just w. Ext corridors. **Pets:** Large, other species. $10 one-time fee/room. Supervision.
SAVE SO X B B

BRUNSWICK

▼▼ Sleep Inn SH
(330) 273-1112. **$62-$99.** 1435 S Carpenter Rd. I-71, exit 226, just w. Ext corridors. **Pets:** Accepted.
ASK SO X B B

BRYAN

▼▼▼ Colonial Manor Motel M
(419) 636-3123. **$73-$115.** 924 E High St. US 127, 0.8 mi e on SR 2/34. Ext corridors. **Pets:** Medium. Designated rooms, no service, crate.
SAVE X B B TI

CAMBRIDGE

▼▼ Best Western Cambridge SH
(740) 439-3581. **$44-$89.** 1945 Southgate Pkwy. I-70, exit 178, 0.3 mi n on SR 209. Ext corridors. **Pets:** Small. $10 daily fee/pet. Service with restrictions, supervision.
SAVE SO X B B

▼ Budget Inn M 🐾
(740) 432-2304. **$30-$50.** 6405 Glenn Hwy. I-70, exit 176, just e on US 40. Ext/int corridors. **Pets:** Small. $10 daily fee/pet. Designated rooms, service with restrictions, supervision.
ASK SO X B B

▼▼ Comfort Inn SH
(740) 435-3200. **$74-$134.** 2327 Southgate Pkwy. I-70, exit 178, just n on SR 209. Int corridors. **Pets:** Medium, other species. $10 one-time fee/pet. Designated rooms, service with restrictions, supervision.
SAVE SO X B B

▼▼ Days Inn-Cambridge SH
(740) 432-5691. **Call for rates.** 2328 Southgate Pkwy. I-70, exit 178, just n on SR 209. Int corridors. **Pets:** $10 daily fee/pet. Service with restrictions.
X B B

▼▼ Deer Creek Motel M 🐾
(740) 432-6391. **$49-$69, 7 day notice.** 2321 Southgate Pkwy. I-70, exit 178, just ne on SR 209. Ext corridors. **Pets:** Medium, other species. $5 one-time fee/pet. Designated rooms, service with restrictions, crate.
ASK SO X B B

▼▼▼ Holiday Inn Cambridge/Salt Fork Area SH
(740) 432-7313. **$59-$99.** 2248 Southgate Pkwy. I-70, exit 178, just n on SR 209. Int corridors. **Pets:** Medium. Service with restrictions, crate.
ASK SO X B B TI

▼▼ Super 8 Motel-Cambridge SH
(740) 435-8080. **$49-$99.** 8779 Georgetown Rd. I-70, exit 178, just n. Ext corridors. **Pets:** Medium. $10 daily fee/pet. Service with restrictions, supervision.
SAVE SO X B B

CANTON

▼▼ Red Roof Inn #7019 M
(330) 499-1970. **Call for rates.** 5353 Inn Circle Ct NW. I-77, exit 109, just w on Everhard Rd. Ext corridors. **Pets:** Accepted.
X B

▼▼▼ Residence Inn by Marriott SH
(330) 493-0004. **$154-$187.** 5280 Broadmoor Cir NW. I-77, exit 109, 0.5 mi e on Everhard Rd. Int corridors. **Pets:** Accepted.
ASK SO X SM B B

CARROLLTON

▼▼▼▼ Carrollton Days Inn SH
(330) 627-9314. $81-$130. 1111 Canton Rd. On SR 43, 0.5 mi n of SR 39. Int corridors. Pets: $20 one-time fee/pet. Service with restrictions, supervision.

ASK S✖ ✕ 🛏 💻 🏊

CEDARVILLE

▼▼▼▼ Hearthstone Inn & Suites SH
(937) 766-3000. $99-$149. 10 S Main St. I-70, exit 54, 11 mi s. Int corridors. Pets: Accepted.

ASK ✕ 🛏 💻

CELINA

▲▲▲▽ ▼◆▼ Americas Best Value Inn-Celina SH
(419) 586-4656. $56-$125. 1421 SR 703 E. Jct SR 29. Ext corridors. Pets: Small, dogs only. $15 daily fee/pet. Designated rooms, service with restrictions, supervision.

SAVE S✖ ✕ 🛏 💻

CINCINNATI METROPOLITAN AREA

BATAVIA

▼▼▼▼ Hampton Inn-Cincinnati Eastgate SH
(513) 752-8584. $79-$129, 3 day notice. 858 Eastgate North Dr. I-275, exit 63B (SR 32), just e, just n on Gleneste Withamsville Rd, then just w; behind Longhorn Steak House. Int corridors. Pets: Medium. Service with restrictions, crate.

ASK S✖ ✕ 🛏 💻 🏊

▼▼▼▼ Holiday Inn-Cincinnati Eastgate LH
(513) 752-4400. Call for rates. 4501 Eastgate Blvd. I-275, exit 63B (SR 32), 0.5 mi e to Eastgate Mall exit, then 0.5 mi n. Int corridors. Pets: Accepted.

✕ 🛏 💻 🍴 🏊 ✕

BLUE ASH

▼▼ Extended StayAmerica-Cincinnati-Blue
Ash-South SH
(513) 793-6750. $63-$125. 4260 Hunt Rd. I-71, exit 14, 1 mi w on Ronald Reagan Hwy, exit Hunt Rd, then just e. Int corridors. Pets: Other species. $75 one-time fee/pet. Service with restrictions.

ASK S✖ ✕ 🛏 💻 🏊

▼▼▼▼ Residence Inn by Marriott-Blue Ash SH 🐾
(513) 530-5060. $175-$195. 11401 Reed-Hartman Hwy. I-275, exit 47, 0.8 mi s. Ext/int corridors. Pets: Medium, other species. $75 one-time fee/room. Service with restrictions.

ASK S✖ ✕ ✖M 🛏 💻 🏊 ✕

▼▼ TownePlace Suites by Marriott Blue Ash SH 🐾
(513) 469-8222. $153-$174. 4650 Cornell Rd. I-275, exit 47, 0.9 mi s on Reed-Hartman Hwy, then just w. Int corridors. Pets: Medium, other species. $75 one-time fee/pet. Service with restrictions.

ASK S✖ ✕ 🛏 💻 🏊

CHERRY GROVE

▲▲▲▽ ▼◆▼ Best Western Clermont M
(513) 528-7702. $63-$90. 4004 Williams Dr. I-275, exit 65, just w, then just s. Ext corridors. Pets: Medium. $25 one-time fee/pet. Service with restrictions, supervision.

SAVE S✖ ✕ 🛏 💻 🏊

CINCINNATI

▲▲▲▽ ▼▼▼◆ Millennium Hotel Cincinnati LH
(513) 352-2100. $79-$209. 150 W 5th St. Between Elm and Race sts. Int corridors. Pets: Accepted.

SAVE S✖ ✕ 🛏 💻 🍴 🏊

CHILLICOTHE

▲▲▲▽ ▼◆▼ Best Western Adena Inn SH
(740) 775-7000. $79-$179. 1250 N Bridge St. US 35, exit Bridge St, 0.8 mi n. Int corridors. Pets: Accepted.

SAVE S✖ ✕ 🛏 💻 🏊

▼▼ ▼▼ Christopher Inn & Suites SH
(740) 774-6835. $83-$190. 30 N Plaza Blvd. US 35, exit Bridge St. Int corridors. Pets: Accepted.

✕ 🛏 💻 🏊

▲▲▲▽ ▼▼▼ ▼▼▼ The Westin Cincinnati LH 🐾
(513) 621-7700. $350-$370. 21 E 5th St. Between Vine and Walnut sts. Int corridors. Pets: Medium. Service with restrictions, supervision.

SAVE S✖ ✕ ✖M 💻 🍴 🏊

FAIRFIELD

▼▼ Extended StayAmerica SH
(513) 860-5733. $68-$125. 9651 Seward Rd. I-275, exit 41, 1.7 mi n on SR 4. Int corridors. Pets: Other species. $75 one-time fee/pet. Service with restrictions.

ASK S✖ ✕ 🛏 💻 🏊

HARRISON

▼▼ Comfort Inn SH
(513) 367-9666. Call for rates. 391 Comfort Dr. I-74, exit 1, just n on New Haven Rd, then just e. Int corridors. Pets: Accepted.

✕ ✖M 🛏 💻 🏊

MASON

▼▼ La Quinta Inn & Suites SH
(513) 459-1111. $119. 9918 Escort Dr. I-71, exit 19, just w, then just s. Int corridors. Pets: Other species. Service with restrictions, supervision.

ASK S✖ ✕ 🛏 💻 🏊

▲▲▲▽ ▼▼ Microtel Inn & Suites Kings Island SH
(513) 754-1500. $55-$169. 5324 Beach Blvd. I-71, exit 25, just nw. Int corridors. Pets: Small, dogs only. $20 daily fee/pet. Service with restrictions, supervision.

SAVE S✖ ✕ ✖M 🛏 💻

▼▼ ▼▼ TownePlace Suites by Marriott SH
(513) 774-0610. $142-$175. 9369 Waterstone Blvd. I-71, exit 19, 0.5 mi e on Mason-Montgomery and Fields-Ertel rds, then 0.9 mi n. Int corridors. Pets: Accepted.

ASK S✖ ✕ ✖M 🛏 💻 🏊

MIDDLETOWN

▲▲▲▽ ▼▼▼▼ Best Western Regency Inn SH
(513) 424-3551. $75-$145. 6475 Culbertson Rd. I-75, exit 32. Int corridors. Pets: Dogs only. $25 daily fee/pet. Designated rooms, service with restrictions, crate.

SAVE S✖ ✕ 🛏 💻 🏊

▼▼ Fairfield Inn by Marriott SH
(513) 424-5444. **$78-$98.** 6750 Roosevelt Pkwy. I-75, exit 32, 0.5 mi w on SR 122. Int corridors. **Pets:** Accepted.

ASK SO X &M H P ~

▼ Super 8 Motel Middletown SH
(513) 422-4888. **$59-$69.** 3553 Commerce Dr. I-75, exit 32, just e, then just n. Int corridors. **Pets:** Dogs only. $10 daily fee/pet. Designated rooms, service with restrictions, supervision.

ASK SO X H

MILFORD

▼▼▼ Homewood Suites by Hilton SH
(513) 248-4663. **Call for rates (no credit cards).** 600 Chamber Dr. I-275, exit 59A, 0.5 mi w on Milford Pkwy, then 0.5 mi s. Int corridors. **Pets:** Accepted.

X &M H P ~

MOUNT ORAB

AAA ▼▼▼ Best Western Mount Orab Inn SH
(937) 444-6666. **$73-$89.** 100 Leininger St. Jct US 68 and SR 32, just n on US 68. Int corridors. **Pets:** Medium. $15 daily fee/pet. Designated rooms, service with restrictions, supervision.

SAVE SO X H P ~

SHARONVILLE

AAA ▼▼▼ Arcadia Residential Suites SH
(513) 354-1000. **$89-$129.** 11180 Dowlin Dr. I-75, exit 15, just e on Sharon Rd, then just n. Int corridors. **Pets:** Medium. $50 one-time fee/room. Service with restrictions, crate.

SAVE SO X H P ~

▼▼▼ Drury Inn & Suites-Cincinnati North SH
(513) 771-5601. **$96-$186.** 2265 Sharon Rd. I-75, exit 15, just e. Int corridors. **Pets:** Large, other species. Service with restrictions, supervision.

ASK X &M H P ~

▼▼▼ Homewood Suites by Hilton-Cincinnati North SH
(513) 772-8888. **$149-$189.** 2670 E Kemper Rd. I-275, exit 44, jct Mosteller Rd. Int corridors. **Pets:** Medium. $100 daily fee/room. Service with restrictions, crate.

X H P ~ X

▼▼▼ La Quinta Inn & Suites SH
(513) 771-0300. **$114.** 11029 Dowlin Dr. I-75, exit 15, just e. Int corridors. **Pets:** Other species. Service with restrictions, supervision.

ASK SO X &M H P ~ X

▼▼▼ Residence Inn by Marriott SH 🐾
(513) 771-2525. **$169-$199.** 11689 Chester Rd. I-75, exit 15, just w on Sharon Rd, then 1 mi n. Ext corridors. **Pets:** Large, other species. $100 one-time fee/room. Service with restrictions.

ASK SO X &M H P ~ X

▼▼▼ Sheraton Cincinnati North Hotel LH 🐾
(513) 771-2080. **$109-$179.** 11320 Chester Rd. I-75, exit 15, just w on Sharon Rd, then 0.5 mi n. Int corridors. **Pets:** Medium, dogs only. Service with restrictions, crate.

ASK SO X &M H P TI ~

SPRINGDALE

▼▼ La Quinta Inn SH
(513) 671-2300. **$84.** 12150 Springfield Pike. I-275, exit 41, just n on SR 4. Int corridors. **Pets:** Other species. Service with restrictions, supervision.

ASK SO X H P

WEST CHESTER

AAA ▼▼▼ Staybridge Suites Cincinnati North SH 🐾
(513) 874-1900. **$99-$169.** 8955 Lakota Dr W. I-75, exit 19, just w on Union Center Blvd, then just n. Int corridors. **Pets:** Other species. Service with restrictions, supervision.

SAVE SO X &M H P ~ X

WILMINGTON

▼▼ AmeriHost Inn & Suites SH
(937) 383-3950. **Call for rates.** 201 Carrie Dr. Jct US 22 and 68, 1.5 mi e on US 22. Int corridors. **Pets:** Accepted.

X H P ~ X

AAA ▼▼▼ Holiday Inn Wilmington & Roberts Conference Centre LH
(937) 283-3200. **Call for rates.** 123 Gano Rd. I-71, exit 50, just w. Int corridors. **Pets:** Accepted.

SAVE X &M H P ~

END METROPOLITAN AREA

CLEVELAND METROPOLITAN AREA

BEACHWOOD

▼▼▼ Extended StayAmerica-Cleveland-Beachwood **SH**
(216) 595-9551. **$90-$120.** 3820 Orange Pl. I-271, exit Chagrin Blvd, just e. Int corridors. **Pets:** Other species. $75 one-time fee/pet. Service with restrictions.

▼▼▼▼ Hilton Cleveland East/Beachwood **LH**
(216) 464-5950. **$109-$289.** 3663 Park East Dr. I-271, exit Chagrin Blvd, just w. Int corridors. **Pets:** Accepted.

▼▼▼ Holiday Inn-Beachwood **SH**
(216) 831-3300. **Call for rates.** 3750 Orange Pl. I-271, exit Chagrin Blvd, just e. Int corridors. **Pets:** Accepted.

▼▼▼ Homestead Studio Suites Hotel-Cleveland/Beachwood **SH**
(216) 896-5555. **$91-$120.** 3625 Orange Pl. I-271, exit Chagrin Blvd, just e. Int corridors. **Pets:** Other species. $75 one-time fee/pet. Service with restrictions.

▼▼▼▼ Residence Inn by Marriott Cleveland-Beachwood **SH**
(216) 831-3030. **$129-$299.** 3628 Park East Dr. Jct US 422 and I-271, exit Chagrin Blvd, just w. Int corridors. **Pets:** Large, other species. $75 one-time fee/room. Service with restrictions, crate.

BROOKLYN

▼▼ Extended StayAmerica **SH**
(216) 267-7799. **$67-$97.** 10300 Cascade Crossing. I-480, exit 13, just s. Int corridors. **Pets:** Other species. $75 one-time fee/pet. Service with restrictions.

BROOK PARK

▼▼ Howard Johnson Cleveland Airport **M**
(216) 676-5200. **Call for rates.** 16644 Snow Rd. I-71, exit 237, just e. Ext/int corridors. **Pets:** Other species. $10 daily fee/room. Service with restrictions.

CLEVELAND

▼▼▼ Cleveland Airport Marriott **LH**
(216) 252-5333. **$175-$197.** 4277 W 150th St. I-71, exit 240, just s. Int corridors. **Pets:** Accepted.

▼▼▼▼ La Quinta Inn & Suites Cleveland Airport **SH**
(216) 251-8500. **$99.** 4222 W 150th St. I-71, exit 240, just n. Int corridors. **Pets:** Other species. Service with restrictions, supervision.

▼▼▼ Residence Inn by Marriott **SH**
(216) 443-9043. **$129-$229.** 527 Prospect Ave. Between E 9th St and Ontario. Int corridors. **Pets:** $100 one-time fee/room. Service with restrictions, supervision.

▼▼▼ The Ritz-Carlton, Cleveland **LH**
(216) 623-1300. **$229-$399.** 1515 W 3rd St. In Tower City Center (3rd St side). Int corridors. **Pets:** Accepted.

▼▼▼▼ Sheraton Cleveland Airport Hotel **SH**
(216) 267-1500. **$235.** 5300 Riverside Dr. I-71, exit 237, follow signs; just s of I-480 on SR 237. Int corridors. **Pets:** Accepted.

INDEPENDENCE

▼▼▼ La Quinta Inn **SH**
(216) 447-1133. **$92.** 6161 Quarry Ln. I-77, exit Rockside Rd, just e. Int corridors. **Pets:** Other species. Service with restrictions, supervision.

▼▼ Red Roof Inn #7028 **M**
(216) 447-0030. **Call for rates.** 6020 Quarry Ln. I-77, exit Rockside Rd, just e. Ext corridors. **Pets:** Accepted.

▼▼▼ Residence Inn by Marriott **SH** 🐾
(216) 520-1450. **$139-$189.** 5101 W Creek Rd. I-77, exit Rockside Rd, just w to W Creek Rd, then just n. Ext corridors. **Pets:** Other species. $100 one-time fee/room. Service with restrictions, supervision.

▼▼▼ Sheraton Independence Hotel **SH**
(216) 524-0700. **$89-$229.** 5300 Rockside Rd. I-77, exit Rockside Rd, just w. Int corridors. **Pets:** Accepted.

LAKEWOOD

▼▼ Days Inn **SH**
(216) 226-4800. **Call for rates.** 12019 Lake Ave. I-90, exit 166, 1 mi n on W 117th St, then just w. **Pets:** Accepted.

▼▼ Travelodge **SH**
(216) 221-9000. **Call for rates.** 11837 Edgewater Dr. I-90, exit 166, 1 mi n on W 117th St, then just w. Int corridors. **Pets:** Accepted.

MACEDONIA

▼▼ Knights Inn-Cleveland/Macedonia **M**
(330) 467-1981. **Call for rates.** 240 E Highland Rd. I-271, exit 18, just s; I-80/90 (Ohio Tpke), exit 180, 3 mi n. Ext corridors. **Pets:** Accepted.

▼▼▼ La Quinta Inn & Suites Cleveland-Macedonia **SH**
(330) 468-5400. **$94.** 268 E Highland Rd. I-271, exit 18, just s; I-80/90 (Ohio Tpke), exit 180, just n. Int corridors. **Pets:** Other species. Service with restrictions, supervision.

MAYFIELD HEIGHTS

▼▼▼ Baymont Inn & Suites-Cleveland (Mayfield Heights) **SH**
(440) 442-8400. **Call for rates.** 1421 Golden Gate Blvd. I-271, exit 34, 0.3 mi w off US 322. Int corridors. **Pets:** Medium, other species. $10 one-time fee/pet. Service with restrictions, crate.

MEDINA

▼▼ Motel 6 4112 **SH**
(330) 723-3322. **Call for rates.** 3122 Eastpointe Dr. I-71, exit 218, just w. Int corridors. **Pets:** Other species. Service with restrictions, supervision.

MIDDLEBURG HEIGHTS

◆◆◆ ▼▼▼▼ **Comfort Inn-Cleveland Airport** SH
(440) 234-3131. **$109-$129.** 17550 Rosbough Dr. I-71, exit 235, 0.3 mi w to Engle Rd, then 0.3 mi n. Int corridors. **Pets:** Accepted.
⟨SAVE⟩ ⟨S🐾⟩ ⟨✕⟩ ⟨&M⟩ ⟨🛏⟩ ⟨💻⟩ ⟨≈⟩

◆◆◆ ▼▼▼▼ **Ramada Airport South** M
(440) 243-2277. **$69-$149.** 7233 Engle Rd. I-71, exit 235, just w. Ext corridors. **Pets:** $10 one-time fee/room. Designated rooms, service with restrictions, supervision.
⟨SAVE⟩ ⟨S🐾⟩ ⟨✕⟩ ⟨🛏⟩ ⟨💻⟩ ⟨≈⟩

▼▼ ▼▼ **Red Roof Inn-Middleburg Heights #7060** SH
(440) 243-2441. **Call for rates.** 17555 Bagley Rd. I-71, exit 235, just w. Ext/int corridors. **Pets:** Accepted.
⟨✕⟩ ⟨🛏⟩

▼▼▼ ▼▼ **Residence Inn by Marriott** SH
(440) 234-6488. **$109-$199.** 17525 Rosbough Dr. I-71, exit 235, just w on Bagley Rd, then just n on Engle Rd. Ext/int corridors. **Pets:** Large, other species. $100 one-time fee/room. Designated rooms, service with restrictions, crate.
⟨ASK⟩ ⟨S🐾⟩ ⟨✕⟩ ⟨🛏⟩ ⟨💻⟩ ⟨≈⟩

▼▼ ▼▼ **StudioPLUS-Cleveland-Middleburg Heights** SH
(440) 243-7024. **$82-$112.** 17552 Rosbough Dr. I-71, exit 235, 0.3 mi w to Engle Rd, then 0.3 mi n. Int corridors. **Pets:** Other species. $75 one-time fee/pet. Service with restrictions.
⟨ASK⟩ ⟨S🐾⟩ ⟨✕⟩ ⟨🛏⟩ ⟨💻⟩

▼▼ ▼▼ **TownePlace Suites** SH
(440) 816-9300. **$164-$186.** 7325 S Engle Rd. I-71, exit 235, just w on Bagley Rd. Int corridors. **Pets:** Accepted.
⟨ASK⟩ ⟨S🐾⟩ ⟨✕⟩ ⟨🛏⟩ ⟨💻⟩ ⟨≈⟩

NORTH OLMSTED

▼▼ ▼▼ **Candlewood Suites** SH
(440) 716-0584. **Call for rates.** 24741 Country Club Blvd. I-480, exit 6B, just n on SR 252. Int corridors. **Pets:** Accepted.
⟨✕⟩ ⟨🛏⟩ ⟨💻⟩

▼▼ ▼▼ **Homestead Studio Suites Hotel-Cleveland/Airport/North Olmsted** SH
(440) 777-8585. **$75-$105.** 24851 Country Club Blvd. I-480, exit 6B, just n on SR 252. Ext corridors. **Pets:** Other species. $75 one-time fee/pet. Service with restrictions.
⟨ASK⟩ ⟨S🐾⟩ ⟨✕⟩ ⟨&M⟩ ⟨🛏⟩ ⟨💻⟩

◆◆◆ ▼▼◆▼ **Radisson Hotel Cleveland Airport** SH
(440) 734-5060. **$129-$199.** 25070 Country Club Blvd. I-480, exit 6B, just n on SR 252. Int corridors. **Pets:** Accepted.
⟨SAVE⟩ ⟨S🐾⟩ ⟨✕⟩ ⟨&M⟩ ⟨🛏⟩ ⟨💻⟩ ⟨🍽⟩ ⟨≈⟩ ⟨✕⟩

▼▼ ▼▼ **StudioPLUS** SH
(440) 716-2412. **$75-$105.** 25801 Country Club Blvd. I-480, exit 6B, just n on SR 252. Int corridors. **Pets:** Other species. $75 one-time fee/pet. Service with restrictions.
⟨ASK⟩ ⟨S🐾⟩ ⟨✕⟩ ⟨🛏⟩ ⟨💻⟩ ⟨≈⟩

NORTH RIDGEVILLE

◆◆◆ ▼▼ **Motel 6 Cleveland/North Ridgeville** M
(440) 327-6311. **Call for rates.** 32751 Lorain Rd. I-80, exit 152, 0.6 mi ne on SR 10. Ext corridors. **Pets:** Other species. Service with restrictions, supervision.
⟨SAVE⟩ ⟨✕⟩

▼▼ **Super 8 Motel** SH
(440) 327-0500. **$59-$89.** 32801 Lorain Rd. I-80, exit 152, 0.5 mi ne on SR 10. Int corridors. **Pets:** Accepted.
⟨ASK⟩ ⟨S🐾⟩ ⟨✕⟩

RICHFIELD

▼▼◆▼ ▼ **Quality Inn & Suites** SH
(330) 659-6151. **Call for rates.** 4742 Brecksville Rd. I-80, exit 173, just s. Int corridors. **Pets:** Other species. $25 one-time fee/pet. Designated rooms, no service, supervision.
⟨✕⟩ ⟨🛏⟩ ⟨💻⟩ ⟨🍽⟩ ⟨≈⟩ ⟨✕⟩

SOLON

▼▼▼ ▼ **Hampton Inn** SH
(440) 542-0400. **Call for rates.** 6035 Enterprise Pkwy. US 422, exit Harper Rd, 0.6 mi s, then 0.4 mi e. Int corridors. **Pets:** Dogs only. Service with restrictions, crate.
⟨✕⟩ ⟨&M⟩ ⟨🛏⟩ ⟨💻⟩ ⟨≈⟩

STRONGSVILLE

▼ **Motel 6-Strongsville #1497** M
(440) 238-0170. **$45-$55.** 15385 Royalton Rd. I-71, exit 231A, just e; I-76 (Ohio Tpke), exit 161, 1 mi s. Ext corridors. **Pets:** Other species. Service with restrictions, supervision.
⟨S🐾⟩ ⟨✕⟩

TWINSBURG

▼▼▼ ▼ **Comfort Suites-Twinsburg** SH 🐾
(330) 963-5909. **$79-$139.** 2715 Creekside Dr. I-480, exit 37 (SR 91), just n. Int corridors. **Pets:** Medium, dogs only. $5 daily fee/room, $15 one-time fee/room. Designated rooms, service with restrictions, crate.
⟨ASK⟩ ⟨S🐾⟩ ⟨✕⟩ ⟨&M⟩ ⟨🛏⟩ ⟨💻⟩ ⟨≈⟩

▼▼ ▼▼ **Twinsburg Super 8 Motel** SH
(330) 425-2889. **Call for rates.** 8848 Twins Hills Dr. I-480, exit 36, just w on SR 82. Int corridors. **Pets:** Small. $6 daily fee/pet. Service with restrictions, supervision.
⟨✕⟩ ⟨🛏⟩ ⟨💻⟩

WESTLAKE

▼▼ ▼▼ **Extended Stay Deluxe** SH
(440) 899-4160. **$82-$112.** 30360 Clemens Rd. I-90, exit 156, just n. Int corridors. **Pets:** Other species. $75 one-time fee/pet. Service with restrictions.
⟨ASK⟩ ⟨S🐾⟩ ⟨✕⟩ ⟨🛏⟩ ⟨💻⟩

▼▼ ▼▼ **Red Roof Inn-Westlake #7094** M
(440) 892-7920. **Call for rates.** 29595 Clemens Rd. I-90, exit 156, just n. Ext corridors. **Pets:** Accepted.
⟨✕⟩ ⟨🛏⟩

▼▼▼ ▼ **Residence Inn by Marriott** SH
(440) 892-2254. **$169-$209.** 30100 Clemens Rd. I-90, exit 156, just n. Ext corridors. **Pets:** Other species. $75 one-time fee/room. Service with restrictions, crate.
⟨ASK⟩ ⟨S🐾⟩ ⟨✕⟩ ⟨🛏⟩ ⟨💻⟩ ⟨≈⟩ ⟨✕⟩

WILLOUGHBY

▼▼ Red Roof Inn-East #7053
(440) 946-9872. **Call for rates.** 4166 SR 306. I-90, exit 193, just s. Ext
corridors. **Pets:** Accepted.

END METROPOLITAN AREA

CLYDE

▼▼ Red Roof Inn 🆂🅷
(419) 547-6660. **$59-$118.** 1363 W McPherson Hwy. 1 mi w on SR 20.
Int corridors. **Pets:** Small, dogs only. $50 deposit/pet. Designated rooms,
service with restrictions, supervision.

COLUMBUS METROPOLITAN AREA

BUCKEYE LAKE

▼ Super 8 Motel-Buckeye Lake 🅼
(740) 928-1015. **$56.** 10780 Hebron Rd. I-70, exit 129A, just s on SR
79. Ext corridors. **Pets:** Service with restrictions, supervision.

CANAL WINCHESTER

▼▼ AmeriHost Inn & Suites Columbus Southeast 🆂🅷
(614) 834-4790. **Call for rates.** 6323 Prentiss School Pl. US 33, exit
Canal Winchester, just w. Int corridors. **Pets:** $15 daily fee/pet. Service
with restrictions, supervision.

CIRCLEVILLE

▼▼ Comfort Inn Circleville 🆂🅷
(740) 477-6116. **$70-$140.** 24517 US 23 S. Jct US 22 and 23, 2 mi s.
Int corridors. **Pets:** Accepted.

▼◆▼▼ Holiday Inn Express Hotel & Suites 🆂🅷
(740) 420-7711. **Call for rates (no credit cards).** 23911 US 23 S. Jct
US 22, 1.2 mi s. Int corridors. **Pets:** Accepted.

COLUMBUS

ⒶⒶⒶ◇ ▼▼▼ Baymont Inn & Suites Columbus Airport 🅼
(614) 237-3403. **Call for rates.** 4240 International Gateway. At Port
Columbus International Airport. Ext corridors. **Pets:** Accepted.

**▼▼ Baymont Inn & Suites Columbus at
Rickenbacker** 🆂🅷
(614) 491-4400. **Call for rates.** 2323 Port Rd. I-270, exit 49, 3.4 mi s,
then just w. Int corridors. **Pets:** Accepted.

ⒶⒶⒶ◇ ▼▼▼ Baymont Inn and Suites Columbus/OSU 🅼
(614) 267-4646. **Call for rates.** 3246 Olentangy River Rd. SR 315, exit
N Broadway, 0.3 mi s. Ext corridors. **Pets:** Accepted.

ⒶⒶⒶ◇ ▼▼▼▼ Best Western Columbus North 🆂🅷
(614) 888-8230. **$90-$100.** 888 E Dublin-Granville Rd. I-71, exit 117,
0.5 mi w on SR 161. Int corridors. **Pets:** Medium, other species. $25
deposit/room. No service, crate.

▼▼▼▼ Candlewood Suites Polaris 🆂🅷 🐾
(614) 436-6600. **$120-$140.** 8515 Lyra Dr. I-71, exit 121, 0.3 mi w on
SR 750. Int corridors. **Pets:** Large, other species. $75 one-time fee/room.
Designated rooms, service with restrictions, crate.

ⒶⒶⒶ◇ ▼▼▼ Comfort Inn 🆂🅷 🐾
(614) 791-9700. **$79-$179.** 8400 Lyra Dr. I-71N, exit 121, just w. Int
corridors. **Pets:** Medium. $25 one-time fee/room. Designated rooms, serv-
ice with restrictions, supervision.

ⒶⒶⒶ◇ ▼▼▼▼ Comfort Suites Fairgrounds 🆂🅷
(614) 586-1001. **$75-$150.** 1690 Clara St. I-71, exit 111, just w. Int
corridors. **Pets:** Medium. $10 daily fee/pet. Service with restrictions, crate.

ⒶⒶⒶ◇ ▼▼ Days Inn-Columbus Worthington 🆂🅷
(614) 436-0556. **$60-$90.** 7500 Vantage Dr. I-270, exit 23, 0.4 mi n on
US 23, just e on Dimension Dr, then just s. Int corridors.
Pets: Accepted.

▼▼▼ DoubleTree Columbus/Worthington 🅻🅷
(614) 885-3334. **Call for rates.** 175 Hutchinson Ave. I-270, exit 23, just
n of jct US 23 N, just e on Dimension Dr, then just s on High Cross
Blvd. Int corridors. **Pets:** Other species. $50 one-time fee/room. Service
with restrictions, crate.

▼▼▼ DoubleTree Guest Suites 🅻🅷
(614) 228-4600. **$109-$209.** 50 S Front St. Corner of Front and State
sts, just n. Int corridors. **Pets:** Accepted.

**▼▼▼▼ Drury Inn & Suites-Columbus Convention
Center** 🅻🅷
(614) 221-7008. **$126-$176.** 88 E Nationwide Blvd. 0.3 mi n on US 23.
Int corridors. **Pets:** Large, other species. Service with restrictions, supervision.

▼▼▼ Extended StayAmerica-Columbus-Easton 🆂🅷
(614) 428-6022. **$104-$114.** 4200 Stelzer Rd. I-270, exit 32, just w on
Morse Rd, then just n. Int corridors. **Pets:** Other species. $75 one-time
fee/pet. Service with restrictions.

▼▼▼ Extended StayAmerica-Columbus-North 🆂🅷
(614) 431-0033. **$59-$69.** 6255 Zumstein Dr. I-71, exit 117, just nw.
Pets: Other species. $75 one-time fee/pet. Service with restrictions.

▼▼▼ Extended StayAmerica-Columbus-Worthington SH
(614) 785-1006. **$74-$84.** 7465 High Cross Blvd. I-270, exit 23, just n on US 23, just e on Dimension Dr, then just s. Int corridors. **Pets:** Other species. $75 one-time fee/pet. Service with restrictions.
ASK S⊘ ⊠ ⊟ ▣

▼▼▼ Extended Stay Deluxe Columbus/Polaris SH
(614) 431-5522. **$99-$109.** 8555 Lyra Dr. I-71N, exit 121, just w on Polaris Pkwy. Int corridors. **Pets:** Other species. $75 one-time fee/pet. Service with restrictions.
ASK S⊘ ⊠ ⊾M ⊟ ▣ ⇌

◀◀◀▷ ▼▼ Holiday Inn Columbus City Center LH
(614) 221-3281. **$109.** 175 E Town St. 4th and E Town sts. Int corridors. **Pets:** Accepted.
SAVE S⊘ ⊠ ⊟ ▣ ⊤⊤ ⇌

◀◀◀▷ ▼◆▼ Holiday Inn on the Lane LH ❖
(614) 294-4848. **$105-$135.** 328 W Lane Ave. 0.5 mi e of SR 315, exit Lane Ave. Int corridors. **Pets:** Designated rooms, service with restrictions, crate.
SAVE S⊘ ⊠ ⊾M ⊟ ▣ ⊤⊤ ⇌ ⊠

◀◀◀▷ ▼▼ Microtel Inn & Suites (West) SH
(614) 851-1745. **$50-$90.** 5655 Feder Rd. I-70, exit 91A, just sw. Int corridors. **Pets:** Accepted.
SAVE S⊘ ⊠ ⊟ ▣

▼▼ Motel 6 #1486 M
(614) 431-2525. **$39-$55.** 7474 N High St. I-270, exit 23, 0.4 mi n on US 23, just e on Dimension Dr, then just s. Ext corridors. **Pets:** Other species. Service with restrictions, supervision.
S⊘ ⊠

◀◀◀▷ ▼◆▼ Ramada North Columbus SH
(614) 890-8111. **$70-$90.** 6767 Schrock Hill Ct. I-270, exit 27, n off Cleveland Ave; enter off Schrock Rd. Int corridors. **Pets:** Medium, other species. $10 daily fee/pet. Service with restrictions, supervision.
SAVE S⊘ ⊠ ⊟ ▣ ⇌

▼▼ Red Roof Inn-Columbus Convention Center SH
(614) 224-6539. **Call for rates.** 111 E Nationwide Blvd. Nationwide Blvd at 3rd St. Int corridors. **Pets:** Accepted.
⊠ ⊾M ⊟

▼▼ Red Roof Inn-OSU #7121 SH
(614) 267-9941. **Call for rates.** 441 Ackerman Rd. SR 315, exit Ackerman Rd, 0.3 mi e. Ext corridors. **Pets:** Accepted.
⊠ ⊾M ⊟

▼▼ Red Roof Inn-West #7009 M
(614) 878-9245. **Call for rates.** 5001 Renner Rd. I-70, exit 91 eastbound; exit 91B westbound, just nw. Ext corridors. **Pets:** Accepted.
⊠ ⊾M ⊟

▼▼ Red Roof Inn-Worthington #7310 SH
(614) 846-3001. **Call for rates.** 7480 N High St. I-270, exit 23, 0.3 mi n on US 23, just w on Dimension Dr, then just s on Vantage Dr. Ext/int corridors. **Pets:** Accepted.
⊠ ⊟

▼▼▼ The Residence Inn by Marriott-Columbus North SH
(614) 431-1819. **$143-$163.** 6191 W Zumstein Dr. I-71, exit 117, just nw. Ext corridors. **Pets:** Accepted.
ASK S⊘ ⊠ ⊟ ▣ ⇌ ⊠

▼▼▼ Residence Inn by Marriott-Columbus Southeast
(614) 864-8844. **$209-$229.** 2084 S Hamilton Rd. I-70, exit 107, just e. Ext corridors. **Pets:** Accepted.
ASK S⊘ ⊠ ⊾M ⊟ ▣ ⇌ ⊠

▼▼▼ Sheraton Suites Columbus LH ❖
(614) 436-0004. **$229-$259.** 201 Hutchinson Ave. I-270, exit 23, 0.3 mi n on US 23, just e on Dimension Dr, then just SE on Vantage Dr. Int corridors. **Pets:** Medium, dogs only. Designated rooms, service with restrictions, crate.
ASK S⊘ ⊠ ⊾M ⊟ ▣ ⊤⊤ ⇌

◀◀◀▷ ▼▼ ▼◆▼ The Westin Columbus LH
(614) 228-3800. **$109-$2500.** 310 S High St. Corner of Main and High sts. Int corridors. **Pets:** Accepted.
SAVE ⊠ ⊟ ▣ ⊤⊤

DELAWARE

▼ Travelodge M
(740) 369-4421. **Call for rates.** 1001 US Rt 23 N. 0.5 mi n of downtown. Ext/int corridors. **Pets:** Accepted.
⊠ ⊟ ▣

DUBLIN

▼▼▼ Drury Inn & Suites-Columbus Northwest SH
(614) 798-8802. **$86-$136.** 6170 Parkcenter Cir. I-270, exit 15 (Tuttle Crossing Blvd), 0.3 mi e, then just n on Blazer Pkwy. Int corridors. **Pets:** Large, other species. Service with restrictions, supervision.
ASK ⊠ ⊾M ⊟ ▣

▼▼ Dublin Homewood Suites by Hilton SH
(614) 791-8675. **Call for rates.** 5300 Parkcenter Ave. I-270, exit 15 (Tuttle Crossing Blvd), just e, just n on Blazer Pkwy, then just e. Int corridors. **Pets:** Accepted.
⊠ ⊾M ⊟ ▣ ⇌ ⊠

▼▼ Extended StayAmerica-Columbus-Dublin SH
(614) 760-0053. **$84-$94.** 450 Metro Pl N. I-270, exit 17A, just e on SR 161, just s on Frantz Rd, then just n. Int corridors. **Pets:** Other species. $75 one-time fee/pet. Service with restrictions.
ASK S⊘ ⊠ ⊟ ▣

▼▼ Extended StayAmerica Columbus-Sawmill SH
(614) 764-0159. **$74-$84.** 6601 Reflections Dr. I-270, exit 20, 0.7 mi s on Sawmill Rd, just e on SR 161, just s on Martin, then just w. Int corridors. **Pets:** Other species. $75 one-time fee/pet. Service with restrictions.
ASK S⊘ ⊠ ⊟ ▣ ⇌

▼▼ Extended Stay Deluxe (Columbus/Tuttle) SH
(614) 760-0245. **$99-$109.** 5530 Tuttle Crossing Blvd. I-270, exit 15 (Tuttle Crossing Blvd), 0.5 mi w. Int corridors. **Pets:** Other species. $75 one-time fee/pet. Service with restrictions.
ASK S⊘ ⊠ ⊟ ▣

▼▼ La Quinta Inn & Suites SH
(614) 792-8300. **$94.** 6145 Parkcenter Cir. I-270, exit 15 (Tuttle Crossing Blvd), just e. Int corridors. **Pets:** Other species. Service with restrictions, supervision.
ASK S⊘ ⊠ ⊾M ⊟ ▣

◀◀◀▷ ▼◆▼ Quality Inn & Suites SH
(614) 764-0770. **$80-$90.** 3950 Tuller Rd. I-270, exit 20, just s on Sawmill Rd, then just w on Dublin Center Dr. Int corridors. **Pets:** Accepted.
SAVE S⊘ ⊠ ⊟ ▣

▼▼ Red Roof Inn-Dublin #7127 M
(614) 764-3993. **Call for rates.** 5125 Post Rd. I-270, exit 17A, just ne. Ext corridors. **Pets:** Accepted.
⊠ ⊾M ⊟

▼▼▼ Residence Inn by Marriott Dublin SH
(614) 791-0403. **$208-$228.** 435 Metro Pl S. I-270, exit 17A, 0.5 mi e to Frantz Rd, then 0.5 mi s. Ext/int corridors. **Pets:** Accepted.
ASK S⊘ ⊠ ⊾M ⊟ ▣ ⇌ ⊠

▼▼▼ Staybridge Suites SH
(614) 734-9882. **Call for rates.** 6095 Emerald Pkwy. I-270, exit 15 (Tuttle Crossing Blvd), just w. Int corridors. **Pets:** Medium. $100 one-time fee/room. Service with restrictions, crate.

🗙 🛅 💻 �というア

ⓐⓐⓐ ▼▼▼ Woodfin Suites Hotel SH ❀
(614) 766-7762. **$99-$179.** 4130 Tuller Rd. I-270, exit 20, 0.3 mi s on Sawmill Rd via Dublin Center Dr. Ext corridors. **Pets:** Other species. $10 daily fee/room. Designated rooms, service with restrictions, supervision.

SAVE S🛅 🗙 🛅 💻 ➔

GAHANNA

▼▼▼ Candlewood Suites Columbus Airport SH
(614) 863-4033. **Call for rates.** 590 Taylor Rd. I-270, exit 37, just e, 0.6 mi s on Morrison Rd, then just e. Int corridors. **Pets:** Accepted.

🗙 🛅 💻

GROVE CITY

ⓐⓐⓐ ▼▼▼ Best Western Executive Inn M
(614) 875-7770. **$64-$90.** 4026 Jackpot Rd. I-71, exit 100, just e. Ext corridors. **Pets:** Medium, dogs only. $10 daily fee/pet. Designated rooms, service with restrictions, crate.

SAVE S🛅 🗙 🛅 💻 ➔

▼▼▼ Drury Inn & Suites-Columbus South SH
(614) 875-7000. **$96-$186.** 4109 Parkway Centre Dr. I-71, exit 100 (Stringtown Rd), just e. Int corridors. **Pets:** Large, other species. Service with restrictions, supervision.

A$K 🗙 🛅 🛅 💻 ➔

ⓐⓐⓐ ▼▼▼ La Quinta Inn South SH
(614) 539-6200. **$87.** 3962 Jackpot Rd. I-71, exit 100, just ne. Int corridors. **Pets:** Other species. Service with restrictions, supervision.

SAVE S🛅 🗙 🛅 💻 ➔ 🗙

▼▼ Motel 6-South Columbus #1492 M
(614) 875-8543. **$41-$55.** 1900 Stringtown Rd. I-71, exit 100, just w. Ext corridors. **Pets:** Other species. Service with restrictions, supervision.

S🛅 🗙

▼▼ Red Roof Inn Columbus/Grove City M
(614) 871-9617. **Call for rates.** 4055 Jackpot Rd. I-71, exit 100, 1.3 mi s of jct I-270. Ext corridors. **Pets:** Accepted.

🗙 🛅 💻

HEATH

ⓐⓐⓐ ▼▼▼ Quality Inn SH
(740) 522-1165. **Call for rates.** 733 Hebron Rd. I-70, exit 129B, 7 mi n on SR 79. Ext corridors. **Pets:** Accepted.

SAVE 🗙 🛅 💻 ➔

HEBRON

▼▼ Red Roof Inn SH
(740) 467-7663. **Call for rates.** 10668 Lancaster Rd SW. I-70, exit 126, just s. Int corridors. **Pets:** Accepted.

🗙 🛅

HILLIARD

▼▼▼ Comfort Suites by Choice Hotels-Columbus SH
(614) 529-8118. **Call for rates.** 3831 Park Mill Run Dr. I-270, exit 13A northbound; exit 13 southbound. Int corridors. **Pets:** Accepted.

🗙 🛅 🛅 💻 ➔

▼▼▼ Homewood Suites by Hilton-Columbus SH
(614) 529-4100. **Call for rates.** 3841 Park Mill Run Dr. I-270, exit 13 southbound; exit 13A northbound. Int corridors. **Pets:** Accepted.

🗙 🛅 🛅 💻 ➔ 🗙

LANCASTER

ⓐⓐⓐ ▼▼▼ Lancaster Inn SH
(740) 653-3040. **$60-$95.** 1858 N Memorial Dr. 2 mi nw on US 33. Ext/int corridors. **Pets:** Accepted.

SAVE S🛅 🗙 🛅 💻 🍴 ➔

MARYSVILLE

▼▼▼ Super 8 Motel-Marysville SH
(937) 644-8821. **$55-$100.** 16510 Square Dr. Just e of US 36, exit off US 33. Ext corridors. **Pets:** Accepted.

🗙 🛅 💻

NEWARK

ⓐⓐⓐ ▼▼▼ Cherry Valley Lodge SH ❀
(740) 788-1200. **$118-$189.** 2299 Cherry Valley Rd. 3.5 mi w on SR 16, then 0.3 mi s. Int corridors. **Pets:** $50 deposit/room. Service with restrictions, crate.

SAVE S🛅 🗙 🛅ᴹ 🛅 💻 🍴 ➔ 🗙

OBETZ

ⓐⓐⓐ ▼▼▼ Comfort Inn SH
(614) 492-9000. **$59-$129.** 4870 Old Rathmell Ct. I-270, exit 49, just e. Int corridors. **Pets:** $20 one-time fee/pet. Designated rooms, service with restrictions, supervision.

SAVE S🛅 🗙 🛅 💻 ➔

REYNOLDSBURG

▼▼▼ Columbus East Fairfield Inn & Suites by Marriott Columbus East SH
(614) 864-4555. **$84-$101.** 2826 Taylor Rd SW. I-70, exit 112 (SR 256 W), just n, then e. Int corridors. **Pets:** Accepted.

A$K S🛅 🗙 🛅 💻 ➔

ⓐⓐⓐ ▼▼▼ Days Inn & Suites Columbus East SH
(614) 864-1280. **$53-$85.** 2100 Brice Rd. I-70, exit 110 westbound; exit 110B eastbound, just n. Int corridors. **Pets:** Other species. $20 daily fee/room. Service with restrictions, supervision.

SAVE S🛅 🗙 🛅 💻 🍴 ➔

▼▼▼ Extended StayAmerica-Columbus-East SH
(614) 759-1451. **$69-$79.** 2200 Lake Club Dr. I-70, exit 110 westbound; exit 110B eastbound, 0.5 mi n on Brice Rd, just w on Channingway, then just s. Int corridors. **Pets:** Other species. $75 one-time fee/pet. Service with restrictions.

A$K S🛅 🗙 🛅 💻 ➔

▼▼▼ La Quinta Inn Columbus East SH
(614) 866-6456. **$78.** 2447 Brice Rd. I-70, exit 110 westbound; exit 110B eastbound, 0.3 mi n. Int corridors. **Pets:** Other species. Service with restrictions, supervision.

A$K S🛅 🗙 🛅 💻 ➔

▼▼ Red Roof Inn-East #7033 M
(614) 864-3683. **Call for rates.** 2449 Brice Rd. I-70, exit 110 westbound; exit 110B eastbound. Ext corridors. **Pets:** Accepted.

🗙 🛅

▼▼ Super 8 Motel Reynoldsburg M
(614) 864-3880. **Call for rates.** 2055 Brice Rd. I-70, exit 110 westbound; exit 110B eastbound. Ext corridors. **Pets:** Accepted.

🗙 🛅 💻 ➔

SUNBURY

ⓐⓐⓐ ▼▼▼ Days Inn of Sunbury SH
(740) 362-6159. **$65-$120.** 7323 SR 37 E. I-71, exit 131, just nw. Int corridors. **Pets:** $10 daily fee/pet. Service with restrictions, supervision.

SAVE 🗙 🛅 💻 ➔

WESTERVILLE

 Baymont Inn & Suites North East **M** ❖
(614) 890-1244. **Call for rates.** 909 S State St. I-270, exit 29, 0.3 mi n on SR 3. Ext corridors. **Pets:** Other species. Service with restrictions, supervision.

SAVE ✕ 🛏 💻 ⇌

WORTHINGTON

 Holiday Inn Columbus/Worthington **SH**
(614) 436-0700. **$109-$139.** 7007 N High St. I-270, exit 23, just s on US 23. Int corridors. **Pets:** Accepted.

ASK ✕ ♿M 🛏 💻 ¶↑ ⇌

END METROPOLITAN AREA

CONNEAUT

 Days Inn of Conneaut **SH**
(440) 593-6000. **$65.** 600 Days Blvd. I-90, exit 241, 0.3 mi n. Int corridors. **Pets:** $10 daily fee/pet. Designated rooms, supervision.

SAVE ✕ ⇌

CUYAHOGA FALLS

Sheraton Suites Akron-Cuyahoga Falls **SH** ❖
(330) 929-3000. **$239-$439.** 1989 Front St. SR 8, exit Broad Blvd, just w. Int corridors. **Pets:** Medium, other species. Designated rooms, service with restrictions, supervision.

SAVE S♦ ✕ ♿M 🛏 💻 ¶↑ ⇌ ✕

DAYTON

Comfort Inn by Choice Hotels-North **SH**
(937) 890-9995. **Call for rates.** 7125 Miller Ln. I-75, exit 59 (Wyse/Benchwood rds), just w on Benchwood Rd, then 0.6 mi n. Int corridors. **Pets:** Accepted.

✕ ♿M 🛏 💻 ⇌

Country Inn & Suites Dayton South **SH**
(937) 425-7400. **$89-$129.** 8277 Yankee St. I-675, exit 2, just e on SR 725, then just s. Int corridors. **Pets:** Large, other species. $20 daily fee/pet. Service with restrictions, supervision.

SAVE S♦ ✕ ♿M 🛏 💻 ⇌

Dayton Marriott Hotel **LH**
(937) 223-1000. **$197-$218.** 1414 S Patterson Blvd. I-75, exit 51 (Edwin C Moses Blvd), 0.8 mi e, just s on Stewart St, then just w. Int corridors. **Pets:** Accepted.

ASK S♦ ✕ 🛏 💻 ¶↑ ⇌ ✕

Drury Inn & Suites-Dayton North **LH**
(937) 454-5200. **$83-$193.** 6616 Miller Ln. I-75, exit 59 (Wyse/Benchwood rds), just w on Benchwood Rd, then just n. Int corridors. **Pets:** Large, other species. Service with restrictions, supervision.

ASK ✕ ♿M 🛏 💻 ⇌

Extended StayAmerica-Dayton North **SH**
(937) 898-9221. **$85-$115.** 6688 Miller Ln. I-75, exit 59 (Wyse/Benchwood rds), just w on Benchwood Rd, then just n. Int corridors. **Pets:** Other species. $75 one-time fee/pet. Service with restrictions.

ASK S♦ ✕ 🛏 💻

Extended StayAmerica Dayton South **SH**
(937) 439-2022. **$85-$115.** 7851 Lois Cir. I-75, exit 44, just e on SR 725; opposite mall. Int corridors. **Pets:** Other species. $75 one-time fee/pet. Service with restrictions.

ASK S♦ ✕ 🛏 💻 ⇌

Hampton Inn-Dayton South **SH**
(937) 436-3700. **Call for rates.** 8099 Old Yankee St. I-675, exit 2, just e on SR 725, then just s. Int corridors. **Pets:** Accepted.

✕ 🛏 💻 ⇌

Howard Johnson Express Inn **SH**
(937) 454-0550. **$40-$60.** 7575 Poe Ave. I-75, exit 59 (Wyse/Benchwood rds), just e on Wyse Rd, just sw on Poe Ave/Wyse Rd connector, then 0.8 mi n. Int corridors. **Pets:** Accepted.

SAVE S♦ ✕ 🛏 💻 ⇌

Red Roof Inn-North #7023 **SH**
(937) 898-1054. **Call for rates.** 7370 Miller Ln. I-75, exit 59 (Wyse/Benchwood rds), just w on Benchwood Rd, then 0.8 mi n. Ext corridors. **Pets:** Accepted.

✕ 🛏

Residence Inn by Marriott-Dayton North **SH**
(937) 898-7764. **$143-$163.** 7070 Poe Ave. I-75, exit 59 (Wyse/Benchwood rds), just e on Wyse Rd, just sw on Poe Ave/Wyse Rd connector, then 0.6 mi n. Ext corridors. **Pets:** Accepted.

ASK S♦ ✕ 🛏 💻 ⇌ ✕

DOVER

Hospitality Inn **M**
(330) 364-7724. **Call for rates.** 889 Commercial Pkwy. I-77, exit 83, just e. Ext corridors. **Pets:** Accepted.

✕ 🛏 ⇌

ELYRIA

Comfort Inn **SH**
(440) 324-7676. **$69-$139.** 739 Leona St. I-80, exit 145, just n on SR 57, exit Midway Blvd. Int corridors. **Pets:** $10 daily fee/pet. Service with restrictions, supervision.

ASK S♦ ✕ 🛏 💻

Red Roof Inn & Suites **SH**
(440) 324-4444. **$59-$99.** 621 Midway Blvd. I-80, exit 145, just n on SR 57, exit Midway Blvd. Int corridors. **Pets:** Accepted.

ASK S♦ ✕ ♿M 🛏 💻 ⇌

Super 8 Motel **SH** ❖
(440) 323-7488. **$59-$99.** 910 Lorain Blvd. I-80, exit 145, 0.5 mi s on SR 57. Int corridors. **Pets:** $10 one-time fee/room. Service with restrictions, supervision.

ASK S♦ ✕ 💻 ⇌

ENGLEWOOD

Holiday Inn-Dayton Northwest Airport **SH**
(937) 832-1234. **$95.** 10 Rockridge Rd. I-70, exit 29, just n. Int corridors. **Pets:** Medium, other species. $10 daily fee/pet. Designated rooms.

ASK S♦ ✕ 💻 ¶↑ ⇌

Red Roof Inn-Dayton (Englewood) **M**
(937) 836-8339. **Call for rates.** 9325 N Main St. I-70, exit 29, just s. Ext corridors. **Pets:** Accepted.

✕ 🛏 ⇌

Super 8 Motel-Englewood **M**
(937) 832-3350. **Call for rates.** 15 Rockridge Rd. I-70, exit 29, just n. Ext corridors. **Pets:** Accepted.

✕ 🛏

FAIRBORN

▼▼▼ Best Western Wright Patterson SH
(937) 879-3920. **$75-$97.** 800 N Broad St. I-675, exit 24, 1.8 mi sw on SR 444. Int corridors. **Pets:** Small, other species. Service with restrictions, supervision.

A$K S♦ ✕ 🛏 💻 🍴 🌊

ǾǾ ▼▼▼ Hawthorn Inn & Suites SH
(937) 754-9109. **Call for rates.** 730 E Xenia Dr. I-675, exit 22, just w. Int corridors. **Pets:** Medium. $75 one-time fee/room. Service with restrictions, crate.

SAVE ✕ 🛏 💻

▼▼▼▼ Holiday Inn Dayton/Fairborn/I-675 SH
(937) 426-7800. **$109-$179.** 2800 Presidential Dr. I-675, exit 17 (N Fairfield Rd), just w. Int corridors. **Pets:** Accepted.

A$K ✕ 🛏 💻 🍴 🌊

▼▼▼▼ Homewood Suites by Hilton-Fairborn/Dayton SH
(937) 429-0600. **Call for rates.** 2750 Presidential Dr. I-675, exit 17 (N Fairfield Rd), just w. Ext/int corridors. **Pets:** Accepted.

✕ 🛏 💻 🌊

▼▼▼▼ Ramada Limited & Suites-Fairborn Ohio SH
(937) 490-2000. **Call for rates.** 2540 University Blvd. I-675, exit 15 (Colonel Glen Hwy), 1.5 mi e, then just s. Int corridors. **Pets:** Medium. $10 daily fee/room. Service with restrictions, crate.

✕ 🛏 💻 🌊

▼▼◆ Red Roof Inn-Fairborn #7205 SH
(937) 426-6116. **Call for rates.** 2580 Colonel Glenn Hwy. I-675, exit 17 (N Fairfield Rd), just w. Ext corridors. **Pets:** Accepted.

✕ 🛏

FAIRLAWN

ǾǾ ▼ Akron Super 8 Motel SH
(330) 666-8887. **$38-$100.** 79 Rothrock Rd. I-77, exit 137A, just e. Int corridors. **Pets:** Other species. $10 daily fee/pet. Service with restrictions.

SAVE S♦ ✕ 🛏 💻

▼▼ Extended StayAmerica SH
(330) 668-9818. **$74-$84.** 185 Montrose Ave W. I-77, exit 137B, just w on SR 18. Int corridors. **Pets:** Other species. $75 one-time fee/pet. Service with restrictions.

A$K S♦ ✕ 🛏 💻

▼ Motel 6 Akron North #2000 M
(330) 666-0566. **$45-$58.** 99 Rothrock Rd. I-77, exit 137A, just e. Ext corridors. **Pets:** Other species. Service with restrictions, supervision.

S♦ ✕

▼▼▼▼ The Residence Inn by Marriott SH
(330) 666-4811. **$198-$218.** 120 W Montrose Ave. I-77, exit 137B, just w. Ext corridors. **Pets:** Accepted.

A$K S♦ ✕ 🛏 💻 🌊 ✕

▼▼▼ StudioPLUS-Akron-Copley SH
(330) 666-3177. **$84-$94.** 170 Montrose Ave W. I-77, exit 137B, just w on SR 18. Int corridors. **Pets:** Other species. $75 one-time fee/pet. Service with restrictions.

A$K S♦ ✕ 🛏 💻 🌊

FINDLAY

ǾǾ ▼▼ Econo Lodge M
(419) 422-0154. **$38-$65.** 316 Emma St. I-75, exit 157, just w. Ext corridors. **Pets:** $10 daily fee/pet. Service with restrictions, crate.

SAVE ✕ 🛏 💻

▼▼▼ Extended Stay Deluxe SH
(419) 425-9696. **$80-$90.** 2355 Tiffin Ave. 3 mi e on US 224. Int corridors. **Pets:** Other species. $75 one-time fee/pet. Service with restrictions.

A$K S♦ ✕ 🛏 💻 🌊 ✕

▼▼◆ Quality Inn M
(419) 423-4303. **$65-$110.** 1020 Interstate Ct. I-75, exit 159, just w. Ext corridors. **Pets:** Medium, dogs only. $15 daily fee/pet. Designated rooms, service with restrictions, crate.

A$K S♦ ✕ 🛏 💻 🌊

▼▼ Red Roof Inn M
(419) 424-0466. **Call for rates.** 1951 Broad Ave. I-75, exit 159, 0.5 mi e. Ext corridors. **Pets:** Accepted.

✕ 🛏 🌊

▼▼ Super 8 Motel-Findlay SH
(419) 422-8863. **Call for rates.** 1600 Fox St. I-75, exit 159, just e. Int corridors. **Pets:** Accepted.

✕ 🛏

FREDERICKTOWN

▼▼▼ Heartland Country Resort CA 🐾
(419) 768-9300. **$120-$195, 7 day notice.** 3020 Township Rd 190. I-71, exit 151, 2 mi e on SR 95, 0.6 mi s on SR 314, then 1.3 mi e. Ext corridors. **Pets:** Other species. $15 daily fee/room.

A$K S♦ ✕ 🛏 💻 ✕

FREMONT

ǾǾ ▼▼◆ Comfort Inn & Suites SH
(419) 355-9300. **$90-$250.** 840 Sean Dr. I-80/90, exit 91, 2 mi s on SR 53. Int corridors. **Pets:** Medium, other species. $25 one-time fee/pet. Service with restrictions, supervision.

SAVE S♦ ✕ 🛏 💻 🌊

▼▼ Days Inn SH
(419) 334-9551. **$64-$119.** 3701 SR 53 N. I-80/90, exit 91, just n. Int corridors. **Pets:** Small, dogs only. $50 deposit/pet. Designated rooms, service with restrictions, supervision.

A$K S♦ ✕ 💻 🍴 🌊

▼▼▼ Holiday Inn-Fremont SH
(419) 334-2682. **Call for rates.** 3422 Port Clinton Rd. I-80/90, exit 91, just s. Int corridors. **Pets:** Accepted.

✕ 🛗M 🛏 💻 🍴 🌊

GENEVA

ǾǾ ▼▼ Howard Johnson Express Inn SH
(440) 466-1168. **$60-$95.** SR 534. I-90, exit 218, just n. Ext/int corridors. **Pets:** Large. $10 daily fee/room. Service with restrictions.

SAVE S♦ ✕ 🛏 💻 🌊

GENEVA-ON-THE-LAKE

ǾǾ ▼▼▼▼ The Lodge & Conference Center at Geneva-on-the-Lake SH 🐾
(440) 466-7100. **$89-$189, 3 day notice.** 4888 N Broadway. I-90, exit 218, 8 mi n. Ext corridors. **Pets:** Other species. $25 one-time fee/room. Designated rooms, service with restrictions, crate.

SAVE S♦ ✕ 🛗M 🛏 💻 🍴 🌊 ✕

GIRARD

ǾǾ ▼▼▼ Days Inn & Suites M
(330) 759-9820. **$42-$99.** 1615 E Liberty St. I-80, exit 229, just s. Int corridors. **Pets:** Medium. $25 deposit/pet. Designated rooms, service with restrictions, crate.

SAVE S♦ ✕ 🛏 💻 🌊

GREEN

ǾǾ ▼▼▼ Super 8 Motel SH
(330) 899-9888. **$66-$100.** 1605 Corporate Woods Pkwy. I-77, exit 118, just w. **Pets:** Large. $10 daily fee/pet. Service with restrictions, supervision.

SAVE S♦ ✕ 🛏 💻 🌊

GREENVILLE

Greenville Inn SH
(937) 548-3613. **$65-$115.** 851 E Martin. Jct US 36 and 127, 0.3 mi w on SR 571. Int corridors. **Pets:** Other species. $10 daily fee/pet. Service with restrictions, supervision.

HOLLAND

Econo Lodge M
(419) 866-6565. **$40-$80.** 1201 E Mall Dr. I-475, exit 8, just w on SR 2. Ext corridors. **Pets:** Small, dogs only. $10 daily fee/pet. Designated rooms, no service, supervision.

Extended StayAmerica SH
(419) 861-1133. **$69-$79.** 6155 Trust Dr. I-475, exit 8, just e to Holland-Sylvania Rd, then just n. Int corridors. **Pets:** Other species. $75 one-time fee/pet. Service with restrictions.

Quality Inn Toledo Airport M
(419) 867-1144. **$59-$149.** 1401 E Mall Dr. I-475, exit 8, just w on SR 2. Ext/int corridors. **Pets:** $10 daily fee/pet. Service with restrictions, supervision.

Red Roof Inn Toledo/Holland #7058 M
(419) 866-5512. **Call for rates.** 1214 Corporate Dr. I-475, exit 8, just e on Holland-Sylvania Rd, then just n to Trust Dr. Ext corridors. **Pets:** Accepted.

Residence Inn by Marriott SH
(419) 867-9555. **$186-$208.** 6101 Trust Dr. I-475, exit 8, just e to Holland-Sylvania Rd, then just n. Ext corridors. **Pets:** Accepted.

HUBBARD

Best Western Penn Ohio Inn & Suites SH
(330) 534-5100. **$90-$129.** 6828 Commerce Dr. I-80, exit 234, just n. Int corridors. **Pets:** Accepted.

HUBER HEIGHTS

Americas Best Value Inn M
(937) 236-9361. **$50-$65.** 7911 Brandt Pike. I-70, exit 38, just s at SR 201. Ext/int corridors. **Pets:** Small. $10 daily fee/pet. Designated rooms, service with restrictions, crate.

Holiday Inn Express Hotel & Suites SH
(937) 235-2000. **$105-$150.** 5612 Merily Way. I-70, exit 36, just se on SR 202. Int corridors. **Pets:** $25 one-time fee/room. Service with restrictions, supervision.

HURON

Microtel Inn & Suites SH
(419) 433-7829. **$50-$150, 3 day notice.** 601 Rye Beach Rd. SR 2, exit Rye Beach, 2.5 mi w on US 6. Int corridors. **Pets:** Medium. $10 daily fee/pet. Service with restrictions, supervision.

JACKSON

Comfort Inn-Jackson SH
(740) 286-7581. **$80-$90, 30 day notice.** 605 E Main St. Jct SR 32, 0.5 mi n on SR 93. Int corridors. **Pets:** Accepted.

Red Roof Inn M
(740) 288-1200. **Call for rates.** 1000 Acy Ave. US 35, exit McCarty Ln, just nw. Int corridors. **Pets:** Accepted.

JEFFERSONVILLE

Quality Inn-Washington Court House SH
(740) 426-6400. **$59-$170.** 10160 Carr Rd NW. I-71, exit 69 (SR 41), just w. Int corridors. **Pets:** $25 daily fee/pet. Designated rooms, service with restrictions, supervision.

KENT

Days Inn-Akron Kent M
(330) 677-9400. **Call for rates.** 4422 Edson Rd. I-76, exit 33. Ext corridors. **Pets:** Accepted.

Super 8 Motel SH
(330) 678-8817. **Call for rates.** 4380 Edson Rd. I-76, exit 33. Int corridors. **Pets:** $10 daily fee/pet. Service with restrictions, supervision.

KENTON

AmeriHost Inn-Kenton SH
(419) 675-1400. **$94-$125.** 902 E Columbus St. Jct US 68 and SR 67, just ne on SR 67. Int corridors. **Pets:** Dogs only. $25 daily fee/pet. Service with restrictions, supervision.

LIMA

Holiday Inn Lima SH
(419) 222-0004. **$94-$159.** 1920 Roschman Ave. I-75, exit 125A, just se. Int corridors. **Pets:** Other species. Service with restrictions, crate.

LOGAN

Baymont Inn and Suites SH
(740) 385-1700. **$69-$179.** 12819 SR 664. Jct US 33, just n. Int corridors. **Pets:** Small, other species. $10 daily fee/pet. Service with restrictions, supervision.

Holiday Inn Express Hocking Hills SH
(740) 385-7700. **$129-$165.** 12916 Grey St. SR 664, just w to Lake Logan Rd, then just n. Int corridors. **Pets:** Small, dogs only. Designated rooms, service with restrictions, supervision.

The Inn At Cedar Falls CI
(740) 385-7489. **$119-$279.** 21190 SR 374. 9.5 mi s on SR 664, 1 mi e. Int corridors. **Pets:** Dogs only. $30 daily fee/pet. Designated rooms, service with restrictions, crate.

LOUDONVILLE

Little Brown Inn M
(419) 994-5525. **$49-$79.** 940 S Market St. 1 mi s on SR 3. Int corridors. **Pets:** Small. $10 daily fee/pet. Designated rooms, no service, supervision.

MANSFIELD

All America Inn Mansfield SH
(419) 756-6670. **$59-$159.** 180 E Hanley Rd. I-71, exit 169, jct SR 13. Int corridors. **Pets:** $25 one-time fee/room. No service, supervision.

▽▽▽ Comfort Inn North 🆂🅷
(419) 529-1000. **$70-$160.** 500 N Trimble Rd. Jct US 30. Int corridors. **Pets:** Medium, other species. $50 deposit/room. Service with restrictions, supervision.
🅰🅂🅺 🆂🖄 ⊠ 🅱 🖵 ⊅ 🖾

🅐🅐🅐 ▽ Econo Lodge 🆂🅷
(419) 589-3333. **$55-$70.** 1017 Koogle Rd. I-71, exit 176, just e. Int corridors. **Pets:** Small. $5 daily fee/pet. Service with restrictions, supervision.
🆂🅰🆅🅴 🆂🖄 ⊠ 🅱

▽ Knights Inn Ⓜ
(419) 529-2100. **Call for rates.** 555 N Trimble Rd. Jct US 30. Ext corridors. **Pets:** Dogs only. $10 deposit/pet. Service with restrictions, supervision.
⊠ 🅱 🖵

🅐🅐🅐 ▽▽▽▽ La Quinta Inns 🆂🅷
(419) 774-0005. **$90.** 120 Stander Ave. I-71, exit 169. Int corridors. **Pets:** Other species. Service with restrictions, supervision.
🆂🅰🆅🅴 🆂🖄 ⊠ 🅗 🅱 🖵 ⊅

🅐🅐🅐 ▽▽ Super 8 Motel 🆂🅷
(419) 756-8875. **Call for rates.** 2425 Interstate Cir. I-71, exit 169. Int corridors. **Pets:** Accepted.
🆂🅰🆅🅴 ⊠ 🅱 🖵

🅐🅐🅐 ▽▽ Travelodge Ⓜ
(419) 756-7600. **$50-$100.** 90 W Hanley Rd. I-71, exit 169, just s. Ext corridors. **Pets:** Medium. $10 daily fee/pet. Service with restrictions, supervision.
🆂🅰🆅🅴 🆂🖄 ⊠ 🅱 🖵

MARIETTA

🅐🅐🅐 ▽▽▽ Americas Best Value Inn Ⓜ
(740) 373-7373. **$42-$48.** 506 Pike St. I-77, exit 1, just w. Ext corridors. **Pets:** Accepted.
🆂🅰🆅🅴 🆂🖄 ⊠ 🅱 🖵 ⊅

▽▽▽ Best Western Marietta Ⓜ
(740) 374-7211. **$66-$139.** 279 Muskingum Dr. I-77, exit 6, 3.5 mi sw on SR 821, then 1 mi s on SR 60. Ext corridors. **Pets:** Accepted.
🅰🅂🅺 🆂🖄 ⊠ 🅱 🖵 🖾

▽▽▽▽ The Lafayette Hotel 🅻🅷
(740) 373-5522. **$55-$160.** 101 Front St. Center. Int corridors. **Pets:** Accepted.
🅰🅂🅺 🆂🖄 ⊠ 🅱 🖵 🍴

▽▽ Super 8 Motel-Marietta 🆂🅷
(740) 374-8888. **$50-$57.** 46 Acme St. I-77, exit 1, just w. Int corridors. **Pets:** Accepted.
🅰🅂🅺 🆂🖄 ⊠ 🅱

MARION

▽▽ Comfort Inn by Choice Hotels 🆂🅷
(740) 389-5552. **$70-$75.** 256 James Way. Jct US 23 and SR 95, just w. Int corridors. **Pets:** Accepted.
🅰🅂🅺 🆂🖄 ⊠ 🅱 🖵 ⊅

MASSILLON

▽▽▽▽ Hampton Inn-Canton/Massillon 🆂🅷
(330) 834-1144. **$94-$124.** 44 First St SW. Downtown. Int corridors. **Pets:** Accepted.
🅰🅂🅺 🆂🖄 ⊠ 🅗 🖵

MAUMEE

🅐🅐🅐 ▽▽▽▽ Comfort Inn West Toledo/Maumee 🆂🅷
(419) 893-2800. **$69-$99.** 1426 S Reynolds Rd. I-80/90, exit 59, just s. Int corridors. **Pets:** Medium. $10 daily fee/pet. Service with restrictions, supervision.
🆂🅰🆅🅴 🆂🖄 ⊠ 🅱 🖵 ⊅

🅐🅐🅐 ▽▽▽ Days Inn-Toledo/Maumee Ⓜ
(419) 897-6900. **Call for rates.** 1704 Tollgate Dr. I-80/90, exit 59, just s. Ext corridors. **Pets:** Other species. $10 daily fee/pet. No service, supervision.
🆂🅰🆅🅴 ⊠ 🅱 🖵 ⊅

▽▽▽▽ Homewood Suites by Hilton-Toledo 🆂🅷
(419) 897-0980. **Call for rates.** 1410 Arrowhead Rd. I-475, exit 6, just e. Int corridors. **Pets:** Accepted.
⊠ 🅗 🅱 🖵 ⊅ 🖾

▽▽ Red Roof Inn-Maumee #7046 Ⓜ
(419) 893-0292. **Call for rates.** 1570 S Reynolds Rd. I-80/90, exit 59, just s. Ext/int corridors. **Pets:** Accepted.
⊠ 🅱

▽▽ StudioPLUS-Toledo-Maumee 🆂🅷
(419) 891-1211. **$79-$89.** 542 W Dussel Dr. I-475, exit 8, just e. Int corridors. **Pets:** Other species. $75 one-time fee/pet. Service with restrictions.
🅰🅂🅺 🆂🖄 ⊠ 🅱 🖵 ⊅

🅐🅐🅐 ▽▽▽ Super 8 Motel-Maumee/Toledo 🆂🅷
(419) 897-3800. **Call for rates.** 1390 Arrowhead Rd. I-475, exit 6, just e. Int corridors. **Pets:** Accepted.
🆂🅰🆅🅴 ⊠ 🅱 🖵

MENTOR

🅐🅐🅐 ▽▽▽▽ Best Western Lawnfield Inn & Suites 🆂🅷 ❀
(440) 205-7378. **$79-$149.** 8434 Mentor Ave. I-90, exit 195, 1.5 mi n to SR 20 (Mentor Ave) then just e. Int corridors. **Pets:** $20 one-time fee/pet. Service with restrictions, supervision.
🆂🅰🆅🅴 🆂🖄 ⊠ 🅗 🅱 🖵 ⊅

▽▽▽▽ Residence Inn by Marriott 🆂🅷
(440) 392-0800. **$129-$209.** 5660 Emerald Ct. Jct SR 2 and Heisley Rd, just s. Int corridors. **Pets:** Other species. $75 one-time fee/room. Service with restrictions, crate.
🅰🅂🅺 🆂🖄 ⊠ 🅱 🖵 ⊅ 🖾

▽▽ Studio 6 #6019 Ⓜ
(440) 946-0749. **$57-$67.** 7677 Reynolds Rd. Just s of SR 2 on SR 306. Ext corridors. **Pets:** Other species. Service with restrictions, supervision.
🆂🖄 ⊠ 🅗 🅱 🖵

🅐🅐🅐 ▽▽▽ Super 8 Motel 🆂🅷
(440) 951-8558. **$49-$89.** 7325 Palisades Pkwy. On SR 306, just s of SR 2. Int corridors. **Pets:** Other species. $15 daily fee/pet. Service with restrictions, supervision.
🆂🅰🆅🅴 ⊠ 🅱

MIAMISBURG

▽▽▽▽ Holiday Inn-Dayton Mall 🆂🅷
(937) 434-8030. **$89-$149.** 31 Prestige Plaza Dr. I-75, exit 44, just e on SR 725, then just s. Int corridors. **Pets:** $30 one-time fee/room. Service with restrictions, crate.
🅰🅂🅺 🆂🖄 ⊠ 🅱 🖵 🍴 ⊅ 🖾

▽▽▽▽ Homewood Suites by Hilton-Dayton South 🆂🅷
(937) 432-0000. **Call for rates.** 3100 Contemporary Ln. I-75, exit 44, just e on SR 725, just se on Prestige Plaza Dr, then just s. Int corridors. **Pets:** Accepted.
⊠ 🅱 🖵 ⊅

Red Roof Inn-South #7006 SH
(937) 866-0705. **Call for rates.** 222 Byers Rd. I-75, exit 44, just w on SR 725. Ext corridors. **Pets:** Accepted.

Residence Inn by Marriott-Dayton South SH
(937) 434-7881. **$172-$192.** 155 Prestige Pl. I-75, exit 44, just e on SR 725, just se on Prestige Plaza Dr, then just s. Ext corridors. **Pets:** Accepted.

Super 8 Miamisburg/South Dayton SH
(937) 866-5500. **Call for rates.** 155 Monarch Ln. I-75, exit 44, 0.5 mi w on SR 725. Int corridors. **Pets:** Medium. $10 one-time fee/pet. Service with restrictions, supervision.

MILAN

Motel 6–4016 SH
(419) 499-8001. **$39-$139, 3 day notice.** 11406 US 250 N. I-80/90, exit 118, 1.5 mi n. Int corridors. **Pets:** Other species. Service with restrictions, supervision.

Red Roof Inn SH
(419) 499-4347. **$49-$159.** 11303 Rt 250/Milan Rd. I-80/90, exit 118, 0.5 mi n. Int corridors. **Pets:** Small, dogs only. $50 deposit/pet. Designated rooms, service with restrictions, supervision.

Super 8 Motel SH
(419) 499-4671. **$44-$149.** 11313 Milan Rd. I-80/90, exit 118, 0.5 mi n on SR 250. Int corridors. **Pets:** Small, dogs only. $50 deposit/pet. Designated rooms, service with restrictions, supervision.

MILLERSBURG

Comfort Inn Millersburg SH
(330) 674-7400. **$69-$149.** 1102 Glen Dr. SR 39, 0.5 mi s on S Clay. Int corridors. **Pets:** Small, dogs only. $15 daily fee/pet. Designated rooms, service with restrictions, supervision.

Hotel Millersburg SH
(330) 674-1457. **$65-$169.** 35 W Jackson St. Downtown. Int corridors. **Pets:** Small. $10 daily fee/room. Designated rooms, supervision.

MONTPELIER

Holiday Inn Express Hotel & Suites Bryan/ Montpelier SH
(419) 485-0008. **$100, 3 day notice.** 13399 SR 15. I-80/90, exit 13, just s. Int corridors. **Pets:** Other species. $10 one-time fee/pet. Service with restrictions, crate.

Ramada Inn & Suites SH
(419) 485-5555. **$79-$99.** 13508 SR 15. I-80/90, exit 13, just s. Int corridors. **Pets:** Other species. Service with restrictions, crate.

MORAINE

Holiday Inn Hotel & Suites Dayton South SH
(937) 294-1471. **Call for rates.** 2455 Dryden Rd. I-75, exit 50A (Dryden Rd), just nw. Int corridors. **Pets:** Small, other species. $10 daily fee/pet. Service with restrictions, supervision.

MOUNT GILEAD

Knights Inn M
(419) 946-6010. **$50-$99.** 5898 SR 95. I-71, exit 151, 0.3 mi w. Ext corridors. **Pets:** $10 daily fee/pet. Service with restrictions, supervision.

MOUNT VERNON

Comfort Inn SH
(740) 392-6886. **$70-$150, 14 day notice.** 150 Howard St. Jct SR 13; south of downtown. Int corridors. **Pets:** Other species. $10 daily fee/pet. Service with restrictions, supervision.

Holiday Inn Express SH
(740) 392-1900. **$99-$129.** 11555 Upper Gilchrist Rd. 3 mi e on US 36, then just s. Int corridors. **Pets:** Accepted.

NAPOLEON

Best Western Napoleon Inn & Suites SH
(419) 599-0850. **$59-$74.** 1290 Independence Dr. From US 6/24, just se. Int corridors. **Pets:** Other species. $12 daily fee/pet. Supervision.

NEWCOMERSTOWN

Hampton Inn SH
(740) 498-9800. **$89-$150.** 200 Morris Crossing. I-77, exit 65, 0.8 mi w. Int corridors. **Pets:** Small, dogs only. Service with restrictions, supervision.

NEW PHILADELPHIA

Holiday Inn-New Philadelphia/Dover SH
(330) 339-7731. **$59-$109.** 131 Bluebell Dr SW. I-77, exit 81, 0.4 mi e. Int corridors. **Pets:** Dogs only. $20 daily fee/pet. Designated rooms, supervision.

NEWTON FALLS

Econo Lodge M
(330) 872-0988. **$45-$99.** 4248 SR 5. I-80, exit 209, just w. Ext corridors. **Pets:** Large, other species. $10 daily fee/pet. Service with restrictions, crate.

NORTH CANTON

Knights Inn Canton M
(330) 492-5030. **$44-$130.** 3950 Convenience Cir NW. I-77, exit 109 southbound, 0.3 mi e on Everhard, then 0.3 mi s on Whipple; exit 109A northbound, 0.3 mi s on Whipple. Ext corridors. **Pets:** Accepted.

NORTH LIMA

Quality Inn and Suites SH
(330) 549-9190. **Call for rates.** 10076 Market St. I-76, exit 232, 0.5 mi n. Ext corridors. **Pets:** Medium, other species. $10 daily fee/pet. Service with restrictions, crate.

NORTHWOOD

Comfort Inn South SH
(419) 666-2600. **$70-$100.** 2426 Oregon Rd. I-75, exit 198, just e; jct Wales and Oregon rds. Int corridors. **Pets:** Accepted.

NORWALK

◆◆ Econo Lodge M
(419) 668-5656. **$44-$144.** 342 Milan Ave. 3 mi n on US 250; 6 mi s of I-80/90 (Ohio Tpke). Ext corridors. **Pets:** Small, dogs only. $50 deposit/pet. Designated rooms, service with restrictions, supervision.

A$K S☉ ✕ 🖬 💻 ⇌

OBERLIN

◆◆◆ Oberlin Inn CI
(440) 775-1111. **$109-$189.** 7 N Main St. On SR 58; jct College and Main sts; center. Int corridors. **Pets:** Accepted.

A$K S☉ ✕ 🖬 💻 �🍴

OREGON

◆◆◆ ◆◆ Comfort Inn East SH ❀
(419) 691-8911. **$79-$99.** 2930 Navarre Ave. I-280, exit 7, just n on access road, then 0.5 mi e on SR 2 (Navarre Ave). Int corridors. **Pets:** $15 one-time fee/room. Designated rooms, service with restrictions, supervision.

SAVE S☉ ✕ 🖬 💻 ⇌

◆◆◆ ◆◆ Sleep Inn & Suites SH ❀
(419) 697-7800. **$79-$109.** 1761 Meijer Cir. I-280, exit 6, just w. Int corridors. **Pets:** $45 one-time fee/room. Designated rooms, service with restrictions, supervision.

SAVE S☉ ✕ 🖬 💻 ⇌

PERRYSBURG

◆◆◆ ◆◆ Howard Johnson Inn Toledo South M
(419) 837-5245. **$39-$79.** 3555 Hanley Rd. I-80/90, exit 71 to I-280, exit 1B. Ext/int corridors. **Pets:** Other species. $10 daily fee/pet. Service with restrictions, supervision.

SAVE S☉ ✕ 🖬 💻 ⇌

◆◆ La Quinta Inn & Suites Toledo-Perrysburg SH
(419) 872-0000. **$90.** 1154 Professional Dr. I-75, exit 193, just w. Int corridors. **Pets:** Other species. Service with restrictions, supervision.

A$K S☉ ✕ 🖬 💻

◆◆◆ ◆◆ Super 8 Motel-Toledo/Perrysburg/Millbury M
(419) 837-6409. **$39-$89.** 3491 Latcha Rd. I-80/90, exit 71 to I-280, exit 1B, just n. Ext corridors. **Pets:** Other species. $10 daily fee/pet. Service with restrictions, supervision.

SAVE S☉ ✕ 🖬

PIQUA

◆◆◆ ◆◆◆ Comfort Inn-Piqua SH
(937) 778-8100. **$84-$94.** 987 E Ash St. I-75, exit 82, just w. Int corridors. **Pets:** Small, other species. $25 daily fee/pet. Service with restrictions, crate.

SAVE S☉ ✕ 🖬 💻 ⇌

◆◆◆ La Quinta Inn Piqua SH
(937) 615-0140. **$72.** 950 E Ash St. I-75, exit 82, just w. Int corridors. **Pets:** Other species. Service with restrictions, supervision.

A$K S☉ ✕ 🖬 💻 ⇌

POLAND

◆◆ Red Roof Inn #7253 SH
(330) 758-1999. **Call for rates.** 1051 Tiffany S. I-680, exit 11, just w. Int corridors. **Pets:** Accepted.

✕ 🖬 💻

◆◆◆ Residence Inn by Marriott-Youngstown SH
(330) 726-1747. **Call for rates.** 7396 Tiffany S. I-680, exit 11, just w. Int corridors. **Pets:** Accepted.

✕ 🖬 💻 ⇌ ⊠

PORT CLINTON

◆◆ Best Western Port Clinton SH
(419) 734-2274. **$49-$159.** 1734 E Perry St. 1.7 mi e on SR 163, w of jct SR 2. Int corridors. **Pets:** Small, dogs only. $50 deposit/pet. Designated rooms, service with restrictions, supervision.

A$K S☉ ✕ 💻 ⇌

◆◆◆ ◆◆ Commodore Perry Inn & Suites SH
(419) 732-2645. **$49-$59, 3 day notice.** 255 W Lakeshore Dr. Just n of bridge. Int corridors. **Pets:** $15 one-time fee/pet.

SAVE ✕ 🖬 💻 🍴 ⇌

◆◆ Country Hearth Inn M
(419) 732-2111. **Call for rates.** 1815 E Perry St. 1.2 mi e on SR 163, w of jct SR 2. Ext/int corridors. **Pets:** Accepted.

✕ 🖬 💻 ⇌

◆◆ Days Inn Port Clinton M
(419) 734-4945. **Call for rates.** 2149 E Gill Rd. SR 2, exit 163, 0.3 mi e to Gill Rd, then 0.3 mi s. Ext corridors. **Pets:** Accepted.

✕ 🖬 💻 ⇌

◆◆ Super 8 SH
(419) 734-4446. **$49-$149.** 1704 E Perry St. 1.7 mi e on SR 163, w of jct SR 2. Int corridors. **Pets:** Small, dogs only. $50 deposit/pet. Designated rooms, service with restrictions, supervision.

A$K S☉ ✕ 💻

PORTSMOUTH

◆◆ Portsmouth Super 8 Motel SH
(740) 353-8880. **Call for rates.** 4266 US Rt 23 N. 5 mi n. Int corridors. **Pets:** Accepted.

✕ 🖬 💻 ⇌

RIO GRANDE

◆ College Hill Motel M
(740) 245-5326. **$69-$79.** 10987 State Rt 588. US 35, exit Rio Grande. Ext corridors. **Pets:** $10 daily fee/pet. No service.

A$K S☉ ✕ 🖬

ST. CLAIRSVILLE

◆◆◆ ◆◆ Americas Best Value Inn St. Clairsville/Wheeling M
(740) 695-5038. **$59-$129.** 51260 National Rd. I-70, exit 218, 0.5 mi ne on US 40. Ext corridors. **Pets:** $10 one-time fee/room. Service with restrictions, supervision.

SAVE S☉ ✕ 🖬 💻 ⇌

◆◆ Red Roof Inn #7101 M
(740) 695-4057. **Call for rates.** 68301 Red Roof Ln. I-70, exit 218, just n. Ext corridors. **Pets:** Accepted.

✕ 🖬

ST. MARYS

◆◆◆ ◆◆ Americas Best Value Inn St Marys SH ❀
(419) 394-2341. **$58-$128.** 1321 Celina Rd. SR 66/29, 0.8 mi w on SR 703. Ext corridors. **Pets:** Small, dogs only. $15 daily fee/pet. Designated rooms, service with restrictions, supervision.

SAVE S☉ ✕ 🖬 💻 ⇌ ⊠

◆◆◆ ◆◆ Country Hearth Inn and Suites SH
(419) 394-2710. **$79-$99, 14 day notice.** 1410 Commerce Dr. Jct US 33 and SR 29, just s. Int corridors. **Pets:** Accepted.

SAVE S☉ ✕ 🖬 💻 ⇌

SANDUSKY

△△△ ▽▽▽ **Best Budget Inn** Ⓜ
(419) 626-3610. **$39-$129.** 2027 Cleveland Rd. US 6, just e of Cedar Point Cswy. Ext/int corridors. **Pets:** Medium, dogs only. $50 deposit/pet. Designated rooms, service with restrictions, supervision.
ⓈⒶⓋⒺ Ⓢ◑ ⓧ ➰

▽▽ **Knights Inn Sandusky** Ⓜ
(419) 621-9000. **$44-$139.** 2405 Cleveland Rd. US 6, 2 mi e of Cedar Point Cswy. Ext/int corridors. **Pets:** Small, dogs only. $25 deposit/room, $10 daily fee/pet. Designated rooms, service with restrictions, supervision.
ⒶⓈⓀ ⓧ 🔋 💻 ➰

SEAMAN

▽▽ **Comfort Inn** 🆂🅷
(937) 386-2511. **$79-$105.** 55 Stern Dr. Jct SR 32 and 247. Int corridors. **Pets:** Accepted.
ⒶⓈⓀ Ⓢ◑ ⓧ 🅐Ⓜ 🔋 💻 ➰

SEVILLE

▽▽▽ **Hawthorn Suites Ltd** 🆂🅷
(330) 769-5025. **$79-$129.** 5025 Park Ave W. SR 224, exit 2, just n. Int corridors. **Pets:** Small. $75 one-time fee/room. Designated rooms, service with restrictions.
ⒶⓈⓀ Ⓢ◑ ⓧ 🔋 💻 ➰

▽▽ **Super 8 Motel-Seville** 🆂🅷
(330) 769-8880. **Call for rates.** 6116 Speedway Dr. Jct SR 224 and Lake Rd. Int corridors. **Pets:** Medium, other species. $25 one-time fee/pet. Service with restrictions, supervision.
ⓧ 🅐Ⓜ 🔋 💻

SIDNEY

△△△ ▽▽▽ **Comfort Inn** 🆂🅷
(937) 492-3001. **$80.** 1959 W Michigan Ave. I-75, exit 92, just sw of SR 47. Int corridors. **Pets:** Medium. $25 one-time fee/pet. Service with restrictions, supervision.
ⓈⒶⓋⒺ Ⓢ◑ ⓧ 🔋 💻 ➰

▽▽ **Econo Lodge** 🆂🅷
(937) 492-9164. **Call for rates.** 2009 W Michigan St. I-75, exit 92, just w on SR 47. Ext/int corridors. **Pets:** Accepted.
ⓧ 🔋 💻

▽▽▽ **Holiday Inn** 🆂🅷
(937) 492-1131. **$85-$119.** 400 Folkerth Ave. I-75, exit 92, just w. Int corridors. **Pets:** Accepted.
ⒶⓈⓀ Ⓢ◑ ⓧ 🔋 💻 🍽 ➰

SPRINGFIELD

▽▽▽ **Holiday Inn South Springfield Ohio** 🆂🅷 🐾
(937) 323-8631. **$105.** 383 E Leffel Ln. I-70, exit 54, just n, then e. Int corridors. **Pets:** Service with restrictions, supervision.
ⒶⓈⓀ Ⓢ◑ ⓧ 🔋 💻 🍽 ➰ ⊠

△△△ ▽▽▽ **Ramada Limited** 🆂🅷
(937) 328-0123. **$60-$110.** 319 E Leffel Ln. I-70, exit 54, just n, then e. Int corridors. **Pets:** Small, dogs only. $10 daily fee/pet. Designated rooms, service with restrictions, supervision.
ⓈⒶⓋⒺ Ⓢ◑ ⓧ 🔋 💻 ➰

△△△ ▽▽▽ **Red Roof Inn** 🆂🅷
(937) 325-5356. **Call for rates.** 155 W Leffel Ln. I-70, exit 54, just n, then w. Int corridors. **Pets:** Accepted.
ⓈⒶⓋⒺ ⓧ 🔋 💻 ➰

STEUBENVILLE

△△△ ▽▽▽▽ **Holiday Inn-Steubenville** 🆂🅷 🐾
(740) 282-0901. **$100-$120.** 1401 University Blvd. Jct US 22 and SR 7, 1 mi sw. Ext/int corridors. **Pets:** Medium. $25 daily fee/room. Service with restrictions, crate.
ⓈⒶⓋⒺ Ⓢ◑ ⓧ 🔋 💻 🍽

STRASBURG

△△△ ▽▽▽ **Ramada Limited Dover/Strasburg** 🆂🅷
(330) 878-1400. **$70-$125.** 509 S Wooster Ave. I-77, exit 87, 0.4 mi n on US 250 and SR 21. Int corridors. **Pets:** Dogs only. $15 daily fee/room. Service with restrictions, supervision.
ⓈⒶⓋⒺ Ⓢ◑ ⓧ 🅐Ⓜ 🔋 💻 ➰

STREETSBORO

△△△ ▽▽▽ **Microtel Inn & Suites of Streetsboro** 🆂🅷 🐾
(330) 422-1234. **$70-$90.** 9371 SR 14. I-80, exit 187, 1.2 mi s. Int corridors. **Pets:** Medium, other species. $35 one-time fee/room. Service with restrictions, crate.
ⓈⒶⓋⒺ Ⓢ◑ ⓧ 🔋 💻 ➰

▽▽ **TownePlace Suites by Marriott** 🆂🅷
(330) 422-1855. **$153-$186.** 795 Mondial Pkwy. I-80, exit 187, 0.8 mi s. Int corridors. **Pets:** Medium, other species. $100 one-time fee/pet. Service with restrictions.
ⒶⓈⓀ Ⓢ◑ ⓧ 🔋 💻 ➰

SWANTON

△△△ ▽▽▽ **Days Inn** 🆂🅷
(419) 865-2002. **Call for rates.** 10753 Airport Hwy. I-80/90, exit 3A, just s, then e. Int corridors. **Pets:** Accepted.
ⓈⒶⓋⒺ ⓧ 💻

TIFFIN

▽▽▽ **Holiday Inn Express** 🆂🅷
(419) 443-5100. **$85-$139.** 78 Shaffer Park Dr. Just w of mall. Int corridors. **Pets:** Other species. $20 one-time fee/room. Service with restrictions, supervision.
ⒶⓈⓀ Ⓢ◑ ⓧ 🔋 💻 ➰

▽▽ **Quality Inn** 🆂🅷
(419) 447-6313. **$80-$135.** 1927 S SR 53. Jct US 224 and SR 53, 2 mi sw. Ext/int corridors. **Pets:** $20 daily fee/pet. Designated rooms, service with restrictions, crate.
ⒶⓈⓀ Ⓢ◑ ⓧ 🔋 💻 🍽 ➰

TOLEDO

△△△ ▽▽▽ **Comfort Inn-North** 🆂🅷
(419) 476-0170. **$74-$94.** 445 E Alexis Rd. I-75, exit 210, 2 mi w on SR 184; just e of jct US 24 and SR 184. Int corridors. **Pets:** Accepted.
ⓈⒶⓋⒺ Ⓢ◑ ⓧ 🔋 💻

△△△ ▽▽▽▽ **Park Inn Hotel** 🆂🅷
(419) 241-3000. **$138-$159.** 101 N Summit St. Between Jefferson and Monroe sts; downtown. Int corridors. **Pets:** Designated rooms, service with restrictions, crate.
ⓈⒶⓋⒺ Ⓢ◑ ⓧ 💻 🍽

▽▽ **Red Roof Inn Toledo University #7196** Ⓜ
(419) 536-0118. **Call for rates.** 3530 Executive Pkwy. I-475, exit 17, 0.5 mi s on Secor Rd, then just e. Ext corridors. **Pets:** Accepted.
ⓧ 🔋

TROY

▽▽▽ **Holiday Inn Express Hotel & Suites** 🆂🅷
(937) 332-1700. **Call for rates.** 60 Troy Town Dr. I-75, exit 74, just w. Int corridors. **Pets:** Small. $25 one-time fee/pet. Service with restrictions, crate.
ⓧ 🔋 💻 ➰

▼▼▼▼ Residence Inn By Marriott 🆂🅷
(937) 440-9303. **$164-$184.** 87 Troy Town Dr. I-75, exit 74, just w. Int corridors. **Pets:** Accepted.

🅰🆂🅺 🆂🕭 ✕ 🅗 🖵 🏊 ✕

UHRICHSVILLE

🅐🅐🅐 ▼▼▼ Best Western Country Inn 🅼
(740) 922-0774. **$50-$79.** 111 McCauley Dr. US 250, exit McCauley Dr. Ext corridors. **Pets:** $5 one-time fee/pet. Service with restrictions, crate.

🆂🅰🆅🅴 🆂🕭 ✕ 🅗 🖵

URBANA

🅐🅐🅐 ▼▼▼ Econo Lodge Urbana 🅼
(937) 652-2188. **Call for rates.** 2551 S US Hwy 68. 1.3 mi s. Ext corridors. **Pets:** Accepted.

🆂🅰🆅🅴 ✕ 🅗 🏊

VANDALIA

🅐🅐🅐 ▼▼▼ Super 8 Motel-Vandalia 🅼
(937) 898-7636. **$37-$100.** 550 E National Rd. I-75, exit 63, just w. Ext corridors. **Pets:** Accepted.

🆂🅰🆅🅴 🆂🕭 ✕ 🅗 🖵 🏊

▼▼ Travelodge Dayton Airport 🅼
(937) 898-8321. **Call for rates.** 75 Corporate Center Dr. I-70, exit 32, 2.5 mi n, then just e. Ext corridors. **Pets:** Accepted.

✕ 🅗 🖵 🏊

VERMILION

▼▼▼▼ Holiday Inn Express 🆂🅷
(440) 967-8770. **$85-$160.** 2417 SR 60. Jct SR 2 and 60. Int corridors. **Pets:** Medium. $15 one-time fee/room. Service with restrictions, supervision.

🅰🆂🅺 🆂🕭 ✕ 🅗 🖵 🏊

▼ Motel Plaza 🅼
(440) 967-3191. **$65-$89.** 4645 Liberty Ave. On US 6, 2 mi e of SR 60. Ext corridors. **Pets:** $20 deposit/pet. Service with restrictions, supervision.

🅰🆂🅺 🆂🕭 ✕ 🅗

WADSWORTH

🅐🅐🅐 ◆ Legacy Inn 🅼
(330) 336-6671. **$39-$51, 3 day notice.** 810 High St. I-76, exit 9, just s. Ext corridors. **Pets:** Medium. $5 daily fee/room. Service with restrictions, crate.

🆂🅰🆅🅴 🆂🕭 ✕ 🅗 🏊

WAPAKONETA

▼▼▼▼ Holiday Inn Express 🆂🅷
(419) 738-2050. **$89-$99.** 1008 Lunar Dr. I-75, exit 111, just w. Int corridors. **Pets:** Accepted.

🅰🆂🅺 🆂🕭 ✕ 🅗 🖵 🏊

WARREN

🅐🅐🅐 ▼▼▼ Americas Best Value Inn 🅼
(330) 392-2515. **$60-$80, 3 day notice.** 777 Mahoning Ave. 0.3 mi n of Courthouse Square. Ext corridors. **Pets:** Other species. Supervision.

🆂🅰🆅🅴 🆂🕭 ✕ 🅗 🖵 🏊

🅐🅐🅐 ▼▼▼▼ Comfort Inn 🆂🅷
(330) 393-1200. **$65-$95.** 136 N Park Ave. Downtown; east side of Courthouse Square. Int corridors. **Pets:** Medium. $10 daily fee/pet. Service with restrictions, supervision.

🆂🅰🆅🅴 🆂🕭 ✕ 🅗 🖵 🍴

WAUSEON

🅐🅐🅐 ▼▼▼ Best Western Del Mar 🅼 🐾
(419) 335-1565. **$65-$95, 14 day notice.** 8319 SR 108. I-80/90, exit 34, just s. Ext corridors. **Pets:** Medium. $15 one-time fee/room. Service with restrictions, crate.

🆂🅰🆅🅴 🆂🕭 ✕ 🅗 🖵 🏊

WINCHESTER

▼▼ Budget Host Inn 🅼
(937) 695-0381. **Call for rates.** 18760 SR 136. Jct US 32. Ext corridors. **Pets:** Accepted.

✕ 🅗

WOOSTER

🅐🅐🅐 ▼▼▼ Econo Lodge 🅼
(330) 264-8883. **$49-$99.** 2137 E Lincoln Way. US 30, 3 mi e. Ext corridors. **Pets:** Small. $10 daily fee/pet. Designated rooms, service with restrictions, supervision.

🆂🅰🆅🅴 🆂🕭 ✕ 🅗 🖵 🏊

XENIA

▼▼▼▼ Holiday Inn-Xenia 🆂🅷
(937) 372-9921. **$79-$89, 30 day notice.** 300 Xenia Towne Square. On W Main St, 0.5 mi w. Int corridors. **Pets:** Accepted.

🅰🆂🅺 🆂🕭 ✕ 🅗 🖵 🍴 🏊

▼▼ Regency Inn 🆂🅷
(937) 372-9954. **$50-$60.** 600 Little Main St. 1 mi w. Ext corridors. **Pets:** Other species. $10 daily fee/room. Designated rooms, service with restrictions, supervision.

🅰🆂🅺 🆂🕭 ✕ 🅗 🖵

ZANESVILLE

🅐🅐🅐 ▼▼▼ Baymont Inn & Suites Zanesville 🆂🅷
(740) 454-9332. **$79-$129.** 230 Scenic Crest Dr. I-70, exit 155, just s. Int corridors. **Pets:** Medium. $25 one-time fee/pet. Service with restrictions, supervision.

🆂🅰🆅🅴 🆂🕭 ✕ 🅗 🖵 🏊 ✕

▼▼ Best Western–B.R. Guest 🆂🅷 🐾
(740) 453-6300. **$74-$134.** 4929 E Pike. I-70, exit 160, just s. Int corridors. **Pets:** Large, other species. $10 daily fee/pet. Service with restrictions, crate.

🅰🆂🅺 🆂🕭 ✕ 🔊🅼 🅗 🖵 🏊

🅐🅐🅐 ▼▼▼ Comfort Inn 🆂🅷
(740) 454-4144. **$69-$199.** 500 Monroe St. I-70, exit 155 westbound; exit 7th St eastbound, e on Elberon to light, just n on Underwood. Int corridors. **Pets:** Medium, other species. $10 one-time fee/room. Designated rooms, service with restrictions, supervision.

🆂🅰🆅🅴 🆂🕭 ✕ 🅗 🖵 🏊

🅐🅐🅐 ▼▼ Econo Lodge-Zanesville 🅼
(740) 452-4511. **$45-$65.** 135 N 7th St. I-70, exit 155, on SR 60 via signs; downtown. Ext corridors. **Pets:** Medium, dogs only. $50 deposit/pet. Service with restrictions, supervision.

🆂🅰🆅🅴 🆂🕭 ✕ 🅗 🖵

▼▼▼▼ Ramada Hotel and Conference Center 🆂🅷
(740) 453-0771. **$79-$140.** 4645 E Pike. I-70, exit 160, on US 22 and 40. Int corridors. **Pets:** Accepted.

🅰🆂🅺 🆂🕭 ✕ 🅗 🖵 🍴 🏊 ✕

▼▼ Super 8 Motel-Zanesville 🆂🅷
(740) 455-3124. **$39-$99.** 2440 National Rd. I-70, exit 152, just n. Int corridors. **Pets:** Medium. $10 daily fee/pet. Service with restrictions, supervision.

🅰🆂🅺 🆂🕭 ✕ 🅗

OKLAHOMA

CITY INDEX

ALTUS

Best Western Altus SH
(580) 482-9300. **$71-$99.** 2804 N Main St. 2 mi n on US 283. Ext corridors. **Pets:** Accepted.

ARDMORE

Holiday Inn SH
(580) 223-7130. **$97-$109.** 2705 W Broadway. I-35, exit 31A, just e. Ext corridors. **Pets:** Small. $20 one-time fee/room. Designated rooms, service with restrictions, crate.

La Quinta Inn Ardmore SH
(580) 223-7976. **$80.** 2432 Veterans Blvd. I-35, exit 33, just e. Ext corridors. **Pets:** Other species. Service with restrictions, supervision.

BARTLESVILLE

Microtel Inn & Suites of Bartlesville SH
(918) 333-2100. **$59-$99.** 2696 SE Washington Blvd. 1.4 mi s of jct US 60 E. Int corridors. **Pets:** Accepted.

BIG CABIN

Super 8 Motel-Big Cabin M
(918) 783-5888. **Call for rates.** 30954 S Hwy 69. I-44, exit 283, just ne. Ext/int corridors. **Pets:** Accepted.

BLACKWELL

Best Western Blackwell Inn SH
(580) 363-1300. **Call for rates.** 4545 W White Ave. I-35, exit 222, just ne. Int corridors. **Pets:** Medium. $10 daily fee/pet. Designated rooms, service with restrictions, supervision.

Comfort Inn SH
(580) 363-7000. **$49-$179.** 1201 N 44th St. I-35, exit 222, just ne. Int corridors. **Pets:** Accepted.

CHICKASHA

Holiday Inn Express Hotel & Suites SH
(405) 224-8883. **$95-$150, 14 day notice.** 2610 S 4th St. I-44, exit 80, just se. Int corridors. **Pets:** Accepted.

DAVIS

Davis Microtel Inn & Suites-Treasure Valley Casino SH
(580) 369-3223. **$78-$110.** Rt 1, Box 7C. I-35, exit 55, just e. Int corridors. **Pets:** Accepted.

DURANT

Holiday Inn Express Hotel & Suites SH
(580) 924-8881. **$99-$169.** 2112 W Main St. Just e of jct US 75/69 and 70. Int corridors. **Pets:** Accepted.

ELK CITY

Holiday Inn SH
(580) 225-6637. **$139-$169.** 101 Meadow Ridge Dr. I-40, exit 38, just sw. Ext/int corridors. **Pets:** Accepted.

ENID

Baymont Inn & Suites SH
(580) 234-6800. **Call for rates.** 3614 W Owen K Garriott Rd. Just off US 412, 2 mi w of US 81. Int corridors. **Pets:** Medium, dogs only. $50 deposit/pet, $10 daily fee/pet. Designated rooms, service with restrictions, supervision.

Holiday Inn Express Hotel & Suites SH
(580) 237-7722. **Call for rates (no credit cards).** 4702 W Garriott Rd. 2.3 mi w of jct US 81. Int corridors. **Pets:** Accepted.

GUYMON

Guymon Super 8 SH
(580) 338-0507. **$70-$100.** 1201 Hwy 54 E. Jct US 54 and 64. Int corridors. **Pets:** Other species. $7 daily fee/pet. Service with restrictions, supervision.

Western Townsman Inn SH
(580) 338-6556. **$67.** 212 NE Hwy 54. 0.7 mi s of jct US 64. Ext corridors. **Pets:** Accepted.

HENRYETTA

Green Country Inn M
(918) 652-9988. **$45-$58.** 2004 Old Hwy 75 W. I-40, exit 237, just ne. Ext corridors. **Pets:** Medium. $5 daily fee/pet. Designated rooms, service with restrictions, supervision.

IDABEL

Comfort Suites SH
(580) 286-9393. **$79-$149.** 400 SE Lincoln Rd. Just s of jct US 70 and 259. Int corridors. **Pets:** Accepted.

LAWTON

(AAA) ▼ ▼ Baymont Inn & Suites SH
(580) 353-5581. **Call for rates.** 1203 NW 40th St. I-44, exit 39A, 3.7 mi w. Int corridors. **Pets:** Large, other species. $25 deposit/room. Service with restrictions, crate.

(SAVE) ✕ ⊟ 🖭 ➡

(AAA) ▼ ▼ ▼ Best Western Hotel & Convention
Center SH
(580) 353-0200. **$89-$99, 14 day notice.** 1125 E Gore Blvd. I-44, exit 37, just e. Ext/int corridors. **Pets:** Medium. $40 one-time fee/pet. Designated rooms, service with restrictions, supervision.

(SAVE) (S🐾) ✕ ⊟ 🖭 ⫴🍴 ➡ ✕

LOCUST GROVE

(AAA) ▼ ▼ ▼ Best Western Locust Grove Inn &
Suites SH
(918) 479-8082. **Call for rates.** 106 Holiday Ln. Just nw of jct US 412 and SR 82. Int corridors. **Pets:** Small. $50 one-time fee/pet. Designated rooms, service with restrictions, crate.

(SAVE) ✕ ⊟ 🖭 ➡

LONE WOLF

▼ ▼ Quartz Mountain Resort Arts & Conference
Center SH 🐾
(580) 563-2424. **$89-$129.** 22469 Lodge Rd. 1.4 mi w of jct SR 44 and 44A, 1.9 mi n. Int corridors. **Pets:** Other species. $100 one-time fee/pet. Service with restrictions, supervision.

(ASK) ✕ ⊟ 🖭 ⫴🍴 ➡

MCALESTER

▼ ▼ Best Western Inn of McAlester SH
(918) 426-0115. **Call for rates.** 1215 George Nigh Expwy. 3 mi s on US 69. Ext corridors. **Pets:** Accepted.

✕ ⊟ 🖭 ➡

▼ ▼ ▼ Comfort Suites SH
(918) 302-0001. **Call for rates.** 650 George Nigh Expwy. 1.2 mi s on US 69. Int corridors. **Pets:** Accepted.

✕ ⊟ 🖭 ➡

▼ Happy Days Hotel SH
(918) 429-0910. **$73-$95.** 1400 S George Nigh Expwy. 3.3 mi s on US 69. Int corridors. **Pets:** Accepted.

(ASK) ✕ ⊟ 🖭 ➡

MIAMI

▼ ▼ Microtel Inn & Suites SH
(918) 540-3333. **$65.** 2015 E Steve Owens Blvd. I-44, exit 313, just w. Int corridors. **Pets:** $25 one-time fee/pet. Service with restrictions, crate.

(ASK) (S🐾) ✕ ⊟ 🖭 ➡

MUSKOGEE

▼ ▼ ▼ La Quinta Inn & Suites Muskogee SH
(918) 687-9000. **$93.** 3031 Military Blvd. Just se of jct US 62 and 69. Int corridors. **Pets:** Other species. Service with restrictions, supervision.

(ASK) (S🐾) ✕ ⊟ 🖭 ⫴🍴 ➡

OKLAHOMA CITY METROPOLITAN AREA

DEL CITY

▼ ▼ ▼ La Quinta Inn Oklahoma City East (Del City) SH
(405) 672-0067. **$67-$87.** 5501 Tinker Diagonal Rd. I-40, exit 156A (Sooner Rd), just nw. Ext/int corridors. **Pets:** Other species. Service with restrictions, supervision.

(ASK) (S🐾) ✕ ⊟ 🖭 ➡

EDMOND

(AAA) ▼ ▼ ▼ Best Western Edmond Inn & Suites SH
(405) 216-0300. **Call for rates.** 2700 E 2nd St. I-35, exit 141, 1.1 mi w. Int corridors. **Pets:** Accepted.

(SAVE) ✕ ⊟ 🖭 ➡

EL RENO

(AAA) ▼ ▼ ▼ Best Western Hensley's SH
(405) 262-6490. **$65-$95.** 2701 S Country Club Rd. I-40, exit 123, just s. Ext corridors. **Pets:** Dogs only. $25 deposit/room, $5 daily fee/pet. Service with restrictions, supervision.

(SAVE) (S🐾) ✕ ⊟ 🖭 ➡

(AAA) ▼ Motel 6 SH
(405) 262-6060. **Call for rates.** 1506 Domino Dr. I-40, exit 123, just ne. Int corridors. **Pets:** Other species. Service with restrictions, supervision.

(SAVE) ✕ ⊟ ➡

GUTHRIE

(AAA) ▼ ▼ ▼ Best Western Territorial Inn SH
(405) 282-8831. **$79-$89.** 2323 Territorial Tr. I-35, exit 157, just sw. Int corridors. **Pets:** Small, other species. Service with restrictions, supervision.

(SAVE) (S🐾) ✕ ⊟ 🖭 ➡

MIDWEST CITY

▼ ▼ ▼ Hawthorn Suites SH
(405) 737-7777. **$105-$125.** 5701 Tinker Diagonal Rd. I-40, exit 156A (Sooner Rd), just n. Int corridors. **Pets:** Accepted.

(ASK) (S🐾) ✕ (🐾M) ⊟ 🖭 ➡

▼ ▼ ▼ Sheraton Midwest City Hotel at the Reed Conference
Center 🏨 🐾
(405) 741-7333. **$99-$229.** 5750 Will Rogers Rd. I-40, exit 156A (Sooner Rd), just ne. Int corridors. **Pets:** Medium, dogs only. $25 one-time fee/pet. Service with restrictions, supervision.

(ASK) (S🐾) ✕ ⊟ 🖭 ⫴🍴 ➡ ✕

▼ Studio 6 #6003 🅼
(405) 737-8851. **Call for rates.** 5801 Tinker Diagonal Rd. I-40, exit 156A (Sooner Rd), just ne. Ext corridors. **Pets:** Other species. Service with restrictions, supervision.

✕ ⊟ 🖭 ➡

MOORE

(AAA) ▼ ▼ ▼ Best Western Green Tree Inn & Suites SH
(405) 912-8882. **$85-$109.** 1811 N Moore Ave. I-35, exit 118, just n on westbound frontage road. Int corridors. **Pets:** Very small. $10 daily fee/pet. Service with restrictions, supervision.

(SAVE) (S🐾) ✕ ⊟ 🖭 ➡

NORMAN

▼ ▼ ▼ La Quinta Inn & Suites Oklahoma City
(Norman) SH
(405) 579-4000. **$99.** 930 Ed Noble Dr. I-35, exit 108B (Lindsey St), just nw. Int corridors. **Pets:** Other species. Service with restrictions, supervision.

(ASK) (S🐾) ✕ ⊟ 🖭 ➡

◆◆ ▼▼▼ Quality Inn **M**
(405) 364-5554. **$95-$105.** 100 SW 26th Dr. I-35, exit 109 (Main St), just se. Ext corridors. **Pets:** Very small. $5 daily fee/pet. Service with restrictions, supervision.
SAVE S◊ ⊠ ▣

◆◆▽ ▼▼▼ Residence Inn by Marriott **SH**
(405) 366-0900. **$176-$196.** 2681 Jefferson St. I-35, exit 108A, just se. Ext corridors. **Pets:** Other species. $100 one-time fee/pet.
SAVE S◊ ⊠ ▤ ▣ ⋙ ⊠

OKLAHOMA CITY

▼▼ Baymont Inn **SH**
(405) 631-8661. **Call for rates.** 8315 I-35 S. I-35, exit 121A (82nd St), just sw. Ext corridors. **Pets:** Other species. Service with restrictions.
⊠ ▤ ▣ ⋙

▼▼▼ Best Western Memorial Inn & Suites **SH**
(405) 286-5199. **Call for rates.** 1301 W Memorial Rd. John Kilpatrick Tpke, exit Western Ave, just nw. Int corridors. **Pets:** Accepted.
⊠ ◊M ▤ ▣ ⋙

◆◆▽ ▼▼▼ Best Western Saddleback Inn & Conference Center **LH**
(405) 947-7000. **Call for rates.** 4300 SW 3rd St. I-40, exit 145 (Meridian Ave), just ne. Ext/int corridors. **Pets:** Small. $50 deposit/pet. Service with restrictions, crate.
SAVE ⊠ ▤ ▣ ⫴ ⋙ ⊠

▼▼ Candlewood Suites Hotel **SH**
(405) 680-8770. **Call for rates.** 4400 River Park Dr. I-40, exit 145 (Meridian Ave), 1.1 mi s. Int corridors. **Pets:** Accepted.
⊠ ◊M ▤ ▣

◆◆▽ ▼▼ Comfort Inn **SH**
(405) 943-4400. **$68-$88.** 4240 W I-40 Service Rd. I-40, exit 145 (Meridian Ave), just e on south frontage road. Ext/int corridors. **Pets:** Accepted.
SAVE S◊ ⊠ ▤ ▣ ⋙

◆◆▽ ▼▼ Comfort Inn at Founders Tower **SH**
(405) 810-1100. **$85-$105.** 5704 Mosteller Dr. 0.5 mi e of jct SR 74 and 3. Int corridors. **Pets:** Accepted.
SAVE S◊ ⊠ ▤ ▣

◆◆▽ ▼▼ Comfort Inn North **SH**
(405) 478-7282. **$69-$140.** 4625 NE 120th. I-35, exit 137 (122nd St), just sw. Int corridors. **Pets:** Large, dogs only. $20 daily fee/pet. Service with restrictions, crate.
SAVE S◊ ⊠ ▤ ▣ ⋙

▼▼▼ Country Inn & Suites By Carlson **SH**
(405) 843-2002. **$89-$125.** 3141 Northwest Expwy. 0.4 mi e of jct SR 74 and 3. Int corridors. **Pets:** Accepted.
ASK S◊ ⊠ ▤ ▣ ⋙

◆◆▽ ▼▼▼ Courtyard by Marriott-Downtown/Bricktown **SH**
(405) 232-2290. **$179-$199.** 2 W Reno Ave. Gaylord and Reno aves; downtown. Int corridors. **Pets:** Small. $75 one-time fee/room. Service with restrictions, crate.
SAVE S◊ ⊠ ◊M ▤ ▣ ⫴ ⋙

▼▼▼ Courtyard by Marriott-NW **SH** ❀
(405) 848-0808. **$139-$160.** 1515 Northwest Expwy. I-44, exit 125C westbound; exit 125B eastbound, just e. Int corridors. **Pets:** Small. $75 one-time fee/pet. Service with restrictions, supervision.
ASK S◊ ⊠ ◊M ▤ ▣ ⫴ ⋙ ⊠

▼▼▼ Embassy Suites **LH**
(405) 682-6000. **Call for rates.** 1815 S Meridian Ave. I-40, exit 145 (Meridian Ave), 1 mi s. Int corridors. **Pets:** Accepted.
⊠ ▤ ▣ ⫴ ⋙ ⊠

▼▼▼▼ Four Points by Sheraton Oklahoma City **SH**
(405) 681-3500. **Call for rates.** 6300 Terminal Dr. I-40, exit 145 (Meridian Ave), 4 mi s. Int corridors. **Pets:** Accepted.
⊠ ▤ ▣ ⫴ ⋙

▼▼▼ La Quinta Inn & Suites Oklahoma City (Northwest Expressway) **SH**
(405) 773-5575. **$115.** 4829 Northwest Expwy. 1.9 mi w of jct SR 3 and 74. Int corridors. **Pets:** Other species. Service with restrictions, supervision.
ASK S◊ ⊠ ▤ ▣ ⋙

▼▼▼ La Quinta Inn and Suites-Quail Springs **SH**
(405) 755-7000. **$103.** 3003 W Memorial Rd. John Kilpatrick Tpke, exit May Ave, just nw. Int corridors. **Pets:** Other species. Service with restrictions, supervision.
ASK S◊ ⊠ ◊M ▤ ▣ ⋙ ⊠

▼▼▼ La Quinta Inn Oklahoma City (Airport) **SH**
(405) 942-0040. **$82.** 800 S Meridian Ave. I-40, exit 145 (Meridian Ave), just se. Ext/int corridors. **Pets:** Other species. Service with restrictions, supervision.
ASK S◊ ⊠ ▤ ▣ ⫴ ⋙

▼ Motel 6 Airport–116 **M**
(405) 946-6662. **Call for rates.** 820 S Meridian Ave. I-40, exit 145 (Meridian Ave), just s. Ext corridors. **Pets:** Accepted.
⊠ ⋙

▼ Motel 6 West–1128 **SH**
(405) 947-6550. **Call for rates.** 4200 I-40 Service Rd. I-40, exit 145 (Meridian Ave), just e on south frontage road. Ext/int corridors. **Pets:** Other species. Service with restrictions, supervision.
⊠ ▤ ⋙

▼▼ Quality Inn **SH**
(405) 632-6666. **$75-$100.** 7800 CA Henderson Blvd. I-240, exit 2A, just s. Ext corridors. **Pets:** Accepted.
ASK S◊ ⊠ ▤ ▣ ⋙

▼▼ Quality Inn At Frontier City **SH**
(405) 478-0400. **Call for rates.** 12001 N I-35 Service Rd. I-35, exit 137, just sw. Ext corridors. **Pets:** Accepted.
⊠ ▣ ⋙

◆◆▽ ▼▼▼▼ Renaissance Oklahoma City Hotel **LH**
(405) 228-8000. **$220-$240.** 10 N Broadway Ave. Sheridan and Broadway aves; downtown. Int corridors. **Pets:** Accepted.
SAVE S◊ ⊠ ◊M ▤ ▣ ⫴ ⋙ ⊠

▼▼▼▼ Residence Inn by Marriott **SH**
(405) 601-1700. **$319-$339.** 400 E Reno Ave. Just se of jct Joe Carter Ave; in Bricktown. Int corridors. **Pets:** Accepted.
ASK S◊ ⊠ ◊M ▤ ▣ ⋙ ⊠

▼▼▼ Residence Inn by Marriott-Oklahoma City West **SH**
(405) 942-4500. **$220-$240.** 4361 W Reno Ave. I-40, exit 145 (Meridian Ave), 0.3 mi n, then just e. Ext corridors. **Pets:** Accepted.
ASK S◊ ⊠ ▤ ▣ ⋙ ⊠

▼▼▼ Residence Inn by Marriott South-Crossroads Mall **SH**
(405) 634-9696. **$143-$187.** 1111 E I-240 Service Rd. I-240, exit 4C eastbound, 0.4 mi nw; exit 5 westbound, 0.8 mi nw. Int corridors. **Pets:** Accepted.
ASK S◊ ⊠ ▤ ▣ ⋙ ⊠

◆◆▽ ▼▼▼ Sheraton Oklahoma City **LH**
(405) 235-2780. **$159-$259.** One N Broadway Ave. Sheridan and Broadway aves; downtown. Int corridors. **Pets:** Accepted.
SAVE S◊ ⊠ ▣ ⫴ ⋙

◆◆◆ ▼▼▼ ▼▼▼ The Skirvin Hilton [LH]
(405) 272-3040. **Call for rates (no credit cards).** 1 Park Ave. Just n of jct Robinson Ave; downtown. Int corridors. **Pets:** Large. $75 one-time fee/room. Service with restrictions, supervision.

[SAVE] [X] [&M] [+] [D] [††] [➧]

SHAWNEE

▼▼▼▼ La Quinta Inn & Suites [SH]
(405) 275-7930. **$99-$109.** 5401 Enterprise Ct. I-40, exit 186, just ne. Int corridors. **Pets:** Other species. Service with restrictions, supervision.

[ASK] [S🔒] [X] [+] [D] [➧]

▼▼▼ Motel 6–1236 [M]
(405) 275-5310. **Call for rates.** 4981 N Harrison. I-40, exit 186, just ne. Int corridors. **Pets:** Other species. Service with restrictions, supervision.

[X] [➧]

YUKON

◆◆◆ ▼▼▼▼ Best Western Inn & Suites Yukon [SH]
(405) 265-2995. **$70-$145.** 11440 W I-40 Service Rd. I-40, exit 138, just sw. Ext/int corridors. **Pets:** Other species. $25 deposit/pet, $6 daily fee/pet. Designated rooms, service with restrictions, supervision.

[SAVE] [S🔒] [X] [+] [D] [➧] [X]

END METROPOLITAN AREA

OKMULGEE

◆◆◆ ▼▼▼▼ Best Western Okmulgee [SH]
(918) 756-9200. **Call for rates.** 3499 N Wood Dr. Just n of jct US 75 and SR 56. Int corridors. **Pets:** Small. $50 deposit/pet. Service with restrictions, supervision.

[SAVE] [X] [+] [D] [➧]

PAULS VALLEY

▼▼▼▼ Comfort Inn & Suites [SH]
(405) 207-9730. **$85-$95.** 103 S Humphrey Blvd. I-35, exit 72, just e. Int corridors. **Pets:** Accepted.

[ASK] [S🔒] [X] [+] [D] [➧]

◆◆◆ ▼▼ ▼ Days Inn [SH]
(405) 238-7548. **Call for rates.** 2606 W Grant Ave. I-35, exit 72, just e. Int corridors. **Pets:** Accepted.

[SAVE] [X] [+] [D]

PONCA CITY

◆◆◆ ▼▼▼▼ Comfort Inn & Suites [SH]
(580) 765-2322. **$93-$160.** 3101 N 14th St. I-35, exit 214, 3 mi n on US 77. Int corridors. **Pets:** Small. $10 one-time fee/pet. Service with restrictions, crate.

[SAVE] [S🔒] [X] [&M] [+] [D] [➧]

PRYOR

▼▼▼▼ Comfort Inn & Suites [SH]
(918) 476-6660. **$80-$130.** 307 Mid America Dr. 5 mi s on US 69. Int corridors. **Pets:** Accepted.

[ASK] [S🔒] [X] [+] [D] [➧]

◆◆◆ ▼▼ ▼ Microtel Inn & Suites [SH]
(918) 476-4661. **$99.** 315 Mid America Dr. 5.1 mi s on US 69. Int corridors. **Pets:** Accepted.

[SAVE] [S🔒] [X] [+] [D]

SALLISAW

◆◆◆ ▼▼ ▼ Best Western Blue Ribbon Inn [SH]
(918) 775-6294. **Call for rates.** 706 S Kerr Blvd (US 59). I-40, exit 308 (US 59), just n. Ext/int corridors. **Pets:** Accepted.

[SAVE] [X] [+] [D] [➧]

▼▼ ▼ Microtel Inn & Suites [SH]
(918) 774-0400. **$49-$90.** 710 S Kerr Blvd. I-40, exit 308 (US 59), just n. Int corridors. **Pets:** Accepted.

[ASK] [S🔒] [X] [+] [D]

SAVANNA

◆◆◆ ▼▼ ▼ Candlelight Inn & Suites [SH]
(918) 548-3676. **$75-$90.** Hwy 69. 1.5 mi sw of jct US 69 and Indian Creek Tpke. Int corridors. **Pets:** Accepted.

[SAVE] [S🔒] [X] [+] [D]

SAYRE

▼▼ ▼ AmericInn Lodge & Suites of Sayre [SH]
(580) 928-2700. **$80-$130, 7 day notice.** 2405 S El Camino Rd. I-40, exit 20, just n. Int corridors. **Pets:** Dogs only. $15 one-time fee/pet. Designated rooms, service with restrictions, supervision.

[ASK] [S🔒] [X] [&M] [+] [D] [➧]

THACKERVILLE

▼▼ ▼ Winstar Microtel Inn and Suites [SH]
(580) 276-4487. **$135-$300.** Rt 1, Box 682. I-35, exit 1, 1.2 mi n on E Service Rd. Int corridors. **Pets:** Accepted.

[ASK] [X] [+] [D] [➧]

TULSA METROPOLITAN AREA

BROKEN ARROW

▼▼▼▼ Clarion Hotel [SH]
(918) 258-7085. **$79-$199.** 2600 N Aspen Ave. Just s of jct SR 51. Int corridors. **Pets:** Accepted.

[ASK] [S🔒] [X] [+] [D] [➧]

◆◆◆ ▼▼▼▼ Homewood Suites by Hilton Tulsa
South [SH]
(918) 392-7700. **Call for rates.** 4900 W Madison Pl. Just ne of jct 71st St and Garnett Ave. Int corridors. **Pets:** Medium, other species. $75 deposit/pet, $75 one-time fee/pet. Service with restrictions, supervision.

[SAVE] [X] [&M] [+] [D] [➧]

CLAREMORE

◆◆◆ ▼▼ Claremore Motor Inn [M]
(918) 342-4545. **$39-$69.** 1709 N Lynn Riggs Blvd. 1.2 mi n on SR 66. Ext/int corridors. **Pets:** Small, dogs only. $100 deposit/room, $7 daily fee/pet. Service with restrictions, supervision.

[SAVE] [S🔒] [X] [+]

▼▼ ▼ Days Inn Claremore [SH]
(918) 343-3297. **Call for rates.** 1720 S Lynn Riggs Blvd. 1.6 mi s on SR 66. Int corridors. **Pets:** Accepted.

[X] [+] [D] [➧]

Microtel Inn & Suites SH
(918) 343-2868. **$53-$96.** 10600 E Mallard Lake Rd. 2.6 mi s on SR 66. Int corridors. **Pets:** Small. $20 daily fee/pet. Designated rooms, service with restrictions, supervision.

Super 8 Motel SH
(918) 341-2323. **$59-$79.** 1100 E Will Rogers Blvd. I-44, exit 255, just w. Ext/int corridors. **Pets:** Small. $10 daily fee/pet. Service with restrictions, supervision.

GLENPOOL

Best Western Glenpool/Tulsa SH
(918) 322-5201. **Call for rates.** 14831 S Casper St. I-44, exit 224, 9.5 mi s on US 75. Ext corridors. **Pets:** Large. $20 one-time fee/pet. Service with restrictions, supervision.

TULSA

Ambassador Hotel SH
(918) 587-8200. **$259-$329.** 1324 S Main St. Jct 14th and Main sts. Int corridors. **Pets:** Other species. Service with restrictions, crate.

Baymont Inn & Suites Tulsa SH
(918) 488-8777. **Call for rates.** 4530 E Skelly Dr. I-44, exit 229 (Yale Ave/SR 66), just s, then w. Int corridors. **Pets:** Small. Designated rooms, no service, supervision.

Best Western Airport SH
(918) 438-0780. **$74-$89.** 222 N Garnett Rd. I-244, exit 14 (Garnett Rd), just s. Ext corridors. **Pets:** Other species. $25 one-time fee/room. Service with restrictions, crate.

Candlewood Suites SH
(918) 294-9000. **$104-$119.** 10008 E 73rd St S. Just sw of jct 71st and 101st E Ave. Int corridors. **Pets:** Accepted.

Days Inn SH
(918) 836-3931. **Call for rates.** 35 N Sheridan Rd. I-244, exit 11 (Sheridan Rd). Ext corridors. **Pets:** Accepted.

Days Inn SH
(918) 496-9300. **Call for rates.** 4724 S Yale Ave. I-44, exit 229 (Yale Ave/SR 66), just s. Ext corridors. **Pets:** Small. $10 daily fee/room. Service with restrictions, supervision.

DoubleTree Hotel At Warren Place LH
(918) 495-1000. **Call for rates.** 6110 S Yale Ave. I-44, exit 229 (Yale Ave/SR 66), 1.3 mi s. Int corridors. **Pets:** Accepted.

DoubleTree Hotel Tulsa Downtown LH
(918) 587-8000. **$99-$189.** 616 W 7th St. Jct 7th St and Houston. Int corridors. **Pets:** Accepted.

Embassy Suites Hotel LH
(918) 622-4000. **$119-$179.** 3332 S 79th E Ave. I-44, exit 231 eastbound; exit 232 (Memorial Dr) westbound, just sw. Int corridors. **Pets:** Accepted.

GuestHouse Suites Plus SH
(918) 664-7241. **$79.** 8181 E 41st St. 1.7 mi w of jct US 169. Ext corridors. **Pets:** Accepted.

Hampton Inn SH
(918) 663-1000. **Call for rates.** 3209 S 79th E Ave. I-44, exit 231 eastbound; exit 232 (Memorial Dr) westbound, just sw. Int corridors. **Pets:** Accepted.

Hilton Tulsa Southern Hills LH
(918) 492-5000. **Call for rates.** 7900 S Lewis Ave. I-44, exit 227, 3 mi s. Int corridors. **Pets:** Accepted.

Holiday Inn-International Airport SH
(918) 437-7660. **$89.** 1010 N Garnett Rd. I-244, exit 14 (Garnett Rd), just n. Int corridors. **Pets:** Accepted.

Holiday Inn Select SH
(918) 622-7000. **$109.** 5000 E Skelly Dr. I-44, exit 229 (Yale Ave/SR 66); on south frontage road. Ext/int corridors. **Pets:** Accepted.

La Quinta Inn & Suites Tulsa Central SH
(918) 665-2630. **$89.** 6030 E Skelly Dr. I-44, exit 230, just s. Int corridors. **Pets:** Other species. Service with restrictions, supervision.

La Quinta Inn Tulsa (East) SH
(918) 665-0220. **$68.** 10829 E 41st St. US 169, exit E 41st St. Ext corridors. **Pets:** Other species. Service with restrictions, supervision.

La Quinta Inn Tulsa (South) SH
(918) 254-1626. **$69.** 12525 E 52nd St S. Broken Arrow Expwy (SR 51), exit 129th and 51st sts, just s. Ext corridors. **Pets:** Other species. Service with restrictions, supervision.

Microtel Inn & Suites SH
(918) 858-3775. **$63-$100.** 4531 E 21st St. Just w of 21st St and Yale Ave. Int corridors. **Pets:** Accepted.

Post Oak Lodge SH
(918) 425-2112. **$89-$109.** 5323 W 31st N. 0.7 mi w of jct Apache/41st St. Int corridors. **Pets:** Accepted.

Radisson Tulsa LH
(918) 627-5000. **$119-$149.** 10918 E 41st St. Just e of US 169. Int corridors. **Pets:** Medium. $50 deposit/room. Service with restrictions, supervision.

Radisson Tulsa Airport SH
(918) 835-9911. **Call for rates.** 2201 N 77th East Ave. SR 11, exit airport terminal. Int corridors. **Pets:** Accepted.

Red Roof Inn M
(918) 622-6776. **Call for rates.** 4717 S Yale Ave. I-44, exit 229 (Yale Ave), just s. Ext corridors. **Pets:** Accepted.

Renaissance Tulsa Hotel & Convention Center LH
(918) 307-2600. **$187-$207.** 6808 S 107th E Ave. Just ne of jct US 169 and 71st St. Int corridors. **Pets:** Accepted.

Residence Inn by Marriott SH
(918) 250-4850. **$133-$154.** 11025 E 73rd St. US 169, exit 71st St, just e. Int corridors. **Pets:** Accepted.

▼▼ ▼▼ **Sleep Inn & Suites Tulsa Central** 🅂🄷
(918) 663-2777. **$79-$149.** 8021 E 33rd St S. I-44, exit 231 eastbound; exit 232 (Memorial Dr) westbound, just sw. Int corridors. **Pets:** Accepted.

A$K S🄳 ✕ 🄴 🖵 ⤳ ✕

▼▼▼ **Staybridge Suites** 🅂🄷
(918) 461-2100. **$159.** 11111 E 73rd St. Just se of jct US 169 and 71st St. Int corridors. **Pets:** Accepted.

A$K S🄳 ✕ ♿ᴹ 🄴 🖵 ⤳ ✕

▼▼ ▼▼ **StudioPLUS Tulsa Central** 🅂🄷
(918) 660-2890. **$70-$95.** 7901 E 31st Ct. I-44, exit 231 eastbound; exit 232 (Memorial Dr) westbound, just sw. Int corridors. **Pets:** Other species. $75 one-time fee/pet. Service with restrictions.

A$K S🄳 ✕ 🄴 🖵 ⤳

END METROPOLITAN AREA

WOODWARD

🄰🄰🄰 ▼▼ ▼▼ **Northwest Inn** 🅂🄷
(580) 256-7600. **$99.** Hwy 270 S & 1st St. 1.4 mi s of jct US 183, 270, SR 3 and 34. Ext/int corridors. **Pets:** Small. $10 one-time fee/room. Service with restrictions, crate.

SAVE S🄳 ✕ 🄴 🖵 🍽 ⤳

OREGON

ALBANY

⬦ ▼▼▼ Best Western Albany Inn SH
(541) 928-6322. $59-$129. 315 Airport Rd SE. I-5, exit 234B southbound; exit 234 northbound, just w, then just s. Ext corridors. Pets: Accepted.
SAVE | 🔊 | ✖ | 🖥 | 💻 | 🏊

▼▼▼ Comfort Suites SH
(541) 928-2053. Call for rates. 100 Opal Ct NE. I-5, exit 234A southbound; exit 234 northbound, just e. Int corridors. Pets: Accepted.
✖ | 🖥 | 💻 | 🏊 | ✖

⬦ ▼▼▼ Econo Lodge M
(541) 926-0170. $49-$89. 1212 SE Price Rd. I-5, exit 233, just e, then just n. Ext corridors. Pets: Medium, dogs only. $10 daily fee/pet. Service with restrictions, supervision.
SAVE | 🔊 | ✖ | 🖥 | 🏊

⬦ ▼▼▼ Holiday Inn Express Hotel & Suites SH 🐾
(541) 928-8820. $69-$129. 105 Opal Ct NE. I-5, exit 234A southbound; exit 234 northbound, 0.4 mi e. Int corridors. Pets: Other species. $30 one-time fee/room. Service with restrictions, supervision.
SAVE | 🔊 | ✖ | 🔊 | 🖥 | 💻 | 🏊 | ✖

⬦ ▼▼▼ La Quinta Inn Albany SH
(541) 928-0921. $98-$108. 251 Airport Rd SE. I-5, exit 234B southbound; exit 234 northbound, just w. Int corridors. Pets: Other species. Service with restrictions, supervision.
SAVE | 🔊 | ✖ | 🖥 | 💻 | 🏊 | ✖

⬦ ▼▼▼ Motel 6 #4124 M
(541) 926-4233. $55-$69. 2735 E Pacific Blvd. I-5, exit 234B southbound; exit 234 northbound, 0.5 mi w. Ext corridors. Pets: Small. $50 deposit/pet. Service with restrictions, supervision.
SAVE | 🔊 | ✖ | 🔊 | 🖥

⬦ ▼▼▼ Phoenix Inn Suites-Albany SH
(541) 926-5696. $79-$139. 3410 Spicer Rd SE. I-5, exit 233, just e. Int corridors. Pets: $15 daily fee/pet. Designated rooms, no service, supervision.
SAVE | ✖ | 🖥 | 💻 | 🏊

⬦ ▼▼▼ Quality Inn SH
(541) 928-5050. $59-$150. 1100 Price Rd SE. I-5, exit 233, just e, then just n. Int corridors. Pets: Accepted.
SAVE | 🔊 | ✖ | 🔊 | 🖥 | 💻 | 🏊

ASHLAND

▼▼▼ Ashland Springs Hotel SH
(541) 488-1700. $89-$259. 212 E Main St. Corner of 1st St; center. Int corridors. Pets: Accepted.
ASK | 🔊 | ✖ | 🖥 | 🍴

⬦ ▼▼▼ Best Western Bard's Inn SH
(541) 482-0049. Call for rates. 132 N Main St. Just n on SR 99 (N Main St) from Downtown Plaza. Ext/int corridors. Pets: Accepted.
SAVE | ✖ | 🔊 | 🖥 | 💻 | 🏊

⬦ ▼▼▼ Best Western Windsor Inn SH
(541) 488-2330. Call for rates. 2520 Ashland St. I-5, exit 14, just e on SR 66. Ext corridors. Pets: Other species. $15 daily fee/pet. Designated rooms, service with restrictions, supervision.
SAVE | ✖ | 🔊 | 🖥 | 💻 | 🏊

⬦ ▼▼▼ Cedarwood Inn M
(541) 488-2000. $59-$119, 3 day notice. 1801 Siskiyou Blvd. I-5, exit 11 northbound, 2.8 mi w; exit 14 southbound, just w on SR 66, 0.6 mi s on Tolman Creek Rd, then 0.6 mi w. Ext corridors. Pets: Small. $10 daily fee/pet. Service with restrictions, supervision.
SAVE | 🔊 | ✖ | 🖥 | 💻 | 🏊

⬦ ▼▼▼ Flagship Inn of Ashland M 🐾
(541) 482-2641. $59-$119, 3 day notice. 1193 Siskiyou Blvd. I-5, exit 14, 1.3 mi w on SR 66, just n on SR 99 (Siskiyou Blvd). Ext corridors. Pets: Medium, other species. $10 daily fee/pet. Designated rooms, service with restrictions.
SAVE | 🔊 | ✖ | 🖥 | 💻 | 🏊

⬦ ▼▼▼ La Quinta Inn & Suites Ashland SH
(541) 482-6932. $126-$146. 434 S Valley View Rd. I-5, exit 19, just w. Int corridors. Pets: Other species. Service with restrictions, supervision.
SAVE | 🔊 | ✖ | 🔊 | 🖥 | 💻 | 🏊

⬦ ▼▼▼ Plaza Inn & Suites At Ashland Creek SH 🐾
(541) 488-8900. $89-$289. 98 Central Ave. I-5, exit 19, 0.5 mi w, 1.9 mi s on SR 99 (N Main St), just e on Water St, then just n. Int corridors. Pets: Medium. $25 daily fee/room. Designated rooms, service with restrictions, supervision.
SAVE | 🔊 | ✖ | 🖥 | 💻

⬦ ▼▼▼ Timbers Motel of Ashland M 🐾
(541) 482-4242. $46-$89, 3 day notice. 1450 Ashland St. I-5, exit 14, 0.8 mi w. Ext corridors. Pets: Other species. Designated rooms, service with restrictions.
SAVE | ✖ | 🖥 | 💻 | 🏊

△△△ ▽▼▽▼ **Windmill Inn & Suites of Ashland** 🆂🅷
(541) 482-8310. **$109-$159.** 2525 Ashland St. I-5, exit 14, just e. Int corridors. **Pets:** Accepted.
[SAVE] [S♦] [✕] [♿M] [🛏] [📺] [⇌] [✕]

ASTORIA

▽▼▽▼ **Astoria Holiday Inn Express Hotel & Suites** 🆂🅷
(503) 325-6222. **$119-$339.** 204 W Marine Dr. On US 30; west side of town. Int corridors. **Pets:** Accepted.
[ASK] [S♦] [✕] [♿M] [🛏] [📺] [⇌] [✕]

△△△ ▽▼▽▼ **Best Western Lincoln Inn** 🆂🅷 ❖
(503) 325-2205. **$89-$399.** 555 Hamburg Ave. On US 101/30; at east end of Young's Bay Bridge. Int corridors. **Pets:** Small, dogs only. $15 daily fee/pet. Designated rooms, service with restrictions, supervision.
[SAVE] [S♦] [✕] [🛏] [📺] [⇌] [✕]

▽▼▽▼ **Clementine's Bed & Breakfast** 🅱🅱
(503) 325-2005. **Call for rates.** 847 Exchange St. At 8th and Exchange sts; in historic downtown. Int corridors. **Pets:** Accepted.
[✕] [🛏] [📺] [🎟] [🦺]

△△△ ▽▼▽▼ **Crest Motel, P.C.** 🅼
(503) 325-3141. **Call for rates.** 5366 Leif Erickson Dr. 4 mi e of Astoria Bridge on US 30. Ext corridors. **Pets:** Other species. Designated rooms, service with restrictions, supervision.
[SAVE] [✕] [🛏] [📺] [🎟]

△△△ ▽▼▽▼ **Red Lion Inn Astoria** 🅼
(503) 325-7373. **$79-$189.** 400 Industry St. Just w of Astoria Bridge on US 30, just n on Basin St (caution: do not turn onto Astoria-Megler Bridge). Ext corridors. **Pets:** Other species. $20 daily fee/pet. Service with restrictions, supervision.
[SAVE] [S♦] [✕] [🛏] [📺] [🎟]

BAKER CITY

△△△ ▽▼▽▼ **Best Western Sunridge Inn** 🆂🅷 ❖
(541) 523-6444. **Call for rates.** 1 Sunridge Ln. I-84, exit 304, just w. Int corridors. **Pets:** Other species. $50 deposit/room, $15 daily fee/room. Designated rooms, service with restrictions, supervision.
[SAVE] [✕] [♿M] [🛏] [📺] [🍽] [⇌]

▽▼▽▼ **Geiser Grand Hotel** 🆂🅷
(541) 523-1889. **$89-$229, 3 day notice.** 1996 Main St. I-84, exit 304, 0.9 mi w on Campbell St, then 0.3 mi s; downtown. Int corridors. **Pets:** Accepted.
[ASK] [S♦] [✕] [🍽]

△△△ ▽▼▽▼ **Super 8 Motel Baker City** 🆂🅷
(541) 523-8282. **Call for rates.** 250 Campbell St. I-84, exit 304, just e. Int corridors. **Pets:** Accepted.
[SAVE] [✕] [♿M] [🛏] [📺] [⇌]

BANDON

△△△ ▽▼ **Bandon Inn** 🅼 ❖
(541) 347-4417. **$74-$139.** 355 Hwy 101. Center. Ext corridors. **Pets:** Medium. $15 daily fee/pet. Designated rooms, service with restrictions, supervision.
[SAVE] [S♦] [✕] [🛏] [📺] [🎟]

△△△ ▽▼ **Best Western Inn at Face Rock** 🆂🅷 ❖
(541) 347-9441. **Call for rates.** 3225 Beach Loop Dr. 1 mi s on US 101, 0.8 mi w on Seabird Rd, then just s. Ext corridors. **Pets:** $15 one-time fee/room. Designated rooms, service with restrictions, supervision.
[SAVE] [✕] [🛏] [📺] [🍽] [⇌] [✕] [🎟]

BEND

▽▼▽▼ **Bend Riverside Motel Suites** 🅼
(541) 389-2363. **$68-$159.** 1565 NW Wall St. US 97, exit 137 (Revere Ave), just s. Ext corridors. **Pets:** Accepted.
[ASK] [S♦] [✕] [🛏] [📺] [⇌]

△△△ ▽▼▽▼ **Best Western Inn & Suites of Bend** 🆂🅷
(541) 382-1515. **Call for rates.** 721 NE 3rd St. Just s of jct US 20 on Business Rt US 97; at jct of Greely Ave. Ext corridors. **Pets:** Accepted.
[SAVE] [✕] [🛏] [📺] [⇌]

▽▼▽▼ **Cricketwood Country Bed & Breakfast** 🅱🅱
(541) 330-0747. **$105-$145, 7 day notice.** 63520 Cricketwood Rd. 3.8 mi se on Deschutes Market Rd, 0.5 mi e on Hamehook Rd, 0.5 mi on Repine Rd, then just n. Ext/int corridors. **Pets:** Accepted.
[✕] [🛏] [📺]

▽▼▽▼ **Days Inn** 🆂🅷
(541) 383-3776. **Call for rates.** 849 NE 3rd St. US 97, just s of jct US 20. Ext corridors. **Pets:** Accepted.
[✕] [♿M] [🛏] [📺] [⇌]

△△△ ▽▼ **Dunes Motel** 🅼
(541) 382-6811. **$39-$125.** 1515 NE 3rd St. Just n on Business Rt US 97 from jct US 20 E. Ext corridors. **Pets:** Accepted.
[SAVE] [S♦] [✕] [🛏]

▽▼▽▼ **Fairfield Inn & Suites by Marriott** 🆂🅷
(541) 318-1747. **$103-$131.** 1626 NW Wall St. US 97, exit 137 (Revere Ave), just s; downtown. Int corridors. **Pets:** Accepted.
[ASK] [S♦] [✕] [♿M] [🛏] [📺] [⇌] [✕]

△△△ ▽▼▽▼ **Hampton Inn** 🆂🅷
(541) 388-4114. **Call for rates.** 15 NE Butler Market Rd. US 97, exit 136 (Butler Market Rd), just n. Ext corridors. **Pets:** Accepted.
[SAVE] [✕] [🛏] [📺] [⇌]

△△△ ▽▼▽▼ **Holiday Inn Express Hotel & Suites** 🆂🅷
(541) 317-8500. **$99-$189.** 20615 Grandview Dr. On US 97; north end of town. Int corridors. **Pets:** Medium. $20 one-time fee/room. Designated rooms, service with restrictions.
[SAVE] [S♦] [✕] [♿M] [🛏] [📺] [⇌] [✕]

△△△ ▽▼▽▼ **La Quinta Inn Bend** 🆂🅷
(541) 388-2227. **$110-$130.** 61200 S Business Hwy 97. Jct US 20 E, 3 mi s. Int corridors. **Pets:** Other species. Service with restrictions, supervision.
[SAVE] [S♦] [✕] [♿M] [🛏] [📺] [⇌]

△△△ ▽▼▽▼ **Quality Inn** 🆂🅷
(541) 318-0848. **$79-$119.** 20600 Grandview Dr. On US 97; north end of town. Int corridors. **Pets:** Medium. $10 daily fee/pet. Designated rooms, supervision.
[SAVE] [✕] [♿M] [🛏] [📺] [⇌]

△△△ ▽▼▽ **Red Lion Hotel Bend** 🆂🅷
(541) 382-7011. **$99-$189.** 1415 NE 3rd St. US 97, just n of jct US 20. Ext corridors. **Pets:** Accepted.
[SAVE] [S♦] [✕] [♿M] [🛏] [📺] [⇌]

△△△ ▽▼▽▼ **The Riverhouse Resort Hotel** 🅻🅷 ❖
(541) 389-3111. **$99-$159.** 3075 N Business 97. US 97, exit 136 (Butler Market Rd) northbound, just n; exit 135B southbound. Ext/int corridors. **Pets:** Other species. Supervision.
[SAVE] [S♦] [✕] [🛏] [📺] [🍽] [⇌] [✕]

▽▼▽▼ **Shilo Inn Suites Hotel Bend** 🆂🅷 ❖
(541) 389-9600. **$190-$200.** 3105 OB Riley Rd. 1.5 mi n on US 97 from jct US 20 E. Ext corridors. **Pets:** $25 one-time fee/room. Designated rooms, service with restrictions, supervision.
[ASK] [S♦] [✕] [🛏] [📺] [🍽] [⇌] [✕]

▽▼▽▼ **Sleep Inn of Bend** 🆂🅷
(541) 330-0050. **$59-$109.** 600 NE Bellevue. On US 20 E, 2 mi e of US 97. Int corridors. **Pets:** Accepted.
[ASK] [S♦] [✕] [♿M] [🛏] [📺] [⇌]

BOARDMAN

AAA ▼▼▼ **Econo Lodge** Ⓜ
(541) 481-2375. **$58-$99.** 105 SW Front St. I-84, exit 164, just s. Ext corridors. **Pets:** Other species. Designated rooms, service with restrictions, supervision.
SAVE Sᴅ ✕ ⊟ ⊒ ⇌

BROOKINGS

AAA ▼◆▼ **Best Western Beachfront Inn** SH ✿
(541) 469-7779. **$119-$299.** 16008 Boat Basin Rd. Jct US 101, 0.6 mi w on Benham Ln. Ext corridors. **Pets:** Large. $10 daily fee/pet. Designated rooms, service with restrictions, supervision.
SAVE Sᴅ ✕ &ᴹ ⊟ ⊒ ⇌ ⒜

AAA ▼ **Westward Inn** Ⓜ
(541) 469-7471. **$55-$99, 3 day notice.** 1026 Chetco Ave. On US 101; north end of town. Ext corridors. **Pets:** Accepted.
SAVE Sᴅ ✕ ⊟ ⒜

BURNS

AAA ▼▼▼ **America's Best Inn** Ⓜ
(541) 573-1700. **$53-$86.** 999 Oregon Ave. 1 mi w on US 395/20 from jct SR 78. Ext/int corridors. **Pets:** Other species. $5 daily fee/pet. Designated rooms, service with restrictions, supervision.
SAVE Sᴅ ✕ ⊟ ⊒ ⇌

AAA ▼ **Silver Spur Motel** Ⓜ
(541) 573-2077. **$42-$52.** 789 N Broadway. US 395/20, at edge of town center. Ext corridors. **Pets:** Large, other species. $5 daily fee/pet. Designated rooms, service with restrictions, supervision.
SAVE ✕ ⊟ ⊒

CANNON BEACH

▼▼ **Cannon Beach Ecola Creek Lodge** Ⓜ
(503) 436-2776. **$72-$230, 3 day notice.** 208 5th St. 0.3 mi w of US 101 via north exit to Ecola State Park. Ext corridors. **Pets:** Accepted.
A$K Sᴅ ✕ &ᴹ ⇌

AAA ▼◆▼ **Inn at Cannon Beach** Ⓜ
(503) 436-9085. **Call for rates.** 3215 S Hemlock St. US 101, exit Tolovana Park, just w, then just n. Ext corridors. **Pets:** Accepted.
SAVE ✕ ⊟ ⊒ ⒜

AAA ▼◆▼ **Ocean Lodge** SH
(503) 436-2241. **Call for rates.** 2864 S Pacific St. US 101, exit Tolovana Park, 1 mi s, then just w on Chisana. Ext/int corridors. **Pets:** Accepted.
SAVE ✕ ⊟ ⊒

AAA ▼▼▼ **Surfsand Resort at Cannon Beach** Ⓜ ✿
(503) 436-2274. **$159-$439, 7 day notice.** Ocean Front & Gower. US 101, exit Cannon Beach (2nd exit); downtown. Ext corridors. **Pets:** $12 daily fee/pet. Designated rooms, service with restrictions, supervision.
SAVE Sᴅ ✕ ⊟ ⊒ ⑪ ⇌ ⊠

AAA ▼▼ **Tolovana Inn** ⒸⓄ ✿
(503) 436-2211. **$69-$399, 3 day notice.** 3400 S Hemlock St. 2 mi s off US 101 Beach Loop. Ext corridors. **Pets:** $15 daily fee/pet. Designated rooms, service with restrictions, supervision.
SAVE Sᴅ ✕ ⊟ ⊒ ⇌ ⊠ ⒜

CANYONVILLE

AAA ▼◆▼ **Best Western Canyonville Inn & Suites** SH
(541) 839-4200. **$74-$170.** 200 Creekside Dr. I-5, exit 99, just w. Int corridors. **Pets:** Small. $15 daily fee/pet. Service with restrictions, supervision.
SAVE Sᴅ ✕ ⊟ ⊒ ⇌

CASCADE LOCKS

AAA ▼▼◆▼ **Best Western Columbia River Inn** SH
(541) 374-8777. **$99-$179.** 735 WaNaPa St. I-84, exit 44. Int corridors. **Pets:** Medium. $10 daily fee/pet. Designated rooms, service with restrictions, supervision.
SAVE Sᴅ ✕ &ᴹ ⊟ ⊒ ⇌

CENTRAL POINT

▼▼ **Super 8 Inn & Suites** SH
(541) 664-5888. **Call for rates (no credit cards).** 4999 Biddle Rd. I-5, exit 33, just e. Int corridors. **Pets:** $25 daily fee/pet. Service with restrictions, supervision.
✕ ⊟ ⇌

CLATSKANIE

AAA ▼ ▼▼ **Clatskanie River Inn** SH
(503) 728-9000. **$89-$149.** 600 E Columbia River Hwy. On US 30. Int corridors. **Pets:** Medium, other species. $20 one-time fee/room. Service with restrictions, supervision.
SAVE Sᴅ ✕ ⊟ ⊒ ⇌

COOS BAY

AAA ▼▼◆▼ **Best Western Holiday Motel** SH
(541) 269-5111. **$99-$189.** 411 N Bayshore Dr. Just n of downtown on US 101. Ext/int corridors. **Pets:** Small, dogs only. $10 daily fee/pet. Service with restrictions, supervision.
SAVE Sᴅ ✕ ⊟ ⊒ ⇌

AAA ▼▼▼ **Red Lion Hotel Coos Bay** SH
(541) 267-4141. **$104-$134.** 1313 N Bayshore Dr. 0.5 mi n of downtown on US 101. Ext corridors. **Pets:** Other species. $10 daily fee/room. Service with restrictions, crate.
SAVE Sᴅ ✕ &ᴹ ⊟ ⊒ ⑪ ⇌

CORVALLIS

AAA ▼▼▼ **Best Western Grand Manor Inn** SH
(541) 758-8571. **$84-$149.** 925 NW Garfield. 1.5 mi n on 9th St; downtown. Int corridors. **Pets:** Small, dogs only. $10 daily fee/pet. Designated rooms, service with restrictions, supervision.
SAVE Sᴅ ✕ &ᴹ ⊟ ⊒ ⇌

AAA ▼▼ **Days Inn** SH
(541) 754-7474. **$54-$159.** 1113 NW 9th St. 1.3 mi n. Int corridors. **Pets:** Medium, other species. $5 daily fee/pet. Designated rooms, service with restrictions, supervision.
SAVE Sᴅ ✕ ⊟ ⇌

AAA ▼▼▼ **Holiday Inn Express On The River** SH ✿
(541) 752-0800. **$69-$199.** 781 NE 2nd St. I-5, exit 228, 9.8 mi w on SR 34, then 0.4 mi nw. Int corridors. **Pets:** $25 daily fee/room. Service with restrictions, supervision.
SAVE Sᴅ ✕ ⊟ ⊒ ⇌ ⊠

AAA ▼ **Motel 6 #4243** SH ✿
(541) 758-9125. **Call for rates.** 935 NW Garfield Ave. 1.5 mi n on 9th St. Int corridors. **Pets:** Very small, dogs only. $20 deposit/pet. Designated rooms, service with restrictions, supervision.
SAVE ✕ &ᴹ ⊟

▼▼ **Super 8 Motel** SH
(541) 758-8088. **Call for rates.** 407 NW 2nd St. US 20, just n of jct SR 34; downtown. Int corridors. **Pets:** Accepted.
✕ &ᴹ ⊟ ⇌

COTTAGE GROVE

AAA ▼▼▼ **Comfort Inn** SH
(541) 942-9747. **$64-$150.** 845 Gateway Blvd. I-5, exit 174, just w. Ext/int corridors. **Pets:** Other species. $10 daily fee/pet. Designated rooms, service with restrictions, supervision.
SAVE Sᴅ ✕ ⊟ ⊒ ⇌

Holiday Inn Express SH
(541) 942-1000. **$99-$129.** 1601 Gateway Blvd. I-5, exit 174, just w. Int corridors. **Pets:** Medium, dogs only. $15 daily fee/pet. Service with restrictions, supervision.

CRESWELL

Best Western Creswell Inn M ☼
(541) 895-3341. **Call for rates.** 345 E Oregon Ave. I-5, exit 182, just w. Ext corridors. **Pets:** Small. $10 one-time fee/pet. Designated rooms, service with restrictions, supervision.

DALLAS

Best Western Dallas Inn & Suites SH
(503) 623-6000. **$90-$120.** 250 Orchard Dr. SR 223, just n. Int corridors. **Pets:** Small, dogs only. $10 daily fee/pet. Designated rooms, supervision.

DEPOE BAY

Crown Pacific Inn M
(541) 765-7773. **$80-$95.** 50 NE Bechill St. Center. Ext/int corridors. **Pets:** Accepted.

Surfrider Resort SH
(541) 764-2311. **$84-$199, 3 day notice.** 3115 NW Hwy 101. North end of Depoe Bay. Ext corridors. **Pets:** Small, dogs only. $20 one-time fee/pet. Designated rooms, service with restrictions, supervision.

ENTERPRISE

Ponderosa Motel M
(541) 426-3186. **$56-$79.** 102 E Greenwood St. Center. Ext corridors. **Pets:** Accepted.

The Wilderness Inn M
(541) 426-4535. **$49-$72.** 301 W North St. Corner of NW 2nd. Ext corridors. **Pets:** Accepted.

EUGENE

Americas Best Value Inn M
(541) 343-0730. **$44-$74.** 1140 W 6th Ave. I-5, exit 194B, 3 mi w on I-105, then just w on SR 99 N (6th Ave). Ext corridors. **Pets:** Medium, dogs only. $10 daily fee/pet. Designated rooms, service with restrictions, supervision.

Best Western Greentree Inn SH ☼
(541) 485-2727. **$95-$110.** 1759 Franklin Blvd. I-5, exit 191 (southbound); exit Glenwood Blvd, 0.6 mi n, then 1.1 mi w; exit 192 northbound, 1 mi w. Ext/int corridors. **Pets:** $50 deposit/pet. Designated rooms, service with restrictions, supervision.

Best Western New Oregon Motel SH ☼
(541) 683-3669. **$95-$110.** 1655 Franklin Blvd. I-5, exit 191 (southbound); exit Glenwood Blvd, 0.6 mi n, then 1.1 mi w; exit 192 northbound, 1 mi w. Ext/int corridors. **Pets:** $50 deposit/pet. Service with restrictions, supervision.

Eugene/Springfield Residence Inn by Marriott SH
(541) 342-7171. **$187-$207.** 25 Club Rd. I-5, exit 194B, 1.3 mi w on I-105, exit 2 (Coburg Rd), go straight through jct Coburg Rd to Southwood Ln, just w, then se on Country Club Rd; follow signs for Autzen Stadium. Int corridors. **Pets:** Accepted.

Express Inn & Suites M
(541) 868-1520. **$65-$85, 3 day notice.** 990 W 6th Ave. I-5, exit 194B, 3 mi w on I-105, then just w on SR 99 N (6th Ave). Ext corridors. **Pets:** Small, dogs only. $10 daily fee/pet. Designated rooms, service with restrictions, supervision.

Hilton Eugene LH
(541) 342-2000. **$119-$209.** 66 E 6th Ave. At 6th Ave and Oak St; center. Int corridors. **Pets:** Accepted.

La Quinta Inn & Suites Waterfront SH
(541) 344-8335. **$110-$130.** 155 Day Island Rd. I-5, exit 194B, 1.3 mi w on I-105, exit 2 (Coburg Rd), go straight through jct Coburg Rd to Southwood Ln, just w, then 0.5 mi se on Country Club Rd; follow signs for Autzen Stadium. Int corridors. **Pets:** Other species. Service with restrictions, supervision.

Motel 6-36 M
(541) 687-2395. **$49-$55 (no credit cards).** 3690 Glenwood Dr. I-5, exit 191, just sw. Ext corridors. **Pets:** Other species. Service with restrictions, supervision.

Red Lion Hotel Eugene M ☼
(541) 342-5201. **$129-$159.** 205 Coburg Rd. I-5, exit 194B, 1.3 mi w on I-105, exit 2 (Coburg Rd), then just n. Ext corridors. **Pets:** Other species. $20 daily fee/room. Service with restrictions, crate.

Valley River Inn SH
(541) 743-1000. **$139-$249.** 1000 Valley River Way. I-5, exit 194B southbound, 2.5 mi w on I-105, exit 1, follow Valley River Center signs. Int corridors. **Pets:** Accepted.

FLORENCE

Best Western Pier Point Inn SH
(541) 997-7191. **$114-$180.** 85625 Hwy 101. Jct SR 126, 1 mi s. Ext corridors. **Pets:** Medium, other species. $10 daily fee/pet. Designated rooms, supervision.

Le Chateau Motel M
(541) 997-3481. **Call for rates.** 1084 Hwy 101 N. SR 126, just n. Ext corridors. **Pets:** Accepted.

Ocean Breeze Motel M
(541) 997-2642. **$50-$139 (no credit cards).** 85165 Hwy 101 S. SR 126, 2 mi s; south end of Siuslaw Bridge. Ext corridors. **Pets:** Dogs only. $10 daily fee/pet. Designated rooms, supervision.

Old Town Inn M
(541) 997-7131. **$65-$99.** 170 Hwy 101. SR 126, 0.5 mi s. Ext corridors. **Pets:** Accepted.

Park Motel M ☼
(541) 997-2634. **$49-$135.** 85034 Hwy 101 S. Jct SR 126 and US 101, 2.2 mi s. Ext corridors. **Pets:** Medium, other species. $10 daily fee/pet. Service with restrictions, supervision.

FOREST GROVE

Best Western University Inn & Suites SH
(503) 992-8888. **$89-$199.** 3933 Pacific Ave. East end of town on SR 8. Int corridors. **Pets:** Medium, dogs only. $15 daily fee/pet. Designated rooms, service with restrictions, supervision.

GARIBALDI

Comfort Inn by Choice Hotels SH
(503) 322-3338. **$89-$189.** 502 Garibaldi Ave. On US 101 at jct 5th St; center. Int corridors. **Pets:** Medium, dogs only. $20 daily fee/pet. Designated rooms, service with restrictions, supervision.

GEARHART

Gearhart By The Sea CO
(503) 738-8331. **$89-$150, 3 day notice.** 1157 N Marion. 1 mi w off US 101, City Center exit, 1 mi w. Ext corridors. **Pets:** $11 daily fee/pet. Designated rooms, service with restrictions, supervision.

GLENEDEN BEACH

Salishan Spa & Golf Resort LH
(541) 764-2371. **Call for rates.** 7760 Hwy 101 N. Just e of US 101; center. Ext corridors. **Pets:** Other species. $25 one-time fee/pet. Supervision.

GLIDE

Illahee Inn and Restaurant M
(541) 496-3338. **Call for rates.** 170 Bar L Ranch Rd. I-5, exit 124, 0.8 mi e, just n to SR 138, then e. Ext corridors. **Pets:** Accepted.

Steelhead Run Bed & Breakfast BB
(541) 496-0563. **$65-$139, 9 day notice.** 23049 N Umpqua (Hwy 138). I-5, exit 124, 0.8 mi e, just n to SR 138, then 20.7 mi e; just e of MM 24. Ext/int corridors. **Pets:** Other species. $20 daily fee/room. Designated rooms, crate.

GOLD BEACH

Clear Sky Lodging VH
(541) 247-6456. **Call for rates.** 29350 Clear Sky Ln. On US 101, just e on 10th St. Ext corridors. **Pets:** Accepted.

Gold Beach Inn M
(541) 247-7091. **$70-$220.** 29346 Ellensburg Ave. On US 101; center. Ext corridors. **Pets:** Accepted.

Inn of the Beachcomber M
(541) 247-6691. **$79-$184.** 29266 Ellensburg Ave. On US 101; south end of town. Ext/int corridors. **Pets:** Accepted.

Jot's Resort M
(541) 247-6676. **$65-$230, 3 day notice.** 94360 Wedderburn Loop. Just w of US 101, north end of bridge. Ext corridors. **Pets:** Other species. $15 daily fee/pet. Service with restrictions, supervision.

Motel 6-4047 M
(541) 247-4533. **Call for rates.** 94433 Jerry's Flat Rd. Just e of jct US 101. Ext corridors. **Pets:** Other species. Service with restrictions, supervision.

GOVERNMENT CAMP

Mt. Hood Inn SH
(503) 272-3205. **$99-$189.** 87450 E Government Camp. 0.5 mi w of center. Int corridors. **Pets:** Other species. $10 daily fee/pet. Service with restrictions, supervision.

GRANTS PASS

Bestway Inn M
(541) 479-2952. **$59-$79.** 1253 NE 6th St. I-5, exit 58, 0.8 mi s on SR 99. Ext corridors. **Pets:** Very small, dogs only. $5 daily fee/pet. Service with restrictions, supervision.

Best Western Grants Pass Inn SH
(541) 476-1117. **Call for rates.** 111 NE Agness Ave. I-5, exit 55, just w. Ext corridors. **Pets:** $10 daily fee/pet. No service, supervision.

Best Western Inn at the Rogue SH
(541) 582-2200. **Call for rates.** 8959 Rogue River Hwy. I-5, exit 48, just w. Int corridors. **Pets:** Other species. $20 daily fee/pet. Designated rooms, service with restrictions, supervision.

Buona Sera Inn M
(541) 476-4260. **$58-$125, 3 day notice.** 1001 NE 6th St. I-5, exit 58, 1.2 mi s on SR 99. Ext corridors. **Pets:** Accepted.

Comfort Inn SH
(541) 479-8301. **$60-$130.** 1889 NE 6th St. I-5, exit 58, just s on SR 99. Int corridors. **Pets:** $10 one-time fee/pet. Service with restrictions, supervision.

Holiday Inn Express SH
(541) 471-6144. **$92-$159.** 105 NE Agness Ave. I-5, exit 55, just w. Int corridors. **Pets:** Medium, other species. $10 daily fee/pet. Designated rooms, service with restrictions, supervision.

Knights Inn Motel M
(541) 479-5595. **$50-$95.** 104 SE 7th St. I-5, exit 58, 1.7 mi s on SR 99 to G St, 1 blk e, then just n. Ext corridors. **Pets:** Small, dogs only. $10 one-time fee/pet. Designated rooms, service with restrictions, supervision.

La Quinta Inn & Suites Grants Pass SH
(541) 472-1808. **$90-$115.** 243 NE Morgan Ln. I-5, exit 58, 0.4 mi s on SR 99, just e on Hillcrest Dr to SR 99 northbound, then just n. Int corridors. **Pets:** Other species. Service with restrictions, supervision.

Motel 6-253 M
(541) 474-1331. **$43-$53 (no credit cards).** 1800 NE 7th St. I-5, exit 58, 0.3 mi s on SR 99. Ext corridors. **Pets:** Other species. Service with restrictions, supervision.

Redwood Motel M
(541) 476-0878. **Call for rates.** 815 NE 6th St. I-5, exit 58, 1.2 mi s on SR 99. Ext corridors. **Pets:** Small, dogs only. $10 daily fee/pet. Designated rooms, no service, supervision.

Riverside Inn Resort SH
(541) 476-6873. **$125-$149, 3 day notice.** 986 SW 6th St. I-5, exit 58, 2.5 mi s on SR 99. Ext corridors. **Pets:** Other species. $10 daily fee/pet. Designated rooms, service with restrictions, crate.

Shilo Inn SH
(541) 479-8391. **$100-$115 (no credit cards).** 1880 NW 6th St. I-5, exit 58, 0.4 mi s on SR 99. Int corridors. **Pets:** $25 one-time fee/room. Designated rooms, service with restrictions, supervision.

◆◆◆ ▼▼▼ **Sunset Inn** Ⓜ
(541) 479-3305. **$55-$135.** 1400 NW 6th St. I-5, exit 58, 0.6 mi s on SR 99. Ext corridors. **Pets:** Medium. $10 deposit/pet. Designated rooms, service with restrictions, supervision.

[SAVE] [S🐾] [✕] [🖥] [💻] [≈]

◆◆◆ ▼▼▼ **Super 8 Motel-Grants Pass** [SH]
(541) 474-0888. **Call for rates.** 1949 NE 7th St. I-5, exit 58, 0.4 mi s on SR 99, just e on Hillcrest Dr to SR 99 northbound, then just n. Int corridors. **Pets:** Small, dogs only. $25 deposit/pet. Service with restrictions, supervision.

[SAVE] [✕] [♿] [🖥] [💻] [≈]

◆◆◆ ▼▼▼ **Sweet Breeze Inn** Ⓜ
(541) 471-4434. **$60-$165.** 1627 NE 6th St. I-5, exit 58, 0.5 mi s on SR 99. Ext/int corridors. **Pets:** Small, dogs only. $5 daily fee/pet. Designated rooms, service with restrictions, supervision.

[SAVE] [S🐾] [✕] [🖥]

◆◆◆ ▼▼▼ **Travelodge** Ⓜ ❖
(541) 479-6611. **$59-$79.** 1950 NW Vine St. I-5, exit 58, just s on SR 99. Ext corridors. **Pets:** Medium, other species. $100 deposit/room, $8 daily fee/pet. Designated rooms, service with restrictions, supervision.

[SAVE] [S🐾] [✕] [♿] [🖥] [💻] [≈]

HALSEY

◆◆◆ ▼▼ **Pioneer Villa Travelodge** Ⓜ
(541) 369-2804. **$72-$85.** 33180 SR 228. I-5, exit 216, just e. Ext corridors. **Pets:** Accepted.

[ASK] [S🐾] [✕] [🖥] [💻] [🍴] [≈]

HERMISTON

▼▼▼ **Comfort Inn & Suites Hermiston** [SH]
(541) 564-5911. **Call for rates.** 77514 Hwy 207. I-84, exit 182, just n. Int corridors. **Pets:** Accepted.

[✕] [🖥] [💻] [≈]

◆◆◆ ▼▼▼ **Oak Tree Inn** [SH]
(541) 567-2330. **$69-$84.** 1110 SE 4th St. 0.4 mi s on US 395, just w. Int corridors. **Pets:** Small. $10 daily fee/pet. Service with restrictions, crate.

[SAVE] [S🐾] [✕] [🖥] [💻]

▼▼▼ **Oxford Suites** [SH]
(541) 564-8000. **$99-$109.** 1050 N 1st St. 0.3 mi n on US 395. Int corridors. **Pets:** Accepted.

[ASK] [S🐾] [✕] [♿] [🖥] [💻] [≈]

HINES

◆◆◆ ▼▼▼ **Best Western Rory & Ryan Inns** [SH]
(541) 573-5050. **$70-$125.** 534 Hwy 20 N. On US 20 (Hines/Burns). Int corridors. **Pets:** Accepted.

[SAVE] [S🐾] [✕] [♿] [🖥] [💻] [≈]

HOOD RIVER

◆◆◆ ▼▼▼ **Best Western Hood River Inn** [SH] ❖
(541) 386-2200. **$80-$179.** 1108 E Marina Way. I-84, exit 64, just n, then just e. Int corridors. **Pets:** Dogs only. $12 daily fee/pet. Designated rooms, service with restrictions, supervision.

[SAVE] [S🐾] [✕] [♿] [🖥] [💻] [🍴] [≈] [✕]

◆◆◆ ▼▼▼ **Columbia Gorge Hotel** [CI] ❖
(541) 386-5566. **$153-$312, 14 day notice.** 4000 Westcliff Dr. I-84, exit 62, just w of overpass. Int corridors. **Pets:** Dogs only. $35 one-time fee/room. Designated rooms, supervision.

[SAVE] [S🐾] [✕] [🖥] [🍴]

◆◆◆ ▼▼ **Vagabond Lodge** Ⓜ ❖
(541) 386-2992. **$52-$102.** 4070 Westcliff Dr. I-84, exit 62, just n, then just w. Ext corridors. **Pets:** Medium. $5 daily fee/pet. Designated rooms, service with restrictions, supervision.

[SAVE] [✕] [🖥] [💻]

JACKSONVILLE

▼▼ **The Stage Lodge** Ⓜ
(541) 899-3953. **$92-$175, 7 day notice.** 830 N 5th St. On N 5th St (SR 238), 0.3 mi ne. Ext corridors. **Pets:** Accepted.

[ASK] [S🐾] [✕] [♿] [🖥] [💻]

JOHN DAY

◆◆◆ ▼▼ **Best Western John Day Inn** Ⓜ
(541) 575-1700. **$80-$100.** 315 W Main St. Just w on jct US 26 and 395. Ext corridors. **Pets:** Medium. $15 daily fee/pet. Service with restrictions, crate.

[SAVE] [S🐾] [✕] [🖥] [💻] [≈]

◆◆◆ ▼ **Dreamers Lodge** Ⓜ ❖
(541) 575-0526. **$42-$99.** 144 N Canyon Blvd. Just n of jct US 26 and 395. Ext corridors. **Pets:** Medium, dogs only. $5 daily fee/pet. Service with restrictions, supervision.

[SAVE] [S🐾] [✕] [🖥] [💻]

KEIZER

◆◆◆ ▼▼▼▼ **Keizer Renaissance Inn** [SH]
(503) 390-4733. **$79-$89.** 5188 Wittenberg Ln N. I-5, exit 260B southbound; exit 260 northbound, 1.5 mi w on Chemawa Rd and Lockhaven Dr, then just s on River Rd. Int corridors. **Pets:** Accepted.

[SAVE] [S🐾] [✕] [♿] [🖥] [💻] [≈] [✕]

KLAMATH FALLS

◆◆◆ ▼▼▼ **Best Western Klamath Inn** Ⓜ
(541) 882-1200. **Call for rates.** 4061 S 6th St. Just w on 6th St (SR 140) from jct SR 140 E/39 S and SR 39 N/US 97 business route. Ext corridors. **Pets:** Accepted.

[SAVE] [✕] [🖥] [💻] [≈]

◆◆◆ ▼ **Econo Lodge** Ⓜ
(541) 884-7735. **$39-$109.** 75 Main St. I-97, exit City Center Dr, 1.3 mi s. Ext corridors. **Pets:** $10 daily fee/pet. Designated rooms, service with restrictions, supervision.

[SAVE] [S🐾] [✕] [🖥]

◆◆◆ ▼ **Golden West Motel** Ⓜ
(541) 882-1758. **$38-$68.** 6402 S 6th St. S 6th St (SR 140) at eastern edge of town. Ext corridors. **Pets:** Accepted.

[SAVE] [S🐾] [✕] [🖥] [💻]

◆◆◆ ▼ **Majestic Inn & Suites** Ⓜ
(541) 883-7771. **$35-$105.** 5543 S 6th St. 1 mi e on 6th St (SR 140) from jct SR 140 E/39 S and SR 39 N/US 97 business route. Ext corridors. **Pets:** $6 daily fee/pet. Designated rooms, service with restrictions, supervision.

[SAVE] [S🐾] [✕] [🖥]

◆◆◆ ▼▼ **Maverick Motel** Ⓜ
(541) 882-6688. **$39-$109.** 1220 Main St. US 97 N to City Center exit, 0.3 mi e. Ext corridors. **Pets:** $6 daily fee/pet. Designated rooms, service with restrictions, supervision.

[SAVE] [S🐾] [✕] [🖥]

▼ **Motel 6–226** [SH]
(541) 884-2110. **$43-$53 (no credit cards).** 5136 S 6th St. 0.5 mi e on 6th St E (SR 140) from jct SR 39/US 97 business route. Ext corridors. **Pets:** Other species. Service with restrictions, supervision.

[S🐾] [✕] [♿] [🖥] [💻]

◆◆◆ ▼▼ **Oregon 8 Motel** Ⓜ ❖
(541) 883-3431. **$38-$98.** 5225 Hwy 97 N. On US 97; between MM 270 and 271; east side of highway. Ext corridors. **Pets:** $10 daily fee/pet. Designated rooms, service with restrictions, supervision.

[SAVE] [S🐾] [✕] [🖥] [💻] [≈]

Quality Inn M
(541) 882-4666. **$75-$135.** 100 Main St. Just e of US 97, exit City Center. Ext corridors. **Pets:** $10 daily fee/pet. Designated rooms, service with restrictions, supervision.

Red Lion Inn Klamath Falls M
(541) 882-8864. **$129.** 3612 S 6th St. 0.3 mi w on 6th St (SR 140) from jct SR 140 E/39 S and SR 39 N/US 97 business route. Ext corridors. **Pets:** Large. Service with restrictions, crate.

The Running y Ranch SH
(541) 850-5500. **$139-$199, 3 day notice.** 5500 Running y Rd. On 6th St (SR 140), 7.2 mi n from jct US 66 and SR 140. Int corridors. **Pets:** Accepted.

Shilo Inn Klamath Falls SH
(541) 885-7980. **$180.** 2500 Almond St. North end of US 97. Int corridors. **Pets:** $25 one-time fee/room. Designated rooms, service with restrictions, supervision.

Super 8 Motel SH
(541) 884-8880. **$74-$80.** 3805 Hwy 97. On US 97, 2 mi n. Int corridors. **Pets:** Accepted.

LA GRANDE

Americas Best Value Sandman Inn SH
(541) 963-3707. **$80-$85.** 2410 E R Ave. I-84, exit 261, just s on Albany, then just e. Int corridors. **Pets:** Other species. $25 one-time fee/room. Designated rooms, supervision.

Royal Motor Inn M
(541) 963-4154. **Call for rates.** 1510 Adams Ave. I-84, exit La Grande on US 30, just n of jct SR 82; downtown. Ext corridors. **Pets:** Dogs only. $10 one-time fee/pet. Designated rooms, service with restrictions, supervision.

LAKEVIEW

Best Western Skyline Motor Lodge M
(541) 947-2194. **Call for rates.** 414 N G St. Jct US 395 and SR 140. Ext corridors. **Pets:** Large, other species. $15 daily fee/pet. Designated rooms, service with restrictions, supervision.

LA PINE

Best Western Newberry Station SH
(541) 536-5130. **$85-$160.** 16515 Reed Rd. North end of town, just off SR 97. Int corridors. **Pets:** Small, dogs only. $15 deposit/room, $10 one-time fee/room. Service with restrictions, supervision.

LINCOLN CITY

Ashley Inn & Suites SH
(541) 996-7500. **$69-$199.** 3430 NE Hwy 101. North side on US 101. Int corridors. **Pets:** Accepted.

Coho Inn M
(541) 994-3684. **$63-$280.** 1635 NW Harbor Ave. US 101, exit N 17th St, just w. Ext corridors. **Pets:** Small. $10 daily fee/pet. Designated rooms, service with restrictions, supervision.

Comfort Inn by Choice Hotels-Lincoln City SH
(541) 994-8155. **$89-$299.** 136 NE Hwy 101. On US 101 near D River. Int corridors. **Pets:** Small, dogs only. $20 daily fee/pet. Designated rooms, service with restrictions, supervision.

Econo Lodge SH
(541) 994-5281. **$52-$229.** 1713 NW 21st St. US 101, just w. Int corridors. **Pets:** Accepted.

Lincoln City Inn SH
(541) 996-4400. **Call for rates.** 1091 SE 1st St. On US 101 at D River. Int corridors. **Pets:** Dogs only. $10 one-time fee/pet. Designated rooms, service with restrictions, supervision.

Looking Glass Inn M
(541) 996-3996. **$84-$229, 3 day notice.** 861 SW 51st St. South side, w of US 101, exit 51 St. Ext corridors. **Pets:** Accepted.

Motel 6-4172 SH
(541) 996-9900. **Call for rates (no credit cards).** 3517 NW Hwy 101. North end of town. Int corridors. **Pets:** Medium, dogs only. $150 deposit/room. Designated rooms, service with restrictions, supervision.

The O'dysius Hotel SH
(541) 994-4121. **$159-$365.** 120 NW Inlet Ct. On US 101 at D River; center. Int corridors. **Pets:** Small. $10 daily fee/pet. Designated rooms, supervision.

Palace Inn & Suites SH
(541) 996-9466. **$69-$209.** 550 SE Hwy 101. Center. Int corridors. **Pets:** Medium, dogs only. $25 one-time fee/pet. Designated rooms, service with restrictions, supervision.

MADRAS

Best Western Madras Inn M
(541) 475-6141. **$79-$119.** 12 SW 4th St. On US 97, at B and 4th sts; downtown. Ext corridors. **Pets:** Medium, other species. $20 daily fee/pet. Designated rooms, service with restrictions, supervision.

Budget Inn M
(541) 475-3831. **$55-$99.** 133 NE 5th St. On US 97/26 northbound; downtown. Ext corridors. **Pets:** Small, other species. $10 daily fee/pet. Service with restrictions, supervision.

MCMINNVILLE

Best Western Vineyard Inn SH
(503) 472-4900. **Call for rates.** 2035 S SR 99 W. Jct SR 99 W and 18. Int corridors. **Pets:** Accepted.

Comfort Inn & Suites SH
(503) 472-1700. **Call for rates.** 2520 SE Stratus Ave. Jct SR 99 W, 3.6 mi e on SR 18. Int corridors. **Pets:** Medium, other species. $10 daily fee/pet. Service with restrictions, crate.

Red Lion Inn & Suites SH
(503) 472-1500. **$122.** 2535 NE Cumulus Ave. Jct SR 99 W, 3.7 mi e on SR 18. Int corridors. **Pets:** Accepted.

AAA ◈◈ Safari Motor Inn **M**
(503) 472-5187. **$70-$90.** 381 NE Hwy 99W. North end of SR 99 W. Ext corridors. **Pets:** Small. $10 daily fee/pet. Designated rooms, service with restrictions, supervision.

SAVE Sδ ✕ 🖪 🖵

MEDFORD

AAA ◈ Cedar Lodge Motor Inn **M**
(541) 773-7361. **Call for rates.** 518 N Riverside Ave. I-5, exit 27, 0.5 mi w on Barnett Rd, then 1.2 mi n on SR 99. Ext corridors. **Pets:** Accepted.

SAVE ✕ 🖪 🥤

◈ Motel 6-Medford North–739 **M**
(541) 779-0550. **$49-$55 (no credit cards).** 2400 Biddle Rd. I-5, exit 30 northbound, just s; exit southbound, follow signs for Biddle Rd. Ext corridors. **Pets:** Other species. Service with restrictions, supervision.

Sδ ✕ ⓛM 🖪 🥤

◈ Motel 6-Medford South–89 **M**
(541) 773-4290. **$49-$59 (no credit cards).** 950 Alba Dr. I-5, exit 27, just e on Barnett Rd, then just n. Ext corridors. **Pets:** Other species. Service with restrictions, supervision.

Sδ ✕ ⓛM 🖪 🥤

AAA ◈◈◈ Red Lion Hotel Medford **SH**
(541) 779-5811. **$109-$139.** 200 N Riverside Ave. I-5, exit 27, 0.4 mi w on Barnett Rd, then 1 mi n. Ext corridors. **Pets:** Medium, other species. $10 daily fee/room. Service with restrictions, supervision.

SAVE Sδ ✕ ⓛM 🖪 🖵 🍴 🥤

AAA ◈◈ Shilo Inn Medford **SH** 🐾
(541) 770-5151. **$80-$115.** 2111 Biddle Rd. I-5, exit 30 northbound, just s; exit southbound, follow signs for Biddle Rd, then just s. Int corridors. **Pets:** $25 one-time fee/room. Designated rooms, service with restrictions, supervision.

SAVE Sδ ✕ 🖪 🖵

◈◈◈ TownePlace Suites by Marriott **SH**
(541) 842-5757. **Call for rates.** 1395 Center Dr. I-5, exit 27 (Barnett Rd) southbound, straight onto Stewart Ave, then just s; northbound, just w on Barnett Rd, just s on Stewart Ave, then just s. Int corridors. **Pets:** Accepted.

✕ ⓛM 🖪 🖵 🥤

AAA ◈◈ Windmill Inn of Medford **SH** 🐾
(541) 779-0050. **$89-$139, 3 day notice.** 1950 Biddle Rd. I-5, exit 30 northbound, just s; exit southbound, follow signs for Biddle Rd, then just s. Int corridors. **Pets:** Other species. Service with restrictions, supervision.

SAVE Sδ ✕ ⓛM 🖪 🖵 🏊 ✕

MYRTLE POINT

AAA ◈ Myrtle Trees Motel **M**
(541) 572-5811. **$58-$64, 5 day notice.** 1010 8th St (Hwy 42). On SR 42, 0.5 mi e. Ext corridors. **Pets:** Accepted.

SAVE Sδ ✕ 🖪 🗲

NEWBERG

AAA ◈◈ Shilo Inn Suites-Newberg **SH** 🐾
(503) 537-0303. **$129.** 501 Sitka Ave. On SR 99 W. Int corridors. **Pets:** $25 one-time fee/room. Designated rooms, service with restrictions, supervision.

SAVE Sδ ✕ 🖪 🖵 🥤 ✕

NEWPORT

AAA ◈◈◈ The Best Western Agate Beach Inn **SH** 🐾
(541) 265-9411. **$99-$225.** 3019 N Coast Hwy. US 20, 1.5 mi n on US 101. Int corridors. **Pets:** $20 one-time fee/pet. Designated rooms, service with restrictions, supervision.

SAVE Sδ ✕ 🖪 🖵 🍴 🥤 ✕ 🗲

◈◈◈ Hallmark Resort Oceanfront **SH**
(541) 265-2600. **$104-$224.** 744 SW Elizabeth St. US 20, 0.7 mi s on US 101, just w on SW Bay St. Ext corridors. **Pets:** Accepted.

ASK Sδ ✕ ⓛM 🖪 🖵 🍴 🥤 ✕ 🗲

AAA ◈◈◈ The Landing at Newport **CO** 🐾
(541) 574-6777. **$109-$229.** 890 SE Bay Blvd. 0.5 mi e on US 20 from jct US 101, just s on John Moore Rd. Ext corridors. **Pets:** Medium. $75 deposit/room, $25 daily fee/pet. Designated rooms, service with restrictions, supervision.

SAVE Sδ ✕ 🖪 🖵 🗲

AAA ◈◈◈ La Quinta Inn & Suites Newport **SH**
(541) 867-7727. **$114.** 45 SE 32nd St. US 101, just s of Yaquina Bay Bridge. Int corridors. **Pets:** Other species. Service with restrictions, supervision.

SAVE Sδ ✕ ⓛM 🖪 🖵 🥤 ✕

◈◈ Shilo Inn Oceanfront Resort **SH** 🐾
(541) 265-7701. **$155-$235 (no credit cards).** 536 SW Elizabeth St. US 20, 0.5 mi s on US 101, just w on SW Falls St. Ext/int corridors. **Pets:** $25 one-time fee/room. Designated rooms, service with restrictions, supervision.

ASK Sδ ✕ 🖪 🖵 🍴 🥤 🗲

AAA ◈◈ The Whaler Motel **M** 🐾
(541) 265-9261. **$95-$175.** 155 SW Elizabeth St. Just s on US 101 from jct US 20, just w on SW 2nd St. Ext corridors. **Pets:** Dogs only. $10 daily fee/pet. Designated rooms, service with restrictions, supervision.

SAVE Sδ ✕ ⓛM 🖪 🖵 🥤 🗲

NORTH BEND

AAA ◈◈ Comfort Inn **M** 🐾
(541) 756-3191. **$79-$159.** 1503 Virginia Ave. 0.5 mi w of US 101. Ext/int corridors. **Pets:** Small, dogs only. $15 daily fee/pet. Designated rooms, service with restrictions, crate.

SAVE ✕ ⓛM 🖪 🖵

OAKLAND

AAA ◈◈ Best Western Rice Hill **M**
(541) 849-3335. **$72-$85.** 621 John Long Rd. I-5, exit 148, just e. Ext corridors. **Pets:** Accepted.

SAVE Sδ ✕ 🖪 🖵 🥤 ✕

OAKRIDGE

AAA ◈◈ Best Western Oakridge Inn **M**
(541) 782-2212. **Call for rates.** 47433 Hwy 58. West end of SR 58. Ext corridors. **Pets:** Accepted.

SAVE ✕ 🖪 🖵 🥤

AAA ◈ Cascade Motel **M**
(541) 782-2489. **$48-$68.** 47487 SR 58. Center. Ext corridors. **Pets:** Small, dogs only. $10 daily fee/room. Designated rooms, service with restrictions, supervision.

SAVE Sδ ✕ 🖪

ONTARIO

◈◈◈ Creek House Bed & Breakfast Inn **BB**
(541) 823-0717. **$89-$129, 7 day notice.** 717 SW 2nd St. I-84, exit 376A, 0.8 mi w on Idaho Ave, then 0.4 mi s. Int corridors. **Pets:** Accepted.

ASK ✕ 🖪 🖵 🗲

Holiday Inn-Ontario, OR SH
(541) 889-8621. **$79-$119.** 1249 Tapadera Ave. I-84, exit 376B, just ne. Int corridors. **Pets:** Accepted.
[SAVE] [S🐾] [✕] [🛏] [💻] [🍴] [🌊]

Rodeway Inn M ☀
(541) 889-9188. **$60-$78.** 615 E Idaho. I-84, exit 376A, just nw. Ext corridors. **Pets:** Medium, other species. $5 one-time fee/pet. Service with restrictions, supervision.
[SAVE] [S🐾] [✕] [🛏] [🍴] [🌊]

Sleep Inn SH
(541) 881-0007. **$59-$129.** 1221 SE 1st Ave. I-84, exit 376B, just se. Int corridors. **Pets:** Dogs only. $10 daily fee/pet. Designated rooms, service with restrictions, supervision.
[SAVE] [S🐾] [✕] [♿M] [🛏] [💻] [🌊]

PACIFIC CITY

Inn at Cape Kiwanda SH ☀
(503) 965-7001. **$119-$329.** 33105 Cape Kiwanda Dr. Just w on Pacific Ave, 1 mi n. Ext corridors. **Pets:** $20 daily fee/pet. Service with restrictions, supervision.
[SAVE] [✕] [♿M] [🛏] [💻] [✕] [🐾]

Pacific City Inn M ☀
(503) 965-6464. **$69-$99, 3 day notice.** 35280 Brooten Rd. Center. Ext corridors. **Pets:** Dogs only. $15 daily fee/pet. Designated rooms, service with restrictions, supervision.
[SAVE] [✕] [🛏] [💻] [🍴] [🐾]

PENDLETON

Americas Best Value Inn SH
(541) 276-1400. **$69-$95.** 201 SW Court Ave. I-84, exit 210 (SR 11), 0.7 mi n, then 1.2 mi w. Ext corridors. **Pets:** Other species. $10 daily fee/room. Designated rooms, service with restrictions, supervision.
[SAVE] [S🐾] [✕] [🛏] [💻] [🌊]

Best Western Pendleton Inn SH
(541) 276-2135. **Call for rates.** 400 SE Nye Ave. I-84, exit 210, just se. Int corridors. **Pets:** Medium. $10 one-time fee/pet. Service with restrictions, supervision.
[SAVE] [✕] [♿M] [🛏] [💻] [🌊]

Holiday Inn Express SH
(541) 966-6520. **$109-$149.** 600 SE Nye Ave. I-84, exit 210, just se. Int corridors. **Pets:** Other species. $10 daily fee/room. Designated rooms, service with restrictions, supervision.
[SAVE] [S🐾] [✕] [🛏] [💻] [🌊]

Motel 6-#349 M
(541) 276-3160. **$45-$55 (no credit cards).** 325 SE Nye Ave. I-84, exit 210, just se. Ext corridors. **Pets:** Other species. Service with restrictions, supervision.
[S🐾] [✕] [🛏] [🌊]

Oxford Suites SH
(541) 276-6000. **$99-$139.** 2400 SW Court Pl. I-84, exit 209, Just n to SW 20th St, just nw to SW Court Ave, then 0.3 mi sw. Int corridors. **Pets:** Accepted.
[ASK] [S🐾] [✕] [♿M] [🛏] [💻] [🌊] [✕]

Red Lion Hotel Pendleton SH
(541) 276-6111. **$99-$139.** 304 SE Nye Ave. I-84, exit 210, just s. Ext/int corridors. **Pets:** Other species. $20 one-time fee/room. Designated rooms, service with restrictions, crate.
[SAVE] [✕] [🛏] [💻] [🍴] [🌊] [✕]

Super 8 Motel SH
(541) 276-8881. **Call for rates.** 601 SE Nye Ave. I-84, exit 210, just se. Int corridors. **Pets:** $10 daily fee/room. Service with restrictions, supervision.
[✕] [🛏] [💻] [🌊]

Travelodge M ☀
(541) 276-7531. **$65-$80.** 411 SW Dorion Ave. I-84, exit 209, just w of town center on corner of SW 4th St; downtown. Ext corridors. **Pets:** Dogs only. $10 daily fee/pet. Designated rooms, service with restrictions.
[SAVE] [S🐾] [✕] [🛏] [💻]

PORTLAND METROPOLITAN AREA

BEAVERTON

Comfort Inn & Suites SH
(503) 643-9100. **Call for rates.** 13455 SW Tualatin Valley Hwy. SR 217, exit Canyon Rd (SR 8), 1 mi w. Int corridors. **Pets:** Accepted.
[✕] [🛏] [💻] [🌊]

Homewood Suites By Hilton SH
(503) 614-0900. **$129-$159.** 15525 NW Gateway Ct. US 26, exit 65, s on 158th Ave, then just e on Waterhouse Ave. Int corridors. **Pets:** Accepted.
[ASK] [S🐾] [✕] [♿M] [🛏] [💻] [🌊]

Phoenix Inn Suites-Beaverton SH
(503) 614-8100. **$89-$149.** 15402 NW Cornell Rd. US 26, exit 65, just n. Int corridors. **Pets:** Medium. $15 daily fee/pet. Designated rooms, service with restrictions, supervision.
[SAVE] [✕] [♿M] [🛏] [💻] [🌊] [✕]

Shilo Inn–Portland/Beaverton SH ☀
(503) 297-2551. **$145.** 9900 SW Canyon Rd. SR 217, exit Canyon Rd/Beaverton Hillsdale Hwy, take feeder road, 0.3 mi e to SR 8 (Canyon Rd), then 0.6 mi e. Int corridors. **Pets:** $25 one-time fee/room. Designated rooms, service with restrictions, supervision.
[ASK] [S🐾] [✕] [🛏] [💻] [🍴] [🌊]

CLACKAMAS

Comfort Suites SH
(503) 723-3450. **Call for rates.** 15929 SE McKinley Ave. I-205, exit 12 northbound, 0.3 mi w; exit 12B southbound, just w. Int corridors. **Pets:** Accepted.
[✕] [🛏] [💻] [🌊] [✕]

GLADSTONE

Oxford Suites SH
(503) 722-7777. **$89-$119.** 75 82nd Dr. I-205, exit 11, just w. Int corridors. **Pets:** Accepted.
[ASK] [S🐾] [✕] [♿M] [🛏] [💻] [🌊] [✕]

GRESHAM

Best Western Pony Soldier Inn SH
(503) 665-1591. **$85-$125.** 1060 NE Cleveland Ave. I-84, exit 14 (Fairview Pkwy), 0.9 mi s, then just 0.4 mi e on NE Glisan St, 1.2 mi s on NE 223rd Ave, 0.7 mi e on Burnside Rd, then just s. Int corridors. **Pets:** Accepted.
[SAVE] [S🐾] [✕] [🛏] [💻] [🌊] [✕]

△△△ ▽▼▼▼ **Days Inn & Suites** 🆂🅷
(503) 465-1515. **$74-$114.** 24124 SE Stark St. I-84, exit 16, 1.5 mi s on NE 238th Dr/242nd, then just n. Int corridors. **Pets:** Accepted.

🆂🅰🆅🅴 🆂🅳 ✕ 🖪 💻 ➷

▽▼▼ **Days Inn-Portland East /Gresham** 🆂🅷
(503) 618-8400. **$64-$100.** 2261 NE 181st Ave. I-84, exit 13, just s. Int corridors. **Pets:** Accepted.

🅰🆂🅺 🆂🅳 ✕ 🕹🅼 🖪 💻 ➷

▽▼▼ **Extended StayAmerica Portland/Gresham** 🆂🅷
(503) 661-0226. **$77-$85.** 17777 NE Sacramento St. I-84, exit 13, just s to NE San Raefael, just w, then just n on NE 178th Ave. Int corridors. **Pets:** Other species. $75 one-time fee/pet. Service with restrictions.

🅰🆂🅺 🆂🅳 ✕ 🖪 💻

△△△ ▽▼▼▼ **Holiday Inn Portland/Gresham** 🆂🅷
(503) 907-1777. **$89-$189.** 2752 NE Hogan Dr. I-84, exit 16, 1.7 mi s on 238th/Hogan drs. Int corridors. **Pets:** Accepted.

🆂🅰🆅🅴 ✕ 🕹🅼 🖪 💻 🍴 ➷

△△△ ▽▼▼ **Super 8 Motel** 🅼
(503) 661-5100. **$60-$70.** 121 NE 181st Ave. I-84, exit 13, 1.4 mi s. Int corridors. **Pets:** Medium, dogs only. $10 daily fee/pet. Designated rooms, service with restrictions, supervision.

🆂🅰🆅🅴 🆂🅳 ✕ 🖪 💻

HILLSBORO

△△△ ▽▼ **The Dunes Motel** 🅼
(503) 648-8991. **$55-$95.** 452 SE 10th Ave (SR 8). US 26, exit 62A westbound; exit 62 eastbound, 1 mi s on NW Cornelius Pass Rd, then 4.4 mi w on NE Cornell Rd. Int corridors. **Pets:** Small, dogs only. $10 daily fee/pet. Service with restrictions, supervision.

🆂🅰🆅🅴 🆂🅳 ✕ 🖪

▽▼ 🔷 **Extended StayAmerica-Portland-Beaverton** 🆂🅷
(503) 439-1515. **$87-$95.** 18665 NW Eider Ct. US 26, exit 64, 0.8 mi s; behind Wendy's. Int corridors. **Pets:** Other species. $75 one-time fee/pet. Service with restrictions.

🅰🆂🅺 🆂🅳 ✕ 🖪 💻

▽▼▼▼ **Extended Stay Deluxe-Portland-Hillsboro-NW Cornell Rd** 🆂🅷
(503) 439-0706. **$95-$105.** 19311 NW Cornell Rd. US 26, exit 64, 0.5 mi s on 185th Ave, then 0.4 mi w. Int corridors. **Pets:** Other species. $75 one-time fee/pet. Service with restrictions.

🅰🆂🅺 🆂🅳 ✕ 🖪 💻 ➷

△△△ ▽▼▼▼ **Larkspur Landing Hillsboro/Portland** 🆂🅷
(503) 681-2121. **$89-$143.** 3133 NE Shute Rd. US 26, exit 61, 1.2 mi s. Int corridors. **Pets:** Other species. $75 one-time fee/room. Designated rooms, service with restrictions, crate.

🆂🅰🆅🅴 🆂🅳 ✕ 🖪 💻

△△△ ▽▼▼▼ **Residence Inn by Marriott Portland West** 🆂🅷
(503) 531-3200. **$199-$219.** 18855 NW Tanasbourne Dr. US 26, exit 64, just s, then just w. Ext/int corridors. **Pets:** Accepted.

🆂🅰🆅🅴 🆂🅳 ✕ 🕹🅼 🖪 💻 ➷ ✖

△△△ ▽▼▼▼ **TownePlace Suites by Marriott-Portland Hillsboro** 🆂🅷
(503) 268-6000. **$169-$186.** 6550 NE Brighton St. US 26, exit 62A westbound; exit 62 eastbound, just s, 1 mi s on Cornelius Pass Rd, 0.7 mi w on Cornell Rd, just n on 229th Ave, then just w. Ext/int corridors. **Pets:** Accepted.

🆂🅰🆅🅴 🆂🅳 ✕ 🕹🅼 🖪 💻 ➷ ✖

KING CITY

△△△ ▽▼▼▼ **Best Western Northwind Inn & Suites** 🆂🅷 ☕
(503) 431-2100. **$89-$139.** 16105 SW Pacific Hwy. I-5, exit 292, just nw on SR 217, exit SR 99W, then 2.5 mi s. Int corridors. **Pets:** $20 daily fee/pet. Service with restrictions, supervision.

🆂🅰🆅🅴 🆂🅳 ✕ 🕹🅼 🖪 💻 ➷

LAKE OSWEGO

△△△ ▽▼▼▼ **Crowne Plaza Hotel** 🆂🅷 ☕
(503) 624-8400. **$79-$249.** 14811 Kruse Oaks Dr. I-5, exit 292B northbound; exit 292 southbound, just e. Int corridors. **Pets:** $20 daily fee/room. Designated rooms, service with restrictions, supervision.

🆂🅰🆅🅴 🆂🅳 ✕ 🖪 💻 🍴 ➷ ✖

▽▼▼ **Residence Inn by Marriott-Portland South** 🆂🅷
(503) 684-2603. **$219-$242.** 15200 SW Bangy Rd. I-5, exit 292B northbound; exit 292 southbound, just e, then 0.3 mi s. Ext corridors. **Pets:** Accepted.

🅰🆂🅺 🆂🅳 ✕ 🕹🅼 🖪 💻 ➷ ✖

MILWAUKIE

△△△ ▽▼▼ **Econo Lodge Suites Inn** 🅼
(503) 654-2222. **$59-$79, 14 day notice.** 17330 SE McLoughlin Blvd. I-205, exit 9 (Oregon City/Gladstone), 2.3 mi n on SR 99 E (McLoughlin Blvd). Ext corridors. **Pets:** Small, dogs only. $10 daily fee/pet. Designated rooms, service with restrictions, supervision.

🆂🅰🆅🅴 🆂🅳 ✕ 🖪 💻 ➷

OREGON CITY

△△△ ▽▼▼ **Best Western Rivershore Hotel** 🆂🅷 ☕
(503) 655-7141. **Call for rates.** 1900 Clackamette Dr. I-205, exit 9, just n. Int corridors. **Pets:** $5 daily fee/pet. Service with restrictions, supervision.

🆂🅰🆅🅴 ✕ 🕹🅼 🖪 💻 🍴 ➷ ✖

PORTLAND

△△△ ▽▼▼ ▽▼▼ **The Benson Hotel, a Coast Hotel** 🅻🅷
(503) 228-2000. **Call for rates.** 309 SW Broadway. At SW Broadway and Oak. Int corridors. **Pets:** Accepted.

🆂🅰🆅🅴 ✕ 🕹🅼 💻 🍴

△△△ ▽▼▼▼ **Best Western Inn At The Meadows** 🆂🅷
(503) 286-9600. **$110-$150.** 1215 N Hayden Meadows Dr. I-5, exit 306B, just e. Int corridors. **Pets:** Small. $15 daily fee/room. Designated rooms, service with restrictions, supervision.

🆂🅰🆅🅴 🆂🅳 ✕ 🖪 💻

△△△ ▽▼▼▼ **Best Western Pony Soldier Inn-Airport** 🆂🅷 ☕
(503) 256-1504. **$99-$159.** 9901 NE Sandy Blvd. I-205, exit 23A, just e. Int corridors. **Pets:** Medium. Designated rooms, service with restrictions, crate.

🆂🅰🆅🅴 🆂🅳 ✕ 🕹🅼 🖪 💻 ➷ ✖

△△△ ▽▼▼ **Briarwood Suites** 🅼
(503) 788-9394. **$59-$99.** 7740 SE Powell Blvd. I-205, exit 19, 1 mi w. Ext corridors. **Pets:** Accepted.

🆂🅰🆅🅴 🆂🅳 ✕ 🖪 💻

△△△ ▽▼▼ **Days Inn-Portland North** 🆂🅷
(503) 289-1800. **Call for rates.** 9930 N Whitaker Rd. I-5, exit 306B, just e. Int corridors. **Pets:** Accepted.

🆂🅰🆅🅴 ✕ 🖪 💻

The Heathman Hotel 🅂🄷 ❀
(503) 241-4100. **$199-$469.** 1001 SW Broadway. At SW Broadway and Salmon St. Int corridors. **Pets:** Medium. $30 daily fee/pet. Designated rooms, service with restrictions, supervision.

Hilton Portland & Executive Tower 🄻🄷
(503) 226-1611. **Call for rates.** 921 SW 6th Ave. I-405, exit 1B (6th Ave); at 6th Ave and Taylor St. Int corridors. **Pets:** Accepted.

Holiday Inn-Portland Airport 🄻🄷
(503) 256-5000. **$119-$229.** 8439 NE Columbia Blvd. I-205, exit 23B, 0.5 mi w. Int corridors. **Pets:** $25 one-time fee/room. Service with restrictions, supervision.

Hotel deLuxe 🅂🄷 ❀
(503) 219-2094. **$289.** 729 SW 15th Ave. I-5 to I-405, exit Salmon St northbound, just n on 14th Ave, w on Morrison St, then s; exit Couch-Burnside southbound; at SW 15th Ave and Yamhill. Int corridors. **Pets:** $45 one-time fee/pet.

Hotel Fifty 🅂🄷
(503) 221-0711. **$159-$229.** 50 SW Morrison St. At Morrison St and Naito Pkwy (formerly Front Ave). Int corridors. **Pets:** Accepted.

Hotel Lucia 🅂🄷 ❀
(503) 225-1717. **$295.** 400 SW Broadway. At SW Broadway and Stark St. Int corridors. **Pets:** $45 one-time fee/pet. Designated rooms, service with restrictions, crate.

Hotel Monaco Portland 🄻🄷 ❀
(503) 222-0001. **$159-$329.** 506 SW Washington St. At SW 5th Ave and SW Washington St. Int corridors. **Pets:** Other species. Service with restrictions, supervision.

Hotel Vintage Plaza 🅂🄷
(503) 228-1212. **Call for rates.** 422 SW Broadway. At Broadway and Washington St. Int corridors. **Pets:** Accepted.

La Quinta Inn & Suites Portland Airport 🅂🄷
(503) 382-3820. **$93.** 11207 NE Holman St. I-205, exit 24B northbound; exit 24 southbound, just e on Airport Way. Int corridors. **Pets:** Other species. Service with restrictions, supervision.

La Quinta Inn Portland Lloyd Center/Convention Center 🅂🄷
(503) 233-7933. **$98.** 431 NE Multnomah St. I-5, exit 302A, just e, then just s on Martin Luther King Blvd. Int corridors. **Pets:** Other species. Service with restrictions, supervision.

La Quinta Inn Portland Northwest 🅂🄷
(503) 497-9044. **$105.** 4319 NW Yeon. I-5 to I-405, exit 3 (US 30), 2.5 mi w on US 30. Int corridors. **Pets:** Other species. Service with restrictions, supervision.

The Mark Spencer Hotel 🅂🄷
(503) 224-3293. **$89-$199.** 409 SW 11th Ave. At SW Stark St and SW 11th Ave. Int corridors. **Pets:** Other species. $10 daily fee/pet. Service with restrictions, supervision.

Motel 6 North Portland #4198 🅂🄷
(503) 247-3700. **$53-$70.** 1125 N Schmeer Rd. I-5, exit 306B, 0.4 mi s on N Whitaker Rd, then just e. Int corridors. **Pets:** Other species. Service with restrictions, supervision.

Oxford Suites 🅂🄷 ❀
(503) 283-3030. **$119-$199.** 12226 N Jantzen Dr. I-5, exit 308, just e on Hayden Island Dr. Int corridors. **Pets:** $10 daily fee/pet, $25 one-time fee/pet. Service with restrictions, supervision.

The Paramount Hotel, a Coast Hotel 🅂🄷
(503) 223-9900. **$195.** 808 SW Taylor St. At SW 8th Ave and SW Taylor St. Int corridors. **Pets:** Medium, dogs only. Service with restrictions, crate.

Park Lane Suites 🄼
(503) 226-6288. **$129-$229.** 809 SW King Ave. I-405, exit Couch/Burnside St southbound, 0.5 mi w on Burnside St, then just s; exit Everett St northbound, 0.4 mi w on Glisan St, just s on NW 21st Ave, just w on Burnside St, then just s. Ext corridors. **Pets:** Accepted.

Quality Inn Portland Airport 🅂🄷 ❀
(503) 256-4111. **$65-$120.** 8247 NE Sandy Blvd. I-84, exit 5, 1.5 mi n on 82nd Ave; I-205, exit 23A southbound; exit 23B northbound (US 30 business route/Sandy Blvd W), 1 mi w. Ext/int corridors. **Pets:** Small. $10 daily fee/room. Designated rooms, service with restrictions, crate.

Ramada Portland 🅂🄷
(503) 255-6511. **$69-$199.** 6221 NE 82nd Ave. I-205, exit 23B (Killingsworth), just w on Columbia Blvd, then just n on 80th Ave. Int corridors. **Pets:** Accepted.

Red Lion Hotel on the River Jantzen Beach-Portland 🄻🄷
(503) 283-4466. **$159.** 909 N Hayden Island Dr. I-5, exit 308, just e. Int corridors. **Pets:** Accepted.

Red Lion Hotel Portland Airport 🅂🄷
(503) 255-6722. **$129.** 7101 NE 82nd Ave. I-205, exit 24A northbound; exit 24 southbound, 1 mi w on NE Airport Way, then just s. Ext/int corridors. **Pets:** Accepted.

Red Lion Hotel Portland-Convention Center 🅂🄷
(503) 235-2100. **$170.** 1021 NE Grand Ave. I-5, exit 302A, just e on Weidler, then just s on Martin Luther King Jr Blvd. Int corridors. **Pets:** Accepted.

Residence Inn by Marriott-Lloyd Center 🅂🄷
(503) 288-1400. **$220-$251.** 1710 NE Multnomah St. I-5, exit 302A, 0.8 mi e on Weidler St, then just s on 15th Ave; I-84, exit 1 (Lloyd Center) westbound, just n on 13th St, then just e. Ext corridors. **Pets:** Accepted.

Residence Inn by Marriott Portland North Harbour 🅂🄷
(503) 285-9888. **$175-$197.** 1250 N Anchor Way. I-5, exit 307, Follow signs to Marine Dr E, then just n. Int corridors. **Pets:** Accepted.

⬥ ▼▼▼▼ Residence Inn Portland Downtown at RiverPlace SH ❧
(503) 552-9500. **$208-$230.** 2115 SW River Pkwy. At SW Moody and SW River Pkwy; on the Willamette River Waterfront. Int corridors. **Pets:** Other species. $10 daily fee/pet. Service with restrictions.
[SAVE] [S🐾] [✕] [🛗] [▦] [🐾] [✕]

⬥ ▼▼▼ ▼▼▼ RiverPlace, a Larkspur Collection Hotel SH ❧
(503) 228-3233. **$219-$519.** 1510 SW Harbor Way. At Naito Pkwy (formerly Front Ave) and SW Harbor Way. Int corridors. **Pets:** Other species. $45 one-time fee/room.
[SAVE] [S🐾] [✕] [&M] [🛗] [▦] [🍴] [✕]

⬥ ▼▼▼▼ Sheraton Portland Airport Hotel LH ❧
(503) 281-2500. **Call for rates.** 8235 NE Airport Way. I-205, exit 24A northbound; exit 24 southbound, 1.5 mi w. Int corridors. **Pets:** $25 one-time fee/room. Service with restrictions, supervision.
[SAVE] [✕] [&M] [▦] [🍴] [🐾] [✕]

▼▼ ▼▼ Shilo Inn Rose Garden SH ❧
(503) 736-6300. **$145.** 1506 NE 2nd Ave. I-5, exit 302A, just e, on NE Weidler, then just s. Int corridors. **Pets:** $25 one-time fee/room. Designated rooms, service with restrictions, supervision.
[ASK] [S🐾] [✕] [🛗] [▦]

▼▼▼▼ Staybridge Suites Portland-Airport SH
(503) 262-8888. **$115-$145.** 11936 NE Glenn Widing Dr. I-205, exit 24B northbound; exit 24 southbound, just e, then just ne. Int corridors. **Pets:** Accepted.
[ASK] [S🐾] [✕] [&M] [🛗] [▦] [🐾] [✕]

⬥ ▼▼▼ ▼▼▼ The Westin Portland LH ❧
(503) 294-9000. **$339.** 750 SW Alder St. At Park Ave and SW Alder St. Int corridors. **Pets:** Large, dogs only. Designated rooms, service with restrictions, supervision.
[SAVE] [S🐾] [✕] [&M] [▦] [🍴]

TIGARD

▼▼▼▼ Embassy Suites Hotel-Portland Washington Square LH
(503) 644-4000. **Call for rates.** 9000 SW Washington Square Rd. SR 217, exit Progress/Scholls Ferry Rd, just e, then just s on Hall Blvd. Int corridors. **Pets:** Accepted.
[✕] [&M] [🛗] [▦] [🍴] [🐾] [✕]

▼▼ ▼▼ Homestead Studio Suites Hotel Portland-Tigard SH
(503) 670-0555. **$81-$90.** 13009 SW 68th Pkwy. I-5, exit 293 (Haines) southbound, 0.5 mi s on SW 68th Ave; exit 293 northbound, just w on Atlanta Ave, then 0.7 mi s; SR 217 S, exit 72nd Ave, just ne, just e on Hampton St, then just s. Ext corridors. **Pets:** Other species. $75 one-time fee/pet. Service with restrictions.
[ASK] [S🐾] [✕] [🛗] [▦]

▼▼ ▼▼ Shilo Inn-Tigard/Washington Square SH ❧
(503) 620-4320. **$95 (no credit cards).** 10830 SW Greenburg Rd. SR 217, exit Greenburg Rd, just w. Int corridors. **Pets:** $25 one-time fee/room. Designated rooms, service with restrictions, supervision.
[ASK] [S🐾] [✕] [🛗] [▦] [✕]

TROUTDALE

⬥ ▼▼ ▼▼ Comfort Inn & Suites, Columbia Gorge West SH
(503) 669-6500. **$69-$174.** 477 NW Phoenix Dr. I-84, exit 17. Int corridors. **Pets:** Accepted.
[SAVE] [S🐾] [✕] [🛗] [▦] [🐾]

▼▼ Holiday Inn Express-Portland East SH
(503) 492-2900. **$89-$159.** 1000 NW Graham Rd. I-84, exit 17 eastbound, e on Frontage Rd, then just n; westbound, just n. Int corridors. **Pets:** Accepted.
[ASK] [S🐾] [✕] [🛗] [▦] [✕]

▼▼ Motel 6-Portland Troutdale–407 M
(503) 665-2254. **$47-$55 (no credit cards).** 1610 NW Frontage Rd. I-84, exit 17 eastbound, just s; westbound, just w on Frontage Rd, then just s. Ext corridors. **Pets:** Other species. Service with restrictions, supervision.
[S🐾] [✕] [&M] [🛗] [🐾]

TUALATIN

⬥ ▼▼▼▼ Comfort Inn & Suites SH ❧
(503) 612-9952. **$99-$199.** 7640 SW Warm Springs St. I-5, exit 289, w on Nyberg Rd then s on Martinazzi; just behind Fred Meyer. Int corridors. **Pets:** Medium, dogs only. $15 daily fee/pet. Designated rooms, service with restrictions, supervision.
[SAVE] [S🐾] [✕] [&M] [🛗] [▦] [🐾]

WILSONVILLE

⬥ ▼▼▼▼ Best Western Willamette Inn SH
(503) 682-2288. **$88-$98.** 30800 SW Parkway Ave. I-5, exit 283, just e, then just s. Int corridors. **Pets:** Small. Designated rooms, service with restrictions, supervision.
[SAVE] [S🐾] [✕] [&M] [🛗] [▦] [🐾] [✕]

▼▼ Holiday Inn-Wilsonville SH
(503) 682-2211. **$140-$180.** 25425 SW 95th Ave. I-5, exit 286, just w. Int corridors. **Pets:** Accepted.
[ASK] [S🐾] [✕] [&M] [🛗] [▦] [🍴] [🐾]

⬥ ▼▼▼▼ La Quinta Inn Wilsonville SH
(503) 682-3184. **$73.** 8815 SW Sun Pl. I-5, exit 286, just e, then just n. Int corridors. **Pets:** Other species. Service with restrictions, supervision.
[SAVE] [S🐾] [✕] [&M] [🛗] [▦]

⬥ ▼▼▼▼ Wilsonville Inn & Suites SH
(503) 570-9700. **Call for rates.** 29769 SW Boones Ferry Rd. I-5, exit 283, just w. Int corridors. **Pets:** Accepted.
[SAVE] [✕] [&M] [🛗] [▦] [🐾] [✕]

END METROPOLITAN AREA

PORT ORFORD

⬥ ▼▼ Castaway by the Sea M
(541) 332-4502. **$65-$160.** 545 W 5th St. Jct US 101, just w on Oregon St. Ext corridors. **Pets:** Medium, dogs only. $10 daily fee/pet. Designated rooms, service with restrictions, supervision.
[SAVE] [✕] [🛗] [▦] [K]

PRINEVILLE

⬥ ▼▼▼▼ Best Western Prineville Inn SH ❧
(541) 447-8080. **Call for rates.** 1475 NE 3rd St. 1.4 mi e on US 26. Int corridors. **Pets:** Medium, dogs only. $10 one-time fee/room. Designated rooms, service with restrictions, supervision.
[SAVE] [✕] [&M] [🛗] [▦] [🐾]

Econo Lodge M
(541) 447-6231. **$60-$110.** 123 NE 3rd St. Center; downtown. Int corridors. **Pets:** Dogs only. $5 one-time fee/pet. Service with restrictions, supervision.
SAVE ⑤ ⊠ 🔒 ▣

Stafford Inn SH
(541) 447-7100. **Call for rates.** 1773 NE 3rd St. 1.6 mi w on US 26. Int corridors. **Pets:** Accepted.
⊠ 🔒 ▣ ⇒

PROSPECT

Prospect Historic Hotel-Motel & Dinner House M
(541) 560-3664. **Call for rates.** 391 Mill Creek Dr. Jct SR 62, 0.3 mi s on 1st St (0.7 mi e of MM 43), just w. Ext/int corridors. **Pets:** Accepted.
⊠ 🔒 ▣ 🍴 ⊠

REDMOND

Comfort Suites-Redmond Airport SH
(541) 504-8900. **$115-$160.** 2243 SW Yew Ave. US 97, just w. Int corridors. **Pets:** Accepted.
ASK ⑤ ⊠ 🔒 ▣ ⇒

Eagle Crest Resort SH
(541) 923-2453. **Call for rates.** 1522 Cline Falls Rd. 4.5 mi w on SR 126, 1 mi s. Int corridors. **Pets:** Accepted.
SAVE ⊠ ⑤M 🔒 ▣ 🍴 ⇒ ⊠

Motel 6 Redmond-4076 SH
(541) 923-2100. **Call for rates.** 2247 S Hwy 97. 1 mi s on US 97 from jct SR 126 W. Int corridors. **Pets:** Other species. Service with restrictions, supervision.
SAVE ⊠ ⑤M 🔒

Redmond Inn M
(541) 548-1091. **$50-$99.** 1545 S Hwy 97. 0.5 mi s on US 97 from jct SR 126 W. Ext corridors. **Pets:** Accepted.
SAVE ⑤ ⊠ 🔒 ▣ ⇒

Redmond Super 8 Motel SH
(541) 548-8881. **Call for rates.** 3629 21st Pl SW. US 97, exit Yew Ave. Int corridors. **Pets:** Accepted.
⊠ ⑤M ⇒

REEDSPORT

Anchor Bay Inn M
(541) 271-2149. **$50-$80.** 1821 Winchester Ave (Hwy 101). On US 101, 0.8 mi s of jct SR 38. Ext corridors. **Pets:** Dogs only. $7 daily fee/pet. Designated rooms, service with restrictions, supervision.
SAVE ⑤ ⊠ 🔒 ▣ ⇒ 🐾

Best Western Salbasgeon Inn M
(541) 271-4831. **Call for rates.** 1400 Hwy Ave 101 S. Just s on US 101 from jct SR 38. Ext corridors. **Pets:** Dogs only. $10 daily fee/pet. Designated rooms, service with restrictions, crate.
SAVE ⊠ 🔒 ▣ ⇒

Economy Inn M
(541) 271-3671. **$55-$120.** 1593 Hwy 101. On US 101; center. Ext corridors. **Pets:** Dogs only. $10 one-time fee/room. Designated rooms, service with restrictions, supervision.
SAVE ⑤ ⊠ 🔒 ⇒ 🐾

Salbasgeon Inn of the Umpqua M
(541) 271-2025. **Call for rates.** 45209 Hwy 38. US 101, 7.3 mi e. Ext corridors. **Pets:** Dogs only. $5 one-time fee/pet. Designated rooms, supervision.
SAVE ⊠ 🔒 ▣ ⊠

ROCKAWAY BEACH

Sea Treasures Inn M
(503) 355-8220. **Call for rates.** 301 N Miller St. Jct 3rd Ave N; center. Ext corridors. **Pets:** $10 one-time fee/pet. Service with restrictions, supervision.
SAVE ⊠ 🔒 ▣ 🐾

Silver Sands Motel M
(503) 355-2206. **Call for rates.** 215 S Pacific St. US 101, exit S 2nd Ave, just w. Ext corridors. **Pets:** Accepted.
⊠ 🔒 ▣ ⇒ ⊠ 🐾

Tradewinds Motel M
(503) 355-2112. **$58-$169, 7 day notice.** 523 N Pacific St. Just w of US 101, off N 6th Ave. Ext corridors. **Pets:** Medium, dogs only. $15 daily fee/pet. Designated rooms, service with restrictions, supervision.
SAVE ⊠ 🔒 ▣ 🐾

ROSEBURG

Best Western Garden Villa Inn M
(541) 672-1601. **$79-$139.** 760 NW Garden Valley Blvd. I-5, exit 125, just w. Ext corridors. **Pets:** Accepted.
SAVE ⑤ ⊠ 🔒 ▣ ⇒

The Douglas County Inn M
(541) 673-6625. **$63-$79.** 511 SE Stephens St. I-5, exit 124, 0.5 mi e, then just n; downtown. Ext corridors. **Pets:** Small. $100 deposit/room. Designated rooms, service with restrictions, supervision.
SAVE ⑤ ⊠ 🔒 ▣

Holiday Inn Express SH
(541) 673-7517. **$129-$199.** 375 W Harvard Ave. I-5, exit 124, just e. Ext/int corridors. **Pets:** Other species. $10 daily fee/room. Designated rooms, service with restrictions, supervision.
SAVE ⊠ ⑤M 🔒 ▣ ⇒

Motel 6 SH
(541) 464-8000. **Call for rates.** 3100 NW Aviation Dr. I-5, exit 127, just ne. Int corridors. **Pets:** Other species. Service with restrictions, supervision.
SAVE ⊠ ⑤M 🔒

Quality Inn M
(541) 673-5561. **$65-$120.** 427 NW Garden Valley Blvd. I-5, exit 125, just e. Ext corridors. **Pets:** Dogs only. $50 deposit/room, $10 daily fee/pet. Designated rooms, service with restrictions, supervision.
SAVE ⑤ ⊠ 🔒 ▣ ⇒

Roseburg Travelodge M
(541) 672-4836. **$65-$99.** 315 W Harvard Ave. I-5, exit 124, just e. Ext corridors. **Pets:** Accepted.
SAVE ⑤ ⊠ 🔒 ▣ ⇒

Shady Oaks Motel M
(541) 672-2608. **$45-$66.** 2954 Old Hwy 99 S. I-5, exit 120, 0.5 mi n. Ext corridors. **Pets:** Medium, dogs only. $8 daily fee/pet. Designated rooms, service with restrictions, supervision.
SAVE ⑤ ⊠ 🔒

Sleep Inn and Suites SH
(541) 464-8338. **$59-$99.** 2855 NW Edenbower Blvd. I-5, exit 127, just n. Int corridors. **Pets:** Accepted.
ASK ⑤ ⊠ 🔒 ▣ ⇒

Super 8 Motel SH
(541) 672-8880. **Call for rates.** 3200 NW Aviation Dr. I-5, exit 127, just ne. Int corridors. **Pets:** Accepted.
⊠ ⑤M 🔒 ⇒

Windmill Inn of Roseburg SH ❖
(541) 673-0901. **$79-$115.** 1450 NW Mulholland Dr. I-5, exit 125, just ne. Int corridors. **Pets:** Other species. Designated rooms, service with restrictions, supervision.

SAVE S⬤ ✕ ⊟ 🖵 ⚊ 🔀

ST. HELENS

Best Western Oak Meadows Inn SH
(503) 397-3000. **Call for rates.** 585 S Columbia River Hwy. South end of town on US 30. Int corridors. **Pets:** $10 one-time fee/pet. Service with restrictions, supervision.

SAVE ✕ ⊟ 🖵 ⚊

SALEM

Best Western Black Bear Inn M ❖
(503) 581-1559. **$69-$159.** 1600 Motor Ct NE. I-5, exit 256, just e. Ext corridors. **Pets:** Medium. $10 daily fee/room. Designated rooms, service with restrictions, supervision.

SAVE S⬤ ✕ ⬥M ⊟ 🖵 ⚊ 🔀

Best Western Pacific Hwy Inn M
(503) 390-3200. **Call for rates.** 4646 Portland Rd NE. I-5, exit 258, just e. Ext corridors. **Pets:** Dogs only. $20 one-time fee/room. Designated rooms, no service, supervision.

SAVE ✕ ⬥M ⊟ 🖵 ⚊ 🔀

Crossland Studios Salem North M
(503) 363-7557. **$59-$65.** 3535 Fisher Rd NE. I-5, exit 258, just n, 0.4 mi s on Ward Dr, then 0.8 mi s. Ext corridors. **Pets:** Other species. $75 one-time fee/pet. Service with restrictions.

ASK S⬤ ✕ ⊟ 🖵 ⚊

Howard Johnson Inn SH
(503) 375-7710. **Call for rates.** 2250 Mission St SE. I-5, exit 253, 1.4 mi w. Int corridors. **Pets:** Small, other species. $10 daily fee/pet. Designated rooms, service with restrictions, crate.

SAVE ✕ ⊟ 🖵 ⚊

Phoenix Inn Suites-North Salem SH
(503) 581-7004. **$79-$119.** 1590 Weston Ct NE. I-5, exit 256, just w, then just s. Int corridors. **Pets:** Small. $15 daily fee/pet. Designated rooms, service with restrictions, supervision.

SAVE S⬤ ✕ ⬥M ⊟ 🖵 ⚊ 🔀

Phoenix Inn Suites-South Salem SH
(503) 588-9220. **$79-$139.** 4370 Commercial SE. I-5, exit 252, 1.5 mi w on Kuebler Rd, then 0.7 mi n. Int corridors. **Pets:** Medium. $15 daily fee/pet. Designated rooms, service with restrictions, supervision.

SAVE S⬤ ✕ ⬥M ⊟ 🖵 ⚊ 🔀

Red Lion Hotel Salem SH
(503) 370-7888. **$124-$169.** 3301 Market St NE. I-5, exit 256, just w. Int corridors. **Pets:** Accepted.

SAVE S⬤ ✕ ⊟ 🖵 ⛾ ⚊ 🔀

Residence Inn by Marriott SH
(503) 585-6500. **$176-$198.** 640 Hawthorne Ave SE. I-5, exit 253, just w, then n. Int corridors. **Pets:** Accepted.

ASK S⬤ ✕ ⬥M ⊟ 🖵 ⚊ 🔀

Salem Super 8 SH
(503) 370-8888. **Call for rates.** 1288 Hawthorne Ave NE. I-5, exit 256, just w, then just s. Int corridors. **Pets:** Accepted.

✕ ⬥M ⊟ ⚊

Shilo Inn Suites-Salem SH ❖
(503) 581-4001. **$140.** 3304 Market St NE. I-5, exit 256, just w. Int corridors. **Pets:** $25 one-time fee/room. Designated rooms, service with restrictions, supervision.

SAVE S⬤ ✕ ⊟ 🖵 ⚊ 🔀

Travelodge Salem Capital M
(503) 581-2466. **Call for rates.** 1555 State St. I-5, exit 253, just w on SR 22/99 (Mission St), 0.6 mi n on Airport Rd SE, then 1 mi w. Ext corridors. **Pets:** Accepted.

SAVE ✕ ⊟ 🖵 ⚊

SANDY

Best Western Sandy Inn SH
(503) 668-7100. **Call for rates.** 37465 Hwy 26. West side of town. Int corridors. **Pets:** Medium, dogs only. $10 daily fee/pet. Service with restrictions, supervision.

✕ ⬥M ⊟ 🖵 ⚊

SEASIDE

Best Western Ocean View Resort SH
(503) 738-3334. **$59-$459, 30 day notice.** 414 N Prom. US 101, exit 1st Ave, just w, just n on Necanicum Dr, then just w on 4th Ave. Ext/int corridors. **Pets:** Accepted.

SAVE S⬤ ✕ ⊟ 🖵 ⛾ ⚊

Comfort Inn Boardwalk SH
(503) 738-3011. **$89-$399.** 545 Broadway. US 101, exit Ave A, just w; downtown. Int corridors. **Pets:** Accepted.

SAVE S⬤ ✕ ⬥M ⊟ 🖵 ⚊

Ebb-Tide Resort SH
(503) 738-8371. **Call for rates.** 300 N Prom. US 101, exit 1st Ave, 0.4 mi w, just n on Columbia St, then just w on 2nd Ave. Ext/int corridors. **Pets:** Other species. $20 daily fee/pet. Service with restrictions, supervision.

SAVE ✕ 🖵 ⚊ 🐾

Inn at Seaside M ❖
(503) 738-9581. **Call for rates.** 441 2nd Ave. US 101, exit 1st Ave, 0.4 mi w. Ext/int corridors. **Pets:** Other species. $10 daily fee/pet. Service with restrictions, crate.

SAVE ✕ ⊟ 🖵 ⚊

Rivertide Suites SH ❖
(503) 717-1100. **$95-$525, 3 day notice.** 102 N Holladay. US 101, exit Broadway, just w, then just n. Int corridors. **Pets:** Medium. $25 daily fee/pet. Service with restrictions, supervision.

SAVE S⬤ ✕ ⬥M ⊟ 🖵 ⚊

Seashore Inn...on the Beach M
(503) 738-6368. **$75-$249.** 60 N Prom. US 101, exit 1st Ave, 0.4 mi w. Ext/int corridors. **Pets:** Medium. $20 daily fee/room. Designated rooms, service with restrictions, supervision.

SAVE S⬤ ✕ ⊟ 🖵 ⚊ 🐾

Sea Side Oceanfront Inn Bed & Breakfast Hotel BB
(503) 738-6403. **Call for rates.** 581 S Prom. US 101, exit Ave G, 0.6 mi w, then just n. Int corridors. **Pets:** Accepted.

✕ ⊟ 🖵 ⛾

Shilo Inn Suites Hotel Seaside Oceanfront SH ❖
(503) 738-9571. **$140-$400.** 30 N Prom. US 101, exit Broadway, 0.4 mi w. Ext corridors. **Pets:** $25 one-time fee/room. Designated rooms, service with restrictions, supervision.

ASK S⬤ ✕ ⊟ 🖵 ⛾ ⚊ 🔀 🐾

SHADY COVE

The Edgewater Inn on the Rogue River SH ❖
(541) 878-3171. **$79-$185.** 7800 Rogue River Dr. Off SR 62. Ext corridors. **Pets:** $7 daily fee/pet. Designated rooms, service with restrictions, supervision.

SAVE S⬤ ✕ ⊟ 🖵 ⚊ 🔀

SISTERS

◬◬◭◭◭◭ Best Western Ponderosa Lodge M ☙
(541) 549-1234. **$99-$250.** 500 Hwy 20 W. West end of town, just w on US 20 from jct SR 242. Ext corridors. **Pets:** $10 daily fee/pet. Designated rooms, service with restrictions, supervision.

SPRINGFIELD

◬◬◭◭◭◭ Best Western Grand Manor Inn M
(541) 726-4769. **$93-$200.** 971 Kruse Way. I-5, exit 195A, just e. Int corridors. **Pets:** Dogs only. $100 deposit/room, $10 daily fee/pet. Designated rooms, service with restrictions, supervision.

◭◭◭◭ Comfort Suites Eugene/Springfield SH
(541) 746-5359. **$109-$179.** 969 Kruse Way. I-5, exit 195A, just e. Int corridors. **Pets:** Accepted.

◬◬◭◭◭◭ Holiday Inn Express Hotel & Suites SH
(541) 746-8471. **$109-$209.** 3480 Hutton St. I-5, exit 195A, just e. Int corridors. **Pets:** Accepted.

◭◭ Motel 6 #418 M
(541) 741-1105. **$49-$59 (no credit cards).** 3752 International Ct. I-5, exit 195A, just e, then just n on Gateway St. Ext corridors. **Pets:** Other species. Service with restrictions, supervision.

◬◬◭◭◭◭ Super 8 Motel SH
(541) 746-1314. **Call for rates.** 3315 Gateway St. I-5, exit 195A, just e, then just s. Int corridors. **Pets:** Accepted.

◬◬◭◭◭◭ Village Inn M
(541) 747-4546. **$74.** 1875 Mohawk Blvd. I-5, exit 194A, 2.5 mi e, then just n. Ext corridors. **Pets:** Accepted.

SUMMER LAKE

◭◭◭ Summer Lake Inn CI
(541) 943-3983. **Call for rates.** 47531 Hwy 31. 10 mi s; between MM 81 and 82. Ext corridors. **Pets:** Accepted.

SUNRIVER

◬◬◭◭◭◭ Sunray Vacation Rentals VH
(541) 593-3225. **$120-$800, 60 day notice.** 56890 Venture Ln. 1 mi w on S Century Dr from jct US 97, then just e. Ext corridors. **Pets:** Accepted.

◬◬◭◭◭◭◭◭ Sunriver Resort LH
(541) 593-1000. **$149-$249, 21 day notice.** 17600 Center Dr. US 97, exit Sunriver/S Century Blvd, 2 mi w. Ext corridors. **Pets:** $75 one-time fee/room. Designated rooms, supervision.

SUTHERLIN

◭◭◭ Sutherlin Inn SH
(541) 459-6800. **Call for rates.** 1400 Hospitality Pl. I-5, exit 136, just se. Int corridors. **Pets:** Accepted.

◬◬◭◭◭◭ Umpqua Regency Inn M
(541) 459-1424. **$75-$125.** 150 Myrtle St. I-5, exit 136, just e. Ext corridors. **Pets:** Medium. $10 daily fee/pet. Service with restrictions, supervision.

SWEET HOME

◬◬◭◭◭◭ Sweet Home Inn M
(541) 367-5137. **$69-$89.** 805 Long St. Just e of jct US 20 and SR 228; just s on 10th Ave, just w. Ext corridors. **Pets:** Medium, dogs only. $10 one-time fee/pet. Designated rooms, service with restrictions, supervision.

THE DALLES

◬◬◭◭◭◭ Best Western River City Inn SH
(541) 296-9107. **Call for rates.** 112 W 2nd St. I-84, exit 84 eastbound, just se; exit 85 westbound, 0.8 mi nw; at Liberty and W 2nd St; downtown. Ext/int corridors. **Pets:** Small, other species. $10 daily fee/pet. Designated rooms, supervision.

◬◬◭◭◭◭ Comfort Inn Columbia Gorge SH
(541) 298-2800. **$85-$174.** 351 Lone Pine Dr. I-84, exit 87, just n. Int corridors. **Pets:** Accepted.

◬◬◭◭◭◭ Cousins Country Inn M ☙
(541) 298-5161. **$79-$109.** 2114 W 6th St. I-84, exit 83 eastbound, just n; exit 84 westbound, just nw on W 2nd St, just sw on Webber St, then just n. Ext corridors. **Pets:** Other species. $10 daily fee/pet. Designated rooms, service with restrictions, supervision.

◬◬◭ Motel 6 #4268 SH
(541) 296-1191. **$59-$135.** 2500 W 6th St. I-84, exit 83 eastbound, just n; exit 84 westbound, just nw on w 2nd St, just sw on Webber St, then just n. Int corridors. **Pets:** Small. $10 daily fee/pet. Service with restrictions, supervision.

◭◭ Super 8 Motel SH
(541) 296-6888. **Call for rates.** 609 Cherry Heights Rd. I-84, exit 84, just se. Int corridors. **Pets:** Medium. $10 daily fee/pet. No service, supervision.

TILLAMOOK

◭ Mar-Clair Inn M
(503) 842-7571. **$86-$106.** 11 Main Ave. US 101, just n of jct SR 6. Ext/int corridors. **Pets:** Accepted.

◬◬◭◭◭◭ Shilo Inn Suites-Tillamook SH ☙
(503) 842-7971. **$150 (no credit cards).** 2515 Main Ave. 1 mi n on US 101. Int corridors. **Pets:** $25 one-time fee/room. Designated rooms, service with restrictions, supervision.

UMATILLA

◬◬◭◭◭◭ Desert River Inn SH
(541) 922-1000. **$91.** 705 Willamette Ave. I-82, exit 1 (US 730), 1.6 mi e, then 0.3 mi n. Int corridors. **Pets:** Accepted.

WARRENTON

◭◭◭ Shilo Inn Suites-Warrenton/Astoria SH ☙
(503) 861-2181. **$200 (no credit cards).** 1609 E Harbor Dr. On US 26/101; near west end of Young's Bay Bridge. Int corridors. **Pets:** $25 one-time fee/room. Designated rooms, service with restrictions, supervision.

WELCHES

◬◬◭◭◭◭ The Resort at the Mountain LH
(503) 622-3101. **$99-$475, 3 day notice.** 68010 E Fairway Ave. 0.8 mi s of US 26 on E Welches Rd. Ext corridors. **Pets:** Accepted.

WHEELER

◆ Wheeler on the Bay Lodge and Marina Ⓜ
(503) 368-5858. **$60-$155, 3 day notice.** 580 Marine Dr. On US 101; center. Ext corridors. **Pets:** Accepted.

WINSTON

◆◆ ◆ Sweet Breeze Inn II Ⓜ 🐾
(541) 679-2420. **$49-$89, 3 day notice.** 251 NE Main St. I-5, exit 119, 3 mi w. Ext corridors. **Pets:** Small. $15 daily fee/pet. Designated rooms, service with restrictions, supervision.

⟨SAVE⟩ ⟨S⟩ ⟨✕⟩ ⟨▪⟩

WOODBURN

◆◆ ◆◆ Best Western Woodburn Inn 🄪 🐾
(503) 982-6515. **Call for rates.** 2887 Newburg Hwy. I-5, exit 271, just e. Int corridors. **Pets:** Other species. $10 daily fee/room. Designated rooms, service with restrictions, supervision.

⟨SAVE⟩ ⟨✕⟩ ⟨M⟩ ⟨▪⟩ ⟨▭⟩ ⟨≈⟩

◆◆ ◆◆◆ La Quinta Inn & Suites Woodburn 🄪
(503) 982-1727. **$92.** 120 Arney Rd NE. I-5, exit 271, just w. Int corridors. **Pets:** Other species. Service with restrictions, supervision.

⟨SAVE⟩ ⟨S⟩ ⟨✕⟩ ⟨▪⟩ ⟨▭⟩ ⟨≈⟩

YACHATS

◆◆◆ ◆◆◆ The Adobe Resort 🄪 🐾
(541) 547-3141. **$105-$405.** 1555 Hwy 101. 0.5 mi n. Int corridors. **Pets:** Other species. $10 daily fee/pet. Designated rooms, service with restrictions, supervision.

⟨SAVE⟩ ⟨S⟩ ⟨✕⟩ ⟨▪⟩ ⟨▭⟩ ⟨🍴⟩ ⟨≈⟩ ⟨⊠⟩ ⟨M⟩

◆◆ The Dublin House Ⓜ
(541) 547-3703. **Call for rates.** 251 W 7th St. US 101 at 7th St; downtown. Ext corridors. **Pets:** Accepted.

⟨✕⟩ ⟨▪⟩ ⟨▭⟩ ⟨≈⟩ ⟨M⟩

◆◆◆ ◆◆ Fireside Motel Ⓜ 🐾
(541) 547-3636. **$70-$140.** 1881 Hwy 101 N. 0.6 mi n; just w of US 101. Ext corridors. **Pets:** $9 daily fee/pet. Service with restrictions, supervision.

⟨SAVE⟩ ⟨S⟩ ⟨✕⟩ ⟨▪⟩ ⟨▭⟩ ⟨⊠⟩ ⟨M⟩

◆◆ Shamrock Lodgettes 🄲
(541) 547-3312. **Call for rates.** 105 Hwy 101 S. On US 101, just s. Ext corridors. **Pets:** Accepted.

⟨✕⟩ ⟨▪⟩ ⟨▭⟩ ⟨⊠⟩ ⟨M⟩

PENNSYLVANIA

CITY INDEX

ABBOTTSTOWN

AAA ▼▼▼ **The Altland House** 🄲🄸
(717) 259-9535. **Call for rates.** Center Square Rt 30. Jct SR 194. Int corridors. **Pets:** Accepted.
🆂🅰🆅🅴 ⊠ 🛉 💻 🍴

ALLENTOWN

AAA ▼▼▼ **Allentown Howard Johnson Inn & Suites** 🆂🅷
(610) 439-4000. **$44-$299.** 3220 Hamilton Blvd. I-78, exit 54 (Hamilton Blvd), 0.8 mi n. Int corridors. **Pets:** Accepted.
🆂🅰🆅🅴 🆂🏋 ⊠ 🅶🅼 🛉 💻 🔁

▼▼▼ **Crowne Plaza Hotel** 🄻🄷 🐾
(610) 433-2221. **$119-$179.** 904 Hamilton Blvd. 9th St and Hamilton Blvd; downtown. Int corridors. **Pets:** Other species. $30 one-time fee/pet. Designated rooms, service with restrictions, crate.
⊠ 🛉 💻 🍴 🔁

▼▼▼ **Four Points by Sheraton Hotel & Suites Allentown Jetport** 🆂🅷 ❄
(610) 266-1000. **$120-$140.** 3400 Airport Rd. On SR 987 N (Airport Rd), 0.5 mi n of jct US 22. Int corridors. **Pets:** Medium. $25 deposit/room, $25 one-time fee/room. Service with restrictions, supervision.
🄰🅂🄺 ⊠ 🅶🅼 🛉 💻 🍴 🔁

AAA ▼▼ **Microtel Inn** 🆂🅷
(610) 266-9070. **$50-$100.** 1880 Steelstone Rd. US 22, exit Airport Rd S. Int corridors. **Pets:** Accepted.
🆂🅰🆅🅴 ⊠ 🅶🅼 🛉 💻

AAA ▼▼▼◆ **Quality Inn-Allentown** 🆂🅷
(610) 435-7880. **$49-$299.** 1715 Plaza Ln. US 22, exit 15th St, just n. Int corridors. **Pets:** Accepted.
🆂🅰🆅🅴 🆂🏋 ⊠ 🛉 💻

▼▼ **Red Roof Inn #7110** 🄼
(610) 264-5404. **Call for rates.** 1846 Catasauqua Rd. US 22, exit Airport Rd S, just s. Ext corridors. **Pets:** Accepted.
⊠ 🅶🅼 🛉

▼▼▼▼ **Staybridge Suites Allentown-Airport** 🆂🅷
(610) 443-5000. **$149-$259.** 1787-A Airport Rd. US 22, exit Airport Rd S, 0.3 mi s. Int corridors. **Pets:** Accepted.
🄰🅂🄺 🆂🏋 ⊠ 🅶🅼 🛉 💻 🔁

AAA ▼▼▼ **Super 8 Motel** 🄼
(610) 434-9550. **$45-$145.** 1033 Airport Rd. US 22, exit Airport Rd S, 1.1 mi s. Int corridors. **Pets:** Accepted.
🆂🅰🆅🅴 ⊠ 🅶🅼 🛉 💻

ALTOONA

▼▼ **Motel 6 #1415** 🄼
(814) 946-7601. **$52-$62.** 1500 Sterling St. I-99/US 220, exit 31 (Plank Rd), just w. Ext corridors. **Pets:** Other species. Service with restrictions, supervision.
🄰🅂🄺 ⊠ 🅶🅼 🔁

▼▼ **Quality Inn of Altoona** 🆂🅷
(814) 944-4581. **$69-$99.** 2915 Pleasant Valley Blvd. I-99/US 220, exit 32 (Frankstown Rd), 0.4 mi w, then 0.5 mi n. Ext corridors. **Pets:** Small. $25 one-time fee/pet. Designated rooms, service with restrictions.
🄰🅂🄺 🆂🏋 ⊠ 🛉 💻 🍴 🔁

▼▼ **Super 8 Motel Altoona** 🄼
(814) 942-5350. **$56-$78.** 3535 Fairway Dr. I-99/US 220, exit 32 (Frankstown Rd), just w. Int corridors. **Pets:** Small. $10 daily fee/pet. Service with restrictions, supervision.
🄰🅂🄺 🆂🏋 ⊠ 🅶🅼 🛉

BARKEYVILLE

AAA ▼▼▼ **Comfort Inn-Barkeyville** 🄼
(814) 786-7901. **$79-$140, 3 day notice.** 137 Gibb Rd. I-80, exit 29, just n on SR 8. Ext corridors. **Pets:** Medium. $15 one-time fee/room. No service, supervision.
🆂🅰🆅🅴 🆂🏋 ⊠ 🛉 💻

▼▼ Super 8 Motel-Barkeyville
(814) 786-8375. **Call for rates.** 1010 Dholu Rd. I-80, exit 29, just n on SR 8. Int corridors. **Pets:** Dogs only. $10 daily fee/pet. Designated rooms, service with restrictions, supervision.

⊗ 🛢 💻

BEDFORD

▼◆▼ Bedford Springs Resort **LH**
(814) 623-8100. **$209-$379, 3 day notice.** 2138 Business Rt 220. I-76, exit 146, 3.9 mi s. Int corridors. **Pets:** Accepted.

A$K S🐾 ⊗ 🛢 💻 ¶¶ ➜ ⊠

◍◍ ▼◆▼ Best Western Bedford Inn **SH** 🐾
(814) 623-9006. **$75-$98.** 4517 Business Rt 220. I-70/76 (Pennsylvania Tpke), exit 146, 0.3 mi n. Ext/int corridors. **Pets:** Medium, other species. $50 deposit/room, $10 daily fee/room. Service with restrictions, supervision.

SAVE S🐾 ⊗ 🛢 💻 ¶¶ ➜ ⊠

◍◍▽ ▼◆▼ Budget Host Inn **M**
(814) 623-8107. **$35-$90.** 4378 Business Rt 220. I-70/76 (Pennsylvania Tpke), exit 146, just n. Ext corridors. **Pets:** $5 one-time fee/pet. Service with restrictions, supervision.

SAVE S🐾 ⊗ 🛢 ➜

◍◍▽ ▼◆▼ Quality Inn Bedford **SH**
(814) 623-5188. **$68-$161.** 4407 Business Rt 220 N. I-70/76 (Pennsylvania Tpke), exit 146, just n. Ext/int corridors. **Pets:** Medium, other species. $50 deposit/room, $15 daily fee/pet. Designated rooms, service with restrictions, supervision.

SAVE S🐾 ⊗ 🛢 💻 ¶¶ ➜

▼ Super 8 Motel **M**
(814) 623-5880. **Call for rates.** 4498 Business Rt 220. I-70/76 (Pennslyvania Tpke), exit 146, 0.3 mi n. Int corridors. **Pets:** Accepted.

⊗ 🛢

◍◍▽ ▼◆▼ Travelodge **M**
(814) 623-7800. **Call for rates.** 4271 Business Rt 220. I-70/76 (Pennsylvania Tpke), exit 146, just s. Ext/int corridors. **Pets:** Accepted.

SAVE ⊗ 🛢 💻

BETHEL

◍◍▽ ▼◆▼▼ Comfort Inn-Bethel/Midway **SH**
(717) 933-8888. **$79-$139.** 41 Diner Dr. I-78, exit 16, just w. Int corridors. **Pets:** Other species. $10 daily fee/pet. Designated rooms, service with restrictions, crate.

SAVE S🐾 ⊗ 🛢M 🛢 💻 ➜

BETHLEHEM

◍◍▽ ▼◆▼▼ Best Western Lehigh Valley Hotel & Conference Center **SH** 🐾
(610) 866-5800. **$89-$109.** 300 Gateway Dr. US 22, exit Center St and SR 512. Ext/int corridors. **Pets:** Medium. $10 one-time fee/pet. Designated rooms, service with restrictions, crate.

SAVE S🐾 ⊗ 🛢M 🛢 💻 ¶¶ ➜

◍◍▽ ▼◆▼ Comfort Inn **SH** 🐾
(610) 865-6300. **$84-$159.** 3191 Highfield Dr. US 22, exit SR 191, just s. Ext/int corridors. **Pets:** Other species. $10 daily fee/pet. Service with restrictions, supervision.

SAVE S🐾 ⊗ 🛢 💻

◍◍▽ ▼◆▼▼ Comfort Suites **SH**
(610) 882-9700. **$99-$179.** 120 W 3rd St. SR 378, exit 3rd St, at W 3rd and Brodhead sts; center. Int corridors. **Pets:** Other species. $10 daily fee/room. Designated rooms, service with restrictions, supervision.

SAVE S🐾 ⊗ 🛢 💻 ¶¶

▼◆▼ Extended StayAmerica-Allentown/Bethlehem **SH**
(610) 866-8480. **$95-$115.** 3050 Schoenersville Rd. US 22, exit SR 378/Schoenersville Rd, follow signs for Schoenersville Rd, just n. Int corridors. **Pets:** Other species. $75 one-time fee/pet. Service with restrictions.

A$K S🐾 ⊗ 🛢 💻

◍◍▽ ▼◆▼▼ Historic Hotel Bethlehem **LH**
(610) 625-5000. **$119-$209.** 437 Main St. SR 378 S, exit 3 (City Center), just n on 3rd Ave, 0.3 mi e on Union, then 0.3 mi s. Int corridors. **Pets:** Accepted.

SAVE S🐾 ⊗ 🛢M 🛢 💻 ¶¶

◍◍▽ ▼◆▼▼ Homewood Suites–Allentown/Bethlehem Airport **SH**
(610) 264-7500. **Call for rates.** 2031 Avenue C. US 22, exit SR 378/Schoenersville Rd, follow signs for Schoenersville Rd, 0.7 mi n. Int corridors. **Pets:** Accepted.

SAVE ⊗ 🛢M 🛢 💻 ➜ ⊠

▼◆▼▼ Residence Inn by Marriott **SH**
(610) 317-2662. **$192-$213.** 2180 Motel Dr. US 22, exit Airport Rd S, 0.8 mi se on Catasauqua Rd. Int corridors. **Pets:** Accepted.

A$K S🐾 ⊗ 🛢 💻 ➜ ⊠

BLOOMSBURG

◍◍▽ ▼◆▼ Econo Lodge at Bloomsburg **SH** 🐾
(570) 387-0490. **$60-$95.** 189 Columbia Mall Dr. I-80, exit 232, just n on SR 42. Int corridors. **Pets:** Large, other species. $20 one-time fee/room. Service with restrictions, supervision.

SAVE S🐾 ⊗ 🛢 💻

▼◆▼▼ The Inn at Turkey Hill **CI** 🐾
(570) 387-1500. **$121-$215.** 991 Central Rd. I-80, exit 236 eastbound; exit 236A westbound, just s. Ext/int corridors. **Pets:** Other species. $20 daily fee/room. Designated rooms, service with restrictions, supervision.

A$K ⊗ 🛢 💻 ¶¶

BLUE MOUNTAIN

◍◍▽ ▼◆▼ Kenmar Motel **M**
(717) 423-5915. **$70-$85.** 17788 Cumberland Hwy. I-76, exit 201, just e on SR 997 N. Ext corridors. **Pets:** Accepted.

SAVE S🐾 ⊗ 🛢

BOYERTOWN

▼◆▼ Mel-Dor Motel **M**
(610) 367-2626. **$36-$70.** 5 Spring Garden Dr. SR 100, exit New Berlinville; 1 mi n of town. Ext corridors. **Pets:** Accepted.

A$K S🐾 ⊗ 💻

BRADFORD

◍◍▽ ▼◆▼▼ Best Western Bradford Inn **SH**
(814) 362-4501. **$100-$175.** 100 Davis St S. US 219, exit Forman St southbound, just w to Davis St, then 0.3 mi s; exit Elm St northbound, just w. Ext/int corridors. **Pets:** $10 daily fee/pet. Designated rooms, service with restrictions, crate.

SAVE ⊗ 🛢 💻 ¶¶ ➜

▼◆▼ Comfort Inn-Bradford **SH**
(814) 368-6772. **$100-$110.** 76 Elm St. US 219, exit Forman St southbound, just w to Davis St, then 0.3 mi s; exit Elm St northbound, just w. Int corridors. **Pets:** $10 daily fee/pet. Service with restrictions, supervision.

A$K S🐾 ⊗ 🛢 💻 ➜

▼◆▼▼ Glendorn **CI** 🐾
(814) 362-6511. **$299-$725, 30 day notice.** 1000 Glendorn Dr. SR 219, exit Forman St, just s on Mechanic St, then 4.3 mi w on W Corydon. Ext/int corridors. **Pets:** Dogs only. $75 daily fee/pet. Designated rooms, service with restrictions, supervision.

A$K ⊗ 🛢 💻 ¶¶ ➜ ⊠

BREEZEWOOD

Best Western Plaza Inn M
(814) 735-4352. **$60-$90.** 16407 Lincoln Hwy. I-76 (Pennsylvania Tpke), exit 161, just w on US 30; I-70, exit 147. Ext corridors. **Pets:** Accepted.
SAVE SO X 📶 💻 ⤵

Breezewood Ramada SH ❀
(814) 735-4005. **$54-$72.** 16620 Lincoln Hwy. I-76 (Pennsylvania Tpke), exit 161, just e on US 30; I-70, exit 147, just e on US 30. Int corridors. **Pets:** Medium. $10 daily fee/pet. Service with restrictions, supervision.
SAVE SO X 📶 💻 🍴 ⤵ ⊠

Howard Johnson of Breezewood M
(814) 735-2200. **$59-$89.** 16550 Lincoln Hwy. I-76 (Pennsylvania Tpke), exit 161, just w on US 30; I-70, exit 147, just e on US 30. Int corridors. **Pets:** Medium, other species. $10 one-time fee/pet. Designated rooms, service with restrictions, supervision.
SAVE SO X 📶 💻 ⤵

Wiltshire Motel M
(814) 735-4361. **Call for rates.** 140 S Breezewood Rd. I-76 (Pennsylvania Tpke), exit 161, just w on US 30; I-70, exit 147. Ext corridors. **Pets:** Accepted.
SAVE X 💻

BROOKVILLE

Budget Host Gold Eagle Inn M
(814) 849-7344. **$48-$85.** 250 W Main St. I-80, exit 78, 0.5 mi s on SR 36. Ext corridors. **Pets:** Service with restrictions, crate.
SAVE X 📶 💻 🍴

Holiday Inn Express M
(814) 849-8381. **$70-$110.** 235 Allegheny Blvd. I-80, exit 78, just s on SR 36. Int corridors. **Pets:** Other species. $15 one-time fee/pet. Service with restrictions, supervision.
SAVE SO X 📶 💻

Super 8 Motel M
(814) 849-8840. **$60-$65.** 251 Allegheny Blvd. I-80, exit 78, just n on SR 36. Int corridors. **Pets:** $10 daily fee/pet. Supervision.
SAVE SO X 📶 💻

CAMBRIDGE SPRINGS

The Riverside Inn CI
(814) 398-4645. **$65-$170, 10 day notice.** 1 Fountain Ave. Just ne of center. Int corridors. **Pets:** Other species. $25 one-time fee/room. Service with restrictions, supervision.
X 📶 🍴 ⤵ ⊠ 🄩

CAMP HILL

Radisson Penn Harris Hotel & Convention Center LH
(717) 763-7117. **$109-$174.** 1150 Camp Hill Bypass. Jct US 11, 15 and Erford Rd. Ext/int corridors. **Pets:** Accepted.
ASK SO X SM 📶 💻 🍴 ⤵

CARLISLE

Comfort Suites Hotel SH
(717) 960-1000. **$114-$194.** 10 S Hanover St. I-81, exit 47, 0.8 mi n on SR 34, just s of the square; downtown. Int corridors. **Pets:** Medium. $10 daily fee/pet. Service with restrictions, crate.
SAVE SO X SM 📶 💻 🍴

Days Inn & Suites-Carlisle SH
(717) 258-4147. **$77-$160, 14 day notice.** 101 Alexander Spring Rd. I-81, exit 45, just sw. Int corridors. **Pets:** Large. $10 daily fee/room. Designated rooms, service with restrictions, supervision.
SAVE SO X SM 📶 💻 ⤵

Hampton Inn Carlisle SH
(717) 240-0200. **$119-$199.** 1164 Harrisburg Pike. I-76 (Pennsylvania Tpke), exit 226, just n; I-81, exit 52 (US 11) southbound; exit 52B northbound, 0.8 mi s. Int corridors. **Pets:** Other species. $25 one-time fee/room. Designated rooms, service with restrictions, supervision.
SAVE SO X SM 📶 💻 ⤵

Holiday Inn Carlisle SH ❀
(717) 245-2400. **$89-$180, 7 day notice.** 1450 Harrisburg Pike. I-81, exit 52 (US 11) southbound; exit 52A northbound, just se; I-76 (Pennsylvania Tpke), exit 226, 0.8 mi n. Int corridors. **Pets:** Small. $10 daily fee/pet. Designated rooms, service with restrictions, supervision.
SAVE SO X 📶 💻 🍴 ⤵ ⊠

Hotel Carlisle & Embers Convention Center LH
(717) 243-1717. **$105-$205.** 1700 Harrisburg Pike. I-81, exit 52 (US 11) southbound; exit 52A northbound, 0.4 mi n; I-76 (Pennsylvania Tpke), exit 226, 1.2 mi n. Int corridors. **Pets:** Accepted.
SAVE SO X 📶 💻 🍴 ⤵ ⊠

Howard Johnson Inn SH
(717) 243-5411. **$43-$149.** 1245 Harrisburg Pike. I-81, exit 52 (US 11) southbound; exit 52B northbound, 0.5 mi s; I-76 (Pennsylvania Tpke), exit 226, 0.8 mi n on US 11. Ext/int corridors. **Pets:** Accepted.
SAVE SO X SM 📶 💻 🍴 ⤵

Pheasant Field Bed & Breakfast BB
(717) 258-0717. **$105-$205, 3 day notice.** 150 Hickorytown Rd. I-76 (Pennsylvania Tpke), exit 226, 0.4 mi n on US 11, 2.3 mi se on S Middlesex Rd, 0.4 mi e on Ridge Dr, then just s (right turn). Ext/int corridors. **Pets:** Accepted.
SAVE X 📶

Quality Inn Carlisle SH
(717) 243-6000. **$79-$160.** 1255 Harrisburg Pike. I-81, exit 52 (US 11) southbound; exit 52B northbound; I-76 (Pennsylvania Tpke), exit 226, 0.8 mi n. Int corridors. **Pets:** Other species. $25 daily fee/pet. Service with restrictions.
SAVE SO X 📶 💻 ⤵

Ramada Limited SH
(717) 243-8585. **Call for rates.** 1252 Harrisburg Pike. I-81, exit 52 (US 11) southbound; exit 52B northbound; I-76 (Pennsylvania Tpke), exit 226, 1 mi n on US 11. Ext/int corridors. **Pets:** Accepted.
SAVE X 📶 💻

Residence Inn by Marriott Harrisburg/Carlisle SH ❀
(717) 610-9050. **$164-$186.** 1 Hampton Ct. I-76, exit 226, just e. Int corridors. **Pets:** Medium. $75 one-time fee/room. Service with restrictions, supervision.
ASK SO X 📶 💻 ⤵ ⊠

Rodeway Inn M ❀
(717) 249-2800. **$45-$150.** 1239 Harrisburg Pike. I-81, exit 52 (US 11) southbound; exit 52B northbound, 0.3 mi s; I-76 (Pennsylvania Tpke), exit 226, 0.8 mi s. Ext corridors. **Pets:** Medium, other species. $10 daily fee/room. Service with restrictions, supervision.
SAVE SO X 📶 💻 ⤵

Sleep Inn Carlisle SH
(717) 249-8863. **Call for rates.** 5 E Garland Dr. I-81, exit 47 northbound, just ne; exit 47A southbound. Int corridors. **Pets:** Accepted.
SAVE X SM 📶 💻 ⤵

Super 8 Motel/Carlisle South M
(717) 245-9898. **$50-$125.** 100 Alexander Spring Rd. I-81, exit 45, just se. Int corridors. **Pets:** Medium, other species. $8 one-time fee/pet.
SAVE SO X SM 📶

AAA ▼ ▼ **Super 8 Motel/North Carlisle** **M**
(717) 249-7000. **Call for rates.** 1800 Harrisburg Pike. I-81, exit 52A northbound; exit 52 (US 11) southbound, 0.5 mi n; I-76 (Pennsylvania Tpke), exit 226, 1.3 mi n. Ext/int corridors. **Pets:** Accepted.

🆂🅰🆅🅴 ✕ 🕭ᴹ 🖥 🖢

CHAMBERSBURG

AAA ▼▼▼ **Best Western Chambersburg** **SH**
(717) 263-4994. 211 Walker Rd. I-81, exit 16, just w on US 30, then just n. Int corridors. **Pets:** Accepted.

🆂🅰🆅🅴 ✕ 🖥 🖢 🖢

▼ ▼ **Comfort Inn-Chambersburg** **SH**
(717) 263-6655. **$63-$150.** 3301 Black Gap Rd. I-81, exit 20, just e, then just s on SR 997. Int corridors. **Pets:** Small. $25 one-time fee/pet. Designated rooms, no service, crate.

A$K 🆂🅾 ✕ 🖥 🖢

AAA ▼ ▼ **Days Inn** **SH**
(717) 263-1288. **$60-$129.** 30 Falling Spring Rd. I-81, exit 16, just e on US 30. Int corridors. **Pets:** Medium, other species. $10 daily fee/pet. Designated rooms, service with restrictions, supervision.

🆂🅰🆅🅴 ✕ 🖥 🖢 🖢

AAA ▼ ▼ **Econo Lodge** **M**
(717) 264-8005. **$59-$68.** 1110 Sheller Ave. I-81, exit 14, just w on SR 316. Int corridors. **Pets:** Other species. $10 one-time fee/pet. Service with restrictions, supervision.

🆂🅰🆅🅴 🆂🅾 ✕ 🖥 🖢

▼ ▼ **Red Carpet Inn** **M**
(717) 267-2323. **$50-$75.** 1175 Wayne Ave. I-81, exit 14, just e on SR 316. Ext corridors. **Pets:** Accepted.

A$K 🆂🅾 ✕ 🖥 🖢

AAA ▼▼▼ **Sleep Inn & Suites** **SH**
(717) 263-0596. **$70-$110, 5 day notice.** 1435 Doron Dr. I-81, exit 20, just w. Int corridors. **Pets:** Medium, other species. $10 daily fee/pet. Designated rooms, service with restrictions, crate.

🆂🅰🆅🅴 🆂🅾 ✕ 🕭ᴹ 🖥 🖢 🖢

CLARION

▼ ▼ **Comfort Inn-Clarion** **SH**
(814) 226-5230. **$59-$129.** 129 Dolby St. I-80, exit 62, 0.6 mi n on SR 68. Int corridors. **Pets:** Dogs only. $10 one-time fee/pet. Service with restrictions, supervision.

A$K 🆂🅾 ✕ 🕭ᴹ 🖥 🖢

▼▼▼ **Holiday Inn** **SH** 🐾
(814) 226-8850. **$109-$169.** 45 Holiday Inn Rd. I-80, exit 62, 0.5 mi n on SR 68. Int corridors. **Pets:** Small, other species. $10 daily fee/pet. Service with restrictions, supervision.

A$K ✕ 🕭ᴹ 🖥 🖢 🍴 🖢 🖾

▼▼▼ **Microtel Inn & Suites-Clarion** **SH**
(814) 227-2700. **$69.** 151 Hotel Dr. I-80, exit 62, just n on SR 68, then just e. Int corridors. **Pets:** Medium. $10 daily fee/pet. Service with restrictions, supervision.

A$K 🆂🅾 ✕ 🕭ᴹ 🖥 🖢

AAA ▼▼▼ **Quality Inn & Suites Clarion** **M**
(814) 226-8682. **$80.** 24 United Dr. I-80, exit 62, just n on SR 68. Int corridors. **Pets:** Other species. $5 one-time fee/pet. Designated rooms, service with restrictions, supervision.

🆂🅰🆅🅴 🆂🅾 ✕ 🖥 🖢 🍴 🖢

▼ ▼ **Super 8 Motel-Clarion** **M**
(814) 226-4550. **Call for rates.** 135 Hotel Rd. I-80, exit 62, just n on SR 68. Ext corridors. **Pets:** Other species. Designated rooms, service with restrictions, supervision.

✕ 🖥 🖢 🖢

CLARKS SUMMIT

AAA ▼ ▼▼ **Comfort Inn-Clarks Summit/Scranton** **SH**
(570) 586-9100. **$69-$159.** 811 Northern Blvd. I-81, exit 194, on US 6 and 11; I-476 (Pennsylvania Tpke), exit 131. Int corridors. **Pets:** Accepted.

🆂🅰🆅🅴 🆂🅾 ✕ 🖥 🖢

AAA ▼ ▼ ◆ **Econo Lodge of Clarks Summit** **M** 🐾
(570) 586-1211. **$44-$149.** 649 Northern Blvd. I-81, exit 194, on US 6 and 11 E; I-476 (Pennsylvania Tpke), exit 131, just e. Ext corridors. **Pets:** Other species. $8 daily fee/pet. Service with restrictions, supervision.

🆂🅰🆅🅴 🆂🅾 ✕ 🖥 🖢

CLEARFIELD

AAA ▼ ▼ **Budget Inn** **M**
(814) 765-2639. **$31-$70.** 6321 Woodland Hwy (US 322 E). I-80, exit 120, 1.5 mi sw on SR 879, then 1.2 mi e. Ext/int corridors. **Pets:** Accepted.

🆂🅰🆅🅴 🆂🅾 ✕ 🖥

▼ ▼ **Comfort Inn Clearfield** **SH**
(814) 768-6400. **$86-$150.** 1821 Industrial Park Rd. I-80, exit 120, just s. Int corridors. **Pets:** Other species. $15 daily fee/room. Service with restrictions, supervision.

A$K 🆂🅾 ✕ 🖥 🖢 🖢

▼ ▼ **Super 8 Motel-Clearfield** **M**
(814) 768-7580. **Call for rates.** 14597 Clearfield/Shawville Hwy (Rt 879). I-80, exit 120, just s. Int corridors. **Pets:** Accepted.

✕ 🕭ᴹ 🖥 🖢

DANVILLE

AAA ▼▼▼ **Best Western Danville Inn** **SH**
(570) 275-5750. **$68-$140, 14 day notice.** 79 Old Valley School Rd. I-80, exit 224, just s. Int corridors. **Pets:** Other species. $15 one-time fee/pet. Service with restrictions, crate.

🆂🅰🆅🅴 🆂🅾 ✕ 🖢 🖢

AAA ▼▼▼ **Quality Inn & Suites Danville** **M** 🐾
(570) 275-5100. **$69-$169.** 15 Valley West Rd. I-80, exit 224, just n on SR 54. Int corridors. **Pets:** Medium, other species. $25 one-time fee/room. Designated rooms, service with restrictions, supervision.

🆂🅰🆅🅴 🆂🅾 ✕ 🖥 🖢 🍴 🖢

DICKSON CITY

▼▼▼ **Residence Inn by Marriott-Scranton** **SH**
(570) 343-5121. **$187-$209.** 947 Viewmont Dr. I-81, exit 190, just e, follow signs to Viewmont Dr. Int corridors. **Pets:** Accepted.

A$K 🆂🅾 ✕ 🖥 🖢 🖢 🖾

DU BOIS

AAA ▼▼▼ **Best Western Inn & Conference Center** **SH** 🐾
(814) 371-6200. **$70-$130.** 82 N Park Pl. I-80, exit 97 eastbound, 2.5 mi e on Du Bois Ave (US 219), then just s; exit 101 westbound, 2.7 mi w on Du Bois Ave (SR 255), then just s on US 219. Int corridors. **Pets:** Other species. $10 daily fee/pet. Service with restrictions, crate.

🆂🅰🆅🅴 🆂🅾 ✕ 🖥 🖾

▼ ▼ **Clarion Hotel DuBois** **SH**
(814) 371-5100. **$84-$99.** 1896 Rich Hwy. I-80, exit 97, just s. Int corridors. **Pets:** Other species. $50 deposit/pet. Service with restrictions, supervision.

A$K 🆂🅾 ✕ 🕭ᴹ 🖥 🖢 🍴 🖢

DUNMORE

㊂ ▽▽ Days Inn SH
(570) 348-6101. **Call for rates.** 1226 O Hwy. I-81, exit 188 (Throop), just n at SR 347. Int corridors. **Pets:** $5 daily fee/pet. Service with restrictions, supervision.
SAVE ⊠ 🖰 💻

▽▽▽▽ Holiday Inn-Scranton East SH
(570) 343-4771. **$79-$199.** 200 Tigue St. I-84/380, exit 1 (Tigue St), 0.3 mi e of jct I-81. Ext/int corridors. **Pets:** Medium. $10 daily fee/pet. Designated rooms, service with restrictions.
ASK S⊘ ⊠ 🖰 💻 🍴 ⇌ ⊠

㊂ ▽▽▽ Sleep Inn & Suites SH ❀
(570) 961-1116. **$69-$159.** 102 Monahan Ave. I-81, exit 188 (Throop), just e at SR 347 N (O'Neill Hwy), then just s. Int corridors. **Pets:** Medium. $10 daily fee/pet. Designated rooms, service with restrictions, supervision.
SAVE S⊘ ⊠ ᴹ 🖰 💻

EASTON

▽▽ Comfort Inn SH
(610) 253-0546. **Call for rates.** 2555 Nazareth Rd. US 22, exit 25th St, just e on N Service Rd. Int corridors. **Pets:** Accepted.
⊠ 🖰

▽▽▽ The Lafayette Inn BB ❀
(610) 253-4500. **$125-$225.** 525 W Monroe St. US 22, exit 4th St (SR 611), just n on 3rd St, 0.3 mi ne on College Ave, then 0.3 mi n on Cattell St to jct Monroe St. Ext/int corridors. **Pets:** $20 daily fee/room. Designated rooms, service with restrictions, crate.
⊠ 🖰 💻

㊂ ▽▽▽▽ Quality Inn-Easton Inn SH
(610) 253-9131. **$39-$179.** 185 S 3rd St. I-78, exit 75, 1 mi n, follow signs; US 22, exit 4th St (SR 611), just e to 3rd St, then 0.5 mi s; downtown. Int corridors. **Pets:** Accepted.
SAVE S⊘ ⊠ 🖰 💻 ⇌

EBENSBURG

▽▽▽ Comfort Inn SH
(814) 472-6100. **Call for rates.** 111 Cook Rd. Jct US 219, just e on US 22. Int corridors. **Pets:** Medium. $25 deposit/room, $15 daily fee/pet. Designated rooms, service with restrictions, supervision.
⊠ ᴹ 🖰 💻 ⇌

ERIE

▽▽▽▽ Country Inn & Suites SH
(814) 864-5810. **$69-$169.** 8040 Oliver Rd. I-90, exit 24, just s, then 0.5 mi w. Int corridors. **Pets:** Accepted.
ASK S⊘ ⊠ 🖰 💻 ⇌

▽▽ Days Inn SH
(814) 868-8521. **$110-$190.** 7415 Schultz Rd. I-90, exit 27, just n on SR 97. Int corridors. **Pets:** Other species. $5 daily fee/pet. Service with restrictions, crate.
ASK S⊘ ⊠ 🖰 💻 ⇌

▽▽▽ Erie Inn & Suites SH
(814) 864-1812. **Call for rates.** 7820 Perry Hwy. I-90, exit 27, just n. Int corridors. **Pets:** Accepted.
⊠ 🖰 💻 ⇌

▽▽▽ Homewood Suites by Hilton SH
(814) 866-8292. **Call for rates.** 2084 Interchange Rd. I-79, exit 180, just e. Int corridors. **Pets:** Accepted.
⊠ 🖰 💻 ⇌

▽▽ Microtel Inn-Erie M ❀
(814) 864-1010. **$60-$120.** 8100 Peach St. I-90, exit 24, just s. Int corridors. **Pets:** Dogs only. $10 daily fee/pet. Designated rooms, service with restrictions, crate.
ASK S⊘ ⊠ 🖰 💻

▽▽ Red Roof Inn #7054 M
(814) 868-5246. **Call for rates.** 7865 Perry Hwy. I-90, exit 27, just n on SR 97. Ext/int corridors. **Pets:** Accepted.
⊠ 🖰

FOGELSVILLE

▽▽▽▽ Comfort Inn Lehigh Valley-West SH
(610) 391-0344. **$85-$130.** 7625 Imperial Way. I-78, exit 49B (SR 100), just n. Int corridors. **Pets:** Other species. $25 one-time fee/pet. Service with restrictions, crate.
ASK S⊘ ⊠ 🖰 💻

▽▽▽▽ Glasbern CI
(610) 285-4723. **$145-$480, 7 day notice.** 2141 Packhouse Rd. I-78, exit 49B (SR 100), 0.3 mi n to 1st light, 0.3 mi w on Main St, 0.6 mi n on Church St, then 0.8 mi ne. Ext/int corridors. **Pets:** Dogs only. $25 daily fee/pet. Designated rooms, service with restrictions, supervision.
ASK ⊠ 🖰 💻 🍴 ⇌ ⊠

▽▽▽▽ Holiday Inn Conference Center SH ❀
(610) 391-1000. **$139-$209.** 7736 Adrienne Dr. I-78, exit 49A, 0.3 mi s on SR 100. Int corridors. **Pets:** $49 one-time fee/room. Service with restrictions, crate.
ASK S⊘ ⊠ ᴹ 🖰 💻 🍴 ⇌ ⊠

▽▽▽ Sleep Inn SH
(610) 395-6603. **$59-$159.** 327 Star Rd. I-78, exit 49A, 0.3 mi s on SR 100, left at 1st traffic light, then immediate left on service road. Int corridors. **Pets:** Medium. $15 daily fee/pet. Designated rooms, no service, supervision.
ASK S⊘ ⊠ ᴹ 🖰 💻

▽▽▽ Staybridge Suites-Allentown West SH
(610) 841-5100. **Call for rates.** 327 C Star Rd. I-78, exit 49A, 0.3 mi s on SR 100, e at traffic light, then n on service road. Int corridors. **Pets:** Accepted.
⊠ 🖰 💻 ⇌ ⊠

FRACKVILLE

㊂ ▽▽ Econo Lodge M
(570) 874-3838. **$53-$109.** 501 S Middle St. I-81, exit 124B, 0.4 mi n on SR 61. Ext corridors. **Pets:** Accepted.
SAVE S⊘ ⊠ 🖰

FRANKLIN

▽▽ Franklin Super 8 Motel SH
(814) 432-2101. **Call for rates.** 847 Allegheny Blvd. 2 mi on SR 8 N. Int corridors. **Pets:** Accepted.
⊠ 🖰 💻

GETTYSBURG

㊂ ▽▽ Americas Best Value Inn M
(717) 334-1188. **$56-$155.** 301 Steinwehr Ave. 1 mi s on US 15 business route, just s of jct SR 134. Ext/int corridors. **Pets:** Medium, dogs only. $50 deposit/room. Service with restrictions, supervision.
SAVE S⊘ ⊠ 🖰 💻

▽▽▽ Battlefield Bed & Breakfast Inn BB ❀
(717) 334-8804. **$199-$349, 7 day notice.** 2264 Emmitsburg Rd. 4 mi s on Steinwehr Ave and Baltimore Pike. Int corridors. **Pets:** Dogs only. Designated rooms.
ASK S⊘ ⊠ 🐾

Eisenhower Hotel, Conference Center and Resort 🄻🄷
(717) 334-8121. **$69-$169.** 2634 Emmitsburg Rd. US 15 business route, 5 mi s. Int corridors. **Pets:** Large. $20 one-time fee/room. Service with restrictions.
(ASK) (S🄳) (✕) (🖃) (💻) (🍴) (➜) (🛇)

Gettysburg Travelodge 🄼
(717) 334-9281. **Call for rates.** 613 Baltimore St. On SR 97 at US 15 business route. Ext/int corridors. **Pets:** Other species. Service with restrictions.
(✕) (🖃) (💻)

Holiday Inn-Battlefield 🅂🄷
(717) 334-6211. **$94-$300.** 516 Baltimore St. Jct US 15 business route and SR 97. Ext/int corridors. **Pets:** Other species. $10 one-time fee/room. Designated rooms, service with restrictions, supervision.
(ASK) (S🄳) (✕) (🖃) (💻) (🍴) (➜)

Holiday Inn Express of Gettysburg 🄼
(717) 337-1400. **$76-$170.** 869 York Rd. 1 mi e on US 30. Int corridors. **Pets:** Service with restrictions, supervision.
(SAVE) (S🄳) (✕) (🄼) (🖃) (💻) (➜)

Wyndham Gettysburg 🄻🄷 🐾
(717) 339-0020. **$119-$199.** 95 Presidential Cir. US 15, exit York St, just e on US 30. Int corridors. **Pets:** Medium, other species. $50 daily fee/room. Service with restrictions, supervision.
(SAVE) (S🄳) (✕) (🄼) (🖃) (💻) (🍴) (➜)

GIRARD

The Green Roof Inn 🄼 🐾
(814) 774-7072. **$57-$154.** 8790 Rt 18. I-90, exit 9, 1.9 mi s. Ext corridors. **Pets:** Other species. $10 daily fee/pet. Designated rooms, service with restrictions, supervision.
(SAVE) (S🄳) (✕) (🖃) (💻)

GRANTVILLE

Days Inn 🄼
(717) 469-0631. **$89-$140.** 252 Bow Creek Rd. I-81, exit 80. Ext corridors. **Pets:** Medium. $10 daily fee/pet. Designated rooms, service with restrictions, supervision.
(SAVE) (S🄳) (✕) (🖃) (💻)

Holiday Inn Harrisburg-Hershey Area, I-81 🅂🄷
(717) 469-0661. **$109-$219.** 604 Station Rd. I-81, exit 80. Int corridors. **Pets:** $75 deposit/room. Service with restrictions, crate.
(SAVE) (S🄳) (✕) (🄼) (🖃) (💻) (🍴) (➜) (🛇)

GREENCASTLE

Comfort Inn 🅂🄷
(717) 597-8164. **$70-$120.** 50 Pine Dr. I-81, exit 3, just s on US 11. Int corridors. **Pets:** Medium. $10 daily fee/pet. Service with restrictions, supervision.
(SAVE) (S🄳) (✕) (🖃) (💻) (🍴) (🛇)

GROVE CITY

Old Arbor Rose Bed & Breakfast 🄱🄱
(724) 458-6425. **Call for rates.** 114 W Main St. Just e. Int corridors. **Pets:** Accepted.
(✕) (🖅)

HAMBURG

Microtel Inn & Suites 🅂🄷
(610) 562-4234. **$74-$150.** 50 Industrial Dr. I-78, exit 29B, 0.3 mi n on SR 61, then just e. Int corridors. **Pets:** Other species. $10 daily fee/pet. Service with restrictions, supervision.
(ASK) (✕) (🄼) (🖃) (💻)

HANOVER

Howard Johnson Inn 🄼
(717) 646-1000. **Call for rates.** 1080 Carlisle St. 1.5 mi n on SR 94, just e. Ext corridors. **Pets:** Accepted.
(SAVE) (✕) (🄼) (🖃) (💻) (➜)

HARRISBURG

Best Western Harrisburg/Hershey Hotel & Suites 🅂🄷
(717) 652-7180. **Call for rates.** 300 N Mountain Rd. I-81, exit 72 southbound; exit 72B northbound. Int corridors. **Pets:** Accepted.
(SAVE) (✕) (🖃) (💻) (🍴) (➜) (🛇)

Comfort Inn Harrisburg East 🅂🄷
(717) 561-8100. **$79-$159, 5 day notice.** 4021 Union Deposit Rd. I-83, exit 48, just w. Int corridors. **Pets:** Accepted.
(SAVE) (S🄳) (✕) (🖃) (💻) (➜)

Comfort Inn Harrisburg/Hershey 🅂🄷 🐾
(717) 540-8400. **$69-$169.** 7744 Linglestown Rd. I-81, exit 77, 0.5 mi w. Int corridors. **Pets:** Other species. $10 daily fee/pet. Service with restrictions, crate.
(SAVE) (S🄳) (✕) (🖃) (💻) (➜) (🛇)

Comfort Inn Riverfront 🅂🄷
(717) 233-1611. **$99-$199.** 525 S Front St. I-83, exit 43, 0.5 mi n. Ext/int corridors. **Pets:** Medium. $25 daily fee/pet. Designated rooms, service with restrictions, supervision.
(SAVE) (S🄳) (✕) (🖃) (💻) (🍴) (➜)

Country Hearth Inn & Suites 🅂🄷
(717) 545-6944. **Call for rates.** 7965 Jonestown Rd. I-81, exit 77, just s. Int corridors. **Pets:** Accepted.
(SAVE) (✕) (🖃) (➜)

Crowne Plaza Harrisburg-Hershey 🄻🄷
(717) 234-5021. **$129-$219.** 23 S 2nd St. Jct Chestnut St; downtown. Int corridors. **Pets:** Accepted.
(SAVE) (S🄳) (✕) (🄼) (🖃) (💻) (🍴) (➜)

Holiday Inn Express Hotel & Suites 🅂🄷
(717) 657-2200. **$69-$169.** 5680 Allentown Blvd. I-81, exit 72, just s on N Mountain Rd, then just w on US 22. Int corridors. **Pets:** Accepted.
(SAVE) (S🄳) (✕) (🄼) (🖃) (💻) (➜)

Holiday Inn Harrisburg East-Airport 🅂🄷
(717) 939-7841. **$140-$200.** 4751 Lindle Rd. I-283, exit 2, just e. Int corridors. **Pets:** Accepted.
(SAVE) (S🄳) (✕) (🄼) (🖃) (💻) (🍴) (➜) (🛇)

Howard Johnson Inn 🅂🄷
(717) 540-9100. **$49-$109.** 7930 Linglestown Rd. I-81, exit 77. Int corridors. **Pets:** Accepted.
(SAVE) (S🄳) (✕) (🖃) (💻)

La Quinta Inn & Suites Harrisburg Airport 🅂🄷
(717) 939-8000. **$85-$99.** 990 Eisenhower Blvd. I-283, exit 2, just se; I-76 (Pennsylvania Tpke), exit 247, 1 mi n. Int corridors. **Pets:** Medium, other species. Service with restrictions, crate.
(ASK) (S🄳) (✕) (🖃) (💻)

Quality Inn 🅂🄷
(717) 540-9339. **$70-$140.** 200 N Mountain Rd. I-81, exit 72A northbound; exit 72 southbound. Int corridors. **Pets:** Accepted.
(SAVE) (S🄳) (✕) (🖃) (💻)

Red Roof Inn-North #7037 🄼
(717) 657-1445. **Call for rates.** 400 Corporate Cir. I-81, exit 69, just n on Progress Ave. Ext/int corridors. **Pets:** Accepted.
(✕) (🖃)

▼▼ Red Roof Inn-South #7027 M
(717) 939-1331. **Call for rates.** 950 Eisenhower Blvd. I-283, exit 2, just e. Ext/int corridors. **Pets:** Accepted.
⊠ 🖥

▼▼ Residence Inn by Marriott Harrisburg-Hershey SH
(717) 561-1900. **$209-$229.** 4480 Lewis Rd. US 322, exit Penhar Dr, just e. Ext corridors. **Pets:** $100 one-time fee/room. Service with restrictions, supervision.
ASK S🖥 ⊠ 🖥 🖵 🏊 ⊠

⬧⬧ ▼▼▼ Sheraton Harrisburg Hershey LH
(717) 564-5511. **Call for rates.** 4650 Lindle Rd. I-283, exit 2, just e. Int corridors. **Pets:** Accepted.
SAVE ⊠ &M 🖥 🖵 ¶¶ 🏊

⬧⬧ ▼ Super 8 Motel-North M
(717) 233-5891. **Call for rates.** 4125 N Front St. I-81, exit 66, 0.8 mi n. Ext corridors. **Pets:** Accepted.
SAVE ⊠ 🖥 🏊

HAZLETON

⬧⬧ ▼▼💎 Best Western Genetti Inn & Suites SH
(570) 454-2494. **$81-$110.** 1441 N Church St. I-80, exit 262, 6 mi s on SR 309. Ext/int corridors. **Pets:** Large. $10 daily fee/pet. Service with restrictions, supervision.
SAVE S🖥 ⊠ 🖥 🖵 🏊

▼▼ Ramada Inn Hazleton SH
(570) 455-2061. **Call for rates.** 1213 N Church St. I-80, exit 262, 6 mi s on SR 309; I-81, exit 145, 0.5 mi s on SR 93, 1 mi e on Airport Rd, then 0.7 mi s. Ext corridors. **Pets:** Medium. $10 daily fee/pet. Designated rooms, no service, supervision.
⊠ 🖥 🖵 ¶¶ 🏊

HERSHEY

⬧⬧ ▼▼▼▼ Days Inn Hershey SH
(717) 534-2162. **$89-$269.** 350 W Chocolate Ave. On US 422; center. Int corridors. **Pets:** Medium, dogs only. $15 daily fee/pet. Designated rooms, service with restrictions, supervision.
SAVE S🖥 ⊠ &M 🖥 🖵 🏊 ⊠

⬧⬧ ▼▼▼▼ Hampton Inn & Suites SH
(717) 533-8400. **$109-$309.** 749 E Chocolate Ave. 0.9 mi e on US 422. Int corridors. **Pets:** Small. $10 daily fee/pet. Designated rooms, service with restrictions, supervision.
SAVE S🖥 ⊠ &M 🖥 🖵 🏊 ⊠

HUMMELSTOWN

⬧⬧ ▼ Hershey Econo Lodge M
(717) 533-2515. **$59-$179.** 115 Lucy Ave. Jct US 322, just e on US 422. Ext corridors. **Pets:** Large, dogs only. $10 daily fee/pet. Designated rooms, crate.
SAVE ⊠ 🖥 🖵

HUNTINGDON

▼▼ Huntingdon Motor Inn M ❀
(814) 643-1133. **$51-$75.** 6920 Motor Inn Dr. On US 22 at SR 26. Ext corridors. **Pets:** Other species. $10 one-time fee/pet. Service with restrictions, supervision.
⊠ 🖥 🖵

INDIANA

▼▼▼ Holiday Inn SH
(724) 463-3561. **Call for rates.** 1395 Wayne Ave. US 422, exit Wayne Ave, 1 mi n. Ext/int corridors. **Pets:** Accepted.
⊠ 🖥 🖵 ¶¶ 🏊

JONESTOWN

⬧⬧ ▼▼ Days Inn Lebanon/Lickdale SH
(717) 865-4064. **Call for rates.** 3 Everest Ln. I-81, exit 90. Int corridors. **Pets:** Small. $10 daily fee/pet. Designated rooms, service with restrictions, supervision.
SAVE ⊠ 🖥 🖵 ⊠

▼▼ Quality Inn Jonestown/Lebanon M
(717) 865-6600. **$55-$150.** 16 Marsanna Ln. I-81, exit 90, just w. Int corridors. **Pets:** Accepted.
ASK S🖥 ⊠ 🖥 🖵 🏊

KITTANNING

▼▼ Comfort Inn SH
(724) 543-5200. **$89-$111.** 13 Hilltop Plaza. SR 28, exit 19A. Int corridors. **Pets:** Small. $15 one-time fee/pet. No service, supervision.
ASK S🖥 ⊠ 🖥 🖵 🏊

⬧⬧ ▼▼▼ Quality Inn Royle SH
(724) 543-1159. **$55-$99.** 405 Butler Rd. SR 28, exit US 422 W (Belmont). Ext/int corridors. **Pets:** Other species. $5 daily fee/pet. Designated rooms, service with restrictions, supervision.
SAVE S🖥 ⊠ 🖥 🖵 ¶¶

▼▼ Rodeway Inn Kittanning M
(724) 543-1100. **$45-$65.** US 422 E. E of jct Business Rt US 422, SR 66 and 28. Ext corridors. **Pets:** Other species. $5 daily fee/pet. Service with restrictions.
ASK S🖥 ⊠ 🖥 🖵

LAUREL HIGHLANDS AREA

CHALK HILL

⬧⬧ ▼▼💎 The Lodge at Chalk Hill M
(724) 438-8880. **$49-$110.** Rt 40 E. Just w. Ext corridors. **Pets:** Accepted.
SAVE S🖥 ⊠ 🖥 🖵 ⊠

DONEGAL

▼▼▼▼ Lesley's Mountain View Country Inn CI
(724) 593-6349. **$160-$210, 7 day notice.** 327 Mountain View Rd. I-76 (Pennsylvania Tpke), exit 91, 1 mi e, then 0.5 mi s. Ext/int corridors. **Pets:** Small. Designated rooms, supervision.
⊠ ¶¶

FARMINGTON

▼▼▼ Historic Summit Inn LH
(724) 438-8594. **$139-$299, 3 day notice.** 101 Skyline Dr. On US 40; center. Int corridors. **Pets:** Small, dogs only. $20 daily fee/pet. Designated rooms, service with restrictions, supervision.
ASK ⊠ 🖥 🖵 ¶¶ 🏊 ⊠

⬧⬧⬧ ▼▼▼▼ Nemacolin Woodlands Resort LH
(724) 329-8555. **$229-$799.** 1001 LaFayette Dr. 1 mi e on US 40. Ext/int corridors. **Pets:** Accepted.
SAVE S🖥 ⊠ 🖥 🖵 ¶¶ 🏊 ⊠

GREENSBURG

▼▼▼▼ Four Points by Sheraton SH
(724) 836-6060. **$105.** 100 Sheraton Dr. I-76 (Pennsylvania Tpke), exit 75, 5.6 mi on US 119 N, 3 mi e on US 30, then just n. Int corridors. **Pets:** Accepted.

(ASK) (Sᴏ) (✕) (◪) (▥) (¶¶) (≈) (✕)

▼ Knights Inn-Greensburg SH
(724) 836-7100. **$60-$80.** 1215 S Main St. I-76 (Pennsylvania Tpke), exit 75, 4 mi s on US 119; just s of US 30. Ext corridors. **Pets:** $10 daily fee/pet. Designated rooms, service with restrictions, supervision.

(ASK) (Sᴏ) (✕) (◪) (▥)

JOHNSTOWN

▼▼▼▼ Comfort Inn & Suites SH
(814) 266-3678. **$99-$159.** 455 Theatre Dr. US 219, exit Elton (SR 756), just e. Int corridors. **Pets:** $15 daily fee/pet. Designated rooms, service with restrictions, supervision.

(ASK) (Sᴏ) (✕) (ᴷᴹ) (◪) (▥) (≈)

▼▼ Econo Lodge M
(814) 536-1114. **$49-$149.** 430 Napoleon Pl. Jct SR 271 and 403; downtown. Int corridors. **Pets:** Accepted.

(ASK) (Sᴏ) (✕) (ᴷᴹ) (◪) (▥)

▼▼ Holiday Inn Downtown SH
(814) 535-7777. **Call for rates.** 250 Market St. Corner of Market and Vine sts; downtown. Int corridors. **Pets:** Accepted.

(✕) (◪) (▥) (¶¶) (≈) (✕)

▼▼ Holiday Inn Express Johnstown M
(814) 266-8789. **Call for rates.** 1440 Scalp Ave. US 219, exit Windber (SR 56 E), just e. Int corridors. **Pets:** $25 one-time fee/room. Designated rooms, service with restrictions, supervision.

(✕) (ᴷᴹ) (◪) (▥)

▼▼ Sleep Inn SH
(814) 262-9292. **$89-$115.** 453 Theatre Dr. US 219, exit Elton (SR 756), just e. Int corridors. **Pets:** $15 daily fee/pet. Designated rooms, service with restrictions, supervision.

(ASK) (Sᴏ) (✕) (ᴷᴹ) (◪) (▥)

▲▲▲ ▼▼▼ Super 8 Motel Johnstown SH
(814) 535-5600. **Call for rates.** 627 Solomon Run Rd. US 219, exit Galleria Dr, just w. Int corridors. **Pets:** Accepted.

(SAVE) (✕) (◪)

LIGONIER

▲▲▲ ▼▼▼▼▼ Lady of the Lake Bed & Breakfast BB
(724) 238-6955. **$85-$135, 14 day notice.** 157 Rt 30 E. US 30 E, just w of jct SR 711; beside Idlewild Park. Ext/int corridors. **Pets:** Accepted.

(SAVE) (Sᴏ) (✕) (◪) (▥) (≈) (✕) (✍)

NEW STANTON

▲▲▲ ▼▼▼ Days Inn New Stanton SH
(724) 925-3591. **$50-$95.** 127 W Byers Ave. I-76, exit 75, 0.5 mi sw; I-70, exit 57B westbound; exit 57 eastbound. Int corridors. **Pets:** Medium. $10 daily fee/pet. Service with restrictions, supervision.

(SAVE) (Sᴏ) (✕) (◪) (▥) (¶¶) (≈)

▲▲▲ ▼▼▼ Howard Johnson Inn M
(724) 925-3511. **$49-$119.** 112 W Byers Ave. I-76, exit 75, 0.5 mi sw; I-70, exit 57B westbound; exit 57 eastbound. Ext/int corridors. **Pets:** Medium, other species. $7 daily fee/pet. Designated rooms, service with restrictions, supervision.

(SAVE) (Sᴏ) (✕) (◪) (▥) (≈)

▲▲▲ ▼▼▼ Super 8 Motel-New Stanton M
(724) 925-8915. **$53-$76.** 103 Bair Blvd. I-76, exit 75, 0.5 mi se; I-70, exit 57B westbound; exit 57 eastbound. Int corridors. **Pets:** $10 daily fee/pet. Service with restrictions, supervision.

(SAVE) (Sᴏ) (✕) (◪)

SOMERSET

▼▼ Best Western Executive Inn SH
(814) 445-3996. **Call for rates.** 165 Water Works Rd. I-70/76 (Pennsylvania Tpke), exit 110, just e. Int corridors. **Pets:** Accepted.

(✕) (◪) (▥) (✕)

▼ Budget Host Inn M
(814) 445-7988. **$45-$95, 3 day notice.** 799 N Center Ave. I-70/76 (Pennsylvania Tpke), exit 110, 0.3 mi s. Ext corridors. **Pets:** Small. $7 daily fee/pet. No service, supervision.

(ASK) (Sᴏ) (✕) (◪)

▼ Days Inn-Somerset M
(814) 445-9200. **Call for rates.** 220 Water Works Rd. I-70/76 (Pennsylvania Tpke), exit 110, just e. Ext corridors. **Pets:** Accepted.

(✕) (◪)

▲▲▲ ▼ Dollar Inn M
(814) 445-2977. **$38-$85.** 1146 N Center Ave. I-70/76 (Pennsylvania Tpke), exit 110, 0.3 mi s, then just n on SR 601/N Central Ave; at top of hill. Ext corridors. **Pets:** Accepted.

(SAVE) (Sᴏ) (✕) (◪)

▼▼ Glades Pike Inn BB
(814) 443-4978. **$65-$125, 7 day notice.** 2684 Glades Pike. I-70/76 (Pennsylvania Tpke), exit 110, 6 mi w on SR 31; exit 91, 13 mi e on SR 31. Int corridors. **Pets:** Accepted.

(✕)

▲▲▲ ▼▼▼▼ Holiday Inn SH
(814) 445-9611. **$94-$149.** 202 Harmon St. I-70/76 (Pennsylvania Tpke), exit 110, just s. Int corridors. **Pets:** Accepted.

(SAVE) (Sᴏ) (✕) (▥) (¶¶) (≈)

▼▼▼▼ The Inn at Georgian Place BB
(814) 443-1043. **$105-$195, 7 day notice.** 800 Georgian Place Dr. I-70/76 (Pennsylvania Tpke), exit 110, 0.5 mi e, then 0.5 mi n on SR 601. Int corridors. **Pets:** Accepted.

(ASK) (Sᴏ) (✕) (¶¶)

▲▲▲ ▼▼▼ Quality Inn Somerset SH
(814) 443-4646. **$69-$199.** 215 Ramada Rd. I-70/76 (Pennsylvania Tpke), exit 110, just s. Int corridors. **Pets:** Accepted.

(SAVE) (Sᴏ) (✕) (◪) (▥) (¶¶) (≈) (✕)

▼ Super 8 Motel M
(814) 445-8788. **$49-$125.** 125 Lewis Dr. I-70/76 (Pennsylvania Tpke), exit 110, just s. Int corridors. **Pets:** Accepted.

(ASK) (Sᴏ) (✕) (◪) (▥)

UNIONTOWN

▼▼▼ Uniontown Holiday Inn SH
(724) 437-2816. **Call for rates.** 700 W Main St. 1.8 mi w on US 40. Int corridors. **Pets:** Other species. $10 daily fee/pet, $50 one-time fee/pet. Designated rooms, service with restrictions, crate.

(✕) (◪) (▥) (¶¶) (≈) (✕)

END AREA

LEBANON

▼▼▼▼ Berry Patch Bed and Breakfast BB
(717) 865-7219. **$125-$219, 14 day notice.** 115 Moore Rd. I-81, exit 90, 2.8 mi s on SR 72, 1 mi on New Bunker Hill St, 0.8 mi s on S Lancastor St, just e, then follow signs. Ext/int corridors. **Pets:** Accepted.
ASK S♦ ✕ 🖥

◢◢◢ ▼▼▼ Quality Inn-Lebanon Valley SH
(717) 273-6771. **$80-$169.** 625 Quentin Rd. 0.5 mi s on SR 72, from jct US 422. Ext/int corridors. **Pets:** Other species. $10 daily fee/pet. Designated rooms, service with restrictions, supervision.
SAVE S♦ ✕ ⓜ 🖥 🖵 🍴 ⇌ ✕

LEWISBURG

▼▼ All Suites Inn M
(570) 523-8882. **$93-$225.** 4663 Westbranch Hwy (US 15). 0.5 mi s on US 15. Ext corridors. **Pets:** Accepted.
ASK S♦ ✕ ⓜ 🖥 🖵 🍴

◢◢◢ ▼▼ Days Inn-Lewisburg SH
(570) 523-1171. **$81-$97.** US Rt 15. 0.5 mi n of jct SR 45. Ext corridors. **Pets:** Other species. Service with restrictions, crate.
SAVE S♦ ✕ 🖥 🖵 ⇌

LINCOLN FALLS

▼▼ Morgan Century Farm BB
(570) 924-4909. **$99-$145.** 30-809 Rt 154. In village. Ext/int corridors. **Pets:** Small. $10 deposit/pet. Service with restrictions, supervision.
S♦ ✕ 🖥 🖵 🅩

LOCK HAVEN

◢◢◢ ▼▼ Best Western-Lock Haven SH
(570) 748-3297. **Call for rates.** 101 E Walnut St. US 220, exit SR 120 W, just w. Int corridors. **Pets:** Other species. $10 daily fee/pet. Service with restrictions, supervision.
SAVE ✕ 🖥 🖵

MANSFIELD

◢◢◢ ▼▼ Comfort Inn SH
(570) 662-3000. **$109-$119.** 300 Gateway Dr. Jct US 6 and 15. Int corridors. **Pets:** $10 daily fee/pet. Service with restrictions, supervision.
SAVE S♦ ✕ 🖥 🖵 ✕

◢◢◢ ▼ Mansfield Inn M
(570) 662-2136. **$55-$80, 3 day notice.** 26 S Main St. Jct US 6, just s on Business Rt 15; downtown. Ext corridors. **Pets:** Accepted.
SAVE S♦ ✕ 🖥 🖵

◢◢◢ ▼ West's Deluxe Motel M
(570) 659-5141. **$65-$80.** 2848 S Main St. SR 15, exit Covington and Canoe Camp, Business Rt 15, 0.8 mi s on 660 W (Main St). Ext corridors. **Pets:** Accepted.
SAVE S♦ ✕ 🖥 🖵 ⇌

MARIENVILLE

▼ The Forest Lodge & Campground M 🐾
(814) 927-8790. **$40-$80, 14 day notice.** SR 66. 6 mi n of Marienville. Ext/int corridors. **Pets:** Dogs only. $10 daily fee/pet. Designated rooms, service with restrictions, supervision.
ASK S♦ ✕ 🖥 🖵

▼▼ Microtel Inn & Suites SH
(814) 927-8300. **$69.** 252 Cherry St. 0.6 mi sw of center, on SR 66. Int corridors. **Pets:** Medium. $10 daily fee/pet. Service with restrictions, supervision.
ASK S♦ ✕ 🖥 🖵

MEADVILLE

▼▼ Quality Inn M 🐾
(814) 333-8883. **$59-$109.** 17259 Conneaut Lake Rd. I-79, exit 147B, just w on US 322. Ext/int corridors. **Pets:** Dogs only. $10 daily fee/pet. Designated rooms, service with restrictions, supervision.
ASK S♦ ✕ 🖥 🖵

MECHANICSBURG

◢◢◢ ▼▼ Comfort Inn Capital City SH 🐾
(717) 766-3700. **$79-$129.** 1012 Wesley Dr. I-76 (Pennsylvania Tpke), exit 236 (US 15), 1 mi n to Wesley Dr exit, then just w. Int corridors. **Pets:** Small. $25 daily fee/pet. Service with restrictions, crate.
SAVE S♦ ✕ ⓜ 🖥 🖵 ⇌

◢◢◢ ▼▼ Comfort Inn West SH 🐾
(717) 790-0924. **$84-$160, 3 day notice.** 6325 Carlisle Pike. Jct Carlisle Pike and US 11, 1 mi w on US 11. Int corridors. **Pets:** Small, other species. $25 deposit/pet. Designated rooms, supervision.
SAVE S♦ ✕ 🖥 🖵

▼▼▼ Hampton Inn-Harrisburg West SH
(717) 691-1300. **$124-$154, 14 day notice.** 4950 Ritter Rd. I-76 (Pennsylvania Tpke), exit 236 (US 15), 1 mi n to Rossmoyne Rd exit. Int corridors. **Pets:** Accepted.
ASK S♦ ✕ ⓜ 🖥 🖵 ⇌ ✕

▼▼▼ Holiday Inn Harrisburg-West SH
(717) 697-0321. **$119-$180.** 5401 Carlisle Pike. Jct Carlisle Pike and US 11, just w. Ext corridors. **Pets:** Medium. $25 one-time fee/room. Service with restrictions, crate.
ASK S♦ ✕ 🖥 🖵 🍴 ⇌ ✕

MERCER

▼ Colonial Inn Motel M
(724) 662-5600. **$37-$49.** 383 N Perry Hwy (US 19). I-80, exit 15, 3.5 mi n; I-79, exit 121, 4.5 mi s on SR 62, then 0.5 mi n on US 19. Ext/int corridors. **Pets:** Other species. $5 daily fee/pet. Service with restrictions, supervision.
ASK S♦ ✕ 🖥 🖵

▼▼ Comfort Inn Mercer SH
(724) 748-3030. **$59-$129.** 835 Perry Hwy. I-80, exit 15, just n on US 19. Int corridors. **Pets:** Accepted.
ASK S♦ ✕ 🖥 🖵 ⇌ ✕

▼▼ Microtel Inn & Suites SH
(724) 748-9920. **Call for rates.** 2049 Leesburg Grove City Rd. I-79, exit 113, 0.9 mi w on SR 208. Int corridors. **Pets:** Accepted.
✕ 🖥 🖵

MIDDLETOWN

▼▼ Days Inn-Harrisburg Airport SH
(717) 939-4147. **Call for rates.** 800 S Eisenhower Blvd. I-76 (Pennsylvania Tpke), exit 247, just n; I-283, exit 1B (Highspire). Ext corridors. **Pets:** Other species. $10 daily fee/pet. Service with restrictions, crate.
✕ 🖥 🖵 ⇌

MIFFLINVILLE

▼▼ Super 8 Motel M
(570) 759-6778. **$55-$125.** 450 3rd St. I-80, exit 242, just n on SR 339. Ext corridors. **Pets:** Accepted.
ASK S♦ ✕ 🖥

MILESBURG

◢◢◢ ▼▼▼ Holiday Inn SH
(814) 355-7521. **$85-$350.** 971 N Eagle Valley Rd. I-80, exit 158, 0.4 mi n. Int corridors. **Pets:** Other species. Service with restrictions, supervision.
SAVE S♦ ✕ ⓜ 🖥 🖵 🍴 ⇌

MILROY

▼▼ ▼▼ Best Western Nittany Inn 🆂🅷
(717) 667-9595. **$69-$199.** 5 Commerce Dr. US 322, exit Milroy, just e.
Int corridors. **Pets:** Accepted.

ⒶⓈ🅺 🆂🄰 ⊠ 🄳 🖵 ⌲

MONTGOMERY

🐠⟍ ▼▼ White Deer Motel 🅼
(570) 547-1007. **$42-$98, 3 day notice.** 6967 Rt 15 Hwy. Jct SR 54,
1.4 mi s. Ext corridors. **Pets:** Accepted.

🆂🄰🆅🄴 🆂🄰 ⊠ 🄳 🖵

MORGANTOWN

▼▼▼▼ Holiday Inn 🆂🅷
(610) 286-3000. **$95-$112.** 6170 Morgantown Rd. I-76, exit 298, just s
on SR 10. Int corridors. **Pets:** Medium. $20 daily fee/pet. Designated
rooms, service with restrictions, supervision.

⊠ 🄳 🖵 🍽 ⌲ ⊠̸

NEW CASTLE

▼▼ ▼▼ Comfort Inn-New Castle 🅼
(724) 658-7700. **$59-$130.** 1740 New Butler Rd (US Business 422). Jct
SR 65, 1 mi e on US 422, then 1 mi w on US 422 business route. Int
corridors. **Pets:** Small. $10 one-time fee/pet. Designated rooms, no serv-
ice, crate.

ⒶⓈ🅺 🆂🄰 ⊠ 🄳 🖵

NEW COLUMBIA

🐠⟍ ▼▼▼▼ Holiday Inn Express 🆂🅷
(570) 568-1100. **$80-$209.** 160 Commerce Park Dr. I-80, exit 210A (US
15/New Columbia), just s. Int corridors. **Pets:** Small, other species. $25
one-time fee/pet. Designated rooms, service with restrictions, supervision.

🆂🄰🆅🄴 ⊠ 🄳ᴹ 🄳 🖵 ⌲

🐠⟍ ▼▼▼▼ New Columbia Comfort Inn 🆂🅷 🐾
(570) 568-8000. **Call for rates.** 330 Commerce Park Dr. I-80, exit 210A
(US 15/New Columbia), just s. Int corridors. **Pets:** Other species.

🆂🄰🆅🄴 ⊠ 🄳ᴹ 🄳 🖵 🍽 ⌲

NEW CUMBERLAND

🐠⟍ ▼▼▼▼ Days Inn Harrisburg South 🆂🅷
(717) 774-4156. **Call for rates.** 353 Lewisberry Rd. I-83, exit 39A, just
ne. Int corridors. **Pets:** Accepted.

🆂🄰🆅🄴 ⊠ 🄳 🖵 ⌲

🐠⟍ ▼▼▼▼ Holiday Inn Hotel & Conference
                  Center-Harrisburg 🆂🅷
(717) 774-2721. **$99-$149.** 148 Sheraton Dr. I-83, exit 40A, just se. Int
corridors. **Pets:** Accepted.

🆂🄰🆅🄴 🆂🄰 ⊠ 🄳 🖵 🍽 ⌲

PENNSYLVANIA DUTCH COUNTRY AREA

AKRON

▼▼▼▼ Boxwood Inn 🄱🄱 🐾
(717) 859-3466. **$110-$235, 7 day notice.** 1320 Diamond St. SR 272,
0.4 mi se on Main St to Diamond St, then 0.3 mi s. Ext/int corridors.
Pets: Medium, dogs only. $25 one-time fee/pet. Designated rooms, service
with restrictions.

ⒶⓈ🅺 🆂🄰 ⊠ 🄳 🖵

DENVER

🐠⟍ ▼▼▼▼ Black Horse Lodge and Suites 🆂🅷
(717) 336-7563. **$59-$199, 3 day notice.** 2180 N Reading Rd. I-76
(Pennsyvlania Tpke), exit 286, 1 mi w to SR 272, then 0.3 mi n. Ext/int
corridors. **Pets:** Other species. Service with restrictions, supervision.

🆂🄰🆅🄴 🆂🄰 ⊠ 🄳 🖵 🍽 ⌲

🐠⟍ ▼▼▼▼ Comfort Inn 🆂🅷
(717) 336-4649. **$80-$170, 3 day notice.** 2017 N Reading Rd. I-76
(Pennsylvania Tpke), exit 286, 1 mi w to SR 272, then just s. Int
corridors. **Pets:** Accepted.

🆂🄰🆅🄴 🆂🄰 ⊠ 🄳 🖵

🐠⟍ ▼▼▼▼ Holiday Inn-Lancaster County 🆂🅷
(717) 336-7541. **$99-$169.** 1 Denver Rd. I-76 (Pennsylvania Tpke), exit
286, 1 mi w to SR 272, then just s. Int corridors. **Pets:** $10 daily fee/pet.
Service with restrictions, supervision.

🆂🄰🆅🄴 🆂🄰 ⊠ 🄳ᴹ 🄳 🖵 🍽 ⌲

EPHRATA

🐠⟍ ▼▼▼▼ Historic Smithton Inn 🄱🄱
(717) 733-6094. **$95-$165, 14 day notice.** 900 W Main St. On US 322,
just w of jct SR 272, then just s on Academy Dr. Int corridors.
Pets: Accepted.

🆂🄰🆅🄴 ⊠ 🄳 🅩

GORDONVILLE

🐠⟍ ▼▼ Motel 6-Lancaster #4174 🅼
(717) 687-3880. **$55-$100.** 2959 Lincoln Hwy E. On US 30; center. Int
corridors. **Pets:** Other species. Service with restrictions, supervision.

🆂🄰🆅🄴 🆂🄰 ⊠ 🄳ᴹ 🄳

LANCASTER

▼▼ ▼▼ Americas Best Value Inn 🅼
(717) 397-4911. **$55-$150.** 1320 Harrisburg Pike. US 30 (Lincoln Hwy),
exit Harrisburg Pike, 0.6 mi s. Ext corridors. **Pets:** Dogs only. $10 daily
fee/pet. Service with restrictions, supervision.

ⒶⓈ🅺 🆂🄰 ⊠ 🄳

🐠⟍ ▼▼▼▼ Best Western Eden Resort Inn & Suites 🅻🅷
(717) 569-6444. **$89-$209.** 222 Eden Rd. Jct US 30 (Lincoln Hwy) and
SR 272 (Oregon Pike). Ext/int corridors. **Pets:** Small, other species. $15
daily fee/pet. Designated rooms, service with restrictions, supervision.

🆂🄰🆅🄴 🆂🄰 ⊠ 🄳ᴹ 🄳 🖵 🍽 ⌲ ⊠̸

🐠⟍ ▼▼▼▼ Hawthorn Inn & Suites 🆂🅷
(717) 290-7100. **$69-$159.** 2045 Lincoln Hwy E. Jct US 30 (Lincoln
Hwy E). Int corridors. **Pets:** Accepted.

🆂🄰🆅🄴 🆂🄰 ⊠ 🄳 🖵

🐠⟍ ▼▼▼▼ Lancaster Host Resort & Conference
                  Center 🅻🅷
(717) 299-5500. **$99-$199.** 2300 Lincoln Hwy E. On US 30 (Lincoln
Hwy), 5 mi e. Int corridors. **Pets:** Accepted.

🆂🄰🆅🄴 ⊠ 🄳 🖵 🍽 ⌲ ⊠̸

▼▼ ▼▼ Red Roof Inn of Lancaster 🆂🅷
(717) 299-9700. **Call for rates.** 2307 Lincoln Hwy E. On US 30 (Lincoln
Hwy), 5 mi e. Ext/int corridors. **Pets:** Accepted.

⊠ 🄳ᴹ 🄳 ⌲

LITITZ

WWWW Holiday Inn Express Hotel & Suites SH
(717) 625-2366. **$109-$246.** 101 Crosswinds Dr. 1.4 mi s on Lititz Pike/SR 501, then just w on Trolley Run Rd. Int corridors. **Pets:** Medium. $25 one-time fee/pet. Service with restrictions, supervision.
ASK ✕ ⓛ ⬛ 🖥 ➿

MANHEIM

WWW W Rodeway Inn M
(717) 665-2755. **$48-$78.** 2931 Lebanon Rd. I-76 (Pennsylvania Tpke), exit 266, just s on SR 72. Ext corridors. **Pets:** Other species. $5 daily fee/pet. Service with restrictions, supervision.
SAVE S✗ ✕ ➿

MOUNTVILLE

WWW WWWW MainStay Suites SH
(717) 285-2500. **$110-$210.** 314 Primrose Ln. US 30 (Lincoln Hwy), exit Mountville. Int corridors. **Pets:** Medium, other species. $10 daily fee/room. Service with restrictions, crate.
SAVE S✗ ✕ ⓛ ⬛ 🖥 ➿

NEW HOLLAND

WWW W Comfort Inn SH
(717) 355-9900. **$89-$179.** 626 W Main St. 0.5 mi w on SR 23. Int corridors. **Pets:** Large, other species. $15 daily fee/pet. Designated rooms, service with restrictions, supervision.
ASK S✗ ✕ ⬛ 🖥

STRASBURG

WWW WWWW Carriage House Motor Inn M
(717) 687-7651. **$49-$99.** 144 E Main St. 0.3 mi e on SR 896 and 741. Ext corridors. **Pets:** Accepted.
SAVE S✗ ✕ ⬛

WWW WWWW Historic Strasburg Inn SH
(717) 687-7691. **$129-$189, 3 day notice.** One Historic Dr. 0.5 mi n on SR 896; 2.5 mi s of US 30 (Lincoln Hwy). Ext/int corridors. **Pets:** Accepted.
SAVE S✗ ✕ ⬛ 🖥 🍽 ➿ ✗

END AREA

PHILADELPHIA METROPOLITAN AREA

AUDUBON

(AAA) ▼▼▼▼ Homewood Suites by Hilton SH
(610) 539-7300. **Call for rates.** 681 Shannondell Blvd. I-422, exit Trooper Rd, 1.2 mi n. Int corridors. **Pets:** Accepted.

BENSALEM

▼▼ Extended StayAmerica-Philadelphia/Bensalem SH
(215) 633-6900. **$105-$125.** 3216 Tillman Dr. I-95, exit 37 (PA 132/Street Rd), 2.5 mi w, then just s; I-276, exit 351, 0.9 mi on US 1, 1.4 mi e, then just s. Int corridors. **Pets:** Other species. $75 one-time fee/pet. Service with restrictions.

(AAA) ▼▼▼▼ Holiday Inn-Philadelphia Northeast SH
(215) 638-1500. **$109-$149.** 3499 Street Rd. I-276 (Pennsylvania Tpke), exit 351, just s on US 1, then 0.3 mi e on SR 132. Ext/int corridors. **Pets:** Medium. $30 one-time fee/pet. Designated rooms, service with restrictions, supervision.

(AAA) ▼▼▼▼ Sleep Inn & Suites-Bensalem SH
(215) 244-2300. **$69-$179.** 3427 Street Rd. I-276 (Pennsylvania Tpke), exit 351, just s on US 1, then 0.3 mi e on SR 132. Int corridors. **Pets:** Medium. $10 daily fee/pet. No service, supervision.

BERWYN

▼▼▼▼ Residence Inn by Marriott SH
(610) 640-9494. **$263-$285.** 600 W Swedesford Rd. US 202, exit Paoli/SR 252, 1 mi n. Ext corridors. **Pets:** Other species. $100 one-time fee/room. Service with restrictions.

CHADDS FORD

(AAA) ▼▼▼▼ Brandywine River Hotel SH
(610) 388-1200. **$129-$179.** 1609 Baltimore Pike. Jct US 1 and SR 100, 2 mi w of US 202. Int corridors. **Pets:** Accepted.

CONSHOHOCKEN

(AAA) ▼▼▼▼ Residence Inn by Marriott
Philadelphia/Conshohocken SH
(610) 828-8800. **$252-$274.** 191 Washington St. I-76 (Schuylkill Expwy), exit 332 (SR 23); I-476, exit 16 (SR 23), 0.3 mi over Fayette Bridge to Elm St, then just se along the river. Int corridors. **Pets:** Accepted.

EAST NORRITON

▼▼▼▼ Hyatt Summerfield Suites-Plymouth Meeting SH
(610) 313-9990. **$89-$229.** 501 E Germantown Pike. I-476, exit 20; I-276 (Pennsylvania Tpke), exit 333, 2.5 mi w. Int corridors. **Pets:** Medium. $5 daily fee/pet, $150 one-time fee/room. Designated rooms, service with restrictions, crate.

ERWINNA

▼▼▼▼ Golden Pheasant Inn CI ❀
(610) 294-9595. **$95-$225, 21 day notice.** 763 River Rd. SR 32, 0.5 mi n of jct Dark Hollow Rd. Ext/int corridors. **Pets:** Medium, other species. $25 daily fee/pet. Designated rooms, service with restrictions, crate.

ESSINGTON

▼▼ Motel 6 M
(610) 521-6650. **$75-$85.** 43 Industrial Hwy. I-95, exit 9A, 0.3 mi sw on SR 291. Ext corridors. **Pets:** Other species. Service with restrictions, supervision.

▼▼ Red Roof Inn-Airport #7119 M
(610) 521-5090. **Call for rates.** 49 Industrial Hwy. I-95, exit 9A, 0.3 mi sw on SR 291. Ext corridors. **Pets:** Accepted.

FORT WASHINGTON

▼▼▼▼ Hilton Garden Inn Philadelphia/Fort
Washington SH
(215) 646-4637. **$109-$259.** 530 Pennsylvania Ave. I-276 (Pennsylvania Tpke), exit 339. Int corridors. **Pets:** Small, dogs only. $25 daily fee/pet. Service with restrictions, supervision.

(AAA) ▼▼▼▼ Holiday Inn Fort Washington SH
(215) 643-3000. **Call for rates.** 432 Pennsylvania Ave. I-276 (Pennsylvania Tpke), exit 339 (SR 309 S), just w. Int corridors. **Pets:** Accepted.

GLEN MILLS

▼▼▼▼ Sweetwater Farm Bed & Breakfast BB
(610) 459-4711. **$135-$325, 14 day notice.** 50 Sweetwater Rd. US 1, 2 mi w on Valley Rd, then 0.6 mi s. Int corridors. **Pets:** Accepted.

HORSHAM

(AAA) ▼▼▼▼ Days Inn-Horsham/Willow Grove SH ❀
(215) 674-2500. **$109-$169.** 245 Easton Rd. I-276 (Pennsylvania Tpke), exit 343, 1 mi n. Int corridors. **Pets:** $10 daily fee/pet. Designated rooms, service with restrictions, supervision.

▼▼ Extended StayAmerica-Philadelphia/Horsham SH
(215) 784-9045. **$103-$125.** 114 Welsh Rd. I-276 (Pennsylvania Tpke), exit 343 (SR 611), s toward Jenkintown, 0.6 mi w on Maryland Rd, 0.5 mi sw on Computer Ave, then just n. Int corridors. **Pets:** Other species. $75 one-time fee/pet. Service with restrictions.

▼▼▼ Homestead Studio Suites Hotel-Horsham/Willow
Grove SH
(215) 956-9966. **$108-$130.** 537 Dresher Rd. I-276 (Pennsylvania Tpke), exit 343, 1.5 mi n on SR 611 (Easton Rd), just w on Horsham Rd, then 0.5 mi s. Int corridors. **Pets:** Other species. $75 one-time fee/pet. Service with restrictions.

▼▼▼▼ Residence Inn by Marriott-Willow Grove SH
(215) 443-7330. **$214-$235.** 3 Walnut Grove Dr. I-276 (Pennsylvania Tpke), exit 343, 1 mi n on SR 611 (Easton Rd), then 1.3 mi w on Dresher Rd; inside Pennsylvania Business Campus. Ext corridors. **Pets:** Other species. $150 one-time fee/room. Service with restrictions, supervision.

KING OF PRUSSIA

▼▼▼ Homestead Studio Suites Hotel Philadelphia-King of Prussia SH
(610) 962-9000. **$105-$125.** 400 American Ave. I-76 (Pennsylvania Tpke), exit 326 (Valley Forge); Schuylkill Expwy, exit 328A (Mall Blvd), 1.3 mi n on N Gulph Rd, then 1 mi ne on 1st Ave. Int corridors. **Pets:** Other species. $75 one-time fee/pet. Service with restrictions.
[ASK] [S🐾] [✕] [🕭M] [☎] [▣]

◭◭◭ ▼▼▼ MainStay Suites SH
(484) 690-3000. **$109-$159, 30 day notice.** 440 American Ave. I-76 (Pennsylvania Tpke), exit 326 (Valley Forge); Schuylkill Expwy, exit 328A (Mall Blvd), 1.3 mi n on N Gulph Rd, 1 mi ne on 1st Ave, then just e. Int corridors. **Pets:** Small, dogs only. $15 daily fee/pet. Service with restrictions, supervision.
[SAVE] [S🐾] [✕] [🕭M] [☎] [▣] [➣]

▼ Motel 6 Philadelphia-King of Prussia #1280 SH
(610) 265-7200. **$75-$85.** 815 W DeKalb Pike. I-76 (Pennsylvania Tpke), exit 326 (Valley Forge), 1.3 mi e to jct US 202 N and S Gulph Rd; Schuylkill Expwy, exit 328A (Mall Blvd), just e. Int corridors. **Pets:** Other species. Service with restrictions, supervision.
[S🐾] [✕] [➣]

▼▼▼ The Sheraton Park Ridge Hotel and Conference Center LH ❀
(610) 337-1800. **$309-$329.** 480 N Gulph Rd. I-76 (Pennsylvania Tpke), exit 327 (Valley Forge), 0.3 mi w. Int corridors. **Pets:** Medium, dogs only. Designated rooms, service with restrictions, supervision.
[ASK] [S🐾] [✕] [🕭M] [☎] [▣] [❢❢] [➣] [✕]

KULPSVILLE

▼▼▼ Best Western-The Inn at Towamencin SH
(215) 368-3800. **$98-$113.** 1750 Sumneytown Pike. I-476, exit 31, just e. Int corridors. **Pets:** Accepted.
[ASK] [S🐾] [✕] [☎] [▣] [❢❢] [➣] [✕]

LANGHORNE

▼▼▼ Sheraton Bucks County Hotel LH
(215) 547-4100. **$229-$332.** 400 Oxford Valley Rd. I-95, exit 46A (Oxford Valley Rd), 0.8 mi e, exit off US 1 N. Int corridors. **Pets:** Accepted.
[ASK] [S🐾] [✕] [🕭M] [☎] [▣] [❢❢] [➣] [✕]

LIONVILLE

▼▼ Extended StayAmerica-Philadelphia/Exton SH
(610) 524-7185. **$100-$120.** 877 N Pottstown Pike (Rt 100). I-76 (Pennslyvania Tpke), exit 312, 1.8 mi s on SR 100. Int corridors. **Pets:** Other species. $75 one-time fee/pet. Service with restrictions.
[ASK] [S🐾] [✕] [☎] [▣]

▼▼▼ Hampton Inn Exton SH
(610) 363-5555. **$119-$159.** 4 N Pottstown Pike. I-76 (Pennsylvania Tpke), exit 312, 0.5 mi s; jct SR 113 and 100. Int corridors. **Pets:** Medium. Service with restrictions, supervision.
[ASK] [S🐾] [✕] [🕭M] [☎] [▣] [➣]

◭◭◭ ▼▼▼ The Inn at Chester Springs Hotel Conference Center SH
(610) 363-1100. **$149-$189.** 815 N Pottstown Pike. I-76 (Pennsylvania Tpke), exit 312, 2 mi s on SR 100. Int corridors. **Pets:** Accepted.
[SAVE] [✕] [☎] [▣] [❢❢] [➣]

▼▼▼ Residence Inn by Marriott-Exton SH
(610) 594-9705. **$209-$242.** 10 N Pottstown Pike. I-76 (Pennsylvania Tpke), exit 312, 1 mi s on SR 100. Int corridors. **Pets:** Accepted.
[ASK] [S🐾] [✕] [☎] [▣] [✕]

MALVERN

▼▼ ▼▼ Extended StayAmerica-Philadelphia/Malvern SH
(610) 240-0455. **$102-$125.** 300 Morehall Rd (US 29). US 202, exit SR 29 N. Int corridors. **Pets:** Other species. $75 one-time fee/pet. Service with restrictions.
[ASK] [S🐾] [✕] [🕭M] [☎] [▣]

▼▼▼ Homestead Studio Suites Hotel Philadelphia-Malvern SH
(610) 695-9200. **$120-$142.** 8 E Swedesford Rd. Just w of US 202 and SR 29 N. Int corridors. **Pets:** Other species. $75 one-time fee/pet. Service with restrictions.
[ASK] [S🐾] [✕] [☎] [▣] [➣]

◭◭◭ ▼▼▼ Homewood Suites by Hilton SH
(610) 296-3500. **Call for rates.** 12 E Swedesford Rd. US 202, exit SR 29, follow signs. Int corridors. **Pets:** Accepted.
[SAVE] [✕] [🕭M] [☎] [▣] [➣]

◭◭◭ ▼▼▼ Sheraton Great Valley Hotel LH
(610) 524-5500. **$169-$194.** 707 Lancaster Pike. Jct US 202 and 30 E. Int corridors. **Pets:** Accepted.
[SAVE] [S🐾] [✕] [🕭M] [☎] [▣] [❢❢] [➣]

▼▼▼ Staybridge Suites SH
(610) 296-4343. **$159-$319.** 20 Morehall Rd. Jct US 30 and SR 29, just nw. Ext/int corridors. **Pets:** Medium. $10 daily fee/room. Service with restrictions, supervision.
[ASK] [S🐾] [✕] [☎] [▣] [➣] [✕]

MONTGOMERYVILLE

▼▼ ▼ Quality Inn Conference Center SH
(215) 699-8800. **$94-$129.** 969 Bethlehem Pike. I-276 (Pennsylvania Tpke), exit 339, 8 mi n on SR 309. Ext corridors. **Pets:** Large, other species. $25 daily fee/room. Designated rooms, service with restrictions, supervision.
[ASK] [S🐾] [✕] [☎] [▣]

▼▼▼ Residence Inn by Marriott SH
(267) 468-0111. **$209-$253.** 1110 Bethlehem Pike. I-276 (Pennsylvania Tpke), exit 339, 6.5 mi n on SR 309. Int corridors. **Pets:** Accepted.
[ASK] [S🐾] [✕] [☎] [▣] [➣] [✕]

NEW HOPE

◭◭◭ ▼▼▼ 1870 Wedgwood Inn of New Hope BB
(215) 862-2570. **$90-$285, 10 day notice.** 111 W Bridge St (SR 179). 0.5 mi w of SR 32; downtown. Ext/int corridors. **Pets:** Accepted.
[SAVE] [✕] [☎] [▣]

▼▼▼ Aaron Burr House Inn & Conference Center BB
(215) 862-2520. **$95-$295, 10 day notice.** 80 W Bridge St (SR 179). 0.5 mi w of SR 32; at W Bridge and Chestnut sts. Int corridors. **Pets:** Small, dogs only. $25 daily fee/pet. Designated rooms, service with restrictions, supervision.
[✕] [☎]

◭◭◭ ▼▼▼ New Hope Inn SH
(215) 862-5221. **Call for rates.** 6426 Lower York Rd. 2 mi s on US 202, 1 mi w of jct SR 179. Ext corridors. **Pets:** Accepted.
[SAVE] [✕] [☎] [▣] [❢❢] [➣] [✕]

PHILADELPHIA

◭◭◭ ▼▼▼ Best Western Center City Hotel SH
(215) 568-8300. **$135-$165.** 501 N 22nd St. Just n of Benjamin Franklin Pkwy. Int corridors. **Pets:** Medium, other species. $10 daily fee/pet. Service with restrictions.
[SAVE] [S🐾] [✕] [☎] [▣] [❢❢] [➣]

Best Western Independence Park Inn SH
(215) 922-4443. **$149-$325.** 235 Chestnut St. Between 2nd and 3rd sts. Int corridors. **Pets:** Accepted.

Extended StayAmerica-Philadelphia-Airport SH
(215) 492-6766. **$110-$130.** 9000 Tinicum Blvd. I-95, exit 12B, just n on Essington Ave, then just w on Bartram Ave. Int corridors. **Pets:** Other species. $75 one-time fee/pet. Service with restrictions.

Four Points by Sheraton Philadelphia Airport SH ❀
(215) 492-0400. **$240.** 4101 Island Ave. Jct I-95 and SR 291, exit 13 northbound; exit 15 southbound. Int corridors. **Pets:** Medium. Service with restrictions, supervision.

Four Seasons Hotel Philadelphia LH
(215) 963-1500. **$370-$495.** 1 Logan Square. Corner of 18th St and Benjamin Franklin Pkwy. Int corridors. **Pets:** Accepted.

Loews Philadelphia Hotel LH
(215) 627-1200. **$199-$329.** 1200 Market St. Corner of 12th and Market sts. Int corridors. **Pets:** Accepted.

Park Hyatt Philadelphia at The Bellevue LH
(215) 893-1234. **$250-$399.** Broad & Walnut. Broad St; between Walnut and Locust sts. Int corridors. **Pets:** Accepted.

Philadelphia Airport Residence Inn by Marriott SH
(215) 492-1611. **$230-$252.** 4630 Island Ave. I-95, exit 13 northbound; exit 15 southbound, 0.5 mi e; just e of SR 291. Ext/int corridors. **Pets:** Accepted.

Philadelphia Downtown Marriott Hotel LH
(215) 625-2900. **$373-$395.** 1201 Market St. Between 12th and 13th sts. Int corridors. **Pets:** Accepted.

The Radisson Plaza-Warwick Hotel Philadelphia LH
(215) 735-6000. **$189-$389.** 1701 Locust St. Jct 17th and Locust sts. Int corridors. **Pets:** Small, dogs only. $50 one-time fee/room. Designated rooms, service with restrictions, crate.

Residence Inn by Marriott Philadelphia City Center LH
(215) 557-0005. **$308-$328.** 1 E Penn Square. Jct Market and Juniper sts. Int corridors. **Pets:** Accepted.

The Rittenhouse Hotel and Condominium Residences LH
(215) 546-9000. **$450-$480.** 210 W Rittenhouse Square. On Rittenhouse Square. Int corridors. **Pets:** Service with restrictions, supervision.

The Ritz-Carlton Philadelphia LH ❀
(215) 523-8000. **Call for rates.** Ten Avenue of the Arts. On Broad St; between Market and Chestnut. Int corridors. **Pets:** $75 one-time fee/room.

The Sheraton Philadelphia City Center Hotel LH
(215) 448-2000. **$359-$379.** 2 Franklin Plaza. Jct 17th and Race sts. Int corridors. **Pets:** Accepted.

Sheraton Society Hill LH ❀
(215) 238-6000. **$329.** One Dock St. Just s of jct 2nd and Walnut sts. Int corridors. **Pets:** Medium, dogs only. Service with restrictions, crate.

Sheraton Suites Philadelphia Airport LH
(215) 365-6600. **$269.** 4101 Island Ave. Jct I-95 and SR 291, exit 13 northbound; exit 15 southbound. Int corridors. **Pets:** Medium, dogs only. Service with restrictions, supervision.

Sheraton University City LH
(215) 387-8000. **$185-$245.** 36th & Chestnut Sts. I-76 (Pennsylvania Tpke), exit 345, 0.5 mi w. Int corridors. **Pets:** Accepted.

Sofitel Philadelphia LH
(215) 569-8300. **$500-$620.** 120 S 17th St. Jct Sansom and 17th sts. Int corridors. **Pets:** Accepted.

The Westin Philadelphia LH
(215) 563-1600. **$499-$509.** 99 S 17th St at Liberty Pl. Between Market and Chestnut sts. Int corridors. **Pets:** Accepted.

PLYMOUTH MEETING

Extended StayAmerica-Philadelphia-Plymouth Meeting SH
(610) 260-0488. **$115-$135.** 437 Irwins Ln. I-276 (Pennslyvania Tpke), exit 333, follow signs for Plymouth Rd (Norristown), just w on Plymouth Rd, then just n. Int corridors. **Pets:** Other species. $75 one-time fee/pet. Service with restrictions.

POTTSTOWN

Comfort Inn SH
(610) 326-5000. **$104-$139.** 99 Robinson St. SR 100, 1 mi n of jct US 422. Int corridors. **Pets:** Other species. $10 daily fee/room. Designated rooms, service with restrictions, supervision.

QUAKERTOWN

Comfort Inn & Suites SH ❀
(215) 538-3000. **$89-$169.** 1905 John Fries Hwy (SR 663). I-476 (Pennsylvania Tpke), exit 44, just e. Ext corridors. **Pets:** Other species. $25 one-time fee/room. Designated rooms, service with restrictions, supervision.

Hampton Inn-Quakertown SH
(215) 536-7779. **$139-$149.** 1915 John Fries Hwy (SR 663). I-476 (Pennsylvania Tpke), exit 44, just e. Int corridors. **Pets:** Medium. $10 daily fee/pet. Service with restrictions, supervision.

TREVOSE

Red Roof Inn #7185 M
(215) 244-9422. **Call for rates.** 3100 Lincoln Hwy. I-276 (Pennsylvania Tpke), exit 351, 0.5 mi s on US 1 at US 132. Ext corridors. **Pets:** Accepted.

UPPER BLACK EDDY

▼▼▼▼ **The Bridgeton House on the Delaware** BB ❖
(610) 982-5856. **$149-$429.** 1525 River Rd. On SR 32; center. Int corridors. **Pets:** Small, dogs only. $100 deposit/pet. Designated rooms, service with restrictions, supervision.
⊠ 🛗 💻

WEST CHESTER

⬥⬥⬥ ▼▼▼ **Microtel Inn & Suites** SH
(610) 738-9111. **$79-$114.** 500 Willowbrook Ln. Just se of US 202, exit Matlack St. Int corridors. **Pets:** Other species. $20 daily fee/pet. Service with restrictions, supervision.
SAVE 🛍 ⊠ 🛗 🛗

END METROPOLITAN AREA

PHILIPSBURG

⬥⬥⬥ ▼ **Main Liner Motel** M
(814) 342-2004. **$39-$75.** 1896 Philipsburg Bigler (US 322 W) Hwy. 1 mi w of jct SR 53 N. Ext corridors. **Pets:** Accepted.
SAVE 🛍 ⊠ 🛗

PINE GROVE

⬥⬥⬥ ▼▼▼ **Comfort Inn** SH
(570) 345-8031. **$79-$140.** SR 443. I-81, exit 100. Int corridors. **Pets:** Other species. $10 daily fee/pet. Designated rooms, service with restrictions.
SAVE 🛍 ⊠ 🛗 🛗 💻 ⇄

▼▼▼▼ **Hampton Inn Pine Grove** SH
(570) 345-4505. **$79-$124.** 481 Suedberg Rd. I-81, exit 100. Int corridors. **Pets:** Service with restrictions, supervision.
ASK 🛍 ⊠ 🛗 🛗 💻 ⇄

PITTSBURGH METROPOLITAN AREA

BEAVER FALLS

▼▼▼▼ **Holiday Inn** SH
(724) 846-3700. **$139-$179.** 7195 Eastwood Rd. I-76 (Pennsylvania Tpke), exit 13, just n. Int corridors. **Pets:** Other species. $35 deposit/ room. Service with restrictions, supervision.
ASK 🛍 ⊠ 🛗 💻 🍴 ⇄ ⊠

BETHEL PARK

⬥⬥⬥ ▼▼▼▼ **Crowne Plaza Pittsburgh South** SH ❖
(412) 833-5300. **$109-$299.** 164 Ft Couch Rd. 1 mi n on US 19. Int corridors. **Pets:** Medium. $50 one-time fee/pet. Designated rooms, service with restrictions, supervision.
SAVE 🛍 ⊠ 🛗 💻 🍴 ⇄

BLAWNOX

▼▼▼▼ **Holiday Inn Hotel & Suites-RIDC Park** SH
(412) 963-0600. **$119-$129.** 180 Gamma Dr. I-76 (Pennsylvania Tpke), exit 48, 3.3 mi s; SR 28, RIDC, exit 10. Int corridors. **Pets:** Small. Designated rooms, service with restrictions, supervision.
ASK 🛍 ⊠ 🛗 💻 🍴 ⇄

BUTLER

▼▼▼ **Comfort Inn** SH
(724) 287-7177. **$90-$190.** 1 Comfort Ln. 4 mi s on SR 8. Int corridors. **Pets:** $20 daily fee/room. Service with restrictions, crate.
ASK 🛍 ⊠ 🛗 💻 ⇄

▼▼▼ **Days Inn Butler** SH
(724) 287-6761. **$79-$84.** 139 Pittsburgh Rd. 2 mi s. Int corridors. **Pets:** Accepted.
ASK 🛍 ⊠ 🛗 💻 🍴 ⇄ ⊠

▼▼▼ **Locust Brook Lodge** BB
(724) 283-8453. **$85-$150.** 179 Eagle Mill Rd. 5 mi w on US 422 to jct Eagle Mill Rd, then 0.8 mi s; I-79, exit 99, 10 mi e on US 422 to jct Eagle Mill Rd, then 0.8 mi s. Ext/int corridors. **Pets:** Large, other species. Designated rooms, no service, supervision.
ASK 🛍 ⊠

▼ **Super 8 Motel** M
(724) 287-8888. **$59-$65.** 138 Pittsburgh Rd. 2 mi s. Int corridors. **Pets:** Medium. $10 daily fee/pet. Designated rooms, service with restrictions, supervision.
ASK 🛍 ⊠ 🛗

CANONSBURG

▼▼ **Super 8 Motel** M
(724) 873-8808. **Call for rates.** 8 Curry Ave. I-79, exit 45, follow signs. Int corridors. **Pets:** Accepted.
⊠ 🛗 💻

CARNEGIE

▼▼ ⬥ **Extended StayAmerica-Pittsburgh-Carnegie** SH
(412) 278-4001. **$75-$90.** 520 N Bell Ave. I-279, exit 1B (Rosslyn exit), just se. Int corridors. **Pets:** Other species. $75 one-time fee/pet. Service with restrictions.
ASK 🛍 ⊠ 🛗 💻

CORAOPOLIS

▼ **Americas Best Value Inn-Pittsburgh Airport** M
(412) 604-2378. **Call for rates.** 8858 University Blvd. 0.5 mi n of Business Rt SR 60. Ext corridors. **Pets:** Accepted.
⊠ 🛗

⬥⬥⬥ ▼▼▼▼ **Crowne Plaza Hotel Pittsburgh International** LH
(412) 262-2400. **$99-$199.** 1160 Thorn Run Rd. Business Rt SR 60, exit Thorn Run Rd. Int corridors. **Pets:** Accepted.
SAVE 🛍 ⊠ 🛗 💻 🍴 ⇄

⬥⬥⬥ ▼▼▼▼ **Embassy Suites-Pittsburgh International Airport** LH ❖
(412) 269-9070. **$129-$289.** 550 Cherrington Pkwy. Business Rt SR 60, exit Thorn Run Rd. Int corridors. **Pets:** Other species. $50 one-time fee/room. Service with restrictions, crate.
SAVE 🛍 ⊠ 🛗 🛗 💻 🍴 ⇄ ⊠

▼▼▼▼ **Hampton Inn Airport-Pittsburgh** SH
(412) 264-0020. **Call for rates.** 8514 University Blvd. Business Rt SR 60, 0.5 mi n. Int corridors. **Pets:** Accepted.
[X] [♿] [☕]

ⒶⒶⒶ▷ ▼▼▼▼ **Holiday Inn-Pittsburgh Airport** LH
(412) 262-3600. **$99-$199.** 8256 University Blvd. Business Rt SR 60, 1 mi n. Int corridors. **Pets:** Accepted.
[SAVE] [S♫] [X] [♿M] [♿] [☕] [¶] [⊷]

▼▼▼▼ **La Quinta Inn Pittsburgh (Airport)** SH
(412) 269-0400. **$89-$95.** 8507 University Blvd. 1 mi n of Business Rt SR 60. Int corridors. **Pets:** Other species. Service with restrictions, supervision.
[ASK] [S♫] [X] [♿M] [♿] [☕]

CRANBERRY TOWNSHIP

▼▼▼▼ **Holiday Inn Express** SH
(724) 772-1000. **Call for rates.** 20003 Rt 19. I-76 (Pennsylvania Tpke), exit 28, jct US 19 and I-76 (Pennsylvania Tpke); I-79, exit 76 northbound; exit 78 southbound, just s. Int corridors. **Pets:** Accepted.
[X] [♿] [☕]

▼▼▼▼ **Pittsburgh Marriott North** LH
(724) 772-3700. **$187-$207.** 100 Cranberry Woods Dr. I-79, exit 78 (SR 228) to Cranberry Woods Dr. Int corridors. **Pets:** Medium, dogs only. $75 one-time fee/room. Designated rooms, service with restrictions, supervision.
[ASK] [S♫] [X] [♿M] [♿] [☕] [¶] [⊷]

▼▼ **Red Roof Inn-Cranberry Township-Pittsburgh North #7079** M
(724) 776-5670. **Call for rates.** 20009 Rt 19. I-76 (Pennsylvania Tpke), exit 28; I-79, exit 76 northbound; exit 78 southbound. Ext corridors. **Pets:** Accepted.
[X] [♿]

▼▼▼▼ **Residence Inn Cranberry** SH 🐾
(724) 779-1000. **$132-$152.** 1308 Freedom Rd. I-76 (Pennsylvania Tpke), exit 28, 0.5 mi n on US 19, then 0.3 mi w; I-79, exit 78 southbound, 0.5 mi w. Int corridors. **Pets:** $75 one-time fee/room. Service with restrictions, supervision.
[ASK] [S♫] [X] [♿] [☕] [⊷] [X]

DELMONT

▼▼▼▼ **Super 8 Motel** M
(724) 468-4888. **Call for rates.** 180 Sheffield Dr. SR 66, just s of US 22. Int corridors. **Pets:** Accepted.
[X] [♿M] [♿]

GIBSONIA

▼▼▼ **Comfort Inn Gibsonia** M
(724) 444-8700. **$69-$149.** 5137 Rt 8. I-76 (Pennsylvania Tpke), exit 39, just n. Ext corridors. **Pets:** Other species. $10 daily fee/pet. Service with restrictions, supervision.
[ASK] [S♫] [X] [♿] [☕]

GREEN TREE

▼▼▼▼ **Hampton Inn Hotel Green Tree** SH
(412) 922-0100. **$109-$129.** 555 Trumbull Dr. I-279, exit 4A, northbound; exit 4B southbound, jct US 22 and 30, 1 mi nw via Mansfield Ave. Int corridors. **Pets:** Large. $25 one-time fee/room. Service with restrictions, supervision.
[ASK] [X] [♿] [☕]

ⒶⒶⒶ▷ ▼▼▼ **Quality Suites** SH
(412) 279-6300. **$99-$169.** 700 Mansfield Ave. I-279, exit 4A to jct US 22 and 30, 1.5 mi nw. Ext corridors. **Pets:** Accepted.
[SAVE] [S♫] [X] [♿] [☕] [⊷] [X]

ⒶⒶⒶ▷ ▼▼▼▼ **The Radisson Hotel Pittsburgh/Green Tree** LH
(412) 922-8400. **$99-$359.** 101 Radisson Dr. I-279, exit 4A to jct US 22 and 30, 1.1 mi nw via Mansfield Ave. Int corridors. **Pets:** Other species. $100 deposit/room. Designated rooms, service with restrictions, supervision.
[SAVE] [S♫] [X] [♿M] [♿] [☕] [¶] [⊷] [X]

MARS

▼▼▼ **Comfort Inn Cranberry Township** SH
(724) 772-2700. **$74-$150.** 924 Sheraton Dr. I-76 (Pennsylvania Tpke), exit 28; I-79, exit 76 (US 19 N) northbound; exit 78 southbound, 0.5 mi s on US 19. Int corridors. **Pets:** Accepted.
[ASK] [S♫] [X] [♿]

▼ **Motel 6 Pittsburgh North Cranberry #42** M
(724) 776-4333. **$45-$55.** 19025 Perry Hwy. I-76 (Pennsylvania Tpke), exit 28, jct US 19; I-79, exit 76 (US 19 N) northbound; exit 78 southbound on US 19. Ext corridors. **Pets:** Other species. Service with restrictions, supervision.
[S♫] [X] [♿]

MONACA

▼▼▼▼ **Hampton Inn Beaver Valley/Pittsburgh** SH
(724) 774-5580. **$119-$138.** 202 Fairview Dr. SR 60, exit 12, just n. Int corridors. **Pets:** Medium, other species. Service with restrictions, supervision.
[ASK] [S♫] [X] [♿] [☕] [⊷]

▼▼▼▼ **Holiday Inn Express Hotel & Suites-Center Township** SH
(724) 728-5121. **$99-$104.** 105 Stone Quarry Rd. SR 60, exit 12, just n. Int corridors. **Pets:** Accepted.
[ASK] [S♫] [X] [♿] [☕] [⊷]

MONROEVILLE

▼▼▼▼ **Comfort Inn Pittsburgh East** SH
(412) 244-1600. **$79-$159.** 699 Rodi Rd. I-376, exit 11, just n. Int corridors. **Pets:** Accepted.
[ASK] [S♫] [X] [♿] [☕] [¶] [⊷] [X]

▼▼▼ **Days Inn-Monroeville** M
(412) 856-1610. **$48-$99.** 2727 Mosside Blvd. I-76 (Pennsylvania Tpke), exit 57; I-376, exit 14A, 1 mi s on SR 48. Ext corridors. **Pets:** Dogs only. $10 daily fee/room. Service with restrictions, supervision.
[ASK] [X] [♿]

▼▼▼ **Extended StayAmerica-Pittsburgh-Monroeville** SH
(412) 856-8400. **$80-$95.** 3851 Northern Pike. I-76 (Pennsylvania Tpke), exit 57 (Monroeville), 1.2 mi w on Business Rt 22. Int corridors. **Pets:** Other species. $75 one-time fee/pet. Service with restrictions.
[ASK] [S♫] [X] [♿] [☕]

▼▼▼▼ **Hampton Inn Monroeville/Pittsburgh** SH
(412) 380-4000. **Call for rates.** 3000 Mosside Blvd. I-76 (Pennsylvania Tpke), exit 57; I-376, exit 14A, 0.3 mi s on SR 48. Int corridors. **Pets:** Accepted.
[X] [♿] [☕] [⊷]

▼▼▼ **Red Roof Inn-Monroeville #7174** M
(412) 856-4738. **Call for rates.** 2729 Mosside Blvd. I-76 (Pennsylvania Tpke), exit 57; I-376, exit 14A, 0.8 mi s on SR 48. Ext corridors. **Pets:** Accepted.
[X] [♿]

▼▼▼ **Super 8 Motel Pittsburgh/Monroeville** M 🐾
(724) 733-8008. **Call for rates.** 1807 Rt 286. I-76 (Pennsylvania Tpke), exit 57; I-376, exit 14A, 2 mi e on US 22 E, then 2 mi e. Int corridors. **Pets:** Other species. $10 daily fee/pet. Designated rooms, service with restrictions, supervision.
[X] [♿]

MOON RUN

AAA ▼▼▼ Comfort Inn-Pittsburgh Airport SH
(412) 787-2600. **$74-$124.** 7011 Old Steubenville Pike. US 22 and 30, jct SR 60; 4 mi w of jct I-279 and 79. Ext/int corridors. **Pets:** Other species. $15 daily fee/pet. Designated rooms, service with restrictions, supervision.
SAVE S X ⊟ ▣ ⊞

AAA ▼▼▼ Days Inn Pittsburgh International Airport SH
(412) 859-4000. **$70-$80.** 2500 Marketplace Blvd. SR 60, exit 2 (Montour Run Rd), 0.5 mi e, then 0.5 mi n. Int corridors. **Pets:** Accepted.
SAVE S X ⊟ ▣ ⊷

▼▼ Extended Stay Deluxe Pittsburgh Airport SH
(412) 490-0979. **$100-$115.** 200 Chauvet Dr. SR 60, exit 1, just s. Int corridors. **Pets:** Other species. $75 one-time fee/pet. Service with restrictions.
ASK S X ⊟ ▣ ⊷

▼▼▼ Four Points by Sheraton Pittsburgh Airport SH
(724) 695-0002. **$95-$205.** 1 Industry Ln. SR 60, exit 2 (Montour Run Rd). Int corridors. **Pets:** Accepted.
ASK S X ⊟ ▣ ⊞ ⊷

AAA ▼▼▼ Holiday Inn Express Pittsburgh Airport SH
(412) 788-8400. **Call for rates.** 5311 Campbells Run Rd. US 22 and 30 W, exit Crafton (SR 60) S, just w. Int corridors. **Pets:** Accepted.
SAVE X ⊟ ▣ ⊷

▼ Motel 6 Pittsburgh #657 M
(412) 922-9400. **$45-$55.** 211 Beecham Dr. I-79, exit 60A, just s on Steubenville Pike (SR 60), then e. Ext corridors. **Pets:** Other species. Service with restrictions, supervision.
S X ⊾M

AAA ▼▼▼ Pittsburgh Airport Marriott LH
(412) 788-8800. **$230-$263.** 777 Aten Rd. SR 60, exit 2 (Montour Run Rd). Int corridors. **Pets:** Accepted.
SAVE S X ⊟ ▣ ⊞ ⊷ X

▼▼ Red Roof Inn South Airport #7030 M
(412) 787-7870. **Call for rates.** 6404 Steubenville Pike. I-79, exit 60A, 3.2 mi w on SR 60. Ext/int corridors. **Pets:** Accepted.
X ⊟

▼▼▼ Residence Inn-Pittsburgh Airport SH
(412) 787-3300. **$187-$207.** 1500 Park Lane Dr. SR 60, exit 2 (Montour Run Rd), just w on Cliff Mine Dr to Summit Park Dr,- just s to Park Lane Dr, then just e. Int corridors. **Pets:** Accepted.
ASK S X ⊾M ⊟ ▣ ⊷ X

NEW KENSINGTON

▼▼▼ Clarion Hotel SH
(724) 335-9171. **$77-$99, 3 day notice.** 300 Tarentum Bridge Rd. SR 366, 1.5 mi s of SR 28, exit 14; at south end of Tarentum Bridge. Int corridors. **Pets:** Other species. Service with restrictions, supervision.
ASK S X ⊟ ▣ ⊞ ⊷

PITTSBURGH

AAA ▼▼▼ Hilton Pittsburgh LH
(412) 391-4600. **Call for rates.** 600 Commonwealth Pl. Jct I-279/376/SR 885; in Gateway Center. Int corridors. **Pets:** Accepted.
SAVE X ⊾M ⊟ ▣ ⊞

▼▼▼ Omni William Penn Hotel LH
(412) 281-7100. **Call for rates.** 530 William Penn Pl. Jct 6th St and William Penn Pl. Int corridors. **Pets:** Accepted.
X ⊟ ▣ ⊞ X

AAA ▼▼▼ Residence Inn by Marriott Pittsburgh University/Medical Center SH
(412) 621-2200. **$197-$219.** 3896 Bigelow Blvd. On SR 380. Int corridors. **Pets:** Accepted.
SAVE S X ⊟ ▣ ⊷ X

▼▼▼ Sheraton Station Square Hotel LH 🐾
(412) 261-2000. **Call for rates.** 300 W Station Square St. I-376, exit Grant St, south end of Smithfield St Bridge; across river. Int corridors. **Pets:** Medium, dogs only. Service with restrictions, supervision.
X ⊟ ▣ ⊞ ⊷ X

▼▼▼ The Westin Convention Center Pittsburgh LH 🐾
(412) 281-3700. **$159-$335.** 1000 Penn Ave. Jct 10th St; at Liberty Center. Int corridors. **Pets:** Other species. Service with restrictions, supervision.
ASK S X ⊟ ▣ ⊞ ⊷ X

▼▼▼ Wyndham Pittsburgh University Place LH
(412) 683-2040. **Call for rates.** 3454 Forbes Ave. Jct Forbes Ave and McKee Pl. Int corridors. **Pets:** Accepted.
X ⊟ ▣ ⊞

WASHINGTON

AAA ▼▼▼ Ramada Inn SH
(724) 225-9750. **$75-$125.** 1170 W Chestnut St. I-70, exit 15, 0.5 mi e on US 40. Ext/int corridors. **Pets:** Small. $30 one-time fee/room. Designated rooms, service with restrictions, crate.
SAVE S X ⊟ ▣ ⊞ ⊷

▼▼ Red Roof Inn #7048 M
(724) 228-5750. **Call for rates.** 1399 W Chestnut St. I-70, exit 15, just e on US 40. Ext/int corridors. **Pets:** Accepted.
X ⊟

WEST MIFFLIN

▼▼ Comfort Inn-West Mifflin SH
(412) 653-6600. **$80-$165.** 1340 Lebanon Church Rd. 0.6 mi e of jct SR 51. Int corridors. **Pets:** $10 daily fee/room. Designated rooms, service with restrictions, supervision.
ASK S X ⊟ ▣ ⊷

▼▼ Extended StayAmerica-Pittsburgh-West Mifflin SH
(412) 650-9096. **$75-$85.** 1303 Lebanon Churck Rd. 0.5 mi e of jct SR 51. Int corridors. **Pets:** Other species. $75 one-time fee/pet. Service with restrictions.
ASK S X ⊟ ▣

▼▼▼ Holiday Inn Express Hotel & Suites SH
(412) 469-1900. **$105.** 3122 Lebanon Church Rd. 1.5 mi e of jct SR 51. Int corridors. **Pets:** Other species. $10 daily fee/pet. Service with restrictions, crate.
ASK S X ⊟ ▣

END METROPOLITAN AREA

PITTSTON

AAA' ▼▼▼ Knights Inn-Scranton/Pittston M
(570) 654-6020. **Call for rates.** 310 SR 315. I-81, exit 175 northbound, just s on SR 315; exit 175A southbound; I-476 (Northeast Extension Pennslyvania Tpke), exit 115. Ext corridors. **Pets:** Very small. Service with restrictions, supervision.
[SAVE] [X] [🔲]

POCONO MOUNTAINS AREA

BLAKESLEE

AAA' ▼▼▼▼ Best Western Inn-Blakeslee/Pocono SH
(570) 646-6000. **$70-$175.** New Ventures Business Park. I-80, exit 284, just n. Int corridors. **Pets:** $50 deposit/room. Service with restrictions, supervision.
[SAVE] [S🔒] [X] [&M] [🔲] [💻] [⇔]

EAST STROUDSBURG

AAA' ▼▼▼▼ Budget Inn & Suites SH
(570) 424-5451. **$67-$106, 3 day notice.** I-80, exit 308. I-80, exit 308, just se on Greentree Rd. Ext/int corridors. **Pets:** Medium. $50 deposit/room. Designated rooms, service with restrictions, supervision.
[SAVE] [S🔒] [X] [🔲] [🍽]

▼▼▼ Super 8 Motel M
(570) 424-7411. **Call for rates.** 340 Greentree Dr. I-80, exit 308, just se. Int corridors. **Pets:** $10 daily fee/pet. Designated rooms, service with restrictions, supervision.
[X] [&M] [🔲]

LAKE HARMONY

AAA' ▼▼▼ Ramada Inn-Pocono SH
(570) 443-8471. **Call for rates.** Rt 940. I-80, exit 277, 0.5 mi e; I-476 (Northeast Extension Pennsylvania Tpke), exit 95 (Pocono). Int corridors. **Pets:** Accepted.
[SAVE] [X] [🔲] [💻] [🍽] [⇔] [X]

MARSHALLS CREEK

AAA' ▼ Value Inn M
(570) 588-1100. **$45-$129.** 5219 Milford Rd, Rt 209. I-80, exit 309, 7.9 mi n on SR 209. Ext corridors. **Pets:** Accepted.
[SAVE] [S🔒] [X] [🔲] [⇔] [X]

MILFORD

AAA' ▼▼▼ Hotel Fauchere SH ❀
(570) 409-1212. **$275-$350, 4 day notice.** 401 Broad St. Downtown; in historic Milford. Int corridors. **Pets:** $15 daily fee/pet. Service with restrictions, supervision.
[SAVE] [X] [🍽]

AAA' ▼▼▼ Milford Motel M
(570) 296-6411. **$45-$110, 3 day notice.** 591 Rt 6 & 209. On US 6 and 209 N, 0.7 mi e. Ext corridors. **Pets:** Accepted.
[SAVE] [S🔒] [X] [🔲]

AAA' ▼▼▼ Red Carpet Inn-Milford M
(570) 296-9444. **$55-$125, 7 day notice.** 240 Rt 6. I-84, exit 46, just s. Ext corridors. **Pets:** Medium. $10 daily fee/pet. Designated rooms, no service, supervision.
[SAVE] [S🔒] [X] [🔲]

AAA' ▼▼ Scottish Inns M
(570) 491-4414. **$50-$100.** 274 Rt 6 & 209. I-84, exit 53, 1 mi s. Ext corridors. **Pets:** Accepted.
[SAVE] [S🔒] [X] [🔲] [💻]

STARLIGHT

▼▼ The Inn at Starlight Lake CI
(570) 798-2519. **$115-$195, 14 day notice.** 289 Starlight Lake Rd. Off SR 370, 1 mi n, follow signs. Ext/int corridors. **Pets:** Accepted.
[ASK] [X] [🍽] [X] [🎿] [🐾] [☎]

END AREA

PUNXSUTAWNEY

▼▼▼ Pantall Hotel SH
(814) 938-6600. **$54-$99.** 135 E Mahoning St. On US 119/SR 36; downtown. Int corridors. **Pets:** Medium. $20 one-time fee/pet. Designated rooms, service with restrictions, supervision.
[ASK] [S🔒] [X] [🔲] [🍽]

READING

AAA' ▼▼▼ Quality Inn Airport SH
(610) 736-0400. **Call for rates.** 2017 Bernville Rd. US 222, exit SR 183, 2 mi s. Int corridors. **Pets:** Small. $20 one-time fee/pet. Designated rooms, service with restrictions, supervision.
[SAVE] [X] [🔲] [💻]

ST. MARYS

▼▼ Comfort Inn SH
(814) 834-2030. **$81-$89.** 195 Comfort Ln. 1.8 mi s of center on SR 255, just w. Int corridors. **Pets:** Other species. $15 daily fee/pet. Service with restrictions, supervision.
[ASK] [S🔒] [X] [🔲] [💻] [⇔]

SAYRE

AAA' ▼▼▼ Best Western Grand Victorian SH
(570) 888-7711. **Call for rates.** 255 Spring St. SR 17, exit 61, just s. Int corridors. **Pets:** Small. $25 deposit/pet. Designated rooms, service with restrictions, supervision.
[SAVE] [X] [🔲] [💻] [🍽] [⇔] [X]

SCRANTON

▼▼▼ Clarion Hotel LH
(570) 344-9811. **$79-$139.** 300 Meadow Ave. I-81, exit 184, just w. Int corridors. **Pets:** Accepted.
[ASK] [S🔒] [X] [🔲] [💻] [🍽] [⇔] [X]

▼▼▼ Hilton Scranton & Conference Center LH
(570) 343-3000. **$99-$199.** 100 Adams Ave. I-81, exit 185, just w of jct Lackawanna Ave, Jefferson Ave and Spruce St; downtown. Int corridors. **Pets:** Medium. $50 deposit/room. Designated rooms, service with restrictions, supervision.
[ASK] [S🔒] [X] [&M] [🔲] [💻] [🍽] [⇔]

SELINSGROVE

Comfort Inn SH
(570) 374-8880. **$79-$179.** 613 N Susquehanna Tr. On US 11 and 15, just n of jct US 522. Int corridors. **Pets:** Accepted.

SHAMOKIN DAM

Econo Lodge Inn & Suites SH
(570) 743-1111. **$59-$169.** 3249 N Susquehanna Tr. US 11 and 15; just n of jct SR 61. Ext corridors. **Pets:** Small, other species. $10 daily fee/pet. Designated rooms, service with restrictions, crate.

Hampton Inn SH
(570) 743-2223. **Call for rates.** 3 Stettler Ave. US 11 and 15, 1 mi s of jct SR 61. Int corridors. **Pets:** Other species. $25 one-time fee/room. Designated rooms, service with restrictions, supervision.

SHICKSHINNY

The Blue Heron Bed & Breakfast BB
(570) 864-3740. **$60-$90 (no credit cards), 7 day notice.** 1270 Bethel Hill Rd. Jct US 11, 6.2 mi n on SR 239, then 2 mi n on CR 4016 (Harveyville/Bethel Hill Rd). Int corridors. **Pets:** Accepted.

SHIPPENSBURG

Best Western Shippensburg Hotel SH
(717) 532-5200. **$62-$109.** 125 Walnut Bottom Rd. I-81, exit 29, 0.5 mi w on SR 174. Int corridors. **Pets:** Small. $10 daily fee/pet. Designated rooms, service with restrictions, crate.

SOUTH WILLIAMSPORT

Quality Inn Williamsport SH
(570) 323-9801. **$59-$219.** 234 US Hwy 15. 0.8 mi s on US 15. Int corridors. **Pets:** Accepted.

Ridgemont Motel M
(570) 321-5300. **$39-$55.** 637 Rt 15 Hwy. 1.2 mi s on US 15. Ext corridors. **Pets:** Accepted.

STATE COLLEGE

The Autoport Motel & Restaurant Inc SH
(814) 237-7666. **Call for rates.** 1405 S Atherton St. US 322 business route, 1.4 mi e of jct SR 26. Ext/int corridors. **Pets:** Accepted.

Days Inn Penn State LH
(814) 238-8454. **$69-$129.** 240 S Pugh St. Just e of SR 26 northbound; 0.4 mi n of jct US 322 business route; downtown. Int corridors. **Pets:** $10 daily fee/pet. Service with restrictions, supervision.

Motel 6 State College#4101 M
(814) 234-1600. **Call for rates.** 1274 N Atherton St. US 322, 1 mi w of jct SR 26. Int corridors. **Pets:** Other species. Service with restrictions, supervision.

Nittany Budget Motel M
(814) 238-0015. **Call for rates.** 2070 Cato Ave. SR 26, 2.6 mi s of jct US 322 business route. Ext corridors. **Pets:** Accepted.

Residence Inn by Marriott SH
(814) 235-6960. **$126-$152.** 1555 University Dr. US 322 business route, 1.5 mi e of jct SR 26. Int corridors. **Pets:** Accepted.

Super 8 State College SH
(814) 237-8005. **$56-$76.** 1663 S Atherton St. US 322 business route, 1.6 mi e of jct SR 26. Int corridors. **Pets:** Accepted.

TOWN HILL

Days Inn Breezewood SH
(814) 735-3860. **$53-$68.** 9648 Old Rt 126. I-70, exit 156, just n. Int corridors. **Pets:** $10 daily fee/pet. Designated rooms, supervision.

WARREN

Holiday Inn of Warren SH
(814) 726-3000. **$114.** 210 Ludlow St. Jct US 6, just n on Ludlow St (US 62 N). Int corridors. **Pets:** Accepted.

Warren Super 8 Motel SH
(814) 723-8881. **Call for rates.** 204 Struthers St. 1.5 mi w on US 6, exit Ludlow St, w on Allegheny, then s. Ext/int corridors. **Pets:** Accepted.

WAYNESBORO

Best Western of Waynesboro M
(717) 762-9113. **Call for rates.** 239 W Main St. 0.5 mi w on SR 16. Ext corridors. **Pets:** Small. $20 daily fee/pet. Designated rooms, service with restrictions, supervision.

WAYNESBURG

Comfort Inn SH
(724) 627-3700. **Call for rates.** 100 Comfort Ln. I-79, exit 14, just e. Int corridors. **Pets:** Accepted.

Econo Lodge M
(724) 627-5544. **$63-$69.** 126 Miller Ln. I-79, exit 14, just w. Ext corridors. **Pets:** Accepted.

Super 8 Motel-Waynesburg M
(724) 627-8880. **Call for rates.** 100 Stanley Dr. I-79, exit 14, just w. Int corridors. **Pets:** Accepted.

WELLSBORO

Penn Wells Lodge M
(570) 724-3463. **$60-$127.** 4 Main St. Just n on US 6 and SR 287. Ext/int corridors. **Pets:** Accepted.

WEST HAZLETON

Comfort Inn Hazleton/West Hazleton SH
(570) 455-9300. **$79-$169.** 58 SR 93. I-81, exit 145, 0.3 mi se; I-80, exit 256, 3.8 mi se. Int corridors. **Pets:** Other species. Service with restrictions.

WEST MIDDLESEX

Super 8 Motel-West Middlesex/Sharon SH
(724) 528-3888. **Call for rates.** 3369 New Castle Rd. I-80, exit 4B (SR 60), just w to SR 18, then just s. Int corridors. **Pets:** Accepted.

WILKES-BARRE

Best Western Genetti Hotel & Conference Center SH
(570) 823-6152. **$94-$114.** 77 E Market St. Jct Washington St; downtown. Int corridors. **Pets:** Medium, other species. $10 one-time fee/pet. Designated rooms, service with restrictions, crate.

Days Inn SH
(570) 826-0111. **$50-$175.** 760 Kidder St. I-81, exit 170B, exit 1 (SR 309 S business route), just w; I-76 (Pennsylvania Tpke), exit 105, exit 1 (SR 115 N). Int corridors. **Pets:** Small, dogs only. $50 deposit/room, $10 daily fee/pet. Designated rooms, service with restrictions, supervision.

Econo Lodge SH
(570) 823-0600. **$59-$179.** 1075 Wilkes-Barre Township Blvd. I-81, exit 165 southbound; exit 165B northbound, on SR 309 business route. Int corridors. **Pets:** Large, other species. $50 deposit/room, $10 daily fee/pet. Designated rooms, service with restrictions, supervision.

Extended Stay Deluxe SH
(570) 970-2500. **Call for rates (no credit cards).** 1067 Hwy 315. I-81, exit 170B, 0.3 mi n. Int corridors. **Pets:** Other species. $75 one-time fee/pet. Service with restrictions.

Host Inn All Suites Hotel SH
(570) 270-4678. **Call for rates.** 860 Kidder St. I-81, exit 170B to exit 1 (SR 309 S business route) off expressway, then 0.5 mi w. Int corridors. **Pets:** Medium, other species. $15 one-time fee/pet. Service with restrictions, crate.

Red Roof Inn #7139 M
(570) 829-6422. **Call for rates.** 1035 Hwy 315. I-81, exit 170B, jct SR 115, 0.7 mi w, exit 1 (SR 309 S business route) to SR 315, then just n. Ext corridors. **Pets:** Accepted.

The Woodlands Inn & Resort LH
(570) 824-9831. **$119-$199.** 1073 Hwy 315. I-81, exit 170B to exit 1 (SR 309 S business route), then 0.3 mi n. Int corridors. **Pets:** Accepted.

WILLIAMSPORT

Best Western Williamsport Inn SH
(570) 326-1981. **$70-$180, 14 day notice.** 1840 E Third St. I-180, exit 25 (Faxon St), just e; 1 mi w of W 3rd St. Ext corridors. **Pets:** Large. $15 one-time fee/pet. Service with restrictions, crate.

Candlewood Suites SH
(570) 601-9100. **$89-$259.** 1836 E Third St. I-180, exit 25 (Faxon St), 0.5 mi e. Int corridors. **Pets:** Large, other species. $75 one-time fee/room. Service with restrictions, supervision.

Econo Lodge M
(570) 326-1501. **Call for rates.** 2019 E Third St. I-180, exit 25 (Faxon St) eastbound, 0.8 mi e, just n on Westminster St; exit 23 (3rd St) westbound, 0.3 mi w. Ext corridors. **Pets:** Dogs only. $10 daily fee/room.

Genetti Hotel & Suites SH
(570) 326-6600. **$71-$195, 7 day notice.** 200 W Fourth St. Jct William St; downtown. Ext/int corridors. **Pets:** Accepted.

Holiday Inn Downtown Williamsport SH
(570) 327-8231. **$89-$149.** 100 Pine St. Jct US 220 and SR 15 S; downtown. Int corridors. **Pets:** Accepted.

WIND GAP

Red Carpet Inn M
(610) 863-7782. **$50-$135.** 1395 Jacobsburg Rd. SR 33, exit Wind Gap/Bath SR 512 S, just s on Jacobsburg Rd, follow signs. Ext/int corridors. **Pets:** Accepted.

WYOMISSING

Econo Lodge SH
(610) 378-5105. **$65-$140, 3 day notice.** 635 Spring St. Just off US 422, exit Papermill Rd. Int corridors. **Pets:** Small. $15 daily fee/pet. Designated rooms, service with restrictions, supervision.

Homewood Suites-Reading/Wyomissing SH
(610) 736-3100. **Call for rates.** 2801 Papermill Rd. US 422, exit Papermill Rd, 1.8 mi nw; US 222, exit Spring Ridge Rd. Int corridors. **Pets:** Accepted.

The Inn at Reading SH
(610) 372-7811. **$83-$145.** 1040 Park Rd. US 222, exit N Wyomissing Blvd, just n, then 0.3 mi e. Int corridors. **Pets:** Accepted.

Sheraton Reading Hotel SH
(610) 376-3811. **$259.** 1741 W Papermill Rd. US 422, exit Papermill Rd. Int corridors. **Pets:** Accepted.

WYSOX

Comfort Inn SH
(570) 265-5691. **$115.** US 6. On US 6; center. Int corridors. **Pets:** Other species. $20 one-time fee/room. Service with restrictions, supervision.

YORK

Budget Host Inn M
(717) 755-1068. **$54-$59.** 1162 Haines Rd. I-83, exit 18, just e on SR 124. Ext corridors. **Pets:** Dogs only. $25 deposit/pet. Service with restrictions, supervision.

Holiday Inn Conference Center of York SH
(717) 846-9500. **Call for rates.** 2000 Loucks Rd. I-83, exit 21B northbound, 2.5 mi w on US 30, then just n; exit 22 southbound, 0.5 mi s on SR 181, 2.2 mi w on US 30, then just n. Int corridors. **Pets:** Accepted.

Red Roof Inn #315 M
(717) 843-8181. **Call for rates.** 125 Arsenal Rd. I-83, exit 21B northbound, 0.3 mi w on US 30; exit 21 southbound, 0.5 mi s on SR 181 to US 30. Int corridors. **Pets:** Accepted.

RHODE ISLAND

EAST PROVIDENCE

Extended StayAmerica Providence-East Providence SH
(401) 272-1661. **$107-$160.** 1000 Warren Ave. I-195, exit 8 eastbound, just e; exit 6 westbound, 1.1 mi e via Warren Ave. Int corridors. **Pets:** Other species. $75 one-time fee/pet. Service with restrictions.

MIDDLETOWN

Econo Lodge M
(401) 849-2718. **Call for rates.** 1359 W Main Rd. On SR 114, just n of jct SR 214. Int corridors. **Pets:** Accepted.

Howard Johnson Inn-Newport SH
(401) 849-2000. **$49-$254.** 351 W Main Rd. On SR 114, 0.3 mi s of jct SR 138. Int corridors. **Pets:** Other species. $10 daily fee/pet. Designated rooms, service with restrictions, supervision.

Residence Inn by Marriott-Newport/Middletown SH
(401) 845-2005. **$99-$319, 3 day notice.** 325 W Main Rd. On SR 114, 0.3 mi s of jct SR 138. Int corridors. **Pets:** Other species. $100 one-time fee/room. Designated rooms, service with restrictions.

SeaView Inn M
(401) 324-6200. **$59-$199, 7 day notice.** 240 Aquidneck Ave (SR 138A). Jct SR 214. Ext corridors. **Pets:** $10 daily fee/pet. Designated rooms, service with restrictions, supervision.

NEWPORT

Beech Tree Inn BB
(401) 847-9794. **$125-$350, 14 day notice.** 34 Rhode Island Ave. Just e of SR 114; 0.8 mi s of jct SR 138. Int corridors. **Pets:** Other species. $25 daily fee/pet. Designated rooms, no service, crate.

The Burbank Rose BB
(401) 849-9457. **$89-$240.** 111 Memorial Blvd W. Just e on SR 138A. Int corridors. **Pets:** Accepted.

The Hotel Viking LH
(401) 847-3300. **$109-$499, 7 day notice.** One Bellevue Ave. Corner of Kay St, Church and Bellevue Ave. Int corridors. **Pets:** Large. $75 one-time fee/room. Designated rooms, service with restrictions, crate.

Hyatt Regency Newport Hotel & Spa LH
(401) 851-1234. **$119-$479, 3 day notice.** 1 Goat Island. 0.8 mi w of America's Cup Ave, follow signs to Goat Island. Int corridors. **Pets:** Other species. $75 one-time fee/room. Service with restrictions.

NORTH KINGSTOWN

Hamilton Village Inn M
(401) 295-0700. **$79-$129, 7 day notice.** 642 Boston Neck Rd. SR 1A, 1.3 mi s of jct SR 102. Ext corridors. **Pets:** Other species. Designated rooms, service with restrictions, supervision.

PROVIDENCE

The Hotel Providence SH
(401) 861-8000. **$249-$349.** 311 Westminster St. I-95, exit 22A, 0.5 mi se on Memorial Blvd, then 0.3 mi sw; entrance on Mathewson St. Int corridors. **Pets:** Very small. $75 one-time fee/room. Service with restrictions, supervision.

Marriott Providence Downtown LH
(401) 272-2400. **$263-$285.** One Orms St. I-95, exit 23 to state offices. Int corridors. **Pets:** Accepted.

The Westin Providence LH
(401) 598-8000. **$149-$419.** One W Exchange St. I-95, exit 22A; downtown. Int corridors. **Pets:** Medium, dogs only. $75 one-time fee/room. Service with restrictions, supervision.

WAKEFIELD

The Kings' Rose Inn BB
(401) 783-5222. **$150-$175, 7 day notice.** 1747 Mooresfield Rd (SR 138). I-95, exit 3A, 11 mi e on SR 138; 3.3 mi w of US 1. Int corridors. **Pets:** Large. Service with restrictions, supervision.

WARWICK

Best Western Airport Inn SH
(401) 737-7400. **$89-$125.** 2138 Post Rd. I-95, exit 13, e to US 1, then just ne. Int corridors. **Pets:** Small. $15 daily fee/room. Designated rooms, service with restrictions, supervision.

Crowne Plaza Hotel at the Crossings LH
(401) 732-6000. **$129-$179.** 801 Greenwich Ave. I-95, exit 12A southbound; exit 12 northbound, 0.3 mi se on SR 5. Int corridors. **Pets:** Small. $50 one-time fee/room. Service with restrictions, supervision.

Extended StayAmerica Providence-Airport-Warwick SH
(401) 732-2547. **$100-$155.** 245 W Natick Rd. I-295, exit 2 northbound; just sw; exit 3A southbound, 1.1 mi e on SR 37, 2 mi s on SR 2, then just sw. Int corridors. **Pets:** Other species. $75 one-time fee/pet. Service with restrictions.

Hampton Inn & Suites Providence-Warwick Airport SH
(401) 739-8888. **$119-$199.** 2100 Post Rd. I-95, exit 13, e to US 1, then just n. Int corridors. **Pets:** Accepted.

Holiday Inn Express Hotel & Suites SH
(401) 736-5000. **$104-$162.** 901 Jefferson Blvd. I-95, exit 13, 0.4 mi on Airport Connector Rd, then exit Jefferson Blvd. Int corridors. **Pets:** Large, other species. Service with restrictions, supervision.

Homestead Studio Suites
Hotel-Providence/Airport/Warwick 🆂🅷
(401) 732-6667. **$107-$160.** 268 Metro Center Blvd. I-95, exit 12A, 0.4
mi e on SR 113, 0.4 mi n on SR 5, then 0.4 mi e. Int corridors.
Pets: Other species. $75 one-time fee/pet. Service with restrictions.

ⒶⓈⓀ 🆂⬛ ⓧ 🅜 ⬛ 🖵 ⬜

◆◆◆ Residence Inn by Marriott 🆂🅷
(401) 737-7100. **$187-$275.** 500 Kilvert St. I-95, exit 13 to Jefferson
Blvd, 0.4 mi n, then 0.6 mi w. Ext corridors. **Pets:** Accepted.

ⒶⓈⓀ 🆂⬛ ⓧ ⬛ 🖵 ≈ ⬜

◆◆◆ Sheraton Providence Airport Hotel 🅻🅷
(401) 738-4000. **$99-$179.** 1850 Post Rd. I-95, exit 13, 0.6 mi n on US
1. Int corridors. **Pets:** Accepted.

ⒶⓈⓀ 🆂⬛ ⓧ 🅜 ⬛ 🖵 🍴 ≈ ⬜

WEST WARWICK

◆ ◆ Extended StayAmerica Providence-Airport-West
Warwick 🆂🅷
(401) 885-3161. **$100-$155.** 1235 Division St. I-95, exit 8A northbound,
just s on SR 2, then just w; exit 8 southbound, just s on SR 2, then
just w. Int corridors. **Pets:** Other species. $75 one-time fee/pet. Service
with restrictions.

ⒶⓈⓀ 🆂⬛ ⓧ 🅜 ⬛ 🖵

WYOMING

🆎🅰🅰 ◆◆◆ Stagecoach House Inn 🅱🅱
(401) 539-9600. **$100-$199.** 1136 Main St (SR 138). I-95, exit 3B
northbound, 0.7 mi nw; exit southbound, 0.4 mi nw. Ext/int corridors.
Pets: Accepted.

🆂🅰🆅🅴 ⓧ ⬛ 🖵

SOUTH CAROLINA

AIKEN

◆ ▼▼◆ Econo Lodge Ⓜ
(803) 649-3968. **$55-$225.** 3560 Richland Ave W. Jct US 1/78 and SR 19, 2.6 mi w on US 1/78. Ext corridors. **Pets:** Accepted.
[SAVE] [S0] [X] [🅗] [💷] [🏊]

▼▼◆ Holiday Inn Express Ⓜ
(803) 648-0999. **$82-$275.** 155 Colony Pkwy/Whiskey Rd. Jct US 1/78 and SR 19, 1.8 mi s on SR 19. Ext corridors. **Pets:** Other species. $45 one-time fee/room. Service with restrictions, crate.
[ASK] [S0] [X] [🅗] [💷] [🏊] [X]

▼▼ Knights Inn Ⓜ
(803) 648-6821. **Call for rates.** 1850 Richland Ave W. Jct US 1/78 and SR 19, 1.6 mi w on US 1/78. Ext corridors. **Pets:** Accepted.
[X] [🅗] [💷] [🏊]

◆ ▼▼ Quality Inn & Suites Ⓢ🅗
(803) 641-1100. **$55-$80.** 3608 Richland Ave W. Jct US 1/78 and SR 19, 2.9 mi w on US 1/78. Ext corridors. **Pets:** Large. $10 daily fee/pet. Service with restrictions, supervision.
[SAVE] [S0] [X] [🅗] [💷] [🏊]

▼▼◆ The Town & Country Inn Bed, Breakfast and Stables Ⓑ🅑
(803) 642-0270. **Call for rates.** 2340 Sizemore Cir. Jct US 78 and SR 302/19 (Whiskey Rd), 2.3 mi s on SR 19, then just w. Int corridors. **Pets:** Accepted.
[X] [🏊] [🇿]

ANDERSON

▼▼◆ Country Inn & Suites Ⓢ🅗
(864) 622-2200. **$80-$89.** 116 Interstate Blvd. I-85, exit 19B, just n, then just se. Int corridors. **Pets:** Small. $25 daily fee/pet. Service with restrictions, supervision.
[ASK] [S0] [X] [♿M] [🅗] [💷] [🏊]

▼▼ Days Inn Ⓜ
(864) 375-0375. **Call for rates.** 1007 Smith Mill Rd. I-85, exit 19A, just se. Ext corridors. **Pets:** Small. $10 daily fee/pet. Service with restrictions, supervision.
[X] [♿M] [🅗] [💷] [🏊]

◆ ▼▼◆ Holiday Inn Express Ⓢ🅗
(864) 231-0231. **$75-$159.** 410 Alliance Pkwy. I-85, exit 27, just s on SR 81. Int corridors. **Pets:** Small, dogs only. $5 daily fee/room, $25 one-time fee/room. Service with restrictions, supervision.
[SAVE] [S0] [X] [♿M] [🅗] [💷] [🏊]

◆ ▼▼▼ La Quinta Inn Anderson Ⓢ🅗
(864) 225-3721. **$55-$85.** 3430 Clemson Blvd. I-85, exit 19A, 2.9 mi se on US 76/SR 28; exit 21 southbound, 2.6 mi s on US 178. Ext corridors. **Pets:** Other species. Service with restrictions, supervision.
[SAVE] [S0] [X] [🅗] [💷] [🏊]

BENNETTSVILLE

◆ ▼▼◆ Best Western Bennettsville Inn Ⓜ
(843) 479-1700. **$75-$105.** 213 US Hwy 15 & 401 Bypass E. 0.6 mi s of center, just ne on US 15/401/SR 9. Ext corridors. **Pets:** $10 daily fee/room. Service with restrictions, supervision.
[SAVE] [S0] [X] [🅗] [💷] [🏊]

BLUFFTON

◆ ▼▼◆ Holiday Inn Express Hotel & Suites Ⓢ🅗
(843) 757-2002. **$69-$139.** 35 Bluffton Rd. Jct William Hilton Pkwy (US 278/Bluffton Rd US 46), just se. Int corridors. **Pets:** Medium. $40 one-time fee/pet. Service with restrictions, supervision.
[SAVE] [S0] [X] [♿M] [🅗] [💷] [🏊]

▼▼◆▼◆ The Inn at Palmetto Bluff Ⓒ🅐
(843) 706-6500. **Call for rates (no credit cards).** 476 Mount Pelia Rd. Jct US 278/SR 170, 4.4 mi sw on SR 170 to SR 46, then 2.2 mi e to Palmetto Bluff Rd; check-in at gatehouse. Ext corridors. **Pets:** Accepted.
[X] [🅗] [💷] [🍽] [🏊] [X]

CAMDEN

◆ ▼▼▼ Colony Inn Ⓜ
(803) 432-5508. **$65-$75.** 2020 W DeKalb St. Jct US 521/1/601, 1.6 mi w on US 1/601. Ext/int corridors. **Pets:** Medium, dogs only. Designated rooms, service with restrictions, supervision.
[SAVE] [S0] [X] [🅗] [💷] [🍽] [🏊]

CAYCE

◆ ▼▼▼ Riverside Inn Ⓜ
(803) 939-4688. **$62.** 111 Knox Abbott Dr. US 21, just w of Congaree River Bridge. Ext corridors. **Pets:** $20 one-time fee/room. Service with restrictions, crate.
[SAVE] [S0] [X] [🅗] [💷] [🏊] [X]

CHARLESTON METROPOLITAN AREA

CHARLESTON

Best Western Charleston-Downtown 🏨 ❖
(843) 722-4000. **$79-$209.** 250 Spring St. I-26, exit 221A (US 17 S), 1.2 mi sw; just e of Ashley River. Int corridors. **Pets:** $25 daily fee/room. Service with restrictions, crate.

Best Western Sweetgrass Inn 🏨
(843) 571-6100. **$49-$199.** 1540 Savannah Hwy. US 17 S, 3.6 mi w of Ashley River Bridge; jct I-526 W (end) and US 17 N, 1.7 mi e. Ext corridors. **Pets:** Accepted.

The Inn at Middleton Place 🏨 ❖
(843) 556-0500. **Call for rates.** 4290 Ashley River Rd. I-526, exit 11 (Ashley River Rd/SR 61), then 10.3 mi on SR 61 N. Ext corridors. **Pets:** Medium. $50 one-time fee/pet. Designated rooms, service with restrictions, crate.

La Quinta Inn Riverview 🏨
(843) 556-5200. **$129-$179.** 11 Ashley Point Dr. US 17 S, just over Ashley River Bridge to Albermarle Rd, 0.4 mi s to Ashley Pointe Dr. Ext/int corridors. **Pets:** Other species. Service with restrictions, supervision.

Residence Inn by Marriott 🏨
(843) 571-7979. **$129-$149.** 90 Ripley Point Dr. US 17 S, just over Ashley River Bridge to Albermarle Rd, just s. Int corridors. **Pets:** Medium. $100 one-time fee/room. Service with restrictions, supervision.

Sleep Inn-Charleston 🏨
(843) 556-6959. **$49-$199.** 1524 Savannah Hwy. US 17 S, 3.6 mi w of Ashley River Bridge; jct I-526 W (end) and US 17 N, 1.7 mi e. Int corridors. **Pets:** Accepted.

Town & Country Inn & Conference Center 🏨
(843) 571-1000. **Call for rates.** 2008 Savannah Hwy. US 17 S, 3.5 mi nw of Ashley River Bridge; jct I-526 W (end) and US 17 N, just se. Ext corridors. **Pets:** Accepted.

Vendue Inn 🏨
(843) 577-7970. **$199-$459, 3 day notice.** 19 Vendue Range. Off E Bay St, 1 blk from Waterfront Park; in historic district. Int corridors. **Pets:** Accepted.

FOLLY BEACH

"Charleston On The Beach" Holiday Inn 🏨
(843) 588-6464. **$109-$309, 3 day notice.** 1 Center St. Terminus of SR 171; center. Ext corridors. **Pets:** Accepted.

KIAWAH ISLAND

Courtside Villas-Kiawah Island Golf Resort-Villas 🏨
(843) 768-2121. **Call for rates.** 1 Sanctuary Beach Dr. 2 mi ne of main gate. Ext corridors. **Pets:** Dogs only. $25 daily fee/room. Designated rooms, service with restrictions.

Fairway Oaks-Kiawah Island Golf Resort-Villas 🏨
(843) 768-2121. **Call for rates.** 1 Sanctuary Beach Dr. 2 mi ne of main gate. Ext corridors. **Pets:** Dogs only. $25 daily fee/room. Designated rooms.

Mariners Watch Villas-Kiawah Island Golf Resort-Villas 🏨
(843) 768-2121. **Call for rates.** 1 Sanctuary Beach Dr. 2 mi ne of main gate. Ext corridors. **Pets:** Dogs only. $25 daily fee/room. Designated rooms.

Parkside Villas-Kiawah Island Golf Resort-Villas 🏨
(843) 768-2121. **Call for rates.** 1 Sanctuary Beach Dr. 2 mi ne of main gate. Ext corridors. **Pets:** Dogs only. $25 daily fee/room. Designated rooms.

Seascape Villas-Kiawah Island Golf Resort-Villas 🏨
(843) 768-2121. **Call for rates.** 1 Sanctuary Beach Dr. 2 mi ne of main gate. Ext corridors. **Pets:** Dogs only. $25 daily fee/room. Designated rooms, service with restrictions.

Shipwatch Villas-Kiawah Island Golf Resort-Villas 🏨
(843) 768-2121. **Call for rates.** 1 Sanctuary Beach Dr. 2 mi ne of main gate. Ext corridors. **Pets:** Dogs only. $25 daily fee/room. Designated rooms.

Turtle Cove Villas-Kiawah Island Golf Resort-Villas 🏨
(843) 768-2121. **Call for rates.** 1 Sanctuary Beach Dr. 2 mi ne of main gate. Ext corridors. **Pets:** Accepted.

Turtle Point Villas-Kiawah Island Golf Resort-Villas 🏨
(843) 768-2121. **Call for rates.** 1 Sanctuary Beach Dr. 2 mi ne of main gate. Ext corridors. **Pets:** Dogs only. $25 daily fee/room. Designated rooms.

Windswept Villas-Kiawah Island Golf Resort-Villas 🏨
(843) 768-2121. **Call for rates.** 1 Sanctuary Beach Dr. 2 mi ne of main gate. Ext corridors. **Pets:** Dogs only. $25 daily fee/room. Designated rooms.

MOUNT PLEASANT

Charleston Harbor Resort & Marina 🏨
(843) 856-0028. **$99-$289.** 20 Patriots Point Rd. Base of Cooper River Bridge, 0.6 mi se on Coleman Blvd (SR 703), then 0.8 mi sw; past museum. Int corridors. **Pets:** Accepted.

Days Inn Patriots Point 🏨
(843) 881-1800. **Call for rates.** 261 Johnnie Dodds Blvd. Just e of base of Cooper River Bridge. Ext corridors. **Pets:** Small, dogs only. $10 daily fee/pet. Designated rooms, service with restrictions, supervision.

▼▼ **Extended StayAmerica-Charleston-Mount Pleasant** SH
(843) 884-4453. **$81-$104.** 304 Wingo Way. Just e of Cooper River Bridge on US 17, then just n. Int corridors. **Pets:** Other species. $75 one-time fee/pet. Service with restrictions.

ASK 🅢 ✕ 🛈 🖥

▼▼ **Homewood Suites by Hilton** SH
(843) 881-6950. **$99-$239, 5 day notice.** 1998 Riviera Dr. I-526, exit 32 (Georgetown/US 17 N), 1.4 mi ne on US 17, 1 mi se on Isle of Palms connector (SR 517), then just sw. Int corridors. **Pets:** Small, dogs only. $75 one-time fee/room. Designated rooms, service with restrictions, crate.

ASK 🅢 ✕ 🖫 🛈 🖥 ⇌ ✕

▼▼ **Lands Inn East** SH
(843) 884-5853. **Call for rates.** 310 Hwy 17 (Johnnie Dodds Blvd). US 17, 0.7 mi n of Cooper River Bridge. Ext corridors. **Pets:** Small. $20 one-time fee/room. Service with restrictions.

✕ 🛈 🖥 ⇌

▼▼ **Red Roof Inn** M
(843) 884-1411. **Call for rates.** 301 Johnnie Dodds Blvd. Just e of base of Cooper River Bridge, on US 17 (Johnnie Dodds Blvd), then just s on McGrath-Darby Blvd. Ext corridors. **Pets:** Medium. Service with restrictions, crate.

✕ 🛈 ⇌

▼▼▼ **Residence Inn by Marriott** SH
(843) 881-1599. **$149-$179.** 1116 Isle of Palms Connector. I-526, exit 32 (Georgetown/US 17 N), 1.4 mi ne on US 17 to Isle of Palms connector (SR 517), then just se. Int corridors. **Pets:** Accepted.

ASK 🅢 ✕ 🖫 🛈 🖥 ⇌

▼▼ **Sleep Inn Mt Pleasant** SH
(843) 856-5000. **Call for rates.** 299 Wingo Way. Just e of base of Cooper River Bridge, then just n at McGrath-Darby Blvd. Int corridors. **Pets:** Medium. $15 daily fee/pet. Designated rooms, service with restrictions.

✕ 🖫 🛈 🖥 ⇌

NORTH CHARLESTON

▼▼ **Comfort Inn Coliseum** M
(843) 554-6485. **$80-$129.** 5055 N Arco Ln. I-26, exit 213 westbound; exit 213A eastbound, just s, then n. Ext corridors. **Pets:** Accepted.

ASK 🅢 ✕ 🛈 🖥 ⇌

▼▼ **Comfort Suites Charleston/N Charleston, SC** SH
(843) 725-5400. **$89-$169.** 2520 N Forest Dr. I-26, exit 209 (Ashley Phosphate Rd), just w of Northside Dr. Int corridors. **Pets:** Accepted.

ASK 🅢 ✕ 🖫 🛈 🖥 ⇌

ⱯⱯⱯ ▼ **Country Hearth Inn & Suites** M
(843) 572-2228. **Call for rates.** 2311 Ashley Phosphate Rd. I-26, exit 209 (Ashley Phosphate Rd), just e. Ext corridors. **Pets:** Accepted.

SAVE ✕ 🛈 🖥 ⇌

▼▼ **Extended StayAmerica Charleston-North Charleston-Airport** M
(843) 747-3787. **$73-$91.** 5059 N Arco Ln. I-26, exit 213, just s on Montague Ave, then just nw. Ext corridors. **Pets:** Other species. $75 one-time fee/pet. Service with restrictions.

ASK 🅢 ✕ 🛈 🖥

▼▼ **Homestead Studio Suites Hotel-Charleston/Airport** SH
(843) 740-3440. **$90-$110.** 5045 N Arco Ln. I-26, exit 213 westbound; exit 213A eastbound, just s, then n. Int corridors. **Pets:** Other species. $75 one-time fee/pet. Service with restrictions.

ASK 🅢 ✕ 🖫 🛈 🖥 ⇌

ⱯⱯⱯ ▼▼▼ **La Quinta Inn Charleston** SH
(843) 797-8181. **$89-$119.** 2499 La Quinta Ln. I-26, exit 209 (Ashley Phosphate Rd), just w. Ext corridors. **Pets:** Other species. Service with restrictions, supervision.

SAVE 🅢 ✕ 🛈 🖥 ⇌

▼ **Motel 6 #642** M
(843) 572-6590. **$49-$61.** 2551 Ashley Phosphate Rd. I-26, exit 209 (Ashley Phosphate Rd), just w. Ext corridors. **Pets:** Other species. Service with restrictions, supervision.

🅢 ✕ ⇌

ⱯⱯⱯ ▼▼▼ **Quality Suites Convention Center** SH 🐾
(843) 747-7300. **$89-$149, 30 day notice.** 5225 N Arco Ln. I-26, exit 213 westbound; exit 213A eastbound, just s, then n. Int corridors. **Pets:** Medium. $49 one-time fee/room. Designated rooms.

SAVE 🅢 ✕ 🛈 🖥 ⇌

▼▼ **Red Roof Inn** M
(843) 572-9100. **Call for rates.** 7480 Northwoods Blvd. I-26, exit 209 (Ashley Phosphate Rd), just e, then just n. Ext corridors. **Pets:** Accepted.

✕ 🛈

▼▼▼ **Residence Inn by Marriott** SH 🐾
(843) 572-5757. **$145.** 7645 Northwoods Blvd. I-26, exit 209 (Ashley Phosphate Rd), just e, then n. Ext corridors. **Pets:** $100 one-time fee/room. Service with restrictions.

ASK 🅢 ✕ 🛈 🖥 ⇌ ✕

ⱯⱯⱯ ▼▼▼ **Residence Inn Charleston Airport** SH 🐾
(843) 266-3434. **$169-$189.** 5035 International Blvd. I-26, exit 213A eastbound, 0.4 mi s, then just w; exit westbound, 0.4 mi s, then just w; I-526, exit International Blvd, 0.8 mi e. Int corridors. **Pets:** Other species. $100 one-time fee/room. Service with restrictions.

SAVE 🅢 ✕ 🖫 🛈 🖥 ⇌ ✕

ⱯⱯⱯ ▼▼▼ **Sheraton Hotel North Charleston Convention Center** LH 🐾
(843) 747-1900. **$99-$159.** 4770 Goer Dr. I-26, exit 213 westbound; exit 213B eastbound, just n. Int corridors. **Pets:** Medium, dogs only. $40 one-time fee/pet. Service with restrictions, supervision.

SAVE 🅢 ✕ 🛈 🖥 🍴 ⇌

▼▼ **Sleep Inn Charleston North** SH
(843) 572-8400. **$69-$159.** 7435 Northside Dr. I-26, exit 209 (Ashley Phosphate Rd), just w. Int corridors. **Pets:** Medium. $10 daily fee/pet. Designated rooms, service with restrictions, crate.

ASK 🅢 ✕ 🛈 🖥

▼▼ **StudioPlus** SH
(843) 553-0036. **$90-$110.** 7641 Northwoods Blvd. I-26, exit 209 (Ashley Phosphate Rd), just e, then just n. Int corridors. **Pets:** Other species. $75 one-time fee/pet. Service with restrictions.

ASK 🅢 ✕ 🛈 🖥 ⇌

SUMMERVILLE

▼▼▼ **Country Inn & Suites** SH
(843) 285-9000. **$94-$104.** 220 Holiday Dr. I-26, exit 199A, just w on US 17 alternate route to Holiday Dr, then just n. Int corridors. **Pets:** Medium, other species. $10 daily fee/room. Service with restrictions, supervision.

ASK 🅢 ✕ 🛈 🖥 ⇌

ⱯⱯⱯ ▼▼▼ **Holiday Inn Express-Charleston/Summerville** SH 🐾
(843) 875-3300. **Call for rates.** 120 Holiday Dr. I-26, exit 199A, just w. Int corridors. **Pets:** Service with restrictions, supervision.

SAVE ✕ 🖫 🛈 🖥 ⇌

Summerville Econo Lodge ▥
(843) 875-3022. **$64-$84.** 110 Holiday Dr. I-26, exit 199A, just w on US 17A, then just n. Ext corridors. **Pets:** Small. $10 daily fee/room. Service with restrictions, crate.

⟦ASK⟧ ⟦S🐾⟧ ⟦✕⟧ ⟦▯⟧ ⟦▭⟧

Woodlands Resort & Inn ⟦CI⟧ ❧
(843) 875-2600. **$325-$890, 7 day notice.** 125 Parsons Rd. I-26, exit 199A, 2 mi s on US 17 alternate route, 1.5 mi w on W Richardson Ave (SR 165), then just s. Int corridors. **Pets:** $25 daily fee/room.

⟦SAVE⟧ ⟦S🐾⟧ ⟦✕⟧ ⟦¶⟧ ⟦⤳⟧ ⟦✕⟧

END METROPOLITAN AREA

CHARLOTTE METROPOLITAN AREA (NEARBY NORTH CAROLINA)

FORT MILL

The Plaza Hotel at Carowinds ⟦LH⟧
(803) 548-2400. **$70-$90.** 225 Carowinds Blvd. I-77, exit 90, just nw. Int corridors. **Pets:** Accepted.

⟦SAVE⟧ ⟦S🐾⟧ ⟦✕⟧ ⟦▯⟧ ⟦▭⟧ ⟦¶⟧ ⟦⤳⟧ ⟦✕⟧

ROCK HILL

Baymont Inn & Suites ⟦SH⟧
(803) 329-1330. **$72-$115.** 1106 N Anderson Rd. I-77, exit 82B (US 21), 0.4 mi sw to US 21 Bypass, then just s. Int corridors. **Pets:** Medium. $10 daily fee/pet. Service with restrictions, supervision.

⟦SAVE⟧ ⟦S🐾⟧ ⟦✕⟧ ⟦▯⟧ ⟦▭⟧ ⟦⤳⟧

The Book & the Spindle ⟦BB⟧ ❧
(803) 328-1913. **$85-$105, 10 day notice.** 626 Oakland Ave. I-77, exit 82B (US 21), 3.1 mi s; before Aiken. Int corridors. **Pets:** Small, other species. $10 deposit/room. Service with restrictions, crate.

⟦✕⟧ ⟦▯⟧ ⟦▭⟧

Howard Johnson Inn ▥
(803) 329-7900. **Call for rates.** 911 Riverview Rd. I-77, exit 82B (US 21), just sw, then just s. Ext corridors. **Pets:** Small. $10 one-time fee/pet. Service with restrictions, supervision.

⟦✕⟧ ⟦▯⟧ ⟦▭⟧

Super 8 Motel ⟦SH⟧
(803) 980-0400. **Call for rates.** 888 Riverview Rd. I-77, exit 82B (US 21), just sw, then just s. Int corridors. **Pets:** Medium. $10 daily fee/pet. Service with restrictions, supervision.

⟦✕⟧ ⟦⌖M⟧ ⟦▯⟧ ⟦▭⟧

END METROPOLITAN AREA

CHERAW

Days Inn ▥
(843) 537-5554. **Call for rates.** 820 Market St. Jct US 52/1/SR 9. Ext corridors. **Pets:** Very small. $10 daily fee/pet. Designated rooms, service with restrictions, supervision.

⟦SAVE⟧ ⟦✕⟧ ⟦▯⟧ ⟦▭⟧ ⟦⤳⟧

Jameson Inn ▥
(843) 537-5625. **$70-$100.** 885 Chesterfield Hwy. Jct US 1/52/SR 9, 1.6 mi w on SR 9. Ext corridors. **Pets:** Small. $15 daily fee/room. Service with restrictions, crate.

⟦ASK⟧ ⟦S🐾⟧ ⟦✕⟧ ⟦▯⟧ ⟦▭⟧ ⟦⤳⟧

CLEMSON

Comfort Inn-Clemson ⟦SH⟧
(864) 653-3600. **$85-$175.** 1305 Tiger Blvd. Jct SR 133 and US 76/123, 0.5 mi e. Int corridors. **Pets:** Small, other species. $10 daily fee/room. Designated rooms, service with restrictions.

⟦SAVE⟧ ⟦S🐾⟧ ⟦✕⟧ ⟦▯⟧ ⟦▭⟧ ⟦⤳⟧

Ramada Inn of Clemson ⟦SH⟧
(864) 654-7501. **Call for rates.** 1310 Tiger Blvd. Jct SR 133 and US 76/123, 0.5 mi e. Int corridors. **Pets:** Accepted.

⟦SAVE⟧ ⟦✕⟧ ⟦▯⟧ ⟦▭⟧ ⟦¶⟧ ⟦⤳⟧

CLINTON

Comfort Inn ▥
(864) 833-5558. **$79-$99.** 105 Trade St. I-26, exit 52, just n; behind truck stop. Ext corridors. **Pets:** Small. $10 daily fee/pet. Service with restrictions, supervision.

⟦SAVE⟧ ⟦S🐾⟧ ⟦✕⟧ ⟦▯⟧ ⟦▭⟧ ⟦⤳⟧

Days Inn ▥
(864) 833-6600. **$59-$99.** 12374 Hwy 56 N. I-26, exit 52, just s. Ext corridors. **Pets:** Small. $10 daily fee/pet. Service with restrictions, supervision.

⟦SAVE⟧ ⟦S🐾⟧ ⟦✕⟧ ⟦▯⟧ ⟦▭⟧ ⟦⤳⟧

COLUMBIA

Chestnut Cottage Bed & Breakfast ⟦BB⟧ ❧
(803) 256-1718. **Call for rates.** 1718 Hampton St. SR 12 (Taylor St), just s; between Henderson and Barnwell sts; downtown. Int corridors. **Pets:** Large, other species.

⟦✕⟧ ⟦▯⟧ ⟦▭⟧

Econo Lodge ▥
(803) 772-7275. **$50-$125.** 773 St Andrews Rd. I-26, exit 106A westbound; exit 106 eastbound, just w. Ext corridors. **Pets:** Small. $10 daily fee/pet. Service with restrictions, supervision.

⟦ASK⟧ ⟦S🐾⟧ ⟦✕⟧ ⟦▯⟧ ⟦▭⟧ ⟦⤳⟧

Extended StayAmerica Columbia-Fort Jackson ▥
(803) 782-2025. **$77-$87.** 5430 Forest Dr. I-77, exit 12, just ne, then just s along service road; behind mall. Ext corridors. **Pets:** Other species. $75 one-time fee/pet. Service with restrictions.

⟦ASK⟧ ⟦S🐾⟧ ⟦✕⟧ ⟦▯⟧ ⟦▭⟧

Extended StayAmerica-Columbia-West ⟦SH⟧
(803) 251-7878. **$64-$74.** 450 Gracern Rd. I-126, exit Greystone Blvd, just n to Stoneridge Dr, just w to Gracern Rd, then s. Ext corridors. **Pets:** Other species. $75 one-time fee/pet. Service with restrictions.

⟦ASK⟧ ⟦S🐾⟧ ⟦✕⟧ ⟦▯⟧ ⟦▭⟧

Jameson Suites 🅂🅷
(803) 736-6666. **Call for rates.** 7525 Two Notch Rd. I-20, exit 74 (Two Notch Rd), just ne; I-77, exit 17 (Two Notch Rd), 0.5 mi sw. Int corridors. **Pets:** Accepted.
⊠ 🖪 💻 🌊

La Quinta Inn & Suites Columbia NE/Ft. Jackson Area 🅂🅷
(803) 736-6400. **$84-$122.** 1538 Horseshoe Dr. I-20, exit 74 (Two Notch Rd), just n; I-77, exit 17 (Two Notch Rd), 0.5 mi s. Int corridors. **Pets:** Other species. Service with restrictions, supervision.
🆂🅰🆅🅴 🆂 ⊠ 🖪 💻 🌊

La Quinta Inn-Maingate Ft. Jackson 🅂🅷
(803) 783-5410. **$107-$137.** 7333 Garners Ferry Rd. I-77, exit 9A southbound; exit 9 northbound, just se on US 76/378. Int corridors. **Pets:** Other species. Service with restrictions, supervision.
🆂🅰🆅🅴 🆂 ⊠ 🖪 💻 🌊

Motel 6 #1291 🅂🅷
(803) 736-3900. **$50-$61.** 7541 Nates Rd. I-20, exit 74 (Two Notch Rd), just n, then just e; I-77, exit 17 (Two Notch Rd), 0.5 mi s, then e. Int corridors. **Pets:** Other species. Service with restrictions, supervision.
🆂 ⊠ 🅛🅜 🌊

Radisson Hotel Columbia & Conference Center 🅻🅷
(803) 731-0300. **$89-$199.** 2100 Bush River Rd. I-20, exit 63 (Bush River Rd), just e; I-26, exit 108 (Bush River Rd), 0.7 mi w. Int corridors. **Pets:** $50 one-time fee/room. Designated rooms, service with restrictions, supervision.
🆂🅰🆅🅴 🆂 ⊠ 🖪 💻 🍽 🌊

Red Roof Inn-West 🅜
(803) 798-9220. **Call for rates.** 10 Berryhill Rd. I-26, exit 106A westbound; exit 106 eastbound, just w. Ext corridors. **Pets:** Accepted.
⊠ 🖪

Residence Inn by Marriott 🅂🅷
(803) 779-7000. **$139-$159.** 150 Stoneridge Dr. I-126, exit Greystone Blvd, just n, then just e. Ext corridors. **Pets:** Accepted.
🅰🆂🅺 🆂 ⊠ 🖪 💻 🌊 🅧

Residence Inn by Marriott 🅂🅷
(803) 788-8850. **$129-$149.** 2320 Legrand Rd. I-77, exit 19 southbound, just ne on Farrow Rd to Rabon Rd, then just se; exit 18 northbound. Int corridors. **Pets:** $75 one-time fee/room. Service with restrictions, crate.
🅰🆂🅺 🆂 ⊠ 🖪 💻 🌊 🅧

StudioPLUS Greystone Columbia 🅂🅷
(803) 771-0303. **$77-$87.** 180 Stoneridge Dr. I-126, exit Greystone Blvd, just n, then just e. Int corridors. **Pets:** Other species. $75 one-time fee/pet. Service with restrictions.
🅰🆂🅺 🆂 ⊠ 🖪 💻 🌊

Super 8 🅜
(803) 735-0008. **$70-$95.** 5719 Fairfield Rd. I-20, exit 70, just s. Ext corridors. **Pets:** Accepted.
🆂🅰🆅🅴 🆂 ⊠ 🖪

TownePlace Suites by Marriott 🅂🅷
(803) 781-9391. **$119-$139.** 350 Columbiana Dr. I-26, exit 103 (Harbison Blvd), just sw to Columbiana Dr, then 0.7 mi nw. Int corridors. **Pets:** Accepted.
🅰🆂🅺 🆂 ⊠ 🅛🅜 🖪 💻 🌊

DILLON

Comfort Inn 🅜
(843) 774-4137. **$68-$135.** 810 Radford Blvd. I-95, exit 193, just s. Ext/int corridors. **Pets:** Accepted.
🆂🅰🆅🅴 🆂 ⊠ 🖪 💻 🌊

DUNCAN

Jameson Inn 🅜
(864) 433-8405. **$60-$90.** 1546 E Main St. I-85, exit 63, 0.4 mi se on SR 290. Ext corridors. **Pets:** Small. $15 daily fee/room. Service with restrictions, crate.
🅰🆂🅺 🆂 ⊠ 🖪 💻 🌊

EASLEY

Comfort Inn 🅜
(864) 859-7520. **$74-$79.** 5539 Calhoun Memorial Hwy. Jct US 123 and SR 93, just e on US 123. Ext corridors. **Pets:** Accepted.
🆂🅰🆅🅴 🆂 ⊠ 🖪 💻 🌊

Jameson Inn 🅜
(864) 306-9000. **$63-$95.** 211 Dayton School Rd. Jct US 123 and SR 93, 0.6 mi e on US 123; jct US 123 and SR 153, 1.4 mi w. Ext corridors. **Pets:** Small. $15 daily fee/room. Service with restrictions, crate.
🅰🆂🅺 🆂 ⊠ 🖪 💻 🌊

FLORENCE

Comfort Inn 🅜 🐾
(843) 665-4558. **$59-$89.** 1916 W Lucas St. I-95, exit 164, just se. Ext/int corridors. **Pets:** Other species. $10 daily fee/pet. Designated rooms, service with restrictions, supervision.
🆂🅰🆅🅴 🆂 ⊠ 🖪 💻 🌊

Country Hearth Inn & Suites 🅜
(843) 662-9421. **Call for rates.** 831 S Irby St. 1.3 mi s on US 301 and 52. Ext corridors. **Pets:** Accepted.
🆂🅰🆅🅴 ⊠ 🖪 💻 🍽 🌊

Econo Lodge 🅜
(843) 665-8558. **$35-$70.** 1811 W Lucas St. I-95, exit 164, just se. Ext corridors. **Pets:** Other species. $15 daily fee/pet. Designated rooms, service with restrictions, supervision.
🆂🅰🆅🅴 🆂 ⊠ 🖪 💻 🌊

Holiday Inn Hotel & Suites 🅂🅷
(843) 665-4555. **$85-$160.** 1819 W Lucas St. I-95, exit 164, just se. Ext corridors. **Pets:** Other species. $25 one-time fee/pet. Designated rooms, service with restrictions.
🆂🅰🆅🅴 🆂 ⊠ 🅛🅜 🖪 💻 🍽 🌊

Howard Johnson Express Inn & Suites 🅜 🐾
(843) 664-9494. **$69.** 3821 Bancroft Rd. I-95, exit 157, just ne on US 76. Ext corridors. **Pets:** Medium. $10 one-time fee/room. Service with restrictions, crate.
🆂🅰🆅🅴 🆂 ⊠ 🖪 💻 🌊

Motel 6 #1250 🅜
(843) 667-6100. **$41-$53.** 1834 W Lucas St. I-95, exit 164, just sw. Ext corridors. **Pets:** Other species. Service with restrictions, supervision.
🆂 ⊠ 🌊

Quality Inn & Suites 🅜
(843) 664-2400. **$69-$100.** 150 Dunbarton Dr. I-95, exit 160A, just e, then just n. Ext corridors. **Pets:** Other species. $20 one-time fee/room. Designated rooms, service with restrictions, supervision.
🆂🅰🆅🅴 🆂 ⊠ 🖪 💻 🌊

Ramada Inn 🅂🅷
(843) 669-4241. **$59-$79.** 2038 W Lucas St. I-95, exit 164, just nw. Ext/int corridors. **Pets:** Accepted.
🆂🅰🆅🅴 🆂 ⊠ 🖪 💻 🍽 🌊 🅧

Red Roof Inn 🅜
(843) 678-9000. **Call for rates.** 2690 David McLeod Blvd. I-95, exit 160A, just e on service road. Ext corridors. **Pets:** Accepted.
⊠ 🅛🅜

▼▼▼ Super 8 Motel M
(843) 661-7267. **$56-$180.** 1832 1/2 W Lucas St. I-95, exit 164, just se. Ext corridors. **Pets:** Small. $10 daily fee/pet. No service, supervision.
[SAVE] [S&] [✕] [🛏] [⇆]

▼▼▼ Thunderbird Inn M
(843) 669-1611. **$45-$55.** 2004 W Lucas St. I-95, exit 164, just nw. Ext corridors. **Pets:** Accepted.
[SAVE] [S&] [✕] [🛏] [💻] [🍽] [⇆]

GAFFNEY

▼▼ Jameson Inn M
(864) 489-0240. **$58-$90.** 101 Stuard St. I-85, exit 92, 0.5 mi se on SR 11/W Floyd Baker Blvd. Ext corridors. **Pets:** Small. $15 daily fee/room. Service with restrictions, crate.
[ASK] [S&] [✕] [🛏] [💻] [⇆]

THE GRAND STRAND AREA

GEORGETOWN

▼▼ Jameson Inn Georgetown M
(843) 546-6090. **Call for rates.** 120 Church St. Jct US 17/17 alternate route/701, 1.2 mi se on US 17; just w of ICW Bridge at Georgetown Landing. Ext corridors. **Pets:** Small. $15 daily fee/room. Service with restrictions, crate.
[✕] [🛏] [💻] [⇆]

LITTLE RIVER

▼▼▼▼ Holiday Inn Hotel & Suites-North Myrtle Beach SH
(843) 281-9400. **Call for rates.** 722 Hwy 17. Jct SR 9/US 17, 1 mi e; at Coquina Harbor. Int corridors. **Pets:** Accepted.
[SAVE] [✕] [🛏] [💻] [🍽] [⇆]

MYRTLE BEACH

▼▼▼▼ La Quinta Inn & Suites Myrtle Beach SH
(843) 916-8801. **$95-$149.** 1561 21st Ave N. Jct US 17 Bypass, just se. Int corridors. **Pets:** Other species. Service with restrictions, supervision.
[SAVE] [S&] [✕] [&M] [🛏] [💻] [⇆]

▼▼▼▼ La Quinta Inn Myrtle Beach SH
(843) 449-5231. **$94-$139.** 4709 N Kings Hwy. Jct 48th Ave N and US 17 business route. Int corridors. **Pets:** Other species. Service with restrictions, supervision.
[SAVE] [S&] [✕] [🛏] [💻] [⇆]

▼▼▼ Sea Mist Oceanfront Resort LH
(843) 448-1551. **$32-$199, 14 day notice.** 1200 S Ocean Blvd. Jct 12th Ave S. Ext/int corridors. **Pets:** Accepted.
[SAVE] [✕] [🛏] [🍽] [⇆] [✕]

▼▼▼▼ Staybridge Suites-Fantasy Harbour SH 🐾
(843) 903-4000. **Call for rates.** 3163 Outlet Blvd. Jct US 17 Bypass, 0.7 mi n on US 501, exit River Oaks Rd/George Bishop Pkwy, just w on River Oaks Rd, then 0.4 mi s. Int corridors. **Pets:** Medium. $20 daily fee/room. Service with restrictions.
[✕] [🛏] [💻] [⇆] [✕]

PAWLEYS ISLAND

▼▼ Best Western Hammock Inn M
(843) 237-4261. **$79-$99.** 7903 Ocean Hwy. 2.6 mi sw on US 17. Ext corridors. **Pets:** Accepted.
[ASK] [S&] [✕] [🛏] [💻] [🍽] [⇆]

SURFSIDE BEACH

▼▼▼▼ Holiday Inn SunSpree SH
(843) 238-5601. **Call for rates.** 1601 N Ocean Blvd. Jct 16th Ave N and N Ocean Blvd. Int corridors. **Pets:** Medium. $100 one-time fee/pet. Service with restrictions, crate.
[SAVE] [✕] [🛏] [💻] [🍽] [⇆] [✕]

END AREA

GREENVILLE

▼▼▼▼ Crowne Plaza Hotel and Resort Greenville LH
(864) 297-6300. **$159-$189.** 851 Congaree Rd. I-385, exit 37, just s, then just nw. Int corridors. **Pets:** Accepted.
[ASK] [S&] [✕] [&M] [🛏] [💻] [🍽] [⇆] [✕]

▼▼▼ Drury Inn & Suites-Greenville SH
(864) 288-4401. **$95-$160.** 10 Carolina Point Pkwy. I-85, exit 51, just se; I-385, exit 35, 0.6 mi nw. Int corridors. **Pets:** Large, other species. Service with restrictions, supervision.
[ASK] [✕] [🛏] [💻]

▼▼ Extended StayAmerica-Greenville Airport SH
(864) 213-9698. **$73-$83.** 3715 Pelham Rd. I-85, exit 54 (Pelham Rd), 0.5 mi w. Int corridors. **Pets:** Other species. $75 one-time fee/pet. Service with restrictions.
[ASK] [S&] [✕] [🛏] [💻]

▼▼▼ Hawthorn Suites SH
(864) 297-0099. **Call for rates.** 48 McPrice Ct. I-385, exit 39 (Haywood Rd), just n, just e on Orchard Park Rd, then just s. Ext corridors. **Pets:** Very small. $150 one-time fee/room. Service with restrictions, crate.
[✕] [🛏] [💻] [⇆] [✕]

▼▼▼ Holiday Inn Express Hotel & Suites SH 🐾
(864) 213-9331. **$99-$155.** 2681 Dry Pocket Rd. I-85, exit 54 (Pelham Rd), just w to The Parkway, just n to Parkway E, then just se. Int corridors. **Pets:** Small. $25 one-time fee/room. Service with restrictions, supervision.
[ASK] [S&] [✕] [🛏] [💻] [⇆] [✕]

▼▼▼ Holiday Inn I-85/Augusta Rd SH 🐾
(864) 277-8921. **$100-$110.** 4295 Augusta Rd. I-85, exit 46A, just s. Int corridors. **Pets:** $30 one-time fee/room. Service with restrictions, crate.
[SAVE] [S&] [✕] [&M] [🛏] [💻] [🍽] [⇆]

▼▼▼ La Quinta Inn Greenville (Woodruff Rd.) SH
(864) 297-3500. **$89-$129.** 31 Old Country Rd. I-85, exit 51A, just n on SR 146; I-385, exit 35, just n. Ext/int corridors. **Pets:** Other species. Service with restrictions, supervision.
[SAVE] [S&] [✕] [🛏] [💻] [⇆]

▼▼▼ La Quinta Inns & Suites Greenville (Haywood) SH
(864) 233-8018. **$109-$144.** 65 W Orchard Park Dr. I-385, exit 39 (Haywood Rd), just n, then w. Int corridors. **Pets:** Other species. Service with restrictions, supervision.
[SAVE] [S&] [✕] [🛏] [💻] [⇆] [✕]

▼▼ 💎 MainStay Suites-Greenville 🆂🅷
(864) 987-5566. **$100-$126.** 2671 Dry Pocket Rd. I-85, exit 54 (Pelham Rd), just w to The Parkway, just n to Parkway E, then just se. Int corridors. **Pets:** Accepted.
(A$K) 🆂🔟 ✕ 🍽 💻 🏊

▼▼ Microtel Inn & Suites 🆂🅷
(864) 297-3811. **$56-$79, 7 day notice.** 1024 Woodruff Rd. I-85, exit 51A, 0.5 mi n on SR 146. Int corridors. **Pets:** Accepted.
(A$K) 🆂🔟 ✕ 🍽 💻

▲▲▲ ▼▼▼ The Phoenix Greenville's Inn 🆂🅷
(864) 233-4651. **$89-$295.** 246 N Pleasantburg Dr. I-385, exit 40B, 0.6 mi s on SR 291. Ext corridors. **Pets:** Other species. $25 one-time fee/room. Service with restrictions, crate.
(SAVE) ✕ 🍽 💻 🍴 🏊

▼▼ Red Roof Inn Ⓜ
(864) 297-4458. **Call for rates.** 2801 Laurens Rd. I-85, exit 48A, just se frontage road, then just e to end. Ext corridors. **Pets:** Accepted.
✕ 🅶🅼 🍽

▲▲▲ ▼▼ Sleep Inn Palmetto Expo Center 🆂🅷 🐾
(864) 240-2006. **$59-$109.** 231 N Pleasantburg Dr (SR 291). I-385, exit 40B, 0.6 mi s on SR 291. Int corridors. **Pets:** Medium. $20 one-time fee/room. No service, supervision.
(SAVE) 🆂🔟 ✕ 🅶🅼 🍽 💻

▼▼ StudioPLUS-Greenville-Haywwod Mall 🆂🅷
(864) 288-4300. **$77-$87.** 530 Woods Lake Rd. I-385, exit 39, just s, then just w. Int corridors. **Pets:** Other species. $75 one-time fee/pet. Service with restrictions.
(A$K) 🆂🔟 ✕ 🍽 💻 🏊

GREENWOOD

▲▲▲ ▼▼▼ Inn on the Square, a Clarion Collection 🆂🅷
(864) 330-1010. **$85-$95.** 104 E Court Ave. Jct Montague St, just s of center; downtown. Int corridors. **Pets:** Accepted.
(SAVE) 🆂🔟 ✕ 🍽 💻 🍴 🏊

GREER

▼▼ 💎 Super 8 🆂🅷
(864) 848-1626. **$55-$65.** 1515 Hwy 101 S. I-85, exit 60, just nw. Int corridors. **Pets:** Accepted.
(A$K) 🆂🔟 ✕ 🅶🅼 🍽 🏊

HARDEEVILLE

▲▲▲ ▼▼ Quality Inn & Suites Ⓜ
(843) 784-7060. **$50-$170.** 19000 Whyte Hardee Blvd. I-95, exit 5 (US 17), just n. Ext corridors. **Pets:** $10 daily fee/pet. Service with restrictions, supervision.
(SAVE) 🆂🔟 ✕ 🅶🅼 🍽 💻 🏊

▲▲▲ ▼▼▼ Sleep Inn Hardeeville 🆂🅷
(843) 784-7181. **$59-$149.** 16553 Whyte Hardee Blvd. I-95, exit 5 (US 17), just se. Int corridors. **Pets:** Small. $20 daily fee/pet. Designated rooms, service with restrictions.
(SAVE) ✕ 🅶🅼 🍽 💻 🏊

HILTON HEAD ISLAND

▲▲▲ ▼▼▼ Beachwalk Hotel & Condominiums 🆂🅷 🐾
(843) 842-8888. **$59-$149.** 40 Waterside Dr. Sea Pines Cir, 0.7 mi se on Pope Rd, just e. Ext corridors. **Pets:** Medium. $40 one-time fee/pet. Designated rooms, service with restrictions, crate.
(SAVE) 🆂🔟 ✕ 🍽 💻 🏊

▲▲▲ ▼▼▼ Comfort Inn 🆂🅷
(843) 842-6662. **$49-$179.** 2 Tanglewood Dr. Sea Pines Cir, 1.1 mi se on Pope Ave, just sw; at Coligny Plaza. Int corridors. **Pets:** Medium. $10 daily fee/pet, $25 one-time fee/pet. Service with restrictions, supervision.
(SAVE) 🆂🔟 ✕ 🍽 💻 🏊 ✕

▼▼ Motel 6-#1129 Ⓜ
(843) 785-2700. **$46-$58.** 830 William Hilton Pkwy. J Wilton Graves Bridge, 9 mi e on US 278 business route. Ext corridors. **Pets:** Accepted.
🆂🔟 🍽 💻 🏊

▲▲▲ ▼▼▼ Park Lane Hotel & Suites 🆂🅷
(843) 686-5700. **$60-$150.** 12 Park Ln. 10 mi of J Wilton Graves Bridge on US 278 business route. Int corridors. **Pets:** Large. $50 one-time fee/room. Service with restrictions.
(SAVE) 🆂🔟 ✕ 🍽 💻 🏊 ✕

▼▼▼ Quality Inn & Suites of Hilton Head Island 🆂🅷
(843) 681-3655. **$59-$139.** 200 Museum St. 3.3 mi e of J Wilton Graves Bridge on US 278 business route. Ext corridors. **Pets:** Medium. $10 daily fee/room, $25 one-time fee/room. Designated rooms, service with restrictions, supervision.
(A$K) 🆂🔟 ✕ 🍽 💻 🏊

▼▼ Red Roof Inn-Hilton Head Ⓜ
(843) 686-6808. **Call for rates.** 5 Regency Pkwy. Over bridge, 9 mi e on US 278 business route; between Shipyard Plantation and Palmetto Dunes. Ext corridors. **Pets:** Accepted.
✕ 🍽 🏊

IRMO

▼▼💎 Extended Stay Deluxe (Columbia-Harbison) 🆂🅷
(803) 781-8590. **$86-$96.** 1170 Kinley Rd. I-26, exit 102B, just e, then n. Int corridors. **Pets:** Other species. $75 one-time fee/pet. Service with restrictions.
(A$K) 🆂🔟 ✕ 🅶🅼 🍽 💻 🏊

LANCASTER

▼▼ Jameson Inn Ⓜ
(803) 283-1188. **$60-$90.** 114 Commerce Blvd. Jct SR 9 Bypass and US 521, 1.3 mi w on SR 9 Bypass. Ext corridors. **Pets:** Small. $15 daily fee/room. Service with restrictions, crate.
(A$K) 🆂🔟 ✕ 🅶🅼 🍽 💻 🏊

LANDRUM

▼▼▼ The Red Horse Inn Cottages 🅲🅰 🐾
(864) 895-4968. **$155-$280, 7 day notice.** 310 N Campbell Rd. Jct SR 14/414, 1.5 mi w on SR 414 to Campbell Rd, then 0.7 mi n. Ext corridors. **Pets:** Medium, other species. $35 one-time fee/pet. Designated rooms, service with restrictions, supervision.
(A$K) 🆂🔟 ✕ 🍽 💻 ✕

LUGOFF

▼▼💎 Quality Inn & Suites 🆂🅷 🐾
(803) 438-9441. **$70-$80.** 850 Hwy 1 S. I-20, exit 92 (US 601), 2.9 mi n. Ext corridors. **Pets:** Very small. $20 one-time fee/pet. No service, supervision.
(A$K) 🆂🔟 ✕ 🍽 💻 🍴 🏊

▼▼💎 Ramada Limited Ⓜ
(803) 438-1807. **Call for rates.** 542 Hwy 601 S. I-20, exit 92 (US 601), just n. Ext corridors. **Pets:** Accepted.
✕ 🍽 💻 🏊

MANNING

▲▲▲ ▼▼▼ Best Western Palmetto Inn Ⓜ
(803) 473-4021. **$45-$99.** 2825 Paxville Hwy. I-95, exit 119 (SR 261), just se. Ext corridors. **Pets:** Other species. $5 one-time fee/pet. Service with restrictions, crate.
(SAVE) ✕ 🍽 💻 🏊

▼💎 Econo Lodge Ⓜ
(803) 473-2596. **$44-$69.** 6137 Alex Harvin Hwy. I-95, exit 115, just sw. Ext corridors. **Pets:** Accepted.
(A$K) 🆂🔟 ✕ 🍽 🏊

AAA ▼▼ Ramada Inn M
(803) 473-5135. **Call for rates.** 2816 Paxville Hwy. I-95, exit 119 (SR 261), just se. Ext corridors. **Pets:** Accepted.
[SAVE] [X] [B] [P] [≈]

NEWBERRY

AAA ▼ Days Inn-Newberry M
(803) 276-2294. **$52-$72.** 50 Thomas Griffin Rd. I-26, exit 74 (SR 34), just sw. Ext corridors. **Pets:** Medium, other species. $10 daily fee/pet. Service with restrictions, supervision.
[SAVE] [S/D] [X] [B]

AAA ▼▼ Newberry Inn M
(803) 276-5850. **$55-$65.** 11701 S Carolina Hwy 34. I-26, exit 74 (SR 34), just ne. Ext corridors. **Pets:** Small, dogs only. $5 daily fee/pet. Service with restrictions, supervision.
[ASK] [S/D] [X] [B] [P] [≈]

ORANGEBURG

AAA ▼▼ Jameson Inn Orangeburg M
(803) 534-1611. **Call for rates.** 2350 Chestnut St NE. I-26, exit 145A (US 601), 3.9 mi sw to jct US 601 and 21/178 Bypass, then 2 mi nw. Ext corridors. **Pets:** Small. $15 daily fee/room. Service with restrictions, crate.
[X] [B] [P] [≈]

AAA ▼▼ Traveler's Inn M
(803) 531-2590. **$54-$110.** 3691 St Matthews Rd. I-26, exit 145A (US 601), just sw. Ext corridors. **Pets:** $10 daily fee/pet. Service with restrictions, supervision.
[SAVE] [S/D] [X] [B] [≈]

RICHBURG

AAA ▼▼ Super 8 Motel M
(803) 789-7888. **$59-$89, 7 day notice.** 3085 Lancaster Hwy. I-77, exit 65, just w on SR 9. Ext corridors. **Pets:** Small, other species. $10 daily fee/pet. Designated rooms, service with restrictions, supervision.
[SAVE] [S/D] [X] [B] [P] [≈]

RIDGELAND

AAA ▼▼▼ Comfort Inn SH
(843) 726-2121. **$79-$109.** Hwy 336 & I-95. I-95, exit 21 (US 336), just nw. Ext/int corridors. **Pets:** Large, dogs only. $10 one-time fee/pet. Service with restrictions, supervision.
[SAVE] [S/D] [X] [B] [P] [≈]

ST. GEORGE

AAA ▼▼ Comfort Inn M
(843) 563-4180. **$54-$110.** 139 Motel Dr. I-95, exit 77 (US 78), just e. Ext corridors. **Pets:** Accepted.
[SAVE] [X] [B] [P] [≈]

AAA ▼ Econo Lodge M
(843) 563-4195. **$55-$80.** 5971 W Jim Bilton Blvd. I-95, exit 77 (US 78), just e. Ext corridors. **Pets:** Small. $5 daily fee/pet. Service with restrictions, supervision.
[SAVE] [S/D] [X] [B] [P] [≈]

AAA ▼▼ Quality Inn- St George M ❁
(843) 563-4581. **$60-$150.** 6014 W Jim Bilton Blvd. I-95, exit 77 (US 78), just e. Ext corridors. **Pets:** $10 daily fee/room. Designated rooms, service with restrictions, crate.
[SAVE] [S/D] [X] [⌖M] [B] [P] [≈]

SANTEE

▼▼ Baymont Inn & Suites M
(803) 854-3221. **Call for rates.** 249 Britain St. I-95, exit 98 (SR 6), just nw, then just s. Ext corridors. **Pets:** Accepted.
[X] [B] [P] [≈]

AAA ▼▼▼ Holiday Inn Santee SH
(803) 854-9800. **$62-$135.** 139 Bradford Blvd. I-95, exit 98 (SR 6), just nw, then just sw. Int corridors. **Pets:** Small, other species. $20 daily fee/pet. Designated rooms, service with restrictions, supervision.
[SAVE] [X] [⌖M] [B] [P] [¶] [≈]

AAA ▼▼ Howard Johnson Express Inn M
(803) 854-3870. **Call for rates.** 9112 Old Hwy 6. I-95, exit 98 (SR 6), 0.4 mi se. Ext corridors. **Pets:** Small, dogs only. $10 daily fee/room. Service with restrictions, supervision.
[SAVE] [X] [B] [P] [≈]

AAA ▼▼ Super 8 Motel M
(803) 854-3456. **$65-$75.** 9125 Old Hwy 6. I-95, exit 98 (SR 6), 0.4 mi se. Ext corridors. **Pets:** Medium. $10 daily fee/pet. Designated rooms, service with restrictions, supervision.
[SAVE] [S/D] [X] [B] [P] [≈]

SENECA

▼▼ Jameson Inn M
(864) 888-8300. **$68-$100.** 226 Hi-Tech Rd. Jct SR 28 and US 76/123, 0.9 mi w on US 76/123, just se. Ext corridors. **Pets:** Small. $15 daily fee/room. Service with restrictions, crate.
[ASK] [S/D] [X] [⌖M] [B] [P] [≈]

SIMPSONVILLE

▼▼ Days Inn M
(864) 963-7701. **$65.** 45 Ray E Talley Ct. I-385, exit 27, just s, then just e. Ext corridors. **Pets:** Accepted.
[ASK] [S/D] [X] [B] [P] [≈]

▼ Motel 6 SH
(864) 962-8484. **Call for rates.** 3706 Grandview Dr. I-385, exit 27, just s, then just w. Int corridors. **Pets:** Other species. Service with restrictions, supervision.
[X] [⌖M] [B]

AAA ▼▼ Quality Inn M
(864) 963-2777. **$79-$119.** 3755 Grandview Dr. I-385, exit 27, just s. Ext corridors. **Pets:** Small. $7 daily fee/pet. Service with restrictions, supervision.
[SAVE] [S/D] [X] [B] [P] [≈]

SPARTANBURG

▼▼ Extended StayAmerica-Spartanburg-Asheville Hwy M
(864) 573-5949. **$58-$68.** 130 Mobile Dr. I-85 business loop, exit 4 northbound, just se, then just ne on service road; exit 4B southbound, just se, then just ne on service road. Ext corridors. **Pets:** Other species. $75 one-time fee/pet. Service with restrictions.
[ASK] [S/D] [X] [B] [P]

▼▼▼ Holiday Inn Express Hotel & Suites SH
(864) 699-7777. **Call for rates.** 895 Spartan Blvd. I-26, exit 21B (US 29), just e to Blackstock Rd, then 0.7 mi n; adjacent to Westgate Mall. Int corridors. **Pets:** Accepted.
[X] [⌖M] [B] [P] [≈]

SUMMERTON

AAA ▼▼▼ Days Inn of Summerton M
(803) 485-2865. **$34-$65.** 400 Bluff Blvd. I-95, exit 108, just n. Ext corridors. **Pets:** Medium. $5 daily fee/pet. Service with restrictions, supervision.
[SAVE] [S/D] [X] [B] [P] [≈]

SUMTER

AAA ▼▼▼ Ramada Inn SH
(803) 775-2323. **$69-$73.** 226 N Washington St. US 76 business route/521, just n. Ext corridors. **Pets:** $50 deposit/pet, $10 daily fee/pet. Designated rooms, service with restrictions.
[SAVE] [S/D] [X] [B] [P] [¶] [≈] [X]

AAA **W** Travelers Inn & Suites **M**
(803) 469-9210. **Call for rates.** 1210 Camden Rd. Jct US 521/US 76. Ext corridors. **Pets:** Medium. $7 daily fee/pet. Designated rooms, service with restrictions, supervision.

[SAVE] [X] [🛏] [💻] [➰]

TRAVELERS REST

W W Sleep Inn **SH**
(864) 834-7040. **Call for rates.** 110 Hawkins Rd. US 25, exit Hawkins Rd. Int corridors. **Pets:** Other species. $15 daily fee/room. Service with restrictions, supervision.

[X] [♿M] [🛏] [➰]

WALTERBORO

AAA **W W** Best Western of Walterboro **SH** ❧
(843) 538-3600. **$59-$89.** 1428 Sniders Hwy. I-95, exit 53 (SR 63), just e. Ext corridors. **Pets:** Small. $15 daily fee/pet. Designated rooms, service with restrictions, supervision.

[SAVE] [♿] [X] [🛏] [💻] [➰]

AAA **W W** Econo Lodge **M**
(843) 538-3830. **$49-$99.** 1145 Sniders Hwy. I-95, exit 53 (SR 63), just e. Ext corridors. **Pets:** Accepted.

[SAVE] [♿] [X] [🛏] [💻]

W W Ramada Inn of Walterboro **SH**
(843) 538-5403. **$65.** 1245 Sniders Hwy. I-95, exit 53 (SR 63), just e. Ext corridors. **Pets:** Small. $10 daily fee/pet. Service with restrictions, supervision.

[ASK] [♿] [X] [🛏] [💻] [➰]

AAA **W** Rice Planters Inn **M**
(843) 538-8964. **Call for rates.** 97 Ladson Ln. I-95, exit 53 (SR 63), just e. Ext corridors. **Pets:** Other species. $5 daily fee/pet. Service with restrictions, supervision.

[SAVE] [X] [➰]

AAA **W W** Super 8 Motel **M**
(843) 538-5383. **Call for rates.** 1972 Bells Hwy. I-95, exit 57 (SR 64), just nw. Ext corridors. **Pets:** Accepted.

[SAVE] [X] [🛏] [➰]

WEST COLUMBIA

AAA **W W** Quality Inn **SH**
(803) 791-5160. **$59-$89.** 2516 Augusta Rd. I-26, exit 111B, just e. Ext/int corridors. **Pets:** Accepted.

[SAVE] [♿] [X] [🛏] [💻] [➰]

WINNSBORO

W W Days Inn **M**
(803) 635-1447. **$55.** 1894 US Hwy 321 Bypass. I-77, exit 34 (SR 34), 6.5 mi w; jct US 321/SR 34/213. Ext corridors. **Pets:** Small. $7 daily fee/pet. Designated rooms, service with restrictions, supervision.

[ASK] [♿] [X] [🛏] [💻] [➰]

AAA **W W** Fairfield Motel **M**
(803) 635-3458. **$45-$60.** 56 US 321 Bypass S. Jct SR 213/US 321 Bypass S, 1.8 mi n. Ext corridors. **Pets:** Small, dogs only. $5 daily fee/pet. Service with restrictions, supervision.

[SAVE] [♿] [X] [🛏] [➰]

YEMASSEE

W W W Holiday Inn Express Point South/Yemassee **SH**
(843) 726-9400. **$69-$159.** 138 Frampton Dr. I-95, exit 33 (US 17), just ne. Int corridors. **Pets:** Small. $20 one-time fee/room. Service with restrictions, supervision.

[ASK] [♿] [X] [♿M] [🛏] [💻] [➰]

SOUTH DAKOTA

ABERDEEN

◇◇ Aberdeen East Super 8 Motel SH
(605) 229-5005. **$80-$125, 60 day notice.** 2405 6th Ave SE. 1.8 mi e on US 12. Int corridors. **Pets:** Accepted.
[A$K] [X] [&M] [H] [L] [≈] [X]

◇◇ Aberdeen North Super 8 Motel SH
(605) 226-2288. **Call for rates.** 770 NW Hwy 281. On US 281, 1.5 mi nw. Int corridors. **Pets:** Accepted.
[X]

◇◇ Aberdeen West Super 8 Motel SH
(605) 225-1711. **Call for rates.** 714 S Hwy 281. Jct US 12 and 281. Int corridors. **Pets:** Accepted.
[X] [H]

◇◇◇ AmericInn Lodge & Suites of Aberdeen SH
(605) 225-4565. **$100-$250.** 310 Centennial St. 2.2 mi e on US 12, just n. Int corridors. **Pets:** Accepted.
[A$K] [S6] [X] [&M] [H] [L] [≈] [X]

◇◇ Best Western Ramkota Hotel SH
(605) 229-4040. **$90-$100.** 1400 8th Ave NW. 1.5 mi nw on US 281. Ext/int corridors. **Pets:** Designated rooms, service with restrictions, supervision.
[SAVE] [S6] [X] [&M] [H] [L] [†1] [≈] [X]

◇◇ Comfort Inn SH
(605) 226-0097. **$84-$106.** 2923 6th Ave SE. 2 mi e on US 12. Int corridors. **Pets:** $30 deposit/room. No service, supervision.
[SAVE] [S6] [X] [H] [L] [≈] [X]

◇◇◇ Holiday Inn Express Hotel & Suites SH
(605) 725-4000. **$95-$140.** 3310 7th Ave SE. 2.1 mi e on US 12. Int corridors. **Pets:** Accepted.
[A$K] [X] [&M] [H] [L] [≈] [X]

ARLINGTON

◇◇ Arlington Inn SH
(605) 983-4609. **$51-$65.** 402 S Hwy 81. 1 mi s on US 81. Int corridors. **Pets:** Accepted.
[A$K] [S6] [X] [H]

BERESFORD

◇◇ Super 8 Motel SH
(605) 763-2001. **Call for rates.** 1410 W Cedar. I-29, exit 47 (SR 46), just e. Int corridors. **Pets:** Accepted.
[X] [H] [L] [≈] [X]

BLACK HILLS AREA

BELLE FOURCHE

◇ Ace Motel M
(605) 892-2612. **$38-$58.** 109 6th Ave. 0.5 mi n via US 85, just e; just s of US 212 Bypass. Ext corridors. **Pets:** Accepted.
[X] [H]

BLACKHAWK

◇◇ Ramada SH
(605) 787-4844. **Call for rates.** 7900 Stagestop Rd. I-90, exit 48, just s. Int corridors. **Pets:** Accepted.
[X] [H] [L] [≈]

CUSTER

◇◇◇ Bavarian Inn Motel SH
(605) 673-2802. **$59-$119, 3 day notice.** 907 N 5th St. 1 mi n on US 16 and 385. Ext/int corridors. **Pets:** Accepted.
[SAVE] [S6] [X] [H] [L] [†1] [≈] [X]

◇◇ Rock Crest Lodge and Cabins CA ❀
(605) 673-4323. **$49-$99, 14 day notice.** 15 W Mt. Rushmore Rd. US 16, 0.5 mi w. Ext/int corridors. **Pets:** Medium, dogs only. $25 deposit/pet, $8 daily fee/pet. Designated rooms, service with restrictions, crate.
[SAVE] [S6] [X] [H] [L] [≈] [X]

◇ Rocket Motel M
(605) 673-4401. **$40-$90.** 211 Mt. Rushmore Rd. On US 16; center. Ext corridors. **Pets:** Small. $20 one-time fee/pet. Designated rooms, service with restrictions, supervision.
[SAVE] [S6] [X] [H]

◇◇ Super 8 Custer SH
(605) 673-2200. **$55-$99.** 415 W Mt. Rushmore Rd. US 16, 0.8 mi w. Int corridors. **Pets:** Accepted.
[SAVE] [X] [H] [L] [≈]

DEADWOOD

◇ Black Hills Inn & Suites M
(605) 578-7791. **$40-$70, 3 day notice.** 206 Mountain Shadow Ln. 0.3 mi s of jct US 385 and 85. Int corridors. **Pets:** Accepted.
[A$K] [X] [H] [L] [≈]

◇◇ First Gold Hotel & Gaming SH
(605) 578-9777. **$59-$299, 7 day notice.** 270 Main St. 0.7 mi n on US 85. Int corridors. **Pets:** Medium. $15 one-time fee/room. Designated rooms, service with restrictions.
[SAVE] [S6] [X] [L] [†1]

HILL CITY

Best Western Golden Spike Inn & Suites SH
(605) 574-2577. **$70-$203.** 106 Main St. Just n on US 16 and 385. Ext/int corridors. **Pets:** Medium, other species. $10 daily fee/pet. Designated rooms, service with restrictions, supervision.

Lantern Inn M
(605) 574-2582. **$54-$130.** 580 E Main St. On north side of town, on US 16 and 385. Ext corridors. **Pets:** Very small. $4 daily fee/pet. Service with restrictions, supervision.

The Lodge at Palmer Gulch SH
(605) 574-2525. **$50-$695, 10 day notice.** 12620 SR 244. On SR 244, 5 mi w of Mt. Rushmore. Int corridors. **Pets:** $20 daily fee/pet. Designated rooms, service with restrictions, supervision.

HOT SPRINGS

Americas Best Value Inn By The River M
(605) 745-4292. **$40-$90.** 602 W River. On US 385; downtown. Ext corridors. **Pets:** Accepted.

Best Western Sundowner Inn SH
(605) 745-7378. **$70-$180.** 737 S 6th St. 0.5 mi se off US 18 and 385. Int corridors. **Pets:** Designated rooms, service with restrictions, supervision.

Budget Host Hills Inn M
(605) 745-3130. **$49-$154.** 640 S 6th St. 0.5 mi se off US 18 and 385. Ext corridors. **Pets:** Small. Designated rooms, service with restrictions, supervision.

Hot Springs Super 8 Motel SH
(605) 745-3888. **$52-$124.** 800 Mammoth St. Jct US 18 and 385, 1 mi w on US 18 Bypass. Int corridors. **Pets:** Other species. $10 one-time fee/room. Supervision.

KEYSTONE

Best Western Four Presidents Lodge SH
(605) 666-4472. **$80-$200.** 24075 Hwy 16A. On US 16A, 1 mi n. Int corridors. **Pets:** Large, dogs only. $10 daily fee/pet. Designated rooms, service with restrictions, supervision.

Holy Smoke Resort CA
(605) 666-4616. **$40-$140, 3 day notice.** 24105 Hwy 16A. On US 16A, 1 mi n. Ext corridors. **Pets:** Dogs only. $8 daily fee/pet. Designated rooms, service with restrictions, supervision.

Keystone Boardwalk Inn & Suites SH
(605) 666-4990. **$50-$100.** 250 Winter St. On US 16A; downtown. Ext/int corridors. **Pets:** Accepted.

Mt. Rushmore's Washington Inn SH
(605) 666-5070. **$39-$199, 3 day notice.** 231 Winter St. On US 16A; downtown. Ext/int corridors. **Pets:** Medium, dogs only. Designated rooms, service with restrictions, supervision.

Mt. Rushmore's White House Resort SH
(605) 666-4917. **$39-$199, 3 day notice.** 115 Swanzey St. Jct US 16A and SR 40. Ext/int corridors. **Pets:** Accepted.

Powder House Lodge CA
(605) 666-4646. **$70-$200, 3 day notice.** 24125 Hwy 16A. On US 16A, 1.5 mi n. Ext corridors. **Pets:** Accepted.

LEAD

Spearfish Canyon Lodge SH
(605) 584-3435. **$89-$169, 5 day notice.** 10619 Roughlock Falls Rd. I-90, exit 14 (Spearfish Canyon), 13 mi s. Int corridors. **Pets:** $15 daily fee/pet. Service with restrictions, supervision.

RAPID CITY

Alex Johnson Hotel SH
(605) 342-1210. **$89-$179.** 523 6th St. I-90, exit 57, s on I-190, then left at Omaha; downtown. Int corridors. **Pets:** Small. $35 one-time fee/room. Designated rooms, service with restrictions, crate.

Americas Best Value Inn SH
(605) 343-5434. **$59-$119.** 620 Howard St. I-90, exit 58, just nw of Haines Ave. Int corridors. **Pets:** Other species. $10 daily fee/pet. Service with restrictions, supervision.

Best Western Ramkota Hotel SH
(605) 343-8550. **$97-$189.** 2111 N LaCrosse St. I-90, exit 59 (LaCrosse St), just n. Ext/int corridors. **Pets:** Service with restrictions, supervision.

Big Sky Lodge M
(605) 348-3200. **$49-$109.** 4080 Tower Rd. 3 mi s on US 16, 0.3 mi n on Skyline Dr, take service road off US 16. Ext corridors. **Pets:** Accepted.

Budget Host Inn M
(605) 343-5126. **Call for rates.** 2101 Mt. Rushmore Rd. 1 mi s on US 16. Ext corridors. **Pets:** Accepted.

Days Inn I-90 SH
(605) 348-8410. **$59-$299.** 1570 Rapp St. I-90, exit 59 (LaCrosse St), just s. Int corridors. **Pets:** Small, other species. $10 daily fee/pet. Designated rooms, service with restrictions, supervision.

Fair Value Inn M
(605) 342-8118. **$45-$75.** 1607 LaCrosse St. I-90, exit 59 (LaCrosse St), 0.3 mi s. Ext corridors. **Pets:** Dogs only. Designated rooms, service with restrictions, supervision.

Foothills Inn SH
(605) 348-5640. **$49-$299.** 1625 N LaCrosse St. I-90, exit 59 (LaCrosse St), just s. Int corridors. **Pets:** Accepted.

Gold Star Motel M
(605) 341-7051. **$45-$78.** 801 E North. I-90, exit 60, 1.5 mi sw on I-90 business loop, 1.2 mi s, then just e, from exit 59 (LaCrosse St). Ext corridors. **Pets:** Small, other species. $5 daily fee/pet. Service with restrictions, supervision.

▼▼▼ GrandStay Residential Suites 🆂🅷
(605) 341-5100. **$130-$180.** 660 Disk Dr. I-90, exit 58C (Haines Ave), just n, then w. Int corridors. **Pets:** Accepted.
🅰🆂🅺 ☒ ♿ 🛏 💻 🏊

▼▼ Happy Holiday Resort Motel Ⓜ
(605) 342-8101. **Call for rates.** 8990 S Hwy 16. On US 16, 7 mi s. Ext corridors. **Pets:** Accepted.
🆂🅰🆅🅴 ☒ 🛏 💻 🏊 ☒

▼▼▼ Holiday Inn Express Hotel & Suites, I-90 🆂🅷
(605) 355-9090. **$94-$269.** 645 E Disk Dr. I-90, exit 59 (LaCrosse St), just ne. Int corridors. **Pets:** Accepted.
☒ ♿ 🛏 💻 🏊

▼▼▼ Holiday Inn-Rushmore Plaza 🅻🅷
(605) 348-4000. **Call for rates.** 505 N 5th St. I-90, exit 58, 1.3 mi s on Haines. Int corridors. **Pets:** Accepted.
🆂🅰🆅🅴 ☒ ♿ 🛏 💻 🍽 🏊 ☒

▼▼▼ La Quinta Inn & Suites 🆂🅷
(605) 718-7000. **$114.** 1416 N Elk Vale Rd. I-90, exit 61 (Elk Vale Rd), just s, then just e. Int corridors. **Pets:** Other species. Service with restrictions, supervision.
🆂🅰🆅🅴 🆂🅾 ☒ ♿ 🛏 💻 🍽 🏊 ☒

▼ Lazy U Motel Ⓜ 🐾
(605) 343-4242. **$42-$72.** 2215 Mt. Rushmore Rd. 1 mi s on US 16. Ext corridors. **Pets:** Small, dogs only. $5 daily fee/pet. Service with restrictions, supervision.
🆂🅰🆅🅴 🆂🅾 ☒ 🛏

▼▼ Microtel Inn & Suites 🆂🅷
(605) 348-2523. **$57-$259.** 1740 Rapp St. I-90, exit 59 (LaCrosse St), just se. Int corridors. **Pets:** Accepted.
🆂🅰🆅🅴 ☒ ♿ 🛏 💻 🏊

▼▼ Quality Inn 🆂🅷
(605) 342-3322. **$50-$330.** 1902 LaCrosse St. I-90, exit 59 (LaCrosse St), just s. Ext/int corridors. **Pets:** Accepted.
🅰🆂🅺 🆂🅾 ☒ ♿ 🛏 💻 🍽 🏊 ☒

▼▼▼ Super 8 Motel-I-90 🆂🅷
(605) 348-8070. **Call for rates.** 2124 LaCrosse St. I-90, exit 59 (LaCrosse St), just n. Int corridors. **Pets:** Accepted.
🆂🅰🆅🅴 ☒ ♿ 🛏

▼▼ Super 8 Motel-South 🆂🅷
(605) 342-4911. **$40-$160.** 2520 Tower Rd. 1.4 mi s on US 16, then just e. Int corridors. **Pets:** Accepted.
🆂🅰🆅🅴 🆂🅾 ☒ 🛏

SPEARFISH

▼▼▼ Best Western Black Hills Lodge 🆂🅷
(605) 642-7795. **$69-$240, 30 day notice.** 540 E Jackson Blvd. I-90, exit 12, just s. Ext/int corridors. **Pets:** Dogs only. $5 daily fee/pet. Designated rooms, service with restrictions, supervision.
🆂🅰🆅🅴 🆂🅾 ☒ 💻 🏊

▼▼ Days Inn 🆂🅷
(605) 642-7101. **Call for rates.** 240 Ryan Rd. I-90, exit 10, 1.2 mi s. Ext/int corridors. **Pets:** Accepted.
☒ 🛏 💻

▼▼▼▼ Holiday Inn Hotel & Convention Center 🆂🅷 🐾
(605) 642-4683. **$80-$120.** 305 N 27th St. I-90, exit 14 (Spearfish Canyon), just n. Ext/int corridors. **Pets:** $25 one-time fee/pet. Designated rooms, service with restrictions, supervision.
🆂🅰🆅🅴 ☒ ♿ 🛏 💻 🍽 🏊 ☒

▼▼▼ Howard Johnson Express Inn 🆂🅷
(605) 642-8105. **Call for rates.** 323 S 27th St. I-90, exit 14 (Spearfish Canyon), just s. Int corridors. **Pets:** Medium, other species. $10 daily fee/pet. Service with restrictions, supervision.
🆂🅰🆅🅴 ☒ 🛏 💻 🍽 🏊

▼▼ Spearfish Super 8 Motel 🆂🅷
(605) 642-4721. **Call for rates.** 440 Heritage Dr. I-90, exit 14 (Spearfish Canyon), just s, then e, then s. Int corridors. **Pets:** Accepted.
☒ 🛏 💻 🏊

STURGIS

▼▼▼ Best Western of Sturgis 🆂🅷
(605) 347-3604. **$50-$120.** 2431 S Junction Ave. I-90, exit 32. Ext/int corridors. **Pets:** Other species. Designated rooms, service with restrictions, crate.
🆂🅰🆅🅴 🆂🅾 ☒ 🛏 💻 🍽 🏊

END AREA

BRANDON

▼▼▼ Comfort Inn 🆂🅷
(605) 582-5777. **$79-$159.** 1105 N Splitrock Blvd. I-90, exit 406, just s. Int corridors. **Pets:** Accepted.
🆂🅰🆅🅴 🆂🅾 ☒ ♿ 🛏 💻 🏊

BROOKINGS

▼▼ Brookings Super 8 Motel 🆂🅷
(605) 692-6920. **Call for rates.** 3034 Lefevre Dr. I-29, exit 132, just e. Int corridors. **Pets:** Accepted.
☒ 🛏 🏊

▼▼▼ Holiday Inn Express Hotel & Suites 🆂🅷
(605) 692-9060. **$110-$150.** 3020 Lefevre Dr. I-29, exit 132, just se. Int corridors. **Pets:** Accepted.
🅰🆂🅺 🆂🅾 ☒ ♿ 🛏 💻 🏊 ☒

BUFFALO

▼ Tipperary Lodge Ⓜ
(605) 375-3721. **$50.** 604 1st St W. 0.5 mi n on US 85, turn at sign. Int corridors. **Pets:** Accepted.
🅰🆂🅺 🆂🅾 ☒ 🛏

CANISTOTA

▼▼▼ Best Western U-Bar Motel Ⓜ
(605) 296-3466. **$60-$96, 3 day notice.** 130 Ash St. I-90, exit 368, 6 mi s, follow signs. Ext corridors. **Pets:** Very small, dogs only. $15 one-time fee/room. Designated rooms, service with restrictions, supervision.
🆂🅰🆅🅴 🆂🅾 ☒ 🛏 💻

CHAMBERLAIN

▼▼▼ AmericInn Lodge & Suites of Chamberlain 🆂🅷
(605) 734-0985. **$60-$150.** 1981 E King St. I-90, exit 265, just e. Int corridors. **Pets:** Accepted.
🆂🅰🆅🅴 🆂🅾 ☒ ♿ 🛏 💻 🏊

Bel Aire Motel M
(605) 734-5595. **$45-$70.** 312 E King St. On US 16 and I-90 business loop; downtown. Ext/int corridors. **Pets:** Accepted.
(SAVE) (S) (X) (🔌)

Best Western Lee's Motor Inn SH
(605) 734-5575. **$50-$90, 3 day notice.** 220 W King St. US 16 and I-90 business loop; downtown. Ext/int corridors. **Pets:** Accepted.
(SAVE) (S) (X) (🔌) (🔌) (X)

Cedar Shore Resort LH
(605) 734-6376. **$80-$210.** 1500 Shoreline Dr. I-90, exit 260, 2.5 mi e on Business Rt I-90, then 1 mi ne on Mickelson county road, follow signs. Int corridors. **Pets:** $10 daily fee/room. Service with restrictions, supervision.
(SAVE) (S) (X) (&M) (🔌) (🔌) (11) (🔌) (X)

Holiday Inn Express SH
(605) 734-5593. **Call for rates.** 100 W Hwy 16. I-90, exit 260, just n. Int corridors. **Pets:** Accepted.
(X) (&M) (🔌)

Oasis Inn SH
(605) 734-6061. **$59-$109.** 1100 E Hwy 16. I-90, exit 260, 0.4 mi e on US 16 and I-90 business loop. Ext/int corridors. **Pets:** Medium, other species. Service with restrictions, crate.
(SAVE) (S) (X) (&M) (🔌) (🔌)

DELL RAPIDS

Bilmar Inn & Suites SH
(605) 428-4288. **$56-$110.** 510 N Hwy 77. I-29, exit 98 (SR 115), 3 mi e, then just n. Int corridors. **Pets:** Accepted.
(SAVE) (S) (X) (🔌)

DE SMET

De Smet Super Deluxe Inn & Suites SH
(605) 854-9388. **$59-$135.** 288 Hwy 14 E. US 14, just e. Int corridors. **Pets:** Accepted.
(X) (🔌) (🔌) (🔌)

FAITH

Prairie Vista Inn SH
(605) 967-2343. **$66-$86.** Hwy 212 & E 1st. On US 212; at east city edge. Int corridors. **Pets:** Medium. $10 daily fee/pet. Designated rooms, supervision.
(SAVE) (S) (X) (🔌) (🔌)

FAULKTON

Super 8 Motel SH
(605) 598-4567. **Call for rates.** 700 Main St. On US 212; center. Int corridors. **Pets:** Accepted.
(X) (🔌) (🔌)

FLANDREAU

Royal River Casino & Hotel SH
(605) 997-3746. **$55-$199.** 607 S Veterans St. I-29, exit 114, 7 mi e, follow signs. Int corridors. **Pets:** Medium. $50 deposit/pet. Designated rooms, service with restrictions, supervision.
(SAVE) (X) (&M) (🔌) (🔌) (11) (🔌) (X)

FORT PIERRE

Fort Pierre Motel M
(605) 223-3111. **$58-$78, 3 day notice.** 211 S 1st Ave. On US 83, 1.2 mi s of jct US 14. Ext corridors. **Pets:** Accepted.
(X) (🔌)

FREEMAN

Freeman Country Inn SH
(605) 925-4888. **$58-$75.** 1019 S Hwy 81. On US 81, just s. Int corridors. **Pets:** Accepted.
(ASK) (S) (X) (🔌)

HURON

Best Western of Huron SH
(605) 352-2000. **$86-$101.** 2000 Dakota Ave. 1.3 mi s on SR 37. Ext/int corridors. **Pets:** Medium, dogs only. $10 daily fee/room. Service with restrictions, supervision.
(ASK) (S) (X) (&M) (🔌) (🔌) (X)

Comfort Inn SH
(605) 352-6655. **$69-$99.** 100 21st St SW. 1.3 mi s on SR 37. Ext/int corridors. **Pets:** Large. $30 one-time fee/room. Service with restrictions, supervision.
(SAVE) (S) (X) (&M) (🔌) (🔌) (X)

INTERIOR

Badlands Budget Host Inn M
(605) 433-5335. **$41-$63.** 900 SD Hwy 377. Jct SR 44 and 377, 2 mi s of Badlands National Park. Ext corridors. **Pets:** Other species. $5 daily fee/pet. Service with restrictions, supervision.
(SAVE) (S) (🔌) (🔌) (🔌)

KADOKA

Budget Host Sundowner Motor Inn M
(605) 837-2296. **$50-$145.** 510 SR 73. I-90, exit 150, just s. Ext corridors. **Pets:** Small. $15 daily fee/room. Designated rooms, supervision.
(SAVE) (S) (X) (🔌) (🔌)

H & H El Centro M
(605) 837-2287. **$59-$109.** 105 E Hwy 16. 1.5 mi w on I-90 business route from exit 152, 1.3 mi e from exit 150. Ext corridors. **Pets:** Other species. Service with restrictions, crate.
(SAVE) (S) (X) (🔌) (11) (🔌) (X)

West Motel M
(605) 837-2427. **$42-$80, 3 day notice.** 306 Hwy 16 W. I-90, exit 150, 1 mi e on I-90 business route. Ext corridors. **Pets:** $10 daily fee/room. Service with restrictions, supervision.
(SAVE) (X) (🔌)

MADISON

AmericInn Lodge & Suites SH
(605) 256-3076. **$74-$123.** 504 10th St SE. SR 34, 0.5 mi se; south side of town. Int corridors. **Pets:** Accepted.
(ASK) (X) (&M) (🔌) (🔌) (🔌)

MITCHELL

AmericInn Lodge & Suites SH
(605) 996-9700. **$72-$135.** 1421 S Burr St. I-90, exit 332, just n. Int corridors. **Pets:** Medium. $20 daily fee/pet. Designated rooms, service with restrictions, supervision.
(SAVE) (X) (&M) (🔌) (🔌) (🔌)

Anthony Motel M
(605) 996-7518. **$38-$99.** 1518 W Havens St. I-90, exit 330, 0.6 mi n on I-90 business loop. Ext corridors. **Pets:** Accepted.
(SAVE) (S) (X) (🔌) (🔌)

Best Western Motor Inn M
(605) 996-5536. **$45-$99.** 1001 S Burr St. I-90, exit 332 (SR 37), 0.6 mi n. Ext corridors. **Pets:** Medium. $25 deposit/pet. Designated rooms, service with restrictions.
(SAVE) (S) (X) (🔌) (🔌)

⚸ ▼▼◆ Days Inn Mitchell SH
(605) 996-6208. **$79-$99.** 1506 S Burr St. I-90, exit 332, just n. Int corridors. **Pets:** Medium, dogs only. $20 deposit/pet, $10 one-time fee/pet. Designated rooms, service with restrictions, supervision.
[SAVE] [S6] [✕] [🛢] [💻] [⇌] [⊠]

⚸ ▼▼◆ Hampton Inn SH
(605) 995-1575. **$79-$135, 30 day notice.** 1920 Highland Way. I-90, exit 332 (SR 37), just se. Int corridors. **Pets:** Large, dogs only. $20 daily fee/room. Service with restrictions, supervision.
[SAVE] [✕] [&M] [🛢] [💻] [⇌] [⊠]

⚸ ▼▼◆ Holiday Inn SH
(605) 996-6501. **$89-$109.** 1525 W Havens St. I-90, exit 330, 0.5 mi n. Ext/int corridors. **Pets:** $10 daily fee/room. Service with restrictions, crate.
[SAVE] [S6] [✕] [&M] [🛢] [💻] [¶¶] [⇌] [⊠]

⚸ ▼◆◆ Kelly Inn & Suites SH
(605) 995-0500. **$69-$130.** 1010 Cabela Dr. I-90, exit 332, just sw. Ext/int corridors. **Pets:** Large, other species. Service with restrictions, supervision.
[SAVE] [✕] [🛢] [💻] [⇌] [⊠]

⚸ ▼◆◆ Thunderbird Lodge M
(605) 996-6645. **$55-$109.** 1601 S Burr St. I-90, exit 332, just n. Ext/int corridors. **Pets:** Large. $10 daily fee/pet. Designated rooms, service with restrictions, supervision.
[SAVE] [S6] [✕] [&M] [🛢] [💻]

MOBRIDGE

▼◆◆ Wrangler Inn SH
(605) 845-3641. **$69-$139.** 820 W Grand Crossing. 0.5 mi w on US 12. Ext/int corridors. **Pets:** Accepted.
[ASK] [S6] [✕] [🛢] [💻] [¶¶] [⇌] [⊠]

MURDO

⚸ ▼▼◆ Best Western Graham's M
(605) 669-2441. **$49-$119.** 301 W 5th. On I-90 business loop, 0.5 mi w of jct US 83; I-90, exits 191 and 192. Ext corridors. **Pets:** Other species. Service with restrictions, supervision.
[SAVE] [S6] [✕] [💻] [⇌]

⚸ ▼▼◆ Days Inn Range Country SH
(605) 669-2425. **Call for rates.** 302 W 5th. On I-90 business loop, 0.5 mi w of jct US 83, exits 192 and 191. Ext/int corridors. **Pets:** Other species. Designated rooms, service with restrictions, supervision.
[SAVE] [✕] [🛢] [💻] [⇌]

NORTH SIOUX CITY

▼▼◆ Hampton Inn SH
(605) 232-9739. **Call for rates.** 101 S Sodrac Dr. I-29, exit 2, just w. Int corridors. **Pets:** Accepted.
[✕] [&M] [🛢] [💻] [⇌] [⊠]

PICKSTOWN

▼◆◆ Fort Randall Inn M
(605) 487-7801. **$65-$70.** 116 US Hwy 18. On US 18/281; just e of the dam. Ext corridors. **Pets:** Accepted.
[S6] [✕] [🛢]

PIERRE

⚸ ▼▼◆ Best Western Ramkota Hotel SH
(605) 224-6877. **$98-$115.** 920 W Sioux Ave. 1 mi w on US 14/83. Ext/int corridors. **Pets:** Other species. Service with restrictions, supervision.
[SAVE] [S6] [✕] [&M] [🛢] [💻] [¶¶] [⇌]

⚸ ▼▼◆ Comfort Inn of Pierre SH
(605) 224-0377. **$65-$120.** 410 W Sioux Ave. 0.3 mi w on US 14/83 and SR 34. Int corridors. **Pets:** Dogs only. $10 daily fee/pet. Service with restrictions, supervision.
[SAVE] [S6] [✕] [&M] [🛢] [💻] [⇌]

⚸ ▼▼◆ Governor's Inn SH
(605) 224-4200. **$70-$135.** 700 W Sioux Ave. 0.8 mi w on US 14/83 and SR 34. Ext/int corridors. **Pets:** Other species. $10 one-time fee/room. Service with restrictions, supervision.
[SAVE] [✕] [🛢] [💻] [⇌]

▼▼ Kelly Inn SH
(605) 224-4140. **$62-$69.** 713 W Sioux Ave. 0.8 mi w on US 14/83. Int corridors. **Pets:** Accepted.
[ASK] [S6] [✕] [🛢] [💻]

PLANKINTON

▼▼ Super 8 Motel SH
(605) 942-7722. **Call for rates.** 801 S Main St. I-90, exit 308, just n. Int corridors. **Pets:** Accepted.
[⊠] [🛢]

SIOUX FALLS

▼▼ Baymont Inn SH
(605) 362-0835. **Call for rates.** 3200 Meadow Ave. I-29, exit 77 (41st St), just w, then just n. Int corridors. **Pets:** Accepted.
[⊠] [&M] [🛢] [💻] [⇌]

⚸ ▼▼ Best Western Empire Towers SH
(605) 361-3118. **$65-$135.** 4100 W Shirley Pl. I-29, exit 77 (41st St), just ne. Int corridors. **Pets:** Large, other species. $15 daily fee/room. Service with restrictions, supervision.
[SAVE] [S6] [✕] [🛢] [💻] [⇌]

⚸ ▼▼◆ Best Western Ramkota Hotel & Conference Center LH ✤
(605) 336-0650. **$110-$150.** 3200 W Maple. I-29, exit 81 (Airport/Russell St), just e. Ext/int corridors. **Pets:** Other species. Service with restrictions, supervision.
[SAVE] [S6] [✕] [&M] [🛢] [💻] [¶¶] [⇌] [⊠]

⚸ ▼▼◆ ClubHouse Hotel & Suites SH 🐾
(605) 361-8700. **$129-$169.** 2320 S Louise Ave. I-29, exit 78 (26th St), just e. Ext/int corridors. **Pets:** Other species. Service with restrictions, supervision.
[SAVE] [S6] [✕] [&M] [🛢] [💻] [⊠]

▼▼ Comfort Inn by Choice Hotels South SH
(605) 361-2822. **Call for rates.** 3216 S Carolyn Ave. I-29, exit 77 (41st St), just e, then n. Int corridors. **Pets:** Accepted.
[⊠] [🛢] [💻] [⇌]

⚸ ▼▼ Comfort Inn North SH
(605) 331-4490. **Call for rates.** 5100 N Cliff Ave. I-90, exit 399 (Cliff Ave), 0.3 mi s. Int corridors. **Pets:** Other species. $10 one-time fee/pet. Service with restrictions, supervision.
[SAVE] [✕] [&M] [🛢] [💻] [⇌]

▼◆▼ Comfort Suites by Choice Hotels SH
(605) 362-9711. **Call for rates.** 3208 S Carolyn Ave. I-29, exit 77 (41st St), just e, then n. Int corridors. **Pets:** Accepted.
[⊠] [🛢] [💻] [⇌]

⚸ ▼▼◆▼ Country Inn & Suites By Carlson SH
(605) 373-0153. **$84-$159.** 200 E 8th St. Just e of Phillips Ave; downtown. Int corridors. **Pets:** Medium. $10 daily fee/room. Designated rooms, service with restrictions, supervision.
[SAVE] [S6] [✕] [&M] [🛢] [💻] [¶¶] [⇌]

Days Inn Airport SH
(605) 331-5959. **Call for rates.** 5001 N Cliff Ave. I-90, exit 399 (Cliff Ave), just s. Int corridors. **Pets:** Other species. $10 daily fee/room. Service with restrictions, supervision.
SAVE ✕ ᴹ 🖥 💷

Days Inn-Empire SH
(605) 361-9240. **Call for rates.** 3401 Gateway Blvd. I-29, exit 77 (41st St), just w. Int corridors. **Pets:** Dogs only. $10 daily fee/pet. Service with restrictions, supervision.
SAVE ✕ 🖥 💷

Homewood Suites By Hilton SH ✤
(605) 338-8585. **Call for rates.** 3620 W Avera Dr. I-229, exit 1C (Louise Ave), just s. Int corridors. **Pets:** Other species. $5 daily fee/pet, $15 one-time fee/room. Service with restrictions, crate.
SAVE ✕ ᴹ 🖥 💷 ⊅ ⊠

Kelly Inn SH
(605) 338-6242. **$64-$79.** 3101 W Russell St. I-29, exit 81 (Airport/Russell St), 0.3 mi e. Ext/int corridors. **Pets:** Accepted.
SAVE ᔕ ✕ 🖥 💷

Microtel Inn & Suites SH
(605) 361-7484. **Call for rates.** 2901 S Carolyn Ave. I-29, exit 77 (41st St), just e, then n. Int corridors. **Pets:** Accepted.
✕ ᴹ 🖥

Quality Inn & Suites SH
(605) 336-1900. **$89-$149.** 5410 N Granite Ln. I-29, exit 83, just e, then 0.3 mi n. Int corridors. **Pets:** Medium, other species. $10 daily fee/pet. Designated rooms, service with restrictions, supervision.
SAVE ᔕ ✕ ᴹ 🖥 💷 ⊅

Red Roof Inn SH
(605) 361-1864. **Call for rates.** 3500 S Gateway Blvd. I-29, exit 77 (41st St), just w. Int corridors. **Pets:** Accepted.
✕ 🖥

Residence Inn by Marriott SH
(605) 361-2202. **$110-$143.** 4509 W Empire Pl. I-29, exit 77 (41st St), 0.5 mi se. Int corridors. **Pets:** Accepted.
ASK ᔕ ✕ ᴹ 🖥 💷 ⊅ ⊠

Sheraton Sioux Falls Hotel LH
(605) 331-0100. **$159.** 1211 N West Ave. I-29, exit 81 (Airport/Russell St), 1.3 mi e. Int corridors. **Pets:** Accepted.
SAVE ✕ ᴹ 🖥 💷 🍴 ⊅ ⊠

Sleep Inn Airport SH
(605) 339-3992. **$50-$81.** 1500 N Kiwanis Ave. I-29, exit 81 (Airport/Russell St), 0.7 mi e. Int corridors. **Pets:** Small. $10 daily fee/room. Designated rooms, service with restrictions, supervision.
SAVE ᔕ ✕ ᴹ 🖥 💷 ⊅ ⊠

Staybridge Suites SH ✤
(605) 361-2298. **$119-$219, 10 day notice.** 2505 S Carolyn Ave. I-29, exit 78, just se. Int corridors. **Pets:** Medium, other species. $25 daily fee/pet. Designated rooms, service with restrictions, crate.
SAVE ᔕ ✕ ᴹ 🖥 💷 ⊅ ⊠

Super 8/I-90/Airport East SH ✤
(605) 339-9212. **Call for rates.** 4808 N Cliff Ave. I-90, exit 399 (Cliff Ave), 0.3 mi s. Int corridors. **Pets:** Other species. $10 daily fee/pet. Designated rooms, supervision.
✕ 🖥 💷

Super 8 Motel-East SH
(605) 338-8881. **Call for rates.** 2616 E 10th St. I-229, exit 6, just e. Int corridors. **Pets:** Accepted.
✕ ᴹ 🖥 💷 ⊅

TownePlace Suites by Marriott SH
(605) 361-2626. **$104-$125.** 4545 W Homefield Dr. I-29, exit 78 (26th St), just w. Int corridors. **Pets:** Accepted.
ASK ᔕ ✕ ᴹ 🖥 💷 ⊅ ⊠

SISSETON

Sisseton Super 8 SH
(605) 742-0808. **$70-$110.** 2104 SD Hwy 10. I-29, exit 232 (SR 10), 1.5 mi w; just w of jct SR 127. Int corridors. **Pets:** Accepted.
ASK ᔕ ✕ ᴹ 🖥 💷 ⊅

VERMILLION

Comfort Inn SH
(605) 624-8333. **$69-$89.** 701 W Cherry St. I-29, exit 26 (SR 50), 7.5 mi w on Business Rt SR 50. Int corridors. **Pets:** Medium. $10 daily fee/pet. Service with restrictions, supervision.
SAVE ᔕ ✕ 🖥 💷 ⊅ ⊠

Holiday Inn Express Hotel & Suites-Vermillion SH
(605) 624-7600. **Call for rates.** 1200 N Dakota St. I-29, exit 26, 7 mi w. Int corridors. **Pets:** Accepted.
✕ ᴹ 🖥 💷 ⊅

WALL

Best Western Plains Motel M
(605) 279-2145. **$60-$135.** 712 Glenn St. I-90, exit 110, just n. Ext corridors. **Pets:** Other species. $10 one-time fee/pet. Service with restrictions, supervision.
SAVE ᔕ ✕ 🖥 💷 ⊅ ⊠

Days Inn SH
(605) 279-2000. **Call for rates.** 212 10th Ave. I-90, exit 110, just n, then just w. Int corridors. **Pets:** Accepted.
✕ 🖥 💷 ⊠

Econo Lodge M
(605) 279-2121. **$59-$169.** 804 Glenn St. I-90, exit 110, just n. Ext corridors. **Pets:** Accepted.
SAVE ᔕ ✕ 🖥 💷 ⊅

Sunshine Inn M
(605) 279-2178. **$49-$69.** 608 Main St. Downtown. Ext corridors. **Pets:** Other species. $5 one-time fee/room. Service with restrictions.
SAVE ᔕ ✕

WATERTOWN

Best Western Ramkota Hotel SH ✤
(605) 886-8011. **$96-$175.** 1901 9th Ave SW. I-29, exit 177 (US 212), 4 mi w. Int corridors. **Pets:** Medium, dogs only. Designated rooms, service with restrictions, supervision.
SAVE ᔕ ✕ ᴹ 🖥 💷 🍴 ⊅ ⊠

Comfort Inn SH
(605) 886-3010. **$69-$129.** 800 35th St Cir. I-29, exit 177 (US 212), just w. Ext/int corridors. **Pets:** $15 one-time fee/room. Designated rooms, service with restrictions, supervision.
SAVE ᔕ ✕ ᴹ 🖥 💷 ⊅

Country Inn & Suites By Carlson SH ✤
(605) 886-8900. **$75-$140.** 3400 8th Ave SE. I-29, exit 177 (US 212), just w. Int corridors. **Pets:** Medium, dogs only. $20 one-time fee/room. Designated rooms, service with restrictions, supervision.
SAVE ᔕ ✕ ᴹ 🖥 💷 ⊅

Days Inn SH
(605) 886-3500. **Call for rates.** 2900 9th Ave SE. I-29, exit 177 (US 212), 0.5 mi w. Ext/int corridors. **Pets:** Large, other species. $10 one-time fee/room. Service with restrictions, supervision.
SAVE ✕ ᴹ 🖥 💷 ⊅

▼▼▼▼ Holiday Inn Express Hotel & Suites SH
(605) 882-3636. **$104-$144.** 3901 9th Ave SE. I-29, exit 177 (US 212), just e. Int corridors. **Pets:** Accepted.
ASK SD X ⛨ ⬛ ⇒ ⊠

▼ Super 8 Motel-Watertown SH
(605) 882-1900. **$56-$73.** 503 14th Ave SE. On US 81, 0.3 mi s of jct US 212. Int corridors. **Pets:** Small. $10 daily fee/pet. Designated rooms, no service, crate.
ASK SD X ⛨ ⬛ ⇒

▲▲▲▲ ▼▼ Travelers Inn Motel SH
(605) 882-2243. **$52-$59.** 920 14th St SE. I-29, exit 177 (US 212), 1.5 mi w, then just s. Int corridors. **Pets:** Other species. $6 daily fee/pet. Designated rooms, supervision.
SAVE SD X ⛨ ⬛

▲▲▲ ▼ Travel Host Motel M
(605) 886-6120. **$41-$65.** 1714 9th Ave SW. I-29, exit 177 (US 212), 4 mi w. Int corridors. **Pets:** Dogs only. $5 daily fee/room. Designated rooms, no service, supervision.
SAVE SD X ⛨

WINNER

▼▼▼▼ Holiday Inn Express Hotel & Suites SH
(605) 842-2255. **$84-$199.** 1360 E Hwy 44. Just ne of jct US 18 and 183. Int corridors. **Pets:** Accepted.
ASK X ⛨M ⛨ ⬛ ⇒

YANKTON

▼▼ Best Western Kelly Inn-Yankton SH
(605) 665-2906. **$69-$109.** 1607 Hwy 50 E. On US 50, 1.8 mi e. Ext/int corridors. **Pets:** Medium, other species. Service with restrictions, crate.
ASK SD X ⛨M ⛨ ⬛ ⑪ ⇒ ⊠

▼▼ Days Inn SH
(605) 665-8717. **Call for rates.** 2410 Broadway. US 81, 1.7 mi n. Int corridors. **Pets:** Accepted.
X ⛨ ⬛

▼▼ Lewis & Clark Resort M
(605) 665-2680. **$65-$115, 30 day notice.** 43496 Shore Dr. 4 mi w on SR 52; in Lewis and Clark State Park, turn into park, just w of Marina. Ext corridors. **Pets:** Accepted.
X ⛨ ⬛ ⇒ ⊠ ⎙

TENNESSEE

ALCOA

Family Inns of America M
(865) 970-2006. **$49-$59.** 2450 Airport Hwy. US 129, just e. Ext corridors. **Pets:** Very small, dogs only. Service with restrictions, supervision.

Jameson Inn Alcoa SH
(865) 984-6800. **Call for rates.** 206 Corporate Pl. US 129, just s. Int corridors. **Pets:** Small. $15 daily fee/room. Service with restrictions, crate.

MainStay Suites SH
(865) 379-7799. **$89-$179.** 361 Fountain View Cir. US 129, just s. Int corridors. **Pets:** Small, other species. $100 one-time fee/room. Service with restrictions, supervision.

ATHENS

Athens Inn SH
(423) 745-1212. **Call for rates.** 115 CR 247. I-75, exit 52, just w. Ext corridors. **Pets:** Accepted.

Days Inn-Athens M
(423) 745-5800. **Call for rates.** 2541 Decatur Pike. I-75, exit 49, 0.3 mi e. Ext corridors. **Pets:** Medium. $5 daily fee/pet. Service with restrictions, supervision.

BRENTWOOD

Baymont Inn & Suites SH
(615) 376-4666. **Call for rates.** 111 Penn Warren Dr. I-65, exit 74B, 1.5 mi w, then just s on West Park. Int corridors. **Pets:** Medium, other species. $10 daily fee/pet. Designated rooms, service with restrictions, crate.

Candlewood Suites SH
(615) 309-0600. **Call for rates.** 5129 Virginia Way. I-65, exit 74B, 0.5 mi w, 0.5 mi s on Franklin Rd, 1.2 mi w on Maryland Way, just s on Ward Cir, then just s. Int corridors. **Pets:** Medium, other species. $75 one-time fee/room. Service with restrictions, crate.

Holiday Inn Brentwood SH
(615) 373-2600. **$99-$159.** 760 Old Hickory Blvd. I-65, exit 74A. Int corridors. **Pets:** Small. $75 one-time fee/room. Designated rooms, service with restrictions, supervision.

MainStay Suites-Brentwood SH
(615) 371-8477. **$80-$150.** 107 Brentwood Blvd. I-65, exit 74B, 1 mi w. Int corridors. **Pets:** Small, other species. $10 daily fee/pet. Service with restrictions, crate.

Residence Inn Brentwood SH
(615) 371-0100. **$154-$174.** 206 Ward Cir. I-65, exit 74B, 0.3 mi s on Franklin Pike Cir (US 31 S), 0.5 mi w on Maryland Way. Ext/int corridors. **Pets:** Accepted.

Sleep Inn SH
(615) 376-2122. **Call for rates.** 1611 Galleria Blvd. I-65, exit 69 northbound, 0.4 mi, then just n; exit 69W southbound, just n. Int corridors. **Pets:** Accepted.

StudioPlus Brentwood SH
(615) 373-4272. **$65.** 9025 Church St E. I-65, exit 74B, 0.5 mi s on US 31, then e. Int corridors. **Pets:** Other species. $75 one-time fee/pet. Service with restrictions.

BULLS GAP

Best Western Executive Inn SH
(423) 235-9111. **$49-$190.** 50 Speedway Ln. I-81, exit 23. Int corridors. **Pets:** Other species. $15 daily fee/pet. Designated rooms, service with restrictions.

Super 8 Motel M
(423) 235-4112. **Call for rates.** 90 Speedway Ln. I-81, exit 23. Ext corridors. **Pets:** Medium. $9 daily fee/room. Service with restrictions, supervision.

BUTLER

Iron Mountain Inn B&B and Creekside Chalet BB
(423) 768-2446. **Call for rates.** 138 Moreland Dr. 1.6 mi w on Pine Orchard Rd from SR 67 at Stout Store, follow signs; 13 mi w on SR 67 from US 421 in Mountain City, follow sign at Stout Store area; 15.1 mi from Shell Station in Hampton to Pine Orchard, 1.6 mi to Moreland Dr. Ext/int corridors. **Pets:** $50 one-time fee/pet. Designated rooms, no service, supervision.

CARYVILLE

▲▲▲◇ **◆** Budget Host Inn **M**
(423) 562-9595. **$33-$55, 7 day notice.** 115 Woods Ave. I-75, exit 134, just w. Ext corridors. **Pets:** Small. $10 one-time fee/pet. Designated rooms, service with restrictions, supervision.
SAVE **X**

CENTERVILLE

▼▼▼ Stay Inn **SH**
(931) 729-5600. **$50-$60.** 634 David St. On SR 100, 3 mi w of jct SR 48. Int corridors. **Pets:** Accepted.
ASK **S** **X** **fi** **P** **≈**

CHATTANOOGA

▼▼ America's Best Inn-Hamilton Mall Area **M**
(423) 894-5454. **Call for rates.** 7717 Lee Hwy. I-75, exit 7B northbound; exit 7 southbound. Ext corridors. **Pets:** Accepted.
X **fi** **P** **≈**

▼◆▼ Baymont Inn & Suites-Chattanooga **SH**
(423) 821-1090. **Call for rates.** 3540 Cummings Hwy. I-24, exit 174, 0.4 mi s. Int corridors. **Pets:** Accepted.
X **fi** **P** **≈**

▲▲▲◇ **▼▼** Best Western Heritage Inn **SH**
(423) 899-3311. **$59-$99.** 7641 Lee Hwy. I-75, exit 7B northbound; exit 7 southbound. Ext corridors. **Pets:** Small, dogs only. $10 daily fee/pet. Service with restrictions, supervision.
SAVE **S** **X** **fi** **P** **Y1** **≈**

▲▲▲◇ **▼▼** Best Western Royal Inn **SH**
(423) 821-6840. **$70-$100.** 3644 Cummings Hwy. I-24, exit 174, 0.4 mi s. Ext corridors. **Pets:** Small. $10 daily fee/pet. Service with restrictions, supervision.
SAVE **S** **X** **fi** **P** **≈**

▲▲▲◇ **▼▼** Comfort Inn **SH**
(423) 499-1993. **$62-$99.** 7620 Hamilton Park Dr. I-75, exit 7B northbound; exit 7 southbound, just w to Lee Hwy, just s, then just e. Int corridors. **Pets:** Accepted.
SAVE **S** **fi** **P** **≈**

▲▲▲◇ **▼▼** Days Inn-Lookout Mountain Tiftonia West **SH**
(423) 821-6044. **Call for rates.** 3801 Cummings Hwy. I-24, exit 174, just n. Ext corridors. **Pets:** Medium. $10 daily fee/pet. Designated rooms, service with restrictions, supervision.
SAVE **X** **fi** **P** **≈**

▼▼ Extended StayAmerica-Chattanooga-Airport **SH**
(423) 892-1315. **$55-$65.** 6240 Airport Dr. SR 153, exit 1 (Lee Hwy), 0.3 mi s to Vance Rd, then just w. Ext corridors. **Pets:** Other species. $75 one-time fee/pet. Service with restrictions.
ASK **S** **X** **fi** **P**

▲▲▲◇ **▼▼▼** Holiday Inn Chattanooga Choo-Choo **LH**
(423) 266-5000. **$139-$159.** 1400 Market St. I-24, exit 178 (Broad St) eastbound, then E Main St; exit 178 (Market St) westbound, 0.5 mi n. Ext/int corridors. **Pets:** Small. $25 one-time fee/room. Service with restrictions, supervision.
SAVE **S** **X** **fi** **P** **Y1** **≈** **X**

▲▲▲◇ **▼▼▼** La Quinta Inn Chattanooga **SH**
(423) 855-0011. **Call for rates.** 7015 Shallowford Rd. I-75, exit 5 (Shallowford Rd), just w. Ext corridors. **Pets:** Other species. Service with restrictions, supervision.
SAVE **X** **fi** **P** **≈**

▼◆▼ MainStay Suites-Chattanooga **SH**
(423) 485-9424. **$74-$104.** 7030 Amin Dr. I-75, exit 5 (Shallowford Rd), just w, then s. Int corridors. **Pets:** Medium. $50 one-time fee/pet. Designated rooms, service with restrictions, crate.
ASK **S** **X** **fi** **P**

▼▼ Microtel Inn-Chattanooga **SH** **❀**
(423) 510-0761. **$50-$70.** 7014 McCutcheon Rd. I-75, exit 5 (Shallowford Rd), just w, 0.3 mi n on Shallowford Village Dr, then just w. Int corridors. **Pets:** Small, other species. $10 one-time fee/pet. Service with restrictions, supervision.
ASK **S** **X** **fi**

▼▼ Motel 6 Downtown **SH**
(423) 265-7300. **Call for rates.** 2440 Williams St. I-24, exit 178 (Market St). Int corridors. **Pets:** Other species. Service with restrictions, supervision.
X **fi**

▲▲▲◇ **▼▼▼** Quality Inn **SH**
(423) 821-1499. **$69-$145.** 3109 Parker Ln. I-24, exit 175, just s. Ext corridors. **Pets:** Other species. $15 daily fee/pet. Designated rooms, service with restrictions, supervision.
SAVE **S** **X** **fi** **P** **≈**

▲▲▲◇ **▼▼▼** Quality Suites **SH** **❀**
(423) 892-1500. **$75-$99.** 7324 Shallowford Rd. I-75, exit 5 (Shallowford Rd), just e. Ext corridors. **Pets:** Small. $15 daily fee/pet. Service with restrictions, supervision.
SAVE **S** **X** **fi** **P** **≈**

▼▼ Ramada Limited-Lookout Mountain West **SH**
(423) 821-7162. **Call for rates.** 30 Birmingham Hwy. I-24, exit 174, just s. Ext/int corridors. **Pets:** Dogs only. $10 daily fee/pet. Service with restrictions, supervision.
X **fi** **P** **≈**

▼▼ Red Roof Inn-Chattanooga **M**
(423) 899-0143. **Call for rates.** 7014 Shallowford Rd. I-75, exit 5 (Shallowford Rd), just w. Ext corridors. **Pets:** Accepted.
X

▼◆▼ Residence Inn by Marriott **SH**
(423) 266-0600. **$134-$159.** 215 Chestnut St. US 27, exit 1C (4th St), just n. Int corridors. **Pets:** Accepted.
ASK **S** **X** **S M** **fi** **P** **≈**

▲▲▲◇ **▼▼▼** The Sheraton Read House Hotel **LH** **❀**
(423) 266-4121. **$249-$269.** 827 Broad St. US 27, exit 1A, just e. Int corridors. **Pets:** Medium. $50 one-time fee/pet. Service with restrictions, supervision.
SAVE **S** **X** **fi** **P** **Y1** **≈**

▼◆▼ Staybridge Suites **SH**
(423) 267-0900. **$119-$319.** 1300 Carter St. US 27 N, exit 1A (Martin Luther King Blvd), just e to Carter St, then 0.3 mi s. Int corridors. **Pets:** Other species. $25 one-time fee/room. Service with restrictions.
ASK **S** **X** **S M** **fi** **P** **≈**

▼▼ Super 8 Motel/Lookout Mountain **SH**
(423) 821-8880. **Call for rates.** 20 Birmingham Hwy. I-24, exit 174. Int corridors. **Pets:** Medium, other species. $30 daily fee/pet. Designated rooms, service with restrictions, supervision.
X **fi** **≈**

CLARKSVILLE

▲▲▲◇ **▼▼▼** Best Western Executive Inn **SH**
(931) 552-3330. **$55-$99.** 250 Holiday Dr. I-24, exit 4, just se. Ext corridors. **Pets:** Accepted.
SAVE **S** **X** **S M** **fi** **P** **≈**

▼◆▼ Candlewood Suites **SH**
(931) 906-0900. **Call for rates.** 3050 Clay Lewis Rd. I-24, exit 4, 0.3 mi s. Int corridors. **Pets:** Accepted.
X **S M** **fi** **P**

▼◆▼ Days Inn North **SH**
(931) 552-1155. **Call for rates.** 130 Westfield Ct. I-24, exit 4, just s. Ext corridors. **Pets:** Accepted.
X **S M** **fi** **P** **≈**

Days Inn of Clarksville SH
(931) 358-3194. **Call for rates.** 1100 Hwy 76 Connector Rd. I-24, exit 11. Ext corridors. **Pets:** Other species. $6 daily fee/pet. Supervision.

Econo Lodge Inn & Suites SH
(931) 647-2002. **$60-$70.** 3065 Wilma Rudolph Blvd. I-24, exit 4, 0.3 mi w. Ext corridors. **Pets:** Medium. $10 daily fee/pet. Designated rooms, service with restrictions, supervision.

Holiday Inn-I-24 SH 🐾
(931) 648-4848. **Call for rates.** 3095 Wilma Rudolph Blvd. I-24, exit 4, just e. Ext corridors. **Pets:** Medium. $15 daily fee/room, $49 one-time fee/room. Designated rooms, service with restrictions, crate.

Red Roof Inn SH
(931) 905-1555. **Call for rates.** 197 Holiday Dr. I-24, exit 4, just se. Ext corridors. **Pets:** Accepted.

CLEVELAND

America's Best Inn & Suites M
(423) 472-3281. **$40-$70.** 2655 Westside Dr NW. I-75, exit 25, just e. Ext corridors. **Pets:** Medium. $10 daily fee/pet. Designated rooms, service with restrictions, supervision.

Baymont Inn & Suites-Cleveland SH
(423) 339-1000. **Call for rates.** 107 Interstate Dr NW. I-75, exit 25, just w. Int corridors. **Pets:** Small. $15 daily fee/pet. Service with restrictions, supervision.

Colonial Inn M
(423) 472-6845. **$35-$45, 7 day notice.** 1555 25th St. I-75, exit 25, 0.3 mi e. Ext corridors. **Pets:** Accepted.

Comfort Inn SH
(423) 478-5265. **$65-$105.** 153 James Asbury Dr. I-75, exit 27, just w. Ext/int corridors. **Pets:** Accepted.

Douglas Inn & Suites SH
(423) 559-5579. **$55-$115.** 2600 Westside Dr NW. I-75, exit 25, just e. Ext/int corridors. **Pets:** Medium. $10 daily fee/pet. Service with restrictions, supervision.

Holiday Inn Mountain View SH
(423) 472-1500. **$85-$176.** 2400 Executive Park Dr. I-75, exit 25, just w. Ext/int corridors. **Pets:** Small. $25 one-time fee/room. Designated rooms, service with restrictions, supervision.

Howard Johnson Chalet SH
(423) 476-8511. **$65-$85.** 2595 Georgetown Rd. I-75, exit 25, just e. Ext corridors. **Pets:** Small, other species. $10 daily fee/room. Service with restrictions, supervision.

Jameson Inn SH
(423) 614-5583. **Call for rates.** 360 Paul Huff Pkwy. I-75, exit 27, 1 mi e. Ext corridors. **Pets:** Accepted.

Ramada Limited SH
(423) 472-5566. **Call for rates.** 156 James Asbury Dr. I-75, exit 27, just w. Ext corridors. **Pets:** Medium. $10 daily fee/pet. Service with restrictions, crate.

Super 8 Motel SH
(423) 476-5555. **Call for rates.** 163 Bernham Dr. I-75, exit 27, just w. Ext/int corridors. **Pets:** Accepted.

CLINTON

Super 8 Motel M
(865) 457-2311. **Call for rates.** 720 Park Pl. I-75, exit 122, just w. Ext corridors. **Pets:** Medium. $7 daily fee/pet. Service with restrictions, supervision.

COLUMBIA

Americas Best Value Inn SH
(931) 381-1410. **$66-$76.** 1548 Bear Creek Pike. I-65, exit 46, just w. Ext corridors. **Pets:** Other species. $6 daily fee/pet. Service with restrictions, supervision.

Holiday Inn Express SH
(931) 380-1227. **$89-$145.** 1554 Bear Creek Pike. I-65, exit 46, just w. Ext corridors. **Pets:** Small, dogs only. $15 one-time fee/pet. Service with restrictions, supervision.

Jameson Inn SH
(931) 388-3326. **Call for rates.** 715 James M Campbell Blvd. 0.9 mi w jct SR 50 and US 31. Int corridors. **Pets:** Small. $15 daily fee/room. Service with restrictions, crate.

COOKEVILLE

Alpine Lodge & Suites SH
(931) 526-3333. **$40-$64.** 2021 E Spring St. I-40, exit 290, just s. Int corridors. **Pets:** Medium, other species. $5 daily fee/pet. Designated rooms, supervision.

Baymont Inn & Suites Cookeville SH
(931) 525-6668. **Call for rates.** 1151 S Jefferson Ave. I-40, exit 287, just s. Int corridors. **Pets:** Medium, other species. Designated rooms, service with restrictions, crate.

Best Western Thunderbird Motel SH
(931) 526-7115. **$54-$120.** 900 S Jefferson Ave. I-40, exit 287, just n. Ext corridors. **Pets:** $10 daily fee/pet. Service with restrictions.

Clarion Inn SH
(931) 526-7125. **Call for rates.** 970 S Jefferson Ave. I-40, exit 287, just n. Ext/int corridors. **Pets:** Medium, other species. $10 one-time fee/room. Designated rooms, service with restrictions, supervision.

Country Hearth Inn & Suites SH 🐾
(931) 528-1040. **$30-$104.** 1100 S Jefferson Ave. I-40, exit 287. Ext corridors. **Pets:** Medium, other species. $10 daily fee/pet. Service with restrictions, crate.

Days Inn SH
(931) 528-1511. **Call for rates.** 1296 S Walnut Ave. I-40, exit 287. Ext corridors. **Pets:** Small, dogs only. $10 one-time fee/pet. Service with restrictions, supervision.

Hampton Inn SH
(931) 520-1117. **Call for rates.** 1025 Interstate Dr. I-40, exit 287, 0.5 mi n. Ext corridors. **Pets:** Accepted.

CORNERSVILLE

 Econo Lodge **M**
(931) 293-2111. **$69-$79.** 3731 Pulaski Hwy. I-65, exit 22 at US 31A. Ext corridors. **Pets:** Medium, dogs only. $7 daily fee/pet. Designated rooms, service with restrictions, supervision.

SAVE SÔ X 🔧 🔁

CROSSVILLE

La Quinta Inn-Crossville **SH**
(931) 456-9338. **Call for rates.** 4038 Hwy 127 N. I-40, exit 317, just n. Int corridors. **Pets:** Other species. Service with restrictions, supervision.

SAVE X Ġᴹ 🔧 🖥 🔁

DANDRIDGE

Holiday Inn Express **SH**
(865) 397-1910. **$59-$79.** 119 Sharon Dr. I-40, exit 417, just s. Int corridors. **Pets:** Medium, other species. $25 one-time fee/pet. Designated rooms, service with restrictions, crate.

SAVE SÔ X Ġᴹ 🔧 🖥 🔁

Jefferson Inn **SH**
(865) 940-5042. **$50-$60.** 127 Sharon Dr. I-40, exit 417, just s. Int corridors. **Pets:** Small, dogs only. $10 daily fee/pet, $10 one-time fee/pet. Designated rooms, service with restrictions, supervision.

ASK SÔ X 🔧 🖥 🔁

Super 8 Motel **SH**
(865) 397-1200. **Call for rates.** 125 Sharon Dr. I-40, exit 417, just s. Int corridors. **Pets:** Large, other species. $10 daily fee/pet. Designated rooms, service with restrictions.

X 🔧 🖥 🔁

DECHERD

Jameson Inn **SH**
(931) 962-0130. **Call for rates.** 1838 Decherd Blvd. Jct Main St and SR 41A, just s. Ext corridors. **Pets:** Small. $15 daily fee/room. Service with restrictions, crate.

X 🔧 🖥 🔁

DICKSON

Best Western Executive Inn **SH**
(615) 446-0541. **$69-$99.** 2338 Hwy 46. I-40, exit 172, just n. Ext corridors. **Pets:** Accepted.

SAVE SÔ X 🔧 🖥 🔁

Comfort Inn **SH**
(615) 441-5252. **Call for rates.** 1025 E Christi Rd. I-40, exit 172, just s. Int corridors. **Pets:** Small, dogs only. $10 daily fee/pet. Designated rooms, service with restrictions, supervision.

SAVE X 🔧 🖥 🔁

Holiday Inn Express **SH**
(615) 446-2781. **$90-$100.** 100 Barzani Blvd. I-40, exit 172, just n. Int corridors. **Pets:** Accepted.

ASK SÔ X Ġᴹ 🔧 🖥 🔁

Ramada Inn **SH**
(615) 446-9081. **Call for rates.** 2420 Hwy 46 S. I-40, exit 172, just s. Ext corridors. **Pets:** Other species. $10 daily fee/pet. Designated rooms, service with restrictions, crate.

SAVE X 🔧 🖥 🍴 🔁

Super 8 Motel **SH**
(615) 446-1923. **Call for rates.** 150 Suzanne Dr. I-40, exit 172, just n on SR 46, then just e. Int corridors. **Pets:** Accepted.

SAVE X 🔧 🖥 🔁

DYERSBURG

Best Western Dyersburg **SH** 🐾
(731) 285-8601. **$75.** 770 Hwy 51 Bypass W. I-155, exit 13, 0.5 mi s; jct of US 51 Bypass and SR 78. Ext corridors. **Pets:** Other species. $10 daily fee/pet. Service with restrictions, supervision.

ASK SÔ X 🔧 🖥 🍴 🔁

Comfort Inn **SH**
(731) 285-6951. **Call for rates.** 815 Reelfoot Dr. I-155, exit 13, just s. Ext corridors. **Pets:** Accepted.

X 🔧 🖥 🔁

Executive Inn & Suites **SH**
(731) 287-0044. **$45-$55.** 2331 Lake Rd. I-155, exit 13, 0.5 mi s. Ext corridors. **Pets:** $10 one-time fee/pet. Service with restrictions, crate.

SÔ X 🔧

Hampton Inn **SH**
(731) 285-4778. **Call for rates.** 2750 Mall Loop Rd. I-155, exit 13, just s. Int corridors. **Pets:** Medium. Designated rooms, service with restrictions, supervision.

X Ġᴹ 🔧 🖥 🔁

EAST RIDGE

Americas Best Value Inn **SH**
(423) 894-6110. **$45-$90.** 639 Camp Jordan Pkwy. I-75, exit 1A (Ringgold Rd), 0.3 mi e. Ext/int corridors. **Pets:** Accepted.

ASK SÔ X 🔧 🖥 🔁

Howard Johnson Plaza Hotel **SH**
(423) 892-8100. **Call for rates.** 6700 Ringgold Rd. I-75, exit 1A (Ringgold Rd), just e. Int corridors. **Pets:** Accepted.

X 🔧 🖥 🍴 🔁

Ramada Limited **SH** 🐾
(423) 894-1860. **$49-$79.** 6650 Ringgold Rd. I-75, exit 1 (Ringgold Rd). Int corridors. **Pets:** Medium. $10 daily fee/pet. Designated rooms, service with restrictions, supervision.

SAVE X 🔧 🖥 🔁

Super 8 Motel **M**
(423) 894-6720. **Call for rates (no credit cards).** 6521 Ringgold Rd. I-75, exit 1B (Ringgold Rd), just w. Ext corridors. **Pets:** Accepted.

X Ġᴹ 🔧 🔁

ETOWAH

Sleep Inn **SH**
(423) 263-4343. **$69-$169.** 600 N Tennessee Ave (US 411). I-75, exit 49 (SR 30), jct US 411 and SR 30, just s. Int corridors. **Pets:** Large. $25 daily fee/pet. Designated rooms, service with restrictions, supervision.

SAVE SÔ X Ġᴹ 🔧 🖥

FAIRVIEW

Deerfield Inn & Suites **SH**
(615) 799-4700. **$60-$80.** 1407 Hwy 96 N. I-40, exit 182. Ext corridors. **Pets:** Small. $15 daily fee/pet. Designated rooms, service with restrictions, supervision.

SAVE SÔ X 🔧 🖥

FARRAGUT

Super 8-West **SH**
(865) 675-5566. **$50-$70.** 11748 Snyder Rd. I-40/75, exit 373 (Campbell Station Rd), just ne. Ext corridors. **Pets:** Medium. $10 daily fee/pet. Designated rooms, service with restrictions, supervision.

ASK SÔ X Ġᴹ 🔧 🖥 🔁

FAYETTEVILLE

Best Western-Fayetteville Inn SH
(931) 433-0100. **$77-$95.** 3021 Thornton Taylor Pkwy. 0.7 mi e of US
431, on US 64 and 231 Bypass. Ext corridors. **Pets:** Accepted.

FRANKLIN

Best Western Franklin Inn SH
(615) 790-0570. **Call for rates.** 1308 Murfreesboro Rd. I-65, exit 65,
just w. Ext corridors. **Pets:** $10 one-time fee/room. Service with restrictions, supervision.

Days Inn SH
(615) 790-1140. **Call for rates.** 4217 S Carothers Rd. I-65, exit 65, just
e. Ext corridors. **Pets:** Medium. $5 daily fee/pet. Designated rooms, service with restrictions, supervision.

**Homestead Studio Suites Hotel-Nashville/Franklin-Cool
Springs** SH
(615) 771-7600. **$65-$75.** 680 Bakers Bridge Ave. I-65, exit 69 (Galleria
Blvd), 0.3 mi e on Moore's Ln to Carothers Pkwy, 0.5 mi s, then 0.3 mi
w. Ext corridors. **Pets:** Other species. $75 one-time fee/pet. Service with
restrictions.

**La Quinta Inn & Suites
Nashville-Franklin** M
(615) 791-7700. **$89-$119.** 4207 Franklin Commons Ct. I-65, exit 65,
just e. Int corridors. **Pets:** Other species. Service with restrictions, supervision.

GALLATIN

Jameson Inn SH
(615) 451-4494. **Call for rates.** 1001 Village Green Crossing. 2 mi s on
US 31. Ext corridors. **Pets:** Small. $15 daily fee/room. Service with restrictions, crate.

GATLINBURG

Cobbly Nob Rentals Inc CA
(865) 436-5298. **$85-$800, 30 day notice.** 3722 E Parkway. On US
321, 10.3 mi n of jct US 441. Ext corridors. **Pets:** Medium, other
species. $15 daily fee/pet. Designated rooms, no service, supervision.

**Greenbrier Valley Resorts at Cobbly
Nob** CA
(865) 436-2015. **Call for rates.** 3629 E Parkway. On US 321, 10.1 mi n
of jct US 441. Ext corridors. **Pets:** Other species. $100 deposit/room, $15
daily fee/pet. Designated rooms, service with restrictions, crate.

Holiday Inn SunSpree Resort M
(865) 436-9201. **$59-$129.** 520 Historic Nature Tr. 0.4 mi e of US 441
at traffic light 8. Ext/int corridors. **Pets:** Medium, other species. $15
one-time fee/pet. Service with restrictions, crate.

Microtel Gatlinburg SH
(865) 436-0107. **$45-$159, 3 day notice.** 211 Historic Nature Tr. Just e
of US 441 at traffic light 8. Int corridors. **Pets:** Small. $10 daily fee/pet.
Designated rooms, service with restrictions, supervision.

The Park Vista Hotel & Convention Center LH
(865) 436-9211. **$70-$169, 3 day notice.** 705 Cherokee Orchard Rd.
0.6 mi e of jct US 441 at traffic light 8. Int corridors. **Pets:** Accepted.

Sleep Inn & Suites SH
(865) 436-9945. **Call for rates.** 335 E Parkway. On US 321, just n of jct
US 441 at traffic light 3. Int corridors. **Pets:** Accepted.

Terrace on the Water M
(865) 436-4965. **Call for rates.** 396 Parkway. On US 441; between
traffic lights 2 and 3. Ext corridors. **Pets:** Accepted.

GREENEVILLE

Comfort Inn of Greeneville SH
(423) 639-4185. **$60-$200.** 1790 E Andrew Johnson Hwy. US 11 E, 2.9
mi ne. Ext/int corridors. **Pets:** Other species. $10 daily fee/room. Designated rooms, service with restrictions, supervision.

Days Inn M
(423) 639-2156. **Call for rates.** 935 E Andrew Johnson Hwy. US 11 E,
2 mi ne. Ext corridors. **Pets:** Medium, other species. $10 daily fee/pet.
Designated rooms, service with restrictions, crate.

Jameson Inn SH
(423) 638-7511. **Call for rates.** 3160 E Andrew Johnson Hwy. US 11 E
Bypass, 3.6 mi ne. Int corridors. **Pets:** Small. $15 daily fee/room. Service
with restrictions, crate.

HARRIMAN

Best Western Sundancer Motor Lodge M
(865) 882-6200. **Call for rates.** 120 Childs Rd. I-40, exit 347, just n. Ext
corridors. **Pets:** Small. $10 daily fee/pet. Service with restrictions, supervision.

Caney Creek Inn SH
(865) 882-5340. **$75.** 1845 S Roane St. I-40, exit 347, just s on US
27/SR 61. Ext corridors. **Pets:** Accepted.

Super 8 Motel M
(865) 882-6600. **Call for rates.** 1867 S Roane St. I-40, exit 347, just s
on US 27/SR 61. Ext corridors. **Pets:** Small. $10 daily fee/pet. Designated rooms, service with restrictions, supervision.

HIXSON

Comfort Inn SH
(423) 877-8388. **$69-$99.** 4833 Hixson Pike. SR 153 and 315, just s.
Int corridors. **Pets:** Accepted.

Home Away Extended Stay Studios SH
(423) 643-4663. **Call for rates.** 1949 North Point Blvd. Jct SR 153 and
Hixson Pike, just w. Ext corridors. **Pets:** Accepted.

HURRICANE MILLS

Best Western of Hurricane Mills M
(931) 296-4251. **$79-$99.** 15542 Hwy 13 S. I-40, exit 143. Ext corridors. **Pets:** Large. $15 daily fee/pet. Designated rooms, service with restrictions, supervision.

JACKSON

Best Western Inn & Suites SH
(731) 664-3030. **$60-$125.** 1936 Hwy 45 Bypass. I-40, exit 80A, just s.
Ext corridors. **Pets:** Accepted.

▼▼▼▼ Jameson Inn SH
(731) 660-8651. **Call for rates.** 1292 Vann Dr. I-40, exit 80B, 0.6 mi w. Int corridors. **Pets:** Small. $15 daily fee/room. Service with restrictions, crate.

[X] [✆] [▣] [≈]

AAA ▼▼▼▼ La Quinta Inn of Jackson SH
(731) 664-1800. **$89-$119.** 2370 N Highland Ave. I-40, exit 82A. Int corridors. **Pets:** Other species. Service with restrictions, supervision.

[SAVE] [S◐] [X] [✆] [▣] [≈]

▼▼ Quality Inn SH
(731) 668-1400. **$60-$75.** 535 Wiley Parker Rd. I-40, exit 80A, just s, then e on Carriage House Dr. Ext/int corridors. **Pets:** Accepted.

[ASK] [S◐] [X] [✆] [▣] [≈]

AAA ▼▼▼ Supertel Inn-Jackson SH
(731) 664-4312. **$79-$114.** 1890 Hwy 45 Bypass. I-40, exit 80A, just s. Ext corridors. **Pets:** Small. $10 daily fee/pet. Designated rooms, no service, crate.

[SAVE] [S◐] [X] [&M] [✆] [▣] [≈]

JOHNSON CITY

▼▼ Comfort Inn of Johnson City SH
(423) 928-9600. **$60-$280.** 1900 S Roan St. I-26, exit 31, just w on US 321. Ext corridors. **Pets:** Other species. $15 daily fee/pet. Service with restrictions, supervision.

[ASK] [S◐] [X] [✆] [▣] [≈]

▼▼▼▼ DoubleTree Hotel SH
(423) 929-2000. **Call for rates.** 211 Mockingbird Ln. I-26, exit 35 eastbound; exit 35B westbound, 0.6 mi e on N Roan St. Int corridors. **Pets:** Medium. $50 one-time fee/room. Service with restrictions, supervision.

[X] [✆] [▣] [¶¶] [≈]

AAA ▼▼▼ Holiday Inn-Johnson City SH
(423) 282-4611. **$85-$350.** 101 W Springbrook Dr. I-26, exit 35A westbound; exit 35 eastbound, just e on N Roan St, then just n. Int corridors. **Pets:** Accepted.

[SAVE] [S◐] [X] [✆] [▣] [¶¶] [≈]

▼▼ Jameson Inn SH
(423) 282-0488. **Call for rates.** 119 Pinnacle Dr. I-26, exit 38, just w on CR 354, then just s. Ext corridors. **Pets:** Small. $15 daily fee/room. Service with restrictions, crate.

[X] [✆] [▣] [≈]

▼▼ Red Roof Inn-Johnson City SH
(423) 282-3040. **Call for rates.** 210 Broyles Dr. I-26, exit 35B westbound; exit 35 eastbound, just w on N Roan St. Ext corridors. **Pets:** Accepted.

[X] [✆]

▼▼ Sleep Inn & Suites SH
(423) 915-0081. **$72-$250.** 2020 Franklin Terrace Ct. I-26, exit 36, just w, then just n, follow signs; entrance on Oakland Ave at light. Int corridors. **Pets:** Accepted.

[ASK] [S◐] [X] [&M] [✆] [▣]

JONESBOROUGH

AAA ▼▼▼▼ AmericInn Lodge & Suites SH
(423) 753-3100. **Call for rates.** 376 E Jackson Blvd. I-26, exit 38 (Boones Creek Rd), Jct US 32 and SR 81. Int corridors. **Pets:** Accepted.

[SAVE] [X] [&M] [✆] [▣] [≈]

KIMBALL

AAA ▼▼ Country Hearth Inn & Suites M ❀
(423) 837-7185. **$35-$90.** 395 Main St. I-24, exit 152, 0.5 mi n. Ext corridors. **Pets:** Dogs only. $10 one-time fee/pet. Service with restrictions, supervision.

[SAVE] [S◐] [X] [✆] [≈]

KINGSPORT

▼▼▼ Americourt Hotel SH
(423) 245-0271. **Call for rates.** 1900 American Way. On US 11 W at SR 93. Ext corridors. **Pets:** Accepted.

[X] [✆] [▣] [¶¶] [≈]

▼▼▼▼ Jameson Inn SH
(423) 230-0534. **Call for rates.** 3004 Bay Meadow Pl. I-181, exit 51 westbound; exit 51B eastbound, just n on SR 93. Int corridors. **Pets:** Small. $15 daily fee/room. Service with restrictions, crate.

[X] [✆] [▣] [≈]

AAA ▼▼▼ La Quinta Inn Kingsport SH
(423) 323-0500. **$89-$119.** 10150 Airport Pkwy. I-81, exit 63, just e. Int corridors. **Pets:** Other species. Service with restrictions, supervision.

[SAVE] [S◐] [X] [&M] [✆] [▣] [≈]

▼▼▼ Sleep Inn SH
(423) 279-1811. **$72-$250.** 200 Hospitality Pl. I-81, exit 63, just s. Int corridors. **Pets:** Accepted.

[ASK] [S◐] [X] [✆] [▣]

KINGSTON

AAA ▼▼▼ Comfort Inn of Kingston M
(865) 376-4965. **$70-$90.** 905 N Kentucky St. I-40, exit 352, 0.3 mi s. Ext corridors. **Pets:** Small, other species. $10 daily fee/pet. Service with restrictions, supervision.

[SAVE] [S◐] [X] [✆] [▣]

AAA ▼▼▼ Days Inn M
(865) 376-2069. **Call for rates.** 495 Gallaher Rd. I-40, exit 356, just n. Ext corridors. **Pets:** Medium. $5 daily fee/pet. Service with restrictions, supervision.

[SAVE] [X] [✆] [▣] [≈]

KINGSTON SPRINGS

AAA ▼▼▼ Best Western Harpeth Inn SH
(615) 952-3961. **Call for rates.** 116 Luy Ben Hills Rd. I-40, exit 188, just n. Ext corridors. **Pets:** Accepted.

[SAVE] [X] [✆] [▣] [≈]

KNOXVILLE

▼▼▼▼ Best Western Knoxville Suites SH
(865) 687-9922. **$59-$119.** 5317 Pratt Rd. I-75, exit 108 (Merchants Dr), just e, then n. Int corridors. **Pets:** Accepted.

[ASK] [S◐] [X] [&M] [✆] [▣] [≈]

▼▼▼ Best Western West M
(865) 675-7666. **$69-$99.** 500 Lovell Rd. I-40, exit 374 (Lovell Rd), just n. Ext corridors. **Pets:** Accepted.

[ASK] [S◐] [X] [&M] [✆] [▣] [≈]

▼▼▼ Candlewood Suites-Knoxville SH
(865) 777-0400. **Call for rates.** 10206 Parkside Dr. I-40/75, exit 374 (Lovell Rd), 0.5 mi s, then 1 mi e. Int corridors. **Pets:** Medium. $75 one-time fee/room. Service with restrictions, crate.

[X] [&M] [✆] [▣]

AAA ▼▼▼▼ The Clarion Inn SH
(865) 687-8989. **$69-$99.** 5634 Merchants Center Blvd. I-75, exit 108 (Merchants Dr), just w, then just n. Int corridors. **Pets:** Accepted.

[SAVE] [S◐] [X] [&M] [✆] [▣] [≈]

▼▼▼▼ Crowne Plaza Knoxville SH ❀
(865) 522-2600. **$129-$164.** 401 W Summit Hill Dr. Corner of Walnut St; downtown. Int corridors. **Pets:** Other species. $25 one-time fee/room. Service with restrictions.

[ASK] [S◐] [X] [&M] [✆] [▣] [¶¶] [≈]

Econo Lodge Inn & Suites–East Knoxville M
(865) 932-1217. **$49-$129.** 7424 Strawberry Plains Pike. I-40, exit 398 (Strawberry Plains), just n. Ext corridors. **Pets:** Small, other species. $10 daily fee/room. Service with restrictions, supervision.

SAVE S X 🔒 💻 ⇌

Econo Lodge-North SH
(865) 687-5680. **$49-$99.** 5505 Merchants Center Blvd. I-75, exit 108 (Merchants Dr), just w, then just n. Ext corridors. **Pets:** Accepted.

SAVE S X 🔒

Econo Lodge West M
(865) 693-6061. **$50-$109.** 9240 Park West Blvd. I-40/75, exit 378 (Cedar Bluff Rd), just n to Park West Blvd, then just w. Ext corridors. **Pets:** Medium. Designated rooms, service with restrictions, supervision.

SAVE X 🔒 💻 ⇌

Extended StayAmerica Knoxville-Cedar Bluff M
(865) 769-0822. **$63-$73.** 214 Langley Pl. I-40, exit 378 (Cedar Bluff), just s, then 1 mi w on N Peters Rd. Ext corridors. **Pets:** Other species. $75 one-time fee/pet. Service with restrictions.

ASK S X S 🔒 💻 ⇌

Extended StayAmerica Knoxville-West Hills SH
(865) 694-4178. **$68-$78.** 1700 Winston Rd. I-40, exit 380 (West Hills), just w on Kingston Pike, then just s. Int corridors. **Pets:** Other species. $75 one-time fee/pet. Service with restrictions.

ASK S X S 🔒 💻 ⇌

Holiday Inn-Central/Papermill Road LH
(865) 584-3911. **$89-$189.** 1315 Kirby Rd. I-40/75, exit 383 (Papermill Rd), 0.5 mi e. Int corridors. **Pets:** Other species. $75 one-time fee/room. Designated rooms, service with restrictions, crate.

SAVE S X S 🔒 💻 🍴 ⇌

Holiday Inn Express Knoxville-East SH ❖
(865) 525-5100. **$99-$159.** 730 Rufus Graham Rd. I-40, exit 398 (Strawberry Plains), just n. Int corridors. **Pets:** Other species. $15 daily fee/pet. Service with restrictions, crate.

ASK S X S 🔒 💻 ⇌

Holiday Inn Select-Cedar Bluff LH
(865) 693-1011. **$109-$159.** 304 Cedar Bluff Rd. I-40/75, exit 378 (Cedar Bluff Rd) eastbound; exit 378B westbound, just n to Executive Park Dr. Int corridors. **Pets:** Other species. $50 one-time fee/room. Designated rooms, service with restrictions, crate.

ASK X 🔒 💻 🍴 ⇌ X

Homewood Suites by Hilton SH
(865) 777-0375. **Call for rates.** 10935 Turkey Dr. I-40, exit 374 (Lovell Rd), just s to Parkside Dr, then 0.5 mi n on Snow Goose. Int corridors. **Pets:** Accepted.

X 🔒 💻 ⇌ X

La Quinta Inn Knoxville (West) SH
(865) 690-9777. **$99-$129.** 258 N Peters Rd. I-40, exit 378 (Cedar Bluff Rd), just s, then just e. Ext corridors. **Pets:** Other species. Service with restrictions, supervision.

SAVE S X S 🔒 💻 ⇌

Motel 6–1252 M
(865) 675-7200. **$43-$55.** 402 Lovell Rd. I-40/75, exit 374 (Lovell Rd), just s. Ext corridors. **Pets:** Other species. Service with restrictions, supervision.

S X S ⇌

Red Roof Inn SH
(865) 688-1010. **$65-$99.** 5334 Central Ave Pike. I-75, exit 108 (Merchants Dr), just e. Ext corridors. **Pets:** Accepted.

ASK S X 💻 ⇌

Red Roof Inn-West M
(865) 691-1664. **Call for rates.** 209 Advantage Pl. I-40/75, exit 378 (Cedar Bluff Rd), just s to N Peters Rd, then w. Ext corridors. **Pets:** Accepted.

X S 🔒

Super 8 East M
(865) 524-0855. **Call for rates.** 7585 Crosswood Blvd. I-40, exit 398 (Strawberry Plains), just n, then w. Ext corridors. **Pets:** Medium. $15 daily fee/pet. Service with restrictions, supervision.

X S 🔒 💻 ⇌

LAKE CITY

Days Inn M
(865) 426-2816. **Call for rates.** 221 Colonial Ln. I-75, exit 129, just w. Ext corridors. **Pets:** Medium. $10 daily fee/pet. Service with restrictions, supervision.

X 🔒 💻 ⇌

LAWRENCEBURG

Best Western Villa Inn SH
(931) 762-4448. **$76-$100.** 2126 N Locust Ave. On US 43, 2.2 mi n of jct US 64. Ext corridors. **Pets:** Medium. $10 daily fee/pet. Designated rooms, service with restrictions, supervision.

ASK X 🔒 💻 ⇌

LEBANON

Americas Best Value Inn & Suites M
(615) 449-5781. **$40-$100.** 822 S Cumberland St. I-40, exit 238, just n. Ext corridors. **Pets:** Very small. $12 daily fee/pet. Designated rooms, service with restrictions, crate.

ASK S X 🔒 💻 ⇌

Comfort Inn M
(615) 444-1001. **$49-$89.** 829 S Cumberland St. I-40, exit 238, just n. Ext corridors. **Pets:** Other species. $10 daily fee/pet. Designated rooms, service with restrictions, crate.

ASK S X 🔒 💻 ⇌

Days Inn M
(615) 444-5635. **Call for rates.** 914 Murfreesboro Rd. I-40, exit 238, just n. Ext corridors. **Pets:** Accepted.

X 🔒 💻 ⇌

Sleep Inn & Suites-Lebanon SH
(615) 449-7005. **$75-$159.** 150 S Eastgate Ct. I-40, exit 232. Int corridors. **Pets:** Small. $25 one-time fee/pet. Service with restrictions, supervision.

SAVE S X 🔒 💻 ⇌

Super 8 Motel M
(615) 444-5637. **Call for rates.** 914 Murfreesboro Rd. I-40, exit 238, just s. Ext corridors. **Pets:** Accepted.

X 🔒 ⇌

LENOIR CITY

Days Inn SH
(865) 986-2011. **Call for rates.** 1110 Hwy 321 N. I-75, exit 81, just e. Ext corridors. **Pets:** Small. $10 daily fee/pet. Service with restrictions, supervision.

SAVE X 🔒 💻 ⇌

Econo Lodge SH
(865) 986-0295. **$52-$89.** 1211 Hwy 321 N. I-75, exit 81, just w. Ext corridors. **Pets:** Medium. $5 daily fee/pet. Service with restrictions, supervision.

SAVE S X 🔒 ⇌

LEWISBURG

▼▼ A Richland Inn Hotel [SH]
(931) 359-1800. **$50-$70.** 723 E Commerce St. Jct US 431 and 31A, just w; just e of town. Ext corridors. **Pets:** Accepted.

⊠ 🛢 💻

LOUDON

△△△ ▽ Americas Best Value Inn [M]
(865) 458-5855. **$50-$65.** 15100 Hwy 72. I-75, exit 72, just w. Ext corridors. **Pets:** Medium. $6 daily fee/pet. Service with restrictions, supervision.

[SAVE] [S🔊] ⊠ 🛢 ⇒

MANCHESTER

▼▼ Ambassador Inn [SH]
(931) 728-2200. **$45-$89.** 925 Interstate Dr. I-24, exit 110, just n. Ext/int corridors. **Pets:** Small, dogs only. Designated rooms, service with restrictions.

[A$K] [S🔊] ⊠ 🛢 💻 ⇒

▼▼▼ Country Inn & Suites By Carlson [SH]
(931) 728-7551. **Call for rates.** 126 Expressway Dr. I-24, exit 114, just w. Int corridors. **Pets:** Accepted.

⊠ [🔊M] 🛢 💻 ⇒

△△△ ▽▽ Days Inn & Suites [M]
(931) 728-9530. **Call for rates.** 2259 Hillsboro Blvd. I-24, exit 114, just w. Ext corridors. **Pets:** Medium. $15 daily fee/pet. No service, supervision.

[SAVE] ⊠ [🔊M] 🛢 💻 ⇒

△△△ ▽▽ Ramada Limited [SH]
(931) 728-0800. **$54-$79.** 2314 Hillsboro Blvd. I-24, exit 114, just n. Ext corridors. **Pets:** Small. $10 one-time fee/pet. Designated rooms, service with restrictions, supervision.

[SAVE] [S🔊] ⊠ 🛢 💻 ⇒

MARTIN

△△△ ▽▽ Days Inn [SH]
(731) 587-9577. **Call for rates.** 800 University St. Jct US 431 and 43 Bypass. Ext corridors. **Pets:** Accepted.

[SAVE] ⊠ 🛢 💻 ⇒

MCMINNVILLE

△△△ ▽▽▽ Best Western Tree City Inn [SH]
(931) 473-2159. **$59-$75.** 809 Sparta Hwy. Jct US 70 S Bypass and Red Rd, 1 mi s, follow signs. Ext corridors. **Pets:** Small, dogs only. $10 daily fee/pet. Service with restrictions, supervision.

[SAVE] [S🔊] ⊠ 🛢 💻 ⇒

▽▽ McMinnville Inn [M]
(931) 473-7338. **Call for rates.** 2545 Sparta Hwy. I-24, exit 111, n on SR 55 to US 70 S Bypass. Ext corridors. **Pets:** Accepted.

⊠ 🛢 💻 ⇒

MEMPHIS METROPOLITAN AREA

COLLIERVILLE

▼▼▼▼ Hampton Inn Collierville [SH]
(901) 854-9400. **Call for rates.** 1280 W Poplar Ave. 0.9 mi w of jct CR 175 on US 72. Int corridors. **Pets:** Accepted.

⊠ [🔊M] 🛢 💻 ⇒

CORDOVA

▼▼▼▼ Quality Suites-Wolfchase [SH]
(901) 386-4600. **Call for rates.** 8166 Varnavas Dr. I-40, exit 16, 0.3 mi s on Germantown Pkwy, then e. Int corridors. **Pets:** Accepted.

⊠ 🛢 💻 ⇒

▼▼ StudioPLUS-Cordova [SH]
(901) 754-4030. **$60-$70.** 8110 Cordova Centre Dr. I-40, exit 16, 0.8 mi s. Int corridors. **Pets:** Other species. $75 one-time fee/pet. Service with restrictions.

[A$K] [S🔊] [🔊M] 🛢 💻 ⇒

COVINGTON

▼▼ Comfort Inn [SH]
(901) 475-0380. **Call for rates.** 901 Hwy 51 N. 1 mi n of jct US 59. Ext corridors. **Pets:** Small. $10 one-time fee/pet. Designated rooms, service with restrictions, supervision.

⊠ 🛢 💻 🏊

GERMANTOWN

▼▼ Comfort Inn & Suites-Germantown [SH]
(901) 757-7800. **Call for rates.** 7787 Wolf River Blvd. I-40, exit 16, 5 mi s on Germantown Pkwy. Int corridors. **Pets:** Accepted.

⊠ [🔊M] 🛢 💻 ⇒

▼▼▼▼ Homewood Suites by Hilton-Germantown [SH]
(901) 751-2500. **Call for rates.** 7855 Wolf River Blvd. I-40, exit 16, 5.8 mi s on CR 177; at Germantown Pkwy and Wolf River Blvd. Int corridors. **Pets:** Accepted.

⊠ 🛢 💻 ⇒

▽▽▽▽ Residence Inn [SH]
(901) 752-0900. **$129-$149.** 9314 Poplar Pike. I-240, exit 15 (Poplar Ave), 7 mi e. Int corridors. **Pets:** Other species. $100 one-time fee/room. Service with restrictions, supervision.

[A$K] [S🔊] ⊠ [🔊M] 🛢 💻 ⇒ ⊠

LAKELAND

△△△ ▽▽ Super 8 Motel [SH]
(901) 372-4575. **Call for rates.** 9779 Huff Puff Rd. I-40, exit 20. Ext corridors. **Pets:** Small, dogs only. $10 daily fee/pet. Designated rooms, service with restrictions, supervision.

[SAVE] ⊠ 🛢 ⇒

MEMPHIS

▼▼▼▼ Baymont Inn & Suites Memphis East [SH]
(901) 377-2233. **Call for rates.** 6020 Shelby Oaks Dr. I-40, exit 12, just n. Int corridors. **Pets:** Accepted.

⊠ 🛢 💻 ⇒

▼▼▼▼ Drury Inn & Suites-Memphis Northeast [SH]
(901) 373-8200. **$143.** 1556 Sycamore View. I-40, exit 12, just n. Int corridors. **Pets:** Large, other species. Service with restrictions, supervision.

[A$K] ⊠ 🛢 💻 ⇒

▼▼ Econo Lodge Inn & Suites [M]
(901) 396-1000. **Call for rates.** 2745 Airways Blvd. I-240, exit 23B (Airways Blvds), just s. Ext corridors. **Pets:** Accepted.

⊠ 🛢 💻 ⇒

▼▼ Extended StayAmerica [SH]
(901) 362-0338. **$65-$75.** 6520 Mt Moriah Rd. Jct SR 385 and Kirby Pkwy, just s. Int corridors. **Pets:** Other species. $75 one-time fee/pet. Service with restrictions.

[A$K] [S🔊] ⊠ [🔊M] 🛢 💻

▼▼ **Extended StayAmerica-Poplar Ave** SH
(901) 685-7575. **$80-$90.** 6325 Quail Hollow. I-240, exit 15 (East Poplar Ave), 0.4 mi e, then just n on Briarcrest. Int corridors. **Pets:** Other species. $75 one-time fee/pet. Service with restrictions.

ASK S♦ ✕ ↻M ⊟ ⌨

▼▼ **Extended StayAmerica-Sycamore View** SH
(901) 386-0026. **$60-$70.** 5885 Shelby Oaks Dr. I-40, exit 12, 0.3 mi n, then just w. Ext corridors. **Pets:** Other species. $75 one-time fee/pet. Service with restrictions.

ASK S♦ ✕ ⊟ ⌨

▼▼ **Extended Stay Deluxe Memphis-Wolfchase Galleria** SH
(901) 380-1525. **$75-$85.** 2520 Horizon Lake Dr. I-40, exit 16B, just n, then just w. Int corridors. **Pets:** Other species. $75 one-time fee/pet. Service with restrictions.

ASK S♦ ✕ ⊟ ⌨ ⇔

▼▼▼▼ **Holiday Inn Select Memphis Airport** LH
(901) 332-1130. **$99-$149.** 2240 Democrat Rd. I-240, exit 23B (Airways Blvd S), just s to Democrat Rd, then just w. Int corridors. **Pets:** Accepted.

✕ ↻M ⊟ ⌨ ⍟ ⇔ ⍟

▼▼ **Homestead Studio Suites Hotel-Memphis/Airport** SH
(901) 344-0010. **$90-$100.** 2541 Corporate Ave E. I-240, exit 23B (Airways Blvd S), just s to Democrat Rd, just w to Nonconnah Blvd, then 0.4 mi n to Corporate Ave, follow signs. Int corridors. **Pets:** Other species. $75 one-time fee/pet. Service with restrictions.

ASK S♦ ✕ ↻M ⊟ ⌨

▼▼ **Homestead Studio Suites Hotel-Memphis/Poplar Ave** SH
(901) 767-5522. **$85-$95.** 6500 Poplar Ave. I-240, exit 15 (Poplar Ave), 1 mi e. Int corridors. **Pets:** Other species. $75 one-time fee/pet. Service with restrictions.

ASK S♦ ✕ ↻M ⊟ ⌨

▼▼▼▼ **Homewood Suites** SH
(901) 763-0500. **Call for rates.** 5811 Poplar Ave. I-240, exit 15 (Poplar Ave). Ext/int corridors. **Pets:** Accepted.

✕ ⊟ ⌨ ⇔

▼▼▼▼ **Homewood Suites by Hilton** SH ✿
(901) 758-5018. **Call for rates.** 3583 Hacks Cross Rd. I-240, exit 16, 4 mi e on SR 385, then 1 mi n. Int corridors. **Pets:** Other species. $25 daily fee/room. Designated rooms, service with restrictions.

✕ ↻M ⊟ ⌨ ⇔

AAA ▼▼▼▼ **La Quinta Inn & Suites Memphis (Primacy Parkway)** SH
(901) 374-0330. **$109-$149.** 1236 Primacy Pkwy. I-240, exit 15 (Poplar Ave), 0.3 mi e, s on Ridgeway, just w, then just s. Int corridors. **Pets:** Other species. Service with restrictions, supervision.

SAVE S♦ ✕ ↻M ⊟ ⌨ ⇔

AAA ▼▼▼▼ **La Quinta Inn & Suites Sycamore View-Memphis** SH
(901) 381-0044. **$115-$145.** 6069 Macon Cove. I-40, exit 12, just s. Int corridors. **Pets:** Other species. Service with restrictions, supervision.

SAVE S♦ ✕ ↻M ⊟ ⌨ ⇔

AAA ▼▼▼ **Quality Inn** SH ✿
(901) 382-2323. **$69-$169.** 6068 Macon Cove Rd. I-40, exit 12, just s. Ext/int corridors. **Pets:** Small, other species. $10 daily fee/pet. Service with restrictions, supervision.

SAVE S♦ ✕ ⊟ ⌨ ⇔

AAA ▼▼▼ **Quality Inn Airport/Graceland** SH
(901) 345-3344. **$70-$140.** 1581 E Brooks Rd. I-55, exit 5A (Brooks Rd), 0.3 mi e. Ext corridors. **Pets:** Accepted.

SAVE S♦ ✕ ⊟ ⌨ ⇔

▼▼▼ **Red Roof Inn-East** SH
(901) 388-6111. **Call for rates.** 6055 Shelby Oaks Dr. I-40, exit 12, just n. Ext corridors. **Pets:** Accepted.

✕ ⊟ ⌨

▼▼▼▼ **Residence Inn by Marriott Memphis Downtown** SH
(901) 578-3700. **$189-$209.** 110 Monroe Ave. I-40, exit 1; I-55, exit Riverside Dr, 0.6 mi s, then just e. Int corridors. **Pets:** Accepted.

ASK S♦ ✕ ↻M ⌨ ⍟

▼▼▼▼ **Staybridge Suites** SH
(901) 682-1722. **Call for rates.** 1070 Ridge Lake Blvd. I-240, exit 15 (Poplar Ave), just e, then n under overpass. Int corridors. **Pets:** Accepted.

✕ ↻M ⊟ ⌨ ⇔ ⍟

AAA ▼▼▼▼ **The Westin Memphis Beale St** LH ✿
(901) 334-5900. **Call for rates.** 170 Lt. George W. Lee Ave. Jct S 3rd St and Lt. George W. Lee Ave. Int corridors. **Pets:** Medium, dogs only. Supervision.

SAVE ✕ ↻M ⌨ ⍟

MILLINGTON

▼▼ **Admiralty of Plantation Oaks** SH
(901) 872-8000. **Call for rates.** 6656 Hwy 51 N. On US 51, 2 mi s. Ext/int corridors. **Pets:** Accepted.

✕ ⊟ ⌨ ⇔

END METROPOLITAN AREA

MONTEAGLE

▼▼▼▼ **Best Western Smoke House Lodge** SH
(931) 924-2091. **$70-$95.** 850 W Main St. I-24, exit 134, just s. Ext corridors. **Pets:** Accepted.

ASK S♦ ✕ ⊟ ⌨ ⍟ ⇔ ⍟

▼▼▼▼ **Edgeworth Inn** BB
(931) 924-4000. **Call for rates.** Monteagle Assembly, Cottage 23. I-24, exit 134, 0.4 mi e on US 41A, 2nd left through assembly gates, follow signs. Ext/int corridors. **Pets:** Accepted.

✕ ⊟ ⌨ ⍟

MORRISTOWN

AAA ▼▼▼ **Days Inn** M
(423) 587-2200. **Call for rates.** 2512 E Andrew Johnson Hwy. I-81, exit 8, 6 mi n on US 25 E to exit 2B (Greenville-Morristown), then just w. Ext corridors. **Pets:** Accepted.

SAVE ✕ ⊟ ⌨ ⇔

AAA ▼▼▼ **Holiday Inn Morristown Conference Center** SH
(423) 587-2400. **$115-$269, 7 day notice.** 5435 S Davy Crockett Pkwy. I-81, exit 8, just n. Int corridors. **Pets:** Accepted.

SAVE S♦ ✕ ⌨ ⍟ ⇔

▼▼ Super 8 Motel
(423) 318-8888. **Call for rates.** 5400 S Davy Crockett Pkwy. I-81, exit 8, just n. Int corridors. **Pets:** Small. $9 one-time fee/pet. Service with restrictions, supervision.

⊗ ⌂ᴹ ▯ ▭

MOUNT JULIET

Quality Inn & Suites SH
(615) 773-3600. **$70-$120.** 1000 Hershel Dr. I-40, exit 226. Int corridors. **Pets:** Large. $25 one-time fee/room. Service with restrictions, supervision.

SAVE S◊ ⊗ ▯ ▭ ⌒

MURFREESBORO

▼▼ Baymont Inn & Suites M ❀
(615) 896-1172. **Call for rates.** 2230 Armory Dr. I-24, exit 78B, just n. Ext corridors. **Pets:** Other species. $10 daily fee/pet. Designated rooms, service with restrictions.

⊗ ⌂ᴹ ▯ ▭ ⌒

▼▼ Best Western Chaffin Inn M ❀
(615) 895-3818. **$79-$159, 7 day notice.** 168 Chaffin Pl. I-24, exit 78B. Ext corridors. **Pets:** Medium. $15 daily fee/pet. Designated rooms, service with restrictions, crate.

SAVE S◊ ⊗ ▯ ▭ ⌒

▼▼▼ DoubleTree Hotel Murfreesboro SH
(615) 895-5555. **Call for rates.** 1850 Old Fort Pkwy. I-24, exit 78B. Int corridors. **Pets:** Small. $50 one-time fee/room. Service with restrictions, supervision.

⊗ ▯ ▭ ⊺⊺ ⌒

▼▼▼ Howard Johnson Express Inn SH
(615) 896-5522. **$50-$100.** 2424 S Church St. I-24, exit 81A eastbound; exit 81 westbound. Int corridors. **Pets:** Small. $10 daily fee/pet. Service with restrictions, supervision.

SAVE S◊ ⊗ ▯ ▭ ⊺⊺ ⌒

▼▼▼ Quality Inn Murfreesboro SH
(615) 890-1006. **$85.** 2135 S Church St. I-24, exit 81 westbound; exit 81B eastbound. Int corridors. **Pets:** Medium, other species. $10 one-time fee/pet. Service with restrictions, supervision.

ASK S◊ ⊗ ▯ ▭ ⌒

▼▼▼ Ramada Limited SH ❀
(615) 896-5080. **Call for rates.** 1855 S Church St. I-24, exit 81. Int corridors. **Pets:** Large, other species. $10 daily fee/pet. Service with restrictions, supervision.

SAVE ⊗ ▯ ▭ ⌒

▼▼▼ Vista Inn and Suites SH
(615) 848-9030. **$55-$200 (no credit cards), 3 day notice.** 118 Westgate Blvd. I-24, exit 81A eastbound; exit 81 westbound. Int corridors. **Pets:** Small. $10 daily fee/pet. Designated rooms, service with restrictions, crate.

SAVE S◊ ⊗ ▯ ▭ ⌒

NASHVILLE METROPOLITAN AREA

ANTIOCH

▼▼▼ Holiday Inn-The Crossings SH
(615) 731-2361. **$94-$115.** 201 Crossings Pl. I-24, exit 60, 0.5 mi e. Int corridors. **Pets:** Accepted.

ASK S◊ ⊗ ⌂ᴹ ▯ ▭ ⊺⊺ ⌒

GOODLETTSVILLE

▼▼▼ Best Western Fairwinds Inn SH
(615) 851-1067. **$69-$99.** 100 Northcreek Blvd. I-65, exit 97 (Long Hollow Pike), 0.5 mi e. Ext corridors. **Pets:** Small. $10 daily fee/pet. Service with restrictions, supervision.

SAVE S◊ ⊗ ▯ ▭ ⌒

▼▼▼ Holiday Inn Express Hotel & Suites SH
(615) 851-1891. **$99-$179.** 120 Cartwright St. I-65, exit 97 (Long Hollow Pike), just w. Int corridors. **Pets:** Accepted.

ASK S◊ ⊗ ⌂ᴹ ▯ ▭ ⌒

HERMITAGE

▼▼ Motel 6 SH
(615) 889-5060. **Call for rates.** 5768 Old Hickory Blvd. I-40, exit 221 westbound; exit 221B eastbound, just n. Ext corridors. **Pets:** Other species. Service with restrictions, supervision.

⊗ ▯ ⌒

NASHVILLE

▼▼▼▼ Best Western Music Row SH
(615) 242-1631. **$79-$199.** 1407 Division St. I-40, exit 209B (Broadway), just w around circle, then just e. Int corridors. **Pets:** Small, other species. $10 daily fee/pet. Service with restrictions.

SAVE S◊ ⊗ ▯ ▭ ⌒

▼▼▼ Comfort Inn Opryland SH
(615) 889-0086. **$69-$109.** 2516 Music Valley Dr. I-40, exit 215 (Briley Pkwy), 4 mi n; I-65, exit 90, exit McGavock Pike off Briley Pkwy. Int corridors. **Pets:** Accepted.

SAVE S◊ ⊗ ▭ ⌒

▼▼ Crossland Studios Nashville SH
(615) 366-0559. **$55-$65.** 1210 Murfreesboro Rd. I-40, exit 215 (Briley Pkwy), 2 mi s to exit 4, then 0.8 mi n. Ext corridors. **Pets:** Other species. $75 one-time fee/pet. Service with restrictions.

ASK S◊ ⊗ ⌂ᴹ ▯ ▭

▼▼▼ Drury Inn & Suites-Nashville Airport SH
(615) 902-0400. **$136.** 555 Donelson Pike. I-40, exit 216 (Donelson Pike). Int corridors. **Pets:** Large, other species. Service with restrictions, supervision.

ASK ⊗ ⌂ᴹ ▯ ▭ ⌒

▼▼▼ Days Inn SH
(615) 889-0090. **Call for rates.** 2460 Music Valley Dr. I-40, exit 215B (Briley Pkwy), 4 mi n to exit 11 (McGavock Pike). Int corridors. **Pets:** Accepted.

SAVE ⊗ ▭ ⌒

▼▼ Extended StayAmerica SH
(615) 383-7490. **$105.** 3311 W End Ave. I-440, exit 1A, then just e. Int corridors. **Pets:** Other species. $75 one-time fee/pet. Service with restrictions.

ASK ⊗ ⌂ᴹ ▯ ▭

▼▼▼ **GuestHouse International Inn & Suites** 🆂🅷 🐾
(615) 885-4030. **$99-$139.** 2420 Music Valley Dr. Briley Pkwy, exit 12, 0.3 mi w, then 0.3 mi n. Int corridors. **Pets:** $25 one-time fee/room. Designated rooms, service with restrictions, crate.

A$K 🆂 ⊠ 🖪 🖵 🕭

📖 ▼▼▼▼ **The Hermitage Hotel** 🅻🅷
(615) 244-3121. **Call for rates.** 231 6th Ave N. Corner of Union St; center. Int corridors. **Pets:** Accepted.

SAVE ⊠ 🖓 🖪 🍴 🕱

▼▼ **Homestead Studio Suites Hotel-Nashville/Airport** 🆂🅷
(615) 316-9020. **$65-$75.** 727 McGavock Pike. I-40, exit 215B (Briley Pkwy), 1 mi n to exit 7 (Elm Hill Pike), then just e. Ext corridors. **Pets:** Other species. $75 one-time fee/pet. Service with restrictions.

A$K 🆂 ⊠ 🖓 🖪 🖵

📖 ▼▼▼ **Homewood Suites by Hilton** 🆂🅷
(615) 884-8111. **Call for rates.** 2640 Elm Hill Pike. I-40, exit 216C (Donelson Pike). Int corridors. **Pets:** Accepted.

SAVE ⊠ 🖓 🖪 🖵 🕭

📖 ▼▼▼ **Hotel Preston** 🅻🅷 🐾
(615) 361-5900. **$79-$199, 3 day notice.** 733 Envious Ln. I-40, exit 215 (Briley Pkwy). Int corridors. **Pets:** Large, other species. $30 one-time fee/room. Designated rooms, service with restrictions, crate.

SAVE 🆂 ⊠ 🖪 🖵 🍴 🕭

📖 ▼▼▼ **La Quinta Inn & Suites Nashville-Airport** 🆂🅷
(615) 885-3100. **$89-$119.** 531 Donelson Pike. I-40, exit 216C (Donelson Pike). 0.3 mi n. Int corridors. **Pets:** Other species. Service with restrictions, supervision.

SAVE 🆂 ⊠ 🖪 🖵 🕭

📖 ▼▼▼ ▼▼▼ **Loews Vanderbilt Hotel Nashville** 🅻🅷 🐾
(615) 320-1700. **Call for rates.** 2100 West End Ave. I-40, exit 209B (Broadway), 1.3 mi w. Int corridors. **Pets:** Other species. Service with restrictions, crate.

SAVE ⊠ 🖪 🖵 🍴 🕱

📖 ▼▼ ◆ **Microtel Inn & Suites** 🆂🅷
(615) 662-0004. **Call for rates.** 100 Coley Davis Ct. I-40, exit 196. Int corridors. **Pets:** Small. $10 daily fee/pet. Service with restrictions, supervision.

SAVE ⊠ 🖪 🖵 🕭

📖 ▼▼▼ **Radisson Hotel Nashville Airport** 🆂🅷
(615) 889-9090. **$199.** 1112 Airport Center Dr. I-40, exit 216C (Donelson Pike N). Int corridors. **Pets:** Medium. $50 one-time fee/pet. Designated rooms, service with restrictions, supervision.

SAVE 🆂 ⊠ 🖓 🖪 🖵 🍴 🕭

▼▼ ▼▼ **Red Roof Inn Airport** 🅼
(615) 872-0735. **Call for rates.** 510 Claridge Dr. I-40, exit 216C (Donelson Pike), 0.3 mi n. Ext corridors. **Pets:** Accepted.

⊠ 🖪

📖 ▼▼▼ **Residence Inn** 🆂🅷 🐾
(615) 889-8600. **$169-$189.** 2300 Elm Hill Pike. I-40, exit 215B (Briley Pkwy), 1.5 mi n. Int corridors. **Pets:** Other species. $100 one-time fee/room. Service with restrictions.

SAVE 🆂 ⊠ 🖪 🖵 🕭

📖 ▼▼▼ **Sheraton Music City Hotel** 🅻🅷
(615) 885-2200. **$249.** 777 McGavock Pike. I-40, exit 215B (Briley Pkwy), 1 mi n to exit 7 (Elm Hill Pike), 0.5 mi e, then s. Int corridors. **Pets:** Large, other species. Designated rooms, service with restrictions, supervision.

SAVE 🆂 ⊠ 🖓 🖪 🖵 🍴 🕭 🕱

📖 ▼▼▼ **Sheraton Nashville Downtown Hotel** 🅻🅷 🐾
(615) 259-2000. **Call for rates.** 623 Union St. I-40, exit 209, just s of State Capitol. Int corridors. **Pets:** Medium. Service with restrictions, supervision.

SAVE ⊠ 🖓 🖪 🖵 🍴 🕭 🕱

📖 ▼▼ ▼ **Super 8 Motel** 🆂🅷
(615) 889-8887. **Call for rates.** 720 Royal Pkwy. I-40, exit 216C (Donelson Pike N), 0.5 mi n, then just e. Int corridors. **Pets:** Medium, other species. $10 daily fee/pet. Designated rooms, service with restrictions, supervision.

SAVE ⊠ 🖓 🖪 🕭

📖 ▼▼ ▼ **Super 8 Motel-West** 🆂🅷
(615) 356-6005. **Call for rates.** 6924 Charlotte Pike. I-40, exit 201. Ext corridors. **Pets:** Medium, dogs only. $10 daily fee/pet. Service with restrictions, supervision.

SAVE ⊠ 🖪

▼▼ ◆ **Thrifty Inn-Nashville South** 🆂🅷
(615) 834-4242. **$73.** 343 Harding Pl. I-24, exit 56 (Harding Pl). Ext corridors. **Pets:** Large, other species. Service with restrictions, supervision.

A$K ⊠ 🖵 🕭

END METROPOLITAN AREA

NEWPORT

📖 ▼▼ ▼ **Best Western Newport Inn** 🅼 🐾
(423) 623-8713. **$49-$169, 14 day notice.** 1015 Cosby Hwy. I-40, exit 435, just w. Ext corridors. **Pets:** Medium, other species. No service, crate.

SAVE 🆂 ⊠ 🖓 🖪 🖵 🕭

📖 ▼▼ ▼ **Comfort Inn** 🆂🅷
(423) 623-5355. **$49-$150.** 1149 Smokey Mountain Ln. I-40, exit 432B. Int corridors. **Pets:** Other species. $10 daily fee/pet. Designated rooms, service with restrictions, crate.

SAVE 🆂 ⊠ 🖓 🖪 🖵 🕭

▼▼ ▼ **Holiday Inn** 🆂🅷
(423) 623-8622. **$75-$140.** 1010 Cosby Hwy. I-40, exit 435. Ext/int corridors. **Pets:** Accepted.

A$K ⊠ 🖪 🖵 🍴 🕭 🕱

📖 ▼▼ ▼ **Motel 6-4090** 🅼 🐾
(423) 623-1850. **$35-$70.** 255 Heritage Blvd. I-40, exit 435. Int corridors. **Pets:** Other species. Designated rooms, service with restrictions, supervision.

SAVE 🆂 ⊠ 🖓 🖪 🖵 🕭

▼ **Relax Inn** 🅼
(423) 625-1521. **Call for rates.** 1148 W Hwy 25-70. I-40, exit 432B. Ext corridors. **Pets:** Other species. $5 one-time fee/pet. Service with restrictions, crate.

⊠ 🖪 🖵

OAK RIDGE

▼▼ Comfort Inn 🆂🅷
(865) 481-8200. **$80-$150.** 433 S Rutgers Ave. 0.9 mi se of SR 95 on SR 62. Int corridors. **Pets:** Accepted.
[A$K] [S🐾] [✕] [🕹M] [🛏] [💻] [🏊]

▼▼▼ DoubleTree Oak Ridge 🆂🅷
(865) 481-2468. **Call for rates.** 215 S Illinois Ave. 0.3 mi se of SR 95 on SR 62. Int corridors. **Pets:** Small. $50 one-time fee/pet. Service with restrictions, supervision.
[✕] [🛏] [💻] [🍴] [🏊]

▼▼▼ Jameson Inn 🆂🅷
(865) 483-6809. **Call for rates.** 216 S Rutgers Ave. Jct SR 95 and 62, 0.9 mi se on SR 62 to Rutgers Ave, then 0.7 mi n. Int corridors. **Pets:** Small. $15 daily fee/room. Service with restrictions, crate.
[✕] [🛏] [💻] [🏊]

ONEIDA

▼ The Galloway Inn Ⓜ
(423) 569-8835. **Call for rates.** 299 Galloway Dr. Jct SR 63, 3.3 mi n on US 27, just e. Ext corridors. **Pets:** Medium, other species. $10 daily fee/pet. Service with restrictions, supervision.
[✕] [🛏] [💻]

OOLTEWAH

▼ Super 8 Motel Ⓜ
(423) 238-5951. **Call for rates.** 5111 Hunter Rd. I-75, exit 11, just w. Ext corridors. **Pets:** Accepted.
[✕] [🛏] [💻]

PARIS

▼▼▼ Hampton Inn 🆂🅷
(731) 642-2838. **Call for rates.** 1510 E Wood St. 1.5 mi ne on US 79. Ext corridors. **Pets:** Accepted.
[✕] [🕹M] [🛏] [💻] [🏊]

PICKWICK DAM

▼▼▼ Pickwick Landing State Resort Park Inn 🅻🅷
(731) 689-3135. **$68-$82.** 220 Playground Loop. Intersection of US 57 and SR 128. Ext/int corridors. **Pets:** $10 daily fee/pet. Designated rooms, service with restrictions, supervision.
[A$K] [S🐾] [✕] [🕹M] [🛏] [💻] [🍴] [🏊] [✕]

PIGEON FORGE

▼▼▼ Blackberry Ridge-Accommodations by Sunset Cottage 🅲🅰
(865) 429-8478. **Call for rates (no credit cards).** 3630 S River Rd. Just e of jct US 441 at traffic light 8, just n. Ext corridors. **Pets:** $100 deposit/pet, $50 one-time fee/room. Designated rooms, no service, crate.
[✕] [🛏] [💻]

◈◈◈ ▼▼▼ Briarstone Inn Ⓜ
(865) 453-4225. **$40-$90.** 3626 Parkway. On US 441; between traffic lights 7 and 8. Ext corridors. **Pets:** Accepted.
[SAVE] [S🐾] [✕] [🛏] [💻] [🏊]

◈◈◈ ▼▼◈ Eden Crest Vacation Rentals 🅲🅰 🐾
(865) 774-0059. **$110-$380 (no credit cards), 90 day notice.** 652 Wears Valley Rd. US 321 to light 3, just w. Ext corridors. **Pets:** Medium, dogs only. $135 one-time fee/pet. Designated rooms, service with restrictions, crate.
[SAVE] [S🐾] [✕] [🛏] [💻] [🏊]

▼▼▼ Hampton Inn & Suites 🆂🅷 🐾
(865) 428-1600. **$64-$219.** 2025 Parkway. On US 441 at traffic light 0. Int corridors. **Pets:** Large, other species. $20 daily fee/room. Designated rooms, service with restrictions.
[A$K] [✕] [🕹M] [🛏] [💻] [🏊]

▼▼▼ Holiday Inn Resort 🆂🅷
(865) 428-2700. **$50-$180.** 3230 Parkway. On US 441; between traffic lights 2 and 3. Int corridors. **Pets:** Accepted.
[A$K] [S🐾] [✕] [🛏] [💻] [🍴] [🏊]

◈◈◈ ▼▼◈ La Quinta Inn 🆂🅷
(865) 429-3010. **$70-$100.** 219 Emert St. Just w of jct US 441; between traffic lights 7 and 8. Int corridors. **Pets:** Other species. Service with restrictions, supervision.
[SAVE] [S🐾] [✕] [🕹M] [🛏] [💻] [🏊]

▼▼ Microtel Suites at Music Road 🆂🅷
(865) 453-1116. **Call for rates.** 2045 Parkway. On US 441, just s of traffic light 0. Int corridors. **Pets:** Accepted.
[✕] [🕹M] [🛏] [💻] [🏊]

◈◈◈ ◈ Motel 6 #4021 🆂🅷 🐾
(865) 908-1244. **$29-$99.** 336 Henderson Chapel Rd. From jct US 441, just w at traffic light 1. Int corridors. **Pets:** Small. Designated rooms, service with restrictions, supervision.
[SAVE] [S🐾] [✕] [🕹M] [🛏] [💻] [🏊]

◈◈◈ ▼▼▼ National Parks Resort Lodge 🆂🅷
(865) 453-4106. **$30-$130.** 2385 Parkway. On US 441 at traffic light 1. Int corridors. **Pets:** Large, other species. $20 deposit/room, $20 one-time fee/room. Designated rooms, service with restrictions.
[SAVE] [✕] [🛏] [💻] [🏊]

◈◈◈ ▼ Rodeway Inn Mountain Sky Ⓜ
(865) 453-3530. **$29-$139.** 4236 Parkway. On US 441, at traffic light 10. Ext corridors. **Pets:** Accepted.
[SAVE] [✕] [🛏] [💻] [🏊]

◈◈◈ ▼▼◈ Smoky Shadows Motel & Conference Center 🆂🅷
(865) 453-7155. **$39-$119, 3 day notice.** 4215 Parkway. On US 441, just n of traffic light 10. Ext/int corridors. **Pets:** Small, dogs only. $10 daily fee/pet. Service with restrictions, crate.
[SAVE] [S🐾] [✕] [🛏] [💻] [🏊]

◈◈◈ ▼▼◈ Starr Crest Resort Cabin Rentals 🆅🅷
(865) 429-0156. **$89-$1209, 30 day notice.** 1431 Upper Middle Creek Rd. I-40, US 441, e at traffic light 8, 1.5 mi on Dollywood Ln. Ext corridors. **Pets:** Accepted.
[SAVE] [S🐾] [✕] [🛏] [💻] [🏊]

POWELL

▼▼ Comfort Inn Ⓜ
(865) 938-5500. **Call for rates.** 323 E Emory Rd. I-75, exit 112. Ext corridors. **Pets:** Accepted.
[✕] [🛏] [💻] [🏊]

PULASKI

◈◈◈ ▼▼ Super 8 Motel 🆂🅷
(931) 363-4501. **Call for rates.** I-65 & Hwy 64, Exit 14 East. I-65, exit 14, just e. Ext corridors. **Pets:** Accepted.
[SAVE] [✕] [🛏] [💻] [🏊]

RICEVILLE

▼ Rice Inn Ⓜ
(423) 462-2224. **Call for rates.** 3692 Hwy 11. I-75, exit 42, 1.5 mi e, then just n. Ext corridors. **Pets:** Accepted.
[✕] [🛏]

ROGERSVILLE

▼▼ Holiday Inn Express 🆂🅷
(423) 272-1842. **Call for rates.** 7139 Hwy 11 W. Jct SR 66 and US 11, 0.5 mi sw. Int corridors. **Pets:** Accepted.
[✕] [🛏] [💻] [🏊]

SELMER

▼▼ Super 8 Motel-Selmer SH
(731) 645-8880. **Call for rates.** 644 Mulberry Ave. Jct SR 64 and 45, just s on SR 45. Ext corridors. **Pets:** Accepted.

SEVIERVILLE

▼▼▼ Best Western Dumplin Valley Inn M
(865) 933-3467. **$44-$129.** 3426 Winfield Dunn Pkwy. I-40, exit 407, 0.4 mi s on SR 66. Ext corridors. **Pets:** Other species. $10 daily fee/room. Service with restrictions.

▼▼▼ Comfort Inn Mountain River Suites M
(865) 428-5519. **$59-$139.** 860 Winfield Dunn Pkwy. I-40, exit 407, 7 mi s on SR 66; 1.3 mi n of jct US 411. Ext corridors. **Pets:** Other species. $10 daily fee/pet. Designated rooms, service with restrictions, supervision.

▼▼ Holiday Inn Express Hotel & Suites SH
(865) 933-9448. **$49-$149.** 2863 Winfield Dunn Pkwy. I-40, exit 407, 2.3 mi s on SR 66. Int corridors. **Pets:** Very small. $10 fee/pet. Designated rooms, service with restrictions.

▼▼ Quality Inn Interstate M
(865) 933-1719. **$50-$199.** 155 Dumplin Valley Rd. I-40, exit 407, just s on SR 66, then just w. Ext corridors. **Pets:** Medium, other species. $10 daily fee/pet. Designated rooms, service with restrictions, supervision.

▼▼ Sleep Inn SH
(865) 429-0484. **$49-$119.** 1020 Parkway. On US 441, 1.2 mi s of jct US 411. Int corridors. **Pets:** Large, other species. $10 daily fee/room. Designated rooms, service with restrictions, crate.

SMYRNA

▼▼ Rodeway Inn & Suites M
(615) 355-6161. **$58-$65.** 1300 Plaza Dr. I-24, exit 66B, 2.5 mi ne. Ext corridors. **Pets:** $10 daily fee/pet. Designated rooms, service with restrictions, supervision.

SWEETWATER

▼▼▼ Best Western Sweetwater Inn SH
(423) 337-3541. **$69-$99.** 1421 Murray Rd. I-75, exit 60, just w. Ext/int corridors. **Pets:** Small. $15 one-time fee/room. Designated rooms, service with restrictions, supervision.

▼▼ Comfort Inn SH
(423) 337-6646. **$53-$100.** 731 S Main St. On US 11, jct SR 68. Ext/int corridors. **Pets:** Medium. $10 daily fee/pet. Service with restrictions, supervision.

▼▼ Comfort Inn West SH
(423) 337-3353. **$60-$169.** 249 Hwy 68. I-75, exit 60, just e. Ext/int corridors. **Pets:** Medium. $10 daily fee/pet. Service with restrictions, supervision.

▼▼ Knights Inn M
(423) 337-9357. **Call for rates.** 207 Hwy 68. I-75, exit 60. Ext corridors. **Pets:** Medium. $5 one-time fee/pet. Service with restrictions, supervision.

▼▼▼ Quality Inn & Suites SH
(423) 337-4900. **$70-$153.** 1116 Hwy 68. I-75, exit 60. Int corridors. **Pets:** Other species. $10 one-time fee/pet. Service with restrictions.

TOWNSEND

▼▼ Econo Lodge Inn & Suites M
(865) 448-9000. **$39-$189.** 7824 E Lamar Alexander Pkwy. On US 321, 0.7 mi s of jct SR 73. Ext corridors. **Pets:** Small, dogs only. $20 daily fee/pet. Designated rooms, service with restrictions, supervision.

▼▼ Valley View Lodge M
(865) 448-2237. **Call for rates.** 7726 E Lamar Alexander Pkwy. On US 321, 1.1 mi s of jct SR 73. Ext corridors. **Pets:** $10 one-time fee/pet. Designated rooms, service with restrictions, supervision.

TULLAHOMA

▼▼ Jameson Inn SH
(931) 455-7891. **Call for rates.** 2113 N Jackson St. 3 mi n on SR 41A (N Jackson St). Ext corridors. **Pets:** Small. $15 daily fee/room. Service with restrictions, crate.

VONORE

▼▼▼ Grand Vista Hotel & Suites SH
(423) 884-6200. **$80-$90.** 117 Grand Vista Dr. I-75, exit 172, 14 mi e. Int corridors. **Pets:** Medium. $10 deposit/pet. Designated rooms, supervision.

WHITE HOUSE

▼▼ Holiday Inn Express SH
(615) 672-7200. **$80-$90.** 354 Hester Ln. I-65, exit 108, just e. Ext corridors. **Pets:** Accepted.

WHITEVILLE

▼▼ Super 8 SH
(731) 254-8884. **Call for rates.** 2040 Hwy 64. US 64 and SR 179. Ext corridors. **Pets:** Small. $5 daily fee/pet. Service with restrictions, supervision.

WILDERSVILLE

▼▼ Best Western Crossroads Inn SH
(731) 968-2532. **Call for rates.** 21045 Hwy 22 N. I-40, exit 108, just s. Ext corridors. **Pets:** Accepted.

TEXAS

ABILENE

Best Western Mall South SH
(325) 695-1262. $79-$95. 3950 Ridgemont Dr. US 83/84, exit Ridgemont Dr, just s. Ext corridors. Pets: Medium. $30 daily fee/pet. Designated rooms, service with restrictions, crate.

Budget Host Colonial Inn M
(325) 677-2683. Call for rates. 3210 Pine St. Jct I-20 and US 83 business route, exit 286A. Ext/int corridors. Pets: Medium. $10 daily fee/pet. Designated rooms, no service, supervision.

Civic Plaza Hotel SH
(325) 676-0222. $49-$65. 505 Pine St. Downtown. Ext corridors. Pets: $20 one-time fee/pet. Designated rooms, service with restrictions.

Comfort Suites SH
(325) 795-8500. $90-$110. 3165 S Danville Dr. I-20, exit 279, s on US 83/84/277 to Southwest Dr, then just e. Int corridors. Pets: $30 daily fee/pet. Service with restrictions, crate.

Days Inn M
(325) 672-6433. Call for rates. 1702 E Hwy 20. I-20, exit 288. Ext corridors. Pets: Accepted.

Econo Lodge M
(325) 673-5424. $45-$55. 1633 W Stamford. S Frontage Rd off I-20 and US 80, exit 285 eastbound; exit 286A westbound. Ext corridors. Pets: Accepted.

Holiday Inn Express Mall South SH
(325) 695-0500. $99-$139. 3112 S Clark. US 83/277 and Southwest Dr, just e to Catclaw, then just n. Int corridors. Pets: Small. $30 one-time fee/room. Designated rooms, service with restrictions, supervision.

La Quinta Inn Abilene SH
(325) 676-1676. $99-$119. 3501 W Lake Rd. I-20, exit 286C. Ext corridors. Pets: Other species. Service with restrictions, supervision.

Motel 6 Abilene #79 M
(325) 672-8462. $43-$56. 4951 W Stamford St. I-20, exit 282, on eastbound frontage road. Ext corridors. Pets: Other species. Service with restrictions, supervision.

Super 8 Motel Abilene North M
(325) 673-5251. $60-$75. 1525 E I-20. I-20, exit 288. Ext corridors. Pets: Accepted.

ALAMO

Super 8 Motel SH
(956) 787-9444. Call for rates. 714 N Alamo Rd. US 83, exit FM 907, just n. Ext corridors. Pets: Accepted.

ALICE

Days Inn SH
(361) 664-6616. Call for rates. 555 N Johnson St. On US 281 business route, n of Johnson St. Int corridors. Pets: Accepted.

ALPINE

Oak Tree Inn SH
(432) 837-5711. **Call for rates.** 2407 E Holland (Hwy 90/67). US 90, 2 mi e. Int corridors. **Pets:** Accepted.

ALVIN

Americas Best Value Inn & Suites M
(281) 331-0335. **Call for rates.** 1588 S Hwy 35 Loop. SR 35 Bypass, 0.5 mi sw of SR 6. Ext corridors. **Pets:** Accepted.

AMARILLO

Ambassador Hotel LH ❖
(806) 358-6161. **$139-$169.** 3100 I-40 W. I-40, exit 68, just w on north frontage road. Int corridors. **Pets:** Medium. $50 one-time fee/pet. Designated rooms, no service, supervision.

Baymont Inn & Suites SH
(806) 356-6800. **Call for rates.** 3411 I-40 W. I-40, exit 67, 0.3 mi e on south frontage road. Int corridors. **Pets:** Accepted.

Best Western Amarillo Inn SH
(806) 358-7861. **Call for rates.** 1610 Coulter Dr. I-40, exit 65 (Coulter Dr), 0.6 mi n. Ext/int corridors. **Pets:** Small. $15 daily fee/pet. Designated rooms, service with restrictions, supervision.

Best Western Santa Fe SH
(806) 372-1885. **Call for rates.** 4600 I-40 E. I-40, exit 73 (Eastern St) eastbound; exit 73 (Bolton St) westbound, U-turn on south frontage road. Int corridors. **Pets:** Medium. $25 one-time fee/pet. Service with restrictions, supervision.

Big Texan Motel M ❖
(806) 372-5000. **$60-$75, 7 day notice.** 7701 I-40 E. I-40, exit 75 (Lakeside Dr), 0.3 mi w on north frontage road. Ext corridors. **Pets:** Other species. $30 deposit/pet, $10 daily fee/pet. Designated rooms, service with restrictions, supervision.

Days Inn SH ❖
(806) 379-6255. **Call for rates.** 1701 I-40 E. I-40, exit 71 (Ross-Osage), just w on north frontage road. Int corridors. **Pets:** Other species. $10 one-time fee/pet. Designated rooms, service with restrictions, supervision.

Days Inn SH
(806) 359-9393. **Call for rates.** 2102 S Coulter Dr. I-40, exit 65 (Coulter Dr), just n. Ext corridors. **Pets:** Medium. $20 daily fee/pet. Service with restrictions, supervision.

Drury Inn & Suites SH
(806) 351-1111. **$141.** 8540 W I-40. I-40, exit 64. Int corridors. **Pets:** Large, other species. Service with restrictions, supervision.

Extended StayAmerica Amarillo West SH
(806) 351-0117. **$67-$75.** 2100 Cinema Dr. I-40, exit 64, just n. Int corridors. **Pets:** Other species. $75 one-time fee/pet. Service with restrictions.

Hampton Inn SH
(806) 372-1425. **$89-$129.** 1700 I-40 E. I-40, exit 71 (Ross-Osage), just e on south frontage road. Int corridors. **Pets:** Large, other species. Service with restrictions, supervision.

Holiday Inn-I-40 SH
(806) 372-8741. **Call for rates.** 1911 I-40 at Ross-Osage. I-40, exit 71 (Ross-Osage), on north frontage road. Int corridors. **Pets:** Other species. $50 deposit/room. Designated rooms, service with restrictions, crate.

Howard Johnson SH
(806) 374-2020. **Call for rates.** 1620 I-40 E. I-40, exit 71 (Ross-Osage), just e on south frontage road. Ext corridors. **Pets:** Accepted.

La Quinta Inn Amarillo (East/Airport Area) SH
(806) 373-7486. **$92-$112.** 1708 I-40 E. I-40, exit 71 (Ross-Osage), just e on south frontage road. Ext corridors. **Pets:** Other species. Service with restrictions, supervision.

La Quinta Inn Amarillo (West/Medical Center) SH
(806) 352-6311. **$92-$112.** 2108 S Coulter Dr. I-40, exit 65 (Coulter Dr), just n. Ext corridors. **Pets:** Other species. Service with restrictions, supervision.

Microtel Inn & Suites SH
(806) 372-8373. **$59-$119.** 1501 S Ross St. I-40, exit 71 (Ross-Osage), just n. Int corridors. **Pets:** Small, dogs only. $20 one-time fee/pet. Designated rooms, service with restrictions, supervision.

Motel 6 Amarillo East #409 M
(806) 374-6444. **$41-$55.** 3930 I-40 E. I-40, exit 72B, on eastbound frontage road. Ext corridors. **Pets:** Other species. Service with restrictions, supervision.

Motel 6 Amarillo West #1146 M
(806) 359-7651. **$42-$55.** 6030 I-40 W. I-40, exit 66 (Bell St), just w, on north frontage road. Ext corridors. **Pets:** Other species. Service with restrictions, supervision.

Quality Inn & Suites West SH
(806) 358-7943. **$69-$109.** 6800 I-40 W. I-40, exit 66 (Bell St), 0.5 mi w on north frontage road. Ext corridors. **Pets:** Medium. Designated rooms, service with restrictions, supervision.

Quality Inn-East SH
(806) 376-9993. **Call for rates.** 1515 I-40 E. I-40, exit 71 (Ross-Osage), just w on north frontage road. Ext corridors. **Pets:** Accepted.

Residence Inn by Marriott SH
(806) 354-2978. **$155-$175.** 6700 I-40 W. I-40, exit 66 (Bell St), 0.5 mi w on north frontage road. Int corridors. **Pets:** Accepted.

Travelodge West SH
(806) 353-3541. **$55-$59.** 2035 Paramount Blvd. I-40, exit 68A (Paramount Blvd), just s. Ext corridors. **Pets:** Small. $5 daily fee/room. Service with restrictions, supervision.

ANTHONY

Best Western Oasis of the Sun SH
(915) 886-3333. **$81-$99.** 9401 S Desert Blvd. I-10, exit 0. Ext corridors. **Pets:** Accepted.

ARLINGTON

▼▼▼ Arlington TownePlace Suites by Marriott SH
(817) 861-8728. **$132-$152.** 1709 E Lamar Ave. 2 mi w of SR 360. Int corridors. **Pets:** Accepted.

ASK Sⓐ ✕ ⓕM 🖶 🖵 ⬿

▼▼ Country Inn & Suites By Carlson SH
(817) 261-8900. **Call for rates.** 1075 Wet N Wild Way. I-30, exit 28 (Collins St/FM 157), just e. Ext corridors. **Pets:** Accepted.

✕ ⓕM 🖶 🖵 ✕

ⒶⒶⒶ ▼▼▼ Days Inn Ameriquest Field/Six Flags SH
(817) 261-8444. **$56-$88, 3 day notice.** 910 N Collins St. I-30, exit 28 (Collins St/FM 157), 1 mi s. Int corridors. **Pets:** Accepted.

SAVE Sⓐ ✕ 🖶 🖵 ⬿

▼▼▼ Hawthorn Suites SH
(817) 640-1188. **$79-$249.** 2401 Brookhollow Plaza Dr. I-30, exit 30 (SR 360), just n to Lamar Blvd, just w to Brookhollow Plaza Dr, then just n. Ext corridors. **Pets:** Medium. $58 one-time fee/pet. Service with restrictions, supervision.

ASK Sⓐ ✕ 🖶 🖵 ⬿ ✕

▼▼▼ Homewood Suites by Hilton SH
(817) 633-1594. **Call for rates.** 2401 E Rd to Six Flags St. I-30, exit 30 (SR 360), 0.5 mi sw. Int corridors. **Pets:** Accepted.

✕ ⓕM 🖶 🖵 ⬿ ✕

▼▼▼ Howard Johnson Express Inn SH
(817) 461-1122. **Call for rates.** 2001 E Copeland Rd. I-30, exit 30 (SR 360) westbound, just s to Six Flags Dr, just w to Copeland Rd, then 0.9 mi w; exit 29 (Ball Pkwy) eastbound. Int corridors. **Pets:** Accepted.

✕ 🖶 🖵 ⬿

▼▼▼ La Quinta Inn & Suites Dallas/Arlington North SH
(817) 640-4142. **$125-$145.** 825 N Watson Rd. I-30, exit 30 (SR 360), exit Six Flags Dr northbound; exit Ave H/Lamar Blvd southbound. Int corridors. **Pets:** Other species. Service with restrictions, supervision.

ASK Sⓐ ✕ 🖶 🖵 ⬿

ⒶⒶⒶ ▼▼▼ Microtel Inn SH
(817) 557-8400. **$55-$75.** 1740 Oak Village Blvd. I-20, exit 449 (Cooper St) westbound; exit 449A (Cooper St) eastbound, just s. Int corridors. **Pets:** Small, dogs only. $15 daily fee/pet. Service with restrictions, supervision.

SAVE Sⓐ ✕ 🖶 ⬿

ⒶⒶⒶ ▼▼▼ Sleep Inn Main Gate-Six Flags SH
(817) 649-1010. **$50-$130.** 750 Six Flags Dr. I-30, exit 30 (SR 360), 0.5 mi s. Int corridors. **Pets:** Large, other species. $10 one-time fee/pet. Service with restrictions, supervision.

SAVE Sⓐ ✕ 🖶 🖵 ⬿

▼▼ Studio 6-South Arlington #6036 SH
(817) 465-8500. **$61-$75.** 1980 W Pleasant Ridge Rd. I-20, exit 449 (Cooper St), 0.3 mi n, then just w. Ext corridors. **Pets:** Other species. Service with restrictions, supervision.

Sⓐ ✕ 🖶 🖵

▼▼ StudioPLUS SH
(817) 649-0021. **$58-$65.** 2420 E Lamar Blvd. I-30, exit 30 (SR 360), just n to Lamar Blvd; just w of SR 360. Int corridors. **Pets:** Other species. $75 one-time fee/pet. Service with restrictions.

ASK Sⓐ ✕ 🖶 🖵 ⬿

AUSTIN

▼▼▼ Baymont Inn Highland Mall SH
(512) 452-9401. **Call for rates.** 7100 I-35 N. I-35, exit 239, on west frontage road. Ext corridors. **Pets:** Medium. Service with restrictions, supervision.

✕ 🖶 🖵 ⬿

ⒶⒶⒶ ▼▼▼ Best Western Atrium North SH
(512) 339-7311. **$89-$104.** 7928 Gessner Dr. I-35, exit 240A, 0.4 mi w on Anderson Ln. Int corridors. **Pets:** Small, other species. $25 one-time fee/room. Service with restrictions, supervision.

SAVE Sⓐ ✕ 🖶 🖵 ⬿

ⒶⒶⒶ ▼▼▼ Best Western Seville Plaza Inn SH
(512) 447-5511. **$89-$139.** 4323 I-35 S. I-35, exit 230A (Stassney Rd) southbound; exit 230 (Ben White Blvd) northbound. Int corridors. **Pets:** Accepted.

SAVE Sⓐ ✕ 🖶 🖵 ⓣ ⬿

▼▼▼ Candlewood Suites Austin Northwest SH
(512) 338-1611. **Call for rates.** 9701 Stonelake Blvd. Jct SR 360 (Capital of Texas Hwy) and Stonelake Blvd, just s. Int corridors. **Pets:** Medium, other species. $75 one-time fee/room. Service with restrictions, crate.

✕ ⓕM 🖶 🖵

▼▼▼ Candlewood Suites-South SH 🐾
(512) 444-8882. **$109-$159.** 4323 I-35 S. I-35, exit 230 northbound; exit 230B southbound, on southbound frontage road. Int corridors. **Pets:** Large. $75 one-time fee/room. Service with restrictions, crate.

ASK Sⓐ ✕ ⓕM 🖶 🖵

ⒶⒶⒶ ▼▼▼ Clarion Inn & Suites Conference Center SH
(512) 444-0561. **$109-$189.** 2200 S I-35. I-35, exit 232A (Oltorf Blvd), on west side access road. Ext/int corridors. **Pets:** Accepted.

SAVE Sⓐ ✕ 🖶 🖵 ⓣ ⬿

▼▼▼ Comfort Suites Airport SH
(512) 386-6000. **$109-$139.** 7501 E Ben White Blvd. I-35, exit 230B (Ben White Blvd/SR 71), 3.6 mi e. Int corridors. **Pets:** Accepted.

ASK Sⓐ ✕ ⓕM 🖶 🖵 ⬿

▼ Crossland Studios Austin West SH
(512) 331-4747. **$60-$70.** 12621 Hymeadow Rd. US 183 N, exit Lake Creek, just n, then just e. Ext corridors. **Pets:** Other species. $75 one-time fee/pet. Service with restrictions.

ASK Sⓐ ✕ 🖶 🖵

▼▼▼ DoubleTree Guest Suites-Austin LH
(512) 478-7000. **Call for rates.** 303 W 15th St. Just nw of state capitol building. Int corridors. **Pets:** Large, other species. $40 one-time fee/room. Service with restrictions, crate.

✕ 🖶 🖵 ⓣ ⬿

▼▼▼ DoubleTree Hotel Austin LH
(512) 454-3737. **Call for rates.** 6505 I-35 N. I-35, exit 238A, on east frontage road. Int corridors. **Pets:** Accepted.

✕ ⓕM 🖶 🖵 ⓣ ⬿

ⒶⒶⒶ ▼▼▼▼ The Driskill LH 🐾
(512) 474-5911. **$199-$509.** 604 Brazos St. Jct 6th St. Int corridors. **Pets:** Small. $50 one-time fee/pet. Designated rooms, service with restrictions, supervision.

SAVE Sⓐ ✕ ⓣ

▼▼▼ Drury Inn & Suites-Austin North SH
(512) 467-9500. **$131.** 6711 I-35 N. I-35, exit 238A, on east frontage road. Int corridors. **Pets:** Large, other species. Service with restrictions, supervision.

ASK ✕ 🖶 🖵 ⬿

▼▼ Econo Lodge SH
(512) 835-7070. **$60-$90.** 9102 Burnet Rd. US 183 and Burnet Rd; on northeast corner. Ext corridors. **Pets:** Accepted.

ASK Sⓐ ✕ 🖶 🖵

▼▼ Econo Lodge SH
(512) 458-4759. **Call for rates.** 6201 Hwy 290 E. I-35, exit 238, 0.3 mi e of jct I-35 and US 290 E. Ext corridors. **Pets:** Accepted.

✕ 🖶 🖵 ⬿

▼▼▼▼ **Embassy Suites Austin North** 🇱🇭
(512) 454-8004. **Call for rates.** 5901 I-35 N. I-35, exit 238A, on east frontage road. Int corridors. **Pets:** Accepted.
⊠ 🛇 🖵 🍴 ⇌ ⊠

▼▼▼▼ **Embassy Suites Hotel-Downtown** 🇱🇭
(512) 469-9000. **Call for rates.** 300 S Congress Ave. Just s of Congress Ave Bridge. Int corridors. **Pets:** Accepted.
⊠ 🛇 🖵 🍴 ⇌

💥 ▼▼▼ **Exel Inn Of Austin** 🇸🇭
(512) 462-9201. **$53-$69.** 2711 I-35 S. I-35, exit 231 (Woodward Ave) southbound; exit 232A (Oltorf St) northbound, on northbound frontage road; just n of jct I-35 and US 290/SR 71. Int corridors. **Pets:** Accepted.
SAVE S☉ ⊠ 🛇 ⇌

▼▼ **Extended StayAmerica Austin Arboretum** 🇸🇭
(512) 231-1520. **$85-$95.** 10100 Capital of Texas Hwy. Jct Loop 1 (Mo-Pac) and Capital of Texas Hwy (SR 360), just w. Int corridors. **Pets:** Other species. $75 one-time fee/pet. Service with restrictions.
ASK S☉ ⊠ 🛇M 🛇 🖵

▼▼ **Extended StayAmerica Austin Downtown** 🇸🇭
(512) 457-9994. **$115-$125.** 600 Guadalupe St. Jct 6th and Guadalupe sts; on northwest corner. Int corridors. **Pets:** Other species. $75 one-time fee/pet. Service with restrictions.
ASK S☉ ⊠ 🛇M 🛇 🖵

▼▼ **Extended StayAmerica Austin Northwest Lakeline Mall** 🇸🇭
(512) 258-3365. **$80-$90.** 13858 US Hwy 183 N. Jct US 183 and SR 620; on southwest corner. Int corridors. **Pets:** Other species. $75 one-time fee/pet. Service with restrictions.
ASK S☉ ⊠ 🛇M 🛇 🖵

▼▼▼▼ **Extended StayAmerica (Austin/Northwest/Research Park)** 🇸🇭
(512) 219-6500. **$90-$100.** 12424 Research Blvd. US 183, exit Oak Knoll, on eastbound frontage road. Int corridors. **Pets:** Other species. $75 one-time fee/pet. Service with restrictions.
ASK S☉ ⊠ 🛇M 🛇 🖵 ⇌

▼▼ **Extended StayAmerica Austin Southwest** 🇸🇭
(512) 892-4272. **$90-$100.** 5100 US Hwy 290 W. I-35, exit 230, US 290 W to Brodie Lane exit, then 1 mi w. Int corridors. **Pets:** Other species. $75 one-time fee/pet. Service with restrictions.
ASK S☉ ⊠ 🛇M 🛇 🖵

▼▼▼▼ **Extended StayAmerica Deluxe** 🇸🇭
(512) 339-6005. **$85-$95.** 8221 N I-35. I-35, exit 241, on east frontage road. Int corridors. **Pets:** Other species. $75 one-time fee/pet. Service with restrictions.
ASK S☉ ⊠ 🛇 🖵 ⇌

▼▼▼▼ **Extended Stay Deluxe Austin-Arboretum-North** 🇸🇭
(512) 833-0898. **$90-$100.** 2700 Gracy Farms Ln. 2 mi n of US 183 on Loop 1 (Mo-Pac Expwy), exit Burnet Rd (FM 1325). Int corridors. **Pets:** Other species. $75 one-time fee/pet. Service with restrictions.
ASK S☉ ⊠ 🛇 🖵 ⇌

▼▼ **Extended Stay Deluxe Austin Metro** 🇸🇭
(512) 452-0880. **Call for rates.** 6300 US Hwy 290 E. Jct I-35 and US 290 E. Int corridors. **Pets:** Other species. $75 one-time fee/pet. Service with restrictions.
⊠ 🛇 🖵 ⇌

▼▼▼▼ **Fairfield Inn & Suites Austin NW** 🇸🇭 🐾
(512) 527-0734. **$132-$152.** 11201 N Mo-Pac Blvd. US 183 N, 1.5 mi n on Loop 1 (Mo-Pac Expwy) to Braker Ln exit, on east frontage road. Int corridors. **Pets:** Medium. $75 one-time fee/room. Service with restrictions, supervision.
ASK S☉ ⊠ 🛇M 🛇 🖵 ⇌ ⊠

▼▼▼ ▼▼▼ **Four Seasons Hotel** 🇱🇭
(512) 478-4500. **$410-$2300.** 98 San Jacinto Blvd. Bordering Town Lake. Int corridors. **Pets:** Accepted.
⊠ 🛇 🖵 🍴 ⇌ ⊠

▼▼▼▼ **Hampton Inn Northwest** 🇸🇭
(512) 349-9898. **$139.** 3908 W Braker Ln. 1 mi n of US 183 on Loop 1 (Mo-Pac Expwy) to Braker Ln exit. Int corridors. **Pets:** Accepted.
ASK S☉ ⊠ 🛇M 🖵 ⇌

💥 ▼▼▼ **Hawthorn Suites Ltd-Austin-Bergstrom International Airport** 🇸🇭
(512) 247-6166. **Call for rates.** 7800 E Riverside Dr. I-35, exit 230B (Ben White Blvd/SR 71), 3.2 mi e. Int corridors. **Pets:** Accepted.
SAVE ⊠ 🛇M 🛇 🖵 ⇌ ⊠

▼▼▼ **Holiday Inn Express Hotel & Suites** 🇸🇭
(512) 251-9110. **$120-$140.** 14620 N I-35. I-35, exit 247, on west frontage road. Int corridors. **Pets:** Accepted.
ASK ⊠ 🛇M 🛇 🖵 ⇌

▼▼▼ **Holiday Inn Northwest/Arboretum** 🇸🇭
(512) 343-0888. **$89-$149.** 8901 Business Park Dr. Jct US 183 and Loop 1 (Mo-Pac Expwy), on southwest corner. Int corridors. **Pets:** Accepted.
ASK S☉ ⊠ 🛇 🖵 🍴 ⇌

▼▼ **Homestead Studio Suites Hotel-Austin/Arboretum-South** 🇸🇭
(512) 837-6677. **$70-$80.** 9100 Waterford Centre Blvd. US 183, exit Burnet Rd, on westbound frontage road. Ext corridors. **Pets:** Other species. $75 one-time fee/pet. Service with restrictions.
ASK S☉ ⊠ 🛇 🖵

▼▼▼ **Homestead Studio Suites Hotel-Austin/Downtown/Town Lake** 🇸🇭
(512) 476-1818. **$95-$105.** 507 S 1st St. I-35, exit 234B southbound; exit 234A northbound, 1.8 mi w on Cesar Chavez/E 1st St, then 0.5 mi s. Int corridors. **Pets:** Other species. $75 one-time fee/pet. Service with restrictions.
ASK S☉ ⊠ 🛇 🖵

▼▼▼ **Homewood Suites-Austin South** 🇸🇭
(512) 445-5050. **Call for rates.** 4143 Governor's Row. I-35, exit 231 (Ben White Blvd/SR 71) southbound; exit 229 northbound, at Ben White Blvd. Int corridors. **Pets:** Accepted.
⊠ 🛇M 🛇 🖵 ⇌

▼▼▼▼ **Homewood Suites by Hilton Arboretum NW** 🇸🇭
(512) 349-9966. **$189.** 10925 Stonelake Blvd. US 183 N to Loop 1 (Mo-Pac Expwy), 1.5 mi n to Braker Ln; on northwest corner. Int corridors. **Pets:** Accepted.
ASK S☉ ⊠ 🛇M 🛇 🖵 ⇌ ⊠

▼▼▼ **Howard Johnson Plaza Hotel** 🇸🇭
(512) 836-8520. **$114-$122.** 7800 I-35 N. I-35, exit 240A, on west frontage road at US 183. Int corridors. **Pets:** Accepted.
ASK S☉ ⊠ 🛇 🖵 🍴 ⇌

💥 ▼▼▼ ▼▼▼ **Hyatt Regency Austin** 🇱🇭 🐾
(512) 477-1234. **$159-$309.** 208 Barton Springs Rd. At south end of Congress Bridge; on south bank of Town Lake. Int corridors. **Pets:** Large. $35 daily fee/pet. Service with restrictions, supervision.
SAVE ⊠ 🛇M 🛇 🖵 🍴 ⇌ ⊠

▼▼▼ ▼▼▼ **Hyatt Regency Lost Pines Resort and Spa** 🇱🇭 🐾
(512) 308-1234. **$179-$409, 3 day notice.** 575 Hyatt Lost Pines Rd. SR 71, 13 mi e of Austin Airport; 9 mi w of Bastrop. Int corridors. **Pets:** Dogs only. $100 daily fee/pet. Service with restrictions, supervision.
ASK ⊠ 🛇M 🛇 🖵 🍴 ⇌ ⊠

La Quinta Inn & Suites SH
(512) 246-2800. **$89-$109.** 150 Parker Dr. I-35, exit 250, on west frontage road. Int corridors. **Pets:** Other species. Service with restrictions, supervision.
ASK S⊘ ✕ &M ⛝ ⬛ ⇌

La Quinta Inn & Suites Austin (Airport) SH
(512) 386-6800. **$129-$149.** 7625 E Ben White Blvd. I-35, exit 230B (Ben White Blvd/SR 71), 3.8 mi e. Int corridors. **Pets:** Other species. Service with restrictions, supervision.
ASK S⊘ ✕ &M ⛝ ⬛ ⇌

La Quinta Inn & Suites Austin (Mopac North) SH
(512) 832-2121. **$105-$125.** 11901 N Mo-Pac Expwy. US 183, 2 mi n on Loop 1 (Mo-Pac Expwy) to Duval exit. Int corridors. **Pets:** Other species. Service with restrictions, supervision.
ASK S⊘ ✕ &M ⛝ ⬛ ⇌

La Quinta Inn & Suites Austin (Southwest at Mopac) SH
(512) 899-3000. **$149-$169.** 4424 S Loop 1 (Mo-Pac Expwy). Jct Loop 1 (Mo-Pac Expwy), US 290 and SR 71 E, on southbound frontage road. Int corridors. **Pets:** Other species. Service with restrictions, supervision.
ASK S⊘ ✕ &M ⛝ ⬛ ⇌

La Quinta Inn Austin (Capitol) SH
(512) 476-1166. **$119-$139.** 300 E 11 St. Just e of state capitol building. Ext/int corridors. **Pets:** Other species. Service with restrictions, supervision.
ASK S⊘ ✕ ⛝ ⬛ ⇌

La Quinta Inn Austin (Highland Mall) SH
(512) 459-4381. **$95-$115.** 5812 I-35 N. I-35, exit 238A, on west frontage road. Ext corridors. **Pets:** Other species. Service with restrictions, supervision.
ASK S⊘ ✕ ⛝ ⬛ ⇌

La Quinta Inn Austin (I-35 South/Ben White) SH
(512) 443-1774. **$89-$109.** 4200 I-35 S. I-35, exit 231 (St. Edwards/Woodward Ave) southbound; exit 230 northbound, just s of jct I-35, US 290 and SR 71, on frontage road. Ext corridors. **Pets:** Other species. Service with restrictions, supervision.
ASK S⊘ ✕ &M ⛝ ⬛ ⇌

La Quinta Inn Austin (Oltorf) SH
(512) 447-6661. **$99-$119.** 1603 E Oltorf Blvd. I-35, exit 232A (Oltorf Blvd), just s. Ext/int corridors. **Pets:** Other species. Service with restrictions, supervision.
ASK S⊘ ✕ ⛝ ⬛ ⇌

La Quinta Inn North SH
(512) 467-1701. **$94-$114.** 7622 N I-35 & 183. I-35, exit 240A, on west frontage road. Int corridors. **Pets:** Other species. Service with restrictions, supervision.
SAVE S⊘ ✕ ⛝ ⬛ ⇌

The Mansion at Judge's Hill SH
(512) 495-1800. **$139-$399.** 1900 Rio Grande. Jct Rio Grande and Martin Luther King Jr Blvd. Int corridors. **Pets:** Accepted.
SAVE ✕ S⊘ ⬛ ⑪

Northcross Suites SH
(512) 452-9391. **Call for rates.** 7685 Northcross Dr. Loop 1 (Mo-Pac Expwy), exit Anderson Rd, just e to Northcross Dr, then just s. Ext corridors. **Pets:** Accepted.
SAVE ✕ ⛝ ⬛ ⇌ ⊠

Omni Austin Hotel & Suites LH
(512) 476-3700. **$259-$309.** 700 San Jacinto Blvd. 8th St and San Jacinto Blvd. Int corridors. **Pets:** Accepted.
ASK S⊘ ✕ &M ⛝ ⬛ ⑪ ⇌ ⊠

Omni Austin Hotel Southpark LH ❀
(512) 448-2222. **$188-$249.** 4140 Governor's Row. I-35, exit 230B southbound; exit 230 northbound, on east frontage road. Int corridors. **Pets:** Medium, other species. $50 deposit/room. Service with restrictions, supervision.
SAVE S⊘ ✕ ⛝ ⬛ ⑪ ⇌ ⊠

Ramada Austin Central SH
(512) 454-1144. **$85-$95.** 919 E Koenig Ln. I-35, exit 238A, on west frontage road. Int corridors. **Pets:** $10 daily fee/pet. Service with restrictions, crate.
ASK S⊘ ✕ &M ⛝ ⬛ ⇌

Red Roof Inn Austin North M
(512) 835-2200. **Call for rates.** 8210 I-35 N. I-35, exit 241 northbound; exit 240A southbound, on west frontage road. Ext corridors. **Pets:** Accepted.
✕ ⛝ ⑪ ⇌

Renaissance Austin Hotel LH
(512) 343-2626. **$319-$339.** 9721 Arboretum Blvd. Jct US 183 and Capital of Texas Hwy (SR 360); southwest corner. Int corridors. **Pets:** Accepted.
SAVE S⊘ ✕ &M ⛝ ⬛ ⑪ ⇌ ⊠

Residence Inn by Marriott Austin Airport/South SH
(512) 912-1100. **$165-$185.** 4537 S I-35. I-35, exit 229 (Stassney Rd) southbound; exit 230 (Ben White Blvd/SR 71) northbound, on northbound frontage road. Int corridors. **Pets:** Accepted.
ASK S⊘ ✕ ⛝ ⬛ ⇌ ⊠

Residence Inn by Marriott Austin/Downtown/Convention Center LH
(512) 472-5553. **$241-$252.** 300 E 4th St. Between Trinity and San Jacinto Blvd. Int corridors. **Pets:** Accepted.
ASK S⊘ ✕ ⛝ ⬛ ⑪ ⇌

Residence Inn by Marriott-Austin North/Parmer Lane SH
(512) 977-0544. **$175-$186.** 12401 N Lamar Blvd. I-35, exit 245, just w. Int corridors. **Pets:** Accepted.
ASK S⊘ ✕ &M ⛝ ⬛ ⇌ ⊠

Sheraton Austin LH
(512) 478-1111. **$169-$359.** 701 E 11th St. I-35, exit 234B, 0.3 mi e. Int corridors. **Pets:** Accepted.
✕ ⛝ ⬛ ⑪ ⇌ ⊠

Staybridge Suites Hotel SH
(512) 349-0888. **$169-$189.** 10201 Stonelake Blvd. Jct US 183 and Capital of Texas Hwy (SR 360); northwest corner. Int corridors. **Pets:** Accepted.
ASK S⊘ ✕ &M ⛝ ⬛ ⇌ ⊠

Studio 6-Northwest #6032 M
(512) 258-3556. **$54-$61.** 11901 Pavillon Blvd. US 183, exit Oak Knoll westbound; exit Duval/Balcones Woods eastbound, on eastbound frontage road. Ext corridors. **Pets:** Other species. Service with restrictions, supervision.
S⊘ ✕ ⛝ ⬛

Super 8 Austin North SH
(512) 339-1300. **$45-$60.** 8128 N I-35. I-35, exit 241, on west frontage road. Int corridors. **Pets:** Medium, other species. $20 one-time fee/pet. Service with restrictions, supervision.
SAVE S⊘ ✕ ⛝ ⬛ ⇌

Super 8 Central M
(512) 472-8331. **$75-$200.** 1201 N I-35. I-35, exit 234, at 12th St. Ext corridors. **Pets:** Accepted.
SAVE S⊘ ✕ ⛝ ⬛ ⇌

▼▼▼▼ **Wyndham Garden Hotel** 🅛🅗
(512) 448-2444. **$119-$189.** 3401 I-35 S. I-35, exit 231 (Woodward St) southbound; exit 230 (Ben White Blvd/SR 71) northbound; on northbound frontage road. Ext/int corridors. **Pets:** Accepted.
(A$K) [S🄳] [✕] 🔒 [💻] [🍴] [🌊] [✕]

BASTROP

🔶🔶 ▼▼▼ **Days Inn Bastrop** 🅢🅗
(512) 321-1157. **Call for rates.** 4102 Hwy 71 E. On SR 71, 2 mi e of river at Loop 150 E. Ext corridors. **Pets:** $10 daily fee/pet. Designated rooms, service with restrictions.
(SAVE) [✕] 🔒 [💻] [🌊]

▼▼▼▼ **Holiday Inn Express Hotel & Suites** 🅢🅗
(512) 321-1900. **$129-$189.** 491 Agnes St. Jct SR 71/95, 2 mi w. Int corridors. **Pets:** Accepted.
(A$K) [S🄳] [✕] [&M] 🔒 [💻] [🌊]

BEAUMONT

🔶🔶 ▼▼▼ **Best Western Jefferson Inn** 🅢🅗
(409) 842-0037. **$69-$99.** 1610 I-10 S. I-10, exit 851 (College St), westbound service road; 0.5 mi s of jct US 90. Ext corridors. **Pets:** Accepted.
(SAVE) [S🄳] [✕] 🔒 [💻] [🌊]

🔶🔶 ▼▼▼▼ **Holiday Inn Beaumont Midtown** 🅢🅗
(409) 892-2222. **Call for rates.** 2095 N 11th St. I-10, exit 853B (11th St), just n. Int corridors. **Pets:** Accepted.
(SAVE) [✕] [&M] 🔒 [💻] [🍴] [🌊]

🔶🔶 ▼▼▼▼ **Holiday Inn Beaumont Plaza** 🅛🅗
(409) 842-5995. **Call for rates.** 3950 I-10 S. I-10, exit 848 (Walden Rd), just n. Int corridors. **Pets:** Accepted.
(SAVE) [✕] 🔒 [💻] [🍴] [🌊]

▼▼▼▼ **La Quinta Inn & Suites** 🅢🅗
(409) 842-0002. **$109-$129.** 5820 Walden Rd. I-10, exit 848, just n. Int corridors. **Pets:** Accepted. Service with restrictions, supervision.
(A$K) [S🄳] [✕] [&M] 🔒 [💻] [🌊]

▼▼ **La Quinta Inn Beaumont (Midtown)** 🅢🅗
(409) 838-9991. **$99-$119.** 220 I-10 N. I-10, exit 852B (Calder Ave) eastbound; exit 852A (Laurel Ave) westbound, on eastbound service road. Ext corridors. **Pets:** Other species. Service with restrictions, supervision.
(A$K) [S🄳] [✕] 🔒 [💻] [🌊]

BEDFORD

🔶🔶 ▼▼▼ **Baymont Inn DFW West** 🅢🅗
(817) 267-5200. **$69.** 1450 W Airport Frwy. SR 121/183, 0.3 mi e of jct Bedford Rd/Forest Ridge Dr exit. Ext corridors. **Pets:** Accepted.
(SAVE) [S🄳] [✕] 🔒 [💻] [🌊]

▼▼ **Comfort Inn DFW Airport West** 🅢🅗
(817) 545-2555. **Call for rates.** 2904 Crystal Springs St. SR 121, exit Harwood Rd. Ext/int corridors. **Pets:** Accepted.
[✕] 🔒 [💻]

▼▼ **Extended Stay Hotels** 🅢🅗
(817) 354-5210. **Call for rates.** 1908 Forest Ridge Dr. SR 183, exit Forest Ridge Dr, just n. Int corridors. **Pets:** Other species. $75 one-time fee/pet. Service with restrictions.
[✕] 🔒 [💻] [🌊]

BEEVILLE

▼▼ **Best Western Texan Inn** 🅢🅗
(361) 358-9999. **$75-$105.** 2001 Hwy 59. US 181 at US 59, just e. Ext/int corridors. **Pets:** Large, other species. $10 daily fee/pet.
(A$K) [S🄳] [✕] 🔒 [💻] [🌊]

▼▼ **Motel 6** 🅢🅗
(361) 358-4000. **Call for rates.** 400 S US 181 Bypass. 0.3 mi s of jct US 59 and 181. Ext corridors. **Pets:** Other species. Service with restrictions, supervision.
[✕] 🔒 [🌊]

BELTON

🔶🔶 ▼▼▼ **Budget Host Inn** 🅢🅗 ✿
(254) 939-0744. **$49-$75, 3 day notice.** 1520 S I-35. I-35, exit 292 southbound; exit 293A northbound. Ext corridors. **Pets:** Medium. $7 one-time fee/pet. Service with restrictions, supervision.
(SAVE) [S🄳] [✕] 🔒 [💻] [🌊]

▼▼▼▼ **La Quinta Inn & Suites** 🅢🅗
(254) 939-2772. **$99-$119.** 229 W Loop 121. I-35, exit 292, just w. Int corridors. **Pets:** Other species. Service with restrictions, supervision.
(A$K) [S🄳] [✕] 🔒 [💻] [🌊]

🔶🔶 ▼▼▼ **Ramada Limited** 🅢🅗
(254) 939-3745. **$76-$84.** 1102 E 2nd Ave. I-35, exit 294A southbound; exit 294B northbound. Ext corridors. **Pets:** Accepted.
(SAVE) [S🄳] [✕] 🔒 [💻] [🌊]

BENBROOK

🔶🔶 ▼▼▼▼ **Best Western Winscott Inn & Suites** 🅢🅗
(817) 249-0076. **$99-$189.** 590 Winscott Rd. I-20, exit 429B. Int corridors. **Pets:** Small. $10 daily fee/pet. Service with restrictions, supervision.
(SAVE) [S🄳] [✕] 🔒 [💻] [🌊]

▼ **Motel 6–4051** 🅢🅗
(817) 249-8885. **$56-$68.** 8601 Benbrook Blvd (Hwy 377 S). I-20, exit 429A, 0.7 mi s. Int corridors. **Pets:** Other species. Service with restrictions, supervision.
(A$K) [✕] [&M] 🔒 [🌊]

BIG SPRING

🔶🔶 ▼▼▼ **Comfort Inn** 🅜
(432) 267-4553. **Call for rates.** 2900 E I-20. I-20, exit 179. Ext corridors. **Pets:** Small, other species. $25 one-time fee/pet. Service with restrictions, supervision.
(SAVE) [✕] 🔒 [💻] [🌊]

🔶🔶 ▼▼▼ **Quality Inn & Suites** 🅢🅗
(432) 264-7086. **$80-$130.** 300 Tulane Ave. I-20, exit 179, just s. Ext corridors. **Pets:** Small. $20 daily fee/pet. Service with restrictions, supervision.
(SAVE) [S🄳] [✕] [&M] 🔒 [💻] [🌊]

🔶🔶 ▼▼▼ **Whitten Inn** 🅜
(432) 267-1601. **Call for rates.** 700 W I-20. I-20, exit 177, just n. Ext corridors. **Pets:** Accepted.
[✕] 🔒 [💻] [🌊]

BOERNE

🔶🔶 ▼▼▼ **Best Western Texas Country Inn** 🅢🅗
(830) 249-9791. **$99-$139.** 35150 I-10 W. I-10, exit 540 (SR 46), westbound access road. Ext corridors. **Pets:** Medium. $20 one-time fee/pet. Service with restrictions, supervision.
(SAVE) [S🄳] [✕] 🔒 [💻] [🌊]

🔶🔶 ▼▼▼▼ **Holiday Inn Express Hotel & Suites-Six Flags West** 🅢🅗
(830) 249-6800. **Call for rates.** 35000 I-10 W. I-10, exit 540 (SR 46), just e to Norris Ln, then just s. Int corridors. **Pets:** Accepted.
(SAVE) [✕] 🔒 [💻] [🌊]

BONHAM

AAA ▼ **5 Star Inn**
(903) 583-3121. **$57-$67.** 1515 Old Ector Rd. Jct SR 56 W and 121 S. Ext corridors. **Pets:** Medium. $25 deposit/room. Designated rooms, service with restrictions, supervision.

⬛ ⬛ ⬛ ⬛ ⬛ ⬛

BORGER

AAA ▼▼▼ **Best Western Borger Inn** 🆂🅷
(806) 274-7050. **$82-$120.** 206 S Cedar. Jct SR 136 and 207, just n. Int corridors. **Pets:** Small. $10 one-time fee/pet. Service with restrictions, supervision.

⬛ ⬛ ⬛ ⬛ ⬛ ⬛

BOWIE

AAA ▼▼ **Days Inn** 🆂🅷
(940) 872-5426. **$65-$75.** 2436 S US 287. Jct SR 59. Ext corridors. **Pets:** Medium. $5 daily fee/pet. Designated rooms, service with restrictions, supervision.

⬛ ⬛ ⬛ ⬛ ⬛

AAA ▼ **Park's Inn** Ⓜ
(940) 872-1111. **Call for rates.** 708 W Wise St. 0.5 mi n of jct SR 59; downtown. Ext corridors. **Pets:** Other species. $5 daily fee/pet. Service with restrictions, supervision.

⬛ ⬛ ⬛ ⬛

BRADY

AAA ▼▼ **Best Western Brady Inn** 🆂🅷
(325) 597-3997. **Call for rates.** 2200 S Bridge St. 1.1 mi s on US 87/377. Ext corridors. **Pets:** Accepted.

⬛ ⬛ ⬛ ⬛ ⬛

AAA ▼▼ **Days Inn** Ⓜ
(325) 597-0789. **Call for rates.** 2108 S Bridge St. 1 mi s on US 87/377 at US 190. Ext corridors. **Pets:** Accepted.

⬛ ⬛ ⬛ ⬛ ⬛

BRENHAM

AAA ▼▼▼ **Best Western Inn of Brenham** 🆂🅷
(979) 251-7791. **$89-$139.** 1503 Hwy 290 E. Eastbound, 0.7 mi w of jct US 290 E and SR 577; westbound, 1.3 mi e of jct SR 36 and US 290. Ext corridors. **Pets:** Very small. $10 one-time fee/pet. No service, supervision.

⬛ ⬛ ⬛ ⬛ ⬛ ⬛ ⬛

AAA ▼▼▼ **Comfort Suites** 🆂🅷
(979) 421-8100. **$79-$199.** 2350 S Day St. US 290, exit SR 36 S, just n on Business Rt SR 36. Int corridors. **Pets:** Small. $20 daily fee/pet. Service with restrictions, supervision.

⬛ ⬛ ⬛ ⬛ ⬛ ⬛

BROWNFIELD

▼▼ **Best Western Caprock Inn** 🆂🅷
(806) 637-9471. **Call for rates.** 321 Lubbock Rd. Jct US 385 and 82, 2 blks n. Ext corridors. **Pets:** Accepted.

⬛ ⬛ ⬛ ⬛

BROWNSVILLE

▼▼▼ **Hawthorn Suites** 🆂🅷
(956) 574-6900. **Call for rates.** 3759 North Expwy. US 77, exit McAllen Rd; on southbound access road. Int corridors. **Pets:** Accepted.

⬛ ⬛ ⬛ ⬛ ⬛ ⬛

▼▼ **La Quinta Inn** 🆂🅷
(956) 350-8855. **$85-$105.** 8280 North Expwy. US 77/83, exit SR 511, just e. Int corridors. **Pets:** Other species. Service with restrictions, supervision.

⬛ ⬛ ⬛ ⬛ ⬛ ⬛

▼▼▼▼ **La Quinta Inn & Suites** 🆂🅷
(956) 350-2118. **$105-$125.** 5051 North Expwy US 77. US 77, exit Alton Gloor Rd southbound; exit Cameron Rd northbound U-turn; on southbound access road. Int corridors. **Pets:** Other species. Service with restrictions, supervision.

⬛ ⬛ ⬛ ⬛ ⬛ ⬛

AAA ▼▼▼ **Red Roof Inn** 🆂🅷
(956) 504-2300. **$42-$99.** 2377 North Expwy 83. US 83, exit FM 802, just s. Ext corridors. **Pets:** Other species. $25 deposit/room. Service with restrictions, supervision.

⬛ ⬛ ⬛ ⬛ ⬛ ⬛

▼▼▼▼ **Residence Inn by Marriott** 🆂🅷
(956) 350-8100. **$132-$152.** 3975 North Expwy. US 77 and 83, exit McAllen Rd. Int corridors. **Pets:** Accepted.

⬛ ⬛ ⬛ ⬛ ⬛ ⬛ ⬛

▼▼▼▼ **Staybridge Suites** 🆂🅷
(956) 504-9500. **$99-$119.** 2900 Pablo Kisel Blvd. US 77/83 exit FM 802, 0.8 mi n on access road to Pablo Kisel Blvd, 0.5 mi e. Int corridors. **Pets:** Accepted.

⬛ ⬛ ⬛ ⬛ ⬛ ⬛ ⬛

BURKBURNETT

▼▼▼ **Burkburnett Hampton Inn** 🆂🅷
(940) 569-8109. **Call for rates.** 1008 Sheppard Rd. I-44, exit 12, just e. Int corridors. **Pets:** Accepted.

⬛ ⬛ ⬛ ⬛

BURLESON

AAA ▼▼▼ **Comfort Suites** 🆂🅷
(817) 426-6666. **$100.** 321 S Burleson Blvd. I-35W, exit 34 southbound, 2 mi s to crossover, U-turn; exit 36 northbound, on northbound access road. Int corridors. **Pets:** Medium. $25 daily fee/pet. Service with restrictions, supervision.

⬛ ⬛ ⬛ ⬛ ⬛ ⬛ ⬛

BURNET

AAA ▼▼▼ **Best Western Post Oak Inn** Ⓜ
(512) 756-4747. **$70-$120.** 908 Buchanan Dr. Jct US 281 and FM 29, 1 mi w. Ext corridors. **Pets:** $15 daily fee/pet. Service with restrictions, supervision.

⬛ ⬛ ⬛ ⬛ ⬛ ⬛

CANTON

AAA ▼▼ **Best Western Canton Inn** 🆂🅷
(903) 567-6591. **$72-$190.** 2251 N Trade Days Blvd. Jct I-20 and SR 19, exit 527. Ext corridors. **Pets:** Medium. $5 daily fee/pet. Service with restrictions, crate.

⬛ ⬛ ⬛ ⬛ ⬛ ⬛

▼▼ **Comfort Inn & Suites** 🆂🅷
(903) 567-0909. **Call for rates.** 2406 N Trade Days Blvd. I-20, exit 527. Ext corridors. **Pets:** Accepted.

⬛ ⬛ ⬛ ⬛

▼▼ **Super 8 Motel** 🆂🅷
(903) 567-6567. **Call for rates.** 17350 I-20. I-20, exit 527. Ext corridors. **Pets:** Accepted.

⬛ ⬛ ⬛ ⬛

CANYON

▼▼▼▼ **Best Western Palo Duro Canyon** 🆂🅷
(806) 655-1818. **Call for rates.** 2801 4th Ave. I-27, exit 106, 1 mi w. Int corridors. **Pets:** Accepted.

⬛ ⬛ ⬛ ⬛ ⬛

◇◇ ▼▼▼ Holiday Inn Express Hotel & Suites SH
(806) 655-4445. **$80-$177.** 2901 4th Ave. I-27, exit 106, 2 mi w. Int corridors. **Pets:** Other species. $25 one-time fee/room. Service with restrictions, supervision.
SAVE SO ✕ &M 🔲 🔲 ⇔

CEDAR PARK

◇◇ ▼▼▼ Comfort Inn SH
(512) 259-1810. **$82-$117.** 300 E Whitestone Blvd. I-35, exit 256, 8 mi w on FM 1431. Int corridors. **Pets:** Other species. $10 daily fee/pet. Service with restrictions, supervision.
SAVE SO ✕ &M 🔲 🔲 ⇔

CHILDRESS

◇◇ ▼▼▼ Comfort Inn SH
(940) 937-6363. **$90-$95.** 1804 Ave F NW (Hwy 287). On US 287, just s of jct US 62/83. Ext corridors. **Pets:** Medium, other species. $10 daily fee/pet. Service with restrictions, supervision.
SAVE SO ✕ &M 🔲 🔲 ⇔

◇◇ ▼ Rodeway Inn SH
(940) 937-3695. **$39-$59.** 1612 Ave F NW. On US 287, just s of jct US 62/83. Ext corridors. **Pets:** Accepted.
SAVE SO ✕ 🔲

◇◇ ▼▼▼ Super 8 Motel Childress M ❀
(940) 937-8825. **Call for rates.** 411 Ave F NE (Hwy 287 S). Jct US 83/287, 1.5 mi e. Ext corridors. **Pets:** Other species. $13 daily fee/pet. Service with restrictions, supervision.
SAVE ✕ 🔲 🔲 ⇔

CISCO

▼▼ Americas Best Value Inn M
(254) 442-3735. **Call for rates.** 1898 Hwy 206 W. I-20, exit 330. Ext corridors. **Pets:** Accepted.
✕ 🔲 🔲 ⇔

CLARENDON

◇◇ ▼▼▼ Best Western Red River Inn SH
(806) 874-0160. **$99-$109, 7 day notice.** 902 W 2nd St. Jct US 287 and SR 70. Int corridors. **Pets:** Medium. $10 daily fee/pet. Designated rooms, service with restrictions, crate.
SAVE SO ✕ &M 🔲 🔲 ⇔

◇◇ ▼▼▼ Western Skies Motel M
(806) 874-3501. **$45-$99.** 800 W 2nd St. 0.5 mi nw on US 287 and SR 70. Ext corridors. **Pets:** Other species. $5 daily fee/pet. Designated rooms, service with restrictions, supervision.
SAVE SO ✕ 🔲 ⇔

CLAUDE

◇◇ ▼ L a Motel M
(806) 226-4981. **$35-$50.** Hwy 287/200 E 1st St. 0.3 mi s. Ext corridors. **Pets:** Other species. Service with restrictions.
SAVE SO ✕ 🔲 🍴

CLEBURNE

◇◇ ▼▼ Budget Host Inn-Sagamar Inn M
(817) 556-3631. **$75-$90.** 2107 N Main St. US 67, exit SR 174 (Main St), just e. Ext corridors. **Pets:** Accepted.
SAVE SO ✕ 🔲 ⇔

▼▼▼ Comfort Inn SH
(817) 641-4702. **$95-$175.** 2117 N Main St. On SR 174, just s of jct US 67. Int corridors. **Pets:** Accepted.
ASK SO ✕ &M 🔲 🔲 ⇔

CLUTE

◇◇ ▼▼▼ Best Western Clute Inn & Suites SH
(979) 388-0055. **$80-$100, 7 day notice.** 900 Hwy 332. Just w of jct SR 288. Int corridors. **Pets:** Small. $15 daily fee/pet. Service with restrictions, supervision.
SAVE SO ✕ 🔲 🔲 ⇔

▼▼▼ La Quinta Inn Clute/Lake Jackson M
(979) 265-7461. **$92-$112.** 1126 Hwy 332 W. On SR 288/332, just w of jct Business Rt SR 288. Ext corridors. **Pets:** Other species. Service with restrictions, supervision.
ASK SO ✕ 🔲 🔲 ⇔

◇◇ ▼▼▼ Mainstay Suites Clute/Lake Jackson SH
(979) 388-9300. **$119-$212.** 1003 W Hwy 332. Just w of jct SR 288. Int corridors. **Pets:** Accepted.
SAVE SO ✕ 🔲 🔲 ⇔

COLLEGE STATION

▼▼▼ Clarion Hotel College Station SH
(979) 693-1736. **$59-$299.** 1503 Texas Ave S. 1.3 mi s of jct SR 60. Int corridors. **Pets:** Accepted.
ASK SO ✕ 🔲 🔲 🍴 ⇔

▼▼▼ Hilton College Station and Conference Center LH
(979) 693-7500. **Call for rates.** 801 University Dr E. SR 6, exit University Dr, 1.1 mi w. Int corridors. **Pets:** Accepted.
✕ 🔲 🔲 🍴 ⇔

▼▼▼ Homewood Suites–College Station SH
(979) 846-0400. **Call for rates.** 950 University Dr E. Jct SR 6 and 60 (Texas Ave), 1.5 mi e. Int corridors. **Pets:** Accepted.
✕ &M 🔲 🔲 ⇔ ✕

◇◇ ▼▼▼ Howard Johnson SH
(979) 693-6810. **$55-$150.** 3702 Hwy 6 S. SR 6 S, exit Rock Prairie Rd. Ext corridors. **Pets:** Medium, dogs only. $10 daily fee/pet. Service with restrictions, supervision.
SAVE SO ✕ 🔲 🔲 ⇔

▼▼▼ La Quinta Inn College Station SH
(979) 696-7777. **$102-$122.** 607 Texas Ave. Just s on jct SR 60 and 6 business route to Live Oak St, then just e. Ext corridors. **Pets:** Other species. Service with restrictions, supervision.
ASK SO ✕ 🔲 🔲 ⇔

▼▼ Manor House Inn SH
(979) 764-9540. **Call for rates.** 2504 Texas Ave S. 2.4 mi s of jct SR 60. Ext corridors. **Pets:** Accepted.
✕ 🔲 🔲 ⇔

◇◇ ▼▼ Ramada Inn SH
(979) 693-9891. **$65-$125, 3 day notice.** 1502 Texas Ave S. 1.3 mi s of jct SR 60. Int corridors. **Pets:** $15 one-time fee/room. Service with restrictions, crate.
SAVE SO ✕ 🔲 🔲 🍴 ⇔

▼▼▼ TownePlace Suites By Marriott SH ❀
(979) 260-8500. **$110-$130.** 1300 E University Dr. SR 6, exit University Dr, 1 mi w. Ext corridors. **Pets:** Other species. $100 one-time fee/room. Service with restrictions.
ASK SO ✕ 🔲 🔲 ⇔

COLUMBUS

◇◇ ▼▼▼ Country Hearth Inn SH
(979) 732-6293. **$78-$150.** 2436 Hwy 71 S. I-10, exit 696 (SR 71). Ext corridors. **Pets:** Small, dogs only. $20 one-time fee/room. Designated rooms, service with restrictions, supervision.
SAVE ✕ 🔲 🔲 ⇔

Holiday Inn Express Hotel & Suites SH
(979) 733-9300. **$110-$130.** 4321 I-10. I-10, exit 696 (SR 71), just w on westbound service road. Int corridors. **Pets:** Accepted.

CONWAY

Budget Host S & S Motel M
(806) 537-5111. **Call for rates.** I-40 & SR 207. I-40, exit 96 (SR 207), 0.3 mi w on southbound access road. Ext corridors. **Pets:** $20 deposit/ pet. Service with restrictions, supervision.

CORPUS CHRISTI

Best Western Garden Inn SH
(361) 241-6675. **$69-$129.** 11217 I-37. I-37, exit 11B (Violet Rd); on southbound access road. Ext corridors. **Pets:** Accepted.

Best Western Marina Grand Hotel SH
(361) 883-5111. **$79-$195.** 300 N Shoreline Blvd. Center of downtown. Int corridors. **Pets:** Accepted.

Best Western on the Island SH
(361) 949-2300. **$69-$149.** 14050 S Padre Island Dr. On Park Rd 22. Ext corridors. **Pets:** Accepted.

Christy Estate Suites CO
(361) 854-1091. **Call for rates.** 3942 Holly Rd. SR 358, exit Weber Rd, 0.5 mi s. Ext/int corridors. **Pets:** Medium. $500 deposit/pet, $45 one-time fee/pet. Designated rooms, service with restrictions, crate.

Days Inn-Airport SH
(361) 888-8599. **$59-$99.** 901 Navigation Blvd. I-37, exit 3A (Navigation Blvd), just w. Ext corridors. **Pets:** Other species. $15 daily fee/pet. Service with restrictions, crate.

Days Inn Corpus Christi South SH
(361) 854-0005. **Call for rates.** 2838 S Padre Island Dr. On SR 358 westbound access road, 0.4 mi w, exit Kostoryz Rd. Ext corridors. **Pets:** Accepted.

Drury Inn-Corpus Christi SH
(361) 289-8200. **$113.** 2021 N Padre Island Dr. I-37, exit SR 358, just se at Leopard St. Int corridors. **Pets:** Large, other species. Service with restrictions, supervision.

Econo Lodge M
(361) 884-2485. **$60-$150.** 801 S Shoreline Blvd. I-37, exit Shoreline, Between Park and Fuman aves. Ext corridors. **Pets:** Small. $15 one-time fee/room. Service with restrictions, crate.

Holiday Inn-Airport and Conference Center LH
(361) 289-5100. **$109-$129.** 5549 Leopard St. Jct SR 358 and Leopard St, 5.5 mi w. Int corridors. **Pets:** Medium. $25 one-time fee/pet. No service, crate.

Holiday Inn-Emerald Beach LH
(361) 883-5731. **$125-$193.** 1102 S Shoreline Blvd. 1.5 mi s on bay from downtown marina. Ext/int corridors. **Pets:** Accepted.

Homewood Suites by Hilton SH
(361) 854-1331. **Call for rates.** 5201 Crosstown Expwy (SR 286). I-37, exit SR 358 E (Greenwood), 0.6 mi e on eastbound access road. Int corridors. **Pets:** Accepted.

La Quinta Inn Corpus Christi (North) SH
(361) 888-5721. **$92-$112.** 5155 I-37 N. I-37, exit 3A (Navigation Blvd), on southbound access road. Ext corridors. **Pets:** Other species. Service with restrictions, supervision.

La Quinta Inn Corpus Christi (South) SH
(361) 991-5730. **$105-$125.** 6225 S Padre Island Dr. SR 358, exit Airline Rd. Ext corridors. **Pets:** Other species. Service with restrictions, supervision.

Motel 6 #231 M
(361) 289-9397. **$42-$55.** 845 Lantana St. I-37, exit 4B (Lantana St), on southbound access road. Ext corridors. **Pets:** Other species. Service with restrictions, supervision.

Motel 6 SPI Drive–413 SH
(361) 991-8858. **$45-$58.** 8202 S Padre Island Dr. S Padre Island Dr at Paul Jones St. Ext corridors. **Pets:** Other species. Service with restrictions, supervision.

Omni Corpus Christi Hotel-Bayfront Tower LH
(361) 887-1600. **$189.** 900 N Shoreline Blvd. In town across from bay; downtown; in the marina district. Int corridors. **Pets:** Small. $50 one-time fee/room. Service with restrictions, supervision.

Omni Corpus Christi Hotel-Marina Tower LH
(361) 887-1600. **Call for rates.** 707 N Shoreline Blvd. Just n across from bay. Int corridors. **Pets:** Accepted.

Quality Inn & Suites Sandy Shores SH
(361) 883-7456. **$79-$129, 3 day notice.** 3202 Surfside Blvd. 1 mi n on US 181; at north end of Harbor Bridge, exit Bridge St. Ext/int corridors. **Pets:** Accepted.

Red Roof Inn SH
(361) 992-9222. **$45-$149.** 6805 S Padre Island Dr. SR 358, exit Nile Dr. Ext corridors. **Pets:** Other species. $25 deposit/room. Service with restrictions, supervision.

Rodeway Inn SH
(361) 883-6161. **$69-$104.** 5224 I-37 (Navigation Blvd). I-37, exit 3A (Navigation Blvd), on northbound access road. Ext corridors. **Pets:** Medium. $25 one-time fee/room. Designated rooms, service with restrictions, crate.

Surfside Condominiums CO
(361) 949-8128. **$130-$185, 3 day notice.** 15005 Windward Dr. Park Rd 22 on N Padre Island Dr, jct Whitecap Blvd, 0.6 mi n to Winward Dr, then 0.8 mi w. Ext corridors. **Pets:** Small. $15 daily fee/pet. Designated rooms, service with restrictions, supervision.

DALHART

Best Western Nursanickel Motel SH
(806) 244-5637. **$69-$99.** 102 Scott Ave (Hwy 87 S). Just s of jct US 54 and 87. Ext corridors. **Pets:** Accepted.

Budget Inn M
(806) 244-4557. **$45-$55 (no credit cards).** 415 Liberal St (Hwy 54). On US 54, just e of US 87 and 385. Ext corridors. **Pets:** Medium. $20 deposit/pet. Service with restrictions, supervision.

Comfort Inn M
(806) 249-8585. **$85-$100.** 1110 Hwy 54 E (Liberal St). 0.5 mi e of jct US 54 and 87. Ext corridors. **Pets:** Service with restrictions, supervision.

Days Inn SH
(806) 244-5246. **Call for rates.** 701 Liberal St (Hwy 54). On US 54, 0.5 mi e. Int corridors. **Pets:** Other species. $10 one-time fee/room. Crate.

Holiday Inn Express SH
(806) 249-1145. **Call for rates.** 801 Liberal St (Hwy 54). 1 mi e of jct US 54 and 87. Int corridors. **Pets:** Accepted.

Sands Motel M
(806) 244-4568. **$30-$65.** 301 Liberal St (Hwy 54). On US 54, just e of US 87 and 385. Ext corridors. **Pets:** Service with restrictions, crate.

Super 8 Motel M
(806) 249-8526. **$60-$90.** 403 Tanglewood Rd. Jct US 87/54, 0.5 mi e. Int corridors. **Pets:** Accepted.

DALLAS METROPOLITAN AREA

ADDISON

Homewood Suites by Hilton SH
(972) 788-1342. **Call for rates.** 4451 Belt Line Rd. Just e of jct Belt Line and Midway rds. Ext/int corridors. **Pets:** Small. $75 one-time fee/room. Service with restrictions, supervision.

Hyatt Summerfield Suites-Addison SH ❖
(972) 661-3113. **Call for rates.** 4900 Edwin Lewis Dr. Just n of jct Belt Line Rd and Quorum Dr to Edwin Lewis Dr, then just w. Ext/int corridors. **Pets:** Medium. $150 one-time fee/pet. Service with restrictions, crate.

La Quinta Inn & Suites Dallas (Addison-Galleria Area) SH
(972) 404-0004. **$105-$125.** 14925 Landmark Blvd. Jct Belt Line Rd and Landmark Blvd, just s. Int corridors. **Pets:** Other species. Service with restrictions, supervision.

Quality Inn & Suites SH ❖
(972) 991-8888. **$60-$199.** 4103 Belt Line Rd. Between Midway Rd and Marsh Ln. Ext corridors. **Pets:** Medium. $50 one-time fee/pet. Designated rooms, service with restrictions, supervision.

Residence Inn by Marriott-Addison SH
(972) 866-9933. **$198-$218.** 14975 Quorum Dr. Just s of jct Beltline Rd and Quorum Dr. Int corridors. **Pets:** $75 one-time fee/room. Service with restrictions.

BALCH SPRINGS

La Quinta Inn SH
(972) 286-1010. **$79-$99.** 12875 Seagoville Rd. I-20, exit 481 (Seagoville Rd), just n. Int corridors. **Pets:** Other species. Service with restrictions, supervision.

COMMERCE

Holiday Inn Express Hotel & Suites SH
(903) 886-4777. **$89-$159.** 2207 Culver St. 0.9 mi e of jct SR 224, 24 and 50. Int corridors. **Pets:** Small. $25 one-time fee/pet. Service with restrictions, crate.

DALLAS

Baymont Inn & Suites SH
(214) 350-5577. **Call for rates.** 2370 W Northwest Hwy. I-35E, exit 436 Northwest Hwy (Loop 12), 0.8 mi e. Int corridors. **Pets:** Accepted.

Best Western City Place Inn SH
(214) 827-6080. **$69-$119.** 4150 N Central Expwy. US 75, exit 1B (Fitzhugh Ave) southbound; exit 2 (Fitzhugh Ave) northbound. Ext corridors. **Pets:** Small. $50 one-time fee/room. Designated rooms, service with restrictions, supervision.

Bradford HomeSuites North Dallas SH
(972) 726-9990. **Call for rates.** 16060 North Dallas Pkwy. North Dallas Tollway northbound, exit Keller Springs, just n on north access road; exit Keller Springs southbound, just e to Noel Tr, then just s. Int corridors. **Pets:** Accepted.

Candlewood Dallas Market Center SH
(214) 631-3333. **Call for rates.** 7930 N Stemmons Frwy. I-35, exit 433B (Mockingbird Ln), on northbound frontage road. Int corridors. **Pets:** Accepted.

Candlewood Suites-Dallas by the Galleria SH
(972) 233-6888. **$95-$115.** 13939 Noel Rd. Jct Dallas Pkwy and Spring Valley, just e to Noel Rd, then just s. Int corridors. **Pets:** Accepted.

Candlewood Suites Dallas North/Richardson SH
(972) 669-9606. **Call for rates.** 12525 Greenville Ave. I-635, exit 18A (Greenville Ave), just n. Int corridors. **Pets:** Accepted.

Comfort Inn & Suites Market Center SH
(214) 461-2677. **$99-$129.** 7138 N Stemmons Frwy. I-35E, exit 433B (Mockingbird Ln) northbound; exit 432B (Commonwealth Dr) southbound, turn under freeway, 0.7 mi on north access road. Int corridors. **Pets:** Accepted.

Country Inn & Suites Dallas Park Central SH
(972) 907-9500. **$87.** 13185 N Central Expwy. US 75 N, exit 22 (Midpark Rd). Int corridors. **Pets:** Accepted.

Crowne Plaza Hotel Dallas Market Center LH
(214) 630-8500. **$169-$189.** 7050 Stemmons Frwy. I-35E, exit 433B northbound; exit 432B southbound. Int corridors. **Pets:** Accepted.

Crowne Plaza Suites Hotel Dallas Park Central LH
(972) 233-7600. **$169-$219.** 7800 Alpha Rd. I-635, exit 19C (Coit Rd) eastbound; exit 19B (Coit Rd) westbound, 0.3 mi nw of jct US 75. Int corridors. **Pets:** $100 deposit/room, $25 one-time fee/room. Designated rooms, service with restrictions.

Dallas Marriott Suites Market Center SH
(214) 905-0050. **$275-$295.** 2493 N Stemmons Frwy. I-35E, exit 431 (Motor St). Int corridors. **Pets:** Accepted.

Extended StayAmerica SH
(972) 238-1133. **$58-$65.** 12270 Greenville Ave. I-635, exit 18A (Greenville Ave), just s. Int corridors. **Pets:** Other species. $75 one-time fee/pet. Service with restrictions.

Extended StayAmerica Dallas-North-Park Central SH
(972) 671-7722. **$54-$60.** 9019 Vantage Point Rd. I-635, exit 18A (Greenville Ave), just sw. Ext corridors. **Pets:** Other species. $75 one-time fee/pet. Service with restrictions.

Extended Stay Delux SH
(214) 630-0154. **$67-$75.** 2979 N Stemmons Frwy. I-35E, exit 432B, on eastbound access road. Int corridors. **Pets:** Other species. $75 one-time fee/pet. Service with restrictions.

Fairfield Inn by Marriott Dallas North SH
(972) 661-9800. **$93-$113.** 13900 Parkside Center Blvd. I-635, exit 23, 0.9 mi n to Spring Valley, just w, then just s. Int corridors. **Pets:** Other species. $75 one-time fee/room. Service with restrictions.

Fairfield Inn by Marriott-Park Central SH
(972) 437-9905. **$84-$104.** 9230 LBJ Frwy. I-635, exit 18A (Greenville Ave S), just s, then just e. Int corridors. **Pets:** Accepted.

The Fairmont Dallas LH
(214) 720-2020. **$99-$469.** 1717 N Akard St. Corner of Ross Ave and N Akard St. Int corridors. **Pets:** Medium. $35 one-time fee/pet. Designated rooms, service with restrictions, supervision.

Holiday Inn Select Dallas Central LH
(214) 373-6000. **Call for rates.** 10650 N Central Expwy. US 75, exit 6 (Walnut Hill Ln/Meadow Rd), 0.5 mi n on northbound access road. Int corridors. **Pets:** Accepted.

Homestead Studio Suites Hotel-Dallas/North Addison/Tollway SH
(972) 447-1800. **$58-$65.** 17425 North Dallas Pkwy. North Dallas Tollway, exit Trinity Mills, just s of jct Trinity Mills and Dallas Pkwy, on southbound access road. Ext corridors. **Pets:** Other species. $75 one-time fee/pet. Service with restrictions.

Homestead Studio Suites Hotel-Dallas/Plano SH
(972) 248-2233. **$76-$85.** 18470 N Dallas Pkwy. North Dallas Tollway, exit Frankford, just ne. Int corridors. **Pets:** Other species. $75 one-time fee/pet. Service with restrictions.

Homewood Suites by Hilton SH
(214) 819-9700. **Call for rates.** 2747 N Stemmons Frwy. I-35E, exit 432A (Inwood Rd), just s. Int corridors. **Pets:** Accepted.

Homewood Suites by Hilton-I-635 SH
(972) 437-6966. **Call for rates.** 9169 Markville Dr. I-635, exit 18A (Greenville Ave S), just s, then just e. Int corridors. **Pets:** Accepted.

Hotel Crescent Court, a Rosewood Hotel LH
(214) 871-3200. **$525-$3000.** 400 Crescent Ct. Corner of Crescent Ct and McKinney Ave; uptown. Int corridors. **Pets:** Accepted.

Hotel Indigo Dallas Downtown SH
(214) 741-7700. **Call for rates.** 1933 Main St. Main and Harwood sts; northwest corner. Int corridors. **Pets:** Accepted.

Hotel Lawrence SH
(214) 761-9090. **$139-$189.** 302 S Houston St. I-35E, exit 428A (Commerce St), 0.8 mi to Griffin, just s to Jackson St, then just w. Int corridors. **Pets:** Medium. $25 one-time fee/pet. Service with restrictions.

Hotel Palomar LH
(214) 520-7969. **Call for rates.** 5300 E Mockingbird Ln. US 75 and Mockingbird Ln; on southeast corner. Int corridors. **Pets:** Other species. Designated rooms, service with restrictions.

Hotel St. Germain CI
(214) 871-2516. **$290-$650, 7 day notice.** 2516 Maple Ave. I-35, exit 430A (Oak Lawn Ave), 0.5 mi e, then 1 mi s. Int corridors. **Pets:** Small, dogs only. $50 daily fee/pet. Designated rooms, service with restrictions, supervision.

Hotel ZaZa SH
(214) 468-8399. **Call for rates.** 2332 Leonard St. Jct Maple Ave/Routh St and McKinney Ave, southeast corner. Int corridors. **Pets:** Medium, dogs only. $50 one-time fee/room.

La Quinta Inn & Suites Dallas (North Central) SH
(214) 361-8200. **$119-$139.** 10001 N Central Expwy. US 75, exit 6 (Walnut Hill Ln/Meadow Rd) northbound, 0.5 mi n to Meadow Rd, then U-turn under highway; exit 7 (Royal/Meadow Rd) southbound, 1 mi s on feeder. Int corridors. **Pets:** Other species. Service with restrictions, supervision.

La Quinta Inn & Suites Dallas Northwest SH
(214) 904-9955. **$99-$119.** 2380 W Northwest Hwy. I-35, exit 436 Northwest Hwy (Loop 12), 0.8 mi e. Int corridors. **Pets:** Other species. Service with restrictions, supervision.

La Quinta Inn Dallas (City Place) SH
(214) 821-4220. **$109-$129.** 4440 N Central Expwy. N off US 75, exit 2 (Henderson-Knox) northbound; exit 1B (Haskell/Blackburn) southbound. Ext corridors. **Pets:** Other species. Service with restrictions, supervision.

La Quinta Inn Dallas (East) SH
(214) 324-3731. **$95-$115.** 8303 E R L Thornton Frwy. I-30, exit 52A (Jim Miller Rd). Ext corridors. **Pets:** Other species. Service with restrictions, supervision.

The Mansion On Turtle Creek, a Rosewood Hotel LH
(214) 559-2100. **$495-$2400.** 2821 Turtle Creek Blvd. 2 mi nw, entrance on Gillespie St, just e of jct Gillespie St and Oak Lawn Ave. Int corridors. **Pets:** Accepted.

Motel 6–560 SH
(972) 620-2828. **$43-$55.** 2753 Forest Ln. I-635, exit 26 (Josey Ln) eastbound; exit 25 (Josey Ln) westbound, just s to Forest Ln, then just w. Ext corridors. **Pets:** Other species. Service with restrictions, supervision.

◆ **Motel 6 Forest Lane-South #1119** SH
(972) 484-9111. **$45-$61.** 2660 Forest Ln. I-635, exit 26 (Josey Ln) eastbound, 0.5 mi s to Forest Ln, then just w; exit 25 (Josey Ln) westbound, just s to Forest Ln, then just w. Ext corridors. **Pets:** Other species. Service with restrictions, supervision.
⑤ ⊠ ⊇

◆◆◆◆ **Quality Inn & Suites-North Dallas** SH
(972) 484-3330. **$89-$129.** 2421 Walnut Hill Ln. I-35E, exit 438 (Walnut Hill Ln). Int corridors. **Pets:** Accepted.
A$K ⑤ ⊠ ⊟ ⊇ ⊇

◆◆ **Quality Inn Dallas Market Center** SH
(214) 747-9551. **$81-$99, 3 day notice.** 1955 Market Center Blvd. I-35E, exit 430B (Market Center Blvd), 0.3 mi w. Ext corridors. **Pets:** Medium, other species. $10 daily fee/pet. Service with restrictions.
A$K ⑤ ⊠ ⊟ ⊇ ⊇

◆◆◆ **Radisson Dallas Love Field** LH
(214) 630-7000. **$103-$129.** 1241 W Mockingbird Ln. I-35E, exit 433B, just ne of jct I-35E and W Mockingbird Ln. Int corridors. **Pets:** $25 one-time fee/pet. Service with restrictions, supervision.
SAVE ⑤ ⊠ ⊟ ⊇ ⊺ ⊇

◆◆◆ **Radisson Hotel Central/Dallas** LH
(214) 750-6060. **$109-$199.** 6060 N Central Expwy. US 75, exit 3 (Mockingbird Ln), on northbound frontage road. Int corridors. **Pets:** Small, dogs only. $50 one-time fee/room. Service with restrictions, supervision.
SAVE ⑤ ⊠ ⊟ ⊇ ⊺ ⊇

◆◆◆ **Red Roof Inn Dallas (Richardson) #8474** SH
(972) 234-1016. **Call for rates.** 13685 N Central Expwy. US 75 N, exit 22 (Midpark Rd). Ext/int corridors. **Pets:** Accepted.
SAVE ⊠ ⊟ ⊇

◆ **Red Roof Inn-Market Center** M
(214) 638-5151. **Call for rates.** 1550 Empire Central Dr. I-35E, exit 434A (Empire Central Dr), 0.3 mi e. Ext corridors. **Pets:** Accepted.
⊠

◆◆◆◆ **Renaissance Dallas Hotel** LH
(214) 631-2222. **$286-$306.** 2222 Stemmons Frwy. I-35E, exit 430B (Market Center Blvd), 0.3 mi nw on access road. Int corridors. **Pets:** Accepted.
SAVE ⑤ ⊠ ⊇ ⊺ ⊇ ⊠

◆◆◆◆ **Residence Inn by Marriott at Dallas Central** SH
(214) 750-8220. **$186-$197.** 10333 N Central Expwy. US 75, exit 6 (Walnut Hill Ln/Meadow Rd) northbound, 0.5 mi n to Meadow Rd, U-turn under highway; exit 7 (Royal/Meadow Rd) southbound, 1 mi s on access road. Ext corridors. **Pets:** Accepted.
SAVE ⑤ ⊠ ⊟ ⊇ ⊇ ⊠

◆◆◆◆ **Residence Inn by Marriott-Dallas Market Center** SH
(214) 631-2472. **$187-$207.** 6950 N Stemmons Frwy. I-35E, exit 432B (Commonwealth Ln), 0.6 mi n on northbound frontage road. Ext/int corridors. **Pets:** Accepted.
A$K ⑤ ⊠ ⊟ ⊇ ⊇ ⊠

◆◆◆◆ **Residence Inn by Marriott-Dallas Park Central** SH
(972) 503-1333. **$143-$163.** 7642 LBJ Frwy. I-635, exit 20 (Hillcrest), just e, on eastbound access road. Int corridors. **Pets:** Accepted.
A$K ⑤ ⊠ ⊑M ⊟ ⊇ ⊇ ⊠

◆◆◆◆ **Sheraton Suites Market Center-Dallas** LH ❀
(214) 747-3000. **$89-$269.** 2101 Stemmons Frwy. Nw off I-35E and US 77, exit 430B (Market Center Blvd). Int corridors. **Pets:** Dogs only. Service with restrictions, supervision.
A$K ⑤ ⊠ ⊟ ⊇ ⊺ ⊇

◆◆◆◆ **Staybridge Suites Dallas By The Galleria** SH
(972) 391-0000. **Call for rates.** 7880 Alpha Rd. I-635, exit 19B (Coit Rd), 0.3 mi n, then just w. Int corridors. **Pets:** Accepted.
⊠ ⊟ ⊇ ⊇

◆◆ **Super 8 Motel** SH
(972) 572-1030. **Call for rates.** 8541 S Hampton Rd. I-20, exit 465, 0.3 mi e to S Hampton Rd, then just s. Ext corridors. **Pets:** Accepted.
⊠ ⊟ ⊇ ⊇

◆◆◆ ◆◆◆ **Warwick Melrose Hotel** SH
(214) 521-5151. **$325.** 3015 Oak Lawn Ave. I-35E, exit 430 (Oak Lawn Ave), 0.8 mi n; entrance off Cedar Springs, just n. Int corridors. **Pets:** Accepted.
SAVE ⑤ ⊠ ⊟ ⊇ ⊺

◆◆◆◆ **The Westin City Center, Dallas** LH ❀
(214) 979-9000. **$109-$359.** 650 N Pearl St. Between San Jacinto and Bryan St, 0.3 mi w of US 75 Central Expwy. Int corridors. **Pets:** Medium. Service with restrictions, supervision.
A$K ⑤ ⊠ ⊟ ⊇ ⊺

DENTON

◆◆◆ ◆◆ **Exel Inn of Denton** SH
(940) 383-1471. **$45-$55.** 4211 I-35 N. Jct US 380 and I-35, exit 469, just n. Int corridors. **Pets:** Accepted.
SAVE ⑤ ⊠ ⊟ ⊇ ⊇

◆◆ **La Quinta Inn Denton** SH
(940) 387-5840. **$99-$119.** 700 Fort Worth Dr. I-35E, exit 465B (Fort Worth Dr), just n. Ext corridors. **Pets:** Other species. Service with restrictions, supervision.
A$K ⑤ ⊠ ⊑M ⊟ ⊇ ⊇

◆ **Motel 6 Denton #97** M
(940) 566-4798. **$43-$56.** 4125 I-35 N. I-35, exit 469. Ext corridors. **Pets:** Other species. Service with restrictions, supervision.
⑤ ⊠ ⊇

◆◆◆ ◆◆ **Quality Inn & Suites Denton** SH
(940) 387-3511. **$65-$219.** 1500 Dallas Dr. 2 mi se of jct I-35E and US 77 business route, exit 464 westbound; exit 465A (Teasley Ln) eastbound, 0.4 mi n to Dallas Dr, then 0.5 mi e. Ext corridors. **Pets:** Other species. $20 one-time fee/pet. Service with restrictions.
SAVE ⑤ ⊠ ⊟ ⊇ ⊇

◆◆◆ **Radisson Hotel Denton** SH
(940) 565-8499. **$99-$109.** 2211 I-35E N. Off I-35E and US 77, exit 466B (N Texas Blvd), 2.5 mi sw. Int corridors. **Pets:** Accepted.
A$K ⑤ ⊠ ⊟ ⊇ ⊺ ⊇

◆◆◆ ◆◆◆ **Super 8 Motel-Denton** SH
(940) 380-8888. **Call for rates.** 620 S I-35 E. I-35, exit 465A (Teasley Ln). Int corridors. **Pets:** Accepted.
SAVE ⊠ ⊟

DESOTO

◆◆◆ ◆◆◆ **McM Grande Hotel FUNDome** SH ❀
(972) 224-9100. **$99-$119.** 1515 N I-35 E. I-35E, exit 416 (Wintergreen Rd), just s. Ext/int corridors. **Pets:** Service with restrictions.
SAVE ⑤ ⊠ ⊟ ⊇ ⊺ ⊇ ⊠

◆ **Red Roof Inn Dallas/DeSoto** SH
(972) 224-7100. **Call for rates.** 1401 N Beckley Ave. I-35E, exit 416, just s. Ext/int corridors. **Pets:** Accepted.
⊠ ⊟

DUNCANVILLE

◆ **Motel 6–#1130** 🅢🅗
(972) 296-0345. **$45-$61.** 202 Jellison Blvd. I-20, exit 462A (Duncanville Rd) eastbound; exit 462B (Main St) westbound, just s to Camp Wisdom, just w to Duncanville Rd, just n to Jellison Blvd, then just w. Ext/int corridors. **Pets:** Other species. Service with restrictions, supervision.
🆂🗙🔲🔚

ENNIS

◈ ◆◆ **Best Western Ennis** 🅢🅗
(972) 875-3390. **Call for rates.** 100 S I-45. I-45, exit 251B. Ext/int corridors. **Pets:** Accepted.
🅢🅐🆅🗙🔲💻🔚

FARMERS BRANCH

◆◆ **Comfort Inn of North Dallas** 🅢🅗
(972) 406-3030. **$59-$99.** 14040 Stemmons Frwy. I-35E, exit 442 (Valwood Pkwy). Int corridors. **Pets:** Accepted.
🅐🆂🗙🔲💻🔚

◈ ◆◆◆ **Holiday Inn Select North Dallas** 🅢🅗
(972) 243-3363. **$109-$129.** 2645 LBJ Frwy. I-635, exit 26 (Josey Ln) eastbound, just n; exit 25 westbound, 0.4 mi w. Int corridors. **Pets:** Medium. $25 deposit/pet, $25 one-time fee/pet. Service with restrictions, supervision.
🅢🅐🆂🗙🔲💻🔚

◆◆ ◆◆ **La Quinta Inn Dallas (NW-Farmers Branch)** 🅢🅗
(972) 620-7333. **$82-$102.** 13235 Stemmons Frwy N. I-35E, exit 441 (Valley View Ln), on southbound frontage road. Ext corridors. **Pets:** Other species. Service with restrictions, supervision.
🅐🆂🗙🔲💻🔚

◆◆◆ ◆◆◆ **Omni Dallas Hotel Park West** 🅛🅗
(972) 869-4300. **Call for rates.** 1590 LBJ Frwy. Nw off I-635, 1.5 mi w of jct I-35E, exit 29 (Luna Rd). Int corridors. **Pets:** Small. $50 one-time fee/room. Service with restrictions, crate.
🗙🔲💻🔚🗙

◆◆ ◆◆ **StudioPLUS Hotel** 🅢🅗
(972) 385-6006. **$65-$85.** 4022 Parkside Center Blvd. I-635, exit 23 (Midway Rd), 0.9 mi n to Parkside Center Blvd. Int corridors. **Pets:** Other species. $75 one-time fee/pet. Service with restrictions.
🅐🆂🗙🔲💻🔚

FRISCO

◈ ◆◆◆◆ **The Westin Stonebriar Resort** 🅛🅗 🐾
(972) 668-8000. **$149-$399.** 1549 Legacy Dr. 0.3 mi n of jct SR 121. Int corridors. **Pets:** Small, dogs only. $100 deposit/room. Designated rooms, service with restrictions, crate.
🅢🅐🗙🔲🔲💻🔚🗙

GARLAND

◈ ◆◆ **Best Western Executive Inn** 🅢🅗
(972) 613-5000. **$50-$65.** 12670 E Northwest Hwy. I-635, exit 11B, just s. Ext corridors. **Pets:** Other species. $10 one-time fee/pet. Service with restrictions, supervision.
🅢🅐🆂🗙🔲💻🔚

◈ ◆◆ **Best Western Lakeview Inn** 🅢🅗
(972) 303-1601. **$69-$99.** 1635 E I-30 at Bass Pro Dr. I-30, exit 62 (Chaha Rd). Ext corridors. **Pets:** Medium. $8 daily fee/pet. Service with restrictions, supervision.
🅢🅐🆂🗙🔲💻🔚

◆◆ ◆◆ **La Quinta Inn Dallas (Garland)** 🅢🅗
(972) 271-7581. **$85-$105.** 12721 I-635. I-635, exit 11B, just nw. Ext/int corridors. **Pets:** Other species. Service with restrictions, supervision.
🅐🆂🗙🔲💻🔚

◆ **Motel 6–0620** 🅢🅗
(972) 226-7140. **$41-$57.** 436 W I-30. I-30, exit 59 (Belt Line Rd). Ext corridors. **Pets:** Other species. Service with restrictions, supervision.
🆂🗙🔚

◆◆◆◆ **Radisson Hotel Dallas East** 🅢🅗
(214) 341-5400. **$79-$199, 3 day notice.** 11350 LBJ Frwy. I-635, exit 13 (Jupiter/Kingsley rds), just sw. Int corridors. **Pets:** Small. $25 one-time fee/room. Service with restrictions, crate.
🅐🆂🗙🔲💻🔚🔚

GRAND PRAIRIE

◆◆ ◆◆ **La Quinta Inn Dallas (Grand Prairie)** 🅢🅗
(972) 641-3021. **$85-$105.** 1410 NW 19th St. I-30, exit 32, just e. Ext corridors. **Pets:** Other species. Service with restrictions, supervision.
🅐🆂🗙🔲🔲💻🔚

◆ **Motel 6–446** 🅢🅗
(972) 642-9424. **$39-$51.** 406 E Palace Pkwy. I-30, exit 34 (Belt Line Rd), just n to Safari Pkwy, then 0.6 mi w. Ext corridors. **Pets:** Other species. Service with restrictions, supervision.
🆂🗙🔲💻🔚

GREENVILLE

◆◆◆ **Holiday Inn Express Hotel & Suites** 🅢🅗
(903) 454-8680. **$85.** 2901 Mustang Crossing. I-30, exit 93A. Int corridors. **Pets:** Accepted.
🅐🆂🗙🔲🔲💻🔚

◈ ◆◆◆ **La Quinta Inn & Suites** 🅢🅗
(903) 454-3700. **$109-$129.** 3001 Mustang Crossing. I-30, exit 93A. Int corridors. **Pets:** Other species. Service with restrictions, supervision.
🅢🅐🆂🗙🔲🔲💻🔚

◆◆◆ **Quality Inn** 🅢🅗
(903) 454-7000. **$75.** 1215 E I-30. I-30, exit 94B, just e of jct I-30 and US 69. Int corridors. **Pets:** Accepted.
🅐🆂🗙🔲💻🔚

IRVING

◆◆◆◆ **Candlewood Dallas/Las Colinas** 🅢🅗
(972) 714-9990. **$115-$140.** 5300 Greenpark Dr. SR 114, exit Walnut Hill Ln, just s. Int corridors. **Pets:** Accepted.
🅐🆂🗙🔲🔲🔲

◆◆◆ **Days Inn DFW North** 🅢🅗 🐾
(972) 621-8277. **Call for rates.** 4325 W Hwy 114. SR 114, exit Belt Line Rd, on westbound service road. Ext corridors. **Pets:** Medium. $25 one-time fee/pet. Service with restrictions, supervision.
🗙🔲💻🔲🔚

◈ ◆◆◆ **DFW North Super 8 Motel** 🅢🅗
(214) 441-9000. **$49-$79.** 4770 W John Carpenter Frwy (SR 114). SR 114, exit Freeport Pkwy. Int corridors. **Pets:** Accepted.
🅐🆂🗙🔲🔲

◆◆◆ **Drury Inn & Suites-DFW Airport** 🅢🅗
(972) 986-1200. **$136.** 4210 W Airport Frwy. SR 183, exit Esters Rd, on southbound access road. Int corridors. **Pets:** Large, other species. Service with restrictions, supervision.
🅐🗙🔲💻🔚

◆◆◆ **Extended Stay Deluxe (Dallas-Las Colinas-Green Park Dr.)** 🅢🅗
(972) 751-0808. **$72-$80.** 5401 Green Park Dr. SR 114, exit Walnut Hill Ln, just s. Int corridors. **Pets:** Other species. $75 one-time fee/pet. Service with restrictions.
🅐🆂🗙🔲🔲💻🔚

Four Seasons Resort and Club LH
(972) 717-0700. **$395-$2500.** 4150 N MacArthur Blvd. SR 114, exit MacArthur Blvd, 1.5 mi s. Int corridors. **Pets:** Accepted.

Hampton Inn-DFW Airport South SH
(972) 986-3606. **Call for rates.** 4340 W Airport Frwy. SR 183, exit Valley View Ln, on southbound access road. Int corridors. **Pets:** Accepted.

Homestead Studio Suites Hotel-Dallas/DFW Airport North SH
(972) 929-3333. **$54-$60.** 7825 Heathrow Dr. SR 114, exit Esters Blvd, s to Plaza Dr, then just w. Int corridors. **Pets:** Other species. $75 one-time fee/pet. Service with restrictions.

Homewood Suites by Hilton Las Colinas SH
(972) 556-0665. **Call for rates.** 4300 Wingren Dr. Ne off SR 114, exit O'Connor Rd/Wingren Dr eastbound, just n to Las Colinas Blvd, 0.4 mi e to Rochelle Rd, then just s; exit Rochelle Rd westbound. Ext/int corridors. **Pets:** Accepted.

Hyatt Summerfield Suites-Las Colinas SH
(972) 831-0909. **$79-$199.** 5901 N MacArthur Blvd. SR 114, exit MacArthur Blvd, northwest corner. Ext/int corridors. **Pets:** Accepted.

La Quinta Inn & Suites Dallas (DFW-Airport North) SH
(972) 915-4022. **$115-$135.** 4850 W John Carpenter Frwy. SR 114, exit Freeport Pkwy, on eastbound service road. Int corridors. **Pets:** Other species. Service with restrictions, supervision.

La Quinta Inn & Suites Dallas DFW Airport South (Irving) SH
(972) 252-6546. **$129-$149.** 4105 W Airport Frwy. 3 mi nw off SR 183, exit Esters Rd; on northbound access road. Int corridors. **Pets:** Other species. Service with restrictions, supervision.

Motel 6 #1274 DFW North M
(972) 915-3993. **$47-$60.** 7800 Heathrow Dr. SR 114, exit Freeport Pkwy, just se. Int corridors. **Pets:** Other species. Service with restrictions, supervision.

Omni Mandalay Hotel at Las Colinas LH
(972) 556-0800. **Call for rates.** 221 E Las Colinas Blvd. Nw off SR 114, exit O'Connor Rd. Int corridors. **Pets:** Small, dogs only. $50 one-time fee/room. Service with restrictions, supervision.

Quality Inn & Suites DFW Airport North SH
(972) 929-4008. **$49-$179.** 4100 W John Carpenter Frwy. SR 114, exit Esters Blvd, s to Reese St, then e. Ext corridors. **Pets:** Accepted.

Ramada DFW South LH
(972) 399-1010. **Call for rates.** 4440 W Airport Frwy. SR 183, exit Valley View Ln, on eastbound access road. Int corridors. **Pets:** Accepted.

Red Roof Inn/DFW Airport North M
(972) 929-0020. **Call for rates.** 8150 Esters Blvd. SR 114, exit Esters Blvd, just n. Ext corridors. **Pets:** Accepted.

Residence Inn by Marriott at Las Colinas SH
(972) 580-7773. **$198-$218.** 950 W Walnut Hill Ln. SR 114, exit MacArthur Blvd, 0.5 mi s, then just e. Ext corridors. **Pets:** Accepted.

Residence Inn by Marriott-DFW/Irving SH
(972) 871-1331. **$176-$196.** 8600 Esters Blvd. SR 114, exit Esters Blvd, 0.9 mi n. Int corridors. **Pets:** Accepted.

Sheraton Grand Hotel LH
(972) 929-8400. **$319-$379.** 4440 W John Carpenter Frwy. SR 114, exit Esters Blvd, just s. Int corridors. **Pets:** Accepted.

Staybridge Suites Dallas-Las Colinas SH
(972) 465-9400. **$125-$135.** 1201 Executive Cir. SR 114, exit MacArthur Blvd, just s to W Walnut Hill Ln, then just w. Int corridors. **Pets:** Accepted.

The Westin Dallas Fort Worth Airport LH
(972) 929-4500. **$319.** 4545 W John Carpenter Frwy. Nw off SR 114, exit Esters Blvd. Int corridors. **Pets:** Accepted.

Wyndham-Las Colinas SH
(972) 650-1600. **$179-$199.** 110 W John Carpenter Frwy. Sw off SR 114, exit O'Connor Rd. Int corridors. **Pets:** Accepted.

LEWISVILLE

Comfort Suites by Choice Hotels SH
(972) 315-6464. **Call for rates.** 755A Vista Ridge Mall Dr. I-35E, exit 448A (Round Grove Rd) southbound, 0.5 mi s of jct I-35 and Round Grove Rd on southbound service road to Vista Ridge Mall Dr, then just w; exit 447B northbound, just w on SR 121 Bypass. Int corridors. **Pets:** Accepted.

Country Inn & Suites by Carlson SH
(972) 315-6565. **Call for rates.** 755B Vista Ridge Mall Dr. I-35E, exit 448A (Round Grove Rd) southbound, 0.5 mi s on service road to Vista Ridge Rd, then just w; exit 447B northbound, just w on SR 121 Bypass. Int corridors. **Pets:** Accepted.

Extended Stay Hotel SH
(972) 315-7455. **$54-$60.** 1900 Lake Pointe Dr. I-35E, exit 449 (Corporate Dr), just e to Lake Pointe Dr, then just s. Int corridors. **Pets:** Other species. $75 one-time fee/pet. Service with restrictions.

La Quinta Inn Dallas (Lewisville) SH
(972) 221-7525. **$85-$105.** 1657 S Stemmons Frwy. I-35E, exit 449 (Corporate Dr), just w. Ext corridors. **Pets:** Other species. Service with restrictions, supervision.

Motel 6-1288 SH
(972) 436-5008. **$42-$55.** 1705 Lakepointe Dr. I-35E, exit 449, just n on access road. Int corridors. **Pets:** Other species. Service with restrictions, supervision.

Residence Inn by Marriott Dallas SH
(972) 315-3777. **$165-$185.** 755C Vista Ridge Mall Dr. I-35E, exit 448A (Round Grove Rd), 0.5 mi s on service road; jct I-35 and Round Grove Rd to Vista Ridge Rd, just w. Int corridors. **Pets:** Accepted.

Rodeway Inn SH
(972) 221-2121. **$49-$54.** 1102 Texas St. I-35E, exit 450 (SR 121), just e. Ext corridors. **Pets:** Accepted.

MCKINNEY

▼ ▼ Days Inn McKinney SH
(972) 548-8888. **Call for rates.** 2104 N Central Expwy. US 75, 0.5 mi n of jct US 380, exit 41. Ext corridors. **Pets:** Accepted.

▼ ▼ Super 8 Motel-McKinney SH
(972) 548-8880. **$60-$80.** 910 N Central Expwy. US 75, exit 40A (Virginia St/Louisiana St), 0.5 mi n on northbound service road. Int corridors. **Pets:** Accepted.

MESQUITE

▼▼▼▼ Comfort Inn SH
(972) 285-6300. **Call for rates.** 923 Windbell Cir. I-635, exit 5, just e. Int corridors. **Pets:** Other species. $10 daily fee/pet. Designated rooms, service with restrictions.

▼ Crossland Economy Studios SH
(972) 270-3630. **$49-$55.** 2544 US Hwy 67. I-30, exit 56A, on eastbound access road. Ext corridors. **Pets:** Other species. $75 one-time fee/pet. Service with restrictions.

▼▼▼▼ La Quinta Inn and Suites SH
(972) 216-7460. **$89-$109.** 118 E Hwy 80. US 80 E, exit Belt Line Rd. Int corridors. **Pets:** Other species. Service with restrictions, supervision.

⨁ ▼▼▼ Super 8 Motel SH
(972) 289-5481. **Call for rates.** 121 Grand Junction Blvd. I-635, exit 4 (Military Pkwy). Ext corridors. **Pets:** $10 daily fee/pet. Service with restrictions, supervision.

MIDLOTHIAN

⨁ ▼▼▼ Best Western Midlothian Inn SH
(972) 775-1891. **$69-$149.** 220 N Hwy 67. On US 67, just n of jct US 287. Ext corridors. **Pets:** Medium. $10 daily fee/pet. Service with restrictions, supervision.

PLANO

▼▼▼▼ Best Western Park Suites Hotel SH
(972) 578-2243. **$99-$104.** 640 Park Blvd E. US 75, exit 29A northbound, just e; exit 29 southbound, 0.5 mi s on access road, just e on 15th St, then 0.5 mi n on access road. Int corridors. **Pets:** Dogs only. $50 one-time fee/pet. Service with restrictions, supervision.

▼▼▼▼ Candlewood Suites-Plano SH
(972) 618-5446. **Call for rates.** 4701 Legacy Dr. Jct SR 289 (Preston Rd) and Legacy Dr, just e. Int corridors. **Pets:** Accepted.

▼▼ Extended Stay Deluxe SH
(972) 398-0135. **$85-$95.** 4636 W Plano Pkwy. Jct SR 289 (Preston Rd) and W Plano Pkwy, 0.4 mi e. Int corridors. **Pets:** Other species. $75 one-time fee/pet. Service with restrictions.

▼▼ Extended Stay Deluxe (Dallas/Plano) SH
(972) 378-9978. **$85-$95.** 2900 Dallas Pkwy. Dallas Pkwy, exit Park Blvd northbound; exit Parker Rd southbound, on northbound service road. Int corridors. **Pets:** Other species. $75 one-time fee/pet. Service with restrictions.

▼▼▼ Hampton Inn Plano SH
(972) 519-1000. **Call for rates.** 4901 Old Shepherd Pl. 0.4 mi n of jct SR 289 (Preston Rd) and W Plano Pkwy, just e. Int corridors. **Pets:** Accepted.

▼▼▼▼ Holiday Inn Express Hotel & Suites Plano East SH
(972) 881-1881. **$119-$129.** 700 Central Pkwy E. Just e of US 75, 0.5 mi ne of jct FM 544, exit 29A northbound; exit 29 southbound, 0.5 mi s on access road, just e on 15th St, then 0.5 mi n on access road. Int corridors. **Pets:** Accepted.

▼▼ Homestead Studio Suites Hotel-Dallas/Plano Parkway SH
(972) 596-9966. **$76-$85.** 4709 W Plano Pkwy. Just n of jct Plano Pkwy and SR 289 (Preston Rd), then just e. Int corridors. **Pets:** Other species. $75 one-time fee/pet. Service with restrictions.

▼▼▼ Homewood Suites by Hilton SH
(972) 758-8800. **Call for rates.** 4705 Old Shepherd Pl. Jct Plano Pkwy and SR 289 (Preston Rd), 0.4 mi n, then just e. Int corridors. **Pets:** Accepted.

▼▼▼▼ La Quinta Inn & Suites Dallas (West Plano) SH
(972) 599-0700. **$115-$135.** 4800 W Plano Pkwy. Just n of jct SR 289 (Preston Rd), then just e. Int corridors. **Pets:** Other species. Service with restrictions, supervision.

▼▼ La Quinta Inn Dallas (Plano) SH
(972) 423-1300. **$85-$105.** 1820 N Central Expwy. US 75, exit 29A (Park Blvd), northbound, just ne; exit 29 southbound, 0.5 mi s on access road, just e on 15th St, then just n on northbound access road. Ext corridors. **Pets:** Other species. Service with restrictions, supervision.

▼ Motel 6–1121 SH
(972) 578-1626. **$43-$56.** 2550 N Central Expwy. US 75, exit 29A (Park Blvd) northbound; exit 29 southbound, 1 mi n of jct Park Rd (SR 544), on east side of US 75. Ext/int corridors. **Pets:** Other species. Service with restrictions, supervision.

▼▼ Motel 6 #4309 SH
(972) 867-1111. **Call for rates.** 4801 W Plano Pkwy. Just n of jct SR 289 (Preston Rd) and N Plano Pkwy, just e. Int corridors. **Pets:** Accepted.

▼▼ Red Roof Inn Dallas-Plano SH
(972) 881-8191. **Call for rates.** 301 Ruisseau Dr. SR 75, exit 30 (Parker Rd), 0.5 mi w to Premier, then just n. Ext/int corridors. **Pets:** Accepted.

⨁ ▼▼▼ Southfork Hotel SH
(972) 578-8555. **$89-$99.** 1600 N Central Expwy. US 75, exit 29A northbound; exit 29 southbound, on northbound access road. Int corridors. **Pets:** Large. $50 one-time fee/pet. Service with restrictions, supervision.

▼▼ Super 8 Motel-Plano SH
(972) 423-8300. **Call for rates.** 1704 N Central Expwy. US 75, exit 29A (Park Blvd) northbound, just e; exit 29 southbound, 0.5 mi s on access road, just e on 15th St, then just n on access road. Int corridors. **Pets:** Accepted.

▼▼ **TownePlace Suites by Marriott** SH
(972) 943-8200. **$175-$186.** 5005 Whitestone Ln. North Dallas Tollway, exit Spring Creek Pkwy, 1.9 mi e, just n on SR 289 (Preston Rd), to Whitestone Ln, then just w. Int corridors. **Pets:** $75 one-time fee/room. Service with restrictions, crate.

ASK S☐ ✕ ⭨M 🛏 💻 ⌒

RICHARDSON

▼▼ **Econo Lodge Inn & Suites** SH
(972) 470-9440. **$55-$65.** 2458 N Central Expwy. US 75, exit 27 northbound; exit 26 southbound, 0.8 mi n on access road. Int corridors. **Pets:** Accepted.

ASK S☐ ✕ 🛏 💻

▼▼▼ **Homestead Studio Suites Hotel-Dallas/Richardson** SH
(972) 479-0500. **$67-$75.** 901 E Campbell Rd. US 75, exit 26 (Campbell Rd), just e. Int corridors. **Pets:** Other species. $75 one-time fee/pet. Service with restrictions.

ASK S☐ ✕ ⭨M 🛏 💻 ⌒

◈◈◈ ▼▼▼ **The Radisson Hotel Dallas North At Richardson** LH
(972) 644-4000. **$179-$199.** 1981 N Central Expwy. US 75, exit 26 (Campbell Rd), 1.8 mi n; jct SR 5. Int corridors. **Pets:** Medium, other species. $50 one-time fee/room. Service with restrictions, crate.

SAVE S☐ ✕ ⭨M 🛏 💻 🍽 ⌒

◈◈◈ ▼▼ ▼▼ **Renaissance Dallas-Richardson Hotel** LH
(972) 367-2000. **$209-$229.** 900 E Lookout Dr. US 75, exit 27A (Gallatin Pkwy/Renner Rd) northbound; exit 26 (Gallatin Pkwy/Campbell Rd) southbound, just e. Int corridors. **Pets:** Other species. $50 one-time fee/room. Service with restrictions, supervision.

SAVE S☐ ✕ 🛏 💻 🍽 ⌒ ✕

▼▼▼ **Residence Inn by Marriott Richardson** SH
(972) 669-5888. **$186-$197.** 1040 Waterwood Dr. US 75, exit 26 (Campbell Rd), just e to Greenville Ave, 0.4 mi n to Glenville Rd, then just w. Int corridors. **Pets:** Accepted.

ASK S☐ ✕ 🛏 💻 ⌒ ✕

ROANOKE

◈◈◈ ▼▼▼ **Speedway Sleep Inn & Suites** SH
(817) 491-3120. **$70-$109.** 13471 Raceway Dr. I-35, exit 70 (SR 114), just e, then just s. Int corridors. **Pets:** Accepted.

SAVE S☐ ✕ ⭨M 🛏 💻 ⌒

ROCKWALL

◈◈◈ ▼▼▼▼ **La Quinta Inn & Suites** SH
(972) 771-1685. **$99-$119.** 689 E I-30. I-30, exit 67 westbound; exit 67B eastbound. Int corridors. **Pets:** Other species. Service with restrictions, supervision.

SAVE S☐ ✕ ⭨M 🛏 💻 ⌒

ROWLETT

◈◈◈ ▼▼▼ **Comfort Suites Lake Ray Hubbard** SH
(972) 463-9595. **$89.** 8701 E I-30. I-30, exit 64 (Dalrock Rd). Int corridors. **Pets:** Accepted.

SAVE S☐ ✕ ⭨M 🛏 💻 ⌒

TERRELL

◈◈◈ ▼▼ ◈ **Best Western Country Inn** SH
(972) 563-1521. **$59-$89.** 1604 Hwy 34 S. I-20, exit 501 (SR 34), just n. Ext corridors. **Pets:** Accepted.

SAVE S☐ ✕ 🛏 💻 ⌒

THE COLONY

◈◈◈ ▼▼▼ **Comfort Suites** SH
(972) 668-5555. **$99-$160.** 4796 Memorial Dr. Just n of jct SR 121. Int corridors. **Pets:** Medium. $10 daily fee/room. Service with restrictions, supervision.

SAVE S☐ ✕ ⭨M 🛏 💻 ⌒

UNIVERSITY PARK

◈◈◈ ▼▼▼ **Hotel Lumen** SH ❀
(214) 219-2400. **Call for rates.** 6101 Hillcrest Ave. Just n of jct Mockingbird Ln and Hillcrest Ave. Int corridors. **Pets:** Other species. Service with restrictions, crate.

SAVE ✕ 🛏 🍽

END METROPOLITAN AREA

DECATUR

◈◈◈ ▼▼ ▼ **Best Western Decatur Inn** M
(940) 627-5982. **$70-$110.** 1801 S Hwy 287. 0.6 mi s of jct Business Rt SR 380. Ext corridors. **Pets:** Medium. $15 daily fee/pet. Service with restrictions, supervision.

SAVE S☐ ✕ 🛏 💻 ⌒

◈◈◈ ▼▼▼ **Comfort Inn** SH
(940) 627-6919. **$115-$150.** 1709 S US 287. 0.6 mi s of jct Business Rt SR 380. Ext corridors. **Pets:** Accepted.

SAVE S☐ ✕ 🛏 💻 ⌒

◈◈◈ ▼▼▼▼ **Holiday Inn Express Hotel & Suites** SH
(940) 627-0776. **Call for rates.** 1051 N Hwy 287. US 380, exit US 287 N, just n. Int corridors. **Pets:** Accepted.

SAVE ✕ 🛏 💻 ⌒

◈◈◈ ▼▼ **Super 8 Motel** SH
(940) 627-0250. **Call for rates.** 1600 US S 81/287. 0.4 mi s of jct Business Rt US 380. Int corridors. **Pets:** Accepted.

SAVE ✕ 🛏 ⌒

DEL RIO

◈◈◈ ▼▼ **Comfort Inn & Suites** SH
(830) 775-2933. **$70-$90, 3 day notice.** 3616 Veterans Blvd. 3.2 mi nw on US 90. Ext/int corridors. **Pets:** Medium. $10 daily fee/pet. Service with restrictions, supervision.

SAVE S☐ ✕ 🛏 💻 ⌒

◈◈◈ ▼▼▼ **Days Inn and Suites** SH
(830) 775-0585. **$53-$71.** 3808 Veterans Blvd. 3.5 mi nw on US 90. Ext corridors. **Pets:** Accepted.

SAVE S☐ ✕ 🛏 💻 ⌒

▼▼▼▼ La Quinta Inn Del Rio 🆂🅷
(830) 775-7591. **$85-$105.** 2005 Veterans Blvd. 1.8 mi nw on US 90, 277 and 377. Ext/int corridors. **Pets:** Other species. Service with restrictions, supervision.

A$K 🔊 ⊠ 🖥 💻 🏊

▼ Motel 6 Del Rio #323 🆂🅷
(830) 774-2115. **$39-$51.** 2115 Veterans Blvd. Jct US 90/277 and Garner Dr. Ext corridors. **Pets:** Other species. Service with restrictions, supervision.

🔊 ⊠ 🏊

⨁ ▼▼▼▼ Ramada Inn 🆂🅷
(830) 775-1511. **$108-$121.** 2101 Veterans Blvd. 1.8 mi nw on US 90, 277 and 377. Ext/int corridors. **Pets:** Accepted.

SAVE 🔊 ⊠ 🖥 💻 🍴 🏊 ⊠

DONNA

⨁ ▼▼▼▼ Victoria Palms Inn & Suites 🆂🅷
(956) 464-4656. **$50-$90, 90 day notice.** 602 N Victoria Rd. US 83, exit Victoria Rd. Ext corridors. **Pets:** Accepted.

SAVE ⊠ 🖥 💻 🍴 🏊 ⊠

DUMAS

⨁ ▼▼▼ Best Western Windsor Inn 🆂🅷
(806) 935-9644. **$69-$119.** 1701 S Dumas Ave. US 287, 2 mi s of US 87 and SR 152. Ext corridors. **Pets:** Dogs only. $20 deposit/pet, $10 daily fee/pet. Designated rooms, service with restrictions, supervision.

SAVE 🔊 ⊠ 🖥 💻 🏊 ⊠

⨁ ▼▼▼ Econo Lodge 🆂🅷
(806) 935-9098. **Call for rates.** 1719 S Dumas Ave. US 287, 2 mi s of US 87 and SR 152. Int corridors. **Pets:** Accepted.

SAVE ⊠ 🖥

▼▼▼ Holiday Inn Express 🆂🅷
(806) 935-4000. **Call for rates.** 1525 S Dumas Ave. US 87, 1.1 mi s of US 87 and SR 152. Int corridors. **Pets:** Accepted.

⊠ 🖥 💻 🏊

▼▼ Super 8 Motel 🅼 🐾
(806) 935-6222. **Call for rates.** 119 W 17th St. US 287, 2 mi s of jct US 87 and SR 152. Ext corridors. **Pets:** Medium. $20 daily fee/pet. Designated rooms, service with restrictions, supervision.

⊠ 🖥 💻

EAGLE PASS

⨁ ▼▼▼▼ Holiday Inn Express Hotel & Suites 🆂🅷
(830) 757-3050. **$84-$89.** 2007 Veterans Blvd. 1.5 mi n on Loop 431 (US 277). Int corridors. **Pets:** Accepted.

SAVE ⊠ ⓜ 🖥 💻 🏊

▼▼▼▼ La Quinta Inn Eagle Pass 🆂🅷
(830) 773-7000. **$95-$115.** 2525 E Main St. US 57 and 277 at Loop 431. Ext corridors. **Pets:** Other species. Service with restrictions, supervision.

A$K 🔊 ⊠ 🖥 💻 🏊

▼▼ Super 8 Motel 🆂🅷
(830) 773-9531. **Call for rates.** 2150 N US Hwy 277. On US 277, 4 mi n. Ext corridors. **Pets:** Accepted.

⊠ 🖥 🏊

EASTLAND

▼ Super 8 Motel & RV Park 🅼
(254) 629-3336. **Call for rates.** 3900 I-20 E. I-20, exit 343, on north service road. Ext corridors. **Pets:** Accepted.

⊠ 🖥 💻 🏊

EDINBURG

⨁ ▼▼▼▼ Comfort Inn Edinburg 🅼
(956) 318-1117. **$65-$70.** 4001 Closner Blvd. US 281, exit Trenton Rd, just w, then just n on Business Rt US 281. Int corridors. **Pets:** Accepted.

SAVE 🔊 ⊠ 🖥 💻 🏊

⨁ ▼▼▼ Super 8 🆂🅷
(956) 381-8888. **$62-$80.** 1210 E Canton Rd. US 281, exit Canton Rd, just off southbound access road. Ext corridors. **Pets:** Medium, other species. $10 daily fee/pet. Service with restrictions, supervision.

SAVE 🔊 ⊠ 🖥 🏊

⨁ ▼▼▼ Super 8 Motel 🆂🅷
(956) 381-1688. **$71-$90.** 202 N Hwy 281. US 281, exit University Dr. Ext/int corridors. **Pets:** Accepted.

SAVE 🔊 ⊠ 🖥 🏊

EL PASO

⨁ ▼▼▼ Best Western Sunland Park Inn 🅼
(915) 587-4900. **$89-$109.** 1045 Sunland Park Dr. I-10, exit 13, just s. Ext corridors. **Pets:** Small. Designated rooms, service with restrictions, supervision.

SAVE 🔊 ⊠ 🖥 💻 🏊

⨁ ▼▼▼▼ Chase Suites by Woodfin 🆂🅷
(915) 772-8000. **$155-$169.** 6791 Montana Ave. I-10, exit 25 (Airway Blvd), 1 mi n, then just e. Ext corridors. **Pets:** Accepted.

SAVE 🔊 ⊠ 🖥 💻 🏊

▼▼ Comfort Inn Airport East 🆂🅷 🐾
(915) 594-9111. **$84.** 900 Yarbrough Dr. I-10, exit 28B. Ext corridors. **Pets:** Small, other species. $20 one-time fee/room. Service with restrictions, supervision.

A$K 🔊 ⊠ 🖥 💻 🏊

⨁ ▼▼▼ Econo Lodge 🅼
(915) 778-3311. **$60-$70.** 6363 Montana Ave. I-10, exit 24 (Geronimo Dr) westbound; exit 24B eastbound, 0.5 mi n on Geronimo Dr, 0.5 mi e. Ext corridors. **Pets:** Accepted.

SAVE 🔊 ⊠ 🖥 💻 🏊

▼▼ Extended StayAmerica-El Paso-Airport 🆂🅷
(915) 772-5754. **$58-$65.** 6580 Montana Ave. I-10, exit 24 (Geronimo Dr), westbound, exit 24B (Geronimo Dr) eastbound, 0.5 mi n, then 0.5 mi e. Ext corridors. **Pets:** Other species. $75 one-time fee/pet. Service with restrictions.

A$K 🔊 ⊠ 🖥 💻

▼▼▼ Hawthorn Inn & Suites 🆂🅷 🐾
(915) 778-6789. **$89-$129.** 6789 Boeing. 7 mi e on US 62 and 180 to Airway Blvd, then just n. Int corridors. **Pets:** $125 one-time fee/room. Service with restrictions, supervision.

A$K 🔊 ⊠ ⓜ 🖥 💻 🏊

⨁ ▼▼▼▼ Holiday Inn-Airport 🆂🅷 🐾
(915) 778-6411. **$159-$179.** 6655 Gateway Blvd W. I-10, exit 25 (Airway Blvd). Ext/int corridors. **Pets:** Medium, other species. $49 one-time fee/pet. Service with restrictions, supervision.

SAVE ⊠ 🖥 💻 🍴 🏊

⨁ ▼▼▼▼ Holiday Inn El Paso Sunland Park 🆂🅷
(915) 833-2900. **$99-$165.** 900 Sunland Park Dr. I-10, exit 13. Ext corridors. **Pets:** Medium, other species. $25 one-time fee/room. Service with restrictions, supervision.

SAVE 🔊 ⊠ 🖥 💻 🍴 🏊

▼▼ Howard Johnson Inn 🆂🅷
(915) 591-9471. **Call for rates.** 8887 Gateway Blvd W. I-10, exit 26 (Hawkins Blvd). Int corridors. **Pets:** Accepted.

⊠ 🖥 💻 🍴 🏊

La Quinta Inn Airport East 🅂🅷
(915) 593-8400. **$104-$124.** 9125 Gateway Blvd W. I-10, exit 28B westbound; exit 27 eastbound. Ext corridors. **Pets:** Other species. Service with restrictions, supervision.
(A$K) 🛇 ⊠ 🖥 🖵 ⌕

La Quinta Inn & Suites El Paso East 🅂🅷
(915) 591-3300. **Call for rates.** 7944 Gateway Blvd E. I-10, exit 28B. Int corridors. **Pets:** Other species. Service with restrictions, supervision.
⊠ 🅖ᴹ 🖥 🖵 ⌕

La Quinta Inn & Suites El Paso West 🅂🅷
(915) 585-2999. **Call for rates.** 7620 N Mesa St. I-10, exit 11 (Mesa St). Int corridors. **Pets:** Other species. Service with restrictions, supervision.
⊠ 🖥 🖵 ⌕

La Quinta Inn El Paso (Airport) 🅼
(915) 778-9321. **$99-$119.** 6140 Gateway Blvd E. I-10, exit 24B (Geronimo Dr) eastbound; exit 24 westbound. Ext corridors. **Pets:** Other species. Service with restrictions, supervision.
(A$K) 🛇 ⊠ 🖥 🖵 ⌕

La Quinta Inn El Paso (Lomaland) 🅂🅷
(915) 591-2244. **$85-$105.** 11033 Gateway Blvd W. I-10, exit 29 eastbound; exit 30 westbound, 1 mi w. Ext corridors. **Pets:** Other species. Service with restrictions, supervision.
(A$K) 🛇 ⊠ 🅖ᴹ 🖥 🖵 ⌕

La Quinta Inn El Paso (West) 🅼
(915) 833-2522. **$99-$119.** 7550 Remcon Cir. I-10, exit 11 (Mesa St). Ext corridors. **Pets:** Other species. Service with restrictions, supervision.
(A$K) 🛇 ⊠ 🖥 🖵 ⌕

Microtel Inn & Suites West 🅼
(915) 584-2026. **$56-$69.** 6185 S Desert Blvd. I-10, exit 8 (Artcraft Rd/Paseo del Norte), on eastbound frontage road. Int corridors. **Pets:** Accepted.
(A$K) 🛇 ⊠ 🅖ᴹ 🖥 🖵 ⌕

Microtel Inn & Suites 🅂🅷
(915) 772-3650. **$76-$94.** 2001 Airway Blvd. I-10, exit 25 (Airway Blvd), 1.3 mi n. Int corridors. **Pets:** Accepted.
(A$K) ⊠ 🅖ᴹ 🖥 🖵

Microtel Inn & Suites El Paso East 🅂🅷
(915) 858-1600. **Call for rates.** 12211 Gateway W at Don Haskins Rd. I-10, exit 34 (Joe Battle), on westbound frontage road. Int corridors. **Pets:** Accepted.
⊠ 🅖ᴹ 🖥 🖵 ⌕

Quality Inn & Suites 🅂🅷
(915) 772-3300. **Call for rates.** 6099 Montana Ave. I-10, exit 24 (Geronimo Dr) westbound; exit 24B (Geronimo Dr) eastbound, 0.5 mi n. Ext corridors. **Pets:** Accepted.
⊠ 🖥 🖵 🍴 ⌕

Red Roof Inn West 🅂🅷
(915) 587-9977. **Call for rates.** 7530 Remcon Cir. I-10, exit 11 (Mesa St). Ext/int corridors. **Pets:** Accepted.
⊠ 🅖ᴹ 🖥 ⌕

Residence Inn by Marriott El Paso 🅂🅷
(915) 771-0504. **$183-$203.** 6355 Gateway Blvd W. I-10, exit 24B (Geronimo Dr) eastbound, n to Edgemere, then just e; exit 25 (Airway Blvd) westbound on westbound frontage road. Int corridors. **Pets:** Accepted.
(A$K) 🛇 ⊠ 🖥 🖵 ⌕ ⊠

Sleep Inn by Choice Hotels 🅂🅷
(915) 585-7577. **Call for rates.** 953 Sunland Park Dr. I-10, exit 13. Int corridors. **Pets:** Accepted.
⊠ 🖥 🖵 ⌕

Studio 6 El Paso #6001 🅼
(915) 594-8533. **$60-$73 (no credit cards).** 11049 Gateway Blvd W. I-10, exit 29 eastbound; exit 30 westbound. Ext corridors. **Pets:** Other species. Service with restrictions, supervision.
🛇 ⊠ 🖥 🖵 ⌕

Super 8 Motel 🅂🅷
(915) 584-4030. **Call for rates.** 7840 N Mesa St. I-10, exit 11 (N Mesa), just s. Ext corridors. **Pets:** Accepted.
⊠ 🖵 ⌕

Wyndham El Paso Airport 🅻🅷
(915) 778-4241. **$129-$172, 6 day notice.** 2027 Airway Blvd. I-10, exit 25 (Airway Blvd), 1.3 mi n. Int corridors. **Pets:** Accepted.
(A$K) ⊠ 🖥 🖵 🍴 ⌕ ⊠

EULESS

La Quinta DFW Airport West-Euless 🅂🅷
(817) 540-0233. **$82-$102.** 1001 W Airport Frwy. SR 183, exit Industrial Blvd (FM 157). Ext corridors. **Pets:** Other species. Service with restrictions, supervision.
(SAVE) 🛇 ⊠ 🖥 🖵 ⌕

Microtel Inn and Suites 🅂🅷
(817) 545-1111. **$64-$99.** 901 W Airport Frwy. SR 183, exit Industrial Blvd (FM 157), just e. Int corridors. **Pets:** Accepted.
(A$K) 🛇 ⊠ 🅖ᴹ 🖥 🖵 ⌕

Motel 6-Euless #1345 🅂🅷
(817) 545-0141. **$41-$55.** 110 Airport Frwy. SR 183, exit Euless/Main St, on westbound access road. Ext corridors. **Pets:** Other species. Service with restrictions, supervision.
🛇 ⊠ ⌕

FALFURRIAS

Days Inn 🅼
(361) 325-2515. **Call for rates.** 2116 Hwy 281 S. 1.5 mi s of SR 285. Ext corridors. **Pets:** Accepted.
⊠ 🅖ᴹ 🖥 🖵

FORT DAVIS

Historical Prude Guest Ranch 🆁🅰
(432) 426-3202. **$51-$80, 3 day notice.** 6 mi n Hwy 118. 4.5 mi n of jct SR 118 and 17. Ext corridors. **Pets:** Accepted.
(A$K) 🛇 ⊠ 🖥 🍴 ⌕ ⊠ 🅦 🎱

FORT STOCKTON

Best Western Swiss Clock Inn 🅂🅷
(432) 336-8521. **$109.** 3201 W Dickinson Blvd. I-10, exit 256, 0.5 mi e. Ext corridors. **Pets:** Accepted.
(A$K) 🛇 ⊠ 🖥 🖵 🍴 ⌕

Days Inn 🅂🅷
(432) 336-7500. **$79-$99.** 1408 N US Hwy 285. I-10, exit 257, just s. Ext corridors. **Pets:** Small. $6 daily fee/pet. Designated rooms, service with restrictions, supervision.
(SAVE) 🛇 ⊠ 🖥 🖵 ⌕

La Quinta Inn Fort Stockton 🅂🅷
(432) 336-9781. **$89-$109.** 1537 N Hwy 285. I-10, exit 257. Ext corridors. **Pets:** Other species. Service with restrictions, supervision.
(A$K) 🛇 ⊠ 🖥 🖵 ⌕

Quality Inn 🅂🅷
(432) 336-5955. **$65-$130.** 1308 N US Hwy 285. I-10, exit 257, just s. Ext corridors. **Pets:** Medium. $25 daily fee/pet. Designated rooms, service with restrictions, supervision.
(SAVE) 🛇 ⊠ 🖥 🖵 ⌕

Super 8 Motel SH
(432) 336-8531. **$59-$99.** 3200 W Dickinson Blvd. I-10, exit 256, just s. Int corridors. **Pets:** Accepted.

SAVE S✪ ✕ 🛏 🖵 🏊

FORT WORTH

The Ashton Hotel SH 🐾
(817) 332-0100. **$290-$810.** 610 Main St. Jct of 6th and Main sts; center. Int corridors. **Pets:** Medium. $150 deposit/room. Service with restrictions, crate.

A$K S✪ ✕ ⑪

Best Western InnSuites Hotel & Suites-Fort Worth SH
(817) 534-4801. **$75-$125.** 2000 Beach St. I-30, exit 16C (Beach St), just s. Ext/int corridors. **Pets:** Medium. $25 one-time fee/pet. Designated rooms, service with restrictions, supervision.

SAVE S✪ ✕ 🛏 🖵 🏊 ✕

Candlewood Suites SH
(817) 838-8229. **$99-$131, 3 day notice.** 5201 Endicott Ave. I-820, exit 17B, just s. Int corridors. **Pets:** Medium. $150 one-time fee/pet. Service with restrictions, supervision.

A$K S✪ ✕ 🛏 🖵

Comfort Inn-North SH
(817) 834-8001. **Call for rates.** 4850 North Frwy. I-35W, exit 56A. Int corridors. **Pets:** Accepted.

✕ 🛏 🖵 🏊

Comfort Suites Hotel SH
(817) 731-9600. **$119-$169.** 6851 West Frwy. I-30, exit 7B, 0.8 mi e to Green Oaks Rd exit. Int corridors. **Pets:** Accepted.

A$K S✪ ✕ ⑭M 🛏 🖵 🏊

Country Inn & Suites By Carlson SH
(817) 831-9200. **$109-$219.** 2200 Mercado Dr. I-35W, exit 53, just w. Int corridors. **Pets:** Small. $25 one-time fee/pet. No service, supervision.

SAVE S✪ ✕ ⑭M 🛏 🖵 🏊

Crossland Economy Suites SH
(817) 838-3500. **$54-$60.** 3804 Tanacross Dr. I-820, exit 17B (Beach St), just s. Ext corridors. **Pets:** Other species. $75 one-time fee/pet. Service with restrictions.

A$K S✪ ✕ 🛏 🖵

Extended StayAmerica SH
(817) 263-9006. **$67-$75.** 5831 Overton Ridge Blvd. I-20, exit 431, 0.5 mi s to Overton Ridge Blvd. Int corridors. **Pets:** Other species. $75 one-time fee/pet. Service with restrictions.

A$K S✪ ✕ 🛏 🖵

Extended Stay Deluxe SH
(817) 263-8700. **Call for rates.** 4701 City Lake Blvd W. I-20, exit 431 (Bryant Irvin), just e. Int corridors. **Pets:** Other species. $75 one-time fee/pet. Service with restrictions.

✕ 🛏 🖵 🏊

Extended Stay Deluxe Hotel SH
(817) 232-1622. **Call for rates.** 3261 NE Loop 820. I-820, exit 17B (N Beach St), 0.5 mi w. Int corridors. **Pets:** Other species. $75 one-time fee/pet. Service with restrictions.

✕ 🛏 🖵 🏊

Green Oaks Hotel SH
(817) 738-7311. **Call for rates.** 6901 West Frwy. I-30, exit 8A westbound; exit 7B eastbound. Ext/int corridors. **Pets:** Accepted.

SAVE ✕ 🛏 🖵 ⑪ 🏊 ✕

Hampton Inn & Suites-FW Alliance Airport SH
(817) 439-0400. **Call for rates.** 13600 North Frwy. I-35W, exit 66 (Westport Pkwy). Int corridors. **Pets:** Accepted.

✕ ⑭M 🛏 🖵 🏊

Holiday Inn Express Hotel & Suites-Fort Worth West SH
(817) 560-4200. **$117-$139.** 2730 Cherry Ln. I-30, exit 7A. Int corridors. **Pets:** Accepted.

A$K ✕ 🛏 🖵 🏊

Homestead Studio Suites Hotel-Fort Worth/Medical Center SH
(817) 338-4808. **$63-$70.** 1601 River Run. I-30, exit 12 (University Dr), just s. Ext corridors. **Pets:** Other species. $75 one-time fee/pet. Service with restrictions.

A$K S✪ ✕ 🛏 🖵

La Quinta Inn & Suites Fort Worth (North) SH
(817) 222-2888. **$105-$125.** 4700 North Frwy. I-35W, exit 56A, just n. Int corridors. **Pets:** Other species. Service with restrictions, supervision.

A$K S✪ ✕ 🛏 🖵 🏊

La Quinta Inn & Suites Fort Worth (Southwest) SH
(817) 370-2700. **$109-$129.** 4900 Bryant Irvin Rd. I-20, exit 431. Int corridors. **Pets:** Other species. Service with restrictions, supervision.

A$K S✪ ✕ ⑭M 🛏 🖵 🏊

La Quinta Inn Fort Worth (West/Medical Center) SH
(817) 246-5511. **$95-$115.** 7888 I-30 W. I-30, exit 7A. Ext/int corridors. **Pets:** Other species. Service with restrictions, supervision.

A$K S✪ ✕ 🛏 🖵 🏊

Microtel Inn & Suites SH
(817) 222-3740. **Call for rates.** 3740 Tanacross Dr. I-820, exit 17B (Beach St), just s. Int corridors. **Pets:** Accepted.

✕ 🛏 🖵

Motel 6–#117 SH
(817) 244-9740. **$39-$52.** 8701 I-30 W. I-30, exit 6, just s on Las Vegas. Ext corridors. **Pets:** Other species. Service with restrictions, supervision.

S✪ ✕ 🛏 🏊

The Renaissance Worthington Hotel LH 🐾
(817) 870-1000. **$275-$295.** 200 Main St. Northwest corner of 2nd and Main sts. Int corridors. **Pets:** Medium. Service with restrictions, supervision.

SAVE S✪ ✕ 🛏 🖵 ⑪ 🏊 ✕

Residence Inn-Alliance Airport SH
(817) 750-7000. **$132-$152.** 13400 North Frwy. I-35W, exit 66. Int corridors. **Pets:** Accepted.

A$K S✪ ✕ 🛏 🖵 🏊 ✕

Residence Inn by Marriott Fort Worth Cultural District SH 🐾
(817) 885-8250. **$209-$229.** 2500 Museum Way. I-30, exit 12A, just e of jct University and 7th St, to Stayton St, just s. Int corridors. **Pets:** Other species. $75 one-time fee/pet. Supervision.

A$K S✪ ✕ ⑭M 🛏 🖵 🏊 ✕

Residence Inn By Marriott Fort Worth-River Plaza SH
(817) 870-1011. **$198-$218.** 1701 S University Dr. I-30, exit 12 (University Dr), 0.4 mi s. Ext corridors. **Pets:** Accepted.

A$K S✪ ✕ ⑭M 🛏 🖵 🏊 ✕

TownePlace Suites by Marriott-Fort Worth SH
(817) 732-2224. **$143-$163.** 4200 International Plaza Dr. I-820, exit 433. Int corridors. **Pets:** Large, other species. $100 one-time fee/pet. Service with restrictions, crate.

A$K S✪ ✕ 🛏 🖵 🏊

FREDERICKSBURG

Best Western Fredericksburg SH
(830) 992-2929. **Call for rates.** 314 E Highway St. Jct US 87 and 290, 6 blks s. Int corridors. **Pets:** Small. $15 one-time fee/pet. Designated rooms, service with restrictions, supervision.

Budget Host Deluxe Inn M
(830) 997-3344. **Call for rates.** 901 E Main St. US 290, 0.5 mi e. Ext corridors. **Pets:** Accepted.

Comfort Inn & Suites SH
(830) 990-2552. **Call for rates.** 723 S Washington St. W on Main St, then s. Int corridors. **Pets:** Accepted.

Dietzel Motel M
(830) 997-3330. **$49-$89.** 1141 W US 290. 1 mi w on US 290 at US 87. Ext corridors. **Pets:** Other species. $10 daily fee/pet. Service with restrictions.

Fredericksburg Econo Lodge M
(830) 997-3437. **$49-$109.** 810 S Adams St. Jct US 290 and SR 165, 1 mi s. Ext corridors. **Pets:** Other species. $10 daily fee/pet. Service with restrictions, supervision.

Fredericksburg Inn & Suites SH
(830) 997-0202. **Call for rates.** 201 S Washington. US 290 and 87, 3 blks s. Ext corridors. **Pets:** Accepted.

Holiday Inn Express SH
(830) 990-4200. **Call for rates.** 1220 N Hwy 87. 1 mi w on US 290 at US 87. Int corridors. **Pets:** Accepted.

La Quinta Inn & Suites SH
(830) 990-2899. **$109-$129.** 1465 E Main St. 1 mi e of downtown. Int corridors. **Pets:** Other species. Service with restrictions, supervision.

Quality Inn SH
(830) 997-9811. **$80-$116.** 908 S Adams St. 0.8 mi sw on SR 16; 0.8 mi sw of jct US 87 and 290. Ext corridors. **Pets:** Accepted.

Sunday House Inn & Suites SH
(830) 997-4484. **$99-$249.** 501 E Main St. 0.4 mi e on US 290. Ext corridors. **Pets:** Accepted.

Sunset Inn M
(830) 997-9581. **$49-$64.** 900 S Adams St. 0.8 mi sw of jct US 290 and SR 16. Ext corridors. **Pets:** Dogs only. No service, crate.

Super 8 Fredericksburg M
(830) 997-6568. **Call for rates.** 514 E Main St. US 290, just e of jct US 87. Ext corridors. **Pets:** Small. $10 one-time fee/pet. Service with restrictions, supervision.

FULTON

Best Western Inn by the Bay M
(361) 729-8351. **$94-$149.** 3902 N Hwy 35. SR 35, 0.5 mi n of jct Business Rt SR 35 and FM 3063. Ext corridors. **Pets:** $10 daily fee/pet. Service with restrictions, supervision.

GAINESVILLE

Best Western Southwinds M
(940) 665-7737. **Call for rates.** 2103 N I-35. I-35, exit 499 northbound, 1.4 mi n on access road to S Frontage Rd; exit 498B southbound. Ext corridors. **Pets:** Accepted.

Budget Host Inn M
(940) 665-2856. **Call for rates.** 1900 N I-35. I-35, exit 499 northbound; exit 498B southbound. Ext corridors. **Pets:** Other species. $5 daily fee/pet. No service, supervision.

Super 8 SH
(940) 665-5599. **$55-$65.** 1936 I-35 N. I-35, exit 499 northbound, exit 498A southbound. Int corridors. **Pets:** Accepted.

GEORGETOWN

La Quinta Inn Georgetown SH
(512) 869-2541. **$82-$102.** 333 I-35 N. I-35, exit 264 northbound; exit 262 southbound; on west frontage road. Ext corridors. **Pets:** Other species. Service with restrictions, supervision.

GEORGE WEST

Best Western George West Executive Inn SH
(361) 449-3300. **Call for rates.** 208 N Nueces St. Just n of US 59 on SR 281. Ext corridors. **Pets:** Large. $25 one-time fee/pet. Service with restrictions, crate.

GLEN ROSE

Best Western Dinosaur Valley Inn & Suites SH
(254) 897-4818. **Call for rates.** 1311 NE Big Ben Tr. On US 67. Int corridors. **Pets:** Small. $20 daily fee/pet. Service with restrictions, supervision.

GRANBURY

Comfort Inn SH
(817) 573-2611. **Call for rates.** 1201 Plaza Dr N. 2 mi e on US 377 Bypass. Ext corridors. **Pets:** Medium. $15 daily fee/pet. Service with restrictions.

Plantation Inn on the Lake SH
(817) 573-8846. **$75-$100.** 1451 E Pearl St. 0.3 mi w of Business Rt US 377 at US 377 Bypass. Ext/int corridors. **Pets:** Medium, dogs only. $10 daily fee/pet. Service with restrictions, supervision.

GRAPEVINE

Baymont Inn-Dallas-Ft Worth/Airport North SH
(817) 329-9300. **Call for rates.** 301 Capitol St. SR 114, exit Main St. Int corridors. **Pets:** Accepted.

Embassy Suites Outdoor World LH
(972) 724-2600. **$129-$349.** 2401 Bass Pro Dr. US 121, exit Bass Pro Dr. Int corridors. **Pets:** Medium. $200 deposit/room, $50 one-time fee/room. Service with restrictions, supervision.

Homewood Suites by Hilton SH
(972) 691-2427. **Call for rates.** 2214 Grapevine Mills Cir W. SR 121 N, exit Bass Pro Dr. Int corridors. **Pets:** Accepted.

▼▼ Super 8 Motel-Grapevine SH
(817) 329-7222. **$80-$94.** 250 E Hwy 114. SR 114, exit Main St. Int corridors. **Pets:** Accepted.

ASK S⌀ ✕ ⌖M 🛏 🖵 🏊

GROOM

⟨AAA⟩ ▼▼▼ Chalet Inn M
(806) 248-7524. **$39-$60.** I-40 FM 2300. I-40, exit 113, just s. Ext corridors. **Pets:** Medium. $5 daily fee/pet. Designated rooms, service with restrictions, supervision.

SAVE S⌀ ✕ ⌖M

HANKAMER

⟨AAA⟩ ▼▼▼ Americas Best Value Inn SH
(409) 374-2424. **$70-$90.** 25941 I-10, Box-57. I-10, exit 813 west-bound; exit 812 eastbound, just n to frontage road, then just e. Ext corridors. **Pets:** Accepted.

SAVE S⌀ ✕ 🛏 🖵

HARLINGEN

⟨AAA⟩ ▼▼▼ America's Best Inn & Suites SH
(956) 425-1040. **Call for rates.** 1821 W Tyler. 0.8 mi e of US 77, exit downtown. Ext corridors. **Pets:** Accepted.

SAVE ✕ 🛏 🖵 🏊

▼▼▼▼ Country Inn & Suites By Carlson SH
(956) 428-0043. **$80-$105.** 3825 S Expwy 83. US 83 and 77, exit Ed Carrey. Int corridors. **Pets:** Medium. $25 one-time fee/pet. Designated rooms, service with restrictions, supervision.

ASK S⌀ ✕ 🛏 🖵 🏊

▼▼ Howard Johnson Inn SH
(956) 425-7070. **Call for rates.** 6779 W Expwy 83. Jct US 77, 2.3 mi w on US 83, exit Stuart Place Rd. Ext corridors. **Pets:** Accepted.

✕ 🛏 🖵 🍴 🏊

▼▼ La Quinta Inn Harlingen SH
(956) 428-6888. **$99-$119.** 1002 S Expwy 83. US 83 and 77, exit M St. Ext corridors. **Pets:** Other species. Service with restrictions, supervision.

ASK S⌀ ✕ ⌖M 🛏 🏊

⟨AAA⟩ ▼▼▼ Super 8 Motel SH
(956) 412-8873. **Call for rates.** 1115 S Expwy 83. US 83 and 77, exit M St, just n. Int corridors. **Pets:** Small. $10 daily fee/pet. Service with restrictions, supervision.

SAVE ✕ 🛏 🖵 🏊

HEARNE

⟨AAA⟩ ▼▼▼ Oak Tree Inn SH
(979) 279-5599. **$77-$82.** 1051 N Market St. 0.6 mi n of jct US 79 and SR 6. Ext/int corridors. **Pets:** Accepted.

SAVE S⌀ ✕ 🛏 🖵 🍴

HENDERSON

⟨AAA⟩ ▼▼▼ Best Western Inn of Henderson SH
(903) 657-9561. **$65-$119.** 1500 Hwy 259 S. 2 mi s on US 259, 0.7 mi s of jct US 79 and 259 S. Ext/int corridors. **Pets:** Accepted.

SAVE S⌀ ✕ 🛏 🖵 🏊

HEREFORD

⟨AAA⟩ ▼▼▼ Best Western Red Carpet Inn SH ❋
(806) 364-0540. **$75-$80.** 830 W 1st St. Just w of jct US 385 and 60. Ext corridors. **Pets:** Medium, other species. Service with restrictions, supervision.

ASK S⌀ ✕ 🛏 🖵 🏊

⟨AAA⟩ ▼▼▼ Holiday Inn Express SH
(806) 364-3322. **Call for rates.** 1400 W 1st St. Jct US 385/60, just w. Int corridors. **Pets:** Small. $20 daily fee/pet. Designated rooms, service with restrictions, supervision.

SAVE ✕ ⌖M 🛏 🖵 🏊

HILLSBORO

⟨AAA⟩ ▼▼▼ Best Western Hillsboro Inn SH
(254) 582-8465. **$72-$86.** 307 I-35. I-35, exit 368A northbound; exit 368B southbound, just w. Ext corridors. **Pets:** Accepted.

SAVE S⌀ ✕ 🛏 🖵 🏊

▼▼ Comfort Inn of Hillsboro SH
(254) 582-3333. **$50-$200.** 1515 Old Brandon Rd. I-35, exit 368A north-bound; exit 368B southbound, just w. Ext corridors. **Pets:** Accepted.

ASK S⌀ ✕ ⌖M 🛏 🖵 🏊

▼▼ Motel 6–4136 SH
(254) 580-9000. **Call for rates.** 1506 Hillview Dr. I-35, exit 368 south-bound; exit 368A northbound. Int corridors. **Pets:** Other species. Service with restrictions, supervision.

✕ ⌖M 🛏 🏊

▼▼▼ Super 8 SH
(254) 580-0404. **Call for rates.** 1512 Hillview Dr. I-35, exit 368A north-bound; 368 southbound, just e. Int corridors. **Pets:** Accepted.

✕ 🛏 🖵 🏊

HONDO

⟨AAA⟩ ▼▼◆ Americas Best Value Inn M
(830) 426-3031. **$40-$90.** 401 Hwy 90 E. Jct SR 173. Ext corridors. **Pets:** Other species. $10 one-time fee/pet. Service with restrictions, crate.

SAVE S⌀ ✕ 🛏 🏊

⟨AAA⟩ ▼▼▼ Hondo Executive Inn M
(830) 426-2535. **$45-$95.** 102 E 19th St. On US 90 W. Ext corridors. **Pets:** Dogs only. $15 one-time fee/pet. Service with restrictions, supervision.

SAVE S⌀ ✕ 🛏 🖵 🏊

HOUSTON METROPOLITAN AREA

BAYTOWN

⟨AAA⟩ ▼▼▼▼ Comfort Suites Baytown SH
(281) 421-9764. **$110-$199.** 7209 Garth Rd. I-10, exit 792 (Garth Rd), just n. Int corridors. **Pets:** Small. $25 one-time fee/pet. Service with restrictions, supervision.

SAVE S⌀ ✕ ⌖M 🛏 🖵 🏊

▼▼ La Quinta Inn Baytown East SH
(281) 421-5566. **$69-$89.** 5215 I-10 E. I-10, exit 792 (Garth Rd). Int corridors. **Pets:** Other species. Service with restrictions, supervision.

ASK S⌀ ✕ 🛏 🖵 🏊

▼▼ La Quinta Inn Houston/Baytown SH
(281) 421-7300. **Call for rates.** 4911 I-10 E. I-10, exit 792 (Garth Rd). Ext corridors. **Pets:** Other species. Service with restrictions, supervision.

✕ 🛏 🖵 🏊

CHANNELVIEW

▼▼ Days Inn & Suites of Channelview SH
(281) 457-0140. **$69-$89.** 15765 I-10 E Frwy. I-10, exit 783 (Sheldon Rd), on westbound frontage road. Ext corridors. **Pets:** Accepted.

ASK S⌀ ✕ 🛏 🖵

CLEVELAND

▼▼▼ Super 8 Motel 🆂🅷
(281) 432-8800. **Call for rates.** 427 W Southline. US 59, exit SR 105, just e to W Southline, then just s. Int corridors. **Pets:** Accepted.

❌ 🛅 💻

CONROE

🅐🅐🅐 ▼▼▼ Baymont Inn and Suites-Conroe/Woodlands 🆂🅷
(936) 539-5100. **Call for rates.** 1506 I-45 S. I-45, exit 85 (Gladstell St) northbound; exit 84 (Frazier St) southbound. Int corridors. **Pets:** Medium, other species. $15 daily fee/pet. Service with restrictions.

🆂🅰🆅🅴 ❌ 🛅 💻 ⇌

▼▼▼▼ La Quinta Inn & Suites 🆂🅷
(936) 228-0790. **$90-$110.** 4006 Sprayberry Ln. I-45, exit 91 (League Line Rd), just e. Int corridors. **Pets:** Other species. Service with restrictions, supervision.

🅰🆂🅺 🆂🅰 ❌ 🅻🅼 🛅 💻 ⇌

◈ Motel 6 Conroe #385 🅼
(936) 760-4003. **$43-$55.** 820 I-45 S. I-45, exit 85 (Gladstell Rd). Ext corridors. **Pets:** Other species. Service with restrictions, supervision.

🆂🅰 ❌ ⇌

DEER PARK

▼▼▼ Best Western Deer Park Inn & Suites 🆂🅷
(281) 476-1900. **$89-$109.** 1401 Center St. SR 225 (La Porte Rd), exit Center St, 0.9 mi s. Ext corridors. **Pets:** Accepted.

🅰🆂🅺 🆂🅰 ❌ 🛅 💻 ⇌

HOUSTON

🅐🅐🅐 ▼▼▼ Americas Best Value Inn 🆂🅷
(281) 866-8686. **Call for rates.** 609 FM 1960 W. I-45, exit 66 (FM 1960) southbound; exit 66A northbound, just w. Int corridors. **Pets:** Accepted.

🆂🅰🆅🅴 ❌ 🛅 ⇌

▼▼▼ Baymont Inn 🆂🅷
(713) 941-0900. **$79-$99.** 9902 Gulf Frwy. I-45 S, exit 36 (Airport Blvd/College Rd), just s on southbound frontage road. Ext corridors. **Pets:** Accepted.

🅰🆂🅺 🆂🅰 ❌ 🅻🅼 💻 ⇌

▼▼▼ Baymont Inn & Suites (Brookhollow) 🅼
(713) 688-2581. **$59-$99.** 11002 Northwest Frwy. Nw on US 290, exit Magnum Rd-Watonga Blvd. Ext corridors. **Pets:** Accepted.

🅰🆂🅺 🆂🅰 ❌ 🛅 💻 ⇌

🅐🅐🅐 ▼▼▼▼ Best Western Westchase Mini Suites 🆂🅷
(713) 782-1515. **Call for rates.** 2950 W Sam Houston Pkwy S. Just w of Sam Houston Pkwy (Beltway 8) and Westheimer Rd, on southbound frontage road. Int corridors. **Pets:** Small. Service with restrictions, supervision.

🆂🅰🆅🅴 ❌ 🅻🅼 🛅 💻 ⇌

▼▼▼▼ Candlewood Suites Houston by the Galleria 🆂🅷
(713) 839-9411. **Call for rates.** 4900 Loop Central Dr. I-610, exit 7 (Fournace Pl), on northbound frontage road. Int corridors. **Pets:** Accepted.

❌ 🛅 💻

▼▼▼▼ Candlewood Suites-Houston-Clear Lake 🆂🅷
(281) 461-3060. **Call for rates.** 2737 Bay Area Blvd. I-45, exit 26, 3.7 mi e. Int corridors. **Pets:** Accepted.

❌ 🛅 💻

▼▼▼ Candlewood Suites-Town & Country 🆂🅷
(713) 464-2677. **Call for rates.** 10503 Town & Country Way. I-10, exit 755 eastbound, 1.1 mi on frontage road to Town & Country Blvd, then 0.4 mi s; exit 756A westbound, U-turn under I-10, just e to Town & Country Blvd, then 0.4 mi s. Int corridors. **Pets:** Medium. $75 one-time fee/pet. Service with restrictions, crate.

❌ 🅻🅼 🛅 💻

▼▼▼▼ Candlewood Suites-Westchase 🆂🅷
(713) 780-7881. **Call for rates.** 4033 W Sam Houston Pkwy S. Sam Houston Pkwy (Beltway 8), exit Westpark, southeast corner of Westpark and Sam Houston Pkwy (Beltway 8) on northbound frontage road. Int corridors. **Pets:** Accepted.

❌ 🅻🅼 🛅 💻

▼▼▼▼ Comfort Suites 🆂🅷
(281) 440-4448. **$89-$94.** 150 Overland Tr. I-45, exit 66 (FM 1960), on southbound frontage road. Int corridors. **Pets:** Accepted.

🅰🆂🅺 🆂🅰 ❌ 🅻🅼 🛅 💻 ⇌

🅐🅐🅐 ▼▼▼▼ Comfort Suites Galleria 🆂🅷
(713) 787-0004. **$100-$229.** 6221 Richmond Ave. US 59, exit Hillcroft St, 1 mi n to Richmond Ave, then 0.6 mi e. Int corridors. **Pets:** Accepted.

🆂🅰🆅🅴 🆂🅰 ❌ 🛅 💻 ⇌

▼▼▼▼ Comfort Suites Intercontinental Plaza 🆂🅷
(281) 442-0600. **$69-$129.** 15555 John F Kennedy Blvd. Sam Houston Pkwy (Beltway 8), exit John F Kennedy Blvd, just n. Int corridors. **Pets:** Accepted.

🅰🆂🅺 🆂🅰 ❌ 🅻🅼 🛅 💻 ⇌

🅐🅐🅐 ▼▼▼▼ Courtyard by Marriott Houston Brookhollow 🆂🅷 ❀
(713) 688-7711. **$153-$175.** 2504 N Loop W. I-610, exit 13C (TC Jester), just nw. Int corridors. **Pets:** Medium, dogs only. $75 one-time fee/room. Service with restrictions, supervision.

🆂🅰🆅🅴 🆂🅰 ❌ 🛅 💻 🍴 ⇌

▼ Crossland Economy Studios 🆂🅷
(713) 934-7600. **Call for rates.** 5959 Guhn Rd. US 290, exit Fairbanks, just e on eastbound frontage road, then just s. Ext corridors. **Pets:** Other species. $75 one-time fee/pet. Service with restrictions.

❌ 🅻🅼 🛅 💻

🅐🅐🅐 ▼▼▼▼ Crowne Plaza Northwest Hotel 🅻🅷 ❀
(713) 462-9977. **$80-$179.** 12801 Northwest Frwy. Nw on US 290, exit Hollister Rd, 0.7 mi e on south service road. Ext/int corridors. **Pets:** Small, other species. $25 one-time fee/pet. Designated rooms, service with restrictions, crate.

🆂🅰🆅🅴 🆂🅰 ❌ 🛅 💻 🍴 ⇌ ⊠

▼▼▼▼ DoubleTree Guest Suites 🅻🅷
(713) 961-9000. **Call for rates.** 5353 Westheimer Rd. I-610, exit 8C (Westheimer Rd) northbound; exit 9A (San Felipe Rd/Westheimer Rd) southbound, 0.8 mi w. Int corridors. **Pets:** Accepted.

❌ 🛅 💻 🍴 ⇌ ⊠

▼▼▼▼ DoubleTree Houston Downtown 🅻🅷
(713) 759-0202. **$119-$329, 7 day notice.** 400 Dallas St. At Dallas and Bagby sts. Int corridors. **Pets:** Accepted.

🅰🆂🅺 ❌ 🛅 💻 🍴

▼▼▼▼ Drury Inn & Suites-Houston Hobby 🆂🅷
(713) 941-4300. **$158.** 7902 Mosley Rd. I-45, exit 36 (Airport Blvd/College Rd) northbound, just w on Airport Blvd, then just n; exit southbound, follow frontage road to Mosley Rd. Int corridors. **Pets:** Large, other species. Service with restrictions, supervision.

🅰🆂🅺 ❌ 🅻🅼 🛅 💻 ⇌

⚑ ▼▼▼▼ Drury Inn & Suites-Houston Near the Galleria SH
(713) 963-0700. **$196.** 1615 W Loop S. I-610, exit 9 (San Felipe Rd) northbound; exit 9A (San Felipe Rd/Westheimer Rd) southbound, on east service road. Int corridors. **Pets:** Large, other species. Service with restrictions, supervision.

▼▼▼▼ Drury Inn & Suites-Houston West SH
(281) 558-7007. **$151.** 1000 N Hwy 6. I-10, exit 751 (Addicks/SR 6), just n on SR 6. Int corridors. **Pets:** Large, other species. Service with restrictions, supervision.

⚑ ▼▼ Executive Inn & Suites Houston/Hobby Airport M
(713) 645-7666. **$51-$95.** 6711 Telephone Rd. I-610, exit 33, 2.1 mi s; 0.5 mi s of jct Telephone and Bellfort rds. Ext corridors. **Pets:** Accepted.

▼▼ ▼▼ Extended StayAmerica SH
(713) 521-0060. **Call for rates.** 2330 Southwest Frwy. US 59, exit Greenbriar/Shephard; on southbound frontage road. Int corridors. **Pets:** Other species. $75 one-time fee/pet. Service with restrictions.

▼▼ Extended Stay Deluxe SH
(713) 895-0965. **Call for rates.** 5454 Hollister St. US 290, exit Tidwell/Hollister, just s. Int corridors. **Pets:** Other species. $75 one-time fee/pet. Service with restrictions.

▼▼ ▼▼ Extended Stay Deluxe Houston Medical Center/Reliant Park SH
(713) 790-9753. **Call for rates.** 1303 La Concha. I-610, exit 1C (Kirby Dr), just n. Int corridors. **Pets:** Other species. $75 one-time fee/pet. Service with restrictions.

⚑ ▼▼▼▼ Four Seasons Hotel Houston LH
(713) 650-1300. **Call for rates.** 1300 Lamar St. Lamar and Austin sts. Int corridors. **Pets:** Accepted.

▼▼▼ ▼▼ Hilton Americas-Houston LH
(713) 739-8000. **$154-$424.** 1600 Lamar St. At George R Brown Convention Center; between Crawford and Avenida De Las Americas. Int corridors. **Pets:** Accepted.

⚑ ▼▼▼▼ Hilton Houston Post Oak LH ☙
(713) 961-9300. **$139-$289.** 2001 Post Oak Blvd. I-610, exit 8C (Westheimer Rd) northbound, just w; exit 9A (San Felipe Rd/Westheimer Rd) southbound; between San Felipe and Westheimer rds. Int corridors. **Pets:** Service with restrictions.

⚑ ▼▼▼▼ Holiday Inn Astrodome at Reliant Park SH
(713) 790-1900. **$120-$180.** 8111 Kirby Dr. I-610, exit 1C (Kirby Dr), 0.3 mi n. Int corridors. **Pets:** No service, crate.

⚑ ▼▼▼▼ Holiday Inn Express Hotel & Suites-Intercontinental SH
(281) 372-1000. **$89-$159.** 1330 N Sam Houston Pkwy. Off Sam Houston Pkwy (Beltway 8), exit Aldine Westfield eastbound, 0.8 mi e on service road; exit Hardy Toll Rd westbound, U-turn, then 1 mi e on service road. Int corridors. **Pets:** Accepted.

⚑ ▼▼▼▼ Holiday Inn Express Hotel & Suites Memorial Area SH
(713) 688-2800. **$119-$155.** 7625 Katy Frwy. I-10, exit 762 (Silber Rd), on eastbound frontage road. Int corridors. **Pets:** Small. $20 one-time fee/pet. Service with restrictions, supervision.

⚑ ▼▼▼▼ Holiday Inn Houston Hobby Airport SH
(713) 946-8900. **$129-$149.** 8611 Airport Blvd. I-45, exit 36 (Airport Blvd), 1.3 mi w. Int corridors. **Pets:** Medium. $50 one-time fee/room. Service with restrictions, supervision.

▼▼▼▼ Holiday Inn Houston Intercontinental Airport LH
(281) 449-2311. **$99-$209.** 15222 John F Kennedy Blvd. Jct N Sam Houston Pkwy (Beltway 8) E and John F Kennedy Blvd. Int corridors. **Pets:** Accepted.

⚑ ▼▼▼▼ Holiday Inn Select-Greenway Plaza SH
(713) 523-8448. **$109-$299.** 2712 Southwest Frwy. US 59, exit Kirby Dr. Int corridors. **Pets:** Accepted.

▼▼▼ ▼▼ Homestead Studio Suites Hotel-Houston/Galleria Area SH
(713) 960-9660. **$85-$95.** 2300 W Loop S. Loop 610, exit 9A (San Felipe Rd/Westheimer Rd) southbound; exit 9 (San Felipe Rd) northbound, on southbound frontage road. Int corridors. **Pets:** Other species. $75 one-time fee/pet. Service with restrictions.

▼▼▼▼ Homewood Suites by Hilton Intercontinental SH
(281) 219-9100. **Call for rates.** 1340 N Sam Houston Pkwy E. Sam Houston Pkwy (Beltway 8), exit Aldine Westfield eastbound, 0.8 mi e on frontage road; exit Hardy Toll Rd westbound, U-turn, then 1 mi e on frontage road. Int corridors. **Pets:** Accepted.

▼▼▼▼ Homewood Suites by Hilton-Westchase SH
(713) 334-2424. **Call for rates.** 2424 Rogerdale Rd. Sam Houston Pkwy (Beltway 8), exit Westheimer Rd, just w to Rogerdale Rd, then just n. Int corridors. **Pets:** Accepted.

▼▼▼▼ Homewood Suites by Hilton-Willowbrook SH
(281) 955-5200. **Call for rates.** 7655 W FM 1960. Just e of jct SR 249 and FM 1960. Int corridors. **Pets:** Accepted.

▼▼▼ ▼▼ Hotel Icon SH
(713) 224-4266. **Call for rates (no credit cards).** 220 Main St. Between Travis and Main sts; entrance on Congress St. Int corridors. **Pets:** Accepted.

⚑ ▼▼▼▼ Houston Marriott Medical Center Hotel LH
(713) 796-0080. **$274-$296.** 6580 Fannin St. I-610, exit 2 (Main St), 2.5 mi ne to Holcombe St, 0.3 mi e, then just n. Int corridors. **Pets:** Accepted.

▼▼▼▼ La Quinta Inn SH
(713) 680-8282. **$79-$99.** 11130 Northwest Frwy. US 290 W, exit W 34th St, on southeast corner. Int corridors. **Pets:** Other species. Service with restrictions, supervision.

▼▼▼▼ La Quinta Inn & Suites Houston (Bush Intercontinental Airport) SH
(281) 219-2000. **$129-$149.** 15510 John F Kennedy Blvd. Sam Houston Pkwy (Beltway 8), exit John F Kennedy Blvd/Vickery, just n. Int corridors. **Pets:** Other species. Service with restrictions, supervision.

▼▼▼▼ **La Quinta Inn & Suites Houston (Galleria Area)** 🆂🅷
(713) 355-3440. **$149-$169.** 1625 W Loop S. I-610, exit 9 (San Felipe Rd) northbound; exit 9A (San Felipe Rd/Westheimer Rd) southbound, on northbound service road. Int corridors. **Pets:** Other species. Service with restrictions, supervision.
Ⓐ🆂🅚 🆂🄳 ⊠ 🕭🅼 🛗 🖵 🈯

▼▼▼▼ **La Quinta Inn & Suites Houston North Beltway** 🆂🅷
(832) 554-5000. **$95-$115.** 10137 North Frwy. I-45, exit 59 (West Rd), on southbound frontage road. Int corridors. **Pets:** Other species. Service with restrictions, supervision.
Ⓐ🆂🅚 🆂🄳 ⊠ 🛗 🖵 🈯

▼▼▼▼ **La Quinta Inn & Suites Houston (Park 10)** 🆂🅷
(281) 646-9200. **$109-$129.** 15225 Katy Frwy. I-10, exit 748 (Barker Cypress Rd) eastbound, 2.6 mi on eastbound service road; exit 751 (SR 6) westbound, just s to Grisby Rd, then 0.5 mi w. Int corridors. **Pets:** Other species. Service with restrictions, supervision.
Ⓐ🆂🅚 🆂🄳 ⊠ 🛗 🖵 🈯

▼▼▼ **La Quinta Inn & Suites Houston Southwest** 🆂🅷
(713) 784-3838. **Call for rates.** 6790 Southwest Frwy. US 59 (Southwest Frwy), exit Hillcroft St/W Park eastbound; exit Hillcroft St westbound. Int corridors. **Pets:** Other species. Service with restrictions, supervision.
⊠ 🛗 🖵 🈯

▼▼▼ **La Quinta Inn Houston (Cyfair)** 🆂🅷
(281) 469-4018. **$105-$125.** 13290 FM 1960 W. Just w of jct US 290 and FM 1960. Ext corridors. **Pets:** Other species. Service with restrictions, supervision.
Ⓐ🆂🅚 🆂🄳 ⊠ 🛗 🖵 🈯

▼▼ **La Quinta Inn Houston (East)** 🆂🅷
(713) 453-5425. **$89-$109.** 11999 East Frwy. I-10, exit 778A (Federal Rd) eastbound; exit 776B (Holland Ave) westbound, just n. Ext corridors. **Pets:** Other species. Service with restrictions, supervision.
Ⓐ🆂🅚 🆂🄳 ⊠ 🛗 🖵 🈯

▼▼ **La Quinta Inn Houston (I-45 North)** 🆂🅷
(281) 444-7500. **$62-$69.** 17111 North Frwy. I-45, exit 66, on southbound service road, 0.4 mi s of jct FM 1960 and I-45. Ext corridors. **Pets:** Other species. Service with restrictions, supervision.
Ⓐ🆂🅚 🆂🄳 ⊠ 🛗 🖵 🈯

▼▼ **La Quinta Inn Houston (Wilcrest)** 🆂🅷
(713) 932-0808. **$94-$114.** 11113 Katy Frwy. I-10, exit 754 (Kirkwood Dr) westbound; exit 755 (Wilcrest Rd) eastbound, on eastbound service road. Ext corridors. **Pets:** Other species. Service with restrictions, supervision.
Ⓐ🆂🅚 🆂🄳 ⊠ 🛗 🖵 🈯

🅐🅐🅐 ▼▼▼ **Marriott Houston Hobby Airport** 🅻🅷
(713) 943-7979. **$209-$229.** 9100 Gulf Frwy. I-45, exit 36 (Airport Blvd/College Rd) southbound; exit 38 (Monroe) northbound, on southbound frontage road. Int corridors. **Pets:** Small. $50 one-time fee/room. Service with restrictions, supervision.
🆂🄰🅅🄴 🆂🄳 ⊠ 🛗 🖵 🍴 🈯

🅐🅐🅐 ▼▼▼ ▼▼▼ **Omni Houston Hotel** 🅻🅷
(713) 871-8181. **$323-$399.** Four Riverway. I-610, exit 10 (Woodway Dr), 0.3 mi w. Int corridors. **Pets:** Accepted.
🆂🄰🅅🄴 🆂🄳 ⊠ 🛗 🖵 🍴 🈯 🈯

🅐🅐🅐 ▼▼▼ ▼▼▼ **Omni Houston Hotel Westside** 🅻🅷 🐾
(281) 558-8338. **$129-$329.** 13210 Katy Frwy. I-10, exit 753A (Eldridge St), just n. Int corridors. **Pets:** Small. $50 one-time fee/room. Service with restrictions, supervision.
🆂🄰🅅🄴 🆂🄳 ⊠ 🛗 🖵 🍴 🈯 🈯

🅐🅐🅐 ▼▼▼ ▼▼▼ **Renaissance Houston Hotel Greenway Plaza** 🅻🅷
(713) 629-1200. **$242-$262.** 6 Greenway Plaza E. US 59 (Southwest Frwy), exit Buffalo Speedway. Int corridors. **Pets:** Accepted.
🆂🄰🅅🄴 🆂🄳 ⊠ 🛗 🖵 🍴 🈯 🈯

▼▼▼▼ **Residence Inn by Marriott** 🆂🅷
(832) 366-1000. **$275-$295.** 904 Dallas St. At Main St. Int corridors. **Pets:** Accepted.
Ⓐ🆂🅚 🆂🄳 ⊠ 🕭🅼 🛗 🖵 🈯

▼▼▼▼ **Residence Inn by Marriott Houston by the Galleria** 🆂🅷
(713) 840-9757. **$209-$229.** 2500 McCue. I-610, exit 8C (Westheimer Rd) northbound; exit 9A (San Felipe Rd/Westheimer Rd) southbound, just w to McCue, then just n. Ext/int corridors. **Pets:** Accepted.
Ⓐ🆂🅚 🆂🄳 ⊠ 🛗 🖵 🈯

▼▼▼▼ **Residence Inn by Marriott Houston Westchase** 🆂🅷
(713) 974-5454. **$209-$229.** 9965 Westheimer Rd. Sam Houston Pkwy (Beltway 8), exit Westheimer Rd, 0.7 mi e to Elmside Dr, then just s. Int corridors. **Pets:** Accepted.
Ⓐ🆂🅚 🆂🄳 ⊠ 🛗 🖵 🈯 🈯

▼▼▼▼ **Residence Inn by Marriott-Medical Center/Reliant Park** 🆂🅷
(713) 660-7993. **$165-$185.** 7710 Main St. I-610, exit 2 (S Main St/Buffalo Speedway), 1.5 mi n. Ext corridors. **Pets:** Accepted.
Ⓐ🆂🅚 🆂🄳 ⊠ 🛗 🖵 🈯 🈯

▼▼▼▼ **Residence Inn by Marriott-West University** 🆂🅷 🐾
(713) 661-4660. **$219-$230.** 2939 Westpark Dr. US 59, exit Kirby Dr, just s, then just w. Int corridors. **Pets:** Medium, other species. $100 one-time fee/room. Service with restrictions, supervision.
Ⓐ🆂🅚 🆂🄳 ⊠ 🕭🅼 🛗 🖵 🈯 🈯

▼▼▼▼ **Residence Inn by Marriott Willowbrook** 🆂🅷
(832) 237-2002. **$166-$186.** 7311 W Greens Rd. SR 249, exit Greens Rd, just e. Int corridors. **Pets:** Accepted.
Ⓐ🆂🅚 🆂🄳 ⊠ 🛗 🖵 🈯 🈯

▼▼▼▼ **Residence Inn-Houston Clear Lake** 🆂🅷
(281) 486-2424. **$176-$196.** 525 Bay Area Blvd. I-45 S, exit 26 (Bay Area Blvd), 1.2 mi e. Ext/int corridors. **Pets:** Accepted.
Ⓐ🆂🅚 🆂🄳 ⊠ 🛗 🖵 🈯 🈯

🅐🅐🅐 ▼▼▼▼ **The St. Regis Hotel, Houston** 🆂🅷 🐾
(713) 840-7600. **$525-$5000.** 1919 Briar Oaks Ln. I-610, exit 9A (San Felipe Rd/Westheimer Rd), 0.3 mi e. Int corridors. **Pets:** Large, dogs only. Service with restrictions, supervision.
🆂🄰🅅🄴 🆂🄳 ⊠ 🛗 🖵 🍴 🈯 🈯

▼▼▼▼ **Sheraton Houston Brookhollow** 🅻🅷 🐾
(713) 688-0100. **$169-$279.** 3000 N Loop W. I-610, exit 13C (TC Jester Blvd). Int corridors. **Pets:** Service with restrictions.
Ⓐ🆂🅚 🆂🄳 ⊠ 🛗 🖵 🍴 🈯 🈯

🅐🅐🅐 ▼▼▼▼ **Sheraton North Houston Hotel** 🅻🅷
(281) 442-5100. **Call for rates.** 15700 John F Kennedy Blvd. Sam Houston Pkwy (Beltway 8), exit John F Kennedy Blvd, just n. Int corridors. **Pets:** Accepted.
🆂🄰🅅🄴 ⊠ 🕭🅼 🛗 🖵 🍴 🈯

▼▼▼▼ **Sheraton Suites Houston Near The Galleria** 🆂🅷
(713) 586-2444. **Call for rates.** 2400 W Loop S. I-610, exit 9 (San Felipe Rd) northbound; exit 9A (San Felipe Rd/Westheimer Rd) southbound. Int corridors. **Pets:** Accepted.
⊠ 🛗 🖵 🍴 🈯

▼▼▼▼ **Staybridge Suites Houston-Near The Galleria** 🆂🅷
(713) 355-8888. **$190-$195.** 5190 Hidalgo St. I-610, exit 9A (San Felipe Rd/Westheimer Rd) southbound; exit 8C (Westheimer Rd) northbound, 0.4 mi w to Sage Rd, then just s. Int corridors. **Pets:** Accepted.
Ⓐ🆂🅚 🆂🄳 ⊠ 🛗 🖵 🈯 🈯

▼▼ **TownePlace Suites by Marriott-Central** 🆂🅷
(713) 690-4035. **$111-$131.** 12820 Northwest Frwy (US 290). US 290, exit Bingle/43rd St eastbound; exit Bingle/Pinemont/43rd St westbound, on westbound feeder. Int corridors. **Pets:** Accepted.
Ⓐ🆂🅚 🆂🄳 ⊠ 🕭🅼 🛗 🖵 🈯

▼▼ TownePlace Suites by Marriott-West 🆂🅷
(281) 646-0058. **$111-$131.** 15155 Katy Frwy. I-10, exit 751, just s on SR 6 to Grisby Rd, then w. Int corridors. **Pets:** Accepted.
🅰🆂🅺 🆂🔌 ✕ 🔲 🛏 ⌇

◈◈◇ ▼▼▼▼ The Westin Galleria, Houston 🅻🅷
(713) 960-8100. **$170-$379.** 5060 W Alabama St. I-610, exit 8C (Westheimer Rd) northbound; exit 9A (San Felipe Rd/Westheimer Rd) southbound, 0.5 mi w on Westheimer Rd to Sage, just s, then just e. Int corridors. **Pets:** Accepted.
🆂🅰🆅🅴 ✕ ♿ 🔲 🍽 ⌇

◈◈◇ ▼▼▼▼ The Westin Oaks, Houston 🅻🅷
(713) 960-8100. **Call for rates.** 5011 Westheimer Rd. I-610, exit 8C (Westheimer Rd) northbound; exit 9A (San Felipe Rd/Westheimer Rd) southbound, just w. Int corridors. **Pets:** Accepted.
🆂🅰🆅🅴 ✕ 🔲 🍽 ⌇

SEABROOK

◈◈◇ ▼▼▼ La Quinta Inn & Suites #618 🆂🅷
(281) 326-7300. **Call for rates.** 3636 NASA Pkwy. I-45, exit 25 (NASA Rd One), 6 mi e; SR 146, 2 mi w. Int corridors. **Pets:** Other species. Service with restrictions, supervision.
🆂🅰🆅🅴 ✕ ♿ 🔲 ⌇

STAFFORD

▼▼ La Quinta Inn Houston (Stafford/Sugarland) 🆂🅷
(281) 240-2300. **$99-$119.** 12727 Southwest Frwy. US 59 eastbound service road, exit Corporate Dr southbound; exit Airport Blvd/Kirkwood Rd northbound. Int corridors. **Pets:** Other species. Service with restrictions, supervision.
🅰🆂🅺 🆂🔌 ✕ ♿ 🔲 ⌇

▼▼▼ Residence Inn by Marriott Houston/Sugar Land 🆂🅷
(281) 277-0770. **$165-$185.** 12703 Southwest Frwy. US 59, exit Corporate Dr southbound; exit Airport Blvd/Kirkwood Rd northbound; on northbound service road. Int corridors. **Pets:** Accepted.
🅰🆂🅺 🆂🔌 ✕ ♿ 🔲 ⌇ 🔲

SUGAR LAND

▼▼▼ Drury Inn & Suites-Houston/Sugar Land 🆂🅷
(281) 277-9700. **$151.** 13770 Southwest Frwy. Sw on US 59, exit Dairy Ashford/Sugar Creek southbound; exit Dairy Ashford/Sugar Creek northbound, left under US 59. Int corridors. **Pets:** Large, other species. Service with restrictions, supervision.
🅰🆂🅺 ✕ ♿ 🔲 ⌇

THE WOODLANDS

▼▼▼ Drury Inn & Suites-Houston/The Woodlands 🆂🅷
(281) 362-7222. **$151.** 28099 I-45 N. I-45, exit 76 southbound; exit 77 northbound, on west service road. Int corridors. **Pets:** Large, other species. Service with restrictions, supervision.
🅰🆂🅺 ✕ ♿ ♿ 🔲 ⌇

◈◈◇ ▼▼▼▼ Holiday Inn Express Hotel & Suites 🆂🅷
(281) 681-8088. **$109.** 24888 I-45 N. I-45, exit 73 (Rayford/Sawdust Rd), on northbound access road. Int corridors. **Pets:** Accepted.
🆂🅰🆅🅴 🆂🔌 ✕ ♿ 🔲 ⌇ ✕

▼▼▼ Residence Inn by Marriott 🆂🅷
(281) 292-3252. **$177-$197.** 1040 Lake Front Cir. I-45, exit 78 southbound; exit 79 (SR 242) northbound, 0.8 mi s of jct I-45 and Research Forest Dr, just w. Int corridors. **Pets:** Accepted.
🅰🆂🅺 🆂🔌 ✕ ♿ 🔲 ⌇ ✕

TOMBALL

◈◈◇ ▼▼ Holiday Inn Express 🆂🅷
(281) 351-4114. **$84-$115.** 1437 Keefer St. SR 249 and FM 2920; northeast corner. Ext corridors. **Pets:** Accepted.
🆂🅰🆅🅴 🆂🔌 ✕ ♿ 🔲 ⌇

WEBSTER

▼▼▼▼ Extended Stay Deluxe Houston NASA-Bay Area Blvd 🆂🅷
(281) 338-7711. **$90-$100.** 720 W Bay Area Blvd. I-45, exit 26 (Bay Area Blvd), just e. Int corridors. **Pets:** Other species. $75 one-time fee/pet. Service with restrictions.
🅰🆂🅺 🆂🔌 ✕ ♿ 🔲 ⌇

▼▼▼ La Quinta Inn & Suites Webster 🆂🅷
(281) 554-5290. **$129-$149.** 520 W Bay Area Blvd. I-45, exit 26 (Bay Area Blvd), just e. Int corridors. **Pets:** Other species. Service with restrictions, supervision.
🅰🆂🅺 🆂🔌 ✕ ♿ 🔲 ⌇

WINNIE

◈◈◇ ▼▼ Holiday Inn Express 🆂🅷
(409) 296-2866. **$59-$149.** 14932 FM 1663. I-10, exit 829, just n. Ext corridors. **Pets:** Accepted.
🆂🅰🆅🅴 🆂🔌 ✕ ♿ 🔲 ⌇

◈◈◇ ▼▼ Quality Inn 🆂🅷
(409) 296-9292. **$60-$75.** 46318 I-10 E. I-10, exit 829, on eastbound frontage road. Ext corridors. **Pets:** $25 deposit/pet, $10 daily fee/pet. Service with restrictions, supervision.
🆂🅰🆅🅴 🆂🔌 ✕ ♿ 🔲 ⌇

◈◈◇ ▼▼ Winnie Inn & Suites 🆂🅷
(409) 296-2947. **$50-$90.** 205 Spur 5, Hwy 124. I-10, exit 829, just s. Ext corridors. **Pets:** Accepted.
🆂🅰🆅🅴 🆂🔌 ✕ ♿ 🔲 ⌇

END METROPOLITAN AREA

HUNTSVILLE

▼▼▼ Holiday Inn Express (Sam Houston) 🆂🅷
(936) 293-1900. **$99-$109, 10 day notice.** 201 W Hill Park Cir. I-45, exit 116, just w on US 190. Ext corridors. **Pets:** Accepted.
🅰🆂🅺 🆂🔌 ✕ ♿ ♿ 🔲 ⌇

▼▼▼ La Quinta Inn Huntsville 🆂🅷
(936) 295-6454. **$89-$109.** 124 I-45 N. I-45, exit 116. Ext corridors. **Pets:** Other species. Service with restrictions, supervision.
🅰🆂🅺 🆂🔌 ✕ ♿ 🔲 ⌇

JACKSONVILLE

◈◈◇ ▼▼▼▼ Best Western Executive Inn 🆂🅷
(903) 586-0007. **$72-$84, 4 day notice.** 1659 S Jackson St. 1.7 mi s of jct US 69 and 79, on US 69. Int corridors. **Pets:** Accepted.
🆂🅰🆅🅴 🆂🔌 ✕ ♿ 🔲 ⌇

▼▼▼ Holiday Inn Express 🆂🅷
(903) 589-8500. **Call for rates.** 1848 S Jackson St. On US 69, 2 mi s of jct US 69 and 79. Int corridors. **Pets:** Accepted.
✕ ♿ 🔲 ⌇

JUNCTION

▼▼▼▼ Best Western Dos Rios SH
(325) 446-3700. **$80-$100.** 244 Dos Rios Dr. I-10, exit 456, just s. Ext corridors. **Pets:** Accepted.
A$K S✺ ✕ ⊟ ⬚ 🏊

▼▼ Days Inn SH
(325) 446-3730. **Call for rates.** 111 S Martinez St. I-10, exit 457, 0.3 mi s. Ext corridors. **Pets:** Accepted.
✕ ⊟ ⬚ 🏊

▼ The Hills Motel M
(325) 446-2567. **$40-$48.** 1520 Main St. I-10, exit 456, 1.3 mi s on US 377. Ext corridors. **Pets:** Accepted.
A$K S✺ ✕ ⊟ 🏊

▼▼ Rodeway Inn SH
(325) 446-4588. **$55-$69.** 2343 N Main St. I-10, exit 456, just s on US 377. Ext corridors. **Pets:** Accepted.
A$K S✺ ✕ ⊟ ⬚ 🏊

AAA ▼ Sun Valley Motel M
(325) 446-2505. **$30-$39, 3 day notice.** 1611 Main St. I-10, exit 456 eastbound, 1 mi s on US 377; exit 460 westbound, 3 mi w on Loop 481 to jct US 377, then just n. Ext corridors. **Pets:** Small, other species. $50 one-time fee/pet. Service with restrictions, crate.
SAVE S✺ ✕ ⊟ 🏊

KERRVILLE

AAA ▼▼ Americas Best Value Inn M
(830) 896-8200. **$60-$80.** 1804 Sidney Baker St. I-10, exit 508 (SR 16), 0.5 mi s on SR 16. Ext corridors. **Pets:** Small, dogs only. $10 one-time fee/room. Service with restrictions, supervision.
SAVE S✺ ✕ ⊟ 🏊

AAA ▼▼▼ Best Western Sunday House Inn SH
(830) 896-1313. **$80-$110.** 2124 Sidney Baker St. I-10, exit 508 (SR 16), just s. Ext corridors. **Pets:** Medium. $10 daily fee/pet. Designated rooms, service with restrictions, supervision.
SAVE S✺ ✕ ⬚ ⑪ 🏊

▼▼ Days Inn of Kerrville M
(830) 896-1000. **Call for rates.** 2000 Sidney Baker St. I-10, exit 508 (SR 16), 0.5 mi s. Ext/int corridors. **Pets:** Accepted.
✕ ⊟ ⬚ 🏊

▼▼ Econo Lodge of Kerrville SH
(830) 896-1711. **$52-$84.** 2105 Sidney Baker St. I-10, exit 508 (SR 16), just s. Int corridors. **Pets:** Accepted.
A$K S✺ ✕ ⊟ ⬚ 🏊

AAA ▼▼▼ Y. O. Ranch Resort Hotel & Conference Center LH
(830) 257-4440. **$109-$119.** 2033 Sidney Baker St. I-10, exit 508 (SR 16), 0.3 mi s. Ext/int corridors. **Pets:** Large, other species. Service with restrictions, supervision.
SAVE S✺ ✕ ⊟ ⬚ ⑪ 🏊 ✕

KILGORE

AAA ▼▼▼ Best Western Inn of Kilgore SH
(903) 986-1195. **$79-$125.** 1411 N Hwy 259. I-20, exit 589, 3.9 mi s. Ext corridors. **Pets:** Accepted.
SAVE S✺ ✕ ⊟ ⬚ 🏊

KILLEEN

AAA ▼▼▼ Holiday Inn Express SH
(254) 554-2727. **$65-$99.** 1602 E Central Texas Expwy. US 190, exit Trimmier Rd. Ext corridors. **Pets:** Accepted.
SAVE ✕ ⊟ ⬚

▼▼ ▼▼ La Quinta Inn Killeen SH
(254) 526-8331. **$109-$129.** 1112 S Fort Hood St. US 190, exit Fort Hood St, on westbound access road. Ext corridors. **Pets:** Other species. Service with restrictions, supervision.
A$K S✺ ✕ ⊟ ⬚ 🏊

KINGSLAND

▼▼ Rio Vista Resort CO
(325) 388-6331. **Call for rates.** 234 Rio Vista Dr. Colorado River Bridge, 0.5 mi nw on FM 1431, 0.5 mi s on Reynolds St. Ext corridors. **Pets:** Accepted.
✕ ⊟ ⬚ 🏊 ✕

KINGSVILLE

AAA ▼▼ Quality Inn SH
(361) 592-5251. **$69-$89.** 221 S Hwy 77 Bypass. On US 77, just s of jct SR 141. Ext corridors. **Pets:** Very small, dogs only. $50 deposit/pet. Designated rooms, service with restrictions, supervision.
SAVE S✺ ✕ ⊟ ⬚ 🏊

AAA ▼▼▼ Rodeway Inn SH
(361) 595-5753. **$75.** 3430 Hwy 77. 4.5 mi s on US 77. Ext corridors. **Pets:** Accepted.
SAVE S✺ ✕ ⊟ ⬚ ⑪ 🏊

AAA ▼▼▼ Super 8 Motel M
(361) 592-6471. **$65-$90.** 105 S 77 Bypass. 0.8 mi e on US 77. Ext corridors. **Pets:** Large. $25 one-time fee/pet. No service, supervision.
SAVE S✺ ✕ ⊟ ⬚ 🏊

LA GRANGE

▼▼▼ Best Western La Grange Inn and Suites SH
(979) 968-6800. **Call for rates.** 600 E State Hwy 71 Bypass. Jct US 77 and SR 71, just e on N Frontage Rd. Int corridors. **Pets:** Accepted.
✕ ⊟ ⬚ 🏊

LAJITAS

▼▼ ▼▼ Lajitas The Ultimate Hideout SH
(432) 424-5000. **Call for rates.** 1 Main St. Center. Ext/int corridors. **Pets:** $50 one-time fee/pet. Designated rooms, service with restrictions, crate.
✕ ⊟ ⬚ ⑪ 🏊 ✕

LAKE JACKSON

▼▼▼▼ Cherotel Brazosport Hotel & Conference Center SH
(979) 297-1161. **Call for rates.** 925 Hwy 332. On SR 228/332, just w of jct Business Rt SR 288. Int corridors. **Pets:** Accepted.
✕ ⊟ ⬚ ⑪ 🏊

LAKE WORTH

▼▼▼ Holiday Inn Express Hotel & Suites SH
(817) 624-0303. **Call for rates.** 3541 NW Loop 820. I-820, exit 10A eastbound; exit 10B westbound. Int corridors. **Pets:** Accepted.
✕ ⍟ ⊟ ⬚ 🏊

LAMESA

AAA ▼▼ Shiloh Inn M
(806) 872-6721. **$63-$79, 3 day notice.** 1707 Lubbock Hwy. Jct US 87 and 180, 1 mi n. Ext corridors. **Pets:** Other species. $10 daily fee/pet. Service with restrictions, supervision.
SAVE S✺ ✕ ⊟ ⬚ ⑪ 🏊

LAREDO

Days Inn & Suites SH
(956) 724-8221. **Call for rates.** 7060 N San Bernardo Ave. I-35, exit 4 (San Bernardo Ave), just s on southbound access road. Ext/int corridors. **Pets:** Medium. $10 daily fee/pet. Designated rooms, service with restrictions, supervision.

Extended StayAmerica CO
(956) 724-1920. **Call for rates.** 106 W Village. I-35, exit 3B (Mann Rd), just n on northbound access road to W Village, then just e. Int corridors. **Pets:** Other species. $75 one-time fee/pet. Service with restrictions.

La Posada Hotel & Suites SH
(956) 722-1701. **Call for rates.** 1000 Zaragoza St. I-35, exit downtown; just e of International Bridge. Ext/int corridors. **Pets:** Accepted.

La Quinta Inn Laredo (I-35) SH
(956) 722-0511. **$115-$135.** 3610 Santa Ursula Ave. I-35, exit 2 (US 59). Ext corridors. **Pets:** Other species. Service with restrictions, supervision.

Motel 6 South-142 M
(956) 725-8187. **$55-$64.** 5310 San Bernardo Ave. I-35, exit 3B (Mann Rd). Ext corridors. **Pets:** Other species. Service with restrictions, supervision.

Red Roof Inn Laredo M
(956) 712-0733. **Call for rates.** 1006 W Calton Rd. I-35, exit 3A, 0.3 mi w. Ext/int corridors. **Pets:** Accepted.

SpringHill Suites SH
(956) 717-0800. **$79-$159.** 5940 San Bernardo Ave. From airport; n onto Bob Bullock (Loop 20), left on E Del Mar Blvd past IH 35, left on San Bernardo (IH 35 Frontage Rd), then s on San Bernardo 2 blks, just right. **Pets:** Other species. $75 one-time fee/room. Service with restrictions, supervision.

Staybridge Suites-Laredo SH
(956) 722-0444. **$120-$130.** 7010 Bob Bullock Loop. US 83, exit onto Loop 20 (Bob Bullock Loop); hotel is on west side. Int corridors. **Pets:** Medium, other species. $150 one-time fee/room. Service with restrictions, crate.

LITTLEFIELD

Crescent Park Motel & Suites M
(806) 385-4464. **$45-$70.** 2021 Hall Ave. Jct US 84, just n on SR 385. Ext corridors. **Pets:** Accepted.

LLANO

Best Western Llano SH
(325) 247-4101. **$70-$100.** 901 W Young St. 1 mi w on SR 71 and 29. Ext corridors. **Pets:** Accepted.

Hill Country Suites SH
(325) 247-1141. **Call for rates.** 609 Bessemer Ave. Jct SR 29 and 16/71, 2 blks s. Ext corridors. **Pets:** Accepted.

LONGVIEW

Baymont Inn SH
(903) 757-3663. **$69-$77.** 502 S Access Rd. I-20, exit 595. Ext corridors. **Pets:** Accepted.

Motel 6–158 M
(903) 758-5256. **$45-$58.** 110 S Access Rd. I-20, exit 595A. Ext corridors. **Pets:** Other species. Service with restrictions, supervision.

LUBBOCK

Best Western Lubbock Windsor Inn SH
(806) 762-8400. **Call for rates.** 5410 I-27. 3.5 mi s on I-27, exit 1B southbound; U-turn at exit 1A (50th St) northbound. Int corridors. **Pets:** Large, dogs only. $10 daily fee/pet. Service with restrictions, supervision.

Extended StayAmerica Lubbock Southwest SH
(806) 785-9881. **$67-$75.** 4802 S Loop 289. S Loop 289, exit Slide Rd, on north access road. Int corridors. **Pets:** Other species. $75 one-time fee/pet. Service with restrictions.

La Quinta Inn and Suites SH
(806) 749-1600. **$109-$129.** 5006 Auburn St. Jct Loop 289 W and Quaker Ave, 1.5 mi w on N Frontage Rd. Int corridors. **Pets:** Other species. Service with restrictions, supervision.

La Quinta Inn Lubbock SH
(806) 763-9441. **$95-$115.** 601 Ave Q. 0.8 mi nw on US 84 (Ave Q). Ext corridors. **Pets:** Other species. Service with restrictions, supervision.

La Quinta Inn Lubbock (West/Medical Center) SH
(806) 792-0065. **$99-$119.** 4115 Brownfield Hwy. 3.3 mi sw; 2.5 mi ne of Loop 289 on US 62 and 82. Int corridors. **Pets:** Other species. Service with restrictions, supervision.

Lubbock Super 8 Motel M
(806) 762-8726. **$40-$100, 3 day notice.** 501 Ave Q. 1 mi nw on US 84. Ext corridors. **Pets:** Accepted.

Radisson Hotel SH
(806) 747-0171. **$99-$157.** 505 Ave Q. I-27, exit 4, 0.9 mi w to US 84 (Ave Q), then just s. Int corridors. **Pets:** Very small, dogs only. $25 deposit/pet. No service, supervision.

Residence Inn by Marriott SH
(806) 745-1963. **$143-$163.** 2551 S Loop 289. Loop 289, exit University, 3 mi s, on south frontage road. Ext corridors. **Pets:** Small, other species. $100 one-time fee/room. Service with restrictions.

Staybridge Suites SH
(806) 765-8900. **$119-$129.** 2515 19th St. Jct University Ave and 19th St; on southwest corner. Int corridors. **Pets:** Accepted.

TownePlace Suites by Marriott SH
(806) 799-6226. **$111-$131.** 5310 W Loop 289. W Loop 289, exit US 62/82 (Brownfield Rd), 0.5 mi s on west frontage road. Int corridors. **Pets:** Accepted.

LUFKIN

Best Western Crown Colony Inn & Suites 🆂🅷
(936) 634-3481. **$109-$139.** 3211 S 1st St. 2 mi s of Jct US 59 and Loop 287. Int corridors. **Pets:** Small. $25 one-time fee/pet. No service, crate.
🆂🅰🆅🅴 🆂🄳 ❌ 🔋 💻 🌊

La Quinta Inn Lufkin 🆂🅷
(936) 634-3351. **$104-$124.** 2119 S 1st St. US 59, exit Carriageway northbound, 0.3 mi s of jct S Loop 287 and US 59 business route. Ext corridors. **Pets:** Other species. Service with restrictions, supervision.
🄰🆂🅺 🆂🄳 ❌ 🔋 💻 🌊

MADISONVILLE

Best Western Executive Inn & Suites 🆂🅷
(936) 349-1700. **Call for rates.** 3307 E Main St. I-45, exit 142, just e. Int corridors. **Pets:** Accepted.
❌ 🅶🅼 🔋 💻 🌊

Western Lodge Ⓜ
(936) 348-7654. **Call for rates.** 2007 E Main St. I-45, exit 142, 0.3 mi w. Ext corridors. **Pets:** Very small. $7 daily fee/pet. Service with restrictions, supervision.
🆂🅰🆅🅴 ❌ 🔋 🌊

MANSFIELD

Comfort Inn 🆂🅷
(817) 453-8848. **$79-$139.** 175 N Hwy 287. US 287 S, exit E Broad St. Int corridors. **Pets:** Accepted.
🄰🆂🅺 🆂🄳 ❌ 🅶🅼 🔋 💻 🌊

MARBLE FALLS

Best Western Marble Falls Inn 🆂🅷
(830) 693-5122. **$69-$139.** 1403 Hwy 281 N. 0.4 mi n of jct SR 281 and FM 1431. Ext/int corridors. **Pets:** Medium. $10 daily fee/pet. Designated rooms, service with restrictions, supervision.
🆂🅰🆅🅴 🆂🄳 ❌ 🔋 💻 🌊

MARSHALL

Best Western Executive Inn 🆂🅷
(903) 935-0707. **Call for rates.** 5201 E End Blvd S. I-20, exit 617, 0.4 mi n on US 59. Ext corridors. **Pets:** Small, dogs only. $15 daily fee/pet. No service, supervision.
🆂🅰🆅🅴 ❌ 🔋 💻 🌊

La Quinta Inn & East Texas Conference Center 🆂🅷
(903) 927-0009. **$89-$109.** 5301 E End Blvd S. I-20, exit 617, just n on US 59. Int corridors. **Pets:** Other species. Service with restrictions, supervision.
🆂🅰🆅🅴 🆂🄳 ❌ 🔋 💻 🌊

Motel 6 Marshall #422 Ⓜ
(903) 935-4393. **$43-$56.** 300 I-20 E. I-20, exit 617, just e on access road. Ext corridors. **Pets:** Other species. Service with restrictions, supervision.
🆂🄳 ❌ 🌊

Quality Inn Marshall 🆂🅷
(903) 935-7923. **$77-$85.** 4911 E End Blvd S. I-20, exit 617, 0.5 mi n on US 59. Ext corridors. **Pets:** Small. $30 one-time fee/room. Service with restrictions, supervision.
🆂🅰🆅🅴 🆂🄳 ❌ 🔋 💻 🌊

MCALLEN

Drury Inn-McAllen 🆂🅷
(956) 687-5100. **$129.** 612 W Expwy 83. US 83, exit 2nd St, on northwest frontage road. Int corridors. **Pets:** Large, other species. Service with restrictions, supervision.
🄰🆂🅺 ❌ 🔋 💻 🌊

Drury Suites-McAllen 🆂🅷
(956) 682-3222. **$217.** 228 W Expwy 83. At US 83 and 6th St. Int corridors. **Pets:** Large, other species. Service with restrictions, supervision.
🄰🆂🅺 ❌ 🔋 💻 🌊

Four Points Hotel by Sheraton 🆂🅷
(956) 984-7900. **Call for rates.** 2721 S 10th St. 2.5 mi s on SR 336 (S 10th St). Int corridors. **Pets:** Accepted.
❌ 🔋 💻 🍽 🌊 ❌

Hampton Inn-McAllen 🆂🅷
(956) 682-4900. **$98-$115.** 300 W Expwy 83. US 83, exit 2nd St, on northwest frontage road. Int corridors. **Pets:** Small. Service with restrictions, crate.
🄰🆂🅺 ❌ 🔋 💻 🌊

La Quinta Inn McAllen 🆂🅷
(956) 687-1101. **$99-$119.** 1100 S 10th St. 1.5 mi s on SR 336 (S 10th St); just n of jct US 83. Ext corridors. **Pets:** Other species. Service with restrictions, supervision.
🄰🆂🅺 🆂🄳 ❌ 🅶🅼 🔋 💻 🌊

Motel 6 McAllen #212 Ⓜ
(956) 687-3700. **$45-$58.** 700 W Expwy 83. US 83, exit 2nd St, on northwest frontage road. Ext corridors. **Pets:** Other species. Service with restrictions, supervision.
🆂🄳 ❌ 🌊

Posada Ana Inn 🆂🅷
(956) 631-6700. **$77.** 620 W Expwy 83. US 83, exit 2nd St, on northwest frontage road. Int corridors. **Pets:** Large, other species. Service with restrictions, supervision.
🄰🆂🅺 ❌ 💻

Residence Inn by Marriott 🆂🅷
(956) 994-8626. **$121-$141.** 220 W Expwy 83. US 83, exit 2nd St, just w, then just n on 2nd St. Int corridors. **Pets:** Accepted.
🄰🆂🅺 🆂🄳 ❌ 🔋 💻 🌊 ❌

Super 8 🆂🅷
(956) 688-6666. **$55-$89.** 6420 S 23rd St. SR 83, exit 23rd St, 0.8 mi s. Ext corridors. **Pets:** Accepted.
❌ 🔋 💻 🌊

Super 8 Motel 🆂🅷
(956) 682-1190. **Call for rates.** 1420 E Jackson Ave. US 83, exit Jackson Ave/Sam Houston St, just s. Int corridors. **Pets:** Accepted.
❌ 🔋 🌊

MEMPHIS

Travelodge Ⓜ
(806) 259-3583. **$49-$99.** 1600 Boykin Dr. On US 287, 1.3 mi n of jct SR 256. Ext corridors. **Pets:** Small. $10 daily fee/pet. No service, supervision.
🆂🅰🆅🅴 🆂🄳 ❌ 🔋 💻 🍽 🌊

MIDLAND

Americas Best Value Inn 🆂🅷
(432) 694-7774. **$79.** 3904 W Wall St. I-20, exit 134, 1 mi n on Midkiff Rd, 0.3 mi w on I-20 business route. Ext/int corridors. **Pets:** Accepted.
🆂🅰🆅🅴 🆂🄳 ❌ 🔋 💻 🌊 ❌

♨ ❖❖❖ Clarion Inn **SH**
(432) 697-3181. **$99.** 4300 W Wall St. I-20, exit 134 (Midkiff Rd), 1 mi n to I-20 business loop, then 0.7 mi w. Ext/int corridors. **Pets:** Very small, dogs only. $30 one-time fee/pet. Designated rooms, service with restrictions, supervision.
SAVE Sᴅ ✕ 🗄 🖥 ⁇ 🍴 ⥲ ✕

❖❖❖❖ Hilton Midland Plaza **LH** ❖
(432) 683-6131. **Call for rates.** 117 W Wall St. Jct Wall and Loraine sts; downtown. Int corridors. **Pets:** Other species. $25 one-time fee/room. Designated rooms, service with restrictions, crate.
✕ ᵹᴹ 🗄 🖥 🍴 ⥲ ✕

❖❖❖❖ La Quinta Inn Midland **SH**
(432) 697-9900. **$95-$115.** 4130 W Wall St. I-20, exit 131, 0.9 mi n on SR 250 Loop to exit 1A; 1.2 mi e on I-20 business route. Ext corridors. **Pets:** Other species. Service with restrictions, supervision.
ASK Sᴅ ✕ 🗄 🖥 ⥲

❖❖ Plaza Inn **SH**
(432) 686-8733. **Call for rates.** 4108 N Big Spring St. I-20, exit 144, 6.1 mi on SR 250 Loop to SR 349 (Big Spring St), then just s on SR 349. Ext corridors. **Pets:** Accepted.
✕ 🗄 🖥 ⥲

MINERAL WELLS

♨ ❖❖❖❖ Best Western Clubhouse Inn &
Suites **SH** ❖
(940) 325-2270. **$96-$160.** 4410 Hwy 180 E. Jct US 180 and SR 1195; in East Mineral Wells. Int corridors. **Pets:** Other species. $10 one-time fee/pet. Service with restrictions, supervision.
SAVE Sᴅ ✕ ᵹᴹ 🗄 🖥 ⥲

MISSION

❖❖❖❖ El Rocio Retreat **BB**
(956) 584-7432. **$75-$250.** 2519 S Inspiration Rd. Jct US 83 at Inspiration Rd, 2 mi s. Ext/int corridors. **Pets:** Accepted.
ASK Sᴅ ✕

❖❖❖ Hawthorn Suites **SH**
(956) 519-9696. **$111-$118.** 3700 Plantation Grove Blvd. US 83, exit Sharyland Rd, 2.1 mi s to Plantation Grove Blvd. Ext corridors. **Pets:** Accepted.
ASK Sᴅ ✕ 🖥 ⥲

MONAHANS

❖❖ Americas Best Value Colonial Inn **M**
(432) 943-4345. **$72-$99.** 702 W I-20. I-20, exit 80, just s. Ext/int corridors. **Pets:** Accepted.
ASK Sᴅ ✕ 🗄 🖥 ⥲

❖❖❖ Best Western Monahans Inn and Suites **SH**
(432) 943-3360. **$110-$150.** 2101 S Betty St. I-20, exit 80, just s. Int corridors. **Pets:** Accepted.
ASK Sᴅ ✕ 🗄 🖥 ⥲

MOUNT PLEASANT

♨ ❖❖❖ Comfort Inn **SH**
(903) 577-7553. **$75-$100.** 2515 W Ferguson Rd. I-30, exit 160. Ext corridors. **Pets:** Other species. $15 one-time fee/room. Service with restrictions, supervision.
SAVE Sᴅ ✕ 🗄 🖥 ⥲

❖❖❖ Holiday Inn Express Hotel & Suites **SH**
(903) 577-3800. **Call for rates.** 2306 Greenhill Rd. I-30, exit 162, just n. Int corridors. **Pets:** Accepted.
✕ ᵹᴹ 🗄 🖥 ⥲

MOUNT VERNON

♨ ❖❖❖ Super 8 Motel of Mount Vernon **SH**
(903) 588-2882. **Call for rates.** 401 W I-30. I-30, exit 146 (SR 37). Ext corridors. **Pets:** Small. $8 daily fee/pet. Service with restrictions, supervision.
SAVE ✕ 🗄 🖥

NACOGDOCHES

♨ ❖❖❖ Best Western Northpark Inn **SH**
(936) 560-1906. **Call for rates.** 4809 NW Stallings Dr. Jct US 59 N and Loop 224, exit Westward Dr. Ext corridors. **Pets:** Accepted.
✕ 🗄 🖥 ⥲

❖❖ La Quinta Inn Nacogdoches **SH**
(936) 560-5453. **Call for rates.** 3215 South St. US 59, jct Loop 224 and US 59 business route, s of town. Ext corridors. **Pets:** Other species. Service with restrictions, supervision.
✕ 🗄 🖥 ⥲

NEW BOSTON

♨ ❖❖❖ Best Western Inn of New Boston **SH**
(903) 628-6999. **Call for rates.** 1024 N Center. I-30, exit 201, on westbound access road. Ext corridors. **Pets:** Small, other species. $10 daily fee/pet. Supervision.
SAVE ✕ 🗄 🖥 ⥲

NORTH RICHLAND HILLS

❖❖ Studio 6 #6034 **SH**
(817) 788-6000. **$61-$75.** 7450 NE Loop 820. I-820, exit 21 (Holiday Ln), 0.4 mi e on south access road. Ext corridors. **Pets:** Other species. Service with restrictions, supervision.
Sᴅ ✕ 🗄 🖥

ODEM

♨ ❖❖ Days Inn-Odem **M**
(361) 368-2166. **Call for rates.** 1505 Voss Ave (US 77). US 77, 1 mi s of jct 631. Ext corridors. **Pets:** Accepted.
SAVE ✕ 🗄 🖥 ⥲

ODESSA

❖❖ Best Western Garden Oasis **SH**
(432) 337-3006. **Call for rates (no credit cards).** 110 W I-20. Jct I-20 and US 385, exit 116, just w. Ext/int corridors. **Pets:** Other species. Designated rooms, service with restrictions, supervision.
✕ 🗄 🖥 🍴 ⥲ ✕

♨ ❖❖❖ Days Inn **SH**
(432) 335-8000. **$60-$99.** 3075 E Business Loop 20. I-20, exit 121, 0.7 mi n on Loop 338, then 0.5 mi w. Int corridors. **Pets:** Accepted.
SAVE Sᴅ ✕ 🗄 ⥲

❖❖ La Quinta Inn Odessa **SH**
(432) 333-2820. **$99-$119.** 5001 E Business Loop I-20. I-20, exit 121, 0.8 mi n on Loop 338, then just w. Ext corridors. **Pets:** Other species. Service with restrictions, supervision.
ASK Sᴅ ✕ 🗄 🖥 ⥲

❖❖ McM Grande Hotel **SH**
(432) 362-2311. **$90-$170.** 6201 E Business I-20. I-20, exit 121, 0.8 mi n on Loop 338, then 1 mi e. Ext/int corridors. **Pets:** Accepted.
ASK ✕ 🗄 🖥 🍴 ⥲ ✕

❖ Motel 6 Odessa #439 **M**
(432) 333-4025. **$45-$58.** 200 E I-20 Service Rd. I-20, exit 116, on eastbound frontage road. Ext corridors. **Pets:** Other species. Service with restrictions, supervision.
Sᴅ ✕ ⥲

▼▼ Quality Inn & Suites 🆂🄷
(432) 333-3931. **Call for rates.** 3001 E Business I-20. I-20, exit 121, 0.7 mi n on Loop 338, then 0.5 mi w. Ext/int corridors. **Pets:** Accepted.
⊠ 🛢 💻 ➰

OZONA

🔺 ▼▼▼ Travelodge Ⓜ
(325) 392-2656. **$65-$70.** 8 11th St. I-10, exit 368 westbound, 2 mi w; exit 365 eastbound to Loop 466, 1 mi e. Ext corridors. **Pets:** Other species. $10 daily fee/pet. Service with restrictions, supervision.
🆂🅰🆅🄴 🔊 ⊠ 🛢 💻 ➰

PALESTINE

🔺 ▼▼▼ Best Western Palestine Inn 🆂🄷
(903) 723-4655. **$79-$109.** 1601 W Palestine Ave. Jct US 287/SR 19, 0.7 mi sw on US 79. Ext corridors. **Pets:** Accepted.
🆂🅰🆅🄴 🔊 ⊠ 🛢 💻 🍴 ➰

PARIS

🔺 ▼▼▼ Best Western Inn of Paris 🆂🄷
(903) 785-5566. **$64-$74.** 3755 NE Loop 286. Jct US 82 and E Loop 286, just n. Ext corridors. **Pets:** Medium. $15 daily fee/pet. Designated rooms, service with restrictions.
🆂🅰🆅🄴 🔊 ⊠ 🛢 💻 ➰

🔺 ▼▼▼ Days Inn 🆂🄷
(903) 784-8164. **$75-$95, 14 day notice.** 2650 N Main. NE Loop 286, exit US 271, just n. Ext corridors. **Pets:** Accepted.
🆂🅰🆅🄴 🔊 ⊠ 🛢 💻 ➰

🔺 ▼▼▼ Holiday Inn 🆂🄷
(903) 785-5545. **$81.** 3560 NE Loop 286. E Loop 286, 0.3 mi n of jct US 82. Ext corridors. **Pets:** Accepted.
🆂🅰🆅🄴 🔊 ⊠ 🛢 💻 🍴 ➰

PECOS

🔺 ▼▼▼ Knights Inn Laura Lodge Motel & Suites Ⓜ
(432) 445-4924. **$59-$99.** 1000 E Business 20. I-20, exit 42 (US 285), 1 mi nw to Business Rt I-20, then 0.5 mi e. Ext corridors. **Pets:** Small. $15 daily fee/pet. Designated rooms, service with restrictions, supervision.
🆂🅰🆅🄴 🔊 ⊠ 🛢 💻 ➰

🔺 ▼▼▼ Oak Tree Inn 🆂🄷
(432) 447-0180. **Call for rates.** 22 N Frontage Rd. I-20, exit 42, just w on north access road. Int corridors. **Pets:** Accepted.
🆂🅰🆅🄴 ⊠ 🛢 ➰

PERRYTON

▼▼▼ Best Western Perryton Inn 🆂🄷
(806) 434-2850. **$75-$130.** 3505 S Main St (US 83). US 83, just s of town. Int corridors. **Pets:** Accepted.
🄰🅂🄺 🔊 ⊠ 🛢 💻 🍴 ➰

PHARR

▼▼▼ Americas Best Value Inn 🆂🄷
(956) 702-3330. **Call for rates.** 1130 E Expwy 83. Jct US 83, exit I Rd. Ext corridors. **Pets:** Accepted.
⊠ 🛢 💻 ➰

PLAINVIEW

▼▼ Best Western Conestoga 🆂🄷
(806) 293-9454. **$66-$100.** 600 N I-27. I-27, exit 49, just s of US 70, on eastbound access road. Ext corridors. **Pets:** Accepted.
🄰🅂🄺 🔊 ⊠ 🛢 💻 ➰

▼▼▼ Holiday Inn Express Hotel & Suites 🆂🄷
(806) 296-9900. **$100.** 4213 W 13th St. I-27, exit 49 northbound, just w to Mesa, then just n; exit 50 southbound, just s to 13th St, then just w. Int corridors. **Pets:** Accepted.
⊠ 🅶🄼 🛢 💻 ➰

PORT ARANSAS

▼▼ Beachgate CondoSuites & Motel 🄲🄾
(361) 749-5900. **Call for rates.** 2000 On the Beach. Beach access; between markers 8 and 9; street access on Anchor Rd off 11th St. Ext/int corridors. **Pets:** Accepted.
⊠ 🛢 💻 ➰

▼▼ Executive Keys 🄲🄾
(361) 749-6272. **$69-$399, 30 day notice.** 820 Access Rd 1A. 2.5 mi s on SR 361. Ext corridors. **Pets:** Accepted.
💻 ➰

🔺 ▼▼▼▼ Plantation Suites & Conference Center Ⓜ
(361) 749-3866. **$59-$350.** 1909 Hwy 361. On SR 361, 0.4 mi s. Ext corridors. **Pets:** Other species. $100 deposit/room, $50 one-time fee/room. Service with restrictions, crate.
🆂🅰🆅🄴 🔊 ⊠ 🛢 💻 ➰

POST

▼▼ Best Western Post Inn 🆂🄷
(806) 495-9933. **$91-$119.** 1011 N Broadway. 1 mi n on US 84. Int corridors. **Pets:** Accepted.
🄰🅂🄺 🔊 ⊠ 🛢 💻 ➰

QUANAH

🔺 ▼▼▼ Best Western Quanah Inn & Suites 🆂🄷
(940) 663-5407. **$89-$139.** 1100 W 11th St (Hwy 287). On north end of town. Int corridors. **Pets:** Very small. $10 daily fee/pet. Designated rooms, no service, supervision.
🆂🅰🆅🄴 🔊 ⊠ 🅶🄼 🛢 💻 ➰

RAYMONDVILLE

🔺 ▼▼▼ Americas Best Value Inn & Suites 🆂🄷
(956) 689-5900. **$39-$89.** 450 S Hwy 77/I-69. US 77/I-69, exit 186 (Raymondville), on frontage road. Ext corridors. **Pets:** Other species. No service, crate.
🆂🅰🆅🄴 🔊 ⊠ 🛢 💻 ➰

🔺 ▼▼▼ Best Western 🆂🄷
(956) 689-4141. **$59-$119.** 16 N Hwy 77. US 77, jct FM 186 on southbound access road. Ext corridors. **Pets:** Small. $20 deposit/room, $10 one-time fee/pet. Service with restrictions, supervision.
🆂🅰🆅🄴 🔊 ⊠ 🛢 💻 ➰

ROBSTOWN

🔺 ▼▼ Executive Inn 🆂🄷
(361) 387-9416. **$56.** 620 Hwy 77 S. On US 77, 1 mi s. Ext corridors. **Pets:** Accepted.
🆂🅰🆅🄴 ⊠ 🛢 ➰

ROCKPORT

▼▼ Days Inn Ⓜ
(361) 729-6379. **$59-$150.** 1212 Laurel St @ Bus 35 Hwy. Jct Laurel St and Business Rt SR 35; center. Ext corridors. **Pets:** Accepted.
🄰🅂🄺 🔊 ⊠ 🛢 💻 ➰

🔺 ▼▼▼ Hunt's Castle 🆂🄷
(361) 729-5002. **$99-$179.** 725 S Water St. Business SR 35, jct Market St, 1.6 mi e to Water St, then just s. Ext corridors. **Pets:** Accepted.
🆂🅰🆅🄴 🔊 ⊠ 🛢 💻 ➰

△△△ ▽▽▽▽ **Laguna Reef Hotel** 🚲 ❀
(361) 729-1742. **$85-$325, 3 day notice.** 1021 Water St. 0.5 mi s, just e of Business Rt SR 35; entrance on S Austin St. Ext corridors. **Pets:** Medium, dogs only. $10 daily fee/pet. Service with restrictions.
🆂 🆂 ✕ 📋 💻 ♒ ✕

△△△▽ ▽▽▽▽ **Sportsman Manor Motel** Ⓜ
(361) 729-5331. **$50-$100.** 1075 N Fulton Beach Rd. SR 35; across from airport. Ext corridors. **Pets:** Accepted.
🆂 ✕ ♒

△△△▽ ▽▽▽ **The Village Inn** Ⓜ
(361) 729-6370. **$45-$149, 5 day notice.** 503 N Austin St. Just w of jct SR 35 and Business Rt SR 35. Ext corridors. **Pets:** Accepted.
🆂 🆂 ✕ 📋 💻 ♒

ROUND ROCK

△△△▽ ▽▽▽ **Best Western Executive Inn** 🆂🅷
(512) 255-3222. **$99-$138.** 1851 N I-35. I-35, exit 253 northbound; exit 253A U-turn southbound. Ext corridors. **Pets:** Accepted.
🆂 🆂 ✕ 🆂 📋 💻 ♒

▽▽▽▽ **Candlewood Suites** 🆂🅷
(512) 828-0899. **$99-$159.** 521 S I-35. I-35, exit 252A, just n on northbound frontage road. Int corridors. **Pets:** Medium, other species. $150 one-time fee/room. Service with restrictions.
🅰🆂🅺 ✕ 📋 💻

▽▽▽▽ **La Quinta Inn Austin (Round Rock)** 🆂🅷
(512) 255-6666. **$95-$115.** 2004 I-35 N. I-35, exit 254, on west frontage road. Int corridors. **Pets:** Other species. Service with restrictions, supervision.
🅰🆂🅺 🆂 ✕ 📋 💻 ♒ ✕

▽▽ **Red Roof Inn** 🆂🅷
(512) 310-1111. **Call for rates.** 1990 I-35 N. I-35, exit 254, on west frontage road. Int corridors. **Pets:** Accepted.
✕ 📋 ♒

▽▽▽▽ **Residence Inn by Marriott Austin Round Rock** 🆂🅷
(512) 733-2400. **$176-$196.** 2505 S I-35. I-35, exit 250 southbound; exit 251 northbound, on east frontage road. Int corridors. **Pets:** Accepted.
🅰🆂🅺 🆂 ✕ 🆂 📋 💻 ♒ ✕

▽▽▽▽ **Staybridge Suites Austin-Round Rock** 🆂🅷
(512) 733-0942. **$149.** 520 I-35 S. I-35, exit 252B northbound; exit 252AB southbound, on west frontage road. Int corridors. **Pets:** Accepted.
🅰🆂🅺 🆂 ✕ 🆂 📋 💻 ♒

SALADO

▽▽▽▽ **Holiday Inn Express** 🆂🅷
(254) 947-4004. **Call for rates.** 1991 N Stagecoach Rd. I-35, exit 286. Int corridors. **Pets:** Accepted.
✕ 🆂 📋 💻 ♒

SAN ANGELO

△△△▽ ▽▽▽ **Americas Best Value Inn** Ⓜ
(325) 653-1323. **Call for rates.** 1601 S Bryant Blvd. US 87 and 277 at Ave L. Ext/int corridors. **Pets:** Accepted.
🆂 ✕ 📋 💻 ♒

△△△▽ ▽▽▽ **Benchmark Comfort Inn** 🆂🅷
(325) 944-2578. **Call for rates.** 2502 Loop 306. Loop 306, exit Knickerbocker Rd. Ext corridors. **Pets:** Accepted.
🆂 ✕ 📋 💻 ♒

△△△▽ ▽▽▽ **Days Inn San Angelo** 🆂🅷
(325) 658-6594. **Call for rates.** 4613 S Jackson St. Jct US 87 and Jackson St. Ext corridors. **Pets:** Accepted.
🆂 ✕ 📋 💻 🍽 ♒

△△△▽ ▽▽▽ **Howard Johnson San Angelo** 🆂🅷
(325) 653-2995. **$58-$75.** 415 W Beauregard. Just w on US 67 business route at US 87 southbound. Ext/int corridors. **Pets:** Accepted.
🆂 🆂 ✕ 📋 💻 🍽 ♒

▽▽▽▽ **La Quinta Inn San Angelo (Conference Center)** 🆂🅷
(325) 949-0515. **$89-$109.** 2307 Loop 306. Loop 306, exit Knickerbocker Rd, just s. Ext corridors. **Pets:** Other species. Service with restrictions, supervision.
🅰🆂🅺 🆂 ✕ 📋 💻 ♒

▽▽▽▽ **San Angelo Inn & Conference Center** 🆂🅷
(325) 658-2828. **Call for rates.** 441 Rio Concho Dr. US 87 to Concho Ave, 0.5 mi e; downtown. Int corridors. **Pets:** Accepted.
✕ 📋 💻 🍽 ♒

▽▽▽▽ **Staybridge Suites** 🆂🅷
(325) 653-1500. **Call for rates.** 1355 Knickerbocker Rd. US 87 S, 1 mi w. Int corridors. **Pets:** Accepted.
✕ 📋 💻 ♒

SAN ANTONIO METROPOLITAN AREA

ELMENDORF

△△△▽ ▽▽▽ **Comfort Inn & Suites Braunig Lake** 🆂🅷
(210) 633-1833. **$90-$110.** 13800 I-37 S. I-37, exit 130 (Donop, Southton Rd), on northbound access lane. Ext corridors. **Pets:** Medium, other species. $7 daily fee/pet. Service with restrictions, supervision.
🆂 🆂 ✕ 📋 💻 ♒

FLORESVILLE

△△△▽ ▽▽▽▽ **Best Western Floresville Inn** 🆂🅷
(830) 393-0443. **$71-$92.** 1720 S 10th St. US 181, just s of downtown. Ext corridors. **Pets:** Small. $15 one-time fee/pet. Service with restrictions, crate.
🆂 🆂 ✕ 📋 💻 ♒

LIVE OAK

▽▽▽▽ **La Quinta Inn San Antonio (I-35 North at Toepperwein)** 🆂🅷
(210) 657-5500. **$95-$115.** 12822 I-35 N. I-35, exit 170B (Toepperwein), on northbound access road. Ext/int corridors. **Pets:** Other species. Service with restrictions, supervision.
🅰🆂🅺 🆂 ✕ 🆂 📋 💻

NEW BRAUNFELS

△△△▽ ▽▽▽▽ **Best Western Inn & Suites** 🆂🅷
(830) 625-7337. **$60-$190.** 1493 I-35 N. I-35, exit 190, on southbound access lane. Ext/int corridors. **Pets:** Other species. $10 daily fee/pet. Service with restrictions, crate.
🆂 🆂 ✕ 📋 💻 ♒

▼▼ **Executive Inn & Suites** SH
(830) 625-3932. **$199.** 808 Hwy 46 S. I-35, exit 189, 0.4 mi e. Ext corridors. **Pets:** Accepted.
Ⓐ$Ⓚ S⊿ ✕ ⚷M 🗎 💻 ⇝

ⒶⒶⒹ ▼▼▼ **Holiday Inn** SH
(830) 625-8017. **Call for rates.** 1051 I-35 E. I-35, exit 189, on southbound access road. Ext corridors. **Pets:** $25 one-time fee/room. Service with restrictions, crate.
SAVE ✕ ⚷M 🗎 💻 ¶ ⇝

▼▼▼ **Quality Inn & Suites** SH
(830) 643-9300. **$59-$400.** 1533 IH-35 N. I-35, exit 190, on southbound access road. Int corridors. **Pets:** Accepted.
Ⓐ$Ⓚ S⊿ ✕ 🗎 💻 ⇝

ⒶⒶⒹ ▼▼▼ **Rodeway Inn** SH
(830) 629-6991. **$39-$150.** 1209 I-35 N. I-35, exit 189, on southbound access road. Ext corridors. **Pets:** Accepted.
SAVE S⊿ ✕ 🗎 💻 ⇝

▼▼ **Super 8 Motel-New Braunfels** M
(830) 629-1155. **Call for rates.** 510 Hwy 46 S. I-35, exit 189 (SR 46), just e. Ext corridors. **Pets:** Accepted.
✕ 🗎 💻 ⇝

SAN ANTONIO

ⒶⒶⒹ ▼▼▼ **Arbor House Suites Bed & Breakfast** BB
(210) 472-2005. **$129-$207, 7 day notice.** 109 Arciniega St. Just s of E Nueva; between S Presa and S St Marys sts; near La Villita Historic District. Ext/int corridors. **Pets:** Medium. Service with restrictions, supervision.
SAVE ✕ 🗎 💻

▼▼▼ **Baymont Inns & Suites** SH
(210) 593-0338. **$68-$76 (no credit cards).** 9542 I-10 W. I-10, exit Wurzbach Rd, just e on eastbound access road. Ext corridors. **Pets:** Accepted.
Ⓐ$Ⓚ S⊿ ✕ 🗎 💻 ⇝

▼▼▼ **Best Western Casa Linda Inn-San Antonio Airport** SH
(210) 366-1800. **$70-$118.** 8818 Jones Maltsberger Rd. I-410, exit 21B (Jones Maltsberger Rd), on westbound access road. Int corridors. **Pets:** Medium, other species. Service with restrictions, supervision.
Ⓐ$Ⓚ ✕ 🗎 💻 ⇝

▼▼▼ **Best Western Fiesta Inn** SH
(210) 696-2400. **Call for rates.** 13535 I-10 W. I-10, exit 557 westbound; exit 558 eastbound, on westbound access road. Ext corridors. **Pets:** Accepted.
✕ 🗎 💻 ⇝

▼▼▼ **Best Western-Garden Inn** SH
(210) 599-0999. **$89-$299.** 11939 N I-35. I-35, exit 170, on southbound access road, 0.5 mi s to Judson Rd exit. Ext corridors. **Pets:** Accepted.
Ⓐ$Ⓚ S⊿ ✕ 🗎 💻 ⇝

▼▼▼ **Best Western Posada Ana Inn-Medical Center** SH
(210) 691-9550. **$73-$106.** 9411 Wurzbach Rd. I-10 NW, exit 561 (Wurzbach Rd), on eastbound access road. Int corridors. **Pets:** Medium, other species. Service with restrictions, supervision.
Ⓐ$Ⓚ ✕ 🗎 💻 ⇝

▼▼▼ **Best Western Posada Ana Inn-San Antonio Airport** SH
(210) 342-1400. **$82-$122.** 8600 Jones Maltsberger Rd. I-410, exit 21A (Jones Maltsberger Rd), 0.5 mi s. Int corridors. **Pets:** Small, other species. $50 one-time fee/pet. Service with restrictions, crate.
Ⓐ$Ⓚ ✕ 🗎 💻 ⇝

▼▼▼ **Brackenridge House B & B** BB
(210) 271-3442. **$125-$300, 14 day notice.** 230 Madison. Just s of S St. Marys St at Durango St. Ext/int corridors. **Pets:** Accepted.
✕ 🗎 💻 ⇝

▼▼▼ **Candlewood Suites Hotel** SH
(210) 615-0550. **$100-$140.** 9350 I-10 W. I-10 W, exit 561 (Wurzbach Rd), eastbound access road; between Wurzbach Rd and Callaghan. Int corridors. **Pets:** Accepted.
Ⓐ$Ⓚ S⊿ ✕ 🗎 💻 ⇝

ⒶⒶⒹ ▼▼▼ **Comfort Inn & Suites Airport** SH
(210) 249-2000. **$99-$159.** 8640 Crownhill Blvd. I-410, exit Airport Blvd, just off I-410 westbound access road; 0.3 mi e of Airport Blvd exit. Int corridors. **Pets:** Accepted.
SAVE S⊿ ✕ 🗎 💻 ⇝

ⒶⒶⒹ ▼▼ **Comfort Inn Sea World** SH
(210) 684-8606. **$69-$159.** 4 Piano Pl. I-410, exit Evers Rd westbound, U-turn; exit 14 Callahan/Babocks Rd eastbound. Ext corridors. **Pets:** Small, dogs only. $25 daily fee/pet. Designated rooms, service with restrictions, supervision.
SAVE S⊿ ✕ 🗎 💻 ⇝

ⒶⒶⒹ ▼▼▼ ▼▼▼ **Crowne Plaza San Antonio Riverwalk** LH
(210) 354-2800. **$189-$269.** 111 Pecan St E. Corner of Pecan and Soledad sts. Int corridors. **Pets:** Small. $50 one-time fee/room. Service with restrictions, crate.
SAVE ✕ 🗎 💻 ¶ ⇝ ⊠

ⒶⒶⒹ ▼▼▼ **Days Inn Coliseum/AT&T Center** SH
(210) 225-4040. **$55-$300.** 3443 I-35 N. I-35, exit 160 (Splashtown), on southbound access road. Ext corridors. **Pets:** Accepted.
SAVE S⊿ ✕ 🗎 💻 ⇝

ⒶⒶⒹ ▼▼▼ **Days Inn Downtown Riverwalk** SH
(210) 271-3334. **$70-$350.** 1500 I-35 S. I-10/35, exit 154 (Laredo St). Ext/int corridors. **Pets:** Accepted.
SAVE S⊿ ✕ 🗎 💻 ⇝

▼▼▼ **Drury Inn & Suites-San Antonio Airport** SH
(210) 308-8100. **$194.** 95 NE Loop 410. I-410, exit 21A (Jones Maltsberger Rd), 1.8 mi w of airport. Int corridors. **Pets:** Large, other species. Service with restrictions, supervision.
Ⓐ$Ⓚ ✕ ⚷M 🗎 💻 ⇝

▼▼▼ **Drury Inn & Suites-San Antonio North** SH
(210) 404-1600. **$208.** 801 N Loop 1604 E. On FM 1604, 0.4 mi w on US 281. Int corridors. **Pets:** Large, other species. Service with restrictions, supervision.
Ⓐ$Ⓚ ✕ 🗎 💻 ⇝

▼▼▼ **Drury Inn & Suites-San Antonio Northwest** SH
(210) 561-2510. **$306.** 9806 I-10 W. I-10, exit Wurzbach Rd, on southeast corner. Int corridors. **Pets:** Large, other species. Service with restrictions, supervision.
Ⓐ$Ⓚ ✕ 🗎 💻 ⇝

ⒶⒶⒹ ▼▼▼ **Drury Inn & Suites-San Antonio Riverwalk** SH
(210) 212-5200. **$286.** 201 N St. Mary's St. Just s of College St. Int corridors. **Pets:** Large, other species. Service with restrictions, supervision.
SAVE ✕ 🗎 💻 ⇝

▼▼▼ **Drury Plaza Hotel-San Antonio Riverwalk** SH
(210) 270-7799. **$121-$291.** 105 S Saint Marys St. Commerce and St. Mary's and Market sts. **Pets:** Large, other species. Service with restrictions, supervision.
Ⓐ$Ⓚ ✕ 🗎 💻 ⇝

▼▼ **Econo Lodge Inn & Suites Fiesta Park** Ⓜ
(210) 690-5500. **$49-$159.** 13575 I-10 W. I-10, exit 557, westbound access road. Ext corridors. **Pets:** Accepted.

Ⓐ𝐒𝐊 ⓢ▽ ✕ 🛏 💻 🏊

◆◆◆ ▼▼▼▼ **Emily Morgan Hotel** Ⓛ𝐇 ❖
(210) 225-8486. **$239-$509, 3 day notice.** 705 E Houston St. On Houston St, just n of Bonham St. Int corridors. **Pets:** Other species. Service with restrictions.

Ⓢ𝐀𝐕𝐄 ⓢ▽ ✕ ♿ 💻 🍴 🏊 ✕

◆◆◆◇ ▼▼▼▼ **The Fairmount Hotel** Ⓢ𝐇 🐾
(210) 224-8800. **Call for rates.** 401 S Alamo St. Opposite convention center and Hemisfair Plaza. Ext/int corridors. **Pets:** Large, other species. $75 one-time fee/pet. Service with restrictions, crate.

Ⓢ𝐀𝐕𝐄 ✕ 🛏 💻 ✕

◆◆◆ ▼▼▼ **Hallmark Inn & Suites Windsor Park** Ⓜ
(210) 646-6336. **$59-$99.** 6370 I-35 N. I-410/35, exit 164A (Rittiman Rd), on northbound access road. Ext corridors. **Pets:** Small. $15 one-time fee/pet. Designated rooms, service with restrictions, crate.

Ⓢ𝐀𝐕𝐄 ⓢ▽ ✕ 🛏 🏊

▼▼▼▼ **Hampton Inn Six Flags Area** Ⓢ𝐇
(210) 561-9058. **Call for rates.** 11010 I-10 W. I-10, exit 560 westbound; exit 559 (Huebner Rd) eastbound. Int corridors. **Pets:** Accepted.

✕ 🛏 💻 🏊

◆◆◆ ▼▼▼▼ **Holiday Inn-Downtown-Market Square** Ⓛ𝐇
(210) 225-3211. **$85-$499.** 318 W Durango St. I-35, exit Durango St, 2 blks e. Int corridors. **Pets:** Accepted.

Ⓢ𝐀𝐕𝐄 ⓢ▽ ✕ ♿ 💻 🍴 🏊 ✕

▼▼▼▼ **Holiday Inn Express-San Antonio Airport** Ⓢ𝐇
(210) 308-6700. **$109-$169.** 91 NE Loop 410. I-410, exit 21A (Jones Maltsberger Rd) eastbound; exit 20B westbound, on westbound access road; between San Pedro Ave and Jones Maltsberger Rd. Int corridors. **Pets:** Medium, other species. Service with restrictions, supervision.

Ⓐ𝐒𝐊 ✕ ♿ 🛏 💻 🏊

◆◆◆ ▼▼▼ **Holiday Inn Select** Ⓢ𝐇
(210) 349-9900. **$119-$189.** 77 NE Loop 410. I-410, exit 20B (McCullough St), on westbound access road. Int corridors. **Pets:** $25 one-time fee/room. Service with restrictions, supervision.

Ⓢ𝐀𝐕𝐄 ⓢ▽ ✕ ♿ 🛏 💻 🍴 🏊

▼▼ **HomeGate Studios & Suites** Ⓢ𝐇
(210) 342-4800. **$49-$99.** 11221 San Pedro Ave. I-410, exit US 281 (San Pedro Ave), 2.3 mi n on US 281, exit Nakoma, on west frontage road. Ext corridors. **Pets:** Other species. $50 one-time fee/pet. Designated rooms, service with restrictions, crate.

Ⓐ𝐒𝐊 ⓢ▽ ✕ 💻 🏊 ✕

▼▼ **Homestead Studio Suites Hotel-San**
　　Antonio-Airport Ⓜ
(210) 491-9009. **$75-$85.** 1015 Central Pkwy S. I-410, exit US 281 (San Pedro Ave), 4 mi n on US 281, exit Bitters Rd, on northbound access road. Ext corridors. **Pets:** Other species. $75 one-time fee/pet. Service with restrictions.

Ⓐ𝐒𝐊 ⓢ▽ ✕ 🛏 💻

▼▼ **Hotel Marquis Airport** Ⓢ𝐇
(210) 653-9110. 2635 NE Loop 410. I-410, exit 25B (Perrin-Beitel Rd), on westbound access road. Ext/int corridors. **Pets:** Accepted.

Ⓐ𝐒𝐊 ⓢ▽ ✕ 🛏 💻 🏊

▼▼ **Howard Johnson Inn & Suites Fort Sam AT&T**
　　Center Ⓢ𝐇
(210) 224-3030. **Call for rates.** 3817 I-35 N. I-35, exit 161 (Binz-Engleman Rd), follow signs to I-35 S access road northbound; exit Binz-Engleman Rd, continue southbound. Int corridors. **Pets:** Accepted.

✕ 🛏 💻 🏊

◆◆◆◇ ▼▼▼ **Howard Johnson Inn & Suites Hotel** Ⓢ𝐇
(210) 738-1100. **Call for rates.** 6901 I-10 W. I-10, exit 565A (Crossroads), exit 565A (Crossroads); on westbound access road. Ext corridors. **Pets:** Accepted.

Ⓢ𝐀𝐕𝐄 ✕ 🛏 💻 🏊

◆◆◆ ▼▼▼ **Howard Johnson Lackland Inn & Suites** Ⓢ𝐇
(210) 675-9690. **$61-$90.** 6815 Hwy 90 W. I-410, exit US 90 to Military Dr, 0.5 mi e on westbound access road. Ext corridors. **Pets:** Small. $25 one-time fee/room. Service with restrictions.

Ⓢ𝐀𝐕𝐄 ⓢ▽ ✕ 🛏 💻 🏊

▼▼ **Inn on the River** Ⓑ𝐁
(210) 225-6333. **$99-$225, 7 day notice.** 129 Woodward Pl. Just n of W Durango St. Ext/int corridors. **Pets:** Medium, other species. $20 daily fee/pet. No service, supervision.

Ⓐ𝐒𝐊 ⓢ▽ ✕ 🛏 💻 🏊

▼▼▼ **La Quinta Inn** Ⓢ𝐇
(210) 661-4545. **$89-$109.** 6075 IH 10 E Foster Rd. I-10, exit 583 (Foster Rd), on westbound access road. Int corridors. **Pets:** Other species. Service with restrictions, supervision.

Ⓐ𝐒𝐊 ⓢ▽ ✕ 🛏 💻 🏊

▼▼▼ **La Quinta Inn & Suites San Antonio (Convention**
　　Center) Ⓢ𝐇
(210) 222-9181. **$169-$189.** 303 Blum St. 0.5 mi ne. Ext/int corridors. **Pets:** Other species. Service with restrictions, supervision.

Ⓐ𝐒𝐊 ⓢ▽ ✕ 🛏 💻 🏊

▼▼▼ **La Quinta Inn Alamo South** Ⓢ𝐇
(210) 337-7171. **$99-$119.** 3180 Goliad Rd. I-37, exit 135 (Brooks City Base/SE Military Dr), just w of interstate. Int corridors. **Pets:** Other species. Service with restrictions, supervision.

Ⓐ𝐒𝐊 ⓢ▽ ✕ 🛏 💻 🏊

▼▼▼▼ **La Quinta Inn & Suites San Antonio Airport** Ⓢ𝐇
(210) 342-3738. **$129-$149.** 850 Halm. I-410, exit US 281 S, southwest corner. Int corridors. **Pets:** Other species. Service with restrictions, supervision.

Ⓐ𝐒𝐊 ⓢ▽ ✕ 🛏 💻 🏊

▼▼▼▼ **La Quinta Inn & Suites San Antonio-Downtown** Ⓢ𝐇
(210) 212-5400. **$129-$149.** 100 W Durango Blvd. I-35, exit 155B (Durango Blvd), 3 blks e of jct E Flores St. Int corridors. **Pets:** Other species. Service with restrictions, supervision.

Ⓐ𝐒𝐊 ⓢ▽ ✕ ♿ 🛏 💻 🏊

▼▼▼ **La Quinta Inn San Antonio (I-35 North @ Windsor**
　　Park Mall) Ⓢ𝐇
(210) 653-6619. **$99-$119.** 6410 I-35 N. I-35, exit 163B northbound, on I-35 northbound access road; between Rittiman and Eisenhauer rds; exit 164A (Rittiman Rd) southbound. Ext corridors. **Pets:** Other species. Service with restrictions, supervision.

Ⓐ𝐒𝐊 ⓢ▽ ✕ 🛏 💻 🏊

▼▼ **La Quinta Inn San Antonio (Lackland)** Ⓢ𝐇
(210) 674-3200. **$95-$115.** 6511 Military Dr W. Sw of jct US 90 and Military Dr W. Ext corridors. **Pets:** Other species. Service with restrictions, supervision.

Ⓐ𝐒𝐊 ⓢ▽ ✕ 🛏 💻 🏊

▼▼▼ **La Quinta Inn San Antonio (Market Square)** Ⓢ𝐇
(210) 271-0001. **$104-$124.** 900 Dolorosa. I-10/35, exit Durango St, just n on Santa Rosa St, then just w on Nueva St. Ext corridors. **Pets:** Other species. Service with restrictions, supervision.

Ⓐ𝐒𝐊 ⓢ▽ ✕ ♿ 🛏 💻 🏊

▼▼▼▼ **La Quinta Inn San Antonio (SeaWorld/Ingram**
　　Park) Ⓢ𝐇
(210) 680-8883. **$99-$119.** 7134 NW Loop 410. I-410, exit 10 (Culebra Rd), on eastbound access road. Ext corridors. **Pets:** Other species. Service with restrictions, supervision.

Ⓐ𝐒𝐊 ⓢ▽ ✕ 🛏 💻 🏊

▼▼▼▼ **La Quinta Inn San Antonio (South Park)** 🆂🅷
(210) 922-2111. **$102-$122.** 7202 S Pan American Expwy. I-35, exit 150A (Military Dr) northbound; exit 150B southbound, southeast of jct I-35 and Military Dr SW. Ext corridors. **Pets:** Other species. Service with restrictions, supervision.
🄰🅂🄺 🆂🄳 🗙 🕭 🛏 🖵 🌊

▼▼▼▼ **La Quinta Inn San Antonio (Vance Jackson)** 🆂🅷
(210) 734-7931. **$99-$119.** 5922 I-10 W. I-10, exit 565B eastbound; exit 565C (Vance Jackson Rd) westbound, on eastbound access road. Ext corridors. **Pets:** Other species. Service with restrictions, supervision.
🄰🅂🄺 🆂🄳 🗙 🛏 🖵 🌊

▼▼▼ ▼▼▼ **Marriott Plaza San Antonio** 🅻🅷
(210) 229-1000. **$329-$340.** 555 S Alamo St. Opposite convention center and Hemisfair Plaza. Int corridors. **Pets:** Accepted.
🄰🅂🄺 🆂🄳 🗙 🕭 🖵 🍴 🌊 🐾

▼▼ **Motel 6–1122** Ⓜ
(210) 225-1111. **$51-$65.** 211 N Pecos St. I-10/35, exit 155 B (Pecos St), on I-10 E/35 S access road. Ext corridors. **Pets:** Other species. Service with restrictions, supervision.
🆂🄳 🗙 🛏 🌊

▼▼ **Motel 6–134** Ⓜ
(210) 650-4419. **$39-$53.** 9503 I-35 N. I-35, exit 167A (Randolf Blvd) southbound; exit 167 (Starlight Terr) northbound. Ext corridors. **Pets:** Other species. Service with restrictions, supervision.
🆂🄳 🗙 🌊

▼ **Motel 6–651** Ⓜ
(210) 673-9020. **$45-$58.** 2185 SW Loop 410. I-410, exit 7 (Marbach Rd), 0.7 mi w; on westbound access road. Ext corridors. **Pets:** Other species. Service with restrictions, supervision.
🆂🄳 🗙 🛏 🌊

▼ **Motel 6 East #183** 🆂🅷
(210) 333-1850. **$39-$52.** 138 N WW White Rd. I-10, exit 580 (WW White Rd), just off westbound access road. Ext corridors. **Pets:** Other species. Service with restrictions, supervision.
🆂🄳 🗙 🌊

▼ **Motel 6 Fort Sam Houston #1350** Ⓜ
(210) 661-8791. **$41-$55.** 5522 N PanAm Expwy. I-35/410, exit 164 (Rittiman Rd), just s on northbound access road; just off Goldfield St. Ext corridors. **Pets:** Other species. Service with restrictions, supervision.
🆂🄳 🗙 🌊

▼ **Motel 6 San Antonio #1188** Ⓜ
(210) 653-8088. **$39-$53.** 4621 E Rittiman Rd. I-35, exit 164 (Rittiman Rd); on north side of Rittiman Rd. Ext corridors. **Pets:** Other species. Service with restrictions, supervision.
🆂🄳 🗙 🌊

▼▼ **Oak Hills Medical Center Inn & Suites** 🆂🅷
(210) 614-9900. **$75-$80.** 7401 Wurzbach Rd. 1.5 mi s of jct I-10 and Wurzbach Rd, just ne of Babcock Rd. Ext/int corridors. **Pets:** Accepted.
🆂🄳 🗙 🛏 🖵 🍴 🌊

🄰🄰🄰ⁿ ▼▼▼ ▼▼▼ **Omni La Mansion del Rio** 🅻🅷 🌸
(210) 518-1000. **$219-$389, 3 day notice.** 112 College St. Just s on the Riverwalk. Ext/int corridors. **Pets:** Small. $50 one-time fee/pet. Designated rooms, service with restrictions, supervision.
🆂🄰🆅🄴 🆂🄳 🗙 🛏 🖵 🍴 🌊

🄰🄰🄰ⁿ ▼▼▼ ▼▼▼ **Omni San Antonio Hotel** 🅻🅷
(210) 691-8888. **$149-$249.** 9821 Colonnade Blvd. I-10, exit Wurzbach Rd, 12 mi nw on westbound access road. Int corridors. **Pets:** Accepted.
🆂🄰🆅🄴 🆂🄳 🗙 🖵 🍴 🌊 🐾

▼▼▼ **Pear Tree Inn by Drury-San Antonio Northeast** 🆂🅷
(210) 654-1144. **$113.** 8300 I-35 N. I-35, exit 165 (Walzem Rd), northbound access road. Ext/int corridors. **Pets:** Large, other species. Service with restrictions, supervision.
🄰🅂🄺 🗙 🕭 🛏 🖵

▼▼▼ **Pear Tree Inn San Antonio Airport** 🆂🅷
(210) 366-9300. **$123.** 143 NE Loop 410. Loop 410 W, exit 21 (Jones Maltsberger Rd), on westbound access road; between Airport Blvd and Jones Maltsberger Rd. Int corridors. **Pets:** Large, other species. Service with restrictions, supervision.
🄰🅂🄺 🗙 🛏 🖵 🌊

🄰🄰🄰ⁿ ▼▼▼ ▼▼▼ **Quality Inn & Suites Bandera Point** 🆂🅷
(210) 372-9900. **$65-$250.** 9522 Brimhall Rd. Loop 1640, exit Bandera Rd, on westbound access road. Int corridors. **Pets:** Small. $35 one-time fee/pet. Designated rooms, no service, supervision.
🆂🄰🆅🄴 🆂🄳 🗙 🛏 🖵 🌊

🄰🄰🄰ⁿ ▼▼▼ ▼▼▼ **Quality Inn & Suites North Airport** 🆂🅷
(210) 545-5400. **$80-$150.** 1505 Bexar Crossing. US 281, exit 1604 (Anderson Loop), on southbound access road. Int corridors. **Pets:** Small. $25 one-time fee/pet. Designated rooms, service with restrictions, supervision.
🆂🄰🆅🄴 🆂🄳 🗙 🛏 🖵 🌊

🄰🄰🄰ⁿ ▼▼▼ **Quality Inn Northwest** 🆂🅷
(210) 736-1900. **$49-$159.** 6023 NW I-10 W. I-10, exit 565B eastbound; exit 565C (Vance Jackson Rd) westbound, just n. Ext corridors. **Pets:** Accepted.
🆂🄰🆅🄴 🆂🄳 🗙 🛏 🖵

🄰🄰🄰ⁿ ▼▼▼ **Red Roof Inn** 🆂🅷
(210) 333-9430. **Call for rates.** 4403 I-10 E. I-10, exit 580 (WW White Rd), on westbound access road. Ext corridors. **Pets:** Accepted.
🆂🄰🆅🄴 🗙 🛏 🖵 🍴 🌊

🄰🄰🄰ⁿ ▼▼▼ **Red Roof Inn Lackland** 🆂🅷
(210) 675-4120. **Call for rates.** 6861 Hwy 90 W. Northeast jct of US 90 and Military Dr W; access via Renwick St, off Military Dr, just n of jct US 90. Ext corridors. **Pets:** Accepted.
🆂🄰🆅🄴 🗙 🛏 🖵 🌊

▼▼ ▼▼ **Red Roof Inn-San Antonio Airport** 🆂🅷
(210) 340-4055. **Call for rates.** 333 Wolfe Rd. On southbound access road, just s of US 281 at Isom Rd. Ext/int corridors. **Pets:** Accepted.
🗙 🕭 🛏

▼▼ ▼▼ **Red Roof Inn San Antonio (Downtown)** Ⓜ
(210) 229-9973. **Call for rates.** 1011 E Houston St. I-37, exit 141 northbound; exit 141B southbound. Int corridors. **Pets:** Accepted.
🗙 🛏 🌊

▼▼ ▼▼ **Red Roof Inn San Antonio (NW-SeaWorld)** 🆂🅷
(210) 509-3434. **Call for rates.** 6880 NW Loop 410. I-410, exit 11 (Alamo Downs Pkwy), on eastbound access road. Ext/int corridors. **Pets:** Accepted.
🗙 🕭 🛏 🌊

▼▼▼▼ **Residence Inn Alamo Plaza** 🆂🅷
(210) 212-5555. **$253-$273.** 425 Bonham St. I-37/281, exit Commerce St, just w to Bowie St, then 4 blks n. Int corridors. **Pets:** Accepted.
🄰🅂🄺 🆂🄳 🗙 🛏 🖵 🌊

▼▼▼▼ **Residence Inn by Marriott San Antonio Downtown/ Market Square** 🆂🅷
(210) 231-6000. **$176-$196.** 628 S Santa Rosa. I-10/35, exit Durango St, 0.5 mi e. Int corridors. **Pets:** Accepted.
🄰🅂🄺 🆂🄳 🗙 🛏 🖵 🌊 🐾

▼▼▼▼ **Residence Inn NW/Six Flags** 🆂🅷
(210) 561-9660. **$132-$152.** 4041 Bluemel Rd. I-10, exit Wurzbach Rd, 0.3 mi w on eastbound access road. Ext corridors. **Pets:** Accepted.
🄰🅂🄺 🆂🄳 🗙 🖵 🌊 🐾

▼▼▼▼ **Residence Inn San Antonio-Airport** 🆂🅷
(210) 805-8118. **$198-$218.** 1014 NE Loop 410. Loop 410, exit Broadway St, 0.4 mi e on access road. Ext corridors. **Pets:** Accepted.
🄰🅂🄺 🆂🄳 🗙 🖵 🌊 🐾

▼▼ Rittiman Inn & Suites 🅂🅷
(210) 657-0808. **Call for rates.** 6364 I-35 N. I-35, exit 163B (Rittiman Rd) northbound, on northbound access road; exit 164A (Rittiman Rd) southbound. Ext corridors. **Pets:** Accepted.

🔲

AAA ▼▼ Rodeway Inn Downtown 🅂🅷
(210) 223-2951. **$70-$100.** 900 N Main Ave. I-35, exit San Pedro/Main aves; northeast corner. Ext corridors. **Pets:** Accepted.

[SAVE] [S🔥] [✕] [🔲] [🖵] [🐾]

▼▼ Royal Hawaiian Continental Inn 🅂🅷
(210) 655-3510. **Call for rates.** 9735 I-35 N. I-35, exit 167 (Starlight Terr) northbound; exit 167A (Randolph Blvd) southbound; just n of Loop 410 NE; on southbound access road. Ext corridors. **Pets:** Accepted.

[✕] [&M] [🔲] [🖵] [🍴] [🐾]

AAA ▼▼▼▼ San Antonio Marriott Rivercenter 🅻🅷
(210) 223-1000. **$380-$396.** 101 Bowie St. Corner of Bowie and Commerce sts. Int corridors. **Pets:** Accepted.

[SAVE] [S🔥] [✕] [🔲] [🖵] [🍴] [🐾] [🐕]

AAA ▼▼▼▼ San Antonio Marriott Riverwalk 🅻🅷
(210) 224-4555. **$380-$396.** 711 E Riverwalk. Opposite convention center and Hemisfair Plaza; across from Marriott River Center. Int corridors. **Pets:** Accepted.

[SAVE] [S🔥] [✕] [🔲] [🖵] [🍴] [🐾] [🐕]

AAA ▼▼▼▼ Sheraton Gunter 🅂🅷 ❀
(210) 227-3241. **$289-$329.** 205 E Houston St. Center. Int corridors. **Pets:** Medium, dogs only. Service with restrictions, supervision.

[SAVE] [✕] [🖵] [🍴] [🐾]

▼▼▼▼ Staybridge Suites San Antonio-Airport 🅂🅷
(210) 341-3220. **$129-$297.** 66 NE Loop 410. I-410, exit 20B (McCullough St), on eastbound access road; next to Texas Land & Cattle Restaurant. Int corridors. **Pets:** Accepted.

[ASK] [✕] [&M] [🔲] [🖵] [🐾]

▼▼▼▼ Staybridge Suites San Antonio NW-Colonnade 🅂🅷
(210) 558-9009. **$129-$279.** 4320 Spectrum One. I-10 W, exit 560 (Wurzbach Rd), follow westbound access road through light, then just n. Int corridors. **Pets:** Accepted.

[ASK] [S🔥] [✕] [🔲] [🖵] [🐾]

▼▼▼ Studio 6 #6046 🅼
(210) 691-0121. **$61-$75.** 11802 I-10 W. I-10, exit 558 (De Zavala Rd), 0.6 mi e on eastbound access road. Ext corridors. **Pets:** Other species. Service with restrictions, supervision.

[S🔥] [✕] [🔲]

AAA ▼▼ Super 8 Downtown Riverwalk 🅼
(210) 222-8833. **$70-$350.** 1614 N St. Mary's St. I-35, exit 157B (Brooklyn/McCullough St), 4 blks n on Quincey. Ext corridors. **Pets:** Accepted.

[SAVE] [S🔥] [✕] [&M] [🔲] [🐾]

AAA ▼▼▼ Super 8 Motel on Roland 🅂🅷
(210) 798-5500. **Call for rates.** 302 Roland Ave. I-10, exit 577 (Roland Ave) eastbound. Ext corridors. **Pets:** Medium. $10 daily fee/pet. Service with restrictions, supervision.

[SAVE] [✕] [🔲] [🐾]

▼▼▼▼ Super 8 Motel SBC/Coliseum Area 🅼
(210) 227-8888. **Call for rates.** 3617 N PanAm Expwy. I-35, exit 160 (Splashtown), on southbound access road. Ext corridors. **Pets:** Accepted.

[✕] [&M] [🔲] [🐾]

▼▼▼▼ Super 8 Motel-Six Flags Fiesta 🅂🅷
(210) 696-6916. **Call for rates.** 5319 Casa Bella. I-10, exit 557 westbound; exit 558 eastbound, on westbound access road. Int corridors. **Pets:** Accepted.

[✕] [🔲] [🐾]

▼▼▼▼ Travelodge 🅂🅷
(210) 224-5114. **Call for rates (no credit cards).** 3821 IH 35 N. I-35, exit 161 (Binz-Engleman Rd), follow signs to I-35 S access road. Int corridors. **Pets:** Accepted.

[✕] [🔲] [🐾]

AAA ▼▼▼▼ The Westin Riverwalk 🅻🅷 ❀
(210) 224-6500. **$459-$529.** 420 W Market St. 2 blks w of Navarro St. Int corridors. **Pets:** Small, dogs only. Service with restrictions, crate.

[SAVE] [✕] [&M] [🔲] [🍴] [🐾] [🐕]

SEGUIN

▼▼▼▼ Holiday Inn Seguin 🅂🅷
(830) 372-0860. **$84-$109.** 2950 N 123 Bypass. I-10, exit 610 (SR 123). Ext corridors. **Pets:** Accepted.

[ASK] [S🔥] [✕] [🔲] [🖵] [🍴] [🐾]

▼▼▼▼ La Quinta Inn & Suites 🅂🅷
(830) 372-0567. **Call for rates.** 1501 Hwy 46 N. I-10, exit 607. Int corridors. **Pets:** Other species. Service with restrictions, supervision.

[✕] [🔲] [🐾]

▼▼▼ Super 8 Motel of Seguin 🅂🅷
(830) 379-6888. **$59-$179.** 1525 N Hwy 46. I-10, exit 607 (SR 46), on eastbound access road. Int corridors. **Pets:** Accepted.

[ASK] [S🔥] [✕] [🔲]

UNIVERSAL CITY

AAA ▼▼▼ Clarion Suites Hotel 🅂🅷
(210) 655-9491. **$89-$139.** 13101 E Loop, 1604 N. Loop 1604 at Pat Booker Rd; 0.8 mi e of I-35. Ext corridors. **Pets:** Medium. $25 one-time fee/pet. Designated rooms, service with restrictions, crate.

[SAVE] [S🔥] [✕] [🔲] [🐾]

END METROPOLITAN AREA

SAN JUAN

▼▼▼ Days Inn San Juan 🅂🅷
(956) 782-1510. **Call for rates.** 112 W Expwy 83. US 83, exit Raul Longoria, just w on westbound access road. Ext corridors. **Pets:** Accepted.

[✕] [🔲] [🖵] [🐾]

SAN MARCOS

AAA ▼▼▼ Days Inn 🅂🅷
(512) 353-5050. **$49-$135.** 1005 I-35 N. I-35, exit 205 northbound; exit 204B southbound, on southbound frontage road, jct SR 80. Ext corridors. **Pets:** Dogs only. $10 one-time fee/pet. Designated rooms, service with restrictions, supervision.

[SAVE] [S🔥] [✕] [🔲] [🐾]

♦♦♦♦ ▼▼▼ Econo Lodge SH
(512) 353-5300. **$39-$120.** 811 S Guadalupe St. I-35, exit 204 northbound; exit 204A southbound, on west frontage road. Ext corridors. **Pets:** Small, other species. $15 one-time fee/room. Designated rooms, service with restrictions, crate.
SAVE ⬛ ⊠ 🖥 💻 🏊

▼▼▼▼ La Quinta Inn San Marcos SH
(512) 392-8800. **$94-$114.** 1619 I-35 N. I-35, exit 206 southbound, 0.5 mi s, on west frontage road; exit northbound, 1 mi n to turnaround to west frontage road, then 1.5 mi s. Ext/int corridors. **Pets:** Other species. Service with restrictions, supervision.
ASK ⬛ ⊠ ⬛M 🖥 💻 🏊

♦♦♦ ▼▼▼ Ramada Limited SH
(512) 395-8000. **$69-$99.** 1701 I-35 N. I-35, exit 206 southbound, 0.4 mi s on west frontage road; exit northbound, 1 mi n to turnaround for west frontage road, then 1.4 mi s. Ext corridors. **Pets:** Very small, dogs only. $20 daily fee/pet. Designated rooms, service with restrictions, supervision.
SAVE ⬛ ⊠ 🖥 💻 🏊

▼▼ Rodeway Inn SH
(512) 353-8011. **Call for rates.** 1635 Aquarena Springs Dr. I-35, exit 206, 0.5 mi s. Ext corridors. **Pets:** Accepted.
⊠ 🖥 🏊

SEALY

▼▼ Best Western Inn of Sealy SH
(979) 885-3707. **$77-$87.** 2107 Hwy 36. I-10, exit 720. Ext corridors. **Pets:** Accepted.
ASK ⬛ ⊠ 💻 🏊

SEGOVIA

♦♦♦ ▼▼▼ Econo Lodge M 🐾
(325) 446-2475. **$44-$66.** 311 S Segovia Access Rd. I-10, exit 465; on south access road. Ext corridors. **Pets:** $10 one-time fee/pet. Designated rooms, service with restrictions, supervision.
SAVE ⬛ ⊠ 🖥 💻 🏊

SHAMROCK

♦♦♦ ▼▼▼▼ Best Western Shamrock Inn & Suites SH
(806) 256-1001. **$90-$125.** 1802 N Main St. I-40, exit 163, just n. Int corridors. **Pets:** $10 daily fee/pet. Designated rooms, service with restrictions, supervision.
SAVE ⬛ ⊠ ⬛M 🖥 💻 🏊

♦♦♦ ▼▼▼ Econo Lodge M
(806) 256-2111. **$50-$70.** 1006 E 12th St. I-40, exit 164 westbound; exit 161 or 163 eastbound, just e of US 83. Ext corridors. **Pets:** Accepted.
SAVE ⬛ ⊠ 🖥 💻 🏊

♦♦♦ ▼▼▼ Irish Inn SH
(806) 256-2106. **$57-$74, 7 day notice.** 301 I-40 E. I-40, exit 163, 0.3 mi e on north service road. Ext/int corridors. **Pets:** Other species. $9 one-time fee/room. Designated rooms, service with restrictions, supervision.
SAVE ⬛ ⊠ 🖥 💻 🍴 🏊

♦♦♦ ▼▼ Western Motel M
(806) 256-3244. **$89.** 104 E 12th St. Business Rt I-40 and US 83. Ext corridors. **Pets:** Medium. $5 daily fee/pet. Service with restrictions, supervision.
SAVE ⬛ ⊠ 🖥 🍴

SHERMAN

▼▼▼▼ Comfort Suites of Sherman SH
(903) 893-0499. **$99-$145, 14 day notice.** 2900 US Hwy 75 N. US 75, exit 63; 0.3 mi s of jct US 82. Int corridors. **Pets:** Accepted.
ASK ⬛ ⊠ 🖥 💻 🏊

▼▼▼▼ La Quinta Inn & Suites Sherman/Denison SH
(903) 870-1122. **$99-$119.** 2912 US 75 N. US 75, exit 63; just sw of jct US 82. Int corridors. **Pets:** Other species. Service with restrictions, supervision.
ASK ⬛ ⊠ 🖥 💻 🏊

♦♦♦ ▼▼▼▼ Stonebridge Hotel & Suites SH
(903) 868-0555. **$70-$80.** 3605 Hwy 75 S. US 75, exit 56. Int corridors. **Pets:** Accepted.
SAVE ⬛ ⊠ 🖥 💻 🍴 🏊

SMITHVILLE

▼▼ Pine Point Inn SH
(512) 237-2040. **Call for rates.** 1503 Dorothy Nichols Ln. Jct SR 71 and Dorothy Nichols Ln. Ext corridors. **Pets:** Accepted.
⊠ 🖥 🏊

SNYDER

▼▼▼ Best Western Snyder Inn M
(325) 574-2200. **Call for rates.** 810 E Coliseum Dr. 1.5 mi w of US 84/80. Ext corridors. **Pets:** Accepted.
⊠ 🖥 💻 🏊

♦♦♦ ▼▼▼ Purple Sage Motel M
(325) 573-5491. **Call for rates.** 1501 E Coliseum Dr. 1 mi w on US 180 from jct US 84. Ext corridors. **Pets:** Accepted.
SAVE ⊠ 🖥 💻 🏊

SONORA

♦♦♦ ▼▼ Americas Best Value Inn-Twin Oaks Motel M
(325) 387-2551. **$45-$60.** 1009 N Crockett Ave. I-10, exit 400 westbound; exit 399 eastbound, 0.5 mi e, then 0.3 mi s on US 277. Ext corridors. **Pets:** Accepted.
SAVE ⬛ ⊠ 🖥

♦♦♦ ▼▼▼ Best Western Sonora Inn SH
(325) 387-9111. **$85-$90.** 270 Hwy 277 N. I-10, exit 400. Ext corridors. **Pets:** Medium. $10 daily fee/pet. Designated rooms, service with restrictions, supervision.
SAVE ⬛ ⊠ 🖥 💻 🏊

▼▼▼▼ Comfort Inn of Sonora SH
(325) 387-5800. **$73-$96.** 311 N Hwy 277. I-10, exit 400. Ext corridors. **Pets:** Accepted.
ASK ⬛ ⊠ ⬛M 🖥 💻 🏊

♦♦♦ ▼▼ Holiday Host Motel M
(325) 387-2532. **$34-$50.** 127 Loop 467 (Hwy 290). Loop 467, exit 404 westbound, 3 mi w; exit 399 eastbound, 3 mi e. Ext corridors. **Pets:** Medium. $10 deposit/pet. No service, supervision.
SAVE ⊠ 🖥 🏊

SOUTH PADRE ISLAND

♦♦♦ ▼▼▼ Best Western Fiesta Isles Hotel SH
(956) 761-4913. **Call for rates.** 5701 Padre Blvd. 3 mi n of Queen Isabella Cswy. Ext corridors. **Pets:** $25 one-time fee/pet. Service with restrictions, supervision.
SAVE ⊠ 🖥 💻 🏊

▼▼▼▼ Howard Johnson Inn SH
(956) 761-5658. **Call for rates.** 1709 Padre Blvd. SR 100, 0.9 mi n at corner of W Palm St. Int corridors. **Pets:** Accepted.
⊠ ⬛M 🖥 💻 🏊

♦♦♦ ▼▼▼▼ La Copa Beach Resort SH 🐾
(956) 761-6000. **$49-$399, 3 day notice.** 350 Padre Blvd. Just s of Queen Isabella Cswy. Int corridors. **Pets:** Small. $10 daily fee/pet. Service with restrictions, supervision.
SAVE ⬛ ⊠ 🖥 💻 🏊

◆ La Quinta Inn and Suites South Padre Island [SH]
(956) 772-7000. **Call for rates.** 7000 Padre Blvd. I-77, exit SR 100, over Queen Isabella Cswy, then 3 mi n. Int corridors. **Pets:** Other species. Service with restrictions, supervision.

[✕] [🛢M] [🛢] [💻] [🏊] [✕]

◆ Motel 6 South Padre Island #1237 [M]
(956) 761-7911. **$35-$55.** 4013 Padre Blvd. 2 mi n of Queen Isabella Cswy. Ext corridors. **Pets:** Other species. Service with restrictions, supervision.

[S🛢] [✕] [🏊]

◆◆ Ramada Limited [SH]
(956) 761-4097. **$66-$309.** 4109 Padre Blvd. 2 mi n of Queen Isabella Cswy. Ext corridors. **Pets:** Accepted.

[SAVE] [✕] [🛢] [💻] [🏊]

◆◆ Super 8 Motel [SH]
(956) 761-6300. **$99-$249.** 4205 Padre Blvd. 2.7 mi n of Queen Isabella Cswy. Ext corridors. **Pets:** Accepted.

[ASK] [S🛢] [✕] [🛢M] [🛢] [💻] [🏊]

◆◆ The Tiki Condominium Hotel [CO]
(956) 761-2694. **$79-$325, 3 day notice.** 6608 Padre Blvd. 3.8 mi n of Queen Isabella Cswy. Ext corridors. **Pets:** Accepted.

[S🛢] [✕] [🛢] [💻] [🏊] [✕]

◆◆ Travelodge [SH]
(956) 761-4744. **Call for rates.** 6200 Padre Blvd. 3 mi n of Queen Isabella Cswy. Ext corridors. **Pets:** $10 daily fee/pet. Service with restrictions, supervision.

[✕] [🛢M] [🛢] [💻] [🏊]

STEPHENVILLE

◆◆ Best Western Cross Timbers [SH]
(254) 968-2114. **$67-$89.** 1625 W South Loop (US 377). 1.8 mi sw on US 377 Bypass and 67. Ext corridors. **Pets:** $10 daily fee/room. Supervision.

[SAVE] [S🛢] [✕] [🛢] [💻] [🏊]

◆◆ Holiday Inn Stephenville [SH]
(254) 968-5256. **$72-$119.** 2865 W Washington St. 1.5 mi s on US 377/167. Ext corridors. **Pets:** Accepted.

[ASK] [S🛢] [✕] [🛢] [💻] [🍴] [🏊]

SULPHUR SPRINGS

◆◆ Best Western Trail Dust Inn & Suites [SH] ❀
(903) 885-7515. **$79-$99.** 1521 Shannon Rd. Jct I-30 and Loop 301, exit 127. Ext/int corridors. **Pets:** Small. $10 daily fee/pet. Service with restrictions.

[SAVE] [S🛢] [✕] [🛢] [💻] [🏊]

◆◆ Comfort Suites [SH]
(903) 438-0918. **$79, 3 day notice.** 1521 E Industrial Dr. I-30, exit 127, just n. Int corridors. **Pets:** Other species. $5 daily fee/pet. No service, supervision.

[SAVE] [✕] [🛢M] [🛢] [💻] [🏊]

SWEETWATER

◆◆ Days Inn [SH]
(325) 235-4853. **Call for rates (no credit cards).** 701 SW Georgia Ave. I-20, exit 244, just w on south frontage road. Ext corridors. **Pets:** Accepted.

[SAVE] [✕] [🛢] [💻] [🍴] [🏊]

◆◆ La Quinta Inn [SH]
(325) 236-6887. **$95-$115.** 500 NW Georgia St. I-20, exit 244, just w of jct SR 70 on north access road. Ext/int corridors. **Pets:** Other species. Service with restrictions, supervision.

[ASK] [S🛢] [✕] [🛢] [💻] [🍴] [🏊]

◆◆ Ranch House Motel & Restaurant [SH]
(325) 236-6341. **$59-$69.** 301 SW Georgia Ave. I-20, exit 244, just w of jct SR 70 on south access road. Ext/int corridors. **Pets:** Medium. Designated rooms, service with restrictions, supervision.

[SAVE] [✕] [🛢] [💻] [🍴] [🏊]

◆◆ Super 8 [SH]
(325) 235-5234. **Call for rates.** 216 SE Georgia Ave. I-20, exit 244. Ext corridors. **Pets:** $25 one-time fee/room. Designated rooms, service with restrictions.

[SAVE] [✕] [🛢] [💻] [🏊]

TEMPLE

◆◆ La Quinta Inn Temple [SH]
(254) 771-2980. **$89-$109.** 1604 W Barton Ave. SR 53, just e; jct I-35 and US 81, exit 301. Ext/int corridors. **Pets:** Other species. Service with restrictions, supervision.

[ASK] [S🛢] [✕] [🛢] [💻] [🏊]

TERLINGUA

◆◆◆ Big Bend Motor Inn [M]
(432) 371-2218. **$90-$95, 7 day notice.** Hwy 118/170. SR 118, 2 mi from entrance of Big Bend National Park. Ext corridors. **Pets:** Small. $5 daily fee/pet. Designated rooms, no service, supervision.

[SAVE] [✕] [🛢] [💻]

TEXARKANA

◆◆ Country Plaza Inn [SH]
(903) 792-3366. **Call for rates.** 5401 N State Line Ave. I-30, exit 223B, 0.3 mi n on US 71. Int corridors. **Pets:** Accepted.

[SAVE] [✕] [🛢] [💻] [🏊]

◆◆ La Quinta Inn [SH]
(903) 794-1900. **$89-$109.** 5201 State Line Ave. I-30, exit 223A, sw of jct US 59 and 71. Ext corridors. **Pets:** Other species. Service with restrictions, supervision.

[ASK] [S🛢] [✕] [🛢] [💻] [🏊]

◆ Motel 6–201 [SH]
(903) 793-1413. **$43-$55.** 1924 Hampton Rd. I-30, exit 222 (Summerhill Rd). Ext corridors. **Pets:** Other species. Service with restrictions, supervision.

[S🛢] [✕] [🏊]

◆◆ Texarkana Inn [SH]
(903) 792-6688. **$52-$70.** 5105 N State Line Ave. I-30, exit 223A, just sw. Ext corridors. **Pets:** Accepted.

[SAVE] [S🛢] [✕] [🛢] [💻] [🏊]

TEXAS CITY

◆◆◆ Best Western Mainland Inn & Suites [SH]
(409) 986-6600. **Call for rates.** 10620 Emmett Lowry Expwy. I-45, exit 16, 1 mi w to Century Blvd exit, then 0.5 mi w. Int corridors. **Pets:** Accepted.

[✕] [🛢] [🏊]

THREE RIVERS

◆◆ Econo Lodge [M]
(361) 786-3563. **$59-$89.** 1401 N Harborth Ave. I-37, exit 72 (US 281), 3.8 mi s. Ext corridors. **Pets:** Accepted.

[ASK] [S🛢] [✕] [🛢] [💻] [🏊]

TULIA

◆◆ Select Inn of Tulia [M]
(806) 995-3248. **$54-$75.** 1591 I-27. I-27, exit 74. Ext corridors. **Pets:** Accepted.

[ASK] [✕] [🛢M] [🛢] [💻]

TYLER

♦♦♦♦♦ Candlewood Suites SH
(903) 509-4131. **$95.** 315 E Rieck Rd. 1.1 mi s of jct Loop 323 and US 69 (S Broadway) to Rieck Rd, just e. Int corridors. **Pets:** Accepted.
SAVE ⊠ &M ▤ ▣

♦♦♦ Holiday Inn Select SH
(903) 561-5800. **$129.** 5701 S Broadway. 1.1 mi s of jct Loop 323 and US 69 (S Broadway). Int corridors. **Pets:** Accepted.
ASK S⊙ ⊠ ▤ ▣ ¶ ⇌ ⊠

♦♦ La Quinta Inn Tyler SH
(903) 561-2223. **$99-$119.** 1601 W SW Loop 323. 1 mi w of S US 69. Ext corridors. **Pets:** Other species. Service with restrictions, supervision.
ASK S⊙ ⊠ ▤ ▣ ⇌

♦♦♦♦ Ramada Tyler Conference Center SH
(903) 593-3600. **Call for rates.** 3310 Troup Hwy. 0.3 mi n of jct E Loop 323 and SR 110. Ext corridors. **Pets:** Accepted.
SAVE ⊠ ▤ ▣ ¶ ⇌

♦♦♦ Residence Inn by Marriott SH
(903) 595-5188. **$143-$163.** 3303 Troup Hwy. 0.3 mi n of jct E Loop 323 and SR 110. Ext corridors. **Pets:** Medium, other species. $100 one-time fee/room. Service with restrictions, supervision.
ASK S⊙ ⊠ ▤ ▣ ⇌ ⊠

UVALDE

♦♦ Holiday Inn SH
(830) 278-4511. **$88-$106.** 920 E Main St. 0.5 mi e on US 90. Ext corridors. **Pets:** Accepted.
ASK S⊙ ⊠ ▤ ▣ ¶ ⇌

VAN HORN

♦♦♦ Americas Best Value Inn M
(432) 283-2410. **$55-$120.** 1705 W Broadway St. I-10, exit 138, 0.3 mi e, then 1 mi w on US 80. Ext corridors. **Pets:** Accepted.
SAVE S⊙ ⊠ ▤ ⇌

♦♦ Budget Inn M
(432) 283-2019. **$36-$40.** 1303 W Broadway. I-10, exit 138, 0.7 mi e. Ext corridors. **Pets:** Accepted.
SAVE S⊙ ⊠ ▤

♦♦ Days Inn M
(432) 283-1007. **$65-$105.** 600 E Broadway St. I-10, exit 140B, just w. Ext corridors. **Pets:** Other species. $10 daily fee/pet. Service with restrictions, supervision.
SAVE S⊙ ⊠ ▤ ▣ ⇌

♦♦ Econo Lodge SH
(432) 283-2211. **$60-$95.** 1601 W Broadway St. I-10, exit 138, 0.5 mi e on Business Rt I-10. Ext corridors. **Pets:** Small. $10 daily fee/pet. Service with restrictions, supervision.
SAVE S⊙ ⊠ ▤ ▣ ⇌

♦♦ Economy Inn M
(432) 283-2754. **$38-$42.** 1500 W Broadway St. I-10, exit 138, 0.5 mi e on US 80. Ext corridors. **Pets:** $5 one-time fee/pet. No service, supervision.
SAVE S⊙ ⊠ ▤

♦♦♦ Holiday Inn Express SH
(432) 283-7444. **$89-$109.** 1905 SW Frontage Rd. I-10, exit 138 (Golf Course Dr). Ext corridors. **Pets:** Small, other species. $10 daily fee/pet. Service with restrictions, supervision.
SAVE ⊠ &M ▤ ▣ ⇌

♦♦ Knights Inn & Suites M
(432) 283-2030. **$55-$99.** 1309 W Broadway. I-10, exit 138, 1 mi e. Ext corridors. **Pets:** $10 daily fee/pet. Designated rooms, no service, supervision.
SAVE S⊙ ⊠ ▤ ▣ ⇌

♦ Motel 6-4024 M
(432) 283-2992. **$46-$56.** 1805 W Broadway St. I-10, exit 138. Ext corridors. **Pets:** Small, other species. Service with restrictions, supervision.
SAVE S⊙ ⊠

♦♦ Ramada Inn SH
(432) 283-2780. **$76-$89.** 200 Golf Course Dr. I-10, exit 138 (Golf Course Dr). Ext/int corridors. **Pets:** Accepted.
SAVE S⊙ ⊠ ▤ ▣ ⇌

♦♦ Van Horn Super 8 M
(432) 283-2282. **$65-$80.** 1807 E Service Rd. I-10, exit 138 (Golf Course Dr). Ext corridors. **Pets:** Accepted.
SAVE S⊙ ⊠ ▤ ▣

VEGA

♦♦♦ Best Western Country Inn M
(806) 267-2131. **Call for rates.** 1800 W Vega Blvd. 0.5 mi w on US 40 business loop. Ext corridors. **Pets:** Medium, other species. $10 daily fee/pet. Designated rooms, service with restrictions, supervision.
SAVE ⊠ ▤ ▣ ⇌

♦♦♦ Comfort Inn SH
(806) 267-0126. **$65-$89.** 1005 S Main. I-40, exit 36. Int corridors. **Pets:** Small. $10 daily fee/pet. Service with restrictions, supervision.
SAVE S⊙ ⊠ ▤ ▣ ⇌

VERNON

♦♦♦ Best Western Village Inn M
(940) 552-5417. **$74-$119.** 1615 US Hwy 287 E. US 287, exit Main St, just w. Ext/int corridors. **Pets:** Accepted.
ASK S⊙ ⊠ ▤ ▣ ¶ ⇌

♦♦♦ Holiday Inn Express Hotel and Suites SH
(940) 552-0200. **$99-$104.** 700 Hillcrest Dr. Jct US 287 and 70. Int corridors. **Pets:** Accepted.
ASK S⊙ ⊠ ▤ ▣ ⇌

VICTORIA

♦♦♦ Holiday Inn Holidome SH
(361) 575-0251. **Call for rates.** 2705 E Houston Hwy (Business Rt 59). On Business Rt US 59, 2.5 mi ne. Ext/int corridors. **Pets:** Accepted.
⊠ ▤ ▣ ¶ ⇌ ⊠

♦♦ La Quinta Inn Victoria SH
(361) 572-3585. **$99-$119.** 7603 N Navarro St (US 77 N). 4 mi n; at Loop 463. Ext corridors. **Pets:** Other species. Service with restrictions, supervision.
ASK S⊙ ⊠ ▤ ▣ ⇌

♦♦♦ Lone Star Inn & Suites SH
(361) 579-0225. **$65-$70.** 1907 US 59 N. US 59, exit Bloomington (US 185); on northeast corner. Ext corridors. **Pets:** $25 daily fee/pet. Service with restrictions, supervision.
SAVE S⊙ ⊠ ▤ ▣ ⇌

♦ Motel 6 Victoria #225 M
(361) 573-1273. **$45-$58.** 3716 Houston Hwy. On Business Rt US 59. Ext corridors. **Pets:** Other species. Service with restrictions, supervision.
S⊙ ⊠ ⇌

♦♦ Quality Inn-Victoria SH
(361) 578-2030. **$75-$90, 7 day notice.** 3112 E Houston Hwy (Business Rt 59). On Business Rt US 59, 2 mi ne. Ext corridors. **Pets:** Accepted.
ASK S⊙ ⊠ ▤ ▣ ⇌

VIDOR

La Quinta Inn & Suites SH
(409) 783-2600. **$89-$109.** 165 E Courtland St. I-10, exit 861A, just s. Int corridors. **Pets:** Other species. Service with restrictions, supervision.

SAVE SD X ⬛ 🖥 🏊

WACO

Best Western Old Main Lodge SH
(254) 753-0316. **$95-$105.** I-35 & 4th St. I-35 and US 81, exit 335A (4th-5th sts). Ext corridors. **Pets:** Small. Service with restrictions, supervision.

SAVE SD X ⬛ 🖥 🏊

Days Inn SH ❖
(254) 799-8585. **$69-$125.** 1504 I-35 N. I-35, exit 338B (Behrens Cir), just n. Ext corridors. **Pets:** Medium, dogs only. $10 daily fee/pet. Service with restrictions.

SAVE SD X ⬛ 🖥 🏊

Hotel Waco SH ❖
(254) 753-0261. **$69-$99.** 1001 Martin Luther King Blvd. I-35, exit 335C (Lake Brazos Dr), just n. Int corridors. **Pets:** Small. $25 one-time fee/pet. Designated rooms, service with restrictions, supervision.

SAVE SD X ⬛ 🖥 🍴 🏊

La Quinta Inn Waco (University) SH
(254) 752-9741. **$102-$122.** 1110 S 9th St. I-35, exit 334 (17th St) southbound; exit 334A (18th St) northbound. Ext corridors. **Pets:** Other species. Service with restrictions, supervision.

ASK SD X ⬛ 🖥 🏊

Residence Inn by Marriott SH
(254) 714-1386. **$144-$164.** 501 S University Parks Dr. I-35, exit 335B, 0.3 mi w. Int corridors. **Pets:** Accepted.

ASK SD X ⬛ 🖥 🏊 ⊠

Super 8 Motel-Waco SH
(254) 754-1023. **Call for rates.** 1320 S Jack Kultgen Frwy. I-35, exit 334, just e. Int corridors. **Pets:** Accepted.

⊠ ⬛

WAXAHACHIE

Super 8 Motel SH
(972) 938-9088. **$67-$99, 7 day notice.** 400 I-35E. I-35E, exit 401B. Int corridors. **Pets:** Accepted.

ASK SD X ⬛ 🖥 🏊

WEATHERFORD

Best Western Santa Fe Inn SH
(817) 594-7401. **$84-$99.** 1927 Santa Fe Dr. I-20, exit 409 (Clear Lake Rd/FM 2552), 0.3 mi nw. Ext corridors. **Pets:** Accepted.

SAVE SD X ⬛ 🖥 🏊

Hampton Inn SH
(817) 599-4800. **$105-$200.** 2524 S Main St. I-20, exit 408. Int corridors. **Pets:** Accepted.

ASK SD X ⬛ 🖥 🏊

Holiday Inn Express Hotel & Suites SH
(817) 599-3700. **$110-$150.** 2500 S Main St. I-20, exit 408. Ext/int corridors. **Pets:** Accepted.

ASK SD X ♿M ⬛ 🖥 🏊

La Quinta Inn & Suites SH
(817) 594-4481. **$109-$129.** 1915 Wall St. I-20, exit 408, just se. Int corridors. **Pets:** Other species. Service with restrictions, supervision.

ASK SD X ♿M ⬛ 🖥 🏊

WEIMAR

Czech Inn SH
(979) 725-9788. **$61-$71.** 102 Townsend Ln. I-10, exit 682, just w on north access road. Int corridors. **Pets:** $10 daily fee/room. Service with restrictions.

SAVE X ⬛ 🖥 🏊

WELLINGTON

Cherokee Inn & Restaurant M
(806) 447-2508. **$39-$75.** 1105 Houston St. US 83, just n of jct FM 338. Ext corridors. **Pets:** Accepted.

ASK SD X 🍴

WESLACO

Best Western Palm Aire Hotel & Suites SH
(956) 969-2411. **$64-$118.** 415 S International Blvd. US 83, exit International Blvd. Ext corridors. **Pets:** Accepted.

SAVE SD X ⬛ 🖥 🍴 🏊 ⊠

Super 8 Motel SH
(956) 969-9920. **Call for rates.** 1702 E Expwy 83. US 83, exit Airport Dr. Ext corridors. **Pets:** Accepted.

⊠ ⬛ 🖥 🏊

WICHITA FALLS

Best Western Northtown Inn SH
(940) 766-3300. **Call for rates.** 1317 Kenley Ave. I-44, exit 2, just w. Int corridors. **Pets:** Accepted.

SAVE X ⬛ 🖥 🏊

Best Western Wichita Falls Inn SH
(940) 766-6881. **$60-$80.** 1032 Central Frwy. I-44, exit 2, just w. Ext corridors. **Pets:** Small. $10 daily fee/pet. Service with restrictions, supervision.

SAVE SD X ⬛ 🖥 🏊

Hawthorn Suites Limited SH
(940) 692-7900. **$99-$189.** 1917 Elmwood Ave N. US 281 S, exit Southwest Pkwy (CR 369), 2.3 mi w to Kemp Blvd, 2 blks n to Elmwood Ave, then just e. Int corridors. **Pets:** Accepted.

ASK SD X ♿M ⬛ 🖥 🏊

Holiday Inn LH
(940) 761-6000. **$80.** 100 Central Frwy. I-287, exit 1C, on west side access road. Int corridors. **Pets:** Accepted.

ASK SD X ⬛ 🖥 🍴 🏊

La Quinta Inn Wichita Falls SH
(940) 322-6971. **$92-$112.** 1128 Central Frwy N. I-44, exit 2, just w. Ext corridors. **Pets:** Other species. Service with restrictions, supervision.

ASK SD X ⬛ 🖥 🏊

Motel 6 #130 M
(940) 322-8817. **$39-$51.** 1812 Maurine St. I-44, exit 2, just e. Ext corridors. **Pets:** Other species. Service with restrictions, supervision.

SD X 🏊

Ramada Limited M
(940) 855-0085. **$67-$74.** 3209 Northwest Frwy. US 287, exit Beverly (CR 11), just w. Ext corridors. **Pets:** Other species. $10 one-time fee/room. Service with restrictions, crate.

SAVE SD X ⬛ 🖥 🏊

WOODWAY

Extended StayAmerica SH
(254) 399-8836. **$72-$80.** 5903 Woodway Dr. I-35, exit 330 (SR 6), 5 mi sw; Loop 340, exit 330 to jct SR 84. Int corridors. **Pets:** Other species. $75 one-time fee/pet. Service with restrictions.

ASK SD X ⬛ 🖥

Travelodge Waco SH
(254) 751-7400. **$75-$110, 14 day notice.** 7007 Woodway Dr. I-35, exit 330 (SR 6 N), 2.4 mi w to exit US 84, then 1.1 mi s. Int corridors. **Pets:** Other species. $100 deposit/room, $25 one-time fee/room. Service with restrictions, supervision.

ZAPATA

Best Western Inn by the Lake SH
(956) 765-8403. **$85-$99.** Hwy 83 S. On US 83, 0.5 mi se. Ext corridors. **Pets:** Accepted.

UTAH

BEAVER

Best Western Butch Cassidy Inn 🅼
(435) 438-2438. **$71-$110.** 161 S Main St. I-15, exit 109, 1.5 mi e. Ext corridors. **Pets:** Other species. $5 daily fee/pet. Service with restrictions, supervision.

Best Western Paradise Inn 🅼
(435) 438-2455. **$84.** 1451 N 300 W. I-15, exit 112, just e; north end of town. Ext corridors. **Pets:** Accepted.

Country Inn 🅼
(435) 438-2484. **$55-$80.** 1450 N 300 W. I-15, exit 112, 2 blks e. Ext corridors. **Pets:** Accepted.

Quality Inn 🅼
(435) 438-5426. **$50-$75.** 781 W 1800 S. I-15, exit 109, just w. Int corridors. **Pets:** Accepted.

BICKNELL

Aquarius Motel and Restaurant 🆂🅷
(435) 425-3835. **$52-$64.** 240 W Main St. SR 24, 9 mi w of Capitol Reef National Park; downtown. Ext/int corridors. **Pets:** Large, other species. $25 deposit/pet, $5 daily fee/room. Service with restrictions, crate.

BLANDING

Four Corners Inn 🅼
(435) 678-3257. **$55-$67.** 131 E Center St. On US 191. Ext corridors. **Pets:** Other species. $3 daily fee/room. Crate.

Gateway Inn 🅼
(435) 678-2278. **$55-$70.** 88 E Center St. East side on US 191. Ext corridors. **Pets:** Large. Designated rooms, service with restrictions, supervision.

BLUFF

Kokopelli Inn 🅼
(435) 672-2322. **$50-$60.** 160 E Main St. On US 191. Int corridors. **Pets:** Medium. $11 daily fee/pet. Service with restrictions, supervision.

Recapture Lodge 🅼
(435) 672-2281. **$45-$65 (no credit cards).** 220 E Main St. On US 191. Ext corridors. **Pets:** Other species. Designated rooms, supervision.

BOULDER

Boulder Mountain Lodge 🆂🅷
(435) 335-7460. **$72-$175 (no credit cards), 14 day notice.** 20 N Hwy 12. Just n of jct SR 12 and Burr Trail Rd. Ext/int corridors. **Pets:** Accepted.

BRIGHAM CITY

Crystal Inn 🆂🅷
(435) 723-0440. **$118-$138.** 480 Westland Dr. I-15 and 84, exit 362 (Logan and Brigham City), 1 mi e. Int corridors. **Pets:** Other species. $75 deposit/pet. Designated rooms, service with restrictions, supervision.

BRYCE CANYON CITY

Best Western Ruby's Inn 🅻🅷
(435) 834-5341. **$60-$189.** UT Hwy 63. On SR 63, 1 mi s of SR 12, 1 mi n of Bryce Canyon National Park entrance. Ext/int corridors. **Pets:** Medium. $100 deposit/pet, $10 daily fee/pet. No service, supervision.

Bryce Canyon Resort 🆂🅷
(435) 834-5351. **$50-$179.** 139 W SR 12. Jct of SR 12 and 63. Ext corridors. **Pets:** Accepted.

Bryce View Lodge 🆂🅷
(435) 834-5180. **$60-$110.** SR 63. On SR 63, 1 mi s of SR 12; 1 mi n of Bryce Canyon National Park entrance. Ext corridors. **Pets:** Medium. $100 deposit/pet, $10 daily fee/pet. No service, supervision.

CEDAR CITY

Anniversary House Bed & Breakfast 🅱🅱
(435) 865-1266. **$90-$129, 14 day notice.** 133 S 100 W. I-15, exit 59, 1 mi e to 100 W, then just s. Int corridors. **Pets:** Accepted.

Cedar Rest Motel 🅼
(435) 586-9471. **Call for rates.** 479 S Main St. I-15, exit 59, just e. Ext corridors. **Pets:** Accepted.

Crystal Inn Cedar City 🆂🅷
(435) 586-8888. **$129-$139.** 1575 W 200 N. I-15, exit 59, just w. Ext/int corridors. **Pets:** $25 one-time fee/pet. Service with restrictions, supervision.

Days Inn 🅼
(435) 867-8877. **$59-$109.** 1204 S Main St. I-15, exit 57, 0.4 mi ne. Ext corridors. **Pets:** $10 daily fee/pet. Designated rooms, service with restrictions, supervision.

▼▼▼▼ Holiday Inn Express Hotel & Suites Ⓜ
(435) 865-7799. **$81-$129.** 1555 S Old Hwy 91. I-15, exit 57, just e, then s. Int corridors. **Pets:** Accepted.
ⒶⓈⓀ Ⓢ Ⓧ Ⓛ Ⓜ 🛏 🖵 🏊

▼▼ Knights Inn Ⓜ
(435) 586-9916. **$49-$139.** 281 S Main St. I-15, exit 57, just e. Ext corridors. **Pets:** Accepted.
ⒶⓈⓀ Ⓢ Ⓧ 🛏 🖵 🏊

▼▼ Motel 6 of Cedar City–4041 Ⓜ
(435) 586-9200. **Call for rates.** 1620 W 200 N. I-15, exit 59, just w. Int corridors. **Pets:** Other species. Service with restrictions, supervision.
Ⓧ

ⒶⒶⒶ ▼▼▼▼ Quality Inn Ⓜ
(435) 586-2082. **$49-$129.** 250 N 1100 W. I-15, exit 59, just w. Ext corridors. **Pets:** Other species. $10 daily fee/room. Designated rooms, service with restrictions, crate.
Ⓢ Ⓢ Ⓧ 🛏 🖵 🏊

ⒶⒶⒶ ▼▼▼ Super 7 Motel Ⓜ
(435) 586-6566. **$35-$95.** 190 S Main St. I-15, exit 57, just e. Ext corridors. **Pets:** Small, dogs only. $10 daily fee/pet. Designated rooms, service with restrictions, supervision.
Ⓢ Ⓢ Ⓧ 🛏

▼▼ Super 8 Motel Ⓜ
(435) 586-8880. **Call for rates.** 145 N 1550 W. I-15, exit 59, just w. Int corridors. **Pets:** Accepted.
Ⓧ Ⓛ 🛏

CLEARFIELD

▼▼ Days Inn Ⓜ
(801) 825-8000. **Call for rates.** 572 N Main St. I-15, exit 335, just w. Int corridors. **Pets:** Accepted.
Ⓧ 🛏 🖵

COALVILLE

▼▼▼▼ Best Western Holiday Hills Ⓢ⌂
(435) 336-4444. **$71-$99, 3 day notice.** 210 S 200 W. I-80, exit 162, just w. Int corridors. **Pets:** Accepted.
ⒶⓈⓀ Ⓢ Ⓧ 🛏 🖵 🏊 Ⓧ

DELTA

ⒶⒶⒶ ▼▼▼▼ Best Western Motor Inn Ⓜ
(435) 864-3882. **Call for rates.** 527 E Topaz Blvd. US 6, at US 50. Ext corridors. **Pets:** Medium, other species. $10 one-time fee/pet. Designated rooms, service with restrictions, supervision.
Ⓢ Ⓧ 🛏 🖵 🏊

DUCK CREEK VILLAGE

ⒶⒶⒶ ▼▼▼ Pinewoods Resort Ⓜ
(435) 682-2512. **$75-$495, 30 day notice.** 121 Duck Creek Ridge Rd. Just s of SR 14 via Cedar Mountain Rd, 31 mi e of Cedar City; in Cedar Mountain Village; 10 mi w of jct US 89. Ext/int corridors. **Pets:** Medium. $25 deposit/pet, $10 daily fee/pet. Designated rooms, no service, supervision.
Ⓢ Ⓢ Ⓧ 🛏 🖵 Ⓣ Ⓧ Ⓩ

ESCALANTE

▼▼ Rainbow Country Bed & Breakfast ⒷⒷ
(435) 826-4567. **$59-$89, 3 day notice.** 585 E 300 S. Just off SR 12; east end of town. Int corridors. **Pets:** Accepted.
ⒶⓈⓀ Ⓢ Ⓧ Ⓦ Ⓩ

FILLMORE

ⒶⒶⒶ ▼▼▼▼ Best Western Paradise Resort Ⓜ
(435) 743-6895. **$69-$89.** 905 N Main St. I-15, exit 167, just e. Ext corridors. **Pets:** Accepted.
Ⓢ Ⓢ Ⓧ 🛏 🖵 Ⓣ 🏊

▼▼ Inn at Apple Creek Ⓜ
(435) 743-4334. **$69-$100.** 940 S Hwy 99. I-15, exit 163, just e. Int corridors. **Pets:** Accepted.
ⒶⓈⓀ Ⓢ Ⓧ 🛏 🖵 🏊

GARDEN CITY

▼▼ Canyon Cove Inn Ⓜ
(435) 946-3565. **Call for rates.** 315 W Logan (Hwy 89). On US 89, 0.5 mi w of jct US 89 and SR 30. Int corridors. **Pets:** Accepted.
Ⓧ 🛏 🏊

GLENDALE

▼▼ Historic Smith Hotel Bed & Breakfast ⒷⒷ
(435) 648-2156. **$58-$84.** 295 N Main St. US 89; north end of town. Int corridors. **Pets:** Accepted.
ⒶⓈⓀ Ⓢ Ⓧ Ⓩ

GREEN RIVER

▼▼▼▼ Holiday Inn Express Ⓜ
(435) 564-4439. **$79-$104.** 1845 E Main St. I-70, exit 160, 2.6 mi ne. Int corridors. **Pets:** Large, other species. $10 daily fee/pet. Designated rooms, service with restrictions, supervision.
ⒶⓈⓀ Ⓢ Ⓧ 🛏 🖵 🏊

▼▼ Motel 6 #289 Ⓜ
(435) 564-3436. **$41-$55.** 1860 E Main St. I-70, exit 160, 2.7 mi ne. Ext corridors. **Pets:** Other species. Service with restrictions, supervision.
Ⓢ Ⓧ 🛏 🏊

▼▼▼▼ Ramada Limited Ⓜ
(435) 564-8441. **Call for rates.** 1117 E Main St. I-70, exit 164, 1 mi nw. Ext/int corridors. **Pets:** Accepted.
Ⓧ 🛏 🖵 🏊

ⒶⒶⒶ ▼▼▼ Super 8 Motel Ⓜ
(435) 564-8888. **Call for rates.** 1248 E Main St. I-70, exit 160, 3.1 mi ne. Int corridors. **Pets:** Accepted.
Ⓢ Ⓧ 🛏 🖵 🏊

HATCH

ⒶⒶⒶ ▼▼▼ Riverside Resort & RV Park Ⓜ
(435) 735-4223. **Call for rates.** 594 US Hwy 89. On US 89, 1 mi n. Ext corridors. **Pets:** $50 deposit/room, $5 daily fee/pet. Designated rooms, service with restrictions, supervision.
Ⓢ Ⓧ 🛏 Ⓣ Ⓩ

HEBER CITY

ⒶⒶⒶ ▼▼▼ Swiss Alps Inn Ⓜ
(435) 654-0722. **$80-$100.** 167 S Main St. I-80, exit 148 (US 40), 15 mi s. Ext corridors. **Pets:** Designated rooms, service with restrictions, supervision.
Ⓢ Ⓧ 🛏 🖵 🏊 Ⓧ

HUNTSVILLE

▼▼ Jackson Fork Inn ⒷⒷ
(801) 745-0051. **$80-$140, 3 day notice.** 7345 E 900 S. I-15, exit 344 (12th St), 12 mi e on SR 39. Int corridors. **Pets:** Accepted.
ⒶⓈⓀ Ⓢ Ⓧ Ⓣ Ⓩ

HURRICANE

▼▼ Super 8
(435) 635-0808. **Call for rates.** 65 S 700 W. Just s of SR 9. Ext corridors. **Pets:** Accepted.
⊠ 🖪 🖵 ⌘

▼▼ Travelodge 🖩
(435) 635-4647. **$39-$125.** 280 W State St. Just w on SR 9. Ext corridors. **Pets:** Accepted.
🅰️🆂🅺 🆂🅳 ⊠ 🖪 🖵 ⌘

KANAB

⚠️ ▼▼▼ Aikens Lodge 🖩
(435) 644-2625. **$62-$100, 3 day notice.** 79 W Center St. On US 89. Ext corridors. **Pets:** Small, dogs only. $10 daily fee/pet. Designated rooms, service with restrictions, supervision.
🆂🅰️🆅🅴 🆂🅳 ⊠ 🖪 ⌘

⚠️ ▼▼▼ Best Western Red Hills 🖩
(435) 644-2675. **$50-$125.** 125 W Center St. Center. Ext/int corridors. **Pets:** Other species. $10 one-time fee/room. Service with restrictions.
🆂🅰️🆅🅴 🆂🅳 ⊠ 🖪 🖵 ⌘

⚠️ ▼▼▼ Bob-Bon Inn 🖩
(435) 644-5094. **$39-$60.** 236 Hwy 89 N. On US 89. Ext corridors. **Pets:** $5 daily fee/pet. Designated rooms, service with restrictions, supervision.
🆂🅰️🆅🅴 🆂🅳 ⊠ 🖪 ⌘

▼▼▼ Clarion Collection-Victorian Charm Inn 🖩
(435) 644-8660. **$69-$119.** 190 N Hwy 89. North end of town. Int corridors. **Pets:** Accepted.
🅰️🆂🅺 🆂🅳 ⊠

▼▼ Four Seasons Motel 🖩
(435) 644-2635. **$49-$149.** 36 N 300 W. N of downtown, on US 89. Ext corridors. **Pets:** Accepted.
🅰️🆂🅺 🆂🅳 ⊠ 🖪

⚠️ ▼▼ Kanab Mission Inn 🖩
(435) 644-5373. **Call for rates.** 386 E 300 S. E on US 89. Int corridors. **Pets:** Accepted.
🆂🅰️🆅🅴 ⊠

⚠️ ▼▼▼ Parry Lodge 🖩
(435) 644-2601. **$62-$92 (no credit cards).** 89 E Center St. On US 89; corner of 100 E; center. Ext/int corridors. **Pets:** $10 daily fee/pet. Designated rooms, service with restrictions.
🆂🅰️🆅🅴 🆂🅳 ⊠ 🖵 🍴 ⌘

⚠️ ▼▼▼ Quail Park Lodge 🖩
(435) 644-8700. **$36-$65.** 125 Hwy 89 N. On US 89. Ext corridors. **Pets:** Medium, other species. $10 one-time fee/room. Designated rooms, supervision.
🆂🅰️🆅🅴 🆂🅳 ⊠ 🖪 ⌘

▼▼▼▼ Quality Inn 🖩
(435) 644-8888. **$79-$159.** 815 E Hwy 89. On US 89, just e. Int corridors. **Pets:** Medium, other species. $10 daily fee/room. Designated rooms, service with restrictions, supervision.
🅰️🆂🅺 🆂🅳 ⊠ 🆎 🖪 🖵 ⌘

⚠️ ▼▼▼ Shilo Inn 🆂🅷 🐾
(435) 644-2562. **$125 (no credit cards).** 296 W 100 N. N of downtown, on US 89. Int corridors. **Pets:** $25 one-time fee/room. Designated rooms, service with restrictions, supervision.
🆂🅰️🆅🅴 🆂🅳 ⊠ 🖪 🖵 ⌘

▼▼ Super 8 🖩
(435) 644-5500. **$49-$149.** 70 S 200 W. Just s of US 89. Ext corridors. **Pets:** Accepted.
🅰️🆂🅺 🆂🅳 ⊠ 🖪 ⌘

LAKE POWELL

⚠️ ▼▼▼ Defiance House Lodge-Bullfrog Marina 🆂🅷
(435) 684-3000. **Call for rates.** Hwy 276. 1 mi from entrance at Bullfrog sign. Int corridors. **Pets:** Accepted.
🆂🅰️🆅🅴 ⊠ 🖪 🖵

LAYTON

▼▼▼ Comfort Inn 🆂🅷
(801) 544-5577. **$50-$125.** 877 N 400 W. I-15, exit 331, then e. Int corridors. **Pets:** Medium, other species. $25 deposit/room. Designated rooms, service with restrictions, supervision.
🅰️🆂🅺 🆂🅳 ⊠ 🖪 🖵 ⌘

⚠️ ▼▼▼ Hampton Inn 🆂🅷
(801) 775-8800. **Call for rates.** 1700 Woodland Park Dr. I-15, exit 332, 0.3 mi se. Int corridors. **Pets:** Other species. Service with restrictions, supervision.
🆂🅰️🆅🅴 ⊠ 🖪 🖵 ⌘

▼▼▼ Holiday Inn Express 🆂🅷
(801) 773-3773. **$124-$149.** 1695 Woodland Park Dr. I-15, exit 332, 0.3 mi se. Int corridors. **Pets:** Accepted.
🅰️🆂🅺 🆂🅳 ⊠ 🖪 🖵 ⌘

▼▼▼ La Quinta Inn Salt Lake City (Layton) 🆂🅷
(801) 776-6700. **$84.** 1965 N 1200 W. I-15, exit 332, 1 blk e; corner of Antelope Dr and Angel Rd. Int corridors. **Pets:** Other species. Service with restrictions, supervision.
🅰️🆂🅺 🆂🅳 ⊠ 🖪 🖵 ⌘ ⊠

▼▼▼ TownePlace Suites 🖩
(801) 779-2422. **$132-$152.** 1743 Woodland Park Dr. I-15, exit 332, 0.3 mi se. Int corridors. **Pets:** Accepted.
🅰️🆂🅺 🆂🅳 ⊠ 🖪 🖵 ⌘

LEHI

⚠️ ▼▼▼ Best Western Timpanogos Inn 🆂🅷 🐾
(801) 768-1400. **$67-$96, 3 day notice.** 195 S 850 E. I-15, exit 279; southwest side. Int corridors. **Pets:** Medium, other species. $10 one-time fee/room. Designated rooms, service with restrictions, supervision.
🆂🅰️🆅🅴 🆂🅳 ⊠ 🖪 🖵 ⌘

▼▼▼ Motel 6–1405 🖩
(801) 768-2668. **Call for rates.** 210 S 1200 E. I-15, exit 279, just e. Int corridors. **Pets:** Other species. Service with restrictions, supervision.
⊠ 🖪 ⌘

▼▼ Super 8 🖩
(801) 766-8800. **Call for rates.** 125 S 850 E. I-15, exit 279; southwest side. Int corridors. **Pets:** Accepted.
⊠ 🖪 ⌘

LOGAN

⚠️ ▼▼▼ Best Western Baugh Motel 🆂🅷
(435) 752-5220. **Call for rates.** 153 S Main St. On US 89 and 91. Ext corridors. **Pets:** Accepted.
🆂🅰️🆅🅴 ⊠ 🖪 🖵 ⌘

⚠️ ▼▼▼ Best Western Weston Inn 🆂🅷
(435) 752-5700. **$90-$120.** 250 N Main St. I-15, exit 362, on US 89 and 91; downtown. Ext corridors. **Pets:** Small, dogs only. $10 daily fee/pet. Designated rooms, service with restrictions, supervision.
🆂🅰️🆅🅴 🆂🅳 ⊠ 🖪 🖵 ⌘ ⊠

▼▼ Logan Super 8 🆂🅷
(435) 753-8883. **$45-$71.** 865 S Hwy 89 and 91. I-15, exit 362 (Logan and Brigham City), on US 89 and 91; south end of town. Int corridors. **Pets:** Other species. $10 daily fee/pet. Designated rooms, service with restrictions, supervision.
🅰️🆂🅺 🆂🅳 ⊠ 🖪 ⌘

MANTI

▼▼ **Manti Country Village Motel** Ⓜ
(435) 835-9300. **$69-$99.** 145 N Main St. On US 89. Ext corridors.
Pets: Accepted.
Ⓐ𝐒𝐊 ☒ 🖪 🍴

MARYSVALE

▼▼ **Big Rock Candy Mountain Resort** Ⓜ
(435) 326-2000. **$69-$199, 3 day notice.** 4479 N Hwy 89. On US 89,
6 mi n. Ext corridors. **Pets:** Accepted.
Ⓐ𝐒𝐊 𝐒🖥 ☒ 🖪 🖵 🍴 ☒

MEXICAN HAT

◆◆◆ ▼ **San Juan Inn & Trading Post** Ⓜ
(435) 683-2220. **$58-$80.** Hwy 163 & San Juan River. On US 163. Ext
corridors. **Pets:** Dogs only. $10 one-time fee/pet. Designated rooms, serv-
ice with restrictions, supervision.
𝐒𝐀𝐕𝐄 𝐒🖥 ☒ 🖪 🍴

MOAB

◆◆◆ ▼ **Apache Motel** Ⓜ
(435) 259-5727. **$39-$79.** 166 S 400 E. Jct US 191 and 100 S, just e,
then just s. Ext corridors. **Pets:** Other species. Service with restrictions,
supervision.
𝐒𝐀𝐕𝐄 𝐒🖥 ☒ 🖪 🏊

◆◆◆ ▼▼ **Big Horn Lodge** 𝐒𝐇 🐾
(435) 259-6171. **$39-$100.** 550 S Main St. South end of town. Ext
corridors. **Pets:** Other species. $5 daily fee/pet. Designated rooms, service
with restrictions, supervision.
𝐒𝐀𝐕𝐄 ☒ 🖪 🖵 🍴 🏊

◆◆◆ ▼▼▼ **Cedar Breaks Condos** 🄲🄾 🐾
(435) 259-5125. **$100-$205, 7 day notice.** 400 East & Center St. Jct
Main and Center sts, just e, then just s. Ext corridors. **Pets:** Other
species. $10 daily fee/pet. Designated rooms, service with restrictions,
supervision.
𝐒𝐀𝐕𝐄 ☒ 🖪 🖵

▼ **Days Inn** Ⓜ
(435) 259-4468. **$40-$180.** 426 N Main St. On US 191; town center. Int
corridors. **Pets:** Accepted.
Ⓐ𝐒𝐊 𝐒🖥 ☒ 🖪 🖵 🏊

◆◆◆ ▼▼▼ **The Gonzo Inn** Ⓜ 🐾
(435) 259-2515. **$91-$330.** 100 W 200 S. Downtown. Ext/int corridors.
Pets: $25 daily fee/room. Designated rooms, service with restrictions,
supervision.
𝐒𝐀𝐕𝐄 𝐒🖥 ☒ 🖪 🖵 🏊

▼▼▼ **La Quinta Inn Moab** Ⓜ
(435) 259-8700. **$99.** 815 S Main St. South end of town. Int corridors.
Pets: Other species. Service with restrictions, supervision.
Ⓐ𝐒𝐊 𝐒🖥 ☒ 🖪 🖵 🏊

▼▼ **Moab Valley Inn** Ⓜ
(435) 259-4419. **$59-$130.** 711 S Main St. 1 mi s on US 191. Int
corridors. **Pets:** Accepted.
Ⓐ𝐒𝐊 𝐒🖥 ☒ 🖪 🖵 🏊 ☒

▼ **Motel 6 Moab #4119** Ⓜ
(435) 259-6686. **$49-$149.** 1089 N Main St. North end of town; west
side of street. Int corridors. **Pets:** Other species. Service with restrictions,
supervision.
Ⓐ𝐒𝐊 𝐒🖥 ☒ 🏊

▼ **Nichol's Lane Accommodations** 🄲🄾
(435) 259-5125. **$75-$150, 7 day notice.** 543 Nichol Ln. Jct Center and
Main sts, e to 400 E, just s, then just e. Ext corridors. **Pets:** Accepted.
☒ 🖪 🖵

◆◆◆ ▼▼▼ **Ramada of Downtown Moab** Ⓜ
(435) 259-7141. **$59-$169.** 182 S Main St. At 200 S; downtown. Ext/int
corridors. **Pets:** Small. $20 one-time fee/pet. Designated rooms, service
with restrictions, supervision.
𝐒𝐀𝐕𝐄 𝐒🖥 ☒ 🖪 🖵 🍴 🏊

◆◆◆ ▼▼▼ **Red Cliffs Adventure Lodge** 🄡🄐
(435) 259-2002. **$99-$299, 30 day notice.** Milepost 14 Hwy 128. 2 mi
n to jct US 191 and SR 128, 14.5 mi e. Ext corridors. **Pets:** Medium.
$20 daily fee/pet. Designated rooms, service with restrictions, supervision.
𝐒𝐀𝐕𝐄 𝐒🖥 ☒ 🖪 🖵 🍴 🏊 ☒

◆◆◆ ▼▼ **Red Stone Inn** Ⓜ 🐾
(435) 259-3500. **$35-$95.** 535 S Main St. Downtown. Ext/int corridors.
Pets: $5 daily fee/pet. Designated rooms, service with restrictions, supervi-
sion.
𝐒𝐀𝐕𝐄 𝐒🖥 ☒ 🖪 🖵

◆◆◆ ▼▼ **River Canyon Lodge, An Extended Stay Inn &**
Suites Ⓜ 🐾
(435) 259-8838. **$59-$280.** 71 W 200 N. Jct 200 N and Main St, just w;
downtown. Int corridors. **Pets:** Small. $20 one-time fee/pet. Designated
rooms, service with restrictions, supervision.
𝐒𝐀𝐕𝐄 𝐒🖥 ☒ 🖪 🖵 🏊

▼▼ **Riverside Inn** 𝐒𝐇
(435) 259-8848. **Call for rates.** 988 N Main St. 1 mi n on US 191. Int
corridors. **Pets:** Accepted.
☒ 🖪 🏊

◆◆◆ ▼▼ **Silver Sage Inn** Ⓜ
(435) 259-4420. **$45-$90.** 840 S Main St. South end of town on US
191. Int corridors. **Pets:** Medium, other species. $5 daily fee/pet. Service
with restrictions.
𝐒𝐀𝐕𝐄 𝐒🖥 ☒ 🖪 🖵

▼▼ **Sleep Inn** Ⓜ
(435) 259-4655. **$59-$189.** 1051 S Main St. South end of town. Int
corridors. **Pets:** Accepted.
Ⓐ𝐒𝐊 𝐒🖥 ☒ 🅼 🖪 🖵 🏊

◆◆◆ ▼▼▼ **Super 8 Motel, Moab** Ⓜ
(435) 259-8868. **$52-$159.** 889 N Main St. US 191, 1 mi n. Int corridors. **Pets:** Small. $20 one-time fee/pet. Designated rooms, service with
restrictions, supervision.
𝐒𝐀𝐕𝐄 𝐒🖥 ☒ 🖪 🏊

◆◆◆ ▼ **The Virginian Motel** Ⓜ
(435) 259-5951. **$25-$89.** 70 E 200 S. Just e of US 191. Ext corridors.
Pets: Large, other species. $10 daily fee/pet. No service, supervision.
𝐒𝐀𝐕𝐄 𝐒🖥 ☒ 🖪 🖵

MONTICELLO

◆◆◆ ▼▼ **Best Western Wayside Inn** Ⓜ
(435) 587-2261. **Call for rates.** 197 E Central St. On US 491, just e of
US 191. Ext corridors. **Pets:** $10 one-time fee/pet. Designated rooms,
service with restrictions, supervision.
𝐒𝐀𝐕𝐄 ☒ 🖪 🖵 🏊

◆◆◆ ▼▼ **Rodeway Inn & Suites** Ⓜ
(435) 587-2489. **$39-$79.** 649 N Main St. On US 191 N; end of town.
Int corridors. **Pets:** Accepted.
𝐒𝐀𝐕𝐄 𝐒🖥 ☒ 🖪 🖵 🏊

MONUMENT VALLEY

◆◆◆ ▼▼ **Goulding's Trading Post & Lodge** 𝐒𝐇
(435) 727-3231. **$80-$189, 3 day notice.** 1000 Main St. Just n of
Arizona border; 2 mi w of US 163. Ext corridors. **Pets:** $20 daily fee/pet.
Service with restrictions, crate.
𝐒𝐀𝐕𝐄 ☒ 🖪 🖵 🍴 🏊

NEPHI

◆◆◆ ▼▼▼ Best Western Paradise Inn M
(435) 623-0624. **Call for rates.** 1025 S Main St. I-15, exit 222, 0.5 mi n.
Ext corridors. **Pets:** $25 deposit/room, $7 daily fee/pet. Designated rooms,
service with restrictions, supervision.

SAVE ✕ 🖭 🖳 🏊

◆◆◆ ▼▼▼ Safari Motel M
(435) 623-1071. **$55-$61.** 413 S Main St. I-15, exit 228, 3.2 mi s. Ext
corridors. **Pets:** Accepted.

SAVE S🖭 ✕ 🖭 🏊

OGDEN

◆◆◆ ▼▼▼ Best Rest Inn M
(801) 393-8644. **$110-$120.** 1206 W 2100 S. I-15, exit 343, just e. Int
corridors. **Pets:** Other species. $20 deposit/room. Designated rooms, serv-
ice with restrictions, supervision.

SAVE S🖭 ✕ 🖭 🖳 🍴 🏊

◆◆◆ ▼▼▼▼ Best Western High Country Inn SH ❀
(801) 394-9474. **$69-$109.** 1335 W 12th St. I-15, exit 344 (12th St), just
e. Ext/int corridors. **Pets:** Other species. Supervision.

SAVE S🖭 ✕ 🖭 🖳 🍴 🏊 ✕

▼▼▼▼ Comfort Suites of Ogden SH
(801) 621-2545. **$79-$150.** 2250 S 1200 W. I-15, exit 343, just e. Int
corridors. **Pets:** Accepted.

ASK S🖭 ✕ 🖭 🖳 🍴 🏊 ✕

▼▼▼▼ Holiday Inn Express Hotel & Suites SH
(801) 392-5000. **$89-$129.** 2245 S 1200 W. I-15, exit 343, just e. Int
corridors. **Pets:** Accepted.

ASK S🖭 ✕ 🖭 🖳

▼▼ Motel 6 #1082 M
(801) 627-2880. **Call for rates.** 1500 W Riverdale Rd. I-15, 340 southbound; exit 339 northbound, just w. Ext/int corridors. **Pets:** Other species. Service with restrictions, supervision.

✕ 🖭 🏊

▼ Motel 6 Ogden #0111 M
(801) 627-4560. **Call for rates.** 1455 Washington Blvd. I-15, exit 344, 3
mi e, then just s. Int corridors. **Pets:** Other species. Service with restrictions, supervision.

✕ 🖭 🏊

◆◆◆ ▼▼▼ Sleep Inn M ❀
(801) 731-6500. **$55-$70.** 1155 S 1700 W. I-15, exit 344, just w. Int
corridors. **Pets:** Large. $10 daily fee/pet. Service with restrictions, supervi-
sion.

SAVE S🖭 ✕ 🖭 🖳

◆◆◆ ▼▼▼ Super 8 Motel M ❀
(801) 731-7100. **$55-$80.** 1508 W 2100 S. I-15, exit 343, just w. Int
corridors. **Pets:** Medium. $6 daily fee/pet. Designated rooms, service with
restrictions, supervision.

SAVE S🖭 ✕ 🖭

OREM

◆◆◆ ▼▼▼▼ Comfort Inn M
(801) 431-0405. **$80-$100.** 427 W University Pkwy. I-15, exit 269, 0.5
mi e. Int corridors. **Pets:** $25 one-time fee/pet. No service, crate.

SAVE S🖭 ✕ 🖭 🖳 🏊

▼▼▼▼ La Quinta Inn & Suites Orem (University
    Parkway) SH
(801) 226-0440. **$104-$114.** 521 W University Pkwy. I-15, exit 269, 0.5
mi e. Int corridors. **Pets:** Other species. Service with restrictions, supervision.

ASK S🖭 ✕ 🖭 🖳 🏊

◆◆◆ ▼▼▼▼ La Quinta Inn Orem (North/Provo) M
(801) 235-9555. **$72.** 1100 W 780 N. I-15, exit 272, east side. Int
corridors. **Pets:** Small. Service with restrictions, supervision.

SAVE S🖭 ✕ 🖭 🖳 🏊

PANGUITCH

◆◆◆ ▼▼▼ Bryce Way Motel M
(435) 676-2400. **$29-$75.** 429 N Main St. On US 89. Ext corridors.
Pets: Accepted.

SAVE S🖭 ✕ 🖭 🖳

◆◆◆ ▼▼▼ Color Country Motel M ❀
(435) 676-2386. **$39-$66.** 526 N Main St. On US 89. Ext corridors.
Pets: Other species. $10 one-time fee/room. Designated rooms, no service,
supervision.

SAVE ✕ 🏊

▼▼ Harold's Place Cabins CA
(435) 676-2350. **$85-$95.** 3066 Hwy 12. 1 mi e off US 89 at SR 12; 17
mi w of Bryce Canyon. Ext corridors. **Pets:** Accepted.

ASK S🖭 ✕ 🖭 🍴 ☎

▼▼ Harold's Place Inn M
(435) 676-2350. **$65-$85.** 3068 Hwy 12. 0.5 mi e off US 89 at SR 12.
Int corridors. **Pets:** Accepted.

ASK S🖭 ✕ ☎

▼▼ Horizon Motel M
(435) 676-2651. **Call for rates.** 730 N Main St. On US 89. Ext corridors. **Pets:** Accepted.

✕ 🖭 🖳 ☎

◆◆◆ ▼▼▼ Marianna Inn Motel M
(435) 676-8844. **$35-$85.** 699 N Main St. On US 89. Ext corridors.
Pets: Accepted.

SAVE S🖭 ✕ 🖭 🖳

PARK CITY

◆◆◆ ▼▼▼▼ Best Western Landmark Inn SH
(435) 649-7300. **Call for rates.** 6560 N Landmark Dr. I-80, exit 145, at
Kimball Junction. Int corridors. **Pets:** Accepted.

SAVE ✕ 🖭 🖳 🏊 ✕

▼▼▼▼ Holiday Inn Express Hotel & Suites SH
(435) 658-1600. **$117-$216.** 1501 W Ute Blvd. I-80, exit 145 (Kimball
Juncton). Int corridors. **Pets:** Accepted.

ASK S🖭 ✕ 🖭 🖳 🏊 ✕

PAYSON

▼▼▼▼ Comfort Inn SH
(801) 465-4861. **Call for rates.** 830 N Main St. I-15, exit 250, just e. Int
corridors. **Pets:** Accepted.

✕ 🖭 🖳 🏊 ✕

PRICE

◆◆◆ ▼▼▼ Budget Host Inn M
(435) 637-2424. **$54-$125.** 145 N Carbonville Rd. US 6, exit 240, just
e, then just n on Main St. Ext corridors. **Pets:** Accepted.

SAVE S🖭 ✕ 🖭 🖳

◆◆◆ ▼▼ National 9-Price River Inn M
(435) 637-7000. **$54-$84.** 641 W Price River Dr. US 6, exit 240, just e.
Ext/int corridors. **Pets:** $25 deposit/room, $7 daily fee/room. Designated
rooms, service with restrictions, supervision.

SAVE S🖭 ✕ 🖭 🖳

PROVO

△△△ **▽▽▽** **Days Inn** **M**
(801) 375-8600. **Call for rates.** 1675 N 200 W. I-15, exit 269, 3.5 mi e on University Pkwy. Ext corridors. **Pets:** Large. $25 one-time fee/room. Service with restrictions, supervision.

⟨SAVE⟩ ⟨✕⟩ ⟨☎⟩ ⟨💻⟩ ⟨➳⟩

▽▽▽ **Econo Lodge Provo Airport** **M**
(801) 373-0099. **$69-$79.** 1625 W Center St. I-15, exit 265A southbound; exit 265B northbound, 0.3 mi w. Ext corridors. **Pets:** Accepted.

⟨ASK⟩ ⟨S⟩ ⟨✕⟩ ⟨☎⟩ ⟨💻⟩

▽▽▽ **Hampton Inn** ⟨SH⟩
(801) 377-6396. **Call for rates.** 1511 S 40 E. I-15, exit 266, just e. Int corridors. **Pets:** Accepted.

⟨✕⟩ ⟨☎⟩ ⟨💻⟩

▽▽▽ **La Quinta Inn** ⟨SH⟩
(801) 374-9750. **$69-$189.** 1460 S University Ave. I-15, exit 263, just e. Int corridors. **Pets:** Medium. $10 daily fee/pet. Service with restrictions, supervision.

⟨ASK⟩ ⟨S⟩ ⟨✕⟩ ⟨☎⟩ ⟨💻⟩ ⟨🍴⟩ ⟨➳⟩

▽▽▽ **Residence Inn by Marriott** ⟨SH⟩
(801) 374-1000. **$143-$163.** 252 W 2230 N. I-15, exit 269, 3.1 mi e via University Pkwy. Int corridors. **Pets:** Accepted.

⟨ASK⟩ ⟨S⟩ ⟨✕⟩ ⟨&M⟩ ⟨☎⟩ ⟨💻⟩ ⟨➳⟩ ⟨✕⟩

△△△ **▽▽▽** **Sleep Inn** **M**
(801) 377-6597. **$55-$229.** 1505 S 40 E. I-15, exit 263, just e. Int corridors. **Pets:** Medium. $10 daily fee/pet. Service with restrictions, supervision.

⟨SAVE⟩ ⟨S⟩ ⟨✕⟩ ⟨☎⟩ ⟨💻⟩ ⟨➳⟩

△△△ **▽▽▽** **Super 8 Provo BYU/Orem UVSC** **M**
(801) 374-6020. **$49-$200.** 1555 N Canyon Rd. I-15, exit 269, 3.5 mi e. Ext/int corridors. **Pets:** Small. $10 one-time fee/pet. Service with restrictions, supervision.

⟨SAVE⟩ ⟨S⟩ ⟨✕⟩ ⟨☎⟩ ⟨💻⟩ ⟨➳⟩

RICHFIELD

△△△ **▽▽▽** **Best Western Richfield Inn** **M**
(435) 893-0100. **$55-$99.** 1275 N Main St. I-70, exit 40, just s. Int corridors. **Pets:** Accepted.

⟨SAVE⟩ ⟨S⟩ ⟨✕⟩ ⟨☎⟩ ⟨💻⟩

△△△ **▽▽▽** **Budget Host Nights Inn** **M**
(435) 896-8228. **$36-$53.** 69 S Main St. I-70, exit 37 or 40; center of downtown. Ext corridors. **Pets:** Accepted.

⟨SAVE⟩ ⟨✕⟩ ⟨☎⟩ ⟨➳⟩

△△△ **▽▽▽** **Days Inn** ⟨SH⟩ 🐾
(435) 896-6476. **Call for rates.** 333 N Main St. I-70, exit 40, 1 mi s on US 89. Int corridors. **Pets:** Other species. $50 deposit/pet, $10 one-time fee/room. Designated rooms, service with restrictions, supervision.

⟨SAVE⟩ ⟨✕⟩ ⟨☎⟩ ⟨💻⟩ ⟨🍴⟩ ⟨➳⟩

▽▽▽ **New West Motel 1** **M**
(435) 896-4076. **$30-$42.** 447 S Main St. I-70, exit 37 or 40; downtown. Ext corridors. **Pets:** Accepted.

⟨ASK⟩ ⟨S⟩ ⟨✕⟩ ⟨☎⟩ ⟨💻⟩

△△△ **▽▽▽** **Richfield Travelodge** **M**
(435) 896-9271. **Call for rates.** 647 S Main St. I-70, exit 37; south end of town. Int corridors. **Pets:** Medium, other species. $10 one-time fee/room. Designated rooms, supervision.

⟨SAVE⟩ ⟨✕⟩ ⟨☎⟩ ⟨💻⟩ ⟨🍴⟩ ⟨➳⟩

▽▽▽ **Super 8 Motel** **M**
(435) 896-9204. **Call for rates.** 1377 N Main St. I-70, exit 40, just s. Ext/int corridors. **Pets:** Accepted.

⟨✕⟩ ⟨☎⟩ ⟨💻⟩

ROOSEVELT

△△△ **▽▽▽** **Frontier Motel** **M**
(435) 722-2201. **$80.** 75 S 200 E. On US 40. Ext corridors. **Pets:** Accepted.

⟨SAVE⟩ ⟨S⟩ ⟨✕⟩ ⟨☎⟩ ⟨🍴⟩ ⟨➳⟩

ST. GEORGE

▽▽▽ **America's Best Inn & Suites** **M**
(435) 652-3030. **$54-$120.** 245 N Red Cliffs Dr. I-15, exit 8, just e. Ext corridors. **Pets:** Accepted.

⟨ASK⟩ ⟨S⟩ ⟨✕⟩ ⟨☎⟩ ⟨💻⟩ ⟨➳⟩

▽▽ **Americas Best Value Inn** **M**
(435) 673-4666. **$35-$79.** 60 W St. George Blvd. 1 blk w of Main St; downtown. Ext corridors. **Pets:** Accepted.

⟨ASK⟩ ⟨S⟩ ⟨✕⟩ ⟨☎⟩ ⟨➳⟩

△△△ **▽▽▽** **Budget Inn & Suites** ⟨SH⟩
(435) 673-6661. **Call for rates.** 1221 S Main St. I-15, exit 6 (Bluff St), just w. Ext corridors. **Pets:** Medium. $15 daily fee/room. Designated rooms, service with restrictions, supervision.

⟨SAVE⟩ ⟨✕⟩ ⟨☎⟩ ⟨💻⟩ ⟨➳⟩ ⟨✕⟩

△△△ **▽▽▽** **Coronada Inn & Suites** ⟨SH⟩
(435) 628-4436. **$44-$190, 3 day notice.** 559 E St. George Blvd. Downtown. Ext corridors. **Pets:** Accepted.

⟨ASK⟩ ⟨S⟩ ⟨✕⟩ ⟨☎⟩ ⟨➳⟩

△△△ **▽▽▽** **Crystal Inn St. George** ⟨SH⟩
(435) 688-7477. **$129-$149.** 1450 S Hilton Dr. I-15, exit 6 (Bluff St), just w. Int corridors. **Pets:** Very small. $25 one-time fee/pet. Designated rooms, service with restrictions, supervision.

⟨SAVE⟩ ⟨S⟩ ⟨✕⟩ ⟨☎⟩ ⟨💻⟩ ⟨🍴⟩ ⟨➳⟩ ⟨✕⟩

▽▽ **Econo Lodge** **M**
(435) 673-4861. **$40-$120.** 460 E St. George Blvd. I-15, exit 8, cross streets 500 E and St. George Blvd; downtown. Ext corridors. **Pets:** Accepted.

⟨S⟩ ⟨✕⟩ ⟨☎⟩ ⟨💻⟩ ⟨➳⟩

△△△ **▽▽▽** **Fairfield Inn by Marriott** **M**
(435) 673-6066. **$62-$129.** 1660 S Convention Center Dr. I-15, exit 6 (Bluff St), just e. Int corridors. **Pets:** Other species. $75 one-time fee/room. Service with restrictions, supervision.

⟨SAVE⟩ ⟨S⟩ ⟨✕⟩ ⟨☎⟩ ⟨➳⟩

△△△ **▽▽▽** **▽▽▽** **The Green Valley Spa & Resort** ⟨SH⟩ 🐾
(435) 628-8060. **$112-$325, 30 day notice.** 1871 W Canyon View Dr. Bluff and S Main sts, 4 mi sw via Hilton Dr to Dixie Dr, then to Canyon View Dr. Ext corridors. **Pets:** $500 deposit/room, $25 daily fee/room. Service with restrictions.

⟨SAVE⟩ ⟨✕⟩ ⟨&M⟩ ⟨☎⟩ ⟨💻⟩ ⟨🍴⟩ ⟨➳⟩ ⟨✕⟩

△△△ **▽▽▽** **Holiday Inn** ⟨SH⟩
(435) 628-4235. **$89-$139.** 850 S Bluff St. I-15, exit 6 (Bluff St), just w. Ext/int corridors. **Pets:** Small, other species. $25 one-time fee/pet. Designated rooms, supervision.

⟨SAVE⟩ ⟨S⟩ ⟨✕⟩ ⟨☎⟩ ⟨💻⟩ ⟨🍴⟩ ⟨➳⟩ ⟨✕⟩

▽▽▽ **Knights Inn & Suites** **M**
(435) 628-6699. **$50-$110.** 1140 S Bluff St. I-15, exit 6 (Bluff St), just w. Ext corridors. **Pets:** Accepted.

⟨ASK⟩ ⟨S⟩ ⟨✕⟩ ⟨☎⟩ ⟨💻⟩ ⟨➳⟩

△△△ **▽▽▽** **Red Cliffs Inn & Suites** **M**
(435) 673-3537. **$55-$110.** 912 Red Cliffs Dr. I-15, exit 10, just e. Ext/int corridors. **Pets:** Accepted.

⟨SAVE⟩ ⟨S⟩ ⟨✕⟩ ⟨☎⟩ ⟨💻⟩ ⟨🍴⟩ ⟨➳⟩

▼▼▼▼ Seven Wives Inn 🅱🅱
(435) 628-3737. **$95-$195, 7 day notice.** 217 N 100 W. I-15, exit 8, 2.1 mi w, then n. Ext/int corridors. **Pets:** Accepted.

(ASK) ✕ 🛏 ⇔

▼▼▼▼ Shuttle Lodge Inn Ⓜ 🐾
(435) 688-8383. **Call for rates.** 915 S Bluff St. I-15, exit 6 (Bluff St), just w. Int corridors. **Pets:** Other species. $10 daily fee/pet. Designated rooms, service with restrictions, supervision.

✕ 🛏 ⇔

SALINA

▼▼▼▼ Rodeway Inn Ⓜ
(435) 529-1300. **$53-$85.** 1400 S State. I-70, exit 56, just n. Int corridors. **Pets:** Accepted.

(ASK) (S🅾) ✕ 🛏 🖥 ⇔

SALT LAKE CITY METROPOLITAN AREA

COTTONWOOD HEIGHTS

▼▼▼▼ Candlewood Suites Hotel 🆂🅷
(801) 567-0111. **Call for rates.** 6990 S Park Centre Dr. I-15, exit 297, 2.5 mi via 7200 S and Fort Union Blvd. Int corridors. **Pets:** Large, other species. $150 one-time fee/pet. Designated rooms, service with restrictions, supervision.

✕ 🛏 🖥

▼▼▼▼ Residence Inn by Marriott at The Cottonwoods 🆂🅷
(801) 453-0430. **$230-$395.** 6425 S 3000 E. I-215 S, exit 6 (6200 S), 0.3 mi se. Int corridors. **Pets:** Accepted.

(ASK) (S🅾) ✕ 🛏 🖥 ⇔ ✕

DRAPER

▼▼▼▼ Comfort Inn Ⓜ
(801) 571-2511. **$79-$120.** 12033 S Factory Outlet Dr. I-15, exit 291, just n; on east side of interstate. Int corridors. **Pets:** Accepted.

(ASK) ✕ 🛏 🖥 ⇔

▼▼▼▼ Ramada Limited Ⓜ
(801) 571-1122. **$75-$90.** 12605 S Minuteman Dr. I-15, exit 291, 0.3 mi s on frontage road. Int corridors. **Pets:** Accepted.

(ASK) (S🅾) ✕ 🛏 🖥

MIDVALE

▲▲▲▽ ▼▼▼▼▼ Best Western Executive Inn 🆂🅷
(801) 566-4141. **Call for rates.** 280 W 7200 S. I-15, exit 297, just e. Int corridors. **Pets:** Small. $15 daily fee/pet. Service with restrictions, supervision.

(SAVE) ✕ 🛏 🖥 ⇔

▼▼ ▼▼ Extended StayAmerica-Salt Lake City-Union Park Ⓜ
(801) 567-0404. **Call for rates.** 7555 S Union Park Ave. I-215, exit 9 (Union Park Ave), 0.3 mi s. Int corridors. **Pets:** Other species. $75 one-time fee/pet. Service with restrictions.

✕ 🛏 🖥

▼▼▼▼▼ La Quinta Inn Salt Lake City (Midvale) Ⓜ
(801) 566-3291. **$59-$74.** 7231 S Catalpa St. I-15, exit 297, just e. Int corridors. **Pets:** Other species. Service with restrictions, supervision.

(ASK) (S🅾) ✕ 🛏 🖥 ⇔

▼▼ Motel 6 #476 Ⓜ
(801) 561-0058. **Call for rates.** 7263 S Catalpa St. I-15, exit 297, just e, then just s. Ext corridors. **Pets:** Other species. Service with restrictions, supervision.

✕ 🛏 ⇔

▲▲▲▽ ▼▼▼ Scenic Hills Super 8 Ⓜ 🐾
(435) 529-7483. **$65-$95.** 75 E 1500 S. I-70, exit 56, just n. Ext corridors. **Pets:** Dogs only. $15 one-time fee/pet. Designated rooms, service with restrictions, supervision.

(SAVE) (S🅾) ✕ 🛏 ⇔

▲▲▲▽ ▼▼▼ National 9 Discovery Inn Ⓜ
(801) 561-2256. **$59-$89 (no credit cards).** 380 W 7200 S. I-15, exit 297, just e. Ext/int corridors. **Pets:** $25 deposit/room, $7 daily fee/room. Designated rooms, service with restrictions, supervision.

(SAVE) (S🅾) ✕ 🛏 🖥 ⇔

▲▲▲▽ ▼▼▼ Super 8 Ⓜ
(801) 255-5559. **$69-$99.** 7048 S 900 E. I-15, exit 297, 1.5 mi e on 7200 S to 900 E, then just n. Int corridors. **Pets:** Medium. Service with restrictions, supervision.

(SAVE) (S🅾) ✕ 🛏 🖥

MURRAY

▲▲▲▽ ▼▼▼▼ Holiday Inn Express 🆂🅷
(801) 268-2533. **$89-$139.** 4465 S Century Dr. I-15, exit 301, just w. Int corridors. **Pets:** Accepted.

(SAVE) (S🅾) ✕ 🛏 🖥 ⇔

▼▼▼▼ Pavilion Inn 🆂🅷
(801) 506-8000. **$69-$79.** 5335 S 440 W. I-15, exit 300, 0.3 mi w. Int corridors. **Pets:** Accepted.

(ASK) (S🅾) ✕ 🛏 ⇔

▼▼ ▼▼ Studio 6 #6038 Ⓜ
(801) 685-2102. **$61-$71.** 975 E 6600 S. I-215, exit 9, on 900 E, then 0.5 mi e. Ext corridors. **Pets:** Other species. Service with restrictions, supervision.

(S🅾) ✕ 🛏 🖥

NORTH SALT LAKE

▲▲▲▽ ▼▼▼▼ Best Western Cottontree Inn 🆂🅷
(801) 292-7666. **$110-$170, 21 day notice.** 1030 N 400 E. I-15, exit 315, just e. Int corridors. **Pets:** Large. Service with restrictions, crate.

(SAVE) (S🅾) ✕ 🛏 🖥 ⇔

SALT LAKE CITY

▼▼▼▼ Airport Comfort Inn 🆂🅷
(801) 746-5200. **$79-$159.** 200 N Admiral Byrd Rd. I-80, exit 113, 0.8 mi n via 5600 W, Amelia Earhart Dr, then s. Int corridors. **Pets:** $30 one-time fee/room. Designated rooms, service with restrictions, supervision.

(ASK) (S🅾) ✕ 🛏 🖥 🍴 ⇔

▲▲▲▽ ▼▼▼▼ Best Western Airport Inn 🆂🅷
(801) 539-5005. **Call for rates.** 315 N Admiral Byrd Rd. I-80, exit 113, 0.8 mi n, then just e. Int corridors. **Pets:** Accepted.

(SAVE) ✕ 🛏 🖥 ⇔

▼▼▼ **Candlewood Suite Hotel** SH
(801) 359-7500. **Call for rates.** 2170 W N Temple. 3 mi w of Temple Square. Int corridors. **Pets:** Accepted.

⊠ 🖪 🖵

(AAA) ▼▼▼ **Chase Suite Hotel by Woodfin** SH
(801) 532-5511. **$99-$169.** 765 E 400 S. Cross streets 700 E and 400 S. Ext corridors. **Pets:** Accepted.

SAVE S✆ ⊠ 🖪 🖵 ➡ ⊠

(AAA) ▼▼▼ **City Creek Inn** M
(801) 533-9100. **$43-$89.** 230 W N Temple St. Cross street 200 W. Ext corridors. **Pets:** Accepted.

SAVE S✆ ⊠ 🖪

▼▼▼ **Days Inn-Salt Lake City Airport** SH
(801) 539-8538. **$63-$165.** 1900 W N Temple. 2.5 mi w of Temple Square. Int corridors. **Pets:** Accepted.

A$K S✆ ⊠ 🖪 🖵 ➡

(AAA) ▼▼▼ **Econo Lodge Downtown** M
(801) 363-0062. **$60-$130.** 715 W N Temple. West from Temple Square, 1 mi. Ext corridors. **Pets:** Medium. $25 deposit/room, $10 daily fee/room. Service with restrictions, supervision.

SAVE S✆ ⊠ 🖪 🖵 ➡

(AAA) ▼▼▼▼ **Hilton Salt Lake City Airport** LH
(801) 539-1515. **$89-$242.** 5151 Wiley Post Way. I-80, exit 114 westbound, 0.4 mi nw via Wright Brothers Dr and Wiley Post; exit 113 eastbound, 1.3 mi n via 5600 W, Amelia Earhart Dr, then just s on Charles Lindbergh Dr. Int corridors. **Pets:** $50 deposit/room. Service with restrictions, crate.

SAVE S✆ ⊠ 🖪 🖵 ⑪ ➡ ⊠

(AAA) ▼▼▼▼ **Hilton Salt Lake City Center** LH
(801) 328-2000. **$99-$329.** 255 S W Temple. On W Temple, just s of Temple Square. Int corridors. **Pets:** Medium. $50 one-time fee/room. Designated rooms, service with restrictions, supervision.

SAVE S✆ ⊠ 🖪 🖵 ⑪ ➡ ⊠

▼▼▼ **Holiday Inn Express Airport East** SH
(801) 741-1500. **$129-$189.** 200 N 2100 W. I-80, exit 18 westbound; exit N Temple St eastbound, just n on 2200 W, then just n on corner of N Temple and 2100 W. Int corridors. **Pets:** Accepted.

A$K S✆ ⊠ 🖪 🖵 ➡

▼▼◇ **Homestead Studio Suites Salt Lake City-Sugar House** M
(801) 474-0771. **Call for rates.** 1220 E 2100 S. I-80, exit 126, cross streets 1300 E and 2100 S. Ext corridors. **Pets:** Other species. $75 one-time fee/pet. Service with restrictions.

⊠ 🖪 🖵

(AAA) ▼▼▼▼ **Hotel Monaco** LH
(801) 595-0000. **$119-$299.** 15 W 200 South. Cross streets 200 S and Main St. Int corridors. **Pets:** Accepted.

SAVE S✆ ⊠ 🖵 ⑪

(AAA) ▼▼◇ **Howard Johnson Express Inn** M
(801) 521-3450. **$69-$89.** 121 N 300 W. At N Temple and 300 W. Ext/int corridors. **Pets:** Medium. $10 one-time fee/pet. Designated rooms, service with restrictions, supervision.

SAVE S✆ ⊠ 🖪 🖵 ➡

(AAA) ▼▼▼ **Metropolitan Inn** SH
(801) 531-7100. **$79.** 524 SW Temple. Cross streets 500 S and W Temple. Ext corridors. **Pets:** Accepted.

SAVE S✆ ⊠ 🖪 🖵 ➡

(AAA) ▼▼◇ **Peery Hotel** SH
(801) 521-4300. **$129-$300.** 110 W Broadway. W Temple and 300 S. Int corridors. **Pets:** Accepted.

SAVE S✆ ⊠ 🖪 🖵 ⑪

(AAA) ▼▼▼ **Quality Inn Airport** SH
(801) 533-9000. **$99.** 1659 W N Temple. 3 mi w of Temple Square. Ext corridors. **Pets:** Accepted.

SAVE S✆ ⊠ 🖪 🖵 ⑪ ➡

(AAA) ▼▼◇ **Radisson Hotel Salt Lake City Downtown** LH
(801) 531-7500. **$115-$349.** 215 W South Temple. Opposite Delta Center. Int corridors. **Pets:** Small, other species. $25 one-time fee/room. Service with restrictions, supervision.

SAVE S✆ ⊠ 🖪 🖵 ⑪ ➡ ⊠

(AAA) ▼▼◇ **Red Lion Hotel Salt Lake Downtown** LH
(801) 521-7373. **$170.** 161 W 600 S. At W Temple and 600 S. Int corridors. **Pets:** Small. $15 daily fee/room. Service with restrictions, supervision.

SAVE S✆ ⊠ 🖪 🖵 ⑪ ➡ ⊠

▼▼▼ **Residence Inn by Marriott-City Center** SH
(801) 355-3300. **$198-$218.** 285 W Broadway (300 S). Cross streets 300 W and 300 S. Int corridors. **Pets:** Accepted.

A$K S✆ ⊠ 🖪 🖵 ➡ ⊠

▼▼▼ **Residence Inn by Marriott Salt Lake City Airport** SH
(801) 532-4101. **$137-$157.** 4883 W Douglas Corrigon Way. I-80, exit 114 westbound, via Wright Brothers Dr; exit 113 eastbound, via Amelia Earhart and Wright Brothers drs, then 2.6 mi se. Int corridors. **Pets:** Accepted.

A$K S✆ ⊠ 🖾-M 🖪 🖵 ➡ ⊠

(AAA) ▼▼▼ **Royal Garden Inn** SH
(801) 521-2930. **$79-$139.** 154 W 600 S. Between cross streets 100 and 200 W. Ext/int corridors. **Pets:** Other species. $20 daily fee/room. Designated rooms, service with restrictions, crate.

SAVE S✆ ⊠ 🖪 🖵 ⑪ ➡

▼▼▼ **Sheraton City Centre** LH
(801) 401-2000. **Call for rates.** 150 W 500 S. At 200 W and 500 S. Int corridors. **Pets:** Accepted.

⊠ 🖪 🖵 ⑪ ➡ ⊠

(AAA) ▼▼▼ **Shilo Inn Suites Hotel** LH ❧
(801) 521-9500. **$180.** 206 S W Temple. Cross streets 200 S and W Temple. Int corridors. **Pets:** $25 one-time fee/room. Designated rooms, service with restrictions, supervision.

SAVE S✆ ⊠ 🖪 🖵 ⑪ ➡ ⊠

(AAA) ▼▼▼ **Super 8 Airport** M
(801) 533-8878. **Call for rates.** 223 N Jimmy Doolittle Rd. I-80, exit 113, 0.8 mi ne, then just s. Int corridors. **Pets:** Accepted.

SAVE ⊠ 🖪 🖵 ➡

SANDY

(AAA) ▼▼▼ **Best Western CottonTree Inn** SH
(801) 523-8484. **Call for rates.** 10695 S Auto Mall Dr. I-15, exit 293 eastbound, 0.3 mi e. Int corridors. **Pets:** Accepted.

SAVE ⊠ 🖪 🖵 ➡

▼▼▼ **Comfort Inn** M
(801) 255-4919. **$60-$160.** 8955 S 255 W. I-15, exit 295, just ne. Int corridors. **Pets:** Accepted.

A$K S✆ ⊠ 🖪 🖵 ➡

▼▼▼ **Holiday Inn Express Hotel & Suites** SH
(801) 495-1317. **$99-$169.** 10680 S Auto Mall Dr. I-15, exit 293 eastbound, 0.3 mi e. Int corridors. **Pets:** Accepted.

A$K S✆ ⊠ 🖪 🖵 ➡

▼▼▼ **Residence Inn by Marriott** SH
(801) 561-5005. **$264-$284.** 270 W 10000 S. I-15, exit 293, from State St, 0.3 mi w. Int corridors. **Pets:** Accepted.

A$K S✆ ⊠ 🖪 🖵 ➡ ⊠

▼▼ **Sleep Inn** Ⓜ
(801) 572-2020. **Call for rates.** 10676 S 300 W. I-15, exit 293 westbound, just w. Int corridors. **Pets:** Accepted.
⊠ 🛢 💻 ≈

▼▼ **Super 8 Motel South Jordan/Sandy** Ⓜ
(801) 553-8888. **Call for rates.** 10722 S 300 W. I-15, exit 293 westbound, just w. Int corridors. **Pets:** Accepted.
⊠ 🛢 💻 ≈

TAYLORSVILLE

▼▼ **Homestead Studio Suites Hotel-Salt Lake City/Mid Valley** Ⓜ
(801) 269-9292. **Call for rates.** 5683 S Redwood Rd. I-215, exit 13, 0.5 mi n. Ext corridors. **Pets:** Other species. $75 one-time fee/pet. Service with restrictions.
⊠ 🛢 💻

WEST VALLEY CITY

▼▼▼ **Baymont Inn & Suites Salt Lake City-West Valley City** 🆂🅷
(801) 886-1300. **$79-$119.** 2229 W City Center Ct. I-215, exit 18, just e. Int corridors. **Pets:** Medium. Service with restrictions, supervision.
A$K 🅢 ⊠ 🛢 💻 ≈

▼▼▼ **Country Inn & Suites By Carlson** 🆂🅷
(801) 908-0311. **$109-$129.** 3422 S Decker Lake Dr. I-215, exit 18, just e, then just n. Int corridors. **Pets:** Accepted.
A$K 🅢 ⊠ 🛢 💻 ≈

▼▼ **Extended StayAmerica-Salt Lake City-West Valley Center** Ⓜ
(801) 886-2400. **Call for rates.** 2310 W City Center Ct. I-215, exit 18A, just e, then just n. Int corridors. **Pets:** Other species. $75 one-time fee/pet. Service with restrictions.
⊠ 🛢 💻

▼▼▼▼ **La Quinta Inn West Valley City (Salt Lake-West)** 🆂🅷
(801) 954-9292. **$62.** 3540 S 2200 W. I-215, exit 18, just e. Int corridors. **Pets:** Other species. Service with restrictions, supervision.
A$K 🅢 ⊠ 🛢 💻 ≈

▼▼ **Sleep Inn** Ⓜ
(801) 975-1888. **Call for rates.** 3440 S 2200 W. I-215, exit 18, just e, then just n. Int corridors. **Pets:** Accepted.
⊠ 🛢 💻

WOODS CROSS

▼▼▼ **Hampton Inn** 🆂🅷
(801) 296-1211. **Call for rates.** 2393 S 800 W. I-15, exit 315, just w of freeway. Int corridors. **Pets:** Accepted.
⊠ 🛢 💻 ≈

▼ **Motel 6 #1205** Ⓜ
(801) 298-0289. **$45-$65.** 2433 S 800 W. I-15, exit 315 westbound, just w. Ext corridors. **Pets:** Accepted.
🅢 ⊠ 🛢 ≈

END METROPOLITAN AREA

SCIPIO

▼▼ **Super 8** Ⓜ
(435) 758-9188. **$69-$94.** 230 W 400 N. I-15, exit 188, just ne. Int corridors. **Pets:** Accepted.
A$K 🅢 ⊠ 🛢 💻 ≈

SPANISH FORK

▲▲▲ ▼▼▼ **Western Inn** Ⓜ
(801) 798-9400. **$50-$80.** 632 Kirby Ln. I-15, exit 258 southbound, 0.5 mi e; exit 257 northbound, 1 mi ne. Int corridors. **Pets:** Dogs only. $12 daily fee/pet. Designated rooms, service with restrictions, supervision.
SAVE 🅢 ⊠ 🛢

SPRINGDALE

▲▲▲ ▼▼▼▼ **Best Western Zion Park Inn** Ⓜ
(435) 772-3200. **$70-$123.** 1215 Zion Park Blvd. 2 mi s of park entrance. Int corridors. **Pets:** Accepted.
SAVE 🅢 ⊠ 🛢 💻 🍴 ≈ ⊠

▼▼ **Canyon Ranch Motel** Ⓜ
(435) 772-3357. **$49-$99.** 668 Zion Park Blvd. SR 9, just s of south gate to Zion National Park. Ext corridors. **Pets:** Accepted.
⊠ 🛢 ≈

▲▲▲ ▼▼▼▼ **Driftwood Lodge & Suites** Ⓜ ❀
(435) 772-3262. **$59-$199, 3 day notice.** 1515 Zion Park Blvd. SR 9, 2 mi s of south gate to Zion National Park. Ext corridors. **Pets:** Large, other species. $20 daily fee/pet. Designated rooms, service with restrictions, supervision.
SAVE ⊠ 🛢 💻 🍴 ≈

SPRINGVILLE

▲▲▲ ▼▼▼▼ **Best Western Mountain View Inn** Ⓜ ❀
(801) 489-3641. **Call for rates.** 1455 N 1750 W. I-15, exit 261, just e. Int corridors. **Pets:** Medium, other species. $10 daily fee/pet. Designated rooms, service with restrictions, supervision.
SAVE ⊠ 🛢 💻 ≈

TEASDALE

▼▼ **Cactus Hill Ranch Motel** Ⓜ
(435) 425-3578. **Call for rates.** 830 S 1000 E. 3 mi s of SR 24 at Teasdale; 5 mi w of SR 12, exit Teasdale; 13 mi w of Capitol Reef National Park, 1.5 mi se of town center. Ext corridors. **Pets:** Accepted.
⊠ 🛢 💻

TOOELE

▼▼▼ **Holiday Inn Express Hotel & Suites** 🆂🅷
(435) 833-0500. **$119-$179.** 1531 N Main St. I-80, exit 99, 11 mi s on SR 36. Int corridors. **Pets:** Accepted.
A$K 🅢 ⊠ 🛢 💻 ≈

TORREY

▲▲▲ ▼▼▼▼ **Best Western Capitol Reef Resort** 🆂🅷
(435) 425-3761. **$59-$139.** 2600 E Hwy 24. On SR 24, 2 mi e of jct SR 12 and 24, 1 mi w of Capitol Reef National Park. Ext corridors. **Pets:** Small. $10 daily fee/room. Designated rooms, service with restrictions, supervision.
SAVE 🅢 ⊠ 🛢 💻 🍴 ≈ ⊠

▼▼▼ **Comfort Inn at Capitol Reef/Torrey** 🆂🅷
(435) 425-3866. **Call for rates.** 2424 E Hwy 24. On SR 24, 1.5 mi e of jct SR 12 and 24, 1.5 mi w of Capitol Rd. Ext corridors. **Pets:** Accepted.
⊠ 🛢 💻

▼▼ **Rim Rock Inn** M
(435) 425-3398. **Call for rates.** 2523 E Hwy 24. 2.5 mi e of jct SR 12 and 24; east end of town. Ext corridors. **Pets:** Accepted.
⊠ ⑪

▼▼ **Torrey/Capitol Reef-Econo Lodge** M
(435) 425-3688. **$49-$125.** 600 E Hwy 24. On SR 24, 0.3 mi w of SR 12; 3.3 mi w of Capitol Reef National Park. Int corridors. **Pets:** Accepted.
ASK S☼ ⊠ ⬛ ⤢

▲▲ ▼▼ **Torrey Days Inn** M
(435) 425-3111. **$70-$85.** 675 E Hwy 24. Jct SR 12 and 24. Int corridors. **Pets:** Other species. $10 daily fee/room. Designated rooms, service with restrictions.
SAVE S☼ ⊠ ᴟᴹ ⬛ ▣ ⤢

▲▲ ▼▼ **Wonderland Inn** SH
(435) 425-3775. **$54-$95.** 875 E Hwy 24. Jct SR 12 and 24; 3 mi w of Capitol Reef National Park. Ext corridors. **Pets:** $10 one-time fee/pet. Designated rooms, service with restrictions, crate.
SAVE ⊠ ⬛ ⑪ ⤢

TREMONTON

▲▲ ▼ **Sandman Motel** M
(435) 257-7149. **$48-$58.** 585 W Main St. I-15/84 N, exit 376, 2.1 mi ne to 4-way stop, then 1.5 mi w; I-15 S, exit 381, 0.6 mi e to 4-way stop, s to Main St, then 0.5 mi e; I-84, exit 40, 1.5 mi e. Ext corridors. **Pets:** Medium, other species. $10 deposit/room. Designated rooms, service with restrictions, supervision.
SAVE S☼ ⊠

TROPIC

▲▲ ▼▼ **Americas Best Value Inn & Suites-Bryce Valley Inn** SH
(435) 679-8811. **$85.** 199 N Main St. SR 12, 10 mi e of Bryce Canyon Park. Ext/int corridors. **Pets:** Other species. $20 one-time fee/pet. Designated rooms, service with restrictions, crate.
SAVE S☼ ⊠ ⬛ ▣ ⑪

VERNAL

▼▼ **Econo Lodge** M
(435) 789-2000. **Call for rates.** 311 E Main St. On US 40; east end of town. Ext corridors. **Pets:** Accepted.
⊠ ⬛ ▣

▼ **Sage Motel & Restaurant** M
(435) 789-1442. **$80.** 54 W Main St. On US 40; center. Ext corridors. **Pets:** Accepted.
ASK S☼ ⊠ ⬛ ⑪

WELLINGTON

▲▲ ▼ **National 9 Inn** M
(435) 637-7980. **$50-$76.** 50 S 700. On US 6. Ext/int corridors. **Pets:** $25 deposit/room, $7 daily fee/room. Designated rooms, service with restrictions, supervision.
SAVE S☼ ⊠ ⬛ ⑪ ⤢

ALBURG

▼▼ Ransom Bay Inn [BB]
(802) 796-3399. **$95-$105.** 4 Center Bay Rd. 0.5 mi s on US 2, from jct SR 78. Int corridors. **Pets:** Small. $10 one-time fee/room. Service with restrictions, supervision.

BARRE

◆◆◇ ▼▼▼ The Hollow Inn & Motel [M] ❀
(802) 479-9313. **$80-$139.** 278 S Main St. Jct US 302, 1 mi s on SR 14; I-89, exit 6, 4.3 mi e on SR 63, then 0.7 mi n on SR 14. Ext/int corridors. **Pets:** Medium. $15 daily fee/pet. Designated rooms, service with restrictions, supervision.

◆◆◇ ▼▼ Pierre Motel [M]
(802) 476-3188. **$58-$95.** 362 N Main St. I-89, exit 7, 4 mi e on SR 62; jct US 302. Ext corridors. **Pets:** Accepted.

BENNINGTON

◆◆◇ ▼▼ Americas Best Value Inn [M]
(802) 442-2322. **$65-$129, 3 day notice.** 357 US 7 S. Jct SR 9 and US 7, 1.2 mi s. Ext corridors. **Pets:** Accepted.

◆◆◇ ▼▼▼ Bennington Motor Inn [M]
(802) 442-5479. **$69-$165, 3 day notice.** 143 W Main St. Jct US 7, 0.4 mi w on SR 9. Ext corridors. **Pets:** Accepted.

◆◆◇ ▼▼ Harwood Hill Motel [M]
(802) 442-6278. **$53-$85, 3 day notice.** 864 Harwood Hill Rd (Historic Rt 7A). Jct SR 9, 1.2 mi n on US 7, then 1.7 mi n. Ext corridors. **Pets:** Accepted.

▼▼ Knotty Pine Motel [M]
(802) 442-5487. **$75-$115.** 130 Northside Dr (SR 7A). Jct SR 9, 1.2 mi n on US 7, then just n on Historic SR 7A. Ext corridors. **Pets:** Service with restrictions, supervision.

BOLTON VALLEY

◆◆◇ ▼▼▼▼ Black Bear Inn [CI]
(802) 434-2126. **$104-$325, 21 day notice.** 4010 Bolton Access Rd. I-89, exit 10 northbound, 6.2 mi w on US 2, then 4 mi n; exit 11 southbound, 8.4 mi e on US 2, then 4 mi n. Ext/int corridors. **Pets:** Accepted.

BRANDON

◆◆◇ ▼▼▼ Brandon Motor Lodge [M]
(802) 247-9594. **$69-$139.** 2095 Franklin St. 2 mi s on US 7. Ext corridors. **Pets:** Accepted.

◆◆◇ ▼▼ Cozy Cottages [CA]
(802) 247-6644. **Call for rates.** 1246 Franklin St. Jct SR 73 and US 7, 1.2 mi s on US 7. Ext corridors. **Pets:** Accepted.

▼▼▼▼ The Lilac Inn [CI] ❀
(802) 247-5463. **$125-$315, 30 day notice.** 53 Park St. Just e on SR 73. Int corridors. **Pets:** Dogs only. $35 one-time fee/pet. Service with restrictions, supervision.

BRATTLEBORO

▼▼▼ Colonial Motel & Spa [SH]
(802) 257-7733. **$79-$145.** 889 Putney Rd. I-91, exit 3, just e on SR 9, then 0.5 mi s on US 5. Ext corridors. **Pets:** Dogs only. $10 daily fee/pet. Service with restrictions, supervision.

◆◆◇ ▼▼▼ Econo Lodge [M]
(802) 254-2360. **$45-$175.** 515 Canal St. I-91, exit 1, 0.3 mi n on US 5. Ext/int corridors. **Pets:** Accepted.

◆◆◇ ▼▼▼ Super 8 Motel [M]
(802) 254-8889. **$50-$195.** 1043 Putney Rd. I-91, exit 3, just e on SR 9, then just s on US 5. Int corridors. **Pets:** Other species. $20 one-time fee/room.

CAVENDISH

◆◆◇ ▼◆◆◆◆ The Pointe at Castle Hill Resort & Spa [SH]
(802) 226-7688. **$109-$449, 14 day notice.** 2940 SR 103. On SR 103, just n of jct SR 131. Int corridors. **Pets:** Dogs only. $20 daily fee/room. Designated rooms, service with restrictions, supervision.

COLCHESTER

▼▼ Days Inn [SH]
(802) 655-0900. **$50-$135.** 124 College Pkwy. I-89, exit 15 northbound, just e on SR 15; exit 16 southbound, 1.1 mi s on US 7, then 1 mi e on SR 15. Int corridors. **Pets:** Dogs only. $10 daily fee/pet. Designated rooms, service with restrictions, crate.

▼▼▼ Hampton Inn & Conference Center [SH]
(802) 655-6177. **$119-$249.** 42 Lower Mountain View Dr. I-89, exit 16, just n on US 7. Int corridors. **Pets:** Other species. Designated rooms, service with restrictions, supervision.

▼▼ Motel 6 #1407 [SH]
(802) 654-6860. **Call for rates.** 74 S Park Dr. I-89, exit 16, just s on US 7. Int corridors. **Pets:** Other species. Service with restrictions, supervision.

EAST ST. JOHNSBURY

◆◆ Echo Ledge Farm Inn BB
(802) 748-4750. **Call for rates (no credit cards).** 87 US Rt 2. I-93, exit 1, 0.5 mi n, then 2.2 mi e. **Pets:** Accepted.
[X] [Z]

ESSEX JUNCTION

◆◆◆ Handy Suites SH
(802) 872-5200. **$74-$249.** 27 Susie Wilson Rd. I-89, exit 15 northbound, 2 mi e, then just n. Int corridors. **Pets:** Accepted.
[ASK] [S⊘] [X] [&M] [✆] [▤] [≈]

◆◇ ◆◆◆◆ The Inn at Essex SH ❀
(802) 878-1100. **$169-$299, 7 day notice.** 70 Essex Way. SR 289, exit 10, 0.3 mi s. Int corridors. **Pets:** $25 daily fee/room. Designated rooms, service with restrictions.
[SAVE] [S⊘] [X] [&M] [✆] [▤] [¶¶] [≈] [X]

FAIRLEE

◆◇ ◆◆◆ Silver Maple Lodge & Cottages BB
(802) 333-4326. **$72-$109, 14 day notice.** 520 US 5 S. I-91, exit 15, 0.5 mi s. Ext/int corridors. **Pets:** Other species. Designated rooms.
[SAVE] [S⊘] [X] [✆] [▤] [Z]

FLETCHER

◆◆◆◆ The Inn at Buck Hollow Farm BB
(802) 849-2400. **$93-$105, 14 day notice.** 2150 Buck Hollow Rd. 6.4 mi n of jct SR 104 via Buck Hollow Rd. Int corridors. **Pets:** $20 daily fee/pet. Supervision.
[ASK] [X] [≈] [X] [Z]

JAMAICA

◆◇ ◆◆◆◆ Three Mountain Inn CI
(802) 874-4140. **$165-$370, 21 day notice.** 3732 Main St. On SR 30; center. Ext/int corridors. **Pets:** Accepted.
[SAVE] [X] [¶¶] [≈] [X]

KILLINGTON

◆◇ ◆◆◆◆ The Cascades Lodge SH
(802) 422-3731. **$84-$229, 21 day notice.** 58 Old Mill Rd. 3.6 mi s on Killington Rd, from jct SR 100/US 4, then just e. Int corridors. **Pets:** Accepted.
[SAVE] [S⊘] [X] [✆] [▤] [¶¶] [≈] [X]

LONDONDERRY

◆ Snowdon Motel M
(802) 824-6047. **Call for rates.** 4071 VT Rt 11. Jct SR 100, 2 mi e. Ext corridors. **Pets:** Accepted.
[X] [✆] [Z]

LUDLOW

◆◇ ◆◆ All Seasons Motel SH
(802) 228-8100. **$70-$250, 14 day notice.** 112 Main St. On SR 103; center. Ext/int corridors. **Pets:** Accepted.
[SAVE] [X] [✆] [▤] [≈]

◆◇ ◆◆◆ The Andrie Rose Inn BB
(802) 228-4846. **$110-$350, 20 day notice.** 13 Pleasant St. Corner of Depot St; center. Int corridors. **Pets:** Accepted.
[SAVE] [X] [✆] [¶¶] [Z]

◆◇ ◆◆◆ Best Western Ludlow Colonial Motel SH
(802) 228-8188. **$100-$350, 14 day notice.** 93 Main St. On SR 103; center. Ext/int corridors. **Pets:** Small, dogs only. $25 daily fee/pet. Service with restrictions, supervision.
[SAVE] [S⊘] [X] [✆] [▤] [≈]

◆◆ Timber Inn Motel M
(802) 228-8666. **$69-$229, 14 day notice.** 112 Rt 103 S. On SR 103 S, 1 mi e. Ext corridors. **Pets:** Accepted.
[SAVE] [X] [✆] [▤] [≈] [X]

MANCHESTER CENTER

◆◆◆ Casablanca Motel CA ❀
(802) 362-2145. **$70-$108, 7 day notice.** 5927 Main St (Rt 7A). Jct SR 11/30 N, 1 mi n on Historic SR 7A. Ext corridors. **Pets:** $15 daily fee/pet. Designated rooms, service with restrictions.
[ASK] [S⊘] [X] [✆] [≈]

MANCHESTER VILLAGE

◆◇ ◆◆◆◆ The Equinox LH
(802) 362-4700. **$209-$999, 21 day notice.** 3567 Main St. 1.3 mi s on Historic SR 7A, from jct SR 11/30. Int corridors. **Pets:** Accepted.
[SAVE] [S⊘] [X] [✆] [▤] [¶¶] [≈] [X]

◆◆◆◆ The Village Country Inn, a Clarion Collection Hotel CI
(802) 362-1792. **Call for rates.** 3835 Main St. On Historic SR 7A, 1 mi s of jct SR 11/30. Ext/int corridors. **Pets:** Accepted.
[X] [✆] [▤] [≈]

MENDON

◆◆◆◆ Cortina Inn and Resort SH
(802) 773-3333. **Call for rates.** 103 US Rt 4. Jct SR 100 N, 3 mi w. Int corridors. **Pets:** Accepted.
[X] [✆] [▤] [¶¶] [≈] [X]

◆◇ ◆◆◆ Econo Lodge-Killington Area SH
(802) 773-6644. **$55-$145, 14 day notice.** 51 US 4. Jct US 7, 5.3 mi e. Int corridors. **Pets:** $10 one-time fee/room. Designated rooms, service with restrictions, supervision.
[SAVE] [S⊘] [X] [✆] [▤] [≈]

◆◆ Mendon Mountainview Lodge SH
(802) 773-4311. **$59-$242, 7 day notice.** 78 US 4. On US 4, 6 mi e of jct US 7. Int corridors. **Pets:** Accepted.
[ASK] [S⊘] [X] [✆] [≈] [X]

MIDDLEBURY

◆◇ ◆◆◆ The Middlebury Inn SH
(802) 388-4961. **$119-$299, 3 day notice.** 14 Court Square. On US 7; center. Ext/int corridors. **Pets:** Accepted.
[SAVE] [X] [✆] [▤] [¶¶]

◆◇ ◆◆◆ Swift House Inn CI
(802) 388-9925. **$120-$285, 14 day notice.** 25 Stewart Ln. 0.3 mi n on US 7 from jct SR 125 W. Ext/int corridors. **Pets:** Accepted.
[SAVE] [S⊘] [X] [✆] [▤] [¶¶] [X]

MONTGOMERY CENTER

◆◇ ◆◆◆ Phineas Swann Bed & Breakfast BB ❀
(802) 326-4306. **$89-$395, 30 day notice.** 195 Main St. Center. Ext/int corridors. **Pets:** Other species.
[SAVE] [X] [✆] [X]

MORRISVILLE

◆◇ ◆◆◆ Sunset Motor Inn M
(802) 888-4956. **$68-$168, 7 day notice.** 160 VT Rt 15 W. On SR 15, just w of jct SR 100. Ext/int corridors. **Pets:** Accepted.
[SAVE] [S⊘] [X] [&M] [✆] [≈]

◆◆◆◆ Village Victorian Bed & Breakfast BB
(802) 888-8850. **$80-$170, 15 day notice.** 107 Union St. From center, just e, then just n. Int corridors. **Pets:** Small. $10 daily fee/pet. Designated rooms, service with restrictions, supervision.
[ASK] [S⊘] [X] [Z]

NORTH HERO

Shore Acres Inn SH
(802) 372-8722. **$95-$225, 14 day notice.** 237 Shore Acres Dr. 0.5 mi s on US 2. Ext/int corridors. **Pets:** Dogs only. $5 daily fee/pet, $15 one-time fee/pet. Crate.

SAVE ✕ 🖥 ❚❙ ✕ 🏊

PUTNEY

The Putney Inn SH
(802) 387-5517. **$118-$188.** 57 Putney Landing Rd. I-91, exit 4, just e. Ext corridors. **Pets:** $10 daily fee/pet. Designated rooms, service with restrictions.

SAVE ✕ 🖥 ❚❙

RUTLAND

Holiday Inn Rutland/Killington LH
(802) 775-1911. **$119-$249.** 476 US Rt 7 S. 2.4 mi s on US 7, from US 4 W; 0.4 mi n, US 7 from US 4 E. Int corridors. **Pets:** Medium. $25 daily fee/pet. Service with restrictions, supervision.

SAVE 🐾 ✕ 🦽 🖥 🖥 ❚❙ 🏊 ✕

Ramada Limited of Rutland SH
(802) 773-3361. **$59-$99.** 253 S Main St, US 7. 1.3 mi s on US 7, from US 4 W; 1.5 mi n on US 7, from US 4 E. Int corridors. **Pets:** $10 one-time fee/room. Service with restrictions, supervision.

ASK 🐾 ✕ 🖥 🖥 🏊

Red Roof Inn Rutland-Killington SH
(802) 775-4303. **Call for rates.** 401 US Hwy 7 S. On US 7/4. Int corridors. **Pets:** Accepted.

SAVE ✕ 🖥 🖥 🏊

Rodeway Inn M
(802) 775-2575. **$49-$169, 5 day notice.** 138 N Main St. 0.5 mi n of jct US 4 E. Ext corridors. **Pets:** Medium, dogs only. $10 daily fee/pet. Designated rooms, service with restrictions, supervision.

SAVE 🐾 ✕ 🖥 🖥 🏊

Rodeway Inn M
(802) 773-9176. **$49-$169.** 115 Woodstock Ave. Jct US 7, 0.5 mi e on US 4. Ext/int corridors. **Pets:** Accepted.

SAVE ✕ 🖥 🏊

ST. ALBANS

Econo Lodge M
(802) 524-5956. **$55-$120.** 287 S Main St. I-89, exit 19, 1 mi w to US 7, then 0.5 mi s. Ext/int corridors. **Pets:** Accepted.

SAVE 🐾 ✕ 🖥 🖥

La Quinta Inn & Suites SH
(802) 524-3300. **$85-$130.** 813 Fairfax Rd. I-89, exit 19, just w, then just s on SR 104. Int corridors. **Pets:** Other species. Service with restrictions, supervision.

ASK 🐾 ✕ 🦽 🖥 🖥 🏊

ST. JOHNSBURY

Fairbanks Inn M
(802) 748-5666. **$95-$145.** 401 Western Ave. I-91, exit 21, 1 mi e on US 2. Ext corridors. **Pets:** Accepted.

SAVE 🐾 ✕ 🖥 🖥 🏊

SAXTONS RIVER

The Inn at Saxtons River CI
(802) 869-2110. **$99-$189, 10 day notice.** 27 Main St. Center. **Pets:** Medium. $20 daily fee/room. Designated rooms, service with restrictions, supervision.

SAVE ✕ 🖥 ✕

SHAFTSBURY

Governor's Rock Motel M
(802) 442-4734. **$55-$105.** 4325 Rt 7A. 3.3 mi n on Historic SR 7A, from jct SR 67. Ext corridors. **Pets:** Dogs only. $5 daily fee/pet. Designated rooms, supervision.

✕ 🖥

Hillbrook Motel M
(802) 447-7201. **$65-$90, 3 day notice.** 2629 Rt 7A. SR 7, exit 2, 2 mi n on SR 7A. Ext corridors. **Pets:** Medium, dogs only. $5 one-time fee/pet. Service with restrictions, supervision.

ASK 🐾 ✕ 🖥 🖥 🏊

Serenity Motel CA
(802) 442-6490. **Call for rates.** 4379 Rt 7A. 3.3 mi n on Historic SR 7A, from jct SR 67. Ext corridors. **Pets:** Large, other species. Designated rooms, service with restrictions, supervision.

✕ 🖥 🖥

SOUTH BURLINGTON

Best Western Windjammer Inn & Conference Center SH 🐾
(802) 863-1125. **$90-$200.** 1076 Williston Rd. I-89, exit 14E, 0.3 mi e on US 2. Int corridors. **Pets:** $10 daily fee/pet. Designated rooms, service with restrictions, supervision.

ASK 🐾 ✕ 🦽 🖥 🖥 ❚❙ 🏊 ✕

DoubleTree Hotel Burlington SH
(802) 658-0250. **$119-$274.** 1117 Williston Rd. I-89, exit 14E, just e on US 2. Int corridors. **Pets:** Accepted.

SAVE ✕ 🦽 🖥 🖥 ❚❙ 🏊

Hawthorn Suites Hotel SH
(802) 860-1212. **$129-$209.** 401 Dorset St. I-89, exit 14E, just e on US 2, then 0.8 mi s. Int corridors. **Pets:** Accepted.

SAVE ✕ 🦽 🖥 🖥 🏊

Holiday Inn Burlington LH
(802) 863-6363. **$89-$219.** 1068 Williston Rd. I-89, exit 14E, just e on US 2. Int corridors. **Pets:** Accepted.

SAVE 🐾 ✕ 🖥 🖥 ❚❙ 🏊

La Quinta Inn & Suites SH
(802) 865-3400. **$99-$135.** 1285 Williston Rd. I-89, exit 14E, 0.5 mi e on US 2. Int corridors. **Pets:** Other species. Service with restrictions, supervision.

ASK 🐾 ✕ 🦽 🖥 🖥 🏊

Sheraton Burlington Hotel & Conference Center LH
(802) 865-6600. **$269-$299.** 870 Williston Rd. I-89, exit 14W, just w on US 2. Int corridors. **Pets:** Accepted.

SAVE ✕ 🖥 🖥 ❚❙ 🏊

SOUTH WOODSTOCK

Kedron Valley Inn CI
(802) 457-1473. **Call for rates.** 10671 South Rd. Jct US 4, 5 mi s. Ext/int corridors. **Pets:** Accepted.

SAVE ✕ 🖥 🖥 ❚❙ ✕ 🏊

SPRINGFIELD

The Hartness House CI
(802) 885-2115. **Call for rates.** 30 Orchard St. 0.4 mi n on Summer St, bear left at old cemetery. Int corridors. **Pets:** Accepted.

✕ 🖥 ❚❙ 🏊 ✕

Holiday Inn Express SH
(802) 885-4516. **Call for rates.** 818 Charlestown Rd. I-91, exit 7. Int corridors. **Pets:** Accepted.

✕ 🦽 🖥 🖥 🏊

STOWE

1066 Ye Olde England Inne CI
(802) 253-7558. **$109-$189, 15 day notice.** 433 Mountain Rd. 0.4 mi w on SR 108, from jct SR 100. Ext/int corridors. **Pets:** Accepted.
SAVE SD X 🛡 💻 🍴 🏊 🐾

Commodores Inn LH
(802) 253-7131. **$98-$198.** 823 S Main St. Jct SR 108, 0.8 mi s on SR 100. Int corridors. **Pets:** Accepted.
SAVE SD X 🛡 🍴 🏊 🐾

Edson Hill Manor CI
(802) 253-7371. **$159-$219, 15 day notice.** 1500 Edson Hill Rd. Jct SR 100, 3.5 mi w on SR 108, then 1.3 mi n. Ext/int corridors. **Pets:** Accepted.
X 🍴 🏊 🐾

Golden Eagle Resort M
(802) 253-4811. **$99-$259, 5 day notice.** 511 Mountain Rd. 0.5 mi w on SR 108, from jct SR 100. Ext corridors. **Pets:** Other species. $25 one-time fee/room. Designated rooms, service with restrictions, crate.
SAVE X 🛡 💻 🍴 🏊 🐾

Hob Knob Inn & Restaurant M 🐾
(802) 253-8549. **$89-$280, 14 day notice.** 2364 Mountain Rd. Jct SR 100, 2.5 mi w on SR 108. Ext/int corridors. **Pets:** $20 daily fee/pet. Designated rooms, service with restrictions.
ASK X 🛡 💻 🍴 🏊

Honeywood Country Lodge M
(802) 253-4124. **$79-$139, 15 day notice.** 4527 Mountain Rd. Jct SR 100, 4.5 mi w on SR 108. Ext corridors. **Pets:** Accepted.
SAVE SD X 🛡 💻 🏊 🐾

Innsbruck Inn at Stowe M
(802) 253-8582. **$84-$199, 15 day notice.** 4361 Mountain Rd. 4.5 mi w on SR 108, from jct SR 100. Ext/int corridors. **Pets:** Accepted.
SAVE SD X 🛡 💻 🏊 🐾

The Mountain Road Resort at Stowe M
(802) 253-4566. **Call for rates.** 1007 Mountain Rd. 1 mi w on SR 108, from jct SR 100. Ext corridors. **Pets:** Accepted.
X 🛡 💻 🏊 🐾

The Snowdrift Motel M
(802) 253-7305. **$75-$140, 15 day notice.** 2135 Mountain Rd. Jct SR 100, 2.1 mi w on SR 108. Ext/int corridors. **Pets:** Dogs only. $10 daily fee/pet. Designated rooms, service with restrictions, crate.
X 🛡 💻 🏊 🐾

Ten Acres Lodge CI
(802) 253-7638. **Call for rates.** 14 Barrows Rd. Jct SR 100, 2.1 mi w on SR 108, then 0.5 mi s on Luce Hill Rd. Ext/int corridors. **Pets:** Accepted.
SAVE X 🏊 🐾

Topnotch Resort and Spa LH
(802) 253-8585. **$300-$1600, 14 day notice.** 4000 Mountain Rd. 4.2 mi w on SR 108, from jct SR 100. Ext/int corridors. **Pets:** Accepted.
SAVE SD X 🛡 💻 🍴 🏊 🐾

SUNDERLAND

Arcady at the Sunderland M
(802) 362-1176. **$50-$165, 3 day notice.** 6249 Rt 7A. On Historic SR 7A, 6.3 mi s of jct SR 11. Ext corridors. **Pets:** Accepted.
SD X 🛡 💻 🏊

WARREN

PowderHound Inn & Condominiums CO 🐾
(802) 496-5100. **$89-$169, 14 day notice.** 203 Powderhound Rd. On SR 100, 0.3 mi s of jct Sugarbush Access Rd. Ext corridors. **Pets:** Dogs only. $10 daily fee/pet. No service, crate.
SAVE X 🛡 💻 🏊 🐾

WEST BRATTLEBORO

Molly Stark Motel M
(802) 254-2440. **$45-$85.** 829 Marlboro Rd. I-91, exit 2, 3.3 mi w on SR 9. Ext corridors. **Pets:** Dogs only. $5 daily fee/pet.
X 🛡 💻

WEST DOVER

Big Bear's Lodge M
(802) 464-5591. **$70-$210, 15 day notice.** 344 Rt 100 N. 8.7 mi n on SR 100, from jct SR 9. Ext/int corridors. **Pets:** $10 daily fee/pet. Designated rooms, service with restrictions, crate.
SAVE SD X 🏊 🐾 🐾 🐾

The Gray Ghost Inn SH
(802) 464-2474. **$88-$157, 14 day notice.** 290 Rt 100 N. 7.8 mi n on SR 100, from jct SR 9. Int corridors. **Pets:** Service with restrictions, supervision.
X 🍴 🏊 🐾

Red Oak Inn CI
(802) 464-8817. **$79-$149, 7 day notice.** 45 Rt 100. 5 mi n. Int corridors. **Pets:** Medium. $25 one-time fee/room. Designated rooms, service with restrictions, supervision.
ASK X 🛡 💻 🏊 🐾

WESTMORE

WilloughVale Inn on Lake Willoughby CI
(802) 525-4123. **Call for rates.** 793 VT Rt 5A. Just s on SR 5A, from jct SR 16. Ext/int corridors. **Pets:** Accepted.
SAVE X 🛡 💻 🍴 🐾

WHITE RIVER JUNCTION

Comfort Inn SH
(802) 295-3051. **$99-$189.** 56 Ralph Lehman Dr. I-91, exit 11, just e. Int corridors. **Pets:** Service with restrictions, supervision.
ASK SD X SM 🛡 💻 🏊

Econo Lodge SH
(802) 295-3015. **Call for rates.** 91 Ballardvale Dr. I-91, exit 11, just s on US 5. Int corridors. **Pets:** Accepted.
SAVE X 🛡 💻 🏊 🐾

Super 8 Motel-White River Junction SH
(802) 295-7577. **$67-$119.** 442 N Hartland Rd. US 5, just w of jct I-89 and 91. Ext corridors. **Pets:** Other species. Service with restrictions, supervision.
ASK SD X 🏊

WILLISTON

Residence Inn by Marriott SH 🐾
(802) 878-2001. **$253-$273.** 35 Hurricane Ln. I-89, exit 12, just s on SR 2A, then just e. Ext corridors. **Pets:** $75 one-time fee/room. Service with restrictions, crate.
ASK SD X 🛡 💻 🏊 🐾

TownePlace Suites by Marriott SH
(802) 872-5900. **$136-$175.** 66 Zephyr Rd. I-89, exit 12, 1.1 mi n on SR 2A. Int corridors. **Pets:** $10 daily fee/pet. Service with restrictions.
ASK SD X SM 🛡 💻 🏊

WILMINGTON

🔺 ♦♦ Nordic Hills Lodge 🆂🅷
(802) 464-5130. **$95-$209.** 34 Look Rd. 2.5 mi n on SR 100, from jct SR 9, then 0.6 mi w on Colbrook Rd. Int corridors. **Pets:** Accepted.
[SAVE] 🔳 ⊠ 🍽️ 🏊 ⊠

WOODSTOCK

🔺 ♦ Braeside Motel 🅼
(802) 457-1366. **$88-$148, 15 day notice.** 432 US 4 E (Woodstock Rd). 1 mi e. Ext corridors. **Pets:** Accepted.
[SAVE] ⊠ 📠 🏊

VIRGINIA

ABINGDON

🔺 🔷🔷🔷🔷 Holiday Inn Express SH
(276) 676-2829. **$89-$129.** 940 E Main St. I-81, exit 19 (US 11), just w. Int corridors. **Pets:** Accepted.
SAVE ✕ ⟨M 🛏 🖵 ⟲

🔷 Super 8 Motel of Abingdon M
(276) 676-3329. **Call for rates.** 298 Towne Centre Dr. I-81, exit 17, just ne. Int corridors. **Pets:** Accepted.
✕ 🛏 🖵

ALTAVISTA

🔷🔷🔷 Comfort Inn SH
(434) 369-4000. **$63-$200.** 1558 Main St. US 29 business route, at jct US 29. Int corridors. **Pets:** Other species. $6 daily fee/pet. Service with restrictions, supervision.
ASK S🔒 ✕ 🛏 🖵 ⟲ ⊗

BIG STONE GAP

🔺 🔷 Country Inn Motel M
(276) 523-0374. **$45-$52.** 627 Gilley Ave. US 23, 1 mi w on US 23 business route and 58A. Ext corridors. **Pets:** $3 daily fee/pet. Service with restrictions, supervision.
SAVE S🔒 ✕ 🛏

BLACKSBURG

🔺 🔷🔷🔷 Comfort Inn SH 🐾
(540) 951-1500. **$80-$160, 7 day notice.** 3705 S Main St. 3.5 mi s on US 460, jct US 460 Bypass. Int corridors. **Pets:** Other species. Service with restrictions.
SAVE S🔒 ✕ 🛏 🖵 ⟲

BRISTOL

🔺 🔷 Econo Lodge M
(276) 466-2112. **$69-$109.** 912 Commonwealth Ave. I-81, exit 3, 1.5 mi e. Ext corridors. **Pets:** Medium, dogs only. $20 one-time fee/pet. Service with restrictions, supervision.
SAVE S🔒 ✕ 🛏 🖵

🔺 🔷🔷🔷 Holiday Inn Hotel & Suites LH 🐾
(276) 466-4100. **$104.** 3005 Linden Dr. I-81, exit 7, just w. Int corridors. **Pets:** Large, other species. $50 daily fee/room. Designated rooms, service with restrictions, supervision.
SAVE S🔒 ✕ ⟨M 🛏 🖵 ¶ ⟲

🔷 Knights Inn M
(276) 591-5090. **Call for rates.** 2221 Euclid Ave. I-81, exit 1, just e. Ext corridors. **Pets:** Accepted.
✕ 🛏 🖵

🔷🔷🔷 La Quinta Inn Bristol SH
(276) 669-9353. **$89-$129.** 1014 Old Airport Rd. I-81, exit 7, just e. Ext corridors. **Pets:** Other species. Service with restrictions, supervision.
ASK S🔒 ✕ ⟨M 🛏 🖵 ⟲

🔷 Motel 6 #4125 SH
(276) 466-6060. **$58-$75.** 21561 Clear Creek Rd. I-81, exit 7, 0.3 mi w. Int corridors. **Pets:** Small. $20 daily fee/pet. Designated rooms, no service, supervision.
✕ ⟨M 🛏

🔺 🔷 Super 8 Motel SH
(276) 466-8800. **Call for rates.** 2139 Lee Hwy. I-81, exit 5, just s. Int corridors. **Pets:** Other species. $10 one-time fee/room. Service with restrictions, supervision.
SAVE ✕ 🛏

BURKEVILLE

🔺 🔷🔷🔷 Comfort Inn Burkeville SH
(434) 767-3750. **$72-$121.** 419 N Agnew St. On US 460, just e of jct US 360. Int corridors. **Pets:** Small, other species. $25 one-time fee/pet. No service, supervision.
SAVE S🔒 ✕ 🛏 🖵 ¶ ⟲

CAPE CHARLES

🔺 🔷🔷🔷 Sunset Beach Resort SH
(757) 331-1776. **$79-$109.** 32246 Lankford Hwy. US 13, just n of the Chesapeake Bay Bridge Tunnel. Ext corridors. **Pets:** $10 daily fee/room. Designated rooms, service with restrictions, crate.
SAVE ✕ ⟨M 🛏 🖵 ¶ ⟲ ⊗

CHARLOTTESVILLE

🔺 🔷🔷🔷 Comfort Inn SH 🐾
(434) 293-6188. **$72-$129.** 1807 Emmet St. Jct US 250 Bypass, just n on US 29. Int corridors. **Pets:** $10 daily fee/pet. Designated rooms, service with restrictions, supervision.
SAVE S🔒 ✕ 🛏 🖵 ⟲

🔺 🔷🔷🔷 DoubleTree Hotel Charlottesville SH
(434) 973-2121. **Call for rates.** 990 Hilton Heights Rd. I-64, exit 118B (US 29), 4 mi n of jct US 250 Bypass. Int corridors. **Pets:** Accepted.
SAVE ✕ 🛏 🖵 ¶ ⟲ ⊗

▼▼▼▼ Holiday Inn-Monticello/Charlottesville LH ❖
(434) 977-5100. **$84-$199.** 1200 5th St SW. I-64, exit 120, just n on SR 631. Int corridors. **Pets:** Medium, other species. $15 daily fee/pet. Service with restrictions, supervision.
ASK 🛇 ✕ 🛏 💻 🍽 ➤

▲▲▲ ▼▼▼▼ Omni Charlottesville Hotel LH
(434) 971-5500. **$199-$299.** 235 W Main St. I-64, exit 120, 2.3 mi n on SR 631; downtown. Int corridors. **Pets:** Small. Service with restrictions, crate.
SAVE 🛇 ✕ 🛏 💻 🍽 ➤ ✕

▲▲▲ ▼▼▼ Quality Inn-University Area SH
(434) 971-3746. **$84-$169.** 1600 Emmet St. US 29 (Emmet St), just n of jct US 250 Bypass, then just e on Holiday Dr. Ext corridors. **Pets:** $15 daily fee/pet. Supervision.
SAVE 🛇 ✕ 🛏 💻

▼▼ Red Roof Inn of Charlottesville SH
(434) 295-4333. **Call for rates.** 1309 W Main St. US 29 (Emmet St), 1 mi e on US 250 (University Ave). Int corridors. **Pets:** Accepted.
✕ 🛏

▲▲▲ ▼▼▼▼ Residence Inn by Marriott SH
(434) 923-0300. **$142-$174.** 1111 Millmont St. I-64, exit 118B (US 29), 2.5 mi n on US 29/250 E, just s on Barracks Rd, then just se. Int corridors. **Pets:** Accepted.
SAVE 🛇 ✕ 🛏 💻 ➤ ✕

▲▲▲ ▼▼▼▼ Sleep Inn & Suites Monticello SH
(434) 244-9969. **$89-$239.** 1185 5th St. I-64, exit 120, just n. Int corridors. **Pets:** Other species. $15 daily fee/pet. Service with restrictions.
SAVE 🛇 ✕ 🛏 💻 ➤

CHINCOTEAGUE

▲▲▲ ▼▼▼▼ Americas Best Value Inn & Suites M
(757) 336-6562. **$65-$199, 10 day notice.** 6151 Maddox Blvd. 0.5 mi n on N Main St, just e. Ext corridors. **Pets:** Medium, dogs only. $10 daily fee/pet. Designated rooms, service with restrictions, supervision.
SAVE 🛇 ✕ 🛏 💻 ➤

CHRISTIANSBURG

▲▲▲ ▼▼ Econo Lodge M ❖
(540) 382-6161. **$49-$179.** 2430 Roanoke St. I-81, exit 118, just w on US 11/460. Ext corridors. **Pets:** Small. $10 daily fee/pet. Designated rooms, service with restrictions, supervision.
SAVE 🛇 ✕ 🛦M 🛏 💻 ➤

▲▲▲ ▼▼▼▼ Quality Inn SH
(540) 382-2055. **$69-$170.** 50 Hampton Blvd. I-81, exit 118C, just e. Ext corridors. **Pets:** Other species. $10 daily fee/room. Service with restrictions, crate.
SAVE 🛇 ✕ 🛏 💻 ➤

▼▼ Super 8 Motel-Christiansburg West SH
(540) 382-5813. **Call for rates.** 55 Laurel St NE. I-81, exit 118, 1 mi w on US 11/460, then 3.5 mi nw on US 460 Bypass; jct SR 114. Int corridors. **Pets:** Accepted.
✕ 🛏

CLARKSVILLE

▼▼▼▼ Best Western On The Lake SH
(434) 374-5023. **$76-$124, 3 day notice.** 103 Second St. Just n of US 58 business route. Int corridors. **Pets:** Other species. $100 deposit/pet, $10 daily fee/pet, $20 one-time fee/pet. Designated rooms, service with restrictions.
ASK 🛇 ✕ 🛦M 🛏 💻 ➤

COLLINSVILLE

▲▲▲ ▼▼ Knights Inn M
(276) 647-3716. **Call for rates.** 2357 Virginia Ave. Jct US 58, 3 mi n on US 220 business route. Ext corridors. **Pets:** Medium. $10 daily fee/room. Designated rooms, no service, supervision.
SAVE ✕ 🛏 ➤

▼▼▼▼ Quality Inn-Dutch Inn Hotel and Convention Center SH
(276) 647-3721. **$80-$300.** 2360 Virginia Ave. Jct US 58, 3 mi n on US 220 business route. Ext corridors. **Pets:** Small. $10 daily fee/pet. Service with restrictions, crate.
ASK 🛇 ✕ 🛏 💻 🍽 ➤

COVINGTON

▼▼▼▼ Best Western Mountain View SH
(540) 962-4951. **Call for rates.** 820 E Madison St. I-64, exit 16, just n. Ext corridors. **Pets:** Other species. $10 one-time fee/room. Service with restrictions, crate.
✕ 🛏 💻 🍽 ➤

▼▼ Compare Inn & Suites SH
(540) 962-2141. **$98-$115.** 203 Interstate Dr. I-64, exit 16, just sw. Int corridors. **Pets:** Other species. $10 one-time fee/room. Service with restrictions, crate.
ASK 🛇 ✕ 🛏 💻 ➤

CULPEPER

▼▼▼ Comfort Inn-Culpeper SH
(540) 825-4900. **$90-$100.** 890 Willis Ln. 2 mi s on US 29 business route; jct US 29, then just e. Ext corridors. **Pets:** Other species. $15 daily fee/pet. Service with restrictions, supervision.
ASK 🛇 ✕ 🛏 💻 ➤

DALEVILLE

▼▼ Howard Johnson Express Inn SH
(540) 992-1234. **Call for rates.** 437 Roanoke Rd. I-81, exit 150B, just nw on US 220. Ext corridors. **Pets:** Accepted.
✕ 🛏 💻 ➤ ✕

DANVILLE

▼▼▼▼ Comfort Inn & Suites SH
(434) 793-2000. **$79-$139, 14 day notice.** 100 Tower Dr. US 58, just w of jct US 29 business route. Int corridors. **Pets:** $10 daily fee/pet. Supervision.
ASK 🛇 ✕ 🛏 💻 🍽 ➤

▼▼▼▼ Courtyard by Marriott SH
(434) 791-2661. **$99-$114, 3 day notice.** 2136 Riverside Dr. On US 58, just w of jct US 29 business route. Int corridors. **Pets:** Small, other species. $10 one-time fee/room. Service with restrictions.
ASK 🛇 ✕ 🛦M 🛏 💻 🍽 ➤

▼▼ Innkeeper Danville North M
(434) 836-1700. **$50-$65, 3 day notice.** 1030 Piney Forest Rd. US 29 N business route, 0.5 mi n of US 58. Ext corridors. **Pets:** Small, other species. $10 one-time fee/room. Service with restrictions.
ASK 🛇 ✕ 🛏 ➤

▼▼ Super 8 Motel M
(434) 799-5845. **Call for rates.** 2385 Riverside Dr. On US 58, just e of jct US 29 business route. Int corridors. **Pets:** Small. $20 daily fee/pet. Service with restrictions, supervision.
✕ 🛏

DISTRICT OF COLUMBIA METROPOLITAN AREA

ALEXANDRIA

▼▼▼ Extended StayAmerica-Washington, DC-Alexandria SH
(703) 941-9440. **$164-$174.** 205 N Breckinridge Pl. I-395, exit 3B, 0.3 mi w on SR 236, 0.4 mi ne on Beauregard St, just e on Gloucester Rd, then just s. Int corridors. **Pets:** Other species. $75 one-time fee/pet. Service with restrictions.
(ASK) (S) (X) (M) (B) (P)

▼▼ Hawthorn Suites LTD-Alexandria SH
(703) 370-1000. **$180-$240.** 420 N Van Dorn St. I-395, exit 3A, 0.3 mi e on SR 236 to S Van Dorn St, then 0.5 mi n. Int corridors. **Pets:** Accepted.
(ASK) (S) (X) (B) (P) (≈)

⟨AAA⟩ ▼▼▼▼ Holiday Inn Hotel & Suites-Historic District Alexandria SH
(703) 548-6300. **$119-$259.** 625 First St. George Washington Memorial Pkwy, just e of jct First and Washington sts. Int corridors. **Pets:** Accepted.
(SAVE) (X) (B) (P) (¶) (≈) (⊠)

▼▼ Homestead Studio Suites Hotel-Alexandria SH
(703) 329-3399. **$164-$174.** 200 Bluestone Rd. I-95/495, exit 174 (Eisenhower Ave Connector), just n to Eisenhower Ave, then 1.2 mi e. Int corridors. **Pets:** Other species. $75 one-time fee/pet. Service with restrictions.
(ASK) (S) (X) (M) (B) (P)

⟨AAA⟩ ▼▼▼ ▼▼▼ Morrison House SH ✿
(703) 838-8000. **$169-$469.** 116 S Alfred St. Jct King and S Alfred sts, just s; in Old Town. Int corridors. **Pets:** Large, other species. Designated rooms, supervision.
(SAVE) (S) (X) (¶)

▼▼ Red Roof Inn-Alexandria M
(703) 960-5200. **Call for rates.** 5975 Richmond Hwy. I-95/495, exit 177A, 0.5 mi s on US 1. Ext corridors. **Pets:** Accepted.
(X) (M) (B)

▼▼▼ Residence Inn by Marriott Alexandria-Old Town SH
(703) 548-5474. **$307-$340.** 1456 Duke St. I-95/495, exit 176, 0.5 mi n on SR 241, then 0.7 mi e on SR 236. Int corridors. **Pets:** Accepted.
(ASK) (S) (X) (M) (B) (P) (≈)

⟨AAA⟩ ▼▼▼ Sheraton Suites Old Town Alexandria SH ✿
(703) 836-4700. **$119-$379.** 801 N St Asaph St. Just e of Washington St. Int corridors. **Pets:** Medium, dogs only. Designated rooms, service with restrictions, supervision.
(SAVE) (X) (B) (P) (¶) (≈)

⟨AAA⟩ ▼▼▼ Washington Suites-Alexandria SH
(703) 370-9600. **$159-$409.** 100 S Reynolds St. I-395, exit 3A, 0.8 mi e on SR 236 E (Duke St), then just s; near a shopping center. Int corridors. **Pets:** Medium, other species. $20 daily fee/pet. Designated rooms.
(SAVE) (S) (X) (M) (B) (P) (¶) (≈)

ARLINGTON

⟨AAA⟩ ▼▼▼▼ Arlington Residence Court a Clarion Collection SH
(703) 524-4000. **$99-$399.** 1200 N Courthouse Rd. 1.5 mi sw of Theodore Roosevelt Bridge on US 50. Int corridors. **Pets:** Medium. $10 daily fee/pet, $75 one-time fee/pet. Designated rooms, service with restrictions, crate.
(SAVE) (S) (X) (B) (P)

▼▼▼ Residence Inn by Marriott Arlington At Rosslyn SH ✿
(703) 812-8400. **$296-$362.** 1651 N Oak St. I-66, exit 73, 0.3 mi s on Fort Myer Dr, 0.3 mi w on Wilson Blvd to N Pierce St, then 2 blks e on Clarendon Blvd; 2 blks from Rosslyn Metro Station. Int corridors. **Pets:** Other species. $100 one-time fee/room.
(ASK) (S) (X) (B) (P)

⟨AAA⟩ ▼▼▼▼ Residence Inn by Marriott-Pentagon City SH
(703) 413-6630. **$329-$351.** 550 Army Navy Dr. I-395, exit 8C, just 1 mi s of 14th St Bridge. Int corridors. **Pets:** Accepted.
(SAVE) (S) (X) (M) (B) (P) (≈)

▼▼▼ The Ritz-Carlton, Pentagon City LH
(703) 415-5000. **Call for rates.** 1250 S Hayes St. 1 mi s of 14th St Bridge. Int corridors. **Pets:** Accepted.
(X) (M) (B) (P) (¶) (≈) (⊠)

▼▼▼ Sheraton Crystal City Hotel LH
(703) 486-1111. **$109-$319.** 1800 Jefferson Davis Hwy. I-395, exit 8C, 1.4 mi s of 14th St Bridge on US 1; hotel entrance, corner of Eads St. Int corridors. **Pets:** Accepted.
(X) (B) (P) (¶) (≈)

⟨AAA⟩ ▼▼▼▼ Sheraton National Hotel LH
(703) 521-1900. **$329.** 900 S Orme St. I-395, exit 8A, at SR 27 and 244; 1.3 mi s of 14th St Bridge. Int corridors. **Pets:** Accepted.
(SAVE) (S) (X) (B) (P) (¶) (≈)

▼▼▼ The Westin Arlington Gateway LH
(703) 717-6200. **$139-$499.** 801 N Glebe Rd. I-66, exit 71, just e on Fairfax Dr to Vermont Ave; just n of jct SR 120 and Wilson Blvd; 2 blks from metro station. Int corridors. **Pets:** Accepted.
(ASK) (S) (X) (M) (B) (P) (¶) (≈)

ASHBURN

⟨AAA⟩ ▼▼▼ Homewood Suites by Hilton/Dulles North SH
(703) 723-7500. **Call for rates.** 44620 Waxpool Rd. 1.7 mi w of jct SR 28 and Waxpool Rd (SR 625); SR 7, 3.4 mi s on Loudoun County Pkwy (CR 607), 0.3 mi w. Int corridors. **Pets:** Accepted.
(SAVE) (X) (M) (B) (P) (≈)

CENTREVILLE

▼▼ Extended StayAmerica-Centreville SH
(703) 988-9955. **$119-$129.** 5920 Fort Dr. I-66, exit 53, 0.9 mi s on SR 28; off SR 28, 0.3 mi s of jct US 29. Int corridors. **Pets:** Other species. $75 one-time fee/pet. Service with restrictions.
(ASK) (S) (X) (B) (P)

CHANTILLY

▼▼ Extended StayAmerica-Chantilly SH
(703) 263-7173. **$154-$164.** 14420 Chantilly Crossing Ln. On US 50, 0.4 mi w of jct SR 28; at Chantilly Crossing Shopping Complex. Int corridors. **Pets:** Other species. $75 one-time fee/pet. Service with restrictions.
(ASK) (S) (X) (M) (B) (P)

▼▼ Extended Stay Deluxe Chantilly SH
(703) 263-7200. **$164-$174.** 4506 Brookfield Corporate Dr. I-66, exit 53, 3 mi n on SR 28; 1 mi s of jct SR 28 and US 50. Int corridors. **Pets:** Other species. $75 one-time fee/pet. Service with restrictions.
(ASK) (S) (X) (M) (B) (P) (≈)

▼▼▼▼ Holiday Inn Select Chantilly-Dulles Expo
Center 🅻🅷
(703) 815-6060. **Call for rates.** 4335 Chantilly Shopping Center. I-66,
exit 53, 3 mi n on SR 28; 1 mi s of jct US 50 and SR 28. Int corridors.
Pets: Accepted.

❌ 🔳 🔳 🔳 🔳 🔳

▼▼▼ Residence Inn by Marriott Chantilly Dulles
South 🆂🅷
(703) 263-7900. **$252-$274.** 14440 Chantilly Crossing Ln. I-66, exit
57B, on US 50, just w of jct SR 28. Int corridors. **Pets:** Accepted.

🅰🆂🅺 🆂 ❌ 🔳 🔳 🔳 🔳

▼▼▼▼ Staybridge Suites Hotel Chantilly/Dulles International
Airport 🆂🅷
(703) 435-8090. **$79-$229.** 3860 Centerview Dr. Jct SR 28, just e on
US 50. Int corridors. **Pets:** Medium, other species. $150 one-time fee/
room. Designated rooms, service with restrictions, crate.

🅰🆂🅺 🆂 ❌ 🔳 🔳 🔳

▼▼ TownePlace Suites by Marriott-Chantilly 🆂🅷
(703) 709-0453. **$186-$208.** 14036 Thunderbolt Pl. Jct SR 28, just e on
US 50. Int corridors. **Pets:** Accepted.

🅰🆂🅺 🆂 ❌ 🔳 🔳 🔳

▼▼▼▼ Wingate Inn Dulles Airport-Chantilly 🆂🅷
(571) 203-0999. **$145-$269.** 3940 Centerview Dr. Jct SR 28, just e on
US 50. Int corridors. **Pets:** Accepted.

🅰🆂🅺 🆂 ❌ 🔳 🔳 🔳

FAIRFAX

▼▼ Candlewood Suites Fairfax-Washington, D.C. 🆂🅷
(703) 359-4490. **$179.** 11400 Random Hills Rd. I-66, exit 57A, 0.5 mi e
on US 50, just s on Waples Mill Rd, then 0.4 mi w. Int corridors.
Pets: Accepted.

🅰🆂🅺 🆂 ❌ 🔳 🔳 🔳

🅰🅰🅰 ▼▼▼▼ Comfort Inn University Center 🆂🅷 🌿
(703) 591-5900. **$109-$179, 45 day notice.** 11180 Fairfax Blvd. I-66,
exit 57A, 0.8 mi se on US 50, then 0.5 mi nw of jct US 29. Int
corridors. **Pets:** Medium, other species. $25 one-time fee/pet. Service with
restrictions, crate.

🆂🅰🆅🅴 🆂 ❌ 🔳 🔳 🔳 🔳 ❌

▼▼ Extended Stay Deluxe Fairfax 🆂🅷
(703) 359-5000. **$164-$174.** 3997 Fair Ridge Dr. I-66, exit 57B, 1.2 mi
w on US 50. Int corridors. **Pets:** Other species. $75 one-time fee/pet.
Service with restrictions.

🅰🆂🅺 🆂 ❌ 🔳 🔳 🔳

▼▼ Homestead Studio Suites Hotel-Fair Oaks 🆂🅷
(703) 273-3444. **$144-$154.** 12104 Monument Dr. I-66, exit 57B, 0.8 mi
w on US 50, 0.3 mi s on SR 620 (West Ox Rd), then just se. Ext
corridors. **Pets:** Other species. $75 one-time fee/pet. Service with restric-
tions.

🅰🆂🅺 🆂 ❌ 🔳 🔳 🔳

▼▼▼ Homestead Studio Suites Hotel-Falls
Church/Merrifield 🅼
(703) 204-0088. **$149-$159.** 8281 Willow Oaks Corporate Dr. I-495, exit
50A, just w on US 50 to Gallows Rd, then just s. Ext corridors.
Pets: Other species. $75 one-time fee/pet. Service with restrictions.

🅰🆂🅺 🆂 ❌ 🔳 🔳 🔳

▼▼▼▼ Residence Inn by Marriott-Fair Lakes 🆂🅷 🌿
(703) 266-4900. **$252-$274.** 12815 Fair Lakes Pkwy. I-66, exit 55 (Fairfax County Pkwy N), just w. Int corridors. **Pets:** Medium, other species.
$150 one-time fee/room.

🅰🆂🅺 🆂 ❌ 🔳 🔳 🔳 🔳 ❌

FALLS CHURCH

▼▼▼▼ Homewood Suites by Hilton-Falls Church 🆂🅷
(703) 560-6644. **Call for rates.** 8130 Porter Rd. I-495, exit 50A, just w
to SR 650; 0.4 mi n of SR 650. Int corridors. **Pets:** Accepted.

❌ 🔳 🔳 🔳 🔳 ❌

▼▼▼▼ Residence Inn by Marriott Fairfax-Merrifield 🆂🅷
(703) 573-5200. **$296-$318.** 8125 Gatehouse Rd. I-495, exit 50A, just
w to SR 640 N. Int corridors. **Pets:** Accepted.

🅰🆂🅺 🆂 ❌ 🔳 🔳 🔳 ❌

▼▼ TownePlace Suites by Marriott-Falls Church 🆂🅷
(703) 237-6172. **$166-$252.** 205 Hillwood Ave. I-495, exit 50B, 2.5 mi e
on US 50, 0.6 mi n on Annandale Rd, then e; just s of US 29. Int
corridors. **Pets:** Accepted.

🅰🆂🅺 🆂 ❌ 🔳 🔳 🔳

▼▼▼▼ The Westin Tysons Corner 🅻🅷
(703) 893-1340. **$289.** 7801 Leesburg Pike. I-495, exit 47B, just e on
SR 7. Int corridors. **Pets:** Accepted.

🅰🆂🅺 🆂 ❌ 🔳 🔳 🔳 🔳

HERNDON

▼▼▼▼ Candlewood Suites Washington-Dulles Herndon 🆂🅷
(703) 793-7100. **$207-$215.** 13845 Sunrise Valley Dr. SR 28, 0.4 mi e
on Frying Pan Rd, 0.7 mi nw. Int corridors. **Pets:** Accepted.

🅰🆂🅺 🆂 ❌ 🔳 🔳 🔳

▼▼▼ Extended StayAmerica-Herndon 🆂🅷
(703) 481-5363. **$164-$174.** 1021 Elden St. 0.8 mi n on SR 657 from
jct SR 267 (Dulles Toll Rd), exit 10. Int corridors. **Pets:** Other species.
$75 one-time fee/pet. Service with restrictions.

❌ 🔳 🔳 🔳

▼▼▼▼ Hawthorn Suites Herndon 🆂🅷
(703) 437-5000. **Call for rates.** 467 Herndon Pkwy. SR 267 (Dulles Toll
Rd), exit 11 CR 7100 (Fairfax County Pkwy), just n to Spring St exit,
just s to Herndon Pkwy (CR 606), just w on CR 606. Int corridors.
Pets: Accepted.

❌ 🔳 🔳 🔳 ❌

🅰🅰🅰 ▼▼▼▼ Hilton Washington Dulles Airport 🅻🅷
(703) 478-2900. **Call for rates.** 13869 Park Center Rd. SR 267 (Dulles
Toll Rd), exit 9, 3 mi s on SR 28; at McLearen Blvd (SR 668). Int
corridors. **Pets:** Accepted.

🆂🅰🆅🅴 ❌ 🔳 🔳 🔳 🔳 🔳 ❌

▼▼▼▼ Residence Inn by Marriott-Herndon/Reston 🆂🅷
(703) 435-0044. **$249-$269.** 315 Elden St. 0.4 mi w on CR 606 from jct
CR 7100 (Fairfax County Pkwy). Int corridors. **Pets:** Accepted.

🅰🆂🅺 🆂 ❌ 🔳 🔳 🔳 ❌

▼▼▼▼ Staybridge Suites Herndon Dulles 🆂🅷
(703) 713-6800. **$89-$284.** 13700 Coppermine Rd. SR 267 (Dulles Toll
Rd), exit 10, 0.7 mi s on Centreville Rd (SR 657), then 0.4 mi w. Int
corridors. **Pets:** Medium. $150 one-time fee/room. Service with restrictions,
crate.

🅰🆂🅺 🆂 ❌ 🔳 🔳 🔳 ❌

LEESBURG

🅰🅰🅰 ▼▼▼ Best Western Leesburg Hotel & Conference
Center 🆂🅷 🌿
(703) 777-9400. **$89-$149.** 726 E Market St. 0.5 mi e on SR 7 business route. Int corridors. **Pets:** Small, dogs only. $10 one-time fee/pet.
Designated rooms, service with restrictions, supervision.

🆂🅰🆅🅴 🆂 ❌ 🔳 🔳 🔳

🅰🅰🅰 ▼▼▼▼ Holiday Inn Leesburg 🆂🅷
(703) 771-9200. **$149-$169.** 1500 E Market St. 2 mi e on SR 7. Int
corridors. **Pets:** Accepted.

🆂🅰🆅🅴 🆂 ❌ 🔳 🔳 🔳 🔳 🔳

LORTON

Comfort Inn Gunston Corner SH ✿
(703) 643-3100. **$99-$129.** 8180 Silverbrook Rd. I-95, exit 163, just w.
Int corridors. **Pets:** Large, other species. $25 one-time fee/room. Service
with restrictions, supervision.

MANASSAS

Best Western Battlefield Inn SH
(703) 361-8000. **Call for rates.** 10820 Balls Ford Rd. I-66, exit 47A
westbound; exit 47 eastbound, just s on SR 234 business route. Ext
corridors. **Pets:** Accepted.

Red Roof Inn-Manassas M
(703) 335-9333. **Call for rates.** 10610 Automotive Dr. I-66, exit 47
eastbound; exit 47A westbound, just s on SR 234 business route, then
just e on Balls Ford Rd. Ext corridors. **Pets:** Accepted.

Residence Inn by Marriott Manassas Battlefield SH
(703) 330-8808. **$168-$206.** 7345 Williamson Blvd. I-66, exit 47A westbound; exit 47 eastbound, 0.5 mi s on SR 234 business route, then
just e. Int corridors. **Pets:** Accepted.

MCLEAN

Best Western Tysons Westpark Hotel LH
(703) 734-2800. **Call for rates.** 8401 Westpark Dr. I-495, exit 47A, 1.3
mi w on SR 7. Int corridors. **Pets:** Accepted.

Crowne Plaza Tysons Corner LH
(703) 893-2100. **$69-$369.** 1960 Chain Bridge Rd. I-495, exit 46A, 0.5
mi s on SR 123, just nw on International Dr, then just sw on Greensboro Dr. Int corridors. **Pets:** Accepted.

**Staybridge Suites-McLean/Tysons
Corner** SH
(703) 448-5400. **$229-$289.** 6845 Old Dominion Dr. I-495, exit 46B, 2
mi n on SR 123, then 0.3 mi e on SR 309. Int corridors.
Pets: Accepted.

RESTON

Homestead Studio Suites Hotel-Reston M
(703) 707-9700. **$164-$174.** 12190 Sunset Hills Rd. SR 267 (Dulles Toll
Rd), exit 12 (Reston Pkwy), just n, then just w. Ext corridors.
Pets: Other species. $75 one-time fee/pet. Service with restrictions.

Sheraton Reston Hotel LH
(703) 620-9000. **$399.** 11810 Sunrise Valley Dr. SR 267 (Dulles Toll
Rd), exit 12 (Reston Pkwy), just s. Int corridors. **Pets:** Accepted.

SPRINGFIELD

Comfort Inn Washington DC/Springfield SH
(703) 922-9000. **$99-$149.** 6560 Loisdale Ct. I-95, exit 169A, just e on
SR 644 E; jct I-395 and 495, 0.8 mi s. Int corridors. **Pets:** Accepted.

**Extended StayAmerica-Washington,
DC-Springfield** SH
(703) 822-0992. **$164-$174.** 6800 Metropolitan Center Dr. I-95, exit
169A, just e on SR 644, 0.6 mi s on Loisdale Rd, then just e. Int
corridors. **Pets:** Other species. $75 one-time fee/pet. Service with restric-
tions.

Hampton Inn Washington DC/Springfield SH
(703) 924-9444. **Call for rates.** 6550 Loisdale Ct. I-95, exit 169A, just e
on SR 644 E; jct I-395 and 495, 0.8 mi s. Int corridors. **Pets:** Accepted.

Red Roof Inn Springfield SH
(703) 644-5311. **Call for rates.** 6868 Springfield Blvd. I-95, exit 169B,
just sw of SR 644; jct I-395 and 495, 0.8 mi s. Int corridors.
Pets: Accepted.

TownePlace Suites by Marriott Springfield SH
(703) 569-8060. **$210-$241.** 6245 Brandon Ave. I-95, exit 169B, just nw
of SR 644; jct I-395 and 495, 0.8 mi s. Int corridors. **Pets:** Accepted.

STERLING

**Best Western Washington-Dulles
Airport** SH
(703) 471-8300. **$79-$189.** 45440 Holiday Dr. 1.7 mi n on SR 28 from
jct SR 267 (Dulles Toll Rd), just e on CR 846, then just s on Shaw Rd.
Ext corridors. **Pets:** Large. $75 one-time fee/room. Service with restric-
tions, supervision.

Candlewood Suites Washington Dulles/Sterling SH
(703) 674-2288. **$65-$289.** 45520 E Severn Way. 1.6 mi s on SR 28
from jct SR 7, 0.3 mi e. Int corridors. **Pets:** Accepted.

Extended StayAmerica-Sterling SH
(703) 444-7240. **$154-$164.** 46001 Waterview Plaza. 1.3 mi e on SR 7
from jct SR 28. Int corridors. **Pets:** Other species. $75 one-time fee/pet.
Service with restrictions.

Hampton Inn-Dulles/Cascades SH
(703) 450-9595. **$219-$249.** 46331 McClellan Way. 1.7 mi e on SR 7,
from jct SR 28, 0.5 mi n on CR 1794 (Cascades Pkwy) to Palisade
Pkwy, just e, then 0.4 mi s on Whitfield Pl. Int corridors. **Pets:** Medium.
$25 one-time fee/pet. Service with restrictions, crate.

**Holiday Inn Washington Dulles International
Airport** LH
(703) 471-7411. **$99-$279.** 1000 Sully Rd. 1.7 mi n on SR 28 from jct
SR 267 (Dulles Toll Rd), just e on CR 846, then just s on Shaw Rd.
Ext/int corridors. **Pets:** Other species. $50 one-time fee/pet. Service with
restrictions, crate.

**Residence Inn by Marriott Dulles Airport @ Dulles 28
Center** SH
(703) 421-2000. **$274-$296.** 45250 Monterey Pl. SR 28, exit CR 625
(Waxpool Rd), just w, just n on Pacific Blvd, then just e on Commercial
Dr. Int corridors. **Pets:** Medium. $150 one-time fee/room. Service with
restrictions.

**Suburban Extended Stay Hotel
Washington-Dulles/Sterling** SH
(703) 674-2299. **$55-$179.** 45510 Severn Way. 1.6 mi s on SR 28 from
jct SR 7, 0.3 mi e. Int corridors. **Pets:** Accepted.

**TownePlace Suites by Marriott at Dulles
Airport** SH
(703) 707-2017. **$202-$246.** 22744 Holiday Park Dr. 1.7 mi n on SR 28
from jct SR 267 (Dulles Toll Rd), just e on CR 846, then just s on
Shaw Rd. Int corridors. **Pets:** Accepted.

▲▲▲ ▼▼▼ **TownePlace Suites by Marriott Sterling** SH
(703) 421-1090. **$214-$256.** 21123 Whitfield Pl. 1.7 mi e on SR 7 from jct SR 28, 0.5 mi n on SR 1794 (Cascades Pkwy) to Palisades Pkwy, just e, then just s. Int corridors. **Pets:** Other species. $100 one-time fee/room. Service with restrictions, crate.

[SAVE] [S🐾] [✕] [🛏] [🍽] [🐾]

VIENNA

▲▲▲ ▼▼▼ **Comfort Inn Tysons Corner** M
(703) 448-8020. **$79-$199.** 1587 Spring Hill Rd. I-495, exit 47A, 1.8 mi w on SR 7, then just s; just e of jct SR 267 (Dulles Toll Rd). Ext corridors. **Pets:** Accepted.

[SAVE] [S🐾] [✕] [🛏] [🍽] [🐾]

▼▼ **Homestead Studio Suites Hotel-Tysons Corner** SH
(703) 356-6300. **$174-$184.** 8201 Old Courthouse Rd. I-495, exit 47A, 0.6 mi w on SR 7, then just s on Gallows Rd. Int corridors. **Pets:** Other species. $75 one-time fee/pet. Service with restrictions.

[ASK] [S🐾] [✕] [🖥M] [🛏] [🍽]

▼▼▼ **Residence Inn by Marriott-Tysons Corner** SH
(703) 893-0120. **$287-$317.** 8616 Westwood Center Dr. I-495, exit 47A, 1.9 mi w on SR 7, then just s. Ext corridors. **Pets:** Accepted.

[ASK] [S🐾] [✕] [🛏] [🍽] [🐾] [✕]

▼▼▼▼ **Residence Inn by Marriott Tysons Corner Mall** SH
(703) 917-0800. **$296-$362.** 8400 Old Courthouse Rd. I-495, exit 46A, 1.1 mi s on SR 123; 0.3 mi s of jct SR 7 and 123. Int corridors. **Pets:** Accepted.

[ASK] [S🐾] [✕] [🖥M] [🛏] [🍽] [🐾]

▼▼▼▼ **Sheraton Premiere At Tysons Corner** LH
(703) 448-1234. **$349.** 8661 Leesburg Pike. SR 7, just e of jct SR 267 (Dulles Toll Rd). Int corridors. **Pets:** Accepted.

[ASK] [✕] [🛏] [🍽] [🍽] [🐾] [✕]

WOODBRIDGE

▼▼▼▼ **Residence Inn by Marriott Potomac Mills** SH
(703) 490-4020. **$189-$219.** 14301 Crossing Pl. I-95, exit 158B (Prince William Pkwy), 0.5 mi sw. Int corridors. **Pets:** Accepted.

[ASK] [S🐾] [✕] [🖥M] [🛏] [🍽] [🐾] [✕]

END METROPOLITAN AREA

EMPORIA

▲▲▲ ▼▼ **Best Western Emporia** SH
(434) 634-3200. **Call for rates.** 1100 W Atlantic St. I-95, exit 11B, just w on US 58. Ext corridors. **Pets:** Other species. $10 daily fee/pet. Service with restrictions, supervision.

[SAVE] [✕] [🛏] [🍽] [🐾]

▲▲▲ ▼▼▼ **Days Inn-Emporia** SH
(434) 634-9481. **Call for rates.** 921 W Atlantic St. I-95, exit 11B, just w on US 58. Ext corridors. **Pets:** Medium. $8 daily fee/pet. Designated rooms, service with restrictions, supervision.

[SAVE] [✕] [🛏] [🍽] [🐾]

▲▲▲ ▼▼▼▼ **Hampton Inn** SH
(434) 634-9200. **Call for rates.** 898 Wiggins Rd. I-95, exit 11B (US 58), just w. Int corridors. **Pets:** Accepted.

[SAVE] [✕] [🖥M] [🛏] [🍽] [🐾]

▲▲▲ ▼▼▼ **Quality Inn** SH
(434) 348-8888. **$65-$99.** 1207 W Atlantic St. I-95, exit 11B, just w on US 58. Ext corridors. **Pets:** Accepted.

[SAVE] [S🐾] [✕] [🛏] [🍽] [🐾]

EXMORE

▲▲▲ ▼▼▼▼ **Best Western Eastern Shore Inn** SH
(757) 442-7378. **$75-$107.** 2543 Lankford Hwy. US 13, just n of SR 178. Ext/int corridors. **Pets:** Accepted.

[SAVE] [S🐾] [✕] [🖥M] [🛏] [🐾]

FREDERICKSBURG

▲▲▲ ▼▼▼ **Best Western Central Plaza** M
(540) 786-7404. **Call for rates.** 3000 Plank Rd. I-95, exit 130B on SR 3. Ext corridors. **Pets:** Small, other species. $10 daily fee/pet. Service with restrictions, supervision.

[SAVE] [✕] [🖥M] [🛏] [🍽]

▲▲▲ ▼▼▼▼ **Best Western Fredericksburg** SH
(540) 371-5050. **$69-$89.** 2205 William St. I-95, exit 130A, 0.3 mi e on SR 3. Ext corridors. **Pets:** $10 daily fee/pet. Designated rooms, service with restrictions, crate.

[SAVE] [S🐾] [✕] [🖥M] [🛏] [🍽] [🐾]

▲▲▲ ▼▼▼▼ **Country Inn & Suites**
Fredericksburg SH 🐾
(540) 898-1800. **$98-$108.** 5327 Jefferson Davis Hwy. I-95, 126 south-bound; exit 126A northbound; just n on US 1. Int corridors. **Pets:** Small. Service with restrictions, supervision.

[SAVE] [S🐾] [✕] [🛏] [🍽] [🐾]

▲▲▲ ▼▼▼ **Dunning Mills Inn All Suites Hotel** CO
(540) 373-1256. **$59-$89.** 2305-C Jefferson Davis Hwy. I-95, exit 126, 3 mi n on US 1. Ext corridors. **Pets:** Medium. $200 deposit/room, $5 daily fee/pet. Service with restrictions, supervision.

[SAVE] [S🐾] [✕] [🛏] [🐾]

▼▼▼▼ **Fredericksburg Hospitality House & Conference**
Center LH
(540) 786-8321. **$119-$129.** 2801 Plank Rd. I-95, exit 130B, on SR 3. Int corridors. **Pets:** Small. $50 one-time fee/pet. Service with restrictions, supervision.

[ASK] [S🐾] [✕] [🖥M] [🛏] [🍽] [🍽] [🐾]

▲▲▲ ▼▼▼▼ **Holiday Inn-Fredericksburg North** SH 🐾
(540) 371-5550. **$75-$115.** 564 Warrenton Rd. I-95, exit 133, just nw on US 17. Ext corridors. **Pets:** Medium. Service with restrictions, crate.

[SAVE] [S🐾] [✕] [🛏] [🍽] [🍽] [🐾] [✕]

▼▼▼ **Quality Inn Central Park** SH 🐾
(540) 371-0330. **$75-$125.** 2310 William St. I-95, exit 130A on SR 3 E. Ext corridors. **Pets:** Other species. Designated rooms, service with restrictions, supervision.

[ASK] [S🐾] [✕] [🛏] [🍽] [🐾]

▲▲▲ ▼▼▼ **Quality Inn Fredericksburg** SH
(540) 373-0000. **$59-$109.** 543 Warrenton Rd. I-95, exit 133, just n on US 17. Ext corridors. **Pets:** Other species. $10 daily fee/pet. Service with restrictions, supervision.

[SAVE] [S🐾] [✕] [🛏] [🍽] [🍽]

▲▲▲ ▼▼▼ **Ramada Inn South** SH
(540) 898-1102. **Call for rates.** 5324 Jefferson Davis Hwy. I-95, exit 126, just n on US 1. Ext/int corridors. **Pets:** Very small, other species. $10 daily fee/pet. Designated rooms, service with restrictions, crate.

[SAVE] [✕] [🛏] [🍽] [🍽] [🐾] [✕]

▼▼▼▼ TownePlace Suites by Marriott 🅂🄷
(540) 891-0775. **$73-$89.** 4700 Market St. I-95, exit 126 southbound; exit 126A northbound, just n on US 1, then just e. Int corridors. **Pets:** Other species. $10 daily fee/pet. Service with restrictions.
🆂🅰🆅🄴 🆂🄳 ☒ 🄴 💻 🌊

FRONT ROYAL

▲▲▲▽ ▼ Budget Inn 🄼
(540) 635-2196. **$45-$65.** 1122 N Royal Ave. I-66, exit 6, 2.2 mi s on US 340/522 and SR 55. Ext corridors. **Pets:** Small, dogs only. $8 daily fee/pet. Designated rooms, service with restrictions, supervision.
🆂🅰🆅🄴 🆂🄳 ☒ 🄴

▲▲▲▽ ▼ Relax Inn 🄼
(540) 635-4101. **$45-$75.** 1801 Shenandoah Ave. I-66, exit 6, 1.5 mi s on US 340/522. Ext corridors. **Pets:** Accepted.
🆂🅰🆅🄴 🆂🄳 ☒ 🄴 💻 🌊

▲▲▲▽ ▼ Twi-Lite Motel 🄼
(540) 635-4148. **$39-$89.** 53 W 14th St. I-66, exit 6, 2.3 mi s on US 340/522. Ext corridors. **Pets:** Very small. $10 daily fee/pet. Designated rooms, service with restrictions, supervision.
🆂🅰🆅🄴 🆂🄳 ☒ 🄴 🌊

GLADE SPRING

▲▲▲▽ ▼ Swiss Inn Motel & Suites 🄼
(276) 429-5191. **$39-$79.** 33361 Lee Hwy. I-81, exit 29, just e. Ext corridors. **Pets:** Accepted.
🆂🅰🆅🄴 🆂🄳 ☒ 🄴

GRUNDY

▼▼▼▼ Comfort Inn 🅂🄷
(276) 935-5050. **$74-$175.** 22006 Riverside Dr. On US 460, 0.5 mi e. Int corridors. **Pets:** Small, dogs only. $30 one-time fee/room. Designated rooms, service with restrictions, supervision.
🄰🅂🄺 🆂🄳 ☒ 🆂🄼 🄴 💻

HAMPTON ROADS AREA

CHESAPEAKE

▼▼ Extended StayAmerica Chesapeake-Crossways Blvd 🄼
(757) 424-8600. **$82-$150.** 1540 Crossways Blvd. I-64, exit 289B (Greenbrier Pkwy), 0.3 mi s, just w on Jarman Rd (at Crossways Center) to Crossways Blvd, then 0.3 mi n. Ext corridors. **Pets:** Other species. $75 one-time fee/pet. Service with restrictions.
🄰🅂🄺 🆂🄳 ☒ 🄴 💻

▼▼ Extended StayAmerica Chesapeake-Greenbrier Circle 🅂🄷
(757) 523-7377. **$95-$145.** 809 Greenbrier Cir. I-64, exit 289A (Greenbrier Pkwy), just n. Int corridors. **Pets:** Other species. $75 one-time fee/pet. Service with restrictions.
🄰🅂🄺 🆂🄳 ☒ 🆂🄼 🄴 💻

▼▼ Extended StayAmerica Hotel 🅂🄷
(757) 483-9200. **$95-$145.** 3214 Churchland Blvd. I-664, exit 9B northbound; exit 8B southbound, 1 mi s on US 17. Int corridors. **Pets:** Other species. $75 one-time fee/pet. Service with restrictions.
🄰🅂🄺 🆂🄳 ☒ 🄴 💻

▼▼▼ Residence Inn by Marriott, Chesapeake-Greenbrier 🅂🄷
(757) 502-7300. **$153-$186.** 1500 Crossways Blvd. I-64, exit 289B (Greenbrier Pkwy), just s to Jarman Rd (at Crossways Center) to Crossways Blvd, then 0.6 mi n. Int corridors. **Pets:** Accepted.
🄰🅂🄺 🆂🄳 ☒ 🄴 💻 🌊 ⊠

▼▼▼ TownePlace Suites By Marriott 🅂🄷
(757) 523-5004. **$120-$153.** 2000 Old Greenbrier Rd. I-64, exit 289A (Greenbrier Pkwy), just n on Greenbrier Pkwy. Int corridors. **Pets:** Accepted.
🄰🅂🄺 🆂🄳 ☒ 🆂🄼 🄴 💻 🌊

GLOUCESTER

▼▼▼▼ Comfort Inn Gloucester 🅂🄷
(804) 695-1900. **$84-$179.** 6639 Forest Hill Ave. US 17, just s. Int corridors. **Pets:** Medium, dogs only. $10 daily fee/pet. Service with restrictions, crate.
🄰🅂🄺 🆂🄳 ☒ 🄴 💻 🌊

HAMPTON

▼▼ Candlewood Suites 🅂🄷
(757) 766-8976. **Call for rates.** 401 Butler Farm Rd. I-64, exit 261B (Hampton Roads Center Pkwy) eastbound; exit 262B (Magruder Blvd) westbound, then n. Int corridors. **Pets:** Accepted.
☒ 🆂🄼 🄴 💻

▲▲▲▽ ▼▼▼▼ Clarion Hotel-Hampton Roads Convention Center 🅂🄷
(757) 838-5011. **$89-$159.** 1809 W Mercury Blvd. I-64, exit 263B (Mercury Blvd), jct SR 58. Int corridors. **Pets:** Accepted.
🆂🅰🆅🄴 🆂🄳 ☒ 🆂🄼 🄴 💻 🍴 🌊

▼▼ Extended StayAmerica-Hampton Coliseum 🄼
(757) 896-3600. **$77-$140.** 1915 Commerce Dr. I-64, exit 263 (Mercury Blvd), just n, then just e. Int corridors. **Pets:** Other species. $75 one-time fee/pet. Service with restrictions.
🄰🅂🄺 🆂🄳 ☒ 🆂🄼 🄴 💻

▲▲▲▽ ▼▼▼▼ Holiday Inn Hampton Hotel & Conference Center 🄻🄷 🐾
(757) 838-0200. **$104-$159.** 1815 W Mercury Blvd. I-64, exit 263B (Mercury Blvd) westbound; exit 263 eastbound. Ext/int corridors. **Pets:** Medium, other species. $25 one-time fee/pet. Service with restrictions, supervision.
🆂🅰🆅🄴 🆂🄳 ☒ 🆂🄼 🄴 💻 🍴 🌊 ⊠

▼▼▼ Ramada Hampton Coliseum & Convention Center 🅂🄷
(757) 827-7400. **Call for rates.** 1905 Coliseum Dr. I-64, exit 263 (Mercury Blvd) eastbound, just n, then just e towards Hampton Coliseum; exit 263B westbound. Ext/int corridors. **Pets:** Small. $10 daily fee/pet. Designated rooms, service with restrictions, supervision.
☒ 🄴 💻 🌊

▼▼▼ Super 8 Motel 🄼
(757) 723-2888. **Call for rates.** 1330 Thomas St. I-64, exit 265B westbound; exit 265C eastbound. Int corridors. **Pets:** Accepted.
☒ 🄴

NEWPORT NEWS

▼▼▼ Comfort Inn SH
(757) 249-0200. **$109-$149.** 12330 Jefferson Ave. I-64, exit 255A, just s on Clarie Ln (mall parking lot). Int corridors. **Pets:** $50 daily fee/room. Designated rooms, service with restrictions, supervision.

ASK S X &M 🛏 💻 �

◆ ◆ Crestwood Suites M ❖
(757) 951-1017. **$65-$130.** 11 Old Oyster Point Rd. I-64, exit 256A, just s on Oyster Point Rd to Canon Blvd, just e, then just n. Int corridors. **Pets:** Small, other species. $50 one-time fee/room. Service with restrictions, crate.

X 🛏 💻

◆◆◆ ▼▼ ◆ Days Inn-Oyster Point at City Center SH
(757) 873-6700. **$89-$119.** 11829 Fishing Point Dr. I-64, exit 255A, 2.5 mi s to Thimble Shoals Dr E, then 1 blk. Int corridors. **Pets:** Medium. $25 one-time fee/pet. Designated rooms, service with restrictions.

SAVE S X 🛏 💻 ➞

▼▼ Extended StayAmerica Newport News-Oyster Point SH
(757) 873-2266. **$77-$145.** 11708 Jefferson Ave. I-64, exit 258A (Jefferson Ave), 1 mi s. Ext corridors. **Pets:** Other species. $75 one-time fee/pet. Service with restrictions.

ASK S X 🛏 💻

◆◆◆ ◆ Host Inn M
(757) 599-3303. **$45-$59.** 985 J Clyde Morris Blvd. I-64, exit 258B, 0.8 mi n. Ext corridors. **Pets:** Accepted.

SAVE X 🛏 ➞

◆◆◆ ▼▼▼◆ Omni Newport News Hotel LH
(757) 873-6664. **$136-$159.** 1000 Omni Blvd. I-64, exit 258A (US 17), just s to Oyster Point Rd. Int corridors. **Pets:** Small, other species. $50 one-time fee/room. Service with restrictions, supervision.

SAVE X 🛏 💻 ❤ ➞

◆◆◆ ▼▼▼◆ Point Plaza-Suites at City Center SH
(757) 599-4460. **$69-$139.** 950 J Clyde Morris Blvd. I-64, exit 258B, just n on US 17. Ext/int corridors. **Pets:** $50 one-time fee/room. Designated rooms, service with restrictions, crate.

SAVE X 🛏 💻 ❤ ➞

▼▼ StudioPLUS-Newport News SH
(757) 882-8847. **$95-$155.** 12359 Hornsby Ln. I-64, exit 255A, just s on Jefferson Ave. Int corridors. **Pets:** Other species. $75 one-time fee/pet. Service with restrictions.

ASK S X 🛏 💻 ➞

◆◆◆ ◆ Travelodge M
(757) 874-4100. **Call for rates.** 13700 Warwick Blvd. I-64, exit 255B, 1 mi w to Bland Blvd, 1 mi s to Warwick Blvd, then just n. Ext corridors. **Pets:** Accepted.

SAVE X &M 🛏 💻

NORFOLK

◆◆◆ ▼▼▼ ◆ B & B @ Historic Page House Inn BB ❖
(757) 625-5033. **$139-$154 (no credit cards), 7 day notice.** 323 Fairfax Ave. I-264, exit 9, 1.4 mi n on Waterside Dr to Olney Rd, just w to Mowbray Arch, then just s; in Ghent historic district. Int corridors. **Pets:** Medium, other species. $25 daily fee/pet. Service with restrictions, crate.

SAVE X 🛏 X

◆◆◆ ▼▼▼◆ Quality Suites Lake Wright SH ❖
(757) 461-6251. **$109-$159.** 6280 Northampton Blvd. I-64, exit 282, just w on US 13. Int corridors. **Pets:** $35 one-time fee/room. Service with restrictions.

SAVE S X &M 🛏 💻 ❤ ➞

◆◆◆ ▼▼▼ Radisson Hotel Norfolk SH
(757) 627-5555. **$129-$169.** 700 Monticello Ave. Jct Brambleton Ave and St. Pauls Blvd; downtown. Int corridors. **Pets:** Medium, dogs only. $100 deposit/room. Designated rooms, service with restrictions, supervision.

SAVE S X &M 🛏 💻 ❤ ➞

▼▼▼ Residence Inn by Marriott Norfolk Airport SH
(757) 333-3000. **$158-$186.** 1590 N Military Hwy. I-64, exit 281B (Military Hwy). Int corridors. **Pets:** Accepted.

ASK S X &M 🛏 💻 ➞ X

◆◆◆ ▼▼▼ Sleep Inn Lake Wright SH ❖
(757) 461-1133. **$89-$139.** 6280 Northampton Blvd. I-64, exit 282, just w on US 13. Int corridors. **Pets:** $25 one-time fee/room. Service with restrictions.

SAVE S X 🛏 💻 ❤ ➞

◆◆◆ ▼▼▼▼ Tazewell Hotel and Suites SH
(757) 623-6200. **$109-$269, 3 day notice.** 245 Granby St. Jct Tazewell St; downtown. Int corridors. **Pets:** Accepted.

SAVE S X 🛏 💻 ❤

PORTSMOUTH

◆◆◆ ▼▼▼ Holiday Inn-Olde Towne Portsmouth SH ❖
(757) 393-2573. **$110-$130.** 8 Crawford Pkwy. Just nw from High St. Int corridors. **Pets:** Other species. $10 daily fee/room. Service with restrictions, supervision.

SAVE S X 🛏 💻 ❤ ➞

SUFFOLK

▼▼ Quality Inn SH
(757) 934-2311. **$89-$109.** 2864 Pruden Blvd. US 460 at jct US 58 Bypass. Ext corridors. **Pets:** Small. $50 deposit/pet, $15 daily fee/pet. Service with restrictions, supervision.

ASK S X 🛏 💻 ❤ ➞

◆◆◆ ▼▼▼ TownePlace Suites by Marriott SH ❖
(757) 483-5177. **$118-$144.** 8050 Harbour View Blvd. I-664, exit 8A (College Dr), just n. Int corridors. **Pets:** Medium, other species. $100 one-time fee/room. Service with restrictions, crate.

ASK S X &M 🛏 💻 ➞

VIRGINIA BEACH

◆◆◆ ▼▼◆ Best Western Beach Quarters Inn M
(757) 437-1200. **Call for rates.** 300 Atlantic Ave. I-264, 1.2 mi s of terminus at Rudee Inlet. Ext corridors. **Pets:** Accepted.

SAVE X 🛏 💻 ➞

▼▼▼ Candlewood Suites SH
(757) 213-1500. **$69-$199, 3 day notice.** 4437 Bonney Rd. I-264, exit 17B (Independence Blvd/Pembroke Area), just n to Bonney Rd, then just e. Int corridors. **Pets:** Accepted.

ASK S X 🛏 💻

◆◆◆ ▼▼▼▼ DoubleTree Hotel Virginia Beach LH
(757) 422-8900. **Call for rates.** 1900 Pavilion Dr. I-264, exit 22 (Birdneck Rd). Int corridors. **Pets:** Small. $25 one-time fee/pet. Designated rooms, service with restrictions, supervision.

SAVE X 🛏 💻 ❤ ➞ X

▼▼ Extended StayAmerica-Virginia Beach-Independence Blvd M
(757) 473-9200. **$100-$165.** 4548 Bonney Rd. I-264, exit 17B (Independence Blvd/Pembroke Area), just n to Bonney Rd, then just e. Ext corridors. **Pets:** Other species. $75 one-time fee/pet. Service with restrictions.

ASK S X 🛏 💻

Holiday Inn-Executive Center 🏨
(757) 499-4400. **$104-$200.** 5655 Greenwich Rd. I-64, exit 284B (Newtown Rd); jct I-64 and 264. Int corridors. **Pets:** Medium, other species. $50 deposit/room. Designated rooms, service with restrictions, supervision.

Howard Johnson Inn Ⓜ
(757) 460-1151. **Call for rates.** 5173 Shore Dr. Just w of jct Independence Blvd (SR 225) at Gate 5 of Naval Amphibious Base. Ext corridors. **Pets:** Accepted.

La Quinta Inn Norfolk (Virginia Beach) 🅂🄷
(757) 497-6620. **$99-$129.** 192 Newtown Rd. I-64, exit 284B to I-264 (Virginia Beach-Norfolk Expwy), exit Newtown Rd S. Int corridors. **Pets:** Other species. Service with restrictions, supervision.

Red Roof Inn VA Beach (Norfolk Airport) Ⓜ
(757) 460-6700. **Call for rates.** 5745 Northampton Blvd. I-64, exit 282, 1 mi n on US 13 (Northampton Blvd). Ext corridors. **Pets:** Accepted.

Residence Inn Virginia Beach Oceanfront 🅂🄷
(757) 425-1141. **$186-$351, 3 day notice.** 3217 Atlantic Ave. I-264, 1.5 mi n of terminus; Atlantic Ave and 33rd St. Int corridors. **Pets:** Accepted.

Sheraton Oceanfront Hotel 🅂🄷 🐾
(757) 425-9000. **$109-$259, 3 day notice.** 3501 Atlantic Ave. I-264, 1 mi n of terminus; jct 36th St. Int corridors. **Pets:** Medium, dogs only. Designated rooms, service with restrictions, supervision.

TownePlace Suites By Marriott 🅂🄷
(757) 490-9367. **$125-$164.** 5757 Cleveland St. I-64, exit 284B to I-264 (Virginia Beach-Norfolk Expwy), exit Newtown Rd N. Int corridors. **Pets:** Accepted.

Wyndham Virginia Beach Oceanfront 🏨
(757) 428-7025. **$189-$249, 3 day notice.** Atlantic Ave & 57th St. I-264, 2.2 mi n of terminus. Int corridors. **Pets:** Medium, dogs only. $25 daily fee/pet. Designated rooms, service with restrictions, crate.

END AREA

HARRISONBURG

Comfort Inn 🅂🄷
(540) 433-6066. **$79-$130.** 1440 E Market St. I-81, exit 247A, just e. Int corridors. **Pets:** Other species. $10 daily fee/pet. Service with restrictions, supervision.

Days Inn Harrisonburg 🅂🄷
(540) 433-9353. **$79-$120.** 1131 Forest Hill Rd. I-81, exit 245, just e. Int corridors. **Pets:** Medium, dogs only. $20 one-time fee/pet. Service with restrictions, supervision.

Harrisonburg Econo Lodge Ⓜ
(540) 433-2576. **$70-$150.** 1703 E Market St. I-81, exit 247A, 0.5 mi e on US 33. Ext/int corridors. **Pets:** Small. $20 daily fee/pet. Designated rooms, service with restrictions, supervision.

Ramada Limited 🅂🄷
(540) 434-9981. **Call for rates.** 1 Pleasant Valley Rd. I-81, exit 243, just w, then just n on US 11. Ext corridors. **Pets:** Accepted.

Super 8 Motel Ⓜ
(540) 433-8888. **Call for rates.** 3330 S Main St. I-81, exit 243, just e, then just s on US 11. Int corridors. **Pets:** Small. $10 daily fee/pet. Designated rooms, no service, supervision.

The Village Inn 🅂🄷
(540) 434-7355. **$74-$79.** 4979 S Valley Pike. I-81, exit 240 southbound, 0.6 mi w on SR 257, then 1.5 mi n on US 11; exit 243 northbound, just w to US 11, then 1.7 mi s. Ext corridors. **Pets:** Other species. $10 daily fee/pet. Service with restrictions, supervision.

HILLSVILLE

Best Western Four Seasons South 🅂🄷
(276) 728-4136. **$65-$140.** 57 Airport Rd. I-77, exit 14, just w on US 58 and 221. Ext corridors. **Pets:** $10 daily fee/pet. Designated rooms, service with restrictions, supervision.

Quality Inn 🅂🄷
(276) 728-2120. **$69-$169.** 85 Airport Rd. I-77, exit 14, just w on US 58 and 221. Ext corridors. **Pets:** Accepted.

HOPEWELL

Candlewood Suites 🅂🄷
(804) 541-0200. **$119-$145.** 5113 Plaza Dr. I-295, exit 9B (SR 36), just w; adjacent to Oak Lawn Plaza. Int corridors. **Pets:** Accepted.

Econo Lodge 🅂🄷
(804) 541-4849. **$69-$99.** 4096 Oaklawn Blvd. I-295, exit 9A, just e on SR 36. Int corridors. **Pets:** Small. $20 one-time fee/room. Service with restrictions, supervision.

HUDDLESTON

Mariners Landing 🄲🄾
(540) 297-4900. **$135-$270, 7 day notice.** 1217 Graves Harbor Tr. On SR 626; on Smith Mountain Lake. Ext/int corridors. **Pets:** Accepted.

IRVINGTON

The Tides Inn 🅂🄷 🐾
(804) 438-5000. **$189-$375, 7 day notice.** 480 King Carter Dr. 0.3 mi w of CR 200. Ext/int corridors. **Pets:** Medium, dogs only. $25 daily fee/pet. Designated rooms, service with restrictions, supervision.

KESWICK

◆◇ ▽▽▽▽ **Keswick Hall at Monticello** 🆂🅷 ❀
(434) 979-3440. **$325-$425 (no credit cards).** 701 Club Dr. I-64, exit 129, just n. Int corridors. **Pets:** Large. $75 one-time fee/pet. Designated rooms, service with restrictions, crate.
[SAVE] [✕] [♿M] [🛏] [❚ㅣ] [🏊] [✕]

LAWRENCEVILLE

▽▽▽▽ **Brunswick Mineral Springs B & B Circa**
1785 🅱🅱 ❀
(434) 848-4010. **$90-$200, 5 day notice.** 14910 Western Mill Rd. 5 mi e on US 58, 1 mi s on SR 712, then just e. Int corridors. **Pets:** Large, dogs only. $25 one-time fee/pet. Designated rooms, service with restrictions, supervision.
[ASK] [✕] [🛏] [🖵]

LEXINGTON

◆◇ ▽▽▽▽ **Best Western Inn at Hunt Ridge** 🆂🅷
(540) 464-1500. **$56-$175.** 25 Willow Spring Rd. I-64, exit 55, just n on US 11 to SR 39; I-81, exit 191, 6 mi w. Int corridors. **Pets:** Large, other species. $25 one-time fee/room. Service with restrictions.
[SAVE] [S🌙] [✕] [♿M] [🛏] [🖵] [❚ㅣ] [🏊]

◆◇ ▽▽▽▽ **Best Western Lexington Inn** 🆂🅷
(540) 458-3020. **$64-$150.** 850 N Lee Hwy. I-64, exit 55, just s on US 11; I-81, exit 191, 1.6 mi w. Ext corridors. **Pets:** Medium, other species. $25 one-time fee/room. Service with restrictions, crate.
[SAVE] [S🌙] [✕] [🛏] [🖵]

◆◇ ▽▽▽ **Comfort Inn-Virginia Horse Center** 🆂🅷
(540) 463-7311. **$64-$175.** 62 Comfort Way. I-64, exit 55, just s on US 11; I-81, exit 191, 0.6 mi w. Int corridors. **Pets:** Large, other species. $25 one-time fee/room. Designated rooms, supervision.
[SAVE] [S🌙] [✕] [🛏] [🖵] [🏊]

◆◇ ▽▽▽ **Days Inn** 🆂🅷
(540) 463-9131. **Call for rates.** 2809 N Lee Hwy. I-81, exit 195, just sw on US 11. Ext corridors. **Pets:** Accepted.
[SAVE] [✕] [🛏] [🖵] [❚ㅣ] [🏊]

▽▽▽ **Econo Lodge** Ⓜ
(540) 463-7371. **$50-$150.** 65 Econo Ln. I-81, exit 191, just s on US 11. Ext corridors. **Pets:** Medium. $10 daily fee/pet. Designated rooms, service with restrictions, supervision.
[ASK] [S🌙] [✕] [🛏] [🖵]

◆◇ ▽▽▽▽ **Holiday Inn Express** 🆂🅷
(540) 463-7351. **$99-$200.** 880 N Lee Hwy. I-64, exit 55, just s on US 11; I-81, exit 191, 1 mi w. Int corridors. **Pets:** Medium, other species. $25 one-time fee/room. Service with restrictions, supervision.
[SAVE] [S🌙] [✕] [🛏] [🖵]

◆◇ ▽▽▽ **Howard Johnson Inn** 🆂🅷
(540) 463-9181. **Call for rates.** 2836 N Lee Hwy. I-81, exit 195, just s on US 11. Int corridors. **Pets:** Other species. $10 daily fee/pet. Designated rooms, service with restrictions, supervision.
[SAVE] [✕] [🛏] [🖵] [🏊]

▽▽▽ **Super 8 Motel** Ⓜ
(540) 463-7858. **Call for rates.** 1139 N Lee Hwy. I-64, exit 55, just n. Int corridors. **Pets:** Accepted.
[✕] [🛏] [🖵]

LURAY

▽▽▽ **Days Inn-Luray** 🆂🅷
(540) 743-4521. **Call for rates.** 138 Whispering Hill Rd. US 211 Bypass, 1.7 mi e of jct US 340. Ext/int corridors. **Pets:** Medium. $10 daily fee/pet. Designated rooms, service with restrictions, crate.
[✕] [🛏] [🖵] [🏊] [✕]

LYNCHBURG

▽▽▽▽ **Days Inn of Lynchburg** 🆂🅷
(434) 847-8655. **$75-$150.** 3320 Candlers Mountain Rd. US 29, exit US 501, just e. Int corridors. **Pets:** Accepted.
[ASK] [S🌙] [✕] [🛏] [🖵] [❚ㅣ] [🏊]

◆◇ ▽▽▽ **Econo Lodge** Ⓜ
(434) 847-1045. **$80-$140, 4 day notice.** 2400 Stadium Rd. US 29, exit 4 southbound; exit 6 northbound, just w on James St, then just n. Ext corridors. **Pets:** Very small, dogs only. $25 daily fee/pet. Designated rooms, service with restrictions.
[SAVE] [S🌙] [✕] [🛏] [🖵]

▽▽▽ **Extended StayAmerica–University Blvd** Ⓜ
(434) 239-8863. **$77-$175.** 1910 University Blvd. US 460, exit Candlers Mountain Rd/University Blvd. Int corridors. **Pets:** Other species. $75 one-time fee/pet. Service with restrictions.
[ASK] [S🌙] [✕] [♿M] [🛏] [🖵]

▽▽▽▽ **Holiday Inn Select** 🆂🅷
(434) 528-2500. **$119.** 601 Main St. US 29 Expwy, exit 1 (Main St), just w; downtown. Int corridors. **Pets:** Accepted.
[ASK] [S🌙] [✕] [🛏] [🖵] [❚ㅣ] [🏊]

▽▽ **Lynchburg Super 8 Motel** 🆂🅷
(434) 846-1668. **Call for rates.** 3736 Candlers Mountain Rd. US 29, exit 8B, just e. Int corridors. **Pets:** $10 daily fee/pet, $25 one-time fee/pet. Service with restrictions, supervision.
[✕] [♿M] [🛏]

◆◇ ▽▽▽▽ **Quality Inn** 🆂🅷
(434) 847-9041. **$59-$99, 15 day notice.** 3125 Albert Lankford Dr. US 29, exit 7, just s. Int corridors. **Pets:** Other species. $25 one-time fee/room. Designated rooms, service with restrictions.
[SAVE] [S🌙] [✕] [🛏] [🖵] [🏊]

MARION

◆◇ ▽▽▽ **Best Western-Marion** 🆂🅷
(276) 783-3193. **Call for rates.** 1424 N Main St. I-81, exit 47, 0.3 mi s on US 11. Ext corridors. **Pets:** Small. $10 daily fee/pet. Designated rooms, service with restrictions, supervision.
[SAVE] [✕] [🛏] [🖵] [❚ㅣ] [🏊]

◆◇ ▽▽ **Econo Lodge** 🆂🅷 🐾
(276) 783-6031. **$59-$89, 10 day notice.** 1420 N Main St. I-81, exit 47, 0.3 mi s on US 11. Ext corridors. **Pets:** Other species. $6 daily fee/pet. Service with restrictions, supervision.
[SAVE] [S🌙] [✕] [🛏] [🖵]

MARTINSVILLE

▽ **Best Lodge** Ⓜ
(276) 647-3941. **$48-$68.** 1985 Virginia Ave. Jct US 58, 2.5 mi n on US 220 business route. Ext corridors. **Pets:** Small. $10 daily fee/pet. Designated rooms, service with restrictions, supervision.
[ASK] [S🌙] [✕] [🛏] [🖵]

◆◇ ▽▽▽ **Best Western Martinsville Inn** 🆂🅷
(276) 632-5611. **$85.** US 220 Business Rt S. Jct US 58, 2.3 mi n. Ext corridors. **Pets:** Other species. $10 daily fee/room. Service with restrictions.
[SAVE] [S🌙] [✕] [🛏] [🖵] [❚ㅣ] [🏊]

MIDDLETOWN

▽▽ **Super 8 Motel** 🆂🅷
(540) 868-1800. **Call for rates.** 2120 Reliance Rd. I-81, exit 302. Int corridors. **Pets:** Accepted.
[✕] [🛏] [🏊]

MOUNT JACKSON

Super 8 Motel SH
(540) 477-2911. **Call for rates.** 250 Conicville Blvd. I-81, exit 273, just e. Ext corridors. **Pets:** Accepted.

The Widow Kip's BB
(540) 477-2400. **$90-$125, 5 day notice.** 355 Orchard Dr. I-81, exit 273, 1.5 mi s on US 11, just w on SR 263, then just sw on SR 698. Int corridors. **Pets:** Other species. $15 daily fee/pet. Designated rooms, service with restrictions.

NEW CHURCH

The Garden & The Sea Inn BB
(757) 824-0672. **Call for rates.** 4188 Nelson Rd. US 13, 0.3 mi n, just w on CR 710 (Nelson Rd). Int corridors. **Pets:** Other species.

NEW MARKET

Budget Inn M
(540) 740-3105. **$29-$69, 3 day notice.** 2192 Old Valley Pike. I-81, exit 264, 1 mi n on US 11. Ext corridors. **Pets:** Small. $6 daily fee/pet. Designated rooms, no service, supervision.

Days Inn SH
(540) 740-4100. **Call for rates.** 9360 George Collins Pkwy. I-81, exit 264, just w on US 211. Ext corridors. **Pets:** Small, dogs only. $10 daily fee/pet. Service with restrictions, supervision.

NORTON

Days Inn SH
(276) 679-5340. **Call for rates.** 375 Wharton Ln. Jct US 58 and 23. Int corridors. **Pets:** Accepted.

ONANCOCK

Spinning Wheel Bed & Breakfast BB
(757) 787-7311. **$75-$125, 3 day notice.** 31 North St. Just n of jct Market (SR 179) and North sts. Int corridors. **Pets:** Other species. $10 daily fee/pet. Service with restrictions, crate.

PETERSBURG

Days Inn SH
(804) 733-4400. **Call for rates.** 12208 S Crater Rd. I-95, exit 45, jct US 301. Ext corridors. **Pets:** Accepted.

Howard Johnson Steven Kent SH
(804) 733-0600. **Call for rates.** 12205 S Crater Rd. I-95, exit 45, jct US 301. Ext/int corridors. **Pets:** Accepted.

Quality Inn SH
(804) 732-2900. **$60-$139.** 11974 S Crater Rd. I-95, exit 45, just n. Ext corridors. **Pets:** Large. Designated rooms, service with restrictions, supervision.

POUNDING MILL

Claypool Hill Holiday Inn Express Hotel & Suites SH
(276) 596-9880. **$140-$160.** 180 Clay Dr. 0.5 mi e of US 460 and 19. Int corridors. **Pets:** Accepted.

RADFORD

Best Western Radford Inn SH
(540) 639-3000. **$69-$119.** 1501 Tyler Ave. I-81, exit 109, 2.7 mi nw on SR 177. Int corridors. **Pets:** Small. $10 daily fee/pet. Designated rooms, service with restrictions, supervision.

Super 8 Motel-Radford M
(540) 731-9355. **Call for rates.** 1600 Tyler Ave. I-81, exit 109, just w. Int corridors. **Pets:** Accepted.

RICHMOND METROPOLITAN AREA

ASHLAND

Days Inn Ashland M
(804) 798-4262. **Call for rates.** 806 England St. I-95, exit 92B, just w on SR 54. Ext corridors. **Pets:** Accepted.

DOSWELL

Best Western-Kings Quarters SH
(804) 876-3321. **$59-$189, 3 day notice.** 16102 Theme Park Way. I-95, exit 98, just e on SR 30; entrance to theme park. Ext corridors. **Pets:** Accepted.

GLEN ALLEN

Candlewood Suites Richmond-West SH
(804) 364-2000. **$109-$179.** 4120 Brookriver Dr. I-64, exit 178, just w on W Broad St. Int corridors. **Pets:** Accepted.

Holiday Inn Express SH
(804) 934-9300. **$119-$134, 3 day notice.** 9933 Mayland Dr. I-64, exit 180B, just n to Mayland Dr, then just w. Int corridors. **Pets:** Small, other species. $10 one-time fee/room. Service with restrictions.

Homestead Studio Suites Hotel-Richmond-Innsbrook M
(804) 747-8898. **$77-$140.** 10961 W Broad St. I-64, exit 178B, just e on W Broad St, then just s on Cox Rd. Ext corridors. **Pets:** Other species. $75 one-time fee/pet. Service with restrictions.

Homewood Suites by Hilton Richmond West End-Innsbrook SH
(804) 217-8000. **Call for rates.** 4100 Innslake Dr. I-64, exit 178B, just e on W Broad St to Cox Rd, then just n. Int corridors. **Pets:** Small. $150 one-time fee/room. Service with restrictions, crate.

▼▼▼ **Residence Inn by Marriott** 🆂🅷
(804) 762-9852. **$204-$234.** 3940 Westerre Pkwy. I-64, exit 180, n on Gaskins Rd to W Broad St. Int corridors. **Pets:** Accepted.
🅰🅂🅺 🆂🐾 ✕ 🖳 🅼 🔋 🖵 ➿ 🖾

RICHMOND

▼▼ **Candlewood Suites** 🆂🅷
(804) 271-0016. **$129-$189.** 4301 Commerce Rd. I-95, exit 69, just n. Int corridors. **Pets:** Accepted.
🅰🅂🅺 🆂🐾 ✕ 🖳 🅼 🔋 🖵

▼▼ **Extended StayAmerica-I-64-West Broad** 🅼
(804) 285-2065. **$64-$135.** 6811 Paragon Pl. I-64, exit 183C (W Broad St), just w to Glenside Dr, just n. Ext corridors. **Pets:** Other species. $75 one-time fee/pet. Service with restrictions.
🅰🅂🅺 🆂🐾 ✕ 🔋 🖵

▼▼ **Extended Stay Deluxe Hotel** 🆂🅷
(804) 285-7050. **$95-$165.** 6807 Paragon Pl. I-64, exit 183C (W Broad St), just w to Glenside Dr, just n. Int corridors. **Pets:** Other species. $75 one-time fee/pet. Service with restrictions.
🅰🅂🅺 🆂🐾 ✕ 🔋 🖵 ➿

♨♨ ▼▼▼ **Holiday Inn Central** 🆂🅷
(804) 359-9441. **$109-$159.** 3207 N Boulevard. I-64/95, exit 78, just n. Ext/int corridors. **Pets:** Accepted.
🆂🅰🆅🅴 🆂🐾 ✕ 🖳 🅼 🔋 🖵 🍴 ➿

▼▼ **Homestead Studio Suites Hotel-Richmond/Midlothian** 🆂🅷
(804) 272-1800. **$77-$140.** 241 Arboretum Pl. Jct Powhite Pkwy (US 76) and Midlothian Tpke (US 60), just w. Int corridors. **Pets:** Other species. $75 one-time fee/pet. Service with restrictions.
🅰🅂🅺 🆂🐾 ✕ 🖳 🅼 🔋 🖵

♨♨ ▼▼▼▼ **The Jefferson Hotel** 🅻🅷
(804) 788-8000. **$245-$375.** 101 W Franklin St. Franklin and Adams sts; center. Int corridors. **Pets:** Accepted.
🆂🅰🆅🅴 🆂🐾 ✕ 🔋 🍴 ➿

▼▼▼ **Omni Richmond Hotel** 🅻🅷
(804) 344-7000. **$169-$299.** 100 S 12th St. I-95, exit 74A; I-195, exit Canal St. Int corridors. **Pets:** Small. $50 one-time fee/room. Service with restrictions, crate.
🅰🅂🅺 🆂🐾 ✕ 🔋 🖵 🍴 ➿

♨♨ ▼▼▼▼ **Quality Inn West End** 🆂🅷
(804) 346-0000. **$79-$159.** 8008 W Broad St. I-64, exit 183C westbound; exit 183 eastbound, 1.5 mi w. Int corridors. **Pets:** Medium. $10 daily fee/pet, $35 one-time fee/pet. Service with restrictions, crate.
🆂🅰🆅🅴 🆂🐾 ✕ 🔋 🖵 ➿

▼▼▼▼ **Sheraton Park South Hotel** 🆂🅷
(804) 323-1144. **Call for rates.** 9901 Midlothian Tpke. US 60, 1 mi w of Powhite Pkwy (US 76). Int corridors. **Pets:** Accepted.
✕ 🅼 🔋 🖵 🍴 ➿ 🖾

♨♨ ▼▼▼▼ **Sheraton Richmond West** 🅻🅷 🐾
(804) 285-2000. **$249-$255.** 6624 W Broad St. I-64, exit 183 eastbound; exit 183B westbound. Int corridors. **Pets:** Medium. Service with restrictions, crate.
🆂🅰🆅🅴 🆂🐾 ✕ 🅼 🔋 🖵 🍴 ➿ 🖾

▼▼ **Super 8 Motel** 🅼
(804) 262-8880. **Call for rates.** 5615 Chamberlayne Rd. I-95, exit 82. Int corridors. **Pets:** Accepted.
🖾 🔋

SANDSTON

♨♨ ▼▼▼ **Red Roof Inn** 🅼
(804) 440-5770. **$49-$79.** 5209 Williamsburg Rd. I-64, exit 195, 1.5 mi s to Williamsburg Rd, then just e. Ext corridors. **Pets:** Accepted.
🆂🅰🆅🅴 🆂🐾 ✕ 🔋 🖵

END METROPOLITAN AREA

ROANOKE

♨♨ ▼▼▼▼ **Best Western Inn at Valley View** 🆂🅷
(540) 362-2400. **$74-$180.** 5050 Valley View Blvd. I-581, exit 3E, just e, then just s via shopping center exit. Int corridors. **Pets:** Small, dogs only. $25 one-time fee/room. Service with restrictions, crate.
🆂🅰🆅🅴 🆂🐾 ✕ 🔋 🖵 ➿

♨♨ ▼▼▼ **Comfort Inn Airport** 🆂🅷
(540) 527-2020. **$79-$190.** 5070 Valley View Blvd. I-81, exit 143 to I-581, exit 3, e to Hershberger Rd. Int corridors. **Pets:** Medium, dogs only. $25 one-time fee/room. Service with restrictions, supervision.
🆂🅰🆅🅴 🆂🐾 ✕ 🔋 🖵 ➿

♨♨ ▼▼▼ **Days Inn** 🆂🅷
(540) 366-0341. **Call for rates.** 8118 Plantation Rd. I-81, exit 146, just e on SR 115. Ext/int corridors. **Pets:** Other species. $15 one-time fee/room. Service with restrictions, supervision.
🆂🅰🆅🅴 ✕ 🔋 🖵 ➿

▼ **Extended StayAmerica Roanoke-Airport** 🅼
(540) 366-3216. **$68-$135.** 2705 W Frontage Rd NW. I-581, exit 3W, just w to Ordway Dr, then 0.4 mi n via service frontage road. Ext corridors. **Pets:** Other species. $75 one-time fee/pet. Service with restrictions.
🅰🅂🅺 🆂🐾 ✕ 🔋 🖵

♨♨ ▼▼▼ **Holiday Inn Hotel Tanglewood** 🆂🅷
(540) 774-4400. **$99-$149.** 4468 Starkey Rd. I-581, exit Franklin Rd/Salem, 0.8 mi n on SR 419. Int corridors. **Pets:** Medium. $35 one-time fee/room. Service with restrictions, supervision.
🆂🅰🆅🅴 🆂🐾 ✕ 🔋 🖵 🍴 ➿

▼▼▼ **Holiday Inn Roanoke** 🆂🅷
(540) 362-4500. **$129-$139.** 3315 Ordway Dr. I-581, exit 3W, just w to Ordway Dr, then 0.6 mi n via service road. Int corridors. **Pets:** Medium. $10 daily fee/room, $25 one-time fee/room. Service with restrictions, supervision.
🅰🅂🅺 🆂🐾 ✕ 🔋 🖵 🍴 ➿ 🖾

♨♨ ▼▼▼▼ **MainStay Suites Roanoke Airport** 🆂🅷
(540) 527-3030. **$99-$175.** 5080 Valley View Blvd. I-581, exit 3E, just n. Int corridors. **Pets:** Medium, dogs only. $40 one-time fee/room. Service with restrictions, supervision.
🆂🅰🆅🅴 🆂🐾 ✕ 🔋 🖵

♨♨ ▼▼▼ **Quality Inn Airport** 🆂🅷
(540) 366-8861. **$59-$149.** 6626 Thirlane Rd. I-581, exit 2 southbound, just s on SR 117 (Peters Creek Rd), then just w. Ext corridors. **Pets:** Other species. $15 one-time fee/pet. Service with restrictions.
🆂🅰🆅🅴 🆂🐾 ✕ 🖵 🍴 ➿ 🖾

▼▼▼ **Super 8 Motel** 🆂🅷
(540) 563-8888. **Call for rates.** 6616 Thirlane Rd. I-581, exit 25, s on SR 117 (Peters Creek Rd), then just w. Int corridors. **Pets:** Medium. $10 daily fee/pet. Service with restrictions, supervision.
🖾 🔋

ROCKY MOUNT

Franklin Motel M
(540) 483-9962. **$45-$90.** 20281 Virgil H Goode Hwy. 6.5 mi n on US 220. Ext corridors. **Pets:** Very small, dogs only. $10 daily fee/pet. Designated rooms, service with restrictions, supervision.

SAVE [S🐾] [✕] [📶]

Rocky Mount Holiday Inn Express Hotel & Suites SH ❖
(540) 489-5001. **$90-$175.** 395 Old Franklin Tpke. US 220 S and SR 40, 0.3 mi e. Int corridors. **Pets:** $25 daily fee/pet. Service with restrictions, supervision.

A$K [S🐾] [✕] [📶] [📠] [➤]

RUTHER GLEN

Comfort Inn & Suites SH
(804) 448-1144. **$68-$199.** 24058 Welcome Way Dr. I-95, exit 104 (SR 207), just w. Int corridors. **Pets:** Accepted.

SAVE [S🐾] [✕] [♿M] [📶] [📠] [➤]

Super 8 Motel-Ruther Glen SH
(804) 448-2608. **Call for rates.** 24011 Ruther Glen Rd. I-95, exit 104 (SR 207), just e on Rogers Clark Blvd. Ext corridors. **Pets:** Other species. $15 one-time fee/room. Service with restrictions, supervision.

[✕] [📠] [➤]

SALEM

Comfort Suites Inn at Ridgewood Farm SH
(540) 375-4800. **$80-$130.** 2898 Keagy Rd. I-81, exit 141, 4.7 mi s on SR 419, then just w. Int corridors. **Pets:** Accepted.

SAVE [✕] [📶] [📠] [➤]

Days Inn SH
(540) 986-1000. **Call for rates.** 1535 E Main St. I-81, exit 141, 2 mi s on SR 419, then just w on US 460. Ext/int corridors. **Pets:** Medium, other species. $25 one-time fee/pet. Service with restrictions.

SAVE [✕] [📶] [📠]

Econo Lodge-Roanoke/Salem M
(540) 389-0280. **$34-$99.** 301 Wildwood Rd. I-81, exit 137, just e on SR 112. Ext corridors. **Pets:** Small. $5 daily fee/pet. Designated rooms, service with restrictions, crate.

SAVE [S🐾] [✕] [📶] [📠]

Quality Inn Roanoke/Salem SH
(540) 562-1912. **Call for rates.** 179 Sheraton Dr. I-81, exit 141, 0.4 mi e on SR 419. Int corridors. **Pets:** Medium. $50 one-time fee/room. Designated rooms, service with restrictions, supervision.

SAVE [✕] [📶] [📠] [➤]

SOUTH BOSTON

Holiday Inn-Express SH
(434) 575-4000. **$90-$129, 14 day notice.** 1074 Bill Tuck Hwy. Just e on US 58, from jct US 501. Int corridors. **Pets:** Accepted.

[✕] [♿M] [📶] [📠] [➤]

Quality Inn South Boston SH
(434) 572-4311. **$60-$100.** 2001 Seymour Dr. Jct US 58, 501 and 360, 1 mi e on US 360. Ext corridors. **Pets:** Accepted.

SAVE [S🐾] [✕] [📶] [📠] [➤]

SOUTH HILL

Comfort Inn SH
(434) 447-2600. **$60-$90.** 918 E Atlantic St. I-85, exit 12B, just w. Ext corridors. **Pets:** Other species. $10 daily fee/room. No service, crate.

SAVE [S🐾] [✕] [📶] [📠]

Super 8 Motel SH
(434) 447-2313. **Call for rates.** 250 Thompson St. I-85, exit 12A, just n. Int corridors. **Pets:** Accepted.

[✕] [♿M] [📶]

STAFFORD

Holiday Inn Express SH
(540) 657-5566. **$99-$139.** 28 Greenspring Dr. I-95, exit 143B, just w on Garrisonville Rd. Int corridors. **Pets:** Small. $20 daily fee/pet. Service with restrictions, supervision.

A$K [S🐾] [✕] [📶] [📠]

TownePlace Suites by Marriott SH
(540) 657-1990. **$78-$96.** 2772 Jefferson Davis Hwy. I-95, exit 143A, just s on US 1. Int corridors. **Pets:** Other species. $10 daily fee/pet. Designated rooms, supervision.

A$K [S🐾] [✕] [♿M] [📶] [📠] [➤]

STAUNTON

Best Western Staunton Inn SH
(540) 885-1112. **$64-$175.** 92 Rowe Rd. I-81, exit 222, just e on US 250. Int corridors. **Pets:** Medium. $25 one-time fee/room. Service with restrictions, supervision.

SAVE [S🐾] [✕] [📶] [📠] [➤]

Budget Host-Historic Hessian House SH
(540) 337-1231. **$49-$85, 3 day notice.** 3554 Lee Jackson Hwy. I-81, exit 213, 0.3 mi e. Ext corridors. **Pets:** $6 daily fee/pet. Designated rooms, service with restrictions, supervision.

SAVE [S🐾] [✕] [📶]

Comfort Inn SH ❖
(540) 886-5000. **$72-$135.** 1302 Richmond Ave. I-81, exit 222, just w on US 250. Int corridors. **Pets:** Small. $10 daily fee/pet. Designated rooms, service with restrictions, supervision.

SAVE [S🐾] [✕] [📶] [📠] [➤]

Days Inn-Staunton M
(540) 337-3031. **Call for rates.** 372 White Hill Rd. I-81, exit 217, just e on SR 654. Ext corridors. **Pets:** Accepted.

[✕] [📶] [📠] [➤]

Econo Lodge Staunton SH
(540) 885-5158. **$45-$109, 3 day notice.** 1031 Richmond Ave. I-81, exit 222, 0.7 mi w on US 250. Ext/int corridors. **Pets:** Medium. $10 daily fee/pet. Service with restrictions, supervision.

SAVE [S🐾] [✕] [📶] [📠]

GuestHouse International Inn SH
(540) 885-3117. **$60-$120.** 42 Sangers Ln. I-81, exit 222, just e on US 250. Ext corridors. **Pets:** Small. $10 one-time fee/pet. Designated rooms, service with restrictions, supervision.

A$K [S🐾] [✕] [📶] [📠] [➤] [✕]

Holiday Inn Golf & Conference Center SH
(540) 248-6020. **$99-$200.** 152 Fairway Ln. I-81, exit 225, 0.3 mi w on SR 275 (Woodrow Wilson Pkwy). Int corridors. **Pets:** Large. $15 one-time fee/room. Designated rooms, service with restrictions, supervision.

SAVE [S🐾] [✕] [📶] [📠] [🍽] [➤]

Howard Johnson Express Inn SH
(540) 886-5330. **Call for rates.** 268 N Central Ave. I-81, exit 222, 2.2 mi w on SR 250 into downtown; between Pine and Baldwin sts. Ext corridors. **Pets:** Accepted.

[✕] [📶] [📠]

Quality Inn-Conference Center SH
(540) 248-5111. **$59-$139.** 96 Baker Ln. I-81, exit 225, just e on SR 275 (Woodrow Wilson Pkwy). Ext corridors. **Pets:** Large. $10 daily fee/pet. Designated rooms, service with restrictions, supervision.

SAVE [S🐾] [✕] [📶] [📠] [➤]

Sleep Inn SH
(540) 887-6500. **$69-$125, 7 day notice.** 222 Jefferson Hwy. I-81, exit 222, just e on US 250. Int corridors. **Pets:** Medium. $25 one-time fee/room. Service with restrictions, supervision.

SAVE [S🐾] [✕] [📶] [📠]

STEPHENS CITY

ⒶⒶⒶ ▼▼▼▼ Comfort Inn-Stephens City 🅂🅷
(540) 869-6500. **$85-$125.** 167 Town Run Ln. I-81, exit 307, just se. Int corridors. **Pets:** Other species. $15 daily fee/pet. Service with restrictions, supervision.

🆂🅰🆅🅴 🆂🔴 ⊠ 🎛 🖥 🔜

STONY CREEK

ⒶⒶⒶ ▼▼▼▼ Hampton Inn-Stony Creek 🅂🅷
(434) 246-5500. **Call for rates.** 10476 Blue Star Hwy. I-95, exit 33, 0.3 mi s on SR 301. Int corridors. **Pets:** Small. $15 daily fee/pet. Service with restrictions, supervision.

🆂🅰🆅🅴 ⊠ ⑯ 🎛 🖥 🔜

ⒶⒶⒶ ▼▼▼▼ Sleep Inn & Suites 🅂🅷 ❀
(434) 246-5100. **$69-$149.** 11019 Blue Star Hwy. I-95, exit 33, 0.3 mi s on SR 301. Int corridors. **Pets:** Medium. $15 one-time fee/pet. Designated rooms, service with restrictions, supervision.

🆂🅰🆅🅴 🆂🔴 ⊠ 🎛 🖥 🔜

STRASBURG

ⒶⒶⒶ ▼▼▼▼ Hotel Strasburg 🅲🅸
(540) 465-9191. **$83-$180.** 213 S Holliday St. I-81, exit 298, 2.2 mi s on US 11, then just s. Int corridors. **Pets:** Medium, dogs only. $10 daily fee/pet. No service, supervision.

🆂🅰🆅🅴 ⊠ 🍽

▼▼ Ramada 🅂🅷
(540) 465-2444. **Call for rates.** 21 Signal Knob Dr. I-81, exit 298, just e. Int corridors. **Pets:** Small, other species. $10 daily fee/pet. Service with restrictions, supervision.

⊠ 🎛 🖥 🍽 🔜 ⊠

TAPPAHANNOCK

▼▼▼▼ The Essex Inn 🅱🅱
(804) 443-9900. **$145-$200, 7 day notice.** 203 Duke St. 0.3 mi s on US 17, then just s. Ext/int corridors. **Pets:** Medium, other species. $30 daily fee/pet. Designated rooms, service with restrictions, crate.

⊠ 🎛 🖥

▼ Super 8 Motel 🅼
(804) 443-3888. **Call for rates.** 1800 Tappahannock Blvd. US 17 and 360. Int corridors. **Pets:** Accepted.

⊠ 🎛 🖥

THORNBURG

▼▼ Quality Inn 🅂🅷
(540) 582-1097. **Call for rates.** 6409 Dan Bell Ln. I-95, exit 118 (SR 606), just w. Ext corridors. **Pets:** Accepted.

⊠ 🎛 🖥 🔜

TROUTVILLE

ⒶⒶⒶ ▼▼▼▼ Comfort Inn Troutville 🅂🅷
(540) 992-5600. **$64-$125.** 2545 Lee Hwy S. I-81, exit 150A, just s on US 11. Int corridors. **Pets:** Medium. $25 one-time fee/room. Service with restrictions, crate.

🆂🅰🆅🅴 🆂🔴 ⊠ 🎛 🖥 🔜

VERONA

ⒶⒶⒶ ▼▼▼▼ Knights Inn 🅂🅷
(540) 248-8981. **Call for rates.** 70 Lodge Ln. I-81, exit 227, just w, then just n. Ext corridors. **Pets:** Medium, other species. $10 daily fee/pet. Designated rooms, service with restrictions, supervision.

🆂🅰🆅🅴 ⊠ 🎛 🖥 🔜

WARRENTON

ⒶⒶⒶ ▼▼▼ Comfort Inn 🅼
(540) 349-8900. **$129-$179.** 7379 Comfort Inn Dr. 1.5 mi n on US 15/29, on service road. Ext/int corridors. **Pets:** Medium. $10 daily fee/pet. Designated rooms, service with restrictions, supervision.

🆂🅰🆅🅴 🆂🔴 ⊠ 🎛 🖥 🔜

WARSAW

▼▼▼▼ Best Western Warsaw 🅂🅷
(804) 333-1700. **Call for rates.** 4522 Richmond Rd. US 360, just w of town. Int corridors. **Pets:** Small. $10 daily fee/pet. Designated rooms, service with restrictions, supervision.

⊠ 🎛 🖥 🔜

WAYNESBORO

ⒶⒶⒶ ▼▼▼ Days Inn Waynesboro 🅂🅷
(540) 943-1101. **Call for rates.** 2060 Rosser Ave. I-64, exit 94, 0.5 mi n on US 340. Ext corridors. **Pets:** Other species. $10 daily fee/room. Service with restrictions, supervision.

🆂🅰🆅🅴 ⊠ 🎛 🖥 🔜

ⒶⒶⒶ ▼▼▼ Quality Inn Waynesboro 🅂🅷
(540) 942-1171. **$66-$130.** 640 W Broad St. I-64, exit 96, 3 mi w on SR 624; jct US 250 and 340. Ext/int corridors. **Pets:** $10 daily fee/pet. Service with restrictions, crate.

🆂🅰🆅🅴 🆂🔴 ⊠ 🎛 🖥 🔜

ⒶⒶⒶ ▼ Super 8 Motel 🅂🅷
(540) 943-3888. **Call for rates.** 2045 Rosser Ave. I-64, exit 94, n on US 340 to Lew Dewitt Blvd, then just w to Apple Tree Ln. Int corridors. **Pets:** $5 daily fee/pet. Service with restrictions, supervision.

🆂🅰🆅🅴 ⊠ 🎛 🖥

WILLIAMSBURG, JAMESTOWN & YORKTOWN AREA

WILLIAMSBURG

ⒶⒶⒶ ▼▼▼▼ America's Best Inn Williamsburg 🅂🅷
(757) 229-1134. **$49-$109.** 1600 Richmond Rd. Jct US 60/Richmond Rd and SR 612 (Ironbound Rd). Ext/int corridors. **Pets:** Accepted.

🆂🅰🆅🅴 🆂🔴 ⊠ ⑯ 🎛 🖥 🔜

ⒶⒶⒶ ▼▼▼▼ Crowne Plaza Williamsburg at Fort Magruder 🅻🅷 ❀
(757) 220-2250. **$69-$279.** 6945 Pocahontas Tr. US 60, 0.8 mi e of jct SR 5 and 31. Int corridors. **Pets:** Medium. $45 one-time fee/room. Designated rooms, service with restrictions, supervision.

🆂🅰🆅🅴 ⊠ 🎛 🖥 🍽 🔜 ⊠

ⒶⒶⒶ ▼▼▼ Days Inn Colonial Downtown 🅂🅷
(757) 229-5060. **$39-$129.** 902 Richmond Rd. Just w of Colonial Williamsburg on US 60. Ext corridors. **Pets:** Small. $15 daily fee/pet. Designated rooms, no service, supervision.

🆂🅰🆅🅴 🆂🔴 ⊠ 🎛 🔜

ⒶⒶⒶ ▼▼▼▼ Four Points by Sheraton Hotel & Suites Williamsburg Historic District 🅂🅷
(757) 229-4100. **$50-$160.** 351 York St. US 60 E, 0.3 mi se of jct SR 5 and 31. Ext/int corridors. **Pets:** Medium. $25 daily fee/pet. Designated rooms, service with restrictions, crate.

🆂🅰🆅🅴 🆂🔴 ⊠ ⑯ 🎛 🖥 🍽 🔜 ⊠

▼▼▼▼ Holiday Inn Patriot SH
(757) 565-2600. **$79-$149.** 3032 Richmond Rd. I-64, exit 234 (SR 199 E) to US 60, 2.5 mi e. Int corridors. **Pets:** Small, dogs only. $15 daily fee/pet. Service with restrictions, supervision.
SAVE Sꙸ ✕ 🛌 🖵 🍴 🏊 ⊠

▼▼▼▼ La Quinta Inn Williamsburg (Historic Area) SH
(757) 253-1663. **$85-$115.** 119 Bypass Rd. US 60 Bypass Rd, 0.3 mi e of Richmond Rd. Ext corridors. **Pets:** Other species. Service with restrictions, supervision.
ASK Sꙸ ✕ 🛌 🖵 🏊

▼▼▼▼ Patrick Henry Inn SH
(757) 229-9540. **$64-$104.** 249 York St. E on US 60/Richmond Rd at jct SR 5 and 31; 1 blk from Colonial Williamsburg. Int corridors. **Pets:** Large, other species. $15 one-time fee/room. Designated rooms, service with restrictions.
SAVE Sꙸ ✕ 🛌 🖵 🏊

▼▼▼ Quarterpath Inn M
(757) 220-0960. **$39-$109.** 620 York St. I-64, exit 242 (SR 199 W), 0.6 mi w to US 60 E, then just w. Ext corridors. **Pets:** Medium. No service.
SAVE Sꙸ ✕ 🛌

▼▼▼ Ramada Inn 1776 SH ✿
(757) 220-1776. **Call for rates.** 725 Bypass Rd. US 60 (Bypass Rd), 0.5 mi w of jct SR 132. Int corridors. **Pets:** Medium, other species. $10 daily fee/room. No service, crate.
✕ 🛌 🖵 🍴 🏊

▼▼▼ Red Roof Inn-Williamsburg M
(757) 259-1948. **Call for rates.** 824 Capitol Landing Rd. I-64, exit 238, 0.9 mi se on SR 143, then just w on SR 5. Ext corridors. **Pets:** Accepted.
SAVE ✕ 🛌 🏊

▼▼▼▼ Residence Inn by Marriott Williamsburg SH
(757) 941-2000. **$110-$241.** 1648 Richmond Rd. US 60, just w of jct Bypass Rd. Int corridors. **Pets:** Accepted.
ASK Sꙸ ✕ 🛌 🖵 🏊 ⊠

▼▼▼ Super 8 Motel-Historic M
(757) 229-0500. **Call for rates.** 304 2nd St. I-642, exit 242 (SR 199 W), 0.6 mi w on SR 199 to SR 143, 1.6 mi w to SR 162, then just w. Ext corridors. **Pets:** Medium, dogs only. $10 daily fee/pet. Service with restrictions, supervision.
SAVE ✕ 🛌 🏊

YORKTOWN

▼▼▼ Candlewood Suites-Yorktown SH
(757) 952-1120. **Call for rates.** 329 Commonwealth Dr. I-64, exit 256B, just n, then just e. Int corridors. **Pets:** Medium, other species. $75 one-time fee/room. Service with restrictions, crate.
✕ 🛌 🖵 🏊

▼▼▼ Days Inn SH
(757) 283-1111. **Call for rates (no credit cards).** 4531 George Washington Memorial Hwy. I-64, exit 256B, 0.8 mi ne on Victory Blvd (SR 171), 2.4 mi n on US 17. Int corridors. **Pets:** Accepted.
✕ 🛌 🏊

▼▼▼ TownePlace Suites by Marriott SH ✿
(757) 874-8884. **$154-$185.** 200 Cybernetics Way. I-64, exit 256B, e to Kiln Creek Pkwy. Int corridors. **Pets:** Other species. $100 one-time fee/room. Crate.
SAVE Sꙸ ✕ 🛌 🖵 🏊

END AREA

WINCHESTER

▼▼▼ Best Western Lee-Jackson Motor Inn SH
(540) 662-4154. **$62-$72.** 711 Millwood Ave. I-81, exit 313B, just nw on US 50/522/17. Ext corridors. **Pets:** Small. $5 daily fee/pet. Service with restrictions, supervision.
SAVE Sꙸ ✕ 🛌 🖵 🍴 🏊

▼▼▼ Days Inn SH
(540) 667-1200. **Call for rates.** 2951 Valley Ave. I-81, exit 310, just w, then 1.8 mi n on US 11. Ext/int corridors. **Pets:** Large. $5 daily fee/pet. Designated rooms, service with restrictions, supervision.
SAVE ✕ 🛌 🖵 🏊

▼▼▼ Red Roof Inn SH
(540) 667-5000. **Call for rates.** 991 Millwood Pike. I-81, exit 313 northbound; exit 313A southbound, just se on US 50/17. Ext corridors. **Pets:** Accepted.
SAVE ✕ 🛌

▼▼▼ Super 8 Motel SH
(540) 665-4450. **Call for rates.** 1077 Millwood Pike. I-81, exit 313 northbound; exit 313A southbound, 0.3 mi se on US 50/17. Int corridors. **Pets:** Other species. $12 one-time fee/pet. Service with restrictions, supervision.
SAVE ✕ 🛌

▼▼▼ Tourist City Motel M
(540) 662-9011. **Call for rates.** 214 Millwood Ave. I-81, exit 313 northbound; exit 313B southbound, 1 mi nw on US 50/522. Ext corridors. **Pets:** Accepted.
SAVE ✕ 🛌

▼▼▼ Travelodge of Winchester SH
(540) 665-0685. **Call for rates.** 160 Front Royal Pike. I-81, exit 313 northbound; exit 313A southbound, just s on US 522. Int corridors. **Pets:** Accepted.
SAVE ✕ 🛌 🖵 🏊

WOODSTOCK

▼▼ Budget Host Inn M
(540) 459-4086. **$50-$77.** 1290 S Main St. I-81, exit 283, 0.8 mi se on SR 42, then 0.6 mi s on US 11. Ext corridors. **Pets:** Medium. $5 daily fee/pet. Service with restrictions, supervision.
SAVE ✕ 🛌 🏊

▼▼▼ Comfort Inn Shenandoah SH
(540) 459-7600. **$72-$139.** 1011 Motel Dr. I-81, exit 283, just e. Int corridors. **Pets:** Accepted.
SAVE Sꙸ ✕ 🛌 🖵 🏊

WYTHEVILLE

▼▼▼ Best Western Wytheville Inn SH
(276) 228-7300. **Call for rates.** 355 Nye Rd. I-77, exit 41, just e. Int corridors. **Pets:** $10 daily fee/pet. Designated rooms, service with restrictions, supervision.
SAVE ✕ 🛌 🖵 🏊

▼▼ Budget Host Inn/Interstate Inn M
(276) 228-8618. **$55-$155.** 705 Chapman Rd. I-77/81, exit 73, just w. Ext corridors. **Pets:** Small. $10 daily fee/pet. Service with restrictions, supervision.
ASK Sꙸ ✕ 🛌

Comfort Inn SH
(276) 637-4281. **Call for rates.** 2594 E Lee Hwy. I-77/81, exit 80, just w. Int corridors. **Pets:** Accepted.

Days Inn SH
(276) 228-5500. **Call for rates.** 150 Malin Dr. I-81, exit 73, just w. Ext corridors. **Pets:** Small. $10 daily fee/room. Service with restrictions, supervision.

La Quinta Inn SH
(276) 228-7400. **$89-$129.** 1800 E Main. I-77/81, exit 73, just w. Int corridors. **Pets:** Other species. Service with restrictions, supervision.

Ramada SH
(276) 228-6000. **Call for rates.** 955 Peppers Ferry Rd. I-77, exit 41, just e. Ext corridors. **Pets:** Accepted.

Red Carpet Inn M
(276) 228-5525. **$45-$90, 7 day notice.** 280 Lithia Rd. I-77/81, exit 73, just w. Ext corridors. **Pets:** Small, other species. $10 daily fee/pet. Designated rooms, service with restrictions, supervision.

Red Roof Inn & Suites SH
(276) 223-1700. **$53-$129.** 1900 E Main St. I-77/81, exit 73, just w. Ext corridors. **Pets:** Accepted.

Super 8 Motel SH
(276) 228-6620. **Call for rates.** 130 Nye Cir. I-77, exit 41, just e. Ext corridors. **Pets:** Other species. $10 one-time fee/room. Service with restrictions, crate.

WASHINGTON

ABERDEEN

◆◆◆◆ GuestHouse International Inn & Suites ⑤Ⓗ
(360) 537-7460. **Call for rates.** 701 E Heron St. Just e on US 12, cross
street to Kansas St; downtown. Int corridors. **Pets:** Small. $50 deposit/
room, $10 daily fee/pet. Designated rooms, service with restrictions, super-
vision.

⊠ 🛏 🖵 🏊

◆◆◆ ◆ Olympic Inn Motel Ⓜ
(360) 533-4200. **$56-$90.** 616 W Heron St. 0.5 mi w; downtown. Ext
corridors. **Pets:** Other species. $10 daily fee/pet. Service with restrictions,
supervision.

SAVE S🐾 ⊠ 🛏

AIRWAY HEIGHTS

◆◆◆ Stratford Suites ⑤Ⓗ
(509) 321-1600. **$135-$165.** 11808 W Center Ln. I-90, exit 277, 4 mi w
on SR 2. Ext corridors. **Pets:** Accepted.

ASK S🐾 ⊠ 🛏 🖵

ANACORTES

◆◆◆ ◆◆ Anacortes Inn Ⓜ
(360) 293-3153. **$67-$125.** 3006 Commercial Ave. Just s of downtown.
Ext corridors. **Pets:** Dogs only. $10 one-time fee/room. Designated rooms,
service with restrictions.

SAVE S🐾 ⊠ 🛏 🖵 🏊

◆◆◆ ◆◆ Anacortes Ship Harbor Inn Ⓜ
(360) 293-5177. **$79-$179, 3 day notice.** 5316 Ferry Terminal Rd. 0.3
mi s of ferry landing. Ext corridors. **Pets:** Medium, dogs only. $10 one-
time fee/pet. Designated rooms, service with restrictions, supervision.

SAVE ⊠ 🛏 🖵 🐾

◆◆◆ ◆◆◆ Cap Sante Inn Ⓜ ☘
(360) 293-0602. **$66-$95.** 906 9th St. On 9th St, just e. Ext corridors.
Pets: Dogs only. $10 daily fee/pet. Service with restric-
tions, supervision.

SAVE ⊠ 🛏 🐾

◆◆◆ ◆◆◆◆ Fidalgo Country Inn & Suites ⑤Ⓗ
(360) 293-3494. **$90-$200.** 7645 SR 20. Jct Fidalgo Bay Rd. Ext/int
corridors. **Pets:** Accepted.

SAVE ⊠ ♿M 🛏 🖵 🏊

◆◆◆ Islands Inn Ⓜ
(360) 293-4644. **$79-$99 (no credit cards).** 3401 Commercial Ave.
Just s of downtown. Ext corridors. **Pets:** Dogs only. $5 daily fee/room.
Service with restrictions, supervision.

ASK S🐾 ⊠ 🛏 🖵 🐾

◆◆◆◆ Majestic Inn & Spa ⑤Ⓗ
(360) 299-1400. **Call for rates (no credit cards).** 419 Commercial Ave.
Downtown. Int corridors. **Pets:** Small, dogs only. $50 one-time fee/pet.
Designated rooms, service with restrictions, supervision.

⊠ 🛏 🖵 🍴 🐾

ASHFORD

◆◆◆ Mountain Meadows Inn Bed & Breakfast ⒷⒷ
(360) 569-2788. **$99-$165, 14 day notice.** 28912 SR 706 E. West end
of town. Ext/int corridors. **Pets:** Accepted.

⊠ 🛏 🖵 🐾 🐾 🐾

BELLINGHAM

◆◆◆ ◆◆◆ Best Western Heritage Inn ⑤Ⓗ ☘
(360) 647-1912. **Call for rates.** 151 E McLeod Rd. I-5, exit 256A, just
e. Int corridors. **Pets:** $20 daily fee/pet. Service with restrictions, supervi-
sion.

SAVE ⊠ 🛏 🖵 🏊

◆◆◆ ◆◆◆◆ Best Western Lakeway Inn & Conference
Center ⑤Ⓗ
(360) 671-1011. **Call for rates.** 714 Lakeway Dr. I-5, exit 253 (Lakeway
Dr), just se. Int corridors. **Pets:** Small. $25 daily fee/room. Designated
rooms, service with restrictions, supervision.

SAVE ⊠ 🛏 🖵 🍴 🐾 🐾

◆◆◆ ◆◆◆◆ Fairhaven Village Inn ⑤Ⓗ ☘
(360) 733-1311. **$149-$289.** 1200 10th St. I-5, exit 250, 1.5 mi w. Int
corridors. **Pets:** Small. $20 daily fee/pet. Designated rooms, service with
restrictions, supervision.

SAVE ⊠ ♿M 🛏 🖵

◆◆◆ ◆◆◆◆ Holiday Inn Express-Bellingham ⑤Ⓗ
(360) 671-4800. **$120-$140.** 4160 Meridian St. I-5, exit 256A, 0.7 mi e.
Int corridors. **Pets:** Small. $15 one-time fee/pet. Service with restrictions,
supervision.

SAVE S🐾 ⊠ ♿M 🛏 🖵 🏊

AAA ◆◆◆◆ **Hotel Bellwether** SH
(360) 392-3100. **$151-$649, 3 day notice.** One Bellwether Way. I-5, exit 253 (Lakeway Dr), 0.9 mi nw via Lakeway Dr and E Holly St, just w on Bay St, 0.6 mi n via W Chestnut St and Roeder Ave, then just w. Int corridors. **Pets:** Medium. $20 daily fee/room. Designated rooms, service with restrictions, crate.
SAVE S♦ ✕ ▣ ❗️ ✕

◆◆◆ **La Quinta Inn Bellingham** SH
(360) 671-6200. **$109.** 125 E Kellogg Rd. I-5, exit 256A, 1 mi ne via Meridian St. Int corridors. **Pets:** Medium. Service with restrictions, supervision.
ASK S♦ ✕ ▤ ▣ ➛

◆ **Motel 6–44** M
(360) 671-4494. **$55-$65 (no credit cards).** 3701 Byron Ave. I-5, exit 252, just nw. Ext corridors. **Pets:** Other species. Service with restrictions, supervision.
S♦ ✕ &M ▤ ➛

AAA ◆◆◆◆ **Quality Inn Baron Suites** SH 🐾
(360) 647-8000. **$85-$219.** 100 E Kellogg Rd. I-5, exit 256A, 1 mi ne via Meridian St. Ext/int corridors. **Pets:** Medium, other species. $25 one-time fee/room. Designated rooms, service with restrictions, supervision.
SAVE S♦ ✕ ▤ ▣ ➛

AAA ◆◆◆ **Travel House Inn** SH
(360) 671-4600. **$64-$99.** 3750 Meridian St. I-5, exit 256A, just w. Ext corridors. **Pets:** Small, dogs only. $10 daily fee/room. Designated rooms, service with restrictions, supervision.
SAVE S♦ ✕ ▤ ➛

◆◆ **Val-U Inn** SH
(360) 671-9600. **$73-$104.** 805 Lakeway Dr. I-5, exit 253 (Lakeway Dr), just ne. Int corridors. **Pets:** Accepted.
ASK S♦ ✕ ▤ ▣

BLAINE

◆ **Anchor Inn Motel** M
(360) 332-5539. **$57-$72, 3 day notice.** 250 Cedar St. I-5, exit 276, 0.6 mi sw via Peace Portal Dr. Ext corridors. **Pets:** Accepted.
ASK S♦ ✕ ▤

AAA ◆◆◆◆ **Semiahmoo Resort** SH
(360) 318-2000. **Call for rates.** 9565 Semiahmoo Pkwy. I-5, exit 270, 9.5 mi nw on Semiahmoo Spit. Int corridors. **Pets:** Medium, dogs only. $50 daily fee/room. Designated rooms, service with restrictions, supervision.
SAVE ✕ ▤ ▣ ❗️ ➛ ✕

BURLINGTON

AAA ◆◆◆ **Cocusa Motel** SH
(360) 757-6044. **$58-$135.** 370 W Rio Vista. I-5, exit 230, just e. Ext corridors. **Pets:** $20 one-time fee/room. Designated rooms, service with restrictions, supervision.
SAVE S♦ ✕ ▤ ▣ ➛

CASHMERE

AAA ◆◆◆ **Village Inn Motel** M
(509) 782-3522. **$54-$89, 7 day notice.** 229 Cottage Ave. On Business Rt US 2 and 97; downtown. Ext corridors. **Pets:** Small, dogs only. $10 daily fee/pet. Designated rooms, no service, supervision.
SAVE S♦ ✕ ▤

CASTLE ROCK

AAA ◆◆◆ **Timberland Inn & Suites** M
(360) 274-6002. **$60-$200.** 1271 Mount St. Helens Way. I-5, exit 49, just ne. Ext corridors. **Pets:** Small, dogs only. $10 daily fee/pet. Designated rooms, service with restrictions, supervision.
SAVE S♦ ✕ ▤ ▣

CENTRALIA

◆ **Motel 6–394** M
(360) 330-2057. **$45-$55 (no credit cards).** 1310 Belmont Ave. I-5, exit 82, just w on Harrison Ave, then just n. Ext corridors. **Pets:** Other species. Service with restrictions, supervision.
S♦ ✕ ▤ ➛

CHEHALIS

AAA ◆◆◆◆ **Best Western Park Place Inn & Suites** SH 🐾
(360) 748-4040. **$95-$124, 3 day notice.** 201 SW Interstate Ave. I-5, exit 76, just se. Int corridors. **Pets:** Small, dogs only. $10 daily fee/pet. Designated rooms, service with restrictions, supervision.
SAVE S♦ ✕ &M ▤ ▣ ➛

CHELAN

AAA ◆◆◆◆ **Best Western Lakeside Lodge** SH
(509) 682-4396. **$79-$329.** 2312 W Woodin Ave. West end of town. Ext corridors. **Pets:** Accepted.
SAVE S♦ ✕ ▤ ▣ ➛ ✕

CHEWELAH

AAA ◆◆◆ **Nordlig Motel** M
(509) 935-6704. **Call for rates.** W 101 Grant Ave. North edge of town on US 395. Ext corridors. **Pets:** Dogs only. $3 one-time fee/room. Service with restrictions, supervision.
SAVE ✕ ▤

CLARKSTON

◆◆ **Best Western Rivertree Inn** SH 🐾
(509) 758-9551. **$89-$159.** 1257 Bridge St. 0.9 mi w of Snake River Bridge on US 12. Ext corridors. **Pets:** Other species. $20 one-time fee/room. Designated rooms, service with restrictions, supervision.
ASK S♦ ✕ &M ▤ ▣ ➛ ✕

◆ **Motel 6** M
(509) 758-1631. **Call for rates (no credit cards).** 222 Bridge St. Just w of Snake River Interstate Bridge. Ext corridors. **Pets:** Other species. Service with restrictions, supervision.
✕ ▤ ➛

CLE ELUM

AAA ◆◆ **Cle Elum Travelers Inn** M
(509) 674-5535. **$56-$80.** 1001 E 1st St. I-90, exit 85, 1 mi w on SR 903. Ext/int corridors. **Pets:** Accepted.
SAVE S♦ ✕ ▤

◆◆ **Timber Lodge Inn** M
(509) 674-5966. **Call for rates.** 301 W 1st St. I-90, exit 84 eastbound, 1 mi ne; exit westbound, just w; downtown. Ext/int corridors. **Pets:** Small. $15 one-time fee/pet. Designated rooms, service with restrictions, supervision.
✕ ▤

COLFAX

◆◆◆ **Wheatland Inn** SH
(509) 397-0397. **Call for rates.** 701 N Main. Downtown. Int corridors. **Pets:** Medium, dogs only. $10 daily fee/pet. Service with restrictions, supervision.
✕ &M ▤ ▣ ➛

CONCRETE

AAA ◆◆◆◆ **Ovenell's Heritage Inn B&B and Log Cabins** BB
(360) 853-8494. **$100-$160 (no credit cards), 3 day notice.** 46276 Concrete Sauk Valley Rd. 0.5 mi w of downtown on SR 20, 3 mi se. Ext/int corridors. **Pets:** Dogs only. $25 daily fee/pet. Designated rooms, service with restrictions, supervision.
SAVE ✕ ▤ ▣ ✕

COUGAR

▽ Lone Fir Resort **M**
(360) 238-5210. **$55-$85, 3 day notice.** 16806 Lewis River Rd. Center. Ext corridors. **Pets:** Accepted.
(A$K) ⊠ 🛢 💻 📶 🏊 ❌ ☎

COULEE DAM

◈◈ ▽▽▽ Coulee House Inn & Suites **M**
(509) 633-1101. **Call for rates.** 110 Roosevelt Way. Just e of river bridge. Ext corridors. **Pets:** Other species. $15 daily fee/pet. Designated rooms, service with restrictions, supervision.
(SAVE) ⊠ 🛢 💻 🏊 ❌

DAYTON

▽▽▽▽ The Weinhard Hotel **SH**
(509) 382-4032. **Call for rates.** 235 E Main St. Downtown. Int corridors. **Pets:** Accepted.
⊠

EAST WENATCHEE

▽▽▽◈ Cedars Inn, East Wenatchee **SH**
(509) 886-8000. **Call for rates.** 80 Ninth St NE. Just e of SR 28. Int corridors. **Pets:** Accepted.
⊠ 🛢 💻 🏊

EATONVILLE

◈◈ ▽▽ Mill Village Motel **M**
(360) 832-3200. **$80-$100.** 210 Center St E. Just e of jct SR 161; center. Ext corridors. **Pets:** Small. $10 one-time fee/room. Designated rooms, service with restrictions, supervision.
(SAVE) ⊠ 🛢 💻

ELLENSBURG

◈◈ ▽▽◈ Best Western Lincoln Inn & Suites **SH** ❀
(509) 925-4244. **$99-$299.** 211 W Umptanum Rd. I-90, exit 109, just n, then just w. Int corridors. **Pets:** Small, dogs only. $25 daily fee/pet. Designated rooms, service with restrictions, supervision.
(SAVE) 🅂🄳 ⊠ 🛢 💻 🏊 ❌

▽▽▽ Ellensburg Comfort Inn **SH**
(509) 925-7037. **$89-$139.** 1722 Canyon Rd. I-90, exit 109. Int corridors. **Pets:** Accepted.
(A$K) 🅂🄳 ⊠ 🛢 💻 🏊

▽▽▽ Holiday Inn Express **SH**
(509) 962-9400. **$139-$169.** 1620 Canyon Rd. I-90, exit 109, just n. Int corridors. **Pets:** Accepted.
(A$K) 🅂🄳 ⊠ 🛢 💻 🏊

◈◈ ▽▽ I-90 Inn Motel **M**
(509) 925-9844. **$58-$78.** 1390 Dollar Way N. I-90, exit 106, just n. Ext corridors. **Pets:** Medium, dogs only. $10 one-time fee/pet. Service with restrictions, supervision.
(SAVE) 🅂🄳 ⊠ 🛢

▽▽ Nites Inn **M**
(509) 962-9600. **$56-$68.** 1200 S Ruby. I-90, exit 109, 0.5 mi n. Ext corridors. **Pets:** Accepted.
(A$K) 🅂🄳 ⊠ 🛢 💻

◈◈ ▽▽◈ Quality Inn & Conference Center **SH**
(509) 925-9800. **Call for rates.** 1700 Canyon Rd. I-90, exit 109, just n. Int corridors. **Pets:** Accepted.
(SAVE) ⊠ 🛢 💻 📶 🏊

ELMA

▽▽▽ Microtel Inn & Suites-Elma **SH**
(360) 482-6868. **Call for rates.** 800 E Main St. Just ne of jct US 12 and SR 8. Int corridors. **Pets:** Accepted.
⊠ 🛢 💻

FERNDALE

▽▽ ◈ Ferndale Super 8 **SH**
(360) 384-8881. **Call for rates.** 5788 Barrett Ave. I-5, exit 262, just ne. Int corridors. **Pets:** Accepted.
⊠ 🅶🄼 🛢 🏊

◈◈ ▽▽▽▽ Silver Reef Hotel Casino & Spa **SH** ❀
(360) 383-0777. **Call for rates.** 4876 Haxton Way. I-5, exit 260, 3.6 mi w. Int corridors. **Pets:** Small. $15 one-time fee/pet. Designated rooms, service with restrictions.
(SAVE) ⊠ 🛢 💻 📶 🏊 ❌

FORKS

◈◈ ▽▽▽ Forks Motel **M**
(360) 374-6243. **$54-$145.** 351 US 101 (Forks Ave S). Just s. Ext corridors. **Pets:** Small. $15 daily fee/pet. Service with restrictions, crate.
(SAVE) ⊠ 🛢 💻 🏊

▽▽ Manitou Lodge **BB**
(360) 374-6295. **$99-$179, 14 day notice.** 813 Kilmer Rd. 7.7 mi sw on SR 110 (LaPush Rd), 0.7 mi w on Mora Rd, then 0.8 mi n. Ext/int corridors. **Pets:** Accepted.
⊠ 🛢 💻 🅰 🚫 ☎

▽▽ Miller Tree Inn Bed & Breakfast **BB**
(360) 374-6806. **$95-$195, 7 day notice.** 654 E Division St. 0.3 mi e of US 101 (S Forks Ave). Ext/int corridors. **Pets:** Accepted.
⊠ 🛢 💻 🅰 ☎

◈◈ ▽▽▽ Olympic Suites Inn **M** ❀
(360) 374-5400. **$49-$119.** 800 Olympic Dr. North end of town, just ne off US 101 (S Forks Ave). Ext corridors. **Pets:** Dogs only. $5 daily fee/pet. Designated rooms, service with restrictions, supervision.
(SAVE) ⊠ 🛢 💻 🅰

▽▽ Pacific Inn Motel **M**
(360) 374-9400. **$54-$150.** 352 US 101 (S Forks Ave). Just s. Ext corridors. **Pets:** Accepted.
(A$K) 🅂🄳 ⊠ 🛢 💻

GOLDENDALE

◈◈ ▽▽▽ Quality Inn & Suites **M**
(509) 773-5881. **$89-$149.** 808 E Simcoe Dr. US 97, exit Simcoe Dr, just sw. Ext corridors. **Pets:** Accepted.
(SAVE) 🅂🄳 ⊠ 🛢 💻 📶 🏊

ILWACO

◈◈ ▽ Heidi's Inn **M**
(360) 642-2387. **$55-$85.** 126 Spruce St. Downtown. Ext corridors. **Pets:** Small, dogs only. $8 one-time fee/pet. Designated rooms, service with restrictions, supervision.
(SAVE) ⊠ 🛢 💻 🅰

KALALOCH

◈◈ ▽▽▽ Kalaloch Lodge **CA**
(360) 962-2271. **$99-$300, 3 day notice.** 157151 US 101. At MM 157. Ext/int corridors. **Pets:** Accepted.
(SAVE) 🅂🄳 ⊠ 🛢 💻 📶 🅰 ☎

KALAMA

◈◈ ▽ Kalama River Inn **M**
(360) 673-2855. **$53-$70.** 602 NE Frontage Rd. I-5, exit 30 northbound, 0.4 mi n; exit southbound, 0.4 mi s. Ext corridors. **Pets:** Very small, dogs only. $5 daily fee/pet. Service with restrictions, supervision.
(SAVE) 🅂🄳 ⊠ 🛢

KELSO

▼▼ **Best Western Aladdin** SH
(360) 425-9660. **$90-$109.** 310 Long Ave. I-5, exit 39, 1.1 mi w via Allen St and W Main St, then just n on 5th Ave NW. Int corridors. **Pets:** Very small, dogs only. $15 daily fee/pet. Designated rooms, service with restrictions, supervision.

ASK S♦ ✕ 🛏 💻 ➴

▼▼▼ **GuestHouse Inn & Suites** SH
(360) 414-5953. **Call for rates.** 501 Three Rivers Dr. I-5, exit 39, 0.3 mi w on Allen St, then 0.3 mi s. Int corridors. **Pets:** Accepted.

✕ 🛏 💻 ➴

▼ **Motel 6–43** M
(360) 425-3229. **$55-$65 (no credit cards).** 106 Minor Rd. I-5, exit 39, 0.3 mi ne. Ext corridors. **Pets:** Other species. Service with restrictions, supervision.

S♦ ✕ 🛏 ➴

▲▲▲ ▼▼▼ **Red Lion Hotel & Conference Center Kelso/Longview** SH
(360) 636-4400. **$150.** 510 Kelso Dr. I-5, exit 39, 0.3 mi se. Int corridors. **Pets:** Accepted.

SAVE S♦ ✕ 🛏 💻 ¶¶ ➴

▼▼ **Super 8 Motel** SH
(360) 423-8880. **Call for rates.** 250 Kelso Dr. I-5, exit 39, just se. Int corridors. **Pets:** Accepted.

✕ 🖧M 🛏 ➴

KENNEWICK

▲▲▲ ▼▼▼ **Best Western Kennewick Inn** SH
(509) 586-1332. **$95-$150, 3 day notice.** 4001 W 27th Ave. I-82, exit 113 (US 395), 0.8 mi n. Int corridors. **Pets:** Small. $10 one-time fee/room. Service with restrictions, crate.

SAVE S♦ ✕ 🖧M 🛏 💻 ➴ ⊠

▼▼▼ **Clover Island Inn** SH
(509) 586-0541. **$109-$349.** 435 Clover Island Dr. US 395, exit Port of Kennewick, 1 mi e on Columbia Dr, then just n. Int corridors. **Pets:** Accepted.

ASK S♦ ✕ 🛏 💻 ➴ ⊠

▼▼▼ **Comfort Inn** M
(509) 783-8396. **$85-$130.** 7801 W Quinault Ave. 0.5 mi s on Columbia Center Blvd from SR 240. Int corridors. **Pets:** Accepted.

ASK S♦ ✕ 🖧M 🛏 💻 ➴

▲▲▲ ▼▼ **Days Inn Kennewick** SH
(509) 735-9511. **$69-$109.** 2811 W 2nd Ave. Jct US 395 and Clearwater Ave, just s, just w. Ext/int corridors. **Pets:** Small. $10 daily fee/pet.

SAVE S♦ ✕ 🛏 💻 ➴

▼▼▼ **Fairfield Inn by Marriott** SH ❧
(509) 783-2164. **$98-$119.** 7809 W Quinault Ave. 0.5 mi s on Columbia Center Blvd from SR 240. Int corridors. **Pets:** $10 daily fee/pet. Service with restrictions, supervision.

ASK S♦ ✕ 🛏 💻 ➴

▲▲▲ ▼▼ **Guesthouse International Suites** SH
(509) 735-2242. **Call for rates.** 5616 W Clearwater Ave. US 395, 1.9 mi w. Int corridors. **Pets:** Medium. $10 deposit/pet. Designated rooms, service with restrictions, crate.

SAVE ✕ 🛏 💻

▼▼ **Kennewick Super 8** SH
(509) 736-6888. **$71-$91, 10 day notice.** 626 N Columbia Center Blvd. 1.1 mi s of SR 240. Int corridors. **Pets:** Accepted.

ASK S♦ ✕ 🖧M 🛏 ➴

▲▲▲ ▼▼▼ **La Quinta Inn & Suites Kennewick** SH
(509) 736-3326. **$119.** 4220 W 27th Pl. I-82, exit 113 (US 395), 0.8 mi n. Int corridors. **Pets:** Other species. Service with restrictions, supervision.

SAVE S♦ ✕ 🖧M 🛏 💻 ➴ ⊠

▲▲▲ ▼▼▼ **Red Lion Hotel Columbia Center-Kennewick** SH
(509) 783-0611. **$130.** 1101 N Columbia Center Blvd. SR 240, 0.5 mi s. Int corridors. **Pets:** Medium, other species. $25 deposit/pet. Service with restrictions, crate.

SAVE S♦ ✕ 🖧M 🛏 💻 ¶¶ ➴

LACEY

▲▲▲ ▼▼ **La Quinta Inn** SH
(360) 412-1200. **$103.** 4704 Park Center Ave NE. I-5, exit 109, just sw. Int corridors. **Pets:** Other species. Service with restrictions, supervision.

SAVE S♦ ✕ 🛏 💻 ➴

▼▼ **Quality Inn & Suites** SH
(360) 493-1991. **$65-$115, 30 day notice.** 120 College St SE. I-5, exit 109, just sw. Int corridors. **Pets:** Accepted.

ASK S♦ ✕ 🛏 💻

LA CONNER

▲▲▲ ▼▼▼ **La Conner Country Inn** SH ❧
(360) 466-3101. **$109-$210.** 107 S 2nd St. 2nd and Morris sts; downtown. Ext/int corridors. **Pets:** Other species. $50 one-time fee/room. Designated rooms, service with restrictions, supervision.

SAVE S♦ ✕ 🛏 💻 ¶¶ 🅰🄲

LANGLEY

▼▼▼ **Island Tyme Bed & Breakfast** BB
(360) 221-5078. **Call for rates.** 4940 S Bayview Rd. SR 525 at MM 15, just e on Marshview, 2.1 mi n. Int corridors. **Pets:** Accepted.

✕ 🅰🄲

LEAVENWORTH

▼▼ **Alpine Rivers Inn** SH
(509) 548-8888. **$79-$109, 7 day notice.** 1505 Alpensee Strasse. East edge of town. Ext corridors. **Pets:** Accepted.

✕ 🛏 💻 ➴

▲▲▲ ▼▼▼ **Bavarian Ritz Hotel** SH
(509) 548-5455. **$89-$269, 3 day notice.** 633 Front St. Center. Ext/int corridors. **Pets:** Accepted.

SAVE S♦ ✕ 🛏 💻

▲▲▲ ▼▼▼ **Der Ritterhof Motor Inn** SH ❧
(509) 548-5845. **$60-$97, 3 day notice.** 190 US 2. 0.3 mi w. Ext corridors. **Pets:** Dogs only. $10 daily fee/pet, $10 one-time fee/pet. Service with restrictions, supervision.

SAVE S♦ ✕ 🛏 💻 ➴

▼ **The Evergreen Inn** M
(509) 548-5515. **Call for rates.** 1117 Front St. US 2, just s. Ext corridors. **Pets:** Accepted.

✕ 🛏 💻

▼▼▼ **Howard Johnson Inn** M
(509) 548-4326. **Call for rates.** 405 W US 2. West end of town. Ext corridors. **Pets:** Accepted.

✕ 🛏 💻 ➴

▲▲▲ ▼▼ **Obertal Inn** M ❧
(509) 548-5204. **$79-$149.** 922 Commercial St. Off US 2; center. Ext corridors. **Pets:** Other species. $15 daily fee/pet. Designated rooms, service with restrictions.

SAVE ✕ 🛏 💻

▼▼▼▼ Quality Inn & Suites 🆂🅷
(509) 548-7992. **Call for rates.** 185 US 2. 0.3 mi w. Ext corridors.
Pets: Accepted.
[✕] [⚙M] [🛏] [💻] [⇌]

▼▼ River's Edge Lodge Ⓜ
(509) 548-7612. **$74-$225, 7 day notice.** 8401 US 2. 3.5 mi e. Ext
corridors. **Pets:** Accepted.
[A$K] [✕] [🛏] [💻] [⇌]

LIBERTY LAKE

▲▲ ▼▼▼▼ Best Western Peppertree Liberty Lake
Inn 🆂🅷
(509) 755-1111. **Call for rates.** 1816 N Pepper Ln. I-90, exit 296. Int
corridors. **Pets:** Very small, dogs only. $10 daily fee/pet. Service with
restrictions, supervision.
[SAVE] [✕] [⚙M] [🛏] [💻] [⇌]

▲▲ ▼▼▼▼ Days Inn Spokane at Liberty Lake 🆂🅷
(509) 340-3333. **Call for rates.** 2327 N Madson Rd. I-90, exit 296, 1 mi
e on Appleway, then just n. Int corridors. **Pets:** Accepted.
[SAVE] [✕] [⚙M] [🛏] [💻] [⇌]

LONG BEACH

▲▲ ▼▼▼ Anchorage Cottages Ⓒ🅰
(360) 642-2351. **Call for rates.** 2209 Boulevard N. Just w of SR 103.
Ext corridors. **Pets:** Medium. $10 daily fee/pet. Designated rooms, service
with restrictions, supervision.
[SAVE] [✕] [🛏] [💻] [🅺] [🏊]

▲▲ ▼▼▼ The Breakers Ⓒ🅾
(360) 642-4414. **$58-$278, 20 day notice.** 26th & SR 103. North end
of downtown. Ext corridors. **Pets:** Dogs only. $10 daily fee/room. Desig-
nated rooms, service with restrictions, supervision.
[SAVE] [S🅳] [✕] [🛏] [💻] [⇌] [🅺] [🅐🅒]

▲▲ ▼▼▼ Edgewater Inn 🆂🅷
(360) 642-2311. **$64-$119.** 409 Sid Snyder Dr. Just w of SR 103. Ext/int
corridors. **Pets:** $10 daily fee/pet. Designated rooms, service with restric-
tions, supervision.
[SAVE] [✕] [🛏] [💻] [🍽] [🅐🅒]

▲▲ ▼▼ Our Place at the Beach 🆂🅷
(360) 642-3793. **$59-$130.** 1309 South Blvd. Just w of SR 103 at south
end of town. Ext corridors. **Pets:** Large, other species. $5 one-time
fee/pet. Service with restrictions, supervision.
[SAVE] [S🅳] [✕] [🛏] [💻] [🅺] [🅐🅒]

▲▲ ▼▼▼ Rodeway Inn & Suites 🆂🅷 🐾
(360) 642-3714. **$70-$140.** 115 3rd St SW. Downtown. Ext corridors.
Pets: $7 daily fee/pet. Service with restrictions, supervision.
[SAVE] [S🅳] [✕] [🛏] [💻] [⇌] [🅐🅒]

▲▲ ▼▼▼▼ Super 8 Motel 🆂🅷
(360) 642-8988. **$79-$199.** 500 Ocean Beach Blvd. On SR 103; downtown. Int corridors. **Pets:** Accepted.
[SAVE] [S🅳] [✕] [⚙M] [🛏] [💻] [🅐🅒]

LONGVIEW

▲▲ ▼▼▼ Hudson Manor Inn & Suites Ⓜ
(360) 425-1100. **$60-$90.** 1616 Hudson St. Downtown. Ext corridors.
Pets: Medium, other species. $15 one-time fee/room. Service with restric-
tions, supervision.
[SAVE] [S🅳] [✕] [🛏] [💻]

▲▲ ▼▼ Longview Travelodge Ⓜ
(360) 423-6460. **Call for rates.** 838 15th Ave. Downtown; opposite
Medical Center. Ext corridors. **Pets:** Dogs only. $15 daily fee/pet. Service
with restrictions.
[SAVE] [✕] [🛏] [💻]

▲▲ ▼▼ The Townhouse Motel Ⓜ
(360) 423-7200. **$50-$95 (no credit cards).** 744 Washington Way.
Downtown. Ext corridors. **Pets:** Large, other species. $7 daily fee/pet.
Service with restrictions, supervision.
[SAVE] [S🅳] [✕] [🛏] [💻] [⇌]

MOCLIPS

▲▲ ▼▼▼ Ocean Crest Resort 🆂🅷 🐾
(360) 276-4465. **$79-$199, 7 day notice.** 4651 SR 109 N. South edge
of town. Ext corridors. **Pets:** Other species. $18 daily fee/pet. Designated
rooms, service with restrictions, supervision.
[SAVE] [S🅳] [✕] [🛏] [💻] [🍽] [⇌] [🅺] [🅐🅒]

MONTESANO

▲▲ ▼▼▼ Monte Square Motel Ⓜ
(360) 249-4424. **$49-$99.** 100 Brumfield Ave W. US 12, exit SR 107
(Montesano/Raymond), just nw. Ext corridors. **Pets:** Accepted.
[SAVE] [S🅳] [✕] [⚙M] [🛏] [💻]

MORTON

▲▲ ▼▼▼ The Seasons Motel Ⓜ
(360) 496-6835. **$70-$100.** 200 Westlake Ave. On US 12, at jct SR 7.
Ext corridors. **Pets:** Small. $10 one-time fee/room. Service with restric-
tions, supervision.
[SAVE] [✕] [🛏] [💻]

MOSES LAKE

▼▼▼ AmeriStay Inn & Suites 🆂🅷
(509) 764-7500. **Call for rates.** 1157 N Stratford Rd. I-90, exit 179, 1 mi
n to SR 17, 2.8 mi nw to Stratford exit, just n, then just e. Int corridors.
Pets: Accepted.
[✕] [⚙M] [🛏] [💻] [⇌]

▲▲ ▼▼▼▼ Best Western Lake Front Hotel 🆂🅷
(509) 765-9211. **$60-$225.** 3000 Marina Dr. I-90, exit 176, just nw. Int
corridors. **Pets:** Medium. $20 one-time fee/room. Designated rooms, serv-
ice with restrictions, supervision.
[SAVE] [S🅳] [✕] [⚙M] [🛏] [💻] [🍽] [⇌] [🅺]

▼▼▼ Inn at Moses Lake 🆂🅷
(509) 766-7000. **$79-$109.** 1741 E Kittleson Rd. I-90, exit 179, just n,
then just w. Int corridors. **Pets:** Accepted.
[A$K] [S🅳] [✕] [🛏] [💻] [⇌]

▲▲ ▼▼▼ Moses Lake Super 8 🆂🅷
(509) 765-8886. **$81-$151.** 449 Melva Ln. I-90, exit 176, just n. Int
corridors. **Pets:** Accepted.
[SAVE] [S🅳] [✕] [🛏] [⇌]

▼▼ Shilo Inn Suites-Moses Lake 🆂🅷 🐾
(509) 765-9317. **$120 (no credit cards).** 1819 E Kittleson Rd. I-90, exit
179, just n. Int corridors. **Pets:** $25 one-time fee/room. Designated rooms,
service with restrictions, supervision.
[A$K] [S🅳] [✕] [⚙M] [🛏] [💻] [⇌] [🅺]

MOUNT VERNON

▲▲ ▼▼▼ Best Western College Way Inn 🆂🅷
(360) 424-4287. **$89-$110.** 300 W College Way. I-5, exit 227, just w. Ext
corridors. **Pets:** Large. $20 daily fee/pet. Designated rooms, service with
restrictions, supervision.
[SAVE] [S🅳] [✕] [🛏] [💻] [⇌]

▲▲ ▼▼▼ Best Western CottonTree Inn & Convention
Center 🆂🅷
(360) 428-5678. **$99-$180.** 2300 Market St. I-5, exit 227, 0.3 mi e on
College Way, then 0.5 mi n on Riverside Dr. Int corridors.
Pets: Accepted.
[SAVE] [S🅳] [✕] [⚙M] [🛏] [💻] [⇌]

⚫⚫⚫ ♦♦♦ **Quality Inn-Mount Vernon** 🆂🅷
(360) 428-7020. **$95-$180.** 1910 Freeway Dr. I-5, exit 227, just w on College Way, then just n. Ext corridors. **Pets:** Large. $10 daily fee/room. Designated rooms, service with restrictions, supervision.
🆂🅰🆅🅴 ⓢ⊘ ⊠ 🗋 🖃 ⇜

⚫⚫⚫ ♦ **Tulip Inn** Ⓜ
(360) 428-5969. **$60-$90.** 2200 Freeway Dr. I-5, exit 227, just w on College Way, then just n. Ext corridors. **Pets:** Medium, other species. $10 one-time fee/pet. Designated rooms, service with restrictions, supervision.
🆂🅰🆅🅴 ⓢ⊘ ⊠ 🗋 🖃

OAK HARBOR

⚫⚫⚫ ♦♦♦ **Acorn Motor Inn** 🆂🅷
(360) 675-6646. **$46-$109.** 31530 SR 20. On SR 20 at 300th Ave W (SE Barrington Dr). Int corridors. **Pets:** Other species. $10 daily fee/room. Designated rooms, service with restrictions, supervision.
🆂🅰🆅🅴 ⓢ⊘ ⊠ 🗋

⚫⚫⚫ ♦♦♦♦ **Coachman Inn** 🆂🅷
(360) 675-0727. **$84-$209.** 32959 SR 20. Jct Goldie Rd and Midway Blvd. Ext corridors. **Pets:** Medium. $8 daily fee/pet. Designated rooms, service with restrictions, supervision.
🆂🅰🆅🅴 ⓢ⊘ ⊠ 🗋 🖃 ⇜ ⊠

OCEAN PARK

⚫⚫⚫ ♦ **Ocean Park Resort** Ⓜ
(360) 665-4585. **Call for rates.** 25904 R St. Just e of SR 103; downtown. Ext corridors. **Pets:** Small. $7 daily fee/pet. Designated rooms, service with restrictions, supervision.
🆂🅰🆅🅴 ⊠ 🗋 🖃 ⇜ ⊠ 🐾 ☎

OCEAN SHORES

⚫⚫⚫ ♦♦♦♦ **The Canterbury Inn** 🅒🅞
(360) 289-3317. **$82-$198.** 643 Ocean Shores Blvd NW. 0.3 mi s of Chance a La Mer Blvd. Int corridors. **Pets:** Medium, dogs only. $150 deposit/room, $15 daily fee/pet. Designated rooms, supervision.
🆂🅰🆅🅴 ⊠ 🗋 🖃 ⇜ 🐾

⚫⚫⚫ ♦♦♦♦ **The Grey Gull Resort** 🅒🅞 🐾
(360) 289-3381. **$130-$350, 3 day notice.** 651 Ocean Shores Blvd NW. Just s of Chance a La Mer Blvd. Ext corridors. **Pets:** Small, dogs only. $10 daily fee/pet. Designated rooms, service with restrictions, supervision.
🆂🅰🆅🅴 ⓢ⊘ ⊠ 🗋 🖃 ⇜ 🐾

♦♦ **The Nautilus** 🅒🅞
(360) 289-2722. **Call for rates.** 835 Ocean Shores Blvd NW. 0.3 mi s of Chance a La Mer Blvd. Ext corridors. **Pets:** Accepted.
⊠ 🗋 🖃 🐾

⚫⚫⚫ ♦♦♦♦ **The Polynesian Condominium Resort** 🅒🅞
(360) 289-3361. **$99-$239, 3 day notice.** 615 Ocean Shores Blvd NW. 0.3 mi s of Chance a La Mer Blvd. Ext/int corridors. **Pets:** Accepted.
🆂🅰🆅🅴 ⓢ⊘ ⊠ 🗋 🖃 ⊺⊺ ⇜ ⊠ 🐾

OKANOGAN

⚫⚫⚫ ♦♦♦ **Okanogan Inn & Suites** 🆂🅷 🐾
(509) 422-6431. **$60-$65.** 1 Apple Way. SR 97, exit SR 20, just w. Int corridors. **Pets:** Other species. Service with restrictions, supervision.
🆂🅰🆅🅴 ⓢ⊘ ⊠ 🗋 ⊺⊺ ⇜

⚫⚫⚫ ♦♦♦♦ **Ponderosa Motor Lodge** Ⓜ
(509) 422-0400. **Call for rates.** 1034 S 2nd Ave. 0.3 mi n on SR 215 from jct SR 20. Ext corridors. **Pets:** Accepted.
🆂🅰🆅🅴 ⊠ 🗋 🖃 ⇜

OLYMPIA

♦♦ ♦♦ **Clarion Hotel-Olympia** 🆂🅷
(360) 352-7200. **$89-$159.** 900 Capitol Way S. I-5, exit 105 (City Center) northbound; exit 105A southbound, 0.4 mi w on 14th Ave, then 0.5 mi n; downtown. Int corridors. **Pets:** Small, other species. $25 daily fee/pet. Designated rooms, service with restrictions, supervision.
🅰🆂🅺 ⓢ⊘ ⊠ 🖑Ⓜ 🗋 🖃 ⊺⊺ ⇜

♦♦ ♦♦ **Governor Hotel** 🆂🅷
(360) 352-7700. **$130-$140.** 621 Capitol Way S. I-5, exit 105 (City Center) northbound; exit 105A southbound, 0.4 mi w on 14th Ave, then 0.6 mi n; downtown. Int corridors. **Pets:** Accepted.
🅰🆂🅺 ⓢ⊘ ⊠ 🗋 🖃 ⊺⊺ ⇜ ⊠

♦♦ ♦♦ **Quality Inn–Olympia** 🆂🅷
(360) 943-4710. **$70-$129.** 1211 S Quince St SE. I-5, exit 105B, just n, follow Port of Olympia signs, just n on Plum St, then e on Union Ave. Int corridors. **Pets:** Accepted.
🅰🆂🅺 ⓢ⊘ ⊠ 🗋 🖃 ⇜

♦♦♦ ♦♦♦ **Red Lion Hotel Olympia** 🆂🅷
(360) 943-4000. **$179.** 2300 Evergreen Park Dr SW. I-5, exit 104, 0.7 mi w on US 101, just n on Cooper Point Rd N, 0.7 mi e on S Evergreen Park Dr SW, then just n on Lakeridge Way SW. Int corridors. **Pets:** Accepted.
🅰🆂🅺 ⓢ⊘ ⊠ 🖑Ⓜ 🗋 🖃 ⊺⊺ ⇜

OLYMPIC NATIONAL PARK

⚫⚫⚫ ♦♦♦ **Lake Crescent Lodge** 🆂🅷
(360) 928-3211. **$68-$231, 7 day notice.** 416 Lake Crescent Rd. 22 mi w of Port Angeles on US 101. Ext/int corridors. **Pets:** Accepted.
🆂🅰🆅🅴 ⊠ 🗋 🖃 ⊺⊺ ⇜ ⊠ 🐾 🐾 ☎

♦ **Log Cabin Resort** 🅒🅐
(360) 928-3325. **Call for rates.** 3183 E Beach Rd. 3.3 mi nw of US 101 (MM 232). Ext corridors. **Pets:** Accepted.
⊠ 🗋 🖃 ⊺⊺ ⊠ 🐾 🐾 ☎

OMAK

⚫⚫⚫ ♦♦♦♦ **Omak Inn** 🆂🅷
(509) 826-3822. **$70-$85.** 912 Koala Dr. On US 97, just n of Riverside Dr. Int corridors. **Pets:** Accepted.
🆂🅰🆅🅴 ⊠ 🗋 🖃 ⇜

OTHELLO

⚫⚫⚫ ♦♦♦♦ **Best Western Lincoln Inn Othello** 🆂🅷
(509) 488-5671. **$79-$179.** 1020 E Cedar St. Just off Main St at 10th and Cedar sts. Int corridors. **Pets:** Accepted.
🆂🅰🆅🅴 ⓢ⊘ ⊠ 🗋 🖃 ⇜

PACIFIC BEACH

♦ **Sandpiper Beach Resort** 🅒🅞
(360) 276-4580. **Call for rates.** 4159 SR 109. 1.8 mi s. Ext corridors. **Pets:** Accepted.
⊠ 🗋 🖃 🐾 🐾 ☎

PACKWOOD

♦ **Inn of Packwood** Ⓜ
(360) 494-5500. **Call for rates.** 13032 US 12. Center. Ext corridors. **Pets:** Accepted.
⊠ 🗋 🖃 ⇜

PASCO

⚫⚫⚫ ♦♦♦♦ **Best Western Pasco Inn & Suites** 🆂🅷
(509) 543-7722. **$110-$160, 14 day notice.** 2811 N 20th Ave. I-182, exit 12B, just n. Int corridors. **Pets:** Small. $10 one-time fee/room. Designated rooms, service with restrictions, crate.
🆂🅰🆅🅴 ⓢ⊘ ⊠ 🖑Ⓜ 🗋 🖃 ⇜

Budget Inn M
(509) 546-2010. **Call for rates.** 1520 N Oregon St. I-182, exit 14A (SR 395 S). Ext corridors. **Pets:** Accepted.
[SAVE] [X] [🔲] [≈]

Holiday Inn Express Pasco at TRAC SH
(509) 543-7000. **$119-$159.** 4525 Convention Pl. I-182, exit 9 (Rd 68), just n, then just e. Int corridors. **Pets:** Accepted.
[ASK] [S6] [X] [&M] [🔲] [🔲] [≈]

Red Lion Hotel Pasco LH
(509) 547-0701. **$129.** 2525 N 20th Ave. I-182, exit 12B, just n. Int corridors. **Pets:** Accepted.
[SAVE] [S6] [X] [&M] [🔲] [🔲] [TI] [≈]

Sleep Inn SH
(509) 545-9554. **$80-$164.** 9930 Bedford St. I-182, exit 7, just ne. Int corridors. **Pets:** Medium. $10 daily fee/room. Designated rooms, service with restrictions, supervision.
[SAVE] [S6] [X] [&M] [🔲] [🔲] [≈]

PORT ANGELES

Portside Inn SH
(360) 452-4015. **$59-$169, 3 day notice.** 1510 E Front St. Front St at Alder, on east side. Ext corridors. **Pets:** Large, other species. $10 daily fee/room. Designated rooms, service with restrictions, supervision.
[SAVE] [S6] [X] [🔲] [🔲] [≈]

Quality Inn-Uptown M ❀
(360) 457-9434. **$79-$219.** 101 E 2nd St. At Laurel St, just w of US 101; on bluff. Ext corridors. **Pets:** Small, dogs only. $10 daily fee/pet. Designated rooms, service with restrictions, supervision.
[SAVE] [S6] [X] [🔲] [🔲] [K]

Red Lion Hotel Port Angeles SH
(360) 452-9215. **$249.** 221 N Lincoln St. On US 101 westbound; at ferry landing. Ext/int corridors. **Pets:** Medium, other species. $15 daily fee/pet. Service with restrictions, supervision.
[SAVE] [S6] [X] [🔲] [🔲] [TI] [≈]

Riviera Inn M
(360) 417-3955. **$59-$149.** 535 E Front St. On US 101 W; downtown. Ext corridors. **Pets:** Small, dogs only. $15 daily fee/pet. Designated rooms, service with restrictions, supervision.
[SAVE] [X] [🔲] [K]

Super 8 Motel M
(360) 452-8401. **Call for rates.** 2104 E 1st St. 1.8 mi e of downtown, just s of US 101. Int corridors. **Pets:** Accepted.
[X] [&M] [🔲] [🔲]

PORTLAND METROPOLITAN AREA (NEARBY OREGON)

VANCOUVER

Comfort Inn SH ❀
(360) 574-6000. **$60-$100.** 13207 NE 20th Ave. I-5, exit 7, just e; I-205, exit 36, just w. Int corridors. **Pets:** Other species. $15 daily fee/room. Service with restrictions, supervision.
[SAVE] [S6] [X] [🔲] [🔲] [≈]

Extended StayAmerica-Portland-Vancouver SH
(360) 604-8530. **$72-$80.** 300 NE 115th Ave. I-205, exit 28 (Mill Plain Blvd E), just ne. Int corridors. **Pets:** Other species. $75 one-time fee/pet. Service with restrictions.
[ASK] [S6] [X] [🔲] [🔲]

Hilton Vancouver Washington and Vancouver Convention Center LH
(360) 993-4500. **$105-$219 (no credit cards).** 301 W 6th St. I-5, exit 1C (Mill Plain Blvd) southbound, 0.3 mi w, then 0.3 mi s on W Columbia St; exit 1B northbound, 0.5 mi, follow signs to City Center/6th St. Int corridors. **Pets:** Medium, other species. $35 one-time fee/room. Service with restrictions.
[SAVE] [X] [&M] [🔲] [🔲] [TI] [≈]

Homewood Suites by Hilton SH
(360) 750-1100. **Call for rates.** 701 SE Columbia Shores Blvd. SR 14, exit 1, just s. Ext/int corridors. **Pets:** Accepted.
[X] [🔲] [🔲] [≈] [X]

Phoenix Inn Suites-Vancouver SH
(360) 891-9777. **$79-$149.** 12712 SE 2nd Cir. I-205, exit 28 (Mill Plain Blvd E), 0.8 mi e, then just n on SE 126th Ave. Int corridors. **Pets:** Medium, other species. $15 daily fee/pet. Designated rooms, service with restrictions, supervision.
[SAVE] [X] [🔲] [🔲] [≈] [X]

Quality Inn & Suites SH
(360) 696-0516. **$69-$109.** 7001 NE Hwy 99. I-5, exit 4, 0.5 mi se. Int corridors. **Pets:** Other species. $10 daily fee/room. Service with restrictions, supervision.
[SAVE] [S6] [X] [🔲] [🔲] [≈]

Red Lion Hotel Vancouver @ the Quay SH
(360) 694-8341. **$129-$179.** 100 Columbia St. 0.5 mi s on dock at foot of Columbia St. Int corridors. **Pets:** Accepted.
[ASK] [S6] [X] [&M] [🔲] [🔲] [TI] [≈] [X]

Residence Inn Vancouver SH
(360) 253-4800. **$177-$195.** 8005 NE Parkway Dr. I-205, exit 30 (SR 500 W), 0.5 mi w to Thurston Way, just n to NE Parkway Dr, then just w. Ext corridors. **Pets:** Accepted.
[ASK] [S6] [X] [&M] [🔲] [🔲] [≈] [X]

Salmon Creek Inn & Suites SH
(360) 566-1100. **Call for rates.** 1500 NE 134th St. I-5, exit 7, just w; I-205, exit 36, 0.5 mi w. Int corridors. **Pets:** Accepted.
[X] [&M] [🔲] [🔲] [≈]

Shilo Inn-Salmon Creek SH ❀
(360) 573-0511. **$120 (no credit cards).** 13206 Hwy 99. I-5, exit 7, just e; I-205, exit 36, just w. Int corridors. **Pets:** $25 one-time fee/room. Designated rooms, service with restrictions, supervision.
[ASK] [S6] [X] [🔲] [🔲] [≈] [X]

▼▼▼▼ Staybridge Suites Vancouver-Portland 🅂🅷
(360) 891-8282. **Call for rates.** 7301 NE 41st St. I-205, exit 30 (SR 500 W), 1.5 mi w to NE Andresen Rd, just n to NE 40th St, just e to NE 72nd St, just n to NE 41st St, then just e. Int corridors. **Pets:** Accepted.

[X] [&M] [🛏] [💻] [🏊] [X]

END METROPOLITAN AREA

PORT TOWNSEND

🌢🌢🌢 ▼▼▼▼ Bishop Victorian Hotel 🅂🅷
(360) 385-6122. **$105-$215, 3 day notice.** 714 Washington St. Corner of Washington and Quincy sts. Int corridors. **Pets:** Medium, dogs only. $15 daily fee/pet. Designated rooms, service with restrictions, supervision.

[SAVE] [S🐾] [X] [🛏] [💻] [🕱]

▼▼ Harborside Inn 🅂🅷
(360) 385-7909. **$60-$180.** 330 Benedict St. Just e of SR 20. Ext corridors. **Pets:** Accepted.

[ASK] [S🐾] [X] [🛏] [💻] [🏊] [🕱]

🌢🌢🌢 ▼▼▼ Palace Hotel 🅂🅷 ❖
(360) 385-0773. **$59-$289.** 1004 Water St. Downtown. Int corridors. **Pets:** Other species. $10 one-time fee/pet. Service with restrictions, supervision.

[SAVE] [S🐾] [X] [🛏] [💻] [🕱]

🌢🌢🌢 ▼▼▼ The Swan Hotel 🅼
(360) 385-1718. **$85-$495, 3 day notice.** 216 Monroe St. Downtown. Ext corridors. **Pets:** Medium, dogs only. $15 daily fee/pet. Designated rooms, service with restrictions, supervision.

[SAVE] [S🐾] [X] [🛏] [💻] [🕱]

PROSSER

▼▼▼ Best Western Inn at Horse Heaven 🅂🅷
(509) 786-7977. **Call for rates.** 259 Merlot Dr. I-82, exit 80, just s. Int corridors. **Pets:** Accepted.

[X] [&M] [🛏] [💻] [🏊]

PULLMAN

🌢🌢🌢 ▼▼▼▼ Hawthorn Inn & Suites 🅂🅷 ❖
(509) 332-0928. **$70-$199.** 928 NW Olsen St. 1.6 mi e on SR 270 from US 195. Int corridors. **Pets:** $15 one-time fee/room. Designated rooms, supervision.

[SAVE] [S🐾] [X] [&M] [🛏] [💻] [🏊] [X]

▼▼▼ Holiday Inn Express Hotel & Suites 🅂🅷
(509) 334-4437. **$109.** SE 1190 Bishop Blvd. Jct US 195 business route, 0.5 mi s, 1 mi e on SR 270. Int corridors. **Pets:** Accepted.

[ASK] [S🐾] [X] [&M] [🛏] [💻] [🏊]

🌢🌢🌢 ▼▼▼ Quality Inn Paradise Creek 🅂🅷
(509) 332-0500. **Call for rates.** 1400 SE Bishop Blvd. Jct US 195 business route, just s, 1 mi e on SR 270. Int corridors. **Pets:** Dogs only. Designated rooms, service with restrictions, supervision.

[SAVE] [X] [🛏] [💻] [🏊] [X]

QUINAULT

🌢🌢🌢 ▼▼▼ Lake Quinault Lodge 🅂🅷
(360) 288-2900. **$117-$268, 3 day notice.** 345 S Shore Rd. 2 mi off US 101. Ext/int corridors. **Pets:** $25 daily fee/room. Designated rooms, no service, supervision.

[SAVE] [S🐾] [X] [💻] [🍴] [🏊] [X] [🕱] [🗲]

QUINCY

▼▼ Traditional Inns 🅼
(509) 787-3525. **$85-$149.** 500 F St SW. West end of town on SR 28. Ext corridors. **Pets:** Accepted.

[ASK] [S🐾] [X] [🛏] [💻]

REPUBLIC

🌢🌢🌢 ▼▼▼ Prospector Inn 🅂🅷 ❖
(509) 775-3361. **$55-$125.** 979 S Clark Ave. Downtown. Int corridors. **Pets:** $12 daily fee/pet. Designated rooms, service with restrictions, supervision.

[SAVE] [S🐾] [X] [🛏] [💻] [X]

RICHLAND

▼▼▼▼ Clarion Hotel & Conference Center 🅂🅷
(509) 946-4121. **Call for rates.** 1515 George Washington Way. I-182, exit 5B, 2.5 mi n. Int corridors. **Pets:** Accepted.

[X] [&M] [🛏] [💻] [🍴] [🏊] [X]

🌢🌢🌢 ▼▼▼ Days Inn 🅼
(509) 943-4611. **Call for rates.** 615 Jadwin Ave. I-182, exit 5B, 0.9 mi n; just w of SR 240 business route; downtown. Ext corridors. **Pets:** Other species. $10 daily fee/pet. No service.

[SAVE] [X] [🛏] [💻] [🏊]

▼▼▼▼ Holiday Inn Express Hotel & Suites 🅂🅷
(509) 737-8000. **Call for rates.** 1970 Center Pkwy. Just s on Columbia Center Blvd from SR 240, just w. Int corridors. **Pets:** Accepted.

[X] [&M] [🛏] [💻] [🏊]

▼▼▼▼ Red Lion Hotel Richland Hanford House 🅂🅷
(509) 946-7611. **$139.** 802 George Washington Way. I-182, exit 5B, 1.3 mi n on SR 240 business route. Ext/int corridors. **Pets:** Accepted.

[ASK] [S🐾] [X] [&M] [🛏] [💻] [🍴] [🏊] [X]

▼▼▼▼ Shilo Inn Hotel Richland Conference Center 🅂🅷 ❖
(509) 946-4661. **$145.** 50 Comstock St. I-182, exit 5B, 0.5 mi n. Ext corridors. **Pets:** $25 one-time fee/room. Designated rooms, service with restrictions, supervision.

[ASK] [S🐾] [X] [🛏] [💻] [🍴] [🏊] [X]

RITZVILLE

🌢🌢🌢 ▼▼▼ Americas Best Value Inn- Colwell 🅼
(509) 659-1620. **Call for rates.** 501 W 1st Ave. I-90, exit 220, 0.9 mi n; downtown. Ext corridors. **Pets:** Accepted.

[SAVE] [X] [🛏] [💻] [🏊]

🌢🌢🌢 ▼▼▼ Best Western Bronco Inn 🅂🅷
(509) 659-5000. **$89-$169.** 105 W Galbreath Way. I-90, exit 221, go over overpass, take second left. Int corridors. **Pets:** Other species. $10 daily fee/room. Service with restrictions, supervision.

[SAVE] [S🐾] [X] [🛏] [💻] [🏊]

🌢🌢🌢 ▼▼▼ La Quinta Inn Ritzville 🅂🅷
(509) 659-1007. **$104.** 1513 Smitty's Blvd. I-90, exit 221, just n. Int corridors. **Pets:** Other species. Service with restrictions, supervision.

[SAVE] [S🐾] [X] [&M] [🛏] [💻] [🏊] [X]

▼▼ Top Hat Motel 🅼
(509) 659-1100. **$38-$64.** 210 E 1st Ave. I-90, exit 221, 1 mi ne via Division St. Ext corridors. **Pets:** Accepted.

[ASK] [S🐾] [🛏]

ROCHESTER

(AAA) ▼▼▼▼ Eagles Landing Hotel 🆂🅷
(360) 273-8640. **Call for rates.** 12840 188th Ave SW. 3 mi w on US 12, 0.8 mi s on Anderson Rd, then just e. Int corridors. **Pets:** Other species. $25 one-time fee/room. Designated rooms, service with restrictions.

[SAVE] [✕] [🛏] [💻] [🐾]

SAN JUAN ISLANDS AREA

DEER HARBOR

▼▼ ▼▼ Deer Harbor Inn 🅲🅸
(360) 376-4110. **Call for rates.** 33 Inn Ln. 7 mi sw of ferry landing; 3.5 mi sw of Westsound. Ext/int corridors. **Pets:** Accepted.

[✕] [🛏] [💻] [🍽] [🐾] [🐾]

FRIDAY HARBOR

(AAA) ▼▼▼ Elements Hotel & Spa 🆂🅷
(360) 378-4000. **Call for rates.** 410 Spring St. 0.5 mi w of ferry dock. Ext corridors. **Pets:** Other species. $15 daily fee/pet. Designated rooms, service with restrictions, supervision.

[SAVE] [✕] [🛏] [💻] [🐾] [✕]

(AAA) ▼▼▼▼ Lakedale Resort 🆂🅷 🐾
(360) 378-2350. **$179-$489, 7 day notice.** 4313 Roche Harbor Rd. 4 mi n of Friday Harbor via Tucker Ave. Ext/int corridors. **Pets:** Dogs only. $25 one-time fee/pet. Designated rooms, service with restrictions, supervision.

[SAVE] [S🐾] [✕] [🛏] [💻] [✕] [🍽]

END AREA

SEATTLE METROPOLITAN AREA

ARLINGTON

(AAA) ▼▼▼ Quality Inn 🆂🅷
(360) 403-7222. **$91-$120.** 5200 172nd St NE, Bldg E. I-5, exit 206, 1.3 mi e. Int corridors. **Pets:** Accepted.

[SAVE] [S🐾] [✕] [🛏] [💻]

AUBURN

(AAA) ▼▼▼▼ Best Western Peppertree Auburn Inn 🆂🅷 🐾
(253) 887-7600. **Call for rates.** 401 8th St SW. SR 18, exit C St, just s, then just w. Int corridors. **Pets:** Very small, dogs only. $10 daily fee/pet. Service with restrictions, supervision.

[SAVE] [✕] [🛏] [💻] [🐾] [✕]

(AAA) ▼▼▼ Travelodge Suites 🆂🅷
(253) 833-7171. **$59-$149.** Nine 16th St NW. SR 167, exit 15th St NW, 0.8 mi e, then just n on a St NE. Int corridors. **Pets:** Large, other species. $10 daily fee/pet. Service with restrictions, supervision.

[SAVE] [S🐾] [✕] [🛏] [🛏] [💻]

▼▼ ▼▼ Val-U Inn 🆂🅷
(253) 735-9600. **$85-$95.** Nine 14th St NW. SR 167, exit 15th St NW, 0.8 mi e, just s on a St NE, then just w. Int corridors. **Pets:** Accepted.

[ASK] [S🐾] [✕] [🛏] [💻]

BAINBRIDGE ISLAND

▼▼ ▼▼ Best Western Bainbridge Island Suites 🆂🅷 🐾
(206) 855-9666. **$109-$169.** 350 NE High School Rd. 0.8 mi n of ferry dock on SR 305, then just w. Int corridors. **Pets:** Medium, other species. $50 one-time fee/room. Designated rooms, service with restrictions, crate.

[ASK] [S🐾] [✕] [🛏] [💻]

BELLEVUE

(AAA) ▼▼▼ ▼▼▼ Bellevue Club Hotel 🆂🅷 🐾
(425) 454-4424. **$285-$345.** 11200 SE 6th St. I-405, exit 12, 0.4 mi nw. Int corridors. **Pets:** Small, dogs only. $50 one-time fee/room. No service, supervision.

[SAVE] [✕] [🅼] [🛏] [🍽] [🐾] [✕]

(AAA) ▼▼▼ Days Inn Bellevue 🆂🅷
(425) 643-6644. **$92.** 3241 156th Ave SE. I-90, exit 11 westbound; exit 11A (156th Ave SE) eastbound, just ne. Ext corridors. **Pets:** Medium. $25 one-time fee/pet. Service with restrictions, supervision.

[SAVE] [✕] [🛏] [💻]

▼▼ ▼▼ Extended StayAmerica-Seattle-Bellevue 🆂🅷
(425) 453-8186. **$119-$135.** 11400 Main St. I-405, exit 13A, just se. Int corridors. **Pets:** Other species. $75 one-time fee/pet. Service with restrictions.

[ASK] [S🐾] [✕] [🛏]

▼▼ ▼▼ Homestead Studio Suites Hotel-Seattle-Bellevue 🅼
(425) 865-8680. **$117-$135.** 3700 132nd Ave SE. I-90, exit 11A westbound; exit 10B eastbound, 0.5 mi se. Ext corridors. **Pets:** Other species. $75 one-time fee/pet. Service with restrictions.

[ASK] [S🐾] [✕] [🛏] [💻]

▼▼ ▼▼ Homestead Studio Suites Seattle-Redmond 🅼
(425) 885-6675. **$125-$145.** 15805 NE 28th St. I-405, exit 14 (SR 520), 3.3 mi e to 148th Ave NE (south exit), just e on 24th St, just ne on Bel-Red Rd, just n on 156th Ave, then just e. Ext corridors. **Pets:** Other species. $75 one-time fee/pet. Service with restrictions.

[ASK] [S🐾] [✕] [🛏] [💻]

(AAA) ▼▼▼ La Residence Suite Hotel 🆂🅷
(425) 455-1475. **Call for rates.** 475 100th Ave NE. I-405, exit 13B, 0.9 mi w on NE 8th St, then just s. Int corridors. **Pets:** Accepted.

[SAVE] [✕] [🛏] [💻]

AAA ▼▼▼▼ **Larkspur Landing Bellevue/Seattle** SH
(425) 373-1212. **$169-$219.** 15805 SE 37th St. I-90, exit 11 westbound; exit 11A (150th Ave SE) eastbound, 0.9 mi se on south frontage road. Int corridors. **Pets:** Large, other species. $75 one-time fee/room. Designated rooms.
SAVE S⃞ X⃞ 🖫 🖵

AAA ▼▼▼▼ **Red Lion Bellevue Inn** SH
(425) 455-5240. **$239.** 11211 Main St. I-405, exit 12, 0.4 mi n on 114th St. Int corridors. **Pets:** Accepted.
SAVE S⃞ X⃞ 🖫 🖵 ▯▮ ⇌

▼▼▼▼ **Residence Inn by Marriott, Bellevue-Redmond** SH
(425) 882-1222. **$260-$288.** 14455 NE 29th Pl. I-405, exit 14 (SR 520), 2.3 mi e to 148th Ave NE (north exit), then just nw. Ext corridors. **Pets:** Accepted.
ASK S⃞ X⃞ 🖫 🖵 ⇌ X⃞

AAA ▼▼▼▼ **Sheraton Bellevue Hotel** LH
(425) 455-3330. **$139-$409.** 100 112th Ave NE. I-405, exit 12 northbound; exit 13 southbound, just s. Int corridors. **Pets:** Accepted.
SAVE S⃞ X⃞ ♿M 🖫 🖵 ▯▮ ⇌ X⃞

▼▼▼ ▼▼▼ **The Westin Bellevue** LH ❀
(425) 638-1000. **Call for rates.** 600 Bellevue Way NE. I-405, exit 13B, 1.5 mi w on NE 8th St. Int corridors. **Pets:** Large, other species. Service with restrictions, supervision.
X⃞ 🖵 ▯▮ ⇌

BOTHELL

▼▼▼ ▼ **Extended StayAmerica-Seattle-Bothell** SH
(425) 402-4252. **$117-$130.** 923 228th St SE. I-405, exit 26, just sw. Int corridors. **Pets:** Other species. $75 one-time fee/pet. Service with restrictions.
ASK S⃞ X⃞ 🖫 🖵

▼▼▼▼ **Extended Stay Deluxe Seattle-Bothell** SH
(425) 482-2900. **$126-$140.** 22122 17th Ave SE. I-405, exit 26, just n on Bothell Everett Hwy, just e on Canyon Park Blvd SE, then just s. Int corridors. **Pets:** Other species. $75 one-time fee/pet. Service with restrictions.
ASK S⃞ X⃞ ♿M 🖫 🖵 ⇌

▼▼▼▼ **Residence Inn by Marriott Seattle NE** SH
(425) 485-3030. **$252-$296.** 11920 NE 195th St. I-405, exit 24, 0.4 mi ne. Ext corridors. **Pets:** Accepted.
ASK S⃞ X⃞ 🖫 🖵 ⇌ X⃞

BREMERTON

AAA ▼▼ **Flagship Inn** SH
(360) 479-6566. **$75-$115.** 4320 Kitsap Way. 3.5 mi w of ferry terminal; SR 3, exit Kitsap Way, 0.5 mi e. Int corridors. **Pets:** Small, dogs only. $6 daily fee/pet. Supervision.
SAVE S⃞ X⃞ 🖫 🖵 ⇌

AAA ▼▼▼▼ **Illahee Manor Bed & Breakfast** BB
(360) 698-7555. **$120-$255, 10 day notice.** 6680 Illahee Rd NE. Downtown/ferry terminal, just n on Washington Ave, across Manette Bridge, 0.7 mi e on 11th St, then 3.9 mi n via Trenton Ave and Illahee Rd. Ext/int corridors. **Pets:** Accepted.
SAVE X⃞ 🖫 🖵 ⚿

AAA ▼▼ **Midway Inn** SH
(360) 479-2909. **$89-$104.** 2909 Wheaton Way. SR 303, 2 mi n. Int corridors. **Pets:** Accepted.
SAVE S⃞ X⃞ 🖫 🖵

▼▼ ▼ **Super 8 Motel** SH
(360) 377-8881. **Call for rates.** 5068 Kitsap Way. 4.2 mi w of ferry terminal; SR 3, exit Kitsap Way, just ne. Int corridors. **Pets:** Accepted.
X⃞ ♿M 🖫

EDMONDS

AAA ▼▼▼▼ **Edmonds Harbor Inn** SH ❀
(425) 771-5021. **$129-$159.** 130 W Dayton St. Just s at Port of Edmonds. Ext/int corridors. **Pets:** Medium. $20 daily fee/pet. Designated rooms, service with restrictions, supervision.
SAVE S⃞ X⃞ 🖫 🖵

AAA ▼ **K & E Motor Inn** M
(425) 778-2181. **Call for rates.** 23921 Hwy 99. I-5, exit 177, 1 mi w on SR 104, exit SR 99 (Everett-Lynnwood), then just n. Ext corridors. **Pets:** Very small. $25 daily fee/pet. Designated rooms, service with restrictions, supervision.
SAVE X⃞ 🖫

AAA ▼▼▼ **Travelodge Seattle/Edmonds** SH
(425) 771-8008. **Call for rates.** 23825 Hwy 99. I-5, exit 177, 1 mi w on SR 104, exit SR 99 (Everett-Lynnwood), then just n. Ext corridors. **Pets:** Medium. $25 one-time fee/pet. Service with restrictions, supervision.
SAVE X⃞ 🖫 🖵

EVERETT

▼▼▼ **Days Inn Everett-Seattle** SH
(425) 355-1570. **$70-$121.** 1602 SE Everett Mall Way. I-5, exit 189 northbound, 0.5 mi w on SR 527, then 0.5 mi s; exit southbound, 0.7 mi s. Ext corridors. **Pets:** Accepted.
ASK S⃞ X⃞ 🖫 🖵 ⇌

▼▼▼ **Extended StayAmerica-Seattle-Everett** SH
(425) 355-1923. **$105-$115.** 8410 Broadway. I-5, exit 189, follow signs towards Broadway, just nw. Int corridors. **Pets:** Other species. $75 one-time fee/pet. Service with restrictions.
ASK S⃞ X⃞ 🖫 🖵

▼▼▼ **Extended Stay Deluxe-Seattle-Everett** SH
(425) 337-1341. **$122-$135.** 1431 112th St SE. I-5, exit 189 (Hwy 527), 1.5 mi se on 19th Ave SE, then 0.3 mi w. Int corridors. **Pets:** Other species. $75 one-time fee/pet. Service with restrictions.
ASK S⃞ X⃞ 🖫 🖵

AAA ▼▼▼▼ **Holiday Inn Downtown Everett** SH ❀
(425) 339-2000. **$129-$159.** 3105 Pine St. I-5, exit 193 northbound; exit 194 southbound, just sw. Int corridors. **Pets:** Other species. $40 one-time fee/pet. Service with restrictions.
SAVE S⃞ X⃞ 🖫 🖵 ▯▮ ⇌

AAA ▼▼▼▼ **Inn at Port Gardner** SH ❀
(425) 252-6779. **$139-$289.** 1700 W Marine View Dr. I-5, exit 193 northbound, 1.2 mi w on Pacific Ave, then 1.2 mi n; exit 194 southbound, 1.2 mi w on Everett Ave, then 1 mi n; in Everett Marina Village. Int corridors. **Pets:** Medium. $25 one-time fee/room. Supervision.
SAVE S⃞ X⃞ 🖵

FEDERAL WAY

▼▼ ▼ **Extended StayAmerica-Seattle-Federal Way** SH
(253) 946-0553. **$86-$95.** 1400 S 320th St. I-5, exit 143, 0.6 mi w. Int corridors. **Pets:** Other species. $75 one-time fee/pet. Service with restrictions.
ASK S⃞ X⃞ 🖫 🖵

▼▼ **Federal Way Super 8** SH
(253) 838-8808. **Call for rates.** 1688 S 348th St. I-5, exit 142B, just w. Int corridors. **Pets:** Accepted.
X⃞ 🖫

AAA ▼▼▼ **La Quinta Inn & Suites** SH
(253) 529-4000. **$155.** 32124 25th Ave S. I-5, exit 143, just sw. Int corridors. **Pets:** Other species. Service with restrictions, supervision.
SAVE S⃞ X⃞ 🖫 🖵 ▯▮ ⇌

◈◈ ▼▼▼ Quality Inn & Suites 🆂🆗
(253) 835-4141. **$80-$120.** 1400 S 348th St. I-5, exit 142B, 0.5 mi w. Int corridors. **Pets:** Accepted.
🆂🅰🆅🅴 🆂🅾 ✖ 🅶🅼 🎮 💻 🏊

FIFE

◈◈ ▼▼▼ Emerald Queen Hotel & Casino 🆂🆗
(253) 922-2000. **$89-$119.** 5700 Pacific Hwy E. I-5, exit 137, just ne. Int corridors. **Pets:** Accepted.
🆂🅰🆅🅴 🆂🅾 ✖ 🅶🅼 🎮 💻 🍴

▼▼ Extended StayAmerica-Tacoma-Fife 🆂🆗
(253) 926-6316. **$86-$95.** 2820 Pacific Hwy E. I-5, 136B northbound; exit 136 southbound, just nw. Int corridors. **Pets:** Other species. $75 one-time fee/pet. Service with restrictions.
🅰🅺 🆂🅾 ✖ 🎮 💻

◈◈ ▼▼▼ GuestHouse Royal Coachman, Fife 🆂🆗
(253) 922-2500. **$70-$100.** 5805 Pacific Hwy E. I-5, exit 137, just ne. Ext corridors. **Pets:** Medium. $10 daily fee/pet, $25 one-time fee/pet. Designated rooms, supervision.
🆂🅰🆅🅴 🆂🅾 ✖ 🎮 💻

◈◈ ▼▼▼ Howard Johnson Ⓜ
(253) 926-1000. **Call for rates.** 3501 Pacific Hwy E. I-5, exit 136B northbound; exit 136 southbound, just ne. Ext corridors. **Pets:** Accepted.
🆂🅰🆅🅴 ✖ 🎮 💻

◈◈ ▼▼▼ Quality Inn Ⓜ
(253) 926-2301. **$72-$90.** 5601 Pacific Hwy E. I-5, exit 137, just ne. Ext corridors. **Pets:** Medium. $15 daily fee/pet. Designated rooms, service with restrictions, supervision.
🆂🅰🆅🅴 🆂🅾 ✖ 🎮 💻

GIG HARBOR

◈◈ ▼▼▼ Best Western Wesley Inn 🆂🆗 🐾
(253) 858-9690. **$154-$275, 3 day notice.** 6575 Kimball Dr. SR 16, exit City Center, just e on Pioneer Way, then 0.3 mi s. Int corridors. **Pets:** Other species. $10 daily fee/pet. Designated rooms, supervision.
🆂🅰🆅🅴 🆂🅾 ✖ 🅶🅼 🎮 💻 🏊

◈◈ ▼▼▼ The Inn at Gig Harbor 🆂🆗 🐾
(253) 858-1111. **$149-$205.** 3211 56th St NW. SR 16, exit Olympic Dr, just w, then 0.4 mi n. Int corridors. **Pets:** Other species. $25 one-time fee/pet. Designated rooms, service with restrictions, supervision.
🆂🅰🆅🅴 🆂🅾 ✖ 🅶🅼 🎮 💻 🍴 ✖

ISSAQUAH

▼ Motel 6–295 Ⓜ
(425) 392-8405. **$71-$81 (no credit cards).** 1885 15th Pl NW. I-90, exit 15, 0.3 mi n on 17th Ave NW, then just w on NW Sammamish Rd. Ext corridors. **Pets:** Other species. Service with restrictions, supervision.
🆂🅾 ✖ 🎮 🏊

KENT

◈◈ ▼▼▼ Best Western Plaza By The Green 🆂🆗
(253) 854-8767. **$99-$159.** 24415 Russell Rd. I-5, exit 149 southbound; exit 149A northbound, 2 mi ne via Kent Des Moines Rd (SR 516) and Meeker St. Int corridors. **Pets:** Accepted.
🆂🅰🆅🅴 🆂🅾 ✖ 🎮 💻 ✖

◈◈ ▼▼▼ Comfort Inn Kent 🆂🆗
(253) 872-2211. **Call for rates.** 22311 84th Ave S. SR 167, exit 84th Ave S, just n. Int corridors. **Pets:** Accepted.
🆂🅰🆅🅴 ✖ 🎮 💻 🏊

▼▼▼ Extended StayAmerica-Seattle-Kent 🆂🆗
(253) 872-6514. **$86-$95.** 22520 83rd Ave S. SR 167, exit 84th Ave S, just nw. Int corridors. **Pets:** Other species. $75 one-time fee/pet. Service with restrictions.
🅰🅺 🆂🅾 ✖ 🎮 💻

▼▼▼ Hawthorn Suites 🆂🆗
(253) 395-3800. **$129-$199.** 6329 S 212th St. I-5, exit 152, 2.6 mi se via Orilla Rd and 212th St. Ext corridors. **Pets:** Accepted.
🅰🅺 🆂🅾 ✖ 🎮 💻 🏊 ✖

◈◈ ▼▼▼▼ TownePlace Suites by Marriott-Seattle Southcenter 🆂🆗
(253) 796-6000. **$208-$230.** 18123 72nd Ave S. I-405, exit 1 (SR 181), 1.6 mi s on W Valley Hwy, just e on S 180th, then just s. Ext corridors. **Pets:** Accepted.
🆂🅰🆅🅴 🆂🅾 ✖ 🅶🅼 🎮 💻 🏊 ✖

KIRKLAND

◈◈ ▼▼▼ Baymont Inn & Suites 🆂🆗
(425) 822-2300. **$82-$105.** 12223 NE 116th St. I-405, exit 20A northbound; exit 20 southbound, just e; in Totem Lake area. Ext corridors. **Pets:** Accepted.
🆂🅰🆅🅴 🆂🅾 ✖ 🎮 💻 🏊

▼▼▼ La Quinta Inn Seattle (Bellevue/Kirkland) 🆂🆗
(425) 828-6585. **$132.** 10530 NE Northup Way. I-405, exit 14 (SR 520) via 108th Ave exit, n on 108th Ave, then just w. Int corridors. **Pets:** Other species. Service with restrictions, supervision.
🅰🅺 🆂🅾 ✖ 🎮 💻 🏊

▼ Motel 6–687 Ⓜ
(425) 821-5618. **$65-$75 (no credit cards).** 12010 120th Pl NE. I-405, exit 20B northbound; exit 20 southbound, just se. Ext corridors. **Pets:** Other species. Service with restrictions, supervision.
🆂🅾 ✖ 🏊

◈◈ ▼▼▼▼ Woodmark Hotel, Yacht Club & Spa 🅻🅷 🐾
(425) 822-3700. **$279-$1800.** 1200 Carillon Point. On Lake Washington Blvd, 1 mi n of SR 520. Int corridors. **Pets:** Large, other species. Service with restrictions, supervision.
🆂🅰🆅🅴 🆂🅾 ✖ 💻 🍴 ✖

LAKEWOOD

▼▼▼ La Quinta–Lakewood Inn & Suites 🆂🆗
(253) 582-7000. **Call for rates (no credit cards).** 11751 Pacific Hwy SW. I-5, exit 125, just nw. Int corridors. **Pets:** Other species. Service with restrictions, supervision.
✖ 🎮 💻 🏊

◈◈ ▼▼▼ Western Inn 🆂🆗
(253) 588-5241. **Call for rates.** 9920 S Tacoma Way. I-5, exit 127 (S Tacoma Way), just w on SR 512, then just n. Ext corridors. **Pets:** Accepted.
🆂🅰🆅🅴 ✖ 🎮 💻

LYNNWOOD

◈◈ ▼▼▼ Best Western Alderwood 🆂🆗 🐾
(425) 775-7600. **Call for rates.** 19332 36th Ave W. I-5, exit 181B northbound, just n on Poplar Way, just w on 196th St SW, then just n; exit 181 (SR 524 W) southbound, just nw. Int corridors. **Pets:** Very small, dogs only. Designated rooms, service with restrictions.
🆂🅰🆅🅴 ✖ 🎮 💻 🏊

▼▼▼ Embassy Suites Hotel Seattle North/Lynnwood 🅻🅷
(425) 775-2500. **$129-$219.** 20610 44th Ave W. I-5, exit 181A northbound, just se; exit 181 (SR 524 W) southbound, 0.5 w on 196th St SW, then 0.6 mi s. Int corridors. **Pets:** Accepted.
✖ 🅶🅼 🎮 💻 🍴 🏊 ✖

▼▼ Extended StayAmerica-Seattle-Lynnwood 🔣
(425) 670-2520. **$95-$105.** 3021 196th St SW. I-5, exit 181E southbound; exit 181B northbound, just ne. Int corridors. **Pets:** Other species. $75 one-time fee/pet. Service with restrictions.

(A$K) (S₆) (X) 🔲 💻

(AAA) ▼▼▼▼ La Quinta Inn Lynnwood 🔣
(425) 775-7447. **$119.** 4300 Alderwood Mall Blvd. I-5, exit 181A northbound, just w; exit 181 (SR 524 W) southbound, 0.5 mi w on 196th St SW, just s on 44th Ave SW, then just e. Int corridors. **Pets:** Other species. Service with restrictions, supervision.

(SAVE) (S₆) (X) 🔲 💻 🏊

▼▼▼▼ Residence Inn by Marriott-Seattle North/Lynnwood 🔣
(425) 771-1100. **$197-$219.** 18200 Alderwood Mall Pkwy. I-5, exit 183 southbound, just w on 164th St SW, then 1.5 mi se on 28th St W; exit 182 northbound on SR 525, exit 1, then just s; just n of Alderwood Mall Shopping Center. Ext corridors. **Pets:** Accepted.

(A$K) (S₆) (X) 🔲 💻 🏊 (X)

MONROE

(AAA) ▼▼▼▼ Best Western Sky Valley Inn 🔣
(360) 794-3111. **$88-$200.** 19233 US 2. West end of town. Int corridors. **Pets:** $15 daily fee/pet. Service with restrictions, supervision.

(SAVE) (S₆) (X) 🔲 💻 🏊

▼▼▼▼ GuestHouse International Inn & Suites 🔣
(360) 863-1900. **$114-$144.** 19103 US 2. West end of town. Int corridors. **Pets:** $20 daily fee/room. Service with restrictions, supervision.

(A$K) (S₆) (X) 🔲 💻 🏊

MOUNTLAKE TERRACE

▼▼ Studio 6 #6042 Ⓜ
(425) 771-3139. **Call for rates.** 6017 244th St SW. I-5, exit 177, just ne. Ext corridors. **Pets:** Other species. Service with restrictions, supervision.

(X) (&M) 🔲 💻

MUKILTEO

▼▼ Extended StayAmerica-Seattle-Mukilteo 🔣
(425) 493-1561. **$117-$130.** 3917 Harbour Pointe Blvd SW. Jct SR 526 and 525 (Mukilteo Speedway), 1.5 mi s, then just w. Int corridors. **Pets:** Other species. $75 one-time fee/pet. Service with restrictions.

(A$K) (S₆) (X) 🔲 💻

(AAA) ▼▼▼▼ TownePlace Suites by Marriott-Mukilteo 🔣
(425) 551-5900. **$177-$195.** 8521 Mukilteo Speedway. Just se of jct 84th St SW and SR 525 (Mukilteo Speedway). Ext corridors. **Pets:** Medium, other species. $10 daily fee/pet. Designated rooms, service with restrictions, crate.

(SAVE) (S₆) (X) (&M) 🔲 💻 🏊 (X)

POULSBO

▼▼▼▼ Holiday Inn Express 🔣
(360) 697-4400. **$99-$199.** 19801 NE 7th Ave. On SR 305. Int corridors. **Pets:** Accepted.

(A$K) (S₆) (X) (&M) 🔲 💻

PUYALLUP

(AAA) ▼▼▼▼ Best Western Park Plaza 🔣 ❀
(253) 848-1500. **$130-$215.** 620 S Hill Park Dr. SR 512 southbound, exit S Hill/Eatonville, just w; northbound, exit 9th St SW, just w. Int corridors. **Pets:** Dogs only. $25 one-time fee/room. Service with restrictions, supervision.

(SAVE) (S₆) (X) (&M) 🔲 💻 🏊

▼▼▼▼ Holiday Inn Express Hotel & Suites Puyallup 🔣
(253) 848-4900. **$189.** 812 S Hill Park Dr. SR 512 southbound, exit S Hill/Eatonville, just w; northbound, exit 9th St SW, just w. Int corridors. **Pets:** Accepted.

(A$K) (S₆) (X) 🔲 💻 🏊

RENTON

▼▼ 💎 Clarion Hotel 🔣
(425) 251-9591. **Call for rates.** 3700 E Valley Rd. SR 167, exit E Valley Rd, just nw. Int corridors. **Pets:** Accepted.

(X) 🔲 💻

▼▼ Extended Stay Deluxe-Seattle 🔣
(425) 228-2454. **$123-$145.** 1150 Oakesdale Ave SW. I-405, exit 1 southbound, just s; exit Renton northbound, just n on Interurban, 0.6 mi e on SW Grady Way, then just n. Int corridors. **Pets:** Other species. $75 one-time fee/pet. Service with restrictions.

(A$K) (S₆) (X) 🔲 💻 🏊

(AAA) ▼▼ Guest House Inn & Suites Ⓜ
(425) 228-2858. **Call for rates.** 4710 Lake Washington Blvd NE. I-405, exit 7, just ne. Ext corridors. **Pets:** Accepted.

(SAVE) (X) 🔲 🏊

(AAA) ▼▼▼▼ Holiday Inn-Renton 🔣 ❀
(425) 226-7700. **Call for rates.** One S Grady Way. I-405, exit 2 (SR 167/Rainier Ave), jct SR 167 N. Int corridors. **Pets:** Medium. $50 deposit/room. Service with restrictions, crate.

(SAVE) (X) 🔲 💻 (¶) 🏊

(AAA) ▼▼▼▼ Larkspur Landing Renton/Seattle 🔣 ❀
(425) 235-1212. **$149-$179.** 1701 E Valley Rd. SR 167, exit E Valley Rd, 1 mi nw. Int corridors. **Pets:** Medium. $75 one-time fee/room. Designated rooms, service with restrictions, supervision.

(SAVE) (S₆) (X) 🔲 💻

SEATAC

(AAA) ▼▼▼ Clarion Hotel 🔣
(206) 242-0200. **$99-$119.** 3000 S 176th St. Just e of SR 99. Int corridors. **Pets:** Medium, other species. $20 daily fee/pet. Crate.

(SAVE) (S₆) (X) (&M) 🔲 💻 (¶) 🏊

▼▼▼▼ Doubletree Hotel Seattle Airport 🔣
(206) 246-8600. **Call for rates.** 18740 International Blvd. On SR 99. Int corridors. **Pets:** Accepted.

(X) 🔲 💻 (¶) 🏊

▼▼▼▼ Hilton Seattle Airport & Conference Center 🔣
(206) 244-4800. **Call for rates.** 17620 International Blvd. On SR 99. Int corridors. **Pets:** Accepted.

(X) 🔲 💻 (¶) 🏊

▼▼▼▼ Holiday Inn Express Hotel & Suites-Seattle Sea-Tac Airport 🔣
(206) 824-3200. **$109-$179.** 19621 International Blvd. On SR 99. Int corridors. **Pets:** Accepted.

(A$K) (S₆) (X) 🔲 💻

(AAA) ▼▼▼▼ Holiday Inn Seattle SeaTac International Airport 🔣
(206) 248-1000. **$89-$209.** 17338 International Blvd. On SR 99. Int corridors. **Pets:** Small. $20 daily fee/pet. Designated rooms, service with restrictions.

(SAVE) (X) (&M) 🔲 💻 (¶) 🏊

▼▼▼▼ La Quinta Inn Seattle (Sea-Tac International) 🔣
(206) 241-5211. **$122.** 2824 S 188th St. On SR 99. Int corridors. **Pets:** Other species. Service with restrictions, supervision.

(A$K) (S₆) (X) 🔲 💻 🏊

▼ Motel 6–1332 **M**
(206) 246-4101. **$55-$65 (no credit cards).** 16500 International Blvd. On SR 99. Ext corridors. **Pets:** Other species. Service with restrictions, supervision.
🛇🅂 ✖

▼ Motel 6–736 **M**
(206) 824-9902. **$49-$59 (no credit cards).** 20651 Military Rd. I-5, exit 151, just se. Ext corridors. **Pets:** Other species. Service with restrictions, supervision.
🛇🅂 ✖ 📳 ➿

▼ Motel 6–90 **SH**
(206) 241-1648. **$49-$59 (no credit cards).** 18900 47th Ave S. I-5, exit 152, just sw. Int corridors. **Pets:** Other species. Service with restrictions, supervision.
🛇🅂 ✖ 📳 ➿

▼◆▼ Radisson Hotel Gateway Seattle-Tacoma
Airport **LH**
(206) 244-6666. **$98-$170.** 18118 International Blvd. On SR 99. Int corridors. **Pets:** Accepted.
(A$K) 🛇🅂 ✖ 🅼 📳 💻 🍴 ➿

▼◆▼ Red Lion Hotel Seattle Airport **SH**
(206) 246-5535. **$229.** 18220 International Blvd. On SR 99. Int corridors. **Pets:** Accepted.
(A$K) 🛇🅂 ✖ 📳 💻 🍴 ➿ ✖

▼◆▼ Super 8 Motel Sea-Tac **SH**
(206) 433-8188. **Call for rates.** 3100 S 192nd St. Just e of SR 99. Int corridors. **Pets:** Accepted.
✖

SEATTLE

⟨AAA⟩ ▼◆▼ ▼◆▼ Alexis Hotel **LH** 🐾
(206) 624-4844. **Call for rates.** 1007 1st Ave. Corner of Madison St and 1st Ave. Int corridors. **Pets:** Other species. Designated rooms, service with restrictions, supervision.
(SAVE) ✖ 💻 🍴 ✖

⟨AAA⟩ ▼◆▼ Comfort Inn & Suites **SH**
(206) 361-3700. **$74-$119.** 13700 Aurora Ave N. I-5, exit 175, 1.1 mi w on NE 145th St, then 0.3 mi s. Int corridors. **Pets:** Medium. $15 daily fee/pet. Designated rooms, service with restrictions, supervision.
(SAVE) 🛇🅂 ✖ 📳 💻 ✖

▼◆▼ Crowne Plaza Seattle **LH**
(206) 464-1980. **Call for rates.** 1113 6th Ave. Corner of 6th Ave and Seneca St. Int corridors. **Pets:** Accepted.
✖ 📳 💻 🍴

⟨AAA⟩ ▼◆▼ Days Inn Town Center **SH**
(206) 448-3434. **$79-$199.** 2205 7th Ave. Between Bell and Blanchard sts. Int corridors. **Pets:** Other species. Service with restrictions, supervision.
(SAVE) 🛇🅂 ✖ 📳 🍴

⟨AAA⟩ ▼◆▼ ▼◆▼ The Edgewater **LH**
(206) 728-7000. **$459-$659, 3 day notice.** 2411 Alaskan Way, Pier 67. On waterfront at Pier 67; at base of Wall St. Int corridors. **Pets:** Service with restrictions, supervision.
(SAVE) 🛇🅂 ✖ 📳 💻 🍴 ✖

▼◆▼ Executive Hotel Pacific **SH**
(206) 623-3900. **$159-$249.** 400 Spring St. Between 4th and 5th aves. Int corridors. **Pets:** Accepted.
(A$K) 🛇🅂 ✖ 💻

▼◆▼ Extended StayAmerica-Seattle-Northgate **SH**
(206) 365-8100. **$86-$95.** 13300 Stone Ave N. I-5, exit 175, 1 mi w on n 145th St, 0.5 mi s on Aurora Ave, then just e on 135th St. Int corridors. **Pets:** Other species. $75 one-time fee/pet. Service with restrictions.
(A$K) 🛇🅂 ✖ 📳 💻

⟨AAA⟩ ▼◆▼◆▼ The Fairmont Olympic Hotel **LH**
(206) 621-1700. **$299-$3000.** 411 University St. Corner of 4th Ave and University St. Int corridors. **Pets:** Medium. $35 one-time fee/pet. Designated rooms, service with restrictions, supervision.
(SAVE) 🛇🅂 ✖ 📳 💻 🍴 ➿ ✖

▼◆▼◆▼ Homewood Suites by Hilton-Seattle Downtown **SH**
(206) 281-9393. **$139-$599.** 206 Western Ave W. I-5, exit 167 (Mercer St), 0.3 mi w, 0.5 mi s on Fairview Ave, 1.2 mi w on Denny Way, then just n. Int corridors. **Pets:** Accepted.
(A$K) 🛇🅂 ✖ 📳 💻

▼◆▼ ▼◆▼ Hotel 1000 **LH**
(206) 957-1000. **Call for rates (no credit cards).** 1000 First Ave. Northeast corner of 1st Ave and Madison St. Int corridors. **Pets:** Accepted.
✖ 💻 🍴

⟨AAA⟩ ▼◆▼ Hotel Max **SH** 🐾
(206) 728-6299. **$269.** 620 Stewart St. Corner of 7th Ave and Stewart St. Int corridors. **Pets:** Large. $35 one-time fee/room. Service with restrictions, crate.
(SAVE) 🛇🅂 ✖ 🅼 📳 💻 🍴

⟨AAA⟩ ▼◆▼ Hotel Monaco **LH**
(206) 621-1770. **Call for rates.** 1101 4th Ave. Corner of 4th Ave and Spring St. Int corridors. **Pets:** Accepted.
(SAVE) ✖ 📳 💻 🍴 ✖

⟨AAA⟩ ▼◆▼ Hotel Nexus Seattle **SH**
(206) 365-0700. **$99-$149.** 2140 N Northgate Way. I-5, exit 173, just nw. Ext corridors. **Pets:** Accepted.
(SAVE) ✖ 📳 💻 🍴 ➿

⟨AAA⟩ ▼◆▼◆▼ Hotel Vintage Park **LH** 🐾
(206) 624-8000. **$299.** 1100 5th Ave. Corner of Spring St and 5th Ave. Int corridors. **Pets:** Other species. Service with restrictions.
(SAVE) 🛇🅂 ✖ 🍴 ✖

⟨AAA⟩ ▼◆▼ La Quinta Inn & Suites Seattle
Downtown **SH**
(206) 624-6820. **$149.** 2224 8th Ave. Corner of 8th Ave and Blanchard St. Int corridors. **Pets:** Other species. Service with restrictions, supervision.
(SAVE) 🛇🅂 ✖ 📳 💻 ✖

⟨AAA⟩ ▼◆▼ ▼◆▼ Pan Pacific Hotel Seattle **LH**
(206) 264-8111. **$195-$425.** 2125 Terry Ave. Just s of jct E Denny Way. Int corridors. **Pets:** Large, other species. $50 one-time fee/room. Designated rooms, service with restrictions, supervision.
(SAVE) 🛇🅂 ✖ 💻 🍴 ✖

⟨AAA⟩ ▼◆▼ Red Lion Hotel on Fifth
Avenue-Seattle **LH** 🐾
(206) 971-8000. **$329.** 1415 5th Ave. Between Pike and Union sts. Int corridors. **Pets:** Small. $50 one-time fee/room. Service with restrictions, crate.
(SAVE) 🛇🅂 ✖ 📳 💻 🍴

⟨AAA⟩ ▼◆▼ Residence Inn Marriott Seattle Downtown/
Lake Union **SH**
(206) 624-6000. **$219-$329.** 800 Fairview Ave N. I-5, exit 167 (Mercer St), south end of Lake Union. Int corridors. **Pets:** Other species. $10 daily fee/pet.
(SAVE) 🛇🅂 ✖ 📳 💻 ➿ ✖

(AAA) ▼▼▼▼ The Roosevelt, a Coast Hotel SH ❀
(206) 621-1200. **$159-$279.** 1531 7th Ave. Corner of 7th Ave and Pine St. Int corridors. **Pets:** Medium. $75 one-time fee/pet. Service with restrictions, supervision.
SAVE S❂ ✕ 🖪 💻 🍽

(AAA) ▼▼▼▼ Sheraton Seattle Hotel LH
(206) 621-9000. **Call for rates.** 1400 6th Ave. Corner of 6th Ave and Pike St. Int corridors. **Pets:** Accepted.
SAVE ✕ 🖪 💻 🍽 ⤳ ✕

(AAA) ▼▼▼ The Sixth Avenue Inn SH
(206) 441-8300. **$69-$179.** 2000 6th Ave. Downtown. Int corridors. **Pets:** Other species. Service with restrictions, supervision.
SAVE S❂ ✕ 🖪 💻 🍽

(AAA) ▼▼▼▼ Sorrento Hotel SH ❀
(206) 622-6400. **Call for rates.** 900 Madison St. I-5, exit Madison St, just e; at 9th Ave and Madison St. Int corridors. **Pets:** Dogs only. $50 one-time fee/room. Designated rooms, service with restrictions, crate.
SAVE ✕ 💻 🍽 ✕

(AAA) ▼▼▼ University Inn SH
(206) 632-5055. **$135-$175.** 4140 Roosevelt Way NE. I-5, exit 169, 0.5 mi e, then just s. Int corridors. **Pets:** Medium, dogs only. $20 daily fee/pet. Designated rooms, service with restrictions, supervision.
SAVE ✕ 🖪 💻 🍽 ⤳

(AAA) ▼▼▼▼ The Westin Seattle LH ❀
(206) 728-1000. **Call for rates.** 1900 5th Ave. Corner of 5th Ave and Stewart St. Int corridors. **Pets:** Large. Service with restrictions, supervision.
SAVE ✕ ⛟M 🖪 💻 🍽 ⤳

▼▼▼▼ W Seattle LH ❀
(206) 264-6000. **Call for rates.** 1112 4th Ave. Corner of 4th Ave and Seneca St. Int corridors. **Pets:** Large, other species. $100 one-time fee/room. Service with restrictions, supervision.
✕ 🍽

SILVERDALE

▼▼▼ Oxford Inn SH
(360) 692-7777. **$89.** 9734 NW Silverdale Way. SR 3, exit Newberry Hill Road, just e, then 1.2 mi n. Int corridors. **Pets:** Accepted.
ASK ✕ 🖪 💻

(AAA) ▼▼▼▼ Silverdale Beach Hotel SH ❀
(360) 698-1000. **Call for rates.** 3073 NW Bucklin Hill Dr. SR 3, exit Newberry Hill Rd, just e, 1 mi n on Silverdale Way, then just e. Int corridors. **Pets:** Medium. $20 daily fee/pet. Service with restrictions, supervision.
SAVE ✕ 🖪 💻 🍽 ⤳ ✕

SNOHOMISH

(AAA) ▼▼▼ Inn At Snohomish M
(360) 568-2208. **$69-$130.** 323 2nd St. East end of town. Ext corridors. **Pets:** Other species. $100 deposit/room. Service with restrictions, crate.
SAVE S❂ ✕ 🖪 💻

TACOMA

▼ Crossland Studios-Tacoma-Hosmer M
(253) 538-9448. **$68-$75.** 8801 S Hosmer St. I-5, exit 128 northbound, just se; exit 129 southbound, just e on 72nd St, then 1.0 mi s. Ext corridors. **Pets:** Other species. $75 one-time fee/pet. Service with restrictions.
ASK S❂ ✕ 🖪 💻

▼▼▼ Extended StayAmerica-Tacoma-South SH
(253) 475-6565. **$95-$105.** 2120 S 48th St. I-5, exit 130, 0.4 mi nw. Int corridors. **Pets:** Other species. $75 one-time fee/pet. Service with restrictions.
ASK S❂ ✕ 🖪 💻

▼▼▼▼ La Quinta Inn & Suites Tacoma (Conference Center) SH
(253) 383-0146. **$122.** 1425 E 27th St. I-5, exit 135 southbound; exit 134 northbound, just n. Int corridors. **Pets:** Other species. Service with restrictions, supervision.
ASK S❂ ✕ 🖪 💻 🍽 ⤳

(AAA) ▼▼▼▼ Red Lion Hotel Tacoma SH
(253) 548-1212. **$139.** 8402 S Hosmer St. I-5, exit 128 northbound, just ne; exit 129 southbound, just e on 72nd St, then 1 mi s. Int corridors. **Pets:** Accepted.
SAVE S❂ ✕ 🖪 💻

▼▼▼ Shilo Inn-Tacoma SH ❀
(253) 475-4020. **$155.** 7414 S Hosmer St. I-5, exit 129, just se. Int corridors. **Pets:** $25 one-time fee/room. Designated rooms, service with restrictions, supervision.
ASK S❂ ✕ 🖪 💻 ⤳ ✕

TUKWILA

▼▼▼ Extended StayAmerica-Seattle-Tukwila SH
(206) 244-2537. **$81-$90.** 15451 53rd Ave S. I-5, exit 153 (northbound), Just n on Southcenter Pkwy, just n on 61st St, just w on Southcenter Blvd, then just sw; exit 154B (Southcenter Mall) southbound, just sw. Ext corridors. **Pets:** Other species. $75 one-time fee/pet. Service with restrictions.
ASK S❂ ✕ 🖪 💻

▼▼▼ Homestead Studio Suites Hotel-Seattle-Southcenter M
(425) 235-7160. **$90-$100.** 15635 W Valley Hwy. I-405, exit 1 (SR 181), just s. Ext corridors. **Pets:** Other species. $75 one-time fee/pet. Service with restrictions.
ASK S❂ ✕ ⛟M 🖪 💻

▼▼▼ Homewood Suites by Hilton SH
(206) 433-8000. **Call for rates.** 6955 Fort Dent Way. I-405, exit 1 (SR 181), just ne. Ext/int corridors. **Pets:** Accepted.
✕ 🖪 💻 ⤳ ✕

▼▼▼ Ramada Limited Sea-Tac Airport SH
(206) 244-8800. **Call for rates.** 13900 Tukwila International Blvd. I-5, exit 158 southbound, 2 mi s; exit 154A (SR 518 W) northbound, 1 mi n on SR 99. Int corridors. **Pets:** Accepted.
✕ 🖪 💻

▼▼▼ Residence Inn by Marriott-Seattle South SH
(425) 226-5500. **$263-$318.** 16201 W Valley Hwy. I-405, exit 1 (SR 181), just s. Ext corridors. **Pets:** Accepted.
ASK S❂ ✕ ⛟M 🖪 💻 ⤳ ✕

VASHON

▼ The Swallow's Nest Guest Cottages CA
(206) 463-2646. **$115-$310.** 6030 SW 248th St. From north end Ferry Landing, 7.8 mi s on Vashon Hwy; from south end (Tahlequah) Ferry Landing, 5.8 mi n on Vashon Hwy, 1.4 mi e on Quartermaster Dr, 1.5 mi s on Dockton Rd, 0.4 mi s on 75th Ave, then 1 mi e. Ext corridors. **Pets:** Accepted.
✕ 🖪 💻 🎍

END METROPOLITAN AREA

SEDRO-WOOLLEY

▼▼▼▼ South Bay Bed and Breakfast @ Lake Whatcom BB
(360) 595-2086. **Call for rates.** 4095 S Bay Dr. I-5, exit 240, 5.5 mi ne via Lake Samish and Cain Lake rds, then 3.2 mi e. Int corridors. **Pets:** Medium, dogs only. $20 daily fee/room. Designated rooms, service with restrictions, supervision.
[✕] [🐾] [📺] [🐾]

SEQUIM

AAA ▼▼▼▼ Econo Lodge SH
(360) 683-7113. **$69-$179.** 801 E Washington St. US 101, exit Sequim Ave, 0.4 mi n, then 0.6 mi e; east end of downtown. Int corridors. **Pets:** Medium, dogs only. $10 daily fee/pet. Designated rooms, service with restrictions, supervision.
[SAVE] [S🐾] [✕] [🛏] [📺]

AAA ▼▼▼▼ Quality Inn & Suites–Sequim SH ❧
(360) 683-2800. **$80-$180.** 134 River Rd. US 101, exit River Rd, just nw. Int corridors. **Pets:** Dogs only. $10 daily fee/pet. Designated rooms, service with restrictions, supervision.
[SAVE] [✕] [🛏] [📺] [🏊]

AAA ▼▼▼ Sequim West Inn M
(360) 683-4144. **$54-$125.** 740 W Washington St. US 101, exit River Rd, 0.9 mi ne via River Rd and W Washington St. Ext corridors. **Pets:** Small. $10 daily fee/pet. Service with restrictions, supervision.
[SAVE] [✕] [🛏] [📺]

SHELTON

AAA ▼▼▼▼ Little Creek Casino Resort SH
(360) 427-7711. **$75-$226.** West 91 SR 108. Jct US 101 and SR 108. Int corridors. **Pets:** Other species. $30 one-time fee/room. Service with restrictions.
[SAVE] [✕] [📶] [🛏] [📺] [🍴] [🏊]

▼▼▼▼ Super 8 Motel of Shelton SH ❧
(360) 426-1654. **Call for rates.** 2943 Northview Cir. US 101, exit Wallace-Kneeland Blvd, just se. Int corridors. **Pets:** Large. $15 daily fee/pet. Supervision.
[✕] [🛏] [📺]

SNOQUALMIE PASS

▼▼▼ Summit Lodge at Snoqualmie Pass SH
(425) 434-6300. **$89-$279, 3 day notice.** 603 SR 906. I-90, exit 52 eastbound, 0.3 mi e; exit 53 westbound, 0.3 mi w. Int corridors. **Pets:** Accepted.
[ASK] [S🐾] [✕] [🛏] [📺] [🍴] [🏊]

SOAP LAKE

▼▼▼▼ Notaras Lodge M
(509) 246-0462. **Call for rates.** 236 E Main Ave. Just w of SR 17. Ext corridors. **Pets:** Accepted.
[✕] [🛏] [📺]

SOUTH BEND

AAA ▼▼▼▼ The Russell House BB
(360) 875-6487. **$100-$250.** 902 E Water St. 0.5 mi s on Harrison. Int corridors. **Pets:** Accepted.
[SAVE] [S🐾] [✕] [🐾]

SPOKANE

AAA ▼▼▼ Apple Tree Inn M
(509) 466-3020. **$49-$69.** 9508 N Division St. Jct US 2 and 395, just n. Ext/int corridors. **Pets:** Accepted.
[SAVE] [S🐾] [✕] [🛏] [🏊]

AAA ▼▼▼ Best Western Peppertree Airport Inn SH ❧
(509) 624-4655. **Call for rates.** 3711 S Geiger Blvd. I-90, exit 276, just n. Int corridors. **Pets:** Very small, dogs only. $10 daily fee/pet. Service with restrictions, supervision.
[SAVE] [✕] [📶] [🛏] [📺] [🏊]

▼▼▼ Comfort Inn North SH
(509) 467-7111. **$51-$89.** 7111 N Division St. I-90, exit 281 (Division St), 4.6 mi n. Int corridors. **Pets:** Accepted.
[ASK] [S🐾] [✕] [📺] [🏊] [🐾]

AAA ▼▼▼ ▼▼▼ The Davenport Hotel and Tower LH
(509) 455-8888. **$319-$2500.** 10 S Post St. Downtown. Int corridors. **Pets:** Accepted.
[SAVE] [S🐾] [✕] [📶] [🛏] [🍴] [🏊] [🐾]

▼▼▼ Days Inn City Center SH
(509) 747-2011. **$54-$79.** 120 W 3rd Ave. I-90, exit 281 (Division St), just n, then just w on 2nd Ave. Ext corridors. **Pets:** Accepted.
[ASK] [S🐾] [✕] [🛏] [📺] [🍴] [🏊]

▼▼▼ Doubletree Hotel Spokane City Center LH
(509) 455-9600. **$109-$189, 3 day notice.** 322 N Spokane Falls Ct. I-90, exit 281 (Division St), just n; downtown. Int corridors. **Pets:** Accepted.
[ASK] [✕] [🛏] [📺] [🍴] [🏊] [🐾]

▼▼▼ Holiday Inn Express-Downtown SH
(509) 328-8505. **Call for rates.** 801 N Division St. I-90, exit 281 (Division St), 0.8 mi n. Ext/int corridors. **Pets:** Accepted.
[✕] [📶] [🛏] [📺]

▼▼▼ Holiday Inn Spokane Airport SH
(509) 838-1170. **Call for rates.** 1616 S Windsor Dr. I-90, exit 277 westbound; exit 277B eastbound, just w on US 2, then just s. Int corridors. **Pets:** Accepted.
[✕] [📶] [🛏] [📺] [🍴] [🏊]

▼▼▼ Howard Johnson Inn SH
(509) 838-6630. **Call for rates.** 211 S Division St. I-90, exit 281 (Division St), just n. Int corridors. **Pets:** Accepted.
[✕] [🛏] [📺]

AAA ▼▼▼ Howard Johnson Inn North M
(509) 326-5500. **$61-$275.** 3033 N Division St. I-90, exit 281 (Division St), 2.3 mi n on US 2 and 395. Int corridors. **Pets:** Accepted.
[SAVE] [S🐾] [✕] [🛏] [📺] [🏊]

AAA ▼▼▼ Madison Inn SH
(509) 474-4200. **$70-$85.** 15 W Rockwood Blvd. I-90, exit 281 (Division St) eastbound, just e to Cowley, 0.4 mi s, then just w; exit westbound, just n to 2nd Ave, just w to Browne St, 0.5 mi s to 9th Ave, then just e. Int corridors. **Pets:** Other species. $10 daily fee/pet. Designated rooms, service with restrictions, supervision.
[SAVE] [S🐾] [✕] [📶] [🛏] [📺]

▼▼▼ Oxford Suites-Downtown Spokane SH
(509) 353-9000. **$129-$199.** 115 W North River Dr. I-90, exit 281 (Division St), 1 mi n, then just n. Int corridors. **Pets:** Accepted.
[ASK] [S🐾] [✕] [🛏] [📺] [🏊] [🐾]

AAA ▼▼▼ Ramada Limited M ❧
(509) 838-8504. **$65-$150.** 123 S Post St. I-90, exit 280B (Lincoln St), just n to 1st Ave W, just e to Post St, then just s. Ext corridors. **Pets:** Other species. $25 one-time fee/room. Service with restrictions, crate.
[SAVE] [S🐾] [✕] [🛏] [📺]

▼▼▼ Ramada Limited Suites SH
(509) 468-4201. **Call for rates.** 9601 N Newport Hwy. US 2 and 395, just n on US 2 (Newport Hwy). Int corridors. **Pets:** Accepted.
[✕] [📶] [🛏] [📺] [🏊] [🐾]

▼▼▼▼ **Ramada Spokane Airport & Indoor Waterpark** SH
(509) 838-5211. **$120-$125.** 8909 Airport Dr. I-90, exit 277B eastbound; exit 277 westbound, 3.4 mi n. Int corridors. **Pets:** Accepted.
ASK SÒ ⊠ 🛏 🖵 ♟ ⊠ ⊠

♦♦♦⁷ ▼▼▼▼ **Red Lion Hotel at the Park-Spokane** LH
(509) 326-8000. **$199.** 303 W North River Dr. I-90, exit 281 (Division St), 1.5 mi n on US 195, then just w. Int corridors. **Pets:** Accepted.
SAVE SÒ ⊠ 🛏 🖵 ♟ ⊠

▼▼▼▼ **Red Lion River Inn-Spokane** SH
(509) 326-5577. **$175.** N 700 Division St. I-90, exit 281 (Division St), 0.8 mi n; downtown. Int corridors. **Pets:** Accepted.
ASK SÒ ⊠ ⅘M 🛏 🖵 ♟ ⊠

♦♦♦⁷ ▼ **Shangri-La Motel** M
(509) 747-2066. **Call for rates.** 2922 W Government Way. I-90, exit 277A eastbound; exit 277 westbound, Garden Springs Rd to Sunset Blvd, 1 mi e to Government Way, then just n to Hartson. Ext corridors. **Pets:** Accepted.
SAVE ⊠ 🛏 🖵 ♟

▼▼ **Shilo Inn Hotel** SH ❀
(509) 535-9000. **$130.** 923 E 3rd Ave. I-90, exit 281 (Division St), just n to E 3rd Ave, then 0.7 mi e. Int corridors. **Pets:** $25 one-time fee/room. Designated rooms, service with restrictions, supervision.
ASK SÒ ⊠ ⅘M 🛏 🖵 ♟ ⊠ ⊠

♦♦♦⁷ ▼▼▼ **Super 8 Airport West** SH
(509) 838-8800. **Call for rates.** 11102 W Westbow Blvd. I-90, exit 272 (Medical Lake), just s. Int corridors. **Pets:** Accepted.
SAVE ⊠ ⅘M 🛏 🖵 ♟

▼▼◈ **Travelodge** SH
(509) 623-9727. **$89.** W 33 Spokane Falls Blvd. I-90, exit 281 (Division St), 0.5 mi n, then just w. Int corridors. **Pets:** Accepted.
ASK SÒ ⊠ ⅘M 🛏 🖵

SPOKANE VALLEY

♦♦♦⁷ ▼▼▼ **Best Western Pheasant Hill** SH ❀
(509) 926-7432. **Call for rates.** 12415 E Mission. I-90, exit 289, just se. Int corridors. **Pets:** $15 one-time fee/room. Crate.
SAVE ⊠ ⅘M 🛏 🖵 ♟

▼▼ **Comfort Inn Valley** SH
(509) 924-3838. **$61-$120.** 905 N Sullivan Rd. I-90, exit 291B, just s. Int corridors. **Pets:** Accepted.
ASK SÒ ⊠ 🛏 🖵 ♟

▼◈ **Crossland Studios-Spokane Valley** SH
(509) 928-5948. **$59-$65.** 12803 E Sprague. I-90, exit 289, 1.1 mi s, just e. Ext corridors. **Pets:** Other species. $75 one-time fee/pet. Service with restrictions.
ASK SÒ ⊠ 🛏 🖵

▼▼◈ **Holiday Inn Express-Valley** SH
(509) 927-7100. **$109-$209.** 9220 E Mission. I-90, exit 287, just s. Ext/int corridors. **Pets:** Accepted.
ASK SÒ ⊠ ⅘M 🛏 🖵

▼▼◈ **La Quinta Inn & Suites Spokane** SH
(509) 893-0955. **$129.** 3808 N Sullivan Rd. I-90, exit 291B, 1.3 mi n. Int corridors. **Pets:** Other species. Service with restrictions, supervision.
ASK SÒ ⊠ ⅘M 🛏 🖵 ♟

♦♦♦⁷ ▼▼▼▼ **Mirabeau Park Hotel and Convention Center** SH
(509) 924-9000. **$96-$169.** 1100 N Sullivan Rd. I-90, exit 291B, just s. Int corridors. **Pets:** Large, other species. $25 one-time fee/room. Designated rooms, service with restrictions, crate.
SAVE SÒ ⊠ 🛏 🖵 ♟ ⊠ ⊠

♦♦♦⁷ ▼▼▼▼ **Oxford Suites Spokane Valley** SH ❀
(509) 847-1000. **$115-$195.** 15015 E Indiana Ave. I-90, exit 291A eastbound; exit 291B westbound, just nw. Int corridors. **Pets:** Medium, dogs only. $25 one-time fee/room. Service with restrictions, supervision.
SAVE SÒ ⊠ ⅘M 🛏 🖵 ♟ ⊠

▼▼▼ **Quality Inn Valley Suites** SH
(509) 928-5218. **$89-$129.** 8923 E Mission. I-90, exit 287. Int corridors. **Pets:** Accepted.
ASK SÒ ⊠ ⅘M 🛏 🖵 ♟ ⊠

▼▼▼ **Residence Inn by Marriott** SH
(509) 892-9300. **$120-$142.** 15915 E Indiana. I-90, exit 291 westbound, just e; exit 291B eastbound, just n, then just e. Int corridors. **Pets:** Accepted.
ASK SÒ ⊠ ⅘M 🛏 🖵 ♟ ⊠

♦♦♦⁷ ▼▼▼ **Rodeway Inn & Suites** SH
(509) 535-7185. **$49-$99, 7 day notice.** 6309 E Broadway. I-90, exit 286, just w. Ext/int corridors. **Pets:** Accepted.
SAVE SÒ ⊠ 🛏 🖵 ♟

▼▼◈ **Super 8 Motel** SH
(509) 928-4888. **Call for rates.** N 2020 Argonne Rd. I-90, exit 287, just n. Int corridors. **Pets:** Accepted.
⊠ 🛏 🖵 ♟ ⊠

STEVENSON

♦♦♦⁷ ▼▼▼▼ **Skamania Lodge** LH ❀
(509) 427-7700. **$169-$249, 5 day notice.** 1131 SW Skamania Lodge Way. 1 mi w on SR 14, just n on Rock Creek Dr, then just w. Int corridors. **Pets:** Other species. $50 one-time fee/room. Designated rooms, service with restrictions, supervision.
SAVE SÒ ⊠ 🛏 🖵 ♟ ⊠ ⊠

SULTAN

♦♦♦⁷ ◈ **Dutch Cup Motel** M
(360) 793-2215. **$77-$88, 3 day notice.** 819 Main St. Jct US 2 and Main St. Ext corridors. **Pets:** Medium, other species. $10 daily fee/pet. Designated rooms, service with restrictions, supervision.
SAVE SÒ ⊠ 🛏

SUNNYSIDE

▼▼◈ **Best Western Grapevine Inn** SH
(509) 839-6070. **Call for rates.** 1849 Quail Ln. I-82, exit 69, just n, then just w. Int corridors. **Pets:** Medium, dogs only. $25 one-time fee/pet. Service with restrictions, supervision.
⊠ 🛏 🖵 ♟

♦♦♦⁷ ▼◈ **Country Inn & Suites** M
(509) 837-7878. **$45-$60.** 408 Yakima Valley Hwy. Downtown. Ext corridors. **Pets:** Accepted.
SAVE SÒ ⊠ 🛏 🖵 ♟

♦♦♦⁷ ▼◈ **Rodeway Inn** SH
(509) 837-5781. **$69-$89.** 3209 Picard Pl. I-82, exit 69, just n. Int corridors. **Pets:** Other species. $10 daily fee/pet. Supervision.
SAVE SÒ ⊠ 🛏 🖵 ♟

TOPPENISH

♦♦♦⁷ ▼▼◈ **Best Western Toppenish Inn** SH
(509) 865-7444. **$70-$130.** 515 S Elm St. I-82, exit 50, 3.1 mi e. Int corridors. **Pets:** Other species. $10 daily fee/pet. Supervision.
SAVE SÒ ⊠ ⅘M 🛏 🖵 ♟

TUMWATER

Best Western Tumwater Inn SH
(360) 956-1235. **Call for rates.** 5188 Capitol Blvd. I-5, exit 102, just e. Int corridors. **Pets:** Medium, other species. $15 daily fee/pet. Service with restrictions, supervision.
SAVE X 🛏 💻 X

Comfort Inn and Conference Center SH
(360) 352-0691. **$89-$120.** 1620 74th Ave SW. I-5, exit 101, just se. Int corridors. **Pets:** Accepted.
ASK S X 🛏 💻 ⚊

Extended StayAmerica-Olympia-Tumwater SH
(360) 754-6063. **$90-$100.** 1675 Mottman Rd SW. I-5, exit 104, 0.4 mi nw on US 101, just s on Crosby Blvd, then just se. Int corridors. **Pets:** Other species. $75 one-time fee/pet. Service with restrictions.
ASK S X 🛏 💻

GuestHouse Inn & Suites SH 🐾
(360) 943-5040. **$89-$120.** 1600 74th Ave SW. I-5, exit 101, just se. Int corridors. **Pets:** Medium. $10 daily fee/pet. Designated rooms, service with restrictions, supervision.
ASK S X �&M 🛏 💻 ⚊

Motel 6–77 M
(360) 754-7320. **$47-$57 (no credit cards).** 400 W Lee St. I-5, exit 102, just e on Trosper Rd, just s on Capitol Blvd, then just w. Ext corridors. **Pets:** Accepted.
S X 🛏 ⚊

TWISP

Idle-A-While Motel M
(509) 997-3222. **$55-$120.** 505 N SR 20. Just n of town. Ext corridors. **Pets:** Accepted.
ASK S X 🛏 💻 X

UNION

Alderbrook Resort & Spa SH 🐾
(360) 898-2200. **Call for rates.** 10 E Alderbrook Dr. On SR 106, just e of town. Ext/int corridors. **Pets:** Other species. $25 daily fee/pet. Service with restrictions, supervision.
X 🛏 💻 ⑪ ⚊ X

UNION GAP

Best Western Ahtanum Inn SH
(509) 248-9700. **$109-$299.** 2408 Rudkin Rd. I-82, exit 36, just n. Int corridors. **Pets:** Accepted.
ASK S X �&M 🛏 💻 ⚊ X

Quality Inn-Yakima Valley M
(509) 248-6924. **$69-$169.** 12 E Valley Mall Blvd. I-82, exit 36, just s. Ext corridors. **Pets:** Accepted.
SAVE S X �&M 🛏 💻 ⚊

Super 8 Motel Yakima SH
(509) 248-8880. **$76-$110.** 2605 Rudkin Rd. I-82, exit 36, just s. Int corridors. **Pets:** Accepted.
ASK S X ⚊

WALLA WALLA

Best Western Walla Walla Suites Inn SH 🐾
(509) 525-4700. **$110-$140.** 7 E Oak St. US 12, exit 2nd Ave, just s. Int corridors. **Pets:** Dogs only. $10 daily fee/pet. Service with restrictions, supervision.
SAVE S X �&M 🛏 💻 ⚊

Budget Inn M
(509) 529-4410. **$55-$110.** 305 N 2nd Ave. US 12, exit 2nd Ave, 0.3 mi s. Ext corridors. **Pets:** Medium. $10 daily fee/pet. Service with restrictions, supervision.
SAVE X 🛏 ⚊

Holiday Inn Express SH 🐾
(509) 525-6200. **$119.** 1433 W Pine St. US 12, exit Pendleton/Prescott. Int corridors. **Pets:** Other species. $20 daily fee/pet. Service with restrictions, supervision.
SAVE X 🛏 💻 ⚊ X

La Quinta Inn Walla Walla SH
(509) 525-2522. **$82.** 520 N 2nd Ave. US 12, exit 2nd Ave, just s. Int corridors. **Pets:** Other species. Service with restrictions, supervision.
SAVE S X 🛏 💻 ⚊ X

Marcus Whitman Hotel & Conference Center LH
(509) 525-2200. **$109-$294.** Six W Rose. Downtown. Int corridors. **Pets:** Accepted.
SAVE S X 🛏 💻 ⑪

Walla Walla Motor Hotel SH
(509) 529-4360. **$59-$119.** 325 E Main St. US 12, exit 2nd Ave, 0.5 mi s, then just e. Ext/int corridors. **Pets:** Accepted.
ASK S X 🛏 💻 ⚊ X

Walla Walla Super 8 SH
(509) 525-8800. **Call for rates.** 2315 Eastgate St N. US 12, exit Wilbur Ave, just s. Int corridors. **Pets:** Accepted.
X �&M 🛏 ⚊

Walla Walla Travelodge M
(509) 529-4940. **$50-$75.** 421 E Main St. US 12, exit 2nd Ave, 0.5 mi s, then just e. Ext/int corridors. **Pets:** Medium. $7 daily fee/pet. Service with restrictions, supervision.
SAVE X 🛏 💻 ⚊

WENATCHEE

Avenue Motel M
(509) 663-7161. **$50-$76.** 720 N Wenatchee Ave. On US 2 business loop; just nw of downtown. Ext/int corridors. **Pets:** Accepted.
X 🛏 💻 ⚊

Coast Wenatchee Center Hotel LH 🐾
(509) 662-1234. **$79-$155.** 201 N Wenatchee Ave. Downtown. Int corridors. **Pets:** $10 one-time fee/room. Service with restrictions, supervision.
SAVE X 🛏 💻 ⑪ ⚊

Comfort Inn SH
(509) 662-1700. **Call for rates.** 815 N Wenatchee Ave. Downtown. Int corridors. **Pets:** Small. $10 daily fee/pet. Service with restrictions, supervision.
SAVE X 🛏 💻 ⚊

Econo Lodge M
(509) 663-7121. **$55-$120.** 232 N Wenatchee Ave. Downtown. Ext corridors. **Pets:** Small, dogs only. $10 daily fee/pet. Service with restrictions, supervision.
SAVE S X 🛏 💻 ⚊

Holiday Inn Express SH
(509) 663-6355. **$99-$189.** 1921 N Wenatchee Ave. Northwest side of town. Int corridors. **Pets:** Accepted.
ASK S X ᏚM 🛏 💻 ⚊

La Quinta Inn & Suites Wenatchee SH
(509) 664-6565. **$139.** 1905 N Wenatchee Ave. West end of town. Int corridors. **Pets:** Other species. Service with restrictions, supervision.
SAVE S X 🛏 💻 ⚊ X

▼▼▼▼ Red Lion Hotel Wenatchee 🄻🄷 ❀
(509) 663-0711. **$180.** 1225 N Wenatchee Ave. Just nw of downtown.
Int corridors. **Pets:** Service with restrictions, supervision.
[SAVE] [S🐾] [✕] [🛢] [📶] [🍴] [≈]

▼▼ Super 8 🅂🄷
(509) 662-3443. **Call for rates.** 1401 N Miller St. 1.5 mi n on US 2. Int
corridors. **Pets:** Accepted.
[SAVE] [✕] [🛢] [≈]

▼▼▼ Travelodge-Wenatchee 🄼
(509) 662-8165. **$62-$72.** 1004 N Wenatchee Ave. Downtown. Ext
corridors. **Pets:** Other species. $25 deposit/room. Service with restrictions,
supervision.
[SAVE] [S🐾] [✕] [🛢] [📶] [≈]

WESTPORT

▼ Albatross Motel 🄼
(360) 268-9233. **$45-$79, 3 day notice.** 200 E Dock St. Just s from
boat basin. Ext corridors. **Pets:** Accepted.
[✕] [🛢] [📶] [ℐ]

▼▼▼ Chateau Westport 🅂🄷
(360) 268-9101. **$85-$358.** 710 W Hancock. Just w of SR 105 Spur N;
1.5 mi n of Twin Harbors State Park. Int corridors. **Pets:** $25 daily
fee/room. Designated rooms, service with restrictions, supervision.
[SAVE] [S🐾] [✕] [🛢] [📶] [≈] [✕] [ℐ]

WINTHROP

▼▼▼ Americas Best Value Cascade Inn 🄼
(509) 996-3100. **$70-$150.** 1006 SR 20. 1 mi e. Ext corridors.
Pets: Accepted.
[SAVE] [S🐾] [✕] [🛢] [📶] [≈] [✕]

▼▼▼▼ River Run Inn 🄼
(509) 996-2173. **$65-$145, 10 day notice.** 27 Rader Rd. 0.5 mi w on
SR 20. Ext corridors. **Pets:** Dogs only. $13 daily fee/pet. Service with
restrictions, supervision.
[SAVE] [✕] [🛢] [📶] [≈]

▼▼▼ Winthrop Inn 🄼
(509) 996-2217. **$75-$110, 3 day notice.** 960 SR 20. 0.9 mi e. Int
corridors. **Pets:** Medium, dogs only. $10 daily fee/pet. Service with restric-
tions, supervision.
[SAVE] [✕] [🛢] [≈] [✕]

▼▼▼▼ Winthrop Mtn View Chalets 🄲🄰
(509) 996-3113. **$70-$125, 7 day notice.** 1120 SR 20. South end of
town. Ext corridors. **Pets:** Dogs only. $25 daily fee/room. Designated
rooms, no service, supervision.
[SAVE] [✕] [🛢] [📶] [⚡]

WOODLAND

▼▼▼ Cedars Inn Woodland 🅂🄷 ❀
(360) 225-6548. **$60-$100 (no credit cards).** 1500 Atlantic Ave. I-5, exit
21, just ne. Ext corridors. **Pets:** Medium. $10 daily fee/pet. Service with
restrictions, supervision.
[SAVE] [S🐾] [✕] [🛢] [≈]

▼▼▼ Lewis River Inn 🄼
(360) 225-6257. **$64-$105.** 1100 Lewis River Rd. I-5, exit 21, just e. Ext
corridors. **Pets:** Accepted.
[SAVE] [✕] [🛢] [📶]

YAKIMA

▼▼▼▼ Best Western Lincoln Inn 🅂🄷 ❀
(509) 453-8898. **$99-$299.** 1614 N 1st St. I-82, exit 31, just s. Int
corridors. **Pets:** Small, dogs only. $20 daily fee/pet. Service with restric-
tions, supervision.
[SAVE] [S🐾] [✕] [🛢] [📶] [≈]

▼▼▼▼ Cedars Suites Yakima Downtown 🄼
(509) 452-8101. **$70-$100.** 1010 E a St. I-82, exit 33B eastbound; exit
33 westbound, just w to 9th St, just n to a St, then just e. Ext corridors.
Pets: Small. $10 daily fee/pet. Designated rooms, service with restrictions,
supervision.
[SAVE] [S🐾] [✕] [🛢]

▼▼▼▼ Clarion Hotel & Conference Center 🅂🄷
(509) 248-7850. **$69-$99.** 1507 N 1st St. I-82, exit 31, 0.5 mi s. Int
corridors. **Pets:** Accepted.
[✕] [🛒M] [🛢] [📶] [🍴] [≈] [✕]

▼▼▼▼ Comfort Suites 🅂🄷 ❀
(509) 249-1900. **$99-$299.** 3702 Fruitvale Blvd. US 12, exit 40th Ave,
just s. Int corridors. **Pets:** Small, dogs only. $15 daily fee/pet. Designated
rooms, service with restrictions, supervision.
[SAVE] [S🐾] [✕] [🛒M] [🛢] [📶] [≈]

▼▼ Days Inn Yakima 🅂🄷
(509) 248-3393. **Call for rates.** 1504 N 1st St. I-82, exit 31, 0.6 mi s. Int
corridors. **Pets:** Accepted.
[✕] [🛒M] [🛢] [📶] [≈]

▼▼▼▼ Fairfield Inn & Suites by Marriott 🅂🄷
(509) 452-3100. **$99-$119.** 137 N Fair Ave. I-82, exit 33A eastbound,
just s; exit 33 westbound, just w to 9th St, just n to B St, then just e.
Int corridors. **Pets:** Accepted.
[ASK] [S🐾] [✕] [🛒M] [🛢] [📶]

▼▼▼▼ Holiday Inn Express Yakima 🅂🄷
(509) 249-1000. **$129-$169.** 1001 E a St. I-82, exit 33B eastbound; exit
33 westbound, just w to 9th St, just n to a St, then just e. Int corridors.
Pets: Small. $10 daily fee/pet. Designated rooms, service with restrictions,
supervision.
[ASK] [S🐾] [✕] [🛒M] [🛢] [📶] [≈]

▼▼▼▼ Howard Johnson Plaza Yakima Gateway 🅂🄷
(509) 452-6511. **Call for rates.** 9 N 9th St. I-82, exit 33 westbound; exit
33B eastbound, just s. Int corridors. **Pets:** Accepted.
[✕] [🛒M] [🛢] [📶] [🍴] [≈]

▼▼▼ Oxford Inn 🅂🄷
(509) 457-4444. **$79-$89.** 1603 E Yakima Ave. I-82, exit 33 westbound,
just e; exit 33B eastbound. Int corridors. **Pets:** Small. $20 one-time
fee/room. Designated rooms, service with restrictions, supervision.
[ASK] [S🐾] [✕] [🛒M] [🛢] [📶] [≈] [✕]

▼▼▼ Oxford Suites 🅂🄷
(509) 457-9000. **$115-$125.** 1701 E Yakima Ave. I-82, exit 33 westbound; 33B eastbound. Int corridors. **Pets:** Accepted.
[ASK] [S🐾] [✕] [🛒M] [🛢] [📶] [≈] [✕]

▼▼▼ Ramada Limited 🄼
(509) 453-0391. **Call for rates.** 818 N 1st St. I-82, exit 31, 1.2 mi s. Ext
corridors. **Pets:** Accepted.
[✕] [🛢] [📶] [≈]

▼▼▼▼ Red Lion Hotel Yakima Center 🅂🄷
(509) 248-5900. **$129.** 607 E Yakima Ave. I-82, exit 33 westbound;
33B eastbound, 0.8 mi w. Ext/int corridors. **Pets:** Accepted.
[ASK] [S🐾] [✕] [🛢] [📶] [🍴] [≈]

▼▼▼ Sun Country Inn 🄼
(509) 248-5650. **$58-$70, 3 day notice.** 1700 N 1st St. I-82, exit 31,
just s. Ext corridors. **Pets:** Accepted.
[ASK] [S🐾] [✕] [🛢] [📶] [≈]

ZILLAH

▼▼▼ Comfort Inn 🅂🄷
(509) 829-3399. **$104-$160.** 911 Vintage Valley Pkwy. I-82, exit 52, just
n. Int corridors. **Pets:** Accepted.
[ASK] [S🐾] [✕] [🛒M] [🛢] [📶] [≈]

WEST VIRGINIA

CITY INDEX

BARBOURSVILLE

▽▼▽▼ Comfort Inn by Choice Hotels 🆂🅷
(304) 733-2122. **Call for rates.** 249 Mall Rd. I-64, exit 20, 0.4 mi n. Int corridors. **Pets:** Accepted.
❌ 🅼 🎗 💻 🏊

BECKLEY

🐾 ▽▼▽ Best Western Four Seasons Inn 🆂🅷
(304) 252-0671. **$63-$110, 7 day notice.** 1939 Harper Rd. I-64/77, exit 44, just e on SR 3. Ext/int corridors. **Pets:** Other species. $5 daily fee/pet. Service with restrictions, supervision.
🆂🅰🆅🅴 🆂 ❌ 💻

🐾 ▽▼▽ Country Inn & Suites By Carlson 🆂🅷
(304) 252-5100. **$99-$199.** 2120 Harper Rd. I-64/77, exit 44, just w on SR 3. Int corridors. **Pets:** Medium. $30 one-time fee/room. Designated rooms, service with restrictions, supervision.
🆂🅰🆅🅴 🆂 ❌ 🅼 🎗 💻 🏊 🗙

▽▼▽ Econo Lodge 🆂🅷 🐾
(304) 255-2161. **$49-$100.** 1909 Harper Rd. I-64/77, exit 44, 0.3 mi e on SR 3. Ext/int corridors. **Pets:** Other species. Service with restrictions.
🅰🆂🅺 🆂 ❌ 🎗 💻

🐾 ▽▼▽ Howard Johnson Express Inn 🆂🅷
(304) 255-5900. **Call for rates.** 1907 Harper Rd. I-64/77, exit 44, 0.4 mi e on SR 3. Int corridors. **Pets:** Medium, dogs only. $15 daily fee/pet. Designated rooms, service with restrictions, supervision.
🆂🅰🆅🅴 ❌ 🎗 💻 🏊

🐾 ▽▼▽ Microtel Inn 🆂🅷
(304) 256-2000. **$55-$129 (no credit cards), 3 day notice.** 2130 Harper Rd. I-64/77, exit 44. Int corridors. **Pets:** Other species. $25 one-time fee/room. Designated rooms, service with restrictions, supervision.
🆂🅰🆅🅴 🆂 ❌ 🎗 🏊

🐾 ◆ Super 8 Motel 🆂🅷
(304) 253-0802. **Call for rates.** 2014 Harper Rd. I-64/77, exit 44, just e. Int corridors. **Pets:** Small. $10 one-time fee/pet. Service with restrictions, crate.
🆂🅰🆅🅴 ❌ 🎗

BLUEFIELD

🐾 ▽▼▽ Holiday Inn Bluefield-On The Hill 🆂🅷
(304) 325-6170. **$80-$110 (no credit cards).** 3350 Big Laurel Hwy. I-77, exit 1, 3.8 mi nw via US 52/460. Int corridors. **Pets:** Accepted.
🆂🅰🆅🅴 🆂 ❌ 🎗 💻 🍴 🏊 🗙

BRIDGEPORT

▽▼ Sleep Inn 🆂🅷
(304) 842-1919. **$79.** 115 Tolley Dr. I-79, exit 119, just e on US 50. Int corridors. **Pets:** Other species. Service with restrictions, supervision.
🅰🆂🅺 🆂 ❌ 🎗 💻

CHARLESTON

▽▼▽ Charleston Comfort Suites 🆂🅷 🐾
(304) 925-1171. **$110-$130.** 107 Alex Ln. I-77, exit 95, just s on SR 61. Int corridors. **Pets:** Medium, other species. $25 one-time fee/pet.
🅰🆂🅺 🆂 ❌ 🎗 💻 🏊

▽▼▽ Country Inn & Suites By Carlson 🆂🅷 🐾
(304) 925-4300. **$110-$130.** 105 Alex Ln. I-77, exit 95, just s on SR 61. Int corridors. **Pets:** Medium, other species.
🅰🆂🅺 🆂 ❌ 🎗 💻 🏊

▽▼▽ Days Inn Charleston East 🅼
(304) 925-1010. **Call for rates.** 6400 MacCorkle Ave SE. I-77, exit 95, just s on SR 61. Int corridors. **Pets:** Accepted.
❌ 🎗 💻 🏊

▽▼▽ Holiday Inn Express Civic Center 🆂🅷
(304) 345-0600. **$80-$100.** 100 Civic Center Dr. I-64, exit 58B eastbound; exit 58C westbound, just s; downtown. Int corridors. **Pets:** Small. $25 daily fee/room. Designated rooms, service with restrictions, supervision.
🅰🆂🅺 🆂 ❌ 🎗 💻

🐾 ◆ Knights Inn-Charleston East 🅼
(304) 925-0451. **$47-$57.** 6401 MacCorkle Ave SE. I-77, exit 95, just s on SR 61. Ext corridors. **Pets:** Small, dogs only. $10 daily fee/pet. Service with restrictions, supervision.
🆂🅰🆅🅴 🆂 ❌ 🎗 💻 🏊

▽▼▽ Red Roof Inn-Kanawha City 🅼
(304) 925-6953. **Call for rates.** 6305 SE MacCorkle Ave. I-77, exit 95, just s on SR 61. Ext corridors. **Pets:** Accepted.
❌ 🎗

CROSS LANES

🐾 ▽▼▽ Comfort Inn West Charleston 🆂🅷 🐾
(304) 776-8070. **$88.** 102 Racer Dr. I-64, exit 47, just s. Int corridors. **Pets:** Large. $15 daily fee/room. Designated rooms, service with restrictions, supervision.
🆂🅰🆅🅴 🆂 ❌ 🎗 💻 🏊

DANIELS

🐾 ▽▼▽▼ The Resort at Glade Springs 🆂🅷
(304) 763-2000. **$138-$332, 7 day notice.** 255 Resort Dr. I-64, exit 125, 1.5 mi w on SR 307, then 2.8 mi w on US 19. Ext/int corridors. **Pets:** Large, dogs only. $50 daily fee/pet. Designated rooms, service with restrictions, supervision.
🆂🅰🆅🅴 🆂 ❌ 🎗 💻 🍴 🏊 🗙

DAVIS

🐾 ▽▼▽▼ Black Bear Resort 🅲🅰
(304) 866-4391. **$90-$510.** Cortland Rd, Canaan Valley. 7.4 mi s on SR 32. Ext corridors. **Pets:** Dogs only. $35 one-time fee/pet. Designated rooms, no service.
❌ 🎗 💻 🏊 🗙

DUNBAR

◆ Dunbar Super 8 Motel SH
(304) 768-6888. **Call for rates.** 911 Dunbar Ave. I-64, exit 53, just w. Int corridors. **Pets:** Other species. $10 daily fee/pet. Service with restrictions, supervision.

⊠ 🛗

EDRAY

AAA ◆◆◆ Marlinton Motor Inn M
(304) 799-4711. **$65-$115, 3 day notice.** US 219 N. Center. Ext corridors. **Pets:** Small. $12 daily fee/pet. Designated rooms, no service, supervision.

SAVE S🐕 ⊠ 🛗 ▣ ¶ ⇆

ELKINS

AAA ◆◆◆◆ Cheat River Lodge & Inn CA
(304) 636-2301. **$73-$88.** Rt 1, Box 115, Faulkner Rd. 4.8 mi e on US 33, then 1.5 mi ne. Ext corridors. **Pets:** Dogs only. $10 daily fee/pet. Service with restrictions, supervision.

SAVE ⊠ 🛗 ▣ ¶ ⊠

◆ Econo Lodge M
(304) 636-5311. **Call for rates.** US 33 E. 1 mi e. Ext/int corridors. **Pets:** Accepted.

⊠ 🛗 ⇆

◆◆ Elkins Super 8 Motel SH
(304) 636-6500. **Call for rates.** 350 Beverly Pike. 0.8 mi s on SR 219. Int corridors. **Pets:** Medium. $10 daily fee/pet. Designated rooms, service with restrictions, supervision.

⊠ 🛗 ▣

FAIRMONT

◆◆ Super 8 Motel SH
(304) 363-1488. **Call for rates.** 2208 Pleasant Valley Rd. I-79, exit 133, just e. Int corridors. **Pets:** Accepted.

⊠ 🛗

FALLING WATERS

◆◆◆ Holiday Inn Express Martinsburg North SH
(304) 274-6100. **Call for rates.** 1220 TJ Jackson Dr. I-81, exit 20, just w. Int corridors. **Pets:** Accepted.

⊠ 🛗 ▣ ⇆

FROST

◆◆◆ The Inn at Mountain Quest CI ✿
(304) 799-7267. **$130-$150.** Rt 92 Frost. On SR 92, 0.4 mi n. Ext corridors. **Pets:** Other species. $10 daily fee/pet. Designated rooms, service with restrictions, supervision.

ASK S🐕 ⊠ ¶ ⊠

HUNTINGTON

◆◆ Red Roof Inn SH
(304) 733-3737. **Call for rates.** 5190 US Rt 60 E. I-64, exit 15, just s. Ext corridors. **Pets:** Accepted.

⊠ 🛗

HURRICANE

◆◆◆ Red Roof Inn M
(304) 757-6392. **Call for rates.** 500 Putnam Village Dr. I-64, exit 39, just n on SR 34, then just e. Ext corridors. **Pets:** Accepted.

⊠ 🛗

KEYSER

AAA ◆◆◆ Keyser Inn SH
(304) 788-0913. **$54-$60.** Rt 220 S. On US 220, 2.3 mi s. Int corridors. **Pets:** Medium. $25 one-time fee/room. Service with restrictions, supervision.

SAVE S🐕 ⊠ 🛗 ▣

LEWISBURG

AAA ◆◆ Americas Best Value Inn M
(304) 645-7070. **Call for rates.** 107 W Fair St. I-64, exit 169, 3.1 mi s on US 219, then just e. Ext corridors. **Pets:** Small. $10 daily fee/pet. Service with restrictions.

SAVE ⊠ 🛗 ▣

AAA ◆◆◆ Brier Inn SH
(304) 645-7722. **$64-$110.** 540 N Jefferson St. I-64, exit 169, just s on US 219. Ext corridors. **Pets:** Other species. $10 daily fee/pet. Designated rooms, crate.

SAVE S🐕 ⊠ 🛗 ▣ ¶ ⇆

◆◆ Super 8 Motel SH
(304) 647-3188. **Call for rates.** 550 N Jefferson St. I-64, exit 169, just s on US 219. Int corridors. **Pets:** Large, other species. $10 daily fee/pet. Service with restrictions, supervision.

⊠ 🛗

LOGAN

◆ Super 8 Motel-Logan M
(304) 752-8787. **Call for rates (no credit cards).** 316 Riverview Ave. 1.8 mi e on SR 73. Int corridors. **Pets:** Accepted.

⊠ 🛗 ▣

MARTINSBURG

◆◆ Days Inn Martinsburg SH
(304) 263-1800. **Call for rates.** 209 Viking Way. I-81, exit 13, just e on W King St (CR 15). Ext/int corridors. **Pets:** Small. $10 daily fee/pet. Service with restrictions, supervision.

⊠ 🛗

AAA ◆◆ Econo Lodge M
(304) 274-2181. **$60-$62.** 5595 Hammonds Mill Rd. I-81, exit 20, just e. Ext/int corridors. **Pets:** Other species. Service with restrictions, supervision.

SAVE S🐕 ⊠ ▣

AAA ◆ Knights Inn-Martinsburg M
(304) 267-2211. **Call for rates.** 1997 Edwin Miller Blvd. I-81, exit 16E, 0.4 mi e on SR 9. Ext corridors. **Pets:** Other species. $10 daily fee/pet. Designated rooms.

SAVE ⊠

AAA ◆◆◆ Rodeway Inn SH
(304) 263-8811. **$55-$80.** 94 McMillan Ct. I-81, exit 16E, just e. Ext/int corridors. **Pets:** Medium. $10 daily fee/pet. Service with restrictions.

SAVE S🐕 ⊠ 🛗 ▣ ⇆

◆ Super 8 Motel-Martinsburg SH
(304) 263-0801. **Call for rates.** 2048 Edwin Miller Blvd. I-81, exit 16E, just e on SR 9. Int corridors. **Pets:** Accepted.

⊠ 🛗

MORGANTOWN

AAA ◆◆◆ Comfort Inn-Morgantown SH
(304) 296-9364. **$69-$125.** 225 Comfort Inn Dr. I-68, exit 1, 0.3 mi n on US 119. Int corridors. **Pets:** Other species. $25 deposit/pet. Designated rooms, service with restrictions, supervision.

SAVE ⊠ 🛗 ▣ ¶ ⇆

Friends Inn M
(304) 599-4850. **$50-$150, 14 day notice.** 452 Country Club Rd. I-79, exit 155, s on US 19 to SR 705, then e on University Ave. Ext corridors. **Pets:** Small. $5 one-time fee/pet. Designated rooms, service with restrictions, supervision.

Ramada Conference Center SH
(304) 296-3431. **Call for rates.** 20 Scott Ave. I-68, exit 1, 0.3 mi n. Int corridors. **Pets:** Other species. Service with restrictions, supervision.

Residence Inn by Marriott Morgantown SH
(304) 599-0237. **$128-$156.** 1046 Willowdale Rd. I-79, exit 155, 2 mi s on US 19, then 0.9 mi e on SR 705. Int corridors. **Pets:** Other species. $75 one-time fee/room.

NITRO

Econo Lodge M
(304) 755-8341. **$50-$60.** 4115 1st Ave. I-64, exit 45, 0.8 mi e on SR 25. Ext corridors. **Pets:** Large, dogs only. $10 daily fee/pet. Designated rooms, service with restrictions, supervision.

PARKERSBURG

The Blennerhassett SH
(304) 422-3131. **$109-$269.** 320 Market St. Between Fourth and Fifth sts; downtown. Int corridors. **Pets:** Accepted.

Holiday Inn Parkersburg SH
(304) 485-6200. **Call for rates.** 225 Holiday Hills Dr. I-77, exit 176, just e. Int corridors. **Pets:** Accepted.

Red Carpet Inn M
(304) 485-1851. **$45-$65.** 6333 Emerson Ave. I-77, exit 179, 0.4 mi sw on SR 68. Ext corridors. **Pets:** Dogs only. $5 daily fee/pet. Service with restrictions, supervision.

Red Roof Inn M
(304) 485-1741. **Call for rates.** 3714 E 7th St. I-77, exit 176, just w on US 50. Ext corridors. **Pets:** Accepted.

Travelodge Parkersburg M
(304) 424-5100. **Call for rates.** 3604 E 7th St. I-77, exit 176, just w. Ext corridors. **Pets:** Other species. $5 daily fee/pet. Designated rooms, service with restrictions, supervision.

PHILIPPI

Philippi Lodging M
(304) 457-5888. **$46-$83.** Rt 4, Box 155. 2.5 mi s on US 250. Int corridors. **Pets:** Accepted.

PRINCETON

Days Inn SH
(304) 425-8100. **Call for rates.** 347 Meadowfield Ln. I-77, exit 9, 0.3 mi w on US 460, just s on Ambrose Ln, then just e. Ext corridors. **Pets:** Accepted.

Holiday Inn Express Princeton SH
(304) 425-8156. **$85-$125.** 805 Oakvale Rd. I-77, exit 9, just w. Int corridors. **Pets:** Medium. $20 daily fee/pet. Designated rooms, service with restrictions, supervision.

Sleep Inn & Suites SH
(304) 431-2800. **$99-$225.** 1015 Oakvale Rd. I-77, exit 9, just w on US 460, then just n via service road. Int corridors. **Pets:** Accepted.

RIPLEY

Best Western McCoys Inn & Conference Center SH
(304) 372-9122. **Call for rates.** 701 W Main St. I-77, exit 138, just e. Ext/int corridors. **Pets:** Small. $10 one-time fee/pet. Designated rooms, service with restrictions, supervision.

Holiday Inn Express SH
(304) 372-5000. **$89.** 1 Hospitality Dr. I-77, exit 138, just w on SR 33, then 0.3 mi n. Ext/int corridors. **Pets:** Designated rooms, service with restrictions, supervision.

Ripley Super 8 Motel M
(304) 372-8880. **Call for rates.** 102 Duke Dr. I-77, exit 138, just e on SR 33. Int corridors. **Pets:** Accepted.

SNOWSHOE

Inn at Snowshoe SH
(304) 572-6520. **Call for rates.** SR 66. 0.5 mi e on SR 66, from US 219 jct, follow signs. Int corridors. **Pets:** Accepted.

SOUTH CHARLESTON

Ramada Plaza Hotel Charleston SH
(304) 744-4641. **$89-$139.** 400 2nd Ave. I-64, exit 56, just nw. Int corridors. **Pets:** Accepted.

STAR CITY

Econo Lodge-Coliseum SH
(304) 599-8181. **$64-$75.** 3506 Monongahela Blvd. I-79, exit 155, 1.4 mi s on US 119/SR 7. Ext corridors. **Pets:** Accepted.

SUMMERSVILLE

Best Western Summersville Lake Motor Lodge SH
(304) 872-6900. **Call for rates.** 1203 S Broad St. US 19 and Broad St; 0.6 mi s of jct SR 39. Ext corridors. **Pets:** Medium. $10 daily fee/pet. Designated rooms, service with restrictions, supervision.

Comfort Inn SH
(304) 872-6500. **$75-$180.** 903 Industrial Dr N. US 19, 1.9 mi n of jct SR 39. Int corridors. **Pets:** Accepted.

Sleep Inn of Summersville SH
(304) 872-4500. **$65-$155.** 701 Professional Park Dr. US 19, 1.7 mi n of jct SR 39. Int corridors. **Pets:** Medium, other species. $10 daily fee/pet. Designated rooms, service with restrictions, supervision.

Super 8 Motel-Summersville SH
(304) 872-4888. **Call for rates.** 306 Merchants Walk. US 19, just n. Int corridors. **Pets:** Accepted.

TRIADELPHIA

 Comfort Inn-Wheeling SH

(304) 547-0610. $69-$129. 675 Fort Henry Rd. I-70, exit 11, just n. Int corridors. Pets: $10 daily fee/pet. Service with restrictions, supervision.

SAVE S⦿ ⊠ 🛏 🖥 🏊

WEIRTON

 Holiday Inn SH

(304) 723-5522. $105-$109. 350 Three Springs Dr. 4.5 mi e on US 22, exit Three Springs Dr. Int corridors. Pets: $50 one-time fee/room. Service with restrictions, supervision.

ASK ⊠ 🛏 🖥 🍴 🏊 ⊠

WESTON

 Comfort Inn SH

(304) 269-7000. $65-$130. 2906 US Hwy 33 E. I-79, exit 99, just e. Ext corridors. Pets: Medium, dogs only. $10 daily fee/room. Designated rooms, service with restrictions, supervision.

SAVE ⊠ 🛏 🖥 🏊

 Weston Super 8 Motel SH

(304) 269-1086. Call for rates. 100 Market Place Mall, Suite 12. I-79, exit 99, just e. Int corridors. Pets: Very small, other species. $10 daily fee/pet. Service with restrictions, supervision.

⊠ 🛏

WHITE SULPHUR SPRINGS

 The Greenbrier LH 🐾

(304) 536-1110. $299-$729, 15 day notice. 300 W Main St. I-64, exit 181 westbound, 1.8 mi w on US 60; exit 175 eastbound, just n, then 3.2 mi e on US 60. Ext/int corridors. Pets: Small. $150 one-time fee/pet. Designated rooms, service with restrictions, crate.

SAVE ⊠ &M 🛏 🖥 🍴 🏊 ⊠

WILLIAMSTOWN

 Days Inn SH 🐾

(304) 375-3730. Call for rates. 1339 Highland Ave. I-77, exit 185, just w on SR 31. Int corridors. Pets: Large, other species. $5 daily fee/pet, $10 one-time fee/pet. Designated rooms, service with restrictions, supervision.

SAVE ⊠ 🛏 🖥 🏊

WISCONSIN

ABBOTSFORD

▼▼ Sleep Inn SH
(715) 223-3337. **$70-$90.** 300 E Elderberry Rd. SR 29, exit 132 (SR 13), just se. Int corridors. **Pets:** Accepted.

ALGOMA

◆◆◆ ▼ Algoma Beach Motel SH
(920) 487-2828. **$79-$159, 3 day notice.** 1500 Lake St. Jct SR 54, 0.4 mi s on SR 42. Ext/int corridors. **Pets:** Accepted.

▼ Scenic Shore Inn M
(920) 487-3214. **$49-$65, 3 day notice.** 2221 Lake St. Jct SR 54, 0.8 mi s on SR 42. Ext corridors. **Pets:** Accepted.

ANTIGO

▼▼ Northwoods Birch Inn SH
(715) 623-0506. **Call for rates.** 525 Memory Ln. 0.4 mi n of jct SR 64 E and US 45, then just w. Int corridors. **Pets:** Accepted.

▼▼ Super 8 Motel-Antigo SH
(715) 623-4188. **$59-$112.** 535 Century Ave. On US 45 at SR 64 E. Int corridors. **Pets:** Accepted.

APPLETON

▼▼ Best Western Midway Hotel SH
(920) 731-4141. **$69-$189, 3 day notice.** 3033 W College Ave. US 41, exit 137 (SR 125), 0.5 mi e. Int corridors. **Pets:** Accepted.

▼▼ Candlewood Suites SH
(920) 739-8000. **$100-$145.** 4525 W College Ave. Just w of US 41. Int corridors. **Pets:** Accepted.

▼▼▼ Comfort Suites Appleton Airport SH
(920) 730-3800. **$89-$149.** 3809 W Wisconsin Ave. US 41, exit 138 (Wisconsin Ave), just e. Int corridors. **Pets:** Accepted.

◆◆◆ ▼▼ Country Inn & Suites By Carlson SH
(920) 830-3240. **Call for rates.** 355 Fox River Dr. US 41, exit 137 (SR 125), just nw. Int corridors. **Pets:** Small, other species. $15 daily fee/pet. Designated rooms, service with restrictions, supervision.

◆◆◆ ▼ Exel Inn of Appleton M
(920) 733-5551. **$51-$71.** 210 Westhill Blvd. US 41, exit 137 (SR 125), just e. Int corridors. **Pets:** Accepted.

▼▼ Extended StayAmerica-Appleton-Fox Cities SH
(920) 830-9596. **$68-$75.** 4141 Boardwalk Ct. US 41, exit 137 (SR 125), w on College Ave, then s on Nicolet Rd. Int corridors. **Pets:** Other species. $75 one-time fee/pet. Service with restrictions.

▼▼ Fairfield Inn by Marriott SH
(920) 954-0202. **$89-$109.** 132 Mall Dr. US 41, exit 137 (SR 125), just nw. Int corridors. **Pets:** Accepted.

▼▼▼ La Quinta Inn & Suites College Ave SH
(920) 734-7777. **$99-$112.** 3730 W College Ave. US 41, exit 137 (SR 125), just e. Int corridors. **Pets:** Other species. Service with restrictions, supervision.

▼▼ La Quinta Inn Appleton Fox River Mall Area M
(920) 734-6070. **$62-$70.** 3920 W College Ave. US 41, exit 137 (SR 125), just e. Ext/int corridors. **Pets:** Other species. Service with restrictions, supervision.

▼▼ Microtel Inn & Suites SH
(920) 997-3121. **Call for rates.** 321 Metro Dr. US 41, exit 137 (SR 125), just nw. Int corridors. **Pets:** Accepted.

▼▼▼ Residence Inn by Marriott SH
(920) 954-0570. **$210-$230.** 310 Metro Dr. US 41, exit 137 (SR 125), just nw on Mall Dr. Int corridors. **Pets:** Accepted.

ARKDALE

Northern Bay Golf Resort & Marina **CO**
(608) 339-2090. **Call for rates.** 1844 20th Ave. 2.9 mi nw on SR 21, 4 mi s on CR Z, then 1.5 nw via Dakota Ave and 20th Ave. Int corridors. **Pets:** Accepted.

ASHLAND

AmericInn of Ashland **SH**
(715) 682-9950. **$99-$259.** 3009 Lake Shore Dr E. On US 2, 2.1 mi e of jct SR 13 S. Int corridors. **Pets:** Accepted.

Ashland Motel **M**
(715) 682-5503. **Call for rates.** 2300 W Lake Shore Dr. 1.8 mi w on US 2. Ext corridors. **Pets:** Accepted.

Best Western Lake Superior Lodge **SH**
(715) 682-5235. **$80-$140.** 30600 US Hwy 2. 2.5 mi w. Ext/int corridors. **Pets:** Small. $50 deposit/room, $10 one-time fee/pet. Designated rooms, service with restrictions, supervision.

BALDWIN

AmericInn of Baldwin **SH**
(715) 684-5888. **Call for rates.** 500 Baldwin Plaza Dr. I-94, exit 19 (US 63), just ne. Int corridors. **Pets:** Medium, dogs only. $10 daily fee/pet. Designated rooms, service with restrictions, crate.

Super 8 Motel **SH**
(715) 684-2700. **Call for rates.** 2110 10th Ave. I-94, exit 19 (US 63), just se. Int corridors. **Pets:** Accepted.

BARABOO

Park Plaza Baraboo **SH**
(608) 356-6422. **$67-$129.** 626 W Pine St. On US 12, 0.3 mi n of SR 33. Int corridors. **Pets:** Accepted.

BAYFIELD

Old Rittenhouse Inn **CI**
(715) 779-5111. **Call for rates.** 301 Rittenhouse Ave. Just w on SR 13. Int corridors. **Pets:** Accepted.

BEAVER DAM

Super 8 Motel **SH**
(920) 887-8880. **Call for rates.** 711 Park Ave. US 151, exit 132 (SR 33), just w. Int corridors. **Pets:** Accepted.

BELMONT

Baymont Inn & Suites **SH**
(608) 762-6900. **Call for rates.** 103 W Moundview Ave. US 151, exit 26, just w. Int corridors. **Pets:** Accepted.

BELOIT

Americas Best Value Inn **SH**
(608) 365-8680. **$69-$89.** 3002 Milwaukee Rd. I-90, exit 185A, just sw at I-43 and SR 81. Int corridors. **Pets:** Dogs only. $10 one-time fee/room. Designated rooms, service with restrictions, supervision.

Beloit Inn **SH**
(608) 362-5500. **$89-$189.** 500 Pleasant St. Downtown. Int corridors. **Pets:** Other species. $100 deposit/room, $10 daily fee/room. Designated rooms, service with restrictions, crate.

Comfort Inn of Beloit **SH**
(608) 362-2666. **$69-$99.** 2786 Milwaukee Rd. I-90, exit 185A, just w at I-43 and SR 81. Int corridors. **Pets:** Medium. $10 daily fee/room. Service with restrictions, supervision.

Econo Lodge **M**
(608) 364-4000. **$51-$79.** 2956 Milwaukee Rd. I-90, exit 185A, 0.3 mi w. Ext/int corridors. **Pets:** Medium, other species. $6 daily fee/pet. Service with restrictions.

BERLIN

Best Western Countryside **M**
(920) 361-4411. **$89-$94.** 227 Ripon Rd. On SR 49, at CR F. Int corridors. **Pets:** Accepted.

BIRCHWOOD

Cobblestone Bed & Breakfast **BB**
(715) 354-3494. **$87-$135, 10 day notice.** 319 S Main St. 0.8 mi e of jct SR 48 and Main St; center. Int corridors. **Pets:** Accepted.

BLACK RIVER FALLS

Best Western-Arrowhead Lodge & Suites **SH**
(715) 284-9471. **$65-$165.** 600 Oasis Rd. I-94, exit 116, jct SR 54. Int corridors. **Pets:** Medium, other species. $10 daily fee/room. Service with restrictions, supervision.

Days Inn **SH**
(715) 284-4333. **Call for rates.** 919 Hwy 54 E. I-94, exit 116, just w. Int corridors. **Pets:** Small. $15 daily fee/room. Designated rooms, service with restrictions, supervision.

BURLINGTON

AmericInn Lodge & Suites **SH**
(262) 534-2125. **$79-$109.** 2059 S Browns Lake Rd. 3 mi n on SR 36 and 83, jct CR W. Int corridors. **Pets:** Medium. $25 one-time fee/pet. Designated rooms, service with restrictions, supervision.

CADOTT

Countryside Motel **M**
(715) 289-4000. **$56-$95.** 545 Lavorata Rd. SR 29, exit 91 (SR 27), just s. Int corridors. **Pets:** Accepted.

CHILTON

Best Western Stanton Inn **SH**
(920) 849-3600. **$79-$179, 3 day notice.** 1101 E Chestnut St. Jct US 151 and SR 32/57. Int corridors. **Pets:** Small, dogs only. $50 deposit/room. Designated rooms, service with restrictions, supervision.

CHIPPEWA FALLS

AmericInn of Chippewa Falls **SH**
(715) 723-5711. **$75-$135.** 11 W South Ave. 2 mi s on SR 124, access via CR J. Int corridors. **Pets:** Accepted.

ABA **♦♦♦** Avalon Hotel & Conference Center **SH**
(715) 723-2281. **$80-$100.** 1009 W Park Ave. Jct SR 124 and CR J. Ext/int corridors. **Pets:** Small, dogs only. $10 daily fee/pet. Designated rooms, service with restrictions.

COLUMBUS

♦♦ Super 8 Motel-Columbus **SH**
(920) 623-8800. **$70-$118.** 219 Industrial Dr. US 151, exit 118 (SR 16/60), just ne. Int corridors. **Pets:** Accepted.

DE FOREST

♦♦♦♦ Comfort Inn & Suites **SH**
(608) 846-9100. **$89-$109, 14 day notice.** 5025 County Hwy V. I-90/94, exit 126 (CR V), just w. Int corridors. **Pets:** Accepted.

♦♦♦♦ Holiday Inn Express **SH**
(608) 846-8686. **$89-$109, 7 day notice.** 7184 Morrisonville Rd. I-90/94, exit 126 (CR V), just e. Int corridors. **Pets:** Accepted.

DE PERE

ABA **♦♦♦♦** Kress Inn–Clarion Collection **SH**
(920) 403-5100. **$109-$499.** 300 Grant St. US 41, exit 163 (Main St), 1 mi e, then just s on 3rd St. Int corridors. **Pets:** Accepted.

DODGEVILLE

ABA **♦♦♦** Best Western Quiet House & Suites **SH**
(608) 935-7739. **Call for rates.** 1130 N Johns St. On US 18, just e of jct SR 23. **Pets:** $13 daily fee/pet. Designated rooms, supervision.

ABA **♦♦** Pine Ridge Motel **M**
(608) 935-3386. **$30-$79.** 405 CR YZ. On CR YZ, 0.5 mi e of jct SR 23. Ext corridors. **Pets:** Very small, dogs only. $20 deposit/pet. Designated rooms, service with restrictions, crate.

ABA **♦♦♦** Super 8 Motel of Dodgeville **SH**
(608) 935-3888. **$60-$90.** 1308 Johns St. Just n of US 18. Int corridors. **Pets:** $50 deposit/pet. Supervision.

DOOR COUNTY AREA

EGG HARBOR

ABA **♦♦** The Shallows **M**
(920) 868-3458. **$75-$410, 30 day notice.** 7353 Horseshoe Bay Rd, Hwy G. On CR G, 2.5 mi s. Ext corridors. **Pets:** Small, dogs only. $20 daily fee/pet. Service with restrictions, supervision.

FISH CREEK

♦♦ Julie's Park Cafe & Motel **M**
(920) 868-2999. **$45-$116, 10 day notice.** 4020 Hwy 42. On SR 42, 0.3 mi n. Ext corridors. **Pets:** Accepted.

GILLS ROCK

♦♦ Harbor House Inn **BB**
(920) 854-5196. **$79-$199, 21 day notice.** 12666 SR 42. On SR 42; center. Ext/int corridors. **Pets:** Accepted.

♦ Maple Grove Motel **M** ❖
(920) 854-2587. **Call for rates.** 809 SR 42. On SR 42, 0.3 mi e; 1.5 mi w of car ferry. Ext corridors. **Pets:** $10 daily fee/room. Service with restrictions, crate.

STURGEON BAY

♦♦ AmericInn of Sturgeon Bay **SH**
(920) 743-5898. **$69-$169.** 622 S Ashland Ave. On SR 42/57, 0.5 mi s of jct CR C/S. Int corridors. **Pets:** Accepted.

ABA **♦♦** Best Western Maritime Inn **SH**
(920) 743-7231. **Call for rates.** 1001 N 14th Ave. 1 mi n on Business Rt SR 42/57. Int corridors. **Pets:** Accepted.

ABA **♦♦** Super 8 Motel **SH**
(920) 743-9211. **Call for rates.** 409 Green Bay Rd. 1 mi s on Business Rt SR 42/57. Int corridors. **Pets:** Accepted.

END AREA

EAGLE RIVER

ABA **♦♦♦** Best Western Derby Inn **SH**
(715) 479-1600. **$76-$190, 3 day notice.** 1800 Hwy 45 N. On US 45, 1 mi n. Int corridors. **Pets:** Small. $50 deposit/room. Designated rooms, service with restrictions, supervision.

♦♦ Days Inn **SH**
(715) 479-5151. **Call for rates.** 844 Railroad St N. 0.5 mi n on US 45. Int corridors. **Pets:** Accepted.

EAST TROY

▼▼▼▼ Country Inn & Suites by Carlson SH
(262) 642-2100. **Call for rates.** 2921 O Ln. I-43, exit 36, at jct SR 120. Int corridors. **Pets:** Accepted.
⊠ ⑤M 🖥 💻 ⇌

EAU CLAIRE

ΦΦΦ ▼▼ AmericInn Motel & Suites SH
(715) 874-4900. **$75-$175.** 6200 Texaco Dr. I-94, exit 59, jct US 12. Int corridors. **Pets:** Medium, dogs only. $10 one-time fee/pet. Service with restrictions, supervision.
SAVE S⑥ ⊠ 🖥 💻 ⇌

▼▼▼▼ Best Western Trail Lodge Hotel & Suites SH
(715) 838-9989. **$80-$110.** 3340 Mondovi Rd. I-94, exit 65, just n. Int corridors. **Pets:** Other species. $100 deposit/room, $20 daily fee/pet. Designated rooms, service with restrictions, crate.
A$K S⑥ ⊠ ⑤M 🖥 💻 ⇌ ⊠

▼▼ Comfort Inn SH
(715) 833-9798. **$59-$119.** 3117 Craig Rd. I-94, exit 65, 1.3 mi n on SR 37; just s of jct US 12. Int corridors. **Pets:** Accepted.
A$K S⑥ ⊠ 🖥 💻 ⇌

▼▼ Days Inn-West SH
(715) 874-5550. **Call for rates.** 6319 Truax Ln. I-94, exit 59, jct US 12. Int corridors. **Pets:** Accepted.
⊠ 🖥 💻 ⇌

▼▼ Econo Lodge SH
(715) 833-8818. **$60-$100.** 4608 Royal Dr. I-94, exit 68, just n on SR 93, just w on Golf Rd, then just s. Int corridors. **Pets:** Accepted.
A$K S⑥ ⊠ 🖥 💻

ΦΦΦ ▼ Exel Inn of Eau Claire SH
(715) 834-3193. **$46-$66.** 2305 Craig Rd. I-94, exit 65, 1.3 mi n on SR 37; just w of jct US 12. Int corridors. **Pets:** Accepted.
SAVE S⑥ ⊠ 🖥 💻

▼▼▼ Grandstay Residential Suites SH
(715) 834-1700. **$84-$109.** 5310 Prill Rd. I-94, exit 70, 0.8 mi n on US 53. Int corridors. **Pets:** Accepted.
A$K S⑥ ⊠ ⑤M 🖥 💻 ⇌ ⊠

▼▼▼▼ Holiday Inn Campus Area SH
(715) 835-2211. **$98-$109.** 2703 Craig Rd. I-94, exit 65, 1.3 mi n on SR 37; just w of jct US 12. Int corridors. **Pets:** Accepted.
A$K S⑥ ⊠ ⑤M 🖥 💻 ⑪ ⇌ ⊠

▼▼▼▼ The Plaza Hotel & Suites LH
(715) 834-3181. **$62-$199.** 1202 W Clairemont Ave. I-94, exit 65, 1.3 mi n on SR 37; just w of jct US 12. Int corridors. **Pets:** Accepted.
A$K S⑥ ⊠ 🖥 💻 ⑪ ⇌ ⊠

▼▼▼▼ Ramada Convention Center LH
(715) 835-6121. **Call for rates.** 205 S Barstow St. Jct S Barstow and Gibson sts; downtown. Int corridors. **Pets:** Accepted.
⊠ 🖥 💻 ⑪ ⇌

▼▼▼▼ Sleep Inn & Suites Conference Center SH
(715) 874-2900. **$85-$160.** 5872 N 33rd Ave. I-29, exit 69 Hwy T, just s. Int corridors. **Pets:** Accepted.
A$K S⑥ ⊠ 🖥 💻 ⑪ ⇌ ⊠

EDGERTON

▼▼ Comfort Inn SH
(608) 884-2118. **$59-$129.** 11102 N Goede Rd. I-90, exit 163, just e. Int corridors. **Pets:** Accepted.
A$K S⑥ ⊠ 🖥 💻 ⇌

ELKHORN

▼▼ ▼ AmericInn Lodge & Suites SH
(262) 723-7799. **$79-$109.** 210 E Commerce Ct. I-43, exit 25, just s. Int corridors. **Pets:** Medium. $25 one-time fee/pet. Designated rooms, service with restrictions, supervision.
A$K S⑥ ⊠ ⑤M 🖥 💻 ⇌

FITCHBURG

▼▼▼▼ Candlewood Suites SH 🐾
(608) 271-3400. **Call for rates.** 5421 Caddis Bend. US 12/18, exit 260, 1.5 mi s. Int corridors. **Pets:** Other species. $25 one-time fee/room. Service with restrictions, crate.
⊠ ⑤M 🖥 💻 ⇌ ⊠

ΦΦΦ ▼▼▼▼ Quality Inn & Suites SH
(608) 274-7200. **$79-$159, 3 day notice.** 2969 Cahill Main. US 12/18, exit 260 (Fish Hatchery/CR PD) at CR PD (McKee Rd). Int corridors. **Pets:** Other species. $13 daily fee/room. Service with restrictions.
SAVE S⑥ ⊠ 🖥 💻 ⇌ ⊠

FOND DU LAC

▼▼▼ Comfort Inn Fond du Lac SH
(920) 921-4000. **Call for rates.** 77 Holiday Ln. Sw of jct US 41 and 151. Int corridors. **Pets:** Service with restrictions, crate.
⊠ 🖥 💻 ⇌ ⊠

▼▼▼ Executive Lodge of Fond du Lac SH
(920) 923-2020. **$53-$89.** 649 W Johnson St. On SR 23, 0.3 mi e jct of US 41. Int corridors. **Pets:** Accepted.
A$K S⑥ ⊠ 🖥 💻 ⇌

▼▼▼ Holiday Inn SH
(920) 923-1440. **$79-$239.** 625 W Rolling Meadows Dr. On US 151, just sw of jct US 41. Int corridors. **Pets:** Accepted.
A$K S⑥ ⊠ ⑤M 🖥 💻 ⑪ ⇌ ⊠

▼▼▼ Microtel Inn & Suites SH
(920) 929-4000. **Call for rates.** 920 S Military Rd. Jct US 41 and 151. Int corridors. **Pets:** Medium. $10 daily fee/room. Service with restrictions, supervision.
⊠ 🖥 💻 ⊠

ΦΦΦ ▼▼▼▼ Ramada Plaza Hotel LH
(920) 923-3000. **$69-$299.** 1 N Main St. Downtown. Int corridors. **Pets:** Small, dogs only. $20 daily fee/pet. Designated rooms, service with restrictions, crate.
SAVE S⑥ ⊠ 🖥 💻 ⑪ ⇌ ⊠

ΦΦΦ ▼▼▼ Super 8 Motel-FOND du LAC SH
(920) 922-1088. **$55-$105, 3 day notice.** 391 N Pioneer Rd. US 41, exit SR 23, just n on east frontage road (CR VV). Int corridors. **Pets:** Medium, dogs only. $15 daily fee/room. Designated rooms, service with restrictions, supervision.
SAVE S⑥ ⊠ 🖥 💻

GRANTSBURG

ΦΦΦ ▼ Wood River Motel M
(715) 463-2541. **$63-$115, 3 day notice.** 703 W SR 70. 1 mi w on SR 70. Ext corridors. **Pets:** Medium. $10 one-time fee/pet. Designated rooms, service with restrictions, supervision.
SAVE S⑥ ⊠ ⑤M 🖥

GREEN BAY

ΦΦΦ ▼▼▼ AmericInn SH
(920) 434-9790. **$85-$160, 30 day notice.** 2032 Velp Ave. US 41, exit 170, 0.3 mi w. Int corridors. **Pets:** Small. $10 daily fee/pet. Designated rooms, service with restrictions, supervision.
SAVE S⑥ ⊠ ⑤M 🖥 💻 ⇌

AmeriHost Inn-Green Bay SH
(920) 406-8200. **$79-$165.** 2911 Voyager Dr. I-43, exit 183 (Mason St), just e. Int corridors. **Pets:** Accepted.
SAVE S X &M 🛢 ▣ 🐾 ⊠

Baymont Inn-Green Bay SH
(920) 494-7887. **Call for rates.** 2840 S Oneida St. US 41, exit 164 (Oneida St), just e. Int corridors. **Pets:** Accepted.
SAVE X 🛢 ▣

Bay Motel M
(920) 494-3441. **$45-$73.** 1301 S Military Ave. US 41, exit 167 (Lombardi Ave), 0.4 mi e to Marlee, then 0.6 mi n. Ext corridors.
Pets: Accepted.
SAVE S X 🛢 ▣ ⑪

Best Western Midway Hotel SH 🐾
(920) 499-3161. **$79-$89.** 780 Armed Forces Dr. US 41, exit 167 (Lombardi Ave), 1.4 mi e to Holmgren Way, just s. Int corridors. **Pets:** Small, dogs only. $35 one-time fee/room. Designated rooms, service with restrictions, supervision.
ASK S X 🛢 ▣ ⑪ 🐾 ⊠

Candlewood Suites SH
(920) 430-7040. **$79-$199.** 1125 E Mason St. US 41, exit 168 (Mason St), 4 mi e. Int corridors. **Pets:** Accepted.
ASK S X 🛢 ▣

Comfort Inn by Choice Hotels SH
(920) 498-2060. **$65-$199.** 2841 Ramada Way. US 41, exit 164 (Oneida St), just e to Ramada Way, then just n. Int corridors.
Pets: Accepted.
ASK S X 🛢 ▣ 🐾

Country Inn & Suites By Carlson SH
(920) 336-6600. **Call for rates.** 2945 Allied St. US 41, exit 164 (Oneida St), just nw. Int corridors. **Pets:** Small, other species. $15 daily fee/pet. Designated rooms, service with restrictions, supervision.
X 🛢 ▣ 🐾 ⊠

Days Inn-Lambeau Field SH
(920) 498-8088. **$69-$125.** 1978 Holmgren Way. US 41, exit 167 (Lombardi Ave), 1.4 mi e, then just s. Int corridors. **Pets:** Accepted.
SAVE S X 🛢 ▣ 🐾

Exel Inn of Green Bay SH
(920) 499-3599. **$52-$72.** 2870 Ramada Way. US 41, exit 164 (Oneida St), just e. Int corridors. **Pets:** Accepted.
SAVE S X 🛢 🛢

Holiday Inn City Centre LH
(920) 437-5900. **Call for rates.** 200 Main St. Downtown. Int corridors.
Pets: Accepted.
X 🛢 ▣ ⑪ 🐾 ⊠

Quality Inn & Suites SH
(920) 437-8771. **Call for rates.** 321 S Washington St. On east side of Fox River, just s of Walnut St (SR 29); downtown. Int corridors.
Pets: Accepted.
X 🛢 ▣ 🐾 ⊠

Ramada Plaza Hotel SH
(920) 499-0631. **$84-$199.** 2750 Ramada Way. US 41, exit 164 (Oneida St), just e to Ramada Way, then 0.3 mi n. Int corridors.
Pets: Accepted.
ASK S X 🛢 ▣ ⑪ 🐾 ⊠

Residence Inn by Marriott SH
(920) 435-2222. **$187-$207.** 335 W St Joseph St. SR 172, exit Riverside Dr, 1.1 mi n on SR 57, then just e. Ext corridors. **Pets:** Accepted.
ASK S X 🛢 ▣ 🐾 ⊠

Super 8 Motel SH
(920) 494-2042. **$75-$92.** 2868 S Oneida St. US 41, exit 164 (Oneida St), just e. Int corridors. **Pets:** Other species. $15 one-time fee/room. Service with restrictions, supervision.
SAVE S X 🛢 ▣ ⊠

HAYWARD

AmericInn of Hayward SH
(715) 634-2700. **Call for rates.** 15601 US Hwy 63. On US 63, just n of jct SR 77. Int corridors. **Pets:** Accepted.
X 🛢 ▣ 🐾

Comfort Suites SH
(715) 634-0700. **$89-$189.** 15586 CR B. On CR B, 0.5 mi s of jct SR 27. Int corridors. **Pets:** Other species. $13 daily fee/room. Designated rooms, service with restrictions, supervision.
SAVE S X &M 🛢 ▣ 🐾 ⊠

Northern Pine Inn SH 🐾
(715) 634-4959. **$60-$100.** 9966 N Hwy 27. On SR 27 S, 1.7 mi s of jct US 63. Ext/int corridors. **Pets:** Medium. $5 daily fee/pet. Service with restrictions, supervision.
SAVE S X 🛢 ▣ 🐾 ⊠

Ramada-Hayward SH
(715) 634-4100. **$120-$145, 3 day notice.** 10290 Hwy 27 S. On SR 27 S, 0.7 mi s of jct US 63. Int corridors. **Pets:** Accepted.
X 🛢 ▣ ⑪ 🐾

Ross' Teal Lake Lodge and Teal Wing Golf Club CA
(715) 462-3631. **$160-$340, 21 day notice.** 12425 N Ross Rd. On SR 77, 20 mi ne of jct US 63. Ext corridors. **Pets:** Accepted.
SAVE X 🛢 ▣ ⑪ 🐾 ⊠ 🖢

Super 8 Motel SH
(715) 634-2646. **Call for rates.** 10444 N SR 27. On SR 27, 0.3 mi s of jct US 63. Ext/int corridors. **Pets:** Accepted.
X 🛢 ▣ 🐾

HILLSBORO

Sleep Inn Hillsboro SH
(608) 489-3000. **$70-$110.** 1235 Water Ave (Hwy 33). SR 33 and 80/82, just w. Int corridors. **Pets:** Large. $10 one-time fee/pet. Designated rooms, service with restrictions, supervision.
ASK S X 🛢 ▣ 🐾 ⊠

HUDSON

Comfort Inn SH
(715) 386-6355. **$75-$90.** 811 Dominion Dr. I-94, exit 2 (CR F), 1 mi w on south frontage road (Crestview Dr). Int corridors. **Pets:** Accepted.
ASK S X 🛢 ▣ 🐾

Super 8 Motel of Hudson SH
(715) 386-8800. **$70-$110.** 808 Dominion Dr. I-94, exit 2 (CR F), 1 mi w on south frontage road (Crestview Dr). Int corridors. **Pets:** Medium. $15 daily fee/pet. Designated rooms, service with restrictions, supervision.
SAVE S X 🛢 ▣ 🐾

HURLEY

Days Inn of Hurley SH
(715) 561-3500. **Call for rates.** 13355 N US Hwy 51. Jct US 2 and 51, 0.4 mi s on US 51. Int corridors. **Pets:** Small, other species. $15 daily fee/room. Designated rooms, service with restrictions, supervision.
X 🛢 ▣ 🐾 ⊠

JANESVILLE

Best Western Janesville SH
(608) 756-4511. **$75-$189.** 3900 Milton Ave. I-90, exit 171A (SR 26), just e. Int corridors. **Pets:** Accepted.
SAVE S X 🛢 ▣ ⑪ 🐾 ⊠

AAA ▼▼ **Microtel Inn** 🆂🅷
(608) 752-3121. **$56-$80.** 3121 Wellington Pl. I-90, exit 171C (US 14), just se. Int corridors. **Pets:** $25 daily fee/pet. Designated rooms, service with restrictions, supervision.
🆂🅰🆅🅴 ❌ 🔥🅼 🔋

JEFFERSON

▼▼ **Rodeway Inn** Ⓜ
(920) 674-4404. **Call for rates.** 1456 S Ryan Ave. On SR 26, 1.2 mi s of jct US 18. Int corridors. **Pets:** Accepted.
❌ 🔥🅼 🔋 💻 ⊇

JOHNSON CREEK

AAA ▼▼ **Days Inn–Johnson Creek** 🆂🅷
(920) 699-8000. **Call for rates.** W4545 Linmar Ln. I-94, exit 267 (SR 26), just ne. Int corridors. **Pets:** Accepted.
🆂🅰🆅🅴 ❌ 🔋 💻 ⊇ ❌

KENOSHA

AAA ▼▼ **Best Western Harborside Inn & Kenosha**
Convention Center 🆂🅷
(262) 658-3281. **$99-$279.** 5125 6th Ave. Just ne of jct SR 32 and 158; downtown. Int corridors. **Pets:** Small. $25 one-time fee/pet. Designated rooms, service with restrictions, supervision.
🆂🅰🆅🅴 🆂🅳 ❌ 🔋 💻 ⊇ ❌

▼▼▼ **Country Inn & Suites By Carlson** 🆂🅷
(262) 857-3680. **Call for rates.** 7011 122nd Ave. I-94, exit 344 (SR 50), just nw. Int corridors. **Pets:** Small, other species. $15 daily fee/pet. Designated rooms, service with restrictions, supervision.
❌ 🔥🅼 🔋 💻 ⊇ ❌

LA CROSSE

AAA ▼▼ **Americas Best Value Inn** 🆂🅷
(608) 781-3070. **$48-$94.** 2622 Rose St. I-90, exit 3, just s. Int corridors. **Pets:** Medium. $50 deposit/pet, $10 daily fee/pet. Designated rooms, service with restrictions, supervision.
🆂🅰🆅🅴 🆂🅳 ❌ 🔋 💻

AAA ▼▼▼ **Best Western-Midway Hotel Riverfront**
Resort 🆂🅷 🐾
(608) 781-7000. **$89-$145.** 1835 Rose St. I-90, exit 3, 1 mi s on US 53. Int corridors. **Pets:** Medium, dogs only. $25 deposit/room. Designated rooms, service with restrictions, supervision.
🆂🅰🆅🅴 🆂🅳 ❌ 🔋 💻 🍴 ⊇ ❌

AAA ▼▼ **Days Inn Hotel & Conference Center** 🆂🅷
(608) 783-1000. **Call for rates.** 101 Sky Harbour Dr. I-90, exit 2, just sw; on French Island. Int corridors. **Pets:** Accepted.
🆂🅰🆅🅴 ❌ 🔋 💻 🍴 ⊇ ❌

AAA ▼▼ **Econo Lodge** 🆂🅷 🐾
(608) 781-0200. **$50-$130.** 1906 Rose St. I-90, exit 3, 0.9 mi s on US 53. Int corridors. **Pets:** Small, other species. $50 deposit/pet. Designated rooms, service with restrictions, supervision.
🆂🅰🆅🅴 🆂🅳 ❌ 🔋 💻

AAA ▼▼▼ **Exel Inn of La Crosse** 🆂🅷
(608) 781-0400. **$49-$74.** 2150 Rose St. I-90, exit 3, 0.8 mi s on US 53. Int corridors. **Pets:** Accepted.
🆂🅰🆅🅴 🆂🅳 ❌ 🔋 💻

▼▼▼ **Grandstay Residential Suites of La Crosse** 🆂🅷
(608) 796-1615. **$85-$179.** 525 Front St N. I-90, exit 3; downtown. Int corridors. **Pets:** Accepted.
A$K ❌ 🔋 💻 ⊇ ❌

AAA ▼▼▼ **Holiday Inn Hotel & Suites** 🆂🅷
(608) 784-4444. **Call for rates.** 200 Pearl St. Downtown. Int corridors. **Pets:** Accepted.
🆂🅰🆅🅴 ❌ 🔋 💻 🍴 ⊇

AAA ▼▼▼ **The Radisson Hotel La Crosse** 🅻🅷
(608) 784-6680. **$149-$199.** 200 Harborview Plaza. Just w of US 53; downtown. Int corridors. **Pets:** Accepted.
🆂🅰🆅🅴 🆂🅳 ❌ 🔋 💻 🍴 ⊇

LADYSMITH

AAA ▼▼ **AmericInn Motel & Suites** 🆂🅷
(715) 532-6650. **Call for rates.** 800 W College Ave. On SR 27, 0.5 mi s of US 8. Int corridors. **Pets:** $10 daily fee/pet. Service with restrictions, crate.
🆂🅰🆅🅴 ❌ 🔋 💻 ⊇

LAND O'LAKES

▼▼▼ **Sunrise Lodge** 🅲🅰
(715) 547-3684. **$85-$210, 21 day notice.** 5894 W Shore Dr. 2 mi s on US 45, 2.8 mi e on CR E, then 1 mi n. Ext corridors. **Pets:** Accepted.
A$K 🔋 💻 🍴 ❌ 🅿

LODI

AAA ▼▼▼ **Best Western Countryside Inn** 🆂🅷 🐾
(608) 592-1450. **$59-$109.** W 9250 Prospect Dr. I-90/94, exit 119, just w. Int corridors. **Pets:** Other species. $15 one-time fee/pet. Designated rooms, service with restrictions.
🆂🅰🆅🅴 🆂🅳 ❌ 🔥🅼 🔋 💻 ⊇ ❌

▼▼▼ **Lodi Valley Suites** 🆂🅷
(608) 592-7331. **$65-$85.** 1440 N Hwy 113. On SR 113; 1.5 mi n of jct SR 60. Int corridors. **Pets:** Accepted.
A$K 🆂🅳 ❌ 🔋 💻

LUCK

AAA ▼▼ **Luck Country Inn** 🆂🅷
(715) 472-2000. **$55-$139.** 10 Robertson Rd. Jct SR 35 and 48. Int corridors. **Pets:** Very small. $5 daily fee/pet. Designated rooms, service with restrictions, supervision.
🆂🅰🆅🅴 🆂🅳 ❌ 🔋 💻 🍴 ⊇

MADISON

AAA ▼▼▼ **Best Western East Towne Suites** 🆂🅷
(608) 244-2020. **Call for rates.** 4801 Annamark Dr. I-90/94, exit 135A southbound, exit 135C northbound, just sw on US 151. Int corridors. **Pets:** Medium. $15 one-time fee/pet. Designated rooms, service with restrictions, supervision.
🆂🅰🆅🅴 ❌ 🔋 💻 ⊇

AAA ▼▼ **Best Western West Towne Suites** 🆂🅷 🐾
(608) 833-4200. **$74-$179.** 650 Grand Canyon Dr. US 12 and 14, exit 255 (Gammon Rd), just e on Odana Rd, then just sw. Int corridors. **Pets:** Medium. $25 deposit/pet. Designated rooms, service with restrictions, supervision.
🆂🅰🆅🅴 🆂🅳 ❌ 🔋 💻

AAA ▼▼▼ **Clarion Suites Madison-Central** 🆂🅷
(608) 284-1234. **$94-$179.** 2110 Rimrock Rd. US 12 and 18, exit 262 (Rimrock Rd), just nw. Int corridors. **Pets:** $25 daily fee/pet. Designated rooms, service with restrictions, supervision.
🆂🅰🆅🅴 🆂🅳 ❌ 🔋 💻 ⊇

▼▼▼ **Comfort Suites-Madison** 🆂🅷
(608) 836-3033. **Call for rates.** 1253 John Q Hammons Dr. US 12 and 14, exit 252 (Greenway Blvd), just sw. Int corridors. **Pets:** Accepted.
❌ 🔋 💻 ⊇ ❌

AAA ▼▼▼ **Crowne Plaza Hotel and Resort** 🅻🅷 🐾
(608) 244-4703. **$139-$179.** 4402 E Washington Ave. I-90/94, exit 135A (US 151), 0.4 mi w. Int corridors. **Pets:** Other species. $20 one-time fee/room. Designated rooms, service with restrictions.
🆂🅰🆅🅴 🆂🅳 ❌ 🔋 💻 🍴 ⊇ ❌

Days Inn-Madison SH
(608) 223-1800. **$72-$160.** 4402 E Broadway Service Rd. US 12 and 18, exit 266 (US 51), just ne. Int corridors. **Pets:** Medium. $10 daily fee/pet. Service with restrictions, supervision.

Econo Lodge of Madison SH
(608) 241-4171. **$55-$99, 30 day notice.** 4726 E Washington Ave. I-90/94, exit 135A (US 151), just w. Int corridors. **Pets:** Accepted.

Exel Inn of Madison SH
(608) 241-3861. **$53-$73.** 4202 E Towne Blvd. I-90/94, exit 135A (US 151), 0.5 mi w. Int corridors. **Pets:** Accepted.

ExtendedStay Deluxe SH
(608) 833-2121. **Call for rates.** 45 Junction Ct. SR 12, exit 253 (Old Sauk Rd), just w. Int corridors. **Pets:** Other species. $75 one-time fee/pet. Service with restrictions.

GrandStay Residential Suites SH
(608) 241-2500. **$89-$169.** 5317 High Crossing Blvd. I-90/94, exit 135C (US 151), 0.5 mi e. Int corridors. **Pets:** Accepted.

Holiday Inn Express-Madison SH
(608) 255-7400. **$95-$200.** 722 John Nolen Dr. US 12 and 18, exit 263 (John Nolen Dr), just ne. Int corridors. **Pets:** Accepted.

Howard Johnson Plaza SH
(608) 244-2481. **$99-$149.** 3841 E Washington Ave. I-90/94, exit 135A (US 151), 1 mi w. Int corridors. **Pets:** Accepted.

La Quinta Inn & Suites SH
(608) 245-0123. **$109-$135.** 5217 E Terrace Dr. US 151, exit 98B (American Pkwy), just sw. Int corridors. **Pets:** Other species. Service with restrictions, supervision.

Microtel Inn & Suites SH
(608) 242-9000. **$59-$89.** 2139 E Springs Dr. I-90/94, exit 135A, just s, then 0.5 mi e. Int corridors. **Pets:** Medium, other species. $10 daily fee/pet. Designated rooms, service with restrictions, supervision.

Red Roof Inn-Madison #7052 M
(608) 241-1787. **Call for rates.** 4830 Hayes Rd. I-90/94, exit 135A, just sw on US 151. Ext corridors. **Pets:** Accepted.

Residence Inn by Marriott SH
(608) 244-5047. **$199-$219.** 4862 Hayes Rd. I-90/94, exit 135A (US 151), just sw to Hayes Rd, then just ne. Int corridors. **Pets:** Accepted.

Select Inn SH
(608) 249-1815. **$65-$105.** 4845 Hayes Rd. I-90/94, exit 135A, just sw on US 151. Int corridors. **Pets:** $25 deposit/room, $15 daily fee/pet. Service with restrictions, supervision.

Sheraton Madison Hotel LH ❀
(608) 251-2300. **$275-$295.** 706 John Nolen Dr. US 12/18, exit 263 (John Nolen Dr), just n. Int corridors. **Pets:** Large. Service with restrictions.

Staybridge Suites SH
(608) 241-2300. **$129-$229.** 3301 City View Dr. I-90/94, exit 135C (US 151), just e on High Crossing Blvd. Int corridors. **Pets:** Small. $150 one-time fee/pet. Service with restrictions, crate.

Super 8 Motel-Madison SH
(608) 258-8882. **$60-$140.** 1602 W Beltline Hwy. US 12 and 18, exit 260B (CR D), just w on North Frontage Road. Int corridors. **Pets:** Accepted.

MANITOWOC

Best Western Lakefront Hotel SH
(920) 682-7000. **$129-$169.** 101 Maritime Dr. I-43, exit 152, 4.2 mi e on SR 42 N, then 1 mi s. Int corridors. **Pets:** Accepted.

Comfort Inn by Choice Hotels SH
(920) 683-0220. **$65-$85.** 2200 S 44th St. I-43, exit 149, just e. Int corridors. **Pets:** Accepted.

Holiday Inn SH
(920) 682-6000. **$105-$189.** 4601 Calumet Ave. I-43, exit 149, just e. Int corridors. **Pets:** Accepted.

MARSHFIELD

Baymont Inn and Suites-Marshfield SH
(715) 384-5240. **$69-$79.** 2107 N Central Ave. On SR 97; 1.6 mi n of SR 13. Int corridors. **Pets:** Accepted.

Comfort Inn SH
(715) 387-8691. **$59-$99.** 114 E Upham St. On SR 97; 0.8 mi n of jct SR 13. Int corridors. **Pets:** Accepted.

Holiday Inn & Conference Center SH
(715) 486-1500. **$99-$104.** 750 S Central Ave. Jct SR 13 and 97, 0.5 mi s on Business Rt 13. Int corridors. **Pets:** Medium, dogs only. $50 one-time fee/room. Designated rooms, service with restrictions, supervision.

Park Motel M
(715) 387-1741. **$35-$46.** 1806 S Roddis Ave. Jct SR 13 and 97, 1.0 mi s on Business Rt 13. Ext corridors. **Pets:** Accepted.

MAUSTON

Best Western Park Oasis Inn SH
(608) 847-6255. **$85-$109.** W5641 Hwy 82 E. I-90/94, exit 69, just se. Int corridors. **Pets:** Medium, other species. $50 deposit/pet, $5 daily fee/pet. Supervision.

Country Inn By Carlson SH ❀
(608) 847-5959. **Call for rates.** 1001 SR 82. I-90/94, exit 69, just ne. Int corridors. **Pets:** $10 one-time fee/room. Designated rooms, service with restrictions, crate.

Super 8 Motel M
(608) 847-2300. **Call for rates.** 1001A Hwy 82 E. I-90/94, exit 69, just ne. Int corridors. **Pets:** Accepted.

MEDFORD

▼ Malibu Inn Motel 🅜
(715) 748-3995. **Call for rates.** 854 N 8th St. On SR 13, 0.6 mi n of jct SR 64. Int corridors. **Pets:** Accepted.

[⊠] [🛏] [💻] [🏊]

MENOMONIE

▼▼ AmericInn Lodge & Suites 🆂🅷
(715) 235-4800. **Call for rates.** 1915 N Broadway. I-94, exit 41 (SR 25), just sw. Int corridors. **Pets:** Accepted.

[⊠] [🛏] [💻] [🏊]

▼▼ Comfort Inn 🆂🅷
(715) 233-1500. **$59-$200.** 1721 Plaza Dr NE. I-94, exit 45 (CR B), just sw. Int corridors. **Pets:** Accepted.

[A$K] [🆂🗖] [⊠] [🕭M] [🛏] [💻] [🏊]

⟨AAA⟩ ▼ Menomonie Motel 6 #4109 🆂🅷
(715) 235-6901. **$40-$59.** 2100 Stout St. I-94, exit 41 (SR 25), just se. Int corridors. **Pets:** Medium. Service with restrictions, supervision.

[SAVE] [🆂🗖] [⊠]

▼▼ Super 8 Motel-Menomonie 🆂🅷
(715) 235-8889. **$60-$100.** 1622 N Broadway. I-94, exit 41 (SR 25), just s. Int corridors. **Pets:** Small. $10 daily fee/pet. Designated rooms, no service, crate.

[A$K] [🆂🗖] [⊠] [🛏] [💻] [🏊]

MERRILL

⟨AAA⟩ ▼▼ AmericInn Lodge & Suites of Merrill 🆂🅷
(715) 536-7979. **$89-$149.** 3300 E Main St. US 51, exit 208, 0.5 mi w on SR 64. Int corridors. **Pets:** Large. $10 daily fee/pet. Service with restrictions, supervision.

[SAVE] [⊠] [🛏] [💻] [🏊] [☒]

▼▼ Super 8 Motel 🆂🅷
(715) 536-6880. **Call for rates.** 3209 E Main St. US 51, exit 208, 0.5 mi w on SR 64. Int corridors. **Pets:** Accepted.

[⊠] [🕭M] [🛏] [💻] [🏊]

MIDDLETON

⟨AAA⟩ ▼▼▼ Country Inn & Suites 🆂🅷
(608) 831-6970. **$114-$169.** 2212 Deming Way. I-12/14, exit 252 (Greenway Blvd), just w. Int corridors. **Pets:** Medium. $35 daily fee/pet. Designated rooms, no service, supervision.

[SAVE] [🆂🗖] [⊠] [🛏] [💻] [🏊]

⟨AAA⟩ ▼▼▼ Marriott Madison West 🅛🅷
(608) 831-2000. **$159-$179.** 1313 John Q Hammons Dr. US 12/14, exit 252 (Greenway Blvd), just w. Int corridors. **Pets:** Accepted.

[SAVE] [🆂🗖] [⊠] [💻] [🍴] [🏊]

▼▼▼ Residence Inn by Marriott-Madison West/Middleton 🆂🅷
(608) 662-1100. **$198-$218.** 8400 Market St. US 12/14 (Beltline), exit 252 (Greenway Blvd), just w, then just n; in Greenway Station. Int corridors. **Pets:** Accepted.

[A$K] [🆂🗖] [⊠] [🕭M] [🛏] [💻] [🏊] [☒]

⟨AAA⟩ ▼▼▼ Staybridge Suites by Holiday Inn 🆂🅷
(608) 664-5888. **$159-$179.** 7790 Elmwood Ave. US 12/14, exit 251 (University Ave), just nw. Int corridors. **Pets:** Medium. $150 one-time fee/room. Service with restrictions, crate.

[SAVE] [🆂🗖] [⊠] [🕭M] [🛏] [💻] [🏊]

MILWAUKEE METROPOLITAN AREA

BROOKFIELD

⟨AAA⟩ ▼▼▼▼ Best Western Midway Hotel 🆂🅷
(262) 786-9540. **$120-$160.** 1005 S Moorland Rd. I-94, exit 301A (Moorland Rd), just s. Int corridors. **Pets:** Medium. $50 deposit/room. Service with restrictions, supervision.

[SAVE] [🆂🗖] [⊠] [🛏] [💻] [🍴] [🏊] [☒]

⟨AAA⟩ ▼▼▼▼ Country Inn & Suites Milwaukee West 🅛🅷
(262) 782-1400. **$109-$239.** 1250 S Moorland Rd. I-94, exit 301A (Moorland Rd), just se. Int corridors. **Pets:** Medium. $75 one-time fee/room. Service with restrictions, crate.

[SAVE] [🆂🗖] [⊠] [🛏] [💻] [🍴] [🏊] [☒]

▼▼ Homestead Studio Suites Hotel-Milwaukee/Brookfield 🆂🅷
(262) 782-9300. **$95-$105.** 325 N Brookfield Rd. I-94, exit 297, 1.1 mi e on US 18, then just e. Int corridors. **Pets:** Other species. $75 one-time fee/pet. Service with restrictions.

[A$K] [🆂🗖] [⊠] [🛏] [💻]

▼▼▼ La Quinta Inn 🆂🅷
(262) 782-9100. **$85-$97.** 20391 W Bluemound Rd. I-94, exit 297, just e on US 18. Int corridors. **Pets:** Other species. Service with restrictions, supervision.

[A$K] [🆂🗖] [⊠] [🛏] [💻]

⟨AAA⟩ ▼▼▼▼ Sheraton Milwaukee Brookfield 🅛🅷
(262) 786-1100. **$99-$229.** 375 S Moorland Rd. I-94, exit 301B (Moorland Rd), just n. Int corridors. **Pets:** Accepted.

[SAVE] [🆂🗖] [⊠] [🕭M] [🛏] [💻] [🍴] [🏊] [☒]

▼▼ TownePlace Suites by Marriott 🆂🅷
(262) 784-8450. **$176-$215.** 600 N Calhoun Rd. I-94, exit 297 eastbound, 2.1 mi e on US 18; exit 301B (Moorland Rd) westbound, 1.5 mi n, then 0.4 mi w on US 18. Int corridors. **Pets:** Accepted.

[A$K] [🆂🗖] [⊠] [🛏] [💻] [🏊]

DELAFIELD

▼▼ La Quinta Inn & Suites Milwaukee-Delafield 🆂🅷
(262) 646-8500. **$85-$104.** 2801 Hillside Dr. I-94, exit 287, just s on SR 83, then just e. Int corridors. **Pets:** Other species. Service with restrictions, supervision.

[A$K] [🆂🗖] [⊠] [🕭M] [🛏] [💻] [🏊]

GERMANTOWN

⟨AAA⟩ ▼▼▼▼ Holiday Inn Express Milwaukee NW-Germantown 🆂🅷
(262) 255-1100. W 177 N9675 Riversbend Ln. US 41 and 45, exit CR Q (County Line Rd), then just w. Int corridors. **Pets:** Accepted.

[SAVE] [🆂🗖] [⊠] [🕭M] [🛏] [💻] [🏊] [☒]

⟨AAA⟩ ▼▼▼ Super 8 Motel-Germantown/Milwaukee 🆂🅷 ❀
(262) 255-0880. **$70-$159.** N96 W17490 County Line Rd. US 41 and 45, exit CR Q (County Line Rd), then just w. Int corridors. **Pets:** Large. $5 daily fee/pet. Service with restrictions, supervision.

[SAVE] [🆂🗖] [⊠] [🛏] [💻] [🏊] [☒]

GLENDALE

Exel Inn of Milwaukee Northeast SH
(414) 961-7272. **$66-$94.** 5485 N Port Washington Rd. I-43, exit 78A (Silver Spring Dr), just se. Int corridors. **Pets:** Accepted.
SAVE S6 X 8 8 💻

La Quinta Inn & Suites-Bayshore Town Center SH
(414) 962-6767. **$115-$149.** 5423 N Port Washington Rd. I-43, exit 78A (Silver Spring Dr), just se. Int corridors. **Pets:** Other species. Service with restrictions, supervision.
ASK S6 X 5M 8 💻 ➰ 🚫

Residence Inn by Marriott SH
(414) 352-0070. **$186-$230, 9 day notice.** 7275 N Port Washington Rd. I-43, exit 80 (Good Hope Rd), just e. Ext corridors. **Pets:** Accepted.
ASK S6 X 8 💻 ➰ 🚫

GRAFTON

Baymont Inn & Suites Milwaukee-Grafton SH
(262) 387-1180. **Call for rates.** 1415 Port Washington Rd. I-43, exit 92 (SR 60), just w, then just s. Int corridors. **Pets:** Medium. $10 daily fee/pet. Designated rooms, service with restrictions, supervision.
X 8 💻 ➰

HARTFORD

Super 8 Motel-Hartford SH
(262) 673-7431. **Call for rates.** 1539 E Sumner St. On SR 60, 1.1 mi e of center. Int corridors. **Pets:** Small. $50 deposit/pet. Designated rooms, service with restrictions, supervision.
SAVE X 8 💻

JACKSON

Comfort Inn & Suites of Jackson SH
(262) 677-1133. **Call for rates.** W227 N16890 Tillie Lake Ct. Nw of jct US 45 and SR 60. Int corridors. **Pets:** Accepted.
SAVE X 8 💻 ➰ 🚫

MEQUON

Best Western Quiet House & Suites SH
(262) 241-3677. **$86-$215.** 10330 N Port Washington Rd. I-43, exit 85 (Mequon Rd), just w on SR 167, then 1 mi s. Int corridors. **Pets:** Large. $15 daily fee/pet. Designated rooms, service with restrictions, supervision.
SAVE S6 X 5M 8 💻 ➰

The Chalet Motel of Mequon M
(262) 241-4510. **$62-$159.** 10401 N Port Washington Rd. I-43, exit 85 (Mequon Rd), just w on SR 167, then 1 mi s. Ext corridors. **Pets:** Accepted.
ASK S6 X 8 💻 🍴

MILWAUKEE

Best Western Inn Towne Hotel SH
(414) 224-8400. **$59-$129.** 710 N Old World 3rd St. Corner of Wisconsin Ave and N Old World 3rd St. Int corridors. **Pets:** Small, other species. Designated rooms, service with restrictions, supervision.
SAVE S6 X 8 💻 🍴

Country Inn & Suites By Carlson SH
(414) 762-6018. **Call for rates.** 6200 S 13th St. I-94, exit 319, just e on College Ave (CR ZZ). Int corridors. **Pets:** Small, other species. $15 daily fee/pet. Designated rooms, service with restrictions, supervision.
X 8 💻 ➰ 🚫

Holiday Inn Express Hotel & Suites Milwaukee Airport SH
(414) 563-4000. **Call for rates (no credit cards).** 1400 W Zellman Ct. I-94, exit 319, 0.4 mi e on College Ave (CR 22) to S 13th St, then just s. Int corridors. **Pets:** Medium. Designated rooms, service with restrictions, crate.
X 8 💻 ➰ 🚫

Holiday Inn Hotel and Suites SH 🐾
(414) 482-4444. **$119-$149.** 545 W Layton Ave. I-94, exit 317, 1.3 mi e. Int corridors. **Pets:** $25 one-time fee/pet. Designated rooms, service with restrictions, supervision.
SAVE S6 X 8 💻 🍴 ➰ 🚫

Hotel Metro-Milwaukee SH 🐾
(414) 272-1937. **$209-$349.** 411 E Mason St. Corner of Mason and Milwaukee sts. Int corridors. **Pets:** Small, other species. $25 one-time fee/pet. Designated rooms, service with restrictions, crate.
SAVE S6 X 5M 💻 🍴 🚫

Howard Johnson Milwaukee Airport Inn SH
(414) 282-7000. **Call for rates.** 1716 W Layton Ave. I-94, exit 317. Int corridors. **Pets:** Accepted.
X 8 💻 🍴 ➰

OAK CREEK

Comfort Suites Milwaukee Airport SH
(414) 570-1111. **$99-$159.** 6362 S 13th St. I-94, exit 319 (College Ave), just e on CR 22, then just s. Int corridors. **Pets:** Accepted.
ASK S6 X 5M 8 💻 ➰ 🚫

Exel Inn of Milwaukee South SH
(414) 764-1776. **$56-$79.** 1201 W College Ave. I-94, exit 319 (College Ave), just e. Int corridors. **Pets:** Accepted.
SAVE S6 X 8 💻

La Quinta Inn & Suites Milwaukee-Airport SH
(414) 762-2266. **$69-$94.** 7141 S 13th St. I-94, exit 320 (Rawson Ave), just se. Int corridors. **Pets:** Other species. Service with restrictions, supervision.
ASK S6 X 8 💻

MainStay Suites Oak Creek SH
(414) 571-8800. **$70-$190.** 1001 W College Ave. I-94, exit 319 (College Ave), just e. Int corridors. **Pets:** Large. $25 one-time fee/room. Service with restrictions, crate.
SAVE S6 X 8 💻

Red Roof Inn-Milwaukee #7031 M
(414) 764-3500. **Call for rates.** 6360 S 13th St. I-94, exit 319 (College Ave), just e. Ext corridors. **Pets:** Accepted.
X 8

OCONOMOWOC

Olympia Resort, Spa & Conference Center LH
(262) 369-4999. **$149.** 1350 Royale Mile Rd. I-94, exit 282 (SR 67), 1 mi n. Int corridors. **Pets:** Other species. $10 one-time fee/room. Service with restrictions, crate.
SAVE S6 X 8 💻 🍴 ➰ 🚫

PORT WASHINGTON

Holiday Inn Harborview SH 🐾
(262) 284-9461. **$79-$229.** 135 E Grand Ave. On SR 33, waterfront of Lake Michigan; downtown. Int corridors. **Pets:** Medium, dogs only. $25 one-time fee/room. Designated rooms, service with restrictions, crate.
SAVE S6 X 5M 8 💻 🍴 ➰ 🚫

SAUKVILLE

Saukville Super 8 Motel SH
(262) 284-9399. **$60-$125.** 180 Foster Rd. I-43, exit 96, just s. Int corridors. **Pets:** Accepted.
SAVE S6 X 8 💻 🚫

WAUKESHA

AAA ♦♦♦ Best Western Waukesha Grand SH
(262) 524-9300. **$74-$199.** 2840 N Grandview Blvd. I-94, exit 293, just
s on CR T. Int corridors. **Pets:** $10 one-time fee/room. Service with
restrictions, supervision.

SAVE SA ✕ &M 🛏 📺 ≋

♦♦ Extended StayAmerica-Milwaukee-Waukesha SH
(262) 798-0217. **$90-$100.** 2520 Plaza Ct. I-94, exit 297, just e on SR
18, then just s. Int corridors. **Pets:** Other species. $75 one-time fee/pet.
Service with restrictions.

ASK SA ✕ 🛏 📺

AAA ♦♦♦ Select Inn SH
(262) 786-6015. **$55-$140.** 2510 Plaza Ct. I-94, exit 297, just w on CR
JJ (Bluemound Rd). Int corridors. **Pets:** Medium. $25 deposit/room, $10
daily fee/room. Designated rooms, service with restrictions, supervision.

SAVE SA ✕ 🛏 📺

WAUWATOSA

AAA ♦♦♦ Exel Inn of Milwaukee West SH
(414) 257-0140. **$61-$94.** 115 N Mayfair Rd. I-94, exit 304B, just n on
SR 100. Int corridors. **Pets:** Accepted.

SAVE SA ✕ 🛏 📺

AAA ♦♦♦ Holiday Inn Express-Medical Center SH
(414) 778-0333. **Call for rates.** 11111 W North Ave. US 45, exit 42A,
just n on SR 100, then just w. Int corridors. **Pets:** Accepted.

SAVE ✕ 🛏 📺

END METROPOLITAN AREA

MINERAL POINT

♦♦♦ Comfort Inn SH
(608) 987-4747. **$50-$150.** 1345 Business Park Rd. On US 151; 0.6 mi
n of jct SR 23 and 39. Int corridors. **Pets:** Accepted.

ASK SA ✕ 🛏 📺 ≋

MINOCQUA

AAA ♦♦♦ AmericInn of Minocqua SH
(715) 356-3730. **$76-$192.** 700 Hwy 51. On US 51; downtown. Int
corridors. **Pets:** Accepted.

SAVE SA ✕ 🛏 📺 ≋ ✕

♦♦ Comfort Inn-Minocqua SH
(715) 358-2588. **$61-$115.** 8729 US 51 N. On US 51 at SR 70 W. Int
corridors. **Pets:** Other species. $10 daily fee/pet. Crate.

ASK SA ✕ 🛏 📺 ≋

AAA ♦ Super 8 Motel M
(715) 356-9541. **$53-$89.** 8730 Hwy 51 N. On US 51 at SR 70 W.
Ext/int corridors. **Pets:** Accepted.

SAVE SA ✕

MONONA

♦♦ AmericInn of Madison South/Monona SH
(608) 222-8601. **$99-$199.** 101 W Broadway. US 12/18, exit 265
(Monona Dr), just nw. Int corridors. **Pets:** Accepted.

ASK ✕ 🛏 📺 ≋ ✕

♦♦♦♦ Country Inn & Suites By Carlson SH
(608) 221-0055. **Call for rates.** 400 River Pl. US 12/18, exit 265
(Monona Dr), just nw. Int corridors. **Pets:** Small, other species. $15 daily
fee/pet. Designated rooms, service with restrictions, supervision.

✕ 🛏 📺 ≋ ✕

MONROE

AAA ♦♦♦ Gasthaus Motel M
(608) 328-8395. **$59-$99.** 685 30th St. 1.5 mi s on SR 69. Ext corridors. **Pets:** Other species. $10 daily fee/pet. Designated rooms, no service,
supervision.

SAVE ✕ &M 🛏 📺

♦♦ Super 8 Motel SH
(608) 325-1500. **$59-$70.** 500 6th St. On SR 69 S, 0.5 mi s of jct SR
81/11. Int corridors. **Pets:** Accepted.

ASK SA ✕ 🛏

NEENAH

♦♦♦♦ Holiday Inn Neenah Riverwalk SH
(920) 725-8441. **Call for rates.** 123 E Wisconsin Ave. US 41, exit 132
(Main St), 2 mi e; downtown. Int corridors. **Pets:** Accepted.

✕ 🛏 📺 🍴 ≋ ✕

NEILLSVILLE

♦♦ Super 8 Motel-Neillsville SH
(715) 743-8080. **Call for rates.** 1000 E Division St. US 10, jct Boon
and Division St. Int corridors. **Pets:** Accepted.

✕ 🛏 📺

NEW GLARUS

♦♦♦ Chalet Landhaus Inn SH
(608) 527-5234. **$89-$215.** 801 Hwy 69. On SR 69. Int corridors.
Pets: Accepted.

ASK SA ✕ 🛏 📺 🍴 ≋ ✕

AAA ♦♦ Swiss Aire Motel SH
(608) 527-2138. **$59-$99.** 1200 Hwy 69. Just s of jct SR 39/69.
Pets: Other species. $10 daily fee/pet. Designated rooms, no service,
supervision.

SAVE ✕ 🛏 📺

NEW LISBON

AAA ♦♦♦ Travelers Inn of New Lisbon SH
(608) 562-5141. **$58-$159.** 1700 E Bridge St. I-90/94, exit 61 (SR 80),
just ne. Int corridors. **Pets:** Other species. $50 deposit/pet. Designated
rooms, service with restrictions, supervision.

SAVE SA ✕ 🛏 📺 ≋

NEW LONDON

AAA ♦ Americas Best Value Inn New London SH
(920) 982-5820. **$49-$115.** 1409 N Shawano St. US 45, exit US 54,
just n. Int corridors. **Pets:** Dogs only. $8 daily fee/pet. Service with restric-
tions, supervision.

SAVE SA ✕ 🛏 📺 ≋

♦♦♦ AmericInn Lodge & Suites of New London SH
(920) 982-5700. **$69-$189.** 1404 N Shawano St. US 45, exit US 54,
just n. Int corridors. **Pets:** Accepted.

ASK SA ✕ &M 🛏 📺 ≋

NEW RICHMOND

▼▼ **AmericInn Motel & Suites** SH
(715) 246-3993. **$69-$95.** 1020 S Knowles Ave. Just s on SR 65. Int corridors. **Pets:** Accepted.
(ASK) (S6) (✕) (🛏) (📺) (🏊) (✕)

▼▼ **Super 8 Motel** SH
(715) 246-7829. **Call for rates.** 1561 Dorset Ln. Just s on SR 65. Int corridors. **Pets:** Accepted.
(✕) (🛏) (📺)

ONALASKA

▼▼ **Comfort Inn by Choice Hotels** SH
(608) 781-7500. **Call for rates.** 1223 Crossing Meadows Dr. I-90, exit 4, just e on SR 157, then w on CR SS. Int corridors. **Pets:** Accepted.
(✕) (🛏) (📺) (🏊)

▼▼▼ **Holiday Inn Express** SH
(608) 783-6555. **$80-$110.** 9409 Hwy 16. I-90, exit 5, 1 mi e. Int corridors. **Pets:** Accepted.
(ASK) (S6) (✕) (🛏) (📺) (🏊) (✕)

▼▼ **Microtel Inn** SH
(608) 783-0833. **$60-$70.** 3240 N Kinney Coulee Rd. I-90, exit 5, just ne. Int corridors. **Pets:** Accepted.
(ASK) (S6) (✕) (🛏) (📺)

OSCEOLA

AAA ▼▼ **River Valley Inn** SH
(715) 294-4060. **$69-$129.** 1030 Cascade St. Just n on SR 35. Int corridors. **Pets:** Small, dogs only. $10 daily fee/pet. Service with restrictions, supervision.
(SAVE) (S6) (✕) (🛏) (📺) (🏊)

OSHKOSH

▼▼ **Fairfield Inn by Marriott** SH
(920) 233-8504. **$72-$93.** 1800 S Koeller Rd. US 41, exit 117 (9th Ave), 0.8 mi s on east frontage road. Int corridors. **Pets:** Accepted.
(ASK) (S6) (✕) (🛏) (📺) (🏊)

▼▼▼ **Hawthorn Inn & Suites** SH
(920) 303-1133. **$109-$449.** 3105 S Washburn St. US 41, exit 116 (SR 44), just w, then just s. Int corridors. **Pets:** Accepted.
(ASK) (S6) (✕) (🛏M) (🛏) (📺) (🍴) (🏊) (✕)

AAA ▼▼▼ **Holiday Inn Express Hotel & Suites** SH
(920) 303-1300. **$105-$275.** 2251 Westowne Ave. US 41, exit 119, 0.4 mi w of jct SR 21. Int corridors. **Pets:** Accepted.
(SAVE) (✕) (🛏M) (🛏) (📺) (🏊) (✕)

▼▼ **La Quinta Inn Oshkosh** SH
(920) 233-4190. **$65-$70.** 1950 Omro Rd. US 41, exit 119, jct SR 21. Int corridors. **Pets:** Other species. Service with restrictions, supervision.
(ASK) (S6) (✕) (🛏) (📺)

PLATTEVILLE

▼▼ **Mound View Inn** SH
(608) 348-9518. **$65-$85, 3 day notice.** 1755 E Business Hwy 151. On US 151, exit 21, just w. Int corridors. **Pets:** Accepted.
(✕) (🛏) (✕)

AAA ▼▼ **Super 8 Motel** SH ❀
(608) 348-8800. **Call for rates.** 100 Hwy 80/81 S. Jct US 151 and SR 80. Int corridors. **Pets:** Other species. $10 one-time fee/pet. Service with restrictions, supervision.
(SAVE) (✕) (🛏) (📺)

PLEASANT PRAIRIE

▼▼ **Holiday Inn Express Hotel & Suites** SH
(262) 942-6000. **Call for rates.** 7887 94th Ave. I-94, exit 344 (SR 50), 1.5 mi e, then 0.3 mi s. Int corridors. **Pets:** Accepted.
(✕) (🛏M) (🛏) (📺) (🏊) (✕)

▼▼ **La Quinta Inn-Pleasant Prairie** SH
(262) 857-7911. **$69-$80.** 7540 118th Ave. I-94, exit 344 (SR 50), just e. Int corridors. **Pets:** Other species. Service with restrictions, supervision.
(ASK) (S6) (✕) (🛏) (📺)

PLOVER

AAA ▼▼ **Sleep Inn & Suites** SH
(715) 342-0400. **$80-$130.** 1560 American Dr. I-39, exit 153, just w. Int corridors. **Pets:** Medium. $15 daily fee/room. Designated rooms, service with restrictions, supervision.
(SAVE) (✕) (🛏) (📺) (🏊)

PORTAGE

▼▼ **Super 8 Motel-Portage** SH
(608) 742-8330. **$55-$85.** 3000 New Pinery Rd. I-39, exit 92, just s. Int corridors. **Pets:** Other species. $10 daily fee/pet. Service with restrictions, supervision.
(ASK) (S6) (✕) (🛏) (📺)

PRAIRIE DU CHIEN

AAA ▼▼ **Best Western Quiet House & Suites** SH
(608) 326-4777. **$60-$180.** US 18 and SR 35. On US 18, 1.9 mi e of jct SR 27 N. Ext/int corridors. **Pets:** Accepted.
(SAVE) (✕) (🛏) (📺) (🏊)

▼▼ **Bridgeport Inn** SH
(608) 326-6082. **Call for rates.** Hwy 18, 35 & 60 S. On US 18, 2.2 mi e of jct SR 27 N. Int corridors. **Pets:** Accepted.
(✕) (🛏) (🏊)

AAA ▼ **Brisbois Motor Inn** M ❀
(608) 326-8404. **Call for rates.** 533 N Marquette Rd. On SR 35 N, 0.5 mi n of jct US 18/SR 35 S and 27 N. Ext/int corridors. **Pets:** $10 one-time fee/room. Designated rooms, service with restrictions, supervision.
(SAVE) (✕) (🛏) (📺) (🏊)

AAA ▼▼▼ **Country Inn & Suites By Carlson** SH
(608) 326-5700. **$80-$149.** 1801 Cabela's Dr. On SR 35; 2 mi n of jct US 18/SR 35 S and 27 N. Int corridors. **Pets:** Other species. Service with restrictions, supervision.
(SAVE) (S6) (✕) (🛏) (📺) (🍴) (🏊) (✕)

AAA ▼ **Holiday Motel** M
(608) 326-2448. **$35-$135.** 1010 S Marquette Rd. On US 18, 1 mi e of jct SR 27 N. Ext corridors. **Pets:** Medium, other species. $15 daily fee/pet. Service with restrictions, supervision.
(SAVE) (S6) (✕) (🛏)

AAA ▼▼ **Super 8 Motel-Prairie Du Chien** SH
(608) 326-8777. **Call for rates.** 1930 S Marquette Rd. On US 18, 1.9 mi e of jct SR 27 N. Ext/int corridors. **Pets:** Accepted.
(SAVE) (✕) (🛏) (📺)

RACINE

▼▼▼ **Racine Marriott Hotel** LH
(262) 886-6100. **$198-$218.** 7111 Washington Ave. I-94, exit 333, 4 mi e on SR 20. Int corridors. **Pets:** Accepted.
(ASK) (S6) (✕) (🛏) (📺) (🍴) (🏊) (✕)

▼▼ **Super 8-Racine** SH
(262) 884-0486. **Call for rates.** 1150 Oakes Rd. I-94, exit 333, 4 mi e on SR 20. Int corridors. **Pets:** Accepted.
(✕) (🛏)

REEDSBURG

Copper Springs Motel M
(608) 524-4312. **$48-$68, 5 day notice.** E7278 Hwy 23 & 33. 2 mi e on SR 23 and 33. Ext corridors. **Pets:** Accepted.

RHINELANDER

Best Western Claridge Motor Inn SH
(715) 362-7100. **$84-$150.** 70 N Stevens St. Between Davenport and Rives St; downtown. Int corridors. **Pets:** Other species. $25 deposit/room, $10 daily fee/pet. Designated rooms, service with restrictions, supervision.

Comfort Inn SH
(715) 369-1100. **$59-$159.** 1490 Lincoln St. On Business Rt US 8, 2.6 mi e of jct SR 47. Int corridors. **Pets:** Accepted.

Holiday Acres Resort SH
(715) 369-1500. **$69-$139.** 4060 S Shore Dr. 4.5 mi e on Business Rt US 8, 2.3 mi n on W Lake George Rd. Ext/int corridors. **Pets:** Accepted.

Holiday Inn Express SH
(715) 369-3600. **$76-$176.** 668 W Kemp St. On Business Rt US 8, just e of jct SR 47. Int corridors. **Pets:** Accepted.

RICE LAKE

Microtel Inn & Suites SH
(715) 736-2010. **$60-$90.** 2771 Decker Dr. US 53, exit 140 (CR O), just ne. Int corridors. **Pets:** Accepted.

RICHLAND CENTER

The Center Lodge SH
(608) 647-8988. **$70-$90, 10 day notice.** 100 Foundry Dr. 0.9 mi e on US 14. Int corridors. **Pets:** Accepted.

RIPON

AmericInn of Ripon SH
(920) 748-7578. **$69-$185.** 1219 W Fond du Lac St. 1.8 mi w on SR 23. Int corridors. **Pets:** Accepted.

Comfort Suites at Royal Ridges SH
(920) 748-5500. **$69-$179.** 2 Westgate Dr. 2 mi w on SR 23. Int corridors. **Pets:** Accepted.

RIVER FALLS

Super 8 Motel SH
(715) 425-8388. **Call for rates.** 1207 St. Croix St. On SR 65, 0.5 mi w jct SR 35. Int corridors. **Pets:** Medium. $5 daily fee/pet, $15 one-time fee/room. Supervision.

ROTHSCHILD

Comfort Inn SH
(715) 355-4449. **$75-$120.** 1510 County Hwy XX. I-39, exit 185 (Business Rt US 51), just se. Int corridors. **Pets:** Medium, dogs only. $15 daily fee/room. Designated rooms, service with restrictions, supervision.

SHAWANO

Comfort Inn & Suites SH
(715) 524-9090. **$79-$169.** W7393 River Bend Rd. SR 29, exit 225, just n on SR 22. Int corridors. **Pets:** Accepted.

Super 8 Motel-Shawano SH
(715) 526-6688. **$46-$90.** 211 Waukechon St. 1.2 mi e on SR 29 business route; SR 29, exit 227, 1.8 mi n. then 1.1 mi w. Int corridors. **Pets:** Other species. $25 deposit/pet. Service with restrictions, supervision.

SHEBOYGAN

Americas Best Value Inn-Sheboygan SH
(920) 458-8080. **$79-$99.** 3402 Wilgus Rd. I-43, exit 126, just ne. Int corridors. **Pets:** Dogs only. $10 one-time fee/room. Designated rooms, service with restrictions, supervision.

Comfort Inn-Sheboygan SH
(920) 457-7724. **$70-$190.** 4332 N 40th St. I-43, exit 128, 0.3 mi e on Business Rt SR 42. Int corridors. **Pets:** Other species. $10 daily fee/pet. Designated rooms, service with restrictions, supervision.

La Quinta Inn Sheboygan SH
(920) 457-2321. **$69-$94.** 2932 Kohler Memorial Dr. I-43, exit 126, 1 mi e on SR 23. Int corridors. **Pets:** Other species. Service with restrictions, supervision.

SHEBOYGAN FALLS

Days Inn & Suites SH
(920) 467-4314. **$50-$170.** 600 Hwy 32 N. On SR 32, just s of jct SR 23. Int corridors. **Pets:** Accepted.

SHELL LAKE

AmericInn of Shell Lake SH
(715) 468-4494. **$69-$189.** 315 Hwy 63 S. On SR 63, just s. Int corridors. **Pets:** Accepted.

SIREN

The Lodge at Crooked Lake SH
(715) 349-2500. **$89-$265.** 24271 SR 35 N. On SR 35, 0.5 mi n of jct SR 70. Int corridors. **Pets:** Dogs only. $50 deposit/room, $10 one-time fee/pet. Service with restrictions, supervision.

Pine Wood Motel M
(715) 349-5225. **$45-$65.** 23862 Hwy 35 S. On SR 35, 0.3 mi s of jct SR 70 W and CR B E. Ext corridors. **Pets:** Accepted.

SPARTA

Best Nights Inn M
(608) 269-3066. **$39-$139.** 303 W Wisconsin St. I-90, exit 25 (SR 27), 0.5 mi n; exit 28 (SR 16), 1 mi w. Ext corridors. **Pets:** Small, other species. $7 daily fee/pet. Designated rooms, service with restrictions, supervision.

Best Western Sparta Trail Lodge SH
(608) 269-2664. **Call for rates.** 4445 Theatre Rd. I-90, exit 28 (US 16), just w. Int corridors. **Pets:** Accepted.

⚹⚹⚹ ▼▼▼ **Country Inn By Carlson** SH ❀
(608) 269-3110. **$79-$180.** 737 Avon Rd. I-90, exit 25 (SR 27), just n.
Int corridors. **Pets:** Other species. $10 daily fee/pet. Service with restrictions, supervision.
SAVE S♦ ✕ ♿ ♦ 🛏 ≈

▼▼ **Super 8 Sparta** SH
(608) 269-8489. **$60-$155.** 716 Avon Rd. I-90, exit 25 (SR 27), just n.
Int corridors. **Pets:** Accepted.
ASK S♦ ✕ ♦ 🛏 ≈

SPOONER

▼▼ **Best Western American Heritage Inn** SH
(715) 635-9770. **Call for rates.** 101 E Maple St. On SR 70 just e of US
63, 1 mi w of US 53. Int corridors. **Pets:** Small, other species. $15 daily
fee/room. Designated rooms, service with restrictions, supervision.
✕ ♦ 🛏 ≈ ✕

⚹⚹⚹ ▼▼▼ **Country House Motel & RV Park** M
(715) 635-8721. **$55-$109.** 717 South River. On US 63, 0.5 mi s of jct
SR 70. Ext/int corridors. **Pets:** Large, other species. $6 daily fee/pet.
Designated rooms, service with restrictions, supervision.
SAVE ✕ ♿ ♦ 🛏

STEVENS POINT

⚹⚹⚹ ▼▼ **Americas Best Value Inn** SH ❀
(715) 341-8888. **$60-$80.** 247 N Division St. I-39, exit 161 (US 51
business route), 0.6 mi s. Int corridors. **Pets:** Dogs only. $10 one-time
fee/room. Designated rooms, service with restrictions, supervision.
SAVE S♦ ✕ ♦ 🛏

⚹⚹⚹ ▼▼▼ **Comfort Suites Stevens Point** SH
(715) 341-6000. **$69-$149, 3 day notice.** 300 Division St N. I-39, exit
161 (US 51 business route), 0.6 mi s. Int corridors. **Pets:** Accepted.
SAVE S♦ ✕ ♦ 🛏 ≈

▼▼▼ **Country Inn & Suites By Carlson** SH
(715) 345-7000. **$79-$139.** 301 Division St N. I-39, exit 161 (US 51
business route), 0.6 mi s. Int corridors. **Pets:** Accepted.
ASK S♦ ✕ ♦ 🛏 ≈

▼▼▼ **Fairfield Inn by Marriott** SH
(715) 342-9300. **$73-$93.** 5317 Hwy 10 E. I-39, exit 158A (US 10), just
se. Int corridors. **Pets:** Accepted.
ASK S♦ ✕ ♦ 🛏 ≈

▼▼ **Holiday Inn Express** SH
(715) 344-0000. **$89.** 1100 Amber Ave. I-39, exit 158 (US 10), 1 mi e
on US 10, then just n. Int corridors. **Pets:** Accepted.
✕ ♿ ♦ 🛏 ≈

▼▼▼ **La Quinta Inn & Suites Stevens Point** SH
(715) 344-1900. **$72-$87.** 4917 Main St. I-39, exit 158B (US 10), just
sw. Int corridors. **Pets:** Other species. Service with restrictions, supervision.
ASK S♦ ✕ ♦ 🛏 ≈

▼ **Point Motel** M
(715) 344-8312. **Call for rates.** 209 Division St. I-39, exit 161 (US 51
business route), 0.7 mi s. Ext corridors. **Pets:** Accepted.
✕ ♦ 🛏

⚹⚹⚹ ▼▼ **Stay Inn & Suites** SH
(715) 341-9090. **$45-$120.** 159 Division St N. I-39, exit 161 (US 51
business route), 0.6 mi s. Int corridors. **Pets:** Small, dogs only. $10
one-time fee/pet. Designated rooms, service with restrictions, supervision.
SAVE S♦ ✕ ♦

STURTEVANT

⚹⚹⚹ ▼▼▼ **Grandview Inn** SH
(262) 886-0385. **$70-$135.** 910 S Sylvania Ave. I-94, exit 333 (SR 20),
just s on west frontage road. Int corridors. **Pets:** Small. $5 daily fee/pet.
No service, supervision.
SAVE S♦ ✕ ♦ 🛏 ≈

⚹⚹⚹ ▼▼▼ **Holiday Inn Express-Racine** SH
(262) 884-0200. **Call for rates.** 13339 Hospitality Ct. I-94, exit 333 (SR
20), just se. Int corridors. **Pets:** Accepted.
SAVE ✕ ♿ ♦ 🛏 ≈

SUN PRAIRIE

⚹⚹⚹ ▼▼▼ **AmeriHost Inn & Suites-Sun Prairie** SH
(608) 834-9889. **Call for rates.** 105 Business Park Dr. US 151, exit 103
(CR N), just n. Int corridors. **Pets:** Medium, dogs only. $10 daily fee/pet.
Service with restrictions, supervision.
SAVE ✕ ♿ ♦ 🛏

⚹⚹⚹ ▼ **McGovern's Motel & Suites** M
(608) 837-7321. **$59-$92.** 820 W Main St. On US 151, exit 101, 1.2 mi
ne. Ext/int corridors. **Pets:** Accepted.
SAVE S♦ ✕ ♦ 🛏 ⑪

SUPERIOR

⚹⚹⚹ ▼▼▼ **Barkers Island Inn** SH
(715) 392-7152. **$100-$190.** 300 Marina Dr. Just ne of US 2/53; on
Barkers Island. Int corridors. **Pets:** Accepted.
SAVE S♦ ✕ ♦ 🛏 ⑪ ≈ ✕

⚹⚹⚹ ▼▼▼ **Best Western Bay Walk Inn** SH
(715) 392-7600. **$60-$170.** 1405 Susquehanna Ave. Just e of US 2 on
Belknap St. Int corridors. **Pets:** Accepted.
SAVE S♦ ✕ ♦ 🛏 ≈ ✕

⚹⚹⚹ ▼▼▼ **Best Western Bridgeview Motor Inn** SH
(715) 392-8174. **$59-$152.** 415 Hammond Ave. 0.8 mi n at south end
of Blatnik Bridge. Int corridors. **Pets:** Other species. Service with restrictions, supervision.
SAVE S♦ ✕ ♦ 🛏 ≈ ✕

⚹⚹⚹ ▼▼▼ **Superior Inn** SH
(715) 394-7706. **$45-$165.** 525 Hammond Ave. 0.8 mi n at south end
of Blatnik Bridge. Int corridors. **Pets:** Other species. Designated rooms,
service with restrictions, supervision.
SAVE S♦ ✕ ♦ 🛏 ✕

THORP

▼▼ **AmericInn Lodge & Suites** SH
(715) 669-5959. **$74-$84.** 203 1/2 W Hill St. US 29, exit 108 (SR 73),
just nw. Int corridors. **Pets:** Accepted.
ASK S♦ ✕ ♦ 🛏 ≈ ✕

TOMAH

⚹⚹⚹ ▼▼▼ **AmericInn Lodge and Suites** SH
(608) 372-4100. **$69-$139.** 750 Vandervort St. I-94, exit 143 (SR 21),
just e. Int corridors. **Pets:** $50 deposit/room. Designated rooms, service
with restrictions, supervision.
SAVE S♦ ✕ ♦ 🛏 ≈

▼▼ **Comfort Inn by Choice Hotels** SH
(608) 372-6600. **$50-$124, 7 day notice.** 305 Wittig Rd. I-94, exit 143
(SR 21), just w. Int corridors. **Pets:** Accepted.
ASK S♦ ✕ ♦ 🛏 ≈

▼▼▼ **Cranberry Country Lodge Convention Center and
Water Park** SH
(608) 374-2801. **Call for rates.** 319 Wittig Rd. I-94, exit 143 (SR 21),
just w. Int corridors. **Pets:** Accepted.
✕ ♦ 🛏 ≈ ✕

Econo Lodge SH ❀
(608) 372-9100. **$60-$146.** 2005 N Superior Ave. I-94, exit 143 (SR 21), just w. Ext/int corridors. **Pets:** Medium, other species. $10 daily fee/pet. Service with restrictions, supervision.

Holiday Inn SH
(608) 372-3211. **$89-$104.** 1017 E McCoy Blvd. I-94, exit 143 (SR 21), just e. Int corridors. **Pets:** Accepted.

Lark Inn M ❀
(608) 372-5981. **$59-$125.** 229 N Superior Ave. I-94, exit 143 (SR 21), 1.5 mi s on US 12; I-90, exit 41, 2 mi n on US 12. Ext/int corridors. **Pets:** Medium. $7 daily fee/pet. Service with restrictions, supervision.

Microtel Inn & Suites SH
(608) 374-2050. **$60-$84.** 115 W Andres St. I-94, exit 143 (SR 21), just nw. Int corridors. **Pets:** Accepted.

Super 8 Motel-Tomah SH
(608) 372-3901. **$50-$120.** 1008 E McCoy Blvd. I-94, exit 143 (SR 21), just e. Int corridors. **Pets:** Small. $10 daily fee/pet. Designated rooms, no service, supervision.

TOMAHAWK

Comfort Inn SH
(715) 453-8900. **$70-$130.** 1738 E Comfort Dr. US 51, exit 229, just nw. Int corridors. **Pets:** Accepted.

Super 8 Motel-Tomahawk SH
(715) 453-5210. **Call for rates.** 108 W Mohawk Dr. On US 51 business route, 0.6 mi n of downtown. Int corridors. **Pets:** Accepted.

VIROQUA

Hickory Hill Motel M
(608) 637-3104. **$54-$75.** US 14 S 3955. 1.8 mi se on US 14 and SR 27 and 82. Ext corridors. **Pets:** Accepted.

WATERFORD

Baymont Inns & Suites-Waterford SH
(262) 534-4100. **Call for rates.** 750 Fox Ln. On SR 36, 1 mi s of jct SR 164. Int corridors. **Pets:** Other species. $15 daily fee/room. Service with restrictions.

WATERTOWN

Super 8 Motel SH
(920) 261-1188. **Call for rates.** 1730 S Church St. On SR 26, 1.5 mi s of jct SR 19. Int corridors. **Pets:** Accepted.

WAUPACA

Best Western Grand Seasons Hotel SH
(715) 258-9212. **$78-$259.** 110 Grand Seasons Dr. Jct US 10 and SR 54 W. Int corridors. **Pets:** Accepted.

WAUPUN

Inn Town Motel M
(920) 324-4211. **$49-$89.** 27 S State St. US 151, exit 146 (SR 49), 1 mi w on Main St, then just s. Ext corridors. **Pets:** Accepted.

WAUSAU

Best Western Midway Hotel SH
(715) 842-1616. **$79-$149.** 2901 Hummingbird Rd. I-39, exit 190 (CR NN), just sw. Int corridors. **Pets:** Accepted.

Days Inn-Wausau SH
(715) 355-5501. **Call for rates.** 4700 Rib Mountain Dr. I-39, exit 188, just ne. Int corridors. **Pets:** Dogs only. $10 daily fee/pet. Designated rooms, service with restrictions, supervision.

Exel Inn of Wausau M
(715) 842-0641. **$51-$71.** 116 S 17th Ave. I-39, exit 192, just ne. Int corridors. **Pets:** Accepted.

La Quinta Inn-Wausau SH
(715) 842-0421. **$62-$74.** 1910 Stewart Ave. I-39, exit 192, just se. Int corridors. **Pets:** Other species. Service with restrictions, supervision.

Rib Mountain Inn SH
(715) 848-2802. **$69-$499, 3 day notice.** 2900 Rib Mountain Way. I-39, exit 190 (CR NN), 1 mi w on N Mountain Rd (CR NN), then just s. Ext/int corridors. **Pets:** Accepted.

Stewart Inn Bed and Breakfast BB
(715) 849-5858. **$150-$215, 10 day notice.** 521 Grant St. Just n on N 6th St (SR 52), then just w. Int corridors. **Pets:** Accepted.

Super 8 Motel SH
(715) 848-2888. **$62-$80.** 2006 Stewart Ave W. I-39, exit 192, just se. Int corridors. **Pets:** Dogs only. $10 daily fee/pet. Designated rooms, service with restrictions, supervision.

WAUTOMA

AmericInn SH
(920) 787-5050. **$78-$158.** W7696 SR 21/73. On SR 21 and 73, 1.2 mi e. Int corridors. **Pets:** Accepted.

Super 8 Motel-Wautoma SH
(920) 787-4811. **$70-$91.** W7607 SR 21 and 73. On SR 21 and 73, 1.5 mi e. Int corridors. **Pets:** Accepted.

WEST SALEM

AmericInn SH
(608) 786-3340. **$83-$153.** 125 Buol Rd. I-90, exit 12, just sw on CR C. Int corridors. **Pets:** Accepted.

WHITEWATER

AmeriHost Inn & Suites SH
(262) 472-9400. **Call for rates.** 1355 W Main St. On US business 12, 0.5 mi w of jct SR 59 W. Int corridors. **Pets:** Accepted.

Super 8 Motel SH
(262) 473-8818. **Call for rates.** 917 E Milwaukee St. On US business 12, east end of town. Int corridors. **Pets:** Accepted.

WINDSOR

AAA 🔻🔻 **Days Inn** SH
(608) 846-7473. **$59-$110.** 6311 Rostad Cir. I-90/94, exit 131 (SR 19). Int corridors. **Pets:** Small, dogs only. $10 daily fee/pet. Designated rooms, service with restrictions, supervision.
SAVE ✖ ⛟ 🚽 💻 ⇌ ✕

WISCONSIN DELLS

AAA 🔻 **Americas Best Value Day's End Motel** M
(608) 254-8171. **$34-$125, 3 day notice.** N 604 Hwy 12-16. I-90/94, exit 85 (US 12), 0.8 mi nw. Ext corridors. **Pets:** Other species. $7 daily fee/pet. Designated rooms, service with restrictions, crate.
SAVE ⛟ ✖ 🚽 💻 ⇌ ✕

AAA 🔻 **Black Hawk Motel** M 🐾
(608) 254-7770. **$38-$240, 3 day notice.** 720 Race St. I-90/94, exit 87 (SR 13), 2 mi e on SR 13, 16 and 23. Ext corridors. **Pets:** Small. $10 daily fee/pet. Designated rooms, service with restrictions, crate.
SAVE ✖ 🚽 💻 ⇌ ✕

🔻 **Bridge View Motel** M
(608) 254-6114. **$49-$118, 3 day notice.** 1020 River Rd. Just n of SR 13; center. Ext corridors. **Pets:** Accepted.
ASK ⛟ ✖ 🚽 💻 ⇌

AAA 🔻🔻 **Days Inn of Wisconsin Dells** SH
(608) 254-6444. **$48-$159, 3 day notice.** 944 Hwy 12 N. I-90/94, exit 87 (SR 13), 1 mi n at jct US 12 and SR 16. Int corridors. **Pets:** Large, dogs only. $50 deposit/pet, $10 daily fee/pet. Designated rooms, service with restrictions, supervision.
SAVE ⛟ ✖ 🚽 ⇌

AAA 🔻🔻 **Howard Johnson Hotel and Antiqua Bay**
Waterpark SH
(608) 254-8306. **Call for rates.** 655 Frontage Rd. I-90/94, exit 87 (SR 13), just e. Int corridors. **Pets:** Accepted.
SAVE ✖ 🚽 💻 ⛙ ⇌ ✕

AAA 🔻🔻 **Motel 6** SH
(608) 355-0700. **Call for rates.** E 10892 Fern Dell Rd. I-90/94, exit 92 (US 12), 0.3 mi s. Int corridors. **Pets:** Other species. Service with restrictions, supervision.
SAVE ✖ ⛟ 🚽 ⇌

🔻🔻 **Super 8 Motel-Wisconsin Dells** SH
(608) 254-6464. **Call for rates.** 800 CR H. I-90/94, exit 87 (SR 13), just e. Int corridors. **Pets:** Accepted.
✖ 💻 ⇌ ✕

WISCONSIN RAPIDS

AAA 🔻🔻 **Americas Best Value Inn** SH 🐾
(715) 423-8080. **$65-$85.** 3410 8th St S. 1.9 mi s on SR 13 of jct SR 54 W. Int corridors. **Pets:** Dogs only. $10 one-time fee/room. Designated rooms, service with restrictions, supervision.
SAVE ⛟ ✖ 🚽 💻

AAA 🔻🔻🔻 **Hotel Mead** LH
(715) 423-1500. **Call for rates.** 451 E Grand Ave. Just e of downtown. Int corridors. **Pets:** Accepted.
SAVE ✖ 🚽 💻 ⛙ ⇌ ✕

🔻🔻🔻 **Quality Inn** SH
(715) 423-5506. **$70-$85.** 3120 8th St S. 1.5 mi s on SR 13. Int corridors. **Pets:** Accepted.
ASK ⛟ ✖ 🚽 💻 ⇌

🔻🔻🔻 **Sleep Inn & Suites** SH
(715) 424-6800. **$90-$145.** 4221 8th St S. I-39, exit 136 (SR 73), 16.6 mi w; 3.5 mi n on SR 13. Int corridors. **Pets:** Accepted.
ASK ⛟ ✖ ⛟ 🚽 💻 ⇌

WITTENBERG

🔻🔻🔻 **Comfort Inn & Wilderness Conference Center** SH
(715) 253-3755. **$69-$109.** W17267 Red Oak Ln. US 29, exit 198, just se. Int corridors. **Pets:** Accepted.
ASK ⛟ ✖ ⛟ 🚽 💻 ⇌ ✕

WYOMING

AFTON

◆ The Corral Motel [CA]
(307) 885-5424. **Call for rates.** 161 Washington St (US 89). On US 89; center. Ext corridors. **Pets:** Accepted.

◆◆ Lazy B Motel [M] ❀
(307) 885-3187. **$70-$95.** 219 Washington St (US Hwy 89). On US 89; center. Ext corridors. **Pets:** Other species. Service with restrictions, supervision.

BUFFALO

◆ Big Horn Motel [M]
(307) 684-7822. **Call for rates.** 209 N Main St, US Hwy 16. On US 16; downtown. Ext corridors. **Pets:** Accepted.

◆◆ Comfort Inn [SH]
(307) 684-9564. **$69-$144.** 65 Hwy 16 E. I-25, exit 299 (Hwy 16) E, just e; I-90, exit 58, 1.3 mi w. Ext/int corridors. **Pets:** Accepted.

◆◆◆ The Occidental Hotel [SH] ❀
(307) 684-0451. **$50-$210, 14 day notice.** 10 N Main St. Center. Int corridors. **Pets:** Other species. Service with restrictions.

◆◆ Rodeway Inn [M]
(307) 684-2219. **$59-$159.** 333 E Hart St. I-25, exit 299 (US 16), just w. Ext corridors. **Pets:** Small. $10 daily fee/pet. Designated rooms, service with restrictions, supervision.

◆◆ Super 8 Motel of Buffalo [SH]
(307) 684-2531. **$55-$135.** 655 E Hart St. I-25, exit 299 (US 16), just w; I-90, exit 58, 1.3 mi w. Int corridors. **Pets:** $5 daily fee/pet. Designated rooms, service with restrictions, supervision.

◆◆ WYO Motel [M] ❀
(307) 684-5505. **$49-$169.** 610 E Hart St. I-25, exit 299 (US 16), just w; I-90, exit 58, 1.3 mi w. Ext corridors. **Pets:** Medium. $5 one-time fee/pet. Designated rooms, service with restrictions, supervision.

CASPER

◆◆ Best Western Ramkota [LH] ❀
(307) 266-6000. **$109-$129.** 800 N Poplar St. I-25, exit 188B, just e. Int corridors. **Pets:** Other species. $50 deposit/pet. Designated rooms, service with restrictions, supervision.

◆◆ Days Inn Casper [SH]
(307) 234-1159. **Call for rates.** 301 E 'E' St. I-25, exit 188A, just s. Int corridors. **Pets:** Accepted.

◆◆ Parkway Plaza Hotel & Convention Centre [SH]
(307) 235-1777. **$90-$129.** 123 W 'E' St. I-25, exit 188A, just w. Ext/int corridors. **Pets:** Accepted.

◆◆ Quality Inn & Suites [SH] ❀
(307) 266-2400. **$90-$200.** 821 N Poplar St. I-25, exit 188B, just e. Int corridors. **Pets:** Dogs only. $10 one-time fee/room. Designated rooms, service with restrictions, supervision.

◆◆ Ramada Plaza [SH]
(307) 235-2531. **Call for rates.** 300 W 'F' St. I-25, exit 188A, just e. Int corridors. **Pets:** Accepted.

◆ The Royal Inn [M]
(307) 234-3501. **$45-$50.** 440 E 'A' St. I-25, exit 188A, just s to 'A' St, then just e. Ext corridors. **Pets:** Medium, other species. $25 deposit/room, $4 one-time fee/pet. Designated rooms, service with restrictions, supervision.

◆◆ Skyler Inn [SH]
(307) 232-5100. **$84.** 111 S Wilson St. I-25, exit 186, 0.5 mi s to Yellowstone Hwy, then 1 mi w, jct 1st St. Int corridors. **Pets:** Accepted.

◆◆ Super 8 Motel [SH]
(307) 266-3480. **$81-$89.** 3838 CY Ave. I-25, exit 188B, 1.7 mi w on S Poplar St (SR 220), then 1.8 mi n. Int corridors. **Pets:** Accepted.

CHEYENNE

◆◆ Best Western Hitching Post Inn Resort & Conference Center [SH] ❀
(307) 638-3301. **Call for rates.** 1700 W Lincolnway. I-25, exit 9, 0.8 mi e. Ext/int corridors. **Pets:** Other species. $25 one-time fee/room. Designated rooms, service with restrictions, supervision.

◆◆ Cheyenne Super 8 Motel [M]
(307) 635-8741. **Call for rates.** 1900 W Lincolnway. I-25, exit 9, 0.7 mi e. Int corridors. **Pets:** Accepted.

◆◆ Days Inn Cheyenne [SH]
(307) 778-8877. **$69-$199.** 2360 W Lincolnway. I-25, exit 9, just e. Int corridors. **Pets:** Other species. $10 one-time fee/room. Designated rooms, service with restrictions, supervision.

◆◆ Historic Plains Hotel [SH]
(307) 638-3311. **$99-$259.** 1600 Central Ave. I-80, exit 362, 1 mi n on I-180/I-25 business loop/US 85/87 business route, then just w on I-80 business loop/US 30; downtown. Int corridors. **Pets:** Other species. $25 one-time fee/pet. Designated rooms, service with restrictions, supervision.

▼▼ La Quinta Inn Cheyenne 🆂🅷
(307) 632-7117. **$81.** 2410 W Lincolnway. I-25, exit 9, just e. Int corridors. **Pets:** Other species. Service with restrictions, supervision.
(ASK) 🆂🅳 ☒ 🅲🅼 🔳 💻 ⊃

△△△ ▼▼▼▼ Nagle Warren Mansion B & B 🅱🅱 ❀
(307) 637-3333. **$158-$192, 3 day notice.** 222 E 17th St. I-80, exit 362, 1.2 mi n on I-25 business loop/US 85/87 business route, then just e; jct House St; downtown. Int corridors. **Pets:** Designated rooms, service with restrictions, supervision.
(SAVE) ☒ 🇽

△△△ ▼ Oak Tree Inn 🆂🅷
(307) 778-6620. **Call for rates.** 1625 Stillwater. 1.2 mi e of jct Dell Range Blvd and Yellowstone Rd, 0.4 mi s. Ext/int corridors. **Pets:** Accepted.
(SAVE) ☒ 🔳 🍴

▼▼ Porch Swing Bed & Breakfast 🅱🅱
(307) 778-7182. **$75-$85.** 502 E 24th St. I-80, exit 362, 1.8 mi n on I-25 business loop/US 85/87 business route, then just e; downtown. Int corridors. **Pets:** Accepted.
☒ 🇽

▼▼▼ Windy Hills Guest House 🅱🅱
(307) 632-6423. **$125-$255, 3 day notice.** 393 Happy Jack Rd. I-25, exit 10B, 22 mi w on SR 210 (Happy Jack Rd), then 1 mi s on private gravel road. Ext corridors. **Pets:** Accepted.
🆂🅳 ☒ 🔳 💻 🇽 🇽

CODY

△△△ ▼▼▼ Beartooth Inn of Cody 🆂🅷
(307) 527-5505. **$59-$169.** 2513 Greybull Hwy. 1.5 mi e on US 14/16/20. Ext/int corridors. **Pets:** Medium, dogs only. Designated rooms, service with restrictions, supervision.
(SAVE) 🆂🅳 ☒ 🔳 💻 🇽

△△△ ▼▼▼▼ Best Western Sunset Motor Inn 🆂🅷
(307) 587-4265. **$69-$179.** 1601 8th St. 0.8 mi w on US 14/16/20. Ext corridors. **Pets:** Small. $25 one-time fee/pet. Designated rooms, service with restrictions, supervision.
(SAVE) 🆂🅳 ☒ 🔳 💻 🍴 ⊃ 🇽

△△△ ▼ Big Bear Motel 🅼 ❀
(307) 587-3117. **$49-$99.** 139 W Yellowstone Ave. 2 mi w on US 14/16/20, from city center. Ext corridors. **Pets:** Other species. $10 daily fee/pet. Designated rooms, supervision.
(SAVE) ☒ 🔳 💻 ⊃ 🇿

△△△ ▼ Cody Motor Lodge 🅼
(307) 527-6291. **$69-$115, 7 day notice.** 1455 Sheridan Ave. Just w on US 14/16/20 and SR 120. Int corridors. **Pets:** Other species. Designated rooms, service with restrictions, supervision.
(SAVE) 🆂🅳 ☒

△△△ ▼▼▼ Sunrise Motor Inn 🅼
(307) 587-5566. **$54-$160.** 1407 8th St. 0.8 mi w on US 14/16/20. Ext corridors. **Pets:** Small, dogs only. $15 one-time fee/room. Designated rooms, service with restrictions, supervision.
(SAVE) 🆂🅳 ☒ 🔳 💻 ⊃

DOUGLAS

△△△ ▼▼▼ Best Western Douglas Inn & Conference Center 🆂🅷 ❀
(307) 358-9790. **$73-$94, 60 day notice.** 1450 Riverbend Dr. I-25, exit 140, 0.8 mi e. Int corridors. **Pets:** $10 daily fee/room. Designated rooms, service with restrictions, supervision.
(SAVE) 🆂🅳 ☒ 🅲🅼 🔳 💻 🍴 ⊃ 🇽

△△△ ▼▼▼ Holiday Inn Express Hotel & Suites 🆂🅷
(307) 358-4500. **$110-$120.** 900 W Yellowstone Hwy. I-25, exit 140, 0.5 mi e. Int corridors. **Pets:** Medium. $20 daily fee/pet. Designated rooms, service with restrictions, supervision.
(SAVE) 🆂🅳 ☒ 🅲🅼 🔳 💻 ⊃

DUBOIS

△△△ ▼ Branding Iron Inn 🅲🅰
(307) 455-2893. **Call for rates.** 401 W Ramshorn St. 0.3 mi w on US 26 and 287. Ext corridors. **Pets:** Accepted.
(SAVE) ☒ 🔳 💻 🇽

△△△ ▼▼▼ Longhorn RV & Motel 🅼
(307) 455-2337. **$52-$99.** 5810 US Hwy 26. 3 mi e on US 26 and 287. Ext corridors. **Pets:** Dogs only. $10 daily fee/room. Designated rooms, service with restrictions, supervision.
(SAVE) 🆂🅳 ☒ 🔳 💻 🇽

▼ Rocky Mountain Lodge 🅼
(307) 455-2844. **$60-$100, 3 day notice.** 1349 W Ramshorn St. 1.6 mi w on US 26 and 287. Ext corridors. **Pets:** Accepted.
(ASK) ☒ 🔳 💻 🇽

△△△ ▼▼▼ Stagecoach Motor Inn 🆂🅷 ❀
(307) 455-2303. **$58-$98.** 103 Ramshorn St. On US 26 and 287; center. Ext corridors. **Pets:** Medium, dogs only. $10 daily fee/pet. Designated rooms, service with restrictions.
(SAVE) 🆂🅳 ☒ 🔳 💻 ⊃ 🇽 🇽

EVANSTON

▼▼ Comfort Inn 🆂🅷 ❀
(307) 789-7799. **$75-$135.** 1931 Harrison Dr. I-80, exit 3, just n. Int corridors. **Pets:** Other species. $10 one-time fee/pet. Designated rooms, service with restrictions, supervision.
(ASK) 🆂🅳 ☒ 🔳 💻 ⊃

△△△ ▼▼▼ Days Inn 🆂🅷
(307) 789-0783. **$69-$109.** 1983 Harrison Dr. I-80, exit 3 (Harrison Dr), just n. Int corridors. **Pets:** Medium. $10 daily fee/pet. Designated rooms, service with restrictions, supervision.
(SAVE) 🆂🅳 ☒ 🔳 💻 ⊃

△△△ ▼ Prairie Inn 🅼
(307) 789-2920. **$65-$90.** 264 Bear River Dr. I-80, exit 6, 0.3 mi n. Ext/int corridors. **Pets:** Small. $10 daily fee/pet. Designated rooms, service with restrictions, supervision.
(SAVE) ☒ 🔳

EVANSVILLE

▼▼ Comfort Inn by Choice Hotels-Casper 🆂🅷
(307) 235-3038. **Call for rates.** 480 Lathrop Rd. I-25, exit 185, just e. Int corridors. **Pets:** Accepted.
☒ 🅲🅼 🔳 💻 ⊃

▼▼▼ Sleep Inn & Suites 🆂🅷
(307) 235-3100. **$80-$160.** 6733 Bonanza. I-25, exit 182, n on Hat Six Rd, then w. Int corridors. **Pets:** Accepted.
(ASK) 🆂🅳 ☒ 🔳 💻 ⊃

▼▼▼ Super 8 East Casper 🆂🅷
(307) 237-8100. **$99-$109.** 269 Miracle Dr. I-25, exit 185, just e. Int corridors. **Pets:** Accepted.
(ASK) 🆂🅳 ☒ 🅲🅼 🔳 💻 ⊃

GILLETTE

△△△ ▼▼▼ Best Western Tower West Lodge 🆂🅷
(307) 686-2210. **$79-$229.** 109 N US Hwy 14-16. I-90, exit 124, just n. Int corridors. **Pets:** Accepted.
(SAVE) 🆂🅳 ☒ 🔳 💻 🍴 ⊃ 🇽

Budget Inn Express M
(307) 686-1989. **$69-$159.** 2011 Rodgers Dr. I-90, exit 124, just n. Int corridors. **Pets:** Medium. $5 daily fee/pet. Designated rooms, service with restrictions, supervision.

Comfort Inn & Suites of Gillette SH
(307) 685-2223. **$89-$300.** 1607 W 2nd Ave. I-90, exit 124, just ne. Int corridors. **Pets:** Accepted.

Holiday Inn Express Hotel & Suites SH
(307) 686-9576. **$159-$239.** 1908 Cliff Davis Dr. I-90, exit 126. Int corridors. **Pets:** Accepted.

GREEN RIVER

Oak Tree Inn SH
(307) 875-3500. **$105-$115.** 1170 W Flaming Gorge Way. I-80, exit 89, just s. Ext/int corridors. **Pets:** Accepted.

GREYBULL

Yellowstone Motel M
(307) 765-4456. **$55-$99.** 247 Greybull Ave. 0.4 mi e on US 14. Ext corridors. **Pets:** Accepted.

GUERNSEY

The Bunkhouse Motel M
(307) 836-2356. **$57-$70, 7 day notice.** 350 W Whalen. On US 26; center. Ext corridors. **Pets:** $10 one-time fee/pet. Designated rooms, service with restrictions, supervision.

HULETT

Hulett Motel M
(307) 467-5220. **$65-$85.** 202 Main St. SR 24 at north end of town. Ext corridors. **Pets:** Dogs only. $20 one-time fee/room. Designated rooms, service with restrictions, supervision.

JACKSON HOLE AREA

ALPINE

Alpen Haus Resort Hotel SH
(307) 654-7545. **$80-$95.** 50 W Hwy 26. Jct US 26 and 89. Int corridors. **Pets:** Small. $10 daily fee/room. Designated rooms, service with restrictions, supervision.

Best Western Flying Saddle Resort SH
(307) 654-4422. **Call for rates.** 118878 Jct US 26 & 89. 0.5 mi e of jct US 26 and 89. Ext corridors. **Pets:** Accepted.

GRAND TETON NATIONAL PARK

Flagg Ranch Resort LH
(307) 543-2861. **$175-$185, 6 day notice.** Hwy 89. US 89 and 191; 2 mi s of Yellowstone National Park south entrance; 5 mi n of Grand Teton National Park north entrance. Ext corridors. **Pets:** Accepted.

Jackson Lake Lodge LH
(307) 543-2811. **$189, 7 day notice.** US 89 and 287. 5 mi nw of Moran. Ext/int corridors. **Pets:** Accepted.

Signal Mountain Lodge SH
(307) 543-2831. **$125-$299, 7 day notice.** Inner Park Rd. Teton Park Rd, 2 mi s of US 89, 191 and 287. Ext corridors. **Pets:** Other species. $10 daily fee/room. Designated rooms, service with restrictions, crate.

Togwotee Mountain Lodge CA
(307) 543-2847. **$89-$219, 7 day notice.** 27655 Hwys US 26 & 287. 16.5 mi e of Moran at jct US 26 and 287. Ext/int corridors. **Pets:** Other species. $20 one-time fee/pet. Designated rooms, service with restrictions, crate.

JACKSON

49'er Inn and Suites (Quality Inn and Suites) SH ❀
(307) 733-7550. **$79-$159, 14 day notice.** 330 W Pearl St. Just w and just s of town square. Ext/int corridors. **Pets:** Service with restrictions, supervision.

Antler Inn SH
(307) 733-2535. **$72-$220.** 43 W Pearl St. Just s of town square. Ext/int corridors. **Pets:** Dogs only. Designated rooms, service with restrictions, supervision.

Cowboy Village Resort CA ❀
(307) 733-3121. **$86-$186.** 120 S Flat Creek Dr. 0.3 mi w on Broadway to Flat Creek Dr, just s; downtown. Ext corridors. **Pets:** Large, dogs only. Service with restrictions, supervision.

Elk Country Inn M ❀
(307) 733-2364. **$68-$148, 14 day notice.** 480 W Pearl St. Just w, then just s of town square. Ext/int corridors. **Pets:** Designated rooms, service with restrictions, supervision.

Homewood Suites by Hilton SH
(0) 000-0000. **Call for rates.** 260 N Millward. Just nw of town square, n on Millward St or w on Mercil Ave, from US 26/89/191 (Broadway). Int corridors. **Pets:** Accepted.

Jackson Hole Lodge SH
(307) 733-2992. **$94-$319, 15 day notice.** 420 W Broadway. 0.3 mi w on US 26/89/191. Ext corridors. **Pets:** Accepted.

Painted Buffalo Inn SH
(307) 733-4340. **$85-$189.** 400 W Broadway. Just w of town square. Ext corridors. **Pets:** Other species. $10 one-time fee/pet. Service with restrictions, supervision.

Snow King Resort LH
(307) 733-5200. **$150-$760, 3 day notice.** 400 E Snow King Ave. Just se of town square. Ext/int corridors. **Pets:** Accepted.

TETON VILLAGE

◈◈◈ ▼▼▼▼▼ **Four Seasons Resort Jackson Hole** 🄻🄷
(307) 732-5000. **$575-$6000, 30 day notice.** 7680 Granite Loop Rd.
Located at the base of Jackson Hole Mountain Resort. Int corridors.
Pets: Very small, dogs only. Service with restrictions, supervision.
⊠ 🔊M 🛏 💻 🍴 ➷ ⊠

END AREA

LANDER

◈◈◈ ▼ **Holiday Lodge** Ⓜ
(307) 332-2511. **$60-$75.** 210 McFarlane Dr. Just e of jct US 287 and
SR 789. Ext corridors. **Pets:** Dogs only. $10 daily fee/pet. Designated
rooms, service with restrictions, crate.
(SAVE) ⊠ 🛏

◈◈◈ ▼▼▼ **Rodeway Inn & Suites/Pronghorn Lodge** 🅂🄷
(307) 332-3940. **$60-$125.** 150 E Main St. Just n of jct US 287 and SR
789. Ext corridors. **Pets:** Small, dogs only. $10 daily fee/room. Designated
rooms, service with restrictions, supervision.
(SAVE) (S🔊) ⊠ 🛏 💻 🍴

LARAMIE

▼▼▼ **Days Inn** 🅂🄷
(307) 745-5678. **Call for rates.** 1368 McCue St. I-80, exit 310, just e.
Int corridors. **Pets:** Accepted.
⊠ 🔊M 🛏 💻 ➷

◈◈◈ ▼ **Gas Lite Inn Motel** Ⓜ
(307) 742-6616. **$46-$66.** 960 N 3rd St. I-80, exit 313, 1.6 mi n on US
287; downtown. Ext corridors. **Pets:** Other species. $5 daily fee/pet.
Designated rooms, no service, supervision.
(SAVE) (S🔊) ⊠ 🛏 ➷

▼▼▼▼ **Holiday Inn-Laramie-University of Wyoming** 🅂🄷
(307) 721-9000. **Call for rates.** 204 30th St. I-80, exit 316 (Grand Ave),
2.5 mi w; jct 30th St. Int corridors. **Pets:** Accepted.
⊠ 🔊M 🛏 💻 🍴 ➷

◈◈◈ ▼ **Sunset Inn** Ⓜ
(307) 742-3741. **$58-$85.** 1104 S 3rd St. I-80, exit 313, just n on US
287. Ext corridors. **Pets:** Medium, dogs only. $100 deposit/room. Service
with restrictions, supervision.
(SAVE) (S🔊) ⊠ 🛏 ➷

◈◈◈ ▼ **Travelodge Downtown** Ⓜ
(307) 742-6671. **$65-$100.** 165 N 3rd St. I-80, exit 313, 1 mi n on US
287; downtown. Ext corridors. **Pets:** Medium, other species. $50 deposit/
room. Designated rooms, service with restrictions, supervision.
(SAVE) (S🔊) ⊠ 🛏 💻

LUSK

◈◈◈ ▼ **Town House Motel** Ⓜ 🐾
(307) 334-2376. **$45-$90.** 525 S Main St. Just n of jct US 20/85. Ext
corridors. **Pets:** Other species. $5 one-time fee/pet. Designated rooms,
service with restrictions.
(SAVE) (S🔊) ⊠ 🛏 💻

NEWCASTLE

◈◈◈ ▼ **Auto Inn Motel** Ⓜ
(307) 746-2734. **$49-$89.** 2503 W Main St. West end of town on US
16. Ext corridors. **Pets:** Other species. $6 daily fee/pet. Designated rooms,
no service, supervision.
(SAVE) (S🔊) ⊠ 🛏 💻

◈◈◈ ▼ **Sage Motel** Ⓜ
(307) 746-2724. **$50-$75, 3 day notice.** 1227 S Summit Ave. 0.3 mi s
of jct US 16 on US 85, just w. Ext corridors. **Pets:** Small, dogs only. $10
daily fee/pet. Designated rooms, service with restrictions, supervision.
(SAVE) (S🔊) ⊠ 🛏 💻

PAINTER

▼ **Hunter Peak Ranch** 🅁🄰
(307) 587-3711. **Call for rates.** 4027 Crandall Rd. SR 296, 5 mi s of
US 212; 40 mi n of SR 120. Ext corridors. **Pets:** Accepted.
⊠ 🛏 💻 🍴 ⊠ 🎿 🐾 🎣

PINEDALE

▼▼ **AmeriHost Inn & Suites** 🅂🄷
(307) 367-8300. **$109-$169.** 1624 W Pine St. 1 mi n on US 191. Int
corridors. **Pets:** Accepted.
(ASK) (S🔊) ⊠ 🔊M 🛏 💻 ➷

◈◈◈ ▼▼▼ **Best Western Pinedale Inn** 🅂🄷
(307) 367-6869. **$85-$185.** 850 W Pine St. 0.5 mi n on US 191. Int
corridors. **Pets:** Dogs only. Designated rooms, service with restrictions,
supervision.
(SAVE) (S🔊) ⊠ 🛏 💻 ➷

◈◈◈ ▼▼▼ **The Lodge at Pinedale** 🅂🄷
(307) 367-8800. **$75-$115.** 1054 W Pine St. 0.7 mi n on US 191. Int
corridors. **Pets:** Medium. $10 daily fee/room. Designated rooms, service
with restrictions, crate.
(SAVE) (S🔊) ⊠ 🛏 💻 ➷

◈◈◈ ▼ **Sun Dance Motel** Ⓜ
(307) 367-4336. **Call for rates.** 148 E Pine St. US 191; city center. Ext
corridors. **Pets:** Accepted.
(SAVE) ⊠ 🛏 💻

POWELL

▼▼ **Americas Best Value Inn** Ⓜ
(307) 754-5117. **Call for rates.** 777 E 2nd St. 0.3 mi e on US 14A. Ext
corridors. **Pets:** Other species. Designated rooms, service with restrictions.
⊠ 🛏 💻 ➷

RAWLINS

◈◈◈ ▼▼▼ **Best Western CottonTree Inn** 🅂🄷
(307) 324-2737. **Call for rates.** 2221 W Spruce St. I-80, exit 211, just n.
Ext/int corridors. **Pets:** Medium, other species. $10 daily fee/room. Desig-
nated rooms, service with restrictions, supervision.
(SAVE) ⊠ 🛏 💻 🍴 ➷ ⊠

▼▼▼ **Holiday Inn Express** 🅂🄷
(307) 324-3760. **Call for rates.** 201 Airport Rd. I-80, exit 215, just w. Int
corridors. **Pets:** Accepted.
⊠ 🔊M 🛏 💻 ➷

◈◈◈ ▼▼▼ **Oak Tree Inn** 🅂🄷
(307) 324-4700. **$69-$99.** 2005 E Daley St. I-80, exit 215, 0.5 mi w,
then just n on US 287. Int corridors. **Pets:** Accepted.
(SAVE) (S🔊) ⊠ 🔊M 🛏 💻 🍴

RIVERTON

▼▼ Comfort Inn & Suites 🆂🅷
(307) 856-8900. **$89-$139.** 2020 N Federal Blvd. 1.5 mi ne on US 26/SR 789. Int corridors. **Pets:** Accepted.
🅰️$🅺 🆂🅓 ⊠ 🗎 🖵 🏊

▼ Days Inn 🆂🅷
(307) 856-9677. **Call for rates.** 909 W Main St. 0.5 mi nw on US 26. Ext corridors. **Pets:** Accepted.
⊠ 🗎 🖵

AAA ▼▼◆ Holiday Inn Convention Center 🆂🅷
(307) 856-8100. **$99-$129.** 900 E Sunset Dr. 0.8 mi ne on US 26/SR 789. Int corridors. **Pets:** $20 one-time fee/room. Designated rooms, service with restrictions, supervision.
🆂🅐🆅🅴 🆂🅓 ⊠ 🕭ᴹ 🗎 🖵 🍴 🏊

▼ Super 8 Motel 🆂🅷
(307) 857-2400. **$50-$110.** 1040 N Federal Blvd. 1 mi ne on US 26/SR 789. Int corridors. **Pets:** Accepted.
🅰️$🅺 🆂🅓 ⊠ 🗎 🖵

ROCK SPRINGS

▼▼ Econo Lodge 🆂🅷
(307) 382-4217. **$90-$140.** 1635 Elk St. I-80, exit 104 (Elk St), just n. Ext corridors. **Pets:** Accepted.
🅰️$🅺 🆂🅓 ⊠ 🗎 🖵 🏊

▼▼▼ Hampton Inn 🆂🅷
(307) 382-9222. **Call for rates.** 1901 Dewar Dr. I-80, exit 102 (Dewar Dr), 1 mi s. Int corridors. **Pets:** Accepted.
⊠ 🗎 🖵 🏊

▼▼▼ Holiday Inn 🆂🅷
(307) 382-9200. **$135.** 1675 Sunset Dr. I-80, exit 102 (Dewar Dr), 0.3 mi sw. Ext/int corridors. **Pets:** Accepted.
🅰️$🅺 🆂🅓 ⊠ 🗎 🖵 🍴 🏊

▼▼ La Quinta Inn 🆂🅷
(307) 362-1770. **$129.** 2717 Dewar Dr. I-80, exit 102 (Dewar Dr), just n. Int corridors. **Pets:** Other species. Service with restrictions, supervision.
🅰️$🅺 🆂🅓 ⊠ 🗎 🖵 🏊

▼ Motel 6–#395 🅼
(307) 362-1850. **Call for rates.** 2615 Commercial Way. I-80, exit 102 (Dewar Dr), n to Foothills Blvd, then just e. Ext corridors. **Pets:** Other species. Service with restrictions, supervision.
⊠ 🗎 🏊

▼▼ Quality Inn 🆂🅷
(307) 382-9490. **$109-$129.** 1670 Sunset Dr. I-80, exit 102 (Dewar Dr), 0.3 mi s, then just w. Ext corridors. **Pets:** Accepted.
🅰️$🅺 🆂🅓 ⊠ 🗎 🖵 🏊 ⊠

SARATOGA

▼ Hacienda Motel 🅼
(307) 326-5751. **$75-$85, 7 day notice.** 1500 S First St. 0.5 mi s on SR 130. Int corridors. **Pets:** Accepted.
🅰️$🅺 🆂🅓 ⊠ 🗎

SHERIDAN

AAA ▼ Americas Best Value Inn 🅼
(307) 672-9757. **$54-$92.** 580 E 5th St. I-90, exit 23, 0.4 mi w. Ext corridors. **Pets:** Other species. Designated rooms, supervision.
🆂🅐🆅🅴 🆂🅓 ⊠ 🗎

AAA ▼▼◆ Best Western Sheridan Center 🆂🅷
(307) 674-7421. **$69-$169.** 612 N Main St. I-90, exit 23 (5th St), 1 mi w, then just s. Ext/int corridors. **Pets:** Other species. $20 one-time fee/room. Designated rooms, service with restrictions, supervision.
🆂🅐🆅🅴 🆂🅓 ⊠ 🗎 🖵 🍴 🏊

▼ Budget Host Inn 🅼
(307) 674-7496. **$55-$115.** 2007 N Main St. I-90, exit 20, 0.7 mi s; on I-90 business loop. Ext corridors. **Pets:** Accepted.
🅰️$🅺 🆂🅓 ⊠ 🗎 🖵

AAA ▼▼◆ Holiday Inn Atrium & Convention Center 🆂🅷 🐾
(307) 672-8931. **$119-$139.** 1809 Sugarland Dr. I-90, exit 25, 0.3 mi nw. Int corridors. **Pets:** Other species. $50 deposit/room. Service with restrictions, supervision.
🆂🅐🆅🅴 🆂🅓 ⊠ 🗎 🖵 🍴 🏊 ⊠

AAA ▼▼◆ Mill Inn 🅼
(307) 672-6401. **$65-$130.** 2161 Coffeen Ave. I-90, exit 25, 0.3 mi w. Ext/int corridors. **Pets:** Accepted.
🆂🅐🆅🅴 🆂🅓 ⊠ 🗎 🖵

SUNDANCE

AAA ▼▼◆ Best Western Inn at Sundance 🆂🅷
(307) 283-2800. **$65-$175, 30 day notice.** 2719 E Cleveland Ave. I-90, exit 189, just n, then just w on I-90 business loop. Int corridors. **Pets:** Small, other species. $10 daily fee/pet. Designated rooms, service with restrictions, supervision.
🆂🅐🆅🅴 🆂🅓 ⊠ 🗎 🖵 🏊

AAA ▼▼ Budget Host Arrowhead Motel 🅼
(307) 283-3307. **$49-$69.** 214 Cleveland Ave. I-90 business loop and US 14. Ext corridors. **Pets:** Dogs only. Service with restrictions, supervision.
🆂🅐🆅🅴 ⊠

AAA ▼▼ Rodeway Inn Sundance Mountain 🅼
(307) 283-3737. **$59-$199.** 26 Hwy 585. I-90, exit 187, 0.4 mi n. Ext corridors. **Pets:** Accepted.
🆂🅐🆅🅴 🆂🅓 ⊠ 🗎 🖵 🏊

THERMOPOLIS

▼▼◆ Holiday Inn of the Waters 🆂🅷
(307) 864-3131. **$89-$149.** 115 E Park St. In Hot Springs State Park. Ext/int corridors. **Pets:** Accepted.
🅰️$🅺 ⊠ 🖵 🍴 🏊 ⊠

▼▼ Hot Springs Super 8 🆂🅷
(307) 864-5515. **Call for rates.** Lane 5, Hwy 20 S. On US 20, just se. Int corridors. **Pets:** Accepted.
⊠ 🕭ᴹ 🗎 🖵 🏊

TORRINGTON

▼▼◆ Holiday Inn Express Hotel & Suites 🆂🅷
(307) 532-7600. **$84-$190.** 1700 E Valley Rd. US 85, e on US 26. Int corridors. **Pets:** Accepted.
🅰️$🅺 ⊠ 🕭ᴹ 🗎 🖵 🏊 ⊠

WAPITI

AAA ▼ Green Creek Inn 🅼
(307) 587-5004. **$45-$159.** 2908 Northfork Hwy. 2.8 mi w on US 14/16/20. Ext corridors. **Pets:** Accepted.
🆂🅐🆅🅴 🆂🅓 ⊠ 🗎 🅿

▼ Yellowstone Valley Inn 🅼
(307) 587-3961. **$59-$169, 21 day notice.** 3324 Yellowstone Park Hwy. 3.3 mi w on US 14/16/20. Ext corridors. **Pets:** Accepted.
🅰️$🅺 🆂🅓 ⊠ 🗎 🖵 🍴 🏊 ⊠ 🅿

WHEATLAND

AAA ▼▼▼ Best Western Torchlite Motor Inn 🆂🅷 🐾
(307) 322-4070. **$72-$114.** 1809 N 16th St. I-25, exit 78, just e; 1.5 mi n on US 87/I-25 business loop (16th St). Ext corridors. **Pets:** Other species. $15 daily fee/pet. Service with restrictions, supervision.
🆂🅐🆅🅴 🆂🅓 ⊠ 🗎 🖵 🏊

WORLAND

🔻🔻 Days Inn M
(307) 347-4251. **Call for rates.** 500 N 10th St. 0.5 mi n on US 20. Ext corridors. **Pets:** Accepted.
⊠ 🔲 🖵

YELLOWSTONE NATIONAL PARK

AAA 🔻🔻🔻 Elephant Head Lodge CA
(307) 587-3980. **$135-$300, 30 day notice.** 1170 Yellowstone Hwy. 11.7 mi e of Yellowstone National Park East Gate on US 14/16/20. Ext corridors. **Pets:** $10 one-time fee/pet. Designated rooms, crate.
SAVE S6 ⊠ 🔲 🖵 ⧗ ⊠ 🐾 🕅 ✉

🔻🔻 Shoshone Lodge CA
(307) 587-4044. **$90-$300, 30 day notice.** 349 Yellowstone Hwy. 3.5 mi e of Yellowstone National Park East Gate on US 14/16/20. Ext corridors. **Pets:** Accepted.
ASK ⊠ 🔲 🖵 ⧗ ⊠ 🕅 🐾 ✉

Canadian Lodgings

ALBERTA

CITY INDEX

BANFF

◆◆ Banff Rocky Mountain Resort CO
(403) 762-5531. **$165-$380, 3 day notice.** 1029 Banff Ave. Banff Ave and Tunnel Mountain Rd; just s of Trans-Canada Hwy 1. Ext corridors. **Pets:** Accepted.

ASK S◊ ☒ 🛏 💻 🍴 🏊 ✗ 🐾

◆◆ Best Western Siding 29 Lodge SH
(403) 762-5575. **$99-$349.** 453 Marten St. 0.6 mi (1 km) ne, just off Banff Ave. Int corridors. **Pets:** Other species. $10 one-time fee/room. Service with restrictions, supervision.

SAVE S◊ ☒ 🛏 💻 🏊

◆◆ Castle Mountain Chalets CA
(403) 762-3868. **$150-$345, 14 day notice.** Bow Valley Pkwy (Hwy 1A). 20 mi (32 km) w on Trans-Canada Hwy 1, jct Castle, 0.6 mi (1 km) ne on Hwy 1A (Bow Valley Pkwy). Ext corridors. **Pets:** Accepted.

SAVE S◊ ☒ 🛏 💻 ✗ 🐾 ✗

◆◆ Douglas Fir Resort & Chalets CO 🐾
(403) 762-5591. **$177-$459, 5 day notice.** 525 Tunnel Mountain Rd. From centre, 1 mi (1.6 km) ne. Ext/int corridors. **Pets:** Medium, dogs only. $25 daily fee/pet. Designated rooms, service with restrictions, supervision.

SAVE ☒ 🛏 💻 🏊 ✗

◆◆◆◆ The Fairmont Banff Springs LH
(403) 762-2211. **$233-$593, 3 day notice.** 405 Spray Ave. Just s on Banff Ave over the bridge, 0.3 mi (0.5 km) e. Int corridors. **Pets:** Medium. $35 one-time fee/pet. Designated rooms, service with restrictions, supervision.

SAVE S◊ ☒ 🛏 💻 🍴 🏊 ✗

◆◆ Johnston Canyon Resort CA
(403) 762-2971. **$119-$318, 3 day notice.** Hwy 1A. 15 mi (24 km) nw on Hwy 1A (Bow Valley Pkwy). Ext corridors. **Pets:** Other species. $10 daily fee/room. Supervision.

SAVE ☒ 🛏 💻 🍴 ✗ 🐾 ✗

◆◆ Red Carpet Inn SH
(403) 762-4184. **$75-$169.** 425 Banff Ave. N of Rabbit St. Ext/int corridors. **Pets:** $10 daily fee/room. Designated rooms, service with restrictions, supervision.

SAVE ☒ 🛏 💻

BROOKS

◆◆ Best Western Brooks Inn SH
(403) 363-0080. **Call for rates.** 115 Fifteenth Ave W. Just s off Trans-Canada Hwy 1. Ext/int corridors. **Pets:** Accepted.

SAVE ☒ 🛏 💻 🏊 ✗

◆◆ Heritage Inn SH
(403) 362-6666. **$105-$120.** 1217 2nd St W. Trans-Canada Hwy 1, exit Hwy 873, 0.5 mi (0.8 km) s. Int corridors. **Pets:** Accepted.

ASK S◊ ☒ 🛏 💻 🍴 🏊 ✗

◆◆ Lakeview Inn & Suites SH
(403) 362-7440. **$139-$179.** 1307 2nd St W. Trans-Canada Hwy 1, exit Hwy 873, 0.5 mi (0.8 km) s. Int corridors. **Pets:** Accepted.

ASK S◊ ☒ 🛏 💻 🏊

◆◆ Travelodge Brooks SH
(403) 362-8000. **$91-$119.** 1240 Cassils Rd E. Trans-Canada Hwy 1, just sw on SR 542, exit E Brooks. Ext/int corridors. **Pets:** Accepted.

ASK S◊ ☒ ⬛ 🛏 💻

CALGARY METROPOLITAN AREA

AIRDRIE

◆◆◆ Ramada Inn & Suites SH 🐾
(403) 945-1288. **$149-$289.** 191 E Lake Crescent. Hwy 2, exit E Airdrie. Int corridors. **Pets:** Medium, other species. $20 daily fee/pet. Service with restrictions, supervision.

SAVE ☒ ⬛ 🛏 💻 🍴 🏊

◆◆ Super 8 Motel-Airdrie SH
(403) 948-4188. **Call for rates.** 815 E Lake Blvd. Hwy 2, exit E Airdrie, 0.5 mi (0.8 km) e on Hwy 587 E. Int corridors. **Pets:** Accepted.

☒ 🛏 💻

CALGARY

◆◆ 5 Calgary Downtown Suites LH
(403) 263-0520. **$99-$369.** 618 5th Ave SW. Corner of 5th Ave SW and 5th St SW. Int corridors. **Pets:** Accepted.

ASK S◊ ☒ 🛏 💻 🍴 🏊 ✗

◆◆◆ Blackfoot Inn SH
(403) 252-2253. **$195-$325.** 5940 Blackfoot Tr SE. At 58th Ave SE; access to property from 58th Ave only. Int corridors. **Pets:** Accepted.

ASK S◊ ☒ 💻 🍴 🏊 ✗

◆◆◆ Calgary Marriott Hotel LH
(403) 266-7331. **$318-$340.** 110 9th Ave SE. Jct 9th Ave and Centre St; adjacent to Telus Convention Centre. Int corridors. **Pets:** Other species. Service with restrictions.

SAVE S◊ ☒ 🛏 💻 🍴 🏊 ✗

◆◆◆ Calgary Westways Guest House BB 🐾
(403) 229-1758. **$110-$170, 4 day notice.** 216 25th Ave SW. 1.1 mi (1.7 km) s on Hwy 2A (MacLeod Trail S), 0.2 mi (0.5 km) w. Int corridors. **Pets:** Other species. $8 daily fee/pet.

SAVE S◊ ☒

Carriage House Inn SH ❀
(403) 253-1101. **$145-$225.** 9030 MacLeod Tr S. On Hwy 2A (MacLeod Trail); corner of 90th Ave SW. Int corridors. **Pets:** Other species. $10 daily fee/pet. Service with restrictions, crate.

Coast Plaza Hotel & Conference Centre LH
(403) 248-8888. **$139-$249.** 1316 33rd St NE. Just s of jct 16th Ave (Trans-Canada Hwy 1) and 36th St NE, just w on 12th Ave NE. Int corridors. **Pets:** Accepted.

Days Inn Calgary Airport SH
(403) 250-3297. **$129-$159.** 2799 Sunridge Way NE. Barlow Trail, just e of Sunridge Way NE. Int corridors. **Pets:** Accepted.

Delta Bow Valley LH ❀
(403) 266-1980. **$139-$469.** 209 4th Ave SE. 1st St SE and 4th Ave SE. Int corridors. **Pets:** Small, other species. $35 one-time fee/room. Designated rooms, service with restrictions, supervision.

Delta Calgary Airport LH ❀
(403) 291-2600. **$159-$550.** 2001 Airport Rd NE. At Calgary International Airport. Int corridors. **Pets:** Large. $35 one-time fee/pet. Service with restrictions, supervision.

Delta Calgary South SH ❀
(403) 278-5050. **$389-$399.** 135 Southland Dr SE. On Hwy 2A (MacLeod Trail); corner of Southland Dr. Int corridors. **Pets:** Medium. $35 one-time fee/room. Service with restrictions, supervision.

Econo Lodge South M
(403) 252-4401. **$89-$209.** 7505 MacLeod Tr S. Corner of MacLeod Tr and 75th Ave. Ext/int corridors. **Pets:** Accepted.

Executive Royal Inn North Calgary SH
(403) 291-2003. **$144-$205.** 2828 23rd St NE. 27th Ave NE and Barlow Trail. Int corridors. **Pets:** Accepted.

The Fairmont Palliser LH
(403) 262-1234. **$179-$449.** 133 9th Ave SW. 9th Ave SW and 1st St SW. Int corridors. **Pets:** Medium. $35 one-time fee/pet. Designated rooms, service with restrictions, supervision.

Holiday Inn Express Hotel & Suites Calgary Downtown SH
(403) 269-8262. **$189-$259.** 1020 8th Ave SW. 8th Ave at 10th St SW. Int corridors. **Pets:** Small, other species. $25 one-time fee/room. Designated rooms, service with restrictions, supervision.

Holiday Inn Express Hotel & Suites Calgary-South SH
(403) 225-3000. **Call for rates.** 12025 Lake Fraser Dr SE (MacLeod Trail S). Hwy 2 (Deerfoot Trail), exit Anderson Rd W, then just s on MacLeod Trail. Int corridors. **Pets:** Accepted.

Hotel Arts SH
(403) 266-4611. **$129-$309.** 119 12th Ave SW. At 1st St SW; centre. Int corridors. **Pets:** Accepted.

International Hotel of Calgary LH
(403) 265-9600. **Call for rates.** 220 4th Ave SW. Corner of 4th Ave and 2nd St SW. Int corridors. **Pets:** Accepted.

Lakeview Signature Inn SH ❀
(403) 735-3336. **$139-$199.** 2622 39th Ave NE. Corner of Barlow Trail and 39th Ave NE. Int corridors. **Pets:** Small. $100 one-time fee/pet. Service with restrictions, supervision.

Radisson Hotel Calgary Airport SH
(403) 291-4666. **$240.** 2120 16th Ave NE. Just e of jct 16th Ave NE (Trans-Canada Hwy 1) and Hwy 2 (Deerfoot Trail). Int corridors. **Pets:** Accepted.

Sandman Hotel Downtown Calgary LH
(403) 237-8626. **$179-$199.** 888 7th Ave SW. Corner of 7th Ave SW and 8th St SW. Int corridors. **Pets:** Accepted.

Sandman Hotel Suites & Spa Calgary Airport SH
(403) 219-2475. **$189.** 25 Hopewell Way NE. Just n of jct Barlow Trail and McKnight Blvd. Int corridors. **Pets:** Accepted.

Sheraton Cavalier Hotel LH
(403) 291-0107. **$469.** 2620 32nd Ave NE. Barlow Trail at 32nd Ave NE. Int corridors. **Pets:** Accepted.

Sheraton Suites Calgary Eau Claire LH
(403) 266-7200. **Call for rates.** 255 Barclay Parade SW. At 3rd St SW and 2nd Ave SW. Int corridors. **Pets:** Accepted.

Super 8 Motel Calgary Airport SH
(403) 291-9888. **$120-$240.** 3030 Barlow Tr NE. Corner of 32nd Ave and Barlow Trail NE. Int corridors. **Pets:** Accepted.

Travelodge Calgary Macleod Trail SH ❀
(403) 253-7070. **$131-$167.** 9206 MacLeod Tr S. On MacLeod Tr just s of 90th Ave SW. Int corridors. **Pets:** Small. $20 one-time fee/room. Designated rooms, service with restrictions, supervision.

Travelodge Calgary-University SH ❀
(403) 289-6600. **$98-$187.** 2227 Banff Tr NW. 16th Ave NW (Trans-Canada Hwy 1) and Banff Trail NW. Int corridors. **Pets:** Other species. $10 daily fee/pet. Designated rooms, supervision.

Travelodge Hotel Calgary Airport SH
(403) 291-1260. **$129-$229.** 2750 Sunridge Blvd NE. Just se of jct 32nd Ave NE and Barlow Trail NE. Int corridors. **Pets:** Other species. $100 deposit/room. Service with restrictions, crate.

The Westin Calgary LH
(403) 266-1611. **$129-$489.** 320 4th Ave SW. Corner of 4th Ave SW and 3rd St. Int corridors. **Pets:** Accepted.

Wingate Inn SH
(403) 514-0099. **$147-$169, 4 day notice.** 400 Midpark Way. Hwy 2A (MacLeod Trail), 0.3 mi (0.5 km) e on Sun Valley, just n on Midpark Way, then just s. Int corridors. **Pets:** Accepted.

COCHRANE

Best Western Harvest Country Inn SH
(403) 932-1410. **$129-$149.** 11 West Side Dr. Hwy 1A, 0.6 mi (1 km) sw on Hwy 22. Ext/int corridors. **Pets:** Small, other species. $10 daily fee/pet. Designated rooms, service with restrictions, supervision.

▼▼◆◆ **Super 8 Motel-Cochrane** 🆂🅷
(403) 932-6355. **$155-$175.** 10 Westside Dr. Hwy 1A, 0.6 mi (1 km) sw on Hwy 22. Int corridors. **Pets:** Accepted.
🅰🆂🅺 🆂🌀 ⊠ 🔒 💻 🏊 ⊠

▼▼ **Travelodge Cochrane** 🆂🅷
(403) 932-5588. **$98-$129.** 5 West Side Dr. Hwy 1A, 0.6 mi (1 km) sw on Hwy 22. Int corridors. **Pets:** Accepted.
🅰🆂🅺 🆂🌀 ⊠ 🔒 💻 🏊

OKOTOKS

▼▼▼▼ **Lakeview Inns & Suites** 🆂🅷
(403) 938-7400. **$129-$149.** 22 Southridge Dr. Hwy 2, exit 2A, 2.5 mi (4 km) s to Southridge Dr. Int corridors. **Pets:** Accepted.
⊠ 🔒 💻

STRATHMORE

🅐🅐 ▼▼▼ **Best Western Strathmore Inn** 🆂🅷
(403) 934-5777. **Call for rates.** 550 Hwy 1. Trans-Canada Hwy 1, jct SR 817; centre. Int corridors. **Pets:** Accepted.
🆂🅰🆅🅴 ⊠ 🔒 💻 🏊

▼▼▼▼ **Travelodge Strathmore** 🆂🅷
(403) 901-0000. **$134-$154.** 350 Ridge Rd. Just n of Trans-Canada Hwy 1 at Ridge Rd. Int corridors. **Pets:** Accepted.
🅰🆂🅺 🆂🌀 ⊠ 🔒 💻 🏊 ⊠

END METROPOLITAN AREA

CAMROSE

▼▼◆ **Norsemen Inn** 🆂🅷
(780) 672-9171. **$95.** 6505 48th Ave. Hwy 13 (48th Ave) at 65th St; west end of town. Int corridors. **Pets:** Accepted.
🅰🆂🅺 🆂🌀 ⊠ 🔒 💻 🍴

CANMORE

🅐🅐 ▼▼◆◆ **Banff Boundary Lodge** 🅲🅾
(403) 678-9555. **$89-$239, 3 day notice.** 1000 Harvie Heights Rd. Just e of Banff National Park east gate, parallel to Trans-Canada Hwy 1, exit Harvie Heights Rd. Ext corridors. **Pets:** Accepted.
🆂🅰🆅🅴 🆂🌀 ⊠ 🔒 💻 🎿

🅐🅐 ▼▼▼▼ **Best Western Pocaterra Inn** 🆂🅷
(403) 678-4334. **Call for rates.** 1725 Mountain Ave. 3.6 mi (5.8 km) e of Banff National Park east gate on Hwy 1A (Bow Valley Trail). Int corridors. **Pets:** Accepted.
🆂🅰🆅🅴 ⊠ 🔒 💻 🏊 ⊠

🅐🅐 ▼▼◆◆ **Canmore Inn & Suites** 🆂🅷
(403) 609-4656. **Call for rates.** 1402 Bow Valley Tr. 3.5 mi (5.6 km) e of Banff National Park east gate on Hwy 1A (Bow Valley Trail); Trans-Canada Hwy 1, exit Canmore. Int corridors. **Pets:** Other species. $15 daily fee/pet. Designated rooms, service with restrictions.
🆂🅰🆅🅴 ⊠ 🔒 💻 🏊 ⊠

▼▼ **The Lodges at Canmore** 🆂🅷
(403) 678-9350. **$175-$339.** 107 Montane Rd. Trans-Canada Hwy 1, exit 1A (Bow Valley Trail), 0.6 mi (1.6 km) w to Montane Rd. Int corridors. **Pets:** Accepted.
🅰🆂🅺 ⊠ 🔒 💻 🏊

▼▼▼▼ **Mystic Springs Chalets & Hot Pools** 🅲🅾 ♣
(403) 609-0333. **$245-$369.** 140 Kananaskis Way. Trans-Canada Hwy 1, exit 1A (Bow Valley Trail), 0.6 mi (1 km) w, then n at Montane Dr. Ext corridors. **Pets:** Medium. $20 daily fee/pet. Designated rooms, service with restrictions, supervision.
🅰🆂🅺 🆂🌀 ⊠ 🔒 💻 🏊 ⊠

🅐🅐 ▼▼▼ **Radisson Hotel & Conference Centre** 🆂🅷 ♣
(403) 678-3625. **$169-$249.** 511 Bow Valley Tr. Trans-Canada Hwy 1, exit Canmore, just e. Ext/int corridors. **Pets:** Other species. $50 one-time fee/room. Service with restrictions, supervision.
🆂🅰🆅🅴 🆂🌀 ⊠ 🔒 💻 🍴 🏊 ⊠

🅐🅐 ▼▼▼ **Rocky Mountain Ski Lodge** 🅼
(403) 678-5445. **$120-$205.** 1711 Bow Valley Tr. Trans-Canada Hwy 1, exit Canmore; 3 mi (4.8 km) e of Banff National Park east gate on Hwy 1A (Bow Valley Trail). Ext corridors. **Pets:** Medium. $10 daily fee/room. Designated rooms, service with restrictions, supervision.
🆂🅰🆅🅴 🆂🌀 ⊠ 🔒 💻 ⊠

🅐🅐 ▼▼▼ **Rundle Mountain Lodge** 🅼
(403) 678-5322. **$75-$125, 7 day notice.** 1723 Bow Valley Tr. Trans-Canada Hwy 1, exit Canmore; 3 mi (4.8 km) e of Banff National Park east gate on Hwy 1A (Bow Valley Trail). Ext corridors. **Pets:** Medium, other species. $10 one-time fee/pet. Designated rooms, service with restrictions, supervision.
🆂🅰🆅🅴 🆂🌀 ⊠ 🔒 💻 🏊

🅐🅐 ▼▼▼ **Windtower Lodge & Suites** 🅲🅾 ♣
(403) 609-6600. **$139-$399, 3 day notice.** 160 Kananaskis Way. Trans-Canada Hwy 1, exit 1A (Bow Valley Trail), 0.6 mi (1 km) w, then n at Montane Dr. Int corridors. **Pets:** $35 one-time fee/pet. Designated rooms, service with restrictions, supervision.
🆂🅰🆅🅴 ⊠ 🔒 💻 🍴 🎿

CLAIRMONT

🅐🅐 ▼▼▼▼ **Ramada Inn & Suites** 🆂🅷 ♣
(780) 814-7448. **$169-$299.** 7201 99 St. Jct Hwy 43 and 2, just n. Int corridors. **Pets:** Other species. $25 one-time fee/room. Service with restrictions, crate.
🆂🅰🆅🅴 🆂🌀 ⊠ 🔒 💻

CLARESHOLM

▼▼ **Bluebird Motel** 🅼
(403) 625-3395. **$80-$90.** 5505 1st St W. 0.3 mi (0.5 km) n on Hwy 2. Ext corridors. **Pets:** Accepted.
⊠ 🔒 💻

DEAD MAN'S FLATS

🅐🅐 ▼▼ **Pigeon Mountain Motel** 🅼
(403) 678-5756. **$75-$135, 3 day notice.** 250 1st Ave. On Trans-Canada Hwy 1. Ext corridors. **Pets:** Accepted.
🆂🅰🆅🅴 🆂🌀 ⊠ 🔒 💻 🎿

DRAYTON VALLEY

▼▼ **Lakeview Inns & Suites** 🆂🅷
(780) 542-3200. **Call for rates.** 4302 50th St. Hwy 22, exit Drayton Valley, just n. Int corridors. **Pets:** Accepted.
⊠ 🔒 💻 🍴 ⊠

DRUMHELLER

🅐🅐 ▼▼▼ **Best Western Jurassic Inn** 🆂🅷
(403) 823-7700. **$114-$153.** 1103 Hwy 9 S. Hwy 9, southeast access to town. Ext/int corridors. **Pets:** Accepted.
🆂🅰🆅🅴 🆂🌀 ⊠ 🔒 💻 🍴 🏊

🅐🅐 ▼▼▼▼ **Inn and Spa at Heartwood** 🅱🅱
(403) 823-6495. **$99-$280, 3 day notice.** 320 N Railway Ave E. Downtown. Ext/int corridors. **Pets:** Accepted.
🆂🅰🆅🅴 ⊠ 🔒 💻

▼▼▼ **Ramada Inn & Suites** 🆂🅷
(403) 823-2028. **Call for rates.** 680 2nd St SE. Off Hwy 9. Ext/int corridors. **Pets:** Accepted.
☒ ♿ 🛏 💻 ⇆ ⊠

▼▼ **Super 8 Motel** 🆂🅷
(403) 823-8887. **Call for rates.** 600-680 2nd St SE. Off Hwy 9. Ext/int corridors. **Pets:** Accepted.
☒ 🛏 💻 ⇆ ⊠

EDMONTON METROPOLITAN AREA

EDMONTON

🆑🅐 ▼▼▼ **Best Western Cedar Park Inn** 🆂🅷
(780) 434-7411. **Call for rates.** 5116 Gateway Blvd. Hwy 2 (Gateway Blvd) at 51st Ave. Int corridors. **Pets:** Accepted.
[SAVE] ☒ 🛏 💻 🍴 ⇆

🆑🅐 ▼▼▼ **Chateau Louis Hotel & Conference Centre** 🆂🅷
(780) 452-7770. **$119-$209.** 11727 Kingsway. On Kingsway and 117th St. Int corridors. **Pets:** Accepted.
[SAVE] [S♿] ☒ ♿ 🛏 💻 🍴

▼▼ **Coast Edmonton House** 🅲🅾
(780) 420-4000. **$105-$245.** 10205 100th Ave. Just se of jct 102nd St and 100th Ave. Int corridors. **Pets:** Accepted.
[ASK] [S♿] ☒ 🛏 💻 🍴 ⇆ ⊠

🆑🅐 ▼▼ **Comfort Inn West** 🆂🅷
(780) 484-4415. **$109-$154.** 17610 100th Ave. At 176th St. Int corridors. **Pets:** Medium. $10 daily fee/pet. Service with restrictions, supervision.
[SAVE] [S♿] ☒ 🛏 💻 🍴

🅐🅐 ▼▼ **Continental Inn** 🆂🅷
(780) 484-7751. **$110-$135, 6 day notice.** 16625 Stony Plain Rd. On Hwy 16A (Stony Plain Rd) at 166th St. Int corridors. **Pets:** Accepted.
[SAVE] ☒ 🛏 💻 🍴

▼▼▼ **Delta Edmonton Centre Suite Hotel** 🅻🅷 ❖
(780) 429-3900. **$99-$389.** 10222 102nd St. At 102nd St at 103rd Ave. Int corridors. **Pets:** Dogs only. $35 one-time fee/room. Service with restrictions, crate.
☒ 💻 🍴 ⊠

▼▼▼ **Delta Edmonton South Hotel and Conference Centre** 🅻🅷 ❖
(780) 434-6415. **$160-$270.** 4404 Gateway Blvd. Jct Calgary Trail (Hwy 2) and Whitemud Dr. Int corridors. **Pets:** Small, other species. $35 one-time fee/pet. Service with restrictions.
[ASK] [S♿] ☒ 🛏 💻 🍴 ⇆

▼▼ **Executive Royal Inn West Edmonton** 🆂🅷
(780) 484-6000. **$105.** 10010 178th St. Corner of 178th St and 100th Ave. Int corridors. **Pets:** Accepted.
[ASK] ☒ 🛏 💻 🍴 ⊠

🅐🅐 ▼▼▼▼ **The Fairmont Hotel Macdonald** 🅻🅷
(780) 424-5181. **$159-$465.** 10065 100th St. Just s of Jasper Ave. Int corridors. **Pets:** Medium. $35 one-time fee/pet. Designated rooms, service with restrictions, supervision.
[SAVE] ☒ ♿ 💻 🍴 ⇆ ⊠

🅐🅐 ▼▼▼▼ **Four Points by Sheraton Edmonton South** 🅻🅷
(780) 465-7931. **$205-$225.** 7230 Argyll Rd. Hwy 2 (Gateway Blvd), 2.3 mi (3.7 km) e at 63rd Ave (which becomes Argyll Rd); at 75th St. Int corridors. **Pets:** Accepted.
[SAVE] ☒ 🛏 💻 🍴 ⇆

🅐🅐 ▼▼▼ **Greenwood Hotel & Suites** 🆂🅷
(780) 431-1100. **$129-$249.** 4485 Gateway Blvd. Hwy 2 (Gateway Blvd), just n of Whitemud Dr. Int corridors. **Pets:** Other species. $10 daily fee/room. Designated rooms, service with restrictions, supervision.
[SAVE] [S♿] ☒ ♿ 🛏 💻 🍴 ⊠

▼▼▼ **Holiday Inn Edmonton-The Palace** 🆂🅷
(780) 438-1222. **Call for rates.** 4235 Gateway Blvd. Just s of Whitemud Dr. Int corridors. **Pets:** Accepted.
☒ 🛏 💻 🍴

🅐🅐 ▼▼▼ **Holiday Inn Express Edmonton-Downtown** 🆂🅷
(780) 423-2450. **$128.** 10010 104th St. Corner of 100th Ave; centre. Int corridors. **Pets:** Small. $25 one-time fee/pet. Designated rooms, service with restrictions, supervision.
[SAVE] ☒ 🛏 💻 ⇆ ⊠

🅐🅐 ▼▼▼ **Mayfield Inn & Suites at West Edmonton** 🅻🅷 ❖
(780) 484-0821. **$150-$225.** 16615 109th Ave. 1 mi (1.6 km) n of jct Hwy 2 (Gateway Blvd) and 16A on Mayfield Rd. Int corridors. **Pets:** Small, dogs only. $25 one-time fee/pet. Designated rooms, service with restrictions, supervision.
[SAVE] ☒ 🛏 💻 🍴 ⇆ ⊠

▼▼▼ **Metterra Hotel on Whyte** 🆂🅷
(780) 465-8150. **$170-$350.** 10454 82nd Ave (Whyte Ave). Just e of 105th St. Int corridors. **Pets:** Accepted.
[ASK] ☒ 💻

🅐🅐 ▼▼▼ **Rosslyn Inn & Suites** 🆂🅷 ❖
(780) 476-6241. **$111.** 13620 97 St. Hwy 16 (Yellowhead Hwy), exit 97th St, 1 mi (1.6 km) n. Int corridors. **Pets:** Medium. $10 one-time fee/pet. Designated rooms, service with restrictions, crate.
[SAVE] [S♿] ☒ 🛏 💻 🍴

🅐🅐 ▼▼▼ **Super 8 Hotel** 🆂🅷
(780) 433-8688. **$129-$149.** 3610 Gateway Blvd. Jct 36th Ave. Int corridors. **Pets:** Accepted.
[SAVE] ☒ ♿ 🛏 💻 ⇆

▼▼▼ **The Sutton Place Hotel, Edmonton** 🅻🅷
(780) 428-7111. **$325-$355.** 10235 101st St. 102nd Ave at 101st St. Int corridors. **Pets:** Accepted.
[ASK] ☒ 🛏 💻 🍴 ⇆ ⊠

🅐🅐 ▼▼▼ **Travelodge Edmonton West** 🆂🅷 ❖
(780) 483-6031. **$109-$159.** 18320 Stony Plain Rd. Hwy 16A (Stony Plain Rd) at 184th St. Int corridors. **Pets:** $50 deposit/room. Designated rooms, service with restrictions, supervision.
[SAVE] [S♿] ☒ 🛏 💻 🍴 ⇆ ⊠

▼▼▼▼ **Varscona Hotel on Whyte** 🆂🅷
(780) 434-6111. **$150-$300.** 8208 106th St. Corner of 82nd Ave (Whyte Ave) and 106th St. Int corridors. **Pets:** Accepted.
[ASK] ☒ 🛏 💻 🍴

🅐🅐 ▼▼▼ **The Westin Edmonton** 🅻🅷
(780) 426-3636. **$119-$399.** 10135 100th St. 101st Ave at 100th St. Int corridors. **Pets:** Accepted.
[SAVE] [S♿] ☒ 💻 🍴 ⇆ ⊠

🅐🅐 ▼▼▼▼ **Wingate Inn Edmonton West** 🆂🅷 ❖
(780) 443-1000. **$135-$150.** 18220 100th Ave. 100th Ave at 182nd St. Int corridors. **Pets:** $25 one-time fee/pet. Service with restrictions, supervision.
[SAVE] [S♿] ☒ ♿ 🛏 💻 ⇆ ⊠

FORT SASKATCHEWAN

Lakeview Inns & Suites SH
(780) 998-7888. **Call for rates.** 10115 88th Ave. Just w of Hwy 15/21 and 101st St. Int corridors. **Pets:** Accepted.

NISKU

Holiday Inn Express Edmonton Int'l Airport SH
(780) 955-1000. **$150-$160.** 1102 4th St. Hwy 2, exit Edmonton International Airport/Nisku Business Park (10th Ave), 0.5 mi (0.8 km) e. Int corridors. **Pets:** Accepted.

SHERWOOD PARK

Franklin's Inn SH
(780) 467-1234. **$105-$149.** 2016 Sherwood Dr. At Granada Blvd. Int corridors. **Pets:** Accepted.

Ramada Limited-Edmonton East/Sherwood Park SH
(780) 467-6727. **Call for rates.** 30 Broadway Blvd. Hwy 16, exit Broadmoor Blvd, 1.2 mi (2 km) s. Int corridors. **Pets:** Accepted.

Roadking Inns SH
(780) 464-1000. **$129-$149.** 26 Strathmoor Dr. Just sw of Hwy 16, exit Broadmoor Blvd. Int corridors. **Pets:** Other species. $39 one-time fee/room. Designated rooms, service with restrictions, supervision.

STONY PLAIN

Ramada Inn & Suites SH
(780) 963-0222. **$63-$115.** 3301 43rd Ave. Hwy 16A, exit Dunmore Rd, just s. Ext/int corridors. **Pets:** Other species. $15 daily fee/room. Designated rooms, service with restrictions, supervision.

END METROPOLITAN AREA

EDSON

Best Western High Road Inn SH
(780) 712-2378. **$133-$229.** 300 52nd St. On 2nd Ave; centre. Int corridors. **Pets:** Accepted.

Guest House Inn & Suites M
(780) 723-4486. **$101-$122.** 4411 4th Ave. 0.6 mi (1 km) e on Hwy 16. Ext/int corridors. **Pets:** Other species. Service with restrictions, crate.

Lakeview Inns & Suites SH
(780) 723-2500. **$120.** 4300 2nd Ave. 0.6 mi (1.1 km) e on Hwy 16. Int corridors. **Pets:** Accepted.

FORT MACLEOD

Sunset Motel M
(403) 553-4448. **$54-$74.** 104 Hwy 3 W. 0.6 mi (1 km) w on Hwy 2 and 3. Ext corridors. **Pets:** Accepted.

FORT MCMURRAY

Super 8 Motel SH
(780) 799-8450. **$144-$185.** 321 Sakitawaw Tr. Just w of Hwy 63, 3.1 mi (5 km) s. Int corridors. **Pets:** Accepted.

GRANDE PRAIRIE

Best Western Grande Prairie Hotel & Suites SH
(780) 402-2378. **Call for rates.** 10745 117th Ave. Corner of Hwy 43 and 117th Ave. Int corridors. **Pets:** Accepted.

Pomeroy Inn & Suites SH
(780) 831-2999. **$179-$189.** 11710 102nd St. 102nd St at 117th Ave. Int corridors. **Pets:** Medium, other species. $10 daily fee/pet. Service with restrictions, supervision.

Quality Hotel & Conference Centre Grande Prairie LH
(780) 539-6000. **$203-$300.** 11201 100th Ave. 1.8 mi (2.9 km) w on Hwy 2. Int corridors. **Pets:** Accepted.

Service Plus Inns and Suites SH
(780) 538-3900. **$159-$300.** 10810 107th a Ave. 1.4 mi (2.2 km) w on Hwy 2, just n. Int corridors. **Pets:** Accepted.

Stanford Inn SH
(780) 539-5678. **$139-$149.** 11401 100th Ave. 1.8 mi (2.8 km) w on Hwy 2. Ext/int corridors. **Pets:** Other species. $8 daily fee/pet. Service with restrictions, supervision.

Super 8 Motel SH
(780) 532-8288. **$129-$169.** 10050 116 Ave. 102nd St at 117th Ave. Int corridors. **Pets:** Accepted.

HIGH RIVER

Heritage Inn SH
(403) 652-3834. **$119-$225.** 1104 11th Ave SE. Trans-Canada Hwy 2, exit 23, 0.5 mi (0.8 km) w of Hwy 2. Int corridors. **Pets:** Accepted.

Super 8 Motel SH
(403) 652-4448. **$140-$200.** 1601 13th Ave SE. Trans-Canada Hwy 2, exit High River, just w. Int corridors. **Pets:** Accepted.

HINTON

Best Western White Wolf Inn SH
(780) 865-7777. **$126-$160.** 828 Carmichael Ln. At west end of town; just off Hwy 16. Ext corridors. **Pets:** Accepted.

Lakeview Inns & Suites SH
(780) 865-2575. **Call for rates.** 500 Smith St. 1.1 mi (1.7 km) e on Hwy 16. Ext/int corridors. **Pets:** Accepted.

JASPER

Amethyst Lodge SH
(780) 852-3394. **$85-$285.** 200 Connaught Dr. 0.3 mi (0.5 km) e. Ext/int corridors. **Pets:** Other species. $10 daily fee/room. Designated rooms, service with restrictions, crate.

SAVE S❄ ✕ ▣ ❚❙

The Coast Pyramid Lake Resort SH
(780) 852-4900. **$209-$364, 3 day notice.** Pyramid Lake Rd. Jct Connaught Dr and Cedar St, 3.75 mi (6 km) nw via Pyramid Lake Rd. Ext corridors. **Pets:** Accepted.

SAVE S❄ ✕ 🛏 ▣ ❚❙ ✕ ⚲

The Fairmont Jasper Park Lodge LH
(780) 852-3301. **$169-$629, 3 day notice.** Lodge Rd. 3 mi (4.8 km) ne via Hwy 16; 2 mi (3.2 km) se off highway via Maligne Rd, follow signs. Ext corridors. **Pets:** Medium. $35 one-time fee/pet. Designated rooms, service with restrictions, supervision.

SAVE S❄ ✕ 🛏 ▣ ❚❙ ⇆ ✕ ⚲

Jasper Inn Alpine Resort SH
(780) 852-4461. **$118-$413, 3 day notice.** 98 Geikie St. Corner of Geikie and Bonhomme sts. Ext/int corridors. **Pets:** Accepted.

SAVE S❄ ✕ 🛏 ▣ ❚❙ ⇆ ✕ ⚲

Lobstick Lodge SH
(780) 852-4431. **$99-$255.** 94 Geikie St. Corner of Geikie and Juniper sts. Int corridors. **Pets:** Other species. $10 daily fee/room. Designated rooms, service with restrictions.

SAVE S❄ ✕ 🛏 ▣ ❚❙ ✕ ⚲

Maligne Lodge M
(780) 852-3143. **$99-$400.** 900 Connaught. 0.6 mi (1 km) sw. Ext/int corridors. **Pets:** Accepted.

SAVE S❄ ✕ 🛏 ▣ ❚❙ ⇆

Marmot Lodge M
(780) 852-4471. **$89-$255.** 86 Connaught Dr. 1 mi (1.6 km) ne. Ext corridors. **Pets:** Other species. $10 daily fee/room. Designated rooms, service with restrictions, crate.

SAVE S❄ ✕ 🛏 ▣ ❚❙ ⇆

Patricia Lake Bungalows CA
(780) 852-3560. **$75-$325, 7 day notice.** Pyramid Lake Rd. 3 mi (4.8 km) nw via Pyramid Lake Rd. Ext corridors. **Pets:** Accepted.

✕ 🛏 ▣ ✕ ⚲ ⚡

The Sawridge Inn and Conference Centre SH
(780) 852-5111. **$139-$289, 3 day notice.** 82 Connaught Dr. 1.1 mi (1.7 km) e. Int corridors. **Pets:** Accepted.

SAVE S❄ ✕ ❙M ▣ ⇆ ✕

Sunwapta Falls Resort M
(780) 852-4852. **$89-$389, 7 day notice.** Hwy 93. 34.75 mi (55 km) s on Icefields Pkwy (Hwy 93). Ext corridors. **Pets:** Accepted.

SAVE S❄ ✕ 🛏 ▣ ❚❙ ✕ ⚲ ⚡

Tonquin Inn M 🐾
(780) 852-4987. **$135-$260.** 100 Juniper St. Corner of Juniper and Geikie sts. Ext/int corridors. **Pets:** Medium. $25 one-time fee/room. Service with restrictions, supervision.

SAVE ✕ 🛏 ▣ ❚❙ ⇆

KANANASKIS

Delta Lodge at Kananaskis LH 🐾
(403) 591-7711. **Call for rates.** Kananaskis Village. Trans-Canada Hwy 1, 14.7 mi (23.5 km) s on Hwy 40 (Kananaskis Trail), then 1.8 mi (3 km) on Kananaskis Village access road, follow signs. Int corridors. **Pets:** Medium. $85 one-time fee/room. Designated rooms, service with restrictions, supervision.

✕ 🛏 ▣ ❚❙ ⇆ ✕

LAKE LOUISE

The Fairmont Chateau Lake Louise LH
(403) 522-3511. **$249-$659, 3 day notice.** 111 Lake Louise Dr. 1.8 mi (3 km) up the hill from the village. Int corridors. **Pets:** Medium. $35 one-time fee/pet. Designated rooms, service with restrictions, supervision.

SAVE S❄ ✕ ▣ ❚❙ ⇆ ✕

Lake Louise Inn SH
(403) 522-3791. **Call for rates.** 210 Village Rd. Just w of 4-way stop. Ext/int corridors. **Pets:** Accepted.

✕ 🛏 ▣ ❚❙ ⇆ ✕

LETHBRIDGE

Comfort Inn SH
(403) 320-8874. **Call for rates.** 3226 Fairway Plaza Rd S. Southeast end of city; Mayor Magrath Dr, exit n at Scenic Dr. Int corridors. **Pets:** Accepted.

✕ 🛏 ▣ ⇆

Days Inn Lethbridge SH
(403) 327-6000. **$90-$180.** 100 3rd Ave S. Corner of 3rd Ave and Scenic Dr; centre. Ext/int corridors. **Pets:** Accepted.

SAVE ✕ 🛏 ▣ ⇆

Holiday Inn Express Hotel & Suites Lethbridge SH
(403) 394-9292. **$129-$229.** 120 Stafford Dr S. Hwy 3, exit Stafford Dr, just s; downtown. Int corridors. **Pets:** Accepted.

ASK S❄ ✕ 🛏 ▣ ⇆ ✕

Lethbridge Lodge Hotel and Conference Centre LH
(403) 328-1123. **$109-$189.** 320 Scenic Dr. Scenic Dr at 4th Ave S; centre. Int corridors. **Pets:** Accepted.

SAVE S❄ ✕ 🛏 ▣ ❚❙ ⇆

Pepper Tree Inn M
(403) 328-4436. **$55-$90.** 1142 Mayor Magrath Dr S. 2.5 mi (4 km) se on Hwy 4 and 5, exit Mayor Magrath Dr S. Ext corridors. **Pets:** Accepted.

SAVE ✕ 🛏 ⇆

Ramada Hotel & Suites LH
(403) 380-5050. **$140-$150.** 2375 Mayor Magrath Dr S. 2.6 mi (4.5 km) se on Hwy 4 and 5, exit Mayor Magrath Dr S. Int corridors. **Pets:** Accepted.

ASK S❄ ✕ 🛏 ▣ ❚❙ ⇆ ✕

Sandman Hotel Lethbridge SH
(403) 328-1111. **$129.** 421 Mayor Magrath Dr. Hwy 3, exit Mayor Magrath Dr, just s. Int corridors. **Pets:** Accepted.

ASK S❄ ✕ 🛏 ▣ ❚❙ ⇆

MEDICINE HAT

Best Western Inn SH
(403) 527-3700. **$99-$249.** 722 Redcliff Dr. On Trans-Canada Hwy 1, 0.3 mi (0.4 km) w of jct Hwy 3, access 7th St SW. Ext/int corridors. **Pets:** Accepted.

ASK S❄ ✕ ♿ 🛏 ▣ ⇆ ✕

Medicine Hat Lodge Hotel Casino Convention Centre Health Spa & Indoor LH
(403) 529-2222. **$119-$136.** 1051 Ross Glen Dr SE. East end approach to city on Trans-Canada Hwy 1, at Dunmore Rd. Int corridors. **Pets:** Accepted.

ASK S❄ ✕ 🛏 ▣ ❚❙ ⇆ ✕

Motel 6-Medicine Hat SH
(403) 527-1749. **Call for rates.** 20 Strochon Ct SE. Trans-Canada Hwy 1, exit Dunmore Rd, just sw. Int corridors. **Pets:** Other species. Service with restrictions, supervision.

✕ ❙M 🛏

▼▼◆ Super 8 Motel 🅂🄷
(403) 528-8888. **$82-$89.** 1280 Trans-Canada Way SE. Trans-Canada Hwy 1 at 13 Ave SE; just n off Trans-Canada Hwy 1. Ext/int corridors. **Pets:** Accepted.

🄰🅂🄺 🅂🄸 ⊠ 🔋 💻 ⇌

PINCHER CREEK

▼▼ Heritage Inn 🅂🄷
(403) 627-5000. **$95-$149.** 919 Waterton Ave (Hwy 6). SR 3, 2.9 mi (4.7 km) s. Int corridors. **Pets:** Accepted.

🄰🅂🄺 🅂🄸 ⊠ 🔋 💻 🍴

RED DEER

🄰 ▼▼◆ Best Western Red Deer Inn & Suites 🅂🄷
(403) 346-3555. **$115-$135.** 6839 66th St. Hwy 2, exit 67th St, just e. Int corridors. **Pets:** Accepted.

🆂🅰🆅🅴 🅂🄸 ⊠ 🔋 💻 ⇌

🄰 ▼▼◆ Capri Hotel Trade & Convention Centre 🄻🄷
(403) 346-2091. **Call for rates.** 3310 50th Ave. 1.3 mi (2 km) n on Hwy 2A (Gaetz Ave). Int corridors. **Pets:** Accepted.

🆂🅰🆅🅴 ⊠ 🔋 💻 🍴 ⇌ ⊠

🄰 ▼▼◆ Comfort Inn & Suites 🅂🄷 🐾
(403) 348-0025. **$99-$149.** 6846 66th St. Hwy 2, exit 67th St, just e. Int corridors. **Pets:** Small. $20 one-time fee/room. Service with restrictions, supervision.

🆂🅰🆅🅴 🅂🄸 ⊠ 🔋 💻 ⇌ ⊠

🄰 ▼▼◆ Holiday Inn 67th Street 🅂🄷
(403) 342-6567. **$130.** 6500 67th St. Hwy 2, exit 67th St, 0.5 mi (0.8 km) e. Int corridors. **Pets:** Small. $15 daily fee/room. Designated rooms, service with restrictions, supervision.

🆂🅰🆅🅴 🅂🄸 ⊠ 🔋 💻 🍴 ⇌ ⊠

▼ Motel 6–Red Deer 🅂🄷
(403) 340-1749. **$60-$80.** 900-5001 19th St. Hwy 2, exit 394 (Gaetz Ave), just n, then just w; in Southpointe Common Shopping District. Int corridors. **Pets:** Other species. Service with restrictions, supervision.

⊠ 🔋

▼▼ Sandman Hotel Red Deer 🅂🄷
(403) 343-7400. **$124-$179.** 2818 Gaetz Ave. 1 mi (1.6 km) n on Hwy 2A (Gaetz Ave). Int corridors. **Pets:** Accepted.

🄰🅂🄺 🅂🄸 ⊠ 🔋 💻 🍴 ⇌

ROCKY MOUNTAIN HOUSE

🄰 ▼ Chinook Inn 🄼
(403) 845-2833. **$70-$90.** 5321 59th Ave. 0.8 mi (1.3 km) w on Hwy 11, then s. Int corridors. **Pets:** $10 daily fee/pet. Designated rooms, service with restrictions, supervision.

🆂🅰🆅🅴 🅂🄸 ⊠ 🔋 💻

🄰 ▼▼ Holiday Inn Express Rocky Mountain House 🅂🄷
(403) 845-2871. **$119-$129.** 4715 45th St. Just nw of jct 47th Ave and 45th St. Int corridors. **Pets:** $15 daily fee/pet. Service with restrictions, supervision.

🆂🅰🆅🅴 ⊠ 🔋 💻

▼▼◆ Super 8 Motel 🅂🄷
(403) 846-0088. **Call for rates.** 4406 41st Ave. Just off Hwy 11 at east end of town. Int corridors. **Pets:** Accepted.

⊠ 🔋 💻 ⇌ ⊠

TABER

▼▼ Heritage Inn 🅂🄷
(403) 223-4424. **$89-$125.** 4830 46th Ave. 0.6 mi (1 km) e of jct Hwy 3 and 36 S, on Hwy 3. Int corridors. **Pets:** Accepted.

🄰🅂🄺 🅂🄸 ⊠ 🔋 💻 🍴 ⊠

WATERTON PARK

🄰 ▼▼◆ Bayshore Inn 🄼
(403) 859-2211. **$119-$249, 3 day notice.** 111 Waterton Ave. Centre. Ext corridors. **Pets:** Accepted.

🆂🅰🆅🅴 ⊠ 🔋 💻 🍴 🄰🄲

🄰 ▼▼◆ Waterton Lakes Resort 🄻🄷
(403) 859-2150. **$114-$219, 3 day notice.** 101 Clematis Ave. Centre. Ext/int corridors. **Pets:** Accepted.

🆂🅰🆅🅴 ⊠ 🅼 🔋 💻 ⇌ ⊠

WESTEROSE

▼▼ Village Creek Country Inn 🄼
(780) 586-0006. **Call for rates.** 9 Village Dr. Hwy 2, exit 482, 17.5 mi (28 km) w on Hwy 13. Ext/int corridors. **Pets:** Accepted.

⊠ 🔋 💻 ⊠

WETASKIWIN

🄰 ▼▼◆ Best Western Wayside Inn 🅂🄷
(780) 352-6681. **$120-$130.** 4103 56 St. Just n of Hwy 13 W, on Hwy 2A. Int corridors. **Pets:** Large, other species. $100 deposit/room. Designated rooms, service with restrictions, supervision.

🆂🅰🆅🅴 🅂🄸 ⊠ 💻 🍴

▼▼ Super 8 Motel 🅂🄷
(780) 361-3808. **Call for rates.** 3820 56th St. On Hwy 2A, just s of jct Hwy 13 W. Ext/int corridors. **Pets:** Accepted.

⊠ 🅼 🔋

WHITECOURT

🄰 ▼▼▼ Super 8 Motel 🅂🄷
(780) 778-8908. **$129-$139.** 4121 Kepler St. On Hwy 43, just e of Hwy 32. Int corridors. **Pets:** Other species. $25 daily fee/room. Designated rooms, service with restrictions, crate.

🆂🅰🆅🅴 🅂🄸 ⊠ 🔋 💻

BRITISH COLUMBIA

CITY INDEX

100 MILE HOUSE

100 Mile House Super 8 ☒
(250) 395-8888. **$100-$150, 7 day notice.** 989 Alder Ave. 0.6 mi (1 km) s on Hwy 97. Ext corridors. **Pets:** Accepted.

ASK ☒ ☒ ☒ ☒

Ramada Limited ☒
(250) 395-2777. **$80-$179.** 917 Alder Ave. 0.6 mi (1 km) s on Hwy 97. Int corridors. **Pets:** Accepted.

ASK ☒ ☒ ☒ ☒

Red Coach Inn ☒
(250) 395-2266. **Call for rates.** 170 Cariboo Hwy N. On Hwy 97, on north end of town. Ext/int corridors. **Pets:** Accepted.

☒ ☒ ☒ ☒ ☒ ☒

108 MILE HOUSE

108 Resort & Conference Centre ☒
(250) 791-5211. **$80-$140.** 4816 Telqua Dr. From Hwy 97, 1 mi (1.6 km) nw on access road, follow signs. Ext corridors. **Pets:** Accepted.

☒ ☒ ☒ ☒ ☒ ☒ ☒ ☒

ABBOTSFORD

Best Western Bakerview Inn ☒ ☒
(604) 859-1341. **$109-$159.** 1821 Sumas Way. Trans-Canada Hwy 1, exit 92 (Town Centre), just n on Hwy 11. Ext corridors. **Pets:** Large, other species. Service with restrictions, supervision.

☒ ☒ ☒ ☒ ☒ ☒

Coast Abbotsford Hotel & Suites ☒
(604) 853-1880. **$99-$260.** 2020 Sumas Way. Trans-Canada Hwy 1, exit 92 (Town Centre), just n on Hwy 11. Int corridors. **Pets:** Accepted.

ASK ☒ ☒ ☒ ☒ ☒ ☒

Ramada Plaza & Conference Centre-Abbotsford ☒
(604) 870-1050. **$109-$149.** 36035 N Parallel Rd. Trans-Canada Hwy 1, exit 95 (Whatcom Rd). Int corridors. **Pets:** Accepted.

ASK ☒ ☒ ☒ ☒ ☒ ☒ ☒

Super 8 Motel Abbotsford ☒ ☒
(604) 853-1141. **$99-$229.** 1881 Sumas Way. Trans-Canada Hwy 1, exit 92 (Town Centre), just n on Hwy 11. Ext/int corridors. **Pets:** Medium, other species. $10 daily fee/pet. Designated rooms, service with restrictions, supervision.

☒ ☒ ☒ ☒ ☒ ☒ ☒ ☒

BLUE RIVER

Glacier Mountain Lodge ☒
(250) 673-2393. **$89-$159.** 869 Shell Rd. On Hwy 5 (Yellowhead Hwy) at Shell Rd, follow signs. Int corridors. **Pets:** Other species. $10 daily fee/room. Designated rooms, service with restrictions, supervision.

☒ ☒ ☒

BOWEN ISLAND

Wildwood Lane Cottages ☒
(604) 947-2253. **Call for rates.** 1291 Adams Rd. From ferry terminal, 3.5 mi (5.6 km) w on Grafton Rd, then 0.6 mi (1 km) n. Ext corridors. **Pets:** Accepted.

☒ ☒ ☒ ☒

CACHE CREEK

Bonaparte Motel ☒
(250) 457-9693. **$49-$120.** 1395 Hwy 97 N. Just n of jct Trans-Canada Hwy 1. Ext corridors. **Pets:** Small, dogs only. $10 daily fee/pet. Designated rooms, service with restrictions, supervision.

☒ ☒ ☒ ☒

CAMPBELL RIVER

Anchor Inn & Suites ☒
(250) 286-1131. **$119-$289.** 261 Island Hwy. On Island Hwy 19A, 1.3 mi (2 km) s. Int corridors. **Pets:** Accepted.

☒ ☒ ☒ ☒ ☒ ☒ ☒ ☒

Best Western Austrian Chalet ☒
(250) 923-4231. **$114-$147.** 462 S Island Hwy. 2 mi (3.2 km) s on Island Hwy 19A. Ext/int corridors. **Pets:** Small, other species. $6 one-time fee/pet. Designated rooms, service with restrictions, supervision.

☒ ☒ ☒ ☒ ☒ ☒ ☒ ☒ ☒

Campbell River Lodge Fishing & Adventure Resort ☒ ☒
(250) 287-7446. **$75-$115, 3 day notice.** 1760 N Island Hwy. On Island Hwy 19A, 1.3 mi (2 km) nw of downtown; just e from Hwy 19 and 28. Ext/int corridors. **Pets:** $15 one-time fee/pet. Service with restrictions, supervision.

☒ ☒ ☒ ☒ ☒

Ocean Resort ☒
(250) 923-4281. **Call for rates.** 4834 S Island Hwy. 11 mi (18 km) s on Hwy 19A. Int corridors. **Pets:** Accepted.

☒ ☒ ☒

▼▼ Town Centre Inn **M**
(250) 287-8866. **$74-$89.** 1500 Dogwood St. Follow Island Hwy 19A through town, watch for signs, just e on Dogwood St; corner of 16th Ave. Ext corridors. **Pets:** Accepted.
ASK ⊠ 🔒 💻 ✗

▼ Travelodge Campbell River **M**
(250) 286-6622. **$78-$145.** 340 S Island Hwy. 1.9 mi (3 km) s on Island Hwy 19A. Int corridors. **Pets:** Accepted.
ASK S☐ ⊠ ⑤M 🔒 💻 ⊇

CASTLEGAR

ⒸⒶ ▼▼ Quality Inn Castlegar **M**
(250) 365-2177. **Call for rates.** 1935 Columbia Ave. Jct Hwy 3A and 3B, just s. Ext/int corridors. **Pets:** Accepted.
SAVE ⊠ 🔒 💻 ⑪

▼▼ Super 8 Motel-Castlegar **SH**
(250) 365-2700. **Call for rates.** 651 18th St. Hwy 3, exit city centre. Int corridors. **Pets:** Accepted.
⊠ 🔒 💻

CHASE

▼▼ Chase Country Inn Motel **M**
(250) 679-3333. **$59-$99.** 576 Coburn St. Trans-Canada Hwy 1 and Coburn St. Ext corridors. **Pets:** Accepted.
ASK S☐ ⊠ 🔒 💻 ⑪

▼▼ Talking Rock at Quaaout Lodge **SH**
(250) 679-3090. **$99-$219.** Trans-Canada Hwy 1, exit Squilax Bridge, 1.5 mi (2.5 km) w on Little Shuswap Rd. Int corridors. **Pets:** Accepted.
⊠ ⑤M 🔒 💻 ⑪ ⊇ ✗

CHEMAINUS

ⒸⒶ ▼▼▼ Best Western Chemainus Festival
Inn **SH** 🐾
(250) 246-4181. **$128-$158, 3 day notice.** 9573 Chemainus Rd. Trans-Canada Hwy 1, exit Henry Rd, 0.9 mi (1.4 km) e. Int corridors. **Pets:** Medium, other species. $15 daily fee/room. Designated rooms, service with restrictions, supervision.
SAVE S☐ ⊠ ⑤M 🔒 💻 ⊇

CHILLIWACK

ⒸⒶ ▼▼ Best Western Rainbow Country Inn **SH**
(604) 795-3828. **$100-$130.** 43971 Industrial Way. Trans-Canada Hwy 1, exit 116 (Lickman Rd). Int corridors. **Pets:** Accepted.
SAVE S☐ ⊠ ⑤M 🔒 💻 ⑪ ⊇

ⒸⒶ ▼▼ Chilliwack Travelodge **SH**
(604) 792-4240. **$79-$99.** 45466 Yale Rd W. Trans-Canada Hwy 1, exit 119, just n. Int corridors. **Pets:** Accepted.
SAVE S☐ ⊠ ⑤M 🔒 💻 ⑪ ⊇

▼▼ Comfort Inn **M**
(604) 858-0636. **$100-$145.** 45405 Luckakuck Way. Trans-Canada Hwy 1, exit 119, s on Vedder Rd, then 0.6 mi (1 km) w. Int corridors. **Pets:** Accepted.
ASK S☐ ⊠ ⑤M 💻

CHRISTINA LAKE

▼▼ New Horizon Motel **M**
(250) 447-9312. **$95-$185.** 2037 Hwy 3. Just e. Ext corridors. **Pets:** Accepted.
⊠ ⑤M 🔒 💻

CLEARWATER

ⒸⒶ ▼▼▼ Clearwater Valley Resort & KOA
Kampground **CA**
(250) 674-3909. **$85-$135.** 373 Clearwater Valley Rd. Jct Hwy 5 (Yellowhead Hwy) and Clearwater Valley Rd. Ext corridors. **Pets:** Accepted.
SAVE ⊠ 🔒 💻 ⑪ ⊇ ✗

ⒸⒶ ▼ Loons at The Lakeshore Motel **M**
(250) 674-3345. **$50-$90.** 57 E Old N Thompson Hwy. 0.6 mi (1 km) w on Old N Thompson Hwy, just off Hwy 5 (Yellowhead Hwy). Ext corridors. **Pets:** Small, dogs only. Service with restrictions, supervision.
SAVE S☐ ⊠ 🔒 💻 ✗

COMOX

ⒸⒶ ▼▼ Port Augusta Inn & Suites **M**
(250) 339-2277. **$85-$165.** 2082 Comox Ave. From Hwy 19A (Cliffe Ave), follow signs to Comox Ave, then 2.5 mi (4 km) e. Ext/int corridors. **Pets:** Medium, dogs only. $10 one-time fee/pet. Designated rooms, service with restrictions, supervision.
SAVE S☐ ⊠ ⑤M 🔒 💻 ⑪ ⊇

COURTENAY

ⒸⒶ ▼▼ Best Western The Westerly Hotel **SH**
(250) 338-7741. **$144-$289.** 1590 Cliffe Ave. Corner of Cliffe Ave and Island Hwy 19A N. Int corridors. **Pets:** Large. $10 daily fee/pet. Service with restrictions, supervision.
SAVE S☐ ⊠ ⑤M 💻 ⑪ ⊇ ✗

ⒸⒶ ▼▼▼ Kingfisher Oceanside Resort & Spa **SH**
(250) 338-1323. **Call for rates.** 4330 S Island Hwy. 3.8 mi (6 km) s on Island Hwy 19A S, watch for signs. Ext corridors. **Pets:** Accepted.
SAVE ⊠ ⑤M 🔒 💻 ⑪ ⊇ ✗ ✗

ⒸⒶ ▼ Travelodge Courtenay **M**
(250) 334-4491. **$93-$118.** 2605 Cliffe Ave. 0.8 mi (1.2 km) s on Island Hwy 19A S. Ext corridors. **Pets:** $5 daily fee/pet. Designated rooms, service with restrictions, supervision.
SAVE S☐ ⊠ 🔒 💻 ⊇

CRANBROOK

▼▼▼ Best Western Cranbrook Hotel **SH**
(250) 417-4002. **Call for rates.** 1019 Cranbrook St N. Hwy 3 and 95; centre. Int corridors. **Pets:** Small, dogs only. $20 daily fee/pet. Designated rooms, service with restrictions, crate.
⊠ 🔒 💻 ⊇

▼▼ Heritage Inn **SH**
(250) 489-4301. **$120-$229.** 803 Cranbrook St N. Hwy 3 and 95; centre. Int corridors. **Pets:** Accepted.
ASK S☐ ⊠ 🔒 💻 ⑪ ⊇

ⒸⒶ ▼▼▼ St. Eugene Golf Resort & Casino **LH**
(250) 420-2000. **$105-$179.** 7731 Mission Rd. Hwy 3, exit Kimberley/Airport (Hwy 95A) to Mission Rd, 2.8 mi (4.5 km) n. Int corridors. **Pets:** Accepted.
SAVE S☐ ⊠ 🔒 💻 ⑪ ⊇ ✗

▼▼ Super 8 Motel **SH**
(250) 489-8028. **$95-$115.** 2370 Cranbrook St N. Just w of jct Hwy 93 and 95. Int corridors. **Pets:** Accepted.
ASK S☐ ⊠ ⑤M 🔒

CRESTON

▼ Downtowner Motor Inn **SH**
(250) 428-2238. **$48-$79.** 1218 Canyon St. Corner of 12th Ave N. Int corridors. **Pets:** Accepted.
⊠ 🔒

ⒸⒶ ▼▼▼ Skimmerhorn Inn Ⓜ
(250) 428-4009. **$87-$157.** 2711 Hwy 3. 0.5 mi (0.8 km) e on Hwy 3.
Ext corridors. **Pets:** Small, dogs only. $100 deposit/pet, $25 daily fee/room.
Designated rooms, service with restrictions, supervision.
[SAVE] ⊠ 🖬 🖵 ≈

ⒸⒶ ▼ Sunset Motel Ⓜ
(250) 428-2229. **$63-$99.** 2705 Canyon St, Hwy 3 E. On Hwy 3, 0.6 mi
(1 km) e. Ext corridors. **Pets:** Accepted.
[SAVE] [S$] ⊠ 🖬 🖵 ≈

DAWSON CREEK

▼▼▼ Dawson Creek Super 8 🆂🅷
(250) 782-8899. **$133-$220.** 1440 Alaska Ave. Just s of jct Hwy 97 S
(Hart Hwy) and 97 N (Alaska Hwy). Int corridors. **Pets:** Accepted.
[ASK] [S$] ⊠ 🖬 🖵 ⑪

DUNCAN

ⒸⒶ ▼▼▼ Best Western Cowichan Valley Inn 🆂🅷
(250) 748-2722. **Call for rates.** 6474 Trans-Canada Hwy 1. 1.8 mi (3
km) n. Int corridors. **Pets:** Accepted.
[SAVE] ⊠ 🖬 🖵 ⑪ ≈

▼ Falcon Nest Motel Ⓜ
(250) 748-8188. **$58-$84.** 5867 Trans-Canada Hwy 1. 0.9 mi (1.5 km)
n. Ext corridors. **Pets:** Accepted.
[ASK] [S$] ⊠ 🖬 🖵 ≈

▼▼▼ Travelodge Silver Bridge Inn Duncan 🆂🅷
(250) 748-4311. **$109-$199.** 140 Trans-Canada Hwy 1. Just n of Silver
Bridge. Ext corridors. **Pets:** Accepted.
[ASK] [S$] ⊠ 🖬 🖵 ⑪

FERNIE

ⒸⒶ ▼▼▼▼ Best Western Fernie Mountain Lodge 🆂🅷
(250) 423-5500. **Call for rates.** 1622 7th Ave. Jct Hwy 3 and 7th Ave;
east end of town. Int corridors. **Pets:** $20 daily fee/room. Designated
rooms, supervision.
[SAVE] ⊠ 🖬 🖵 ⑪ ≈

ⒸⒶ ▼▼▼ Park Place Lodge 🆂🅷
(250) 423-6871. **$109-$249.** 742 Hwy 3. At 7th St. Int corridors.
Pets: Designated rooms, supervision.
[SAVE] [S$] ⊠ 🖬 🖵 ⑪ ≈ ⊠

▼▼▼ Stanford Hotels & Resorts 🅲🅾
(250) 423-5000. **Call for rates.** 100 Riverside Way. From centre, 1.2 mi
(2 km) on Hwy 3. Ext/int corridors. **Pets:** Accepted.
⊠ 🖬 🖵 ⑪ ≈ ⊠

▼▼ Super 8 Motel-Fernie 🆂🅷
(250) 423-6788. **Call for rates.** 2021 Hwy 3. On Hwy 3; west end of
town. Int corridors. **Pets:** Accepted.
⊠ 🖬

FORT ST. JOHN

ⒸⒶ ▼▼▼ Best Western Coachman Inn 🆂🅷
(250) 787-0651. **Call for rates.** 8540 Alaska Rd. 1.2 mi (2 km) s on
Hwy 97. Int corridors. **Pets:** Accepted.
[SAVE] ⊠ 🖬 🖵 ⑪ ⊠

ⒸⒶ ▼▼▼ Lakeview Inn & Suites 🆂🅷
(250) 787-0779. **$96-$106.** 10103 98th Ave. Corner of 100th Ave; centre of downtown. Int corridors. **Pets:** Accepted.
[SAVE] [S$] ⊠ [&M] 🖬 🖵 ⑪

▼▼▼ Pomeroy Inn & Suites 🆂🅷
(250) 262-3030. **$179-$199.** 9304 Alaska Rd. Just s on Hwy 97 (Alaska
Hwy). Int corridors. **Pets:** Accepted.
[ASK] [S$] ⊠ 🖬 🖵

▼▼▼ Quality Inn Northern Grand 🅻🅷 🐾
(250) 787-0521. **$119-$159, 30 day notice.** 9830 100th Ave. Centre. Int
corridors. **Pets:** Large. $20 daily fee/pet. Designated rooms.
[ASK] [S$] ⊠ 🖬 🖵 ⑪ ≈ ⊠

ⒸⒶ ▼▼▼▼ Super 8 Motel-Fort St. John 🆂🅷
(250) 785-7588. **$160-$200.** 9500 Alaska Hwy. Just s on Hwy 97
(Alaska Hwy). Int corridors. **Pets:** Accepted.
[SAVE] [S$] ⊠ [&M] 🖬 🖵 ⑪ ≈ ⊠

FORT STEELE

▼▼▼ Bull River Guest Ranch 🆁🅰
(250) 429-3760. **Call for rates.** Hwy 95, 21.9 km se of town on Ft
Steele-Wardner Rd, 12 km ne on gravel road, follow signs; Hwy 3 W,
41 km e of Cranbrook, use Ft Steele Rd. Ext corridors. **Pets:** Accepted.
⊠ 🖬 🖵 ⊠ [K] [W] [Z]

GIBSONS

▼▼▼ Bonniebrook Lodge Bed & Breakfast 🅶🅸
(604) 886-2887. **Call for rates.** 1532 Ocean Beach Esplanade. Hwy
101, 3.8 mi (6 km) s on Veterans Rd to Fichett St, just sw to King St,
0.6 mi (1 km) sw to Chaster, then 5 mi (8 km) sw to Gowers Pt Rd,
follow signs. Ext/int corridors. **Pets:** Accepted.
⊠ 🖬 🖵 [K] [Z]

ⒸⒶ ▼▼▼ Cedars Inn Hotel & Convention Centre Ⓜ
(604) 886-3008. **$94-$156.** 895 Gibsons Way. Hwy 101 and Shaw Rd;
3.8 mi (6 km) n from ferry terminal. Ext/int corridors. **Pets:** Accepted.
[SAVE] [S$] ⊠ 🖬 🖵 ⑪ ≈ ⊠

GOLD BRIDGE

▼▼▼ Morrow Chalets 🅲🅰
(250) 238-2462. **$225-$350.** Tyaughton Lake. 5 mi (8 km) n from the
Tyaughton Lake turnoff, follow signs. Ext corridors. **Pets:** Accepted.
⊠ 🖬 🖵 [K]

▼▼ Tyax Mountain Lake Resort 🆂🅷
(250) 238-2221. **$118-$286.** Tyaughton Lake Rd. 5 mi (8 km) n from
the Tyaughton Lake turnoff, follow signs. Int corridors. **Pets:** Accepted.
⊠ 🖬 ⑪ ⊠ [K]

GOLDEN

ⒸⒶ ▼▼▼▼ Best Western Mountain View Inn 🆂🅷
(250) 344-2333. **$129-$179.** 1024 11th St N. Just w of jct Hwy 95 and
Trans-Canada Hwy 1; on S Service Rd. Int corridors. **Pets:** Accepted.
[SAVE] [S$] ⊠ 🖬 🖵 ≈

▼▼ Golden Rim Motor Inn Ⓜ
(250) 344-2216. **$69-$185.** 1416 Golden View Rd. On Trans-Canada
Hwy 1, 1 mi (1.6 km) e of jct Hwy 95. Ext corridors. **Pets:** Accepted.
[ASK] [S$] ⊠ 🖬 🖵 ⑪ ≈ ⊠

ⒸⒶ ▼▼▼ Hillside Lodge & Chalets 🅲🅰
(250) 344-7281. **$125-$165, 5 day notice.** 1740 Seward Frontage Rd.
9.4 mi (15 km) w on Hwy 1, follow signs; n off highway. Ext corridors.
Pets: Accepted.
[SAVE] ⊠ 🖬 🖵 ⊠ [K] [Z]

GRAND FORKS

▼▼▼ Ramada Limited Ⓜ
(250) 442-2127. **Call for rates.** 2729 Central Ave. West end of town on
Hwy 3. Ext corridors. **Pets:** Accepted.
⊠ 🖬 🖵 ⑪ ≈

ⒸⒶ ▼▼▼ Western Traveller Motel Ⓜ
(250) 442-5566. **$64-$139.** 1591 Central Ave. West end of town on
Hwy 3. Ext corridors. **Pets:** Small, dogs only. $7 one-time fee/pet. Desig-
nated rooms, no service, supervision.
[SAVE] [S$] ⊠ 🖬 🖵

GULF ISLANDS NATIONAL PARK RESERVE AREA

PENDER ISLAND

▼▼▼ Poets Cove Resort & Spa SH ❄
(250) 629-2100. **Call for rates.** 9801 Spalding Rd, South Pender Island. From Otter Bay Ferry Terminal, follow signs to South Pender Island, then 10 mi (16 km) s; Otter Bay Rd to Bidwell Harbour Rd to Canal Rd. Ext/int corridors. **Pets:** Medium. $50 one-time fee/pet. Designated rooms, service with restrictions, supervision.

⊠ ᴸᴹ 🛢 🖨 ᵀᴵ ➳ ⊠ 🐾

QUADRA ISLAND

▼▼ Taku Resort & Marina M
(250) 285-3031. **$89-$295, 15 day notice.** 616 Taku Rd. From Campbell River ferry terminal, 4.1 mi (6.6 km) n on West Rd, then just e on Heriot Bay Rd, follow signs to Heriot Bay. Ext corridors. **Pets:** Accepted.

⊠ 🛢 🖨 ⊠ 🐾 🅩

SALT SPRING ISLAND

▼▼ Harbour House SH
(250) 537-5571. **$59-$295.** 121 Upper Ganges Rd. 0.6 mi (1 km) n on Lower Ganges Rd, then just e, towards Long Harbour ferry terminal. Ext/int corridors. **Pets:** Accepted.

ASK Sᴅ ⊠ ᴸᴹ 🖨 ᵀᴵ 🐾

▼▼ Old Farmhouse Bed & Breakfast BB
(250) 537-4113. **Call for rates.** 1077 North End Rd. From Ganges township, 2.5 mi (4 km) n on Lower Ganges North End Rd. Int corridors. **Pets:** Accepted.

⊠ 🐾 🎞 🅩

END AREA

HARRISON HOT SPRINGS

㉺ ▼▼▼ Harrison Beach Hotel SH
(604) 796-1111. **$145-$265.** 160 Esplanade Ave. Just w; on the lakefront. Int corridors. **Pets:** Medium. $15 daily fee/pet. Designated rooms, service with restrictions, supervision.

SAVE Sᴅ ⊠ ᴸᴹ 🛢 🖨 ᵀᴵ 🐾

㉺ ▼▼▼ Harrison Hot Springs Resort & Spa LH
(604) 796-2244. **$139-$599, 3 day notice.** 100 Esplanade Ave. Just w; on lakefront. Int corridors. **Pets:** Large, dogs only. Designated rooms, service with restrictions, supervision.

SAVE ⊠ 🛢 🖨 ᵀᴵ 🐾 ⊠

HOPE

㉺ ▼▼ Alpine Motel M
(604) 869-9931. **$78-$110.** 505 Old Hope-Princeton Way. Trans-Canada Hwy 1, exit 173 westbound; exit 170 eastbound, just n from lights. Ext corridors. **Pets:** Small. $100 deposit/room, $10 daily fee/room. No service, supervision.

SAVE Sᴅ ⊠ 🛢 🖨

㉺ ▼ Best Continental Motel M
(604) 869-9726. **$59-$125.** 860 Fraser Ave. Trans-Canada Hwy 1, exit 170 to downtown; at Fort St. Ext corridors. **Pets:** Small, dogs only. $6 daily fee/pet. Designated rooms, no service, supervision.

SAVE Sᴅ ⊠ 🛢 🖨

㉺ ▼ Quality Inn M
(604) 869-9951. **$75-$145.** 350 Old Hope-Princeton Way. Trans-Canada Hwy 1, exit 173 westbound; exit 170 eastbound, just n from lights. Int corridors. **Pets:** Medium. Service with restrictions, supervision.

SAVE Sᴅ ⊠ ᴸᴹ 🛢 🖨 🐾

INVERMERE

▼▼ Best Western Invermere Inn SH
(250) 342-9246. **$119-$199, 3 day notice.** 1310 7th Ave. 1.8 mi (3 km) w of Hwy 93 and 95 at Invermere exit; centre. Int corridors. **Pets:** Accepted.

ASK Sᴅ ⊠ 🛢 🖨 ᵀᴵ

▼▼ Invermere Super 8 SH
(250) 342-8888. **$110-$180.** 8888 Arrow Rd. On Hwy 95. Int corridors. **Pets:** Accepted.

ASK ⊠ 🛢 🖨 ᵀᴵ

KAMLOOPS

㉺ ▼▼▼ Accent Inns M ❄
(250) 374-8877. **$99-$169.** 1325 Columbia St W. Trans-Canada Hwy 1, exit 369 (Columbia St) eastbound, at Notre Dame Dr; exit 370 (Summit Dr) westbound, at Notre Dame Dr. Ext corridors. **Pets:** Other species. $15 daily fee/room. Service with restrictions, supervision.

SAVE Sᴅ ⊠ ᴸᴹ 🛢 🖨 🐾 ⊠

▼▼▼ Best Western Kamloops LH ❄
(250) 828-6660. **Call for rates.** 1250 Rogers Way. Trans-Canada Hwy 1, exit 368 (Hillside Ave), just s. Int corridors. **Pets:** Medium, other species. $15 one-time fee/room. Designated rooms, service with restrictions, supervision.

⊠ ᴸᴹ 🛢 🖨 ᵀᴵ 🐾 ⊠

㉺ ▼▼ Econo Lodge Inn & Suites M ❄
(250) 372-8533. **$69-$99.** 1773 Trans-Canada Hwy E. 1.5 mi (2.4 km) e on Trans-Canada Hwy 1, south side of service access road. Ext corridors. **Pets:** Medium. $10 daily fee/pet. Service with restrictions, supervision.

SAVE Sᴅ ⊠ 🛢 🖨 🐾

㉺ ▼ Grandview Motel M
(250) 372-1312. **$55-$105.** 463 Grandview Terr. Trans-Canada Hwy 1, exit 369 (Columbia St) eastbound, 1.3 mi (2 km) n; exit 370 (Summit Dr) westbound to Columbia St, via City Centre. Ext corridors. **Pets:** Medium. $5 daily fee/pet. Designated rooms, service with restrictions, supervision.

SAVE Sᴅ ⊠ 🛢 🖨 🐾

㉺ ▼▼▼ Hampton Inn SH ❄
(250) 571-7897. **$109-$179.** 1245 Rogers Way. Trans-Canada Hwy 1, exit 368 (Hillside Ave), just s via Hillside Way. Int corridors. **Pets:** Medium, dogs only. $20 daily fee/pet. Designated rooms, service with restrictions, supervision.

SAVE Sᴅ ⊠ ᴸᴹ 🛢 🖨 🐾 ⊠

▼ Hospitality Inn M
(250) 374-4164. **$77-$101.** 500 W Columbia St. Trans-Canada Hwy 1, exit 369 (Columbia St) eastbound, 1.3 mi (2 km) n; exit 370 (Summit Dr) westbound to Columbia St via City Centre. Ext corridors. **Pets:** Accepted.

ASK Sᴅ ⊠ 🛢 🖨 🐾

▼▼ Kamloops Super 8 Motel M
(250) 374-8688. **$100-$150.** 1521 Hugh Allan Dr. Trans-Canada Hwy 1, exit 367 (Pacific Way). Int corridors. **Pets:** Accepted.

ASK Sᴅ ⊠ ᴸᴹ 🛢 🖨

Ⓐ 💎💎💎 **Ramada Inn-Kamloops** 🆂🅷
(250) 374-0358. **$89-$189.** 555 W Columbia St. Trans-Canada Hwy 1, exit 369 (Columbia St) eastbound, 1.3 mi (2 km) n; exit 370 (Summit Dr) westbound to Columbia St via City Centre. Int corridors. **Pets:** Accepted.

🆂🅰🆅 🆂🅳 ☒ 🛢 💻 🍽 ➷

💎 **Ranchland Motel** Ⓜ
(250) 828-8787. **$65-$89.** 2357 Trans-Canada Hwy E. 2.8 mi (4.5 km) e on Trans-Canada Hwy 1, exit River Rd, then just w along service access road. Ext corridors. **Pets:** Accepted.

🅰🆂🅺 🆂🅳 ☒ 🛢 💻

Ⓐ 💎💎💎 **Scott's Inn & Restaurant** Ⓜ
(250) 372-8221. **$80-$120.** 551 11th Ave. Trans-Canada Hwy 1, exit 369 (Columbia St) eastbound, 3.1 mi (5 km) n; exit City Centre westbound, 1 mi (1.6) km s on Columbia St. Ext corridors. **Pets:** Small. $6 daily fee/pet. Designated rooms, service with restrictions, supervision.

🆂🅰🆅 🆂🅳 ☒ 🛢 💻 🍽 ➷

KIMBERLEY

Ⓐ 💎💎💎💎 **Trickle Creek Residence Inn by Marriott** 🆂🅷 🐾
(250) 427-5175. **$115-$135.** 500 Stemwinder Dr. From Gerry Sorensen Way, follow signs. Int corridors. **Pets:** $75 one-time fee/room. Designated rooms, service with restrictions, crate.

🆂🅰🆅 🆂🅳 ☒ 🛢 💻 🍽 ➷ ☒

LOGAN LAKE

💎 **Logan Lake Lodge** Ⓜ
(250) 523-9466. **$70-$99, 7 day notice.** 111 Chartrand Ave. At Meadow Creek Rd and Chartrand Cresent; centre. Int corridors. **Pets:** Accepted.

🅰🆂🅺 🆂🅳 ☒ 🛢 💻 🍽 🐾

LUND

Ⓐ 💎 **The Historic Lund Hotel** 🆂🅷
(604) 414-0474. **$95-$250, 3 day notice.** 1436 Hwy 101. End of Hwy 101; on Sunshine Coast (Hwy 101). Ext/int corridors. **Pets:** Accepted.

🆂🅰🆅 ☒ 🛢 💻 🍽

MADEIRA PARK

💎💎💎 **Sunshine Coast Resort & Marina** 🅲🅾
(604) 883-9177. **$95-$495, 21 day notice.** 12695 Sunshine Coast (Hwy 101). Just n of Madeira Park Rd, follow signs. Ext/int corridors. **Pets:** Accepted.

☒ 🐾 🛢 💻 ☒ 🐾

MANNING PARK

Ⓐ 💎💎💎 **Manning Park Resort** 🆂🅷
(250) 840-8822. **$134-$164, 14 day notice.** 7500 Hwy 3. Crowsnest Hwy 3; between Hope and Princeton. Ext/int corridors. **Pets:** Accepted.

🆂🅰🆅 ☒ 🛢 💻 🍽 ➷ ☒ 🐾

MCBRIDE

Ⓐ 💎💎💎 **North Country Lodge** Ⓜ
(250) 569-0001. **Call for rates.** 868 Frontage Rd N. Just w of village main exit, on Hwy 16 north service road. Ext corridors. **Pets:** Other species. $10 daily fee/pet. Designated rooms, service with restrictions, crate.

🆂🅰🆅 ☒ 🛢 💻 🍽

MERRITT

Ⓐ 💎💎💎💎 **Best Western Nicola Inn** 🆂🅷
(250) 378-4253. **$79-$179.** 4025 Walters St. Hwy 5, exit 290, 0.6 mi (1 km) w. Ext corridors. **Pets:** Small. $10 daily fee/pet. Designated rooms, service with restrictions, supervision.

🆂🅰🆅 🆂🅳 ☒ 🛢 💻 🍽 ➷

💎💎 **Super 8 Motel** Ⓜ
(250) 378-9422. **$95-$130.** 3561 Voght St. Hwy 5, exit 290, just w. Ext corridors. **Pets:** Accepted.

🅰🆂🅺 🆂🅳 ☒ 🛢 💻 🍽 ➷

NAKUSP

Ⓐ 💎💎💎 **The Selkirk Inn** 🆂🅷
(250) 265-3666. **$52-$90.** 210 W 6th Ave. Centre. Int corridors. **Pets:** Medium. $8 daily fee/room. Designated rooms, service with restrictions, crate.

🆂🅰🆅 ☒ 🛢 💻

NANAIMO

Ⓐ 💎💎💎 **Best Western Dorchester Hotel** 🆂🅷 🐾
(250) 754-6835. **$135-$200, 30 day notice.** 70 Church St. Island Hwy 19A to Comox Rd; downtown. Int corridors. **Pets:** Large, dogs only. $15 daily fee/pet. Designated rooms, service with restrictions, supervision.

🆂🅰🆅 🆂🅳 ☒ 🛢 💻 🍽

💎💎 **Best Western Northgate Inn** 🆂🅷
(250) 390-2222. **$102-$190.** 6450 Metral Dr. Hwy 19A (Island Hwy), just w on Aulds Rd, then just s. Int corridors. **Pets:** Medium. $20 daily fee/room. Designated rooms, service with restrictions, supervision.

🆂🅰🆅 🆂🅳 ☒ 🛢 💻 🍽 ☒

💎💎 **Days Inn Nanaimo Harbourview** 🆂🅷
(250) 754-8171. **$113-$148.** 809 Island Hwy S. On Island Hwy 1, 1.3 mi (2 km) s. Int corridors. **Pets:** Accepted.

🅰🆂🅺 🆂🅳 ☒ 🛢 💻 🍽 ➷

Ⓐ 💎💎💎💎 **Inn on Long Lake** 🆂🅷 🐾
(250) 758-1144. **$109-$189.** 4700 Island Hwy N. 3.1 mi (5 km) n on Hwy 19A (Island Hwy) from Departure Bay ferry terminal. Ext corridors. **Pets:** Large, other species. $20 one-time fee/pet. Designated rooms, service with restrictions, supervision.

🆂🅰🆅 🆂🅳 ☒ 🅼 🛢 💻 ☒

Ⓐ 💎💎💎 **Travelodge Nanaimo** Ⓜ
(250) 754-6355. **$120-$146.** 96 Terminal Ave N. Jct Terminal Ave and Island Hwy 19A. Int corridors. **Pets:** Accepted.

🆂🅰🆅 🆂🅳 ☒ 🛢 💻

NELSON

Ⓐ 💎💎 **Best Western Baker Street Inn & Convention Centre** 🆂🅷 🐾
(250) 352-3525. **$109-$259.** 153 Baker St. Jct Hwy 6 and 3A. Int corridors. **Pets:** $10 daily fee/pet. Designated rooms, service with restrictions, supervision.

🆂🅰🆅 🆂🅳 ☒ 🅼 🛢 💻 🍽

NEW DENVER

💎💎 **Sweet Dreams Guesthouse** 🅲🅸
(250) 358-2415. **Call for rates.** 702 Eldorado St. Just w of Hwy 6 on Slocan Ave. Int corridors. **Pets:** Accepted.

☒ 🍽 🐾 📺 🖨

OKANAGAN VALLEY AREA

ENDERBY

(AA) ▼▼▼ Howard Johnson Inn Fortunes Landing M ❖
(250) 838-6825. **$79-$109.** 1510 George St. 0.6 mi (1 km) n on Hwy 974. Ext corridors. **Pets:** Other species. $5 daily fee/pet. Service with restrictions, supervision.
⬛ 🔲 ❌ 🔲 🔲 🔲 🔲

KELOWNA

(AA) ▼▼▼ Accent Inns SH ❖
(250) 862-8888. **$99-$179.** 1140 Harvey Ave. Corner of Hwy 97 N (Harvey Ave) and Gordon Dr. Ext corridors. **Pets:** Medium. $15 daily fee/room. Designated rooms, service with restrictions, supervision.
⬛ 🔲 ❌ 🔲 🔲 🔲 🔲 🔲

(AA) ▼▼▼▼ Best Western Inn-Kelowna SH ❖
(250) 860-1212. **$129-$229.** 2402 Hwy 97 N. 0.6 mi (1 km) s of jct Hwy 33 and 97 N (Harvey Ave); corner of Leckie Rd. Ext/int corridors. **Pets:** Medium. $25 daily fee/pet. Designated rooms, service with restrictions, crate.
⬛ 🔲 ❌ 🔲 🔲 🔲 🔲 🔲

(AA) ▼▼▼ Comfort Inn Kelowna-Westside SH
(250) 769-2355. **Call for rates.** 1655 Westgate Rd. Jct Hwy 97 (Harvey Ave) and Bartley Rd, s to Ross Rd. Int corridors. **Pets:** Medium, other species. $10 daily fee/pet. Designated rooms, service with restrictions, supervision.
⬛ ❌ 🔲 🔲 🔲 🔲

(AA) ▼▼▼ Days Inn M
(250) 868-3297. **$99-$174.** 2649 Hwy 97 N. Jct Hwy 97 (Harvey Ave) and 33, just n. Ext/int corridors. **Pets:** Medium. $10 one-time fee/pet. Service with restrictions, supervision.
⬛ 🔲 ❌ 🔲 🔲 🔲

▼▼▼ The Grand Okanagan Lakefront Resort & Conference Centre LH
(250) 763-4500. **$189-$569.** 1310 Water St. Hwy 97 (Harvey Ave), 0.6 mi (1 km) w along Water St. Int corridors. **Pets:** Accepted.
❌ 🔲 🔲 🔲 🔲 🔲 🔲

▼▼▼ Ramada Lodge Hotel SH
(250) 860-9711. **$99-$189.** 2170 Harvey Ave. Hwy 97 N (Harvey Ave) at Dilworth Dr. Ext/int corridors. **Pets:** Accepted.
❌ 🔲 🔲 🔲

(AA) ▼▼▼ The Royal Anne Hotel SH
(250) 763-2277. **$89-$189.** 348 Bernard Ave. Corner of Pandosy and Bernard Ave; downtown. Int corridors. **Pets:** Small. $20 daily fee/pet. Designated rooms, service with restrictions, supervision.
⬛ 🔲 ❌ 🔲

▼▼▼ Vineyard Inn M
(250) 860-5703. **$84-$184.** 2486 Hwy 97 N. Southwest corner of jct Hwy 97 (Harvey Ave) and 33. Ext corridors. **Pets:** Accepted.
🔲 🔲 ❌ 🔲 🔲 🔲 🔲

NARAMATA

▼▼▼ The Village Motel M
(250) 496-5535. **$76-$145, 14 day notice.** 244 Robinson Dr. 8.8 mi (14 km) n on Naramata Rd from Penticton. Ext corridors. **Pets:** Accepted.
🔲 ❌ 🔲 🔲 🔲 🔲

OSOYOOS

▼▼▼▼ Spirit Ridge Vineyard Resort & Spa CO
(250) 495-5445. **$215-$429.** 1200 Rancher Creek Rd. Hwy 97 S, e on Hwy 3 (Main St), cross bridge, left on 45th St. Ext corridors. **Pets:** Accepted.
🔲 🔲 ❌ 🔲 🔲 🔲 🔲 🔲

PENTICTON

(AA) ▼▼▼▼ Best Western Inn at Penticton SH
(250) 493-0311. **Call for rates.** 3180 Skaha Lake Rd. 2.5 mi (4 km) s. Ext corridors. **Pets:** Accepted.
⬛ ❌ 🔲 🔲 🔲 🔲

▼▼ Days Inn Penticton SH
(250) 493-6616. **Call for rates.** 152 Riverside Dr. Hwy 97, just n. Ext/int corridors. **Pets:** Accepted.
❌ 🔲 🔲 🔲 🔲

(AA) ▼▼▼▼ Penticton Lakeside Resort, Convention Centre & Casino LH ❖
(250) 493-8221. **$165-$225, 7 day notice.** 21 Lakeshore Dr W. Main St at Lakeshore Dr W. Int corridors. **Pets:** Other species. $10 daily fee/room. Designated rooms, service with restrictions, supervision.
⬛ 🔲 ❌ 🔲 🔲 🔲 🔲 🔲

(AA) ▼▼▼▼ Ramada Inn & Suites SH ❖
(250) 492-8926. **$89-$269.** 1050 Eckhardt Ave W. 0.8 mi (1.2 km) w on Hwy 97. Ext corridors. **Pets:** Large, other species. $15 daily fee/pet. Designated rooms, service with restrictions, supervision.
⬛ 🔲 ❌ 🔲 🔲 🔲 🔲 🔲

(AA) ▼▼▼ Spanish Villa Resort M
(250) 492-2922. **$68-$350, 14 day notice.** 890 Lakeshore Dr W. Corner of Power St and Lakeshore Dr W. Ext corridors. **Pets:** Medium, dogs only. $10 daily fee/pet. Designated rooms, service with restrictions, supervision.
⬛ ❌ 🔲 🔲 🔲

▼▼▼ Super 8 Motel Penticton M
(250) 492-3829. **Call for rates.** 1706 Main St. Jct Main St and Industrial. Ext/int corridors. **Pets:** Accepted.
❌ 🔲 🔲 🔲

SUMMERLAND

(AA) ▼▼▼ Summerland Motel M
(250) 494-4444. **$80-$150.** 2107 Tait St. 3.1 mi (5 km) s on Hwy 97. Ext corridors. **Pets:** Dogs only. $10 daily fee/pet. Designated rooms, service with restrictions, supervision.
⬛ 🔲 ❌ 🔲 🔲 🔲

VERNON

(AA) ▼▼▼ Best Western Vernon Lodge & Conference Centre SH ❖
(250) 545-3385. **$109-$193.** 3914 32nd St. 1 mi (1.5 km) n on Hwy 97 (32nd St). Int corridors. **Pets:** Other species. $15 daily fee/room. Designated rooms, service with restrictions, supervision.
⬛ 🔲 ❌ 🔲 🔲 🔲 🔲 🔲

(AA) ▼▼▼▼ Holiday Inn Express Hotel & Suites Vernon SH
(250) 550-7777. **$119-$199.** 4716 34th St. Hwy 97 (32nd St) northbound at 48th Ave. Int corridors. **Pets:** Large. $20 one-time fee/room. Designated rooms, service with restrictions, supervision.
⬛ 🔲 ❌ 🔲 🔲 🔲

▼▼ **Super 8 Vernon** SH
(250) 542-4434. **$80-$175.** 4204 32nd St. Hwy 97 (32nd St); jct 43rd Ave. Int corridors. **Pets:** Accepted.

ASK SĐ ⊠ 🔒 ▣ ⇶

▼ **Vernon Travelodge** SH
(250) 545-2161. **$79-$159.** 3000 28th Ave. Hwy 97 (32nd St), just e on 28th Ave; near Polson Park. Ext corridors. **Pets:** Accepted.

ASK SĐ ⊠ 🔒 ▣ ⇶

WESTBANK

CAA ▼▼▼ **Holiday Inn Westbank (Kelowna)** SH
(250) 768-8879. **$99-$275.** 2569 Dobbin Rd. Hwy 97 (Dobbin Rd) and Herbert Rd. Int corridors. **Pets:** Accepted.

SAVE SĐ ⊠ 🔒 🔒 ▣ ❘❙ ⇶

END AREA

PARKSVILLE

▼▼▼ **Oceanside Village Resort** CA
(250) 248-8961. **$110-$295, 30 day notice.** 1080 Resort Dr. Island Hwy 19, exit 46 (Parksville), 1.8 mi (2.5 km) n on Hwy 19A. Ext corridors. **Pets:** Accepted.

⊠ 🔒 ▣ ⇶ 🞰

CAA ▼▼▼ **Quality Resort Bayside** SH ❧
(250) 248-8333. **$119-$259.** 240 Dogwood St. Island Hwy 19, exit 51 (Parksville/Coombs), 1.3 mi (2 km) e, then 0.6 mi (1 km) n on Hwy 19A. Int corridors. **Pets:** Dogs only. $15 daily fee/pet. Designated rooms, service with restrictions, supervision.

SAVE SĐ ⊠ 🔒 ▣ ❘❙ ⇶ 🞰

▼ **Skylite Motel** M
(250) 248-4271. **$69-$129.** 459 E Island Hwy. Island Hwy 19, exit 46 (Parksville), 2.2 mi (3.5 km) n on Hwy 19A. Ext corridors. **Pets:** Accepted.

ASK SĐ ⊠ 🔒

CAA ▼▼▼ **Tigh-Na-Mara Seaside Spa Resort & Conference Center** LH ❧
(250) 248-2072. **$119-$359, 5 day notice.** 1155 Resort Dr. Island Hwy 19, exit 46 (Parksville), 1.3 mi (2 km) n on Hwy 19A. Ext corridors. **Pets:** Dogs only. $30 one-time fee/room. Designated rooms, service with restrictions, supervision.

SAVE ⊠ 🔒 ▣ ❘❙ ⇶ 🞰 🞰

▼▼ **Travelodge Parksville** SH
(250) 248-2232. **$99-$189.** 424 W Island Hwy. Island Hwy 19, exit 51 (Parksville/Coombs), 1.3 mi (2 km) e, then just n on Hwy 19A. Int corridors. **Pets:** Accepted.

SĐ ⊠ 🔒 ▣ ⇶

CAA ▼▼▼ **V.I.P. Motel** M
(250) 248-3244. **$69-$169.** 414 W Island Hwy. Island Hwy 19, exit 51 (Parksville/Coombs), 1.3 mi (2 km) e, then just n on Hwy 19A. Ext corridors. **Pets:** $10 one-time fee/pet. Service with restrictions, supervision.

SAVE SĐ ⊠ 🔒 ▣ 🞰

PARSON

▼▼ **Alexa Chalets-Timber Inn & Restaurant** SH
(250) 348-2228. **$75-$180, 30 day notice.** 3483 Hwy 95. Just off Hwy 95; 21.3 mi (34 km) s of Golden. Ext/int corridors. **Pets:** Accepted.

⊠ 🔒 ▣ ❘❙ 🞰 🞰 🞰 🞰

PEMBERTON

CAA ▼▼▼ **Pemberton Valley Lodge** SH ❧
(604) 894-2000. **$129-$339.** 1490 Portage Rd. Just e on Hwy 99 from Pioneer Junction. Int corridors. **Pets:** Medium, dogs only. $45 one-time fee/room. Supervision.

SAVE ⊠ 🔒 🔒 ▣ ⇶

PORT ALBERNI

CAA ▼▼▼ **Best Western Barclay Hotel** SH
(250) 724-7171. **Call for rates.** 4277 Stamp Ave. Johnston Rd (Hwy 4), just s on Gertrude St. Int corridors. **Pets:** Accepted.

SAVE ⊠ 🔒 ▣ ❘❙ ⇶ 🞰

▼▼▼ **The Hospitality Inn** SH
(250) 723-8111. **$129-$155.** 3835 Redford St. 2 mi (3.2 km) sw of jct Hwy 4 via City Centre/Port Alberni South Route. Int corridors. **Pets:** Accepted.

ASK SĐ ⊠ ▣ ❘❙ ⇶

CAA ▼ **Riverside Motel** M
(250) 724-9916. **$79-$99.** 5065 Roger St. Johnston Rd (Hwy 4), just s on Gertrude St, then just w. Ext corridors. **Pets:** Accepted.

SAVE SĐ ⊠ 🔒 ▣ 🞰

PORT HARDY

▼▼ **Glen Lyon Inn** SH
(250) 949-7115. **$105-$180, 3 day notice.** 6435 Hardy Bay Rd. Hwy 19, 0.9 mi (1.5 km) n, follow signs. Ext corridors. **Pets:** Accepted.

⊠ 🔒 ▣ ❘❙ 🞰

POWELL RIVER

▼▼ **Powell River Town Centre Hotel** SH
(604) 485-3000. **$135-$180.** 4660 Joyce Ave. 0.5 mi (0.8 km) e on Duncan St (BC ferry terminal), then 0.6 mi (1 km) n. Int corridors. **Pets:** Accepted.

ASK SĐ ⊠ 🔒 ▣ ❘❙

PRINCE GEORGE

CAA ▼▼▼ **Best Western City Centre** M ❧
(250) 563-1267. **Call for rates.** 910 Victoria St. Just n of Victoria St (Hwy 16) and Patricia Blvd; downtown. Ext corridors. **Pets:** $25 daily fee/room. Designated rooms, service with restrictions, supervision.

SAVE ⊠ 🔒 ▣ ❘❙ ⇶

▼▼▼ **Four Points by Sheraton Prince George** SH ❧
(250) 564-7100. **$129-$209.** 1790 Hwy 97 S. Hwy 97 N, exit Spruce; Hwy 97 S, exit city centre via Queensway. Int corridors. **Pets:** Small, dogs only. $10 daily fee/pet. Designated rooms, service with restrictions, supervision.

⊠ 🔒 🔒 ▣

CAA ▼ **P.G. Hi-Way Motel** M
(250) 564-6869. **$60-$90.** 1737 20th Ave. Jct Hwy 97, 0.7 mi (1.2 km) e on Trans-Canada Hwy 16 (Yellowhead Hwy). Ext corridors. **Pets:** Accepted.

SAVE SĐ ⊠ 🔒 ▣

PRINCE RUPERT

CAA ▼ **Aleeda Motel** M
(250) 627-1367. **$55-$110.** 900 3rd Ave W. Corner of 3rd Ave W and 8th St. Int corridors. **Pets:** Other species. $5 daily fee/pet. Designated rooms, service with restrictions, supervision.

SAVE SĐ ⊠ 🔒 ▣ 🞰

▼▼ ◆ **The Coast Prince Rupert Hotel** SH
(250) 624-6711. **$119-$189.** 118 6th St. Between 1st and 2nd aves W. Int corridors. **Pets:** Accepted.
(ASK) (S6) (X) (&M) ⬛ (▥) (¶)

▼▼ **Inn on the Harbour** M
(250) 624-9107. **$75-$135.** 720 1st Ave W. Corner of 6th St. Int corridors. **Pets:** Accepted.
(ASK) (S6) (X) (&M) 🔒 (▥) (K)

CAA ▼ **Totem Lodge Motel** M
(250) 624-6761. **$69-$99.** 1335 Park Ave. 1 mi (1.6 km) w on Hwy 16 (2nd Ave W) from downtown. Int corridors. **Pets:** Accepted.
(SAVE) (S6) (X) 🔒 (▥) (K)

PRINCETON

CAA ▼▼▼ **Best Western Princeton Inn** M
(250) 295-3537. **$99-$139.** 169 Hwy 3. On Hwy 3. Ext corridors. **Pets:** Accepted.
(SAVE) (S6) (X) 🔒 (▥) (≈)

CAA ▼ **Villager Inn** M
(250) 295-6996. **$65-$95.** 244 4th St. Just off Hwy 3. Ext corridors. **Pets:** Accepted.
(SAVE) (S6) (X) 🔒 (▥)

QUALICUM BEACH

▼▼ **Casa Grande Inn** M
(250) 752-4400. **Call for rates.** 3080 W Island Hwy. Hwy 19, exit 60 (Qualicum Beach/Port Alberni), 2 mi (4 km) e on Memorial Ave, then 1.2 mi (2 km) n on Hwy 19A. Ext corridors. **Pets:** Accepted.
(X) (&M) 🔒 (▥) (K)

▼▼ **Old Dutch Inn (By The Sea)** SH
(250) 752-6914. **$80-$140.** 2690 Island Hwy W. Hwy 19, exit 60 (Qualicum Beach/Port Alberni), 2.5 mi (4 km) on Memorial Ave at jct Hwy 19A. Int corridors. **Pets:** Accepted.
(ASK) (S6) (X) 🔒 (▥) (¶) (≈) (K)

QUESNEL

CAA ▼▼ **Talisman Inn** M ❀
(250) 992-7247. **$69-$139.** 753 Front St. Hwy 97, 0.6 mi (1 km) n of Carson Ave. Int corridors. **Pets:** Small, dogs only. $10 one-time fee/pet. Designated rooms, no service, supervision.
(SAVE) (S6) (X) 🔒 (▥)

RADIUM HOT SPRINGS

▼▼ **Chalet Europe** M
(250) 347-9305. **$89-$189, 7 day notice.** 5063 Madsen Rd. 0.6 mi (1 km) off Hwy 93; up the hill. Ext corridors. **Pets:** Accepted.
(S6) (X) 🔒 (▥) (X)

▼ **Lido Motel** M
(250) 347-9533. **$55-$85, 7 day notice.** 4876 McKay St. Jct Hwy 93 and 95, just w along Main St, then just s. Ext corridors. **Pets:** Accepted.
(X) 🔒 (▥) (Z)

REVELSTOKE

CAA ▼▼ **Best Western Wayside Inn** SH
(250) 837-6161. **$89-$169, 30 day notice.** 1901 LaForme Blvd. North side of Trans-Canada Hwy 1, at intersection nearest east end of Columbia River Bridge. Ext/int corridors. **Pets:** Accepted.
(SAVE) (S6) (X) 🔒 (▥) (¶) (≈)

CAA ▼▼ ◆ **The Coast Hillcrest Resort Hotel** LH ❀
(250) 837-3322. **$155-$239.** 2100 Oak Dr. 2.7 mi (4.3 km) e on Trans-Canada Hwy 1, 0.6 mi (0.9 km) sw. Int corridors. **Pets:** $15 daily fee/room. Designated rooms, service with restrictions, crate.
(SAVE) (S6) (X) 🔒 (▥) (¶) (X)

CAA ▼▼ **Monashee Lodge** M
(250) 837-6778. **$79-$89.** 1601 3rd St W. South side of Trans-Canada Hwy 1, just e of Columbia River Bridge at Victoria Rd, then just se on Wright Ave. Ext corridors. **Pets:** Medium, dogs only. $10 daily fee/pet. Service with restrictions.
(SAVE) (X) 🔒 (▥)

CAA ▼▼ **Swiss Chalet Motel** M
(250) 837-4650. **$74-$109.** 1101 Victoria Rd. 0.6 mi (1 km) s from Trans-Canada Hwy 1. Ext corridors. **Pets:** Accepted.
(SAVE) (X) 🔒 (▥)

ROSSLAND

▼ **Thriftlodge Rossland** M
(250) 362-7364. **$79-$99, 3 day notice.** 1199 Nancy Green Hwy. 0.6 mi (1 km) w on Hwy 3B, jct Hwy 22. Ext corridors. **Pets:** Accepted.
(ASK) (X) 🔒 (▥)

SALMON ARM

CAA ▼▼ ◆ **Best Western Salmon Arm Inn** M
(250) 832-9793. **$99-$169.** 61 10th St SW. From centre, 0.7 mi (1.1 km) w on Trans-Canada Hwy 1. Ext corridors. **Pets:** Medium. $20 daily fee/pet. Designated rooms, service with restrictions, supervision.
(SAVE) (S6) (X) 🔒 (▥) (≈)

▼▼ ◆ **Holiday Inn Express Hotel & Suites Salmon Arm** SH
(250) 832-7711. **$139-$299.** 1090 22nd St NE. 0.5 mi (0.8 km) on Trans-Canada Hwy 1. Int corridors. **Pets:** Accepted.
(ASK) (S6) (X) (&M) 🔒 (▥) (≈) (X)

▼ **Super 8 Motel** SH
(250) 832-8812. **Call for rates.** 2901 10th Ave NE. 0.6 mi (1 km) e on Trans-Canada Hwy 1. Int corridors. **Pets:** Accepted.
(X) (&M) 🔒

SICAMOUS

▼▼ **Sicamous Super 8 Motel** SH
(250) 836-4988. **$60-$150.** 1120 Riverside Ave. Trans-Canada Hwy 1, s on Hwy 97A, just w on Main St to traffic circle, then just s. Ext corridors. **Pets:** Accepted.
(ASK) (X) (&M) 🔒

SILVERTON

▼▼ **William Hunter Cabins** CA
(250) 358-2844. **Call for rates.** 303 Lake Ave. Centre. Ext corridors. **Pets:** Accepted.
(X) 🔒 (▥) (X) (K)

SMITHERS

▼▼ **Aspen Inn & Suites** M
(250) 847-4551. **Call for rates.** 4628 Yellowhead Hwy. 0.9 mi (1.5 km) w on Hwy 16 (Yellowhead Hwy). Ext corridors. **Pets:** Accepted.
(X) 🔒 (▥) (¶) (≈)

SQUAMISH

CAA ▼▼ **Mountain Retreat Hotel & Suites** SH
(604) 815-0883. **$129.** 38922 Progress Way. 0.9 mi (1.5 km) n on Hwy 99 at Industrial Way. Int corridors. **Pets:** Medium, other species. $25 one-time fee/room. Designated rooms, service with restrictions, supervision.
(SAVE) (S6) (X) (&M) 🔒 (▥) (¶) (≈) (X)

SUN PEAKS

CAA ▼▼ ▼▼ **Delta Sun Peaks Resort** LH ❀
(250) 578-6000. **$99-$329.** 3240 Village Way. Hwy 5, 19.4 mi (31 km) ne on Todd Mountain Rd, follow signs to village. Int corridors. **Pets:** Large, other species. $35 one-time fee/room. Designated rooms, service with restrictions.
(SAVE) (S6) (X) (&M) 🔒 (▥) (¶) (≈) (X)

TERRACE

(CAA) ▼▼▼▼ Best Western Terrace Inn SH
(250) 635-0083. **$90-$208.** 4553 Greig Ave. Hwy 16, just e on Greig Ave, follow City Centre signs. Int corridors. **Pets:** Accepted.
SAVE 🅂 ✕ 🛗 🖵 ¶

TOFINO

(CAA) ▼▼▼▼ Best Western Tin Wis Resort Lodge SH
(250) 725-4445. **$116-$420.** 1119 Pacific Rim Hwy. 1.8 mi (3.5 km) s on Hwy 4. Ext corridors. **Pets:** Accepted.
SAVE 🅂 ✕ 🛗 🖵 ¶ 🎿

▼▼▼▼ Long Beach Lodge Resort SH
(250) 725-2442. **$299-$569.** 1441 Pacific Rim Hwy. 4.7 mi (7.5 km) s on Hwy 4. Ext/int corridors. **Pets:** Accepted.
ASK ✕ 🛗 🖵 ¶ 🎿

(CAA) ▼▼▼▼ Pacific Sands Beach Resort SH 🐾
(250) 725-3322. **$170-$585.** 1421 Pacific Rim Hwy. 4.7 mi (7.5 km) s on Hwy 4. Ext corridors. **Pets:** Other species. $25 daily fee/pet. Supervision.
SAVE 🅂 ✕ 🛗 🖵 🎿

(CAA) ▼▼▼▼ Wickaninnish Inn SH 🐾
(250) 725-3100. **$280-$1500, 14 day notice.** Osprey Ln at Chesterman Beach. 2.7 mi (4.3 km) e on Hwy 4. Int corridors. **Pets:** $40 daily fee/pet. Designated rooms, service with restrictions, crate.
SAVE ✕ 🛗 🖵 ¶ ✕ 🎿

VALEMOUNT

(CAA) ▼▼▼▼ Best Western Valemount Inn & Suites SH 🐾
(250) 566-0086. **Call for rates.** 1950 Hwy 5 S. 0.9 mi (1.5 km) s on Hwy 5 (Yellowhead Hwy). Int corridors. **Pets:** $35 one-time fee/room. Designated rooms, service with restrictions, supervision.
SAVE ✕ 🛗 🖵 ¶ ⟲ ✕

(CAA) ▼▼▼ Canoe Mountain Lodge SH
(250) 566-9171. **$72-$124.** 1465 5th Ave. Just e of Hwy 5 (Yellowhead Hwy). Int corridors. **Pets:** Accepted.
SAVE 🅂 ✕ 🛗 🖵

(CAA) ▼▼▼ Chalet Continental Motel SH
(250) 566-9787. **$79-$135.** 1450 5th Ave. Off Hwy 5 (Yellowhead Hwy), just e. Int corridors. **Pets:** Dogs only. $10 daily fee/pet. Service with restrictions, supervision.
SAVE 🅂 ✕ 🛗 🖵 ⟲ ✕

VANCOUVER METROPOLITAN AREA

ALDERGROVE

(CAA) ▼▼▼▼ Best Western Country Meadows SH 🐾
(604) 856-9880. **$89-$229.** 3070 264th St. Trans-Canada Hwy 1, exit 73 (264th St/Aldergrove), 3.1 mi (5 km) s on 264th St (Hwy 13). Int corridors. **Pets:** Medium. $15 daily fee/pet. Designated rooms, service with restrictions, supervision.
SAVE 🅂 ✕ 🛗 🖵 ¶ ⟲

BURNABY

(CAA) ▼▼▼ Accent Inns M 🐾
(604) 473-5000. **$119-$179.** 3777 Henning Dr. Trans-Canada Hwy 1, exit 28 (Grandview Hwy), just n on Boundary Rd. Ext corridors. **Pets:** Small. $15 daily fee/pet. Designated rooms, service with restrictions, supervision.
SAVE 🅂 ✕ 🛗 🖵 ¶ ✕

(CAA) ▼▼▼▼ Best Western Kings Inn and Conference Centre SH
(604) 438-1383. **Call for rates.** 5411 Kingsway. Trans-Canada Hwy 1, exit 29 (Willingdon Ave), 1.9 mi (3 km) s to Kingsway, then 1.2 mi (2 km) e. Ext corridors. **Pets:** Small. $15 daily fee/room. Designated rooms, service with restrictions, supervision.
SAVE ✕ 🛗 🖵 ¶ ⟲

(CAA) ▼▼▼▼ Hilton Vancouver Metrotown LH
(604) 438-1200. **$140-$239.** 6083 McKay Ave. Trans-Canada Hwy 1, exit 29 (Willingdon Ave), 1.8 mi (3 km) s to Kingsway, then just e. Int corridors. **Pets:** $75 deposit/room. No service, supervision.
SAVE 🅂 ✕ 🛗 🖵 ¶ ⟲

▼▼▼ Lake City Motor Inn M
(604) 294-5331. **$94-$179.** 5415 Lougheed Hwy. Trans-Canada Hwy 1, exit 29 (Willingdon Ave), just n, 0.6 mi (1 km) e on Lougheed Hwy, just n on Springer Ave, then just e on Broadway. Ext corridors. **Pets:** Accepted.
ASK ✕ 🛗 🖵 ⟲

COQUITLAM

(CAA) ▼▼▼▼ Best Western Chelsea Inn SH
(604) 525-7777. **$109-$139.** 725 Brunette Ave. Trans-Canada Hwy 1, exit 40B (Brunette Ave N). Int corridors. **Pets:** Medium. $20 daily fee/pet. Designated rooms, service with restrictions, crate.
SAVE 🅂 ✕ 🛗 🖵 ⟲

▼▼▼ Ramada Inn Coquitlam SH
(604) 931-4433. **$90-$150.** 631 Lougheed Hwy. Trans-Canada Hwy 1, exit 44 (Coquitlam), 1.9 mi (3 km) w on Lougheed Hwy (Hwy 7). Ext/int corridors. **Pets:** Accepted.
✕ 🛗 🛗 🖵 ¶ ⟲

DELTA

(CAA) ▼▼▼▼ The Coast Tsawwassen Inn SH 🐾
(604) 943-8221. **$122-$240.** 1665 56th St. Hwy 99, exit 28 (Tsawwassen Ferries), 5 mi (8 km) w on Hwy 17; 3.1 mi (5 km) from the BC ferry terminal. Int corridors. **Pets:** Medium. $10 daily fee/pet. Service with restrictions, supervision.
SAVE 🅂 ✕ 🛗 🛗 🖵 ¶ ⟲ ✕

▼▼▼ River Run Cottages BB
(604) 946-7778. **$129-$210, 21 day notice.** 4551 River Rd W. Hwy 17, 1.6 mi (2.5 km) n on Ladner Trunk Rd (which becomes 47A St, then becomes River Rd W). Ext corridors. **Pets:** Accepted.
ASK 🅂 ✕ 🛗 🖵 🎿 ⟲ ⟲

LANGLEY

(CAA) ▼▼ Best Value Westward Inn M
(604) 534-9238. **$75-$95.** 19650 Fraser Hwy. Trans-Canada Hwy 1, exit 58 (200th St/Langley City), 3.1 mi (5 km) s on 200th St, 0.6 mi (1 km) w on Hwy 10, then just w. Ext corridors. **Pets:** $6 daily fee/pet. Service with restrictions, supervision.
SAVE ✕ 🛗 🖵

(AA) ▼▼▼▼ **Best Western Langley Inn** SH
(604) 530-9311. **Call for rates.** 5978 Glover Rd. Trans-Canada Hwy 1, exit 66 (232nd St), 6 km s, follow signs. Int corridors. **Pets:** Accepted.
SAVE ✕ 🅱 💻 ▥ 🍴 ➰

(AA) ▼▼▼▼ **Coast Hotel & Convention Centre** SH
(604) 530-1500. **$115-$165.** 20393 Fraser Hwy. Trans-Canada Hwy 1, exit 58 (200th St/Langley City), 3.9 mi (6.3 km) s on 200th St, then just e. Int corridors. **Pets:** Accepted.
SAVE Sᴏ̃ ✕ &ᴹ ▥ 🍴

(AA) ▼▼▼▼ **Holiday Inn Express Hotel & Suites**
Langley SH
(604) 882-2000. **$114-$144.** 8750 204th St. Trans-Canada Hwy 1, exit 58 (200th St/Langley City), just e on 88th Ave. Int corridors. **Pets:** Accepted.
SAVE Sᴏ̃ ✕ &ᴹ ▥ 🅱 💻 ➰ ✕▤

▼▼ **Sandman Hotel Langley** SH
(604) 888-7263. **Call for rates.** 8855 202nd St. Trans-Canada Hwy 1, exit 58 (200th St/Langley City), just e on 88th Ave. Int corridors. **Pets:** Accepted.
✕ 🅱 💻 🍴

▼▼ **Super 8 Langley/Aldergrove** M
(604) 856-8288. **$71-$99.** 26574 Gloucester Way. Trans-Canada Hwy 1, exit 73 (264th St/Aldergrove), just e on 56th Ave. Int corridors. **Pets:** Accepted.
ASK Sᴏ̃ ✕ &ᴹ 💻 ➰ ✕▤

▼▼ **Super 8 Langley City** M
(604) 514-3111. **$80-$90.** 6722 Glover Rd. Trans-Canada Hwy 1, exit 66 (232nd St), 2.5 mi (4 km) s on Glover Rd, follow signs. Int corridors. **Pets:** Accepted.
ASK Sᴏ̃ ✕

MAPLE RIDGE

(AA) ▼▼▼▼ **Best Western Maple Ridge** SH
(604) 463-5111. **Call for rates.** 21735 Lougheed Hwy. 1.2 mi (2 km) w on Lougheed Hwy (Hwy 7). Ext corridors. **Pets:** Accepted.
SAVE ✕ 🅱 💻 🍴

(AA) ▼▼▼ **Travelodge Maple Ridge** M
(604) 467-1511. **$90-$110.** 21650 Lougheed Hwy. 1.2 mi (2 km) w on Lougheed Hwy (Hwy 7). Int corridors. **Pets:** Accepted.
SAVE Sᴏ̃ ✕ 🅱 💻 ✕▤

MISSION

(AA) ▼▼▼ **Best Western Mission City Lodge** SH
(604) 820-5500. **Call for rates.** 32281 Lougheed Hwy. Just w of Hwy 11; corner of Lougheed Hwy (Hwy 7) and Hurd St. Int corridors. **Pets:** Accepted.
SAVE ✕ &ᴹ 🅱 💻 🍴 ➰ ✕▤

NORTH VANCOUVER

(AA) ▼▼▼▼ **Holiday Inn Hotel & Suites North**
Vancouver LH ☙
(604) 985-3111. **$199-$329.** 700 Old Lillooet Rd. Trans-Canada Hwy 1, exit 22 (Mt Seymour Pkwy), follow signs. Int corridors. **Pets:** Medium, dogs only. $25 daily fee/pet. Designated rooms, service with restrictions, supervision.
SAVE Sᴏ̃ ✕ &ᴹ 🅱 💻 🍴 ➰ ✕▤

▼ **Lionsgate Travelodge** M
(604) 985-5311. **$69-$149.** 2060 Marine Dr. Trans-Canada Hwy 1, exit 14 (Capilano Rd), 0.9 mi (1.5 km) s, then just w; from north end of Lions Gate Bridge, just e. Ext corridors. **Pets:** Accepted.
ASK Sᴏ̃ ✕ 🅱 💻 ➰

(AA) ▼▼▼ **North Vancouver Hotel** M
(604) 987-4461. **$79-$159.** 1800 Capilano Rd. Trans-Canada Hwy 1, exit 14 (Capilano Rd), 0.9 mi (1.5 km) s; from north end of Lions Gate Bridge, 0.6 mi (1 km) e on Marine Dr, then just n. Ext corridors. **Pets:** Medium. $20 daily fee/room. Designated rooms, service with restrictions, supervision.
SAVE Sᴏ̃ ✕ &ᴹ 🅱 💻 ➰

RICHMOND

(AA) ▼▼▼ **Accent Inns** SH ☙
(604) 273-3311. **$99-$169.** 10551 St. Edwards Dr. Hwy 99, exit 39 (Bridgeport/Airport) northbound to St. Edwards Dr; exit 39A (Richmond/Airport) southbound to St. Edwards Dr. Ext corridors. **Pets:** Medium. $15 daily fee/room. Designated rooms, service with restrictions.
SAVE Sᴏ̃ ✕ &ᴹ 🅱 💻 🍴

(AA) ▼▼▼ **Best Western Abercorn Inn** SH ☙
(604) 270-7576. **$119-$219.** 9260 Bridgeport Rd. Hwy 99, exit 39 (Bridgeport/Airport) northbound; exit 39A (Richmond/Airport) southbound. Int corridors. **Pets:** Medium, other species. $15 daily fee/pet. Service with restrictions, supervision.
SAVE Sᴏ̃ ✕ &ᴹ 🅱 💻 🍴

(AA) ▼▼▼ **Best Western Richmond Hotel & Convention**
Center LH
(604) 273-7878. **Call for rates.** 7551 Westminster Hwy. Corner of Minoru Blvd and Westminster Hwy. Int corridors. **Pets:** Accepted.
SAVE ✕ &ᴹ 🅱 💻 🍴 ➰ ✕▤

(AA) ▼▼▼ **Delta Vancouver Airport** LH
(604) 278-1241. **$149-$300.** 3500 Cessna Dr. Corner of Russ Baker Way and Cessna Dr; near Moray Bridge. Int corridors. **Pets:** Medium. $35 daily fee/pet. Designated rooms, service with restrictions, crate.
SAVE Sᴏ̃ ✕ &ᴹ 💻 🍴 ➰

(AA) ▼▼▼▼ **The Fairmont Vancouver Airport** LH
(604) 207-5200. **$279-$900.** 3111 Grant McConachie Way. In Vancouver International Airport. Int corridors. **Pets:** Medium. $35 one-time fee/pet. Designated rooms, service with restrictions, supervision.
SAVE Sᴏ̃ ✕ &ᴹ 💻 🍴 ➰ ✕▤

▼▼▼ **Holiday Inn Express Vancouver-Airport** SH
(604) 273-8080. **$109-$179.** 9351 Bridgeport Rd. Hwy 99, exit 39 (Bridgeport Rd/Airport) northbound; exit 39A (Richmond/Airport) southbound. Int corridors. **Pets:** Medium. $10 daily fee/pet. Service with restrictions, supervision.
ASK Sᴏ̃ ✕ &ᴹ 🅱 💻

▼▼▼ **Holiday Inn International Vancouver Airport** SH
(604) 821-1818. **$109-$179.** 10720 Cambie Rd. Hwy 99, exit 39 (Bridgeport/Airport) northbound to St. Edwards Dr, just 0.6 mi (1 km) n; southbound exit 39B (No. 4 Rd), just e. Int corridors. **Pets:** Medium. $15 daily fee/pet. Service with restrictions, supervision.
ASK Sᴏ̃ ✕ &ᴹ 🅱 💻 🍴

(AA) ▼▼▼▼ **River Rock Casino Resort** LH
(604) 247-8900. **Call for rates.** 8831 River Rd. Hwy 99, exit 39 (Bridgeport Rd/Airport) northbound; exit 39A (Richmond/Airport) southbound, just w on Bridgeport Rd, then just n on Great Canadian Way. Int corridors. **Pets:** Accepted.
SAVE ✕ &ᴹ 💻 🍴 ➰ ✕▤

(AA) ▼▼▼ **Sandman Hotel Vancouver Airport** SH ☙
(604) 303-8888. **$99-$159.** 3233 St. Edwards Dr. Hwy 99, exit 39 (Bridgeport Rd/Airport) northbound to St. Edwards Dr; exit 39A (Richmond/Airport) southbound. Int corridors. **Pets:** $10 daily fee/pet. Designated rooms, service with restrictions, supervision.
SAVE Sᴏ̃ ✕ &ᴹ 🅱 💻 🍴 ➰

ⒶⒶ ▼▼▼▼ **Vancouver Airport Marriott** 🆂🅷 ❖
(604) 276-2112. **$219-$263.** 7571 Westminster Hwy. Corner of Minoru Blvd and Westminster Hwy. Int corridors. **Pets:** Other species. $60 one-time fee/room. Service with restrictions, supervision.
🆂🅰🆅🅴 🆂🅳 ✕ ♿M 🅗 ▣ ¶¶ ⌐

SURREY

ⒶⒶ ▼▼ **Days Inn Surrey** 🆂🅷
(604) 588-9511. **Call for rates.** 9850 King George Hwy. Jct Fraser Hwy (Hwy 1A) and Hwy 99A (King George Hwy). Int corridors. **Pets:** Accepted.
🆂🅰🆅🅴 ✕ ♿M 🅗 ▣ ¶¶ ⌐

▼▼ **Ramada Hotel & Suites Surrey/Guildford** 🆂🅷
(604) 930-4700. **$99-$159.** 10410 158th St. Trans-Canada Hwy 1, exit 50 (160th St), just w on 104th Ave. Int corridors. **Pets:** Accepted.
✕ ♿M 🅗 ▣ ¶¶ ⌐

▼▼ **Ramada Inn Langley-Surrey** 🆂🅷
(604) 576-8388. **Call for rates.** 19225 Hwy 10. Trans-Canada Hwy 1, exit 58, 3.1 mi (5 km) s on 200th St, then 1.2 mi (2 km) w on Rt 10; corner of 192nd St and Rt 10. Int corridors. **Pets:** Accepted.
✕ ♿M 🅗 ▣ ¶¶ ⌐

ⒶⒶ ▼▼▼ **Sheraton Vancouver Guildford Hotel** 🅛🅗 ❖
(604) 582-9288. **Call for rates.** 15269 104th Ave. Trans-Canada Hwy 1, exit 48 eastbound, 0.6 mi (1 km) s on 152nd St, then just e; exit 50 westbound, 104th Ave, then just w. Int corridors. **Pets:** Large, dogs only. $50 deposit/pet. Designated rooms, service with restrictions, crate.
🆂🅰🆅🅴 ✕ ♿M ▣ ¶¶ ⌐

VANCOUVER

▼ **2400 Motel** 🅜
(604) 434-2464. **$70-$110.** 2400 Kingsway. 4.5 mi (7.2 km) se on Hwy 1A and 99A (Kingsway and 33rd Ave). Ext corridors. **Pets:** Accepted.
✕ 🅗 🅺

ⒶⒶ ▼▼▼ **Best Western Chateau Granville** 🆂🅷
(604) 669-7070. **$99-$249.** 1100 Granville St. Between Davie and Helmcken sts. Int corridors. **Pets:** Accepted.
🆂🅰🆅🅴 🆂🅳 ✕ ♿M 🅗 ▣ ¶¶

ⒶⒶ ▼▼▼ **Best Western Sands** 🆂🅷 ❖
(604) 682-1831. **$119-$259.** 1755 Davie St. Between Bidwell and Denman sts. Int corridors. **Pets:** $15 daily fee/pet. Designated rooms, supervision.
🆂🅰🆅🅴 🆂🅳 ✕ 🅗 ▣ ¶¶

ⒶⒶ ▼▼▼ **Delta Vancouver Suites** 🆂🅷 ❖
(604) 689-8188. **$174-$234.** 550 W Hastings St. Between Seymour and Richards sts; entrance in alley way. Int corridors. **Pets:** Medium. $35 one-time fee/pet. Service with restrictions, supervision.
🆂🅰🆅🅴 ✕ ♿M ▣ ¶¶ ⌐ ✕

ⒶⒶ ▼▼▼▼ **The Fairmont Hotel Vancouver** 🅛🅗
(604) 684-3131. **$229-$429.** 900 W Georgia St. Corner of Burrard at W Georgia St; enter from Hornby St. Int corridors. **Pets:** Medium. $35 one-time fee/pet. Designated rooms, service with restrictions, supervision.
🆂🅰🆅🅴 🆂🅳 ✕ ♿M ▣ ¶¶ ⌐ ✕

ⒶⒶ ▼▼▼▼ **The Fairmont Waterfront** 🅛🅗
(604) 691-1991. **$249-$429.** 900 Canada Place Way. Howe St at Cordova St. Int corridors. **Pets:** Medium. $35 one-time fee/pet. Designated rooms, service with restrictions, supervision.
🆂🅰🆅🅴 ✕ ♿M ▣ ¶¶ ⌐ ✕

ⒶⒶ ▼▼▼▼ **Four Seasons Hotel Vancouver** 🅛🅗 ❖
(604) 689-9333. **$240-$815.** 791 W Georgia St. Between Howe and W Georgia sts. Int corridors. **Pets:** Small. Designated rooms, service with restrictions, supervision.
🆂🅰🆅🅴 ✕ ♿M ¶¶ ⌐ ✕

ⒶⒶ ▼▼▼ **The Georgian Court Hotel** 🆂🅷
(604) 682-5555. **$189-$359.** 773 Beatty St. Between Georgia and Robson sts. Int corridors. **Pets:** Accepted.
🆂🅰🆅🅴 ✕ ♿M ▣ ¶¶ ✕

ⒶⒶ ▼▼▼ **Granville Island Hotel** 🆂🅷
(604) 683-7373. **$160-$475.** 1253 Johnston St. Granville Island; below the bridge, follow signs. Int corridors. **Pets:** $25 daily fee/room. Designated rooms, service with restrictions, supervision.
🆂🅰🆅🅴 🆂🅳 ✕ ♿M ▣ ¶¶ ✕

ⒶⒶ ▼▼▼ **Holiday Inn Express Vancouver** 🆂🅷 ❖
(604) 254-1000. **$89-$209.** 2889 E Hastings St. Between Renfrew and Kaslo sts. Int corridors. **Pets:** Medium. $15 daily fee/pet. Service with restrictions, supervision.
🆂🅰🆅🅴 🆂🅳 ✕ ♿M 🅗 ▣

ⒶⒶ ▼▼▼ **Holiday Inn Hotel & Suites Vancouver-Downtown** 🅛🅗 ❖
(604) 684-2151. **$119-$379.** 1110 Howe St. Between Helmcken and Davie sts. Int corridors. **Pets:** Medium. Service with restrictions, supervision.
🆂🅰🆅🅴 🆂🅳 ✕ ♿M 🅗 ▣ ¶¶ ⌐

▼▼▼ **Holiday Inn Vancouver-Centre (Broadway)** 🆂🅷
(604) 879-0511. **$119-$209.** 711 W Broadway. Between Heather and Willow sts. Int corridors. **Pets:** Accepted.
🅰🆂🅺 🆂🅳 ✕ ♿M 🅗 ▣ ¶¶ ⌐

ⒶⒶ ▼▼▼ **Hotel Le Soleil** 🆂🅷 ❖
(604) 632-3000. **$365-$465.** 567 Hornby St. Between Dunsmuir and Pender sts. Int corridors. **Pets:** $75 one-time fee/room. Service with restrictions, crate.
🆂🅰🆅🅴 🆂🅳 ✕ ♿M ▣ ¶¶

ⒶⒶ ▼▼▼ **Howard Johnson Hotel** 🆂🅷
(604) 688-8701. **$79-$259.** 1176 Granville St. Between Davie and Helmcken sts. Int corridors. **Pets:** Accepted.
🆂🅰🆅🅴 🆂🅳 ✕ 🅗 ▣ ¶¶

ⒶⒶ ▼▼▼ ◆ **Hyatt Regency Vancouver** 🅛🅗
(604) 683-1234. **$159-$439.** 655 Burrard St. Between W Georgia and Melville sts. Int corridors. **Pets:** $50 one-time fee/room. Service with restrictions, supervision.
🆂🅰🆅🅴 ✕ ♿M ▣ ¶¶ ⌐

ⒶⒶ ▼▼▼ **Pacific Palisades Hotel** 🅛🅗 ❖
(604) 688-0461. **$370-$420.** 1277 Robson St. Between Jervis and Bute sts. Int corridors. **Pets:** Designated rooms, service with restrictions.
🆂🅰🆅🅴 🆂🅳 ✕ ♿M 🅗 ▣ ¶¶ ⌐ ✕

ⒶⒶ ▼▼▼▼ ◆ **Pan Pacific Vancouver** 🅛🅗 ❖
(604) 662-8111. **$179-$449.** 300-999 Canada Place. Motor entrance off Burrard St. Int corridors. **Pets:** Medium. $30 daily fee/room. Service with restrictions, supervision.
🆂🅰🆅🅴 🆂🅳 ✕ ♿M 🅗 ▣ ¶¶ ⌐ ✕

▼▼ **Quality Hotel Downtown-The Inn at False Creek** 🆂🅷
(604) 682-0229. **$89-$209.** 1335 Howe St. Between Drake and Pacific sts. Int corridors. **Pets:** Accepted.
🅰🆂🅺 🆂🅳 ✕ ♿M 🅗 ▣ ¶¶ ⌐

ⒶⒶ ▼▼▼ **Ramada Inn & Suites Downtown Vancouver** 🆂🅷
(604) 685-1111. **$79-$259.** 1221 Granville St. Between Davie and Drake sts. Int corridors. **Pets:** Other species. $20 daily fee/room. Service with restrictions, supervision.
🆂🅰🆅🅴 🆂🅳 ✕ 🅗 ▣ ¶¶

ⒶⒶ ▼▼ **Ramada Limited Downtown Vancouver** 🆂🅷
(604) 488-1088. **$129-$229.** 435 W Pender St. Between Homer and Richards sts. Int corridors. **Pets:** Accepted.
🆂🅰🆅🅴 🆂🅳 ✕ ♿M ▣

CAA ▽▽▽▽ **Residence Inn by Marriott Vancouver** SH
(604) 688-1234. **$252-$384.** 1234 Hornby St. Between Drake and
Davie sts. Int corridors. **Pets:** Other species. $75 one-time fee/room.
Service with restrictions.

SAVE ⌖ ✕ ℶM ⌘ ▯ ⑪ ⫘

▽▽ **Sandman Hotel Vancouver City Center** LH
(604) 681-2211. **Call for rates.** 180 W Georgia St. Between Cambie
and Beatty sts. Int corridors. **Pets:** Accepted.

✕ ▯ ⑪ ⫘

CAA ▽▽▽▽ **Sheraton Vancouver Wall Centre**
Hotel LH ❀
(604) 331-1000. **$359-$459.** 1088 Burrard St. Between Helmcken and
Nelson sts. Int corridors. **Pets:** Large, dogs only. $60 one-time fee/room.
Service with restrictions.

SAVE ⌖ ✕ ℶM ⌘ ▯ ⑪ ⫘ ✕

CAA ▽▽▽▽ **The Sutton Place Hotel** LH ❀
(604) 682-5511. **$209-$599.** 845 Burrard St. Between Smithe and Robson sts. Int corridors. **Pets:** Other species. $150 one-time fee/room.

SAVE ⌖ ✕ ℶM ▯ ⑪ ⫘ ✕

▽▽ **Sylvia Hotel** SH
(604) 681-9321. **$115-$200, 30 day notice.** 1154 Gilford St. Beach Ave
and Gilford St; across from English Bay. Int corridors. **Pets:** Accepted.

✕ ⌘ ⑪ ⫔

CAA ▽▽▽ ▽▽ **Vancouver Marriott Pinnacle**
Downtown LH
(604) 684-1128. **$219-$340.** 1128 W Hastings St. Between Thurlow and
Bute sts. Int corridors. **Pets:** Accepted.

SAVE ⌖ ✕ ℶM ⌘ ▯ ⑪ ⫘ ✕

CAA ▽▽▽ ▽▽ **The Westin Bayshore Vancouver** LH
(604) 682-3377. **$460.** 1601 Bayshore Dr. W Georgia and Cardero sts.
Int corridors. **Pets:** Medium, dogs only. Designated rooms, service with
restrictions, supervision.

SAVE ⌖ ✕ ℶM ▯ ⑪ ⫘ ✕

CAA ▽▽▽ ▽▽ **The Westin Grand, Vancouver** LH
(604) 602-1999. **$429-$749.** 433 Robson St. Between Homer and Richards sts. Int corridors. **Pets:** Accepted.

SAVE ✕ ℶM ▯ ⑪ ⫘ ✕

WHITE ROCK

CAA ▽▽▽ **Ocean Promenade Hotel** SH
(604) 542-0102. **$129-$469.** 15611 Marine Dr. Hwy 99, exit 2B southbound; exit 2 (White Rock/8th Ave) northbound, 1.3 mi (2 km) w.
Ext/int corridors. **Pets:** Accepted.

SAVE ✕ ℶM ⌘ ▯

END METROPOLITAN AREA

VICTORIA METROPOLITAN AREA

ESQUIMALT

CAA WWWW Comfort Inn & Suites M ❖
(250) 388-7861. **$89-$299.** 101 Island Hwy. Douglas St, 3.1 mi (5 km) w on Gorge Rd, then just s on Admirals Rd. Ext/int corridors. **Pets:** Small, dogs only. $15 daily fee/pet. Designated rooms, service with restrictions, supervision.
(SAVE) (S/D) (X) (&M) (🛏) (💻) (≈)

MALAHAT

CAA WWWW The Aerie Resort CI ❖
(250) 743-7115. **$175-$825, 7 day notice.** 600 Ebadora Ln. 20 mi (32 km) n of Victoria off Trans-Canada Hwy 1, use Spectacle Lake turn off, follow signs. Int corridors. **Pets:** Small. $25 daily fee/pet. Designated rooms, service with restrictions, crate.
(SAVE) (S/D) (X) (💻) (🍴) (X)

WWW Malahat Bungalows Motel M
(250) 478-3011. **$62-$500, 3 day notice.** 300 Trans-Canada Hwy. Trans-Canada Hwy 1, 16.3 mi (26 km) n of Victoria, watch for signs. Ext corridors. **Pets:** Accepted.
(X) (🛏) (&M) (Z)

SAANICH

WWW Howard Johnson Hotel & Suites SH
(250) 704-4656. **Call for rates.** 4670 Elk Lake Dr. Blanshard St (Hwy 17), just w on Royal Oak Dr, then just n. Ext/int corridors. **Pets:** Accepted.
(X) (&M) (🛏) (💻) (🍴) (≈)

SAANICHTON

CAA WW Quality Inn Waddling Dog SH
(250) 652-1146. **$99-$169.** 2476 Mt Newton Crossroad. Corner of Hwy 17 and Mt Newton Crossroad. Int corridors. **Pets:** Dogs only. $15 daily fee/pet. Service with restrictions, supervision.
(SAVE) (S/D) (X) (💻) (🍴)

CAA WW Victoria Airport Super 8 SH
(250) 652-6888. **Call for rates.** 2477 Mt Newton Crossroad. Just e of Hwy 17. Int corridors. **Pets:** Accepted.
(SAVE) (X) (&M) (💻)

SIDNEY

CAA WWWW Best Western Emerald Isle Motor Inn SH ❖
(250) 656-4441. **$99-$181.** 2306 Beacon Ave. Hwy 17, exit Sidney, just e. Int corridors. **Pets:** Medium, other species. $15 daily fee/pet. Designated rooms, service with restrictions, supervision.
(SAVE) (S/D) (X) (&M) (🛏) (💻) (🍴)

WWWW The Cedarwood Inn & Suites SH
(250) 656-5551. **$85-$249.** 9522 Lochside Dr. Hwy 17, just e on McTavish Rd, then 0.8 mi (1.4 km) n. Ext corridors. **Pets:** Accepted.
(X) (🛏) (💻) (X)

WWWW Miraloma on the Cove SH
(250) 656-6622. **$119-$399.** 2326 Harbour Rd. Beacon Ave, 1.3 mi (2 km) n on Resthaven Dr, then 0.6 mi (1 km) e. Int corridors. **Pets:** Accepted.
(ASK) (S/D) (X) (&M) (🛏) (💻) (X) (X)

WWWW The Sidney Pier Hotel & Spa SH
(250) 655-9445. **$109-$649.** 9805 Seaport Pl. From Hwy 17, 0.6 mi (1 km) e on Beacon Ave. Int corridors. **Pets:** Accepted.
(ASK) (S/D) (X) (&M) (🛏) (💻) (🍴) (X)

SOOKE

CAA WWWW Markham House Bed & Breakfast BB
(250) 642-7542. **$120-$250, 7 day notice.** 1775 Connie Rd. 6.2 mi (10 km) e on Hwy 14. Int corridors. **Pets:** Accepted.
(SAVE) (S/D) (X) (🛏) (X)

WW Ocean Wilderness Inn BB
(250) 646-2116. **$120-$210, 7 day notice.** 9171 W Coast Rd. 8.6 mi (14 km) w on Hwy 14. Ext/int corridors. **Pets:** Accepted.
(ASK) (S/D) (X) (🛏) (X) (W) (Z)

CAA WWWW Sooke Harbour House CI ❖
(250) 642-3421. **$269-$599, 7 day notice.** 1528 Whiffen Spit Rd. 1.2 mi (2 km) w on Hwy 14. Ext/int corridors. **Pets:** Other species. $40 daily fee/pet.
(SAVE) (X) (&M) (🛏) (💻) (🍴) (X) (W)

VICTORIA

CAA WWWW Abigail's Hotel BB ❖
(250) 388-5363. **$209-$450, 7 day notice.** 906 McClure St. Blanshard St (Hwy 17), just e on Fairfield Rd, then just n on Vancouver St. Int corridors. **Pets:** Dogs only. $25 one-time fee/pet. Designated rooms, service with restrictions, crate.
(SAVE) (S/D) (X) (🛏) (💻)

CAA WW Accent Inns SH ❖
(250) 475-7500. **$99-$179.** 3233 Maple St. 1.9 mi (3 km) n on Blanshard St (Hwy 17); corner of Blanchard St and Cloverdale Ave. Ext corridors. **Pets:** Small. $15 daily fee/room. Designated rooms, service with restrictions, crate.
(SAVE) (S/D) (X) (&M) (🛏) (💻) (🍴)

CAA WWWW Admiral Inn M ❖
(250) 388-6267. **$99-$609.** 257 Belleville St. Corner of Belleville and Quebec sts. Ext corridors. **Pets:** Other species. $10 daily fee/pet. Designated rooms, crate.
(SAVE) (S/D) (X) (🛏) (💻)

CAA WWWW Best Western Carlton Plaza Hotel SH ❖
(250) 388-5513. **$89-$189.** 642 Johnson St. Between Douglas and Broad sts. Int corridors. **Pets:** $10 daily fee/pet. Designated rooms, service with restrictions, supervision.
(SAVE) (S/D) (X) (&M) (🛏) (💻) (🍴)

CAA WW Blue Ridge Inns M ❖
(250) 388-4345. **$69-$129.** 3110 Douglas St. Between Finlayson St and Speed Ave. Ext corridors. **Pets:** $10 daily fee/room. Designated rooms, service with restrictions, supervision.
(SAVE) (S/D) (X) (🛏) (💻) (🍴) (≈) (X)

WWWW Chateau Victoria Hotel and Suites LH
(250) 382-4221. **$89-$229.** 740 Burdett Ave. Between Douglas and Blanshard sts. Int corridors. **Pets:** Accepted.
(ASK) (X) (🛏) (💻) (🍴) (≈)

CAA WWWW Delta Victoria Ocean Pointe Resort & Spa LH ❖
(250) 360-2999. **$159-$398.** 45 Songhees Rd. Just w of Johnson St Bridge, Esquimalt at Tyee Rd. Int corridors. **Pets:** Medium, dogs only. $35 one-time fee/room. Designated rooms, service with restrictions, supervision.
(SAVE) (S/D) (X) (&M) (🛏) (💻) (🍴) (≈) (X)

WWW Executive House Hotel SH ☙
(250) 388-5111. **$195-$215.** 777 Douglas St. Between Blanshard and Douglas sts; downtown. Int corridors. **Pets:** $15 daily fee/pet. Designated rooms, service with restrictions, crate.
[SAVE] [X] [🛏] [▣] [🍴] [⊠] [🐾]

WWW WWW The Fairmont Empress LH
(250) 384-8111. **$169-$569.** 721 Government St. Between Belleville and Humboldt sts. Int corridors. **Pets:** Medium. $35 one-time fee/pet. Designated rooms, service with restrictions, supervision.
[ASK] [🛏] [X] [M] [🛏] [▣] [🍴] [🏊] [⊠] [🐾]

WWW Harbour Towers Hotel & Suites LH ☙
(250) 385-2405. **$94-$450.** 345 Quebec St. Between Oswego and Pendray sts. Int corridors. **Pets:** Small. $20 daily fee/pet. Designated rooms, service with restrictions, supervision.
[SAVE] [🛏] [X] [M] [🛏] [▣] [🍴] [🏊] [⊠] [🐾]

WWW Hotel Grand Pacific LH ☙
(250) 386-0450. **$149-$319.** 463 Belleville St. Between Oswego and Menzies sts. Int corridors. **Pets:** Medium. $50 one-time fee/room. Designated rooms, service with restrictions, crate.
[SAVE] [🛏] [X] [M] [▣] [🍴] [🏊] [⊠]

WWW Howard Johnson Hotel-City Centre SH
(250) 382-2151. **$59-$159.** 310 Gorge Rd E. From Douglas St, 0.6 mi (1.4 km) w; between Jutland St and Washington Ave. Int corridors. **Pets:** Accepted.
[SAVE] [X] [🛏] [▣] [🍴] [🏊]

WWW Huntingdon Hotel & Suites SH
(250) 381-3456. **$99-$379.** 330 Quebec St. Between Oswego and Pendray sts. Int corridors. **Pets:** $15 daily fee/pet. Designated rooms, service with restrictions, crate.
[SAVE] [🛏] [X] [🛏] [▣] [🍴]

WWW WWW The Magnolia Hotel & Spa SH ☙
(250) 381-0999. **$175-$335.** 623 Courtney St. Corner of Courtney and Gordon sts. Int corridors. **Pets:** $80 one-time fee/room. Service with restrictions, crate.
[SAVE] [🛏] [X] [M] [▣] [🍴] [⊠]

WWW WWW Marriott Victoria Inner Harbour LH ☙
(250) 480-3800. **$208-$307.** 728 Humboldt St. Between Blanshard and Douglas sts. Int corridors. **Pets:** Small, other species. $50 one-time fee/room. Designated rooms, service with restrictions, supervision.
[SAVE] [🛏] [X] [M] [🛏] [▣] [🍴] [🏊] [⊠]

WWW WWW The Oswego Hotel SH
(250) 294-7500. **$195-$650.** 500 Oswego St. Between Kingston and Quebec sts. Int corridors. **Pets:** Accepted.
[ASK] [🛏] [X] [🛏] [▣] [🍴] [🐾]

WWW WWW Prior House B&B Inn BB ☙
(250) 592-8847. **$129-$299, 14 day notice.** 620 St. Charles St. Blanshard St (Hwy 17), 1.2 mi (2 km) e on Fort St, then just s. Int corridors. **Pets:** Medium, dogs only. $20 one-time fee/room. Designated rooms, service with restrictions, supervision.
[SAVE] [X] [🛏] [▣] [🐾]

WWW WWW Ramada Victoria SH ☙
(250) 386-1422. **$65-$185.** 123 Gorge Rd E. From Douglas St, 1.2 mi (2.4 km) w. Int corridors. **Pets:** Small, dogs only. $20 daily fee/room. Designated rooms, service with restrictions, supervision.
[SAVE] [🛏] [X] [🛏] [▣] [🍴] [🏊]

WWW Robin Hood Motel M
(250) 388-4302. **$66-$104.** 136 Gorge Rd E. Douglas St, 1.2 mi (2.4 km) w. Ext corridors. **Pets:** Dogs only. $5 daily fee/pet. Designated rooms, service with restrictions, supervision.
[SAVE] [🛏] [X] [🛏] [▣]

WWW WWW Travelodge Victoria SH
(250) 388-6611. **$74-$174.** 229 Gorge Rd E. From Douglas St, 1.2 mi (2 km) w on Gorge Rd E; at Washington Ave. Ext corridors. **Pets:** Medium. $10 daily fee/pet. Service with restrictions.
[SAVE] [🛏] [X] [🛏] [▣] [🍴] [🏊]

WWW WWW The Westin Bear Mountain Victoria Golf Resort & Spa SH ☙
(250) 391-7160. **$169-$419.** 1999 Country Club Way. Trans-Canada Hwy 1, exit 14 (Highlands), 1.1 mi (1.7 km) n on Millstream Rd, then 1.9 mi (3 km) ne on Bear Mountain Pkwy, follow signs. Int corridors. **Pets:** Small. $60 one-time fee/room. Designated rooms, service with restrictions, supervision.
[SAVE] [🛏] [X] [M] [🛏] [▣] [🍴] [🏊] [⊠]

END METROPOLITAN AREA

WHISTLER

WWW Best Western Listel Whistler Hotel SH
(604) 932-1133. **Call for rates.** 4121 Village Green. Hwy 99, just e on Village Gate Blvd, then follow Whistler Way. Int corridors. **Pets:** Medium, other species. $25 daily fee/room. Designated rooms, service with restrictions, crate.
[SAVE] [X] [🛏] [▣] [🍴] [🏊]

WWW Crystal Lodge SH ☙
(604) 932-2221. **$108-$1225.** 4154 Village Green. Hwy 99, just e on Village Gate Blvd, then follow Whistler Way. Int corridors. **Pets:** $20 daily fee/pet. Service with restrictions, crate.
[SAVE] [🛏] [X] [M] [🛏] [▣] [🍴] [🏊] [⊠]

WWW Delta Whistler Village Suites LH ☙
(604) 905-3987. **$99-$399, 45 day notice.** 4308 Main St. Hwy 99, just e on Village Gate Blvd, just n on Northlands Blvd, then just e. Int corridors. **Pets:** Other species. $35 one-time fee/pet. Designated rooms, service with restrictions.
[SAVE] [🛏] [X] [M] [🛏] [▣] [🍴] [🏊] [⊠]

WWW Edgewater Lodge M ☙
(604) 932-0688. **$124-$225, 14 day notice.** 8020 Alpine Way. 2.5 mi (4 km) n of Whistler Village via Hwy 99, then e. Ext corridors. **Pets:** Dogs only. $25 one-time fee/pet. Service with restrictions, supervision.
[SAVE] [X] [▣] [🍴] [🐾]

WWW The Fairmont Chateau Whistler LH
(604) 938-8000. **$199-$3099, 3 day notice.** 4599 Chateau Blvd. Hwy 99, 0.6 mi (1 km) e on Lorimer Rd (Upper Village), just w on Blackcomb Way. Int corridors. **Pets:** Medium. $35 one-time fee/pet. Designated rooms, service with restrictions, supervision.
[SAVE] [🛏] [X] [M] [▣] [🍴] [🏊] [⊠]

WWW WWW Four Seasons Resort Whistler LH ☙
(604) 935-3400. **Call for rates.** 4591 Blackcomb Way. Hwy 99, 0.6 mi (1 km) e on Lorimer Rd (Upper Village). Int corridors. **Pets:** Large. Service with restrictions.
[SAVE] [X] [M] [🛏] [▣] [🍴] [🏊] [⊠]

ⒶⒶ ◆◆ ◆◆ **Hilton Whistler Resort & Spa** 🏨
(604) 932-1982. **$149-$899.** 4050 Whistler Way. Hwy 99, just e on Village Gate Blvd, then follow Whistler Way. Int corridors. **Pets:** Accepted.
SAVE Ⓢ╳ Ⓚᴹ 🔌 📺 ❯❮ ⌁ ╳

ⒶⒶ ◆◆◆ **Pan Pacific Whistler Village Centre** 🏨
(604) 966-5500. **$159-$2699, 7 day notice.** 4299 Blackcomb Way. Hwy 99, just e on Village Gate Blvd. Int corridors. **Pets:** Accepted.
SAVE ╳ Ⓚᴹ 🔌 📺 ⌁ ╳

◆◆◆ **Residence Inn by Marriott** 🄲🄾
(604) 905-3400. **$164-$329.** 4899 Painted Cliff Rd. Hwy 99, 0.6 mi (1 km) e on Lorimer Rd (Upper Village), just se on Blackcomb Way, then just w, follow road all the way to the end. Int corridors. **Pets:** Accepted.
A$K Ⓢ╳ 🔌 📺 ⌁ ╳

ⒶⒶ ◆◆◆ **Summit Lodge & Spa** 🏨 🐾
(604) 932-2778. **$119-$425, 30 day notice.** 4359 Main St. Hwy 99, just n on Village Gate Blvd, just w on Northlands Blvd. Int corridors. **Pets:** Other species. Service with restrictions, supervision.
SAVE Ⓢ╳ Ⓚᴹ 🔌 📺 ⌁ ╳

◆◆ **Tantalus Resort Lodge** 🄲🄾 🐾
(604) 932-4146. **$129-$829.** 4200 Whistler Way. Hwy 99, just e on Village Gate Blvd, then follow Whistler Way to the end. Int corridors. **Pets:** Medium. $35 one-time fee/pet. Designated rooms, service with restrictions, crate.
A$K Ⓢ╳ 🔌 📺 ⌁ ╳ ⍾

ⒶⒶ ◆◆◆ **The Westin Resort & Spa** 🏨 🐾
(604) 905-5000. **Call for rates.** 4090 Whistler Way. Hwy 99, just e on Village Gate Blvd, then s. Int corridors. **Pets:** Medium, dogs only. Service with restrictions, supervision.
SAVE ╳ Ⓚᴹ 🔌 📺 ❯❮ ⌁ ╳

WILLIAMS LAKE

◆ **Drummond Lodge Motel** Ⓜ
(250) 392-5334. **$69-$135.** 1405 Cariboo Hwy. 0.6 mi (1 km) s on Hwy 97. Ext corridors. **Pets:** Accepted.
╳ 🔌 📺

MANITOBA

BEAUSEJOUR

▼▼ Superior Inn SH
(204) 268-9050. $90-$95. 1055 Park Ave. Jct Hwy 44, 12 and 302. Int corridors. Pets: Accepted.
(ASK) (S🐾) (✕) (📶) (🖥) (🏊)

BRANDON

(CAA) ▼▼▼ Canad Inns-Brandon SH
(204) 727-1422. $109-$159. 1125 18th St. On Hwy 10 (18th St) at jct Brandon Ave. Int corridors. Pets: Accepted.
(SAVE) (S🐾) (✕) (📶) (🖥) (🍴) (🏊)

▼▼ Comfort Inn SH
(204) 727-6232. $98-$130. 925 Middleton Ave. Northside Trans-Canada Hwy 1 service road; between Hwy 10 N and 10 S; just e of McDonald's Restaurant. Int corridors. Pets: Accepted.
(ASK) (S🐾) (✕) (🔧) (📶) (🖥)

(CAA) ▼▼ Days Inn SH 🐾
(204) 727-3600. $90-$104. 2130 Currie Blvd. Jct Trans-Canada Hwy 1, 5 mi (8 km) s on Hwy 10 S (18th St). Int corridors. Pets: Other species. $10 daily fee/pet. Designated rooms, service with restrictions, crate.
(SAVE) (S🐾) (✕) (📶) (🖥) (🏊)

▼▼ Royal Oak Inn & Suites SH
(204) 728-5775. $122. 3130 Victoria Ave. 3 mi (5 km) s of Trans-Canada Hwy 1; 0.9 mi (1.4 km) w of jct Hwy 10 (18th St) and 1A (Victoria Ave). Int corridors. Pets: Accepted.
(ASK) (✕) (🔧) (📶) (🖥) (🍴) (🏊) (✕)

▼▼ Super 8 Motel Brandon SH
(204) 729-8024. $86-$101. 1570 Highland Ave. On Trans-Canada Hwy 1, south service road, just e of Hwy 10 (18th St). Int corridors. Pets: Accepted.
(ASK) (✕) (🔧) (📶) (🖥) (🏊)

▼▼◆ Victoria Inn SH
(204) 725-1532. $131. 3550 Victoria Ave. 3 mi (5 km) s of Trans-Canada Hwy 1; 1.1 mi (1.8 km) w of jct Hwy 10 (18th St) and 1A (Victoria Ave). Int corridors. Pets: Accepted.
(ASK) (S🐾) (✕) (🔧) (📶) (🍴) (🏊) (✕)

CHURCHILL

▼▼◆ Polar Inn & Suites M
(204) 675-8878. $135. 153 Kelsey Blvd. Centre. Int corridors. Pets: Accepted.
(ASK) (✕) (🔧) (📶) (🅰)

▼▼◆ The Tundra Inn SH
(204) 675-8831. $95-$205. 34 Franklin St. Centre. Int corridors. Pets: Accepted.
(S🐾) (✕) (🔧) (📶) (🅰)

FLIN FLON

▼▼ Victoria Inn North SH
(204) 687-7555. Call for rates. 160 Hwy 10A N. Jct Hwy 10 and 10A, 0.6 mi (1 km) nw (eastern approach to city). Int corridors. Pets: Accepted.
(✕) (🔧) (📶) (🍴) (🏊)

HECLA

▼▼ Solmundson Gesta Hus BB
(204) 279-2088. $75-$90. Village on Hecla Island. On Hwy 8. Int corridors. Pets: Accepted.
(ASK) (S🐾) (✕) (🅩)

NEEPAWA

▼▼◆ Bay Hill Inns & Suites M
(204) 476-8888. Call for rates. 160 Main St W. Hwy 16, just w of jct Rt 5. Int corridors. Pets: Accepted.
(✕) (🔧) (📶) (🍴) (🏊)

PORTAGE LA PRAIRIE

▼▼◆ Super 8 M
(204) 857-8883. Call for rates. 2668 Hwy 1A W. 0.9 mi (1.5 km) w on Trans-Canada Hwy 1A. Int corridors. Pets: Accepted.
(✕) (🔧) (📶) (🏊)

▼ Westgate Inn Motel M
(204) 239-5200. $60-$89. 1010 Saskatchewan Ave E. 0.6 mi (1 km) e on Trans-Canada Hwy 1A. Ext corridors. Pets: Accepted.
(ASK) (✕) (🔧) (📶)

RUSSELL

▼▼◆ The Russell Inn Hotel & Conference Centre SH
(204) 773-2186. $89-$158. Hwy 16 Russell. 0.8 mi (1.2 km) se on Hwy 16 and 83. Ext/int corridors. Pets: Accepted.
(ASK) (S🐾) (✕) (🔧) (📶) (🍴) (🏊) (✕)

STEINBACH

▼▼ Days Inn SH
(204) 320-9200. Call for rates. 75 Hwy 12 N. Jct Trans-Canada Hwy 1 and 12, 12.5 mi (20 km) s. Int corridors. Pets: Accepted.
(✕) (🔧) (📶) (🏊) (✕)

THE PAS

▼▼ Kikiwak Inn SH
(204) 623-1800. Call for rates. Hwy 10 N. On Hwy 10, 0.4 mi (0.6 km) n. Int corridors. Pets: Accepted.
(✕) (🔧) (📶) (🍴) (🏊)

▼▼ Super 8 SH
(204) 623-1888. Call for rates. 1717 Gordon Ave. At southern approach to town. Int corridors. Pets: Accepted.
(✕) (🔧) (📶) (🏊)

(CAA) ▼ Wescana Inn SH
(204) 623-5446. $106. 439 Fischer Ave. On Hwy 10; centre. Ext/int corridors. Pets: Accepted.
(SAVE) (S🐾) (✕) (🔧) (📶) (🍴)

THOMPSON

▼▼▼ Country Inn & Suites By Carlson SH
(204) 778-8879. $108. 70 Thompson Dr N. Just w of Hwy 6. Int corridors. Pets: Accepted.
(ASK) (S🐾) (✕) (🔧) (📶)

WINNIPEG METROPOLITAN AREA

WINNIPEG

▼▼ ▼▼ Best Western Pembina Inn & Suites SH
(204) 269-8888. **$89-$160, 7 day notice.** 1714 Pembina Hwy. 0.6 mi (1 km) n of jct Bishop Grandin Blvd. Int corridors. **Pets:** Medium. $10 daily fee/pet. Designated rooms, service with restrictions, supervision.

ASK Sô ☒ 🛏 💻 ≈ ☒

CAA ▼▼▼▼ Canad Inns Polo Park SH
(204) 775-8791. **$109-$159.** 1405 St. Matthews Ave. Just e of St James St. Int corridors. **Pets:** Accepted.

SAVE Sô ☒ 🛏 💻 🍴 ≈ ☒

▼▼▼▼ Clarion Hotel & Suites SH
(204) 774-5110. **$139-$299.** 1445 Portage Ave. Jct Empress St. Int corridors. **Pets:** Accepted.

ASK Sô ☒ 🛏 💻 🍴 ≈ ☒

▼▼ ▼▼ Comfort Inn Airport SH
(204) 783-5627. **$116-$135.** 1770 Sargent Ave. At Sargent Ave and King Edward St. Int corridors. **Pets:** Medium. $5 daily fee/room. Designated rooms, service with restrictions, supervision.

ASK Sô ☒ Ꮪᴹ 🛏 💻

CAA ▼▼ ▼▼ Comfort Inn South SH
(204) 269-7390. **$105-$130.** 3109 Pembina Hwy. Just n of jct Perimeter Hwy 100 and 75. Int corridors. **Pets:** Medium. $10 daily fee/room. Designated rooms, service with restrictions, supervision.

SAVE Sô ☒ 🛏 💻

▼▼ ▼▼ Country Inn & Suites By Carlson SH
(204) 783-6900. **$91-$99, 4 day notice.** 730 King Edward St. Just s of jct Wellington Ave. Int corridors. **Pets:** Accepted.

ASK Sô ☒ Ꮪᴹ 🛏 💻

CAA ▼▼ ▼▼ Days Inn SH
(204) 586-8525. **$109-$139.** 550 McPhillips St. Just n of Logan Ave. Int corridors. **Pets:** Accepted.

SAVE Sô ☒ 🛏 💻 🍴 ≈

CAA ▼▼▼▼ Delta Winnipeg LH 🐾
(204) 942-0551. **$89-$349.** 350 St. Mary Ave. At Hargrave St. Int corridors. **Pets:** Medium, other species. $35 one-time fee/room. Crate.

SAVE Sô ☒ Ꮪᴹ 🛏 💻 🍴 ≈ ☒

▼▼▼▼ The Fairmont Winnipeg LH 🐾
(204) 957-1350. **$149-$399.** 2 Lombard Pl. Just e of corner Portage Ave and Main St. Int corridors. **Pets:** Large, other species. $50 one-time fee/room. Service with restrictions, crate.

ASK Sô ☒ 🛏 💻 🍴 ≈ ☒

CAA ▼▼▼▼ Greenwood Inn & Suites SH
(204) 775-9889. **Call for rates.** 1715 Wellington Ave. Wellington Ave at Century St. Int corridors. **Pets:** Accepted.

SAVE ☒ 🛏 💻 🍴 ≈ ☒

CAA ▼▼▼▼ Hilton Suites Winnipeg Airport SH
(204) 783-1700. **$119-$189.** 1800 Wellington Ave. At Berry St. Int corridors. **Pets:** Medium. Service with restrictions, supervision.

SAVE Sô ☒ Ꮪᴹ 🛏 💻 🍴 ≈ ☒

CAA ▼▼▼▼ Holiday Inn Winnipeg-South SH
(204) 452-4747. **$115-$139.** 1330 Pembina Hwy. At McGillivray Blvd. Int corridors. **Pets:** Other species. Designated rooms, service with restrictions, supervision.

SAVE ☒ 🛏 💻 🍴 ≈ ☒

▼▼ ▼▼ The Marlborough Hotel SH
(204) 942-6411. **Call for rates.** 331 Smith St. Just n off Metro Rt 85 (Portage Ave). Int corridors. **Pets:** Accepted.

☒ 🛏 💻 🍴 ≈ ☒

▼▼ ▼▼ Place Louis Riel All-Suite Hotel SH
(204) 947-6961. **$125-$300.** 190 Smith St. At St. Mary Ave. Int corridors. **Pets:** Accepted.

ASK Sô ☒ Ꮪᴹ 🛏 💻 🍴 ☒

CAA ▼▼ ▼▼ Quality Inn & Suites SH 🐾
(204) 453-8247. **$90-$270, 30 day notice.** 635 Pembina Hwy. Jct Grant Ave, just s. Int corridors. **Pets:** Other species. $10 daily fee/pet.

SAVE Sô ☒ 🛏 💻 🍴

▼▼▼▼ Radisson Hotel Winnipeg Downtown LH
(204) 956-0410. **Call for rates.** 288 Portage Ave. At Smith St. Int corridors. **Pets:** Accepted.

☒ 🛏 💻 🍴 ≈ ☒

CAA ▼▼ ▼▼ Travelodge SH 🐾
(204) 255-6000. **$76-$119.** 20 Alpine Ave. Just e of jct Fermor Ave and St. Anne's Rd. Int corridors. **Pets:** Medium. $8 daily fee/room. Designated rooms, service with restrictions, supervision.

SAVE Sô ☒ 🛏 💻 🍴 ≈ ☒

CAA ▼▼▼▼ Victoria Inn Hotel & Convention Centre SH
(204) 786-4801. **$95-$160.** 1808 Wellington Ave. At Berry St. Int corridors. **Pets:** Accepted.

SAVE ☒ 🛏 💻 🍴 ≈ ☒

CAA ▼▼ ▼▼ Viscount Gort Hotel SH
(204) 775-0451. **$87.** 1670 Portage Ave. Portage Ave at Rt 90. Int corridors. **Pets:** Accepted.

SAVE Sô ☒ 🛏 💻 ≈ ☒

END METROPOLITAN AREA

NEW BRUNSWICK

BATHURST

▼▼ ▼▼ Atlantic Host Hotel SH
(506) 548-3335. **$96-$120.** 1450 Vanier Blvd. Rt 11, exit 310 (Vanier Blvd). Int corridors. **Pets:** Accepted.
⊠ 🖃 🍴 ⇌ ⊠

▼▼ ▼▼ Comfort Inn SH
(506) 547-8000. **$90-$110, 7 day notice.** 1170 St Peter's Ave. 2.1 mi (3.4 km) n on Rt 134 (St Peter's Ave). Int corridors. **Pets:** Accepted.
(ASK) 🔊 ⊠ 🛏 🖃

▼▼ ▼▼ Danny's Inn & Conference Centre SH
(506) 546-6621. **$77-$150.** Rt 134. Rt 11, exit 310 (Vanier Blvd) north-bound to Rt 134 (St Peter's Ave), 2.5 mi (4 km) n; exit 318 south-bound to Rt 134 (St Peter's Ave), 2.3 mi (3.8 km) s. Ext/int corridors. **Pets:** Accepted.
🔊 ⊠ 🛏 🖃 🍴 ⇌ ⊠

▼▼ ▼▼ Lakeview Inns & Suites SH
(506) 548-4949. **$96-$108.** 777 St Peter's Ave. 1.8 mi (3 km) n on Rt 134 (St Peter's Ave). Int corridors. **Pets:** Accepted.
(ASK) 🔊 ⊠ (&M) 🛏 🖃

BOUCTOUCHE

▼▼ ▼▼ Auberge Bouctouche Inn & Suites SH
(506) 743-5003. **$79-$139.** 50 Industrielle St. Rt 11, exit 32A/B. Int corridors. **Pets:** Accepted.
(ASK) ⊠ (&M) 🛏

CAMPBELLTON

▼▼ ▼▼ Comfort Inn SH
(506) 753-4121. **$110-$160.** 111 chemin Val D'Amour. Hwy 11, exit 415, 0.6 mi (1 km) e on Sugarloaf St W. Ext/int corridors. **Pets:** Accepted.
(ASK) 🔊 ⊠ 🛏 🖃

(CAA) ▼▼ ▼▼ Howard Johnson SH
(506) 753-4133. **Call for rates.** 157 Water St. Hwy 134; in City Centre Complex. Int corridors. **Pets:** Accepted.
(SAVE) ⊠ 🛏 🖃 🍴

CARAQUET

▼▼ ▼▼ ▼▼ Super 8 Motel SH
(506) 727-0888. **Call for rates.** 9 Carrefour Ave. Just e of jct Rt 11 and St Pierre Blvd E. Int corridors. **Pets:** Small. $10 daily fee/pet. Service with restrictions, supervision.
⊠ (&M) 🛏 🖃 ⇌ ⊠

CHANCE HARBOUR

(CAA) ▼▼ ▼▼ ▼▼ The Mariner's Inn CI
(506) 659-2619. **$109-$139, 3 day notice.** 32 Mawhinney Cove Rd. Hwy 1, exit 96, 5.6 mi (9 km) s on Rt 790; 18.7 mi (30 km) w of Saint John. Int corridors. **Pets:** Medium, dogs only. $15 daily fee/pet. Desig-nated rooms, service with restrictions, supervision.
(SAVE) ⊠ 🛏 🖃 🍴

COCAGNE

▼▼ Cocagne Motel M
(506) 576-6657. **Call for rates.** 1718 Rt 535. Rt 11, exit 15, 0.6 mi (1 km) n on Rt 535. Ext corridors. **Pets:** Accepted.
🛏 (AC)

DALHOUSIE

▼▼ ▼▼ ▼▼ Best Western Manoir Adelaide SH
(506) 684-5681. **$119-$129.** 385 Adelaide St. Centre. Int corridors. **Pets:** Medium. $100 deposit/pet. Service with restrictions, supervision.
(ASK) 🔊 ⊠ 🛏 🖃 🍴

DOAKTOWN

▼▼ ▼▼ The Ledges Inn CI
(506) 365-1820. **Call for rates.** 30 Ledges Inn Ln. On Rt 8; centre. Int corridors. **Pets:** Accepted.
⊠ 🍴

EDMUNDSTON

▼▼ ▼▼ Auberge Les Jardins Inn SH
(506) 739-5514. **$89-$169.** 60 Principale St. Trans-Canada Hwy 2, exit 8. Ext/int corridors. **Pets:** $10 daily fee/pet. Designated rooms, service with restrictions, crate.
⊠ 🛏 🖃 🍴 ⇌

(CAA) ▼▼ ▼▼ Chateau Edmundston Hotel & Suites SH
(506) 739-7321. **$110-$160.** 100 rue Rice. Trans-Canada Hwy 2, exit 18 (Hebert Blvd), 1 mi (1.6 km) sw, then just w on Church Rd. Int corridors. **Pets:** Accepted.
(SAVE) 🔊 ⊠ 🛏 🖃 🍴 ⇌

▼▼ ▼▼ Comfort Inn SH
(506) 739-8361. **$89-$199.** 5 Bateman Ave. Trans-Canada Hwy 2, exit 18 (Hebert Blvd). Int corridors. **Pets:** Accepted.
(ASK) 🔊 ⊠ 🛏 🖃

▼▼ ▼▼ Days Inn Edmundston SH
(506) 263-0000. **$139-$159.** 10 rue Mathieu. Trans-Canada Hwy 2, exit 26. Int corridors. **Pets:** Accepted.
(ASK) 🔊 ⊠ 🛏 🖃

▼▼ ▼▼ Quality Inn SH
(506) 735-5525. **$72-$135.** 919 Canada Rd. Trans-Canada Hwy 2, exit 13B eastbound; exit 13BA westbound. Ext/int corridors. **Pets:** Accepted.
(ASK) 🔊 ⊠ (&M) 🛏 🖃 🍴 ⇌

FREDERICTON

▼▼ ▼▼ Auberge Wandlyn Inn SH
(506) 462-4444. **$90-$120.** 958 Prospect St. Rt 8, exit 3 (Hanwell Rd) eastbound; exit 5 (Smythe St) westbound. Ext/int corridors. **Pets:** Accepted.
(ASK) 🔊 ⊠ 🛏 🖃 🍴 ⇌

(CAA) ▼▼ ▼▼ City Motel SH
(506) 450-9900. **$69-$150.** 1216 Regent St. Trans-Canada Hwy 2, exit 285A and B eastbound; exit 285B westbound, 2 mi (3.3 km) n on Rt 101 (Regent St). Int corridors. **Pets:** Accepted.
(SAVE) 🔊 ⊠ 🛏 🖃 🍴

(CAA) ▼▼ ▼▼ Comfort Inn SH 🐾
(506) 453-0800. **$109-$170.** 797 Prospect St. Rt 8, exit 3 (Hanwell Rd) eastbound; exit 5 (Smythe St) westbound. Int corridors. **Pets:** Accepted.
(SAVE) 🔊 ⊠ 🛏 🖃

ⓐ ▼▼▼▼ **Crowne Plaza Fredericton Lord Beaverbrook** 🆔
(506) 455-3371. **$149-$249.** 659 Queen St. Corner of Regent St. Int corridors. **Pets:** Accepted.
[SAVE] [S🐾] [✕] [💷] [🍴] [⇨] [✕]

ⓐ ▼▼▼▼ **Delta Fredericton** 🆔 🐾
(506) 457-7000. **$164-$294.** 225 Woodstock Rd. 1 mi (1.6 km) n on Rt 102; downtown. Int corridors. **Pets:** Medium, other species. $35 one-time fee/room. Designated rooms, service with restrictions, supervision.
[SAVE] [S🐾] [✕] [♿] [♨] [💷] [🍴] [⇨] [✕]

▼▼▼▼ **Holiday Inn Fredericton** 🆔
(506) 363-5111. **$95-$171.** 35 Mactaquac Rd (Hwy 102). Trans-Canada Hwy 2, exit 258 eastbound, 7 mi (11 km) e; exit 294 westbound, 19 mi (30 km) w. Ext/int corridors. **Pets:** Accepted.
[A$K] [S🐾] [✕] [♿] [♨] [💷] [🍴] [⇨] [✕]

▼▼▼ **Lakeview Inns & Suites-Fredericton** 🆔
(506) 459-0035. **$107-$131.** 665 Prospect St. Rt 8, exit 3 (Hanwell Rd) eastbound; exit 5 (Smythe St) westbound. Int corridors. **Pets:** Small. $10 one-time fee/pet. Designated rooms, service with restrictions, crate.
[A$K] [S🐾] [✕] [♨] [💷]

ⓐ ▼▼▼▼ **Ramada Hotel Fredericton** 🆔 🐾
(506) 460-5500. **Call for rates.** 480 Riverside Dr. On Rt 105 at the north end of Princess Margaret Bridge. Int corridors. **Pets:** $20 one-time fee/room. Designated rooms, service with restrictions, supervision.
[SAVE] [✕] [♨] [💷] [🍴] [⇨] [✕]

GRAND FALLS

▼▼ **Auberge Pres-du-Lac Inn** 🆔
(506) 473-1300. **$110-$152.** 10039 Rt 144. Trans-Canada Hwy 2, exit 75, just w. Ext/int corridors. **Pets:** Accepted.
[A$K] [S🐾] [✕] [♨] [♨] [💷] [🍴] [⇨] [✕]

▼▼▼▼ **Best Western Grand Sault Hotel & Suites** 🆔 🐾
(506) 473-6200. **$113-$225.** 187 Ouellette St. Trans-Canada Hwy 2, exit 79. Int corridors. **Pets:** Large. $25 daily fee/pet. Designated rooms, service with restrictions, supervision.
[A$K] [S🐾] [✕] [♿] [♨] [💷] [⇨]

MIRAMICHI

▼▼▼▼ **Best Value Inn and Suites** 🆔
(506) 622-1215. **$79-$127.** 201 Edward St. 0.6 mi (1 km) w on Rt 8. Int corridors. **Pets:** Accepted.
[A$K] [S🐾] [✕] [♨] [💷]

▼▼ **Lakeview Inns & Suites** 🆔
(506) 627-1999. **$82-$101, 7 day notice.** 333 King George Hwy. 1.1 mi (1.8 km) w on Rt 8. Int corridors. **Pets:** Accepted.
[A$K] [S🐾] [✕] [♨] [💷]

▼▼▼▼ **Rodd Miramichi River-A Rodd Signature Hotel** 🆔
(506) 773-3111. **$113-$175.** 1809 Water St. Hwy 11, exit 120, 0.4 mi (0.6 km) e. Int corridors. **Pets:** Accepted.
[A$K] [S🐾] [✕] [♿] [♨] [💷] [🍴] [⇨]

MONCTON

ⓐ ▼▼▼ **Beacon Light Motel** Ⓜ
(506) 384-1734. **$75-$125.** 1062 Mountain Rd. Trans-Canada Hwy 2, exit 454 (Mapleton Rd), 1.7 mi (2.8 km) to Rt 126 (Mountain Rd), then just s. Ext/int corridors. **Pets:** Accepted.
[SAVE] [✕] [♨] [💷] [🍴] [⇨]

ⓐ ▼▼▼▼ **Best Western Moncton** 🆔
(506) 388-0888. **$112-$129.** 300 Lewisville Rd. Trans-Canada Hwy 2, exit 459A eastbound, s on Rt 115 to Lewisville Rd, then left; exit 467A westbound, 5 mi (8 km) w on Hwy 15, exit 10. Int corridors. **Pets:** Accepted.
[SAVE] [S🐾] [✕] [♿] [♨] [💷] [⇨]

ⓐ ▼▼▼ **Coastal Inn Champlain** 🆔
(506) 857-9686. **$115-$149.** 502 Kennedy St. At Paul St; opposite Champlain Place Shopping Centre. Ext/int corridors. **Pets:** Accepted.
[SAVE] [S🐾] [✕] [♨] [💷] [🍴] [⇨]

▼▼▼ **Colonial Inns** 🆔
(506) 382-3395. **$84-$153.** 42 Highfield St. 1 blk n of Main St; centre. Ext/int corridors. **Pets:** Accepted.
[✕] [♨] [🍴] [⇨]

ⓐ ▼▼▼ **Comfort Inn** 🆔
(506) 859-6868. **$95-$295.** 20 Maplewood Dr. Trans-Canada Hwy 2, exit 459A on Hwy 115 S, left on Rt 134 E (Lewisville Rd). Int corridors. **Pets:** Other species. Service with restrictions.
[SAVE] [S🐾] [✕] [♨] [💷]

▼▼ **Comfort Inn** 🆔
(506) 384-3175. **$89-$295.** 2495 Mountain Rd. Trans-Canada Hwy 2, exit 450. Int corridors. **Pets:** Accepted.
[A$K] [S🐾] [✕] [♨] [💷]

▼▼▼ **Country Inn & Suites By Carlson** 🆔 🐾
(506) 852-7000. **$89-$200.** 2475 Mountain Rd. Trans-Canada Hwy 2, exit 450. Int corridors. **Pets:** Other species. $50 deposit/room, $5 daily fee/pet. Designated rooms, supervision.
[A$K] [S🐾] [✕] [♨] [💷]

ⓐ ▼▼▼▼ **Crowne Plaza Moncton Downtown** 🆔
(506) 854-6340. **$299-$369.** 1005 Main St. Highfield and Main sts; downtown. Int corridors. **Pets:** Other species. $10 one-time fee/room. Designated rooms, supervision.
[SAVE] [S🐾] [✕] [♨] [💷] [🍴] [⇨] [✕]

▼▼▼▼ **Delta Beausejour** 🆔 🐾
(506) 854-4344. **$185-$329.** 750 Main St. Main and Bacon sts; downtown. Int corridors. **Pets:** Dogs only. $35 one-time fee/pet. Supervision.
[A$K] [S🐾] [✕] [💷] [🍴] [⇨]

ⓐ ▼▼▼▼ **Holiday Inn Express Hotel & Suites Moncton** 🆔
(506) 384-1050. **$109-$199.** 2515 Mountain Rd. Trans-Canada Hwy 2, exit 450. Ext/int corridors. **Pets:** Accepted.
[SAVE] [✕] [♿] [♨] [💷] [🍴] [⇨] [✕]

▼▼ **Rodd Park House Inn** 🆔
(506) 382-1664. **$115-$150.** 434 Main St. On Rt 106 (Main St) at King St. Ext/int corridors. **Pets:** Accepted.
[A$K] [S🐾] [✕] [💷] [🍴] [⇨]

▼▼▼ **Super 8 Motel Moncton/Dieppe** 🆔 🐾
(506) 858-8880. **$129-$199, 14 day notice.** 370 Dieppe Blvd. Hwy 15, exit 16, 0.6 mi (1 km) s. Int corridors. **Pets:** Medium. $10 daily fee/room. Service with restrictions, supervision.
[A$K] [S🐾] [✕] [♿] [♨] [💷] [⇨] [✕]

OROMOCTO

▼▼▼ **Days Inn Oromocto** 🆔
(506) 357-5657. **Call for rates.** 60 Brayson Blvd. Trans-Canada Hwy 2, exit 301 eastbound; exit 303 westbound, just s to Pioneer Ave, then 1 mi (1.6 km) w. Int corridors. **Pets:** Accepted.
[✕] [♿] [♨] [💷] [🍴] [⇨]

PERTH-ANDOVER

ⓐ ▼▼▼ **The Castle Inn** Ⓒ🆔
(506) 273-9495. **$100-$290, 4 day notice.** 21 Brentwood Dr. Trans-Canada Hwy 2, exit 115, follow signs over St. John River. Int corridors. **Pets:** Accepted.
[SAVE] [S🐾] [✕] [♿] [💷] [🍴]

ROTHESAY

◆◆◆◆ **Shadow Lawn Inn** **CI**
(506) 847-7539. **Call for rates.** 3180 Rothesay Rd. Hwy 1, exit 137B eastbound; exit 137A westbound, follow signs for Rothesay Rd and Rt 100, 1 mi (1.6 km) left on Old Hampton Rd (Rt 100), then left on Rt 100. Int corridors. **Pets:** Accepted.
☒ 🛏 💻 🍴

SACKVILLE

◆◆◆ **Coastal Inn Sackville** **SH**
(506) 536-0000. **$109-$129.** 15 Wright St. Trans-Canada Hwy 2, exit 504. Int corridors. **Pets:** Accepted.
A$K S🐾 ☒ 🛏

◆◆◆◆ **Marshlands Inn** **CI**
(506) 536-0170. **$95-$205.** 55 Bridge St. On Hwy 106; centre. Int corridors. **Pets:** Accepted.
SAVE ☒ 🍴

ST. ANDREWS

◆◆◆◆ **The Fairmont Algonquin** **LH**
(506) 529-8823. **$119-$569, 3 day notice.** 184 Adolphus St. Off Hwy 127. Int corridors. **Pets:** Medium. $35 one-time fee/pet. Designated rooms, service with restrictions, supervision.
SAVE ☒ 🛏 💻 🍴 🏊 ☒

◆◆◆◆ **St. Andrews Cottages** **CA**
(506) 529-8555. **$95-$139, 14 day notice.** 3889 Rt 127. On Rt 127, 1.5 mi (2.5 km) n. Ext corridors. **Pets:** Accepted.
☒ 🛏 💻 🏊 🐾

SAINT JOHN

◆◆◆ **Colonial Inns** **SH**
(506) 652-3000. **$88-$98.** 175 City Rd. Adjacent to Hwy 1, exit 123. Ext/int corridors. **Pets:** Accepted.
A$K S🐾 ☒ 🛏 🍴 🏊

◆◆◆ **Comfort Inn** **SH**
(506) 674-1873. **$105-$136.** 1155 Fairville Blvd. Hwy 1, exit 117 westbound; exit 119 eastbound, turn left. Int corridors. **Pets:** Accepted.
SAVE S🐾 ☒ 🛏 💻

◆◆◆ **Country Inn & Suites** **SH** 🐾
(506) 635-0400. **Call for rates.** 1011 Fairville Blvd. Hwy 1, exit 119B eastbound, left on Catherwood Dr, left at lights; exit 119A westbound. Int corridors. **Pets:** $10 one-time fee/pet. Supervision.
☒ 🛏 💻

◆◆◆◆ **Delta Brunswick** **LH** 🐾
(506) 648-1981. **$119-$179.** 39 King St. Centre of downtown; in Brunswick Square Mall. Int corridors. **Pets:** Medium. $35 one-time fee/room. Designated rooms, service with restrictions, crate.
A$K S🐾 ☒ S🐾 💻 🍴 🏊 ☒

◆◆◆ **Fort Howe Hotel and Convention Centre** **SH**
(506) 657-7320. **$109-$149, 30 day notice.** 10 Portland St. Hwy 1, exit 121 eastbound off Harbour Bridge; exit 123 westbound. Int corridors. **Pets:** Accepted.
A$K S🐾 ☒ 🛏 💻 🍴 🏊

◆◆◆◆ **Hilton Saint John** **LH**
(506) 693-8484. **Call for rates.** 1 Market Square. Hwy 1, exit 122 at Market Square. Int corridors. **Pets:** Accepted.
SAVE ☒ 💻 🍴 🏊 ☒

◆◆◆◆ **Holiday Inn Express Hotel & Suites** **SH**
(506) 642-2622. **$109-$199.** 400 Main St/Chesley Dr. 0.6 mi (1 km) w on Hwy 1; north end of Chesley Dr, exit 121; off Harbour Bridge. Int corridors. **Pets:** Other species. Service with restrictions.
SAVE S🐾 ☒ 🛏 💻 🏊

◆◆ **Inn on the Cove and Spa** **CI** 🐾
(506) 672-7799. **$145-$225, 7 day notice.** 1371 Sand Cove Rd. Hwy 1 E, exit 119, right on Bleury, right on Sand Cove Rd, then 2 mi (3.2 km) w. Int corridors. **Pets:** Medium, dogs only. $35 one-time fee/room. Designated rooms, service with restrictions, supervision.
SAVE S🐾 ☒ S🐾 💻 🍴 ☒

ST-LEONARD

◆◆◆ **Daigle's Motel** **SH**
(506) 423-6351. **$78-$99.** 68 rue DuPont. Hwy 17, 0.6 mi (1 km) s of Trans-Canada Hwy 2, exit 58. Ext corridors. **Pets:** Small. $7 daily fee/pet. Designated rooms, service with restrictions, supervision.
SAVE S🐾 ☒ 🍴 🏊

ST. STEPHEN

◆ **St. Stephen Inn** **SH**
(506) 466-1814. **Call for rates.** 99 King St. On Hwy 1; centre. Ext/int corridors. **Pets:** Accepted.
☒ 🛏 🍴

SHEDIAC

◆◆ **Gaudet Chalets & Motel** **M**
(506) 533-8877. **Call for rates.** 14 Belleview Heights. On Rt 133, 1.4 mi (2.4 km) w of Rt 15, exit 37. Ext corridors. **Pets:** Large, dogs only. $10 daily fee/pet. Designated rooms, service with restrictions.
☒ 🛏 💻

SUSSEX

◆ **All Seasons Inn** **M**
(506) 433-2220. **$95-$125.** 1015 Main St. Hwy 1, exit 192 eastbound; exit 198 westbound, left towards Sussex Corner; centre. Ext corridors. **Pets:** Accepted.
A$K S🐾 ☒ 🍴

◆◆ **Fairway Inn** **SH**
(506) 433-3470. **$100-$175.** 216 Roachville Rd. Hwy 1, exit 193. Ext/int corridors. **Pets:** Accepted.
A$K S🐾 ☒ 💻 🍴 🏊

◆ **Pine Cone Motel** **M**
(506) 433-3958. **$65-$75.** 12808 Rt 114. Hwy 1, exit 198, 1.2 mi (2 km) e on Rt 114 towards Penobsquis. Ext corridors. **Pets:** Accepted.
☒ ☒

WOODSTOCK

◆◆◆◆ **Best Western Woodstock Inn &**
Suites **SH** 🐾
(506) 328-2378. **$119-$229.** 123 Gallop Ct. Trans-Canada Hwy 2, exit 185. Int corridors. **Pets:** Medium, other species. $25 one-time fee/room. Designated rooms, service with restrictions, supervision.
SAVE S🐾 ☒ 🛏 💻 🏊

◆◆ **Econo Lodge** **SH**
(506) 328-8876. **$80-$170.** 168 Rt 555. Trans-Canada Hwy 2, exit 188 (Houlton Rd). Ext/int corridors. **Pets:** Accepted.
A$K S🐾 ☒ 💻 🍴 🏊

◆◆ **Howard Johnson Inn** **SH**
(506) 328-3315. **Call for rates.** 159 Rt 555, exit 188 TCH. Trans-Canada Hwy 2, exit 188 (Houlton Rd). Ext/int corridors. **Pets:** Accepted.
☒ 💻 🍴 🏊

YOUNGS COVE ROAD

◆◆ **McCready's Motel** **M**
(506) 362-2916. **$56-$65.** 10995 Rt 10. Trans-Canada Hwy 2, exit 365, just w. Ext corridors. **Pets:** Accepted.
SAVE 🍴 🐾 ☒

NEWFOUNDLAND AND LABRADOR

CHANNEL-PORT-AUX-BASQUES

▼▼ Hotel Port Aux Basques ⑤ℍ
(709) 695-2171. **$99-$110.** 1 Grand Bay Rd. Jct Trans-Canada Hwy 1. Int corridors. **Pets:** Accepted.
(A$K) (⊠) (🛏) (🖥) (🍽)

▼▼ St. Christopher's Hotel ⑤ℍ
(709) 695-7034. **$120.** 146 Caribou Rd. Trans-Canada Hwy 1, exit Port Aux Basques (downtown), follow signs 1.2 mi (2 km). Int corridors. **Pets:** Accepted.
(A$K) (S⊘) (⊠) (🛏) (🖥) (🍽)

CLARENVILLE

▼ Restland Motel ⑤ℍ
(709) 466-7636. **$85-$95.** 262 Memorial Dr. Centre. Ext/int corridors. **Pets:** Accepted.
(S⊘) (⊠) (🛏) (🍽) (ⓚ)

▼▼ St. Jude Hotel ⑤ℍ
(709) 466-1717. **$85-$115.** 247 Trans-Canada Hwy. On Trans-Canada Hwy 1; centre. Int corridors. **Pets:** Accepted.
(A$K) (S⊘) (⊠) (🛏) (🖥) (🍽)

CORNER BROOK

▼▼ Comfort Inn ⑤ℍ
(709) 639-1980. **$110-$130.** 41 Maple Valley Rd. Trans-Canada Hwy 1, exit 5 eastbound; exit 6 westbound, via Confederation Ave. Int corridors. **Pets:** Accepted.
(A$K) (S⊘) (⊠) (🛏) (🖥) (🍽)

▼▼▼ Glynmill Inn ⑤ℍ
(709) 634-5181. **$115-$190.** 1B Cobb Ln. Centre. Int corridors. **Pets:** Accepted.
(⊠) (🛏) (🖥) (🍽)

▼▼▼ Greenwood Inn & Suites-Corner Brook ℒℍ
(709) 634-5381. **Call for rates.** 48 West St. Centre. Int corridors. **Pets:** Accepted.
(⊠) (🛏) (🖥) (🍽) (🏊)

▼▼ Mamateek Inn ⑤ℍ
(709) 639-8901. **Call for rates.** 64 Maple Valley Rd. Trans-Canada Hwy 1, exit 5 eastbound; exit 6 westbound via Confederation Ave. Int corridors. **Pets:** Accepted.
(⊠) (🍽)

COW HEAD

▼▼ Shallow Bay Motel & Cabins ⑤ℍ
(709) 243-2471. **$95-$125.** Rt 430, The Viking Trail. Hwy 430, 2.5 mi (4 km) w towards the ocean, follow signs. Ext/int corridors. **Pets:** Accepted.
(⊠) (🛏) (🖥) (🍽) (🏊)

GANDER

▼▼▼ Albatross Hotel ⑤ℍ
(709) 256-3956. **$85-$96.** Trans-Canada Hwy. On Trans-Canada Hwy 1. Ext/int corridors. **Pets:** Accepted.
(A$K) (⊠) (🖥) (🍽)

▼▼ Comfort Inn ⑤ℍ
(709) 256-3535. **Call for rates.** 112 Trans-Canada Hwy 1. Centre. Ext/int corridors. **Pets:** Accepted.
(⊠) (🛏) (🖥) (🍽)

▼▼ Hotel Gander ⑤ℍ
(709) 256-3931. **$125-$240.** 100 Trans-Canada Hwy 1. Centre. Int corridors. **Pets:** Other species. Designated rooms, service with restrictions.
(A$K) (S⊘) (⊠) (🛏) (🖥) (🍽) (🏊)

▼▼ Sinbad's Hotel & Suites ⑤ℍ
(709) 651-2678. **$91-$240.** Bennett Dr. Centre; opposite Gander Mall. Ext corridors. **Pets:** Accepted.
(A$K) (S⊘) (⊠) (🛏) (🖥) (🍽)

GRAND FALLS-WINDSOR

▼▼ Mount Peyton Hotel ⑤ℍ
(709) 489-2251. **Call for rates.** 214 Lincoln Rd. 0.6 mi (1 km) ne on Trans-Canada Hwy 1. Ext/int corridors. **Pets:** Accepted.
(⊠) (🛏) (🖥) (🍽)

LABRADOR CITY

▼▼ Carol Inn ⑤ℍ
(709) 944-7736. **Call for rates.** 215 Drake Ave. Centre. Int corridors. **Pets:** Accepted.
(⊠) (🛏) (🖥) (🍽)

L'ANSE AU CLAIR

▼▼ Northern Light Inn ⑤ℍ
(709) 931-2332. **Call for rates.** Rt 510. On Rt 510; centre. Int corridors. **Pets:** Accepted.
(⊠) (🛏) (🍽)

ST. JOHN'S

▼▼▼ Capital Hotel ⑤ℍ
(709) 738-4480. **$119-$138.** 208 Kenmount Rd. Just w of Pippy Place Rd. Int corridors. **Pets:** Accepted.
(⊠) (🛏) (🖥) (🍽)

ⒶⒶ ▼▼ Comfort Inn Airport ⑤ℍ
(709) 753-3500. **$139-$159.** 106 Airport Rd. Trans-Canada Hwy 1, exit 47A, 0.6 mi (1 km) n on Rt 40 (Portugal Cove Rd). Int corridors. **Pets:** $35 one-time fee/room. Service with restrictions, crate.
(SAVE) (S⊘) (⊠) (🛏) (🖥) (🍽)

▼▼▼ Delta St. John's Hotel and Conference Centre ℒℍ 🐾
(709) 739-6404. **$266-$278.** 120 New Gower St. At Barter's Hill Rd; centre. Int corridors. **Pets:** Other species. $35 one-time fee/room. Service with restrictions, supervision.
(A$K) (S⊘) (⊠) (🛏ᴹ) (🖥) (🍽) (🏊) (⊠)

▼▼▼ The Fairmont Newfoundland ℒℍ
(709) 726-4980. **$189-$530.** 115 Cavendish Square. Centre. Int corridors. **Pets:** Medium. $35 one-time fee/pet. Designated rooms, service with restrictions, supervision.
(A$K) (S⊘) (⊠) (🖥) (🍽) (🏊) (⊠)

▼▼▼ Holiday Inn St. John's-Govt Centre ℒℍ
(709) 722-0506. **$135-$155.** 180 Portugal Cove Rd. Trans-Canada Hwy 1, exit 47A, 0.9 mi (1.4 km) s. Ext/int corridors. **Pets:** Accepted.
(A$K) (S⊘) (⊠) (🛏ᴹ) (🛏) (🖥) (🍽) (🏊)

(AAA) ◆◆◆ **Ramada St. John's** SH
(709) 722-9330. **Call for rates.** 102 Kenmount Rd. Corner of Pippy Place Rd. Int corridors. **Pets:** Accepted.
SAVE ✕ 🗄 💻 ¶

◆◆◆ **Super 8 Motel** SH
(709) 739-8888. **$99-$149.** 175 Higgins Line. Trans-Canada Hwy 1, exit 47A, just s on Rt 40 (Portugal Cove Rd). Int corridors. **Pets:** Accepted.
A$K S✗ ✕ &M 🗄 💻 ➷

(AAA) ◆◆◆ **Travellers Inn St. John's** SH ❀
(709) 722-5540. **$89-$129.** 199 Kenmount Rd. Just w of Pippy Place Rd. Ext/int corridors. **Pets:** Medium. Service with restrictions, supervision.
SAVE S✗ ✕ 🗄 💻 ¶ ➷

STEPHENVILLE

◆◆ **Holiday Inn Stephenville** SH
(709) 643-6666. **$140-$158.** 44 Queen St. Centre. Int corridors.
Pets: Accepted.
A$K S✗ ✕ 🗄 💻 ¶

NORTHWEST TERRITORIES

YELLOWKNIFE

▼▼▼ **Fraser Tower Suite Hotel** SH
(867) 873-8700. **$156-$185.** 5303 52nd St. Corner of 52nd St and 53rd Ave. Int corridors. **Pets:** Accepted.
A$K S⬛ ⊠ 🖥 ⬛ 🅰

▼▼ **Yellowknife Super 8 Motel** M
(867) 669-8888. **$169-$199.** 308 Old Airport Rd. 1.2 mi (2 km) s on Franklin, 0.6 mi (1 km) w; in WalMart Plaza. Int corridors. **Pets:** Accepted.
A$K S⬛ ⊠ 🖥 ⬛

NOVA SCOTIA

AMHERST

Auberge Wandlyn Inn SH
(902) 667-3331. **Call for rates.** W Victoria St. Trans-Canada Hwy 104, exit 3, 0.6 mi (1 km) w. Ext/int corridors. **Pets:** Accepted.

Comfort Inn SH
(902) 667-0404. **$113-$173.** 143 Albion St S. Trans-Canada Hwy 104, exit 4, 1 mi (1.6 km) n on Rt 2. Int corridors. **Pets:** Accepted.

Super 8 Motel SH
(902) 660-8888. **$89-$249.** 40 Lord Amherst Dr. Trans-Canada Hwy 104, exit 4. Int corridors. **Pets:** Accepted.

ANNAPOLIS ROYAL

Annapolis Royal Inn M
(902) 532-2323. **$89-$150, 30 day notice.** 3924 Hwy 1. 0.6 mi (1 km) w. Ext corridors. **Pets:** Accepted.

Champlain Motel M
(902) 532-5473. **Call for rates.** RR 2. 2.5 mi (4.2 km) w on Rt 1. Ext corridors. **Pets:** Accepted.

Hillsdale House Inn BB
(902) 532-2345. **$79-$149.** 519 St George St. Just e of Rt 1; centre. Int corridors. **Pets:** $25 one-time fee/room. Service with restrictions.

The King George Inn BB
(902) 532-5286. **$80-$160.** 548 Upper St George St. Jct Rt 1 and 8, just e on Rt 8. Int corridors. **Pets:** Accepted.

ANTIGONISH

Maritime Inn Antigonish SH
(902) 863-4001. **$109-$149.** 158 Main St. Centre. Ext/int corridors. **Pets:** Designated rooms, service with restrictions, supervision.

AULD'S COVE

The Cove Motel & Restaurant/Gift Shop M
(902) 747-2700. **$99-$118.** 227 Cove Rd. 0.6 mi (1 km) n off Trans-Canada Hwy 104; 1.9 mi (3 km) w of Canso Cswy. Ext corridors. **Pets:** Designated rooms, service with restrictions, supervision.

BADDECK

The Ceilidh Country Lodge M
(902) 295-3500. **$89-$129, 3 day notice.** 357 Shore Rd. Trans-Canada Hwy 105, exit 8, 1 mi (1.6 km) e on Rt 205 (Shore Rd). Ext/int corridors. **Pets:** Accepted.

Hunter's Mountain Chalets CA
(902) 295-3392. **$78-$138, 4 day notice.** 562 Cabot Tr. Trans-Canada Hwy 105, exit 7, 1.6 mi (2.6 km) n. Ext corridors. **Pets:** Small, dogs only. $10 daily fee/pet. No service, supervision.

Inverary Resort SH
(902) 295-3500. **$109-$189, 3 day notice.** 368 Shore Rd. Trans-Canada Hwy 105, exit 8, 1 mi (1.6 km) e on Rt 205 (Shore Rd). Ext/int corridors. **Pets:** Accepted.

McIntyre's Housekeeping Cottages CA
(902) 295-1133. **Call for rates.** 8908 Hwy 105. Trans-Canada Hwy 105, 3 mi (5 km) w. Ext corridors. **Pets:** Other species. $8 daily fee/pet. Designated rooms, service with restrictions, supervision.

Silver Dart Lodge & MacNeil House SH
(902) 295-2340. **$99-$265.** 257 Hwy 205 (Shore Rd). Trans-Canada Hwy 105, exit 8, 0.6 mi (1 km) e on Rt 205 (Shore Rd). Ext/int corridors. **Pets:** Accepted.

BAYFIELD

Sea'Scape Cottages CA
(902) 386-2825. **Call for rates.** Bayfield Antigonish Civil 6. Trans-Canada Hwy 104, exit 36, 3.1 mi (5.1 km) n on Sunrise Tr, then 1 mi (1.6 km) w. Ext corridors. **Pets:** Accepted.

BLACK POINT

Grand View Motel and Cottages M
(902) 857-9776. **Call for rates.** 8414 Hwy 3. Hwy 103, exit 5 westbound, 1.2 mi (2 km) s to Rt 3, then 9 mi (15 km) w; exit 6 eastbound to Rt 3, then 5.4 mi (9 km) e. Ext corridors. **Pets:** Accepted.

BRIDGETOWN

Bridgetown Motor Inn SH
(902) 665-4403. **$72-$85.** 396 Granville St. Hwy 101, exit 20, 0.6 mi (1 km) w on Rt 1. Ext corridors. **Pets:** Accepted.

BRIDGEWATER

Auberge Wandlyn Inn SH
(902) 543-7131. **$100-$130.** 50 North St. Hwy 103, exit 12, 1.1 mi (1.7 km) s on Rt 10. Int corridors. **Pets:** Accepted.

Bridgewater Bogan Villa Inn SH
(902) 543-8171. **Call for rates.** 35 High St. Hwy 103, exit 13, just e. Int corridors. **Pets:** Accepted.

◆◆ Comfort Inn 🏨
(902) 543-1498. **Call for rates.** 49 North St. Hwy 103, exit 12, 1.1 mi (1.7 km) s on Rt 10. Int corridors. **Pets:** Accepted.

⊠ 🔏 🔲 💻

CHESTER

◆ Windjammer Motel Ⓜ
(902) 275-3567. **$55-$85.** 4070 Rt 3. 0.6 mi (1 km) w. Ext corridors. **Pets:** Accepted.

🔏 ⊠ 🔲

CHETICAMP

◆◆ Cabot Trail Sea & Golf Chalets 🅲🅰
(902) 224-1777. **$129-$169, 7 day notice.** 71 Fraser Doucet Ln. Centre. Ext corridors. **Pets:** Accepted.

🅰$🅺 ⊠ 🔲 💻 ⊠ 🐾 🌀

◆◆ Laurie's Motor Inn 🏨
(902) 224-2400. **$79-$169.** 15456 Laurie Rd. Centre. Ext/int corridors. **Pets:** Service with restrictions.

🆂🅰🆅🅴 ⊠ 🔲 🍽

◆◆ ◆ Parkview Motel, Dining Room & Lounge Ⓜ
(902) 224-3232. **$69-$109, 7 day notice.** 16546 Cabot Tr. 4.5 mi (7.2 km) n at West Gate Cape Breton Highlands National Park. Ext corridors. **Pets:** Accepted.

🆂🅰🆅🅴 ⊠ 🔲 💻 🍽 🌀

CHURCH POINT

◆◆ Le Manoir Samson Ⓜ
(902) 769-2526. **Call for rates.** 1768 Rt 1. On Hwy 1; centre. Ext corridors. **Pets:** Accepted.

⊠ 🔲 🅺

DARTMOUTH

◆◆ ◆ Comfort Inn 🏨 🐾
(902) 463-9900. **$130-$180.** 456 Windmill Rd. Hwy 111, exit Shannon Park. Int corridors. **Pets:** Service with restrictions.

🆂🅰🆅🅴 🔏 ⊠ 🔲 💻

◆◆ Country Inn & Suites By Carlson 🏨
(902) 465-4000. **$105-$200.** 101 Yorkshire Ave Ext. Hwy 111, exit Princess Margaret Blvd. Int corridors. **Pets:** Accepted.

🅰$🅺 ⊠ 🔲 💻

◆◆ ◆◆ Holiday Inn Halifax-Harbourview 🏨
(902) 463-1100. **$105-$189, 30 day notice.** 101 Wyse Rd. Adjacent to Angus L MacDonald Bridge. Int corridors. **Pets:** Accepted.

🆂🅰🆅🅴 🔏 ⊠ 🔲 💻 🍽 🌿

◆◆ ◆◆◆ Park Place Hotel & Conference Centre Ramada Plaza 🏨
(902) 468-8888. **$109-$209.** 240 Brownlow Ave. From Murray Mackay Bridge, 0.7 mi (1.2 km) n on Hwy 111, exit 3 (Burnside Dr). Int corridors. **Pets:** Small, other species. $50 deposit/room. Designated rooms, service with restrictions, supervision.

🆂🅰🆅🅴 ⊠ 🔏🄼 🔲 💻 🍽 🌿 ⊠

◆◆ ◆ Quality Inn Halifax/Dartmouth 🏨
(902) 469-5850. **$80-$180.** 313 Prince Albert Rd. Hwy 111, exit 6A, 1 blk s. Int corridors. **Pets:** Medium. Designated rooms, service with restrictions, supervision.

🆂🅰🆅🅴 🔏 ⊠ 🔲 💻 🍽

◆◆ ◆ Super 8 Hotel-Dartmouth 🏨
(902) 463-9520. **Call for rates.** 65 King St. Corner of King and Queen sts; centre. Int corridors. **Pets:** Accepted.

⊠ 🔲 💻

DIGBY

◆◆ ◆◆ Admiral Digby Inn 🏨
(902) 245-2531. **$75-$129.** 441 Shore Rd. Hwy 101, exit 26, 1.5 mi (2.5 km) n, follow St John Ferry signs, 3 mi (5 km) w on Victoria Rd, just e of ferry terminal. Ext corridors. **Pets:** Accepted.

🆂🅰🆅🅴 ⊠ 🔲 💻 🍽 🌿

ECONOMY

◆◆◆ Four Seasons Retreat 🅲🅰
(902) 647-2628. **$79-$109, 7 day notice.** 320 Cove Rd. 3 mi (5 km) e on Rt 2. Ext corridors. **Pets:** Accepted.

⊠ 🔲 💻 🌿 ⊠ 🐾 🌀

HALIFAX

◆ Chebucto Inn 🏨
(902) 453-4330. **$85-$145.** 6151 Lady Hammond Rd. Jct Hwy 111 and Rt 2 (Bedford Hwy), 0.4 mi (0.7 km) e. Ext corridors. **Pets:** Accepted.

🅰$🅺 ⊠ 🍽

◆◆ ◆◆◆ Citadel Halifax Hotel 🏨 🐾
(902) 422-1391. **$124-$311.** 1960 Brunswick St. Between Cogswell and Duke sts. Int corridors. **Pets:** Other species.

🆂🅰🆅🅴 🔏 ⊠ 🔲 💻 🍽 🌿 ⊠

◆◆ ◆◆◆ Comfort Inn Halifax 🏨 🐾
(902) 443-0303. **$75-$175.** 560 Bedford Hwy. On Rt 2 (Bedford Hwy), 6 mi (9.6 km) w. Int corridors. **Pets:** Medium. $10 one-time fee/pet. Designated rooms, service with restrictions, supervision.

🆂🅰🆅🅴 🔏 ⊠ 🔏🄼 🔲 💻 🍽 🌿

◆◆ ◆◆◆ Delta Barrington 🏨 🐾
(902) 429-7410. **$209-$259, 14 day notice.** 1875 Barrington St. Between Cogswell and Duke sts. Int corridors. **Pets:** Other species. $35 one-time fee/room. Designated rooms, service with restrictions, supervision.

🆂🅰🆅🅴 🔏 ⊠ 💻 🍽 🌿 ⊠

◆◆ ◆◆◆ Delta Halifax 🏨 🐾
(902) 425-6700. **$115-$209.** 1990 Barrington St. Corner of Cogswell and Barrington sts. Int corridors. **Pets:** Other species. $35 one-time fee/room. Designated rooms, service with restrictions, supervision.

🆂🅰🆅🅴 ⊠ 🔲 🍽 🌿 ⊠

◆◆ ◆◆◆ Esquire Motel Ⓜ
(902) 835-3367. **$79-$135.** 771 Bedford Hwy. Hwy 102, exit 4A, 3.3 mi (5.3 km) e on Rt 2 (Bedford Hwy). Ext corridors. **Pets:** Accepted.

🆂🅰🆅🅴 ⊠ 🔲 💻 🌿 🅺

◆◆ ◆◆◆ ◆◆◆ Halifax Marriott Harbourfront 🏨
(902) 421-1700. **$175-$219.** 1919 Upper Water St. Adjacent to historic properties and Casino Nova Scotia. Int corridors. **Pets:** $50 one-time fee/room. Service with restrictions.

🆂🅰🆅🅴 🔏 ⊠ 🔏🄼 🔲 💻 🍽 🌿 ⊠

◆◆ ◆◆◆◆ Holiday Inn Express Halifax/Bedford 🏨 🐾
(902) 445-1100. **$109-$159, 14 day notice.** 133 Kearney Lake Rd. Hwy 102, exit 2. Int corridors. **Pets:** Medium. $25 one-time fee/room. Designated rooms, service with restrictions, supervision.

🆂🅰🆅🅴 🔏 ⊠ 🔏🄼 🔲 💻 🌿

◆◆ ◆◆◆◆ Holiday Inn Select Halifax Centre 🏨 🐾
(902) 423-1161. **$130-$190.** 1980 Robie St. Jct Quinpool St. Int corridors. **Pets:** Medium. Designated rooms, service with restrictions, supervision.

🆂🅰🆅🅴 🔏 ⊠ 🔲 💻 🍽 🌿 ⊠

◆◆ ◆ Lakeview Inns & Suites 🏨
(902) 450-3020. **$159-$299.** 98 Chain Lake Dr. Hwy 102, exit 2A eastbound; Hwy 103, exit 2. Int corridors. **Pets:** Accepted.

🅰$🅺 🔏 ⊠ 🔏🄼 🔲 💻 🌿

ⓐ ◈◈◈◈ **The Lord Nelson Hotel & Suites** 🄻🄷 ❁
(902) 423-6331. **$115-$205.** 1515 S Park St. Corner of Park St and Spring Garden Rd; centre. Int corridors. **Pets:** Service with restrictions, supervision.
🆂🅰🆅🅴 ⊠ 🛗 🛉 🖵 ⑾

ⓐ ◈◈◈◈ **The Prince George Hotel** 🄻🄷 ❁
(902) 425-1986. **$155-$279.** 1725 Market St. Between Prince and Carmichael sts. Int corridors. **Pets:** Other species. Service with restrictions, supervision.
🆂🅰🆅🅴 ⊠ 🛗 🖵 ⑾ ⇆ ⊠

◈◈◈◈ **Quality Inn & Suites Halifax** 🅂🄷
(902) 444-6700. **$119-$169.** 980 Parkland Dr. Hwy 102, exit 2. Int corridors. **Pets:** Accepted.
🄰🆂🅺 🆂🄱 ⊠ 🛗 🛉 🖵 ⇆ ⊠

◈◈◈◈ **Residence Inn by Marriott** 🅂🄷
(902) 422-0493. **$175-$208.** 1599 Grafton St. Corner of Sackville St. Int corridors. **Pets:** Accepted.
🄰🆂🅺 🆂🄱 ⊠ 🛗 🛉 🖵

◈ **Travelers Motel** 🄼
(902) 835-3394. **Call for rates.** 773 Bedford Hwy. Hwy 102, exit 4A, 3.3 mi (5.3 km) e on Rt 2 (Bedford Hwy). Ext corridors. **Pets:** Designated rooms, no service, supervision.
⊠ 🛉 🄺

ⓐ ◈◈◈◈ **The Westin Nova Scotian** 🄻🄷 ❁
(902) 421-1000. **$229-$295.** 1181 Hollis St. Between Barrington and Lower Water sts. Int corridors. **Pets:** Other species.
🆂🅰🆅🅴 🆂🄱 ⊠ 🛗 🖵 ⑾ ⇆ ⊠

INGONISH BEACH

◈◈◈ **Keltic Lodge Resort & Spa** 🄻🄷
(902) 285-2880. **$174-$242, 3 day notice.** Middle Head Peninsula. In Cape Breton Highlands National Park; off Cabot Tr. Ext/int corridors. **Pets:** Accepted.
🄰🆂🅺 ⊠ 🛉 🖵 ⑾ ⇆ ⊠

KEMPTVILLE

ⓐ ◈◈◈◈ **Trout Point Lodge** 🄲🄸
(902) 482-8360. **$165-$265, 21 day notice.** 189 Trout Point Rd. 6.6 mi (11 km) e on Rt 203, 2.1 mi (3.5 km) n on gravel entry road. Ext corridors. **Pets:** Accepted.
🆂🅰🆅🅴 🆂🄱 ⊠ ⑾ ⊠ 🄺 🆆 ☑

KENTVILLE

ⓐ ◈ **Sun Valley Motel** 🄼
(902) 678-7368. **$68-$90.** 905 Park St. Hwy 101, exit 14, 0.5 mi (0.8 km) e on Rt 1. Ext corridors. **Pets:** Accepted.
🆂🅰🆅🅴 🆂🄱 ⊠ 🛉 🖵 🄺 ☑

LISCOMB

◈◈◈ **Liscombe Lodge Resort & Conference Centre** 🅂🄷
(902) 779-2307. **$195-$280, 3 day notice.** 2884 Hwy 7 (RR 1). On Hwy 7. Ext/int corridors. **Pets:** Accepted.
🄰🆂🅺 🆂🄱 ⊠ 🛗 🛉 🖵 ⑾ ⇆ ⊠

LUNENBURG

ⓐ ◈◈ **Boscawen Inn** 🄲🄸
(902) 634-3325. **Call for rates.** 150 Cumberland St. Centre. Int corridors. **Pets:** Accepted.
🆂🅰🆅🅴 ⊠ 🖵 ⑾ 🄺

◈◈ **The Homeport Motel** 🄼
(902) 634-8234. **$75-$150.** 167 Victoria Rd. 0.6 mi (1 km) w on Rt 3. Ext corridors. **Pets:** Accepted.
⊠ 🛉 🖵

ⓐ ◈◈◈◈ **Lunenburg Arms Hotel & Spa** 🅂🄷
(902) 640-4040. **$109-$299, 7 day notice.** 94 Pelham St. Corner of Pelham and Duke sts; centre. Int corridors. **Pets:** Accepted.
🆂🅰🆅🅴 ⊠ 🛗 🛉 🖵 ⑾

MAHONE BAY

◈◈◈ **Bayview Pines Country Inn** 🄱🄱
(902) 624-9970. **$90-$150, 5 day notice.** 678 Oakland Rd. Hwy 103, exit 10, 1.2 mi (2 km) w on Rt 3 to Kedy's Landing, 3.6 mi (6 km) e of Mahone Bay. Ext/int corridors. **Pets:** Accepted.
⊠ 🛉 🖵 🄺 ☑

MAVILLETTE

◈ **Cape View Motel & Cottages** 🄼
(902) 645-2258. **$86.** 124 John Doucette Rd. Rt 1, 19.2 mi (32 km) ne of Yarmouth; centre. Ext corridors. **Pets:** Accepted.
🆂🄱 ⊠ 🛉 🖵 🄺 ☑

MIDDLETON

◈◈ **Mid-Valley Motel** 🅂🄷
(902) 825-3433. **Call for rates.** 121 Main St. Hwy 101, exit 18, 0.6 mi (1 km) w on Rt 1. Ext corridors. **Pets:** Accepted.
⊠ 🛉 ⑾ ⇆

MUSQUODOBOIT HARBOUR

◈◈◈ **The Elephant's Nest Bed & Breakfast** 🄱🄱
(902) 827-3891. **$90-$135, 3 day notice.** 127 Pleasant Dr. From jct Hwy 107 and 7, 2.5 mi (4 km) w, follow signs. Ext/int corridors. **Pets:** Accepted.
🄰🆂🅺 🆂🄱 ⊠ ⊠ 🄺

NEW GLASGOW

◈◈ **Comfort Inn** 🅂🄷
(902) 755-6450. **$115-$180.** 740 Westville Rd. On Hwy 289, just e of jct Trans-Canada Hwy 104, exit 23. Int corridors. **Pets:** Accepted.
🄰🆂🅺 🆂🄱 ⊠ 🛉 🖵

◈◈ **Country Inn & Suites By Carlson** 🅂🄷
(902) 928-1333. **$134-$137.** 700 Westville Rd. On Hwy 289, just e of jct Trans-Canada Hwy 104, exit 23. Int corridors. **Pets:** Accepted.
🄰🆂🅺 🆂🄱 ⊠ 🛉 🖵

NEW HARBOUR

◈◈◈ **Lonely Rock Seaside Bungalows** 🄲🄰
(902) 387-2668. **$90-$230, 14 day notice.** 150 New Harbour Rd. Rt 316, 0.4 mi (0.7 km) s. Ext corridors. **Pets:** Accepted.
⊠ 🛉 ⊠ 🄺

NORTH SYDNEY

ⓐ ◈◈◈ **Clansman Motel** 🅂🄷 ❁
(902) 794-7226. **$89-$125.** 9 Baird St. Hwy 125, exit 2, just e on King St. Ext/int corridors. **Pets:** Designated rooms, service with restrictions.
🆂🅰🆅🅴 ⊠ 🛉 🖵 ⑾ ⇆

PARRSBORO

◈◈ **The Sunshine Inn** 🄼
(902) 254-3135. **$76-$96.** Rt 2. 2 mi (3.2 km) n. Ext corridors. **Pets:** Accepted.
⊠ 🛉 ⊠ ☑

PICTOU

◈◈ **Willow House Inn** 🄱🄱
(902) 485-5740. **$60-$120.** 11 Willow St. Corner of Willow and Church sts; centre. Int corridors. **Pets:** Accepted.
⊠ ☑

PORT DUFFERIN

◆ Marquis of Dufferin Seaside Inn Ⓜ
(902) 654-2696. **$76-$94.** 25658 Hwy 7, RR 1. On Hwy 7. Ext corridors. **Pets:** Accepted.

[X] [Ⅱ] [X] [Ⅱ] [Z]

PORT HASTINGS

Ⓐ ◆ Cape Breton Causeway Inn ⑤Ⅱ
(902) 625-0460. **Call for rates.** 21 Old Victoria Rd. E of Canso Cswy on Trans-Canada Hwy 105 rotary; entrance through north side of church. Ext/int corridors. **Pets:** Accepted.

[SAVE] [X] [🛏] [💻] [Ⅱ]

◆ Econo Lodge MacPuffin Ⓜ
(902) 625-0621. **$89-$139.** 373 Hwy 4. 1 mi (1.6 km) n on Hwy 4; 1 mi (1.6 km) s of Canso Cswy. Ext corridors. **Pets:** Accepted.

[ASK] [S] [X] [💻] [🏊]

PORT HAWKESBURY

Ⓐ ◆ Maritime Inn Port Hawkesbury ⑤Ⅱ
(902) 625-0320. **$114-$199.** 717 Reeves St. 4.2 mi (6.4 km) e of Canso Cswy on Hwy 4. Ext/int corridors. **Pets:** Accepted.

[SAVE] [X] [🛏] [💻] [Ⅱ] [🏊]

SCOTSBURN

◆◆◆ Stonehame Lodge & Chalets ⒸⒶ
(902) 485-3468. **$75-$225.** RR 3. Rt 256, 7.5 mi (12 km) w of Pictou via Rt 376, last 1.2 mi (2 km) on gravel entry road. Ext corridors. **Pets:** Accepted.

[ASK] [S] [X] [🛏] [💻] [🏊] [X]

SMITHS COVE

◆◆ Harbourview Inn ⒷⒷ
(902) 245-5686. **$94-$149, 7 day notice.** 25 Harbourview Rd. Hwy 101, exit 25 eastbound; exit 24 westbound. Ext/int corridors. **Pets:** Accepted.

[X] [🛏] [💻] [🏊] [X] [Z]

◆◆ Hedley House Inn By The Sea Ⓜ
(902) 245-2500. **$75-$169.** RR 1. Hwy 101, exit 25 eastbound; exit 24 westbound. Ext corridors. **Pets:** Accepted.

[ASK] [X] [🛏] [💻] [Ⅱ] [Z]

Ⓐ ◆◆ Mountain Gap Inn ⑤Ⅱ
(902) 245-5841. **$79-$350.** 217 Hwy 1, Smiths Cove. Hwy 101, exit 25 eastbound; exit 24 westbound. Ext corridors. **Pets:** Accepted.

[SAVE] [S] [X] [🛏] [💻] [Ⅱ] [🏊] [X]

SYDNEY

Ⓐ ◆◆◆ Cambridge Suites Hotel ⓁⒽ
(902) 562-6500. **$109-$210.** 380 Esplanade. Hwy 4, 3.1 mi (5 km) e of jct Hwy 125, exit 6E; downtown. Int corridors. **Pets:** Accepted.

[SAVE] [S] [X] [🛏] [💻] [Ⅱ]

◆◆ Comfort Inn ⑤Ⅱ
(902) 562-0200. **$109-$189.** 368 Kings Rd. Hwy 4, 2.1 mi (3.5 km) e of jct Hwy 125, exit 6E. Int corridors. **Pets:** Accepted.

[ASK] [S] [X] [🛏] [💻]

Ⓐ ◆◆◆ Days Inn Sydney ⑤Ⅱ
(902) 539-6750. **$89-$119.** 480 Kings Rd. Hwy 4, 1.7 mi (2.8 km) e of jct Hwy 125, exit 6E. Int corridors. **Pets:** Large. Designated rooms, service with restrictions, supervision.

[SAVE] [S] [X] [🛏] [💻] [Ⅱ] [🏊] [X]

Ⓐ ◆◆◆◆ Delta Sydney ⓁⒽ
(902) 562-7500. **$119-$240.** 300 Esplanade. At Prince St; centre. Int corridors. **Pets:** $35 one-time fee/pet. Service with restrictions, crate.

[SAVE] [X] [🛏] [💻] [Ⅱ] [🏊] [X]

◆◆◆ Quality Inn Sydney ⑤Ⅱ
(902) 539-8101. **Call for rates.** 560 Kings Rd. Hwy 4, 2 mi (3.3 km) e of jct Hwy 125. Int corridors. **Pets:** Accepted.

[X] [💻] [Ⅱ] [🏊]

SYDNEY MINES

◆◆◆ Gowrie House Country Inn ⒸⒾ
(902) 544-1050. **$99-$265, 3 day notice.** 840 Shore Rd. Hwy 105, exit 21E, 1.9 mi (3 km) n on Rt 305. Ext/int corridors. **Pets:** Accepted.

[X] [🛏] [💻] [Ⅱ]

TRURO

◆◆ Comfort Inn ⑤Ⅱ
(902) 893-0330. **$109-$199.** 12 Meadow Dr. Hwy 102, exit 14. Int corridors. **Pets:** Accepted.

[ASK] [S] [X] [🛏] [💻]

Ⓐ ◆ The Palliser Motel Ⓜ ✿
(902) 893-8951. **$79-$89.** 103/104 Tidal Bore Rd. Hwy 102, exit 14. Ext corridors. **Pets:** Medium, dogs only. Service with restrictions, supervision.

[SAVE] [S] [X] [Ⅱ] [Z]

◆◆ Super 8 Motel ⑤Ⅱ
(902) 895-8884. **Call for rates.** 85 Treaty Tr. Hwy 102, exit 13A. Int corridors. **Pets:** Accepted.

[X] [S] [🛏] [💻] [🏊]

◆◆ Truro Hotel and Convention Centre ⑤Ⅱ
(902) 895-1651. **$109-$169.** 437 Prince St. Centre. Ext/int corridors. **Pets:** Accepted.

[ASK] [S] [X] [🛏] [💻] [Ⅱ] [🏊]

WHITE POINT

◆◆ White Point Beach Resort ⑤Ⅱ
(902) 354-2711. **$100-$190, 3 day notice.** 75 White Point Rd 2. Hwy 103, exit 20A westbound, 5 mi (8 km) w on Rt 3; exit 20 eastbound, 6 mi (10 km) e on Rt 3. Ext/int corridors. **Pets:** Accepted.

[ASK] [X] [🛏] [💻] [Ⅱ] [X]

WHYCOCOMAGH

◆◆◆ Keltic Quay Bayfront Lodge & Cottages ⒸⒶ
(902) 756-1122. **Call for rates.** 90 Main St. Just se off Trans-Canada Hwy 105; centre. Ext corridors. **Pets:** Accepted.

[X] [🛏] [💻] [X] [Ⅱ]

YARMOUTH

Ⓐ ◆◆◆ Best Western Mermaid Ⓜ
(902) 742-7821. **$79-$180.** 545 Main St. Corner of Main St and Starrs Rd. Ext corridors. **Pets:** Accepted.

[SAVE] [S] [X] [🛏] [💻] [🏊] [Ⅱ]

Ⓐ ◆◆◆ Capri Motel Ⓜ
(902) 742-7168. **$59-$160.** 8-12 Herbert St. Corner of Herbert and Main sts. Ext corridors. **Pets:** Accepted.

[SAVE] [S] [X] [🛏] [💻]

◆◆ Comfort Inn ⑤Ⅱ
(902) 742-1119. **$95-$195.** 96 Starrs Rd. Jct Hwy 101 E and 3. Int corridors. **Pets:** Accepted.

[ASK] [S] [X] [🛏] [💻]

◆ Lakelawn Motel Ⓜ
(902) 742-3588. **$74-$84.** 641 Main St. 0.6 mi (1 km) n on Hwy 1. Ext/int corridors. **Pets:** Accepted.

[ASK] [X] [Ⅱ] [Z]

◆◆ Rodd Colony Harbour Inn ⑤Ⅱ
(902) 742-9194. **$96-$143.** 6 Forest St. At ferry terminal. Int corridors. **Pets:** Accepted.

[ASK] [S] [X] [🛏] [💻] [Ⅱ] [Ⅱ]

Rodd Grand Yarmouth-A Rodd Signature Hotel LH
(902) 742-2446. **$131-$183.** 417 Main St. Near centre of downtown. Int corridors. **Pets:** Accepted.

ASK S⊘ ✕ 🖥 🖵 ⑪ ⇌ ⊠

Voyageur Motel M
(902) 742-7157. **$79-$94.** RR #1. 3 mi (4.8 km) ne on Hwy 1. Ext corridors. **Pets:** Accepted.

ASK S⊘ ✕ 🖥 ⒦

ONTARIO

AJAX

▼▼ Super 8 Motel-Ajax SH
(905) 428-6884. **Call for rates.** 210 Westney Rd S. Jct Bayly St from Hwy 401, exit Westney Rd, 0.6 mi (1 km) s. Int corridors. **Pets:** Accepted.

ALGONQUIN PROVINCIAL PARK

▼▼▼ Killarney Lodge CA
(705) 633-5551. **$318-$618, 3 day notice.** Hwy 60-Lake of Two Rivers-Algonquin. On Hwy 60; 21 mi (33 km) into park from west gate; 14 mi (23 km) from east gate. Ext corridors. **Pets:** Accepted.

ARNPRIOR

▼ Country Squire Motel M
(613) 623-6556. **$59-$120.** 111 Staye Court Dr. Hwy 17, exit White Lake Rd N. Ext corridors. **Pets:** Medium, dogs only. $15 daily fee/pet. Service with restrictions, supervision.

ⒸⒶ ▼▼▼ Quality Inn SH
(613) 623-7991. **$129-$149.** 70 Madawaska Blvd. Hwy 17, exit CR 29 N, 0.5 mi (0.8 km) to Madawasaka Blvd, then 1.5 mi (2.4 km) w. Int corridors. **Pets:** $10 daily fee/room. Service with restrictions, crate.

BANCROFT

ⒸⒶ ▼▼▼ Best Western Sword Motor Inn M
(613) 332-2474. **$113-$153.** 146 Hastings St. On Hwy 62 N; centre. Ext/int corridors. **Pets:** Small. $20 deposit/pet. Designated rooms, service with restrictions, supervision.

BARRIE

▼▼ Comfort Inn SH
(705) 722-3600. **$106-$147.** 75 Hart Dr. Hwy 400, exit 96A E (Dunlop St). Int corridors. **Pets:** Accepted.

ⒸⒶ ▼▼▼ Comfort Inn & Suites SH
(705) 721-1122. **$89-$129.** 210 Essa Rd. Hwy 400, exit 94 (Essa Rd), just e. Int corridors. **Pets:** Other species. Designated rooms, service with restrictions, supervision.

▼▼▼ Days Inn Barrie SH
(705) 733-8989. **$110-$160.** 60 Bryne Dr. Hwy 400, exit 94 (Essa Rd), just s, then just e. Int corridors. **Pets:** Accepted.

ⒸⒶ ▼▼▼ Holiday Inn Barrie-Hotel & Conference Centre SH
(705) 728-6191. **$109-$179.** 20 Fairview Rd. Hwy 400, exit 94 (Essa Rd), just e. Int corridors. **Pets:** Accepted.

ⒸⒶ ▼▼▼ Holiday Inn Express Hotel & Suites Barrie SH
(705) 725-1002. **$117-$185.** 506 Bryne Dr. Hwy 400, exit 90 (Maple-view Dr), just sw. Int corridors. **Pets:** Small. $15 one-time fee/room. Service with restrictions, supervision.

ⒸⒶ ▼▼▼ Travelodge Barrie SH
(705) 734-9500. **$90-$120.** 55 Hart Dr. Hwy 400, exit 96A E (Dunlop St). Int corridors. **Pets:** Accepted.

BARRY'S BAY

▼ Mountain View Motel M
(613) 756-2757. **$70-$175, 7 day notice.** 18508 Hwy 60 E. On Hwy 60, 2.5 mi (4 km) e. Ext corridors. **Pets:** Accepted.

BAYFIELD

ⒸⒶ ▼▼▼▼ The Little Inn of Bayfield CI ❀
(519) 565-2611. **$192-$275, 4 day notice.** 26 Main St. Hwy 21, exit Main St, jct Catherine St. Int corridors. **Pets:** Dogs only. $50 one-time fee/room. Designated rooms, service with restrictions, crate.

ⒸⒶ ▼ The Martha Ritz House CI
(519) 565-2325. **$125, 4 day notice.** 27 Main St. Hwy 21, exit Main St, jct Catherine St. Int corridors. **Pets:** Other species. Service with restrictions, supervision.

BELLEVILLE

ⒸⒶ ▼▼▼ Best Western Belleville SH ❀
(613) 969-1112. **$95-$125.** 387 N Front St. Hwy 401, exit 543A, 0.3 mi (0.5 km) s on Hwy 62 (N Front St). Int corridors. **Pets:** Other species. Designated rooms, crate.

▼▼ **Comfort Inn** SH
(613) 966-7703. **$113-$128.** 200 N Park St. Hwy 401, exit 543A, 0.6 mi (1 km) s on Hwy 62 (N Front St). Int corridors. **Pets:** Accepted.
A$K ⊠ 🛏 🖵

⒜ ▼▼▼ **Ramada Inn on the Bay** SH
(613) 968-3411. **Call for rates.** 11 Bay Bridge Rd. Hwy 2, 0.3 mi (0.5 km) s. Int corridors. **Pets:** Accepted.
SAVE ⊠ 🛏 🖵 ▢ ♙ ➤ ⊠

BLIND RIVER

▼ **Lakeview Inn** M
(705) 356-0800. **$90-$99, 3 day notice.** 143 Causley St. On Hwy 17, just e of Hwy 557. Ext corridors. **Pets:** Accepted.
A$K S⦿ ⊠ 🛏 ♙

BRACEBRIDGE

⒜ ▼▼▼ **Travelodge Bracebridge** M
(705) 645-2235. **$80-$159.** 320 Taylor Rd. Hwy 11, exit 189 (Hwy 42/Taylor Rd), 0.6 mi (1 km) w. Ext corridors. **Pets:** Accepted.
SAVE S⦿ ⊠ 🛏 🖵 ➤ ⊠

BRAMPTON

▼▼ **Comfort Inn** SH
(905) 452-0600. **$99-$139.** 5 Rutherford Rd S. Hwy 401, exit Hwy 410 N, 6.9 mi (11 km) to Hwy 7 E (Queen St), then 0.6 mi (1 km) w. Int corridors. **Pets:** Accepted.
A$K S⦿ ⊠ 🛏 🖵

▼▼ **Motel 6 Brampton** SH
(905) 451-3313. **$65-$71 (no credit cards).** 160 Steelwell Rd. Hwy 410, exit Steeles Ave E, s on Tomken, then just w. Int corridors. **Pets:** Other species. Service with restrictions, supervision.
S⦿ ⊠ 🛏

BRANTFORD

▼▼ **Comfort Inn** SH
(519) 753-3100. **$100-$116.** 58 King George Rd. Just s of jct Hwy 403 and 24. Int corridors. **Pets:** Medium. Designated rooms, service with restrictions, crate.
A$K S⦿ ⊠ 🛏 🖵 ♙

▼▼ **Days Inn** SH
(519) 759-2700. **$200.** 460 Fairview Dr. Hwy 403, exit Wayne Gretzky Pkwy, 5 mi (0.8 km) n. Int corridors. **Pets:** Accepted.
⊠ 🛏 🖵 ♙

▼▼▼ **Holiday Inn Brantford** SH
(519) 758-9999. **$94-$99.** 664 Colborne St. Hwy 403, exit Wayne Gretzky Pkwy, 1.3 mi (2 km) s to Colborne St, then just w. Int corridors. **Pets:** Accepted.
⊠ 🛏 🖵 ♙ ➤

BROCKVILLE

⒜ ▼▼ **Comfort Inn** SH
(613) 345-0042. **$144-$234.** 7777 Kent Blvd. Hwy 401, exit 696, just nw. Int corridors. **Pets:** Other species. $5 daily fee/pet. Service with restrictions, supervision.
SAVE S⦿ ⊠ 🛏 🖵

⒜ ▼ **Travelodge** SH
(613) 345-3900. **$78-$130, 30 day notice.** 7789 Kent Blvd. Hwy 401, exit 696, just nw. Int corridors. **Pets:** Accepted.
SAVE S⦿ ⊠ 🛏 🖵

BURLINGTON

⒜ ▼▼▼ **Comfort Inn** SH ❀
(905) 639-1700. **$109-$150.** 3290 S Service Rd. QEW, exit Walker's Line Rd westbound, just s to Harvester Rd, then just w; exit Guelph Line Rd eastbound, just s to Harvester Rd, then just e. Int corridors. **Pets:** Designated rooms, service with restrictions, supervision.
SAVE S⦿ ⊠ 🛏 🖵

⒜ ▼▼▼ **Homewood Suites by Hilton** SH
(905) 631-8300. **$149-$199.** 975 Syscon Rd. QEW, exit Burloak Dr S, w on Harvester Rd. Int corridors. **Pets:** Small. $100 one-time fee/room. Designated rooms, service with restrictions, crate.
SAVE S⦿ ⊠ 🛏 🖵 ➤

▼▼▼ **Motel 6 Burlington** SH
(905) 331-1955. **Call for rates.** 4345 N Service Rd. QEW, exit Walker's Line Rd N to N Service Rd. Int corridors. **Pets:** Other species. Service with restrictions, supervision.
⊠ 🛏

▼▼▼ **Travelodge Burlington** SH
(905) 639-9290. **Call for rates.** 950 Walker Rd. QEW, exit Walker's Line Rd, just s. Int corridors. **Pets:** Accepted.
⊠ 🛏 🖵 ➤

⒜ ▼▼▼ **Travelodge Hotel Burlington on the Lake** SH
(905) 681-0762. **Call for rates.** 2020 Lakeshore Rd. Jct Brant. Int corridors. **Pets:** Accepted.
SAVE ⊠ 🛏 🖵 ♙ ➤ ⊠

CAMBRIDGE

⒜ ▼▼ **Comfort Inn** SH ❀
(519) 658-1100. **$122-$164.** 220 Holiday Inn Dr. Hwy 401, exit 282, just n to Groh Ave. Int corridors. **Pets:** Other species. Service with restrictions, supervision.
SAVE S⦿ ⊠ 🛏 🖵 ⊠

⒜ ▼▼▼▼ **Langdon Hall Country House Hotel & Spa** CI
(519) 740-2100. **$229-$629, 3 day notice.** 1 Langdon Dr. Hwy 401, exit 275, 0.8 mi (1.3 km) se on Fountain St, 0.6 mi (1 km) s on Blair Rd, then follow signs. Ext/int corridors. **Pets:** Accepted.
SAVE ⊠ 🛏 🖵 ♙ ➤ ⊠

⒜ ▼▼▼ **Travelodge Cambridge Hotel** SH
(519) 622-1180. **$75-$140.** 605 Hespeler Rd. Hwy 401, exit 282, 0.6 mi (1 km) s. Int corridors. **Pets:** Accepted.
SAVE S⦿ ⊠ 🛏 🖵 ♙

CHAPLEAU

▼ **Riverside Motel** M
(705) 864-0440. **Call for rates.** 116 Cherry St. Corner of Grey and Cherry sts. Ext corridors. **Pets:** Accepted.
⊠ 🛏 ⊠

CHATHAM

▼▼ **Comfort Inn** SH
(519) 352-5500. **$139-$159.** 1100 Richmond St. Hwy 401, exit 81 (Bloomfield Rd), 3.1 mi (5 km) n. Int corridors. **Pets:** Accepted.
A$K S⦿ ⊠ 🛏

CHATSWORTH

▼▼ **Key Motel** M
(519) 794-2350. **$60-$85.** 317051 Hwy 6/10. On Hwy 6 and 10. Ext/int corridors. **Pets:** Accepted.
⊠ 🛏 ➤ ⊠

COBOURG

(CAA) ▼▼▼ Best Western Cobourg Inn and Convention Centre SH
(905) 372-2105. **$149-$159, 3 day notice.** 930 Burnham St. Hwy 401, exit 472 (Burnham St S). Int corridors. **Pets:** Other species. Service with restrictions, crate.

[SAVE] 🛏 ✕ 🖥 🖵 🍴 🏊

▼▼ Comfort Inn SH
(905) 372-7007. **$100-$155.** 121 Densmore Rd. Hwy 401, exit 474, just se. Int corridors. **Pets:** Accepted.

[ASK] 🛏 ✕ 🖥 🖵

CORNWALL

(CAA) ▼▼▼ Best Western Parkway Inn & Conference Centre SH
(613) 932-0451. **$129-$239.** 1515 Vincent Massey Dr. Hwy 401, exit 789 (Brookdale Ave), 1.8 mi (2.8 km) s, then just w. Int corridors. **Pets:** Medium. Designated rooms, service with restrictions.

[SAVE] 🛏 ✕ 🖵 🍴 🏊

(CAA) ▼▼ Comfort Inn-Cornwall SH
(613) 937-0111. **$99-$225.** 1625 Vincent Massey Dr. Hwy 401, exit 789 (Brookdale Ave), 1.8 mi (2.8 km) s, then 0.4 mi (0.7 km) w. Int corridors. **Pets:** Other species. $20 one-time fee/room. Designated rooms, service with restrictions, supervision.

[SAVE] 🛏 ✕ 🖥 🖵 🏊

(CAA) ▼ Econo Lodge SH
(613) 936-1996. **$59-$110.** 1142 Brookdale Ave. Hwy 401, exit 789 (Brookdale Ave), 1.9 mi (3 km) s. Ext/int corridors. **Pets:** Accepted.

[SAVE] 🛏 ✕ 🖥

DRYDEN

(CAA) ▼▼▼ Best Western Motor Inn SH
(807) 223-3201. **$116-$130, 7 day notice.** 349 Government St. On Hwy 17. Ext/int corridors. **Pets:** Accepted.

[SAVE] 🛏 ✕ 🖥 🖵 🍴 🏊 ✕

▼▼ Comfort Inn M
(807) 223-3893. **$117-$136.** 522 Government St. On Hwy 17. Int corridors. **Pets:** Other species. Service with restrictions, supervision.

[ASK] 🛏 ✕ 🖥 🖵

FONTHILL

▼ Hipwell's Motel M
(905) 892-3588. **$45-$75.** 299 Reg Rd 20 W. 1 mi (1.6 km) w; centre. Ext corridors. **Pets:** Accepted.

[ASK] 🛏 ✕ 🖥 🏊

FORT FRANCES

▼▼ Super 8 SH
(807) 274-4945. **Call for rates.** 810 Kings Hwy. On Hwy 11. Int corridors. **Pets:** Accepted.

✕ 🖥 🖵 🏊 ✕

FRENCH RIVER

(CAA) ▼ French River Trading Post Motel M
(705) 857-2115. **$70-$80.** 20112 Hwy 69. On Trans-Canada Hwy 69, 0.6 mi (1 km) n of French River Bridge. Ext corridors. **Pets:** Medium, other species. $10 daily fee/pet. Designated rooms, service with restrictions, crate.

[SAVE] 🛏 ✕ 🖥 🖵 🍴 ✕ 🏊

GANANOQUE

(CAA) ▼▼▼ Best Western Country Squire Resort SH
(613) 382-3511. **$69-$249.** 715 King St E. Hwy 401, exit 647 eastbound; exit 648 westbound, 0.6 mi (1 km) w on Hwy 2 (King St). Ext/int corridors. **Pets:** $11 daily fee/pet. Designated rooms, service with restrictions.

[SAVE] 🛏 ✕ 🖥 🖵 🍴 🏊 ✕

(CAA) ▼▼▼ Clarion Inn & Conference Centre 1000 Islands SH
(613) 382-7272. **$79-$249.** 50 Main St. Corner of Hwy 2 (King St); centre. Int corridors. **Pets:** Accepted.

[SAVE] ✕ 🖥 🖵 🍴 🏊

(CAA) ▼▼▼ Comfort Inn 1000 Islands M
(613) 382-4728. **$69-$249.** 785 King St E. Hwy 401, exit 647 eastbound; exit 648 westbound, 0.3 mi (0.5 km) w on Hwy 2 (King St). Ext/int corridors. **Pets:** Accepted.

[SAVE] ✕ 🖥 🖵 🏊

▼▼▼ Trinity House Inn CI
(613) 382-8383. **$90-$235, 7 day notice.** 90 Stone St S. Corner of Pine St; centre. Int corridors. **Pets:** Accepted.

✕ 🖥 🖵 🍴 🏊

GRIMSBY

(CAA) ▼▼▼ Super 8 Motel-Grimsby SH
(905) 309-8800. **$99-$169.** 11 Windward Dr. QEW, exit 74 (Casablanca N). Int corridors. **Pets:** Medium, other species. $10 daily fee/pet. Service with restrictions, crate.

[SAVE] 🛏 ✕ 🖥 🖵 🏊

GUELPH

(CAA) ▼▼ Comfort Inn Guelph SH
(519) 763-1900. **$118-$148.** 480 Silvercreek Pkwy. Jct Hwy 6 and 7. Int corridors. **Pets:** Service with restrictions, supervision.

[SAVE] 🛏 ✕ 🖥 🖵

(CAA) ▼▼ Holiday Inn Guelph LH 🐾
(519) 836-0231. **$135-$189.** 601 Scottsdale Dr. Jct Hwy 6 N and Stone Rd E; 5 mi (8 km) n of jct Hwy 401. Int corridors. **Pets:** Other species. Designated rooms, service with restrictions, supervision.

[SAVE] 🛏 ✕ 🖥 🖵 🍴 🏊 ✕

(CAA) ▼▼▼ Ramada Guelph SH
(519) 836-1240. **Call for rates.** 716 Gordon St. Jct Gordon St and Stone Rd; 5 mi (8 km) n of Hwy 401 via Brock Rd. Int corridors. **Pets:** Medium. $12 daily fee/room. Designated rooms, service with restrictions, crate.

[SAVE] ✕ 🖥 🖵 🍴 🏊

HALIBURTON

▼▼ Lakeview Motel M
(705) 457-1027. **$95-$190, 5 day notice.** 4951 CR 21. Jct Hwy 118, 1.6 mi (2.5 km) w on CR 21. Ext corridors. **Pets:** Accepted.

[ASK] ✕ 🖥 🖵 🍴 🏊 ✕

HAMILTON

(CAA) ▼▼▼ Sheraton Hamilton LH 🐾
(905) 529-5515. **$129-$299.** 116 King St W. On Hwy 6 and 8 W; downtown. Int corridors. **Pets:** Service with restrictions.

[SAVE] ✕ 🛏 🖥 🖵 🍴

▼▼▼ Staybridge Suites SH
(905) 577-9000. **Call for rates.** 118 Market St. Hwy 403, exit King St, then e across from Jackson Square, jct Caroline. Int corridors. **Pets:** Accepted.

✕ 🖥 🖵 🏊

▼▼ Super 8 Motel-Hamilton Airport/Mount Hope SH
(905) 679-3355. **Call for rates.** 2975 Homestead Dr. Jct Hwy 6 S
(Upper James St) and Homestead Dr. Int corridors. **Pets:** Accepted.
⊠ 🛢

HANOVER

▼▼▼▼ The Victorian Manor Bed & Breakfast BB
(519) 364-1117. **$70-$95.** 500 9th Ave. Just n of 10th St. Int corridors.
Pets: Accepted.
⊠ 🗷

HUNTSVILLE

▼▼ Comfort Inn SH 🐾
(705) 789-1701. **$100-$142.** 86 King William St. Jct Hwy 60. Int corridors. **Pets:** Other species. Designated rooms, service with restrictions,
supervision.
A$K S🐾 ⊠ 🛢 🖢

⊕ ▼▼▼ HV Hidden Valley Resort SH 🐾
(705) 789-2301. **$89-$239, 5 day notice.** 1755 Valley Rd. Jct Hwy 11,
4 mi (6.5 km) e on Hwy 60 to Hidden Valley Rd, follow signs. Int
corridors. **Pets:** Large. $35 daily fee/room. Designated rooms, service with
restrictions.
SAVE S🐾 ⊠ 🛢 🖢 ¶¶ 🌊 🗶

⊕ ▼▼▼ King William Inn M
(705) 789-9661. **$69-$129.** 23 King William St. Hwy 60, 0.6 mi (1 km)
s. Ext corridors. **Pets:** Accepted.
SAVE S🐾 ⊠ 🛢 🖢

▼▼ Motel 6-Huntsville SH
(705) 787-0118. **$65-$130.** 70 Howland Dr. Jct Hwy 11 and 60, just se.
Int corridors. **Pets:** Other species. Service with restrictions, supervision.
A$K S🐾 ⊠ 🛢 🌊

▼ Tulip Inn M
(705) 789-4001. **$60-$130, 3 day notice.** 211 Arrowhead Park Rd. Hwy
11, exit 226 (Muskoka Rd 3), follow signs for Arrowhead Park. Ext
corridors. **Pets:** Accepted.
A$K S🐾 ⊠ 🛢 🖢

INGERSOLL

▼▼▼ Comfort Inn & Suites SH
(519) 425-1100. **$79-$159.** 20 Samnah Crescent. Hwy 401, exit 216
(Culloden Rd). Int corridors. **Pets:** Accepted.
A$K S🐾 ⊠ 🛢 🖢 🌊

KAPUSKASING

▼▼ Comfort Inn SH
(705) 335-8583. **$104-$118, 30 day notice.** 172 Government Rd E.
Hwy 11; corner of Brunelle Rd. Int corridors. **Pets:** Accepted.
A$K S🐾 ⊠ 🛢 🖢

KENORA

⊕ ▼▼▼ Best Western Lakeside Inn & Conference
Centre SH
(807) 468-5521. **$109-$269.** 470 First Ave S. Centre. Int corridors.
Pets: Accepted.
SAVE S🐾 ⊠ 🛢 🖢 ¶¶ 🌊

▼▼▼ Comfort Inn M
(807) 468-8845. **$95-$135.** 1230 Hwy 17 E. 0.9 mi (1.5 km) e. Int
corridors. **Pets:** Accepted.
A$K S🐾 ⊠ 🛢 🖢

▼▼ Days Inn SH
(807) 468-2003. **Call for rates.** 920 Hwy 17 E. On Hwy 17, 0.6 mi (1
km) e. Ext/int corridors. **Pets:** Accepted.
⊠ 🛢 🖢 ¶¶ 🌊 🗶

⊕ ▼▼ Kenora Travelodge SH
(807) 468-3155. **$85-$150.** 800 Hwy 17 E. 0.6 mi (1 km) e. Int corridors. **Pets:** Accepted.
SAVE S🐾 ⊠ 🛢 🖢 ¶¶ 🌊 🗶

KILLALOE

▼▼▼ Annie's Inn BB
(613) 757-0950. **$65-$200 (no credit cards), 7 day notice.** 67 Roche
St. Hwy 60, exit Maple St, 1 blk to Roche St, then w; driveway
entrance is at the end of the street. Int corridors. **Pets:** Accepted.
A$K S🐾 ⊠ 🛢 🗷

KINGSTON

▼▼ Comfort Inn SH
(613) 549-5550. **$90-$160.** 1454 Princess St. Hwy 401, exit 613
(Sydenham Rd), 2.5 mi (4 km) se. Int corridors. **Pets:** Accepted.
A$K S🐾 ⊠ 🛢 🖢

⊕ ▼▼ Comfort Inn SH
(613) 546-9500. **$100-$185.** 55 Warne Crescent. Hwy 401, exit 617
(Division St), just s to Dalton Ave. Int corridors. **Pets:** Service with
restrictions, crate.
SAVE S🐾 ⊠ 🛢 🖢

▼▼ Confederation Place Hotel SH
(613) 549-6300. **$99-$199.** 237 Ontario St. Centre of downtown. Int
corridors. **Pets:** Accepted.
A$K S🐾 ⊠ 🛢 🖢 ¶¶ 🌊

⊕ ▼▼▼ The Executive Inn & Suites M
(613) 549-1620. **$99-$149, 3 day notice.** 794 Hwy 2 E. Hwy 401, exit
623, 5 mi (8 km) s, then 1.3 mi (2 km) e. Ext corridors. **Pets:** Small,
dogs only. $10 daily fee/pet. Designated rooms, service with restrictions,
supervision.
SAVE S🐾 ⊠ 🛢 🖢 🌊

⊕ ▼▼▼▼ Holiday Inn Kingston-Waterfront SH
(613) 549-8400. **$140-$250.** 2 Princess St. Corner of Ontario St; centre
of downtown. Int corridors. **Pets:** Other species. $20 daily fee/room.
Designated rooms, service with restrictions, supervision.
SAVE S🐾 ⊠ 🛢�ᴹ 🛢 🖢 ¶¶ 🌊 🗶

▼▼ Super 8 Motel SH
(613) 542-7395. **Call for rates.** 720 Princess St. Centre. Int corridors.
Pets: Accepted.
⊠ 🛢

KIRKLAND LAKE

▼▼ Comfort Inn SH
(705) 567-4909. **$109-$199.** 455 Government Rd W. Rt 66, just w of
centre. Int corridors. **Pets:** Accepted.
A$K S🐾 ⊠ 🛢 🖢

KITCHENER

⊕ ▼▼▼▼ Delta Kitchener-Waterloo LH 🐾
(519) 744-4141. **$145-$219.** 105 King St E. Corner of King and Benton
sts; downtown. Int corridors. **Pets:** $35 one-time fee/room. Service with
restrictions, crate.
SAVE S🐾 ⊠ 🛢 🖢 ¶¶ 🌊 🗶

⊕ ▼▼▼▼ Holiday Inn Kitchener-Waterloo Hotel &
Conference Centre LH
(519) 893-1211. **Call for rates.** 30 Fairway Rd S. Hwy 401, exit 278,
3.5 mi (5.6 km) w on Hwy 8, exit Weber St, then just e on King St. Int
corridors. **Pets:** Accepted.
SAVE ⊠ 🛢ᴹ 🛢 🖢 ¶¶ 🌊 🗶

⊕ ▼▼▼▼ Radisson Hotel Kitchener-Waterloo SH
(519) 894-9500. **$99-$169.** 2960 King St E. Hwy 401, exit 278, 3.8 mi
(6 km) w on Hwy 8, exit Weber St. Int corridors. **Pets:** Accepted.
SAVE S🐾 ⊠ 🛢 🖢 ¶¶ 🌊

▼▼ Sunbridge Crescent B&B BB
(519) 743-4557. **$95-$140.** 11 Sunbridge Crescent. Hwy 86 N, exit University E, 0.6 mi (1 km) to Bridge St, 0.3 mi (0.5 km) to Bridal Tr, then 0.5 mi (0.9 km) e. Int corridors. **Pets:** Accepted.

`ASK` `S/D` `X` `⊟` `🖭` `➥` `⊘`

▼▼▼ Walper Terrace Hotel SH
(519) 745-4321. **$99-$179.** 1 King St W. Corner of King and Queen sts; downtown. Int corridors. **Pets:** Accepted.

`ASK` `S/D` `X` `⊟` `🖭` `⊞`

LEAMINGTON

▼▼ Comfort Inn SH
(519) 326-9071. **$93-$142.** 279 Erie St S. 0.6 mi (1 km) s of jct Talbot and Erie sts; on direct route to Point Pelee National Park. Int corridors. **Pets:** Accepted.

`ASK` `S/D` `X` `⊟` `🖭`

CAA ▼▼▼ Ramada Leamington SH
(519) 325-0260. **$100-$300, 3 day notice.** 201 Erie St N. 0.6 mi (1 km) n of Talbot St. Int corridors. **Pets:** Medium, other species. $15 daily fee/pet. Designated rooms, service with restrictions, crate.

`SAVE` `S/D` `X` `⊟` `🖭` `➥` `⊠`

LISTOWEL

▼▼ Country Inn Motel M
(519) 291-1580. **$89-$119, 3 day notice.** RR 1 Hwy 23 N-8500 Rd 164. On Hwy 23 N, 2.2 mi (3.5 km) n of Main St. Ext/int corridors. **Pets:** Accepted.

`ASK` `S/D` `X` `⊟` `🖭` `⊠`

LONDON

▼▼▼ Airport Inn & Suites SH
(519) 457-1200. **$99.** 2230 Dundas St E. Hwy 401, exit Airport Rd, 4.8 mi (7.7 km) n; corner of Airport Rd and Dundas St E. Int corridors. **Pets:** Accepted.

`ASK` `S/D` `X` `⊟` `🖭`

CAA ▼▼▼ Best Western Lamplighter Inn & Conference Centre SH
(519) 681-7151. **$144-$259.** 591 Wellington Rd S. 2.3 mi (3.7 km) n off Hwy 401, exit 186 (Wellington Rd). Int corridors. **Pets:** Small, other species. $10 daily fee/pet. Designated rooms, service with restrictions, supervision.

`SAVE` `S/D` `X` `⊟` `🖭` `�△` `➥` `⊠`

▼▼ Comfort Inn SH
(519) 685-9300. **$97-$120.** 1156 Wellington Rd. Hwy 401, exit 186B (Wellington Rd), just n. Int corridors. **Pets:** Accepted.

`ASK` `S/D` `X` `⊟` `🖭`

CAA ▼▼ Days Inn London SH
(519) 681-1240. **$69-$149.** 1100 Wellington Rd S. Hwy 401, exit 186B (Wellington Rd), 0.9 mi (1.5 km) n. Int corridors. **Pets:** Accepted.

`SAVE` `S/D` `X` `⊟` `🖭` `�△` `➥`

CAA ▼▼▼ Delta London Armouries LH
(519) 679-6111. **$119-$229.** 325 Dundas St. Between Wellington and Waterloo sts. Int corridors. **Pets:** Large, other species. $35 one-time fee/room. Service with restrictions, crate.

`SAVE` `S/D` `X` `⊟` `🖭` `�△` `➥` `⊠`

CAA ▼▼▼ Holiday Inn Hotel & Suites-London SH
(519) 680-0077. **$139.** 864 Exeter Rd. Hwy 401, exit 186 (Wellington Rd) westbound; exit 186B eastbound. Int corridors. **Pets:** Accepted.

`SAVE` `S/D` `X` `⊟` `🖭` `�△` `➥`

▼▼▼ Homewood Suites by Hilton London SH
(519) 686-7700. **Call for rates.** 45 Bessemer Rd. Hwy 401, exit 186 (Wellington Rd). Int corridors. **Pets:** $10 daily fee/room, $75 one-time fee/room. Service with restrictions, supervision.

`X` `&M` `⊟` `🖭` `➥`

▼▼ Motel 6 London SH
(519) 680-0900. **$76-$110.** 810 Exeter Rd. Hwy 401, exit 186 (Wellington Rd), just n. Int corridors. **Pets:** Other species. Service with restrictions, supervision.

`ASK` `S/D` `X` `⊟` `➥`

CAA ▼▼▼ Quality Suites SH 🐾
(519) 680-1024. **$138-$165.** 1120 Dearness Dr. Hwy 401, exit 186B (Wellington Rd), 1 mi (1.6 km) n. Int corridors. **Pets:** Other species. Service with restrictions, supervision.

`SAVE` `S/D` `X` `⊟` `🖭`

▼▼▼ Residence Inn by Marriott London Downtown SH
(519) 433-7222. **$165-$185.** 383 Colborne St. Jct King St. Int corridors. **Pets:** Other species. $75 one-time fee/room. Service with restrictions, crate.

`ASK` `S/D` `X` `⊟` `🖭` `⊠`

CAA ▼▼▼ StationPark All Suite Hotel LH 🐾
(519) 642-4444. **$194.** 242 Pall Mall St. Hwy 401, exit 186B (Wellington Rd), 5.6 mi (9 km) n to Pall Mall St. Int corridors. **Pets:** Other species. Designated rooms, service with restrictions.

`SAVE` `S/D` `X` `⊟` `⊠`

CAA ▼▼▼ Staybridge Suites SH
(519) 649-4500. **$139-$169.** 824 Exeter Rd. Hwy 401, exit 186 (Wellington St). Int corridors. **Pets:** $35 one-time fee/room. Supervision.

`SAVE` `S/D` `X` `&M` `⊟` `🖭` `➥`

MARATHON

CAA ▼ Peninsula Inn M
(807) 229-0651. **$85-$98.** Hwy 17. 1.5 mi (2.4 km) w of jct Hwy 626. Ext corridors. **Pets:** Small. $10 one-time fee/pet. Designated rooms, service with restrictions, supervision.

`SAVE` `S/D` `X` `⊟` `�△`

▼▼▼ Travelodge Marathon SH
(807) 229-1213. **Call for rates.** Hwy 17. On Hwy 17, jct Peninsula Rd. Int corridors. **Pets:** Accepted.

`X` `⊟` `🖭` `�△`

MASSEY

CAA ▼ Mohawk Motel Canada M
(705) 865-2722. **$70-$155.** 335 Sable St. Centre. Ext/int corridors. **Pets:** Accepted.

`SAVE` `S/D` `X` `⊟` `🖭`

MCKELLAR

CAA ▼▼▼ ▼▼ The Inn at Manitou SH
(705) 389-2171. **$590-$990, 30 day notice.** 81 The Inn Rd. Hwy 124, exit McKellar Centre Rd, 5 mi (8 km) s, follow signs. Ext corridors. **Pets:** Accepted.

`SAVE` `X` `⊟` `�△` `➥` `⊠`

MIDLAND

▼▼ Comfort Inn SH
(705) 526-2090. **$100-$180.** 980 King St. Jct King St and Hwy 12. Int corridors. **Pets:** Accepted.

`ASK` `S/D` `X` `⊟` `🖭`

MINDEMOYA

▼ Mindemoya Motel M
(705) 377-4779. **$82-$109, 3 day notice.** 6375 Hwy 542. 0.6 mi (1 km) w of jct Hwy 551 and 542. Ext corridors. **Pets:** Accepted.

`S/D` `X` `⊟` `🖭`

MISSISSAUGA

⬥ ▼▼▼ **Best Western Admiral Hotel & Suites @ Conference Centre-Mississauga Airport** 🆂🅷
(905) 795-1011. **Call for rates.** 40 Admiral Blvd. Hwy 401, exit Hwy 10 (Hurontario St), 0.9 mi (1.5 km) n; just s of Derry Rd. Int corridors. **Pets:** Small. $25 daily fee/pet. Designated rooms, service with restrictions, supervision.
🆂🅰🆅🅴 ⊠ 🖰 🖵 🔁 ⊠

⬥ ▼▼ **Comfort Inn Airport West** 🆂🅷 🐾
(905) 624-6900. **$119-$169.** 1500 Matheson Blvd. Hwy 401, exit Dixie Rd, then s. Int corridors. **Pets:** Designated rooms, service with restrictions, supervision.
🆂🅰🆅🅴 🆂🅳 ⊠ 🖰 🖵 🍴

⬥ ▼▼▼▼ **Delta Meadowvale Resort and Conference Centre** 🅻🅷 🐾
(905) 821-1981. **$99-$299.** 6750 Mississauga Rd. Hwy 401 W, exit 336 (Mississauga Rd), just s. Int corridors. **Pets:** Other species. $35 one-time fee/room. Service with restrictions, crate.
🆂🅰🆅🅴 🆂🅳 ⊠ 🆕 🖰 🖵 🍴 🔁 ⊠

⬥ ▼▼▼▼ **Delta Toronto Airport West** 🅻🅷
(905) 624-1144. **$99-$278.** 5444 Dixie Rd. 0.6 mi (1 km) s of jct Hwy 401 and Dixie Rd. Int corridors. **Pets:** Medium. $35 one-time fee/room. Service with restrictions, crate.
🆂🅰🆅🅴 🆂🅳 ⊠ 🖰 🖵 🍴 🔁 ⊠

⬥ ▼▼ **Econo Lodge Inn & Suites Toronto Airport** 🆂🅷
(905) 677-7331. **$109-$119.** 6355 Airport Rd. 1.3 mi (2 km) s of Derry Rd. Ext/int corridors. **Pets:** Medium, other species. $150 deposit/room, $10 daily fee/pet. Service with restrictions, supervision.
🆂🅰🆅🅴 🆂🅳 ⊠ 🖰 🖵 🍴

▼▼▼ **Four Points by Sheraton Mississauga Meadowvale** 🅻🅷
(905) 858-2424. **$90-$150.** 2501 Argentia Rd. Sw of Hwy 401 and Mississauga Rd; corner of Derry and Argentia rds. Int corridors. **Pets:** Accepted.
🅰🆂🅺 🆂🅳 ⊠ 🆕 🖰 🖵 🍴 🔁 ⊠

⬥ ▼▼▼ **Four Points by Sheraton Toronto Airport** 🅻🅷
(905) 678-1400. **$109-$149.** 6257 Airport Rd. 7 mi (11.2 km) n of jct QEW and Hwy 427 N, exit Hwy 401 via airport expressway. Int corridors. **Pets:** Accepted.
🆂🅰🆅🅴 🆂🅳 ⊠ 🆕 🖰 🖵 🍴 🔁 ⊠

▼▼▼ **Holiday Inn Toronto-Mississauga** 🅻🅷
(905) 855-2000. **$99-$149.** 2125 N Sheridan Way. QEW, exit Erin Mills Pkwy. Int corridors. **Pets:** Accepted.
🅰🆂🅺 🆂🅳 ⊠ 🆕 🖰 🖵 🍴

⬥ ▼▼▼ **Homewood Suites by Hilton Toronto-Mississauga** 🆂🅷
(905) 564-5529. **$189-$329.** 6430 Edwards Blvd. Hwy 401, exit Hwy 10 (Hurontario St), 0.3 mi (0.5 km) n to Annagem Blvd, then just e. Int corridors. **Pets:** Accepted.
🆂🅰🆅🅴 🆂🅳 ⊠ 🖰 🖵 🔁 ⊠

▼▼ **Motel 6 Mississauga** 🆂🅷
(905) 814-1664. **Call for rates.** 2935 Argentia Rd. Hwy 401, exit 333 (Winston Churchill Blvd), just s. Int corridors. **Pets:** Other species. Service with restrictions, supervision.
⊠ 🗚 🖰

⬥ ▼▼▼ **Novotel Toronto Mississauga Centre** 🅻🅷 🐾
(905) 896-1000. **$259.** 3670 Hurontario St. On Hwy 10 at Burnhamthorpe Rd; Hwy 401, exit Hwy 10 S (Hurontario St), 3.1 mi (5 km). Int corridors. **Pets:** Small. Designated rooms, service with restrictions, supervision.
🆂🅰🆅🅴 🆂🅳 ⊠ 🖰 🖵 🍴 🔁 ⊠

⬥ ▼▼▼ **Quality Inn and Suites** 🆂🅷
(905) 624-9500. **$100-$110.** 5599 Ambler Dr. Hwy 401, exit 346 (S Dixie Rd), w on Aerowood Dr, then just n. Int corridors. **Pets:** Small. $10 daily fee/pet. Designated rooms, service with restrictions, supervision.
🆂🅰🆅🅴 🆂🅳 ⊠ 🖰 🖵 🍴 🔁

▼▼▼ **Residence Inn by Marriott** 🆂🅷
(905) 567-2577. **$198-$218.** 7005 Century Ave. Hwy 401, exit Erin Mills Pkwy/Mississauga Rd, s to Argentia Rd. Int corridors. **Pets:** Accepted.
🅰🆂🅺 🆂🅳 ⊠ 🗚 🖰 🖵 🔁 ⊠

⬥ ▼▼▼▼ **Residence Inn by Marriott Mississauga Airport Corporate Centre West** 🆂🅷
(905) 602-7777. **$205-$225.** 5070 Creekbank Rd. Hwy 401 W, exit Dixie Rd S, 0.9 mi (1.5 km) to Eglinton Ave, then 0.6 mi (1 km). Int corridors. **Pets:** Accepted.
🆂🅰🆅🅴 🆂🅳 ⊠ 🖰 🖵 🍴 🔁 ⊠

⬥ ▼▼▼▼ **Sandalwood Suites Hotel Toronto Airport** 🆂🅷
(905) 238-9600. **$89-$159.** 5050 Orbitor Dr. Jct Eglinton Ave and Renforth Dr, 1.4 mi (2.3 km) w on Eglinton Ave. Int corridors. **Pets:** Medium, dogs only. $100 one-time fee/room. Designated rooms, service with restrictions, crate.
🆂🅰🆅🅴 ⊠ 🖰 🖵

⬥ ▼▼▼ ▼▼ **Sheraton Gateway Hotel in Toronto International Airport** 🅻🅷 🐾
(905) 672-7000. **$349.** Terminal 3, Toronto AMF. In Lester B. Pearson International Airport. Int corridors. **Pets:** Service with restrictions, supervision.
🆂🅰🆅🅴 🆂🅳 ⊠ 🗚 🖰 🖵 🍴 🔁 ⊠

⬥ ▼▼▼ **Staybridge Suites Mississauga** 🆂🅷
(905) 564-6892. **$129-$299.** 6791 Hurontario St. Hwy 401 W, exit Hwy 10 (Hurontario St), then n, 0.9 mi (1.5 km); just s of Derry Rd. Int corridors. **Pets:** Accepted.
🆂🅰🆅🅴 🆂🅳 ⊠ 🖰 🖵 🔁

▼▼ **Studio 6 Mississauga #1908** 🅼
(905) 502-8897. **$69-$79.** 60 Brittannia Rd E. Hwy 401, exit Hwy 10 (Hurontario St). Int corridors. **Pets:** Other species. Service with restrictions, supervision.
🆂🅳 ⊠ 🖰 🖵

▼▼▼ **Toronto Airport Hilton** 🅻🅷
(905) 677-9900. **Call for rates.** 5875 Airport Rd. Hwy 401, exit Dixon Rd, 2.2 mi (3.5 km) w. Int corridors. **Pets:** Accepted.
⊠ 🗚 🖰 🍴 🔁

MONETVILLE

▼▼ **Memquisit Lodge** 🅲🅰
(705) 898-2355. **Call for rates.** 506 Memquisit Rd. 13 mi (20.8 km) ne on west arm of Lake Nipissing, on Hwy 64 and Memquisit Lodge Rd; 23 mi (36.8 km) sw off Hwy 17, on Hwy 64. Ext corridors. **Pets:** Accepted.
🖰 🖵 🍴 ⊠ 🗚 🖊

MORRISBURG

⬥ ▼▼ **The McIntosh Country Inn & Conference Centre** 🆂🅷
(613) 543-3788. **$69-$129.** 12495 Hwy 2 E. Hwy 401, exit 750, 1.2 mi (2 km) s on Rt 31, then 0.6 mi (1 km) e. Int corridors. **Pets:** $20 one-time fee/pet. Designated rooms, service with restrictions, supervision.
🆂🅰🆅🅴 🆂🅳 ⊠ 🖰 🖵 🍴 🔁 ⊠

NEWMARKET

▼▼ **Comfort Inn** 🆂🅷
(905) 895-3355. **$115-$158.** 1230 Journey's End Cir. Hwy 404, exit 51 (Davis Dr), just w on Davis Dr, then just n on Harry Walker Pkwy. Int corridors. **Pets:** Accepted.
🅰🆂🅺 🆂🅳 ⊠ 🖰 🖵

NIAGARA FALLS METROPOLITAN AREA

FORT ERIE

Ⓐ ▼▼ Comfort Inn 🆂🅷
(905) 871-8500. **$85-$100.** 1 Hospitality Dr. QEW, exit 2 (Berti St) westbound; exit 1B (Concession Rd S) eastbound. Int corridors. **Pets:** Accepted.

[SAVE] [S/D] [✕] [🛎] [💻]

Ⓐ ▼▼▼ Holiday Inn Fort Erie/Niagara-Convention Centre 🆂🅷
(905) 871-8333. **$109-$299, 14 day notice.** 1485 Garrison Rd. QEW, exit Gilmore Rd. Int corridors. **Pets:** Medium. $30 daily fee/pet. Designated rooms, service with restrictions, supervision.

[SAVE] [S/D] [✕] [🛎] [💻] [🍴] [🏊] [🐾]

LINCOLN

Ⓐ ▼▼ Best Western Beacon Harbourside Inn & Conference Centre 🆂🅷
(905) 562-4155. **$110-$170.** 2793 Beacon Blvd. QEW, exit 57. Int corridors. **Pets:** Accepted.

[SAVE] [S/D] [✕] [🛎] [💻] [🍴] [🏊]

▼▼ Prudhommes Inn 🆂🅷
(905) 562-4101. **Call for rates.** 3305 N Service Rd. QEW, exit 57. Int corridors. **Pets:** Accepted.

[✕] [🛎] [💻] [🏊]

NIAGARA FALLS

Ⓐ ▼▼ Best Western Fallsview 🆂🅷
905) 356-0551. **$94-$352, 3 day notice.** 6289 Fallsview Blvd. Jct Niagara River Pkwy, just n on Murray St. Ext/int corridors. Pets: Accepted.

[SAVE] [S/D] [✕] [💻] [🍴] [🏊]

▼▼ Econo Lodge near the Falls Ⓜ
(905) 358-6243. **$50-$180.** 6000 Stanley Ave. 0.8 mi (1.3 km) w on Hwy 20, just s. Ext/int corridors. **Pets:** Accepted.

[ASK] [S/D] [✕] [🛎] [🏊]

Ⓐ ▼▼ Flamingo Inn Ⓜ
(905) 356-4646. **Call for rates.** 7701 Lundy's Ln. QEW, exit Hwy 20, 2.1 mi (3.4 km) w. Ext corridors. **Pets:** Accepted.

[SAVE] [✕] [🛎] [🏊]

Ⓐ ▼▼ Howard Johnson Express Inn Ⓜ
(905) 358-9777. **$40-$200.** 8100 Lundy's Ln. QEW, exit Hwy 20, 3.1 mi (5 km) w. Ext corridors. **Pets:** Accepted.

[SAVE] [S/D] [✕] [🛎] [💻] [🏊]

Ⓐ ▼▼ Howard Johnson Hotel by the Falls 🆂🅷 🐾
(905) 357-4040. **$49-$349.** 5905 Victoria Ave. On Hwy 20; 0.4 mi (0.6 km) from the falls. Int corridors. **Pets:** Small, dogs only. $15 daily fee/pet. Designated rooms, service with restrictions, supervision.

[SAVE] [S/D] [✕] [🛎] [💻] [🍴] [🏊] [🐾]

▼▼ Motel 6 Niagara Falls 🆂🅷
(905) 356-6696. **$59-$169.** 5700 Stanley Ave. Just n of Hwy 20, just s of Hwy 420. Int corridors. **Pets:** Other species. Service with restrictions, supervision.

[ASK] [S/D] [✕] [🛎] [🏊]

Ⓐ ▼▼ Niagara Parkway Court Motel Ⓜ
(905) 295-3331. **$39-$149.** 3708 Main St (Niagara Pkwy S). 1.6 mi (2.5 km) s of the falls. Ext corridors. **Pets:** Small. $10 daily fee/pet. Designated rooms, service with restrictions, crate.

[SAVE] [S/D] [✕] [🛎] [💻]

Ⓐ ▼▼▼ Peninsula Inn & Resort 🆂🅷
(905) 354-8812. **$59-$339.** 7373 Niagara Square Dr. QEW, exit McLeod Rd, just w. Int corridors. **Pets:** Small. $10 daily fee/pet. Designated rooms, service with restrictions, crate.

[SAVE] [✕] [🛎M] [🛎] [💻] [🍴] [🏊] [🐾]

Ⓐ ▼▼▼▼ Sheraton Fallsview Hotel & Conference Centre 🅻🅷
(905) 374-1077. **$99-$699.** 6755 Fallsview Blvd. Near Konica Minolta Tower. Int corridors. **Pets:** Accepted.

[SAVE] [S/D] [✕] [🛎M] [🛎] [💻] [🍴] [🏊] [🐾]

Ⓐ ▼▼▼▼ Sheraton on the Falls 🅻🅷
(905) 374-4445. **$129-$999.** 5875 Falls Ave. Entrance to Rainbow Bridge on Hwy 20. Int corridors. **Pets:** Accepted.

[SAVE] [S/D] [✕] [🛎] [💻] [🍴] [🏊]

Ⓐ ▼▼ Stanley Motor Inn Ⓜ
(905) 358-9238. **$60-$180.** 6220 Stanley Ave. 2 blks from the falls; w of Skylon Tower. Ext/int corridors. **Pets:** Small, dogs only. $10 daily fee/pet. Service with restrictions.

[SAVE] [✕] [🛎] [🏊] [🛁]

Ⓐ ▼ Thriftlodge Clifton Hill Ⓜ
(905) 357-4330. **$69-$299.** 4945 Clifton Hill. Just s on jct Victoria Ave. Ext corridors. **Pets:** Small, dogs only. Designated rooms, service with restrictions, supervision.

[SAVE] [S/D] [✕] [🛎] [💻]

NIAGARA-ON-THE-LAKE

▼▼▼ Gate House Hotel 🅲🅸
(905) 468-3263. **$145-$245.** 142 Queen St. Jct Gate. Int corridors. **Pets:** Accepted.

[✕] [🍴]

▼▼▼▼ Harbour House Hotel 🅱🅱
(905) 468-4683. **$215-$445, 10 day notice.** 85 Melville St. Jct Ricardo St. Int corridors. **Pets:** Accepted.

[ASK] [S/D] [✕] [💻]

Ⓐ ▼▼▼▼ The Oban Inn and OSpa 🆂🅷
(905) 468-2165. **$150-$410, 7 day notice.** 160 Front St. Jct Gate. Ext/int corridors. **Pets:** Small. $50 daily fee/pet. Designated rooms, supervision.

[SAVE] [S/D] [✕] [🍴] [🏊] [🐾]

▼▼▼ Old Bank House 🅱🅱
(905) 468-7136. **$149-$249, 28 day notice.** 10 Front St. Corner of King and Front sts; centre. Int corridors. **Pets:** Accepted.

[ASK] [S/D] [✕] [🛁]

Ⓐ ▼▼▼▼ The Pillar and Post Hotel 🅲🅸
(905) 468-2123. **$150-$550.** 48 John St. Just n on Hwy 55 (Mississauga St), then just e; 13 mi from QEW. Ext/int corridors. **Pets:** Accepted.

[SAVE] [✕] [🛎] [💻] [🍴] [🏊] [🐾]

Ⓐ ▼▼▼▼ Prince of Wales Hotel 🆂🅷
(905) 468-3246. **$170-$570.** 6 Picton St. Jct Picton and King sts; 9 mi (14.4 km) e of jct QEW and Hwy 55, via Hwy 55. Ext/int corridors. **Pets:** Medium, other species. $35 daily fee/pet. Designated rooms, service with restrictions, supervision.

[SAVE] [✕] [🛎] [💻] [🍴] [🏊] [🐾]

Ⓐ ▼▼▼▼ Queen's Landing Hotel 🆂🅷
(905) 468-2195. **$150-$550.** 155 Byron St. Just n on King St, then just e. Int corridors. **Pets:** Small, dogs only. $100 daily fee/room. Service with restrictions, crate.

[SAVE] [✕] [🛎] [💻] [🍴] [🏊] [🐾]

▼▼▼▼ **Shaw Club Hotel and Spa** 🆂🅷 ❖
(905) 468-5711. **$105-$455, 10 day notice.** 92 Picton St. Jct Wellington St. Int corridors. **Pets:** Dogs only. $25 daily fee/pet. Designated rooms, service with restrictions, supervision.
🅰🆂🅺 🆂🔏 ⊠ 🛡 💻 🍽

ST. CATHARINES

🆂🅰 ▼▼▼ **Comfort Inn** 🆂🅷
(905) 687-8890. **$89-$179.** 2 Dunlop Dr. QEW, exit 46 (Lake St); between Lake and Geneva sts. Int corridors. **Pets:** Designated rooms, service with restrictions, supervision.
🆂🅰🆅🅴 🆂🔏 ⊠ 🛡 💻 🍽

🆂🅰 ▼▼▼▼ **Holiday Inn St. Catharines/Niagara** 🆂🅷
(905) 934-8000. **$139-$179.** 2 N Service Rd. QEW, exit 46 (Lake St), just e. Int corridors. **Pets:** Medium, dogs only. $15 daily fee/pet. Designated rooms, service with restrictions.
🆂🅰🆅🅴 🆂🔏 ⊠ 🛡 💻 🍽 🛌 ⊠

🆂🅰 ▼▼▼ **Howard Johnson Hotel & Conference Centre** 🆂🅷
(905) 934-5400. **$89-$289.** 89 Meadowvale Dr. QEW, exit 46 (Lake St). Int corridors. **Pets:** Large. $10 daily fee/room. Designated rooms, service with restrictions, supervision.
🆂🅰🆅🅴 🆂🔏 ⊠ 🛡 💻 🍽 🛌 ⊠

🆂🅰 ▼▼▼▼ **Quality Hotel Parkway Convention Centre** 🅻🅷 ❖
(905) 688-2324. **$100-$160.** 327 Ontario St. QEW, exit 47 (Ontario St), 0.5 mi (0.8 km) s. Int corridors. **Pets:** $10 daily fee/room.
🆂🅰🆅🅴 🆂🔏 ⊠ 🛡 💻 🍽 🛌 ⊠

🆂🅰 ▼▼▼ **The Travelodge St. Catharines** 🅼
(905) 688-1646. **Call for rates.** 420 Ontario St. QEW, exit 47 (Ontario St). Ext corridors. **Pets:** Accepted.
🆂🅰🆅🅴 ⊠ 🛡 💻 🍽 🛌

WELLAND

▼▼ **Comfort Inn-Niagara Falls/Welland** 🆂🅷
(905) 732-4811. **$50-$150.** 870 Niagara St. 1.5 mi (2.5 km) n. Int corridors. **Pets:** Accepted.
🅰🆂🅺 🆂🔏 ⊠ 🛡 💻

END METROPOLITAN AREA

NORTH BAY

🆂🅰 ▼▼▼ **Best Western North Bay** 🆂🅷
(705) 474-5800. **$99-$199.** 700 Lakeshore Dr. Hwy 11, exit Lakeshore Dr, 2.5 mi (4 km) n on Hwy 11B. Int corridors. **Pets:** Accepted.
🆂🅰🆅🅴 🆂🔏 ⊠ 🛡 💻 🍽 🛌 ⊠

🆂🅰 ▼▼▼▼ **Clarion Resort Pinewood Park** 🆂🅷
(705) 472-0810. **$119-$199.** 201 Pinewood Park Dr. Hwy 11, exit Lakeshore Dr, immediately turn s on Pinewood Park Dr, then 0.4 mi (0.7 km). Int corridors. **Pets:** Accepted.
🆂🅰🆅🅴 🆂🔏 ⊠ 🛡 💻 🍽 🛌 ⊠

▼▼ **Comfort Inn** 🆂🅷
(705) 494-9444. **$92-$129.** 676 Lakeshore Dr. Hwy 11B, exit Lakeshore Dr; 2.5 mi (4 km) n of jct Hwy 11. Int corridors. **Pets:** Accepted.
🅰🆂🅺 🆂🔏 ⊠ 🛡 💻

▼▼ **Comfort Inn-Airport** 🆂🅷
(705) 476-5400. **$115-$165.** 1200 O'Brien St. 1.8 mi (3 km) e on Hwy 11 and 17 Bypass; at O'Brien St exit. Int corridors. **Pets:** Designated rooms, service with restrictions, supervision.
🅰🆂🅺 🆂🔏 ⊠ 🛡 💻

▼▼ **Super 8** 🆂🅷
(705) 495-4551. **Call for rates.** 570 Lakeshore Dr. Hwy 11, exit Lakeshore Dr, 2.8 mi (4.5 km) n on Hwy 11B. **Pets:** Accepted.
⊠ 🛡 💻

🆂🅰 ▼▼▼ **Travelodge** 🆂🅷 ❖
(705) 472-7171. **$82-$102.** 718 Lakeshore Dr. Hwy 11B, exit Lakeshore Dr, 2.2 mi (3.5 km) n of jct Hwy 11. Int corridors. **Pets:** Small. Service with restrictions, supervision.
🆂🅰🆅🅴 🆂🔏 ⊠ 🛡 💻

🆂🅰 ▼▼▼ **Travelodge-Airport** 🆂🅷
(705) 495-1133. **$109-$189.** 1525 Seymour St. Jct Hwy 11, 17 and Seymour St. Int corridors. **Pets:** Accepted.
🆂🅰🆅🅴 🆂🔏 ⊠ 🛡 💻 🛌

OAKVILLE

▼▼▼ **Holiday Inn Oakville-Centre** 🆂🅷
(905) 842-5000. **$49-$200.** 590 Argus Rd. QEW, exit 118 (Trafalgar Rd), just s. Int corridors. **Pets:** Accepted.
🅰🆂🅺 🆂🔏 ⊠ 🛡 💻 🍽 🛌 ⊠

▼▼▼ **Homewood Suites by Hilton Toronto-Oakville** 🆂🅷
(905) 829-9998. **Call for rates.** 2095 Winston Park Dr. QEW, exit 124 (Winston Churchill Blvd), just n to Upper Middle Rd E. Int corridors. **Pets:** Accepted.
⊠ 🛡 💻 🛌 ⊠

ORILLIA

▼▼ **Comfort Inn** 🆂🅷
(705) 327-7744. **$121-$148.** 75 Progress Dr. Hwy 11 N, exit Hwy 12, s on Memorial Ave; corner of Progress Dr and Memorial Ave. Int corridors. **Pets:** Accepted.
🅰🆂🅺 🆂🔏 ⊠ 🛡 💻

OSHAWA

▼▼ **Comfort Inn** 🆂🅷
(905) 434-5000. **$100-$170.** 605 Bloor St W. Hwy 401, exit 416 (Park Rd), s to Bloor St, then 0.5 mi (0.8 km) w. Int corridors. **Pets:** Accepted.
🅰🆂🅺 🆂🔏 ⊠ 🛡 💻

🆂🅰 ▼▼▼ **Holiday Inn Oshawa** 🆂🅷
(905) 576-5101. **$129-$199.** 1011 Bloor St E. Hwy 401, exit 419 (Harmony Rd). Int corridors. **Pets:** Other species. $15 daily fee/pet. Designated rooms, service with restrictions, crate.
🆂🅰🆅🅴 🆂🔏 ⊠ 🛡 💻 🍽 🛌 ⊠

▼▼▼ **Oshawa Travelodge** 🆂🅷
(905) 436-9500. **$99-$139.** 940 Champlain Ave. Hwy 401, exit 412 (Thickson Rd N). Int corridors. **Pets:** Medium. $25 one-time fee/room. Designated rooms, service with restrictions, supervision.
🅰🆂🅺 🆂🔏 ⊠ 🛡 💻 🛌

OTTAWA METROPOLITAN AREA

OTTAWA

Ⓐ ▼▼ Adam's Airport Inn 🆂🅷
(613) 738-3838. **$89-$109.** 2721 Bank St. Jct Hunt Club Rd and Bank St, 0.6 mi (1 km) s. Int corridors. **Pets:** Accepted.

Ⓐ ▼▼ Best Western Barons Hotel & Conference Centre 🆂🅷
(613) 828-2741. **Call for rates.** 3700 Richmond Rd. Hwy 417, exit 130, 1.3 mi (2 km) s. Int corridors. **Pets:** Accepted.

▼▼▼ Bostonian Executive Suites 🆂🅷
(613) 594-5757. **Call for rates.** 341 MacLaren St. Between Bank and O'Connor sts. Int corridors. **Pets:** Accepted.

Ⓐ ▼▼▼ Brookstreet 🅻🅷
(613) 271-1800. **$149-$399.** 525 Legget Dr. Hwy 417, exit 138 (March Rd), 2.3 (3.7 km) n, just e on Solandt Dr to Legget Dr, then just n. Int corridors. **Pets:** Small. $250 deposit/pet, $25 daily fee/pet. Designated rooms, service with restrictions, supervision.

Ⓐ ▼▼▼ Cartier Place Suite Hotel 🆂🅷
(613) 236-5000. **$139-$219.** 180 Cooper St. Between Elgin and Cartier sts. Int corridors. **Pets:** $15 daily fee/room, $65 one-time fee/room. Service with restrictions, crate.

Ⓐ ▼▼ Comfort Inn 🆂🅷
(613) 744-2900. **$99-$200.** 1252 Michael St. Hwy 417, exit 115 (St. Laurent Blvd), just ne. Int corridors. **Pets:** Medium, other species. Service with restrictions, supervision.

Ⓐ ▼▼▼ Comfort Inn Ottawa West 🆂🅷
(613) 592-2200. **$128-$155.** 222 Hearst Way. Hwy 417, exit 138 (Eagleson Rd), 0.4 mi (0.6 km) s, then just w on Katimavik Rd. Int corridors. **Pets:** Accepted.

Ⓐ ▼▼ Days Inn-Downtown (Ottawa) 🆂🅷
(613) 789-5555. **$109-$149.** 319 Rideau St. Between Nelson St and King Edward Ave. Ext/int corridors. **Pets:** Accepted.

▼▼▼ The Days Inn Ottawa West 🆂🅷
(613) 726-1717. **$130-$210.** 350 Moodie Dr. Hwy 417, exit 134, 0.9 mi (1.5 km) s. Int corridors. **Pets:** Accepted.

Ⓐ ▼▼▼ Delta Ottawa Hotel and Suites 🅻🅷 ❀
(613) 238-6000. **$290-$350.** 361 Queen St. Corner of Lyon St. Int corridors. **Pets:** Large, other species. $35 one-time fee/room. Service with restrictions, supervision.

Ⓐ ▼▼▼ Extended Stay Deluxe Ottawa Downtown 🆂🅷
(613) 236-7500. **$100-$150.** 141 Cooper St. Between Elgin and Cartier sts. Int corridors. **Pets:** Other species. $75 one-time fee/pet. Service with restrictions.

Ⓐ ▼▼▼ Fairmont Chateau Laurier 🅻🅷
(613) 241-1414. **$179-$399.** 1 Rideau St. Just e of Parliament buildings. Int corridors. **Pets:** Medium. $35 one-time fee/pet. Designated rooms, service with restrictions, supervision.

Ⓐ ▼▼▼ Holiday Inn Hotel & Suites Ottawa Downtown 🆂🅷 ❀
(613) 238-1331. **$134-$179.** 111 Cooper St. Corner of Cartier St. Int corridors. **Pets:** Other species. Designated rooms.

Ⓐ ▼▼▼ Les Suites Hotel Ottawa 🆂🅷
(613) 232-2000. **$139-$239.** 130 Besserer St. Between Nicholas and Waller sts. Int corridors. **Pets:** $35 one-time fee/pet. Designated rooms, service with restrictions, crate.

▼▼▼ Lord Elgin Hotel 🅻🅷
(613) 235-3333. **$139-$189.** 100 Elgin St. Between Laurier Ave and Slater St. Int corridors. **Pets:** Accepted.

Ⓐ ▼▼▼ Marriott Ottawa Hotel 🅻🅷
(613) 238-1122. **$219-$285.** 100 Kent St. Corner of Queen St. Int corridors. **Pets:** Other species. Service with restrictions, crate.

Ⓐ ▼▼ Monterey Inn Resort & Conference Centre 🆂🅷
(613) 288-3500. **$109-$139.** 2259 Prince of Wales Dr. 0.5 mi (0.8 km) s of Hunt Club Rd. Ext corridors. **Pets:** Accepted.

Ⓐ ▼▼▼ Novotel Ottawa Hotel 🆂🅷
(613) 230-3033. **$159-$259.** 33 Nicholas St. Corner of Daly Ave. Int corridors. **Pets:** Accepted.

Ⓐ ▼▼ Quality Hotel Ottawa, Downtown 🆂🅷
(613) 789-7511. **$159-$169, 30 day notice.** 290 Rideau St. Corner of King Edward Ave. Int corridors. **Pets:** Accepted.

▼▼▼ Radisson Hotel Ottawa Parliament Hill 🆂🅷
(613) 236-1133. **$135-$159.** 402 Queen St. Corner of Bay and Queen sts. Int corridors. **Pets:** Medium. Designated rooms, service with restrictions, crate.

▼▼▼ Residence Inn by Marriott 🆂🅷
(613) 231-2020. **$227-$247.** 161 Laurier Ave W. Corner of Elgin St. Int corridors. **Pets:** Accepted.

Ⓐ ▼▼ Rideau Heights Motor Inn 🅼
(613) 226-4152. **$99-$129.** 72 Rideau Heights Dr. Hwy 16 (Prince of Wales Dr), 0.3 mi (0.5 km) n of Hunt Club Rd. Ext corridors. **Pets:** Small, other species. $10 daily fee/pet. Designated rooms, service with restrictions, supervision.

Ⓐ ▼▼▼ Sheraton Ottawa Hotel 🅻🅷
(613) 238-1500. **$149-$169.** 150 Albert St. Corner of O'Connor St. Int corridors. **Pets:** Small. Designated rooms, service with restrictions, supervision.

Ⓐ ▼▼▼ Southway Inn of Ottawa 🆂🅷 ❀
(613) 737-0811. **$133-$148.** 2431 Bank St. On Hwy 31; corner of Hunt Club Rd. Int corridors. **Pets:** Medium. $30 daily fee/pet. Designated rooms, service with restrictions, crate.

(AA) ▼▼▼ **Travelodge Ottawa East** SH
(613) 745-1133. **$104-$149.** 1486 Innes Rd. Hwy 417, exit 112 (Innes Rd), just e. Int corridors. **Pets:** $25 deposit/room. Designated rooms, service with restrictions, crate.
[SAVE] [S🐾] [✕] [🔌] [💻] [📶] [⛲]

(AA) ▼▼▼▼ **Travelodge Ottawa Hotel & Conference Centre** SH
(613) 722-7600. **$129-$149.** 1376 Carling Ave. Just e of jct Kirkwood Ave. Int corridors. **Pets:** Accepted.
[SAVE] [S🐾] [✕] [🔌] [💻] [📶] [⛲]

(AA) ▼▼ **Webb's Motel** M
(613) 728-1881. **$85-$125.** 1705 Carling Ave. Hwy 417, exit 126, 0.3 mi (0.5 km) n on Maitland Ave, then 0.3 mi (0.5 km) e. Ext/int corridors. **Pets:** Accepted.
[SAVE] [✕] [🔌]

▼▼ **WelcomINNS** SH
(613) 748-7800. **$99-$115.** 1220 Michael St. Hwy 417, exit 115 (St. Laurent Blvd), just ne. Int corridors. **Pets:** Accepted.
[ASK] [S🐾] [✕] [🔌] [💻] [⛲]

(AA) ▼▼▼▼ **The Westin Ottawa** LH
(613) 560-7000. **$179-$449.** 11 Colonel By Dr. Corner of Rideau St. Int corridors. **Pets:** Accepted.
[SAVE] [✕] [🔌] [💻] [📶] [⛲]

END METROPOLITAN AREA

OWEN SOUND

▼▼ **Comfort Inn** SH 🐾
(519) 371-5500. **$85-$250.** 955 9th Ave E. Jct Hwy 6, 10, 21 and 26. Int corridors. **Pets:** Medium. Designated rooms, service with restrictions, supervision.
[ASK] [S🐾] [✕] [🔌] [💻]

(AA) ▼▼▼▼ **Days Inn and Conference Centre** SH 🐾
(519) 376-1551. **$99-$250.** 950 6th St E. Jct Hwy 6 and 10. Int corridors. **Pets:** Other species. $20 daily fee/room. Service with restrictions.
[SAVE] [S🐾] [✕] [🔌] [💻] [⛲] [📶] [⛲]

▼▼ **Owen Sound Inn** SH
(519) 371-3011. **$59-$200.** 485 9th Ave E. Jct Hwy 6, 10, 26 and 21; follow Hwy 6 and 10, 0.6 mi (1 km) s. Int corridors. **Pets:** Accepted.
[ASK] [S🐾] [✕] [🔌] [💻]

PARRY SOUND

▼▼ **Comfort Inn** SH
(705) 746-6221. **$156-$174.** 120 Bowes St. Hwy 69, exit 224 (Bowes St), just w. Int corridors. **Pets:** Accepted.
[ASK] [S🐾] [✕] [🔌] [💻]

(AA) ▼▼▼ **Microtel Inn & Suites** SH
(705) 746-2700. **$99-$169.** 292 Louisa St. Hwy 69, exit 224 (Bowes St), just w. Int corridors. **Pets:** Small, other species. $10 daily fee/room. Designated rooms, supervision.
[SAVE] [S🐾] [✕] [🔌] [💻]

▼▼ **Resort Tapatoo** SH
(705) 378-2208. **Call for rates.** Otter Lake Rd. Hwy 69, exit 217, 3.9 mi (6.2 km) sw. Ext/int corridors. **Pets:** Accepted.
[✕] [🔌] [💻] [📶] [⛲] [⛲]

PEMBROKE

▼▼ **Colonial Fireside Inn** M
(613) 732-3623. **$59-$120.** 1350 Pembroke St W. Jct Hwy 17, 3.1 mi (5 km) n on Forest Lea Rd, just e. Ext corridors. **Pets:** Accepted.
[ASK] [S🐾] [✕] [🔌] [💻] [📶]

▼▼ **Comfort Inn** SH
(613) 735-1057. **$109-$210.** 959 Pembroke St E. 1 mi (1.6 km) e on Old Hwy 17. Int corridors. **Pets:** Accepted.
[ASK] [S🐾] [✕] [🔌] [💻]

PETAWAWA

(AA) ▼▼▼ **Petawawa River Inn & Suites** SH 🐾
(613) 687-4686. **$110-$200.** 3520 Petawawa Blvd. Hwy 17, exit Paquette Rd, 1.5 mi (2.4 km) e, then just s. Int corridors. **Pets:** Other species. $10 daily fee/pet. Service with restrictions, supervision.
[SAVE] [S🐾] [✕] [🔌] [💻]

PETERBOROUGH

▼▼ **King Bethune House, Guest House & Spa** BB
(705) 743-4101. **$129-$299, 14 day notice.** 270 King St. From Charlotte and George sts (clock tower), 1 blk s on George St to King St, then just w. Int corridors. **Pets:** Accepted.
[✕] [🔌] [💻]

▼▼ **Motel 6 Peterborough** SH
(705) 748-0550. **$69-$109.** 133 Landsdowne St E. 1.6 mi (2.6 km) e of The Parkway. Int corridors. **Pets:** Other species. Service with restrictions, supervision.
[ASK] [S🐾] [✕] [🔌]

(AA) ▼▼▼ **Quality Inn** SH
(705) 748-6801. **$92-$120.** 1074 Lansdowne St W. 1.9 mi (3 km) from jct Hwy 115 and Bypass. Int corridors. **Pets:** Accepted.
[SAVE] [S🐾] [✕] [🔌] [💻]

PICKERING

▼▼ **Comfort Inn** SH
(905) 831-6200. **$99-$165.** 533 Kingston Rd. Hwy 401, exit 394 N (White's Rd) to Hwy 2, 0.3 mi (0.5 km) w. Int corridors. **Pets:** Designated rooms, service with restrictions.
[ASK] [S🐾] [✕] [🔌] [💻]

PLANTAGENET

▼▼ **Motel de Champlain** M
(613) 673-5220. **$64-$110.** 5999 Hwy 17. Jct CR 9. Ext/int corridors. **Pets:** Accepted.
[✕] [🔌] [📶]

PORT CARLING

(AA) ▼▼▼▼ **Delta Sherwood Inn** SH 🐾
(705) 765-3131. **Call for rates.** 1090 Sherwood Rd. Hwy 169, just n of jct Hwy 118; on Lake Joseph. Ext/int corridors. **Pets:** Medium. Designated rooms, service with restrictions, supervision.
[SAVE] [✕] [🔌] [💻] [📶] [⛲]

PORT HOPE

▼▼▼ Comfort Inn ⚠️
(905) 885-7000. **$109-$149.** Hwy 401 & 28. Hwy 401, exit 464, just n. Int corridors. **Pets:** Accepted.

⎡ASK⎤ ⎡S🐾⎤ ☒ 🔋 💻

PROVIDENCE BAY

(CAA) ▼▼ Huron Sands Motel 🅼
(705) 377-4616. **$70-$140, 3 day notice.** 5216 Hwy 551. On Hwy 551, 17 mi (27.2 km) w of South Baymouth via 10th Side Rd, follow signs; centre. Ext corridors. **Pets:** Other species. $10 one-time fee/pet. Service with restrictions, supervision.

⎡SAVE⎤ ☒ 🔋 🍴 ✍️

RENFREW

(CAA) ▼▼▼ Best Western-Renfrew Inn and Conference
        Centre ⚠️
(613) 432-8109. **$149-$156.** 760 Gibbons Rd. Hwy 17, exit O'Brien Rd. Int corridors. **Pets:** Accepted.

⎡SAVE⎤ ⎡S🐾⎤ ☒ 🔋 💻 🍴 ✍️ ☒

▼ The Rocky Mountain House 🅼
(613) 432-5801. **Call for rates.** 409 Stewart St N. Jct Bruce St. Ext corridors. **Pets:** Accepted.

☒ 🔋 💻 🍴

ROSSPORT

▼▼ The Willows Inn Bed & Breakfast 🆖
(807) 824-3389. **$100-$120, 10 day notice.** 1 Main St. Centre. Int corridors. **Pets:** Accepted.

☒ 🐾 ✍️

ST. THOMAS

(CAA) ▼▼▼ Comfort Inn ⚠️
(519) 633-4082. **Call for rates.** 100 Centennial Ave. 4.1 mi (6.5 km) e on Hwy 3. Int corridors. **Pets:** Accepted.

⎡SAVE⎤ ☒ 🔋 💻

SARNIA

(CAA) ▼▼▼▼ Best Western Guildwood Inn and Conference
        Centre ⚠️
(519) 337-7577. **$110.** 1400 Venetian Blvd. 0.6 mi (1 km) e of Bluewater Bridge. Ext/int corridors. **Pets:** Accepted.

⎡SAVE⎤ ⎡S🐾⎤ ☒ 🔋 💻 🍴 ✍️

▼▼▼ Holiday Inn Sarnia-Point Edward ⚠️
(519) 336-4130. **$115-$230.** 1498 Venetian Blvd. E of Bluewater Bridge. Int corridors. **Pets:** Accepted.

⎡ASK⎤ ⎡S🐾⎤ ☒ 🔋 💻 🍴 ✍️ ☒

▼▼▼ Super 8 Motel-Sarnia ⚠️
(519) 337-3767. **Call for rates.** 420 Christina St N. Between Exmouth and London rds. Ext/int corridors. **Pets:** Accepted.

☒ 🐾M 🔋 💻

SAULT STE. MARIE

▼ Adams Motel 🅼
(705) 254-4345. **$59-$99.** 647 Great Northern Rd. 2.8 mi (4.4 km) n on Hwy 17B. Ext corridors. **Pets:** Accepted.

⎡ASK⎤ ⎡S🐾⎤ ☒ 🔋 💻

(CAA) ▼▼▼▼ Algoma's Water Tower Inn ⚠️
(705) 949-8111. **$115-$145.** 360 Great Northern Rd. Jct Hwy 17 and Second Line. Int corridors. **Pets:** Accepted.

⎡SAVE⎤ ⎡S🐾⎤ ☒ 🔋 💻 🍴 ✍️ ☒

▼ Ambassador Motel 🅼
(705) 759-6199. **$59-$89.** 1275 Great Northern Rd. 4 mi (6.4 km) n on Hwy 17. Ext corridors. **Pets:** Accepted.

☒ 🔋 💻 🐾 ☒

(CAA) ▼ Bel-Air Motel 🅼
(705) 945-7950. **$55-$99.** 398 Pim St. 1.3 mi (2 km) n on Hwy 17B. Ext corridors. **Pets:** $5 daily fee/pet. Designated rooms, no service.

⎡SAVE⎤ ⎡S🐾⎤ ☒ 🔋 💻

(CAA) ▼ Catalina Motel 🅼
(705) 945-9260. **$92-$136.** 259 Great Northern Rd. 2 mi (3.2 km) n on Hwy 17B. Ext corridors. **Pets:** $10 daily fee/room. No service.

⎡SAVE⎤ ⎡S🐾⎤ ☒ 🔋 💻

(CAA) ▼▼▼ City Centre Travelodge ⚠️
(705) 759-1400. **$95-$130.** 332 Bay St. Opposite Station Mall. Int corridors. **Pets:** Medium. Designated rooms, service with restrictions, supervision.

⎡SAVE⎤ ⎡S🐾⎤ ☒ 🔋 💻 🍴

(CAA) ▼▼▼ Comfort Inn ⚠️
(705) 759-8000. **$101-$155.** 333 Great Northern Rd. 2.3 mi (3.6 km) n on Hwy 17B. Ext/int corridors. **Pets:** $15 daily fee/room. Designated rooms, supervision.

⎡SAVE⎤ ⎡S🐾⎤ ☒ 🔋 💻

▼▼ Glenview Cottages 🆑
(705) 759-3436. **$99-$150, 5 day notice.** 2611 Great Northern Rd. 6 mi (9.6 km) n on Hwy 17. Ext corridors. **Pets:** Accepted.

⎡ASK⎤ ☒ 🔋 💻 🐾 ☒

(CAA) ▼▼▼▼ Holiday Inn Sault Ste. Marie-Waterfront ⚠️
(705) 949-0611. **$109-$169, 7 day notice.** 208 St. Marys River Dr. On the waterfront. Int corridors. **Pets:** Accepted.

⎡SAVE⎤ ⎡S🐾⎤ ☒ 🔋 💻 🍴 🐾 ☒

▼ Holiday Motel 🅼
(705) 759-8608. **$55-$70.** 435 Trunk Rd. Jct Hwy 17 and 17B, just e. Ext corridors. **Pets:** Accepted.

☒ 🔋 💻

(CAA) ▼ Northlander Motel 🅼
(705) 254-6452. **$55-$80.** 243 Great Northern Rd. 1.9 mi (3 km) n on Hwy 17B. Ext corridors. **Pets:** Medium. Service with restrictions, supervision.

⎡SAVE⎤ ⎡S🐾⎤ ☒ 🔋 💻

▼ Satelite Motel 🅼
(705) 759-2897. **$55-$95.** 248 Great Northern Rd. 1.9 mi (3 km) n on Hwy 17B. Ext corridors. **Pets:** Accepted.

☒ 🔋 💻

(CAA) ▼ Skyline Motel 🅼
(705) 942-1240. **$65-$85.** 232 Great Northern Rd. 1.9 mi (3 km) n on Hwy 17B. Ext corridors. **Pets:** Accepted.

⎡SAVE⎤ ⎡S🐾⎤ ☒ 🔋 💻

▼▼ Sleep Inn ⚠️
(705) 253-7533. **$79-$139.** 727 Bay St. Between East and Church sts; downtown. Int corridors. **Pets:** Accepted.

⎡ASK⎤ ⎡S🐾⎤ ☒ 🔋 💻 ☒

(CAA) ▼▼▼ Super 8 ⚠️
(705) 254-6441. **$75-$135.** 184 Great Northern Rd. 1.3 mi (2 km) n on Hwy 17B. Int corridors. **Pets:** Other species. $15 one-time fee/room. Service with restrictions, supervision.

⎡SAVE⎤ ⎡S🐾⎤ ☒ 🔋 💻

▼ Villa Inn Motel 🅼
(705) 942-2424. **$55-$75.** 724 Great Northern Rd. 2.9 mi (4.6 km) n on Hwy 17B. Ext corridors. **Pets:** Accepted.

☒ 🔋 💻

SIMCOE

▼▼ Comfort Inn SH ❁
(519) 426-2611. **$94-$180.** 85 Queensway E. 0.3 mi (0.5 km) e on Hwy 3. Int corridors. **Pets:** Medium, other species. Designated rooms, service with restrictions, supervision.

ASK S⊘ ✕ 🔟 💻 💻

▼▼ Travelodge Simcoe SH
(519) 426-4751. **$109-$159.** 385 Queensway W (Hwy 3). 0.6 mi (1 km) w. Ext/int corridors. **Pets:** Accepted.

ASK S⊘ ✕ ⌖M 🔟 💻 💻 ⑪ 🕿 ⌧

SMITHS FALLS

CAA ▼▼ Best Western Colonel By Inn SH
(613) 284-0001. **$87-$140.** 88 Lombard St. 1.8 mi (1.2 km) s on Hwy 15. Ext/int corridors. **Pets:** Medium. $10 daily fee/pet. Designated rooms, service with restrictions, supervision.

SAVE S⊘ ✕ 🔟 💻 🕿

SOUTH BAYMOUTH

CAA ▼ Huron Motor Lodge SH
(705) 859-3131. **$89-$155.** 24 Water St N. Centre; opposite ferry terminal dock. Ext corridors. **Pets:** Other species. $10 daily fee/pet. Designated rooms, service with restrictions, supervision.

SAVE ✕ 🔟 🕿 ⌧ ⌧

STRATFORD

▼▼▼ Arden Park Hotel SH
(519) 275-2936. **$139-$199.** 552 Ontario St. Jct Romeo St. Int corridors. **Pets:** Accepted.

ASK ✕ ⌖M 🔟 💻 ⑪ 🕿

STURGEON FALLS

▼▼▼ Comfort Inn SH
(705) 753-5665. **$100-$130.** 11 Front St. On Hwy 17 at western approach to town. Int corridors. **Pets:** Accepted.

ASK S⊘ ✕ 🔟 💻 🕿

SUDBURY

CAA ▼▼▼ Best Western Downtown Sudbury Centre-Ville SH
(705) 673-7801. **$99-$139.** 151 Larch St. Centre. Int corridors. **Pets:** Other species. $100 deposit/pet, $15 daily fee/pet. Designated rooms, service with restrictions, supervision.

SAVE S⊘ ✕ 🔟 💻 ⑪

CAA ▼▼▼ Comfort Inn SH
(705) 522-1101. **$126-$180.** 2171 Regent St S. 3 mi (5 km) s on Hwy 46. Int corridors. **Pets:** Service with restrictions.

SAVE S⊘ ✕ 🔟 💻

CAA ▼▼▼ Comfort Inn East SH ❁
(705) 560-4502. **$80-$195.** 440 Second Ave N. Kingsway Hwy at Second Ave. Int corridors. **Pets:** Medium. $20 daily fee/pet. Service with restrictions, supervision.

SAVE S⊘ ✕ ⌖M 🔟 💻

▼▼ Days Inn Sudbury SH
(705) 674-7517. **Call for rates.** 117 Elm St. Centre of downtown. Int corridors. **Pets:** Accepted.

✕ 🔟 💻 ⑪ 🕿

CAA ▼▼▼▼ Holiday Inn Hotel Sudbury SH
(705) 522-3000. **$109-$152.** 1696 Regent St S. Hwy 69 (Regent St), just n of Paris St. Ext/int corridors. **Pets:** Designated rooms, service with restrictions, supervision.

SAVE S⊘ ✕ 🔟 💻 ⑪ 🕿 ⌧

CAA ▼▼▼ Quality Inn & Conference Centre SH
(705) 675-1273. **$114-$164.** 390 Elgin St S. Jct Kingsway Hwy and Paris St, 0.3 mi (0.5 km) s, just e. Int corridors. **Pets:** Accepted.

SAVE S⊘ ✕ 🔟 💻 🕿

▼▼▼ Radisson Hotel, Sudbury SH
(705) 675-1123. **$135-$175.** 85 St. Anne Rd. Jct St. Anne Rd and Notre Dame Ave; downtown. Int corridors. **Pets:** Accepted.

ASK S⊘ ✕ 🔟 💻 ⑪ 🕿

CAA ▼▼▼ Travelodge Hotel Sudbury SH
(705) 522-1100. **$109-$189.** 1401 Paris St. 0.9 mi (1.5 km) n of jct Hwy 69 (Regent St). Int corridors. **Pets:** Accepted.

SAVE S⊘ ✕ 🔟 💻 🕿

THESSALON

CAA ▼ Carolyn Beach Motor Inn M
(705) 842-3330. **$90-$125.** 1 Lakeside Dr. Just w on Hwy 17; jct Hwy 17B. Ext corridors. **Pets:** $12 daily fee/pet. Service with restrictions, supervision.

SAVE ✕ 🔟 💻 ⑪ ⌧

THUNDER BAY

CAA ▼▼▼ Best Western Crossroads Motor Inn SH
(807) 577-4241. **$119-$170.** 655 W Arthur St. Jct Hwy 61, 17 and 11, just e. Int corridors. **Pets:** Medium. $15 one-time fee/room. Designated rooms, service with restrictions, supervision.

SAVE S⊘ ✕ 🔟 💻

CAA ▼▼▼ Best Western Nor'Wester Resort Hotel SH
(807) 473-9123. **$139-$169.** 2080 Hwy 61. 5.8 mi (9.2 km) sw of jct Hwy 11, 17 and 61, exit Loch Lomond Rd. Int corridors. **Pets:** Medium. $20 one-time fee/pet. Designated rooms, service with restrictions, supervision.

SAVE S⊘ ✕ 🔟 💻 ⑪ 🕿 ⌧

CAA ▼▼▼ Comfort Inn M
(807) 475-3155. **$95-$155.** 660 W Arthur St. Jct Hwy 11, 17 and 61, just e. Int corridors. **Pets:** Other species. Service with restrictions, crate.

SAVE S⊘ ✕ 🔟 💻

CAA ▼▼▼ Super 8 Motel SH
(807) 344-2612. **Call for rates.** 439 Memorial Ave. Jct Hwy 11, 17 and Harbour Expwy, 1.9 mi (3 km) e on Harbour Expwy, 1.3 mi (2 km) n. Int corridors. **Pets:** Other species. $10 one-time fee/room. Designated rooms, service with restrictions, supervision.

SAVE ✕ 🔟 💻

▼▼ Victoria Inn SH
(807) 577-8481. **$110.** 555 W Arthur St. 0.5 mi (0.8 km) e of jct Hwy 11B, 17B and 61 (western access to town). Int corridors. **Pets:** Accepted.

ASK ✕ 🔟 💻 ⑪ 🕿 ⌧

TILLSONBURG

CAA ▼▼▼ Super 8 Motel-Tillsonburg SH
(519) 842-7366. **$110-$140.** 92 Simcoe St. Hwy 19, just e. Int corridors. **Pets:** $10 daily fee/pet. Service with restrictions, supervision.

SAVE S⊘ ✕ 🔟 💻 ⑪

TIMMINS

CAA ▼▼ Comfort Inn SH
(705) 264-9474. **$111-$132, 31 day notice.** 939 Algonquin Blvd E. Hwy 101, 0.3 mi (0.5 km) e of Hwy 655. Int corridors. **Pets:** Accepted.

SAVE S⊘ ✕ 🔟 💻

▼ ▼ Travelodge **SH**
(705) 360-1122. **Call for rates.** 1136 Riverside Dr. Hwy 101, 2.8 mi (4.4 km) w on Hwy 655. Int corridors. **Pets:** Accepted.

TOBERMORY

▼ Coach House Inn **M**
(519) 596-2361. **$59-$105.** 7189 Hwy 6. Hwy 6, 1.2 mi (2 km) s of ferry docks. Ext corridors. **Pets:** Accepted.

TORONTO METROPOLITAN AREA

MARKHAM

🅐🅐 ▼▼▼ Comfort Inn **SH**
(905) 477-6077. **$109-$129.** 8330 Woodbine Ave. Hwy 401, exit 375, 5.6 mi (9 km) n; Hwy 404, exit Hwy 7, just e, then s. Int corridors. **Pets:** Accepted.

▼▼▼ Delta Markham **LH** ❖
(905) 477-2010. **$99-$189.** 50 E Valhalla Dr. Hwy 404, exit Hwy 7, then e. Int corridors. **Pets:** Medium. $35 one-time fee/room. Service with restrictions, supervision.

🅐🅐 ▼▼▼ Howard Johnson Hotel Toronto-Markham **SH**
(905) 479-5000. **$99-$169.** 555 Cochrane Dr. Hwy 404 N, exit Hwy 7 E to E Valhalla Dr. Int corridors. **Pets:** Other species. $50 deposit/room. Service with restrictions, supervision.

▼▼▼ Residence Inn by Marriott **SH**
(905) 707-7933. **$181-$207.** 55 Minthorn Blvd. Directly s of jct Hwy 7 and Leslie St. Int corridors. **Pets:** Accepted.

▼▼▼ Staybridge Suites Toronto-Markham **SH**
(905) 771-9333. **$170-$175.** 355 S Park Rd. Jct Hwy 404 and 7, w on Hwy 7, then e. Int corridors. **Pets:** Accepted.

RICHMOND HILL

🅐🅐 ▼▼ ▼▼ Sheraton Parkway Toronto North Hotel, Suites & Conference Centre **LH** ❖
(905) 881-2121. **$109-$189.** 600 Hwy 7 E. Jct Hwy 401 and Don Valley Pkwy (Hwy 404), exit 375 via Don Valley Pkwy (Hwy 404), 5 mi (8 km) n to jct Hwy 7, then 0.6 mi (1 km) w. Int corridors. **Pets:** Medium, dogs only. $100 one-time fee/room. Designated rooms, service with restrictions, supervision.

TORONTO

🅐🅐 ▼▼▼ Best Western Roehampton Hotel & Suites **SH**
(416) 487-5101. **$109-$159.** 808 Mt. Pleasant Rd. Just n of Eglinton Ave. Int corridors. **Pets:** Medium. $35 one-time fee/room. Service with restrictions, supervision.

▼▼ Carlingview Airport Inn **SH**
(416) 675-3303. **$95.** 221 Carlingview Dr. QEW, exit Hwy 427 N to Dixon Rd E, 0.6 mi (1 km) to Carlingview Dr, then just s. Ext/int corridors. **Pets:** Accepted.

▼▼▼ Cawthra Square Inn **BB**
(416) 966-0013. **Call for rates.** 10 Cawthra Square. Directly w of Jarvis St. Int corridors. **Pets:** Accepted.

🅐🅐 ▼▼▼ Comfort Inn **SH**
(416) 736-4700. **$100.** 66 Norfinch Dr. Hwy 400, exit Finch Ave E, just n. Int corridors. **Pets:** Accepted.

🅐🅐 ▼▼▼ Cosmopolitan Toronto Hotel and Spa **SH** ❖
(416) 350-2000. **$179-$460.** 8 Colborne St. Between King and Wellington sts. Int corridors. **Pets:** Small. $25 daily fee/room, $75 one-time fee/room. Service with restrictions, supervision.

🅐🅐 ▼▼▼ Crowne Plaza Toronto Don Valley **LH**
(416) 449-4111. **$117-$189.** 1250 Eglinton Ave E. Don Valley Pkwy, exit 375 (Wynford Dr); jct Don Valley Pkwy and Eglinton Ave E. Int corridors. **Pets:** Other species. $25 one-time fee/pet. Designated rooms, service with restrictions, supervision.

🅐🅐 ▼▼▼ Days Hotel & Conference Centre-Toronto Downtown **LH**
(416) 977-6655. **$119-$189.** 30 Carlton St. Adjacent to Maple Leaf Gardens. Int corridors. **Pets:** Medium. $50 one-time fee/room. Designated rooms, service with restrictions, supervision.

🅐🅐 ▼▼▼ Delta Chelsea Hotel **LH**
(416) 595-1975. **$139-$429.** 33 Gerrard St W. Just w of Yonge St; just s of College St. Int corridors. **Pets:** Medium. $35 one-time fee/room. Service with restrictions, supervision.

▼▼▼ Delta Toronto East **LH**
(416) 299-1500. **$119-$299.** 2035 Kennedy Rd. Just ne of jct Hwy 401 and Kennedy Rd, exit 379. Int corridors. **Pets:** Medium, other species. $35 one-time fee/room. Designated rooms, service with restrictions, crate.

🅐🅐 ▼▼▼ DoubleTree International Plaza Hotel Toronto Airport **LH**
(416) 244-1711. **$134.** 655 Dixon Rd. Jct Hwy 27 N, just w of jct Hwy 401. Int corridors. **Pets:** Other species. Service with restrictions, supervision.

🅐🅐 ▼▼ ▼▼ The Fairmont Royal York **LH**
(416) 368-2511. **$170-$332.** 100 Front St W. QEW/Gardiner Expwy, exit n on York or Bay sts; entrance on Wellington St. Int corridors. **Pets:** Medium. $35 one-time fee/pet. Designated rooms, service with restrictions, supervision.

🅐🅐 ▼▼ ▼▼ Four Seasons Hotel **LH**
(416) 964-0411. **$390-$4500.** 21 Avenue Rd. Corner of Avenue Rd and Cumberland Ave. Int corridors. **Pets:** Accepted.

▼▼▼ Gloucester Square Inns of Toronto **BB**
(416) 966-0013. **Call for rates.** 512-514 Jarvis St. Jct Gloucester. Int corridors. **Pets:** Accepted.

▼▼▼ **Hilton Toronto** 🄻🄷
(416) 869-3456. **$149-$349.** 145 Richmond St W. Jct University Ave. Int corridors. **Pets:** Medium, dogs only. $50 one-time fee/room. Service with restrictions, supervision.
🆂🄳 ☒ 🔋 🖳 ⑪ ⇌ ☒

🅒🅐🅐 ▼▼▼ **Holiday Inn Express Toronto Downtown** 🅂🄷
(416) 367-5555. **$119-$199.** 111 Lombard St. West side of Jarvis St; between Adelaide and Richmond sts; 0.6 mi (1 km) n off Gardiner Expwy at Jarvis St exit. Int corridors. **Pets:** Medium. Service with restrictions, supervision.
🆂🄰🆅🄴 🆂🄳 ☒ 🔋 🖳

🅒🅐🅐 ▼▼▼ **Holiday Inn Express Toronto-North York** 🅂🄷
(416) 665-3500. **$109-$169.** 30 Norfinch Dr. Hwy 400, exit Finch Ave E. Int corridors. **Pets:** Accepted.
🆂🄰🆅🄴 🆂🄳 ☒ 🔋🄼 🔋 🖳

🅒🅐🅐 ▼▼▼ **Holiday Inn Toronto Midtown** 🅂🄷
(416) 968-0010. **$129-$249.** 280 Bloor St W. Just w of St. George. Int corridors. **Pets:** Accepted.
🆂🄰🆅🄴 🆂🄳 ☒ 🔋 🖳 ⑪

🅒🅐🅐 ▼▼▼ **Holiday Inn Toronto On King**
(Downtown) 🄻🄷 🐾
(416) 599-4000. **$179-$309.** 370 King St W. Between Spadina Ave and Peter St. Int corridors. **Pets:** Medium, dogs only. $35 one-time fee/room. Designated rooms, service with restrictions, supervision.
🆂🄰🆅🄴 🆂🄳 ☒ 🔋 🖳 ⑪ ⇌ ☒

▼▼▼ **Hotel Le Germain** 🅂🄷
(416) 345-9500. **Call for rates.** 30 Mercer St. Between John St and Blue Jays Way. Int corridors. **Pets:** Accepted.
☒ 🔋🄼 🖳 ⑪

🅒🅐🅐 ▼▼▼ ▼▼▼ **InterContinental Toronto Yorkville** 🄻🄷 🐾
(416) 960-5200. **$229-$3000.** 220 Bloor St W. Just w of Avenue Rd. Int corridors. **Pets:** Large. $25 daily fee/room, $50 one-time fee/room. Designated rooms, service with restrictions.
🆂🄰🆅🄴 🆂🄳 ☒ 🔋 🖳 ⑪ ⇌ ☒

🅒🅐🅐 ▼▼▼ ▼▼▼ **Le Royal Meridien King Edward**
Hotel 🄻🄷 🐾
(416) 863-9700. **$425.** 37 King St E. Just e of Yonge St. Int corridors. **Pets:** Other species. Service with restrictions, supervision.
🆂🄰🆅🄴 ☒ 🔋 ⑪

🅒🅐🅐 ▼▼▼▼ **Metropolitan Hotel** 🄻🄷
(416) 977-5000. **$155-$255.** 108 Chestnut St. Just s of Dundas St. Int corridors. **Pets:** Accepted.
🆂🄰🆅🄴 🆂🄳 ☒ 🔋 🖳 ⑪ ⇌ ☒

▼▼▼ **Montecassino Hotel & Suites** 🅂🄷
(416) 630-8100. **$105-$145.** 3710 Chesswood Dr. At Sheppard Ave. Int corridors. **Pets:** Accepted.
🄰🆂🄺 🆂🄳 ☒ 🔋 🖳

🅒🅐🅐 ▼▼▼▼ **Novotel Toronto Centre** 🄻🄷 🐾
(416) 367-8900. **$155-$335.** 45 The Esplanade. Just ne of Gardiner Expwy via Yonge St. Int corridors. **Pets:** Other species. Designated rooms, service with restrictions, supervision.
🆂🄰🆅🄴 🆂🄳 ☒ 🔋 🖳 ⑪ ⇌ ☒

🅒🅐🅐 ▼▼▼▼ **Novotel Toronto North York** 🄻🄷
(416) 733-2929. **$295-$335.** 3 Park Home Ave. Hwy 401, exit Yonge St, 0.6 mi (1 km) n, then just w. Int corridors. **Pets:** Accepted.
🆂🄰🆅🄴 🆂🄳 ☒ 🔋 🖳 ⑪ ⇌

🅒🅐🅐 ▼▼▼▼ **Pantages Suites Hotel and Spa** 🅂🄷 🐾
(416) 362-1777. **$179-$440.** 200 Victoria St. Jct Shuter. Int corridors. **Pets:** Medium. $25 daily fee/room, $75 one-time fee/room. Service with restrictions, supervision.
🆂🄰🆅🄴 🆂🄳 ☒ 🔋 🖳 ⑪

🅒🅐🅐 ▼▼▼ **Quality Hotel & Suites Toronto Airport East** 🅂🄷
(416) 240-9090. **$112-$185.** 2180 Islington Ave. Hwy 401, exit 356. Int corridors. **Pets:** Accepted.
🆂🄰🆅🄴 🆂🄳 ☒ 🔋 🖳 ⑪

🅒🅐🅐 ▼▼▼▼ **Quality Suites Toronto Airport** 🄻🄷
(416) 674-8442. **$164-$187.** 262 Carlingview Dr. 0.6 mi (1 km) w of jct Hwy 27 N and Dixon Rd. Int corridors. **Pets:** Other species. Service with restrictions, supervision.
🆂🄰🆅🄴 🆂🄳 ☒ 🔋 🖳 ⑪

🅒🅐🅐 ▼▼▼▼ **Radisson Hotel Toronto East** 🄻🄷
(416) 493-7000. **$149-$275.** 55 Hallcrown Pl. Hwy 401, exit Victoria Park N to Consumers Rd, then w. Int corridors. **Pets:** Very small. Designated rooms, service with restrictions, supervision.
🆂🄰🆅🄴 🆂🄳 ☒ 🔋🄼 🔋 🖳 ⑪ ⇌

🅒🅐🅐 ▼▼▼▼ **Radisson Suite Hotel Toronto Airport** 🄻🄷
(416) 242-7400. **$129-$189.** 640 Dixon Rd. Just e of jct Hwy 27; just w of jct Hwy 401. Int corridors. **Pets:** Accepted.
🆂🄰🆅🄴 🆂🄳 ☒ 🖳 ⑪

🅒🅐🅐 ▼▼▼ ▼▼▼ **Renaissance Toronto Airport Hotel and**
Conference Centre 🄻🄷
(416) 675-6100. **$253-$273.** 801 Dixon Rd. Jct Hwy 27 N and Dixon Rd. Int corridors. **Pets:** Accepted.
🆂🄰🆅🄴 🆂🄳 ☒ 🔋🄼 🔋 🖳 ⑪ ⇌

🅒🅐🅐 ▼▼▼ ▼▼▼ **Renaissance Toronto Hotel Downtown** 🄻🄷
(416) 341-7100. **$259-$289.** 1 Blue Jays Way. Jct Front St. Int corridors. **Pets:** Medium, dogs only. $50 one-time fee/room. Service with restrictions, supervision.
🆂🄰🆅🄴 🆂🄳 ☒ 🔋 🖳 ⑪ ⇌ ☒

▼▼▼ **Residence Inn by Marriott Downtown Toronto/**
Entertainment District 🅂🄷
(416) 581-1800. **$199-$349.** 255 Wellington St. Jct of Blue Jays Way. Int corridors. **Pets:** Accepted.
🄰🆂🄺 🆂🄳 ☒ 🔋 🖳 ⇌

▼▼▼ **Residence Inn by Marriott Toronto Airport** 🅂🄷
(416) 798-2900. **$242-$262.** 17 Reading Ct. Just w of jct Hwy 27 and Dixon Rd. Int corridors. **Pets:** Accepted.
🄰🆂🄺 🆂🄳 ☒ 🔋🄼 🔋 🖳 ⇌ ☒

🅒🅐🅐 ▼▼▼ ▼▼▼ **The Sheraton Centre Toronto**
Hotel 🄻🄷 🐾
(416) 361-1000. **$350-$459.** 123 Queen St W. Opposite Toronto Civic Centre and City Hall. Int corridors. **Pets:** Medium, dogs only. Service with restrictions, crate.
🆂🄰🆅🄴 ☒ 🔋🄼 🖳 ⑪ ⇌ ☒

🅒🅐🅐 ▼▼▼ ▼▼▼ **SoHo Metropolitan Hotel** 🅂🄷 🐾
(416) 599-8800. **$420-$850.** 318 Wellington St W. Jct Blue Jays Way. Int corridors. **Pets:** Small. Service with restrictions, crate.
🆂🄰🆅🄴 ☒ 🔋 🖳 ⑪ ⇌ ☒

🅒🅐🅐 ▼▼▼ ▼▼▼ **The Sutton Place Hotel** 🄻🄷
(416) 924-9221. **$168-$515.** 955 Bay St. Jct Wellesley St. Int corridors. **Pets:** Accepted.
🆂🄰🆅🄴 ☒ 🔋 🖳 ⑪ ⇌ ☒

🅒🅐🅐 ▼▼▼ ▼▼▼ **Toronto Airport Marriott Hotel** 🄻🄷
(416) 674-9400. **$286-$306.** 901 Dixon Rd. Corner of Dixon Rd and Carlingview Dr. Int corridors. **Pets:** Accepted.
🆂🄰🆅🄴 🆂🄳 ☒ 🔋🄼 🔋 🖳 ⇌ ☒

🅒🅐🅐 ▼▼▼ ▼▼▼ **Toronto Marriott Bloor Yorkville** 🄻🄷
(416) 961-8000. **$296-$406.** 90 Bloor St E. Just e of Yonge St. Int corridors. **Pets:** $50 one-time fee/room. Service with restrictions, supervision.
🆂🄰🆅🄴 🆂🄳 ☒ 🔋🄼 🔋 🖳 ⑪ ☒

ⓐ ▼▼▼▼ Travelodge Hotel Toronto Airport (Dixon
    Road) **SH**
(416) 674-2222. **$109-$189.** 925 Dixon Rd. Corner of Carlingview Dr
and Dixon Rd. Int corridors. **Pets:** Accepted.
【SAVE】 ⓢ ☒ 目 ▣ 『 ㋡

ⓐ ▼▼▼▼ Travelodge Toronto East **SH**
(416) 299-9500. **$95-$139.** 20 Milner Business Ct. Jct Hwy 401 and
Markham Rd, just n on Markham Rd. Int corridors. **Pets:** Accepted.
【SAVE】 ⓢ ☒ 目 ▣ 『 ㋡

ⓐ ▼▼▼▼ Travelodge Toronto North (North York) **SH** ❖
(416) 663-9500. **Call for rates.** 50 Norfinch Dr. Hwy 400, exit 25 (Finch
Ave E). Int corridors. **Pets:** Other species. Designated rooms.
【SAVE】 ☒ 目 ▣ 『 ㋡

ⓐ ▼▼▼ ▼▼▼ The Westin Bristol Place Toronto
    Airport **LH**
(416) 675-9444. **$370-$390.** 950 Dixon Rd. 0.6 mi (2.6 km) w of jct
Hwy 401. Int corridors. **Pets:** Accepted.
【SAVE】 ⓢ ☒ ▣ 『 ㋡

ⓐ ▼▼▼ ▼▼▼ The Westin Harbour Castle **LH**
(416) 869-1600. **$319-$519.** One Harbour Sq. At the foot of Bay St; on
shore of Lake Ontario. Int corridors. **Pets:** Medium, dogs only. Service
with restrictions, supervision.
【SAVE】 ☒ ▣ 『 ☇ ㋡

ⓐ ▼▼▼ ▼▼▼ The Westin Prince Toronto **LH** ❖
(416) 444-2511. **$139-$359.** 900 York Mills Rd. Just s of Hwy 401 via
Leslie St exit to York Mills Rd E. Int corridors. **Pets:** Small. Designated
rooms, service with restrictions, crate.
【SAVE】 ⓢ ☒ ⓜ 目 ▣ 『 ㋡ ㋡

ⓐ ▼▼▼ ▼▼▼ Windsor Arms Hotel **SH** ❖
(416) 971-9666. **$295.** 18 St. Thomas St. Jct Bloor St. Int corridors.
Pets: Medium. $30 one-time fee/pet. Service with restrictions, supervision.
【SAVE】 ☒ 『 ㋡ ㋡

VAUGHAN

▼▼▼▼ Residence Inn by Marriott Vaughan **SH**
(905) 695-4002. **$183-$203.** 11 Interchange Way. Hwy 400, exit Hwy 7,
directly e. Int corridors. **Pets:** Accepted.
【ASK】 ⓢ ☒ ⓜ 目 ▣ ㋡ ㋡

END METROPOLITAN AREA

TRENTON

▼▼ ▼▼ Comfort Inn **SH**
(613) 965-6660. **$90-$160.** 68 Monogram Pl. Hwy 401, exit 526 (Glen
Miller Rd), just s. Int corridors. **Pets:** Other species. Designated rooms,
service with restrictions, crate.
【ASK】 ⓢ ☒ ⓜ 目 ▣

ⓐ ▼▼▼▼ Holiday Inn Trenton **SH**
(613) 394-4855. **Call for rates.** 99 Glen Miller Rd. Hwy 401, exit 526
(Glen Miller Rd), just s. Int corridors. **Pets:** Accepted.
【SAVE】 ☒ 目 ▣ 『 ㋡

ⓐ ▼▼ ▼ Park Motel **M**
(613) 392-1251. **$80-$156.** 276 Dundas St E. Hwy 2 (Dundas St), just
e of jct Flindall St. Ext corridors. **Pets:** Medium. $10 daily fee/room.
Designated rooms, service with restrictions, supervision.
【SAVE】 目 ▣

TWEED

ⓐ ▼▼ Park Place Motel **M**
(613) 478-3134. **$75-$90, 4 day notice.** 43 Victoria St. Hwy 37, 0.3 mi
(0.5 km) s of centre. Ext corridors. **Pets:** Large. $10 one-time fee/pet.
Designated rooms, service with restrictions, supervision.
【SAVE】 ⓢ ☒ 目

WALLACEBURG

ⓐ ▼▼ ▼ Days Inn Wallaceburg **SH**
(519) 627-0781. **$90-$149.** 76 McNaughton Ave. On Hwy 40
(McNaughton Ave), south side of town. Int corridors. **Pets:** Dogs only.
$10 daily fee/room. Service with restrictions, supervision.
【SAVE】 ⓢ ☒ 目

WATERLOO

ⓐ ▼▼ ▼ Comfort Inn **SH**
(519) 747-9400. **$99-$169.** 190 Weber St N. East side off Weber St;
just s of Hwy 86. Int corridors. **Pets:** Accepted.
【SAVE】 ⓢ ☒ 目 ▣ 『

▼▼ ▼▼ Les Diplomates B&B (Executive Guest House) **BB**
(519) 725-3184. **$116-$156.** 100 Blythwood Rd. Hwy 85 N, exit King St,
s to Columbia, w to Hazel St, then n. Ext/int corridors. **Pets:** Accepted.
【ASK】 ⓢ ☒ 目 ▣

▼▼ ▼▼ The Waterloo Inn & Conference Centre **SH**
(519) 884-0220. **$179-$209.** 475 King St N. 1.9 mi (3 km) n on King St,
jct Hwy 85. Int corridors. **Pets:** Accepted.
☒ 目 ▣ 『 ㋡ ㋡

WAWA

▼ Best Northern **M**
(705) 856-7302. **$60-$95.** 150 Hwy 17 S. Hwy 17, 3.3 mi (5.3 km) s of
jct Hwy 101. Ext corridors. **Pets:** Accepted.
☒ 目 ▣ ㋡ ㋭

ⓐ ▼ The Mystic Isle Motel **M**
(705) 856-1737. **$70-$90.** 153 Hwy 17 S. On Hwy 17, 3.3 mi (5.2 km)
s of jct Hwy 101. Ext corridors. **Pets:** Accepted.
【SAVE】 ⓢ ☒ 目 ▣ ㋡ ㋭

ⓐ ▼ Parkway Motel **M**
(705) 856-7020. **$75-$105.** 232 Hwy 17 S. Hwy 17, 2.5 mi (4 km) s of
jct Hwy 101. Ext corridors. **Pets:** Other species. $10 daily fee/room.
Designated rooms, service with restrictions, supervision.
【SAVE】 ☒ 目 ▣ ㋭

▼ Sportsman's Motel **M**
(705) 856-2272. **$85.** 171 Mission Rd. Hwy 101, 1.5 mi (2.4 km) e of jct
Hwy 17. Ext corridors. **Pets:** Accepted.
☒ 目 ▣ ㋭

ⓐ ▼ Wawa Northern Lights Motel & Chalets **M** ❖
(705) 856-1900. **$79-$109.** 1014 Hwy 17. On Hwy 17, 5 mi (8 km) n of
jct Hwy 101. Ext corridors. **Pets:** Other species. Designated rooms, service with restrictions, supervision.
【SAVE】 ⓢ ☒ 目 ▣ 『 ㋭

WHITBY

ⓐ ▼▼ Canadiana Inn Ⓜ
(905) 668-3686. **$75-$120.** 732 Dundas St E (Hwy 2). Hwy 401, exit 410 (Brock St/Hwy 12), 1 mi (1.6 km) n to Dundas St, then 0.6 mi (1 km) e. Ext corridors. **Pets:** Medium, dogs only. $250 deposit/pet. Service with restrictions, supervision.

SAVE S🐾 ✕ 🖥 💻 🔀

▼▼ Motel 6 Whitby 🆂🅷
(905) 665-8883. **Call for rates.** 165 Consumers Dr. Hwy 401, exit 410 (Brock St/Hwy 12), just ne. Int corridors. **Pets:** Other species. Service with restrictions, supervision.

✕ 🖥

▼▼▼ Quality Suites 🆂🅷
(905) 432-8800. **$119-$219.** 1700 Champlain Ave. Hwy 401, exit 412 (Thickson Rd), 0.3 mi (0.5 km) n to Champlain Ave, then 0.6 mi (1 km) e. Int corridors. **Pets:** Accepted.

A$K S🐾 ✕ 🖥 💻

▼▼▼ Residence Inn by Marriott 🆂🅷
(905) 444-9756. **$153-$175.** 160 Consumers Dr. Hwy 401, exit 410 (Brock St/Hwy 12). Int corridors. **Pets:** Accepted.

A$K S🐾 ✕ 🅼 🖥 💻 🔀

WIARTON

ⓐ ▼▼ Glen Miller Motel Ⓜ ❁
(519) 534-0175. **$70-$110.** 143 Hwy 6. 1.6 mi (2.5 km) n of town; centre. Ext corridors. **Pets:** $10 daily fee/pet. Designated rooms, service with restrictions, supervision.

SAVE ✕ 🖥 💻 🔀

WINDSOR

▼▼ Comfort Inn 🆂🅷
(519) 972-1331. **$99-$169, 14 day notice.** 2765 Huron Church Rd. West side of Huron Church Rd; 0.5 mi (0.8 km) s of EC Row Expwy. Int corridors. **Pets:** Accepted.

A$K S🐾 ✕ 🖥 💻 🔀

▼▼ Comfort Inn 🆂🅷
(519) 966-7800. **Call for rates.** 2955 Dougall Ave. 3.3 mi (5.3 km) s on Hwy 3B, off Hwy 401 via Detroit-Windsor Tunnel exit. Int corridors. **Pets:** Accepted.

✕ 🖥 💻

▼▼▼ Hampton Inn and Suites 🆂🅷
(519) 972-0770. **$119-$179.** 1840 Huron Church Rd. 0.9 mi (1.5 km) n of EC Row Expwy. Int corridors. **Pets:** Accepted.

A$K S🐾 ✕ 🅼 🖥 💻 🔀

ⓐ ▼▼▼ Hilton Windsor 🅻🅷
(519) 973-5555. **$199-$299.** 277 Riverside Dr W. 0.6 mi (1 km) w of Detroit-Windsor Tunnel; 0.6 mi (1 km) e of Ambassador Bridge; downtown. Int corridors. **Pets:** Accepted.

SAVE S🐾 ✕ 💻 🍴 🔀

ⓐ ▼▼▼▼ Holiday Inn Select Windsor (Ambassador Bridge) 🅻🅷 🐾
(519) 966-1200. **$135-$169.** 1855 Huron Church Rd. Jct Huron Church and Malden rds; 0.9 mi (1.5 km) n of EC Row Expwy. Int corridors. **Pets:** Medium. Service with restrictions, crate.

SAVE S🐾 ✕ 🖥 💻 🍴 🔀

ⓐ ▼▼▼ Ivy Rose Motor Inn Ltd. Ⓜ
(519) 966-1700. **$74-$99.** 2885 Howard Ave. 3 mi (4.8 km) s of downtown; just n of Devonshire Shopping Mall. Ext corridors. **Pets:** Accepted.

SAVE S🐾 ✕ 🖥 🍴 🔀

ⓐ ▼▼▼ Quality Suites Windsor 🆂🅷 🐾
(519) 977-9707. **$119-$199.** 250 Dougall Ave. Jct McDougall Ave and Chatham St; downtown. Int corridors. **Pets:** Service with restrictions, supervision.

SAVE S🐾 ✕ 🅼 🖥 💻

ⓐ ▼▼▼▼ Radisson Riverfront Hotel 🅻🅷
(519) 977-1100. **$142-$199.** 333 Riverside Dr W. 0.6 mi (1 km) w of Detroit-Windsor Tunnel; 0.6 mi (1 km) e of Ambassador Bridge; downtown. Int corridors. **Pets:** Accepted.

SAVE S🐾 ✕ 🖥 💻 🍴 🔀

▼▼▼ Stonecroft Inn 🆂🅷
(519) 969-7600. **$85-$95.** 3032 Dougall Ave. 0.3 mi (0.5 km) s of EC Row Expwy. Int corridors. **Pets:** Accepted.

A$K S🐾 ✕ 🖥 💻 🍴

ⓐ ▼▼▼ Travelodge Windsor Ambassador Bridge 🆂🅷
(519) 972-1100. **$92-$125.** 2330 Huron Church Rd. N of EC Row Expwy. Int corridors. **Pets:** Medium. Service with restrictions, supervision.

SAVE S🐾 ✕ 🖥 💻 🔀

WOODSTOCK

ⓐ ▼▼▼ Quality Hotel and Suites 🆂🅷
(519) 537-5586. **$89-$269.** 580 Bruin Blvd. Hwy 401, exit 232, just n; w of Hwy 59. Int corridors. **Pets:** Service with restrictions, crate.

SAVE S🐾 ✕ 🖥 💻 🍴 🔀

ⓐ ▼▼ Super 8 Motel 🆂🅷
(519) 421-4588. **Call for rates.** 560 Norwich Ave. Jct Hwy 401 and 59, exit 232, just n. Int corridors. **Pets:** Accepted.

SAVE ✕ 🖥 💻

PRINCE EDWARD ISLAND

CAVENDISH

▼▼ Bay Vista Motor Inn **M**
(902) 963-2225. **$56-$105.** 9517 Cavendish Rd. Jct Rt 13, 2.8 mi (4.8 km) w on Rt 6. Ext corridors. **Pets:** Accepted.

▼▼ Cavendish Bosom Buddies Cottages & Suites **CA**
(902) 963-3449. **$85-$295, 14 day notice.** RR 1. Jct Rt 6 and 13, 0.4 mi (0.7 km) e on Rt 6. Ext corridors. **Pets:** Accepted.

CAA ▼▼▼ Cavendish Maples Cottages **CA**
(902) 963-2818. **$72-$290, 30 day notice.** 73 Avonlea Blvd. Jct Rt 6 and 13, 1.5 mi (2.5 km) w on Rt 6. Ext corridors. **Pets:** Accepted.

CHARLOTTETOWN

CAA ▼▼▼ Best Western Charlottetown **SH** ☆
(902) 892-2461. **$102-$200.** 238 Grafton St. Centre. Int corridors. **Pets:** Designated rooms, service with restrictions, supervision.

CAA ▼▼▼ Comfort Inn **SH** ☆
(902) 566-4424. **$109-$169.** 112 Trans-Canada Hwy 1. Trans-Canada Hwy 1, 2.8 mi (4.5 km) w. Int corridors. **Pets:** Service with restrictions, supervision.

▼▼▼ Delta Prince Edward **LH** ☆
(902) 566-2222. **$119-$324.** 18 Queen St. At Water and Queen sts. Int corridors. **Pets:** Medium. $35 one-time fee/room. Service with restrictions, supervision.

▼▼ Econo Lodge **M**
(902) 368-1110. **Call for rates.** 20 Lower Malpeque Rd. Jct Trans-Canada Hwy 1 and Lower Malpeque Rd, 2.8 mi (4.5 km) w. Ext/int corridors. **Pets:** Accepted.

CAA ▼▼▼▼ Holiday Inn Express Hotel & Suites Charlottetown **SH**
(902) 892-1201. **$99-$319.** 200 Trans-Canada Hwy. On Trans-Canada Hwy 1, 3 mi (5 km) w. Int corridors. **Pets:** Accepted.

▼▼▼ Quality Inn on the Hill **SH**
(902) 894-8572. **$124-$270.** 150 Euston St. Just e of University Ave. Int corridors. **Pets:** Accepted.

CAA ▼▼▼▼ Rodd Charlottetown-A Rodd Signature Hotel **SH**
(902) 894-7371. **$113-$225.** 75 Kent St. Corner of Kent and Pownal sts. Int corridors. **Pets:** Accepted.

▼▼▼ Rodd Confederation Inn & Suites **M**
(902) 892-2481. **$78-$137.** Trans-Canada Hwy 1. On Trans-Canada Hwy 1, 2.5 mi (4 km) w. Ext/int corridors. **Pets:** Accepted.

▼▼ ▼▼ Rodd Royalty Inn & Suites **SH**
(902) 894-8566. **$99-$175.** Intersection Hwy 1 & 2. 2.5 mi (4 km) w on Trans-Canada Hwy 1. Ext/int corridors. **Pets:** Accepted.

CORNWALL

▼▼ Sunny King Motel **M**
(902) 566-2209. **$54-$116, 3 day notice.** Trans-Canada Hwy. On Hwy 1; centre. Ext corridors. **Pets:** Accepted.

MAYFIELD

▼▼ ▼▼ Cavendish Gateway Resort by Clarion Collection **M**
(902) 963-2213. **$99-$199, 3 day notice.** 6596 Rt 13. On Rt 13, 3.6 mi (6 km) w of Cavendish; centre. Ext/int corridors. **Pets:** Accepted.

NORTH RUSTICO

CAA ▼▼ St. Lawrence Motel **M**
(902) 963-2053. **$49-$159, 14 day notice.** 351 Gulf Shore Rd. On RR 2. Ext corridors. **Pets:** Accepted.

RICHMOND

CAA ▼▼▼▼ Caernarvon Cottages & Gardens **CA**
(902) 854-3418. **$115, 30 day notice.** 4697 Hwy 12, RR 1. Jct Hwy 2 and Rt 131, 6 mi (10 km) e. Ext/int corridors. **Pets:** No service, supervision.

ROSENEATH

CAA ▼▼▼▼ Rodd Brudenell River-A Rodd Signature Resort **LH**
(902) 652-2332. **$135-$232, 3 day notice.** Rt 3. Jct Rt 4, 3.3 mi (5.5 km) e. Ext/int corridors. **Pets:** Accepted.

ST. PETERS

▼▼ ▼▼ Greenwich Gate Lodge **M**
(902) 961-3496. **$89-$169.** Rt 2. Jct Rt 2 and 16; centre. Ext corridors. **Pets:** Accepted.

CAA ▼▼▼▼ The Inn at St. Peters **CI**
(902) 961-2135. **$240-$315, 7 day notice.** 1668 Greenwich Rd. Jct Rt 16 and 313, 0.6 mi (1 km) w on Rt 313. Ext corridors. **Pets:** Accepted.

SUMMERSIDE

▼▼ ▼▼ Econo Lodge **SH**
(902) 436-9100. **$90-$155.** 80 All Weather Hwy. Jct Hwy 1A and 2, 3.1 mi (5 km) w on Hwy 2. Int corridors. **Pets:** Accepted.

CAA ▼▼ ▼▼ Quality Inn & Suites **M**
(902) 436-2295. **$89-$199.** 618 Water St. 1 mi (1.6 km) e on Hwy 11. Ext/int corridors. **Pets:** $10 one-time fee/pet. Designated rooms, service with restrictions, supervision.

Ⓐ ◆◆ Slemon Park Hotel & Conference Centre SH
(902) 432-1780. **$92-$115.** 12 Redwood Ave. On Rt 2, 3 mi (5 km) w at Summerside Airport. Int corridors. **Pets:** Accepted.

SAVE S▢ ✕ ⚕M ⊟ ⊡ �ιι

WOODSTOCK

Ⓐ ◆◆ Rodd Mill River Resort SH
(902) 859-3555. **$99-$159, 3 day notice.** Rt 136. On Rt 136, just e of jct Rt 2. Int corridors. **Pets:** Other species. $10 daily fee/room. Supervision.

SAVE S▢ ✕ ⊟ ⊡ ιι ⇌ ✕

QUEBEC

ALMA

▼▼ Comfort Inn SH
(418) 668-9221. $82-$155. 870 ave du Pont S. On Hwy 169; centre of town. Int corridors. Pets: Accepted.
[ASK] [S/o] [X] [fridge] [microwave]

(AA) ▼▼▼ Hotel Universal LH
(418) 668-5261. $69-$182. 1000 boul des Cascades. Centre. Int corridors. Pets: Accepted.
[SAVE] [X] [fridge] [microwave] [restaurant] [X]

BAIE-COMEAU

▼▼ Comfort Inn SH
(418) 589-8252. $117-$131. 745 boul Lafleche. On Rt 138. Int corridors. Pets: $25 one-time fee/room. Designated rooms, service with restrictions, supervision.
[ASK] [S/o] [X] [fridge] [microwave]

▼▼▼▼ Hotel Le Manoir SH
(418) 296-3391. $109. 8 ave Cabot. Rt 138, 2.6 mi (4.4 km) e, follow signs. Int corridors. Pets: Accepted.
[ASK] [X] [microwave] [restaurant] [X]

BAIE-ST-PAUL

(AA) ▼▼▼ Hotel Baie-Saint-Paul SH
(418) 435-3683. $59-$124, 7 day notice. 911 boul Mgr-de-Laval. On Rt 138, 0.3 mi (0.5 km) e of Rt 362. Int corridors. Pets: Other species. $5 daily fee/pet. Service with restrictions, supervision.
[SAVE] [X] [fridge] [microwave] [restaurant] [X]

BERTHIERVILLE

▼▼ Days Inn Berthierville SH
(450) 836-1621. $85-$165, 7 day notice. 760 rue Gadoury. Hwy 40, exit 144. Ext/int corridors. Pets: Accepted.
[ASK] [S/o] [X] [fridge] [microwave]

BROMONT

▼▼ Hotel Le Menhir SH
(450) 534-3790. $98-$195. 125 boul Bromont. Hwy 10, exit 78, 1.6 mi (2.7 km) s. Ext/int corridors. Pets: Accepted.
[ASK] [S/o] [X] [fridge] [microwave] [restaurant] [restaurant]

CARLETON-ST-OMER

▼▼ Hostellerie Baie Bleue M
(418) 364-3355. Call for rates. 482 boul Perron. On Hwy 132. Ext corridors. Pets: Accepted.
[X] [fridge] [microwave] [restaurant] [X] [X]

CHICOUTIMI

▼▼▼▼ Centre de Congres et Hotel La Sagueneenne SH
(418) 545-8326. $118-$144. 250 des Sagueneens. Just w of jct Rt 175 (boul Talbot); in Saguenay sector. Int corridors. Pets: Accepted.
[ASK] [S/o] [X] [microwave] [fridge] [microwave] [restaurant] [restaurant] [X]

▼▼ Comfort Inn SH
(418) 693-8686. $96-$128. 1595 boul Talbot. Jct Rt 170, 1.8 mi (2.8 km) n. Int corridors. Pets: Accepted.
[X] [fridge] [microwave]

COWANSVILLE

▼▼ Days Inn-Cowansville SH
(450) 263-7331. $99-$134. 111 Place Jean-Jacques Bertrand. Hwy 10, exit 68, 9.9 mi (15.9 km) s on Rt 139. Int corridors. Pets: Accepted.
[ASK] [X] [fridge] [microwave] [restaurant]

DRUMMONDVILLE

(AA) ▼▼▼▼ Best Western Hotel Universel SH
(819) 478-4971. $109-$399. 915 rue Hains. Hwy 20, exit 177, just s of boul St-Joseph, then just e. Int corridors. Pets: Service with restrictions, supervision.
[SAVE] [S/o] [X] [fridge] [microwave] [restaurant] [restaurant]

▼▼ Comfort Inn SH
(819) 477-4000. Call for rates. 1055 rue Hains. Hwy 20, exit 177, 0.3 mi (0.5 km) s on boul St-Joseph, then just w. Int corridors. Pets: Accepted.
[X] [fridge] [microwave]

▼▼▼ Quality Suites SH
(819) 472-2700. $110-$220. 2125 rue Canadien. Hwy 20, exit 175, just s. Int corridors. Pets: Accepted.
[ASK] [S/o] [X] [fridge] [microwave] [restaurant]

FORESTVILLE

▼▼ Econo Lodge M
(418) 587-2278. $89-$109. 5 Rt 138 est. On Rt 138; centre. Ext/int corridors. Pets: Accepted.
[ASK] [S/o] [X] [fridge] [microwave] [restaurant]

GATINEAU

(AA) ▼▼▼▼ Clarion Hotel & Conference Center SH
(819) 568-5252. $120-$180. 111 rue Bellehumeur. Hwy 50, exit 139, 1 mi (1.6 km) se on boul Maloney ouest (Hwy 148), then just sw. Int corridors. Pets: Accepted.
[SAVE] [S/o] [X] [fridge] [microwave] [restaurant] [restaurant] [X]

(AA) ▼▼▼ Comfort Inn Gatineau SH
(819) 243-6010. $101-$179. 630 boul La Gappe. Hwy 50, exit 140, 1.3 mi (2.6 km) e. Int corridors. Pets: Other species. $25 one-time fee/room. Designated rooms, service with restrictions, supervision.
[SAVE] [S/o] [X] [microwave]

Four Points by Sheraton & Conference Centre Gatineau-Ottawa LH
(819) 778-6111. **Call for rates.** 35 rue Laurier. Corner of rue Victoria, across from Canadian Museum of Civilization; in Hull sector. Int corridors. **Pets:** Other species. Service with restrictions.

 Holiday Inn Plaza La Chaudiere Gatineau-Ottawa LH
(819) 778-3880. **Call for rates.** 2 rue Montcalm. 0.5 mi (0.8 km) w of Portage Bridge at Rt 148 and rue Montcalm; in Hull sector. Int corridors. **Pets:** Large. $35 one-time fee/room. Designated rooms, service with restrictions, supervision.

GRENVILLE-SUR-LA-ROUGE

Hotel du Lac Carling LH
(450) 533-9211. **Call for rates.** 2255 Rt 327 nord. 3.1 mi (5 km) n. Int corridors. **Pets:** Other species. $25 one-time fee/room. Service with restrictions, crate.

LAC-BROME (KNOWLTON)

Auberge Knowlton CI
(450) 242-6886. **$130.** 286 chemin Knowlton. Corner of Hwy 104 and Rt 243; centre. Int corridors. **Pets:** Accepted.

LA MALBAIE

Fairmont Le Manoir Richelieu LH
(418) 665-3703. **$159-$269.** 181 rue Richelieu. On Rt 362, 2.6 mi (4.1 km) w of jct Rt 138. Int corridors. **Pets:** Medium. $35 one-time fee/pet. Designated rooms, service with restrictions, supervision.

La Pinsonniere CI
(418) 665-4431. **$285-$450, 15 day notice.** 124 rue St-Raphael. Just off Rt 138, follow signs; in Cap-a-L'Aigle sector. Int corridors. **Pets:** Medium. Designated rooms, service with restrictions, supervision.

LA POCATIERE

Motel Le Pocatois M
(418) 856-1688. **$79-$119.** 235 Rt 132. Hwy 20, exit 439, 0.5 mi (0.8 km) s. Ext/int corridors. **Pets:** Accepted.

L'ISLET

Auberge La Paysanne CO
(418) 247-7276. **Call for rates.** 497 des Pionniers est. On Rt 132, 2.6 mi (4.2 km) e, jct Rt 285; centre. Ext corridors. **Pets:** Accepted.

LOUISEVILLE

Gite du Carrefour et Maison historique J.L.L. Hamelin BB
(819) 228-4932. **$60-$80 (no credit cards), 15 day notice.** 11 ave St-Laurent ouest. On Rt 138; Hwy 40, exit 174 westbound; exit 166 eastbound; centre. Int corridors. **Pets:** Accepted.

MONTEBELLO

Fairmont Le Chateau Montebello LH
(819) 423-6341. **$189-$289, 3 day notice.** 392 rue Notre-Dame. On Rt 148. Int corridors. **Pets:** Medium. $35 one-time fee/pet. Designated rooms, service with restrictions, supervision.

MONTMAGNY

Manoir des Erables CI
(418) 248-0100. **$89-$225, 10 day notice.** 220 boul Tache est (Rt 132). Hwy 20, exit 376, 1.4 mi (2.2 km) e on Rt 228, 0.9 mi (1.5 km) e. Ext/int corridors. **Pets:** Accepted.

MONTREAL METROPOLITAN AREA

BROSSARD

Best Western Hotel National SH
(450) 466-6756. **$104-$139.** 7746 boul Taschereau. Rt 134, 0.8 mi (1.3 km) w of Hwy 10, exit boul Taschereau ouest. Int corridors. **Pets:** Accepted.

Comfort Inn SH
(450) 678-9350. **$100-$122.** 7863 boul Taschereau. Rt 134, 0.9 mi (1.5 km) w of Hwy 10, exit boul Taschereau ouest. Int corridors. **Pets:** $25 one-time fee/pet. Designated rooms, service with restrictions, supervision.

DORVAL

 Comfort Inn Dorval SH
(514) 636-3391. **$121-$158.** 340 ave Michel-Jasmin. Hwy 520, exit 2 eastbound; exit 1 westbound, just e along service road to ave Marshall, follow to ave Michel-Jasmin. Int corridors. **Pets:** Accepted.

Hampton Inn & Suites SH
(514) 633-8243. **$150-$190.** 1900 Rt Transcanadienne (Hwy 40). Hwy 40, exit 55, 0.5 mi (0.8 km) e of boul des Sources on south side service road. Int corridors. **Pets:** Accepted.

Hilton Montreal Aeroport LH
(514) 631-2411. **Call for rates.** 12505 boul Cote-de-Liesse. Just n of Hwy 520 on northside service road at airport entrance. Int corridors. **Pets:** Medium, other species. $25 one-time fee/room. Service with restrictions, supervision.

Travelodge Aeroport Montreal-Trudeau Airport SH
(514) 631-4537. **$99-$225, 4 day notice.** 1010 chemin Herron. Hwy 20, exit 54 westbound, just s on boul Fenelon to ave Dumont, follow to chemin Herron; exit 56 eastbound, 1.1 mi (1.7 km) along service road. Int corridors. **Pets:** $100 deposit/room. Designated rooms, service with restrictions, crate.

LAVAL

 Comfort Inn SH
(450) 686-0600. **$105-$122.** 2055 Autoroute des Laurentides. Hwy 15, exit 8 (boul St-Martin), e on boul St-Martin, 0.4 mi (0.7 km) n on boul Le Corbusier, then w on boul Tessier. Int corridors. **Pets:** Medium. Designated rooms, service with restrictions, supervision.

▼▼ ▼▼ **Econo Lodge** 🆂🅷
(450) 681-6411. **$74-$124.** 1981 boul Cure-Labelle. Hwy 15, exit 8 (boul St-Martin) northbound; exit 10 southbound, 1.3 mi (2 km) w on boul St-Martin ouest, then 0.3 mi (0.5 km) n. Ext/int corridors. **Pets:** Accepted.

A$K 🆂♿ ✕ 🛏 ▦ ⚊

🄰🄰 ▼▼▼▼ **Hampton Inn & Suites-Laval** 🆂🅷
(450) 687-0010. **$119-$139.** 1961 boul Cure-Labelle. Hwy 15, exit 8 (boul St-Martin) northbound; exit 10 southbound, 1.4 mi (2.3 km) w on boul St-Martin ouest, then just n. Int corridors. **Pets:** Service with restrictions, supervision.

SAVE 🆂♿ ✕ 🛏 ▦ ⚊

🄰🄰 ▼▼ ▼▼ **Quality Suites Laval** 🆂🅷
(450) 686-6777. **$121-$159.** 2035 Autoroute des Laurentides. Hwy 15, exit 8 (boul St-Martin), 0.4 mi (0.7 km) n on boul Le Corbusier, w on boul Tessier. Int corridors. **Pets:** Medium. Designated rooms, service with restrictions, supervision.

SAVE 🆂♿ ✕ 🛏 ▦

▼▼▼▼ **Sheraton Laval Hotel** 🅻🅷 🐾
(450) 687-2440. **$259-$520.** 2440 Autoroute des Laurentides. Hwy 15, exit 10. Int corridors. **Pets:** Small. Service with restrictions, supervision.

✕ 🛏 ▦ 🍽 ⚊ ✕

MONTREAL

🄰🄰 ▼▼ ▼▼ **All Suite VIP Loft** 🆂🅷
(514) 448-4848. **$80-$117, 3 day notice.** 329 rue Ontario est. Just w of rue St-Denis. Int corridors. **Pets:** Accepted.

SAVE 🆂♿ ✕ 🛏 ▦

🄰🄰 ▼▼▼▼ **All Suite VIP Saint-Jacques** 🆂🅷
(514) 667-5052. **Call for rates.** 10 rue Saint Jacques ouest. Corner of boul St-Laurent. Int corridors. **Pets:** Accepted.

SAVE ✕ 🛏 ▦ 🍽 ⚊

▼▼▼▼ **Candlewood Suites** 🆂🅷
(514) 667-5002. **$119-$400.** 191 boul Rene-Levesque est. Corner of rue Hotel-de-ville. **Pets:** Accepted.

✕ 🛏 ▦

🄰🄰 ▼▼▼▼ **Chateau Versailles Hotel** 🆂🅷 🐾
(514) 933-3611. **$169-$375.** 1659 rue Sherbrooke ouest. Corner rue St-Mathieu. Int corridors. **Pets:** Other species. $20 daily fee/room. Designated rooms, service with restrictions, crate.

SAVE ✕ ▦

🄰🄰 ▼▼▼▼ **Days Hotel** 🅻🅷
(514) 938-4611. **$109-$179.** 1005 rue Guy. Just s of boul Rene-Levesque. Int corridors. **Pets:** Small. $15 daily fee/pet. Service with restrictions.

SAVE 🆂♿ ✕ 🛏 ▦ 🍽 ⚊

🄰🄰 ▼▼▼▼ **Delta Montreal** 🅻🅷 🐾
(514) 286-1986. **$145-$322.** 475 ave President-Kennedy. Corner of rue City Councillors. Int corridors. **Pets:** Medium. $35 one-time fee/room. Designated rooms, service with restrictions, supervision.

SAVE 🆂♿ ✕ 🛏 ▦ 🍽 ⚊ ✕

🄰🄰 ▼▼▼▼ **DoubleTree by Hilton Montreal Centre-Ville** 🅻🅷
(514) 842-8581. **Call for rates.** 505 rue Sherbrooke est. Between rue Berri and St-Hubert. Int corridors. **Pets:** Accepted.

SAVE ✕ ▦ 🍽 ⚊

🄰🄰 ▼▼▼▼ **Embassy Suites Montreal** 🅻🅷
(514) 288-8886. **Call for rates.** 208 rue St-Antoine ouest. Corner of rue St-Francois-Xavier. Int corridors. **Pets:** Accepted.

SAVE ✕ 🛏 ▦ 🍽 ⚊

🄰🄰 ▼▼▼▼ ▼▼▼▼ **Fairmont The Queen Elizabeth** 🅻🅷
(514) 861-3511. **$169-$699.** 900 boul Rene-Levesque ouest. Between rue University and Mansfield. Int corridors. **Pets:** Medium. $35 one-time fee/pet. Designated rooms, service with restrictions, supervision.

SAVE 🆂♿ ✕ ♿🄼 🛏 ▦ 🍽 ⚊ ✕

🄰🄰 ▼▼▼▼ **Four Points by Sheraton Montreal Airport** 🅻🅷
(514) 344-1999. **$119-$250.** 6600 Cote-de-Liesse. Hwy 520, exit 5 eastbound on south side service road; exit westbound to rue Ness, follow signs for rue Hickmore and Hwy 520 E; in St-Laurent sector. Int corridors. **Pets:** Accepted.

SAVE 🆂♿ ✕ 🛏 ▦ 🍽 ⚊ ✕

🄰🄰 ▼▼▼▼ **Four Points by Sheraton Montreal Centre-Ville** 🅻🅷
(514) 842-3961. **$125-$199.** 475 rue Sherbrooke ouest. Between rue Durocher and Aylmer. Int corridors. **Pets:** Other species. Service with restrictions.

SAVE ✕ 🛏 ▦ 🍽

🄰🄰 ▼▼▼▼ ▼▼▼▼ **Hilton Montreal Bonaventure** 🅻🅷
(514) 878-2332. **$159-$329.** 900 rue de la Gauchetiere ouest. Corner of Mansfield and de la Gauchetiere. Int corridors. **Pets:** Small. Designated rooms, service with restrictions, supervision.

SAVE 🆂♿ ✕ ♿🄼 🛏 ▦ 🍽 ⚊

🄰🄰 ▼▼▼▼ **Holiday Inn Express Hotel & Suites Montreal Centre-Ville** 🆂🅷
(514) 448-7100. **$119-$400.** 155 boul Rene-Levesque est. Corner de Bullion. Int corridors. **Pets:** Medium. Designated rooms, service with restrictions, crate.

SAVE ✕ 🛏 ▦

🄰🄰 ▼▼▼▼ **Holiday Inn Montreal-Airport** 🆂🅷
(514) 739-3391. **$104-$169.** 6500 Cote-de-Liesse. Hwy 520, exit 5 eastbound on south side service road; exit westbound to rue Ness, follow signs for rue Hickmore and Hwy 520 E; in St-Laurent sector. Ext/int corridors. **Pets:** Other species. $35 one-time fee/room. Designated rooms, service with restrictions, supervision.

SAVE ✕ ♿🄼 🛏 ▦ 🍽 ⚊ ✕

🄰🄰 ▼▼▼▼ **Holiday Inn Montreal-Midtown** 🆂🅷
(514) 842-6111. **$119-$179.** 420 rue Sherbrooke ouest. Between rue Bleury and City Councillors. Int corridors. **Pets:** Small, other species. $35 one-time fee/room. Service with restrictions, supervision.

SAVE 🆂♿ ✕ 🛏 ▦ 🍽 ⚊ ✕

▼▼▼▼ **Hotel Gault** 🆂🅷
(514) 904-1616. **Call for rates.** 449 rue Ste-Helene. Just s of rue Notre-Dame. Int corridors. **Pets:** Accepted.

✕ 🛏 ▦ 🍽

🄰🄰 ▼▼▼▼ ▼▼▼▼ **Hotel InterContinental Montreal** 🅻🅷
(514) 987-9900. **$169-$249, 14 day notice.** 360 rue St-Antoine ouest. Corner of rue St-Pierre. Int corridors. **Pets:** Small. $35 one-time fee/room. Service with restrictions, supervision.

SAVE 🆂♿ ✕ 🛏 ▦ 🍽 ⚊ ✕

▼▼▼▼ **Hotel Kutuma** 🆂🅷
(514) 844-0111. **$115-$350.** 3708 rue St-Denis. Just s of ave des Pins est. Int corridors. **Pets:** Accepted.

A$K 🆂♿ ✕ 🛏 ▦ 🍽

🄰🄰 ▼▼▼▼ **Hotel La Tour Centre-Ville** 🄲🄾
(514) 866-8861. **$104-$350.** 400 boul Rene-Levesque ouest. Corner of rue de Bleury. Int corridors. **Pets:** Accepted.

SAVE ✕ 🛏 ▦ 🍽 ⚊

▼▼▼▼ **Hotel Le Germain** 🆂🅷
(514) 849-2050. **$230-$295.** 2050 rue Mansfield. Just n of ave President-Kennedy. Int corridors. **Pets:** Accepted.

A$K ✕ 🛏 ▦ 🍽

▼▼▼ ▼▼▼ Hotel Le St-James SH ✿
(514) 841-3111. **$400.** 355 rue St-Jacques ouest. Corner of rue St-Pierre. Int corridors. **Pets:** Service with restrictions, supervision.
ASK SD ✕ ▦ 🍴 ✕

▼▼▼ ▼▼▼ Hotel Omni Mont-Royal LH
(514) 284-1110. **$139-$279.** 1050 rue Sherbrooke ouest. Corner of rue Peel. Int corridors. **Pets:** Accepted.
SAVE SD ✕ ▦ 🍴 ⇌ ✕

▼▼▼ ▼▼▼ Hotel St-Paul SH
(514) 380-2222. **Call for rates.** 355 rue McGill. Corner of rue St-Paul. Int corridors. **Pets:** Accepted.
✕ ▦ 🍴

▼▼ ▼▼ Hotel Terrasse Royale SH
(514) 739-6391. **Call for rates.** 5225 chemin Cote-des-Neiges. Just n of chemin Queen Mary. Int corridors. **Pets:** Accepted.
✕ ▦ ▦ 🍴

▼▼ ▼▼ Hotel Travelodge Montreal Centre SH
(514) 874-9090. **$99-$260.** 50 boul Rene-Levesque ouest. Between rue Clark and St-Urbain. Int corridors. **Pets:** Other species. $10 daily fee/pet. Service with restrictions, crate.
SAVE SD ✕ ▦ ▦ 🍴

▼▼ ▼▼ L'Appartement Hotel CO
(514) 284-3634. **$115-$245.** 455 rue Sherbrooke ouest. Corner of rue Durocher. Int corridors. **Pets:** Designated rooms, service with restrictions, crate.
SAVE SD ✕ ▦ ▦ ⇌

▼▼▼ La Presidence Hotel and Suites CO
(514) 842-9988. **Call for rates.** 505 rue Sherbrooke est. Between rue Berri and St-Hubert. Int corridors. **Pets:** Accepted.
✕ ▦ ▦ 🍴 ⇌

▼▼▼ ▼▼▼ Le Centre Sheraton LH ✿
(514) 878-2000. **$179-$599.** 1201 boul Rene-Levesque ouest. Between rue Drummond and Stanley. Int corridors. **Pets:** Medium. Service with restrictions, supervision.
SAVE ✕ ▦ ▦ 🍴 ⇌ ✕

▼▼▼ ▼▼▼ Le Meridien Versailles-Montreal SH ✿
(514) 933-8111. **$159-$375.** 1808 rue Sherbrooke ouest. Corner of rue St-Mathieu. Int corridors. **Pets:** Other species. $20 daily fee/room. Designated rooms, service with restrictions, crate.
SAVE ✕ ▦ ▦ 🍴

▼▼▼ ▼▼▼ Le Saint-Sulpice Hotel Montreal SH ✿
(514) 288-1000. **$179-$539.** 414 rue St-Sulpice. Just n of rue St-Paul. Int corridors. **Pets:** Medium. $50 one-time fee/pet. Service with restrictions, supervision.
SAVE SD ✕ ▦ ▦ 🍴 ✕

▼▼▼ ▼▼▼ Le Square Phillips Hotel & Suites SH
(514) 393-1193. **$141-$323.** 1193 Place Phillips. Between rue Ste-Catherine and boul Rene-Levesque. Int corridors. **Pets:** Designated rooms, service with restrictions, supervision.
SAVE SD ✕ ▦ ▦ 🍴 ⇌

▼▼▼ ▼▼▼ Loews Hotel Vogue LH
(514) 285-5555. **$199-$499.** 1425 rue de la Montagne. Between rue Ste-Catherine and boul de Maisonneuve. Int corridors. **Pets:** Accepted.
SAVE SD ✕ ▦ ▦ 🍴

▼▼▼ ▼▼▼ Marriott Residence Inn Montreal Airport LH
(514) 336-9333. **$285-$307.** 6500 Place Robert-Joncas. Hwy 40, exit 65 (boul Cavendish), 0.3 mi (0.5 km) w on northside service road, then just n on rue Beaulac. Int corridors. **Pets:** Accepted.
ASK SD ✕ ▦M ▦ ▦ 🍴 ⇌ ✕

▼▼▼ Marriott Residence Inn-Montreal Centre-ville/Downtown SH ✿
(514) 982-6064. **$175-$230.** 2045 rue Peel. Between rue Sherbrooke and boul de Maisonneuve. Int corridors. **Pets:** Medium. $100 one-time fee/room. Service with restrictions, crate.
SAVE SD ✕ ▦ ▦ ⇌

▼▼▼ ▼▼▼ Novotel Montreal LH
(514) 337-3222. **$125-$299.** 2599 boul Alfred-Nobel. Hwy 40, exit 60 (boul Alfred-Nobel); in St-Laurent Technoparc, just s of south side service road; in St-Laurent sector. Int corridors. **Pets:** Large. Service with restrictions, supervision.
ASK SD ✕ ▦ ▦ 🍴 ⇌

▼▼▼ ▼▼▼ Novotel Montreal Centre LH ✿
(514) 861-6000. **$129-$450.** 1180 rue de la Montagne. Between rue Ste-Catherine and boul Rene-Levesque. Int corridors. **Pets:** Other species. Service with restrictions, crate.
SAVE SD ✕ ▦ 🍴

▼▼▼ ▼▼▼ Opus Hotel Montreal SH
(514) 843-6000. **$229.** 10 rue Sherbrooke ouest. Corner of boul St-Laurent. Int corridors. **Pets:** Accepted.
SAVE ✕ ▦ ▦ 🍴

▼▼▼ ▼▼▼ Quality Hotel Dorval SH
(514) 731-7821. **Call for rates.** 7700 Cote-de-Liesse. Hwy 520, exit 4 eastbound on south side service road; exit 4 (Montee-de-Liesse) westbound; in St-Laurent sector. Int corridors. **Pets:** Accepted.
SAVE ✕ ▦ ▦ 🍴 ⇌ ✕

▼▼▼ ▼▼▼ Quality Hotel Downtown Montreal SH ✿
(514) 849-1413. **$99-$400.** 3440 ave du Parc. Between rue Sherbrooke and Milton. Int corridors. **Pets:** $25 daily fee/room. No service, supervision.
SAVE SD ✕ ▦ ▦ 🍴

▼▼▼ Residence Inn by Marriott Montreal Westmount SH
(514) 935-9224. **$139-$271.** 2170 ave Lincoln. Just e of rue Atwater. Int corridors. **Pets:** Other species. $75 one-time fee/room. Service with restrictions.
SAVE ✕ ▦M ▦ ▦ ⇌

▼▼▼ ▼▼▼ The Ritz-Carlton, Montreal LH
(514) 842-4212. **Call for rates.** 1228 rue Sherbrooke ouest. Corner de la Montagne. Int corridors. **Pets:** Accepted.
✕ ▦ 🍴 ✕

▼▼▼ ▼▼▼ Sofitel Montreal SH ✿
(514) 285-9000. **$400-$800.** 1155 rue Sherbrooke ouest. Corner of rue Stanley. Int corridors. **Pets:** Medium. Designated rooms.
SAVE SD ✕ ▦ 🍴 ✕

▼▼▼ ▼▼▼ W Montreal LH ✿
(514) 395-3100. **$189-$709.** 901 Square Victoria. Corner of rue St-Antoine. Int corridors. **Pets:** Medium, other species. $25 daily fee/room, $100 one-time fee/room. Service with restrictions, supervision.
SAVE SD ✕ ▦M ▦ 🍴

▼▼▼ ▼▼▼ XIXe siecle Hotel Montreal SH
(514) 985-0019. **$150-$305.** 262 rue St-Jacques ouest. Between rue St-Jean and St-Pierre. Int corridors. **Pets:** Accepted.
SAVE SD ✕ ▦ 🍴

POINTE-CLAIRE

▼▼ ▼▼ Comfort Inn SH
(514) 697-6210. **$79-$144.** 700 boul St-Jean. Hwy 40, exit 52, just s. Int corridors. **Pets:** Service with restrictions, supervision.
SAVE SD ✕ ▦ ▦

⊕ ▼▼▼ **Quality Suites Montreal Aeroport, Pointe-Claire** SH
(514) 426-5060. **$99-$385.** 6300 Rt Transcanadienne. Hwy 40, exit 52 eastbound, south side service road; westbound, follow signs for boul St-Jean sud and Hwy 40 est to access south side service road. Int corridors. **Pets:** Accepted.

SAVE ⬛ ✖ ⬛ ⬛ ⬛ ⬛

ROSEMERE

▼▼▼ **Hotel Le Rivage** SH
(450) 437-2171. **Call for rates.** 125 boul Cure-Labelle. Hwy 15, exit 14, 2.4 mi (4 km) e. Int corridors. **Pets:** Accepted.

✖ ⬛ ⬛ ⬛ ✖

VAUDREUIL-DORION

⊕ ▼▼▼▼ **Chateau Vaudreuil Suites Hotel** LH
(450) 455-0955. **$159-$195.** 21700 Trans-Canada Hwy 40. Hwy 40, exit 36 westbound; exit 35 eastbound. Int corridors. **Pets:** Accepted.

SAVE ✖ ⬛ ⬛ ⬛ ⬛ ✖

END METROPOLITAN AREA

MONT-TREMBLANT CENTRE DE VILLEGIATURE

⊕ ▼▼▼ ▼▼▼ **Fairmont Tremblant** LH
(819) 681-7000. **$149-$609.** 3045 chemin de la Chapelle. In Mont-Tremblant Resort centre. Int corridors. **Pets:** Small, dogs only. $25 daily fee/room. Supervision.

SAVE ⬛ ✖ ⬛ ⬛ ⬛ ⬛ ✖

⊕ ▼▼▼ **Le Grand Lodge Mont-Tremblant** SH
(819) 425-2734. **$100-$340, 8 day notice.** 2396 rue Labelle. On Rt 327, 0.3 mi (0.4 km) s of Montee Ryan. Int corridors. **Pets:** Accepted.

SAVE ⬛ ✖ ⬛ ⬛ ⬛ ⬛ ✖

⊕ ▼▼▼▼ **Le Westin Resort & Spa, Tremblant** LH
(819) 681-8000. **$165-$629, 30 day notice.** 100 chemin Kandahar. Hwy 117 N, exit 119 (Montee Ryan), 6 mi (10 km) e, follow signs; in Mont-Tremblant Resort centre. Int corridors. **Pets:** Accepted.

SAVE ⬛ ✖ ⬛ ⬛ ⬛ ⬛ ✖

NEW RICHMOND

▼▼▼ **Hotel Le Francis** SH
(418) 392-4485. **Call for rates.** 210 chemin Pardiac. Just s of Rt 132. Ext/int corridors. **Pets:** Accepted.

✖ ⬛ ⬛ ⬛ ⬛ ✖

PERCE

▼ **Au Pic de l'Aurore** CA
(418) 782-2151. **$57-$185.** 1 Rt 132. 1.2 mi (2 km) e from village. Ext corridors. **Pets:** Accepted.

✖ ⬛ ⬛

▼▼▼ **Hotel La Normandie** SH
(418) 782-2112. **$79-$239.** 221 Rt 132 ouest. Centre. Int corridors. **Pets:** Accepted.

✖ ⬛ ⬛ ⬛ ⬛

▼▼▼ **Hotel/Motel Le Mirage** M
(418) 782-5151. **$92-$198.** 288 Rt 132 ouest. On Rt 132. Ext corridors. **Pets:** Accepted.

✖ ⬛ ⬛ ⬛

▼ ▼ **Hotel Motel Manoir de Perce** SH
(418) 782-2022. **$66-$168.** 212 Rt 132. Centre. Ext/int corridors. **Pets:** Accepted.

✖ ⬛ ⬛

QUEBEC METROPOLITAN AREA

BEAUPRE

⊕ ▼▼▼ **Auberge La Camarine** CI
(418) 827-5703. **Call for rates.** 10947 boul Ste-Anne. On Hwy 138, 0.9 mi (1.5 km) w of jct Hwy 360. Int corridors. **Pets:** Accepted.

SAVE ✖ ⬛

⊕ ▼▼▼ **Chateau Mont Sainte-Anne** LH ❦
(418) 827-5211. **$109-$499.** 500 boul du Beau-Pre. Hwy 360, 2.3 mi (3.7 km) ne from jct Hwy 138. Int corridors. **Pets:** Dogs only. $20 daily fee/room. Designated rooms, service with restrictions, supervision.

SAVE ✖ ⬛ ⬛ ⬛ ⬛ ✖

⊕ ▼▼▼ **Hotel Val des Neiges** LH
(418) 827-5711. **$92-$249.** 201 rue Val-des-Neiges. Just off Hwy 360. Int corridors. **Pets:** Accepted.

SAVE ⬛ ✖ ⬛ ⬛ ⬛ ⬛ ✖

BOISCHATEL

⊕ ▼ ▼ **Econo Lodge** SH
(418) 822-4777. **$90-$145, 10 day notice.** 5490 boul Ste-Anne. On Rt 138. Int corridors. **Pets:** Accepted.

SAVE ⬛ ✖ ⬛

L'ANCIENNE-LORETTE

▼ ▼ **Comfort Inn** SH
(418) 872-5900. **$110-$173.** 1255 boul Duplessis. Jct boul Duplessis and Wilfrid-Hamel (Hwy 138). Int corridors. **Pets:** Medium. $25 one-time fee/room. Service with restrictions, supervision.

ASK ⬛ ✖ ⬛ ⬛

LEVIS

▼ ▼ **Comfort Inn** SH
(418) 835-5605. **$100-$175.** 10 du Vallon est. Hwy 20, exit 325S eastbound; exit 325 westbound. Int corridors. **Pets:** Accepted.

ASK ⬛ ✖ ⬛ ⬛

QUEBEC

▼▼▼ **ALT Hotel-Quebec** LH
(418) 658-1224. **$129-$169.** 1200 ave Germain-des-Pres. Just n of boul Laurier; in Ste-Foy sector. Int corridors. **Pets:** Accepted.

✖ ⬛ ⬛

▼ ▼ **Appartements La Pergola** CO
(418) 681-1428. **Call for rates.** 405 boul Rene-Levesque ouest. Between aves Moncton and des Erables. Int corridors. **Pets:** Accepted.

⬛ ⬛

(AAA) ▼▼▼ ▼▼▼ **Auberge Saint-Antoine** SH
(418) 692-2211. **$159-$399.** 8 rue St-Antoine. Corner of rue Dalhousie. Int corridors. **Pets:** Accepted.
SAVE ⊠ 🛏 💻 ⍩

(AAA) ▼▼▼ ▼▼▼ **Chateau Bonne Entente** SH
(418) 653-5221. **$189-$499.** 3400 chemin Ste-Foy. Hwy 540 (Autoroute Duplessis), exit chemin Ste-Foy, just w; in Ste-Foy sector. Int corridors. **Pets:** Medium. $60 one-time fee/room. Service with restrictions, supervision.
SAVE ⊠ ⌷M ⍩ ⇒ ⊠

▼▼ ▼▼ **Comfort Inn** SH 🐾
(418) 666-1226. **$99-$199.** 240 boul Ste-Anne. Hwy 440, exit Francois-de-Laval. Int corridors. **Pets:** Large. $15 one-time fee/room. Designated rooms, service with restrictions, supervision.
ASK ⌷ ⊠ 🛏 💻

▼▼ ▼▼ **Comfort Inn de l'Aeroport-Hamel** SH
(418) 872-5038. **$93-$180.** 7320 boul Wilfrid-Hamel. Hwy 138, 0.9 mi (1.5 km) w of boul Duplessis. Int corridors. **Pets:** Medium, other species. $25 one-time fee/pet. Service with restrictions, supervision.
ASK ⌷ ⊠ 🛏 💻

(AAA) ▼▼▼ ▼▼▼ **Delta Quebec** LH
(418) 647-1717. **$129-$270.** 690 boul Rene-Levesque est. Just w of boul Honore-Mercier. Int corridors. **Pets:** Medium. $35 one-time fee/room. Service with restrictions, supervision.
SAVE ⌷ ⊠ 🛏 💻 ⍩ ⇒ ⊠

(AAA) ▼▼▼ ▼▼▼ **Fairmont Le Chateau Frontenac** LH
(418) 692-3861. **$199-$549.** 1 rue des Carrieres. In Old Quebec. Int corridors. **Pets:** Medium. $35 one-time fee/pet. Designated rooms, service with restrictions, supervision.
SAVE ⌷ ⊠ 🛏 💻 ⍩ ⇒ ⊠

▼▼ ▼▼ **Gite du Vieux-Bourg** BB
(418) 661-0116. **Call for rates.** 492 ave Royale. Hwy 440, exit Francois-de-Laval, just n, then 0.3 mi (0.5 km) e; in Beauport sector. Int corridors. **Pets:** No service, supervision.
⊠ 🛏 💻 ⇒

(AAA) ▼▼▼ ▼▼▼ **Hilton Quebec** LH
(418) 647-2411. **$125-$315.** 1100 boul Rene-Levesque est. Corner of ave Honore-Mercier. Int corridors. **Pets:** Medium. $25 one-time fee/room. Service with restrictions, supervision.
SAVE ⌷ ⊠ 🛏 💻 ⍩ ⇒ ⊠

▼▼ ▼▼ **Hotel Clarion Quebec** LH
(418) 653-4901. **$99-$400.** 3125 boul Hochelaga. Hwy 73, exit 136 (Hochelaga ouest); in Ste-Foy sector. Int corridors. **Pets:** Accepted.
ASK ⌷ ⊠ 🛏 💻 ⍩ ⇒ ⊠

▼▼ ▼▼ **Hotel Gouverneur Quebec-Sainte-Foy** LH
(418) 651-3030. **$171-$239.** 3030 boul Laurier. Corner of rue Lavigerie; in Ste-Foy sector. Ext/int corridors. **Pets:** Accepted.
ASK ⌷ ⊠ 🛏 💻 ⇒

(AAA) ▼▼ ▼▼ **Hotel Quality Suites Quebec** SH
(418) 622-4244. **$115-$210.** 1600 rue Bouvier. Hwy 40, exit 312N (Pierre-Bertrand nord), 1.3 mi (2 km) w of jct Rt 358. Int corridors. **Pets:** Other species. $25 one-time fee/room. Service with restrictions, supervision.
SAVE ⌷ ⊠ 🛏 💻

▼▼ ▼▼ **Hotel Super 8 Quebec Ste-Foy** SH
(418) 877-6888. **Call for rates.** 7286 boul Wilfred Hamel. Hwy 138, 0.7 mi (1.1 km) w of boul Duplessis; in Ste-Foy sector. Int corridors. **Pets:** Accepted.
⊠ 🛏 💻 ⇒ ⊠

(AAA) ▼▼ ▼▼ **Hotel Universel** SH
(418) 653-5250. **$100-$150.** 2300 chemin Ste-Foy. Hwy 73, exit 137, 1.4 mi (2.3 km) e on chemin des Quatre-Bourgeois; in Ste-Foy sector. Ext/int corridors. **Pets:** Small. Designated rooms, service with restrictions, supervision.
SAVE ⌷ ⊠ 🛏 💻 ⍩ ⇒

(AAA) ▼▼ ▼▼ **L'Hotel du Vieux Quebec** SH 🐾
(418) 692-1850. **$94-$294.** 1190 rue St-Jean. Corner of rue de l'Hotel-Dieu. Int corridors. **Pets:** $10 daily fee/room. Designated rooms, service with restrictions, supervision.
SAVE ⊠ 🛏 💻 ⍩

(AAA) ▼▼▼ ▼▼▼ **Loews Le Concorde** LH 🐾
(418) 647-2222. **$119-$359.** 1225 Cours du General-de-Montcalm. Corner of Grande Allee est. Int corridors. **Pets:** $25 deposit/room. Designated rooms, service with restrictions, supervision.
SAVE ⌷ ⊠ 🛏 💻 ⍩ ⇒ ⊠

ST-FERREOL-LES-NEIGES

(AAA) ▼▼ ▼▼ **Chalets Montmorency Condominiums** CO
(418) 826-2600. **$99-$159.** 1768 ave Royale. On Hwy 360. Ext corridors. **Pets:** Accepted.
SAVE ⌷ ⊠ 🛏 💻 ⇒ ⊠

▼▼ ▼▼ **Chalets-Village Mont-Sainte-Anne** CA
(418) 826-3331. **$1800-$6500, 60 day notice.** 1815 boul Les Neiges. On north side of Hwy 360; village centre. Ext corridors. **Pets:** Accepted.
⊠ 🛏 ⊠

STE-FOY

(AAA) ▼▼▼ ▼▼▼ **Hotel Quartier** LH 🐾
(418) 650-1616. **$99-$299.** 2955 boul Laurier. Just e of Hwy 73; in Ste-Foy Sector. Int corridors. **Pets:** $30 daily fee/room. Service with restrictions, supervision.
SAVE ⌷ ⊠ 🛏 💻 ⍩ ⇒

END METROPOLITAN AREA

RIGAUD

▼▼ ▼▼ **Howard Johnson** SH
(450) 458-7997. **Call for rates (no credit cards).** 93 Rt 201. Hwy 40, exit 17, then just ne. Int corridors. **Pets:** Accepted.
⊠ 🛏 💻 ⍩

RIMOUSKI

▼▼ ▼▼ **Comfort Inn** SH
(418) 724-2500. **$115-$155.** 455 boul St-Germain ouest. On Rt 132. Int corridors. **Pets:** $25 daily fee/room. Service with restrictions, supervision.
ASK ⌷ ⊠ 🛏 💻

▼▼ ▼▼ **Hotel Rimouski** LH
(418) 725-5000. **$115-$145, 15 day notice.** 225 boul Rene-Lepage est. On Rt 132, corner of rue Julien-Rehel. Int corridors. **Pets:** Accepted.
ASK ⊠ 🛏 💻 ⍩ ⇒ ⊠

RIVIERA-DU-LOUP

▼▼ ▼▼ **Comfort Inn** SH 🐾
(418) 867-4162. **$100-$180.** 85 boul Cartier. Hwy 20, exit 507, just se; Hwy 85, exit 96 (Fraserville); follow signs. Int corridors. **Pets:** Other species. $25 one-time fee/room. Service with restrictions, supervision.
ASK ⌷ ⊠ 🛏 💻

(AA) ▼▼▼▼ Days Inn Riviere-du-Loup SH
(418) 862-6354. **Call for rates.** 182 rue Fraser. Hwy 20, exit 503, 0.6 mi (1 km) e on Rt 132. Ext corridors. **Pets:** Accepted.

[SAVE] [✕] [🛏] [📖]

ROBERVAL

(AA) ▼▼▼▼ Hotel Chateau Roberval LH
(418) 275-7511. **Call for rates.** 1225 boul Marcotte. On Hwy 169; centre. Int corridors. **Pets:** Medium, dogs only. Service with restrictions, supervision.

[SAVE] [✕] [🛏] [🛎] [📖] [🍴] [🏊] [✕]

ROUYN-NORANDA

▼▼▼▼ Comfort Inn SH
(819) 797-1313. **$102-$115.** 1295 rue Lariviere. On Rt 117, 2.5 mi (4 km) s from town centre. Int corridors. **Pets:** Accepted.

[A$K] [S🐾] [✕] [🛏] [📖]

SHAWINIGAN

(AA) ▼▼▼ Auberge Escapade Inn SH
(819) 539-6911. **$88-$165.** 3383 rue Garnier. Hwy 55, exit 217, then 0.3 mi (0.5 km) n on Rt 351. Ext/int corridors. **Pets:** Accepted.

[SAVE] [✕] [🛏] [🍴]

(AA) ▼▼▼▼ Auberge Gouverneur & Centre de Congres Shawinigan SH
(819) 537-6000. **$103-$148.** 1100 Promenade-du-St-Maurice. Hwy 55 N, exit 211, 2.8 mi (4.4 km) n on Hwy 153, follow signs. Int corridors. **Pets:** Accepted.

[SAVE] [S🐾] [✕] [🛏] [📖] [🍴] [🏊] [✕]

▼▼▼▼ Comfort Inn & Suites SH
(819) 536-2000. **$72-$145.** 500 boul du Capitaine. Hwy 55 N, exit 211, 2.8 mi (4.4 km) n on Hwy 153, then 1.3 mi (2 km) s on Rt 157. Int corridors. **Pets:** Accepted.

[A$K] [S🐾] [✕] [🛏] [📖]

SHERBROOKE

(AA) ▼▼▼▼ Delta Sherbrooke Hotel and Conference Centre LH 🐾
(819) 822-1989. **$139-$279.** 2685 rue King ouest. Hwy 410, exit 4E, 0.6 mi (1 km) e on Rt 112. Int corridors. **Pets:** Large. $35 one-time fee/room.

[SAVE] [✕] [🛏] [📖] [🍴] [🏊] [✕]

ST-ANTOINE-DE-TILLY

▼▼▼ Manoir de Tilly CI
(418) 886-2407. **Call for rates.** 3854 chemin de Tilly. Jct Hwy 20, exit 291, 5.3 mi (8.5 km) n on Rt 273; centre. Int corridors. **Pets:** Accepted.

[✕] [🍴]

ST-FAUSTIN-LAC-CARRE

▼ Motel sur la Colline M
(819) 688-2102. **Call for rates.** 357 Rt 117. On Rt 117, 2.5 mi (4 km) n of exit for city. Ext/int corridors. **Pets:** Accepted.

[✕] [🛏] [📖] [🏊]

ST-HONORE-DE-TEMISCOUATA

▼ Motel Jasper M
(418) 497-2322. **$58-$72.** 657 Rt 185. On Rt 185. Ext corridors. **Pets:** Small. Service with restrictions, supervision.

[S🐾] [✕] [🛏] [🍴]

ST-HYACINTHE

▼▼▼▼ Hotel des Seigneurs Saint-Hyacinthe LH
(450) 774-3810. **$188-$240.** 1200 rue Johnson. Hwy 20, exit 130S, just e on rue Gauvin from boul Laframboise. Int corridors. **Pets:** Accepted.

[A$K] [S🐾] [✕] [🛏] [📖] [🍴] [🏊] [✕]

ST-JEAN-PORT-JOLI

▼▼▼ Auberge du Faubourg M
(418) 598-6455. **$99-$220, 10 day notice.** 280 ave de Gaspe ouest (Rt 132). 1.4 mi (2.4 km) w on Rt 132 from jct Rt 204; Hwy 20, exit 414. Ext corridors. **Pets:** Accepted.

[A$K] [✕] [🛏] [📖] [🍴] [🏊] [✕] [🐾]

ST-JEAN-SUR-RICHELIEU

▼▼▼ Comfort Inn SH
(450) 359-4466. **$109-$149.** 700 rue Gadbois. Hwy 35, exit 9, e on rue Pierre-Caisse. Int corridors. **Pets:** Accepted.

[A$K] [S🐾] [✕] [🛏] [🏊]

ST-LIBOIRE

▼▼▼ Econo Lodge SH
(450) 793-4444. **Call for rates.** 110 Rang Charlotte. Hwy 20, exit 147, just s. Int corridors. **Pets:** Accepted.

[✕] [🛏] [📖] [🍴] [🏊]

STE-AGATHE-DES-MONTS

(AA) ▼▼▼▼ Super 8 Hotel SH
(819) 324-8880. **$88-$149.** 500 rue Leonard St. Hwy 15, exit 86, just w on Rt 117 to rue Leonard, then 0.3 mi (0.5 km) s. Int corridors. **Pets:** Medium. $15 daily fee/pet. Designated rooms, service with restrictions, supervision.

[SAVE] [S🐾] [✕] [🛏] [📖] [🏊] [✕]

STE-ANNE-DE--BEAUPRE

(AA) ▼▼▼ Manoir Ste-Anne M
(418) 827-8383. **$65-$125.** 9776 boul Ste-Anne. On Hwy 138. Ext corridors. **Pets:** Accepted.

[SAVE] [S🐾] [✕] [🛏] [📖]

STE-MARTHE

▼▼▼▼ Auberge des Gallant CI
(450) 459-4241. **$175-$225, 7 day notice.** 1171 chemin St-Henri. 5.3 mi (8.5 km) w on chemin St-Henri from Hwy 201. Int corridors. **Pets:** Accepted.

[✕] [📖] [🍴] [🏊] [✕]

THETFORD MINES

▼▼ Comfort Inn SH
(418) 338-0171. **$128-$138.** 123 boul Frontenac ouest. On Rt 112. Int corridors. **Pets:** Accepted.

[A$K] [S🐾] [✕] [🛏] [📖]

TROIS-RIVIERES

▼▼ Comfort Inn SH
(819) 371-3566. **$89-$108.** 6255 rue Corbeil. Hwy 55, exit 183 (boul Jean XXIII); 1.3 mi (2 km) n of Laviolette Bridge, then 0.3 mi (0.5 km) e. Int corridors. **Pets:** Accepted.

[✕] [🛏] [📖]

(AA) ▼▼▼ Days Inn SH
(819) 377-4444. **Call for rates.** 3155 boul Saint-Jean. Hwy 55, exit 183 (boul Jean XXIII), 0.3 mi (0.5 km) w, then 0.3 mi (0.4 km) n. Int corridors. **Pets:** Accepted.

[SAVE] [✕] [🛏] [📖]

(CAA) ▼▼▼▼ **Delta Trois-Rivieres Hotel and Conference Center** [LH] ❀
(819) 376-1991. **$102-$250.** 1620 rue Notre-Dame Centre. Corner of rue St-Roch; centre. Int corridors. **Pets:** $35 one-time fee/room. Service with restrictions, supervision.
[SAVE] [✕] [�] [▼] [🛏] [⏵⏴] [✕]

(CAA) ▼▼▼ **Hotel Du Roy Trois-Rivieres** [SH]
(819) 379-3232. **Call for rates.** 3600 boul Gene H Kruger. On Rt 138, 1.3 mi (2 km) e of Pont Laviolette and jct Hwy 55. Ext/int corridors. **Pets:** Accepted.
[SAVE] [✕] [🔒] [▼] [🛏] [⏵⏴]

(CAA) ▼▼▼▼ **Super 8 Hotel Trois-Rivieres** [SH]
(819) 377-5881. **$109-$139.** 3185 boul St-Jean. Hwy 55, exit 183 (boul Jean XXIII), then just nw. Int corridors. **Pets:** Small. $15 daily fee/pet. Designated rooms, service with restrictions, supervision.
[SAVE] [🔒] [✕] [🔒] [▼] [⏵⏴] [✕]

VAL-D'OR

▼▼▼ **Comfort Inn** [SH]
(819) 825-9360. **Call for rates.** 1665 3ieme Ave. In town centre. Int corridors. **Pets:** Accepted.
[✕] [🔒] [▼]

▼▼ **Hotel Forestel** [LH]
(819) 825-5660. **Call for rates.** 1001 3ieme ave est. On Rt 117. Int corridors. **Pets:** Accepted.
[✕] [🔒] [▼] [🛏]

▼▼▼ **Motel L'Escale Hotel Suite** [SH]
(819) 824-2711. **Call for rates.** 1100 rue L'Escale. In town centre. Ext/int corridors. **Pets:** Accepted.
[✕] [🔒] [▼] [🛏]

WENTWORTH-NORD

(CAA) ▼▼▼ **Domaine de L'Etang** [BB]
(450) 533-6571. **$90-$125, 22 day notice.** 1045 chemin du Lac Louisa. 2.2 mi (3.7 km) e on chemin St-Michel from Hwy 327 N, then 1.6 mi (2.7 km) s. **Pets:** Designated rooms, no service, crate.
[SAVE] [✕] [🔒] [⏵⏴] [✕] [🐾] [🖊]

SASKATCHEWAN

CARONPORT

▼▼ The Pilgrim Inn SH
(306) 756-5002. **$70-$80.** Hwy 1 W. Jct Main Access; on Trans-Canada Hwy 1. Int corridors. **Pets:** Accepted.

(ASK) ⊠ ▤ 🖥

ESTEVAN

◎ ▼▼▼▼ Perfect Inns & Suites SH
(306) 634-8585. **$83-$110.** 134 2nd Ave. Just n of jct Hwy 39 E and 2nd Ave. Int corridors. **Pets:** Accepted.

(SAVE) ⊠ ▤ 🖥

KINDERSLEY

◎ ▼▼▼ Best Western Westridge Inn SH
(306) 463-4687. **Call for rates.** 100 12th Ave NW. Jct of Hwy 7 and 21. Ext/int corridors. **Pets:** Accepted.

(SAVE) ⊠ ▤ 🖥 🍴

MOOSE JAW

▼▼ Comfort Inn SH
(306) 692-2100. **Call for rates.** 155 Thatcher Dr W. Just w of jct Main St. Int corridors. **Pets:** Medium. $15 one-time fee/pet. Designated rooms, service with restrictions, supervision.

⊠ ▤ 🖥

▼▼▼ Days Inn SH
(306) 691-5777. **$101-$130.** 1720 Main St N. From jct Trans-Canada Hwy 1, just s. Int corridors. **Pets:** Accepted.

(ASK) ⊠ ▤ 🖥 ➳ 🐾

▼▼▼ Heritage Inn SH
(306) 693-7550. **Call for rates.** 1590 Main St N. 0.9 mi (1.5 km) s of jct Trans-Canada Hwy 1 and 2; access from Hwy 2 via Thatcher Dr. Int corridors. **Pets:** Accepted.

⊠ ▤ 🖥 🍴 ➳

◎ ▼▼▼ Prairie Oasis Motel M
(306) 692-4894. **$80-$84.** 955 Thatcher Dr E. Just s of jct Trans-Canada Hwy 1 and Thatcher Dr E. Ext corridors. **Pets:** Dogs only. Designated rooms, service with restrictions.

(SAVE) ⊠ ▤ 🖥 ➳ 🐾

▼▼ Super 8 Motel-Moose Jaw M
(306) 692-8888. **$99.** 1706 Main St N. 0.9 mi (1.5 km) s of jct Trans-Canada Hwy 1; access from Hwy 2 via Thatcher Dr. Int corridors. **Pets:** Accepted.

⊠ 🔥M ▤ 🖥

NORTH BATTLEFORD

▼ Super 8 Motel SH
(306) 446-8888. **$80-$100.** 1006 Hwy 16 Bypass. 0.3 mi (0.5 km) nw of jct Hwy 16. Int corridors. **Pets:** Accepted.

(ASK) 🔥ö ⊠ ▤

▼▼ Tropical Inn SH
(306) 446-4700. **Call for rates.** 1001 Hwy 16 Bypass. Corner of Battleford Rd and Hwy 16 Bypass. Int corridors. **Pets:** Accepted.

⊠ ▤ 🖥 🍴 ➳ 🐾

PRINCE ALBERT

▼▼ Comfort Inn SH
(306) 763-4466. **$109.** 3863 2nd Ave W. 1.4 mi (2.3 km) s at jct Hwy 2 and Marquis Rd. Int corridors. **Pets:** Accepted.

(ASK) 🔥ö ⊠ ▤ 🖥

▼▼ Super 8 SH
(306) 953-0088. **$87-$97.** 4444 2nd Ave W. Just s of jct Hwy 2 and Marquis Rd. Int corridors. **Pets:** Accepted.

(ASK) 🔥ö ⊠ ▤ 🖥

▼▼ Travelodge Prince Albert SH
(306) 764-6441. **Call for rates.** 3551 2nd Ave W. 1.4 mi (2.2 km) s at jct Hwy 2 and Marquis Rd. Ext/int corridors. **Pets:** Accepted.

⊠ ▤ 🖥 🍴

REGINA

◎ ▼▼ Best Western Seven Oaks Inn SH
(306) 757-0121. **Call for rates.** 777 Albert St. Jct 2nd Ave. Int corridors. **Pets:** Accepted.

(SAVE) ⊠ ▤ 🖥 🍴 ➳ 🐾

◎ ▼▼ Comfort Inn SH
(306) 789-5522. **$115-$122.** 3221 E Eastgate Dr. Trans-Canada Hwy 1, 1.3 mi (2 km) e of Ring Rd; at eastern approach to city. Int corridors. **Pets:** Accepted.

(SAVE) ⊠ ▤ 🖥

▼▼ Country Inn & Suites By Carlson SH
(306) 789-9117. **Call for rates.** 3321 Eastgate Bay. Trans-Canada Hwy 1, 1.3 mi (2 km) e of Ring Rd; at eastern approach to city. Int corridors. **Pets:** Accepted.

⊠ 🔥M ▤ 🖥

▼▼▼ Delta Regina LH
(306) 525-5255. **$165-$230.** 1919 Saskatchewan Dr. At Rose St; centre. Int corridors. **Pets:** Other species. $35 one-time fee/room. Designated rooms, service with restrictions, crate.

⊠ ▤ 🖥 🍴 ➳ 🐾

◎ ▼▼▼▼ Holiday Inn Express Hotel & Suites Regina SH
(306) 569-4600. **$130.** 1907 11th Ave. Corner of Rose St; centre of downtown. Int corridors. **Pets:** Accepted.

(SAVE) 🔥ö ⊠ ▤ 🖥 🍴

▼▼▼ Holiday Inn Hotel & Suites SH
(306) 789-3883. **$115-$185.** 1800 Prince of Wales Dr. From jct Trans-Canada Hwy 1, just n; at eastern approach to city. Int corridors. **Pets:** Accepted.

(ASK) ⊠ ▤ 🖥 🍴 ➳ 🐾

◎ ▼▼▼ Howard Johnson Inn SH
(306) 565-0455. **$100-$130.** 1110 Victoria Ave E. Trans-Canada Hwy 1, just w of Ring Rd; at eastern approach to city. Int corridors. **Pets:** Accepted.

(SAVE) ⊠ ▤ 🖥 ➳

▼▼▼ Quality Hotel SH
(306) 569-4656. **$109-$149.** 1717 Victoria Ave. Just e of Broad St; downtown. Int corridors. **Pets:** Accepted.

(ASK) 🔥ö ⊠ ▤ 🖥 🍴

◆◆ ▼▼▼ ▼▼▼ **Radisson Plaza Hotel Saskatchewan** 🄻🄷
(306) 522-7691. **$135-$178.** 2125 Victoria Ave. Victoria Ave at Scarth
St; centre. Int corridors. **Pets:** Accepted.
[SAVE] [S🐾] [✕] [🕭M] [🛏] [💻] [🍽] [✕]

▼ ▼ **Ramada Hotel & Convention Centre** 🄻🄷
(306) 569-1666. **Call for rates.** 1818 Victoria Ave. Victoria Ave and
Broad St; centre of downtown. Int corridors. **Pets:** Accepted.
[✕] [🛏] [💻] [🍽] [🌊] [✕]

◆◆ ▼▼▼ ▼▼▼ **Regina Inn Hotel & Conference Centre** 🄻🄷
(306) 525-6767. **$119-$195.** 1975 Broad St. Jct Victoria Ave; centre of
downtown. Int corridors. **Pets:** Large. $35 one-time fee/room. Service with
restrictions.
[SAVE] [S🐾] [✕] [🛏] [💻] [🍽]

▼ **Regina Super 8** 🅂🄷
(306) 789-8833. **Call for rates.** 2730 Victoria Ave E. Trans-Canada
Hwy 1, 1 mi (1.6 km) e of Ring Rd; at eastern approach to city. Int
corridors. **Pets:** Accepted.
[✕] [🕭M] [🛏] [💻]

▼▼ ▼▼ **Sandman Hotel Suites and Spa** 🅂🄷
(306) 757-2444. **Call for rates.** 1800 Victoria Ave E. Just e of Ring Rd;
at eastern approach to city. Int corridors. **Pets:** Accepted.
[✕] [🛏] [💻] [🍽] [🌊]

SASKATOON

◆◆ ▼▼ **Best Western Inn & Suites** 🅂🄷
(306) 244-5552. **$120-$160.** 1715 Idylwyld Dr N. 1.6 mi (2.6 km) n on
Hwy 11 (Idylwyld Dr). Ext/int corridors. **Pets:** Accepted.
[SAVE] [S🐾] [✕] [🛏] [💻] [🍽]

◆◆ ▼▼ **Colonial Square Motel & Suites** 🅂🄷
(306) 343-1676. **$99-$109.** 1301 8th St E. Just w of Cumberland Ave.
Ext/int corridors. **Pets:** Accepted.
[SAVE] [S🐾] [✕] [🛏] [💻]

▼▼ ▼▼ **Comfort Inn** 🅂🄷
(306) 934-1122. **$109, 7 day notice.** 2155 Northridge Dr. 1.9 mi (3 km)
n; just ne of jct Hwy 11 (Idylwyld Dr) and Circle Dr. Int corridors.
Pets: Accepted.
[A$K] [S🐾] [✕] [🕭M] [🛏] [💻]

▼▼ ▼▼ **Country Inn & Suites By Carlson** 🅂🄷 🐾
(306) 934-3900. **$97-$100.** 617 Cynthia St. Just w of jct Hwy 11 (Idylwyld Dr) and Circle Dr. Int corridors. **Pets:** $20 one-time fee/room.
Service with restrictions, crate.
[A$K] [S🐾] [✕] [🕭M] [🛏] [💻]

▼▼▼▼ ▼ **Delta Bessborough** 🄻🄷 🐾
(306) 244-5100. **$122-$340.** 601 Spadina Crescent E. At 21st St E;
centre of downtown. Int corridors. **Pets:** Medium, other species. $35
one-time fee/room. Service with restrictions, crate.
[A$K] [✕] [🛏] [💻] [🍽] [🌊] [✕]

▼▼▼▼ **Holiday Inn Express Hotel & Suites Saskatoon** 🅂🄷
(306) 384-8844. **$114.** 315 Idylwyld Dr N. Jct 25th St W. Int corridors.
Pets: Accepted.
[A$K] [✕] [🕭M] [🛏] [💻] [🌊]

▼▼ **Motel 6 Saskatoon** 🅂🄷
(306) 665-6688. **$79-$101.** 231 Marquis Dr. Jct Trans Canada Hwy 16
W (Yellowhead Hwy). Int corridors. **Pets:** Other species. Service with
restrictions, supervision.
[A$K] [S🐾] [✕] [🛏] [🌊]

▼▼▼▼ **Radisson Hotel Saskatoon** 🅂🄷
(306) 665-3322. **$129-$199.** 405 20th St E. At 4th Ave S; centre. Int
corridors. **Pets:** Accepted.
[A$K] [S🐾] [✕] [🕭M] [🛏] [💻] [🍽] [🌊] [✕]

▼▼ ▼▼ **Sandman Hotel** 🅂🄷
(306) 477-4844. **Call for rates.** 310 Circle Dr W. Jct Ave C N. Int
corridors. **Pets:** Accepted.
[✕] [🛏] [💻] [🍽] [🌊]

◆◆ ▼▼ ▼▼ **Saskatoon Travelodge Hotel** 🅂🄷
(306) 242-8881. **$129-$169, 30 day notice.** 106 Circle Dr W. 1.9 mi (3
km) n, then just w of jct Hwy 11 (Idylwyld Dr). Int corridors.
Pets: Accepted.
[SAVE] [S🐾] [✕] [🛏] [💻] [🍽] [🌊] [✕]

▼▼▼▼ **Sheraton Cavalier** 🅂🄷
(306) 652-6770. **$219.** 612 Spadina Crescent E. At 21st St E; centre of
downtown. Int corridors. **Pets:** Accepted.
[A$K] [S🐾] [✕] [🛏] [💻] [🍽] [🌊] [✕]

▼▼ ▼▼ **Super 8** 🅂🄷
(306) 384-8989. **$110-$122.** 706 Circle Dr E. 1.3 mi (2 km) e of jct Hwy
11 (Idylwyld Dr). Ext/int corridors. **Pets:** Accepted.
[A$K] [S🐾] [✕] [🛏] [💻]

SHAUNAVON

▼ **Hidden Hilten Motel** 🄼
(306) 297-4166. **$58-$73.** 352 5th St W. 0.3 mi (0.5 km) e from jct Hwy
13 and 37, just n. Ext corridors. **Pets:** Accepted.
[✕] [🛏] [💻]

SWIFT CURRENT

▼▼ ▼▼ **Comfort Inn** 🅂🄷
(306) 778-3994. **$103-$144.** 1510 S Service Rd E. Trans-Canada Hwy
1, just w of 22nd Ave NE. Int corridors. **Pets:** Accepted.
[A$K] [S🐾] [✕] [🛏] [💻]

◆◆ ▼▼ **Rodeway Inn Motel** 🅂🄷
(306) 773-4664. **$57-$65.** 1200 S Service Rd E. Trans-Canada Hwy 1,
just w of 22nd Ave NE. Ext/int corridors. **Pets:** Accepted.
[SAVE] [S🐾] [✕] [🛏] [🍽]

◆◆ ▼▼ **Safari Inn Motel** 🄼
(306) 773-4608. **$62-$67.** 810 S Service Rd E. 0.6 mi (1 km) w of jct
Hwy 1 and 4. Ext corridors. **Pets:** Medium. $10 daily fee/pet. Service with
restrictions, supervision.
[SAVE] [S🐾] [✕] [🛏] [💻]

▼▼ ▼▼ **Super 8 Motel** 🅂🄷
(306) 778-6088. **$120-$130.** 405 N Service Rd E. Just e of Central Ave.
Int corridors. **Pets:** Accepted.
[A$K] [S🐾] [✕] [🛏] [💻] [🌊]

◆◆ ▼▼ **Westwind Motel** 🄼
(306) 773-1441. **$60-$78.** 155 N Service Rd W. Trans-Canada Hwy 1,
0.3 mi (0.5 km) w of Central Ave. Ext corridors. **Pets:** Accepted.
[SAVE] [S🐾] [✕] [🛏] [🍽] [🌊]

WEYBURN

◆◆ ▼▼ ▼▼ **Perfect Inns & Suites** 🄼
(306) 842-2691. **$60-$120.** 238 Sims Ave. 0.3 mi (0.5 km) w of jct Hwy
35 and 39. Ext/int corridors. **Pets:** $5 daily fee/room. Designated rooms,
service with restrictions, supervision.
[SAVE] [✕] [🛏] [💻]

YORKTON

▼▼ ▼▼ **Best Western Parkland Inn** 🅂🄷
(306) 783-9781. **Call for rates (no credit cards).** 100 Broadway St E.
On Hwy 9, 10, and 16 (Yellowhead Hwy); downtown. Int corridors.
Pets: Accepted.
[✕] [🛏] [💻] [🍽] [🌊] [✕]

▼▼ ▼▼ **Comfort Inn & Suites** 🅂🄷
(306) 783-0333. **$110-$199.** 22 Dracup Ave. Just w of jct Hwy 9, 10
and 16 (Yellowhead Hwy). Int corridors. **Pets:** Accepted.
[A$K] [S🐾] [✕] [🛏] [💻] [🌊]

YUKON TERRITORY

DAWSON CITY

▼▼ Bonanza Gold Motel Ⓜ
(867) 993-6789. **$89-$189.** Bonanza Creek Rd. 1.5 mi (2.4 km) s on Hwy 2. Ext corridors. **Pets:** Accepted.

⊠ 🖃 ⬛ 🍴 🅰

▼▼ Klondike Kate's Cabins Ⓒ
(867) 993-6527. **$95-$140.** 1103 3rd Ave & King St. Corner of 3rd Ave and King St. **Pets:** Accepted.

ⒶⓈⓀ ⊠ 🖃 ⬛ 🍴 🅰

ⒶⒶ ▼▼ Westmark Inn Dawson City Ⓜ
(867) 993-5542. **$155.** 5th St & Harper. At 5th and Harper sts; downtown. Ext/int corridors. **Pets:** Accepted.

Ⓢ🅰🆅🅴 Ⓢ🔟 ⊠ ⬛ 🍴 🅰

HAINES JUNCTION

ⒶⒶ ▼▼ Alcan Motor Inn Ⓜ
(867) 634-2371. **$110-$160, 3 day notice.** Alaska & Haines Hwys. Jct Hwy 1 (Alaska Hwy) and 3 (Haines Hwy). Ext corridors. **Pets:** Other species. $10 daily fee/pet. Designated rooms, service with restrictions, supervision.

Ⓢ🅰🆅🅴 Ⓢ🔟 ⊠ 🖃 ⬛

WHITEHORSE

ⒶⒶ ▼▼ High Country Inn Ⓢ🅷
(867) 667-4471. **$149-$259, 3 day notice.** 4051 4th Ave. 0.4 mi (0.6 km) e of Main St. Int corridors. **Pets:** Small, other species. $25 one-time fee/pet. Designated rooms, service with restrictions, crate.

Ⓢ🅰🆅🅴 Ⓢ🔟 ⊠ 🖃 ⬛ 🍴

ⒶⒶ ▼▼ Westmark Whitehorse Hotel & Conference Centre Ⓢ🅷
(867) 393-9700. **$159-$179.** 201 Wood St. At 2nd Ave; centre. Int corridors. **Pets:** Designated rooms, service with restrictions, supervision.

Ⓢ🅰🆅🅴 ⊠ ♿🄼 🖃 ⬛ 🍴 🅰

Pet-Friendly Campgrounds

United States
Canada

United States

Alabama

CHILDERSBURG — DESOTO CAVERNS PARK CAMPGROUND. (256) 378-7252. **$27.** 5181 DeSoto Caverns Pkwy, 35044. On SR 76, 5 mi e.

PELHAM — BIRMINGHAM SOUTH CAMPGROUND. (205) 664-8832. **2P $35-$41, XP: $2.** 222 Hwy 33, 35124. I-65, exit 242, 0.5 mi w on CR 52, then 0.3 mi n.

Alaska

ANCHORAGE — ANCHORAGE RV PARK. (907) 338-7275. **Call for rates.** 1200 N Muldoon Rd, 99506. SR 1, exit Muldoon Rd N, 0.5 mi nw.

Arizona

AMADO — DE ANZA TRAILS RV RESORT. (520) 398-8628. **2P $30, XP: $5.** 2869 E Frontage Rd, 85645. I-19, exit 48, just e, then 1.6 mi s. (HC 65 Box 381, TUMACACORI, 85640).

ANTHEM — PIONEER RV PARK. (623) 465-7465. **Call for rates. (no credit cards).** 36408 N Black Canyon Hwy, 85086. I-17, exit 225, 0.3 mi w, follow signs.

APACHE JUNCTION — SUPERSTITION SUNRISE LUXURY RV RESORT. (480) 986-4524. **2P $33-$50. (no credit cards).** 702 S Meridian Rd, 85220. US 60, exit 193 (Signal Butte Rd), 0.4 mi n to Southern, 1 mi e, then 0.5 mi n.

BENSON — PATO BLANCO LAKES RV RESORT. (520) 586-8966. **$19-$28, XP: $2.** 635 E Pearl St, 85602. I-10, exit 306, just s, 0.7 mi w on Frontage Rd, then 0.4 mi n on County Rd.

BENSON — COCHISE TERRACE RV RESORT. (520) 586-0600. **2P $19-$30, XP: $2.** 1030 S Barrel Cactus Ridge, 85602. I-10, exit 302, 1 mi s on SR 90, then just w.

BENSON — BUTTERFIELD RV RESORT. (520) 586-4400. **2P $33-$35, XP: $2.** 251 S Ocotillo Rd, 85602. I-10, exit 304 (Ocotillo Rd), 0.6 mi s.

BENSON — SAN PEDRO RESORT COMMUNITY. (520) 586-9546. **Call for rates. (no credit cards).** 1110 S Hwy 80, Box 1, 85602. I-10, exit 304 (Ocotillo Ave), 0.5 mi s, 1 mi e on 4th St, then 1.3 mi se.

CAMP VERDE — DISTANT DRUMS RV RESORT. (928) 554-8000. **4P $20-$36.** 583 W Middle Verde Rd, 86322. I-17, exit 289, just sw.

CASA GRANDE — FIESTA GRANDE-RV RESORT. (520) 836-7222. **2P $34, XP: $2.** 1511 E Florence Blvd, 85222. I-10, exit 194, 2 mi w.

CASA GRANDE — PALM CREEK GOLF AND RV RESORT. (520) 421-7000. **2P $30-$72, XP: $5.** 1110 N Henness Rd, 85222. I-10, exit 194, 1 mi w, then just n.

ELOY — DESERT VALLEY RV RESORT. (520) 466-4500. **2P $32, XP: $3. (no credit cards).** 4555 W Tonto Rd, 85231. I-10, exit 203 (Toltec Rd), 0.5 mi n on Toltec Rd, then 0.5 mi w.

FORT MCDOWELL — EAGLE VIEW RV RESORT AT FT MCDOWELL. Ⓐ (480) 836-5310. **4P $40-$45, XP: $10.** 9605 N Ft McDowell Rd, 85264. Jct Shea Blvd, 2 mi ne on SR 89, 0.5 mi se.

GOLD CANYON — CANYON VISTAS RV RESORT. (480) 288-8844. **2P $18-$36, XP: $3.** 6601 E US Hwy 60, 85218. 1.2 mi w of Kings Ranch Rd; between MM 202 and 201.

HUACHUCA CITY — TOMBSTONE TERRITORIES RV PARK. Ⓐ (520) 457-2584. **2P $31-$34, XP: $1.** 2111 E Hwy 82, 85616. Jct SR 90, 7.7 mi e on SR 82; between MM 59 and 60.

LAKE HAVASU CITY — HAVASU RV RESORT. (928) 764-2020. **2P $41-$50, XP: $5.** 1905 Victoria Farms Rd, 86404. From London Bridge, 5.3 mi n on SR 95, just e on Chenoweth Dr, then 0.4 mi n.

LAKE HAVASU CITY — ISLANDER RV RESORT. (928) 680-2000. **Call for rates. (no credit cards).** 751 Beachcomber Blvd, 86403. Jct Lake Havasu Blvd, 1.7 mi sw on McCulloch Blvd.

MESA — SUN LIFE VACATION RESORT. (480) 981-9500. **2P $38. (no credit cards).** 5055 E University Dr, 85205. Just w of Higley Rd.

MESA — GOOD LIFE RV RESORT. Ⓐ (480) 832-4990. **2P $25-$36, XP: $3.** 3403 E Main St, 85213. US 60, exit 184 (Val Vista Dr), 2 mi n, then just w.

MESA — TOWERPOINT RV RESORT. Ⓐ (480) 832-4996. **2P $25-$36, XP: $3.** 4860 E Main St, 85205. US 60, exit 186 (Higley Rd), 2 mi n, then just w.

MESA — VIEWPOINT RV & GOLF RESORT. (480) 373-8700. **2P $20-$55, XP: $3.** 8700 E University Dr, 85207. 2.4 mi e of Power Rd.

MESA — MESA REGAL RV RESORT. (480) 830-2821. **Call for rates. (no credit cards).** 4700 E Main St, 85205. Just e of Greenfield Rd.

MESA — VAL VISTA VILLAGE. (480) 832-2547. **2P $20-$60, XP: $3.** 233 N Val Vista Dr, 85213. US 60, exit 184 (Val Vista Dr), 2.2 mi n.

🏕 🏊 🍽

MESA — VALLE DEL ORO RV RESORT. (480) 984-1146. **Call for rates.** 1452 S Ellsworth Rd, 85209. US 60, exit 191, just n.

🏕 🏊 🍽

MESA — MESA SPIRIT RV RESORT. 🆑 (480) 832-1770. **2P $19-$47, XP: $4.** 3020 E Main St, 85213. US 60, exit 184 (Val Vista Dr), 2 mi n to Main St, then 0.8 mi w.

🏕 🏊 🍽

MESA — APACHE WELLS RV RESORT. (480) 832-4324. **Call for rates. (no credit cards).** 2656 N 56th St, 85215. Jct N Higley Rd, 0.4 mi e on E McDowell Rd, just s.

🏕 🏊 🍽

MESA — MONTE VISTA VILLAGE RESORT. (480) 833-2223. **2P $48, XP: $2.** 8865 E Baseline Rd, 85209. US 60, exit 191 (Ellsworth), 0.6 mi s, then just w.

🏕 🏊 🍽

PHOENIX — DESERT SHADOWS RV RESORT. (623) 869-8178. **$30-$34, XP: $3.** 19203 N 29th Ave, 85027. I-17, exit 214A (Union Hills) northbound, 0.3 mi w, then 0.4 mi n; exit 214 A&B southbound, continue 0.5 mi s, 0.3 mi w on Union Hills, then 0.4 mi n.

🏕 🏊 🍽

PICACHO — PICACHO PEAK RV RESORT. 🆑 (520) 466-7841. **2P $27, XP: $2.** 17065 E Peak Ln, 85241. I-10, exit 219, 0.7 mi s on frontage road. (PO Box 300).

🏕 🏊 🍽

SHOW LOW — VOYAGER AT JUNIPER RIDGE. 🆑 (928) 532-3456. **4P $23-$35, XP: $2.** 1993 Juniper Ridge Resort, 85901. Jct US 60, 7.3 mi n on SR 77 to White Mountain Lake Rd, then 3 mi e.

🏕 🏊 🍽

SUN CITY — PARADISE RV RESORT. 🆑 (623) 977-0344. **2P $27-$52, XP: $2-$4.** 10950 W Union Hills Dr, 85373. Loop 101, exit 15 (Union Hills Dr), 3.8 mi w.

🏕 🏊 🍽

TONOPAH — SADDLE MOUNTAIN RV PARK. 🆑 (623) 386-3892. **Call for rates.** 3607 N 411th Ave, 85354. I-10, exit 94, 0.6 mi s.

🏕 🏊 🍽

TUCSON — BEAUDRY RV RESORT. (520) 239-1700. **2P $22-$55.** 5151 S Country Club, 85706. I-10, exit 264B (Palo Verde and Irvington), just n to Irvington, 0.5 mi w, then just s.

🏕 🏊 🍽

TUCSON — VOYAGER RV RESORT. 🆑 (520) 574-5000. **4P $30-$52, XP: $2.** 8701 S Kolb Rd, 85706. I-10, exit 270, 0.7 mi s.

🏕 🏊 🍽

YUMA — SUN VISTA RV RESORT. 🆑 (928) 726-8920. **2P $44, XP: $3.** 7201 E 32nd St (Business 8), 85365. I-8, exit 7 (Araby Rd), just s, then 0.5 mi e.

🏕 🏊 🍽

YUMA — LAS QUINTAS OASIS RESORT. (928) 305-9005. **2P $33, XP: $3.** 10442 E Frontage Rd, 85365. I-8, exit 12 (Fortuna Rd), just n, then 0.6 mi w; north side of interstate.

🏕 🏊 🍽

YUMA — BONITA MESA RV RESORT. (928) 342-2999. **Call for rates. (no credit cards).** 9400 N Frontage Rd, 85365. I-8, exit 12 (Fortuna Rd), just n, then 1.6 mi w.

🏕 🏊 🍽

YUMA — DEL PUEBLO RV PARK & TENNIS RESORT. (928) 341-2100. **Call for rates. (no credit cards).** 14794 Ave 3 E, 85365. I-8, exit 3 (Ave 3 E/SR 280 S), 5.3 mi s.

🏕 🏊 🍽

YUMA — WESTWIND RV & GOLF RESORT. (928) 342-2992. **2P $38-$50, XP: $3.** 9797 E 32nd St (S Frontage Rd), 85365. I-8, exit 12 (Fortuna Rd) on south side, 1 mi w.

🏕 🏊 🍽

YUMA — COCOPAH RV & GOLF RESORT. (928) 343-9300. **2P $32-$37, XP: $2.** 6800 Strand Ave, 85364. I-8, exit Winterhaven/4th Ave eastbound, 0.5 mi s on 4th Ave, 2.4 mi w on 1st St, just s on Ave C, 1.4 mi w on Riverside, then 0.9 mi nw.

🏕 🏊 🍽

YUMA — ARABY ACRES RV RESORT. (928) 344-8666. **2P $35-$55, XP: $2.** 6649 E 32nd St, 85365. I-8, exit 7 (Araby Rd), just s, then just e.

🏕 🏊 🍽

YUMA — HIDDEN SHORES RV VILLAGE. (928) 539-6700. **6P $50-$90.** 10300 Imperial Dam Rd, 85365. I-8, exit 12 (Fortuna Rd), 1.9 mi n, 10.4 mi n on US 95, then 6.5 mi w; Yuma Proving Ground Base.

🏕 🏊 🍽

California

AGUANGA — OUTDOOR RESORTS RANCHO CALIFORNIA. (951) 767-0848. **Call for rates.** 45525 Hwy 79 S, 92536. I-15, exit 58 (SR 79 S), 14 mi e; just e of SR 371.

🏕 🏊 🍽

BIG BEAR LAKE — BIG BEAR SHORES RV RESORT & YACHT CLUB. (909) 866-4151. **6P $60-$140.** 40751 North Shore Ln, 92315. SR 18, 5 mi e of the dam on SR 38 (North Shore Dr), 1.2 mi se. (PO Box 1572).

🏊 🍽

BUELLTON — FLYING FLAGS RV PARK & CAMPGROUND. 🆑 (805) 688-3716. **2P $22-$98, XP: $3.** 180 Ave of the Flags, 93427. Just w of US 101, exit 140A (SR 246).

🏊 🍽

CASTAIC — VALENCIA TRAVEL VILLAGE. 🆑 (661) 257-3333. **6P $51-$75, XP: $2.** 27946 Henry Mayo Rd, 91384. I-5, exit SR 126, 1.3 mi w.

🏕 🏊 🍽

CATHEDRAL CITY — OUTDOOR RESORTS/PALM SPRINGS. (760) 324-4005. **6P $45-$77.** 69-411 Ramon Rd, 92234. I-10, exit 126 (Date Palm Dr), 2.2 mi s, then 0.5 mi e.

🏊 🍽

CHULA VISTA — CHULA VISTA RV RESORT. (619) 422-0111. **4P $46-$69, XP: $3-$10.** 460 Sandpiper Way, 91910. I-5, exit 7B (J St/Marina Pkwy), 4 mi w, then 0.5 mi n.

🏕 🏊 🍽

CHULA VISTA — SAN DIEGO METRO KOA. (619) 427-3601. **2P $39-$99, XP: $5.** 111 N 2nd Ave, 91910. I-5, exit 8B (E St), 1 mi e to 2nd Ave, then 1 mi n; I-805, exit E St, 1 mi w, then just n.

🏊 🍽

COLOMA — COLOMA RESORT. (530) 621-2267. **2P $38-$45, XP: $7-$10.** 6921 Mt Murphy Rd, 95613. E off SR 49 on Mt. Murphy Rd; on South Fork of American River. (PO Box 516).

DEL LOMA — DEL LOMA RV PARK & CAMPGROUND. (530) 623-2834. **2P $25, XP: $2.** Rt 1, Box 54, 96010. US 299, southwest Del Loma.

DESERT HOT SPRINGS — SKY VALLEY RESORT. (760) 329-2909. **2P $38-$49, XP: $5.** 74-711 Dillon Rd, 92241. I-10, exit Palm Dr, 3.3 mi n, then 8.5 mi e.

EL CENTRO — DESERT TRAILS RV PARK. (760) 352-7275. **2P $20-$36, XP: $3.** 225 Wake Ave, 92243. I-8, exit 115 (4th St/SR 86), just s, then just e.

EL CENTRO — SUNBEAM LAKE RV RESORT. (760) 352-7154. **2P $35-$39, XP: $3.** 1716 W Sunbeam Lake Dr, 92243. I-8, exit 107 (Drew Rd), 0.5 mi n.

FORTUNA — RIVERWALK RV PARK & CAMPGROUND. (707) 725-3359. **2P $22-$65, XP: $5.** 2189 Riverwalk Dr, 95540. W of US 101, exit Kenmar Rd.

GARBERVILLE — BENBOW VALLEY RV RESORT & GOLF COURSE. (707) 923-2777. **2P $32-$49, XP: $5.** 7000 Benbow Dr, 95542. US 101, exit Benbow Dr, 2 mi s.

HEMET — GOLDEN VILLAGE PALMS RV RESORT. (951) 925-2518. **2P $38-$52, XP: $10.** 3600 W Florida Ave, 92545. SR 79 N (San Jacinto St), 3 mi w.

INDIO — INDIAN WELLS RV PARK. (760) 347-0895. **2P $38-$45, XP: $2-$5.** 47-340 Jefferson St, 92201. I-10, exit 139 (Jefferson St/Indio Blvd), 3 mi s.

INDIO — OUTDOOR RESORTS INDIO-THE ULTIMATE MOTOR-COACH RESORT. (760) 775-7255. **3P $40-$75, XP: $5.** 80-394 48th Ave, 92201. I-10, exit 139 (Jefferson St/Indio Blvd), 3.5 mi s, then just e.

JULIAN — PINEZANITA TRAILER RANCH & CAMPGROUND. (760) 765-0429. **2P $29-$32, XP: $3.** 4446 SR 79, 92036. On SR 79, 3.6 mi s of SR 78. (PO Box 2380).

LODI — FLAG CITY RV RESORT. (209) 339-8300. **6P $44, XP: $2.** 6120 W Banner St, 95242. I-5, exit SR 12 E, s on Star St, then just e.

NEWPORT BEACH — NEWPORT DUNES WATERFRONT RV RESORT. (949) 729-3863. **6P $60-$350.** 1131 Back Bay Dr, 92660. SR 73, exit 15 (Jamboree Rd) southbound, 3 mi s, then just n on SR 1; exit 13 (Bison Ave) northbound, just w to MacArthur Blvd, 2.5 mi s to SR 1, then 1.5 mi n.

NILAND — FOUNTAIN OF YOUTH SPA. (760) 354-1340. **2P $29-$42, XP: $2-$5.** 10249 Coachella Canal Rd, 92257. 14 mi nw on SR 111, then 2.3 mi ne on Hot Mineral Spa Rd.

ORANGE — ORANGELAND RECREATION VEHICLE PARK. (714) 633-0414. **8P $60-$75, XP: $2.** 1600 W Struck Ave, 92867. SR 57, exit 2 (Katella Ave), 0.5 mi e, then just s.

PASO ROBLES — WINE COUNTRY RV RESORT. (805) 238-4560. **2P $39-$85, XP: $3-$5.** 2500 Airport Rd, 93446. US 101, exit 231B (SR 46/Fresno/Bakersfield), 2 mi e, then just n. (PO Box 2552, 93447).

PETALUMA — SAN FRANCISCO NORTH/PETALUMA KOA. (707) 763-1492. **2P $32-$73, XP: $5-$7.** 20 Rainsville Rd, 94952. US 101, exit Penngrove, just w to Stony Point Rd, then 0.5 mi n.

PISMO BEACH — PACIFIC DUNES RANCH RV PARK. (805) 489-7787. **6P $43-$58, XP: $5.** 1205 Silver Spur Pl, 93445. In Oceano; SR 1, exit 22nd St, 0.3 mi s, then 0.4 mi w.

PISMO BEACH — PISMO COAST VILLAGE RV RESORT. (805) 773-1811. **6P $34-$49, XP: $2.** 165 S Dolliver St, 93449. 0.5 mi s on SR 1.

PLYMOUTH — FAR HORIZONS 49'ER VILLAGE. (209) 245-6981. **4P $37-$62, XP: $5.** 18265 Hwy 49, 95669. On SR 49, 0.3 mi s.

SAN DIEGO — CAMPLAND ON THE BAY. (858) 581-4260. **Call for rates.** 2211 Pacific Beach Dr, 92109. I-5, exit 23A (Grand Ave) northbound, 1 mi w to Olney, then 0.3 mi s; exit 23 (Balboa/Garnet) southbound, s on Mission Bay Dr to Grand Ave, then 1 mi w to Olney.

SAN DIMAS — EAST SHORE RV PARK. (909) 599-8355. **2P $43-$47, XP: $3.** 1440 Camper View Rd, 91773. I-10, exit 44 (Fairplex Dr), 0.6 mi n, 0.6 mi w on Via Verde, then 0.6 mi n; in Frank G Bonelli Regional Park.

SAN JUAN BAUTISTA — BETABEL RV RESORT. (831) 623-2202. **2P $35-$38, XP: $3.** 9664 Betabel Rd, 95045. US 101, exit Betabel Rd, just w.

SANTA BARBARA — OCEAN MESA AT EL CAPITAN. (805) 685-3887. **4P $35-$85, XP: $10.** 11560 Calle Real, 93117. 20 mi nw on north side of US 101; at El Capitan State Beach.

SANTA BARBARA — EL CAPITAN CANYON. (805) 685-3887. **$125-$345.** 11560 Calle Real, 93117. 20 mi nw on north side of US 101 at El Capitan State Beach.

SHAVER LAKE — CAMP EDISON. (559) 841-3134. **Call for rates.** 42696 Tollhouse Rd, 93664. Just ne; lakeside. (PO Box 600).

TEMECULA — PECHANGA RV RESORT. (951) 770-2658. **$42-$52.** 45000 Pechanga Pkwy, 92592. I-15, exit 58 (SR 79 S), 1 mi e, then 2 mi s.

TEMECULA — VAIL LAKE RESORT. (951) 303-0173. **6P $40-$150, XP: $5-$10.** 38000 Hwy 79 S, 92592. I-15, exit 58 (SR 79 S), 9 mi se.

TRINIDAD — EMERALD FOREST OF TRINIDAD. ⟨AAA⟩ (707) 677-3554. **2P $23-$44, XP: $3.** 753 Patricks Point Dr, 95570. US 101, exit Patricks Point Dr W. (PO Box 870).

WEAVERVILLE — TRINITY LAKE RESORTS AT PINEWOOD COVE RV PARK & CAMPGROUND. (530) 286-2201. **Call for rates.** 45110 State Hwy 3, 96091. 14 mi ne of town.

WILLITS — WILLITS-UKIAH KOA. (707) 459-6179. **2P $25-$65, XP: $4.** 1600 Hwy 20, 95490. 1.5 mi w on SR 20, from jct US 101. (PO Box 946).

WINTERHAVEN — RIVER'S EDGE RV RESORT. (760) 572-5105. **2P $28, XP: $2.** 2299 Winterhaven Dr, 92283. I-8, exit 170 (Winterhaven Dr), 0.5 mi e.

Colorado

BRECKENRIDGE — TIGER RUN RESORT. (970) 453-9690. **$34-$59.** 85 Tiger Run Rd, 80424. I-70, exit 203, 6 mi s on SR 9, then just e on Revette Dr.

FORT COLLINS — FORT COLLINS LAKESIDE KOA. (970) 484-9880. **2P $34-$75, XP: $3-$8.** 1910 N Taft Hill Rd, 80524. I-25, exit 269B, 6 mi w to Taft Hill, then 2.2 mi n.

GOLDEN — DAKOTA RIDGE RV PARK. (303) 279-1625. **Call for rates.** 17800 W Colfax Ave, 80401. I-70, exit 262 (W Colfax Ave), 1.8 mi w on US 40.

GRAND LAKE — WINDING RIVER RESORT INC. ⟨AAA⟩ (970) 627-3215. **2P $29-$38, XP: $4-$5.** 1447 CR 491, 80447. 1.5 mi ne on US 34 to CR 491, then 1.5 mi w. (PO Box 629).

LOVELAND — JOHNSON'S CORNER RV RETREAT. (970) 669-8400. **Call for rates.** 3618 SE Frontage Rd, 80537. I-25, exit 254, 0.3 mi se; adjacent to Great Colorado Marketplace.

Florida

ARCADIA — LITTLE WILLIES RV RESORT. (863) 494-2717. **2P $35. (no credit cards).** 5905 NE Cubitus Ave, 34266. 3.8 mi n on US 17, just w on NE McKay St, then 1.4 mi n.

ARCADIA — TOBY'S RV RESORT. (863) 494-1744. **Call for rates.** 3550 NE Hwy 70, 34266. On SR 70, 2.7 mi e.

BRADENTON — MANATEE ENCORE RV RESORT. (941) 745-2600. **2P $27-$65.** 800 Kay Rd NE, 34212. I-75, exit 220 southbound; exit 220B northbound, 0.6 mi w on SR 64, then 0.8 mi n on Cypress Creek Blvd (merges to Kay Rd NE).

BRADENTON — HORSESHOE COVE RV RESORT. (941) 758-5335. **2P $30-$60, XP: $3.** 5100 60th St E, 34203. I-75, exit 217 southbound; exit 217B northbound, 1.7 mi w on SR 70, then just n on Caruso Rd.

CHOKOLOSKEE — OUTDOOR RESORTS OF AMERICA OF CHOKOLOSKEE. (239) 695-2881. **Call for rates.** 100 CR 29 S, 34138. On CR 29; center. (PO Box 39).

CRYSTAL RIVER — ROCK CRUSHER CANYON RV PARK. (352) 795-3870. **Call for rates.** 275 S Rock Crusher Rd, 34429. 1.5 mi s of SR 44.

CRYSTAL RIVER — ENCORE SUPERPARK CRYSTAL RIVER. (352) 795-3774. **Call for rates.** 11419 W Fort Island Tr, 34429. Jct US 19, 4.5 mi w on SR 44 W.

DAVENPORT — DEER CREEK RV RESORT. (863) 424-2839. **2P $45-$65.** 42749 Hwy 27, 33837. I-4, exit 55, 1 mi se.

DAVENPORT — FORT SUMMIT KOA. ⟨AAA⟩ (863) 424-1880. **$44-$75, XP: $4.** 2525 Frontage Rd, 33837. Jct US 27 and I-4, exit 55, on frontage road; behind Best Western.

DEBARY — HIGH BANKS MARINA & CAMP RESORT. (386) 668-4491. **2P $45-$65, XP: $5.** 488 W Highbanks Rd, 32713. 2.7 mi w of US 17-92.

DESTIN — DESTIN RV BEACH RESORT. (850) 837-3529. **Call for rates.** 362 Miramar Beach Dr, 32550. 4.1 mi e of SR 293 (Mid-Bay Bridge), just s.

FORT MYERS — SIESTA BAY RV RESORT. ⟨AAA⟩ (239) 466-8988. **$49, XP: $4.** 19333 Summerlin Rd, 33908. 1.6 mi sw of jct US 41 on Gladiolus Dr (CR 865), 4.8 mi s on Summerlin Rd (CR 869).

FORT MYERS BEACH — GULF WATERS RV RESORT. ⟨AAA⟩ (239) 437-5888. **Call for rates.** 11301 Summerlin Square Rd, 33931. 2.6 mi nw of jct Matanzas Pass Bridge, 0.4 mi e on Summerlin Rd, just s on Pine Ridge Rd, then just w.

FORT MYERS BEACH — INDIAN CREEK PARK RV RESORT & MANUFACTURED HOME COMMUNITY. ⟨AAA⟩ (239) 466-6060. **2P $47-$49, XP: $5.** 17340 San Carlos Blvd, 33931. 2.4 mi nw of jct Matanzas Pass Bridge.

FORT PIERCE — TREASURE COAST RV RESORT. (772) 468-2099. **4P $45-$63.** 2550 Crossroads Pkwy, 34945. I-95, exit 129 (SR 70), just w, then just n.

JACKSONVILLE — FLAMINGO LAKE RV RESORT. ⟨AAA⟩ (904) 766-0672. **2P $42-$48, XP: $3.** 3640 Newcomb Rd, 32218. I-295, exit 32, just nw on SR 115.

JENNINGS — JENNINGS OUTDOOR RESORT CAMPGROUND. (386) 938-3321. **2P $26-$30, XP: $2.** 2039 Hamilton Ave, 32053. I-75, exit 467, just w on SR 143.

JENSEN BEACH — NETTLES ISLAND. (772) 229-1300. **$37-$64.** 9803 S Ocean Dr, 34957. On SR A1A, 2.3 mi n of jct SR 732 (Jensen Beach Cswy); on S Hutchinson Island.

KISSIMMEE — TROPICAL PALMS RV RESORT. (407) 396-4595. **Call for rates.** 2650 Holiday Tr, 34746. I-4, exit 64A, 1.5 mi e on US 192, then 0.8 mi s.

KISSIMMEE — OUTDOOR RESORTS AT ORLANDO. (863) 424-1259. **Call for rates.** On US 192, 1 mi e of jct US 27; jct I-4, exit 64B, 6.3 mi w. (9000 W US 192, CLERMONT, 34711).

LA BELLE — WHISPER CREEK RV RESORT. (863) 675-6888. **2P $35. (no credit cards).** 3745 N SR 29 SW, 33935. On SR 29, 1.8 mi n of jct SR 80.

LAKE BUENA VISTA — DISNEY'S FORT WILDERNESS RESORT & CAMPGROUND. (407) 824-2900. **2P $42-$111, XP: $2.** 4510 N Fort Wilderness Tr, 32830-1000. In Walt Disney World. (PO Box 10000).

LAKELAND — LAKELAND CAREFREE RV RESORT. (863) 687-6146. **2P $32-$36, XP: $3.** 900 Old Combee Rd, 33805. I-4, exit 33 eastbound, 1 mi ne on SR 33, then just w; exit 38 westbound, 5 mi sw on SR 33, then just nw.

LAKELAND — SANLAN RV PARK. (863) 665-1726. **Call for rates.** 3929 US 98 S, 33812. I-4, exit 32, 8.7 mi s on US 98; just s of SR 570 (exit 10).

LEESBURG — HOLIDAY TRAVEL RESORT. (352) 787-5151. **2P $34, XP: $5.** 28229 CR 33, 34748. 3.5 mi s via US 27, 0.5 mi w.

MELBOURNE BEACH — OUTDOOR RESORTS MELBOURNE BEACH LUXURY RV RESORT. (321) 724-2600. **Call for rates.** 214 Horizon Ln, 32951. 2.5 mi s.

MIMS — SEASONS IN THE SUN MOTOR COACH RESORT. (321) 385-0440. **Call for rates.** 2400 Seasons In The Sun Blvd, 32754. I-95, exit 223, 0.5 mi w on SR 46.

NOKOMIS — ENCORE ROYAL COACHMEN. (941) 488-9674. **Call for rates.** 1070 Laurel Rd E, 34275. I-75, exit 195, 1.9 mi w (CR 762).

OCALA — OCALA RV CAMP RESORT. (352) 237-2138. **Call for rates.** 3200 SW 38th Ave, 34474. I-75, exit 350, just w on SR 200, just n on SW 38th Ct, then 0.5 mi e.

OKEECHOBEE — OKEECHOBEE KOA RESORT & GOLF COURSE. (863) 763-0231. **Call for rates.** 4276 Hwy US 441 S, 34974. On US 98 and 441, 3 mi s of jct SR 70; 0.3 mi n of Lake Okeechobee and jct SR 78.

OLD TOWN — YELLOW JACKET CAMPGROUND RESORT. (352) 542-8365. **2P $29-$44, XP: $6-$10.** 55 SE 503 Ave, 32680. 10.7 mi s on SR 349, then 1.2 mi on dirt road.

PANAMA CITY BEACH — EMERALD COAST RV BEACH RESORT. (850) 235-0924. **$48-$66, XP: $3.** 1957 Allison Ave, 32407. US 98/98A and Allison Ave, 1.5 mi w of Hathaway Bridge.

PORT CHARLOTTE — RIVERSIDE RV RESORT & CAMPGROUND. (863) 993-2111. **4P $39-$54, XP: $2-$3.** 9770 SW CR 769, 34269. I-75, exit 170, 4.5 mi ne on Kings Hwy.

PORT CHARLOTTE — ENCORE RV RESORT-PORT CHARLOTTE. (941) 624-4511. **Call for rates.** 3737 El Jobean Rd, 33953. On SR 776, 4.6 mi w of jct US 41.

REDDICK — OCALA NORTH RV PARK. (352) 591-1723. **$29-$33.** 16905 NW CR 225, 32686. I-75, exit 368, just w on CR 318, then 0.8 mi s.

RIVER RANCH — RIVER RANCH RV RESORT. (863) 692-1116. **4P $60-$85, XP: $2.** 3400 River Ranch Blvd, 33867. 3.5 mi s of SR 60; 25 mi e of US 27; 23 mi w of Florida Tpke and US 441; just w of the Kissimmee River. (30529 River Ranch Blvd).

ROCKLEDGE — SPACE COAST RV RESORT. (321) 636-2873. **2P $45-$55, XP: $3.** 820 Barnes Blvd, 32955. I-95, exit 195 (Fiske Blvd), just e, then just s on CR 502.

SARASOTA — SUN-N-FUN RV RESORT. (941) 371-2505. **$32-$75.** 7125 Fruitville Rd, 34240. I-75, exit 210, 1.2 mi e on SR 780.

SEBASTIAN — ENCORE RV PARK-VERO BEACH. (772) 589-7828. **6P $32-$47.** I-95, exit 156, just e on CR 512. (9455 108th Ave, VERO BEACH, 32967-3154).

SEBRING — BUTTONWOOD BAY RV RESORT. (863) 655-1122. **2P $28-$48, XP: $5.** 10001 US 27 S, 33876. 1.5 mi s of SR 98.

SILVER SPRINGS — THE SPRINGS RV RESORT. (352) 236-5250. **2P $27, XP: $3.** 2950 NE 52nd Ct, 34488. On SR 40, 0.5 mi w of Silver Springs attraction, 0.5 mi n.

SILVER SPRINGS — WILDERNESS RV PARK ESTATES. (352) 625-1122. **4P $30-$35, XP: $6.** 10313 E Hwy 40, 34488. On SR 40, 4.5 mi e of Silver Springs attraction.

ST. PETERSBURG — ST. PETERSBURG-MADEIRA BEACH RESORT KOA. (727) 392-2233. **Call for rates.** 5400 95th St N, 33708. Jct 38th Ave N, 1.4 mi n on Tyrone/Bay Pines Blvd (Alternate Rt US 19), 0.5 mi e.

SUMTERVILLE — SHADY BROOK GOLF & RV RESORT. (352) 568-2244. **Call for rates.** 178 N US 301, 33585. I-75, exit 321, 2.5 mi e on CR 470, then 0.7 mi n. (PO Box 130).

TAMPA — BAY BAYOU RV RESORT. (813) 855-1000. **4P $48-$52, XP: $4.** 12622 Old Memorial Hwy, 33635. Jct SR 580 (Hillsborough Ave W), 0.4 mi n on Countryway Blvd, then 0.8 mi w.

TITUSVILLE — THE GREAT OUTDOORS RV & GOLF RESORT. (321) 269-5004. **2P $35-$65, XP: $3.** 125 Plantation Dr, 32780. I-95, exit 215, 0.5 mi w on SR 50, 1.8 mi s on paved entrance road.

UMATILLA — OLDE MILL STREAM RV RESORT. Ⓐ (352) 669-3141. **2P $24-$33, XP: $3.** 1000 N Central Ave, 32784. 0.8 mi n on SR 19.

ZEPHYRHILLS — MAJESTIC OAKS CAREFREE RV RESORT. (813) 783-7518. **2P $26, XP: $2.** 3751 Laurel Valley Blvd, 33542. Jct US 301, 1.5 mi e on Chancey Rd, then just n.

Georgia

PINE MOUNTAIN — PINE MOUNTAIN RV RESORT. (706) 663-4329. **Call for rates.** 8804 Hamilton Rd, 31822. I-185, exit 42, 8 mi s on US 27.

STONE MOUNTAIN — STONE MOUNTAIN PARK CAMPGROUND. (770) 498-5710. **Call for rates.** Stone Mountain, 30086. On east side of Stone Mountain; in Stone Mountain Memorial Park. (PO Box 778).

Idaho

CASCADE — ARROWHEAD R.V. PARK ON THE RIVER. Ⓐ (208) 382-4534. **2P $26-$28, XP: $1.** 955 S Hwy 55, 83611. South end of town. (PO Box 337).

COEUR D'ALENE — BLACKWELL ISLAND RV RESORT. (208) 665-1300. **$38-$46, XP: $2.** 800 S Marina Dr, 83814. I-90, exit 12, 1.5 mi s on US 95.

KAMIAH — LEWIS-CLARK RESORT RV PARK. (208) 935-2556. **Call for rates.** 1.5 mi e on US 12. (Rt 1, Box 17X, 83536).

WHITE BIRD — SWIFTWATER RV PARK & STORE. (208) 839-2700. **2P $22-$24, XP: $3-$5.** HC 01, Box 24, 83554. Just n of Milepost 222, exit Hammer Creek Recreational area, 0.8 mi nw. (PO Box 150).

Illinois

LEE CENTER — O'CONNELL'S YOGI BEAR JELLYSTONE PARK. Ⓐ (815) 857-3860. **2P $35-$60, XP: $15-$20.** 970 Greenwing Rd, 61310. I-39, exit 87 (US 30), 12.8 mi w to CR 1955 E, then 3.3 mi se, follow signs. (PO Box 200, AMBOY).

MILLBROOK — YOGI BEAR'S JELLYSTONE PARK CAMP RESORT. Ⓐ (630) 553-5172. **2P $42-$55, XP: $10-$15.** 8574 Millbrook Rd, 60536. 1.5 mi n of jct SR 71. (PO Box 306).

Indiana

CRAWFORDSVILLE — CRAWFORDSVILLE KOA. (765) 362-4190. **2P $23-$35, XP: $2-$3.** 1600 Lafayette Rd, 47933. I-74, exit 34, 2 mi s on US 231.

FREMONT — YOGI BEAR'S JELLYSTONE PARK CAMP RESORT. Ⓐ (260) 833-1114. **5P $30-$58, XP: $10.** 140 Ln, 201 Barton Lake, 46737-9652. I-69, exit 157 southbound; exit 154 northbound, 3 mi w on SR 120, then 0.5 mi n on CR 300 W; Toll Rd, exit 144 to SR 120.

GRANGER — SOUTH BEND EAST KOA. (574) 277-1335. **2P $28-$47, XP: $3-$4.** 50707 Princess Way, 46530. I-80/90, exit 83, just w on SR 331, 2 mi n on SR 23 (Adams Rd), then just w.

MONTICELLO — YOGI BEAR'S JELLYSTONE PARK AT INDIANA BEACH. (574) 583-8646. **Call for rates. (no credit cards).** 2882 NW Shafer Dr, 47960. 0.5 mi w on US 24, then 3.5 mi n.

MONTICELLO — INDIANA BEACH CAMPGROUND. (574) 583-8306. **$23-$34.** 5224 E Indiana Beach Rd, 47960. 0.5 mi w on US 24, 3.5 mi n on W Shafer Dr (6th St).

PIERCETON — YOGI BEAR'S JELLYSTONE PARK CAMP-RESORT. (574) 594-2124. **5P $20-$55, XP: $5.** 1916 N 850 E, 46562. US 30, 4.3 mi n on SR 13, 1.3 mi e on CR 200.

SANTA CLAUS — LAKE RUDOLPH CAMPGROUND & RV RESORT. (812) 937-4458. **8P $25-$50.** 78 N Holiday Blvd, 47579. I-64, exit 63, 7.9 mi s on SR 162. (PO Box 98).

Louisiana

CARENCRO — BAYOU WILDERNESS RV RESORT. (337) 896-0598. **4P $35-$38, XP: $3.** 201 St Clair Rd, 70520. I-49, exit 2, 2.5 mi e on SR 98, then 1 mi n on Wilderness Trail.

HAMMOND — CALLOWAY RV & CAMPGROUND. (985) 542-8094. **2P $26-$30, XP: $2-$3.** 14154 Club Deluxe Rd, 70403. I-12 to I-55 S, exit 28, 1 blk n, then 0.7 mi w.

KINDER — COUSHATTA CASINO RV RESORT. (337) 738-1200. **$17-$22.** 777 Pow Wow Pkwy, 70648. N of jct US 190 and 165, 4.5 mi on US 165. (PO Box 1240).

ROBERT — YOGI BEAR'S JELLYSTONE PARK CAMP-RESORT. (985) 345-3011. **Call for rates.** 46049 SR 445 N, 70455. I-12, exit 47, 3 mi n. (PO Box 519).

SCOTT — KOA KAMPGROUND OF LAFAYETTE. (337) 235-2739. **4P $33-$42, XP: $5.** 537 Apollo Rd, 70583. I-10, exit 97, 0.5 mi s.

VIDALIA — RIVER VIEW RV PARK. Ⓐ (318) 336-1400. **2P $28-$40, XP: $2.** 100 River View Pkwy, 71373. Jct US 65/84, 0.8 mi s on SR 131.

Maine

CASCO — POINT SEBAGO RESORT. (207) 655-3821. **4P $30-$82, XP: $5-$35.** 261 Point Sebago Rd, 04015. Jct SR 121, 3.7 mi n on US 302, then 1 mi w, follow signs.

DAMARISCOTTA — LAKE PEMAQUID CAMPGROUND. △△△ (207) 563-5202. **4P $24-$46, XP: $10.** 100 Twin Cove Ln, 04543. 0.8 mi n on US 1 business route, 2 mi e on Biscay Rd, then 0.3 mi n on Egypt Rd. (PO Box 967).

NORTH WATERFORD — PAPOOSE POND RESORT & CAMP-GROUND. (207) 583-4470. **6P $23-$65, XP: $5-$10.** 700 Norway Rd, 04088. 1.9 mi w on SR 118 from jct SR 37; from Norway, 10 mi w on SR 118.

OLD ORCHARD BEACH — POWDER HORN FAMILY CAMP-ING RESORT. (207) 934-4733. **2P $27-$61, XP: $4-$10.** 48 Cascade Rd (SR 98), 04064. 1 mi nw on SR 98; jct US 1, 1.8 mi se on SR 98. (PO Box 366).

ORLAND — SHADY OAKS CAMPGROUND & CABINS. (207) 469-7739. **2P $28-$34, XP: $2.** 32 Leaches, 04472. Jct US 1 and SR 175, sharp right, then 0.3 mi. (32 Leaches Pt).

SCARBOROUGH — BAYLEY'S CAMPING RESORT. △△△ (207) 883-6043. **2P $26-$69, XP: $5-$12.** 275 Pine Point Rd, 04074. Jct US 1, 2 mi e via SR 9 (Pine Point Rd), watch for sign.

WELLS — WELLS BEACH RESORT CAMPGROUND. △△△ (207) 646-7570. **2P $32-$70, XP: $7.** 1000 Post Rd (US 1), 04090-4109. Jct SR 109/9, 1.3 mi s.

Maryland

BERLIN — FRONTIER TOWN CAMPGROUND. (410) 641-0880. **Call for rates.** 8428 Stephen Decatur Hwy, 21811. Jct SR 50, 4 mi s on SR 611. (PO Box 691, OCEAN CITY, 21843).

COLLEGE PARK — CHERRY HILL PARK. △△△ (301) 937-7116. **2P $55-$65, XP: $5-$10.** 9800 Cherry Hill Rd, 20740. I-95, exit 29B, 1 mi w on SR 212 (Powder Mill Rd), then 1 mi s; I-495, exit 25, just s to Cherry Hill Rd, then 1 mi nw.

FLINTSTONE — HIDDEN SPRINGS CAMPGROUND. (814) 767-9676. **4P $25-$29, XP: $2.** I-68, exit 50 to Rocky Gap State Park, 3.5 mi n on Pleasant Valley Rd. (PO Box 190, 21530).

FREELAND — MORRIS MEADOWS RECREATION FARM. △△△ (410) 329-6636. **2P $27-$54, XP: $5-$10.** 1523 Freeland Rd, 21053. I-83, exit 36 (SR 439), w to jct SR 45, 1 mi n, then 3 mi w, follow signs.

WILLIAMSPORT — YOGI BEAR'S JELLYSTONE PARK CAMP RESORT HAGERSTOWN. (301) 223-7117. **6P $37-$50.** 16519 Lappans Rd, 21795. I-81, exit 1, 1.2 mi e on SR 68.

Massachusetts

BRIMFIELD — QUINEBAUG COVE CAMPGROUND. (413) 245-9525. **Call for rates.** 49 E Brimfield-Holland Rd, 01010. I-84, exit 3B, 3.8 mi w on US 20, then 0.3 mi s.

FOXBORO — NORMANDY FARMS CAMPGROUND. (508) 543-7600. **2P $25-$69, XP: $5-$10.** 72 West St, 02035. I-495, exit 14A, 1 mi n on US 1, then 1.3 mi e on Thurston and West sts.

OAKHAM — PINE ACRES FAMILY CAMPING RESORT. (508) 882-9509. **2P $28-$43, XP: $8-$15.** 203 Bechan Rd, 01068. Jct SR 122, 2 mi sw on SR 148, then just s via Spencer Rd.

SAVOY — SHADY PINES CAMPGROUND. (413) 743-2694. **2P $30-$32, XP: $8-$10.** 547 Loop Rd, 01256. On SR 8A and 116, 3.1 mi se.

Michigan

BAY VIEW — PETOSKEY KOA RV & CABIN RESORT. (231) 347-0005. **2P $19-$69, XP: $3-$5.** 1800 N US 31, 49770. US 31, 1 mi n of SR 119.

DECATUR — TIMBER TRAILS RV PARK. (269) 423-7311. **2P $28, XP: $6.** 84981 47 1/2 St, 49045. 1.9 mi sw on SR 51, 0.8 mi n.

PORT HURON — PORT HURON KOA KAMPGROUND. (810) 987-4070. **2P $30-$80, XP: $4.** 5111 Lapeer Rd, 48074. I-94, exit 262, 8 mi n on Wadhams Rd, then 0.3 mi e; I-69, exit 196, 0.4 mi n on Wadhams Rd, then 0.3 mi e.

Minnesota

CALEDONIA — DUNROMIN' PARK. (507) 724-2514. **4P $25-$45, XP: $2-$4.** 12757 Dunromin Dr, 55921. 2.8 mi s on SR 76 S from jct SR 44, 0.5 mi e.

CASS LAKE — STONY POINT RESORT, TRAILER PARK CAMP-GROUNDS. △△△ (218) 335-6311. **2P $22-$32, XP: $2.** 5510 US 2 NW, 56633. On US 2, 2 mi e of jct SR 371. (PO Box 518).

COKATO — COKATO LAKE CAMPING & RV RESORT. (320) 286-5779. **Call for rates.** 2945 CR 4 SW, 55321. 2.8 mi n of jct SR 12.

HINCKLEY — GRAND CASINO HINCKLEY RV RESORT & CHA-LETS. △△△ (320) 384-4886. **$13-$23.** 1326 Fire Monument Rd, 55037. I-35, exit 183, 1 mi e on SR 48.

PARK RAPIDS — BREEZE CAMPING & RV RESORT ON EAGLE LAKE. (218) 732-5888. **2P $30-$34, XP: $3.** 25824 CR 89, 56470. 9 mi n on US 71 from jct SR 34.

PARK RAPIDS — VAGABOND VILLAGE CAMPGROUND. (218) 732-5234. **Call for rates. (no credit cards).** 23801 Green Pines Rd, 56470. 2 mi e on SR 34, 5.7 mi n on CR 4, just w on CR 40, then 0.5 mi w via signs.

PRIOR LAKE — DAKOTAH MEADOWS RV PARK. △△△ (952) 445-8800. **$21-$30.** 2341 Park Pl, 55372. Just w of CR 83.

RICHMOND — EL RANCHO MANANA CAMPGROUND & RIDING STABLE. (320) 597-2740. **$20-$45, XP: $2-$3.** 27302 Ranch Rd, 56368. 4 mi n on CR 9 from jct SR 23 and 24, 2 mi ne on Manana and Ranch rds; 9 mi s of jct I-94, exit 153, via CR 9.

WALKER — SHORES OF LEECH LAKE CAMPGROUND & MARINA. (218) 547-1819. **$43, XP: $8.** 6166 Morriss Point Rd, 56484. 2.8 mi nw on SR 371 and 200 from jct SR 34, 0.5 mi e, follow signs.

Mississippi

BILOXI — MAJESTIC OAKS RV RESORT. (228) 436-4200. **4P $38-$44, XP: $2.** 1750 Pass Rd, 39531. I-110, exit 46A, 3.1 mi w on US 90, 0.6 mi n on Rodenberg Ave, then just w.

OCEAN SPRINGS — CAMP JOURNEY'S END. (228) 875-2100. **$38, XP: $3-$5.** 7501 Hwy 57, 39565. I-10, exit 57, 0.5 mi n.

PICAYUNE — SUN ROAMERS RV RESORT. (601) 798-5818. **4P $26-$36, XP: $2.** 41 Mississippi Pines Blvd, 39466. I-59, exit 4, 0.8 mi e on SR 43 S, then 0.5 mi s on Stafford Rd.

TOOMSUBA — MERIDIAN EAST/TOOMSUBA KOA. (601) 632-1684. **Call for rates.** 3953 KOA Campground Rd, 39364. I-20/59, exit 165, 1.5 mi s, follow signs.

TUNICA — GRAND CASINO TUNICA RV RESORT. (662) 363-2788. **$22-$37.** 111 Resort Village Rd, 38664. US 61, just w to Grand Casino Pkwy S.

VICKSBURG — MAGNOLIA RV PARK RESORT. (601) 631-0388. **4P $22-$25, XP: $2.** 211 Miller St, 39180. I-20, exit 1B, 1.1 mi s on US 61, just w.

Missouri

BRANSON — THE WILDERNESS AT SILVER DOLLAR CITY LOG CABINS AND RV'S. (417) 338-8189. **2P $30-$35, XP: $2.** 5125 SR 265, 65616. 0.5 mi s of jct SR 76.

EUREKA — YOGI BEAR'S JELLYSTONE PARK CAMP-RESORT. (636) 938-5925. **2P $25-$49, XP: $3-$4.** 5300 Fox Creek Rd, 63069. I-44, exit 261, 0.5 mi w. (PO Box 626, 63025).

Montana

MISSOULA — JELLYSTONE RV RESORT. (406) 543-9400. **2P $34-$36, XP: $3-$4.** 9900 Jellystone Ave, 59808. I-90, exit 96 (west side entry), 0.9 mi n.

POLSON — POLSON/FLATHEAD LAKE KOA. (406) 883-2151. **2P $25-$55, XP: $3-$5.** 200 Irvine Flats Rd, 59860. 1 mi n on US 93, 0.3 mi w.

WEST GLACIER — WEST GLACIER KOA. (406) 387-5341. **2P $30-$55, XP: $5-$6.** 355 Halfmoon Flats Rd, 59936. 2.5 mi w on US 2, 1 mi s. (PO Box 215).

Nebraska

NORTH PLATTE — HOLIDAY RV PARK & CAMPGROUND. (308) 534-2265. **2P $20-$32, XP: $2.** 601 Halligan Dr, 69101. I-80, exit 177, just n on US 83, immediate right turn on frontage road (Halligan Dr), then 0.5 mi e.

Nevada

BOULDER CITY — BOULDER OAKS RV RESORT. (702) 294-4425. **4P $35, XP: $2.** 1010 Industrial Rd, 89005. Just w of US 93. (PO Box 62364, 89006).

CARSON CITY — COMSTOCK COUNTRY RV RESORT. (775) 882-2445. **2P $28-$48, XP: $2-$4.** 5400 S Carson St, 89701. 3.3 mi s and w off US 395, 0.3 mi s of jct US 50 W.

LAS VEGAS — OASIS LAS VEGAS RV RESORT. (702) 260-2020. **4P $39-$71, XP: $2.** 2711 W Windmill Ln, 89123. I-15, exit 33 (Blue Diamond Rd), 0.5 mi e.

MESQUITE — DESERT SKIES RESORT. (928) 347-6000. **2P $50, XP: $5.** 350 E Hwy 91, 89024. I-15, exit 122, 1.5 mi ne via Hillside Dr. (PO Box 3780).

MINDEN — CARSON VALLEY RV RESORT & CASINO. (775) 782-9711. **2P $22-$42, XP: $6.** 1639 US 395 N, 89423. Center.

MINDEN — SILVER CITY RV RESORT. (775) 267-3359. **2P $35-$38, XP: $4.** 3165 US 395, 89423. 6 mi s of Carson City; 3 mi s of jct US 50 W.

PAHRUMP — SEIBT DESERT RETREAT LUXURY RV RESORT. (775) 751-1174. **4P $28-$45, XP: $10.** 301 W Leslie St, 89060. 10 mi n of SR 160 and 372, jct SR 160.

PAHRUMP — TERRIBLE'S LAKESIDE CASINO & RV RESORT. (775) 751-7770. **6P $24-$40, XP: $2.** 5870 S Homestead Rd, 89048. SR 160, 3.5 mi s.

SPARKS — RIVERS EDGE RV PARK. (775) 358-8533. **2P $33-$46, XP: $3.** 1405 S Rock Blvd, 89431. I-80, exit Rock Blvd S; US 395, exit SR 66 (Mill St).

VERDI — GOLD RANCH CASINO & RV RESORT. (775) 345-8880. **Call for rates.** 320 Gold Ranch Rd, 89439. I-80, exit 2. (PO Box 160).

ZEPHYR COVE — ZEPHYR COVE RESORT CAMPGROUND. (775) 589-4907. **6P $27-$65.** 760 Hwy 50, 89448. US 50, 4 mi n of state line. (PO Box 830).

New Hampshire

BARRINGTON — AYERS LAKE FARM CAMPGROUND. 🟢
(603) 335-1110. **4P $35-$47, XP:** $2-$5. (no credit cards). 557 US 202, 03825. Spaulding Tpke, exit 13, 4.5 mi w.   ⊠

BARRINGTON — BARRINGTON SHORES CAMPGROUND. 🟢
(603) 664-9333. **5P $35-$46, XP:** $3-$12. 70 Hall Rd, 03825. Jct SR 125 and US 4, 2.5 mi w on US 4, then 3 mi n.   ⊠

CHICHESTER — HILLCREST CAMPGROUND. (603) 798-5124. **2P $30-$35, XP:** $5-$12. 78 Dover Rd, 03234. I-93, exit 15, 8 mi e on SR 4; jct SR 28 and 4, 2 mi w on SR 4.   ⇌ ⊠

FREEDOM — DANFORTH BAY CAMPING & RV RESORT. 🟢
(603) 539-2069. **4P $31-$50, XP:** $3-$5. 196 Shawtown Rd, 03836. Jct SR 25/153, 1 mi n on SR 153, 3 mi w on Ossipee Lake Rd.   ⇌ ⊠

GLEN — GLEN ELLIS FAMILY CAMPGROUND. (603) 383-4567. **Call for rates.** US 302, 03838. 0.3 mi w of jct SR 16. (PO Box 397).   ⇌ ⊠

HAMPTON FALLS — WAKEDA CAMPGROUND LLC. 🟢 (603) 772-5274. **5P $30-$42, XP:** $5. 294 Exeter Rd (SR 88), 03844. SR 88, 3.8 mi w of jct US 1.   ⊠

LACONIA — PAUGUS BAY CAMPGROUND. (603) 366-4757. **Call for rates. (no credit cards).** 96 Hilliard Rd, 03246. Jct US 3 and SR 11B, 0.5 mi n on US 3, then w.   ⊠

MEREDITH — CLEARWATER CAMPGROUND. 🟢 (603) 279-7761. **Call for rates.** 26 Campground Rd (SR 104), 03253. I-93, exit 23, 3 mi e.   ⊠

MEREDITH — MEREDITH WOODS 4 SEASON CAMPING AREA. 🟢 (603) 279-5449. **Call for rates.** 26 Campground Rd, 03253. I-93, exit 23, 3 mi e.   ⇌ ⊠

MILTON — MI-TE-JO LAKESIDE FAMILY CAMPGROUND. 🟢
(603) 652-9022. **2P $39-$44, XP:** $5-$8. (no credit cards). 111 Mi-Te Jo Rd, 03851. SR 16, exit 17 northbound, 0.8 mi e on SR 75, 3.3 mi n on SR 125, then 1 mi e on Townhouse Rd; exit southbound, 3.3 mi n on SR 125, 1 mi e on Townhouse Rd. (PO Box 830).   ⊠

NEW HAMPTON — TWIN TAMARACK FAMILY CAMPING & RV RESORT. 🟢 (603) 279-4387. **2P $32-$46, XP:** $2-$8. 41 Twin Tamarack Rd, 03256. I-93, exit 23, 2.5 mi e on SR 104.   ⇌ ⊠

SOUTH WEARE — COLD SPRINGS CAMP RESORT. (603) 529-2528. **2P $46-$52, XP:** $3-$7. 62 Barnard Hill Rd, 03281. Jct SR 77/149, 1.5 mi se, 0.3 mi n on sign posted road; 10 mi nw of jct SR 114/101. (22 Wildlife Dr, SOUTH WEARE).   ⇌ ⊠

TAMWORTH — CHOCORUA CAMPING VILLAGE. 🟢 (603) 323-8536. **4P $25-$62, XP:** $6-$8. 893 White Mountain Hwy, 03817. SR 16, 2.5 mi n of jct SR 25. (PO Box 484, CHOCORUA).   ⇌ ⊠

TWIN MOUNTAIN — TWIN MOUNTAIN KOA KAMPGROUND. 🟢 (603) 846-5559. **2P $30-$43, XP:** $7-$10. 372 SR 115, 03595. Jct US 302, 2.1 mi n on US 3, then 0.8 mi ne. (PO Box 148).   ⇌ ⊠

WOODSTOCK — BROKEN BRANCH KOA. (603) 745-8008. **2P $29-$33, XP:** $3-$10. 1000 Eastside Rd (SR 175), 03293. I-93, exit 31, 2 mi s, follow signs. (PO Box 6, WOODSTOCK).   ⇌ ⊠

New Jersey

CAPE MAY — BEACHCOMBER CAMPING RESORT. (609) 886-6035. **4P $23-$65, XP:** $5-$8. 462 Seashore Rd, 08204. Garden State Pkwy, exit 4A (SR 47 N), w to 3rd traffic light, then 1 mi s; Railroad Ave and Seashore Rd.   ⇌ ⊠

CAPE MAY — SEASHORE CAMPSITES INC. 🟢 (609) 884-4010. **4P $24-$52, XP:** $5. 720 Seashore Rd, 08204. Garden State Pkwy, exit 4A (SR 47 N), 1 mi n to CR 626, then 2.7 mi s.   ⇌ ⊠

CAPE MAY — HOLLY SHORES CAMPGROUND. 🟢 (609) 886-1234. **2P $26-$54, XP:** $5-$8. 491 US 9, 08204. Garden State Pkwy, exit 4A (SR 47 N) to 2nd traffic light, 1 mi s.   ⇌ ⊠

CAPE MAY COURT HOUSE — BIG TIMBER LAKE CAMPING RESORT. 🟢 (609) 465-4456. **4P $41-$60, XP:** $3-$8. 116 Swainton Goshen Rd, 08210. Garden State Pkwy, exit 13 southbound, 0.5 mi w on paved road, 1 mi s on US 9, then 1 mi w (CR 646). (PO Box 366).   ⇌ ⊠

OCEAN VIEW — OCEAN VIEW RESORT CAMPGROUND. 🟢
(609) 624-1675. **4P $39-$68, XP:** $7. 2555 Rt 9, 08230. US 9, 0.8 mi nw of Garden State Pkwy, exit 17 southbound; exit northbound, use service area turnaround. (PO Box 607).   ⇌ ⊠

New Mexico

ALBUQUERQUE — ALBUQUERQUE CENTRAL KOA. (505) 296-2729. **Call for rates.** 12400 Skyline Rd NE, 87123. I-40, exit 166, just s, then 0.4 mi e.   ⇌ ⊠

ALBUQUERQUE — AMERICAN RV PARK OF ALBUQUERQUE. 🟢 (505) 831-3545. **4P $28-$37, XP:** $3. 13500 Central Ave SW, 87121. I-40, exit 149, just s, then w.   ⇌ ⊠

DEMING — LITTLE VINEYARD RV PARK. 🟢 (575) 546-3560. **2P $25, XP:** $3. 2901 E Pine St, 88030. I-10, exit 85, 1 mi w.   ⇌ ⊠

GALLUP — USA RV PARK. 🟢 (505) 863-5021. **2P $27-$29, XP:** $2. 2925 W Hwy 66, 87301. I-40, exit 16, 1 mi e.   ⇌ ⊠

LAS CRUCES — HACIENDA RV RESORT. 🟢 (575) 528-5800. **2P $35-$47, XP:** $2. 740 Stern Dr, 88005. I-10, exit 140, just e.   ⊠

RIO RANCHO — STAGECOACH STOP RV RESORT. (505) 867-1000. **Call for rates.** 3650 SR 528, 87124. I-25, exit 242, w to SR 528, then 0.5 mi s.   ⇌ ⊠

SILVER CITY — SILVER CITY KOA. (575) 388-3351. **4P $18-$37, XP: $3-$4.** 11824 E Hwy 180, 88022. 4.9 mi e on US 180 and SR 90.

New York

BATH — HICKORY HILL CAMPING RESORT. ⏺ (607) 776-4345. **2P $39-$51.** 7531 CR 13, 14810. SR 17, exit 38, 1 mi n on SR 54, then at fork, 2 mi n on Haverling St (CR 13).

DEWITTVILLE — CHAUTAUQUA HEIGHTS CAMPING RESORT CAMPGROUND. (716) 386-3804. **2P $25-$39, XP: $4-$8.** 5652 Thumb Rd, 14728. I-86, exit 10 westbound, 5 mi on CR 430 W; I-90, exit 60 to Mayville, 2.4 mi on CR 430 E, just e.

FARMINGTON — CANANDAIGUA/ROCHESTER KOA CAMP-GROUND. (585) 398-3582. **2P $28-$40, XP: $3.** 5374 Farmington Townline Rd, 14425. I-90, exit 44, 3.2 mi s on SR 332, then 1 mi e.

GARDINER — YOGI BEAR'S JELLYSTONE PARK CAMP-RESORTS AT LAZY RIVER. (845) 255-5193. **4P $56-$61, XP: $4.** 50 Bevier Rd, 12525. 2.5 mi w on US 44 and SR 55, just s on Albany Post, then just e.

GARRATTSVILLE — YOGI BEAR'S JELLYSTONE PARK AT CRYSTAL LAKE. (607) 965-8265. **4P $18-$63, XP: $5-$10.** 111 E Turtle Lake Rd, 13342. Jct SR 80, 6.2 mi s on CR 16, 0.7 mi n on CR 51, then 1.1 mi w on CR 17.

GREENFIELD PARK — YOGI BEAR'S JELLYSTONE PARK CAMP-RESORT AT BIRCHWOOD ACRES. (845) 434-4743. **4P $35-$64, XP: $6-$12.** 85 Martinfeld Rd, 12789. Jct US 209 and SR 52, 8 mi w on SR 52, then 0.5 mi s. (PO Box 482, WOODRIDGE).

GREENFIELD PARK — SKYWAY CAMPING RESORT. (845) 647-5747. **4P $55-$65, XP: $10.** 99 Mountaindale Rd, 12435. Jct US 209 and SR 52, 5.2 mi w on SR 52, then 1.1 mi sw.

LAKE GEORGE — LAKE GEORGE ESCAPE. (518) 623-3207. **2P $24-$67, XP: $6.** 175 E Schroon River Rd, 12845. I-87, exit 23, 0.4 mi e on Diamond Point Rd, then 0.8 mi n. (PO Box 431).

LAKE GEORGE — LAKE GEORGE RV PARK. (518) 792-3775. **2P $47-$71, XP: $7.** 74 SR 149, 12845. I-87 (New York State Thruway), exit 20, 0.5 mi n on US 9, then 0.4 mi e. (74 SR 149, 12845).

OLD FORGE — OLD FORGE CAMPING RESORT. (315) 369-6011. **2P $24-$165, XP: $3-$5.** 3347 SR 28, 13420. 1 mi n of town. (PO Box 51).

PLATTEKILL — NEWBURGH/NEW YORK CITY NORTH KOA. ⏺ (845) 564-2836. **2P $25-$65, XP: $4-$8.** 119 Freetown Hwy, 12568. 1.5 mi n on SR 32, 3 mi s of jct US 44 and SR 55, 0.5 mi e, follow signs.

PULASKI — BRENNAN BEACH RV RESORT. ⏺ (315) 298-2242. **Call for rates.** 80 Brennan Beach, 13142. I-81, exit 36, 4 mi w on SR 13, 1 mi n on SR 3.

QUEENSBURY — LEDGEVIEW VILLAGE RV PARK. (518) 798-6621. **2P $35-$39, XP: $4-$7.** 321 SR 149, 12845. I-87 (New York State Thruway), exit 20, 0.5 mi n on US 9, then 1.5 mi e.

VERONA — THE VILLAGES AT TURNING STONE. (315) 361-7275. **4P $40-$55.** 5065 SR 365, 13478. I-90, exit 33, 1.3 mi w. (PO Box 126).

WATKINS GLEN — WATKINS GLEN-CORNING KOA KAMP-GROUND. (607) 535-7404. **2P $32-$62, XP: $3-$8.** 1710 SR 414, 14891. SR 414, 4.5 mi s of jct SR 14. (PO Box 228).

North Carolina

BOONE — KOA-BOONE. (828) 264-7250. **2P $32-$38, XP: $2-$6.** 123 Harmony Mt Ln, 28607. Jct US 221 and 421, 3 mi n on SR 194, 1 mi w on Ray Brown Rd.

CANDLER — KOA ASHEVILLE WEST. (828) 665-7015. **2P $25-$41, XP: $4-$5.** 309 Wiggins Rd, 28715. I-40, exit 37, just s, 0.5 mi w on US 19/23, then 0.3 mi n.

CEDAR MOUNTAIN — BLACK FOREST CAMPING RESORT. (828) 884-2267. **2P $25-$36, XP: $3-$5.** 100 Summer Rd, 28718. On US 276, 12.6 mi s of Brevard. (PO Box 709).

CHEROKEE — CHEROKEE GREAT SMOKIES KOA. (828) 497-9711. **Call for rates.** 4 mi n on Big Cove Rd. (92 KOA Campground Rd, 28719).

North Dakota

BISMARCK — BISMARCK KOA. (701) 222-2662. **Call for rates.** 3720 Centennial Rd, 58503-8001. I-94, exit 161 (Centennial Rd), 1 mi n.

Ohio

BROOKVILLE — DAYTON TALL TIMBERS RESORT KOA. (937) 833-3888. **Call for rates.** 7796 Wellbaum Rd, 45309. 0.5 mi n on SR 49; jct I-70, exit 24, 0.5 mi w on Pleasant Plain Rd, then 0.3 mi s.

SHELBY — SHELBY/MANSFIELD KOA. (419) 347-1392. **2P $28-$75, XP: $5-$12.** 6787 Baker 47, 44875-9103. 4 mi nw on SR 39, then 4.5 mi n, follow signs.

Oklahoma

GORE — MARVAL RESORT. ⏺ (918) 489-2295. **2P $29-$49, XP: $3-$6.** Rt 3, Box 60 Gore, 74435. I-40, exit 287, 6 mi n on SR 100, then just e.

Oregon

ASHLAND — HOWARD PRAIRIE LAKE RESORT. ⓐⓐⓐ (541) 482-1979. **Call for rates.** 3249 Hyatt Prairie Rd, 97520. I-5, exit 14, 0.7 mi e on SR 66, 17 mi e on Dead Indian Memorial Rd, then 3.4 mi s. 🅚🅧

BEND — CROWN VILLA RV RESORT. (541) 388-1131. **4P $32-$70, XP: $3.** 60801 Brosterhous Rd, 97702. Business Rt US 97, 1 mi e on Murphy Rd, then just s; south end of town. 🅚🅧

CANNON BEACH — RV RESORT AT CANNON BEACH. ⓐⓐⓐ (503) 436-2231. **Call for rates.** 340 Elk Creek Rd, 97110. US 101, exit Sunset Blvd. (PO Box 1037). 🅚➦🅧

EUGENE — PREMIER RV RESORT OF EUGENE. (541) 686-3152. **2P $34-$44, XP: $3.** 33022 Van Duyn Rd, 97408. I-5, exit 199, just e, then 0.4 mi s; n of town at Coburg exit. 🅚➦🅧

HAMMOND — ASTORIA/WARRENTON/SEASIDE KOA. ⓐⓐⓐ (503) 861-2606. **2P $26-$75, XP: $4-$8.** 1100 NW Ridge Rd, 97121. 4.6 mi nw of jct US 101, follow signs to Fort Stevens State Park. ➦🅧

LEBANON — MALLARD CREEK GOLF & RV RESORT. (541) 259-0070. **2P $30-$33.** 31958 Bellinger Scale Rd, 97355. I-5, exit 228, 5.6 mi e on SR 34 (follow south and east truck route), 1.3 mi s on Denny School Rd, 2.2 mi e on Airport Dr, 4.6 mi s on US 20, 1.1 mi ne on Waterloo Rd, just e on Berlin Rd, then 0.4 mi n. 🅚🅧

NETARTS — NETARTS BAY RV PARK & MARINA. (503) 842-7774. **Call for rates.** 2260 Bilyeu, 97143. Just w. (PO Box 218, NETARTS). 🅚🅧

NEWPORT — OUTDOOR RESORTS PACIFIC SHORES MOTORCOACH RESORT. (541) 265-3750. **6P $50-$90, XP: $5.** 6225 N Coast Hwy 101, 97365. On US 101, 3.4 mi n. 🅚➦🅧

SALEM — SALEM PREMIER RV RESORT. (503) 364-7714. **2P $33-$42, XP: $3.** 4700 Salem-Dallas Hwy 22, 97304. I-5, exit 260A (Salem Pkwy), follow signs to city center; 3 mi sw to Commercial St NE, then 1.4 mi s to Marion St; 4.7 mi sw from Marion St Bridge via SR 22; 4.3 mi e of jct SR 22 and 99 W. 🅚➦🅧

SALEM — PHOENIX RV PARK. ⓐⓐⓐ (503) 581-2497. **2P $31, XP: $2.** 4130 Silverton Rd NE, 97305. I-5, exit 256, 0.3 mi e on Market, 1.3 mi n on Lancaster, then just e. 🅚🅧

SISTERS — SISTERS/BEND KOA. (541) 549-3021. **2P $45-$75, XP: $3-$6.** 67667 Hwy 20 W, 97701. On US 20, 3.5 mi e. 🅚➦🅧

WARM SPRINGS — KAHNEETA HIGH DESERT RESORT & CASINO RV PARK. (541) 553-1112. **4P $20-$40, XP: $8.** 6823 Hwy 8, 97761. 11 mi ne off US 26; on Warm Springs Indian Reservation. (PO Box 1240). 🅚➦🅧

WELCHES — MT. HOOD VILLAGE VACATION COTTAGES & RV RESORT. ⓐⓐⓐ (503) 622-4011. **6P $25-$45.** 65000 E Hwy 26, 97067. On US 26, 2 mi w. ➦🅧

WILSONVILLE — PHEASANT RIDGE RV RESORT. ⓐⓐⓐ (503) 682-7829. **2P $33-$36, XP: $1.** 8275 SW Elligsen Rd, 97070. I-5, exit 286, just e. 🅚➦🅧

Pennsylvania

BAKERSVILLE — PIONEER PARK CAMPGROUND. (814) 445-6348. **2P $22-$34, XP: $3.** Just e on SR 31, 0.5 mi s via signs. (273 Trent Rd, 15501). ➦🅧

BEDFORD — FRIENDSHIP VILLAGE CAMPGROUND. ⓐⓐⓐ (814) 623-1677. **$21-$35, XP: $3.** 348 Friendship Village Rd, 15522. 1.3 mi w on US 30 from jct US 220, 0.5 mi n via signs. ➦🅧

BELLEFONTE — BELLEFONTE/STATE COLLEGE KOA. ⓐⓐⓐ (814) 355-7912. **2P $22-$52, XP: $3-$5.** 2481 Jacksonville Rd, 16823. I-80, exit 161, 2 mi ne on SR 26. ➦🅧

BOWMANSVILLE — LAKE IN WOOD CAMPGROUND. (717) 445-5525. **2P $40-$55, XP: $3-$6.** 576 Yellow Hill Rd, 17555. SR 23, 4.5 mi n on SR 625, 1 mi ne on Oaklyn Dr, then 1.5 mi e, follow signs. ➦🅧

BOWMANSVILLE — OAK CREEK CAMPGROUNDS. ⓐⓐⓐ (717) 445-6161. **4P $25-$43, XP: $7.** 400 E Maple Grove Rd, 17507. From SR 625, 1.5 mi e. (PO Box 128). ➦🅧

BOWMANSVILLE — SUN VALLEY CAMPGROUND. (717) 445-6262. **Call for rates.** 451 E Maple Grove Rd, 17507. From SR 625, 1.9 mi e. (PO Box 129). ➦🅧

CLAY — STARLITE CAMPING RESORT. (717) 733-9655. **2P $36-$40, XP: $3-$5.** 1500 Furnace Hill Rd, 17578. US 322, 1.1 mi n on Clay Rd, 2.4 mi ne, follow signs. ➦🅧

COOKSBURG — KALYUMET CAMPGROUND. ⓐⓐⓐ (814) 744-9622. **4P $27-$36, XP: $5.** I-80, exit 62, 2 mi e on SR 68 E to light at Clarion Courthouse, go straight for 9.5 mi. (8630 Miola Rd, LUCINDA, 16235). ➦🅧

ERIE — ERIE KOA KAMPGROUNDS. (814) 476-7706. **$25-$65, XP: $6.** I-90, exit 18, 1.3 mi s on SR 832, then 0.8 mi e; I-79, exit 174, 1.5 mi w. (6645 West Rd, MCKEAN, 16426). ➦🅧

FARMINGTON — BENNER'S MEADOW RUN CAMPING & CABINS. (724) 329-4097. **2P $26-$145, XP: $3-$10.** 315 Nelson Rd, 15437. 2.5 mi n of US 40, follow signs. ➦🅧

GARDNERS — MOUNTAIN CREEK CAMPGROUND. ⓐⓐⓐ (717) 486-7681. **2P $20-$35, XP: $5.** 349 Pine Grove Rd, 17324. 2 mi w of SR 34, follow signs. ➦🅧

GETTYSBURG — GRANITE HILL CAMPING RESORT. ⓐⓐⓐ (717) 642-8749. **4P $20-$44, XP: $2-$8.** 3340 Fairfield Rd, 17325. 5.8 mi w on SR 116. ➦🅧

GETTYSBURG — GETTYSBURG CAMPGROUND. ⓐⓐⓐ (717) 334-3304. **4P $35-$40, XP: $3-$5.** 2030 Fairfield Rd, 17325. 3 mi w on SR 116 W.

GETTYSBURG — GETTYSBURG KOA KAMPGROUND. ⓐⓐⓐ (717) 642-5713. **2P $25-$65, XP: $3-$6.** 20 Knox Rd, 17325. 3 mi w on US 30, 3 mi s on Knoxlyn Rd, follow signs.

GETTYSBURG — DRUMMER BOY CAMPING RESORT. ⓐⓐⓐ (717) 334-3277. **2P $32-$70, XP: $4.** 1300 Hanover Rd, 17325. 2 mi e on SR 116 at US 15 Bypass, exit Hanover Rd.

GETTYSBURG — ROUND TOP CAMPGROUND. (717) 334-9565. **4P $36-$45, XP: $3-$6.** 180 Knight Rd, 17325. 3 mi s on SR 134 at US 15.

HARRISVILLE — KOZY REST KAMPGROUND. ⓐⓐⓐ (724) 735-2417. **4P $28-$35, XP: $2-$4.** 449 Campground Rd, 16038. Jct SR 8/SR 58, 0.5 mi e on SR 58 to Campground Rd, then 1.9 mi ne.

HERSHEY — HERSHEY HIGHMEADOW CAMPGROUND. (717) 534-8999. **2P $31-$46, XP: $4.** 1200 Matlack Rd, 17036. 0.5 mi n on SR 39 W from jct US 322 and 422. (PO Box 866, 17033).

HOLTWOOD — MUDDY RUN RECREATION PARK. (717) 284-5850. **6P $23, XP: $3.** 172 Bethesda Church Rd W, 17532. 1.8 mi ne on SR 372.

JONESTOWN — JONESTOWN KOA. (717) 865-2526. **Call for rates.** 145 Old Rt 22, 17038. 2 mi e on US 22 from jct SR 72, 0.5 mi s; I-81, exit 90, 5 mi se; I-78, exit 6, 5 mi w, follow signs. (PO Box 867).

KNOX — WOLFS CAMPING RESORT. ⓐⓐⓐ (814) 797-1103. **Call for rates.** 308 Timberwolf Run, 16232. I-80, exit 53.

LANCASTER — OLD MILL STREAM CAMPGROUND. (717) 299-2314. **4P $30-$41, XP: $3.** 2249 Lincoln Hwy E, 17602. 5 mi e on US 30.

LENHARTSVILLE — ROBIN HILL CAMPING RESORT. (610) 756-6117. **Call for rates.** 149 Robin Hill Rd, 19534. I-78, exit 40 (Krumsville) or exit 35 (Lenhartsville), follow signs for 3 mi.

LICKDALE — LICKDALE CAMPGROUND. (717) 865-6411. **4P $25-$33, XP: $3-$7.** 11 Lickdale Rd, 17038. I-81, exit 90, just e.

LIVERPOOL — FERRY BOAT CAMPSITES. ⓐⓐⓐ (717) 444-3200. **2P $20-$40.** 32 Ferry Ln, 17045. 2 mi s on US 11/15.

MANHEIM — PINCH POND FAMILY CAMPGROUND & RV PARK. ⓐⓐⓐ (717) 665-7640. **4P $32-$40, XP: $5-$7.** 3075 Pinch Rd, 17545. I-76 (Pennsylvania Tpke), exit 266, 1 mi s on SR 72, 0.5 mi w on Cider Press Rd, then 1 mi n.

MANSFIELD — BUCKTAIL CAMPING RESORT. (570) 662-2923. **4P $19-$49, XP: $11.** 130 Bucktail Rd, 16933. US 15, exit US 6, just e on US 6, 1.5 mi n on Lambs Creek Rd, then 1 mi w.

MARSHALLS CREEK — OTTER LAKE CAMP RESORT. ⓐⓐⓐ (570) 223-0123. **2P $35-$54, XP: $4-$8.** I-80, exit 309, 3 mi n on US 209, just n on SR 402, then 7 mi w on Marshalls Creek Rd. (PO Box 850, 18335).

MEADVILLE — BROOKDALE FAMILY CAMPGROUND. (814) 789-3251. **4P $27-$40, XP: $4-$6.** 25164 State Hwy 27, 16335. On SR 27, 8 mi e.

MERCER — MERCER-GROVE CITY KOA. (724) 748-3160. **2P $30-$60, XP: $3-$5.** 1337 Butler Pike, 16137. I-79, exit 113, 3 mi n on SR 258, follow signs.

MERCER — ROCKY SPRINGS CAMPGROUND. (724) 662-4415. **Call for rates. (no credit cards).** 84 Rocky Spring Rd, Rt 318, 16137. I-80, exit 15 westbound, 2 mi n on US 19 to Butler St (SR 318), then 4.5 mi w; exit eastbound, jct I-80 and exit 4A (SR 318), 6.5 mi ne.

MERCERSBURG — SAUNDEROSA PARK INC. (717) 328-2216. **4P $26-$30, XP: $1-$2.** 5909 Little Cove Rd, 17236. 4.8 mi w on SR 16, 2.5 mi s on SR 456.

MEXICO — BUTTONWOOD CAMPGROUND. (717) 436-8334. **4P $24-$34, XP: $3.** River Rd, 17056. US 322, exit 24 (Port Royal), 0.6 mi s on SR 75 S, 0.8 mi se on Old US 322, then 0.4 mi s on River Rd. (PO Box 223).

MILL RUN — YOGI BEAR'S JELLYSTONE PARK CAMP RESORT. (724) 455-2929. **4P $18-$56, XP: $3-$7.** 839 Mill Run Rd, 15464. Just s on SR 381. (PO Box 91).

NEW COLUMBIA — WILLIAMSPORT SOUTH/NITTANY MOUNTAIN KOA KAMPGROUND. (570) 568-5541. **2P $22-$45, XP: $2-$6.** 2751 Millers Bottom Rd, 17856. I-80, exit 210A, 0.5 mi s on US 15, 4.5 mi w on New Columbia Rd, then 0.4 mi nw.

NEW HOLLAND — SPRING GULCH RESORT. (717) 354-3100. **2P $30-$60, XP: $2-$6.** 475 Lynch Rd, 17557. Jct SR 23 and 897, 4 mi s on SR 897.

NORTHUMBERLAND — SPLASH MAJIC CAMPGROUND & RV RESORT. (570) 473-8021. **4P $33-$48.** 213 Yogi Blvd, 17857. I-80, exit 224, 2 mi e on SR 54, 8 mi s on US 11; 2.5 mi n on US 11.

PINE GROVE — PINE GROVE KOA AT TWIN GROVE PARK. ⓐⓐⓐ (717) 865-4602. **2P $27-$45, XP: $4-$6.** 1445 Suedburg Rd, 17963. I-81, exit 100, 5 mi w on SR 443.

PORTERSVILLE — BEAR RUN CAMPGROUND. ⓐⓐⓐ (724) 368-3564. **2P $25-$47, XP: $3-$10.** 184 Badger Hill Rd, 16051. I-79, exit 96, 0.8 mi n on SR 488.

PORTLAND — DRIFTSTONE ON THE DELAWARE. **AAA** (570) 897-6859. **2P $30-$42, XP: $5-$8.** SR 611, Portland exit, 4 mi s on River Rd, slight left at split. (2731 River Rd, MOUNT BETHEL, 18343).

QUARRYVILLE — YOGI BEAR'S JELLYSTONE PARK. (717) 786-3458. **Call for rates.** 340 Blackburn Rd, 17566. 2.7 mi s on US 222, 1.5 mi se, follow signs.

ROBESONIA — ADVENTURE BOUND CAMPING RESORTS AT EAGLES PEAK. (610) 589-4800. **4P $30-$48, XP: $2-$10.** 397 Eagles Peak Rd, 19551. 1.6 mi s on SR 419 from jct US 422, just s on Main St, 0.5 mi w on Memorial Blvd, then 1.1 mi s on Sheridan Rd, follow signs for Eagles Peak.

ROSE POINT — COOPER'S LAKE. (724) 368-8710. **Call for rates.** 205 Currie Rd, 16057. I-79, exit 99, 0.8 mi w on US 422, then 1 mi n.

SANDY LAKE — GODDARD PARK VACATION LAND CAMPGROUND. (724) 253-4645. **2P $22-$33, XP: $2-$3.** 867 Georgetown Rd, 16145. I-79, exit 130, 0.3 mi w on SR 358, then 3.5 mi n, follow signs.

SHARTLESVILLE — APPALACHIAN CAMPSITES. (610) 488-6319. **Call for rates.** 60 Motel Dr, 19554. I-78, exit 23, 0.5 mi w on service road (entrance just past motel). (PO Box 289).

SHARTLESVILLE — MOUNTAIN SPRINGS CAMPING RESORT INC & ARENA. **AAA** (610) 488-6859. **Call for rates.** 3450 Mountain Rd, 19554. I-78, exit 23, 1 mi n. (PO Box 365).

SIGEL — CAMPERS PARADISE CAMPGROUNDS & CABINS. (814) 752-2393. **2P $25-$35, XP: $5-$10.** 37 Steele Dr, 15860. On SR 949 N, 3 mi n of SR 36.

STRASBURG — WHITE OAK CAMPGROUND. **AAA** (717) 687-6207. **2P $24-$30, XP: $3.** 3156 White Oak Rd, 17566. 3.7 mi s of Centre Square on S Decatur St/May Post Office Rd, then 0.3 mi e. (PO Box 90, 17579).

UPPER BLACK EDDY — COLONIAL WOODS FAMILY CAMPING RESORT. (610) 847-5808. **4P $33-$42, XP: $4-$6.** 545 Lonely Cottage Dr, 18972. 1.5 mi e on Marienstein Rd from jct SR 611, then 1 mi n, follow signs.

WATERFORD — SPARROW POND FAMILY CAMPGROUND AND RECREATION FACILITY. **AAA** (814) 796-6777. **4P $32-$45, XP: $3.** 11103 Route 19 N, 16441. I-90, exit 24, 10 mi s on US 19 (Peach St).

South Carolina

HILTON HEAD ISLAND — HILTON HEAD HARBOR RV RESORT & MARINA. (843) 681-3256. **4P $45-$59, XP: $3.** 43A Jenkins Rd, 29926. 0.9 mi se of Intracoastal Waterway Bridge off US 278, 0.4 mi n, follow signs.

HILTON HEAD ISLAND — HILTON HEAD ISLAND MOTOR-COACH RESORT. **AAA** (843) 785-7699. **4P $47-$53, XP: $2.** 133 Arrow Rd, 29928. 5.6 mi e on Cross Island Pkwy (US 278 toll), then just w. (PO Box 6037, 29938).

MYRTLE BEACH — MYRTLE BEACH TRAVEL PARK. (843) 449-3714. **4P $32-$60, XP: $4.** 10108 Kings Rd, 29572. Jct US 17 business route/SR 22, 1.3 mi s.

MYRTLE BEACH — OCEAN LAKES FAMILY CAMPGROUND. **AAA** (843) 238-5636. **$28-$64.** 6001 S Kings Hwy, 29575. Jct SR 544 and US 17 business route.

MYRTLE BEACH — APACHE FAMILY CAMPGROUND AND PIER. (843) 449-7323. **4P $26-$55, XP: $4.** 9700 Kings Rd, 29572. Jct SR 22, 1.3 mi sw on US 17, then 0.8 mi e on Lake Arrowhead Rd.

MYRTLE BEACH — PIRATELAND FAMILY CAMPING RESORT. (843) 238-5155. **4P $27-$65, XP: $3.** 5401 S Kings Hwy, 29575. Jct SR 544, 1.2 mi ne on US 17 business route.

MYRTLE BEACH — LAKEWOOD CAMPING RESORT. **AAA** (843) 238-5161. **7P $25-$62, XP: $2.** 5901 S Kings Hwy, 29575. Jct SR 544, 0.5 mi ne on US 17 business route.

South Dakota

CHAMBERLAIN — CEDAR SHORE CAMPGROUND. **AAA** (605) 734-5273. **$25-$30.** 1400 Shoreline Dr, 57365. I-90, exit 260, 2.5 mi e on US 16 and I-90 business loop, then 1 mi ne on Mickelson country road, follow signs. (PO Box 308, 57325).

DEADWOOD — WHISTLER GULCH CAMPGROUND & RV PARK. (605) 578-2092. **$25-$40.** 235 Cliff, 57732. 0.7 mi s on US 85.

HILL CITY — RAFTER J BAR RANCH CAMPGROUND. **AAA** (605) 574-2527. **2P $25-$68, XP: $3-$6.** 12325 Rafter J Rd, 57745. 3.3 mi s on US 16 and 385 at SR 87/244. (PO Box 128).

INTERIOR — BADLANDS WHITE RIVER KOA. **AAA** (605) 433-5337. **2P $23-$42, XP: $2-$4.** 20720 SD Hwy 44, 57750. 4 mi e of jct SR 377.

MITCHELL — MITCHELL KOA. (605) 996-1131. **Call for rates.** 41255 SD Hwy 38, 57301-7800. I-90, exit 335, 0.5 mi n, then 0.3 mi w.

NORTH SIOUX CITY — SIOUX CITY NORTH KOA. (605) 232-4519. **2P $20-$43, XP: $3.** 601 Streeter Dr, 57049. I-29, exit 2 northbound, 1 mi n on west service road; exit 4 southbound, 1 mi w on west service road.

SIOUX FALLS — YOGI BEAR CAMP RESORT. (605) 332-2233. **2P $22-$35, XP: $2.** 26014 478th Ave, 57005. I-90, exit 402, just n.

SPEARFISH — ELKHORN RIDGE RV PARK & CAMPGROUND. (605) 722-1800. **Call for rates.** 20189 US 85, 57783. I-90, exit 17 (US 85), 0.5 mi s.

Tennessee

EAST RIDGE — BEST HOLIDAY TRAV-L-PARK/CHATTANOOGA. (706) 891-9766. **2P $23-$33, XP: $3.** 1709 Mack Smith Rd, 37412. I-75, exit 1 southbound; exit 1B northbound, 0.3 mi w, then 1 mi s.

GATLINBURG — OUTDOOR RESORTS OF GATLINBURG. (865) 436-5861. **4P $35-$45, XP: $2.** 11.5 mi e on US 321 N. (4229 Parkway E, 37738).

PIGEON FORGE — RIVEREDGE RV PARK. (865) 453-5813. **2P $26-$36, XP: $4.** 4220 Huskey St, 37863. Just off US 441 at traffic light 10.

TOWNSEND — TOWNSEND/GREAT SMOKIES KOA. (865) 448-2241. **Call for rates.** 8533 State Hwy 73, 37882. On SR 73, 0.4 mi w of entrance to Great Smoky Mountain National Park.

Texas

ABILENE — KOA-ABILENE. (325) 672-3681. **2P $15-$60, XP: $3.** 4851 W Stamford St, 79603. I-20, exit 282 (Shirley Rd), 0.5 mi w of US 83-277, follow signs.

AMARILLO — FORT AMARILLO RV RESORT. (806) 331-1700. **2P $30, XP: $2.** 10101 Amarillo Blvd W, 79124. I-40, exit 64 westbound, 0.3 mi n on Soncy to Amarillo Blvd, then 1 mi w; exit 62B eastbound, 0.7 mi e.

AMARILLO — AMARILLO RV RANCH. (806) 373-4962. **2P $30-$34, XP: $2.** 1414 Sunrise Dr, 79104. I-40, exit 74 (Whitaker Rd), 0.3 mi w on north frontage road.

AUSTIN — AUSTIN LONE STAR CAREFREE RV RESORT. (512) 444-6322. **2P $38-$50, XP: $5.** 7009 I-35 S, 78744. I-35, exit 226B/227 (Slaughter/S Congress aves) southbound; exit 228/229 (Wm Cannon Dr) northbound, on N Frontage Rd.

BEAUMONT — GULF COAST RV RESORT. (409) 842-2285. **2P $35, XP: $4-$6.** 5175 Brooks Rd, 77705. I-10, exit 846 westbound; exit 845 eastbound, follow blue signs.

BOERNE — ALAMO FIESTA RV RESORT. (830) 249-4700. **2P $33-$40, XP: $3.** 33000 IH-10 W, 78006. I-10, exit 543, 1 mi w on westbound access road.

DONNA — VICTORIA PALMS RESORT. (956) 464-7801. **Call for rates.** 602 E Victoria Rd, 78537. Just s of jct US 83.

GOODLETT — OLE TOWNE COTTON GIN RV PARK. (940) 674-2477. **Call for rates.** 230 Market St, 79252. US 287, 1 blk e; in town.

KERRVILLE — KERRVILLE KOA. (830) 895-1665. **Call for rates.** 2400 Goat Creek Rd, 78028. I-10, exit 501, 1.5 mi s on FM 1338.

KERRVILLE — GUADALUPE RIVER RV RESORT. (830) 367-5676. **Call for rates.** 2605 Junction Hwy, 78028. I-10, exit 505 (Harper Rd), 2.5 mi s, then 2.5 mi w on SR 27.

LUBBOCK — LUBBOCK RV PARK. (806) 747-2366. **2P $26-$28, XP: $2.** 4811 N I-27, 79403. I-27, exit 9, 2 mi n of Loop 289. (PO Box 597).

LUBBOCK — LUBBOCK KOA. (806) 762-8653. **Call for rates.** 5502 CR 6300, 79416. 2.5 mi nw of Loop 289 on US 84.

MERCEDES — PARADISE SOUTH R.V. RESORT. (956) 565-2044. **2P $31, XP: $2.** 9099 N Mile 2 Rd W, 78570. On Mile 2 W Rd, just n of US 83.

SAN ANTONIO — ADMIRALTY RV RESORT. (210) 647-7878. **2P $32-$36, XP: $3.** 1485 N Ellison Dr, 78251. Jct Loop 1604 and SR 151, 1.3 mi nw on SR 151 to Military Dr, just w to Ellison Dr, then 0.7 mi n.

SAN ANTONIO — BLAZING STAR RV RESORT. (210) 680-7827. **Call for rates.** 1120 W Loop 1604 N, 78251. Just s of Military Hwy.

SAN ANTONIO — ALAMO KOA KAMPGROUND. (210) 224-9296. **2P $37-$42, XP: $3.** 602 Gembler Rd, 78219. I-35, exit AT&T Center Pkwy, 0.5 mi s, then 0.8 mi e; I-10, exit WW White Rd, 0.3 mi n, then 1 mi w.

SAN BENITO — FUN-N-SUN RV RESORT. (956) 399-5125. **3P $30, XP: $2.** 1400 Zillock Rd, 78586. 4 mi nw from US 83 and 77, exit Paso Real Rd, 0.4 mi s.

SOUTH PADRE ISLAND — LONG ISLAND VILLAGE. (956) 943-6449. **2P $46-$52, XP: $5.** 900 S Garcia St, 78597. On SR 100, turn right before crossing causeway. (PO Box 695, PORT ISABEL, 78578).

UVALDE — QUAIL SPRINGS RV PARK. (830) 278-8182. **Call for rates.** 2727 E Main St, 78801. 2.2 mi e on US 90.

WESLACO — PINE TO PALM RESORT PARK. (956) 968-5760. **2P $22, XP: $2. (no credit cards).** 802 International Blvd, 78596. FM 1015, 0.8 mi s of jct US 83, just s of jct Business Rt US 83.

WICHITA FALLS — WICHITA FALLS RV PARK. (940) 723-1532. **2P $25-$28, XP: $3.** 2944 Seymour Hwy (Business 277 S), 76301. I-44, exit 1A, 1.2 mi s.

Utah

BRYCE CANYON CITY — RUBY'S INN CAMPGROUND TRAILER PARK. (AAA) (435) 834-5301. **2P $31-$43, XP: $2.** 1280 S Hwy 63, 84764. On SR 63, 1 mi n of Bryce Canyon Park entrance. (PO Box 640022).

CANNONVILLE — CANNONVILLE-BRYCE VALLEY KOA. (435) 679-8988. **2P $28-$38, XP: $3.** Hwy 12 at Redrock Rd, 84718. On SR 12, north end of town. (PO Box 50).

FRUIT HEIGHTS — CHERRY HILL CAMPING RESORT. (AAA) (801) 451-5379. **2P $25-$34, XP: $2.** 1325 S Main St, 84037. I-15 N, exit 324 (US 89), exit 297, just w; I-15 S, exit 328, just e, then 2 mi s.

MOAB — MOAB VALLEY RV RESORT. (435) 259-4469. **2P $20-$75, XP: $5.** 1773 N Hwy 191, 84532. 2 mi n, just s of Colorado River Bridge.

RICHFIELD — RICHFIELD KOA. (435) 896-6674. **Call for rates.** 600 W 600 S, 84701. 6 blks w of US 89 (Main St); I-70, exit 40 southbound, 2.5 mi via Main St; exit 37 northbound, 1.5 mi via 1200 S and 400 W.

ST. GEORGE — MCARTHUR'S TEMPLE VIEW RV RESORT. (AAA) (435) 673-6400. **2P $35-$40, XP: $3-$4.** 975 S Main St, 84770. I-15, exit 6 (Bluff St), 0.5 mi w, then just n.

VIRGIN — ZION RIVER RESORT RV PARK & CAMPGROUND. (AAA) (435) 635-8594. **4P $45-$50, XP: $3.** 730 E Hwy 9, 84779. I-15, exit 16 (SR 16) northbound, 22 mi ne; exit 27 southbound, 12 mie ne. (PO Box 790219).

Virginia

BIG ISLAND — WILDWOOD CAMPGROUND. (434) 299-5228. **Call for rates.** SR 130, 1.3 mi e from jct Blue Ridge Pkwy, 14 mi w of SR 29. (6252 Elon Rd, MONROE, 24574).

CHARLOTTESVILLE — CHARLOTTESVILLE KOA. (434) 296-9881. **2P $26-$38, XP: $2-$5.** 3825 Red Hill Rd, 22903. US 29 (s of I-64), 4.2 mi e on CR 708; SR 20, 1.4 mi w on CR 708.

CHERITON — CHERRYSTONE FAMILY CAMPING RESORT. (AAA) (757) 331-3063. **2P $17-$55, XP: $5-$15.** 1511 Townfields Dr, 23316. 1.5 mi w on SR 680 from jct US 13. (PO Box 545).

DOSWELL — KINGS DOMINION CAMPGROUND. (AAA) (804) 876-5355. **4P $30-$41, XP: $8.** 10061 Kings Dominion Blvd, 23047. I-95, exit 98, 1 mi e on SR 30; adjacent to theme park.

FRONT ROYAL — FRONT ROYAL RV CAMPGROUND. (AAA) (540) 635-2741. **2P $30, XP: $2.** 585 KOA Dr, 22630. I-66, exit 6 or 13, entrance is 2 mi s of town on US 340 S. (PO Box 274).

LURAY — YOGI BEAR'S JELLYSTONE PARK. (AAA) (540) 743-4002. **2P $35-$63, XP: $3-$6.** 2250 Hwy 211 E, 22835. On US 211, 3 mi e. (PO Box 191).

LURAY — LURAY RV RESORT COUNTRY WAYE. (AAA) (540) 743-7222. **2P $29-$39, XP: $3-$6.** 3402 Kimball Rd, 22835. Jct US 211, 2 mi n on US 340, then 0.3 mi e on SR 658.

MADISON — SHENANDOAH HILLS CAMPGROUND. (AAA) (540) 948-4186. **2P $27-$45, XP: $3-$5.** 110 Campground Ln, 22727. 2 mi s on US 29.

MINT SPRING — WALNUT HILLS CAMPGROUND. (540) 337-3920. **2P $28-$36, XP: $3.** 484 Walnut Hills Rd, 24463. I-81, exit 217, 0.7 mi w to US 11, 1.5 mi s, then 1.2 mi e on SR 655.

NATURAL BRIDGE — NATURAL BRIDGE KOA KAMP-GROUND. (AAA) (540) 291-2770. **2P $23-$99, XP: $3-$5.** 214 Kildeer Ln, 24578. I-81, exit 180 northbound; exit 180B southbound, just nw on US 11. (PO Box 148).

URBANNA — BETHPAGE CAMP RESORT. (804) 758-4349. **4P $35-$65, XP: $4.** 679 Brown's Ln, 23175. 1 mi n of town on CR 602. (PO Box 178).

VIRGINIA BEACH — HOLIDAY TRAV-L-PARK. (AAA) (757) 425-0249. **6P $21-$70, XP: $3-$5.** 1075 General Booth Blvd, 23451. I-264 terminus to Pacific Ave, 2.5 mi s.

VIRGINIA BEACH — OUTDOOR RESORTS/VIRGINIA BEACH. (757) 721-2020. **4P $40-$70, XP: $5.** 3665 S Sandpiper Rd, 23456. I-264 terminus to Pacific Ave, 2 mi s to Rudee Inlet Bridge/General Booth Blvd, 5.6 mi s to Princess Anne Rd, 0.8 mi e to Sandbridge Rd, 5.5 mi e to Sandpiper Rd, then 3.5 mi s.

Washington

BURLINGTON — BURLINGTON KOA. (360) 724-5511. **2P $24-$41, XP: $3-$4.** 6397 N Green Rd, 98233. I-5, exit 232, 3.5 mi n on Old US 99.

CHENEY — PONDEROSA FALLS RV RESORT. (509) 747-9415. **Call for rates.** 7520 S Thomas Mallen Rd, 99004. I-90, exit 272, 2 mi s.

CLARKSTON — GRANITE LAKE PREMIER RV RESORT. (509) 751-1635. **2P $30-$42, XP: $3.** 306 Granite Lake Dr, 99403. Just w of Snake River Bridge on US 12, just n on 5th St.

COULEE CITY — SUN LAKES PARK RESORT. (509) 632-5291. **Call for rates.** 34228 Park Lake Rd NE, 99115. US 2, 4 mi s on SR 17.

EPHRATA — STARS AND STRIPES RV PARK & DRIVING RANGE. (509) 787-1062. **Call for rates.** 5707 US 28 W, 98823. 5 mi w.

LYNDEN — LYNDEN KOA. (360) 354-4772. **2P $25-$45, XP: $5.** 8717 Line Rd, 98264. 1.7 mi n of downtown on SR 539 (Guide Meridian Rd), 3 mi e on SR 546 (E Badger Rd), then 0.5 mi s.

MOSSYROCK — HARMONY LAKESIDE RV PARK. ⚠ (360) 983-3804. **2P $29-$50, XP: $4.** 563 SR 122, 98585. I-5, exit 68, 21 mi e on US 12, then 2.3 mi n.

OAK HARBOR — NORTH WHIDBEY RV PARK. (360) 675-9597. **2P $29, XP: $2.** 565 W Cornet Bay Rd, 98277. On SR 20, 1 mi s of Deception Pass Bridge, 8 mi n of Oak Harbor.

PORT ANGELES — PORT ANGELES/SEQUIM KOA. (360) 457-5916. **2P $22-$76, XP: $3-$5.** 80 O'Brien Rd & US 101 E, 98362. 7 mi e on US 101; 8 mi w of Sequim on US 101; just e of US 101, MM 255.

SPOKANE — ALDERWOOD RV RESORT. (509) 467-5320. **2P $27-$37, XP: $3.** 14007 N Newport Hwy, 99021. I-90, exit 287, 8 mi n to SR 206, then 1.5 mi w.

SPOKANE VALLEY — SPOKANE KOA. (509) 924-4722. **Call for rates.** I-90, exit 293, 1.5 mi n. (3025 N Barker Rd, 99027).

West Virginia

HARPERS FERRY — HARPERS FERRY/CIVIL WAR BATTLEFIELDS KOA. ⚠ (304) 535-6895. **2P $29-$200, XP: $3-$6.** 343 Campground Rd, 25425. 1 mi sw on US 340 from Shenandoah River Bridge, 0.3 mi s, follow signs.

MILTON — FOX FIRE CAMPING RESORT. (304) 743-5622. **Call for rates.** 660 Fox Fire Rd, 25541. I-64, exit 28, 0.3 mi s, then 2.7 mi w. (Rt 2, Box 655).

Wisconsin

BAGLEY — YOGI BEAR'S JELLYSTONE PARK CAMP RESORT. (608) 996-2201. **4P $20-$45, XP: $3-$6.** 11354 CR X, 53801. 1.3 mi n.

ELKHART LAKE — PLYMOUTH ROCK CAMPING RESORT. (920) 892-4252. **Call for rates.** N7271 Lando St, 53073. 3 mi s on SR 67, 4 mi n of Plymouth. (PO Box 445, 53020).

FORT ATKINSON — JELLYSTONE PARK OF FORT ATKINSON. (920) 568-4100. **4P $20-$40, XP: $5-$9.** N 551 Wishing Well Dr, 53538. 5 mi s on SR 26 from jct US 12, 0.8 mi w on Koshkonong Lake Rd, then just s.

FREMONT — YOGI BEAR'S JELLYSTONE PARK CAMP RESORT. (920) 446-3420. **Call for rates.** E 6506 Hwy 110, 54940. On SR 110 S, 1.5 mi w. (PO Box 497).

WISCONSIN DELLS — YOGI BEAR'S JELLYSTONE PARK CAMP-RESORT. ⚠ (608) 254-2568. **4P $19-$109, XP: $5-$10.** S 1915 Ishnala Rd, 53965. I-90/94, exit 89 eastbound; exit 92 westbound, follow signs. (PO Box 510).

WISCONSIN DELLS — CHRISTMAS MOUNTAIN CAMPGROUND. (608) 253-1000. **Call for rates. (no credit cards).** 944 S Christmas Mountain Rd, 53913. I-90/94, exit 87 (SR 13), 0.4 mi ne to CR H, 4 mi sw, then just s.

Canada

Alberta

EDMONTON — GLOWING EMBERS TRAVEL CENTRE & RV PARK. ⚠ (780) 962-8100. **2P $33-$40.** 26309 Hwy 16A, T7X 5A6. 1.9 mi (3 km) w of city limits; 1.1 mi (1.8 km) sw from Devon exit (Hwy 60 S), follow signs.

HINTON — HINTON/JASPER KOA. ⚠ (780) 865-5062. **2P $27-$42, XP: $3-$5.** Hwy 16, T9B 1X3. On Hwy 16, 2.5 mi (4 km) w. (4720 Vegas Rd NW, CALGARY, T3A 1W3).

OKOTOKS — COUNTRY LANE RV PARK. ⚠ (403) 995-2330. **Call for rates.** E on Hwy 7 and 2A; jct Hwy 2, 7 and 2A. (PO Box 1530, T1S 1B4).

PINE LAKE — LEISURE CAMPGROUNDS. (403) 886-4705. **Call for rates.** On Hwy 42, 15.6 mi (2.6 km) e off Hwy 2. (PO Box 68, T0M 1S0).

SUNDRE — TALL TIMBER LEISURE PARK. (403) 638-3555. **Call for rates.** 0.6 mi (1 km) e of Centre St on Main Ave E (Hwy 27 E). (PO Box 210, T0M 1X0).

British Columbia

BURNABY — BURNABY CARIBOO R.V. PARK. ⚠ (604) 420-1722. **2P $34-$51, XP: $3-$5.** 8765 Cariboo Pl, V3N 4T2. Trans-Canada Hwy 1, exit 37 (Gaglardi Way), follow signs.

CAMPBELL RIVER — RIPPLE ROCK RV PARK. (250) 287-7108. **Call for rates.** 15011 Browns Bay Rd, V9H 1N9. Jct Hwy 19A, 28 and 19, 12 mi (19 km) n on Hwy 19, then 2.8 mi (4.5 km) e.

FAIRMONT HOT SPRINGS — FAIRMONT HOT SPRINGS RV PARK. (250) 345-6033. **Call for rates.** 1 mi (1.6 km) e off Hwy 93 and 95; adjacent to Fairmont Hot Springs Resort. (PO Box 10, V0B 1L0).

MALAHAT — VICTORIA WEST KOA. (250) 478-3332. **2P $33-$149, XP: $4-$6.** On Trans-Canada Hwy 1 (Malahat Dr), 15.9 mi (25.6 km) n of Victoria. (PO Box 103).

NORTH VANCOUVER — CAPILANO RV PARK. ⒶⒶ (604) 987-4722. **2P $33-$50, XP: $3-$4.** 295 Tomahawk Ave, V7P 1C5. Trans-Canada Hwy 1, exit 14 (Capilano Rd), 1 mi (1.6 km) s to Marine Dr, follow signs.

OLIVER — DESERT GEM RV RESORT. ⒶⒶ (250) 498-5544. **2P $21-$35, XP: $5.** 34037 Hwy 97, V0H 1T0. 0.6 mi (1 km) s from 342nd Ave. (PO Box 400).

SURREY — PEACE ARCH RV PARK. (604) 594-7009. **2P $31-$43, XP: $3.** 14601 40th Ave, V3S 0L2. Hwy 99, exit 10, follow signs.

WHISTLER — RIVERSIDE RV RESORT AND CAMPGROUND. (604) 905-5533. **2P $45-$50, XP: $5.** 8018 Mons Rd, V0N 1B8. Hwy 99, from Upper Village, 0.9 mi (1.5 km) n, exit Blackcomb Way, follow signs.

New Brunswick

WOODSTOCK — YOGI BEAR'S JELLYSTONE PARK AT KOZY ACRES. (506) 328-6287. **5P $34-$41, XP: $8.** Trans-Canada Hwy 2, exit 191 (Beardsley Rd). (PO Box 9004, E7M 6B5).

Nova Scotia

BADDECK — BADDECK-CABOT TRAIL CAMPGROUND/GOOD SAM PARK. ⒶⒶ (902) 295-2288. **$23-$32, XP: $3-$4.** 9584 Trans-Canada Hwy 105, B0E 1B0. 5 mi (8 km) w of town. (PO Box 417).

Ontario

AMHERSTBURG — YOGI BEAR JELLYSTONE PARK CAMP RESORTS. (519) 736-3201. **Call for rates.** 4610 County Rd 18, RR 1, N9V 2Y7. 2.5 mi (4 km) e on Pike Rd (Simco St).

BRADFORD — YOGI BEAR'S JELLYSTONE PARK & CAMP-RESORT. ⒶⒶ (905) 775-1377. **2P $35-$55, XP: $6-$8.** 3666 Simcoe Rd 88, L3Z 2A4. Hwy 400, exit 64B, jct Hwy 400 and Simcoe Rd 88. (RR 1, 3666 Simcoe Rd 88).

FOREST — OUR PONDEROSA RV RESORT & GOLF RESORT. (519) 786-2031. **4P $45.** 9338 W Ipperwash Rd, N0N 1J0. 1.9 mi (3 km) n on W Ipperwash Rd from jct CR 7. (RR 2).

KINCARDINE — FISHERMAN'S COVE TENT & TRAILER PARK LTD. (519) 395-2757. **2P $40-$50, XP: $3-$5.** 13 Southline Ave, N2Z 2X5. Jct Hwy 21 and 9, 10.6 mi (17.7 km) e to Kinloss, then 1.9 mi (3 km) s; follow signs. (RR 4).

KITCHENER — BINGEMANS. (519) 744-1002. **Call for rates.** 425 Bingemans Centre Dr, N2B 3X7. 3.5 mi (5.6 km) on Hwy 7; 1 mi (1.6 km) e of jct Hwy 7 and Conestoga Pkwy (Hwy 86).

NIAGARA FALLS — CAMPARK RESORTS. ⒶⒶ (905) 358-3873. **2P $38-$49, XP: $3-$5.** 9387 Lundy's Ln, L2E 6S4. 3.9 mi (6.3 km) w of falls on Hwy 20.

NIAGARA FALLS — YOGI BEAR'S JELLYSTONE PARK CAMP-RESORT. ⒶⒶ (905) 354-1432. **2P $33-$53, XP: $3-$5.** 8676 Oakwood Dr, L2E 6S5. QEW, exit 27 (McLeod Rd), 1.5 mi (2.4 km) se.

NIAGARA FALLS — NIAGARA FALLS KOA KAMPGROUND. (905) 356-2267. **Call for rates.** 8625 Lundy's Ln, L2H 1H5. 3.5 mi (5.6 km) w on Hwy 20.

SAUBLE BEACH — WOODLAND PARK. (519) 422-1161. **2P $32-$50, XP: $3-$20.** 47 Sauble Falls Pkwy, RR 1, N0H 2G0. 0.6 mi (1 km) n on CR 13.

SAUBLE BEACH — CARSON'S CAMP LTD.. (519) 422-1143. **2P $25-$45, XP: $3-$10. (no credit cards).** 110 Southampton Pkwy, N0H 2G0. 0.6 mi (1 km) s on CR 13. (Rt 1).

Québec

FRELIGHSBURG — LE CAMPING DES CHUTES HUNTER. (450) 298-5005. **Call for rates.** 18 chemin des Chutes, J0J 1C0. Jct Rt 237, just w on chemin du Moulin a Scie.

LEVIS — KOA-QUEBEC CITY. (418) 831-1813. **$25-$55, XP: $2-$5.** 684 chemin Olivier, G7A 2N6. Hwy 20, exit 311, 0.9 mi (1.5 km) w, north-side service road; in St-Nicolas sector.

ST-LIBOIRE — CAMPING PLAGE LA LIBERTE. (450) 793-2716. **Call for rates.** 129 Rang Charlotte, J0H 1R0. Hwy 20, exit 147, 0.3 mi (0.5 km) s.

ST-MATHIEU-DE-BELOEIL — CAMPING ALOUETTE. ⒶⒶ (450) 464-1661. **2P $32-$40, XP: $3.** 3449 de l'Industrie, J3G 4S5. Hwy 20, exit 105; follow signs.

STE-SABINE — CAMPING CARAVELLE. (450) 293-7637. **2P $24-$30. (no credit cards).** 180 Rang de la Gare, J0J 2B0. Jct Rt 104, 2.9 mi (4.7 km) s on Rt 235, then 0.5 mi (0.8 km) w on Rang de la Gare; 3.6 mi (6 km) s of Farnham.